August 24–27, 2014
New York, NY, USA

Association for Computing Machinery

Advancing Computing as a Science & Profession

KDD

KDD'14

Proceedings of the 20th ACM SIGKDD International Conference on Knowledge Discovery and Data Mining

Sponsored by:

ACM SIGKDD
ACM SIGMOD

Supported by:

Bloomberg, Bosch, Facebook, Microsoft, Rapidminer, Amazon, AT&T, Baidu, Booking.com, Criteo, Goldman Sachs, Google, Huawei, IBM Research, IBM Watson, SAS, Siemens, Verizon, Yahoo! Labs, eBay, Flipkart.com, Stanford, Collective, Technicolor, Leidos, Zementis, Knime, dstillery, KDnuggets, Big Data Journal, Kaggle, NYU Stern, Donors Choose.org, NSF, American Airlines, Oracle Labs

Association for
Computing Machinery

Advancing Computing as a Science & Profession

The Association for Computing Machinery
2 Penn Plaza, Suite 701
New York, New York 10121-0701

ISBN: 978-1-4503-2956-9 (Digital)

ISBN: 978-1-4503-3271-5 (Print)

Additional copies may be ordered prepaid from:

ACM Order Department
PO Box 30777
New York, NY 10087-0777, USA

Phone: 1-800-342-6626 (USA and Canada)
+1-212-626-0500 (Global)
Fax: +1-212-944-1318
E-mail: acmhelp@acm.org
Hours of Operation: 8:30 am – 4:30 pm ET

ACM Order Number: 618142

Printed in the USA

General Chairs' Welcome

This Year's Theme: Data Science for Social Good

It is our great pleasure to welcome you to the 20th ACM SIGKDD Conference on Knowledge Discovery and Data Mining (KDD). The annual ACM SIGKDD conference is the premier international forum for data science, data mining, knowledge discovery and big data. It brings together researchers and practitioners from academia, industry, and government to share their ideas, research results and experiences KDD-2014 features plenary presentations, paper presentations, poster sessions, workshops, tutorials, exhibits, and the KDD Cup competition. We are happy to announce that this year we are partnering with Bloomberg to emphasize our theme of Data Science for Social Good. To this end, part of our workshop and tutorial program will be held at the Bloomberg facilities together with Bloomberg-specific events, all focusing on issues pertaining to social good.

Today, you hear a lot about data science, big data and data intensive computing. The core of this work is extracting knowledge and useful information from data, which for science leads to beautiful insights, and for applications leads to actions, alerts and decisions. The KDD community has always been at the center of this activity and it is clear from this conference that it will continue to drive this broader field of data science.

This year we had a record number of submissions. There were 1036 submissions to the Research Track, and 151 papers were accepted. There were 197 submissions to the Industry and Government Track, and 44 papers were accepted.

KDD also has a history of inviting talks that are of broad interest to the KDD community. This year we chose to have 4 plenary talks. A program committee also selected 8 talks to present at the Industry and Government track.

A strength of the KDD conference is the number of workshops and tutorials that are co-located with it. This year there were 9 full-day workshops, 16 half-day workshops, and 12 tutorials. As part of our partnership with Bloomberg on the theme of social good, Bloomberg will have 3 workshops jointly located with our workshops at their New York Office.

Our community is a unique blend of industry and academia, ranging from people starting their career to leaders in their respective fields. This year, we are piloting programs to facilitate networking amongst these groups. Specifically, we have a networking lounge for industry and job-seekers to meet and we helped find good matches. We also have a networking event focused on defining what a data science career looks like and have senior members meet young people to help them understand the skills needed and what a job in this discipline might entail.

We would like to thank all sponsors, who are a very important part of the conference, and the members of the Organizing Committee and our other colleagues who volunteered their time during the past year to make this conference a success. Special thanks goes to the Research Track Co-Chairs and the Industry and Government Track Co-Chairs. Also special thanks are due to the Workshops Co-Chairs, the Sponsorship Chair, the Treasurer, the Publications Co-Chairs, and the KDD Cup Committee.

We are grateful to the several program committees that provided the advice necessary to put together a quality program – the Research Track Program Committee, the Research Track Senior Program Committee, the Industry and Government Track Program Committee, the Industry Practice Expo Program Committee, the Workshop Program Committee, and the Tutorial Program Committee.

Please join us for KDD-2014 to gain new knowledge and to exchange exciting new research results, leading practices, high impact applications, and to increase your social network. We hope that you will find this program interesting and thought-provoking and that the conference will provide you with a valuable opportunity to share ideas with other researchers and practitioners from institutions around the world.

Sofus A. Macskassy
KDD 2014 General Co-Chair
Facebook, USA

Claudia Perlich
KDD 2014 General Co-Chair
Dstillery, USA

Research Track Program Chairs' Welcome

The KDD conference has seen remarkable growth since its origins as an IJCAI workshop in Detroit in 1989, evolving into a full-fledged research conference in 1995, underscoring the important role that data mining as a field has played in extracting knowledge and actionable insights from vast troves of data that are being generated in the digital world as well as in the physical world around us. This year, we received a record-high number of 1,036 submissions to the research program, out of which 151 papers were accepted. Overall, the number of submissions has increased 42% over the last year (KDD '13), while the acceptance rate dropped from 17.2% last year to 14.6% this year. This makes KDD 2014 by far the biggest and the most competitive KDD in its 20-year history.

Among academic conferences, the KDD conference typically has more of an emphasis on research motivated by real-world applications. It is important to keep in mind that it is this synergy of research in areas such as algorithms, computational geometry, database, graph theory, machine learning, natural language processing, statistics, visualization, and many others when applied to problems arising in diverse fields, such as the Web, medicine, biology, and marketing, driving our field forward and making it vibrant and fun.

The breadth of topics covered in this year's research program is truly comprehensive and nicely balanced among social and information networks (6.58% of papers), data mining for social good (5.26%), graph mining (5.26%), statistical techniques for big data (5.26%), recommender systems (4.61%), data streams (3.95%), scalable methods (3.95%), Web mining (3.29%), clustering (3.29%), feature selection (3.29%), applications to health care and medicine (3.29%), mining rich data types (2.63%), and many more. In particular, we are happy to observe an increase in the number of papers related to data mining for social good, as well as works on scaling up algorithms to deal with big data. It is extremely encouraging to see that data mining is branching out to many application areas of societal importance: public policy, education, healthcare, medicine, smart cities, the Internet of things, and many others. We hope that this trend of data mining affecting all aspects of our society will definitely continue in the future.

We are also very fortunate to have four world-class keynote speakers this year spanning industry and academia, providing inspirational talks on cutting-edge techniques and issues in big data, automatic knowledge discovery, and decision making in medicine, science, and understanding human behavior.

The process of whittling down the initial 1,036 submissions to the final set of 151 accepted papers required the coordination and time of a large number of willing volunteers. The program committee (PC) consisted of 376 reviewers (PC members) and 46 senior PC members. The selection of the PC members involved quantitative constraints to achieve a well-balanced coverage of expertise matching the expected distribution of the submissions' subject areas, as well as requiring seniority and freshness in the field. In the first review phase, each submitted paper was automatically assigned to three reviewers (after a bidding process). After the first round of reviewing was complete, the papers were assigned to the senior PC members based on their bids. The senior PC members then initiated discussions on many of the papers, e.g., if there was significant divergence in scores among reviewers or if a paper was on the borderline of being accepted. Following the discussion phase, the senior PC members provided a recommendation score and a meta-review for each paper. In the final phase, we (the program chairs) normalized and analyzed all of this information, starting with the obvious accept and reject decisions, and then we gradually focused in more detail on the papers near the borderline, seeking additional reviews and input from the PC and senior PC members where appropriate. The top-rated papers were provided to an awards committee, chaired by Thorsten Joachims and Sunita Sarawagi, who chose the best paper and best student paper award winners.

We conclude with some well-deserved words of thanks to the large supporting cast. We thank all authors for submitting their research to KDD 2014. We are extremely grateful to the PC members and senior PC members for volunteering their time to help in the review process. Diligent peer review is an essential cornerstone for research progress, and we thank you all for the many detailed and conscientious reviews that were generated. Last year's program chairs, Inderjit Dhillon and Yehuda Koren, were generous in providing us with advice and expertise based on lessons learned in 2013. We would also like to convey our sincere thanks to the staff who run the Microsoft CMT system—they were more than willing to answer questions and help us at all times during the submission, review, and decision process. Finally, we would like to thank all of our colleagues on the KDD 2014 organization committee, who were a pleasure to work with and without whom we would not have such a wonderful conference. Let the 20th ACM SIGKDD conference begin—we hope you enjoy it!

Jure Leskovec and Wei Wang
ACM SIGKDD 2014 Program Chairs

Industry & Government Track Program Chairs' Welcome

The 2014 Industry & Government Track continues the focus on real applications of KDD technologies that provide measurable and documented benefits to Industry and Government. One of the changes implemented this year is the merger of the previous years' Industry Practice Expo (IPE) with the Industry & Government Track, to be presented as the Industry Government Track Invited Talk series. We have done this in an effort to better align scheduling and content.

Overall, the Industry & Government Track is focused on highlighting the contributions that KDD researchers and practitioners have made towards solving problems in industry and government organizations, as well as increasing awareness and understanding of practical issues regarding the deployment and use of KDD technologies. We solicited papers in three areas:

(1) Deployed papers that describe the implementation, deployment, and evaluation of KDD systems in industry and government.
(2) Emerging papers that are not about deployed systems but solve a real problem in industry and government using real data, solid evaluation and a clear path to deployment. The expectation is that these applications will be deployed in the future and these papers are reporting on early work.
(3) Discovery papers that describe discoveries of new knowledge that is valuable to an industry or government organization. These papers are typically very rare and the discoveries need to be evaluated by domain experts.

There were several classes of technically sound papers that were not a good fit to the Industry and Government track and were thus rejected. Papers that asserted the existence of a potential problem that could be solved by KDD technologies but provided no evidence of interest from potential users of that problem, and papers that used real data but did not attempt to deal with real-world complexities were rejected. Papers that proposed and applied a novel algorithm to a real dataset that achieved better performance according to some metric, but did not have any evidence of external validation or interest from potential users, were also rejected from this track. Those papers are valuable for the KDD community but not a good fit for the Industry & Government Track which is focused on real, deployed (or on the path to deployment) applications as opposed to applying an algorithm to a data set. As one PC member stated in a review "Using real data is not the same as solving real problems in a real operational setting."

On the other hand, papers that discussed enabling infrastructure or issues of general interest regarding the real-world use of KDD technologies were viewed favorably, even when they did not discuss a specific case study or application. These infrastructure and issue papers were included in the "emerging" category.

The application areas of accepted papers cover a broad range, including the theme this year of social good, public safety, advertising, social analytics, personalization, workforce analytics, health, and others, showing the wide range of fields to which KDD is being applied and adding value.

The track received **193** papers and accepted **44**, for an overall acceptance rate of **22.7%**. All submitted papers received at least three reviews from separate PC members. For papers with divergent recommendations, a discussion among reviewers was held to reach consensus. The Senior PC member assigned to the paper then performed a meta-review of all papers whose ratings and reviews were sufficiently positive that there was a possibility of acceptance. We then made our final decisions based on paper quality, initial reviews, meta-review, and fit to the track's goals as evidenced by the paper's ranking on all of the review criteria.

We would like to thank all our PC and Senior PC members whose reviews were critical in helping us select the best possible program for this year's Industry and Government track.

The Industry & Government Track Invited Talk series features presentations from leading experts who have developed and deployed large-scale data mining applications and systems in their respective fields that have generated measurable and meaningful impact. We trust that this opportunity for the KDD community to hear directly from industry and government practitioners will inspire new advances and broader interdisciplinary collaboration between researchers, industry and government counterparts and organizations leveraging data for social good.

Following in the steps of three previous Industry Practice Expo (IPE) sessions, we have worked hard to live up to the high bar set by previous speakers and to strive for the right balance between business context and technical depth in this year's invited talks.

This year, we present to you world-renowned experts whose talks will help you learn and take key ideas back to your respective professional endeavors. Featured topics include applications in medicine, crime, data collection and compensation in emerging markets, personalization, using unstructured text and imaging data from natural disasters, real-world predictive modeling infrastructure and examples of data science work from the New York Mayor's Office. Attendees will also learn about the new science of Information Environment Security. We're excited that a number of talks align with the conference theme of "Data Science for Social Good". Jake Porway (of DataKind) will host an "ignite"-style session where NGOs and other non-profits will present their applications, goals and issues related to their data assets to further inspire attendees in the area of social good.

It has been a great pleasure to work with our invited talk advisory committee comprising Misha Bilenko, Eric Bloedorn, Usama Fayyad, Johannes Gehrke, Ronny Kohavi, Ying Li, Gabor Melli, Rajesh Parekh, Jian Pei, Gregory Piatetsky, Ramasamy Uthurusamy and Mohammed Zaki. We thank them and the other members of the organizing committee for advice and support throughout the search for candidate speakers.

We warmly welcome you to the KDD 2014 Industry & Government Track, and hope you find these papers and invited talks interesting and insightful. Your suggestions and comments are much appreciated.

Best Regards,
Rayid Ghani, Prem Melville, Brian Dalessandro, and Paul Bradley

Bloomberg Welcome

On behalf of Bloomberg, and particularly the technology and design organizations within Bloomberg, we are pleased to welcome you to "KDD at Bloomberg."

Bloomberg sits at the intersection of technology, data and finance. We recognize that we have a unique opportunity to leverage our strengths to drive meaningful change, while we also create competitive advantage and value for our customers. It is why we are so excited to be a part of the SIGKDD's annual flagship KDD 2014 conference, which has a special focus on applying data science to improve civic and social outcomes.

Data scientists have a tremendous opportunity to contribute to the most pressing problems faced by policy makers today. Since the inception of our company, we've shown that data is crucial to making informed decisions, and that it can also have a broader societal impact. This event presents an excellent opportunity to help bring together communities that are ideally positioned to help address society's greatest challenges.

Through our event researchers and participants will be able to engage with practitioners, policy makers and activists engaged in NGO's. We hope that together they will discover opportunities to utilize data science in socially relevant application domains like public health, medicine, urbanization and geopolitical disparity. Our motivation is to explore how technical innovation around data-driven analytics can identify new opportunities and accelerate solutions to pressing societal issues like climate change or the spread of disease.

We hope that by partnering with KDD, we are creating a platform so that industry and academic research can come together to generate not just a conversation but more importantly concrete, measurable actions that will help make the world a better place.

Vlad K.
Bloomberg Head of R&D

Shawn E.
Bloomberg CTO

Table of Contents

Research Session 3: Applications to Healthcare and Medicine II

Research Session 4: Recommender Systems

Research Session 5: Clustering

Research Session 6: Supervised Learning I

Research Session 7: Supervised Learning II

Research Session 8: Trend, Anomaly and Novelty Detection

Research Session 9: Data Streams

Research Session 10: Active Learning

Research Session 11: Feature Selection

Research Session 15: Web Mining

Research Session 16: Transfer Learning

Research Session 17: Recommendations and Ratings

Research Session 18: Topic Modeling

Research Session 19: Security and Privacy

Research Session 20: Dimensionality Reduction

Research Session 21: Novel Applications

Research Session 22: Crowds and Markets

Research Session 23: Text Mining

Research Session 24: Dynamic Graph Analysis

Research Session 28: Network Community Detection

Research Session 29: Scaling-up Graph Algorithms

Research Session 30: Social Network Analysis

Industry & Government Invited Talks

Industry & Government

Panel

Tutorials

KDD'14 Conference on Knowledge Discovery & Data Mining Organization

General Chairs:	Sofus Macskassy (Facebook) Claudia Perlich (Dstillery)
Research Track Program Chairs:	Jure Leskovec (Stanford University) Wei Wang (UCLA)
Industry & Government Track Program Chairs:	Rayid Ghani (University of Chicago & Edgeflip) Prem Melville (Social Alpha)
Industry & Government Track Invited Talks Chairs:	Paul Bradley (MethodCare) Brian Dalessandro (Dstillery)
Workshop Chairs:	Alejandro Jaimes (Yahoo!) Dragos Margineantu (Boeing)
Tutorial Chairs:	Ying Li (EV Analysis Corporation) Jian Pei (Simon Fraser University)
Poster and Spotlight Chairs:	Aris Gionis (Aalto University) Jie Tang (Tsinghua University)
Local Arrangements Chair:	Shannon Cunningham (Executive Events)
Exhibits and Demo Chair:	Shannon Cunningham (Executive Events)
SIGKDD 2014 Awards Chair:	Gabor Melli (VigLink)
KDD Cup Chairs:	William Cukierski (Kaggle) Ben Hamner (Kaggle)
Media and Publicity Chairs:	Kaitlin Atkinson (PeekAnalytics) Polo Chau (Georgia Tech) Ankur Teredesai (University of Washington)
Panel Chairs:	Raghu Ramakrishnan (Microsoft) Geoff Webb (Monash University)
Publications Chairs:	Jing Gao (University at Buffalo) Xiang Zhang (Case Western Reserve University)
Sponsorship Chair:	Balaji Krishnapuram (Siemens)

Treasurer:	Ted Senator (Leidos)
Best Paper Chairs:	Thorsten Joachims (Cornell University) Sunita Sarawagi (IIT Bombay)
Student Award Chairs:	Tanya Berger-Wolf (University of Illinois at Chicago) Bart Goethals (University of Antwerp)
Webmaster & Web Designers:	Andrej Krevl (Stanford University) Sébastien Robaszkiewicz (Stanford University)
Registration Chair:	Brooke Daley (Executivevents, Inc.)

KDD'14 Research Track Senior Program Committee

Naoki Abe (IBM T. J. Watson Research Center)
Deepak Agarwal (LinkedIn)
Charu C. Aggarwal (IBM T. J. Watson Research Center)
James Bailey (The University of Melbourne)
Arindam Banerjee (University of Minnesota)
Paul Bennett (Microsoft Research)
Francesco Bonchi (Yahoo! Labs)
Deepayan Chakrabarti (Facebook)
Hong Cheng (Chinese University of Hong Kong)
Diane Cook (Washington State University)
W. Bruce Croft (University of Massachusetts)
Ian Davidson (University of California, Davis)
Inderjit Dhillon (University of Texas at Austin)
Tina Eliassi-Rad (Rutgers University)
Martin Ester (Simon Fraser University)
Christos Faloutsos (Carnegie Mellon University)
Evgeniy Gabrilovich (Google)
Lise Getoor (University of California, Santa Cruz)
Aristides Gionis (Aalto University)
Bart Goethals (University of Antwerp)
Dimitrios Gunopulos (University of Athens)
Jiawei Han (University of Illinois at Urbana-Champaign)
Thorsten Joachims (Cornell University)
Eamonn Keogh (University of California, Riverside)
Yehuda Koren (Google)
Ravi Kumar (Google)
Shou-de Lin (National Taiwan University)
Chih-Jen Lin (National Taiwan University)
Christopher Meek (Microsoft Research)
Srinivasan Parthasarathy (Ohio State University)
Jian Pei (Simon Fraser University)
Saharon Rosset (Tel Aviv University)
Sunita Sarawagi (IIT Bombay)
Jimeng Sun (Georgia Tech)
Jie Tang (Tsinghua University)
Evimaria Terzi (Boston University)
Andrew Tomkins (Google)
S. V. N. Vishwanathan (Purdue University)
Geoff Webb (Monash University)
Stefan Wrobel (University of Bonn and Fraunhofer IAIS)
Hui Xiong (Rutgers, the State University of New Jersey)
Kenji Yamanishi (University of Tokyo)
Xifeng Yan (University of California, Santa Barbara)
Qiang Yang (Hong Kong University of Science and Technology)
Philip S. Yu (University of Illinois at Chicago)
Jeffrey Yu (Chinese University of Hong Kong)

KDD'14 Research Track Program Committee

Bruno Abrahao (Cornell University)
Leman Akoglu (Stony Brook University)
Aijun An (York University)
Annalisa Appice (Università degli Studi di Bari)
Ira Assent (Aarhus University)
Tony Bagnall (University of East Anglia)
Fabricio Benevenuto (Federal University of Minas Gerais)
Tanya Berger-Wolf (University of Illinois at Chicago)
Michele Berlingerio (IBM Research Dublin)
Michael Berthold (KNIME)
Smriti Bhagat (Technicolor Palo Alto)
Jinbo Bi (University of Connecticut)
Klemens Bohm (Karlsruhe Institute of Technology (KIT))
Mario Boley (University of Bonn)
Christian Borgelt (European Centre for Soft Computing)
Henrik Bostrom (University of Stockholm)
Christos Boutsidis (IBM)
Pavel Brazdil (University of Porto)
Ulf Brefeld (Technische Universität Darmstadt)
David Buttler (Lawrence Livermore National Laboratory)
Deng Cai (Zhejiang University)
Rui Cai (Microsoft Research)
Berkant Barla Cambazoglu (Yahoo! Research)
Longbing Cao (University of Technology Sydney)
Yunbo Cao (Microsoft Research Asia)
Licia Capra (University College of London)
Lawrence Carin (Duke University)
Carlos Castillo (Qatar Computing Research Institute)
Edward Chang (HTC)
Kai-Wei Chang (University of Illionis)
Duen Horng Chau (Georgia Tech)
Nitesh Chawla (University of Notre Dame)
Sanjay Chawla (University of Sydney)
Bee-Chung Chen (LinkedIn)
Enhong Chen (University of Science and Technology of China)
Haifeng Chen (NEC Research Lab)
Ji Chen (eBay Inc.)
Ming-Syan Chen (Academic Sinica)
Songqing Chen (George Mason University)
Wei Chen (Microsoft Research)
Weizhu Chen (Microsoft)
Ye Chen (Microsoft)
Yixin Chen (Washington University in St Louis)
James Cheng (Chinese Univ. of Hong Kong)
Reynold Cheng (University of Hong Kong)
Wei Cheng (University of North Carolina at Chapel Hill)
Junghoo Cho (University of California)
Peter Christen (The Australian National University)
Wei Chu (Microsoft Research)
Tyson Condie (University of California)
Gao Cong (Nanyang Technological University)
Bin Cui (Institute of Network Computing and Information Systems)
Peng Cui (Tsinghua University)
Mahashweta Das (University of Texas)
Atish Das Sarma (eBay Research Labs)
Anirban Dasgupta (Indian Institute of Technology at Gandhinagar)
Chris Ding (University of Texas at Arlington)
Nan Ding (Google)
Wei Ding (University of Massachusetts Boston)
Carlotta Domeniconi (George Mason University)
Debora Donato (Yahoo! Research)
Anlei Dong (Yahoo! Labs)
Pinar Donmez (Salesforce)
Gideon Dror (Yahoo! Labs)
Saso Dzeroski (J. Stefan Institute)
Dora Erdos (Boston University)
Hui Fang (University of Delaware)
Elena Ferrari (University of Insubria)
Marcus Fontoura (Google)
Ada Fu (The Chinese University of Hong Kong)
Ryohei Fujimaki (NEC Laboratories America)
Benjamin C. M. Fung (McGill University)
Glenn Fung (University of Wisconsin at Madison)
Joao Gama (University of Porto)
Jing Gao (University at Buffalo)
Minos Garofalakis (Technical University of Crete)
Yong Ge (University of North Carolina at Charlotte)
David Gleich (Purdue University)
Manuel Gomez Rodriguez (Max Planck Institute for Intelligent Systems)

Francesco Gullo (Yahoo! Labs)
Asela Gunawardana (Microsoft Research)
Stephan Gunnemann (Carnegie Mellon University)
Rahul Gupta (Google)
Wook-Shin Han (POSTECH)
Jingrui He (Stevens Institute of Technology)
Qi He (LinkedIn)
Steven Hoi (Nanyang Technological University)
Geoff Holmes (The University of Waikato)
Andreas Hotho (University of Kassel)
Vagelis Hristidis (University of California)
Cho-Jui Hsieh (UT Austin)
Chun-Nan Hsu (University of California)
Jun Huan (Information and Telecommunication Technology Center)
Heng Huang (University of Texas)
Ling Huang (Intel Labs)
Seung-won Hwang (POSTECH)
Tomoharu Iwata (NTT Communication Science Laboratories)
Arun Iyer (IIT Bombay)
Prateek Jain (Microsoft Research)
Szymon Jaroszewicz (Polish Academy of Sciences)
Shuiwang Ji (Old Dominion University)
Hongxia Jin (IBM Research)
Ruoming Jin (Kent State University)
Wen Jin (Simon Fraser University)
Xiaoming Jin (Tsinghua University)
Panos Kalnis (KAUST)
Jaap Kamps (University of Amsterdam)
U Kang (KAIST)
Murat Kantarcioglu (University of Texas at Dallas)
Hisashi Kashima (The University of Tokyo)
Kristian Kersting (University of Bonn)
Myunghwan Kim (LinkedIn)
Ron Kohavi (Microsoft)
George Kollios (Boston University)
Christian Konig (Microsoft Research)
Nick Koudas (University of Toronto)
Stefan Kramer (Johannes Gutenberg - Universität Mainz)
Andreas Krause (ETH Zurich)
Peer Kroger (Ludwig-Maximilians-Universität München)
Wai Lam (The Chinese University of Hong Kong)
Theodoros Lappas (Stevens Institute of Technology)
Quoc Le (Google/CMU)
Dongwon Lee (Penn State University)
Mong-Li Lee (National University of Singapore)
Victor Lee (Kent State University)
Kristina Lerman (The University of Southern California)
Cheng-Te Li (National Taiwan University)
Guoliang Li (Tsinghua University)
Hang Li (Huawei Technologies)
Juanzi Li (Tsinghua University)
Ninghui Li (Purdue University)
Xiaoli Li (Institute for Infocomm Research)
Yuefeng Li (Queensland University of Technology)
Zhenhui Li (Penn State University)
Bangyong Liang (Microsoft Incorporation)
Ee-Peng Lim (Singapore Management University)
Hsuan-Tien Lin (National Taiwan University)
Charles Ling (Western University)
Chao Liu (Sogou Inc.)
Fei Liu (Carnegie Mellon University)
Guimei Liu (National University of Singapore)
Nathan Nan Liu (Yahoo! Labs)
Shixia Liu (Microsoft Research)
Tie-Yan Liu (Microsoft Research)
Yan Liu (University of Southern California)
David Lo (Singapore Management University)
Hung-Yi Lo (Shih-Chien University)
Yue Lu (Twitter, Inc.)
Chang-Tien Lu (Virginia Tech)
Dijun Luo (RetailMeNot)
Jiebo Luo (Rochester University)
Ping Luo (HP Lab)
Ashwin Machanavajjhala (Duke University)
Donato Malerba (University of Bari)
Hiroshi Mamitsuka (Kyoto University)
Nikos Mamoulis (University of Hong Kong)
Julian McAuley (Stanford University)
Qiaozhu Mei (University of Michigan)
Wagner Meira Jr (Universidade Federal de Minas Gerais)
Weiyi Meng (Binghamton University)
Vahab Mirrokni (Google Research)
Dunja Mladenic (J. Stefan Institute)
Katharina Morik (University of Dortmund)
Klaus-Robert Muller (TU Berlin)
Emmanuel Muller (Karlsruhe Institute of Technology (KIT))
Mirco Nanni (Istituto I.S.T.I.)

Alexandros Nanopoulos (University of Eichstätt-Ingolstadt)
Vivek Narasayya (Microsoft Research)
Franco Nardini (Information Science and Technologies Institute)
Olfa Nasraoui (University of Louisville)
Jennifer Neville (Purdue University)
Raymond Ng (University of British Columbia)
See-Kiong Ng (Institute for Infocomm Research)
Wilfred Ng (The Hong Kong University of Science and Technology)
Zaiqing Nie (Microsoft Research Asia)
Siegfried Nijssen (Leiden University)
Tim Oates (University of Maryland Baltimore County)
Zoran Obradovic (Temple University)
Iadh Ounis (University of Glasgow)
Gerhard Paass (Fraunhofer IAIS)
Rong Pan (Sun Yat-Sen University)
Spiros Papadimitriou (IBM)
Laurence Park (Univ. of Western Sydney)
Douglass Parker (University of California)
Vladimir Pavlovic (Rutgers University)
Dino Pedreschi (University of Pisa)
Wen-Chih Peng (National Chiao Tung University)
Chang-Shing Perng (IBM Research)
Bernhard Pfahringer (The University of Waikato)
Claudia Plant (The Florida State University)
Aditya Prakash (Virginia Tech)
Kunal Punera (Yahoo! Research)
Weining Qian (East China Normal University)
Kira Radinsky (Sales Predict)
Troy Raeder (Media6Degrees)
Ganesh Ramakrishnan (IIT Bombay)
Sujith Ravi (Google)
Chandan Reddy (Wayne State University)
Steffen Rendle (University of Konstanz)
Matthias Renz (Ludwig-Maximilians-Universität München)
Lior Rokach (Ben-Gurion University of the Negev)
Stefan Ruping (Fraunhofer IAIS)
Ankan Saha (LinkedIn)
Lorenza Saitta (University of Torino)
Yasushi Sakurai (Kumamoto University)
Jorg Sander (University of Alberta)
Maria Sapino (University of Torino)
Tamas Sarlos (Google)
Shin'ichi Satoh (National Institute of Informatics)
Ralf Schenkel (Max-Planck-Institut für Informatik)
Lars Schmidt-Thieme (Stiftung Universität Hildesheim)
Jeff Schneider (Carnegie Mellon University)
Dou Shen (CityGrid Media)
Heng Shen (The University of Queensland)
Jialie Shen (Singapore Management University)
Yelong Shen (Kent State University)
Yi-Dong Shen (Chinese Academy of Sciences)
Kyuseok Shim (Seoul National University)
Fabrizio Silvestri (Yahoo! Labs)
Vikas Sindhwani (IBM T.J.Watson Research Center)
Parag Singla (IIT Delhi)
Le Song (Georgia Institute of Technology)
Yangqiu Song (University of Illinois at Urbana-Champaign)
Myra Spiliopoulou (Otto-von-Guericke-Universitaet Magdeburg)
Rohini Srihari (University at Buffalo)
Gerd Stumme (University of Kassel)
Karthik Subbian (IBM T.J. Watson Labs)
L Subramaniam (IBM Research - India)
Torsten Suel (Polytechnic Institute of NYU)
Masashi Sugiyama (Tokyo Institute of Technology)
Aixin Sun (Nanyang Technological University)
Jian-Tao Sun (Microsoft Research)
Yizhou Sun (Northeastern Univ)
Einoshin Suzuki (Kyushu University)
Partha Talukdar (Carnegie Mellon University)
Ah-Hwee Tan (Nanyang Technological University)
Dacheng Tao (The University of Technology)
Yufei Tao (Chinese University of Hong Kong)
Nikolaj Tatti (Aalto University)
Alex Thomo (University of Victoria)
YongHong Tian (Peking University)
Hanghang Tong (IBM Research)
Agma Traina (University of São Paulo at São Carlos)
Volker Tresp (Ludwig Maximilian University of Munich/Siemens)
Panayiotis Tsaparas (University of Ioannina)
Vincent Tseng (National Cheng Kung University)
Jaideep Vaidya (Rutgers University)
Sergei Vassilvitskii (Google)
Michalis Vazirgiannis (Athens University of Economics and Business)
Suresh Venkatasubramanian (University of Utah)
Michail Vlachos (IBM Zurich Research Laboratory)

Jilles Vreeken (Max-Planck Institute for Informatics and Saarland University)
Slobodan Vucetic (Temple University)
Bai Wang (Bejing University of Posts and Telecommunications)
Fei Wang (IBM T. J. Watson Research Lab)
Hua Wang (Colorado School of Mines)
Jian Wang (LinkedIn)
Jianyong Wang (Tsinghua University)
Ke Wang (Simon Fraser University)
Shaojun Wang (Kno.e.sis)
Shengrui Wang (University of Sherbrooke)
Takashi Washio (Osaka University)
Ingmar Weber (Qatar Computing Research Institute)
Zhen Wen (IBM Research)
Tim Weninger (University of Notre Dame)
Robert West (Stanford University)
Raymond Wong (Hong Kong University of Science and Technology)
Junjie Wu (Beihang University)
Teresa Wu (Arizona State University)
Xintao Wu (University of North Carolina at Charlotte)
Evan Xiang (Baidu)
Xiaokui Xiao (Nanyang Technological University)
Yanghua Xiao (Fudan University)
Xing Xie (Microsoft Research Asia)
Takeshi Yamada (NTT Communication Science Laboratories)
Feng Yan (Facebook)
Rong Yan (Facebook)
De-Nian Yang (Academic Sinica)
Jaewon Yang (LinkedIn)
Jieping Ye (Arizona State University)
Mi-Yen Yeh (Academic Sinica)
Ainur Yesenalina (Amazon)
Dit-Yan Yeung (Hong Kong University of Science and Technology)
Emine Yilmaz (Microsoft Research)
Jie Yin (CSIRO ICT)
Hwanjo Yu (POSTECH)
Lei Yu (Binghamton University)
Shipeng Yu (Siemens Medical Solutions)
Xiao Yu (University of Illinois)
Yang Yu (Nanjing University)
Jing Yuan (Microsoft Research Asia)
Hyokun Yun (Purdue University)
Carlo Zaniolo (University of California)
Gerson Zaverucha (Federal University of Rio de Janeiro)
Dan Zhang (Facebook)
Kun Zhang (Max Planck Institute for Intelligent Systems)
Nan Zhang (The George Washington University)
Peng Zhang (Chinese Academy of Sciences)
Shichao Zhang (University of Technology)
Xiang Zhang (Case Western Reserve University)
Xiangliang Zhang (KAUST)
Xiaodan Zhang (Vertex Pharmaceuticals Inc.)
Xinhua Zhang (NICTA)
Zhaojun Zhang (UNC)
Zhenjie Zhang (ADSC)
Zhongfei Zhang (Binghamton University)
Peng Zhang (Chinese Academy of Science)
Bo Zhao (Microsoft Research)
Yuchen Zhao (Sumo Logic)
Zheng Zhao (SAS)
Yu Zheng (Microsoft)
Wenjun Zhou (University of Tennessee)
Feida Zhu (Singapore Management University)
Jun Zhu (Tsinghua University)
Xingquan Zhu (University of Technology)
Arthur Zimek (Ludwig-Maximilians-Universität München)

KDD'14 Industry & Government Track Senior Program Committee

KDD'14 Industry & Government Track Program Committee

Dean Abbott (Abbott Analytics)
Naoki Abe (IBM T.J. Watson Research Center)
Kareem Aggour (GE Global Research)
Kamal Ali (Grokker)
Ricardo Baeze-Yates (UPF)
Michele Berlingerio (IBM Research Dublin)
Michael Berthold (KNIME)
Kanishka Bhaduri (NASA)
Christos Boutsidis (IBM)
Tilmann Bruckhaus (Outright)
Rui Cai (Microsoft Research)
Berkant Barla Cambazoglu (Yahoo! Research, Barcelona)
Longbing Cao (University of Technology Sydney)
Yunbo Cao (Microsoft Research Asia)
Charlie Catlett (University of Chicago)
Haifeng Chen (NEC Research Lab)
Wei Chen (Microsoft Research)
Weizhu Chen (Microsoft)
Ye Chen (Microsoft)
Ira Cohen (HP)
Rob Cooley (Optimine)
Chad Cumby (PNT Financial)
Michelandgelo D'Agostino (BrainTree)
Brian Dalessandro (Dstillery)
Kamalika Das (NASA Ames Research Center)
Atish Das Sarma (eBay Research Labs)
Wei Ding (University of Massachusetts Boston)
Anlei Dong (Yahoo! Labs)
Pinar Donmez (Salesforce)
Seymour Douglas (Deloitte)
Gideon Dror (Yahoo! Labs)
Wei Fan (IBM Research)
Andrew Fano (Accenture)
Marcus Fontoura (Google)
Dayne Freitag (SRI)
Ryohei Fujimaki (NEC Laboratories America)
Shalini Ghosh (SRI)
David Hardcastle (GCHQ, UK)
Michael Hart (Google)
Qi He (LinkedIn)
Shawndra Hill (U Penn Wharton)
Jianying Hu (IBM T.J. Watson Research Center)
Ling Huang (Intel Labs)
Mario Inchiosa (IBM)
Sergei Izrailev (Collective)
Alex Jaimes (Yahoo!)
Prateek Jain (Microsoft Research - India)
Bin Jiang (Facebook)
Daxin Jiang (Microsoft)
Hongxia Jin (IBM Research)
George John (Rocket Fuel Inc.)
Vanja Josifovski (Google)
Christian Konig (Microsoft Research)
Georgia Koutrika (HP Labs)
Rui Kuang (University of Minnesota)
Mohit Kumar (Accenture)
Mounia Lalmas (Yahoo! Labs Barcelona)
Ming-Long Lam (SAS)
Richard Lawrence (IBM Research)
Aleksandar Lazarevic (Travelers)
Bangyong Liang (Microsoft Incorporation)
Nathan Nan Liu (Yahoo! Labs)
Shixia Liu (Microsoft Research)
Tie-Yan Liu (Microsoft Research)
Yue Lu (Twitter, Inc.)
Jiebo Luo (University of Rochester)
Ping Luo (HP Lab)
Mohammad Mahdian (Google)
Arun Maiya (Institute for Defense Analyses)
Manish Marwah (HP Labs)
Sameep Mehta (IBM Research - India)
Vahab Mirrokni (Google Research)
Thomas Montgomery (Ford Motor Company)
Vivek Narasayya (Microsoft Research)
Suman Nath (Microsoft Research)
Zaiqing Nie (Microsoft Research Asia)
Feng Pan (Microsoft)
Gaurav Pandey (Mount Sinai School of Medicine)
Rina Panigrahy (Microsoft Research)
Spiros Papadimitriou (IBM)
Jan Pedersen (Microsoft)
Ana-Maria Popescu (Consultant)
Ned Porter (Census)

Troy Raeder (Media6Degrees)
Matthew Rattigan (Edgeflip)
Karl Rexer (Rexer Analytics)
Romer Rosales (LinkedIn)
Ramendra Sahoo (Citi)
Krishna Sankar (TCS)
Mohak Shah (GE Global Research)
Jimi Shanahan (Consultant)
Abhishek Sharma (NEC Research Lab)
Dou Shen (CityGrid Media)
Amy Shi-Nash (SingTel)
Alexander Smola (Carnegie Mellon University)
Ramakrishnan Srikant (Google)
L Subramaniam (IBM Research - India)
Gordon Guo-zheng Sun (Sun Tencent Technology)
Jian-Tao Sun (Microsoft Research)
Jimeng Sun (Georgia Tech)
Neel Sundaresan (eBay Research)
Shu Tao (IBM Research)
Wayne Thompson (SAS)
Hanghang Tong (IBM Research)
Volker Tresp (Ludwig Maximilian University of Munich/Siemens)
Ranga Vatsavai (Oak Ridge National Labs)
Darren Vengroff (Rich Relevance)
Michail Vlachos (IBM Zurich Research Laboratory)
Fei Wang (IBM T.J. Watson Research Lab)
Zhen Wen (IBM Research)
Graham Williams (Togaware)
Michael Witbrock (Cyc)
Xing Xie (Microsoft Research Asia)
Oksana Yakhnenko (Google)
Rong Yan (Facebook)
Jiangang Yu (Microsoft)
Shipeng Yu (Siemens Medical Solutions)
Kun Zhang (Max Planck Institute for Intelligent Systems)
Bo Zhao (Microsoft Research)
Zheng Zhao (SAS)
Yu Zheng (Microsoft Research)
Scott Zoldi (FICO)
Peter van der Putten (Pegasystems & Leiden University)

KDD'14 Research Track Additional Reviewers

Sofiane Abbar (Qatar Computing Research Institute)
Ibrahim Abdelaziz (KAUST)
Ehab Abdelhamid (KAUST)
Ameeta Agrawal (York University)
Zahra Ahmadi (University of Mainz)
Cuneyt Gurcan Akcora (Qatar Computing Research Institute)
Shahid Alam (University of Victoria)
Darko Aleksovski (JSI, Ljubljana)
Razen Al-Harbi (KAUST)
Khalil Al-Hussaeni (Concordia University)
Sarah Alkhodair (Concordia University)
Vania Almeida (LIAAD-INESC TEC)
Stefanos Antaris (Aristotle University of Thessaloniki)
Shuang Ao (Western University)
Karim Awara (KAUST)
Yukino Baba (National Institute of Informatics)
Ahmet Bakan (Kabbage Inc.)
Anu Banerjee (Siemens Medical Solutions)
Gabor Bartok (ETH Zurich)
Daniel Bartz (TU Berlin)
Daniel Bengs (DIPF Frankfurt/Main)
Hendrik Blom (TU Dortmund University)
Kenneth Sejdenfaden Bøgh (Aarhus University)
Mohamed Bouguessa (Universite du Quebec at Montreal)
Panagiotis Bouros (Humboldt University Berlin)
Janez Brank (Jozef Stefan Institute)
Mikio Braun (TU Berlin)
Ivan Brugere (University of Illinois at Chicago)
Yilin Cai (University of Hong Kong)
K. Selcuk Candan (Arizona State University)
Xi hang Cao (Temple University)
AlexanFaria de Carvalho (INESC TEC)
Diego Ceccarelli (IMT Institute for Advanced Studies, Lucca)
Janathan Chang (Facebook)
Changyou Chen (National ICT Australia)
Chun-Hao Chen (Tamkang University Taipei)
Danqi Chen (Stanford University)
Lifei Chen (Fujian Normal University)
Ning Chen (SCE, NTU)
Ting Chen (NEU)
Yuxin Chen (ETH Zurich)
Dehua Cheng (USC)
Shiwen Cheng (University of California, Riverside)
Sean Chester (Aarhus University)
Flavio Chierichetti (Sapienza University of Rome)
Belkacem Chikhaoui (University of Toronto)
Freddy Chong-Tat (CHUA)
Maria Christoforaki (NYU Poly)
Paolo Cintia (University of Pisa)
Yang Cong (Chinese Academy of Sciences)
João Paulo Cordeiro (University of Beira Interior / INESC-TEC)
Mario Cordeiro (LIAAD-INESC TEC)
Robson L. F. Cordeiro (University of São Paulo)
Michele Coscia (Harvard University)
Alceu Ferraz Costa (University of Sao Paulo)
Gaby Dagher (Concordia University)
Pradipto Das (University at Buffalo)
Wei-Yen Day (Purdue University)
Elnaz Delpisheh (York University)
Vasil Denchev (Google Inc.)
Hongbo Deng (Yahoo Labs)
Martin Dimkovski (York University)
Costas Dimopoulos (NYU)
Steven H. H. Ding (McGill University)
Huang Dong (Institute for Infocomm Research)
Xiaowen Dong (Ecole Polytechnique Fédérale de Lausanne (EPFL))
João Duarte (LIAAD-INESC)
Wouter Duivesteijn (TU Dortmund)
Ahmed El-Kishky
Nuno Escudeiro (ISEP, Porto)
Cristobal Esteban (Siemens)
Meng Fang (University of Technology, Sydney)
Yuan Fang (University of Illinois at Urbana Champaign)
Zheng Fang (Zhejiang University)
Elaine Faria (University of Uberlandia)
Jing Feng (University of Munich)
Wei Feng (Tsinghua University)
Carlos Ferreira (Liaad-Inesc Tec)

Ricky Fok (York University)
Manoel Vitor Macedo França (City University London)
Alberto De Francesco (ISTI-CNR)
Hao Fu (Microsoft Reserach)
Hao Fu (University of Science and Technology of China)
Fabio Fumarola (Università degli Studi di Bari "Aldo Moro")
Bin Gao (Microsoft Research)
Shi Gao (University of California, Los Angeles)
Tianshi Gao (Facebook)
Michael Geilke (University of Mainz)
Bluma Gelley (NYU)
Djordje Gligorijevic (Temple University)
Jean-Pierre Glouzon (University of Sherbrooke, Canada)
Nico Goernitz (Technical University Berlin)
Neil Zhenqiang Gong (University of California, Berkeley)
Alkis Gotovos (ETH Zurich)
Josif Grabocka (University of Hildesheim)
Yupeng Gu (NEU)
Huan Gui (University of Illinois at Urbana Champaign)
Riccardo Guidotti (University of Pisa)
Hongchen Guo (Tsinghua University)
Nima Haghpanah
Chao Han (Temple University)
Chunhui Han (Tsinghua University)
Melinda Han (Dstillery)
Xiantian Hao (HKUST)
Xiao He (University of Munich)
Zhouzhou He (Zhejiang University)
Shohei Hido (Preferred Infrastructure, Inc.)
Linmei HU (Tsinghua University)
Xiaocheng Hu (Chinese University of Hong Kong)
Shengyu Huang (Arizona State University)
Silu Huang (Chinese University of Hong Kong)
Yi-Hung Huang
Nina Hubig (Helmholtz Zentrum München)
Fuad Jamour (KAUST)
Zongcheng JI (Huawei Technologies)
Lili Jiang (Max Planck Institute for Informatics)
Xueyan Jiang (Ludwig-Maximilian University of Munich)
Ulf Johansson (University of Boras)
Aditya Johri (George Mason University)
Alipio Jorge (Universidade do Porto)
Shafiq Joty (Qatar Research)
Minsuk Kahng (Georgia Institute of Technology)
Hiroshi Kajino (The University of Tokyo)
David Kale (USC)
Michael Kamp (Fraunhofer IAIS)
Lakesh Kansakar (Temple University)
Alex Kantchelian (University of California, Berkeley)
Komal Kapoor (University of Minnesota)
Hima P Karanam (IBM Research-India)
Masayuki Karasuyama (Kyoto University)
Amin Karbasi (ETH Zurich)
Rasoul Karimi (University of Hildeshiem)
Isak Karlsson (Stockholm University)
Andreas Karwath (University of Mainz)
Gilad Katz (Ben Gurion University)
Fabian Keller (Karlsruhe Institute of Technology)
Zuhair Khayyat (KAUST)
Mark Kibanov (University of Kassel)
Doo Soon Kim (Bosch Research and Technology Center)
Mijung Kim (Arizona State University)
Dragi Kocev (Jozef Stefan Institute)
Giorgos Kollias
Xiangnan Kong (University of Illinois at Chicago)
Denis Krompass (Ludwig-Maximilian University of Munich)
Guo-Cheng Lan (National Cheng Kung University)
Ni Lao (Google)
Sangkyun Lee (TU Dortmund University)
Jurica Levatic (JSI, Ljubljana)
Qi Li (University at Buffalo)
Qing Li (University of Sherbrooke, Canada)
Rui Li (PRIME Research)
Xiang Li (University of Western University)
Xiaoyi Li (University at Buffalo)
Xinsheng Li (Arizona State University)
Yaliang Li (University at Buffalo)
Yan Li (Wayne State University)
Yingming Li (Zhejiang University)
Yuemeng Li (University of North Carolina at Charlotte)
Zhixing Li (Tsinghua University)

Defu Lian (University of Science and Technology of China & Microsoft Research)
Jianxun Lian (University of Science and Technology of China)
Hongwei Liang
Hongyu Liang (Facebook)
Yu Liang (Institute for Infocomm Research)
Thomas Liebig (TU Dortmund)
Luiz Alberto Lima (Petrobras)
Kawuu W. Lin (National Kaohsiung University of Applied Sciences)
Tian Lin (Tsinghua University)
Wenqing Lin (Nanyang Technological University)
Bo Liu (quare)
Jing Liu (Harbin Institute of Technology)
Lu Liu (Northwestern University)
Xiang Liu (NYU)
Yandong Liu (Yahoo! Labs)
Tuve Lofstrom (University of Boras)
Corrado Loglisci (University of Bari Aldo Moro)
Nikhil Londhe (University at Buffalo)
Eric Hsueh-Chan Lu (National Taitung University)
Yi Lu (Chinese University of Hong Kong)
Minh Luan (Nguyen Institute for Infocomm Research)
Yan Luo (Western University)
Lin Ma (Noah's Ark Lab, Huawei Technologies)
Zongyang Ma (Nanyang Technological University)
Craig Macdonald (University of Glasgow)
Björn Elmar Macek (University of Kassel)
Gjorgji Madjarov (University Ss. Cyril and Methodius, Skopje)
Hamid Mahini
Son T. Mai (University of Munich)
Silviu Maniu (University of Hong Kong)
Andreas Maunz (Oncotest)
Sam Maurus (Helmholtz-Zentrum München)
Giuseppe M. Mazzeo (University of California, Los Angeles)
Richard McCreadie (University of Glasgow)
Yashar Mehdad (UBC)
Rishabh Mehrotra (University College London)
Yelena Mejova (Qatar Computing Research Institute)
Lei Meng (Nanyang Technological University)
Barbora Micenkova (Aarhus University)
Letizia Milli (University of Pisa)
Luyi Mo (University of Hong Kong)
John Moeller (University of Utah)
Noman Mohammed (McGill University)
Anna Monreale (University of Pisa)
Grégoire Montavon (TU Berlin)
C. Moore (Santa Fe Institute)
Michael Lind Mortensen (Aarhus University)
Benjamin Moseley (TTI Institute)
Shinichi Nakajima (Nikon)
Benjamin Negrevergne (KU Leuven)
Ido Nevat (Institute for Infocomm Research)
M. E. J. Newman (University of Michigan)
Hoang Vu Nguyen (Karlsruhe Institute of Technology)
Rad Niazadeh (Cornell University)
Thomas Niebler
Yung-Kyun Noh (KAIST)
Nozomi Nori (Kyoto University)
Inna Novalija
Alja Osojnik (Josef Stefan Institute)
Panagiotis Papapetrou (Stockholm University)
Peng Peng (The Hong Kong University of Science and Technology)
Ruggero G. Pensa (University of Torino)
Antonio Penta (University of Turin)
Te Pi (Zhejiang University)
Nico Piatkowski (TU Dortmund University)
Gianvito Pio (University of Bari Aldo Moro)
Francesca Pratesi (University of Pisa)
Fang Qiong (HKUST)
Ahsanur Rahman (CS, VT)
Rajiur Rahman (Wayne State University)
Piyush Rai (Duke University)
Karthik Raman (Cornell University)
Dusan Ramljak (Temple University)
Xiang Ren (University of Illinois at Urbana Champaign)
Yazhou Ren (South China University of Technology)
Matt Revelle (George Mason University)
Marcela Xavier Ribeiro (Federal University of Sao Carlos)
Rita Ribeiro (LIAAD-INESC TEC)
Salvatore Rinzivillo (KDDLab-ISTI-CNR)
Jose Fernando Rodrigues (University of Sao Paulo)
Shoumik Roychoudhury
Delia Rusu (Jozef Stefan Institute)

Mrinmaya Sachan (Carnegie Mellon University)
Shouq Sadah (University of California, Riverside)
Tanwistha Saha (George Mason University)
Hiroaki Sasaki (Tokyo Institute of Technology)
Claudio Schifanella (Joint Research Centre - European Commission Ispra)
Nicolas Schilling (University of Hildesheim)
Jana Schmidt (TU München)
Erich Schubert (LMU Munich)
Lena Schwemmlein
Madeleine Seeland (TU München)
Moloud Shahbazi (University of California, Riverside)
Lifeng Shang (Noah's Ark Lab, Huawei Technologies)
Junming Shao (University of Mainz)
Wei Shen (Tsinghua University)
Jieming Shi (University of Hong Kong)
Yanchen Shi
Motoki Shiga (Gifu University)
Zhang Shitao (Tsinghua University)
Alexander Shkapsky
Sergio F. Silva (Federal University of Goias)
Adish Singla (ETH Zurich)
Ng Wee Siong (Institute for Infocomm Research)
George Skoumas
Vinícius M. A. de Souza (Instituto de Ciências Matemáticas e de Computação - ICMC/USP)
Ivan Stojkovic (Temple University)
Marco Stolpe (TU Dortmund University)
Dong Su (Purdue University)
Ja-Hwung Su (Kainan University)
Amar Subramanya (Google Research)
Umar Syed
Andrea Tagarelli (University of Calabria)
Tadej Tajner (Jožef Stefan Institute)
Ben Tan (HKUST)
Jovan Tanevski (JSI, Ljubljana)
Jun Tang (The Hong Kong University of Science and Technology)
Youze Tang (Nanyang Technological University)
Maryam Tavakol (TU Darmstadt)
Teck-Hou Teng (Nanyang Technological University)
Pavel Tokmakov (University of Bonn)
Daniel Trabold (Fraunhofer IAIS)
Caetano Traina, Jr. (University of Sao Paulo)
Mitja Trampus (Jozef Stefan Institute)
Emmanouil Tzouridis (TU Darmstadt)
Alexey Uversky (Temple University)
Hastagiri Vanchinathan (ETH Zurich)
Celine Vens (UGent)
Manisha Verma (University College London)
Sarah Vieweg (Qatar Computing Research Institute)
Bhanukiran Vinzamuri (Wayne State University)
Jan Vosecky (HKUST)
Dawei Wang (University of Massachusetts)
Hao Wang (University of Hong Kong)
Quan Wang (Chinese Academy of Sciences)
Yue Wang (University of North Carolina at Charlotte)
Zhigang WANG (Tsinghua University)
Chen Wei (Institute for Infocomm Research)
Steven Whang (Google Research)
Joerg Wicker (University of Mainz)
Matthew Wiley (University of California, Riverside)
Martin Wistuba (University of Hildesheim)
Dingming Wu (University of Hong Kong)
Huanhuan WU (The Chinese University of Hong Kong)
Le Wu (University of Science and Technology of China)
Wei Wu (Facebook)
Zhiang Wu (Nanjing University of Finance and Economics)
Daniel Xia (University of Victoria)
Houping Xiao (University at Buffalo)
Min Xie (The Hong Kong University of Science and Technology)
Jun Xu (Noah's Ark Lab, Huawei Technologies)
Tianbing Xu (Facebook)
Yanyan Xu (Chinese University of Hong Kong)
Zenglin Xu (Purdue University)
Yang Xuan (The University of Hong Kong)
Makoto Yamada (Yahoo Labs)
Da Yan (HKUST)
Ming Yang (Zhejiang University)
Mohan Yang
Jianhua Yin (Tsinghua University)
Josh Jia-Ching Ying (National Cheng-Kung University)
Jane You (Amazon.com)
Chung-Hsien Yu

Yaoliang Yu (Carnegie Mellon University)
Quan Yuan (Nanyang Technological University)
Kai Zeng
Kay Zeng
Bernard Zenko (Jozef Stefan Institute)
Chenyi Zhang
Fuzheng Zhang (University of Science and Technology of China)
Fuzheng Zhang (Microsoft Research)
Jianfei Zhang (University of Sherbrooke)
Jun Zhang (Nanyang Technological University)
Miao Zhang (University of Texas Arlington)
Ning Zhang (University of California, Berkeley)
Shanshan Zhang (Temple University)
Shaonan Zhang (Amazon.com)
Wangda Zhang (University of Hong Kong)
Wei Zhang (Tsinghua University)
Xian Zhang (Microsoft)
Yao Zhang (CS VT)
Jing Zhao (Stockholm University)
Kaiqi Zhao (Nanyang Technological University)
Kunsheng Zhao
Xueyi Zhao (Zhejiang University)
Vincent Zheng (Advanced Digital Sciences Center (ADSC))
Wen Zhong (Microsoft Research)
Yuan Zhong (Microsoft Research)
Linfei Zhou (University of Munich)
Yan Zhou (University of Texas at Dallas)
Zhao Zhou (HKUST)
Zhuojie Zhou (George Washington University)
Diwen Zhu (Nanyang Technological University)
Haohan Zhu (Boston University)
Linhong ZHU (University of Southern California)
Yin Zhu (Hong Kong University of Science and Technology)
Morteza Zihayat (York University)
Anastasios Zouzias (IBM Research)
Andreas Züfle (Ludwig-Maximilians-Universität München)

KDD'14 Sponsors & Supporters

Sponsors: KDD, ACM SIGMOD

Supporter: Platinum Bloomberg

Supporters: Gold BOSCH Invented for life, facebook, Microsoft, rapidminer

Supporters: Silver amazon, Baidu 百度, Booking.com, Goldman Sachs, Google, HUAWEI, IBM Research, IBM Watson, sas, SIEMENS

Supporters: Silver (continued)

Supporters: Bronze

Supporter: Research Paper Award

Supporter: Best Industry & Government Paper Award

Supporter: Best Test of Time Paper Award

Supporter: Lanyard Sponsor

Supporters: Media

Supporter: WiFi

Supporter: Mobile App

Supporters: KDD CUP

Supporter: Student Travel Awards

Supporter: Travel

Supporter: Program Ad

Exhibitors:

Fast DTT – A Near Linear Algorithm for Decomposing a Tensor into Factor Tensors

Xiaomin Fang
Department of Computer Science
School of Information Science and Technology
Sun Yat-sen University
Guangzhou, China
fangxmin@mail2.sysu.edu.cn

Rong Pan*
Department of Computer Science
School of Information Science and Technology
Sun Yat-sen University
Guangzhou, China
panr@sysu.edu.cn

ABSTRACT

As tensors provide a natural representation for the higher-order relations, tensor factorization techniques such as Tucker decomposition and CANDECOMP/PARAFAC decomposition have been applied to many fields. Tucker decomposition has strong capacity of expression, but the time complexity is unpractical for the large-scale real problems. On the other hand, CANDECOMP/PARAFAC decomposition is linear in the feature dimensionality, but the assumption is so strong that it abandons some important information. Besides, both of TD and CP decompose a tensor into several factor matrices. However, the factor matrices are not natural for the representation of the higher-order relations. To overcome these problems, we propose a near linear tensor factorization approach, which decompose a tensor into factor tensors in order to model the higher-order relations, without loss of important information. In addition, to reduce the time complexity and the number of the parameters, we decompose each slice of the factor tensors into two smaller matrices. We conduct experiments on both synthetic datasets and real datasets. The experimental results on the synthetic datasets validate that our model has strong capacity of expression. The results on the real datasets show that our approach outperforms the state-of-the-art tensor factorization methods.

Categories and Subject Descriptors

H.3.3 [**Information Storage and Retrieval**]: Information Search and Retrieval—*Information filtering*; I.2.6 [**Artificial Intelligence**]: Learning

Keywords

Tensor decomposition; DTT

*Corresponding author

KDD'14, August 24–27, 2014, New York, NY, USA.

http://dx.doi.org/10.1145/2623330.2623713 .

1. INTRODUCTION

Matrix factorization is used for modeling the second-order relations. For example, for the item recommendation problem, we can construct a user-item matrix. The user-item matrix is factorized into two factor matrices, representing the latent features of the users and the items, respectively. From the users' view, matrix factorization assumes the items are divided into D item-groups, where D denote the number of the elements in the vector. For user u, there is a corresponding vector of the factor matrix of the users, describing the relation between that user and the items. Each element of that vector represents the relevance between that user and a item-groups. From the items'view, the situation is similar.

Tensor is a higher-order extension of matrix and tensor factorization is a higher-order extension of matrix factorization. Since tensor decomposition can model the higher-order relations, tensor decomposition techniques are applied to many fields, such are psychology, chemometrics, computer vision and data mining. Traditional tensor decomposition techniques like Tucker decomposition (TD) [21] and CANDECOMP/PARAFAC (CP) [2, 9] decomposition factorize a tensor into several factor matrices. Take the problem of personalized tag recommendation for example. Traditional tensor decomposition techniques decompose a user-item-tag tensor into three factor matrices. Just like matrix factorization, from the users' view, for user u, there is a corresponding vector of the factor matrix of the users, indicating the relation between that user, the items and the tag, but we can not explain the meaning of each element in that vector by the same way we analyzing matrix factorization, since vector is not natural for the representation of the relations between that user, the item-groups and the tag-groups. Moreover, both of Tucker decomposition and CANDECOMP/PARAFAC have some drawbacks. Tucker decomposition has strong capacity of expression but it requires lots of computation power, which is unpractical for large-scale real problems. The other tensor factorization technique CANDECOMP/PARAFAC decomposition is linear in the feature dimensionality, but it makes a strong assumption that limits its capacity of expression.

To tackle all these problems, we propose a novel tensor factorization approach in this paper. We decompose a tensor into several factor tensors instead of factor matrices. From the users' view, for user u, there is a corresponding matrix of the factor tensor of the users, indicating the relation between that user, the items and the tag, and each element of that matrix can be seen as the relevance between that user, a item-group and a tag-group. Thus, the higher-order relations can be modeled by a more natural way. In addition, to reduce the time complexity and the number of the parameters, we decompose each slice of the factor tensors into two smaller matrices. Our proposed model is near linear and has strong capacity of expression.

The contributions of our work are summarized as follows.

- We propose a novel tensor decomposition approach, decomposing a tensor into factor tensors rather than factor matrices, which is more natural for the representation of the higher-order relations
- Our proposed approach has strong capacity of expression and is near linear, which is practical for the large-scale real problems.
- Our experimental results on the synthetic datasets verify that our proposed approach has strong capacity of expression and our proposed approach significantly outperforms other tensor factorization techniques on the real datasets.

The rest of the paper is organized as follows. The related work to tensor factorization techniques is depicted in the next section. The notations and preliminaries of tensor and tensor factorization are presented in section 3. Our proposed tensor decomposition approach is described in section 4. The experimental results on the synthetic datasets and the real datasets are showed and analyzed in section 5. Finally, we conclude our work in section 6.

2. RELATED WORK

Since tensors provide a natural representation for the higher-order relations, they are applied to many fields [12], including chemometrics [1], neuroscience [13], graph analysis [18, 6, 5, 24], personalized recommendation [19, 24, 11, 14, 17, 7, 20, 16, 23] and so on. Tucker decomposition (TD) [21] and CANDECOMP/PARAFAC decomposition (CP) [2, 9] are the most common techniques to decompose a tensor, where Tucker decomposition has stronger capacity of expression and CANDECOMP/PARAFAC decomposition can be trained in linear time.

Some researches are based on Tucker decomposition (TD) [3, 4, 19, 11, 14]. Higher-Order Singular Value Decomposition (HOSVD) [3, 4], a generation of the matrix Singular Value Decomposition (SVD), is introduced for computing Tucker decomposition. Sun et al. [19] construct a user-query-URL tensor from the clickthrough data in the search engines and employ HOSVD to capture the latent factors of users, queries and URLs for personalized web search. Karatzoglou et al. [11] integrate the context information into the traditional collaborative filtering models to improve the recommendation quality by making use of HOSVD as well. However, one of the drawbacks of HOSVD is that it can not deal with the missing data in the sparse tensors. It treats the values of all the missing elements in the tensors as zeros. To fix this problem, Rendle et al. [14] propose a method called RTF, which exploits Bayesian Personalized Ranking (BPR) [15] and learns from pairwise constraints, for personalized tag recommendation. Although TD has a strong capacity of expression for the higher-order relations, the time complexity of which is not feasible for large-scale real problems.

On the other hand, some studies employ CP decomposition (CANDECOMP/PARAFAC decomposition) [5, 23, 17]. Dunlavy, Kolda, and Acar [5] incorporate the time information for link predictions. The first two dimensions of the tensor represent the entities and the third dimension represents the time slices. They decompose the tensor by CP. Similarly, Xiong et al. [23] take the time into consideration and add a special constraint on the time dimension. Work by Rendle and Schmidt-Thieme [17] puts forward a new tensor factorization technique, Pairwise Interaction Tensor Factorization (PITF) for personalized tag recommendation. PITF can be seen as a special case of CP, modeling the pairwise interactions between the three dimensions of the user-item-tag tensor. The CP-based models can be trained in linear time, but it abandons some important information and restricts the capacity of expression.

Furthermore, both TD and CP decompose a tensor into several factor matrices, but the factor matrices are not natural for the representation of the higher-order relations, since matrices can only represent the second-order relations. Therefore, we propose a novel tensor factorization approach in this paper, which decomposes a tensor into several factor tensors instead.

3. NOTATIONS AND PRELIMINARIES

In this section, we first introduce tensor and the notations. Then, we depict two most common tensor factorization techniques, Tucker decomposition and CANDECOMP/PARAFAC, and analyze the advantages and the disadvantages of them.

3.1 Tensor

A tensor is a multidimensional or multi-way array and the order of a tensor is the number of the dimensions or modes. Vectors are first-order tensors, matrices are second-order tensors and tensors of order three or higher are called higher-order tensors. Matrices have column and row, a column and a row of which are called mode-1 vector and mode-2 vector respectively. Similar to matrices, the third-order tensors have column, row and tube and a tube is a mode-3 vector. Since the constructions of the higher-order tensors are similar, we focus on the third-order tensors and the third-order tensors are called tensors for short in the following paper.

Matrices and tensors are denoted by boldface capital letters, e.g., $\mathbf{X}$. Element (i, j) of a matrix $\mathbf{X}$ is denoted by x_{ij} and element (i, j, k) of a tensor $\mathbf{A}$ is denoted by a_{ijk}.

3.2 Tensor Decomposition

Just like matrix factorization, tensor decomposition techniques factorize a tensor into several components. Tucker decomposition (TD) [21] and CANDECOMP/PARAFAC decomposition (CP) [2, 9] are the most common tensor decomposition techniques and can be seen as higher-order generations of the matrix factorization, Singular Value Decomposition (SVD) [8].

Tensor decomposition techniques have been applied to personalized tag recommendation. For the sake of convenience of analysis, let's take the personalized tag recommendation problem for example in the following paper. A user-item-tag tensor $\mathbf{A} \in \mathbb{R}^{I \times J \times K}$ is constructed from the social tagging data, where I, J, K denote the number of the users, the items and the tags, respectively. Element a_{ijk} of tensor $\mathbf{A}$ measures the probability of the i-th user annotat-

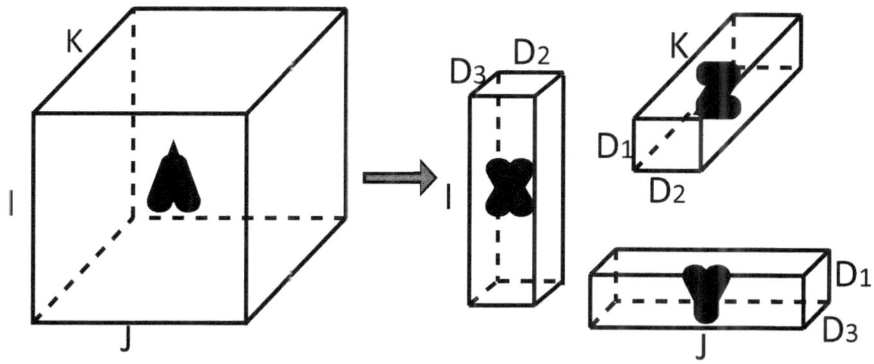

Figure 1: DTT: A novel tensor factorization model

ing the j-th item with the k-th tag. We treat all of the users, the items and the tags as three different types of entities.

Tucker decomposition (TD) [21] was first introduced by Tucker in 1966. It decomposes a tensor into a core tensor multiplied by a matrix along each mode. Element a_{ijk} of tensor $\mathbf{A} \in \mathbb{R}^{I \times J \times K}$ can be written as

$$a_{ijk} = \sum_{p=1}^{D_1} \sum_{q=1}^{D_2} \sum_{r=1}^{D_3} c_{pqr} \cdot x_{ip} \cdot y_{jq} \cdot z_{kr}, \qquad (1)$$

where $\mathbf{X} \in \mathbb{R}^{I \times D_1}$, $\mathbf{Y} \in \mathbb{R}^{J \times D_2}$, $\mathbf{Z} \in \mathbb{R}^{K \times D_3}$ are the factor matrices and $\mathbf{C} \in \mathbb{R}^{D_1 \times D_2 \times D_3}$ is the core tensor. D_1, D_2 and D_3 are the numbers of the latent features. Given a factor matrix, a vector of that matrix represents the latent features of the corresponding entity. For user i, item j and tag k, c_{pqr} of the core tensor $\mathbf{C}$ indicates the relevance between the p-th feature of user i, the q-th feature of item j and the r-th feature of tag k.

CANDECOMP/PARAFAC decomposition (CP) [2, 9] decomposes a tensor into a sum of component rank-one tensors. $a_{i,j,k}$ can be written as

$$a_{ijk} = \sum_{p=1}^{D} x_{ip} \cdot y_{jp} \cdot z_{kp}, \qquad (2)$$

where $\mathbf{X} \in \mathbb{R}^{I \times D}$, $\mathbf{Y} \in \mathbb{R}^{J \times D}$, $\mathbf{Z} \in \mathbb{R}^{K \times D}$ are the factor matrices and D is the number of latent features. For user i, item j and tag k, CP makes a strong assumption that the p-th feature of user i, x_{ip} is only relevant to the p-th feature of item j, y_{jp} and the p-th feature of tag k, z_{kp}. In other words, it assumes x_{ip} is independent of y_{jq} and z_{kr}, where $p \neq q$ and $p \neq r$. As generally $D << I, J, K$ on real problems, the assumption limits CP's capacity of expression.

TD is more flexible and can model the higher-order relations better, but it requires lots of computation power. Therefore, TD is not practical for large-scale real problems. On the other hand, CP is linear in the feature dimensionality, but it gives up some important information. To overcome the drawbacks, we propose a near linear tensor decomposition technique, which is practical for large-scale problems, without lost of information.

4. DECOMPOSING A TENSOR INTO FACTOR TENSORS

In this section, we explain our proposed tensor factorization approach and how to compute our model. Besides, we compare our proposed approach with other tensor factorization techniques on the time complexity, the space complexity and the capacity of expression.

4.1 Tensor Factorization Model DTT

Singular Value Decomposition (SVD) factorize a matrix into two smaller factor matrices and the factor matrices present the the second-order relations. Tensor factorization is a higher-order generation of matrix factorization. Traditional tensor decomposition techniques like TD and CP, decomposing a tensor $\mathbf{A} \in \mathbb{R}^{I \times J \times K}$ into factor matrices, but the factor matrices are not proper for presenting the higher-order relations. Different from TD and CP, we decompose the tensor $\mathbf{A}$ into factor tensors, since the representation of a factor tensor is more natural for the higher-order relations, compared with the representation of a factor matrix. We refer our proposed tensor factorization approach to decomposing a tensor into tensors (DTT). The framework of our proposed tensor factorization model is illustrated in Figure 1. From the figure, we can see that tensor $\mathbf{A}$ is factorized into three smaller factor tensors $\mathbf{X} \in \mathbb{R}^{I \times D_2 \times D_3}$, $\mathbf{Y} \in \mathbb{R}^{J \times D_3 \times D_1}$ and $\mathbf{Z} \in \mathbb{R}^{K \times D_1 \times D_2}$, where D_1, D_2 and D_3 are parameters of the DTT model (e.g., taking personalized social tagging as an example, they can been seen as the numbers of the user groups, the item groups and the tag groups, respectively).

Since we decompose a tensor into factor tensors rather than factor matrices, the latent features of an entity are represented by a matrix rather than a vector. $D_2 \times D_3$ is the size of the factor matrix of a user, $D_3 \times D_1$ is the size of the factor matrix of an item and $D_1 \times D_2$ is the size of the factor matrix of a tag. From the users' view, the factor matrix of user i, the i-th slice in $\mathbf{X}$, which is denoted by $\mathbf{X}_{i::}$, contains D_2 rows and D_3 columns. It can be assumed that for user i, all the items are divided into D_2 item-groups and the q-th row of $\mathbf{X}_{i::}$ represents the characters of the q-th item-group. Similarly, for user i, all the tags are divided into D_3 tag-groups and the r-th column of $\mathbf{X}_{i::}$ represents the characters of the r-th tag-group. Thus, x_{iqr} means the relevance between user i, the items in the q-th item-group and the tags in the r-th tag-group. That is to say, matrix $\mathbf{X}_{i::}$ indicates the preference of user i under different conditions. The analysis from the views of the items and the tags is similar.

Our proposed approach DTT models the higher-order relations by modeling the relations between the user-groups,

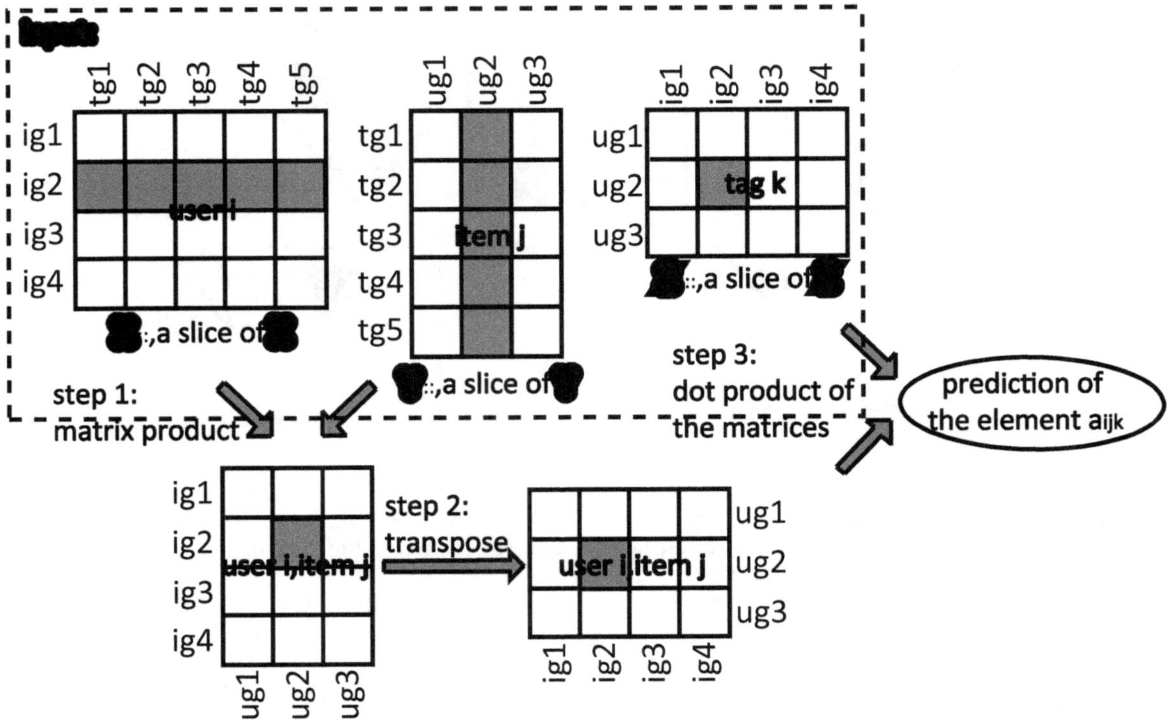

Figure 2: Reconstruction of the tensor elements from the three slices of the factor tensors

the item-groups and the tag-groups. For triplet (i, j, k), the way how we predict the value of that triplet is illustrated in Figure 2, where *ug*, *ig* and *tg* are short for the user-group, the item-group and the tag-group.

- In step 1, we compute the matrix product of the factor matrix of user i, $\mathbf{X}_{i::} \in \mathbb{R}^{D_2 \times D_3}$ and the factor matrix of item j, $\mathbf{Y}_{j::} \in \mathbb{R}^{D_3 \times D_1}$. Thus, the factor matrices of user i and item j are integrated into a new factor matrix $\mathbf{G}^{(ij)} \in \mathbb{R}^{D_2 \times D_1}$ by their multiplication. That is, $\mathbf{G}^{(ij)} = \mathbf{X}_{\mathbf{i}::}\mathbf{Y}_{\mathbf{j}::}$.

- In step 2, we transpose the new factor matrix $\mathbf{G}^{(ij)} \in \mathbb{R}^{D_2 \times D_1}$ to make its dimension be the same as the dimension of the factor matrix of tag k, $\mathbf{Z}_{k::} \in \mathbb{R}^{D_1 \times D_2}$.

- Finally, in step 3, we define the prediction of the tensor element a_{ijk} as the inner product of two matrices $(\mathbf{G}^{(ij)})^{\mathbf{T}} \in \mathbb{R}^{D_1 \times D_2}$ and the factor matrix of tag k, $\mathbf{Z}_{k::} \in \mathbb{R}^{D_1 \times D_2}$. That is,

$$a_{ijk} = \left\langle (\mathbf{G}^{(ij)})^{\mathbf{T}}, \mathbf{Z}_{k::} \right\rangle = \left\langle (\mathbf{X}_{\mathbf{i}::}\mathbf{Y}_{\mathbf{j}::})^{\mathbf{T}}, \mathbf{Z}_{k::} \right\rangle, \quad (3)$$

  where the inner product of matrices $\mathbf{X}, \mathbf{Y} \in \mathbb{R}^{\mathbf{m} \times \mathbf{n}}$ is defined as

$$\langle \mathbf{X}, \mathbf{Y} \rangle = \sum_{i=1}^{m} \sum_{j=1}^{n} x_{ij} y_{ij}.$$

Note that Eq. (3) is equivalent to

$$a_{ijk} = \sum_{p=1}^{D_1} \sum_{q=1}^{D_2} \sum_{r=1}^{D_3} x_{iqr} \cdot y_{jrp} \cdot z_{kpq}, \quad (4)$$

where $\mathbf{X} \in \mathbb{R}^{I \times D_2 \times D_3}$, $\mathbf{Y} \in \mathbb{R}^{J \times D_3 \times D_1}$ and $\mathbf{Z} \in \mathbb{R}^{K \times D_1 \times D_2}$ are the factor tensors. As the order of x_{iqr}, y_{jrp} and z_{kpq} has no influence on computing a_{ijk} in Eq. (4), the order of the factor matrices of user i, item j and tag k in Figure 2 has no influence on computing the relevance score, which is a good property as follows.

Property 1. The prediction of tensor element a_{ijk} is well defined. That is,

$$\begin{aligned} a_{ijk} &= \left\langle (\mathbf{X}_{\mathbf{i}::}\mathbf{Y}_{\mathbf{j}::})^{\mathbf{T}}, \mathbf{Z}_{k::} \right\rangle & (5) \\ &= \left\langle (\mathbf{Y}_{\mathbf{j}::}\mathbf{Z}_{\mathbf{k}::})^{\mathbf{T}}, \mathbf{X}_{i::} \right\rangle & (6) \\ &= \left\langle (\mathbf{Z}_{\mathbf{k}::}\mathbf{X}_{\mathbf{i}::})^{\mathbf{T}}, \mathbf{Y}_{j::} \right\rangle. & (7) \end{aligned}$$

4.2 Fast DTT

Although DTT can capture the higher-order relations, the time complexity to calculate Eq. (4) is $\mathcal{O}(D_1 D_2 D_3)$, which is unacceptable for the large-scale real problems. Besides, there are too many parameters in DTT that it may lead to overfitting, the space complexity of which is $\mathcal{O}(ID_2D_3 + JD_3D_1 + KD_1D_2)$, where I, J and K denote the numbers of the users, the items and the tags, repectively. Note that, for each entity, there is a factor matrix describe the features of that entity. To reduce the number of parameters and the time complexity, we decompose the factor matrix of each entity into two smaller matrices. For user i, the factor matrix $\mathbf{X}_{i::} \in \mathbb{R}^{D_2 \times D_3}$ are decomposed into two smaller matrices $\mathbf{X}^{(l)}_{i::} \in \mathbb{R}^{D_2 \times d_1}$ and $\mathbf{X}^{(r)}_{i::} \in \mathbb{R}^{D_3 \times d_1}$. For item j, the factor matrix $\mathbf{Y}_{j::} \in \mathbb{R}^{D_3 \times D_1}$ are decomposed into two smaller matrices $\mathbf{Y}^{(l)}_{j::} \in \mathbb{R}^{D_3 \times d_2}$ and $\mathbf{Y}^{(r)}_{j::} \in \mathbb{R}^{D_1 \times d_2}$. For tag k, the factor matrix $\mathbf{Z}_{k::} \in \mathbb{R}^{D_1 \times D_2}$ are decomposed into two

Table 1: Comparison between DTT, Tucker decomposition (TD) and CANDECOMP/PARAFAC (CP)

Algorithm	Time Complexity		Space Complexity
	Train	Predict	
DTT	$\mathcal{O}(Dd^2NT)$	$\mathcal{O}(Dd^2)$	$\mathcal{O}(Dd^2I)$
TD	$\mathcal{O}(D^3NT)$	$\mathcal{O}(D^3)$	$\mathcal{O}(D^3I)$
CP	$\mathcal{O}(DNT)$	$\mathcal{O}(D)$	$\mathcal{O}(DI)$

smaller matrices $\mathbf{Z}_{k::}^{(l)} \in \mathbb{R}^{D_1 \times d_3}$ and $\mathbf{Z}_{j::}^{(r)} \in \mathbb{R}^{D_2 \times d_3}$. d_1, d_2 and d_3 are the numbers of latent features of the factor matrices $\mathbf{X}_{i::}$, $\mathbf{Y}_{j::}$ and $\mathbf{Z}_{k::}$, respectively. Additionally, d_1, d_2 and d_3 should satisfy $d_1 \leq min(D_2, D_3)$, $d_2 \leq min(D_3, D_1)$ and $d_3 \leq min(D_1, D_2)$. d_1, d_2 and d_3 depend on the complexity of the pairwise relations. For example, if the relation between the items and the tags is complex for the users, d_1 should be large so as to reconstruct the factor matrices of the users and if the relation between the items and the tags is simple, d_1 is small. Concretely, from the users' view, for user i, matrix $\mathbf{X}_{i::}^{(l)}$ indicates the relations between user i and the item-groups and matrix $\mathbf{X}_{i::}^{(r)}$ indicates the relations between user i and the tag-groups. Thus, the multiplication of $\mathbf{X}_{i::}^{(l)}$ and $\mathbf{X}_{i::}^{(r)}$, $\mathbf{X}_{i::}$, indicates the relations between user i, the item-groups and the tag-groups.

After decomposing each factor matrix into two smaller matrices, a_{ijk} can be rewritten as

$$a_{ijk} = \sum_{p=1}^{D_1}\sum_{q=1}^{D_2}\sum_{r=1}^{D_3}\sum_{u=1}^{d_1} x_{iqu}^{(l)} x_{iru}^{(r)} \sum_{v=1}^{d_2} y_{jrv}^{(l)} y_{jpv}^{(r)} \sum_{w=1}^{d_3} z_{kpw}^{(l)} z_{kqw}^{(r)}, \tag{8}$$

where

$$x_{iqr} = \sum_{u=1}^{d_1} x_{iqu}^{(l)} x_{iru}^{(r)},$$

$$y_{jrp} = \sum_{v=1}^{d_2} y_{jrv}^{(l)} y_{jpv}^{(r)},$$

$$z_{kpq} = \sum_{w=1}^{d_3} z_{kpw}^{(l)} z_{kqw}^{(r)}.$$

Note that, Eq. (8) is equivalent to

$$a_{ijk} = \sum_{u=1}^{d_1}\sum_{v=1}^{d_2}\sum_{w=1}^{d_3} \psi_{jk}^{(1)}(v,w) \cdot \psi_{ki}^{(2)}(w,u) \cdot \psi_{ij}^{(3)}(u,v), \tag{9}$$

where we define

$$\psi_{jk}^{(1)}(v,w) = \sum_{p=1}^{D_1} y_{jpv}^{(r)} \cdot z_{kpw}^{(l)},$$

$$\psi_{ki}^{(2)}(w,u) = \sum_{q=1}^{D_2} z_{kqw}^{(r)} \cdot x_{iqu}^{(l)},$$

$$\psi_{ij}^{(3)}(u,v) = \sum_{r=1}^{D_3} x_{iru}^{(r)} \cdot y_{jrv}^{(l)}.$$

Eq. (9) can be calculated in $\mathcal{O}(D_1d_2d_3 + D_2d_3d_1 + D_3d_1d_2)$ and generally, $d_1, d_2, d_3 << D_1, D_2, D_3$. Therefore, DTT is feasible for large-scale real problems. Besides, the number of parameters is reduced from $\mathcal{O}(ID_2D_3 + JD_3D_1 + KD_1D_2)$ to $\mathcal{O}(Id_1(D_2 + D_3) + Jd_2(D_3 + D_1) + Kd_3(D_1 + D_2))$.

Tensor decomposition techniques are employed to many applications. As for different applications, the objective function are different, let's assume the objective function is F. Gradient-base approaches are common to learn the parameters of the models and we use gradient-based approaches to optimize the objective function F. The gradients are

$$\frac{\partial a_{ijk}}{\partial x_{iqu}^{(l)}} = \sum_{w=1}^{d_3} \phi_{ijk}^{(2)}(w,u) \cdot z_{kqw}^{(r)},$$

$$\frac{\partial a_{ijk}}{\partial x_{iru}^{(r)}} = \sum_{v=1}^{d_2} \phi_{ijk}^{(3)}(u,v) \cdot y_{jrv}^{(l)},$$

$$\frac{\partial a_{ijk}}{\partial y_{jrv}^{(l)}} = \sum_{v=1}^{d_2} \phi_{ijk}^{(3)}(u,v) \cdot x_{iru}^{(r)},$$

$$\frac{\partial a_{ijk}}{\partial y_{jpv}^{(r)}} = \sum_{u=1}^{d_1} \phi_{ijk}^{(1)}(v,w) \cdot z_{kpw}^{(l)},$$

$$\frac{\partial a_{ijk}}{\partial z_{kpw}^{(l)}} = \sum_{u=1}^{d_1} \phi_{ijk}^{(1)}(v,w) \cdot y_{jpv}^{(r)},$$

$$\frac{\partial a_{ijk}}{\partial z_{kqw}^{(r)}} = \sum_{w=1}^{d_3} \phi_{ijk}^{(2)}(w,u) \cdot x_{iqu}^{(l)}$$

where we define

$$\phi_{ijk}^{(1)}(v,w) = \sum_{u=1}^{d_1} \psi_{ki}^{(2)}(w,u) \cdot \psi_{ij}^{(3)}(u,v),$$

$$\phi_{ijk}^{(2)}(w,u) = \sum_{v=1}^{d_2} \psi_{ij}^{(3)}(u,v) \cdot \psi_{jk}^{(1)}(v,w),$$

$$\phi_{ijk}^{(3)}(u,v) = \sum_{w=1}^{d_3} \psi_{jk}^{(1)}(v,w) \cdot \psi_{ki}^{(2)}(w,u).$$

Thus, given a_{ijk} in $\mathbf{A}$, the gradients can be calculated in $\mathcal{O}(D_1d_2d_3 + D_2d_3d_1 + D_3d_1d_2)$. With the gradients, we can optimize the objective function F.

4.3 Comparisons with TD and CP

For the simplicity of the analysis, we assume $D_1 = D_2 = D_3 = D$, $d_1 = d_2 = d_3 = d$ and $I = J = K$, where I, J and K denote the number of the users the items and the tags. Let N denote the number of the triplets in the training set and T denote the number of iterations for training. The comparison of the time complexity and space complexity is summarized in Table 1.

For TD, it makes the assumption that the users, the items and the tags are divided into several groups and uses a core tensor to model the higher-order relations between the user-groups, the item-groups and the tag-groups. Given user i item j, tag k, the higher-order relation between them is or-

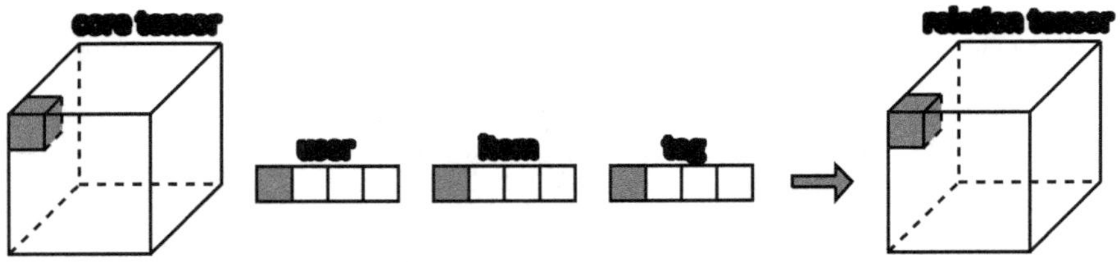

(a) Tucker decomposition

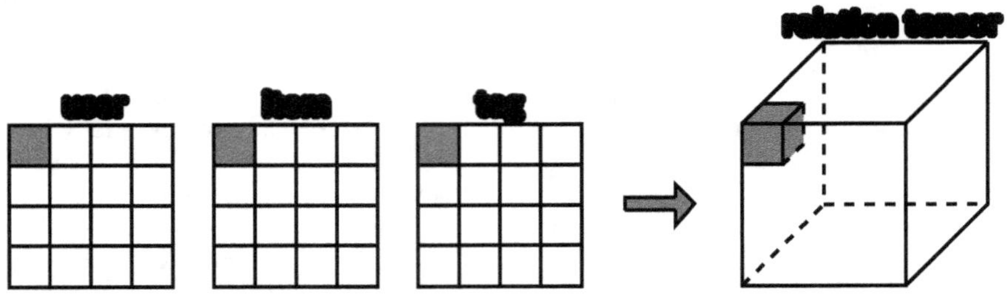

(b) DTT

Figure 3: Comparison of Tucker decomposition and DTT

ganized into a relation tensor. The framework of Tucker decomposition is illustrated in Figure 3(a). The three vectors on the left of the arrow describe the factors of the user, the item and the tag, respectively. The core tensor and the three vectors are integrated into a relation tensor, which is on the right of the tensor. Although Tucker decomposition is flexible and expressive, it takes $\mathcal{O}(D^3NT)$ to train the data and $\mathcal{O}(D^3)$ to predict a triplet. Besides, since the core tensor is shared by all the triplets, it is not suitable to apply parallel computing to training the data. Therefore, TD is unpractical on large-scale datasets.

On the other hand, it takes $\mathcal{O}(DNT)$ to trained a CP-based model and $\mathcal{O}(D)$ to predict a triplet. Thus, CP is efficient. Moreover, CP divides the users, the items and the tags into several groups as well. However, it assumes the users in the p-th user-group are independent of the items in the q-th item-group and the tags in the r-th tag-group, where $p \neq q$ and $p \neq r$. In fact, $D << I$ when solving real problems and it is possible that a user in the first user-group might annotate an item in the first item-group with a tag in the first tag-group and annotate another item in the second item-group with another tag in the third tag-group. Therefore, The assumption is too strong that it reduce the capacity of expression.

For user i, item j, tag k, DTT exploits a special multiplication $x_{iqr}y_{jrp}z_{kpq}$ to model the higher-order relation between them. Just like TD, it organizes the relation into a relation tensor as well, the framework of which is showed in Figure 3(b). The three matrices on the left of the arrow are the factor matrices of the user, the item and the tag and the factor matrices are integrated into a relation tensor, which is on the right of the arrow. Since DTT doesn't make the strong independent assumption like CP, it is more expressive. Moreover, DTT requires $\mathcal{O}(Dd^2NT)$ to train and $\mathcal{O}(Dd^2)$ to predict, where $d << D$. Thus, DTT is near linear. According to the experimental results on the real datasets, $d = 1$ is enough to capture the higher-order relations. Thus, DTT is efficient for large-scale problems. Furthermore, compared with TD and CP, DTT exploits a more natural way to represent the features of an entity, by using a matrix to describe the features of the entity rather than a vector.

5. EXPERIMENTAL RESULTS

In this section, we compare our proposed model with other tensor factorization techniques on the synthetic datasets and the real datasets. The experiments on the synthetic datasets are used to compare the capacity of expression and the experiments on the real datasets are used to compare the accuracy for predicting a triplet of a tensor.

5.1 Experimental Setup

As tensor decomposition techniques are applied to personalized tag recommendation, we use real tag annotation datasets to evaluate the performance of DTT. In addition, we generate synthetic datasets to compare different factorization models' capacity of expression.

Let $\mathbf{A}$ denote the tensor constructed from the training set and P denote the observed user-item posts in the training set. Given post (u, i), $T^+_{(u,i)}$ and $T^-_{(u,i)}$ denote the set of the positive tags and the set of the negative tags for that post, respectively. We construct a candidate set for each post (u, i). If triplet (u, i', t) is observed for some item i' or triplet (u', i, t) is observed for some user u', t is treated as the candidate tag for post (u, i). For tag t in the candidate set of post (u, i), if triplet (u, i, t) is observed, t is treated as the positive tag for post (u, i), otherwise, the negative tag. Following the work of [14], we optimize the pair-wise ranking function Bayesian Personalized Ranking (BPR) [15] for personalized tag recommendation. The objective function

F is defined as

$$F = \sum_{(u,i)\in P} \frac{1}{|T^+_{u,i}||T^-_{u,i}|} \sum_{t^+\in T^+_{u,i}} \sum_{t^-\in T^-_{u,i}} \sigma(a_{uit^+} - a_{uit^-})$$
$$+ \lambda \sum_{\theta\in\Theta} \|\theta - \mu\|^2_F, \quad (10)$$

where λ is the weight of the regularization term, Θ are the model parameters and μ denotes the mean of the parameters. We use Stochastic Gradient Descent (SGD) to optimize the objective function F.

5.2 Evaluation Methodology

We compare our approach with three categories of baselines, CP-based, TD-based and popularity-based. PITF [17], CP are CP-based, RTF [14] and HOSVD [3] are TD-based. For popularity-based, given a post (u, i), method *popularity* ranks the tags based on the frequency item i and the tags co-occur in the training set.

For convenience, we set $D_1 = D_2 = D_3 = D$ and $d_1 = d_2 = d_3 = d$. We performed all the experiments multiple times and tuned the hyper-parameters of all models to achieve the best performance on the first training split for each dataset. Most of the parameters of the tensor factorization models are drawn from normal distribution $N(\mu, 0.01^2)$. For all the parameters in DTT, $\mu = \frac{1}{\sqrt{Dd}}$. For all the parameters in PITF, $\mu = 0.0$. For all the parameters in CP, $\mu = \frac{1}{\sqrt[3]{D}}$. For the parameters of the factor matrices in RTF, $\mu = \frac{1}{D}$ and the parameters of the core tensor in RTF are drawn from normal distribution $N(0, 0.1)$. Besides, the weight of the regularization term $\lambda = 0.0001$ on the synthetic datasets and $\lambda = 0.002$ on the real datasets for DTT and CP, $\lambda = 10^{-6}$ on all the datasets for RTF, and $\lambda = 0.001$ on synthetic datasets and $\lambda = 0.01$ on the real datasets for PITF.

We exploit two widely used metrics in information retrieval, Normalized Discounted Cumulative Gain (NDCG) and Mean Average Precision (MAP), to evaluate the performance of different models.

Discounted Cumulative Gain (DCG) evaluates the gain of a recommendation list based on the positions of the tags in that list. The NDCG accumulated at a particular position p is defined as

$$DCG@p = \sum_{i=1}^{p} \frac{2^{rel(i)} - 1}{log_2(i+1)}, \quad (11)$$

where $rel(i)$ is 1 if the tag at position i i relevant and 0, otherwise. Normalized Discounted Cumulated Gain (NDCG) is defined as

$$NDCG@p = \frac{DCG@p}{IDCG@p} \quad (12)$$

where IDCG (Ideal Discounted Cumulated Gain) is the DCG of the ideal ranked list, which is introduced to normalize the DCG.

Mean Average Precision (MAP) computes the mean of average precision (AP) over all posts in the test set, where AP is the average of precisions computed at all positions with a preferred tag and defined as

$$AP = \frac{\sum_{i=1}^{N} prec(i) \times rel(i)}{\sum_{i=1}^{N} rel(i)}, \quad (13)$$

where $prec(i)$ is the precision of the cutoff rank list from the first tag to the i-th tag and N is the size of the corresponding candidate set.

5.3 Performance on Synthetic Datasets

To evaluate different tensor factorization models' capacity of expression, we generate 10 synthetic datasets. There are 100 users, 100 items and 100 tags in each synthetic dataset. For each dataset, We first randomly divided the users into 10 user-groups, divide the items into 10 item-groups and divide the tags into 10 tag-groups. We assume the users in the i-th user-group always annotate the items in the j-th item-groups with the tags in the $g(i, j)$-th tag-group, where $g(i, j)$ is randomly generated in the range 1 - 10. Thus, to sample a triplet, we first randomly sample a user and an item, and then sample a tag in the $g(i, j)$-th tag group, where i, j denote the IDs of the user-group that user belongs to and the item-group that item belongs to, respectively. For each dataset, we randomly sample 6000 triplets and split the triplets into a training set with 5000 triplets and a test set with 1000 triplets. By this way, we can compare different tensor factorization techniques' capacity of expression and verify whether the independent assumption made by CP limits its capacity.

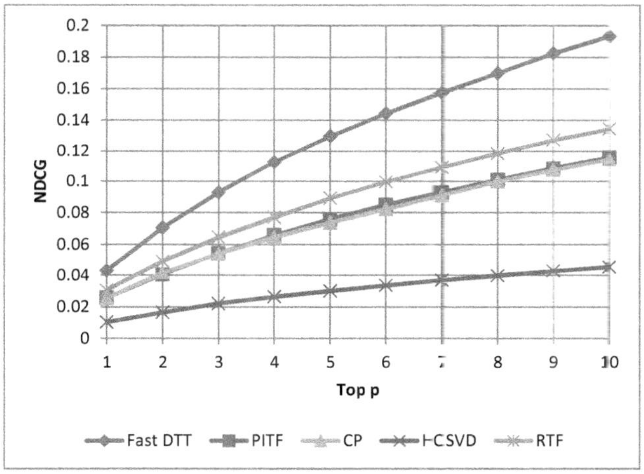

Figure 4: Performance on synthetic datasets

The experiments are repeated 10 times. We compare DTT to other tensor factorization models and for all tensor factorization models, $D = 2$, and for DTT $d = 1$. The results on the synthetic datasets are showed in Figure 4. HOSVD works poorly, since it doesn't handle the missing value in the tensors. As the other TD-based model, RTF, exploits the pair-wise ranking function Bayesian Personalized Ranking (BPR) [15], the performance is much better. Moreover, as we expected, DTT and RTF outperforms the CP-based models, PITF and CP, because the independent assumption constraints CP-based models' capacity. CP-based models assumes the users in the i-th user group will only annotate the items in the i-th item groups and annotate the items with the tags in the i-th tag group, which is not always the truth. Thus, DTT and TD-based models has stronger capacity of expression than CP-based models. Besides, DTT and TD-based models like RTF model the higher-order relation by a relation tensor, but it seems the method DTT exploiting to construct the relation tensor is better.

Table 2: Data statistics

Dataset	Users	Items	Tags	Posts	Triplets	Density	Average Candidates
Delicious	1,681	29,540	7,251	58,114	283,030	7.89×10^{-7}	131.79
Last.fm	1,348	6,927	2,132	59,849	162,047	8.14×10^{-6}	58.90
Movielens	456	1,973	1,222	15,210	27,0126	2.46×10^{-5}	85.96
Delicious-large	433,791	1,241,772	125,455	30,538,733	71,709,640	1.06×10^{-9}	257.10

Table 3: Performance on the smaller real datasets

category	algorithm	#feature		Delicious		Last.fm		Movielens	
		D	d	MAP	NDCG@5	MAP	NDCG@5	MAP	NDCG@5
DTT	DTT	32	1	0.1042	0.2317	0.4184	0.6446	0.4608	0.6028
		64	1	**0.1111**	0.2395	**0.4300**	**0.6561**	**0.4764**	**0.6188**
TD	RTF	32	-	-	-	-	-	0.3285	0.4846
		64	-	-	-	-	-	0.3474	0.5004
	HOSVD	32	-	-	-	-	-	0.0685	0.1442
		64	-	-	-	-	-	0.0790	0.1679
CP	PITF	32	-	0.1050	0.2381	0.4126	0.6463	0.4464	0.6015
		64	-	0.1059	0.2398	0.4146	0.6482	0.4503	0.6058
	CP	32	-	0.1054	0.2419	0.3808	0.6126	0.3920	0.5380
		64	-	0.1040	0.2382	0.3782	0.6115	0.3944	0.5389
popularity	popularity	-	-	0.1004	0.1581	0.3151	0.4995	0.2195	0.3405

5.4 Performance on Real Datasets

In addition to the synthetic datasets, we evaluate the performance of DTT on real datasets *Delicoius*[1], *Last.fm*[2], *Movielens*[3] and *Delicious-large*[4] [22]. The first three smaller datasets come from the 2-nd International Workshop on Information Heterogeneity and Fusion in Recommender Systems (HetRec 2011). The larger dataset *Delicious-large* [22] contains the complete bookmarking activity for almost 2 million users from the launch of the social bookmarking website in 2003 to the end of March 2011. For each real dataset, we removed the infrequent users, items and tags by using a core-based approach [10]. For the smaller datasets, we perform the removal until every user, item and tag occurred in at least 5 triplets. For *Delicious-large*, as the original dataset is too large, we first randomly sample 50% of the users, the items and the tags, and then perform the core-based approach until every user, item and tag occurred in at least 10 triplets. The statistics of the datasets after removal are described in Table 2. *Average Candidates* means the average number of the candidate tags for each post in each dataset.

We perform 10-fold cross-validation for the smaller datasets. The comparison between DTT, PITF, CP, HOSVD, RTF and *popularity* on the smaller real datasets are showed in Table 3. As TD-based models require a lot of computation power, we conducted experiments only on the smallest real dataset *Movielens* for TD-based models, HOSVD and RTF. Although TD-based models have stronger capacity of expression than CP-based models, they work poorer than the CP-based models on the real datasets. Maybe the core tensor of TD is too complex that it leads to overfitting. Both of TD and DTT model the higher-order relations into relation tensors, but it seems DTT works much better. It can be seen from the table that the MAP of DTT is significantly higher than that of the other approaches on all the real dataset and the NDCG@5 of DTT is significantly higher than that of the other approaches on the real datasets *Last.fm* and *Movielens*.

In the next experiment, we split *Delicious-large* into training (90%) and test (10%). As PITF is the most competitive approach on the smaller datasets, we only compare DTT with PITF on *Delicious-large*. The results can be found in Table 4, which show that DTT outperform PITF on the larger dataset as well.

Table 4: Performance on ***Delicious-large***

algorithm	#feature		Delicious-large	
	D	d	MAP	NDCG@5
DTT	64	1	0.4674	0.6847
PITF	64	-	0.4612	0.6803

Finally, we investigate the influence of the number of features to DTT. The results with different number of features on the real datasets are showed in Figure 5. It can be seen from the figure that with the same D, the prediction quality of the models with $d = 1$ is comparable with the models with $d = 2$ on all the real datasets. d has no significant influence to the accuracy of the models on the real datasets. Thus, $d = 1$ is sufficient to capture the higher-order relations on the personalized tag recommendation datasets. As the time complexity of DTT to predict a triplet is $\mathcal{O}(Dd^2)$ and at most of the time $d = 1$, the time complexity is reduced to $\mathcal{O}(D)$. Thus, DTT is near linear and is efficient for the large-scale real problems.

6. CONCLUSION AND FUTURE WORK

We propose a novel tensor factorization technique in this paper. Different from the traditional tensor factorization techniques which decompose a tensor into factor matrices,

[1] http://www.delicious.com
[2] http://www.lastfm.com
[3] http://www.grouplens.org
[4] http://www.zubiaga.org/resources/socialbm0311

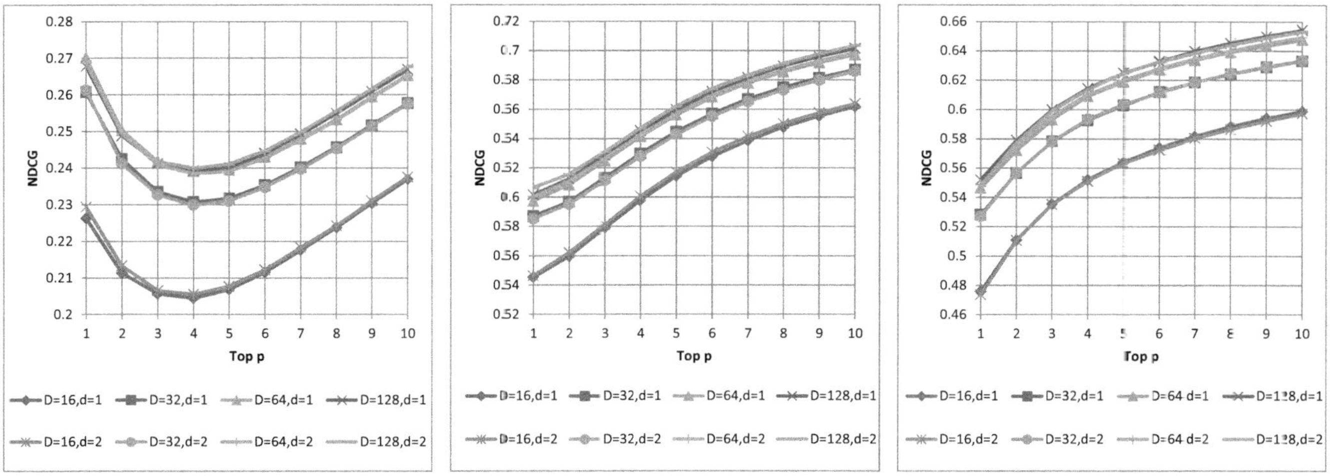

(a) Delicious (b) Last.fm (c) Movielens

Figure 5: Performance with different number of features on the real datasets

we decompose a tensor into factor tensors, since factor tensors can provide a more natural representation for the higher-order relations. Besides, we compare our proposed approach with two commonly used tensor factorization techniques, Tucker decomposition and CANDECOMP/PARAFAC. Our proposed approach overcome some of the drawbacks of Tucker decomposition and CANDECOMP/PARAFAC. It not only has strong capacity of expression, but also is near linear, which is feasible for the large-scale real problems. The experimental results on the synthetic datasets validate that our approach has strong capacity of expression. The results on the real datasets show that our approach outperforms other tensor factorization techniques.

In the future, we plan to further reduce the time complexity and space complexity to compute our proposed approach, by investigating its special case.

Acknowledgements

We would like to thank the many referees of the previous version of this paper for their extremely useful suggestions and comments. This work was supported by Huawei Innovation Research Program (HIRP) and National Science Foundation of China (61033010).

7. REFERENCES

[1] Carl J Appellof and ER Davidson. Strategies for analyzing data from video fluorometric monitoring of liquid chromatographic effluents. *Analytical Chemistry*, 53(13):2053–2056, 1981.

[2] J.D. Carroll and J.J. Chang. Analysis of individual differences in multidimensional scaling via an n-way generalization of "eckart-young" decomposition. *Psychometrika*, 35(3):283–319, 1970.

[3] Lieven De Lathauwer, Bart De Moor, and Joos Vandewalle. A multilinear singular value decomposition. *SIAM journal on Matrix Analysis and Applications*, 21(4):1253–1278, 2000.

[4] Lieven De Lathauwer, Bart De Moor, and Joos Vandewalle. On the best rank-1 and rank-(r 1, r 2,..., rn) approximation of higher-order tensors. *SIAM Journal on Matrix Analysis and Applications*, 21(4):1324–1342, 2000.

[5] Daniel M Dunlavy, Tamara G Kolda, and Evrim Acar. Temporal link prediction using matrix and tensor factorizations. *ACM Transactions on Knowledge Discovery from Data (TKDD)*, 5(2):10, 2011.

[6] Beyza Ermiş, Evrim Acar, and A Taylan Cemgil. Link prediction via generalized coupled tensor factorisation. *arXiv preprint arXiv:1208.6231*, 2012.

[7] Dehong Gao, Renxian Zhang, Wenjie Li, and Yuexian Hou. Twitter hyperlink recommendation with user-tweet-hyperlink three-way clustering. In *Proceedings of the 21st ACM international conference on Information and knowledge management*, pages 2535–2538. ACM, 2012.

[8] Gene H Golub and Christian Reinsch. Singular value decomposition and least squares solutions. *Numerische Mathematik*, 14(5):403–420, 1970.

[9] Richard A. Harshman. Foundations of the PARAFAC procedure: Models and conditions for an "explanatory" multi-modal factor analysis. *UCLA working papers in phonetics*, 16:1, 1970.

[10] Robert Jäschke, Leandro Marinho, Andreas Hotho, Lars Schmidt-Thieme, and Gerd Stumme. Tag recommendations in social bookmarking systems. *Ai Communications*, 21(4):231–247, 2008.

[11] Alexandros Karatzoglou, Xavier Amatriain, Linas Baltrunas, and Nuria Oliver. Multiverse recommendation: n-dimensional tensor factorization for context-aware collaborative filtering. In *Proceedings of the fourth ACM conference on Recommender systems*, pages 79–86. ACM, 2010.

[12] Tamara G Kolda and Brett W Bader. Tensor decompositions and applications. *SIAM review*, 51(3):455–500, 2009.

[13] Fumikazu Miwakeichi, Eduardo Martınez-Montes, Pedro A Valdés-Sosa, Nobuaki Nishiyama, Hiroaki Mizuhara, and Yoko Yamaguchi. Decomposing eeg data into space–time–frequency components using

parallel factor analysis. *NeuroImage*, 22(3):1035–1045, 2004.

[14] Steffen Rendle, Leandro Balby Marinho, Alexandros Nanopoulos, and Lars Schmidt-Thieme. Learning optimal ranking with tensor factorization for tag recommendation. In *Proceedings of the 15th ACM SIGKDD international conference on Knowledge discovery and data mining*, pages 727–736. ACM, 2009.

[15] Steffen Rendle, Christoph Freudenthaler, Zeno Gantner, and Lars Schmidt-Thieme. Bpr: Bayesian personalized ranking from implicit feedback. In *Proceedings of the Twenty-Fifth Conference on Uncertainty in Artificial Intelligence*, pages 452–461. AUAI Press, 2009.

[16] Steffen Rendle, Christoph Freudenthaler, and Lars Schmidt-Thieme. Factorizing personalized markov chains for next-basket recommendation. In *Proceedings of the 19th international conference on World wide web*, pages 811–820. ACM, 2010.

[17] Steffen Rendle and Lars Schmidt-Thieme. Pairwise interaction tensor factorization for personalized tag recommendation. In *Proceedings of the third ACM international conference on Web search and data mining*, pages 81–90. ACM, 2010.

[18] Stephan Spiegel, Jan Clausen, Sahin Albayrak, and Jérôme Kunegis. Link prediction on evolving data using tensor factorization. In *New Frontiers in Applied Data Mining*, pages 100–110. Springer, 2012.

[19] Jian-Tao Sun, Hua-Jun Zeng, Huan Liu, Yuchang Lu, and Zheng Chen. Cubesvd: a novel approach to personalized web search. In *Proceedings of the 14th international conference on World Wide Web*, pages 382–390. ACM, 2005.

[20] Panagiotis Symeonidis, Alexandros Nanopoulos, and Yannis Manolopoulos. Tag recommendations based on tensor dimensionality reduction. In *Proceedings of the 2008 ACM conference on Recommender systems*, pages 43–50. ACM, 2008.

[21] Ledyard R. Tucker. Some mathematical notes on three-mode factor analysis. *Psychometrika*, 31:279–311, 1966.

[22] Robert Wetzker, Carsten Zimmermann, and Christian Bauckhage. Analyzing social bookmarking systems: A del.icio.us cookbook. In *Mining Social Data (MSoDa) Workshop Proceedings*, pages 26–30, 2008.

[23] Liang Xiong, Xi Chen, Tzu-Kuo Huang, Jeff G Schneider, and Jaime G Carbonell. Temporal collaborative filtering with bayesian probabilistic tensor factorization. In *SDM*, volume 10, pages 211–222, 2010.

[24] Nan Zheng, Qiudan Li, Shengcai Liao, and Leiming Zhang. Flickr group recommendation based on tensor decomposition. In *Proceedings of the 33rd international ACM SIGIR conference on Research and development in information retrieval*, pages 737–738. ACM, 2010.

Clustering and Projected Clustering with Adaptive Neighbors

Feiping Nie
Department of Computer Science and Engineering
University of Texas, Arlington
Texas, USA
feipingnie@gmail.com

Xiaoqian Wang
Department of Computer Science and Engineering
University of Texas, Arlington
Texas, USA
xqwang1991@gmail.com

Heng Huang*
Department of Computer Science and Engineering
University of Texas, Arlington
Texas, USA
heng@uta.edu

ABSTRACT

Many clustering methods partition the data groups based on the input data similarity matrix. Thus, the clustering results highly depend on the data similarity learning. Because the similarity measurement and data clustering are often conducted in two separated steps, the learned data similarity may not be the optimal one for data clustering and lead to the suboptimal results. In this paper, we propose a novel clustering model to learn the data similarity matrix and clustering structure simultaneously. Our new model learns the data similarity matrix by assigning the adaptive and optimal neighbors for each data point based on the local distances. Meanwhile, the new rank constraint is imposed to the Laplacian matrix of the data similarity matrix, such that the connected components in the resulted similarity matrix are exactly equal to the cluster number. We derive an efficient algorithm to optimize the proposed challenging problem, and show the theoretical analysis on the connections between our method and the K-means clustering, and spectral clustering. We also further extend the new clustering model for the projected clustering to handle the high-dimensional data. Extensive empirical results on both synthetic data and real-world benchmark data sets show that our new clustering methods consistently outperforms the related clustering approaches.

Categories and Subject Descriptors

H.2.8 [**Database Management**]: Database Applications-Data Mining

General Terms

Algorithms

Keywords

Clustering; Block diagonal similarity matrix; Adaptive neighbors; Clustering with dimensionality reduction

* Corresponding author.

KDD'14, August 24–27, 2014, New York, New York, USA.

http://dx.doi.org/10.1145/2623330.2623726 .

1. INTRODUCTION

Clustering, which partitions the data points into different groups such that the objects in the same group have high similarity to each other, is one of the most fundamental topic in data mining. The clustering technique has been playing an outstanding role in data mining applications. In the past decades, many clustering algorithms have been proposed, such as hierarchical clustering [10], K-means clustering [13], spectral clustering [15], spectral embedded clustering [19], support vector clustering [1], maximum margin clustering [22], initialization independent clustering [18], multi-view clustering [21, 3, 4], *etc.*

Due to the efficiency and simpleness, the most popularly used clustering method is the K-means clustering algorithm, which aims to learn c cluster centroids that minimize the within cluster data distances. The spectral clustering method [15] does a low-dimension embedding of the affinity matrix between samples, followed by a K-means clustering in the low dimensional space. Because the data graph and manifold information are utilized in the clustering model, the graph based clustering methods (such as normalized cut [20], ratio cut [7]) usually show better clustering performance than K-means method. Such methods especially work well for a small number of clusters. More recently, the Nonnegative Matrix Factorization (NMF) has been used as the relaxation technique for clustering with excellent performance [12, 16]. Although the graph-based clustering methods have good performance, they partition the data based on the fixed data graph such that the clustering results are sensitive to the input affinity matrix.

In this paper, we propose to solve the clustering problem from a new point of view and learn the data similarity matrix by assigning the adaptive and optimal neighbors for each data point based on the local connectivity. Our main assumption is that the data points with a smaller distance should have a larger probability to be neighbors. More important, we impose the rank constraint on the Laplacian matrix of the learned similarity matrix to achieve the ideal neighbors assignment, such that the connected components in the data are exact the cluster number and each connected component corresponds to one cluster. Our new model learns the data similarity matrix and cluster structure simultaneously to achieve the optimal clustering results. We derive a novel and efficient algorithm to solve this challenging problem, and show the theoretical analysis on the connections between our method and K-means clustering, and spectral clustering. Moreover, we extend the proposed clustering model for the projected clustering to handle the high-dimensional data. Extensive experiments have been conducted on both synthetic data and real-world benchmark data sets. All empirical results show that our new clustering models consistently outperform the related clustering methods.

Notations: Throughout the paper, all the matrices are written as uppercase. For matrix M, the i-th row (with transpose) and the (i,j)-th element of M are denoted by m_i and m_{ij}, respectively. The trace of matrix M is denoted by $Tr(M)$. The L2-norm of vector v is denoted by $\|v\|_2$, the Frobenius norm of matrix M is denoted by $\|M\|_F$. An identity matrix is denoted by I, and $\mathbf{1}$ denotes a column vector with all the elements as one. For vector v and matrix M, $v \geq 0$ and $M \geq 0$ mean all the elements of M and v are equal to or larger than zero.

2. CLUSTERING WITH ADAPTIVE NEIGHBORS

Exploring the local connectivity of data is a successful strategy for clustering task. Given a data set $\{x_1, x_2, ..., x_n\}$, we denote $X \in \mathbb{R}^{n\times d}$ as the data matrix. The neighbors of $x_i \in \mathbb{R}^{d\times 1}$ can be defined as the k-nearest data points in the data set to x_i. In this paper, we consider the probabilistic neighbors, and use the Euclidean distance as the distance measure for simplicity.

For the i-th data point x_i, all the data points $\{x_1, x_2, ..., x_n\}$ can be connected to x_i as a neighbor with probability s_{ij}. Usually, a smaller distance $\|x_i - x_j\|_2^2$ should be assigned a larger probability s_{ij}, so a natural method to determine the probabilities $s_{ij}|_{j=1}^n$ is solving the following problem:

$$\min_{s_i^T\mathbf{1}=1, 0\leq s_i\leq 1} \sum_{j=1}^n \|x_i - x_j\|_2^2 s_{ij} \tag{1}$$

where $s_i \in \mathbb{R}^{n\times 1}$ is a vector with the j-th element as s_{ij}.

However, the problem (1) has a trivial solution, only the nearest data point can be the neighbor of x_i with probability 1 and all the other data points can not be the neighbors of x_i. On the other hand, if we solve the following problem without involving any distance information in the data:

$$\min_{s_i^T\mathbf{1}=1, 0\leq s_i\leq 1} \sum_{j=1}^n s_{ij}^2 \tag{2}$$

the optimal solution is that all the data points can be the neighbors of x_i with the same probability $\frac{1}{n}$, which can be seen as a prior in the neighbors assignment.

Combining Eq.(1) and (2), we can solve the following problem:

$$\min_{s_i^T\mathbf{1}=1, 0\leq s_i\leq 1} \sum_{j=1}^n \left(\|x_i - x_j\|_2^2 s_{ij} + \gamma s_{ij}^2\right) \tag{3}$$

The second term in Eq.(3) is a regularization and γ is the regularization parameter. Denote $d_{ij}^x = \|x_i - x_j\|_2^2$, and denote $d_i^x \in \mathbb{R}^{n\times 1}$ as a vector with the j-th element as d_{ij}^x, then the problem (3) can be written in vector form as

$$\min_{s_i^T\mathbf{1}=1, 0\leq s_i\leq 1} \left\| s_i + \frac{1}{2\gamma} d_i^x \right\|_2^2 \tag{4}$$

We will see in Subsection 2.4 that this problem can be solved with a closed form solution.

For each data point x_i, we can use Eq.(3) to assign its neighbors. Therefore, we can solve the following problem to assign the neighbors for all the data points:

$$\min_{\forall i, s_i^T\mathbf{1}=1, 0\leq s_i\leq 1} \sum_{i,j=1}^n \left(\|x_i - x_j\|_2^2 s_{ij} + \gamma s_{ij}^2\right) \tag{5}$$

In the clustering task to partition the data into c clusters, an ideal neighbors assignment is that the connected components in the data are exact c. Usually the neighbors assignment with Eq.(5) can not reach the ideal case for any value of γ. In most cases, all the data points are connected as just one connected component. In order to achieve the ideal neighbors assignment, the probabilities $s_{ij}|_{i,j=1}^n$ in the problem (5) should be constrained such that the neighbors assignment becomes an adaptive process to make the connected components are exact c. It seems look like an impossible goal since this kind of structured constraint on the similarities is fundamental but also very difficult to handle. In this paper, we will propose a novel but very simple method to achieve this goal.

The matrix $S \in \mathbb{R}^{n\times n}$ obtained in the neighbors assignment can be seen as a similarity matrix of the graph with the n data points as the nodes. Suppose each node i is assigned a function value as $f_i \in \mathbb{R}^{c\times 1}$, then it can be verified that

$$\sum_{i,j=1}^n \|f_i - f_j\|_2^2 s_{ij} = 2Tr(F^T L_S F) \tag{6}$$

where $F \in \mathbb{R}^{n\times c}$ with the i-th row formed by f_i, $L_S = D_S - \frac{S^T+S}{2}$ is called Laplacian matrix in graph theory, the degree matrix $D_S \in \mathbb{R}^{n\times n}$ is defined as a diagonal matrix where the i-th diagonal element is $\sum_j (s_{ij} + s_{ji})/2$.

If the similarity matrix S is nonnegative, then the Laplacian matrix has an important property as follows [14, 5].

THEOREM 1. *The multiplicity c of the eigenvalue 0 of the Laplacian matrix L_S is equal to the number of connected components in the graph with the similarity matrix S.*

Theorem 1 indicates that if $rank(L_S) = n - c$, then the neighbors assignment is an ideal assignment and we already partition the data points into c clusters based on S, without having to perform K-means or other discretization procedures. Motivated by Theorem 1, we add an additional constraint $rank(L_S) = n - c$ into the problem (5) to achieve the ideal neighbors assignment with clear clustering structure. Thus, our new clustering model is to solve:

$$\begin{aligned} J_{opt} &= \min_S \sum_{i,j=1}^n \left(\|x_i - x_j\|_2^2 s_{ij} + \gamma s_{ij}^2\right) \\ s.t.\ & \forall i, s_i^T\mathbf{1} = 1, 0 \leq s_i \leq 1, rank(L_S) = n - c \end{aligned} \tag{7}$$

It is difficult to solve the problem (7). Because $L_S = D_S - \frac{S^T+S}{2}$ and D_S also depends on S, the constraint $rank(L_S) = n - k$ is not easy to tackle. In the next subsection, we will propose a novel and efficient algorithm to solve this challenging problem.

2.1 Optimization Algorithm Solving Problem (7)

Suppose $\sigma_i(L_S)$ is the i-th smallest eigenvalue of L_S, we know $\sigma_i(L_S) \geq 0$ since L_S is positive semi-definite. It can be seen that the problem (7) is equivalent to the following problem for a large enough value of λ:

$$\begin{aligned}&\min_{S}\sum_{i,j=1}^{n}\left(\|x_i-x_j\|_2^2 s_{ij}+\gamma s_{ij}^2\right)+2\lambda\sum_{i=1}^{c}\sigma_i(L_S)\\&s.t.\quad \forall i, s_i^T\mathbf{1}=1, 0\le s_i\le 1\end{aligned}\tag{8}$$

When λ is large enough, note that $\sigma_i(L_S)\ge 0$ for every i, then the optimal solution S to the problem (8) will make the second term $\sum_{i=1}^{c}\sigma_i(L_S)$ to be zero, and thus the constraint $rank(L_S)=n-c$ in the problem (7) could be satisfied.

According to the Ky Fan's Theorem [6], we have

$$\sum_{i=1}^{c}\sigma_i(L_S)=\min_{F\in\mathbb{R}^{n\times c},F^TF=I}Tr(F^TL_SF)\tag{9}$$

Therefore, the problem (8) is further equivalent to the following problem

$$\begin{aligned}&\min_{S,F}\sum_{i,j=1}^{n}\left(\|x_i-x_j\|_2^2 s_{ij}+\gamma s_{ij}^2\right)+2\lambda Tr(F^TL_SF)\\&s.t.\quad \forall i, s_i^T\mathbf{1}=1, 0\le s_i\le 1, F\in R^{n\times c}, F^TF=I\end{aligned}\tag{10}$$

Compared with the original problem (7), the problem (10) is much easier to solve. We can apply the alternative optimization approach to solve it.

When S is fixed, the problem (10) becomes

$$\min_{F\in\mathbb{R}^{n\times c},F^TF=I}Tr(F^TL_SF)\tag{11}$$

The optimal solution F to the problem (11) is formed by the c eigenvectors of L_S corresponding to the c smallest eigenvalues.

When F is fixed, the problem (10) becomes

$$\begin{aligned}&\min_{S}\sum_{i,j=1}^{n}\left(\|x_i-x_j\|_2^2 s_{ij}+\gamma s_{ij}^2\right)+2\lambda Tr(F^TL_SF)\\&s.t.\quad \forall i, s_i^T\mathbf{1}=1, 0\le s_i\le 1\end{aligned}\tag{12}$$

According to Eq.(6), the problem (12) can be rewritten as

$$\begin{aligned}&\min_{S}\sum_{i,j=1}^{n}\left(\|x_i-x_j\|_2^2 s_{ij}+\gamma s_{ij}^2+\lambda\|f_i-f_j\|_2^2 s_{ij}\right)\\&s.t.\quad \forall i, s_i^T\mathbf{1}=1, 0\le s_i\le 1\end{aligned}\tag{13}$$

Note that the problem (13) is independent between different i, so we can solve the following problem individually for each i:

$$\begin{aligned}&\min_{s_i}\sum_{j=1}^{n}\left(\|x_i-x_j\|_2^2 s_{ij}+\gamma s_{ij}^2+\lambda\|f_i-f_j\|_2^2 s_{ij}\right)\\&s.t.\quad s_i^T\mathbf{1}=1, 0\le s_i\le 1\end{aligned}\tag{14}$$

Denote $d_{ij}^x=\|x_i-x_j\|_2^2$ and $d_{ij}^f=\|f_i-f_j\|_2^2$, and denote $d_i\in\mathbb{R}^{n\times 1}$ as a vector with the j-th element as $d_{ij}=d_{ij}^x+\lambda d_{ij}^f$, then the problem (14) can be written in vector form as

$$\min_{s_i^T\mathbf{1}=1,0\le s_i\le 1}\left\|s_i+\frac{1}{2\gamma}d_i\right\|_2^2\tag{15}$$

We will see in Subsection 2.4 that this problem can be solved with a closed form solution.

The detailed algorithm to solve the problem (7) is summarized in Algorithm 1.

[1]In practice, to accelerate the procedure, the λ can be determined during the iteration. We can initialize $\lambda=\gamma$, then increase λ if the connected components of S is smaller than c and decrease λ if it is greater than c in each iteration.

Algorithm 1 Algorithm to solve problem (7).

input Data matrix $X\in\mathbb{R}^{n\times d}$, cluster number c, parameter γ, a large enough λ[1].
output $S\in\mathbb{R}^{n\times n}$ with exact c connected components.
Initialize S by the optimal solution to the problem (5).
while not converge **do**
1. Update F, which is formed by the c eigenvectors of $L_S=D_S-\frac{S^T+S}{2}$ corresponding to the c smallest eigenvalues.
2. For each i, update the i-th row of S by solving the problem (15), where $d_i\in\mathbb{R}^{n\times 1}$ is a vector with the j-th element as $d_{ij}=\|x_i-x_j\|_2^2+\lambda\|f_i-f_j\|_2^2$.
end while

2.2 Connection to K-means Clustering

Denote the centering matrix by

$$H=I-\frac{1}{n}\mathbf{1}\mathbf{1}^T,\tag{16}$$

and denote $D^x\in\mathbb{R}^{n\times n}$ as a distance matrix where the (i,j)-th element is $d_{ij}^x=\|x_i-x_j\|_2^2$. To analyze the connection of Algorithm 1 to K-means, we first need the following lemma:

LEMMA 1. $HD^xH=-2HXX^TH$

PROOF. Since $d_{ij}^x=\|x_i-x_j\|_2^2=x_i^Tx_i-x_j^Tx_j-2x_i^Tx_j$, we have $D^x=Diag(XX^T)\mathbf{1}\mathbf{1}^T+\mathbf{1}\mathbf{1}^TDiag(XX^T)-2XX^T$, where $Diag(XX^T)$ is a diagonal matrix with the diagonal elements of XX^T. Note that $H\mathbf{1}=\mathbf{1}^TH=\mathbf{0}$ according to the definition of H, we have $HD^xH=-2HXX^TH$. □

Theorem 2 reveals that Algorithm 1 is exactly solving the K-means problem when $\gamma\to\infty$.

THEOREM 2. *When $\gamma\to\infty$, the problem (7) is equivalent to the problem of K-means.*

PROOF. The problem (7) can be written in matrix form as

$$\min_{S\mathbf{1}=\mathbf{1},S\ge 0,rank(L_S)=n-c}Tr(S^TD^x)+\gamma\|S\|_F^2\tag{17}$$

Due to the constraint $rank(L_S)=n-c$, the solution S has exact c components (that is, S is block diagonal with proper permutation). Suppose the i-th component of S is $S_i\in\mathbb{R}^{n_i\times n_i}$, where n_i is the number of data points in the component, then solving problem (17) is to solve the following problem for each i:

$$\min_{S_i\mathbf{1}=\mathbf{1},S_i\ge 0}Tr(S_i^TD_i^x)+\gamma\|S_i\|_F^2\tag{18}$$

When $\gamma\to\infty$, then the problem (18) becomes

$$\min_{S_i\mathbf{1}=\mathbf{1},S_i\ge 0}\|S_i\|_F^2\tag{19}$$

The optimal solution to the problem (19) is that all the elements of S_i are equal to $\frac{1}{n_i}$.

Therefore, the optimal solution S to the problem (17) should be the following form when $\gamma\to\infty$:

$$s_{ij}=\begin{cases}\frac{1}{n_k} & x_i,x_j \text{ are in the same component } k\\ 0 & \text{otherwise}\end{cases}\tag{20}$$

We denote the solution set that satisfies the form in Eq.(20) by $\mathcal{V}$. Note that for any possible partition of the c components such that S has the form as in Eq.(20), $\|S\|_F^2$ has the same value, i.e., $\|S\|_F^2 = c$. Therefore, the problem (17) becomes

$$\min_{S\in\mathcal{V}} Tr(S^T D^x) \tag{21}$$

According to the constraint of S in Eq.(21), S is symmetric and $S\mathbf{1} = \mathbf{1}^T S = \mathbf{1}$. So $Tr(HD^xHS) = Tr(D^xS) - \frac{1}{n}\mathbf{1}^T D^x \mathbf{1}$ and thus the problem (21) is equivalent to the following problem:

$$\min_{S\in\mathcal{V}} Tr(HD^xHS) \tag{22}$$

Define the label matrix $Y \in \mathbb{R}^{n\times c}$, where the (i,j)-th element is

$$y_{ij} = \begin{cases} \frac{1}{\sqrt{n_k}} & x_i \text{ belongs to the } k\text{-th compoment} \\ 0 & otherwise \end{cases} \tag{23}$$

Then according to Eq.(22) and Lemma 1, we have

$$\begin{aligned} &\min_{S\in\mathcal{V}} Tr(HD^xHS) \\ \Leftrightarrow &\max_{S\in\mathcal{V}} Tr(HXX^THS) \\ \Leftrightarrow &\max_{S\in\mathcal{V}} Tr(X^THSHX) \\ \Leftrightarrow &\min_{S\in\mathcal{V}} Tr(X^TH(I-S)HX) \\ \Leftrightarrow &\min_{Y} Tr(X^TH(I-YY^T)HX) \\ \Leftrightarrow &\min_{Y} Tr(S_w) \end{aligned} \tag{24}$$

which is exactly the problem of K-means. The matrix S_w is called within-class scatter matrix in classical Linear Discriminant Analysis (LDA) when the labels Y of data are given. K-means is to find the optimal labels Y such that the trace of the within-class scatter matrix $Tr(S_w)$ is minimized. □

We will see in the next subsection that the proposed method in Algorithm 1 is closely related to spectral clustering. Therefore, although the new algorithm is to solve the K-means problem (which can only partition data with spherical shape) when $\gamma \to \infty$, it can partition data with arbitrary shape when γ is not very large. We will also see in the experiments that this new algorithm can find much better solution to the K-means problem even when γ is not very large.

2.3 Connection to Spectral Clustering

Given a graph with the similarity S, spectral clustering is to solve the following problem:

$$\min_{F\in R^{n\times c}, F^TF=I} Tr(F^TL_SF) \tag{25}$$

The optimal solution is the spectral decomposition of the Laplacian matrix L_S, i.e., the optimal solution F is formed by the c eigenvectors of L_S corresponding to the c smallest eigenvalues, as in Eq.(11).

Usually, given a similarity S, the obtained F can not be directly used for clustering since the graph with S does not has exact c connected components. K-means or other discretization procedures should be performed on F to obtain the final clustering results [9].

In the convergence of Algorithm 1, we also obtain an optimal solution F to the problem (25), the difference is that the similarity S is also learned by the algorithm. Note that in the convergence, the last term $2\lambda Tr(F^TL_SF)$ in the problem (10) will approximate zero, the learned S is mainly achieved by solving problem (5).

Thanks to the constraint $rank(L_S) = n - c$, the graph with the learned S will has exact c connected components. Therefore, the optimal solution F, which is formed by the c eigenvectors of L_S corresponding to the c smallest eigenvalues, can be written as

$$F = YQ \tag{26}$$

where $Y \in \mathbb{R}^{n\times c}$ is the label matrix defined in Eq.(23) and $Q \in \mathbb{R}^{c\times c}$ is an arbitrary orthogonal matrix. That is to say, we can use the obtained F directly to get the final clustering result, without the K-means or other discretization procedures as traditional spectral clustering has to do.

In another viewpoint, it can be seen that the proposed algorithm learns the similarity matrix S and the label matrix F simultaneously, while traditional spectral clustering only learns the F given the similarity matrix S. Therefore, the new algorithm could achieve better performance in practice since it also learns an adaptive graph for clustering.

2.4 Determine The Value of γ

In practice, regularization parameter is difficult to tune since its value could be from zero to infinite. In this subsection, we present an effective method to determine the regularization parameter γ in the problem (7).

For each i, the objective function in the problem (7) is equal to the one in the problem (4). The Lagrangian function of problem (4) is

$$\mathcal{L}(s_i, \eta, \beta_i) = \frac{1}{2}\left\| s_i + \frac{d_i^x}{2\gamma_i}\right\|_2^2 - \eta(s_i^T\mathbf{1} - 1) - \beta_i^T s_i \tag{27}$$

where η and $\beta_i \geq \mathbf{0}$ are the Lagrangian multipliers.

According to the KKT condition [2], it can be verified that the optimal solution s_i should be

$$s_{ij} = (-\frac{d_{ij}^x}{2\gamma_i} + \eta)_+ \tag{28}$$

In practice, usually we could achieve better performance if we focus on the locality of data. Therefore, it is preferred to learn a sparse s_i, i.e., only the k nearest neighbors of x_i could have chance to connect to x_i. Another benefit of learning a sparse similarity matrix S is that the computation burden can be alleviated largely for subsequent processing.

Without loss of generality, suppose $d_{i1}^x, d_{i2}^x, ..., d_{in}^x$ are ordered from small to large. If the optimal s_i has only k nonzero elements, then according to Eq.(28), we know $s_{ik} > 0$ and $s_{i,k+1} = 0$. Therefore, we have

$$\begin{cases} -\frac{d_{ik}^x}{2\gamma_i} + \eta > 0 \\ -\frac{d_{i,k+1}^x}{2\gamma_i} + \eta \leq 0 \end{cases} \tag{29}$$

According to Eq.(28) and the constraint $s_i^T\mathbf{1} = 1$, we have

$$\begin{aligned} &\sum_{j=1}^{k}(-\frac{d_{ij}^x}{2\gamma_i} + \eta) = 1 \\ &\Rightarrow \eta = \frac{1}{k} + \frac{1}{2k\gamma_i}\sum_{j=1}^{k} d_{ij}^x \end{aligned} \tag{30}$$

So we have the following inequality for γ_i according to Eq.(29) and Eq.(30):

$$\frac{k}{2}d_{ik}^x - \frac{1}{2}\sum_{j=1}^{k} d_{ij}^x < \gamma_i \leq \frac{k}{2}d_{i,k+1}^x - \frac{1}{2}\sum_{j=1}^{k} d_{ij}^x \tag{31}$$

Therefore, in order to obtain an optimal solution s_i to the problem (4) that has exact k nonzero values, we could set

γ_i to be

$$\gamma_i = \frac{k}{2} d_{i,k+1}^x - \frac{1}{2} \sum_{j=1}^{k} d_{ij}^x \quad (32)$$

The overall γ could be set to the mean of $\gamma_1, \gamma_2, ..., \gamma_n$. That is, we could set the γ to be

$$\gamma = \frac{1}{n} \sum_{i=1}^{n} \left(\frac{k}{2} d_{i,k+1}^x - \frac{1}{2} \sum_{j=1}^{k} d_{ij}^x \right) \quad (33)$$

The number of neighbors k is much easier to tune than the regularization parameter γ since k is an integer and has explicit meaning.

3. PROJECTED CLUSTERING WITH ADAPTIVE NEIGHBORS

Clustering high-dimensional data is an important and challenging problem in practice. In this section, we propose a projected clustering approach with the adaptive neighbors to solve this problem. The goal is to find an optimal subspace on which the adaptive neighboring is performed such that there are exact c connected components in the data.

Denote the total scatter matrix by $S_t = X^T H X$, where H is the centering matrix defined in Eq.(16). Suppose we are to learn a projection matrix $W \in \mathbb{R}^{d \times m}$. First, we constrain the subspace with $W^T S_t W = I$ such that the data on the subspace are statistically uncorrelated. As in Eq.(5), we assign the neighbors for each data by solving the following problem:

$$\begin{aligned} \min_{S,W} & \sum_{i,j=1}^{n} \left(\left\| W^T x_i - W^T x_j \right\|_2^2 s_{ij} + \gamma s_{ij}^2 \right) \\ s.t. & \ \forall i, s_i^T \mathbf{1} = 1, 0 \le s_i \le 1, W^T S_t W = I \end{aligned} \quad (34)$$

Similarly, to make the neighbors assignment be adaptive such that the connected components in the data are exact c, we impose the constraint on S with $rank(L_S) = n - c$. Therefore, we propose the following problem for learning the projection W and the clustering simultaneously:

$$\begin{aligned} \min_{S,W} & \sum_{i,j=1}^{n} \left(\left\| W^T x_i - W^T x_j \right\|_2^2 s_{ij} + \gamma s_{ij}^2 \right) \\ s.t. & \ \forall i, s_i^T \mathbf{1} = 1, 0 \le s_i \le 1, W^T S_t W = I, \\ & rank(L_S) = n - c \end{aligned} \quad (35)$$

3.1 Optimization Algorithm for Problem (35)

Using the same trick as in Subsection 2.1, we know that solving problem (35) is equivalent to solving the following problem

$$\begin{aligned} \min_{S,W,F} & \sum_{i,j=1}^{n} \left(\left\| W^T x_i - W^T x_j \right\|_2^2 s_{ij} + \gamma s_{ij}^2 \right) \\ & + 2\lambda Tr(F^T L_S F) \\ s.t. & \ \forall i, s_i^T \mathbf{1} = 1, 0 \le s_i \le 1, W^T S_t W = I, \\ & F \in R^{n \times c}, F^T F = I \end{aligned} \quad (36)$$

We can also apply the alternative optimization approach to solve this problem.

When S is fixed, the problem (36) becomes the problem (11), and the optimal solution F is formed by the c eigenvectors of L_S corresponding to the c smallest eigenvalues.

When F is fixed, the problem (36) becomes

$$\begin{aligned} \min_{S,W,F} & \sum_{i,j=1}^{n} \left(\left\| W^T x_i - W^T x_j \right\|_2^2 s_{ij} + \gamma s_{ij}^2 \right) \\ & + 2\lambda Tr(F^T L_S F) \\ s.t. & \ \forall i, s_i^T \mathbf{1} = 1, 0 \le s_i \le 1, W^T S_t W = I \end{aligned} \quad (37)$$

In problem (37), if S is fixed, then the problem becomes

$$\min_{W^T S_t W = I} \sum_{i,j=1}^{n} \left\| W^T x_i - W^T x_j \right\|_2^2 s_{ij} \quad (38)$$

which can be rewritten as the following problem according to Eq.(6):

$$\min_{W^T S_t W = I} Tr(W^T X^T L_S X W) \quad (39)$$

The optimal solution W to the problem (39) is formed by the m eigenvectors of $S_t^{-1} X^T L_S X$ corresponding to the m smallest eigenvalues (we assume the null space of the data X is removed, i.e., S_t is invertible).

In problem (37), if W is fixed, then according to Eq.(6) again, the problem (37) can be rewritten as

$$\begin{aligned} \min_{S} & \sum_{i,j=1}^{n} \left(\left\| W^T x_i - W^T x_j \right\|_2^2 s_{ij} + \gamma s_{ij}^2 \right) \\ & + \lambda \sum_{i,j=1}^{n} \| f_i - f_j \|_2^2 s_{ij} \\ s.t. & \ \forall i, s_i^T \mathbf{1} = 1, 0 \le s_i \le 1 \end{aligned} \quad (40)$$

Note that the problem (40) is independent between different i, so we can solve the following problem individually for each i:

$$\begin{aligned} \min_{s_i} & \sum_{j=1}^{n} \left(\left\| W^T x_i - W^T x_j \right\|_2^2 s_{ij} + \gamma s_{ij}^2 \right) \\ & + \lambda \sum_{j=1}^{n} \| f_i - f_j \|_2^2 s_{ij} \\ s.t. & \ s_i^T \mathbf{1} = 1, 0 \le s_i \le 1 \end{aligned} \quad (41)$$

Denote $d_{ij}^{wx} = \left\| W^T x_i - W^T x_j \right\|_2^2$ and $d_{ij}^f = \| f_i - f_j \|_2^2$, and denote $d_i^w \in \mathbb{R}^{n \times 1}$ as a vector with the j-th element as $d_{ij}^w = d_{ij}^{wx} + \lambda d_{ij}^f$, then the problem (41) can be written in vector form as

$$\min_{s_i^T \mathbf{1} = 1, 0 \le s_i \le 1} \left\| s_i + \frac{1}{2\gamma} d_i^w \right\|_2^2 \quad (42)$$

which is the same problem as in Eq.(15) and can be solved with a closed form solution.

The detailed algorithm to solve the problem (35) is summarized in Algorithm 2. We can also use Eq.(33) to determine the regularization parameter γ.

Algorithm 2 Algorithm to solve problem (35).

input Data matrix $X \in \mathbb{R}^{n\times d}$, cluster number c, reduced dimension m, parameter γ, a large enough λ.
output $S \in \mathbb{R}^{n\times n}$ with exact c connected components, projection $W \in \mathbb{R}^{d\times m}$.
Initialize S by the optimal solution to the problem (3).
while not converge **do**
1. Update $L_S = D_S - \frac{S^T+S}{2}$, where $D_S \in \mathbb{R}^{n\times n}$ is a diagonal matrix with the i-th diagonal element as $\sum_j (s_{ij}+s_{ji})/2$.
2. Update F, whose columns are the c eigenvectors of L_S corresponding to the c smallest eigenvalues.
2. Update W, whose columns are the m eigenvectors of $S_t^{-1}X^T L_S X$ corresponding to the m smallest eigenvalues.
3. For each i, update the i-th row of S by solving the problem (42), where $d_i^w \in \mathbb{R}^{n\times 1}$ is a vector with the j-th element as $d_{ij}^w = \left\|W^T x_i - W^T x_j\right\|_2^2 + \lambda \left\|f_i - f_j\right\|_2^2$.
end while

3.2 Connection to LDA

In this subsection, we show that when $\gamma \to \infty$, the proposed method in Algorithm 2 is to solve the LDA problem with the labels also being optimized at the same time. The result is summarized in the following theorem:

THEOREM 3. *When $\gamma \to \infty$, the problem (35) is equivalent to the problem of LDA, in which the labels are also variables to be optimized.*

PROOF. The problem (35) can be written in matrix form as

$$\min_{\substack{S\mathbf{1}=\mathbf{1},S\geq 0,W^T S_t W=I,\\ rank(L_S)=n-c}} Tr(S^T D^{wx}) + \gamma \left\|S\right\|_F^2 \tag{43}$$

where $D^{wx} \in \mathbb{R}^{n\times n}$ is a distance matrix with the (i,j)-th element as $d_{ij}^{wx} = \left\|W^T x_i - W^T x_j\right\|_2^2$. Due to the constraint $rank(L_S) = n - c$, the solution S has exact c components. Suppose the i-th component of S is $S_i \in \mathbb{R}^{n_i\times n_i}$, where n_i is the number of data points in the component, then solving problem (43) is to solve the following problem for each i:

$$\min_{S_i\mathbf{1}=\mathbf{1},S_i\geq 0,W^T S_t W=I} Tr(S_i^T D_i^{wx}) + \gamma \left\|S_i\right\|_F^2 \tag{44}$$

When $\gamma \to \infty$, then the problem (44) becomes

$$\min_{S_i\mathbf{1}=\mathbf{1},S_i\geq 0} \left\|S_i\right\|_F^2 \tag{45}$$

The optimal solution to the problem (45) is that all the elements of S_i are equal to $\frac{1}{n_i}$.

With similar derivation as in Subsection 2.2, we know the problem (43) is equivalent to the following problem when $\gamma \to \infty$:

$$\min_{S\in\mathcal{V},W^T S_t W=I} Tr(HD^{wx}HS) \tag{46}$$

where $\mathcal{V}$ is the solution set of S that satisfies the form in Eq.(20).

Then according to Eq.(46) and Lemma 1, we have

$$\begin{aligned}
&\min_{S\in\mathcal{V},W^T S_t W=I} Tr(HD^{wx}HS)\\
=&\max_{S\in\mathcal{V},W^T S_t W=I} Tr(HXWW^TX^THS)\\
=&\max_{S\in\mathcal{V},W^T S_t W=I} Tr(W^TX^THSHXW)\\
=&\min_{S\in\mathcal{V},W^T S_t W=I} Tr(W^TX^TH(I-S)HXW)\\
=&\min_{Y,W^T S_t W=I} Tr(W^TX^TH(I-YY^T)HXW)\\
=&\min_{Y,W^T S_t W=I} Tr(W^TS_wW)
\end{aligned} \tag{47}$$

where Y is the label matrix defined as in Eq.(23). If the label matrix Y is given, then the optimal solution to the problem (47) is equal to the solution of LDA. Therefore, when $\gamma \to \infty$, the proposed method in Algorithm 2 is to solve the LDA problem, but the labels are also unknown and are to be optimized at the same time. □

When γ is not very large, the matrix $X^T L_S X$ in Eq.(39) can be viewed as local within-class scatter matrix. In this case, the Algorithm 2 can be viewed as a unsupervised version of local scatter matrices based LDA methods, which are designed for handling multimodal non-Gaussian data [17].

4. EXPERIMENTS

In this part, we will show the performance of the proposed clustering method (Algorithm 1) and the projected clustering method (Algorithm 2) on both synthetic data and real data sets. For simplicity, we denote our clustering method as CAN (Clustering with Adaptive Neighbors), and our projected clustering method as PCAN (Projected Clustering with Adaptive Neighbors) in the following context.

4.1 Experiments on Synthetic Data

4.1.1 Experiments to Evaluate CAN Method

We use two synthetic data sets to measure the clustering efficiency of CAN. Also, we find that CAN is able to obtain an excellent initialization index vector for K-Means, which decreases its objective value and promotes its clustering accuracy to a large extent.

The first toy data set we used is a randomly generated two-moon data. In this data set, there are two clusters of data distributed in the two-moon shape. Our goal is to construct a new similarity matrix to divide the data points into exact two clusters. From Fig. 1 we can easily find the clustering efficiency of the proposed CAN method. In this figure, we set the color of the two clusters to be cyan and blue separately and let the width of the connecting line denote the learned similarity of two corresponding points. In the initial similarity matrix learned by Eq.(5), several pairs of points from different clusters are connected. Whereas, after the learning by Eq.(7), there is not even a single line between these two clusters, which means that the proposed clustering method CAN can successfully partition the original data into two classes.

The second toy data set is a randomly generated multi-cluster data. In this data set, there are 196 clusters distributed in a spherical way. Firstly we run K-Means for 10000 times and report the result with the minimal K-means objective value in the independently 10000 times run. Then we run CAN once to generate an clustering result and use it as initialization for K-means. The comparison results are

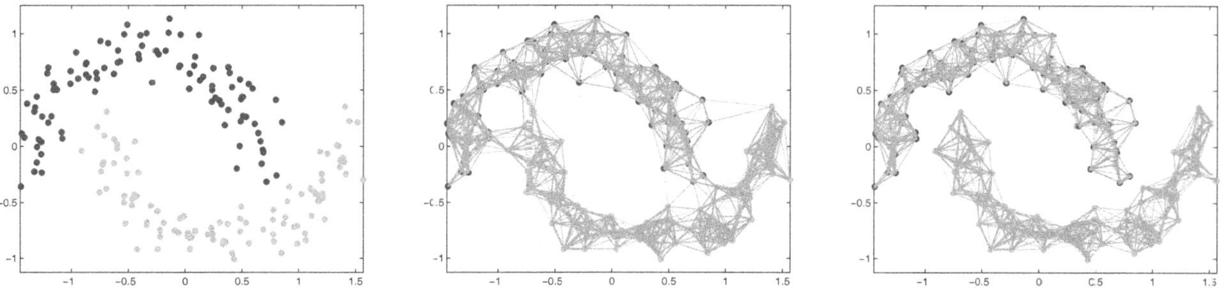

(a) Original Data (b) Learnt Graph by Eq.(5) (c) Learnt Graph by Eq.(7) (CAN)

Figure 1: Learned graph by CAN on the two-moon synthetic data.

shown in Tab. 1 and Fig. 2. It is apparent that even after 10000 times run, the minimal K-means objective value and clustering accuracy obtained by K-means are far behind the result obtained by PCAN with only one run.

Methods	Acc%(min_obj)	Min_obj
K-Means	69.95	318.29
CAN	**98.98**	**106.12**

Table 1: Clustering accuracy and minimal K-Means objective value on multi-cluster synthetic data sets.

4.1.2 *Experiments to Evaluate PCAN Method*

For PCAN method, not only did we measure its clustering efficiency but we also tested its projection ability. The first toy data set for PCAN is a randomly generated three-ring data. In this data set, there are five dimensions, among which the data in the first two dimensions are distributed in a three-circle shape while the data in the other three dimensions are noises.

Since only the first two dimensions contain useful information, it would be important if the method could find a subspace which contains only important dimensions. We compare the PCAN method with two popular dimension reduction methods, Principal Component Analysis (PCA) [11] and Locality Preserving Projections(LPP) [8]. From Fig. 3 we can see the projection results of these three methods. Apparently, PCA and LPP are not powerful enough to find a good subspace for this projection task. In contrast, the proposed method PCAN successfully finds a subspace which is almost the same as the subspace formed by the first two significant dimensions, and also accomplishes the clustering task.

The second toy data set for PCAN is a randomly generated two-Gaussian data. In this data set, there are two clusters of data which obeys the Gaussian distribution. Our goal is to find a good projection direction which helps to partition the two clusters apart. Still, we compare PCAN with PCA and LPP. The comparison results are displayed in Fig. 4. Seen from Fig. 4, we can find out that when these two clusters are far from each other, all these three methods could easily find a good projection direction. However, as the distance between these two clusters lower down, PCA becomes inefficient. As the two clusters become more close, LPP also loses its way to achieve the projection goal. However, the PCAN method always behave well. The reason for this phenomenon is that PCA focus on the global structure thus fail immediately after the two clusters become close. While LPP pays more attention to the local structure, thus could achieve good performance when the two clusters are relatively close. But when the distance of these two clusters are fairly small, LPP is not capable any more. But our method, PCAN, lays more emphasis on the discriminative structure and thus keeps its projection quality all the time.

4.2 Experiments on Real Benchmark Datasets

4.2.1 *Experiments on Clustering*

We evaluated the proposed clustering methods on 15 benchmark datasets: Stock, Pathbased, Movements, Wine, Compound, Spiral, Yeast, Glass, Ecoli, UmistData, COIL25, JAFFE, USPS, Palm and MSRA, among which three are shape data sets, six are biological data sets from UCI Machine Learning Repository and the other six are image data sets. The descriptions of these 15 datasets are summarized in Tab. 2.

We compared our clustering methods CAN and PCAN with K-means, Ratio Cut, Normalized Cut and NMF methods.

In the clustering experiment, we set the number of clusters to be the ground truth in each data set. For those methods calling for an input of an affinity matrix, like Ratio Cut, Normalized Cut and NMF, the graph is constructed with the self-tune Gaussian method [23]. For the methods involving K-means, including K-means, Ratio Cut and Normalized Cut, we use the same initialization and repeat 100 times independently to perform K-means for discretization. For these methods, we record the average performance, standard deviation and the performance corresponding to the best K-Means objective value. As for NMF, CAN and PCAN, we run only once and record the results.

The evaluation of different methods is based on two widely used clustering metrics: accuracy and NMI (normalized mutual information). From Tab. 3 and Tab. 4 we can come into the conclusion that our proposed methods CAN and PCAN outperform other methods on most of the benchmark data sets. We always get a better accuracy and NMI under different circumstances. In addition, the results of other methods are dependent of the initialization, while ours are always stable with a certain setting.

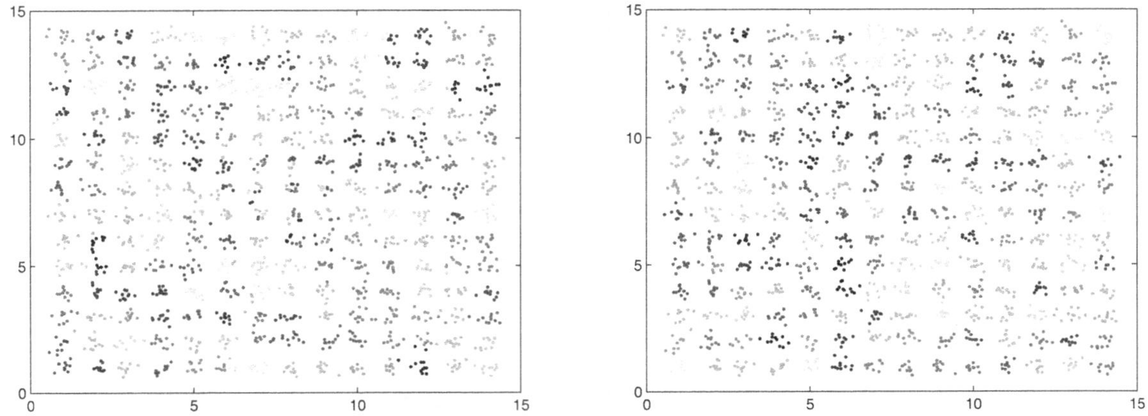

(a) K-Means Result for 196 Clusters (b) CAN Result for 196 Clusters

Figure 2: Clustering results on multi-cluster synthetic data sets.

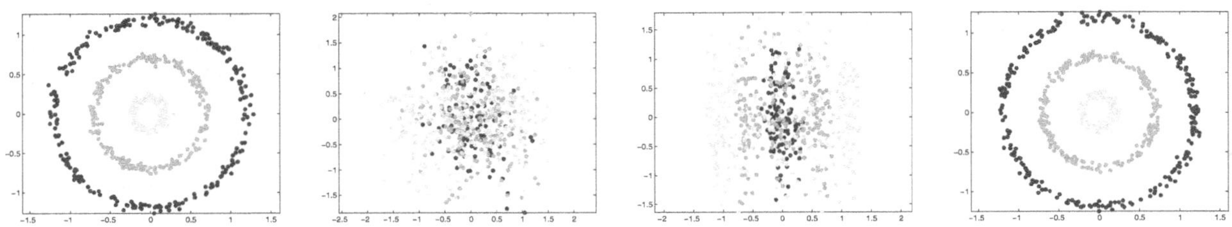

(a) The First Two Dimensions (b) Learnt Subspace by PCA (c) Learnt Subspace by LPP (d) Learnt Subspace by PCAN

Figure 3: Results on the three-ring synthetic data.

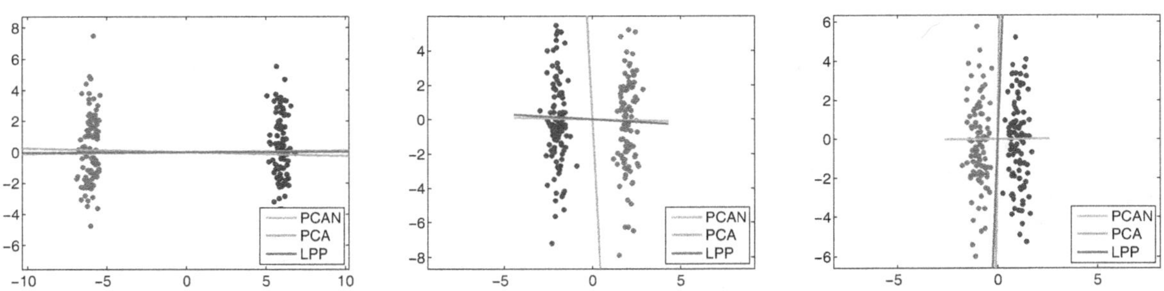

(a) Clusters far away (b) Clusters relatively close (c) Clusters fairly close

Figure 4: Results on the two-Gaussian synthetic data.

4.2.2 Experiments on Projection

In this experiments, we evaluated the projection ability of the proposed PCAN method on 6 benchmark data sets with high dimension: Movements, UmistData, Coil20, Jaffe50, Palm and MSRA50. Similar to that in the synthetic data experiments, we compared PCAN with PCA and LPP methods.

The affinity matrix for LPP is constructed with the self-tune Gaussian method [23]. In order to measure the quality of dimension reduction, we let the three methods learn a projection matrix first and perform K-Means on the projected data for projection ability measurement. For each method, the K-Means method is repeated for 100 times so as to compute the average clustering accuracy and standard deviation.

The results are reported in Fig. 5 and Tab. 5, from which we can see the superiority of the PCAN method for projection task. Moreover, the PCAN method is able to project the original data onto a subspace with quite small dimensions(c-1), where c denotes the number of clusters in each data set. Such a subspace with low dimensions projected by our method would even outperform that obtained by PCA and LPP with higher dimensions. It is worthy to noting that, if we apply PCAN method for only projection task, the c in

	K-Means		Ratio Cut		Normalized Cut		NMF	CAN	PCAN
	%(min_obj)	Average%	%(min_obj)	Average%	%(min_obj)	Average%			
Umist	42.51	43.31±2.66	66.09	60.44±3.81	62.26	59.51±3.50	62.26	**77.57**	68.17
Coil20	71.37	56.54±5.35	77.50	69.42±4.60	79.31	70.30±4.66	70.42	**90.14**	83.33
Jaffe50	91.55	73.70±8.56	96.71	84.78±8.39	96.71	81.63±8.89	96.71	96.71	**100.00**
USPS	65.21	64.27±3.08	69.20	67.59±5.11	69.53	68.43±5.10	67.37	**78.96**	63.81
Palm	72.40	68.43±2.86	65.00	61.35±1.84	63.50	60.97±2.01	61.40	84.85	**88.85**
MSRA50	57.14	53.50±5.00	52.47	49.28±2.67	52.47	47.90±3.53	50.69	**57.87**	**57.87**
Stock	66.74	74.02±11.73	57.68	55.23±4.03	57.68	55.39±5.06	56.21	67.79	**77.16**
Pathbased	74.33	74.34±0.03	77.67	77.67±0.00	77.67	77.67±0.00	78.00	**87.00**	**87.00**
Movements	48.33	44.04±2.27	48.33	46.01±2.29	45.56	44.49±1.90	43.33	**49.17**	**49.17**
Spiral	34.29	34.56±0.26	99.68	96.92±10.10	99.68	96.03±11.82	91.03	**100.00**	**100.00**
Wine	95.51	94.65±0.53	95.51	95.44±0.54	94.94	94.99±4.58	94.94	97.19	**100.00**
Compound	69.42	65.49±9.36	53.63	52.94±3.93	53.13	52.67±3.80	52.38	**80.20**	79.70
Yeast	40.50	38.00±2.13	41.44	38.11±2.18	40.03	36.99±2.81	35.65	**50.27**	50.07
Glass	43.46	45.57±3.51	37.85	38.28±2.27	37.85	38.26±3.00	37.85	**50.00**	49.53
Ecoli	62.50	57.10±6.07	59.23	54.08±5.30	57.44	53.10±4.22	54.17	83.04	**83.33**

Table 3: Clustering Accuracy on Real Datasets

	K-Means		Ratio Cut		Normalized Cut		NMF	CAN	PCAN
	%(min_obj)	Average%	%(min_obj)	Average%	%(min_obj)	Average%			
Umist	66.51	64.44±1.77	81.64	77.78±1.79	78.15	77.26±1.88	78.97	**88.52**	85.60
Coil20	80.56	73.45±2.61	87.10	84.01±1.94	89.17	84.42±1.93	81.22	**94.60**	89.10
Jaffe50	91.75	82.44±5.48	96.23	90.24±4.29	96.23	89.43±4.16	96.23	96.23	**100.00**
USPS	62.99	62.07±1.64	75.80	73.95±2.41	75.78	73.97±2.40	74.15	**80.46**	68.93
Palm	89.42	88.59±1.08	87.17	85.68±0.64	86.53	85.59±0.62	85.73	94.33	**95.14**
MSRA50	66.89	62.79±3.72	59.97	58.59±2.37	59.84	57.38±3.10	63.49	**70.32**	70.10
Stock	73.70	**76.35±6.22**	62.57	56.56±5.69	62.57	56.20±6.40	60.29	74.89	68.30
Pathbased	51.28	51.30±0.04	55.16	55.16±0.00	55.16	55.16±0.00	52.51	**75.63**	**75.63**
Movements	60.43	57.20±1.89	64.76	61.89±2.33	61.39	59.85±2.05	58.95	**64.07**	60.84
Spiral	0.03	0.05±0.02	98.35	94.98±12.34	98.35	94.19±13.95	75.95	**100.00**	**100.00**
Wine	84.89	82.41±1.44	84.47	84.37±1.25	83.24	84.02±3.90	83.24	88.97	**100.00**
Compound	69.68	69.60±5.68	73.37	70.71±4.44	73.34	70.29±4.39	73.26	**79.27**	78.65
Yeast	26.15	25.19±1.06	27.95	24.94±1.37	25.63	23.88±1.35	23.66	30.30	**30.55**
Glass	32.95	33.13±2.60	29.37	29.10±3.05	28.00	28.58±2.49	28.70	26.91	**33.82**
Ecoli	53.34	53.04±3.02	51.26	48.96±3.11	51.26	49.78±2.32	47.12	72.20	**72.44**

Table 4: Clustering NMI on Real Datasets

Data sets	Num of Instances	Dimensions	Classes
Stock	950	10	5
Pathbased	300	2	3
Movements	360	90	15
Spiral	312	2	3
Wine	178	13	3
Compound	399	2	6
Yeast	1484	8	10
Glass	219	9	6
Ecoli	367	7	8
Umist	165	3456	15
Coil20	1440	1024	20
Jaffe50	213	1024	10
USPS	1854	256	10
Palm	2000	256	100
MSRA50	1799	1024	12

Table 2: Descriptions of 15 Benchmark Datasets

PCAN can be viewed as a parameter and thus we can reduce data into arbitrary dimensions. In this experiment, we set the c in PCAN to the class number of data for simplicity.

	PCA	LPP	PCAN
Palm	68.66±2.55	78.77±2.94	**80.03±2.96**
MSRA50	54.65±4.37	52.93±4.31	**62.31±3.68**
Movements	44.46±2.48	47.47±2.55	**55.99±3.06**
Jaffe50	77.45±7.30	79.41±9.61	**81.78±10.15**
Umist	43.85±2.28	64.55±4.66	**67.39±4.53**
Coil20	59.39±4.63	73.32±5.10	**74.93±5.43**

Table 5: The best results with optimal dimensions.

5. CONCLUSIONS

In this paper, we proposed a novel clustering model to simultaneously learn the data similarity matrix and the clustering structure. In our new clustering method, the data similarity matrix is learned by assigning the adaptive neighbors for each data point based on the local connectivity. The new rank constraint is imposed on the Laplacian matrix of the data similarity matrix to create the clustering structure in the similarity matrix as several disconnected components. We derived an efficient algorithm to optimize the proposed challenging problem, and proved the theoretical connections between our method and other clustering approaches. We further extended the proposed clustering model for the projected clustering on high-dimensional data. Extensive experiments have been conducted on both synthetic data and 15

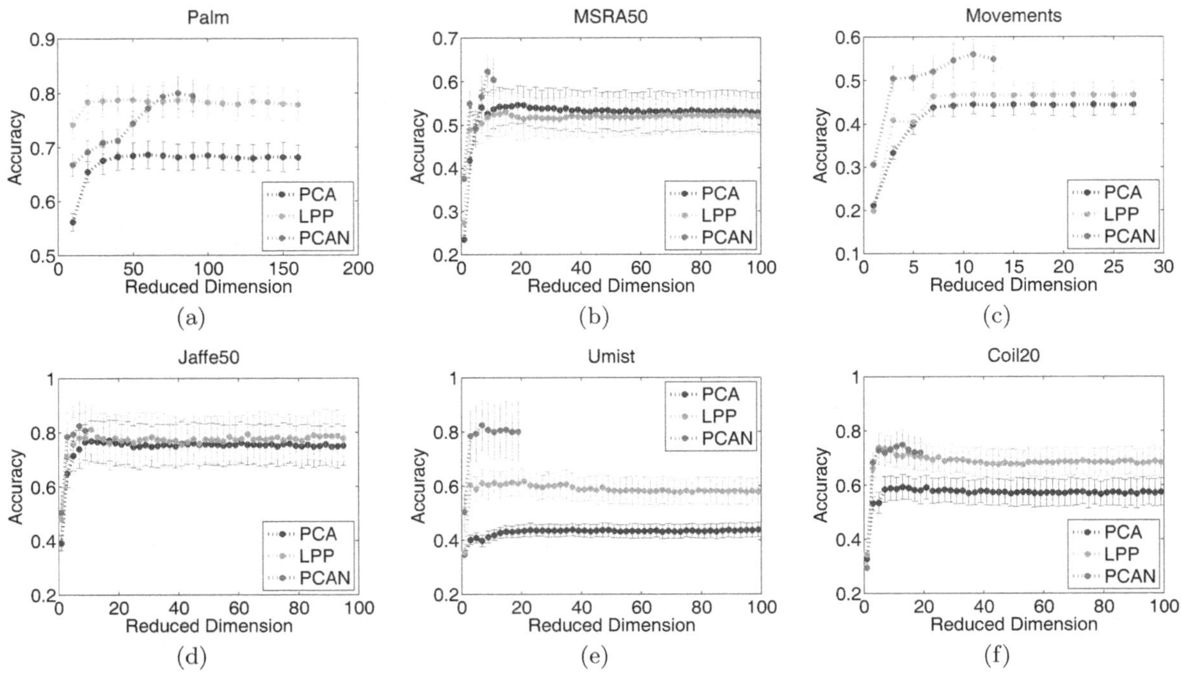

Figure 5: Results of projection methods on 6 benchmark data sets.

real-world benchmark data sets to demonstrate the superior performance of our models.

6. ACKNOWLEDGMENTS

This research was partially supported by NSF-IIS 1117965, NSF-IIS 1302675, NSF-IIS 1344152, NSF-DBI 1356628.

7. REFERENCES

[1] A. Ben-Hur, D. Horn, H. Siegelmann, and V. Vapnik. Support vector clustering. 2:125–137, 2001.

[2] S. Boyd and L. Vandenberghe. *Convex optimization.* Cambridge University Press, 2004.

[3] X. Cai, F. Nie, and H. Huang. Multi-view k-means clustering on big data. *23rd International Joint Conference on Artificial Intelligence (IJCAI)*, pages 2598–2604, 2013.

[4] X. Cai, F. Nie, H. Huang, and F. Kamangar. Heterogeneous image features integration via multi-modal spectral clustering. In *The 24th IEEE Conference on Computer Vision and Pattern Recognition (CVPR 2011)*, pages 1977–1984, 2011.

[5] F. R. K. Chung. *Spectral Graph Theory.* CBMS Regional Conference Series in Mathematics, No. 92, American Mathematical Society, February 1997.

[6] K. Fan. On a theorem of weyl concerning eigenvalues of linear transformations. i. 35(11):652–655, 1949.

[7] L. W. Hagen and A. B. Kahng. New spectral methods for ratio cut partitioning and clustering. *IEEE Transactions on Computer-Aided Design of Integrated Circuits and Systems*, 11(9):1074–1085, 1992.

[8] X. He and P. Niyogi. Locality preserving projections. In *NIPS*, 2003.

[9] J. Huang, F. Nie, and H. Huang. Spectral rotation versus k-means in spectral clustering. In *AAAI*, 2013.

[10] S. C. Johnson. Hierarchical clustering schemes. *Psychometrika*, 2:241–254, 1967.

[11] I. T. Jolliffe. *Principal Component Analysis,2nd Edition.* Springer-Verlag, New York, 2002.

[12] T. Li and C. H. Q. Ding. The relationships among various nonnegative matrix factorization methods for clustering. In *ICDM*, pages 362–371, 2006.

[13] J. B. MacQueen. Some methods for classification and analysis of multivariate observations. In *Proceedings of 5-th Berkeley Symposium on Mathematical Statistics and Probability*, pages 281–297. Berkeley, University of California Press, 1967.

[14] B. Mohar. The laplacian spectrum of graphs. In *Graph Theory, Combinatorics, and Applications*, pages 871–898. Wiley, 1991.

[15] A. Y. Ng, M. I. Jordan, and Y. Weiss. On spectral clustering: Analysis and an algorithm. *Advances in Neural Information Processing Systems (NIPS)*, 14:849–856, 2002.

[16] F. Nie, C. H. Q. Ding, D. Luo, and H. Huang. Improved minmax cut graph clustering with nonnegative relaxation. In *ECML/PKDD*, pages 451–466, 2010.

[17] F. Nie, S. Xiang, and C. Zhang. Neighborhood minmax projections. In *IJCAI*, pages 993–998, 2007.

[18] F. Nie, D. Xu, and X. Li. Initialization independent clustering with actively self-training method. *IEEE Transactions on Systems, Man, and Cybernetics, Part B*, 42(1):17–27, 2012.

[19] F. Nie, Z. Zeng, I. W. Tsang, D. Xu, and C. Zhang. Spectral embedded clustering: A framework for in-sample and out-of-sample spectral clustering. *IEEE Transactions on Neural Networks*, 22(11):1796–1808, 2011.

[20] J. Shi and J. Malik. Normalized cuts and image segmentation. *IEEE Transactions on PAMI*, 22(8):888–905, 2000.

[21] H. Wang, F. Nie, and H. Huang. Multi-view clustering and feature learning via structured sparsity. *The 30th International Conference on Machine Learning (ICML 2013)*, pages 352–360, 2013.

[22] L. Xu, J. Neufeld, B. Larson, and D. Schuurmans. Maximum margin clustering. Cambridge, MA, 2005. MIT Press.

[23] L. Zelnik-Manor and P. Perona. Self-tuning spectral clustering. In *NIPS*, 2004.

LWI-SVD: Low-rank, Windowed, Incremental Singular Value Decompositions on Time-Evolving Data Sets *

Xilun Chen, K. Selçuk Candan
Computer Science and Engineering School of Computing-IDSE (CIDSE), Arizona State University
Tempe, AZ, USA
xilun.chen@asu.edu, candan@asu.edu

ABSTRACT

Singular Value Decomposition (SVD) is computationally costly and therefore a naive implementation does not scale to the needs of scenarios where data evolves continuously. While there are various on-line analysis and incremental decomposition techniques, these may not accurately represent the data or may be slow for the needs of many applications. To address these challenges, in this paper, we propose a *Low-rank, Windowed, Incremental SVD* (LWI-SVD) algorithm, which (a) leverages efficient and accurate *low-rank approximations* to speed up incremental SVD updates and (b) uses a *window-based* approach to aggregate multiple incoming updates (insertions or deletions of rows and columns) and, thus, reduces online processing costs. We also present an *LWI-SVD with restarts* (LWI2-SVD) algorithm which leverages a novel highly efficient *partial reconstruction* based change detection scheme to support timely refreshing of the decomposition with significant changes in the data and prevent accumulation of errors over time. Experiment results, including comparisons to other state of the art techniques on different data sets and under different parameter settings, confirm that LWI-SVD and LWI2-SVD are both efficient and accurate in maintaining decompositions.

1. INTRODUCTION

Feature selection and dimensionality reduction techniques [20] usually involve some (often linear) transformation of the vector space containing the data to help focus on a few features (or combinations of features) that best discriminate the data in a given corpus. For example, the singular value decomposition (SVD [7]) of a data feature matrix A is of the form $A = USV^T$, where the r *orthogonal* column vectors of U form an r dimensional basis in which the n data objects can be described. Also, the r *orthogonal* column vectors of V (or the rows vector of V^T) form an r dimensional basis in which the m features can be placed. These r dimensions are referred to as the *latent variables* [16] or the *latent semantics* of the database [7]: Intuitively, the columns of U can be thought of as the eigen-objects of the data, each corresponding to one independent concept/cluster, and the columns of V can be thought of as the eigen-features of the collection, each, once again, corresponding to a concept/cluster in the database. In other words, SVD can be used for co-clustering both data-objects and features simultaneously. The $r \times r$ diagonal matrix S, can be considered to represent the strength of the corresponding latent concepts in the database: the amount of error caused by the removal of a concept from the database is proportional to the corresponding singular value.

*This work is partially funded by NSF grants #1339835 and #1318788. This work is also supported in part by the NSF I/UCRC Center for Embedded Systems established through the NSF grant #0856090.

KDD'14, August 24–27, 2014, New York, NY, USA.

http://dx.doi.org/10.1145/2623330.2623671.

1.1 Incremental SVD and Related Works

SVD is computationally costly and therefore a naive implementation does not match the real-time needs of scenarios where data evolve continuously: decomposition of an $n \times m$ matrix requires $O(n \times m \times min(n, m))$ time. While there are various on-line techniques, these are often slow or inaccurate. For example, one of the fastest techniques, SPIRIT [13] focuses on row insertions and cannot directly handle row deletions or column insertions/deletions. While a forgetting factor can be introduced to discount old objects it cannot immediately reflect the properties of the removed entries on the decomposition. Moreover, since SPIRIT primarily considers data insertions and deletions, it is not applicable in situations where features of interest themselves evolve with the data (examples include weights of tags extracted from data and proximity to the hubs within an evolving network). As we see in Section 5, it has a higher inaccuracy compared to other incremental techniques, such as [5].

Other incremental SVD algorithms, such as [5, 6, 8, 9, 11, 12, 14, 15, 17], operate on an existing SV decomposition by folding-in new data and features into an existing (often low-rank) SVD; algebraic matrix manipulation techniques are used to rewrite the new SV decomposition matrices in terms of the old SV decomposition and update (including downdating) matrices. [5] showed that a number of database updates (including removal of columns) can all be cast as additive modifications to the original $n \times m$ database matrix, A. These updates then can be reflected on the SVD in $O(nmr)$ time as long as the rank, r, of the matrix A is such that $r \leq \sqrt{min(p, q)}$, where p is the number of new rows and q is the number of new columns. In other words, as long as the latent dimensionality of the database is low, the singular value decomposition can be updated in linear time. [5] further showed that the update to SVD can be computed in a single pass over the data matrix making the process highly efficient for large data. This and other existing algorithms can nevertheless be slow for many real-time applications.

1.2 Contributions of this Paper

In Section 2 we formalize these challenges and in Section 3, we propose a *Low-rank, Windowed, Incremental SVD* (LWI-SVD) algorithm, which leverages efficient and accurate *low-rank approxi-*

mations to speed up incremental SVD updates and uses a *window-based* approach to aggregate multiple incoming updates (insertion or deletions) and, thus reduces on-line costs. We also present, in Section 4, an LWI2-SVD algorithm which leverages a novel partial reconstruction based change detection technique to support timely refreshing of the decompositions to prevent accumulation of errors.

Experiment results reported in Section 5 confirm that LWI-SVD and LWI2-SVD are both efficient and accurate in maintaining decompositions. We conclude the paper in Section 6.

2. BACKGROUND

2.1 Problem Definition

At time stamp i, we are given a set of n data tuples $D_i = \{t_{i,1}, t_{i,2}, ..., t_{i,n}\}$, each with a set, F_i, of m features. We are also given the set, L_i, containing the r latent semantics of D_i (and their weights). As time moves, new tuples arrive and some of the existing tuples expire: at the next time stamp, t_{i+1}, the tuple set is $D_{i+1} = (D_i \backslash \Delta D^-_{i+1}) \cup \Delta D^+_{i+1}$, where ΔD^-_{i+1} are the tuples that expired and ΔD^+_{i+1} are the new tuples that arrived. Moreover, at time $(i+1)$, we have a new set, F_{i+1}, of features, where $F_{i+1} = (F_i \backslash \Delta F^-_{i+1}) \cup \Delta F^+_{i+1}$, where ΔF^-_{i+1} are features that are not of interest anymore and ΔF^+_{i+1} are the new features of interest.

Our goal is to quickly obtain L_{i+1} containing the r latent semantics corresponding to time instance, $i+1$, and efficiently maintain these r latent semantics as time further moves.

2.2 Basic Incremental SVD [5]

Let us be given an $n \times m$ data matrix $X = U_x S_x V_x^T$ and an $n' \times m'$ updated data matrix $X' = X + \Delta$, where Δ is a $max(n, n') \times max(m, m')$ change matrix. Note that if X' has larger dimension than X, X is padded with $n' - n$ rows of zero and $m' - m$ columns of zero to match the dimension of Δ, the removal of rows and columns are modeled by additions that result in zeroing of the corresponding rows and columns (which are then dropped from the matrix). Let us further assume that the change matrix Δ can be decomposed into $\Delta = AB^T$. Note that we can rewrite the matrix X' as

$$X' = X + AB^T = \begin{bmatrix} U_x & A \end{bmatrix} \begin{bmatrix} S_x & 0 \\ 0 & I \end{bmatrix} \begin{bmatrix} V_x & B \end{bmatrix}^T. \quad (1)$$

Given these, [5] incrementally maintains SVD as follows:

2.2.1 QR Decompositions

Let us also define Q_A as the orthogonal basis of $(I - U_x U_x^T)A$ and Q_B as the orthogonal basis of $(I - V_x V_x^T)B$. Both Q_A and Q_B can be obtained through QR decomposition [4] of $(I - U_x U_x^T)A$ and $(I - V_x V_x^T)B$:

$$Q_A R_A = (I - U_x U_x^T)A; \qquad Q_B R_B = (I - V_x V_x^T)B \quad (2)$$

Here Q_A and Q_B are orthogonal matrices and R_A and R_B are upper-triangular. It is easy to see, through basic matrix algebra, that the following holds:

$$\begin{bmatrix} U_x & A \end{bmatrix} = \begin{bmatrix} U_x & Q_A \end{bmatrix} \begin{bmatrix} I & U_x^T A \\ 0 & R_A \end{bmatrix} \quad (3)$$

$$\begin{bmatrix} V_x & B \end{bmatrix} = \begin{bmatrix} V_x & Q_B \end{bmatrix} \begin{bmatrix} I & V_x^T B \\ 0 & R_B \end{bmatrix} \quad (4)$$

Moreover, by substituting Equations 3 and 4 into Equation 1, we can get

$$X' = X + AB^T = \begin{bmatrix} U_x & Q_A \end{bmatrix} K \begin{bmatrix} V_x & Q_B \end{bmatrix}^T \quad (5)$$

where K is equal to

$$K = \begin{bmatrix} I & U_x^T A \\ 0 & R_A \end{bmatrix} \begin{bmatrix} S_x & 0 \\ 0 & I \end{bmatrix} \begin{bmatrix} I & V_x^T B \\ 0 & R_B \end{bmatrix}^T \quad (6)$$

$$= \begin{bmatrix} S_x & 0 \\ 0 & 0 \end{bmatrix} + \begin{bmatrix} U_x^T A \\ R_A \end{bmatrix} \begin{bmatrix} V_x^T B \\ R_B \end{bmatrix}^T \quad (7)$$

2.2.2 Matrix K

Let us remember that X is an $n \times m$ matrix and X' is an $n' \times m'$ matrix. Given this

- if $n \geq n'$ and $m \geq m'$, K is a matrix of size $(n+1) \times (m+1)$. This is because, if $n \geq n'$, then U_x is an orthogonal matrix and $U_x U_x^T$ is equal to I. Consequently, $Q_A R_A = (I - U_x U_x^T)A = 0$ and this implies that R_A is simply 0. The same is true for R_B.
- if $n < n'$ and $m < m'$, K is a matrix of size $n' \times m'$. In Section 3.2.1, we discuss the shape K takes in this case and the resulting properties in detail.
- if $n \geq n'$ and $m < m'$, K is a matrix of size $(n+1) \times m'$.
- if $n < n'$ and $m \geq m'$, K is a matrix of size $n' \times (m+1)$.

2.2.3 Using the Decomposition of K to Obtain the Decomposition of X'

Let us consider the SV decomposition of K; i.e., $K = U_K S_K V_K^T$. Equation 1 can be rewritten [5] as

$$X' = X + AB^T = (\begin{bmatrix} U_x & Q_A \end{bmatrix} U_K) S_K (\begin{bmatrix} V_x & Q_B \end{bmatrix} V_K)^T \quad (8)$$

giving us the SVD of the new tuple matrix, X'.

The challenge, of course, is to obtain the matrices, Q_A and Q_B, and the SV decomposition of K efficiently. In order to keep the complexity down, [5] suggests that A and B should be taken as combination of simple column vectors so that AB^T can be the sum of multiple rank-1 matrices. This, however, may be a significant constraint in real-applications where the change matrix Δ itself can have a large size, indicating great amount of rank-1 matrices it produces and updating a sequence of rank-1 matrix is not effective as treating them as a whole. In the next section, we discuss how to relax this assumption of [5] without impacting efficiency and accuracy.

3. LWI-SVD

We now present our key ideas for efficient incremental SVD operations. As described above, this involves efficiently searching for matrices, Q_A and Q_B, and the SVD of K.

3.1 Efficiently Obtaining Q_A and Q_B

As described above, Q_A is the orthogonal basis of $(I - U_x U_x^T)A$ and Q_B is the orthogonal basis of $(I - V_x V_x^T)B$. These can be obtained using two expensive QR decomposition operations for both Q_A and Q_B. One way to reduce the number of QR decomposition operations would be to seek a decomposition of Δ where $X' = X + \Delta = AA^T$; i.e., $A = B$. However, not all Δ will have such a convenient decomposition. When Δ is negative definite, it cannot be written as the format of $A \times B$ where $A = B$.

Instead, in this paper, we propose to reduce the cost of the overall QR decomposition step by setting A to the identity matrix I and setting B^T to Δ. This does not lose any generality on the algorithn since Δ (B^T) can be any matrix. When we do this, since $A = I$, it would also be the case that $Q_A = \begin{bmatrix} 0 \\ I \end{bmatrix}$. Therefore, we need only one QR decomposition. What is more, if the Δ only reflect a small amount of data insertions and deletions, then it will be a sparse matrix with last few rows and columns of nonzero values. This lead to efficient computation of $(I - V_x V_x^T)B$ and $V_x^T B$ by block matrix multiplication. Let's first find the zero block of B when it is data insertion. Then Δ (B) is a $n' \times m'$ matrix with a block of zero values on the first $n \times m$ position. We can rewrite B as

$$B = \begin{bmatrix} 0 & B_1 \\ B_2 & B_3 \end{bmatrix}$$

Then, we can divide $(I - V_x V_x^T)$ and V_x^T into the same block size as B. For example, we can rewrite V_x^T as

$$V_x^T = \begin{bmatrix} V_{x0}^T & V_{x1}^T \\ V_{x2}^T & V_{x3}^T \end{bmatrix}$$

Then, the multiplication of $V_x^T B$ becomes

$$V_x^T \times B = \begin{bmatrix} V_{x1}^T \times B_2 & V_{x0}^T \times B_1 + V_{x1}^T \times B_3 \\ V_{x3}^T \times B_2 & V_{x2}^T \times B_1 + V_{x3}^T \times B_3 \end{bmatrix}$$

Note that, the multiplication of V_{x0}^T and the corresponding block of B is avoided since the corresponding block of B is all zeros. Also, the other part of V_x^T and B are small size thin matrices. Thus, the multiplication of $V_x^T \times B$ can be done very efficiently. The same applies to $(I - V_x V_x^T) \times B$ and when the data are deleted.

As we experimentally show in Section 5.4.1, this optimization provides significant gains in time, without any noticeable loss in the final accuracy.

3.2 Efficiently Decomposing K

The next challenge is to obtain the singular value decomposition of the matrix, K. Performing SVD on K directly would be costly as the SVD operation is expensive. However, as we prove next, in Section 3.2.1, in the presence of row and column insertions, K takes a special structure:

$$K = \begin{bmatrix} S_x & 0 \\ 0 & 0 \end{bmatrix} + \begin{bmatrix} U_x^T A \\ R_A \end{bmatrix} \begin{bmatrix} V_x^T B \\ R_B \end{bmatrix}^T = \begin{bmatrix} S_x & \Pi \\ \Phi & \Gamma \end{bmatrix}.$$

More specifically, in the presence of insertions, (a) since S_x is diagonal, K is mostly sparse, and (b) it is shaped like an arrow: (aside from the diagonal) there are non-zeros only on its last rows and columns. We verify these next.

3.2.1 Shape of K

Let X be an $n \times m$ matrix and X' be an $n' \times m'$ matrix. In Section 2.2.2, we have seen that K is either of size $n' \times m'$, $(n+1) \times (m+1)$, $(n+1) \times m$, or $n' \times (m+1)$, depending on whether the numbers of rows and columns increase or decrease when the data matrix transforms from X to X'. Let us further assume that $n \leq m$ and $m' > m$ and $n' > n$, which is rows and columns insertion. As we already discussed before, let us set $A = I_{n'}$ and $B^T = \Delta$, where $A \in \mathbb{R}^{n' \times n'}$, $B \in \mathbb{R}^{m' \times n'}$ and $\Delta \in \mathbb{R}^{n' \times m'}$ so that AB^T is equal to the update matrix Δ. Finally, let SVD of X be $X = U_x S_x V_x^T$, or simply $X = USV^T$.

Given the fact that $X' = X + \Delta$, we can also deduce that $X' = U'SV'^T + \Delta$, where

$$U' = \begin{bmatrix} U \\ 0 \end{bmatrix} \in \mathbb{R}^{n' \times n} \text{ and } V' = \begin{bmatrix} V \\ 0 \end{bmatrix} \in \mathbb{R}^{m' \times m}.$$

Intuitively, U and V are augmented by padding $n' - n$ rows of zeros to U and $m' - m$ rows of zeros to V to make it compatible with Δ. This padding gives us

$$X' = \begin{bmatrix} X & 0 \\ 0 & 0 \end{bmatrix} + \Delta = U'SV'^T + \Delta.$$

Secondly, using a similar zero-padding, we can get the following equalities:

$$(I_{n'} - U'U'^T)A = \begin{bmatrix} 0 & 0 \\ 0 & I_{n'-n} \end{bmatrix} \quad (9)$$

$$(I_{m'} - V'V'^T)B = \begin{bmatrix} 0 \\ B_{m'-m} \end{bmatrix} \quad (10)$$

The right hand side of Equation 9 has $n' - n$ independent columns and, thus, it has a simple QR decomposition:

$$Q_A = \begin{bmatrix} 0 \\ I_{n'-n} \end{bmatrix} \text{ and } R_A = \begin{bmatrix} 0 & I_{n'-n} \end{bmatrix}$$

Since the right hand side of the Equation 10 consists of 0s except for the last $m' - m$ rows, the QR decomposition of the left hand side will be such that $Q_B \in \mathbb{R}^{(m'-m) \times m}$ and $R_B \in \mathbb{R}^{(m'-m) \times n'}$. Let us further partition R_B into two,

$$R_B = \begin{bmatrix} R_{B1} & R_{B2} \end{bmatrix},$$

where $R_{B1} \in \mathbb{R}^{(m'-m) \times n}$ and $R_{B2} \in \mathbb{R}^{(m'-m) \times (n'-n)}$.

Given the above, we can rewrite the matrix, K, as

$$K = \begin{bmatrix} S & 0 \\ 0 & 0 \end{bmatrix} + \begin{bmatrix} U'^T A \\ R_A \end{bmatrix} \begin{bmatrix} V'^T B \\ R_B \end{bmatrix}^T$$

where

$$\begin{bmatrix} U'^T A \\ R_A \end{bmatrix} = \begin{bmatrix} U^T & 0 \\ 0 & I_{n'-n} \end{bmatrix}$$

$$\begin{bmatrix} V'^T B \\ R_B \end{bmatrix}^T = \begin{bmatrix} 0 & Y \\ R_{B1} & R_{B2} \end{bmatrix}^T.$$

Here Y is a $m \times (n' - n)$ matrix. Note that we can further rewrite

$$\begin{bmatrix} U'^T A \\ R_A \end{bmatrix} \begin{bmatrix} V'^T B \\ R_B \end{bmatrix}^T = \begin{bmatrix} U'^T A \\ R_A \end{bmatrix} \begin{bmatrix} (V'^T B) \\ R_{B1} \quad R_{B2} \end{bmatrix}^T$$

as

$$\begin{bmatrix} U^T & 0 \\ 0 & I_{n'-n} \end{bmatrix} \begin{bmatrix} 0 & Y \\ R_{B1} & R_{B2} \end{bmatrix}^T = \begin{bmatrix} 0 & U^T R_{B1}^T \\ Y^T & R_{B2}^T \end{bmatrix}.$$

Thus, K simplifies to

$$K = \begin{bmatrix} S & U^T R_{B1}^T \\ Y^T & R_{B2}^T \end{bmatrix} = \begin{bmatrix} S & \Pi \\ \Phi & \Gamma \end{bmatrix}.$$

This confirms that when $m < m'$ and $n < n'$, K is shaped like an arrow: it is diagonal, except for the last $n' - n$ rows and last $m' - m$ columns. This, however, is not true when $m \geq m'$ or $n \geq n'$; in this case K can be a dense matrix, with its last row and columns equal to 0. In the rest of this section, we argue that, especially when $m < m'$ and $n < n'$, we can leverage K's specific structure (sparse, arrow-like) to quickly obtain a highly-accurate approximate decomposition, $K \sim \hat{U}\hat{S}\hat{V}^T$ and use it instead of the exact decomposition $K = U'S'V'^T$. In particular we propose to build on the *SVD through QR decomposition with column pivoting* technique proposed in [4]. Experiment results reported in Section 5 show that this leads to efficient and accurate decompositions even in cases where $m \geq m'$ or $n \geq n'$.

3.2.2 Decomposition of K through Pivoted QR

Pivoted QR Factorization. Let E be a matrix. A pivoted QR factorization of E has the form $EP = Q_e R_e$ where P is a permutation matrix, Q_e is orthonormal and R_e is upper triangular. [4] has shown that a rank-k approximation can be obtained efficiently through a pivoting process where columns of E are considered one at a time and used to compute an additional column of Q_e and row of R_e. The kth round of the process leads to a rank-k approximation of the pivoted QR factorization of E. In particular, let us assume that we are given a QR decomposition of the form $F = Q_f R_f$ and need to compute QR decomposition of $[F\ a]$ for some column vector a:

$$[F\ a] = [Q_f\ q] \begin{bmatrix} R_f & \epsilon \\ 0 & \rho \end{bmatrix}$$

The rank-k approximation can be obtained efficiently by the quasi-Gram-Schmidt method, which further eliminates the need to store dense Q_f matrices [4]: the quasi-Gram-Schmidt process can be applied successively to columns of a given input matrix E to produce a pivoted QR factorization for E.

Low-Rank Decomposition of K. Let us assume that we are targeting a rank-k decomposition of K. We first sample k columns to obtain column-sample matrix $\mathcal{C}$; we then sample k columns from K^T to obtain a row-sample matrix $\mathcal{R}^T$. We then apply the QR decomposition with column pivoting to $\mathcal{C}$ and $\mathcal{R}^T$ to obtain upper triangular matrices, R_c and R_r.

The sampling is done by selecting the longest row and column vectors. We note that when $m < m'$ and $n < n'$, K is not only sparse, but also has an arrow-like shape:

$$K = \begin{bmatrix} S_x & \Pi \\ \Phi & \Gamma \end{bmatrix},$$

where the $n \times m$ matrix S_x is diagonal, whereas $n \times (m' - m)$ matrix Π, $(n' - n) \times m$ matrix Φ, and $(n' - n) \times (m' - m)$ matrix Γ are potentially dense as we discussed in Section 3.2.1. As a result, the sampling is *arrow-sensitive* in the sense that it focuses on the last few rows and columns: The sampled columns usually come from the first few columns (which contain the largest singular values at the top-left corner of the matrix) and the last few columns, which contain entries from the dense, $\begin{bmatrix} \Pi \\ \Gamma \end{bmatrix}$. Similarly, the sampled rows come from the first few rows (which contain large singular values in S_x) and the last few rows from $\begin{bmatrix} \Phi & \Gamma \end{bmatrix}$.

Given these, to obtain a decomposition of K, we need to find a matrix H such that $\|K - \mathcal{C}H\mathcal{R}^T\|$ is minimized. According to [15], the value of H which minimizes this can be computed as

$$(R_c^{-1} R_c^{-T})(\mathcal{C}^T K \mathcal{R})(R_r^{-1} R_r^{-T}).$$

Thus, we can rewrite $\mathcal{C}H\mathcal{R}^T$ as

$$(\mathcal{C}R_c^{-1})(R_c^{-T}\mathcal{C}^T K \mathcal{R} R_r^{-1})(R_r^{-T}\mathcal{R}^T).$$

If we further set $W = R_c^{-T}\mathcal{C}^T K \mathcal{R} R_r^{-1}$ and decompose W into $W = U_w S_w V_w^T$, then we can obtain the SV decomposition of K as $K = U_K S_K, V_K^T$, where

$$U_K = \mathcal{C}R_c^{-1}U_w, \quad V_K^T = V_w^T R_r^{-1} R_r^{-T}, \quad \text{and} \quad S_K = S_w,$$

where U_K and V_K are orthonormal and S_K is diagonal. While this process also involves an SV decomposition step involving W, since W is a much smaller, $k \times k$, matrix, its decomposition is much faster than the direct decomposition of K.

3.3 Pseudocode of LWI-SVD

Algorithm 1 provides the pseudo-code of the proposed Low-rank, Windowed, Incremental Singular Value Decomposition (LWI-SVD) algorithm for incrementally maintaining the SVD of an evolving matrix X. As we later see in Section 5, the LWI-SVD algorithm has a smaller approximation error than other algorithms, such as SPIRIT [13], yet is also much faster than optimal as well as the basic incremental SVD [5] algorithms. Yet, as in any incremental approximate algorithm, in which each step takes the output of

Algorithm 1 LWI-SVD.

Input:

The Base Matrix, X, and its SV decomposition $U_x S_x V_x^T$;

The update matrix, $\Delta = AB^T$, corresponding to a window of updates;

Target rank, r;

Output:

The new SVD results, U_x', S_x', and V_x';

1: Calculate factors R_A and R_B in Equation 2 which, as discussed in Section 3.1, involves a QR Decomposition and several matrix multiplications;

2: Calculate the matrix K in Equation 7;

3: Obtain the low-rank (rank-r) decomposition of K into $K = U_K S_K V_K^T$;

4: Combine the factors as shown in Equation 8 to obtain rank-r decomposition U_x', S_x', and V_x';

5: **return** U_x', S_x', and V_x';

the previous step as its input, there is a likelihood that errors will accumulate over time and the reconstruction error relative to the actual matrix will reach an unacceptable rate. To prevent errors to accumulate, in the next section we propose a novel *LWI-SVD with Restart* (LWI2-SVD) algorithm which restarts the SVD by performing a fresh SVD on the current data matrix.

4. LWI2-SVD: LWI-SVD WITH RESTART

In this section, we build on LWI-SVD and propose a novel *LWI-SVD with Restart* (LWI2-SVD) algorithm which punctuates the incremental SVD sequence by occasionally performing a full SVD on the current data matrix. Obviously, there is a direct, positive correlation between the frequency of restarts and the overall accuracy of the LWI2-SVD algorithm. Unfortunately, however, there is also a strong positive correlation between the cost of LWI2-SVD and the frequency of restarts. Therefore, restart rate should be such that the process is restarted only when the costly SVD is in fact needed to help reduce the overall error.

4.1 Types of Errors

We see that there are two distinct types of errors:

- *Accumulated approximation errors (and periodic restarts):* The first type of error that accumulates over time is due to the various approximation terms, including the low-rank approximation of K as discussed in Section 3.2. While the absolute value of this error will be different from one iteration of the algorithm to the next, its long term behavior will be roughly constant. Therefore, this type of accumulated approximation errors are best dealt with *periodic restarts*.
- *Error bursts due to structural changes in the input data (and on-demand restarts):* The second type of error in the incremental SVD occurs when there is a significant structural (or spectral) change in the data, necessitating large changes in the SVD. Since the incremental process described in Section 3 assumes that the changes are relatively small, a significant structural change in the factor matrices, U_x and V_x, or the core matrix S_x may not be correctly captured, resulting in a large burst of reconstruction error. These bursts are best dealt with *on-demand restarts* that are triggered through a change detection process that tracks the updates to identify when major structural changes in the data occur.

Figure 1 shows an example run with and without restarts. Note that without the restarts errors continuously accumulate due to structural changes in the data. Restarts (both periodic and on-demand)

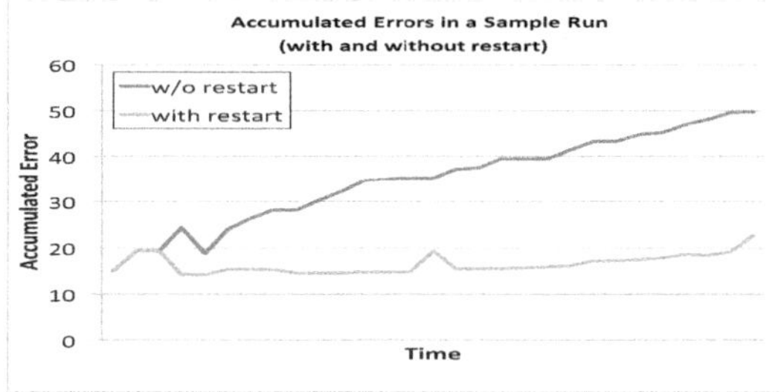

Figure 1: Example runs with and without restarts

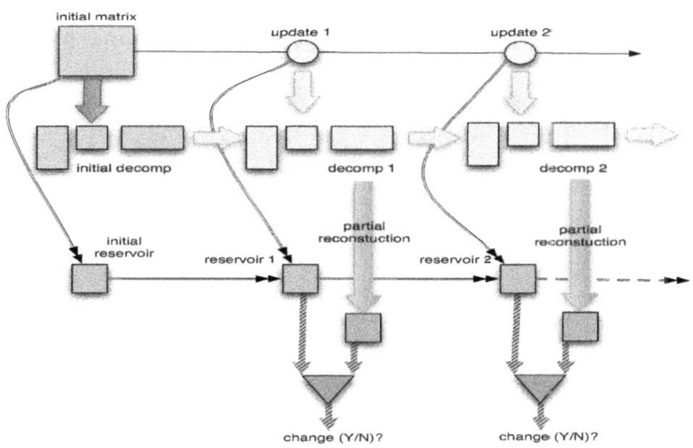

Figure 2: Overview of the change detection process

can limit the accumulation of errors. Error accumulations due to approximations generally show a regular behavior and the frequency with which periodic restarts are scheduled can be set empirically. The structural changes in the data, however, do not necessarily have a regular behavior; therefore, the challenge is to quickly and efficiently detect the structural changes in the data. We will discuss this next.

4.2 Change Detection through Partial Reconstruction

In order to detect major structural changes in the data we need to measure or estimate the reconstruction errors. The naive way to achieve this would be to reconstruct the entire matrix from the incrementally maintained decomposition and compare the reconstructed matrix to the ground truth (which is the actual, revised data matrix). If the difference is high, it means that due to some structural changes, the incrementally maintained decomposition deviated from the true decomposition of the matrix. Obviously, performing a full reconstruction of the matrix at each time step would be extremely costly. Instead, in this section, we propose a change detection scheme which relies on a partial reconstruction as depicted in Figure 2: (a) a fair data matrix sampler, which identifies a small subset of the matrix cells as ground truth and (b) a partial reconstructor, which reconstructs a given subset of matrix cells, without reconstructing the full data matrix.

4.2.1 *Fair Sampling of an Evolving Matrix*

We propose a fair sampler, where all matrix cells have a uniform probability of being selected independently of when they are updated.

Basic Reservoir Sampling. Reservoir sampling [18] is a random sampling method that works well in characterizing data streams. It is especially efficient because (a) it needs to see the data only once

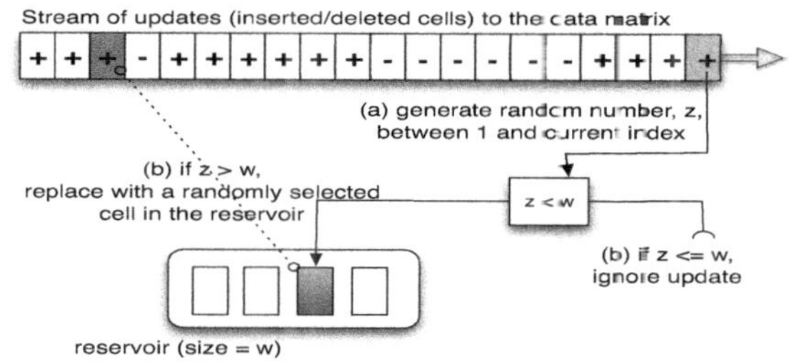

(a) reservoir maintenance for $\mathbf{s_i} = +\langle \mathbf{row_i}, \mathbf{col_i} \rangle$

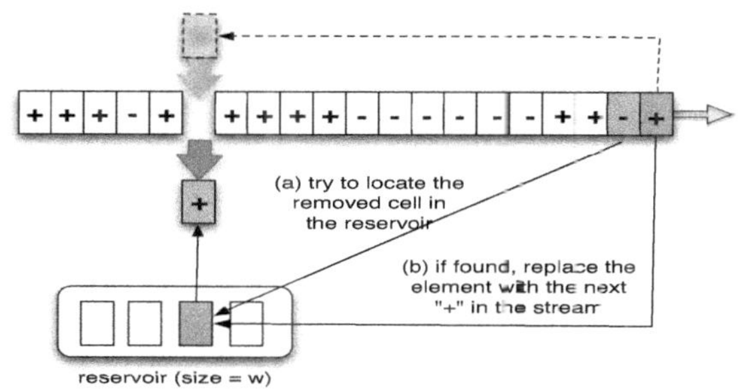

(b) reservoir maintenance for $\mathbf{s_i} = -\langle \mathbf{row_i}, \mathbf{col_i} \rangle$

Figure 3: Overview of the reservoir based matrix sampling

and (b) it uses a fixed (and small) buffer, referred to as the "*reservoir*". Furthermore, while (c) it does not require a priori knowledge of the data size, it (d) ensures that each data element has an equal chance of being represented in the sample. Let $\mathcal{S}$ be a data stream consisting of a sequence of elements s_i. The reservoir sample keeps a fixed reservoir of, say w elements. Once the reservoir is full each new element, s_i, replaces a (randomly) selected element in the reservoir with a decreasing probability, inversely proportional to the index, i, of the new element s_i. More specifically, a random element in the reservoir is replaced by s_i with probability $\frac{w}{i}$. Intuitively, in a fair sampling, each element up to i should have a w/i chance of being in the random sample of size w. Therefore, s_i is selected to be included in the reservoir with probability $\frac{w}{i}$. The sample it replaces, on the other hand, is chosen randomly among the existing w samples in the reservoir to ensure that the reservoir forms a random sample of the first i elements in the stream.

Matrix-Reservoir Model. As we described earlier, we consider the general case where the data matrix can grow or shrink with insertions or deletions of rows and columns. More specifically, we model the evolving data matrix as a stream, $\mathcal{S}$, of $s_i = \pm\langle row_i, col_i \rangle$, where row_i and col_i are the row and columns affected in the update with index i: $+\langle row_i, col_i \rangle$ indicates that the update inserts a new cell in the matrix at location $\langle row_i, col_i \rangle$, whereas $-\langle row_i, col_i \rangle$ indicates that the cell at location $\langle row_i, col_i \rangle$ is being removed.

The reservoir, $\mathfrak{R}_i = \{\mathfrak{r}_{i,1}, \ldots, \mathfrak{r}_{i,w}\}$, at time i consists of w matrix cell positions, which serve as the representatives for the current matrix. In other words, each $\mathfrak{r}_{i,j} \in \mathfrak{R}_i$ is a triple of the form $\mathfrak{r}_{i,j} = \langle index_{i,j}, row_{i,j}, col_{i,j} \rangle$, where $index_{i,j}$ is the index of the update that deposited the cell, located at $row_{i,j}$ and $col_{i,j}$, into the reservoir.

Matrix-Reservoir Maintenance for $\mathbf{s_i} = +\langle \mathbf{row_i}, \mathbf{col_i} \rangle$. As discussed earlier, reservoir sampling randomly selects some of the incoming stream elements for the updating the contents of the reservoir When the (probabilistically) selected incoming stream entry s_i is of the form $+\langle row_i, col_i \rangle$, the basic reservoir sampling process is applied: a random element, $\mathfrak{r}_{i-1,j}$ from the current reservoir

$\mathfrak{R}_{i-1}$ is selected and this is replaced with $\langle i, row_i, col_i\rangle$. This process is visualized in Figure 3(a).

Matrix-Reservoir Maintenance for $\mathbf{s_i = -\langle row_i, col_i\rangle}$. When the (probabilistically) selected incoming entry s_i is of the form $-\langle row_i, col_i\rangle$, on the other hand, the basic reservoir sampling process cannot be applied as this denotes removal of a cell, not insertion. We handle deletions as follows:

- if there exists no
  $$\mathfrak{r}_{i-1,j} = \langle index_{i-1,j}, row_{i-1,j}, col_{i-1,j}\rangle \in \mathfrak{R}_{i-1},$$
  such that $row_{i-1,j} = row_i$ and $col_{i-1,j} = col_i$, then s_i is simply ignored;
- if, on the other hand, there exists a
  $$\mathfrak{r}_{i-1,j} = \langle index_{i-1,j}, row_{i-1,j}, col_{i-1,j}\rangle \in \mathfrak{R}_{i-1},$$
  such that $row_{i-1,j} = row_i$ and $col_{i-1,j} = col_i$, then
  - we drop $\mathfrak{r}_{i-1,j}$ from the reservoir and
  - we keep the jth position reserved for a future update of the form $s_h = +\langle row_h, col_h\rangle$.

Intuitively, the matrix reservoir (and its history) is revised as if the future insertion s_h had in fact arrived *in the past*, instead of $s_{index_{i-1,j}}$, which had originally deposited the cell, $\langle row_{i-1,j}, col_{i-1,j}\rangle$ (which is being deleted) into the reservoir. This process is visualized in Figure 3(b).

4.2.2 Partial Matrix Reconstruction

At time $t = i$, let us have the reservoir $\mathfrak{R}_i = \{\mathfrak{r}_{i,1}, \ldots, \mathfrak{r}_{i,w}\}$, where for all $1 \leq h \leq w$, $\mathfrak{r}_{i,h} = \langle index_{i,h}, row_{i,h}, col_{i,h}\rangle$. Intuitively, the reservoir consists of a set of matrix cell positions (that were fairly sampled from the overall matrix). During the partial reconstruction step, we use the (incrementally maintained) SV decomposition, U_i, S_i, and V_i, of the data matrix X_i to reconstruct only the row and column positions that appear in the reservoir, $\mathfrak{r}_{i,h}$.

More formally, the partially reconstructed matrix value set $\hat{\mathfrak{V}}_i = \{\hat{\mathfrak{v}}_{i,1}, \ldots, \hat{\mathfrak{v}}_{i,w}\}$, is such that for all $1 \leq h \leq w$,

$\hat{\mathfrak{v}}_{i,h} = \hat{X}_i[row_{i,h}, col_{i,h}]$, where

$$\hat{X}_i[row_{i,h}, col_{i,h}] = (U_i[row_{i,h}, *])\, S_i \left(V_i^T[*, col_{i,h}]\right).$$

Note that the cost of the partial reconstruction of the matrix depends on the size of the reservoir and when $|\mathfrak{R}_i| \ll |X_i|$, partial reconstruction is much faster than full reconstruction.

4.2.3 Change Detector

At time $t = i$, given the reservoir $\mathfrak{R}_i = \{\mathfrak{r}_{i,1}, \ldots, \mathfrak{r}_{i,w}\}$, we construct a ground truth value set $\mathfrak{V}_i = \{\mathfrak{v}_{i,1}, \ldots, \mathfrak{v}_{i,w}\}$, where for all $1 \leq h \leq w$, $\mathfrak{v}_{i,h} = X_i[row_{i,h}, col_{i,h}]$. Similarly, we also have the partially reconstructed value set $\hat{\mathfrak{V}}_i = \{\hat{\mathfrak{v}}_{i,1}, \ldots, \hat{\mathfrak{v}}_{i,w}\}$, where for all $1 \leq h \leq w$, $\hat{\mathfrak{v}}_{i,h} = \hat{X}_i[row_{i,h}, col_{i,h}]$, where $\hat{X}_i[row_{i,h}, col_{i,h}]$ is the partially reconstructed value for the cell location $\langle row_{i,h}, col_{i,h}\rangle$. Given these, we detect a major structural change in the data matrix if

$$\sum_{h=1}^{w} (\mathfrak{v}_{i,h} - \hat{\mathfrak{v}}_{i,h})^2 \geq \Theta,$$

where Θ is the inaccuracy threshold.

4.3 Pseudocode of the LWI2-SVD Algorithm

We provide the pseudocode of the LWI-SVD with Restart (LWI2-SVD), which was detailed in this section, in Algorithm 2. In the next section, we evaluate the efficiency and effectiveness gains of LWI2-SVD algorithm on top of the gains provided by LWI-SVD.

Algorithm 2 LWI2-SVD

Input:
The Base Matrix, X, and its SV decomposition $U_x S_x V_x^T$;
The update matrix, $\Delta = AB^T$, corresponding to a window of updates;
Target rank, r;
Reservoir, $\mathfrak{R}$;
Restart Threshold, Θ;
Periodic Restart Flag, f;

Output:
The new SVD results, U_x',S_x', and V_x';
The new Reservoir, $\mathfrak{R}'$;

```
X' = X + Δ
if f = true then
    ⟨U'_x, S'_x, V'_x⟩ = topK_SVD(X', r);
    R' = updateReservoir(R, Δ);
else
    ⟨U'_x, S'_x, V'_x⟩ = LWI-SVD(X, U_x, S_x, V_x, Δ, r);
    R' = updateReservoir(R, Δ);
    V̂ = partialReconstruct(R', U'_x, S'_x V'_x);
    E = measurePartialError(V̂, R', X');
    if E > Θ then
        ⟨U'_x, S'_x, V'_x⟩ = topK_SVD(X', r);
    end if
end if
return U'_x, S'_x, V'_x, R';
```

Table 1: Parameters

Symbol	Desc.	Default	Alternative
$dim(n \times n)$	Initial(for insertions)/Final(for deletions) dimensions of X	100×100	300×300
r	Target rank	5	10
len	Length of the data stream	50	50
num_{upd}	Numbers of columns:rows updated at a given iteration	2:2	6:6
λ_{upd}	Strength of the updates (for synth. data)	5	10
w	Reservoir size	50	150
Θ	On-demand restart threshold	20%	10%
per	Restart period	15	5

5. EXPERIMENTS

In this section, we evaluate the efficiency and effectiveness of LWI-SVD and LWI2-SVD on both synthetic and real datasets and for different scenarios and parameter settings.

Each experiment, consisting of len consecutive update iterations, was run 10 times and averages are reported. Note that to simplify the interpretation of the results we have considered *insertion sequences* and *deletion sequences*; but not hybrid *insertion/deletion* sequences. Also, to make sure that the results for experiments involving sequences of insertions and deletions are comparable, we have set the initial dimensions for an insertion sequence and the final dimensions of a deletion sequence to the same value, dim.

The various parameters varied in the experiments, default values, and value ranges are presented in Table 1. Below we describe the experimental setting, including the data sets, in greater detail.

5.1 Real Data: Digg.com Traces

We use Digg.com data set [2] from Infochimps to evaluate the effectiveness and efficiency for real data. The complete data set was recorded from August to November 2008 and has 3 main components: stories, comments and replies. "Stories" contain 1490 articles that users have posted within the time period. For our experiments, we created data streams by considering the first $n + len \times num_{upd}$ articles in the data set(the first n articles make up the initial data matrix; for each of the len iterations in the update stream, we considered num_{upd} new articles).

Given this data set, we removed the stop words and applied stemming. We then selected the first n stories and identified the most frequent n keywords [1]. X_{ij} denotes occurrence of keyword j in story i. Intuitively, the low-rank decomposition of the data matrix X simultaneously cluster stories and keywords, resulting a co-clustering of the data matrix X. We moved the window at each iteration by inserting or deleting num_{upd} records of the story trace and recomputing the n most frequent keywords (meaning that num_{upd} many rows and columns are inserted and deleted). These correspond to row and column insertions/deletions on X.

5.2 Synthetic Data: Random Traces

We have also experimented with synthetic data sets where we could freely vary the characteristics of the data and updates to observe the accuracy and efficiency of our algorithms under different scenarios. For these experiments, we have created synthetic activity traces which we then converted into data matrices as before. Since the matrices for real data is sparse, we focus on dense matrices.

In particular, we have generated an initial n-length random sequence of 5 dimensional data, where each dimension has a value from 0 to 10. Given these n consecutive records in the trace, we have created a $n \times n$ initial matrix measuring pairwise Euclidean distances of the records in the sequence. Insertions in the random trace were generated by randomly picking numbers with exponential distribution, with the rate parameter, λ_{upd} (i.e., $prob(x) = exp\_dist(x, \lambda_{upd}) = \lambda_{upd}e^{-\lambda_{upd}x}$). Intuitively, if the rate parameter λ_{upd} is large, there is a higher likelihood of having more large amplitude changes. If the rate parameter λ_{upd} is low, there is a lower frequency of large amplitude changes in the trace.

As before, we enlarged or shrank X at each iteration by adding or deleting num_{upd} units of the random activity trace (meaning that num_{upd} many rows and columns are inserted to or deleted from into the matrix, X).

5.3 Evaluation Criteria and Competitors

We evaluate the LWI-SVD and LWI-SVD with Restart (LWI2-SVD) algorithms by comparing them to alternative approaches:

- *Full SVD and SVDS* – SVD is the full SV decomposition of the matrix, we used Matlab's `[U, S, V] = svd(X)` command for this. We also considered with Matlab's `[U, S, V] = svds(X,r)` command which returns the composition results for the top-r components, where r is the desired rank (SVDS tends to perform more efficiently than SVD when r is small and X is large and sparse);
- *Naive Incremental SVD* – this is our implementation of the Brand's algorithm described in [5], it involves a full SVD and pivoted QR based approximation is not leveraged (to implement LWI-SVD and LWI2-SVD, we use this implementation as the basis); and
- *SPIRIT* – this is the algorithm described in [13] which provides fast decompositions, but does not have various desirable properties of incremental SVD; including explicit data deletions and column insertions and deletions (for our experiments, we used the implementation obtained from [3]).

LWI-SVD family of the algorithms extend our implementation of the Brand's algorithm described in [5] along with the Algorithm 844 [4] obtained from [1].

As evaluation criteria, we use three metrics: reconstruction error overhead, execution time, and execution time gain:

- *average relative reconstruction error* (err_{rel}) – this accuracy measure is defined as

$$\frac{1}{len}\sum_{i=1}^{len}\frac{rec\_error(\hat{X}_{i,*}, X_i) - rec\_error(\hat{X}_{i,SVD}, X_i)}{rec\_error(\hat{X}_{i,SVD}, X_i)},$$

  where
  - len is the number of iterations (length of the stream),
  - $\hat{X}_{i,*}$ denotes the decomposition of the data matrix at time i obtained using the algorithm "$*$", and
  - $rec\_error(Y, X)$ denotes the reconstruction error of the decomposition Y against the data matrix X, measured in terms of $Frobenius$ norm.

  Note that a low-rank decomposition of X_i would lead to a reconstruction error, even if it is obtained using full SVD followed by selection of the top r components. Therefore, the denominator of the above term is not equal to 0.
- *absolute execution time* (t_{exec}) – this is the time, in seconds, that is required to complete len consecutive decompositions using the algorithm under consideration.
- *time gain* ($gain_{time}$) – the gain in time is the execution time measured against the execution time of the full SVD; i.e., $\frac{t_{exec,svd} - t_{exec,*}}{t_{exec,svd}}$.

All experiments were conducted using a 4-core Intel Core i5-2400, 3.10GHz, machine with 8GB memory, running 64-bit Windows 7 Enterprise. The codes were executed using Matlab 7.11.0(2010b).

5.4 Evaluation with the Default Settings

5.4.1 Real Trace Data Set

Figure 4 presents the accuracy and efficiency results for the real trace data for the default parameters reported in Table 1.

Accuracy. The first thing to note in Figure 4(a), which reports average relative reconstruction errors for the various versions of the LWI-SVD algorithm proposed in this paper, is that restarts discussed in Section 4 are highly effective in reducing the overall error. While both partial reconstruction-based and periodic restarts used in LWI2-SVD are effective in improving accuracy over the LWI-SVD (which does not use restarts), the best results are obtained when these are used together, bringing down the average relative reconstruction error to 0.3-0.7% of the low-rank decomposition obtained through full SVD.

The second thing to note in Figure 4(a) is that row/column insertions, which bring in new data into the matrix, results in larger relative reconstruction errors than row/column deletions. Note that, when both reservoir-based and periodic restarts are employed, the accuracy penalty relative to the low-rank decomposition of full SVD is negligibly low for both insertions and deletions.

Efficiency. Figure 4(b) shows the efficiency results for this data set under the default parameter configuration.

The first thing to note is that there is minimal time difference between the LWI-SVD and LWI2-SVD algorithm. This indicates

[1]In these experiments, without loss of generality, we kept the matrix in square shape, i.e., $n = m$

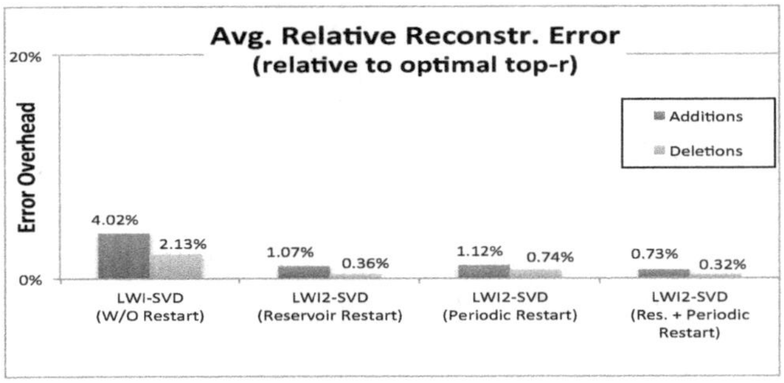

(a) average relative reconstruction error

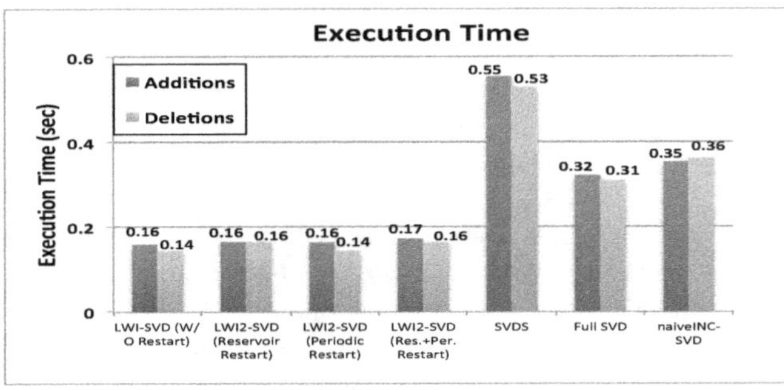

(b) execution time

Figure 4: Accuracy and efficiency for the *real trace data set - default settings*

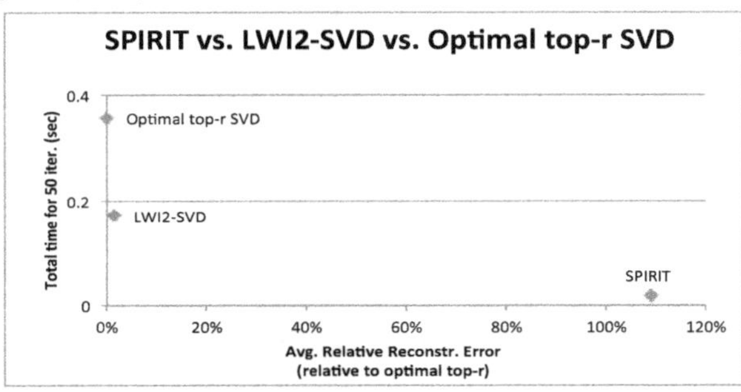

Figure 5: Accuracy and efficiency results for the *synthetic trace data set* for SVD, Spirit, and LWI2-SVD with periodic and on-demand refreshes

Table 2: Impact of setting $A = I$ in Section 3.1

	$A = I$	A is free	Impact
Rec. error	5.786	5.765	+0.36%
Exec time	0.174 sec	0.197 sec	−11.71%

that the time overhead of reservoir maintenance and occasional on-demand full decompositions are negligible in the long run. Secondly, performing full SVD takes $\sim$ 75-100% more than the proposed LWI-SVD family of algorithms. Under this configuration, the naive incremental SVD takes a little more time than full SVD, as the basic algorithm reported in [5] involves a full SVD with same dimension as the original matrix and several matrix multiplications. Further-more, under this configuration, SVDS takes even longer than the full SVD.

Finally, a close look at the LWI-SVD family of algorithms indicates that insertions require slightly longer time to maintain than deletions. This is expected because, as discussed in Section 2.2.1, there is no need for computing R_A and R_B since they are all zero.

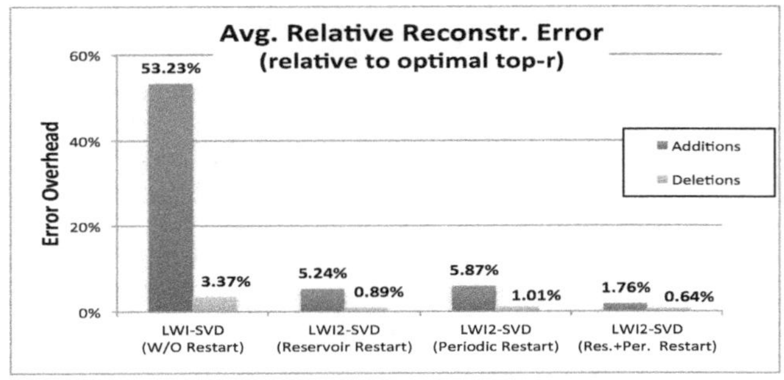

(a) average relative reconstruction error

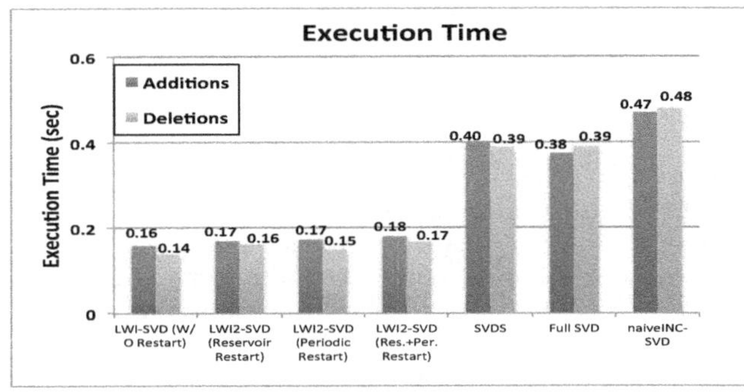

(b) execution time

Figure 6: Accuracy and efficiency for *synthetic trace data set - default settings*

Impact of the QR-Elimination Optimization. In Section 3.1, we had discussed an optimization strategy whereby we eliminate one of the two expensive QR operations by forcing A to be equal to the identity matrix, I. As shown in Table 2, setting $A = I$ causes less than half percentage point impact on the accuracy; on the other hand, this optimization helps save close to 12% in execution time.

5.4.2 Synthetic Trace Data Set

Figure 6 presents results for the synthetic trace data set under the default parameter settings. The key observation from this figure is that the accuracy and efficiency results for the synthetic trace data set are very similar to the results for real trace data set, reported in Figure 4. The similarity is especially pronounced in the execution time results in Figure 6(b). This indicates that the execution time gains of the LWI-SVD family of algorithms (and to a certain degree, the accuracies they provide – especially with the help of periodic and reservoir-based restarts) are inherent properties of these algorithms rather than being highly data specific.

SPIRIT. Since the SPIRIT [13] algorithm approaches the problem differently (e.g. cannot directly handle deletions, cannot handle deletions/insertion of columns), we present it separately from the rest in Figure 5. For these experiments, we use a synthetic data trace that does not include any column insertions or deletions on the data matrix X. As the figure shows, SPIRIT algorithm works much faster than SVD or LWI2-SVD for the default configuration. However, this speed comes with a significant increase in the reconstruction error, relative to the optimal low-rank decomposition using SVD. In contrast, LWI2-SVD achieves an accuracy almost identical to the optimal, yet costs only half as much.

5.5 Impacts of Data and System Parameters

In this subsection, we evaluate the impacts of the various data and systems parameters on the efficiency and effectiveness of the LWI-SVD family of algorithms. As representative, we select the

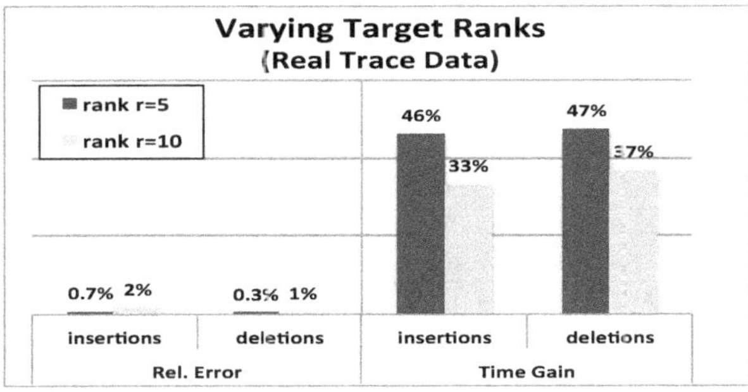

Figure 7: Accuracy and efficiency for *real trace data set* for different *rank*, r

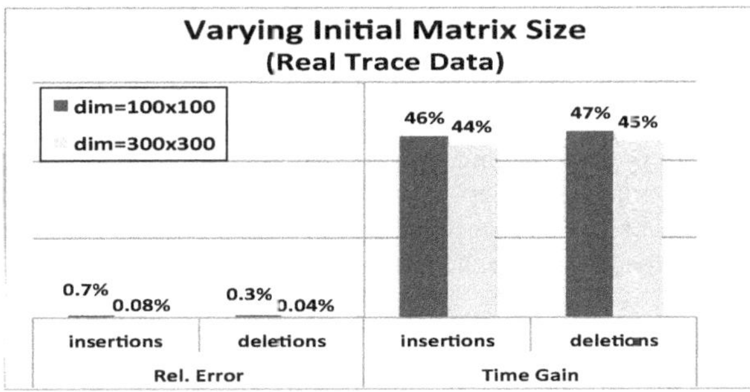

Figure 8: Accuracy and efficiency results for the *real trace data set* varying the *size, dim, of the initial (for insertions) / final (for deletions) matrix*

LWI2-SVD with the default parameters. We then vary, one-by-one, the various data and system parameters, and compare the results against the optimal SVD based rank-r decomposition. Since, as we have seen, the results are similar for real and synthetic data, for the most part we report the results with the real trace data. We use the synthetic trace only for experiments where we vary the strengths of the updates.

5.5.1 *Varying the Target Rank, r*

Figure 7 presents efficiency and accuracy results for the real trace data set where the target rank, r is varied. The results show that, as expected (due to the low-rank nature of the LWI-SVD family of algorithms), as the target rank increases, the time gain drops and the relative error rate slightly increases. The drop in time gains is because the incremental process involves a lot of matrix multiplications where the sizes of matrices are directly related to the target rank. This confirms the observation that LWI-SVD and LWI2-SVD are most effective when the target rank is low.

5.5.2 *Varying the Dimensions, dim, of the Matrix*

Figure 8 presents accuracy and efficiency results when we change the dimensions, dim, of the initial data matrix (for insertions) and the final data matrix (for deletions). Here, we see that increasing the size of matrix does not have a big impact on accuracy and efficiency.

5.5.3 *Varying the Rate of Updates, num_{upd}*

Figure 9 presents efficiency and accuracy results for the real trace data set where the number, num_{upd}, of row and column updates per each iteration is varied. The results indicate that, as expected, an increase in the number of updates per iteration impacts accuracy as well as efficiency. The slight impact on the accuracy is due to

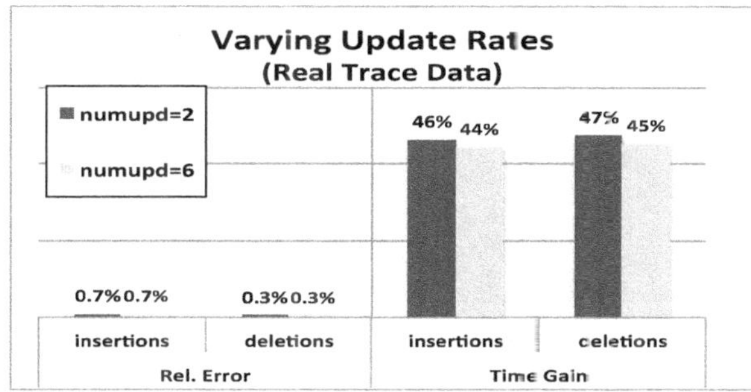

Figure 9: Accuracy and efficiency results for the *real trace data set* varying the *amount updates per iteration*, num_{upd}

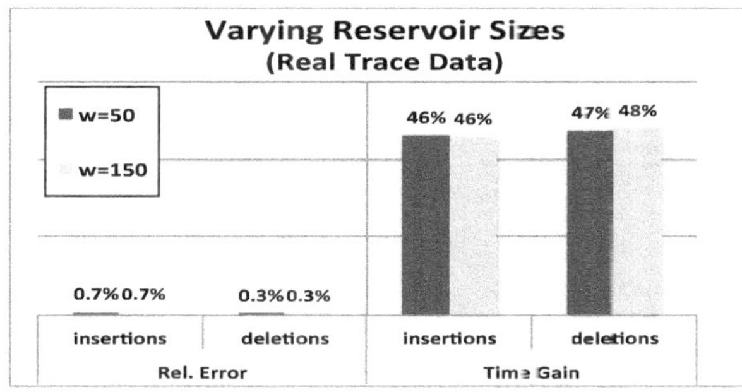

Figure 10: Accuracy and efficiency for *real trace data* varying *reservoir size*, w

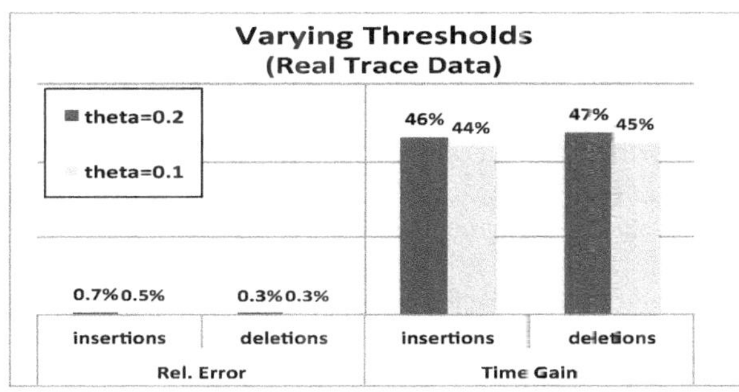

Figure 11: Accuracy and efficiency results for the *real trace data set* varying the *change threshold*, Θ, for on-demand restarts

the approximation nature of the algorithm. The impact on the time gain is due to more on-demand restarts.

5.5.4 *Varying the Reservoir Size, w*

Figure 10 presents efficiency and accuracy results for the real trace data set where the reservoir size, w, is varied. The results confirm that a larger reservoir (even only $\sim 1.5\%$ of the matrix) can help to trigger on-demand restarts more fairly, since larger reservoir has more accurate amortized error measuring.

5.5.5 *Varying the Change Threshold, Θ*

Figure 11 confirms that a slightly tighter threshold, $\Theta = 0.1$ instead of the default $\Theta = 0.2$ will trigger more on-demand restarts and thus can further reduce the error rates (which are already very low), with little impact on execution time gains.

5.5.6 *Varying the Restart Period, per*

Figure 12 confirms that increasing the number of restarts by reducing the restart period, per, may improve the final accuracy. However, unlike the on-demand restarts based on change detec-

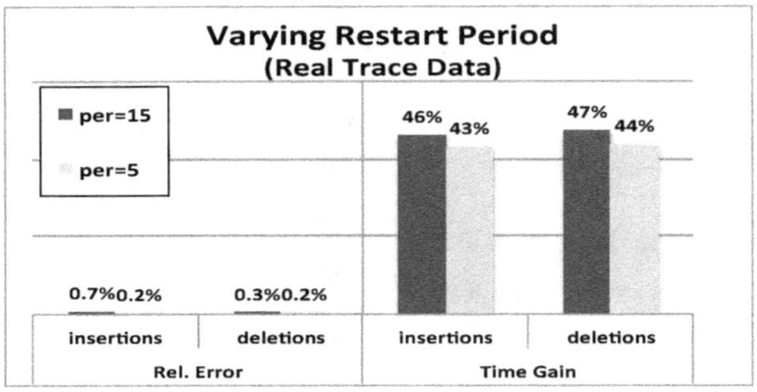

Figure 12: Accuracy and efficiency results for the *real trace data set* varying the *restart period,* per, for periodic restarts

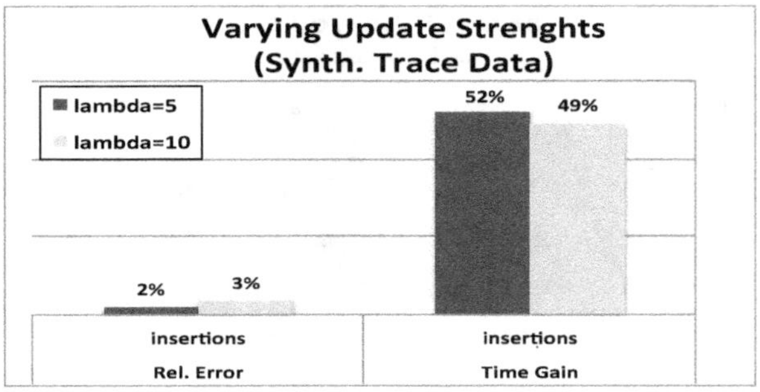

Figure 13: Accuracy and efficiency results for the *synthetic trace data set* varying the *update strength,* λ_{upd}

tion (shown in Figure 11), blindly increasing the frequency of the periodic restarts may negatively impact the time gain.

5.5.7 Varying the Update Strength, λ_{upd}

Finally, in Figure 13, we see the impact of the strength (in amplitude) of the incoming insertions. The figure shows that, when λ_{upd} increases, the LWI2-SVD algorithm adjusts its operation by scheduling more on-demand restarts at a cost of decreasing the time gain.

5.6 Scalability of LWI Algorithms

The results shown above are conducted with small window size, however, in some cases, we need large windows to monitor and analyze a large portion of the data. In this subsection, we analyze the scalability of LWI Algorithm by choosing large base number. Since we have shown that under the small base number condition, SVD out performs SVDS in execution time, however, when the base number is large, seeking a low rank deposition using SVDS is more efficient. Also, as we know that SVDS is very efficient when the data is sparse, but performs less efficient on dense data. We showed that LWI algorithm can concur this short coming when the data is dense. Recall in section 3.2.1, we showed that K is an arrow-like matrix which is very sparse, this leads to the efficiency by using pivoted QR compared to a direct SVDS on the dense data. Therefore, in the incremental maintenance of SVD on a dense matrix, we are actually seeking a second layer reduced rank approximation of a sparse matrix K. It is the main advantage of LWI algorithm compared to SVDS when the data is dense and the base dimension is large. Table 3 shows the execution time and error overhead results under a synthetic dense data, the results confirm that with big base number especially when the base is a thin and tall matrix, LWI algorithm can have advantages in execution time with negligible error overhead .

Table 3: Results for Large Dim

dim	LWI2 Exec. Time(s)	LWI2 Rel. Error	SVDS Exec. Time(s)
$1000 * 100$	8.2604	0.143%	15.91
$1000 * 1000$	6.8087	0.06%	10.839
$1500 * 1500$	17.483	0.03%	23.469
$2000 * 2000$	34.35	0.002%	41.491
$3000 * 3000$	96.577	0.00097%	93.622

6. CONCLUSIONS

In this paper, we presented a *Low-rank, Windowed, Incremental SVD* (LWI-SVD) algorithm, which relies on low-rank approximations to speed up incremental SVD updates. LWI-SVD algorithm also aggregates multiple row/column insertions and deletions to further reduce on-line processing cost. We also presented a *LWI-SVD with restarts* (LWI2-SVD) algorithm which performs periodic and change detection based on-demand refreshing of the decomposition to prevent accumulation of errors. Experiment results on real and synthetic data sets have shown that the LWI-SVD family of incremental SVD algorithms are highly efficient and accurate compared to alternative schemes under different settings.

7. REFERENCES

[1] Algorithm 844. Sparse Reduced-Rank Approximations to Sparse Matrices. *http://dl.acm.org/citation.cfm?id=1067972*. Downloaded 2012.

[2] Digg.com Data Set. *http://www.infochimps.com/datasets/diggcom-data-set*. Downloaded 2013.

[3] SPIRIT *http://www.cs.cmu.edu/afs/cs/project/spirit-1/www/*. Downloaded in 2012.

[4] M.W. Berry, S.A. Pulatova, and G.W. Stewart. Algorithm 844. Computing Sparse Reduced-Rank Approximations to Sparse Matrices. ACM Trans. Math. Softw. 31, 2, pp. 252-269, June 2005.

[5] M. Brand. Fast low-rank modifications of the thin singular value decomposition. Linear Algebra and its Appl., 415(1):20-30, 2006.

[6] S. Chandrasekaran, B.S. Manjunath, Y.F. Wang, J. Winkeler, and H. Zhang. An Eigenspace Update Algorithm for Image Analysis. Graphical Models and Image processing: GMIP, 59(5), 1997.

[7] S. Deerwester, S. Dumais, G.W. Furnas, T.K. Landauer, and R. Harshman. Indexing by Latent Semantic Analysis. Journal of the American Society for Information Science, 41(6):391-407, 1990.

[8] M. Gu and S. Eisenstat. Downdating the Singular Value Decomposition. SIAM J. Matrix Analysis and Applications, 1995.

[9] M. Gu and S.C. Eisenstat. A Stable and Fast Algorithm for Updating the Singular Value Decomposition. Tech. Report YALEU/DCS/RR-966, Department of Computer Science, Yale University, 1993.

[10] T. Kolda and B. Bader. Tensor Decompositions and Applications. SIAM Rev. 51, 3, 455-500. 2009.

[11] A. Levy and M. Lindenbaum. Sequential Karhunen-Loeve Basis Extraction and its Application to Images. IEEE Transactions on Image Processing, 9:1371-1374, 2000.

[12] G. O'Brien. Information Management Tools for Updating an SVD-Encoded Indexing Scheme, MS Thesis. 1994.

[13] S. Papadimitriou, J. Sun, and C. Faloutsos. Streaming Pattern Discovery in Multiple Time-Series. VLDB, pp. 697-708, 2005.

[14] B. Sarwar, G. Karypis, J. Konstan, and J. Riedl. Incremental Singular Value Decomposition Algorithms for Highly Scalable Recommender Systems. ICIS, pp. 27–28, 2002.

[15] G.W. Steward. Four Algorithms for the Efficient Computation of Truncated Pivoted QR Approximations to a Sparse Matrix. Numerische Mathematik 83, 313-323, 1999.

[16] J. Sun, S. Papadimitriou, and C. Faloutsos. Online Latent Variable Detection in Sensor Networks, ICDE, 2005.

[17] D.I. Witter and M.W. Berry. Downdating the Latent Semantic Indexing Model for Conceptual Information Retrieval. The Computer Journal, 1998.

[18] J.S. Vitter. Random Sampling with a Reservoir. ACM Trans. Math. Softw. 11, 1, pp. 37-57, March 1985.

[19] H. Zha and H.D. Simon. On Updating Problems in Latent Semantic Indexing. SIAM J. Sci. Comput., 21(2):782-791, 1999.

[20] Z.A. Zhao and H. Liu. Spectral Feature Selection for Data Mining, Chapman and Hall/CRC Press, 2012.

Provable Deterministic Leverage Score Sampling

Dimitris Papailiopoulos
Electrical and Computer Engineering
UT Texas
dimitris@utexas.edu

Anastasios Kyrillidis
School of Computer and Communication Sciences
EPFL
anastasios.kyrillidis@epfl.ch

Christos Boutsidis
Yahoo! Labs
New York, NY
boutsidis@yahoo-inc.com

ABSTRACT

We explain *theoretically* a curious empirical phenomenon: "Approximating a matrix by *deterministically* selecting a subset of its columns with the corresponding largest leverage scores results in a good low-rank matrix surrogate". In this work, we provide a novel theoretical analysis of *deterministic leverage score sampling*. We show that such sampling can be provably as accurate as its randomized counterparts, if the leverage scores follow a moderately steep power-law decay. We support this power-law assumption by providing empirical evidence that such decay laws are abundant in real-world data sets. We then demonstrate empirically the performance of deterministic leverage score sampling, which many times matches or outperforms the state-of-the-art techniques.

Categories and Subject Descriptors

G.1.3 [**Mathematics of Computing**]: Numerical Analysis-Numerical Linear Algebra; E.m [**Data**]: Miscellaneous

Keywords

Subset selection; low-rank matrix approximation; leverage scores; deterministic sampling; power law distributions

1. INTRODUCTION

Recently, there has been a lot of interest on selecting the "best" or "more representative" columns from a data matrix [13, 26]. Qualitatively, these columns reveal the most important information hidden in the underlying matrix structure. This is similar to what principal components carry, as extracted via Principal Components Analysis (PCA) [23]. In sharp contrast to PCA, using actual columns of the data matrix to form a low-rank surrogate offers interpretability, making it more attractive to practitioners and data analysts [33, 5, 34, 26].

To make the discussion precise and to rigorously characterize the "best" columns of a matrix, let us introduce the following *Column Subset Selection Problem* (CSSP).

KDD'14, August 24–27, 2014, New York, NY, USA.

ACM 978-1-4503-2956-9/14/08 ...$15.00.
http://dx.doi.org/10.1145/2623330.2623698.

Column Subset Selection Problem. *Let $\mathbf{A} \in \mathbb{R}^{m\times n}$ and let $c < n$ be a sampling parameter. Find c columns of $\mathbf{A}$ – denoted as $\mathbf{C} \in \mathbb{R}^{m\times c}$ – that minimize*

$$\|\mathbf{A} - \mathbf{C}\mathbf{C}^\dagger\mathbf{A}\|_F \quad or \quad \|\mathbf{A} - \mathbf{C}\mathbf{C}^\dagger\mathbf{A}\|_2,$$

where $\mathbf{C}^\dagger$ denotes the Moore-Penrose pseudo-inverse.

State of the art algorithms for the CSSP utilize both deterministic and randomized techniques; we discuss related work in Section 5. Here, we describe two algorithms from prior literature that suffice to highlight our contributions.

A central part of our discussion will involve the *leverage scores* of a matrix $\mathbf{A}$, which we define below

Definition 1. *[Leverage scores] Let $\mathbf{V}_k \in \mathbb{R}^{n\times k}$ contain the top k right singular vectors of a $m \times n$ matrix $\mathbf{A}$ with rank $\rho = rank(\mathbf{A}) \geq k$. Then, the (rank-$k$) leverage score of the i-th column of $\mathbf{A}$ is defined as*

$$\ell_i^{(k)} = \|[\mathbf{V}_k]_{i,:}\|_2^2, \quad i = 1, 2, \ldots, n$$

Here, $[\mathbf{V}_k]_{i,:}$ denotes the i-th row of $\mathbf{V}_k$.

One of the first algorithms for column subset selection dates back to 1972: in [21], Joliffe proposes a deterministic sampling of the columns of $\mathbf{A}$ that correspond to the largest leverage scores $\ell_i^{(k)}$, for some $k < \text{rank}(\mathbf{A})$. Although this simple approach has been extremely successful in practice [21, 22, 29, 8], to the best of our knowledge, there has been no theoretical explanation why the approximation errors $\|\mathbf{A} - \mathbf{C}\mathbf{C}^\dagger\mathbf{A}\|_F$ and $\|\mathbf{A} - \mathbf{C}\mathbf{C}^\dagger\mathbf{A}\|_2$ should be small.

One way to circumvent the lack of a theoretical analysis for the above deterministic algorithm is by utilizing randomization. Drineas et al. [13] proposed the following approach: for a target rank $k < \text{rank}(\mathbf{A})$, define a probability distribution over the columns of $\mathbf{A}$, *i.e.*, the ith column is associated with a probability $p_i = \ell_i^{(k)}/k$; observe that $\sum_i p_i = 1$, since $\sum_i \ell_i^{(k)} = \|\mathbf{V}_k\|_F^2 = k$. Then, in c independent and identically distributed passes, sample with replacement c columns from $\mathbf{A}$, with probabilities given by p_i. Drineas et al. [13], using results in [30], show that this random subset of columns $\mathbf{C} \in \mathbb{R}^{m\times c}$ approximates $\mathbf{A}$, with constant probability, within relative error: $\|\mathbf{A} - \mathbf{C}\mathbf{C}^\dagger\mathbf{A}\|_F \leq (1+\varepsilon)\|\mathbf{A} - \mathbf{A}_k\|_F$, when the number of sampled columns is $c = O(k \log k/\varepsilon^2)$, for some $0 < \varepsilon < 1$. Here, $\mathbf{A}_k \in \mathbb{R}^{m\times n}$ is the best rank-k matrix obtained via the SVD.

There are two important remarks that need to be made: *(i)* the randomized algorithm in [13] yields a matrix estimate that is "near optimal", i.e., has error close to that of the best rank-k approximation; and *(ii)* the above random sampling algorithm is a straightforward randomized version of the deterministic algorithm of Joliffe [21].

From a practical perspective, the deterministic algorithm of Joliffe [21] is extremely simple to implement, and is computationally efficient. Unfortunately, as of now, it did not admit provable performance guarantees. An important open question [13, 29, 8] is: *Can one simply keep the columns having the largest leverage scores, as suggested in [21], and still have a provably tight approximation?*

1.1 Contributions

In this work, we establish a new theoretical analysis for the deterministic leverage score sampling algorithm of Joliffe [21]. We show that if the leverage scores $\ell_i^{(k)}$ follow a sufficiently steep power-law decay, then this deterministic algorithm has provably similar or better performance to its randomized counterparts (see Theorems 2 and 3 in Section 2). This means that under the power-law decay assumption, deterministic leverage score sampling provably obtains near optimal low-rank approximations and it can be as accurate as the "best" algorithms in the literature [4, 18].

From an applications point of view, we support the power law decay assumption of our theoretical analysis by demonstrating that several real-world data-sets have leverage scores following such decays. We further run several experiments on synthetic and real data sets, and compare deterministic leverage score sampling with the state of the art algorithms for the CSSP. In most experiments, the deterministic algorithm obtains tight low-rank approximations, and is shown to perform similar, if not better, than the state of the art.

1.2 Notation

We use $\mathbf{A}, \mathbf{B}, \ldots$ to denote matrices and $\mathbf{a}, \mathbf{b}, \ldots$ to denote column vectors. $\mathbf{I}_n$ is the $n \times n$ identity matrix; $\mathbf{0}_{m\times n}$ is the $m \times n$ matrix of zeros; $\mathbf{e}_i$ belongs to the standard basis (whose dimensionality will be clear from the context). Let $\mathbf{C} = [\mathbf{a}_{i_1}, \ldots, \mathbf{a}_{i_c}] \in \mathbb{R}^{m\times c}$ contain c columns of $\mathbf{A}$. We can equivalently write $\mathbf{C} = \mathbf{AS}$, where the *sampling matrix* is $\mathbf{S} = [\mathbf{e}_{i_1}, \ldots, \mathbf{e}_{i_c}] \in \mathbb{R}^{n\times c}$. We define the Frobenius and the spectral norm of a matrix as $\|\mathbf{A}\|_{\mathrm{F}}^2 = \sum_{i,j} \mathbf{A}_{ij}^2$ and $\|\mathbf{A}\|_2 = \max_{\mathbf{x}:\|\mathbf{x}\|_2=1} \|\mathbf{Ax}\|_2$, respectively.

2. DETERMINISTIC COLUMN SAMPLING

In this section, we describe the details of the deterministic leverage score sampling algorithm. In Section 3, we state our approximation guarantees. In the remaining of the text, given a matrix $\mathbf{A}$ of rank ρ, we assume that the "target rank" is $k < \rho$. This means that we wish to approximate $\mathbf{A}$ using a subset of $c \geq k$ of its columns, such that the resulting matrix has an error close to that of the best rank-k approximation.

The deterministic leverage score sampling algorithm can be summarized in the following three steps:

Step 1: Obtain $\mathbf{V}_k$, the top-k right singular vectors of $\mathbf{A}$. This can be carried by simply computing the singular value decomposition (SVD) of $\mathbf{A}$ in $O(\min\{m,n\}mn)$ time.

Step 2: Calculate the leverage scores $\ell_i^{(k)}$. For simplicity, we assume that $\ell_i^{(k)}$ are sorted in descending order, hence the columns of $\mathbf{A}$ have the same sorting as well.[1]

[1]Otherwise, one needs to sort them in $O(n \log n)$ time-cost.

Step 3: Output the c columns of $\mathbf{A}$ that correspond to the largest c leverage scores $\ell_i^{(k)}$ such that their sum $\sum_{i=1}^{c} \ell_i^{(k)}$ is more than θ. This ensures that the selected columns have accumulated "energy" at least θ. In this step, we have to carefully pick θ, our *stopping threshold.* This parameter essentially controls the *quality of the approximation.*

In Section 7, we provide some guidance on how the stopping parameter θ should be chosen. Note that, if θ is such that $c < k$, we force $c = k$. This is a necessary step that prevents the error in the approximation from "blowing up" (see Section 7). The exact steps are given in Algorithm 1.

Algorithm 1 LeverageScoresSampler$(\mathbf{A}, k, \theta)$

Input: $\mathbf{A} \in \mathbb{R}^{m\times n}$, k, θ

Compute $\mathbf{V}_k \in \mathbb{R}^{n\times k}$ (top k right sing. vectors of $\mathbf{A}$)

for $i = 1, 2, \ldots, n$

$\quad \ell_i^{(k)} = \|[\mathbf{V}_k]_{i,:}\|_2^2$

end for

without loss of generality, let $\ell_i^{(k)}$'s be sorted:

$$\ell_1^{(k)} \geq \cdots \geq \ell_i^{(k)} \geq \ell_{i+1}^{(k)} \geq \cdots \geq \ell_n^{(k)}.$$

Find index $c \in \{1, \ldots, n\}$ such that:

$$c = \underset{c}{\operatorname{argmin}} \left(\sum_{i=1}^{c} \ell_i^{(k)} > \theta \right).$$

If $c < k$, set $c = k$.

Output: $\mathbf{S} \in \mathbb{R}^{n\times c}$ s.t. $\mathbf{AS}$ has the top c columns of $\mathbf{A}$.

Algorithm 1 requires $O(\min\{m,n\}mn)$ arithmetic operations. In the full version of this paper [28], we discuss modifications that improve the running time.

3. APPROXIMATION GUARANTEES

Our main technical innovation is a bound on the approximation error of Algorithm 1 in regard to the CSSP; the proof of the following theorem can be found in Section 6.

Theorem 2. *Let $\theta = k - \varepsilon$, for some $\varepsilon \in (0,1)$, and let $\mathbf{S}$ be the $n \times c$ output sampling matrix of Algorithm 1. Then, for $\mathbf{C} = \mathbf{AS}$ and $\xi = \{2, F\}$, we have $\|\mathbf{A} - \mathbf{CC}^{\dagger}\mathbf{A}\|_{\xi}^2 < (1-\varepsilon)^{-1} \cdot \|\mathbf{A} - \mathbf{A}_k\|_{\xi}^2$.*

Choosing $\varepsilon \in (0, 1/2)$ implies $(1-\varepsilon)^{-1} \leq 1 + 2\varepsilon$ and, hence, we have a relative-error approximation:

$$\|\mathbf{A} - \mathbf{CC}^{\dagger}\mathbf{A}\|_{\xi}^2 < (1 + 2\varepsilon) \cdot \|\mathbf{A} - \mathbf{A}_k\|_{\xi}^2.$$

3.1 Bounding the number of sampled columns

Algorithm 1 extracts at least $c \geq k$ columns of $\mathbf{A}$. However, an upper bound on the number of output columns c is not immediate. We study such upper bounds below.

From Theorem 2, it is clear that the stopping parameter $\theta = k - \varepsilon$ directly controls the number of output columns c. This number, extracted for a specific error requirement ε, depends on the decay of the leverage scores. For example, if the leverage scores decay fast, then we intuitively expect $\sum_{i=1}^{c} \ell_i^{(k)} = k - \varepsilon$ to be achieved for a "small" c.

Let us for example consider a case where the leverage scores follow an extremely fast decay:

$$\ell_1^{(k)} = k - 2k \cdot \varepsilon,$$
$$\ell_2^{(k)} = \ldots = \ell_{2k}^{(k)} = \varepsilon,$$
$$\ell_{2k+1}^{(k)} = \ldots = \ell_n^{(k)} = \frac{\varepsilon}{n - 2k}.$$

Then, in this case $\sum_{i=1}^{2k} \ell_i^{(k)} = k - \varepsilon$, and Algorithm 1 outputs the $c = 2k$ columns of $\mathbf{A}$ that correspond to the $2k$ largest leverage scores. Due to Theorem 2, this subset of columns $\mathbf{C} \in \mathbb{R}^{n \times 2k}$ comes with the following guarantee:

$$\|\mathbf{A} - \mathbf{C}\mathbf{C}^\dagger\mathbf{A}\|_\xi^2 < \frac{1}{1-\varepsilon} \cdot \|\mathbf{A} - \mathbf{A}_k\|_\xi^2.$$

Hence, from the above example, we expect that, when the leverage scores decay fast, a small number of columns of $\mathbf{A}$ will offer a good approximation of the form $\mathbf{C}\mathbf{C}^\dagger\mathbf{A}$.

However, in the worst case Algorithm 1 can output a number of columns c that can be as large as $\Omega(n)$. To highlight this subtle point, consider the case where the leverage scores are uniform $\ell_i^{(k)} = \frac{k}{n}$. Then, one can easily observe that if we want to achieve an error of ε according to Theorem 2, we have to set $\theta = k - \varepsilon$. This directly implies that we need to sample $c > (n/k)\theta$ columns. Hence, if $\varepsilon = o(1)$, then,

$$c \geq (n/k)\theta = (1 - \varepsilon/k)n = \Omega(n).$$

Hence, for $\varepsilon \to 0$ we have $c \to n$, which makes the result of Theorem 2 trivial.

We argued above that when the leverage scores decay is "fast" then a good approximation is to be expected with a "small" c. We make this intuition precise below [2]. The next theorem considers the case where the leverage scores follow a power-law decay; the proof can be found in Section 6.

Theorem 3. *Let the leverage scores follow a power-law decay with exponent $\alpha_k = 1 + \eta$, for $\eta > 0$:*

$$\ell_i^{(k)} = \frac{\ell_1^{(k)}}{i^{\alpha_k}}.$$

Then, if we set the stopping parameter to $\theta = k - \varepsilon$, for some ε with $0 < \varepsilon < 1$, the number of sampled columns in $\mathbf{C} = \mathbf{AS}$ that Algorithm 1 outputs is

$$c = \max\left\{\left(\frac{2k}{\varepsilon}\right)^{\frac{1}{1+\eta}} - 1,\ \left(\frac{2k}{\eta \cdot \varepsilon}\right)^{\frac{1}{\eta}} - 1,\ k\right\},$$

and $\mathbf{C}$ achieves the following approximation error

$$\|\mathbf{A} - \mathbf{C}\mathbf{C}^\dagger\mathbf{A}\|_\xi^2 < \frac{1}{1-\varepsilon} \cdot \|\mathbf{A} - \mathbf{A}_k\|_\xi^2, \quad \textit{for } \xi = \{2, \mathrm{F}\}.$$

3.2 Theoretical comparison to state of the art

We compare the number of chosen columns c in Algorithm 1 to the number of columns chosen in the randomized leverage scores sampling case [13]. The algorithm of [13] requires

$$c = O(k \log k/\varepsilon^2)$$

columns for a relative-error bound with respect to the Frobenius error in the CSSP:

$$\|\mathbf{A} - \mathbf{C}\mathbf{C}^\dagger\mathbf{A}\|_\mathrm{F}^2 \leq (1+\varepsilon)\|\mathbf{A} - \mathbf{A}_k\|_\mathrm{F}^2.$$

Assuming leverage scores follow a power-law decay, Algorithm 1 requires fewer columns for the same ε when:

$$\max\left\{\left(\frac{2k}{\varepsilon}\right)^{\frac{1}{1+\eta}},\ \left(\frac{2k}{\eta \cdot \varepsilon}\right)^{\frac{1}{\eta}}\right\} < C \cdot \frac{k \log k}{\varepsilon^2},$$

where C is an absolute constant. Hence, under the power law decay, Algorithm 1 offers provably a matrix approximation similar or better than [13].

Let us now compare the performance of Algorithm 1 with [4], which are the current state of the art for the CSSP. Theorem 1.5 in [4] provides a randomized algorithm which selects

$$c = \frac{2k}{\varepsilon}(1 + o(1))$$

columns in $\mathbf{C}$ such that

$$\|\mathbf{A} - \mathbf{C}\mathbf{C}^\dagger\mathbf{A}\|_\mathrm{F}^2 < (1+\varepsilon) \cdot \|\mathbf{A} - \mathbf{A}_k\|_\mathrm{F}^2$$

holds in expectation. This result is in fact optimal, up to a constant 2, since there is a lower bound indicating that such a relative error approximation is not possible unless $c = k/\varepsilon$ (see Section 9.2 in [4]). The approximation bound of Algorithm 1 is indeed better than the upper/lower bounds in [4] for any $\eta > 1$. We should note here that the lower bound in [4] is for general matrices; however, the upper bound of Theorem 3 is applied to a specific class of matrices whose leverage scores follow a power law decay

Next, we compare the spectral norm bound of Theorem 3 to the spectral norm bound of Theorem 1.1 in [4], which indicates that there exists a deterministic algorithm selecting $c > k$ columns with error

$$\|\mathbf{A} - \mathbf{C}\mathbf{C}^\dagger\mathbf{A}\|_2^2 < O(n/c) \cdot \|\mathbf{A} - \mathbf{A}_k\|_2^2.$$

This upper bound is also tight, up to constants, since [4] provides a matching lower bound. Notice that a relative error upper bound requires $c = \Omega\,(n/(1+\varepsilon))$ in the general case. However, under the power law assumption in Theorem 3, we provide such a relative error bound with asymptotically fewer columns. To our best knowledge, fixing η to a constant, this is the *first* relative-error bound for the spectral norm version of the CSSP with $c = \mathrm{poly}(k, 1/\varepsilon)$ columns.

4. EXPERIMENTS

In this section, we first provide evidence that power law decays are prevalent in real-world data sets. Then, we investigate the empirical performance of Algorithm 1 on real and synthetic data sets.

Our experiments are not meant to be exhaustive; however, they provide clear evidence that: (*i*) the leverage scores of real world matrices indeed follow "sharp" power law decays; and (*ii*) deterministic leverage score sampling in such matrices is particularly effective.

4.1 Power-law decays in real data sets

We demonstrate the leverage score decay behavior of many real-world data sets. These range from social networks and product co-purchasing matrices to document-term bag-of-words data sets, citation networks, and medical imaging

[2]We chose to analyze in detail the case where the leverage scores follow a power law decay; other models for the leverage scores, example, exponential decay, are also interesting, and will be the subject of the full version of this work.

Dataset	$m \times n$	Description	Dataset	$m \times n$	Description
Amazon	262111 × 262111	Purchase netw. [25]	Citeseer	723131 × 723131	Citation netw. [24]
4square	106218 × 106218	Social netw. [36]	Github	56519 × 120867	Soft. netw. [24]
Gnutella	62586 × 62586	P2P netw. [25]	Google	875713 × 875713	Web conn. [24]
Gowalla	875713 × 875713	Social netw. [24]	LJournal	4847571 × 4847571	Social netw. [25]
Slashdot	82168 × 82168	Social netw. [25]	NIPS	12419 × 1500	Word/Docs [2]
Skitter	1696415 × 1696415	System netw. [24]	CT slices	386 × 53500	CT images [2]
Cora	23166 × 23166	Citation netw. [24]	Writer	81067 × 42714	Writers/Works [24]
Youtube	1134890 × 1134890	Video netw. [25]	YT groups	94238 × 30087	Users/Groups [24]

Table 1: Summary of datasets used in the experiments of Subsection 4.1

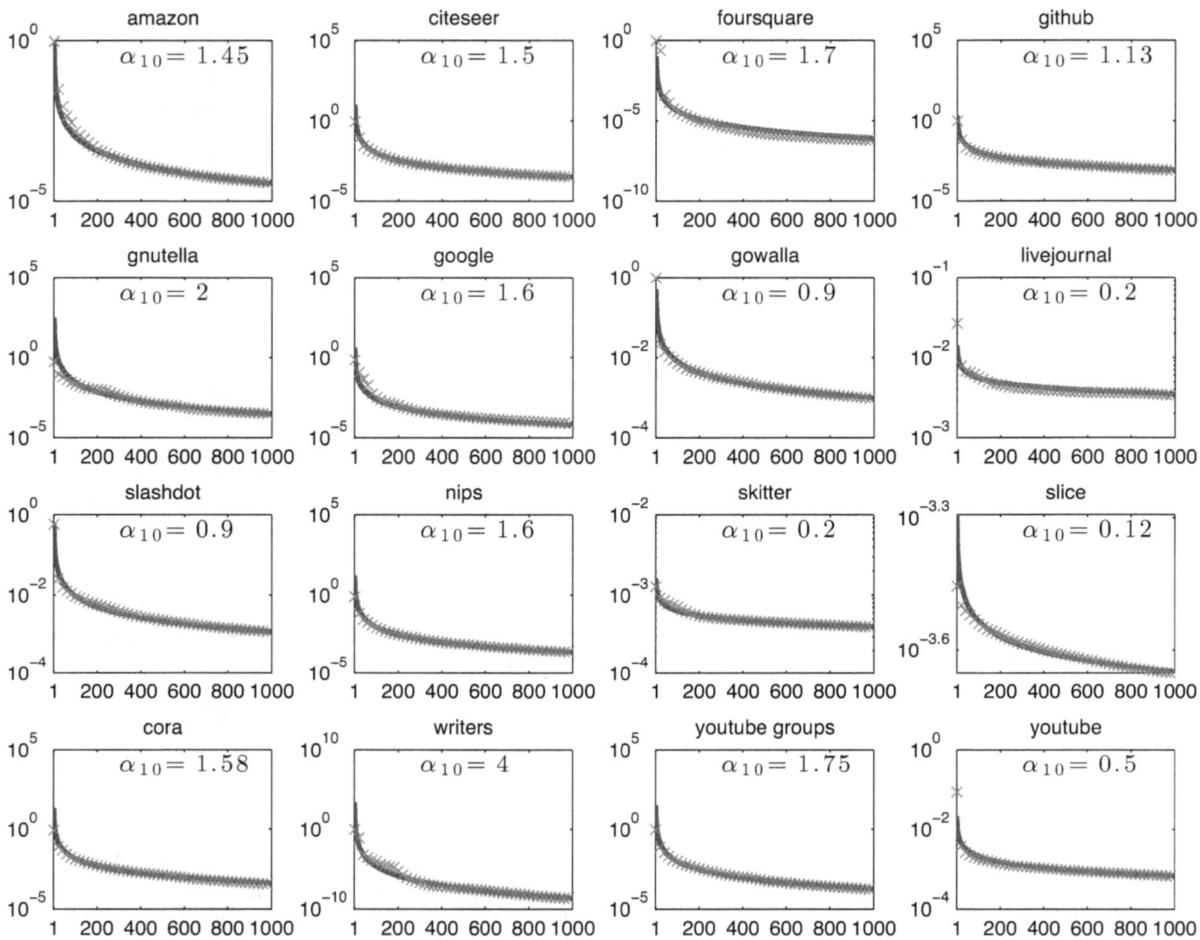

Figure 1: We plot the top $1,000$ leverage scores for 16 different data sets, obtained through $\mathbf{V}_k$ for $k = 10$. The plots are in logarithmic scale. For each data-set, we plot a fitting power-law curve $\beta \cdot x^{-\alpha_k}$. The exponent is listed on each figure as α_{10}. The leverage scores are plotted with a red $\times$ marker, and the fitted curves are denoted with a solid blue line. We observe that the power law fit offers a good approximation of the true leverage scores. We further observe that many data sets exhibit sharp decays ($\alpha_k > 1$), while only a few have leverage scores that decay slowly ($\alpha_k < 1$).

samples. Their dimensions vary from thousands to millions of variables. The data-set description is given in Table 1.

In Figure 1, we plot the top $1,000$ leverage scores extracted from the matrix of the right top-k singular vectors $\mathbf{V}_k$. In all cases we set $k = 10$.[3] For each dataset, we plot a fitting power-law curve of the form $\beta \cdot x^{-\alpha_k}$, where α_k is the exponent of interest.

We can see from the plots that a power law indeed seems to closely match the behavior of the top leverage scores. What is more interesting is that for many of our data sets we observe a decay exponent of $\alpha_k > 1$: this is the regime where deterministic sampling is expected to perform well. It

[3]We performed various experiments for larger k, *e.g.*, $k = 30$ or $k = 100$ (not shown due to space limitations). We found that as we move towards higher k, we observe a "smoothing" of the speed of decay. This is to be expected, since for the case of $k = \text{rank}(\mathbf{A})$ all leverage scores are equal.

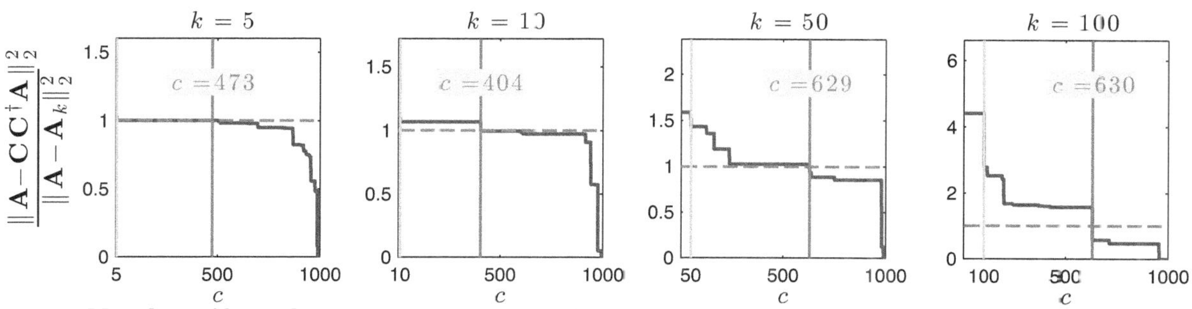

Figure 2: Nearly-uniform leverage scores case: Here, we plot as a blue curve the relative error ratio $\|\mathbf{A}-\mathbf{C}\mathbf{C}^{\dagger}\mathbf{A}\|_2^2/\|\mathbf{A}-\mathbf{A}_k\|_2^2$ achieved by Algorithm 1 as a function of the output columns c. The leftmost vertical cyan line corresponds to the point where $k=c$. When $c<k$ the output error can be large; this justifies why we enforce the algorithm to output $c \geq k$ columns. The rightmost vertical magenta line indicates the point where the c sampled columns offer as good an approximation as that of the best rank-k matrix $\mathbf{A}_k$.

seems that these sharp decays are naturally present in many real-world data sets.

We would like to note that as we move to smaller scores (i.e., after the 10,000-th score), we empirically observe that the leverage scores tail usually decays much faster than a power law. This only helps the bound of Theorem 2.

4.2 Synthetic Experiments

In this subsection, we are interested in understanding the performance of Algorithm 1 on matrices with *(i)* uniform and *(ii)* power-law decaying leverage scores.

To generate matrices with a prescribed leverage score decay, we use the implementation of [20]. Let $\mathbf{V}_k \in \mathbb{R}^{n \times k}$ denote the matrix we want to construct, for some $k<n$. Then, [20] provides algorithms to generate tall-and-skinny orthonormal matrices with specified row norms (i.e., leverage scores). Given the $\mathbf{V}_k$ that is the output of the matrix generation algorithm in [20], we run a basis completion algorithm to find the perpendicular matrix $\mathbf{V}_k^{\perp} \in \mathbb{R}^{n\times(n-k)}$ such that $\mathbf{V}_k^{\mathrm{T}}\mathbf{V}_k^{\perp}=\mathbf{0}_{k\times(n-k)}$. Then, we create an $n \times n$ matrix $\mathbf{V}=[\mathbf{V}_k\mathbf{V}_k^{\perp}]$ where the first k columns of $\mathbf{V}$ are the columns of $\mathbf{V}_k$ and the rest $n-k$ columns are the columns of $\mathbf{V}_k^{\perp}$; hence, $\mathbf{V}$ is a full orthonormal basis. Finally we generate $\mathbf{A} \in \mathbb{R}^{m\times n}$ as $\mathbf{A}=\mathbf{U}\boldsymbol{\Sigma}\mathbf{V}^{\mathrm{T}}$; where $\mathbf{U} \in \mathbb{R}^{m\times m}$ is any orthonormal matrix, and $\boldsymbol{\Sigma} \in \mathbb{R}^{m\times n}$ any diagonal matrix with $\min\{m,n\}$ positive entries along the main diagonal. Therefore, $\mathbf{A}=\mathbf{U}\boldsymbol{\Sigma}\mathbf{V}^{\mathrm{T}}$ is the full SVD of $\mathbf{A}$ with leverage scores equal to the squared ℓ_2-norm of the rows of $\mathbf{V}_k$. In our experiments, we pick $\mathbf{U}$ as an orthonormal basis for an $m\times m$ matrix where each entry is chosen i.i.d. from the Gaussian distribution. Also, $\boldsymbol{\Sigma}$ contains $\min\{m,n\}$ positive entries (sorted) along its main diagonal, where each entry was chosen i.i.d. from the Gaussian distribution.

4.2.1 Nearly-uniform scores

We set the number of rows to $m=200$ and the number of columns to $n=1000$ and construct $\mathbf{A}=\mathbf{U}\boldsymbol{\Sigma}\mathbf{V}^{\mathrm{T}} \in \mathbb{R}^{m\times n}$ as described above. The row norms of $\mathbf{V}_k$ are chosen as follows: First, all row norms are chosen equal to k/n, for some fixed k. Then, we introduce a small perturbation to avoid singularities: for every other pair of rows we add $\beta \in \mathcal{N}(0,1/100)$ to a row norm and subtract the same β from the other row norm – hence the sum of $\ell_i^{(k)}$ equals to k.

We set k to take the values $\{5,10,50,100\}$ and for each k we choose: $c=\{1,2,\ldots,1000\}$. We present our findings in Figure 2, where we plot the relative error achieved $\frac{\|\mathbf{A}-\mathbf{C}\mathbf{C}^{\dagger}\mathbf{A}\|_2^2}{\|\mathbf{A}-\mathbf{A}_k\|_2^2}$, where the $n\times c$ matrix $\mathbf{C}$ contains the first c columns of $\mathbf{A}$ that correspond to the k largest leverage scores of $\mathbf{V}_k$, as sampled by Algorithm 1. Then, the leftmost vertical cyan line corresponds to the point where $k=c$, and the rightmost vertical magenta line indicates the point where the c sampled columns achieve an error of $\|\mathbf{A}-\mathbf{A}_k\|_2^2$, where $\mathbf{A}_k$ is the best rank-k approximation.

In the plots of Figure 2, we see that as we move to larger values of k, if we wish to achieve an error of $\|\mathbf{A}-\mathbf{C}\mathbf{C}^{\dagger}\mathbf{A}\|_2^2 \approx \|\mathbf{A}-\mathbf{A}_k\|_2^2$, then we need to keep in $\mathbf{C}$, approximately almost half the columns of $\mathbf{A}$. This agrees with the uniform scores example that we showed earlier in Subsection 3.1. However, we observe that Algorithm 1 can obtain a moderately small relative error, with significantly smaller c. See for example the case where $k=100$; then, $c\approx 200$ sampled columns suffice for a relative error approximately equal to 2, *i.e.,* $\|\mathbf{A}-\mathbf{C}\mathbf{C}^{\dagger}\mathbf{A}\|_2^2 \approx 2\cdot\|\mathbf{A}-\mathbf{A}_k\|_2^2$. This indicates that our analysis could be loose in the general case

4.2.2 Power-law decay

In this case, our synthetic eigenvector matrices $\mathbf{V}_k$ have leverage scores that follow a power law decay. We choose two power-law exponents: $\alpha_k=0.5$ and $\alpha_k=1.5$. Observe that the latter complies with Theorem 3, that predicts the near optimality of leverage score sampling under such decay.

In the first row of Figure 3, we plot the relative error vs. the number of output columns c of Algorithm 1 for $\alpha_k=0.5$. Then, in the second row of Figure 3, we plot the relative error vs. the number of output columns c of Algorithm 1 for $\alpha_k=1.5$. The blue line represents the relative error in terms of spectral norm. We can see that the performance of Algorithm 1 in the case of the fast decay is surprising: $c\approx 1.5\cdot k$ suffices for an approximation as good as of that of the best rank-k approximation. This confirms the approximation performance in Theorem 3.

4.3 Comparison with other techniques

We will now compare the proposed algorithm to state of the art approaches for the CSSP, both for $\xi=2$ and $\xi=\mathrm{F}$. We report results for the errors $\|\mathbf{A}-\mathbf{C}\mathbf{C}^{\dagger}\mathbf{A}\|_\xi^2/\|\mathbf{A}-\mathbf{A}_k\|_\xi^2$. A comparison of the running time complexity of those algorithms is out of the scope of our experiments.

Table 2 contains a brief description of the datasets used in our experiments. We employ the datasets used in [15], which

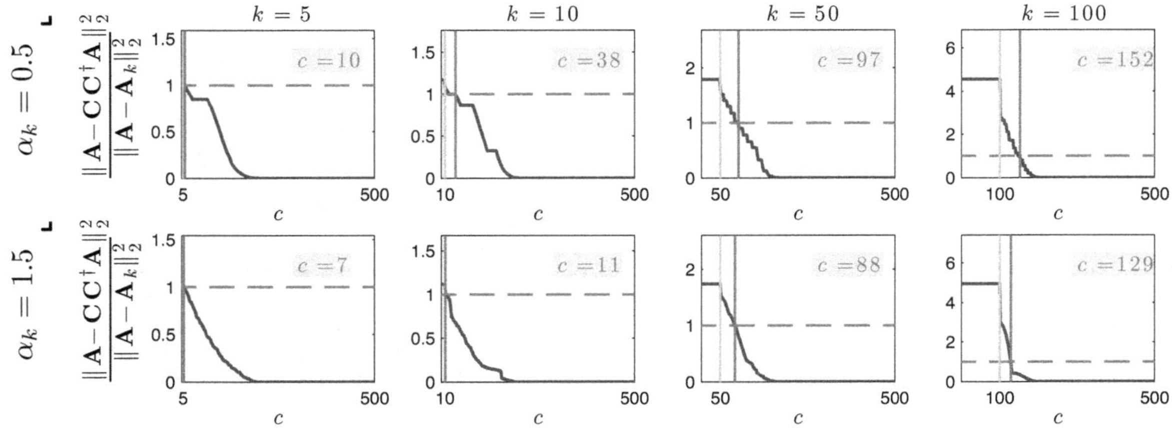

Figure 3: Power-law decaying leverage scores case: We choose two power-law exponents: $\alpha_k = 0.5$ and $\alpha_k = 1.5$. In the first row we plot the relative error of Algorithm 1 vs. c for the first decay profile, and the second row is the error performance of Algorithm 1 for the second, sharpest decay profile. The vertical cyan line corresponds to the point where $k = c$, and the vertical magenta line indicates the point where the c sampled columns offer a better approximation compared to the best rank-k matrix $\mathbf{A}_k$.

Dataset	m	n	rank($\mathbf{A}$)	Description
`Protein`	357	6621	356	Saccharomyces cerevisiae dataset
`SNPS`	46	5523	46	Single Nucleotide - polymorphism dataset
`Enron`	3000	3000	2569	A subgraph of the Enron email graph

Table 2: Summary of datasets used in the experiments of Subsection 4.3 [15]

presents exhaustive experiments for matrix approximations obtained through randomized leverage scores sampling.

4.3.1 List of comparison algorithms

We compare Algorithm 1 against three methods for the CSSP. First, the authors in [4] present a near-optimal deterministic algorithm, as described in Theorem 1.2 in [4]. Given $\mathbf{A}$, $k < \text{rank}(\mathbf{A})$ and $c > k$, the proposed algorithm selects $\tilde{c} \leq c$ columns of $\mathbf{A}$ in $\mathbf{C} \in \mathbb{R}^{m \times \tilde{c}}$ with

$$\|\mathbf{A} - \mathbf{CC}^\dagger\mathbf{A}\|_\text{F} \leq \left(1 + \left(1 - \sqrt{k/c}\right)^{-1}\right) \|\mathbf{A} - \mathbf{A}_k\|_\text{F}.$$

Second, in [16], the authors present a deterministic pivoted QR algorithm such that:

$$\|\mathbf{A} - \mathbf{CC}^\dagger\mathbf{A}\|_2 \leq \left(1 + \sqrt{n-k} \cdot 2^k\right) \|\mathbf{A} - \mathbf{A}_k\|_2.$$

This bound was proved in [17]. In our tests, we use the $\texttt{qr}(\cdot)$ built-in Matlab function, where one can select $c = k$ columns of $\mathbf{A}$ as:

$$[\mathbf{Q},\ \mathbf{R}, \boldsymbol{\pi}] = \texttt{qr}(\mathbf{A}, 0); \quad \mathbf{C} = \mathbf{A}_{:,\boldsymbol{\pi}_{1:c}},$$

where $\mathbf{A} = \mathbf{QR}$, $\mathbf{Q} \in \mathbb{R}^{m \times n}$ contains orthonormal columns, $\mathbf{R} \in \mathbb{R}^{n \times n}$ is upper triangular, and $\boldsymbol{\pi}$ is a permutation information vector such that $\mathbf{A}_{:,\boldsymbol{\pi}} = \mathbf{QR}$.

Third, we also consider the randomized leverage-scores sampling method with replacement, presented in [13]. According to this work and given $\mathbf{A}, k < \text{rank}(\mathbf{A})$, and $c = \Omega(k \log k)$, the bound provided by the algorithm is

$$\|\mathbf{A} - \mathbf{CC}^\dagger\mathbf{A}\|_\text{F} \leq \left(1 + O\left(\sqrt{k \log k/c}\right)\right) \|\mathbf{A} - \mathbf{A}_k\|_\text{F},$$

which holds only with constant probability. In our experiments, we use the software tool developed in [20] for the randomized sampling step.

We use our own Matlab implementation for each of these approaches. For [13], we execute 10 repetitions and report the one that minimizes the approximation error.

4.3.2 Performance Results

Table 3 contains a subset of our results; a complete set is reserved for an extended version of this work. We observe that the performance of Algorithm 1 is particularly appealing: It is almost as good as randomized leverage scores sampling in almost all cases - when randomized sampling is better, the difference is on the first or second decimal digit.

Figure 4 shows the leverage scores for the three matrices used in our experiments. Although the decay for the first data sets does not fit a "sharp" power law as it is required in Theorem 3, the performance of the algorithm is still competitive in practice. Interestingly, we do observe good performance for the third data set (Enron). For this case, the power law decay fits the decay profile needed to establish the near optimality of Algorithm 1.

5. RELATED WORK

One of the first deterministic results regarding the CSSP goes back to the seminal work of Gene Golub on pivoted QR factorizations [16]. Similar algorithms have been developed in [16, 19, 10, 11, 17, 35, 32, 3, 27]; see also [6] for a recent survey. The best of these algorithms is the so-called *Strong Rank-revealing QR* (Strong RRQR) algorithm in [17]:

Model		$\frac{\|\mathbf{A}-\mathbf{CC}^{\dagger}\mathbf{A}\|_2}{\|\mathbf{A}-\mathbf{A}_k\|_2}$			$\frac{\|\mathbf{A}-\mathbf{CC}^{\dagger}\mathbf{A}\|_F}{\|\mathbf{A}-\mathbf{A}_k\|_F}$			
k	c	[13]	[16]	This work	[4]	[13]	[16]	This work
Protein 50	51	**1.7334**	2.2621	2.6809	1.1068	1.0888	1.1017	**1.1000**
	118	**1.3228**	1.4274	2.2536	0.9344	**0.9233**	0.9258	0.9259
	186	1.0846	**1.0755**	1.7357	0.7939	0.7377	0.7423	**0.7346**
	253	**0.9274**	0.9281	1.3858	0.6938	0.5461	0.5326	**0.5264**
	320	0.7899	**0.7528**	0.8176	0.5943	0.2831	0.2303	**0.2231**
Protein 100	101	1.8568	**1.8220**	2.5666	1.1789	**1.1506**	1.1558	1.1606
	156	**1.3741**	1.3987	2.4227	0.9928	**0.9783**	0.9835	0.9820
	211	1.3041	**1.1926**	2.3122	0.8182	0.8100	0.7958	**0.7886**
	265	**1.0270**	1.0459	2.0509	0.6241	0.6004	0.5820	**0.5768**
	320	0.9174	**0.8704**	1.8562	0.3752	0.3648	**0.2742**	0.2874
SNPS 5	6	**1.4765**	1.5030	1.5613	1.1831	**1.0915**	1.1030	1.1056
	12	1.2601	**1.2402**	1.2799	1.0524	0.9649	0.9519	**0.9469**
	18	1.0537	**1.0236**	1.1252	1.0183	0.8283	**0.8187**	0.8281
	24	**0.8679**	0.9063	0.9302	0.9537	0.6943	**0.6898**	0.6975
	30	**0.7441**	0.7549	0.8742	0.9558	0.5827	**0.5413**	0.5789
SNPS 10	11	1.6459	**1.5206**	1.6329	1.2324	1.1708	1.1500	**1.1413**
	16	**1.3020**	1.4265	1.5939	1.1272	1.0386	**1.0199**	1.0420
	21	1.2789	**1.1511**	1.1676	1.0225	0.9170	**0.8842**	0.9011
	25	1.1022	**1.0729**	1.0935	0.9838	0.8091	**0.7876**	0.8057
	30	0.9968	**0.9256**	1.0020	0.8088	0.6636	**0.6375**	0.6707
Enron 10	11	2.2337	1.8320	**1.7217**	1.1096	1.0992	1.0768	**1.0704**
	83	**1.0717**	1.0821	1.1464	1.0123	0.9381	**0.9094**	0.9196
	156	0.8419	**0.8172**	0.8412	1.0044	0.8692	**0.8091**	0.8247
	228	**0.6739**	0.6882	0.6993	0.9984	0.8096	**0.7311**	0.7519
	300	0.6061	**0.6041**	0.6057	1.0000	0.7628	**0.6640**	0.6837
Enron 20	21	2.1726	**1.9741**	2.1669	1.1344	1.1094	**1.0889**	1.0931
	91	1.3502	**1.3305**	1.3344	1.0194	0.9814	**0.9414**	0.9421
	161	1.0242	1.0504	**1.0239**	0.9999	0.9004	**0.8434**	0.8484
	230	0.9099	0.9025	**0.9006**	0.9730	0.8505	**0.7655**	0.7740
	300	0.8211	0.7941	**0.7936**	0.9671	0.8037	**0.6971**	0.7087
Enron 50	51	2.6520	2.2788	**2.2520**	1.1547	1.1436	**1.1053**	1.1076
	113	1.7454	**1.6850**	1.8122	1.0350	1.0425	**0.9902**	0.9929
	176	**1.3524**	1.4199	1.4673	0.9835	0.9718	**0.8999**	0.9011
	238	1.2588	**1.2303**	1.2450	0.9607	0.9187	**0.8251**	0.8282
	300	1.2209	**1.1014**	1.1239	0.9384	0.8806	**0.7593**	0.7651
Enron 100	101	2.2502	**2.2145**	2.2721	1.1938	1.1805	**1.1223**	1.1238
	151	2.2399	**1.8677**	1.8979	1.0891	1.1122	**1.0357**	1.0393
	201	1.7945	1.6350	**1.6332**	1.0236	1.0631	**0.9646**	0.9664
	250	1.6721	**1.5001**	1.5017	0.9885	1.0026	**0.9025**	0.9037
	300	1.3946	**1.3711**	1.3847	0.9485	0.9672	**0.8444**	0.8467

Table 3: We present the performance of Algorithm 1 as compared to the state of the art in CSSP. We run experiments on 3 data sets described in the above table, for various values of k and c. The performance of Algorithm 1, especially in terms of the Frobenius norm error, is very close to optimal, while at the same time similar, if not better, to the performance of the more sophisticated algorithms of the comparison.

Given $\mathbf{A}$, $c = k$, and constant $f \geq 1$, Strong RRQR requires $O(mnk \log_f n)$ arithmetic operations to find k columns of $\mathbf{A}$ in $\mathbf{C} \in \mathbb{R}^{m \times k}$ that satisfy

$$\|\mathbf{A} - \mathbf{CC}^{\dagger}\mathbf{A}\|_2 \leq \left(1 + f^2\sqrt{k(n-k)+1}\right) \cdot \|\mathbf{A} - \mathbf{A}_k\|_2.$$

As discussed in Section 1, [21] suggests column sampling with the largest corresponding leverage scores. A related result in [35] suggests column sampling through selection over $\mathbf{V}_k^{\mathrm{T}}$ with Strong RRQR. Notice that the leverage scores sampling approach is similar, but the column selection is based on the largest Euclidean norms of the columns of $\mathbf{V}_k^{\mathrm{T}}$.

From a probabilistic point of view, much work has followed the seminal work of [14] for the CSSP. [14] introduced the idea of randomly sampling columns based on specific probability distributions. [14] use a simple probability distribution where each column of $\mathbf{A}$ is sampled with probability proportional to its Euclidean norm. The approximation bound achieved, which holds only in expectation, is

$$\|\mathbf{A} - \mathbf{CC}^{\dagger}\mathbf{A}\|_F^2 \leq \|\mathbf{A} - \mathbf{A}_k\|_F^2 + (k/c)\|\mathbf{A}\|_F^2.$$

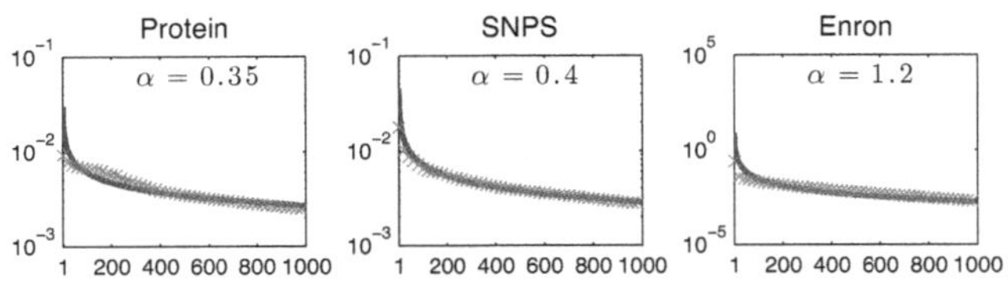

Figure 4: The plots are for $k = 10$ and are in logarithmic scale. The exponent is listed on each figure as α. The leverage scores are plotted with a red $\times$ marker, and the fitted curves are denoted with a solid blue line.

[13] improved upon the accuracy of this result by using a distribution over the columns of $\mathbf{A}$ where each column is sampled with probability proportional to its leverage score. From a different perspective, [12, 18] presented some optimal algorithms using volume sampling. [4] obtained faster optimal algorithms while [7] proposed optimal algorithms that run in input sparsity time.

Another line of research includes row-sampling algorithms for tall-and-skinny orthonormal matrices, which is relevant to our results: we essentially apply this kind of sampling to the rows of the matrix $\mathbf{V}_k$ from the SVD of $\mathbf{A}$. See Lemma 5 in the Section 6 for a precise statement of our result. Similar results exist in [1]. We should also mention the work in [37], which corresponds to a derandomization of the randomized sampling algorithm in [13].

6. PROOFS

Before we proceed, we setup some notation and definitions. For any two matrices $\mathbf{A}$ and $\mathbf{B}$ with appropriate dimensions, $\|\mathbf{A}\|_2 \leq \|\mathbf{A}\|_\mathrm{F} \leq \sqrt{\mathrm{rank}(\mathbf{A})}\|\mathbf{A}\|_2$, $\|\mathbf{AB}\|_\mathrm{F} \leq \|\mathbf{A}\|_\mathrm{F}\|\mathbf{B}\|_2$, and $\|\mathbf{AB}\|_\mathrm{F} \leq \|\mathbf{A}\|_2\|\mathbf{B}\|_\mathrm{F}$. $\|\mathbf{A}\|_\xi$ indicates that an expression holds for both $\xi = 2, \mathrm{F}$. The thin (compact) Singular Value Decomposition (SVD) of a matrix $\mathbf{A} \in \mathbb{R}^{m \times n}$ with $\mathrm{rank}(\mathbf{A}) = \rho$ is:

$$\mathbf{A} = \underbrace{\begin{pmatrix} \mathbf{U}_k & \mathbf{U}_{\rho-k} \end{pmatrix}}_{\mathbf{U_A} \in \mathbb{R}^{m \times \rho}} \underbrace{\begin{pmatrix} \mathbf{\Sigma}_k & \mathbf{0} \\ \mathbf{0} & \mathbf{\Sigma}_{\rho-k} \end{pmatrix}}_{\mathbf{\Sigma_A} \in \mathbb{R}^{\rho \times \rho}} \underbrace{\begin{pmatrix} \mathbf{V}_k^\mathrm{T} \\ \mathbf{V}_{\rho-k}^\mathrm{T} \end{pmatrix}}_{\mathbf{V}_\mathbf{A}^\mathrm{T} \in \mathbb{R}^{\rho \times n}},$$

with singular values $\sigma_1(\mathbf{A}) \geq \ldots \sigma_k(\mathbf{A}) \geq \sigma_{k+1}(\mathbf{A}) \geq \ldots \geq \sigma_\rho(\mathbf{A}) > 0$. The matrices $\mathbf{U_A}$ and $\mathbf{V_A}$ contain the left and right singular vectors, respectively. It is well-known that $\mathbf{A}_k = \mathbf{U}_k\mathbf{\Sigma}_k\mathbf{V}_k^\mathrm{T} = \mathbf{U}_k\mathbf{U}_k^\mathrm{T}\mathbf{A} = \mathbf{A}\mathbf{V}_k\mathbf{V}_k^\mathrm{T} \in \mathbb{R}^{m \times n}$ minimizes $\|\mathbf{A} - \mathbf{X}\|_\xi$ over all matrices $\mathbf{X} \in \mathbb{R}^{m \times n}$ of rank at most $k \leq \mathrm{rank}(\mathbf{A})$. The best rank-$k$ approximation to $\mathbf{A}$ satisfies $\|\mathbf{A} - \mathbf{A}_k\|_2 = \sigma_{k+1}(\mathbf{A})$ and $\|\mathbf{A} - \mathbf{A}_k\|_\mathrm{F}^2 = \sum_{i=k+1}^{\rho} \sigma_i^2(\mathbf{A})$. $\mathbf{A}^\dagger$ denotes the Moore-Penrose pseudo-inverse of $\mathbf{A}$. Let $\mathbf{B} \in \mathbb{R}^{m \times n}$ ($m \leq n$) and $\mathbf{A} = \mathbf{B}\mathbf{B}^\mathrm{T} \in \mathbb{R}^{m \times m}$; then, for all $i = 1, ..., m$, $\lambda_i(\mathbf{A}) = \sigma_i^2(\mathbf{B})$ is the i-th eigenvalue of $\mathbf{A}$.

6.1 Proof of Theorem 2

To prove Theorem 2, we will use the following result.

LEMMA 4. *[Eqn. 3.2, Lemma 3.1 in [4]] Consider* $\mathbf{A} = \mathbf{A}\mathbf{Z}\mathbf{Z}^\mathrm{T} + \mathbf{E} \in \mathbb{R}^{m \times n}$ *as a low-rank matrix factorization of* $\mathbf{A}$*, with* $\mathbf{Z} \in \mathbb{R}^{n \times k}$*, and* $\mathbf{Z}^\mathrm{T}\mathbf{Z} = \mathbf{I}_k$*. Let* $\mathbf{S} \in \mathbb{R}^{n \times c}$ $(c \geq k)$ *be any matrix such that*

$$rank(\mathbf{Z}^\mathrm{T}\mathbf{S}) = k.$$

Let $\mathbf{C} = \mathbf{AS} \in \mathbb{R}^{m \times c}$*. Then, for* $\xi = 2, \mathrm{F}$ *:*

$$\|\mathbf{A} - \mathbf{C}\mathbf{C}^\dagger\mathbf{A}\|_\xi^2 \leq \|\mathbf{E}\|_\xi^2 \cdot \|\mathbf{S}(\mathbf{Z}^\mathrm{T}\mathbf{S})^\dagger\|_2^2.$$

We will also use the following novel lower bound on the smallest singular value of the matrix $\mathbf{V}_k$, after deterministic selection of its rows based on the largest leverage scores.

LEMMA 5. *Repeat the conditions of Theorem 2. Then,*

$$\sigma_k^2(\mathbf{V}_k^\mathrm{T}\mathbf{S}) > 1 - \varepsilon.$$

PROOF. We use the following perturbation result on the sum of eigenvalues of symmetric matrices.

LEMMA 6. *[Theorem 2.8.1; part (i) in [9]] Let* $\mathbf{X}$ *and* $\mathbf{Y}$ *be symmetric matrices of order* k *and, let* $1 \leq i, j \leq n$ *with* $i + j \leq k + 1$*. Then,*

$$\lambda_i(\mathbf{X}) \geq \lambda_{i+j-1}(\mathbf{X} + \mathbf{Y}) - \lambda_j(\mathbf{Y}).$$

Let $\mathbf{S} \in \mathbb{R}^{n \times c}$ sample c columns from $\mathbf{A}$ with $c \geq k$. Similarly, let $\hat{\mathbf{S}} \in \mathbb{R}^{n \times (n-c)}$ sample the rest $n - c$ columns from $\mathbf{A}$. Hence,

$$\mathbf{I}_k = \mathbf{V}_k^\mathrm{T}\mathbf{V}_k = \mathbf{V}_k^\mathrm{T}\mathbf{S}\mathbf{S}^\mathrm{T}\mathbf{V}_k + \mathbf{V}_k^\mathrm{T}\hat{\mathbf{S}}\hat{\mathbf{S}}^\mathrm{T}\mathbf{V}_k.$$

Let

$$\mathbf{X} = \mathbf{V}_k^\mathrm{T}\mathbf{S}\mathbf{S}^\mathrm{T}\mathbf{V}_k, \mathbf{Y} = \mathbf{V}_k^\mathrm{T}\hat{\mathbf{S}}\hat{\mathbf{S}}^\mathrm{T}\mathbf{V}_k, \ i = k, \ \text{and} \ j = 1,$$

in Lemma 6. Notice that $i + j \leq k + 1$, and $\lambda_k(\mathbf{X} + \mathbf{Y}) = 1$; hence:

$$\begin{aligned} \lambda_k(\mathbf{V}_k^\mathrm{T}\mathbf{S}\mathbf{S}^\mathrm{T}\mathbf{V}_k) &\geq 1 - \lambda_1(\mathbf{V}_k^\mathrm{T}\hat{\mathbf{S}}\hat{\mathbf{S}}^\mathrm{T}\mathbf{V}_k) \\ &= 1 - \|\mathbf{V}_k^\mathrm{T}\hat{\mathbf{S}}\|_2^2 \\ &\geq 1 - \|\mathbf{V}_k^\mathrm{T}\hat{\mathbf{S}}\|_\mathrm{F}^2 \\ &> 1 - (k - \theta) \end{aligned}$$

Replacing $\theta = k - \varepsilon$ and $\lambda_k(\mathbf{V}_k^\mathrm{T}\mathbf{S}\mathbf{S}^\mathrm{T}\mathbf{V}_k) = \sigma_k^2(\mathbf{V}_k^\mathrm{T}\mathbf{S})$ concludes the proof. ■

The proof of Theorem 2 is a straightforward combination of the Lemmas 4 and 5. First, by picking $\mathbf{Z} = \mathbf{V}_k$ in Lemma 4 we obtain:

$$\begin{aligned} \|\mathbf{A} - \mathbf{C}\mathbf{C}^\dagger\mathbf{A}\|_\xi^2 &\leq \|\mathbf{A} - \mathbf{A}_k\|_\xi^2 \cdot \|\mathbf{S}(\mathbf{V}_k^\mathrm{T}\mathbf{S})^\dagger\|_2^2 \\ &\leq \|\mathbf{A} - \mathbf{A}_k\|_\xi^2 \cdot \|\mathbf{S}\|_2^2 \cdot \|(\mathbf{V}_k^\mathrm{T}\mathbf{S})^\dagger\|_2^2 \\ &= \|\mathbf{A} - \mathbf{A}_k\|_\xi^2 \cdot \|(\mathbf{V}_k^\mathrm{T}\mathbf{S})^\dagger\|_2^2 \\ &= \|\mathbf{A} - \mathbf{A}_k\|_\xi^2 / \sigma_k^2(\mathbf{V}_k^\mathrm{T}\mathbf{S}) \end{aligned}$$

In the above, we used the facts that

$$\mathbf{E} = \mathbf{A} - \mathbf{A}\mathbf{V}_k\mathbf{V}_k^\mathrm{T} = \mathbf{A} - \mathbf{A}_k,$$

and the spectral norm of the sampling matrix $\mathbf{S}$ equals one. Also, we used that $\mathrm{rank}(\mathbf{V}_k^\mathrm{T}\mathbf{S}) = k$, which is implied from Lemma 5. Next, via the bound in Lemma 5:

$$\|\mathbf{A} - \mathbf{C}\mathbf{C}^\dagger\mathbf{A}\|_\xi^2 < \|\mathbf{A} - \mathbf{A}_k\|_\xi^2 / (1 - \varepsilon).$$

6.2 Proof of Theorem 3

Let $\alpha_k = 1 + \eta$ for some $\eta > 0$. We assume that the leverage scores follow a power law decay such that: $\ell_i^{(k)} = \ell_1^{(k)} / i^{1+\eta}$. According to the proposed algorithm, we select c columns such that $\sum_{i=1}^{c} \ell_i^{(k)} > \theta$. Here, we bound the number of columns c required to achieve an $\varepsilon := k - \theta$ approximation in Theorem 2. To this end, we use the extreme case $\sum_{i=1}^{c} \ell_i^{(k)} = \theta$ which guarantees an $(1 + \varepsilon)$-approximation. For our analysis, we use the following well-known result.

PROPOSITION 7. *[Integral test for convergence] Let $f(\cdot) \geq 0$ be a function defined over the set of positive reals. Furthermore, assume that $f(\cdot)$ is monotone decreasing. Then,*

$$\int_{j}^{J+1} f(i)dx \;\leq\; \sum_{i=j}^{J} f(i) \;\leq\; f(j) + \int_{j}^{J} f(x)dx,$$

over the interval $[j, \dots, J]$ for j, J positive integers.

In our case, consider $f(i) = \frac{1}{i^{1+\eta}}$. By definition of the leverage scores, we have:

$$k = \sum_{i=1}^{n} \ell_i^{(k)} = \ell_1^{(k)} \sum_{i=1}^{n} \frac{1}{i^{1+\eta}} \Longrightarrow \ell_1^{(k)} = \frac{k}{\sum_{i=1}^{n} \frac{1}{i^{1+\eta}}}.$$

By construction, we collect c leverage scores such that $k - \theta = \varepsilon$. This leads to:

$$\begin{aligned} k - \varepsilon &= \ell_1^{(k)} \cdot \sum_{i=1}^{c} \frac{1}{i^{1+\eta}} = \frac{k}{\sum_{i=1}^{n} \frac{1}{i^{1+\eta}}} \cdot \sum_{i=1}^{c} \frac{1}{i^{1+\eta}} \\ &= k \left(\frac{\sum_{i=1}^{n} \frac{1}{i^{1+\eta}} - \sum_{i=c+1}^{n} \frac{1}{i^{1+\eta}}}{\sum_{i=1}^{n} \frac{1}{i^{1+\eta}}} \right) \\ &= k \left(1 - \frac{\sum_{i=c+1}^{n} \frac{1}{i^{1+\eta}}}{\sum_{i=1}^{n} \frac{1}{i^{1+\eta}}} \right) \Longrightarrow \\ \varepsilon &= k \cdot \frac{\sum_{i=c+1}^{n} \frac{1}{i^{1+\eta}}}{\sum_{i=1}^{n} \frac{1}{i^{1+\eta}}}. \end{aligned}$$

To bound the quantity on the right hand side, we observe

$$\begin{aligned} \frac{\sum_{i=c+1}^{n} \frac{1}{i^{1+\eta}}}{\sum_{i=1}^{n} \frac{1}{i^{1+\eta}}} &\leq \frac{\frac{1}{(c+1)^{1+\eta}} + \int_{i=c+1}^{n} \frac{1}{x^{1+\eta}} dx}{\sum_{i=1}^{n} \frac{1}{i^{1+\eta}}} \\ &= \frac{\frac{1}{(c+1)^{1+\eta}} + \left[-\frac{1}{x^{1+\eta}} \right]_{i=c+1}^{n}}{\sum_{i=1}^{n} \frac{1}{i^{1+\eta}}} \\ &= \frac{\frac{1}{(c+1)^{1+\eta}} + \frac{1}{\eta} \left(\frac{1}{(c+1)^{\eta}} - \frac{1}{n^{\eta}} \right)}{\sum_{i=1}^{n} \frac{1}{i^{1+\eta}}} \\ &\leq \frac{\frac{1}{(c+1)^{1+\eta}} + \frac{1}{\eta(c+1)^{\eta}}}{\sum_{i=1}^{n} \frac{1}{i^{1+\eta}}} \\ &= \frac{\frac{1}{(c+1)^{1+\eta}} + \frac{1}{\eta(c+1)^{\eta}}}{1 + \sum_{i=2}^{n} \frac{1}{i^{1+\eta}}} \\ &< \frac{1}{(c+1)\cdot(c+1)^{\eta}} + \frac{1}{\eta(c+1)^{\eta}} \\ &\leq \max \left\{ \frac{2}{(c+1)^{1+\eta}}, \;\; \frac{2}{\eta \cdot (c+1)^{\eta}} \right\} \end{aligned}$$

where the first inequality is due to the right hand side of the integral test and the third inequality is due to $1 + \sum_{i=2}^{n} \frac{1}{i^{1+\eta}} > 1$. Hence, we may conclude:

$$\varepsilon < k \cdot \max \left\{ \frac{2}{(c+1)^{1+\eta}}, \;\; \frac{2}{\eta \cdot (c+1)^{\eta}} \right\}.$$

The above lead to the following two cases: if

$$\varepsilon < \frac{2k}{(c+1)^{1+\eta}},$$

we have:

$$c < \left(\frac{2 \cdot k}{\varepsilon} \right)^{\frac{1}{1+\eta}} - 1,$$

whereas in the case where

$$\varepsilon < \frac{2 \cdot k}{\eta \cdot (c+1)^{\eta}},$$

we get

$$c < \left(\frac{2 \cdot k}{\eta \cdot \varepsilon} \right)^{\frac{1}{\eta}} - 1.$$

7. THE KEY ROLE OF θ

In the proof of Theorem 2, we require that

$$\sigma_k^2(\mathbf{V}_k^{\mathrm{T}}\mathbf{S}) > 1 - (k - \theta) := 1 - \varepsilon.$$

For this condition to hold, the sampling matrix $\mathbf{S}$ should preserve the rank of $\mathbf{V}_k^{\mathrm{T}}$ in $\mathbf{V}_k^{\mathrm{T}}\mathbf{S}$, i.e., choose θ such that $\mathrm{rank}(\mathbf{V}_k^{\mathrm{T}}\mathbf{S}) = k$.

Failing to preserve the rank of $\mathbf{V}_k^{\mathrm{T}}$ has immediate implications for the CSSP. To highlight this, let $\mathbf{A} \in \mathbb{R}^{m\times n}$ of rank $k < \min\{m, n\}$ with SVD $\mathbf{A} = \mathbf{U}_k\mathbf{\Sigma}_k\mathbf{V}_k^{\mathrm{T}}$. Further, assume that the kth singular value of $\mathbf{A}$ is arbitrary large, i.e., $\sigma_k(\mathbf{A}) \to \infty$. Also, let $\mathrm{rank}(\mathbf{V}^{\mathrm{T}}\mathbf{S}) = \gamma < k$ and $\mathbf{C} = \mathbf{AS}$. Then,

$$\begin{aligned} &\|\mathbf{A} - \mathbf{C}\mathbf{C}^{\dagger}\mathbf{A}\|_{\xi} \\ &= \|\mathbf{U}_k\mathbf{\Sigma}_k\mathbf{V}_k^{\mathrm{T}} - \mathbf{U}_k\mathbf{\Sigma}_k\mathbf{V}_k^{\mathrm{T}}\mathbf{S}(\mathbf{U}_k\mathbf{\Sigma}_k\mathbf{V}_k^{\mathrm{T}}\mathbf{S})^{\dagger}\mathbf{U}_k\mathbf{\Sigma}_k\mathbf{V}_k^{\mathrm{T}}\|_{\xi} \\ &= \|\mathbf{\Sigma}_k - \mathbf{\Sigma}_k\mathbf{V}_k^{\mathrm{T}}\mathbf{S}(\mathbf{U}_k\mathbf{\Sigma}_k\mathbf{V}_k^{\mathrm{T}}\mathbf{S})^{\dagger}\mathbf{U}_k\mathbf{\Sigma}_k\|_{\xi} \\ &= \|\mathbf{\Sigma}_k - \mathbf{\Sigma}_k\mathbf{V}_k^{\mathrm{T}}\mathbf{S}(\mathbf{\Sigma}_k\mathbf{V}_k^{\mathrm{T}}\mathbf{S})^{\dagger}(\mathbf{U}_k)^{\dagger}\mathbf{U}_k\mathbf{\Sigma}_k\|_{\xi} \\ &= \|\mathbf{\Sigma}_k - \mathbf{\Sigma}_k\mathbf{V}_k^{\mathrm{T}}\mathbf{S}(\mathbf{\Sigma}_k\mathbf{V}_k^{\mathrm{T}}\mathbf{S})^{\dagger}\mathbf{\Sigma}_k\|_{\xi} \\ &= \|\mathbf{\Sigma}_k - \mathbf{U}_{\mathbf{X}}\mathbf{U}_{\mathbf{X}}^{\mathrm{T}}\mathbf{\Sigma}_k\|_{\xi} \\ &\geq \sigma_k(\mathbf{A}) \end{aligned}$$

The second equality is due to the fact that both spectral and Frobenius norms are invariant to unitary transformations. In the third equality, we used the fact that $(\mathbf{WZ})^{\dagger} = \mathbf{Z}^{\dagger}\mathbf{W}^{\dagger}$ if $\mathbf{W}^{\mathrm{T}}\mathbf{W}$ is the identity matrix. Then, set $\mathbf{X} = \mathbf{\Sigma}_k\mathbf{V}_k^{\mathrm{T}}\mathbf{S} \in \mathbb{R}^{k\times c}$ where $\mathrm{rank}(\mathbf{X}) = \gamma$. Using this notation, let $\mathbf{U}_{\mathbf{X}} \in \mathbb{R}^{m\times\gamma}$ be any orthonormal basis for $span(\mathbf{X})$. Observe $\mathbf{U}_{\mathbf{X}}\mathbf{U}_{\mathbf{X}}^{\mathrm{T}} = \mathbf{X}\mathbf{X}^{\dagger}$. The last inequality is due to $\mathbf{U}_{\mathbf{X}}\mathbf{U}_{\mathbf{X}}^{\mathrm{T}}$ being an $m \times m$ diagonal matrix with γ ones along its main diagonal and the rest zeros. Thus, we may conclude that for this $\mathbf{A}$:

$$\|\mathbf{A} - \mathbf{C}\mathbf{C}^{\dagger}\mathbf{A}\|_{\xi} \geq \sigma_k(\mathbf{A}) \to \infty.$$

8. CONCLUDING REMARKS

We provided a rigorous theoretical analysis of an old and popular *deterministic* feature selection algorithm from the statistics literature [21]. Although randomized algorithms are often easier to analyze, we believe that deterministic algorithms are simpler to implement and explain, hence more attractive to practitioners and data analysts.

One interesting path for future research is understanding the connection of this work with the so-called "spectral graph sparsification problem" [31]. In that case, edge selection in a graph is implemented via randomized leverage scores sampling from an appropriate matrix (see Theorem 1 in [31]). Note that in the context of graph sparsification, leverage scores correspond to the so-called "effective resistances" of the graph. Can deterministic effective resistances sampling be rigorously analyzed? What graphs have effective resistances following a power law distribution?

References

[1] H. Avron and C. Boutsidis. Faster subset selection for matrices and applications. *SIAM Journal on Matrix Analysis and Applications (SIMAX)*, 2013.

[2] K. Bache and M. Lichman. UCI machine learning repository, 2013.

[3] C. H. Bischof and G. Quintana-Ortí. Computing rank-revealing QR factorizations of dense matrices. *ACM Trans. Math. Softw*, 24(2):226–253, 1998.

[4] C. Boutsidis, P. Drineas, and M. Magdon-Ismail. Near optimal column based matrix reconstruction. *SIAM Journal on Computing (SICOMP)*, 2013.

[5] C. Boutsidis, M. W. Mahoney, and P. Drineas. Unsupervised feature selection for principal components analysis. In *KDD*, pages 61–69, 2008.

[6] C. Boutsidis, M. W. Mahoney, and P. Drineas. An improved approximation algorithm for the column subset selection problem. In *SODA*, pages 968–977, 2009.

[7] C. Boutsidis and D. Woodruff. Optimal cur matrix decompositions. *In STOC*, 2014.

[8] M. E. Broadbent, M. Brown, K. Penner, I. Ipsen, and R. Rehman. Subset selection algorithms: Randomized vs. deterministic. *SIAM Undergraduate Research Online*, 3:50–71, 2010.

[9] A. A. E. Brouwer and W. H. Haemers. *Spectra of graphs.* Springer, 2012.

[10] T. F. Chan and P. C. Hansen. Low-rank revealing QR factorizations. *Numerical Linear Algebra with Applications*, 1:33–44, 1994.

[11] S. Chandrasekaran and I. C. F. Ipsen. On rank-revealing factorizations. *SIAM J. Matrix Anal. Appl.*, 15:592–622, 1994.

[12] A. Deshpande and L. Rademacher. Efficient volume sampling for row/column subset selection. In *Proceedings of the 42th Annual ACM Symposium on Theory of Computing (STOC)*, 2010.

[13] P. Drineas, M. W. Mahoney, and S. Muthukrishnan. Relative-error cur matrix decompositions. *SIAM Journal Matrix Analysis and Applications*, 30(2):844–881, 2008.

[14] A. Frieze, R. Kannan, and S. Vempala. Fast Monte-Carlo algorithms for finding low-rank approximations. *Journal of the ACM*, 51(6):1025–1041, 2004.

[15] A. Gittens and M. W. Mahoney. Revisiting the nystrom method for improved large-scale machine learning. In *ICML (3)*, pages 567–575, 2013.

[16] G. H. Golub. Numerical methods for solving linear least squares problems. *Numer. Math.*, 7:206–216, 1965.

[17] M. Gu and S. Eisenstat. Efficient algorithms for computing a strong rank-revealing QR factorization. *SIAM Journal on Scientific Computing*, 17:848–869, 1996.

[18] V. Guruswami and A. K. Sinop. Optimal column-based low-rank matrix reconstruction. In *SODA*. SIAM, 2012.

[19] Y. P. Hong and C. T. Pan. Rank-revealing QR factorizations and the singular value decomposition. *Mathematics of Computation*, 58:213–232, 1992.

[20] I. C. Ipsen and T. Wentworth. The effect of coherence on sampling from matrices with orthonormal columns, and preconditioned least squares problems. *arXiv preprint arXiv:1203.4809*, 2012.

[21] I. Jolliffe. Discarding variables in a principal component analysis. i: Artificial data. *Applied Statistics*, 21(2):160–173, 1972.

[22] I. Jolliffe. Discarding variables in a principal component analysis. ii: Real data. *Applied Statistics*, 22(1):21–31, 1973.

[23] I. Jolliffe. *Principal Component Analysis.* Springer; 2nd edition, 2002.

[24] J. Kunegis. Konect: the koblenz network collection. In *WWW*. International World Wide Web Conferences Steering Committee, 2013.

[25] J. Leskovec. Snap stanford network analysis project. 2009.

[26] M. W. Mahoney and P. Drineas. Cur matrix decompositions for improved data analysis. *Proceedings of the National Academy of Sciences*, 106(3):697–702, 2009.

[27] C. T. Pan. On the existence and computation of rank-revealing LU factorizations. *Linear Algebra and its Applications*, 316:199–222, 2000.

[28] D. Papapailiopoulos, A. Kyrillidis, and C. Boutsidis. Provable Deterministic Leverage Score Sampling. *arXiv preprint arXiv:1404.1530,* 2014

[29] P. Paschou, E. Ziv, E. G. Burchard, S. Choudhry, W. Rodriguez-Cintron, M. W. Mahoney, and P. Drineas. Pca-correlated snps for structure identification in worldwide human populations. *PLoS genetics*, 3(9):e160, 2007.

[30] M. Rudelson and R. Vershynin. Sampling from large matrices: An approach through geometric functional analysis. *JACM: Journal of the ACM*, 54, 2007.

[31] N. Srivastava and D. Spielman. Graph sparsifications by effective resistances. In *STOC*, 2008.

[32] G. Stewart. Four algorithms for the efficient computation of truncated QR approximations to a sparse matrix. *Numerische Mathematik*, 83:313–323, 1999.

[33] J. Sun, Y. Xie, H. Zhang, and C. Faloutsos. Less is more: Compact matrix decomposition for large sparse graphs. In *SDM*. SIAM, 2007.

[34] H. Tong, S. Papadimitriou, J. Sun, P. S. Yu, and C. Faloutsos. Colibri: fast mining of large static and dynamic graphs. In *KDD*. ACM, 2008.

[35] E. Tyrtyshnikov. Mosaic-skeleton approximations. *Calcolo*, 33(1):47–57, 1996.

[36] R. Zafarani and H. Liu. Social computing data repository at ASU, 2009.

[37] A. Zouzias. A matrix hyperbolic cosine algorithm and applications. In *ICALP*. Springer, 2012.

Semantic Visualization for Spherical Representation

Tuan M. V. Le
School of Information Systems
Singapore Management University
vmtle.2012@phdis.smu.edu.sg

Hady W. Lauw
School of Information Systems
Singapore Management University
hadywlauw@smu.edu.sg

ABSTRACT

Visualization of high-dimensional data such as text documents is widely applicable. The traditional means is to find an appropriate embedding of the high-dimensional representation in a low-dimensional visualizable space. As topic modeling is a useful form of dimensionality reduction that preserves the semantics in documents, recent approaches aim for a visualization that is consistent with both the original word space, as well as the semantic topic space. In this paper, we address the semantic visualization problem. Given a corpus of documents, the objective is to simultaneously learn the topic distributions as well as the visualization coordinates of documents. We propose to develop a semantic visualization model that approximates L^2-normalized data directly. The key is to associate each document with three representations: a coordinate in the visualization space, a multinomial distribution in the topic space, and a directional vector in a high-dimensional unit hypersphere in the word space. We join these representations in a unified generative model, and describe its parameter estimation through variational inference. Comprehensive experiments on real-life text datasets show that the proposed method outperforms the existing baselines on objective evaluation metrics for visualization quality and topic interpretability.

Categories and Subject Descriptors

H.4 [**Information Systems Applications**]: Miscellaneous; H.2.8 [**Database Applications**]: Data Mining

Keywords

semantic visualization; topic model; generative model; spherical space; spherical semantic embedding; dimensionality reduction; L2-normalized vector;

1. INTRODUCTION

Visualization is an important and widely applicable tool for exploratory analysis of high-dimensional data. There are various aspects to the study of visualization (e.g., interface, interactivity). Of special interest to data mining and machine learning is the dimensionality reduction aspect of visualization, i.e., finding a low-rank representation in two or three dimensions that preserves as much as possible the properties of the data. These low-rank representations are visualized on a scatterplot, a simple format to reveal the relationship structures among data points. The current state-of-the-art visualization approaches are formulated as finding coordinates whose distances in the visualization space "reflect" the corresponding distances in the original space [12].

While a scatterplot is useful for identifying visualizable structures among data points, it has relatively limited *explanatory* power, because the reduced dimensions have no prescribed semantics. Another type of dimensionality reduction that is focused more on interpretability is topic modeling [17, 5], where the objective is to reduce each document's original representation (e.g., word counts) into a probability distribution over Z (a user-defined quantity) topics. Each topic is associated with a distribution over words. Hence, the reduced dimensions (i.e., topics) have interpretable semantics, revealed by the most important words in each topic. However, topic model is not designed for visualization. In a 2D simplex, we can visualize topic distributions for only 3 topics, which is impractical, because Z is frequently much higher than that (though lower than the vocabulary size).

We are therefore interested in *semantic visualization*, defined as modeling visualization coordinates and topics in an integrated manner [19]. This integration has important benefits not available to either visualization or topic model on their own. On the one hand, it allows the infusion of the scatterplot visualization with topic modeling semantics. Each coordinate in the visualization space can now be associated with both a topic distribution, as well as a list of the most important words. This complements structural observations (e.g., clustering) with semantic explanations (the relevant topics and words). On the other hand, we envision that visualization may eventually serve as a user-friendly interface to explore and tune an underlying topic model, in a way that allows steering the topic model interactively.

In this paper, we propose a semantic visualization model for data with *spherical representation*. This refers to data whose instances can each be represented as a vector of unit length in a high-dimensional hypersphere [1], with dimensionality commensurate with the number of features. In other words, we are dealing with L^2-normalized feature vectors as input. One important category of such data that we focus on in this work is text document. A document can be

KDD'14, August 24–27, 2014, New York, NY, USA.

ACM 978-1-4503-2956-9/14/08 ...$15.00.
http://dx.doi.org/10.1145/2623330.2623620.

naturally represented as a normalized term vector, as done in the classical vector space model [32]. Stated more formally, the input to the problem is a corpus of documents $\mathcal{D} = \{d_1, d_2, \ldots, d_N\}$, where every d_n is represented by an L^2-normalized term vector ν_n. We seek to learn, for each d_n, a probability distribution θ_n over Z topics (*semantic*), and a coordinate x_n on a low-dimensional space (*visualization*). While we frame the discussion here in terms of documents and words, our technique is applicable to other data types for which both visualization and semantic interpretability are important, as long as they can be expressed in terms of spherical representation (i.e., L^2−normalized vectors).

Previous Approach. Jointly modeling topics and visualization coordinates is pioneered by PLSV [19] (reviewed briefly in Section 3). It is aimed at *dyadic data*, whereby every observation involves a couple (d, w) of word w's occurrence in document d. The observations for a document can be summarized as an integer vector of word counts in $\mathbb{N}^{|V|}$, where V is the vocabulary. Like its topic modeling predecessors [17, 5], PLSV uses the word count vectors to maximize the likelihood of generating individual words based on the learned latent multinomial distribution over words $\{\mathrm{P}(w|d_n)\}_{w\in V}$. Here, $\mathrm{P}(w|d_n)$ is obtained from topics' word distribution $\mathrm{P}(w|z)$ and document's topic distribution $\mathrm{P}(z|d_n)$, i.e., $\mathrm{P}(w|d_n) = \sum_{z=1}^{Z} \mathrm{P}(w|z)\mathrm{P}(z|d_n)$.

The stated aim of most visualization approaches is to recover a low-dimensional manifold embedded within the high-dimensional space of the original data [22, 31, 16, 12]. Key to manifold learning is the capacity for approximating the similarities and differences among data instances [2]. In this respect, multinomial modeling of dyadic data has a couple of downsides [30]. For one thing, it primarily models word presences, but does not directly model word absences. The likelihood of a document is defined over only words present in the document. For another thing, it is also sensitive to document lengths. If one document were to contain two copies of each word in another document, the two documents would have different likelihoods, even though the word distributions in the two documents are effectively identical.

Proposed Approach. Spherical representation could address the above-mentioned issues, leading towards better approximation of similarities among documents, and thus towards better manifold learning and visualization. In the spherical space, relationships between documents are measured as cosine similarity $\in [0, 1]$, which is the angular distance between two directional unit vectors. Firstly, two documents would have higher cosine similarity, not only if some words in common are present, but also if some other words in common are absent. Secondly, the normalization of all documents to unit vectors effectively neutralizes the impact of document lengths. Moreover, there is indicative evidence from the literature that a spherical approach will be promising in terms of dimensionality reduction. For instance, the spherical topic model SAM [30] performs significantly better than the multinomial topic model LDA [5], when used as a dimensionality reduction technique.

There are further advantages to spherical representation. For one thing, there is a greater degree of *flexibility* in admitting different L^2-normalized representations, e.g., term frequency *tf* or *tf-idf* or other feature vectors. For another thing, there is a greater degree of *expressiveness*, as an L^2-normalized vector can have both positive and negative elements, representing the degrees of word presences and absences respectively. Inspired by [30], this expressiveness engenders a change in the topic definition, from multinomial word distribution to a unit term vector. Given a topic, we no longer associate a word with a probability value, but rather with a real value that expresses the word's presence or absence (the sign) and relative importance (the weight).

Contributions. Our problem formulation is novel because to the best of our knowledge, we are the first to address semantic visualization for spherical representation (*first contribution*). We propose a generative model called SSE, which stands for *Spherical Semantic Embedding*. In Section 2.1, we develop the full generative process of SSE (*second contribution*). To learn its parameters, we describe an estimation based on variational inference in Section 2.2 (*third contribution*). In Section 3, we review related work in visualization and topic modeling. In Section 4, we validate SSE through experiments on publicly available real-life datasets, showing significant gains in visualization quality and topic interpretability (*fourth contribution*). We conclude in Section 5.

2. SPHERICAL SEMANTIC EMBEDDING

2.1 Generative Model

Document Representations. We associate each document with representations in three different spaces. Table 1 provides a list of notations for reference.

- We model the *visualization space* as a Cartesian plane, where relationships can be visualized spatially in terms of Euclidean distances. This space is low-dimensional, and without loss of generality, we assume it has two dimensions (2D). Each document d_n is associated with 2D coordinates x_n. This is consistent with visualization techniques oriented towards dimensionality reduction [16, 12].
- We model the *topic space* as a $(Z-1)$-simplex, where Z is the number of topics. This is consistent with the practice in most topic models [17, 5, 30]. Each document d_n occupies a point θ_n in the simplex, which codes for a multinomial distribution over the topics $\{\mathrm{P}(z|d_n)\}_{z=1}^{Z}$.
- We model the *word space* as a $(|V|-1)$-dimensional unit sphere in $\mathbb{R}^{|V|}$, where V is the vocabulary. Each document d_n is associated with a directional, unit-length vector ν_n. For instance, ν_n could be a *tf-idf* vector, or other L^2-normalized vector. This is consistent with the vector space model [32], and spherical models [1, 30].

Of the three representations of d_n, only ν_n is observed, while x_n and θ_n are latent. A key step towards integrating visualization and topic modeling is to define a mapping between the spaces to ensure a consistency among the representations. In defining the mapping, we associate each topic z with representations in both the visualization space ϕ_z and the word space τ_z. The coordinate ϕ_z reveals where a topics is in the visualization space, allowing users to observe the relationships between documents and topics. The word vector τ_z reveals the topic semantics in terms of the relative importance of various words within τ_z.

Visualization Space to Topic Space. As both documents and topics have coordinates in the visualization space,

Notation	Description
d_n	a specific document
x_n	coordinate of d_n in the visualization space
θ_n	topic distribution of d_n
$\theta_{n,z}$	probability of topic z in document d_n
ν_n	the observed L^2-normalized word vector of d_n
z	a specific topic
ϕ_z	coordinate of topic z in the visualization space
τ_z	L^2-normalized word vector of topic z
V	the vocabulary (the set of words in the lexicon)
N	total number of documents in the corpus
Z	total number of topics (user-defined)

Table 1: Notations

their relationship can be expressed in terms of distances $||x_n - \phi_z||$. Intuitively, the closer is x_n to a topic's ϕ_z, the higher is $\theta_{n,z}$ or the probability of topic z for document d_n. One framework to relate variables based on distances is Radial Basis Function or RBF [7], which defines a function $\lambda(||x_n - \phi_z||)$ in terms of how far a data point (e.g., x_n) is from a center (e.g., ϕ_z). The function λ may take on various forms, e.g., Gaussian, multi-quadric, polyharmonic spline

RBF network [3] is frequently used to build a function approximation. We use an RBF network as a "kernel" for the mapping between coordinates and topic distributions. To express θ_n as a function of x_n, we consider the normalized architecture of RBF network, with three layers. The input layer consists of one input node (x_n). The hidden layer consists of Z number of normalized RBF activation functions. Each is centered at ϕ_z and computes $\frac{\lambda(||x_n-\phi_z||)}{\sum_{z'=1}^{Z}\lambda(||x_n-\phi_{z'}||)}$. The linear output layer consists of Z output nodes. Each output node $y_z(x_n)$ corresponds to $\theta_{n,z}$, which is a linear combination of the RBF functions, as shown in Equation 1. Here, $w_{z,z'}$ is the weight of influence of the RBF function of z' on the $\theta_{n,z}$, with the constraint $\sum_{z'=1}^{Z} w_{z,z'} = 1$.

$$\theta_{n,z} = y_z(x_n) = \frac{\sum_{z'=1}^{Z} w_{z,z'} \cdot \lambda(||x_n - \phi_{z'}||)}{\sum_{z'=1}^{Z} \lambda(||x_n - \phi_{z'}||)} \quad (1)$$

While Equation 1 is the general form, to instantiate a specific mapping function, we need to determine both the assignment of $w_{z,z'}$ and the form of the function λ. In this work, we will experiment with a special case (λ is Gaussian and $w_{z,z'} = 1$ when $z = z'$ and 0 otherwise), which yields the function in Equation 2, where Φ refers to the collective set of ϕ_z's. This specific function has appeared previously in the baseline [19] that we will compare to, and this design decision helps to establish parity for comparative purposes. In future work, we will explore other function instantiations.

$$\theta_{n,z} = \mathrm{P}(z|x_n, \Phi) = \frac{\exp(\frac{1}{2}||x_n - \phi_z||^2)}{\sum_{z'=1}^{Z} \exp(\frac{1}{2}||x_n - \phi_{z'}||^2)} \quad (2)$$

Topic Space to Word Space. For d_n, we also need to bridge θ_n to its word space representation ν_n. As introduced previously, each topic z also has a word space representation τ_z. Because θ_n is essentially a topic distribution, we adopt a similar practice as in conventional topic model, which represents a document's word distribution as a weighted average (based on topic distribution) of the topics' word distributions. In our context, it means taking a weighted average

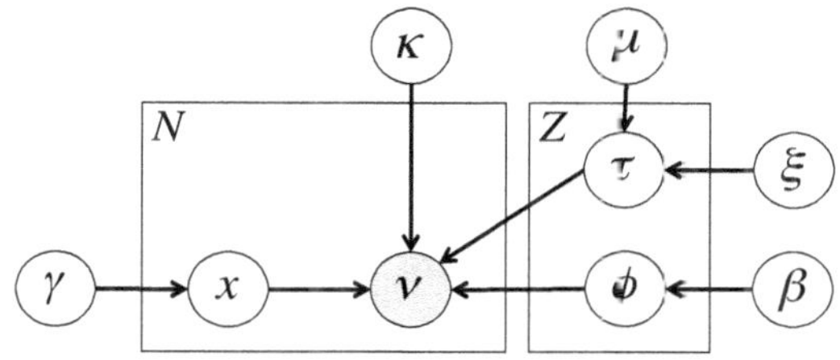

Figure 1: Graphical Model of SSE

of the topics' spherical unit vectors τ_z's, weighted by $\theta_{n,z}$, followed by L^2-normalization to return the mean vector to unit length, i.e., $\tau_n = \frac{\sum_{z=1}^{Z}\theta_{n,z}\cdot\tau_z}{||\sum_{z=1}^{Z}\theta_{n,z}\cdot\tau_z||}$.

To avoid overfitting, instead of equating ν_n to τ_n, we assume a probabilistic process where ν_n is drawn from a distribution centered at τ_n. Because ν_n and τ_n are both directional vectors, we turn to directional statistics [25]. In particular, von Mises-Fisher (vMF) distribution [24] was previously used to model documents [1, 30]. Equation 3 specifies the probability density function (p.d.f.) for a random unit vector ν, given mean directional vector μ, and concentration parameter κ. Note how the p.d.f. is parameterized by the cosine similarity $\mu^T\nu$ between the mean direction μ and ν, which is effectively the angular distance between the two unit vectors. The higher the κ, the more concentrated the distribution is around μ. The distribution is unimodal for $\kappa > 0$, and is uniform for $\kappa = 0$. C_D is the normalization constant, defined in Equation 4, where I_r denotes the modified Bessel function of the first kind and order r.

$$\mathrm{vMF}(\nu; \mu, \kappa) = C_D(\kappa)\exp(\kappa\mu^T\nu) \quad (3)$$

$$C_D(\kappa) = \frac{\kappa^{D/2-1}}{(2\pi)^{D/2} I_{D/2-1}(\kappa)} \quad (4)$$

We can then express ν_n as a draw from a vMF distribution with mean direction τ_n, i.e., $\nu_n \sim \mathrm{vMF}(\tau_n, \kappa)$.

Generative Process. We join the three representations into a generative model, with graphical representation as in Figure 1. The generative process of SSE is as follows:

1. Draw the corpus mean direction: $\mu \sim \mathrm{vMF}(m, \kappa_0)$
2. For each topic $z = 1, \ldots, Z$:
   - Draw z's coordinate: $\phi_z \sim \mathrm{Normal}(0, \beta^{-1}I)$
   - Draw z's spherical direction: $\tau_z \sim \mathrm{vMF}(\mu, \xi)$
3. For each document d_n, where $n = 1, \ldots, N$:
   - Draw d_n's coordinate: $x_n \sim \mathrm{Normal}(0, \gamma^{-1}I)$
   - Derive d_n's topic distribution: $\theta_{n,z} = \mathrm{P}(z|x_n, \Phi) = \frac{\exp(-\frac{1}{2}||x_n-\phi_z||^2)}{\sum_{z'=1}^{Z}\exp(-\frac{1}{2}||x_n-\phi_{z'}||^2)}$
   - Derive d_n's spherical average: $\tau_n = \frac{\sum_{z=1}^{Z}\theta_{n,z}\cdot\tau_z}{||\sum_{z=1}^{Z}\theta_{n,z}\cdot\tau_z||}$
   - Draw d_n's spherical direction: $\nu_n \sim \mathrm{vMF}(\tau_n, \kappa)$

In Step 1, we draw the corpus mean direction μ. In Step 2, we draw, for each topic, a visualization coordinate ϕ_z and a spherical direction τ_z. In Step 3, we draw, for each document, a visualization coordinate x_n, which we use to compute topic distribution θ_n as a function of document and topics' coordinates. θ_n together with different topics' τ_z's are used to compute the weighted average of topics' directions, denoted τ_n. After normalizing τ_n to a unit-length vector, we draw ν_n from a vMF with mean τ_n. Though the observed ν_n is usually positive (e.g., *tf-idf*), the latent τ_n may contain negative elements, which reflect unlikely words.

2.2 Parameter Estimation

To estimate the parameters in SSE, we employ variational EM with maximum a posteriori (MAP) estimation. The unknown parameters are the coordinates for documents (collectively $\chi = \{x_n\}$) and for topics (collectively $\Phi = \{\phi_z\}$), the directional vectors for topics (collectively $\mathcal{T} = \{\tau_z\}$) and the hyperparameters ξ, m. Given a corpus $\mathcal{D}$, which are represented as L^2-normalized term vectors $\mathcal{V} = \{\nu_n\}_{n=1}^N$, we infer the posterior distribution $\mathrm{P}(\mathcal{T}, \mu | \mathcal{V}, \chi, \Phi, \beta, \gamma, \xi, m, \kappa_0, \kappa)$ of the directional vectors for topics (collectively $\mathcal{T} = \{\tau_z\}$) and the corpus mean direction μ.

We approximate the posterior using the following variational distribution:

$$q(\mathcal{T}, \mu | \tilde{\mu}, \xi) = q(\mathcal{T} | \tilde{\mu}, \xi) q(\mu | \tilde{m}, \kappa_0)$$

where $q(\tau_z) = \mathrm{vMF}(\tau_z | \tilde{\mu}, \xi)$, $q(\mu_z) = \mathrm{vMF}(\mu_z | \tilde{m}_z, \kappa_0)$ and the variational parameters are $\tilde{\mu}, \tilde{m}$. Given this variational distribution q, we have a lower bound $\mathcal{L}(\tilde{\mu}, \tilde{m})$ on the log likelihood with priors over the document and topic visualization coordinate x_n, ϕ_z, as follows:

$$\begin{aligned}
\mathcal{L}(\tilde{\mu}, \tilde{m}) &= \mathbb{E}_q\big[\log p(\mathcal{V}, \mathcal{T}, \mu)\big] - \mathbb{E}_q\big[\log q(\mathcal{T}, \mu | \tilde{\mu}, \xi)\big] \\
&+ \sum_{n=1}^{N} \log p(x_n) + \sum_{z=1}^{Z} \log p(\phi_z) \\
&= \mathbb{E}_q\big[\log p(\mathcal{V} | \mathcal{T}, \chi, \Phi)\big] + \mathbb{E}_q\big[\log p(\mathcal{T} | \mu, \xi)\big] \\
&+ \mathbb{E}_q\big[\log p(\mu)\big] - \mathbb{E}_q\big[\log p(\mathcal{T} | \tilde{\mu}, \xi)\big] - \mathbb{E}_q\big[\log p(\mu | \tilde{m}, \kappa_0)\big] \\
&+ \sum_{n=1}^{N} \log p(x_n) + \sum_{z=1}^{Z} \log p(\phi_z)
\end{aligned}$$

In the E-step, we optimize the lower bound $\mathcal{L}(\tilde{\mu}, \tilde{m})$ with respect to the variational parameters $\tilde{\mu}, \tilde{m}$. In the M-step, the lower bound is optimized with respect to the parameters χ, Φ, ξ, m. We alternate E and M-steps until some appropriate convergence criterion is reached. We use gradient-based numerical optimization method such as the quasi-Newton method to update $\tilde{\mu}, \chi, \Phi, \xi$.

E-step. Let $\rho_n = \mathbb{E}\big[\tau_n\big]^T \nu_n$ where $n \in \{1...N\}$ ranges over the documents. Taking the gradients of $\mathcal{L}(\tilde{\mu}, \tilde{m})$ w.r.t $\tilde{\mu}$, we have:

$$\nabla_{\tilde{\mu}_z} \mathcal{L} = A_V(\xi) A_V(\kappa_0) \xi \tilde{m}_z + \kappa \sum_{n=1}^{N} \nabla_{\tilde{\mu}_z} \rho_z$$

where $A_p(c)$ denotes the mean resultant length of a vMF distribution of dimension p with concentration c. Since $\mathbb{E}\big[\tau_n\big]$ does not have a closed form, following [30] we approximate it as:

$$\mathbb{E}\big[\tau_n\big] \approx \mathbb{E}\big[\sum_{z=1}^{Z} \theta_{n,z} \cdot \tau_z\big] \mathbb{E}\big[||\sum_{z=1}^{Z} \theta_{n,z} \cdot \tau_z||^2\big]^{-1/2}$$

We refer to $\mathbb{E}\big[||\sum_{z=1}^{Z} \theta_{n,z} \cdot \tau_z||^2\big]$ as S_n. ρ_n will be approximated as:

$$\rho_n \approx A_V(\xi) S_n^{-1/2} (\tilde{\mu}\theta_n)^T \nu_n$$

where

$$S_n = (1 - A_V(\xi)^2) \sum_z \theta_{nz}^2 + A_V(\xi)^2 ||\tilde{\mu}\theta_n||^2$$

Taking the gradients of ρ_n w.r.t $\tilde{\mu}_j$, yields:

$$\nabla_{\tilde{\mu}_j} \rho_n = A_V(\xi) \big(\frac{\theta_{n,j} \nu_n}{\sqrt{S_n}} - \frac{(\tilde{\mu}\theta_n)^T \nu_n}{2 S_n^{3/2}} \cdot \nabla_{\tilde{\mu}_j} S_n \big)$$

where

$$\nabla_{\tilde{\mu}_j} S_n = 2 A_V(\xi)^2 \theta_{n,j} \tilde{\mu} \theta_n$$

The variational corpus mean $\tilde{m}$ has a closed form update rule:

$$\tilde{m} \propto \kappa_0 m + A_V(\xi) \xi \sum_{z=1}^{Z} \tilde{\mu}_z$$

M-step. In the M-step, taking gradients of $\mathcal{L}(\tilde{\mu}, \tilde{m})$ w.r.t ξ, we have:

$$\nabla_\xi \mathcal{L} = (\nabla_\xi A_V(\xi) \xi + A_V(\xi))(A_V(\kappa_0) \tilde{m}^T \sum_z \tilde{\mu}_z - Z) + \kappa \sum_{n=1}^{N} \nabla_\xi \rho_n$$

where

$$\nabla_\xi \rho_n = \big(\nabla_\xi A_V(\xi) S_n^{-1/2} - \frac{1}{2} A_V(\xi) S_n^{-3/2} \nabla_\xi S_n \big) (\tilde{\mu}\theta_n)^T \nu_n$$

and

$$\nabla_\xi S_n = 2 A_V(\xi) \nabla_\xi A_V(\xi) (||\tilde{\mu}\theta_n||^2 - \sum_z \theta_{nz}^2)$$

The corpus mean m has a closed form update rule as follows:

$$m \propto \sum_z \tilde{\mu}_z$$

Taking the gradients of $\mathcal{L}(\tilde{\mu}, \tilde{m})$ w.r.t x_n, we have:

$$\nabla_{x_n} \mathcal{L} = \kappa A_V(\xi) \big(-\frac{\nabla_{x_n} S_n}{2 S_n^{3/2}} \tilde{\mu} \theta_n + \frac{\tilde{\mu} \nabla_{x_n} \theta_n}{\sqrt{S_n}} \big)^T \nu_n - \gamma x_n$$

where

$$\nabla_{x_n} S_n = 2(1 - A_V(\xi)^2) \sum_z \nabla_{x_n} \theta_{nz} \theta_{nz} + 2 A_V(\xi)^2 \theta_n^T \tilde{\mu}^T \tilde{\mu} \nabla_{x_n} \theta_n$$

Taking the gradients of $\mathcal{L}(\tilde{\mu}, \tilde{m})$ w.r.t ϕ_z, we have:

$$\nabla_{\phi_z} \mathcal{L} = \kappa A_V(\xi) \big(-\frac{\nabla_{\phi_z} S_n}{2 S_n^{3/2}} \tilde{\mu} \theta_n + \frac{\tilde{\mu} \nabla_{\phi_z} \theta_n}{\sqrt{S_n}} \big)^T \nu_n - \beta \phi_z$$

where

$$\nabla_{\phi_z} S_n = 2(1 - A_V(\xi)^2) \sum_{z'} \nabla_{\phi_z} \theta_{nz'} \theta_{nz'} + 2 A_V(\xi)^2 \theta_n^T \tilde{\mu}^T \tilde{\mu} \nabla_{\phi_z} \theta_n$$

3. RELATED WORK

Visualization. The *dimensionality reduction* aspect of visualization is related to such techniques as PCA [20], ICA [11], and Fisher's Linear Discriminant [14], which are frequently used for feature selection. However, they are not designed specifically for visualization, and are concerned more with the relationship between the dimensions (orthogonality or independence), rather than the relationship between instances. Moreover, due to linear projection, PCA and variants do not capture intrinsic non-linearities well, such as

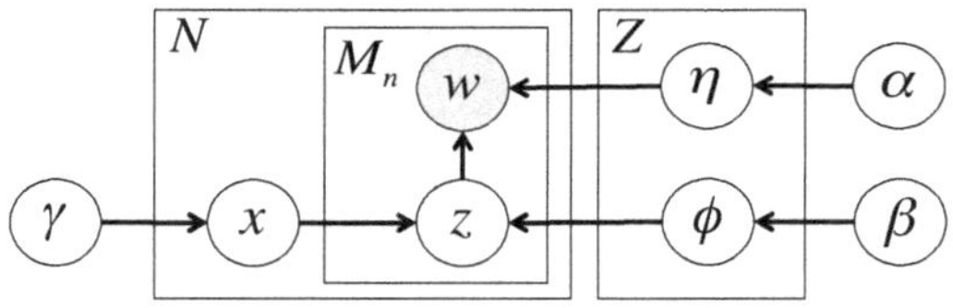

Figure 2: Graphical Model of PLSV

when the data is embedded as a low-dimensional non-linear manifold [2] (frequently-made assumption in visualization).

Therefore, visualization is often formulated as *manifold embedding*, where the objective is to preserve the relationship among data instances in the low-dimensional representation. In most cases, this relationship is expressed in terms of pairwise distance, such as in MDS [22], LLE [31], and Isomap [33]. Recent approaches employ probabilistic formulations, such as PE [18] and t-SNE [12], which we use as baselines. Yet, rather than distances, others seek to preserve the neighborhood information (e.g., SOM [21], GTM [4]).

The related work mentioned above has not incorporated the intermediate topic space. The problem of *semantic visualization* is introduced by PLSV [19]. We briefly review PLSV, whose graphical model is shown in Figure 2. The generative process of PLSV is as follows. For each topic z, we draw its word distribution η_z from a Dirichlet with parameter α, as well as its coordinate ϕ_z from Normal distribution with mean 0 and variance β^{-1}. In turn, for each document d_n, we draw its coordinate from Normal with mean 0 and variance γ^{-1}. To generate each of the M_n words in d_n, we draw a topic z based on Equation 2, and then draw a word from the selected topic's word distribution η_z. The key difference between SSE and PLSV is the representation of a document. Where SSE models the generation of an L^2-normalized vector, PLSV models the multinomial generation of words w. We compare to PLSV in Section 4.

We also describe a few other works in semantic visualization that are related, though not directly comparable. LDA-SOM [26] is a pipeline of LDA [5] followed by SOM [21], whose output is a topographic map not directly comparable to our scatterplot. Semafore [23] introduces manifold regularization to semantic visualization, which is orthogonal to the direction pursued in this paper (spherical representation), as manifold regularization could be applicable to both multinomial as well as spherical representations. CCG [29] is a topic model based on a latent grid space. It seeks to improve topic models, and is not designed specifically for document visualization. For one thing, the grid cells are discrete (unlike PLSV or SSE with continuous visualization space). For another, each document is associated with multiple grid cells, and it is not clear how to visualize such documents.

While semantic visualization deals with visualizing the relationship of documents based on topic modeling, another orthogonal direction is to visualize the topics themselves, such as the prevalence of topics in a corpus [34, 15], or the dominant keywords in topics [9, 10]. These works tend to be on the HCI aspects, such as user interfaces [13], rather than on dimensionality reduction or statistical modeling.

Topic Model. Probabilistic topic modeling is popularized by PLSA [17], and eventually by LDA [5], which provides a fully Bayesian generative model. These probabilistic models associate each document with a multinomial distribution over topics, and indirectly a multinomial distribution over words, effectively a simplex representation.

Recognizing the usefulness of L_2-normalized representations, SAM [30] introduces a topic model, which associates each document with a multinomial distribution of topics, and a directional unit vector in a spherical word space. With SAM, SSE shares a similar modeling of topics in the spherical space. The key difference is that SAM models only topics, whereas SSE also needs to model visualization in addition to topics. This requires a fundamental change in how a document's topic distribution is derived. Unlike SAM, in SSE the topic distribution θ_n is not drawn from a Dirichlet. Instead, to reflect the visualization objective, θ_n is expressed as a function of visualization coordinates (see Equation 1).

4. EXPERIMENTS

We conduct comprehensive experiments to evaluate the effectiveness of SSE, in terms of the quality of its outputs (primarily visualization, but also topic model).

4.1 Experimental Setup

Datasets. We rely on three publicly-available[1], real-life datasets [8]. $20News$ consists of newsgroup documents (in English) belonging to twenty classes. $Reuters8$ consists of newswire articles (in English) from eight classes. $Cade12$ consists of web pages (in Brazilian Portuguese) classified into twelve classes. These datasets are chosen because they represent benchmark datasets for document clustering and classification tasks. Each document in the dataset has a known class label. Because the semantic visualization task is unsupervised, these labels are not required for learning. However, they represent an objective ground truth, which we would use to evaluate visualization quality. In addition, they cover diverse document types, and different languages.

Following the practice in [19], we create balanced datasets by randomly sampling 50 documents from each class, resulting in, *for each sample*, 1000 documents for $20News$, 400 for $Reuters8$, and 600 for $Cade12$. These are of comparable sizes to those used in [19]. Moreover, because the algorithms are statistical, we draw five independent samples from each dataset, and run each sample five times. Hence, for each setting, the reported result is an average of 25 runs. Vocabulary sizes are similar among samples of the same dataset, with a maximum of 5455 for $20News$, 1972 for $Reuters8$, 7622 for $Cade12$. These are the dimensionalities of the word space.

L^2-normalized Representation. SSE admits different options for the L^2 representation of a document. The option that is most well-recognized in the information retrieval literature is *tf-idf*. We experimented with several alternatives, such as word count or term frequency (*tf*), and found *tf-idf* to give the best results. This echoes the finding in [30], which concluded that *tf-idf* was a better document representation than *tf*. Thus, we will use *tf-idf* in the experiments.

4.2 Comparative Methods

The comparative methods, and their attributes, are summarized in Table 2. **SSE** is our proposed method. A proper comparison is to another approach that jointly models visualization and topics, i.e., PLSV [19], which we use as the primary baseline. For completeness, we include other baselines

[1] `http://web.ist.utl.pt/acardoso/datasets/`

	Visualization	Topic model	Joint model	Spherical representation
SSE	✓	✓	✓	✓
PLSV	✓	✓	✓	
t-SNE	✓			✓
PE (SAM)	✓	✓		✓
PE (LDA)	✓	✓		

Table 2: Comparative Methods

in visualization (t-SNE, PE). While not direct competitors, they allow us to highlight certain aspects of our model.

PLSV [19] is a semantic visualization method based on multinomial modeling for dyadic data. Therefore, it is the proper baseline to SSE, allowing us to investigate the effects of SSE's modeling of *spherical representation*. For PLSV, we use the same settings as in the original paper [19] ($\beta = 0.1N$ and $\gamma = 0.1Z$, which we apply to SSE as well). We implement PLSV on our own (its authors have not made their implementation available), and verify that the results are similar to those reported in the original paper [19].

t-SNE [12] stands for t-distributed Stochastic Neighbor Embedding. It is one of the state-of-the-art approaches in visualizing high-dimensional data. Its input are feature vectors in the original dimensions, which in our context are the L^2-normalized *tf-idf* vectors. The idea behind t-SNE is to preserve the pairwise distances in the high dimensions in the visualization space. In addition to benchmarking against direct visualization, including t-SNE allows us to investigate the effects of *topic model* on visualization, by comparing SSE against an approach with the same input (*tf-idf* vectors) and output (visualization), but which does not have an intermediate topic space. We use the R implementation[2] of t-SNE with default settings and perplexity 40 as in [12].

PE [18] stands for Parameteric Embedding. It is also one of the state-of-the-art approaches in visualization, but is aimed at visualizing discrete probability distributions (e.g., class or topic distributions). PE cannot stand alone, as it needs to be coupled with a method that produces topic distributions. Including PE allows us to investigate the effects of modeling visualization and topic model *jointly*, as opposed to obtaining topic model separately before feeding it into PE. To produce the topic distributions, we experiment with two other topic models, as follows. **PE (LDA)** couples PE with LDA [5], which operates in the simplex word space. For LDA, we use the implementation[3] by its first author D. Blei. **PE (SAM)** couples PE with SAM [30], which operates in the spherical word space. For SAM, we use the implementation[4] by an author A. Waters with default settings ($\kappa_0 = 10, \kappa = 5000$, which we apply to SSE as well). [19] showed that PE with PLSA [17] is inferior to PLSV.

For visualization, we will be comparing SSE against PLSV, t-SNE, PE (SAM) and PE (LDA). We also investigate the topic models, comparing SSE against PLSV, and the two topic models used with PE, i.e., SAM and LDA. As input, for models with spherical representation (see Table 2), we use *tf-idf* vector (as explained in Section 4.1). For the multinomial models, we use their regular inputs (word counts).

[2]http://cran.r-project.org/web/packages/tsne/
[3]http://www.cs.princeton.edu/ blei/lda-c
[4]`https://github.com/austinwaters/py-sam`

4.3 Visualization Quality

Metric. The utility of a scatterplot visualization is in allowing the user to perceive similarities between documents through their distances in the visualization space. Our emphasis is on the strength of the dimensionality reduction, rather than on the user interface aspect. Evaluating dimensionality reduction through user studies is hard on the evaluator, may be overly subjective and not repeatable across evaluators. On the other hand, there exists established metrics to measure dimensionality reduction objectively.

One such approach is to rely on the available class labels as ground truth. Intuitively, documents of the same class are more likely to be similar than documents from different classes. A good visualization will "encode" this intuition, by placing documents of the same class nearby, and documents of different classes apart in the visualization space. Since dimensionality reduction means that the lower-dimensional representation still preserves the "properties" of the data, we can measure how well a visualization output reflects this intuition, by employing each document's visualization coordinates as a reduced "feature vector" in a classification task.

The choice of the classification method is not germane, because it is the feature vector that is being evaluated. In favor of simplicity, we employ kNN classification. For each document, we hide its class label, and predict a label by majority voting among its k-nearest neighbors as determined by Euclidean distance on the visualization space. The accuracy at k or $accuracy(k)$ is the fraction of documents whose predicted label based on kNN matches the true label. The higher the accuracy, the better is a visualization at encoding the class information. 1 is the highest possible accuracy, and 0 the lowest. The same metric was also used in [19].

For relative comparison, we set $k = 50$, i.e., measuring $accuracy(50)$, which is appropriate, as the datasets contain 50 documents from each class. Setting $k << 50$ may not sufficiently penalize a visualization that splits documents of the same class into multiple small clusters in different localities.

Vary Number of Topics Z. We now compare the performance of various methods. In Figure 3, we plot the $accuracy(50)$ as we vary the number of topics Z from 10 to 50. The three sub-plots (a), (b), and (c) correspond to the three datasets $20News$, $Reuters8$, and $Cade12$ respectively.

In terms of SSE's performance as the number of topics varies: (#1) As the number of topics Z increases, initially there is an improvement in accuracy, most notably between $Z = 10$ and $Z = 30$. Thereafter, accuracies either remain flat or drop slightly as Z increases further. The best performance by SSE is 0.66 on $20News$ (at $Z = 30$), 0.77 on $Reuters8$ (at $Z = 20$), and 0.41 on $Cade12$ (at $Z = 30$).

(#2) SSE achieves a drastic reduction in dimensionality from thousands (vocabulary size) to two (visualization), while preserving the relationship between data points. The above accuracies as measured in the reduced dimensionality (visualization) approach closely the accuracies of kNN when using the full dimensionality (i.e., *tf-idf* input vectors), which are 0.73 on $20News$, 0.85 on $Reuters8$, and 0.52 on $Cade12$. This shows that SSE's low-dimensional representation has high approximation ratios of 90% for $20News$ and $Reuters8$ and 78% for $Cade12$ in kNN accuracies, underlining the quality of dimensionality reduction achieved.

(#3) The varying accuracies across datasets indicate their relative difficulties, with $20News$ in between $Reuters8$ (the least difficult) and $Cade12$ (the most difficult).

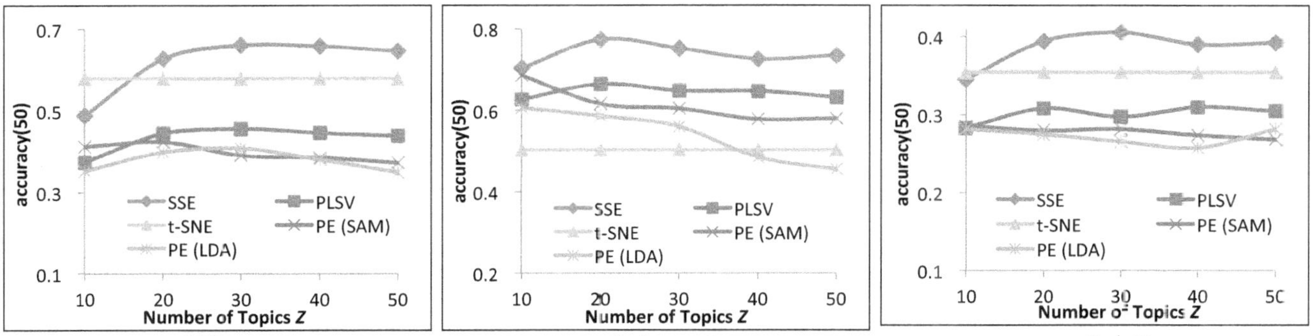

a. *20News* b. *Reuters8* c. *Cade12*

Figure 3: Visualization Quality: Vary Number of Topics Z

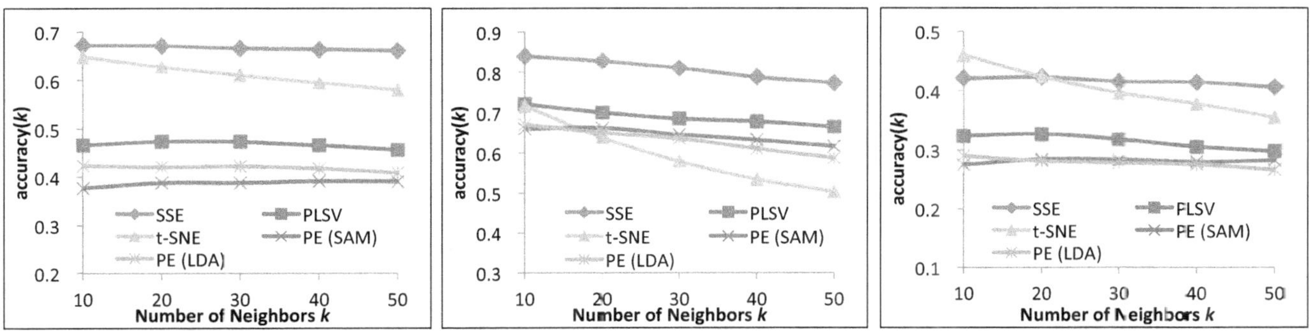

a. *20News* (Z = 30) b. *Reuters8* (Z = 20) c. *Cade12* (Z = 30)

Figure 4: Visualization Quality: Vary Number of Neighbors k

In terms of SSE's comparison to baselines: **(#1)** SSE has significantly higher accuracies than PLSV (the main baseline). In relative terms, SSE improves upon PLSV's accuracy by 30–48% on $20News$, by 12–16% on $Reuters8$, and by 22–36% on $Cade12$. This indicates that *spherical representation* of word space helps to improve the visualization.

(#2) SSE outperforms the visualization method t-SNE that also takes in *tf-idf* vectors as input. t-SNE's accuracy is not affected by the number of topics. A direct visualization technique, t-SNE is competitive, outperforming the other baselines for $20News$ and $Cade12$. However, it performs worst for $Reuters8$ (more on this later). SSE shows significantly higher accuracies than t-SNE in the majority of cases (except for very low number of topics $Z = 10$), with improvements up to 14% on $20News$, 54% on $Reuters8$, and 14% on $Cade12$. Since t-SNE shares the spherical representation of documents but does not model topics, the outperformance by SSE could be attributed in part to the approach of *modeling topics* with visualization.

(#3) SSE also outperforms PE (SAM) by a large margin. Since SSE and SAM share a spherical representation of topics in the word space, this outperformance by SSE can be attributed to *jointly* modeling topics and visualization. This is further suported by how PLSV (which also jointly models topics and visualization) outperforms PE (LDA), even as they share multinomial modeling of topic words.

Vary Number of Neighbors k. In Figure 4 we investigate the effects of different neighborhood size k's at specific settings of topics ($Z = 30$ for $20News$, $Z = 20$ for $Reuters8$, and $Z = 30$ for $Cade12$). These are Z settings where SSE performs best, but similar observations can be drawn for other Z settings. The focus here is on the number of neighbors, rather than on the relative comparison against the baselines again, so we apply the same Z for all methods.

(#1) As k increases from 10 to 50, the $accuracy(k)$ tends to decrease. This is expected because a small k is very conservative, where we are only concerned with the immediate neighbors, which tend to be very similar. As k increases, the neighborhood considered in the kNN is larger, with a higher chance of having neighbors of a different class.

(#2) The gradients of the decrease vary among methods. Most methods, such as SSE, are relatively stable. This stability across different k's is a good sign, indicating that documents of the same class are placed in the same general locality. The most affected is t-SNE, with the greatest difference in accuracies between $k = 10$ and $k = 50$. The sharp difference indicates that t-SNE may splinter documents of the same class into several clusters in different localities, such that neighbors at low k are still of the same class, but neighbors at higher k are of different classes. This is indeed the case, as seen in the qualitative comparison (Section 4.5).

In summary, the experiments show that SSE overall produces a significant gain in visualization quality over the baselines, as measured in terms of its accuracy in kNN classification with coordinates as features.

4.4 Topic Interpretability

We also investigate whether the gain in visualization comes at the expense of the topic model. We compare SSE with baselines PLSV, LDA, and SAM in terms of topic model.

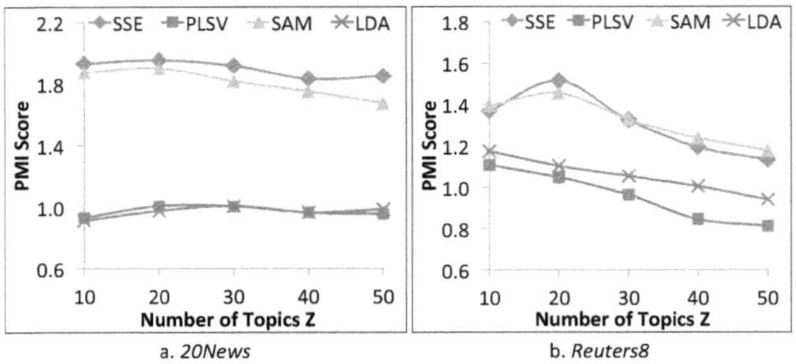

Figure 5: Topic Interpretability (PMI Score)

Metric. There are several evaluation methods for topic models proposed in the literature. One is perplexity [5], which measures the log-likelihood on unseen test data. Perplexity is *intrinsic*, i.e., dependent on the specific probability model, and may be inappropriate when comparing models with drastically different probability models, e.g., PLSV or LDA that uses multinomial models, versus SSE or SAM that uses vMF distributions. We thus need an *extrinsic* evaluation that compares these models using external validation.

In our setting, interpretability is important, because the topic model serves to provide semantics to the visualization of the data at hand. To human subjects, interpretability is closely related to coherence [28], i.e., how much the top keywords in each topic are "associated" with each other. After an extensive study of evaluation methods for coherence, [28] identifies Pointwise Mutual Information (PMI) as the best measure, in terms of having the greatest correlation with human judgments. We therefore adopt PMI as a metric.

PMI is based on term cooccurrences. For a pair of words w_i and w_j, PMI is defined as $\log \frac{p(w_i,w_j)}{p(w_i)p(w_j)}$. For a topic, we average the pairwise PMI's among the top 10 words of that topic. For a topic model, we average PMI across the topics. Intuitively, PMI is higher (better), if each topic features words that are highly correlated with one another.

Key to PMI is the use of an external corpus to estimate $p(w_i, w_j)$ and $p(w_i)$. Following [27], we use *Google Web 1T 5-gram Version 1* [6], a corpus of n-grams generated from 1 trillion word tokens. $p(w_i)$ is estimated from the frequencies of 1-grams. $p(w_i, w_j)$ is estimated from the frequencies of 5-grams, as recommended in [27]. We show the PMI for the English-based $20News$ in Figure 5(a) and $Reuters8$ in Figure 5(b). $Cade12$ is not included because we do not possess a large-scale n-gram corpus for Brazilian Portuguese.

Vary Number of Topics Z. From Figure 5, we draw the following observations on topic interpretability. **(#1)** SSE outperforms PLSV, and SAM outperforms LDA, in terms of PMI scores, across various topic settings, on $20News$ and $Reuters8$. It indicates that spherical models (SSE and SAM) produce topics that are more coherent and interpretable than multinomial models (PLSV and LDA). This is consistent with the conclusion reached in [30], which conducts an evaluation of coherence using human judges. This concurrence helps to show that our automatic evaluation on an external corpus is consistent with human judgments.

(#2) SSE performs similarly to SAM, with slightly higher PMI scores on $20News$, but comparable scores on $Reuters8$. This can be explained by their common modeling of topics in the spherical space. Since SSE also needs to deal with visualization constraints, it is notable that the gains in visualization quality have not hurt, and have even sometimes helped the topic model.

(#3) PLSV performs similarly to LDA on $20News$, but slightly worse on $Reuters8$, which is not surprising since they both share a similar multinomial modeling of topics but PLSV also faces constraints to fit the visualization task.

In summary, the experiments show that by incorporating spherical representation, SSE's significant gain in visualization does not come at the expense of the topic model.

4.5 Qualitative Comparison

To gain a sense of the visualization quality, we show example visualization outputs for $20News$ and $Reuters8$. $Cade12$ is not shown here due to space constraint.

20News. The visualizations for $20News$ are shown in Figure 6 for $Z = 30$ (best viewed in color). Each document has a coordinate in the scatterplot. To aid identification, documents are drawn with a colored marker based on their class (see legend). Topics are drawn as black, hollow circles.

SSE's visualization in Figure 6(a) shows better separation of different classes. For instance, there are distinct blue cluster and purple cluster on the right for *rec.sport.hockey* and *rec.sport.baseball* classes respectively, green and red clusters on the lower right for *rec.motorcycles* and *rec.autos*, etc. Interestingly, not only are documents of the same class placed nearby, but related classes are also neighboring one another, with recreational classes *rec.** on the lower right, computer classes *comp.** on the lower left, science clases *sci.** at the center and upper left, while classes related to politics and religion are on the upper right. Comparatively, PLSV in Figure 6(b) suffers from greater crowding at the mid-section, while t-SNE in Figure 6(c) from splintering of some classes into multiple clusters (e.g., pink square documents denoting *talk.politics.mideast*). PE (LDA) in Figure 6(d) and PE (SAM) in in Figure 6(e) are weaker. The relative ranking in visualization quality largely mirrors the earlier finding on quantitative accuracy, with SSE being the best, followed by t-SNE, PLSV, and then the two PE approaches.

To show that the SSE's visualization is backed by a good topic model, we show some topic words in Table 3. One property of spherical representation is that each topic may have both positive and negative words. We show the five most positive words, and the five most negative words. Only 10 topics out of 30 are shown due to space constraint. Looking at the positive words, we see that the topics cover some classes very well, such as hockey, motorcycle, car, windows, apple, christianity, religion, middle eastern politics, medicine, and space. Looking at the negative words, we see that the topics also define what classes they are not. Topic 0 is about hockey, and not baseball. Topic 1 is about motorcycles, and not cars. Topic 3 is about software, and not hardware.

Reuters8. The visualizations for $Reuters8$ are shown in Figure 7 for $Z = 20$. Generally, it is an easier dataset, and most methods perform better than for $20News$. Comparatively, SSE still produces the clearest separation between classes, and similar observations apply as before. In particular, the splintering issue with t-SNE is even clearer in Figure 7(c). For instance, the *money-fx* class is splintered into two navy-blue diamond clusters (lower left and upper right) separated by other classes. This helps to explain why t-SNE performs even worse (in relative terms) on $Reuters8$ than on other datasets.

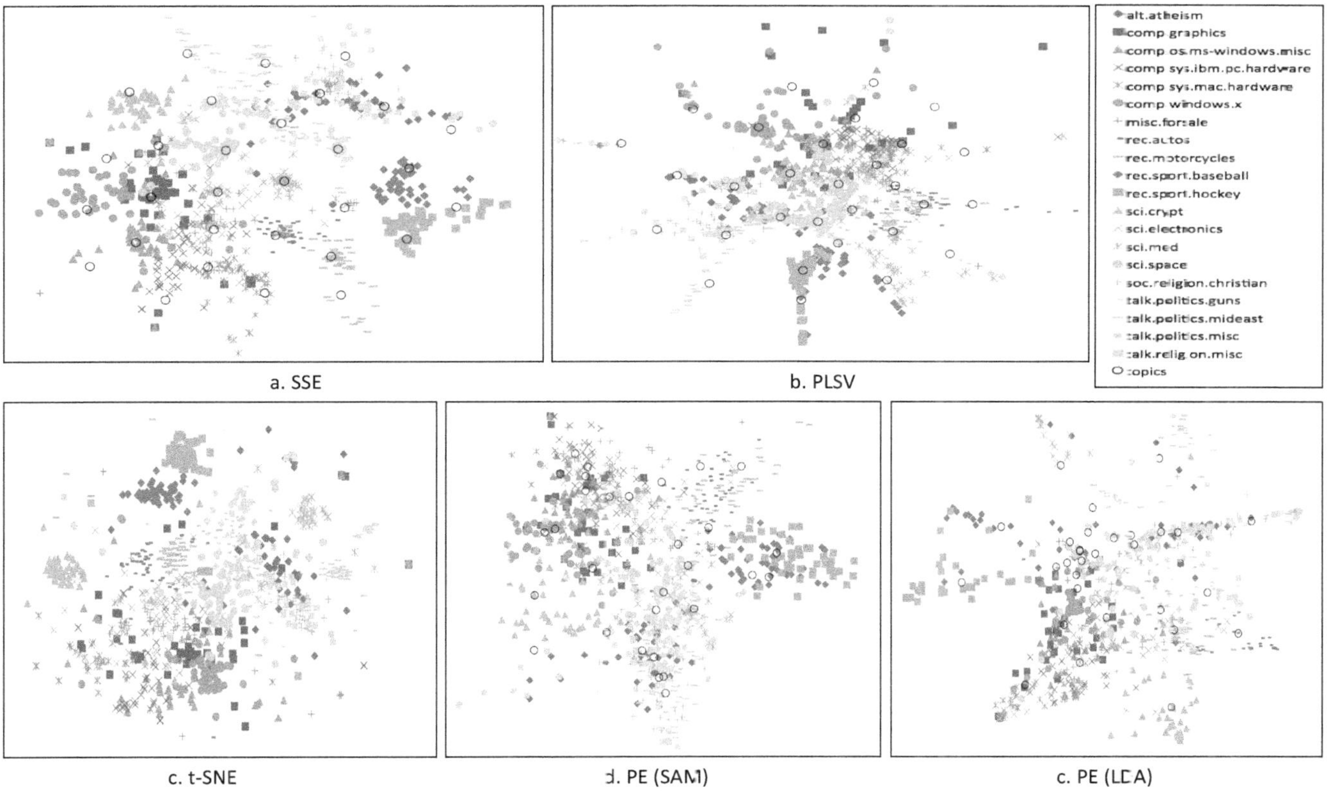

Figure 6: Visualization of 20*News* for $Z = 30$ topics (best viewed in color)

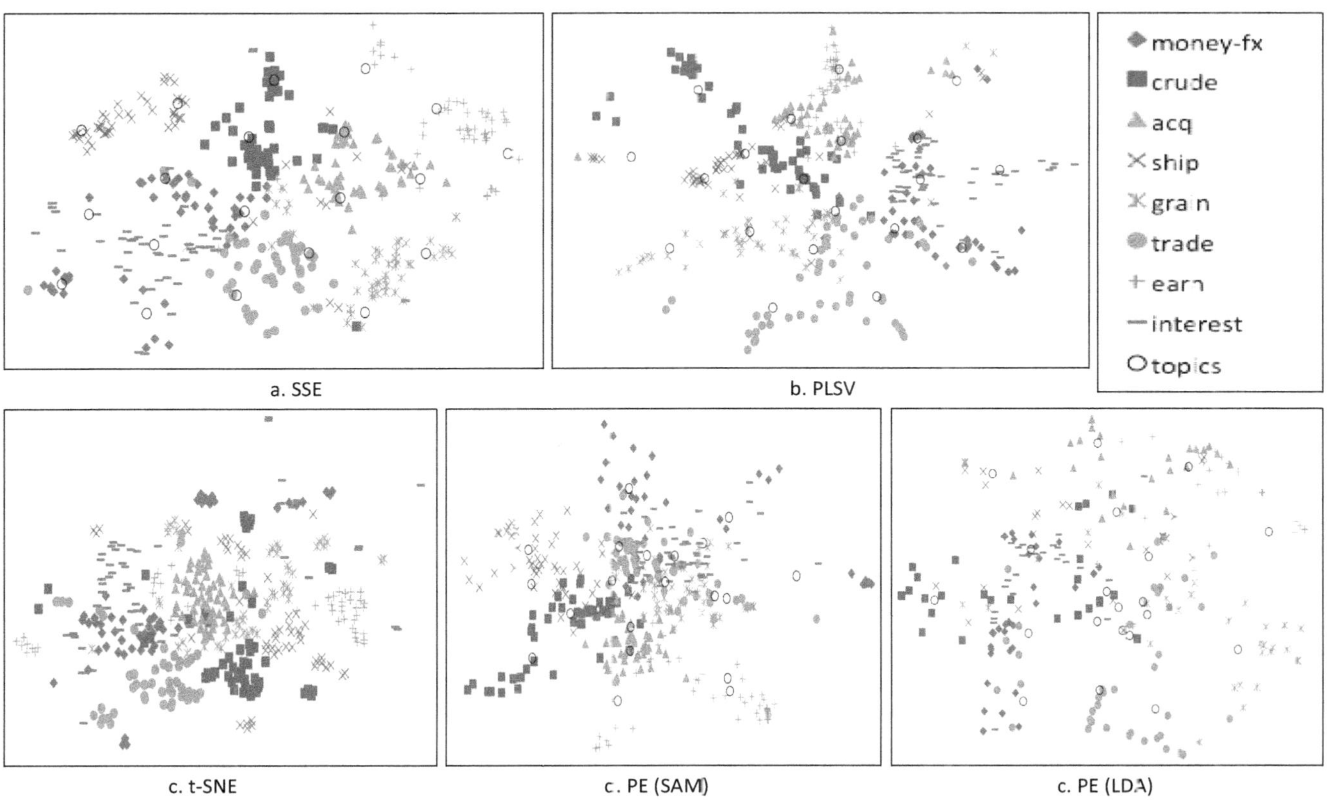

Figure 7: Visualization of *Reuters*8 for $Z = 20$ topics (best viewed in color)

Topic 0	Topic 1	Topic 2	Topic 3	Topic 4	Topic 5	Topic 6	Topic 7	Topic 8	Topic 9
					5 Most Positive Weights				
hockey	bike	car	window	apple	jesus	god	israel	doctor	space
team	dod	engine	software	sale	christ	religion	israeli	patient	launch
cup	motorcycle	mile	product	monitor	christian	truth	arab	treatment	moon
playoff	ride	ford	price	computer	god	belief	jew	medicine	flight
nhl	rider	mustang	user	price	sin	existence	jewish	symptom	nasa
					5 Most Negative Weights				
pitch	ford	circuit	video	scsi-2	scholar	reporter	encryption	objective	algorithm
pitcher	detector	amp	bus	scsi-1	addition	government	armenian	religion	file
inning	oort	board	slot	burst	wingate	livesey	algorithm	jew	driver
bullpen	sensor	lady	wiretap	scsi	sea	corruption	science	key	nice
giant	firearm	1983	ide	16-bit	livesey	theological	armenia	god	motorcycle

Table 3: Positive and Negative Words in Each Topic for 20*News* **by SSE for** $Z = 30$ **(a selection of 10)**

5. CONCLUSION

In this work, we address the problem of semantic visualization that jointly models visualization and topics. Our model, Spherical Semantic Embedding or SSE is designed for data with spherical representation, i.e., L^2−normalized term vectors. Its generative model associates each document with a triplet of representations, namely: a coordinate in the Euclidean visualization space, a multinomial topic distribution in the topic space, as well as a normalized term vector in the spherical word space. Comprehensive experiments on benchmark datasets show that SSE shows significantly improved performance when compared to existing state-of-the-art baselines in terms of visualization quality, as well as topic interpretability.

6. REFERENCES

[1] A. Banerjee, I. S. Dhillon, J. Ghosh, and S. Sra. Clustering on the unit hypersphere using von Mises-Fisher distributions. In *JMLR*, 2005.

[2] M. Belkin and P. Niyogi. Laplacian eigenmaps for dimensionality reduction and data representation. *Neural Computation*, 15(6), 2003.

[3] C. M. Bishop. *Neural Networks for Pattern Recognition.* Oxford University Press, 1995.

[4] C. M. Bishop, M. Svensén, and C. K. I. Williams. GTM: The generative topographic mapping. *Neural Computation*, 10(1), 1998.

[5] D. M. Blei, A. Y. Ng, and M. I. Jordan. Latent dirichlet allocation. *JMLR*, 3, 2003.

[6] T. Brants and A. Franz. Web 1T 5-gram Version 1. 2006.

[7] M. D. Buhmann. Radial basis functions. *Acta Numerica 2000*, 9, 2000.

[8] A. Cardoso-Cachopo. Improving Methods for Single-label Text Categorization. PdD Thesis, Instituto Superior Tecnico, Universidade Tecnica de Lisboa, 2007.

[9] A. J.-B. Chaney and D. M. Blei. Visualizing topic models. In *ICWSM*, 2012.

[10] J. Chuang, C. D. Manning, and J. Heer. Termite: visualization techniques for assessing textual topic models. In *AVI*, 2012.

[11] P. Comon. Independent component analysis, a new concept? *Signal Processing*, 36(3), 1994.

[12] L. V. der Maaten and G. Hinton. Visualizing data using t-SNE. *JMLR*, 9, 2008.

[13] W. Dou, X. Wang, R. Chang, and W. Ribarsky. ParallelTopics: A probabilistic approach to exploring document collections. In *VAST*, 2011.

[14] R. A. Fisher. The use of multiple measurements in taxonomic problems. *Annals of Eugenics*, 7(2), 1936.

[15] B. Gretarsson, J. O'donovan, S. Bostandjiev, T. Höllerer, A. Asuncion, D. Newman, and P. Smyth. TopicNets: Visual analysis of large text corpora with topic modeling. *TIST*, 3(2), 2012.

[16] G. E. Hinton and S. T. Roweis. Stochastic neighbor embedding. In *NIPS*, 2002.

[17] T. Hofmann. Probabilistic latent semantic indexing. In *SIGIR*, 1999.

[18] T. Iwata, K. Saito, N. Ueda, S. Stromsten, T. L. Griffiths, and J. B. Tenenbaum. Parametric embedding for class visualization. *Neural Computation*, 19(9), 2007.

[19] T. Iwata, T. Yamada, and N. Ueda. Probabilistic latent semantic visualization: topic model for visualizing documents. In *KDD*, 2008.

[20] I. Jolliffe. *Principal Component Analysis.* Wiley Online Library, 2005.

[21] T. Kohonen. The self-organizing map. *Proceedings of the IEEE*, 78(9), 1990.

[22] J. B. Kruskal. Multidimensional scaling by optimizing goodness of fit to a nonmetric hypothesis. *Psychometrika*, 29(1), 1964.

[23] T. M. V. Le and H. W. Lauw. Manifold learning for jointly modeling topic and visualization. In *AAAI*, 2014.

[24] K. V. Mardia. Distribution theory for the von Mises-Fisher distribution and its application. In *A Modern Course on Statistical Distributions in Scientific Work.* Springer, 1975.

[25] K. V. Mardia and P. E. Jupp. *Directional Statistics*, volume 494. Wiley.com, 2009.

[26] J. R. Millar, G. L. Peterson, and M. J. Mendenhall. Document clustering and visualization with latent dirichlet allocation and self-organizing maps. In *FLAIRS*, 2009.

[27] D. Newman, S. Karimi, and L. Cavedon. External evaluation of topic models. In *ADCS*, 2009.

[28] D. Newman, J. H. Lau, K. Grieser, and T. Baldwin. Automatic evaluation of topic coherence. In *NAACL HLT*, 2010.

[29] A. Perina, N. Jojic, M. Bicego, and A. Truski. Documents as multiple overlapping windows into grids of counts. In *NIPS*, 2013.

[30] J. Reisinger, A. Waters, B. Silverthorn, and R. J. Mooney. Spherical topic models. In *ICML*, 2010.

[31] S. T. Roweis and L. K. Saul. Nonlinear dimensionality reduction by locally linear embedding. *Science*, 290, 2000.

[32] G. Salton, A. Wong, and C.-S. Yang. A vector space model for automatic indexing. *CACM*, 18(11), 1975.

[33] J. B. Tenenbaum, V. D. Silva, and J. C. Langford. A global geometric framework for nonlinear dimensionality reduction. *Science*, 290, 2000.

[34] F. Wei, S. Liu, Y. Song, S. Pan, M. X. Zhou, W. Qian, L. Shi, L. Tan, and Q. Zhang. Tiara: a visual exploratory text analytic system. In *KDD*, 2010.

Grouping Students in Educational Settings*

Rakesh Agrawal
Microsoft Research
rakesha@microsoft.com

Behzad Golshan
Boston University
behzad@cs.bu.edu

Evimaria Terzi
Boston University
evimaria@cs.bu.edu

ABSTRACT

Given a class of large number of students, each exhibiting a different ability level, how can we group them into sections so that the overall gain for students is maximized? This question has been a topic of central concern and debate amongst social scientists and policy makers for a long time. We propose a framework for rigorously studying this question, taking a computational perspective. We present a formal definition of the grouping problem and investigate some of its variants. Such variants are determined by the desired number of groups as well as the definition of the gain for each student in the group.

We focus on two natural instantiations of the gain function and we show that for both of them the problem of identifying a single group of students that maximizes the gain among its members can be solved in polynomial time. The corresponding partitioning problem, where the goal is to partition the students into non-overlapping groups appear to be much harder. However, the algorithms for the single-group version can be leveraged for solving the more complex partitioning problem. Our experiments with generated data coming from different distributions demonstrate that our algorithm is significantly better than the current strategies in vogue for dividing students in a class into sections.

Categories and Subject Descriptors

H.2.8 [**Database Management**]: Database Applications-Data Mining

Keywords

Clustering; Partitioning; Teams; Groups; Large Classes; Massive Courses; MOOC

*Preliminary ideas related to this work were presented in a poster titled "Forming Beneficial Teams of Students in Massive Online Classes" at the ACM Conference on Learning at Scale (L@S), Atlanta, Georgia, March 2014.

KDD'14, August 24–27, 2014, New York, NY, USA.

http://dx.doi.org/10.1145/2623330.2623748 .

1. INTRODUCTION

That good education is critical for enhancing societal growth and individual prosperity is a widely accepted tenet [18, 33]. While the problem of providing high quality education is multi-faceted and complex [8, 14], one particular problem that has vexed social scientists and policy makers for a long time is how to create groupings of students so that they can augment their learning from the teacher with cooperative learning from each other [3, 30, 32]. Two popular strategies are to group students either homogeneously (stratified by ability level, so low-ability students are in one section, high-ability students in another) or heterogeneously (students of all ability levels in one section) [11, 27]. The verdict from the empirical studies on which of these is more effective is inconclusive [15, 20, 29]. The public sentiment toward these strategies has also swayed back and forth over the years [7, 24].

We endeavour to rigorously study the problem of grouping students in a class, by taking a computational perspective. We consider a setting in which groupings are decided on per subject basis for students within a class. Each student i is associated with *ability* $\theta_i \in [0, 1]$ in the corresponding subject. The ability θ_i can be estimated by administering a test designed using modern practices such as those based on item response theory [9, 16]. Students are able to increase their abilities through interactions and collaborations with more capable peers [19, 31]. The higher ability members also gain as teaching others and giving help has been shown to be positively correlated to increase in ability [5, 32]. We thus strive to form groups such that the overall gain for students is maximized.

We present a formal definition of the grouping problem and describe several of its variants. More specifically, we consider two high-level problems: the 1-GROUP and the ℓ-GROUPS problem. In the former, the goal is to identify a single group from a large set of students such that the gains of the students constituting the group is maximized. In the latter, the goal is to partition a large set of students into smaller groups of approximately the same size such that the sum of the gains of all groups is maximized. Clearly, different definitions of "gain" lead to different instantiations of the 1-GROUP and the ℓ-GROUPS problems.

We consider two types of gain functions – each formalizing different viewpoint. The first maximizes the number of students who improve their abilities by interacting with the higher ability students, while the second incorporates the extent of these improvements. Thus, the former maximizes the number of students that benefit, while the latter is geared towards pulling up the weakest students as much as possible. Depending upon the social goal the school is pursuing, it can accordingly choose the gain function.

For both these functions, we show that the 1-GROUP problem can be solved optimally in polynomial time. For lack of optimum algorithms for the ℓ-GROUPS version, we provide effective heuristics. Our experimental evaluation with generated data demonstrates that our design yields groupings that beat the current strategies. The experiments with different distributions of abilities of students demonstrate that this superior performance is independent of the underlying distribution of the abilities of the students.

Roadmap: The rest of the paper is organized as follows. After reviewing the related work in Section 2, we formally define our framework in Section 3. In Sections 4 and 5, we describe the two problem variants we study and their corresponding algorithms. In Section 6, we describe our experiments. Finally, we conclude with a summary and directions for future work in Section 7.

2. RELATED WORK

Although their importance in the educational process has been identified by educators and social scientists alike, to the best of our knowledge we are the first to introduce the formulations for computationally addressing the problem of grouping students. Naturally, the nature of our problem is related to a large body of work both in the domain of education as well as computer science. We review some of this work below.

Cooperative learning: The origins of the cooperative learning theory can be traced back to at least as early as the 1937 work of May and Doob who found that people who worked together were more successful in attaining the same goals than those who worked independently [26]. Modern cooperative learning theory is heavily influenced by the Vygotsky's idea of co-construction, central to which is the notion of the zone of proximal development (ZPD) – "... the distance between the actual developmental level as determined by independent problem solving and the level of potential development as determined through problem solving under adult guidance or in collaboration with more capable peers" [31]. In our formulation, ZPD for a student can be thought of as the distance between the student's ability and that of the group. One of our objective is striving to maximize the number of students who are able to increase their ability to the group level, while the other maximizes the total increase in the ability of the group members.

Forming teams of experts: Recently, there has been a lot of work on the formation of teams of experts whose goal is to complete a given project task [1, 2, 12, 21, 22, 25]. In these settings, experts are viewed as multi-dimensional vectors describing the expertise of individuals across different aspects. Then the goal is to select a team that best fits the task at hand. In contrast, our students are described by 1-dimensional values – namely their ability in the subject. Moreover, our goal is not to find a single team that can complete a specific task, but to partition the given set of students into teams from which their performance can benefit. These differences in the respective settings lead to different computational problems as well, and therefore the algorithms used for existing team-formation formulations cannot be used for our setting.

Clustering: At a high level, the ℓ-GROUPS version of our problem can be also viewed as a classical clustering problem [17]; afterall, in both cases the goal is to partition an input set of objects. Although in many of these clustering problems each cluster is represented by the *average* of the points in the cluster (exactly as in our setting) their goal is to find a partitioning that minimizes the sum of the distances of each points to its corresponding average. On the other hand, in our ℓ-GROUPS problem the goal is to maximize the number of students that are *below* the corresponding average. This difference in the objective functions makes our problem distinct from existing work on clustering. Specifically, many of the existing clustering problems are solvable in polynomial time for dimensionality 1, while some version of our ℓ-GROUPS problems appear to be NP-hard even though our input consists of 1-dimensional points.

3. FRAMEWORK

Assume there is a population of n students $S = \{1, \ldots, n\}$, studying a particular subject. Each student i is associated with *ability* $\theta_i \in [0, 1]$ (determined using techniques such as item response theory [9, 16]). For simplicity, we will assume that the students have distinct abilities and they are ordered in decreasing order of their abilities, i.e., $\theta_1 > \theta_2 > \ldots > \theta_n$.

We will be interested in forming groups of students $T \subseteq S$, such that students on average benefit by their participation in T. In order to quantify the benefit that a group provides to its members, we need to define the *collective ability* $\widehat{\Theta}_T$ of a group T. Following [28], we assume that the collective ability of a group $T \subseteq S$ is the average ability level of its members. That is, $\widehat{\Theta}_T = 1/|T| \sum_{i \in T} \theta_i$.

We consider the collective ability $\widehat{\Theta}_T$ of a group as being an important characteristic of the group. More specifically, the collective ability $\widehat{\Theta}_T$ of a group T partitions the members of T into two sets: the *leaders* and the *followers*. The set of leaders L_T of group T are all the members of T with ability above $\widehat{\Theta}_T$. That is,

$$L_T = \{i \in T \mid \theta_i \geq \widehat{\Theta}_T\}.$$

Similarly, the set of followers F_T of group T are all the members of T with ability below $\widehat{\Theta}_T$. That is,

$$F_T = \{i \in T \mid \theta_i < \widehat{\Theta}_T\}.$$

When the group T is clear from the context, we drop the subscript T when referring to the set of leaders and followers of T.

The participation in a group amplifies both the leaders and the followers. If we use function $A_f(i, T)$ (resp. $A_\ell(i, T)$) to denote the gain of a follower (resp. leader) i by participating in group T, then we define the gain of a group T as the sum of the gains of its members. That is,

$$\mathcal{A}(T) = \sum_{i \in F_T} A_f(i, T) + \sum_{i \in L_T} A_\ell(i, T). \tag{1}$$

The gain of the followers may be a result of the fact that they are able to increase their abilities through interactions and collaborations with more capable peers [19, 31]. The leaders also gain as teaching others and giving help has been shown to be positively correlated to increase in ability [5, 32].

In this work, we will only focus on the gain of the followers and leave incorporating the gain of leaders for future work.

That is, the gain of a group T

$$A(T) = \sum_{i \in F_T} A_f(i,T). \quad (2)$$

We consider two instances of the $A(T)$ function, namely the *count-based* gain AC and the *value-based* gain AV.

The count-based gain function: Given a group T with leaders L_T and followers F_T, we define the count-based gain $\text{AC}(T)$ as:

$$\text{AC}(T) = \sum_{i \in F_T} \text{AC}_f(i,T), \quad (3)$$

where $\text{AC}_f(i,T) = 1$ for every $i \in F_T$. In other words, the count-based gain of group T is simply the number of followers in the class. These are the students who are able to increase their ability through collaboration with more capable peers [19, 31].

The value-based gain function: A limitation of the count-based gain function is that it considers all followers gaining the same by their participation in T. The value-based gain function takes into consideration the actual values of the followers' abilities as well as the collective ability of the group. More specifically, given a group T with leaders L_T and followers F_T, the value-based gain $\text{AV}(T)$ is defined as:

$$\text{AV}(T) = \sum_{i \in F_T} \text{AV}_f(i,T), \quad (4)$$

where $\text{AV}_f(i,T) = (\widehat{\Theta}_T - \theta_i)$ for every $i \in F_T$. In other words, students with abilities that are further from $\widehat{\Theta}_T$ gain more by their participation in T.

The problems: In this paper we are interested in two problems: the 1-GROUP and the ℓ-GROUPS problems. The former takes as input the set of students and their abilities and aims to identify a single group T that maximizes the value of $A(T)$. The latter focuses on partitioning the input set of students into groups such that the total gain across groups is maximized. The formal definitions of these two problems are given below. We give these definitions in terms of the generic gain functions, but we also discuss their instantiations for the count and value-based functions.

PROBLEM 1 (1-GROUP). *Given a set of n students $S = \{1,\dots,n\}$, identify a group $T \subseteq S$ of at most k students such that $A(T)$ is maximized.*

When we use the count-based (resp. value-based) gain function for computing the gain of the group T, then we refer to the 1-GROUP problem as the COUNT1G (resp. VALUE1G) problem. When the form of the gain function is not important we use the generic 1-GROUP term.

PROBLEM 2 (ℓ-GROUPS). *Given an integer k and a set of n students $S = \{1,\dots,n\}$ (with $n = k\ell$) find a partition of S into groups $T_1, \dots T_\ell$, where each group is of size k and $\sum_{i=1}^{\ell} A(T_i)$ is maximized.*

As before, when we use the count-based (resp. value-based) gain function for computing the gain of the group T, then we refer to the ℓ-GROUPS problem as the COUNTℓG (resp. VALUEℓG) problem. When the form of the gain function is not important we use the generic ℓ-GROUPS term.

4. COUNT-BASED GROUP FORMATION

In this section we study the computational complexity of the COUNT1G and the COUNTℓG problems and we give algorithms for solving them.

4.1 The COUNT1G problem

Clearly, the desired group will consist of a set of *leaders* L of highest ability who will pull up the group's overall ability and a set of *followers* F whose abilities will be below the group's ability yet their abilities will not be as low so as to decrease the overall ability of the group.

EXAMPLE 1. *Consider a set of five students with the following ability scores: $\theta_1 = 0.9$, $\theta_2 = 0.8$, $\theta_3 = 0.6$, $\theta_4 = 0.5$, and $\theta_5 = 0$. Imagine that we need to create a group of three students with maximum possible gain. If students 1 and 2 are picked together (with any other student as the third member), only the third member of this group will be a follower. On the other hand, if we pick students 1, 4 and 5 then the collective group ability would be $\frac{0.9+0.5+0}{3} = 0.466$, which makes only student 5 a follower. Alternatively, grouping student 2, 3 and 4 leads to a collective group ability of $\frac{0.8+0.6+0.5}{3} = 0.633$, which makes students 3 and 4 to be the followers. This example shows that grouping the strongest and weakest students together does not necessarily leads to the maximum possible gain.*

Our algorithm for the COUNT1G problem, which we call the **L&F** algorithm, finds an optimal group composition by efficiently identifying the best sets L and F of leaders and followers that will compose the group $T = L \cup F$. The pseudocode of the **L&F** algorithm is shown in Algorithm 1.

Algorithm 1 L&F

Input: Set of students $S = \{1,\dots,n\}$ with sorted abilities $\theta_1 > \theta_2 > \dots > \theta_n$, Group size k.
Output: Group T with the maximum $\text{AC}(T)$.

```
T = ∅
for i = 1...k do
    L = top-i ability students
    for j = i+1...n − (k − i) + 1 do
        F = students with abilities θ_j, θ_{j+1}, ..., θ_{j+k−i−1}
        if F and L satisfy feasibility constraint then return T = L ∪ F
```

In order to see the intuition behind **L&F** and also understand why it is optimal, we start with the following lemma:

LEMMA 1 (FEASIBILITY CONSTRAINT). $\sum_{i \in F} \theta_i > (k \times \max_{i \in F} \theta_i) - \sum_{i \in L} \theta_i$.

PROOF. Observe that $\widehat{\Theta}_T$ should be larger than the highest ability score of a student in the set F. Thus, if θ_F represents the highest ability in set F, the following condition should be satisfied:

$$\widehat{\Theta}_T = \frac{\sum_{i \in L} \theta_i + \sum_{i \in F} \theta_i}{k} > \theta_F.$$

A simple rewrite of the above inequality yields the lemma. □

We do not know a priori the number of leaders in set L. However, since the gain for a group T is defined to be $\text{AC}(T) = k - |L(T)|$, the optimal solution will have the minimal number of leaders. Our algorithm therefore tries increasing number of leaders, starting with the student of highest ability. The reason for preferring higher ability leaders is that the sum of their abilities appears as a negative term in the right hand side of the inequality in the feasibility constraint. Note that for any fixed set L, all possible sets of followers that satisfy the feasibility constraint lead to the same value of AC. A computationally efficient way to pick the followers is to look for them in $k - |L|$ consecutive positions starting with the first student who is not in L. And that is what our algorithm does.

EXAMPLE 2. *To clarify the details of Algorithm 1, we revisit the students of Example 1. The algorithm starts by placing a single student (i.e., student 1) in the set of leaders. Then, the inner loop (lines 4-5) searches for the consecutive group of students that satisfy the feasibility constraint. First, students 2 and 3 are considered for the followers set, but they do not pass the feasibility test. Next, the algorithm tries students 3 and 4, who pass the test. Thus, the algorithm returns the group consisting of students {1, 3, 4}, having* AC = 2.

Complexity: With a preprocessing step of complexity $O(n)$ for computing the cumulative sums of all the ability levels of all the students sorted in decreasing ability level, `L&F` algorithm has complexity $O(nk)$. If we take a closer look at Algorithm 1, we can observe that the outer loop (line 2) searches for the smallest possible number of students that should be placed in set L to lift students in set F. This linear search, however, can easily be replaced by a binary search. Based on this observation, a more efficient implementation of `L&F` runs in time $O(n \log k)$.

Remark 1: Problem 1 is defined so that the formed group T is of specific size k. A natural question is whether we can form a group T of *any* size. We can observe that the `L&F` algorithm can be used for this problem as well. For example, one can simply run the `L&F` algorithm for all values of $k \in \{1, \ldots, n\}$ and output the group with the best AC score among all those reported for the different values of k.

Remark 2: As stated in Algorithm 1, `L&F` selects the follower set in such a way that the relatively high ability followers are grouped with the highest ability leaders. We will sometime refer to this version of `L&F` as `max-L&F` to emphasize that amongst all the feasible follower sets, the group formed by this algorithm has the highest-ability follower. One can easily modify Algorithm 1 to select the follower set to contain the lowest highest-ability follower or for that matter select a random set amongst all the feasible follower sets. We will refer to these versions as `min-L&F` and `any-L&F` respectively.

4.2 The COUNTℓG problem

In this section, we first show that the COUNTℓG problem is NP-complete and then discuss heuristics for solving it.

LEMMA 2. *When $k = n/2$ then the* COUNTℓG *is NP-complete.*

PROOF. We prove that COUNTℓG is NP-complete by reducing the SUBSET SUM problem [13] to this problem. The SUBSET SUM problem asks whether a given set of positive integers $W = \{w_1, w_2, \cdots, w_N\}$ can be partitioned into two groups W_1, W_2 such that the sum of numbers in W_1 equals the sum of numbers in W_2. In other words, if we use $z = \sum_{i=1}^{N} w_i$ to denote the sum of all numbers in W, we want the sum of the elements in W_1 to be equal to the sum of the elements in W_2 and thus equal to $\frac{z}{2}$.

Now, given an instance of the SUBSET SUM problem we create an instance of the COUNTℓG problem with $n = 2N+6$ students which we want to partition into 2 groups each of size $k = (N+3)$. We create the instance of the COUNTℓG problem as follows: for each number w_i in W, we create a student with ability $\theta_i = -w_i$. Beside these low ability students, we create $n+4$ students with abilities equal to 0, and two strong students with abilities $\frac{z}{2} + \epsilon$ where ϵ is a small value. We claim that (under this construction) the answer to the decision problem of SUBSET SUM is "yes" *iff* the optimal solution to the COUNTℓG would have a total AC of $(2N+4)$.

First, assume that there is a perfect partitioning of W into W_1 and W_2. Now, we can create two groups T_1 and T_2 in the COUNTℓG problem as follows. First, we place a strong student with ability $\frac{z}{2}+\epsilon$ in both T_1 and T_2. Then, we place the low ability students that correspond to the numbers in set W_1 (resp. W_2) in T_1 (resp. T_2). Finally, we distribute the normal students (i.e., those with ability equal to zero) over T_1 and T_2 to make both groups of the same size. Note that the size of each group must be $N+3$ and

$$\widehat{\Theta}_{T_1} = \widehat{\Theta}_{T_2} = \frac{-\frac{z}{2} + \frac{z}{2} + \epsilon}{N+3} = \frac{\epsilon}{N+3} > 0.$$

Since the collective ability levels of both groups are positive, all students except the two strongest students are below the mean. Thus $\text{AC}(T_1) + \text{AC}(T_2) = N+2+N+2 = 2N+4$.

Now, assume that there is an optimal grouping of students into groups T_1 and T_2 each of size $(N+3)$ and total AC equal to $(2N+4)$ for COUNTℓG problem. Let z_1 and z_2 denote the sum of the negative abilities in T_1 and T_2 respectively. We would like to show that $z_1 = z_2$ which further implies a perfect partitioning of the set W. First, observe that due to the pigeon-hole principle, both groups should have at least one student with ability equal to zero. Moreover, one can observe that the two strong students (ability $= \frac{z}{2}+\epsilon$) should be in different groups. This is simply because these are the highest abilities and they can never be below the mean of any group. Thus, if they are placed together there would be at least 3 student above the group average (i.e., the two strong students and the strongest student of the other group).

Given that each group has exactly one student with ability $\frac{z}{2}+\epsilon$ and at least one student with ability equal to 0, the collective ability of both groups must be positive in order to guarantee an overall AC equal to $2N+4$. Formally,

$$\begin{cases} \widehat{\Theta}_{T_1} > 0 \\ \widehat{\Theta}_{T_2} > 0 \\ z_1 + z_2 = z \end{cases} \Rightarrow \begin{cases} \frac{\frac{z}{2}+\epsilon-z_1}{N+3} > 0 \\ \frac{\frac{z}{2}+\epsilon-z_2}{N+3} > 0 \\ z_1 + z_2 = z \end{cases}$$

This implies that

$$\begin{cases} \frac{z_2}{2} - \frac{z_1}{2} + \epsilon > 0 \\ \frac{z_1}{2} - \frac{z_2}{2} + \epsilon > 0 \end{cases} \Rightarrow |z_1 - z_2| < 2\epsilon.$$

Now, it is easy to see that by picking a small value of ϵ one can guarantee z_1 and z_2 to be equal. As mentioned earlier, this further implies that the students with negative abilities in group T_1 and T_2 define a perfect partitioning of the elements in set W. Finally, to guarantee that our reduction take polynomial time, we would like to point that ϵ does not require to be arbitrary small, it can simply be smaller than the precision in which the ability scores are reported.

Given that the ability scores in an instance of CountℓG problem are bound to be between zero and one, it might seem that our reduction is incomplete as it creates students with negative ability scores. However, one can see that the optimal solution to an instance of CountℓG problem would not change if all the ability scores are shifted (i.e., incremented by a constant) or scaled (i.e., multiplied by a constant). Thus, one can simply renormalize the ability scores to be between zero and one without affecting the value of the optimal solution. □

`IterL&F:` Given there is no polynomial-time algorithm for solving CountℓG, we propose `IterL&F`, which is an iterative heuristic. In every iteration of `IterL&F`, one group of size k is formed. The selection of the group is done using the `L&F` algorithm and using as input only those students that have not yet been assigned to any group. Clearly, there are n/k iterations of `IterL&F`, each taking time $O(n \log k)$. Therefore, the overall running time is $O(\frac{n^2 \log k}{k})$.

Depending upon the version of `L&F` algorithm employed (see Remark 2 in Section 4.1), we get three versions of `IterL&F`, namely `max-IterL&F`, `min-IterL&F` and `any-IterL&F`. Our experiments indicate that they obtain similar overall value of the Ac objective, but the structure of the groups built by them exhibit differences. Intuitively, `max-IterL&F` groups the highest ability leaders with relatively high ability followers, whereas `min-IterL&F` groups them with the lowest ability followers, while `any-IterL&F` groups them with mixed ability followers.

5. VALUE-BASED GROUP FORMATION

We next study the Value1G and ValueℓG problems.

5.1 The Value1G problem

We first show that the Value1G problem can be solved in polynomial time with an algorithm, which we call `Endpoints`. Algorithm 2 provides the pseudo-code of `Endpoints`.

Algorithm 2 `Endpoints`

Input: Set of students $S = \{1, \ldots, n\}$ with sorted abilities $\theta_1 > \theta_2 > \ldots > \theta_n$, Group size k.
Output: Group T with the maximum $\text{Av}(T)$.

for $i = 1 \ldots k-1$ **do**
  $L_i = \{1, ..., i\}$
  $F_i = \{(n-i+1), ..., n\}$
  $\widehat{\Theta}_i = ((\theta_1 + ... + \theta_i) + (\theta_{n-i+1} + ... + \theta_n))/k$
  if $\widehat{\Theta}_i > \theta_{n-i+1}$ **then**
    $T_i = L_i \cup F_i$
  else
    $T_i = \phi$
return $\arg\max_{T_i} \text{Av}(T_i)$

We start with the following lemma:

Lemma 3. *Given a group T that maximizes $\text{Av}(T)$ and consists of x leaders and $y = k - x$ followers, it must be the case that $L = \{1, ..., x\}$ and $F = \{(n-y+1), ..., n\}$.*

Proof. We definitely need to pick as followers the y students with the lowest ability since $\text{Av}(T)$ will be strictly worse for any other choice of y students. We also need to select the top-x ability students as the leaders; this is because the top-x ability students maximize the value of $\widehat{\Theta}_T$ and as a result also the value of our objective $\text{Av}(T)$. □

However, since the values of x and y are not known a priori, `Endpoints` iterates over all possible values of x and y that satisfy $x + y = k$ and reports the optimal solution in time $O(k)$. The `IF` condition ensures that the set F under consideration satisfies the constraint imposed by the definition of a follower set.

Example 3. *For the students of Example 1, `Endpoints` returns $L = \{1,2\} \cup F = \{5\}$. Contrast this group with the group formed by `L&F` in Example 2 for the same set of students. The latter uses the top student 1 to lift up the students 3 and 4, whereas `Endpoints` uses the two top students to lift up the very weak student 5.*

5.2 The ValueℓG problem

Determining the exact complexity class of the ValueℓG is still unresolved. Meanwhile, we propose two iterative heuristics for solving the problem: `IterEndpoints` and `RoundRobin`. Their performance characteristics is empirically studied later in the paper.

`IterEndpoints:` This heuristic builds upon the `Endpoints` algorithm. In each iteration, it identifies a group of size k by applying `Endpoints` to the remaining body of students. The running time of `IterEndpoints` is $O(n)$, since there are n/k iterations, each requiring time $O(k)$.

`RoundRobin:` Clearly, `IterEndpoints` does a perfect job of maximizing the gain for the first group. However, the gains for the subsequent groups can decrease considerably. `RoundRobin` tries to balance the gain across all the groups. It works off the sorted list of student abilities and creates the first group consisting of k students at positions 1, $k+1$, $(2k+1)$, etc. The ith group is formed by students at positions i, $k+i$, $(2k+i)$, etc. The running time of `RoundRobin` for a sorted input consisting of n students is $O(n)$. Intuitively, this heuristic mimics how groups are often formed (particularly in recreational team sports) by first selecting the leaders and then letting the leaders take turn in adding members to their respective groups.

Observe that `RoundRobin` can also be used for solving the CountℓG problem. In fact, we use it as a baseline algorithm in our experiments with the CountℓG problem as well.

6. EXPERIMENTS

Our experimental evaluation focuses on studying the performance of our algorithms for the CountℓG and the ValueℓG problems. Moreover, we present some illustrative partitions created by different algorithms and highlight their characteristics.

Datasets: For all the experiments we report here, we experiment with a set of $n = 1024$ students with ability values randomly sampled from (a) normal, (b) uniform and (c) pareto distributions. We refer to the resulting datasets as

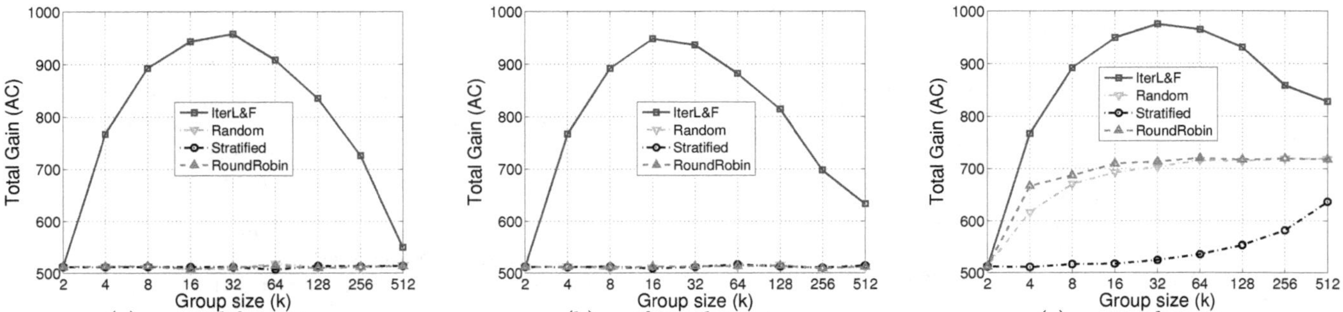

(a) *normal* dataset (b) *uniform* dataset (c) *pareto* dataset

Figure 1: Performance of `IterL&F`, `Random`, `Stratified` and `RoundRobin` for the CountℓG problem; x-axis (log-scale): number of students per group (k); y-axis: sum of the Ac values of the groups.

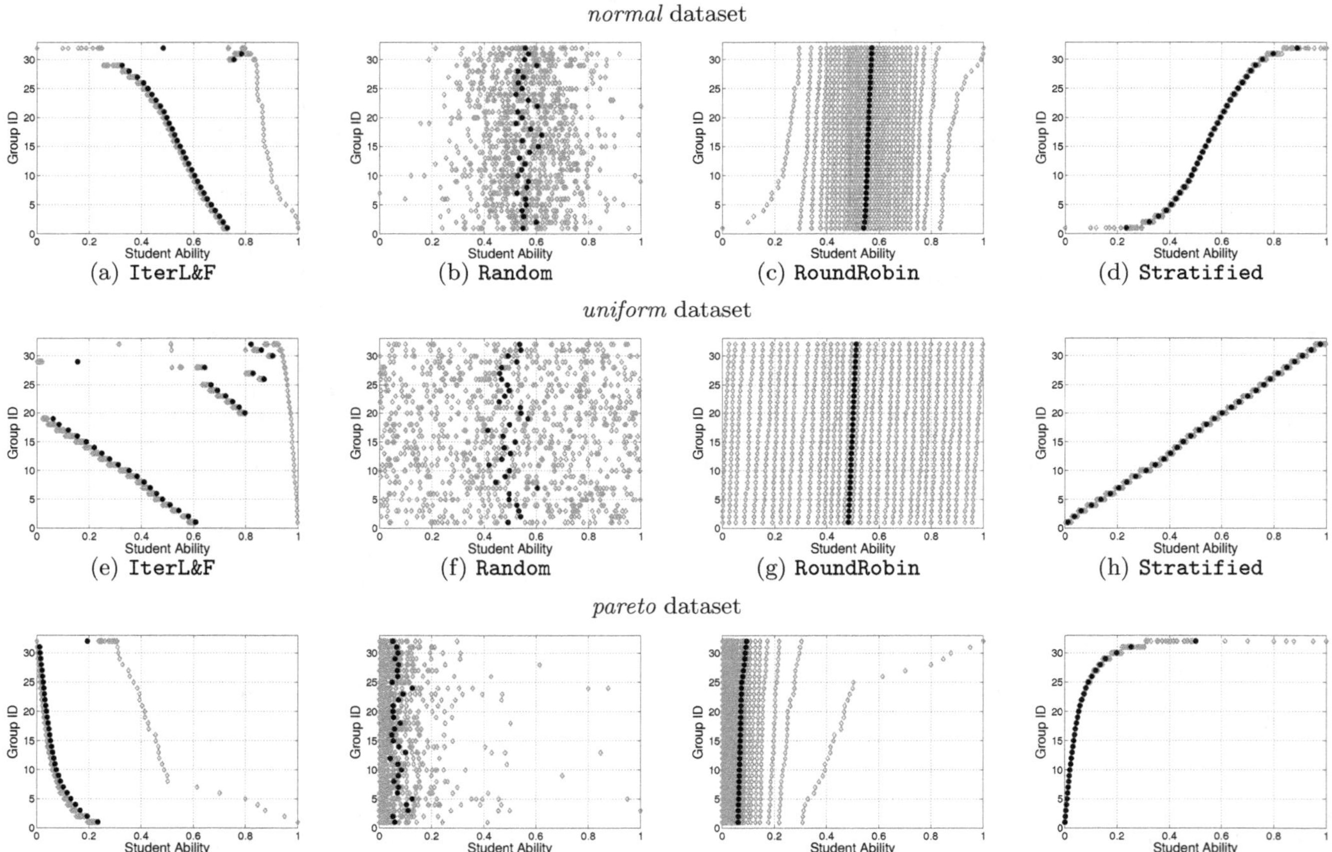

normal dataset

(a) `IterL&F` (b) `Random` (c) `RoundRobin` (d) `Stratified`

uniform dataset

(e) `IterL&F` (f) `Random` (g) `RoundRobin` (h) `Stratified`

pareto dataset

(i) `IterL&F` (j) `Random` (k) `RoundRobin` (l) `Stratified`

Figure 2: CountℓG: Structure of the groups of size $k = 32$ formed by different algorithms for different datasets. Every row of a plot corresponds to a group and the points within a row represent the ability levels of the members of the group; dark points are group abilities.

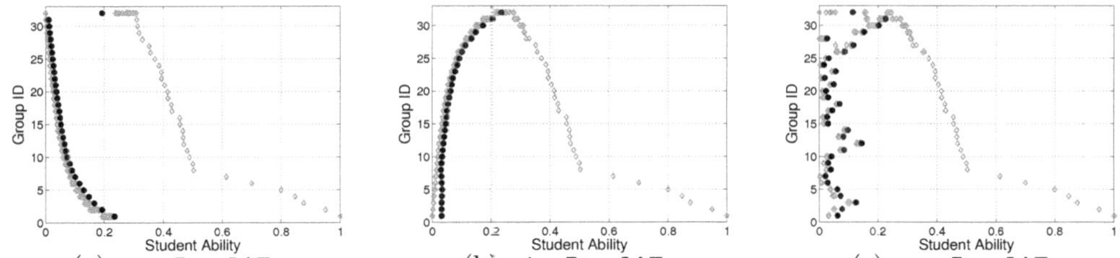

(a) max-IterL&F (b) min-IterL&F (c) any-IterL&F

Figure 3: CountℓG: Structure of the groups of size $k = 32$ formed by different versions of the IterL&F algorithm for the *pareto* dataset.

normal, *uniform* and the *pareto* datasets respectively. The abilities of students in the *normal* dataset are sampled from a normal distribution with mean 0 and standard deviation 1. For the *uniform* dataset the abilities are sampled uniformly from the interval $[0, 1]$. Finally, the abilities of the students in the *pareto* dataset are samples from a pareto distribution, having the shape parameter set to 3. After the datasets are sampled from their respective distributions, we normalize all values to be in $[0, 1]$. This normalization is only done for consistency and plays no role in the conclusions we draw.

Baseline algorithms: In addition to the algorithms we discussed in Sections 4 and 5, we also experiment with two baseline algorithms: `Stratified` and `Random`.

The `Stratified` algorithm sorts the students in decreasing order of their abilities. Then, the first group is created by considering the first k students with the highest abilities and putting them in a group by themselves. The second group is created with the subsequent k students, and so on. The running time of this algorithms for a sorted input consisting of n students is $O(n)$. This algorithm can be thought of as an idealized version of the oft-used, ability-based homogeneous grouping of students [20, 24].

The `Random` algorithm creates ℓ groups of size k by randomly assigning students to groups. The running time of the `Random` algorithm is $O(n)$, since it is adequate to create a random permutation of the students and then create the ℓ groups by considering consecutive members of this permutation. Note that some approximation of `Random` is often used for partitioning a class into heterogeneous sections [27].

6.1 Evaluating algorithms for CountℓG

We study the performance of different algorithms for the CountℓG problem by computing the total gain Ac due to the groups they form. We use the `max-IterL&F` version of `IterL&F` as well as `Random`, `Stratified` and `RoundRobin` in this evaluation. Figure 1 shows their Ac values as a function of the group size $k \in \{2, 4, 8, \ldots, 512\}$ for each one of the three datasets (*normal*, *uniform* and *pareto*).

The results (which are averages over 20 random datasets drawn from the respective distribution) demonstrate that for all values of k (except for $k = 2$), `IterL&F` is significantly better than any other algorithm. In fact, there are values of k (e.g., $k = 32$) for which the `IterL&F` achieves total Ac of more than 950, while the maximum possible value is less than 1024. This means that more than 90% of the students are assigned into groups in which the group ability is higher than their ability.

For $k = 2$, all algorithms have the same total Ac, which is equal to $n/2 = 1024/2 = 512$. The reason is that in groups of size 2 inevitably there is one student who is above and one who is below the group average and therefore the group is beneficial for exactly half of the students, independently of how the group assignment is performed. As k increases, the ability of `IterL&F` to make conscious and judicious use of the high ability students to pull up as many lower ability students as possible starts to shine and the performance gap between `IterL&F` and other algorithms starts to increase. Beyond some value of k (around 32), the law of diminishing return sets in and the performance gap starts to reduce. Note, however, that the x-axis in Figure 1 is in logarithmic scale and the decrease in performance gap is more gradual than it might appear from a cursory glance at the plots.

Turning our attention to the baseline algorithms (i.e., `Random`, `Stratified`, and `RoundRobin`), we observe that for *normal* and *uniform* datasets the performance of these algorithms is almost constant allowing about half of the students to benefit from group participation. The landscape is different for the *pareto* dataset. In this case, `Random` and `RoundRobin` are better than `Stratified` – yet again significantly worse than `IterL&F`. In order to understand that one has to remember that the *pareto* dataset has a small number of exceptionally high-ability students. The `Stratified` algorithm by definition puts these students together in one group and therefore their high abilities cannot be leveraged to lift up the average abilities of other groups. This phenomenon is not observed in the groups formed by `Random` and `RoundRobin` since these algorithms distribute the high-ability individuals into different groups allowing more groups to benefit from them.

Characteristics of groups in CountℓG: Although the plots in Figure 1 demonstrate the superiority of `IterL&F` with respect to the objective function (i.e., total Ac), they do not provide intuition on the types of students that are brought together into groups by different algorithms. We do that in Figure 2 for groups of size 32 using the *normal*, the *uniform* and the *pareto* datasets. The x-axis of all the plots in this figure corresponds to ability values and the y-axis takes values $\{1, 2, \ldots, 32\}$; these y-values correspond to the group IDs. Thus the points on the same horizontal line in a plot represent the abilities of the students that are assigned to the group with ID equal to the value of the y-axis to which this horizontal line corresponds to. The group ID is the same as the order in which the group was output by the corresponding algorithm. For example, the group with ID equal to 1 is the the first group that was built by `IterL&F`,

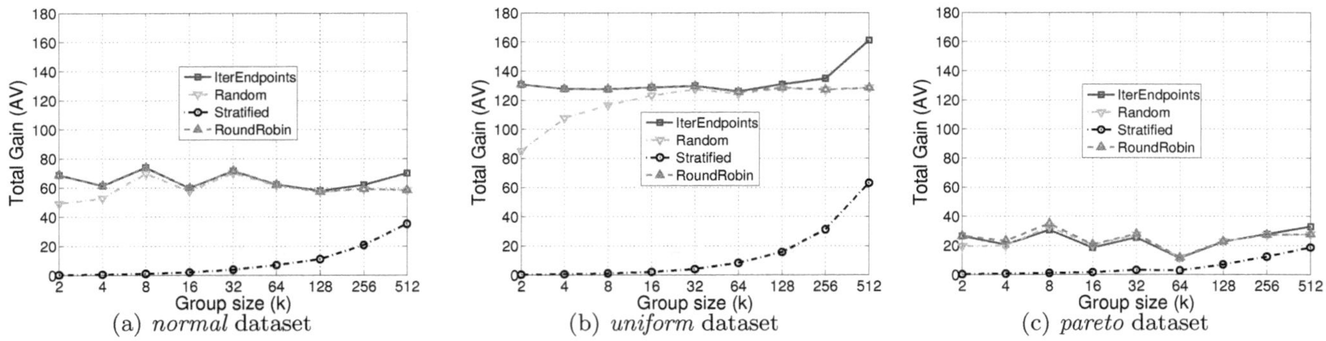

Figure 4: Performance of IterEndpoints, Random, Stratified and RoundRobin for the VALUEℓG problem; x-axis (log-scale): number of students per group (k); y-axis: sum of the Av values of the groups.

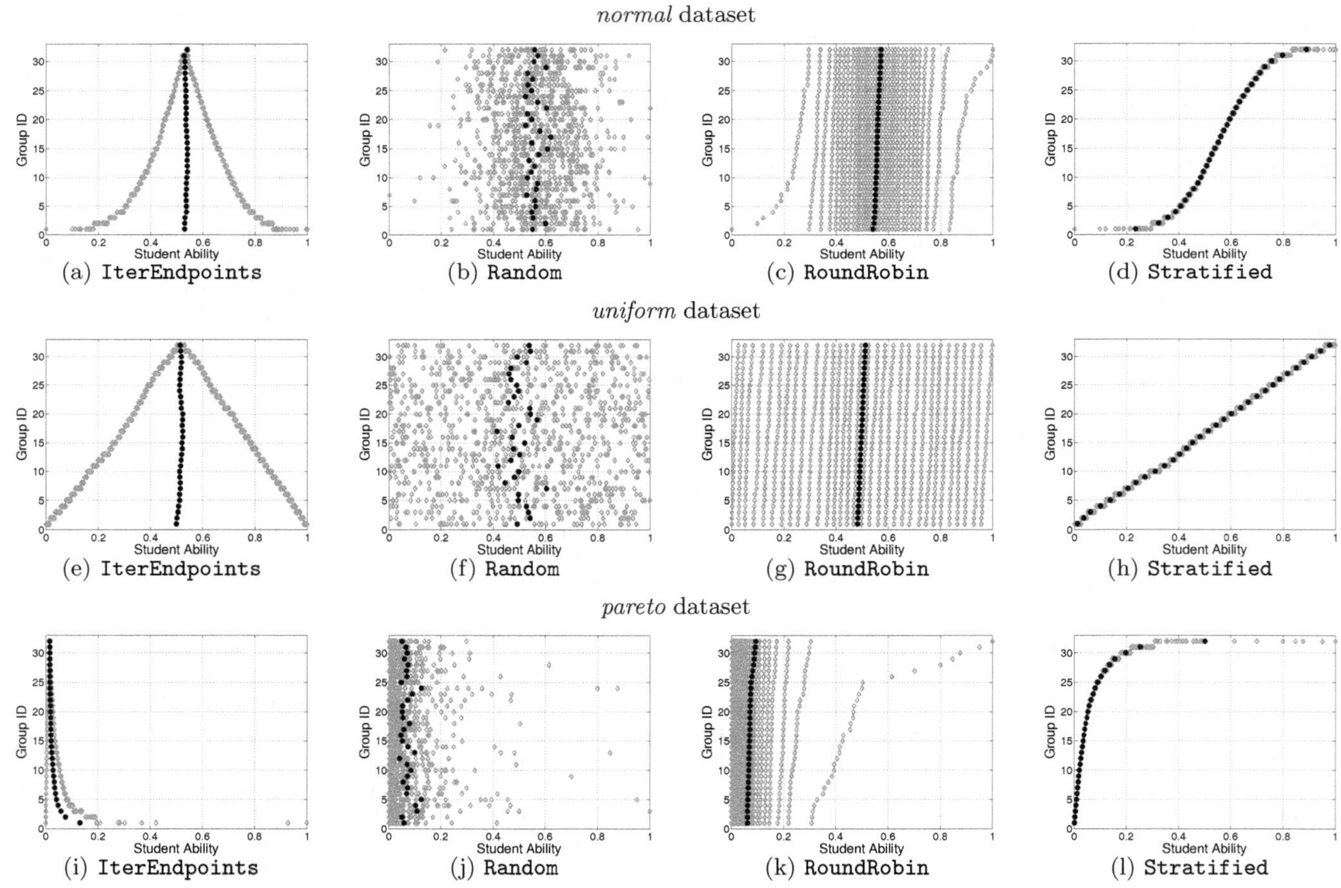

Figure 5: VALUEℓG: Structure of the groups formed for $k = 32$ by different algorithms for different datasets.

and group with ID equal to i was built by `IterL&F` at its i-th iteration. The gray triangles correspond to the members of each group while black dots represent the mean of the abilities within each group. Keep in mind that we are using the `max-IterL&F` version of `IterL&F` in this experiment.

Several interesting observations emerge from this figure. First of all, there is a clear separation between the "leaders" and the "followers" in the groups built by `IterL&F`. We see that `IterL&F` judiciously puts together in each group few strong leaders with followers that are clearly weaker than them, yet they are not as weak as the followers grouped with relatively less strong leaders. The groups formed by `Random` have a mix of students from all ability levels, with no clear separation between leaders and followers. The groups formed by `RoundRobin` are a more deterministic version of the groups built by `Random`. Finally, the groups formed by `Stratified` clearly exhibit ability grouping, where the students with the same ability levels are grouped together. These differences in group composition underlie the superiority of `IterL&F` we see in Figure 1.

Finally, we remark that we found that all three versions of `IterL&F`, namely `max-IterL&F`, `min-IterL&F` and `any-IterL&F`, had similar performance but the structure of the groups they formed differed somewhat. We illustrate in Figure 3 the composition of the groups built by them for $k = 32$ for the *pareto* dataset. As in `max-IterL&F`, there continues be a separation between the "leaders" and the "followers" in the groups constituted by the other two. However, while `max-IterL&F` groups strongest leaders with strongest followers, `min-IterL&F` initially groups the weakest followers with the strongest leaders. Subsequently, it groups decreasingly strong leaders with relatively stronger weak followers until in the final groups the abilities of the leaders and the followers converge. The groups built by `any-IterL&F` are similar to those yielded by `min-IterL&F`, but the followers now have relatively more mixed abilities.

6.2 Evaluating the algorithms for VALUEℓG

Here, we describe our experiments for the VALUEℓG problem. Our experimental methodology is identical to the one we followed for the COUNTℓG problem. We study the performance of `IterEndpoints`, `Random`, `RoundRobin` and `Stratified` with respect to the total Av of the groups they form. We again use *normal*, *uniform* and *pareto* datasets and group sizes $k \in \{2, 4, 8, \ldots, 512\}$.

Figure 4 shows the results. We see that `IterEndpoints`, `Random` and `RoundRobin` consistently outperform `Stratified`. To understand this phenomenon, recall that the goal of VALUEℓG is to maximize the gain for the students in the follower sets. The gain for followers in a particular group depends on the gap between the their abilities and the group ability; the larger the gap the larger will be the value of Av. Thus, an algorithm that forms groups in such a way that the ability of leaders is relatively high compared to the abilities of followers will perform better. Finally, since VALUEℓG aims to maximize the *sum* of the Av values of all the groups, the above property needs to hold only in aggregate.

Examine now Figure 5 that illustrates the abilities of students in each group formed by the different algorithms for the *normal*, the *uniform* and the *pareto* datasets for $k = 32$. As before, the x-axis of all the plots in this figure corresponds to ability values and the y-axis takes values $\{1, 2, \ldots, n/k\}$, which correspond to the group IDs. Clearly, `Stratified` forms homogeneous groups such that in every group there is very little difference in the abilities of the group members and the individual ability of each of the member is quite close to the collective ability of the group. Thus, the total gain for this algorithm is small.

In contrast, the groups formed by `Random` have greater diversity of abilities. It brings together students of varying abilities that has the effect of creating groups having leaders and followers at quite different levels of ability. `RoundRobin` can be viewed as a deterministic version of `Random` and hence its performance characteristics is similar. However, it is interesting to contrast the composition of groups these two heuristics form with those built by `IterEndpoints`. Though they all achieve roughly similar total Av values, particularly for groups of reasonable size, they form very different types of groups. In some of the groups formed by `IterEndpoints`, there is significant difference in the abilities of the leaders and the followers, while in others the difference is small. There is some empirical evidence in support of such structures [23].

7. CONCLUDING REMARKS

We proposed a formal framework for studying the socially important problem of grouping students in a large class into sections so that the gain aggregated over all the students is maximized. Using two different definitions of gain for students, we studied two distinct optimization problems: COUNTℓG and VALUEℓG. Intuitively, COUNTℓG aims to maximize the number of students who can do better by interacting with the higher ability students, while VALUEℓG incorporates the extent of these improvements. From the computational viewpoint, we studied the computational complexity of these grouping problems and provided novel polynomial time heuristics for them.

Our experiments indicate that by appropriately choosing the definition of the gain function, it is possible to achieve different social goals. For example, the groups reported as solutions to COUNTℓG, put strong students together with students who are weaker than them, yet they are not as weak as the students grouped with less strong students. Thus, the group members can learn in their zones of proximal development [19, 31]. On the other hand, groups reported as solutions to VALUEℓG put together the weakest with the strongest students aiming to maximize diversity of the groups. Such groups may provide larger motivation/benefit to the weak students while giving room to the strongest students to learn by teaching and become role models [5, 23, 32]. It is really up to the school to decide its social goals and philosophy and as a result its choice of objective.

The gain functions we studied in this paper are just two of many functions admitted by our framework. In the future, we would like to study other functions particularly those incorporating the gains of strong students and non-linear gains. We would also like to enrich our problem formulation with constraints due to socio-emotional factors such as interpersonal relations [4, 10]. The group dynamics that sets in once a group is formed can have major impact on the outcomes [6]. We would like to explore how to apply computational perspective to studying the group interactions in an educational setting. Finally, we would like to partner with some educational institutions to study the performance characteristics of our work in real-life.

8. ACKNOWLEDGMENTS

This research was partially done when E. Terzi was visiting Microsoft Research. The research was also partially supported by: NSF CAREER #1253393, NSF grants: CNS #1017529, III #1218437, IIS #1320542 and gifts from Microsoft and Hariri Institute of Computing.

9. REFERENCES

[1] Anagnostopoulos, A., Becchetti, L., Castillo, C., Gionis, A., and Leonardi, S. Power in unity: forming teams in large-scale community systems. In *CIKM* (2010), 599–608.

[2] Anagnostopoulos, A., Becchetti, L., Castillo, C., Gionis, A., and Leonardi, S. Online team formation in social networks. In *WWW* (2012), 839–848.

[3] Ashman, A., and Gillies, R. *Cooperative learning: The social and intellectual outcomes of learning in groups.* Routledge, 2003.

[4] Azmitia, M., and Montgomery, R. Friendship, transactive dialogues, and the development of scientific reasoning. *Social Development 2*, 3 (1993), 202–221.

[5] Bargh, J., and Schul, Y. On the cognitive benefits of teaching. *Journal of Educational Psychology 72*, 5 (1980), 593.

[6] Barron, B. When smart groups fail. *Journal of the Learning Sciences 12*, 3 (2003), 307–359.

[7] Boaler, J., Wiliam, D., and Brown, M. Students' experiences of ability grouping-disaffection, polarisation and the construction of failure. *British Educational Research Journal 26*, 5 (2000), 631–648.

[8] Chimombo, J. P. G. Issues in basic education in developing countries: An exploration of policy options for improved delivery. *Journal of International Cooperation in Education 8*, 1 (2005), 129–152.

[9] Crocker, L., and Algina, J. *Introduction to classical and modern test theory.* Wadsworth, 2006.

[10] Da Silva, F. E. D. O., Motta, C. L., Santoro, F. M., and De Oliveira, C. E. T. A social matching approach to support team configuration. In *Groupware: Design, Implementation, and Use.* Springer, 2009, 49–64.

[11] Esposito, D. Homogeneous and heterogeneous ability grouping: Principal findings and implications for evaluating and designing more effective educational environments. *Review of Educational Research 43*, 2 (1973), 163–179.

[12] Gajewar, A., and Sarma, A. D. Multi-skill collaborative teams based on densest subgraphs. In *SDM* (2012), 165–176.

[13] Garey, M., and Johnson, D. S. *Computers and intractability: A guide to the theory of NP-completeness.* W.H. Freeman, 1979.

[14] Gillies, J., and Quijada, J. Opportunity to learn: A high impact strategy for improving educational outcomes in developing countries. *USAID Educational Quality Improvement Program (EQUIP2)* (2008).

[15] Grossen, B. *How should we group to achive excellence with equity.* University of Oregon, July 1996.

[16] Hambleton, R. K., and Jones, R. W. Comparison of classical test theory and item response theory and their applications to test development. *Educational Measurement: Issues and Practice 12*, 3 (1993), 38–47.

[17] Hand, D., Mannila, H., and Smyth, P. *Principles of Data Mining.* MIT Press, 2001.

[18] Hanushek, E. A., and Woessmann, L. The role of education quality for economic growth. *Policy Research Department Working Paper 4122, World Bank* (2007).

[19] Hertz-Lazarowitz, R., and Miller, N. *Interaction in cooperative groups: The theoretical anatomy of group learning.* Cambridge University Press, 1995.

[20] Kulik, J. A. An analysis of the research on ability grouping: Historical and contemporary perspectives. Tech. Rep. 9204, NRC/GT, University of Connecticut, February 1992.

[21] Lappas, T., Liu, K., and Terzi, E. Finding a team of experts in social networks. In *KDD* (2009), 467–476.

[22] Li, C.-T., and Shan, M.-K. Team formation for generalized tasks in expertise social networks. In *SocialCom/PASSAT* (2010), 9–16.

[23] Lou, Y., Abrami, P. C., Spence, J. C., Poulsen, C., Chambers, B., and d'Apollonia, S. Within-class grouping: A meta-analysis. *Review of Educational Research 66*, 4 (1996), 423–458.

[24] Loveless, T. The resurgence of ability grouping and persistence of tracking. Tech. rep., Part II of the 2013 Brown Center Report on American Education, Brookings Institution, March 2013.

[25] Majumder, A., Datta, S., and Naidu, K. V. M. Capacitated team formation problem on social networks. In *KDD* (2012), 1005–1013.

[26] May, M. A., and Doob, L. W. Competition and cooperation. *Social Science Research Council Bulletin* (1937).

[27] McPartland, J. M., Coldiron, J. R., and Braddock, J. H. School structures and classroom practices in elementary, middle, and secondary schools. Tech. Rep. 14, Johns Hopkins University, February 1987.

[28] Mislevy, R. J. Item response models for grouped data. *Journal of Educational Statistics 8*, 4 (1983), 271–288.

[29] Richer, S. Reference-group theory and ability grouping: A convergence of sociological theory and educational research. *Sociology of Education 49*, 1 (1976), 65–71.

[30] Slavin, R. E. *Learning to cooperate.* Springer, 1985.

[31] Vygotsky, L. S. *Mind in society: Development of higher psychological processes.* Harvard University Press, 1978.

[32] Webb, N. M. Peer interaction and learning in small groups. *International Journal of Educational Research 13*, 1 (1989), 21–39.

[33] World-Bank. *Knowledge for Development: World Development Report: 1998/99.* Oxford University Press, 1999.

Inferring Gas Consumption and Pollution Emissions of Vehicles throughout a City

Jingbo Shang[1,2,*], Yu Zheng[2,+], Wenzhu Tong[3,2,*], Eric Chang[2], Yong Yu[1]

[1]Dept. of Computer Science & Engineering, Shanghai Jiao Tong University

[2]Microsoft Research, No.5 Danling Street, Haidian District, Beijing 100080, China

[3]Computer School of Wuhan University, Wuhan, Hubei, China

{v-jishan, yuzheng, v-wetong, echang}@microsoft.com, yyu@apex.sjtu.edu.cn

ABSTRACT

This paper instantly infers the gas consumption and pollution emission of vehicles traveling on a city's road network in a current time slot, using GPS trajectories from a sample of vehicles (e.g., taxicabs). The knowledge can be used to suggest cost-efficient driving routes as well as identifying road segments where gas has been wasted significantly. The instant estimation of the emissions from vehicles can enable pollution alerts and help diagnose the root cause of air pollution in the long run. In our method, we first compute the travel speed of each road segment using the GPS trajectories received recently. As many road segments are not traversed by trajectories (i.e., data sparsity), we propose a Travel Speed Estimation (TSE) model based on a context-aware matrix factorization approach. TSE leverages features learned from other data sources, e.g., map data and historical trajectories, to deal with the data sparsity problem. We then propose a Traffic Volume Inference (TVI) model to infer the number of vehicles passing each road segment per minute. TVI is an unsupervised Bayesian Network that incorporates multiple factors, such as travel speed, weather conditions and geographical features of a road. Given the travel speed and traffic volume of a road segment, gas consumption and emissions can be calculated based on existing environmental theories. We evaluate our method based on extensive experiments using GPS trajectories generated by over 32,000 taxis in Beijing over a period of two months. The results demonstrate the advantages of our method over baselines, validating the contribution of its components and finding interesting discoveries for the benefit of society.

Categories and Subject Descriptors

H.2.8 [Database Management]: Database Applications - data mining, Spatial databases and GIS;

Keywords

Urban computing; traffic pollution; gas consumption; trajectories.

1. INTRODUCTION

While consuming a huge amount of gas, vehicles traveling in cities also generate greenhouse gases (GHG), like CO_2, and air pollution, e.g., PM2.5. Figuring out the answers to challenging questions of emissions, such as how much gas is consumed by vehicles in a given city or on a particular road, or what volume of PM2.5 is generated as a direct result, is strategically important to modeling urban traffic, gas consumption, and pollution emission, in order to help save energy and protect the environment [19]. For instance, if we were to know the gas consumption for traveling any road segment at any time, we can suggest cost-efficient driving routes and identify road segments where gas is being wasted significantly. Such knowledge can impact authorities' decision making on improving a city's transportation infrastructure. In the meantime, real-time estimation of emissions from vehicles can enable pollution alerts. In the long run, this information can help diagnose the root cause of air pollution. For example, whether reducing traffic of vehicles will significantly lower air pollution is still a controversial subject in developing countries. There is no clear method to determine the percentage of PM2.5 in a given air space that is generated by vehicles.

As shown in Figure 1, we instantly estimate the total gas consumption and the corresponding pollution emission of vehicles traveling on any road segment in a city at a particular time slot, using the GPS trajectories of a sample of vehicles (e.g. taxicabs). Specifically, we first infer the average travel speed on each road segment, using sparse GPS data from a few vehicles. We then estimate the traffic volume (i.e., the number of vehicles/minute) traversing a road segment based on the average travel speed and other factors, such as weather and type of roads. Finally, the travel speed and traffic volume of a road segment are used to calculate the total gas consumption and vehicle emissions on the road, allowing us to determine the pulse of traffic, energy consumption, and emission levels throughout a city.

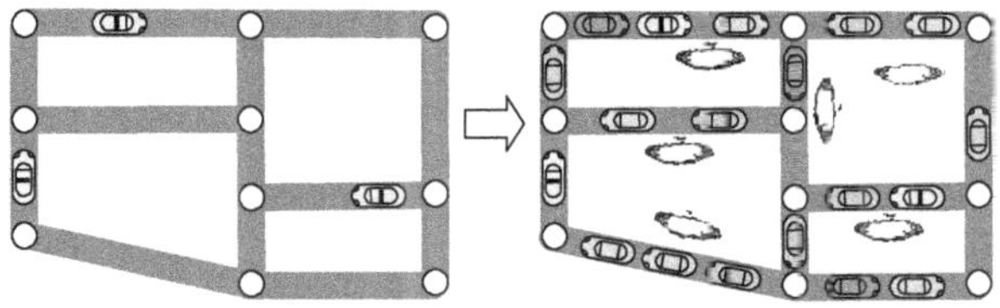

Figure 1. Goals of our Work

Our work faces three main challenges. 1) *Data sparseness*: We can only have a sample of traffic data, as many vehicles do not have a GPS sensor installed. Moreover, in a given time slot, only a small portion of road segments are traversed by GPS-equipped vehicles. For example, according to the statistic on Beijing's taxi data, on average, only 13% of road segments are traversed by taxis in an hour. 2) *From travel speeds to traffic volumes*: The traffic volume on a road segment depends on multiple factors, such as the current travel speeds and density of vehicles, the length, shape, and capacity of the road, as well as weather conditions. Unfortunately, it is not easy to obtain enough training data to learn the mapping between traffic volumes and these factors. In addition, the occurrence of sampled vehicles on roads may be skewed from that of the entire set of vehicles. For example, observing more taxis on a road segment does not mean more occurrences of other vehicles. Consequently, we can neither use the sampled traffic as a training set to learn the

**The paper was done when the first and third authors were an intern in Microsoft Research under the supervision of the second author who contributed the main idea and algorithms of this paper.*

+ Yu Zheng is the correspondence author of this paper.

KDD '14, August 24–27, 2014, New York, New York, USA.

http://dx.doi.org/10.1145/2623330.2623653

aforementioned mapping, nor simply multiply a factor to the volume of sampled vehicles. 3) *Real-time and citywide*: To enable a valuable service, e.g., enabling air pollution alerts, it is better to have real-time information about traffic, gas consumption and emissions, with a city scale. This calls for a knowledge discovery ability that is both efficient (i.e., providing information on the entire city a few minutes after receiving the data) and effective (e.g., consider the traffic conditions not only on a road segment individually but also on a road network systematically).

Given the aforementioned challenges, existing methods for estimating the traffic conditions on a single road do not work well. For instance, traffic detection solutions [5, 7, 13] using loop sensors on roads and surveillance cameras are difficult to scale up to cover an entire city. Some approaches, e.g., fundamental diagram [1, 3], need a lot of training data, or are not applicable to a complex road network [2]. Conventional models using floating car data to estimate traffic conditions do not tackle the data sparsity problem well, which cannot be simply solved by interpolation [18] or just using historical patterns [2] either (refer to the related work section for details). Our research makes three main contributions:

- We infer the travel speed of a road segment throughout a city, using a model (titled *TSE*) based on a context-aware matrix factorization. *TSE* incorporates historical traffic patterns, the correlation between different times of day, and physical features of a road (such as the length), in a framework of collaborative filtering, to tackle the data sparsity problem.
- We propose an unsupervised graphical model for traffic volume inference (titled *TVI*) on a road segment in a given time slot. *TVI* considers multiple factors, such as physical features of a road, travel speed, variance in speed, and weather conditions, in a Bayesian Network.
- We evaluate the effectiveness and efficiency of our method with extensive experiments, using GPS trajectories generated by 32,670 taxis over a period of two months. Our method outperforms baselines significantly. We have share a sample of the experimental data at [20].

The rest of the paper is organized as follows. Section 2 overviews our method. We detail the methodology in Section 3 and evaluate our approach in Section 4. After reviewing related work in Section 5, we conclude this paper in Section 6.

2. OVERVIEW

Definition 1: Trajectory. A spatial *trajectory* Tr is a sequence of time-ordered spatial points, $Tr: p_1 \rightarrow p_2 \rightarrow \cdots \rightarrow p_n$, where each point has a geospatial coordinate set l and a timestamp t, $p = (l, t)$.

Definition 2: POI. A point of interest POI is a venue (like a school and shopping mall) in the physical world, having a name, address, coordinates, category, and other attributes.

Definition 3: Road Network. A road network RN is comprised of a set of road segments $\{r\}$ connected among each other in a graph format. Each road segment r is a directed edge having two terminal points, a list of intermediate points describing the segment, a length $r.len$, a level $r.lev$ (e.g., a highway or a street), a direction $r.dir$ (e.g., one-way or bi-directional) and the number of lanes $r.n$.

Figure 2 presents the framework of our method, which is comprised of five major components: trajectory mapping, context extraction, travel speed estimation, traffic volume inference, and energy & emission calculations, which will be elaborated respectively in Section 3. We first map the GPS trajectories received in the current time slot onto a road network using a map-matching algorithm [6], and then calculate the travel speed on the road segments covered by trajectories. We also extract road features from map data, like Points of Interests (POI) and road networks, and traffic patterns from historical trajectories. The road features and traffic patterns are used as context to improve the accuracy of travel speed estimation, which computes the average travel speeds of road segments that are absent of trajectory data through a context-aware matrix-factorization approach. The road features and inferred travel speed as well as other features (like weather conditions) are then employed as observations in a graphical model to infer traffic volumes on a road segment. Finally, employing existing equations from environmental science, we calculate the gas consumption and emission on each road segment.

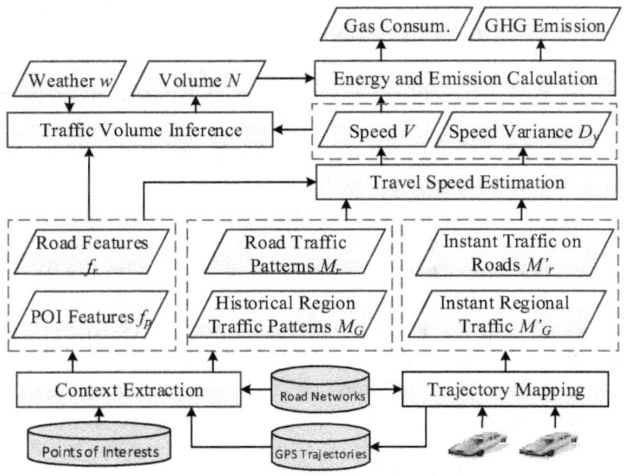

Figure 2. Framework of our method

3. METHODOLOGY

3.1 Trajectory Mapping

The trajectory mapping component receives GPS trajectories from vehicles and projects each trajectory onto a road network using a map-matching algorithm [6]. This component also calculates the average travel speed for road segments currently covered by the trajectory data received. As shown in Figure 3, three vehicles travel four road segments r_1, r_2, r_3 and r_4, generating three trajectories Tr_1, Tr_2, and Tr_3. After map-matching, each point from a trajectory is mapped onto a road segment. Then, we can calculate the travel speed for each point based on Equation 1,

$$v_1 = Dist(p_1.l, p_2.l)/|p_2.t - p_1.t|, \qquad (1)$$

where $Dist$ is a function calculating the road network distance between two points. Likewise, we can calculate the travel speed for other points and then compute the average and variance of travel speed of a road segment as Equation 2 and 3.

$$\bar{v} = \sum_i^n v_i/n; \qquad (2)$$

$$d_v = \sum_i^n \frac{(v_i - \bar{v})^2}{n}, \qquad (3)$$

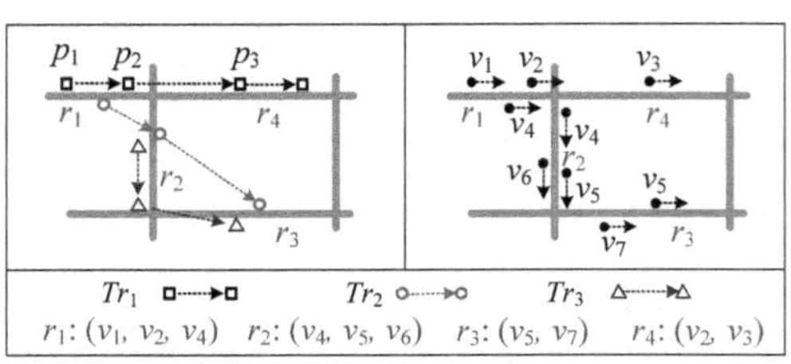

Figure 3. Calculating the average travel speed of a road segment

For instance, the average travel speed of r_1 is $(v_1 + v_2 + v_4)/3$. To ensure the quality of the calculated average speed, we require a road segment to be traveled by vehicles for certain times (e.g., 3 times in the experiments). Otherwise, the road segment is considered absent of data and will later be inferred by our method. The average speed and variance formulate a road segment's traffic conditions, which will be used in both travel speed estimation and traffic volume inference components.

3.2 Context Extraction

This component generates two categories of knowledge. One is a set of physical features extracted from POI and road network databases, describing the geographic contexts of a road segment. The other is the traffic patterns learned from historical trajectories, revealing the correlation between different time slots.

Physical features of a road: As shown in Figure 3 A), the physical features of a road segment r further consist of three parts:

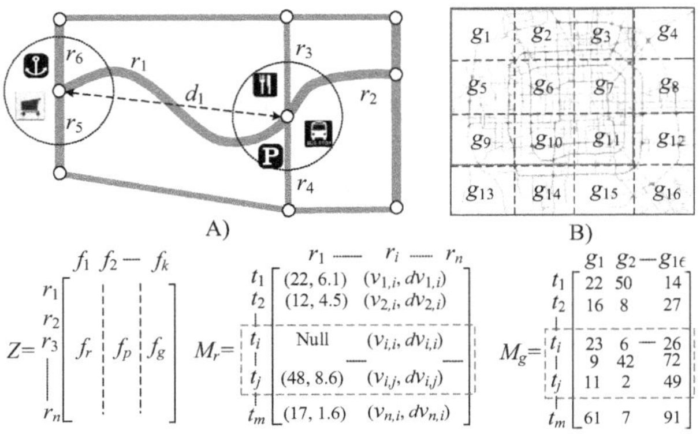

Figure 3. Context Extraction

1) Road network features f_r: $r.len, r.lev, r.dir, r.n$, the number of connections, and a tortuosity τ, which is the ratio between $r.len$ and the Euclidian distance between the two terminals of r. In this example, r_1 has two connections on one terminal and three on the other; $r_1.\tau = r_1.len/d_1$.

2) POI features f_p: For a road segment r, from the POIs around r's terminals (e.g., within a disc of 200 meters), we calculate the distribution of POIs across 10 categories: *Schools*, *Companies & Offices*, *Banks & ATMs*, *Malls & Shopping*, *Restaurants*, *Gas stations & Vehicle services*, *Parking*, *Hotels*, *Residences*, *Transportation,* and *Entertainment & Living Services*. The 10 POI categories are mined from POI and road network datasets, co-occurring with road segments most frequently. For instance, the f_p of r_1 is (0, 0, 1, 1, 0, 1, 0, 0, 2, 0). The feature is further normalized into a distribution.

3) Global position feature f_g: This feature basically indicates which part of the city a road segment falls in. For instance, if we partition a city into 4×4 grids, the f_g of a road segment located in g_6 can be represented by the IDs of its eight neighbors, i.e., (1,1,1,0,1,0,1,0, 1,1,1,0,0,0,0,0), as illustrated in Figure 3 B). If two road segments are geographically close to each other, their f_g will be similar.

We place f_r, f_p, and f_g of each road segment into a matrix Z, where each row denotes a road segment and a column represents a kind of feature. f_r and f_p represent the local features of a road segment, while f_g captures a road segment's global geo-position. The general idea is that road segments with similar f_r and f_p could share a similar traffic condition. If their f_g is also similar (i.e., close to each other), they would have a more similar traffic condition.

Traffic Patterns: While the physical features of a road segment are static, we also extract from historical trajectories two matrices M_r and M_g that respectively represent fine and coarse-grained traffic patterns changing over time of day. Specifically, as shown in the bottom of Figure 3, a row of M_r denotes a time slot (e.g., 2pm-2:10pm), and a column stands for a road segment. Each entry in M_r contains the average traffic condition $(\bar{v}, dv)$ on a particular road segment and in a particular time slot, calculated based on the historical data over a long period (e.g., 2 months). The similarity between two rows reveals the correlation between two time slots. Likewise, matrix M_G reflects coarse-grained traffic patterns in a city, where a row stands for a time slot and a column denotes a grid cell. For example, as shown in Figure 3 B), we partition Beijing into 16 disjoint grids, each of which contains some road segments. Each entry of M_G is the average number of vehicles traversing a specific grid cell in a particular time slot, calculated based on the data over a long period of time. In contrast to M_r, M_g is a higher-level but denser representation of traffic patterns. To model the traffic patterns more accurately, we can maintain M_r and M_g which correspond to workdays and holidays, respectively.

3.3 Travel Speed Estimation (TSE)

This component estimates the traffic condition $(\bar{v}, dv)$ on each road segment, using recently received trajectory data and contexts (extracted in Section 3.2) in a framework of collaborative filtering.

As illustrated in Figure 4, we formulate three matrices X, Y, and Z, where $X = M'_r||M_r$, $Y = M'_G||M_G$, and Z contains the physical features of roads. Specifically, M'_r and M'_G are matrices built based on the recent trajectory data received from t_i to t_j (e.g., 1pm-3pm), where t_j is the current time slot. M_r and M_G are the traffic pattern matrices built over a long period of time, corresponding to the same time slots from t_i to t_j. In the implementation, we build M_r and M_G of an entire day in advance and retrieve the entries from t_i to t_j when constructing X and Y (refer to the broken line box in the bottom of Figure 3). Given the above settings, the goal of estimating current traffic conditions on a road network can be converted into filling the missing values in row t_j of M'_r with the help of M_r, Y and Z.

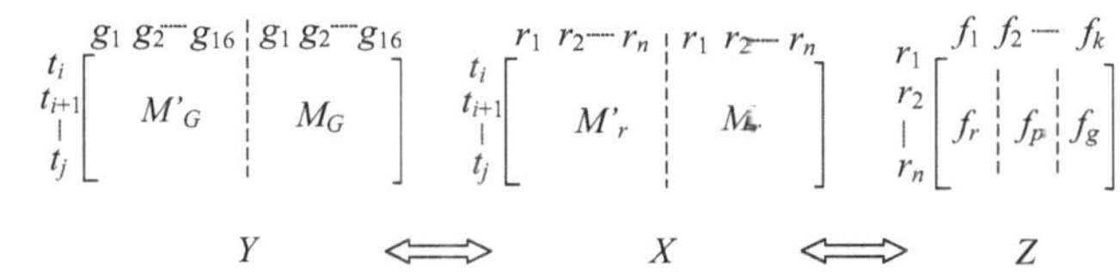

Figure 4. Context-aware Matrix Factorization-based CF

Basically, we can achieve this goal through solely factorizing M'_r into the product of two low-rank matrices based on the non-zero entries of M'_r. However, as we mentioned before, M'_r has very few non-zero entries due to the data sparsity problem. So, the approximation of M'_r by solely factorizing itself is not accurate enough. To tackle the data sparsity problem, we incorporate another two context matrices Y and Z, where Y models the temporal correlations between different time slots and Z models the geographical similarity between two different road segments. Intuitively, M'_r and M'_G represent current traffic conditions in a city, and M_r and M_G denote historical traffic patterns. Putting M'_r together with M_r (and M'_G together with M_G) reveals the deviation of current traffic conditions from the corresponding traffic patterns. Additionally, M_r and M_G built over a long period of time are much denser than the recently received data. As a result, the formulation of X and Y can help tackle the data sparsity problem.

More specifically, we can decompose X, Y and Z as follows:

$$Y \approx T \times (G;G)^T;\ X \approx T \times (R;R)^T;\ Z \approx R \times F^T, \quad (4)$$

where $T, G, R,$ and F are low-rank matrices representing the latent factors; X and Y share latent factor T; X and Z share latent factor R. As Y and Z can be built from other data sources, e.g., historical trajectories and map data, they are much denser than X. Consequently, Y and Z can improve the accuracy of the approximation, if we factorize X, Y and Z collaboratively. After the factorization, we can recover X through the production of T and $(R; R)^T$. The objective function is defined as Equation 5.

$$L(T,R,G,F) = \frac{1}{2}||Y - T(G;G)^T||^2 + \frac{\lambda_1}{2}||X - T(R;R)^T||^2 + \frac{\lambda_2}{2}||Z - RF^T||^2 + \frac{\lambda_3}{2}(||T||^2 + ||R||^2 + ||G||^2 + ||F||^2), \quad (5)$$

where $||\cdot||$ denotes the Frobenius norm. The first three terms in the objective function (5) control the loss in matrix factorization, and the last term controls the regularization over the factorized matrices so as to prevent over fitting. In general, the objective function is not jointly convex to all the variables $R, T, G,$ and F. That is, we cannot get closed-form solutions to minimize the objective function. Therefore, we iteratively minimize the objective function according to the gradient descent algorithm shown in Figure 5. Specifically, we have the gradients (denoted as∇) for each variable:

$$\begin{aligned}
\nabla_T L &= [T(G;G)^T - Y](G;G)^T + \lambda_1(T(R;R)^T - X)(R;R)^T + \lambda_3 T,\\
\nabla_R L &= \lambda_1[T(R;R)^T - X]^T T + \lambda_2(RF^T - Z)F^T + \lambda_3 R,\\
\nabla_G L &= \left(T(G;G)^T - Y\right)^T T + \lambda_3 G, \qquad (6)\\
\nabla_F L &= \lambda_2(RF^T - Z)^T T + \lambda_3 F.
\end{aligned}$$

Algorithm TSE

Input: Incomplete matrix X, context matrices Y and Z
Output: Complete matrix X.

```
t = 1;
While (t < N and L_t − L_{t+1} > ϵ)        // N is #(max iterations)
    Get the gradients ∇_{T_t}, ∇_{R_t}, ∇_{G_t}, and ∇_{F_t} by Eq.(6);
    γ = 1;
    While
      L(T_t − γ∇_{T_t}, R_t − γ∇_{R_t}, G_t − γ∇_{G_t}, F_t − γ∇_{F_t}) ≥ L(T_t, R_t, G_t, F_t)
        γ = γ/2;     // search for the maximal step size
    T_{t+1} = T_t − γ∇_{T_t}, R_{t+1} = R_t − γ∇_{R_t} and
    G_{t+1} = G_t − γ∇_{G_t}, F_{t+1} = F_t − γ∇_{F_t};
    t = t + 1;
Return X;
```

Figure 5. Model for travel speed estimation

3.4 Traffic Volume Inference (TVI)

3.4.1 Model Description

Intrinsically, there exists a certain relationship, e.g., fundamental diagram, among traffic speed, volume and density. Yet to quantify this relationship accurately requires a large amount of traffic volume data. As many road segments are not equipped with in-road devices, collecting such training data with a city-scale is very costly. Thus, it is impractical to use supervised learning algorithms to learn the relationship. In addition, the occurrence of the sampled vehicles (e.g., taxis) on a road segment may be quite different from the entire set of vehicles, though their travel speed could be similar. In other words, observing more taxis on a road segment does not deduce more occurrences of other vehicles. Given this, we cannot infer the total volume of traffic directly based on the sampled traffic data. To address this issue, we propose an unsupervised graphical model, TVI, based on a partially observed Bayesian Network.

Figure 6 presents the graphical structure of TVI model, where a gray node denotes a hidden variable and white nodes are observations. Note that we can train only one TVI model using the data of all road segments. The model is then applied to infer the traffic volume for each road segment respectively. Specifically, the traffic volume on each road lane N_a (i.e., the number of vehicles per minute per lane) of a road segment is influenced by four major factors, consisting of the weather conditions w, time of day t, the type of road θ, and the volume of observed sample vehicles N_t. Furthermore, a road's θ is co-determined by its road network features f_r (such as $r.len$), global position feature f_g, and surrounding POIs α which is influenced by f_p and the total number of POIs N_p. $\bar{v}$ and dv are the average travel speed and speed varriance, respectively, inferred by TSE model. $\bar{v}$ is determined by θ, N_a, and w. dv is co-determined by N_t, N_a, and $\bar{v}$.

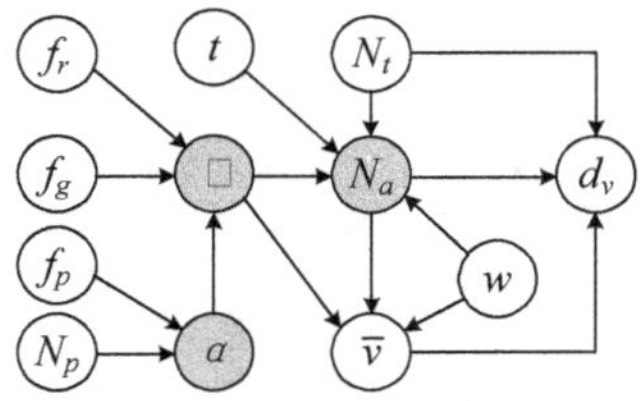

Figure 6. The graphical structure of TVI model

3.4.2 Learning

Due to the hidden nodes, the conditional probability of N_a cannot be drawn simply by counting the occurrence of each condition. Hence, we use the Expectation-Maximization (EM) algorithm to learn the parameters in an unsupervised manner, i.e., without knowing the value of traffic volume N_a, as shown in Figure 7.

Algorithm 2: Parameter Learning of TVI

Input: Bayesian Network structure; observed evidences E
Output: Conditional probability $P(O|Pa(O))$ of each node O

```
1. Randomly initialize P(O|Pa(O)) for each node O
2. While P(O|Pa(O)) does not converge
3.    Foreach evidence e = (f_r, f_g, f_p, N_p, t, w, N_t, v̄, d_v) ∈ E
4.       Foreach value of h = (α, θ, N_a) ∈ H
5.          P(h, e) ← P(α|f_p, N_p)P(θ|α, f_g, f_r) ×
               P(N_a|θ, t, w, N_t)P(v̄|N_a, θ, w)P(d_v|N_a, N_t, v̄)
6.       Foreach value of h = (α, θ, N_a) ∈ H
7.          P(h|e) ← P(h, e)/ Σ_{h∈H} P(h, e);
8.    Foreach node O
9.       ρ ← the occurrences of (O, Pa(O));
10.      P(O|Pa(O)) ← ρ/the occurrence of Pa(O);
11. Return P(O|Pa(O))
```

Figure 7. Parameter learning algorithm of TVI

At the beginning part, this algorithm sets the parameters, i.e., the conditional probabilities, e.g. $P(\alpha|f_p, N_p)$ and $P(\bar{v}|N_a, \theta, w)$, with random values. In the E-step (Line 4-7), we call exact inference method, i.e., use the simple Bayesian rule, to compute the values of the hidden nodes (α, θ, N_a) for each instance of the observed data. This is actually an inference process. In the M-step (Line 8-10), by scanning the inferred results from the E-step, the algorithm recalculates the conditional probabilities, which will replace the old parameters. Keep iterating until the parameters converge, we learn a solution for the unknown parameters.

3.4.3 Discretization

All the variables in our model are discretized. This reduces the inference difficulty, while ensuring the inferred results are statistically useful for gas consumption and emission calculation.

Some nodes are discretized based on commonsense knowledge. For example, speed $\bar{v}$ has 7 categories, i.e., [0,10), [10,20), [20,40), [40,60), [60,80), [80,120), [120, ~) km/h, corresponding to different traffic conditions like free flow and congestion. However, it is difficult to find a proper discretization for traffic volumes (on each lane) N_a, as we do not really have prior knowledge on how big N_a could be on different road segments.

To address this problem, we record 358 video clips on 50 road segments at different times of day, and then manually counted the number of vehicles passing these road segments in a given time slot (i.e. the true traffic volume) (see Table 3 for details) by replaying the video clips. A simple method is to discretize the traffic volume data uniformly according to the range identified from the collected observations. However, the observations are too limited to reveal the true upper bound of the possible volume on road segments. In addition, road segments of different levels may have very different upper bound of traffic volumes. So, we employ the observed true volumes to fit a curve that reveals the distribution of the traffic volumes on different levels of road segments. Then, the fitted distribution is used as a guidance for the discretization of N_a.

As shown in Figure 8, the black data points indicate the observed true volumes, which have been projected onto buckets with a width of 2, i.e., [0, 2), [2, 4), and so on. Significant difference can be observed among the three road levels because of the different road features, such as speed limits and number of lanes. For example, the volume of level 0-1 roads centers in the range of [10, 40), while most volume data of level 3 roads is smaller than 10. To model the traffic volumes on different roads more accurately, we fit a dedicated distributions for each level of road segment (level 0 and 1 share the same distribution as both of them denote highways in Beijing). We adopt normal distribution

$$f(x;\ \mu,\sigma) = \frac{1}{\sigma\sqrt{2\pi}}\exp(-\frac{(x-\mu)^2}{2\sigma^2}) \tag{7}$$

to fit the observed volume data. The parameters are shown in Figure 7, e.g., μ=21.6 and σ=6.38 are good fits for level 0-1 roads (p-value > 0.05 in a chi-square test).

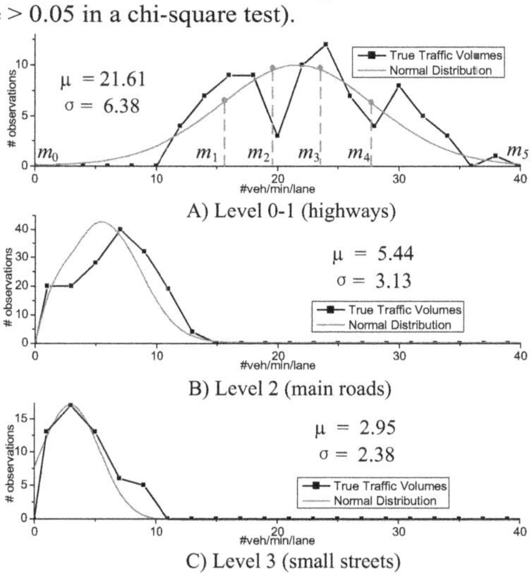

Figure 8. Fitting volume distribution for different road levels

The observations on these road segments can fit the distribution of traffic volume w.r.t. a level of roads for two reasons. First, the selected road segments of a level have a diversity of features (such as length) and traffic volumes. Second, we evenly select the observations from each road segment and in different time slots (82, 163, and 54 observations for level 0-1, 2, and 3 respectively).

Given the fitted distribution of a road level, we find a group of splitting points $m_0, m_1, \cdots, m_5$ that divide the traffic volume into five categories ($c_1, c_2, \ldots, c_5$), such that $\int_{m_{i-1}}^{m_i} f(x;\ \mu,\sigma)\,\mathrm{d}x = 0.2$, where m_{i-1} and m_i are the left and right boundary of category c_i's range respectively; $m_0 = 0$, $m_5 = +\infty$. The five categories may stand for tiny, small, median, big, and very large traffic volumes.

3.4.4 *Inference*

For a more accurate inference, we train three different models for road segments of level 0-1, level 2, and level 3 respectively, based on the data of the corresponding level. Given a road segment r, we select a model according to $r.lev$ and then infer its traffic volume $r.N_a$ according to the E-step in Line 4-7 of Algorithm 2. The output of the inference is a probability distribution over the 5 discretized volume categories.

We choose $argmax_{c\in\{c_1,\cdots,c_5\}}P(N_a \in c)$ as the inferred category and convert the category c to a real traffic volume according to the corresponding volume distribution $f(x;\ \mu,\sigma)$ and the inferred probability $P(N_a \in c)$. Specifically, we find the value N_a (in c's range) such that $P(N_a \in c) = \int_m^{N_a} f(x;\ \mu,\sigma)\,\mathrm{d}x / 0.2$, where m is the left boundary of c's range, and 0.2 is the total probability of category c. The total traffic volume on a road segment r equals $r.N_a \times r.n$.

3.5 Energy and Emission Calculation

The information of traffic speed and volume can be further exploited for estimating real-time gas consumption and emissions on road surfaces. Different models are available in environmental science, which quantify the relationship between emissions and speed, as well as other factors, based on large amounts of data. The most frequently used models include MOBILE and COPERT, which have been developed by scientists in the USA and Europe respectively [11]. We use COPERT model [3] because vehicles in Beijing currently adopt European-3 standards [14].

In the COPERT model, traffic emissions consist of three parts, namely hot emissions, cold start emissions, and evaporative emissions. Hot emissions occur when the engine is at its normal mode, which is the general condition for a running vehicle and thus is our major concern. Cold start emissions denote emissions from transient engine operation, and evaporative emissions come from refueling and temperature changes. The latter two parts are omitted in our estimation due to lack of data; they are also of less significance in overall emissions [2].

Hot emission factor (*EF*), the amount of pollutant a single vehicle emits per kilometer (g/km), is calculated as a function of travel speed v (km/h). The generic function is

$$EF = (a + cv + ev^2)/(1 + bv + dv^2). \tag{8}$$

The parameters are given in Table 1 to calculate different kinds of emissions and gas consumption, which applies for Euro 3 passenger cars (gas consumption calculation additionally requires a vehicle capacity of 1.4-2.0L). Although diversity of vehicles will slightly influence the computation, the results are still statistically useful as we select the most representative cars in the calculation. As for other pollutants like CO_2 and PM2.5, their emission factors are proportional to fuel consumption (*FC*). For instance, the conversion factor of CO_2 is 3.18 for gasoline, i.e. $EF_{CO_2} = 3.18 \times EF_{FC}$; for $PM_{2.5}$ the conversion factor is 3×10^{-5}. The overall emission on a certain road r is:

$$E = EF \times r.N_a \times r.n \times r.len. \tag{9}$$

Table 1. Pollution emission parameters of COPERT model [8]

	a	b	c	d	e
CO	71.7	35.4	11.4	-0.248	0
Hydrocarbon	5.57×10^{-2}	3.65×10^{-2}	- 1.1×	- 1.88×	1.25×10^{-5}
Nox	9.29×10^{-2}	- 1.22×	- 1.49×	3.97×10^{-5}	6.53×10^{-6}
Fuel Consumption	217	9.6×10^{-2}	0.253	- 4.21×	9.65×10^{-3}

4. EXPERIMENTS

As the model introduced in Section 3.5 has already been tested in environmental research, we focus on evaluating TSE and TVI.

4.1 Settings

4.1.1 Datasets

Road networks: We use the road network of Beijing, which is comprised of 148,110 nodes and 196,307 edges. The road network covers a 40×50km spatial range, with a total length (of road segments) of 21,895km. Road segments with level 0 and 1 are highways. The bigger the level number is, the smaller the road is.

POIs: The datasets consist of 273,165 POIs of Beijing, which are classified into 195 tier two categories. We only choose the top 10 categories that are located nearby road segments most frequently.

GPS Trajectories: We use GPS trajectories generated by 33,000 Beijing taxis over a period of 47 days. The number of GPS points reaches 673,469,757, and the total length of the trajectories is over 26,218,407km. The average sampling rate is 96 seconds per point.

After projecting the trajectories onto the road network, we come up with the statistics shown in Table 2. "% covered/time slot" denotes the proportion of road segments traveled by at least one taxi in a given time slot (we set 10 minutes a time slot in the following experiments). The last row of Table 2 presents the average number of traverses by taxis in a time slot. Figure 9 A) presents the proportion of road segments traveled by taxis at different times. Even during the peak hours, the proportion is only about 20% on workdays and 17.5% on holidays, respectively. In reality, the travel speed derived from only one taxi's trajectory (i.e., sup=1) is not reliable. If counting the number of road segments traveled by three taxis (i.e., sup=3) in a time slot, the proportion decreases to 8% on workdays and 5% on holidays, respectively. Figure 9 B) further shows the proportion changing over the number of traverses. For example, over 90 percent of road segments are traversed by less than 5 taxis in a time slot. The data presented in Table 2 and Figure 9 reveals the sparsity problem we are facing.

Table 2. Statistics on Beijing road network with mapped trajectories

	Level 0,1	Level 2	Level 3	others
Num. of segments	5,061	29,803	142,865	18,578
Total length	1,448km	3,537km	14,747km	2,164km
% covered /time slot	9.97%	7.02%	2.07%	2.94%
# of travels/time slot	1.08	0.42	0.11	0.20

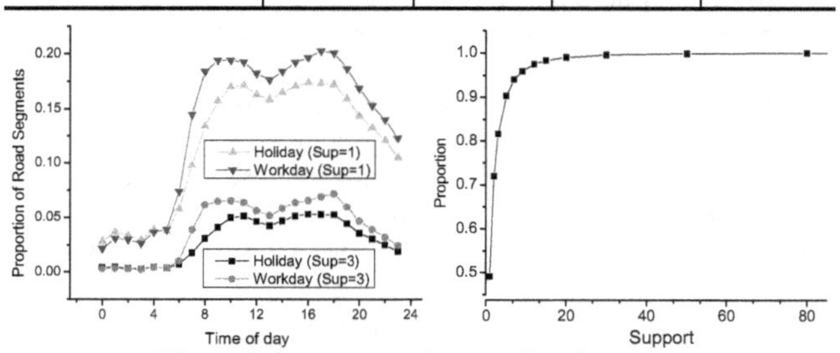

Figure 9. Sparseness of mapped trajectories.

4.1.2 Baselines and Ground Truth

KNN: This baseline uses the average speed and traffic volume of the nearest 3 neighbors to represent a road segment's values.

Kriging is a spatial prediction method with the best linear unbiased estimator [17]. Given a few detected neighbor points $x_i (1 \leq i \leq n)$, Kriging uses a weighted linear combination estimator to predict an unknown point x_0 as follows: $Z^*(x_0) = \sum_{i=1}^{n} \lambda_i Z(x_i)$, where $Z(x_i)$ is a value of location x_i, λ_i is a weight, and n is the number of samples. Using a *Kriging* model with a linear kernel, we interpolate the travel speed of a road segment (absent of taxis) based on its 5 nearest neighbors with data.

Ground Truth: When evaluating TSE, we randomly remove 30% of the non-zero entries from M'_r's last row (i.e., the current time slot) and predict their values using different methods. The 30 percent non-zero entries are then used as a ground truth to measure the accuracy of the predicted values by RMSE (root mean square error), which is defined as

$$RMSE = \sqrt{\frac{\sum_i^n (y_i - \hat{y}_i)^2}{n}} \quad (10)$$

where $\hat{y}_i$is a prediction and y_i is the ground truth.

The ground truth of TVI is collected as introduced in Section 3.4.3. We calculate the mean absolute error (MAE) of volume on each lane (i.e., number of vehicles per minute per lane) as

$$MAE = \left| r.N_a - r.\widehat{N_a} \right| \quad (11)$$

and the mean relative error (MRE) as

$$MRE = \frac{\sum_{r \in RN} |r.N_a - r.\widehat{N_a}| \times r.n}{\sum_{r \in RN} r.N_a \times r.n} \quad (12)$$

where $r.N_a$ is the ground truth of traffic volume on road r's each lane and $r.\widehat{N_a}$ is the prediction; $r.n$ is the number of lanes in r.

Table 3. Ground truth collected for evaluation

Time	7:00 ~ 10:00			10:00~16:00			16:00~20:00			after 20:00			total
Lev.	0,1	2	3	0,1	2	3	0,1	2	3	0,1	2	3	
Holi	0	0	0	6	14	4	6	8	1	4	6	0	49
Work	7	28	8	29	74	9	28	92	7	6	17	4	309
Total	43			136			142			37			358

4.1.3 Configuration of Models

We set 10 minutes as a time slot in our experiment. We partition a city into 4×4 grids and calculate the global position feature f_g and historical traffic pattern M_g (we try different numbers for a partition, finding that 4×4 is slightly better than others). During the experiments, we also found that using 6 time slots (1hour) to formulate M'_r and M'_g results in a relatively higher accuracy. We tried a dynamic extension of our TVI model, and experiment shows that TVI runs much faster without significant accuracy loss. Therefore we keep using the static TVI model in our experiments.

4.2 Evaluation on TSE

In Table 4, we compare the overall performance of TSE with the baseline method that only factorizes current traffic data M'_r, denoted as *MF*(M'_r), or that combines geographic features Z with M'_r, denoted as *MF*($M'_r + Z$), or that combines the temporal correlation between different time slots of M'_G with Z and M'_r, denoted as *MF*($M'_r + M'_g + Z$). As a result, TSE outperforms all the baselines in terms of RMSE of $\bar{v}$ and dv. The historical traffic patterns that TSE incorporates are very helpful, bringing a significant decrease of RMSE (about 0.5) over *MF*($M'_r + M'_g + Z$). In addition, TSE has very good efficiency, much more so than Kriging. By only using one server (with 4-core, 3.4GHz CPU and 8GB RAM), TSE can infer the travel speed of every single road segment in Beijing within 22 seconds.

Table 4. Overall performance of different methods

Methods	RMSE of $\bar{v}$	RMSE of dv	Time (sec)
MF(M'_r)	2.172	1.833	2.2
MF($M'_r + Z$)	1.939	1.385	18.2
MF($M'_r + M'_g + Z$)	1.908	1.314	20.2
TSE	**1.369**	**1.035**	**22.2**
Kriging	2.340	1.300	1,000
KNN	3.360	1.590	0.14

Figure 10 A) further explores the performance of TSE changing over time of day. As there are only a few taxis traveling on road surfaces after 10pm and before 8am (see Figure 9 for a proof), the corresponding estimation error is bigger than other time slots. As time goes by, we observe more taxis in the road network (i.e., more road segments are covered by trajectories). Consequently, the RMSE decreases and reaches its best performance at 4pm. While the number of taxis is approaching to its peak at 4pm, the traffic conditions start stepping into congestions. If focusing on estimating the gas consumption and pollution in daytime, our model is more accurate than the results presented in Table 4.

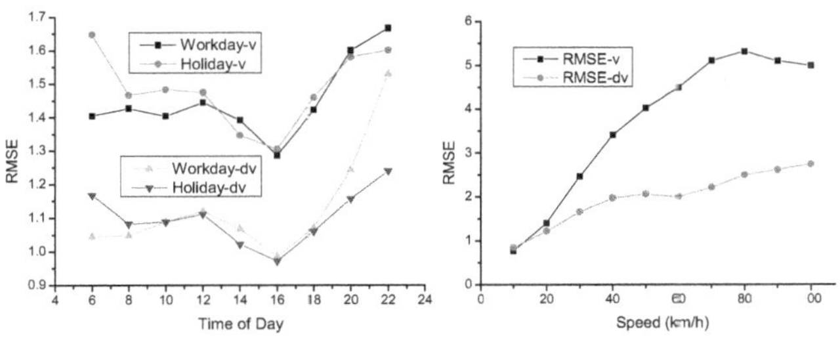

A) Changing over time of day B) Changing over speed

Figure 10. Exploration of TSE's effectiveness

Figure 10 B) shows the RMSE of TSE changing over the (real) travel speed of a road segment to be estimated. Intuitively, a high speed indicates a good traffic condition, in which people have more flexibility in traveling with different speeds. As a result, the variance of speeds (dv) on a road segment can be big and become relatively difficult to estimate. In addition, the number of road segments that allow a high travel speed is small, making it difficult for TSE model to fill in missing values. However, a highway ($\geq$90km/h) usually has the lowest driving speed constraint, or people have the concern in mind when traveling on it. This will reduce the flexibility of driving at different speeds, possibly leading to the drop of RMSE after 90km/h in Figure 10 B).

Table 5. Effectiveness of TSE on different levels of road segments

RMSE	level 0-1	level 2	level 3	level >=4
Speed	2.575	1.189	0.977	1.612
Variance	1.526	1.128	0.628	1.234

We further explore the performance of TSE on different levels of road segments in Table 5. It is worth noting that TSE has a good performance on level 2 and 3 road segments, which covers 88.5% of Beijing's road network. These road segments do not usually have a loop sensor. So, it is important to have a method like TSE that can infer the travel speed on such road segments.

4.3 Evaluation on TVI

Table 6 presents the overall performance of TVI. Using the test data presented in Table 3, we compare TVI with six baselines: we first study not using the variance of speed dv (*TVI w/o* dv) and weather conditions w (*TVI w/o* w) in our model, and then compare TVI with several existing methods, e.g., linear regression (*LR*) and fundamental diagram (*FD*).

Clearly, TVI has better performance beyond *TVI* w/o dv and *TVI* w/o w. As traffic conditions depend on the weather condition, e.g., on rainy days the traffic speed is much slower and thus traffic volume is smaller, information on weather conditions does help improve inference accuracy. Besides, having dv together with $\bar{v}$, we can better reveal the traffic conditions on road segments, thereby inferring traffic volumes more accurately. According to the efficiency study, TVI is very efficient, inferring the traffic volume in Beijing's road network in 0.84 seconds, (i.e., $7\mu s$ each).

Table 6. Overall performance of TVI

Methods	MAE	MRE	Inference time (us/road)
TVI	**3.01**	**29%**	**7.27**
TVI w/o dv	3.19	31%	7.18
TVI w/o w	3.15	29%	7.10
LR	3.06	27%	0.15
FD	2.66	16%	0.13
FD-SC	3.9	42%	0.13
FD-DC	6.7	137%	0.13

We also compare TVI with two supervised methods, consisting of linear regression (*LR*) and Fundamental Diagram (*FD*), which learn a curve simulating the relation between the traffic volume and travel speed on a particular road segment based on a large volume of training data. For *LR*, we use half of the data as a training set and another half for a test. W.r.t. *FD*, we select three road segments with enough labels, using half for training and half for testing. Our TVI model outperforms the supervised LR and has a slightly bigger error than FD. Note that TVI is an unsupervised model that can scale up to the entire road network. Designing an unsupervised method with an accuracy even better than a supervised approach is indeed a contribution. In addition, the performance of *TVI* is tested based on the whole dataset presented in Table 1, while *FD* is only tested on three roads and *LR* is on half roads. Tested on the same three road segments, TVI has a volume error of 2.73 which is even closer to that of *FD*. It should be noted that *FD* needs training for each individual road segment, some of which may have no volume data at all. To address this issue, we first cluster road segments into a few groups in terms of their geographical features in matrix Z. We train a *FD* model based on the data from some road segments in a cluster, and then apply the model to other road segments in the same cluster (*FD-SC*). The performance decreases very quickly. If applying the model trained from one cluster to another cluster, the volume error is even bigger. These results denote that *FD* is not scalable to an entire road network.

Table 7 further explores the performance of TVI on different road levels and in different type of days. It turns out that TVI has a better performance on level 2 road segments which are absent of a loop sensor but with a large volume of traffic, and thus are our major concerns. Additionally, TVI has a better performance on weekdays than weekends, as some taxi drivers do not work on weekends, and traffic conditions on weekends are relatively irregular and complex compared to weekdays.

Table 7. Exploration of the performance of TVI

	level 0-1	level 2	Weekday	Weekend
MAE	5.55	2.23	2.97	3.28
MRE	22%	41%	29%	30%

Table 8 further presents the time that different components spend on processing the data of a time slot (i.e., 10 minutes), if we only use a single core of a single server. Note that we can map-match the trajectories of different drivers separately and infer the traffic volume on different road segments independently. Using five cores of the server to perform the map-matching and TVI in parallel, we can infer the travel speed, traffic volume, energy consumption, and pollution emission throughout Beijing's road network in 1 minute.

Table 8. Efficiency of different components of our method

Online components	Time	Offline components	Time
Map-matching	4.94min	Geo-feature extraction	149s
TSE	22.2s	Historical pattern extraction	240s
TVI (inference)	0.84s	TVI learning	89s
Total	5.32min	Total	478s

4.4 Visualization

Figure 11 visualizes the traffic volume, energy consumption, and pollution emission around Beijing Olympic Park on a weekday (2013/9/17 Tuesday), weekend (2013/9/21 Saturday), and public holiday (2013/10/2), respectively.

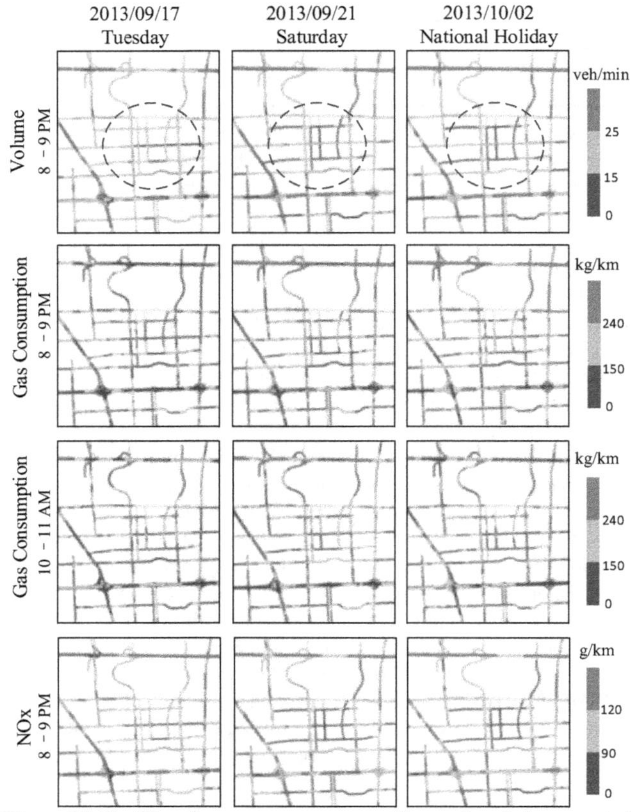

Figure 11. Traffic volume, energy consumption and emissions around Beijing Olympic Park in different time slots

As depicted in the first row, in time slot 8-9pm, the region has a bigger traffic volume during the weekday than during the weekend and holiday. This is aligned with our commonsense knowledge that people usually visit this region in the daytime (rather than in the evening) of weekends or a holiday. The large volume of traffic on a weekday is caused by people who drive home after work passing by this region. Given the same reason, in the second row of Figure 11, we observe more red road segments, which denotes more energy consumption, on the weekday than on the weekend and the national holiday. The latter two days generally have a similar energy consumption pattern except several road segments where the national holiday is slightly higher than the weekend. The former has relatively more sightseeing buses arriving at the park or more tourists taking taxis to this region in the evening (than the latter). On the contrary, in the time slot from 10 to 11am, we observe more energy consumption on the weekend and holiday, as many people drive to the park at these times for fun. On a workday, after morning rush hours (e.g., 8-10am), people barely drive to this place during working time. The emissions of $PM_{2.5}$ and CO_2 have the same pattern as the energy consumption, just having different factors (3×10^{-5} and 3.18 respectively). The last row of Figure 11 presents the emission of NO_x in the region, where the workday has more emission than the weekend and national holiday in 8-9pm.

Figure 12 demonstrates the gas consumption and emission of NO_x around Zhongguancun area, which is a place mixed with many companies and entertainments, in the aforementioned three days, respectively. In the time slot from 3pm to 4pm, the time before evening rush hours, this area has less gas consumption on the workday than during the weekend and holiday, because people are still working indoors. When time goes to weekends and holidays, many people travel to this region for the purpose of entertainment, e.g., go shopping and watch a movie, leading to more energy consumption and emission of CO, as illustrated in the two rows of Figure 12. There is a movie theater, a supermarket, and two shopping centers located in the region marked by the broken curve.

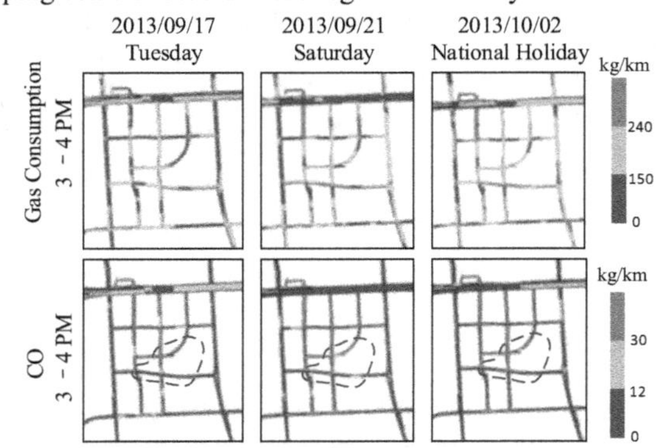

Figure 12. Gas consumption and pollution emission around Zhonguancun area

Figures 13, 14 and 15 show the citywide traffic volume, gas consumption, and NO_x emission on three types of days: weekdays, weekends, and public holidays. The number plotted in the three figures are averaged by day, respectively. Figure 13 presents the average traffic volume on a road segment in one minute, which depends on the travel speed on the road segment and the density of the traffic. Before 7am, a workday has a larger volume of traffic than a weekend or a holiday. At this moment, the travel speed is very fast during the three types of days, while more people travel (to work) on a weekday than a holiday. When time goes to 8-10am (i.e., Beijing's morning rush hours on workdays), however, the travel speed decreases significantly on a weekday, reducing the traffic volume that can pass a road segment. The weekend and holiday have a similar decreasing trend, but do not drop tremendously, because the travel speed is not that slow from 8am to 10am. After morning rush hours, the travel speed increases, leading to an increase of the traffic volume. Then, we see the decreasing pattern repeats in evening rush hours, 5-7pm, during a weekday. After evening rush hours, the traffic volume increases again with the increase of the travel speed on a weekday, until at later night when the traffic density decreases tremendously (we do not show the traffic volume after 11pm in these figures as they are very small and quite similar to each other). The public holiday has a bigger traffic flow than the other two days, as a portion of people leave Beijing for vacation, which reduces the traffic density slightly but enhances the travel speeds on roads significantly.

Figure 14 shows the total energy consumption of the entire road network per hour changing over time of day. For instance, from 12pm to 1pm, about 3,850,000 liters of gasoline are consumed by vehicles in Beijing. Supposing there are 2 million vehicles traveling on the road network in this time slot, each vehicle consumes 1.9 liter gasoline per hour, which is about 19 kilometers per hour. A peak occurs in this time slot due to the bigger traffic volume and travel speed. The reason a public holiday consumes more energy may lie in the fast travel speed and a farther distance that people would travel during holidays.

Figure 15 presents the total emission of NO_x in Beijing's road network, where weekends have the largest volume in the afternoon.

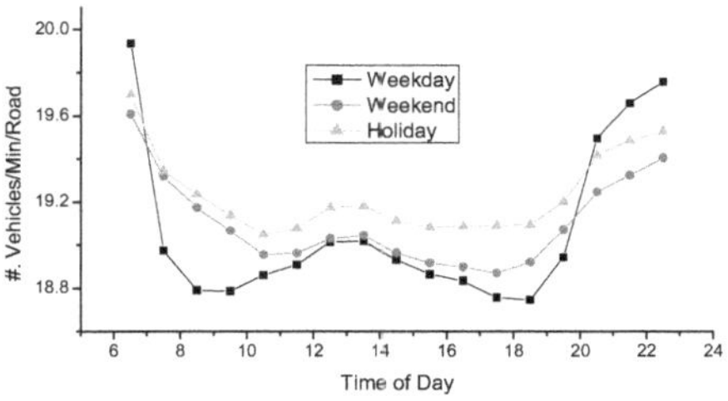

Figure 13. The citywide traffic volume of Beijing

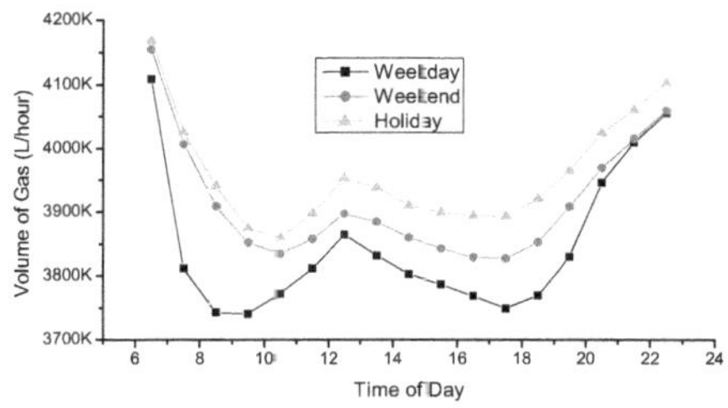

Figure 14. Citywide gas consumption

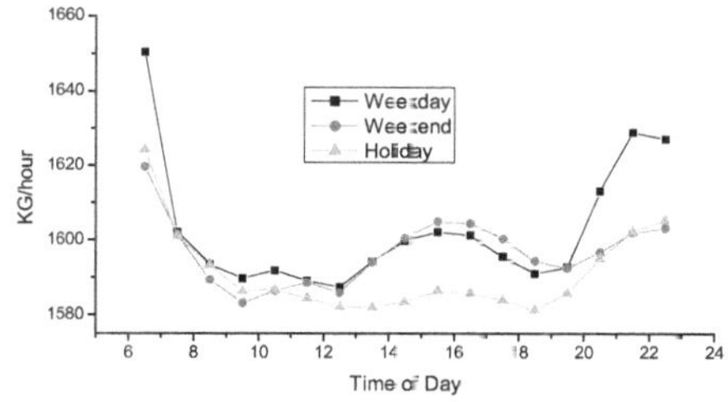

Figure 15. Citywide NOx emission

Figure 16. Geo-distribution of Traffic Volume

Figure 17. Geo-distribution of energy consumption

Figure 18. Geo-distribution of NOx emission

Beijing is running a traffic control policy based on the license ID of a car on workdays. As this policy does not apply to weekends and holidays, the number of people who travel by car is even bigger on a weekend. On public holidays, many people leave the city for vacation, therefore the emissions are not heavy. Combining Figure 14 and 15, we find that public holidays have more gas consumption but less emission than weekdays and weekends, i.e., the energy has been used in a cleaner way.

Figure 16 visualizes the mean traffic volume (i.e., the average number of vehicles per minute) traversing every road segment in Beijing from 6am to 10pm on workdays. The road segments with relatively large volumes of traffic (marked red) are mainly located in the south (e.g., the southern segments of the fifth ring road) and some highways spreading towards rural areas. As the major business and entertainment areas are located in the northern and central part of Beijing, the average travel speed in these places are generally slower than the southern part. The slow speed reduces the traffic volume on corresponding road segments. The traffic volume on the northern segment of the fourth ring road is relatively larger than other road segments in the north part, which well matches our commonsense knowledge. Figure 17 presents the average energy consumption of vehicles on each road segment per hour, from 6am-10pm. As the total energy consumption depends on both travel speed and traffic volume, some road segments marked red in Figure 16 become green in Figure 17. Given this kind of visualization, urban planners and transportation authorities can identify the road segments that have wasted unnecessary energy (e.g., a road segment with small traffic volume while having a large energy consumption), therefore informing future urban planning. Figure 18 displays the total NO_x emission on road segments per hour in the same time slot, where the ring roads and highways have more emissions. When the emission on some road segments exceeds a threshold, we can send alerts to people passing by or living around. The information can also guide drivers for finding the best route in terms of the energy consumption, air quality, and travel time.

5. RELATED WORK

5.1 Traffic Condition Modeling

Traffic modeling on individual roads: Conventional methods use traffic monitoring cameras (usually combined with a speedometer) to observe speed and volume data where relevant instrumentation is installed. This kind of approach usually employs a Fundamental Diagram [1, 3] to learn a specific relation among travel speed, traffic density, and volume for a particular road, from a large amount of data collected by the camera and speedometer. As the number of vehicles traversing a road may not be perfectly detected by using automatic computer vision algorithms, in most cases, human effort is needed to count the vehicles so as to generate training data for the fundamental diagram. Consequently, this kind of methods is difficult to scale up to an entire city, let alone the limited coverage of traffic monitoring camera and speedometers. Later, in-road loop sensors are widely deployed to detect both travel speed and traffic volume. The rich data enables sophisticated modeling to simulate traffic status between the instrument [7, 13], or predict future traffic status [5], for a specific road where the device is installed. Unfortunately, the majority of these models do not incorporate the correlation between the traffic conditions of different road segments (especially those that are geospatially disconnected), when estimating the traffic on a road segment. Some methods [5] model several connected road segments simultaneously with a Markov Model. However, applying these methods to the entire road network will result in a huge model that has very poor efficiency and big issues with training parameters. Additionally, the coverage of loop-sensor systems is also limited due to the high expense for device installation and maintenance.

Traffic modeling on a road network: Recently, more traffic modeling systems have turned to using Floating Car Data [10, 15], which is generated by vehicles traveling around a city with a GPS sensor. The trajectories of these vehicles will be sent to a central system and matched onto the road network for deriving speed on road segments. However, due to the uneven distribution of the probing vehicles as well as the low sampling rate of GPS data (e.g., one point per minute), many road segments are not covered by any trajectory [17]. To address this problem, some interpolation-based methods, such as KNN and Kriging [18], have been proposed to infer the traffic conditions of a road segment based on the values of its spatial neighbors. More advanced methods model the traffic conditions on a road network with a road-time matrix, where each entry stands for the traffic conditions at a specific road segment and in a particular time slot. These methods then adopt Compressive Sensing-based algorithms [16, 17] to fill in the missing entries in the matrix. The interpolation-based methods consider the spatial correlation among different locations' traffic conditions, and the compressive sensing-based approach considers both spatial and temporal correlations. Unlike these methods, our model incorporates two additional (but very helpful) correlations from extra data sources. One is the correlation between road segments in terms of their geographic features, such as the length, POI distributions, and number of connections, learned from road network and POI datasets. The geographic features capture the local and global similarity between two road segments simultaneously. The other is the correlation between the current and historical traffic conditions, learned from historical trajectories over a period of time. Extensive experiments validate the contribution of these correlations beyond the original correlation solely learned from the road-time matrix.

5.2 Energy and Emission Estimation

Vehicular fuel consumption and pollutant emission is a critical environmental issue nowadays. [9] studies the empirical relation between traffic emissions and travel speed as well as the acceleration for a single vehicle. [2] exploited a framework similar to ours to estimate macroscopic pollutant emissions. The main concern with this method is the use of the historical average to deal with the aforementioned data sparsity problem. Consequently, irregular conditions (e.g., congestions caused by accidents) are not well captured. In addition, it applies a homogeneous FD to different roads in the same cluster, which has been compared with our method as a baseline (*FD-SC*).

There also exist crowdsensing-based approaches [4, 12] that sense environmental data using people or vehicles carrying air quality sensors. These methods cannot bypass the data sparsity problem either when scaling up to a citywide application, as the number of sensors is even smaller than the number of GPS-equipped vehicles. These approaches also do not answer the questions, such as how much pollutant is generated from traffic.

6. CONCLUSION

In this paper, we instantly infer the traffic volume, energy consumption, and the emissions of vehicles traveling on a city's road networks, based on the GPS trajectories received from a sample of vehicles, e.g., GPS-equipped taxicabs, in current time slot and over a period of history. The knowledge derived from our research can enable many valuable applications for social good, such as timely road-level pollution alerts, monitoring citywide traffic conditions, improving urban planning, and helping study the root cause of air pollution. This is a very challenging problem, however, considering its efficiency, effectiveness, and scalability. We address this problem through a three step approach, where we first propose TSE model to compute the travel speed on each road segment based on incomplete trajectory data, then infer the volume of a road segment by using TVI model, and finally calculate the energy consumption and pollution emission based on the inferred travel speed and traffic volume. We evaluate our approach based on extensive experiments that use GPS trajectories generated by over 32,000 taxicabs over a period of two months. The results demonstrate the effectiveness, efficiency and scalability of our method, which outperforms baseline approaches, such as Linear Regression, Fundamental Diagram, and Kriging. Using five cores of a server, we can grasp the traffic conditions, energy consumption, and emissions of the past 10 minutes throughout Beijing's road network within 1 minute.

REFERENCES

[1] Greenshields, B. D., Bibbins, J. R., Channing, W. S., and Miller, H. H. 1935. A study of traffic capacity. In Highway research board proceedings (Vol. 14).

[2] Gühnemann, A., Schäfer, R. P., Thiessenhusen, K. U., and Wagner, P. 2004. Monitoring traffic and emissions by floating car data. Institute of Transport Studies Working Paper, (ITS-WP-04-07).

[3] Helbing, D. 2001. Traffic and related self-driven many-particle systems. Reviews of modern physics, 73(4), 1067.

[4] Honicky, R., Brewer, E. A., Paulos, E., and White, R. 2008. N-smarts: networked suite of mobile atmospheric real-time sensors. In Proc. of the second ACM SIGCOMM workshop on Networked systems for developing regions (pp. 25-30).

[5] Kwon, J., and Murphy, K. 2000. Modeling freeway traffic with coupled HMMs. Technical report, Univ. California, Berkeley.

[6] Lou, Y., Zhang, C., Zheng, Y., Xie, X., Wang, W., and Huang, Y. 2009. Map-matching for low-sampling-rate GPS trajectories. In Proc. of ACM SIGSPATIAL GIS, 352-361.

[7] Muñoz, L., Sun, X., Horowitz, R., and Alvarez, L. 2003. Traffic density estimation with the cell transmission model. In Proc. of the 2003 American Control Conference, Vol. 5, 3750-3755.

[8] Ntziachristos, L., Samaras, Z., Eggleston, S., Gorissen, N., Hassel, D., and Hickman, A. J. 2000. COPERT III. Computer Programme to calculate emissions from road transport, methodology and emission factors (version 2.1). European Energy Agency (EEA), Copenhagen.

[9] Panis, L.I., Broekx, S., and Liu, R. 2006. Modelling instantaneous traffic emission and the influence of traffic speed limits. Science of the total environment, 371(1), 270-285.

[10] Schäfer, R. P., Thiessenhusen, K. U., and Wagner, P. 2002. A traffic information system by means of real-time floating-car data. In ITS world congress (Vol. 2).

[11] Smit, R., Ntziachristos, L., and Boulter, P. 2010. Validation of road vehicle and traffic emission models–A review and meta-analysis. Atmospheric environment, 44(25), 2943-2953.

[12] Steed, A., Spinello, S., Croxford, B., and Greenhalgh, C. 2003. E-Science in the streets: urban pollution monitoring. In UK e-science all hands meeting.

[13] Wilkie, D., Sewall, J., and Lin, M. 2013. Flow reconstruction for data-driven traffic animation. ACM Trans. on Graphics, 32(4), 89.

[14] Xie S., Song X., and Shen X. 2006. Calculating Vehicular Emission Factors with COPERTIII Mode in China. Environmental Science, 27(3), 415-419.

[15] Yuan, J., Zheng, Y., Zhang, C., Xie, W., Xie, X., Sun, G., and Huang, Y. 2010. T-drive: driving directions based on taxi trajectories. In Proc. of the 18th SIGSPATIAL GIS, 99-108.

[16] Zhang, Y., Roughan, M., Willinger, W., and Qiu, L. 2009. Spatio-temporal compressive sensing and internet traffic matrices. In ACM SIGCOMM Computer Communication Review, 39(4), 267-278.

[17] Zhu, Y., Li, Z., Zhu, H., Li, M., and Zhang, Q. 2013. A compressive sensing approach to urban traffic estimation with probe vehicles. Mobile Computing, IEEE Transactions on, 12(11), 2289-2302.

[18] Zou, H. X., Yue, Y., Li, Q. Q., and Yeh, A. G. O. 2011. Traffic data interpolation method of non-detection road link based on Kriging interpolation. Jiaotong Yunshu Gongcheng Xuebao, 11(3), 118-126.

[19] Zheng, Y., Capra, Li, Wolfson, O., Yang, H. 2014. Urban computing: concepts, methodologies, and applications. ACM Trans. On Intelligent systems and Technology, 5(3).

[20] Data released: http://research.microsoft.com/apps/pubs/?id=217455

Methods for Ordinal Peer Grading

Karthik Raman
Department of Computer Science
Cornell University, Ithaca NY 14853
karthik@cs.cornell.edu

Thorsten Joachims
Department of Computer Science
Cornell University, Ithaca NY 14853
tj@cs.cornell.edu

ABSTRACT

Massive Online Open Courses have the potential to revolutionize higher education with their wide outreach and accessibility, but they require instructors to come up with scalable alternates to traditional *student evaluation*. Peer grading – having students assess each other – is a promising approach to tackling the problem of evaluation at scale, since the number of "graders" naturally scales with the number of students. However, students are not trained in grading, which means that one cannot expect the same level of grading skills as in traditional settings. Drawing on broad evidence that *ordinal* feedback is easier to provide and more reliable than *cardinal* feedback [5, 38, 29, 9], it is therefore desirable to allow peer graders to make ordinal statements (e.g. "project X is better than project Y") and not require them to make cardinal statements (e.g. "project X is a B-"). Thus, in this paper we study the problem of automatically inferring student grades from ordinal peer feedback, as opposed to existing methods that require cardinal peer feedback. We formulate the ordinal peer grading problem as a type of rank aggregation problem, and explore several probabilistic models under which to estimate student grades and grader reliability. We study the applicability of these methods using peer grading data collected from a real class — with instructor and TA grades as a baseline — and demonstrate the efficacy of ordinal feedback techniques in comparison to existing cardinal peer grading methods. Finally, we compare these peer-grading techniques to traditional evaluation techniques.

Categories and Subject Descriptors

H.4 [**Information Systems Applications**]: Miscellaneous

General Terms

Algorithms, Experimentation, Theory

Keywords

Peer Grading, Ordinal Feedback, Rank Aggregation

KDD'14, August 24–27, 2014, New York, NY, USA.

ACM 978-1-4503-2956-9/14/08 ...$15.00.
http://dx.doi.org/10.1145/2623330.2623654.

1. INTRODUCTION

The advent of *MOOCs* (Massive Online Open Courses) promises unprecedented access to education given their relatively low costs and broad reach, empowering learning across a diverse range of subjects for anyone with access to the Internet. Classes frequently have upwards of 20000 students, which is orders of magnitude larger than a conventional university class. Thus, instructors are forced to rethink classroom logistics and practices so as to scale to MOOCs.

One of the key open challenges is *student evaluation* for such large classes. Traditional assessment practices, such as instructors or teaching assistants (TAs) grading individual student assignments, are simply infeasible at this scale. Consequently, assignments in most current MOOCs take the form of simple multiple-choice questions and other schemes that can be graded automatically. However, relying on such rigid testing schemes does not necessarily serve as a good indicator of learning and falls short of conventional test-design standards [16, 17]. Furthermore, such a restrictive testing methodology limits the learning outcomes that can be tested, or even limits the kinds of courses that can be offered. For example, liberal-arts courses and research-oriented classes require more open-ended assignments and responses (e.g., essays, project proposals, project reports).

Peer grading has the potential to overcome the limitations outlined above while scaling to the size of even the largest MOOCs. In peer grading, students — not instructors or TAs — provide feedback on the work of other students in their class [14, 22], meaning that the number of "graders" naturally grows with the number of students. While the scaling properties of peer grading are attractive, there are several challenges in making peer grading work.

One key challenge lies in the fact that students are not trained graders, which argues for making the feedback process as simple as possible. Given broad evidence that for many tasks *ordinal* feedback is easier to provide and more reliable than *cardinal* feedback [5, 38, 29, 9], it is therefore desirable to base peer grading on ordinal feedback (e.g. "project X is better than project Y"). Unfortunately, all existing methods for aggregating peer feedback into an overall assessment require that students provide *cardinal* feedback (e.g. "project X is a B-"). Furthermore, the efficacy of simple techniques for aggregating cardinal feedback, such as averaging, has been questioned [7, 10, 30]. While probabilistic machine learning methods have recently been proposed to address these challenges [32], they still face the problem that students may be grading on different scales. For example, students may have a preconception of what constitutes a B+

based on the university they come from. These scales may also be non-linear as the difference between an A+ and an A may not be the same as the difference between a C+ and a C.

To overcome the problems of cardinal feedback, we introduce the task of *ordinal peer grading* in this paper. By having students give ordinal statements and not cardinal statements as feedback, we offload the problem of developing a scale from the student onto the peer grading algorithm. The key technical contributions of this paper lie in the development of methods for ordinal peer grading, where the goal is to automatically infer an overall assessment of a set of assignments from ordinal peer feedback. Furthermore, a secondary goal of our methods is to infer how accurately each student provides feedback, so that reliable grading can be incentivized (e.g., as a component of the overall grade). To this effect, we propose several machine learning methods for *ordinal peer grading*, which differ by how probability distributions over rankings are modeled. For these models, we provide efficient algorithms for estimating assignment grades and grader reliabilities.

To study the applicability of our methods in real-world settings, we collected peer-assessment data as part of a university-level course. Using this data, we demonstrate the efficacy of the proposed ordinal feedback techniques in comparison to the existing cardinal feedback techniques. Furthermore, we compare our ordinal peer grading methods with traditional evaluation techniques that were used in the course in parallel. Using this classroom data we also investigate other properties of these techniques, such as their robustness, data dependence and self-consistency. Finally, we analyze the responses to a survey completed by students in the classroom experiment, indicating that most students found the peer grading experience (receiving and providing feedback) helpful and valuable.

2. THE PEER GRADING PROBLEM

We begin by formally defining the peer grading problem, as it presents itself from a machine learning perspective. We are given a set of $|D|$ *assignments* $D = \{d_1, ..., d_{|D|}\}$ (*e.g.*, essays, reports) which need to be graded. Grading is done by a set of $|G|$ graders $G = \{g_1, ..., g_{|G|}\}$ (*e.g.*, student peer grader, reviewers), where each grader receives a subset $D_g \subset D$ to assess. The choice of assignments for each grader can be uniformly random, or can follow a deterministic or sequential design. In either case, the number of assignments that any grader assesses $|D_g|$ is much smaller than the total number of assignments $|D|$ (*e.g.*, $|D_g| \approx 10$).

Each grader provides feedback for his or her set of assignments D_g. Ordinal and cardinal peer grading differ in the type of feedback a grader is expected to give:

Cardinal Peer Grading (CPG): In cardinal peer grading, each grader g provides cardinal-valued feedback for each item $d \in D_g$. Typically, this is a numeric or categorical response which we denote as $y_d^{(g)}$ (*e.g.*, Likert scale, letter grade).

Ordinal Peer Grading (OPG): In ordinal peer grading, each grader g returns an ordering $\sigma^{(g)}$ (possibly with ties) of his or her assignments D_g, indicating relative but not absolute quality. More generally, ordinal feedback could also consist of multiple pairwise preferences, but we focus on the case of a single ordering in this paper.

$D_g(\subset D)$	Set of items graded by grader g
$s_d(\in \Re)$	Predicted grade for item d (larger is better)
$\eta_g(\in \Re^+)$	Predicted reliability of grader g
σ_g	Ranking feedback (with possible ties) from g
$r_d^{(\sigma)}$	Rank of item d in ranking σ (rank 1 is best)
ρ_g	Set of pairwise preference feedback from g
$d_2 \succ_\sigma d_1$	d_2 is preferred/ranked higher than d_1 (in σ)
$\pi(A)$	Set of all rankings over $A \subseteq D$
$\sigma_1 \sim \sigma_2$	$\exists$ way of resolving ties in σ_2 to obtain σ_1

Table 1: Notation overview and reference.

Independent of the type of feedback that graders provide, the goal in peer grading is twofold.

We call the first goal *grade estimation*, which is the task of estimating the true quality of the assignments in D from the grader feedback. We distinguish between two types of grade estimation, which differ by how they express assignment quality. In *ordinal grade estimation*, the goal is to infer a ranking $\hat{\sigma}$ of all assignments in D that most accurately reflects some true ordering (by quality) σ^*. In *cardinal grade estimation*, the goal is to infer a cardinal grade $\hat{s}_d$ for each $d \in D$ that most accurately reflects each true grade s_d^*. Note that the type of feedback does not necessarily determine whether the output of grade estimation is ordinal or cardinal. In particular, we will see that some of our methods can infer cardinal grades even if only given ordinal feedback.

The second goal is *grader reliability estimation*, which is the task of estimating how accurate the feedback of a grader is. Estimating grader reliability is important for at least two reasons. First, identifying unreliable grades allows us to downweight their feedback for grade estimation. Second, and more importantly, it allows us to incentivize good and thorough grading by making peer grading itself part of the overall grade. In the following, we will typically represent the reliability of a grader as a single number $\eta_g \in \Re^+$.

In the following sections, we derive and evaluate methods for grade estimation and grader reliability estimation in the Ordinal Peer Grading setting.

2.1 Related Work in Rank Aggregation

The grade estimation problem in Ordinal Peer Grading can be viewed as a specific type of rank aggregation problem. Rank aggregation describes a class of problem related to combining the information contained in rankings from multiple sources. Many popular methods used today [15, 25, 11] build on classical models and techniques such as the seminal work by Thurstone [39], Mallows [28], Bradley & Terry [8], Luce [27] and Plackett [33]. These techniques have been used in different domains, each of which have branched off their own set of methods.

Search Result Aggregation (also known as **Rank Fusion** or **Metasearch**) has the goal of merging search result rankings from different sources to produce a single output ranking. Such aggregation has been widely used to improve over the performance of any single ranker in both supervised and unsupervised settings [3, 34, 40, 31]. Rank aggregation for search differs from Ordinal Peer Grading in several aspects. First, grader reliability estimation is not a goal in itself. Second, the success of search result aggregation depends mostly on correctly identifying the top items, while grade estimation aims to accurately estimate the full ranking. Third, ties and data sparsity are not an issue in search result aggregation, since (at least in principle) input rankings are total orders over all results.

Algorithm 1 Normal Cardinal-Score (NCS) Algorithm (called $\mathbf{PG}_1$ in [32]) is used as a baseline in our experiments

$s_d \sim \mathcal{N}(\mu_0, \frac{1}{\gamma_0})$ ▷ True Scores
$\eta_g \sim Gamma(\alpha_0, \beta_0)$ ▷ Grader Reliability
$b_g \sim \mathcal{N}(0, \frac{1}{\gamma_1})$ ▷ Grader Bias (Only for NCS+G)
$y_d^{(g)} \sim \mathcal{N}(s_d + b_g, \frac{1}{\eta_g})$ ▷ Observed Cardinal Peer Grade
Estimate $\hat{s}_d, \hat{\eta}_g$ and $\hat{b}_g$ ▷ Using MLE

Social Choice and Voting Systems perform rank aggregation on preferences that a set of individuals stated over competing items/interests/candidates. The goal is to identify the most preferred alternatives given conflicting preferences [2]. Commonly used aggregation techniques are the *Borda count* and other Condorcet voting schemes [3, 13, 26]. These methods are ill-suited for the OPG problem, as they do not model voter reliability, typically assume rankings of all alternatives (or at least leave the choice of alternatives up to the voter), and usually focus on the top of the rankings.

Crowdsourcing is probably the most closely related application domain, where the goal is to merge the feedback from multiple *crowdworkers* [19, 6]. Due to the differing quality of these workers, modeling the worker reliability is essential [35, 11]. The key difference in our setting is that the number of items is large and we would like to correctly order all of them, not just identify the top-few.

Rank-aggregation has also been used for other settings such as multilabel/multiclass classification (by combining different classifiers) [23] or for learning player skills in a gaming environment [18]. Is is impossible to survey the vast literature on this topic and thus we refer the interested reader to a comprehensive survey on the topic [24]. These techniques have also been adapted for educational assessment [4], via a graphical model based approach, for modeling the difficulty of questions and estimating the correct answers in a crowdsourced setting. However these techniques are neither applicable for a peer grading setting nor can they handle open-ended answers (like essays).

2.2 Related Work in Peer Grading

With the advent of online courses, peer grading has been increasingly used for large classes with mixed results [7, 10, 30]. While most previous uses of peer grading have relied on simple estimation techniques like averaging cardinal feedback scores, recently a probabilistic learning algorithms has been proposed for peer grade estimation [32]. However, this method requires that students provide *cardinal* scores as grades. A second limitation of the method in [32] is that they incentivize grader reliability by relating it to the grader's own assignment score. However, such a setup is inappropriate when there are groups (such as our setting) or where external graders/reviewers are used (*e.g.*, conference reviewing). In addition, such an indirect incentive is harder to communicate and justify compared to the direct grader reliability estimates used in our case. Lastly their approach requires that each student grades some assignments that were previously graded by the instructor in order to estimate grader reliability. This seems wasteful, given that students are only able to grade a small number of assignments in total. We empirically compare their cardinal peer grading technique (Algorithm 1, using MLE instead of Gibbs sampling) with the ordinal peer grading techniques proposed in this paper.

Overall, given the limited amount of attention that the peer grading problem has received in the machine learning literature so far, we believe there is ample opportunity to improve on the state-of-the-art and address shortcomings that currently exist [36], which is reinforced by concurrent work on the topic by others [12, 37].

3. ORDINAL PEER GRADING METHODS

In this section, we develop ordinal peer grading methods for grade estimation and then extend these methods to the problem of grader reliability estimation. **Our methods are publicly available as software at `www.peergrading.org`,** where we also provide a **web service for peer grade estimation**. These methods require as data an i.i.d. sample of orderings

$$S = (\sigma^{(g_1)}, ..., \sigma^{(g_{|G|})}), \tag{1}$$

where each ordering sorts a subset of assignments according to the judgment of grader g_i.

3.1 Grade Estimation

Our grade estimation methods are based on models that represent probability distributions over rankings. In particular, we extend Mallow's Model (Sec 3.1.1), the Bradley-Terry model (Sec 3.1.3), Thurstone's model (Sec 3.1.4), and the Plackett-Luce model (Sec 3.1.5) as appropriate for the ordinal peer grading problem.

3.1.1 Mallows Model (MAL and MALBC)

Mallow's model [28] describes a distribution over rankings σ in terms of the distance $\delta(\bar{\sigma}, \sigma)$ from a central ranking $\bar{\sigma}$, which in our setting is the true ranking σ^* of assignments by quality.

$$P(\sigma|\bar{\sigma}) = \frac{e^{-\delta(\bar{\sigma},\sigma)}}{\sum_{\sigma'} e^{-\delta(\bar{\sigma},\sigma')}} \tag{2}$$

While maximum likelihood estimation of σ^* given observed rankings is NP-hard for many distance functions [13, 34], tractable approximations are known for special cases. In this work, we use the following tractable **Kendall-τ distance** [20], which assumes that both rankings are total orderings over all assignments.

Definition 1. *We define the Kendall-τ Distance δ_K between ranking σ_1 and ranking σ_2 as*

$$\delta_K(\sigma_1, \sigma_2) = \sum_{d_1 \succ_{\sigma_1} d_2} \mathbb{I}[[d_2 \succ_{\sigma_2} d_1]] \tag{3}$$

It measures the number of incorrectly ordered pairs between the two rankings. In our case, the rankings that students provide can have ties. We interpret these ties as *indifference* (*i.e.*, agnostic to either ranking), which leads to the following model, where the summation in the numerator is over all total orderings σ' consistent with the weak ordering σ.

$$P(\sigma|\bar{\sigma}) = \frac{\sum_{\sigma' \sim \sigma} e^{-\delta(\bar{\sigma},\sigma')}}{\sum_{\sigma'} e^{-\delta(\bar{\sigma},\sigma')}} \tag{4}$$

Note also that the input ranking σ may only sort a subset of assignments. In such cases, we appropriately restrict the normalization constant in (4). For Kendall-τ distance, this normalization constant can be computed efficiently, and it only depends on the number of elements in the ranking.

$$Z_M(k) = \prod_{i=1}^{k}\left(1+e^{-1}+\cdots+e^{-(i-1)}\right) = \prod_{i=1}^{k} \frac{1-e^{-i}}{1-e^{-1}}$$

Algorithm 2 Computing MLE ranking for Mallows Model

1: $C \leftarrow D$ ▷ C contains unranked items
2: **for** $i = 1 \ldots |D|$ **do**
3: **for** $d \in C$ **do**
4: $x_d \leftarrow \sum_{g \in G} \eta_g |d' \in C : d' \succ_{\sigma_g} d| - |d' \in C : d \succ_{\sigma_g} d'|$
5: $d^* \leftarrow \min_{d \in C} x_d$ ▷ Select highest scoring item
6: $r^{(\hat{\sigma})}_{d^*} \leftarrow i$ ▷ Rank as next item
7: $C \leftarrow C / d^*$ ▷ Remove d^* from candidate set
8: **return** $\hat{\sigma}$

The numerator can likewise be computed efficiently. Note that ties in the grader rankings $\sigma^{(g)}$ do not affect the normalization constant under the interpretation of indifference.

Under this modified Mallow's model, the maximum likelihood estimator of the central ranking $\hat{\sigma}$ is

$$\hat{\sigma} = \texttt{argmax}_{\sigma} \left\{ \prod_{g \in G} \frac{\sum_{\sigma' \sim \sigma^{(g)}} e^{-\delta_K(\sigma, \sigma')}}{Z_M(|D_g|)} \right\}. \quad (5)$$

Computing the maximum likelihood estimate $\hat{\sigma}$ as an estimate of the true ranking by quality σ^* requires finding the *Kemeny-optimal aggregate*, which is known to be NP-hard [13]. However numerous approximations have been studied in the rank aggregation literature [13, 21, 1]. In this work we use a simple greedy algorithm as shown in Algorithm 2.

As an alternative algorithm for computing the estimated ranking, we utilize a Borda count-like approximation for the Mallows model (which we denote as MAL_{BC}), where Line 2 of Algorithm 2 is replaced with

$$x_d \leftarrow \sum_{g \in G} r_d^{(\sigma^{(g)})}.$$

3.1.2 Score-Weighted Mallows (MALS)

Mallow's model presented above has two shortcomings. First, it does not output a meaningful cardinal grade for the assignments, which makes it applicable only to ordinal grade estimation. Second, the distance δ_K does not distinguish between misordering assignments that are similar in quality from those that have a large quality difference.

To address these two shortcomings, we propose an extension which estimates cardinal grades $\hat{s}_d$ for all assignments. To this effect, we introduce the following score-weighted ranking distance, which scales the distance induced by each misranked pairs by its estimated grade difference.

DEFINITION 2. *The* **score-weighted Kendall-τ distance** *δ_{SK} over rankings σ_1, σ_2 given cardinal scores s_d is*

$$\delta_{SK}(\sigma_1, \sigma_2 | s) = \sum_{d_1 \succ_{\sigma_1} d_2} (s_{d_1} - s_{d_2}) \mathbb{I}[[d_2 \succ_{\sigma_2} d_1]]. \quad (6)$$

Treating ties in the grader rankings as described above results in a score-weighted version of the Mallows model (MALS). We use the following maximum a posteriori estimator to estimate the scores $\hat{s}$.

$$\hat{s} = \texttt{argmax}_s \left\{ Pr(\mathbf{s}) \prod_{g \in G} \frac{\sum_{\sigma' \sim \sigma^{(g)}} \exp\left(-\delta_{SK}(\hat{\sigma}, \sigma' | s)\right)}{\sum_{\sigma' \in \pi(D_g)} \exp\left(-\delta_{SK}(\hat{\sigma}, \sigma' | s)\right)} \right\} \quad (7)$$

Note that $\hat{\sigma}$ can be obtained by sorting items as per $\hat{s}_d$. $Pr(\hat{\mathbf{s}}) = \prod_{d \in D} Pr(\hat{s}_d)$ is the prior on the latent item scores. In our experiments we model $Pr(\hat{s}_d) \sim \mathcal{N}(0, 9)$, and use the same prior in all of our methods. While the resulting objective is not necessarily convex, we use Stochastic Gradient Descent (SGD) for grade estimation and initialize the grades using a scaled-down Mallows solution.

3.1.3 Bradley-Terry Model (BT)

The above models define distributions over rankings as a function of a ranking distance, and they require approximate methods for solving the maximum likelihood problem. As an alternative, we can utilize rank aggregation models based on distributions over pairwise preferences, since a ranking of n items can also be viewed as a set of preferences over the $\binom{n}{2}$ item pairs. The Bradley-Terry model [8] is one model for pairwise preferences, and it derives a distribution based on the differences of underlying item scores s_d through a logistic link function.

$$P(d_i \succ_{\rho^{(g)}} d_j | s) = \frac{1}{1 + e^{-(s_{d_i} - s_{d_j})}} \quad (8)$$

Since each preference decision is modeled individually, the feedback from the grader could be a (possibly inconsistent) set of preferences that does not necessarily have to form a consistent ordering. The following is the maximum a posteriori estimator used in this paper.

$$\hat{s} = \texttt{argmax}_s \left\{ Pr(\mathbf{s}) \prod_{g \in G} \prod_{d_i \succ_{\rho^{(g)}} d_j} \frac{1}{1 + e^{-(s_{d_i} - s_{d_j})}} \right\} \quad (9)$$

The resulting objective is (jointly) log-convex in all of the estimated grades $\hat{s}_d$, with the gradients taking a simple form. Hence SGD can be used to estimate the global optimal grades efficiently. We treat ties as the absence of a preference. One can also extend this model to incorporate ties more explicitly, but we do not discuss this for brevity.

3.1.4 Thurstone Model (THUR)

An alternate to the logistic link function of the Bradley-Terry model is to utilize a normal distribution for the pairwise preferences. Like the Bradley-Terry model, the resulting Thurstone model [39] model can be understood as a random utility model using the following process: For each pair of items d_i, d_j, the grader samples (latent) values $x^{(g)}_{d_i} \sim \mathcal{N}(s_{d_i}, \frac{1}{2})$ and $x^{(g)}_{d_j} \sim \mathcal{N}(s_{d_j}, \frac{1}{2})$, and then orders the pair based on the two values. The mean of the normal distribution of d_i is the quality s_{d_i}. Maximum a posteriori estimation of the scores s requires maximization of the following function:

$$\hat{s} = \texttt{argmax}_s \left\{ Pr(\mathbf{s}) \prod_{g \in G} \prod_{d_i \succ_{\rho^{(g)}} d_j} \mathcal{F}(s_{d_i} - s_{d_j}) \right\} \quad (10)$$

$\mathcal{F}$ is the CDF of the standard normal distribution. This objective function is log-convex and we use SGD to optimize it.

3.1.5 Plackett-Luce Model (PL)

A drawback of the pairwise preference models is that they can be less expressive than models built on distributions over rankings. An extension to the Bradley-Terry model (the Plackett-Luce model [33]) allows us to use distributions over rankings, while still retaining convexity and simplicity

Algorithm 3 Alternating SGD-based Minimization

```
Require: N ≥ 0 (Number of iterations), Likelihood L
  Obj ← −log L
  ŝ ← SGD_S(Obj, η=1)          ▷ Est. scores w/o reliabilities
  for i = 1...N do
      η ← SGD_G(Obj, ŝ)        ▷ Estimate reliabilities
      ŝ ← SGD_S(Obj, η)        ▷ Est. scores with reliabilities
  return ŝ, η
```

of gradient computation. This model can be best understood as a multi-stage experiment where at each stage, an item d_i is drawn (w/o replacement) with probability $\propto e^{s_{d_i}}$. The probability of observing ranking $\sigma^{(g)}$ under this process is:

$$P(\sigma^{(g)}|s) = \prod_{d_i \in D_g} e^{s_{d_i}} / \Big(e^{s_{d_i}} + \sum_{d_i \succ_{\sigma^{(g)}} d_j} e^{s_{d_j}} \Big)$$

The resulting maximum a posteriori estimator is

$$\hat{s} = \texttt{argmax}_s \left\{ Pr(\mathbf{s}) \prod_{g \in G} \prod_{d_i \in D_g} \frac{e^{s_{d_i}}}{e^{s_{d_i}} + \sum_{d_i \succ_{\sigma^{(g)}} d_j} e^{s_{d_j}}} \right\}. \quad (11)$$

3.2 Grader Reliability Estimation

While the methods discussed in Section 3.1 allow us to estimate assignment grades from ordinal feedback, they still do not give us means to directly estimate grader reliabilities $\hat{\eta}_g$. However, there is a generic way of extending all methods presented above to incorporate grader reliabilities. Using Mallow's model as an example, we can introduce $\hat{\eta}_g$ as a variability parameter as follows:

$$Pr(\sigma|\bar{\sigma}, \eta_g) = \frac{\sum_{\sigma' \sim \sigma^{(g)}} \exp\left(-\eta_g \delta_K(\bar{\sigma}, \sigma')\right)}{Z_M(\eta_g, |D_g|)} \quad (12)$$

The resulting estimator of both $\hat{\sigma}$ and $\hat{\eta}$ is

$$\hat{\sigma}, \hat{\eta} = \texttt{argmax}_{\sigma,\eta} \left\{ \prod_{g \in G} Pr(\eta_g) \frac{\sum_{\sigma' \sim \sigma^{(g)}} \exp\left(-\eta_g \delta_K(\sigma, \sigma')\right)}{Z_M(\eta_g, |D_g|)} \right\}, \quad (13)$$

where $Pr(\hat{\eta}_g)$ is the prior on the grader reliability. In this work we use a *Gamma* prior $\hat{\eta}_g \sim Gamma(10, 0.1)$.

Similarly, the other objectives can also be extended in this manner as seen in Table 2. While many of the extended objectives, such as the one above in Eq. (13), are convex in the grader reliabilities $\hat{\eta}_g$ (for given $\hat{\sigma}$), they unfortunately are not jointly convex in the reliabilities *and* the estimated grades. We thus use an iterative alternating-minimization technique, which alternates between minimizing the log-objective to estimate the assignment grades and minimizing the log-objective to estimate the grader reliabilities. This iterative alternating approach using stochastic gradient descent is used for all joint estimation tasks in this paper. Note that methods which estimate the reliabilities using Algorithm 3 are denoted by a **+G** suffix to the method, while those that simply estimate the assignment grades are represented by the method name alone.

4. EXPERIMENTS

In the following we present experiments that compare ordinal and cardinal peer grading methods. We evaluate their ability to predict instructor grades, their variability, their robustness to bad peer grading, and their ability to identify bad graders. We also present the results from a qualitative student survey to evaluate how students perceived the peer grading process.

Method	Score	Cnvx	Estimator
MAL+G	No	No	$Pr(\eta)\prod_{g\in G}\sum_{\sigma'\sim\sigma^{(g)}}\exp(-\hat{\eta}_g\delta_K(\hat{\sigma},\sigma'))/Z_M(\hat{\eta}_g,\|D_g\|)$
MALS+G	Yes	No	$Pr(\hat{\mathbf{s}},\eta)\prod_{g\in G}\sum_{\sigma'\sim\sigma^{(g)}}\exp(-\hat{\eta}_g\delta_{SK}(\sigma^{(g)},\hat{\sigma},F))/Z(\cdot)$
BT+G	Yes	Yes	$Pr(\hat{\mathbf{s}},\eta)\prod_{g\in G}\prod_{d_i\succ_{\rho(g)}d_j}1/(1+e^{-\hat{\eta}_g(s_{d_i}-s_{d_j})})$
THUR+G	Yes	Yes	$Pr(\hat{\mathbf{s}},\eta)\prod_{g\in G}\prod_{d_i\succ_{\rho(g)}d_j}\mathcal{F}(\sqrt{\hat{\eta}_g}(s_{d_i}-s_{d_j}))$
PL+G	Yes	Yes	$Pr(\hat{\mathbf{s}},\eta)\prod_{g\in G}\prod_{d_i\in D_g}1/(1+\sum_{d_i\succ_{\rho(g)}d_j}e^{-\hat{\eta}_g(s_{d_i}-s_{d_j})})$

Table 2: Summary of the ordinal methods studied which model the grader's reliabilities, including the ability to output cardinal scores and if the resulting objective is convex in these scores.

4.1 Data Collection in Classroom Experiment

We use a real dataset consisting of peer feedback, TA grades, and instructor grades for evaluating the peer grading methods proposed in this paper. This data was collected as part of a senior-undergraduate and masters-level class with an enrollment of about 170 students. The class was staffed with 9 Teaching Assistants (TAs) that participated in grading, and a single Instructor. This size of class is attractive, since it is large enough for collecting a substantial number of peer grades, while at the same time allowing traditional instructor and TA grading to serve as a baseline. The availability of instructor grades makes our data different from other peer-grading evaluations used in the past (e.g., [32]). We are happy to provide the data to other researchers subject to IRB approval.

The dataset consists of two parts that were graded independently, namely the *poster presentation* and the *final report* of an 8-week long course project. Students worked in groups of 3-4 students for the duration of the project, and there were a total of 44 project groups. While student worked in groups, peer grading was performed individually via the Microsoft Conference Management Toolkit (CMT) system. The peer grading process was performed single-blind for the posters and double-blind for the reports, and the reviewer assignments were made uniformly at random. Students were given clear directives and asked to focus on aspects such as *novelty* and *clarity* (among others) while determining their grade. They were also asked to justify their grade by providing feedback comments. Students were told that a part of their grade depends on the quality of their peer feedback.

All grading was done on a 10-point (cardinal) Likert scale, where 10 was labeled "perfect", 8 "good", 5 "borderline" 3 "deficient" and 1 "unsatisfactory". This will allow us to compare cardinal and ordinal peer grading methods, where ordinal methods merely use the ordering (possibly with ties) implied by the cardinal scores. Note that in a true application of ordinal peer grading accuracy could improve, since it would allow simplifying the grading instructions and reduce cognitive overhead if students did not have to worry about the precise meaning of specific cardinal grades.

The following describes the grading processes used at each stage, and Table 3 summarizes some of the key statistics.

Data Statistic	PO	FR
Number of Assignments	42	44
Number of Peer Reviewers	148	153
Total Peer Reviews	996	586
Total TA Reviews	78	88
Participating TAs	7	9
Per-Item Peer Grade Devn.	1.16	1.03

Set	Who?	Mean	Devn.
PO	Peers	8.16	1.31
	TAs	7.46	1.41
	Meta	7.55	1.53
FR	Peers	8.20	1.35
	TAs	7.59	1.30
	Instructor	7.43	1.16

Table 3: Statistics for the two datasets (PO=Poster, FR=Report) from the classroom experiment along with the staff (TAs/Meta/Instructor) and student grade distributions.

4.1.1 Grading Process for Poster Presentations

The poster presentations took place in a two-hour poster session. Two groups did not present their poster. Students were encouraged to rotate presenting their poster. This likely increased variability of grades, since different reviewers often saw different presenters. Students and TAs took notes and entered their reviews via CMT afterwards.

The *TA Grades* were independent, meaning that the TAs did not see the peer reviews before entering their review. There were on average 1.85 TA reviews for each poster.

The *Peer Grades* totaled on average 23.71 reviews for each poster, with each peer reviewer reviewing 6.73 posters on average.

The final *Meta Grade* for each poster was determined as follows. One of the TAs that already provided an independent review was selected as a meta-reviewer. This TA was asked to aggregate all the arguments brought forward in the reviews and make a final grade on the same 10-point scale. The instructor oversaw this process, but intervened only on very few grades.

4.1.2 Grading Process for Final Projects

At the end of the project, groups submitted a report of about 10 pages in length. The reviewing process was similar to that of the poster presentations, but with one important difference — namely that all project reports were graded by the TAs and the instructor without any knowledge of the peer reviews, as detailed below.

On average each report received 13.32 *Peer Grades* as the overall score on each of the peer reviews (students were also asked for component scores like "clarity", etc.).

Each report also received two *TA Grades*, which the TAs submitted without knowledge of the peer reviews.

Finally, each report received an *Instructor Grade*, following the traditional process of project grading in this class. The instructor and head TA each graded half the projects and determined the grade based on their own reading of the paper, taking the TA reviews as input. These grades were provided without viewing the peer reviews. We can therefore view the instructor grades as an assessment that is entirely independent of the peer grades (in contrast to the Meta Grades for the posters, which have some dependency).

4.2 Evaluation Metrics

A commonly used measure for reporting student performance (among many standardized tests) is the percentile rank relative to all students in the class. Following this practice, we use percentile rank as the grade itself (a letter grade can easily be derived via curving), and report ranking metrics as our main indicators of performance. In particular, we use the following variant of Kendall-τ that accounts for ties.

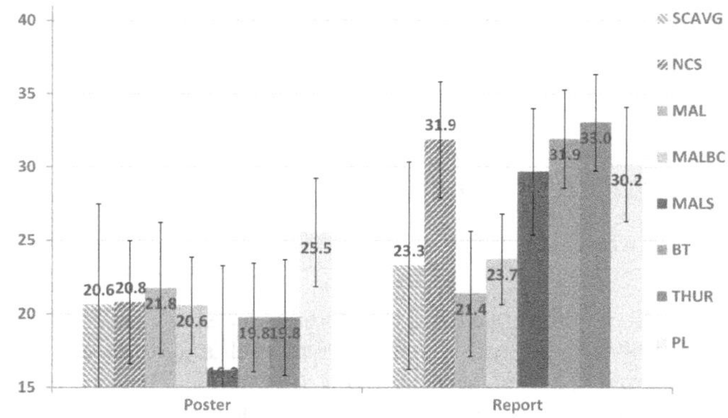

Figure 1: Comparing peer grading methods (w/o grader reliability estimation) against Meta and Instructor Grades in terms of $\mathcal{E}_K$ (lower is better).

$$\tau_{KT}(\sigma_1,\sigma_2)=\sum_{d_1\succ_{\sigma_1}d_2}\mathbb{I}[[d_2\succ_{\sigma_2}d_1]]+\frac{1}{2}\mathbb{I}[[d_1\approx_{\sigma_2}d_2]] \quad (14)$$

Note that this measure is not symmetric, assuming that the first argument is a target ranking and the second argument is a predicted ranking. It treats ties in the target ranking as *indifference*. Ties in the predicted ranking are treating as a lack of information, incurring a $\frac{1}{2}$ error (*i.e.*, equivalent to breaking ties randomly). Such a correction is necessary for evaluation purposes, since otherwise predicted rankings with all ties (which convey no information) would incur no error. Normalizing $\tau_{KT}(\sigma_1,\sigma_2)$ and accounting for the fact that we may have more than one target ranking leads to the following error measure.

DEFINITION 3. *Given a set of target rankings S_g, we define the* **Kendall-τ error** $\mathcal{E}_K$ *of predicted ranking σ_I as:*

$$\mathcal{E}_K(\sigma_I)=\frac{100}{|S_g|}\sum_{\sigma_t\in S_g}\frac{\tau_{KT}(\sigma_t,\sigma_I)}{\max_{\sigma\in\pi(D)}\tau_{KT}(\sigma_t,\sigma)} \quad (15)$$

This error *macro-averages* the (normalized) τ_{KT} errors for each target ranking. Due to the normalization, they lie between 0 (indicating perfect agreement) and 100% (indicating reversal with target rankings). A random ranking has expected $\mathcal{E}_K$ error of 50%.

4.3 How well does Ordinal vs. Cardinal Peer Grading Predict Final Grade?

The first question we address is in how far peer grading resembles the grades given by an instructor. Specifically, we investigate whether ordinal peer grading methods achieve similar performance as cardinal peer grading methods, even though ordinal methods receive strictly less information.

For all methods considered in this paper, Figure 1 shows the Kendall-τ error $\mathcal{E}_K$ compared to the Meta Grades for the Posters, and compared to the Instructor Grades for the Reports. The errorbars show estimated standard deviation using bootstrap-type resampling.

On the posters, none of the methods show significantly worse performance than another method. In particular, there is no evidence that the cardinal methods are performing better than the ordinal methods. A similar conclusion also holds for the reports. However, here the ordinal methods based on Mallow's model perform better than the car-

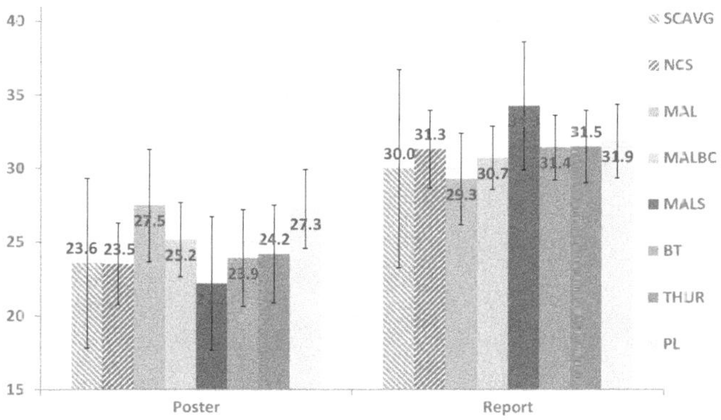

Figure 2: Comparing peer grading methods (w/o grader reliability estimation) against TA Grades in terms of $\mathcal{E}_K$, using TA grades as the target ranking.

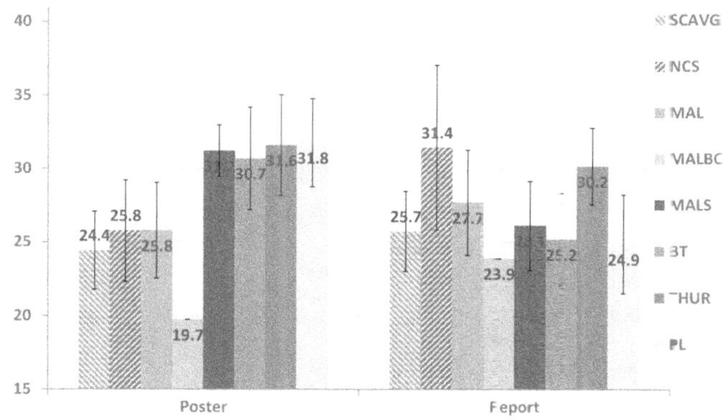

Figure 3: Self-consistency of peer-grading methods (w/o grader reliability estimation) in terms of $\mathcal{E}_K$.

dinal NCS[1] method [32] (see Algorithm 1), as well as some of the other ordinal methods. Simply averaging the cardinal scores of the peer graders, which we call Score Averaging (SCAVG), performs surprisingly well.

In summary, most methods achieve an $\mathcal{E}_K$ between 20% and 30% on both problems, but all have large standard deviations. The $\mathcal{E}_K$ appears lower for the posters than for the projects, which can be explained by the fact that the Meta Grade was influenced by the peer grades. But how good is an $\mathcal{E}_K$ between 20% and 30%?

4.4 How does Peer Grading Compare to TA Grading?

We now consider how Peer Grading compares to having each assignment graded by a TA. For medium sized classes, TA grading may still be feasible. It is therefore interesting to know if TA grading is clearly preferable to Peer Grading when it is feasible. But more importantly, the inter-judge agreement between multiple TAs can give us reference points for the accuracy of Peer Grading.

As a first reference point, we estimate how well the TA Grades reflect the Meta Grades for the posters and the Instructor Grades for the reports. In particular, we consider a grading process where each assignment is graded by a single TA that assigns a cardinal grade. Each TA grades a fraction of the assignments, and a final ranking of the assignments is then computed by sorting all cardinal grades. We call this grading process *TA Grading*.

We can estimate the $\mathcal{E}_K$ of TA grading with the Meta Grades and the Instructor Grades, since we have multiple TA grades for most assignments. We randomly resample a TA grade from the available grades for each assignment, compute the ranking, and then estimate mean and standard deviation of the $\mathcal{E}_K$ over 5000 samples. This leads to a mean $\mathcal{E}_K$ of 22.0 ± 16.0 for the posters and 22.2 ± 6.8 for the reports. Comparing these to the $\mathcal{E}_K$ of the peer grading methods in Figure 1, we see that they are comparable to the performance of many peer grading methods — *even though the $\mathcal{E}_K$ of TA grading is favorably biased. Note that Meta Grades and the Instructor Grades were assigned based on the same TA grades we are evaluating against.*

[1]We tuned the hyperparameters of the NCS model to maximize performance. We also used a fixed grader reliability parameter in the NCS model, since it provided better performance than with reliability estimation (NCS+G).

To avoid this bias and provide a fairer comparison with TA grading, we also investigated how consistent peer grades are with the TA grades, and how consistent TA grades are between different TAs. Figure 2 shows the $\mathcal{E}_K$ of the peer grading methods when using TA Grades as the target ranking for both the Posters and the Reports. Variances were again estimated via bootstrap resampling. Note that TA Grades were submitted without knowledge of the Peer Grades. Overall, the peer grades have an $\mathcal{E}_K$ with the TA Grades that is similar to the $\mathcal{E}_K$ with the respective Final grades considered in the previous subsection. Again, there is no evidence that the ordinal peer grading methods are less predictive of the TA Grades than the cardinal peer grading methods.

To estimate $\mathcal{E}_K$ between different TAs, we use the following resampling procedure. In a leave-one-out fashion, we treat the grades of a randomly selected TA as the target ranking and compute the predicted ranking by sampling from the other TAs grades as described above. Averaging over 5000 repetitions reveals that the $\mathcal{E}_K$ between the TAs is 47.5 ± 21.0 for the posters and 34.0 ± 13.8 for the reports.

These numbers can be compared to the $\mathcal{E}_K$ of peer grading methods in Figure 2. For the Reports, peer grades are roughly as consistent with the TA grades as other TA grades are. For the posters the peer grading methods are substantially more predictive of TA grades than other TA grades. The reason for this is at least twofold. First, the peer grading methods have access to much more data, which reduces variability (especially since presentations were not always given by the same student). Second, the peer grading methods have enough data to correct for different grading scales, while offsets in grading scales can have disastrous consequences in TA grading.

Finally, we also consider the self-consistency of the peer grading methods. Analogous to the self-consistency of TA grading, we ask how similar are the grades we get if we repeat the grading procedure with a different sample of assessments. We randomly partition peer reviewers into two equally sized datasets. For each peer grading method, we perform grade estimation on both datasets, which generates two rankings of the assignments. Ties in these rankings are broken randomly to get total orderings. Figure 3 shows the $\mathcal{E}_K$ between the two rankings (over 20 sampled partitions). For the posters, peer grading is substantially more self consistent than TA grading, and for the reports all peer grading methods have lower $\mathcal{E}_K$ estimates than TA grading as well.

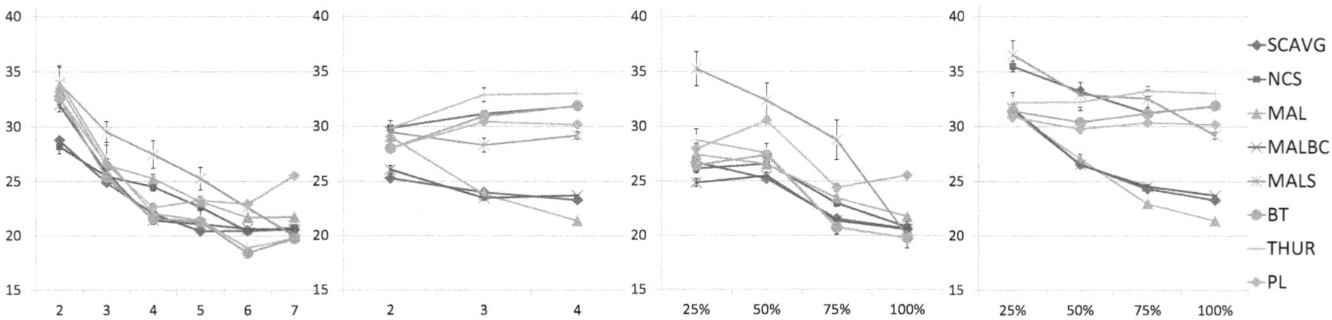

Figure 4: Change in $\mathcal{E}_K$ performance of peer grading methods (using Meta and Instructor Grades as target ranking) when varying the number of assignments assigned to each reviewer for Posters (first from left) & Reports (second), and when varying the number of peer reviewers for Posters (third) Reports (last).

Overall, we conclude that there is no evidence that TA grading would have led to more accurate grading outcomes than peer grading.

4.5 How does Grading Accuracy Scale with the Number of Peer Reviews?

How many reviewers are necessary for accurate peer grading, and how many reviews does each peer grader need to do? To gauge how performance changes with the number of peer reviews, we performed two sets of experiments. First, we created 20 smaller datasets by downsampling the number of peer reviewers. The results are shown in the two rightmost graphs of Figure 4. Overall, the methods degrade gracefully when the number of reviewers is reduced. Overall, we find that most ordinal methods scale as well as cardinal methods for both datasets.

A second way of increasing or reducing the amount of available data lies in the number of assignments that each student grades. Thus we repeated the experiment, but instead downsampled the number of assignments per reviewer (corresponding to a lower workload for each grader). The leftmost two plots of Figure 4 show the results. Again, we find that performance degrades gracefully.

4.6 Can the Peer Grading Methods Identify Unreliable Graders?

Peer grading can only work in practice, if graders are sufficiently incentivised to report an accurate assessment. This can be achieved by giving a grade also for the quality of the grading. In the following, we investigate whether the grader reliability estimators proposed in Section 3.2 can identify graders that are not diligent.

For both the posters and the projects, we add 10 "lazy" peer graders that report random grades drawn from a normal distribution whose mean and variance matches that of the rest of the graders[2]. For the ordinal methods, this results in a random ordering. We then apply the peer grading methods, estimating the respective reliability parameters η_g for each grader using 10 iterations of the alternating optimization algorithm. We then rank graders by their estimated η_g.

Figure 5 (top) shows the percentage of lazy graders that rank among the 20 graders with the lowest η_g. The error bars show standard error over 50 repeated runs with different lazy graders sampled. Most ordinal methods significantly outperform the cardinal NCS method for both the posters and the reports. The variants of Mallow's model perform very well, identifying around 70-80% of the lazy graders for the reports and all 10 lazy graders for the posters. The better performance for the posters than for the reports was to be expected, since students provide 7 instead of 4 grades.

Figure 5 (bottom) shows the results of a heuristic baseline. Here, grade estimation without reliability estimation is performed, and then graders are ranked by their $\mathcal{E}_K$ with the estimated ranking $\hat{\sigma}$. For almost all methods, this performs worse, clearly indicating that reliability estimation is superior in identifying lazy graders. We find similar results even when there are 100+ lazy graders, and we investigate robustness in the following section.

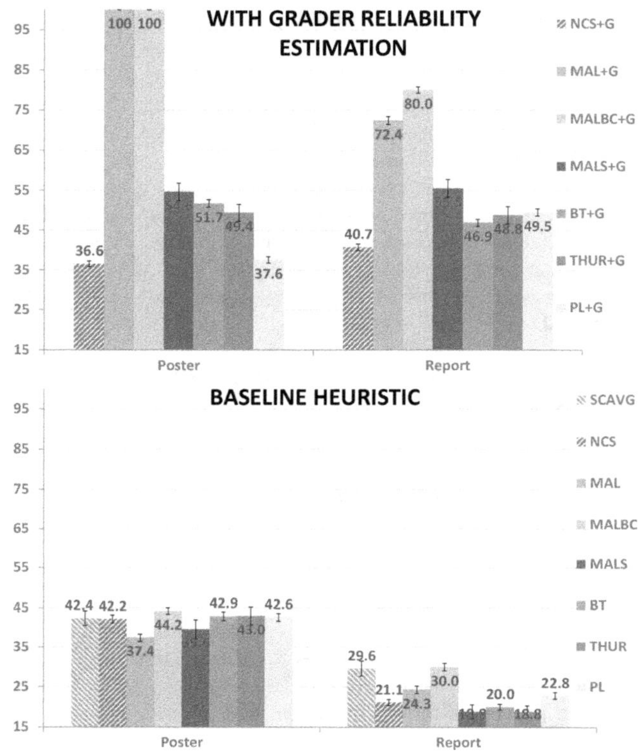

Figure 5: Percentage of times a grader who randomly scores and orders assignments is among the 20 least reliable graders (*i.e.*, bottom 12.5%).

[2]Otherwise it would be easy to identify these graders.

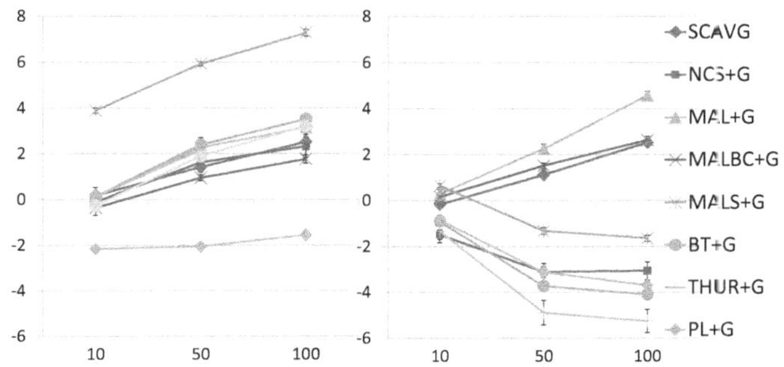

Figure 6: Change in $\mathcal{E}_K$ (using Instructor and Meta Grades as target ranking) for (Left) Posters and (Right) Final Reports with the addition of an increasing number of *lazy* graders *i.e.*, $\mathcal{E}_K$(With Lazy) − $\mathcal{E}_K$(Without Lazy). A negative value indicates that performance improves on adding this noise.

Method	Posters		Reports	
	Runtime	Runtime (+G)	Runtime	Runtime (+G)
NCS	0.32 ±0.03	7.0 ±0.55	0.20 ±0.03	4.6 ±0.25
MAL	0.01 ±0.00	6.1 ±0.11	0.01 ±0.00	2.5 ±0.03
MAL_{BC}	0.01 ±0.00	5.1 ±0.08	0.01 ±0.00	2.5 ±0.03
MALS	151.4 ±12.39	418.7 ±9.10	2.0 ±0.13	4.2 ±0.16
BT	0.46 ±0.06	5.6 ±0.38	0.21 ±0.02	2.2 ±0.10
THUR	57.9 ±0.76	490.1 ±7.45	12.2 ±0.86	120.8 ±1.03
PL	0.36 ±0.03	4.2 ±0.08	0.18 ±0.01	2.0 ±0.10

Table 4: Average runtime (with and without grader reliability estimation) and their standard deviation of different methods in CPU seconds.

4.7 How Robust are the Peer Grading Methods to Lazy Graders?

While Section 4.6 showed that reliability estimation in ordinal peer grading is well-suited for identifying lazy graders, we would also like to know what effect these lazy graders have on grade estimation performance. We study the robustness of the peer grading methods by adding an increasing number of lazy graders. Figure 6 shows the change in $\mathcal{E}_K$ (w.r.t. Instructor/Meta grades) after adding 10/50/100 lazy graders (compared to the $\mathcal{E}_K$ with no lazy graders). We find that in most cases performance does not change much relative to the variability of the methods. Interestingly, in some cases performance also improves on adding this noise. A deeper inspection reveals that noise is most beneficial for methods whose original $\mathcal{E}_K$ performance was weaker than that of the other methods. For example, the Thurstone model showed the weakest performance on the Reports and improves the most.

4.8 How Computationally Efficient are the Peer Grading Methods?

While prediction accuracy is the prime concern of grade inference, computational efficiency needs to be sufficient as well. Table 4 show the average runtimes and their standard deviations for the posters and the reports. All methods are tractable and most finish within seconds. The Score-Weighted Mallows model is less efficient for problems where a each grader assesses many assignments, since the gradient computations involves computing the normalization constant (which involves summing over all rankings). However, training scales linearly with the number of graders. Another method that requires more time is the Thurstone model.

Question A) Was getting peer feedback helpful?		Question B) Was providing peer feedback valuable?	
A_1	Yes, it was helpful.	B_1	Yes it was a valuable experience
A_2	Helpful, but not as much as instructor feedback.	B_2	Yes, it was valuable, but with caveats (e.g. took lot of time).
A_3	Somewhat helpful (e.g. only few comments were helpful).	B_3	Only little value (e.g. was too difficult / lacked the grading skills)
A_4	No / Not really / Did not help much.	B_4	Not valuable / Not really valuable.
A_5	Other / Missing	B_5	Other / Missing

Table 5: Response categories for survey questions.

The main bottleneck here is the computation of the gradient as it involves a lookup of a CDF value from the normal distribution table.

4.9 Do Students Value Peer Grading?

A final point that we would like to explore is that peer grading is not only about grade estimation, but also about generating useful feedback. In particular, the cardinal or ordinal assessments were only a small part of the peer feedback. Peer graders had to write a justification for their assessment and comment on the work more generally.

To assess this aspect of peer grading, a survey was conducted at the end of class as part of the course feedback process. This survey included two questions about the student's peer grading experience in the class; more specifically, about how *helpful* the feedback they received was, and how *valuable* the experience of providing feedback was to them. Both questions were to be answered in free-form text. Of the 161 students that participated in the project, 120 students responded to at least one of the questions, with 119 answering the question about receiving feedback (mean response length in characters: 62.93; stdev: 77.22) and 118 the question about providing feedback (mean: 100.36; stdev: 105.74). Following standard practice from survey analysis, we created five categories for coding these open-ended responses as show in Table 5. While the first four categories (roughly) follow a decreasing scale of approval, the last serves as a catch-all (including missing responses).

All free-text responses were manually assigned to these categories by four external annotators (who were not involved with the class and had not seen the comments before). For all the 237 student comments (*i.e.,* responses), the annotators were asked to choose the category that was *most appropriate/best describes the comment.* To check inter-annotator agreement we used the Fleiss Kappa measure. κ values of 0.8389 and 0.6493 for the two questions indicate high annotator agreement. The final assignment of response to category was done by majority vote among the four annotators (score of 0.5 each if tied between categories).

Table 6 summarizes the results of the survey after coding. Overall, around 68% found it at least somewhat helpful to receive peer feedback, and around 74% found substantial value in providing the peer feedback. Interestingly, of the 26% of the students who expressed that receiving peer feedback was not (really) helpful to them, 17% still found it valuable to provide peer feedback. Overall, we conclude that the vast majority of students found some value in the peer grading process.

5. CONCLUSIONS

In this work we study the problem of student evaluation at scale via peer grading using ordinal feedback. We cast this as a rank aggregation problem and study different probabilistic

%	A_1	A_2	A_3	A_4	A_5	Total
B_1	**34.58**	2.08	5.83	10.00	1.67	**54.17**
B_2	5.42	0.00	5.83	7.08	1.67	20.00
B_3	0.42	2.92	2.08	2.50	0.42	8.33
B_4	2.92	0.83	5.00	5.42	0.00	14.17
B_5	0.00	0.00	0.42	1.67	1.25	3.33
Total	**43.33**	5.83	19.17	26.67	5.00	

Table 6: Results of the student survey, coded according to the categories in Table 5.

models for obtaining student grades, as well as estimating the reliability of the peer graders. Using data collected from a real course, we find that the performance of ordinal peer grading methods is at least competitive with cardinal methods for grade estimation, even though they require strictly less information from the graders. For grader reliability estimation, Mallow's model outperforms all other methods, and it shows consistently good and robust performance for grade estimation as well. In general, we find that ordinal peer grading is robust and scalable, offering a grading accuracy that is comparable to TA grading in our course.

This research was funded in part by NSF Awards IIS-1217686 and IIS-1247696, and the JTCII Cornell-Technion Research Fund.

References

[1] N. Ailon, M. Charikar, and A. Newman. Aggregating inconsistent information: Ranking and clustering. *J. ACM*, 55(5):23:1–23:27, Nov. 2008.

[2] K. J. Arrow. *Social Choice and Individual Values*. Yale University Press, 2nd edition, Sept. 1970.

[3] J. A. Aslam and M. Montague. Models for metasearch. In *SIGIR*, pages 276–284, 2001.

[4] Y. Bachrach, T. Graepel, T. Minka, and J. Guiver. How to grade a test without knowing the answers - a bayesian graphical model for adaptive crowdsourcing and aptitude testing. In *ICML*, 2012.

[5] W. Barnett. The modern theory of consumer behavior: Ordinal or cardinal? *The Quarterly Journal of Austrian Economics*, 6(1):41–65, 2003.

[6] M. Bashir, J. Anderton, J. Wu, P. B. Golbus, V. Pavlu, and J. A. Aslam. A document rating system for preference judgements. In *SIGIR*, pages 909–912, 2013.

[7] L. Bouzidi and A. Jaillet. Can online peer assessment be trusted? *Educational Technology & Society*, 12(4):257–268, 2009.

[8] R. A. Bradley and M. E. Terry. Rank analysis of incomplete block designs: I. the method of paired comparisons. *Biometrika*, 39(3/4):pp. 324–345, 1952.

[9] B. Carterette, P. N. Bennett, D. M. Chickering, and S. T. Dumais. Here or there: Preference judgments for relevance. In *ECIR*, pages 16–27, 2008.

[10] C.-C. Chang, K.-H. Tseng, P.-N. Chou, and Y.-H. Chen. Reliability and validity of web-based portfolio peer assessment: A case study for a senior high school's students taking computer course. *Comput. Educ.*, 57(1):1306–1316, Aug. 2011.

[11] X. Chen, P. N. Bennett, K. Collins-Thompson, and E. Horvitz. Pairwise ranking aggregation in a crowdsourced setting. In *WSDM*, pages 193–202, 2013.

[12] J. Diez, O. Luaces, A. Alonso-Betanzos, A. Troncoso, and A. Bahamonde. Peer assessment in moocs using preference learning via matrix factorization, 2013.

[13] C. Dwork, R. Kumar, M. Naor, and D. Sivakumar. Rank aggregation methods for the web. In *WWW*, pages 613–622, 2001.

[14] S. Freeman and J. W. Parks. How accurate is peer grading? *CBE-Life Sciences Education*, 9(4):482–488, 2010.

[15] J. Guiver and E. Snelson. Bayesian inference for plackett-luce ranking models. In *ICML*, pages 377–384, 2009.

[16] J. Haber. `http://degreeoffreedom.org/between-two-worlds-moocs-and-assessment`.

[17] J. Haber. `http://degreeoffreedom.org/mooc-assignments-screwing/`, Oct. 2013.

[18] R. Herbrich, T. Minka, and T. Graepel. Trueskill^{tm}: A bayesian skill rating system. In *NIPS*, pages 569–576, 2007.

[19] P. G. Ipeirotis and P. K. Paritosh. Managing crowdsourced human computation: a tutorial. In *WWW*, pages 287–288, 2011.

[20] M. Kendall. *Rank correlation methods*. Griffin, London, 1948.

[21] C. Kenyon-Mathieu and W. Schudy. How to rank with few errors. In *STOC*, pages 95–103, 2007.

[22] C. Kulkarni, K. Wei, H. Le, D. Chia, K. Papadopoulos, J. Cheng, D. Koller, and S. Klemmer. Peer and self assessment in massive online classes. *ACM Trans. CHI*, 20(6):33:1–33:31, Dec. 2013.

[23] G. Lebanon and J. D. Lafferty. Cranking: Combining rankings using conditional probability models on permutations. In *ICML*, pages 363–370, 2002.

[24] T.-Y. Liu. Learning to rank for information retrieval. *Found. Trends Inf. Retr.*, 3(3):225–331, Mar. 2009.

[25] T. Lu and C. Boutilier. Learning mallows models with pairwise preferences. In *ICML*, pages 145–152, June 2011.

[26] T. Lu and C. E. Boutilier. The unavailable candidate model: A decision-theoretic view of social choice. In *EC*, pages 263–274, 2010.

[27] R. D. Luce. *Individual Choice Behavior: A theoretical analysis*. Wiley, 1959.

[28] C. L. Mallows. Non-null ranking models. *Biometrika*, 44(1/2):pp. 114–130, 1957.

[29] G. A. Miller. The magical number seven, plus or minus two: Some limits on our capacity for processing information. *The Psychological Review*, 63(2):81–97, March 1956.

[30] M. Mostert and J. D. Snowball. Where angels fear to tread: online peer-assessment in a large first-year class. *Assessment & Evaluation in Higher Education*, 38(6):674–686, 2013.

[31] S. Niu, Y. Lan, J. Guo, and X. Cheng. Stochastic rank aggregation. *CoRR*, abs/1309.6852, 2013.

[32] C. Piech, J. Huang, Z. Chen, C. Do, A. Ng, and D. Koller. Tuned models of peer assessment in MOOCs. In *EDM*, 2013.

[33] R. L. Plackett. The analysis of permutations. *Journal of the Royal Statistical Society. Series C (Applied Statistics)*, 24(2):193–202, 1975.

[34] T. Qin, X. Geng, and T.-Y. Liu. A new probabilistic model for rank aggregation. In *NIPS*, pages 1948–1956, 2010.

[35] V. C. Raykar, S. Yu, L. H. Zhao, G. H. Valadez, C. Florin, L. Bogoni, and L. Moy. Learning from crowds. *JMLR*, 11:1297–1322, Aug. 2010.

[36] J. Rees. `http://www.insidehighered.com/views/2013/03/05/essays-flaws-peer-grading-moocs`.

[37] N. Shah, J. Bradley, A. Parekh, M. Wainwright, and K. Ramchandran. A case for ordinal peer-evaluation in MOOCs, 2013.

[38] N. Stewart, G. D. A. Brown, and N. Chater. Absolute identification by relative judgment. *Psychological Review*, 112:881–911, 2005.

[39] L. L. Thurstone. The method of paired comparisons for social values. *Journal of Abnormal and Social Psychology*, 27:384–400, 1927.

[40] M. N. Volkovs and R. S. Zemel. A flexible generative model for preference aggregation. In *WWW*, pages 479–488, 2012.

Exploiting Geographic Dependencies for Real Estate Appraisal: A Mutual Perspective of Ranking and Clustering

Yanjie Fu[‡], Hui Xiong[‡*], Yong Ge[+], Zijun Yao[‡], Yu Zheng[◇], Zhi-Hua Zhou[†]
[‡]Rutgers University, {yanjie.fu, hxiong, zijun.yao}@rutgers.edu
[+]University of North Carolina at Charlotte, USA, yong.ge@uncc.edu
[◇]Microsoft Research Asia, yuzheng@microsoft.com
[†]Nanjing University, zhouzh@lamda.nju.edu.cn

ABSTRACT

It is traditionally a challenge for home buyers to understand, compare and contrast the investment values of real estates. While a number of estate appraisal methods have been developed to value real property, the performances of these methods have been limited by the traditional data sources for estate appraisal. However, with the development of new ways of collecting estate-related mobile data, there is a potential to leverage geographic dependencies of estates for enhancing estate appraisal. Indeed, the geographic dependencies of the value of an estate can be from the characteristics of its own neighborhood (individual), the values of its nearby estates (peer), and the prosperity of the affiliated latent business area (zone). To this end, in this paper, we propose a geographic method, named ClusRanking, for estate appraisal by leveraging the mutual enforcement of ranking and clustering power. ClusRanking is able to exploit geographic individual, peer, and zone dependencies in a probabilistic ranking model. Specifically, we first extract the geographic utility of estates from geography data, estimate the neighborhood popularity of estates by mining taxicab trajectory data, and model the influence of latent business areas via ClusRanking. Also, we use a linear model to fuse these three influential factors and predict estate investment values. Moreover, we simultaneously consider individual, peer and zone dependencies, and derive an estate-specific ranking likelihood as the objective function. Finally, we conduct a comprehensive evaluation with real-world estate related data, and the experimental results demonstrate the effectiveness of our method.

Categories and Subject Descriptors

H.2.8 [**Database Management**]: Database Applications—*Data mining*

General Terms

Algorithms, Design, Experimentation

Keywords

Real Estate Appraisal; Geographic Dependencies; ClusRanking

1. INTRODUCTION

There are a number of online estate information systems, such as Yahoo! Homes, Zillow.com, and Realtor.com, which provide functions to help people to search estate-related information. In these systems, home buyers can also rank estates based on some criteria, such as prices, the number of bedrooms, and the home size. However, the decision process of buying a house is different from that of buying a regular product. Home buyers not only aim to gain utility from a house, but also seek resale values and long-term capital growth. Therefore, home buyers often need the tool to rank estates based on their investment values. Indeed, the investment value is more related to the potential capital growth in the future. The **return rate**[1] is often used to quantify the investment values of estates instead of using the price. In fact, a high price does not necessarily mean a high investment value, and vice versa.

Traditionally, estate appraisal methods can help for the estimation of the values of estates, but the performances of these methods have been limited by the traditional data sources for estate appraisal. For instance traditional estate price modeling methods exploit the trend, periodicity and volatility of price time series. However, both rigid and speculative demands have a big impact on the prices of estates. It is difficult to identify the true estate values only with the current prices. Also, the comparative estate analysis, e.g. automated valuation models (AVMs), typically aggregates and analyzes the physical characteristics and sales prices of comparable properties to provide property evaluations. However, AVMs could fail to appraise new or planned estates due to the lack of comparable property data.

Indeed, with the development of new ways of collecting estate-related mobile data, there is a potential to exploit geographic dependencies of estates for enhancing estate appraisal. In fact, a large amount of estate-related mobile data, such as urban geographic data and human mobility information near estates, have been accumulated. If properly analyzed, these data could be a source of rich intelligence for finding estates with high investment values.

*Contact author.

[1]http://en.wikipedia.org/wiki/Rate_of_return

KDD'14, August 24–27, 2014, New York, NY, USA.
Copyright 2014 ACM 978-1-4503-2956-9/14/08 ...$15.00.
http://dx.doi.org/10.1145/2623330.2623675.

Specifically, in this paper, we study three types of geographic dependencies, which categorize estate values from three perspectives: (1) the geographic characteristics of its own neighborhood (individual), (2) the values of its nearby estates (estate-estate peer), and (3) the values of its affiliated latent business area (estate-business zone). First, the investment value of an estate is largely determined by the geographic characteristics of its own neighborhood. This is called **individual dependency**. For example, people are usually willing to pay higher prices for estates close to the best public schools. The individual dependency can be captured by correlating the estate investment values with urban geography (e.g. bus stops, subway stations, road network entries, and point of interests (POIs)) as well as human mobility patterns. Second, the estate investment value can be reflected by its nearby estates. This is called **peer dependency**. The peer dependency can be captured by the comparative estate analysis which is a popular method in estate appraisal and evaluates estates based on peer estate comparison. An intuitive understanding along this line is, if the surrounding estates are of high investment values, the targeted estate will usually have a high value as well.

Third, the estate value can also be influenced by the values of its affiliated latent business area. This is called **zone dependency**. A business area is a self-organized region with many estates. The formation of business areas are driven by the long-term commercial activities under two mutually-enhanced effects: (1) estates tend to co-locate in multiple centers, and thus bring human activities to those business areas; (2) prosperous business areas in return lead to more estate constructions. Hence, a prosperous business area represents a high density cluster of human activities, commercial activities, and estates. Here, we assume that each estate is affiliated with a latent business area and each business area is endowed with a value function of estate investment preferences, which measures the prosperity of the estate industry in this business area. The more prosperous the business area is, the easier we can identify a high investment-value estate from this business area.

In summary, the individual dependency shows that the estate investment value can be reflected by urban geography information and human mobility data. This allows us to value real property when we lack of comparable estates. Also, the peer dependency allows to exploit spatial autocorrelation of investment values through the comparison between the targeted estate and its peer estates. Moreover, the zone dependency allows to explore the influence of the associated latent business area of an estate. Based on the above, in this paper, we propose a geographic method, named ClusRanking, for estate appraisal by leveraging the mutual enforcement of ranking and clustering power. ClusRanking is able to exploit geographic individual, peer and zone dependencies into a unified probabilistic ranking model.

Specifically, we first extract the geographic utility from urban geography data. Then, we estimate the neighborhood popularity through spatial propagation and aggregation of passenger visit probabilities by mining taxicab trajectory data. Moreover, we model the influence of latent business areas via ClusRanking. In particular, since we assume there are multiple latent business areas in a city, we embed a dynamic spatial-clustering approach into the ranking process. Here, each business area is treated as a spatial hidden state. A business area not only shows the locations of its estates, but also reflects the influence on estate investment values in terms of geographic proximity between estate and the centroids of the business area. Our method is iteratively updated by mutual enhancement between spatial-clustering and ranking until the boundaries of latent business areas are learned. After this, we fuse the three factors and learn estate investment values for estate ranking. In addition, we derive a mixture likelihood objective, which simultaneously considers the geographic individual, peer and zone dependencies. Here, individual dependency describes the prediction accuracy of estate investment values and locations. Peer dependency captures the ranking consistency of intra-business-area estate pairs. Zone dependency models the ranking consistency of inter-business-area estate pairs. Finally, we conduct a comprehensive performance evaluation on real world estate related data and the experimental results demonstrate the effectiveness of our method.

2. REAL ESTATE RANKING

In this section, we introduce a geographic ClusRanking method for estate appraisal.

2.1 Problem Statement

In estate industry, two concepts are often used for an estate: value-adding capability and value-protecting capability, which are quantified by the investment value of estates in rising and falling markets respectively. In this paper, we focus on estimating the investment value of estates and ranking all estates accordingly during these two markets. Ranking estates is very similar to the traditional information retrieval problem, where documents are ranked according to a defined relevance. Here, each estate is treated as a document and the value-adding capability or the value-protecting capability is considered as the relevance.

Formally, let $E = \{e_1, e_2, ..., e_I\}$ be a set of I estates, each of which is represented by all associated geographic features denoted as e_i as shown in Table 1, where more notation are listed. Our goal is to rank the estates in descending order according to the investment value in two markets. In fact, the essential task of this problem is how to estimate the investment value (denoted as y_i) of each estate i by modeling all associated relevant information of estates in a unified way. In this paper, we consider a group of heterogenous information associated with estates, which include the public transportation information (e.g., bus stop, subway, road network), point of interest (e.g., restaurant and shopping mall), neighborhood popularity, and the influence among estate geographic zone.

Symbol	Size	Description
$\boldsymbol{E}$	$I \times N$	estate geographic feature vector, e_i is the ith estate
$\boldsymbol{Y}$	$1 \times I$	benchmark values, y_i is the benchmark value of e_i
$\boldsymbol{F}$	$1 \times I$	predicted values, f_i is the predicted value of e_i
$\boldsymbol{\Pi}$	$1 \times I$	ranks, π_i is the rank of e_i, smaller is better
$\overline{\boldsymbol{\Pi}}$	$1 \times I$	indexes, $\overline{\pi}_i$ is the index of i-th ranked estate, inverse of Π
$\boldsymbol{\gamma}$	$1 \times I$	geographic utility
$\boldsymbol{\delta}$	$1 \times I$	neighborhood popularity
$\boldsymbol{\rho}$	$1 \times I$	influence of business area
N	I	neighborhood set, n_i is the neighborhood of the i-th estate
D	-	drop-off point set
C	J	POI category set
R	$1 \times I$	business area assignments I estates
$\mathcal{R}$	K	latent business area set
$\boldsymbol{\eta}$	$1 \times K$	business area level prosperity distribution

Table 1: Mathematical Notations

2.2 The Overview of ClusRanking

Assume that each estate i is endowed with an investment value function y_i. We first build a model to predict y_i with the geographic information. Specifically, the estate value is affected by three factors: $y_i \propto \gamma_i + \rho_i + \delta_i$, in which (1) γ_i: the geographic utility extracted from urban geography data F_{geo}; (2) ρ_i: the influence of latent business area F_{area}; (3) δ_i: the neighborhood popularity estimated from human mobility data F_{mobi}. Then, we will be able to get a ranked list of estates based on their predicted investment values, and thus each estate i is associated with an inferred rank π_i. With the ranked list of estates, we formulate a likelihood function, which simultaneously captures the geographic individual (Lik_{id}), peer (Lik_{pd}) and zone (Lik_{zd}) dependencies. This likelihood function unifies both the prediction accuracy based on geographic data of estates and the ranking consistency of the estate ranked list. By maximizing this likelihood function, we could optimize the prediction accuracy of estate investment value and the ranking list of estates at the same time. Finally, we solve the optimization problem using a Expectation Maximization (EM) method. Figure 1 shows the framework of our method.

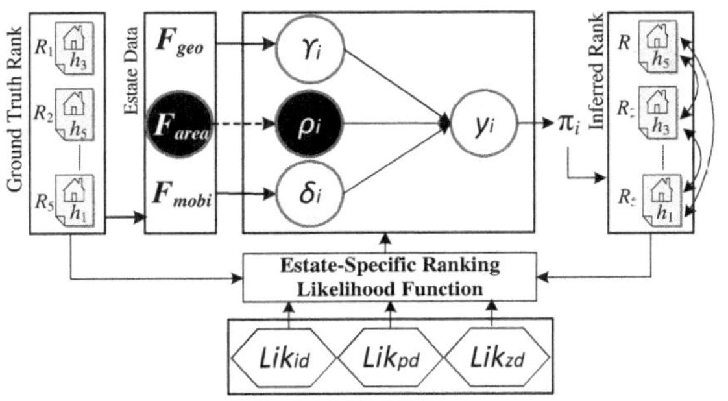

Figure 1: The framework of ClusRanking. (The black plates represent the latent effects.)

2.3 Modeling Estate Investment Value

Before introducing the overall objective function which captures the three dependencies altogether, let us first introduce how to model the investment value of estates with geographic information. Specifically, we will first introduce the modellings of γ_i, ρ_i and δ_i separately, and then state how they are combined together.

2.3.1 Geographic Utility: γ

Data	Feature Design
Transportation	Number of bus stop
	Distance to bus stop
	Number of subway station
	Distance to subway station
	Number of road network entries
	Distance to road network entries
Point of interest	Number of POIs of different POI categories (Shopping, Sports, Education, etc.)

Table 2: Neighbourhood Profiling (a neighborhood is defined as a cell area with a radius of 1km.)

Estate values are largely determined by its geographic location. Therefore, we naturally relate the geographic utility of estate to its location characteristics. More specifically, we first extract geographic features from estate neighborhoods (refer to Table 2) and treat the raw representations of estates as a vector E. The raw representations of estates E are then learned and transformed to the meta representations WE using a single-layer perceptron, where $W \in M \times N$ is indeed a coefficient matrix. Finally, we parameterize geographic utility by a linear aggregation over transferred features in meta representation: $\gamma = qWE^\top$, where $q \in 1 \times M$ are the weights of the transferred features.

According to estate financial theory [16], the estate investment value can be partially approximated by rent-interest ratio from market performances explicitly. We incorporate the rent-interest ratio into $\gamma = \frac{rent}{interest} + qWE^\top$ as side information to strengthen the robustness of our method.

2.3.2 Influence of Latent Business Area: ρ

Since we assume each estate is associated with a latent business area, the estate investment value also depends on the value of the associated business area. Suppose there are K latent business areas, we first choose the business area for each estate. We apply a multinominal distribution over latent business area $r \sim p(r|\boldsymbol{\eta})$, where $\boldsymbol{\eta} \in 1 \times K$ denotes the values (prosperity of estate industry or estate investment preference) of K business areas respectively. Later, each estate location l_i is drawn from a multivariate normal distribution: $l_i \sim \mathcal{N}(\mu_r, \Sigma_r)$, where $\mu_r \in 1 \times 2$ and $\Sigma_r \in 2 \times 2$ is the center and covariance of business area r, respectively. Finally, to model the influence of business area we treat all the K business areas as K latent spatial states. The K latent spatial states together show the influence on each estate. Assume the influence is inversely proportional to the distance between the estate location and the business area center: $d(i,r) = \sqrt{\|\mu_r - l_i\|_2}$, the influence of K business areas over estate i is defined by an aggregate power-law weighted parametric term $\rho_i = \sum_{k=1}^{K} \left(\frac{d_0}{d_0 + d(i, r_k)}\right)^e \frac{\eta_k}{\sum_{k=1}^{K} \eta_k}$ where d_0 as a parameter and e is a mathematical constant.

2.3.3 Neighborhood Popularity: δ

Neighborhood popularity can affect the investment value of an estate to a certain extent. In general, people are willing to live in a popular neighborhood. A popular neighborhood usually has lots of notable POIs, which can be measured from two perspectives: (1) POI numbers, representing the quantitative measurement; (2) POI visit probability, representing the quality of those POIs. We propose to estimate the neighborhood popularity of a targeted estate by strategically combining POI numbers and POI visit probabilities using the taxicab GPS traces via a three-stage algorithm.

Propagating visit probability. In the first stage, given the drop-off point of a taxi trace d , we model the probability of a POI p visited by the passenger as a parametric function, whose input x is the road network distance between d and p: $P(x) = \frac{\beta_1}{\beta_2} \cdot x \cdot exp(1 - \frac{x}{\beta_2})$, where $\beta_1 = \max_x(P(x))$ and $\beta_2 = \operatorname{argmax}_x(P(x))$. The reasons why we adopt this function are as follows. First, when $x = 0$, $P(x) = 0$. Since a taxi could not send passengers into a POI directly, the drop-off point usually is not the same with the destination. A passenger often walks a short distance to reach the destination. Second, the drop-off point usually is close to the destination. Hence, when the distance exceeds a threshold β_2, the probability keeps decreasing with an exponential heavy tail. With this function, we can propagate the visit probability of a passenger from the drop-off point to its surrounding POIs.

Aggregating POI-level visit probability. Given a POI p, the visit probability of p is measured by summarizing all the visit probabilities propagated from all the drop-off points in taxicab trace data via $\kappa(p) = \sum_{d \in D} P(dist(d, p))$.

1 For each estate i:
1.1 Draw a business area $r \sim$ Multinomial(η).
1.2 Draw a location $l_i \sim \mathcal{N}(l_i;\mu,\sigma^2)$
1.3 Generate geographic utility
1.3.1 Draw coefficient matrix of meta representation $w_{mn} \sim \mathcal{N}(w_{mn}\|\mu_w,\sigma_w^2)$
1.3.2 Draw coefficient vector of geography utility $q_m \sim \mathcal{N}(q_m\|\mu_q,\sigma_q^2)$
1.3.3 Estate geographic utility $\gamma_i = \frac{rent_i}{interest} + qWe_i^\top$
1.4 Compute influence given by latent business areas $\rho_i = \sum_{k=1}^K \left(\frac{d_0}{d_0+d(i,r_k)}\right)^e \frac{\eta_k}{\sum_{k=1}^K \eta_k}$
1.5 Compute neighborhood popularity $\delta_i = \frac{1}{J}\sum_{j=1}^J \frac{\phi_{ij}}{max_{i\in r}\{\phi_{ij}\}}$
1.6 Generate the estate investment value $y_i \sim \mathcal{N}(y_i\|f_i,\sigma^2)$ where $f_i = \gamma_i + \delta_i + \rho_i$
2 Compile the ranked list Π of estates in terms of all y_i

Table 3: The generative process of ClusRanking

Aggregating POI-category-level visit probability. In the third stage, we first identify the POIs located in the neighborhood n_i of the i-th estate. Then, we summarize the visit probability of those POIs per category c_j and obtain the category-level aggregated visit probability as $\phi_{ij} = \sum_{p\in c_j \wedge p \in n_i} \kappa(p)$. In this way, we reconstruct the representation of neighborhood popularity as an aggregated visit probability vector $\boldsymbol{\phi_i} =< \phi_{i1},\cdots,\phi_{iJ} >$ over different POI categories for the i-th estate. Finally, we aggregate and normalize the popularity score as $\delta_i = \frac{1}{J}\sum_{j=1}^J \frac{\phi_{ij}}{max_{i\in r}\{\phi_{ij}\}}$.

Finally, we combine all modellings of γ_i, ρ_i and δ_i together and get the overall generative process of estate investment value as shown in Table 3. Specifically, we first assume there are K latent business areas in a city. Each business area is a cluster of estates. We treat K latent business areas as K spatial hidden states, each of which is endowed with a latent value η_k, which represents estate investment preference (or prosperity of estate industry) in the k-th business area. For each estate i, we draw a business area r from all K business areas following a multinomial distribution: Multi($\boldsymbol{\eta}$). The location of estate l_i is drawn from the sampled business area r. Later, given the estate location l_i is drawn, we are able to identify the neighborhood area and represent estate by a geographic feature vector e_i via neighborhood profiling. We then extract geographic utility γ_i from e_i. Moreover, we estimate the neighborhood popularity δ_i by strategically mining the taxicab trajectory traces. Since the estate investment value depends on the value of the associated latent business area, the K business areas together show the value influence on the estate: $\rho_i = \sum_{k=1}^K \left(\frac{d_0}{d_0+d(i,r_k)}\right)^e \frac{\eta_k}{\sum_{k=1}^K \eta_k}$, which is penalized by the distance between area centroid and estate location. After incorporating the three factors, we generate the investment value y_i of real estate i. With all the estate investment values, we compile a ranked list of estates denoted as Π.

2.4 Modeling Three Dependencies

Here, we introduce how to model the geographic individual, peer and zone dependencies of estates together in a unified objective function, as shown in Figure 1. Let us denote all parameters by $\Psi = \{q, W, \eta, \boldsymbol{\mu}, \boldsymbol{\Sigma}\}$, the hyperparamters $\Omega = \{\mu_q, \sigma_q^2, \mu_w, \sigma_w^2, \sigma^2\}$, and the observed data collection $\mathcal{D} = \{Y, \Pi, L\}$ where Y, Π and L are the investment value, ranks and locations of I estates respectively. For simplicity, we first assume that $i = \pi_i = \overline{\pi}_i$. In other words, the real estates in $\mathcal{D}$ are sorted and indexed in a descending order in terms of their investment values, which compiles a descending ranks as well.

By Bayesian inference, we have the posterior probability as

$$Pr(\Psi;\mathcal{D},\Omega) = P(\mathcal{D}|\Psi,\Omega)\,P(\Psi|\Omega) \tag{1}$$

The term $P(\mathcal{D}|\Psi,\Omega)$ is the likelihood of the observed data collection $\mathcal{D}$ as

$$\begin{aligned} P(\mathcal{D}|\Psi,\Omega) &= P(\{Y,\Pi,L\}|\Psi,\Omega) \\ &= P(\{Y,L\}|\Psi,\Omega) \times P(\Pi|\Psi,\Omega), \end{aligned} \tag{2}$$

where $P(\{Y,L\}|\Psi,\Omega)$ denotes the likelihood of the observed investment values and locations of estates given the parameters. $P(\{Y,L\}|\Psi,\Omega)$ can be explained as to be proportional to the individual dependency Lik_{id}. $P(\Pi|\Psi,\Omega)$ denotes the likelihood of the ranking of estates given the parameter, which we argue is proportional to the product of peer dependency Lik_{pd} and zone dependency Lik_{zd}. Next, we introduce the modeling of each dependency in detail.

Individual Dependency. The smaller loss, the higher Lik_{id}. Specifically we model Lik_{id} as a joint probability of the estate investment values, the estate locations, and the business areas to learn the geographic interinfluence between estate investment values and locations. As shown in Table 3, we assume each location of estate is drawn from a business area and all business areas are drawn from a Multinomial distribution. Along this line, Lik_{id} is formulated by

$$\begin{aligned} Lik_{id} &= \prod_i^I P(\{y_i,l_i\}|\Psi,\Omega) = \prod_i^I P(\{y_i,l_i,r_i\}|\Psi,\Omega) \\ &= \prod_{i=1}^I \mathcal{N}(y_i|f_i,\sigma)\prod_{i=1}^I \mathcal{N}(l_i|\mu_{r_i},\Sigma_{r_i})\prod_{i=1}^I Mult(r_i|\boldsymbol{\eta}) \\ &= \prod_{i=1}^I \frac{1}{\sigma}\exp\left(-\frac{(y_i-f_i)^2}{2\sigma^2}\right)\prod_{i=1}^I \frac{1}{\Sigma_{r_i}}\exp\left(-\frac{(l_i-\mu_{r_i})^2}{2\Sigma_{r_i}^2}\right)\prod_{i=1}^I Mult(r_i|\boldsymbol{\eta}) \end{aligned} \tag{3}$$

where we introduce a latent variable $R \in 1\times I$, each of which r_i represents the latent business area assignment of estate i.

Peer and Zone Dependencies.

While directly modeling likelihood of the ranking list of estates cannot comprehensively capture the spatial correlation of estate-estate and estate-business area, we model the ranking consistency by Lik_{pd} and Lik_{zd} instead. In fact, the ranked list of all the estates indeed can be encoded into a directed graph, $G = \{V, E\}$, with the node set V as estates and the edge set E as pairwise ranking orders. For instance, edge $i \to h$ represents an estate i is ranked higher than estate h. From a generative modeling angle, edge $i \to h$ is generated by our model through a likelihood function $P(i \to h)$. The more valuable estate i is than estate h, the larger $P(i \to h)$ should be. Since an estate pair $< i, h >$ can be located inside one business area or cross two different business areas, the edges of G then can be categorized into two sets: (1) edges intra business area which corresponds to peer dependency and (2) edges inter business area which corresponds to zone dependency.

Specifically, Lik_{pd} is defined as the ranking consistencies of estate pairs within the same business area. In other words, peer dependency captures the likelihood of the edges intra business area. Here the generative likelihood of each edge $i \to h$ is defined as Sigmoid($f_i - f_h$): $P(i \to h) = \frac{1}{1+exp(-(f_i-f_h))}$. Therefore, Lik_{pd} is defined by

$$\begin{aligned} Lik_{pd} &= \prod_{i=1}^{I-1}\prod_{h=i+1}^{I} P(i\to h|\Psi,\Omega)^{\mathbb{I}(r_i=r_h)} \\ &= \prod_{i=1}^{I-1}\prod_{h=i+1}^{I}\left(\frac{1}{1+exp(-(f_i-f_h))}\right)^{\mathbb{I}(r_i=r_h)} \end{aligned} \tag{4}$$

where $\mathbb{I}(r_i = r_h)$ is the indicator function with $\mathbb{I}(r_i = r_h) = 1$ when estate i and estate h are in the same business area (or $r_i = r_h$), and $\mathbb{I}(r_i = r_h) = 0$ otherwise.

While the peer dependency considers the estate pairs which are within the same business area, zone dependency yet targets the estate pairs, each of which are within two different business areas. We use the generative likelihood of edges inter business area as the zone dependency. There is investment value conformity between estate and business area. That is, the higher prosperity of estate industry in the associated business area, the higher possibility we can draw a high-value estate from it. Thus, when the estate pair $< i, h >$ is drawn from two different business areas $< r_i, r_h >$, we compare the values of the two associated business areas $(r_i \rightarrow r_h)$ instead of the values of estates $(i \rightarrow h)$. Therefore, the generative likelihood of an inter-business-area edge is define as Sigmoid$(\eta_{r_i} - \eta_{r_h})$: $P(i \rightarrow h) = \frac{1}{1+exp(-(\eta_{r_i}-\eta_{r_h}))}$, where the values of r_i and r_h are represented by η_{r_i} and η_{r_h} respectively (refer to Section 2.3.3). In this way, we capture the spatial dependency between estate and business area. Lik_{zd} is then given by

$$Lik_{zd} = \prod_{i=1}^{I-1}\prod_{h=i+1}^{I} P(r_i \rightarrow r_h|\Psi,\Omega)^{\mathbb{I}(r_i \neq r_h)} = \prod_{i=1}^{I-1}\prod_{h=i+1}^{I}\left(\frac{1}{1+exp(-(\eta_{r_i}-\eta_{r_h}))}\right)^{\mathbb{I}(r_i\neq r_h)}, \quad (5)$$

Second, term $P(\Psi|\Omega)$ is the prior of the parameters Ψ

$$P(\Psi|\Omega) = P(q|\mu_q,\sigma_q^2)P(W|\mu_w,\sigma_w^2) = \prod_{m=1}^{M}\mathcal{N}(q_m|\mu_q,\sigma_q^2) \times \prod_{m=1}^{M}\prod_{n=1}^{N}\mathcal{N}(w_{mn}|\mu_w,\sigma_w^2) = \prod_{m=1}^{M}\frac{1}{\sigma_q}\exp\left(-\frac{(q_m-\mu_q)^2}{2\sigma_q^2}\right)\prod_{m=1}^{M}\prod_{n=1}^{N}\frac{1}{\sigma_w}\exp\left(-\frac{(w_{mn}-\mu_w)^2}{2\sigma_w^2}\right) \quad (6)$$

2.5 Parameter Estimation

With the formulated posterior probability, the learning objective is to find the optimal estimation of the parameters Ψ that maximize the posterior. Specifically, we use EM mixed with a sampling algorithm. The algorithm iteratively updates the parameters by mutually enhancement between Geo-clustering and estate ranking. The Geo-clustering updates the latent business areas based on locations and the three geographic dependencies; estate ranking learns the estate scores and generate a ranked list.

E-Step. In the E-step, we iteratively draw latent business area assignments for all real estates. For each estate i, we treat its latent business area r as a latent variable, which is drawn from the posterior of r in terms of the complete likelihood: $r \sim P\left(r|\mathcal{D}, R^{(t)}, \Psi^{(t)}\right)$. More specifically,

$$r \sim P\left(l_i|r,\Psi^{(t)}\right)P\left(\{Y,\Pi\}|r,\Psi^{(t)}\right)P\left(r|\boldsymbol{\eta}^{(t)}\right) \quad (7)$$

where

$$P\left(l_i|r,\Psi^{(t)}\right) = \mathcal{N}\left(l_i|\mu_r^{(t)},\Sigma_r^{(t)}\right) \quad (8)$$

$$P\left(\{Y,\Pi\}|r,\Psi^{(t)}\right) = P(y_i|f_i,\sigma^2)\prod_{h=i+1}^{I}P(i\rightarrow h|r,\Psi^{(t)})^{\mathbb{I}(r_i=r_h)}\prod_{h=i+1}^{I}P(r_i\rightarrow r_h|r,\Psi^{(t)})^{\mathbb{I}(r_i\neq r_h)} \quad (9)$$

Here the latent business area assignment of real estate e_i is updated by three effects: (1) $P(r|\boldsymbol{\eta}^{(t)})$ updates business area assignment in terms of the prosperity distribution of multiple business areas ; (2) $P\left(l_i|r,\Psi^{(t)}\right)$ is the location emission probability given the latent business area as a hidden spatial state. (3) $P\left(\{Y,\Pi\}|r,\Psi^{(t)}\right)$ updates business area assignment by both prediction accuracy and ranking consistency.

When the latent business area assignment of each estate is updated, we further update the neighborhood popularity $\delta_i = \frac{1}{J}\sum_{j=1}^{J}\frac{\phi_{ij}}{max_{i\in r}\{\phi_{ij}\}}$, because the normalization term is conditional on the updated business area r_i.

M-Step. In the M-step, we maximize the log likelihood of the model given the business area assignments R are fixed in the E-step. Since business area assignments are known, we can update $\boldsymbol{\mu}_r, \boldsymbol{\Sigma}_r, \boldsymbol{\eta}$ directly from the samples.

$$\boldsymbol{\mu}_r = \frac{1}{\#(i,r)}\sum_{i=1}^{I}\mathbb{I}(r_i=r)l_i$$
$$\boldsymbol{\Sigma}_r = \frac{1}{\#(i,r)-1}\sum_{i=1}^{I}\mathbb{I}(r_i=r)\left((l_i-\boldsymbol{\mu}_r)^{\top}(l_i-\boldsymbol{\mu}_r)\right) \quad (10)$$

where $\#(i,r)$ is the number of real states assigned to region r. Through imposing a conjugate Dirichlet prior Dir$(\boldsymbol{\gamma})$. we update $\boldsymbol{\eta}^{(t+1)}$ by

$$\boldsymbol{\eta}_r^{(t+1)} = \frac{C_r^{(t+1)}+\gamma}{C^{(t+1)}+|R|\gamma} \quad (11)$$

where $C_r = \sum_{i\in r} y_i$, $C = \sum y_i$ and $\gamma = \frac{1}{K}$.

Note that the centers ($\boldsymbol{\mu}$) and estate investment values ($\boldsymbol{\eta}$) of latent business areas are updated, so updated is the influence of latent business areas $\rho_i = \sum_{k=1}^{K}\left(\frac{d_0}{d_0+d(i,r_k)}\right)^e\frac{\eta_k}{\sum_{k=1}^{K}\eta_k}$.

After updating the parameters $\{\boldsymbol{\eta},\boldsymbol{\mu},\boldsymbol{\Sigma}\}$ and latent business area assignments R, we update $\Psi^{(t+1)}$ that maximizes the log of posterior

$$\mathcal{L}(q,W|R^{(t+1)},\mathcal{D}) = \sum_{i=1}^{I}\left[-\frac{1}{2}ln\sigma^2 - \frac{(y_i-f_i)^2}{2\delta^2}\right] + \sum_{i=1}^{I-1}\sum_{h=i+1}^{I} ln\frac{1}{1+exp(-(f_i-f_h))}\mathbb{I}(r_i=r_h) + \sum_{m=1}^{M}\left[-\frac{1}{2}ln\sigma_q^2 - \frac{(q_m-\mu_q)^2}{2\sigma_q^2}\right] + \sum_{m=1}^{M}\sum_{n=1}^{N}\left[-\frac{1}{2}ln\sigma_w^2 - \frac{(w_{mn}-\mu_w)^2}{2\sigma_w^2}\right] \quad (12)$$

We apply a gradient descent method to update q, W through $q_m^{t+1} = q_m^t - \epsilon\frac{\partial(-\mathcal{L})}{\partial q_m}$ and $w_{mn}^{t+1} = w_{mn}^t - \epsilon\frac{\partial(-\mathcal{L})}{\partial w_{mn}}$

$$\frac{\partial(\mathcal{L})}{\partial q_m} = \sum_{i=1}^{I}\frac{(y_i-f_i)w_{m\cdot}e_i}{\sigma^2} + \sum_{m=1}^{M}-\frac{q_m-\mu_q}{\sigma_q^2} + \sum_{i=1}^{I-1}\sum_{h=i+1}^{I}\frac{exp(f_h-f_i)w_{m\cdot}(e_i-e_h)}{1+exp(f_h-f_i)}\mathbb{I}(r_i=r_h) \quad (13)$$

$$\frac{\partial(\mathcal{L})}{\partial w_{mn}} = \sum_{i=1}^{I}\frac{(y_i-f_i)q_m e_{in}}{\sigma^2} + \sum_{m=1}^{M}-\frac{w_{mn}-\mu_w}{\sigma_w^2} + \sum_{i=1}^{I-1}\sum_{h=i+1}^{I}\frac{exp(f_h-f_i)q_m(e_{in}-e_{hn})}{1+exp(f_h-f_i)}\mathbb{I}(r_i=r_h) \quad (14)$$

2.6 Ranking Inference

After parameters Ψ are estimated via maximizing the posterior probability, which essentially captures both prediction accuracy of estate investment value and the ranking consistence of estates, we will obtain the learned model for investment value of estate, i.e., $\mathbb{E}(y_i|q,e_i) = \gamma_i + \delta_i - \rho_i$ given a rising or falling market period. For a new coming estate k, we may predict its investment value accordingly. The larger the $\mathbb{E}(y_k|q,e_k)$ is, the higher investment value it has. With the predicted investment values for all new estates, we are able to compile a ranking list of those estate.

3. EXPERIMENTAL RESULTS

In this section, we provide an empirical evaluation of the performances of the proposed ClusRanking method on real-world estate data.

3.1 Experimental Data

Data Sources	Properties	Statistics
Real estates	Number of real estates	2,851
	Size of bounding box (km)	40*40
	Time period of transactions	04/2011 - 09/2012
Bus stop(2011)	Number of bus stop	9,810
Subway(2011)	Number of subway station	215
Road networks (2011)	Number of road segments	162,246
	Total length(km)	20,022
	Percentage of major roads	7.5%
POIs	Number 0f POIs	300,811
	Number of categories	13
Taxi Trajectories	Number of taxis	13,597
	Effective days	92
	Time period	Apr. - Aug. 2012
	Number of trips	8,202,012
	Number of GPS points	111,602
	Total distance(km)	61,269,029

Table 4: Statistics of the experimental data.

Table 4 shows four data sources. The transportation data set includes the data about the bus system, the subway system, and the road network in Beijing, China. Also, we extract POI features from the Beijing POI dataset. Moreover, mobility patterns are extracted from the taxi GPS traces. In Beijing, taxi traffic contributes more than 12 percent of the total traffic, and thus reflects a significant portion of human mobility [30]. Finally, we crawl the Beijing estate data from www.soufun.com, which is the largest real-estate online system in China.

In estate industry, the estate return rate is used to measure the investment value of an estate. The estate return rate is the ratio of the price increase relative to the start price of a market period as $r = \frac{P_f - P_i}{P_i}$, where P_f and P_i denote the final price and the initial price, respectively.

To prepare the benchmark investment values of estates (Y) for training data, we first calculate the return rate of each estate during a given market period. We then sort the return rates of all the estates in a descending order. Finally, we cluster them into five clusters using variance based top-down hierarchical clustering. In this way, we segment the estates into five ordered value categories (i.e., $4 > 3 > 2 > 1 > 0$, the higher the better).

By discretizing estate return rates into five categories, we can understand estate investment potentials and reduce the noise led by the small fluctuations in return rates.

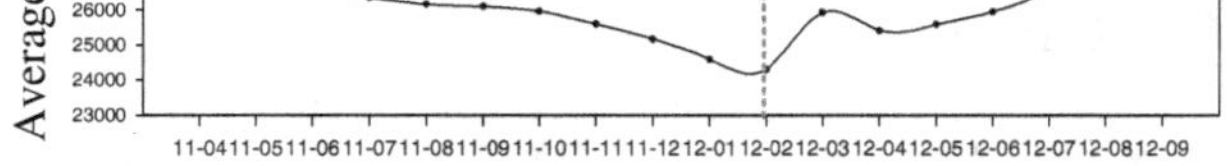

Figure 2: The rising market period and the falling market period in Beijing.

Finally, a list of estates, each of which with the extracted features and investment values, are split into two data sets in terms of the falling market period (from Jul. 2011 to Feb. 2012) and the rising market period (from Feb. 2012 to Sep. 2012) as shown in Figure 2.

3.2 Evaluation Metrics

To show the effectiveness of the proposed model, we use the following metrics for evaluation.

Normalized Discounted Cumulative Gain. The discounted cumulative gain (DCG@N) is given by

$$DCG[n] = \begin{cases} rel_1 & if\, n = 1 \\ DCG[n-1] + \frac{rel_n}{log_2 n}, & if\, n >= 2 \end{cases} \quad (15)$$

Later, given the ideal discounted cumulative gain DCG', NDCG at the n-th position can be computed as NDCG[n]= $\frac{DCG[n]}{DCG'[n]}$. The larger NDCG@N is, the higher top-N ranking accuracy is.

Precision and Recall. Since we use a five-level rating system ($4 > 3 > 2 > 1 > 0$) instead of binary rating, we treat the rating ≥ 3 as "high-value" and the rating < 3 as "low-value". Given a top-N estate list E_N sorted in a descending order of the prediction values, precision and recall are defined as Precision@$N = \frac{|E_N \bigcap E_{\geq 3}|}{N}$ and Recall@$N = \frac{|E_N \bigcap E_{\geq 3}|}{|E_{\geq 3}|}$, where $E_{\geq 3}$ are the estates whose ratings are greater or equal to 3.

Kendall's Tau Coefficient. Kendall's Tau Coefficient (or Tau for short) measures the overall ranking accuracy. Let us assume that each estate i is associated with a benchmark score y_i and a predicted score f_i. Then, for an estate pair $< i, j >$, $< i, j >$ is said to be concordant, if both $y_i > y_j$ and $f_i > f_j$ or if both $y_i < y_j$ and $f_i < f_j$. Also, $< i, j >$ is said to be discordant, if both $y_i < y_j$ and $f_i > f_j$ or if both $y_i < y_j$ and $f_i > f_j$. Tau is given by Tau $= \frac{\#_{conc} - \#_{disc}}{\#_{conc} + \#_{disc}}$.

3.3 Baseline Algorithms

To show the effectiveness of the proposed method, we compare the ranking accuracy of our methods against following baseline algorithms. (1) **MART [10]:** it is a boosted tree model, specifically, a linear combination of the outputs of a set of regression trees. (2) **RankBoost [9]:** it is a boosted pairwise ranking method, which trains multiple weak rankers and combines their outputs as final ranking. (3) **Coordinate Ascent [20]:** it uses domination loss and applies coordinate descent for optimization. (4) **ListNet [4]:** it is a listwise ranking model with permutation top-k ranking likelihood as the objective function.

For the baseline algorithms, we use RankLib[2]. We set the number of trees = 1000, the number of leaves = 10, the number of threshold candidates = 256, and the learning rate = 0.1 for MART. For RankBoost, we set the number of iteration = 300, the number of threshold candidates = 10. Regarding Coordinate Ascent, we set step base = 0.05, step scale = 2.0, tolerance = 0.001, and slack = 0.001. For our model, we set β_1=0.8 and β_2=25m. We set $d_0 = 1$ and $d(i, r_k)$ is computed based on degree (°) instead of mile or km for simplicity. We set latent business areas K=10 and initialize the mean and covariance of the locations of each business area by Kmeans clustering. Finally, we set $\eta = \frac{1}{K}$, $\mu_q = \mu_w = 0$, $\sigma_q = \sigma_w = \sigma = 35$ and M=3 for hyperparameters.

The codes are implemented in R (modeling), Python (preprocessing), and Matlab (visualization). The experiments were performed on a x64 machine with Intel i5 2.60GHz

[2]http://sourceforge.net/p/lemur/wiki/RankLib/

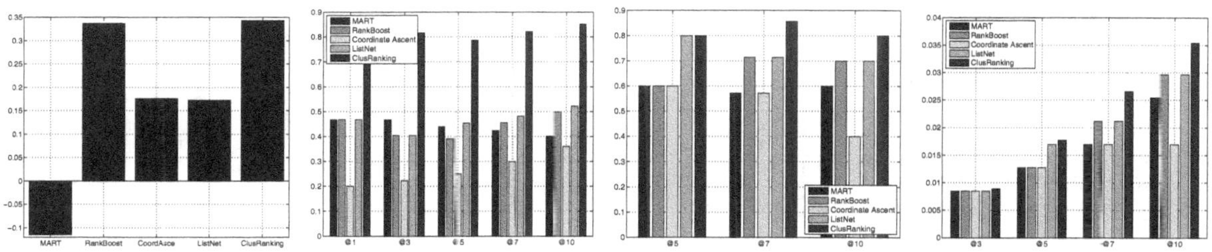

(a) Tau (b) NDCG@N (c) Precision@N (d) Recall@N

Figure 3: The overall performances on the rising market dataset.

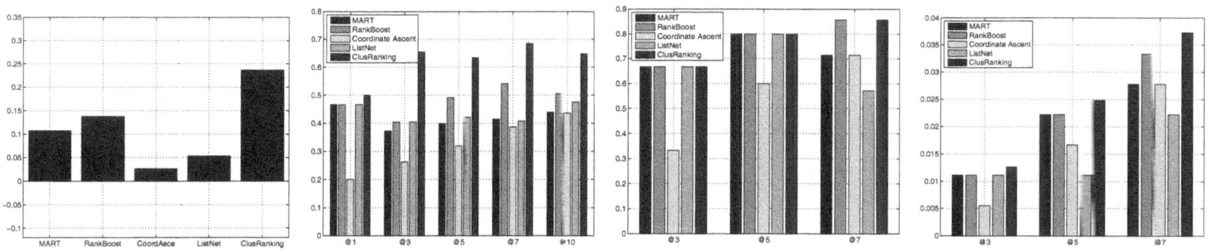

(a) Tau (b) NDCG@N (c) Precision@N (d) Recall@N

Figure 4: The overall performances on the falling market dataset.

dual-core CPU and 16GB RAM. The operation system is Microsoft Windows 7 Professional.

3.4 Overall Performances

We provide the performance comparison on the rising market dataset and the falling market dataset in terms of Tau, NDCG, Precision and Recall.

Rising Market Data. Figure 3(a) shows the comparison of Kendall's Tau Coefficient. Our method achieves 0.3428617 and outperforms the baselines. Figure 3(b) shows the NDCG comparison. Our method achieves 0.75 NDCG@1, 0.81 NDCG@3, 0.78 NDCG@5, 0.82 NDCG@7, and 0.85 NDCG@10 whereas the NDCGs of the four baselines only range from 0.2 to 0.61. Figure 3(c) and Figure 3(d) respectively show the precision@N and recall@N. In Precision, ClusRanking > ListNet > MART, RankBoost, Coordinate Ascent. In Recall, ClusRanking achieves 0.0088 recall@3, 0.017 recall@5, 0.026 recall@7, and 0.035 recall@10, which in overall outperforms ListNet, MART, RankBoost, Coordinate Ascent with a significant margin.

Falling Market Data. Figure 4 shows the comparison in terms of Kendall's Tau. Our method achieves a higher accuracy at 0.2363498 than four baselines. We also compare all the five methods in terms of NDCG, Precision and Recall. Our method achieves around 0.65 NDCG@3, 0.63 NDCG@5, 0.68 NDCG@7, and 0.64 NDCG@10 whereas the NDCGs of the four baselines are lower than 0.6111. Moreover, the Precision@3,5,7 of our method are relatively higher than the baselines in overall. Finally, our method achieves 0.012 recall@3, 0.024 recall@5, and 0.037 recall@7, which are generally better than RankBoost but significantly outperforms MART, Coordinate Ascent and ListNet.

The above overall performances validate the effectiveness of our ClusRanking method.

3.5 The Study on Geographic Dependencies

Here, we study the impact of three geographic dependencies. Specifically, we designed three internal competing methods in terms of variants of posterior likelihood $Pr(\Psi;\mathcal{D},\Omega) = P(\mathcal{D}|\Psi,\Omega)\,P(\Psi|\Omega)$: (1) **Individual Dependency (ID)**, in which we only consider the individual dependency as the objective function. In other words, $P(\mathcal{D}|\Psi,\Omega) = Lik_{id}$. (2) **Peer Dependency (PD)**, in which we only consider the peer dependency as the objective function. (3) **Peer Dependency + Zone Dependency (PD+ZD)**, in which we consider the combination of peer and zone dependencies as the objective function. (4) **Combination (ClusRanking)**, in which we consider individual, peer, and zone dependencies simultaneously. This is exactly our method: $P(\mathcal{D}|\Psi,\Omega) = Lik_{id} \times Lik_{pd} \times Lik_{zd}$.

Rising Market Data. Table 5 shows the performance comparison on the rising market data in terms of Tau and NDCG. It is clear that our method achieves around 0.81 NDCG@3, 0.78 NDCG@5, 0.82 NDCG@7 and 0.85@10 on the rising market data, which outperforms PD+ZD, PD, and ID. In the Tau comparison, the results lead to: ClusRanking > PD > ID > PD+ZD. From Table 5, we conclude that (1) the strategy of capturing three dependencies helps ClusRanking to achieve the highest Tau and NDCG; (2) considering both peer and zone dependencies enhances the top-k accuracy but degrades the overall ranking comparing to individual dependency only. This might be because the peer and zone dependencies better capture the ranking consistency of estates than the individual dependency, as individual dependency indeed models the prediction accuracy of the observed data collection $\{Y, L\}$.

Metric	@N	ID	PD	PD+ZD	ClusRanking
NDCG	3	0.5599531	0.6549766	0.6900469	**0.8166009**
	5	0.5771226	0.6024622	0.6101556	**0.7867076**
	7	0.587992	0.6048394	0.641282	**0.8208795**
	10	0.6518163	0.6723095	0.694175	**0.8513267**
Tau	-	0.2494531	0.2535907	0.2203712	**0.3428617**

Table 5: Performance comparison of different geographic dependencies on the rising market data.

Falling Market Data. Table 6 shows the performance comparison of different geographic dependencies on the falling market data. It is clear that our method outperforms ID, PD and PD+ZD. PD+ZD achieves the second highest NDCG.

Moreover, ClusRanking > PD+ZD > PD > ID in terms of Kendall's Tau.

Metric	@N	ID	PD	PD+ZD	ClusRanking
NDCG	3	0.570193	0.5950234	0.6250234	**0.6549766**
	5	0.6144799	0.6004235	0.6144799	**0.633635**
	7	0.6196808	0.654487	0.6196808	**0.6845354**
	10	0.6415102	0.6252658	0.6307051	**0.6482665**
Tau	-	0.1186736	0.1313437	0.1433408	**0.2363498**

Table 6: Performance comparison of different geographic dependencies on the falling market data.

This experiment not only justifies the spatial autocorrelation of estate investment values (e.g., individual, estate-estate peer, estate-business area), but also shows the advantages of considering three geographical dependencies .

3.6 The Study on Geographic Features

We compare the performances of ClusRanking with different geographic feature sets (i.e., subway, bus stop, POI, and road network) over rising and falling markets.

Rising Market Data. First, Figure 5(a) shows the performance comparison of the five feature sets in terms of Tau: combination > road network > bus stop, subway and poi. Next, Figure 5(b) shows the NDCG@N of different feature sets (N=3, 5, 7, 10 respectively). As can be seen, the combination of all the four feature sets achieves 0.81 NDCG@3, 0.78 NDCG@5, 0.82 NDCG@7, 0.85 NDCG@10, and outperforms the other four individual feature sets. Moreover, the NDCGs of the bus stop and road network feature sets are lower than combination but higher than the POI and subway feature sets. Finally, we can conclude that, in rising market, the combination of all geographic information is the best. Road network outperforms bus stop, subway and POI. Bus stop is more suitable for top-k ranking than road network whereas road network performs better than bus stop in overall ranking.

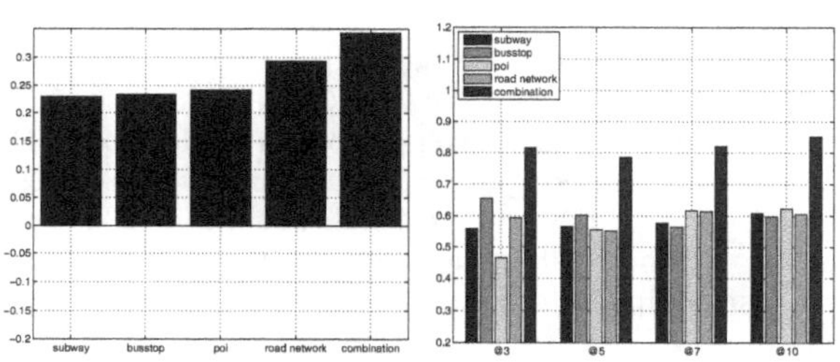

(a) Tau (b) NDCG@N

Figure 5: Performance comparison of different geographic features on rising market data.

Falling Market Data. Figure 6(a) shows a comparison of the five feature sets on Tau: combination > road network > bus stop, subway and poi. This result is consistent with that of rising market data. Regarding top-k ranking, Figure 6(b) shows the NDCG@N (N=3, 5, 7 respectively) of different feature sets in terms of ClusRanking. First, the POI feature set achieves the worst performance in NDCG@5,7. Second, the road network feature set achieves the second highest NDCGs@3,5,7. Finally, the combination of all the four feature sets outperforms all the individual feature sets. In summary, in falling market, combination > bus stop > subway, road network, and POI.

The results validate the effectiveness of using multiple information fusion (subway, bus stop, POI and road network).

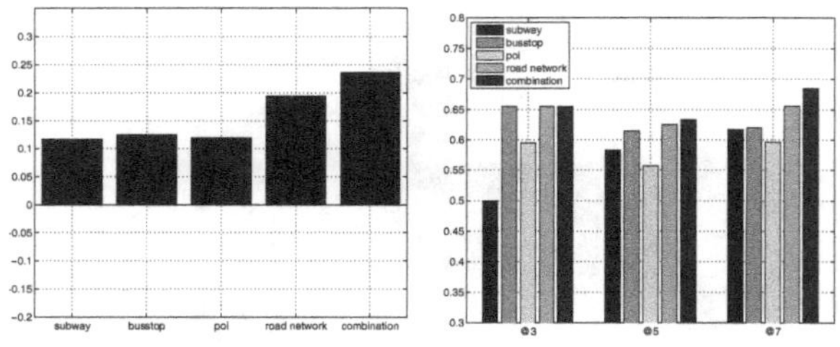

(a) Tau (b) NDCG@N

Figure 6: Performance comparison of different geographic features on falling market data.

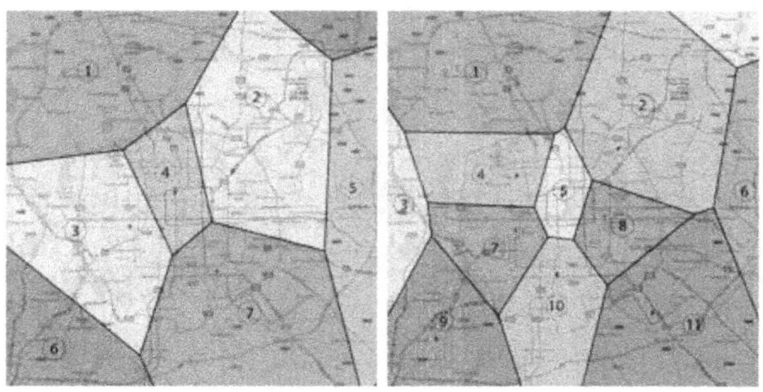

(a) Kmeans (b) ClusRanking

Figure 7: A comparison of the learned business areas within the Beijing Fifth Ring (K=10).

3.7 Implication of Latent Business Areas

Our model also provides a unique understanding of the latent business areas of Beijing from an estate perspective. Figure 7 clearly shows our method, learned from geography, mobility and estate data, is more reasonable than K-means, which simply cluster the estates by location information. For instance, in Figure 7(b), NO.4 area, named Zhongguancun, is the Chinese Silicon Valley and is famous for high-tech companies. This area is a high density cluster of human mobility, estates and POIs. However, in Figure 7(a), the Zhongguancun area is improperly separated into NO.3 and NO.4 area by K-means. Another example is the NO.2 and NO.8 areas, namely Wangjing and CBD respectively, in Figure 7(b). Wangjing is a quick-growing residential sub-center with easy-access transportation and luxury apartments. Currently, about 203,000 young people, including company executives, white-collar workers, expatriates and returnees, are living in Wangjing. CBD is the Center Business District with numerous financial business offices, culture media companies and high-end enterprise information services. However, in Figure 7(a), Wangjing and CBD are improperly united into NO.2 area by K-means. The visualization results show the effectiveness of ClusRanking learned from multi-source estate related data and the effectiveness of capturing the three geographic dependencies as the objective function.

3.8 Hierarchy of Needs for Human Life

We show how our ranking results can be used to understand the hierarchy of human needs from a POI aspect. Figure 8 shows the estate-POI density spectrum. From left to right, x-axis represents the estate rankings in the descending order. From up to down, y-axis represents POI categories in the descending order in terms of POI numbers. Several interesting findings can be drawn from Figure 8. First, the upper half are darker than the lower half. This indicates

POI categories in the upper half are more important than those in the lower half. In other words, people prefer their homes near schools, malls, offices, restaurants, and transits. Whereas, hotels, hospitals, sports and scene spots are not must-have POIs to be located close to living places. Second, along x-axis, the POI density spectrum of the left-side high-ranked estates is evenly distributed for smooth whereas the POI density spectrum of the right-side low-ranked estates are non-smooth. This illustrates high-value estates usually balance the needs of human beings. Third, we calculate the average POI density of each POI category based on the top 2000 estates. We then sort all POI categories in terms of POI densities, show the smoothed POI density curve and find three inflection points. Later, we segment those POI categories into four clusters using the three inflection points. Finally, we present a triangle structure of needs of Beijing citizens as shown in Figure 9. The higher, the more fundamental and urgent in human needs.

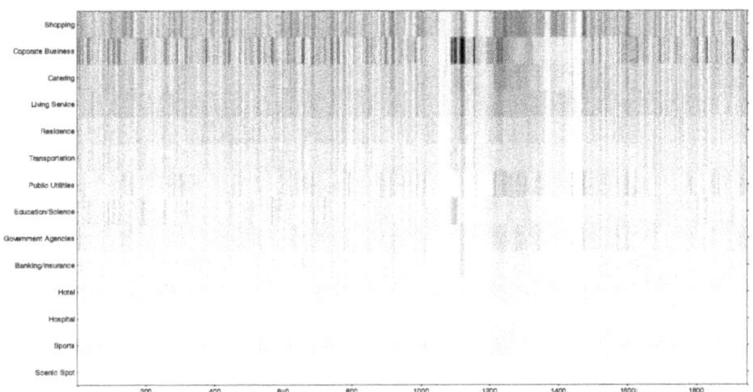

Figure 8: The POI density spectral of estates over multiple poi categories

Figure 9: The triangle need hierarchy of Beijing

3.9 A Case Study

Here, we present a case study. First, we select one high-ranked estate called "Red Hill Family" (RHF) and one low-ranked estate called "Jiuxianqiao Road No. 11" (JR11) from our ranking results. Then, we compare RHF with JR11 from historical transaction prices. As can be seen in Figure 10, during the past 43 months, the prices of RHF increase in both rising and falling markets. However, for the past 15 months, the overall prices of JR11 continuously fall even in the rising market.

To show why, we first check the neighborhood profiles (individual dependency) of two estates. Specifically, we extract geographic and mobility features of the neighborhoods of RHF and JR11, respectively. Table 7 shows RHF has higher road network density, larger amount of POIs (especially schools), bus stops and subway stations, and higher neighborhood popularity than JR11. It thus is reasonable that people are willing to afford higher prices to RHF than JR11. This validates the individual dependency. Besides, RHF is located in the prosperous area of MuXiDi (inside No. 7 area in Figure 7(b)) near the 2nd ring road whereas JR11 is located in the area of DongFengXiang (inside No.2 area in Figure 7(b)) outside the fifth ring road. The average rating of estates in MuXiDi is round to 3, which is higher than that (round to 1) of estates in DongFengXiang. This justifies the zone dependency.

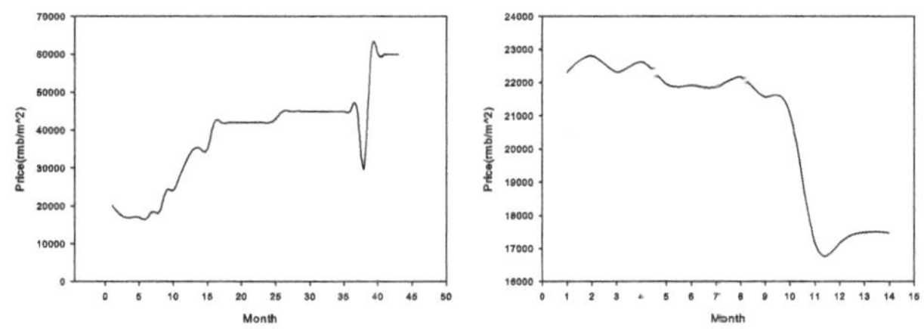

(a) Red Hill Family (b) Jiuxianqiao Road No. 11

Figure 10: Price Trend Comparison.

Type	Name	RHF	JR11
transportation	bus stop(1km)	12	3
	subway(3km)	9	0
	shortest distance to subway	1061	3597
	road network level-2 entry(3km)	102	46
POI number (1km)	catering	143	17
	shopping	127	18
	living	201	16
	sports	27	3
	healthcare	44	2
	education	67	13
	finance	55	1
	public facility	79	10
popularity	average accumulated visit probability	1.64e+7	1.36e+3

Table 7: A comparison of transportation, POI and mobility of RHF and JR11

4. RELATED WORK

Related work can be grouped into two categories. The first one includes the work on estate appraisal. In the second category, we present the ranking related methods.

Traditional research on estate appraisal are based on financial estate theory, typically constructing an explicit index of estate value [16]. More studies rely on financial time series analysis by inspecting the trend, periodicity and volatility of estate prices. Work [8] checks the volatility of estate price and concludes that low investment-valued estate values relatively volatile. Work [5] applies an autoregression method to learn the trend and periodicity of price and predicts estate value. More studies are conducted from an econometric angle, for example, hedonic methods and repeat sales methods. The hedonic methods [27, 1] assume the price of a property depends on its characteristics and location. The repeat sales methods [1, 2, 26] construct a predefined price index based on properties sold more than once during the given period. Recent works [8, 21] study the automated valuation models, which aggregate and analyze physical characteristics and sales prices of comparable properties to provide property valuations. More recent studies [22, 15, 17, 2] shift to computational estate appraisal and apply general additive mode, support vector machine regression, multilayer perceptron and ensemble method to evaluate estate value.

Also, our work can be categorized into Learning-To-Rank (LTR). The LTR methods are threefold: point-wise, pair-wise and list-wise. The point-wise methods [12, 7] reduce the LTR task to a regression problem: given a single query-document pair, predict its score. The pair-wise methods, such as RankBoost [9], RankSVM [14] and LambdaRank [23], approximate the LTR task as a classification problem and learn a binary classifier that can tell which document is better in a given document pair. The list-wise methods, such as AdaRank [29], LambdaMART [3] and ListNet [4], optimize a ranking loss metric over lists instead of document pairs. Works [28, 24, 13] provide full Bayesian explanations and optimize the posterior of point-wise, pair-wise and list-wise ranking models. Study [25] further unifies both rating error and ranking error as objective function to enhance Top-K recommendation. There are also studies that improve ranking performance by semi-supervised learning through exploiting the disagreement between two learners [32] or combining supervised and unsupervised ranking models [18].

Furthermore, our work has a connection with recent studies of exploring the geographic influence for POI recommendation. Works [6, 11] consider the multi-center of user check-in patterns and apply a static pre-clustering method to extract the influence of geographic proximity in choosing a POI. Work [19] exploits multi-center user mobility and embeds a POI clustering method into matrix factorization. Finally, our work is related to studies of city region function via geographic topic modeling using POI and mobility [31].

5. CONCLUSION

In this paper, we proposed a ClusRanking method for ranking estates based on their investment values. Specifically, this method has the ability in capturing the geographic individual, peer, and zone dependencies via ClusRanking by exploiting various estate related data. Also, our method has two advantages. First, for predictive modeling, we establish a hierarchical generative structure to capture both explicit factors (i.g., geographic utility and neighborhood popularity) and latent influences (e.g., the influence of latent business area) based on the estate data. This generative structure profiles, filters, aggregates and fuses multi-source information to predict estate investment values. It helps to take advantage of rich estate-related data sources. Second, in the learning framework, we leverage the mutual enforcement of ranking and clustering power. In addition, we simultaneously consider three dependencies and construct an estate-specific ranking likelihood as the objective function for enhancing model learning. Finally, the experimental study demonstrates the effectiveness of our method on real-world estate-related data over several alternative methods.

Acknowledgement

This research was supported in part by National Science Foundation Grant IIS-1256016, the National Science Foundation of China under Grant number 61333014 and the 111 Project under Grant Number B14020.

6. REFERENCES

[1] E. M. Assil. Constructing a real estate price index: the moroccan experience. 2012.

[2] M. Bailey, R. Muth, and H. Nourse. A regression method for real estate price index construction. *J. Am. Stat. Assoc.*, 58:933–942, 1963.

[3] C. Burges. From ranknet to lambdarank to lambdamart: An overview. *Learning*, 11:23–581, 2010.

[4] Z. Cao, T. Qin, T.-Y. Liu, M.-F. Tsai, and H. Li. Learning to rank: from pairwise approach to listwise approach. In *ICML'07*, 2007.

[5] L. D. B. Chaitra H. Nagaraja and L. H. Zhao. An autoregressive approach to house price modeling, 2009.

[6] C. Cheng, H. Yang, I. King, and M. R. Lyu. Fused matrix factorization with geographical and social influence in location-based social networks. In *AAAI'12*, 2012.

[7] W. S. Cooper, F. C. Gey, and D. P. Dabney. Probabilistic retrieval based on staged logistic regression. In *SIGIR'92*, 1992.

[8] M. L. Downie and G. Robson. Automated valuation models: an international perspective. 2007.

[9] Y. Freund, R. Iyer, R. E. Schapire, and Y. Singer. An efficient boosting algorithm for combining preferences. *The Journal of machine learning research*, 4:933–969, 2003.

[10] J. H. Friedman. Greedy function approximation: a gradient boosting machine. *Annals of Statistics*, pages 1189–1232, 2001.

[11] Y. Fu, B. Liu, Y. Ge, Z. Yao, and H. Xiong. User preference learning with multiple information fusion for restaurant recommendation. In *SDM'14*, 2014.

[12] N. Fuhr. Optimum polynomial retrieval functions based on the probability ranking principle. *ACM Transactions on Information Systems (TOIS)*, 7(3):183–204, 1989.

[13] Z. Gantner, L. Drumond, C. Freudenthaler, and L. Schmidt-Thieme. Personalized ranking for non-uniformly sampled items. *Journal of Machine Learning Research-Proceedings Track*, 18:231–247, 2012.

[14] R. Herbrich, T. Graepel, and K. Obermayer. Large margin rank boundaries for ordinal regression. *Advances in Neural Information Processing Systems*, pages 115–132, 1999.

[15] V. Kontrimas and A. Verikas. The mass appraisal of the real estate by computational intelligence. *Applied Soft Computing*, 11:443 – 448, 2011.

[16] J. Krainer and C. Wei. House prices and fundamental value. *FRBSF Economic Letter*, 2004.

[17] E.-K. Lam. Modern regression models and neural networks for residential property valuation. *RICS Research-The Cutting Edge*, 1996.

[18] M. Li, H. Li, and Z.-H. Zhou. Semi-supervised document retrieval. *Information Processing and Management*, 2009.

[19] B. Liu, Y. Fu, Z. Yao, and H. Xiong. Learning geographical preferences for point-of-interest recommendation. In *KDD'13*, 2013.

[20] D. Metzler and W. B. Croft. Linear feature-based models for information retrieval. *Information Retrieval*, 10:257–274, 2007.

[21] A. Mitropoulos, W. Wu, and G. Kohansky. Criteria for automated valuation models in the uk. *Fitch Ratings*, 2007.

[22] R. K. Pace. Appraisal using generalized additive models. *Journal of Real Estate Research*, 15:77–100, 1998.

[23] C. Quoc and V. Le. Learning to rank with nonsmooth cost functions. *Proceedings of the Advances in Neural Information Processing Systems*, 19:193–200, 2007.

[24] S. Rendle, C. Freudenthaler, Z. Gantner, and L. Schmidt-Thieme. Bpr: Bayesian personalized ranking from implicit feedback. In *UAI '09*, 2009.

[25] Y. Shi, M. Larson, and A. Hanjalic. Unifying rating-oriented and ranking-oriented collaborative filtering for improved recommendation. *Information Sciences*, 2012.

[26] R. J. Shiller. Arithmetic repeat sales price estimators. Technical report, Cowles Foundation for Research in Economics, Yale University, 1991.

[27] L. O. Taylor. The hedonic method. In *A primer on nonmarket valuation*. Springer, 2003.

[28] R. C. Weng and C.-J. Lin. A bayesian approximation method for online ranking. *The Journal of Machine Learning Research*, 12:267–300, 2011.

[29] J. Xu and H. Li. Adarank: a boosting algorithm for information retrieval. In *SIGIR '07*, 2007.

[30] J. Yuan, Y. Zheng, and X. Xie. Discovering regions of different functions in a city using human mobility and pois. In *KDD'12*, 2012.

[31] Y. Zheng, L. Capra, O. Wolfson, and H. Yang. Urban computing: concepts, methodologies, and applications. *ACM TIST*, 2014.

[32] Z.-H. Zhou, K.-J. Chen, and H.-B. Dai. Enhancing relevance feedback in image retrieval using unlabeled data. *ACM Transactions on Information Systems*, 2006.

Towards Scalable Critical Alert Mining

Bo Zong[1] Yinghui Wu[1] Jie Song[2] Ambuj K. Singh[1]
Hasan Cam[3] Jiawei Han[4] Xifeng Yan[1]
[1]UC Santa Barbara [2] LogicMonitor [3]Army Research Lab [4] UIUC
{xyan, bzong, yinghui, ambuj}@cs.ucsb.edu jsong@logicmonitor.com
hasan.cam.civ@mail.mil hanj@cs.uiuc.edu

ABSTRACT

Performance monitor software for data centers typically generates a great number of alert sequences. These alert sequences indicate abnormal network events. Given a set of observed alert sequences, it is important to identify the most critical alerts that are potentially the causes of others. While the need for mining critical alerts over large scale alert sequences is evident, most alert analysis techniques stop at modeling and mining the causal relations among the alerts.

This paper studies the *critical alert mining* problem: Given a set of alert sequences, we aim to find a set of k critical alerts such that the number of alerts potentially triggered by them is maximized. We show that the problem is intractable; therefore, we resort to approximation and heuristic algorithms. First, we develop an approximation algorithm that obtains a near-optimal alert set in quadratic time, and propose pruning techniques to improve its runtime performance. Moreover, we show a faster approximation exists, when the alerts follow certain causal structure. Second, we propose two fast heuristic algorithms based on tree sampling techniques. On real-life data, these algorithms identify a critical alert from up to $270,000$ mined causal relations in 5 seconds; meanwhile, they preserve more than 80% of solution quality, and are up to $5,000$ times faster than their approximation counterparts.

1. INTRODUCTION

System monitoring and analysis in data centers and cyber security applications produces alert sequences to capture abnormal events. For example, performance metrics are posed on hosts in data centers to measure the system activities, and capture alerts such as high CPU usage, memory overflow, or service errors. Understanding the causal and dependency relations among these alerts is critical for data center management [12, 25], cyber security [17], and device network diagnosis [23], among others.

While there exist a variety of approaches for modeling and deriving causal relations [3, 31, 32], another important step is to efficiently suggest critical alerts from a huge amount of observed alerts. Intuitively, these critical alerts indicate the "root causes" that account for the observed alerts, such that if fixed, we may expect a great reduction of other alerts without blindly addressing them one by one. We consider several real-life applications below.

KDD'14, August 24–27, 2014, New York, NY, USA.
Copyright 2014 ACM 978-1-4503-2956-9/14/08 ...$15.00.
http://dx.doi.org/10.1145/2623330.2623729.

Data centers. System monitoring and analysis providers seek efficient and reliable techniques to understand a large number of system performance alerts in data centers. According to LogicMonitor[1], a SaaS network monitor company, a data center of 122 servers generates more than $20,000$ alerts per day. While it is daunting for domain experts to manually check these alerts one by one, it is desirable to automatically suggest a small set of alerts that are potentially causes for a large amount of alerts, for further verification. These critical alerts also help in determining key control points for data center infrastructures [25].

Intrusion detection [2, 16]. State-of-the-art intrusion detection systems produce large numbers of alerts from cyber network sensors, over tens of thousands of security metrics, e.g., Host scan or TCP hijacking [2]. As suggested in [16], it is observed that a few critical alerts generally account for over 90% of the alerts that an intrusion detection system triggers. By handling only a small number of critical alerts, a huge amount of effort and resource can be reduced. On the other hand, critical alerts can reduce the number of "false alerts" and improve alarm quality [2].

Network performance diagnosis [23]. Large-scale IP networks (*e.g.,* North America IPTV network) contain millions of devices, which generate a great number of performance alarms from customer call records and provider logs. Scalable mining of critical alerts for a given set of symptom events benefits fast network diagnosis [23]

These highlight the need for efficient algorithms to mine critical alerts, given the sheer size of observed ones. In this work, we investigate efficient critical alert mining techniques. We focus on a general framework with desirable performance guarantees on alert quality and scalability.

(1) We formulate the *critical alert mining* problem: Given a set of alerts and a number k, it aims to find a set of k critical alerts, such that the number of alerts that are potentially caused by them is maximized. We introduce a generic framework for mining critical alerts. In this framework, we learn and maintain an *alert graph*, a graph representation

[1]http://www.logicmonitor.com/

of causal relations among alerts. Upon users' requests, top critical alerts are mined from alert graphs.

(2) We show that the critical alert mining problem is NP-complete. Nonetheless, we provide an algorithm with approximation ratio $1-\frac{1}{e}$, in time $O(k|V||E|)$, where $|V|$ and $|E|$ are the number of alerts and the number of their causal relations, respectively. To further improve the efficiency of the algorithm, we propose a bound and pruning algorithm that effectively reduces the size of alerts to be verified as critical ones. In addition, we identify a special case: when alert graphs are trees, it is in $O(k|V|)$ time to find k critical alerts, with the same approximation ratio.

(3) The quadratic time approximation may still be expensive for large alert graphs. We further propose two fast heuristics for large-scale critical alert mining. These algorithms induce trees that preserve the most probable causal relations from large alert graphs, and estimate top critical alerts and their impact by only accessing the trees. The first one induces a single tree, while the second algorithm balances alert quality and mining efficiency with multiple sampled trees.

(4) We experimentally verify our critical alert mining framework. Over real-life data center datasets, our algorithms effectively identify critical alerts that trigger a large number of other alerts, as verified by domain experts. We found that our approximation algorithms mine a top critical alert from up to 270,000 causal relations (one day's alert sequences) in 5 seconds. On the other hand, while our heuristics preserve more than 80% of solution quality, they are up to 5,000 times faster than their approximation counterparts. The heuristics also scale well over large synthetic alert graphs, with up to in total 1 million alerts and 10 million relations.

In contrast to conventional causality modeling and mining, our algorithms leverage effecitive pruning and sampling methods for fast critical alert mining. In addition, we do not assume the luxury of accessing rich semantics from the alerts that helps in improving mining efficiency, although our methods immediately benefit from the semantics in specific applications [16, 23, 25], as well as domain experts. Taken together with domain knowledge and causality mining tools, these algorithms are one step towards large-scale critical alert analysis for data centers, intrusion detection systems, and network diagnosis systems.

2. PROBLEM DEFINITION

We start with the notions of alert sequences and alert graphs. Then we introduce the critical alert mining problem.

Performance metrics. A performance metric measures an aspect of system performance. For data centers, common types of performance metrics include CPU and memory usage for virtual machines, error rate of disk writes for a service, or communication time between two hosts. The same type of metrics over different hosts, virtual machines, or services are considered as distinct performance metrics.

In practice, system service providers e.g., LogicMonitor may cope with 2 million metrics from a data center with 5,000 hosts. These metrics could correlate with and cause each other due to functional or resource dependencies.

Alert and alert sequences. For a set of performance metrics $\mathbb{P}$, alerts are determined by aggregating the metric values of interest. For example, in data centers, an alert is raised when the value of a performance metric (*e.g.*, CPU usage) goes beyond a pre-defined threshold (*e.g.*, > 75%). In this work, we define an alert as a triple $u = (p_u, t_u, w_u)$, where $p_u \in \mathbb{P}$ is a performance metric u corresponds to, t_u denotes the timestamp when the alert u happened, and w_u is the weight of u, representing the benefit if u is fixed.

We use a sequence of alerts to characterize abnormal events for a specific performance metric. Indeed, in practice the performance metrics are typically periodically monitored to capture the abnormal events as alerts. We denote as $\vec{s}_p$ an alert series (an ordered sequence of alerts following their timestamps), for a specific performance metric $p \in \mathbb{P}$. Each entry of $\vec{s}_p$ is either 0 (normal) or 1 (alert).

To characterize causal relations between two alerts, we next introduce a notion of *dependency rule*. We also introduce *alert graph* as an intuitive graph representation for multiple dependency rules.

Dependency rule. Let p and q be two distinct performance metrics. A dependency rule $p \xrightarrow{l_{pq}} q$ denotes an alert issued on q at some time t is caused by an alert issued on p at $t' \in [t - l_{pq}, t-1]$, where l_{pq} is a *lag* from p to q (*e.g.*, 5 minutes). Note that we do not specify the time t, as a dependency rule describes a statistical rule for all the observed alerts. Intuitively, a dependency rule indicates that alerts on q occurs if and only if alerts on p occurs as the cause of the alerts on q; that is, the alerts on p will trigger the alerts on q. If certain trouble shooting action is taken to fix p, q is addressed accordingly [2, 23].

Dependency rules can be automatically learned from alert series [3, 31]. They can also be suggested by experts and existing knowledge bases [10]. To smoothen the noise or error brought by rule generation process, we associate an uncertainty to each dependency rule. In particular, we denote the uncertainty by $\Pr(p \xrightarrow{l_{pq}} q)$, which is the probability that the corresponding dependency rule holds.

Alert graph. An alert graph over a set of alerts V is a directed acyclic graph $G = (V, E, f_e)$:

- V is the set of vertices in G, where each vertex $v \in V$ is an alert from V.
- E is a set of edges in G. Let $u = (p_u, t_u, w_u)$ and $v = (p_v, t_v, w_v)$ be two alerts in V. There is an edge $(u, v) \in E$ if and only if there exists a dependency rule $p_u \xrightarrow{l_{p_u p_v}} p_v$, where $t_u < t_v$, and $t_v - t_u \leq l_{pq}$.
- f_e is a function that assigns for each edge (u, v) the probability that u *causes* v, *i.e.*, $\Pr(p_u \xrightarrow{l_{p_u p_v}} p_v)$.

We shall use the following notations. Abusing the notions from tree topology, we say u (resp. v) is a parent (resp. child) of v (resp. u) if $(u, v) \in E$, and the edge (u, v) is an incoming edge of v. The *topological order* r of an alert u in G is defined as follows. (a) $r(u) = 0$ if u has no parent, and (b) $r(u) = 1 + \max r(v)$, for all its parents v.

Following the convention of causal relation and cascading models [29], we assume that an alert is caused by a single alert issued earlier, if any. Intuitively, a path from an alert u to another alert v in the alert graph indicates a potential "causal chain" from u to v, indicated by e.g., the actual dependencies among the vulnerabilities of the servers [5].

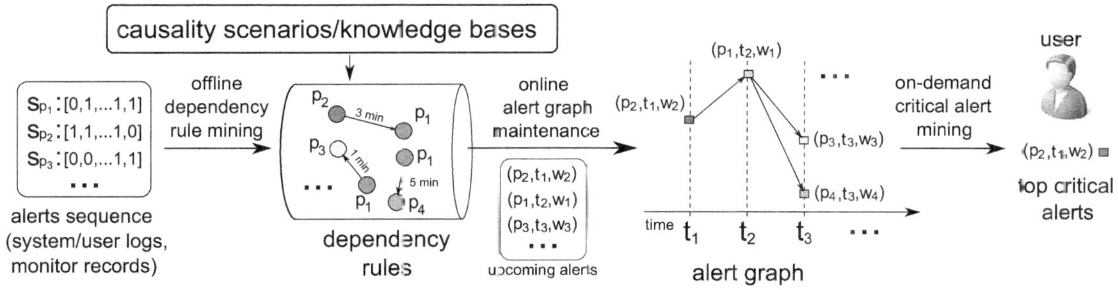

Figure 1: Critical alert mining: pipeline

Critical alerts. We next introduce a metric to characterize critical alerts, in terms of how many alerts are potentially caused by them via a cascading effect (and hence are addressed if the critical ones are fixed). Given $G = (V, E, f_e)$, a set of fixed alerts $S \subseteq V$, and an alert $u \in V$, we use a notion of *alert-fixed probability* P_f to characterize the probability that u is fixed if S is fixed. More specifically,

- $P_f(S, u) = 1$ if $u \in S$,
- otherwise,

$$P_f(S,u) = 1 - \prod_{(u',u)\in E} \Big(1 - P_f(S,u')f_e(u',u)\Big).$$

Based on the alert-fixed probability, we next define a set function, denoted as Gain, to characterize critical alerts. Given an alert graph $G = (V, E, f_e)$ and $S \subseteq V$, the gain of S is a set function

$$\mathsf{Gain}(S) = \sum_{u\in V} w_u \cdot P_f(S,u).$$

As remarked earlier, here w_u refers to the weight of u, *i.e.*, the benfit if u is fixed. Intuitively, $\mathsf{Gain}(S)$ computes the total expected benefits induced via fixing a set of alerts S and subsequently addressing the alerts caused by S. The larger $\mathsf{Gain}(S)$ is, the more "critical" S is.

We next introduce the critical alert mining problem.

DEFINITION 1. *Given an alert graph G and an integer k, the critical alert mining problem (referred to as* CAM*) is to find a set of k critical alerts $S \subset V$ such that $\mathsf{Gain}(S)$ is maximized.*

Finding the best set of k alerts which maximize the gain is desirable albeit intractable.

THEOREM 1. *For a given alert graph G and an integer k, the problem* CAM *is NP-complete.*

PROOF. We prove the NP-completeness of the decision version of CAM as follows. (1) CAM is in NP. Indeed, given an alert graph $G = (V, E)$ and a set of vertices $S \subseteq V$, one can evaluate Gain by computing $P_f(S, v)$ of each alert v in polynomial time. (2) To show that CAM is NP-hard, we construct a reduction from the maximum coverage problem, which is known to be NP-hard [35]. An instance of a maximum coverage problem consists of a set of sets $\mathcal{S}$ and an integer k. It selects at most k of these sets such that the number of elements that are covered is no less than a bound B. A maximum coverage instance can be constructed as a bipartite alert graph, with each "upside" node as a set in $\mathcal{S}$, each "downside" node a distinct element in these sets, and there is an edge from upside node to downside node if the corresponding element is in the set denoted by the upside node. In addition, the weights on edges are uniformly 1. Given the bound B, one may verify that there is a solution for the maximum converage problem if and only if there is a set S of k critical alerts with $\mathsf{Gain}(S) \geq B$. Therefore, CAM is at least as hard as maximum coverage problem, and is NP-hard. Hence, CAM is NP-complete. □

3. MINING FRAMEWORK

In this section, we present a framework for critical alert mining. It consists of three components as illustrated in Figure 1: (1) offline dependency rule mining; (2) online alert graph maintenance; and (3) on-demand critical alert mining.

Offline dependency rule mining. Given a set of observed alert sequences, the system mines the alerts of interest and their causal relations offline, and represent them as a set of dependency rules. As there are a variety of methods to model a causal relation, in this work we adopt Granger causality [3, 31], which can naturally be represented by dependency rules. An alert sequence X is said to Granger-cause another sequence Y if it can be shown, via certain statistic tests on lagged values of X and Y, that the values of X provide statistically significant information to predicate the future values of Y. More specifically,

(1) We collect alert sequences for all performance metrics of interest as training data, following two criteria as follows: (a) the alerts in training data should be the latest ones such that the latest dependency patterns among performance metrics can be captured; and (b) the alert information should be rich enough such that learned dependency rules would be more robust. In our work, we treat the latest one week alert data as the training data.

(2) We apply existing Granger causality analysis tools [31] to mine the dependency rules, and apply conditional probabilities to estimate the uncertainty of the rules [20].

The learned dependency rules are stored in knowledge bases to support online alert graph maintenance. Moreover, existing knowledge bases such as event causality scenarios [10], or vulnerabilities exploitation among cyber assets [5] can also be "plugged" into our critical causal mining framework. The dependency rules are then shipped to the next stage in the system to maintain alert graphs.

Online alert graph maintenance. Using dependency rules, our system constructs and maintains an alert graph G online from a range of newly issued alerts. Upon an alert u from performance metric q is detected at time t, it first marks u as a new alert in G. It then checks (1) if there exists dependency rules in the form of $p \xrightarrow{l_{pq}} q$, and (2) whether there are alerts detected on performance metric p during the time period $[t - l_{pq}, t)$. If there exists such an alert v on p, an directed edge from v to u is inserted, and the rule uncertainty $\Pr(p \xrightarrow{l_{pq}} q)$ is associated to the edge (v, u). Following the above steps, it maintains G online for newly detected alerts.

On-demand critical alert mining. The major task (and the focus of this work) in the pipeline is to identify k critical alerts from alert graphs. In practice, a user may specify a time window of interest, which induces an alert graph from the maintained alert graph. It contains all the alerts detected during the time window. However, the induced alert graphs can still be huge.

In this paper, we propose three algorithms to address the scalability issue: (1) a quadratic time approximation with performance guarantees on the quality of critical alerts, (2) a linear time approximation, which guarantees the alert quality for tree-structured alert graphs; and (3) sampling-based heuristics which can be *tuned* to balance the alert quality and response time. The critical alerts are then returned to users for further analysis and verification.

4. BOUND AND PRUNING ALGORITHM

Theorem 1 tells us that it is unlikely to find a polynomial time algorithm to find the best k alerts with the maximum gain. All is not lost: we can find polynomial time algorithms that approximately identify the most critical alerts. The main result in this section is as follows.

THEOREM 2. *Given an alert graph $G = (V, E, f_e)$ and an integer k, (1) there exists an algorithm in $O(k|V||E|)$ time with approximation ratio $1 - \frac{1}{e}$, where e is the base of natural logarithm, and (2) there exists a $1 - \frac{1}{e}$ approximation algorithm in $O(k|V|)$ time, when G is a tree.*

Here e refers to Euler's number (approximately 2.71828). Denote the optimal k alerts as S^*, we present an efficient algorithm to identify k alerts S where $\mathsf{Gain}(S) \geq (1 - \frac{1}{e})\mathsf{Gain}(S^*)$, in quadratic time.

We start with a greedy algorithm, denoted as Naive.

Naive greedy algorithm. Given an alert graph $G = (V, E, f_e)$ and an integer k, Naive finds k critical alerts in k iterations as follows. (1) It initializes a set S_0 to store the selected alerts. (2) At the ith iteration, Naive checks each alert in V, and greedily picks the alert s_i that maximizes the *incremental gain* $\mathsf{Gain}(S_{i-1} \cup \{s_i\})$, where S_{i-1} is the set of critical alerts found at iteration $i - 1$. (3) It repeats the above step until k alerts are identified.

One may verify that Naive is a $1 - \frac{1}{e}$ approximation algorithm. To see this, observe that the set function $\mathsf{Gain}(\cdot)$ is a *monotonically submodular function.* A function $f(S)$ over a set S is called *submodular* if for any subset $S_1 \subseteq S_2 \subset S$ and $x \in S \setminus S_2$, $f(S_1 \cup \{x\})$ - $f(S_1) \geq f(S_2 \cup \{x\})$ - $f(S_2)$. It is known that for maximizing a submodular function, a greedy strategy achieves $1 - \frac{1}{e}$ approximation ratio [27]. Hence it suffices to show that the function Gain is a monotonically submodular function. Indeed, (1) one may verify that Gain is monotonic: for any $S_1 \subseteq S_2 \subseteq V$, $\mathsf{Gain}(S_1) \leq \mathsf{Gain}(S_2)$; (2) the diminishing return of Gain can be shown by mathematical reduction. We provide the detailed proof in [1].

For complexity, Naive requires k iterations, and in each iteration, it scans all the vertices u and computes $P_f(S_{k-1}, u)$, which takes in total $O(k|V||E|)$ time.

Naive provides a polynomial time algorithm to approximate CAM within $1 - \frac{1}{e}$. Nevertheless, the scalability issue of Naive makes it difficult to use in practice for large alert graphs. For instance, when an alert graph of around $20K$ vertices and $200K$ edges, Naive mines 6 critical alerts in more than 800 seconds. We next present a faster approximation algorithm with the same approximation ratio. By using pruning and verification, the algorithm is 30 times faster than Naive, as verified in our experimental study.

4.1 Pruning and verification

To select a most promising alert at each iteration, Naive evaluates the incremental gain for each alert in $V \setminus S$, and then selects the one of the highest incremental gain, which runs in $O(|V||E|)$ time. Instead of blindly processing every alert, we may efficiently filter "unpromising" alerts, and then evaluate the exact gain for the remaining vertices. In particular, at each iteration i, for two alerts v' and $v \in V \setminus S_{i-1}$, we compute upper bounds U_v', U_v and lower bounds L_v', L_v for $\mathsf{Gain}(S_{i-1} \cup \{v\})$ and $\mathsf{Gain}(S_{i-1} \cup \{v'\})$, respectively. If v' is already not a critical alert, all the alerts v with $L_v' > U_v$ can be safely skipped without losing the alert quality.

We next derive an upper and lower bound for $\mathsf{Gain}(\cdot)$, and present algorithms to compute them efficiently. Instead of visiting each alert and causal relation in G, these algorithms compute the bounds by visiting only local information of each alert in G. This enables a fast estimation of $\mathsf{Gain}(\cdot)$.

4.2 Upper bound

We introduce a notion of *sum gain* (denoted as SGain) to characterize the upper bound for $\mathsf{Gain}(\cdot)$. Given an alert graph $G = (V, E, f_e)$, an alert $v \in V$, and a set of selected critical alerts $S \subseteq V$, an upper bound is computed as $\mathsf{SGain}(S \cup \{v\}) = \sum_{u \in V} w_u \cdot \hat{P}_f(S \cup \{v\}, u)$, where

- $\hat{P}_f(S \cup \{v\}, u) = 1$, if $u \in S$;
- $\hat{P}_f(S \cup \{v\}, u) = \sum_{(u', u) \in E} \hat{P}_f(S \cup \{v\}, u') f_e(u', u)$, if $u \notin S$.

The sum gain SGain (as illustrated in Fig. 2) is an upper bound for $\mathsf{Gain}(\cdot)$. Better still, it can be efficiently computed.

PROPOSITION 1. *Given an alert graph $G = (V, E, f_e)$, a set of critical alert $S \subseteq V$, and an alert $u \in V \setminus S$, (1)* $\mathsf{Gain}(S \cup \{u\}) \leq \mathsf{SGain}(S \cup \{u\})$*; and (2)* SGain *can be computed for* all *alerts in V in $O(|E|)$ time.*

We first prove Proposition 1 (1). We remark that SGain is built upon the following generalization of Bernoulli's inequality [24]. Given $x_i \leq 1$, we have

$$1 - \prod_{i=1}^{n} (1 - x_i) \leq \sum_{i=1}^{n} x_i.$$

We next conduct a mathematical induction over the topological order (Section 2) of the alerts in G as follows.

- Consider the alerts $u_1 \in V$ with topological order 0: (1) if $u_1 \in S$, $\hat{P}_f(S, u_1) = 1$ and $P_f(S, u_1) = 1$; (2) otherwise, $\hat{P}_f(S, u_1) = 0$ and $P_f(S, u_1) = 0$, since u_1 has no parents. In both cases, $P_f(S, u_1) \leq \hat{P}_f(S, u_1)$.

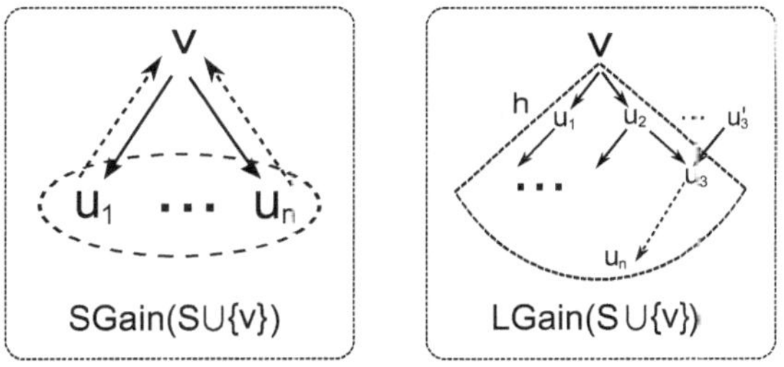

Figure 2: Algorithm BnP: Upper and lower bound

- Assume that alert $u_i \in V$ with topological order i satisfies $P_f(S, u_i) \leq \hat{P}_f(S, u_i)$. For an alert $u_{i+1} \in V$,

$$\begin{aligned} P_f(S, u_{i+1}) &= 1 - \prod_{(u', u_{i+1}) \in E} (1 - P_f(S, u') f_e(u', u_{i+1})) \\ &\leq \sum_{(u', u_{i+1}) \in E} P_f(S, u') f_e(u', u_{i+1}) \\ &\leq \sum_{(u', u_{i+1}) \in E} \hat{P}_f(S, u') f_e(u', u_{i+1}) \\ &= \hat{P}_f(S, u_{i+1}) \end{aligned}$$

Therefore, for any $u \in V$, $P_f(S, u) \leq \hat{P}_f(S, u)$. By definition, $\mathsf{Gain}(S \cup \{u\}) \leq \mathsf{SGain}(S \cup \{u\})$. Hence, SGain is indeed an upper bound for $\mathsf{Gain}(\cdot)$.

Upper bound computation. As a constructive proof for Proposition 1 (2), we present a procedure (denoted as computeUpperBound) for SGain to compute the upper bounds for all vertices in $O(|E|)$ time.

The algorithm (not shown) follows a "bottom up" computation, starting from the alerts with the highest topological order in G. (1) It first computes the topological order for all the alerts in G. (2) Starting from the alert with the highest topological order, it computes SGain for each alert $u \in V \setminus S$ as follows: (a) $\mathsf{SGain}(S \cup \{u\}) = \mathsf{SGain}(S \cup \{u\}) + w_u$, and (b) for each $u' \in N_i(u)$, it updates $\mathsf{SGain}(S \cup \{u'\})$ by $\mathsf{SGain}(S \cup \{u'\}) + f_e(u', u)\mathsf{SGain}(S \cup \{u\})$. (3) It repeats step (2) until all the alerts are processed.

It takes $O(|E|)$ time for computeUpperBound to obtain the topological order by depth-first search in step (1). Each edge in G is visited exactly once in step (2) and (3). Therefore, the algorithm runs in $O(|E|)$ time.

The above analysis completes the proof of Proposition 1.

4.3 Lower bound

To compute the lower bound of $\mathsf{Gain}(\cdot)$, we introduce a notion *local gain* (denoted as LGain). Given an alert graph $G = (V, E)$, an alert $v \in V$, a set of selected alerts $S \subseteq V$, and an integer h, LGain of $S \cup \{v\}$ is defined as follows.

$$\mathsf{LGain}(S \cup \{v\}) = \sum_{u \in V_v^h} w_u \cdot P_f(S \cup \{v\}, u),$$

where h is a tunable integer, and $V_v^h \subseteq V$ is a set of vertices that can be reached from v in no more than h hops. Intuitively, LGain estimates a lower bound of $\mathsf{Gain}(S)$ with the impact of an alert to its local "nearby" alerts in G (as illustrated in Fig.2). One may verify the following.

PROPOSITION 2. *Given $G = (V, E)$, $S \subseteq V$, for any alert $u \in V \setminus S$, (1) $\mathsf{Gain}(S \cup \{v\}) \geq \mathsf{LGain}(S \cup \{v\})$, and (2) LGain can be computed in $O(\sum_{v \in V} |E_v^h|)$ time, where E_v^h is the set of incoming edges in G of the alerts in V_v^h.*

We present a procedure computeLowerBound to compute LGain. For each alert $v \in V \setminus S$ (*e.g.*, u_3 in Fig 2), the algorithm visits the alerts in V_v^h and their incoming edges (*e.g.*, (u_3', u_3)) once, and computes LGain following the definition, in $O(\sum_{v \in V} |E_v^h|)$ time.

4.4 Algorithm BnP

Based on the upper and lower bounds, we propose an approximation, denoted as BnP. BnP enables faster critical alert mining while achieving the approximation ratio $1 - \frac{1}{e}$. The algorithm follows Naive's greedy strategy: given an integer k, it conducts k iterations of search, each determines a top critical alert. The difference is that in each iteration, it invokes a procedure Prune to identify a set C of candidate alerts for consideration.

The procedure Prune (as illustrated in Fig. 3) invokes computeUpperBounds and computeLowerBounds to dynamically update the lower and upper bounds for each alert by accessing their local information (lines 1-2), and filters the alerts that are not critical:

1. it scans the lower bounds LGain of each alert, and find the maximum one as *bar* (line 3);
2. it scans the upper bounds SGain of each alert, and prunes those with $\mathsf{SGain}(u) < bar$, adding the rest to a candidate alert set C.

Input: An alert graph $G = (V, E, f_e)$;
a set of critical alert S.
Output: a set of candidate alerts C.

1. computeUpperBound (G, S);
2. computeLowerBound (G, S);
3. set bar as the largest LGain over alerts in $V \setminus S$;
4. $C \leftarrow \emptyset$;
5. **for each** $u \in V \setminus S$
6.   **if** $\mathsf{SGain}(u) \geq$ bar
7. $C \leftarrow C \cup \{u\}$;
8. **return** C;

Figure 3: The pruning procedure Prune

Correctness and Complexity. The algorithm BnP achieves approximation ratio $1 - \frac{1}{e}$, as it follows the same greedy strategy as Naive. Note that the pruning procedure Prune does not affect the approximation ratio.

For complexity, let C_m be the maximum set of candidate sets in all the iterations after pruning. For the alerts in C_m, it takes BnP $O(|C_m||E|)$ time to find a best alert. The total time for pruning is $O(k(\sum_{u \in V} |E_u^h| + |E|))$. Hence, it takes BnP in total $O(k(\sum_{u \in V} |E_u^h| + |C_m||E|))$ time. Moreover, $|E_u^h|$ is typically small, and is *tunable* by varying h, as indicated by Proposition 2. For example, when $h = 1$, LGain can be computed in $O(d_m|E|)$ for all the alerts, where d_m is the largest in-degree in G. As h gets larger, the computation complexity gets higher, leading to tighter lower bound LGain. In our experimental study, by setting $h = 3$, 95% of the alerts are pruned, which makes BnP 30 times faster than Naive without losing alert quality.

Mining Alert Trees. When G is a directed tree, the algorithm BnP identifies k critical alerts in $O(k|V|)$ as follows.

(1) Starting from the alerts $u \in V$ of the highest topological order, it computes $\mathsf{Gain}(u) = \mathsf{Gain}(u) + w_u$, and makes an update by $\mathsf{Gain}(u') = \mathsf{Gain}(u') + f_e(u', u)\mathsf{Gain}(u)$, if u' is the parent of u. (2) It repeats (1) on the alerts following the decreasing topological order, until all the alerts are processed. One iteration over (1) and (2) identifies a critical alert. (3) BnP repeats (1) and (2) to find k critical alerts.

Following the correctness analysis, BnP preserves the approximation ratio $1 - \frac{1}{e}$ over trees. Moreover, each edge in G is visited once in a single iteration. Hence, it takes $O(k|V|)$ time of BnP over G as trees. Theorem 2 (2) hence follows.

5. TREE APPROXIMATION

Algorithm BnP needs to process all the candidates and their causal relations, which may not be efficient for a large amount of alert sequences. In extreme cases where few alerts are pruned, BnP degrades to its naive greedy counterpart.

As indicated by Theorem 2(2), fast approximation exists for alert graphs as trees. Following this intuition, we may make large alert graphs "small", by sparsifying them into directed trees, which "preserve" most of alert dependency information in an alert graph. This enables both fast algorithms and low quality loss.

5.1 Single-tree approximation

We start by introducing a heuristic algorithm ST. The basic idea is to induce a *maximum directed tree* (forest) T from a given alert graph G, such that for any set of alerts S in G, $\mathsf{Gain}(S)$ in T is "close" as much as possible to $\mathsf{Gain}(S)$ in G, and a fast approximation can be performed over T without much quality loss.

Maximum directed tree. Given an alert graph $G = (V, E, f_e)$, a maximum directed tree of G is a spanning tree $T = (V, E')$, where $E' \subset E$, such that (1) for any $u \in V$, u has at most one incoming edge, and (2) $\sum_{\langle u,v\rangle \in E'} f_e(u, v)$ is maximized. Intuitively, T depicts a "skeleton" of an alert graph G, where causal relations always follow the most likely dependency rules.

Algorithm ST. Given an alert graph $G = (V, E, f_e)$, the single-tree approximation ST mines k critical alerts as follows. (1) ST first finds the maximum directed tree T. To construct T, an algorithm simply selects, for each alert u in G, the incoming edge (u', u) with the maximum $f_e(u', u)$ among all its incoming edges. (2) ST searches the k critical alerts following the algorithm BnP over T.

One may verify that it is in $O(|E|)$ time to construct T. From Theorem 2(2), it is in $O(k|V|)$ time to find k critical alerts in T (as either a tree or a forest). Hence, the algorithm ST takes in total $O(|E| + k|V|)$ time. Note that the induced T can be a set of disjoint trees, where the above complexity still holds.

5.2 Multi-tree sampling

Single-tree approximation provides fast mining method for large scale alerts. On the other hand, using induced trees to approximate causal structures may lead to biased results. For example, more dependency information could be lost for alerts with more incoming edges. To rectify this, we propose a heuristic, denoted as MTS, based on multi-tree sampling.

Algorithm MTS. The algorithm MTS is as illustrated in Fig. 4. Given an alert graph $G = (V, E, f_e)$, integer k and

---

Input: Alert graph $G = (V, E, f_e)$,
integer k, the number of sampled trees N.
Output: A set S of k critical alerts.

1. $S \leftarrow \emptyset$; initializes $P_f(\cdot)$; $i \leftarrow 0$;
2. **while** $i \leq k$ **Do**
3.   **for each** alert u in G **Do**
4.   update $P_f^{(i-1)}(S_{i-1}, u)$;
5. $l \leftarrow 0$;
6.   **while** $l \leq N$ **Do**
7. $T_{i,l} \leftarrow \mathsf{sampleTree}(G)$;
8.   **for each** alert u in G **Do**
9. $\mathsf{Gain}(S_{i-1} \cup \{u\}) \leftarrow \mathsf{Gain}(S_{i-1}) + \frac{\sum_{l=1}^{N} D(u,l)}{N}$;
10.   select u with the maximum $\mathsf{Gain}(S_{i-1} \cup \{u\})$;
11. $S_i \leftarrow S_{i-1} \cup \{u\}$;
12. **return** S_k;

Figure 4: Algorithm MTS

a sample number N, MTS starts by initializing a set S_0 as $\emptyset$, the alert-fixed probability for each node as 0 (line 1), and identify the topological orders of the alerts in G.

Algorithm MTS then finds a set S critical alerts in k iterations as follows. Denote the selected critical set at iteration $i-1$ as S_{i-1}. At each iteration i, (1) MTS updates the alert-fixed probability $P_f^{(i-1)}(S_{i-1}, u)$ for each alert $u \in V$ in G, fixing S_{i-1} as the critical alerts (lines 3-4). (2) It then invokes procedure sampleTree to sample N trees from G (lines 6-7), according to the updated alert-fixed probability in (1). (3) For each alert u, MTS computes the weighted sum of u's descendants $D(u, l)$ in each sampled tree $T_{u,l}$, and takes the average $D(u, l)$ over all sampled tress as an estimation of $\mathsf{Gain}(S_{i-1} \cup \{u\})$ (lines 8-9). It selects the alert u that introduces the maximum improvement, and update S_{i-1} as S_i by adding u (lines 10-11), which is used to update $P_f(\cdot)$ in G in the next iteration.

Procedure sampleTree. Given an alert graph G and an integer N, the procedure sampleTree (line 7) samples N trees (forest) from G at iteration i. More specifically, it generates a single tree (or forest) $T_{i,l}$ as follows. (1) It first samples a set of alerts $V_{i,l}$ as the nodes for tree $T_{i,l}$ following Bernoulli distributions. For each alert $u \in V$ and the updated $P_f^{(i-1)}(u)$, MTS selects u with probability $1 - P_f^{(i-1)}(u)$, and inserts it to $V_{i,l}$. (2) MTS then samples an edge for each alert $u \in V_{i,l}$. It randomly orders u's parents. Starting from the first parent, u tries to build an edge (u', u) to its parent with probability $f_e(u', u)$, where u' ranges over all the parents of u, until an edge is selected (and attached to u), or all the parents are visited. (3) MTS repeats (2) until all the alerts $u \in V_{i,l}$ are visited.

It takes in total $O(k{*}N|E|)$ time for MTS to find k critical alerts. (a) MTS takes in total $O(k|E|)$ time to update P_f in G; (b) the total sampling time is in $O(k * N|E|)$; and (c) it takes in total $O(k * N|V|)$ time to select the critical alerts.

In contrast to its single-tree counterpart, MTS leverages sampling to reduce the bias: alerts with more parents and larger probability are more likely to have a parent in a sampled tree. In addition, it synthesizes the gain estimation from multiple trees, such that the noise from a single tree is smoothed. Indeed, we found that using only 300 samples, MTS finds top 6 critical alerts with $\mathsf{Gain}(\cdot)$ 90% as good as Naive, and is 80 times faster. It reduces 10% more loss on $\mathsf{Gain}(\cdot)$ compared with ST (see Section 6).

6. EXPERIMENT

We applied both real-life and synthetic data to evaluate our algorithms. We first provide a case study (Section 6.2). Using real-life data, we next investigate (1) the efficiency and effectiveness of our algorithms (Section 6.3), (2) the impact of the number of explored hops to the performance of BnP (Section 6.4), and (3) how the number of samples affects MTS (Section 6.5). In addition, we evaluate the scalability of our algorithms, over large synthetic data (Section 6.6).

6.1 Setup

Real-life data. We use real-life data center performance data (referred to as LM), from LogicMonitor, an SaaS network monitoring company. The data spans 53 days from Nov. 23, 2013 to Jan. 14, 2014. It contains the sequences for 50,772 performance metrics from 9,956 services residing in 122 servers. Each metric is reported every 2 minutes. The alerts are identified by specified rules provided by LogicMonitor, where we assign a weight 1.0 to all the metrics.

Dependency rules and alert graphs. Dependency rules were mined from data collected in 7 consecutive days, and are used to construct alert graphs using the data from the following days. We used the tool developed by [31] to mine the Granger causality among performance metrics as dependency rules (with the p-value set to be 0.01 [31]). We then applied conditional probability to estimate the uncertainty of the rules [20]. From the dataset LM, we mined 46 sets of dependency rules, where each set contains on average $2,082$ rules. Each set of rules were mined in less than 60 minutes.

By applying the sets of dependency rules on the alert detected in the next single day, we obtained 46 alert graphs, following the online alert graph construction (Section 3). The number of alerts (resp. edges) ranges from $20,248$ to $25,057$ (resp. $162,000$ to $270,370$) for a single graph.

Synthetic alert graphs. For scalability tests over large alert graphs, we applied the graph model proposed in [18] to generate large synthetic alert graphs (referred to as SYN). In particular, the node degree and edge weights follow the empirical distributions [34] learned from alert graphs over the real-life data LM. We ranged the number of alerts from 100K to 1M, and the average degree of SYN graphs is 9.

Evaluation. To measure the quality of the critical alerts identified by an algorithm A, we investigate a metric *loss ratio* of A defined as

$$\textbf{loss ratio}(A) = 1 - \frac{Gain(S_A)}{Gain(S_{\textsf{Naive}})},$$

where $S_{\textsf{Naive}}$ (resp. S_A) is the set of critical vertices returned by the algorithm Naive (resp. algorithm A). As Naive guarantees the alert quality within a bound, loss ratio suggests how "close" the quality of the alerts from heuristic algorithms and the optimal ones is. The less, the better.

Implementation. In addition to the proposed algorithms BnP, ST, and MTS, we implemented the following baseline algorithms: (1) Naive, the greedy algorithms without pruning strategy; (2) $\textsf{BnP}_{\textsf{UB}}$, a simplified version of BnP, which only uses upper bound to filter unpromising alerts: it skips those alerts with upper bound smaller than an alert with computed $\textsf{Gain}(\cdot)$ in each iteration (Section 4). (3) MaxDeg, a simple strategy that returns the top k alerts with the largest weighted sum of outgoing edges.

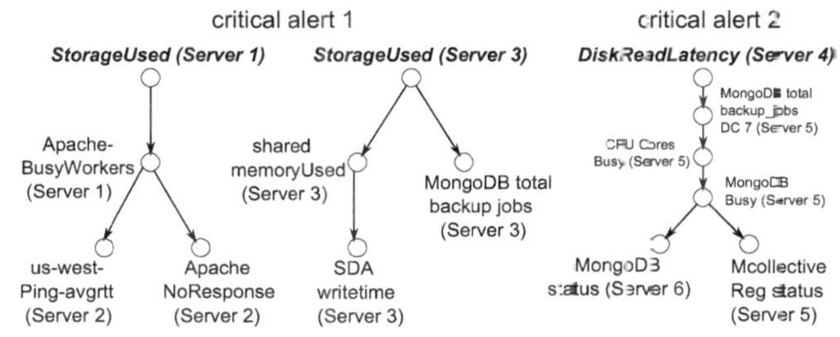

Figure 5: Critical alerts over LM

All the algorithms were implemented in C++, and all experiments were executed on a machine powered by an Intel Core i7-2620M 2.7GHz CPU and 8GB of RAM, using Ubuntu 12.10 with GCC 4.7.2. Each experiment was run 10 times, and their average results are presented.

6.2 Case study

Using real-world data LM, our algorithms suggest reasonable critical alerts that are indeed the source of a range of large amount of alerts, as verified by the domain experts from LogicMonitor. We illustrate three "causality patterns" induced by top two critical alerts and their descendants following the weighted dependency rules in Fig. 5. (1) Our algorithms suggest that StorageUsed, a critical alert that indicates insufficient memory, leads to poor performance of Web servers (Apache), which typically triggers delayed Ping round-trip time (Ping-avgrtt) from other servers. In another set of hosts, it leads to insufficient shared memory over a range of servers, which typically triggers slower Shared Data Access write time (SDA writetime) on their own. (2) A second critical alert DiskReadLatency suggests I/O bottleneck for a range of abnormal status of database applications. The disk access speed alert often triggers the unsolved back up requests from another server, which leads to poor performance of CPU and database servers, and further affects a range of database related requests from more outside servers. These causal patterns are consistent with the workflow of data centers at LogicMonitor.

Our algorithms do not assume prior domain knowledge. On the other hand, external knowledge and rules enable our algorithms to further improve the quality of the critical alerts and causal patterns.

6.3 Overall performance evaluation

We first investigate the efficiency and effectiveness of the proposed algorithms, using alert graphs from LM. In the following tests, we fixed the number of explored hops in BnP as 3, and the number of sampled trees in MTS as 300.

As illustrated in Figure 6(a), the proposed algorithms BnP, MTS, and ST consistently outperform the baseline algorithms Naive and $\textsf{BnP}_{\textsf{UB}}$ in efficiency, while varying k, the number of required critical alerts. They introduce different levels of efficiency improvement. Compared with Naive and $\textsf{BnP}_{\textsf{UB}}$, BnP is 30 times and 17 times faster, respectively, without quality loss on solutions. With some quality loss, ST is 5000 times and 3000 times faster than Naive and $\textsf{BnP}_{\textsf{UB}}$, respectively, and MTS results in 80 times and 50 times speedup. In addition, all the algorithms take more time when k varies from 1 to 6, as expected.

Figure 6(b) shows the loss ratio of ST and MTS, where k varies from 1 to 6. Compared with MaxDeg, MTS and ST

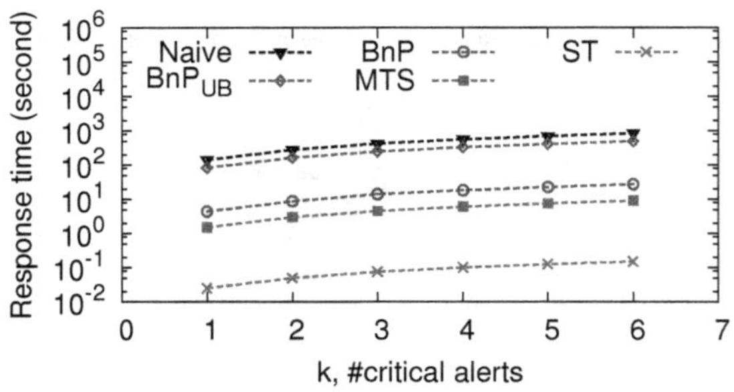

(a) Mining efficiency on different algorithms

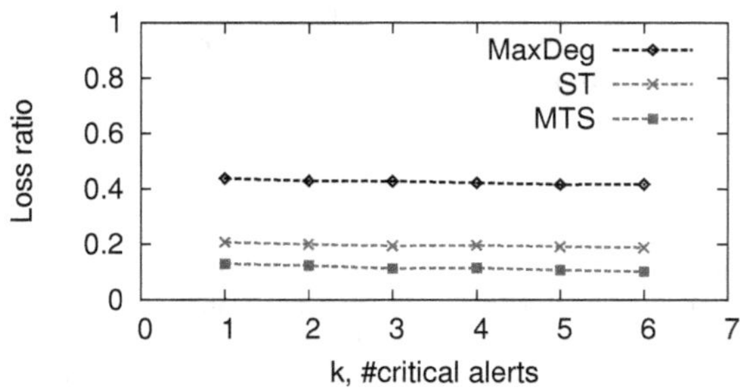

(b) Loss ratio comparison

Figure 6: Mining performance on LM alert graphs

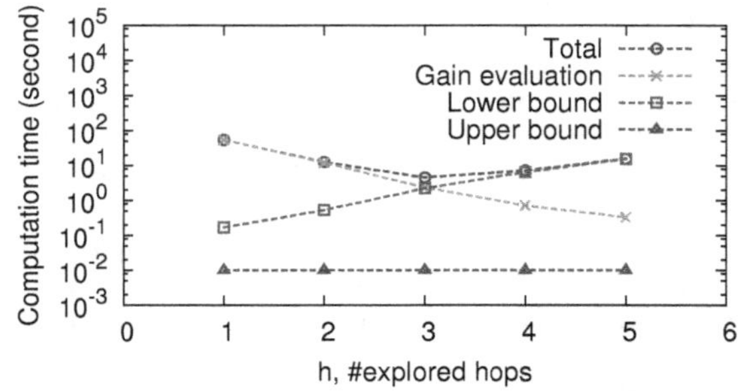

(a) Computation time on different components

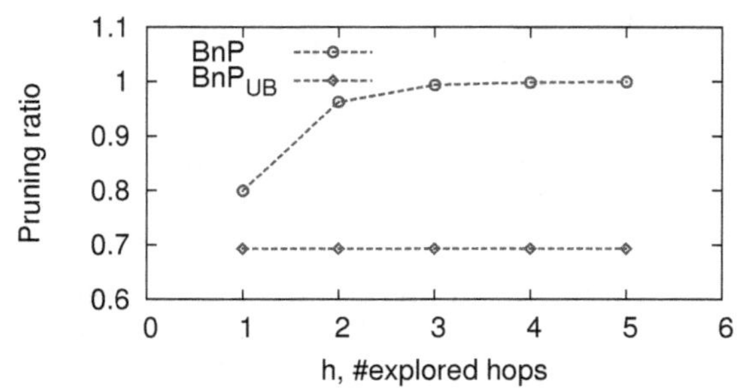

(b) Pruning ratio comparison

Figure 7: BnP performance on LM alert graphs

obtain significant improvement on loss ratio. As k increases, the loss ratio of MaxDeg is consistently more than 0.4; meanwhile, the loss ratio of MTS and ST is around 0.1 and 0.2, respectively. Compared with MTS, ST receives higher efficiency at the cost of solution quality loss. When the number of required critical alerts varies from 1 to 6, MTS and ST share the same trend: the loss ratio decreases. Compared with BnP that returns critical alerts without quality loss, ST and MTS are 180 and 3 times faster, respectively, at the cost of small quality loss.

In all cases, we observe that the total Gain($\cdot$) increases with larger k with diminish return (not shown). This is consistent with its submodularity.

6.4 Performance evaluation of BnP

In this set of experiments, we focus on the impact of the number of hops h (for lower bound computation) to the performance of BnP. We fixed k as 1. Besides running time, we investigate the *pruning ratio* of BnP, defined as $\frac{|V|-|C|}{|V|}$, where $|V|$ is the total alert number in an alert graph G, and $|C|$ is the average size of the candidate set C (Section 4) after pruning, for all the k iterations.

Figure 7(a) and Figure 7(b) illustrate how the computation time of different components in BnP varies, and how the pruning ratio varies, respectively, while the number of explored hops h varies from 1 to 5. The result tells us the following. (1) When h increases from 1 to 3, the response time of BnP drops. Indeed, as observed from Figure 7(b), the efficiency improvement comes from the increasing number of pruned alerts. With more alerts pruned, the amount of time taken on Gain evaluation, which is the dominating cost, drops accordingly. (2) When the number of hops increases from 3 to 5, the response time of BnP increases. As the number of hops grows from 3 to 5, we can see that the pruning ratio of BnP marginally is improved from Figure 7(b); however, the amount of computation time for lower bound in BnP dramatically increases, which becomes the dominating computation cost. According to our result, when the number of explored hops is set to be 3, BnP achieves the best performance on LM alert graphs.

In addition, as shown in Figure 7(b), BnP consistently outperforms $\mathsf{BnP_{UB}}$ in terms of pruning ratio, since the upper and lower bounds in BnP introduce more powerful pruning to reduce unnecessary computation.

6.5 Performance evaluation of MTS

In this set of experiments, we demonstrate how the number of sampled trees affect the performance of MTS.

Figure 8(a) tells us the following. (1) While the number of required critical alerts is fixed, the response time of MTS is proportional to the number of sampled trees (varies from 5 to 500). (2) When the number of samples is fixed, the response time of MTS grows linear to the number of required critical alerts. In all cases, MTS takes no more than 15 seconds.

Figure 8(b) illustrates how the number of sampled trees influences the effectiveness of MTS. When the number of sampled trees increases, the loss ratio of MTS decreases, while the reduction of loss ratio diminishes. As the number of sampled trees changes from 5 to 100, the loss ratio of MTS is significantly improved; meanwhile, as the number of sampled trees changes from 100 to 500, the loss ratio is marginally improved. In addition, fixing the number of sampled trees, when the number of required critical alerts is increased, the loss ratio of all MTS variants decreases.

6.6 Scalability

On SYN alert graphs, we fixed the number of required critical alerts to be 3, and evaluate the scalability of BnP, MTS, ST, Naive, and $\mathsf{BnP_{UB}}$. Note that the number of hops explored in BnP is fixed to be 3, and the number of sampled trees in MTS is fixed to be 300.

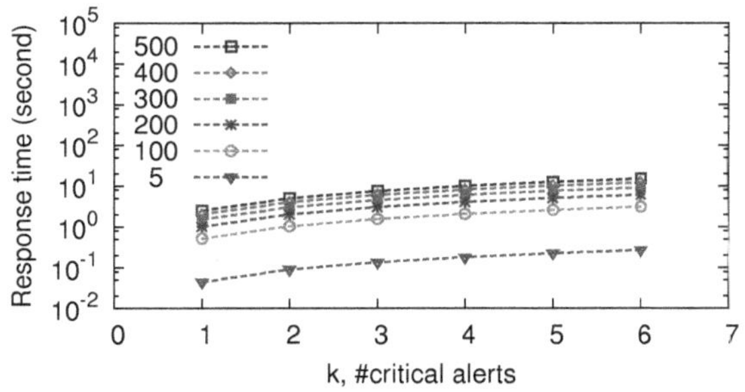

(a) MTS efficiency on varying #sampled trees

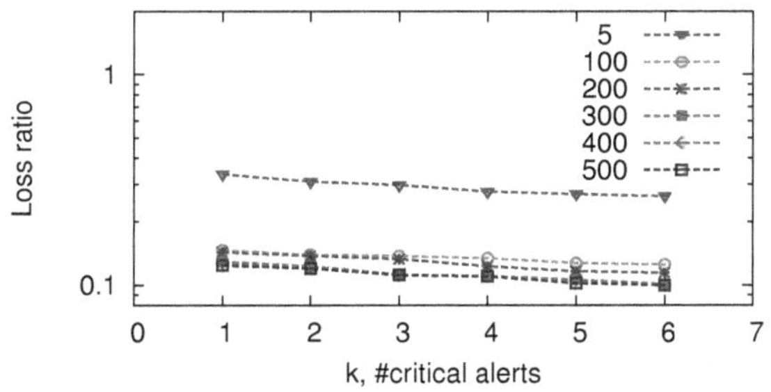

(b) MTS effectiveness on varying #sampled trees

Figure 8: MTS performance on LM alert graphs

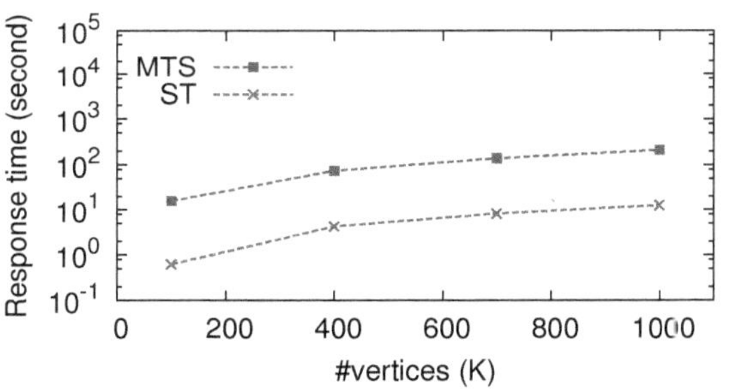

Figure 9: Scalability results on SYN graphs

Figure 9 reports the scalability results. When the number of alerts in SYN graphs increases from 100K to 1000K, the response time of MTS and ST linearly grows. In particular, when a SYN graph has 1M alerts and more than 90M edges, MTS and ST return 3 critical alerts in 4 minutes and 13 seconds, respectively. On the other hand, Naive, BnP_{UB}, and BnP cannot finish the computation in an hour, even for alert graphs with $100K$ alerts (hence are not shown). Indeed, the efficiency of BnP relies on the amount of alerts it can prune. In the worst case, it works as slow as Naive. In contrast, MTS and ST are much less sensitive to the growth of graph size, and are more promising for large alert graphs.

6.7 Summary

We found the following. (1) With pruning strategy, BnP outperforms baseline algorithms in terms of efficiency up to 30 times, without loss of solution quality. (2) While MTS is up to 80 times faster than baseline algorithms, the resulting loss ratio is around 0.1. (3) ST is up to 5000 times faster than baseline algorithms, with loss ratio around 0.2.

7. RELATED WORK

Causality models and analysis. Causal relations among time series data have been modeled with Granger causality [33], lagged correlation [23], Bayesian networks [29, 26], among others. Granger causality measures a cause in terms of whether it passes Granger Test, *i.e.*, whether it helps in predicating the future events, beyond what can be predicted by using only the historical events. Lagged correlation characterizes causal relations with the correlation between two time series shifted in time relative to one another. Causal Bayesian networks interprets causal relations with graphical models, in which the predecessors of a node are interpreted as directly causing the variable associated with that node.

A variety of causality mining techniques have been studied [3, 31, 32], varied with causality models. Silverstein et al. [32] proposed algorithms to mine causal relations in large databases by estimating the conditional probability of rules of interest. For Granger causality, Arnold et al. [3] applied Lasso Granger method to find a set of events that are conditionally dependent with regression, without exhaustively performing pairwise Granger Test. A toolbox for detecting Granger causality is developed [31]. These methods stop at identifying causal relations. Our work, on the contrary, efficiently identifies the most critical alerts rather than suggesting all possible causal relationships. On the other hand, efficient causality mining techniques, as well as existing knowledge bases on event causality scenarios [10] serve as preprocessing in our critical causal mining framework.

Root cause analysis. We are aware of a range of domain-specific studies that aims to find the "root causes". Given a set of observed symptom events, the problem is to identify the set of root causes that can best explain the symptom. In intrusion detection, Julisch [16] leveraged alert clustering techniques to indicate root causes for system alarms. A hierarchical clustering process is iteratively performed over groups of similar alarms, until the top causes are identified. In network performance diagnosis, Mahimkar et al. [23] proposed methods to identify potential root causes as the events that have statistically significant (lagged) correlations with a set of known symptom events. In contrast, we propose a general computational framework for efficient root cause analysis over large-scale alert sequences in networks. While we do not have the luxury to assume the access of rich domain-specific semantics that benefit event filtering, any such knowledge serves as preprocessing to reduce the input size of our problem.

Influence maximization. Node influence evaluation aims to select a group of nodes with maximized influence, under various information diffusion models, such as independent cascade model [21], linear threshold model [19], competing model [4, 15], continuous-time model [11, 30], and credit distribution model [13]. The problem is, however, highly intractable (#P-hard). Sampling methods such as Monte Carlo simulations are usually applied to estimate node influence. Nonetheless, these approaches typically take massive amount of computation time and are hard to scale over large graphs [22]. To improve the scalability, various pruning algorithms have been proposed to reduce the number of Monte Carlo simulations [9, 11, 14, 36], and heuristic algorithms have been studied to estimate node influence [6, 7, 8, 28]. In contrast to these works, we identify efficient algorithms for critical alert mining, with desirable performance guarantees on alert quality and efficiency. Striking a balance between mining quality and efficiency, these algorithms suggest scalable mining for large scale alert analysis.

8. CONCLUSION

We have studied the critical alert mining problem. Despite its intractability, we developed approximation algorithms with quality guarantees, as well as fast heuristics that preserve at least 80% of solution quality, and perform up to 5,000 times faster than their approximation counterparts.

This work is a first step towards large-scale critical alerts mining. We are conducting experiments over various large real-life datasets and causality models. One topic is to extend our techniques for distributed network monitoring systems and data centers. Another topic is to dynamically maintain the alert graphs and mined critical alerts. In addition, to further improve the alert quality, one wants to combine the mining framework with external semantics and knowledge bases, and to automatically interpret the critical alerts for various application domains.

Acknowledgment

We thank Dr. Douglas Kelly at Army Research Lab for valuable comments. This research was sponsored in part by the Army Research Laboratory under cooperative agreements W911NF-09-2-0053, NSF IIS-0954125, and NSF IIS-1219254. The views and conclusions contained herein are those of the authors and should not be interpreted as representing the official policies, either expressed or implied, of the Army Research Laboratory or the U.S. Government. The U.S. Government is authorized to reproduce and distribute reprints for Government purposes notwithstanding any copyright notice herein.

9. REFERENCES

[1] Full version. *http://www.cs.ucsb.edu/~bzong/doc/full.pdf.*

[2] S. O. Al-Mamory and H. Zhang. Intrusion detection alarms reduction using root cause analysis and clustering. *Computer Communications*, 32(2):419–430, 2009.

[3] A. Arnold, Y. Liu, and N. Abe. Temporal causal modeling with graphical granger methods. In *SIGKDD*, 2007.

[4] C. Budak, D. Agrawal, and A. El Abbadi. Limiting the spread of misinformation in social networks. In *WWW*, 2011.

[5] H. Cam and P. Mouallem. Mission-aware time-dependent cyber asset criticality and resilience. CSIIRW, 2013.

[6] W. Chen, C. Wang, and Y. Wang. Scalable influence maximization for prevalent viral marketing in large-scale social networks. In *SIGKDD*, 2010.

[7] W. Chen, Y. Wang, and S. Yang. Efficient influence maximization in social networks. In *SIGKDD*, 2009.

[8] W. Chen, Y. Yuan, and L. Zhang. Scalable influence maximization in social networks under the linear threshold model. In *ICDM*, 2010.

[9] S. Cheng, H. Shen, J. Huang, G. Zhang, and X. Cheng. Staticgreedy: solving the scalability-accuracy dilemma in influence maximization. In *CIKM*, 2013.

[10] O. Dain and R. K. Cunningham. Fusing a heterogeneous alert stream into scenarios. In *ACM workshop on Data Mining for Security Applications*, volume 13, 2001.

[11] N. Du, L. Song, M. Gomez-Rodriguez, and H. Zha. Scalable influence estimation in continuous-time diffusion networks. In *NIPS*, 2013.

[12] P. Gill, N. Jain, and N. Nagappan. Understanding network failures in data centers: measurement, analysis, and implications. In *ACM SIGCOMM Computer Communication Review*, 2011.

[13] A. Goyal, F. Bonchi, and L. V. Lakshmanan. A data-based approach to social influence maximization. *VLDB*, 2011.

[14] A. Goyal, W. Lu, and L. V. Lakshmanan. Celf++: optimizing the greedy algorithm for influence maximization in social networks. In *WWW*, 2011.

[15] X. He, G. Song, W. Chen, and Q. Jiang. Influence blocking maximization in social networks under the competitive linear threshold model. In *SDM*, 2012.

[16] K. Julisch. Clustering intrusion detection alarms to support root cause analysis. *TISSEC*, 2003.

[17] K. Julisch and M. Dacier. Mining intrusion detection alarms for actionable knowledge. In *SIGKDD*, 2002.

[18] B. Karrer and M. E. J. Newman. Random graph models for directed acyclic networks. *Phys. Rev. E*, 2009.

[19] D. Kempe, J. Kleinberg, and É. Tardos. Maximizing the spread of influence through a social network. In *SIGKDD*, 2003.

[20] S. Kim and E. N. Brown. A general statistical framework for assessing granger causality. In *ICASSP*, 2010.

[21] T. Lappas, E. Terzi, D. Gunopulos, and H. Mannila. Finding effectors in social networks. In *SIGKDD*, 2010.

[22] J. Leskovec, A. Krause, C. Guestrin, C. Faloutsos, J. VanBriesen, and N. Glance. Cost-effective outbreak detection in networks. In *SIGKDD*, 2007.

[23] A. A. Mahimkar, Z. Ge, A. Shaikh, J. Wang, J. Yates, Y. Zhang, and Q. Zhao. Towards automated performance diagnosis in a large iptv network. In *ACM SIGCOMM Computer Communication Review*, 2009.

[24] D. S. Mitrinović, J. E. Pečarić, and A. Fink. Bernoulli's inequality. In *Classical and New Inequalities in Analysis*, 1993.

[25] J. Moore, J. Chase, K. Farkas, and P. Ranganathan. Data center workload monitoring, analysis, and emulation. In *Eighth Workshop on Computer Architecture Evaluation using Commercial Workloads*, 2005.

[26] K. P. Murphy. *Dynamic bayesian networks: representation, inference and learning.* PhD thesis, University of California, 2002.

[27] G. L. Nemhauser, L. A. Wolsey, and M. L. Fisher. An analysis of approximations for maximizing submodular set functions-I. *Mathematical Programming*, 14(1):265–294, 1978.

[28] H. Nguyen and R. Zheng. Influence spread in large-scale social networks–a belief propagation approach. In *PKDD*, 2012.

[29] U. H. Nielsen, J.-P. Pellet, and A. Elisseeff. Explanation trees for causal bayesian networks. In *UAI*, pages 427–434, 2008.

[30] M. G. Rodriguez and B. Schölkopf. Influence maximization in continuous time diffusion networks. In *ICML*, 2012.

[31] A. K. Seth. A matlab toolbox for granger causal connectivity analysis. *Journal of neuroscience methods*, 2010.

[32] C. Silverstein, S. Brin, R. Motwani, and J. Ullman. Scalable techniques for mining causal structures. *Data Mining and Knowledge Discovery*, 2000.

[33] J. Tian and J. Pearl. Probabilities of causation: Bounds and identification. *Annals of Mathematics and Artificial Intelligence*, 2000.

[34] A. W. Van der Vaart. *Asymptotic statistics*, volume 3. Cambridge university press, 2000.

[35] V. V. Vazirani. *Approximation Algorithms.* Springer, 2003.

[36] C. Zhou, P. Zhang, J. Guo, X. Zhu, and L. Guo. Ublf: An upper bound based approach to discover influential nodes in social networks. In *ICDM*, 2013.

From Labor to Trader: Opinion Elicitation via Online Crowds as a Market

Caleb Chen Cao † Lei Chen † H. V. Jagadish ‡
†The Hong Kong University of Science and Technology, Hong Kong SAR, PR China
‡University of Michigan, Ann Arbor, MI, USA
{caochen,leichen}@cse.ust.hk, ‡jag@umich.edu

ABSTRACT

We often care about people's degrees of belief about certain events: e.g. causality between an action and the outcomes, odds distribution among the outcome of a horse race and so on. It is well recognized that the best form to elicit opinion from human is probability distribution instead of simple voting, because the form of distribution retains the delicate information that an opinion expresses. In the past, opinion elicitation has relied on experts, who are expensive and not always available. More recently, crowdsourcing has gained prominence as an inexpensive way to get a great deal of human input. However, traditional crowdsourcing has primarily focused on issuing very simple (e.g. binary decision) tasks to the crowd. In this paper, we study how to use crowds for *Opinion Elicitation*. There are three major challenges to eliciting opinion information in the form of probability distributions: *a*) how to measure the quality of distribution; *b*) how to aggregate the distributions; and, *c*) how to strategically implement such a system.

To address these challenges, we design and implement *COPE* (Crowd-powered OPinion Elicitation market). *COPE* models crowdsourced work as a trading market, where the "workers" behave like "traders" to maximize their profit by presenting their opinion. Among the innovative features in this system, we design *COPE updating* to combine the multiple elicited distributions following a Bayesian scheme. Also to provide more flexibility while running *COPE*, we propose a series of efficient algorithms and a *slope* based strategy to manage the ending condition of *COPE*. We then demonstrate the implementation of *COPE* and report experimental results running on real commercial platform to demonstrate the practical value of this system.

Categories and Subject Descriptors

H.2.8 [**DATABASE MANAGEMENT**]: Database Applications—*Data mining*; H.1.2 [**MODELS AND PRINCIPLES**]: User/Machine Systems—*Human information processing*

Keywords

Crowdsourcing; Human Computation; Social Media; Market

KDD'14, August 24–27, 2014, New York, NY, USA.
Copyright 2014 ACM 978-1-4503-2956-9/14/08 ...$15.00.
http://dx.doi.org/10.1145/2623330.2623717.

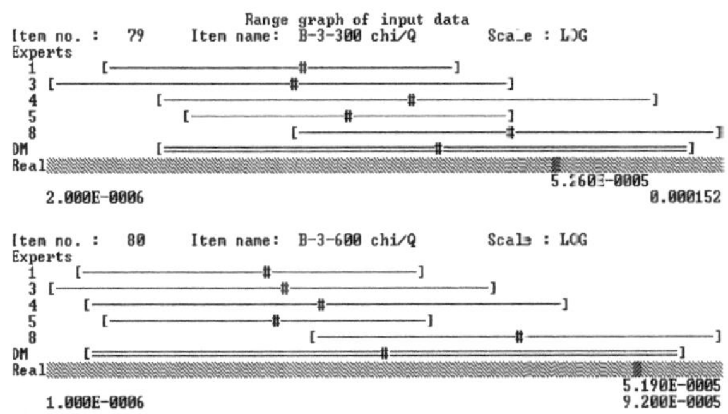

Figure 1: Example of Opinion Elicitation of five participants over two variables(NRC-EU accident uncertainty analysis [4])

1. INTRODUCTION

The application of crowdsourcing has ushered in a brand new age of human-computer collaboration. Online labor markets, such as Amazon MTurk[1], oDesk[2], enable large scale crowdsourcing by providing access to human computation "workers" as well as a programmable infrastructure. The basic assumption in crowdsourcing is that the tasks must be broken down into simple units, such as multiple-choice questions. There is considerable skill in breaking down a complex task into simple units that can be crowd sourced.

Often, we may benefit from getting a richer input from workers. For a very simple example, consider the question 'how many inches of snow will fall tomorrow in city X?' We could discretize this, say into integers, and ask each worker to pick a snipe number as prediction. But such an approach will miss the nuance that the worker predicts 3-6 inches, and chose to predict 4 inches because a single discrete choice was required. For this worker, 6 inches is a likely outcome, while 7 inches is unlikely, but the prediction of 4 inches does not tell us this. In short, simple voting does not suffice because it coarsens the distribution and leads to an extremized opinion expression. What we would like is a framework for eliciting a probability distribution from a worker, and aggregating this with similar distributions obtained from other workers. We call such distributions as *opinions*.

Opinion is a concept of wide extension, which refers to numerical statements expressing an individual's degrees of belief about certain events [17]. Rooted from this definition are such things as prior, posterior, structural distribution, as well as additive probability and belief functions, which can all be expressed in a form of distribution. Such opinion information can then be used not just frivolous pursuits, such as predicting amount of snow, but also as a

[1]www.mturk.com
[2]www.odesk.com

foundation for more advanced decision making procedures and to construct more sophisticated models for risk analysis [4].

In this paper, we focus on exploiting the intrinsic human ability to estimate an opinion, and develop a crowdsourcing framework for this purpose. Specifically, given an event space $\mathcal{S}$, the "workers" are expected to contribute their frank opinion $\vec{r_i}$ in the forms of probability distribution. When the process closes according to certain conditions, the aggregated probability distribution is the elicited consensus opinion.

EXAMPLE 1. *In the standard Probabilistic Risk Analysis [4], during the construction of the Event Trees, one significant step is to provide an accurate probability distribution among many possible outcomes. For certain cases, such probability could be obtained analytically(e.g. failure probability in Circuit Design), but for many sociological or business-related situations, the distributions have to be gathered from a group of related individuals [12]. For example, the Council of Government plans to change the arrangement of public holidays, and before they make the decision, the council board expects a prior distribution among all possible outcomes, e.g. less tourism, more tourism or simply neutral to the alternation. Thus, a crowdsourced application could help to collect the distributed beliefs efficiently.*

EXAMPLE 2. *Another type of applications appears in the causality structure determination, which is widely utilized in building Probabilistic Graphical Models [22]. Given an event, many individuals are invited to describe a set of possible causes for the outcome, along with their probabilistic distributions. Such distribution information can help to build more sophisticated quantitative models such as Bayesian Networks and so on. Figure 1 illustrates an example where 5 expert participants elaborate their probabilistic estimation on two environmental variables B-3-600 and B-3-300 in terms of uniform distribution on selected range over a value space. Then a set of sophisticated inference can be conducted [4].*

There is a crucial challenge for such *Opinion Elicitation* on current crowdsourcing platforms: opinion distribution does not have a "ground truth" with ordinary meaning. Formally, suppose for individual i, the intrinsic opinion for her on an m outcomes event is a probability distribution $\vec{d} = \{d_1, d_2, \ldots, d_m\}$, but during the elicitation process, her reported estimation might be $\vec{r} = \{r_1, r_2, \ldots, r_m\} \neq \vec{d}$. The reason of insincerity might be carelessness or indifference: since the "workers" from online labor markets are essentially money-driven, sloppiness naturally appears when their performance cannot be measured and eventually does not matter. In such cases, we cannot benefit from the correctness based payoff mechanism currently popular on crowdsourcing platforms.

The absence of ground truth knowledge has previously been addressed, most famously in the ESP game [1], where the payoff depends on matching with a partner (or another worker). The basic idea is that if two (or more) individuals independently think of a label for an image, that label is likely to be a good choice. Inappropriate labels are unlikely to qualify. As presented, this is a discrete scheme, there either is a match or there isn't. We would like to extend this idea to find a continuous function to score how well probability distributions match. Furthermore, rather than matching between arbitrarily paired individuals, we do so between each individual and the group 'consensus'.

To address these needs, we propose a 'market' framework for crowdsourcing. Workers trade in this market to earn as high a profit as they can. The concept of variable pay for work is already accepted and widely practiced – many Human Intelligence Tasks (HITs) are offered with a base pay and a (quality-dependent) bonus, with the bonus sometimes being substantially more than the base pay. The quality determination for the bonus is sometimes subjective. We propose instead to have the bonus be determine by the market in a manner that is clearly defined, completely transparent, and reflective of opinion correctness (in a manner we will formally specify below). We implement these ideas in *COPE* (Crowd-powered OPinion Elicitation market). The base pay is provided to workers in the form of seed capital that they invest in an opinion elicitation market with their opinion. We use Bayesian updating, beginning with our initial guess as the prior, to obtain a posterior distribution that reflects the weighted opinions of all the traders in the market. When the task ends, the payoff for each trader is proportional to her contributed modification from the prior to the posterior. Traders that have a zero, or negative contribution, receive no payoff (or a small fixed payoff). In other words, traders have an economic incentive to align their opinion with what they believe will be the consensus direction. Sometimes, individuals may hold opinions that they know are different from the general view. In most opinion elicitation scenarios, we are less interested in such idiosyncratic opinions and more interested in the consensus opinion. The economic incentives of our scheme align well, even for such idiosyncratic individuals, motivating them to express what they truly believe to be popular opinion.

In this paper, we have made the following contributions:

- We formally propose the crowdsourcing application of *Opinion Elicitation*, which treats every crowdsourcing worker as an intrinsic opinion provider and elicits probability distribution information from them.
- We propose *COPE* as the elicitation mechanism, which guarantees the reliability of elicitation and cost control. The *COPE* is built upon a general crowdsourcing worker market, and we strategically induce every involved worker to behave as a risk-neutral trader to achieve honest information elicitation.
- We propose a Bayesian scheme based distribution updating method to incorporate distribution reports from the traders with correctness proof. We also design a series of algorithms to accelerate the incremental merging of causality distribution as well as a *slope* based market running strategy to provide more operational flexibility on *COPE*.
- We practically implement *COPE* on a general labor market and test the system with real datasets. The *COPE* not only serves as a practical information market, but also provides extra human computation resource as a side product.

The rest of the paper is organized as follows. In Section 2 we present a framework overview about the *COPE* system. In Section 3 we formally present the design of *COPE* with necessary preliminaries. In Section 3 we present the algorithmic details about the *COPE* system and a set of core algorithms. In Section 4 we introduce the mechanism of running the system of *COPE*. In Section 5 we elaborate on the non-trivial implementation of *COPE* on Amazon MTurk. In Section 6 we illustrate the experimental results. Then in Section 7 we introduce the recent related work. We conclude the paper with discussion in Section 8.

2. FRAMEWORK OVERVIEW

In this section, we present a system overview of *COPE*(Figure 2). Its three major components are introduced one by one as follows.

Pre-market Building

A running market entails traders and trading capital. In order to turn a crowdsourcing "worker" into an informative "trader", the

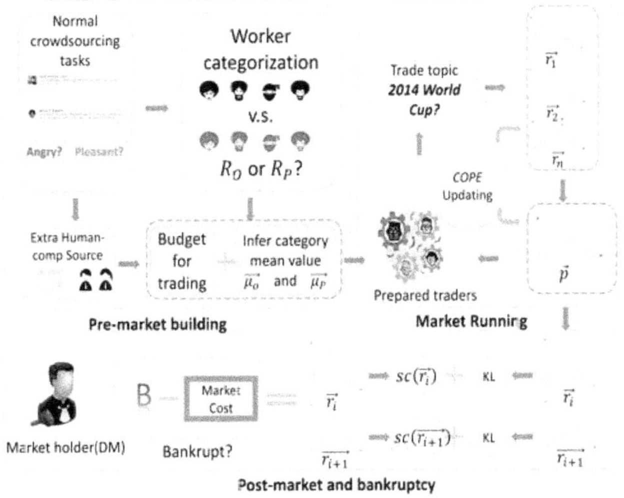

Figure 2: The Framework of *COPE*

Pre-market Building module is designed. First, each "worker" is given a set of normal decision making tasks(termed as *deposit tasks*), e.g. sentiment analysis of short textual messages, image tagging, simple ranking according to image content and so on. After the "worker" finishes these tasks, the promised rewards C_i is retained and set as the *seed capital*. Note that the nature of these tasks will not affect the performance of the market, and these extra crowdsourced tasks are a by-product from running *COPE*.

Meanwhile, among the normal crowdsourcing tasks, a set of testing tasks, of which we know the true answers, are planted. We then examine a workers responses to these testing tasks to find patterns indicating systematic bias, which helps to calibrate the distribution aggregation afterwards. More details can be found in Section 3.2.2.

Market Running

When the traders are prepared, with their *seed capital* and categorical labels, the *COPE* is initiated. The system presents to each trader a trading topic, i.e. a set of exclusive outcomes of one action or possible reasons for one phenomenon, and each trader may specify a distribution among these options. The trader is informed that their later payoff depends on how much their presented answer contributes to the final global distribution of the entire market. The final payoff will be given when the market is closed by the requester or when other conditions are met like *Market Bankruptcy*. Please refer to Section 3.1.2 for more details about the payment. *COPE* then receives a report $\vec{r_i}$ from each trader t_i, and the *COPE* method is incurred to merge the new reports into the global distribution $\vec{p}$.

Market Supervision

The market holder, a.k.a. *decision maker* monitors *COPE* from the *market supervision* module, where the overall cost of the market is calculated whenever a new updating is conducted. We assume that the decision maker is working under the constraint of a patron budget B. She may choose to end *COPE* when the overall cost exceeds the preset budget. In addition, she is allowed to adopt a *slope* based running strategy to flexibly decide the terminating condition. More details can be found in Section 4.

3. DESIGNING *COPE*

In this section, we first present some basic concepts required to define the information market and probability aggregation. Then we formally describe the design of the *COPE*.

3.1 Preliminaries

3.1.1 Trader

The atomic units that build up the *COPE* are the traders. A trader in *COPE*, invests an asset by presenting a report $\vec{r}$ and gets profit by receiving the payoff depending on the presented report $M(\vec{r})$.

Specifically, a *trader* T_i is able to provide a report $\vec{r}$ as a probability distribution over the event space $\mathcal{S}$ of a set of random variables $X = \{X_1, X_2, \ldots, X_m\}$. The report $\vec{r} \in \mathcal{P}$ belongs to the possible report space $\mathcal{P}$, and a trader T_i chooses to present $\vec{r}$ rather than any other possible report $\vec{r'} \in \mathcal{P}$ when the corresponding payoffs $M(\vec{r}) > M(\vec{r'})$. That is, a trader will present a report to maximize his/her payoff according to a certain reward rule.

Without loss of generality, we assume in this work that all *traders* in *COPE* are *Risk-neutral Traders*, which is commonly utilized in Probabilistic Risk Analysis. This property refers to the traders who have no preference between choices with equal expected payoffs(profit), neglecting the risk associated to each option. In other words, a *Risk-neutral Trader* behaves/invests only according to the expected payoffs(profit).

DEFINITION 1 (RISK-NEUTRAL TRADER - T_i). *Given two optional reports $\vec{r}$ and $\vec{r'}$ and their corresponding payoffs $M(\vec{r})$ and $M(\vec{r'})$ as two real-valued random variables, a Risk-neutral Trader T_i considers $\vec{r} \succ \vec{r'}$ iff $E[M(\vec{r})] > E[M(\vec{r'})]$. Here the operation $\succ$ indicates preference among actions.*

For simplicity, in this paper we use simply the term *trader* to refer to a *Risk-neutral Trader*. Note that in the effort of approximating market opinion with the mean beliefs of the traders, risk aversion plays a positive role as well as inevitably introducing certain bias [33]. We consider more detailed tuning on risk-aversion stimulation as the future work, which can be strategically leveraged by adjusting the payoff function in the section below.

3.1.2 Payoff

While *COPE* is running, the market maintains a global probability distribution $\vec{p}$, which combines all previous reports from traders. If the *COPE* stops at step n, i.e. n *traders* have finished their investment by providing reports $\vec{R} = \{\vec{r_1}, \vec{r_2}, \ldots, \vec{r_n}\}$, the *COPE* conducts the *payoff* according to their contributed estimated distribution. In the design of *COPE*, we first use KL-divergence to measure the distance between two discrete distributions:

DEFINITION 2 (KULLBACK-LEIBLER DIVERGENCE [23]) *Let $\vec{r}$ and $\vec{u}$ be two probability mass functions in a discrete domain $\mathcal{S}$ with a finite or countably infinite number of values. The Kullback-Leibler diverge(KL divergence) between $\vec{r}$ and $\vec{u}$ is*

$$D(\vec{r}\|\vec{u}) = \sum_{x \in \mathcal{S}} \vec{r}[x] \log \frac{\vec{r}[x]}{\vec{u}[x]} \quad (1)$$

KL divergence is defined where for any x in space $\mathcal{S}$ if $\vec{r}[x] > 0$ then $\vec{u}[x] > 0$.

There is a wide spectrum of distance measurements that can serve to gauge the "contribution" from prior distribution $\vec{p}$ to posterior distribution $\vec{p^*}$ by a report $\vec{r_i}$. Considering the scenario of *COPE*, we prefer KL-divergence(also formally known as *relative entropy*) to measure the information gain between two distributions. There are two major reasons: *a*) the process of eliciting causality from crowdsourcing traders is an information gaining process, and KL-divergence is one of the natural practices followed in Bayesian inference or updating [22]; *b*) in accordance to the measurement of the intrinsic *goodness* of a report $\vec{r_i}$ introduced in Section 3.1.3), which is in essence a measure of information entropy, the preference of relative entropy seamlessly incorporates the *COPE Updating* and corresponding *payoff*.

The payoff to a trader T_i considers the relative contribution to the final distribution $\vec{p}$ from her(measured as KL-divergence $D(\vec{r_i}||\vec{p})$). Meanwhile, it is designed to guarantee the honesty of each trader as well. Therefore, we propose the following *payoff* mechanism which incorporates a non-linear component that is related to the final outcome:

DEFINITION 3 (PAYOFF). *Given the market estimation $\vec{p}$, a trader T_i, whose proposed report is $\vec{r_i}$, will receive a payoff M_i, when the market is closed.*

$$M_i = C_i \cdot \frac{Odd}{D_i + 1} = C_i \cdot \frac{Odd}{D(\vec{r_i}||\vec{p}) + 1} \tag{2}$$

C_i is the invested capital of T_i, and Odd is the preset parameter such that at most a trader could earn $Odd \times C_i$ as payoff.

In Definition 3 we use $D(\vec{r_i}||\vec{p})$ instead of $D(\vec{p}||\vec{r_i})$ in order to avoid the zero value in $\vec{r_i}$, which may affect the correctness of the KL-divergence. In addition, to enhance the practical usage, currently we assume the *invested capital* C_i for each trader T_i is the same seed capital: $C_1 = C_2 = \ldots = C_i = \ldots = C$, and the payoff can be thus simplified as

$$M_i = \frac{C \cdot Odd}{D(\vec{r_i}||\vec{p}) + 1}$$

The payoff mechanism in Definition 3 enables *COPE* to punish careless or wrong traders by confining the rewards in the range of $(0, Odd \times C_i]$, where the condition for equality is that the report $\vec{r_i} = \vec{p}$ the global posterior distribution. We summarize and provide the following lemma:

LEMMA 1 (PAYOFF RANGE). *The range of payoff for trader T_i is as follow:*

$$0 < M_i \leq Odd \times C_i \tag{3}$$

The maximum equality is observed when $\vec{r_i} = \vec{p}$.

PROOF. Based on Equation 1, we notice that

$$\begin{aligned} D(\vec{r_i}||\vec{p}) = &\quad \textstyle\sum_{j\in\mathcal{S}} \vec{r_i}[j] \log \frac{\vec{r_i}[j]}{\vec{p}[j]} & (4)\\ = &\quad -\textstyle\sum_{j\in\mathcal{S}} \vec{r_i}[j] \log \frac{\vec{p}[j]}{\vec{r_i}[j]} & (5)\\ \geq &\quad -\log \textstyle\sum_{j\in\mathcal{S}} \vec{r_i}[j] \frac{\vec{p}[j]}{\vec{r_i}[j]} & (6)\\ = &\quad \log \textstyle\sum_{j\in\mathcal{S}} \vec{p} & (7)\\ = &\quad 0 & (8) \end{aligned}$$

The inequality in line 6 derives from Jensen's Inequality and the convexity of $\log(\cdot)$ function. Thus, we could obtain that

$$0 < \frac{Odd}{D(\vec{r_i}||\vec{p}) + 1} \leq Odd \tag{9}$$

where Lemma 1 is proved. And without difficulty, we can observe that the turning point for a no-loss-no-gain investment is $Odd - D(\vec{r_i}||\vec{p}) = 1$. □

The introduction of KL-divergence as a leveraging parameter in computing the payoff helps the market holder to encourage informative traders. Obviously, this mechanism converts the labor market into a trader market without introducing real-money gambling settings which constrains the development of information markets in a long list of countries [18]. Moreover, currently the design of *COPE* does not allow traders to forsake the opportunity to become a trader, i.e. that must confront the risk of losing the *seed capital*. The mechanism where abandonment of risking will be explored as future work.

Table 1: Summary of Notations

Notation	Description
T_i	a Risk-neutral trader with index i
$\vec{p}$	the current market estimation
$\vec{r_i}$	the report from trader i
$\vec{d_i}$	the subjective belief of trader i
$sc(\cdot)$	the goodness measure function
Odd	the *boosting parameter* set by market holder
$\vec{\mu_o}$	the mean of optimistic distributions
$\vec{\mu_p}$	the mean of pessimistic distributions
$C(C_i)$	the *seed capital* (of trader T_i)
M_i	the *payoff* of trader T_i
λ	the *adjusting parameter* for *COPE* updating

3.1.3 Goodness of Reported Distribution

To reward the traders who contribute reports with more care and honesty, the *COPE* incorporates the factor $sc(\vec{r_i})$ to evaluate the goodness of the contributed report $\vec{r_i}$.

DEFINITION 4 (GOODNESS). *Given a proposed report $\vec{r_i}$ from trader T_i, we define the goodness of the report $sc(\vec{r_i})$ as its expected score according to scoring rule in logarithm form [30], i.e.*

$$sc(\vec{r_i}) = \sum_j \vec{r_i}[j] \cdot S_j(\vec{r_i}[j]) = \sum_j \vec{r_i}[j] \log \vec{r_i}[j] \tag{10}$$

The definition of *goodness* $sc(\vec{r_i})$ describes the degree to which the trader tends to present a more extreme distribution(which is more informative) than an even one, which helps the *COPE* adjust the incremental update from each new report $\vec{r_i}$. Specifically, we notice that the value of *goodness* $E(sc)$ is mathematically the entropy of the given report $\vec{r_i}$, which reflects the amount of new information that brought in by trader T_i.

Note that we avoid using a traditional strict scoring rule [18] as payoff mechanism mainly for two reasons: *1)* Strict scoring rules-based mechanisms are mostly suitable for verifiable tasks; and *2)* It is too intricate to explain the sophisticated strict scoring rule to workers from Labor Markets, and even with a explicit explanation, the haste while specifying distribution weakens the rule-oriented calibration to a large extent.

We tentatively present the following conjecture for further exploration:

CONJECTURE 1. *The risk-neutral trader invests honestly under the payoff mechanism in COPE, i.e.*

$$\vec{r_i} = \vec{d_i} \tag{11}$$

Since any linear transformation of existing strict scoring rules is also a strict scoring rule, thus, a light modification of the current payoff mechanism on *COPE* may validate the above conjecture.

3.2 Mechanism of *COPE*

The system of *COPE* is an integrated market that is built on a general crowdsourcing platform. It receives trades (bets) as elicited distribution from traders and combines them into a global distribution. In this section, we present the design and mechanism of three major technique steps that enables the *COPE*.

3.2.1 Evaluating $\vec{r_i}$

Each trader T_i will accomplish several normal crowdsourcing tasks before she/he is entitled to participate into a trading. By injecting probe tasks, whose answers are known beforehand, into normal ones, we could evaluate the bias type of the trader T_i .

After finishing the given batch of normal crowdsourcing tasks, each worker is labeled into one of two categories, namely optimistic $R_o = \{\vec{r_1^o}, \vec{r_2^o}, \ldots, \vec{r^o_{|R_o|}}\}$ and pessimistic $R_p = \{\vec{r_1^p}, \vec{r_2^p},$

Algorithm 1: Overall Procedure while Running *COPE*

```
Input: Outcome Space S, Market Holder's Prior Distribution
    p0, Budget B > 0, n Risk-neutral traders
Output: Posterior Distribution p*, payoff M_i to each trader T_i
Initialization: Set the prior distribution p0 = u as uniform
    distribution
Pre-market Building: For each trader T_i, label it according to
    his category, calculate the marginal mean μ_o and μ_p according
    to Equation 12 and 13
Market Running: For each trader T_i, the Market obtains an
    discrete distribution r_i over the outcome space S
for each trader T_i do
    adjust the global posterior p* according to COPE
    updating;
Post-market: Calculate bounds OR exact Market Cost MC
    based on Section 4;
if Bankruptcy conditions are met then
    stop the market;
    conduct payoff to each trader T_i;
return posterior distribution p*;
```

$\ldots, \vec{r^p_{|R_p|}}\}$. For each category, an arithmetic mean is calculated and set as the estimation of the first moment of that category.

Specifically, for the category of optimistic workers, we have:

$$\vec{\mu_o} = \frac{\sum_i \vec{r^o_i}}{|R_o|} \tag{12}$$

And for the pessimistic workers, we have:

$$\vec{\mu_p} = \frac{\sum_i \vec{r^p_i}}{|R_p|} \tag{13}$$

Note that to achieve higher accuracy from *COPE*, more categories can be introduced. And the estimated moment values for each category serve as a clue for the following Bayesian scheme distribution updating.

3.2.2 Updating New Report $\vec{r_i}$ into $\vec{p}$

One of the core technique challenges for building the *COPE* is how it should aggregate the elicited reports from individuals into a universal distribution, while following certain guidance or principles that suits the semantic requirements from the market requester or decision maker. This is a controversial topic that incurs long debates among the community of subjective probability [4, 11, 12], and two major types of updating schemes, namely *Axiomatic* and *Bayesian* both exhibit observable rationales under various updating situations. Therefore, the design of updating scheme should be considered together with the specific application scenario. As mentioned in the introduction, the market holder establishes *COPE* mainly in order to elicit a distribution for further risk analysis tasks, which implies the existence of a latent *decision maker* who would conduct an exclusive decision among the possible outcomes. According to C. Genest and J. Zidek's conclusion in [17], the most appropriate method for updating the distribution under such circumstances should follow the Bayesian scheme with a set of specific constraints. In this section, we present the mechanism of *COPE* to update the current global distribution $\vec{p}$ following such a scheme.

In the combining procedure, the current global distribution is treated as the prior distribution, and the aggregated distribution is then treated as the posterior distribution. Following the Bayesian updating scheme, we have following updating expression:

$$p^* = \Pr(\vec{p}|\vec{r}) \propto \frac{\Pr(\vec{p})L(\vec{r}|\vec{p})}{\Pr(\vec{r})} \tag{14}$$

However, in the setting of *COPE* or other running information market, it is practically impossible for the decision maker to assess a full likelihood function $\Pr(\vec{p})L(\vec{r}|\vec{p})$. Fortunately, powered by the normal deposit tasks finished by each trader, we could partially evaluate their tendency with the estimation of the first moment value of each category. Then we are able to devise the *COPE* combining method following standard Bayesian scheme.

First we introduce two essential properties that describe a normative combining method within Bayesian scheme, the *Unanimity Principle* and *Compromise Principle*.

PROPERTY 1 (UNANIMITY PRINCIPLE). *If the reports are the same, the prior distribution should be same to the posterior distribution.*

PROPERTY 2 (COMPROMISE PRINCIPLE). *The posterior distribution should reside in the range of the two extreme reports.*

It is necessary to follow these two principles in order to design a updating method that confirms with Bayesian Updating. The work in [16] studies the expert opinion combination in terms of forecasting tasks, and the proposed "GS-I" model only entails partial assessment of the forecasters to complete the Bayesian updating. Inspired by this, we design the *COPE* Updating as follows.

DEFINITION 5 (*COPE* UPDATING). *For one step updating, the posterior distribution is defined as below:*

$$p^* = p + \lambda(\vec{r_i} - \vec{\mu}) \tag{15}$$

and the λ *is the confidence from the decision maker for the extreme values in trader's distribution.*

$$\lambda = \frac{sc(\vec{r_i})}{log|\mathcal{S}|} \cdot UB \tag{16}$$

where $|\mathcal{S}|$ *is the size of the possible event space and* $UB = \min\{\frac{p}{\mu}, \frac{1-p}{1-\mu}\}$ *gives the upper bound of the parameter* λ.

Here λ is called *adjusting parameter* which helps the decision maker to gauge the mis-calibration or bias of the reporting individuals. Note that since the *goodness* of a report $sc(\vec{r_i})$ is the entropy of the given report, we can obtain the fact that $\lambda \in [0, \min\{\frac{p}{\mu}, \frac{1-p}{1-\mu}\})$ with the following lemma.

LEMMA 2. *The range of the adjusting parameter* λ *is within* $[0, \min\{\frac{p}{\mu}, \frac{1-p}{1-\mu}\})$.

PROOF. Suppose $U(x) = \frac{1}{|\mathcal{S}|}$ is the probability mass function of a uniform distribution over outcome space $\mathcal{S}$, and $\vec{r_i}$ is the report vector from trader T_i. Then

$$\begin{aligned} D(\vec{r_i}||U) &= \sum_{j=1}^{|\mathcal{S}|} \vec{r_i}[j] \log \frac{\vec{r_i}[j]}{U[j]} & (17)\\ &= \log|\mathcal{S}| - H(\vec{r_i}) & (18)\\ &= \log|\mathcal{S}| - sc(\vec{r_i}) & (19)\end{aligned}$$

Then according to proof 1, we know that $D(\vec{r_i}||U) \geq 0$. Thus we have the following inequality.

$$0 \leq D(\vec{r_i}||U) = \log|\mathcal{S}| - sc(\vec{r_i}) \tag{20}$$

which indicates that

$$0 \leq \lambda = \frac{sc(\vec{r_i})}{log|\mathcal{S}|} \cdot UB \leq UB \tag{21}$$

and Lemma 2 is proved. □

Algorithm 2: Procedure of Computing Market Cost of *COPE*

Input: current global posterior distribution $\vec{p}$, reports from n traders $R_n = \{\vec{r_1}, \vec{r_2}, \ldots, \vec{r_n}\}$, *seed capital* C, preset *boosting parameter Odd*
Output: total Market Cost MC

```
Initialization: zero-valued vector M⃗ with size n, and MC = 0
for each r⃗_i in R_n do
    compute M_i according to Equation 2 ;
    M⃗[i] = M_i ;
    MC+ = M⃗[i] ;
return MC;
```

Then the benefit of introducing *COPE* Updating method can be observed: the design of *COPE* naturally satisfies the aforementioned two basic principles. We then claim the following lemma.

LEMMA 3 (PROPERTIES OF *COPE*). *The COPE updating confirms with the Unanimity Principle and Compromise Principle.*

PROOF. According to Theorem 2.1 in [16], an updating strategy satisfies the two properties when the value of λ observes the following condition:

$$\max\{\frac{p}{\mu-1}, \frac{p-1}{\mu}\} \leq \lambda \leq \min\{\frac{p}{\mu}, \frac{1-p}{1-\mu}\}. \quad (22)$$

Since $\lambda = \frac{sc(\vec{r_i})}{log|S|} \in (0,1)$, it satisfies the requirement above. Thus the two properties are satisfied. □

3.3 Cost of *COPE*

To establish a *COPE*, the market holder has to be willing to be a patron with a budget B: when the overall cost of the *COPE* exceeds this budget, the market has to be closed(termed as *bankruptcy*). Of course, the patron could close the market before this, if a sufficiently good result has been obtained.

DEFINITION 6 (MARKET COST). *Given a COPE, the current distribution $\vec{p}$, the set of reports from n traders $R_n = \{\vec{r_1}, \vec{r_2}, \ldots, \vec{r_n}\}$, the Market Cost is defined as the summation of the payoffs from every trader t_i, i.e.*

$$MC = MC(\vec{p}, R_n) = \sum_{i=1}^{n} M_i \quad (23)$$

The ending condition for one instance of *COPE* is that MC exceeds the preset budget B. And when this condition is reached, the market stops accepting any new report and returns to the market holder with the current global distribution $\vec{p^*}$. This condition has to be checked after every trade report, and can be expensive to compute. In Sec. 4.3 we describe how to do this efficiently.

4. RUNNING *COPE*

In this section, we introduce the essential techniques to keep the *COPE* running. First we introduce the algorithm conducting the *COPE* Updating Strategy in a batching style. Then we introduce the computation of the *Market Cost* given the set of reports $R_n = \{\vec{r_1}, \vec{r_2}, \ldots, \vec{r_n}\}$. Moreover, we further introduce an advanced strategy to run the market with more flexibility. An overall procedure to run the *COPE* is presented in Algorithm 1.

4.1 Batch *COPE* Updating

In Section 3.2.2, we introduce the mechanism of updating the current global distribution $\vec{p}$ from one individual report $\vec{r_i}$. For each iteration of such individual update, the algorithm takes $\mathcal{O}(|S|)$ time complexity. If given an entire set of reports $R_n = \{\vec{r_1}, \vec{r_2}, \ldots, \vec{r_n}\}$, the total time complexity becomes $\mathcal{O}(|S| \cdot n)$. In this section, we introduce a close form of conducting *COPE* updating in batch.

THEOREM 1 (BATCH *COPE* UPDATING). *Given n individual reports $R_n = \{\vec{r_1}, \vec{r_2}, \ldots, \vec{r_n}\}$, and the labeled category mean $\vec{\mu_o}$ and $\vec{\mu_p}$, the posterior global distribution over outcome set S can be computed following the equations below [16]:*

$$\vec{p^*} = \frac{p^{1-n}\prod_{i=1}^{n} n_i}{p^{1-n}\prod_{i=1}^{n} n_i + (1-p)^{1-n}\prod_{i=1}^{n}(1-n_i)} \quad (24)$$

where for each $1 \leq i \leq n, n_i = [p + \lambda_i(\vec{r_i} - \vec{\mu})]$ is between the upper and lower bounds in Equation 22 and $\vec{\mu}$ is to be replaced according to the label of each report.

By conducting the batch-style *COPE* Updating, the time complexity could be reduced to $\mathcal{O}(n + |S|)$.

4.2 Computing Market Cost

The computation of Market Cost MC is another important issue to consider in order to efficiently manage the *COPE*. After obtaining the posterior global distribution $\vec{p}$ by conducting *COPE* Updating, the market goes through all the reports and calculate the exact payoff for each trader. A sketchy procedure of computing the Market Cost MC is given in Algorithm 2. The time cost of exactly calculating a market cost is $\mathcal{O}(n \cdot |S|)$.

Note that the payoff for each trader is positive, but there are traders who suffer from payoff less than the *seed capital* C due to large difference between their report $\vec{r_i}$ and $\vec{p}$.

4.3 Market Running Strategy

When a market holder runs a *COPE*, he acts both as a patron to support the market and a decision maker to determine when to stop the market. The most simple strategy of running the market is to calculate the exact total market cost every time when a new report comes, and shut down the market immediately when $MC \geq B$, which we term as *Bankruptcy*.

Besides the trivial strategy described above, in this section, we propose a ***slope* based running strategy** which grants the market holder more flexibility, as well as improving the efficiency. The *slope* is formed by the upper and lower edges of the market cost: when the upper edge reaches the preset budget B, the system triggers a warning that the Budget is running out and starts to calculate the exact MC; if the lower edges exceeds the Budget, the market is terminated immediately. But while the Budget is running within the *slope* range, the system keeps the market running and returns to the market holder the current result and wait for the decision of the holder.

To facilitate such a *slope* based strategy, we develop a pair of lower and upper bounds of the KL-divergence based on a variant of Pinsker Inequality.

Lower Slope Edge

First we define the concept of *Variational Distance*, a.k.a. $\mathcal{L}_1$-distance, which can be computed faster than the KL-divergence due to the avoidance of computing weighted logarithm value.

DEFINITION 7 (VARIATIONAL DISTANCE). *Let $\vec{v}$ and $\vec{u}$ be two probability mass functions in a discrete domain S with a finite or countably infinite number of values. The Variational Distance*

Algorithm 3: Procedure of determining Market Bankruptcy of *COPE*

Input: current global posterior distribution $\vec{p}$, reports from n traders $R_n = \{\vec{r_1}, \vec{r_2}, \ldots, \vec{r_n}\}$, *seed capital* C, preset *boosting parameter Odd*
Output: Decision of *Bankruptcy*
Initialization: *Bankruptcy* bool flag $F_B K = 0$,
for *each* $\vec{r_i}$ *in* R_n **do**
  for *each* j *in* $\vec{r_i}$ **do**
    compute the $V_i(\vec{r_i}, \vec{p}) += |\vec{r_i}[j] - \vec{p}[j]|$;
    compute the $c_i = \max_j(\vec{r_i}[j]/\vec{p}[j])$;
  $M_i^L = Odd \cdot C/(\log 2 \cdot V(\vec{r_i}, \vec{p}) + \log c_i + 1)$;
  $MC^L += M_i^E$;
if $MC^L - B > 0$ **then**
  return $F_B K = 1$(*Bankruptcy*);
else
  return $F_B K = 0$(still running);

Algorithm 4: Procedure of Warning Trigger of *COPE*

Input: current global posterior distribution $\vec{p}$, reports from n traders $R_n = \{\vec{r_1}, \vec{r_2}, \ldots, \vec{r_n}\}$, *seed capital* C, preset *boosting parameter Odd*
Output: Decision of Warning Trigger
Initialization: *Warning* bool flag $F_W N = 0$,
for *each* $\vec{r_i}$ *in* R_n **do**
  //compute Variational Distance $V_i = V(\vec{r_i}, \vec{p})$ according to Equation 25 ;
  for *each* j *in* $\vec{r_i}$ **do**
    $V_i(\vec{r_i}, \vec{p}) += |\vec{r_i}[j] - \vec{p}[j]|$;
  $M_i^U = Odd \cdot C/(\frac{1}{2}V_i^2 + 1)$;
  $MC^U += M_i^U$;
if $MC^U - B > 0$ **then**
  return $F_W N = 1$(*Warning*);
else
  return $F_W N = 0$(still running);

between $\vec{v}$ and $\vec{u}$ is

$$V(\vec{v}, \vec{u}) = \sum_{j=1}^{n} |\vec{v}[j] - \vec{u}[j]| \tag{25}$$

whose value is always non-negative.

We now present the following *Lower Bounding* theorem.

THEOREM 2 (LOWER BOUNDING). *Given a report $\vec{r_i}$, the current global distribution $\vec{p}$, the lower bound of the payoff to trader T_i can be achieved as follow:*

$$M_i^L = Odd \cdot C/(\log 2 \cdot V(\vec{r_i}, \vec{p}) + \log c + 1) \leq M_i \tag{26}$$

where $c = \max_j(\vec{r_i}[j]/\vec{p}[j])$.

Before we prove the given lower bound, we first define the concept of the *Capacitory Discrimination* as follows:

DEFINITION 8 (CAPACITORY DISCRIMINATION). *Let $\vec{v}$ and $\vec{u}$ be two probability mass functions in a discrete domain $\mathcal{S}$ with a finite or countably infinite number of values. The Capacitory Discrimination between $\vec{v}$ and $\vec{u}$ is*

$$C(\vec{v}, \vec{u}) = D(\vec{v}||\vec{m}) + D(\vec{u}||\vec{m}) \tag{27}$$

where

$$\vec{m} = \frac{1}{2}(\vec{v} + \vec{u}) \tag{28}$$

is the arithmetic mean of the two given vectors.

And we introduce the *Pinsker's Inequality* as follows:

THEOREM 3 (PINSKER'S INEQUALITY). *Given two probability mass functions $\vec{v}$ and $\vec{u}$ with outcome space $\mathcal{S}$, the following inequality is observed:*

$$D(\vec{v}||\vec{u}) \geq \frac{1}{2}V^2(\vec{v}, \vec{u}) \tag{29}$$

The equality holds when $\vec{u} = \vec{v}$.

PROOF. Please refer to [13]. □

Then we prove Theorem 2 based on *Variational Distance* and the *Pinsker's Inequality*:

PROOF (THEOREM 2). According to Theorem 4 in [29], we can obtain that

$$D(\vec{r_i}||\vec{p}) \leq C(\vec{r_i}, \vec{p}) + \log(\frac{1}{2}(1 + c)) \tag{30}$$

where $C(P, Q)$ is the *capacitory discrimination* with $\vec{m} = \frac{1}{2}(\vec{r_i} + \vec{p})$

$$C(\vec{r_i}, \vec{p}) = D(\vec{r_i}||\vec{m}) + D(\vec{p}||\vec{m}) \tag{31}$$

based on the definition of Variational Distance in Equation 25 and Pinsker Equality in Equation 29, we could obtain an upper bound of KL-divergence:

$$D(\vec{r_i}||\vec{p}) \leq \log 2 \cdot V(\vec{r_i}, \vec{p}) + \log c \tag{32}$$

which leads to the inequality in the Theorem 2. □

The lower bounds in Theorem 2 enables the *COPE* with a fast algorithm to determine the *Bankruptcy* situation. We elaborate the procedure in Algorithm 3.

Upper Slope Edge

When the upper edge of the slope reaches the preset budget, the market holder receives an warning, and since then the system starts to calculate the exact market cost.

As a warning function, the upper slope edge is realized based on an upper bound of the KL-divergence:

THEOREM 4 (UPPER BOUNDING). *Given a report $\vec{r_i}$, the current global distribution $\vec{p}$, the upper bound of the payoff to trader T_i can be achieved as follow:*

$$M_i^U = Odd \cdot C/(\frac{1}{2}V^2(\vec{r_i}, \vec{p}) + 1) \geq M_i \tag{33}$$

The proof can be directly inferred from the Pinsker Inequality. Equipped with the upper bound of individual payoff, we are able to estimate the upper edge of the slope. We then present the Warning Trigger technique as described in Algorithm 4. Note that while calculating the lower edge, the variational distance $V(p, r)$ has already been calculated, therefore, with a limited extra space cost, we could obtain the upper slope edge with an $\mathcal{O}(1)$ time cost.

5. IMPLEMENTATION

In this section, we illustrate the non-trivial parts of the implementation of *COPE*.

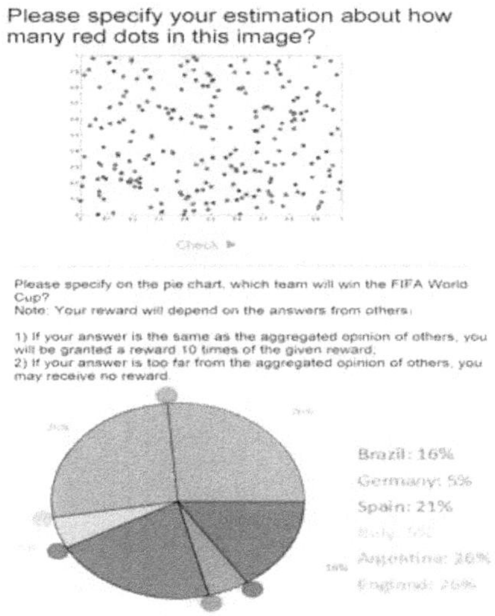

Figure 3: HIT Interface Prototype in a Running *COPE*

5.1 Deposit Task

There are two factors to consider while designing the deposit tasks: the tasks should be with general purpose, and the estimation tendency should be measured for the later Bayesian Updating. Following this requirement, we build up a prototype of *COPE* based on classic jelly-beans-in-a-jar experiment [20]. In this prototype implementation, when a "worker" accepts the task, she is presented with a sample image and informed that the given image contains exactly 200 blue dots. Then another figure is given as shown in the upper part of Figure 3 and the "worker" is required to estimate the number of dots without exhaustively counting them. A set of such tasks could be included in the *pre-market* stage, with a moderate amount of rewards, which makes the "worker" begrudged to forsake. Besides the family of jelly-beans-in-a-jar experiments, many other suitable tasks could be incorporated into the *pre-market* stage. One of the major requirement is that the estimation tendency label of a worker $\vec{r_i}$ should be able to be inferred. As in the prototype, the average over-estimation or under-estimation of the number of dots serves as a measure of the estimation tendency label.

5.2 Opinion Elicitation

After the input from the "worker", another page is presented as shown in the lower part of Figure 3, which is previously hidden. In this new page, the "worker" is required to specify the opinion distribution among a set of options. Due to the "probability-phobia", i.e. common workers feel unwilling or uncomfortable to exactly specify a value of a probability, we use dynamic chart to elicit the probabilistic estimation from a trader. The "worker" is given a set of options where the distribution information is unknown, and she is able to express opinion by swirling the spline of the pie chart. The "worker" is now informed that the final reward depends on how similar her estimation is compared to the aggregated opinion. Under such case, the "worker" is forced into a psychological situation of a "trader", where she confronts a situation of losing certain stake if her answer is not carefully presented. The proposed mechanism in *COPE* is thus activated.

5.3 Payoff Dispatch

The essential technique challenge to implement a *COPE* on general crowdsourcing platform is that the current infrastructure does not support a flexible payment mechanism, which hinters the application of the market. To tackle this challenge, besides the virtual "stake" from the *seed capital*, in *COPE* we also develop an innovative approach to conduct the payoff dispatching. When a "worker" finishes the opinion estimation, a specific task is generated after the closing of the *COPE*, and the task is visible and acceptable only to the "worker" by identifying her worker ID. The reward of the new task is set as the calculated payoff M_i.

6. EXPERIMENTS

In this section, we present the experimental study of the *COPE*. Specifically, we first study the effectiveness of introducing market mechanism in opinion elicitation. We compare the market mechanism with simple voting strategies. After that, we evaluate the relationship between the latency and the number of aggregated traders' information, then we study the characteristic between the distribution properties and the total *Market Cost*. In all figures, we use *ex* to denote the performance of the exact algorithm and *lw* and *up* to denote that of lower and upper bounding algorithms respectively.

6.1 Merits of Market Mechanism

In this section, we compare between the market-based mechanism with simple voting to show the merit of introducing the new mechanism. Note that in a jelly-beans-in-a-jar experiment, the mutual communication among participants impairs the crowd's accuracy [32]. However in the setting of *COPE*, the "investors" only know the existence of other participants but are unaware of others' opinion. Specifically, we set up three set of experiments on Amazon MTurk as follows:

a) We propose to the online crowds a picture with a man's portrait on it, and crowds are asked to estimate the age of the man(ground truth is known to be 40). In the simple voting, we set up two pivots value, e.g. $piv_1 = 35$ and $piv_2 = 45$, and ask the crowds to vote on the option that she think is closest to the real age. Then an answer is achieved by calculating the weighted aggregation. On the contrary, for the value based experiments, crowds are asked to specify a value between piv_1 and piv_2 and their mean is aggregated as the answer. The results are shown in Figure 4(a), where the error rates from simple voting (both $vt1$ and $vt2$) are higher than those of the value estimation ($vl1$ and $vl2$). The experiments are conducted on two independent data sets.

b) We then evaluate the error rates when the crowds are informed with different payoff mechanism, all under value estimation method. The results are shown in Figure 4(b). A first group of crowds are informed that their payoffs are irrelevant to their answers('dir1' and 'dir2'). The last group is encouraged to estimate according to the majority's opinion, i.e. the market mechanism introduced in this paper('mkt1' and 'mkt2'). The results show that the direct payoff incurs highest error rate and the market based method performs best in most cases.

c) Then we test the cost of introducing the market based mechanism. Varying the number of tasks, we record the total payoffs and show the results in Figure 4(c). We set up the price for a single task as 0.02 and 0.05USD respectively. Then the simple direct payoffs are shown in dashed lines and the market based mechanism in solid lines, which saves more payoff for the requester.

6.2 Latency v.s. Market Size

In this and next sections, we mainly study the performance of the proposed algorithms in mainly two aspects: the efficiency according to the number of collected reports, and the value of *Market Cost* according to a varying characteristic of the collected reports. All experiments are conducted on a PC with 2 Intel(R) Core(TM) 2.13GHz CPU and 4GB memory, running on Microsoft 64-bit Win-

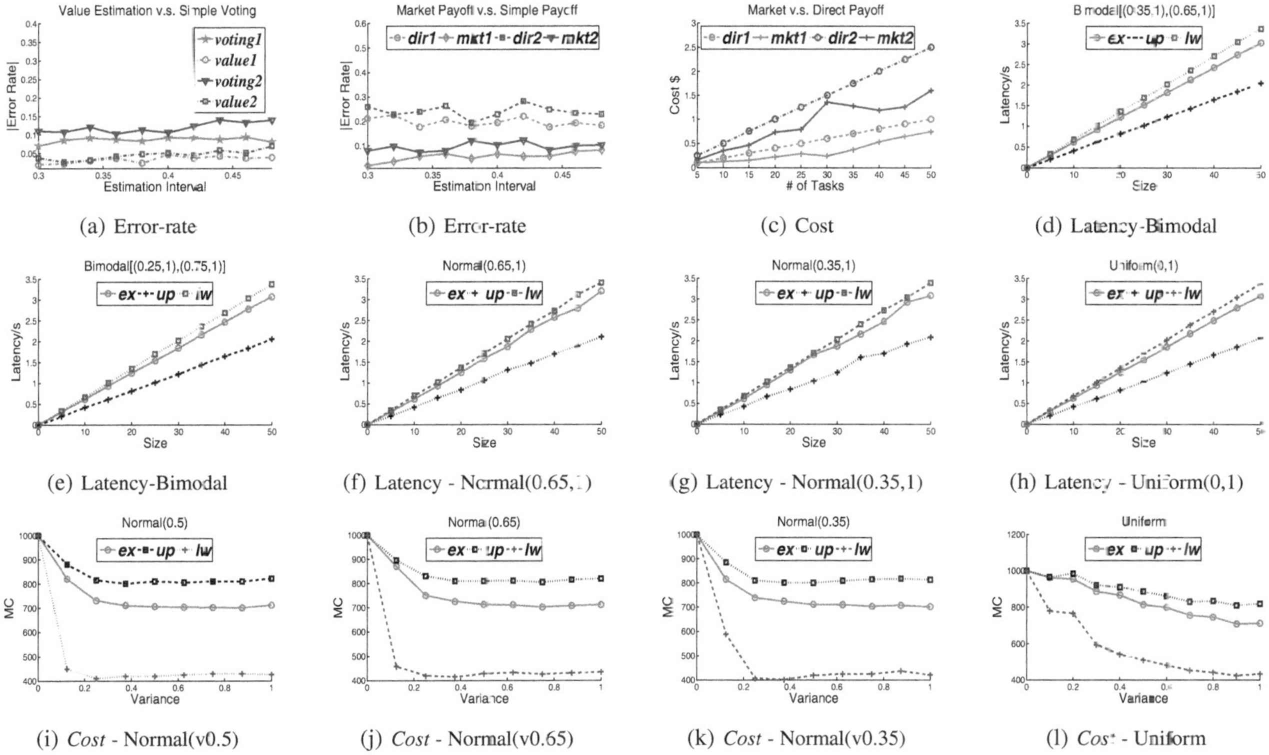

(a) Error-rate (b) Error-rate (c) Cost (d) Latency-Bimodal

(e) Latency-Bimodal (f) Latency - Normal(0.65,1) (g) Latency - Normal(0.35,1) (h) Latency - Uniform(0,1)

(i) *Cost* - Normal(v0.5) (j) *Cost* - Normal(v0.65) (k) *Cost* - Normal(v0.35) (l) *Cost* - Uniform

Figure 4: Experiments Results

dows 8. We generate the data sets following both the family of normal distribution and uniform distribution.

We first present the performance of calculating the *Market Cost* with a varying report number from Figure 4(d) to Figure 4(h). Specifically, we test the performance on Bimodal distribution, Normal distribution and Uniform distribution. As described in Section 4, the time complexity of calculating the *Market Cost* is $\mathcal{O}(n \cdot |\mathcal{S}|)$, thus the latency is roughly linear according to a fixed size of outcome space and an increasing number of reports.

6.3 Market Cost v.s. Distribution Variance

In this experiment, we test the relationship between the *Market Cost* and the variance within a reported distribution. Specifically, we simulate the statistical feature of the crowd with the following four distribution: normal distribution with mean value equal to 0.5 (1), normal distribution with mean value equal to 0.65 (2), normal distribution with mean value equal to 0.35 (3), and uniform distribution (4). For each distribution, the market cost is calculated at every variance value ranging from 0 to its set upper limit.

The results are shown from Figure 4(i) to Figure 4(l). From the tested results, we can clearly observe that, for all the distribution, the *Market Cost* is maximized where the variance equals to 0. Then, the *Market Cost* goes down sharply with the variance increasing. In the final stage, the market cost becomes stable. Such a result is easy to interpret: when the variance of the crowd is small, that people hold similar attitudes toward the given event. Therefore, their reports are likely to resemble the market estimation, which makes the market cost large at first. When the variance gets larger, the crowds' opinions become diversified. Then, we can infer that traders' reports are likely to vary greatly from market estimation, which leads to a lower *Market Cost*. The result here also indicates that the variance of the crowd can serve as a good predictor of the market cost.

7. RELATED WORK

In this section, we summarize the literature of research related to the design of *COPE*. As described in Section 1, the design of *COPE* is a pioneering effort to realize a market-manner information aggregator onto a concrete commercial platform.

7.1 Information Elicitation

Probability distribution elicitation has paved its way in two main branches, Scoring Rules [6] and Information Market [19].

Scoring Rules are first adopted as an incentive mechanism to reward weather forecasters [6], where the reward depends on the designed rules and the final outcomes of the uncertain events. Many different scoring rules are then developed to suit various elicitation scenarios: quadratic strict rules [6], logarithm rules [28], and more recently scoring rule for more complex enviroments [8]. In the work [27] by L. Savage, a functional characterization is presented, and a comprehensive study of Scoring Rule to evaluate probability can be found in work [30] by R. Winkler.

Information Market is developed based on the observation that speculative markets like financial markets or commodity markets reflect the confidence of the investors faithfully. Their chances to reduce information uncertainty are wrapped as tradable products on Information Market, where the stable price reflects the information estimation among the investors. Early prototypes can be found in horse betting [19], political polls [5], science progress [25] and so on. A recent effort [18] by R. Hanson et al. proposes to combine the Information Market and Scoring Rule to facilitate a sequential market. Such a Scoring Market Rule is essentially a cost-function market maker [10] from the perspective of market design. This thread of approach also produces new practice of crowdsourced learning tasks [31], where an iterative and interactive learning procedure is proposed to enhance the prediction performance based on given historical dataset(on the contrary, *COPE* addresses the task of elicit intrinsic opinion of workers without any historical training efforts). Moreover, a recent series of work [9, 26] conducted by Y. Chen et al. provides more sophisticated market mechanism for information elicitation. In the work [9] the authors design a special type of information market that capture the signal structure as informative securities. However, the design of such advanced information markets entails a specially designed speculative market, which is way too complicated and intractable on general labor markets. And in the work [26] the authors implement an information polling tool based on Amazon MTurk by direct polling and payoff, without the support of a market structure.

7.2 Data-driven Human Computation

Human computation is a long-existing concept and has been practiced for centuries. Specifically, whenever a "human" serves to "compute", a human computation is observed. This leads to a history of Human Computation even longer than that of electronic computer. However, with the emergence of Internet web service, especially the one that facilitates online labor recruiting and managing like Amazon MTurk and oDesk, human computation starts to experience a new age where the source of human is broadened to a vast pool of crowds, instead of designated experts or employees. This type of outsourcing to crowds, i.e. *crowdsourcing*, is now receiving countless success in many areas such as fund raising, logistics, monitoring and so on.

In data-driven applications, human cognitive abilities are mainly exploited in two types: voting among many options, and providing contents according to certain requirements. The wide usage of "voting" as a human computing action grows from the observation that humans are better at comparisons rather than evaluation objects by specifying an exact numerical value. Most of basic queries in database [14] and data mining [2] can be decomposed into simple voting as human tasks [7, 14]. Meanwhile, in order to break the *close world assumption* in traditional database, human are enrolled to provide extraneous information to answer certain queries: item enumeration [14], content composing [3, 21], counting [24] and so on. The work in this paper takes effort to explore new usage of human cognitive ability, specifying probability estimation among uncertain events.

8. CONCLUSION

In this paper, we design and propose the *COPE* to facilitate *Opinion Elicitation* functions on general crowdsourcing labor market. We also elaborate the rationale of the design in terms of distribution combination and payoff mechanism. In the end, we theoretically and practically testify the performance of such function.

More general Opinion Elicitation tasks observe multivariate random relationship, whose outcome space may increase exponentially, which render the Market unmanageable. However, human cognitive knowledge is able to help decide the necessity of such dependency, while providing quantitative causality information. We will proceed to extend *COPE* to capture such potential in the future.

Acknowledgment

We thank the anonymous reviewers and area chairs for their in-depth review and constructive comments.

This work is supported in part by the Hong Kong RGC Project N_HKUST637/13, National Grand Fundamental Research 973 Program of China under Grant 2012-CB316200, National Natural Science Foundation of China (NSFC) Grant No. 61232018, NSF grant IIS-1250880, Microsoft Research Asia Gift Grant and Google Faculty Award 2013.

9. REFERENCES

[1] L. von Ahn and L. Dabbish. Labeling images with a computer game. In *CHI Conference*,2004.
[2] Y. Amsterdamer, Y. Grossman, T. Milo, and P. Senellart. Crowd mining. In *SIGMOD*,2013.
[3] Y. Baba and H. Kashima. Statistical quality estimation for general crowdsourcing tasks. In *SIGKDD Conference*, 2013.
[4] T. Bedford and R. Cooke. *Probabilistic risk analysis: foundations and methods*. Cambridge University Press, 2001.
[5] J. Berg, F. Nelson, and T. Rietz. Accuracy and forecast standard error of prediction markets. *Tippie College of Business Administration, University of Iowa*, 2003.
[6] G. Brier. Verification of forecasts expressed in terms of probability. *Monthly weather review*, 78(1):1–3, 1950.
[7] C. C. Cao, J. She, Y. Tong, and L. Chen. Whom to ask? jury selection for decision making tasks on micro-blog services. *VLDB*, 2012.
[8] Y. Chen and I. Kash. Information elicitation for decision making. *AAMAS*, 2011.
[9] Y. Chen, M. Ruberry, and J.W. Vaughan. Designing informative securities. In *UAI*, 2012.
[10] Y. Chen, M. Ruberry, and J.W.Vaughan. Cost function market makers for measurable spaces. In *ACM EC*, 2013.
[11] R. T. Clemen and R. L. Winkler. Unanimity and compromise among probability forecasters. *Management Science*, 36(7):767–779, 1990.
[12] R. T. Clemen and R. L. Winkler. Combining probability distributions from experts in risk analysis. *Risk analysis*, 19(2):187–203, 1999.
[13] T. M Cover and J. A Thomas. *Elements of information theory*. John Wiley & Sons, 2012.
[14] M. J. Franklin, D. Kossmann, T. Kraska, S. Ramesh, and R. Xin. Crowddb: answering queries with crowdsourcing. In *SIGMOD*, 2011.
[15] J. Gao, X. Liu, B. C. Ooi, H. Wang, and G. Chen. An online cost sensitive decision-making method in crowdsourcing systems. In *SIGMOD*, 2013.
[16] C. Genest and M. J Schervish. Modeling expert judgments for bayesian updating. *The Annals of Statistics*, 13(3):1198–1212, 1985.
[17] C. Genest and J. V Zidek. Combining probability distributions: A critique and an annotated bibliography. *Statistical Science*, 1986.
[18] R. Hanson. Combinatorial information market design. *Information Systems Frontiers*, 5(1):107–119, 2003.
[19] D. B. Hausch, V. SY Lo, and W. T Ziemba. Efficiency of Racetrack Betting Markets. *Academic Press New York*, 1994.
[20] J. Howe. Crowdsourcing: Why the power of the crowd is driving the future of business. *Crown Publishing Group*, 2008.
[21] L. Kazemi and C. Shahabi. Geocrowd: enabling query answering with spatial crowdsourcing. In *ACM GIS Conference*, 2012.
[22] D. Kollar and N. Friedman. Probabilistic graphical models: principles and techniques. *The MIT Press*, 2009.
[23] S. Kullback and R. A Leibler. On information and sufficiency. *The Annals of Mathematical Statistics*, 22(1):79–86, 1951.
[24] A. Marcus, D. Karger, S. Madden, R. Miller, and S. Oh. Counting with the crowd. *VLDB*, 2013.
[25] D. M Pennock, S. Lawrence, C L. Giles, F. A. Nielsen, et al. The real power of artificial markets. *Science*, 291(5506):987–988, 2001.
[26] T. Pfeiffer, X. Gao, Y. Chen, A. Mao, and D. G Rand. Adaptive polling for information aggregation. In *AAAI*, 2012.
[27] L. J Savage. Elicitation of personal probabilities and expectations. *Journal of the American Statistical Association*, 1971.
[28] E. H Shuford Jr, A. Albert, and H E. Massengill. Admissible probability measurement procedures. *Psychometrika*, 1966.
[29] F. Topsoe. Some inequalities for information divergence and related measures of discrimination. *Trans. Inf. Theory*, 2000.
[30] R. Winkler, J. Muñoz, José Cervera, José Bernardo, G. Blattenberger, J. Kadane, D. Lindley, A. Murphy, R. Oliver, and D. Ríos-Insua. Scoring rules and the evaluation of probabilities. *JASA*, 1996.
[31] J. Abernethy and R. M. Frongillo. A Collaborative Mechanism for Crowdsourcing Prediction Problems. In *NIPS*, 2011.
[32] J. Lorenz, H. Rauhut, F. Schweitzer and D. Helbing. How social influence can undermine the wisdom of crowd effect. In *PNAS*, 2011.
[33] J. Wolfers and E. Zitzewitz. Interpreting prediction market prices as probabilities. In *NBER Working Paper 12200*, 2006.

Optimal Real-Time Bidding for Display Advertising

Weinan Zhang, Shuai Yuan, Jun Wang
Department of Computer Science, University College London
{w.zhang, s.yuan, j.wang}@cs.ucl.ac.uk

ABSTRACT

In this paper we study bid optimisation for real-time bidding (RTB) based display advertising. RTB allows advertisers to bid on a display ad impression in real time when it is being generated. It goes beyond contextual advertising by motivating the bidding focused on user data and it is different from the sponsored search auction where the bid price is associated with keywords. For the demand side, a fundamental technical challenge is to automate the bidding process based on the budget, the campaign objective and various information gathered in runtime and in history. In this paper, the programmatic bidding is cast as a functional optimisation problem. Under certain dependency assumptions, we derive simple bidding functions that can be calculated in real time; our finding shows that the optimal bid has a non-linear relationship with the impression level evaluation such as the click-through rate and the conversion rate, which are estimated in real time from the impression level features. This is different from previous work that is mainly focused on a linear bidding function. Our mathematical derivation suggests that optimal bidding strategies should try to bid more impressions rather than focus on a small set of high valued impressions because according to the current RTB market data, compared to the higher evaluated impressions, the lower evaluated ones are more cost effective and the chances of winning them are relatively higher. Aside from the theoretical insights, offline experiments on a real dataset and online experiments on a production RTB system verify the effectiveness of our proposed optimal bidding strategies and the functional optimisation framework.

Categories and Subject Descriptors

H.3.5 [**Information Systems**]: Information Storage and Retrieval - Online Information Services

Keywords

Demand-Side Platform, Bid Optimisation, Real-Time Bidding, Display Advertising

1. INTRODUCTION

Real-time bidding (RTB) has recently emerged as a new display advertising paradigm. Unlike traditional sponsored search or contextual advertising, where an advertiser presets a bid price for each keyword chosen for their campaigns, RTB allows an advertiser to submit a bid for each individual impression (based on the impression level features) in a very short time frame, often less than 100ms [38]. RTB has fundamentally changed the landscape of display advertising because (i) allowing per impression transactions scales the buying process across a large number of available ad inventories including the leftovers; (ii) real-time audience data encourages behaviour (re-)targeting and makes a significant shift towards buying that is focused on user data [31], rather than contextual data.

Demand-Side Platforms (DSPs) are thus created to help advertisers manage their campaigns and optimise their real-time bidding activities. Figure 1 briefly illustrates the role of a DSP in the RTB eco-system. In RTB display advertising, once a user visits a webpage and an ad impression is created, a bid request for the impression is immediately triggered by the publisher (usually the Supply-Side Platform, a.k.a. SSP, a technology platform to manage publishers' inventories) and then sent to the DSPs via an ad exchange. On behalf of an advertiser, the DSP will compute a bid for this impression and return a bid response to the exchange, where a second price auction is usually held to select the winner. Finally the winner is notified and his/her ad is displayed to the user through the publisher. A more detailed introduction to RTB is given in [35, 38].

More specifically, after receiving a bid request, the DSP will find all eligible ad creatives from all campaigns[1] and compute a bid for each of them. The DSP uses both contextual [6] (e.g. domain, webpage, keywords, time and date, geographical location, weather, language, operating system, browser, etc.) and behavioural [22] (e.g. search, browsing and purchase history, occupation, income, sentiment, etc.) data to compute a bid. It is common and usually encouraged that advertisers buy user interest segments from third data providers [31]. Note that although we confine our work to the Cost-Per-Mille (CPM) pricing model which is commonly adopted in RTB, other less popular models are also available (e.g. Cost-Per-Click and Cost-Per-Acquisition).

This bid calculation (see the bidding engine in Figure 1) is the most important problem for a DSP. The solution to this problem is referred to as a *bidding strategy*. In pure second price auctions [24] for strategic competitors, theoretically the dominant strategy for advertisers is truth-telling: to bid their private values [15]. When facing a bid request, a DSP will evaluate the value of the impression i.e. to estimate the click-through/conversion rate (CTR/CVR) and

[1]The eligibility of the creative and campaign means their target combinations match the bid request such as placement size, user demographics, geographical location, language, etc. It acts as pre-filtering rules before the bidding process.

KDD'14, August 24–27, 2014, New York, NY, USA.
Copyright 2014 ACM 978-1-4503-2956-9/14/08 ...$15.00.
http://dx.doi.org/10.1145/2623330.2623633.

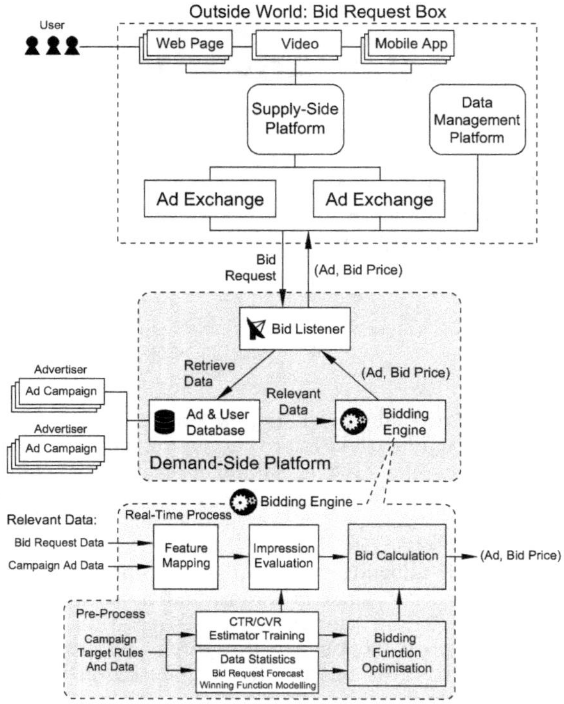

Figure 1: An illustration of a demand-side platform and its bidding engine in RTB display advertising.

multiply it by the value of a click/conversion [26]. Many advertisers simply set this value as their bid [32, 26] and keep using it throughout a campaign's lifetime. However, when computing a bid, practical constraints need to be taken into account including the bid landscape (the expected impressions against the bid price), total budget and the campaign's remaining lifetime. These considerations enable the DSP to optimise towards the overall performance of a campaign (usually referred to as Key Performance Indicator, KPI, e.g. the number of clicks, conversions or total revenue) using stochastic methods rather than assuming advertisers are strategic and have a private "true" value per impression [3].

In this paper, the impression level bidding strategy is formulated as a function that maps the individual impression evaluation to the bid value. A novel functional optimisation framework is proposed to find the optimal bidding function: (i) given the budget constraint and the campaign's lifetime, and (ii) taking into account various statistics such as the probability of winning the auction and the prior distribution of the impression features. Our analytical solution indicates that the auction winning function plays a more critical role in shaping the bidding function, whereas the distribution of the features is less correlated. Simple winning functions derived from practical bidding data result in optimal bidding functions that are *non-linear* and in a *concave* form. Unlike a linear function previously proposed [32], our bidding function encourages to higher bids for impressions with low estimated value because compared to higher evaluated ones, those are more cost-effective and the chance of winning them are relatively higher. Apart from the theoretic insights, both offline experiments on a real dataset and online experiments on a production DSP show that the proposed bidding strategies outperform the strong baselines that have been considered.

To summarise, the contributions of our work are listed below. (i) We propose a novel functional optimisation framework to find the optimal bidding strategy in RTB display advertising. (ii) Based on the auction winning function built from the data, the derived optimal bidding function from our framework is in the concave form against the KPI of each impression, which to our knowledge has never been studied in previous literature on RTB display advertising. (iii) Comprehensive offline and online experiments are conducted to verify the practical effectiveness of our proposed bidding strategy.

2. RELATED WORK

Bid optimisation is a well-studied problem in online advertising [17, 21, 18, 32]. Nonetheless, most research has been so far limited to keyword auction in the context of sponsored search (SS) [15, 4, 28]. Typically, under the scenario of pre-setting the keyword bids (not impression level), the keyword utility, cost and volume are estimated and then an optimisation process is performed to optimise the advertisers' objectives (KPIs) [5, 42, 23, 41]. Given a campaign budget as the cost upper bound, optimising the advertiser performance is defined as a budget optimisation problem [17, 30]. Furthermore, the authors in [7, 16] focus on the bid generation and optimisation on broad matched keywords, where query language features are leveraged to infer the bid price of related keywords. The authors in [40] propose to jointly optimise the keyword-level bid and campaign-level budget allocation under a multi-campaign sponsored search account. Some recent work focuses on periodically changing the pre-setting keyword auction price, taking into account the remaining budget and lifetime. For instance, in [3, 20], Markov decision process is used to perform online decision in tuning the keyword bid price, where the remaining auction volume and budget act as states and the bid price setting as actions. In [23] authors propose to calculate a bid allocation plan during the campaign lifetime, where the bid price on each keyword is set in different discrete time unit by considering the market competition and the CTR on different ad positions. However, none of the work evaluates per-impression auction as in SS, all the bids are associated with keywords and impression level features are seldom considered, especially for advertisers and their agencies. Moreover, in SS bid optimisation, search engines play two roles: setting the keyword bids as well as hosting the auctions. The objective function could be diverted to optimise the overall revenue for the search engine [2, 33, 14, 43], rather than the performance of each individual advertiser's campaigns.

The bid optimisation for RTB display advertising is fundamentally different. First, the bids are not determined by pre-defined keywords [38], but are based on impression level features. Although in general advertisers (or DSPs) are required to set up their target rules, they need to estimate the value of each ad impression that is being auctioned in real time and return the bid price per auction. Second, in RTB, CPM pricing is generally used [38]. Winning an impression directly results in the cost, despite the fact clicks and conversions can now be directly optimised by advertisers and DSPs. Thus, the dependencies over various effectiveness measures such as eCPC[2], CPM and the budget constraints need to be studied in a single framework. In [18] the authors propose an algorithm that learns winning bids distribution from full or partial information of auctions in display advertising. The algorithm then makes bidding decisions to achieve the best delivery (number of impressions) within the budget constraint. In [10], the bid price from each campaign can be adjusted by the publisher side in real time and the target is to maximise the publisher side

[2]Effective cost per click (eCPC) - The cost of a campaign divided by the total number of clicks delivered.

Table 1: Notations and descriptions.

Notation	Description
$\boldsymbol{x}$	The bid request represented by its features.
$p_x(\boldsymbol{x})$	The probability density function of $\boldsymbol{x}$.
$\theta(\boldsymbol{x})$	The predicted KPI if winning the auction of $\boldsymbol{x}$. It could be the CTR, CVR etc.
$p_\theta(\theta)$	The probability density function of KPI θ.
B	The campaign budget.
N_T	The estimated number of bid requests during the lifetime T of the budget.
$b(\theta(\boldsymbol{x}), \boldsymbol{x})$	The bidding strategy is defined as function $b()$. Assume a generative process: $\boldsymbol{x} \rightarrow \theta \rightarrow b$, so $b(\theta(\boldsymbol{x}), \boldsymbol{x}) \equiv b(\theta(\boldsymbol{x}))$. See the text. We occasionally use notation b to refer to a specific bid value.
$w(b(\theta(\boldsymbol{x})), \boldsymbol{x})$	The probability of winning the bid request $\boldsymbol{x}$ with bid price $b(\theta(\boldsymbol{x}))$. We approximate it by the dependency assumption: $\boldsymbol{x} \rightarrow \theta \rightarrow b \rightarrow w$, so $w(b(\theta(\boldsymbol{x})), \boldsymbol{x}) \equiv w(b(\theta(\boldsymbol{x})))$. See the text for details.

revenue. The most relevant work is in [32], where DSP returns the bid price with a linear relationship to the predicted CTR (pCTR) for each ad impression being auctioned. The analytical solution from our proposed functional optimisation framework shows that an optimal bidding function should be non-linear. The non-linearity is closely related to the probability of auction winning, but is loosely correlated with the prior distribution of the impression features.

As a new advertising paradigm, other problems in RTB have also been studied. In [25] the authors focus on the pacing problem, where the target is to smoothly deliver the campaign budget. From the SSP perspective, the reserve price setting in RTB ad auctions is studied in [36]. In [26] the sparsity problem of conversion rate estimation is handled by modelling the conversions at different selected hierarchical levels. In [13] the authors study the evaluation measures of the display advertising performance and they find the site visit turns to be a better proxy than the user click. In addition, there is some work on the ad exchange communication problem [9, 29]. More discussion on related research of RTB can be found in [38].

3. OPTIMAL REAL-TIME BIDDING

Each user visit of a publisher page triggers an ad auction for each ad slot on that page, which, in real time, generates a bid request for each targeting campaign. Given a bid request, along with features covering user, ad, context, and auction information, the DSP bidding engine decides whether to participate this auction, and if participates, returns a bid for this auction. The bid price depends on many factors. It is not only influenced by the predicted KPI (pKPI) value of the ad impression being auctioned, such as the CTR and CVR, that the advertiser wants to achieve, but most importantly, related to many other factors such as the budget constraint, the probability of auction winning, and the features and cost of this particular ad impression. In this section, we consider the problem of optimally generating real-time bids as a functional optimisation problem and propose a novel optimisation framework by taking all these factors into account. We show that solving it leads to a practical bidding function.

3.1 Problem Definition

Let us first mathematically formulate the real-time bidding problem. To launch a campaign in display advertising, the advertiser uploads their ad creatives, sets the targeting rules (e.g. the user segmentation, time, location) and the corresponding budget for the lifetime of the campaign.

After the target rules are set, before optimising the bid, the advertiser would first spend a small amount of budget to bid random impressions in order to learn some statistics. For instance, as studied in [8, 12] the auction volume forecast (e.g. bid landscape prediction) module is usually employed to estimate auction statistics with respect to the current setting and budget constraint. More specifically, we denote the estimated number of bid requests for the target rules during the lifetime T as N_T. Also, each bid request is represented by a high dimensional feature vector $\boldsymbol{x}$, where its entries consist of two sets of features: one is exacted from the campaign ad itself, and the other is related to the impression being auctioned, e.g., the cookie information of the underlying user, location, time, user terminal, browser, the contextual information about the webpage, etc. We use $p_x(\boldsymbol{x})$ to denote the prior distribution of the feature vectors which match the campaign target rules. For each campaign, the advertiser can use the historic bidding and feedback data to predict the KPI for the ad impression being auctioned. We denote the predicted KPI of a bid request $\boldsymbol{x}$ as $\theta(\boldsymbol{x})$. Note that different advertisers might consider different KPIs. For example, if the goal of a campaign is to maximise the direct visits, i.e. the total number of clicks, then $\theta(\boldsymbol{x})$ denotes the pCTR for that impression. For CTR estimation, we refer to [19, 34]. If the goal of a campaign is for conversions, then $\theta(\boldsymbol{x})$ denotes the predicted CVR (pCVR) for that impression. We also denote $p_\theta(\theta)$ as the prior distribution of the predicted KPI per bid request. The notation descriptions are given in Table 1.

Once the major statistics are gathered, our problem now is to devise an optimal bidding strategy such that a certain KPI objective over the budget will be maximised. For the sake of clarity, we consider the number of clicks as the objective here, while a natural extension to covering alternative KPIs and their experimental results are given later in Section 5.5. Mathematically, our optimal bid generation problem is formulated as a *functional* optimisation problem:

$$b()_{\text{ORTB}} = \underset{b()}{\arg\max} \; N_T \int_{\boldsymbol{x}} \theta(\boldsymbol{x}) w(b(\theta(\boldsymbol{x}), \boldsymbol{x}), \boldsymbol{x}) p_x(\boldsymbol{x}) d\boldsymbol{x} \quad (1)$$

$$\text{subject to} \; N_T \int_{\boldsymbol{x}} b(\theta(\boldsymbol{x}), \boldsymbol{x}) w(b(\theta(\boldsymbol{x}), \boldsymbol{x}), \boldsymbol{x}) p_x(\boldsymbol{x}) d\boldsymbol{x} \leq B.$$

where $b(\theta(\boldsymbol{x}), \boldsymbol{x})$ denotes the bidding function we intend to obtain. It depends on the feature vector $\boldsymbol{x}$ and the estimated CTR $\theta(\boldsymbol{x})$. $w(b, \boldsymbol{x})$ denotes the estimated winning rate for a bid price b given the feature $\boldsymbol{x}$ of the impression auction. In Eq. (1), the product of $\theta(\boldsymbol{x})$ and $w(b, \boldsymbol{x})$ produces the probability of click given an impression auction. Marginalising it over the feature space yields the expected click per impression auction. Note that in practice, the impression auctions arrive sequentially, so one can potentially make a sequential bidding rule by taking a feedback loop and employing a dynamical optimisation model such as partially observable Markov decision processes (POMDPs) [37]. However, generally these models are computationally expensive thus not feasible in our case, where bid decisions usually need to be returned within 100ms. We, thus, take a two-stage approach (learning statistics such as $p_x(\boldsymbol{x})$ and N_T, then optimising the bids). Without loss of generality, we consider a simple static model and follow a widely accepted assumption in the previous bid optimisation work [20, 10]: each time the feature vector is independently generated from an identical distribution.

The constraint is made by an upper bound of the expected cost. RTB normally applies the second price auction (pay the second highest bid). However, due to the reserve price setting, the cost is quite often higher than the second highest bid [36, 38]. We thus use the bid price $b(\theta(\boldsymbol{x}), \boldsymbol{x})$ as the upper bound of the cost of winning. Specifically, the product of the cost and the winning rate produces the expected cost per impression auction. Marginalising it over the feature space and multiplying by N_T yields the expected cost, which is set to be not greater than the budget B. Note that by maximising the click number with the budget constraint, the eCPC is minimised, which is a much important measure in display advertising.

To make the above problem solvable, we consider sequential dependency among the variables for each auction by making the following assumptions:

- Assume $b(\theta(\boldsymbol{x}), \boldsymbol{x}) \equiv b(\theta(\boldsymbol{x}))$. That is: $\boldsymbol{x} \rightarrow \theta \rightarrow b$. This allows us to largely reduce the functional decision space for the optimisation, while still gaining the dependency of the impression features through the KPI estimation $\theta(\boldsymbol{x})$. The previous work in [32] also adopts a similar dependency (bid only depends on CTR).
- Assume $w(b, \boldsymbol{x}) \equiv w(b)$. That makes the feature $\boldsymbol{x}$ only influence the winning rate via its generated bid: $\boldsymbol{x} \rightarrow \theta \rightarrow b \rightarrow w$. The assumption as sensible as we found out (shown in Section 4.1) that the dependency over the bid request features is far less than the bid price. Previous SS bid optimisation work [23, 40] also makes such assumption on winning keyword ad slots.

Then the optimisation problem is rewritten as

$$b()_{\text{ORTB}} = \underset{b()}{\arg\max}\ N_T \int_{\boldsymbol{x}} \theta(\boldsymbol{x}) w(b(\theta(\boldsymbol{x}))) p_x(\boldsymbol{x}) d\boldsymbol{x} \tag{2}$$

$$\text{subject to } N_T \int_{\boldsymbol{x}} b(\theta(\boldsymbol{x})) w(b(\theta(\boldsymbol{x}))) p_x(\boldsymbol{x}) d\boldsymbol{x} \leq B.$$

Furthermore, since there is a deterministic relationship between $\boldsymbol{x}$ and $\theta(\boldsymbol{x})$, the relationship between their probability density is also determined:

$$p_\theta(\theta(\boldsymbol{x})) = \frac{p_x(\boldsymbol{x})}{||\nabla\theta(\boldsymbol{x})||}. \tag{3}$$

Thus we can focus on θ via performing integration by substitution

$$\begin{aligned}
&\int_{\boldsymbol{x}} \theta(\boldsymbol{x}) w(b(\theta(\boldsymbol{x}))) p_x(\boldsymbol{x}) d\boldsymbol{x} \\
&= \int_{\boldsymbol{x}} \theta(\boldsymbol{x}) w(b(\theta(\boldsymbol{x}))) p_\theta(\theta(\boldsymbol{x})) ||\nabla\theta(\boldsymbol{x})|| d\boldsymbol{x} \\
&= \int_{\theta(\boldsymbol{x})} \theta(\boldsymbol{x}) w(b(\theta(\boldsymbol{x}))) p_\theta(\theta(\boldsymbol{x})) d\theta(\boldsymbol{x}) \\
&= \int_{\theta} \theta w(b(\theta)) p_\theta(\theta) d\theta
\end{aligned} \tag{4}$$

and the similar substitution for $\int_{\boldsymbol{x}} b(\theta(\boldsymbol{x})) w(b(\theta(\boldsymbol{x}))) p_x(\boldsymbol{x}) d\boldsymbol{x}$. Rewriting the integration with respect to θ leads to our final functional optimisation problem as follows:

$$b()_{\text{ORTB}} = \underset{b()}{\arg\max}\ N_T \int_{\theta} \theta w(b(\theta)) p_\theta(\theta) d\theta \tag{5}$$

$$\text{subject to } N_T \int_{\theta} b(\theta) w(b(\theta)) p_\theta(\theta) d\theta \leq B.$$

3.2 Optimal Solutions

The Lagrangian of the objective function (Eq. (5)) is

$$\begin{aligned}
\mathcal{L}(b(\theta), \lambda) = &\int_{\theta} \theta w(b(\theta)) p_\theta(\theta) d\theta \\
&- \lambda \int_{\theta} b(\theta) w(b(\theta)) p_\theta(\theta) d\theta + \frac{\lambda B}{N_T},
\end{aligned} \tag{6}$$

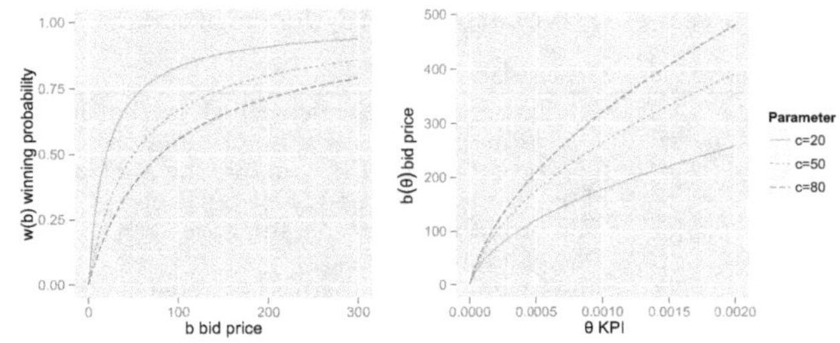

(a) Winning function 1. (b) Bidding function 1.

Figure 2: Winning function 1 and corresponding optimal bidding function $b_{\text{ORTB1}}(\theta)$.

where λ is the Lagrangian multiplier. Based on calculus of variations, the Euler-Lagrange condition of $b(\theta)$ is

$$\theta p_\theta(\theta) \frac{\partial w(b(\theta))}{\partial b(\theta)} - \lambda p_\theta(\theta) \Big[w(b(\theta)) + b(\theta) \frac{\partial w(b(\theta))}{\partial b(\theta)} \Big] = 0 \tag{7}$$

$$\lambda w(b(\theta)) = \Big[\theta - \lambda b(\theta) \Big] \frac{\partial w(b(\theta))}{\partial b(\theta)}, \tag{8}$$

where we can see the KPI probability density $p_\theta(\theta)$ has been eliminated and the *form* of bidding function $b(\theta)$ only depends on the winning function $w(b(\theta))$[3]. This is mainly because both the objective and constraint take the integration over the distribution of $p_\theta(\theta)$. Different winning functions result in different optimal bidding functions. Here we present two winning functions which are typical and fit the curves of real-world data. And we derive the optimal bidding function form for each winning function.

3.2.1 Winning & Bidding Function 1

As depicted in Figure 5 from our experiment on a real data[4], the winning rate $w(b)$ consistently has an (approximately) concave shape: when the bid price is low, adding a unit bid will increase the winning rate more than when the bid is already high. Thus a simple winning function is in the form of

$$w(b(\theta)) = \frac{b(\theta)}{c + b(\theta)}, \tag{9}$$

where c is a constant. An illustration of the winning function with different c's is given in Figure 2(a).

Taking a derivative with respect to the bid gives:

$$\frac{\partial w(b(\theta))}{\partial b(\theta)} = \frac{c}{(c + b(\theta))^2}. \tag{10}$$

Taking Eq. (9) and (10) into Eq. (8) gives:

$$\frac{\theta c}{(c + b(\theta))^2} - \lambda \Big[\frac{b(\theta)}{c + b(\theta)} + c \frac{b(\theta)}{(c + b(\theta))^2} \Big] = 0 \tag{11}$$

$$\Big(b(\theta) + c \Big)^2 = c^2 + \frac{\theta c}{\lambda}. \tag{12}$$

Solving the above equation gives our final optimal bidding function:

$$b_{\text{ORTB1}}(\theta) = \sqrt{\frac{c}{\lambda}\theta + c^2} - c. \tag{13}$$

[3]Later we will show that the optimal value of λ depends on $p_\theta(\theta)$, but λ is only a parameter in $b(\theta)$; thus $p_\theta(\theta)$ does not change the general form of $b(\theta)$.

[4]All the price numbers are presented with the unit of RMB cent. And the bid price is counted on CPM.

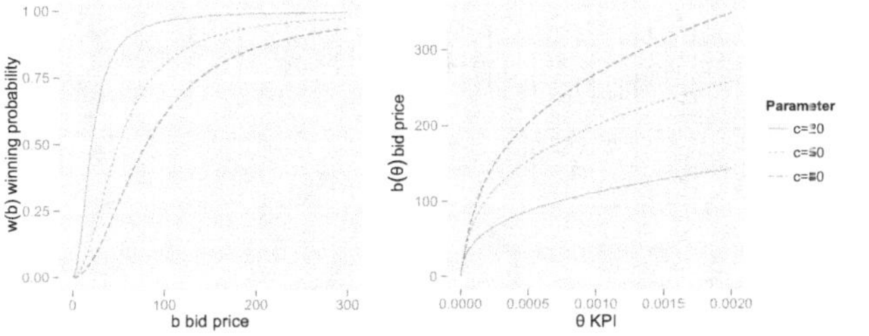

(a) Winning function 2. (b) Bidding function 2.

Figure 3: Winning function 2 and corresponding optimal bidding function $b_{\text{ORTB2}}(\theta)$.

Under the assumption of the winning function 1 in the form of Eq. (9), the optimal bidding function $b_{\text{ORTB1}}(\theta)$ is in a concave form: a square root function form. Figure 2(b) gives an illustration of this bidding function with different parameter c's, fixing $\lambda = 5.2 \times 10^{-7}$.

3.2.2 *Winning & Bidding Function 2*

For some campaigns with competitive targets, or the targeted publishers/SSPs setting a high reserve price, the winning probability will not increase rapidly when the bid price is around 0; only after the bid price becomes larger than some non-zero value the winning probability starts to dramatically increase. Such case usually occurs in high-profile ad slots [40]. To get this feature, we slightly alter it and propose an alternative of winning function:

$$w(b(\theta)) = \frac{b^2(\theta)}{c^2 + b^2(\theta)}, \tag{14}$$

where the parameter c controls the increasing point of the curve[5]. An illustration is given in Figure 3(a).

Following the same token, we solve Eq. (8) using the winning function in Eq. (14), i.e.

$$b_{\text{ORTB2}}(\theta) =$$

$$c \cdot \Big[\Big(\frac{\theta + \sqrt{c^2\lambda^2 + \theta^2}}{c\lambda} \Big)^{\frac{1}{3}} - \Big(\frac{c\lambda}{\theta + \sqrt{c^2\lambda^2 + \theta^2}} \Big)^{\frac{1}{3}} \Big]. \tag{15}$$

Fixing $\lambda = 5.2 \times 10^{-7}$, the bidding functions with different c's are shown in Figure 3(b). Again the $b_{\text{ORTB2}}(\theta)$ is a concave function.

Our optimisation framework is a general one: Eq. (8) shows that different winning functions would lead to different optimal bidding functions. The framework can adapt to various ad markets with different winning functions. Here we estimate the winning functions from real data (Figure 5) and limit our study to the RTB markets only.

3.2.3 *Discussions on Resulting Bidding Functions*

Unlike the linear form bidding function in the previous study [32, 26] (denoted as Lin), our derived bidding functions (denoted as ORTB) Eq. (13) and (15) suggest a non-linear concave form mapping from CTR estimation to the bid value under a budget constraint for RTB. As shown in Figure 4, compared with Lin, ORTB bids higher when the estimated KPI is low, which means ORTB allocates more budget on the low reward and low cost cases.

The strategy of bidding more low cost impressions comes from the shape of the winning functions. In Figure 5 we find that for all the campaigns, when we increase the bid

[5]Actually we can take a more general form of the winning function: $w(b(\theta)) = b^{\alpha}(\theta)/(c^{\alpha} + b^{\alpha}(\theta))$. We investigate the case of $\alpha = 1, 2$ in this paper. When α is larger than 2, there is no analytic solution of $b_{\text{ORTB}}(\theta)$.

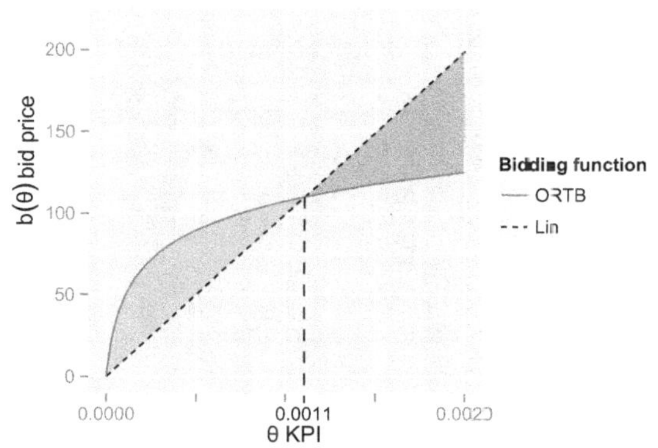

Figure 4: Concave bidding function bids higher on the cases with pCTR less than 0.0011 (example) and vice versa, which allocates more budget on the cases with low bid price and thus low cost.

price from zero, the winning probability will have a high growth rate first and after the bid price surpasses a region, the winning probability starts to converge to 1. As such, the strategy of ORTB will earn much more winning probability while only increase a little CPM because of the concavity of winning rate respective to the bid price.

3.2.4 *Optimal Solution of λ*

The bidding functions in Eq. (13) and (15) also take λ as the parameter; let us explicitly denote them as $b(\theta, \lambda)$. To calculate the optimal λ, the Euler-Lagrange condition of λ from Eq. (6) is

$$\int_{\theta} b(\theta,\lambda) w(b(\theta,\lambda)) p_{\theta}(\theta) d\theta = \frac{B}{N_T}. \tag{16}$$

Given the formula of $b(\theta, \lambda)$, the solution λ can be found. However, in many cases such as using our winning functions, there is no analytic solution of λ. Also we can see the solution depends on $p_{\theta}(\theta)$. Alternatively, one can find the numeric solution using the bidding log data and practically solve it using efficient numeric calculation. In this paper, we take a rather pragmatic approach by regarding λ as a tuning parameter for the bidding functions and learn it from the data. From Eq. (13), (15) and (16), it is easy to see that when λ decreases the value of $\int_{\theta} b(\theta,\lambda) w(b(\theta,\lambda)) p_{\theta}(\theta) d\theta$ monotonically increases. Therefore, with larger per-case budget B/N_T, the solution of λ becomes smaller, which corresponds to a higher bid price. Our experiment will demonstrate the trend of optimal λ corresponding to different per-case budget B/N_T (Figure 11 and 12).

4. EXPERIMENT SETUP

Our methods are tested both by offline evaluation (Section 5) using a real-world dataset and via online evaluation (Section 6) over a commercial DSP with real advertisers and impressions. In this section, we introduce the experiment setup and report the results from our data analysis.

4.1 Dataset and Analysis

Dataset description. We use the real-world bidding feedback log from a well-known DSP company as our dataset[6]. It records more than 15 million impressions and the user feedback of 9 campaigns from different advertisers during ten days in 2013. For each bid request, the log contains the information from the user (e.g. the user segmentation), advertiser (e.g. the creative format and size), publisher (e.g.

[6]The dataset has been publicly released on our website: http://data.computational-advertising.org

Table 2: Dataset statistics.

Cpg.	Imps	Clicks	Cost	CTR	CPM	eCPC
1	3,083,056	2,454	212,400	0.080%	68.89	86.55
2	1,742,104	1,358	160,943	0.078%	92.38	118.52
3	2,593,765	1,926	210,240	0.074%	81.06	109.16
4	2,847,802	2,076	219,067	0.073%	76.93	105.52
5	1,970,360	1,027	156,088	0.052%	79.22	151.99
6	835,556	280	77,755	0.034%	93.06	277.70
7	687,617	207	61,611	0.030%	89.60	297.64
8	1,322,561	843	118,082	0.064%	89.28	140.07
9	312,437	1,386	19,689	0.444%	63.02	14.21
Total	15,395,258	11,557	1,235,876	0.075%	80.28	106.94

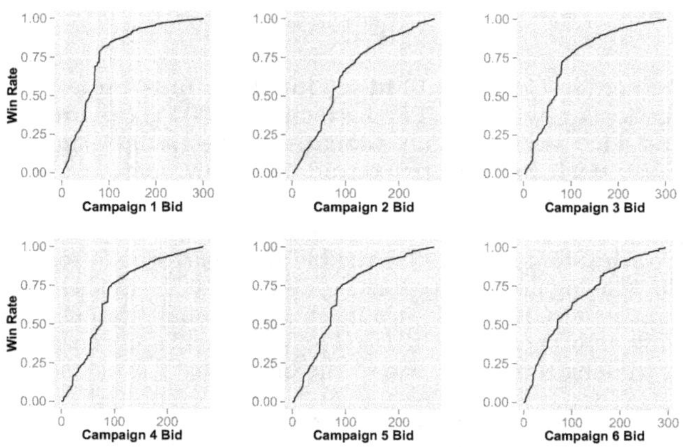

Figure 5: Relationship between auction winning rate and bid value for different campaigns.

the auction reserve price, ad slot, page domain and URL) and the context (e.g. the time, region, the browser and operation system). For each bid request, there is an auction winning bid price, and the user feedback (click, conversion) is recorded if the advertiser won the auction. More details of the dataset is shown in Table 2.

Data analysis on winning bids. Figure 5 depicts the winning rate with respect to the bid price for campaigns 1-6 (due to space limit, campaigns 7-9 are not shown). We observe that all the campaigns follow a similar pattern: as the bid price increases, the campaign winning rate increases dramatically; when the bid price gets larger (e.g. more than 100), the increasing of winning rate slows down and finally the winning rate converges to 1. Thus, it is reasonable to employ concave functions like Eq. (9) and (14) to model the relationships. For each campaign, we fit the winning functions with the parameter c leading the least square error with the real curve.

Next, we study the dependency between the bid request features and the winning bid prices (also named as market prices in [3]). Figure 6 gives the box plot [27] of winning price distribution against the features such as hour, weekday, user browser, operation system and location regions of bid requests to campaign 1 (other campaigns follow the similar pattern). Compared with the clear changing relationship with the bid price shown in Figure 5, Figure 6 shows that the winning price distributions do not have obvious dependency on the categorical feature value. It suggests that the bid price is the key factor influencing the campaign's winning rate in its auctions. Once we have known the bid value, the winning rate is less sensitive to the other bid request features. Thus it is practically reasonable to simplify $w(b, \boldsymbol{x}) \equiv w(b)$ as proposed in Section 3.1.

Training/test split. For each campaign, we perform a 2:1 train/test data split by the time sequence. The training data is mainly used to train the CTR estimator and tune the bidding function parameters. The test data is used to evaluate the compared DSP bidding strategies.

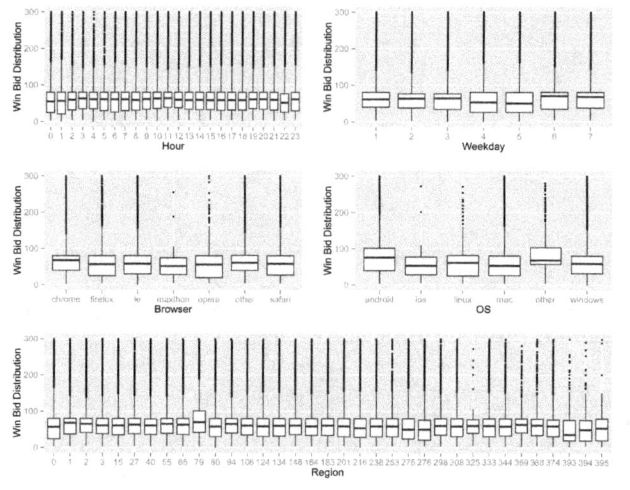

Figure 6: Winning bid distribution against different features for campaign 1.

4.2 Evaluation Measure

The task of DSPs is to optimise each campaign's KPI (such as clicks, conversions etc.) given the budget. Therefore, the KPI is the primary evaluation measure in our experiment. Specifically, we have considered clicks as our primary KPI, while other statistics such as CPM, and eCPC are also monitored. In addition, we also test on an alternative KPI which is the combination of achieved clicks and conversions, as will be discussed in Section 5.5.

4.3 KPI Estimator Training

For each campaign, we use its impression/click/conversion log data to train a KPI estimator for each bid request. Particularly, if the KPI is click, then this task turns to be the well-known CTR estimation [19, 34]. Regression models such as random forest and gradient boosting regression tree can be applied here. Since this work mainly focuses on the bidding strategy instead of the KPI estimator model, we apply the Logistic regression as our CTR estimator as it is a widely used choice [34]. The loss is the cross entropy between the predicted click probability and the ground-truth result. In addition, L2 regularisation is used. For an alternative KPI in our experiment, the KPI estimator training will be discussed in Section 5.5.

Features are extracted from the log data to train the C-TR estimator model. Specifically, we extract 29,408 first-order binary features and based on that generate 657,756 second-order binary features, which yields the total 687,164 features for our training.

4.4 Test Evaluation Setup

Evaluation flow. The evaluation flow is depicted in Figure 7. Given the bidding strategy and a budget for the test period for a particular campaign, we can go through its test data. The test data is a list of records. Each record consists of the features of one bid request, the auction winning price and the user feedback information. Specifically, receiving the bid request features of each record by the timestamp, the bidding strategy generates a bid price for it (if the cost is beyond the budget, just returns 0, i.e. skips the remaining bid requests). If the bid price is higher than the auction winning price of this record, the campaign wins the auction, gets its ad shown. The corresponding user feedback (click) and the corresponding charged price of the record are then referenced to update the performance and cost. After that,

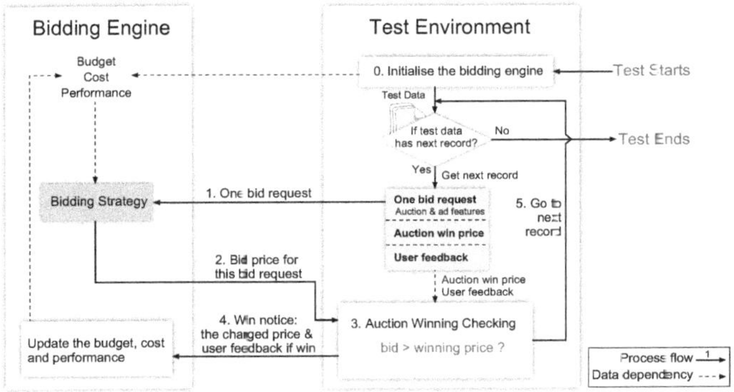

Figure 7: Evaluation flow chart.

if there is no more bid requests in the test data, then the evaluation is over, with the final performance returned.

It is worth mentioning that using user feedback logs for evaluation has limitation. In our case, user feedback only occurs for the winning auctions (having ad impressions); there is no user feedback for the losing bids. We thus do not know whether the user will click or convert even if we bid enough high to win the originally losing ad auction in our offline experiment. In this paper, we follow the convention of the offline evaluations from sponsored search [19], recommender systems [39] and Web search [11] that the objects (auctions) with unseen user feedback are ignored (i.e., considered as auction failure cases). To complement with the offline evaluation, we will further show the online test performance on a production DSP in Section 6.

Budget constraints. It is easy to see that if we set the budget the same as the original total cost in the test log, then just simply bidding as high as possible for each case will exactly run out the budget and get all the logged clicks. In our work, to test the performance against various budget constraints, for each campaign, we respectively run the evaluation test using 1/64, 1/32, 1/16, 1/8, 1/4 and 1/2 of the original total cost in the test log as the budget.

4.5 Compared DSP Bidding Strategies

We compare the following baseline and state-of-the-art bidding strategies in our experiment. The parameters of each bidding strategy are tuned using the training data.

Constant bidding (Const). Bid a constant value for all the bid requests to the campaign. The parameter is the specific constant bid price.

Random bidding (Rand). Randomly choose a bid value in a given range. The parameter is the upper bound of the random bidding range.

Bidding below max eCPC (Mcpc). As discussed in [26], given the advertiser's goal on max eCPC, which is the upper bound of cost per click, the bid price on an impression is obtained by multiplying max eCPC and pCTR. Here we calculate the max eCPC for each campaign by dividing its cost and achieved number of clicks in the training data. No parameter for this bidding strategy.

Linear-form bidding of pCTR (Lin). In the previous work [32], the bid value is linearly proportional to the pCTR. The formula can be generally written as

$$b_{\text{Lin}}(\theta) = b_0 \frac{\theta}{\theta_0}, \tag{17}$$

where θ_0 is the average CTR under a target condition (e.g., a user-inventory pair) and b_0 is the basic bid price for this target condition. We tune b_0 in our experiment.

Optimal real-time bidding (ORTB1 and ORTB2). These are our derived optimal bidding strategies in our framework. As shown in Eq. (13) and (15), the parameters are c and λ, where c is obtained by fitting the winning probability and λ is tuned using the training data.

Table 3: Bid strategy attributes.

Bidding Strategies	Const	Rand	Mcpc	Lin	ORTB
Consider budget conditions	√	√		√	√
Evaluate per impression value			√	√	√
Consider winning function					√

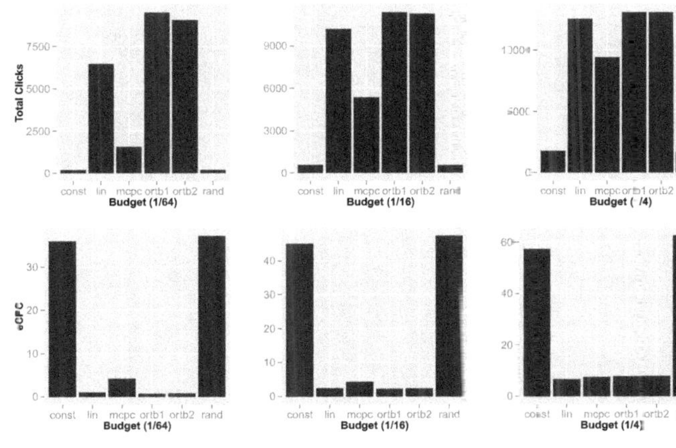

Figure 8: Overall performance comparison.

Table 3 summarises the attributes of the different strategies. Mcpc is not budget-aware to make sure it spends all the budget. Mcpc, Lin and ORTB perform bidding based on impression-level evaluation. Taking winning functions into account, ORTB is the most informative strategy. In Section 5 we will analyse the impact of these attributes in the final performance.

5. OFFLINE EVALUATION

In the experiment, we answer the following questions. (i) Does our derived non-linear bidding function outperform the state-of-the-art linear one? (ii) What are the characteristics of our ORTB algorithms and how do the parameters impact the performance and what are their relationships with the budget conditions?

5.1 Performance Comparison

The performance comparison on total clicks and eCPC under different budget conditions are reported in Figure 8. We observe that (i) under every budget condition, our proposed bidding strategies ORTB1 and ORTB2 have the best performance on total clicks, which verifies the effectiveness of the derived non-linear forms of the bidding function. (ii) Except ORTB, Lin is the best algorithm in the comparison. This algorithm represents the widely used DSP bidding strategies in product [32]. (iii) Mcpc is aware of the upper bound cost for each bid request, and dynamically changes its bid according to the estimated CTR. However, compared to ORTB and Lin, Mcpc has no adaptibility to different budget conditions. For example, when the budget is relatively low for the bid request volume, Mcpc will still bid based on the originally set max eCPC, while ORTB and Lin can adaptively lower the bid to earn the impressions and clicks with higher RIO. (iv) Rand and Const provide very low performance even though their parameters are tuned under different budget conditions. (v) Also from the eCPC performance we can see Rand and Const spend much more money to get one click than the case-value-aware strategy Mcpc, Lin and ORTB. The last two points suggest the benefit of real-time bidding based display advertising: evaluating the

Table 4: **Click improvement of ORTB1 over Lin for each campaign under different budget conditions.**

Cpg.	1/64	1/32	1/16	1/8	1/4	1/2
1	0.68%	1.97%	-0.46%	1.04%	1.25%	0.26%
2	0.70%	0.00%	0.44%	3.38%	0.48%	0.90%
3	27.16%	2.33%	1.45%	0.43%	6.50%	1.11%
4	24.46%	-1.19%	3.11%	2.84%	0.06%	3.14%
5	49.54%	10.85%	0.33%	5.17%	3.82%	1.42%
6	84.07%	49.89%	9.13%	-1.99%	5.67%	3.51%
7	85.67%	51.10%	18.50%	6.27%	2.67%	0.00%
8	58.13%	23.78%	8.82%	1.93%	0.59%	0.65%
9	428.26%	118.78%	103.91%	63.68%	18.82%	6.50%

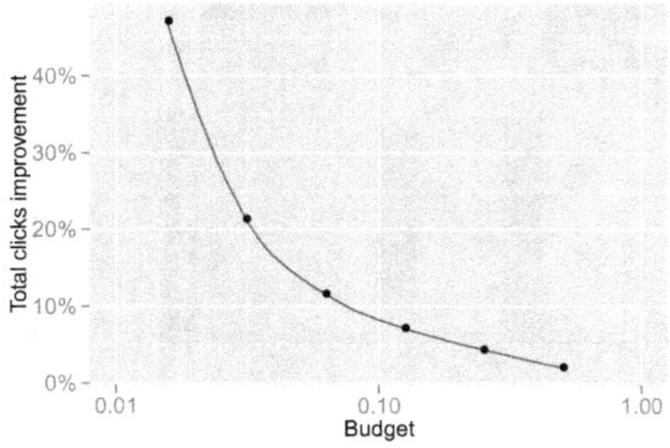

Figure 9: Overall click improvement of ORTB1 over Lin under different budget conditions.

value for each bid request (impression level) plays a significant role in the performance.

Table 4 gives detailed performance improvement on total clicks of ORTB1 over Lin under different campaigns and budget conditions. Among the listed 54 settings, ORTB1 wins Lin in 49 (90.7%) settings, ties in 2 (3.7%) settings, and lose in 3 (5.6%) settings. This shows ORTB1 is fairly robust and the outperformance is stable.

5.2 The Impact of Budget Constraints

It is of great interest to investigate how the bid strategy adapts the changing of the budget constraints. In our experiment, we set the test budget as 1/64, 1/32, 1/16, 1/8, 1/4 and 1/2 of the original total cost in the history log respectively. Figure 9 depicts the percentage improvement on total clicks of ORTB1 over Lin with respect to the budget constraints. As we can see, (i) when the budget is quite low (e.g. 1/64 of the original total cost), the click improvement of ORTB1 over Lin is quite high (more than 45%). This indicates that our proposed bidding strategy performs particularly well under very limited budget conditions. Intuitively, when the budget is quite low (budget on per bid request B/N_T is low), a good bidding strategy should spend relatively low on each bid request. Compared with the linear Lin, ORTB1 allocates more budget on the low cost cases due to the concave form of the bidding function (see Figure 2(b)). This is sensible because from the winning rate functions in Figure 5 we know that lowering the high bid actually does not drop the winning probability too much. By contrast, highering the low bid a little will increase the winning probability a lot. (ii) When the test budget gets higher, the improvement percentage gets lower. This is reasonable: when there is more budget per bid request, the strategy will appropriately reallocate budget from the low cost cases to high cost cases because the high cost cases also mean high value (CTR). Thus the concave degree of the curve in Figure 2(b) will be lower. The curve will relatively approximate to (but not fully change to) the linear form. An extreme case is that when the test budget is set the same as the original total cost in the test log, the improvement is zero. This is because under such condition

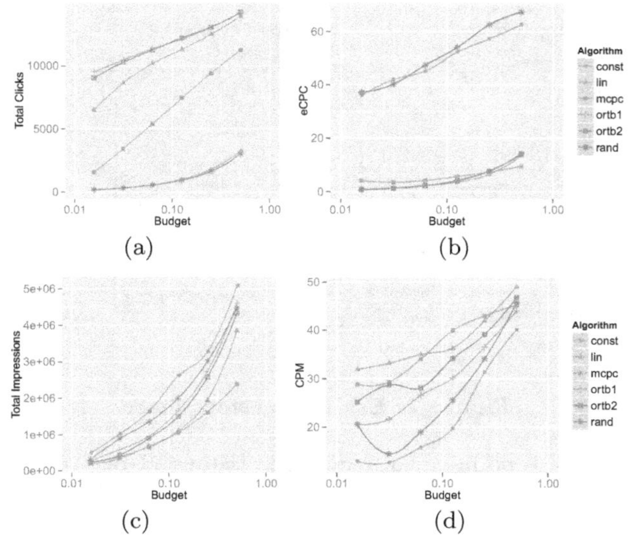

Figure 10: Performance on different measures with different budget conditions.

for every bidding strategy (except Mcpc), just bidding as high as possible will exactly run out the budget and get every impression and click in the test log.

5.3 Clicks vs. Impressions

Figure 10(a) and 10(b) show the total clicks and eCPC of each bidding strategy. We observe that both click number and eCPC increase as the budget increases. This is reasonable because when the budget is low, the optimal setting for each bidding strategy will push the budget to the low cost cases, while the budget is higher, the left budget will be allocated on the relative expensive cases (but with lower ROI), which will higher the eCPC. Mcpc is unaware of the budget condition, and its slight eCPC fluctuation purely depends on the data. Another point is that when the budget is set very low (1/64, 1/32, 1/16 of the original spend), the eCPC of Lin and ORTB is lower than Mcpc, and when the budget increases over 1/4 of the original spend, the eCPC of Lin and ORTB starts to be higher than Mcpc.

Figure 10(c) and 10(d) plot the total impressions and CPM of each bidding strategy. We see that while our ORTB strategies generate the highest clicks, they also produce comparable numbers of impressions against the others. This certainly benefits advertisers who aim to maximising their traffic (clicks) while still want to maintain a good exposure (impressions).

5.4 Parameter Tuning

As explained previously, although parameter λ can be directly solved numerically, for efficiency, in our experiment, we tune it for each campaign using the training data. Figure 11 and 12 shows the corresponding ORTB1 and ORTB2 click performance for the campaign 1[7] when tuning its parameter λ. For each λ, we also try different value of the other parameter c, which makes multiple points to each x-value for volatility checking. However, practically we direct learn c to best fit the winning rate data for each campaign. From Figure 11 and 12 we see that when the given budget is low, the optimal value of λ is high. This is much reasonable. From Eq. (13) and (15) we can see the parameter λ controls the general scale of the bidding price: when λ is higher, the bid price gets lower. Thus it is understandable that when the budget is more limited, the general bidding price level

[7]The trends on other campaigns are quite similar.

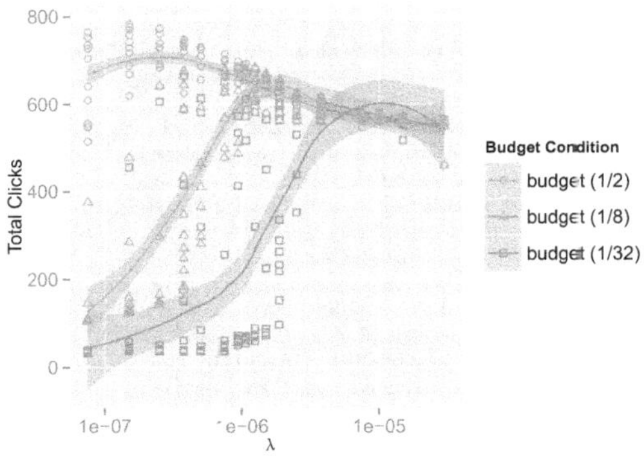

Figure 11: Parameter tuning on λ of ORTB1 under different budget conditions.

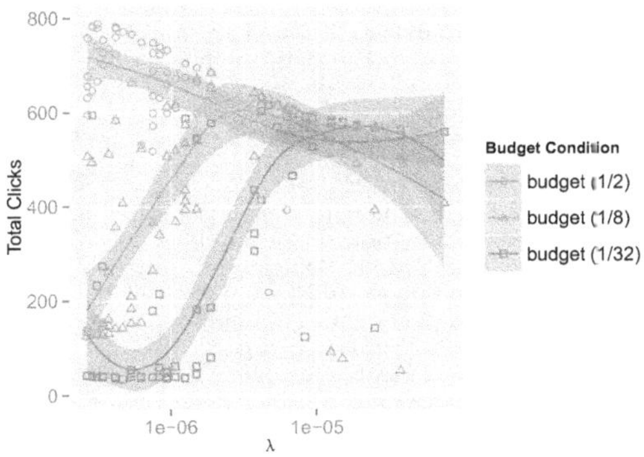

Figure 12: Parameter tuning on λ of ORTB2 under different budget conditions.

should get lower, which corresponds to the higher optimal value of λ.

5.5 Results for An Alternative KPI

As discussed in Section 3.1, our framework is flexible to incorporate different KPIs as our optimisation target. Apart from the number of clicks as the main objective studied in this paper, we also test an alternative KPI as the target by considering conversions, namely, a linear combination of the click number and conversion number, with the parameter k controlling the importance of conversion:

$$\texttt{KPI} = \texttt{\#click} + k \cdot \texttt{\#conversion}. \quad (18)$$

This objective is practically useful [1] since the conversion is a quite important measure for advertisers [32], and such linear combination can address the sparsity problem of conversion counting [26]. In our dataset, only campaign 2 and 8 have sufficient conversion records. Thus we choose them as our optimising campaigns and we set $k = 5$ in our experiment. Specifically, we use two logistic regression models to learn and predict the CTR and CVR (pCTR and pCVR) for each bid request and the pKPI can be calculated by $\texttt{pKPI} = \texttt{pCTR} + k \cdot \texttt{pCVR}$, which is the value of θ in the bidding function.

Figure 13 gives the overall KPI performance and the specific clicks/conversions obtained by each bidding strategy[8]. From the results we see our ORTB strategies still outperform other compared bidding strategies, which verifies the effectiveness of ORTB on the alternative KPI optimisation. Particularly, on 1/64 budget condition, ORTB2 achieves higher KPI and conversion numbers than ORTB1, this is mainly because the winning function 2 fits these two optimised campaigns better than winning function 1.

[8]Here Mcpc is renamed as Mcpi (i.e. bidding under max cost-per-unit-of-KPI).

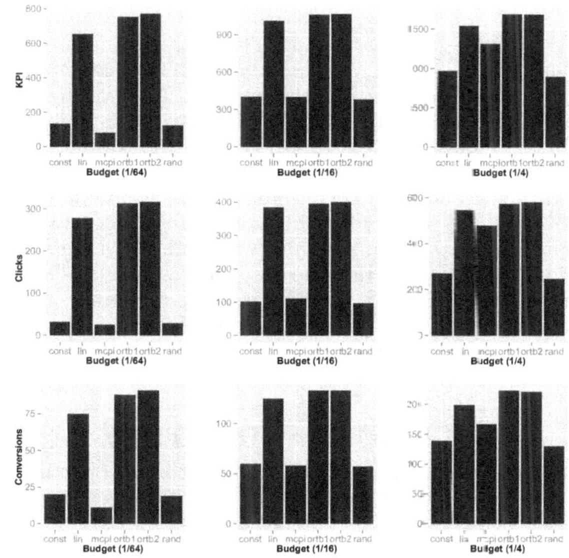

Figure 13: Performance comparison with the new KPI as optimisation target.

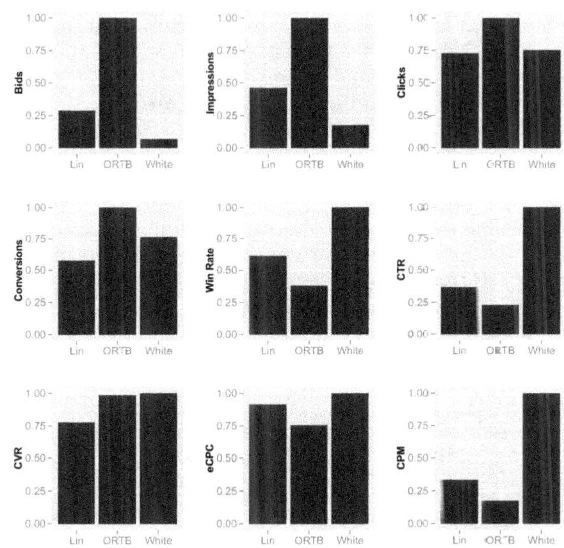

Figure 14: Relative performance for online test.

6. ONLINE EVALUATION

With the strategy of emphasising more on lower CPM impressions than the linear strategy, we conduct an online experiment on iPinYou Optimus platform, which is currently the largest DSP in China. We test on three campaigns during consecutive three days in December 2013. Another two compared bidding strategies are: (i) White list (White), which keeps a list of feature rules and bids much high only when the case satisfies any of the white list rules; (ii) Lin as we discussed before. The target KPI in the optimisation is click. Compared with Lin, White acts like the strategy with a step function in [32]. For each bid request each of the three algorithms has the equal possibility to perform the bidding of iPinYou DSP. The performance comparison with various measures was reported in Figure 14. Due to the data sensitivity, we follow [40] to only present the relative performance here.

From the comparison we can have following observations. (i) ORTB bids much more cases than the other two algorithms (bids lower than the auction reserve price are not counted), and gets the most impressions, clicks and conversions. Also ORTB achieves the lowest eCPC, which indicates it is also the most cost effective algorithm. (ii) ORTB obtains the lowest CPM. These two points show ORTB allocates more budget to the cheap cases. As a result, ORTB bids more cases with lower CPM. (iii) Because of the low CPM on low pCTR cases, ORTB has the lowest auction winning rate and CTR, but this is not that important since our target is the total click number. (iv) White acts oppositely to ORTB. It only bids high on a subset of cases, which results in its low bidding number and high CPM. Due to the carefully made white list, the cases matching the white list do have high CTR. (v) Lin mostly plays moderately, which is in our expectation. In sum, the online test supports our proposed bidding strategies which allocate more budget on the cheap cases to perform more bids with lower CPM.

7. CONCLUSIONS AND FUTURE WORK

In this paper, we proposed a novel functional optimisation framework to find the optimal real-time bidding strategy for display advertising. The derived optimal bidding functions are non-linear and concave with respect to predicted KPI, which to our knowledge has not been studied in the previous literature about real-time bidding strategies. In our experiments, we compared our bidding strategies with other baselines and state-of-the-art bidding strategies under different budget and KPI settings. Apart from the theoretical soundness, the offline and online experiments show that our proposed optimal bidding strategies are also practically the most effective.

In the future work, we plan to further investigate on the bidding function which directly covers the bid request features, not the KPI alone. We also intend to extend our optimisation framework to cover the following three scenarios: (i) As DSPs or ad agencies, how to optimise the overall performance over several advertisers they are managing? Combining auction theory [24] with our functional optimisation framework would possibly provide a sound solution. (ii) Dynamic approaches [3] which tune the bid according to the specific current performance will be considered in our framework. (iii) Modelling the uncertainty and the risk of the bidding. The uncertainty in the CTR prediction, bidding and auction process should be carefully studied to build risk-aware bidding strategies.

8. REFERENCES

[1] DSP bidding optimization task. `http://contest.ipinyou.com/rule.shtml`. Accessed: 2014-02-06.

[2] Z. Abrams. Revenue maximization when bidders have budgets. In *SODA*, pages 1074–1082, 2006.

[3] K. Amin, M. Kearns, P. Key, and A. Schwaighofer. Budget optimization for sponsored search: Censored learning in mdps. In *UAI*, 2012.

[4] A. Animesh, V. Ramachandran, and S. Viswanathan. Online Advertisers Bidding Strategies for Search, Experience, and Credence Goods: An Empirical Investigation. In *Second Workshop on Sponsored Search Auctions. EC*, 2005.

[5] C. Borgs, J. Chayes, N. Immorlica, K. Jain, O. Etesami, and M. Mahdian. Dynamics of bid optimization in online advertisement auctions. In *WWW*, pages 531–540. ACM, 2007.

[6] A. Broder, M. Fontoura, V. Josifovski, and L. Riedel. A semantic approach to contextual advertising. In *SIGIR*, 2007.

[7] A. Broder, E. Gabrilovich, V. Josifovski, G. Mavromatis, and A. Smola. Bid generation for advanced match in sponsored search. In *WSDM*, pages 515–524. ACM, 2011.

[8] S. Cetintas, D. Chen, and L. Si. Forecasting user visits for online display advertising. *Information Retrieval*, 16(3):369–390, 2013.

[9] T. Chakraborty, E. Even-Dar, S. Guha, Y. Mansour, and S. Muthukrishnan. Selective call out and real time bidding. In *Internet and Network Economics*, pages 145–157. 2010.

[10] Y. Chen, P. Berkhin, B. Anderson, and N. R. Devanur. Real-time bidding algorithms for performance-based display ad allocation. *KDD*, 2011.

[11] N. Craswell, O. Zoeter, M. Taylor, and B. Ramsey. An experimental comparison of click position-bias models. In *WSDM*, pages 87–94. ACM, 2008.

[12] Y. Cui, R. Zhang, W. Li, and J. Mao. Bid landscape forecasting in online ad exchange marketplace. In *KDD*, pages 265–273. ACM, 2011.

[13] B. Dalessandro, R. Hook, C. Perlich, and F. Provost. Evaluating and optimizing online advertising: Forget the click, but there are good proxies. 2012.

[14] N. R. Devenur and T. P. Hayes. The adwords problem: online keyword matching with budgeted bidders under random permutations. In *EC*, pages 71–78. ACM, 2009.

[15] B. Edelman, M. Ostrovsky, and M. Schwarz. Internet advertising and the generalized second price auction: Selling billions of dollars worth of keywords. Technical report, National Bureau of Economic Research, 2005.

[16] E. Even Dar, V. S. Mirrokni, S. Muthukrishnan, Y. Mansour, and U. Nadav. Bid optimization for broad match ad auctions. In *WWW*, pages 231–240. ACM, 2009.

[17] J. Feldman, S. Muthukrishnan, M. Pal, and C. Stein. Budget optimization in search-based advertising auctions. In *EC*, 2007.

[18] A. Ghosh, B. I. P. Rubinstein, S. Vassilvitskii, and M. Zinkevich. Adaptive bidding for display advertising. In *WWW*, 2009.

[19] T. Graepel, J. Q. Candela, T. Borchert, and R. Herbrich. Web-scale bayesian click-through rate prediction for sponsored search advertising in microsoft's bing search engine. In *ICML*, pages 13–20, 2010.

[20] R. Gummadi, P. Key, and A. Proutiere. Optimal bidding strategies in dynamic auctions with budget constraints. In *CCC*, pages 588–588. IEEE, 2011.

[21] K. Hosanagar and V. Cherepanov. Optimal bidding in stochastic budget constrained slot auctions. In *EC*, 2008.

[22] J. Jaworska and M. Sydow. Behavioural targeting in on-line advertising: An empirical study. In *WISE*. 2008.

[23] B. Kitts and B. Leblanc. Optimal bidding on keyword auctions. *Electronic Markets*, 14(3):186–201, 2004.

[24] V. Krishna. *Auction theory*. Academic press, 2009.

[25] K.-C. Lee, A. Jalali, and A. Dasdan. Real time bid optimization with smooth budget delivery in online advertising. *ADKDD*, 2013.

[26] K.-C. Lee, B. Orten, A. Dasdan, and W. Li. Estimating conversion rate in display advertising from past performance data. In *KDD*, pages 768–776. ACM, 2012.

[27] R. McGill, J. W. Tukey, and W. A. Larsen. Variations of box plots. *The American Statistician*, 32(1):12–16, 1978.

[28] A. Mehta, A. Saberi, U. V. Vazirani, and V. V. Vazirani. AdWords and Generalized On-line Matching. In *FOCS*, 2005.

[29] S. Muthukrishnan. Ad exchanges: Research issues. In *Internet and network economics*, pages 1–12. Springer, 2009.

[30] S. Muthukrishnan, M. Pál, and Z. Svitkina. Stochastic models for budget optimization in search-based advertising. In *Internet and Network Economics*. 2007.

[31] L. Olejnik, T. Minh-Dung, C. Castelluccia, et al. Selling off privacy at auction. 2013.

[32] C. Perlich, B. Dalessandro, R. Hook, O. Stitelman, T. Raeder, and F. Provost. Bid optimizing and inventory scoring in targeted online advertising. In *KDD*, pages 804–812, 2012.

[33] F. Radlinski, A. Broder, P. Ciccolo, E. Gabrilovich, V. Josifovski, and L. Riedel. Optimizing relevance and revenue in ad search. In *SIGIR*, pages 403–410, 2008.

[34] M. Richardson, E. Dominowska, and R. Ragno. Predicting clicks: estimating the click-through rate for new ads. In *WWW*, pages 521–530. ACM, 2007.

[35] J. Wang, S. Yuan, X. Shen, and S. Seljan. Real-time bidding: A new frontier of computational advertising research. In *CIKM Tutorial*, 2013.

[36] S. Yuan, B. Chen, J. Wang, P. Mason, and S. Seljan. An Empirical Study of Reserve Price Optimisation in Real-Time Bidding. In *KDD*, 2014.

[37] S. Yuan and J. Wang. Sequential selection of correlated ads by pomdps. In *CIKM*, pages 515–524, 2012.

[38] S. Yuan, J. Wang, and X. Zhao. Real-time bidding for online advertising: measurement and analysis. In *ADKDD*, 2013.

[39] W. Zhang, T. Chen, J. Wang, and Y. Yu. Optimizing top-n collaborative filtering via dynamic negative item sampling. In *SIGIR*, pages 785–788. ACM, 2013.

[40] W. Zhang, Y. Zhang, B. Gao, Y. Yu, X. Yuan, and T.-Y. Liu. Joint optimization of bid and budget allocation in sponsored search. In *KDD*, pages 1177–1185. ACM, 2012.

[41] Y. Zhang, W. Zhang, B. Gao, X. Yuan, and T.-Y. Liu. Bid keyword suggestion in sponsored search based on competitiveness and relevance. *IPM*, 2014.

[42] Y. Zhou, D. Chakrabarty, and R. Lukose. Budget constrained bidding in keyword auctions and online knapsack problems. In *Internet and Network Economics*, pages 566–576. 2008.

[43] Y. Zhu, G. Wang, J. Yang, D. Wang, J. Yan, J. Hu, and Z. Chen. Optimizing Search Engine Revenue in Sponsored Search. In *SIGIR*, 2009.

Quantifying Herding Effects in Crowd Wisdom

Ting Wang Dashun Wang Fei Wang
IBM T.J. Watson Research Center
Yorktown Heights, NY
{tingwang, dashun, fwang}@us.ibm.com

ABSTRACT

In many diverse settings, aggregated opinions of others play an increasingly dominant role in shaping individual decision making. One key prerequisite of harnessing the "crowd wisdom" is the independency of individuals' opinions, yet in real settings collective opinions are rarely simple aggregations of independent minds. Recent experimental studies document that disclosing prior collective opinions distorts individuals' decision making as well as their perceptions of quality and value, highlighting a fundamental disconnect from current modeling efforts: How to model social influence and its impact on systems that are constantly evolving? In this paper, we develop a mechanistic framework to model social influence of prior collective opinions (e.g., online product ratings) on subsequent individual decision making. We find our method successfully captures the dynamics of rating growth, helping us separate social influence bias from inherent values. Using large-scale longitudinal customer rating datasets, we demonstrate that our model not only effectively assesses social influence bias, but also accurately predicts long-term cumulative growth of ratings solely based on early rating trajectories. We believe our framework will play an increasingly important role as our understanding of social processes deepens. It promotes strategies to untangle manipulations and social biases and provides insights towards a more reliable and effective design of social platforms.

Categories and Subject Descriptors

H.2.8 [**Database Management**]: Database Applications—*Data mining*; J.4 [**Social and Behavior Sciences**]: Sociology

General Terms

Algorithms, Experimentation

Keywords

Crowd wisdom; social influence; herding effect

KDD'14, August 24–27, 2014, New York, NY, USA.
Copyright 2014 ACM 978-1-4503-2956-9/14/08 ...$15.00.
http://dx.doi.org/10.1145/2623330.2623720.

1. INTRODUCTION

With the explosive growth of information, our decisions are increasingly relying on aggregated opinions contributed by others, with the belief that the aggregations over a large population can successfully harness the "wisdom of crowds" [22]. Indeed, rooting back to Galton [8], many studies have shown that collective opinions of a group are often closer to the truth than the answer of an individual to a question. While the crowd wisdom applies usefully to a spectrum of domains, ranging from product or service recommendation [10] and crowdsourcing [5, 20, 26] to stock markets and political elections [22], one key prerequisite of harnessing the crowd wisdom is the independency of individuals' opinions [22]. Indeed, most if not all of the times, individuals are exposed to others' opinions before forming and expressing their own. As concrete examples, we go to the theater after checking reviews of the movies online; we download songs from the hit list; we purchase products or go to restaurants after researching what others think about them. As a result, the market does not simply aggregate pre-existing individual preferences, but rather creates an environment rich in social influence.

Thanks to the availability of Web-based experiments, recent studies offered convincing evidence that social influence exerts important but counterintuitive effects on collective judgement [16, 19]. Indeed, through carefully designed control experiments in different settings, these studies demonstrate that disclosing prior collective opinions distorts individuals' decision making as well as their perceptions of quality and value, creating herding effects that are irrational and pervasive, yet consequential to market outcome. Despite the significance of these results in experimental settings, there has been no quantitative framework to model social influence and its impact on systems that are constantly evolving. Indeed, models on collective intelligence, from majority voting to collaborating filtering to crowdsourcing [5], all assume independent crowds, representing a critical gap between modeling frameworks and empirical insights.

Here we develop a mechanistic framework to model social influence of prior collective opinions (e.g., product ratings) on subsequent individual decisions, namely, <u>H</u>erding <u>E</u>ffect <u>A</u>ware <u>R</u>ating <u>D</u>ynamics Model (HEARD). Using 28 million ratings spanning over 18 years on over 1.7 million products from *Amazon* [15] as an exemplary case, we demonstrate that our method successfully captures the dynamics of rating growth across different product categories, allowing us to separate social biases introduced by prior ratings from the true values inherent to products. We further show that, comparing with competing methods, our framework not only effectively detects the presence of social biases and gauges less biased values for any given product, but also accurately predicts the long-term cumulative growth of ratings through a scalable estimation model solely based on early rating trajectories. As a result, HEARD can also make testable predictions of collective response to artificial manipulations in rating systems, assisting in further testings through more systematic experiments.

To the best of our knowledge, this work represents one of the first few quantitative framework to model social influence biases introduced from prior opinions. We believe our method is of fundamental importance to studies of social processes, promotes new strategies in untangling manipulations and biases within social environments, and provides significant insights towards design of platforms that aggregate individual opinions, from electoral polling to market analysis to product recommendation.

The remainder of the paper will proceed as follows. Section 2 surveys relevant literature. Section 3 details the model design of HEARD and develops efficient inference algorithms to fit the model. Section 4 presents a scalable algorithm to predict the future rating growth based on HEARD. Section 5 empirically evaluates the proposed models and algorithms. The paper is concluded in Section 6.

2. RELATED WORK

In this section, we review three categories of related work, namely, social network induced influence, measuring social influence in experimental settings, and effect of semantics of prior opinions.

Social networks have attracted significant interest, partly due to the availability of large datasets in many domains. One active line of enquiry in social network studies is how behavior [1, 2], opinion [7], and information [13, 24, 3] spreads through social networks. It is conceivable that microscopic social interactions could induce influence that is visible on an aggregated level [25]. In a way, the process of generating collective opinions is similar to consensus formation [11]. For example, individuals may change their opinions after learning about what their friends think. This is supported by experimental results by Lorenz et al. [14], in which they demonstrated that even mild social interactions can significantly bias simple estimation tasks. Therefore, Das et al. [4] proposed a social sampling method that takes into account individuals' influence from their social neighbors and arrives at a de-biased estimation of collective opinions. While this line of research shows that social interactions can exert influence on overall outcome, their focus on networks inevitably distinguishes themselves from our work. Indeed, often times, the population responsible for collective opinions are not interactive. You choose a restaurant, go watch a movie, or purchase a book, because of the opinions or reviews authored by people you do not know. Therefore, our work focuses on how to model social influence on a macroscopic level and hence predict the outcome of crowd wisdom.

On the other hand, there have been a number of experimental studies on measuring social influence within a population, thanks to the emergence of Web-based experiments. For example, Salganik et al. [19] implemented a music lab, where individuals download and rate songs with or without information about how good the songs are, and they demonstrated that increasing social influence could result in differential outcomes for songs of similar quality. Muchnik et al. [16] ran a large-scale randomized experiment on a reddit like website, finding that prior ratings created significant bias in individual rating behavior, from turnout to binary choices. These studies confirmed experimentally that disclosing prior ratings can create strong herding effects that are irrational and pervasive, leading to significant bias that is consequential to collective outcome. At the same time, they also highlight a fundamental gap between experimental insights and modeling efforts. Our work directly addresses this gap: To the best of our knowledge, this work is among the first few attempt to quantitatively model the herding effects in crowd wisdom and develop effective mechanisms to factor out such bias in estimation.

Finally, there have been a number of interesting studies into the semantics of collective opinions, such as that analyze the text and social aspects of product reviews [10, 15, 21, 9]. While they are useful for review spam detection, customer sentiment analysis, product recommendation, and more, insights extracted from semantic features are, however, not mechanistic, hence not capable of projecting the full rating trajectories. Nevertheless, these studies are complementary to our work, in a sense that the useful semantic features learned can be integrated into our model in forms of prior belief of model parameters. Indeed, one shall see in next sections that incorporating such text and social information into the rating growth model would be a promising future direction.

Our work also draws connections to other modeling efforts. The design of our herding effects model is inspired by the multi-neuron coupled spiking phenomena [17]. The exponential additive generative mechanism has been applied in modeling latent topics for text [6]. Our work differs in proposing a more general form of generative model and developing scalable inference algorithms to fit the model.

3. MODEL AND ALGORITHM

In this section, we detail the design of the HEARD model and present efficient inference algorithms to fit the model. Concretely, we draw an analogy to the coupled spiking phenomena in a multi-neuron system to model the dynamics of rating growth and fit the model parameters using maximum likelihood estimation.

3.1 HEARD Model

Without loss of generality, we consider a discrete K-level rating system, which is extensively used by today's online retailers; for example, *Amazon* adopts a one-to-five star rating system. Consider the sequence of ratings regarding a specific product, with $r_i \in \{1, 2, \ldots, K\}$ being the i-th rating. We assume the first $(i-1)$ ratings form the *history* for r_i: $\boldsymbol{x}_i = [x_{i,1}, x_{i,2}, \ldots, x_{i,K}]^\top$, where $x_{i,k}$ represents the proportion of level-k ratings among the first $(i-1)$ ratings. Clearly, $\sum_{k=1}^{K} x_{i,k} = 1$ for $i > 1$ and $\boldsymbol{x}_1$ is an all-zero vector. We intend to model how disclosing such rating history would influence individual rating behavior on r_i.

Intuitively, the generation of a new level-k rating is driven by multiple factors, including: the intrinsic product quality, the occurrence of preceding level-k ratings, and the history of other ratings. We can draw a close analogy to the spiking activities of a multi-neuron system [17]: the response (i.e., spike) generated by a neuron is jointly determined by the stimulus strength and the preceding spikes of this neuron

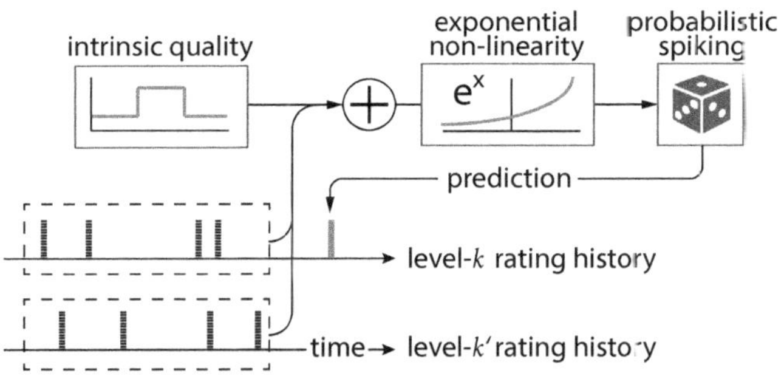

Figure 1: Illustration of HEARD model. The occurrence of a new level-k rating is jointly influenced by (i) the intrinsic quality of product, (ii) the preceding level-k ratings, and (iii) the history of other ratings.

and correlated neurons. We therefore introduce an *additive generative* model to describe the distribution of the i-th rating r_i over different levels:

$$Pr\left(r_i = k|\boldsymbol{x}_i\right) = \frac{\exp\left(\mu_k + f(i)\boldsymbol{\theta}_k^\top \boldsymbol{x}_i\right)}{\sum_{k'=1}^{K}\exp\left(\mu_{k'} + f(i)\boldsymbol{\theta}_{k'}^\top \boldsymbol{x}_i\right)} \quad (1)$$

This conditional distribution describes the likelihood of observing a level-k rating given rating history $\boldsymbol{x}_i$. In this general formulation, we have:

- $\boldsymbol{\mu} = [\mu_1, \mu_2, \ldots, \mu_K]^\top \in \mathbb{R}^K$ represents the coefficients of an *intrinsic distribution*, which is assumed related to the true quality of the product.

- $f(\cdot)$[1] is the *magnitude function*, which describes the relationship between the strength of herding effects and the number of historical ratings; in particular, we have $f(1) = 0$.

- $\boldsymbol{\theta}_k \in \mathbb{R}^K$ weighs the different components of $\boldsymbol{x}_i$. Note that our model captures both positive and negative influence. Concretely, when the k'-th component $\theta_{k,k'} > 0$, the preceding level-k' ratings *excite* the occurrence of level-k ratings; while if $\theta_{k,k'} < 0$, the level-k' ratings *inhibit* the generation of new level-k ratings.

These factors are then integrated in an exponential function, as illustrated in Figure 1.

Note that here we ignore the time dimension in our model because various external factors may abruptly influence the temporal dynamics of rating growth, e.g., low price promotion, emergence of new products, advertisements, etc.

Let $\boldsymbol{\Theta} = [\boldsymbol{\theta}_1, \boldsymbol{\theta}_2, \ldots, \boldsymbol{\theta}_K, \boldsymbol{u}]$ represent all the parameters. Both $\boldsymbol{\Theta}$ and magnitude function $f(\cdot)$ are estimated from data; in particular, $f(\cdot)$ is estimated from an infinite dimensional functional space. Next we elaborate their inference.

3.2 Model Inference

We assume regarding a specific product, a temporally ordered sequence of N ratings $\{r_i\}_{i=1}^N$ has been observed. Note that while we focus on the case of a single product for ease of presentation, the extension to multiple products is straightforward. For notational simplicity, we introduce a set of indicator variables $\boldsymbol{y}_i \in \{0,1\}^K$ with $y_{i,k} = 1$ if $r^{(i)} = k$ and 0 otherwise. Then the log-likelihood of parameters $\boldsymbol{\Theta}$ given this rating sequence is expressed as:

$$\begin{aligned}\mathcal{L}(\boldsymbol{\Theta}) &= \frac{1}{N}\log\prod_{i=1}^{N} Pr\left(r_i|\boldsymbol{x}_i, \boldsymbol{\Theta}\right)\\ &= \frac{1}{N}\sum_{i=1}^{N}\sum_{k=1}^{K} y_{i,k}\log\frac{\exp\left(\mu_k + f_i\boldsymbol{\theta}_k^\top \boldsymbol{x}_i\right)}{\sum_{k'=1}^{K}\exp\left(\mu_{k'} + f_i\boldsymbol{\theta}_{k'}^\top \boldsymbol{x}_i\right)}\end{aligned}$$

We estimate the model parameters by minimizing the penalized log-likelihood function, which is defined as:

$$\mathcal{L}_\lambda(\boldsymbol{\Theta}) = -\mathcal{L}(\boldsymbol{\Theta}) + \frac{\lambda}{2}\left(||\boldsymbol{\Theta}||_F^2 + \mathcal{R}(f)\right) \quad (2)$$

where the first term represents the negative log-likelihood, the second term is a regularizer with λ being the balance parameter to prevent overfitting, and $||\cdot||_F$ denotes the matrix Frobenius norm. In particular, $\mathcal{R}(f)$ is a penalty term preferring smooth functions. Without prior knowledge, we use $\mathcal{R}(f) = \int_0^\infty (f'(t))^2 \mathrm{d}t$, where $f'(\cdot)$ represents the derivative of $f(\cdot)$.

While $\mathcal{L}_\lambda(\boldsymbol{\Theta})$ appears similar to the softmax regression, it contains the integral of an unknown function and meanwhile all the parameters are coupled, which makes it difficult to directly apply off-the-shelf optimization methods (e.g., coordinate descent). Next we propose an iterative algorithm which optimizes $\mathcal{L}_\lambda(\boldsymbol{\Theta})$ by (i) constructing a surrogate function to decouple the parameters and (ii) applying an Euler-Lagrange equation to fit the unknown function.

More specifically, let $\boldsymbol{\Theta}^{(n)} = [\boldsymbol{\theta}_1^{(n)}, \boldsymbol{\theta}_2^{(n)}, \ldots, \boldsymbol{\theta}_K^{(n)}, \boldsymbol{\mu}^{(n)}]$ denote the current parameter setting. We construct the following surrogate function $Q(\boldsymbol{\Theta}; \boldsymbol{\Theta}^{(n)})$, which is a tight upper bound of $\mathcal{L}_\lambda(\boldsymbol{\Theta})$:

$$\begin{aligned}Q(\boldsymbol{\Theta}; \boldsymbol{\Theta}^{(n)}) &= \frac{1}{N}\sum_i\sum_k\left(\phi_{i,k}^2 + \left(\beta_{i,k}^{(n)} - 2\phi_{i,k}^{(n)} - y_{i,k}\right)\phi_{i,k}\right)\\ &\quad -\frac{1}{NK}\sum_i\left(\sum_k\phi_{i,k} - 2\sum_k\phi_{i,k}^{(n)}\right)\left(\sum_k\phi_{i,k}\right)\\ &\quad +\frac{\lambda}{2}\left(||\boldsymbol{\Theta}||_F^2 + \mathcal{R}(f)\right) + \frac{1}{N}\sum_i C_i^{(n)} \quad (3)\end{aligned}$$

where the terms $\phi_{i,k}$, $\phi_{i,k}^{(n)}$, $\beta_{i,k}^{(n)}$ and $C_i^{(n)}$ are defined below:

$$\begin{aligned}\phi_{i,k} &= \mu_k + f_i\boldsymbol{\theta}_k^\top \boldsymbol{x}_i\\ \phi_{i,k}^{(n)} &= \mu_k^{(n)} + f_i^{(n)}\boldsymbol{\theta}_k^{(n)\top}\boldsymbol{x}_i\\ \beta_{i,k}^{(n)} &= \frac{\exp\left(\phi_{i,k}^{(n)}\right)}{\sum_{k'}\exp\left(\phi_{i,k'}^{(n)}\right)}\\ C_i^{(n)} &= \sum_k\left(\phi_{i,k}^{(n)2} - \beta_{i,k}^{(n)}\phi_{i,k}^{(n)}\right) - \frac{1}{K}\left(\sum_k\phi_{i,k}^{(n)}\right)^2\\ &\quad + \log\sum_k\exp\left(\phi_{i,k}^{(n)}\right)\end{aligned}$$

It is noted that $Q(\boldsymbol{\Theta}; \boldsymbol{\Theta}^{(n)})$ possesses the following desirable properties (details in Appendix):

$$\begin{cases} Q(\boldsymbol{\Theta}; \boldsymbol{\Theta}^{(n)}) \geq \mathcal{L}_\lambda(\boldsymbol{\Theta}) & \forall\boldsymbol{\Theta}, \boldsymbol{\Theta}^{(n)}\\ Q(\boldsymbol{\Theta}^{(n)}; \boldsymbol{\Theta}^{(n)}) = \mathcal{L}_\lambda(\boldsymbol{\Theta}^{(n)}) & \forall\boldsymbol{\Theta}^{(n)}\end{cases}$$

which imply that if $\boldsymbol{\Theta}^{(n+1)} = \arg\min_{\boldsymbol{\Theta}} Q(\boldsymbol{\Theta}; \boldsymbol{\Theta}^{(n)})$, then we must have $\mathcal{L}_\lambda(\boldsymbol{\Theta}^{(n)}) \geq \mathcal{L}_\lambda(\boldsymbol{\Theta}^{(n+1)})$. Therefore, minimizing

[1]In the following, we use f_i as a short notation of $f(i)$.

$Q(\mathbf{\Theta};\mathbf{\Theta}^{(n)})$ with respect to $\mathbf{\Theta}$ at each iteration will ensure that $\mathcal{L}_\lambda(\mathbf{\Theta})$ decreases monotonically.

Updating Parameters

The formulation above has the advantage that we can derive the closed form solution of $\mathbf{\Theta}$ for $\arg\min_{\mathbf{\Theta}} Q(\mathbf{\Theta};\mathbf{\Theta}^{(n)})$. Specifically, by deriving the derivatives of $Q(\mathbf{\Theta};\mathbf{\Theta}^{(n)})$ with respect to μ_k and $\theta_{k,k'}$ and set them to zero, we obtain their update rules as follows:

$$\mu_k^{(n+1)} = \frac{K\sum_i\left(y_{i,k}-\beta_{i,k}^{(n)}\right)+2N(K-1)\mu_k^{(n)}}{2N(K-1)+NK\lambda} \tag{4}$$

$$\theta_{k,k'}^{(n+1)} = \frac{K\sum_i f_i x_{i,k'}\left(y_{i,k}-\beta_{i,k}^{(n)}\right)+2(K-1)\sum_i f_i^2 x_{i,k'}^2\theta_{k,k'}^{(n)}}{2(K-1)\sum_i f_i^2 x_{i,k'}^2+NK\lambda} \tag{5}$$

Updating Magnitude Function

Next we derive the update rule for magnitude function $f(\cdot)$ by optimizing it in an infinite dimensional functional space. We extract the parts of $Q(\mathbf{\Theta};\mathbf{\Theta}^{(n)})$ relevant to $f(\cdot)$ and then reformulate the problem of minimizing $Q(\mathbf{\Theta};\mathbf{\Theta}^{(n)})$ with respect to $f(\cdot)$ as follows:

$$\min_{f\in L_1(\mathbb{R})}\sum_i A_i f_i^2+\sum_i B_i f_i+\frac{\lambda}{2}\int_0^{+\infty}(f'(t))^2\mathrm{d}t \tag{6}$$

where terms A_i and B_i are defined below:

$$\begin{aligned} A_i &= \frac{1}{N}\sum_k\left(\boldsymbol{\theta}_k^{(n)\top}\boldsymbol{x}_i\right)^2-\frac{1}{NK}\left(\sum_k\boldsymbol{\theta}_k^{(n)\top}\boldsymbol{x}_i\right)^2 \\ B_i &= \frac{1}{N}\sum_k\left(2\mu_k^{(n)}-2\phi_{i,k}^{(n)}+\beta_{i,k}^{(n)}-y_{i,k}\right)\boldsymbol{\theta}_k^{(n)\top}\boldsymbol{x}_i \\ &+\frac{2}{NK}\left(\sum_k\boldsymbol{\theta}_k^{(n)\top}\boldsymbol{x}_i\right)\left(\sum_k\phi_{i,k}^{(n)}-\sum_k\mu_k^{(n)}\right) \end{aligned}$$

Abusing the notation a little, we introduce two functions: $A(t)=A_t\mathbb{I}\{t\le N\wedge t\in\mathbb{N}\}$ and $B(t)=B_t\mathbb{I}\{t\le N\wedge t\in\mathbb{N}\}$, where $\mathbb{I}\{\cdot\}$ is the indicator function which returns 1 if the predicate is true and 0 otherwise.

Then the solution of the objective function as defined in Eqn.(6) must satisfy the Euler-Lagrange equation [27] (proof referred to Appendix):

$$2A(t)f(t)+B(t)-\lambda f''(t)=0 \tag{7}$$

where $g''(\cdot)$ is the second order derivate of $g(\cdot)$.

Due to the discrete nature of the functions $A(t)$ and $B(t)$, we solve this differential equation numerically using a Seidal type iteration. Specifically, we discretize the differential equations over intervals of length 1:

$$\lambda(f_{i+1}-2f_i+f_{i-1})-2A_if_i-B_i=0$$

Clearly from the equations above we can efficiently solve f_i for $i=1,2,\ldots,N$. We may then perform curve fitting to extrapolate the values of f_i for $i>N$.

Complete Algorithm

To set a proper starting point for optimization, we consider the degenerated case where the prior ratings have no effect on individual rating behaviors. Under this assumption, we have the following setting:

$$\begin{cases} \mu_k=\log\left(\frac{\sum_{i=1}^N y_{i,k}}{N}\right) & k=1,2,\ldots,K \\ f_i=0 & i=1,2,\ldots,N \end{cases} \tag{8}$$

Meanwhile we initialize $\boldsymbol{\theta}_1,\boldsymbol{\theta}_2,\ldots,\boldsymbol{\theta}_K$ randomly.

Putting everything together, Algorithm 1 sketches the procedure of model inference. After initialization, it iterates between updating parameters $\mathbf{\Theta}$ and solving magnitude function $f(\cdot)$ until the objective function converges.

Algorithm 1: Inference of HEARD Model

```
Input: rating history {r_i}_{i=1}^N
Output: setting of parameters Θ and function f
// initialization
initialize Θ and f according to Eqn.(8);
compute statistics {x_i}_{i=1}^N;
// iterative optimization
while not converged yet do
    // update parameter
    for k = 1,2,...,K do
        update μ_k following Eqn.(4);
        for k' = 1,2,...,K do
            update θ_{k,k'} following Eqn.(5);
    // update magnitude function
    compute {f_i}_i by solving differential Eqn.(7);
return setting of Θ and f;
```

4. APPLICATION

In this section we show that equipped with the aforementioned HEARD model, we are able to answer a set of fundamental questions, including:

Debiasing: What is the intrinsic quality of a product after factoring out the herding effects from its collective ratings?

Prediction: Based on its rating history, can we predict the distribution of its next 100 ratings?

What-If Analysis: Given its current ratings, how would its future ratings be "herded" if we could "inject" in 50 five-star ratings?

Next we detail how to answer these questions.

4.1 Debiasing Collective Ratings

To the first question, recall that the HEARD model defined in Eqn.(1) comprises two additive components, namely, the intrinsic distribution and the herding effect distributions. The background intrinsic distribution as controlled by parameters $\{\mu_k\}$ is assumed related to the true quality of a product. Therefore, once we have estimated $\{\mu_k\}$ from the rating history of a product, we can then "debias" the collective ratings by factoring out the components attributed to the herding effects.

More concretely, abusing the notation a little, let $\boldsymbol{\mu}=[\mu_1,\mu_2,\ldots,\mu_K]^\top$. Without the herding effects, each rating is generated by the following unconditional categorical distribution:

$$\boldsymbol{\eta}=\frac{\exp(\boldsymbol{\mu})}{\sum_k\exp(\mu_k)} \tag{9}$$

which represents the intrinsic rating of the product.

The straightforward solution to estimating $\boldsymbol{\mu}$ of a given product is to directly fit the model parameters using its rating history as in Algorithm 1, which however may lead to overfitting. Instead, we introduce an "out-of-sample" extension. As will be detailed in Section 5, the herding effects often follow similar patterns for products of the same category (e.g., books). We therefore use the rating histories of a bulk of products in the same category to train *category-level* parameters $\{\boldsymbol{\theta}_k\}$ and magnitude function $f(\cdot)$. For the query product, we fix $\{\boldsymbol{\theta}_k\}$ and $f(\cdot)$ and focus on learning *product-level* parameter $\boldsymbol{\mu}$. As shown in Algorithm 2, this procedure is similar to Algorithm 1, except that at each iteration we only need to update $\boldsymbol{\mu}$.

Algorithm 2: Out of Sample Extension

```
Input: rating history {r_i}_i of query product, setting of
       {θ_k}_k and f(·)
Output: setting of μ for given product
// initialization
initialize μ according to Eqn.(8);
compute statistics {x_i}_i;
// iterative optimization
while not converged yet do
    // update parameter
    for k = 1, 2, ..., K do
        update μ_k following Eqn.(4);
return μ;
```

4.2 Predicting Rating Growth

Another interesting question one may pose is: given the current rating history of a product, is it possible to predict the distribution of it future ratings? While it is of theoretical interest to discuss the statistical convergence properties of the rating distribution as the number of ratings approaches infinity; in real settings, most products during their lifetimes receive only limited number of ratings. We thus focus on a more concrete question as follows:

Given the first N ratings of a product, can we characterize the distribution of its next M ratings?

Let us first consider the herding effects-agnostic case, in which each rating is independently generated by the categorical distribution as defined in Eqn.(9). Under this assumption, the next M ratings follow a multinomial distribution; specifically, the expected number of level-k rating is given by $M\eta_k$ with variance $M\eta_k(1-\eta_k)$.

Next we incorporate the herding effects. Recall that the distribution of the first $(i-1)$ ratings is given by $\boldsymbol{x}_i$, which also corresponds to the history for the i-th rating. The transition probability from $\boldsymbol{x}_i$ to $\boldsymbol{x}_{i+1}$ can be described as below:

$$Pr\left(\boldsymbol{x}_{i+1} = \frac{i-1}{i}\boldsymbol{x}_i + \frac{\boldsymbol{e}_k}{i} \,\middle|\, \boldsymbol{x}_i\right) = \frac{\exp(\phi_{i,k})}{\sum_{k'}\exp(\phi_{i,k'})} \quad (10)$$

where $\boldsymbol{e}_k$ is a 1-of-K vector with the k-th element being 1.

Note that this transition rule essentially specifies a non-stationary Markov chain in which both the state space and the transition probability change from step to step. This setting is not amenable to exact inference; we thus resort to Monte Carlo methods [18].

Algorithm 3 sketches our prediction model. Starting with current rating distribution $\boldsymbol{x}_{N+1}$ estimated from the given rating history, it iteratively samples the next rating distribution using the transition rule in Eqn.(10). Let $\{\boldsymbol{x}_{N+M+1}^{(i)}\}_{i=1}^{L}$ be the set of samples of target distribution $\boldsymbol{x}_{N+M+1}$ and $\hat{\boldsymbol{x}}_{N+M+1} = \frac{1}{L}\sum_{i=1}^{L}\boldsymbol{x}_{N+M+1}^{(i)}$ be the expectation of target distribution. We can prove that for given thresholds ϵ and δ, if the sample size L satisfies the following condition:

$$L \geq \lfloor \frac{1}{2\epsilon^2}\log\frac{2}{\delta} \rfloor \quad (11)$$

then $|\hat{\boldsymbol{x}}_{N+M+1} - \boldsymbol{x}_{N+M+1}| \leq \epsilon\mathbf{1}$ with probability at least $1-\delta$, where $\mathbf{1}$ denotes a K-dimensional all-ones vector (details given in Appendix).

It is also noted that Algorithm 3 features the complexity of $O\left(\frac{1}{\epsilon^2}\log(\frac{1}{\delta})MK\right)$, thereby scaling up to large M.

Algorithm 3: Prediction of Rating Growth

```
Input: rating history {r_i}_{i=1}^N, prediction range M,
       error threshold ε
Output: estimation of rating distribution x_{N+M+1}
// initialization
estimate Θ and f by Algorithm 1;
compute required sample size L by Eqn.(11) ;
compute x_{N+1} from {r_i}_{i=1}^N;
// random sampling
for i = 1, 2, ... L do
    x_{N+1}^(i) ← x_{N+1};
    for j = 1, 2, ..., M do
        sample x_{N+1+j}^(i) according to Eqn.(10);
    store x_{N+M+1}^(i);
estimate E[x_{N+M+1}] by (1/L) Σ_{i=1}^L x_{N+M+1}^(i);
```

4.3 What-If Analysis

The Markovian nature of the HEARD model also enables us to perform the "what-if" analysis. Concretely, given the current rating distribution $\boldsymbol{x}_i$, one may arbitrarily change $\boldsymbol{x}_i$ to another distribution $\boldsymbol{x}_i'$ to reflect any artificial conditions one wishes to "inject" in (e.g., a burst of 50 five-star ratings due to certain promotion campaigns). Staring from this new state $\boldsymbol{x}_i'$ and applying the prediction method above, one may then gauge the consequences of the injected conditions by predicting the trends of future rating growth.

Such what-if analysis is especially valuable for a range of applications including market profitability estimation, budgeted advertising, and fraudulent manipulation detection.

5. EVALUATION

In this section we present an empirical evaluation on the efficacy of the proposed models and algorithms.

5.1 Experimental Setting

We start with introducing the datasets and the alternative techniques to be evaluated.

Real Customer Rating Data

We evaluate different models using the real customer rating data collected from *Amazon*, which spans a period of approximately 18 years, including around 35 million ratings regarding about 2.4 million products [15]. In particular, we

category	# products	# ratings	avg. # ratings	avg. rating	avg. entropy
Books	929,264	12,886,488	13.9	4.271	0.666
Music	556,814	6,396,350	11.5	4.410	0.555
Movies	212,836	7,850,072	36.9	3.944	0.955
Electronics	82,067	1,241,778	15.1	3.791	0.824
Total	1,780,981	28,374,688	15.9	4.253	0.673

Table 1: Summary of *Amazon* customer rating dataset.

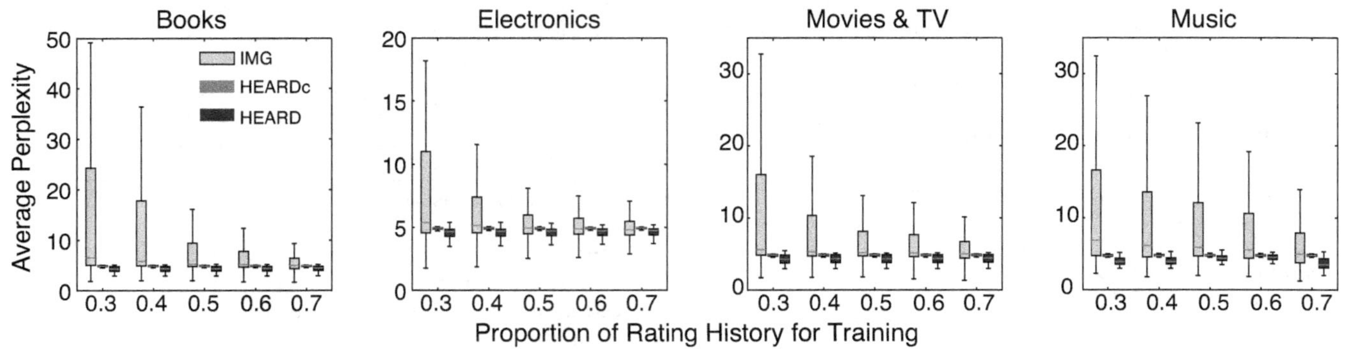

Figure 2: Accuracy of short-term prediction versus the length of rating history used for training.

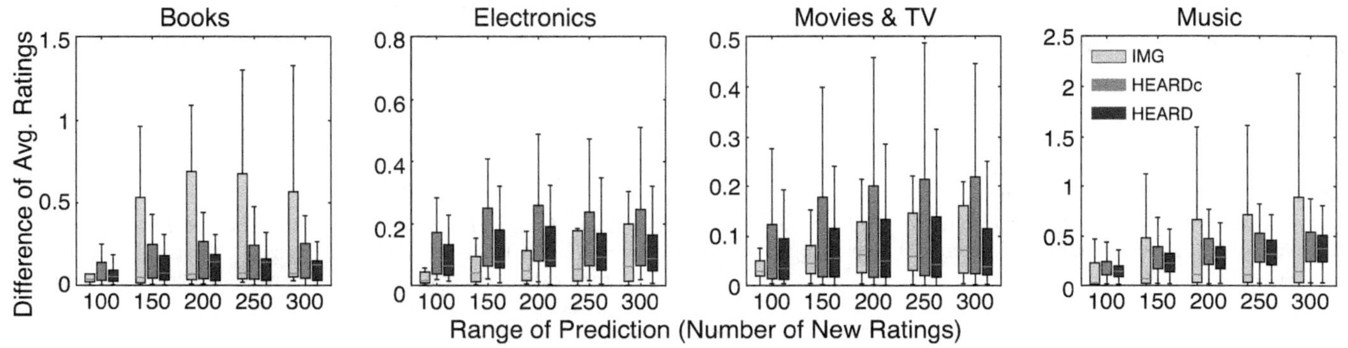

Figure 3: Accuracy of long-term prediction by rating growth models under varying range of prediction.

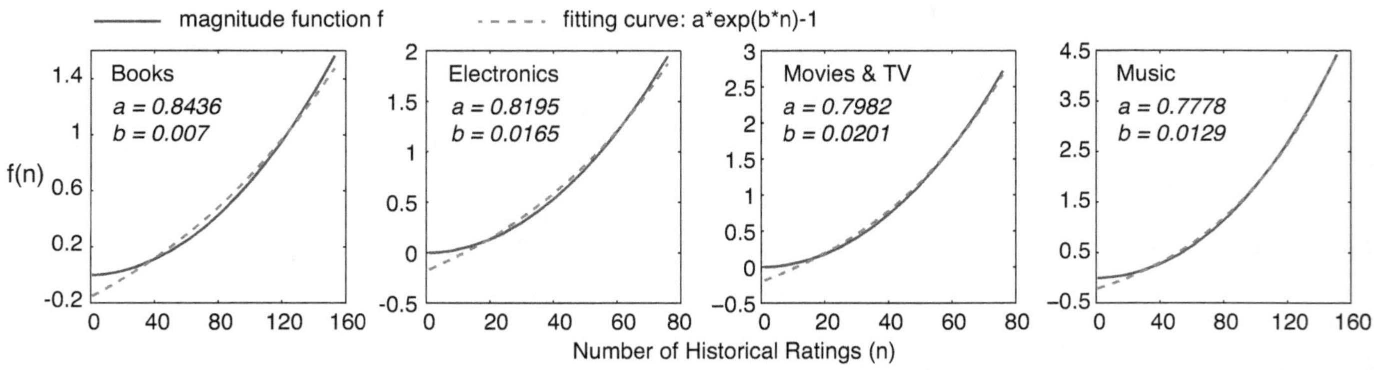

Figure 4: Estimated magnitude function $f(n)$ and fitting curve $a * exp(b * n) - 1$.

focus on the products in four major categories: *Books*, *Music*, *Movies & TV*, and *Electronics*, which cover over 72% of the total number of products in the collection. The statistics of this rating dataset is summarized in Table 1. It is noticed that these four categories demonstrate fairly diverse characteristics, for example, with average rating entropy ranging from 0.56 to 0.96.

Alternative Models

For comparison purposes, besides the HEARD model, we implemented two additional rating growth models:

- Independent Multinomial Generative model (IMG). It is the null hypothesis model, which assumes each new rating is generated according to a fixed multinomial distribution over different rating levels. This multinomial model is estimated from the rating history following the maximum likelihood principle.
- Constant HEARD model (HEARD_C). It is a simplified variant of HEARD, which follows the definition of Eqn.(1), except that the magnitude function is set as $f(x) = 1$ for $x > 1$; that is, it assumes the strength of herding effects stays constant regardless of the cumulative number of ratings.

We implemented all the models and associated algorithms in Matlab and conducted the experiments on a Linux box running 3.5GHz Intel i7 CPU and 16GB RAM. The default parameter setting is: $\lambda = 1$, $\delta = 0.05$, and $\epsilon = 0.01$.

5.2 Validating Rating Growth Models

In this first set of experiments, we intend to evaluate the validity of different rating growth models. For each product in the dataset, we partition its temporally ordered sequence of ratings into two subsequences as the training (i.e., rating history) and testing parts respectively. We use the rating history to train the rating growth models and let them predict the "future" ratings in the testing set. We compare their accuracy in both short-term and long-term prediction.

Short-Term Prediction

In short-term prediction, we vary the length of rating history (as the proportion of the entire rating sequence of a product) and measure the average perplexity of the prediction of the next 50 ratings by different models.

The results are shown in Figure 2. It is noticed that across all four product categories, HEARD and HEARD_C outperform IMG in terms of prediction accuracy. In particular, when only limited data (e.g., 30%) is available for training, the accuracy of IMG can be arbitrarily bad. This is attributed to the fact that the prediction of IMG relies on the overall statistics of the rating history of *each* product, which however has not emerged yet at this early stage. In contrast, HEARD leverages the rating histories of *all* the products in the same category to fit the model, thereby achieving high accuracy even when facing limited training data. This desirable property makes HEARD especially valuable for early-stage prediction, as we will discuss shortly.

It is also noticed that HEARD achieves higher accuracy than HEARD_C but with marginally larger variance. This is consistent with the fact that HEARD adopts a more complicated model than HEARD_C, which enables HEARD to model a wider range of herding effects but at the cost of slightly higher variance.

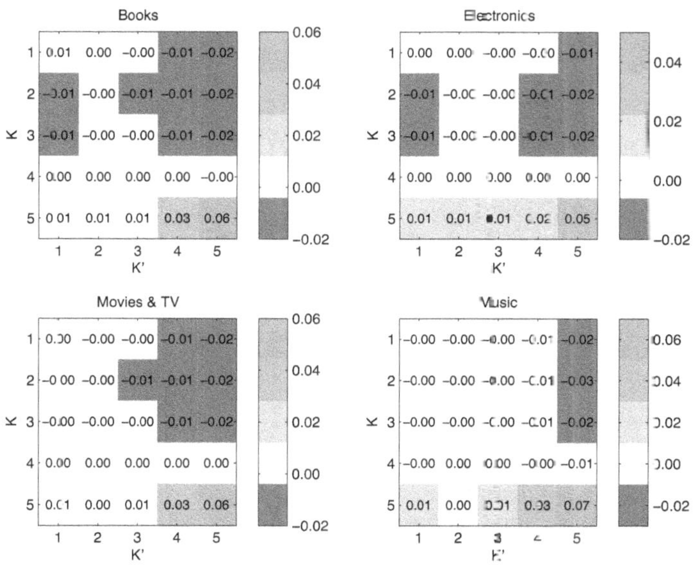

Figure 5: Heat maps of parameters $\{\theta_{k,k'}\}$ for each product category.

Long-Term Prediction

In long-term prediction, we select the products with at least 500 ratings and fix the length of rating history (for training) as 200. We then apply each model to predicting the rating distribution after the next M ratings (M is referred to as the *prediction range*). The accuracy is measured by the difference between predicted and actual average ratings.

The performance of different models is illustrated in Figure 3, wherein we vary prediction range M from 100 to 300. It is observed that compared with IMG and HEARD_C, the prediction accuracy of HEARD is much less sensitive to the setting of M. This can be explained as follows. First, the prediction of IMG depends on the simple statistics (i.e., fraction of ratings at different levels), which however may fluctuate significantly over a large time span. Second, as M increases, the change of the strength of herding effects can no longer be ignored as HEARD_C does.

We can thus conclude that HEARD achieves reliable accuracy in both short-term and long-term prediction tasks, implying that HEARD faithfully captures the growth dynamics of product ratings.

5.3 Characterizing Herding Effect

Next, equipped with the HEARD model as the analytical tool, we conduct a quantitative study on the herding effects observable in real customer rating data. More concretely, for each product category, we apply Algorithm 1 to fitting the model and examine the herding effects as characterized by the estimated magnitude function $f(\cdot)$ and category-level parameters $\{\boldsymbol{\theta}_k\}_k$.

Strength of Herding Effect

Recall that $f(n)$ specifies the strength of herding effects as a function of the number of historical ratings n. Figure 4 illustrates the estimated $f(n)$ for each product category. We further apply curve fitting to $f(n)$ with an exponential model $a * exp(b * n) - 1$ (a and b are parameters). Interestingly, the magnitude functions in all four categories tightly follow the

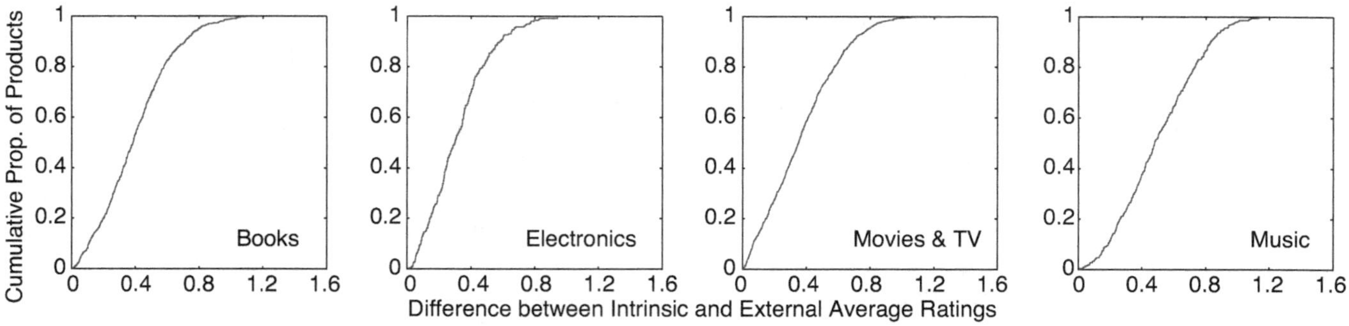

Figure 6: Cumulative proportion of products versus difference between intrinsic and external average ratings.

exponential curves, despite their slightly different parameter settings of a and b.

This finding entails multi-fold implications: First, it confirms our intuition that the strength of herding effects evolves with the cumulative number of historical ratings. Second, it also echoes the results documented by existing experimental studies (e.g., [19]) on the nonlinear relationship between the predicability of individual behaviors and external influence. Third, most importantly, it provides a formula to explicitly quantify the strength of herding effects. For example, comparing the curves for the categories of *Books* and *Movies & TV*, it is observed that the herding effects is stronger in the category of *Movies & TV*, that is, customers are more easily to be influenced by prior ratings when purchasing *Movies & TV* products. Such information can be valuable for applications such as targeted advertising.

Mutual Influence

Now we proceed to examining parameters $\{\boldsymbol{\theta}_k\}$. Recall that these parameters dictate the mutual influence between the ratings at different levels, concretely, with $\theta_{k,k'}$ specifying how preceding level-k' ratings may positively excite or negatively inhibit the generation of level-k ratings.

Figure 5 illustrates the heat maps of $\{\boldsymbol{\theta}_k\}$ estimated for each product category. While each category has its unique traits, certain common patterns are observed. First, high ratings (e.g., five-star ratings) tend to stimulate new high ratings while inhibiting the generation of low ratings. Second, high ratings are more impactful than low ratings in influencing other ratings. These observations are consistent with the finding of the asymmetric herding effects of positive and negative prior opinions as reported in [16].

5.4 Case Studies

As discussed in Section 4, equipped with HEARD, we are able to perform various analytical tasks. In this set of experiments, we showcase how HEARD helps answer two fundamental questions: (i) exposing the rating inherent to the quality of a product (i.e., "intrinsic rating") by factoring out the herding effects from collective ratings, and (ii) performing predicative, what-if analysis by incorporating artificial conditions into the rating growth dynamics model.

Debiasing Collective Ratings

To understand the issue that the simple aggregated (or external) rating of a product deviates from its true quality, we apply HEARD to estimate the intrinsic ratings as in Section 4.1 and then measure for each product the difference between its intrinsic and external average ratings.

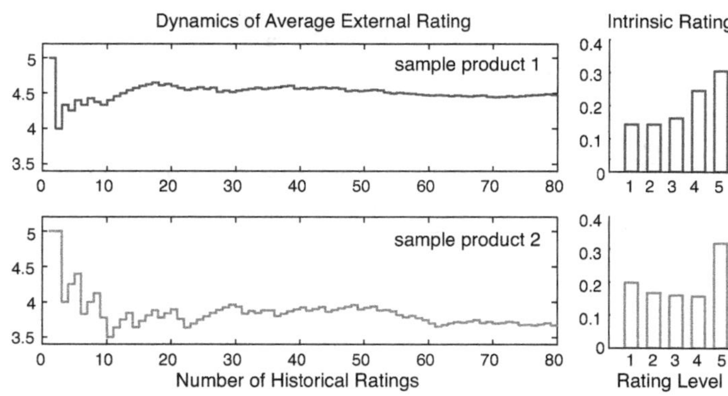

Figure 7: Two sample products with similar intrinsic ratings but with different rating growth histories, leading to significantly distinct external ratings.

Figure 6 shows the cumulative proportion of products with respect to the difference between intrinsic and external ratings in each category. It is observed that in all the cases, over 50% products have their external ratings deviate at least 0.5 from their intrinsic ratings, which is significant considering that *Amazon* uses a five-level rating system.

Endowed with the capability of exposing the intrinsic rating of a product, we can then compare the true quality of two products without being misguided by their external ratings. Figure 7 showcases such an example, in which the dynamics of the average external ratings of two sample products is depicted. Despite that they differ significantly in their external ratings (about 0.9), their intrinsic ratings are indeed fairly similar as shown in the right plot. This is explained by that sample product 2 experiences a sequence of low ratings at the early stage of its history, which considerably changes the dynamics of its rating growth. With the help of HEARD, however, we are able to maximally debias this type of influence caused by the herding effects.

What-If Analysis

As introduced in Section 4.3, the Markovian nature of the HEARD model enables us to perform predicative, "what-if" analysis by artificially incorporating desired conditions into the prediction model and analyze the consequences using simulation. For example, before deciding whether to invest in a promotion campaign for a product, market analysts may

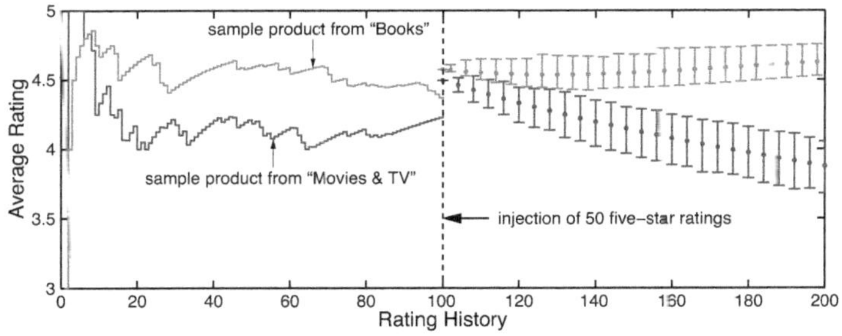

Figure 8: What-if analysis by incorporating artificial conditions into prediction model.

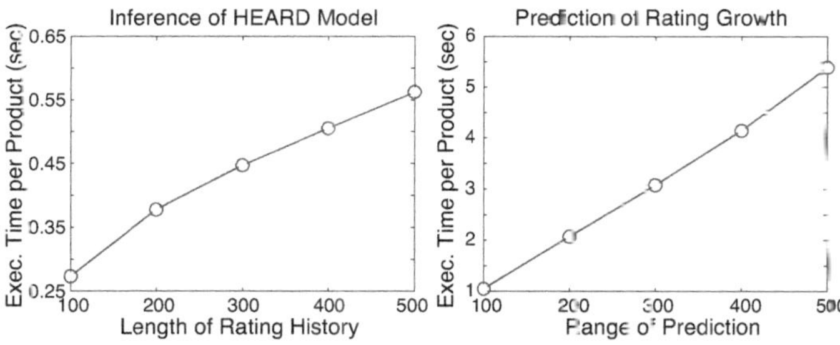

Figure 9: Average execution time per product by HEARD in model inference and rating prediction.

wish to estimate the long-term influence of the burst of high ratings due to the promotion.

Figure 8 shows one concrete example. We pick two sample products respectively from the categories of *Movies & TV* and *Books*, which have fairly close average ratings thus far. Now, assuming the promotion takes effect, we inject 50 five-star ratings into their rating histories. As shown in the right panel of Figure 8, the prediction by HEARD tells us: while both products experience similar short-term bursts in their popularity, in the long run the promotion has much longer-lasting influence on the sample product from the category of *Books*. It is clear that this provides valuable information for the decision making of market analysts.

5.5 Scalability

In the last set of experiments, we evaluate the scalability of HEARD. Specifically, for model inference, we measure the average execution time per product by HEARD under varying length of rating history (for training); meanwhile, for future rating prediction, we measure its average execution time under varying setting of prediction range.

The results are depicted in Figure 9. It is observed that the execution time of HEARD grows approximately linearly with the length of rating history and the range of prediction. This also confirms our theoretical analysis on the complexity of Algorithm 1 and Algorithm 3. We can thus conclude that HEARD scales up to large rating datasets.

6. CONCLUSION

This paper presented a quantitative framework to gauge the herding effects in collective opinions of individuals. We proposed HEARD, a mechanistic modeling framework for the growth dynamics of online product ratings, which explicitly accounts for the herding effects of prior customer opinions. Using massive customer rating datasets, we demonstrated the efficacy of HEARD in capturing the dynamics of rating growth, quantifying social influence and debiasing collective ratings, and further performing what-if analysis against artificial manipulations. HEARD is not limited to product rating systems. Indeed, the mechanistic nature of HEARD makes it applicable for modeling the herding effects in other domains where social influence plays a role, from crowdsourcing and recommender systems to electoral polling.

This work also opens up several directions for future investigations. For example, recent work has shown that the temporal dynamics of collective response to a publication follows rather reproducible patterns, as citations can be captured by a mechanistic model [23]. Hence, incorporating the temporal dynamics in the rating growth model can be fruitful and could potentially shed new light on the nature of crowd wisdom. Furthermore, our framework is orthogonal to studies on the text and social aspects of product reviews and collective opinions, suggesting a rather promising direction by combining the two approaches. Lastly, the model makes falsifiable predictions for collective response against artificial manipulations, making it a viable candidate to assess and guide experimental studies, results of which could feed back to and improve the model with more accurate and realistic predictions.

Acknowledgements

This research was sponsored by the U.S. Army Research Laboratory and the U.K. Ministry of Defense and was accomplished under Agreement Number W911NF-06-3-0001. The views and conclusions contained in this document are those of the authors and should not be interpreted as representing the official policies, either expressed or implied, of the U.S. Army Research Laboratory, the U.S. Government, the U.K. Ministry of Defense or the U.K. Government. The U.S. and U.K. Governments are authorized to reproduce and distribute reprints for Government purposes notwithstanding any copyright notation hereon. The authors would like to thank J. McAuley and J. Leskovec for sharing the Amazon review dataset.

7. REFERENCES

[1] N. A. Christakis and J. H. Fowler. The spread of obesity in a large social network over 32 years. *New England journal of medicine*, 357(4):370–379, 2007.

[2] N. A. Christakis and J. H. Fowler. The collective dynamics of smoking in a large social network. *New England journal of medicine*, 358(21):2249–2258, 2008.

[3] P. Cui, S. Jin, L. Yu, F. Wang, W. Zhu, and S. Yang. Cascading outbreak prediction in networks: A data-driven approach. In *KDD*, 2013.

[4] A. Das, S. Gollapudi, R. Panigrahy, and M. Salek. Debiasing social wisdom. In *KDD*, 2013.

[5] A. P. Dawid and A. M. Skene. Maximum likelihood estimation of observer error-rates using the em algorithm. *Journal of the Royal Statistical Society. Series C (Applied Statistics)*, 28(1):20–28 1979.

[6] J. Eisenstein, A. Ahmed, and E. P. Xing. Sparse additive generative models of text. In *ICML*, 2011.

[7] J. H. Fowler, N. A. Christakis, Steptoe, and D. Roux. Dynamic spread of happiness in a large social network: longitudinal analysis of the framingham heart study social network. *BMJ: British medical journal*, pages 23–27, 2009.

[8] F. Galton. Vox populi. *Nature*, 75(7):450, 1907.
[9] G. Ganu, N. Elhadad, and A. Marian. Beyond the stars: Improving rating predictions using review text content. In *WebDB*, 2009.
[10] M. Hu and B. Liu. Mining and summarizing customer reviews. In *KDD*, 2004.
[11] S. Judd, M. Kearns, and Y. Vorobeychik. Behavioral dynamics and influence in networked coloring and consensus. *Proceedings of the National Academy of Sciences*, 107(34):14978–14982, 2010.
[12] B. Krishnapuram, L. Carin, M. A. T. Figueiredo, and A. J. Hartemink. Sparse multinomial logistic regression: Fast algorithms and generalization bounds. *IEEE Trans. Pattern Anal. Mach. Intell.*, 27(6):957–968, June 2005.
[13] D. Liben-Nowell and J. Kleinberg. Tracing information flow on a global scale using internet chain-letter data. *Proceedings of the National Academy of Sciences*, 105(12):4633–4638, 2008.
[14] J. Lorenz, H. Rauhut, F. Schweitzer, and D. Helbing. How social influence can undermine the wisdom of crowd effect. *Proceedings of the National Academy of Sciences*, 108(22):9020–9025, 2011.
[15] J. McAuley and J. Leskovec. Hidden factors and hidden topics: Understanding rating dimensions with review text. In *RecSys*, 2013.
[16] L. Muchnik, S. Aral, and S. J. Taylor. Social influence bias: A randomized experiment. *Science*, 341(6146):647–651, 2013.
[17] J. W. Pillow, J. Shlens, L. Paninski, A. Sher, A. M. Litke, E. J. Chichilnisky, and E. P. Simoncelli. Spatio-temporal correlations and visual signaling in a complete neuronal population. *Nature*, 454(7206):995–999, 2008.
[18] C. P. Robert and G. Casella. *Monte Carlo Statistical Methods (Springer Texts in Statistics)*. Springer-Verlag New York, Inc., Secaucus, NJ, USA, 2005.
[19] M. J. Salganik, P. S. Dodds, and D. J. Watts. Experimental study of inequality and unpredictability in an artificial cultural market. *Science*, 311(5762):854–856, 2006.
[20] V. S. Sheng, F. Provost, and P. G. Ipeirotis. Get another label? improving data quality and data mining using multiple, noisy labelers. In *KDD*, 2008.
[21] H. Sun, A. Morales, and X. Yan. Synthetic review spamming and defense. In *KDD*, 2013.
[22] J. Surowiecki. *The Wisdom of Crowds*. Anchor, 2005.
[23] D. Wang, C. Song, and A.-L. Barabási. Quantifying long-term scientific impact. *Science*, 342(6154):127–132, 2013.
[24] D. Wang, Z. Wen, H. Tong, C.-Y. Lin, C. Song, and A.-L. Barabási. Information spreading in context. In *WWW*, 2011.
[25] T. Wang, M. Srivatsa, D. Agrawal, and L. Liu. Microscopic social influence. In *SDM*, 2012.
[26] D. Zhou, J. C. Platt, S. Basu, and Y. Mao. Learning from the wisdom of crowds by minimax entropy. In *NIPS*, 2012.
[27] K. Zhou, H. Zha, and L. Song. Learning triggering kernels for multi-dimensional hawkes processes. In *ICML*, 2013.

APPENDIX

Surrogate Function.

We first prove that the objective function $\mathcal{L}_\lambda(\boldsymbol{\Theta})$ as defined in Eqn.(2) and its surrogate function $Q(\boldsymbol{\Theta};\boldsymbol{\Theta}^{(n)})$ as defined in Eqn.(3) satisfy the following relationships:

$$\begin{cases} Q(\boldsymbol{\Theta};\boldsymbol{\Theta}^{(n)}) \geq \mathcal{L}_\lambda(\boldsymbol{\Theta}) & \forall\boldsymbol{\Theta},\boldsymbol{\Theta}^{(n)} \\ Q(\boldsymbol{\Theta}^{(n)};\boldsymbol{\Theta}^{(n)}) = \mathcal{L}_\lambda(\boldsymbol{\Theta}^{(n)}) & \forall\boldsymbol{\Theta}^{(n)} \end{cases}$$

First, according to the definition of Eqn.(1), we have:

$$\begin{aligned}\mathcal{L}_\lambda(\boldsymbol{\Theta}) &= \frac{1}{N}\sum_i\left(\log\sum_k\exp(\phi_{i,k}) - \sum_k y_{i,k}\phi_{i,k}\right)\\ &\quad+\frac{\lambda}{2}\left(||\boldsymbol{\Theta}||_F^2 + \mathcal{R}(f)\right)\end{aligned}$$

We focus on the log-sum-exponential term $\log\sum_k\exp(\phi_{i,k})$ and apply the following quadratic upper bound [12]: for any vectors $\boldsymbol{u}\in\mathbb{R}^K$ and $\boldsymbol{v}\in\mathbb{R}^K$,

$$\begin{aligned}\log\sum_k\exp(u_k) &\leq \sum_k(u_k-v_k)^2 - \frac{1}{K}\left(\sum_k(u_k-v_k)\right)^2\\ &\quad+\sum_k\frac{\exp(v_k)(u_k-v_k)}{\sum_{k'}\exp(v_{k'})} + \log\sum_k\exp(v_k)\end{aligned}$$

In our context, we replace the log-sum-exponential term of $\mathcal{L}_\lambda(\boldsymbol{\Theta})$ with its upper bound and substitute u_k with $\phi_{i,k}$ and v_k with $\phi_{i,k}^{(n)}$, which then leads to the result of $Q(\boldsymbol{\Theta};\boldsymbol{\Theta}^{(n)}) \geq \mathcal{L}_\lambda(\boldsymbol{\Theta})$.

To prove $Q(\boldsymbol{\Theta}^{(n)};\boldsymbol{\Theta}^{(n)}) = \mathcal{L}_\lambda(\boldsymbol{\Theta}^{(n)})$, it is noted that the upper bound above is exact when $\boldsymbol{u}=\boldsymbol{v}$.

Euler-Lagrange Equation.

To derive Eqn.(7), it is first noticed that the optimization problem in Eqn.(6) can be rewritten as:

$$\min_{f\in L_1(\mathbb{R})}\int_0^\infty F(f,f')\mathrm{d}t$$

where $F(f,f')$ is defined by:

$$F(f,f') = A_t\mathbb{I}\{t\in\mathbb{N}\}f(t)^2 + B_t\mathbb{I}\{t\in\mathbb{N}\}f(t) + \frac{\lambda}{2}(f'(t))^2$$

According to Euler-Lagrange equation, the solution of this problem satisfies the following differential equation:

$$\frac{\partial F}{\partial f} - \frac{\mathrm{d}}{\mathrm{d}t}\frac{\partial F}{\partial f'} = 0$$

By substituting F with the definition above, we get the differential equation in Eqn.(7).

Sample Size.

Here we derive the number of samples required for the given thresholds ϵ and δ as in Eqn.(11). Without loss of generality, consider the k-th element of $\boldsymbol{x}_{N+M+1}$, $x_{N+M+1,k}$. Following the Hoeffding's inequality, we have:

$$Pr(|\hat{x}_{N+M+1,k}-\mathbb{E}[\hat{x}_{N+M+1,k}]| \geq \epsilon) \leq \exp\left(-\frac{2L^2\epsilon^2}{\sum_{i=1}^L(b_i-a_i)^2}\right)$$

where $x_{N+M+1,k}^{(i)}$ is bounded by $[a_i,b_i]$.

Notice that $\hat{\boldsymbol{x}}_{N+M+1}$ is an unbiased estimator of $\boldsymbol{x}_{N+M+1}$ and $x_{N+M+1,k}^{(i)}$ is bounded by $[0,1]$. By setting the right side of the inequality above to δ, we obtain Eqn.(11).

Modeling Delayed Feedback in Display Advertising

Olivier Chapelle
Criteo Labs
Palo Alto, CA
o.chapelle@criteo.com

ABSTRACT

In performance display advertising a key metric of a campaign effectiveness is its conversion rate – the proportion of users who take a predefined action on the advertiser website, such as a purchase. Predicting this conversion rate is thus essential for estimating the value of an impression and can be achieved via machine learning. One difficulty however is that the conversions can take place long after the impression – up to a month – and this delayed feedback hinders the conversion modeling. We tackle this issue by introducing an additional model that captures the conversion delay. Intuitively, this probabilistic model helps determining whether a user that has not converted should be treated as a negative sample – when the elapsed time is larger than the predicted delay – or should be discarded from the training set – when it is too early to tell. We provide experimental results on real traffic logs that demonstrate the effectiveness of the proposed model.

Categories and Subject Descriptors

H.3.5 [**Information Storage And Retrieval**]: Online Information Services; I.2.6 [**Artificial Intelligence**]: Learning

Keywords

Display advertising; machine learning; conversion prediction

1. INTRODUCTION

Display advertising is a form of online advertising where advertisers pay publishers for placing graphical ads on their web pages. The traditional method of selling display advertising has been pre-negotiated long term contracts between the advertisers and the publishers. In the last decade spot markets, demand-side platforms (DSP) and real-time bidding exchanges (RTBs) have emerged as a popular alternative due to the promise of increased liquidity for publishers, and increased reach with granular audience targeting capabilities for the advertisers [14].

These markets also offer the advertisers a wide range of payment options. If the goal of an advertising campaign is getting their message to the target audience (for instance in brand awareness campaigns) then paying per impression (CPM) with targeting constraints is normally the appropriate choice for the advertiser. However, many advertisers would prefer not to pay for an ad impression unless that impression leads the user to the advertiser's website. Performance dependent payment models, such as cost-per-click (CPC) and cost-per-conversion (CPA), were introduced to address this concern. The focus of this paper is the CPA model which allows the advertisers to pay only if the user takes a predefined action on their website, such as purchasing a product or subscribing to an email list. A platform that supports such conditional payment options needs to convert advertiser bids to *expected* price per impression (eCPM). The eCPM of a CPC or CPA bid, will depend on the probability that the impression will lead to a click or a conversion event. Estimating these probabilities accurately is critical for an efficient marketplace [10].

There has been significant work in the literature on modeling clicks in the context of search advertising [5, 11] and display advertising [1, 2], but relatively little on conversion prediction [16]. This paper deals with the problem of conversion prediction and more specifically with post-click conversions, these conversions that can be attributed to a preceding click.

The techniques used for click and conversion modeling share some commonalities, but there is an additional difficulty in conversion modeling: whereas a click often occurs in a relatively short time window after an impression, a conversion can happen days or weeks later. This results in the following dilemma when deciding on the matching window length typically used when building a training set: if that window is too short, some of the examples are incorrectly labeled as negatives – those for which a conversion will occur in the future; but if it is too long, the examples in the training set will be impressions that are at least as old as the matching window, hence a risk of generating a stalled model.

The solution proposed in this paper does not involve a matching window: when generating the training set, a click is labeled as positive if it is followed by a conversion and is treated as *unlabeled* otherwise. It cannot indeed be labeled as negative for sure in that latter case because a conversion can happen in the future. The problem of learning from posi-

KDD'14, August 24–27, 2014, New York, NY, USA.

ACM 978-1-4503-2956-9/14/08 ...$15.00.
http://dx.doi.org/10.1145/2623330.2623634.

tive and unlabeled data has already been extensively studied [3, 4]. But most of these works rely on the assumption that the labeled positive examples are chosen randomly from the positive class; or in other words, that the probability of having a positive example with missing label is constant. This assumption does not hold in our setting: the label is much more likely to be missing if the click has just happened.

To tackle this issue of delayed feedback, we introduce a second model that captures the expected delay between the click and the conversion. This model is closely related to the models used in *survival time analysis* [7]. This field studies the distribution of survival times – typically the time between the beginning of a treatment and the death of the patient – but some of these times are *censored*, for instance when a patient drops out of the study or when a patient is still alive at the end of the study. A censored time means that the survival time is *at least* equal to that time. Similarly, for the problem of conversions, some of the delays are censored: if at training time a conversion has not occurred, the delay of the conversion (if any) is known to be at least the time elapsed since the click.

But unlike survival time analysis where a patient will eventually die, the user may not eventually convert. This is the reason why two models are required: one to predict whether the user will convert and the other to predict the delay of the conversion in case he does. These two models are trained *jointly*. It is indeed inherently impossible to separate the two models: when a conversion has not occurred, there is an ambiguity on whether the user will convert but at a later time, or the user will not convert at all. The two models are needed to correctly assign probabilities to both outcomes.

For this work we collected traffic logs of Criteo, a global leader in performance display advertising, specialized in retargeting.[1] Criteo acts as an intermediary between publishers and advertisers by paying publishers on a CPM basis (either through bids on ad exchanges or via direct relationships with publishers) and gets paid by advertisers whenever there is a click on an ad (CPC) or when there is a conversion following that click (CPA).

The paper is organized as follows. Section 2 reviews conversion attributions and introduces some key statistics about the conversions in our data. The model to address the delayed conversion issue is presented in section 3 and its optimization in section 4. We discuss in section 5 related work and finally present experimental results in section 6.

2. CONVERSIONS

This section first describes the mechanism used in this paper to attribute conversions to click and then presents some statistics about the data and conversions in our system.

2.1 Post-Click Attribution

In marketing the attribution is the mechanism used to assign credit for a conversion. The two main mechanisms are post-view attribution in which a conversion is attributed to one or several prior impressions and post-click attribution in which an impression needs to have been clicked to be considered as having led to a conversion. The post-click attribution model is often deemed more reliable in the online advertising industry and is the one considered in this paper.

The attribution mechanism also includes a conversion window: a conversion is attributed to a click only if it occurred within this time window. The window length can be defined by the advertiser, but for the sake of simplicity, we fixed it to 30 days in this paper.[2] In other words, conversions occurring after 30 days are ignored and the delay between a click and a conversion can never be more than 30 days.

The specific rules that we applied for matching a conversion and a click are as follows. In addition to the 30 days window requirement, a match is defined as a conversion event and a click event sharing the same user identifier and the same advertiser. In the case of multiple clicks leading to a conversion, we adopted the industry standard to attribute the conversion to the last click. If several conversions match a click, we keep only the first one, discarding the remaining ones. This means that we are not attempting to model multiple conversions per clicks even though this step may be needed in a production system.

2.2 Conversion Rate Prediction

In a cost-per-conversion (CPA) payment model, the ad exchange or DSP needs to estimate the value of an impression. If CPA is the price the advertiser is willing to pay for a conversion, the expected value of an impression is:[3]

$$\begin{aligned} \text{eCPM} &= \text{CPA} \times \Pr(\text{conversion}, \text{click}) \\ &= \text{CPA} \times \Pr(\text{click}) \times \Pr(\text{conversion} \mid \text{click}). \qquad (1) \end{aligned}$$

The first equation reflects the post-click attribution model while the second one splits that probability into the product of a click probability and a probability of conversion given click. While it is possible to directly model Pr(conversion, click), the decomposition (1) has two advantages: first it reduces the load on the data processing pipeline as there is no need to join impressions and conversions over a long period of time; and second it may predict more accurately campaigns with few or no conversions and a reasonable amount of clicks because in that case the clicks still provide some information on the effectiveness of the campaign.

The modeling of Pr(click) and Pr(conversion | click) present different challenges: training a click model requires a scalable learning architecture – there can be billions of impressions served every day by an ad platform – but the click feedback is almost immediate; on the other hand, the training set of the conversion model is much smaller – it scales as the number of clicks, not impressions – but the conversion feedback can come with a delay of up to 30 days. This paper presents a way to address this delay feedback challenge.

2.3 Analysis of the Conversion Delay

We calculated the percentage of conversion events within different time intervals. As shown in figure 1, a large portion (35%) of the conversions occur within one hour of the clicks, but the rest of them happen much later: about 50% of the conversions occur after 24 hours and 13% after 2 weeks. These delay statistics are quite different from the ones reported in [16, Section 4.2]: on the Yahoo RMX exchange,

[1] `http://en.wikipedia.org/wiki/Behavioral_retargeting`

[2] Most advertisers use in fact a 30 day attribution window.

[3] The eCPM is in fact defined as the value for 1000 impressions so the right hand side of equation (1) should be multiplied by 1000.

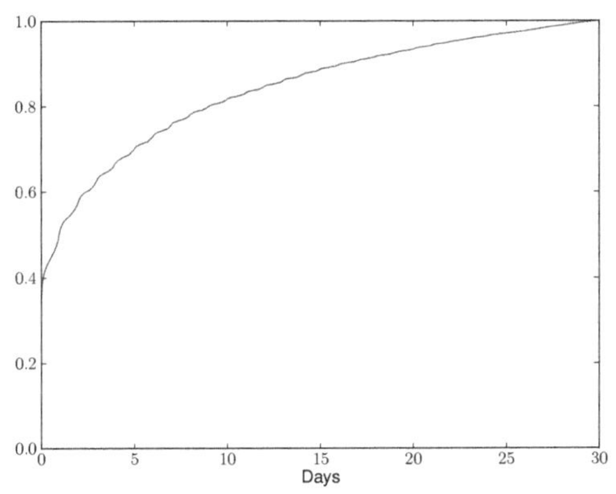

Figure 1: Cumulative distribution of the click to conversion delay. Its oscillating shape is due to daily cyclicality (more visible in figure 5).

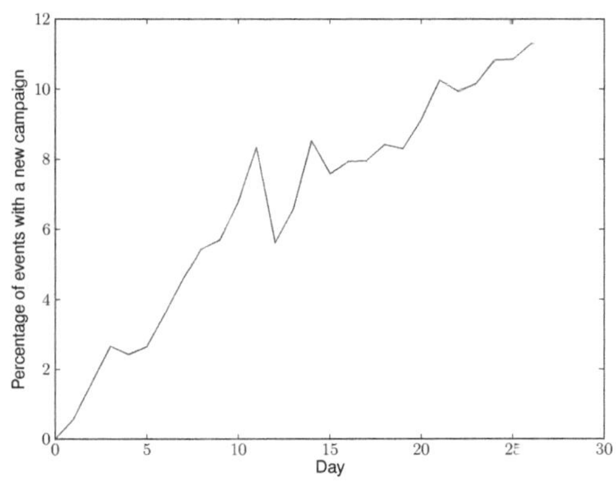

Figure 2: Percentage of traffic with a new campaign for each day following a reference day.

95.5% of the conversion events happen within one hour of the click.

These long delays have implications for learning: this prevents the use of a short matching window – such as the 2 days advocated in [16] – since such a short window would incorrectly label as negatives a large portion of the conversions.

2.4 New campaigns

Display advertising is a non stationary process as the set of active advertisers, campaigns, publishers and users is constantly changing. When new campaigns are added to the system, models built on past data may not perform as well on those new campaigns. Keeping the models fresh can therefore be of critical importance for achieving sustained performance.

We analyzed the rate at which new campaigns are introduced. To this end, we used one day of data as the reference period and computed the percentage of new campaigns introduced in every day of the following next 26 days. Figure 2 shows that the percentage of traffic from new campaigns is increasing steadily day-by-day reaching 11.3% after 26 days. This analysis suggests that waiting 30 days to train a model in order to have a full conversion feedback would probably be harmful: the model would not predict well for a substantial portion of the traffic.

3. MODEL

Before going into the details of our model, we need to introduce some notations regarding the different variables in our training set.

Each past event can be characterized by the outcome of the following 5 random variables:

- X a set of features;
- $Y \in \{0, 1\}$ indicating whether a conversion has already occurred ;
- $C \in \{0, 1\}$ indicating whether the user will eventually convert;
- D the delay between the click and the conversion (undefined[4] if C=0);
- E the elapsed time since the click.

The main relation between these variables is that if a conversion has not been observed, it is either because the user will not convert or because he will convert later, in other words,

$$Y = 0 \iff C = 0 \text{ or } E < D. \quad (2)$$

This obviously implies that if the user has already converted (Y=1) the value of C is observed:

$$Y = 1 \implies C = 1 \quad (3)$$

The only independence assumption required in the following derivation is that the pair (C, D) is independent of E given X,

$$\Pr(C, D \mid X, E) = \Pr(C, D \mid X) \quad (4)$$

This independence makes sense since E, the elapsed time since the click, has an influence only on Y, whether the user has already converted or not.

We denote by lower case letters observed values of these random variables: we are given a data set comprising of triplets$(\mathbf{x}_i, y_i, e_i)$ and in addition, if $y_i = 1$, we are also given the delay d_i between the click and the conversion.

Two parametric models are used to fit this data: a probability of conversion $\Pr(C \mid X)$ and a model of the conversion delay $\Pr(D \mid X, C = 1)$. Once these two models are trained, the former is used to predict the probabilities of conversion while the latter is discarded.

Both models are generalized linear models: the first one is a standard logistic regression model,

$$\Pr(C = 1 \mid X = \mathbf{x}) = p(\mathbf{x}) \quad \text{with} \quad p(\mathbf{x}) = \frac{1}{1 + \exp(-\mathbf{w}_c \cdot \mathbf{x})},$$

and the second one is an exponential distribution of the (nonnegative) delay,

$$\Pr(D = d \mid X = \mathbf{x}, C = 1) = \lambda(\mathbf{x}) \exp(-\lambda(\mathbf{x})d). \quad (5)$$

[4]For the sake of correctness, we can set D to -1 or any other arbitrary value whenever $C = 0$.

Some other distributions can be used to model time between events (e.g. Weibull, Gamma, Log-Normal; see [13, section 2] for an extensive list), but the exponential distribution is a common one and fits quite well the empirical delay distributions as we shall see in section 6.2.

The function $\lambda(\mathbf{x})$ is called the *hazard* function in survival analysis and in order to ensure that $\lambda(\mathbf{x}) > 0$ we use the parametrization $\lambda(\mathbf{x}) = \exp(\mathbf{w}_d \cdot \mathbf{x})$. The parameters of the model are thus the two weight vectors $\mathbf{w}_c$ and $\mathbf{w}_d$.

Under these models, the probability of a conversion event is:

$$\begin{aligned}
&\Pr(Y = 1, D = d_i \mid X = \mathbf{x}_i, E = e_i) \\
&\quad = \Pr(C = 1, D = d_i \mid X = \mathbf{x}_i, E = e_i) \\
&\quad = \Pr(C = 1, D = d_i \mid X = \mathbf{x}_i) \\
&\quad = \Pr(D = d_i \mid X = \mathbf{x}_i, C = 1) \Pr(C = 1 \mid X = \mathbf{x}_i) \\
&\quad = \lambda(\mathbf{x}_i) \exp(-\lambda(\mathbf{x}_i) d_i)\ p(\mathbf{x}_i). \qquad (6)
\end{aligned}$$

The first equality comes from the equivalence (2) and that e_i has to be larger than d_i, while the second equality results from the conditional independence (4).

By the law of total probabilities, and again using the conditional independence (4) of C and E given X, the probability of not having observed a conversion can be written as:

$$\begin{aligned}
&\Pr(Y = 0 \mid X = \mathbf{x}_i, E = e_i) \\
&= \Pr(Y = 0 \mid C = 0, X = \mathbf{x}_i, E = e_i) P(C = 0 \mid X = \mathbf{x}_i) \\
&+ \Pr(Y = 0 \mid C = 1, X = \mathbf{x}_i, E = e_i) P(C = 1 \mid X = \mathbf{x}_i) \qquad (7)
\end{aligned}$$

Furthermore, the probability of delayed conversion is:

$$\begin{aligned}
\Pr(Y = 0 \ &\mid C = 1, X = \mathbf{x}_i, E = e_i) \\
&= \Pr(D > E \mid C = 1, X = \mathbf{x}_i, E = e_i) \\
&= \int_{e_i}^{\infty} \lambda(\mathbf{x}) \exp(-\lambda(\mathbf{x}) t) dt \\
&= \exp(-\lambda(\mathbf{x}) e_i), \qquad (8)
\end{aligned}$$

where the first equality comes from (2). Combining (7), (8) and the fact that $\Pr(Y = 0 \mid C = 0, X = \mathbf{x}_i, E = e_i) = 1$, the likelihood of not observing a conversion can finally be written as:

$$\Pr(Y = 0 \mid X = \mathbf{x}_i, E = e_i) = 1 - p(\mathbf{x}_i) + p(\mathbf{x}_i) \exp(-\lambda(\mathbf{x}_i) e_i). \qquad (9)$$

4. OPTIMIZATION

We propose two ways of optimizing the model presented in the previous section. The first one aims at untangling both models by inferring the value of the hidden variable C. This is achieved through the use of the expectation maximization (EM) algorithm. The second one directly optimizes the log likelihood by gradient descent.

4.1 Expectation-Maximization

The EM algorithm is useful to find the maximum likelihood parameters of a model with hidden variables. In our model, C (whether the user will eventually convert) is a hidden variable. The details of the two steps are given below.

Expectation step.

For a given data point $(\mathbf{x}_i, y_i, e_i)$, we need to compute the posterior probability of the hidden variable,

$$\Pr(C = 1 \mid X = \mathbf{x}_i, Y = y_i) := w_i$$

If $y_i = 1$, this is trivial from equation (3): $w_i = 1$. The interesting case is when $y_i = 0$:

$$\begin{aligned}
&\Pr(C = 1 \mid Y = 0, X = \mathbf{x}_i, E = e_i) \\
&\quad = \Pr(Y = 0 \mid C = 1, X = \mathbf{x}_i, E = e_i) \Pr(C = 1 \mid X = \mathbf{x}_i) \\
&\quad = \exp(-\lambda(\mathbf{x}_i) e_i) p(\mathbf{x}_i), \qquad (10)
\end{aligned}$$

where the last equation comes from (8).

Maximization step.

As for any EM algorithm, the quantity to be maximized during the M step is an expected log-likelihood according to the distribution computed during the E step:

$$\begin{aligned}
&\sum_{i,\ y_i=1} \log \Pr(Y = 1, D = d_i \mid X = \mathbf{x}_i, E = e_i) + \\
&\sum_{i,\ y_i=0} (1 - w_i) \log \Pr(Y = 0, C = 0 \mid X = \mathbf{x}_i, E = e_i) \qquad (11) \\
&\qquad + w_i \log \Pr(Y = 0, C = 1 \mid X = \mathbf{x}_i, E = e_i)
\end{aligned}$$

Using a similar derivation as the one to obtain (9), the expected log likelihood of a unlabeled sample turns out to be:

$$\begin{aligned}
&(1 - w_i) \log \Pr(Y = 0, C = 0 \mid X = \mathbf{x}_i, E = e_i) \\
&\qquad + w_i \log \Pr(Y = 0, C = 1 \mid X = \mathbf{x}_i, E = e_i) \qquad (12) \\
&= (1 - w_i) \log(1 - p(\mathbf{x}_i)) + w_i \left[\log(p(\mathbf{x}_i)) - \lambda(\mathbf{x}_i) e_i\right]
\end{aligned}$$

Plugging (6) and (12) into (11), the quantity to be maximized during the M step over the parameters of p and λ (w being fixed) can finally be summarized as (remember that $w_i = 1$ for $y_i = 1$):

$$\begin{aligned}
&\sum_i w_i \log p(\mathbf{x}_i) + (1 - w_i) \log(1 - p(\mathbf{x}_i)) \\
&+ \sum_i \log(\lambda(\mathbf{x}_i)) y_i - \lambda(\mathbf{x}_i) t_i w_i
\end{aligned} \qquad (13)$$

with

$$t_i := \begin{cases} e_i & \text{if } y_i = 0 \\ d_i & \text{if } y_i = 1 \end{cases}.$$

Equation 13 has two interesting properties:

1. It is easy to optimize since the log-likelihood decomposes, in other words p and λ can be optimized independently. And each of these optimization problems is convex.

2. It is easily interpretable: the optimization on p is a weighted logistic regression, while the optimization on λ is a standard exponential regression in survival models [7, Section 3.5] where the unlabeled samples have their censored times multiplied by w_i.

The drawback of this EM algorithm is that it is a nested optimization problem: each M step requires an optimization on the parameters of p and λ. This typically implies slow convergence. To speed-up training, the M step can be solved approximately [8] or the likelihood can be directly optimized as described below.

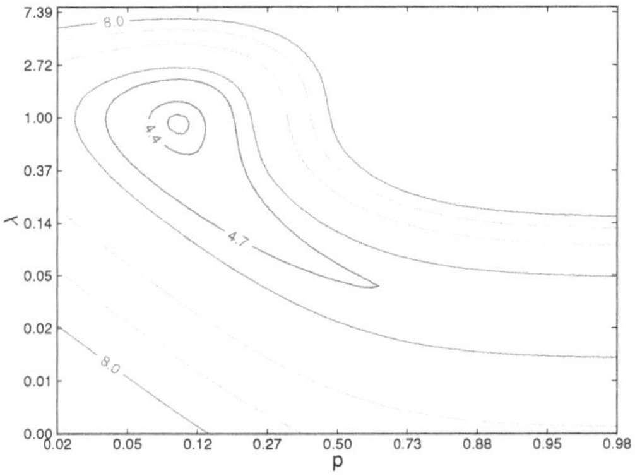

Figure 3: Negative log-likelihood as a function of λ and p on a toy example consisting of one positive sample with a delay of 1 and 10 negatives samples with a delay of 4.

4.2 Joint optimization

The optimization method we implemented for the experiments in this paper is a gradient descent algorithm on the regularized negative log likelihood with respect to the parameters of p and λ:

$$\arg\min_{\mathbf{w}_c,\mathbf{w}_d} L(\mathbf{w}_c,\mathbf{w}_d) + \frac{\mu}{2}(\|\mathbf{w}_c\|_2^2 + \|\mathbf{w}_d\|_2^2), \tag{14}$$

where μ is a regularization parameter and L is the negative log likelihood,

$$\begin{aligned} L(\mathbf{w}_c,\mathbf{w}_d) = &- \sum_{i,\ y_i=1} \log p(\mathbf{x}_i) + \log\lambda(\mathbf{x}_i) - \lambda(\mathbf{x}_i)d_i \\ &- \sum_{i,\ y_i=0} \log[1 - p(\mathbf{x}_i) + p(\mathbf{x}_i)\exp(-\lambda(\mathbf{x}_i)e_i)] \\ \text{with}\ \ p(\mathbf{x}) = &\frac{1}{1+\exp(-\mathbf{w}_c\cdot\mathbf{x})}, \quad \lambda(\mathbf{x}) = \exp(\mathbf{w}_d\cdot\mathbf{x}). \end{aligned} \tag{15}$$

This likelihood is the probability (6) of observing Y and D in the case of a conversion and the probability (9) of observing Y otherwise, these probabilities being conditioned on X, E and the model parameters.

Note that the objective function (15) is not convex as illustrated on the toy example of figure 3. The non-convexity can be understood intuitively because of the potential ambiguity when observing a majority of clicks without conversion: is the conversion rate low or are the delays long? As seen on figure 3 there are indeed two solutions which explain the data almost equally well: low conversion rate and short delay (upper left hand corner) or high conversion rate and long delay (lower right hand corner). This ambiguity typically vanishes as the number of data increases and we have not encountered any local minimum issue in our experiments.

Using the chain-rule, the gradients of the negative log-likelihood with respect to $\mathbf{w}_c$ and $\mathbf{w}_d$ are:

$$\begin{aligned} \frac{\partial L}{\partial \mathbf{w}_c} = &\sum_{i,\ y_i=1} -\frac{1}{p(\mathbf{x}_i)}\frac{\partial p(\mathbf{x}_i)}{\partial \mathbf{w}_c} \\ &+ \sum_{i,\ y_i=0} \frac{1-\exp(-\lambda(\mathbf{x}_i)e_i)}{1-p(\mathbf{x}_i)+p(\mathbf{x}_i)\exp(-\lambda(\mathbf{x}_i)e_i)}\frac{\partial p(\mathbf{x}_i)}{\partial \mathbf{w}_c} \end{aligned} \tag{16}$$

$$\begin{aligned} \frac{\partial L}{\partial \mathbf{w}_d} = &\sum_{i,\ y_i=1} \left(d_i - \frac{1}{\lambda(\mathbf{x}_i)}\right)\frac{\partial \lambda(\mathbf{x}_i)}{\partial \mathbf{w}_d} \\ &+ \sum_{i,\ y_i=0} \frac{p(\mathbf{x}_i)e_i\exp(-\lambda(\mathbf{x}_i)e_i)}{1-p(\mathbf{x}_i)+p(\mathbf{x}_i)\exp(-\lambda(\mathbf{x}_i)e_i)}\frac{\partial \lambda(\mathbf{x}_i)}{\partial \mathbf{w}_d} \end{aligned} \tag{17}$$

Since the optimization problem is unconstrained and twice differentiable, it can be solved with any gradient based optimization technique. We use L-BFGS [15], a state-of-the-art optimizer.

The effect of an unlabeled sample ($y_i = 0$) on the conversion model is best understood by examining its contribution to the gradient (16) of the conversion model parameters in two extreme cases:

1. When $\lambda(\mathbf{x}_i)e_i \ll 1$, that is when the elapsed time since the click is short compared to the predicted mean delay $\lambda(\mathbf{x}_i)^{-1}$: the numerator in (16) is close to 0 and that sample has almost no influence on the conversion model. This is expected since the click is too recent and it cannot be inferred that the user will not convert.

2. When $\lambda(\mathbf{x}_i)e_i \gg 1$, that is when the elapsed time is much longer than the predicted mean delay: the gradient contribution is $1/(1-p(\mathbf{x}_i))$, which is the same as the gradient of a negative sample in logistic regression. In that case the model effectively considers that sample as a negative one since there is enough evidence to believe that the user will not convert.

5. RELATED WORK

As pointed in the introduction, our work is closely related to learning from positive and unlabeled data and to survival analysis. The negatives samples should indeed be considered as unlabeled since a conversion can take place in the future. There has been a substantial amount of research on this topic: see [4] and references therein. Equation (3) of that paper is identical to the first part of our equation (13): all positive examples are counted with a weight of 1, while an unlabeled example is considered to be a mixture of a positive example (with weight w_i) and of a negative example (with weight $1 - w_i$). However these papers rely on the assumption that the labels of a positive sample is missing at random. This assumption does not hold in our scenario since the probability of a conversion not having been observed yet depends on the elapsed time since the click. This is the reason why that time is present in the weight (10).

The link between our model and survival analysis is easy to establish in the extreme case of users always converting: in that case $w_i = 1$ in (10) and the second part of equation (13) is a standard exponential regression [7, Section 3.5]. There is a closed form solution for a model without features:

$$\frac{1}{\lambda} = \frac{\sum t_i}{\sum y_i}.$$

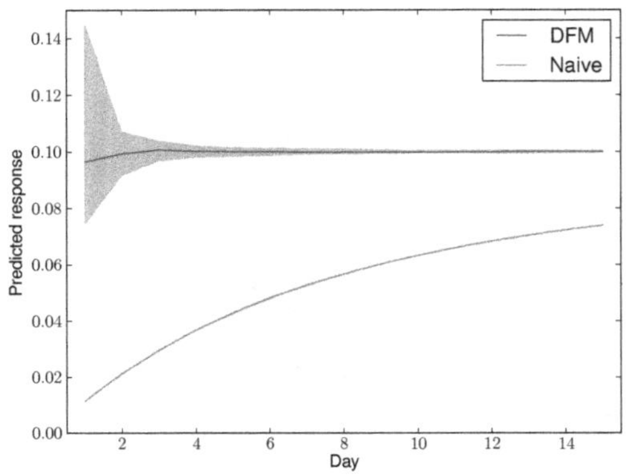

Figure 4: Convergence of the predicted conversion rate on a toy example with a true conversion rate 0.1 and an average conversion delay of 4 days. The error bars are at 25% and 75%. The NAIVE method treats all clicks without conversion as negatives.

Our delay model can thus been seen as an extension of a survival analysis model in which the censored times t_i are weighted by the probability of conversions w_i (see equation (13)). When w_i is small, the corresponding time t_i has almost no influence on the likelihood function.

There has been several prior works on predicting conversion rates for display advertising [1, 12, 9, 16], but none of them address the problem of conversion delay. Since we are unaware of any method for this delayed feedback issue, we are not comparing our algorithm against previously published algorithms, but against a reasonable heuristic that will be presented in the next section.

6. EXPERIMENTAL EVALUATION

6.1 Toy example

As discussed in section 2.4, the emergence of new campaigns every day entails frequent updates of the model in order to learn the statistics of these campaigns. We consider the following simulated example in order to assess how fast a model can react to a single new campaign. Data are generated with a conversion rate $p = 0.1$ and with conversion delays following an exponential distribution with mean 4 days. There are no features associated with the training examples and we just learn constant predictors for p and λ.

The model is retrained every day and the predicted conversion rate as a function of the number of days of available data is shown in figure 4. This simulation has been ran 100 times and the plot includes median, 25% and 75% quantiles. The proposed model, *Delayed Feedback Model* (DFM) correctly predicts the conversion rate after just two days of data, which is less than mean delay (4 days). After one day of data the median predicted value is quite accurate, but the error bars are large. This is due to the ambiguity illustrated in figure 3: when few conversions have been observed, it is unclear whether the conversion rate is low or the delays are long.

As a comparison, the NAIVE method that treats the no-conversions as negatives underpredicts the conversion rate, especially at the beginning of the campaign.

6.2 Conversion delays

We have already analyzed the overall distribution of conversion delays in figure 1. Next, we want to assess whether the exponential distribution (5) used in our delay modeling is reasonable. Note that (5) is a *conditional* distribution (conditioned on the feature vector) whereas figure 1 plots the marginal distribution. Even if the conditional distributions are exponential, the marginal may not be. Since it is impossible to inspect the full conditional distribution (not enough samples for a given feature vector), we plotted instead in figure 5 delay distributions conditioned on the campaign only.

Four observations can be drawn from these plots. First, there is a 24 hours cyclicality; this can easily be explained by the fact that people tend to use their computer at a certain time of day, and thus a conversion is more likely to happen at the same hour of the day as the click. Second, notwithstanding this cyclicality, the empirical distributions (blue lines) are rather close to the matched exponential distributions (green lines). Third, the exponential model has a tendency to under-predict short delays (<1h) and over-predict long delays; in other words, it seems that the delay distribution is a mixture of a short delay and a long one. And finally, the previous observation seems more pronounced for campaigns with shorter average delays (first row of figure 5).

6.3 Competing models

Since we are unaware of an algorithm addressing the delayed feedback issue, we implemented the following heuristic, that we call the *Short Term Conversion model* (STC). A first model is trained to predict the conversions that occur in a short time frame after the click; and another one applies a correction factor to account for conversions occurring afterwards. More specifically these two models are

1. A probability of converting within a day,

$$\Pr(C = 1, D \leq 1 \text{ day} \mid X = \mathbf{x}) \tag{18}$$

2. A model predicting the ratio of short term conversions among all conversions,

$$\frac{\Pr(C = 1, D \leq 1 \text{ day} \mid X = \mathbf{x})}{\Pr(C = 1 \mid X = \mathbf{x})} = \Pr(D \leq 1 \text{ day} \mid C = 1, X = \mathbf{x}). \tag{19}$$

The final predicted probability is defined as the ratio of the predictions from these models. The motivation behind STC is that the first model can be reactive to change of distributions, new campaigns, etc. since the lag between a click and its inclusion in the training set is only one day. As for the second model, there is still a 30 day lag to construct its training set, but hopefully this model is relatively stable over time and the lag would not hinder its performance.

The second model is a classification problem but it is closely related to our delay model. Indeed, according to that model, it is equal to $1 - \exp(-\lambda(\mathbf{x}) \times 1 \text{ day})$. The potential benefit of our proposed approach is that both the conversion and the delay models can be updated shortly after an event.

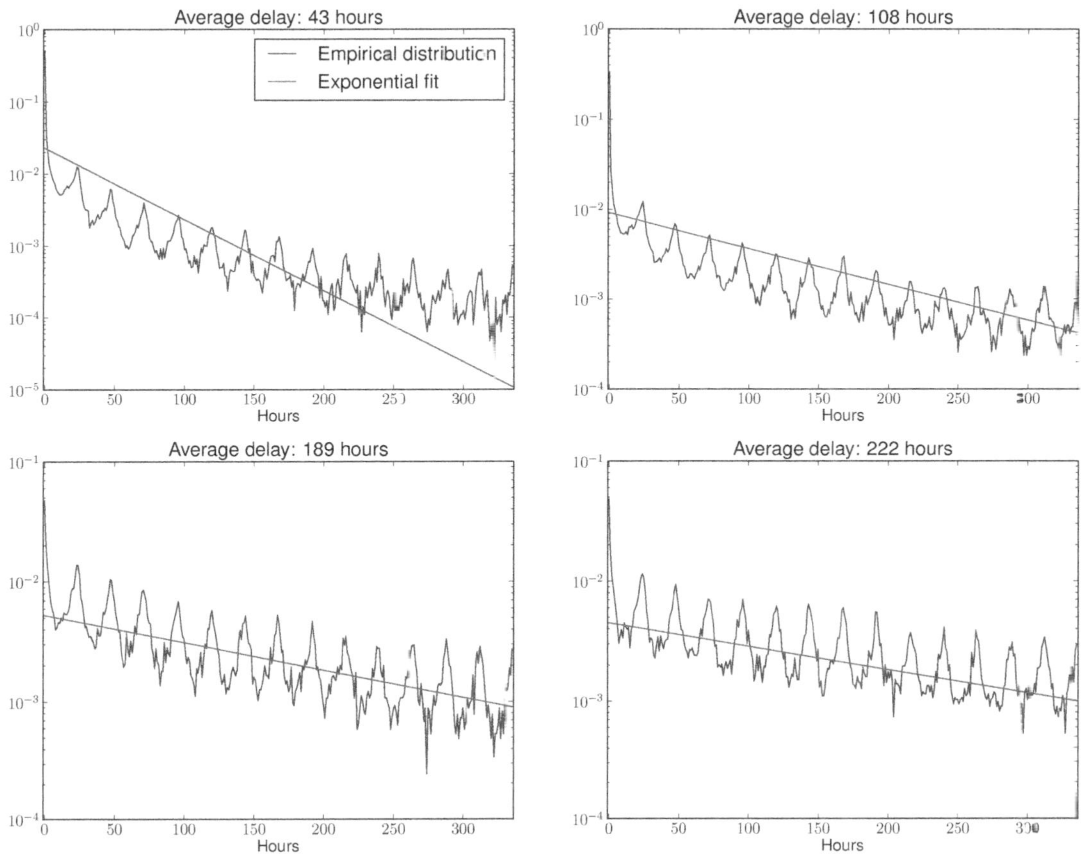

Figure 5: Probability density functions of the delays between clicks and conversions for 4 different campaigns (blue curves) along with the best exponential fits (green curves). The caption indicates the average delay for the corresponding campaign.

In addition to the above STC model and our proposed *Delayed Feedback Model* (DFM), the following baselines have been evaluated:

NAIVE Classification algorithm where the clicks without associated conversion so far are treated as negatives. It has the drawback of underestimating the conversion rate (see figure 4) because it incorrectly considers as negative a click for which a conversion will happen in the future.

ORACLE Same as above, but the labels are given by an oracle that can look into the future to determine if there will be a conversion. This is an upper bound on the best achievable performance as it is oblivious to the delay issue.

SHIFTED The training set is shifted 30 days in the past in order to correctly label all the clicks. There is thus no more uncertainty in the labels, but the dataset is 30 days old.

RESCALE Same as NAIVE, but the probabilities of conversion are divided by a constant, which is the overall probability of having a missing label on the test set. This is in fact the method of choice when learning with positive and unlabeled data and the labels are missing at random (see [4, Lemma 1]).

Because the RESCALE and the STC models involve ratios, they may predict probabilities larger than 1. To avoid this issue their predictions have been truncated to 0.99.

6.4 Features and setting

Most of the features considered in these experiments are categorical and the continuous features and have been made categorical through appropriate quantization. The model also includes cross-features, defined as the cartesian product of two categorical features. These features are useful to introduce non-linearities in the model. All the features are mapped into a sparse binary feature vector of dimension 2^{24} via the *hashing trick* [17]. More details about the data representation and the hashing trick can be found in [2].

		SHIFTED	NAIVE	RESCALE	STC	DFM	ORACLE
Overall	NLL	0.4004	0.4076	0.4042	0.4111	**0.3960**	0.3889
	Diff	0.0115	0.0187	0.0154	0.0222	**0.0072**	—
Recent	NLL	0.4176	0.4398	0.4248	0.4117	**0.4006**	0.3640
	Diff	0.0537	0.0758	0.0608	0.0477	**0.0366**	—

Table 1: Negative log likelihood of different methods (lower is better) and difference with respect to the ORACLE **method. In the lower part of the table, the test set is restricted to the *recent* campaigns.**

The experimental setting is as follows: there are 7 days of test data and for each test day, a model is trained with the previous 3 weeks. Each training set contains a bit less than 6M examples. For reproducibility of the results, the dataset used in these experiments can be downloaded from `http://labs.criteo.com/tag/dataset`.

The metric used for evaluation is the average negative log-likelihood (NLL). We are not reporting standard predictions metrics for classification such as the average area under the ROC curve or precision/recall curve because these metrics are insensitive to the absolute value of the predictions. In our setting, the predicted probabilities are important because they are directly used in (1) to compute the value of an impression .

We provide two set of results in our evaluation: a global one on the entire test set, and another one on the *recent* campaigns only. Recent campaigns are defined as the ones which have more volume in the one week test set than in the preceding 3 week training set. This portion of the traffic is more challenging to predict as there is fewer historical data to learn from.

All of our models have an L_2 regularization on the weights (see equation (14)). We did not use L_1 regularization as a dimensionality reduction technique because, as advocated in [2], the hashing trick is more convenient and as efficient as L_1 regularization for this purpose. We set the regularization parameter with a rule of thumb,

$$\mu := \frac{1}{n}\sum_{i=1}^{n} \|\mathbf{x}_i\|_2^2.$$

This heuristic has also been used as the default choice in SVMLight [6].

Finally all the models have been trained using an L-BFGS optimizer, including our DFM model (see section 4.2).

6.5 Results

The results are provided in table 1. Our proposed DFM method improves the NLL of almost 3% compared to the NAIVE baseline, which is considered substantial for our application. It is also not too far from the upper bound given by the ORACLE method. On the most recent campaigns, the difference between methods is, as expected, more pronounced and DFM does better than the SHIFTED method that has a 30 days old training set. As for the NAIVE method, it underpredicts on average by 21%, confirming the analysis done on the simulated example (see figure 4). The RESCALE method is much better calibrated: it underpredicts by only 5.9% overall, but this number goes to 30% on the recent campaigns. This is because the labels for recent campaigns are more likely to be missing than for the other campaigns. Finally the STC model achieved mixed results: it is the best competing method on the recent campaigns, but the worse one overall.

7. CONCLUSION

We have presented in this paper a technique that addresses the lag in conversions by modeling the conversion delay. This technique is rather simple to implement as it only relies on gradient descent optimization and it provides more accurate conversion predictions than several baselines. It is however not specific to display advertising and could by applied to any problem where the model needs to be updated with recent data, but where the associated labels may come with a delay.

8. REFERENCES

[1] D. Agarwal, R. Agrawal, R. Khanna, and N. Kota. Estimating rates of rare events with multiple hierarchies through scalable log-linear models. In *Proceedings of the 16th ACM SIGKDD international conference on Knowledge discovery and data mining*, pages 213–222. ACM, 2010.

[2] O. Chapelle, E. Manavoglu, and R. Rosales. Simple and scalable response prediction for display advertising. *Transactions on Intelligent Systems and Technology*, 2014. To appear.

[3] F. Denis, R. Gilleron, and F. Letouzey. Learning from positive and unlabeled examples. *Theoretical Computer Science*, 348(1):70–83, 2005.

[4] C. Elkan and K. Noto. Learning classifiers from only positive and unlabeled data. In *Proceedings of the 14th ACM SIGKDD international conference on Knowledge discovery and data mining*, pages 213–220. ACM, 2008.

[5] D. Hillard, S. Schroedl, E. Manavoglu, H. Raghavan, and C. Leggetter. Improving ad relevance in sponsored search. In *Proceedings of the third ACM international conference on Web search and data mining*, pages 361–370, 2010.

[6] T. Joachims. Making large-scale support vector machine learning practical. In *Advances in kernel methods*, pages 169–184. MIT Press, 1999. `svmlight.joachims.org`.

[7] J. D. Kalbfleisch and R. L. Prentice. *The statistical analysis of failure time data*, volume 360 of *Wiley Series in Probability and Statistics*. John Wiley & Sons, 2nd edition, 2002.

[8] K. Lange. A gradient algorithm locally equivalent to the EM algorithm. *Journal of the Royal Statistical Society. Series B (Methodological)*, 57(2):425–437, 1995.

[9] K.-C. Lee, B. Orten, A. Dasdan, and W. Li. Estimating conversion rate in display advertising from past erformance data. In *Proceedings of the 18th ACM SIGKDD international conference on Knowledge discovery and data mining*, pages 768–776. ACM, 2012.

[10] R. P. McAfee. The design of advertising exchanges. *Review of Industrial Organization*, 39(3):169–185, 2011.

[11] H. B. McMahan, G. Holt, D. Sculley, et al. Ad click prediction: a view from the trenches. In *Proceedings of the 19th ACM SIGKDD international conference on Knowledge discovery and data mining*, pages 1222–1230. ACM, 2013.

[12] A. K. Menon, K.-P. Chitrapura, S. Garg, D. Agarwal, and N. Kota. Response prediction using collaborative filtering with hierarchies and side-information. In *Proceedings of the 17th ACM SIGKDD international conference on Knowledge discovery and data mining*, 2011.

[13] R. G. Miller Jr. *Survival analysis*, volume 66. Wiley-Interscience, 2nd edition, 1998.

[14] S. Muthukrishnan. Ad exchanges: Research issues. In *Proceedings of the 5th International Workshop on Internet and Network Economics*, 2009.

[15] J. Nocedal. Updating quasi-newton matrices with limited storage. *Mathematics of computation*, 35(151):773–782, 1980.

[16] R. Rosales, H. Cheng, and E. Manavoglu. Post-click conversion modeling and analysis for non-guaranteed delivery display advertising. In *Proceedings of the fifth ACM international conference on Web search and data mining*, pages 293–302. ACM, 2012

[17] K. Weinberger, A. Dasgupta, J. Langford, A. Smola, and J. Attenberg. Feature hashing for large scale multitask learning. In *Proceedings of the 26th Annual International Conference on Machine Learning*, pages 1113–1120, 2009.

Networked Bandits with Disjoint Linear Payoffs

Meng Fang
Centre for Quantum Comp. & Intelligent Syst.
University of Technology, Sydney
235 Jones Street, Ultimo, NSW 2007, Australia
Meng.Fang@student.uts.edu.au

Dacheng Tao
Centre for Quantum Comp. & Intelligent Syst.
University of Technology, Sydney
235 Jones Street, Ultimo, NSW 2007, Australia
Dacheng.Tao@uts.edu.au

ABSTRACT

In this paper, we study 'networked bandits', a new bandit problem where a set of interrelated arms varies over time and, given the contextual information that selects one arm, invokes other correlated arms. This problem remains under-investigated, in spite of its applicability to many practical problems. For instance, in social networks, an arm can obtain payoffs from both the selected user and its relations since they often share the content through the network. We examine whether it is possible to obtain multiple payoffs from several correlated arms based on the relationships. In particular, we formalize the networked bandit problem and propose an algorithm that considers not only the selected arm, but also the relationships between arms. Our algorithm is 'optimism in face of uncertainty' style, in that it decides an arm depending on integrated confidence sets constructed from historical data. We analyze the performance in simulation experiments and on two real-world offline datasets. The experimental results demonstrate our algorithm's effectiveness in the networked bandit setting.

Categories and Subject Descriptors

H.3.5 [**Information Systems**]: Social and Information Networks; I.2.6 [**Computing Methodologies**]: [Learning]

General Terms

Algorithm, Theory

Keywords

Networked bandits; social network; exploration/exploitation dilemma

1. INTRODUCTION

A multi-armed bandit problem (or bandit problem) is a sequential decision problem defined by a set of actions (or arms). The term 'bandit' originates from the colloquial term for a casino slot machine ('a one-armed bandit'), in which a player (or a forecaster) faces a finite number of slot machines (or arms). The player sequentially allocates coins (one at a time) to different machines and earns money (or payoff) depending on the machine selected. The goal is to earn as high a payoff as possible.

Robbins formalized this problem in 1952 [20]; in the multi-armed bandit problem, K arms exist that are associated with unknown payoff distributions, and a forecaster can select an arm sequentially. In each round of play, a forecaster selects one arm and then receives the payoff from the selected arm. The forecaster's aim is to maximize the total cumulative payoff, i.e., the sum of the payoffs of the chosen arms in total. Since the forecaster does not know the process generating the payoffs but has historical payoffinformation, the bandit problem highlights the fundamental difficultly of decision making in the face of uncertainty: balancing the decision of whether to exploit past choices or make new choices with the hope of discovering a better one.

The bandit problem has been studied for many years, with works primarily focusing on the theory and designing different algorithms based on different settings, such as the stochastic setting, adversarial setting, and contextual setting [9]. In real-world applications, the multi-armed bandit problem is an effective way of solving situations where one encounters an exploration-exploitation dilemma. It has historically been used to decide which clinical trial is better when multiple treatments are available for a given disease and there is a need to decide which treatment to use on the next patient.

Modern technologies have created many opportunities for use of the bandit problem, and it has a wide range of applications including advertising, recommendation systems, online systems, and games. For example, an advertising task may be the choice of which advertisement to display to the next visitor to a web page, where the payoff is associated with the visitor's actions. More recently, the bandit algorithm has been used in personalized recommendation tasks [17], where a user visits a website and the system collects the user's information. The system selectively provides content from a content pool through the user's current and past behaviors analyzing to best satisfy the user's needs, and the payoff is based on user-click feedback.

All the above bandit problems have the major underlying assumption that all the arms are independent, which is inappropriate for web-based social network applications. In a network, including social networks, the users are connected by relationships [2, 22]. Contextual information can

KDD'14, August 24–27, 2014, New York, NY, USA.
Copyright 2014 ACM 978-1-4503-2956-9/14/08 ...$15.00.
http://dx.doi.org/10.1145/2623330.2623672.

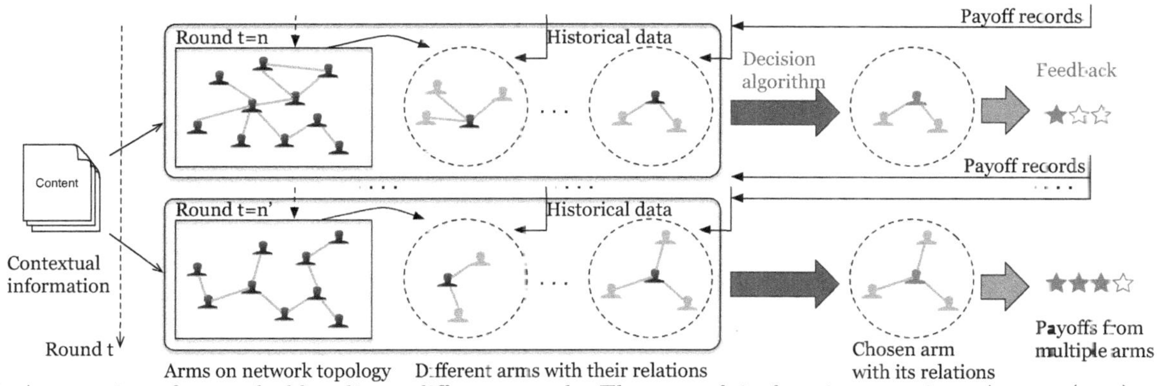

Figure 1: An overview of networked bandits at different rounds. The network is changing over time. An arm (user) can invoke other arms (relations) and have different relations at different rounds. Given the contextual information an arm is chosen by the decision algorithm for getting multiple payoffs (feedback). The algorithm improves the selection strategy after collecting new payoffinformation.

be obtained from other users and can be spread via these relationships. Content promoted to one user provides feedback, not only from that user, but also from his/her relations. For example, a user of Twitter or Facebook can read a tweet/message and can re-post someone else's tweet/message, allowing the user to quickly share it with his/her followers. Impact can be assessed by counting the number of 'favorites/likes' from different users' pages. Therefore, careful selection of a user for tweet/message posting can maximize the number of 'favorites/likes'.

Our study is motivated by the observation that even when a user is randomly selected for promotion, other users close to the selected user in the network will be influenced [18, 22]. Specifically, as shown in Figure 1, in a social network, if we promote a content to a user, the user may share it with others and the payoffs can be collected from the user and its relations. The goal is to gain higher payoffs. The process is similar to share-then-like, which occurs daily in social networks and needs to be considered for optimized recommendation and advertising tasks, the important point being that the context is extended from the selected user to all other invoked users. There are several challenges to realizing this problem. First, only partial information is available about the chosen users when content is posted, and the information of other users is unknown. Therefore, there is a dilemma of whether the system should select a user with the best payoff history or a new user in order to explore more possibilities. Second, the content may frequently change and few overlapping historical records may exist. Furthermore, relationships exist between users and these relationships may change over time. These challenges inspire us to formalize the networked bandit problem.

The above problem can be considered a balance of the trade-off between exploration (discovering a new user) and exploitation (using the current best user) when network topology is known.

We formalize a well-defined but simple setting for the networked bandit problem, in which there exist K arms connected by network topology G. We propose an approach in which a learning algorithm optimally selects an arm at each round based on contextual information and the network topology information of arms. The networked bandit problem can be considered an extension of the contextual multi-armed bandit problem, the difference being that in our problem the arm can be connected to other arms and the payoffs come from the multiple arms.

Our contribution is three-fold: first, we formalize a new networked bandit problem motivated by real network applications; second, we provide an algorithm based on confidence sets to solve it along with theoretical analysis; and third, we design a set of experiments to test and evaluate the algorithm. To the best of our knowledge, we define and solve this problem for the first time and answer the fundamental question of how to define regret when payoffs come from interrelated multiple arms. We design an effective strategy to select arms in order to increase payoffs over time, known as NetBandits, which provides a solution to this problem. Our approach is an 'optimism in the face of uncertainty'-style algorithm that considers the integrated confidence sets and we prove a regret bound for it. Finally, we analyze empirically the performance, which shows that our algorithm is effective in the networked bandit setting.

2. RELATED WORK

The traditional multi-armed bandit problem does not assume that side information is observed. The forecaster's goal is to maximize the sum of payoffs over time based on the historical payoff information. There are two basic settings. In the first, the stochastic setting, the payoffs are i.i.d. drawn from an unknown distribution. The upper confidence bound (UCB) strategy has been used to explore the exploration-exploitation trade-off [4, 6, 16], in which an upper bound estimate is constructed on the mean of each arm at a fixed confidence level, and then the arm with the best estimate is selected. In the second, the adversarial setting, the i.i.d. assumption does not exist. Auer et al. [7] proposed the EXP3 algorithm for the adversarial setting, which was later improved by Bubeck and Audibert [3].

The contextual multi-armed bandit problem is a natural extension of the original bandit problem. Our setting addresses bandit problem with contextual information. Compared to the traditional K-armed bandit problem the forecaster may use action features to infer the payoff in the contextual setting. This problem largely considers the linear model assumption about payoff of action [1, 5, 12, 14, 21]. Auer [5] proposed the LinRel algorithm, a UCB-style algorithm that has a regret of $\tilde{O}(\sqrt{Td})$. Dani et al [14] studied the LinRel and provided an $\tilde{O}(d\sqrt{T})$ regret bound and proved this upper bound is tight. Chu et al. [12] provided the LinUCB and SupLinUCB algorithms, and proved an $O(\sqrt{Td\log^3(KT\log(T)/\delta)})$ regret bound for SupLinUCB that holds with probability $1-\delta$. Abbasi-Yadkori et al. [1] proposed an algorithm that modified the UCB-style algorithm based on the confidence sets, and showed a regret of $O(d\log(1/\delta)/\Delta)$.

Recently, the bandit problem has been used in real-life problems, such as recommendation systems and advertising. Li et al. [17] first introduced the bandit problem to recommendation systems by considering a personalized recommendation as a feature-based exploration-exploitation problem. This problem was formalized as a contextual bandit problem with disjoint linear payoffs and by focusing on the article-selection strategy based on user-click feedback, maximizing the total number of clicks. The features of the users and articles were defined as contextual information, and the expected payoff of an arm was assumed to be a linear function of its contextual features, including the user and article information. Finally, the LinUCB algorithm was proposed to solve this problem and attained a good empirical regret. They further extended the algorithm as SupLinUCB and provided the theoretical analysis [12].

There are limited studies that consider the networked bandit problem or that combine bandit problem and network. Buccapatnam et al. [10] considered the bandit problem in social networks, and assumed that the forecaster can take advantage of side observations of neighbors, except for the selected user (arm). The side observations were used to update the sample mean of other related users and the payoff of the selected arm was collected each time, the goal once again being to maximize the total cumulative payoff of selected arms. Bnaya et al. [8] considered a bandit view for network exploration and proposed VUCB1 to handle the dynamic changes in arms when crawling the network. More recently, Cesa-Bianchi et al. [11] considered the recommendation problem by taking advantage of the relationships between users in the network. They proposed GOB.Lin, which models the similarity between users and used this similarity to help predict the behavior of other users.

Our work belongs to the contextual bandit setting. However, in contrast to these previous studies we assume that the arms (actions) are correlated in the network. The selected arm can invoke other related arms and the forecaster obtains multiple payoffs from these arms. It is a more general setting in networked bandit problem.

3. NETWORKED BANDITS

We consider a network G. Let $\mathcal{V}$ indicate the nodes in the network and $\mathcal{E}$ indicate the edges of the network. We can then use $G=(\mathcal{V},\mathcal{E})$ to represent the networked bandits where $v\in\mathcal{V}$ can be considered as an arm and $e\in\mathcal{E}$ indicates the relationship between arms; nodes here are correlated. Thus, given the network G and a node v, it is possible to obtain the information for the node v and its relations $N(v)$.

In our formulation, we consider a sequential decision problem with contextual information. At round t, except for contextual information x_t, we have a network topology of arms denoted by G_t. Given v we let $N_t(v)$ be its relations and $N_t(v)$ may change over time. If v is selected then $N_t(v)$ will also be invoked. We define this setting as networked bandits. Formally, a networked bandit algorithm $\mathcal{A}$ proceeds as follows: at each round t, the algorithm observes a set of arms $\mathcal{K}_t=\{1,2,\cdots,k\}_t$, contextual information x_t, and the network topology G_t of arms associated with the relationships of arms. The set of relations of arm a is denoted by $N_t(a)$. If we also consider the information of arms, we can redefine the context as a set $\mathcal{C}_t=\{x_{1,t},\cdots,x_{k,t}\}$ by adding arms' information. When the algorithm selects an arm a_t, the a_t will invoke other related arms $N_t(a_t)$. $N_t(a_t)$ can be observed based on the network topology of arms. Before the decision algorithm selects the arm, it observes G_t, $\mathcal{C}_t$, and $\mathcal{K}_t$. Based on historical payoff records, the algorithm selects an arm a_t and receives a set of payoffs $\{y_{a_t}\}\cup\{y_a|a\in N_t(a_t)\}$. The algorithm will improve the selection strategy after collecting new payoff information. It then proceeds to the next round $t+1$. Note that traditional contextual bandit problems usually assume that the arms are independent. However, in our problem, we assume that the correlation exists between the chosen arm and its relations. After a total T rounds the cumulative payoff is defined as $\sum_{t=1}^{T} g_{a_t,t}$, where $g_{a_t,t}=\sum_{a\in N_t(a_t)} y_a + y_{a_t}$ and y_a is the payoff from arm a. For simplicity, we use $N_t(a)$ to indicate both a and its relations. We rewrite $g_{a_t,t}$ as $g_{a_t,t}=\sum_{a\in N_t(a_t)} y_a$.

For this networked bandit problem, the algorithm $\mathcal{A}$ selects an arm a_t at each round $t=1,2,\cdots$ and receives the associate payoff $g_{a_t,t}$. After n selections $a_1,a_2,\cdots,a_n$ we define the regret as follows:

$$\mathcal{R}_n=\max_{a=1,\cdots,k}\sum_{t=1}^{n} g_{a,t}-\sum_{t=1}^{n} g_{a_t,t}. \tag{1}$$

The regret can now be used to compare the best decision with the algorithm $\mathcal{A}$. In this problem, $\mathcal{R}_n$ is a random variable; therefore, the goal is to calculate the expectation of $\mathcal{R}_n$ with high probability, and it is not easy to obtain expectation directly since its search space is large. Normally we try to bound the pseudo-regret, i.e.,

$$\overline{\mathcal{R}}_n=\max_{a=1,\cdots,k}\mathbb{E}\sum_{t=1}^{n} g_{a,t}-\mathbb{E}\sum_{t=1}^{n} g_{a_t,t}, \tag{2}$$

where the pseudo-regret competes against the optimal action in the expectation.

There are two important issues in the networked bandit problem: arms and their network topology. In the context of a social network, the users in the pool may be viewed as arms, the provided message or article as context, and the user's information as additional contextual information. The new context vector then summarizes information of both user and context. A payoff of 1 is incurred when a provided message is 'favorited' or 'liked'; otherwise, the payoff is 0. The network topology of a social network naturally constructs the relationships between users. When a message is posted to a user, the message can be seen by relations (followers). The payoff can be collected from the user's page (selected arm). Furthermore, any 'like', 'share', or 'comment' action by a follower will allow the message to be reposted on the follower's page and to be seen by the follower's friends. The payoff can then be collected from the followers' pages (invoked arms). In the special case that the follower does not repost the message, the payoff can be considered as 0 or the arm is not invoked. For simplicity, we only consider the selected arm and its relations. With these definitions of payoff, arm, and invoked arms, the collected payoff after selecting an arm involves the selected user and his/her relations. Thus, the payoff at round t is defined as $g_{a_t,t} = \sum_{a \in N_t(a_t)} y_a$.

It is assumed that algorithm $\mathcal{A}$ can observe the network topology prior to make a decision. This is intuitive, since network structure information between users can easily be collected or the network structure information can be obtained in advance. In practice, given an arm, we only need concern itself with the invoked arms, and therefore knowledge of full network topology is unnecessary. The invoked arms depend on how we define $N_t(a)$. The worst case scenario is that the whole network needs to be searched to find the invoked arms and feedback; however, we do not concern how to constrict $N_t(a)$ using such a network propagation model since, as stated above, we only focus on the selection strategy and we simplify the problem by only observing the invoked arms.

4. ALGORITHM

In this work, we propose an algorithm to solve the networked bandit problem and show that an integrated confidence bound can efficiently be computed in a closed form when the payoff model of an arm is linear. As with previous contextual bandit work [17], we assume that the expected payoff of an arm a is linear in context x_t and coefficient w_a. At round t, for arm a given context $x_{a,t}$, we assume that the expected payoff of the arm a is a linear function:

$$\mathbb{E}\left[y_{a,t}|x_{a,t}\right] = x_{a,t}^\top w_a + \epsilon_a, \tag{3}$$

where different arms have different w_a and ϵ_a is conditionally R-sub-Gaussian when $R \leq 0$ is a fixed constant. Formally, this means that $\forall\lambda$ and we have

$$\mathbb{E}\left[e^{\lambda\epsilon_{a,t}}|x_{a,1:t}, \epsilon_{a,1:t-1}\right] \leq \exp\left(\frac{\lambda^2 R^2}{2}\right), \tag{4}$$

where $x_{a,1:t}$ denotes the sequence $x_{a,1}, x_{a,2}, \cdots, x_{a,t}$ and, similarly $\epsilon_{a,1:t-1}$ denotes the sequence $\epsilon_{a,1}, \cdots, \epsilon_{a,t-1}$. The arms therefore have disjoint linear payoffs. The decision of the algorithm lies on w with distribution ϵ. Based on our R-sub-Gaussian assumption of the noise, we can obtain meaningful upper bound on the regret. According to this sub-Gaussian condition, we know that $\mathbb{E}\left[\epsilon_{a,t}|x_{a,1:t}, \epsilon_{a,1:t-1}\right] = 0$ and $\mathbb{VAR}[\epsilon_{a,t}|x_{a,1:t}, \epsilon_{a,1:t-1}] \leq R^2$. The conditions therefore show that $\epsilon_{a,t}$ is bounded by a zero-mean noise lying in an interval of length of at most $2R$.

As the networked bandit problem, the algorithm faces a set of uncertainties of arms which involve $N_t(a)$. We design a new algorithm which is the 'optimism in the face of uncertainty' principle, by maintaining confidence of parameter w for each arm. The basic idea is to construct the confidence sets for parameters of each disjoint payoff function and then provide an integrated upper bound.

We use technology from the 'self-normalized bound for vector-valued martingales' [19] and confidence sets [1]. For each arm $\hat{w}_a$ is defined as the L^2-regularized least-squares estimate of w_a^* with regularization parameter $\lambda > 0$:

$$\hat{w}_a = (X_a^\top X_a + \lambda)^{-1} X_a^\top Y_a, \tag{5}$$

where X_a is the matrix whose rows are $x_1, \cdots, x_{n_a(t)}$ corresponding to historical contexts of an arm a and $Y_a \in \mathbb{R}^{n_a(t)}$ is the corresponding historical payoff vector. For a positive definite self-adjoint operator V, we define $\|x\|_V = \sqrt{\langle x, Vx\rangle}$ as the weighted norm of vector x. It can be proved that $\hat{w}$ lies with high probability in an ellipsoid centered at w^* as follows:

THEOREM 1. [1, 19] *According to the 'self-normalized bound for vector-valued martingales', let $V = \lambda I, \lambda > 0$, and $\overline{V}_t = V + \sum_{n=1}^{t-1} x_n \otimes x_n$ be the regularized design matrix underlying the covariates. Define $y_t = x_t^\top w^* + \epsilon_t$ and assume that $\|w^*\|_2 \leq S$. Then, for any $0 < \delta < 1$, with probability at least $1-\delta$, for all $t \geq 1$ we can bound w^* in such a confidence set:*

$$C_t = \left\{ w^* \in \mathbb{R}^d : \right.$$
$$\left. \|\hat{w}_t - w^*\|_{\overline{V}_t} \leq R\sqrt{2\log\left(\frac{|\overline{V}_t|^{1/2}|\lambda I|^{-1/2}}{\delta}\right)} + \lambda^{1/2} S \right\}. \tag{6}$$

In addition, if $\|x_t\| \leq L$ then with probability at least $1-\delta$, for all $t \geq 1$, we can bound w^* in a new confidence set:

$$C_t' = \left\{ w^* \in \mathbb{R}^d : \right.$$
$$\left. \|\hat{w}_t - w^*\|_{\overline{V}_t} \leq R\sqrt{d\log\left(\frac{1 + tL^2/\lambda}{\delta}\right)} + \lambda^{1/2} S \right\}. \tag{7}$$

The above bound provides the confidence region at time t. It shows that with good choice of the right parts of the equation, w^* always remains inside this ellipsoid for all times t with probability $1-\delta$. Next, we show the bound of the arm with a single linear payoff.

THEOREM 2. *Let $(x_1, y_1), \cdots, (x_{t-1}, y_{t-1})$, $x_i \in \mathbb{R}^d, y_i \in \mathbb{R}$ satisfy the linear model assumption. Furthermore, we have the same assumption as Theorem 1. Then, for any $0 < \delta < 1$, with probability at least $1-\delta$, for all $t \geq 1$ we can have:*

$$\|x^\top \hat{w} - x^\top w^*\| \leq$$
$$\|x\|_{\overline{V}_t^{-1}} \left(R\sqrt{2\log\left(\frac{|\overline{V}_t|^{1/2}|\lambda I|^{-1/2}}{\delta}\right)} + \lambda^{1/2} S \right). \tag{8}$$

In addition, if $\|x_t\| \leq L$ then for all $t \geq 1$, with probability $1-\delta$ we can have:

$$\|x^\top \hat{w} - x^\top w^*\| \leq$$
$$\|x\|_{\overline{V}_t^{-1}} \left(R\sqrt{d\log\left(\frac{1 + tL^2/\lambda}{\delta}\right)} + \lambda^{1/2} S \right). \tag{9}$$

PROOF.

$$\|x^\top \hat{w} - x^\top w^*\| = \|x^\top(\hat{w} - w^*)\|$$
$$\leq \|x\|\|\hat{w} - w^*\| = \|x\|_{\overline{V}_t^{-1}}\|\hat{w} - w^*\|_{\overline{V}_t}.$$

According to (6), with probability at least $1-\delta$, for all $t \geq 1$, we have:

$$\|x^\top \hat{w} - x^\top w^*\| \leq$$
$$\|x\|_{\overline{V}_t^{-1}} \left(R\sqrt{2\log\left(\frac{|\overline{V}_t|^{1/2}|\lambda I|^{-1/2}}{\delta}\right)} + \lambda^{1/2} S \right).$$

According to (7), with probability at least $1-\delta$, for all $t \geq 1$ we have:

$$\|x^\top \hat{w} - x^\top w^*\| \leq$$
$$\|x\|_{\overline{V}_t^{-1}} \left(R\sqrt{d \log\left(\frac{1+tL^2/\lambda}{\delta}\right)} + \lambda^{1/2} S \right).$$

□

LEMMA 1. *Given an arm $a \in \mathcal{K}_t$ with the context feature x, let $(x_{a,1}, y_{a,1}), (x_{a,2}, y_{a,2}), \cdots, (x_{a,n_a(t-1)}, y_{a,n_a(t-1)})$ be history records of arm a before t and $x_a \in X_a$ and $y_a \in Y_a$, and let $\hat{w}_a = (X_a^\top X_a + \lambda I)^{-1} X_a^\top Y_a$. We have*

$$x^\top w_a^* \leq x^\top \hat{w}_a +$$
$$\|x\|_{\overline{V}_t^{-1}} \left(R\sqrt{2 \log\left(\frac{|\overline{V}_t|^{1/2} |\lambda I|^{-1/2}}{\delta}\right)} + \lambda^{1/2} S \right). \quad (10)$$

As shown in (10), we have a possible upper bound of $x^\top w_a^*$, which has two parts. The first term can be deemed as empirical expected estimation of payoff of the arm, and the second term can be considered as a penalty. This penalty is typically a high probability upper confidence bound on the payoff of the arm.

Thus, given an arm a and its relations $N_t(a)$, we face the exploitation-exploration problem. We use the integrated confidence bound on the payoffs of these invoked arms.

LEMMA 2. *In the networked bandits, given an arm $a \in \mathcal{K}_t$ and the network relationship $N_t(a)$, we obtain:*

$$\sum_{a \in N_t(a)} x_a^\top w_a^* \leq \sum_{a \in N_t(a)} x_a^\top \hat{w}_a +$$
$$\sum_{a \in N_t(a)} \|x_a\|_{\overline{V}_t^{-1}} \left(R\sqrt{2 \log\left(\frac{|\overline{V}_t|^{1/2} |\lambda I|^{-1/2}}{\delta}\right)} + \lambda^{1/2} S \right). \quad (11)$$

We believe that the confidence bound can be successfully applied to this situation with the exploitation-exploration trade-off. We use the confidence bound generated by the confidence sets of parameters, defined by:

$$B_{a,t} = \nu_{a,t} + \xi_a(t), \quad (12)$$

$\nu_{a,t} = \sum_{a \in N_t(a)} x^\top \hat{w}_{a,t}$ indicates the expected value, and $\xi_a(t)$ is the last term of (11) and indicates the penalty of the estimation. Figure 2 shows the upper bound of arms from our illustrative example. Each arm has the empirical payoff and a potential value. Thus, in each round, our algorithm selects an arm based on the estimation from the confidence bound, such that the predicted payoff is maximized. Our algorithm is shown in Algorithm 1.

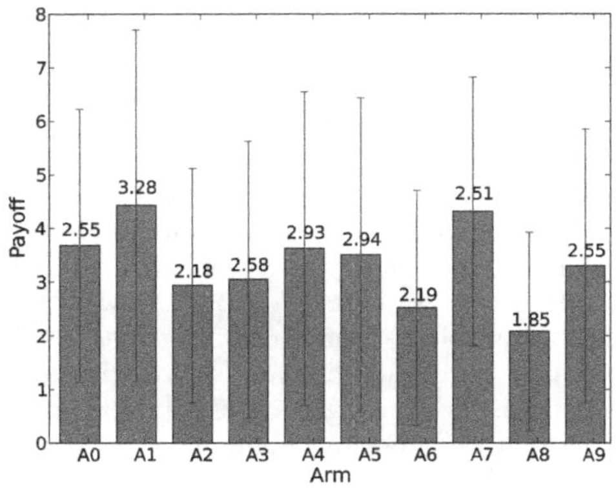

Figure 2: An example of the upper bound B in 10-arm networked bandits when $t = 120$. Bar denotes the payo ff estimation and vertical line denotes the penalty of the estimation.

Algorithm 1 NetBandits

Input: $\mathcal{K}_t$, G_t, $\mathcal{C}_t$, $t = 1, \cdots, T$

for round $t = 1, 2, \cdots, T$ **do**

  For each arm we can observe the features $x_{a,t}, a \in \mathcal{K}_t$, and the invoked arms $N_t(a)$ based on G_t

  for each $a \in \mathcal{K}_t$ **do**

    Compute $\hat{w}_a$ according to (5)

    Compute the quality

$$B_{a,t} = \sum_{a \in N_t(a)} x_{a,t}^\top \hat{w}_a +$$
$$\sum_{a \in N_t(a)} \|x_{a,t}\|_{\overline{V}_t^{-1}} \left(R\sqrt{2 \log\left(\frac{|\overline{V}_t|^{1/2} |\lambda I|^{-1/2}}{\delta}\right)} + \lambda^{1/2} S \right)$$

  end for

  Choose arm $a_t = \arg\max_{a \in \mathcal{K}_t} B_{a,t}$

  Observe the multiple payoffs $\{y_{a,t} | a \in N_t(a_t)\}$

  for each node $a \in N_t(a_t)$ **do**

    Update X_a, Y_a

  end for

end for

THEOREM 3. *On the networked bandits, assume that each arm's payoff function satisfies the linear model, and assume that the contextual vector is $x_{a,t}$ for each arm $a \in \mathcal{K}_t, |\mathcal{K}_t| \leq K$ and $t = 1, \cdots, T$. Then, for any $0 < \delta < 1$, with probability at least $1 - \delta$, the cumulative regret satisfies*

$$\overline{\mathcal{R}}_T \leq 2K\sqrt{2\beta_T(\delta) T \log |I + XX^\top/\lambda|}, \quad (13)$$

where

$$\beta_T(\delta) = \left(R\sqrt{2 \log\left(\frac{|I + XX^\top/\lambda|^{1/2}}{\delta}\right)} + \lambda^{1/2} S \right)^2.$$

5. REGRET ANALYSIS

We next provide a bound on the regret of our algorithm when run through the confidence sets constructed in Theorem 1. We assume that the expected estimation of payoffis bounded. We can view this as a bound on parameters and the bound on the arms set. We state a bound on the regret of the algorithm as follows:

PROOF. Considering the instantaneous regret at round t, we select an optimal arm according to our algorithm. Thus, we have optimistic $(a_t, \tilde{w}_a)$ and $\hat{w}_a$ for the $N(a_t)$. For round

t, we rely on [1] to have:

$$\begin{aligned}
r_t &= \sum_{a\in N(a_t)} x_{a,t}^\top w_a^* - \sum_{a\in N(a^*)} x_{a,t}^\top w_a^* \\
&\le \sum_{a\in N(a_t)} x_{a,t}^\top w_a^* - \sum_{a\in N(a_t)} x_{a,t}^\top \tilde{w}_a \\
&= \sum_{a\in N(a_t)} x_{a,t}^\top w_a^* - \sum_{a\in N(a_t)} x_{a,t}^\top \hat{w}_a \\
&+ \sum_{a\in N(a_t)} x_{a,t}^\top \hat{w}_a - \sum_{a\in N(a_t)} x_{a,t}^\top \tilde{w}_a \\
&= \sum_{a\in N(a_t)} x_{a,t}^\top (w_a^* - \hat{w}_a) + \sum_{a\in N(a_t)} x_{a,t}^\top (\hat{w}_a - \tilde{w}_a) \\
&= \sum_{a\in N(a_t)} \|x_t\|_{\overline{V}_t^{-1}} \|w^* - \hat{w}_t\|_{\overline{V}_t^{-1}} \\
&+ \sum_{a\in N(a_t)} \|x_t\|_{\overline{V}_t^{-1}} \|\hat{w}_t - \tilde{w}_t\|_{\overline{V}_t^{-1}} \\
&\le \sum_{a\in N(a_t)} 2\sqrt{\beta_t(\delta)} \|x_t\|_{\overline{V}_t^{-1}}. \qquad (14)
\end{aligned}$$

For each arm $a \in N_t(a)$, we define

$$r_{a,t} = x_{a,t}^\top w_a^* - x_{a,t}^\top \hat{w}_a + x_{a,t}^\top \hat{w}_a - x_{a,t}^\top \tilde{w}_a, \qquad (15)$$

and we have

$$r_{a,t} \le 2\sqrt{\beta_t(\delta)} \|x_{a,t}\|_{\overline{V}_t^{-1}}. \qquad (16)$$

We then rewrite the instantaneous regret (14) as

$$r_t \le \sum_{a\in N(a_t)} r_{a,t}. \qquad (17)$$

Regarding to the fact that $r_{a,t} \le 2$, we have

$$\begin{aligned}
r_{a,t} &\le 2\min\left(\sqrt{\beta_t(\delta)} \|x_{a,t}\|^2_{\overline{V}_t^{-1}}, 1\right) \\
&\le 2\sqrt{\beta_t(\delta)} \min\left(\|x_{a,t}\|^2_{\overline{V}_t^{-1}}, 1\right). \qquad (18)
\end{aligned}$$

Given arms $N_t(a)$, we define $a' = \arg\max_a \|x_{a,t}\|^2_{\overline{V}_t^{-1}}$. Then we have

$$\begin{aligned}
r_t &\le |N_t(a)| 2\sqrt{\beta_t(\delta)} \|x_{a',t}\|_{\overline{V}_t^{-1}} \\
&\le |N_t(a)| 2\sqrt{\beta_t(\delta)} \min\left(\|x_{a',t}\|^2_{\overline{V}_t^{-1}}, 1\right). \qquad (19)
\end{aligned}$$

Thus, with probability at least $1-\delta$, for any $T \ge 1$.

$$\begin{aligned}
\overline{\mathcal{R}}_T &= \sum_{t=1}^T r_t \le \sum_{t=1}^T |N_t(a)| 2\sqrt{\beta_t(\delta)} \left(\|x_{a',t}\|_{\overline{V}_t^{-1}} \wedge 1\right) \\
&\le 2K \sum_{t=1}^T \sqrt{\beta_t(\delta)} \left(\|x_{a',t}\|_{\overline{V}_t^{-1}} \wedge 1\right) \\
&\le 2K \sqrt{T \sum_{t=1}^T \left(\sqrt{\beta_t(\delta)} \left(\|x_{a',t}\|_{\overline{V}_t^{-1}} \wedge 1\right)\right)^2} \\
&\le 2K \sqrt{T\beta_T(\delta) \sum_{t=1}^T \left(\|x_{a,t}\|^2_{\overline{V}_t^{-1}} \wedge 1\right)}. \qquad (20)
\end{aligned}$$

According to $\log(1+z) \le z$, we have:

$$\log|I + XV^{-1}X| \le \sum_{k=1}^{t-1} \|x_k\|^2_{\overline{V}_k^{-1}}. \qquad (21)$$

Then according to $z \le 2\log(1+z), z \in [0,1]$, we have

$$\sum_{k=1}^{t-1} \left(\|x_k\|^2_{\overline{V}_k^{-1}} \wedge 1\right) \le 2\log|I + XV^{-1}X|. \qquad (22)$$

We choose $V = \lambda I$, then we rewrite $\overline{\mathcal{R}}_T$ as

$$\overline{\mathcal{R}}_T \le 2K\sqrt{2T\beta_T(\delta)\log|I + XX^\top/\lambda|}. \qquad (23)$$

□

LEMMA 3. *Assume that $x \in \mathbb{R}^d$ and $V = \lambda I$. Then, for any $0 < \delta < 1$, with probability at least $1-\delta$, the bound is*

$$\overline{\mathcal{R}}_T \le 2K\sqrt{2Td\log\left(\lambda - \frac{(T-1)L}{d}\right)} \cdot \left(\lambda^{1/2}S + R\sqrt{2\log\left(\frac{1}{\delta}\right) + d\log\left(1 + \frac{(T-1)L}{\lambda d}\right)}\right). \quad (24)$$

We are mainly interested in the interrelated arms. Our regret bound depends on the number of invoked arms $|N_t(a)|$ or loose K. Figure 3 shows experimentation of our bound applied to the networked bandit problem. Our algorithm keeps the regret as low as possible, and can reach $\overline{\mathcal{R}}_t/t \to 0$ with high probability when t is large enough.

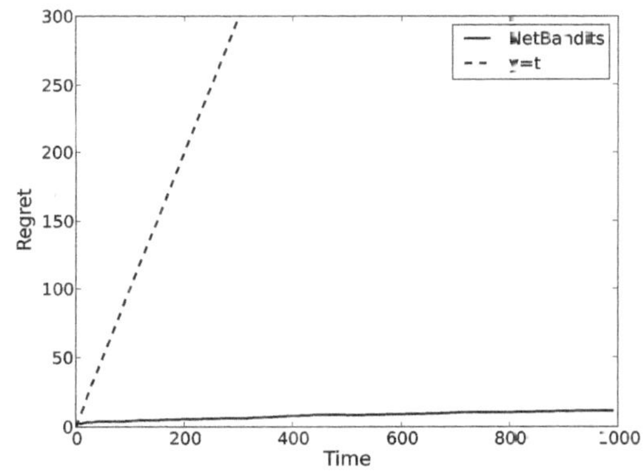

Figure 3: An example of the regret value in 10-arm networked bandits. The experiments are repeated 100 times and the average regrets are shown. $y = x$ is provided for comparison.

6. PRACTICAL ISSUES

In real-world applications, according to different assumptions about the network topology of arms, we can consider special cases of the networked bandit problem. We focus on $N_t(a)$. In our algorithm, we make the very loose assumption that $N_t(a)$ varies over time. However, the network topology is sometimes stable over a fixed duration. For example, a school social network is stable for the duration of a semester. This means that $N_t(a) = N_0(a)$, which is a special case of network bandits. In other cases, for example when inquiring users in the same company, we only need to consider their colleagues or a group of interest.

6.1 Dynamic network

In the networked bandit problem the network topology of arms is usually dynamic over time, which means for each round t we have different $N_t(a)$. Although we assume that $N_t(a)$ will be active after the forecaster selects a, we omit how to generate $N_t(a)$ and how arm a invokes $N_t(a)$, which are not our primary concerns. Instead, we simplify our problem using the simple setting of selecting an arm and then receiving payoffs from invoked arms. We assume that we can observe invoked arms $N_t(a)$. In practice, we can directly obtain $N_t(a)$ by predefining the arms, for example as neighbors or groups, or by observing feedback and collecting arms which provide feedback. We focus on how to select arms in order to maximize the total payoff, and therefore we concern the arms of $N_t(a)$ and the forecaster can obtain the invoked bandits over the course of collecting the payoffs from the network. In particular, at each round the algorithm observes the network topology of arms; it then decides which arm to select using the knowledge of the network topology and historical payoffinformation.

In Algorithm 2, we provide a pseudo-code for the selection at each round in a dynamic network.

Algorithm 2 Selection at round t in dynamic network

For each arm we have $\hat{w}_a$ and observer the context $x_{a,t}$
For each arm we collect $N_t(a)$
for each $a \in \mathcal{K}_t$ **do**
  Compute $B_{a,t}$
end for
Select arm $a_t = \arg\max_{a \in \mathcal{K}_t} B_{a,t}$
Observe the payoffs $\{y_{a,t} | a \in N_t(a_t)\}$ from the network
For each arm $a \in N_t(a_t)$ update X_a, Y_a and $\hat{w}_a$

6.2 Static network

We make the simple assumption that the network topology is fixed. In other words, the relationships between arms do not change. For all t, we have $G_t = G_0$, $\mathcal{K}_t = \mathcal{K}_0$ and $N_t(a) = N_0(a)$. For example, DBLP, Last.FM, and many offline social network datasets are of fixed duration. This is a degenerate version of our problem and can be solved using our algorithm.

In Algorithm 3, we provide a pseudo-code for the selection at each round in a static network.

Algorithm 3 Selection at round t in static network

For each arm we have $\hat{w}_a$ and $N_0(a)$, and observer the context $x_{a,t}$
for $a \in \mathcal{K}_0$ **do**
  Compute $B_{a,t}$
end for
Select arm $a_t = \arg\max_{a \in \mathcal{K}_0} B_{a,t}$
Observe the payoffs $\{y_{a,t} | a \in N_0(a_t)\}$ from the network
For each arm $a \in N_0(a_t)$ update X_a, Y_a and $\hat{w}_a$

6.3 Neighborhood or group

In networks, especially in social networks, a simple yet common assumption is that the node largely influences its neighborhoods or community [13, 15]. Moreover, some applications only focus on people who have the same interest or are in a group. This makes it possible to assume that the selected arm only invokes its neighbors or a group; that is, $N_t(a) = Neig_t(a)$, where $Neig_t(a)$ indicates the neighbors of a. We can only collect the payoffs of neighbors of an arm, and therefore $N_t(a)$ is appropriate. Although there are also two cases in this situation - static and dynamic - here we focus only on the neighborhood.

In Algorithm 4, we provide a pseudo-code for the selection at each round with specific $N_t(a)$.

Algorithm 4 Selection at round t with neighborhood

For each arm we have $\hat{w}_a$ and observer the context $x_{a,t}$
For each arm we collect $Neig_t(a)$
for $a \in \mathcal{K}_t$ **do**
  Compute $B_{a,t}$
end for
Select arm $a_t = \arg\max_{a \in \mathcal{K}_t} B_{a,t}$
Observe the payoffs $\{y_{a,t} | a \in Neig_t(a_t)\}$ from the network
For each arm $a \in Neig_t(a_t)$ update X_a, Y_a and $\hat{w}_a$

7. EXPERIMENTS

7.1 Illustrative Example

We first illustrate our model by a synthetic example (Figure 4), which contains 10 arms (A0-A9) randomly connected at each round. At different rounds, the networks are different. At rounds $t = 11$ and $t = 20$, the upper bound B (the second row, blue) is large; however, the expected estimation is small (the third row, red) because the variance is large. Our algorithm selects the arm with maximal upper bound. We also show the real payoffs of all the arms, which are not known to the algorithm. At an early stage, the selection is poor compared to the real payoff (the fourth row, green). At round $t = 20$, our algorithm chooses A0 however, the best is A1, illustrating that the expected estimation is small and the algorithm can try another arm that has potential, but with uncertainty. Later, selection becomes efficient and at $t = 120$ the algorithm chooses A1 since more information has been learned and the upper bound becomes more stable with lower penalty. This is close to the real situation and provides a good estimation.

7.2 Baselines and Performance Metric

In this section we evaluate the proposed NetBandits strategy on four synthetic datasets and two public real-world datasets. We perform two types of experiments: simulation experiments and offline evaluation of two real applications.

We compare our proposed method against two baselines: a state-of-art algorithm for the contextual bandit problem, referred to as TraBandits, and the random strategy. Since there is no existing method for the networked bandit problem, these methods are little altered for networked bandits. The details are follows:

- **TraBandits:** a state-of-art method for contextual bandits with linear payoff models [17]. The algorithm is a UCB style method with the linear payoff assumption that always selects the arm using highest UCB at each round.
- **Random:** a simple strategy that just randomly selects an arm.

We use two methods to assess the performance of our algorithm. We first analyze the average payoff at each round,

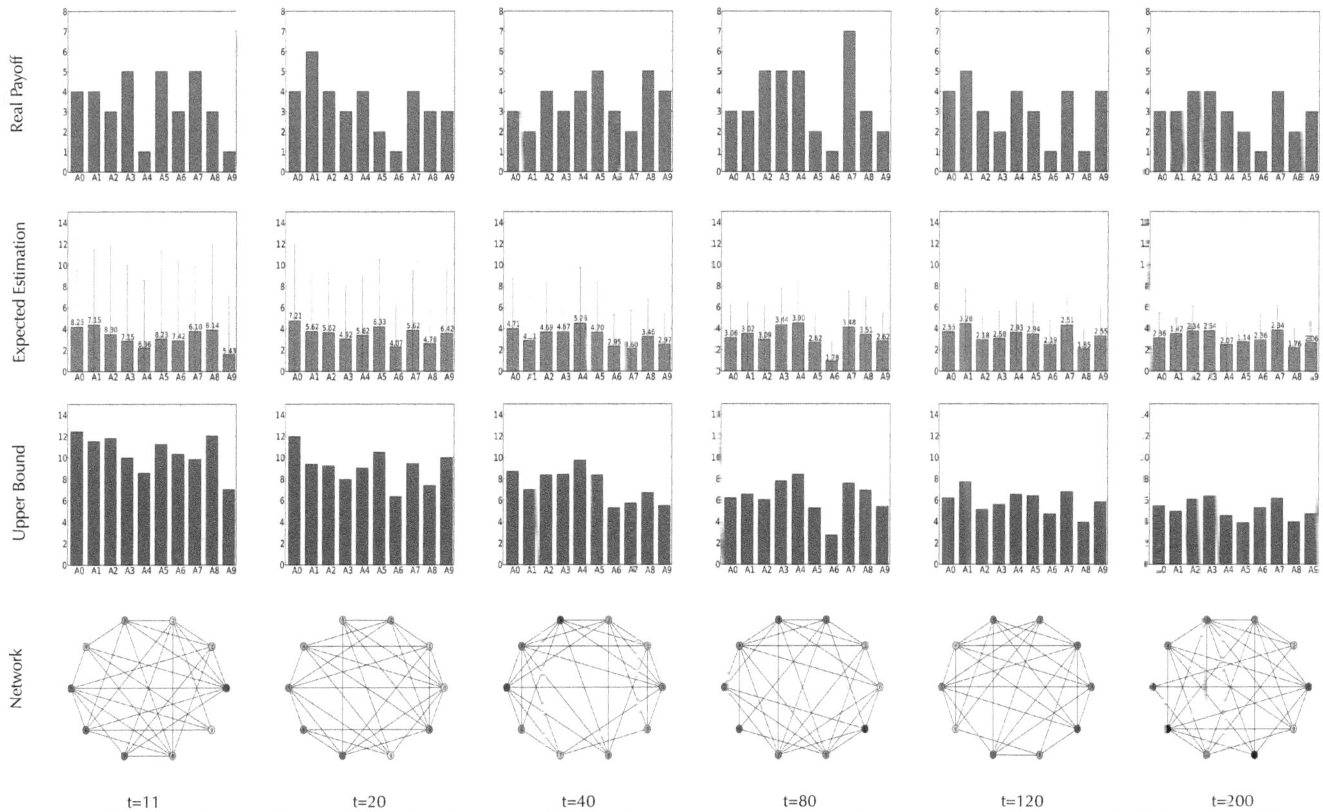

Figure 4: Illustrative synthetic example of exploration-explcitation trade-off. Bottom, arms with networked topology. Second row: the upper bound B for each arm computed using NetBandits. Third row: the expected estimation ν, where bar denotes the estimation and vertical line denotes the penalty of estimation. Fourth row: the real payoff of each arm.

and then we analyze the cumulative payoff at each round, which ignores the performance of the algorithm at each fixed round but gives an overall view of the lifetime performance of the algorithm.

7.3 Simulation Experiments

We test our algorithm on a series of synthetic datasets. In contrast to previous work, we need to construct the network topology, which can be either static or dynamic. Static network is a special case of dynamic situation and static network is generated in advance and remains unchanged. We therefore construct the networked bandits based on the dynamic network as follows: we first construct a fixed number of nodes k, which are considered as arms. We then randomly create edges between them, which are used to generate the relations for each arm. Neighborhood is considered as relationship. For every node, we assign different norm random vector $u_i, u_i \in \mathbb{R}^{10}$ and we use the following stochastic model to generate its payoffs: $y_a(x) = x^\top u_a + \epsilon_a$, where ϵ_a is uniformly distributed in a bounded interval centered around zero and u_a and ϵ_a are not known to the decision algorithm. For contextual information, at each round t we randomly create a set of context vectors $\{x_{1,t}, \cdots, x_{k,t}\}, x_{k,t} \in \mathbb{R}^{10}$. The network topology does not have strict assumptions and is created simply: in the dynamic situation, we generate the network topology at each round (relationships between the nodes change at each round). We randomly create $k^2/3$ edges between the nodes, and therefore for most nodes the relations will be no greater than $k/3$.

We present the results from k =10, 100, 1000, and 10000 arms with dynamic network topology. In Figure 5 and Figure 6 we present the results of average payoff and cumulative payoff; our NetBandits outperforms the other baselines TraBandits does not work well, indicating that best single arm does not always have the best payoff in a network but also depends on its relations. As per the network construction, the average payoff for each node is around $k/3$ if the node and its relations provide feedback, and the average payoff of TraBandits and Random is around $k/3$. For example, as shown in Figure 5, when $k = 10$ the payoff ranges from 3.2 to 3.6; when $k = 100$ the payoff ranges from 34 to 35; when $k = 1000$ the payoff ranges from 340 to 350; when $k = 10000$ the payoff ranges from 3450 to 3550. However, NetBandits usually performs better except the earliest time points, and its value is greater than 4.2 when $k = 10$, 40 when $k = 100$, 400 when $k = 1000$, and 4500 when $k = 10000$. This is because NetBandits performs more exploration than exploitation to begin with. Figure 6 shows that our algorithm obtains the best cumulative payoff over all rounds. As average payoff improves, NetBandits also exhibits higher cumulative payoff. This indicates that more early exploration improves later selections, leading to a fairer assessment of the performance of the different algorithms.

The running time of NetBandits according to different numbers of arms and network topology is also shown in Table 1, and demonstrates the running time increases rapidly as the number of the scale of the networks increase. For example $k = 100$ is slower than $k = 10$ by more than k^2 but

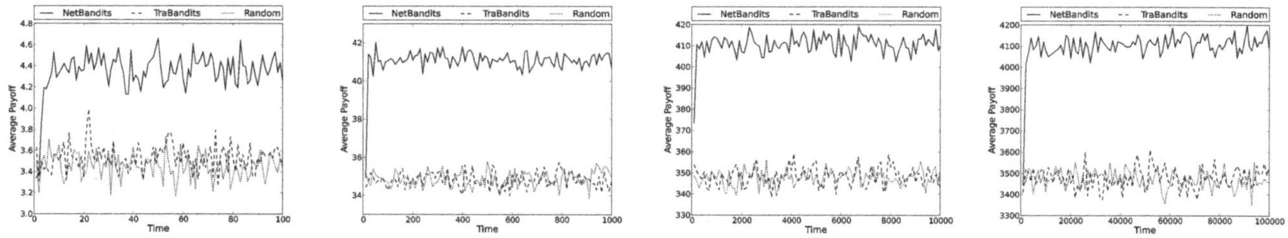

(a) *k=10* (b) *k=100* (c) *k=1000* (d) *k=10000*

Figure 5: The average payoff at each round in dynamic networks.

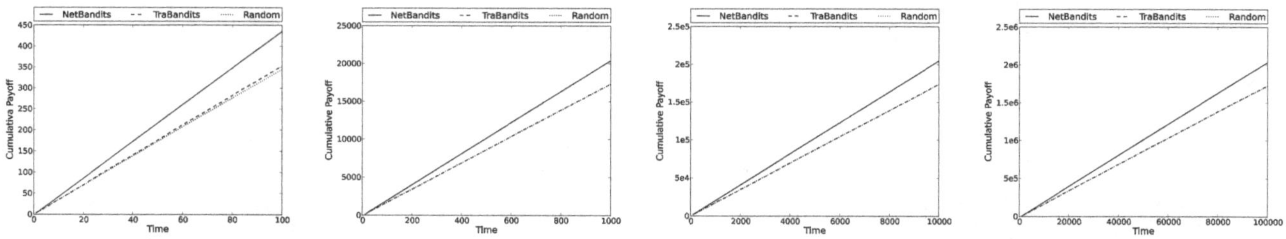

(a) *k=10* (b) *k=100* (c) *k=1000* (d) *k=10000*

Figure 6: The cumulative payoff at each round in dynamic networks.

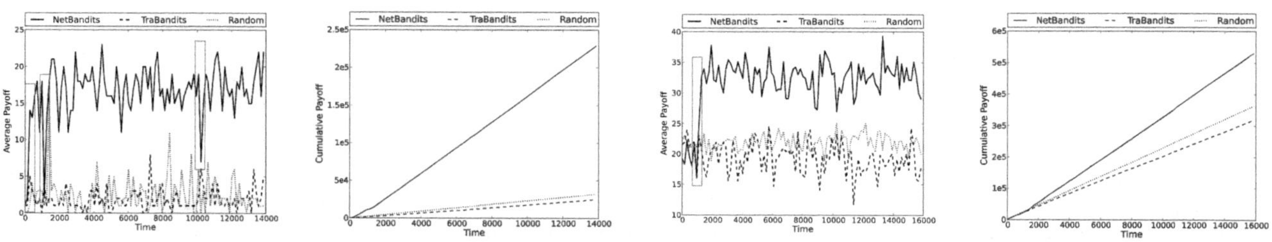

(a) Average payoff(Del) (b) Cumulative payoff(Del) (c) Average payoff(LFM) (d) Cumulative payoff(LFM)

Figure 7: The average payoff and cumulative payoff for two real-world datasets.

Arms	10	100	1,000	10,000
Avg of invoked arms	3	33	333	3333
Total round	100	1,000	10,000	100,000
Time (second)	0.1	23.4	2034.2	173,628.3

Table 1: Running time results of NetBandits on four synthetic datasets.

less than k^3. The time taken depends on the size of the network, including the number of nodes and edges. The time complexity of NetBandits is $O(TKN\Omega)$, where T is the total number of rounds, K is the number of arms, N indicates the average number of invoked arms, and Ω indicates the time taken to compute the parameters; it is no more than $O(TK^2\Omega)$ where $N = K$. It can be improved by calculating each arm in parallel for a large number of arms.

7.4 Real-world Datasets Experiments

We also test our algorithm on two publicly available real-world datasets[1]: Delicious Bookmarks, a dynamic dataset, denoted by Del; and Last.FM, a static dataset, denoted by LFM.

Delicious Bookmarks is a social network for storing, sharing, and discovering web bookmarks. The Del dataset contains 1,861 nodes and 7,668 edges and 69,226 URLs described by 53,388 tags. Payoffs are created using the information about the bookmarked URLs for each user: the payoff is 1 if the user bookmarked the URL, otherwise the payoff is 0. Pre-processing is performed by breaking the tags down into smaller fragile items made up of single words, ignoring the underscores, hyphens, and dashes. Each word is represented using the TF-IDF context vector based on the words of all tags, i.e., these feature vectors are the context vectors. PCA was performed on the dataset and the first 16 principle components selected as context vectors building a linear function based on payoff records for each user. This linear function generates a payoff when given a new context. At each round t, we provide $x_{k,t} \in \mathbb{R}^{16}$ for all users k.

The Last.FM dataset is a music website that builds a detailed profile of each user's musical taste by recording details of the tracks that the user listened to from a range of digital devices. LFM contains 1,892 nodes and 12,717 edges and has 17,632 artists described by 11,946 tags. We use the listened-to artists information to construct payoffs: if the user listened to an artist at least once the payoff is 1, otherwise the payoff is 0. Similar pre-processing is performed as Delicious Bookmarks. Compound tags are broken down into several corresponding single words resulting in 6,036 words. We represent context features using the TF-IDF features, and after PCA the first 16 principle components are selected as context vectors. For each user we then build a linear function based on payoff records. This linear function

[1]http://grouplens.org/node/462

can generate a payoff when given a new context. At each round, we provide $x_{k,t} \in \mathbb{R}^{16}$ for all users k.

We construct the network topology according to the social network of the users. Neighborhood is considered as relationship. The linear payoff function for each user is learned in advance and unknown to the algorithm, which decides its next selection according to previous feedback.

For the Del dataset, there exists the timestamp information that records when contact relationships were created, and we can therefore construct a dynamic network according to the timestamps. Timestamps are from 1146752335000 to 1288104100000; we therefore divide them into 14 groups according to the first three numbers (114, 115, ..., 128). We set the total rounds $T = 14000$ and update the network every 1000 rounds. For the Last.FM dataset, there is no time information, thus we construct a static network.

The results of average payoff and cumulative payoffare shown in Figure 7. Our algorithm outperforms the other baselines. Although the two networks have a similar number of users, LFM has more relationships and the average and cumulative payoff results are higher than Del. For the average payoff of Del, there exist three low intervals marked by (red) rectangles in Figure 7(a). These occurred at the beginning and close to round $t = 1000$ and $t = 10000$. Since many new nodes and edges are added at these rounds and NetBandits performs more exploration than exploitation. The payoffs improve after exploration. For the average payoffresults of LFM, there is a low interval at the start, denoted by the (red) rectangle in Figure 7(c), because NetBandits is trying to select possible better arms and perform exploration; then later the performance improves. Figure 7(b)(d) show that the cumulative payoff results of NetBandits increase faster, and are much greater than the other algorithms, and demonstrate that exploration does not hurt the total performance.

8. CONCLUSION AND FUTURE WORK

In this paper we formalize a new bandit problem, termed networked bandits. We presented the novel problem of how to select the arm with multiple payoffs in networked bandits by considering a multi-armed bandit of interconnected arms, one of which can invoke other related arms at each round. After selecting an arm, we can obtain payoffs from this arm and its relations.

We consider this approach in the contextual bandit setting and assume disjoint linear payoffs for arms. We propose a new networked bandit algorithm NetBandits that considers the uncertainty of the payoffs using integrated confidence sets. We also provide a regret bound for our solution. Our experiments show that it is better to consider both the network topology and the payoffs of arms, and we observe that our approach performs well in this setting.

The networked bandit problem requires further work. Some interesting problems still remain, such as how to model $N_t(a)$. In our work we do not make any assumption about the structure of the network topology; for example the hub may have higher priority, and it is possible to find a more efficient method for some fixed structures.

Another problem is arm complexity. We assume that one arm invokes other arms, which in turn can invoke other arms sequentially, with processing occurring at the same time. However in some real applications, the structure is possible to be much more complex and evolve over time, which is likely to delay the payoffs.

9. ACKNOWLEDGMENTS

This work is supported by Australian Research Council Projects FT-130101457 and DP-140102164.

10. REFERENCES

[1] Y. Abbasi-Yadkori, C. Szepesvári, and D. Tax. Improved algorithms for linear stochastic bandits In *NIPS*, pages 2312–2320, 2011.

[2] A. Anagnostopoulos, R. Kumar, and M. Mahdian. Influence and correlation in social networks. In *KDD*, pages 7–15. ACM, 2008.

[3] J.-Y. Audibert and S. Bubeck. Regret bounds and minimax policies under partial monitoring. *JMLR*, 9999:2785–2826, 2010.

[4] J.-Y. Audibert, R. Munos, and C. Szepesvári. Exploration-exploitation tradeoff using variance estimates in multi-armed bandits. *Theor. Comput. Sci.*, 410(19):1876–1902, 2009.

[5] P. Auer. Using confidence bounds for exploitation-exploration trade-offs. *JMLR*, 3:397–422, 2003.

[6] P. Auer, N. Cesa-Bianchi, and P. Fischer. Finite-time analysis of the multiarmed bandit problem. *Machine Learning*, 47(2-3):235–256, 2002.

[7] P. Auer, N. Cesa-Bianchi, Y. Freund, and R. E. Schapire The nonstochastic multiarmed bandit problem. *SIAM J COMPUT*, 32(1):48–77, 2002.

[8] Z. Bnaya, R. Puzis, R. Stern, and A. Felner. Social network search as a volatile multi-armed bandit problem. *HUMAN*, 2(2):pp–84, 2013.

[9] S. Bubeck and N. Cesa-Bianchi. Regret analysis of stochastic and nonstochastic multi-armed bandit problems. *Foundations and Trends in Machine Learning*, 5(1):1–122, 2012.

[10] S. Buccapatnam, A. Eryilmaz, and N. B. Shroff. Multi-armed bandits in the presence of side observations in social networks. *OSU, Tech. Rep*, 2013.

[11] N. Cesa-Bianchi, C. Gentile, and G. Zappella. A gang of bandits. In *NIPS*, 2013.

[12] W. Chu, L. Li, L. Reyzin, and R. E. Schapire. Contextual bandits with linear payoff functions. In *AISTAS*, pages 208–214, 2011.

[13] D. Crandall, D. Cosley, D. Huttenlocher, J. Kleinberg, and S. Suri. Feedback effects between similarity and social influence in online communities. In *KDD*, pages 160–168. ACM, 2008.

[14] V. Dani, T. P. Hayes, and S. M. Kakade. Stochastic linear optimization under bandit feedback. In *COLT*, pages 355–366, 2008.

[15] T. Iwata, A. Shah, and Z. Ghahramani. Discovering latent influence in online social activities via shared cascade poisson processes. In *KDD*, pages 266–274. ACM, 2013.

[16] T. L. Lai and H. Robbins. Asymptotically efficient adaptive allocation rules. *ADV APPL PROBAB*, 6(1):4–22, 1985.

[17] L. Li, W. Chu, J. Langford, and R. E. Schapire. A contextual-bandit approach to personalized news article recommendation. In *WWW*, pages 661–670. ACM 2010.

[18] S. A. Myers, C. Zhu, and J. Leskovec. Information diffusion and external influence in networks. In *KDD*, pages 33–41. ACM, 2012.

[19] V. H. Peña, T. L. Lai, and Q.-M. Shao. *Self-normalized processes: Limit theory and Statistical Applications.* Springer, 2008.

[20] H. Robbins. Some aspects of the sequential design of experiments. In *Herbert Robbins Selected Papers*, pages 169–177. Springer, 1985.

[21] P. Rusmevichientong and J. N. Tsitsiklis. Linearly parameterized bandits. *MATH OPER RES*, 35(2):395–411, 2010.

[22] J. Tang, J. Sun, C. Wang, and Z. Yang. Social influence analysis in large-scale networks. In *KDD*, pages 807–816. ACM, 2009.

Mining Topics in Documents: Standing on the Shoulders of Big Data

Zhiyuan Chen and Bing Liu
Department of Computer Science
University of Illinois at Chicago
czyuanacm@gmail.com, liub@cs.uic.edu

ABSTRACT

Topic modeling has been widely used to mine topics from documents. However, a key weakness of topic modeling is that it needs a large amount of data (e.g., thousands of documents) to provide reliable statistics to generate coherent topics. However, in practice, many document collections do not have so many documents. Given a small number of documents, the classic topic model LDA generates very poor topics. Even with a large volume of data, unsupervised learning of topic models can still produce unsatisfactory results. In recently years, knowledge-based topic models have been proposed, which ask human users to provide some prior domain knowledge to guide the model to produce better topics. Our research takes a radically different approach. We propose to *learn as humans do*, i.e., retaining the results learned in the past and using them to help future learning. When faced with a new task, we first mine some reliable (prior) knowledge from the past learning/modeling results and then use it to guide the model inference to generate more coherent topics. This approach is possible because of the big data readily available on the Web. The proposed algorithm mines two forms of knowledge: *must-link* (meaning that two words should be in the same topic) and *cannot-link* (meaning that two words should not be in the same topic). It also deals with two problems of the automatically mined knowledge, i.e., wrong knowledge and knowledge transitivity. Experimental results using review documents from 100 product domains show that the proposed approach makes dramatic improvements over state-of-the-art baselines.

Categories and Subject Descriptors

H.3.1 [**Information Storage and Retrieval**]: Content Analysis and Indexing

Keywords

Topic Model; Lifelong Learning; Opinion Aspect Extraction.

1. INTRODUCTION

Topic models, such as LDA [4], pLSA [12] and their extensions, have been popularly used for topic extraction from text documents. However, these models typically need a large amount of data, e.g., thousands of documents, to provide reliable statistics for generating coherent topics. This is a major shortcoming because in practice few document collections have so many documents. For example, in the task of finding product features or aspects from online reviews for opinion mining [13, 19], most products do not even have more than 100 reviews (documents) in a review website. As we will see in the experiment section, given 100 reviews, the classic topic model LDA produces very poor results.

To deal with this problem, there are three main approaches:

1. *Inventing better topic models*: This approach may be effective if a large number of documents are available. However, since topic models perform unsupervised learning, if the data is small, there is simply not enough information to provide reliable statistics to generate coherent topics. Some form of supervision or external information beyond the given documents is necessary.
2. *Asking users to provide prior domain knowledge*: An obvious form of external information is the prior knowledge of the domain from the user. For example, the user can input the knowledge in the form of must-link and cannot-link. A must-link states that two terms (or words) should belong to the same topic, e.g., *price* and *cost*. A cannot-link indicates that two terms should not be in the same topic, e.g., *price* and *picture*. Some existing *knowledge-based topic models* (e.g., [1, 2, 9, 10, 14, 15, 26, 28]) can exploit such prior domain knowledge to produce better topics. However, asking the user to provide prior domain knowledge can be problematic in practice because the user may not know what knowledge to provide and wants the system to discover for him/her. It also makes the approach non-automatic.
3. *Learning like humans* (*lifelong learning*): We still use the *knowledge-based approach* but mine the prior knowledge automatically from the results of past learning. This approach works like human learning. We humans always retain the results learned in the past and use them to help future learning. That is why whenever we see a new situation, few things are really new because we have seen many aspects of it in the past in some other contexts. In machine learning, this paradigm is called *lifelong learning* [30, 31]. The proposed technique takes this approach. It represents a major step forward as it closes the learning or modeling loop in the sense that the whole process is now fully automatic and can learn or model continuously. However, our approach is very different from existing lifelong learning methods (see Section 2).

Existing research has focused on the first two approaches. We believe it is high time to create algorithms and build systems that learn as humans do. Lifelong learning is possible in our context due to two key observations:

KDD'14, August 24–27, 2014, New York, NY, USA.

ACM 978-1-4503-2956-9/14/08 ...$15.00.
http://dx.doi.org/10.1145/2623330.2623622.

1. Although every domain is different, there is a fair amount of topic overlapping across domains. For example, every product review domain has the topic of *price*, most electronic products share the topic of *battery* and some also have the topic of *screen*. From the topics learned from these domains, we can mine frequently shared terms among the topics. For example, we may find *price* and *cost* frequently appear together in some topics, which indicates that they are likely to belong to the same topic and thus form a must-link. Note that we have the frequency requirement because we want reliable knowledge.
2. From the previously generated topics from many domains, it is also possible to find that *picture* and *price* should not be in the same topic (a cannot-link). This can be done by finding a set of topics that have *picture* as a top topical term, but the term *price* almost never appear at the top of this set of topics, i.e., they are negatively correlated.

Such knowledge can clearly help modeling in a related new domain. The observations also indicate that we need document collections from a large number of domains, which we call the *big data*, to mine enough relevant and reliable must-links and cannot-links to help topic modeling in new domains.

The proposed lifelong learning approach works as follows:

Phrase 1 (*Initialization*): Given n prior document collections $D = \{D_1, \ldots, D_n\}$, a topic model (e.g., LDA) is run on each collection $D_i \in D$ to produce a set of topics S_i. Let $S = \cup_i S_i$, which we call the *prior topics* (or *p-topics* for short). It then mines must-links M from S using a multiple minimum supports frequent itemset mining algorithm [20].

Phase 2 (*Lifelong learning*): Given a new document collection D^t, a knowledge-based topic model (KBTM) with the must-links M is run to generate a set of topics A^t. Based on A^t, the algorithm finds a set of cannot-links C. The KBTM then continues, which is now guided by both must-links M and cannot-links C, to produce the final topic set A^t. We will explain why we mine cannot-links based on A^t in Section 4.2. To enable lifelong learning, A^t is incorporated into S, which is used to generate a new set of must-links M.

About knowledge-based topic models, there are two existing ones, DF-LDA [1] and MC-LDA [10], that can use both must-links and cannot-links to help generate better topics. However, both of them assume that the user-provided must-links and cannot-links are correct and there is no conflict among them. However, these assumptions are violated in our case because of the following issues:

(1) The automatically generated must-links and cannot-links can have errors. Blindly trusting them as in DF-LDA and MC-LDA generates poor results (see Section 6).

(2) A term may have multiple senses or meanings. This can cause the *transitivity problem*. That is, if A and B form a must-link, and B and C form a must-link, a topic model, such as DF-LDA, will put all three terms in one topic, which is clearly not always correct. For example, the term *light* can have two distinct meanings and the system may find two must-links, {light, weight} and {light, bright}. It is clearly unreasonable to put these three terms together under the same topic. MC-LDA has difficulty with this problem too because it only chooses one must-link for each term in each document and ignores the rest, which is undesirable because it can miss a lot of good must-link knowledge.

In this paper, we propose a new topic model, called AMC (topic modeling with Automatically generated Must-links and Cannot-links), whose inference can exploit the automatically mined knowledge and deal with the issues of wrong knowledge and transitivity to produce superior topics. Our experiments, using review collections from 100 domains, show that the proposed AMC model outperforms state-of-the-art baseline models significantly.

2. RELATED WORK

Knowledge-based topic models have been proposed to incorporate prior domain knowledge from the user to improve model performance. Existing works such as [1, 9, 26] considered only the must-link type of knowledge (e.g., *price* and *cost*) while [1, 10] also used the cannot-link type of knowledge (e.g., *price* and *picture*). Most of the above models also assume the input knowledge to be correct. [9] is the first work to address the issue of wrong knowledge in topic models by using the ratio of probabilities of two words under each topic. However, [9] only assigns one piece of knowledge (in the form of link or set) to each term, which ignores many pieces of useful knowledge. As shown in Section 6, AMC outperforms it significantly. Other types of knowledge, such as document labels have also been used in [3, 29].

Our work is closely related to transfer learning and lifelong learning. Topic models have been used to help transfer learning [27, 34]. However, transfer learning in these papers is for traditional supervised classification, which is very different from our work of topic extraction. [17] transferred labeled documents from the source domain to the target domain to produce topic models with better fitting. However, we do not use any labeled data. [35] modeled the language gap between topics using a user provided parameter indicating the degree of technicality of the domain. In contrast, our proposed AMC model is fully automatic with no human intervention. Another key difference is that transfer learning typically uses the data from one source domain to help the target domain classification, while we use the knowledge obtained from a large number of past (source) domains to help the new (target) domain learning or modeling. In terms of lifelong learning [31, 30], LTM [7] is the first topic model that performs lifelong learning or modeling. It also improves the model in [8], which was not proposed as a lifelong learning model. However, LTM only considers must-links. AMC considers both must-links and cannot-links. AMC also has a more effective must-link mining method and deals with the transitivity or multiple sense problem, which was not tackled in [7]. As we will see in Section 6, AMC achieves dramatic improvements.

Since our experiments are carried out using product reviews, aspect extraction in opinion mining [19] is related. A topic is basically an aspect. Topic models have been used for the task by many researchers [5, 10, 16, 21, 23, 25, 26, 32, 33, 37]. However, none of these models mines must-links or cannot-links automatically to help modeling.

3. OVERALL ALGORITHM

This section introduces the proposed overall algorithm, which follows the lifelong learning idea described in the introduction section. The algorithm consists of two phases:

Phase 1 - Initialization: Given a set of prior document collections $D = \{D_1, \ldots, D_n\}$ from n domains, this step first runs the standard LDA on each domain collection $D_i \in D$ to generate a set of topics S_i. The resulting topics from all n domains are unionized to produce the set of all topics S, i.e.,

Algorithm 1 AMC(D^t, S, M)

```
1: A^t ← GibbsSampling(D^t, N, M, ∅); // ∅: no cannot-links.
2: for r = 1 to R do
3:    C ← C ∪ MineCannotLinks(S, A^t);
4:    A^t ← GibbsSampling(D^t, N, M, C);
5: end for
6: S ← Incorporate(A^t, S);
7: M ← MiningMustLinks(S);
```

$S = \cup_i S_i$. We call S the *prior topic* (or *p-topic*) set. A set of must-links are then mined from S, which will be detailed in Section 4.1. Note that this initialization phase is only applied at the beginning. It will not be used for modeling of each new document collection.

Phase 2 - Lifelong learning with AMC: Given a new/test document collection D^t, this phase employs the proposed AMC model to generate topics from D^t. To distinguish these topics from p-topics, we call them the *current topics* (or *c-topics* for short). AMC is given in Algorithm 1. Line 1 runs the proposed Gibbs sampler (introduced in Section 5.3) using only the must-links M generated from the p-topic set (S) so far to produce a set of topics A^t, where N is the number of Gibbs sampling iterations. Line 3 mines cannot-links based on the current topics A^t and the p-topics S (see Section 4.2). Then line 4 uses both must-links and cannot-links to improve the resulting topics. Note that this process can run iteratively. We call these iterations the *learning iterations*, which are different from the Gibbs iterations. In each learning iteration, we hope to obtain better topic results. We will experiment with the number of learning iterations in Section 6. Currently, the function *Incorporate*(A^t, S) (line 6 in Algorithm 1) is very simple. If the domain of A^t exists in S, replace those topics of the domain in S with A^t; otherwise, A^t is added to S. With the updated S, a new set of must-links is mined (line 7), which will be used in the next new modeling task by calling AMC.

4. MINING KNOWLEDGE

In this section, we present the algorithms for mining must-links and cannot-links, which form our prior knowledge to be used to guide future modeling.

4.1 Mining Must-Link Knowledge

A must-link means that two terms w_1 and w_2 in it should belong to the same topic. That is, there should be some semantic correlation between them. We thus expect w_1 and w_2 to appear together in a number of p-topics in several domains due to the correlation. For example, for a must-link *price*, *cost*, we should expect to see *price* and *cost* as topical terms in the same topic across many domains. Note that they may not appear together in every topic about *price* due to the special context of the domain or past topic modeling errors. Thus, it is natural to use a frequency-based approach to mine frequent sets of terms (words) as reliable must-links.

Before going further, let us first discuss the representation of a topic to be used in mining. Recall that each topic generated from a topic model, such as LDA, is a distribution over terms (or words), i.e., terms with their associated probabilities. Terms are commonly ranked based on their probabilities in a descending order. In practice, top terms under a topic are expected to represent some similar semantic meaning. The lower ranked terms usually have very low probabilities due to the smoothing effect of the Dirichlet hyper-parameters rather than true correlations within the topic, leading to their unreliability. Thus, in this work, only top 15 terms are employed to represent a topic. For mining the must-link and cannot-link knowledge, we use this topic representation.

Given a set of prior topics (p-topics) S, we find sets of terms that appear together in multiple topics using the data mining technique *frequent itemset mining* (FIM). Each itemset is simply a set of terms. The resulting frequent itemsets serve as must-links. However, this technique is insufficient due to the problem with the single minimum support threshold used in classic FIM algorithms.

A single minimum support is not appropriate because generic topics, such as *price* with topic terms like *price* and *cost*, are shared by many (even all) product review domains, but specific topics such as *screen*, occur only in product domains having such features. This means that different topics may have very different frequencies in the data. Thus, using a single minimum support threshold is unable to extract both generic and specific topics because if we set this threshold too low, the generic topics will result in numerous spurious frequent itemsets (which results in wrong must-links) and if we set it too high we will not find any must-link from less frequent topics. This is called the *rare item problem* in data mining and has been well documented in [18].

Due to this problem, we cannot use a traditional frequent item mining algorithm. We actually experimented with one such algorithm, but it produced very poor must-links. We thus use the multiple minimum supports frequent itemset mining (MS-FIM) algorithm in [20]. MS-FIM is stated as follows: Given a set of transactions T, where each transaction $t_i \in T$ is a set of items from a global item set I, i.e., $t_i \subseteq I$. In our context, t_i is the topic vector comprising the top terms of a topic (no probability attached). An item is a term (or word). T is thus the collection of all p-topics in S and I is the set of all terms in S. In MS-FIM, each item/term is given a minimum itemset support (MIS). The minimum support that an itemset (a set of items) must satisfy is not fixed. It depends on the MIS values of all the items in the itemset. MS-FIM also has another constraint, called the support difference constraint (SDC), expressing the requirement that the supports of the items in an itemset must not be too different. MIS and SDC together can solve the above rare item problem. For details about MS-FIM, please refer to [20].

The goal of MS-FIM is to find all itemsets that satisfy the user-specified MIS thresholds. Such itemsets are called *frequent itemsets*. In our context, a frequent itemset is a set of terms which have appeared multiple times in the p-topics. The frequent itemsets of length two are used as our learned must-link knowledge, e.g.,

{battery, life}, {battery, power}, {battery, charge},
{price, expensive}, {price, pricy}, {cheap, expensive}

Note that we use must-links with only two terms in each as they are sufficient to cover the semantic relationship of terms belonging to the same topic. Larger sets tend to contain more errors, i.e., the terms in a set may not belong to the same topic. Such errors are also harder to deal with than those in pairs. The same rationale applies to cannot-links.

4.2 Mining Cannot-Link Knowledge

Following the same intuition as must-link knowledge mining, we also utilize a frequency based approach to mine the cannot-link knowledge. However, there is a major difference. It is prohibitive to find all cannot-links based on the prior document collections D. For a term w, there are usually only a few terms w_m that share must-links with w while there are a huge number of terms w_c that can form cannot-links with w. For example, only the terms related with *price* or *money* share must-links with *expensive*, but the rest of the terms in the vocabulary of D can form potential cannot-links. Thus, in general, if there are V terms in the vocabulary, there are $O(V^2)$ potential cannot-links. However, for a new or test domain D^t, most of these cannot-links are not useful because the vocabulary size of D^t is much smaller than V. Thus, we focus only on those terms that are relevant to D^t.

Formally, given p-topics S from all domain collections D and the current c-topics A^t from the test domain D^t, we extract cannot-links from each pair of top terms w_1 and w_2 in each c-topic $A_j^t \in A^t$. Based on this formulation, to mine cannot-links, we enumerate every pair of top terms w_1 and w_2 and check whether they form a cannot-link or not. Thus, our cannot-link mining is targeted to each c-topic with the aim to improve the c-topic using the discovered cannot-links.

To determine whether two terms form a cannot-link, if the terms seldom appear together in p-topics, they are likely to have distinct semantic meanings. Let the number of prior domains that w_1 and w_2 appear in different p-topics be N_{diff} and the number of prior domains that w_1 and w_2 share the same topic be N_{share}. N_{diff} should be much larger than N_{share}. We need to use two conditions or thresholds to control the formation of a cannot-link:

1. The ratio $N_{diff}/(N_{share} + N_{diff})$ (called the *support ratio*) is equal to or larger than a threshold π_c. This condition is intuitive because p-topics may contain noise due to errors of topic models.
2. N_{diff} is greater than a support threshold π_{diff}. This condition is needed because the above ratio can be 0, but N_{diff} can be very small, which may not give reliable cannot-links.

Some extracted cannot-link examples are listed below:

{battery, money}, {life, movie}, {battery, line}
{price, digital}, {money, slow}, {expensive, simple}

5. AMC MODEL

We now present the proposed AMC model. As noted earlier, due to errors in the results of topic models, some of the automatically mined must-links and cannot-links may be wrong. AMC is capable of handling such incorrect knowledge. The idea is that the semantic relationships reflected by correct must-links and cannot-links should also be reasonably induced by the statistical information underlying the domain collection. If a piece of knowledge (a must-link or a cannot-link) is inconsistent with a domain collection, this piece of knowledge is likely to be either incorrect in general or incorrect in this particular test domain. In either case, the model should not trust or utilize such knowledge.

AMC still uses the graphical model of LDA and its generative process. Thus, we do not give the graphical model. However, the inference mechanism of AMC is entirely different from that of LDA. The inference mechanism cannot be reflected in the graphical model using the plate notation.

Below we first discuss how to handle issues with must-links and cannot-links and then put everything together to present the proposed Gibbs sampler extending the *Pólya urn* model, which we call the *multi-generalized Pólya urn* (M-GPU) model.

5.1 Dealing with Issues of Must-Links

There are two major challenges in incorporating the must-link knowledge:

1. A term can have multiple meanings or senses. For example, *light* may mean "something that makes things visible" or "of little weight." Different senses may lead to distinct must-links. For example, with the first sense of *light*, the must-links can be {light, bright}, {light, luminance}. In contrast, {light, weight}, {light, heavy} indicate the second sense of light. The existing knowledge-based topic model DF-LDA [1] cannot distinguish multiple senses because its definition of must-link is transitive. That is, if terms w_1 and w_2 form a must-link, and terms w_2 and w_3 form a must-link, it implies a must-link between w_1 and w_3, i.e., w_1, w_2, and w_3 should be in the same topic. We call it the *transitivity* problem. DF-LDA would incorrectly assume that *light*, *bright*, and *weight* are in the same topic. MC-LDA [10] assumes each must-link represents a distinct sense, and thus assigns each term only one relevant must-link and ignores the rest. This misses a lot of good must-links. We propose a method in Section 5.1.1 to distinguish multiple senses embedded in must-links and deal with the transitivity problem.
2. Not every must-link is suitable for a domain. First, a must-link may not be correct in general due to errors in topic modeling and knowledge mining, e.g., {battery, beautiful} is not a correct must-link generally. Second, a must-link may be correct in some domains but wrong in others. For example, {card, bill} is a correct must-link in the domain of restaurant (the card here refers to credit cards), but unsuitable in the domain of camera. We will introduce a method to deal with such inappropriate knowledge in Section 5.1.2.

To deal with the first issue, we construct a must-link graph to distinguish multiple senses in must-links to deal with the transitivity problem. To tackle the second problem, we utilize Pointwise Mutual Information (PMI) to estimate the word correlations of must-link terms in the domain collection. These techniques will be introduced in the next two sub-sections and incorporated in the proposed Gibbs sampler in Section 5.3.

5.1.1 Recognizing Multiple Senses

In order to handle the transitivity problem, we need to distinguish multiple senses of terms in must-links. As our must-links are automatically mined from a set of p-topics, the p-topics may also give us some guidance on whether the mined must-links share the same word sense or not. Given two must-links m_1 and m_2, if they share the same word sense, the p-topics that cover m_1 should have some overlapping with the p-topics that cover m_2. For example, must-links {light, bright} and {light, luminance} should be mostly coming from the same set of p-topics related to the semantic meaning "something that makes things visible" of *light*. On the other hand, little topic overlapping indicates likely different word senses. For example, must-links {light, bright} and {light, weight} may come from two different sets of p-topics as they usually refer to different topics.

Following this idea, we construct a must-link graph G where a must-link is a vertex. An edge is formed between two vertices if the two must-links m_1 and m_2 have a shared term. For each edge, we check how much their original p-topics overlap to decide whether the two must-links share the same sense or not. Given two must-links m_1 and m_2, we denote the p-topics in S covering each of them as T_1 and T_2 respectively. m_1 and m_2 share the same sense if

$$\frac{\#T_1 \cap T_2}{Max(\#T_1, \#T_2)} > \pi_{overlap} \tag{1}$$

where $\pi_{overlap}$ is the *overlap threshold* for distinguishing senses. This threshold is necessary due to errors of topic models. The edges that do not satisfy the above inequality (Equation 1) are deleted.

The final must-link graph G gives us some guidance in selecting the right must-links sharing the same word sense in the Gibbs sampler in Section 5.3 for dealing with the transitivity problem.

5.1.2 Detecting Possible Wrong Knowledge

To measure the correctness of a must-link in a particular domain, we apply Pointwise Mutual Information (PMI), which is a popular measure of word associations in text. In our case, it measures the extent to which two terms tend to co-occur, which corresponds to "the higher-order co-occurrence" on which topic models are based [11]. PMI of two words (or terms) is defined as follows:

$$PMI(w_1, w_2) = log\frac{P(w_1, w_2)}{P(w_1)P(w_2)} \tag{2}$$

where $P(w)$ denotes the probability of seeing term w in a random document, and $P(w_1, w_2)$ denotes the probability of seeing both terms co-occurring in a random document. These probabilities are empirically estimated from the current document collection D^t:

$$P(w) = \frac{\#D^t(w)}{\#D^t} \tag{3}$$

$$P(w_1, w_2) = \frac{\#D^t(w_1, w_2)}{\#D^t} \tag{4}$$

where $\#D^t(w)$ is the number of documents in D^t that contain the term w and $\#D^t(w_1, w_2)$ is the number of documents that contain both terms w_1 and w_2. $\#D^t$ is the total number of documents in D^t. A positive PMI value implies a semantic correlation of terms, while a non-positive PMI value indicates little or no semantic correlation. Thus, we only consider the positive PMI values, which will be used in the proposed Gibbs sampler in Section 5.3.

5.2 Dealing with Issues of Cannot-Links

The main issue here is incorrect cannot-links. Similar to must-links, there are also two cases: a) A cannot-link contains terms that have semantic correlations. For example, {battery, charger} is not a correct cannot-link. b) A cannot-link does not fit for a particular domain. For example, {card, bill} is a correct cannot-link in the camera domain, but not appropriate for restaurants.

Wrong cannot-links can also cause conflicts with must-links. For example, the system may find two must-links {price, cost} and {price, pricy} and a cannot-link {pricy, cost}. Existing knowledge-based models, such as DF-LDA [1] and MC-LDA [10], cannot solve these problems. A further challenge for these systems is that the number of automatically mined cannot-links is large (more than 400 cannot-links on average). Both DF-LDA and MC-LDA are incapable of using so many cannot-links. As we will see in Section 6, DF-LDA crashed and MC-LDA generated a large number of additional (wrong) topics with very poor results.

Wrong cannot-links are usually harder to detect and to verify than wrong must-links. Due to the power-law distribution of natural language words [38], most words are rare and will not co-occur with most other words. The low co-occurrences of two words do not necessarily mean a negative correlation (cannot-link). Thus, we detect and balance cannot-links inside the sampling process. More specifically, we extend Pólya urn model to incorporate the cannot-link knowledge, and also to deal with the issues above.

5.3 Proposed Gibbs Sampler

This section introduces the Gibbs sampler for the proposed AMC model, which differs from LDA as AMC needs the additional mechanism to leverage the prior knowledge and to also deal with the problems with the prior knowledge during sampling. We propose the *multi-generalized Pólya urn* (M-GPU) model for the task. Below, we first introduce the Pólya urn model which serves as the basic framework to incorporate knowledge, and then enhance it to address the challenges mentioned in the above sub-sections.

5.3.1 Pólya Urn Model

Traditionally, the Pólya urn model works on colored balls and urns. In the topic model context, a term can be seen as a ball of a certain color and a topic as an urn. The distribution of a topic is reflected by the color proportions of balls in the urn. LDA follows the simple Pólya urn (SPU) model in the sense that when a ball of a particular color is drawn from an urn, the ball is put back to the urn along with a new ball of the same color. The content of the urn changes over time, which gives a self-reinforcing property known as "the rich get richer". This process corresponds to assigning a topic to a term in Gibbs sampling.

The generalized Pólya urn (GPU) model [22, 24] differs from SPU in that, when a ball of a certain color is drawn, two balls of that color are put back along with a certain number of balls of some other colors. These additional balls of some other colors added to the urn increase their proportions in the urn. This is the key technique for incorporating must-links as we will see below.

Instead of involving only one urn at a time as in the SPU and GPU model, the proposed *multi-generalized Pólya urn* (M-GPU) model considers a set of urns in the sampling process simultaneously. M-GPU allows a ball to be transferred from one urn to another, enabling multi-urn interactions. Thus, during sampling, the populations of several urns will evolve even if only one ball is drawn from one urn. This capability makes the M-GPU model more powerful and suitable for solving our complex problems.

5.3.2 Proposed M-GPU Model

In M-GPU, when a ball is randomly drawn, certain numbers of additional balls of each color are returned to the urn, rather than just two balls of the same color as in SPU. This is inherited from GPU. As a result, the proportions of these colored balls are increased, making them more likely to be drawn in this urn in the future. We call this the *promotion* of these colored balls. Applying the idea to our case, when a term w is assigned to a topic k, each term w' that shares a must-link with w is also assigned to topic k by a certain amount, which is decided by the matrix $\lambda_{w',w}$ (see Equation 5). w' is thus promoted by w. As a result, the probability of w' under topic k is also increased.

To deal with multiple senses problem in M-GPU, we exploit the fact that each term usually has only one correct sense or meaning under one topic. Since the semantic concept of a topic is usually represented by some top terms under it, we refer the word sense that is the most related to the concept as the correct sense. If a term w does not have must-links, then we do not have the multiple sense problem caused by must-links. If w has must-links, the rationale here is to sample a must-link (say m) that contains w to be used to represent the likely word sense from the must-link graph G (built in Section 5.1.1). The sampling distribution will be given in Section 5.3.3. Then, the must-links that share the same word sense with m, including m, are used to promote the related terms of w.

To deal with possible wrong must-links, we leverage the PMI measure (in Section 5.1.2) to estimate knowledge correctness in the M-GPU model. More specifically, we add a parameter factor μ to control how much the M-GPU model should trust the word relationship indicated by PMI. Formally, the amount of promotion for term w' when seen w is defined as follows:

$$\lambda_{w',w} = \begin{cases} 1 & w = w' \\ \mu \times PMI(w, w') & (w, w') \text{ is a must-link} \\ 0 & \text{otherwise} \end{cases} \quad (5)$$

To deal with cannot-links, M-GPU defines two sets of urns which will be used in sampling in the AMC model. The first set is the set of topic urns $U^K_{d \in \{1...D^t\}}$, where each urn is for one document and contains balls of K colors (topics) and each ball inside has a color $k \in \{1...K\}$. This corresponds to the document-topic distribution in AMC. The second set of urns is the set of term urns $U^W_{k \in \{1...K\}}$ corresponding to the topic-term distributions, with balls of colors (terms) $w \in \{1...V\}$ in each term urn.

Based on the definition of cannot-link, two terms in a cannot-link cannot both have large probabilities under the same topic. As M-GPU allows multi-urn interactions, when sampling a ball representing term w from a term urn U^W_k, we want to transfer the balls representing the cannot-terms of w, say w_c (sharing cannot-links with w) to other urns (see Step 5 below), i.e., decreasing the probabilities of those cannot-terms under this topic while increasing their corresponding probabilities under some other topic. In order to correctly transfer a ball that represents term w_c, it should be transferred to an urn which has a higher proportion of w_c. That is, we randomly sample an urn that has a higher proportion of w_c to transfer w_c to (Step 5b below). However, there is a situation when there is no other urn that has a higher proportion of w_c. [10] proposed to create a new urn to move w_c to under the assumption that the cannot-link knowledge is correct. As discussed in Section 5.2, the cannot-link knowledge may not be correct. For example, consider that the model puts battery and life in the same topic k where both *battery* and *life* have the highest probability (or proportion), a cannot-link {battery, life} wants to separate them after seeing them in the same topic. In such a case, we should not trust the cannot-link as it may split the correlated terms into different topics.

Based on all the above ideas, we now present the M-GPU sampling scheme as follows:

1. Sample a topic k from U^K_d and a term w from U^W_k sequentially, where d is the dth document in D^t.
2. Record k and w, put back two balls of color k into urn U^K_d, and two balls of color w into urn U^W_k.
3. Sample a must-link m that contains w from the prior knowledge base. Get a set of must-links $\{m'\}$ where m' is either m or a neighbor of m in the must-link graph G.
4. For each must-link $\{w, w'\}$ in $\{m'\}$, we put back $\lambda_{w',w}$ number of balls of color w' into urn U^W_k based on matrix $\lambda_{w',w}$ (in Equation 5).
5. For each term w_c that shares a cannot-link with w:
   (a) Draw a ball q_c of color w_c (to be transferred) from U^W_k and remove it from U^W_k. The document of ball q_c is denoted by d_c. If no ball of color w_c can be drawn (i.e., there is no ball of color w_c in U^W_k), skip steps b) and c).
   (b) Produce an urn set $\{U^W_{k'}\}$ such that each urn in it satisfies the following conditions:
   i) $k' \neq k$
   ii) The proportion of balls of color w_c in $U^W_{k'}$ is higher than that of balls of color w_c in U^W_k.
   (c) If $\{U^W_{k'}\}$ is not empty, randomly select one urn $U^W_{k'}$ from it. Put the ball q_c drawn from Step a) into $U^W_{k'}$. Also, remove a ball of color k from urn $U^K_{d_c}$ and put back a ball of k' into urn $U^K_{d_c}$. If $\{U^W_{k'}\}$ is empty, put the ball q_c back to U^W_k.

5.3.3 Sampling Distributions

Based on the above sampling scheme of M-GPU, this subsection gives the final Gibbs sampler with the conditional distributions and algorithms for the AMC model. Inference of topics can be computationally expensive due to the non-exchangeability of words under the M-GPU models. We thus take the same approach as that for GPU in [24] which approximates the true Gibbs sampling distribution by treating each word as if it were the last.

For each term w_i in each document d, there are two phases corresponding to the M-GPU sampling process (Section 5.3.2):

Phase 1 (Steps 1-4 in M-GPU): calculate the conditional probability of sampling a topic for term w_i. We enumerate each topic k and calculate its corresponding probability, which is decided by three sub-steps:

a) Sample a must-link m_i that contains w_i, which is likely to have the word sense consistent with topic k, which is based on the following conditional distribution:

$$P(m_i = m|k) \propto P(w_1|k) \times P(w_2|k) \quad (6)$$

where w_1 and w_2 are the terms in must-link m and one of them is the same as w_i. $P(w|k)$ is the probability of term w under topic k given the current status of the Markov chain in the Gibbs sampler, which is defined as:

$$P(w|k) \propto \frac{\sum_{w'=1}^{V} \lambda_{w',w} \times n_{k,w'} + \beta}{\sum_{v=1}^{V}(\sum_{w'=1}^{V} \lambda_{w',v} \times n_{k,w'} + \beta)} \quad (7)$$

where $\lambda_{w',w}$ is the promotion matrix in Equation 5. $n_{k,w}$ refers to the number of times that term w appears under topic k. β is the predefined Dirichlet hyper-parameter.

b) After getting the sampled must-link m_i, we create a set of must-links $\{m'\}$ where m' is either m_i or a neighbor of m_i in the must-link graph G. The must-links in this set $\{m'\}$ are likely to share the same word sense of term

w_i according to the corresponding edges in the must-link graph G.

c) The conditional probability of assigning topic k to term w_i is defined as below:

$$p(z_i = k|\boldsymbol{z}^{-i}, \boldsymbol{w}, \alpha, \beta, \lambda) \propto \frac{n_{d,k}^{-i} + \alpha}{\sum_{k'=1}^{K}(n_{d,k'}^{-i} + \alpha)} \times \frac{\sum_{\{w',w_i\}\in\{m'\}} \lambda_{w',w_i} \times n_{k,w'}^{-i} + \beta}{\sum_{v=1}^{V}(\sum_{\{w',v\}\in\{m'_v\}} \lambda_{w',v} \times n_{k,w'}^{-i} + \beta)} \quad (8)$$

where n^{-i} is the count excluding the current assignment of z_i, i.e., $\boldsymbol{z}^{-i}$. $\boldsymbol{w}$ refers to all the terms in all documents in the document collection D^t and w_i is the current term to be sampled with a topic denoted by z_i. $n_{d,k}$ denotes the number of times that topic k is assigned to terms in document d. $n_{k,w}$ refers to the number of times that term w appears under topic k. α and β are predefined Dirichlet hyper-parameters. K is the number of topics, and V is the vocabulary size. $\{m'_v\}$ is the set of must-links sampled for each term v following Phase 1 a) and b), which is recorded during the iterations. $\lambda_{w',w}$ is the promotion matrix in Equation 5.

Phase 2 (Step 5 in M-GPU): this sampling phase deals with cannot-links. There are two sub-steps:

a) For every cannot-term (say w_c) of w_i, we sample one instance (say q_c) of w_c from topic z_i, where z_i denotes the topic assigned to term w_i in Phase 1, based on the following conditional distribution:

$$P(q = q_c|\boldsymbol{z}, \boldsymbol{w}, \alpha) \propto \frac{n_{d_c,k} + \alpha}{\sum_{k'=1}^{K}(n_{d_c,k'} + \alpha)} \quad (9)$$

where d_c denotes the document of the instance q_c. If there is no instance of w_c in z_i, skip step b).

b) For each drawn instance q_c from Phase 2 a), resample a topic k (not equal to z_i) based on the conditional distribution below:

$$P(z_{q_c} = k|\boldsymbol{z}^{-q_c}, \boldsymbol{w}, \alpha, \beta, \lambda, q = q_c) \propto \boldsymbol{I}_{[0,p(w_c|k))]}(P(w_c|z_c)) \times \frac{n_{d,k}^{-q_c} + \alpha}{\sum_{k'=1}^{K}(n_{d,k'}^{-q_c} + \alpha)} \times \frac{\sum_{\{w',w_i\}\in\{m'_c\}} \lambda_{w',w_i} \times n_{k,w'}^{-q_c} + \beta}{\sum_{v=1}^{V}(\sum_{\{w',v\}\in\{m'_v\}} \lambda_{w',v} \times n_{k,w'}^{-q_c} + \beta)} \quad (10)$$

where z_c (the same as z_i sampled from Equation 8) is the original topic assignment. $\{m'_c\}$ is the set of must-links sampled for term w_c. Superscript $-q_c$ denotes the counts excluding the original assignments. $\boldsymbol{I}()$ is an indicator function, which restricts the ball to be transferred only to an urn that contains a higher proportion of term w_c. If there is no topic k has a higher proportion of w_c than z_c, then keep the original topic assignment, i.e., assign z_c to w_c.

6. EVALUATION

This section evaluates the proposed AMC model and compares it with five state-of-the-art baseline models:

LDA [4]: The classic unsupervised topic model.

DF-LDA [1]: A knowledge-based topic model that can use both must-links and cannot-links, but it assumes all the knowledge is correct.

MC-LDA [10]: A knowledge-based topic model that also use both the must-link and the cannot-link knowledge. It assumes that all knowledge is correct as well.

GK-LDA [9]: A knowledge-based topic model that uses the ratio of word probabilities under each topic to reduce the effect of wrong knowledge. However, it can only use the must-link type of knowledge.

LTM [7]: A lifelong learning topic model that learns only the must-link type of knowledge automatically. It outperformed [8].

Note that although DF-LDA, MC-LDA and GK-LDA can take prior knowledge from the user, they cannot mine any prior knowledge, which make them not directly comparable with the proposed AMC model. We have to feed them the knowledge produced using the proposed knowledge mining algorithm. This enables us to assess the knowledge handling capability of each model. LTM uses its own way to mine and incorporate must-links.

6.1 Experimental Settings

Datasets. We have created two large datasets for our experiments. The first dataset contains reviews from 50 types of electronic products or domains (given in the first row of Table 1). The second dataset contains reviews from 50 mixed types of non-electronic products or domains (given in the second row of Table 1). Each domain has 1000 reviews. Using the first dataset, we want to show the performance of AMC when there is a reasonably large topic overlapping. Using the second dataset, we want to show AMC's performance when there is not much topic overlapping. We followed [9] to pre-process the dataset. The datasets are publicly available at the authors' websites.

Parameter Setting. All models were trained using 2000 iterations with an initial burn-in of 200 iterations. The parameters of all topic models are set to $\alpha = 1$, $\alpha = 0.1$, $K = 15$ (#Topics). The other parameters for the baselines were set as suggested in their original papers. For parameters of AMC, we estimated its parameters using a development set from the domain, Calculator, which was not used in the evaluation. The minimum item support count (MIS) for each term is set to $Max(4$, 35% of its actual support count in the data) and the support difference is 8% [18]. The support ratio threshold (π_c) and support threshold (π_{diff}) for cannot-link mining is 80% and 10 respectively. The overlap ratio threshold $\pi_{overlap}$ for forming a must-link graph edge is 17%. The parameter μ in Equation 5 is set to 0.5, which determines the extent of promotion of words in must-links using the M-GPU model.

6.2 Topic Coherence

This sub-section evaluates the topics generated by each model based on the Topic Coherence measure in [24]. Traditionally, topic models are evaluated using perplexity. However, as shown in [6], perplexity does not reflect the semantic coherence of individual topics. It can sometimes be contrary to human judgments. The Topic Coherence measure [24] was proposed as a better alternative for assessing topic quality. It was shown in [24] that Topic Coherence correlates well with human expert labeling. A higher Topic Coherence indicates a higher quality of topics.

Alarm Clock, Amplifier, Battery, Blu-Ray Player, Cable Modem, Camcorder, Camera, Car Stereo, CD Player, Cell Phone, Computer, DVD Player, Fan, GPS, Graphics Card, Hard Drive, Headphone, Home Theater System, Iron, Keyboard, Kindle, Lamp, Laptop, Media Player, Memory Card, Microphone, Microwave, Monitor, Mouse, MP3Player, Network Adapter, Printer, Projector, Radar Detector, Remote Control, Rice Cooker, Scanner, Speaker, Subwoofer, Tablet, Telephone, TV, Vacuum, Video Player, Video Recorder, Voice Recorder, Watch, Webcam, Wireless Router, Xbox
Android Appstore, Appliances, Arts Crafts Sewing, Automotive, Baby, Bag, Beauty, Bike, Books, Cable, Care, Clothing, Conditioner, Diaper, Dining, Dumbbell, Flashlight, Food, Gloves, Golf, Home Improvement, Industrial Scientific, Jewelry, Kindle Store, Kitchen, Knife, Luggage, Magazine Subscriptions, Mat, Mattress, Movies TV, Music, Musical Instruments, Office Products, Patio Lawn Garden, Pet Supplies, Pillow, Sandal, Scooter, Shoes, Software, Sports, Table Chair, Tent, Tire, Toys, Video Games, Vitamin Supplement, Wall Clock, Water Filter

Table 1: List of 100 domain names: electronic products (1st row) and non-electronic products (2nd row).

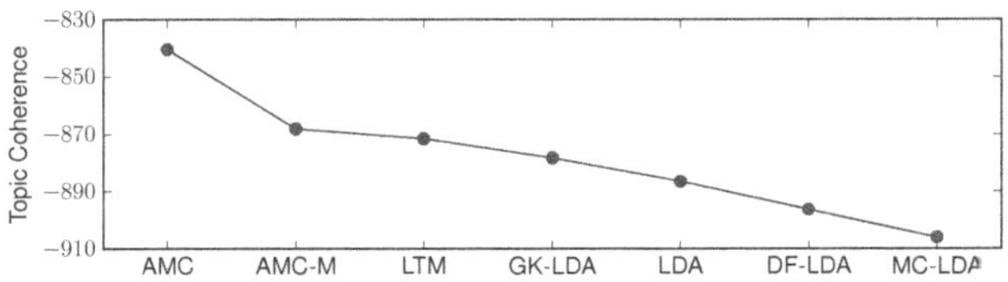

Figure 1: Average Topic Coherence of each model.

In this and the next two sub-sections, we experiment with the 50 Electronics domains, which have a large amount of topic overlapping. We treat each domain as a test set (D^t) while the knowledge is mined from the rest 49 domains. Since our main aim is to improve topic modeling with small datasets, each test set consists of 100 reviews randomly sampled from the 1000 reviews of the domain. We extract knowledge from topics generated from the full data (1000 reviews) of all other 49 domains. Since we have 50 domains, we have 50 small test sets. Figure 1 shows the average Topic Coherence value of each model over the 50 test sets. From Figure 1, we can observe the following:

1. AMC performs the best with the highest Topic Coherence value. In the Figure, "AMC" refers to the AMC model with both must-links and cannot-links and "AMC-M" refers to the AMC model with must-links only. We can see that AMC-M is already better than all baseline models, showing the effectiveness of must-links. AMC is much better than AMC-M which demonstrates that cannot-links are very helpful. These results show that AMC finds higher quality topics than the baselines.

   Note that in our experiments, we found DF-LDA and MC-LDA cannot deal with a large number of cannot-links. We have more than 400 automatically mined cannot-links on average for each test set. For DF-LDA, the number of maximum cliques grows exponentially with the number of cannot-links. The program thus crashed on our data. This issue was also noted in [36]. For MC-LDA, it increases the number of topics whenever there is not a good topic to put a cannot-link term in. This results in a large number of topics (more than 50), which are unreasonable and give very poor results. Thus, for both DF-LDA and MC-LDA, we can only show their results with must-links,
2. LTM is better than LDA while clearly worse than AMC. The additional information from the cannot-links is shown to help produce much more coherent topics. GK-LDA is slightly better than LDA. The wrong knowledge handling method in GK-LDA can cope with some wrong knowledge, but not as effective as AMC.
3. We also notice that both DF-LDA and MC-LDA are worse than LDA. This is because they assume the knowledge to be correct and lack the necessary mechanism to deal with wrong knowledge. Also, for MC-LDA, it assumes each must-link (or must-set in [10]) represents a distinct sense or meaning. Thus, it assigns only one must-link to each word and ignores the rest. Then most must-links are not used. This explains also why MC-LDA is worse than DF-LDA.

Iterative improvement (lines 2-5 in Algorithm 1): We found that accumulating cannot-links iteratively is beneficial to AMC. The Topic Coherence value increases slightly from $r = 1$ to 3 and stabilizes at $r = 3$ (Algorithm 1). Figure 1 shows the AMC's result for $r = 3$.

Comparing with LTM using 1000 reviews: To further compare with LTM, we also conducted experiments in the same setting as [7], i.e., each test document collection contains also 1,000 reviews (not 100 as in Figure 1). AMC still improves LTM by 47 points in Topic Coherence, showing that AMC can also produce more coherent topics with a large number of test documents.

In summary, we can say that the proposed AMC model generates more coherent topics than all baseline models. Even though DF-LDA, GK-LDA and MC-LDA used our method for knowledge mining, without an effective wrong knowledge handling method, they gave poorer results. The improvements of AMC over all baselines are significant ($p < 0.0001$) based on paired t-tests.

6.3 Human Evaluation

Here we want to evaluate the topics based on human judgment. Two human judges who are familiar with Amazon products and reviews were asked to label the generated topics. Since we have a large number of domains (50), we selected 10 domains for labeling. The selection was based on the knowledge of the products of the two human judges. Without enough knowledge, labeling will not be reliable. We labeled the topics generated by AMC, LTM and LDA. LDA is the basic knowledge-free topic model and LTM is our earlier lifelong learning model that achieves the highest Topic Coherence among the baselines in Figure 1. For labeling, we followed the instructions in [24].

Topic Labeling. We first asked the judges to label each topic as *coherent* or *incoherent*. The models that generated the topics for labeling were obscure to the judges. In general, a topic was labeled as coherent if its topical words/terms are semantically *coherent* and together represent a semantic concept; otherwise *incoherent*.

Word Labeling. The topics that were labeled as coherent by both judges were used for word labeling. Each topical word was labeled as *correct* if it was coherently related to the concept represented by the topic (identified in the topic labeling step); otherwise *incorrect*.

The Cohen's Kappa agreement scores for topic labeling and word labeling are 0.873 and 0.860 respectively.

Evaluation Measures. Since topics are rankings of words based on their probabilities, without knowing the exact num-

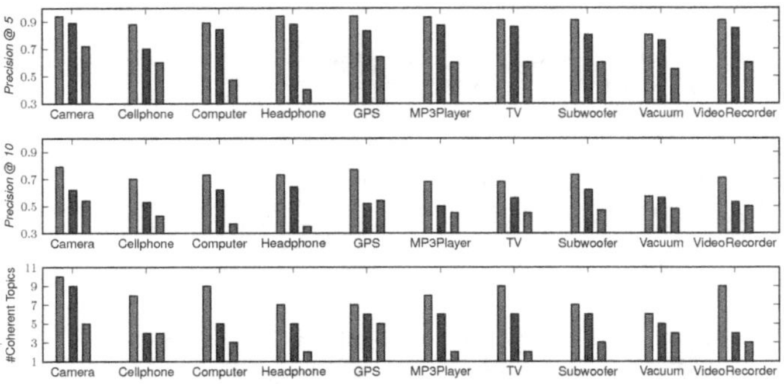

Figure 2: Top & Middle: Topical words ***Precision*@5 & *Precision*@10 of coherent topics of each model respectively; Bottom: number of coherent (#Coherent) topics found by each model. The bars from left to right in each group are for AMC, LTM, and LDA.**

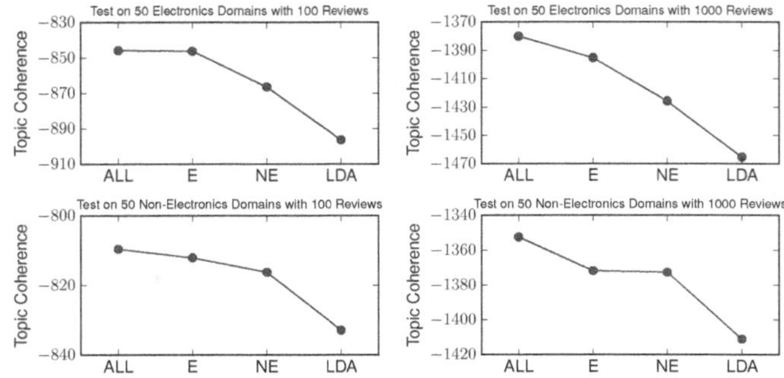

Figure 3: Average Topic Coherence of AMC compared to LDA in different settings (see Section 6.5). ALL means Electronics (E) + Non-Electronics (NE) and LDA is equivalent to no knowledge.

Price			Size & Weight		
AMC	LTM	LDA	AMC	LTM	LDA
money	*shot*	*image*	size	small	*easy*
buy	money	price	small	big	small
price	*review*	*movie*	smaller	size	*canon*
range	price	*stabilization*	weight	pocket	pocket
cheap	cheap	*picture*	compact	*lcd*	*feature*
expensive	*camcorder*	*technical*	hand	*place*	*shot*
deal	*condition*	*photo*	big	*screen*	*lens*
point	*con*	*dslr*	pocket	*kid*	*dslr*
performance	*sony*	*move*	heavy	*exposure*	compact
extra	*trip*	*short*	*case*	*case*	*reduction*

Table 2: Example topics of AMC, LTM and LDA from the Camera domain. Errors are italicized and marked in red.

ber of correct topical words/terms, a natural way to evaluate these rankings is to use *Precision*@n (or p@n) which was also used by other researchers, e.g., [9, 37], where n is a rank position. Apart from p@n, we also report the number of coherent topics found by each model.

Results. Figure 2 gives the average *Precision*@5 (top chart) and *Precision*@10 (middle chart) of topical words of only coherent topics (incoherent topics are not considered) for each model in each domain. It is clear that AMC achieves the highest p@5 and p@10 values for all 10 domains. LTM is also better than LDA in general but clearly inferior to AMC. This is consistent with the Topic Coherence results in Section 6.2. LDA's results are very poor without a large amount of data. On average, for p@5 and p@10, AMC improves LTM by 8% and 14%, and LDA by 33% and 25% respectively. Significance testing using paired t-tests shows that the improvements of AMC are significant over LTM ($p < 0.0002$) and LDA ($p < 0.0001$) on p@5 and p@10.

The bottom chart of Figure 2 shows that AMC also discovers many more coherent topics than LTM and LDA. On average, AMC discovers 2.4 more coherent topics than LTM and 4.7 more coherent topics than LDA over the 10 domains. These results are remarkable. In many domains, LDA only finds 2-4 coherent topics and never more than 5 (out of 15), which again shows that with a small number of documents (reviews), LDA's results are very poor.

6.4 Example Topics

This section shows some example topics produced by AMC, LTM, and LDA in the Camera domain to give a flavor of the kind of improvements made by AMC. Each topic is shown with its top 10 terms. Errors are italicized and marked in red. From Table 2, we can see that AMC discovers many more correct and meaningful topical terms at the top than the baselines. Note that for AMC's topics that were not discovered by the baseline models, we tried to find the best possible matches from the topics of the baseline models. The topic we show for LDA under "Price" is the only one that contains a "Price" related word. Here, the term *price* is mixed with other terms related to the topic "Picture Quality". From the table, we can clearly see that AMC discovers more coherent topics than LTM and LDA. In fact, the coherent topics of AMC are all better than their corresponding topics of LTM and LDA.

6.5 Experiments Using Both Datasets

The above experiments focused on 50 Electronics domains, which have a great deal of topic overlapping. Now we also want to see how AMC performs when the test domain does not have a lot of topic overlapping with the past/prior domains. We use two test data settings: the test set is from (1) an Electronics domain or (2) an non-Electronics domain. For each test set setting, we mine knowledge from topics of (a) 50 Electronics domains (E), (b) 50 non-Electronics domains (NE), and (c) all 100 domains (ALL). For each test set, we use both 100 and 1000 reviews. Figure 3 shows the performance of AMC in each of these settings compared to LDA in terms of Topic Coherence. We can clearly see that AMC performs the best with the knowledge mined from topics of all 100 domains. 50 non-Electronics domains are helpful too because they also share some topics such as *price* and *size*. The improvement of AMC in each setting is significant over LDA using paired t-test ($p < 0.0001$). This clearly shows that AMC is able to leverage the useful knowledge from different domains even if the domains are not so related.

7. CONCLUSIONS

This paper proposed an advanced topic model AMC that is able to perform lifelong learning. For such learning, it mines prior knowledge from the results of past modeling and uses the knowledge to help future modeling. Our system mines two forms of prior knowledge, i.e., must-links and cannot-links, automatically from topics generated from a large number of prior document collections (the big data). The system also identifies some issues with the automatically mined knowledge. The proposed model AMC not only can exploit the learned knowledge but also can deal with the issues of the mined knowledge to generate more accurate topics. Experimental results using review collections from 100 domains showed that the proposed AMC model outperforms existing state-of-the-art models significantly. In our future work, we plan to study other aspects of lifelong learning in the topic modeling context, e.g., how to maintain the prior topics and how to incrementally update the must-links knowledge when new topics are added to the prior topic set.

8. ACKNOWLEDGMENTS

This work was supported in part by a grant from National Science Foundation (NSF) under grant no. IIS-1111092.

References

[1] D. Andrzejewski, X. Zhu, and M. Craven. Incorporating domain knowledge into topic modeling via Dirichlet Forest priors. In *ICML*, pages 25–32, 2009.

[2] D. Andrzejewski, X. Zhu, M. Craven, and B. Recht. A framework for incorporating general domain knowledge into latent Dirichlet allocation using first-order logic. In *IJCAI*, pages 1171–1177, 2011.

[3] D. M. Blei and J. D. McAuliffe. Supervised Topic Models. In *NIPS*, pages 121–128, 2007.

[4] D. M. Blei, A. Y. Ng, and M. I. Jordan. Latent Dirichlet Allocation. *Journal of Machine Learning Research*, 3:993–1022, 2003.

[5] S. R. K. Branavan, H. Chen, J. Eisenstein, and R. Barzilay. Learning Document-Level Semantic Properties from Free-Text Annotations. In *ACL*, pages 263–271, 2008.

[6] J. Chang, J. Boyd-Graber, W. Chong, S. Gerrish, and D. M. Blei. Reading Tea Leaves: How Humans Interpret Topic Models. In *NIPS*, pages 288–296, 2009.

[7] Z. Chen and B. Liu. Topic Modeling using Topics from Many Domains, Lifelong Learning and Big Data. In *ICML*, 2014.

[8] Z. Chen, A. Mukherjee, and B. Liu. Aspect Extraction with Automated Prior Knowledge Learning. In *ACL*, pages 347–358, 2014.

[9] Z. Chen, A. Mukherjee, B. Liu, M. Hsu, M. Castellanos, and R. Ghosh. Discovering Coherent Topics Using General Knowledge. In *CIKM*, pages 209–218, 2013.

[10] Z. Chen, A. Mukherjee, B. Liu, M. Hsu, M. Castellanos, and R. Ghosh. Exploiting Domain Knowledge in Aspect Extraction. In *EMNLP*, pages 1655–1667, 2013.

[11] G. Heinrich. A Generic Approach to Topic Models. In *ECML PKDD*, pages 517 – 532, 2009.

[12] T. Hofmann. Probabilistic Latent Semantic Analysis. In *UAI*, pages 289–296, 1999.

[13] M. Hu and B. Liu. Mining and Summarizing Customer Reviews. In *KDD*, pages 168–177, 2004.

[14] Y. Hu, J. Boyd-Graber, and B. Satinoff. Interactive Topic Modeling. In *ACL*, pages 248–257, 2011.

[15] J. Jagarlamudi, H. D. III, and R. Udupa. Incorporating Lexical Priors into Topic Models. In *EACL*, pages 204–213, 2012.

[16] Y. Jo and A. H. Oh. Aspect and sentiment unification model for online review analysis. In *WSDM*, pages 815–824, Feb. 2011.

[17] J.-h. Kang, J. Ma, and Y. Liu. Transfer Topic Modeling with Ease and Scalability. In *SDM*, pages 564–575, 2012.

[18] B. Liu. *Web data mining*. Springer, 2007.

[19] B. Liu. *Sentiment Analysis and Opinion Mining*. Morgan & Claypool Publishers, 2012.

[20] B. Liu, W. Hsu, and Y. Ma. Mining association rules with multiple minimum supports. In *KDD*, pages 337–341. ACM, 1999.

[21] Y. Lu and C. Zhai. Opinion integration through semi-supervised topic modeling. In *WWW*, pages 121–130, 2008.

[22] H. Mahmoud. *Polya Urn Models*. Chapman & Hall/CRC Texts in Statistical Science, 2008.

[23] Q. Mei, X. Ling, M. Wondra, H. Su, and C. Zhai. Topic sentiment mixture: modeling facets and opinions in weblogs. In *WWW*, pages 171–180, 2007.

[24] D. Mimno, H. M. Wallach, E. Talley, M. Leenders, and A. McCallum. Optimizing semantic coherence in topic models. In *EMNLP*, pages 262–272, 2011.

[25] S. Moghaddam and M. Ester. The FLDA Model for Aspect-based Opinion Mining: Addressing the Cold Start Problem. In *WWW*, pages 909–918, 2013.

[26] A. Mukherjee and B. Liu. Aspect Extraction through Semi-Supervised Modeling. In *ACL*, pages 339–348, 2012.

[27] S. J. Pan and Q. Yang. A Survey on Transfer Learning. *IEEE Trans. Knowl. Data Eng.*, 22(10):1345–1359, 2010.

[28] J. Petterson, A. Smola, T. Caetano, W. Buntine, and S. Narayanamurthy. Word Features for Latent Dirichlet Allocation. In *NIPS*, pages 1921–1929, 2010.

[29] D. Ramage, D. Hall, R. Nallapati, and C. D. Manning. Labeled LDA: a supervised topic model for credit attribution in multi-labeled corpora. In *EMNLP*, pages 248–256, 2009.

[30] D. L. Silver, Q. Yang, and L. Li. Lifelong Machine Learning Systems: Beyond Learning Algorithms. In *AAAI Spring Symposium: Lifelong Machine Learning*, 2013.

[31] S. Thrun. Lifelong Learning Algorithms. In S. Thrun and L. Pratt, editors, *Learning To Learn*. Kluwer Academic Publishers, 1998.

[32] I. Titov and R. McDonald. Modeling online reviews with multi-grain topic models. In *WWW*, pages 111–120, 2008.

[33] H. Wang, Y. Lu, and C. Zhai. Latent aspect rating analysis on review text data: a rating regression approach. In *KDD*, pages 783–792, 2010.

[34] G. Xue, W. Dai, Q. Yang, and Y. Yu. Topic-bridged PLSA for cross-domain text classification. In *SIGIR*, pages 627–634, 2008.

[35] S. H. Yang, S. P. Crain, and H. Zha. Bridging the Language Gap: Topic Adaptation for Documents with Different Technicality. In *AISTATS*, volume 15, pages 823–831, 2011.

[36] Z. Zhai, B. Liu, H. Xu, and P. Jia. Constrained LDA for grouping product features in opinion mining. In *PAKDD*, pages 448–459, May 2011.

[37] W. X. Zhao, J. Jiang, H. Yan, and X. Li. Jointly Modeling Aspects and Opinions with a MaxEnt-LDA Hybrid. In *EMNLP*, pages 56–65, 2010.

[38] G. K. Zipf. *Selective Studies and the Principle of Relative Frequency in Language*. Harvard University Press, 1932.

Integrating Spreadsheet Data via Accurate and Low-Effort Extraction

Zhe Chen
University of Michigan
Ann Arbor, MI 48109-2121
chenzhe@umich.edu

Michael Cafarella
University of Michigan
Ann Arbor, MI 48109-2121
michjc@umich.edu

ABSTRACT

Spreadsheets contain valuable data on many topics. However, spreadsheets are difficult to integrate with other data sources. Converting spreadsheet data to the relational model would allow data analysts to use relational integration tools.

We propose a two-phase *semiautomatic* system that extracts accurate relational metadata while minimizing user effort. Based on an undirected graphical model, our system enables downstream spreadsheet integration applications. First, the *automatic extractor* uses hints from spreadsheets' graphical style and recovered metadata to extract the spreadsheet data as accurately as possible. Second, the *interactive repair* identifies similar regions in distinct spreadsheets scattered across large spreadsheet corpora, allowing a user's single manual repair to be amortized over many possible extraction errors. Our experiments show that a human can obtain the accurate extraction with just 31% of the manual operations required by a standard classification based technique on two real-world datasets.

Categories and Subject Descriptors

H.2.8 [**Database Management**]: Database applications-Data Mining

Keywords

Information extraction; spreadsheets; graphical model

1. INTRODUCTION

Spreadsheets are a critical data management tool that are diverse and widely used: Microsoft estimates the number of worldwide Excel users at more than 400 million, and Forrester Research estimates 50 to 80% of businesses use spreadsheets[1]. Moreover, there is a large amount of data on the Web that is, practically speaking, only available via spreadsheets. For example, the United States government for many years published a compilation of thousands of spreadsheets about economic development, transportation, public health,

5			
6	Sex, age, and race	1990 \1	2000
7			
19	**Total smokers \3**	**25.5**	**23.2**
20	Male, total	28.4	25.6
21	18 to 24 years	26.6	28.1
22	25 to 34 years	31.6	28.9
23	35 to 44 years	34.5	30.2
24	45 to 64 years	29.3	26.4
25	65 years and over	14.6	10.2
26	White, total	28.0	25.7
27	18 to 24 years	27.4	30.4
28	25 to 34 years	31.6	29.7
29	35 to 44 years	33.5	30.6
30	45 to 64 years	28.7	25.8
31	65 years and over	13.7	9.8
32	Black, total	32.5	26.2
33	18 to 24 years	21.3	20.9
34	25 to 34 years	33.8	23.2
35	35 to 44 years	42.0	30.7
36	45 to 64 years	36.7	32.2
37	65 years and over	21.5	14.2

(a)

Relational Tuples:

1990	Total smokers	Male	White	45 to 64 years	28.7
1990	Total smokers	Male	White	65 years and over	13.7
2000	Total smokers	Male	White	45 to 64 years	25.8
2000	Total smokers	Male	Black	65 years and over	14.2

(b)

Figure 1: A spreadsheet about smoking rates, from the Statistical Abstract of the United States.

and other important social topics; a spreadsheet was the only data format used.

However, there is at least one area where spreadsheet functionality badly trails the relational world: data integration. For example, imagine that a policy expert wants to see whether the strength of the connection between smoking and lung cancer is consistent across all U.S. states. Different branches of the government have published data relevant to his task, and he is likely to obtain the data via two downloadable spreadsheets, one for the smoking statistics and one for the lung cancer statistics. Unfortunately, the policy expert may have to write tedious customized code to combine the two spreadsheets for the analysis.

If spreadsheet data could be easily converted to the relational model, many researchers — in public policy, public health, economics, and other areas — could benefit from society's huge investment in relational integration tools. There has been a substantial amount of work in converting grid-style data to the relational model much of it in connection to Web HTML tables [4, 14], rather than spreadsheets. However, projects to date [1, 2, 12, 18] have either been extremely labor-intensive, or they have ignored data layouts that are very typical of spreadsheets.

For example, Figure 1(a) shows a portion of a spreadsheet downloaded from the government's Statistical Abstract of

[1] http://www.cutimes.com/2013/07/31/rethinking-spreadsheets-and-performance-management

KDD'14, August 24–27, 2014, New York, NY, USA.
Copyright 2014 ACM 978-1-4503-2956-9/14/08 ...$15.00.
http://dx.doi.org/10.1145/2623330.2623617.

the United States.[2] A human reader can easily tell that the *data* value 28.7 is annotated by the *annotations* 1990, Male, White, and 45 to 64 years. We call this implicit relationship between annotations and data a ***mapping***. By repeatedly finding such mappings, a human could eventually reconstruct the *relational tuples* seen in Figure 1(b).

This annotation-to-data mapping is common in tabular data such as Web HTML tables and financial reports, but is especially common in spreadsheets. We manually examined 200 randomly selected spreadsheets from the Web and found that more than 32% of the spreadsheets in a general English-language Web crawl contain an implicit mapping between annotations and data. When examining the top ten Internet domains that publish the greatest number of spreadsheets, more than 60% of spreadsheets do so [7].

Our Goal — This paper is to study a critical problem in spreadsheets: recovering *mappings* between annotations and data ***accurately*** and with ***low effort***. Doing so opens up the opportunities for an *ad-hoc* spreadsheet integration tool [9], which a variety of people in society can use for data analysis.

Finding all the *accurate* mappings is important to avoid misleading results in our downstream spreadsheet integration tool. But even a high-quality automatic extractor will eventually make a mistake, and obtaining fully accurate mappings is hard to achieve without incorporating user interactions into our extraction system. Thus, our goal is to extract fully accurate mappings with low human effort.

Technical Challenges — Unfortunately, we face a number of challenges. First, the annotation relationship shown in Figure 1 is clear to a human because of the textual formatting, but many other spreadsheets use different or contradictory formatting; methods based on formatting heuristics will be quite poor at reconstructing these relationships.

Second, many implicit mappings rely on human understanding of domain-specific metadata. Consider a spreadsheet of US states that does not use any stylistic cues to distinguish *Michigan* from *Midwest*; the human reader's domain knowledge is what makes the annotations recoverable.

Finally, our extraction system is designed to be interactive; the user will likely give the system very little labeled data. The system must be able to repair extraction errors and obtain accurate annotation mappings with an unusually small amount of user input.

Our Approach – We propose a new two-phase *semiautomatic* approach based on an undirected graphical model to extracting spreadsheet annotation-to-data mappings accurately and with little human effort.

First, the *automatic extractor* receives spreadsheets as input and computes a mapping without human interaction. Based on an undirected graphical model, it exploits single-spreadsheet graphical style hints, such as the font and typographic alignment, that are obvious to a human observer. It also identifies and exploits correlated extraction decisions; these correlated decisions can appear within one spreadsheet or between two unrelated spreadsheets. Our resulting automatic extractor obtains accuracy that beats a baseline approach by up to 91% on a large workload of spreadsheets.

Second, our system offers an *interactive repair* phase, in which a human repeatedly reviews and corrects the automatic extractor's output until no errors remain. We expect a human will review the automatic extractor's output. But

[2]http://www.census.gov/compendia/statab/2012/tables/12s0204.xls

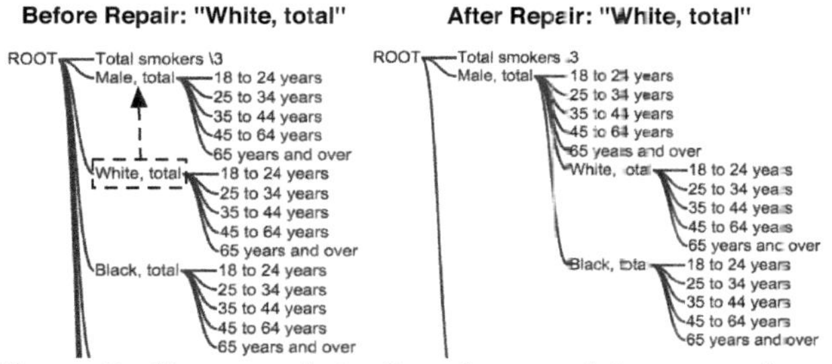

Figure 2: Our user interface for repairing mappings.

our interactive repair is more than simply asking a human to fix every single extraction error. We again exploit the correlations among different extraction decisions to make more effective use of each user repair operation. A user's single repair can be silently and probabilistically applied to multiple possible errors, allowing us to *amortize* the user's effort over many likely extractor mistakes. Building a model that can perform this amortization, and managing the inadvertent errors that such an approach might introduce (a problem we call *backtracking*), is one of this paper's core contributions.

Figure 2 shows an example of the user interface for applying repairs. (We discussed this interface in more detail previously [9].) The left side of the diagram indicates the initial hierarchy obtained by the automatic extractor for Figure 1. The dashed arrow shows that a user performs a repair by clicking and dragging White so that it becomes a child of Male, indicating that Male annotates White. This one repair operation triggers multiple error fixes, including setting Male to also annotate Black. By making our system part of the user's natural review-and-repair loop, we can reduce the number of manual repairs by up to 71% when compared to our already-effective automatic extractor.

A critical component of both the automatic extractor and interactive repair is the detection of similar extraction decisions. By automatically constructing our own domain-specific metadata resource, we can more effectively detect these decisions than when using no metadata or when using an off-the-shelf resource such as Freebase [3].

Background – In our previous work, we described the Web spreadsheet corpus and a basic form of the extractor [7]; we compared against and beat that basic extractor (see Section 7 for more detail). We also demonstrated the ad hoc integration application [9]. We have not previously described the graphical model based extraction and repair technique that forms our core technical contribution in this paper.

Contributions — In this paper, we focus on extracting the annotation-to-data mapping in spreadsheets. To the best of our knowledge, we are the first to present the semiautomatic extraction approach. Our contributions include

- A graphical model based automatic extractor for obtaining spreadsheet annotation mappings. (Section 4.)
- An extended graphical model to implement interactive repair. This technique amortizes each user repair over many extraction errors at once. (Section 5.)
- A method for building a *domain-specific* metadata resource that assists with the above steps. (Section 6.)
- An evaluation of our overall extraction system on two distinct spreadsheet corpora. (Section 7.)

We cover related work in Section 2, and define the annotation-to-data mapping extraction task in Section 3. Finally, we conclude with a discussion of future work in Section 8.

2. RELATED WORK

There are three main areas of related work:

Spreadsheet Management – Existing approaches for transforming spreadsheet data into databases fall into a few broad categories. First, *rule-based* approaches [2, 16, 18, 25] often require users to learn a newly defined language to describe the transformation process. The approaches are flexible but often require explicit conversion rules that are difficult and time-consuming for the user to compose. Second, there is a range of *visualization* systems [27] that help the user navigate and understand spreadsheets with visualization techniques, but the mechanisms are not able to extract relational data from spreadsheets. Finally, *automated* approaches are the most similar to ours. Abraham and Erwig [1] attempted to recover spreadsheet tuples, and Cunha *et al.* [12] primarily focused on the problem of data normalization. But their work assumes a simple type of spreadsheets and they did not address the hierarchical structures that are key to understanding a huge portion of the online spreadsheet data.

Tabular Data Extraction – There has been a large amount of work centered on extracting tabular data on the Web [4, 5, 14]. Most of these projects have focused on the details of identifying data-centric tables or on applications that can be built on top of them. HTML tables likely contain hierarchical-style data examples, but we are not aware of any research to date focused on this problem.

Programming By Demonstration – The interactive repair component of our work is part of an intellectual thread that ties programming by demonstration [15, 20, 21, 28], mixed-initiative systems [17], and incorporation of user feedback into extraction systems [6]. Many of these systems are driven by a programming language that the user must learn; our system does not require the user to learn a language, just to use a "drag-and-release" interface. Our solution's design, which alternates automatic and human-driven effort, is similar in spirit to Wrangler [15, 21] and mixed initiative systems [17, 19, 20, 28]. However, Wrangler-style techniques cannot be applied to our situation directly, as they generally process data with standard textual cues that are often missing from real-world spreadsheets.

3. PRELIMINARIES

In this section, we briefly describe the spreadsheet data model and provide a short summary of a graphical model.

3.1 Data Model & Problem Definition

In its most generic incarnation, a spreadsheet is simply an $M \times N$ grid of cells, in which each cell can contain a string, a number, or nothing. In practice, most spreadsheets, especially the high-quality ones that carry data that we want to extract, have substantially more structures. We make two assumptions about the spreadsheets we will process without seriously compromising our approach's generality.

Data Frames – First, we focus on a prototypical form of spreadsheet that we call a **data frame**. Figure 3 shows the three components that make up a data frame: two rectangular *annotation regions* (*left* and *top*) and a single rectangular *data region*. We previously addressed the problem of finding data frames in spreadsheets using a linear chain CRF [7].

Hierarchies – Second, we focus on **hierarchical** spreadsheets. We assume a spreadsheet is *hierarchical* if the annotations in the *top* or *left* annotation region exhibit a hierarchical tree structure of at least two layers. For example, the *left* annotation region of the spreadsheet in Figure 3 shows a hierarchical structure of three layers. In this paper, we primarily discuss *left* annotation hierarchies, but hierarchies also exist in *top*. However, *top* annotation hierarchies are generally easier to recover than *left*, as the row and column number in *top* are very strong and reliable clues [7].

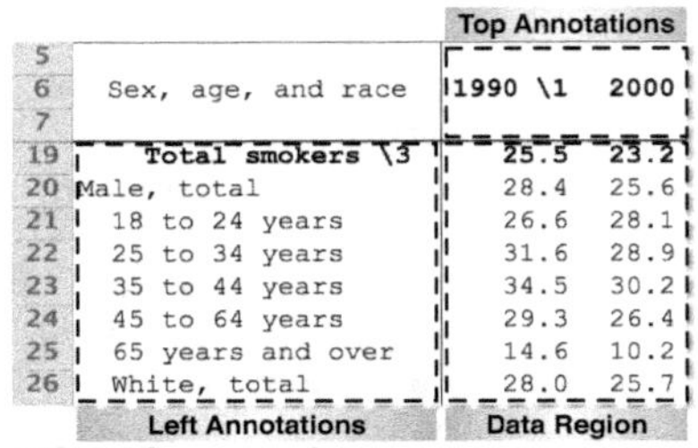

5			
6	Sex, age, and race	1990 \1	2000
7			
19	Total smokers \3	25.5	23.2
20	Male, total	28.4	25.6
21	18 to 24 years	26.6	28.1
22	25 to 34 years	31.6	28.9
23	35 to 44 years	34.5	30.2
24	45 to 64 years	29.3	26.4
25	65 years and over	14.6	10.2
26	White, total	28.0	25.7

Figure 3: The three primary components of a *data frame* spreadsheet.

Problem Statement — Thus, we now formally describe our implicit mappings recovery task.

Let $A = \{a_1, ..., a_N, root\}$ be a set of annotations in an annotation region, where *root* is a synthetic node as the root of every hierarchical tree. Given $a_p, a_c \in A$, we say (a_p, a_c) is a *ParentChild* pair if a_p is the parent of a_c in the annotation hierarchy. For example, in Figure 1, *(row-20, row-26)* (the strings (Male, White)) is a *ParentChild* pair, while *(row-25, row-26)* (the strings (65 years and over, White)) is not.

The spreadsheet annotation-to-data mapping task, thus, amounts to recovering all the *ParentChild* pairs for its annotation regions. For example in Figure 1, the solution for mappings in *left* is a set of all its *ParentChild* pairs {*(row-19, row-20)*, ..., *(row-32, row-37)*}. We also call this the hierarchy extraction task.

3.2 Graphical Model

A graphical model G [22] describes a joint distribution over a set of n random variables $\mathbf{x} = \{x_1, ..., x_n\}$, where each variable x_i takes a label l_i from a set of labels L. The model captures properties of each variable and dependencies among variables in the graph by defining *potential functions* on cliques of correlated variables.

A common method to define the potentials is as a dot function between the *weight* parameters and a *feature* vector [26]. A node potential captures the features that correspond to a single variable. The node potential is usually defined on a variable x_i as $\theta(x_i) = \mathbf{w_1}^T\mathbf{f}(x_i, l_i)$, where $\mathbf{f}(x_i, l_i)$ is a feature vector and $\mathbf{w_1}$ is the associated weight parameters. Similarly, the edge potential is usually defined on pairwise variables x_i and x_j to describe their correlation as $\theta(x_i, x_j) = \mathbf{w_2}^T\mathbf{f}(x_i, l_i, x_j, l_j)$. Users generally provide domain knowledge via the feature vectors $\mathbf{f}$, while the parameters $\mathbf{w} = \{\mathbf{w_1}, \mathbf{w_2}\}$ are *trained* from labeled data. In the *training* stage, the feature vector is derived from a set of labeled data in order to obtain the optimal value for the *weight* parameters $\mathbf{w}$. In the *inference* stage, the optimal labeling can be obtained by finding the maximum joint probability. As our model is conditionally trained, it belongs to the class of general graph conditional random fields [24].

4. AUTOMATIC EXTRACTION

In this section, we describe how to exploit the different sources of information and how to encode the automatic extraction as an undirected graphical model.

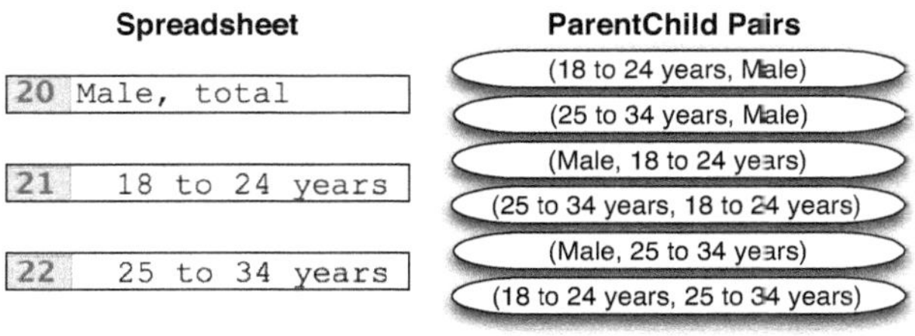

Figure 4: A sample of *ParentChild* variables.

4.1 Encoding Hierarchy Extraction

We now formally describe our problem and observations. The task of hierarchy extraction is to detect all of the *ParentChild* pairs $P = \{ParentChild(a_i, a_j)\}$ in an annotation region A. One way to model this problem is to create a Boolean variable x to represent a *ParentChild* pair candidate (a_p, a_c) for every annotation pair $a_p, a_c \in A$. Each variable x takes a label $l \in L = \{true, false\}$, and x holds true if a_p is the parent of a_c. For example, Figure 4 shows a portion of the created variables for Figure 1's *left* metadata. Each oval node corresponds to a single boolean *ParentChild* decision. For example, setting the node (18 to 24 years, Male) to true indicates that 18 to 24 years is the hierarchy *parent* of Male.

However, simply enumerating all pairs in a region A can yield thousands of variables. In practice, it is possible to greatly reduce the set of *ParentChild* candidates with a few heuristics. [3] Failing to create a node for a true *ParentChild* relationship is bad, but not catastrophic: the user can still describe the correct relationship during interactive repair.

A true *ParentChild* variable may be indicated by the surrounding style and layout information. For example, a variable that describes annotations which are physically close is likelier to be true than a variable that describes annotations that are physically distant. We formulated 32 features for evaluating a *ParentChild* variable. The full set of features can be refered in our technical report version [8].

4.2 Correlating ParentChild Decisions

ParentChild decisions can be correlated; knowing the assignment of one *ParentChild* variable sheds light on some others. We found the following four types of correlations.

Correlation (i) — Stylistic Affinity. When two *ParentChild* variables in the same spreadsheet have identical visual style for parents and for children, it is likely that the two variables should be decided together. For example in Figure 5 (a), the two *ParentChild* variables ((White, College) and (Male, 18 to 24 years)) should be decided together because the parents (White and Male) share the same typographic style, as do the children (College and 18 to 24 years). We say that two variables have stylistic affinity when the parents and children share a range of visual qualities: alignment, indentation, capitalization, typeface, type size, type style (*i.e.*, bold or italicized), and use of certain special strings (*i.e.*, a colon, a number, or the word "total"). Note that stylistic affinity only makes sense when testing *ParentChild* pairs ***within a single spreadsheet***; different

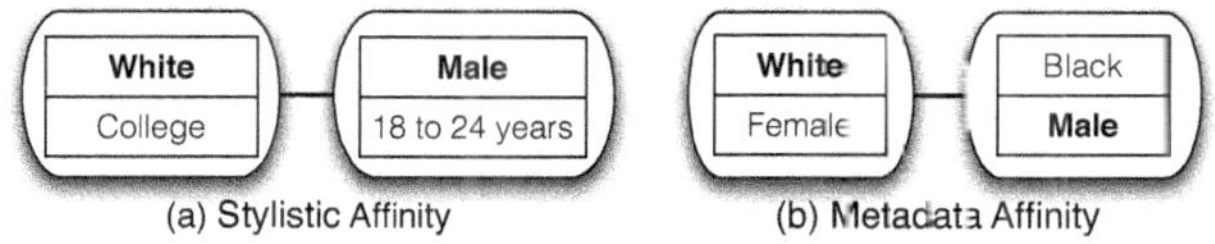

Figure 5: An example of stylistic affinity shown in (a) and metadata affinity shown in (b).

spreadsheets may have different or contradictory ways of visually indicating the *ParentChild* relationship.

Correlation (ii) — Metadata Affinity. If we have a metadata resource available, we can use it to find additional correlations between *ParentChild* variables both ***within and between*** spreadsheets. For example in Figure 5 (b), the two *ParentChild* candidates, (White, Female) and (Black, Male), should be decided together because the parents (White and Black) belong to the same semantic category *race*; similarly the children (Female and Male) belong to *gender*. The details of how to test whether two variables have metadata affinity are discussed in Section 6.

Correlation (iii) — Adjacent Dependency. If we consider the *ParentChild* pairs of a ***single spreadsheet*** as a sequence, adjacent variables often follow a transition pattern of the labels.

Correlation (iv) — Aggregate Design. There are two further constraints that reflect typical overall spreadsheet design and ensure that the resulting variable assignment yields a legal hierarchy (*i.e.*, a tree).

The first is the *orientation constraint*. Spreadsheets tend to have an "upward" or "downward" orientation; that is, parents do not appear above their children in some cases and below their children in other cases. For example in Figure 4, the pairs (Male, 18 to 24 years) and (25 to 34 years, 18 to 24 years) cannot simultaneously be *true*.

The second is the *one-parent constraint*. We enforce our assumption that *ParentChild* relationships genuinely form a tree; one annotation can only have one parent. Put another way, for all of the variables sharing the same child, only one of them is *true* and the rest are *false*. For example in Figure 4, (Male, 25 to 34 years) and (18 to 24 years, 25 to 34 years) could not both be true.

4.3 Graphical Model Potentials

Now we describe how we encode the *ParentChild* pair properties and their correlations into the graphical model.

Node Potentials – Each variable x in the graphical model represents a *ParentChild* decision, which takes a label $l \in L = \{true, false\}$. We define the **node potential** $\theta(x, l)$ on each variable x assigned the label l. The node potentials depend on Boolean feature functions $\{f_k(x, l)\}$ (The 32 features mentioned in Section 4.1) and trained weights $\{w_k\}$ associated with the feature functions:

$$\theta(x, l) = \sum_k w_k f_k(x, l) \qquad (1)$$

Edge Potentials – The correlations (i) (ii) and (iii) mentioned in Section 4.2 are encoded in the graphical model as pairwise *edge potentials*. The **edge potential** $\theta(x, l, x', l')$ is defined on two variables x and x' in the graphical model on their assignments l and l' if the variables x and x' are found to be correlated in one of the three ways mentioned above. We define,

[3] We prioritize *ParentChild* candidates in which the typographic styles of the two nodes differ. We also prioritize pairs that are geometrically close to each other in the spreadsheet. Testing on our 200 testbed spreadsheets for SAUS and WEB, our heuristics only incorrectly filtered out just 0.01% and 0.13% of correct pairs, respectively.

$$\theta(x, l, x', l') = [\![l = l']\!] \sum_e w_e f_e(x, x') \quad (2)$$

where $[\![l = l']\!]$ takes the value 1 when $l = l'$ and 0 otherwise; $\{w_e\}$ are the associated weights. The edge features $\{f_e(x, x')\}$ test which type of correlation x and x' belong to and whether x and x' have the same child/parent.

Global Potentials – Finally we encode the correlation (iv) mentioned in Section 4.2 as *global potentials*. Let $x = (a_p, a_c)$ and $x' = (a'_p, a'_c)$ be two arbitrary variables in the graphical model with the assigned labels l and l', and $R(a)$ represents the row number of an annotation a. We now define two **global potentials:** $\phi_a(\mathbf{x}, \mathbf{l})$ to encode the *orientation constraint* and $\phi_b(\mathbf{x}, \mathbf{l})$ to encode the *one-parent constraint*:

$$\phi_a(\mathbf{x}, \mathbf{l}) = [\![\exists x, x' \in \mathbf{x} \; s.t. \; l = true, l' = true, \\ R(a_p) > R(a_c), R(a'_p) < R(a'_c)]\!]^{0}_{-\infty} \quad (3)$$

$$\phi_b(\mathbf{x}, \mathbf{l}) = [\![\forall c, \sum_p [\![l = true]\!]^{0}_{1} = 1]\!]^{-\infty}_{0} \quad (4)$$

where $[\![C]\!]^{value2}_{value1}$ takes the *value 1* when condition C is true and *value 2* otherwise.

5. INTERACTIVE REPAIR

The interactive repair phase allows the user to check and fix any *ParentChild* decision mistakes made by the system. The goal of interactive repair is to save user effort by using each explicit user-given repair to fix not just the error in question, but also additional extraction errors that the user never directly inspects. In this section, we describe the interactive repair workflow in more detail, plus how to modify the graphical model to support the repair process. Finally, we describe the training and inference methods.

5.1 User Repairs

During interactive repair, we assume a user always fixes extraction errors correctly. We do not focus on the problem of noisy human-labeled data, and there is crowdsourcing literature on how to ensure trustworthy answers [13].

We now discuss our model workflow for interactive repair. The system starts by presenting to the user the initial extraction results computed by the automatic extraction and then enters the interactive repair interaction loops (shown in Figure 6). For each loop, the system takes two steps:

1. Review and Repair — A user is able to repair an error in the extracted hierarchy by dragging and releasing an annotation node on the interface. One ***user repair*** action changes an annotation's parent from one to another. For example in Figure 2, a user changes the parent annotation of White from Root to Male.

A *user repair* operation has two implications. First, the variable x that represents the new *correct ParentChild* relationship is set to *true*. In the case of Figure 2, the variable (Male, White) is *true*. Second, all the other variables that represent *ParentChild* relationships sharing the same child with x are set to *false*. In the case of Figure 2, variables (Root, White) and (Total smoker, White) are *false*.

As a result, a user's repair to an extraction error yields a set of label assignments to some *ParentChild* variables.

2. Spread Repairs — The system now aims to save user effort by repairing other similar extraction errors.

Of course, the system has already given its best extraction estimate in the automatic extraction phase, so it does not know where any latent extraction errors are. But we have

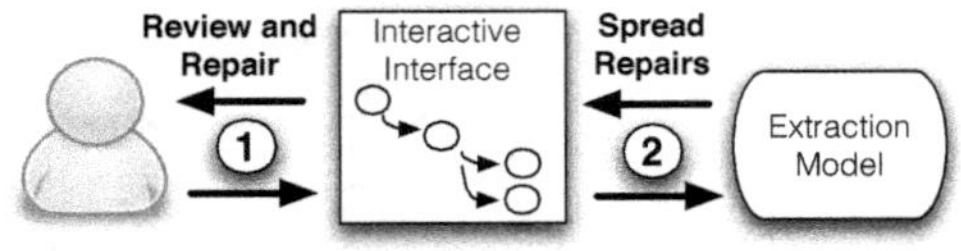

Figure 6: Interaction cycle for interactive repair.

Algorithm 1 SpreadRepair

Input: All user repairs R, and automatic extraction model G
Output: New assignments $\mathbf{l}$ to all variables of G.

From user repairs R, create repair-induced variables $\mathbf{x_r}$ with labels $\mathbf{l_r}$ (as described in Section 5.1 Step 1).
Build new model G' by adding to G the new repair potentials based on $\mathbf{x_r}$. G' has the same set of nodes (variables) as G.
Condition on $\mathbf{x_r}$ and infer assignments $\mathbf{l}$ to G' (and thus, G)

already used different kinds of affinity to connect two *ParentChild* decisions that are highly likely to share the same label; it is a shame to forget about this information just when the user is providing a new source of correct labels.

It is appealing to spread each user-repaired label on a variable to other variables that are identified by affinity correlations (i) and (ii). But simply propagating assignments might introduce errors where none previously exist, which we call the ***backtracking*** problem. We want to leverage the graphical model to integrate probability information with the node, edge, and global correlations to prevent backtracking.

5.2 Encoding User Repairs

Here, we describe how to encode the user repair interaction to the graphical model. Algorithm 1 shows the **SpreadRepair** function that is invoked after each user repair operation (described in step 2 of the previous section). First, when a new repair arrives, we translate this new repair and all the previous repairs to the assignments on a set of variables $\mathbf{x_r} = \{x_{r_1}, ..., x_{r_n}\}$ with labels $\mathbf{l_r} = \{l_{r_1}, ..., l_{r_n}\}$. Second, we generate a new graphical model G' by adding the *repair potentials* to the original automatic extraction graphical model G. The repair potentials capture the pairwise correlation between variables, and we describe the repair potentials later. Finally, we condition on the known variables $\mathbf{x_r}$ and infer labels for the variables of G'. The inferred labels are returned as the updated answer.

Note that by adding repair potentials only to nodes that we also condition on, we add information to the inference process without increasing any inference-time computational complexity. The conditioning process essentially removes the observed nodes and their edges prior to the inference [22].

There is nothing in principle that prevents our system from ***backtracking***, unless we can find heuristics to propagate the assignments fully correctly, which is often hard especially on real-world datasets. However, our mechanism is designed to prevent it. First, we only probabilistically propagate known variable assignments to others, via the repair potentials. Second, this probabilistic repair information is combined with all our previous information sources: the node potentials, edge potentials and global potentials. The hope is that adding high quality new information to the automatic extraction graphical model (instead of treating spreading repairs as a non-probabilistic post-processing stage) will yield better outcomes overall.

We now discuss how to generate the repair potentials.

Repair Potentials — The **repair potential** $\varphi(x, l, x_r, l_r)$ describes the likelihood that the repaired node's label should be spread to a similar *ParentChild* node. A repair potential exists between an observed variable $x_r \in \mathbf{x_r}$ and a variable $x \in \mathbf{x}$ if x_r and x exhibit either stylistic affinity or metadata affinity. In other words, repair potentials do not introduce any novel edges to the graphical model: the edges of repair potentials are a subset of the edges derived from correlations (i) and (ii). The repair potentials are defined as:

$$\varphi(x,l,x_r,l_r) = [\![Stylistic(x,x_r)]\!] f_s(x,l,x_r,l_r) + [\![Metadata(x,x_r)]\!] f_m(x,l,x_r,l_r) \quad (5)$$

$[\![C]\!]$ takes the value 1 when condition C is true; otherwise 0. $Stylistic(x, x_r)$ and $Metadata(x, x_r)$ test whether x and x_r have stylistic or metadata affinity. The two feature functions f_s and f_m weigh the strength of influence from observed variables to unobserved ones. They characterize how similar the unobserved variables are to the observed ones. To be precise, we define $f_s(x,l,x_r,l_r) = logP_s(x = l \mid x_r = l_r)$. where $P_s(x = l \mid x_r = l_r)$ represents the probability of a variable x taking the label l once we observe a variable x_r with the label l_r. This probability can be derived from training data. For example, in the training data, among 1000 *stylistic affinity* edges detected, 900 of them connect two variables with the same assignment. We then set $P_s(x = true|x_r = true) = 0.9$ and $P_s(x = false|x_r = true) = 0.1$. The f_m potentials are defined in the same way.

Summary — We can now formally define the spreadsheet annotation hierarchy extraction framework, which supports both automatic extraction and interactive repair.

Let G be a graphical model that has a set of variables $\mathbf{x} = \{x_1, ..., x_n\}$ where each $x_i \in \mathbf{x}$ represents a *ParentChild* candidate in an *annotation region* and takes a label l_i from $L = \{true, false\}$. Let $\mathbf{l_r}$ be the set of repair-induced labels on variables $\mathbf{x_r}$. We define node potentials (Equation 1), edge potentials (Equation 2), global potentials (Equation 3 and 4), and repair potentials (Equation 5) in G. The joint distribution of the graphical model G is:

$$P(\mathbf{l} \mid \mathbf{l_r}, \mathbf{x}) = \frac{1}{Z(\mathbf{w})} exp(\sum_x \theta(x,l) + \sum_x \sum_{x'} \theta(x,l,x',l') + \sum_{k\in\{a,b\}} \phi_k(\mathbf{x},\mathbf{l}) + \sum_x \sum_{x_r \in \mathbf{x_r}} \varphi(x,l,x_r,l_r))$$

5.3 Training and Inference

In this section, we discuss how to train model parameters and infer assignments to variables in the graphical model.

5.3.1 Parameter Estimation

In the graphical model, we only have unknown parameters for *node* and *edge potentials*. Assuming that no user repairs are involved, we can write the joint probability as,

$$\frac{1}{Z(\mathbf{w})} exp(\sum_x \theta(x,l) + \sum_x \sum_{x'} \theta(x,l,x',l') + \sum_{k\in\{a,b\}} \phi_k(\mathbf{x},\mathbf{l}))$$

Let $\mathbf{w} = \{w\}$ be the set of parameters for *node* and *edge potentials*. Given training data $D = \{\mathbf{x}, \mathbf{l}\}$ that describes hand-labeled correct hierarchies of the training spreadsheets, we estimate $\mathbf{w}$ for node and edge potential functions, $\theta(x,l)$ and $\theta(x,l,x',l')$. A common choice of regularization to avoid overfitting is to add a penalty on weight vectors, based on the Euclidean norm of $\mathbf{w}$ and on a *regularization parameter* $\frac{1}{2\sigma^2}$. The goal is to maximize the regularized log likelihood:

$$\max_{\mathbf{w}} \sum_x \theta(x,l) + \sum_x \sum_{x'} \theta(x,l,x',l') - logZ(\mathbf{w}) - \sum_i \frac{w_i^2}{2\sigma^2} + C$$

Algorithm 2 EnforcedTreeInference

Input: The variables $\mathbf{x} = \{x\}$ and the annotations $A = \{a_1, ..., a_N\}$ in an annotation region.
Output: The *ParentChild* pairs $P = \{(a_p, a_c)\}$ in the annotation hierarchy and its confidence $confidence$.

```
P ← {}, confidence ← 0
for each a_c ∈ A do
    maxprob ← 0, a_p0 ← root
    for each a_p ∈ A do
        Find x ∈ x for the ParentChild pair (a_p, a_c)
        Obtain the probability cprob that x = true
        if cprob > maxprob then
            maxprob ← cprob, a_p0 ← a_p
        end if
    end for
    P ← P ∪ {(a_p0, a_c)}
    confidence ← confidence + log(maxprob)
end for
```

where C is a constant. This is a standard form for parameter estimation, and known techniques, such as conjugate gradient and L-BFGS, can be used to find the optimal parameters for this formula. Previous work [22, 24] discusses this optimization problem and its solution in more detail.

5.3.2 Inference Technique

The graphical model described poses a serious computational challenge. Inference is NP-hard if no assumptions are made about the structure of the graph [11], yet our application requires that we infer labels after each user repair to redisplay the updated hierarchy. In order to infer variables in interactive time, we first simplify the graphical model.

Model Simplification — The potential stumbling blocks to efficient inference are the edge and global potentials. (The repair potentials do not complicate the inference because the conditioning algorithm [22] erases observed variables along with all the repair potential edges.) The edge potentials alone can yield more than a million edges on a graph with 37,386 nodes derived from just 100 randomly-chosen WEB spreadsheets (see Table 3 for details).

We considered two methods for conducting inference in a limited amount of time: running the tree-reweighted belief propagation algorithm [23] on the full graph, or running an exact inference method on a simplified tree-structured model. Our experiments show that when running on a model derived from 100 random SAUS spreadsheets and repeating this process 10 times, tree-reweighted belief propagation is 48 times slower and 5.4% worse on F1 than the tree-structured model. Thus, at inference time we convert our graphical model into a tree-structured model.

It is not easy to find the tree-structured graphical model that yields the highest-quality results. Exhaustively enumerating all the possible trees in a graph with more than a million edges and 37,000 nodes is impractical. We simply randomly sample edges from each type of pairwise correlation (stylistic, metadata, and adjcency), rejecting any edge that would induce a cycle. We terminate when all nodes are connected. We add all possible metadata edges before adding any stylistic edges, and add all stylistic edges before adding any adjacency edges. We found experimentally that this ordering helped slightly, though different orderings do not change F1 very much: testing on 100 random spreadsheets of SAUS, different orderings changed F1 from 0.8808 to 0.8867 and from 0.8237 to 0.8363 when testing on WEB.

Inference — We can now present our method for approximating the graphical model's optimal assignment. First, we build the model with *node* potentials, tree-structured *edge potentials*, and all the *repair potentials* if there exist any. Given a set of observed variables $\mathbf{x_r}$ with labels $\mathbf{l_r}$ translated from users' repairs (we assume $\mathbf{x_r}$ is empty if no repairs are observed), the *conditioning* algorithm yields a forest-structured model.

Second, we run a standard inference algorithm on this new model to obtain the assignment to all the variables. Because the model is now a forest-structured, a variety of existing algorithms, such as belief propagation, can perform exact inference on such a structure.

Finally, we treat the *global potentials* as a post-processing stage to ensure that the inferred variable assignment yields legal hierarchical trees for the input annotation regions. The goal of *global potentials* is to handle the *orientation* and *one-parent* constraints. Thus, we first enumerate all of the *ParentChild* candidates of each orientation, "upward" or "downward," and compute two separate annotation hierarchies with **EnforcedTreeInference**, seen in Algorithm 2. For all the *ParentChild* candidates with a given annotation as the child, the algorithm selects the one with the maximal probability (derived from the graphical model), thereby handling the *one-parent constraint.* We obtain two possible hierarchies, one "upward" and one "downward," each with computed $confidence$. We select the one with the higher confidence to handle the *orientation constraint.* Therefore, our algorithm yields legal annotation hierarchies.

6. THE METADATA RESOURCE

A critical part of both automatic extraction and interactive repair is detecting metadata affinity. As described in Section 4.2, *ParentChild* variables might be correlated because they describe data belonging to one semantic category. This information is useful for examining annotations within a single spreadsheet, and is the *only* way to tie *ParentChild* decisions across multiple spreadsheets.

General-purpose schema resources, such as Freebase [3], can be used to detect metadata affinity between two annotations. But spreadsheet domains can be quite narrow. Fortunately, we are able to synthesize a *domain-specific metadata resource* from a corpus of spreadsheets. Our central observation is that any useful category of annotations — whether a general-purpose one like gender or a hyper-specific one such as chemicalPrecursor — will likely appear in many datasets. Further, annotations drawn from the same category (such as Male and Female) often appear as siblings in an extracted annotation hierarchy. We measure whether two annotations belong to the same category by testing how strongly the annotations appear as siblings in a large number of extracted hierarchies. We perform the test as follows:

1. Extract all annotation hierarchies from a corpus of spreadsheets using a simple classifier or a version of our automatic extractor that does not use metadata information. For each parent annotation, we create a *sibling set* that contains all of its child annotations.
2. Count the number of sibling sets where an annotation a is observed. Divide by the number of sibling sets to obtain $p(a)$, the probability that a randomly chosen sibling set contains a.
3. Count the number of sibling sets where the annotation pair a_i and a_j co-occur together. Divide by the number of sibling sets to obtain $p(a_i, a_j)$, the probability that a randomly chosen sibling set contains both a_i and a_j.

Dataset		Hierarchy Levels			# Left Annotations		
		Min	Mean	Max	Min	Mean	Max
SAUS	R200	2	3.8	8	4	37.8	224
	health	2	3.6	6	12	34.5	76
	fin.	3	3.7	6	6	32.4	81
	trans.	3	4.0	8	5	36.1	73
WEB	R200	2	3.4	10	2	59.3	669
	bts	2	2.6	4	4	10.7	26
	nsf	2	4.0	7	9	83.9	331
	usda	2	3.2	4	5	34.5	56

Table 1: Basic statistics of our eight test sets.

We can then measure the extent to which two annotations a_i and a_j are observed as siblings (and thus are likely to be in the same category) by computing the pointwise mutual information (PMI): $PMI(a_i, a_j) = log\frac{p(a_i,a_j)}{p(a_i)p(a_j)}$.

Let $x_1 = (a_{p1}, a_{c1})$ and $x_2 = (a_{p2}, a_{c2})$ be two variables in the CRF. The two variables x_1 and x_2 have **metadata affinity** if and only if $PMI(a_{p1}, a_{p2}) > \delta$ and $PMI(a_{c1}, a_{c2}) > \delta$, where δ is a predefined threshold.

7. EXPERIMENTS

We now evaluate the performance of automatic extraction (Section 4) and interactive repair (Section 5). We also evaluate the quality of our *metadata resource* (Section 6).

7.1 Experimental Setup

Our experiments are based on two spreadsheet corpora [4]:

- ***SAUS*** – The 2010 Statistical Abstract of the United States (SAUS) consists of 1,369 spreadsheet files totaling 70MB. We downloaded the dataset from the U.S. Census Bureau. It covers a variety of topics of general public interest, such as state-level finances, educational attainment, levels of public health, and so on.
- ***WEB*** – Our Web dataset consists of 410,554 Microsoft Excel files from 51,252 distinct Internet domains. They total 101 GB. We found the spreadsheets by looking for Excel-style file endings among the roughly 10 billion URLs in the ClueWeb09 Web crawl [10].

From each of the two datasets, SAUS and WEB, we randomly selected 200 *hierarchical spreadsheets.* We call these test sets SAUS **R200** and WEB **R200**. We constructed them by randomly sampling from SAUS or WEB and retaining only the hierarchical ones (*i.e.*, ones that have either hierarchical *left* or *top* annotations). In addition, we constructed a series of topic-specific test sets. For SAUS, we used government-provided category labels to identify spreadsheets for each of three topic areas: **health**, **finance**, and **transportation**; we chose 10 random hierarchical spreadsheets from each topic. For WEB, we used URL domain names as a rough proxy for the category label, choosing 10 random hierarchical spreadsheets from each of **bts.gov**, **usda.gov**, and **nsf.gov**. We asked a human expert to manually examine the above spreadsheets and create ground truth hierarchies. Details about the test sets are shown in Table 1.

We used the Python xlrd library to access data and formatting details of spreadsheet files. Our graphical model was implemented with UGM [29].

7.2 Automatic Extraction

In this section, we evaluate the performance of the automatic extraction phase. We evaluate the automatic extrac-

[4]Downloadable:www.eecs.umich.edu/db/sheets/datasets.html

Dataset	Methods	Precision	Recall	F1
SAUS	AutoBasic	0.4641	0.4641	0.4641
	AutoLR	0.8753	0.8750	0.8751
	AutoEdge	0.8801	0.8787	0.8794
	AutoGlobal	0.8834	0.8834	0.8834
	AutoFull	**0.8860**	**0.8860**	**0.8860**
WEB	AutoBasic	0.4736	0.4736	0.4736
	AutoLR	0.7886	0.7898	0.7892
	AutoEdge	0.7979	0.7968	0.7973
	AutoGlobal	0.8122	0.8122	0.8122
	AutoFull	**0.8327**	**0.8327**	**0.8327**

Table 2: Performance of the automatic extractor on SAUS **and** WEB **R200 datasets.**

tion's accuracy in predicting correct *ParentChild* relationships by using standard metrics of Precision, Recall, and F1. We trained and tested automatic extraction using SAUS **R200** and WEB **R200**. We randomly split each of the two datasets equally for training and testing. We trained parameters on the training set and constructed one graphical model for the test set. We repeated the split-and-test process 10 times, computing average Precision, Recall and F1.

We have previously discussed the simple classification based approaches for automatic extraction [7], and the approaches proposed are equivalent to AutoLR and AutoGlobal as below.

Automatic Models — A naive method AutoBasic to solve the hierarchy extraction problem is to use simple features (i.e. local alignment and indentation information) to classify two annotations as having a *ParentChild* relationship or not and assigns the most probable parent to each child.

We compared four different configurations of the automatic extraction graphical model with AutoBasic to demonstrate the power of each component of our automatic extractor: AutoLR uses node potentials only (with no edge or global potentials, the model is equivalent to the logistic regression, or LR, method)[5]. AutoEdge uses node potentials and edge potentials. AutoGlobal uses node potentials and global potentials. Finally, AutoFull uses all three potential types and reflects the entire contents of Section 4.3. [6]

Table 2 shows the performance of the five methods. We can see that all of our four graphical models significantly outperformed the baseline AutoBasic. Both partial models — AutoEdge and AutoGlobal — performed better than AutoLR, indicating that both *edge* and *global potentials* independently helped to improve the performance of automatic extraction. AutoFull, the model that includes all three potential types, is the best of all (though AutoFull's margin is small in the case of SAUS). We noticed that many extraction errors are due to contradictory spreadsheet formatting; designers of different spreadsheets may have conflicting designs, but even the format within one spreadsheet may not be consistent.

Training Data — We wanted to know if our supply of training data was limiting the automatic extractor's accuracy. We conducted a test in which we artificially constrained the training set size derived from SAUS **R200** and WEB **R200**, building a series of automatic extraction models with varying amounts of training data. Figure 7 shows the F1 of the *ParentChild* pairs for AutoFull as we change the size of the training set. The growth in both SAUS and

[5]We also tried support vector machines and other non-joint-inference techniques, but they offered no significant gains over AutoLR

[6]For AutoLR and AutoEdge we chose the probability threshold to maximize F1. For the rest two methods, there is no such flexibility, as the algorithms always select the parent with the maximum *ParentChild* probability for each child.

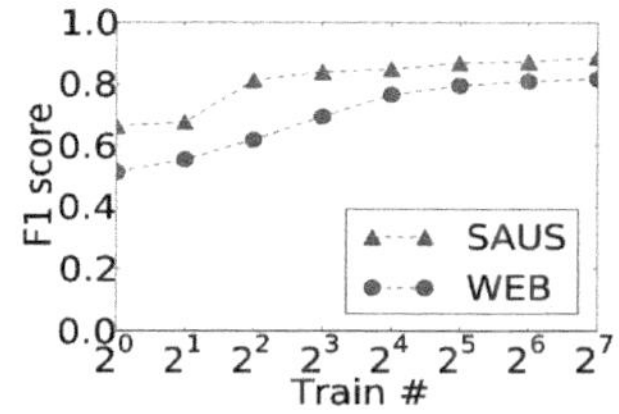

Figure 7: Performance for automatic extractor using different amounts of training data.

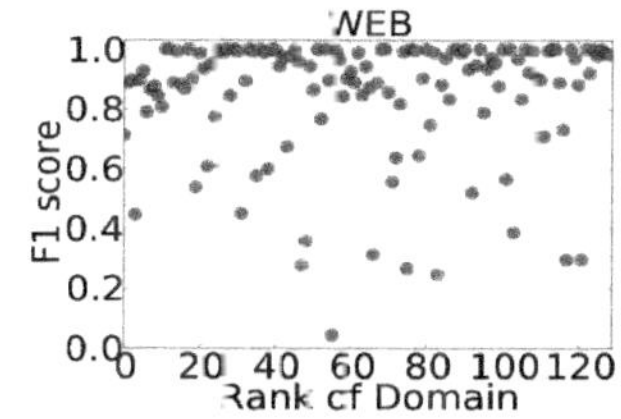

Figure 8: Performance for automatic extractor on different domains in WEB.

WEB accuracy plateaus after a certain size. This analysis does not mean more training data cannot help, but does indicates that additional gains will likely be expensive.

Domain Sensitivity — We also examined whether the WEB automatic extractor's accuracy varies with the quality of the spreadsheet. It is difficult to precisely describe a spreadsheet's quality, so as a proxy we use the rank of the spreadsheet URL's Internet domain, when sorted in descending order of the number of spreadsheets hosted by the domain. Figure 8 shows the average F1 within each Internet domain's spreadsheets. We followed the same training and testing procedure as in the ***Automatic Models*** part above. The figure shows that the publisher's rank (or the quantity of spreadsheets it publishes) does not correlate with extraction performance. However we *did* find that spreadsheets from lower ranked domains are less likely to pass our initial "hierarchical data frame spreadsheet" filter.

In summary, our system shows substantially better performance than the baseline AutoBasic method, a 91% improvement in F1 on SAUS and a 76% improvement in F1 on WEB. We now turn to interactive repair to shrink the user's burden even further.

7.3 User Repairs

We now evaluate the performance of the interactive repair phase. We use the eight datasets described in Section 7.1. For each **R200** of SAUS and WEB, we again randomly split the dataset into 100 training spreadsheets and 100 testing spreadsheets. We further randomly split the 100 testing spreadsheets into 10 subgroups with 10 spreadsheets in each, as **R10**; we then averaged the performance over the 10 subgroups. We created one model for each test set (health, finance, *etc*), except **R10**, where we created one model for each subgroup. Table 3 shows basic statistics for the interactive repair graphical models constructed for our test sets.

The metric of success for interactive repair is the amount of user work reduced when compared to simply fixing all the errors made by automatic extractor. We evaluate the amount of user effort by counting the required number of drag-and-drop repair operations to fix all the extraction errors in an annotation hierarchy, via our visual repair tool (seen in Figure 2). In the experiments, we simulated a user who randomly chooses extraction errors to repair, and who never makes a mistake. The user repairs errors until no errors remain. For each dataset, we ran this process 20 times and counted the average number of repairs performed. Notice that the maximum number of possible repair operations for a given hierarchy is the number of annotations in it.

For each result shown in Figure 9, Figures 10 and 11, we normalize the number of required repairs by the maximum possible number of repairs in that dataset (*i.e.*, the number

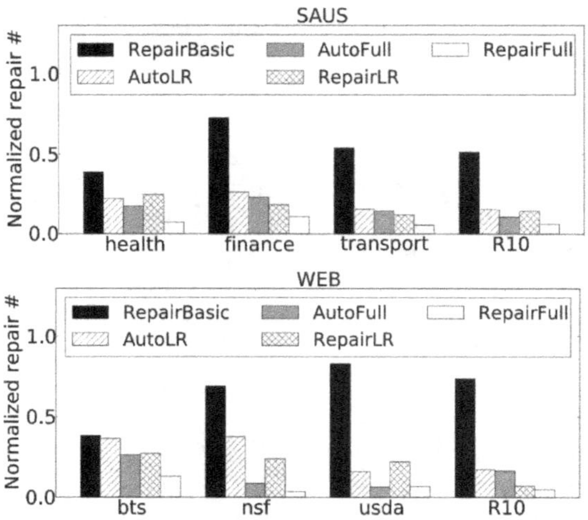

Figure 9: The normalized repair number for interactive repair on SAUS and WEB test sets.

		Sheet #	Node #	Correlation Edge # (×1000) Stylistic	Metadata	Total
SAUS	train	100	11269	87.5	115.7	177.6
	health	10	874	4.9	1.7	5
	fin.	10	1228	8.6	5.5	11.1
	trans.	10	1334	9.5	5.7	12.3
	R10	100	13866	144.4	43.3	161.3
WEB	train	100	31925	724.2	566.9	1069.0
	bts	10	249	0.5	0.0	0.5
	nsf	10	10698	265.1	22.9	283.3
	usda	10	1786	15.1	1.7	15.1
	R10	100	37386	1522.0	289.8	1677.6

Table 3: Basic statistics for each test set's interactive repair model.

of annotations). Thus, smaller bars are better, and results should be comparable across datasets.

Repair Models — A baseline method RepairBasic to incorporate interactive repair is to tie the *ParentChild* variables in one spreadsheet if the parents share the same formatting and so do the children: if a user changes one decision, the system automatically applies the change to the tied ones.

We also evaluated six different versions of our extraction system. AutoLR and AutoFull are the automatic extractors described in the above section; we assume a user simply fixes all of their extraction errors one after another. RepairLR, RepairEdge, RepairGlobal and RepairFull are created by adding repair potentials to the previous four automatic extraction models. RepairFull is the full system described in Section 5.

Figure 9 shows the normalized number of repair operations of different interactive repair systems. RepairFull performed the best of all, requiring just *7.2%* of the maximum number of possible repairs when averaged over all test sets. In contrast, AutoFull (itself a dramatic improvement over the automatic extraction baseline) requires *15.4%* of the maximum; our exploitation of user repairs thus allows us to reduce the user burden by an additional 53%. AutoLR, an automatic extractor without joint inference, yields an even worse average of *23.3%*; we improve by 69%. The absolute number of user repairs is reasonable: RepairFull requires between 2 and 3.5 repairs per sheet for SAUS, and between 1.38 and 2.94 repairs per sheet for WEB.

Note that applying user repair information naively yields terrible results: RepairBasic requires *60.2%* of the maximum possible number of repairs, much worse than even AutoLR.

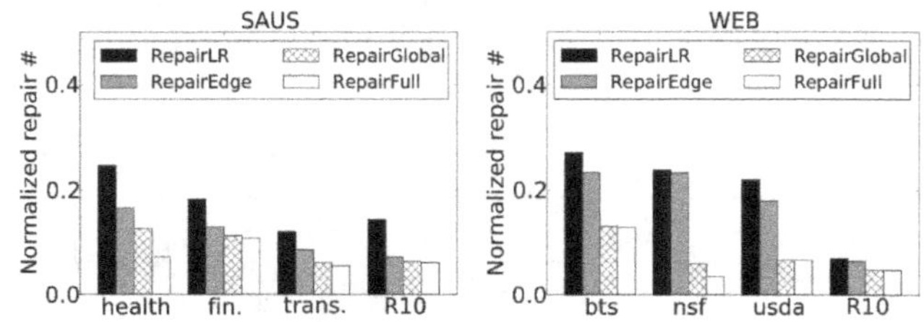

Figure 10: The normalized repair number for four interactive repair configurations.

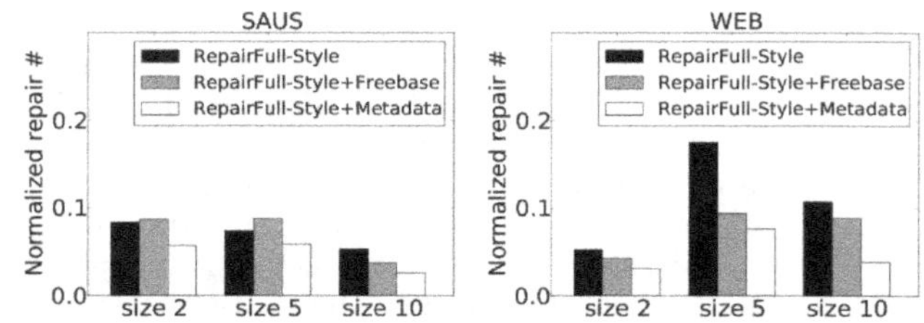

Figure 11: The normalized repair number required by different configurations of metadata links.

In all the datasets, RepairFull always improves or matches AutoFull, which indicates that our repair mechanism is genuinely beneficial to users; we managed to prevent backtracking and did not create more work for users. The same is *not* true for AutoLR *vs* RepairLR, which backtracks in the cases of SAUS/health and WEB/usda.

We further investigated interactive repair by considering different possible configurations of the interactive repair model on different test sets (shown in Figure 10). The Figure shows that both edge and global potentials are useful in reducing user burden, and using all of them helps the most.

Spreadsheet Grouping — We also investigated the influence of two spreadsheet grouping methods on interactive repair performance. (1) ***By topic***: We group spreadsheets according to their human-given topic labels (such as finance and health) or their URL hostnames (such as bts.gov and nsf.gov); and (2) ***By Jaccard similarity***: We compute the clusters by creating a graph in which each spreadsheet is a node, and edges exist when two spreadsheets have Jaccard similarity (computed over the non-numeric strings from each spreadsheet) greater than a threshold of 0.6. We find all weakly connected components in the graph as the spreadsheet groups. Note that grouping spreadsheets should only impact metadata affinity, as metadata affinity is the only way to connect *ParentChild* decisions across spreadsheets.

For both SAUS and WEB, we ran each grouping technique, then randomly selected 3 groups of size 2, 3 groups of size 5, and 3 groups of size 10. For each group, we first built one RepairFull on this group of spreadsheets and computed the number of repairs required to eliminate all the extraction errors. We then compared against the sum of repairs needed by RepairFull when running on each spreadsheet of the group in isolation. We found that grouping by topic only reduces repairs up to 5.8% on SAUS and 2.1% on WEB, while grouping by Jaccard similarity reduces repairs by up to 64.0% in SAUS and 84.6% in WEB.

Thus, Jaccard similarity grouping yields a massive reduction in necessary user repairs when compared to topic grouping. We did not present these results in Figures 9 and 10 because we believe that highly coherent clusterings will only be possible in certain situations. Shared spreadsheet templates is one such situation; another is when the metadata resource is of especially high quality (perhaps even curated by hand), allowing interactive repair to find otherwise invisible connections among independent spreadsheets.

Metadata Resources – The quality of our metadata resource clearly impacts metadata affinity. Figure 11 shows the normalized number of repairs required by different metadata resource configurations of RepairFull, when run on Jaccard-clustered spreadsheets mentioned above in ***Spreadsheet Grouping***. We compared the approach based on our metadata resource from Section 6 (RepairFull-Metadata) against a no-metadata technique (RepairFull-Style) and a technique that uses Freebase to discover metadata affinity (RepairFull-Freebase). (In that last case, two annotations have metadata affinity if they share the same Freebase topic.) The figure shows that in all cases, our RepairFull-Metadata technique performs the best, usually followed by RepairFull-Freebase. On average, our induced metadata resource reduces user effort by 34.4% when compared to the Freebase resource. Note that some of the spreadsheets we process are on extremely technical topics (such as currency trading, health care, and minerals processing) that are unlikely to be captured in a general-purpose metadata resource such as Freebase.

Runtime Performance — After each user repair operation, users have to wait for the model to recompute the new result. In our experiments, each repair's inference took 0.7s on **R10** in SAUS and 3.2s on **R10** in WEB on average. All other test datasets took less than 0.7s, except for **nsf** (at 4.7s). The results indicate that interactive repair is computationally feasible, at least for relatively small datasets.

Overall, we have demonstrated that our RepairFull extraction system can extract accurate spreadsheet hierarchies using just 7.2% of the maximum possible human effort, a reduction of 53% compared to AutoFull, our automatic extraction system (itself a significant improvement over previous automatic extraction techniques). These numbers apply to real-world datasets; in certain cases where spreadsheets share a large amount of metadata, we can improve the factor even further. Moreover, our system works well on domain-specific datasets with no explicit user-provided metadata.

8. CONCLUSIONS AND FUTURE WORK

We have described a *semiautomatic* framework for extracting data from spreadsheets. This system can derive accurate extractions with dramatically lower user effort than required by a traditional system. It should enable individuals and organizations to better exploit the large amount of data currently locked away in spreadsheet files.

In the future work, we would like to automatically and preemptively integrate spreadsheets with the data resources in an organization: relational databases, unstructured documents, even data-centric images, such as plots. The resulting cross-type integrated database could be used as the basis of a general query tool that can ignore distracting details of how each data item happened to be stored.

9. ACKNOWLEDGMENTS

The authors are grateful for feedback from Michael Anderson, Dolan Antenucci, Matthew Burgess, Jun Chen, H. V. Jagadish, Barzan Mozafari, Yongjoo Park, Alex Roper, Jian Tang, and especially Bob Vogel. This work was supported by National Science Foundation grants IIS-1054913 and IIS-1064606, and gifts from Dow, Google, and Yahoo!.

10. REFERENCES

[1] R. Abraham and M. Erwig. Ucheck: A spreadsheet type checker for end users. *J. Vis. Lang. Comput.*, 18(1):71–95, 2007.

[2] Y. Ahmad, T. Antoniu, S. Goldwater, and S. Krishnamurthi. A type system for statically detecting spreadsheet errors. In *ASE*, pages 174–183, 2003.

[3] K. Bollacker, C. Evans, P. Paritosh, T. Sturge, and J. Taylor. Freebase: a collaboratively created graph database for structuring human knowledge. In *SIGMOD*, pages 1247–1250, 2008.

[4] M. J. Cafarella, A. Halevy, D. Z. Wang, E. Wu, and Y. Zhang. Webtables: Exploring the power of tables on the web. In *VLDB*, pages 538–549, 2008.

[5] M. J. Cafarella, A. Y. Halevy, and N. Khoussainova. Data integration for the relational web. *PVLDB*, 2(1):1090–1101, 2009.

[6] X. Chai, B.-Q. Vuong, A. Doan, and J. F. Naughton. Efficiently incorporating user feedback into information extraction and integration programs. In *SIGMOD*, pages 87–100, 2009.

[7] Z. Chen and M. Cafarella. Automatic web spreadsheet data extraction. In *VLDB workshop on SSW*, Trento, Italy, 2013.

[8] Z. Chen and M. Cafarella. A semiautomatic approach for accurate and low-effort spreadsheet data extraction. Technical report, University of Michigan, 2014.

[9] Z. Chen, M. Cafarella, J. Chen, D. Prevo and J. Zhuang. Senbazuru: A prototype spreadsheet database management system. In *VLDB Demo*, 2013.

[10] 2009. ClueWeb09, http://lemurproject.org/clueweb09.php/.

[11] G. F. Cooper. The computational complexity of probabilistic inference using bayesian belief networks. *Artif. Intell.*, 42(2-3):393–405, 1990.

[12] J. Cunha, J. Saraiva, and J. Visser. From spreadsheets to relational databases and back. In *PEPM*, pages 179–188, 2009.

[13] O. Dekel and O. Shamir. Vox populi: Collecting high-quality labels from a crowd. In *COLT*, 2009.

[14] W. Gatterbauer, P. Bohunsky, M. Herzog, B. Krüpl, and B. Pollak. Towards domain-independent information extraction from web tables. In *WWW*, pages 71–80, 2007.

[15] P. J. Guo, S. Kandel, J. M. Hellerstein, and J. Heer. Proactive wrangling: Mixed-initiative end-user programming of data transformation scripts. In *UIST*, pages 65–74, 2011.

[16] M. Gyssens, L. V. S. Lakshmanan, and I. N. Subramanian. Tables as a paradigm for querying and restructuring. In *PODS*, pages 93–103, 1996.

[17] E. Horvitz. Principles of mixed-initiative user interfaces. In *CHI*, pages 159–166, 1999.

[18] V. Hung, B. Benatallah, and R. Saint-Paul. Spreadsheet-based complex data transformation. In *CIKM*, pages 1749–1754, 2011.

[19] D. F. Huynh, R. C. Miller, and D. R. Karger. Potluck: Data mash-up tool for casual users. In *ISWC/ASWC*, pages 239–252, 2007.

[20] Z. G. Ives, C. A. Knoblock, S. Minton, M. Jacob, P. P. Talukdar, R. Tuchinda, J. L. Ambite, M. Muslea, and C. Gazen. Interactive data integration through smart copy & paste. In *CIDR*, 2009.

[21] S. Kandel, A. Paepcke, J. Hellerstein, and J. Heer. Wrangler: interactive visual specification of data transformation scripts. In *CHI*, pages 3363–3372, 2011.

[22] D. Koller and N. Friedman. *Probabilistic Graphical Models - Principles and Techniques*. MIT Press, 2009.

[23] V. Kolmogorov. Convergent tree-reweighted message passing for energy minimization. *IEEE Trans. Pattern Anal. Mach. Intell.*, 28(10):1568–1583, 2006.

[24] J. Lafferty, A. McCallum, and F. Pereira. Conditional random fields: Probabilistic models for segmenting and labeling sequence data. In *ICML*, pages 282–289, 2001.

[25] L. V. S. Lakshmanan, S. N. Subramanian, N. Goyal, and R. Krishnamurthy. On query spreadsheets. In *ICDE*, pages 134–141, 1998.

[26] R. Pimplikar and S. Sarawagi. Answering table queries on the web using column keywords. *PVLDB*, 5(10):908–919, 2012.

[27] M. Spenke, C. Beilken, and T. Berlage. Focus: The interactive table for product comparison and selection. In *UIST*, pages 41–50, 1996.

[28] R. Tuchinda, P. A. Szekely, and C. A. Knoblock. Building data integration queries by demonstration. In *IUI*, pages 170–179, 2007.

[29] 2007. http://www.di.ens.fr/ mschmidt/Software/UGM.html.

Sentiment Expression Conditioned by Affective Transitions and Social Forces

Moritz Sudhof* Andrés Gómez Emilsson† Andrew L. Maas* Christopher Potts‡
*Computer Science †Psychology ‡Linguistics
Stanford University
{sudhof, nc07agom, amaas, cgpotts}@stanford.edu

ABSTRACT

Human emotional states are not independent but rather proceed along systematic paths governed by both internal, cognitive factors and external, social ones. For example, anxiety often transitions to disappointment, which is likely to sink to depression before rising to happiness and relaxation, and these states are conditioned by the states of others in our communities. Modeling these complex dependencies can yield insights into human emotion and support more powerful sentiment technologies.

We develop a theory of conditional dependencies between emotional states in which emotions are characterized not only by valence (polarity) and arousal (intensity) but also by the role they play in state transitions and social relationships. We implement this theory using conditional random fields (CRFs) that synthesize textual information with information about previous emotional states and the emotional states of others. To assess the power of affective transitions, we evaluate our model in a collection of 'mood' updates from the Experience Project. To assess the power of social factors, we use a corpus of product reviews from a website in which the community dynamics encourage reviewers to be influenced by each other. In both settings, our models yield improvements of statistical and practical significance over ones that classify each text independently of its emotional or social context.

Categories and Subject Descriptors

I.2.7 [**Natural Language Processing**]: Discourse; Text analysis

Keywords

multidimensional sentiment analysis; sentiment as social; sentiment transitions

KDD'14, August 24–27, 2014, New York, NY, USA.

ACM 978-1-4503-2956-9/14/08 ...$15.00.
http://dx.doi.org/10.1145/2623330.2623687.

1. INTRODUCTION

Human emotional states are not independent, nor are they experienced in isolation. Rather, they proceed along systematic paths and cohere into psychologically important groups. Anxiety often transitions to disappointment, which is likely to sink to depression, often a long-lasting state. Happiness amplifies to elation or settles down to contentment. States like anxiety, optimism, and worry are inherently transitional; one's optimism might be vindicated, leading to positive states, or crushed, leading to disappointment. All these states are also conditioned by the states of others in our communities; complex social forces can push our emotions closer to those around us or pull them farther away.

Our goal is to show that modeling dependencies between emotional states can yield insights into human emotion and support more powerful sentiment technologies. In our first set of experiments (Section 3), we concentrate on the affective transitions that individuals experience. Using a collection of users' 'mood' updates from the Experience Project,[1] we develop a simple probability model for capturing the conditional dependencies between emotional states. The ideas are founded in dimensional models of emotion [10, 28, 29, 34] based in valence (polarity) and arousal (intensity), but we emphasize the role that emotions play in transitions between states. We implement this theory using conditional random fields (CRFs; [13, 32]) that synthesize textual information with information about temporally organized sequences of emotions, and we show that this delivers improvements of statistical and practical significance over models that classify each text independently of its emotional or social context. The improvements are largest for transitional emotional states, which are often particularly important for industry applications, since moments of emotional inflection often coincide with changing opinions or attitudes.

We then extend our model to social influences (Section 4). Using a corpus of product reviews from a website with rich community interactions [8, 18, 19], we present evidence that the current reviewer for a product is influenced by the sequence of reviews already posted about that product. Here, the sequences come, not from a specific individual, but rather from group-level actions and reactions. Once again, CRFs incorporating this sequence information out-perform simple classifiers by a large margin. This is an important counterpart to our moods study, not only because of its social dimension, but also because it highlights the value of transition information for common polarity-based sentiment tasks.

[1] `http://www.experienceproject.com`

2. RELATED WORK

Our goal is to understand and make use of the dependencies between emotional states, which derive from both personal and social factors. Our work thus finds precedent in diverse areas of natural language processing, social network analysis, and cognitive psychology, including models of social influence and multidimensional sentiment expression. This section provides a high-level summary of these connections with the existing literature.

Our view of sentiment is a *dimensional* one [10, 28, 29, 34], in which emotions are characterized by a small number of more basic dimensions, usually valence and arousal but sometimes much more abstract ones (e.g., [15]). Valence roughly corresponds to polarity (like/dislike, pleasure/pain, pleasant/unpleasant), and arousal corresponds to intensity of experience, mirroring the amount of energy exhibited, spent, or available during a given emotional state. For example, ecstatic and serene are both emotions of positive valence but opposite arousal levels, just as angry and sad are both negative valence emotions of opposite arousal levels. Our own model can be seen as having valence and arousal as its foundation, but we focus on the patterns found in the transition dynamics between emotions through time.

Our moods data take us well beyond the basic polarity classifications or scales that dominate in computational sentiment analysis [11, 25, 26, 27, 30] and are thus more reminiscent of the multidimensional categories of [2, 14, 16, 22, 31, 35]. Even our star-ratings-based experiments with product reviews (Section 4) highlight the importance of having a 'neutral' category along the valence dimension [12], especially in communities that might be polarized in their opinions but nonetheless seek cohesion, a social force that can push evaluations away from the extremes.

We also study the social factors that influence the attitudes and emotions of community members. This can be thought of as part of a growing literature that seeks to understand online, user-provided metadata as both reflecting and shaping complex social processes concerning influence, group cohesion, individual assertion of identity, and sentiment diffusion in networks [1, 5, 8, 20, 21, 38]. Our general approach is also influenced by [24], who use social variables together with textual ones to predict expressed preferences in political speeches. A related model is used by [33] to capture the ways in which social relationships pattern with attitudes and evaluations. Our CRFs are conceptually different from the graph-based models in these papers, but they aim to capture similar insights about how sentiment predictions should be made partly on the basis of high-level emotional and contextual cues (see also [4]).

Our quantitative evaluations use conditional random fields (CRFs; [13, 32]), which are discriminative models in which it is possible to model complex dependencies not only between the input and output variables, as in typical classification problems, but also among the output variables themselves. General CRFs can model essentially any kind of graphical structure, but we concentrate on the more tractable special case of a linear-chain CRF, in which the output variables are arranged in a linear sequence, creating a discriminative counterpart to the generative Hidden Markov Model. Linear-chain CRFs have been used for a wide variety of sequence-labeling phenomena relating to linguistic structure, and they have been successfully applied to more social and contextual tasks of the sort we study here, including opinion-source identification [6], sentiment transitions inside documents [17], and social network extraction [7].

3. AFFECTIVE TRANSITIONS

We now address the personal, internal factors that shape the temporal flow of emotions people experience.

3.1 Experience Project Moods

Our 'moods' dataset is derived from community-member updates at the Experience Project (EP) social networking site. When logged in, EP members can post short texts describing their moods and also choose from a variety of different mood labels, which we use to classify the texts into emotional categories. Mood status updates are visible on member profiles. Table 1 gives an example of a sequence of three posts by the same user; the corpus contains additional metadata, but we use only the information in this table.

We work with a sample of about 2 million anonymized mood posts with unique author identifiers and 174 different mood labels for emotional, evaluative, and attitudinal states. Figure 1 summarizes the distribution of the top 20 moods by update frequency. This fragment of the full dataset shows that the corpus can be used to study sentiment analysis in the broadest terms, since individual pairs of labels or clusters of labels can be used to develop familiar polarity models [27], polarity models with different levels of intensity [3, 35, 36], models of sentiment based in social emotions like sympathy and solidarity [16, 31], and many others. For our purposes, the mix of valence and arousal with transitional emotions like anxiety and optimism is the most important aspect of the data set. In the next section, we study the entire distribution, seeking to motivate a high-level classification of the moods into distinct categories based on their transition relationships with other moods.

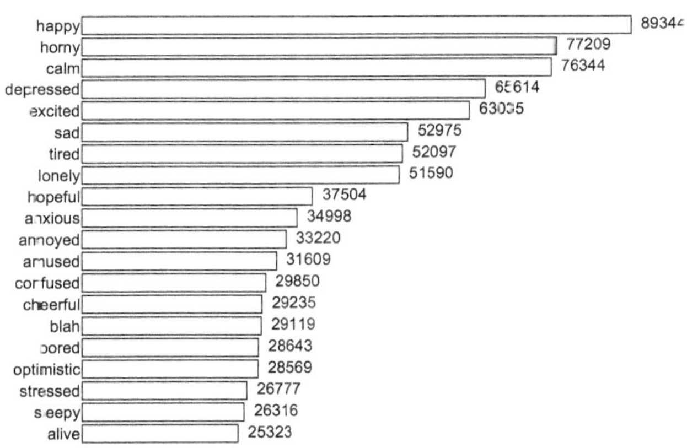

Figure 1: Top 20 mood labels by frequency, accounting for about 40% of the updates in our sample.

3.2 Mood Transitions

One's current emotional state will be heavily influenced by one's previous emotional state. The state before that will also exert an influence on the present, but less so. More generally, we expect previous states to influence current ones, with the influences weakening (becoming less direct) the farther back in time we go.

Time	Mood	Text
2013-07-28 11:56:56	sad	no one wants me . feeling sad cause i dont want me either
2013-07-28 22:41:40	lonely	Laying in this hospital bed I thought I wanted to be here I don't , take me home
2013-07-29 02:32:01	depressed	im sorry i need someone to talk to i need to not be a sub for 5 mins i just need a friend. please
		⋮

Table 1: A partial sequence of mood updates from a single user.

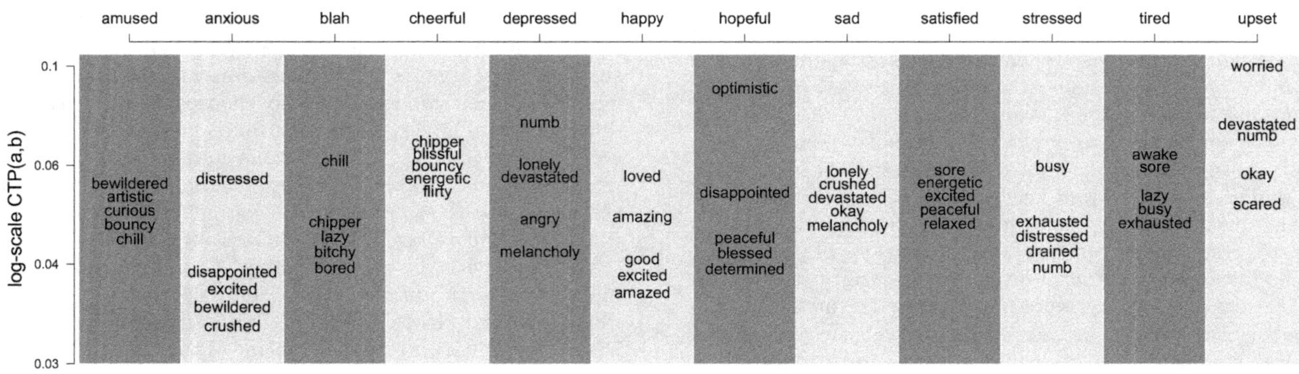

Figure 2: Mood compressed transition probabilities (*CTP* values). Each column labeled with emotion a shows the emotions b with largest *CTP*(a,b), as defined in equation 2.

To capture this pattern of influences, we first define emotional transition probabilities in a way that encompasses the full set of historical relationship between emotions. Let E be the full set of emotions, and let $C(a,t,b)$ be the number of times a user posted emotion $a \in E$ and then posted emotion $b \in E$ exactly t days later. Crucially, these transitions are counted whether or not there is an update between a and b. Then the conditional probability of b given a after t days is given by equation 1.

$$P(b \mid a,t) = \frac{C(a,t,b)}{\sum_{b' \in E} C(a,t,b')} \tag{1}$$

Using these values, we then define the *compressed transition probability* between emotions a and b as follows:

$$CTP(a,b) = (c-1)\sum_{t=0}^{\infty} \frac{P(b \mid a,t)}{c^{t+1}} \tag{2}$$

Here, c is a dampening constant that gives a higher weight to recent transitions. In practice, c can range between 1.5 to 2.5 without significantly changing *CTP* values; in this paper, we use $c = 2$. We choose an exponential decay function so that distant transitions affect the *CTP* value without outweighing more recent transitions. Other dampening functions can also be used; the exact method seems not to matter as long as recent transitions are preferentially weighted and distant transitions are allowed to exert some influence.

The *CTP* measure has a second noteworthy advantage. There is significant diversity in the way EP members interact with the moods update feature. Some users post updates at roughly regular intervals, whereas others do so in less predictable patterns. In taking into account the temporal distance between updates, the *CTP* captures the way influence varies with time, making it more robust to this kind of behavioral variation than interval-blind methods are.

Figure 2 depicts a sample of *CTP*(a,b) values. The conditioning emotions a are given along the top. For each, the emotions b with highest *CTP* to them are given in rank order, according to the log *CTP*(a,b) values, normalized by the frequency of b to correct for differing usage levels. Self-transitions generally have dramatically larger *CTP* values than do other emotions, so those are not depicted. Frequency normalization and the log-scale of the y-axis are intended to make the plot more readable and to facilitate comparisons within and across columns.

The patterns in Figure 2 are intuitive, highlighting valence, arousal, and transition as important ingredients. For instance, the likely next states after a simple positive state like 'happy' have the same polarity, differing largely in intensity (and other social components). In contrast, the transition state 'hopeful', while positive in its own right, has a much more mixed set of later states associated with it, reflecting the uncertainty of this emotion. The emotions 'sad' and 'anxious' are rough negative duals of these: 'sad' emerges as a fairly standard negative valence category, whereas 'anxiety' is itself negative but transitions to both positive and negative outcomes. There are numerous other patterns like these in the data, reflecting not only emotional but also interactional and real-world factors (e.g., 'bored' to 'bitchy'; 'tired' to 'sore'; 'stressed' to 'busy').

To try to get a comprehensive, high-level view of how emotions relate to each other, we can also represent our entire data set as a directed graph based on the full matrix of *CTP* values, as in Figure 3. For any two emotions a and b, the edge from a to b has weight *CTP*(a,b). The resulting graph represents the flow between emotional states of the mood updates population, thereby describing the affective space as a dynamic system. This abstraction is helpful for revealing the dynamic structure of the space. In particular, it is possible to use this graph to identify clusters of emotions that are densely connected with each other.

In order to cluster the emotions into disjoint partitions, we employ a variant of weighted label propagation [37] that

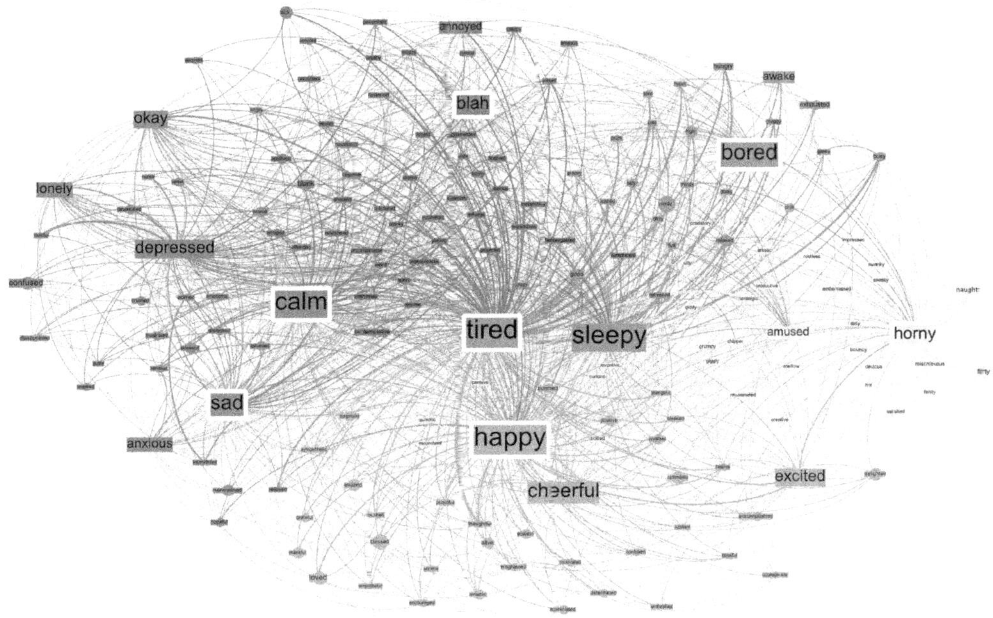

Figure 3: The moods represented as a weighted, directed graph in which edge labels are determined by *CTP* values, and cluster assignments (indicated by color) are also made based on those values. Node sizes are determined by the node's PageRank. White bounding boxes indicate prominent cluster moods.

is tailored specifically for highly dense graphs (by taking the average edge weight from each cluster instead of its sum). The main idea underpinning the algorithm is to identify groups of emotions with a higher than expected within-group transition probability. Unlike other weighted label propagation algorithms, our variant predetermines the number of clusters, and each emotion is iteratively assigned to the cluster from which the average *CTP* to it is the highest (as opposed to obtaining the label of the single heaviest incoming edge). The algorithm works as follows:

1. Initialize n clusters C_i randomly.
2. For each cluster C_i and each emotion e_j, compute the mean of the values $CTP(e_i, e_j)$ for $e_i \in C_i$ and assign e_j to the cluster with the highest such value.
3. Repeat 2 until the cluster assignments stabilize.

Self-transitions are dampened by multiplying them by a small constant s (here, 0.005) and normalizing accordingly. In our experience, large values of s (e.g., 0.01) generally lead to faster and more reliable convergence, but the resulting clusters are less compelling, whereas smaller values of s deliver substantially more plausible clusters but sometimes lead to non-convergence due to cyclic label assignments. We ran the algorithm 100 times using the parameters from Figure 3 ($s = 0.005$, 5 clusters) and it converged 67% of the time, with convergent runs taking an average of 25.40 iterations. Given that our primary goal is to explore the structure of the data set, these rates are more than acceptable.

Figure 3 uses color to represent a clustering of the mood space into five cells. Node sizes are scaled by a node's PageRank, which correlates with frequency but reduces the effect of self-transitions. Given the way in which the algorithm is defined, clusters have a higher than expected within-cluster transition probability. Thus they can be interpreted as enduring emotional states. If we label them based on their prominent members (by PageRank), we get clusters 'tired/bored' (orange), 'horny' (yellow), 'sad/calm' (purple), 'happy' (green), and 'blah' (red), which is an intuitive set of groups based primarily on valence but further structured by other social and emotional factors. By varying the number of clusters, we achieve different levels of resolution. For example, with three clusters, the partitions show a near perfect division between negative, neutral/mixed, and positive valence emotions. With ten clusters, rarefied clusters emerge relating to erotic states, lack of energy ('lethargic', 'exhausted'), high-valence positive emotions ('ecstatic', 'delighted', 'blissful'), and so forth.

The directed nature of the graph also highlights the role emotions play in affective transitions. At a high level, we see the densest pathways between 'sad/calm' and 'blah' (purple, red), between 'blah' and 'tired/bored' (red, orange), and between 'happy' and 'horny' (green, yellow). The pathways are more asymmetrical between 'horny' and 'tired/bored', typically running from the first to the second rather than the other way around. Some pairwise paths are extremely unlikely in either direction. For instance, direct 'happy' to 'sad/calm' (green to purple) transitions are rare; emotional paths that begin with 'happy' and end with 'sad/calm' are likely to travel through other emotional states along the way. These patterns match well with our intuitions about human experiences, and they further support our contention that emotions are defined as much by their transitions as they are by their inherent properties.

3.3 Models

We apply CRFs as a modeling technique to capture emotion structure of the sort we just identified in our moods data. Specifically, we use linear-chain CRF models, as they efficiently represent temporal relationships among emotion labels as well as the mapping from text features of a document to its emotion label. Formally, we have a collection of document sequences $\mathcal{D}$, where each document sequence $d \in \mathcal{D}$ is a sequence of tuples, $d = [(x_1, e_1), (x_2, e_2), \ldots, (x_T, e_T)]$. Each tuple (x_t, e_t) is a vector of document features x_t along with the associated emotion label e_t. The sequence length T can vary for each sequence.

We construct a linear-chain CRF with potential functions $\phi_{j,k}(x_t, e_t)$ between an input feature $x_{t,j}$ and possible emotion $e_{t,k}$. Each $\phi_{j,k}$ is a binary indicator function, with $\phi_{j,k}(x_t, e_t) = 1$ when both feature j and label k are present in a document and 0 otherwise. This type of potential function is equivalent to the binary presence feature functions often used in sentiment classification [27]. However, the CRF goes beyond relationships between a single document's text features and its label. A second set of potential functions $\tau_{l,k}(e_{t-1}, e_t)$ serve as binary indicators for whether emotion l was present in the previous document at time $t-1$ and emotion k is present in the current document at time t.

We use a standard log-linear parameterization, which makes the learning problem convex. Having defined our potential functions and chosen a log-linear CRF approach, our model derivation exactly follows those of other linear chain CRF models in the literature [13, 32]. We do not restate the likelihood and learning problem here; see [32] for the full details.

To evaluate the effect of modeling temporal emotion label relationships, we compare our CRF approach to a time-independent classification approach. This model treats each tuple (x_t, e_t) as independent from other documents in the sequence and estimates the emotion label probability $P(e_t \mid x_t)$. To estimate this probability we use a maximum entropy (MaxEnt) classifier. The MaxEnt model is a standard choice for classification tasks in sentiment analysis and other NLP tasks. Furthermore, the MaxEnt model is a special case of our linear chain CRF approach where we remove the potential functions $\tau_{l,k}(e_{t-1}, e_t)$. In removing these potential functions from our CRF, we are left with only potential functions relating the current text features x_t to the emotion label e_t. Comparing these two models allows us to identify the value in including sequence information.

We use the CRFsuite software package for both the CRF and MaxEnt models [23]. For both models, we use ℓ_2 regularization. We choose the regularization penalty by cross-validating over possible values and evaluating development set performance. We then run 20 trials in which we randomly split the data 80%/20% into training and testing sets and evaluate performance for both models. We use the non-parametric Wilcoxon rank-sums test to measure the significance of the difference between CRF and baseline performance. In order to focus on the effects of sequence structure, we restrict our textual features to simple unigrams.

3.4 Experimental Set-up

We conducted experiments on two different subsets of our moods data: a simple valence/polarity subset and a multi-dimensional subset involving valence/polarity, arousal, and affective transitions. The polarity experiments are relatively easy to interpret and permit general comparisons with more familiar sentiment tasks, while the multidimensional experiments highlight the nuances of our moods data and reveal more of the power of affective transitions.

We built a polarity label set by clustering high-volume moods with unambiguous valence, drawn from the green and purple clusters in Figure 3:

- 'positive' = {'happy', 'excited', 'thankful'}
- 'negative' = {'sad', 'lonely', 'depressed', 'angry'}

Figure 4 summarizes the transition structure of the polarity data set. Each square depicts the probability of seeing a sequence consisting of the row polarity and then the column polarity. The overall structure of the polarity transitions is clear: polarity states are generally enduring, with a slight trend towards positivity. One concern one might raise is that this trend could reflect, not affective transitions, but rather an overall tendency for individuals to be consistently positive or consistently negative. With Figure 4(b), we seek to address this by limiting attention just to high-variance sequences, defined as the top 20% of polarity sequences by label diversity. Thus, these sequences definitely come from users with variable emotional states. The same structure is evident here, though with the additional finding that, for these variable individuals, transitions from 'negative' to 'positive' are more likely than the other way around. As another point of comparison, we include, in Figure 4(c), a version of these heatmaps in which the mood sequences have been randomly shuffled. This destroys all transition structure, revealing instead only the percentages of 'positive' and 'negative' items in the data set.

For our multidimensional experiments, we would ideally study the entire set of moods, since Figure 3 suggests that they have intricate internal structure. However, the resulting models would be intractable to analyze and impractical to report on. Thus, we hand-selected six moods, with the goal of capturing valence, arousal, and the transitional characteristics of emotions, thereby preserving many of the rich inter-emotion dynamics of the full set. The moods we chose for this are 'cheerful', 'satisfied', 'hopeful', 'anxious', 'stressed', and 'depressed'.

Although we focus only on a subset of the moods presented in Figure 2, this visualization provides insights into the transition structure we hypothesize that our CRF can leverage. Overall, since some emotions are more common than others, the label distribution for the multidimensional sentiment classification experiments are not uniform. The emotions 'depressed', 'hopeful', and 'stressed' are the most common, and 'satisfied', 'anxious', and 'cheerful' are the least common. These differing relative frequencies probably reflect deeper underlying facts about the frequency or duration of these experiences.

In Section 3.2, we argued that one's current emotion is affected by one's previous emotions, with influences diminishing rapidly over time. The structure of our CRF model forces us to make a simplifying Markov assumption that only the previous state influences the current one. Since this discretizes the time element, we impose an additional restriction that any two consecutive mood posts in mood sequences can be no more than 24 hours apart, to ensure that we model true affective transitions rather than individuals' general behavior on the site (e.g., users who log on infrequently and only when anxious). After enforcing this restriction, our polarity data set consists of 30,000 sequences containing approximately 70,000 posts, and our multidimensional mood

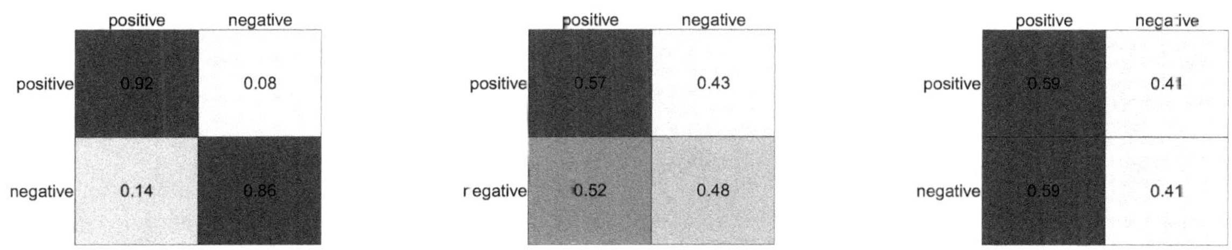

(a) All actual sequences. (b) High-variance sequences. (c) Randomized sequences (averaged over 20 randomizations).

Figure 4: Mood polarity transition probabilities, from the row state to the column state.

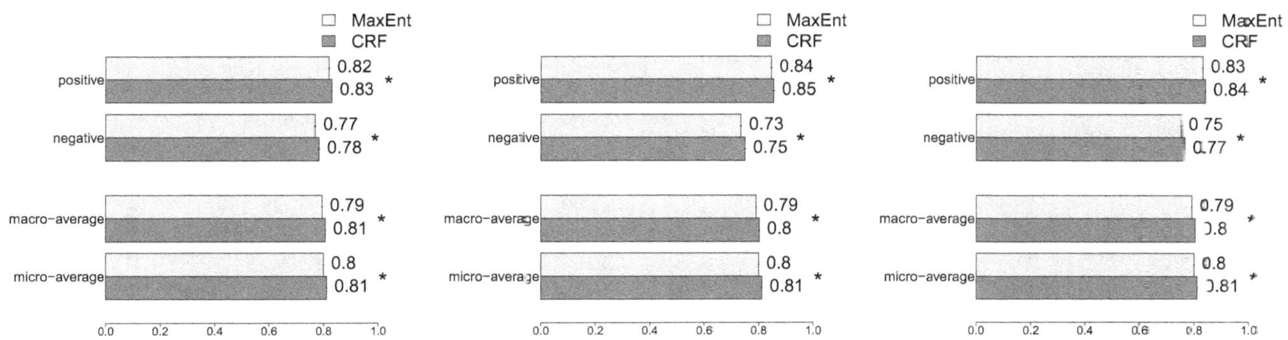

(a) Precision. (b) Recall. (c) F1.

Figure 5: Moods polarity performance with bootstrapped 95% confidence intervals (often very small). Stars mark statistically significant differences ($p < 0.001$) according to a Wilcoxon rank-sums test.

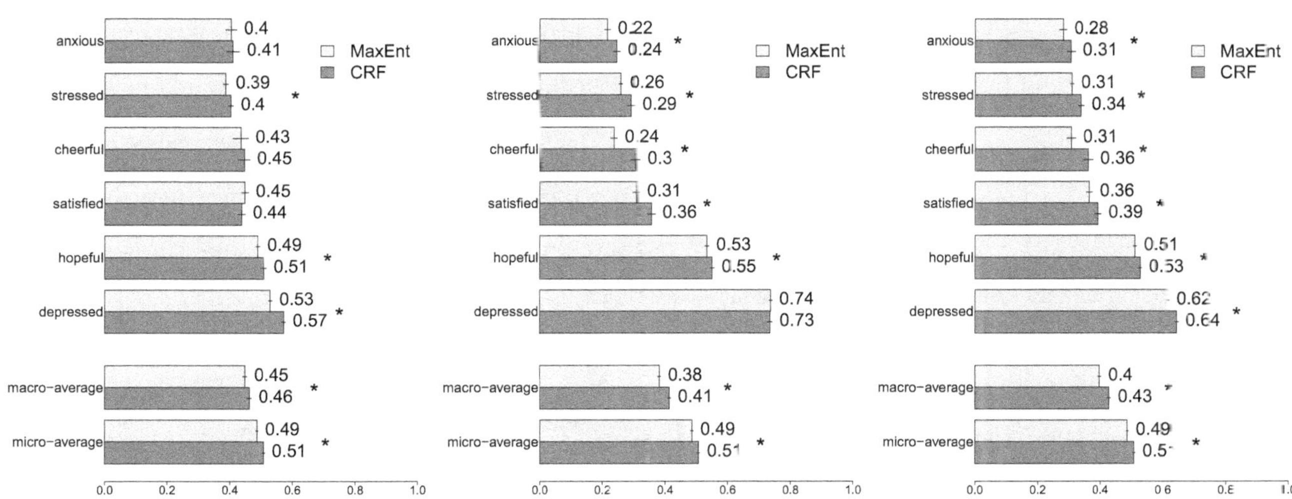

(a) Precision. (b) Recall. (c) F1.

Figure 6: Multidimensional moods performance with bootstrapped 95% confidence intervals (often very small). Stars mark statistically significant differences ($p < 0.001$) according to a Wilcoxon rank-sums test.

dataset consists of approximately 20,000 sequences containing 60,000 posts overall.

3.5 Results

The polarity and multidimensional CRF models achieve absolute micro-average F1 gains of 2% over the MaxEnt baselines, and performance on individual labels improves across the board. All gains are statistically significant ($p < 0.001$) according to a Wilcoxon rank-sums test. Figure 5 summarizes polarity results, and Figure 6 summarizes multidimensional moods results. The results are presented with bootstrapped 95% confidence intervals [9], often very small because of the large amount of data and consistent model performance.

Since the multidimensional moods model must navigate a decision space of six labels, its overall performance is lower than that of the two-label polarity model, and inter-label performance disparities are greater. The advantage of the multidimensional moods model, however, is its ability to identify granular emotions that are richer indications of a person's current and future affective states than the non-specific classes 'positive' and 'negative'. For example, 'anxious' and 'depressed' are both negative valence mood states, but they have different implications for a user's future state: 'anxious' is a transitory mood state that tends towards resolution, either positive or negative, whereas 'depressed' is a more enduring affective state with more limited possible future states. In many applications, these distinctions are particularly relevant. In the customer experience industry, for example, it is often most valuable not to characterize a user's valence but rather to identify moments of emotional inflection, which mark the points of volatility when a user is in the process of changing opinions or attitudes.

One measure of a mood's volatility is the entropy of the probability distributions over previous and subsequent mood states, referred to as $H(prev)$ and $H(next)$, respectively. Moods with high $H(prev)$ and $H(next)$ are crossroads, in that they arise from and transition to diverse sets of other mood states. Because such moods are transitory, they are relatively infrequent and therefore systematically harder to model. For instance, a mood's $H(prev)$ is inversely related to its volume (linear regression; $R^2 = 0.80$, $p < 0.05$), and a mood's volume is inversely related to its F1 score (linear regression; $R^2 = 0.86$, $p < 0.01$). Nonetheless, the CRF models are notably better at identifying them than the MaxEnt models are, especially in terms of recall (linear regression; $R^2 = 0.71$, $p < 0.05$).

For example, 'anxious' is the most high-entropy mood state of the six we model, and it is the second most infrequent. Confusion matrices show that the MaxEnt baseline frequently misclassifies 'anxious' posts: given sparse or ambiguous 'anxious' documents, the contextually-unaware MaxEnt baseline tends toward the more frequent classes 'stressed' and 'depressed'. Our CRF, however, is less susceptible to this mistake because it incorporates knowledge of the particular transition characteristics of 'anxious'. CRF gains in recall for 'anxious' are above average, and, conversely, precision gains for 'stressed' and 'depressed' are also higher than average.

Overall, these experiments validate that a CRF model can incorporate the affective transition structure described in Section 3.2 to improve performance on both the more conventional polarity prediction task and the more complicated multidimensional prediction task. The strong performance gains on infrequent labels, which are often of particular interest, is reflected by the macro-average F1 score, which shows greater CRF gains over the baseline than the micro-average F1 score.

4. SOCIAL FORCES

We now extend the above model of affective transitions to a social setting in which the evidence suggests that current sentiment evaluations are influenced by previous ones.

4.1 RateBeer Data

We develop our basic model of social influences on sentiment evaluations using the RateBeer corpus, a collection of 2.9 million user-supplied beer reviews.[2] With respect to its structure, this corpus is like most corpora of user-supplied product reviews. The review texts are typically just a few sentences long and have associated with them a number of different kinds of rating, including aspects of the beer (e.g., aroma, palate, taste) and an overall rating. (For discussion of these multi-aspect ratings, see [19].) The overall ratings are on the scale 1–20, which we rescale into a more familiar space of 5 star ratings (with fractions of a star possible).

4.2 Social forces

The RateBeer corpus reflects complex social phenomena that make it especially useful for our purposes. First, individual community members often write many reviews (4,798 wrote more than 50; [8]). Second, we know from [18] that reviewers themselves vary greatly in their level of expertise about beers. Third, we know from [8] that the community dynamics of the site are complex, with specific kinds of users influencing the evaluative and communicative norms in complex ways that find many counterparts in off-line communities. These factors lead us to expect reviewers to be influenced by each other when making rating choices. For instance, if the current reviewer is new to the site, she might shift her judgments towards those of more expert members who already posted reviews. Conversely, experts might feel the need to push back against overly positive or negative reviews by newcomers. We do not at present have a deep understanding of the social forces at work, but we require only that forces like these be active.

Figure 8 provides additional information about the rating distribution and how we construe it. For the purposes of our classification experiments, 'positive' reviews are those with ratings 4 or above, 'negative' reviews are those with ratings 2.5 or below, and 'neutral' ones fall in the middle, as indicated in the figure. These boundaries were chosen with the underlying rating distribution in mind. The distribution is noteworthy for being much more skewed to the middle of the rating scale than is typical for corpora of user-supplied reviews, which are usually dominated by positive reviews ([26], p. 74). We think that this too reflects the underlying social dynamics of the site: extreme evaluations (at either end of the scale) are socially riskier; for example, one doesn't want to appear too glowing about a beer that is perceived as mundane, nor too critical of one that is perceived as requiring expertise.

Figure 7 provides a high-level picture of the extent of these influences, using the label categories indicated in Figure 8.

[2]http://snap.stanford.edu/data/web-RateBeer.html

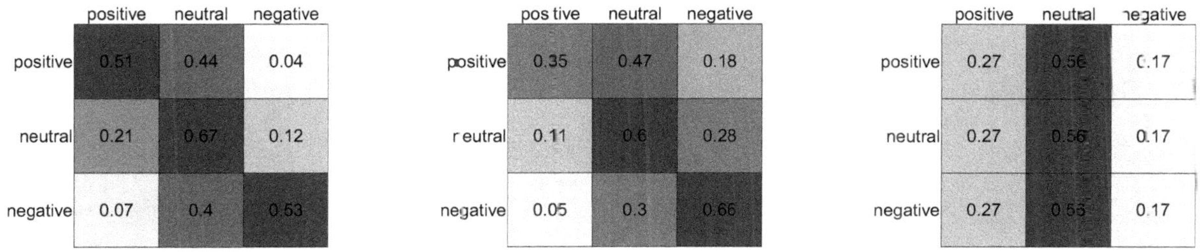

(a) All actual sequences. (b) High-variance products. (c) Randomized sequences (averaged over 20 randomizations).

Figure 7: By-product transition probabilities, from the row state to the column state.

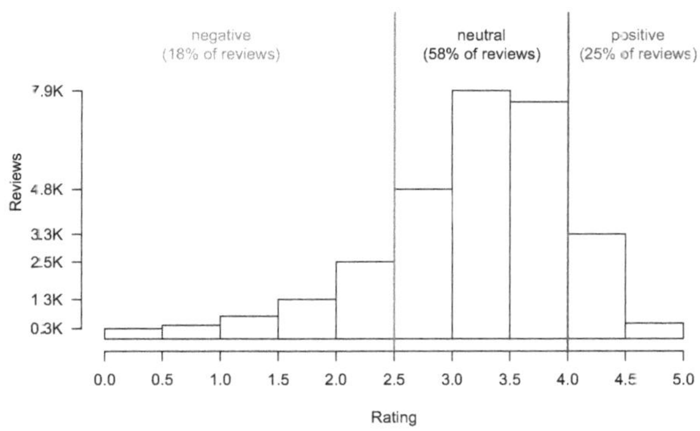

Figure 8: RateBeer ratings and label categories.

Each square depicts the probability of seeing a sequence consisting of the row evaluation and then the column evaluation, using the probability model from our moods study (Section 3.2). The overall picture is easily characterized: self-transitions are most likely for all three categories, polarity reversing sequences are least-likely, and 'neutral'-to-'positive' sequences are more likely than 'neutral'-to-'negative'. This pattern makes sense if we assume that there are generally social costs to disagreeing with others. Importantly, Figure 7(b) shows that the general pattern holds even when we restrict attention to products with extremely highly variable ratings, defined as those with rating standard deviation in the third quartile for those values. This suggests that the patterns are not merely a consequence of overall community agreement. Indeed, the higher-variance reviews seem to reflect the ways in which disagreements are negotiated. Figure 7(c) shows that the pattern disappears when we randomize the sequences; the only remaining pattern is fully explained by the overall label distribution.

4.3 Models

The CRF model is the same as it was for the moods data (see Section 3.3), except label sequence features are now product-level rating sequences. Once again, we compare the CRFs to MaxEnt classifiers with the same textual features. For both, regularization parameters are optimized independently using cross-validation on development sets.

4.4 Experimental Set-up

To study the gains achieved by incorporating social influences into our model, we run 20 classification trials. In each trial, we randomly sample sequences such that the data set consists of roughly 500,000 reviews. We train on 80% of the sampled sequences and test on the remaining 20%.

4.5 Results

The CRF model achieves an absolute micro-average F1 gain of 1% over the MaxEnt baseline, which translates to roughly 1,000 additional correct classifications over the baseline. Figure 9 summarizes by-label performance for both the MaxEnt and CRF models.

Although performance improves for all labels, we observe stronger performance gains for 'positive' and 'negative' documents than 'neutral' ones. This trend is reflective of the sequence structures described in Figure 7: the probability distributions of states that transition to and arise from 'positive' and 'negative' states are more discriminating than those for 'neutral' states. 'Negative' reviews are highly unlikely to follow 'positive' ones and vice versa, and 'neutral' is often the intermediate step in sequences that do transition from one polarity to the other. As a result, given an ambiguous or sparse review that the MaxEnt baseline may, for example, predict to be 'neutral' or 'negative' with equal likelihood, the CRF model can use the previous review's predicted class to help discriminate. In this example, if the previous review is predicted to be 'positive', the CRF will be particularly unlikely to decide that the ambiguous review in question is 'negative'.

5. CONCLUSION

Many sentiment models and technologies make the simplifying assumption that each sentiment expression (emotion, evaluation, perspective) was produced independently of all others. Our central observation is that this simplifying assumption ignores information that is psychologically and socially important, particularly for inherently transitional emotions like hope and anxiety. Using linear-chain CRFs, we showed furthermore that this information has significant predictive value, not only for multidimensional sentiment data, but also in more traditional polarity tasks. To highlight the independent value of internal, cognitive factors and external, social ones, we kept these two kinds of influence apart in our models, but the CRF approach is flexible enough to accommodate the complex graphical structure needed to bring these two kinds of influence together into a single predictive model. We look forward to future experi-

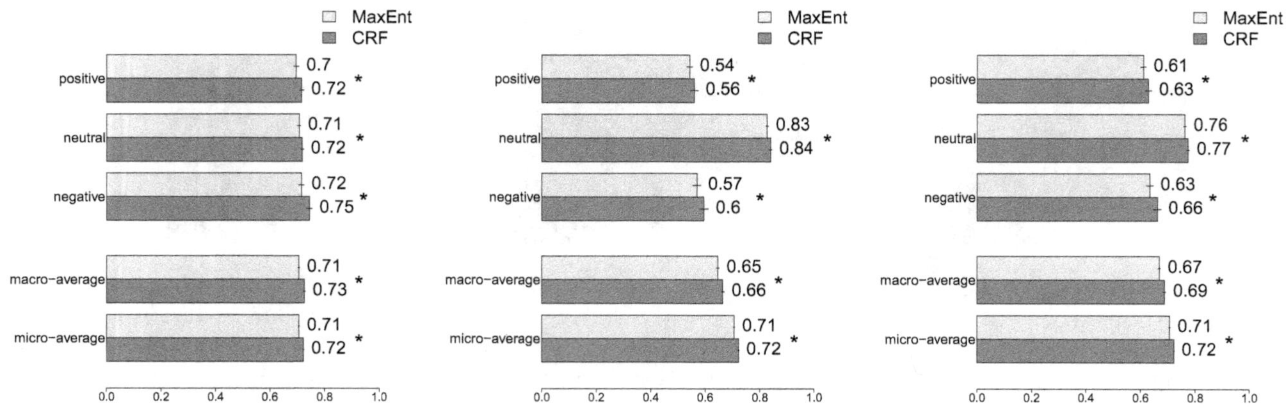

(a) Precision. (b) Recall. (c) F1.

Figure 9: RateBeer results with bootstrapped 95% confidence intervals (often very small). Stars mark statistically significant differences ($p < 0.001$) according to a Wilcoxon rank-sums test.

ments that combine personal affective transitions and social forces to further improve sentiment prediction.

Acknowledgements

We thank Experience Project for providing us with the sample of moods data and for being encouraging about our research. This work was supported in part by ONR grant N00014-13-1-0287 and NSF grant IIS-1016909.

References

[1] A. Aji and E. Agichtein. The "nays" have it: Exploring effects of sentiment in collaborative knowledge sharing. In *Proceedings of the NAACL HLT 2010 Workshop on Computational Linguistics in a World of Social Media*, pages 1–2, Los Angeles, California, USA, June 2010. Association for Computational Linguistics.

[2] C. O. Alm, D. Roth, and R. Sproat. Emotions from text: Machine learning for text-based emotion prediction. In *Proceedings of the Human Language Technology Conference and the Conference on Empirical Methods in Natural Language Processing (HLT/EMNLP)*, 2005.

[3] S. Blair-Goldensohn, K. Hannan, R. McDonald, T. Neylon, G. A. Reis, and J. Reynar. Building a sentiment summarizer for local service reviews. In *WWW Workshop on NLP in the Information Explosion Era (NLPIX)*, Beijing, China, 2008.

[4] J. Blitzer, M. Dredze, and F. Pereira. Biographies, bollywood, boom-boxes and blenders: Domain adaptation for sentiment classification. In *Proceedings of the 45th Annual Meeting of the Association of Computational Linguistics*, pages 440–447, Prague, June 2007. Association for Computational Linguistics.

[5] A. Chmiel, J. Sienkiewicz, M. Thelwall, G. Paltoglou, K. Buckley, A. Kappas, and J. A. Hołyst. Collective emotions online and their influence on community life. *PLoS ONE*, 6(7):e22207, July 2011.

[6] Y. Choi, C. Cardie, E. Riloff, and S. Patwardhan. Identifying sources of opinions with conditional random fields and extraction patterns. In *Proceedings of Human Language Technology Conference and Conference on Empirical Methods in Natural Language Processing*, pages 355–362, Vancouver, October 2005. Association for Computational Linguistics.

[7] A. Culotta, R. Bekkerman, and A. McCallum. Extracting social networks and contact information from email and the web. In *Conference on Email and Spam*, 2004.

[8] C. Danescu-Niculescu-Mizil, R. West, D. Jurafsky, J. Leskovec, and C. Potts. No country for old members: User lifecycle and linguistic change in online communities. In *Proceedings of the 22nd International World Wide Web Conference*, pages 307–317, New York, 2013. ACM.

[9] B. Efron and R. Tibshirani. Bootstrap methods for standard errors, confidence intervals, and other measures of statistical accuracy. *Statistical Science*, 1(1):54–57, February 1986.

[10] L. Feldman Barrett and J. A. Russell. Independence and bipolarity in the structure of affect. *Journal of Personality and Social Psychology*, 74(4):967–984, 1998.

[11] A. B. Goldberg and J. Zhu. Seeing stars when there aren't many stars: Graph-based semi-supervised leaarning for sentiment categorization. In *TextGraphs: HLT/NAACL Workshop on Graph-based Algorithms for Natural Language Processing*, 2006.

[12] M. Koppel and J. Schler. The importance of neutral examples for learning sentiment. *Computational Intelligence*, 22(2):100–109, 2006.

[13] J. Lafferty, A. McCallum, and F. Pereira. Conditional random fields : Probabilistic models for segmenting and labeling sequence data. In *Proceedings of ICML-01*, pages 282–289, 2001.

[14] H. Liu, H. Lieberman, and T. Selker. A model of textual affect sensing using real-world knowledge. In *Proceedings of Intelligent User Interfaces (IUI)*, pages 125–132, 2003.

[15] H. Lövheim. A new three-dimensional model for emotions and monoamine neurotransmitters. *Medical Hypotheses*, 78(2):341–348, 2012.

[16] A. Maas, A. Ng, and C. Potts. Multi-dimensional sentiment analysis with learned representations. Ms., Stanford University, 2011.

[17] Y. Mao and G. Lebanon. Isotonic conditional random fields and local sentiment flow. In B. Schölkopf, J. Platt, and T. Hoffman, editors, *Advances in Neural Information Processing Systems 19*, pages 961–968, Cambridge, MA, 2006. MIT Press.

[18] J. McAuley and J. Leskovec. From amateurs to connoisseurs: Modeling the evolution of user expertise through online reviews. In *Proceedings of the 22nd International World Wide Web Conference*, pages 897–907, New York, 2013. ACM.

[19] J. McAuley, J. Leskovec, and D. Jurafsky. Learning attitudes and attributes from multi-aspect reviews. In *12th International Conference on Data Mining*, pages 1020–1025, Washington, D.C., 2012. IEEE Computer Society.

[20] M. Miller, C. Sathi, D. Wiesenthal, J. Leskovec, and C. Potts. Sentiment flow through hyperlink networks. In *Proceedings of the 5th International AAAI Conference on Weblogs and Social Media*, Barcelona, Spain, July 2011. Association for the Advancement of Artificial Intelligence.

[21] L. Muchnik, S. Aral, and S. J. Taylor. Social influence bias: A randomized experiment. *Science*, 341(6146):647–651, 2013.

[22] A. Neviarouskaya, H. Prendinger, and M. Ishizuka. Recognition of affect, judgment, and appreciation in text. In *Proceedings of the 23rd International Conference on Computational Linguistics (COLING 2010)*, pages 806–814, Beijing, China, August 2010. COLING 2010 Organizing Committee.

[23] N. Okazaki. Crfsuite: a fast implementation of conditional random fields (crfs), 2007.

[24] B. Pang and L. Lee. A sentimental education: Sentiment analysis using subjectivity summarization based on minimum cuts. In *Proceedings of the 42nd Annual Meeting of the Association for Computational Linguistics*, pages 271–278, Barcelona, Spain, July 2004.

[25] B. Pang and L. Lee. Seeing stars: Exploiting class relationships for sentiment categorization with respect to rating scales. In *Proceedings of the 43rd Annual Meeting of the Association for Computational Linguistics*, pages 115–124, Ann Arbor, MI, June 2005. Association for Computational Linguistics.

[26] B. Pang and L. Lee. Opinion mining and sentiment analysis. *Foundations and Trends in Information Retrieval*, 2(1):1–135, 2008.

[27] B. Pang, L. Lee, and S. Vaithyanathan. Thumbs up? sentiment classification using machine learning techniques. In *Proceedings of the Conference on Empirical Methods in Natural Language Processing (EMNLP)*, pages 79–86, Philadelphia, July 2002. Association for Computational Linguistics.

[28] D. C. Rubin and J. M. Talerico. A comparison of dimensional models of emotion. *Memory*, 17(8):802–808, 2009.

[29] J. A. Russell. A circumplex model of affect. *Journal of Personality and Social Psychology*, 39(6):1161–1178, 1980.

[30] B. Snyder and R. Barzilay. Multiple aspect ranking using the Good Grief algorithm. In *Proceedings of the Joint Human Language Technology/North American Chapter of the ACL Conference (HLT-NAACL)*, pages 300–307, 2007.

[31] R. Socher, J. Pennington, E. H. Huang, A. Y. Ng, and C. D. Manning. Semi-supervised recursive autoencoders for predicting sentiment distributions. In *Proceedings of the 2011 Conference on Empirical Methods in Natural Language Processing*, pages 151–161, Edinburgh, Scotland, UK., July 2011. ACL.

[32] C. Sutton and A. McCallum. An introduction to conditional random fields. *Foundations and Trends in Machine Learning*, 4(4):267–373, 2012.

[33] C. Tan, L. Lee, J. Tang, L. Jiang, M. Zhou, and P. Li. User-level sentiment analysis incorporating social networks. In *Proceedings of the 17th ACM SIGKDD International Conference on Knowledge Discovery and Data Mining*, pages 1397–1405, San Diego, CA, August 2011. ACM Digital Library.

[34] D. Watson and A. Tellegen. Toward a consensual structure of mood. *Psychological Bulletin*, 98(2):219–235, 1985.

[35] J. Wiebe, T. Wilson, and C. Cardie. Annotating expressions of opinions and emotions in language. *Language Resources and Evaluation*, 39(2–3):165–210, 2005.

[36] T. Wilson, J. Wiebe, and R. Hwa. Just how mad are you? Finding strong and weak opinion clauses. *Computational Intelligence*, 2(22):73–99, 2006

[37] Y. Yang, C. Chen, and S. Pang. WLPA: A novel algorithm to detect community structures in social networks. *Journal of Computational Information Systems*, 7(2):515–522, 2011.

[38] R. Zafarani, W. Cole, and H. Liu. Sentiment propagation in social networks: A case study in livejournal. In S.-K. Chai, J. Salerno, and P. Mabry, editors, *Advances in Social Computing*, volume 6007 of *Lecture Notes in Computer Science*, pages 413–420. Springer Berlin / Heidelberg, 2010.

Entity Profiling with Varying Source Reliabilities

Furong Li
National University of Singapore
Computing 1, Computing Drive
furongli@comp.nus.edu.sg

Mong Li Lee
National University of Singapore
Computing 1, Computing Drive
leeml@comp.nus.edu.sg

Wynne Hsu
National University of Singapore
Computing 1, Computing Drive
whsu@comp.nus.edu.sg

ABSTRACT

The rapid growth of information sources on the Web has intensified the problem of data quality. In particular, the same real world entity may be described by different sources in various ways with overlapping information, and possibly conflicting or even erroneous values. In order to obtain a more complete and accurate picture for a real world entity, we need to *collate* the data records that refer to the entity, as well as *correct* any erroneous values. We observe that these two tasks are often tightly coupled: rectifying erroneous values will facilitate data collation, while linking similar records provides us with a clearer view of the data and additional evidence for error correction.

In this paper, we present a framework called COMET that interleaves record linkage with error correction, taking into consideration the source reliabilities on various attributes. The proposed framework first utilizes confidence based matching to discriminate records in terms of ambiguity and source reliability. Then it performs adaptive matching to reduce the impact of erroneous values. Experiment results demonstrate that COMET outperforms the state-of-the-art techniques and is able to build complete and accurate profiles for real world entities.

Categories and Subject Descriptors

H.2.8 [**Information Systems**]: Database Management—*data mining*

Keywords

Record linkage; source reliability; truth discovery; entity profiling

1. INTRODUCTION

In the age of Big Data, a real world entity's information is, more often than not, published by more than one data source. Each of the data source may describe the same entity with name variations and provide incomplete and overlapping information. In order to obtain a complete picture of a real world entity, we need to collate the data records that refer to this entity. To complicate matters, not all the data sources are reliable and may publish erroneous information.

While the problem of record linkage has been well-studied [7, 15], linking and merging information from multiple sources remains a challenging task [20, 18]. The work in [20] observes that sources have varying semantic ambiguity and proposes a framework to apply either a relaxed or a conservative matching criteria depending on how ambiguous is the source. On the other hand, [18] develops a transfer learning approach to learn a unified matching function to link records from multiple sources. These works do not explicitly consider the erroneous information in the data.

The work in [12] is the first attempt to link records in the presence of erroneous values. The authors transform the problem into a k-partite graph clustering problem where each node in the graph represents an attribute value and each edge associates a pair of values from the same record. This approach is computationally expensive and its performance degrades when the percentage of erroneous values increases, as shown in our experiments.

In this paper, we present an effective and efficient framework called COMET to *collate* data records from multiple sources, *correct* any erroneous attribute values, and *construct* profiles for real world entities.

EXAMPLE 1. *Suppose we want to collate information on researchers in Computer Science. We could first obtain a set of reference records from some well-established source such as the acm.org website. Table 1 shows the names and affiliations of selected Computer Science researchers. Since the information in these reference records is limited, we would look at other data sources, such as university home pages, object-level search engines, LinkedIn, to harvest more information. Table 2 shows the information crawled from different sources, after transforming them into structured records. Note that records may contain ambiguous name representations and conflicting attribute values.*

In order to get a more complete profile of each researcher, a typical solution consists of two main steps. First, compute the similarity between the records in Tables 1 and 2, and form three clusters:

$$c_1 = \{q_1, r_1, r_3, r_5\}$$
$$c_2 = \{q_2, r_6, r_7, r_9, r_{10}\}$$
$$c_3 = \{q_3, r_2, r_4, r_8\}$$

Then determine the correct attribute values within each cluster by majority vote, and construct the following profiles:

KDD'14, August 24–27, 2014, New York, NY, USA.
Copyright 2014 ACM 978-1-4503-2956-9/14/08 ...$15.00.
http://dx.doi.org/10.1145/2623330.2623685.

Table 1: Reference Records

	Name	Affiliation
q_1	Rakesh Agrawal	MS
q_2	Charu Aggarwal	IBM
q_3	Alon Y. Halevy	Google

Table 2: Input Records from Various Data Sources

	Name	Affiliation	Field	Education	Source
r_1	Rakesh Agrawal	*Bell*	DM	Wisconsin	src_1
r_2	Alon Halevy	Google	DB	Stanford	
r_3	Rakesh Agrawal	MS	DM		src_2
r_4	A. Halevy	Google	DB		
r_5	Agrawal	MS		Wisconsin	src_3
r_6	Charu Aggarwal	IBM		MIT	
r_7	Agrawal	*IBM*		Wisconsin	src_4
r_8	Halevy	*UW*	DB	Stanford	
r_9	Charu Aggarwal	*UIC*	DM	MIT	
r_{10}	Agrawal	IBM	DM	*Wisconsin*	src_5

True matchings: $\{q_1, r_1, r_3, r_5, r_7\}$, $\{q_2, r_6, r_9, r_{10}\}$, $\{q_3, r_2, r_4, r_8\}$

p_1 =<*Rakesh Agrawal, MS, DM, Wisconsin*>
p_2 =<*Charu Aggarwal, IBM, DM, MIT*>
p_3 =<*Alon Y. Halevy, Google, DB, Stanford*>

However, a closer examination would reveal that records r_3 and r_9 which are published by source src_4 contain affiliations that differ from the corresponding profile records. This leads us to suspect that the affiliation information in record r_7 is highly likely to be incorrect since it is provided by the same source src_4.

On the other hand, the education information published by src_4 for r_8 and r_9 are both correct, giving us the confidence that the value "Wisconsin" in r_7 can be trusted. With this key insight on src_4 providing unreliable affiliation information, and more reliable education information, we could infer that r_7 is more likely to refer to "Rakesh Agrawal" rather than "Charu Aggarwal".

The above example illustrates that rectifying errors in attribute values and taking into consideration the reliability of data sources can provide additional evidence for linking records, leading to a more complete and accurate profile of an entity. So how can we utilize this observation to improve the accuracy of data collation, and do that efficiently in practice?

First, we introduce the notion of a reliability matrix to capture the reliability of each source for various attributes. Second, we interleave the processes of record linkage and error correction so that they can benefit from each other: rectifying errors in attribute values will facilitate record comparison and linkage, while linking similar records will provide a clearer view of the data and additional evidence of any erroneous values.

The proposed framework COMET consists of two main phases. The first phase is a confidence based matching that links each input record to one or more reference records. This yields a soft clustering of records and reduces the search space for the next phase. Based on the clustering results, we obtain an initial assessment of the reliability of the sources. Then the second phase, adaptive matching, leverages on the source reliability to iteratively determine the correct attribute values within each cluster and eliminate unlikely matches for the input records.

Experiment results on real world multiple source datasets demonstrate that COMET can build more complete and accurate entity profiles efficiently, and outperforms the state-of-the-art techniques.

The rest of the paper is organized as follows. Section 2 summarizes the related work. Section 3 gives the problem definition. The COMET framework is presented in Section 4. Section 5 describes the experimental evaluation and we conclude in Section 6.

2. RELATED WORK

Constructing structured profiles of real world entities is a challenging task and has been addressed from various aspects. [17, 10] extract entity-related facts from web pages, which form the input records in our framework. [21] proposes a holistic approach to solve the schema matching problem of web tables. Our work builds upon these information extraction and schema matching techniques, and we focus on resolving the ambiguous references and erroneous values contained in the data records.

Record linkage, also known as entity resolution, aims to identify records that refer to the same real world entity [7, 15]. Techniques to match records can be categorized into learning-based algorithms and non-learning methods. Learning-based algorithms [1] train a classifier to label each record pair as match or unmatch, while non-learning methods [9, 8] utilize a set of rules to link records. Based on the pairwise matching results, clustering algorithms are used to find sets of records where each set refers to a unique entity [14, 3]. The works in [20, 18] examine the problem of linking records from multiple sources. [20] transforms the records into a graph to estimate the ambiguity of each source and finds an optimized matching execution plan. [13] adopts transfer learning to learn a classifier which can capture the common characteristics of all the sources as well as the specific characteristics of individual source pairs. All these methods are not aware of source reliabilities and their performance deteriorates when the data is noisy.

There is a line of research to resolve conflicts and find true values from data provided by different sources [13, 16]. These truth discovery algorithms usually adopt an iterative approach to let the data sources and attribute values vote for each other. The similarity between values [22] and the dependence between sources [6] can be taken into account to better model the complexities in the real world. Apart from these voting-based algorithms, the work in [19] constructs probabilistic models where the true values are regarded as latent variables, while [5] deduces the relative accuracy of attributes based on the available master data and a set of pre-defined rules. These works assume that record linkage has already been done and the input set of records refer to the same real world entity.

The work closest to ours, [12], proposes to link records with uniqueness constraints and erroneous values by modeling it as a k-partite graph clustering problem. This approach assumes the existence of a key attribute that can uniquely identify an entity. It is computationally expensive as it compares all the records in each iteration, and its recall rate suffers when the percentage of erroneous values increases. In contrast, the two-phase approach in our proposed framework is efficient and remains robust when the percentage of errors and the degree of ambiguity vary.

3. DEFINITIONS AND NOTATIONS

In this section, we define the notations used as well as a formal definition of the problem addressed.

Let $\mathcal{E}$ be a set of real world *entities*. Each entity $e \in \mathcal{E}$ is described by a set of *attributes* $\mathcal{A}$.

Let $\mathcal{S}$ be a set of *data sources*. Each source $s \in \mathcal{S}$ may publish some information on a subset of the entities in $\mathcal{E}$.

Let $\mathcal{R}$ be a set of *input records* with attributes $\mathcal{A}$. Each input record $r \in \mathcal{R}$ is published by some source $s \in \mathcal{S}$, and refers to some entity $e \in \mathcal{E}$. A published record may have missing or erroneous attribute values. Note that the records from different sources have been mapped to a uniform schema.

Let $\mathcal{Q}$ be a set of *reference records* with attributes $\mathcal{A}_{\mathcal{Q}} \subset \mathcal{A}$. Each reference record $q \in \mathcal{Q}$ is known to be clean, and refers to some unique entity $e \in \mathcal{E}$.

Let $\mathcal{C}$ be a set of clusters. Each cluster $c \in \mathcal{C}$ comprises of a reference record $q \in \mathcal{Q}$ and a set of input records $\mathcal{R}_c \subset \mathcal{R}$. Each cluster c has a signature $H_c = \{<a, v, pr> \mid \forall a \in \mathcal{A}\}$, where pr is the probability for v being the correct value on attribute a.

Problem Definition. Given a set of reference records $\mathcal{Q}$ and a set of input records $\mathcal{R}$ published by data sources $\mathcal{S}$, the goal is to augment the records in $\mathcal{Q}$ with the true values (if any) of the attributes $\mathcal{A} - \mathcal{A}_{\mathcal{Q}}$.

4. COMET FRAMEWORK

This section describes the proposed framework COMET that collates data from different sources, corrects any erroneous values, and constructs entity profiles. An overview of COMET is given in Figure 1. The framework is designed to facilitate robust record matching, and leverage on the knowledge from truth discovery to improve its performance. COMET has two main phases: (a) confidence based matching and (b) adaptive matching.

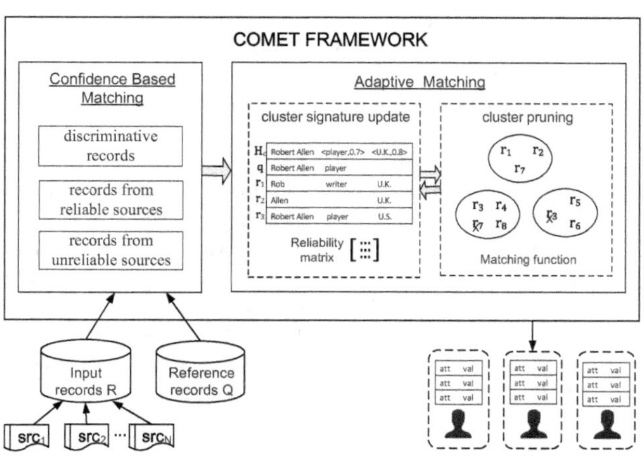

Figure 1: Overview of COMET

The first phase finds a set of entities that an input record may potentially describe by linking each input record to one or more reference records. Each reference record and its set of associated records form a cluster. At the same time, it initializes a matrix to capture the reliability of the data sources for various attributes.

The second phase aims to determine the correct attribute values for each entity. It first finds the most accurate attribute values within each cluster to form the cluster signature, and then updates the source reliability. Subsequently, clusters are refined by removing the records whose attribute values deviate significantly from the cluster signatures. This process is repeated until there is no change to the clusters.

Finally, we augment the reference record in each cluster with the values in cluster signature to construct the profile for the corresponding entity.

4.1 Confidence Based Matching

In this phase, we generate a set of candidate reference records for each input record. Due to the possible erroneous values contained in the records, we would need a relatively low similarity threshold so that the true matches are not missed. However, the low threshold will affect the quality of the resulting clusters, which will in turn impact the discovery of correct attribute values in the next phase (as shown in Section 5.3).

We overcome this dilemma by adopting a confidence based matching approach such that records which clearly reference some real world entity are linked first, while the decisions on difficult cases are postponed until we have gathered more information about the reliability of the data sources. This leads to a smaller set of candidate matches without sacrificing the recall.

We first create a cluster for each reference record q. Then we bootstrap the framework with a small set of *confident matches* between the input records $\mathcal{R}$ and reference records $\mathcal{Q}$. Specifically, we measure the similarity between records using any existing record linkage method, e.g., the Fellegi-Sunter algorithm [9], and link a record r to a reference record q if r is highly similar to q and differs greatly to the records in $\mathcal{Q} \setminus \{q\}$. In other words, we are confident that r refers to q. We formalize this into the following definition.

Definition 1. Given two thresholds δ_H and δ_L, where $\delta_H > \delta_L$, and a similarity function sim(), an input record r and a reference record q form a *confident match* if $\exists q \in \mathcal{Q}$ where $\text{sim}(r, q) > \delta_H$, and $\forall q' \in \mathcal{Q} \setminus \{q\}$, $\text{sim}(r, q') < \delta_L$. Then the record r is called a *discriminative record.*

For each confident match, we compare the attribute values of record r with its matching reference record q to obtain an initial assessment of the reliability of the corresponding data source.

We define a *reliability matrix* M where each entry $M[s, a]$ is the reliability of source s on attribute a, and initialize M as follows. Let $\mathcal{D}_s$ be the set of discriminative records published by s. We first process the sources that have published some discriminative records, that is, $\mathcal{D}_s \neq \emptyset$. Let $\mathcal{D}_s^a \subset \mathcal{D}_s$ be the set of records where both the attribute values $r.a$ and its matching $q.a$ are not null. Then we have

$$M[s, a] = \frac{1}{|\mathcal{D}_s^a|} \sum_{r \in \mathcal{D}_s^a} \text{sim}(r.a, q.a), \quad \text{if } \mathcal{D}_s^a \neq \emptyset \qquad (1)$$

Then for each attribute a where $\mathcal{D}_s^a = \emptyset$, we set its $M[s, a]$ to be the average of the non-null entries in $M[s]$. Finally, for the sources that have not published any discriminative record, we set their entries in M to some small value ϵ.

Table 3: Clusters Obtained by Confidence Based Matching

q_1	Rakesh Agrawal	MS			
r_1	Rakesh Agrawal	*Bell*	DM	Wisconsin	src_1
r_3	Rakesh Agrawal	MS	DM		src_2
r_5	Agrawal	MS		Wisconsin	src_3
r_7	Agrawal	*IBM*		Wisconsin	src_4
r_{10}	Agrawal	IBM	DM	*Wisconsin*	src_5

(a) Cluster c_1

q_2	Charu Aggarwal	IBM			
r_6	Charu Aggarwal	IBM		MIT	src_3
r_9	Charu Aggarwal	*UIC*	DM	MIT	src_4
r_5	Agrawal	MS		Wisconsin	src_3
r_7	Agrawal	*IBM*		Wisconsin	src_4
r_{10}	Agrawal	IBM	DM	*Wisconsin*	src_5

(b) Cluster c_2

q_3	Alon Y. Halevy	Google			
r_2	Alon Halevy	Google	DB	Stanford	src_1
r_4	A. Halevy	Google	DB		src_2
r_8	Halevy	*UW*	DB	Stanford	src_4

(c) Cluster c_3

EXAMPLE 2. *Consider the reference records in Table 1 and the input records in Table 2. Suppose the set of confident matches are* $\{(r_1, q_1), (r_3, q_1), (r_6, q_2), (r_9, q_2), (r_2, q_3)\}$. *We compute the reliability of the five sources on attribute Affiliation by comparing these record pairs. Based on the reference records, we observe that records r_1 and r_9 provide wrong affiliations, while the others are all correct. Then by Equation 1 we have*

$M[src_1, \text{Affiliation}] = 0.5$,
$M[src_2, \text{Affiliation}] = M[src_3, \text{Affiliation}] = 1.0$,
$M[src_4, \text{Affiliation}] = 0.2$,
$M[src_5, \text{Affiliation}] = \epsilon$.

After initializing the reliability matrix, we want to *distinguish* records that originate from the sources which are significantly more unreliable than the others. If we consider the source reliability[1] as a random variable X, then we say a source s is *unreliable* if

$$\frac{1}{|\mathcal{A}|}\sum_{a\in\mathcal{A}} M[s,a] < \mu - \sigma \qquad (2)$$

where μ and σ is the mean and standard deviation of X. Otherwise, we consider the source as *reliable*.

For each record r published by a reliable source, we use all the attribute values to compare r with the reference records $\mathcal{Q}$. We link r with a $q \in \mathcal{Q}$ if the similarity between them exceeds a pre-defined threshold δ.

Finally, we process the records from less reliable sources. For these records, since their attribute values are expected to be more error-prone, we may miss the correct matchings if we simply compare the attribute values. As such, we use the name references, and compare each record r with all the records in each cluster on name. We add r to a cluster if it is similar to some record in that cluster. This approach is similar to the merge closure described in [2].

[1]This is the average reliability of a source on all the attributes.

Algorithm 1: Confidence Based Matching

```
input  : Input records R from data sources S with
         attributes A, reference records Q, threshold δ
output: Set of clusters C, reliability matrix M
1  foreach q ∈ Q do
2      create cluster c containing q;
3      add c to C;
   /* confident matches */
4  foreach r ∈ R do
5      if r and q form a confident match then
6          add r to the cluster of q;
   /* initialize reliability matrix M */
7  let D_s be the set of discriminative records from s;
8  foreach s ∈ S where D_s ≠ ∅ do
9      let D_s^a ⊂ D_s be the set of records where
       r.a ≠ null ∧ q.a ≠ null;
10     foreach a ∈ A where D_s^a ≠ ∅ do
11         set M[s, a] using Equation 1;
12     foreach a ∈ A where D_s^a = ∅ do
13         let n be the number of non-null entries in M[s];
14         M[s, a] = (1/n) Σ_{a∈A} M[s, a];
15 foreach s ∈ S where D_s = ∅ do
16     foreach a ∈ A do
17         M[s, a] = ε;
   /* records from reliable sources */
18 foreach unprocessed r ∈ R do
19     if Equation 2 does not hold then
20         foreach q ∈ Q do
21             if sim(r, q) > δ then
22                 add r to the cluster of q;
   /* records from unreliable sources */
23 foreach unprocessed r ∈ R do
24     foreach c ∈ C do
25         foreach r' in cluster c do
26             if sim(r.N, r'.N) > δ then
27                 add r to cluster c;
28                 break;
```

EXAMPLE 3. *Table 3 shows the three clusters obtained by the confidence based matching phase. Discriminative records r_1 and r_3 are assigned to cluster c_1, r_6 and r_9 are put in c_2, while r_2 is placed in c_3. We next compare these records with their associated reference records to obtain the source reliabilities . Sources src_4 and src_5 are found to be unreliable while the others are reliable. Thus records r_4 and r_5 are processed first. Record r_4 is put in cluster c_3, while r_5 is placed in both c_1 and c_2 as it is similar to both q_1 and q_2.*

For the remaining records r_7, r_8 and r_{10} published by unreliable sources (src_4 and src_5), we compare them with all the records in each cluster on attribute Name. Records r_7 and r_{10} have identical name with r_5 and are assigned to clusters c_1 and c_2; r_8 is highly similar to r_4 and is put in c_3.

Algorithm 1 gives the details of this confidence based matching phase. We first create a cluster for each reference record (lines 1-3). Then we establish the confident matches between reference records and input records (lines 4-6). Lines 7-17 initialize the reliability matrix. Based on the source reliabilities, we process records that originate from the reliable sources (lines 19-22) before those from the less reliable sources (lines 23-28). The output is a set of clusters. Note that an input record may not be placed in any cluster if it cannot be linked to any reference record.

4.2 Adaptive Matching

After clustering the records, the next phase iteratively refines the clusters by interleaving truth discovery with record matching. There are three main steps in this adaptive matching phase: (a) compute the cluster signatures, (b) update the reliability matrix and (c) refine the clusters.

First, for each cluster c obtained in the previous phase, we build its signature H_c based on the accuracy of the attribute values of the records in c. The reliability matrix is updated subsequently. Then each record r is compared with the signatures of the clusters it is associated with, and pruned from the cluster that it is the most dissimilar to. The above steps are repeated until there is no change to the clusters.

In order to form a cluster signature, we need to assign an accuracy score to each attribute value in the cluster. Intuitively, a value published by more reliable sources tends to be more accurate, while a source that provides more accurate values tends to be more reliable. Thus we can let the values and the sources vote for each other. However, since our framework allows records to belong to multiple clusters, these records may skew the value accuracy and source reliability computations with repeated votes. Therefore a likelihood function is introduced to address the issue.

Let $L(r,c)$ be the likelihood of a record r belonging to a cluster c, and q be the reference record in c. $L(r,c)$ is initialized as follows:

$$L(r,c) = \text{sim}(r,q) \tag{3}$$

We now discuss how we use this likelihood function to compute the cluster signatures and update the reliability matrix.

Let $\mathcal{V}_c^a$ be the set of values on attribute a within cluster c. The accuracy of a value $v \in \mathcal{V}_c^a$ is given by the sum of the reliabilities of its sources, weighted by the likelihood:

$$acc(a,v,c) = \sum_{r \in c, r.a=v} L(r,c) \cdot M[s_r, a] \tag{4}$$

where s_r is the source that publishes r. The value accuracies are normalized such that they represent the probabilities of the values being true.

The signature H_c for a cluster c contains a triplet $<a,v,pr>$ for each $a \in \mathcal{A}$ such that

$$<a,v,pr> = \begin{cases} <a,\ q.a,\ 1.0> & \text{if } q.a \neq null \\ <a,\ v_m,\ acc(a,v_m,c)> & \text{otherwise} \end{cases} \tag{5}$$

where $v_m = \arg\max_{v \in \mathcal{V}_c^a} acc(a,v,c)$.

EXAMPLE 4. *Let us calculate the accuracy of the two Education values "MIT" and "Wisconsin" in cluster c_2. Suppose all the sources are equally reliable with a score of* 0.8, *and* $L(r_5,c_2) = L(r_{10},c_2) = L(r_7,c_2) = 0.5$. *Then the accuracy of "MIT" and "Wisconsion" are* 1.6 *and* 1.2 *respectively. We normalize them into probabilities and insert the triplet* <Education, *"MIT"*, 0.6> *into the cluster signature of* c_2.

After obtaining the signatures for all the clusters in $\mathcal{C}$, we update the reliability of a source s for attribute a as the average accuracy of the values it publishes:

$$M[s,a] = \frac{1}{|\mathcal{R}_s|} \sum_{r \in \mathcal{R}_s} \sum_{c \in \mathcal{C}_r} L(r,c) \cdot acc(a, r.a, c) \tag{6}$$

where $\mathcal{R}_s$ is the set of records published by s, and $\mathcal{C}_r$ is the set of clusters that contain r.

Note that a value may have different accuracy scores in different clusters. Hence for a value $r.a$, we calculate its accuracy as the sum of all its accuracy scores weighted by the likelihood.

EXAMPLE 5. *Consider the entry* $M[src_4, \text{Affiliation}]$. *Suppose we have determined* $acc(\text{Affiliation}, \text{"IBM"}, c_1) = 0.4$ *and* $acc(\text{Affiliation}, \text{"IBM"}, c_2) = 0.6$. *Then the accuracy of the Affiliation value in* r_7 *is given by* $0.5 \times 0.4 + 0.5 \times 0.6 = 0.5$. *We repeat the computation for the other records published by* src_4, *which are* r_8 *and* r_9, *and obtain* 0.3 *and* 0.2 *respectively. Then* $M[src_4, \text{Affiliation}] = \frac{0.5+0.3+0.2}{3} = 0.33$.

Once we have computed the cluster signatures and updated the reliability matrix, we prune the clusters by removing records that are unlikely to belong to them. While a record is unlikely to belong to a cluster if its similarity with the cluster signature is low, however, a direct comparison of the record with a cluster signature may lead to incorrect pruning due to the possible erroneous values in the record. As such, we incorporate the reliability matrix to adaptively lower the impact of inaccurate attributes on the matching decisions.

Given a record r and a cluster c, we define a matching function match(r,c) as follows:

$$\text{match}(r,c) = \frac{\sum_{a \in \mathcal{A}} M[s_r,a] \cdot \text{sim}(r.a, H_c.a)}{\sum_{a \in \mathcal{A}} M[s_r,a]} \tag{7}$$

where $\text{sim}(r.a, H_c.a)$ is the similarity between the values in record r and signature H_c on attribute a. Note that this similarity may be weighted.

For each record r that associated with multiple clusters, we compute its match scores with all the clusters in $\mathcal{C}_r$ using Equation 7, and remove r from the cluster with the lowest match score.

EXAMPLE 6. *Consider record* r_7 *which is associated with clusters* c_1 *and* c_2. *We have determined*
$M[src_4, \text{Affiliation}] = 0.33$, $M[src_4, \text{Education}] = 0.8$.
Further, we have
<Affiliation, *"MS"*,1.0>, <Education, *"Wisconsin"*,1.0> *in* H_{c_1},
<Affiliation, *"IBM"*,1.0>, <Education, *"MIT"*,0.6> *in* H_{c_2}.
We compare r_7 *with both* H_{c_1} *and* H_{c_2} *to calculate the match scores by Equation 7. Clearly, the match score with cluster* c_1 *is higher, so we remove* r_7 *from* c_2.

Finally, we update the likelihood $L(r,c)$ for the record r w.r.t. each cluster $c \in \mathcal{C}_r$ as follows:

$$L(r,c) = \frac{\text{match}(r,c)}{\sum_{c' \in \mathcal{C}_r} \text{match}(r,c')} \tag{8}$$

Algorithm 2 shows the details of this adaptive matching phase. We first initialize the likelihood for each record in the clusters (lines 1-4). Then we repeat the steps of cluster signature computation (lines 7-11), reliability matrix update (lines 12-13) and cluster pruning (lines 14-21) until there is no more change to the clusters.

```
Algorithm 2: Adaptive Matching
input : Reliability matrix M, set of clusters C
output: Set of refined clusters C
foreach r ∈ R do
    Let C_r be the set of clusters that contain r;
    foreach c ∈ C_r do
        initialize L(r, c) using Equation 3;
repeat
    /* cluster signature and reliability matrix update */
    foreach a ∈ A do
        foreach c ∈ C do
            foreach v ∈ V_c^a do
                calculate acc(a, v, c) using Equation 4;
            normalization;
            update cluster signature using Equation 5;
        foreach s ∈ S do
            update M[s, a] using Equation 6;
    /* cluster pruning */
    foreach r ∈ R do
        if |C_r| > 1 then
            foreach c ∈ C_r do
                calculate match(r, c) using Equation 7;
            c ← arg min_{c∈C_r} match(r, c);
            remove r from c;
        foreach c ∈ C_r do
            update L(r, c) using Equation 8;
until there is no change to the clusters C;
```

4.3 Time Complexity

Let n be the number of input records $\mathcal{R}$, m be the number of reference records $\mathcal{Q}$, and p be the number of non-discriminative records from unreliable sources.

In the confidence based matching phase, the time complexity for matching the discriminative records and records from reliable sources are both $O(nm)$, as they compare record pairs from $\mathcal{R}$ and $\mathcal{Q}$. In contrast, matching the records from unreliable sources requires comparing each record to every other record in all the clusters. Let k is the largest number of clusters that a record is associated with. Then this step requires a time complexity of $O(knp)$. Hence the time complexity of the confidence based matching phase is $O(nm + knp)$.

For the adaptive matching phase, each iteration involves cluster signature computation and cluster pruning. Each of these steps has a complexity of $O(kn)$. Since this phase takes k iterations to terminate, the time complexity is $O(k^2n)$.

In practice, k is usually a small constant. Hence the complexity of COMET is $O(nm + np)$.

5. PERFORMANCE STUDY

In this section, we present the results of extensive experiments to evaluate the performance of COMET.

Datasets. We use two real world multiple source datasets:

- *Restaurant dataset.*
  We construct a Restaurant dataset by crawling 6 websites for restaurants with zip code 78701. 1082 records on 384 restaurants are obtained. Each record has the attributes Name, Address, Phone, Website, etc. We pre-process this dataset by removing the restaurants that do not have inconsistent values from multiple websites. Finally, we obtain 581 records on 222 restaurants with 380 name values. The ratio of erroneous values to the total number of attribute values is 18.7%. About 9.1% of the records have ambiguous names (a name is ambiguous if there are at least two records with this name but refer to different entities).
  We extract information from *www.yellowpages.com* as true attribute values, and form a reference table consisting of 478 records with attributes Name and Phone. We manually determine the true matchings between records.
- *Football dataset.*
  The Football data in [4] contains 7492 records on the bio-data of football players from 20 websites. Each record contains attributes Name, Birthday, Height, Weight, Position and BirthPlace. The ground truth of the attribute values were collected from official websites of the players or the corresponding football clubs. We pre-process the data by removing the records with less than 3 non-null attribute values. Finally, we have 5031 records on 976 players from 12 websites. The ratio of erroneous values to the total number of attribute values is 32.7%.
  We extract information from *Wikipedia* to get biodata on 12419 players and form reference table with attributes Name, Birthday and BirthPlace.

Based on the Football dataset, we generate a series of datasets by varying the accuracy of attribute values and the ambiguity of name references. We vary the following parameters to obtain different datasets.

- $\%err$, the ratio of erroneous values to the total number of attribute values;
- $\%ambi$, the probability to abbreviate the name reference of a record[2].

Table 4 shows the default values and the ranges for these parameters.

Table 4: Parameter Settings

Parameter	Default	Range
$\%err$	0.33	0.1-0.5
$\%ambi$	0.5	0.4-0.9

When varying $\%err$, if the desired error rate is higher than that of the original data, we introduce errors to the attribute values; otherwise, we correct some errors contained in the original data. We generate errors as follows: for attribute Birthday, we randomly generate an erroneous value; for the other 3 attributes, we randomly select a value from the domain of that attribute. The erroneous values of the generated data have the same distribution as the original data, that is, the relative accuracy among different sources and attributes remain unchanged.

When varying $\%ambi$, we abbreviate the names of the records in the original data and keep the other attributes unchanged. We use one of the following forms of abbreviation with equal probability: remove first name; remove last

[2]The original dataset provides the full name of each player.

name; keep first name initial and last name; remove last name and the last letter of first name.

Methods. We compare the following methods in our performance study:

- MATCH [12]. This is the state-of-the-art method that combines record linkage and truth discovery with uniqueness constraints. For the Football dataset, we concatenate the non-unique attributes, Height and Weight, with Name to form a super-identifier. For the Restaurant dataset, we combine Name and Address to form a multi-attribute identifier.
- PIPELINE. This is the baseline method that performs record linkage and truth discovery sequentially. We use TRANSFER [18], a learning-based method designed to link records from multiple sources, to perform record linkage. Learning-based methods have been shown to provide superior performance [15]. For truth discovery, we employ TRUTHFINDER [22] as the representative method among those surveyed in [16]. We transform the pairwise results of TRANSFER into clusters using the techniques in [11] before calling TRUTHFINDER. To improve performance, records from each pair of data sources are compared, instead of just comparing input records with reference records.
- COMET, the proposed framework. To be fair, we also utilize the TRANSFER method to establish confident matches in the first matching phase.

Note that the reference records are used in both MATCH and PIPELINE where the attribute values in these records are regarded as true values. The same blocking criteria is applied to all the methods to reduce the number of record comparisons. TF-IDF metric is used to measure the similarity of strings, where each token is measured by Jaro-Winkler distance. Levenshtein distance is used for Birthday and Phone. We set $\delta = 0.8$, $\delta_H = 0.95$ and $\delta_L = 0.65$ for COMET.

All the algorithms were implemented in Java, and the experiments were conducted in a Windows 7 machine with 3.40 GHz Intel CPU and 8 GB of RAM. Each experiment was repeated 3 times and the average performance is reported.

5.1 Experiments on Record Linkage

We first evaluate whether each input record can be linked to the correct reference record. The evaluation metrics include *Precision* and *Recall*.

Let *Ground* be the set of correct matchings between input records and reference records, and *Result* be the set of matchings returned from the algorithms. Then we have

$$Precision = \frac{|Ground \cap Result|}{|Result|}$$

$$Recall = \frac{|Ground \cap Result|}{|Ground|}$$

Table 5 shows the performance of various methods on the Restaurant dataset. We observe that both COMET and MATCH outperform PIPELINE, demonstrating that combining record linkage with truth discovery can lead to more robust record comparisons. COMET gives the best precision and recall since it leverages on the more reliable attributes to reduce the impact of erroneous values.

PIPELINE fails to link a considerable amount of records. We found that 57% of these records contain wrong phone

Table 5: Record Linkage on Restaurant Dataset

	Precision	Recall
COMET	**96.6**	**96.6**
MATCH	93.0	88.1
PIPELINE	89.1	83.5

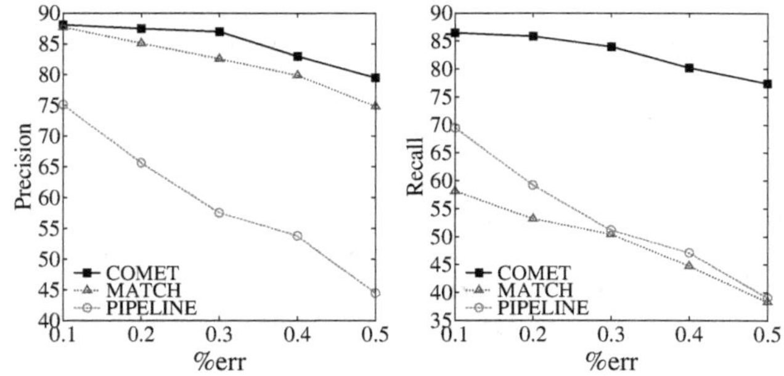

(a) Vary %err

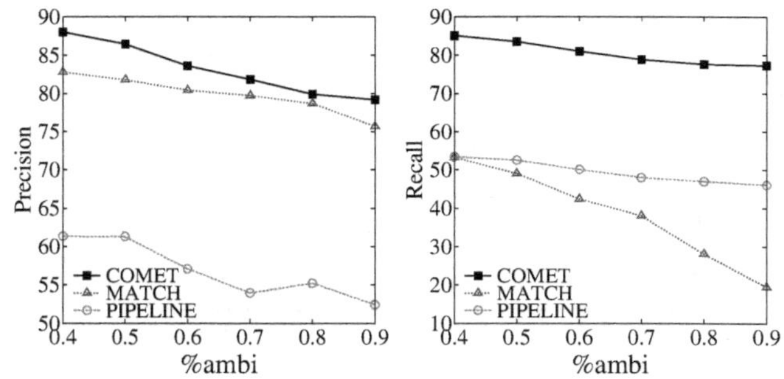

(b) Vary %ambi

Figure 2: Record linkage on Football dataset

numbers, yet the TRANSFER model still assigns a high weight to this attribute. This indicates that the learning-based record linkage methods do not perform well in the presence of erroneous values. In contrast, COMET explicitly considers the source reliabilities and improves the performance significantly.

Figure 2 shows the results on the Football dataset as we vary $\%err$ and $\%ambi$. We observe that the performance of MATCH and PIPELINE drop significantly as the percentage of errors increases. However, COMET remains robust and outperforms the others. Even when $\%err = 0.5$, COMET still achieves a recall of 0.77, which is 97% higher than the second best. This demonstrates its ability to correctly link records in the presence of erroneous values. Compared to MATCH, PIPELINE is less sensitive to $\%ambi$ but more sensitive to $\%err$. That is because the various ambiguities can be learnt more effectively.

5.2 Experiments on Truth Discovery

Next, we evaluate whether COMET constructs an accurate and complete profile for each entity. The evaluation metrics are *Accuracy* and *Coverage*.

Let $TrueValue$ be the set of attribute values in the ground truth that contained in the input records, and $ReturnValue$

Table 6: **Truth Discovery on Restaurant Dataset**

	Accuracy	Coverage
COMET	**86.4**	**83.2**
MATCH	75.3	76.8
PIPELINE	82.3	71.2

be the set of attribute values returned by the methods and are not present in the reference records. Then we define

$$Accuracy = \frac{|TrueValue \cap ReturnValue|}{|ReturnValue|}$$

$$Coverage = \frac{|TrueValue \cap ReturnValue|}{|TrueValue|}$$

Table 6 shows the results on Restaurant dataset. We observe that COMET outperforms MATCH by 15% on accuracy and 8% on coverage. One of the reasons for the low accuracy of MATCH is that it is unaware of the source reliabilities. PIPELINE gives the lowest coverage since many input records are not linked to any reference record. As a result, it fails to find all the attribute values of an entity.

Figure 3 shows the results on Football dataset as we vary *%err* and *%ambi*. Again, both COMET and MATCH outperform PIPELINE, indicating the advantage of integrating record linkage with truth discovery. However, MATCH is highly sensitive to the percentage of erroneous values. We observe that COMET improves the coverage significantly when *%err* and *%ambi* become large. Even when $\%err = 0.5$, COMET can still recover 78% of the correct attribute values. This contributes to its robust record linkage. Overall, COMET consistently constructs both complete and accurate profiles for the entities when *%err* and *%ambi* vary.

5.3 Sensitivity Experiments

In this section, we study the impact of the two main components in the COMET framework, namely, confidence based matching and adaptive matching. We use the Football dataset for this set of experiments and implement the following variants of COMET:

- COM-CM. This method does not utilize confidence based matching. In other words, when we form the initial clustering, records are processed in an arbitrary order and linked to a reference record if their similarity exceeds the threshold δ.
- COM-AM. This method does not utilize adaptive matching. In other words, neither the reliability matrix nor the likelihood function is used to refine the clusters.

To evaluate the effect of confidence based matching, we measure the recall of the matchings established in the first phase of the framework, as the goal of this phase is to achieve a high recall.

Figure 4 shows the recall of record linkage after the first phase as we vary *%err* and *%ambi*. We observe that the confidence based matching has more impact when *%err* increases. It discriminates records from unreliable sources and thus significantly improves the recall. When *%ambi* becomes higher, by postponing the decisions to link the ambiguous records, COMET remains robust.

To evaluate the effect of adaptive matching, we measure the error rate of the cluster pruning process. We define error rate as the ratio of the number of true matchings being pruned to the total number of pruned matchings. The main purpose of the adaptive matching is to reduce errors in cluster pruning.

Figure 5 shows the error rate of the cluster pruning when we vary *%err* and *%ambi*. When *%err* increases, adaptive

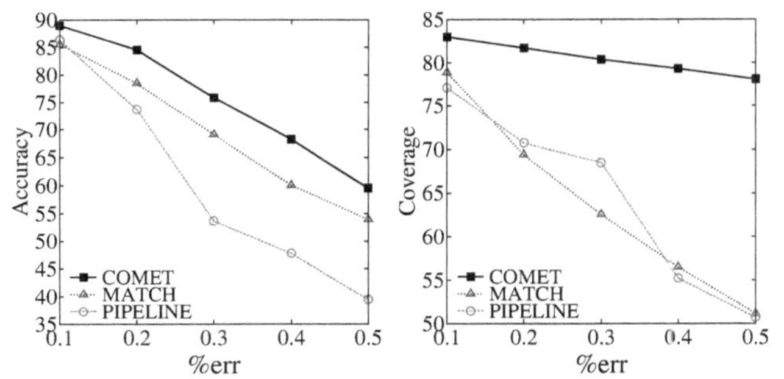

(a) Vary %err

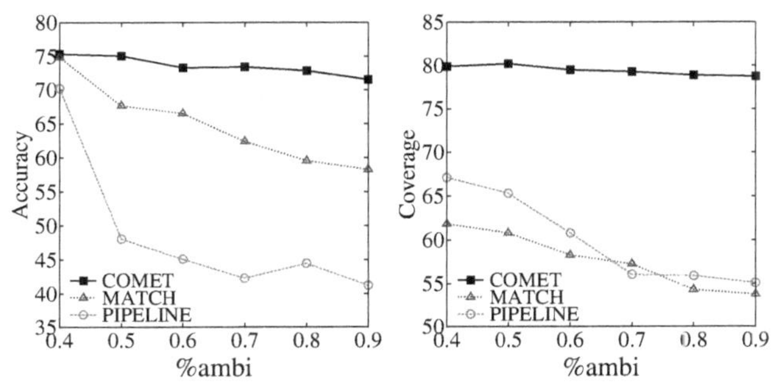

(b) Vary %ambi

Figure 3: Truth discovery on Football dataset

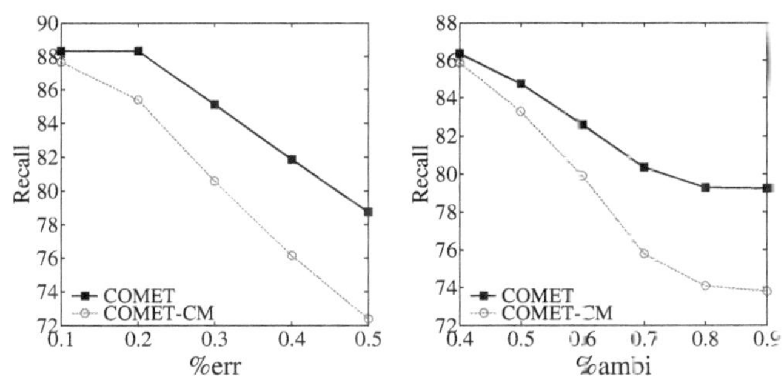

Figure 4: Effect of confidence based matching

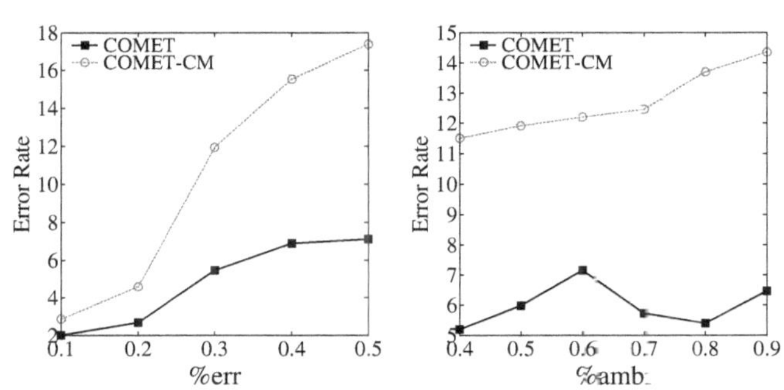

Figure 5: Effect of adaptive matching

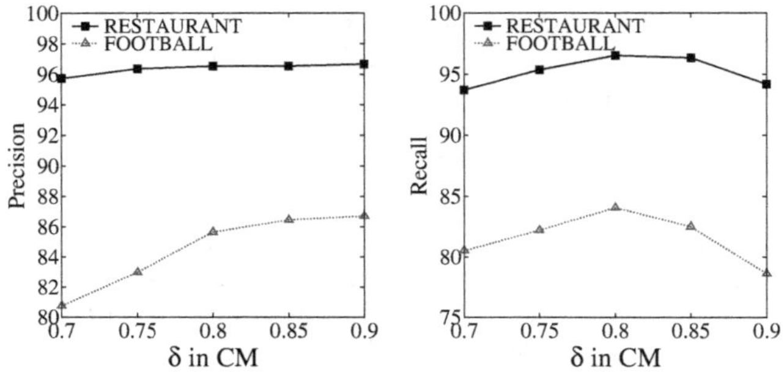

Figure 6: Effect of similarity threshold δ

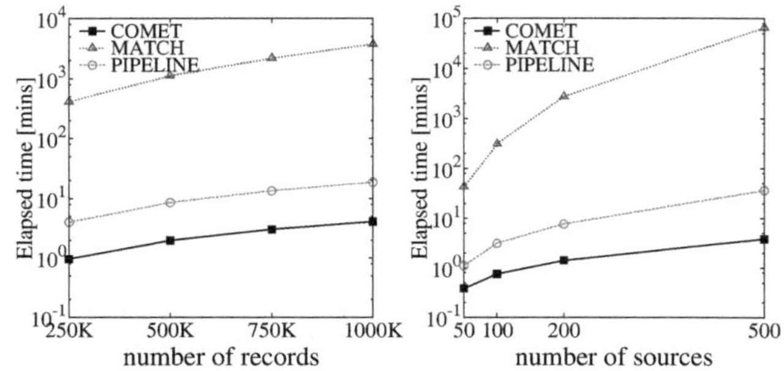

(a) Vary number of entities (b) Vary number of sources

Figure 7: Scalability results

matching avoids up to 59% of the errors by incorporating the reliability matrix to reduce the impact of erroneous values on matching decisions. We observe the gap between COMET and COM-AM widens as *%ambi* increases. This is because a record will be associated with more clusters, while the likelihood function in COMET is able to alleviate the bias brought by these records.

We also examine the effect of the similarity threshold δ in confidence based matching of COMET. We vary δ from 0.7 to 0.9 and report the performance of record linkage on both the Restaurant and Football datasets in Figure 6. In both datasets, we obtain the best results at 0.8. A lower δ generates a larger set of candidates for each input record, which hurts the purity of the resultant clusters. Then the cluster signatures computed in the subsequent phase will be less accurate, leading to incorrect pruning. On the other hand, if δ is too high, correct matchings may be missed in the first phase, resulting in lower recall. We observe similar behaviour when varying δ_H and δ_L and we omit the graphs due to lack of space.

5.4 Scalability Experiments

We also carried out experiments to compare the scalability of COMET, MATCH and PIPELINE. We generate synthetic records using the Football dataset schema by varying the number of entities and number of data sources. Each source will publish a record on each entity. We partition the records and process them in parallel using a cluster with 10 nodes.

We first fix the number of sources at 100 and vary the number of entities from 2,500 to 10,000, thus increasing the number of records from 250k to 1 million. Figure 7(a) shows that the runtime of all the methods increase almost linearly, since the cluster size for each entity remains the same.

Figure 7(b) shows the runtime as we fix the number of entities at 2,000 and increase the number of sources from 50 to 500. We see that COMET remains scalable, while MATCH becomes computationally expensive when the number of sources is large. This is because there will be more nodes in the encoded graph and its complexity is quadratic to the number of nodes. Further, MATCH will require more iterations to terminate.

5.5 Case Studies

Finally, we demonstrate the effectiveness of COMET by case studies. Table 7 shows a sample of the reference records extracted from *www.yellowpages.com*. Each reference record has two attributes: Name and Phone.

Table 7: Sample of Reference Records

Name	Phone
Frank Restaurant	512-494-6894
Frank & Angie's Pizzeria	512-472-3534

Table 8 shows a subset of the input records obtained from 6 websites. We transform the crawled data into a uniform schema, standardize attributes such as Address and Phone, and map range values to categorical values. We observe that the input records have ambiguous names and each provides a subset of attributes. Further, incorrect values are found in the address, phone, opening hours, etc.

Table 9 shows the profile records of two restaurants constructed by COMET after collating data records from the various sources and correcting the erroneous values. We see that each profile record contains more complete information than any of the input record in Table 8 and is more accurate. Further, the prices and ratings in the profiles reduce the bias found in the different websites. Interestingly, we notice that *TripAdvisor* provides more reliable rating information, while *Foursquare* and *Urbanspoon* tend to provide higher ratings.

6. CONCLUSION AND FUTURE WORK

In this paper, we have addressed the problem of building entity profiles by collating data records from multiple sources in the presence of erroneous values. We have designed a framework called COMET that interleaves record linkage with truth discovery to facilitate robust record matching and takes into account the reliability of the data sources to improve performance. The proposed framework first generates a soft clustering of records, and then iteratively determines the cluster signatures and refines the clusters. Extensive experimental results show that our approach significantly outperforms the state-of-the-art techniques on record linkage and truth discovery, and is both scalable and effective. Case studies demonstrate that the proposed framework can construct entity profiles that are both complete and accurate.

In the future, we plan to integrate the information extraction and schema matching processes into the framework, to provide a holistic approach. We believe that taking into account the source reliabilities can improve the performance of them, and an integrated approach will lead to more effective knowledge discovery.

Table 8: Sample Input Records from Various Websites

Name	Address	Phone	Cuisine	Recommend	Price	Weekday Hours	Weekend Hours	Rating	Source
Frank	407 Colorado St	512-494-6894		Hot dog		Normal[1]	Extend[2]	8.7	Urbanspoon[4]
Frank	407 Colorado St	512-494-6916			$	Normal	Normal	6.0	Find Me GF[5]
Frank Restaurant	btw 4th & 5th	512-494-6894			$	Normal	Extend	9.4	Foursquare[6]
Frank	407 Colorado St	512-494-6916			$				LocalEats[7]
Frank	407 Colorado St	512-494-6894			$$	Normal	Extend	8.2	Yelp[8]
Frank	407 Colorado St	512-494-6894	American	Hot dog	$			8.2	TripAdvisor[9]
Frank&Angie's Pizzeria	508 West Ave	512-472-3534	Italian	Pizza	$	Normal	Night[3]	8.8	Urbanspoon
Frank & Angie's	508 West Ave	512-472-3534		Pizza		Normal	Night	8.6	Foursquare
Frank&Angie's Pizzeria	508 West Ave	512-472-3524			$$	Normal	Night		LocalEats
Frank & Angie's	508 West Ave	512-472-3534			$$	Normal	Night	7.0	Yelp
Frank&Angie's Pizzeria	508 West Ave	512-472-3534	Italian	Pizza	$$			8.0	Tripadvisor

[1] Normal: 10am-10pm. [2] Extend: 10am-2am. [3] Night: 5pm-10pm.
[4] www.urbanspoon.com [5] www.findmeglutenfree.com [6] www.foursquare.com
[7] www.localeats.com [8] www.yelp.com [9] www.tripadvisor.com

Table 9: Profile Records Constructed for the Two Restaurants in Table 7

Name	Address	Phone	Cuisine	Recommend	Price	Weekday Hours	Weekend Hours	Rating
Frank Restaurant	407 Colorado St	512-494-6894	American	Hot dog	$	Normal	Extend	8.2
Frank & Angie's Pizzeria	508 West Ave	512-472-3524	Italian	Pizza	$$	Normal	Night	8.0

7. REFERENCES

[1] K. Bellare, S. Iyengar, A. G. Parameswaran, and V. Rastogi. Active sampling for entity matching. In *KDD*, 2012.

[2] O. Benjelloun, H. Garcia-Molina, D. Menestrina, Q. Su, S. E. Whang, and J. Widom. Swoosh: a generic approach to entity resolution. *The VLDB Journal*, pages 255–276, 2009.

[3] I. Bhattacharya and L. Getoor. Collective entity resolution in relational data. *ACM Transactions on Knowledge Discovery from Data (TKDD)*, page 5, 2007.

[4] L. Blanco, V. Crescenzi, P. Merialdo, and P. Papotti. Web data reconciliation: Models and experiences. In *Search Computing*, pages 1–15. 2012.

[5] Y. Cao, W. Fan, and W. Yu. Determining the relative accuracy of attributes. In *SIGMOD*, 2013.

[6] X. L. Dong, L. Berti-Equille, and D. Srivastava. Integrating conflicting data: the role of source dependence. *VLDB*, 2009.

[7] A. K. Elmagarmid, P. G. Ipeirotis, and V. S. Verykios. Duplicate record detection: A survey. *IEEE Transactions on Knowledge and Data Engineering (TKDE)*, pages 1–16, 2007.

[8] W. Fan, H. Gao, X. Jia, J. Li, and S. Ma. Dynamic constraints for record matching. *The VLDB Journal*, pages 495–520, 2011.

[9] I. P. Fellegi and A. B. Sunter. A theory for record linkage. *Journal of the American Statistical Association*, pages 1183–1210, 1969.

[10] N. Garera and D. Yarowsky. Structural, transitive and latent models for biographic fact extraction. In *Proceedings of the 12th Conference of the European Chapter of the Association for Computational Linguistics*, 2009.

[11] J. Gemmell, B. I. Rubinstein, and A. K. Chandra. Improving entity resolution with global constraints. *Microsoft Research Technical Report*, 2011.

[12] S. Guo, X. L. Dong, D. Srivastava, and R. Zajac. Record linkage with uniqueness constraints and erroneous values. *VLDB*, 2010.

[13] M. Gupta and J. Han. Heterogeneous network-based trust analysis: a survey. *ACM SIGKDD Explorations Newsletter*, pages 54–71, 2011.

[14] O. Hassanzadeh, F. Chiang, H. C. Lee, and R. J. Miller. Framework for evaluating clustering algorithms in duplicate detection. *VLDB*, 2009.

[15] H. Köpcke, A. Thor, and E. Rahm. Evaluation of entity resolution approaches on real-world match problems. *VLDB*, 2010.

[16] X. Li, X. L. Dong, K. Lyons, W. Meng, and D. Srivastava. Truth finding on the deep web: is the problem solved? In *VLDB*, 2013.

[17] X. Liu, Z. Nie, N. Yu, and J.-R. Wen. Biosnowball: automated population of wikis. In *KDD*, 2010.

[18] S. N. Negahban, B. I. Rubinstein, and J. G. Gemmell Scaling multiple-source entity resolution using statistically efficient transfer learning. In *CIKM*, 2012.

[19] J. Pasternack and D. Roth. Latent credibility analysis. In *WWW*, 2013.

[20] W. Shen, P. DeRose, L. Vu, A. Doan, and R. Ramakrishnan. Source-aware entity matching: A compositional approach. In *ICDE*, 2007.

[21] M. Yakout, K. Ganjam, K. Chakrabarti, and S. Chaudhuri. Infogather: entity augmentation and attribute discovery by holistic matching with web tables. In *SIGMOD*, 2012.

[22] X. Yin, J. Han, and P. S. Yu. Truth discovery with multiple conflicting information providers on the web. In *KDD*, 2007.

Open Question Answering Over Curated and Extracted Knowledge Bases

Anthony Fader*
Allen Institute for AI
Seattle, WA
afader@gmail.com

Luke Zettlemoyer
University of Washington
Seattle, WA
lsz@cs.washington.edu

Oren Etzioni
Allen Institute for AI
Seattle, WA
orene@allenai.org

ABSTRACT

We consider the problem of open-domain question answering (Open QA) over massive knowledge bases (KBs). Existing approaches use either manually curated KBs like Freebase or KBs automatically extracted from unstructured text. In this paper, we present OQA, the first approach to leverage both curated and extracted KBs.

A key technical challenge is designing systems that are robust to the high variability in both natural language questions and massive KBs. OQA achieves robustness by decomposing the full Open QA problem into smaller sub-problems including question paraphrasing and query reformulation. OQA solves these sub-problems by mining millions of rules from an unlabeled question corpus and across multiple KBs. OQA then learns to integrate these rules by performing discriminative training on question-answer pairs using a latent-variable structured perceptron algorithm. We evaluate OQA on three benchmark question sets and demonstrate that it achieves up to twice the precision and recall of a state-of-the-art Open QA system.

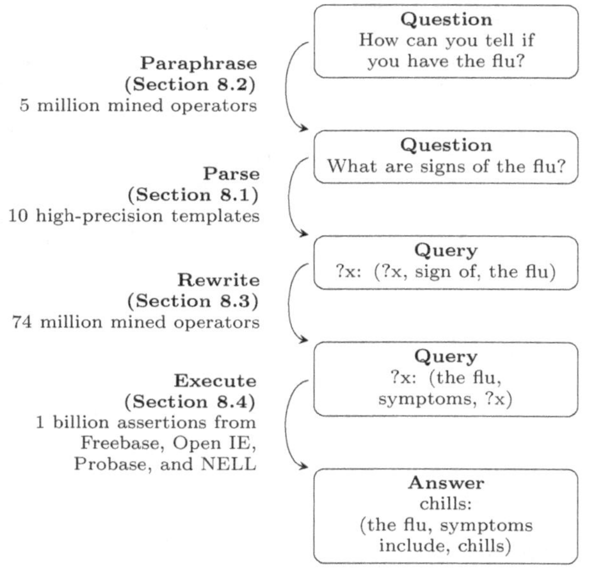

Figure 1: OQA automatically mines millions of operators (left) from unlabeled data, then learns to compose them to answer questions (right) using evidence from multiple knowledge bases.

1. INTRODUCTION

Open-domain question answering (Open QA) is a longstanding problem that has been studied for decades [12, 13]. Open QA systems need broad knowledge to achieve high coverage. Early systems took an information retrieval approach, where question answering is reduced to returning passages of text containing an answer as a substring [24]. Recent advances in constructing large-scale knowledge bases (KBs) [21, 2, 5] have enabled new systems that return an exact answer from a KB [4, 28, 23, 25, 10, 15, 3]. Some such systems have used curated KBs like Freebase,[1] which are high-precision but incomplete. Other systems have used extracted KBs like Open Information Extraction,[2] which have higher coverage but generally lower precision. In this paper, we present OQA, the first Open QA system to leverage both curated and extracted KBs.

A key challenge in Open QA is to be robust to the high variability found in natural language and the many ways of expressing knowledge in large-scale KBs. OQA achieves this robustness by decomposing the full QA problem into smaller sub-problems that are easier to solve. Figure 1 shows an example of how OQA maps the question "How can you tell if you have the flu?" to the answer "chills" over four steps. The first step rewrites the input question to "What are signs of the flu?" using a paraphrase operator mined from a large corpus of questions. The second step uses a hand-written template to parse the paraphrased question to the KB query "?x : (?x, signs of, the flu)." These two steps are synergistic; paraphrase operators effectively reduce the variance of the input questions, allowing OQA to use a small set of high-precision parsing rules while maintaining recall. The third step uses a query-rewrite operator to reformulate the query as "?x : (the flu, symptoms, ?x)." Query-rewrite operators are automatically mined from the KB, and allow the vocabulary mismatch between question words and KB

*Work completed while at the University of Washington.
[1] `http://freebase.com`
[2] `http://openie.cs.washington.edu`

KDD'14, August 24–27, 2014, New York, New York, USA.
Copyright 2014 ACM 978-1-4503-2956-9/14/08 ...$15.00.
http://dx.doi.org/10.1145/2623330.2623677 .

symbols to be solved independent of parsing. Finally, the fourth step executes the rewritten query against the KB, returning the final answer.

The operators and KB are noisy, so it is possible to construct many different sequences of operations (called derivations), very few of which will produce a correct answer. OQA learns from a small amount of question-answer data to find the best derivations. Because the derivations are unobserved in the training data, we use a latent-variable structured perceptron algorithm [31, 17, 22]. OQA uses a small set of general features that allow it to generalize from a limited number of training examples. Experiments on three benchmark question sets show that OQA outperforms the state-of-the-art Open QA system PARALEX [10], achieving twice the precision and recall.

In summary, we make the following contributions:

- We introduce OQA, the first Open QA system to leverage multiple, large-scale curated and extracted KBs.
- We describe an inference algorithm for deriving high-confidence answers (Section 6) and a hidden-variable structured perceptron algorithm for learning a scoring function from data (Section 7).
- We present algorithms for automatically mining paraphrase operators from a question corpus (Section 8.2) and KB-query rewrite operators (Section 8.3) from multiple KBs.
- We provide an empirical evaluation (Section 9), showing the relative contributions of different KBs and different system components across three question sets. We also compare OQA to the state-of-the-art QA systems PARALEX [10] and SEMPRE [3].
- We release the code and data from this work.[3]

In Section 2, we describe related work in more detail before moving on to the description of OQA (Sections 3–8) and experiments (Section 9).

2. RELATED WORK

Early work in Open QA used search engines as a source of background knowledge and relied on hand-written templates to map questions to search engine queries [16, 1]. In contrast, OQA utilizes a set of KBs, which enable it to combine knowledge extracted from Web text with curated knowledge. The KB abstraction also allows OQA to join multiple pieces of evidence to arrive at an answer, a technique that is not possible using just a search engine.

A major research thread in QA has been scaling up semantic parsing systems from small, single-domain KBs [30, 31, 26, 18, 7] to larger, multi-domain KBs like YAGO2 [28], DBpedia [23], and Freebase [4, 3, 15]. Curated KBs like Freebase are attractive for QA because they allow systems to reason over high-precision knowledge and return accurate answers. However, these systems have limited recall due to the inherent incompleteness of curated KBs. This phenomenon can be understood as a power-generality tradeoff: QA systems can rely on the accuracy and conciseness of a curated KB, but incomplete knowledge limits their generality.

[3] `https://github.com/afader/oqa`

The PARALEX system [10] was the first Open QA system to operate over a noisy, extracted KB. The biggest difference between PARALEX and OQA is how they decompose the QA problem. PARALEX uses self-labeled data to learn templates that directly map questions to queries—essentially performing paraphrasing, parsing, and query-rewriting in one step. OQA treats these as separate problems, which allows it to combine high-recall data mining techniques (for paraphrasing and query rewriting) with high-precision, hand-written rules (for parsing).

OQA's feature representation also differs from previous work. Previous systems use a large number of lexicalized features—those involving specific lexemes or KB symbols. OQA uses unlexicalized features that operate on the level of function words, part-of-speech tags, and corpus statistics. We found that the an unlexicalized feature representation generalizes better to questions involving relationships that were never seen during training.

3. TASK DEFINITION AND OVERVIEW

In this section, we define the QA task and give a high-level outline of OQA and our experiments.

Task and Metrics: We focus on the task of factoid QA, where the system takes a natural language question like "How can you tell if you have the flu?" as input and returns a short string answer like "chills" from a KB, or "no answer." We use precision (fraction of answered questions that are correct) and recall (fraction of questions that are correctly answered) as our primary evaluation metrics.

Knowledge Base: OQA uses a simple KB abstraction where ground facts are represented as string triples (argument1, relation, argument2). We use triples from curated and extracted knowledge sources (Section 4.1) and provide a lightweight query language to access the KB (Section 4.2).

Operators and Scoring Function: OQA models QA as a process where answers are derived from questions using operators Ops (Section 5.1). A sequence of operators linking a question to an answer is called a derivation. OQA computes the confidence of an answer derivation d using a linear scoring function score$(d|\mathbf{f}, \mathbf{w})$, which is parameterized by a feature function $\mathbf{f}$ and feature weights $\mathbf{w}$ (Section 5.2).

Inference: In practice, the space of derivations defined by Ops is too large to enumerate. OQA uses heuristic search over partial derivations, guided by score$(d|\mathbf{f}, \mathbf{w})$, to generate high-scoring candidate answers for an input question (Section 6).

Learning: OQA learns the weights $\mathbf{w}$ from a small set of question-answer pairs. Because annotated answer derivations are difficult to obtain, we use a latent-variable structured perceptron algorithm that treats answer derivations as unobserved variables in the training data (Section 7).

Operators and Features: OQA uses four types of operators: a small set of parsing operators (Section 8.1), a large set of paraphrase operators mined from a question corpus (Section 8.2), a large set of query-rewrite rules mined from the KB (Section 8.3), and an execution operator that interfaces with the KB (Section 8.4). Each operator is paired with a small set of features used to compute $\mathbf{f}$. Using a small feature set results in better generalization from limited training data.

Source	Type	# Triples	# Relation Phrases
Freebase	Curated	300M	18K
Open IE [9]	Extracted	500M	6M
Probase [27]	Extracted	200M	1
NELL [5]	Extracted	2M	300

Table 1: Knowledge bases used by OQA.

System Evaluation: We evaluate OQA using three question sets. We compare OQA to the Open QA system PARALEX and the Freebase QA system SEMPRE. We then test the contributions of each knowledge source and system component via ablation.

4. KNOWLEDGE BASE

This section describes where OQA's knowledge comes from and the query language it uses to access the knowledge.

4.1 Knowledge Base Sources

Table 1 summarizes the knowledge sources in OQA. OQA uses one curated KB (Freebase) and three extracted KBs (Open IE, Probase, and NELL).

Freebase is an open-domain, collaboratively edited KB. Freebase has relatively comprehensive coverage of certain domains like film or geography, but does not contain informal assertions like "chicken is high in protein." Freebase maintains canonical string representations of its entities and relations, which we use to coerce facts into string triples.[4]

Open IE [2, 9] is a family of techniques used to extract binary relationships from billions of web pages containing unstructured text. Open IE has the unique property that its relations are unnormalized natural language, which results in over two orders of magnitude more relation phrases than Freebase. The Open IE assertions are noisy and lack the comprehensive domain coverage found in Freebase. However, Open IE contains many of the informal assertions that are not found in curated KBs. For example, Open IE produces assertions like (pepper, provides a source of, vitamins a and c). Open IE triples are annotated with metadata including extractor confidence and corpus frequency, and some triple arguments are linked to Freebase entities [20].

Probase [27] is an extracted KB containing "is-a" relations, *e.g.*, (paris, is-a, beautiful city) or (physicist, is-a, scientist). Probase triples are annotated with statistical metadata that measure the confidence of each extraction.

NELL [5] is an extracted KB that contains approximately 300 relation phrases. NELL generally has high precision, but low recall.

The union of these KBs forms a single resource containing a billion noisy, redundant, and inconsistent assertions. While there is a vast body of literature exploring the problem of data-integration [8], these techniques require a target schema, which does not exist for our knowledge sources. Instead of making an offline commitment to a single schema, at runtime OQA hypothesizes many interpretations for each question. These hypotheses are encoded using the query language described in the next section.

4.2 Query Language

The query language used in OQA provides a lightweight interface between natural language and KB assertions. In contrast to the semantic parsing literature [30], a OQA query is not intended to represent the complete, formal semantic interpretation of a question. Instead, the query language is used to separate the parsing problem (identifying predicate-argument structure) from the vocabulary-matching problem (matching natural language symbols to KB symbols) [12, 15]. This factorization is at the core of the OQA approach, which uses different operators to solve each problem.

OQA's query language is capable of representing conjunctive queries [6]. Because our KB is unnormalized and contains only strings, OQA uses keyword matching and string similarity as primitive operations. Figure 2 shows how the question "What fruits are a source of vitamin C?" can be represented as the query ?x : (?x, is-a, fruit) (?x, source of, vitamin c). This particular query represents one possible mapping of the question to a predicate-argument structure. The middle box of Figure 2 shows how the semantics of the query can be interpreted as a SQL expression over a single table `triples` with string columns `arg1`, `rel`, and `arg2`. A OQA query consists of a projection variable (*e.g.*, ?x) and a list of conjuncts. Each conjunct contains a mix of string literals (*e.g.*, fruit) and variables. String literals correspond to keyword-matching constraints on the table columns, while variables correspond to string-similarity join constraints.

Having keyword matching and string similarity incorporated into the query semantics leads to another useful factorization. The query language provides a general, high-recall solution to the problem of minor surface-form variations (*e.g.*, joining "star-fruit" with "starfruit" or matching "source of" with "provides a source of" in Figure 2). OQA can then increase precision by computing question- or KB-specific features as soft constraints on the output. For example, it uses a feature that checks whether two join keys are linked to the same Freebase entity, if this information is available. This lets OQA maintain a simple data model (entity-linking is not required) while allowing for domain knowledge to be modeled via features.

What fruits are a source of vitamin C?
?x : (?x, is-a, fruit) (?x, source of, vitamin c)

```
SELECT t0.arg1 FROM triples AS t0, triples AS t1
  WHERE
    keyword-match(t0.rel, "is-a")          AND
    keyword-match(t0.arg2, "fruit")        AND
    keyword-match(t1.rel, "source of")     AND
    keyword-match(t1.arg2, "vitamin c")    AND
    string-similarity(t0.arg1, t1.arg1) > 0.9
```

t0.arg1	t0.rel	t0.arg2	t1.arg1	t1.rel	t1.arg2
Lychee	is a	fruit	Lychees	good source of	vitamin c
star-fruit	is a	tropical fruit	starfruit	source of	vitamin c
pepper	is a	fresh fruit	pepper	provides a source of	vitamins c and a

Figure 2: Top: An example question and query used by OQA. Middle: The query semantics expressed as SQL. Bottom: The results when executed against a knowledge base (answers highlighted).

5. DERIVING AND SCORING ANSWERS

OQA factors question answering into a set of smaller, related problems including paraphrasing, parsing, and query

[4]We discard Freebase facts that are not binary relations.

reformulation. The solutions to each of these sub-problems can then be applied in sequence to give a complete mapping from question to answer. Figure 3 shows example derivations for the question "How can you tell if you have the flu?" Our approach consists of two parts: (1) derivation operators, which define the space of possible answers for a given question, and (2) a scoring function, which returns a real-valued confidence for a derivation.

5.1 Derivation Operators

More formally, we model question answering as the process of mapping a question q to an answer a by applying operators from some set Ops. Each operator $o \in \mathsf{Ops}$ takes a state object $s \in \mathsf{States}$ as input and returns a set $o(s) \subseteq \mathsf{States}$ of successor states as output. State objects encode intermediate values that are used during the question-answering procedure. In Figure 3, the intermediate question "What are signs of the flu?" is a state object that is related to the query "?x : (?x, sign of, flu)" via a parsing operator. We use three types of states: question states, query states, and answer states.

Operations can be chained together into a derivation. A single derivation step encodes the process of applying an operator o to some state s and picking a successor state $s' \in o(s)$ from the output. A derivation $d = (\mathbf{o}, \mathbf{s}, k)$ consists of a sequence of k operators $\mathbf{o} = (o_1, \ldots, o_k)$ and a sequence of $k+1$ states $\mathbf{s} = (s_0, s_1, \ldots, s_k)$ satisfying $s_i \in o_i(s_{i-1})$ for all $1 \leq i \leq k$.[5]

An answer a is derivable from a question q under the operator set Ops if there exists some derivation $(\mathbf{o}, \mathbf{s}, k)$ such that $s_0 = q$ and $s_k = a$. We use the notation $\mathsf{Derivs}(q, \mathsf{Ops})$ to represent the space of all possible derivations from the question q under the operations Ops ending at answer a.

In our implementation of OQA, the operator set Ops contains millions of operators, combining both hand-written operators and operators learned from data. These operators are noisy: incorrect answers can be derived from most questions. Thus, estimating the confidence of a derivation is necessary for returning answers with high precision.

5.2 Scoring Function

To compute the confidence of a derivation, OQA uses a scoring function. The scoring function computes a real value for a given derivation, where large, positive scores are assigned to high-confidence derivations.

We make two assumptions about the form of the scoring function. First, we assume that the score is a linear function over features computed from a derivation. This will allow us to use familiar algorithms to learn the function from data. Second, we assume that the feature function decomposes over derivation steps. This allows us to use the scoring function to score partial derivations, which is useful for searching over $\mathsf{Derivs}(q, \mathsf{Ops})$ (discussed further in Section 6).

Under these assumptions, the score of a derivation $d = (\mathbf{o}, \mathbf{s}, k)$ can be written as

$$\text{score}(d|\mathbf{f}, \mathbf{w}) = \sum_{i=1}^{k} \mathbf{w} \cdot \mathbf{f}(s_0, s_{i-1}, o_i, s_i), \qquad (1)$$

where $\mathbf{f}$ is an n-dimensional feature function that maps a

[5]In OQA, $2 \leq k \leq 4$: parsing and execution steps are required to derive an answer, and we limit derivations to have at most one paraphrase step and one query-rewrite step.

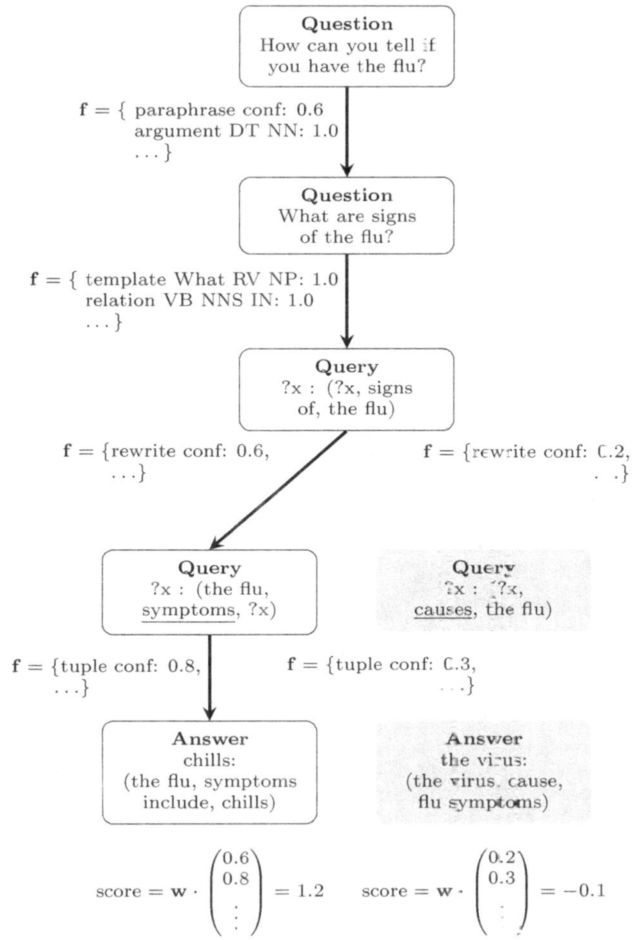

Figure 3: OQA compute operator-specific features to discriminate between correct derivations (left) and incorrect derivations (right).

derivation step into $\mathbb{R}^n$ and $\mathbf{w}$ is an n-dimensional weight vector. Because s_0 (the input question) is a constant in all derivations, we pass it as an argument to the feature function. This allows features to compute properties relating derivation steps to the input question.

Figure 3 shows an example of how the scoring function can discriminate between a correct answer (left) and an incorrect answer (right). The derivation on the left rewrites the original query using a high-confidence rule and uses high-confidence evidence returned from the KB. The derivation on the right uses a low-confidence rewrite rule and low-confidence evidence—and is thus assigned a lower score.

In our implementation of OQA, we learn $\mathbf{w}$ from a small set of question-answer pairs (Section 7) and define $\mathbf{f}$ to compute operator-specific features (Section 8).

6. INFERENCE

We focus on the task of finding a single answer with the highest confidence under the scoring function, which amounts to solving the following equation for an input question q:

$$d^* = \arg\max_{d \in \mathsf{Derivs}(q, \mathsf{Ops})} \text{score}(d|\mathbf{f}, \mathbf{w}) \qquad (2)$$

The underlying knowledge base and set of operators are both large enough that exhaustively enumerating $\mathsf{Derivs}(q, \mathsf{Ops})$ is not feasible. Instead, OQA uses beam search informed by the scoring function to explore $\mathsf{Derivs}(q, \mathsf{Ops})$. We refer to the beam search routine as DERIVEANSWERS.

The algorithm takes a question q as input and returns a set of derivations $D \subseteq \mathsf{Derivs}(q, \mathsf{Ops})$. The output set D is constructed by iteratively growing partial derivations starting at the initial question state $s_0 = q$. The algorithm maintains a beam of partial derivations, each scored by the function $\text{score}(d|\mathbf{f}, \mathbf{w})$. At every iteration, a partial derivation is selected to be extended. Extending a derivation $d = (\mathbf{o}, \mathbf{s}, k)$ amounts to computing successors to the state s_k and appending the successors to construct new derivations. This process is repeated until there are no partial derivations left to extend or until a time limit is reached.

In practice, the scoring function $\text{score}(d|\mathbf{f}, \mathbf{w})$ generally assigns higher scores to short derivations, *e.g.* derivations that do not use a query-rewrite operator. We found that this bias will flood the beam with high-scoring partial derivations occurring early in the search, and later options will not be considered. To avoid this problem, we maintain separate beams for each state-type in the search, similar to the decoding algorithms used in statistical machine translation [14]. OQA uses beam search both at runtime and during learning, which we describe in the next section.

7. LEARNING

A key challenge in learning $\text{score}(d|\mathbf{f}, \mathbf{w})$ is that obtaining labeled answer derivations requires expert annotators and is extremely time consuming. Following recent work in semantic parsing [7, 3, 15], we use question-answer pairs as indirect supervision and treat answer derivations as unobserved variables in the training data. Question-answer pairs like $q =$ "How can you tell if you have the flu?", $A = \{$"chills", "fever", "aches"$\}$ are significantly easier to obtain and do not require expert annotators.

We use the latent-variable structured perceptron algorithm [31, 17, 22] to learn $\mathbf{w}$ from example question-answer pairs. Figure 4 shows the pseudocode for the LEARNWEIGHTS algorithm.

The algorithm takes as input a set of N pairs (q_i, A_i) for $i = 1, \ldots, N$, where A_i is a set containing string answers to q_i. For each training example, the algorithm calls DERIVEANSWERS to generate a candidate set of answer derivations D. The algorithm then chooses a derivation $\hat{d}$ that has the highest score according to the current weights and makes the prediction $\hat{a} = \text{answer}(\hat{d})$. If $\hat{a}$ is correct (*i.e.*, it is in A_i), the algorithm proceeds to the next example. If $\hat{a}$ is incorrect, then the learner picks the highest scoring derivation d^* such that $\text{answer}(d^*)$ is in A_i. The algorithm then performs an additive update $\mathbf{w} = \mathbf{w} + \mathbf{f}(d^*) - \mathbf{f}(\hat{d})$. If there are no derivations with a correct answer in D, then the learner immediately proceeds to the next example without performing an update. Finally, the algorithm returns the average value of $\mathbf{w}$ over all iterations, which improves generalization [11].

8. OPERATORS AND FEATURES

In this section, we describe the operators that OQA uses to derive answers. The operators factor the end-to-end QA problem into smaller subproblems:

```
function LEARNWEIGHTS
  Inputs:
    Number of iterations T
    N example questions with answers (q_1, A_1), ..., (q_N, A_N)
    Initial model (Ops, f, w) (Defined in Section 5)
    Function DERIVEANSWERS (Defined in Section 6)
  Output:
    Learned weights w
  for t = 1, ..., T
    for i = 1, ..., N
      D = DERIVEANSWERS(q_i, Ops, f, w)
      d̂ = arg max_{d∈D} score(d|f, w)
      if answer(d̂) ∉ A_i
        D* = {d ∈ D : answer(d) ∈ A_i}
        d* = arg max_{d∈D*} score(d|f, w)
        w = w + f(d*) − f(d̂)
  return average of w over all iterations
```

Figure 4: The weight-learning algorithm.

Parsing operators (Section 8.1) are responsible for interfacing between natural language questions and the KB query language described in Section 4.2. OQA uses a small number of high-precision templates to map questions to queries.

Paraphrase operators (Section 8.2) are responsible for rewording the input question into the domain of a parsing operator. In an offline process, OQA mines 5 million lexicalized paraphrase-templates from an unlabeled corpus of open-domain questions.

Query-rewrite operators (Section 8.3) are responsible for interfacing between the vocabulary used in the input question and the internal vocabulary used by the KBs. OQA implements its query-rewrite operators by mining a set of 75 million relation-entailment pairs from the knowledge bases described in Section 4.1.

The execution operator (Section 8.4) is responsible for fetching and combining evidence from the KB, given a query.

For each operator, OQA computes general, domain independent features that are used in the scoring function. These features are *unlexicalized* in the sense that they do not compute any values associated with content words in either the question or the KB.

In the following subsections, we describe each type of operator in detail and describe the operator-specific features used by the scoring function.

8.1 Parsing Operators

To map questions to queries, we use the set of 10 hand-written operators shown in Table 2. Each operator consists of a question pattern and a query pattern.

A question pattern is expressed as a regular expression over part-of-speech (POS) tags and function words. To detect noun phrases (NPs), we use a POS pattern that matches a sequence of nouns, determiners, and adjectives. We use the REVERB pattern [9] to detect relation phrases. Each question pattern uses named capture-groups to select substrings from the input question.

A query pattern consists of a query (defined in Section 4.2) containing pointers to capture groups from the question pattern. When a question pattern matches a question, the captured strings are substituted into the query pattern to generate a complete query. For example, the question

Question Pattern	Query Pattern	Example Question	Example Query
Who/What RV_{rel} NP_{arg}	(?x, rel, arg)	Who invented papyrus?	(?x, invented, papyrus)
Who/What Aux NP_{arg} RV_{rel}	(arg, rel, ?x)	What did Newton discover?	(Newton, discover, ?x)
Where/When Aux NP_{arg} RV_{rel}	(arg, rel in, ?x)	Where was Edison born?	(Edison, born in, ?x)
Where/When is NP_{arg}	(arg, is in, ?x)	Where is Detroit?	(Detroit, is in, ?x)
Who/What is NP_{arg}	(arg, is-a, ?x)	What is potassium?	(potassium, is-a, ?x)
What/Which NP_{rel2} Aux NP_{arg} RV_{rel1}	(arg, rel1 rel2, ?x)	What sport does Sosa play?	(Sosa, play sport, ?x)
What/Which NP_{rel} is NP_{arg}	(arg, rel, ?x)	What ethnicity is Dracula?	(Dracula, ethnicity, ?x)
What/Who is NP_{arg}'s NP_{rel}	(arg, rel, ?x)	What is Russia's capital?	(Russia, capital, ?x)
What/Which NP_{type} Aux NP_{arg} RV_{rel}	(?x, is-a, type) (arg rel, ?x)	What fish do sharks eat?	(?x, is-a, fish) (sharks, eat, ?x)
What/Which NP_{type} RV_{rel} NP_{arg}	(?x, is-a, type) (?x, rel, arg)	What states make oil?	(?x, is-a, states) (?x, make, oil)

Table 2: High-precision parsing operators used to map questions to queries. Question templates are expressed using noun phrases (NP), auxiliary verbs (Aux), and ReVerb patterns (RV). Subscripts denote regex-style capture groups.

Source Template	Target Template
How does _ affect your body?	What body system does _ affect?
What is the latin name for _?	What is _'s scientific name?
Why do we use _?	What did _ replace?
What to use instead of _?	What is a substitute for _?
Was _ ever married?	Who has _ been married to?

Table 3: Example paraphrase operators that extracted from a corpus of unlabeled questions.

Source Query	Target Query
(?x, children, ?y)	(?y, was born to, ?x)
(?x, birthdate, ?y)	(?x, date of birth, ?y)
(?x, is headquartered in, ?y)	(?x, is based in, ?y)
(?x, invented, ?y)	(?y, was invented by, ?x)
(?x, is the language of, ?y)	(?y, languages spoken, ?x)

Table 4: Example query-rewrite operators mined from the knowledge bases described in Section 4.1.

pattern in the first row of Table 2 matches "Who invented papyrus?" and captures the substrings {rel → invented, arg → papyrus}. These are substituted into the query pattern (?x, rel, arg) to produce the output (?x, invented, papyrus).

Features: Because some question patterns may be more reliable than others, we include an indicator feature for each question pattern. We also include indicator features for the POS sequence of the capture groups and the POS tags to the left and right of each capture group.

8.2 Paraphrasing Operators

The parsing operators in Table 2 have high precision but low recall. To increase recall, we use paraphrase operators to map questions onto the domain of the parsing operators. Each paraphrase operator is implemented as a pair of paraphrase templates like the examples in Table 3.

Each paraphrase template consists of a natural language string with a slot that captures some argument. For example, the first source template in Table 3 matches the question "How does nicotine affect your body?" This question can then be paraphrased by substituting the argument "nicotine" into the target template, yielding the new question "What body system does nicotine affect?"

We follow the work of PARALEX and automatically mine these source/target template pairs from the WikiAnswers[6] paraphrase corpus [10]. The WikiAnswers paraphrase corpus consists of 23 million question-clusters that WikiAnswers users have grouped as synonymous. Each question cluster contains an average of 25 questions. In general, the clusters have low precision due to mistakes or users grouping related, but non-synonymous questions (*e.g.*, "How to say shut up in french?" is grouped with "Is it nice to say shut up?").

We extracted 200,000 templates that occurred in at least 10 question clusters. For each pair of templates (t, t'), we define the co-occurrence count $c(t, t')$ to be the number of clusters where t and t' both occur with the same argument. For example, if a cluster contains the questions "Why do we use computers?" and "What did computers replace?" we would increment the count c(Why do we use _?, What did _ replace?) by 1. For each template pair (t, t') such that $c(t, t') \geq 5$, we define paraphrase operators $t \to t'$ and $t' \to t$. This generates a set of 5 million paraphrase operators. During inference, all possible paraphrases of a question q are computed by considering all substrings of q (up to 5 tokens) as the argument.

Features: The paraphrase operators are automatically extracted from a noisy corpus, and are not always reliable. We compute statistical and syntactic features to estimate the confidence of using the operator $t \to t'$ to paraphrase a question q to a new question q' using argument a. The statistical features include the pointwise mutual information (PMI) between t and t' in the WikiAnswers corpus and a language model score of q'. The syntactic features include the POS sequence of the matched argument a, and the POS tags to the left and right of a in q.

8.3 Query-Rewrite Operators

To handle the mismatch between natural language vocabulary and the KB vocabulary, we mine query rewrite rules. We focus on handling the mismatch between relation words in the question and relation words in the KB.[7] Table 4 lists example query rewrite rules. Each rule encodes a translation from one relation phrase to another, with a possible re-ordering of the arguments. For example, the first row in Table 4 is an operator that allows the relation phrase "children" to be rewritten as "was born to^{-1}," where the superscript denotes inverted argument ordering.

We follow previous work on mining equivalent relations [19, 29] and count the number of shared argument-pairs between two relation phrases. For example, the tuples (hermann einstein, children, albert einstein) and (albert einstein, was born to, hermann einstein) both appear in the KB, so "children" and "was born to^{-1}" share the argument pair

[6]`http://wiki.answers.com`

[7]Rewriting arguments is future work.

(hermman einstein, albert einstein). We construct a query rewrite operator for each pair of relation phrases (r, r') that share at least 10 argument pairs. This results in a set of 74 million (r, r') pairs that we include as operators.

Features: As with the paraphrase templates (Section 8.2), we compute the PMI for each pair of relation phrases as a feature.

8.4 Execution Operator

The execution operator takes a query as input and returns a set of tuples, as shown in Figure 2. We store the KB (arg1, relation, arg2) triples in an inverted index[8] that allows for efficient keyword search over the three triple fields. We implemented a simple query optimizer that performs joins over triples by making multiple queries to the KB. Due to the size of the KB, we limit each keyword search over the triples to return the top 100 hits. The output of the execution operator is an answer state, containing a string answer and a joined tuple of evidence.

Features: We use features to estimate the reliability of the KB output. The features examine properties of the query, the returned tuple evidence, and the answer.

We measure the keyword similarity between two strings by lemmatizing them, removing stopwords, and computing the cosine similarity. We then include the keyword similarity between the query and the input question, the keyword similarity between the query and the returned evidence, and an indicator feature for whether the query involves a join.

The evidence features compute KB-specific properties. Extracted triples have confidence scores, which are included as features. We compute the join-key string similarity measured using the Levenshtein distance. We also include indicator features for the source of each triple (*e.g.*, whether the triple is from Open IE or Freebase).

The answer features compute conjunctions of properties of the input question and the answer. We compute whether the question begins with some common prefixes (*e.g.*, Who, What, When, How many, *etc.*). For the answer, we compute word-shape features (*e.g.*, "Kansas" has the word shape "Aaaa" and "December 1941" has the word shape "Aaaa 1111"). This allows the system to learn that features like *question starts with When* $\wedge$ *answer has shape 1111* are indicative of a correct answer.

9. EXPERIMENTAL SETUP

We are interested in answering three questions: (1) How does OQA compare to the state-of-the-art systems PARALEX and SEMPRE? (2) How do the different knowledge sources affect performance? (3) How do the different system components affect performance?

We investigate these questions by comparing performance on three question sets. Given a question q, each system returns an answer a with confidence $c \in \mathbb{R}$ or "no answer." We then measure the precision (correct answers/answers returned), recall (correct answers/questions), and F1 score (harmonic mean of precision and recall). We also compute precision-recall curves that show how precision is traded for recall as the minimum confidence to return an answer is varied. We describe the three question sets in Section 9.1 and the system settings in Section 9.2.

[8]`https://lucene.apache.org/solr/`

Question set	Example questions
WebQuestions 3,778 train 2,032 test	who influenced wolfgang amadeus mozart? who won the super bowl xliv 2010? where was nicki minaj born? what is in liverpool england? who is the leader of france 2012?
TREC 962 train 517 test	What other countries do Kurds live in? What year was Barry Manilow born? What format was VHS's main competition? Who is the chairman of WWE? What is Muscular Dystrophy?
WikiAnswers 1,334 train 7,310 test	What is Matthew henson's mothers name? Who is a retired gay nfl football player? Do beluga whales eat penguins? Why were the conquistadors important? How does psychiatry benefit society?

Table 5: The three question sets used in our experiments.

9.1 Question Sets

In our experiments, we use three question sets: WebQuestions, TREC, and WikiAnswers. Figure 5 shows statistics and example questions from each set.

WebQuestions was introduced by the authors of the SEMPRE system [3]. The questions were generated from Google Autocomplete using a seed set of Freebase entities. Amazon Mechanical Turk users then provided answers in the form of Freebase concepts. Questions that could not be answered using Freebase were filtered out. Out of the three test sets, WebQuestions has the unique property that the questions are known *a priori* to be answerable using Freebase.

TREC was introduced for the purpose of evaluating information retrieval QA systems [24]. We re-purpose the TREC questions to test our KB-based Open QA systems. While the TREC questions were designed to be answerable using a small collection of test documents, they are not guaranteed to be answerable using any of the KBs described in Section 4.1.

WikiAnswers is a set of questions that were randomly sampled from a crawl of WikiAnswers. The WikiAnswers question set is completely disjoint from the corpus used to extract the paraphrasing operators described in Section 8.2. WikiAnswers questions are very challenging and ambiguous, and are not necessarily answerable by any KB.

WebQuestions and TREC both have gold-standard answer sets for each question, and WikiAnswers questions often have no answers available. However, due to the open-domain nature of our experiments, the gold-standard answer sets are incomplete. If a system's top answer was not already included in the provided gold-standard sets, we manually tagged the answers as correct or incorrect.

9.2 System Settings

OQA: We examine two different training settings for OQA. In the first setting, we trained OQA on each question set independently, resulting three different sets of weights. In the second setting, we trained OQA on the union of the WebQuestions, TREC, and WikiAnswers training sets, resulting in one set of weights.

For inference, we used a beam capacity of 1,000 and a search time limit of 20 seconds. For learning, we initialized

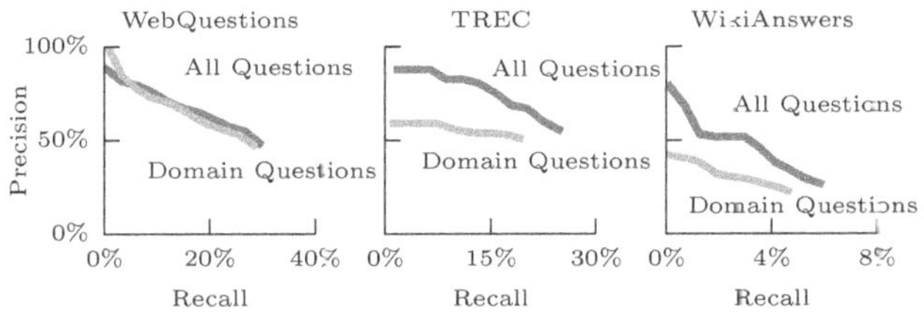

Figure 5: Training OQA on questions from all question sets leads to greater precision and recall than training on domain questions only.

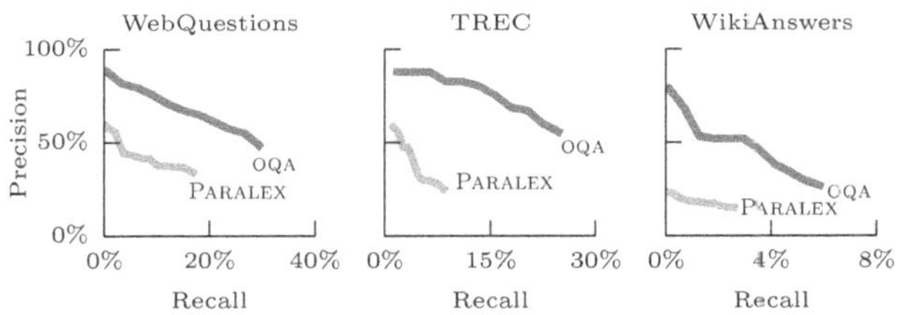

Figure 6: OQA has higher precision and recall than the Open QA system Paralex.

10 of the feature weights to be +1/-1 based on whether the features are indicative of good derivations (*e.g.*, PMI scores) or bad derivations (*e.g.*, verbs as paraphrase-template arguments). We set the number of perceptron iterations (between 1 and 5) using a fraction of held-out training data. For the first perceptron iteration, we interactively trained the system by providing the set D^* in Figure 4.

Paralex: The authors of PARALEX provide a learned model.[9] We used PARALEX to parse questions to queries, and then execute them against the same KB as OQA. PARALEX provides a score for each query. For each answer that the query returns, we use the score from the query as a measure of confidence.

Sempre: The authors of SEMPRE also make it available for download.[10] SEMPRE comes with a model trained on the WebQuestions question set. We attempted to train SEMPRE with questions from TREC and WikiAnswers, but found that the WebQuestions model had higher performance on held-out development questions, so we use the WebQuestions model in our experiments.

10. EXPERIMENTAL RESULTS

Figure 5 shows the precision-recall curves comparing OQA under the two different training settings. Training the scoring function on questions from all three question sets resulted in higher precision and recall on TREC and WikiAnswers, but had no effect on WebQuestions performance. This is likely due to the fact that OQA is unable to derive correct answers for many of the questions in TREC and WikiAnswers, so the effective number of training examples is smaller than WebQuestions.

Figure 6 shows the precision-recall curves of OQA and PARALEX on the test questions. OQA achieves both higher precision and recall than PARALEX across all three question

[9]`http://knowitall.cs.washington.edu/paralex/`
[10]`https://github.com/percyliang/sempre`

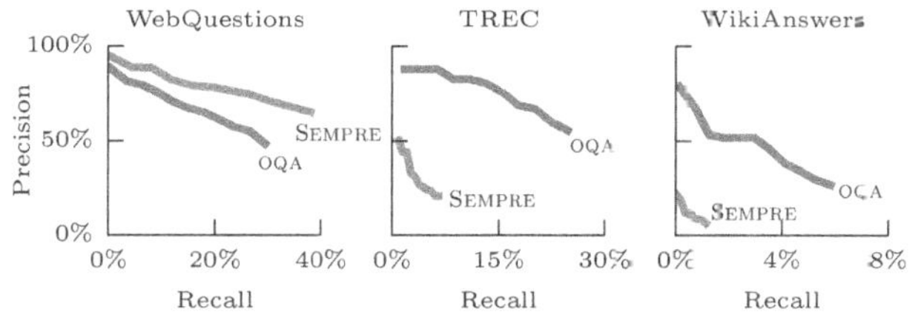

Figure 7: Sempre has higher precision and recall on WebQuestions, which are known to be answerable in Freebase. However, OQA outperforms Sempre on TREC and WikiAnswers, which were not developed for any particular KB.

sets. OQA's scoring function was able to avoid many of the errors made by PARALEX. For example, PARALEX made a systematic error confusing "Where" and "When" questions, *e.g.*, it was unable to tell that "1985" is an unlikely answer to a question that begins with "Where." In contrast, OQA was able to compute features of the full derivation (including the answer), which allowed it to learn not to make this type of error.

Figure 7 shows the precision-recall curves of OQA and SEMPRE on the test questions. In this case, SEMPRE is has higher precision and recall than OQA on WebQuestions. SEMPRE performs better on WebQuestions through its use of lexicalized features, *e.g.*, there is a single feature indicating that the string "see in" corresponds to the Freebase relation "tourist attraction." These features allow SEMPRE to better fit the distribution of relations and entities in WebQuestions. In contrast, OQA uses only unlexicalized features like POS tags and corpus statistics like PMI, which limit OQA's ability to fit the WebQuestions training data.

However, OQA performs significantly better on TREC and WikiAnswers for two reasons. First, OQA is uses both extracted and curated knowledge sources, so it is more likely to have an answer in its KB. Second, SEMPRE requires significant lexical overlap in its training and testing set, which is not satisfied in the TREC and WikiAnswers questions.

Figure 8 shows the effects of removing different components from OQA. The weight-learning algorithm significantly improves performance over the default weights defined in the experimental setup.

The paraphrase operators improve performance on WebQuestions and WikiAnswers, but not on TREC. We found that many TREC questions were covered by the parser operators in Table 2, so the paraphrase operators did not add much. In contrast, the WebQuestions and WikiAnswers questions exhibit much more lexical and syntactic variation, so the paraphrase operators were more useful.

The query-rewrite operators led to only a slight improvement on the TREC question set, and had at best no effect on WebQuestions and WikiAnswers. We examined the output and found some high-confidence examples where the query-rewrite operators helped, *e.g.*, the question "When did the Big Dig begin?" was answered by rewriting "(big dig, begin in, ?x)" to "(big dig, broke ground in, ?x)." However, most derivations that used a query-rewrite operator were assigned low confidence, and had limited effect on recall.

Figure 9 shows the effects of removing a knowledge source from OQA on system performance. Removing Open IE from the KB lowers the F1 score across all test sets. Freebase

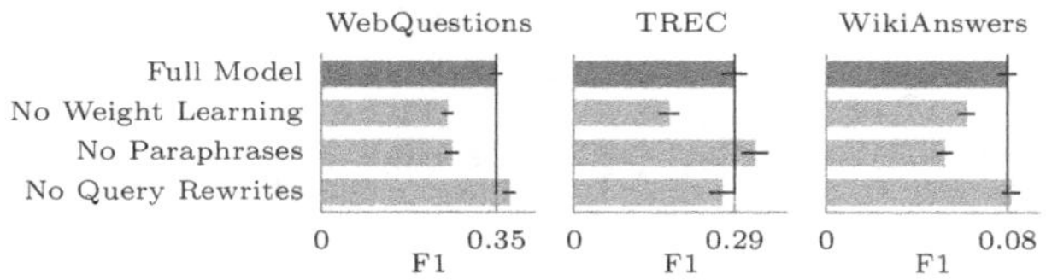

Figure 8: The relative contributions of each system component depend on the distribution of test questions. (Error bars represent one standard deviation from the mean, computed over 10,000 bootstrap samples of test data.)

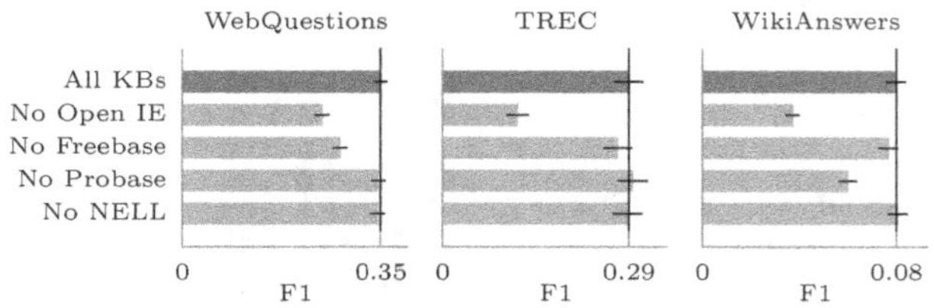

Figure 9: OQA performs best using multiple knowledge sources, in particular Open IE, Freebase, and Probase.

helps the most on the WebQuestions set (which was designed specifically for Freebase), but is less useful for TREC and WikiAnswers. Probase is most useful for WikiAnswers, which contains many "What is..." questions that can be answered using Probase's is-a relations. NELL is largely a subset of the other KBs, so it had no effect on OQA's performance.

11. DISCUSSION

The experimental results in the previous section exemplify the power-generality tradeoff discussed in the introduction: OQA uses a small number of general, unlexicalized features, which provided better generalization. However, this limits OQA's ability to take full advantage of the training data. For example, OQA was unable to answer questions like "What time zone is in South Africa have?" despite seeing several nearly-identical questions in the WebQuestions training data. A challenge for the future is to engineer OQA to take advantage of lexical cues when they are available. Extending OQA to induce higher-precision operators during discriminative training may be one way.

One problem that has gone unaddressed by all of the discussed QA systems is modeling whether a given question is answerable with the given KB and operators. For example, OQA currently has no way to answer truth-false questions like "Are dogs mammals?" Yet OQA systematically chains low-confidence operators together to derive incorrect answers for them, which hurts precision. A measure of answerability would be useful in scenarios where high-precision is required.

Table 6 shows examples from the test data where OQA derives correct answers. The first example shows a query rewrite operator that modifies the relation "marry" to "has wife." The second example shows a paraphrase operator that maps "What are _ made of?" to "What material are _ made of?" In this case, the paraphrase operator introduces a type constraint that does not appear in the input question,

Operator	State
Input	Who did Michael J Fox marry?
Parse	?x: (Michael J Fox, marry, ?x)
Rewrite	?x: (Michael J Fox, has wife, ?x)
Execute	**Tracy Pollan:** (Michael J. Fox, has wife, Tracy Pollan)
Input	What are brake pads made of?
Paraphrase	What material are brake pads made of?
Parse	?x: (?x, is-a, material) (brake pads, made of, ?x)
Execute	**copper:** (copper, is-a, material) (The brake pads, were made of, copper)
Input	What are some examples of building maintenance jobs?
Parse	?x: (?x, example of, building maintenance jobs)
Rewrite	?x: (?x, is-a, building maintenance jobs)
Execute	**changing light bulb:** (changing light bulb, is-a, small building maintenance job)

Table 6: Examples from the test data where OQA derives a correct answer.

Operator	State
Input	What animal represents California?
Paraphrase	What are California's symbols?
Parse	?x: (california, symbols, ?x)
Execute	**CWT:** (California Water Service, Trading symbol, CWT)
Input	Who did George Washington admire?
Parse	?x: (George Washington, admire, ?x)
Execute	**presidents and generals:** (George Washington, was admired by, presidents and generals)

Table 7: Example derivations from the test data where OQA derives an incorrect answer.

which is beneficial for selecting the correct answer. The third example highlights the benefit of extracted knowledge, which contains obscure assertions like "(changing light bulb, is-a, small building maintenance job)."

Table 7 shows examples where OQA derives incorrect answers. The first example shows that the paraphrase operators can be too general, in this case overgeneralizing "animal" to "symbol." This combines with "California Water Service" incorrectly matching "California," resulting in the incorrect answer "CWT." The second example shows that better features are needed to prevent errors like matching an active voice ("admire") with the passive voice ("was admired by").

12. CONCLUSION

We introduced OQA, a novel Open QA system that is the first to leverage both curated and extracted knowledge. We described inference and learning algorithms that OQA uses to derive high-confidence answers. Our experiments demonstrate that OQA generalizes well to unseen questions and makes significant improvements over a state-of-the-art Open

QA baseline. The data and code for this work is available at `https://github.com/afader/oqa`.

Acknowledgements

This research was supported in part by ONR grant N00014-11-1-0294, DARPA contract FA8750-13-2-0019, and ARO grant W911NF-13-1-0246, and was carried out at the University of Washington's Turing Center.

13. REFERENCES

[1] M. Banko, E. Brill, S. Dumais, and J. Lin. AskMSR: Question answering using the worldwide web. In *2002 AAAI Spring Symposium on Mining Answers from Texts and Knowledge Bases*, 2002.

[2] M. Banko, M. J. Cafarella, S. Soderland, M. Broadhead, and O. Etzioni. Open Information Extraction from the Web. In *IJCAI*, 2007.

[3] J. Berant, A. Chou, R. Frostig, and P. Liang. Semantic parsing on Freebase from question-answer pairs. In *EMNLP*, 2013.

[4] Q. Cai and A. Yates. Large-scale Semantic Parsing via Schema Matching and Lexicon Extension. In *ACL*, 2013.

[5] A. Carlson, J. Betteridge, B. Kisiel, B. Settles, E. H. Jr., and T. Mitchell. Toward an architecture for never-ending language learning. In *AAAI*, 2010.

[6] A. K. Chandra and P. M. Merlin. Optimal implementation of conjunctive queries in relational data bases. In *STOC*, 1977.

[7] J. Clarke, D. Goldwasser, M.-W. Chang, and D. Roth. Driving Semantic Parsing from the World's Response. In *CoNLL*, 2010.

[8] A. Doan, A. Y. Halevy, and Z. G. Ives. *Principles of Data Integration*. Morgan Kaufmann, 2012.

[9] A. Fader, S. Soderland, and O. Etzioni. Identifying relations for open information extraction. In *EMNLP*, 2011.

[10] A. Fader, L. Zettlemoyer, and O. Etzioni. Paraphrase-Driven Learning for Open Question Answering. In *ACL*, 2013.

[11] Y. Freund and R. E. Schapire. Large margin classification using the perceptron algorithm. *Mach. Learn.*, 37(3):277–296, 1999.

[12] B. J. Grosz, D. E. Appelt, P. A. Martin, and F. C. N. Pereira. TEAM: An Experiment in the Design of Transportable Natural-Language Interfaces. *Artificial Intelligence*, 32(2):173–243, 1987.

[13] B. Katz. Annotating the World Wide Web using Natural Language. In *RIAO*, pages 136–159, 1997.

[14] P. Koehn. Pharaoh: A beam search decoder for phrase-based statistical machine translation models. In *AMTA*, Lecture Notes in Computer Science, pages 115–124. Springer, 2004.

[15] T. Kwiatkowski, E. Choi, Y. Artzi, and L. Zettlemoyer. Scaling semantic parsers with on-the-fly ontology matching. In *EMNLP*, 2013.

[16] C. Kwok, O. Etzioni, and D. S. Weld. Scaling question answering to the web. *ACM Trans. Inf. Syst.*, 19(3):242–262, 2001.

[17] P. Liang, A. Bouchard-Côté, D. Klein, and B. Taskar. An end-to-end discriminative approach to machine translation. In *ACL*, 2006.

[18] P. Liang, M. Jordan, and D. Klein. Learning Dependency-Based Compositional Semantics. In *ACL*, 2011.

[19] D. Lin and P. Pantel. DIRT – Discovery of inference rules from text. In *KDD*, 2001.

[20] T. Lin, Mausam, and O. Etzioni. Entity linking at web scale. AKBC-WEKEX, 2012.

[21] M. Mintz, S. Bills, R. Snow, and D. Jurafsky. Distant Supervision for Relation Extraction Without Labeled Data. In *ACL*, 2009.

[22] X. Sun, T. Matsuzaki, D. Okanohara and J. Tsujii. Latent variable perceptron algorithm for structured classification. In *IJCAI*, 2009.

[23] C. Unger, L. Bühmann, J. Lehmann, A.-C. N. Ngomo, D. Gerber, and P. Cimiano. Template-Based Question Answering over RDF Data. In *WWW*, 2012.

[24] E. M. Voorhees and D. M. Tice. Building a question answering test collection. In *SIGIR*, 2000.

[25] S. Walter, C. Unger, P. Cimiano, and D. Bär. Evaluation of a Layered Approach to Question Answering over Linked Data. In *ISWC*, 2012.

[26] Y. W. Wong and R. J. Mooney. Learning synchronous grammars for semantic parsing with lambda calculus. In *ACL*, 2007.

[27] W. Wu, H. Li, H. Wang, and K. Q. Zhu. Probase: a probabilistic taxonomy for text understanding. In *SIGMOD*, 2012.

[28] M. Yahya, K. Berberich, S. Elbassuoni, M. Ramanath, V. Tresp, and G. Weikum. Natural Language Questions for the Web of Data. In *EMNLP*, 2012.

[29] A. Yates and O. Etzioni. Unsupervised methods for determining object and relation synonyms on the web. *JAIR*, 34:255–296, March 2009.

[30] J. M. Zelle and R. J. Mooney. Learning to Parse Database Queries Using Inductive Logic Programming. In *AAAI*, 1996.

[31] L. S. Zettlemoyer and M. Collins. Learning to Map Sentences to Logical Form: Structured Classification with Probabilistic Categorial Grammars. In *UAI*, 2005.

Non-Parametric Scan Statistics for Event Detection and Forecasting in Heterogeneous Social Media Graphs

Feng Chen
Department of Computer Science
State University of New York at Albany
fchen5@albany.edu

Daniel B. Neill
H.J. Heinz III College
Carnegie Mellon University
neill@cs.cmu.edu

ABSTRACT

Event detection in social media is an important but challenging problem. Most existing approaches are based on burst detection, topic modeling, or clustering techniques, which cannot naturally model the implicit heterogeneous network structure in social media. As a result, only limited information, such as terms and geographic locations, can be used. This paper presents Non-Parametric Heterogeneous Graph Scan (NPHGS), a new approach that considers the entire heterogeneous network for event detection: we first model the network as a "sensor" network, in which each node senses its "neighborhood environment" and reports an empirical p-value measuring its current level of anomalousness for each time interval (e.g., hour or day). Then, we efficiently maximize a nonparametric scan statistic over connected subgraphs to identify the most anomalous network clusters. Finally, the event represented by each cluster is summarized with information such as type of event, geographical locations, time, and participants. As a case study, we consider two applications using Twitter data, civil unrest event detection and rare disease outbreak detection, and present empirical evaluations illustrating the effectiveness and efficiency of our proposed approach.

Categories and Subject Descriptors

H.2.8 [**Database Management**]: Database Applications—*Data Mining*

Keywords

Non-Parametric Scan Statistics; Event Detection and Forecasting; Social Media; Heterogeneous Graphs

1. INTRODUCTION

Social microblogs such as Twitter and Weibo are experiencing explosive growth, with billions of users globally sharing their daily observations and thoughts online. Unlike traditional channels, where collection of information such as patient data, crimes, and financial transactions is costly and time consuming, social media provides the vast amount of data available in real time on the internet at almost no cost. Social media also helps spread information earlier and faster than traditional media. For example, Twitter first leaked credible word of Osama bin Laden's death before President Obama's announcement, and there were a half million tweets (and only 800 news mentions) one hour after the event [1]. As a social "sensor" which can identify emerging patterns in sentiments and opinions, the use of social media holds great promise for detection and forecasting of significant societal events.

However, the size and complexity of social media datasets create a number of technical challenges. First, the language used in social media is highly informal, ungrammatical, and dynamic, and thus traditional natural language processing (NLP) techniques cannot be directly applied. Second, social media is naturally structured as a heterogeneous graph, with entities such as user, post, geographic location, term, hashtag, and link; and relationships such as follower, friendship, reply, retweet, and spatial neighborhood. In addition, the attributes of each entity type could be heterogeneous as well. For example, a user may have daily attributes such as the numbers of active followers, posts, and retweets, while a tweet may have attributes such as the number of terms and the sentiment score. Finally, the size of data necessitates development of new, scalable detection methods.

This paper focuses on the problem of domain-specific event detection and forecasting, for events such as disease outbreaks, civil unrests, and financial crises. Most existing approaches to event detection can be classified into three categories, including burst detection, geographic topic modeling, and clustering. **Burst detection**-based approaches search for space-time regions where the aggregated counts of some predefined terms are abnormally high compared with the counts outside the regions [9, 10, 13]. Sakaki et al. consider spatial-temporal Kalman filtering, which is similar to space-time burst detection, to track the geographical trajectory of hot spots of tweets related to earthquakes [19]. **Geographic topic model**-based approaches estimate language distributions (over a predefined vocabulary) that are distinct in some geographic regions [25, 11, 8]. **Clustering**-based approaches search for novel clusters of documents or terms using predefined similarity metrics, such as cosine similarity and social similarity for documents [22], or autocorrelations [24] and co-occurrences [20, 23] for terms. Similarly, [21] uses features related to text content and link information to cluster tweets. For each cluster identified, the re-

KDD'14, August 24–27, 2014, New York, NY, USA.
Copyright 2014 ACM 978-1-4503-2956-9/14/08 ...$15.00.
http://dx.doi.org/10.1145/2623330.2623619.

lated documents may have different geographical locations, which can be combined by weighted voting [22].

We note that these domain-specific event detection approaches differ in focus from general-domain event detection methods such as RW-Event [3], which attempt to distinguish events from non-event patterns (such as memes) rather than identifying events of a specific type. Such methods do not use content of tweets but only features such as temporal trends of term volume, rely on a large amount of labeled training data (as opposed to the unsupervised problem we consider here), and require extensive parameter tuning.

Each of the aforementioned methods only exploits partial information from social media that is useful for event detection. However, there is very limited work that is able to model the entire social media graph for event detection, due to the computational challenge of modeling the complicated heterogeneous relationships between entities and attributes, and the risk of overfitting [6]. Our approach, described below, incorporates three types of heterogeneity in the social media graph, including heterogeneous 1) entity types; 2) entity attributes; and 3) entity relationships. In addition, the highly informal, ungrammatical, and dynamic language used in social media motivates our use of nonparametric statistical models to provide more accurate detection and forecasting [18].

To address the above technical challenges, we propose a Non-Parametric Heterogeneous Graph Scan (NPHGS) approach for event detection and forecasting using social media data. We attempt to consider all potentially useful information in social media in a unified nonparametric statistical framework, to facilitate the early detection and accurate forecasting of societal events. Specifically, we first model a heterogeneous graph, in which: 1) each node can be of different types, such as user, tweet, geographic location, and hashtag; 2) the relationships between nodes can be of different types, such as retweet, reply, and follower; and 3) each node type can have different attributes, such as the numbers of tweets and users for a given geographic location; the numbers of followers, tweets, and retweets for a given user; and the number of terms and the sentiment score for a given tweet. Second, we further model the network as a "sensor" network, in which each node senses its "neighborhood environment" and reports an empirical p-value measuring the current anomalousness levels of various neighborhood-related attributes. Third, we efficiently maximize a nonparametric scan statistic over connected subgraphs to identify the most anomalous network clusters. Each cluster is returned as the indicator of an ongoing or upcoming event, and is summarized with information such as type of event, geographic locations, time, and participants. The main contributions of our study are summarized as follows:

- **Formulation of the NPHGS framework**. To the best of our knowledge, this is the first work that models the whole heterogeneous social media graph as a "sensor" network, enabling the use of novel, nonparametric graph scan statistics for accurate and scalable event detection and forecasting.
- **Design of two-stage empirical p-value calibration process.** The heterogeneity of different node types and node attributes, and the correlations between different attributes of a node, are well addressed by calibrating all node types and attributes on the same scale using the proposed two-stage empirical calibration process.
- **Development of an approximate algorithm for non-parametric graph scanning.** The nonparametric scan statistic over connected subgraphs is approximately maximized by iterative subgraph expansion and linear time subset scanning, with time complexity $O(|\mathcal{V}| \log |\mathcal{V}|)$, where $|\mathcal{V}|$ refers to the total number of graph nodes.
- **Evaluation of theoretical properties**: Our proposed approximate algorithm is guaranteed to find the globally optimal solution if the data contains no "breaktire" entities (see Subsection 3.3), and is equivalent to percolation-based graph scan under certain simplifying assumptions.
- **Comprehensive experiments to validate the effectiveness and efficiency of the proposed techniques**. NPHGS was evaluated by extensive experiments on real Twitter datasets. The results demonstrate that NPHGS outperforms existing representative techniques for both event detection and forecasting, increasing detection power, forecasting accuracy, and forecasting lead time while reducing time to detection.

The rest of this paper is organized as follows. Section 2 discusses heterogeneous graph modeling for social media, and considers Twitter data as a case study. Section 3 proposes nonparametric scan statistics for heterogeneous graphs. Experiments on real Twitter datasets are presented in Section 4, and Section 5 describes future work.

2. HETEROGENEOUS GRAPH MODELING

A heterogeneous graph is composed of nodes, attributes, and relations that could be of multiple different types. The formal definition of a heterogeneous graph is as follows:

DEFINITION 1 (HETEROGENEOUS GRAPH). *A heterogeneous graph is defined as a directed graph $\mathcal{G} = (\mathcal{V}, \mathcal{E}, f, \psi)$ where $\mathcal{V} = \{\mathcal{V}_1 \cup \cdots \cup \mathcal{V}_C\}$, $\mathcal{V}_c$ refers to the set of entities of type c, C refers to the total number of entity types, $\mathcal{E} \subseteq \mathcal{V} \times \mathcal{V}$ refers to the set of edges, $f = \{f_1 \ldots f_C\}$ is a set of C mapping functions, $f_c : \mathcal{V} \rightarrow \mathcal{R}^{D_c}$ defines a D_c-dimensional feature vector $(f_c(v))$ for each node v of type c, ψ refers to a mapping function such that each $e \in \mathcal{E}$ belongs to a particular type of relation $\psi(e) \in \{1 \ldots Q\}$, and Q refers to the number of different relation types.*

Throughout the paper, we consider the detection of civil unrest events and rare disease outbreaks using Twitter data as a case study. For this application, we assume that a heterogeneous graph $\mathcal{G} = (\mathcal{V}, \mathcal{E}, f, \psi)$ has been extracted from the Twitter data. Additionally, we assume historical data $f_c(v^{(t)})$ (for $t = 1 \ldots T$), corresponding to each feature vector $f_c(v)$, which will be used to estimate the anomalousness of the current feature values. Given these data, we will return the most anomalous connected sub-graphs $\max_{S \subseteq \mathcal{V}} F(S)$, where F is the nonparametric heterogeneous graph scan statistic defined below. Our goal is to identify subsets S corresponding to events of interest, as given by a separate gold standard dataset and as measured by the performance metrics defined in Section 4.

The selected set of entity types includes User, Location, Term, Tweet, Link, and Hashtag. The selected entity relation types and entity attributes are summarized in Figure 1 and Table 1. The sentiment (polarity) score was calculated using the python sentiment analysis package named "Pattern" [27]. The klout score [28] is an overall measure of the tweet author's influence on a scale from 1 to 100. It is assumed that domain-specific content filtering has been conducted as a preprocessing step, and the majority of unrelated tweets have been removed. In our study, domain-specific dictionaries for civil unrest events and hantavirus outbreaks were obtained from domain experts, and tweets that match less than three terms in the dictionary were removed. More complicated content filtering techniques can be applied, such as the training of a SVM classifier [19]. We note that identical pre-processing steps were applied for all methods in our experiments below, and we do not expect the relative performance of methods to be strongly dependent on this pre-processing.

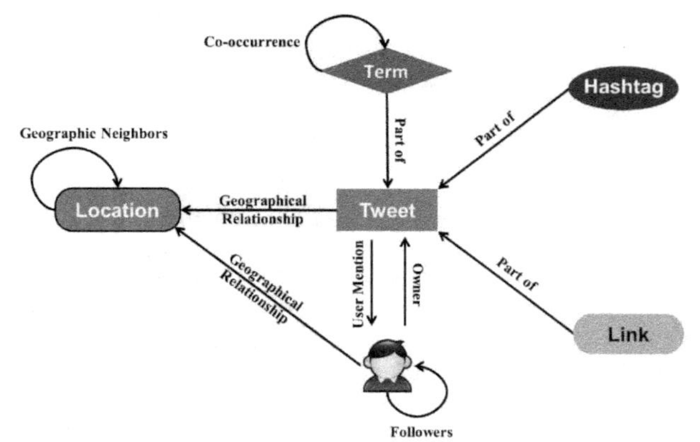

Figure 1: Entity Diagram for Twitter Data Modeling

Node Type	Features Used
User	#tweets, #retweets, #active-followers, #active-followees, #mentions, #replies
Tweet	klout, sentiment, replied-by-graph-size, reply-graph-size, retweet-graph-size, retweet-graph-depth
State	#tweets, #active-users
Term	#tweets
Link	#tweets
Hashtag	#tweets

Table 1: Twitter Node Attributes

3. NON-PARAMETRIC SCAN STATISTICS FOR HETEROGENEOUS GRAPHS

This section presents non-parametric scan statistics for heterogeneous social media graphs. Specifically, Subsection 3.1 discusses the modeling of the heterogeneous graph as a "sensor" network by estimating an empirical p-value

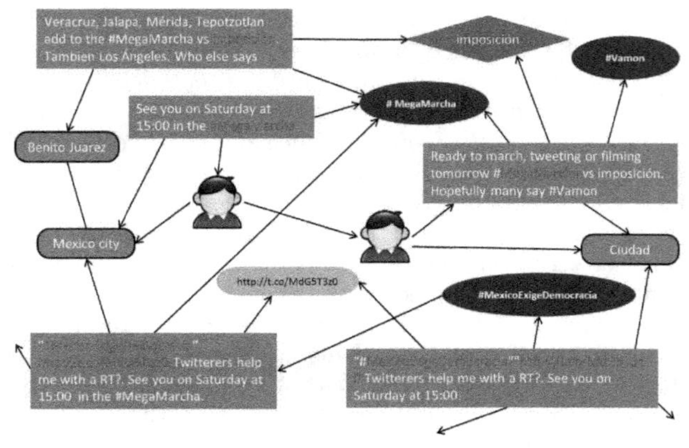

Figure 2: An Example of Twitter Heterogeneous Network

for each graph node; Subsection 3.2 presents nonparametric scan statistics; and Subsection 3.3 presents an efficient approximate algorithm that maximizes the nonparametric scan statistic over connected subgraphs to identify the most anomalous graph clusters, which can be regarded as indicators of ongoing or new events.

3.1 Two-Stage Empirical Calibration Process

To deal with the heterogeneity of node attributes for different entity types, we propose to model the heterogeneous graph as a "sensor" network. Each entity senses its local "neighborhood" in the graph and reports measurements of some predefined features. For event detection, it is necessary to estimate a baseline distribution for each attribute that characterizes its behavior when there is no event occurring. Given these baseline distributions, it is then possible to estimate an *empirical p-value* representing the degree of anomalousness for each node. This empirical p-value can be regarded as the signal strength of the node's current attribute values as an indicator of some ongoing or newly emerging event.

In order to estimate the baseline distribution of each attribute for each entity, the key component is to collect a good training sample for distribution estimation. We first define an appropriate time granularity for event detection (e.g., hourly, daily, or weekly). We then collect a set of historical observations for each entity and attribute. We consider three scenarios:

- **Entities with sufficient observations**: For Twitter data, these include locations, regular users, and existing keywords, hashtags, and links.
- **Entities with insufficient observations**: For Twitter data, these include new users and newly occurring keywords, hashtags, and links.
- **Entities with single observations**: For Twitter data, the related entities mainly include tweets.

For the first category of entities, it is possible to collect enough historical records for that specific entity to estimate its baseline distribution. For example, if a given user, who has used Twitter for more than a month, tweeted 100 times today, that value would be compared to her daily numbers of tweets in historical data. For the second and third categories, there are not sufficient historical observations available for each entity. In this situation, we consider all historical records of the same entity type as the training sample, calibrated based on time since first occurrence. For example, if a given tweet is retweeted 50 times on the third day since its creation, that value would be compared to the numbers of retweets for *all* tweets on their third day.

Once the set of historical observations $\{v^{(1)}, \ldots, v^{(T)}\}$ is defined for a given node v, we can then compute the empirical p-values $p_d(v)$ for each attribute of node v, and an overall empirical p-value $p(v)$ for node v, by comparing the current and historical attribute values. Here we assume one-tailed p-values, which answer the question: under the null hypothesis that no events of interest are occurring, what is the probability that a randomly selected sample would have an observed value greater than or equal to the current observation. (The proposed approach can be easily extended to incorporate two-tailed p-values as well.) For *empirical* p-values, we assume that the set of historical observations represent the null distribution of interest, thus testing the null hypothesis of exchangeability of past and current observations. The empirical p-value of a specific feature d for a node v of type c is defined as:

$$p_d(v) = \frac{1}{T}\sum_{t=1}^{T} I\left(f_{c,d}(v^{(t)}) \geq f_{c,d}(v)\right), d = 1 \ldots D_c, \quad (1)$$

where $f_{c,d}(v)$ refers to the d-th component of the feature vector $f_c(v)$. The empirical value $p_d(v)$ defined above can be interpreted as the proportion of historical observations $f_{c,d}^{(t)}(v)$ when there was no event occurring with observed values that are greater than or equal to the current observation $f_{c,d}(v)$. The empirical p-value of node v is then defined as:

$$p(v) = \frac{1}{T}\sum_{t=1}^{T} I\left(\min_{d=1\ldots D_c} p_d(v^{(t)}) \leq \min_{d=1\ldots D_c} p_d(v)\right). \quad (2)$$

The proposed two-stage empirical p-value p(v) has the nice theoretical property of uniformity as shown in Theorem 1:

THEOREM 1 (UNIFORMITY OF P(V)). *The two-stage empirical p-value $p(v)$ defined by Equations (1) and (2) follows a uniform distribution on [0,1] under the assumption that the current multivariate observations for a single node are exchangeable with the reference set given the null hypothesis that no events of interest are occurring.*

PROOF. The assumption of exchangeability of multivariate observations for a single node implies that each feature's observations are exchangeable with the reference set, so that the first-stage p-values are uniform on [0,1]. Moreover, the features of a node are assumed to have the same correlation structure as the reference set, so the minimum of the first-stage p-values is exchangeable with the corresponding minima in the reference set; and thus the second-stage p-values are uniform on [0,1]. □

The challenge of heterogeneity of different node types and node attributes is well addressed from the following three perspectives: First, it deals with network heterogeneity by calibrating all node types on the same scale, such that all p-values $p(v)$ are drawn uniformly on [0,1] under the null hypothesis that no events of interest are occurring. Second, it allows us to consider multiple attributes for a single User, Tweet, or State node without knowing *a priori* which ones will be most indicative of the events of interest. Finally, it accounts for correlation between the first-stage empirical p-values $p_d(v)$ when computing the overall empirical p-value $p(v)$.

To better understand the advantages of our proposed two-stage solution, we briefly compare it to two alternative approaches. First, we could have simply used a one-stage calibration process where the feature-level p-values $p_d(v)$ are passed directly into the nonparametric scan statistic described below. The nonparametric scan computes the score $F(S)$ of a subgraph S as a function of the number of p-values in S which are significant at level α and the total number of p-values in S. However, we expect the p-values for the various features of a given node to be highly correlated. As a result, the one-stage calibration process would be biased toward detecting nodes with more features. For example, suppose that nodes of type 1 have 100 redundant (fully correlated) features, while nodes of type 2 have only a single feature. In this case, a node of type 1 with all 100 p-values equal to .05 would have a much higher score (given one-stage calibration) than a node of type 2 with p-value equal to .05. The two-stage calibration correctly accounts for the correlation structure and would give both nodes the same score.

A second alternative approach would be to define $p(v)$ as the minimum p-value $\min_{d=1\ldots D_c} p_d(v)$ without re-calibrating the significance of $p(v)$ using the historical data. Clearly this naive approach does not account for multiple hypothesis testing; it can be readily proved that this estimator does not follow a uniform distribution under the null and is biased, tending to underestimate the empirical p-value. For example, if 100 p-values for a node were independently drawn from [0,1], we would expect the minimum p-value to be less than $\alpha = .05$ with probability $1-(1-0.05)^{100} = 0.994$. Moreover, the naive approach would again be biased toward giving higher scores to nodes with more features, since the minimum p-value can only be decreased (made more significant) by adding features. Re-calibrating using the historical data in our two-stage process correctly adjusts for this bias. Finally, we note that our two-stage process is sufficiently flexible so that other p-value combination methods (such as Fisher's method) could easily have been used in Equation 2 instead of the minimum p-value, while still satisfying Theorem 1.

3.2 Non-Parametric Scan Statistics

As described above, we obtain a "sensor" network $\mathcal{H} = (\mathcal{V}, \mathcal{E}, p)$ that is the same as the heterogeneous graph $\mathcal{G}$, except that the mapping function $p : \mathcal{V} \rightarrow [0, 1]$ now defines a single empirical p-value corresponding to each node v of the heterogeneous network. Note that the mapping function ψ has been removed: all relation types will be treated identically in the discussion below.

To determine which connected subgraphs are most anomalous, we generalize the nonparametric scan statistic [17], which extends Kulldorff's spatial scan [12] and was originally proposed for modeling spatial-temporal count data, to heterogeneous graphs. The nonparametric scan has also been used for anomalous pattern detection in general categorical datasets [14], but we note that the present work is the first work to generalize nonparametric scan statistic to heterogeneous graphs, requiring both the novel two-stage calibration procedure described above (to obtain p-values) and the novel graph scan algorithm described below (to identify subgraphs with surprisingly high numbers of low, significant p-values). Ignoring the graph constraints as in [14] leads to the identification of unconnected subsets consisting of unrelated, individually anomalous nodes from different parts of the heterogeneous network, resulting in substantially reduced detection performance.

The general form of the proposed Non-Parametric Heterogeneous Graph Scan (NPHGS) statistic is defined as:

$$F(S) = \max_{\alpha \leq \alpha_{max}} F_\alpha(S) = \max_{\alpha \leq \alpha_{max}} \phi(\alpha, N_\alpha(S), N(S)), \quad (3)$$

where $S \subseteq \mathcal{V}$ refers to a connected set of nodes, $N_\alpha(S) = \sum_{v \in S} I(p(v) \leq \alpha)$ is the number of p-values significant at level α, and $N(S) = \sum_{v \in S} 1$ is the total number of p-values in subset S. The significance level α can be optimized between 0 and some constant $\alpha_{max} < 1$. The function $\phi(\alpha, N_\alpha(S), N(S))$ refers to a nonparametric scan statistic, i.e., a function that compares the observed number of p-values N_α that are significant at level α to the expected number of significant p-values $E[N_\alpha(S)] = \alpha N(S)$, under the null hypothesis that p-values are uniformly distributed on $[0, 1]$. In this work, we explore the use of one nonparametric scan statistic $\phi(\alpha, N_\alpha(S), N(S))$: the Berk-Jones (BJ) statistic [4]. The BJ statistic is defined as:

$$\phi_{BJ}(\alpha, N_\alpha(S), N(S)) = N \times \mathrm{KL}\left(\frac{N_\alpha}{N}, \alpha\right), \quad (4)$$

where KL is the Kullback-Liebler divergence between the observed and expected proportions of p-values less than α:

$$\mathrm{KL}(a, b) = a \log\left(\frac{a}{b}\right) + (1-a) \log\left(\frac{1-a}{1-b}\right).$$

The BJ statistic can be interpreted as the log-likelihood ratio statistic for testing whether the empirical p-values follow a uniform or piecewise constant distribution. Berk and Jones [4] demonstrated that this statistic fulfills several optimality properties and has greater power than any weighted Kolmogorov statistic.

It is important to consider a range of α in NPHGS, rather than a single threshold for significance. For a fixed α such as $\alpha = 0.05$, the resulting statistic may lose the power to detect a small number of highly anomalous p-values (much smaller than 0.05) or a larger number of subtly anomalous p-values (slightly greater than 0.05). The selection of α_{max} is in practice slightly greater than typical significance levels predefined by users; here we use $\alpha_{max} = 0.15$.

We note that the subsets of p-values identified by our algorithm are affected by multiple testing on two dimensions: we maximize $F(S)$ over subgraphs S and over thresholds $\alpha \leq \alpha_{max}$. To adjust for multiple testing and correctly measure the significance of the detected clusters, we could apply a permutation test, shuffling the temporal component of the data (assuming the null hypothesis of exchangeability), identifying the maximum subgraph score for each permuted sample, and finally comparing the detected cluster score to the distribution of maximum cluster scores for the permuted samples to obtain the p-value of the detected cluster.

3.3 Efficient Non-Parametric Scanning

Based on the proposed NPHGS statistic, the detection of the most anomalous connected subgraph from $\mathcal{V}$ can be formalized as the following optimization problem:

$$\max_{S \subseteq \mathcal{V}: S \text{ is connected}} \max_{\alpha \leq \alpha_{max}} \phi(\alpha, N_\alpha(S), N(S)). \quad (5)$$

It can be shown that the time cost of exact solution to the above optimization problem (5) is exponential in the total number of graph nodes $|\mathcal{V}|$ in the worst case. Therefore, it is necessary to develop approximate solutions. We first observe that it is possible to solve a relaxed version of this problem efficiently by removing the connectivity constraint. Note that we will use this efficient unconstrained optimization as a building block to solve the optimization problem with connectivity constraints. The relaxed problem is formalized as follows:

$$\max_{S \subseteq \mathcal{V}} \max_{\alpha \leq \alpha_{max}} \phi(\alpha, N_\alpha(S), N(S)), \quad (6)$$

which is equivalent to the problem:

$$\max_{\alpha \in U(\mathcal{V}, \alpha_{max})} \max_{S \subseteq \mathcal{V}} \phi(\alpha, N_\alpha(S), N(S)), \quad (7)$$

where $U(S, \alpha_{max})$ refers to the union of $\{\alpha_{max}\}$ and the set of distinct p-values less than α_{max} in S. Because the BJ scan statistic satisfies the linear time subset scanning (LTSS) property [16], the subproblem

$$\max_{S \subseteq \mathcal{V}} \phi(\alpha, N_\alpha(S), N(S)) \quad (8)$$

can be solved in $O(|\mathcal{V}|)$ time, assuming that the entities $v \in \mathcal{V}$ have already been sorted by priority. Specifically, the LTSS property guarantees that the only subsets S with the potential to be optimal are those consisting of the top-n highest priority nodes $\{v_{(1)}, \cdots, v_{(n)}\}$, for some n between 1 and $|\mathcal{V}|$. In this case, a lower (more significant) p-value corresponds to a higher priority. Therefore, the relaxed version (6) of the original problem (5) can be solved in the time complexity $O(|\mathcal{V}| \times |U(\mathcal{V}, \alpha_{max})| + |\mathcal{V}| \log |\mathcal{V}|)$, where the additional $|\mathcal{V}| \log |\mathcal{V}|$ is required to sort the entities by priority. Based on the computational efficiency of the relaxed problem, we propose an efficient approximate algorithm by targeted seeding, iterative subgraph expansion, and relaxation. The proposed algorithm, described in Algorithm 1, will return a connected subgraph of the heterogeneous graph that approximately maximizes the proposed non-parametric scan statistic.

The time complexity of Algorithm 1 is dominated by the computation of the relaxed problem (6) for the updated subgraph $S \cup G$ in each iteration of graph expansion. This computation must be performed at most $KCZ = KC \log |\mathcal{V}|$ times, each requiring $O(|\mathcal{V}| \times |U(\mathcal{V}, \alpha_{max})|)$ time assuming that nodes have already been sorted by priority. Here K is the number of seed entities considered for each of the C entity types, and Z is the number of iterative subgraph expansions performed for each seed entity. Computing the empirical p-values is $O(|\mathcal{V}| T \log T)$, and sorting the nodes by priority is $O(|\mathcal{V}| \log |\mathcal{V}|)$. Therefore, the total computational complexity equals $O(KC \times |U(\mathcal{V}, \alpha_{max})| \times |\mathcal{V}| \log |\mathcal{V}| + |\mathcal{V}| T \log T)$. Furthermore, we note that $|U(\mathcal{V}, \alpha_{max})|$ can be considered a constant, since only at most $\alpha_{max} T$ distinct p-values less than α_{max} will be generated by the empirical p-value estimation method described above, and thus the algorithm scales as $O(|\mathcal{V}| \log |\mathcal{V}|)$. For our civil unrest and

Algorithm 1 Non-Parametric Heterogeneous Graph Scan

Input: $\mathcal{G} = (\mathcal{V}, \mathcal{E}, f, \phi)$
Output: The most anomalous subgraph $S^\star$
Obtain "sensor" network $\mathcal{H} = (\mathcal{V}, \mathcal{E}, p)$ as above;
Set $\alpha_{max} = 0.15$, $K = 5$, $Z = \log |\mathcal{V}|$, and $S^\star = \emptyset$;
for $(k, c) \in [1, \cdots, K] \times [1, \cdots, C]$ **do**
  Select seed node v_0 from $\mathcal{V}_c$, where v_0 is the kth highest-priority node of that type;
  Set $S = \{v_0\}$;
  for $z \in [1, \cdots, Z]$ **do**
    Set $G = \{v \mid \exists e \in S, v \notin S, (v, e) \text{ or } (e, v) \in \mathcal{E}\}$;
    Obtain the highest-scoring subset $B \subseteq S \cup G$, where $S \subseteq B$, by solving the relaxed problem (6);
  end for
  if $B - S \neq \emptyset$ **then**
    Set $S = B$;
  else
    Break;
  end if
end for

rare disease detection experiments below, we have $\alpha_{max}T = (.15)(215) \approx 32$.

In addition to its computational efficiency, our proposed algorithm also has two nice theoretical properties, as follows

THEOREM 2 (OPTIMALITY). *Consider the simplified case in which we fix α instead of allowing α to vary between 0 and $\alpha_{\max}$. Let $S^\star = \arg\max_S F_\alpha(S)$ denote the optimal connected subgraph. Assume that K is set sufficiently large to select some $v \in S^\star$ as a seed entity, and Z is set greater than the diameter of $S^\star$. If $S^\star$ satisfies the property that there is no "break-tire" entity $v \in S^\star$ (i.e., a node v with p-value greater than α and whose deletion will break the connectivity of $S^\star$), then Algorithm 1 is guaranteed to identify the optimal connected subgraph $S^\star$.*

PROOF. The BJ scan statistic satisfies three intuitive properties: 1) monotonically increasing with respect to N_α; 2) monotonically decreasing with respect to N and α; and 3) convex. Therefore, if $S^\star$ contains no "break-tire" entities, we know that two properties hold: a) $S^\star$ consists entirely of p-values less than or equal to α, and b) no neighbor of $S^\star$ has p-value less than or equal to α. Property a) holds since any leaf node with p-value greater than α could be deleted without disconnecting $S^\star$, increasing the score. Property b) holds since any neighbor with p-value less than or equal to α could be added without disconnecting $S^\star$, increasing the score. Now, when $v \in S^\star$ is selected as a seed entity, each successive graph expansion will add all and only those neighbor entities with p-values less than or equal to α. If Z is greater than the diameter of $S^\star$, the iteration continues until no remaining neighbors have p-values less than or equal to α, at which point $S = S^\star$. Therefore Algorithm 1 is guaranteed to identify the optimal connected subgraph $S^\star$. □

Note that another popular nonparametric scan statistic, the Higher Criticism (HC) statistic [7], also satisfies the above three properties and Theorem 2 still holds. Our preliminary analysis (omitted due to space limitations) demonstrates that the BJ statistic outperforms the HC statistic for heterogeneous graphs and hence we focus on the BJ statistic for the remainder of our study. We also show an interesting connection to the percolation-based scan statistic defined by Arias-Castro et al. [2], which provides nice asymptotic decision-theoretical properties.

THEOREM 3 (PERCOLATION-BASED SCAN STATISTIC). *As in Theorem 1, we consider the simplified case with fixed α, and again assume that K and Z are set sufficiently large. Following [2], let $F_\alpha(S) = |S|$ if all p-values in S are less than or equal to α, and 0 otherwise. Algorithm 1 is guaranteed to find the optimal subgraph $S^\star = \arg\max_S F_\alpha(S)$.*

PROOF. As in Theorem 2, we know that two properties hold: a) $S^\star$ consists entirely of p-values less than or equal to α, and b) no neighbor of $S^\star$ has p-value less than or equal to α. Property a) holds since the inclusion of any p-value greater than α would reduce $F_\alpha(S)$ to zero. Property b) holds since any neighbor with p-value less than or equal to α could be added without disconnecting $S^\star$, increasing $F_\alpha(S)$ by 1. The remainder of our proof proceeds identically to the proof of Theorem 2; note that we do not need the additional assumption that no "break-tire" entities exist, since this follows directly from the definition of the percolation-based scan statistic $F_\alpha(S)$. □

Note that we have chosen to use the BJ nonparametric scan statistic because of its superior detection power, in comparison with other test statistics such as the percolation-based scan. Nevertheless, this theorem shows the applicability of our work to percolation-based approaches as well. The computational cost of maximizing BJ over connected subgraphs is high, but we have proposed an efficient, approximate algorithm to address this issue. The approximation quality has also been validated by extensive experiments on real-world datasets, as described below.

4. EXPERIMENTS

This section evaluates the effectiveness and efficiency of the proposed NPHGS approach based on comprehensive experiments on four countries' Twitter data. We considered the detection and forecasting of civil unrest events such as protests and strikes, and detection of rare disease (hantavirus) outbreaks as two case study scenarios, but the proposed techniques can also be directly applied to other applications, such as the detection and forecasting of human rights violations and financial crises.

4.1 Experiment Design

Datasets: We randomly collected ten percent of all the raw Twitter data from June 1, 2012 to June 30, 2013 across four countries: Argentina, Chile, Columbia, and Ecuador. Sampling was conducted at the tweet level, instead of user level. The civil unrest event labels, called Golden Standard Report (GSR), were collected and confirmed from the local newspapers that are accessible from internet. The collected tweet volume, news sources, and number of civil unrest events reported for each country are summarized in Table 2. An example of a labeled GSR event is: (PROVINCE = "El Loa", COUNTRY = "Chile", DATE = "2012-05-18", TITLE = "A large-scale march was staged by inhabitants of the northern city of Calama, considered the mining capital of Chile, who demand the allocation of more resources to copper mining cities", NEWS-LINK = "http://www.pressenza.c

om/2012/05/march-of-dignity-in-mining-capital-of-chile/"). For rare disease outbreaks, we considered hantavirus outbreaks in Chile as a case study, because there was a spread of hantavirus outbreaks there last year that greatly threatened public safety and stability. The outbreak labels were reported by Chilean Ministry of Health [26] and local news reports. Specifically, there were 17 rare Hantavirus disease outbreaks in more than eight different states from January 1, 2013 to June 30, 2013. We post-processed both the civil unrest and the disease outbreak data to create binary variables representing whether or not a GSR event occurred in each province (state) for each date.

Country	# tweets	News sources	# events
Argentina	48 million	Clarin; La Nacion; Infobae	302
Chile	25 million	La Tercera; Las Ultimas Noticias; El Mercurio	216
Colombia	37 million	El Espectador; El Tiempo; El Colombiano	251
Ecuador	12 million	El Universo; El Comercio; Hoy	149

Table 2: Description of civil unrest data by country

Data Preprocessing: After we collected the raw tweets, several preprocessing steps were conducted for our proposed approach and all the comparison methods, including:

1) **Vocabulary Generation**: We first generated a vocabulary of ~1000 terms related to civil unrests and a vocabulary of 25 terms related to hantavirus from domain experts;

2) **Content Filtering**: Only the raw tweets that match more than two terms from the vocabulary were preserved;

3) **Tweet Geocoding**: We implemented a geocoding library for tweets based on three major rules with priorities. For each tweet, we first searched for location and landmark mentions in the tweet text, then for geotags that are available if the user enabled the geocoding function in his/her phone, and finally for location information from the user's profile. The first location information identified was returned as the geographic location of this tweet.

Comparison Methods: We compared our proposed NPHGS approach with five existing representative methods, including Spatio-Temporal (ST) Burst Detection [13], Graph Partition [24], Earthquake Detection [19], Real-World (RW) Event Identification [3], and Geographic Topic Modeling [25]. The first method returns an alert for each spatio-temporal burst that is detected. The second method applies wavelet analysis to build signals for individual words, and then clusters the signals based on their auto-correlations using modularity based graph partitioning. Each cluster is returned as an alert, with the most frequent location in the related tweets identified as the event location. The third method classifies tweets based on predefined features, and develops a probabilistic spatiotemporal model to identify the geographic center and date of the event. The fourth method considers the framework of online clustering for event detection, but designs a new similarity function in order to capture features related to time, topical coherence, and social interactions. The fifth method detects geographic topics day by day, each of which is returned as an alert.

Implementations of the first and the fifth methods were obtained from the authors, the second method was replicated under the authors' instructions, and the other two methods were implemented based on the published papers [3, 19]. We strictly followed the strategies recommended by the authors in their papers to select features and estimated the related model parameters. Specifically, the parameters of Earthquake Detection, Graph Partition, and Spatio-Temporal Burst Detection were trained using cross validation. The Twitter data from June 2012 to December 2012 were used as training data, data from January 2013 to April 2013 were considered as the test dataset for the detection and forecasting of civil unrest events, and data from January 1, 2013 to June 30, 2013 were considered as the test dataset for the detection and forecasting of rare disease outbreaks. As an unsupervised approach, the geographic topic model has two major parameters, including the numbers of geographic regions and topics. These two parameters were predefined based on our interpretation of the data distribution. Given the statistics of GSR event labels, the numbers of cities with high frequencies of civil unrest events in the four countries are mostly smaller than 20. The two parameters were set to 20 and 2, respectively. RW-Event has a number of parameters, including the number of most frequent cluster terms, the parameters related to the incremental clustering algorithm, and the parameters related to the classification model used. In our implementation, we considered linear weighted support vector machine (SVM) to handle the issue of unbalanced class labels. We used 10-fold cross validation to identify the best combination of all the related parameters.

Our NPHGS and Baseline Homogeneous Graph Scan Methods: Our proposed NPHGS is designed in a nonparametric statistical framework and the specification of parameters is hence relatively straightforward. Values of α_{max} and the number of seed entities K were set to 0.15 and 5, respectively. We observed that performance of our method is not sensitive to the settings of these two parameters. In addition to the above five comparison methods, we also compared our proposed NPHGS with four different homogeneous versions of NPHGS, including tweet, location, keyword, and user level homogeneous networks. In order to make fair comparisons, for each homogeneous graph, we defined a connection between two entities if they have direct relationships or if they share some neighbors in the heterogeneous graph. For example, two tweets are connected if they have retweet or reply relationships, or if they are connected to the same geographic location or the same terms. In each case, we assume that the system alerts when detecting a subgraph with score $F(S)$ above some threshold, allowing us to consider the tradeoffs between false positive rate and the other four performance metrics defined below by varying the alert threshold.

Performance Metrics: This study focuses on the evaluation of both event detection and forecasting for different methods. The related performance metrics include: 1) false positive rate (FPR), 2) true positive rate (TPR) for forecasting, 3) true positive rate for both detection and forecasting, 4) average lead time for forecasting, and 5) average lag time for detection. For each method, the reported alerts are structured as tuples of (date, location), where "location" is defined at the province level.

For each gold standard event, we determine whether the method: a) Had an alert in that province from 1 to 7 days before the event (such events are considered to be "success-

Method	FPR (FP/Day)	TPR (Forecasting)	TPR (Forecasting & Detection)	Lead Time (Days)	Lag Time (Days)	Run Time (Hours)
ST Burst Detection	0.65	0.07	0.42	1.10	4.57	30.1
Graph Partition	0.29	0.03	0.15	0.59	6.13	18.9
Earthquake	0.04	0.06	0.17	0.49	5.95	18.9
RW Event	0.10	0.22	0.25	0.93	5.83	16.3
Geo Topic Modeling	0.09	0.06	0.08	0.01	6.94	9.7
NPHGS (FPR=.05)	0.05	0.15	0.23	0.65	5.65	38.4
NPHGS (FPR=.10)	0.10	0.31	0.38	1.94	4.49	38.4
NPHGS (FPR= .15)	0.15	0.37	0.42	2.28	4.17	38.4
NPHGS (FPR=.20)	0.20	0.39	0.46	2.36	3.98	38.4

Table 3: Comparison between NPHGS and Existing Methods on the civil unrest datasets

Method	FPR (FP/Day)	TPR (Forecasting)	TPR (Forecasting & Detection)	Lead Time (Days)	Lag Time (Days)
ST Burst Detection	0.57	0.25	0.63	1.13	3.81
Graph Partition	0.57	0.06	0.19	0.19	3.10
Earthquake	0.92	0.13	0.19	0.75	3.69
RW Event	0.40	0.19	0.41	0.43	4.91
Geo Topic Modeling	0.43	0.19	0.50	0.62	4.31
NPHGS (FPR=.05)	0.05	0.20	0.78	0.71	2.44
NPHGS (FPR=.10)	0.10	0.22	0.85	0.76	1.90
NPHGS (FPR= .15)	0.15	0.25	0.93	0.80	1.36
NPHGS (FPR=.20)	0.20	0.29	0.94	0.82	1.24

Table 4: Comparison between NPHGS and Existing Methods on the Hantavirus dataset

fully predicted" at the given threshold). In this case, we record the number of days of lead time for that event based on the earliest such alert; b) Did not have an alert in that province from 1 to 7 days before the event, but did have an alert in that province from 0 to 7 days after the event (such events are considered to be "successfully detected" at the given threshold). In this case, we record the number of days of lag time for that event based on the earliest such alert; or c) Did not have an alert in that province between 7 days before and 7 days after the event (such events are considered to be "undetected" at the given threshold).

Based on the preceding results, we compute how many alerts were triggered that were not within the 7-day window before and after any event (this is the number of "false positives" at the given threshold). Now, as a function of the number of false positives (we scale this by time, e.g., "1 FP per day"), we can determine: 1) Proportion of gold standard events that were successfully predicted; 2) Proportion of gold standard events that were successfully predicted or detected (this is one minus the proportion of undetected gold standard events); 3) Average lead time for all gold standard events higher is better. Note that we average in a "0" lead time for each event that is not successfully predicted; and 4) Average lag time for all gold standard events: lower is better. Note that we average in a "0" lag time for each event that is successfully predicted OR is detected on the event day, and for undetected events we average in a "7" day lag time. Finally, we note that the maximum false positive rate that we consider, 1 FP per day, is non-trivial because we consider each unique combination of a province and a date as one binary variable, and thus the number of potential false positives per day could be up to the total number of provinces in a given country.

4.2 Comparison between NPHGS and Existing Methods

Table 3 presents the comparison between the proposed NPHGS approach and five competing methods for the task of forecasting civil unrest events. All measurements were averaged over the results of the four tested countries. For NPHGS, we show the performance metrics at various false positive rates. For comparable false positive rates, NPHGS achieved much higher forecasting TPR and detection TPR than all competing methods. The average lead time of NPHGS was at least one day greater than the other methods, and average lag time was consistently smaller than the other methods by 1 to 2 days. Run time of NPHGS was comparable to other methods but slightly higher because it considers all node types in the heterogeneous network rather than just tweets. We note that the true positive rates of all tested methods were lower than 50%, perhaps because some GSR events did not produce strong signals in the noisy Twitter data, or because an alert was only considered "correct" if it matched both the date and location of a GSR event.

Table 4 presents the comparison results for the task of detecting hantavirus outbreaks. The results indicate consistent patterns as observed in Table 3. For comparable false positive rates, NPHGS outperformed the competitive methods in all the metrics. Specifically, NPHGS achieved 10% to 30% higher forecasting TPR and detection TPR than all competing methods. The lead time of NPHGS was ten percent to twenty percent (0.2 to 0.5 days) greater than those of competitive methods, and the lag time of NPHGS was 50% (1 to 2 days) lower than those of competing methods. By comparing Table 3 and Table 4, we observe that the true positive rate of NPHGS for forecasting alone on the Hantavirus disease data was 10% lower than that of NPHGS on the civil unrest data. Consistently, the lead time of NPHGS

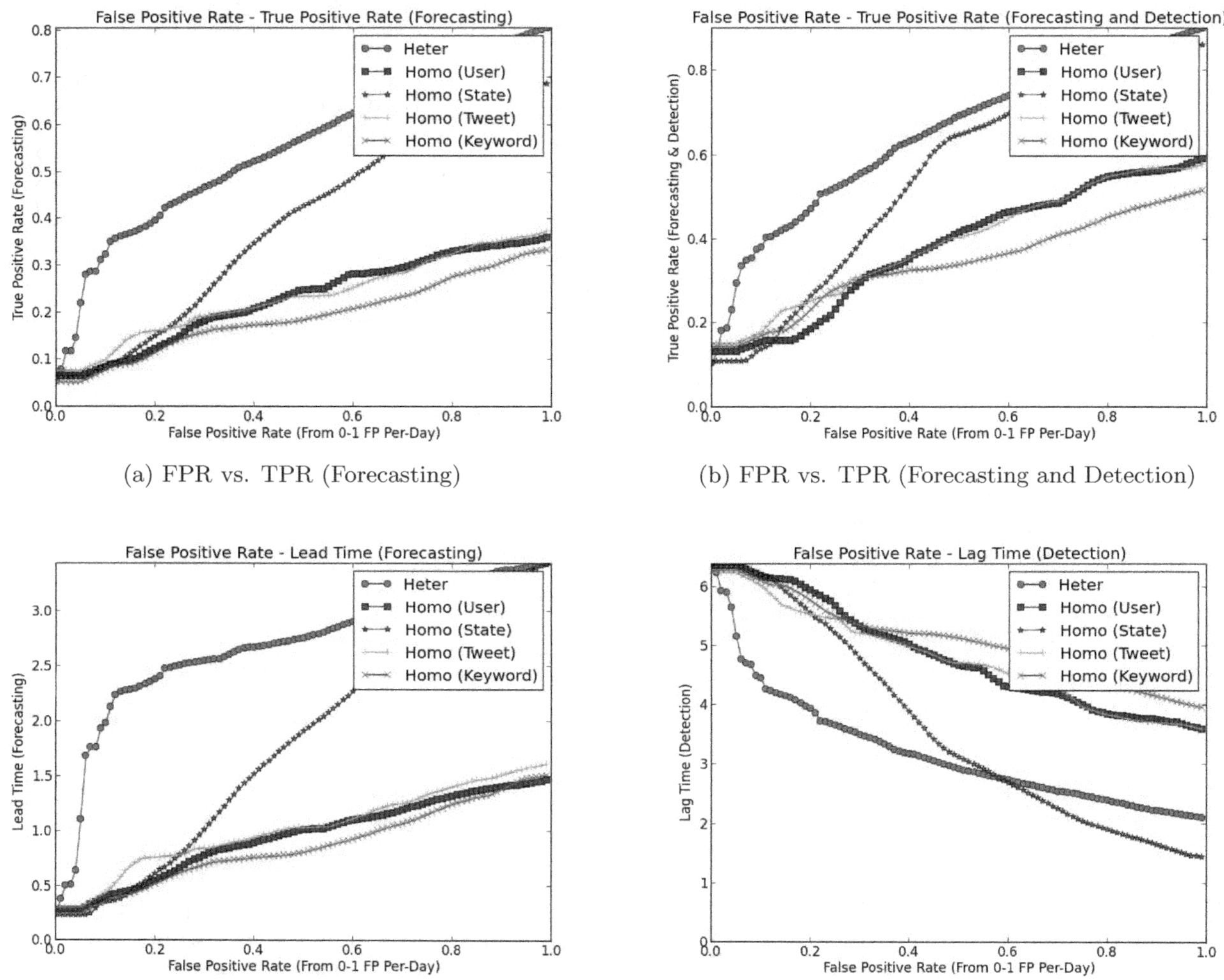

(a) FPR vs. TPR (Forecasting)

(b) FPR vs. TPR (Forecasting and Detection)

(c) FPR vs. Lead Time (Forecasting)

(d) FPR vs. Lag Time (Detection)

Figure 3: Comparison between heterogeneous and homogeneous graph scans. True positive rates for forecasting and detection, forecasting lead time, and detection lag time, all measured as a function of the false positive rate (from 0 to 1 false positive per day).

on the Hantavirus disease data is 1 day less than that of NPHGS on the civil unrest data. One potential interpretation is that civil unrest events tend to have stronger signals in Twitter data leading up to the event, since inflamed public sentiments and emotions, as well as advance planning and organization of strikes and protests, may be visible in the Twitter data. Nevertheless, our results demonstrate that we can achieve very early detection of emerging rare disease outbreaks. Table 4 shows that at a reasonably low false positive rate of 0.2 FP/day, NPHGS has detection lag time of only 1.24 days, which is better than the typical 3 to 4 days lag time using traditional public health surveillance data.

4.3 Comparison between NPHGS and homogeneous graph scans

This section compares NPHGS and different versions of homogeneous graph scan methods on the civil unrest datasets, with results shown in Figure 3. We applied the same framework of NPHGS to homogeneous networks of different entity types as the baseline methods. Hence, we label NPHGS as "Heter" in this case, and label the baseline methods as "Homo-(entity type)". The results in Figure 3 clearly demonstrate that NPHGS consistently outperforms all the homogeneous graph scan methods for all performance metrics. When the false positive rate was low (e.g., between 0 and 0.2 FP per day), NPHGS achieved huge ($\sim$30%) absolute improvements in TPR, provided two days of additional lead time for forecasting, and detected events two days earlier.

5. CONCLUSIONS

This paper presents a nonparametric approach to the problem of event detection and forecasting for heterogeneous social media graphs. The direct statistical modeling of heterogeneous relationships between entities and attributes is very complicated and computationally challenging. Our work avoids this complicated modeling process by transforming the heterogeneous graph into a "sensor" network, where we convert the heterogeneous entities and attributes into empirical p-values (using a novel, two-stage empirical calibration procedure). We then use a novel graph scan algorithm to maximize a non-parametric scan statistic over subgraphs, enabling early detection and advance forecasting of emerging societal events. In addition to evaluation of the theoretical properties of our method, we perform extensive experiments on real Twitter data. Our empirical results demonstrate that we can effectively forecast civil unrest events and achieve very early detection of rare disease outbreaks, outperforming competing methods by a substantial margin for both detection (power and timeliness) and forecasting (accuracy and lead time). For future work, we plan to extend NPHGS to do storytelling and causality analysis, since NPHGS is able to provide rich information related to ongoing or new events, such as the users, geographical locations, and key terms involved. In addition, we plan to extend NPHGS to a Bayesian framework so that rich domain knowledge can be naturally integrated.

6. ACKNOWLEDGMENTS

This work was partially supported by National Science Foundation grants IIS-0916345, IIS-0911032, and IIS-0953330. Additional support was provided by the John D. and Catherine T. MacArthur Foundation.

7. REFERENCES

[1] How fast the news spreads through social media. In *http://blog.sysomos.com/2011/05/02/how-fast-the-news-spreads-through-social-media/*, 2012.

[2] Ery Arias-Castro and Geoffrey R. Grimmett. Cluster detection in networks using percolation. *Bernoulli*, vol. 19, no. 2, pages 676–719, 2013.

[3] Hila Becker, Mor Naaman, and Luis Gravano. Beyond trending topics: Real-world event identification on Twitter. In *AAAI-ICWSM*, 2011.

[4] Robert H. Berk and Douglas H. Jones. Goodness-of-fit test statistics that dominate the Kolmogorov statistics. *Mathematical Reviews*, pages 47–59, 1979.

[5] Carlos Castillo, Marcelo Mendoza, and Barbara Poblete. Information credibility on Twitter. In *WWW*, pages 675–684, 2011.

[6] Lise Getoor. Tutorial: Representation, inference and learning in structured statistical models. In *NIPS*, 2012.

[7] David Donoho and Jiashun Jin. Higher criticism for detecting sparse heterogeneous mixtures. *Annals of Statistics*, vol. 32, no. 3, pages 962–994, 2004.

[8] Jacob Eisenstein, Brendan O'Connor, Noah A. Smith, and Eric P. Xing. A latent variable model for geographic lexical variation. In *EMNLP*, pages 1277–1287, 2010.

[9] Gabriel Pui Cheong Fung, Jeffrey Xu Yu, Philip S. Yu, and Hongjun Lu. Parameter free bursty events detection in text streams. In *VLDB*, pages 181–192, 2005.

[10] Jon Kleinberg. Bursty and hierarchical structure in streams. In *KDD*, pages 91–101, 2002.

[11] Liangjie Hong, Amr Ahmed, Siva Gurumurthy, Alexander J. Smola, and Kostas. Tsioutsiouliklis. Discovering geographical topics in the Twitter stream. In *WWW*, pages 769–778, 2012.

[12] Martin Kulldorff. A spatial scan statistic. *Communications in Statistics: Theory and Methods*, vol. 26, issue 6, pages 1481–1496, 1997.

[13] Theodoros Lappas, Marcos R. Vieira, Dimitrios Gunopulos, and Vassilis J. Tsotras. On the spatiotemporal burstiness of terms. In *PVLDB*, vol. 5, issue 9, pages 836–847, 2012.

[14] Edward McFowland III, Skyler Speakman, and Daniel B. Neill. Fast generalized subset scan for anomalous pattern detection. *Journal of Machine Learning Research*, vol. 14, pages 1533-1561, 2013.

[15] Daniel B. Neill. An empirical comparison of spatial scan statistics for outbreak detection. *International Journal of Health Geographics*, vol. 8, no. 20, 2009.

[16] Daniel B. Neill. Fast subset scan for spatial pattern detection. *Journal of the Royal Statistical Society: Series B*, vol.74, pages 337–360, 2012.

[17] Daniel B. Neill and Jeff Lingwall. A nonparametric scan statistic for multivariate disease surveillance. *Advances in Disease Surveillance*, 2007.

[18] Stanislav Nikolov and Devavrat Shah. A nonparametric method for early detection of trending topics. In *WIDS*, 2012.

[19] Takeshi Sakaki, Makoto Okazaki, and Yutaka Matsuo. Earthquake shakes Twitter users: real-time event detection by social sensors. In *WWW*, pages 851–860, 2010.

[20] Hassan Sayyadi, Matthew Hurst, and Alexey Maykov. Event detection and tracking in social streams. In *AAAI-ICWSM*, 2009.

[21] Charu C. Aggarwal and Karthik Subbian Event Detection in Social Streams In *SDM*, pages 624–635, 2012.

[22] Benjamin E. Teitler, Michael D. Lieberman, Daniele Panozzo, Jagan Sankaranarayanan, Hanan Samet, and Jon Sperling. Newsstand: a new view on news. In *GIS*, no. 18, pages 1–10, 2008.

[23] Kazufumi Watanabe, Masanao Ochi, Makoto Okabe, and Rikio Onai. Jasmine: a real-time local-event detection system based on geolocation information propagated to microblogs. In *CIKM*, pages 2541–2544, 2011.

[24] Jianshu Weng and Bu-Sung Lee. Event detection in Twitter. In *AAAI-ICWSM*, 2011.

[25] Zhijun Yin, Liangliang Cao, Jiawei Han Chengxiang Zhai, and Thomas Huang. Geographical topic discovery and comparison. In *WWW*, pages 247–256, 2011.

[26] http://epi.minsal.cl/vigilancia-epidemiologica/enfermedades-de-notificacion-obligatorial/vigilancia-hantavirus

[27] http://www.clips.ua.ac.be/pattern

[28] http://en.wikipedia.org/wiki/Klout

Event Detection in Activity Networks

Polina Rozenshtein
Aalto University
Espoo, Finland
polina.rozenshtein@aalto.fi

Aris Anagnostopoulos
Sapienza University of Rome
Italy
aris@dis.uniroma1.it

Aristides Gionis
Aalto University and HIIT
Espoo, Finland
aristides.gionis@aalto.fi

Nikolaj Tatti
Aalto University and HIIT
Espoo, Finland
nikolaj.tatti@aalto.fi

ABSTRACT

With the fast growth of smart devices and social networks, a lot of computing systems collect data that record different types of activities. An important computational challenge is to analyze these data, extract patterns, and understand activity trends. We consider the problem of mining activity networks to identify interesting events, such as a big concert or a demonstration in a city, or a trending keyword in a user community in a social network.

We define an *event* to be a subset of nodes in the network that are close to each other and have high activity levels. We formalize the problem of event detection using two graph-theoretic formulations. The first one captures the compactness of an event using the sum of distances among all pairs of the event nodes. We show that this formulation can be mapped to the MaxCut problem, and thus, it can be solved by applying standard semidefinite programming techniques. The second formulation captures compactness using a minimum-distance tree. This formulation leads to the prize-collecting Steiner-tree problem, which we solve by adapting existing approximation algorithms. For the two problems we introduce, we also propose efficient and effective greedy approaches and we prove performance guarantees for one of them. We experiment with the proposed algorithms on real datasets from a public bicycling system and a geolocation-enabled social network dataset collected from twitter. The results show that our methods are able to detect meaningful events.

Categories and Subject Descriptors

H.3.4 [**Database Management**]: Database Applications—*Data mining*

General Terms

Algorithms, Experimentation

KDD'14, August 24–27, 2014, New York, NY, USA.

ACM 978-1-4503-2956-9/14/08 ...$15.00.
http://dx.doi.org/10.1145/2623330.2623674 .

Keywords

Event detection; Submodular function maximization; Prize-collecting Steiner tree; Maximum cut.

1. INTRODUCTION

Detecting events is a fundamental problem in data mining and numerous methods have been applied to a variety of scenarios, including time series and data streams [19], point clouds and vector spaces [12], and networks [11]. The work in this paper concentrates on the latter category: discovering events in networks.

At a high level, our goal is to identify parts of the network with unusual high activity confined in a small space or in a dense part of the graph. We consider a network $G = (V,E)$ whose nodes monitor and record a certain activity. Such a network can represent a sensor network, a social-media site, activity levels from brain imaging, and so on. Given a *time instance* t, each node $v \in V$ in the network keeps a value $w_t(v)$ with the measurement value for the monitored activity. The objective of our approach is to detect an event happening in the network at time instance t. The event is defined with respect to activity values $w_t(\cdot)$ as well as network connectivity. In particular, we aim at finding a subset of network nodes S, such that all nodes in S are close to each other and they all have high levels of activity.

The activity values $w_t(v)$ may be absolute or normalized. Normalization here can be used to capture the abnormality level of a node at a certain time with respect to the routine operation of the network. In general, arbitrarily complex models can be used to define appropriately normalized activity values $w_t(v)$. For instance, periodicity phenomena can be taken into account; for example, when monitoring the traffic activity in a city, the reference values for weekend 8AM traffic are much lower than that of a week day. In this paper, we assume that the activity values $w_t(v)$ are provided as input to our problem. Devising models to obtain finely tuned and appropriately normalized activity values $w_t(v)$ depends on the application at hand and we consider it as an orthogonal problem, outside the scope of this paper.

The problems we define can be applied to a variety of scenarios, such as medical diagnosis, performance monitoring, image or video surveillance, and fraud detection. In this paper we experiment with two applications, event detection in *sensor networks* and *social networks*.

Sensor networks. Consider a network of sensors deployed in a certain region and recording a measurement of interest, such as traffic, pollution, or water-quality level. In some cases, the network nodes are geolocated so that a distance measure is defined among all nodes, whereas in other cases only a list of direct neighbors is known for each node. Events are defined with respect to the activity value monitored: we are interested in finding compact subareas where the traffic measurements are abnormal, the pollution levels are unusually high, and so on.

Social networks. Social networks model social interactions between individuals. The values recorded at each node correspond to a type of activity we are interested in monitoring, for example, the number of messages posted by an individual during the last few hours, an average sentiment score of those messages, or the frequency of keywords associated with a topic of interest. In this application, the events discovered by our methods will correspond to dense network subgraphs that exhibit high values with respect to the activity monitored.

Motivated by the previous discussion, we formalize event detection as a problem of finding a subgraph $S \subseteq V$ in a graph $G = (V,E,w)$ with node weights $w(v)$, for each $v \in V$. The subgraph S needs to be compact in terms of graph distances, and the sum of weights of the nodes of S needs to be large. We express subgraph compactness using two different definitions: *sum of pairs of distances* and *Steiner-tree* cost. The first definition leads to a graph-cut problem. We show that the optimization function is submodular and we provide two simple greedy algorithms with provable approximation guarantees. We also show how we can transform the problem to a variant of the MAXCUT problem to obtain an algorithm that is less practical but has better approximation guarantee than the greedy algorithms.

The second subgraph-compactness definition, which is based on the cost of the minimum Steiner tree, leads to a prize-collecting Steiner-tree problem. For that problem we apply a well known 2-approximation algorithm, which is based on the primal–dual paradigm. We also experiment with a greedy heuristic, which in practice gives almost as good solutions as the primal–dual algorithm.

We evaluate our problem formulation and the proposed algorithms on three sensor-network datasets and two social-network datasets. The former are real-world datasets from public bicycling systems from three large cities, Barcelona, Washington D.C., and Minneapolis, while the latter are datasets collected from twitter on two cities, New York City and Los Angeles. Using our methods allows to successfully discover real events in the cities, as reflected on the usage of shared bikes or twitter volume.

1.1 Related work

Statistical methods. A statistical approach for finding anomalies is the *spatial scan statistic* [23]. The method typically assumes that the data are distributed according to some distribution on a Euclidean space. The goal is then to detect whether there exists a subarea where the data are distributed according to the same distribution but with a higher density parameter. This approach is related to our setting but it has important differences. First, the statistical approach defines a null hypothesis, therefore, it assumes an underlying distribution over the data. Instead, our approach is formalized through an optimization function, and no such assumptions are needed. Second, the classical approaches are rather heuristic in nature: the methods detecting the most diverse subareas are usually based on Monte Carlo sampling, even though there have been approaches to formulate them as optimization problems and provide algorithmic solutions [1, 2]. Yet a third difference is that usually these approaches assume that the shape is predefined (e.g., a circle or an axis-parallel rectangle), which allows for the design of algorithms that can search the space of shapes. Statisticians have proposed generalizations where the shape of the dense cluster is not fixed a priori [7, 25, 27], however this forces the solution of the detection problem to be heuristic (e.g., Monte Carlo simulations). Finally, all these approaches assume that there exists an underlying Euclidean geometry on the space. For several of the applications we are interested, such as social networks, such Euclidean geometry is not present, thus requiring alternative approaches.

In summary, the approach of this paper is conceptually different from all the related work on spatial scan statistics. Here we provide a formal graph-theoretic definition of the problem and algorithms that have theoretical quality guarantees and are efficient in practice.

Event detection in social media. Event detection based on geospatial information from social media and twitter is a research area that has attracted significant attention in the last years. Baldwin et al. [8] developed an interactive system, in which a user can insert some queries and obtain the volume of tweets containing these terms at different granularities of space and time. Walther and Kaisser [30] developed a system for detecting events that take place from the twitter stream. It gathers tweets as they are created and it clusters them online based on geolocation. A machine-learning module evaluates whether a cluster of tweets refer to an event. Also Watanabe et al. [31] develop a similar system that identifies tweets that are created close in time and space and by looking at co-occurring terms it attempts to discover if they refer to the same event. Olson et al. [24] designed a system that aims at detecting very rapidly large *rare* events: events that happen with very low frequency but with large consequences, such as an earthquake or a tsunami. The difference of this line of work with our approach is that we offer a graph-theoretic formulation to the problem, which can be applied to any graph, not just geography-induced graphs. Additionally, our method does not uses text, but it assumes numerical measurements on the graph nodes.

Anomaly and outlier detection. Our problem has also resemblance with problems related to outlier and anomaly detection in networks. The main objective of these works is to identify patterns that are different than normal. For instance, Heard et al. [20] apply statistical techniques to discover a subset of the nodes that in a small period of time change significantly their communication patterns. Bhuyan et al. [9] apply clustering on network data for detecting intrusion attacks. The tutorial of Akoglu and Faloutsos [3] has an extensive reference list with related publications.

Dense subgraphs. Our problem is related to finding dense subgraphs [6, 14, 16, 22, 29]. Here, the goal is to find small parts of the network with a high number of edges. We are interested in small subgraphs with high number of nodes, thus obtaining different objective functions.

Finally, in a work related to the Steiner-tree problem formulation presented in this paper, Seufert et al. [26]

consider the problem of finding a subtree with k nodes such that the total node weight is maximized. Their approach also relies on the prize-collecting Steiner-tree, but their methods focus on identifying a heavy tree of exactly k nodes.

2. PROBLEM FORMULATION

We consider a graph $G = (V,E,w,c)$, with V being a set of n vertices and E being a set of m edges. The weight function $w : V \to \mathbb{R}$ assigns a nonnegative value $w(v)$ to each vertex v, whereas the distance function $c : E \to \mathbb{R}$ assigns a distance value $c(u,v)$ to each edge (u,v). The edge distance function c can be used to define a new distance function over all pairs of vertices $(u,v) \in V \times V$. This can be done by considering the *shortest-path distance closure* between vertices. Namely, for each $u,v \in V$ we define $d(u,v)$ to be equal to the distance of a shortest path from u to v using edges of G, or ∞ if no such path exists. Unless specified otherwise, in the rest of the paper we assume that the shortest-path distance d is used, and that a finite distance value is defined for all pairs of vertices in the graph.

Our goal is to find a subset of vertices $S \subseteq V$ that has *large total weight* according to the weight function w, and it is sufficiently *compact*, that is, the vertices in S are close to each other according to the distance function d.

To capture our objective we need to define appropriate weight and distance functions for subsets of vertices. Given $S \subseteq V$ we denote such weight and distance functions by $W(S)$ and $D(S)$, respectively. As a set weight function we consider simply the sum of all the weights in the set, that is,

$$W(S) = \sum_{v \in S} w(v).$$

For measuring the total distance of a set S we consider two options. The first option is to sum the distances of all pairs of vertices in S, namely

$$D_{\mathrm{AP}}(S) = \frac{1}{2} \sum_{v \in S} \sum_{u \in S} d(u,v).$$

This type of objective function is suitable for events that are concentrated in a small area in a round-shaped area, for instance a football game. But events might have different shapes, such as a parade, a street concert, a firework show, and so on; for such events, we need a distance function that does not penalize long distances, as long as points in between are also active. This leads to using the *minimum Steiner tree* of the subgraph induced by the set of vertices S. We denote this total-distance measure by $D_{\mathrm{T}}(S)$. Thus, we have

$$D_{\mathrm{T}}(S) = \min_{T \in \mathcal{T}(G[S])} \sum_{(u,v) \in T} d(u,v),$$

where $G[S]$ denotes the subgraph of G induced by a subset of vertices $S \subseteq V$, and $\mathcal{T}(H)$ denotes the set of all the trees of a graph H.

Subsets of vertices $S \subseteq V$ that correspond to meaningful events need to have *large* weight value $W(S)$ and *small* total distance value $D(S)$. To combine the two measures in a way that allows to maximize simultaneously $W(S)$ and minimize $D(S)$ there are many different options, for example, optimizing the one measure while setting a budget constraint on the other or taking a linear combination of the two measures. The former approach induces difficulties in devising approximation algorithms. To avoid them, we consider a linear combination of the two measures into a single objective with a normalization coefficient λ. The coefficient λ provides an easy way to control the relative importance of the two measures. In addition, as we will see in the next section, such a linear combination leads to neat mathematical forms, which can be viewed as a quadratic integer program or as well studied tree-based problems.

Thus, we consider the following problem formulation.

PROBLEM 1 (EVENT). *Given a graph $G = (V,E,w,c)$ with vertex weights w and edge distance c, and a normalization coefficient λ, find a subset of vertices $S \subseteq V$ that maximizes the objective function*

$$Q(S) = \lambda W(S) - D(S). \tag{1}$$

Problem 1 is a generic problem. The exact structure of the problem and solution methods depend on which distance function D is used. We obtain two instantiations of Problem 1 by considering the two set distance functions D_{AP} and D_{T} that we discussed previously. Thus, we consider the following two specific problems.

PROBLEM 2 (EVENTALLPAIRS). *Given a graph $G = (V, E,w,c)$ with vertex weights w and edge distance c, and a normalization coefficient λ, find a subset of vertices $S \subseteq V$ that maximizes the objective function*

$$Q_{\mathrm{AP}}(S) = \lambda W(S) - D_{\mathrm{AP}}(S). \tag{2}$$

PROBLEM 3 (EVENTTREE). *Given a graph $G = (V,E, w,c)$ with vertex weights w and edge distance c, and a normalization coefficient λ, find a subset of vertices $S \subseteq V$ that maximizes the objective function*

$$Q_{\mathrm{T}}(S) = \lambda W(S) - D_{\mathrm{T}}(S). \tag{3}$$

One should note that in the above problem formulations, the objective functions Q, Q_{AP}, and Q_{T} can take negative values. Negative values do not create any problems as long as one is after exact solutions. However, in the context of approximation algorithms, objective functions with negative values are problematic because it becomes more difficult to apply the concept of multiplicative approximation guarantee. To overcome this problem we modify the objective functions to ensure that they take nonnegative values. We do so by adding a constant term, and we thus consider a *shifted* version of our objective functions.

First, for the problem EVENTALLPAIRS we consider the shifted function $Q^{+}_{\mathrm{AP}}(S) = Q_{\mathrm{AP}}(S) + D_{\mathrm{AP}}(V)$. It is easy to see that the function Q^{+}_{AP} is nonnegative for all $S \subseteq V$. This makes it easier to design approximation algorithms with multiplicative approximation guarantees. A modified version of the EVENTALLPAIRS problem, which we denote by EVENTALLPAIRS+, is now defined as follows.

PROBLEM 4 (EVENTALLPAIRS+). *Given a graph $G = (V,E,w,c)$ with vertex weights w and edge distance c, and a normalization coefficient λ, find a subset of vertices $S \subseteq V$ that maximizes the objective function*

$$\begin{aligned} Q^{+}_{\mathrm{AP}}(S) &= Q_{\mathrm{AP}}(S) + D_{\mathrm{AP}}(V) \\ &= \lambda W(S) - D_{\mathrm{AP}}(S) + D_{\mathrm{AP}}(V). \end{aligned} \tag{4}$$

For the EVENTTREE problem we follow a different approach: first we note that with respect to finding an exact solution, maximizing the function Q_{T} is equivalent to minimizing $-Q_T$. We choose to work with this minimization problem, and we consider minimizing the shifted function $Q^+_T(S) = -Q_T(S) + \lambda W(V)$, which is a nonnegative for all $S \subseteq V$. For this shifted objected function it holds:

$$\begin{aligned} Q^+_T(S) &= \lambda W(V) - \lambda W(S) + D_T(S) \\ &= \lambda W(V \setminus S) + D_T(S). \end{aligned}$$

The interpretation of the above objective function is to find a set S so that the tree cost $D_T(S)$ and the (scaled by λ) weight of the vertices *not included* in S is minimized. This problem is known as the *prize-collecting Steiner-tree* (PCST) problem [4, 21]. The term "prize collecting" comes from thinking of the weights on the vertices of the graph as *prizes* and the goal is to find a tree that minimizes the tree cost and the total value of prizes not spanned by it. The shifted version of the EVENTTREE problem, denoted by EVENTTREE+, is now defined as follows.

PROBLEM 5 (EVENTTREE+). *Given a graph $G = (V, E, w, c)$ with vertex weights w and edge distance c, and a normalization coefficient λ, find a subset of vertices $S \subseteq V$ that minimizes the objective function*

$$Q^+_T(S) = \lambda W(V \setminus S) + D_T(S). \quad (5)$$

For general graphs, the problem EVENTALLPAIRS+ is **NP**-hard. The proof of the next lemma is obtained by a reduction from the INDEPENDENTSET problem and is omitted because of lack of space.

LEMMA 1. *The problem* EVENTALLPAIRS+ *is* **NP**-*hard for graphs with general edge distance functions.*

In the more restricted version in which the input graph is a metric the complexity of the problem is open.

On the other hand, the problem EVENTTREE+ is **NP**-hard even for metric edge distances as it generalizes the Steiner-tree problem:

LEMMA 2. *The problem* EVENTTREE+ *is* **NP**-*hard.*

3. ALGORITHMS FOR THE EVENTALLPAIRS+ PROBLEM

In this section we present our algorihtms for the EVENTALLPAIRS+ problem, starting with efficient greedy approaches and continuing with a slower but more effective approach based on the MAXCUT problem.

3.1 Greedy algorithms

We start our discussion on the EVENTALLPAIRS+ problem by considering the properties of the underlying objective function Q^+_{AP}. In particular, we can show that the function Q^+_{AP} is submodular. Submodularity is a desirable property because a number of approximation algorithms rely on it. The approximability of a submodular function depends on other properties as well, in particular whether the function is monotone and/or symmetric. We recall that if V is a ground set, a set function $f : 2^V \to \mathbb{R}$ is submodular if for all $S, T \subseteq V$ we have that $f(S) + f(T) \geq f(S \cap T) + f(S \cup T)$. The function f is monotone if for all $S \subseteq T \subseteq V$ it holds that $f(S) \leq f(T)$. It is symmetric if for all $S \subseteq V$ we have that $f(S) = f(V \setminus S)$.

LEMMA 3. *The function Q^+_{AP} is submodular.*

Algorithm 1: BFNS: Greedy algorithm for EVENTALLPAIRS+ using the approach of Buchbinder et al. [13]

```
X_0 ← ∅, Y_0 ← V
for i = 1 to n do
    a_i ← Q+_AP(X_{i-1} ∪ {u_i}) − Q+_AP(X_{i-1})
    b_i ← Q+_AP(Y_{i-1} \ {u_i}) − Q+_AP(Y_{i-1})
    a'_i ← max{a_i,0}, b'_i ← max{b_i,0}
    with probability a'_i/(a'_i + b'_i) do
        X_i ← X_{i-1} ∪ {u_i}, Y_i ← Y_{i-1}
    else with compliment probability b'_i/(a'_i + b'_i) do
        Y_i ← Y_{i-1} \ {u_i}, X_i ← X_{i-1}
return X_n (or equally Y_n)
```

PROOF. (Sketch) We set $I(S) \triangleq \lambda W(S)$ and $D(S) \triangleq D_{AP}(V) - D_{AP}(S)$. It is $Q^+_{AP}(S) = I(S) - D(S)$. It is easy to see that both functions I and D are positive and submodular. The lemma follows from the fact that the sum of two positive submodular functions is submodular. □

Thus we want to approximate a submodular function without any constraints. A recent paper by Buchbinder et al. [13] provides a linear-time $\frac{1}{2}$-approximation algorithm for this problem, which we explain below.

The algorithm of Buchbinder et al. is based on a *randomized double-greedy* approach. The technique utilizes the fact that for a submodular function f, the function $\bar{f}(S) = f(V \setminus S)$ is also submodular. Furthermore, if a set S^* is optimal for f then $V \setminus S^*$ is also optimal for $\bar{f}$ and the optimal values of the two functions are equal.

The suggested approach is a randomized algorithm, which performs two types of greedy steps, searching for the optimal solution for f and $\bar{f}$. The search strategy can be viewed as running two greedy algorithms simultaneously. We start with an arbitrary order of the elements in V, say $u_1, \ldots, u_n$. The two greedy processes traverse the sequences of sets $\{X_0, X_1, \ldots\}$ and $\{Y_0, Y_1, \ldots\}$, respectively. The one greedy process starts from the empty set $X_0 = \emptyset$ and grows it to optimize f, while the other greedy process starts from the ground set $Y_0 = V$ and shrinks it to optimize $\bar{f}$. The algorithm guarantees that the growing set X_i is always included into the shrinking set Y_i. Which of the two steps (grow X_i or reduce Y_i) is a random choice, which depends on the marginal improvement obtained from each move. The algorithm stops when the sets are equal. A formal description of the algorithm, which we call BFNS, is shown in Algorithm 1. We have the following.

THEOREM 1 (BUCHBINDER ET AL. [13]). *The* BFNS *algorithm provides a $\frac{1}{2}$-factor approximation for the* EVENTALLPAIRS+ *problem.*

For the EVENTALLPAIRS+ problem the BFNS algorithm has the following interpretation: It examines each graph vertex v one by one and decides whether to keep v in the solution or remove it. The decision is randomized and the probabilities depend on the marginal gains incurred in the Q^+_{AP} function with respect to the current lower and upper set solutions, X_i and Y_i.

Our objective has additional structure, which leads to a trivial $\frac{1}{2}$-approximation algorithm. Recall the definitions of the functions I and D in the proof of Lemma 3. Both functions are positive and $I(S)$ is increasing in S, whereas

$D(S)$ is decreasing in S. Therefore, for the optimal value S^* we have that

$$\begin{aligned} Q^{+}_{\text{AP}}(S^*) &= I(S^*) + D(S^*) \\ &\leq (I(V) + D(V)) + (I(\emptyset) + D(\emptyset)) \\ &= Q^{+}_{\text{AP}}(V) + Q^{+}_{\text{AP}}(\emptyset) \\ &\leq 2\max\{Q^{+}_{\text{AP}}(\emptyset), Q^{+}_{\text{AP}}(V)\}. \end{aligned}$$

This means that simply taking the best of the empty set or the entire node set V also provides a $\frac{1}{2}$ approximation. We call this algorithm Trivial.

We finally propose the standard greedy algorithm, which starts from the empty set, adds one vertex at a time, and stops when the solution cannot be improved. We refer to this simple greedy as GreedyAP.

For general unconstrained submodular functions, the greedy algorithm does not provide any guarantee. Here we are able to exploit the specific structure of the objective, and we prove that also GreedyAP provides a $\frac{1}{2}$ approximation. The result follows from the following lemma.

LEMMA 4. *Consider a submodular function F and let S be the solution given by the greedy algorithm optimizing F. Then, $F(S) \geq F(V)$.*

PROOF. We prove a more general statement. We prove that any hill-climbing algorithm, that is, any algorithm that starts with the empty set and increasingly adds elements for as long as the marginal gain is positive, if it returns solution S we have that $F(S) \geq F(V)$.

Assume that $V \setminus S = \{x_1, x_2, \ldots, x_r\}$. Then we have

$$\begin{aligned} F(S) - F(V) &= \sum_{i=1}^{r} (F(S \cup \{x_1, \ldots, x_{i-1}) - F(S \cup \{x_1, \ldots, x_i\})) \\ &\geq \sum_{i=1}^{r} (F(S) - F(S \cup \{x_i\})) \geq 0, \end{aligned}$$

where the first inequality follows from the submodularity of F and the second from the fact that the algorithm returned S without adding any element x_i, so each term in the sum is positive. □

COROLLARY 1. *The* GreedyAP *algorithm provides a $\frac{1}{2}$-factor approximation for the* EVENTALLPAIRS+ *problem. This bound is tight.*

PROOF. By the discussion just before Lemma 4, it suffices to show that $F(S) \geq F(\emptyset)$ and $F(S) \geq F(V)$. The former is trivially true, otherwise the algorithm would have returned $S = \emptyset$ and the latter follows from Lemma 4. The counterexample that shows that the greedy cannot, in the worst case, achieve approximation better than 1/2, will appear in the full version of this work. □

Although all three algorithms, BFNS, Trivial, and GreedyAP, have the same theoretical performance, our experiments show that GreedyAP produces solutions of higher quality, even slightly better or equal to MAXCUT-based algorithm, which is theoretically superior and which we discuss next.

3.2 MaxCut formulation

In this section we reduce the EVENTALLPAIRS+ problem to a variant of the MAXCUT problem. This allows us to use a well known algorithm by Goemans and Williamson [18], which has a 0.868-approximation guarantee. For the reduction we need the following variant of MAXCUT.

PROBLEM 6 ((*s*,*t*)-MAXCUT). *Given a graph G and two vertices s and t, partition the vertices of G into two sets A and B such that $s \in A$ and $t \in B$ and the total weight of cross edges is maximized. We denote the cost of such a solution A, B by $Q(A, B)$.*

The only difference between (s,t)-MAXCUT and the traditional MAXCUT is that there are two vertices s and t, for which it is forbidden to be in the same cut. This technicality does not have any complexity consequences.

To reduce EVENTALLPAIRS+ to the (s,t)-MAXCUT problem, assume that we are given a graph $G = (V, E)$ equipped with the distance function c. Assume also that we are given a parameter λ. We then construct a new graph H by adding two special vertices s and t into G. We connect s to each $v \in V$ with a weight $c(s, v) = \sum_{u \in V} d(v, u)$. We connect t to each $v \in V$ with a weight $c(t, v) = 2\lambda w(v)$.

Consider an A, B cut of H such that $s \in A$ and $t \in B$. Let $S = A \setminus \{s\}$ and let $T = B \setminus \{t\}$. We argue that the cost of the cut is twice the cost of EVENTALLPAIRS+, that is, $Q(A, B) = 2\, Q^{+}_{\text{AP}}(S)$. To see this, notice that each vertex $v \in S$ will contribute $2\,\lambda\, w(v)$ to the cost, and each vertex $v \in T$ will contribute $c(s, v) = \sum_{u \in V} d(v, u)$ to the cost. Additional costs will come from edges (u, v), where $v \in S$ and $u \in T$. Combining these costs gives us

$$\begin{aligned} Q(A, B) &= \sum_{v \in S} 2\,\lambda\, w(v) + \sum_{v \in T} \sum_{u \in V} d(v, u) + \sum_{v \in T} \sum_{u \in S} d(v, u) \\ &= 2\,\lambda\, W(S) + \sum_{v \in T} \sum_{u \in T} d(v, u) \\ &\quad + \sum_{v \in T} \sum_{u \in S} d(v, u) + \sum_{v \in T} \sum_{u \in S} d(v, u) \\ &= 2\,\lambda\, W(S) + \sum_{v \in V} \sum_{u \in V} d(v, u) - \sum_{v \in S} \sum_{u \in S} d(v, u) \\ &= 2\,\lambda\, W(S) + 2\, D_{\text{AP}}(V) - 2\, D_{\text{AP}}(S) \\ &= 2\, Q^{+}_{\text{AP}}(S). \end{aligned}$$

Thus, solving (s,t)-MAXCUT also solves EVENTALLPAIRS+. Moreover, since the costs of both problems are the same, up to a scaling factor, any approximation guarantee for (s,t)-MAXCUT yields the same approximation guarantee for EVENTALLPAIRS+.

Our final step is to solve (s,t)-MAXCUT. Following the seminal algorithm of Goemans and Williamson [18], the problem can be formulated as the following integer program:

$$\begin{aligned} \max \quad & \sum_{u,v \in V(H)} c(u,v) \frac{1 - x_u x_v}{2} \\ \text{such that} \quad & x_u \in \{-1, +1\}, \text{ for all } u \in V(H), \\ & x_s x_t = -1 \quad . \end{aligned}$$

The only difference with the original MAXCUT formulation is the additional constraint $x_s x_t = -1$. This constraint ensures that the vertices s and t are in different partitions and the resulting cut is a feasible solution for (s,t)-MAXCUT.

The algorithm of Goemans and Williamson proceeds by making a semidefinite relaxation, and then rounds the solution based on a random projection. Fortunately, the additional constraint $x_s x_t = -1$ can be easily added to the semidefinite program, and the constraint has no effect on the rounding step. Consequently, we can use the same semidefinite-programming algorithm to approximate the (s,t)-MAXCUT problem, which leads to the following.

THEOREM 2. *The (s,t)-MAXCUT problem can be solved by the Goemans-Williamson algorithm [18] with an approximation guarantee $\beta > 0.868$. This also provides a β-factor approximation to the* EVENTALLPAIRS+ *problem.*

The proof for the approximation guarantee for the (s,t)-MAXCUT problem is virtually the same as the proof for the MAXCUT problem [18], and because of space limitations we omit it from this version.

Even though the aforementioned approach uses the function d, which is a metric function (i.e., it satisfies the triangle inequality), note that the approach is general and holds even if the underlying edge cost is not a metric. Specifically, the approach can be applied to arbitrary distance functions and provides the same approximation guarantee. In the case where d is a metric function, as in our case, we can obtain a stronger approximation guarantee.

THEOREM 3. *Assuming that d is a metric, then there exists a polynomial-time approximation scheme (PTAS) for solving* EVENTALLPAIRS+. *In other words, for each $\epsilon > 0$, there is a polynomial algorithm with an approximation guarantee of $1 - \epsilon$.*

The proof of the theorem, which relies on the work of Arora et al. [5] for *dense* MAXCUT instances, is omitted from this version. Whereas this theorem provides a more tight approximation bound, the involved algorithm is impractical even for large values of ϵ. Consequently, this result serves mostly as a theoretical contribution.

4. ALGORITHMS FOR THE EVENTTREE+ PROBLEM

Next we discuss the EVENTTREE+ problem. Recall that in this case we want to minimize the objective function

$$Q_{\mathrm{T}}^{+}(S) = \lambda W(V \setminus S) + D_{\mathrm{T}}(S).$$

This is known as the *prize-collection Steiner-tree* problem (PCST) [17]: we are given a weighted graph with distances between the nodes and prizes for the nodes. The objective is to select a subset of the nodes such that the cost of the tree to connect them plus the prizes of the nodes not in the tree is minimized.

PCST was first considered by Bienstock et al. [10], who provided a 3-approximation. Goemans and Williamson [17] designed a $(2 - \frac{1}{n-1})$-approximation algorithm using a primal–dual schema. In this paper we use a modified version of the algorithm by Johnson et al. [21], which gives 2-approximation, and we call it PD. We choose this algorithm because it is quite fast (runs in time $O(n^2 \log n)$, whereas Goemans and Williamson's algorithm takes $O(n^3 \log n)$ in time) and it is straightforward to implement. The currently best algorithm [4] improves the approximation ratio to $(2 - \epsilon)$, which is more important rather from a theoretical perspective.

Algorithm PD has two phases. In the first phase it *grows* a tree by maintaining and joining components. Each component has a *surplus* and each edge has a *deficit*. Initially every node v is a single component with surplus equal to its weight, and each edge is initialized with a deficit equal to the corresponding distance. The idea is that the surpluses of the components pay for the deficit in the edges inside. The algorithm starts lowering surpluses and deficits until (1) the deficit of an edge becomes zero, in which case the two endpoints are merged into a single component (if the edge is not part of the same component) with the new surplus being the sum of the surpluses of the two components, or (2) the surplus of a component becomes zero, in which case the component is not considered any more to form part of the Steiner tree.

The second phase involves some *pruning* of the tree constructed in the first phase. Starting from the leaves, we move towards the root of the tree, removing a subtree T if the weight of the nodes in T is higher than the cost to connect T to the rest of the tree. The entire algorithm is explained in detail in [21].

We also experiment with a greedy heuristic, similar to GreedyAP, which we call GreedyT. It works as follows: it maintains a set of nodes S, initialized to the empty set. In each iteration it adds to S the node in $V \setminus S$ that provides the maximum decrease to the objective $Q_{\mathrm{T}}^{+}(S)$. The algorithm terminates when $S = V$, or when every node in $V \setminus S$ leads to an increase of $Q_{\mathrm{T}}^{+}(S)$.

5. EXPERIMENTAL EVALUATION

We evaluate our methods on synthetic and real datasets. The real-world datasets are extracted from city sensors (public-bike sharing) and social media (geolocated tweets). We start by describing our datasets.

5.1 Datasets

Synthetic data. We use three synthetic datasets, which we generate as follows. We place the network nodes uniformly at random into the unit square and set the distance between two nodes to their Euclidean distance. The objective with these synthetic datasets is to study whether our methods can detect the planted ground-truth events.

We plant events to the datasets by setting to 1 the values of nodes that occur within the event and to 0 the volues of nodes outside the planted event. Nodes that are close to the border of the events receive a smaller weight. In *Plant1* we plant one spherical event, in *Plant2* we plant two spherical events, and in *Curve* we plant a snake-like event.

To test the robustness of the algorithms, we choose a fraction of the network nodes at random, and assign them an arbitrary weight from a uniform distribution [0, 1]. We refer to the size of the fraction as a level of noise.

In addition, we create semi-synthetic datasets by using the coordinates from real-world datasets (see more detailed description below), and by generating synthetic weights as described above. We plant a cross pattern to the Barcelona data (*PlantB*), and two clusters to the NY data (*PlantNY*).

We show the synthetic datasets with 20% noise level at the top row of Figure 1, where the generated event clusters are colored black.

City-sensor data. We use public-bike sharing data from three systems: Barcelona Bicing,[1] Minneapolis Nice Ride,[2]

[1]http://www.bicing.cat

[2]http://www.niceridemn.org

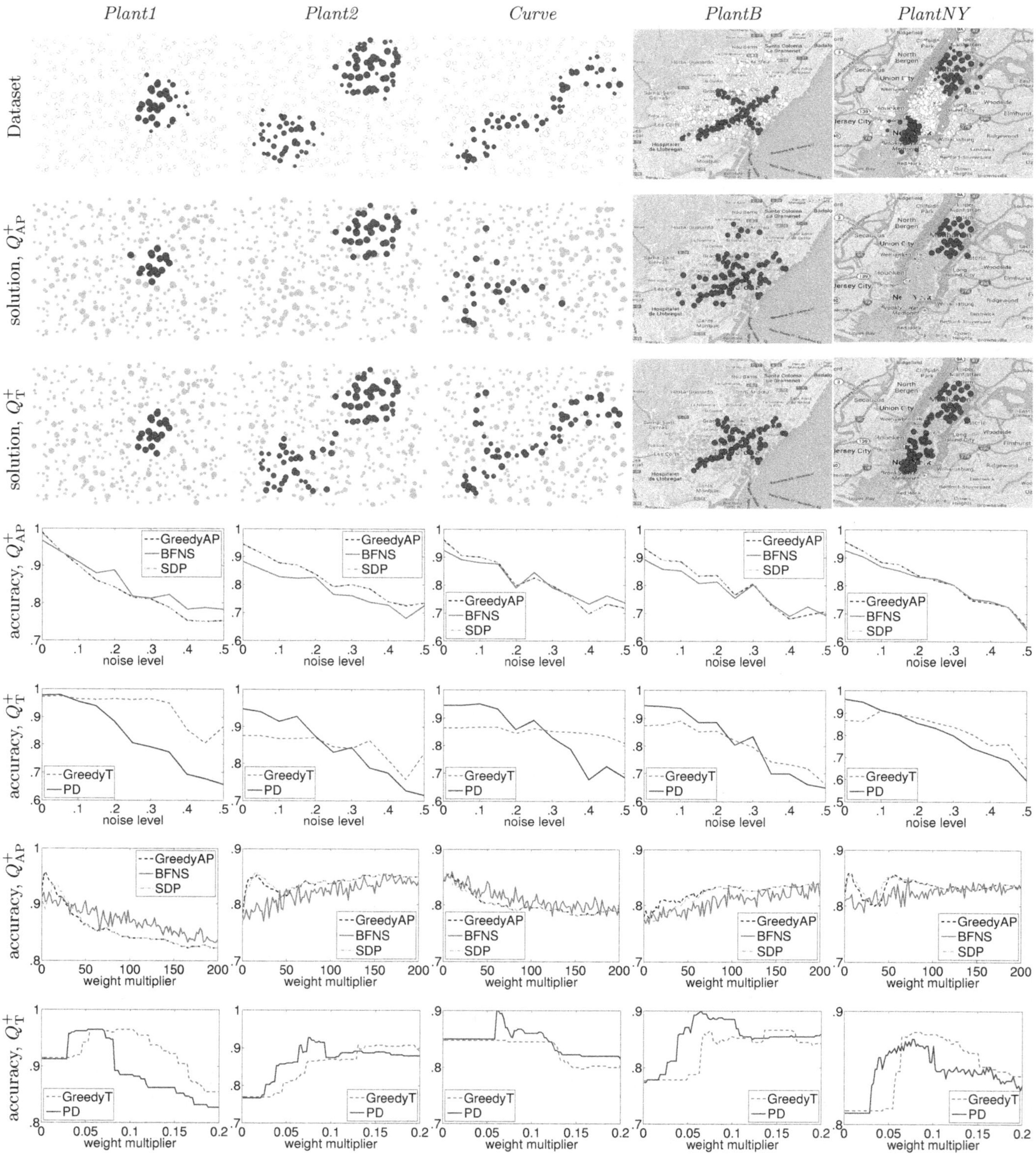

Figure 1: Experiments for synthetic and planted datasets. Each column represents a single dataset. First row contains the datasets and the planted events, contaminated by noise of 20%. Row 2 and 3 row contain events discovered by algorithms for EVENTALLPAIRS+ and EVENTTREE+ respectively that achieve the best accuracy on the particular dataset (with corresponding lambdas). Rows 4–5 contain accuracy as a function of noise level ($\lambda = 100$ for Q^+_{AP} and $\lambda = 0.1$ for Q^+_T). Rows 6–7 contain accuracy as a function of λ (20% noise level).

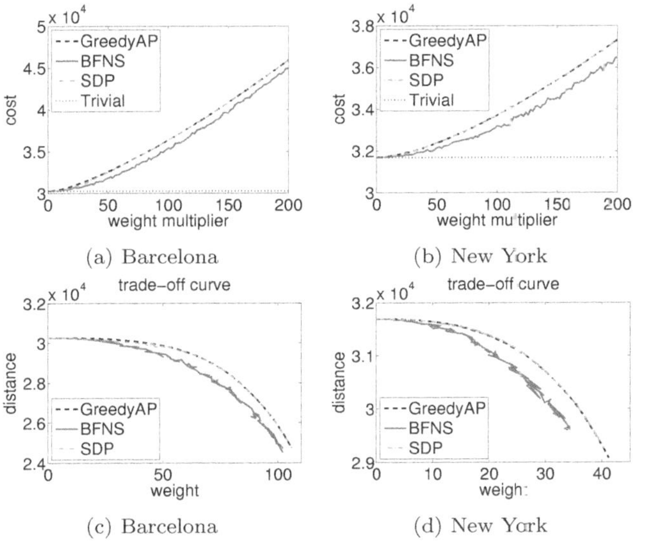

(a) Barcelona (b) New York

(c) Barcelona (d) New York

Figure 2: Performance of different algorithms for the EVENTALLPAIRS+ problem on Barcelona and NY datasets. The top row shows Q^{+}_{AP} as a function of the weight multiplier λ. The bottom row shows a scatter plot of weight $W(S)$ and the distance $D_{\mathrm{AP}}(V) - D_{\mathrm{AP}}(S)$, parameterized by λ; in both dimensions, larger values are better.

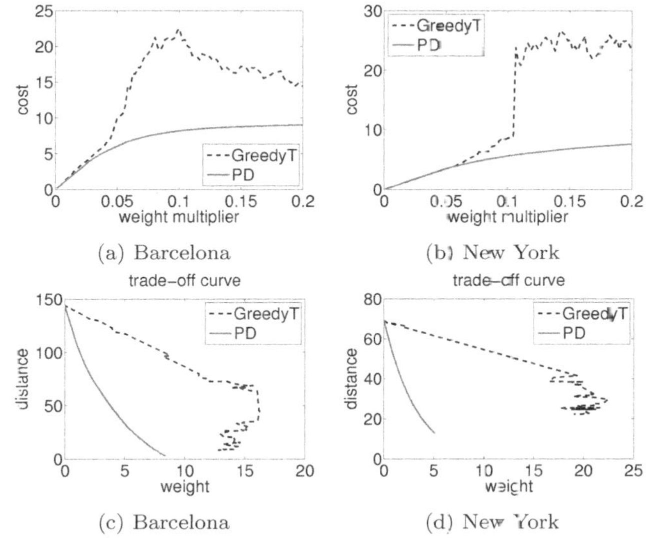

(a) Barcelona (b) New York

(c) Barcelona (d) New York

Figure 3: Performance of different algorithms for the EVENTTREE+ problem on Barcelona and New York datasets. The top row contains Q^{+}_{T} as a function of the weight multiplier λ. The bottom row contains a scatter plot of weight $W(V \setminus S)$ and the distance $D_{\mathrm{T}}(\mathcal{E})$, parameterized by λ; in both dimensions, smaller values are better.

and Washington D.C. Capital bikeshare.[3] In each case, a network node corresponds to a bike station. The activity level of a bike station is the fraction of bikes in the station with respect to the full capacity of the station. To improve the quality of the events discovered by our algorithms we set the weight of a node to be $|x - m|$, where x is the current activity level of a station and m is the typical activity level of the station. As typical activity level we chose the average activity of the station at the same time of the week, over the observation period. The number of stations in the three cities we consider is 420, 145, and 248, respectively, and the data are collected over an observation period of 227, 217, and 273 days, respectively.

Social-media data. We obtain a dataset of geolocated twitter messages for 100 cities. The dataset has been made public by Cheng et al. [15]. For our experiments we focus on the cities of New York and Los Angeles. We start with 302 121 and 254 852 tweets for NY and LA, respectively, which span a period of 329 days. For each city we collapse the locations of the input tweets to centroids, based on proximity, and we use those centroids as network nodes. The activity level of each centroid is the number of tweets during a day. As with the bike-sharing data, we adjust the activity level by considering the difference with respect to the average level at each centroid. The number of centroids is 490 and 487, for NY and LA, respectively. The reason that we collapse tweet locations to centroids is for having enough data at each location to make inferences. The spatial distribution of tweets is highly uneven. To ensure that all the centroids have about the same number of points and, thus, can represent activity of the particular neighborhood correctly, we construct them with the k-means algorithm. The granularity of the result centroids is sufficient to capture accurately the map of activity: in the areas with dense activity, such as city centers, each city block is covered by 2-3 centroids, while in the suburbs one centroid represents several blocks.

[3] `http://www.capitalbikeshare.com`

5.2 Experimental results

Comparison of different algorithms. We have implemented all the algorithms described in the previous sections. For the EVENTALLPAIRS+ problem we use the Trivial algorithm as a *baseline*. For the SDP approach, we solve the corresponding semidefinite program using the SDPT3 solver [28], and we round the solution as described in Section 3.2.

We first compare different algorithms in terms of the objective function. The results are shown in Figures 2 and 3 for the Barcelona and NY datasets, respectively. For the EVENTALLPAIRS+ problem we see that all algorithms, except Trivial, achieve similar results. In particular, GreedyAP and SDP show almost the same performance and outperform BFNS. For the EVENTTREE+ problem we see that the PD algorithm is far superior to the GreedyT algorithm. Similar trends are observed in all other datasets, and are omitted for paucity of space.

Accuracy on planted events. We test the ability of our algorithms to detect planted events. These events are given at the top row in Figure 1. Because the ground-truth events are known we measure the accuracy of our algorithms, as the fraction of points classified correctly as event points.

Our results, shown in rows 4–5 of Figure 1, provide evidence that our algorithms are capable of discovering the ground-truth events with high accuracy. As expected, accuracy decreases with the noise level, but it remains high, always around 70% even for noise levels of 50%.

With respect to comparing the different algorithms, for the EVENTALLPAIRS+ problem, as in the previous experiments, all tested algorithms achieve similar accuracy.

On the other hand, for the EVENTTREE+ problem, the PD algorithm performs better for smaller levels of noise, whereas the GreedyT seems to be more robust for higher noise levels.

We also contrast the solutions found by the two different problem formulations (rows 2–3 of Figure 1), EVENTALLPAIRS+ and EVENTTREE+. It is expected that algorithms for the EVENTALLPAIRS+ problem will be better suited for round-shaped events, whereas algorithms for the EVENTTREE+ problem will be better in recovering events of arbitrary shape. Our experiments confirm this intuition and show that the algorithms for the tree-based model are more versatile and in general achieve higher accuracy.

Effect of weight multiplier, λ. As we can see from rows 6–7 of Figure 1, the accuracy of the methods depends on the value of the weight multiplier λ. Different values of λ force the algorithms to weight differently the distances with respect to vertex weights, and discover events of different sizes. One way of selecting the parameter is to execute the algorithms with different values of λ, plot the Pareto curve for those values and choose a value that yields the desired trade-off between spanned weight and distance.

Case study. Our next step is to highlight some of the events discovered by our method. For all the events shown as case studies we use the SDP algorithm. To help with selecting λ, we normalize the weights of the vertices so that the maximum weight of each day is equal 1 and the edge distances represent actual kilometric distances. We then use the same value of λ for all the experiments ($\lambda = 20$).

We select top events that correspond to major holidays, shown in Figure 4. The discovered events correspond to places where people would gather in such days, for example, in the city center in Barcelona, and in the National Mall in Washington D.C. In New York City the discovered event is located in the Central Park and the nearby Metropolitan Museum and American Museum of Natural History.

To demonstrate that different days may produce diverse events, we focused on the Barcelona dataset. We aim at reporting k days that have high event score and whose event clusters are spatially non-overlapping (do not have any shared nodes). First we find event clusters and corresponding scores for each day in the dataset and then we sort the days by score in descend order. We select the first day from the list and we keep it in a running set of top days. Then we go through the list and greedily search for a day with an event cluster that does not overlap with any of the clusters of the already obtained top days. If such a day is found, we add it to the top set and we continue traversing the list until the size of the selected top days becomes k. We show the top-3 events in Figure 5. The first event indicates a concert by the Cure music band and the event is around the concert hall, the second event corresponds to the festival of the Poblenou neighborhood, and the third event points out to Halloween activities in el Raval, a famous nightlife spot.

Scalability. The proposed greedy algorithms are efficient and can scale to large networks. We report the scalability behavior of the GreedyAP algorithm. We use the twitter dataset, with tweets from the whole US, to create larger activity networks and we apply the GreedyAP algorithm. Our implementation, executed on an Intel Core i7 machine, with 8 GB RAM and processor running at 2.30GHz, is able to find a solution under 10 seconds when we applied to a fully connected network with 10,000 nodes.

6. CONCLUSION

We formalize the problem of detecting events in activity networks, as a problem of finding compact subgraphs in graphs with vertex weights. Depending on the notion of compactness used—sum of all pairs of distances or Steiner-tree distance—we obtain two different optimization problems. By a reduction to a variant of the MAXCUT problem, which we solve with semidefinite programming, and by the use of the primal–dual scheme, we provide approximation algorithms for the two problems considered. In addition, we provide simpler and faster greedy algorithms, for one of which we are able to show approximation guarantees, which rely on the submodularity property of the objective function. Our experiments show that the greedy approaches are more lightweight and perform as well as the more sophisticated approximation algorithms.

The event-detection setting that we consider has many applications. Here we experimented with real-world datasets from city sensors and social media, and we showed that our methods were able to discover successfully real events.

Our work opens many interesting directions for future research. One such direction is to incorporate the temporal dimension of the activity network in the graph-theoretic framework and discover events of varying temporal support.

Acknowledgements

This work was supported by the Academy of Finland grant 118653 (ALGODAN), the EU IP project MULTIPLEX 317532, and the EU FET project SIMPOL 610704. Part of the work was done while Aris Anagnostopoulos was visiting Aalto University under the Aalto Science Institute visiting professor programme.

7. REFERENCES

[1] D. Agarwal, A. McGregor, J. M. Phillips, S. Venkatasubramanian, and Z. Zhu. Spatial scan statistics: Approximations and performance study. *KDD*, 2006.

[2] D. Agarwal, J. M. Phillips, and S. Venkatasubramanian. The hunting of the bump: On maximizing statistical discrepancy. *SODA*, 2006.

[3] L. Akoglu and C. Faloutsos. What is strange in large networks? graph-based irregularity and fraud detection, 2012. Tutorial presented at ICDM.

[4] A. Archer, M. H. Bateni, M. T. Hajiaghayi, and H. Karloff. Improved approximation algorithms for prize-collecting Steiner tree and TSP. *SIAM Journal on Computing*, 40(2), 2011.

[5] S. Arora, D. Karger, and M. Karpinski. Polynomial time approximation schemes for dense instances of NP-hard problems. *JCSS*, 58(1), 1999.

[6] Y. Asahiro, K. Iwama, H. Tamaki, and T. Tokuyama. Greedily finding a dense subgraph. *SWAT*, pages 136–148, 1996.

[7] R. Assunção, M. Costa, A. Tavares, and S. Ferreira. Fast detection of arbitrarily shaped disease clusters. *Statistics in medicine*, 25, 2006.

[8] T. Baldwin, P. Cook, B. Han, A. Harwood, S. Karunasekera, and M. Moshtaghi. A support platform for event detection using social intelligence. *EACL*, 2012.

(a) Barcelona: 11.09.12 National Day of Catalonia (b) Minneapolis: 4.07.12 Independence Day (c) Washington, DC: 27.05.13 Memorial Day (d) Los Angeles: 31.05.10 Memorial Day (e) New York: 6.09.10 Labor Day

Figure 4: Public holiday city-events discovered using the SDP algorithm.

(a) 01.06.12 Primavera sound music festival (b) 18.09.12 festival of the Poblenou neighborhood (c) 31.10.12 Halloween

Figure 5: Top-3 diverse events discovered from Barcelona bicing data using the SDP algorithm.

[9] M. H. Bhuyan, D. K. Bhattacharyya, and J. K. Kalita. An effective unsupervised network anomaly detection method. *ICACCI*, 2012.

[10] D. Bienstock, M. X. Goemans, D. Simchi-Levi, and D. Williamson. A note on the prize-collecting traveling salesman problem. *Mathematical programming*, 59(1-3), 1993.

[11] B. Boden, S. Günnemann, H. Hoffmann, and T. Seidl. Mining coherent subgraphs in multi-layer graphs with edge labels. *KDD*, 2012.

[12] M. M. Breunig, H.-P. Kriegel, R. T. Ng, and J. Sander. LOF: identifying density-based local outliers. *SIGMOD*, 2000.

[13] N. Buchbinder, M. Feldman, J. S. Naor, and R. Schwartz. A tight linear time (1/2)-approximation for unconstrained submodular maximization. *FOCS*, 2012.

[14] M. Charikar. Greedy approximation algorithms for finding dense components in a graph. *APPROX*, 2000.

[15] Z. Cheng, J. Caverlee, K. Lee, and D. Z. Sui. Exploring millions of footprints in location sharing services. *ICWSM*, 2011.

[16] U. Feige, G. Kortsarz, and D. Peleg. The dense k-subgraph problem. *Algorithmica*, 29(3), 2001.

[17] M. X. Goemans and D. P. Williamson. A general approximation technique for constrained forest problems. *SIAM Journal on Computing*, 24(2), 1995.

[18] M. X. Goemans and D. P. Williamson. Improved approximation algorithms for maximum cut and satisfiability problems using semidefinite programming. *JACM*, 42(6), 1995.

[19] V. Guralnik and J. Srivastava. Event detection from time series data. *KDD*, 1999.

[20] N. A. Heard, D. J. Weston, K. Platanioti, and D. J. Hand. Bayesian anomaly detection methods for social networks. *Ann. Appl. Stat.*, 4(2), 2010.

[21] D. S. Johnson, M. Minkoff, and S. Phillips. The prize-collecting Steiner tree problem: theory and practice. *SODA*, 2000.

[22] S. Khuller and B. Saha. On finding dense subgraphs. *ICALP*, 2009.

[23] M. Kulldorff. A spatial scan statistic. *Communications in Statistics-Theory and Methods*, 26(6), 1997.

[24] M. Olson, A. Liu, M. Faulkner, and K. M. Chandy. Rapid detection of rare geospatial events: earthquake warning applications. *DEBS*, 2011.

[25] G. P. Patil and C. Taillie. Upper level set scan statistic for detecting arbitrarily shaped hotspots. *Environmental and Ecological Statistics*, 11. 2004.

[26] S. Seufert, S. J. Bedathur, J. Mestre, and G. Weikum. Bonsai: Growing interesting small trees In *ICDM*, pages 1013–1018, 2010.

[27] T. Tango and K. Takahashi. A flexibly shaped spatial scan statistic for detecting clusters. *International Journal of Health Geographics*, 4-11, 2005.

[28] K.-C. Toh, M. J. Todd, and R. H. Tütüncü. SDPT3 — a Matlab software package for semidefinite programming, version 1.3. *Optimization methods and software*, 11(1-4), 1999.

[29] C. Tsourakakis, F. Bonchi, A. Gionis, F. Gullo, and M. Tsiarli. Denser than the densest subgraph: extracting optimal quasi-cliques with quality guarantees. *KDD*, 2013.

[30] M. Walther and M. Kaisser. Geo-spatial event detection in the twitter stream. *ECIR*, 2013.

[31] K. Watanabe, M. Ochi, M. Okabe, and R. Onai. Jasmine: a real-time local-event detection system based on geolocation information propagated to microblogs. *CIKM*, 2011.

FEMA: Flexible Evolutionary Multi-faceted Analysis for Dynamic Behavioral Pattern Discovery

Meng Jiang[123], Peng Cui[123], Fei Wang[4], Xinran Xu[123], Wenwu Zhu[123], Shiqiang Yang[123]

[1]Tsinghua National Laboratory for Information Science and Technology
[2]Department of Computer Science and Technology, Tsinghua University, Beijing, China
[3]Beijing Key Laboratory of Networked Multimedia, Tsinghua University, China
[4]IBM Watson Research Center, Yorktown Heights, NY, USA
jm06@mails.tsinghua.edu.cn, cuip@tsinghua.edu.cn, feiwang03@gmail.com
xxr10@mails.tsinghua.edu.cn, wwzhu@tsinghua.edu.cn, yangshq@tsinghua.edu.cn

ABSTRACT

Behavioral pattern discovery is increasingly being studied to understand human behavior and the discovered patterns can be used in many real world applications such as web search, recommender system and advertisement targeting. Traditional methods usually consider the behaviors as simple user and item connections, or represent them with a static model. In real world, however, human behaviors are actually complex and dynamic: they include correlations between user and multiple types of objects and also continuously evolve along time. These characteristics cause severe data sparsity and computational complexity problem, which pose great challenge to human behavioral analysis and prediction. In this paper, we propose a Flexible Evolutionary Multi-faceted Analysis (FEMA) framework for both behavior prediction and pattern mining. FEMA utilizes a flexible and dynamic factorization scheme for analyzing human behavioral data sequences, which can incorporate various knowledge embedded in different object domains to alleviate the sparsity problem. We give approximation algorithms for efficiency, where the bound of approximation loss is theoretically proved. We extensively evaluate the proposed method in two real datasets. For the prediction of human behaviors, the proposed FEMA significantly outperforms other state-of-the-art baseline methods by 17.4%. Moreover, FEMA is able to discover quite a number of interesting multi-faceted temporal patterns on human behaviors with good interpretability. More importantly, it can reduce the run time from hours to minutes, which is significant for industry to serve real-time applications.

Categories and Subject Descriptors

I.5.3 [**Computing Methodologies**]: Pattern Recognition - Clustering; J.4 [**Computer Applications**]: Social and Behavioral Sciences

Keywords

Behavior Modeling; Behavioral Pattern; Evolutionary Analysis; Tensor Factorization; Flexible Regularizers

KDD'14, August 24–27, 2014, New York, NY, USA.
Copyright 2014 ACM 978-1-4503-2956-9/14/08 ...$15.00.
http://dx.doi.org/10.1145/2623330.2623644.

1. INTRODUCTION

Scientists study human behavior from a variety of cultural, political, and psychological perspectives, looking for consistent patterns of individual and social behavior and for scientific explanations on those patterns. It is well accepted that human behavior is the product of a multitude of interrelated factors. The factors such as physical environment, social interaction, and social identity, affect how the behavior takes place with our personalities and interests. As an example, if a researcher changes his affiliation, he will start to collaborate with new friends, join in new projects and eventually study new topics. Given the complexity of multi-faceted factors influencing human behaviors, it is difficult to concisely summarize what they are and how they interact. Moreover, psychological studies [21] demonstrate that human behaviors naturally evolve with the changing of both endogenous factors (e.g., personality) and exogenous factors (e.g, environment), resulting in different dynamic (temporal) behavioral patterns over time. For example, in early 1990s, many researchers focused on database systems and query processing. In late 1990s, with various data collective methods emerging and scales of unlabeled data increasing, they turned to work on clustering and pattern mining problems. In 2000s, people started to focus on social networks and communities since Facebook and Twitter become popular. Consequently, the patterns of human behaviors differ from place to place, era to era and across environments. The complexity and dynamic characteristics pose great challenges to understanding and predicting human behaviors. However, there is a lack of research to support behavioral modeling with both multi-faceted and temporal information.

Traditional methods of data analysis have long been used to discover patterns of human behaviors. Sun *et al.* [27] perform 3-mode analysis on the click-through data with user, query and web page. Chen *et al.* [2] models tagging behavior with the decomposition of ternary relationships of user, tag and item. However, their static views on human behavior are not able to learn from temporal information, or capture the dynamic characteristic. Radinsky *et al.* [22] use several time-series models for representing and predicting web search behavior and content change. Xiang *et al.* [33] use session nodes to capture short-term interests of paper-tagging behavior through session-item connections. However, their representations cannot learn from multi-faceted information, or fully describe the complex characteristic of human behavior. Hence, temporal multi-faceted behavioral patterns are rarely investigated, and how to accurately predict these behaviors still remains as an open problem.

There are two key challenges to learn human behavioral patterns from the multi-faceted and temporal information.

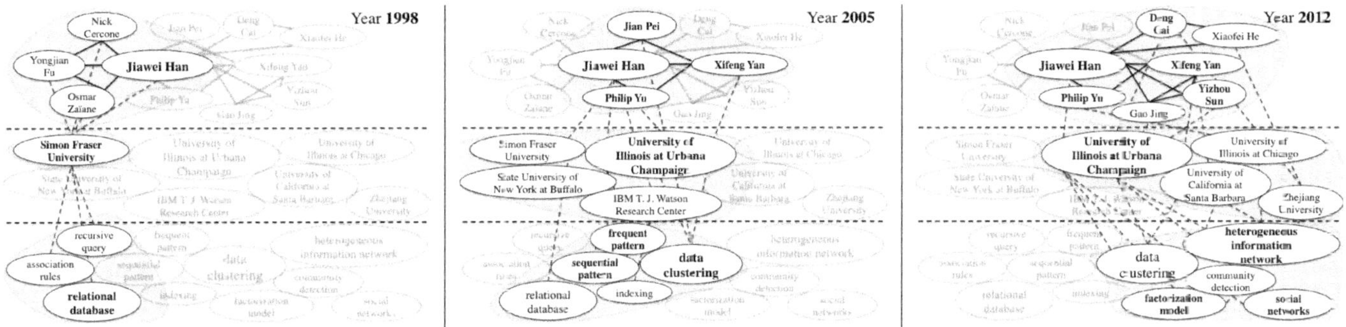

(a) When he was a professor at Simon Fraser University and worked on database systems and data warehousing

(b) When he was a professor at University of Illinois at Urbana-Champaign and worked on data mining from spatio-temporal data

(c) When he was a professor at University of Illinois at Urbana-Champaign and focused on mining social/information network data

Figure 1: A showcase of temporal behavioral pattern discovery: how and why Professor Jiawei Han and his group change their academic research topics? The research behavior includes author, affiliation and keyword (3 layers), and evolves over time.

- **High sparsity.** Multi-faceted data in real applications is often very sparse. In researcher-affiliation-topic case, for example, researchers cannot work in many affiliations or study many problems. The problem is even disastrous when we add the temporal dimension to the multi-faceted behavioral information.
- **High complexity.** Considering the dynamic characteristic, new multi-faceted human behaviors continuously generate along time. The continuously generated data of high volume, high dimension and high sparsity pose great challenge for modeling and analysis due to high computational complexity. Sun *et al.* proposed a tensor based method DTA [26], which saves time of matricizing tensors by storing and updating unfolded matrices. But it still costs too much time on computing eigenvalues and eigenvectors. The issue of fast processing increments is still critical for modeling and predicting human behavior.

To address these challenges, in this paper, we propose a *Flexible Evolutionary Multi-faceted Analysis* (FEMA) method based on a dynamic scheme of tensor factorization for temporal multi-faceted behavior prediction and pattern mining, where flexible regularizers are imposed to alleviate the problems brought by high sparsity. In order to fast decompose high-order tensor sequences, we give approximation algorithms to factorize the new tensor with sparse increments, where the bound of approximation loss is theoretically proved. We evaluate FEMA on two real datasets: publication data from Microsoft Academic Search database and tweet data from Tencent Weibo, a Twitter style website in China. The proposed method achieves 30.8% higher accuracy when it uses multi-faceted factors and 17.4% higher accuracy when it uses flexible regularizers. Moreover, it can reduce the run time from hours to minutes, which is of significant interest to serve real-time applications.

Fig. 1 is a showcase of temporal patterns of academic research behavior discovered by FEMA. It can be seen that the evolutions in Professor Jiawei Han's group from database systems, data clustering to social/information networks can be effectively and efficiently discovered by FEMA. And the pattern clearly shows the co-evolution and interplay between affiliations and his co-authorships, which gives us comprehensive understanding on the temporal and multi-faceted characteristics of behavioral patterns.

The main contributions of this paper are:

(1) Enlightened by the psychological studies on human behaviors, we move one step forward to incorporate temporal dimension into multi-faceted analysis for temporal multi-faceted behavior prediction and pattern mining, which is of paramount importance for various applications, such as web search and recommendation.

(2) We propose the FEMA framework based on tensor factorization to predict temporal multi-faceted behaviors. The model incorporates flexible regularizers to alleviate the sparsity problem. We design approximation algorithms to fast conduct evolutionary analysis of human behaviors.

(3) Our algorithm is efficient and has a theoretical guarantee: it runs in near-quadratic time compared to the near-cubic time of the existing algorithms (see Section 4).

(4) We conduct extensive experiments to predict human behaviors in academic research and social networks. The results show that the proposed FEMA can outperforms other methods on both datasets. More importantly, we demonstrate that the approximation algorithms lead to significant time reduction and the loss is small.

We have the usual organization: Survey, problem definition, proposed method, experiments and conclusions.

2. RELATED WORKS

There is a significant body on research related to our problem, which we categorize into three groups: behavior modeling, behavioral dynamics, and tensor factorization.

Behavior modeling: Matrix factorization has long been used for modeling and predicting human behavior when it includes two types of objects, such as user-item adoption [18] and drug-target interaction [35]. When the number of types is more than two, there has been a great deal of interest in using high-order tensors to model behaviors, for example, web search [27], image and book tagging [29, 23], and recommender systems [11, 12, 2, 10, 20]. These works summarize a static view of the behavioral pattern, but they cannot capture its temporal characteristics.

Behavioral dynamics: There have been attempts to use temporal information to understand past users' behaviors in order to predict future ones in different applications such as recommender systems [6, 3], research themes [32], semantic graphs [28], and online media topics [19, 5, 34]. Xiang *et al.* [33] divide user interests into long-term and short-term and make use of the difference, using a time factor. In contrast to this approach, we consider the group-level dynamics instead of an individual user behavior. Radinsky *et al.* [22] develop a learning algorithm capable of selecting an appropriate model depending on the time. However, how to appropriately use the time information to discover the underlying dynamics of human behavior still remains an important research challenge.

Matrix/tensor factorization: There has been active research on matrix factorization [30, 31], tensor analysis [4, 26, 13], tensor decompositions [15, 16, 9] and scalable methods [17, 1]. Here we focus on how to efficiently process the increments in tensor decomposition by matrix and tensor perturbation theory [25].

3. PROBLEM FORMULATION

In this section, we first give the modeling of two different types of human behavior including academic research and mentioning to someone in tweets. Then we give a general definition of our problem or the task of our method.

Modeling the behavior of academic research.

Let the bibliographic dataset be an example of our problem: we focus on finding temporal patterns of academic research behavior. Let the dataset be a list of tuples (a, f, k, t) denoting that an author a in an affiliation f (university, research center, etc.) publishes about a keyword k at time t ($t = 1, \ldots, T$). We model the data as a 3-order tensor sequence $\mathcal{X}_\mathbf{t} \in \mathbb{R}^{n^{(a)} \times n^{(f)} \times n^{(k)}}$, where $n^{(a)}$ is the number of authors, $n^{(f)}$ is the number of affiliations, and $n^{(k)}$ is the number of keywords. $\mathcal{X}_\mathbf{t}(a, f, k)$ has a value of the number of existing tuples (a, f, k, t') ($t' \leq t$). Our goal is to factorize the tensor sequence

$$\mathcal{X}_\mathbf{t} \approx \mathcal{Y}_\mathbf{t} \times_{(a)} \mathbf{A}_\mathbf{t} \times_{(f)} \mathbf{F}_\mathbf{t} \times_{(k)} \mathbf{K}_\mathbf{t} \quad (1)$$

where

- $\mathcal{Y}_\mathbf{t} \in \mathbb{R}^{r^{(a)} \times r^{(f)} \times r^{(k)}}$ is the core tensor sequence, which encodes the temporal behavioral patterns, i.e., the relationship among author, affiliation and keyword groups. $\mathcal{Y}_\mathbf{t}(j^{(a)}, j^{(f)}, j^{(k)})$ indicates the probability of the behavior before time t if the $j^{(a)}$-th author group in the $j^{(f)}$-th affiliation group publishes the $j^{(k)}$-th keyword group.
- $\mathbf{A}_\mathbf{t} \in \mathbb{R}^{n^{(a)} \times r^{(a)}}$ is the authors' projection matrix before time t. $\mathbf{A}(i^{(a)}, j^{(a)})$ represents the probability that the $i^{(a)}$-th author belongs to the $j^{(a)}$-th group before time t.
- $\mathbf{F}_\mathbf{t} \in \mathbb{R}^{n^{(f)} \times r^{(f)}}$ is the affiliations' projection matrix before time t. $\mathbf{F}_\mathbf{t}(i^{(f)}, j^{(f)})$ represents the probability that the $i^{(f)}$-th affiliation belongs to the $j^{(f)}$-th group before time t.
- $\mathbf{K}_\mathbf{t} \in \mathbb{R}^{n^{(k)} \times r^{(k)}}$ is the keywords' projection matrix before time t. $\mathbf{K}_\mathbf{t}(i^{(k)}, j^{(k)})$ represents the probability that the $i^{(k)}$-th keyword belongs to the $j^{(k)}$-th group before time t.

Note that the key to solving the sparsity problem in tensor decompositions is to learn the flexible regularizers such as the authors' co-authorship, the affiliations' geographical distance and the keywords' semantic information. The regularizers can be encoded as Laplacian matrices $\mathbf{L^{(a)}}$, $\mathbf{L^{(f)}}$, $\mathbf{L^{(k)}}$, where the (i, j)-th element represents the similarity between the i-th and j-th entities (authors, affiliations, keywords): the similarity can be how many papers the authors collaborate or how close the affiliations locate.

The problem is now how to compute the factorizations for the core tensor sequence and projection matrices, given the tensor sequence and constraints. Note that the scale of the tensors are large but the changes are very small. We denote by $\Delta\mathcal{X}_\mathbf{t}$ the increment at time t, which is very sparse: for any $1 \leq t < T$, $\Delta\mathcal{X}_\mathbf{t} = \mathcal{X}_\mathbf{t+1} - \mathcal{X}_\mathbf{t}$. The problem can be summarized into two steps:

- **Given** the first tensor $\mathcal{X}_\mathbf{1}$ and the constraints $\mathbf{L^{(a)}}$, $\mathbf{L^{(f)}}$, $\mathbf{L^{(k)}}$, **find** the projection matrix $\mathbf{A_1}$, $\mathbf{F_1}$, $\mathbf{K_1}$, and the first core tensor $\mathcal{Y}_\mathbf{1}$.
- At time t ($1 \leq t < T$), **given** the tensor $\mathcal{X}_\mathbf{t}$, the increment $\Delta\mathcal{X}_\mathbf{t}$, the old projection matrices $\mathbf{A_t}$, $\mathbf{F_t}$, $\mathbf{K_t}$, and the constraints $\mathbf{L^{(a)}}$, $\mathbf{L^{(f)}}$, $\mathbf{L^{(k)}}$, **find** the new projection matrices $\mathbf{A_{t+1}}$, $\mathbf{F_{t+1}}$, $\mathbf{K_{t+1}}$, and the new core tensor $\mathcal{Y}_\mathbf{t+1}$.

Modeling the behavior of "mentions" in tweets.

Let the tweet dataset be another example of our problem and thus we come to find temporal patterns of the mention in tweets. Let the dataset be a list of tuples (s, d, w, t) denoting that a Twitter user s ("source") uses the "@username" format to mention a user d ("target", or "destination") in the body of a tweet which includes a word w at time t ($t = 1, \ldots, T$), so that the user d will see the tweet in his/her "Mentions" tab. Similarly to the modeling of academic research behavior, we model the data as a 3-order tensor sequence $\mathcal{X}_\mathbf{t} \in \mathbb{R}^{n^{(s)} \times n^{(d)} \times n^{(w)}}$, where $n^{(s)}$ is the number of sources, $n^{(d)}$ is the number of targets, and $n^{(w)}$ is the number of words. $\mathcal{X}_\mathbf{t}(s, d, w)$ is the number of tuples (s, d, w, t') ($t' \leq t$). Our goal is to factorize the tensor sequence

$$\mathcal{X}_\mathbf{t} \approx \mathcal{Y}_\mathbf{t} \times_{(s)} \mathbf{S}_\mathbf{t} \times_{(d)} \mathbf{D}_\mathbf{t} \times_{(w)} \mathbf{W}_\mathbf{t} \quad (2)$$

where $\mathcal{Y}_\mathbf{t} \in \mathbb{R}^{r^{(s)} \times r^{(d)} \times r^{(w)}}$ is the core tensor sequence; $\mathbf{S}_\mathbf{t} \in \mathbb{R}^{n^{(s)} \times r^{(s)}}$ is the source users' projection matrix, $\mathbf{D}_\mathbf{t} \in \mathbb{R}^{n^{(d)} \times r^{(d)}}$ is the target users' projection matrix, and $\mathbf{W}_\mathbf{t} \in \mathbb{R}^{n^{(w)} \times r^{(w)}}$ is the words' projection matrix.

Here, to solve the sparsity problem, the flexible regularizers such as the users' social relations (e.g., the number of common friends), and the words' semantic information, can be encoded as Laplacian matrices $\mathbf{L^{(s)}}$, $\mathbf{L^{(d)}}$, $\mathbf{L^{(w)}}$. Similarly, the problem can be summarized into two steps:

- **Given** the first tensor $\mathcal{X}_\mathbf{1}$ and constraints $\mathbf{L^{(s)}}$, $\mathbf{L^{(d)}}$, $\mathbf{L^{(w)}}$, **find** projection matrix $\mathbf{S_1}$, $\mathbf{D_1}$, $\mathbf{W_1}$, and core tensor $\mathcal{Y}_\mathbf{1}$.
- At time t ($1 \leq t < T$), **given** the tensor $\mathcal{X}_\mathbf{t}$, the increment $\Delta\mathcal{X}_\mathbf{t}$, the old projection matrices $\mathbf{S_t}$, $\mathbf{D_t}$, $\mathbf{W_t}$, and the constraints $\mathbf{L^{(s)}}$, $\mathbf{L^{(d)}}$, $\mathbf{L^{(w)}}$, **find** the new projection matrices $\mathbf{S_{t+1}}$, $\mathbf{D_{t+1}}$, $\mathbf{W_{t+1}}$, and the new core tensor $\mathcal{Y}_\mathbf{t+1}$.

The general problem definition.

Our problem is quite different from previous research. First, we incorporate multi-faceted information and constraints into a unified framework. Second, we conduct evolutionary analysis to efficiently deal with sparse increments, which is in contrast with the majority of existing works that decompose a single tensor. We extend the formulation from 3 to M dimensions and give a general definition.

Definition 1 (Flexible Evolutionary Multi-faceted Analysis (FEMA))
(1) Initialization:
Given *the first* M*-way tensor* $\mathcal{X}_\mathbf{1} \in \mathbb{R}^{n^{(1)} \times \ldots \times n^{(M)}}$ *and the constraints* $\mathbf{L^{(m)}}|_{m=1}^{M} \in \mathbb{R}^{n^{(m)} \times n^{(m)}}$, **find** *the first projection matrices* $\mathbf{A_1^{(m)}}|_{m=1}^{M} \in \mathbb{R}^{n^{(m)} \times r^{(m)}}$ *and the first core tensor* $\mathcal{Y}_\mathbf{1} \in \mathbb{R}^{r^{(1)} \times \ldots \times r^{(M)}}$.
(2) Evolutionary analysis:
At time t ($1 \leq t < T$), **given** *the tensor* $\mathcal{X}_\mathbf{t} \in \mathbb{R}^{n^{(1)} \times \ldots \times n^{(M)}}$, *the increment* $\Delta\mathcal{X}_\mathbf{t}$, *the old projection matrices* $\mathbf{A_t^{(m)}}|_{m=1}^{M}$, *and the constraints* $\mathbf{L^{(m)}}|_{m=1}^{M}$, **find** *the new projection matrices* $\mathbf{A_{t+1}^{(m)}}|_{m=1}^{M}$ *and the new core tensor* $\mathcal{Y}_\mathbf{t+1}$.

4. ALGORITHM

In this section, we provide approximation algorithms for the two steps in Flexible Evolutionary Multi-faceted Analysis (FEMA). We also give a discussion on the computational efficiency and approximation quality.

Initialization.

Here we present how we incorporate the multi-faceted information and constraints into the tensor decomposition. We denote by $\mu^{(m)}$ the weight of the mode-m Laplacian matrix $\mathbf{L^{(m)}}$. The covariance matrix of the m-th mode at time $t = 1$ is

$$\mathbf{C_1^{(m)}} = \mathbf{X_1^{(m)}}\mathbf{X_1^{(m)T}} + \mu^{(m)}\mathbf{L^{(m)}} \quad (3)$$

where $\mathbf{X_1^{(m)}} \in \mathbb{R}^{n^{(m)} \times \prod_{i \neq m} n^{(i)}}$ is the mode-m matricizing of the tensor $\mathcal{X}_1$. The projection matrices $\mathbf{A_1^{(m)}}|_{m=1}^{M}$ can be computed by diagonalization: they are the top $r^{(m)}$ eigenvectors of the covariance matrix $\mathbf{C_1^{(m)}}|_{m=1}^{M}$. The pseudocode is listed in Algorithm 1.

Algorithm 1 Initialization in FEMA

Require: $\mathcal{X}_1, \mathbf{L^{(m)}}|_{m=1}^{M}$
  for $m = 1, \ldots, M$ **do**
    Construct covariance matrix $\mathbf{C_1^{(m)}}$ using Eq.3;
    $\lambda_1^{(m)}$/$\mathbf{A_1^{(m)}}$ are the top $r^{(m)}$ eigenvalue/eigenvector of $\mathbf{C_1^{(m)}}$
  end for
  $\mathcal{Y}_1 = \mathcal{X}_1 \prod_{m=1}^{M} \times_{(m)} \mathbf{A_1^{(m)T}}$;
  return $\mathbf{A_1^{(m)}}|_{m=1}^{M}, \lambda_1^{(m)}|_{m=1}^{M}, \mathcal{Y}_1$

Evolutionary analysis.
Next we introduce an efficient technique based on tensor perturbation to adjust the projection matrices according to changes of the tensor. We denote by $\mathbf{X_t^{(m)}} \in \mathbb{R}^{n^{(m)} \times \prod_{i \neq m} n^{(i)}}$ the mode-m matricizing of the tensor $\mathcal{X}_t$. We define the covariance matrix $\mathbf{C_t^{(m)}} = \mathbf{X_t^{(m)}}\mathbf{X_t^{(m)}}^\top + \mu^{(m)}\mathbf{L^{(m)}}$ and define $(\lambda_{t,i}^{(m)}, \mathbf{a_{t,i}^{(m)}})$ as one eigenvalue-eigenvector pair of the matrix $\mathbf{C_t^{(m)}}$. The vector $\mathbf{a_{t,i}^{(m)}}$ is exactly the i-th column of the projection matrix $\mathbf{A_t^{(m)}}$. Then we can rewrite $(\lambda_{t+1,i}^{(m)}, \mathbf{a_{t+1,i}^{(m)}})$ as

$$\lambda_{t+1,i}^{(m)} = \lambda_{t,i}^{(m)} + \Delta\lambda_{t,i}^{(m)} \quad (4)$$

$$\mathbf{a_{t+1,i}^{(m)}} = \mathbf{a_{t,i}^{(m)}} + \Delta\mathbf{a_{t,i}^{(m)}} \quad (5)$$

To simplify the denotions, we omit "t" in the terms and equations when it is unnecessary. Thus we can obtain

$$\begin{aligned}&[(\mathbf{X^{(m)}} + \Delta\mathbf{X^{(m)}})(\mathbf{X^{(m)}} + \Delta\mathbf{X^{(m)}})^\top + \mu^{(m)}\mathbf{L^{(m)}}] \quad (6)\\ &\cdot(\mathbf{a_i^{(m)}} + \Delta\mathbf{a_i^{(m)}}) = (\lambda_i^{(m)} + \Delta\lambda_i^{(m)})(\mathbf{a_i^{(m)}} + \Delta\mathbf{a_i^{(m)}})\end{aligned}$$

Now the key questions are how to compute changes to the eigenvalue $\Delta\lambda_i^{(m)}$ and eigenvector $\Delta\mathbf{a_i^{(m)}}$, respectively.
Expanding Eq.6, we obtain

$$\begin{aligned}&\mathbf{X^{(m)}}\mathbf{X^{(m)}}^\top\mathbf{a_i^{(m)}} + \mathbf{X^{(m)}}\mathbf{X^{(m)}}^\top\Delta\mathbf{a_i^{(m)}} \quad (7)\\ &+\mathbf{X^{(m)}}\Delta\mathbf{X^{(m)}}^\top\mathbf{a_i^{(m)}} + \mathbf{X^{(m)}}\Delta\mathbf{X^{(m)}}^\top\Delta\mathbf{a_i^{(m)}}\\ &+\Delta\mathbf{X^{(m)}}\mathbf{X^{(m)}}^\top\mathbf{a_i^{(m)}} + \Delta\mathbf{X^{(m)}}\mathbf{X^{(m)}}^\top\Delta\mathbf{a_i^{(m)}}\\ &+\Delta\mathbf{X^{(m)}}\Delta\mathbf{X^{(m)}}^\top\mathbf{a_i^{(m)}} + \Delta\mathbf{X^{(m)}}\Delta\mathbf{X^{(m)}}^\top\Delta\mathbf{a_i^{(m)}}\\ &+\mu^{(m)}\mathbf{L^{(m)}}\mathbf{a_i^{(m)}} + \mu^{(m)}\mathbf{L^{(m)}}\Delta\mathbf{a_i^{(m)}}\\ &= \lambda_i^{(m)}\mathbf{a_i^{(m)}} + \lambda_i^{(m)}\Delta\mathbf{a_i^{(m)}} + \Delta\lambda_i^{(m)}\mathbf{a_i^{(m)}} + \Delta\lambda_i^{(m)}\Delta\mathbf{a_i^{(m)}}\end{aligned}$$

In this paper, we concentrate on first-order approximation, i.e., we assume all high order perturbation terms (such as $\mathbf{X^{(m)}}\Delta\mathbf{X^{(m)}}^\top\Delta\mathbf{a_i^{(m)}}$, $\Delta\mathbf{X^{(m)}}\mathbf{X^{(m)}}^\top\Delta\mathbf{a_i^{(m)}}$, $\Delta\mathbf{X^{(m)}}\Delta\mathbf{X^{(m)}}^\top\mathbf{a_i^{(m)}}$, $\Delta\mathbf{X^{(m)}}\Delta\mathbf{X^{(m)}}^\top\Delta\mathbf{a_i^{(m)}}$ in the above equation) are neglectable. By further using the fact that $(\mathbf{X^{(m)}}\mathbf{X^{(m)}}^\top + \mu^{(m)}\mathbf{L^{(m)}})\mathbf{a_i^{(m)}} = \lambda_i^{(m)}\mathbf{a_i^{(m)}}$, we can obtain

$$\begin{aligned}&\mathbf{X^{(m)}}\mathbf{X^{(m)}}^\top\Delta\mathbf{a_i^{(m)}} + (\mathbf{X^{(m)}}\Delta\mathbf{X^{(m)}}^\top + \Delta\mathbf{X^{(m)}}\mathbf{X^{(m)}}^\top)\mathbf{a_i^{(m)}} \quad (8)\\ &+\mu^{(m)}\mathbf{L^{(m)}}\Delta\mathbf{a_i^{(m)}} = \lambda_i^{(m)}\Delta\mathbf{a_i^{(m)}} + \Delta\lambda_i^{(m)}\mathbf{a_i^{(m)}}\end{aligned}$$

Now multiplying both sides of Eq.8 with $\mathbf{a_i^{(m)}}^\top$ and because of the symmetry of $\mathbf{X^{(m)}}\mathbf{X^{(m)}}^\top$ and $\mathbf{L^{(m)}}$, we get

$$\Delta\lambda_i^{(m)} = \mathbf{a_i^{(m)}}^\top(\mathbf{X^{(m)}}\Delta\mathbf{X^{(m)}}^\top + \Delta\mathbf{X^{(m)}}\mathbf{X^{(m)}}^\top)\mathbf{a_i^{(m)}} \quad (9)$$

Since the eigenvectors are orthogonal to each other, we assume that the change of the eigenvector $\Delta\mathbf{a_i^{(m)}}$ is in the subspace spanned by those original eigenvectors, i.e.,

$$\Delta\mathbf{a_i^{(m)}} \approx \sum_{j=1}^{r^{(m)}} \alpha_{ij}\mathbf{a_j^{(m)}} \quad (10)$$

where $\{\alpha_{ij}\}$ are small constants to be determined. Bringing Eq.10 into Eq.8, we obtain

$$\begin{aligned}&(\mathbf{X^{(m)}}\mathbf{X^{(m)}}^\top + \mu^{(m)}\mathbf{L^{(m)}})\sum_{j=1}^{r^{(m)}} \alpha_{ij}\mathbf{a_j^{(m)}} \quad (11)\\ &+(\mathbf{X^{(m)}}\Delta\mathbf{X^{(m)}}^\top + \Delta\mathbf{X^{(m)}}\mathbf{X^{(m)}}^\top)\mathbf{a_i^{(m)}}\\ &= \lambda_i^{(m)}\sum_{j=1}^{r^{(m)}} \alpha_{ij}\mathbf{a_j^{(m)}} + \Delta\lambda_i^{(m)}\mathbf{a_i^{(m)}}\end{aligned}$$

which is equivalent to

$$\begin{aligned}&\sum_{j=1}^{r^{(m)}} \lambda_j^{(m)}\alpha_{ij}\mathbf{a_j^{(m)}} + \mathbf{X^{(m)}}\Delta\mathbf{X^{(m)}}^\top\mathbf{a_i^{(m)}} \quad (12)\\ &+\Delta\mathbf{X^{(m)}}\mathbf{X^{(m)}}^\top\mathbf{a_i^{(m)}} = \lambda_i^{(m)}\sum_{j=1}^{r^{(m)}} \alpha_{ij}\mathbf{a_j^{(m)}} + \Delta\lambda_i^{(m)}\mathbf{a_i^{(m)}}\end{aligned}$$

Multiplying $\mathbf{a_k^{(m)}}^\top$ $(k \neq i)$ on both sides of the above equation, we get

$$\begin{aligned}&\lambda_k^{(m)}\alpha_{ik} + \mathbf{a_k^{(m)}}^\top\mathbf{X^{(m)}}\Delta\mathbf{X^{(m)}}^\top\mathbf{a_i^{(m)}} \quad (13)\\ &+\mathbf{a_k^{(m)}}^\top\Delta\mathbf{X^{(m)}}\mathbf{X^{(m)}}^\top\mathbf{a_i^{(m)}} = \lambda_i^{(m)}\alpha_{ik}\end{aligned}$$

Therefore,

$$\alpha_{ik} = \frac{\mathbf{a_k^{(m)}}^\top(\mathbf{X^{(m)}}\Delta\mathbf{X^{(m)}}^\top + \Delta\mathbf{X^{(m)}}\mathbf{X^{(m)}}^\top)\mathbf{a_i^{(m)}}}{\lambda_i^{(m)} - \lambda_k^{(m)}} \quad (14)$$

To get α_{ii}, we use the fact that

$$\begin{aligned}(\mathbf{a_i^{(m)}} + \Delta\mathbf{a_i^{(m)}})^\top(\mathbf{a_i^{(m)}} + \Delta\mathbf{a_i^{(m)}}) &= 1\\ \Longleftrightarrow 1 + 2\mathbf{a_i^{(m)}}^\top\Delta\mathbf{a_i^{(m)}} + O(\|\Delta\mathbf{a_i^{(m)}}\|^2) &= 1\end{aligned}$$

Discarding the high order term, and bringing in Eq.10, we get $\alpha_{ii} = 0$. Therefore,

$$\Delta\mathbf{a_i^{(m)}} = \sum_{j \neq i} \frac{\mathbf{a_j^{(m)}}^\top(\mathbf{X^{(m)}}\Delta\mathbf{X^{(m)}}^\top + \Delta\mathbf{X^{(m)}}\mathbf{X^{(m)}}^\top)\mathbf{a_i^{(m)}}}{\lambda_i^{(m)} - \lambda_j^{(m)}}\mathbf{a_j^{(m)}} \quad (15)$$

Note that the constraints $\mathbf{L^{(m)}}$ do not appear in the eigenvalue and eigenvector updating functions Eq.9 and Eq.15. Note that the constraints have to be learnt only *once*.

Algorithm 2 Evolutionary Analysis in FEMA

Require: $\mathcal{X}_t$, $\Delta\mathcal{X}_t$, $\mathbf{A}_t^{(m)}|_{m=1}^M$, $\lambda_t^{(m)}|_{m=1}^M$
  for $m = 1, \ldots, M$ **do**
    for $i = 1, \ldots, r^{(m)}$ **do**
      Compute $\Delta\lambda_{t,i}^{(m)}$ using Eq.9, and compute $\lambda_{t+1,i}^{(m)} = \lambda_{t,i}^{(m)} + \Delta\lambda_{t,i}^{(m)}$;
      Compute $\Delta\mathbf{a}_{t,i}^{(m)}$ using Eq.15, and compute $\mathbf{a}_{t+1,i}^{(m)} = \mathbf{a}_{t,i}^{(m)} + \Delta\mathbf{a}_{t,i}^{(m)}$ and $\mathbf{A}_{t+1}^{(m)} = \{\mathbf{a}_{t+1,i}^{(m)}\}$;
    end for
  end for
  $\mathcal{Y}_{t+1} = (\mathcal{X}_t + \Delta\mathcal{X}_t)\prod_{m=1}^M \times_{(m)} \mathbf{A}_{t+1}^{(m)\mathbf{T}}$;
  return $\mathbf{A}_{t+1}^{(m)}|_{m=1}^M$, $\lambda_{t+1}^{(m)}|_{m=1}^M$, $\mathcal{Y}_{t+1}$

Computational complexity.

Here we analyze the computational complexity of Algorithm 2 before the computation of the core tensor. For the m-th mode, we define $D^{(m)}$ as the number of features of each point on the m-th dimension. Since the tensors are usually extremely sparse, we know $D^{(m)} \leq E \ll \prod_{m' \neq m} n^{(m')}$, where E is the number of non-zero entries in the tensors. In order to compute the increment on the eigenvalue and eigenvector using Eq.9 and Eq.15 for the m-th mode, we need to compute $\mathbf{v}_i^{(m)}$, which requires $O(n^{(m)}D^{(m)})$ time. As $\Delta\mathbf{X}^{(m)}$ is very sparse, $\Delta\mathbf{X}^{(m)}\mathbf{v}_i^{(m)}$ only requires constant time $O(D^{(m)})$. Therefore, for computing $\Delta\lambda_i^{(m)}$ and $\Delta\mathbf{a}_i^{(m)}$, we need $O(r^{(m)}n^{(m)}D^{(m)} + r^{(m)}D^{(m)})$ time, and updating eigenvalues and eigenvectors for T times requires $O(T\sum_{m=1}^M r^{(m)}(n^{(m)}+1)D^{(m)})$ time. In comparison, if we redo the eigenvalue decomposition on $\mathcal{X}_{t+1}$, it costs $O(T\sum_{m=1}^M (D^{(m)}(n^{(m)})^2 + (n^{(m)})^3))$ time, which is much higher.

Approximation quality.

We now present two theorems that bound the magnitude of $\Delta\lambda_i^{(m)}$ and $\Delta\mathbf{a}_i^{(m)}$. Both theorems confirm our intuition that the magnitude of $\Delta\lambda_i^{(m)}$ and $\Delta\mathbf{a}_i^{(m)}$ is directly related to the norm of $\Delta\mathbf{X}^{(m)}$. Also since the higher order terms are ignored in the approximation, FEMA algorithms only works when those terms are relatively small.

Theorem 1 *The magnitude of the variation on the eigenvalue, i.e., $|\Delta\lambda_i^{(m)}|$, $(\forall i = 1, \ldots, r^{(m)})$, satisfies the following inequality*

$$|\Delta\lambda_i^{(m)}| \leq 2(\lambda^{\max}_{\mathbf{X}^{(m)\top}\mathbf{X}^{(m)}})^{\frac{1}{2}}\|\Delta\mathbf{X}^{(m)}\|_2 \tag{16}$$

where $\lambda^{\max}_{\mathbf{X}^{(m)\top}\mathbf{X}^{(m)}}$ is the maximum eigenvalue of the data inner product matrix $\mathbf{X}^{(m)\top}\mathbf{X}^{(m)}$, $\|\Delta\mathbf{X}^{(m)}\|_2$ is the 2-norm of $\Delta\mathbf{X}^{(m)}$.

PROOF. According to Eq.9, we have

$$|\Delta\lambda_i^{(m)}| = |\mathbf{a}_i^{(m)\top}(\mathbf{X}^{(m)}\Delta\mathbf{X}^{(m)\top} + \Delta\mathbf{X}^{(m)}\mathbf{X}^{(m)\top})\mathbf{a}_i^{(m)}| \tag{17}$$

By Cauchy-Schwarz inequality,

$$\begin{aligned}&|\mathbf{a}_i^{(m)\top}(\mathbf{X}^{(m)}\Delta\mathbf{X}^{(m)\top} + \Delta\mathbf{X}^{(m)}\mathbf{X}^{(m)\top})\mathbf{a}_i^{(m)}| \\ &\leq 2\|\Delta\mathbf{X}^{(m)}\mathbf{X}^{(m)\top}\mathbf{a}_i^{(m)}\|_2\|\mathbf{a}_i^{(m)}\|_2 = 2\|\Delta\mathbf{X}^{(m)}\mathbf{X}^{(m)\top}\mathbf{a}_i^{(m)}\|_2\end{aligned} \tag{18}$$

where in the first step we use the symmetry of $\mathbf{X}^{(m)}\Delta\mathbf{X}^{(m)\top} + \Delta\mathbf{X}^{(m)}\mathbf{X}^{(m)\top}$ and in the second step we use the fact that $\|\mathbf{a}_i^{(m)}\| = 1$. By the definition of matrix 2-norm, we have that

$$\|\Delta\mathbf{X}^{(m)}\mathbf{X}^{(m)\top}\|_2 = \sup_{\|\mathbf{w}\|_2=1}\|\Delta\mathbf{X}^{(m)}\mathbf{X}^{(m)\top}\mathbf{w}\|_2 \tag{19}$$

Therefore

$$\begin{aligned}&|\mathbf{a}_i^{(m)\top}(\mathbf{X}^{(m)}\Delta\mathbf{X}^{(m)\top} + \Delta\mathbf{X}^{(m)}\mathbf{X}^{(m)\top})\mathbf{a}_i^{(m)}| \\ &\leq 2\|\Delta\mathbf{X}^{(m)}\mathbf{X}^{(m)\top}\|_2 \leq 2\|\mathbf{X}^{(m)}\|_2\|\Delta\mathbf{X}^{(m)}\|_2 \\ &= 2(\lambda^{\max}_{\mathbf{X}^{(m)\top}\mathbf{X}^{(m)}})^{\frac{1}{2}}\|\Delta\mathbf{X}^{(m)}\|_2 \quad \square\end{aligned} \tag{20}$$

Theorem 2 *The magnitude of the variation on the eigenvector, i.e., $|\Delta\mathbf{a}_i^{(m)}|$, $(\forall i = 1, \ldots, r^{(m)})$, satisfies the following inequality*

$$|\Delta\mathbf{a}_i^{(m)}| \leq 2\|\Delta\mathbf{X}^{(m)}\|_2\sum_{j\neq i}\frac{(\lambda^{\max}_{\mathbf{X}^{(m)\top}\mathbf{X}^{(m)}})^{\frac{1}{2}}}{|\lambda_i^{(m)} - \lambda_j^{(m)}|} \tag{21}$$

where $\lambda^{\max}_{\mathbf{X}^{(m)\top}\mathbf{X}^{(m)}}$ is the maximum eigenvalue of the data inner product matrix $\mathbf{X}^{(m)\top}\mathbf{X}^{(m)}$, $\|\Delta\mathbf{X}^{(m)}\|_2$ is the 2-norm of $\Delta\mathbf{X}^{(m)}$.

PROOF. From Eq.15, we have that

$$\begin{aligned}|\Delta\mathbf{a}_i^{(m)}| &= 2\left|\sum_{j\neq i}\frac{\mathbf{a}_j^{(m)\top}\Delta\mathbf{X}^{(m)}\mathbf{X}^{(m)\top}\mathbf{a}_i^{(m)}}{\lambda_i^{(m)} - \lambda_j^{(m)}}\mathbf{a}_j^{(m)}\right| \\ &\leq 2\sum_{j\neq i}\left\|\frac{\mathbf{a}_j^{(m)\top}\Delta\mathbf{X}^{(m)}\mathbf{X}^{(m)\top}\mathbf{a}_i^{(m)}}{\lambda_i^{(m)} - \lambda_j^{(m)}}\mathbf{a}_j^{(m)}\right\| \\ &\leq 2\sum_{j\neq i}\frac{\|\mathbf{a}_j^{(m)}\|}{|\lambda_i^{(m)} - \lambda_j^{(m)}|}\|\mathbf{a}_j^{(m)\top}\Delta\mathbf{X}^{(m)}\mathbf{X}^{(m)\top}\mathbf{a}_i^{(m)}\| \\ &\leq 2\|\Delta\mathbf{X}^{(m)}\|_2\sum_{j\neq i}\frac{(\lambda^{\max}_{\mathbf{X}^{(m)\top}\mathbf{X}^{(m)}})^{\frac{1}{2}}}{|\lambda_i^{(m)} - \lambda_j^{(m)}|} \quad \square\end{aligned} \tag{22}$$

5. EXPERIMENTS

In this section, we evaluate the effectiveness, efficiency and robustness of our proposed FEMA for the tasks of behavior prediction. We also provide interesting discovery of the temporal behavioral patterns for strong additional evidence of the effectiveness.

5.1 Datasets and Experimental Settings

We use the following two real-world datasets in our experiments:

- MAS data [24]: This is a publicly available dataset from Microsoft Academic Search database, which comprises of three files. The first file contains profile information about 250K authors such as author name and affiliation. The second file contains data about 2.5M papers, such as paper title, year and keywords. The third file contains data of corresponding paper-author connections. We first join these three files over author, affiliation, keyword and year of the paper, and then pre-process the data to generate a subset such that each author, affiliation and keyword occur at least 10 times in the dataset. The resulting dataset has 171,519 tuples (author,affiliation,keyword,year) with 7,777 authors, 651 affiliations and 4,566 keywords in 32 years (from 1980 to 2012). The average density of the tensor in each year is less than $3 \times 10^{-5}\%$, while the density of the co-authorship matrix is as large as 0.2%.
- WEIBO data: Tencent Weibo is one of the largest microblogging platforms in China, on which users can post a mention

Statistics	MAS	Statistics	WEIBO
Author	7,777	Source user	6,200
Affiliation	651	Target user	1,813
Keyword	4,566	Word in tweet	6,435
Time	32 years	Time	43 days
Co-authorship	98,671	Social relation	465,438
Number of tuples	171,519	Number of tuples	519,624

Table 1: Characteristics of datasets.

by typing their tweets with "@username". This dataset comprises of two files. The first file contains posting time, user and content of the tweet. From the content, we can recognize the mentioned (target) users. The second file contains social network information of the source and target users. After the preprocessing, we have 519,624 tuples (source,target,word,time) with 6,200 source users, 1,813 target users and 6,435 words in 43 days (from Nov. 9, 2011 to Dec. 21, 2011). The average density of the tensor in each week is less than $2\times10^{-5}\%$, while the density of the social relation matrix is 0.7%.

Tab. 1 summarizes the characteristics of these academic and tweet datasets. We use the two datasets to perform on two different *behavior prediction* tasks. Both the tasks are set up to continuously predict the future behaviors using new-arriving data.

- **2W** (Who-What and Who-Whom) **prediction:** It is to predict the behaviors of the given *author* u to study the given *keyword* v, or the behaviors of the given *source user* u to mention the given *target user* v in their tweets, no matter where the author is or what the tweet content is.
- **3W** (Who-Where-What and Who-Whom-What) **prediction:** The goal is to predict the behaviors of the given *author* u to study the given *keyword* v in the given *affiliation* w, or the behaviors of the given *source user* u to mention the given *target user* v in tweets of the given *word* w.

Fig. 2 shows how we use the data to set up the experiments. The two datasets were split into three parts: training for initialization, training for evolutionary analysis and testing. We use the earliest 30% for initialization, and then let the behavioral data come 5% by 5% for evolutionary analysis, and use the next 20% for testing. In other words, we will test the performance for $T = 10$ times that the percents of the *training* parts are the first $\alpha_t = 35\%, 40\%$ to 80%, for $t = 1, 2, \ldots, T$.

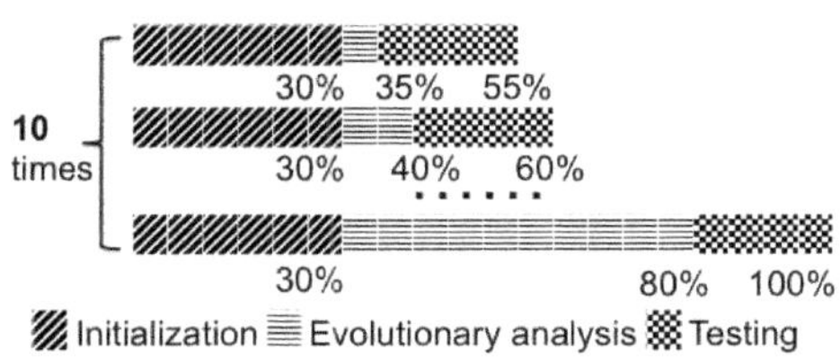

Figure 2: Experimental settings: we use the first 30% data for initialization, and set up 10 times of predictions that each time we train 5% more data, predict and test with the next 20%.

5.2 Competing Algorithms

We evaluate the effectiveness and efficiency of the proposed method. To evaluate the effectiveness, we implement 3 versions of FEMA:

- FEMA models academic research behavior with tensors of authors, affiliations and keywords, and uses the co-authorship regularization. Similarly, it models the behavior of mentioning in tweets with tensors of source users, target users and words, and uses the social regularization.
- EMA models with multi-way tensors but does not utilize regularization. It does not use the co-authorship and social network information.
- EA models the behavior with author-keyword and source-target matrix and uses the standard matrix factorization to predict the missing values. It does not use the multi-faceted information and will only be used for 2W prediction.

To compare with the state-of-the-art methods, we implement the following popular methods:

- CP (CANDECOMP/PARAFAC) [16] decomposes the updated tensor as a sum of rank-one tensors every time. It requires a unified value for the number of groups in each dimension: $r^{(1)} = r^{(2)} = r^{(3)} = R$.
- HOSVD (high-order SVD) [8] is Tucker decomposition of the updated tensor, which is a high-order form of principal component analysis.
- DTA (Dynamic tensor analysis) [26] updates the covariance matrices for quick tensor dimensionality reduction. It does not store any historical tensor but still has to decompose the huge covariance matrix. We will test the online processing ability of our method with it.

To evaluate the approximation quality and efficiency, we also implement an offline learning version of FEMA:

- FMA utilizes the same knowledge as FEMA, however, it merges increments with previous data and processes the decomposition with the updated tensor every time.

We implement our framework in MATLAB and perform the experiments on a single machine with Intel Xeon CPU at 2.40GHz and 32GB RAM, running Windows Server 2008.

By default, the parameters are $r^{(i)} = 50$ and $\mu^{(i)} = 0.3$, for $i = 1, 2, 3$. The discussion for the performances of different parameter settings is given later in Section 5.6.

5.3 Evaluation Methods

For the first task, complex behavior prediction, we use the standard evaluation metrics Mean Absolute Error (*MAE*) and Root Mean Square Error (*RMSE*) [3] defined as:

$$MAE = \frac{\sum_{(u,v,w)\in D} |r_{u,v,w} - \hat{r}_{u,v,w}|}{|D|}$$

$$RMSE = \frac{\sum_{(u,v,w)\in D} (r_{u,v,w} - \hat{r}_{u,v,w})^2}{|D|}$$

where D denotes the testing set; $r_{u,v,w}$ is the predicted probability of the behavior that author u publishes keyword v in affiliation w or user u mentions user v in tweets of word w; and $\hat{r}_{u,v,w}$ is the frequency of the behaviors in the testing set and 0 if not. Small *MAE* and *RMSE* will be a better model.

Also we use two frequently used metrics, *Precision* and *Recall* [7], to evaluate the quality of ranking for prediction values. Let $T(u, v, w)$ be the set of behaviors in the testing set and let $P(u, v, w)$ be the set of the predicted behaviors. *Precision* considers the positively predicted entries within all the predictions, and *Recall* considers the positively predicted entries within all the positive ones in the testing set, so that we can plot the *Precision-Recall* curves by changing the lower limit of the predicted values for $P(u, v, w)$:

$$Precision = \frac{|P(u,v,w) \cap T(u,v,w)|}{|P(u,v,w)|}$$

$$Recall = \frac{|P(u,v,w) \cap T(u,v,w)|}{|T(u,v,w)|}$$

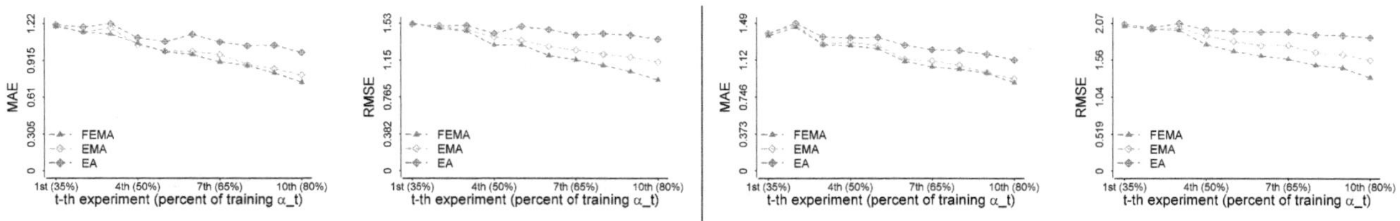

(a) MAE on MAS data (b) RMSE on MAS data (c) MAE on WEIBO data (d) RMSE on WEIBO data

Figure 3: Multi-faceted analysis improve the 2W prediction performance: FEMA and EMA perform much better than EA that formulate human behavior as matrices instead of high-order tensors. The model is better if the MAE and RMSE are smaller.

High *Precision* and *Recall* will be a better model.

When make prediction on the mentioned (target) users in the tweet data, we generate a list of N ($N = 5$) target users named $R_{u,w}$ for each source user u to mention in his/her tweets of a given word w. If the target user v appears in the list, we call it a hit. The *Hit Ratio* [14] is calculated in the following way:

$$Hit\ Ratio = \frac{\sum_{u,v,w} I(v \in R_{u,w})}{|U|}$$

where $I(\cdot)$ is an indicator function, $R_{u,w}$ is a set of top-N mentioned users to user u in tweet of word w, and v is the hold-off user in the testing set that u posts a tweet with "@v". A high *Hit Ratio* will be a better model.

For the second task, simplex behavior prediction, we sum the entries of the tensor along with the dimension of affiliation or word in tweet w as the result of prediction. Then we define similar definitions of *MAE, RMSE, Precision, Recall*, and *Hit Ratio*, using (u, v) as subscripts instead of (u, v, w) and (u) instead of (u, w).

5.4 Experiments on Behavior Prediction

In this section, we conduct three different experiments to demonstrate the effectiveness and efficiency of the model settings of our FEMA. First, we present the usefulness of leveraging multi-faceted information with 2W prediction tasks on learning behavioral patterns on the academic research data MAS and tweet data WEIBO. Second, we present the usefulness of leveraging flexible regularizations with 3W prediction tasks. And finally, we show the effectiveness and efficiency of our evolutionary analysis.

5.4.1 Usefulness of Leveraging Multi-faceted Information: 2W Prediction

In this subsection, we show the results of 2W prediction: predicting author-keyword behaviors on MAS, and source-target behaviors on WEIBO. We compare our FEMA with EMA and EA, while EA uses matrix instead of high-order tensor to formulate the human behaviors. In other words, EA does not learn from the information of affiliation and word in tweets. Fig. 3 shows MAE and RMSE of the above methods on the 10 experiments varying the percent of training data α_t from 35% to 80% by 5%: Fig. 3a and 3b plot the results of MAS, while Fig. 3c and 3d plot the results of WEIBO. FEMA has the smallest MAE and RMSE, while even EMA is much better than EA. Furthermore, we show the numbers of MAE and RMSE in Tab. 2, when we set the percents of the training part as $\alpha_t = 80\%$. FEMA decreases the RMSE of EA by 30.8% on MAS and 30.0% on WEIBO.

Fig. 4 plots the precision-recall curves to test the ranking results of predicted human behaviors. We show that the tensor-based method EMA performs much better than the matrix-based one EA, and the FEMA performs the best on both MAS and WEIBO data.

EA uses author-keyword matrix to model the academic research behavior, while EMA and FEMA use author-affiliation-keyword tensors to model it, and perform better than EA. The information of affiliation has strong impacts in the keywords: when an author changes his/her affiliation, his/her research topics may change because he/she has got new collaborators and new projects. For example, in Fig. 1 we know that when Professor Jiawei Han moves from Simon Fraser University to University of Illinois at Urbana-Champaign, his main research topics change from the area of database systems to data mining. The methods of multi-faceted analysis EMA and FEMA learn the affiliation information from the MAS dataset and better predict what topic an author will study.

Similarly, EMA and FEMA use the *words in tweets* as the third facet to model the mentioning behavior on the microblogging dataset WEIBO. Weibo users usually mention different accounts in their tweets of different content. For example, sports fans usually mention their favorite players when they post messages to send their congratulations, comforts or best wishes; they mention their friends in life when they hear some interesting news like marriage, graduation, travelling and shopping discounts. Multi-faceted analysis can better model this kind of user behavior and predict who will be mentioned later for a Weibo user.

5.4.2 Usefulness of Leveraging Flexible Regularizations: 3W Prediction

As mentioned before, here we predict author-affiliation-keyword

	MAS data		WEIBO data	
	MAE	RMSE	MAE	RMSE
FEMA (+flexible)	**0.735**	**0.944**	**0.894**	**1.312**
EMA (tensor)	0.794	1.130	0.932	1.556
EA (matrix)	0.979	1.364	1.120	1.873

Table 2: The tensor-based methods FEMA and EMA have the smaller MAE and RMSE than the matrix-based method EA on 2W Prediction tasks. FEMA models the behavior as tensors, learns from flexible regularizers, and reaches the smallest errors. The model is better if the MAE and RMSE are smaller.

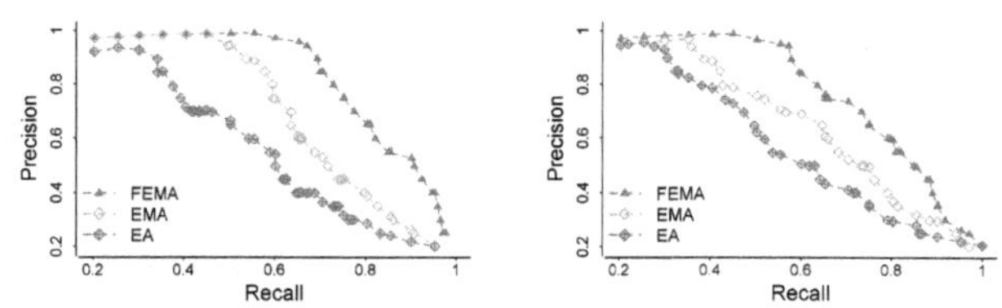

(a) Precision-recall on MAS (b) Precision-recall on WEIBO

Figure 4: FEMA and EMA that use high-order tensors to model human behavior performs the better than the matrix-based EA on 2W Prediction tasks when $t = 10$ and $\alpha_t = 80\%$. The model is better if the precision and recall are higher.

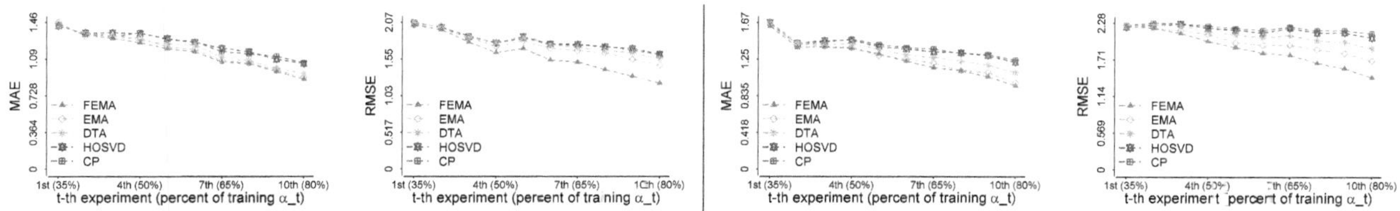

(a) MAE on MAS data (b) RMSE on MAS data (c) MAE on WEIBO data (d) RMSE on WEIBO data

Figure 5: Flexible regularizers alleviate the sparsity problem: on 3W prediction tasks, FEMA performs better than other methods that do not use regularizers. The model is better if the MAE or RMSE is smaller.

behaviors on the academic research dataset MAS, and source (user)-target (user)-word (in tweet) behaviors on the social dataset WEIBO. We compare our FEMA with EMA and three related methods DTA, HOSVD and CP that do not use flexible regularizers on the decompositions. Similarly with Fig. 3, Fig. 5 shows MAE and RMSE of the methods on the 10 experiments varying the percent of training data α_t from 35% to 80% by 5%: Fig. 5a and 5b plot the results of MAS, while Fig. 5c and 5d plot the results of WEIBO. With the size of the training data increasing, the models can learn more from it and thus the MAE and RMSE often decrease by the size. FEMA often reaches the smallest values of MAE and RMSE, which shows that flexible regularizers can alleviate the sparsity problem and thus can help in the prediction task. Furthermore, we show the numbers of MAE and RMSE in Tab. 3, when we set up the experiments with the largest piece of training part $\alpha_t = 80\%$. FEMA decreases the RMSE of the best of the other methods by 17.1% on MAS and 15.4% on WEIBO.

	MAS data		WEIBO data	
	MAE	RMSE	MAE	RMSE
FEMA	**0.893**	**1.215**	**0.954**	**1.437**
EMA	0.909	1.466	0.986	1.698
DTA [26]	0.950	1.556	1.105	1.889
HOSVD [8]	1.047	1.618	1.220	2.054
CP [16]	1.055	1.612	1.243	2.117

Table 3: Flexible FEMA has the smallest MAE and RMSE on 3W Prediction tasks when $t = 10$ and $\alpha_t = 80\%$. The model is better if the MAE and RMSE are smaller.

Similarly with Fig. 4, we also plot the precision-recall curves to test their abilities of ranking the predicted probabilities of human behaviors. In Fig. 6, we show FEMA performs the best when we operate all the algorithms on both MAS data and WEIBO data.

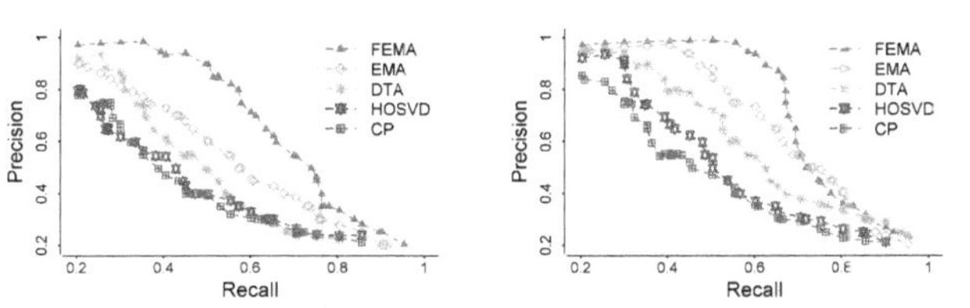

(a) Precision-recall on MAS (b) Precision-recall on WEIBO

Figure 6: FEMA that uses flexible regularizers performs the best on 3W Prediction tasks when $t = 10$ and $\alpha_t = 80\%$. The model is better if the precision and recall are higher.

FEMA uses the *co-authorship* information to constrain the projection matrices on the dimension of *author*. The co-author network is a complementary graph to the authors' affiliation network. It also has strong impacts in determining the topics of authors' academic research. Though the author-affiliation-keyword tensor is too sparse, learning the co-authorship matrix can better understand and predict the authors' behaviors.

Similarly, on the social dataset WEIBO, FEMA uses the *social network* information to constrain the grouping of both the *source users* and *target users*. When a source user u looks for an appropriate target user v from millions of accounts to mention in his/her tweets, u has often already connected to v and followed up v's messages. Therefore, learning the social information can help predict the users' behaviors of mentioning in tweet.

5.4.3 *Effectiveness and Efficiency*

Here we first test the run time of FEMA by changing the following three factors: (1) the number of objects in each dimension, i.e., the scale of tensors $N = n^{(1)} = n^{(2)} = n^{(3)}$; (2) the number of groups in each dimension $R = r^{(1)} = r^{(2)} = r^{(3)}$; (3) the number of tensor increments T. For convenience, let the number of objects/groups be the same in all the dimensions. Second, we show that the loss of FEMA from FMA is quite small, while FEMA saves lots of time.

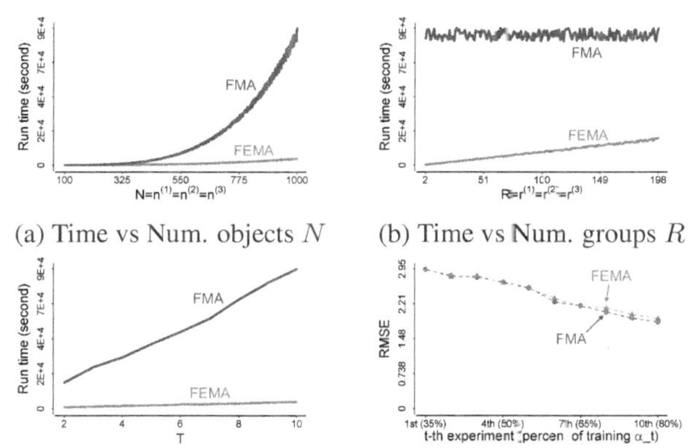

(a) Time vs Num. objects N (b) Time vs Num. groups R (c) Time vs Num. increments T (d) The loss is small.

Figure 7: FEMA saves lots of time and the loss is small: FEMA runs much faster than FMA.

Fig. 7a shows how much time FEMA and FMA cost by changing the number of objects N in each dimension. We random sample $N \times N \times N$ tensors from WEIBO data, for $N = 100, \ldots, 1000$, so that the density of tensors is stable. We set $R = 50$ and $T = 10$ as default. The run time of FEMA goes up much slower than that of FMA. When FMA takes 25 hours (more than one day) to process, FEMA needs only 51 minutes (less than one hour). Fig. 7b shows the time cost by changing the number of groups R from 2 to 100 in each dimension. We use the $1000 \times 1000 \times 1000$ sample tensors and let T be 10. Though the run time of FEMA is proportional to R, it is still much smaller than that of FMA. Fig. 7c shows that the time cost is linear to the number of tensor increments T. The evolutionary analysis method FEMA updates the projection matrices with sparse increments, saving lots of time on decomposition.

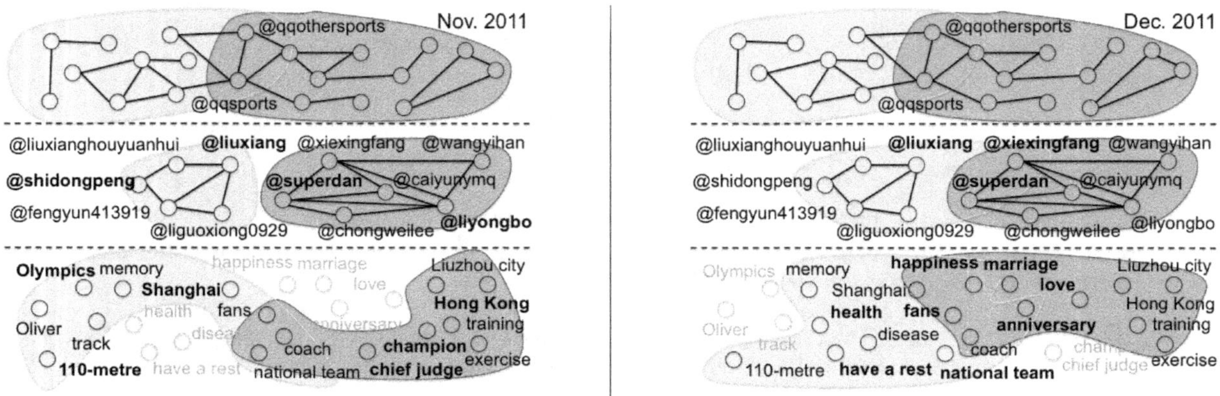

(a) In November 2011, Xiang Liu's fans talk about his championship of Olympics 2004, and a badminton match ended in Hong Kong

(b) In December 2011, Xiang Liu reported his health problem, while Dan Lin and Xingfang Xie celebrated their first marriage anniversary

Figure 8: The temporal pattern of Weibo users' mentioning to someone in tweets: FEMA discovers the groups of hurdle fans and badminton fans in China who use "@" to mention their idols in different words of topics at different times.

In Fig. 7d, we check the loss of FEMA using 3W prediction tasks on the $1000 \times 1000 \times 1000$ sampled tensors and find that FMA achieves smaller RMSE than FEMA but the loss is quite small. Since high-order terms in Eq. 8 are small, though FEMA omits the terms, the result is close to that of FMA.

5.5 Discovery of Behavioral Patterns

In this section, we present interesting discovery from the behaviors of both academic research and mentions in tweet. In the Introduction, we have shown the temporal behavioral pattern of the research groups led by Prof. Jiawei Han in Fig. 1.

Similarly, in Fig. 8, we give a showcase of our discovery from WEIBO data, where the three layers are source users, target (mentioned) users and words in tweets. Fig. 8a shows that the left yellow groups in the three layers are fans of 110-metre hurdle, hurdle runners including the Olympics 2004 champion Xiang Liu (*@liuxiang*), and words about the sport of hurdle and the runners. The right blue groups are fans of badminton, Chinese famous badminton players and the related words. In November 2011, Xiang's fans mentioned Xiang and his friends like Dongpeng Shi (*@shidongpeng*), talking about their sweet memories of welcoming them back to "Shanghai" in 2004. At the same time, the badminton team of China has just finished their matches in Hong Kong. Their most famous player Dan Lin (*@superdan*) and related words like "champion" get high weights in their corresponding groups.

Fig. 8b shows the temporal behavioral patterns of these two group clusters in December 2011. Xiang Liu reported his sickness, and his fans sent their best wishes by mentioning to him. Dan Lin posted a message, saying it was the first anniversary of marriage with Xingfang Xie (*@xiexingfang*) who is also a badminton player. Therefore, we can see the words "love", "marriage" get higher weights than "training" and "exercise". Note that first, the weights of *@qqsports* and *@qqothersports* increase in the two source user groups. Second, the weights of Dan and Xingfang increase in the two target user groups. We examine the data and find out the reason that *@qqsports*, *@qqothersports* and even some of Xiang's fans congratulated to Dan and Xingfang for their good news.

5.6 Parameter Settings

In this section, we discuss how we set the parameters in our experiments: one is the number of groups R and the other is the weight of regularizers μ.

On both datasets, we change the number of groups in each dimension R from 2 to 100 and observe that the RMSE decreases and reaches the bottom when R is larger than 30. In WEIBO, we spot the RMSE decreases much when $R = 23$. As mentioned before, FEMA updates the eigenvectors with the other eigenvectors multiplied by some weights. When R is smaller than 23, if the testing entries have objects in the 23-th cluster, the values of objects are 0 in all the eigenvectors. Thus, the entries will be always zero. We let the default number of groups R to be 50 for the trade-off between better accuracy (smaller RMSE) and faster computing.

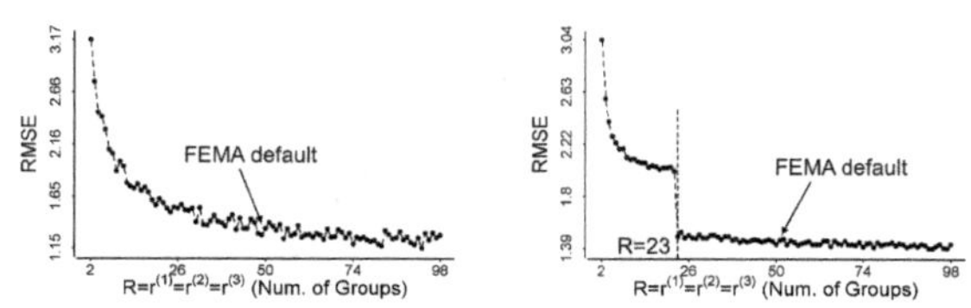

(a) Academic data MAS (b) Tweet data WEIBO

Figure 9: FEMA sets the default number of groups R in each dimension as 50: RMSE decreases when R changes from 2 to 100. In WEIBO, the RMSE decreases much when $R = 23$.

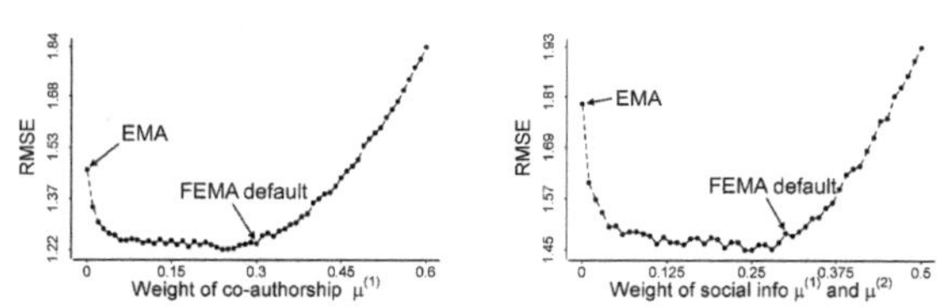

(a) Academic data MAS (b) Tweet data WEIBO

Figure 10: FEMA sets the default weight of regularizers μ as 0.3: the performance of our FEMA is insensitive to μ.

Next, we change the weight of the regularizers in our FEMA μ from 0 to 1: when $\mu = 0$, FEMA is actually EMA that does not use the flexible regularizers; when $\mu = 1$, FEMA uses only the regularizers but none information from the tensors. On both MAS and WEIBO datasets, we observe that the RMSE first decreases and reaches the bottom when μ is from 0.1 to 0.3. The RMSE increases fast when μ is larger than 0.3. Note that our FEMA is insensitive to the weight μ. For convenience, we set the default value of the weight as 0.3. We demonstrate that it would be a better model to understand human behavior if it learns from both the sparse high-order tensors and dense flexible regularizers.

6. CONCLUSION

In this work, we present a novel tensor factorization based framework FEMA for temporal multi-faceted behavior prediction and behavioral pattern mining. The model uses flexible regularizers to alleviate the sparsity problem and gives approximation algorithms to fast process the increments with a theoretical guarantee. Extensive experiments performed on real world datasets demonstrate that our framework is effective and efficient in behavior prediction tasks. The fast speed can support real-time applications of behavior prediction and pattern mining.

7. ACKNOWLEDGEMENT

This work is supported by National Natural Science Foundation of China, No. 61370022, No. 61210008, and No. 61303075; International Science and Technology Cooperation Program of China, No. 2013DFG12870; National Program on Key Basic Research Project, No. 2011CB302206; NExT Research Center funded by MDA, Singapore, WBS:R-252-300-001-490.

8. REFERENCES

[1] E. Acar, D. M. Dunlavy, T. G. Kolda, and M. Mørup. Scalable tensor factorizations for incomplete data. *Chemometrics and Intelligent Laboratory Systems*, 106(1):41–56, 2011.

[2] W. Chen, W. Hsu, and M. L. Lee. Making recommendations from multiple domains. In *KDD'13*, pages 892–900.

[3] W. Chen, W. Hsu, and M. L. Lee. Modeling user's receptiveness over time for recommendation. In *SIGIR'13*, pages 373–382.

[4] A. Cichocki and R. Zdunek. Regularized alternating least squares algorithms for non-negative matrix/tensor factorization. In *Advances in Neural Networks–ISNN 2007*, pages 793–802.

[5] P. Cui, S. Jin, L. Yu, F. Wang, W. Zhu, and S. Yang. Cascading outbreak prediction in networks: a data-driven approach. In *KDD'13*, pages 901–909.

[6] P. Cui, F. Wang, S. Liu, M. Ou, S. Yang, and L. Sun. Who should share what? item-level social influence prediction for users and posts ranking. In *SIGIR'11*, pages 185–194.

[7] J. Davis and M. Goadrich. The relationship between precision-recall and roc curves. In *ICML'06*, pages 233–240.

[8] L. De Lathauwer, B. De Moor, and J. Vandewalle. A multilinear singular value decomposition. *SIAM journal on Matrix Analysis and Applications*, 21(4):1253–1278, 2000.

[9] D. M. Dunlavy, T. G. Kolda, and E. Acar. Temporal link prediction using matrix and tensor factorizations. *TKDD*, 5(2):10, 2011.

[10] L. Hu, J. Cao, G. Xu, L. Cao, Z. Gu, and C. Zhu. Personalized recommendation via cross-domain triadic factorization. In *WWW'13*, pages 595–606.

[11] M. Jiang, P. Cui, R. Liu, Q. Yang, F. Wang, W. Zhu, and S. Yang. Social contextual recommendation. In *CIKM'12*, pages 45–54.

[12] M. Jiang, P. Cui, F. Wang, Q. Yang, W. Zhu, and S. Yang. Social recommendation across multiple relational domains. In *CIKM'12*, pages 1422–1431.

[13] U. Kang, E. Papalexakis, A. Harpale, and C. Faloutsos. Gigatensor: scaling tensor analysis up by 100 times-algorithms and discoveries. In *KDD'12*, pages 316–324.

[14] G. Karypis. Evaluation of item-based top-n recommendation algorithms. In *CIKM'01*, pages 247–254.

[15] T. G. Kolda. Orthogonal tensor decompositions. *SIAM Journal on Matrix Analysis and Applications*, 23(1):243–255, 2001.

[16] T. G. Kolda and B. W. Bader. Tensor decompositions and applications. *SIAM review*, 51(3):455–500, 2009.

[17] T. G. Kolda and J. Sun. Scalable tensor decompositions for multi-aspect data mining. In *ICDM'08*, pages 363–372.

[18] Y. Koren, R. Bell, and C. Volinsky. Matrix factorization techniques for recommender systems. *Computer*, 42(8):30–37, 2009.

[19] L. Liu, J. Tang, J. Han, M. Jiang, and S. Yang. Mining topic-level influence in heterogeneous networks. In *CIKM'10*, pages 199–208.

[20] K. Narang, S. Nagar, S. Mehta, L. Subramaniam, and K. Dey. Discovery and analysis of evolving topical social discussions on unstructured microblogs. In *Advances in Information Retrieval*, pages 545–556. 2013.

[21] H. Rachlin. The value of temporal patterns in behavior. *Current Directions in Psychological Science*, 1995.

[22] K. Radinsky, K. M. Svore, S. T. Dumais, M. Shokouhi, J. Teevan, A. Bocharov, and E. Horvitz. Behavioral dynamics on the web: Learning, modeling, and prediction. *TOIS*, 31(3):16, 2013.

[23] S. Rendle and L. Schmidt-Thieme. Pairwise interaction tensor factorization for personalized tag recommendation. In *WSDM'10*, pages 81–90.

[24] S. B. Roy, M. De Cock, V. Mandava, S. Savanna, B. Dalessandro, C. Perlich, W. Cukierski, and B. Hamner. The microsoft academic search dataset and kdd cup 2013. In *Proceedings of the KDD Cup 2013 Workshop*.

[25] G. W. Stewart and J.-g. Sun. Matrix perturbation theory.

[26] J. Sun, D. Tao, S. Papadimitriou, P. S. Yu, and C. Faloutsos Incremental tensor analysis: Theory and applications. *TKDD*, 2(3):11, 2008.

[27] J.-T. Sun, H.-J. Zeng, H. Liu, Y. Lu, and Z. Chen. Cubesvd: a novel approach to personalized web search. In *WWW'05*, pages 382–390.

[28] Y. Sun, J. Tang, J. Han, C. Chen, and M. Gupta. Co-evolution of multi-typed objects in dynamic star networks. *TKDE*, 2013.

[29] P. Symeonidis, A. Nanopoulos, and Y. Manolopoulos. Tag recommendations based on tensor dimensionality reduction. In *RecSys'08*, pages 43–50.

[30] F. Wang, J. Sun, J. Hu, and S. Ebadollahi. imet: interactive metric learning in healthcare applications. In *SDM'11*, pages 944–955.

[31] F. Wang, H. Tong, and C.-Y. Lin. Towards evolutionary nonnegative matrix factorization. In *AAAI'11*, pages 501–506.

[32] X. Wang, C. Zhai, and D. Roth. Understanding evolution of research themes: a probabilistic generative model for citations. In *KDD'13*, pages 1115–1123.

[33] L. Xiang, Q. Yuan, S. Zhao, L. Chen, X. Zhang, Q. Yang, and J. Sun. Temporal recommendation on graphs via long-and short-term preference fusion. In *KDD'10*, pages 723–732.

[34] Q. Yuan, G. Cong, Z. Ma, A. Sun, and N. M. Thalmann. Who, where, when and what: Discover spatio-temporal topics for twitter users. In *KDD'13*, pages 605–613.

[35] X. Zheng, H. Ding, H. Mamitsuka, and S. Zhu. Collaborative matrix factorization with multiple similarities for predicting drug-target interactions. In *KDD'13*, pages 1025–1033.

Profit-maximizing Cluster Hires

Behzad Golshan
Boston University
behzad@cs.bu.edu

Theodoros Lappas
Stevens Institute of Technology
tlappas@stevens.edu

Evimaria Terzi
Boston University
evimaria@cs.bu.edu

ABSTRACT

Team formation has been long recognized as a natural way to acquire a diverse pool of useful skills, by combining experts with complementary talents. This allows organizations to effectively complete beneficial projects from different domains, while also helping individual experts position themselves and succeed in highly competitive job markets. Here, we assume a collection of projects $\mathcal{P}$, where each project requires a certain set of skills, and yields a different benefit upon completion. We are further presented with a pool of experts $\mathcal{X}$, where each expert has his own skillset and compensation demands. Then, we study the problem of hiring a cluster of experts $\mathcal{T} \subseteq \mathcal{X}$, so that the overall compensation (cost) does not exceed a given budget B, and the total benefit of the projects that this team can collectively cover is maximized. We refer to this as the ClusterHire problem. Our work presents a detailed analysis of the computational complexity and hardness of approximation of the problem, as well as heuristic, yet effective, algorithms for solving it in practice. We demonstrate the efficacy of our approaches through experiments on real datasets of experts, and demonstrate their advantage over intuitive baselines. We also explore additional variants of the fundamental problem formulation, in order to account for constraints and considerations that emerge in realistic cluster-hiring scenarios. All variants considered in this paper have immediate applications in the cluster hiring process, as it emerges in the context of different organizational settings.

Categories and Subject Descriptors

H.2.8 [**Database Management**]: Database Applications-Data Mining

Keywords

Team Formation; Online Marketplaces

KDD'14, August 24–27, 2014, New York, NY, USA.
Copyright 2014 ACM 978-1-4503-2956-9/14/08 ...$15.00.
http://dx.doi.org/10.1145/2623330.2623690.

1. INTRODUCTION

When searching for a group of experts to hire, organizations and decision-makers aim to find the most cost-effective team that can accomplish their goals. The hiring process includes allocating an available budget toward the recruitment of a set of experts from a collection of candidates, in order to form a team that has all the required expertise to perform a large number of profitable projects.

As an example, consider the recruitment of a cluster of college professors by a university. In this setting, the university has to hire individuals that allow it to maximize its academic benefit, given the current opportunities and trends in terms of research and funding options. Given the available budget, the goal is to recruit a cluster of professors that can collectively provide the expertise required to capitalize on such opportunities and maximize the university's benefit. The benefit can be measured in terms of the number of publications or citations, the amount of dollars at grants, or any other function that the university wants to optimize.

In an industry setting, cluster hiring scenarios are even more prevalent. Perhaps the most characteristic example is a typical startup company, where the founders need to select a team of experts with the combined expertise required to capitalize on the different opportunities that have been identified within the market that the company targets.

Another relevant setting comes from the domain of online labor markets, such as oDesk (`www.odesk.com`), Freelancer (`www.freelancer.com`), and Guru (`www.guru.com`). In these online portals, employers hire freelancers with various skills to work remotely on different types of projects. In the early stages of this model, freelancers registered and worked independently. However, as the competition grew, experts realized that it is in their best interest to form "hives", known as agencies, with people of complementary skillsets [11]. This allows them to diversify their talent pool, and go after a larger number of more profitable projects. This trend, has also been recognized by major companies in this area, such as `oDesk.com`, which are already offering team-hiring services to their enterprise customers[1].

In this paper, we formalize the cluster hiring problem as follows: we assume a pool of n experts $\mathcal{X}$, where each expert i is associated with the set of skills X_i that he masters. Additionally, we assume a set of m projects $\mathcal{P}$, where each project $P \in \mathcal{P}$ is also associated with a set of skills; these are the skills that are required for the project to be completed. Finally, every project is associated with a profit $F(P)$ and every expert is associated with a cost $C(X_i)$,

[1] `https://www.odesk.com/info/enterprise/`

which corresponds to X's compensation. Given a budget B, our goal is to form a team of experts $\mathcal{T} \subseteq \mathcal{X}$ such that $\sum_{X \in \mathcal{T}} C(X) \leq B$ and the sum of the profits of the projects that $\mathcal{T}$ can perform is maximized. In the basic version of the problem, we assume that $\mathcal{T}$ can perform a project P only if for every required skill in P, there exists at least one worker in $\mathcal{T}$ that has this skill. We call this problem the CLUSTERHIRE problem.

In addition to this fundamental definition, we consider variants of the CLUSTERHIRE problem that take into consideration (i) a probabilistic version of project profits, based on how likely it is for the team to actually acquire and complete the project, and (ii) constraints on the usage of the experts with respect to how many projects they are willing and able o participate in simultaneously.

Contributions: To the best of our knowledge we are the first to define and study the CLUSTERHIRE problem and its variants. More specifically, we show that this problem is NP-hard to solve and even approximate. We then proceed to design effective heuristics and demonstrate their efficacy in practical settings. For our experiments we use data from Freelancer and Guru. These are two of the largest players in the rapidly growing area of *online labor*, which has been identified as a clear candidate for the cluster hire setting [11]. In addition to experimentally evaluating our algorithms and investigating the characteristics of their solutions, we also provide an extensive data-analytic and visual study of these datasets that provides a much deeper understanding of the nature and dynamics of expert communities.

Roadmap: The rest of the paper is organized as follows: we review the related work in Section 2. In Section 3, we define the CLUSTERHIRE problem and study its computational complexity. Our algorithms for the problem are described in Section 4, and in Section 5 we provide a thorough analysis of our datasets. An extensive experimental evaluation of our methods is given in Section 6. We conclude the paper in Section 7.

2. RELATED WORK

To the best of our knowledge we are the first to introduce and study the CLUSTERHIRE problem and its variants. However, our work is clearly related to other recently-studied team formation problems as well as literature on studying team dynamics and predicting the performance of teams, as well as work on inferring the abilities of the team members based on their team performance. We give an overview of this body of related work below.

Our previous work [14] was the first to introduce the problem of team formation in the context of social networks. Given a pool of experts and a set of skills that needed to be covered, the goal was to select a team of experts that can collectively cover all required skills, while ensuring efficient communication between the team's members. Over the last years, this work has been extended in multiple directions. For example, there exists recent work that focuses on incorporating different definitions of communication costs between experts [1, 6, 8, 13, 15, 19]. Others take into consideration different levels of users' abilities and capacity to participate in different projects [18]. Finally, more recently, the online version of the problem was introduced where the goal is to create multiple teams that can address multiple projects that arrive in an online fashion [3]. The common characteristic of all the above works is that they assume a network of experts and therefore, all these formulations have a graph-theoretic component. Our work does not assume the existence of a graph and therefore our setting raises different computational questions than the ones addressed in the above papers.

Probably the most related to ours is the recent work by Anagnostopoulos et al. [2]. This paper considers a pool of experts, with each expert associated with a set of skills, and a collection of projects arriving one at a time in an online fashion. Each project is characterized by the set of skills required for its completion. In the version of their problem that is most related to ours, Anagnostopoulos et al. aim to create one team for each project, such that over time, the maximum number of teams that each expert participates in is minimized. There are two significant differences between their setting and ours. First, our goal is to create a single team that can address many projects, while the goal of Anagnostopoulos et. al. is to choose a single team per project. Second, we do not assume that projects arrive online: in our setting the set of projects is known apriori. Therefore, again, the computational issues we face and address here are distinct.

In the area of online gaming and robot team formation, the problem of inferring the performance of a teams of players has been investigated at length [17, 16]. Most recently Liemhetcharat and Velose [17] explore a version of the problem in which each expert has a non-deterministic capability with respect to each project. The expected performance of the team is then evaluated based on the synergy of the participating experts, rather than their coverage of skills. Other relevant works [5, 7] evaluate team performance from an anthropological/sociological perspective. We consider these complementary to our computational approach

Recently Gionis et al. [10] have proposed a combinatorial method for computing the skillset of individual experts, based on their participation in successful teams. Their problem setting can be thought as inverse to ours, since our goal is to compute teams based on the skillsets of experts.

3. PROBLEM DEFINITIONS

In this section, we provide the notation we will use throughout the paper, and present the formal definitions and complexity results for different versions of our problem.

3.1 Preliminaries

Throughout the discussion we will assume that there is a set of ℓ skills S, a set of n experts $\mathcal{X}$ and a set of m projects $\mathcal{P}$. Each expert $X \in \mathcal{X}$, is represented by a subset of skills, i.e., $X \subseteq S$; these are the skills that the expert possesses. Similarly, every project $P \in \mathcal{P}$ is characterized by the set of skills that are required in order for the project to be completed (i.e., $P \subseteq S$).

In addition to the above, we have a *profit function* (F), such that for every $P \in \mathcal{P}$, $F(P)$ gives the (expected) profit that completing P with incur. Similarly, for every expert X, function $C(X)$ gives the cost of hiring a particular expert.

For a team of experts $\mathcal{T} \subseteq \mathcal{X}$, we say that team $\mathcal{T}$ has a skill s if there exist at least one expert $X \in \mathcal{T}$, such that X has skill s, i.e., $s \in X$. For a project $P \in \mathcal{P}$, we say that team $\mathcal{T}$ *covers* P if $\mathcal{T}$ (as a team) has all the skills required for P. Clearly, a team of experts may cover more than one projects; in fact the more such projects being covered by a single team the better the team. That is, we define the *coverage* of team $\mathcal{T}$ to be the set of distinct projects that the team can cover. That is,

$$\text{Cov}(\mathcal{T}) = \{P \in \mathcal{P} \mid \mathcal{T} \text{ covers } P\}. \quad (1)$$

Given the projects that a team $\mathcal{T}$ can cover, we define the profit of the team to be the summation of the profits of the projects that $\mathcal{T}$ covers. That is,

$$F(\text{Cov}(\mathcal{T})) = \sum_{P \in \text{Cov}(\mathcal{T})} F(P). \quad (2)$$

In addition, every team incurs a certain cost, computed as the sum of the costs of its members. That is,

$$C(\mathcal{T}) = \sum_{X \in \mathcal{T}} C(X). \quad (3)$$

Dollar profit: In real applications, there is typically a pre-specified gain (in terms of dollars) that the completion of a project will yield for the team (or for the organization that has hired the team). This dollar amount can thus naturally serve as the profit of that project, which we refer to as F_d.

Competition-based profit: The above dollar-based assignment of profits to projects does not consider the uncertainty that is involved in the process of trying to acquire and complete a project. Consider the following example: we are presented with two projects P_1 and P_2 that are worth the same dollar amount. However, assume that P_1 requires a set of "mundane" skills, i.e., skills that are very popular among the pool experts, while P_2 requires a rare skill s^*. Clearly, there is larger competition for project P_1, since there are many possible teams that can contribute the required skills. On the other hand, the competition for P_2 is smaller due to the rare skill that it requires. Therefore, a team that has s^* in its combined skillset has a higher probability of being assigned project P_2, if it chooses to pursue it.

This competitive setting is simply one of the alternative instantiations of uncertainty, which is present in all the applications we consider. Alternatively, one could consider the probability of completing a project even after it has been secured, given the deadlines and other constraints placed by the employer. Our framework is compatible with any method that computes the probability of success for each project. For our own experiments, we compute the *dollar-based* profit of a project P as follows:

$$F_c(P) = \frac{1}{\mathit{freq}(s^*(P))} F_d(P),$$

where $s^*(P)$ is the rarest skill among the skills required for P and $\mathit{freq}(s^*(P))$ is the number of experts that actually possess this skill. While we experimented with other alternatives, including the median and average frequency of the skills required by a project, we found that using the minimum frequency yielded the most intuitive results.

Throughout the paper, we use the generic notation (F) to refer to projects' profits and only use F_d and F_c when we need to explicitly compare them.

3.2 The CLUSTERHIRE problem

Given the above notation, we can now define the main problem addressed in this paper as follows:

PROBLEM 1 (CLUSTERHIRE). *Given a set of projects $\mathcal{P}$, a pool of experts $\mathcal{X}$, cost and profit functions $C()$ and $F()$, respectively, and a budget $B \in \mathbb{R}^+$ find $\mathcal{T} \subseteq \mathcal{X}$ such that $F(\text{Cov}(\mathcal{T}))$ is maximized and $C(\mathcal{T}) \leq B$.*

From the computational point of view, we have the following results for the CLUSTERHIRE problem.

LEMMA 1. *The decision version of the* CLUSTERHIRE *problem is NP-complete.*

PROOF. For our proof, we will consider a simplified version of the problem where $\mathcal{P}$ consists of a single project P and $F(P) = 1$. Moreover, $C(X) = 1$ for every expert $X \in \mathcal{X}$. In the decision version of this simplified instance of the CLUSTERHIRE problem the question is if there exist a team of K experts that covers project P.

Now, we will reduce the decision version of the SETCOVER problem [9] to this simplified version of the CLUSTERHIRE problem. In the classical SETCOVER problem there is a universe of items U and a set of sets $\mathcal{Q}$ such that for every $Q \in \mathcal{Q}$, $Q \subseteq U$. The question in the decision version of the problem is whether there exist L sets from $\mathcal{Q}$, forming $\mathcal{Q}'$ such that $\cup_{Q \in \mathcal{Q}'} Q_i = U$.

Clearly, if we map every set $Q_i \in \mathcal{Q}$ from SETCOVER into an expert $X_i \in \mathcal{X}$ of CLUSTERHIRE, the two problems become identical. That is, there exists a solution of size L in the SETCOVER problem if and only if there exists a solution of cost L in the CLUSTERHIRE problem. □

LEMMA 2. *The* CLUSTERHIRE *problem is NP-hard to approximate.*

PROOF. The proof of the above lemma uses the same simplified decision version of the CLUSTERHIRE problem used in the proof of Lemma 1, as well as some intuition we gained from that proof.

More specifically, we will prove the lemma by contradiction. That is, assume that there exists an α-factor approximation algorithm for this simplified version of the CLUSTERHIRE problem such that if $\mathcal{T}^A$ is the solution of this algorithm and $\mathcal{T}^*$ is the optimal solution, we have that: $F(\mathcal{T}^A) \geq \alpha F(\mathcal{T}^*)$.

Now observe that such an algorithm can be used to decide whether there exists a solution consisting of K experts that could perform the project P of the CLUSTERHIRE problem. However, as we showed above, the decision version of this problem is NP-complete. Therefore, such an α-approximation algorithm cannot exist. □

The T-CLUSTERHIRE problem: Observe that the CLUSTERHIRE problem as defined in Problem 1 allows for solutions where a single expert $X \in \mathcal{T}$ can use a particular skill in multiple projects in $\text{Cov}(\mathcal{T})$. In practice, however, this setting can lead to an expert being overworked, especially if he is one of the few members (or even the sole member) in the team who possesses a frequently required skill.

In order to avoid such shortcomings, we propose a variant of CLUSTERHIRE that places an upper bound $t(X, s)$ on the number of projects for which an expert X can utilize a skill s. By allowing for a different threshold for each expert-skill combination, this formulation is a natural fit for scenarios where certain skills are much easier to apply than others, especially for specific experts. For example, while it is very difficult for a software engineer to be the "development leader" for more than one project, the same person can use his "software consulting" expertise to assist in numerous ongoing efforts. In the same consulting setting, it is easier for a more experienced engineer to participate in more projects.

Computing $\text{Cov}_t(\mathcal{T})$: In practice, such a threshold corresponds to a different definition of the coverage of projects by teams. We refer to this alternative definition as t-coverage and we define it below. If use $\text{Cov}_t(\mathcal{T})$ to denote the set projects that are t-covered by team $\mathcal{T}$, then this set has the following characteristic:

$$F(\text{Cov}_t(\mathcal{T})) \text{ is maximized} \tag{4}$$

such that for all $s \in S$,

$$|\{P \in \text{Cov}_t(\mathcal{T}) | s \in \mathcal{P}\}| \leq \sum_{X \in \mathcal{T}} \sum_{s \in X} t(X, s). \tag{5}$$

The constraints encoded by the inequalities in Equation (5) are essentially the threshold constraints imposed by the experts.

We observe that given a team $\mathcal{T}$, computing $\text{Cov}_t(\mathcal{T})$ as described by Equations 4 and 5 is also an NP-hard problem. In fact, in the special case where $t(X, s) = 1$ for all skills s and experts X, then the problem described by the above equation is identical to the SetPacking problem [9].

4. ALGORITHMS

In this section, we describe our algorithms for the basic version of the ClusterHire problem. We then demonstrate how to adapt these algorithms to solve t-ClusterHire.

The `ExpertGreedy` algorithm: The `ExpertGreedy` algorithm is a greedy algorithm on the space of experts. That is, it greedily picks experts — one at a time — so that the budget constraint is satisfied while at the same time the F objective is maximized. Specifically, the algorithm starts with an empty team and at iteration i, it forms $\mathcal{T}^i$. The expert X, picked at iteration $(i+1)$ needs to be among the qualified candidates $\mathcal{Q}$, where:

$$\mathcal{Q} = \{X \mid X \notin \mathcal{T}^i \text{ and } C(\mathcal{T}^i \cup \{X\}) \leq B\},$$

while X maximizes:

$$\frac{F(\text{Cov}(\mathcal{T}^i \cup \{X\})) - F(\text{Cov}(\mathcal{T}^i))}{C(X)}.$$

Note that that the set of qualified candidates $\mathcal{Q}$ is different at every iteration. The set consists of all the remaining experts that can be added to the current solution without violating the budget constraint B. In case of a tie between candidate experts, the algorithm picks an expert at random.

Algorithm 1 The `ExpertGreedy` algorithm.

Input: Experts $\mathcal{X}$, projects $\mathcal{P}$, budget B.
Output: $\mathcal{T} \subseteq \mathcal{X}$
$\mathcal{T} = \emptyset$, $b = 0$, $\mathcal{Q} = \mathcal{X}$
while $b < B$ and $\mathcal{Q} \neq \emptyset$ **do**
  $\mathcal{Q} = \{X \mid \notin \mathcal{T} \text{ and } C(\mathcal{T} \cup \{X\}) \leq B\}$
  $X = \arg\max_{X' \in \mathcal{Q}} \frac{F(\text{Cov}(\mathcal{T} \cup \{X'\})) - F(\text{Cov}(\mathcal{T}))}{C(X')}$
  $\mathcal{T} = \mathcal{T} \cup \{X\}$
  $b = b + C(X)$
return $\mathcal{T}$

The pseudocode of `ExpertGreedy` is shown in Algorithm 1. The worst-case running time of each iteration of `ExpertGreedy` is $O(nm\ell)$. However, careful implementation and bookkeeping that takes into consideration the sparsity of the data allow for much better running times in practice.

The `ProjectGreedy` algorithm: In contrast to `ExpertGreedy`, which picks experts greedily, `ProjectGreedy` operates by greedily selecting the projects to be covered – one a time – and then finding the best set of experts that can cover the selected project.

Algorithm 2 The `ProjectGreedy` algorithm.

Input: Experts $\mathcal{X}$, projects $\mathcal{P}$, budget B.
Output: $\mathcal{T} \subseteq \mathcal{X}$
1: $\mathcal{T} = \emptyset$, $b = 0$
2: **while** $b < B$ and $\mathcal{P} \neq \emptyset$ **do**
3:   $\mathcal{P}$: set of projects *not covered* by $\mathcal{T}$
4:   **for** $P \in \mathcal{P}$ **do**
5:     $\mathcal{X}_P$: experts from $\mathcal{X}$ required to cover P
6:     **if** $C(\mathcal{X}_P) + b \geq B$ **then**
7:       $\mathcal{P} = \mathcal{P} \setminus \{P\}$
8:   $P = \arg\max_{P \in \mathcal{P}} \frac{F(\text{Cov}(\mathcal{T}^i \cup \mathcal{X}_P)) - F(\text{Cov}(\mathcal{T}^i))}{C(\mathcal{X}_P)}$
9:   $\mathcal{T} = \mathcal{T} \cup \mathcal{X}_P$
10:   $b = b + C(\mathcal{X}_P)$
11: return $\mathcal{T}$

Assume that, at iteration i, `ProjectGreedy` has formed a team $\mathcal{T}^i$. Then, at iteration $(i+1)$, the algorithm picks a project P that is not covered by the skills in team $\mathcal{T}^i$. The selection of P is done so that, if $\mathcal{X}_P$ is the set of additional experts required to cover P, the ratio

$$\frac{F(\text{Cov}(\mathcal{T}^i \cup \mathcal{X}_P)) - F(\text{Cov}(\mathcal{T}^i))}{C(\mathcal{X}_P)}$$

is maximized and the budget constraint, i.e , $C(\mathcal{T}^i \cup \mathcal{X}_P) \leq B$ is satisfied. Similar to `ExpertGreedy`, any ties are broken arbitrarily.

The pseudocode of `ProjectGreedy` is shown in Algorithm 2. We draw attention to line 5 of this pseudocode. This step finds a subset of experts, $\mathcal{X}_P$, who together with the current members of $\mathcal{T}$ can collectively cover the skills of project P Clearly, the formation of $\mathcal{X}_P$ needs to be budget-efficient. Thus, this step involves solving an instance of the *weighted set-cover* problem for the skills of P which are not currently covered by $\mathcal{T}$. For this, we use the standard greedy approximation algorithm for weighted set cover. Thus, a different set-cover problem needs to be solved for each one of the candidate projects.

If I is the number of iterations of the outer `while` loop and T_G the running time required for finding $\mathcal{X}_P$ (i.e., the running time of the greedy algorithm for weighted-set cover on the space of experts), the worst-case running time of `ProjectGreedy` is $O(ImT_G)$. Next, we introduce a method that reduces the number of candidate projects m and consequently leads, in practice, to smaller running times.

The `CliqueGreedy` algorithm: By greedily selecting a single project at every iteration, the `ProjectGreedy` algorithm is forced to repeatedly solve an instance of the weighted set cover problem. At the same time, by evaluating the profit-cost ratio of each project independently, the algorithm fails to identify sets of projects that require similar or even near-identical skillsets, which could lead to even higher ratios if selected together.

Motivated by these observations, we design the `CliqueGreedy` algorithm. `CliqueGreedy` can be thought of as an extension of `ProjectGreedy`, which operates on *groups* of projects, rather than individual projects. Essentially, a group can be viewed as a larger project that requires the union of the skills required by the projects in the group. Next, we describe a 2-step method for grouping projects.

In the first step, we consider the grouping benefit for each pair of projects. Given two project P_1 and P_2, we consider them *compatible* if the profit-to-cost ratio for both projects increases by at least a factor of $(1+\alpha)$ if they are merged. Formally, if

$$R_i = \frac{F(P_i)}{C(P_i)},$$

for $i = 1, 2$, and

$$R = \frac{F(P_1 \cup P_2)}{C(P_1 \cup P_2)} \tag{6}$$

then P_1 and P_2 are in the same group if the following *compatibility condition* holds:

$$R > (1+\alpha)R_i \text{ for both } i = 1, 2. \tag{7}$$

In the second step, we compute the maximal cliques in the graph that has a node for every project and edges between every two compatible projects. The computed cliques then serve as the groups that are considered by `CliqueGreedy`.

Note that a clique is maximal if it is not included in any other possible clique. This allows to avoid trivial candidates and limit the number of cliques that need to be considered. In practice, even the enumeration of all maximal cliques is possible. In our experiments, we use the efficient implementation of the algorithm proposed by Bron and Kerbosch [4] that is included in the NetworkX library [12].

As we saw in our experiments, the computational time of the grouping phase is dominated by the first step, since checking the compatibility condition for a pair of projects requires solving yet another set-cover problem. Therefore, checking the compatibility between all $\binom{m}{2}$ pairs of projects requires solving as many set-cover problems. In order to address this, we effectively eliminate a large number of such pair-wise checks by making the following observations:

OBSERVATION 1. *Any two projects P_1 and P_2 are not compatible if $P_1 \cap P_2 = \emptyset$.*

OBSERVATION 2. *Any two projects P_1 and P_2 are not compatible if*

$$\frac{F(P_i)}{C(P_i)} \leq (1+\alpha)\frac{F(P_1)+F(P_2)}{\max\{C(P_1), C(P_2)\}}.$$

Both these observations are direct consequences of the compatibility condition and can be evaluated in constant time given that $C(P_i)$ is computed for every project – which is required anyway even in the simple version of `ProjectGreedy`. In practice, we have observed that these two pruning mechanisms are extremely effective, as they promptly dismiss many project pairs as incompatible.

Another factor that affects the running time of the grouping phase is the value of the parameter α. This has a direct effect on the applicability of the second pruning criterion, as well as on the density (and thus the clique computation) of the resulting project graph. Larger values of α lead to sparser graphs and reduce the number of cliques.

In our experiments, we found that the value of α is dataset dependent, but tuning this parameter is easy if the dataset characteristics are studied appropriately.

Algorithms for T-CLUSTERHIRE: All three algorithms we designed for T-CLUSTERHIRE, i.e., `ExpertGreedy`, `ProjectGreedy` and `CliqueGreedy` can be modified to take into consideration the threshold on the number of times every expert can use each skill, as stipulated by the definition of the T-CLUSTERHIRE problem. In all cases, the greedy heuristic is modified to maximize the marginal gain at the profit level, while satisfying the threshold constraints. Considering the pseudocode for `ExpertGreedy` given by Algorithm 1, the only required modification is to alter line 4 so that it computes the t-coverage of the teams, and thus use Cov_t instead of simple Cov. Finally, the `ProjectGreedy` for this version is similarly obtained by modifying line 8 of Algorithm 2 to compute the t-coverages instead of the simple coverages.

5. EXPERTISE DATASETS

In our experiments, we used data collected from two large online labor markets: `guru.com` and `freelancer.com`. We refer to these datasets as *Guru* and *Freelancer* respectively.

The business model for labor markets: Both websites follow the same business model: employer post a description of a project that needs to be completed, including the required skills and the monetary reward that they are willing to pay. Experts with various skillsets and salary demands apply for each project, and are evaluated by the employer.

Data analytics: From each website, we collect the following artifacts: (i) the set of skills and the salary demands (in dollars per hour) for each expert, and (ii) the set of required skills and the monetary reward (in dollars) for each posted project. For the *Guru* dataset, we collected data on 6 473 experts and 1 764 projects. For the *Freelancer* dataset, we collected data on 1 763 experts and 721 projects.

Project analytics: Figures 1 and 2 provide some descriptive analytics on the projects from *Freelancer* and *Guru* datasets, respectively.

Figures 1(a) and 2(a) display the distribution of the size of the skillset required for the projects in *Freelancer* and *Guru* respectively. From Figure 2(a), we observe that while the majority of projects in *Guru* require up to 10 skills, larger projects of 30 skills or more are also posted. For *Freelancer* the distribution is different. This is due to the fact in `freelancer.com` employers are only allowed to specify at most 5 skills per project; this fact clearly manifests itself in Figure 1(a).

Figures 1(b) and 2(b) show the distribution of project profits for *Freelancer* and *Guru*, respectively, under the F_d profit function (amount of dollars). Similarly, figures 1(c) and 2(c) show the distribution of project profits under the F_c (expected amount of dollars, based on competition). The x-axis holds the profits, sorted from lowest to highest, and the y-axis the number of projects associated with each profit value. For both figures, both axes are in a logarithmic scale.

For the F_d scheme, we observe only 9 distinct profit values for *Guru* (due to the quantization of profits made by the website), which also follow a distribution that resembles a power law (given the almost straight line and the log-log scale). On the other hand, for *Freelancer*, we observe a much higher variance in the distribution of profits.

As anticipated, the F_c scheme introduces much larger variance in the profit distribution for both datasets, with no clearly identifiable distribution shape. This is reasonable,

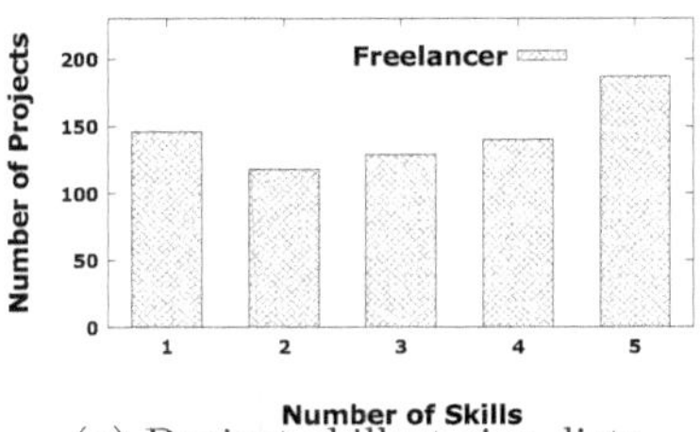

(a) Project skillset size distr.

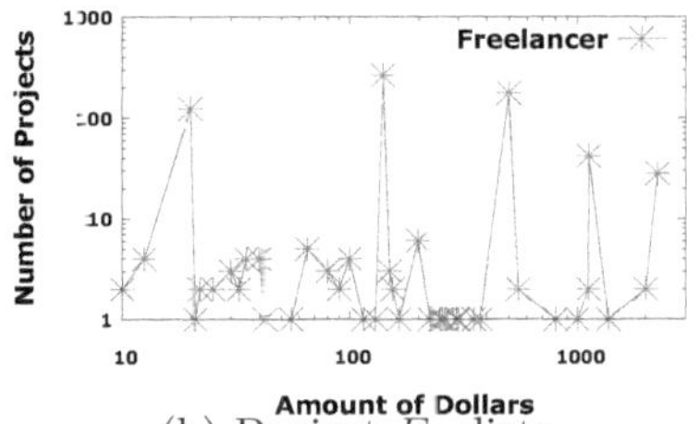

(b) Project F_d distr.

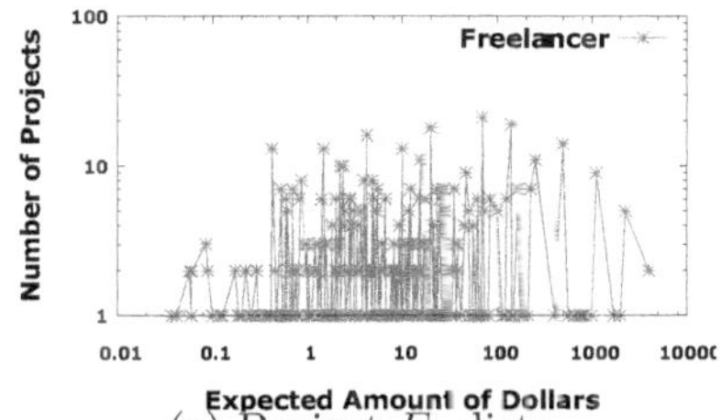

(c) Project F_c distr.

Figure 1: Project analytics for the *Freelancer* dataset.

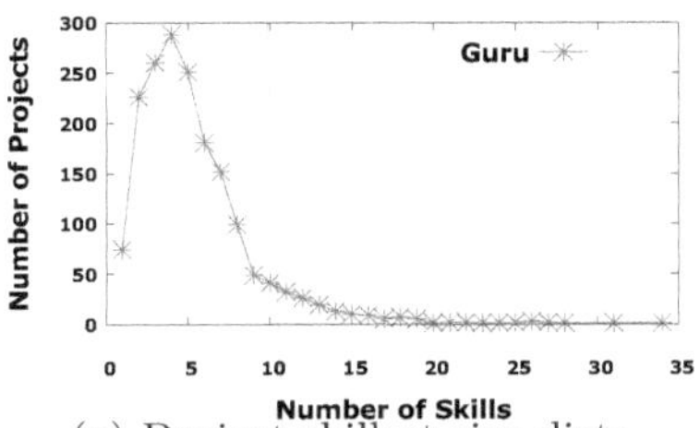

(a) Project skillset size distr.

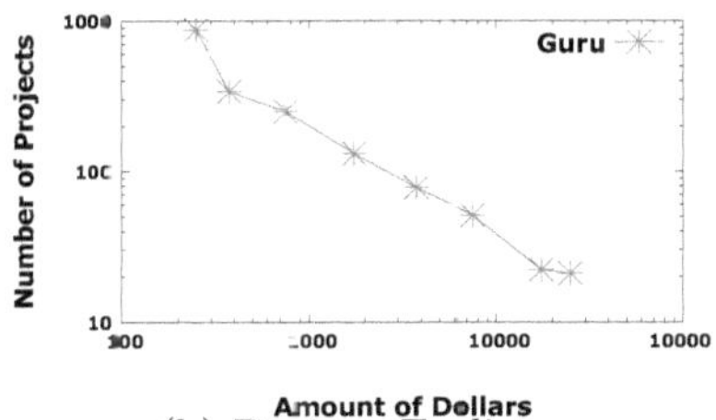

(b) Project F_d distr.

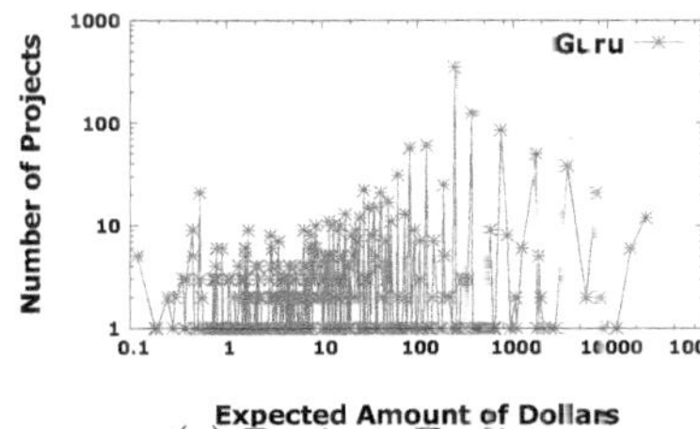

(c) Project F_c distr

Figure 2: Project analytics for the *Guru* dataset.

since this function is based on the rarity of the required skills. which can vary a lot more across projects.

Expert analytics: Figure 3 shows different analytics for the experts from *Freelancer* and *Guru*. Figures 3(a) and 3(b) show the distribution of the skillset size (i.e., number of skills) of the experts in each dataset: the x-axis corresponds to the size of skillset and the y-axis to the number of experts that have skillsets of that size. For *Guru*, Figure 3(b), this distribution is a power-law distribution, with most users having less than 20 skills. On the other hand, the majority of experts on *Freelancer* have five skills, while the remaining skillsets are almost uniformly distributed over 1,2,3, and 4 skills. This difference is explained by the skill verification mechanism that is in place by `freelancer.com` where an expert can declare any number of skills, however on each expert's only at most 6 most verified skills are displayed; a skill of an expert gets a verification every time the expert participates in a project that utilizes this skill. Such a mechanism is absent from `guru.com` (at least at the time the data was collected), and thus the distribution of skillset sizes is different.

Finally, Figures 3(c) and 3(d) show the distribution of salaries for *Freelancer* and *Guru* experts respectively. The x-axis holds the salaries, sorted from lowest to highest, and the y-axis the number of experts with a given salary. Both figures display a "power law"-like distribution, with the majority of experts asking for an hourly salary of at most 50.

Visualization: In an attempt to gain a deeper understanding of the two datasets in the context of our problem, we display the *similarity graphs* for experts in Figures 4 and 6.

Expert graph: In the graphs in Figure 4, nodes correspond to experts. There is an edge between two experts if their Jaccard similarity, computed on their skillsets, is higher than 0.7. For the graph we removed all nodes with

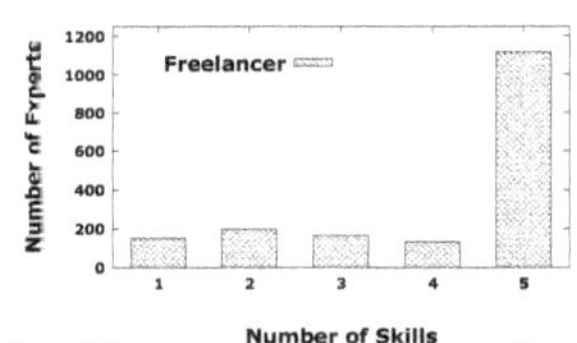

(a) Expert skillset size distr. for *Freelancer*

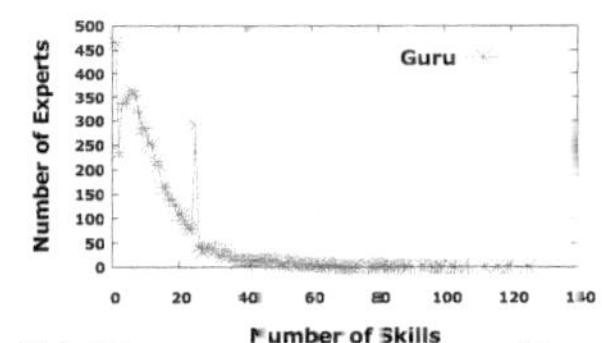

(b) Expert skillset size distr. for *Guru*

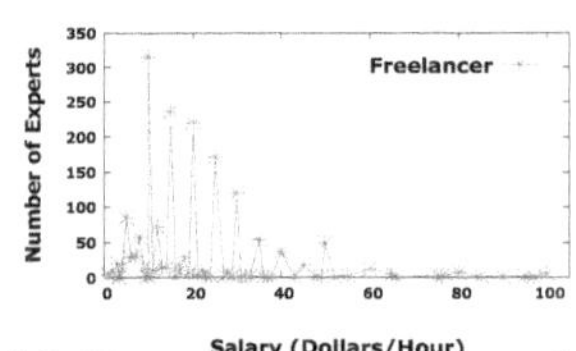

(c) Expert salary distr. for *Freelancer*

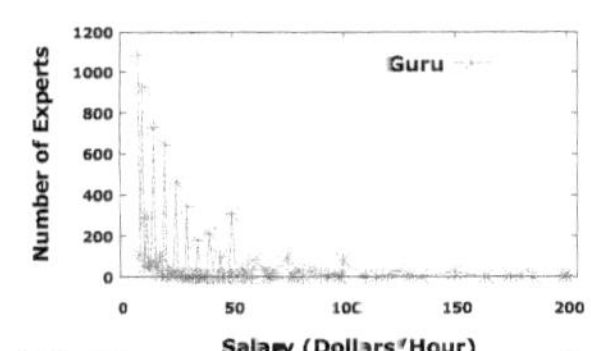

(d) Expert salary distr. for *Guru*

Figure 3: Expert analytics for *Freelancer* and *Guru* datasets.

degree less than 2.[2] The figure demonstrates that the latent similarity structure among experts differs dramatically in the two datasets For *Freelancer* (Figure 4(a)) we observe a number of dense neighborhoods of different sizes, representing clusters of similar experts. At the same time, the graph is well-connected, with several edges often bridging the observed neighborhoods. On the other hand, for *Guru*, (Figure 4(b)), we observe a single large dense component, as well as several smaller components that are not connected to each other. This difference stems from the different na-

[2]Experimenting with lower and higher values of the thresholds had the expected results of producing larger and smaller cliques, respectively, for both datasets.

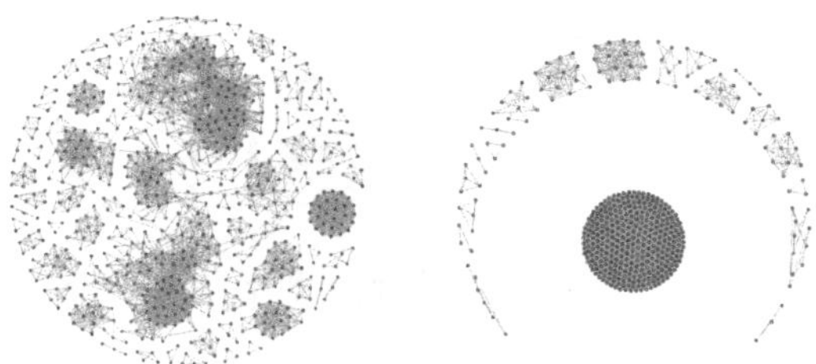

(a) *Freelancer* (b) *Guru*

Figure 4: Expert graphs: Similarity graphs for *Guru* and *Freelancer* experts.

ture of the two websites; `guru.com` hosts a diverse spectrum of experts with skillsets in different domains ranging from IT to legal services, financial consulting etc. On the other hand, the majority of the experts in `freelancer.com` are technology-oriented professionals who are more likely to have overlapping skillsets.

Project graphs: In the graphs in Figure 6, nodes correspond to projects. The graphs were constructed as follows: there is an edge between two projects if the compatibility condition described in Equation (7) is satisfied. We visualize the compatibility graphs for both the F functions: F_d (the dollar amount attached to each project) and F_c (the expected dollar amount, given the competition a team has to face in the process of acquiring the project). Figures 6(a) and 6(b) display the graphs for both functions for the *Freelancer* dataset for $\alpha = 0.2$. Figures 6(c) and 6(d) display the same graphs for *Guru* and $\alpha = 0.7$.

Comparing the graphs across datasets, we observe the same trends found in the expert graphs: *Freelancer* includes a number of distinct (but still connected) neighborhoods. On the other hand, the *Guru* graphs are dominated by 1-2 large components which correspond to experts from disciplines with more dominant representation on the website.

The figures also reveal some interesting facts when considered in the contexts of the two different profit functions. For *Guru*, introducing the competition factor in the profitability of a project leads to a sparser graph. As we saw in Figures 2(a) and 1(a), the average project on *Guru* requires a significantly higher number of skills than the average *Freelancer* project. This makes the occurrence of rare skills more likely, which has a direct effect on the competitive-driven F_c function: as these competitive projects emerge, they are less likely to improve their profit-to-cost ratio by being grouped with other projects, leading to less edges in the graph. On the other hand, the effects of competition on the *Freelancer* project-graph are less prevalent, which is likely to be due to the lower diversity of skillsets required by each project (limited to at most 5).

6. EXPERIMENTS

In our experiments we study the relative performance of our algorithms for the *Freelancer* and the *Guru* datasets, which we extensively analyzed in the previous section.

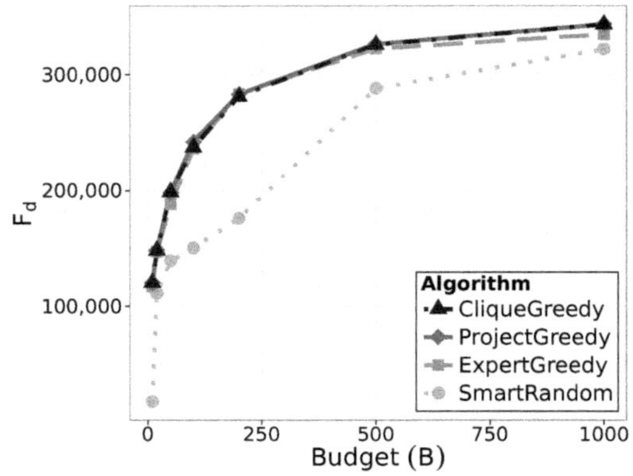

(a) Dollar profit (F_d)

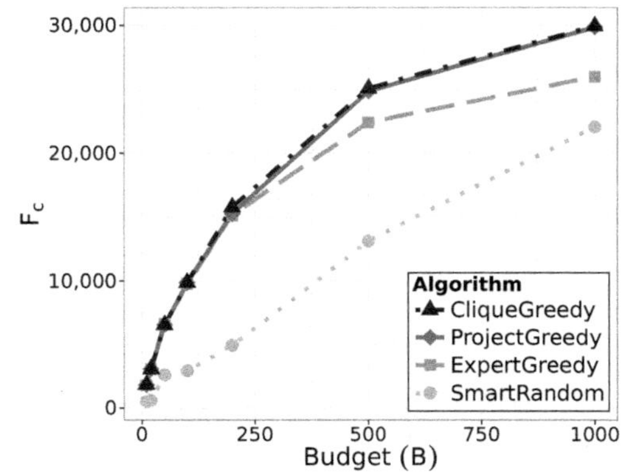

(b) Competition-based profit (F_c)

Figure 5: Performance of different algorithms for the ClusterHire problem (*Freelancer* dataset).

6.1 Evaluating algorithms for ClusterHire

First, we focus on the evaluation of our algorithms for the ClusterHire problem, i.e., **`ExpertGreedy`**, **`ProjectGreedy`** and **`CliqueGreedy`**. To do so, we report the overall profit achieved by each algorithm, for increasing values of the available budget, i.e., $B \in \{10, 20, 50, 100, 200, 500, 1000\}$.

The `SmartRandom` baseline: As an additional baseline, we also evaluate an iterative randomized algorithm, which we refer to as `SmartRandom`. `SmartRandom` is essentially a random version of `ProjectGreedy` and at each iteration it selects a random project, and then proceeds to hire the cheapest set of experts who can fully cover this project. This set of experts is again identified by the greedy algorithm for set cover. In order to ensure that `SmartRandom` exhausts the available budget, only projects that can be covered using the current budget are considered on every iteration. The algorithm then terminates when no such projects exist. Although we use `SmartRandom` as our baseline, it really makes much more educated guesses than a naive random algorithm that forms random teams of experts.

Results for the *Freelancer* dataset: Figures 5(a) and 5(b) show the performance of different algorithms on the *Freelancer* dataset, in terms of the dollar (F_d) and competition-based (F_c) profit functions respectively. The y-axis shows

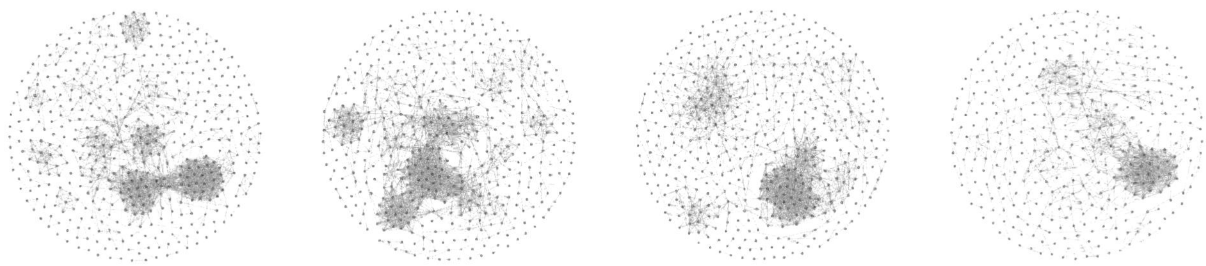

(a) (F_d); *Freelancer* (b) (F_c); *Freelancer* (c) (F_d); *Guru* (d) (F_c); *Guru*

Figure 6: Project graphs: Compatibility graphs for *Guru* and *Freelancer* projects.

the profit achieved by each algorithm, and the x-axis holds the budget that was used to hire experts.

Starting with the results for the dollar profit model, shown in Figure 5(a), we observe that, given a budget of 500$, every algorithm except `SmartRandom` achieves a profit around $32K\$$, while `SmartRandom` reaches a value of $29K\$$. The fact that all algorithms perform well implies that the dataset contains many profitable projects and many low-cost experts who can accomplish these projects. We also observe that `SmartRandom` performs similar to other algorithms under a limited budget (i.e., $0 \leq B \leq 200$), which is reasonable since all algorithms are restricted to a limited set of projects that can actually be covered given the budget.

Under the competition-based profit model the results are different, as illustrated by Figure 5(b). What we observe in this case is that both `ProjectGreedy` and `CliqueGreedy` start to diverge and outperform other methods for budgets above 200$. To understand why `ExpertGreedy` is not as efficient as before, one has to remember that many projects with high dollar profit values will no longer be profitable once the competition of the market is taken into consideration in the evaluation of the profit. The effect of this function is that it changes the space of projects so that there are less projects that are both profitable and cost-effective. This gives `ProjectGreedy` and `CliqueGreedy` an advantage over `ExpertGreedy`. This is because the former evaluate and search for *profitable* projects (or groups of projects) as opposed to `ExpertGreedy` that searches for individual workers who alone can only do projects with small profits.

Results for the *Guru* dataset: To check the consistency of our results, we repeated the same experiment for both profit functions for the *Guru* dataset. The results are shown in Figure 7. Similar to our observations for *Freelancer* dataset, we observe that, while all algorithms perform well in the dollar-based setting, `ExpertGreedy` falls short once the notion of competition is introduced. In fact, the gap between `ExpertGreedy` and the two algorithms based on project selection, i.e., `ProjectGreedy` and `CliqueGreedy`, is even greater than the one observed for *Freelancer*. A similar trend can be observed for `SmartRandom`: the algorithm is again consistently outperformed for both profit functions, with the difference in profit being significantly greater for this dataset, especially under the competition-based profit scheme. As re-

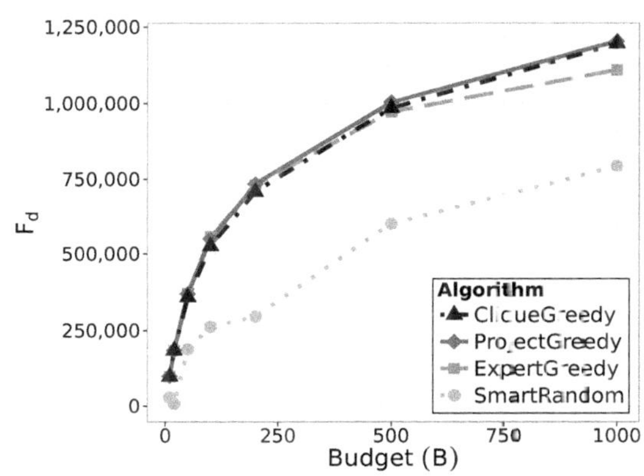

(a) Dollar profit (F_d)

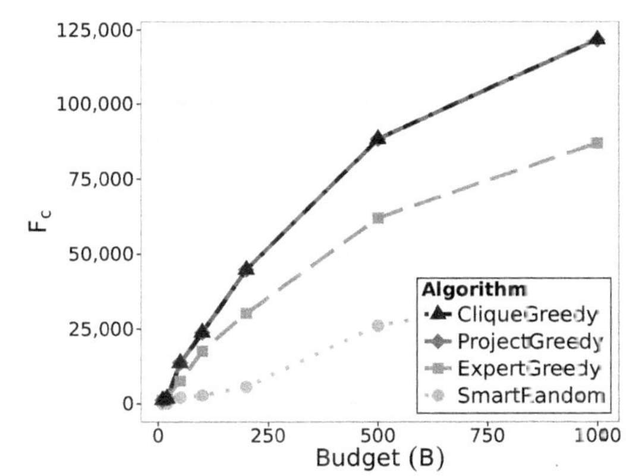

(b) Competition-based profit (F_c)

Figure 7: Performance of different algorithms for CLUSTER-HIRE problem (*Guru* dataset).

vealed in the project analytics presented in Figures 1 and 2, the competitive-based profit function results in a much higher variance in the profits of the available projects. This has a negative effect on `SmartRandom` and `ExpertGreedy`, which do not take into consideration the profitability of the projects when they make their selections. This negative effect is even stronger for the *Guru* dataset, since the competitive profit function dramatically increases the number of less profitable projects. In fact, as can be seen by Figures 2(b) and 2(c), the F_c function introduces very large number of projects with a profit less than 100\$, while no such projects existed for the simple dollar F_d function.

The characteristics of the solutions: In order to gain a deeper understanding of the results, we compute the average profit of the projects covered by the teams reported by the different algorithms for fixed budget $B = 500\$$. The results are summarized in Table 1. The main message of this table is that the average profit of the projects that can be covered by the solutions of `ProjectGreedy` and `CliqueGreedy` is higher than the corresponding average profit achieved by `ExpertGreedy` only in the case where profit is computed by the competition-based profit function. This observation is true for both our datasets. As we have already explained, the reason for that is that `ProjectGreedy` and `CliqueGreedy` are able to identify profitable projects and pick them even if these projects cannot be performed by a single worker. On the other hand, even in the presence of competition, `ExpertGreedy` cannot ignore projects that can be performed by single workers, which are also projects that typically require common skills.

Table 1: Average profit of covered projects for $B = 500\$$

	Freelancer		*Guru*	
	F_d	F_c	F_d	F_c
`ExpertGreedy`	569.0	40.3	1528.3	110.4
`ProjectGreedy`	594.9	47.7	1701.9	186.0
`CliqueGreedy`	594.0	47.5	1667.3	186.0

Performance of `CliqueGreedy`: Figures 5 and 7 show that the `CliqueGreedy` algorithm performs only slightly better in terms of profit, when compared to `ProjectGreedy`. Therefore, a natural question to ask is whether there are any benefits that this algorithm has to offer. Our answer to this question is the following: although `CliqueGreedy` offers smalls gains in terms of profit, there are datasets for which it offers significant computational speedups. We provide evidence for this statement in Table 2.

The table reports the number of candidates that need to be evaluated by `CliqueGreedy` and `ProjectGreedy` for both datasets. The number of candidates per iteration that an algorithm has to evaluate is an important measure of its running time. This is because for every candidate project (or group of projects) the algorithm picks, it needs to solve a set cover problem for this candidate.

The results in Table 2 show that `CliqueGreedy` consistently evaluates less candidates during its computation, especially for the *Freelancer* dataset. This essentially means that for this dataset about 1/3 of the candidates are eliminated and thus 1/3 less set cover computations need to be made by `CliqueGreedy`. Therefore, from the computational point of view for the *Freelancer* `CliqueGreedy` is beneficial

Table 2: Number of candidate (groups) of projects.

	Freelancer		*Guru*	
	F_d	F_c	F_d	F_c
`ProjectGreedy`	721	721	1764	1764
`CliqueGreedy`	520	570	1732	1660

since it offers a significant speedup while giving solutions with (approximately) the same profit. On the other hand, for the *Guru* dataset `CliqueGreedy` does not appear to offer significant computational savings. All these results were computed for $\alpha = 0.2$ for *Freelancer* and $\alpha = 0.7$ for *Guru*.

A visual analysis of the available projects in a dataset, such as the one we presented in Figure 6, can be used prior to running the algorithms, to evaluate if the underlying graph structures justifies the use of `CliqueGreedy`. For example, if multiple dense neighborhoods (which are likely to include cliques) can be identified, then the algorithm can indeed lead to significant computational savings. This is indeed the case for the *Freelancer* dataset and thus the savings.

6.2 Evaluating algorithms for T-CLUSTERHIRE

In this section, we evaluate the performance of for our methods for the T-CLUSTERHIRE problem. For this we use the same experimental setup and evaluation methodology as in the previous section. For T-CLUSTERHIRE, we need to set the value of the threshold on the number of times that a user is willing to utilize each one of his skills. We set this value to $t = 3$ for all users and all skills. However, our experiments suggest that despite the fact that the actual profits change for different thresholds, the relative performance of algorithms is independent of this threshold.

Figure 8 shows the profit achieved by the different algorithms for both datasets and for both our profit models, i.e., dollar profit and competition-based profit. Most of the observations we made in the previous section are true here as well. More specifically, Figures 8(a) and 8(c) show how different algorithms perform under the dollar-based profit model for *Freelancer* and *Guru* datasets respectively. Similar to our previous results for CLUSTERHIRE , we can see that all algorithms perform significantly better than `SmartRandom`. However, unlike our previous results, we can see that the performance of `ExpertGreedy` is significantly lower than the performance of both `ProjectGreedy` and `CliqueGreedy` algorithms. This is due to the utilization constraint which limits the number of cost-effective projects. That is, a set of projects with many overlapping skills are profitable in the CLUSTERHIRE problem since few cheap experts can cover all of the at once, while in the CLUSTERHIRE the profit one can get from this overlapping projects is bounded due to the utility constraint. Therefore, `ExpertGreedy`, that essentially prefers cheap experts looses its power because these experts cannot be used over and over again for multiple projects.

Figures 8(b) and 8(d) show how different algorithms perform under the competition-based profit model. As discussed in the previous section, adjusting the profits based on the competition in the market leads to significantly smaller number of cost-effective jobs. This gives both `ProjectGreedy` and `CliqueGreedy` an advantage as they effectively search for good projects. On the other hand, `ExpertGreedy` does not perform well because due to its myopic nature selects cheap experts that can only do "trivial" projects.

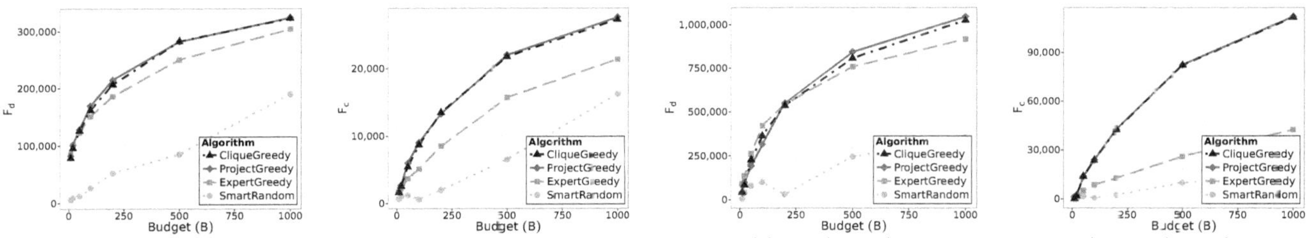

(a) F_d (*Freelancer*) (b) F_c (*Freelancer*) (c) F_d (*Guru*) (d) F_c (*Guru*)

Figure 8: Performance of different algorithms for the T-CLUSTERHIRE problem (*Guru* and *Freelancer* datasets)

Overall, for the T-CLUSTERHIRE problem `ProjectGreedy` and `CliqueGreedy` are consistently and significantly better than `ExpertGreedy`. Despite the computational speedups achieved by `CliqueGreedy` for this problem, the profit it obtained in this case is slightly less than the profit achieved by `ProjectGreedy`. The reason for the slight degradation of the profit achieved by `CliqueGreedy` can be explained as follows: once projects are grouped into clusters, they need to be picked together. However, given the utilization constraints, the set of workers that can satisfy a group of projects may end up being expensive and hence less profitable. In this case, one has to find the balance between computational efficiency and profit that one wants to achieve.

7. CONCLUSIONS

In this paper, we proposed formalizations and algorithmic solutions for the CLUSTERHIRE problem, where the goal is to hire a profit-maximizing team of experts with the ability to complete multiple projects, given a fixed budget. This problem repeatedly emerges in organizational settings, and it has become prevalent due to the establishment of the collaboration paradigm in online labor markets. We provided a detailed analysis of the computational complexity and hardness of approximation of the problem, and presented algorithms that take into consideration the unique nature of expertise data. Our methodology was evaluated on data from two of large players in the domain of online labor.

8. ACKNOWLEDGMENTS

This research was supported by: NSF CAREER #1253393, NSF grants: CNS #1017529, III #1218437, IIS #1320542 and gifts from Microsoft and Hariri Institute of Computing.

9. REFERENCES

[1] A. An, M. Kargar, and M. ZiHayat. Finding affordable and collaborative teams from a network of experts. In *SDM*, pages 587–595, 2013.

[2] A. Anagnostopoulos, L. Becchetti, C. Castillo, A. Gionis, and S. Leonardi. Power in unity: forming teams in large-scale community systems. In *CIKM*, pages 599–608, 2010.

[3] A. Anagnostopoulos, L. Becchetti, C. Castillo, A. Gionis, and S. Leonardi. Online team formation in social networks. In *WWW*, pages 839–848, 2012.

[4] C. Bron and J. Kerbosch. Algorithm 457: Finding all cliques of an undirected graph. *Commun. ACM*, 16(9):575–577, 1973.

[5] S.-J. Chen and L. Lin. Modeling team member characteristics for the formation of a multifunctional team in concurrent engineering. *IEEE Transactions on Engineering Management*, 2004.

[6] C. Dorn and S. Dustdar. Composing near-optimal expert teams: A trade-off between skills and connectivity. In *OTM Conferences (1)*, pages 472–489, 2010.

[7] E. L. Fitzpatrick and R. G. Askin. Forming effective worker teams with multi-functional skill requirements. *Ind. Eng.*, 2005.

[8] A. Gajewar and A. D. Sarma. Multi-skill collaborative teams based on densest subgraphs. In *SDM*, pages 165–176, 2012.

[9] M. Garey and D. Johnson. *Computers and Intractability: A Guide to the Theory of NP-Completeness*. 1979.

[10] A. Gionis, T. Lappas, and E. Terzi. Estimating entity importance via counting set covers. In *KDD*, pages 687–695, 2012.

[11] R. Greenwald. Freelancers find it pays to team up. *The Wall Street Journal*, 2014.

[12] A. A. Hagberg, D. A. Schult, and P. J. Swart. Exploring network structure, dynamics, and function using NetworkX. In *Proceedings of the 7th Python in Science Conference (SciPy2008)*, pages 11–15, 2008.

[13] M. Kargar and A. An. Discovering top-k teams of experts with/without a leader in social networks. In *CIKM*, pages 985–994, 2011.

[14] T. Lappas, K. Liu, and E. Terzi. Finding a team of experts in social networks. In *ACM SIGKDD*, pages 467–476, 2009.

[15] C.-T. Li and M.-K. Shan. Team formation for generalized tasks in expertise social networks. In *SocialCom/PASSAT*, pages 9–16, 2010.

[16] S. Liemhetcharat and M. Veloso. Forming an effective multi-robot team robust to failures. In *IROS*, 2013.

[17] S. Liemhetcharat and M. Veloso. Weighted synergy graphs for effective team formation with heterogeneous ad hoc agents. *Artif. Intell.*, 208:41–65, 2014.

[18] A. Majumder, S. Datta, and K. V. M. Naidu. Capacitated team formation problem on social networks. In *KDD*, pages 1005–1013, 2012.

[19] M. Sozio and A. Gionis. The community-search problem and how to plan a successful cocktail party. In *ACM SIGKDD*, pages 939–948, 2010.

On Social Event Organization

Keqian Li[†] Wei Lu[†] Smriti Bhagat[‡] Laks V.S. Lakshmanan[†] Cong Yu[II]

[†]University of British Columbia
Vancouver, B.C., Canada
{keqianli,welu,laks}@cs.ubc.ca

[‡]Technicolor Research
Palo Alto, CA, USA
smriti.bhagat@technicolor.com

[II]Google Research
New York, NY, USA
congyu@google.com

ABSTRACT

Online platforms, such as Meetup and Plancast, have recently become popular for planning gatherings and event organization. However, there is a surprising lack of studies on how to effectively and efficiently organize social events for a large group of people through such platforms. In this paper, we study the key computational problem involved in organization of social events, to our best knowledge, for the first time.

We propose the Social Event Organization (SEO) problem as one of assigning a set of events for a group of users to attend, where the users are socially connected with each other and have innate levels of interest in those events. As a first step toward Social Event Organization, we introduce a formal definition of a restricted version of the problem and show that it is NP-hard and is hard to approximate. We propose efficient heuristic algorithms that improve upon simple greedy algorithms by incorporating the notion of phantom events and by using look-ahead estimation. Using synthetic datasets and three real datasets including those from the platforms Meetup and Plancast, we experimentally demonstrate that our greedy heuristics are scalable and furthermore outperform the baseline algorithms significantly in terms of achieving superior social welfare.

Categories and Subject Descriptors

H.2.8 [**Database Applications**]: Data Mining

Keywords

Social Networks; Event Organization; Assignment Problems

1. INTRODUCTION

The problem of organizing social events for a large group of people can resonate with the academic community: we are all familiar with the "canned" social events offered by conference organizers, which are often a simple list of activities to choose from and attendance at each event is organically decided by people at the conference based on who they know and how interested they are in the events.

KDD'14, August 24–27, 2014, New York, NY, USA.
Copyright 2014 ACM 978-1-4503-2956-9/14/08 ...$15.00.
http://dx.doi.org/10.1145/2623330.2623724.

More broadly, event organization is one of the most important social activities online, with many companies, established giants and startups alike, such as Meetup[1] and Plancast[2], offering platforms for their users to plan and organize events. The social networks data and the data indicating the interests of the users on these platforms offer a rich setting in which events can be organized effectively and efficiently. Despite its importance, there are few academic studies on this topic: most of the existing research is focused on event detection through time series analysis (e.g., burst detection). Our goal in this paper is to provide a first principled definition of Social Event Organization (SEO) and a platform of algorithmic solutions for addressing this problem. To the best of our knowledge, this is the first paper on *organizing* events, instead of *detecting* events.

The tasks of organizing various social events share many common characteristics. First, each user often has his or her unique preference for the events being offered, a numeric measure which we call a user's *innate affinity* towards an event. Innate affinities can be stated explicitly: e.g., a user can mark his preference for a game of chess as 9 out of 10. Or they can be categorically stated by the users and computed by the organizer: e.g., a user can list outdoor activities in her profile and the organizer can deduce that she will likely prefer hiking to playing chess. Finally, they can be predicted by a recommender system based on the past events that the user has participated in. Regardless of how innate affinities are computed, they are one of the two key ingredients for users' happiness, for purposes of successful organization of social events.

The other key ingredient is the social connections among users – individuals often enjoy an activity more if they attend it along with their friends or others whom they would like to be around with. This connection is often defined between a pair of users and we call this pairwise *social affinity*. Similar to innate affinities, social affinities can be stated explicitly by the users. For example, users on social networks explicitly provide their friendship connections. They can also be deduced based on users' interests or past activities. For instance, two users who share lots of interests and past activities are more likely to enjoy each other's company. Thus, similar to innate affinity, social affinity is represented by a numerical measure.

Importantly, in real world situations, events typically come with natural *cardinality constraints*. For example, most sports activities need a certain number of participants: two or four for tennis, two for chess, and two to nine for poker games.

We illustrate aforementioned characteristics more concretely through the following motivating example. Academic conferences and business conventions often provide networking opportunities for attendees by offering social events. Planning them involves gathering individuals with similar interests to facilitate interactions

[1]http://www.meetup.com
[2]http://www.plancast.com

as well as ensuring that they have a good time. The current practice is to offer these events as a "canned" list of options: e.g., everybody selects from a small set of event choices based on their interests, perhaps uses ad hoc conversations among friends for coordination. Being able to automatically assign people to events from a large list of options, in a *centralized* manner, taking into account both users' interests and friendships will likely lead to people enjoying those events more.

The above example illustrates the core technical challenge inherent in event organization, viz., the *assignment problem*, where the system has to *assign* a given set of users to events, with the goal of making users happy. Other examples in this category include organization of activities at a reunion party, corporate activity day, community fund raising, or volunteering gatherings.

In this first paper towards Social Event Organization, we focus on the assignment problem illustrated above. Specifically, we are given a set of users, who are socially connected and have varying inherent interests in the events being offered. We need to assign users to events so as to maximize the "overall happiness" of the users, while respecting the event cardinality constraints (min and max). In event organization over a wide area, in addition to cardinality constraints, time and location also play a role. E.g., user's proximity to the event's location may affect the user's innate affinity for the event. A similar remark holds for the time at which the event is organized. In order to allow us to focus on the key technical problem of assignment, we assume that users' proximity to the location of events as well as availability of users for the events are factored in while determining the innate affinity of a user to an event. Consequently, *our focus is squarely on finding good assignments of users to events as opposed to scheduling of events.*

One critical aspect of the solution is to define the overall happiness as a combination innate and social affinities. We provide an intuitive definition of *social welfare*, as a linear combination of (i) the total innate affinities enjoyed by the users to the events they are assigned, and (ii) the aggregate social affinities enjoyed by pairs of users assigned to the same event (exact definition in §3.1). This focus allows us to cast the Social Event Organization problem as a constrained discrete optimization problem, for which we can explore algorithmic solutions.

Our event organization problem has close connections with several major bodies of work – generalized assignment problem (GAP) [20, 7, 6, 12], a family of two-sided matching problems including the National Resident Matching Problem (NRMP) [19], and community-search problems [21]. We depart from them by taking both innate and social affinities into account and solving the event organization problem under a unified framework. A detailed comparison with these related works appears in §2.

Specifically, we make the following contributions.

- We formally define social event organization as a constrained discrete optimization problem that asks for an assignment with maximum social welfare while respecting cardinality constraints of events (§3.1).
- The problem is shown to be NP-hard. Given this, we analyze its approximability: we establish close connections between restricted versions of our problem and the SUBSET-SUM problem and DENSE k-SUBGRAPH problem We exploit these connections to offer strong evidence that the problem is hard to approximate (§3.2).
- We then develop several heuristics including a greedy hill-climbing strategy and several improvements. Our improvements are based on a notion of "phantom events" which refer to tentatively scheduled events which have yet to meet their lower cardinality constraint, and a look-ahead based technique (§4).
- We conduct a comprehensive experimental study on both synthetic and real data sets from Plancast, Meetup and SIGCOMM 2009. Our results show that our methods with look ahead estimation far exceed the baseline methods in terms of the social welfare achieved and the regret attained. Furthermore, our most sophisticated algorithm completes event assignments on a dataset consisting of 100,000 users and 500 events in under 17 minutes (§5).

Finally, we conclude the paper and summarize interesting directions for future work in §6.

2. RELATED WORK

Our problem has close connections to the generalized assignment problem (GAP) [20, 7, 6, 12]: there are multiple bins with capacity constraints, multiple objects with a size and a profit for placing an object in a bin; the problem is to find an assignment of objects to bins respecting capacity such that the total profit is maximized. In a special case, all objects have the same size and capacity is replaced by (maximum) cardinality. Differences between GAP and event organization are two-fold. First, events typically have lower bound constraints on cardinality: e.g., a game of Mahjong cannot be played by fewer than four people. Both lower and upper cardinality constraints must be respected by the solutions we propose. Very recently, lower bound constraints have been studied in the context of GAP [12], and the precise relationship between event organization and [12] will be made clear in §3.2. Second, social affinity is not considered in GAP, whereas it is a key ingredient in social event organization.

Our problem is also related to the National Resident Matching Problem (NRMP) and other two-sided matching problems such as college admissions [19, 9, 8, 5]. In NRMP, medical school graduates are matched with residency programs offered by hospitals throughout the U.S. The differences with event organization are three-fold. First, graduates choose residency programs as individuals, and social affinity is almost never a concern, except in rare cases where two graduates are a couple. Second, in NRMP, every graduate provides an ordered list of programs she'd like to join *and* every program has its own preference list over graduates. *Stability* is an important concern. A matching is stable if there is no pair of a graduate and a program so that they both prefer each other over the current assignment they get. While stability is similar in spirit to avoiding regrets (i.e., assigning a user to an event she does not enjoy) in event organization, in event organization stability is not important as events treat all users alike! Third, in contrast to the objectives in NRMP, our goal is to maximize social welfare (defined in §3.1) of the assignment, taking both innate and social affinities into account, while respecting the cardinality constraints of events In §4, we adapt the NRMP solution to solve our problem, and empirically compare it in §5.

In a sense, event organization is also similar to group recommendations: so long as we know which set of users will attend the same event, i.e., group memberships, but not which one, we can, in principle, determine that event using group recommendations [2]. However, we do not know these groups and part of the challenge is to find them. Besides, our assignment of users (and hence of groups) to events is more "holistic" in considering not only innate, but also social affinity: it is their combination that drives our assignment. Thus, group recommendations cannot solve our problem

Team formation problems in social networks [13, 3] assume for each user a set of skills and for each pair of users a compatibility measure. The problem is to put together teams that satisfy the skill requirements of a given task while minimizing the communication overhead of the team, e.g., the diameter or weight of the minimum spanning tree of the graph of the formed team. The problem is NP-hard and many of the works resort to approximation algorithms. Superficially, the team formation problem seems similar to ours. However, while social affinity has a counterpart in compatibility, there is no direct innate affinity between users and tasks, except indirectly via skills. More importantly, cardinality constraints in event organization make the problem significantly more challenging. Finally, a user may be assigned to more than one task whereas users are assigned to at most one event in our problem.

Also relevant to our work is the community search problem [21], where given a set of query nodes, the task is to find a community containing the query nodes that maximizes the overall social affinity, subject to a maximum cardinality constraint. However, there is no notion of events, nor users' innate affinities towards events in [21]. In contrast, our problem involves a combination of social and innate affinities and thus a *holistic approach* is needed which at once pays attention to the innate aspect (matching quality) and the social aspect. There have also been studies on geo-social query processing [4]. Though both our problem and theirs consider social effects, the SEO problem is inherently an assignment problem and cannot be solved by issuing queries.

3. SOCIAL EVENT ORGANIZATION

We now formulate Social Event Organization (SEO) as an assignment problem and study its hardness and approximation.

3.1 Problem Definition

Consider a setting where organizers of a large gathering (e.g., an international conference or a company-wide retreat) are planning social activities for the conference attendees. Or a scenario in which or an event planning platform (e.g., Meetup) is being used to plan social events for its users over a wide local area such as a city. In both cases, there is a set of users U who must be assigned to events or activities from a given set of possible events A. We assume the presence of a social network, through which the friendships among those users can be obtained. Let $G = (U, E)$ be the friendship graph induced on U. Each event $a \in A$ is associated with a *minimum cardinality bound* γ_a and a *maximum cardinality bound* δ_a, as motivated in §1.

There is a function $\sigma : U \times A \to \mathbb{R}_+$ such that for each user u and event a, $\sigma(u, a)$ models the user's *innate affinity* for the event. We often denote $\sigma(u, a)$ as $\sigma_{u,a}$ for simplicity. As mentioned in the introduction, we assume that the innate affinity $\sigma_{u,a}$ factors in u's proximity to a's location and u's availability w.r.t. the time at which a is held. In addition to their innate affinity to events, users have pair-wise social affinity with each other, and we capture this by a function $w : U \times U \to \mathbb{R}_+$, such that $w(u, v)$ is the social affinity between u and v. Both innate affinity to events and social affinity to other users attending the same event contribute to a user's sense of "utility" for attending an event. Note that as discussed in §1, social affinity is important because an individual may enjoy an event more when she is joined by her friends. We assume in this paper that social affinity is non-negative and that social affinity values are symmetric, i.e., $w(u, v) = w(v, u)$, for all $u, v \in U$.

Suppose a set of users $S \subset U$ is assigned to an event $a \in A$. We define the *utility* of this assignment as:

$$\mu(S, a) = (1 - \alpha) \sum_{u \in S} \sigma_{u,a} + \alpha \sum\nolimits_{u,v \in S, u \neq v} w(u, v), \quad (1)$$

where $\alpha \in [0, 1]$ can be chosen by the user of the SEO system, i.e., the organizer, to adjust the relative importance of the two affinities.

That is, the overall utility of the set of participants of an event is a linear combination of the total innate affinity of the participants for the event and the total social affinity of all pairs of participants. As a special case, we define $\mu(\emptyset, a) = 0$: when nobody is assigned to an event, it results in zero utility. As mentioned in the introduction, both innate affinity $\sigma_{u,a}$ and social affinity $w(u, v)$ can be provided by the users explicitly through stated interests and friendships. However, in case such explicit information is not available, those values can be estimated from a user's implicit interests and past activities. For example, social affinity can be computed using well-studied social distance measures (e.g., graph distance, Katz, or hitting time) [14]. We defer the details to §5.

An *assignment* is a (possibly partial) function $M : U \to A$. For $a \in A$, we denote by $M^{-1}(a)$ the (possibly empty) subset of users assigned to a, i.e., $M^{-1}(a) = \{u \in U \mid M(u) = a\}$. An assignment M is said to be *feasible* provided all cardinality constraints are satisfied, i.e., $\forall a \in A$ for which $M^{-1}(a) \neq \emptyset$, we have $\gamma_a \leq |M^{-1}(a)| \leq \delta_a$, in words, for all events to which at least one user is assigned, the number of users assigned to that event lies within its lower and upper bounds. Notice that owing to the cardinality constraints and the number of users and events in an instance of the assignment problem, it may not be possible to find a feasible assignment that covers all users: e.g., we may have 10 users and 1 event such that the event can accommodate at most 5 people. This is the reason we allow partial functions above. Similarly, not all events may be scheduled by an assignment, i.e., M need not be onto. We define the *social welfare* of a feasible assignment M as

$$\omega(M) = \sum\nolimits_{a \in A} \mu(M^{-1}(a), a). \quad (2)$$

The overall social welfare of an assignment is thus determined by the sum of utilities of the assignments made to each event. Our objective is to find a feasible assignment that maximizes the overall social welfare. Our definition of overall social welfare reflects the following intuition. A user's personal utility for an assignment increases with her innate affinity for the event, as well as the social affinity she has toward other users attending the same event. Besides, the more such fellow attendees, the higher her utility. The definition of overall social welfare is a simple extension of this intuition. Note that other definitions of social welfare, using other aggregate functions, are possible: we prefer to use a simple definition here that captures the intuition above. We formally define the Social Event Organization (SEO) problem as follows.

PROBLEM 1 (SOCIAL EVENT ORGANIZATION (SEO)). *Given a set U of users with a social graph $G = (U, E)$, a set A of events where each $a \in A$ has a minimum and maximum cardinality bound, denoted $\gamma_a \in \mathbb{N}$ and $\delta_a \in \mathbb{N}$ respectively ($\gamma_a \leq \delta_a$), innnate affinity function $\sigma(\cdot, \cdot)$, and social affinity function $w(\cdot, \cdot)$, produce a feasible assignment $M : U \to A$ that has the maximum overall social welfare $\omega(M)$, i.e., find*

$$M^* = \arg\max\{\omega(M) \mid M \textit{ is feasible}\}.$$

The number of scheduled events (i.e., those have at least one user assigned and cardinality constraints satisfied) is not fixed in advance, but rather determined by the solution, in which some events may receive zero users. However, the cardinality constraints for each event that has non-zero participants assigned must be respected. It is possible to have multiple groups performing the same event, e.g., there may be four groups of two participants each that are suggested the event of playing chess. This is easily handled by technically treating different instances of a given event as different events. We can consider weighting the two terms in Eq. (1), corresponding to the innate and social contributions to social welfare, differently. Our results in the next section show that the problem remains hard regardless of the weights chosen.

3.2 Hardness Results

Not surprisingly, our first result is that Social Event Organization is NP-hard. Our reduction is from the recently studied Seminar Assignment Problem (SAP). SAP is obtained by adding lower bound constraints to a restricted version of GAP where all objects have the same size, and is formally stated as follows. Given a set of n students and and a set of m seminars with maximum cardinality $B_1, B_2, \ldots, B_m \in \mathbb{N}$ and minimum cardinality $q_1, q_2, \ldots, q_m \in \mathbb{N}$, $q_i \leq B_i$, a profit $p_{i,j} \in \mathbb{N}$ of assigning student i to seminar j, we want to find an assignment of students to seminars that satisfies the cardinality constraints and maximizes the total profit. Krumke and Thielen [12] recently showed that this problem is NP-hard. We have the following easy result:

THEOREM 1. *The decision version of Social Event Organization is NP-complete.*

PROOF. Clearly, SAP is isomorphic to a restricted version of SEO where all innate affinities are natural numbers, all social affinities are zero (and $\alpha = 0$). The NP-hardness of SEO follows from this. Membership in NP is straightforward: given an assignment, both checking its feasibility and whether its social welfare exceeds a given threshold can be done in polynomial time. □

Next, we analyze how hard it is to approximate SEO. Our analysis involves two special cases of the problem, one with only innate affinities (which is isomorphic to the SAP problem) and the other with only social affinity.

Special Case 1: Innate Utility Only. In this case, we only consider instances of SEO where $w(u, v) = 0$, for all users u and v (and $\alpha = 0$). Thus, the problem is to find a feasible assignment $M : U \to A$ that maximizes the social welfare, which is solely determined by innate affinities. We call this version SEO-Innate.

THEOREM 2. *It is NP-hard to approximate SEO-Innate within a factor of* $(1 - 1/n + \epsilon)$ $(\forall \epsilon > 0)$ *in polynomial time, where* n *is the number of users.*

PROOF. We prove the result by showing that if such an algorithm existed, it could solve the SUBSET-SUM problem, an NP-complete problem, in polynomial time. Since this is impossible unless P = NP, the theorem follows. Consider an arbitrary instance $\mathcal{I}$ of SUBSET-SUM consisting of a set of integers $T = \{t_1, t_2, \ldots, t_N\}$ and a target number τ. We must find out if there is a subset of T whose elements sum to exactly τ. Algorithm $\mathcal{B}$ first creates an instance $\mathcal{J}$ of the SEO problem with τ users and N events, and for each event $a \in [1, N]$, it sets $\gamma_a = \delta_a := t_a$. Also, $\sigma_{u,a} = 1$ for all $u \in U, a \in A$ and $w(u, v) = 0$ for all $u, v \in U$. Then $\mathcal{B}$ runs $\mathcal{A}$ on $\mathcal{J}$, and outputs YES (indicating there is a subset of T summing to exactly τ) if and only if $\mathcal{A}$ outputs an assignment with social welfare τ. We next prove that algorithm $\mathcal{B}$ can correctly distinguish between the YES- and NO-instances of SUBSET-SUM.

If $\mathcal{I}$ is a YES-instance, then by the above reduction, $OPT_{\mathcal{J}} = \tau$, i.e., the maximum possible social welfare of any feasible assingment on instance $\mathcal{J}$ is τ. By assumption, $\mathcal{A}$ will output an assignment with welfare $\geq (1 - 1/\tau + \epsilon)\tau > \tau - 1$. Since all utility values are 1, the output of $\mathcal{A}$ will be exactly τ, and thus $\mathcal{B}$ answers correctly: YES.

If $\mathcal{I}$ is a NO-instance, then for $\mathcal{J}$, by construction, not all users can be fit into an event, implying $OPT_{\mathcal{J}} < \tau$. Since the output of $\mathcal{A}$ is always $\leq OPT_{\mathcal{J}}$, it will be surely $< \tau$. Again, algorithm $\mathcal{B}$ answers correctly: NO. This was to be shown. □

We note that complementarily, Krumke and Thielen [12] show that it is NP-hard to approximate SAP within a factor of $1 - \epsilon_0/3$ even when all profits are in $\{0, 1\}$, where $\epsilon_0 > 0$ is a constant associated with the hardness gap of the 3-Bounded 3-Dimensional Matching problem [16]. As a consequence, they show that SAP does not admit PTAS (polynomial time approximation scheme). This hardness is clearly inherited by SEO-Innate as well. Note that both $1 - \epsilon_0/3$ and $(1 - 1/n)$ are close to 1 (the latter when n is large). This raises the question whether coarser approximations exist for SEO. Our result in the next section suggests it is unlikely.

Special Case 2: Pair-wise Affinity Only. In this case, we restrict attention to instances of SEO where $\sigma_{u,a} = 0$ for all users and all events (and $\alpha = 1$). We refer to this restricted version of SEO as SEO-Social. We show that this restricted problem is hard to approximate within any constant factor under hardness assumptions about certain combinatorial problems. Specifically, our result is achieved by a reduction from the DENSE k-SUBGRAPH problem. That problem, given a graph $G = (V, E)$ and a parameter k, asks to find a subgraph G' of G induced by k nodes such that average degree of nodes in G' is maximum. The average degree of a node in $G' = (V', E')$ is given by $2|E'|/|V'|$. By assuming the hardness of a conjecture known as Unique Games with Small Set Expansion Conjecture [11], Raghavendra and Streurer [18] show that DENSE k-SUBGRAPH is hard to approximate within any constant factor. We "lift" this to show a similar hardness of approximation of SEO-Social. For lack of space, we refer the reader to [18] for details and history of this conjecture.

THEOREM 3. *Assuming the Unique Games with Small Set Expansion Conjecture, it is NP-hard to approximate SEO-Social within any constant factor in polynomial time.*

PROOF. Given an instance $\mathcal{I}$ of DENSE k-SUBGRAPH defined by $G = (V, E)$ and a positive integer k, create an SEO instance $\mathcal{J}$ by setting $A = \{a\}$, $\gamma_a = \delta_a = k$, and $U = V$. I.e., there is just one event whose lower and upper bound on cardinality is k and there is a user corresponding to each node of G. For all $u \in U$, set $\sigma_{u,a} = 0$, and for all $u, v \in U$, $w(u, v) = 1$. By construction, $OPT_{\mathcal{I}} = OPT_{\mathcal{J}}$, i.e., the maximum social welfare of a feasible assignment on instance $\mathcal{J}$ is identical to the maximum average degree of a k-vertex induced subgraph of G in instance $\mathcal{I}$. Suppose there is a PTIME algorithm $\mathcal{A}$ approximating SEO within a factor of $c \in (0, 1)$. Then, $\mathcal{B}$ can approximate DENSE k-SUBGRAPH within the same factor by converting $\mathcal{I}$ to $\mathcal{J}$ as above, running $\mathcal{A}$ on $\mathcal{J}$, and outputting the nodes corresponding to the users chosen by $\mathcal{A}$ to attend event a. This is impossible unless the Unique Games with Small Set Expansion Conjecture doesn't hold. □

To conclude this section, not only is SEO NP-complete, it is also made up of two hard subproblems. Our results show that it is unlikely to be approximable within any constant factor in polynomial time, unless some hardness assumptions about important combinatorial problems break down. It should be clear from the proof of Theorems 2 and 3 that this is true regardless of the choice of α in Eq. (1).

4. PROPOSED SOLUTIONS

Given that SEO is NP-hard to even approximate, we propose a variety of heuristics that give emphasis to different aspects of the problem, such as the social affinity, the innate affinity, and the cardinality constraints. Before diving into the details of the algorithms, it is important to first understand what constitutes a feasible (valid) solution to the SEO problem.

Characterizing Feasible Solutions. For any event, if the event has reached its minimum cardinality, we refer to it as a *real event*; otherwise, we call it a *phantom event*. For example, a tennis or chess game with only one player is a phantom event, that will become real only after one other person is assigned to the event. An event is *open* and can accept more participants if the maximum cardinality has not been reached yet, otherwise it is declared *closed*. By definition, all phantom events are open. However, a real event can be either open or closed. A user u is *available* if u has not been assigned to a real event yet. A user-event assignment is valid if it involves an available user and an open event. During the assignment process, if the event to which a user was assigned becomes real, then the user's assignment is fixed, and she is marked *unavailable*. Consequently, all other previous and future assignments involving that particular user are deemed invalid. Recall that the final solution must be feasible, i.e., respect cardinality constraints. As shown in §3, in some instances it is not possible to find an assignment for every user, so the assignment function may be partial. In practice, we can deal with this by supposing that there are sufficiently many events with large capacity such as movies or theatrical shows to which users left unassigned by the algorithm may be assigned.

Notice that each assignment decision impacts the utility received from future assignments, due to the coupling effect with other users in the form of social affinity. Therefore, it is non-trivial to achieve a (feasible) solution to SEO that achieves a high social welfare.

Solution Template. In the remainder of this section we discuss a variety of algorithms. At a high level, each algorithm (except *Random* and NRMP+) follows the following template. First, a sorted list $\mathcal{L}$ of potential assignments of users to events is generated. The additional contents of the list may vary depending on the algorithm. This list may be updated and re-ordered several times during a run of the algorithm. Second, users are assigned to events by making one pass on this list, and the "state" of users (available, unavailable), and events (phantom, real open, real closed) is updated appropriately. In particular, it marks an event a as "real" when it reaches its minimum cardinality γ_a, and "closed" when it reaches its maximum cardinality δ_a. These assignments are tentative and are recorded by membership in the "S" sets, e.g., $u \in S_a$ means u is tentatively assigned to event a, and possibly to other events. All events are "open" and "phantom" to start with. Once an event a becomes real, the users in the set S_a are marked "unavailable" for future assignments and we set $M(u) = a, \forall u \in S_a$. Additionally, the algorithm invalidates any previous and future assignments of each user $u \in M^{-1}(a)$, by cleaning up other "S" sets as needed. Finally, the algorithm performs post-processing to ensure that the output is a feasible solution, i.e., no phantom events are left behind.

4.1 Baselines

In this section, we present a set of intuitive baseline solutions, in increasing level of sophistication. We build on these baselines and present our proposed algorithms in §4.2.

Random. Our first baseline is called *Random*, which randomly assigns users to events while respecting the cardinality constraints. Specifically, the algorithm first randomly shuffles the list $\mathcal{L}$ containing user-event pairs $\langle u, a\rangle$. It then traverses the list and at each tuple $\langle u, a\rangle$ assigns user u to event a if u is available and a is open. It appropriately marks an event as real when it reaches its minimum cardinality constraint. Clearly, this is a "straw man" approach, which does not take into account the "utility" of any assignment.

Algorithm 1 Dynamic Greedy $(U, A, \sigma, w, \alpha)$

$M(u) \leftarrow \perp, \forall u \in U$; $S_a \leftarrow \emptyset, \forall a \in A$
for all $(u, a) \in U \times A$ s.t. $\sigma_{u,a} > 0$ **do**
  $g(u, a \mid S_a) \leftarrow (1-\alpha)\sigma_{u,a}$
  $\mathcal{L}.\mathsf{insert}(\langle u, a, g(u, a \mid S_a)\rangle)$
while $\langle u, a, g(u, a \mid S_a)\rangle \leftarrow \mathcal{L}.\mathsf{pop}()$ **do**
  if $M(u) = \perp$ and $|S_a| < \delta_a$ **then**
    $S_a \leftarrow S_a \cup \{u\}$
    if $|S_a| > \gamma_a$ **then**
      $M(u) \leftarrow a$
      for all $a' \in A$ s.t. $a' \neq a \wedge u \in S_{a'}$ **do**
        $S_{a'} \leftarrow S_{a'} - \{u\}$
    if $|S_a| = \gamma_a$ **then**
      for all $v \in S_a$ **do**
        $M(v) \leftarrow a$
        for all $a' \in A$ s.t. $a' \neq a \wedge v \in S_{a'}$ **do**
          $S_{a'} \leftarrow S_{a'} - \{v\}$
    for all v : $(w(u, v) > 0 \wedge M(v) = \perp)$ **do**
      $\mathcal{L}.\mathsf{update}(\langle v, a, g(v, a \mid S_a)\rangle)$ // Using Eq. (3)
Reassign available users $\{u | M(u) = \perp\}$
return M

NRMP+. Given the connection between SEO and NRMP, a natural question is whether we can leverage algorithms developed for NRMP. We next describe an adaptation of the NRMP algorithm [8] for handling the lower bound constraints present in SEO. In this adaptation, called NRMP+, we cast SEO in the NRMP framework by associating a preference list of events for each user, ordered by the innate affinity, and a preference list of users for each event, ordered by the innate affinity.[3]

NRMP+ repeats the following procedure until each user is either "accepted" by an event or is "rejected" by all events she applied to. Initially, all users are unassigned and no acceptance or rejection has been made yet. In each round, each unassigned user "applies" to the most preferred event that has not rejected her. Each event a then picks the δ_a most preferred users who applied to it, or all applicants if there are fewer than δ_a of them, and puts them on a waiting list. Users who failed to get on the waiting list are rejected and are thus unassigned after this round. After this iterative process stops, we check if there exists any phantom event. If yes, redistribute users assigned to phantom events to existing real open events in a greedy manner, based on innate affinity. After that, either no user is left unassigned or there are no real events to which unassigned users can be assigned, and we stop.

It is unclear how NRMP can be directly adapted to take social affinity into account in deciding acceptances. In Section 5, we empirically compare NRMP+ with the more sophisticated baselines we develop next, as well as with our main algorithm.

Static Pairwise Greedy. Our next baseline, called Static Pairwise Greedy (SG), assigns pairs of users to events, taking into account both innate event and pairwise social affinities. Specifically, a sorted list $\mathcal{L}$ containing tuples $\langle u, v, a\rangle$ representing potential assignment of pairs of users to events is generated. The list is ordered by non-increasing potential gain (of "utility"), defined as

$$g((u, v), a) = (1-\alpha)(\sigma_{u,a} + \sigma_{v,a}) + 2\,\alpha\, w(u, v).$$

The list is traversed and at each tuple $\langle u, v, a\rangle$ users u and v are assigned to event a if both users are available, and a is open with at least two spots. User and event states are appropriately updated.

[3]Events don't have independent preference lists: we induce them from user-event affinities for the sake of simulation of NRMP.

Finally, any users that are in phantom events at the end of one pass over the list $\mathcal{L}$ are redistributed greedily among remaining open events. We call this a *static* approach as the function g is computed only once. Therefore, the partial ordering of the $\mathcal{L}$ is static, and it only incurs deletions (with some assignments being invalidated). Therefore, the assignment of a pair of users to an event is oblivious to which users are already assigned to that event.

Dynamic Greedy. Our next algorithm, called Dynamic Greedy (DG), is more sophisticated. It updates its estimation of the "utility" a user will attain from an assignment, based on the current set of assignments. To achieve this, the algorithm updates the list $\mathcal{L}$ at each assignment, where $\mathcal{L}$ is composed of tuples $\langle u, a, g(u, a|S_a)\rangle$, $S_a = \emptyset$ initially, and the potential gain g is

$$g(u, a \mid S_a) = (1-\alpha)\sigma_{u,a} + \alpha \sum\nolimits_{v \in S_a} w(u, v). \quad (3)$$

Clearly, when no users are assigned to an event a, $g(u, a \mid \emptyset) = (1-\alpha)\sigma_{u,a}$. Algorithm 1 presents the pseudocode for the DG method. At each step, the assignment that gives the largest potential gain $g(.)$ is performed. Let N_u be the set of users v: $w_{u,v} > 0$. Now, whenever a user u is assigned to an event a, we need to recompute the potential gain $g(v, a \mid S_a)$ for all neighbors $v \in N_v$ of user u in the network, since their utility for event a increases after the assignment of u to that event. In practice, the algorithm maintains the list $\mathcal{L}$ as a priority queue of tuples in non-increasing order of $g(u, a \mid S_a)$. We use the notation $M(u) = \perp$ to denote that the user u is available. We remark that the update operation (line 18) is in charge of not only updating the existing entries in the priority queue but also checking whether the pair (v, a) is already in the heap and if not, adding it.

The post-processing in Line 19 is done in a greedy manner. Let A' be the set of currently open real events, i.e., $A' = \{a \mid \gamma_a \leq |S_a| < \delta_a\}$ and U' be the set of users assigned to phantom events. The list $\mathcal{L}$ is re-constructed with users from U' and events from A', and we rerun the DG algorithm over this list. This process can be repeated as needed. The post-processing stops when either all users are assigned or there are not enough real events (i.e., all real events are closed). In the latter case, from a practical perspective, the remaining users may be assigned to new events with a large capacity, e.g., watching a movie or a theatrical show.

Implementation Notes and Time and Space Complexity. We remark that in our implementation, we optimize the algorithm for better performance. In particular, we tune our implementation to suit a Fibonacci heap based realization of the priority queue. Specifically, we commit to making an assignment for new users right after line 7. This allows us to avoid assigning users to multiple phantom events. Thus, when the priority queue is updated, "decrease key" operation will not be needed, permitting us to implement the priority queue using a Fibonacci heap. We note, however, in this case the assignment function M no longer corresponds to only real events since some phantom events may be left behind by the algorithm at termination. For ease of exposition, we have chosen to present our algorithm in a conceptually simpler way.

When the priority queue $\mathcal{L}$ is implemented using a Fibonacci heap, then for each assignment (u, a), the algorithms performs $O(|N_u|)$ `update` operations (Line 18), each of which is constant time. Summing over all users, the total running time of all `update` operations is $O(|E|)$, where E is the edge set of the social network of users, or more precisely the set of pairs (u, v) with $w(u, v) > 0$. Next, since the number of all possible (u, a) pairs is bounded by $|\mathcal{L}|$, we need at most that many pop operations, which in total takes $O(|\mathcal{L}| \log(|\mathcal{L}|))$ time. In addition, insertion is constant time for Fibonacci heaps so the initialization step takes $O(|\mathcal{L}|)$. Hence, the total time complexity for Dynamic Greedy is $O(|\mathcal{L}| \log(|\mathcal{L}|) + |E|)$. Finally, the space complexity is $\Omega(|\mathcal{L}| + |E|)$.

Algorithm 2 PCADG $(U, A, \sigma, w, \alpha)$

1: $M(u) \leftarrow \perp, \forall u \in U$; $S_a \leftarrow \emptyset, \forall a \in A$; $\mathcal{P} \leftarrow \emptyset$
2: `deficit` $\leftarrow 0$; $V \leftarrow U$
3: **for** each $(u, a) \in U \times A$ s.t. $\sigma_{u,a} > 0$ **do**
4:   $g(u, a \mid S_a) \leftarrow (1-\alpha)\sigma_{u,a}$
5:   $\mathcal{L}$.insert($\langle u, a, g(u, a \mid S_a)\rangle$)
6: **while** $\langle u, a, g(u, a \mid S_a)\rangle \leftarrow \mathcal{L}$.pop() **do**
7:   **if** $M(u) = \perp$ and $|S_a| < \delta_a$ **then**
8:     **if** $|S_a| = 0$ **then**
9:       **if** `deficit` $+ \gamma_a \leq |V|$ **then**
10:         `deficit` $\leftarrow$ `deficit` $+ \gamma_a - 1$
11:         $\mathcal{P} \leftarrow \mathcal{P} \cup \{a\}$
12:       **else**
13:         **continue**
14:     **else**
15:       **if** $a \in \mathcal{P}$ **then**
16:         `deficit` $\leftarrow$ `deficit` $- 1$
17:     $S_a \leftarrow S_a \cup \{u\}$
18:     $V \leftarrow V \setminus \{u\}$
19:     **if** $|S_a| > \gamma_a$ **then**
20:       $M(u) \leftarrow a$
21:       **for all** $a' \in A$ s.t. $a' \neq a \wedge u \in S_{a'}$ **do**
22:         $S_{a'} \leftarrow S_{a'} - \{u\}$
23:     **if** $|S_a| = \gamma_a$ **then**
24:       $\mathcal{P} \leftarrow \mathcal{P} \setminus \{a\}$;
25:       **for all** $v \in S_a$ **do**
26:         $M(v) \leftarrow a$
27:         **for all** $a' \in A$ s.t. $a' \neq a \wedge v \in S_{a'}$ **do**
28:           $S_{a'} \leftarrow S_{a'} - \{v\}$
29:     **for all** v : $(w(u, v) > 0 \wedge M(v) = \perp)$ **do**
30:       $\mathcal{L}$.update($\langle v, a, g(v, a \mid S_a)\rangle$)   // Using Eq. (4)
31: **return** M

4.2 Greedy with Look Ahead Estimation

The Dynamic Greedy algorithm is intuitive: it tries to make assignments based on the largest estimated gain, given the current state of the assignment. However, it has its limitations: (i) it is oblivious to which events a user's friends are likely to be assigned; (ii) the first pass may result in a large number of phantom events as it is ignorant of which events are likely to materialize. To address these limitations, we propose the *Phantom- and Community-Aware Dynamic Greedy or PCADG* (pseudocode in Algorithm 2). A key feature of this algorithm is that it looks ahead at the forthcoming assignments to inform the decision at each step.

Community Awareness. The earlier algorithms do not take into account the potential gain that future assignments of friends to an event may bring to a user. In our Phantom- and Community-Aware Dynamic Greedy algorithm, the awareness of friends' potential assignments is incorporated into the decision making process. More specifically, here, the potential gain g is defined as

$$\begin{aligned} g(u, a|S_a) =& (1-\alpha)\sigma_{u,a} + \alpha \sum\nolimits_{v \in S_a} w(u, v) \\ &+ \alpha(\delta_a - |S_a|) \sum\nolimits_{v \in V} w(u, v)/(|V| - 1), \quad (4) \end{aligned}$$

where V is the set of users that have not yet been assigned to any event, phantom or real: $V = \{u \mid u \in U \wedge M(u) = \perp \wedge u \notin \bigcup_{a \in A} S_a\}$.

Notice that the first two terms in this equation are identical to the two terms in Equation 3 of the Dynamic Greedy method. The third term corresponds to the "look-ahead" whereby it is optimistically assumed that the remaining spots in the event a will be filled with friends of u, with an average social affinity toward u. The average is computed over users in V. While the first two terms are based on the current membership of S_a, the third term is based on anticipation. Thus, this algorithm gives equal importance to both innate affinity and social affinity in gauging the potential gain that could come from an assignment. Other variants can be easily designed to weigh the importance of the innate and social affinities differently.

Phantom Awareness. Another observation about Dynamic Greedy is that it tends to be somewhat indiscriminate in the creation of phantom events: it never restricts the creation of new events as the condition $|S_a| < \delta_a$ (line 6 of Algorithm 1) will always be true for new events, for which $|S_a| = 0$ by definition. All phantom events that are left behind after a pass over the list $\mathcal{L}$ have to be cleaned up later. PCADG tries to limit the creation of phantom events, by employing a stronger condition for phantom event creation. Intuitively, it keeps track of phantom events as it proceeds, and procrastinates on creating new events if the number of unassigned users is less than the currently unfilled spots in existing phantom events that need to be filled in order for the events to materialize.

To achieve this, PCADG maintains a variable called `deficit`, defined to be

$$\texttt{deficit} = \sum_{a \in \mathcal{P}} (\gamma_a - |S_a|),$$

where $\mathcal{P}$ is the set of phantom events and S_a is the set of users assigned to event a. If, at any point of the execution of PCADG, it happens that `deficit` $> |V|$, then there must be at least one phantom event at the end of one pass over $\mathcal{L}$, thus requiring reassignment. Therefore, the algorithm performs an assignment based on a tuple $\langle u, a, g(.)\rangle$ *only if* it does *not* push `deficit` over $|V|$ (Line 9). Otherwise, it will skip that tuple and continue to the next one in $\mathcal{L}$. As can be seen, by using `deficit` and V, the algorithm does limit the creation of new phantom events.

We now give more details about the PCADG algorithm. At the beginning, when $\mathcal{P} = \emptyset$, `deficit` $= 0$ and $V = U$. The size of V is non-increasing throughout the algorithm. For any assignment $\langle u, a, g(u, a \mid S_a)\rangle$ that consists of an available user u and open event a, if a is a new event with no users, i.e., $|S_a| = 0$, we increment `deficit` by $\gamma_a - 1$ (because a is a phantom event and it would take $\gamma_a - 1$ more users to make a real). Otherwise, we decrease `deficit` by 1 (since u removes one "unit" of `deficit`). Furthermore, u is removed from V, if $u \in V$ before this assignment was made.

It is worth noting that PCADG may consider user-event combinations for which the innate affinity may be zero, as this assignment may potentially result in a large gain owing to the social affinity with other users assigned to this event, as per Equation 4. This is in keeping with our stated objective of maximizing social welfare. Therefore, it is possible that some users may be assigned to low innate affinity events as a result. We measure this tradeoff empirically in §5 by measuring the "regret ratio" (defined in §5) of the assignment returned by the various algorithms.

In order to explicitly study the impact of community and phantom awareness, we will compare PCADG with a lesser variant called *Phantom-Aware Dynamic Greedy (PADG)* that only takes into account phantom awareness. As such, the PADG algorithm is identical to Algorithm 2, with the one change that the potential gain is defined using Eq. (3) instead of Equation 4. In §5, we compare the running times and scalability of different proposed algorithms, in addition to comparing them on their quality.

We close this section by noting that the time and space complexity of the PCADG algorithm is the same as that of DG (and PADG) except that the size of the list $\mathcal{L}$ may potentially become $O(|U| \times |A|)$ in the worst case.

5. EXPERIMENTAL ANALYSIS

We evaluate our Phantom- and Community-Aware Dynamic Greedy (PCADG) method against the Phantom-Aware variant (PADG) and the baselines described in §4.1, i.e., Random, NRMP+, Static Greedy (SG) and Dynamic Greedy (DG).

Evaluation Metrics. The most natural evaluation metric is the *total social welfare*, $\omega(M)$ defined in Eq. ((2)). In addition, since optimal or near-optimal solution cannot be found in polynomial time, we measure the effectiveness of each algorithm "indirectly" by comparing the utility a user gets against a *coarse upper bound*, which is the maximum utility she could have enjoyed by going to her favorite event with her best friends. Formally, we define the *regret ratio* for a user u, denoted $\rho(u)$, to be

$$\rho(u) = 1 - \frac{(1-\alpha)\sigma_{u,M(u)} + \alpha \sum_{v \in S_{M(u)}} w(u,v)}{\max_{a \in A}((1-\alpha)\sigma_{u,a} + \alpha \sum_{v \in B_u} w(u,v))}, \quad (5)$$

where M is the assignment made by an algorithm, and $B_u \subseteq N_u$ is the set of top-$K_{u,a}$ friends of u in terms of social affinity $w(u, v)$, and $K_{u,a} = \min\{|N_u|, \delta_a - 1\}$.

Ideally an algorithm that performs well w.r.t. this metric should assign users to events in such a way that many users experience low regret in the assignment made. Note that $\sum_{u \in U} \max_{a \in A}(\sigma_{u,a} + \sum_{v \in B_u} w(u, v))$ is guaranteed to be greater than the optimal social welfare, except when the favorite event of all users is the *same*, in which case the optimal welfare may reach this quantity. Moreover, ρ is a very pessimistic ratio, as the denominator is an upper bound on the maximum possible utility that the user can achieve. Also, it is worth pointing out that our algorithms are not designed to directly minimize individual regrets of users, but rather social welfare that is the overall utility enjoyed by all users. The purpose here is to gain some insights about to what extent our algorithms would lead to a compromise w.r.t. regret.

We set α to 0.5 in Eq. (1) and (5) for all experiments unless otherwise mentioned. We also conduct a detailed experiment on real data, where we vary α and study its effect, illustrated in Figure 5.

5.1 Experiments on Synthetic Datasets

To better understand the impact of various parameters on our proposed algorithms, we first perform rigorous evaluations on synthetically generated data. We also conduct scalability tests on large synthetic data to show that our algorithms are scalable and efficient.

For all events $a \in A$, δ_a is sampled from a normal distribution with mean 20 and variance 10, and given that, γ_a is sampled uniformly at random from the interval $[1, \delta_a]$. The social network $G = (U, E)$ is generated by a random power-law graph model with a power-law exponent of 1.5 [1]. The data generated has 500 users and 50 events. A user is interested in an event with probability 0.05, and thus the average number of events he is interested is 2.5. For each $(u, v) \in E$, the social affinity value is sampled from a normal distribution with mean 1.5 and variance 3, as is innate affinity $\sigma_{u,a}$, for each (u, a) pair in the user-event relation. All values less than 10^{-5} are set to be zero: all affinity values are thus non-negative. This gives the default setting for the parameters used to generate the data, however, throughout this section, we vary these parameters to understand their effect on the performance of

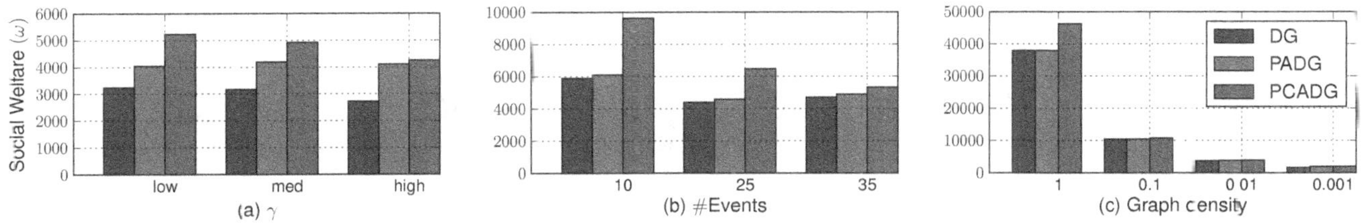

Figure 1: Effects of parameter choices on the performance of PADG and PCADG

Algorithm	$\|U\|$	Number of Events				
		50	100	150	200	500
PADG	1K	0.085	0.085	0.108	0.152	0.187
	10K	0.343	0.435	0.572	1.54	1.6
	100K	2.75	4.61	6.63	15.0	27.1
	1K	0.315	0.759	1.46	3.17	9.05
PCADG	10K	2.09	10.07	14.47	32.1	77.2
	100K	22.10	64.50	166	207	1085

Table 1: Running time (in seconds) of PADG and PCADG

	Random	NRMP+	SG	DG	PADG	PCADG
Time (s)	0.98	0.14	12.7	0.31	0.43	10.1

Table 2: Running time (in seconds) of all algorithms with 10K users and 100 events

our three dynamic greedy methods, DG, PADG and PCADG. Figure 1 shows the social welfare achieved by these algorithms with three types of comparisons: minimum cardinality constraints, total number of events, and density of the social network graph.

Effect of Minimum Cardinality. We alter minimum cardinality constraint (γ) and evaluate its effect on PADG and PCADG. We keep the maximum cardinality constraint δ_a's unchanged from the basic setting for each event $a \in A$, and vary their γ_as. We generate three groups of data, by sampling the minimum cardinality constraint γ_a uniformly at random from $[\delta_a/2, \delta_a]$ (low mean), $[\delta_a - \delta_a/4, \delta_a]$ (medium mean), and $[\delta_a - \delta_a/8, \delta_a]$ (high mean) respectively. As seen in Figure 1(a), there is a noticeable improvement in social welfare for PADG and PCADG over DG (which does not account for phantom events). As γ increases, more phantom events may be created, which increases the gain of PADG.

Effect of the Number of Events. We vary the number of events as 10, 25 and 35, for a 500-user dataset. From Figure 1(b), as the number of events increases, each event needs to accommodate fewer users and thus the effect of social affinity decreases. With fewer events, PCADG is at an advantage over PADG and DG, as it is community aware and takes into account social affinity values by looking ahead.

Effect of Graph Density. Next, we test various graph densities of the underlying social network graph by generating four different graphs using Erdős-Rényi model $G(500, p)$ where the edge existence probability being p = 0.001, 0.01, 0.1, and 1 respectively. For denser graphs, more social affinity values are present and hence we observe that the margin between PCADG and the other two is higher in comparison with sparse graphs (Figure 1(c)).

Running Time. Finally, we evaluate the scalability of the algorithms by varying the number of users (1K, 10K and 100K) and events (50, 100, 150, 200, and 500). We maintain the default settings for all other parameters. Table 1 shows the running time of PADG and PCADG. Overall, both algorithms achieve good efficiency, finishing within seconds or minutes in all cases, and PADG always runs faster than PCADG. As the trend is similar, we show the running time comparison with Random, NRMP+, SG, and DG for one case of 10K users and 100 events. Random, DG, and SG take 0.98, 0.31, and 12.7 seconds to finish, while PADG takes 0.43 and PCADG takes 10.07 seconds respectively (see Table 2). SG was consistently the slowest algorithm in all cases that we tested. For our largest simulation of 100K users and 500 events, PCADG takes 20 mins. This is a reasonable for large scale event organization, where real-time response is not critical.

5.2 Experiments on Real Event Datasets

5.2.1 Data Description and Preprocessing

We evaluate our algorithms on the following three real datasets. *Plancast* and *Meetup* are local event organization websites that allow groups of users to interact and plan events. We use the data[4] released by [15]. Since in Plancast and Meetup users and events are from all over the world, we select several big cities and project the data to such locations. The third dataset is *SIGCOMM2009* (referred to as SIG), collected by Pietilainen et al. [17] (details later). The following pre-processing was performed on the datasets to match our problem setting.

Plancast. We extract two subsets from the Plancast dataset in [15] corresponding to users and events in the vicinity of Chicago (CHI) and Vancouver (VAN). The two datasets CHI and VAN have 2338 and 2327 users, and 339 and 360 events, respectively. For computing the innate affinity, we set $\sigma_{u,a}$ to 1 for events located within 0.01 units of Euclidian distance from the user's geolocation. Plancast allows users to subscribe to each other and receive updates on friends' activities, which gives us a ground-truth social network. We compute the Katz distance [10] for each adjacent pair of users in the subscription graph to learn social affinities $w(u, v)$. By definition of Katz, we have $w(u, v) := \sum_{\ell=1}^{\infty} \beta^{\ell} \cdot |P_{u,v}^{(\ell)}|$, where $P_{u,v}^{(\ell)}$ is the set of paths of length ℓ between u and v in the graph, and β is a damping factor so that the measure counts short path more heavily, and is set to 0.01 in our case. Higher Katz score intuitively implies that two nodes are more connected, and hence gives a higher social affinity value.

Meetup. Similarly, we project Meetup data from [15] on events and users located in San Francisco and New York City and refer to these datasets as SFO and NYC. SFO contains 6438 users and 59 events, while NYC contains 10328 users and 127 events. Meetup allows users to create and participate in groups, which in turn organize events. For both locations, we consider the labeled heterogeneous tripartite graph between users, groups, and events, with edges labeled by the relation that connects the pairs of nodes: e.g., if user u is a member of group g that organized event a which the user attended, we draw edges (u, g) and (g, a). We then define $\sigma_{u,a}$ as the Katz distance between the user node u and event node a in

[4]http://www.largenetwork.org/ebsn

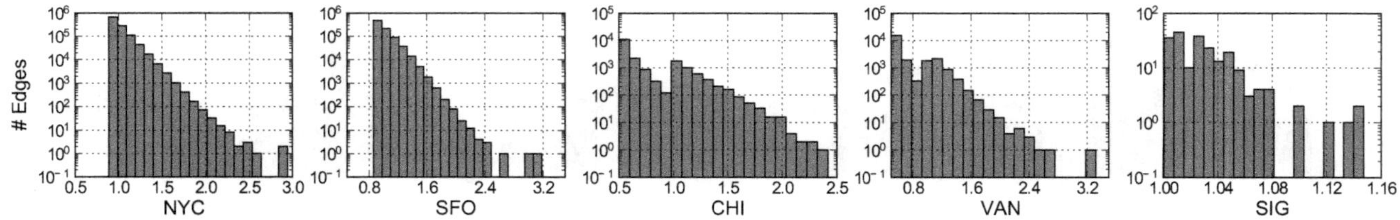

Figure 2: Distributions of social affinity values

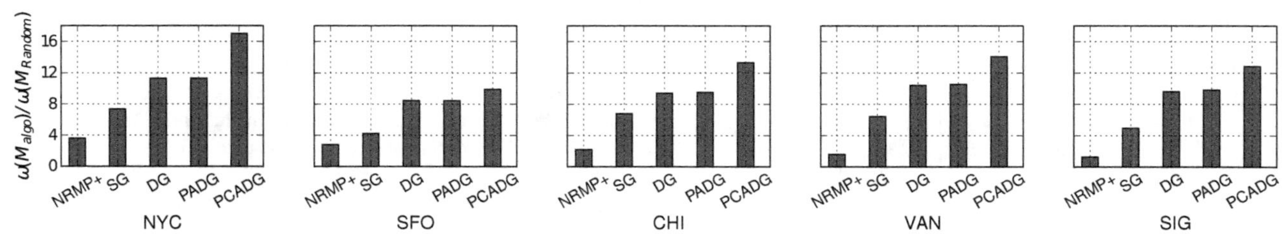

Figure 3: Improvement of social welfare yielded by various algorithms over Random

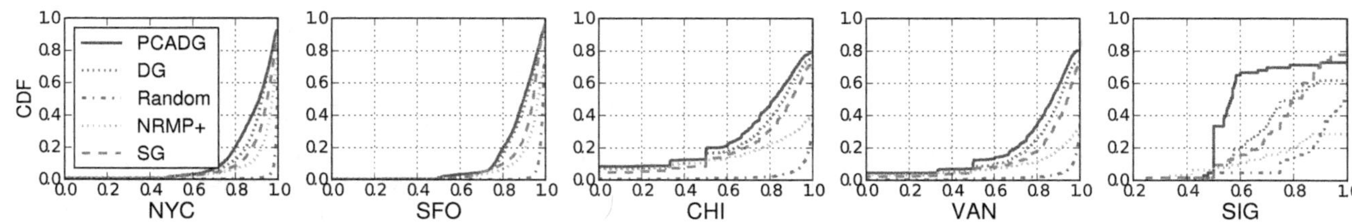

Figure 4: CDF showing regret ratio ρ for different algorithms

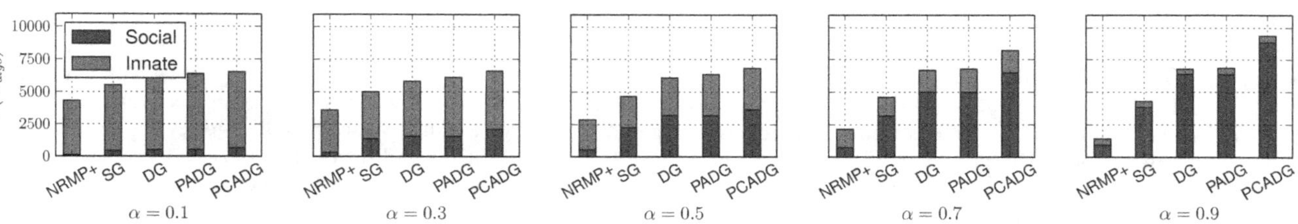

Figure 5: Dominance of PCADG is preserved on varying contributions of social and innate affinities (VAN)

the heterogeneous graph, with higher Katz score indicating higher affinity. For social affinity between users, we utilize tags provided in the data. More specifically, users on Meetup can attach tags in their profiles to indicate preferences and interests. Intuitively, users sharing common interests may enjoy being with each other in activities they both like. Thus, for each $(u, v) \in E$, we compute $w(u, v)$ as the Jaccard similarity coefficient of u's tag sets and v's tag sets: $w(u, v) := \frac{|T_u \cap T_v|}{|T_u \cup T_v|}$, where T_u and T_v is are sets of tags of u and v respectively. Note that users without any tags in their profile are filtered out.

SIGCOMM2009. This is a small dataset with 76 users, and 11 events, collected by a mobile application that records bluetooth device discovery information. Users' innate utility for events is 1 if a user attends an event as indicated by the data, and 0 otherwise. The data includes ground-truth Facebook friendship information, and thus as in the case of Plancast, we take this underlying social network and compute the Katz scores for social affinities.

Finally, for all five datasets described above, the user-event innate affinity is set to 1 if the user attends the event as indicated by the data, and to 0 otherwise. Also due to lack of ground-truth data, we generate the maximum and minimum cardinality constraints on the events as in the basic synthetic case, i.e., let r be the ratio between the number of users and the number of events; then for all $a \in A$, maximum cardinality constraint δ_a is sampled from a normal distribution with mean $2r$ and variance r, while minimum cardinality γ_a is sampled uniformly at random from $[1, \delta_a]$. Figure 2 shows the distributions of social affinity values for all datasets.

5.2.2 *Evaluations and Analysis*

Social Welfare. Figure 3 shows the social welfare (Eq. (2)) obtained by the various methods considered relative to the welfare obtained using a Random assignment. It shows the ratio between the social welfare yielded by assignments made by NRMP+, SG, DG, PADG, PCADG and that by Random. PCADG consistently has the highest social welfare, followed by PADG, DG, SG and NRMP+. The margin between PCADG and the rest of the algorithms is significant in all cases, indicting its overall effectiveness. The biggest lead of PCADG is observed in NYC, 17 times better than Random, while the smallest happens in SIG, in which it is still 4 times better. On all datasets PADG and DG have similar values, with PADG outperforming only slightly. This is because the generated minimum cardinality constraints for events are much smaller than maximum cardinality constraints. Recall from Figure 1(a) that when γs are high, the gap between PADG and DG is also high.

Regret Ratio. Figure 4 shows the cumulative distribution function (CDF) of the regret ratio $\rho(u)$ (see Eq. (5)) achieved by the various methods (PADG skipped for clarity) on the five datasets. The general trend is similar to that of social welfare, where PCADG outperforms all baselines. For instance, in NYC, 20% of the users have a regret below 0.8 using PCADG, while only 8% have that regret with NRMP+. This gap is even more pronounced in CHI and VAN, with the largest difference in SIG. In particular, 70% of users have a regret ratio below 0.7 using PCADG, while only 18% have that regret using NRMP+.

Varying Contribution of Social and Innate Affinities. A possible concern about our definition of social welfare (Eq. (1)) is that it may be dominated by social affinity. However, Eq. (1) allows the organizer to control the relative importance of social and innate affinities and not let the overall objective be undesirably dominated by either. To analyze this, in this final experiment, we first boost the innate affinities such that at $\alpha = 0.5$, innate and social affinities (found by PADG) are nearly equal, and stress-test the various algorithms on VAN by varying α. This allows us to vary the relative contribution of social and innate affinities to the overall welfare achieved and study its impact on the algorithms. Figure 5 shows the absolute value of the total welfare and the individual contribution of the two affinities for $\alpha = 0.1, 0.3, 0.5, 0.7$ and 0.9. As can be seen, the dominance of PCADG over other algorithms is maintained across all values of α, with higher overall welfare for larger α. We also measured regret ratios in all cases. The trend was found to be the same as in Figure 4 and the plot is omitted for brevity.

In summary, through extensive experiments on both synthetic and real world data, we have demonstrated the effectiveness (in terms of social welfare and regret) and efficiency (in terms of running time) of our proposed solutions to the SEO problem.

6. DISCUSSION AND CONCLUSIONS

While there has been considerable work on detecting emerging events from social media, the related, equally important area of organizing events has received much less research attention. In this paper, motivated by popular social event organization platforms like Meetup and Plancast and by applications such as organizing events using these platforms over a wide local area, and organizing events co-located with large conferences and conventions, we study the novel research direction of Social Event Organization (SEO).

Our focus in this work has been on the assignment problem, where we consider two critical factors: *innate affinity*, which captures a user's intrinsic preferences for the events being offered, and *social affinity*, which captures the social connections among the users themselves. We formally define the overall measure of *social welfare* in event organization and formalize the SEO problem as the problem of maximizing social welfare subject to constraints on the participation cardinality of the events. We show that this problem is not only NP-hard, but also hard to approximate. We propose a set of heuristic solutions that leverage the notion of *phantom events* and the technique of *looking ahead* the potential gain that may accrue as a result of future assignments to the current event for which a user is being assigned. Using an extensive set of experiments over synthetic datasets and three real datasets including those from the platforms Meetup and Plancast, we demonstrate that our heuristic algorithms are scalable and furthermore outperform the baseline algorithms significantly in terms of social welfare and regret ratio.

Several interesting questions remain. Innate and social affinities may be interdependent. E.g., Al and Ed are close friends but don't like to play poker together since they know each other's tells, while Al may like going to a hockey game (for which she has low innate affinity) with Bo who is knowledgeable and keeps her engaged. Handling such interdependency is important. Predicting which events a user will attend in the future is also an interesting problem. It is also worth comparing the assignments made by SEO to ground-truth from event participations, which may be challenging to obtain. Also, a systematic study of alternative ways of aggregating innate and social affinities for defining social welfare is worthwhile.

7. REFERENCES

[1] W. Aiello, F. R. K. Chung, and L. Lu. A random graph model for massive graphs. In *STOC*, pages 171–180, 2000.

[2] S. Amer-Yahia, S. B. Roy, A. Chawla, G. Das, and C. Yu. Group recommendation: Semantics and efficiency. *PVLDB*, 2(1), 2009.

[3] A. Anagnostopoulos et al. Online team formation in social networks. In *WWW*, 2012.

[4] N. Armenatzoglou, S. Papadopoulos, and D. Papadias. A general framework for geo-social query processing. *PVLDB*, 6(10), 2013.

[5] P. Biró et al. The college admissions problem with lower and common quotas. *Theor. Comput. Sci*, 411(34-36):3136–3153, 2010.

[6] C. Chekuri and S. Khanna. A ptas for the multiple knapsack problem. In *SODA*, 2000.

[7] L. Fleischer et al. Tight approximation algorithms for maximum general assignment problems. In *SODA*, 2006.

[8] D. Gale and L. S. Shapley. College admissions and the stability of marriage. *Amer. Math. Monthly*, 69, 1962.

[9] K. Hamada, K. Iwama, and S.Miyazaki. The hospitals/residents problem with quota lower bounds. In *MATCH-UP: Matching Under Preferences Workshop at ICALP*, 2008.

[10] L. Katz. A new status index derived from sociometric analysis. *Psychometrika*, 18(1), 1953.

[11] S. Khot. On the power of unique 2-prover 1-round games. STOC, 2002.

[12] S. O. Krumke and C. Thielen. The generalized assignment problem with minimum quantities. *European Journal of Operational Research*, 2013.

[13] T. Lappas, K. Liu, and E. Terzi. Finding a team of experts in social networks. In *KDD*, 2009.

[14] D. Liben-Nowell and J. Kleinberg. The link-prediction problem for social networks. *Journal of the American society for information science and technology*, 58(7), 2007.

[15] X. Liu et al. Event-based social networks: linking the online and offline social worlds. In *KDD*, 2012.

[16] E. Petrank. The hardness of approximations : Gap location *Computational Complexity*, 4:133–157, 1994.

[17] A.-K. Pietilainen and C. Diot. CRAWDAD data set thlab/sigcomm2009 (v. 2012-07-15). Downloaded from http://crawdad.cs.dartmouth.edu/thlab/sigcomm2009, 2012

[18] P. Raghavendra and D. Steurer. Graph expansion and the unique games conjecture. In *STOC*, 2010.

[19] A. E. Roth. The evolution of the labor market for medical interns and residents: a case study in game theory. *Journal of Political Economy*, 6(4):991–1016, 1984.

[20] D. B. Shmoys et al. An approximation algorithm for the generalized assignment problem. *Math. Program.*, 62:461–474, 1993.

[21] M. Sozio and A. Gionis. The community-search problem and how to plan a successful cocktail party. In *KDD*, pages 939–948, 2010.

A Bayesian Framework for Estimating Properties of Network Diffusions

Varun R Embar*
IBM Research Division
IBM India Research Lab
Bangalore 560045, India
varembar@in.ibm.com

Rama Kumar Pasumarthi*
IBM Research Division
IBM India Research Lab
Bangalore 560045, India
sarpasum@in.ibm.com

Indrajit Bhattacharya
IBM Research Division
IBM India Research Lab
Bangalore 560045, India
indrajitb@in.ibm.com

ABSTRACT

The analysis of network connections, diffusion processes and cascades requires evaluating properties of the diffusion network. Properties of interest often involve variables that are not explicitly observed in real world diffusions. Connection strengths in the network and diffusion paths of infections over the network are examples of such hidden variables. These hidden variables therefore need to be estimated for these properties to be evaluated. In this paper, we propose and study this novel problem in a Bayesian framework by capturing the posterior distribution of these hidden variables given the observed cascades, and computing the expectation of these properties under this posterior distribution. We identify and characterize interesting network diffusion properties whose expectations can be computed exactly and efficiently, either wholly or in part. For properties that are not 'nice' in this sense, we propose a Gibbs Sampling framework for Monte Carlo integration. In detailed experiments using various network diffusion properties over multiple synthetic and real datasets, we demonstrate that the proposed approach is significantly more accurate than a frequentist plug-in baseline. We also propose a map-reduce implementation of our framework and demonstrate that this can analyze cascades with millions of infections in minutes.

Categories and Subject Descriptors

H.2.8 [**Database Management**]: Database Application—*Data mining*

Keywords

Social Influence Analysis; Information Cascades; Networks of Diffusion; Bayesian Analysis; Gibbs Sampling

1. INTRODUCTION

The study of networks and diffusions over them has a long history in epidemiology, sociology, econometrics and marketing. Interest in the problem has increased many fold over the last two decades in the context of information diffusion and social networks, first because of the growth of the internet, and then the social media revolution [2, 13]. The study typically involves three different objects of interest: a *network* that defines connection strengths between entities, a *diffusion process* that defines how 'infections' spread randomly over the network, and *cascades* that trace the spread of specific infections over the network. Many different problems have been studied in the context of these three objects of interest. A problem that has received a lot of attention is that of network inference [21, 7, 6, 8, 4, 9, 19, 22, 15], where the task is to infer the hidden network of connection strengths from the cascades.

However, inferring the network of diffusions is often an intermediate task in the analysis. The main objective is often to compute some *property* of the network and/or the cascades, such as centrality and reach of individual nodes, optimal seeds for viral marketing [14, 12, 10], community structures [17, 1], the likelier diffusion mechanism [18], etc.

An example of such a property is the identity of 'tribe leaders' [10], who are well connected to a large tribe of nodes in the network, and whose tribe members follow their actions frequently in the cascades. Computing this notion of node influence is expensive even when the cascades are completely observed, but consider a simplification that is still interesting. Consider the out-degree of a node in the network, counting only those edges that are strong and also frequently used in the cascades. This influence score is much simpler to compute given completely observed networks and cascades, and yet is useful for marketers and epidemiologists.

In Fig. 1, we show the strength-frequency distribution of edges in four different synthetically-generated network diffusions. The x-axis shows edge strength (α) and the y-axis transmission frequency (ρ), which is the number of times an edge was used to transmit infections in the cascades. The distribution only considers actual edges used in the cascades. Fig. 1(a) through Fig. 1(d) correspond to Forest Fire, Core-Periphery, Random and Hierarchical graphs respectively, each with 1024 nodes and ~ 2000 edges. In each case, we generated 20 splitting, independent cascades [22] over these graphs with 2 randomly chosen seeds for each cascade. The plots can also be interpreted as the distribution of the simpler node influence score discussed above. The plots clearly show that these distributions look very different depending on the underlying network connections and possibly also the diffusion mechanism. Thus, given network diffusion data from some network with unknown structure

*The first two authors have contributed equally to this work

KDD'14, August 24–27, 2014, New York, NY, USA.
Copyright 2014 ACM 978-1-4503-2956-9/14/08 ...$15.00.
http://dx.doi.org/10.1145/2623330.2623693 .

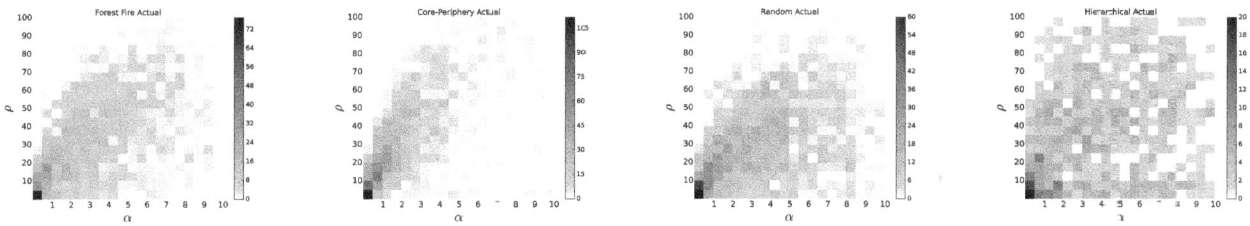

(a) Forest fire (FF) (b) Core-Periphery (CP) (c) Random (Rnd) (d) Hierarchical (HI)

Figure 1: Actual strength-frequency distribution for cascades from synthetic graphs

and diffusion mechanism, it is clearly of interest to construct and study such distributions.

In this paper, we investigate such joint properties of networks and cascades. The main difficulty in evaluating such properties for real-world network diffusions is that the connections strengths in the network are unknown. Additionally, the diffusion edges are also unknown — the cascades only record the catchers of the infections and the infection times, but not the actual path traced by specific infections. For example, in social information flows, the friends and followers are known, but not the extent of influence between them, and often users do not reveal the sources of information. Therefore, to evaluate the properties, these hidden variables need to be inferred from the observed cascades.

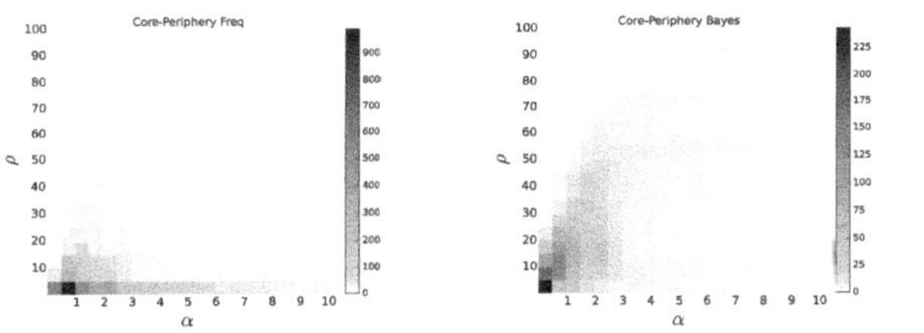

(a) Frequentist (b) Bayesian Expectation

Figure 2: Reconstructed distribution: CP

One way to evaluate a property is to take the 'frequentist plug-in approach', that finds point estimates of the network and the diffusion edges in the cascades, and then evaluates the property using these point estimates. The most popular point estimate used for network inference is the maximum likelihood estimate [6, 22]. This approach for evaluating properties has two drawbacks. The first is the well known problem of overfitting for a frequentist approach. More importantly, for properties that are not one-to-one functions of the network and the diffusion paths, the most likely value of the property need not correspond to the most likely network and diffusion paths. Fig. 2(a) shows the reconstructed edge distribution for the Core-Periphery diffusion data using this frequentist approach. It has failed to recover the signature shape of the distribution.

In this paper, we motivate and propose a Bayesian solution to this problem, where both the network and the diffusion paths are modeled as random variables. This makes network diffusion properties functions of random variables, and our problem becomes one of computing the expectation of the property under the posterior distribution of the hidden variables given the observed features of the cascade.

An obvious challenge for the Bayesian approach is the cost of computing expectations. This seems daunting for the network inference problem with its large number of coupled discrete and continuous hidden variables. However, our analysis shows that for the popular independent cascade model, many interesting network diffusion properties are 'nice', in that their expectations can be computed exactly and efficiently, at least in part. For parts of the expectations that are not 'nice', we propose a Gibbs Sampling technique for efficient Monte Carlo integration. Fig. 2(b) shows the reconstruction of the Core-Periphery strength-frequency distribution using our proposed approach. It has recovered the distinctive shape to a much better extent.

In detailed experiments using various network diffusion properties over multiple synthetic and real datasets, we demonstrate that the proposed approach is significantly more accurate than the MLE plug-in baseline, and is useful for traditional network inference as well. We show that the approach scales easily to very large datasets using a map-reduce implementation.

2. RELATED WORK

Different problems have been studied in the context of diffusion networks [2, 13]. The network inference problem [21, 7, 6, 8, 4, 9, 19, 22, 15] has been investigated in depth, starting with stationary discrete time models [19], to the more recent models that consider features [22] and time-varying networks [9]. The solutions have mostly been based on maximum-likelihood estimation.

Apart from inferring the complete network structure, there has been work on inferring summaries of the network, such as community structures [17, 1]. Other investigated properties are estimating influence of nodes [3], and subsequently selecting a subset of nodes that maximize influence [12]. Sadikov et. al. [20] study various properties of cascades assuming completely missing infections.

Milling et. al. [18] study the problem of deciding which of two given networks caused a specific diffusion with its path properties observed. Efficient algorithms have been designed for identifying leaders and tribes [10] and mining propagation summaries [16] from cascades, assuming the underlying network and the diffusion paths to be known. These problems may be seen as computing joint properties of networks and cascades, with all variables observed.

In summary, we are not aware of any general framework for estimating joint properties of networks and diffusion processes in the context of hidden network and diffusions paths. We are also not aware of any Bayesian framework for network diffusion analysis.

3. PROBLEM DEFINITION

In this section, we first review the network diffusion problem and the independent cascade model. Then we define network diffusion properties and their expectations.

Network Diffusion and Independent Cascade Model: We assume a *network* $G = (V, E)$ with nodes V and edges E. For $(u, v) \in E$, let $\alpha_{uv} \in \mathcal{R}_+$ denote the connection strength between nodes u and v. We have a set C of *cascades* corresponding to spreading infections over the network G. Each cascade $c \in C$ consists of a set of time-stamped infections: $c = \{(u_i, z_i, t_i)\}$. The ith infection records that node u_i got infected at time t_i by its parent infection z_i. We will assume that $t_i < t_j$ for $i < j$. Let $\pi_i \subseteq \{1 \ldots i-1\}$ denote the set of 'potential parents' for the ith infection, so that $z_i \in \pi_i$. Observe that the infecting parent z_i provides edge information for reconstructing the infection paths over the network. We also know that the cascades were observed for time T, which is at least as large as the final infection time.

The joint distribution $p(C|\alpha)$ on the cascades C given the network strengths is typically defined using a *generative process* that captures the dynamics of spreading infections. While many diffusion models have been proposed, we follow the popular *Continuous-Time Independent Cascade Model* [6]. Under this model, each cascade starts with an initial set of seed nodes getting infected. Each infected node proposes an infection times for each currently uninfected neighbor in the network. An uninfected node catches its infection from that infected neighbor who has proposed the earliest infection time for it. We consider the setting where nodes can get infected multiple times in the same cascade, and the *splitting model* for this [22], where all infections between the current and the previous infections of a node are considered as its potential parents.

The main building block of the model is the probability density function $f(t_i|u_i, u_j, t_j; \alpha_{u_j u_i})$, which models the conditional likelihood of node u_i getting infected at time t_i by node u_j which got infected at time t_j for $t_j < t_i$. [6, 22]:

$$p(c|\alpha) = \prod_i H(t_i|t_{z_i}; \alpha_{u_{z_i} u_i}) \prod_{j \in \pi_i} S(t_i|t_j; \alpha_{u_{z_j} u_i}) \prod_{v: l_v < t_i} S(T|t_i; \alpha_{u_i v})$$

where $S(t) = 1 - F(t)$ is the survival function, $H(t) = f(t)/S(t)$ is the hazard function corresponding to the CDF $F(t) = \int_0^t f(t)dt$, l_v is the time of last infection of node v. Assuming cascades to be generated *iid*, the likelihood of C becomes $p(C|\alpha) = \prod_{c \in C} p(c|\alpha)$.

In real-world network diffusions, many of the variables above are unobserved. We will assume that the observed trace $C^o = \{c^o\}$ of the cascade C only contains the infected node u_i and the infection time t_i: $c^o = \{(u_i, t_i)\}$. The infecting parent z_i is not observed. The posterior distribution $p(z|\{c^o\}, \alpha)$ over infection parents, conditioned on observed cascades $\{c^o\}$ and α, has the following form:

$$p(z \mid \{c^o\}, \alpha) = \prod_i \frac{H(t_i|t_{z_i}; \alpha_{u_{z_i} u_i})}{\sum_{j \in \pi_i} H(t_i|t_j; \alpha_{u_j u_i})} \qquad (1)$$

Observe that this decouples into terms involving individual infection parents z_i. This will be a key property for efficient computation of network diffusion properties in Sec. 5.

The network connection strengths α_{uv} are also typically unobserved. Further, we assume that the set of network edges E is also not known. Therefore, we consider α to be a $|V| \times |V|$ matrix of unknown variables. The goal of the popular network inference problem is to reconstruct this α matrix using $\{c^o\}$ [6, 22]. The state-of-the-art approach is to obtain a maximum likelihood estimate:

$$\hat{\alpha} = \arg\max_\alpha \log p(\{c^o\}|\alpha) = \arg\max_\alpha \log \sum_z p(C|\alpha) \qquad (2)$$

For modeling $f(t_i|u_i, u_j, t_j; \alpha)$, the Exponential, Power-law and Rayleigh distributions have been proposed [6, 22]. For the Exponential distribution,

$$f(t_i|t_j; \alpha) = \alpha e^{-\alpha(t_i - t_j)}$$
$$H(t_i|t_j) = \alpha; \quad S(t_i|t_j) = e^{-\alpha(t_i - t_j)}$$

and for the Rayleigh distribution,

$$f(t_i|t_j; \alpha) = \alpha(t_i - t_j) e^{-\frac{1}{2}\alpha(t_i - t_j)^2}$$
$$H(t_i|t_j) = \alpha(t_i - t_j); \quad S(t_i|t_j) = e^{-\frac{1}{2}\alpha(t_i - t_j)^2}$$

Network Diffusion Properties and Expectations: Given this background, we now define our problem. We are interested in computing properties $f(\alpha, C)$ of the cascades C and the network connections α. Two examples properties are the strength-frequency distribution of edges, and influence of leader nodes. We will see more examples in Sec. 5.

Since α and z are unobserved, the properties are not directly computable. We investigate a fully Bayesian solution to the problem, where we model both α and z to be random variables, so that the property $f(\alpha, z)$ is a function of random variables. Assuming a joint distribution $p(C, \alpha)$ to be defined on the cascade C and the network connections strengths α, we consider the posterior distribution $p(z, \alpha|\{c^o\})$ over the hidden variables z and α conditioned on the observed trace $c^o = \{(u_i, t_i)\}$ of the cascades. Then we evaluate the expectation $\bar{f}(C, \alpha)$ of $f(C, \alpha)$ under this posterior distribution:

$$\bar{f}(C, \alpha) = E_{p(z, \alpha|\{c^o\})}[f(C, \alpha)] \qquad (3)$$

For properties that do not involve z, we consider the expectation under the marginal posterior distribution $p(\alpha|\{c^o\}) = \sum_z p(z, \alpha|\{c^o\})$. We similarly define expectations of properties that do not involve α.

Recall that existing approaches for network inference only model the conditional distribution $p(C|\alpha)$ assuming α to be given. In the rest of this paper, our goal is two fold: (a) augment this conditional using a prior $p(\alpha)$ to model the joint distribution $p(C, \alpha)$, (b) investigate tractability of this expectation for interesting network diffusion properties. We look at the first aspect in Sec. 4 and the second in Sec. 5.

4. A BAYESIAN FRAMEWORK

In this section, we introduce a Bayesian framework that will enable us to compute expectations of network diffusion properties. For a Bayesian analysis, we need to model α as a random variable, with a prior distribution. Assuming an *iid* prior $p(\alpha) = \prod_{uv} p(\alpha_{uv})$, the joint distribution is simply $p(C, \alpha) = p(C|\alpha) \prod_{uv} p(\alpha_{uv})$, and the posterior distribution $p(\alpha|\{c^o\}, z)$ looks as follows:

$$p(\alpha \mid \{c^o\}, z) = \prod_{uv} \frac{\bar{H}_{uv} \bar{S}_{uv} p(\alpha_{uv})}{\int_{\alpha_{uv}} \bar{H}_{uv} \bar{S}_{uv} p(\alpha_{uv}) d\alpha_{uv}} \qquad (4)$$

where $\bar{H}_{uv} = \prod_{i \in A_{uv}} H(t_i|t_{z_i}; \alpha_{uv}, z)$ with $A_{uv}(z) = \{i : u_i = v, u_{z_i} = u\}$ denoting infections of v by u, $\bar{S}_{uv} = \prod_{i,j \in P_{uv}} S(t_i|t_j; \alpha_{uv}) \prod_{j \in T_{uv}} S(T|t_j; \alpha_{uv})$, with $P_{uv} = \{i, j : u_i = u, u_j = v; j \in \pi_i\}$ denoting potential infections of v by u and $T_{uv} = \{j : u_j = u, l_v < t_j\}$ denoting survivals of v from u. Observe that this decouples into terms involving individual network strengths α_{uv}. Efficient computation of network properties in Sec. 5 hinges critically on this, as on the decoupling in Eqn. 1.

Another requirement for efficient computation is analytical integration of network properties with respect to α_{uv}. For this, we need *conjugate priors*. Both Rayleigh and Exponential are special cases of the Weibull distribution (corresponding to shape parameters 1 and 2) [3]. For likelihoods involving the Weibull distribution with given shape parameter, the conjugate distribution is the *Gamma distribution*:

$$Gamma(\alpha_{uv}; a, b) = \frac{b^a}{\Gamma(a)} \alpha_{uv}^{a-1} \exp\{-b\alpha_{uv}\} \qquad (5)$$

Substitution into Eqn. 4 gives us the following:

$$p(\alpha|\{c^o\}, z) = \prod_{uv} Gamma(a + \rho_{uv}(z), b + \Delta_{uv}) \qquad (6)$$

where $\rho_{uv}(z) = |A_{uv}(z)|$, $\Delta_{uv} = \sum_{i,j \in P_{uv}} \delta(t_i, t_j) + \sum_{j \in T_{uv}} \delta(T, t_j)$, and $\delta(t_i, t_j) = (t_i - t_j)$ for the Exponential distribution and $\frac{1}{2}(t_i - t_j)^2$ for the Rayleigh distribution. From now on we refer to $\rho_{uv}(z)$ as ρ_{uv}.

This posterior is suitable for the network inference problem. Consider $a < 1$. Then using a suitable b, for no transmissions across an edge, $\rho_{uv} = 0$, and the posterior distribution is peaked sharply at 0. This implies that in the absence of any transmission evidence in the cascade, there is very little belief in the existence of an edge. Once an observation is made and we have $\rho_{uv} \geq 1$, the posterior distribution is unimodal and peaked at $(a + \rho_{uv})/(b + \Delta_{uv})$.

When we have large volumes of data so that $\rho_{uv} \gg a$ and $\Delta_{uv} \gg b$, the mean of the posterior approaches the MLE. While the parameterization $a < 1$ models prior belief in sparse network connections, it is also possible to make the Gamma prior noninformative if necessary, using $a, b \ll 1$ [5].

5. NETWORK DIFFUSION PROPERTIES

In this section, we consider multiple types of network diffusion properties, and analyze the tractability of computing their expectations under the posterior distribution $p(z, \alpha|\{c^0\})$. Consider, as a motivation, the network diffusion property in the introduction that counts leaders of tribes. Computing this properties is hard even when all the network diffusion variables are observed, and we will see that computing the expectations with unobserved variables is not tractable. However, we will investigate simplifications of this properties that are interesting and useful, and at the same time allow their expectations to be computed efficiently.

We consider two different categories of network diffusion properties — network centric and cascade centric. In a network-centric property, the focus is on entities in the network, such as nodes, or edges, which satisfy some constraints in the network as well as in the cascade. The 'counting leaders' property is an example in this category, with nodes in the network being the focus. A cascade-centric property, on the other hand, is about entities in the cascade, such as individual infections, which satisfy certain cascade constraints and additionally some network constraints. Before discussing more about such properties in Sec 5.2 and Sec 5.3, we first investigate conditions under which expectations of network diffusion properties are efficiently computable.

5.1 Niceness of Properties

Given the large size of real-world network diffusion data, in all of the following discussion, we consider a computation to be efficient if it is linear in the size of the network and the size of the cascade. Computing the expectation involves marginalizing out two variables: an integration over possible network strengths α, and a summation over possible network paths defined by the infection parent variables z. We first analyze these two marginalizations separately, before looking at computing the complete expectation.

Integrating over α: First, we characterize properties for which the integration over α can be performed efficiently. We call such properties *nice-α*. Intuitively, a *nice-α* property decomposes into terms that involve the parent variables z, and individual connection strengths α_{uv}. Additionally, the functions involving α_{uv} should be amenable to analytical integration with $p(\alpha_{uv}|z, \{c^o\})$ which is in the Gamma form.

DEFINITION 5.1. *A property $f(\alpha, z)$ is nice-α if it can be written as $g(z) \prod_{u,v} h_{uv}(\alpha_{uv}, z)$ or as $g(z) \sum_{u,v} h_{uv}(\alpha_{uv}, z)$ where $\int h_{uv}(\alpha_{uv}, z)\, p(\alpha_{uv}|z, \{c^o\}) d\alpha_{uv}$ can be performed analytically $\forall$ u, v.*

THEOREM 5.1. *Let $f(\alpha, z)$ be nice-α. Then computing the z-marginal $\bar{f}_z(z) = \int_\alpha f(\alpha, z) p(\alpha|z, \{c^o\}) d\alpha$ is $O(|\mathbf{V}|^2)$.*

The notion of *nice-α* can be extended to properties that depend only on α and not on z. Such properties $f(\alpha)$ need to be of the form $\prod_{u,v} h_{uv}(\alpha_{uv})$ or $\sum_{u,v} h_{uv}(\alpha_{uv})$, where $\int h_{uv}(\alpha_{uv}) p(\alpha_{uv}|z, \{c^o\}) d\alpha_{uv}$ can be performed analytically for *all* z. Note that the z-marginal $\bar{f}_z(z)$ is still a function of z through $p(\alpha|z, \{c^o\})$ Also, properties that are independent of α are trivially *nice-α*. Finally, this complexity corresponds to the scenario when no edge information is available. Given a set E of potential edges, the complexity is $O(|E|)$.

Summing over z: Now we characterize properties for which the summation over infection parents z can be performed efficiently. We call such properties *nice-z*. Recall from Eqn. 1 that the posterior distribution $p(z|\alpha, \{c^o\})$ decomposes into terms involving individual z_i variables. Intuitively, the summation over z can be performed efficiently if the property $f(\alpha, z)$ also decomposes over z.

DEFINITION 5.2. *A property $f(\alpha, z)$ is nice-z if it can be written either as $g(\alpha) \prod_i h_i(z_i, \alpha)$ or as $g(\alpha) \sum_i h_i(z_i, \alpha)$*

THEOREM 5.2. *Let $f(\alpha, z)$ be nice-z. Then the α-marginal $\bar{f}_\alpha(\alpha) = \sum_z f(\alpha, z) p(z|\alpha, \{c^o\})$ can be computed in $O(\pi|C|)$ time, where $\pi = \max_i \pi_i$ is the maximum number of potential parents over all infections.*

As for *nice-α*, the notion of *nice-z* can be extended to properties that involve only z and ignore α. Note that for such properties, the α-marginal $\bar{f}_\alpha(\alpha)$ still depends on α through the posterior distribution $p(z|\alpha, \{c^o\})$. Also, a function which is independent of z is trivially *nice-z*.

Marginalizing both α and z: For computing the complete expectation in Eqn. 3, both marginalizations need to be performed. We now investigate strategies for doing this.

Interestingly, it turns out that the complete expectation can be computed efficiently and exactly for some network diffusion properties, which we call *nice-z*, α.

DEFINITION 5.3. *A property $f(\alpha, z)$ is nice-z, α if it can be written as $\prod_{u,v} g_{uv}(\alpha_{uv}) \prod_{i=1}^{|D|} \frac{h_i(z_i)}{\alpha_{u_{z_i} u_i}}$ where analytical solutions exist for $\int g_{uv}(\alpha_{uv}) p(\alpha_{uv}|z, \{c^o\}) d\alpha_{uv}$ $\forall u, v$.*

LEMMA 5.3. *A property that is nice-z, α is both nice-α according to Defn. 5.1 and nice-z according to Defn 5.2.*

In addition to being *nice-α* and *nice-z*, *nice-z*, α properties require decoupling of α and z variables, not just in the property, but also in the posterior distribution $p(\alpha, z|\{c^o\})$. This is achieved by the $\alpha_{u_{z_i} u_i}$ terms in the property definition. These cancel out the corresponding terms in $p(\alpha, z|\{c^o\})$, which are responsible for the coupling.

THEOREM 5.4. *Let $f(\alpha, z)$ be nice-z, α. Then the expectation $\bar{f}(\alpha, z)$ can be computed in $O(\pi|\mathbf{C}|)) + O(|\mathbf{V}|^2)$ time, up to a multiplicative constant.*

The multiplicative constant in question is the inverse of the likelihood $p(\{c^o\})$ of the observed variables in the cascades. This implies that we may not be able to compute the exact value of any *nice-z*, α efficiently, but we may efficiently *compare* two different *nice-z*, α properties.

In general, there will be properties for which any one or both marginalizations cannot be performed analytically or efficiently. In such cases, we resort to Monte Carlo techniques. Here, we will assume that it is possible to draw *iid* samples $(\alpha^{(s)}, z^{(s)})$ from the joint distribution $p(\alpha, z|\{c^o\})$, and similarly $(\alpha^{(s)}) \sim p(\alpha|\{c^o\})$ and $(z^{(s)}) \sim p(z|\{c^o\})$ from the marginal distributions. In Sec 6, we describe a Gibbs Sampling algorithm for drawing such samples.

First consider properties which are *nice-α* but for which the subsequent marginalization $\sum_z f_z(z) p(z|\{c^o\})$ over z cannot be performed efficiently. For such properties, we first obtain the z-marginal $\bar{f}_z(z)$ efficiently, and then use Monte Carlo summation for z:

$$\bar{f}(\alpha, z) \approx \frac{1}{S} \sum_s \bar{f}_z(z^{(s)}), \text{ where } z^{(s)} \sim p(z|\{c^o\}),\ s = 1 \dots S$$

Similarly, consider properties which are *nice-z* but for which the subsequent marginalization $\int f_\alpha(\alpha) p(\alpha|\{c^o\}) d\alpha$ over α cannot be performed efficiently. For such properties, we first obtain the α-marginal $\bar{f}_\alpha(\alpha)$ efficiently, and then use Monte Carlo integration for α:

$$\bar{f}(\alpha, z) \approx \frac{1}{S} \sum_s \bar{f}_\alpha(\alpha^{(s)}), \text{ where } \alpha^{(s)} \sim p(\alpha|\{c^o\}),\ s = 1 \dots S$$

Finally, for properties where neither of the two marginalizations can be performed efficiently, we use Monte Carlo integration for both α and z:

$$\bar{f}(\alpha, z) \approx \frac{1}{S} \sum_s f(\alpha^{(s)}, z^{(s)}),$$
$$\text{where } (\alpha^{(s)}, z^{(s)}) \sim p(\alpha, z|\{c^o\}),\ s = 1 \dots S$$

Having characterized the notion of niceness for network diffusion properties in terms of computing expectations, we now return to our motivating properties, and analyze them in this light.

5.2 Network-centric Properties

We first discuss network-centric properties, which involve computing scores for specific entities in the network, such as nodes, edges, etc. These scores are functions of the network connection strengths α and also of the cascade C. Recall that the network and the cascades are connected through the node index u_i in the individual infections.

The basic building block for network scores of network entities is the *direct* connection strength α_{uv} between nodes u and v. Using this, we can define the *second-order* network connection strength $\alpha_{uv}^{(2)}$ between u and v as $\sum_w \alpha_{uw}\alpha_{wv}$ or its approximation $\max_w \min(\alpha_{uw}, \alpha_{wv})$. Generalizing further, the rth-order connection strength $\alpha_{uv}^{(r)}$ between them is $\sum_w \alpha_{uw}^{(r-1)} \alpha_{wv}$, and $\alpha_{uv}^* = \sum_{r=1}^{R} \alpha_{uv}^{(r)}$.

On the other hand, the building block for cascade scores of network entities is the *direct* transmission frequency ρ_{uv} between u and v in the cascades, defined as $\sum_{ij} I(u_i = v, z_i = j, u_j = u)$. This can be similarly generalized to define the *second-order* transmission frequency $\rho_{uv}^{(2)}$ between u and v in the cascades as $\sum_w \rho_{uw}\rho_{wv}$ or its approximation $\max_w \min(\rho_{uw}, \rho_{wv})$. The interpretation is that u frequently infects some node w, who in turn frequently infects v in the cascades. This can be similarly generalized further to define the rth-order transmission frequency $\rho_{uv}^{(r)}$, and finally ρ_{uv}^*.

Node-centric Properties: We now formally define our first motivating network diffusion property, that of finding influential nodes considering both network strengths α_{uv}^* and transmission frequencies ρ_{uv}^*.

Node influence score: Intuitively, a node's influence score $f_u(\alpha, z)$ is high if it has many 'followers' v with high α_{uv}^* and high ρ_{uv}^*. One way to capture this is to define

$$f_u(\alpha, z; a, r) = \sum_v I(\alpha_{uv}^* > a) I(\rho_{uv}^*(z) \geq r) \tag{7}$$

Alternatively, we may couple α_{uv}^* and ρ_{uv}^* as $\sum_v \alpha_{uv}^* \rho_{uv}^*$ or $\sum_v {\alpha_{uv}^*}^{\rho_{uv}^*}$ Unfortunately, all of these forms are neither *nice-α* nor *nice-z* even when we consider only first and second order infections ($R = 2$). So their computation requires sampling over both α and z. But it turns out that the definition for $R = 1$ is more tractable, as we see next.

Node influence score for direct infections: This is the special case of node influence score considering only directly connected nodes in the network who are also directly infected in the cascades:

$$f_u(\alpha, z; a, r) = \sum_v I(\alpha_{uv} > a) I(\rho_{uv}(z) \geq r) \tag{8}$$

It turns out that this property is *nice-α*, so that the expectation can be calculated efficiently and exactly, in part. Though $\rho_{uv}(z)$ is itself *nice-z*, Eqn. 8 is not *nice-z* since discretization of $\rho_{uv}(z)$ through $I(\rho_{uv}(z) \geq r)$ leads to coupling across z_i variables. This implies that the alternatives $f_u(\alpha, z; a) = \sum_v I(\alpha_{uv} > a) \rho_{uv}(z)$ and $f_u(\alpha, z) = \sum_v {\alpha_{uv}}^{\rho_{uv}(z)}$ are both *nice-α* and *nice-z*, though not *nice-z*, α, providing two different routes for partly approximating their expectations.

As a further simplification of Eqn. 8, we may restrict the node influence score to consider only the network connections and ignore the cascade:

$$f(\alpha; a)_u = \sum_v I(\alpha_{uv} > a) \tag{9}$$

Interestingly this still remains *nice-α* and (trivially) *nice-z*, but not *nice-z, α*. Alternatively, we could consider only the transmission frequencies:

$$f(z,r)_u = \sum_v I(\rho_{uv}(z) \geq r) \tag{10}$$

This is (trivially) *nice-α* but not *nice-z* because of the discretization.

Edge-centric Properties: Edge-centric properties compute scores for an edge (u, v) in the network. As before, we will focus on scores involving connection strengths α_{uv} and transmission frequencies ρ_{uv}.

Edge Distribution: Given a range (r_1, r_2) for the transmission frequency, and a range (a_1, a_2) for the connection strength, this counts the number of edges (u, v) in the network whose connection strength α_{uv} and transmission frequency ρ_{uv} lie in this range.

$$f(\alpha, z) = \sum_{u,v} I(a_1 < \alpha_{uv} < a_2) I(r_1 \leq \rho_{uv}(z) < r_2) \tag{11}$$

The resultant distribution of the edges over the (α, ρ) space can be suggestive of the effectiveness of viral marketing strategies for this network, or the susceptibility of this network to epidemics. Eqn. 11 can also be viewed as the distribution of the summed (or averaged) direct node influence scores. Recall that the plots in the introduction correspond to this property.

Marginals or projections of this distribution along the ρ and α dimensions can also be useful.

$$f(z) = \sum_{u,v} I(r_1 \leq \rho_{uv}(z) < r_2); \quad f(\alpha) = \sum_{u,v} I(a_1 < \alpha_{uv} < a_2)$$

The first two edge-centric properties are *nice-α but not nice-z. The last property is both nice-α and nice-z but not nice-z, α.*

Observe that removing the binning for the α-projection recovers the well studied network inference problem.

$$f(\alpha, z) = \alpha \tag{12}$$

Computing the expectation of this score is the Bayesian formulation of the network inference problem, where we are seeking the expected network connection strengths given the cascades. This is again *nice-α*, and *nice-z*.

All the network-centric properties introduced so far are at best partly *nice*. We conclude this discussion by presenting an interesting property that is *nice-z, α*. Imagine that we are interested in finding strong edges that are not frequent, and weak edges that are frequent. For this, the following score is useful:

$$f_{uv}(\alpha, z) = \alpha_{uv}^{-\rho_{uv}(z)} \tag{13}$$

This function satisfies Def. 5.3, and therefore the complete expectation can be computed efficiently upto a multiplicative constant.

5.3 Cascade-centric Properties

For cascade centric properties, the focus is on entities in the cascade, such as individual infections, for which we compute some score based on the network as well as the cascade. We illustrate such properties using individual infections.

Infections due to Strongest Neighbor: The strongest neighbor of a node v in the network is the one with the maximum connection strength α_{uv}. We may count the number of infections for which the infecting parent u_{z_i} is the strongest neighbor for u_i in the network:

$$f(\alpha, z) = \sum_i I(u_{z_i} = \arg\max_v \alpha_{vu_i}) \tag{14}$$

We can similarly count number of infections by the nth-strongest neighbor, for $n > 1$. Both properties are *nice-z*, but not *nice-α*.

As an even simpler example of a cascade property, we can consider checking the parents nodes for individual infections.

Infection parent identification: This indicates if node v is the parent of infection i.

$$f(\alpha, z)_{iu} = 1 \text{ if } z_i = u; \quad = 0 \text{ otherwise} \tag{15}$$

This is equivalent to computing the diffusion paths for a cascade. This infection-centric property is *nice-z* and also trivially *nice-α*.

It is worth observing that the *complete likelihood* $p(\{c^o\}, z \mid \alpha)$ of a cascade C given network strengths α can be seen as a cascade-centric property, where the entity of interest is the entire cascade.

$$f(\alpha, z) = p(\{c^o\}, z \mid \alpha) = \prod_{u,v} e^{-\alpha_{uv}\Delta_{uv}} \prod_i \alpha_{u_{z_i} u_i} \tag{16}$$

The *likelihood* can be viewed similarly as a cascade-centric property. Unlike complete likelihood, the likelihood is a function of only the observed infection variables, and the parent variables z are summed out.

$$f(\alpha) = p(\{c^o\} \mid \alpha) = \prod_{u,v} e^{-\alpha_{uv}\Delta_{uv}} \prod_i \sum_{j \in \pi_i} \alpha_{u_j u_i} \tag{17}$$

Both of these properties are *nice-z* (the likelihood trivially so), but not *nice-α*. In the context of test cascades, the expectation of this property can be interpreted as considering the entire posterior distribution over α, learnt from the training cascades, to explain the test cascades. In contrast, the frequentist strategy uses only a point estimate.

6. INFERENCE

We have seen in Sec. 5 that computing the expectation for network diffusion properties that are not completely *nice* requires drawing samples from the posterior distribution $p(\alpha, z|\{c^o\})$ over network strengths α and infection parents z conditioned on the observed cascades $\{c^o\}$. In this section, we propose a Gibbs Sampling framework for this. In this framework, we iterate over all latent variables, sampling a new value for it from its conditional distribution, given the current values of all other variables. Asymptotically, the samples are from the joint posterior distribution over all latent variables. For our problem, we need to draw samples from $p(z_i|\{c^o\}, \alpha, z_{-i})$ and from $p(\alpha_{uv}|\{c^o\}, z, \alpha_{-uv})$, where z_{-i} and α_{-uv} denote variables other than z_i and α_{uv}. All expressions below are for the Exponential Distribution. Expressions for Rayleigh can be derived in a similar manner.

First, the posterior distribution $p(z, \alpha \mid \{c^o\})$ over both z and α looks as follows:

$$p(z, \alpha \mid \{c^o\}) \propto \prod_{uv} \alpha_{uv}^{\rho_{uv}(z)+a-1} e^{-\alpha_{uv}(\Delta_{uv}+b)}$$

Given this, the conditional distribution for the ith infection parent z_i turns out to have a very simple form:

$$p(z_i = j \mid z_{-i}, \alpha, \{c^o\}) \sim \alpha_{ji}$$

The conditional distribution for individual network strengths α_{uv} also has a simple *Gamma* density form:

$$p(\alpha_{uv} \mid \{c^o\}, z, \alpha_{-uv}) \sim Gamma(\rho_{uv} + a, \Delta_{uv} + b)$$

For network properties that are *nice-α*, only samples of z are required. In such cases, an alternative is to perform *collapsed Gibbs Sampling*, by analytically integrating out α:

$$p(z|\{c^o\}) \propto \int_\alpha p(z, \{c^o\} \mid \alpha) p(\alpha) d\alpha \propto \prod_{uv} \frac{\Gamma(\rho_{uv}(z) + a)}{(\Delta_{uv} + b)^{(\rho_{uv}(z)+a)}}$$

Given this conditional, the conditional distribution for individual infection parents z_i looks as follows:

$$p(z_i = j \mid z_{-i}, \{c^o\}) \propto \frac{(\rho^{-i}_{u_j u_i}(z) + a)}{\Delta_{u_j u_i} + b}$$

where $\rho^{-i}_{u_j u_i}(z)$ ignores the ith infection for pair-wise infection counts over nodes. The collapsed Gibbs Sampling algorithm is remarkably simple. It repeatedly samples the parents of the individual infections from Multinomial distributions and updating infection counts for pairs of nodes.

The posterior over α_{uv} when $\rho_{uv} = 0$ is given by Gamma(a,b + Δ_{uv}). Since this is peaked sharply at 0, we sample α_{uv} only when $\rho_{uv} > 0$. This is significantly smaller than $|V|^2$.

Recently, the independent cascade model has been extended to handle features of individual infections [22], which is useful to capture contents of social media posts when inferring influences. Our approach can be extended in a straightforward manner to incorporate features in this way. The analysis in Sec. 5 remains unchanged since the decoupling in Eqns. 1 and 6 still hold. The Gibbs Sampling conditional distributions acquire an additional feature term. We omit further details due to space constraints.

Map-Reduce Implementation: For computing the Δ_{uv} values, each cascade can be processed in parallel. The final value for each for each u, v pair can be obtained by adding across cascades. This is exploited by the Mapper. Each Mapper computes Δ_{uv} for the set of cascades given to it and emits (v:Δ_{uv}) pairs. Each Mapper also generates a list of possible parents for each infection and emits (v:[i,π_i]) pairs.

Sampling a parent for an infection of node v requires ρ_{*v} and Δ_{*v} in case of collapsed sampler, and α_{*v} in the case of uncollapsed sampler. Sampling α_{*v} requires only ρ_{*v} and Δ_{*v}. Moreover, after sampling only ρ_{*v} and α_{*v} are needed to be updated. As a result, the sampler for each node v can be run in parallel if the set of possible parents of each infection is known. The sampling is performed in the Reducer, which exploits this parallelism. Each Reducer performs sampling for a subset of nodes. For each node v assigned, a Reducer combines information from different mappers to compute the final Δ_{uv}, and the complete list of infections of node v. It performs sampling for these infections and generates the samples. The samples from all Reducers are combined to get the complete set of samples.

7. EXPERIMENTS

In this section, we present experimental evaluations of various network diffusion properties defined in Sec. 5 using our Bayesian approach on synthetic and real world datasets. We focus on the accuracy of the properties computations and on the scalability of our algorithms for large datasets.

Baseline: We note at the outset that this general problem has not been studied before, and that there exists no baseline for comparison. However, one potential strategy is to first recover a point estimate $\hat{\alpha}$ (e.g. MLE) of the network strengths α using a state-of-the-art approach, consider the most likely infection parents $\hat{z} = \arg\max_z p(z|\hat{\alpha}, \{c^o\})$ for $\hat{\alpha}$, and then evaluate the property $f(\hat{\alpha}, \hat{z})$ at $(\hat{\alpha}, \hat{z})$. While this suffers from deficiencies outlined in Sec. 3, this is the best possible baseline using existing network inference techniques. As the state-of-the-art network inference approach for the continuous time independent cascade model, we used the featureless version of MONET [22]. We do not use NETRATE [6], since it does not support multiple infections of a node in a cascade. In the rest of this section, we will refer to this approach as the frequentist plug-in approach (**FP**), and to our proposed approach of computing expectations as the Bayesian Expectation approach (**BE**). We have used the Exponential distribution for all experiments. For the Gamma prior we use a = 0.00001 and b = 0.1.

Synthetic data experiments: We first conducted experiments on multiple synthetic datasets. These experiments allowed us to evaluate accuracy against a gold-standard, which is unavailable for most real-world network diffusion datasets. Secondly, these helped us analyze our proposed approach for different families of graphs. Following earlier experiments on network inference [7, 6], we created synthetic graphs with 1024 nodes using Forest Fire (FF), Random (Rnd), Hierarchical (HI) and Core-Periphery (CP) Graph models, the last three being instances of Kronecker Graph models. We used parameter values [0.5, 0.5; 0.5, 0.5] for Rnd, [0.9,0.1;0.1,0.9] for HI, [0.9,0.5;0.5,0.9] for CP, following Gomez-Rodriguez et. al. [6]. To generate weights α_{uv} for each edge (u, v), we sampled uniformly from (0.01, 10) [3]. We then generated 20 *splitting* cascades over these graphs with 2 randomly chosen seeds for each cascade. Finally, we obtained 2046 edges and 48947 infections for the Random graph, 1496 and 38046 for the Hierarchical, 2042 and 58062 for the Core-Periphery, and 2023 and 55274 for the Forest Fire graph.

Recall that one of the reasons behind the synthetic data experiments is to be able to evaluate accuracy. For the infection parents z, we considered the true parents as the gold-standard. However, for the real-valued network connections α_{uv}, the true values are not always possible to recover from finite length cascades. For example, it is impossible to recover the strength for any edge that has no transmission in the cascade. Therefore, we considered as our gold-standard the best achievable α_{uv} given the true infection parents in the cascades: $\alpha^* = \arg\max_\alpha f(\{c^o\}, z^*; \alpha)$. For accuracy in case of a scalar property, we used absolute error between the gold-standard $f(\alpha^*, z^*)$ and the computed value of the property, and for vectors and matrices the root mean squares of the individual errors.

(A) Network-centric Properties: In this category, we first evaluate the edge-distribution (Eqn. 11) as an example of a **property on edges**. Evaluating accuracy for this property is challenging because of the threshold parameters a and r. We discretized the α and the ρ ranges, and within each region of the (α, ρ) space, computed the actual, BE and FP values of these properties, and the errors for BE and FP.

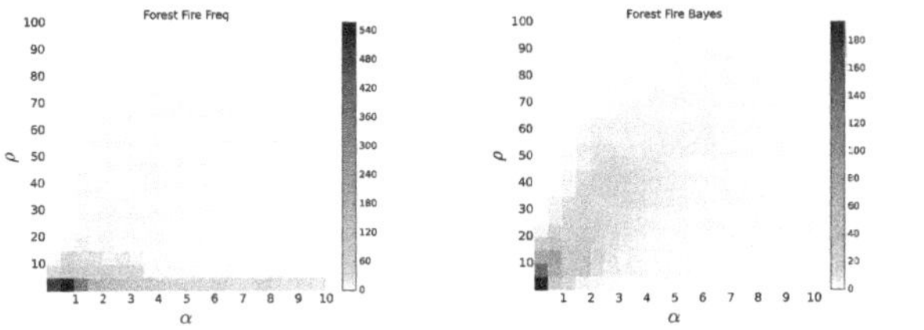

(a) Frequentist (b) Bayesian Expectation

Figure 3: Reconstructed edge distribution: FF

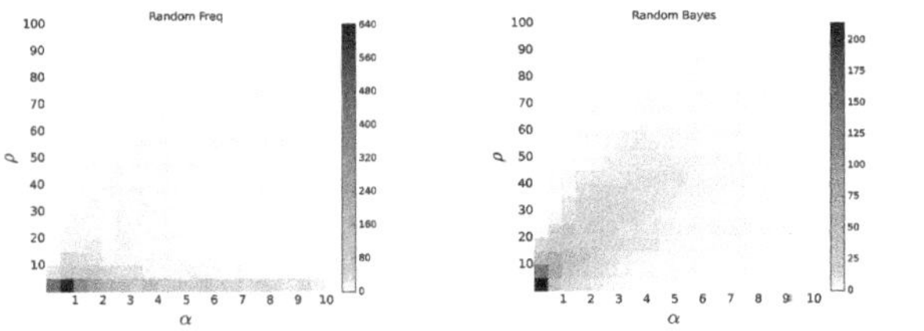

(a) Frequentist (b) Bayesian Expectation

Figure 4: Reconstructed edge distribution: Rnd

The actual plots for the four networks were introduced in Fig. 1. The FE and BE reconstructions for the Core-Periphery graph were also introduced earlier in Fig. 2. The reconstructions for the other three graphs are shown in Figs. 3, 4, and 5. It can be seen quite clearly that while BE is able to reconstruct the actual distributions to a reasonable extent for all 4 graphs, FP does quite poorly. In fact, the FP reconstruction looks similar in all 4 cases, and fails to pick up the signatures for the different graphs.

We also calculated the actual errors for the two approaches over the (α, ρ) space. Since it is difficult to visualize the plots in 2D, we evaluated the projections on the α-dimension and z-dimension (Eqn. 5.2) for the edge distribution for the 4 graphs.

Table 1: α-proj. for edge distribution: abs. error

NW	CP		HI		Rnd		FF	
α	BE	FE	BE	FE	BE	FE	BE	FE
0 1	591	6514	156	1501	470	4004	432	4008
1 2	169	1587	5	287	34	1085	30	1039
2 3	13	618	18	166	6	497	8	379
3 4	9	340	1	87	6	265	15	196
4 5	8	159	2	57	32	139	9	101
5 6	6	138	1	51	14	127	11	61
6 7	3	75	1	34	7	86	13	62
7 8	1	82	**14**	**9**	9	70	4	64
8 9	2	48	8	17	13	45	1	38
9 10	1	46	1	16	4	44	4	36

Table 2: ρ-proj. for edge distribution: abs. error

NW	CP		HI		Rnd		FF	
ρ	BE	FE	BE	FE	BE	FE	BE	FE
0 10	524	4373	69	1032	344	3339	287	2903
10 20	**348**	**228**	14	15	**108**	**8**	89	21
20 30	20	82	3	0	40	87	20	51
30 40	59	91	1	14	28	64	29	73
40 50	47	100	3	19	13	44	10	43
50 60	43	59	5	16	6	16	8	34
60 70	19	27	0	3	1	13	9	12
70 80	1	1	1	0	2	6	2	3
80 90	4	4	2	0	0	4	2	12
90 100	3	5	2	1	1	2	2	8

In Tab. 1, we record the errors for BE α-projection and the FP α-projection for different α-intervals. We can see

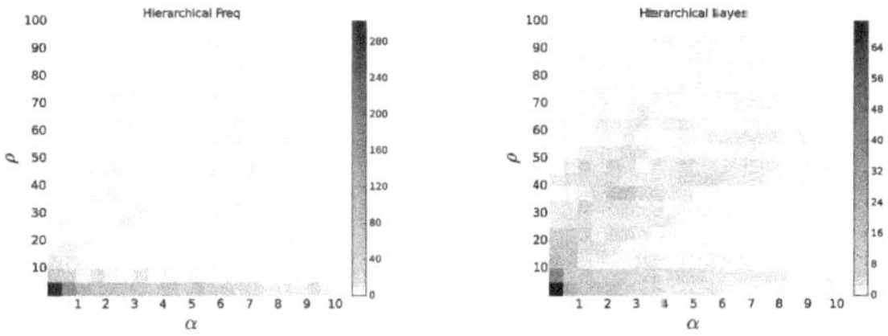

(a) Frequentist (b) Bayesian Expectation

Figure 5: Reconstructed edge distribution: HI

that for the α-projection, the FP errors are an order of magnitude bigger for all intervals, except for $\alpha \in (7, 8)$ for Hierarchical. Similarly, in Tab. 2, we record the errors for BE ρ-projection and the FP ρ-projection for different ρ-intervals. In this case as well, FP error is significantly lower only for the (10, 20) interval for CP and Rnd.

Finally, we come to **properties of nodes**. We evaluated direct node influence (Eqn. 8), and indirect node influence for 2nd-order neighbors (Eqn. 7) for the 4 graphs. Again, we partitioned the (α, ρ)-space into regions. However, reporting detailed results is even harder here, since we have actual, BE and FP scores *for each node* in each α, ρ-region. We consider the sum (or average) of the influence scores over all nodes. Recall that one interpretation of the edge-distribution is the distribution of the sum of direct influence scores over all nodes. So the edge-distribution evaluation above additionally serves as an evaluation of the *direct node influence scores* at an aggregate level.

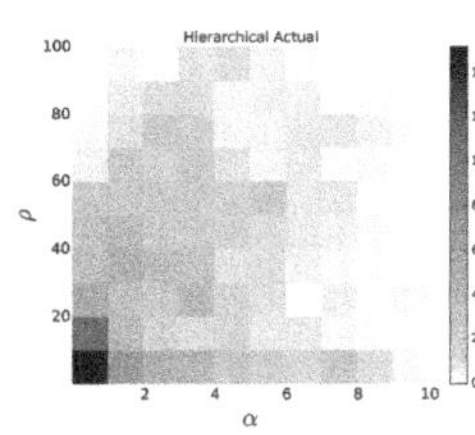

(a) Actual

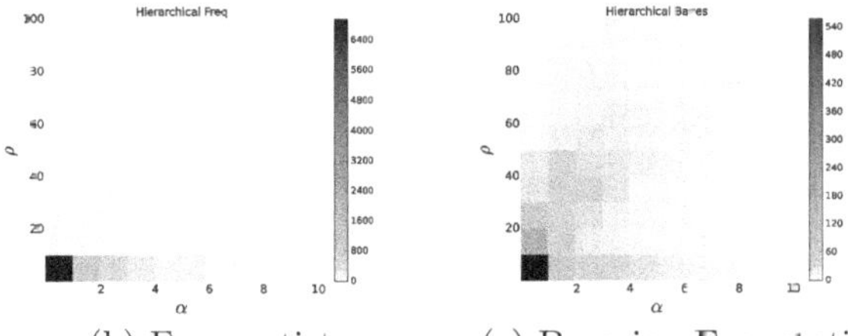

(b) Frequentist (c) Bayesian Expectation

Figure 6: Indirect node influence distribution: HI

For *indirect node influence*, due to space constraints, we show the (averaged) indirect node influence distribution only for the Hierarchical graph in Fig. 6. Again we see that BE is able to pick up the signature of the distribution to a reasonable extent, whereas FP has failed completely.

In Tab. 3, we report the aggregated errors over all nodes and over all (α, ρ) regions for both direct and indirect influence scores. We have scaled down the values by the total number of nodes, which is 1024. We again see that the BE

Table 3: Node influence scores: agg. error

NW	CP		HI		Rnd		FF	
	BE	FP	BE	FP	BE	FP	BE	FP
Dir	29	124	22	46	30	104	30	98
InDir	62	417	15	98	27	288	27	273

errors are significant smaller than the FP errors across the board.

(B) Cascade-centric Properties: Under cascade-centric properties, we evaluate infections due to n^{th} strongest neighbor (Eqn. 14) for $n = 1, 2, 3$.

Table 4: Infections by n^{th}-strongest nbr: abs. error

NW	CP		HI		Rnd		FF	
n	BE	FP	BE	FP	BE	FP	BE	FP
1	3711	22090	631	13537	578	21613	127	23476
2	2374	6171	691	2506	1352	3533	1284	**712**
3	191	**59**	194	3924	152	4825	388	6828

Tab. 4 records the absolute error for the number of infections by the nth-strongest neighbor for $n = 1, 2, 3$. Notice that FP has very high errors for $n = 1$. There are just two instances where FP works better than BE: for $n = 2$ in Forest Fire and for $n = 1$ in Core-Periphery, where the values are comparable. In all other cases, FP has significantly higher error than BE.

Likelihood, Network Inference and Parent Identification: The performance improvement of BE over FP in the experiments so far is attributable to two reasons: (a) the Bayesian approach of using the full posterior distribution instead of the frequentist point estimate, and (b) many-to-one mapping of network variables to property values. We now look at experiments using the basic inference problems for network analysis, and generalization ability on held-out data, which are one-to-one network diffusion properties in our formulation.

Table 5: Loglikelihood for synthetic data

NW	CP	HI	Rnd	FF
	BE, FP	BE, FP	BE, FP	BE, FP
Test	1.0e4, 0.6e4	6.5e3, 2.4e3	1.1e4, -1.5e4	1.2e4, 926
Train	2.8e4, 3.6e4	2.0e4, 2.2e4	2.3e4, 2.9e4	2.8e4, 3.3e4

In Tab. 5, we record the train and test likehoods for the 4 synthetic datasets. We see that BE consistently has higher test likelihood, while the train likelihood is higher for FP, suggesting overfitting.

Table 6: Network Inf. (NI) & Parent Id. (PI)

NW	CP		HI		Rnd		FF	
	BE	FP	BE	FP	BE	FP	BE	FP
NI	0.116	2.553	0.884	3.210	0.147	17.483	0.329	736.821
PI	0.533	0.406	0.861	0.783	0.757	0.646	0.770	0.674

In Tab. 6, we record the errors in recovery of α for BE and FP. Observe that the errors are consistently lower for BE across the 4 datasets. In fact, the FP errors are very high for the Random and Forest Fire datasets. In Tab. 6, we also see that parent identification accuracy of BE is consistently around 10% more than that of FP. These three experiments demonstrate that the Bayesian approach for network diffusion analysis has advantages even for one-to-one properties.

(C) Iterations vs Error: Before moving on to experiments on real-world data, we make a note about Gibbs Sampling iterations. Gibbs Sampling algorithms often take thousands of iterations to converge, which can be a serious problem for large real-world datasets. The number of iterations required for the Gibbs Sampler to converge can be greatly reduced by choosing a good initialization. We use $\hat{z} = \arg\max_z p(z \mid \{c^o\}; \hat{\alpha})$ as the initial z, where $\hat{\alpha_{uv}} = |P(u,v)|/\Delta_{uv}$. $\hat{\alpha}$ is an approximation of α_{MLE} where we use $|P(u,v)|$ which is purely a function of that data instead of ρ_{uv} in the numerator. In our experiments, we observe that the accuracy increases very sharply in the initial iterations, and is close to the best value within 100-200 iterations.

Experiments on real-world data: We now report experiments on real-world data, where the graph structures are more complex than the synthetic settings. The underlying diffusion process is also likely to be different from the Independent Cascade model, which our models assume, and which we used for generating the synthetic cascades.

The **Meme Tracker** dataset[1] records the diffusion of "memes" or catch-phrases across 5000 most active blogs and news sites between March 2011 and February 2012. The flow of each meme corresponds to one cascade. Related memes are grouped into one topics. For our experiments, we selected 5 topics, 2 of which have been used in earlier experiments involving non-stationary networks [9], and 3 others for which the networks are likely to be stationary. Basketball has 1187 Nodes, 130317 Infections and 2663 cascades, Alcohol has 1549 nodes, 151136 infections and 3018 cascades, Technology has 1797 nodes, 338931 infections and 6658 cascades, NBA has 1891 nodes, 179864 infections and 3637 cascades, and Occupy has 1601 nodes, 147135 infections and 2851 cascades. In each topic, we consider all sufficiently long cascades (length > 30). We split the cascades randomly to generate the training and test cascades(80-20), and then prune infections of those users in test cascades who are not present in the training cascades.

Table 7: Loglikelihood for Meme Tracker

	Bball	Alcohol	Tech.	NBA	Occupy
BE	-1.5e6	-5.8e5	-6.6e5	-8.9e5	-5.1e5
FP	-3.5e6	-8.9e5	-2.6e6	-1.1e7	-1.2e6

Since no gold-standard is available for α or z for this dataset, we compared BE and FP using loglikelihood on held-out test data, with the knowledge of α learnt from training data. In Tab. 7, we report the loglikelihood values for the 5 selected topics. We can see that the BE values are significantly better than the FP values. Recall that this is the best scenario for the baseline since likelihood, as a network diffusion property, is a one-to-one function of α for this problem. This suggests that BE is likely to outperform FP to a larger extent for other properties on real-world datasets.

We also computed the proposed network-centric and cascade-centric properties for Meme Tracker using BE. In Fig. 7, we plot the edge distribution for two of the topics. Recall that there is no gold-standard for this. We can see that the nature of the plots is different from all of the synthetic datasets. The mass is more concentrated towards weaker, infrequent edges. We suspect that this is because of the way users were sampled for this dataset.

Scaling experiments: We also experimented with larger volumes of the Meme Tracker data using our map-reduce implementation. We created increasingly larger dataset sizes by randomly sampling cascades and checking the execution

[1] http://snap.stanford.edu/infopath//data.html

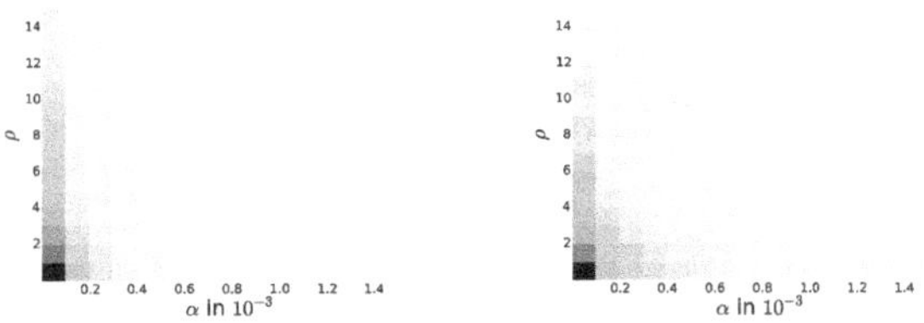

(a) Tech (b) Alcohol

Figure 7: Edge distribution for Meme Tracker topics

Table 8: Millions of Infections vs time (secs)

# Infections	Time (12 nodes)	Time (1 node)
15	552	3635
31	888	6873
43	1311	10277
63	1948	14783

time for 100 iterations of Gibbs Sampling. We performed experiments on a Intel Xeon server with 100GB RAM, which supports 12 mapper/ reducer tasks in parallel.

In Tab. 8, we record execution time with increasing data size on 12 processor nodes and compare against the time taken on a single node. We can see that the map-reduce implementation allows us to scale our analysis by providing a (roughly) linear speed-up in terms of number or processor nodes.

In summary, the experiments clearly demonstrate that computing expectations under the posterior distribution leads to significantly better reconstruction of a wide variety of network diffusion properties. The proposed Bayesian framework that combines exact efficient computation with Gibbs Sampling based approximations outperforms state-of-the-art algorithms even for the well-studied network inference and parent identification problems, and in generalizing to held-out test data. The map-reduce implementation is promising in terms of scaling up the analysis to study properties of large network diffusion datasets.

8. CONCLUSIONS

In this paper, we have investigated the novel problem of computing expectations of properties of network diffusions involving hidden variables. We have proposed a Bayesian framework for computing such expectations, and proposed and characterized network diffusion properties that can be handled efficiently in this framework. In experiments over synthetic and real world datasets, we have shown that we are able to reconstruct network properties significantly more accurately than a frequentist baseline.

9. REFERENCES

[1] N. Barbieri, F. Bonchi, and G. Manco. Influence-based network-oblivious community detection. In *ICDM*, 2013.

[2] F. Bonchi. Influence propagation in social networks: A data mining perspective. *IEEE Intelligent Informatics Bulletin*, 12(1), 2011.

[3] N. Du, L. Song, M. Gomez-Rodriguez, and H. Zha. Scalable influence estimation in continuous-time diffusion networks. In *NIPS*, 2013.

[4] N. Du, L. Song, A. Smola, and M. Yuan. Learning networks of heterogeneous influence. In *NIPS*, 2012.

[5] A. Elfessi and D. Reineke. A bayesian look at classical estimation: The exponential distribution. *Journal of Statistics Education*, 9(1), 2001.

[6] M. Gomez-Rodriguez, D. Balduzzi, and B. Schölkopf. Uncovering the temporal dynamics of diffusion networks. In *ICML*, 2011.

[7] M. Gomez-Rodriguez, J. Leskovec, and A. Krause. Inferring networks of diffusion and influence. In *KDD*, 2010.

[8] M. Gomez-Rodriguez, J. Leskovec, and B. Schölkopf. Modeling information propagation with survival theory. In *ICML*, 2013.

[9] M. Gomez-Rodriguez, J. Leskovec, and B. Schölkopf. Structure and dynamics of information pathways in online media. In *WSDM*, 2013.

[10] A. Goyal, F. Bonchi, and L. Lakshmanan. Discovering leaders from community actions. In *CIKM*, 2008.

[11] A. Goyal, F. Bonchi, and L. Lakshmanan. Learning influence probabilities in social networks. In *WSDM*, 2010.

[12] A. Goyal, F. Bonchi, and L. Lakshmanan. A data-based approach to social influence maximization. *PVLDB*, 2011.

[13] A. Guille, H. Hacid, C. Favre, and D. A. Zighed. Information diffusion in online social networks: A survey. *SIGMOD Rec.*, 42(2), July 2013.

[14] D. Kempe, J. Kleinberg, and E. Tardos. Maximizing the spread of influence through a social network. In *KDD*, 2003.

[15] K. Kutzkov, A. Bifet, F. Bonchi, and A. Gionis. Strip: Stream learning of influence probabilities. In *KDD*, 2013.

[16] L. Macchia, F. Bonchi, F. Gullo, and L. Chiarandini. Mining summaries of propagations. In *ICDM*, 2013.

[17] Y. Mehmood, N. Barbieri, F. Bonchi, and A. Ukkonen. Csi: Community-level social influence analysis. In *ECML PKDD*, 2013.

[18] C. Milling, C. Caramanis, M. S., and S. Shakkottai. Network forensics: Random infection vs spreading epidemic. In *ACM Sigmetrics*, 2012.

[19] P. Netrapalli and S. Sanghavi. Finding the graph of epidemic cascades. In *ACM SIGMETRICS*, 2012.

[20] E. Sadikov, M. Medina, J. Leskovec, and H. Garcia-Molina. Correcting for missing data in information cascades. In *WSDM*, 2011.

[21] K. Saito, M. Kimura, K. Ohara, and H. Motoda. Learning continuous-time information diffusion model for social behavioral data analysis. In *Adv. in Mach. Learning*, 2009.

[22] L. Wang, S. Ermon, and J. Hopcroft. Feature-enhanced probabilistic models for diffusion network inference. In *ECML-PKDD*, 2012.

Scalable Diffusion-Aware Optimization of Network Topology

Elias Khalil
lyes@gatech.edu

Bistra Dilkina
bdilkina@cc.gatech.edu

Le Song
lsong@cc.gatech.edu

School of Computational Science & Engineering
College of Computing
Georgia Institute of Technology
Atlanta, GA 30332-0765

ABSTRACT

How can we optimize the topology of a networked system to bring a flu under control, propel a video to popularity, or stifle a network malware in its infancy? Previous work on information diffusion has focused on modeling the diffusion dynamics and selecting nodes to maximize/minimize influence. Only a paucity of recent studies have attempted to address the network modification problems, where the goal is to either facilitate desirable spreads or curtail undesirable ones by adding or deleting a small subset of network nodes or edges. In this paper, we focus on the widely studied *linear threshold diffusion model*, and prove, for the first time, that the network modification problems under this model have *supermodular* objective functions. This surprising property allows us to design efficient data structures and scalable algorithms with provable approximation guarantees, despite the hardness of the problems in question. Both the time and space complexities of our algorithms are *linear* in the size of the network, which allows us to experiment with millions of nodes and edges. We show that our algorithms outperform an array of heuristics in terms of their effectiveness in controlling diffusion processes, often beating the next best by a significant margin.

Categories and Subject Descriptors: H.2.8 [Database Management]: Database Applications — *Data Mining*

General Terms: Algorithms, Theory, Experimentation

Keywords: diffusion networks; network optimization; supermodularity; approximation

1. INTRODUCTION

The diffusion of physical, conceptual or digital substances over networks has been studied in many domains such as epidemiology [10], social media [16], and computer and mobile [19] networks. These studies have resulted in an array of models aiming to capture the diffusion dynamics, among which the most well-known are the linear threshold (LT) model, the independent cascade (IC) model, and the Susceptible Infected Recovered (SIR) model. Starting with the work of Domingos and Richardson on viral marketing [6], a lot of research has concentrated on how one can pick a small set of source nodes, whose initial adoption of a given substance would trigger maximal spread in the network. The seminal work of Kempe et al. [12] showed that *source node selection for influence maximization* is a submodular maximization problem under the IC and LT diffusion models, and therefore admits a simple greedy algorithm with approximation guarantees. Their result was followed by a whole line of research on source node selection in various related information diffusion contexts [4, 7, 9].

In contrast to these previous works where *the diffusion networks remain unchanged*, we are rather interested in problems of *modifying the topology of a diffusion network* to either facilitate the spread of desirable substances, or curtail the spread of undesirable ones. One can consider deleting edges or nodes to minimize possible undesirable spread, such as that of a virus, disease or rumor, or one can consider adding edges or nodes to facilitate, for example, the spread of information or dispersal of endangered species. For instance, in disease control, authorities may consider disallowing travel between certain pairs of cities to curb the spread of a flu epidemic. On the other hand, social media websites can recommend to users additional information outlets to follow to increase the spread of ideas and memes. The modification setting is particularly relevant when the agent optimizing the topology does not have control over the sources of the spread, but is able to change some subset of the edges or nodes that he has access to. Hence, our setting is most relevant when the agent in question is looking to *strategically design* the topology, as opposed to reacting to a particular event. Thus, we will later assume that the set of nodes that are likely to be sources of diffusion are known, but which ones among them are the sources of a particular diffusion event follows some probability distribution (e.g. uniform). For example, in an information network, we may know which popular news sites are typically the sources of viral news, but are uncertain as to which of these sites will be the source of a particular piece of news. Despite the broad practical relevance of the diffusion network modification problems, existing results are very limited, and lack in either formal optimality guarantees or in algorithmic efficiency.

Related work. Under the SIR model, some positive network optimization results exist: Tong et al. [22] address the edge deletion (addition) problem by approximately minimizing (maximizing) the eigenvalue of the adjacency matrix. In addition, methods have been designed to optimize surrogates for diffusion spread under SIR [8, 20]. Instead of maximizing/minimizing the spread of substances directly,

KDD'14, August 24–27, 2014, New York, NY, USA.

ACM 978-1-4503-2956-9/14/08 ...$15.00.
http://dx.doi.org/10.1145/2623330.2623704 .

these methods typically optimize a static property of the network, in the hope of optimizing diffusion. For instance, Schneider et al. [20] proposed "betweenness centrality" as a heuristic for immunizing nodes or removing edges under the SIR model, while "degree centrality" was adopted in [8] to protect against virus propagation in email networks.

Under the IC model, existing results are negative: Sheldon et al.[21] study the problem of node addition to maximize spread, and provide a counter-example showing that the objective function is *not* submodular. Thus, they resort to a principled but expensive approach based on sample average approximation and mixed integer programming, which provides provable optimality guarantees but cannot scale to large networks. Bogunovic [1] addresses the node deletion problem. For the edge deletion problem under the IC model, Kimura et al.[14] apply the greedy algorithm used by Kempe et al. [12] for source node selection, but do not provide any approximation guarantees. We note that the edge deletion objective that we consider is not supermodular under IC; a simple counter-example is provided in the extended version of this paper.

Network optimization under the LT model is still largely unexplored, and this paper seeks to fill that gap. The greedy approach has been used in [13] to delete edges under the LT model, albeit without any analysis of the supermodularity of the objective, nor formal approximation guarantees. More recently, Kuhlman et al. [15] propose heuristic algorithms for edge removal under a simpler deterministic variant of the LT model. In contrast, we describe *principled algorithms* for edge deletion and addition by exploiting supermodularity of the objectives under the more general *stochastic* LT model. Most related are [3, 9], where node deletion under the "competitive" LT model (a variant of stochastic LT) is addressed using supermodularity. The node deletion problem can be considered a special case of the "influence blocking maximization" problem described in [3, 9]. However, the supermodularity results in those works are limited to node deletion, whereas our theoretical framework leads to supermodularity results for edge deletion and addition, node deletion and addition.

Our contributions. In this paper, we will address network topology optimization for diffusion under the *linear threshold model*. We will focus on two network modification problems involving the deletion of edges for minimizing spread and the addition of edges for maximizing spread [1] :

> **Edge deletion problem:** Given a set of source nodes X, find a set of k edges to remove s.t. the spread of a certain substance is minimized.

> **Edge addition problem:** Given a set of source nodes X, find a set of k edges to add s.t. the spread of a certain substance is maximized.

Proof techniques used in the source node selection literature are inadequate for our more complex network modification problems. Instead, we propose a novel theoretical framework (Section 3) that yields surprising results, namely that the objective function in both problems is *supermodular*, a property that has positive algorithmic implications. In particular, minimization of a supermodular function under cardinality constraints, although typically an NP-hard problem, admits a greedy algorithm with approximation guarantees [18]. Similarly, cardinality-constrained supermodular maximization has recently been shown to admit a simple modular approximation scheme [11]. Our finding, combined with these combinatorial optimization results allows, for the first time, the design of efficient diffusion-aware algorithms with approximation guarantees for the network modification problems under the LT model, filling a gap in the existence research literature on this topic.

We address several challenges in transforming the two general supermodular approximation algorithms into efficient and practical approaches for our setting. Directly implementing the supermodular optimization algorithms is impractical, since evaluating the objective function given a set of source nodes is #P-hard in general [4]. We exploit the correspondence between the LT model and the "live-edge graph" construction [12], and estimate the objective function using a sample of random live-edge graphs. Nevertheless, a naive application of the supermodular approximation schemes to the sample of random live-edge graphs will result in runtime quadratic in the network size, an approach that does not scale to modern problems with millions of nodes and edges. To tackle this issue, we design two data structures, the descendant-count trees for the edge deletion problem, and the neighbor-counting graphs for the edge addition problem, in order to support approximate evaluation of the objective function. These data structures can be *constructed in time linear in the network size*, and *queried in constant time*, allowing us to scale the supermodular optimization algorithms to networks with millions of nodes.

Finally, we evaluate our algorithms on both synthetic and real-world diffusion networks and compare the quality of the solutions to scalable alternative approaches, based on optimizing structural properties of the networks. Our algorithms can lead to as large as 10-20% additional efficacy for edge deletion, and up to 100% for edge addition, compared to the other approaches. In terms of scalability, our algorithms can scale to large networks with millions of nodes and edges.

2. LINEAR THRESHOLD MODEL

In this section, we will provide background on the linear threshold (LT) model for diffusion processes [12], which will be at the center of this study. This model is well-suited for representing threshold behavior, where entities in a network have a "tipping point" in terms of the fraction of neighboring nodes that have to adopt the diffusing substance, beyond which they would adopt it themselves. For instance, in a social setting, an individual may refrain from voicing his opinion, until a significant fraction (e.g. half) of his friends have voiced a similar opinion.

2.1 Cascade Generative Process

Underlying the LT model is a weighted directed graph $G = (V, E, w)$, called the *influence graph*, where V is a set of n nodes and E is a set of m directed edges, and $w : V \times V \to [0, 1]$ is a weight function. For edges $(u, v) \notin E$ we ignore the value of $w(u, v)$. We further require that $\sum_{u:(u,v)\in E} w(u, v) \leq 1$ for each node v. Starting from a source node (or an initially activated node) $S_0 = \{a\}$, a *cascade* then proceeds in discrete time steps $t = 0, 1, 2, \ldots$ as follows: (1) at $t = 0$, every node v first independently selects a threshold θ_v uniformly at random in the range $[0, 1]$, reflecting the uncertainty as to users' true thresholds; (2) subsequently, an inactive node v becomes activated at time $t + 1$ if $\sum_{u:u\in S_t,(u,v)\in E} w(u, v) \geq \theta_v$ where S_t is the set of nodes activated up to time t; (3) finally, the process terminates if no more activations are possible.

[1] One can also consider the analogous node deletion and addition problems, and our theoretical and algorithmic results on the finer-scale edge problems can be extended trivially.

Given an influence graph $G = (V, E, w)$, the *influence function* $\sigma(a, G)$ of a source node $a \in V$ is defined as the expected number of active nodes at the end of the diffusion process, $\sigma(a, G) = \mathbb{E}_{\theta_v}[|S_\infty|]$, where the expectation is taken with respect to the randomness of the node thresholds θ_v.

2.2 Live-Edge Graph Representation

Kempe et al. [12] showed that the influence function can be computed in an alternative way using what is referred to as "live-edge graphs", a construction that is more amenable to mathematical analysis. More specifically, a random live-edge graph X is generated as follows: Independently for each node $v \in V$, at most one of its incoming edges is selected with probability $w(u, v)$, and no edge is selected with probability $1 - \sum_{u:(u,v)\in E} w(u, v)$. Note that the set of nodes of X is equal to V, the set of "live" (or sampled) edges E_X of X is a subset of E, *i.e.*, $E_X \subseteq E$, and these edges are unweighted. Then, the influence function can be alternatively computed as

$$\sigma(a, G) = \mathbb{E}_X[r(a, X)] = \sum\nolimits_{X\in\mathcal{X}_G} \Pr[X|G] \cdot r(a, X), \quad (1)$$

where $\mathcal{X}_G$ is the space of all possible live-edge graphs based on G, $\Pr[X|G]$ is the probability of sampling a particular live-edge graph X, and $r(a, X)$ is the set of all reachable nodes in X from source a. If we define function

$$p(v, X, G) := \begin{cases} w(u, v), & \text{if } \exists u : (u, v) \in E_X \\ 1 - \sum_{u:(u,v)\in E} w(u, v), & \text{otherwise} \end{cases}$$

which is the probability of the configuration of incoming edges for node v in X; then, the probability of a particular live-edge graph X is

$$\Pr[X|G] = \prod\nolimits_{v\in V} p(v, X, G). \quad (2)$$

3. SPACE OF LIVE-EDGE GRAPHS

We will show that the objective functions of the edge deletion and addition problems are supermodular in the next section. However, the proofs require some properties beyond those used in [12]. Thus, we will first give some intuition as to why these properties are needed. We will denote the modification of an influence graph G by deleting or adding a set of edges S respectively by

$$G \setminus S := (V, E \setminus S, w), \text{ and } G \cup S := (V, E \cup S, w).$$

Consider the monotonicity of the influence function as defined in Eq. (1), with respect to the set of source nodes A: $\sigma(A \cup a, G) - \sigma(A, G)$ is a sum over $\mathcal{X}_G$, and so proving that $\Pr[X|G] \cdot r(A \cup a, X) - \Pr[X|G] \cdot r(A, X) \geq 0$ for the single live-edge graph $X \in \mathcal{X}_G$ suffices to prove monotonicity, in this case. In contrast, consider the monotonicity of the influence function, with respect to the set of edges in the graph: $\sigma(a, G\setminus S) - \sigma(a, G\setminus(S\cup\{e\}))$. The issue here lies in that the former function sums over $\mathcal{X}_{G\setminus S}$, whereas the latter sums over $\mathcal{X}_{G\setminus(S\cup\{e\})}$: since the set of live-edge graphs and the associated probabilities involved in the computation of the influence function will change as edges are deleted, it is not obvious that this function is monotone at all. Similar difficulties apply to proving supermodularity.

In this section, we will prove four properties related to the space of live-edge graphs, which will form the basis of our later analysis. More specifically, we are concerned with

- a subset S of the edge set E in the original influence graph G, *i.e.*, $S \subseteq E$; and
- two distinct edges $e = (u, v) \in E \setminus S$ and $g = (u', v') \in E \setminus S$ outside S, where v may or may not equal v'.

Deleting a set S from E will result in a new influence graph $G \setminus S$, which will generate a new space of live-edge graphs, $\mathcal{X}_{G\setminus S}$, and the associated live-edge graph probabilities, $\Pr[X|G \setminus S]$. Furthermore, we will divide the space $\mathcal{X}_{G\setminus S}$, according to the edge e, into three disjoint partitions (see Fig. 1(left)):

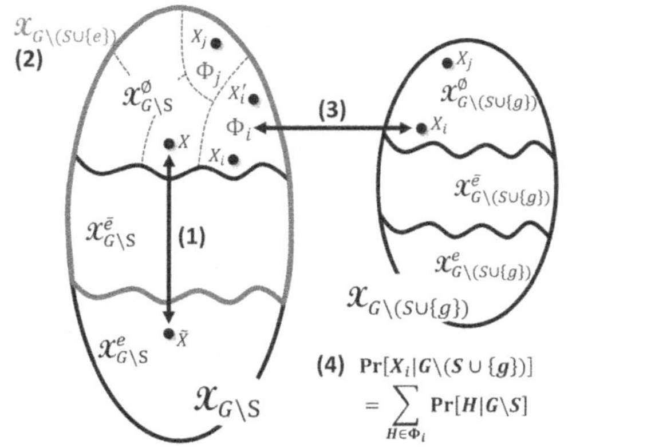

Figure 1: Four properties of the space of live-edge graphs: (1) within space mapping, (2) space inclusion, (3) across space mapping, and (4) across space probability mapping.

- $\mathcal{X}^e_{G\setminus S}$, the set of live-edge graphs where incoming edge $e = (u, v)$ is selected for node v;
- $\mathcal{X}^{\bar{e}}_{G\setminus S}$, the set of live-edge graphs where a different incoming edge $\bar{e} = (y, v)$ is selected for node v;
- $\mathcal{X}^{\emptyset}_{G\setminus S}$, the set of live-edge graphs where no incoming edge is selected for v.

Note that the probabilities of a live-edge graph X common to both $\mathcal{X}_G$ and $\mathcal{X}_{G\setminus\{e\}}$ may or may not change. Specifically, if node v has another incoming edge $g = (u', v)$ in X, then

$$\Pr[X|G] - \Pr[X|G \setminus \{e\}] = 0.$$

Otherwise, if node v has no incoming edge in X, then

$$\Pr[X|G] - \Pr[X|G \setminus \{e\}] = -w(u, v) \prod_{v'\neq v} p(v', X, G) \quad (3)$$

since all terms in Eq. (2) for $\Pr[X|G]$ and $\Pr[X|G \setminus \{e\}]$ concerning nodes $v' \neq v$ are exactly the same, and

$$p(v, X, G) = 1 - \sum_{u':(u',v)\in E\setminus\{e\}} w(u', v) - w(u, v)$$
$$= p(v, X, G \setminus \{e\}) - w(u, v).$$

We establish the following four relations between the spaces of live-edge graphs, and defer their proofs to the appendix. See Fig. 1 for illustrations.

3.1 Within Space Mapping

Our first result establishes a one-to-one mapping between the elements in partition $\mathcal{X}^e_{G\setminus S}$ and $\mathcal{X}^{\emptyset}_{G\setminus S}$.

PROPOSITION 1. *For every live-edge graph $X \in \mathcal{X}^{\emptyset}_{G\setminus S}$, there exists a corresponding live-edge graph $\widetilde{X} \in \mathcal{X}^e_{G\setminus S}$, and vice versa. If $X = (V, E_X)$, then $\widetilde{X} = (V, E_X \cup \{e\})$.*

3.2 Space Inclusion

Our second result relates partitions $\mathcal{X}^{\bar{e}}_{G\setminus S}$ and $\mathcal{X}^{\emptyset}_{G\setminus S}$ of the space $\mathcal{X}_{G\setminus S}$, to the space $\mathcal{X}_{G\setminus(S\cup\{e\})}$. We note that this second space of live-edge graphs, $\mathcal{X}_{G\setminus(S\cup\{e\})}$, is generated from the influence graph $G \setminus (S \cup \{e\})$ with an additional edge e deleted from $G \setminus S$. This result also shows that the space $\mathcal{X}_{G\setminus(S\cup\{e\})}$ is included in the space $\mathcal{X}_{G\setminus S}$.

PROPOSITION 2. *$\mathcal{X}_{G\setminus(S\cup\{e\})} \subseteq \mathcal{X}_{G\setminus S}$, and furthermore $\mathcal{X}_{G\setminus(S\cup\{e\})} = \mathcal{X}^{\bar{e}}_{G\setminus S} \cup \mathcal{X}^{\emptyset}_{G\setminus S}$.*

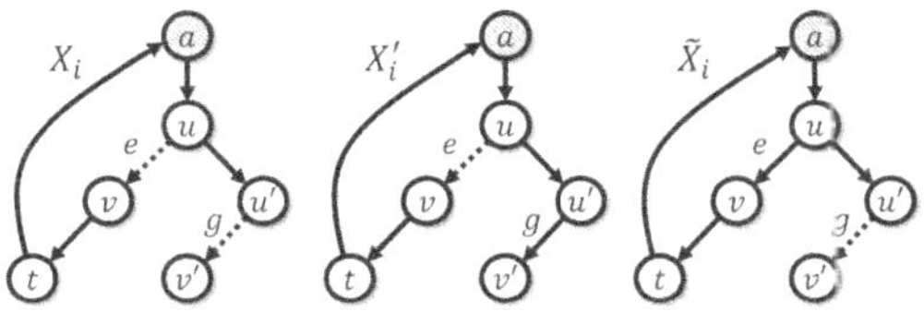

Figure 2: A dashed line means the edge has been deleted.

3.3 Across Space Mapping

Our third result further partitions $\mathcal{X}^{\emptyset}_{G\setminus S}$ into a collection of sets $\{\Phi_i\}$, and establishes a one-to-one mapping between Φ_i and element X_i in the space $\mathcal{X}^{\emptyset}_{G\setminus(S\cup\{g\})}$, where $g = (u', v')$ is an edge in $E \setminus S$ with $v' \neq v$.

PROPOSITION 3. *Let $t = |\mathcal{X}^{\emptyset}_{G\setminus(S\cup\{g\})}|$, then $\mathcal{X}^{\emptyset}_{G\setminus S}$ can be partitioned into t sets $\{\Phi_i\}_{i=1}^t$ such that, for every Φ_i, there exists a corresponding $X_i \in \mathcal{X}^{\emptyset}_{G\setminus(S\cup\{g\})}$, and vice versa.*

3.4 Across Space Probability Mapping

Our fourth result relates the probability of the partition $\Phi_i \subseteq \mathcal{X}^{\emptyset}_{G\setminus S}$ to the probability of the corresponding live-edge graph $X_i \in \mathcal{X}^{\emptyset}_{G\setminus(S\cup\{g\})}$. This result is a sequel to the across space mapping property in the last section. Essentially, we show that the sum of the probabilities of the elements in Φ_i is equal to the probability of X_i.

PROPOSITION 4. *For every $\Phi_i \subseteq \mathcal{X}^{\emptyset}_{G\setminus S}$ and its associated $X_i \in \mathcal{X}^{\emptyset}_{G\setminus(S\cup\{g\})}$, $\Pr[X_i|G\setminus(S\cup\{g\})] = \sum_{H\in\Phi_i}\Pr[H|G\setminus S]$.*

4. NETWORK OPTIMIZATION

In this section, we will prove a set of results for the LT model, namely that the objective functions are *supermodular* in both the edge deletion and the edge addition problems. These results will form the basis for our algorithm design.

A set function $f : 2^E \mapsto \mathbb{R}$ defined over the power set 2^E of a set E is called *supermodular* iff $\forall S \subseteq T \subset E, \forall e \in E\setminus T$

$$f(S\cup\{e\}) - f(S) \leq f(T\cup\{e\}) - f(T). \quad (4)$$

Intuitively, for a monotone increasing supermodular function f, the marginal gain of adding a new element e to a set T is greater than the gain of adding e to any subset S of T. This property is referred to as the *increasing differences* property, as opposed to *diminishing returns* in the case of a submodular function. If f is a monotone decreasing function (as will be the case when we consider deleting edges or nodes), then the marginal loss in adding e to T would be smaller than that of adding e to S.

We define the *susceptibility* of an influence graph G to a set of potential sources A as $\sum_{a\in A}\sigma(a, G)$, which is the sum of the influence function for each node a. Intuitively, one can think of each node $a \in A$ as having equal probability of being the source, and the susceptibility of G as the expected value of the influence function with respect to the randomness of picking an a from A. Our definition of susceptibility can also be generalized to the case where each node a has a different probability of being the source. In this case, all our subsequent theorems would still hold. Furthermore, we assume that the size of the source set is only poly-logarithmic in the total number of nodes in the network, *i.e.*, $|A| \ll |V|$.

4.1 Edge Deletion Problem

In this problem, given an influence graph $G = (V, E, w)$ and a set of sources A, we want to delete a set of edges S^* of size k from G such that the susceptibility of the resulting influence graph is minimized. That is

$$S^* := \operatorname*{argmin}_{S\subseteq E:|S|=k} \sum_{a\in A}\sigma(a, G\setminus S), \quad (5)$$

where the objective function is a set function over the edges S to be deleted. We will show that each $\sigma(a, G\setminus S)$ is a monotonically decreasing and supermodular function of S, and hence their positive sum, $\sum_{a\in A}\sigma(a, G\setminus S)$, also is.

Monotonicity. In this section, we prove that $\sigma(a, G\setminus S)$ is a monotonically decreasing function of S. We will use the within space mapping property in Prop. 1 and the space inclusion property in Prop. 2 to prove the following result:

THEOREM 5. *$\sigma(a, G\setminus S)$ is a monotonically decreasing function of the set of edges S to be deleted.*

PROOF. Given the influence graph $G = (V, E, w)$, we need to show that for any set $S \subseteq E$ and $e = (u, v) \in E\setminus S$:

$$\sigma(a, G\setminus S) - \sigma(a, G\setminus(S\cup\{e\})) \geqslant 0$$

Using the fact that the space $\mathcal{X}_{G\setminus S}$ is partitioned into three sets, $\mathcal{X}^{e}_{G\setminus S}$, $\mathcal{X}^{\bar{e}}_{G\setminus S}$ and $\mathcal{X}^{\emptyset}_{G\setminus S}$, and the space $\mathcal{X}_{G\setminus(S\cup\{e\})}$ is partitioned into two sets $\mathcal{X}^{\bar{e}}_{G\setminus S}$ and $\mathcal{X}^{\emptyset}_{G\setminus S}$ (space inclusion property in Prop. 2), we can write the difference as

$$\sigma(a, G\setminus S) - \sigma(a, G\setminus(S\cup\{e\})) \quad (6)$$

$$= \sum\nolimits_{X\in\mathcal{X}^{e}_{G\setminus S}} \Pr[X|G\setminus S]\cdot r(a, X)$$

$$+ \sum\nolimits_{X\in\mathcal{X}^{\emptyset}_{G\setminus S}} (\Pr[X|G\setminus S] - \Pr[X|G\setminus(S\cup\{e\})])\cdot r(a, X)$$

$$+ \sum\nolimits_{X\in\mathcal{X}^{\bar{e}}_{G\setminus S}} (\Pr[X|G\setminus S] - \Pr[X|G\setminus(S\cup\{e\})])\cdot r(a, X)$$

Recall that $e = (u, v)$. We will simplify the last two summands in the above equation using the following two facts:

- For $X \in \mathcal{X}^{\emptyset}_{G\setminus S}$ based on Eq. (3): $\Pr[X|G\setminus S] - \Pr[X|G\setminus(S\cup\{e\})] = -w(u, v)\prod_{v'\neq v} p(v', X, G\setminus S)$.
- For $X \in \mathcal{X}^{\bar{e}}_{G\setminus S}$, the probability is the same, $p(v, X, G\setminus S) = p(v, X, G\setminus(S\cup\{e\})) = w(\bar{e})$.

Then Eq. (6) simplifies to $\sum_{X\in\mathcal{X}^{e}_{G\setminus S}}\Pr[X|G\setminus S]\cdot r(a, X)$ $+ \sum_{X\in\mathcal{X}^{\emptyset}_{G\setminus S}} -w(u, v)\prod_{v'\neq v} p(v', X, G\setminus S)\cdot r(a, X)$. Since any $\widetilde{X} \in \mathcal{X}^{e}_{G\setminus S}$ has probability $\Pr[\widetilde{X}|G\setminus S] = w(u, v)\cdot \prod_{v'\neq v} p(v', \widetilde{X}, G\setminus S)$, then using Prop. 1 to match $\widetilde{X} \in \mathcal{X}^{e}_{G\setminus S}$ to $X \in \mathcal{X}^{\emptyset}_{G\setminus S}$, we have that Eq. (6) is equal to

$$\sum\nolimits_{X\in\mathcal{X}^{\emptyset}_{G\setminus S}} \Pr[\widetilde{X}|G\setminus S]\cdot\left(r(a, \widetilde{X}) - r(a, X)\right). \quad (7)$$

Since the live-edge graph $\widetilde{X}$ has one more edge than X, clearly $r(a, \widetilde{X}) - r(a, X) \geqslant 0$, which completes the proof. □

Supermodularity. We will use the across space mapping property in Prop. 3 (also Prop. 4) and the probability mapping property in Prop. 1 to prove the following result:

THEOREM 6. *The function $\sigma(a, G\setminus S)$ is a supermodular function of the set of edges S to be deleted.*

PROOF. Let $t = |\mathcal{X}^{\emptyset}_{G\setminus(S\cup\{g\})}|$, then using the across space mapping property in Prop. 3, we can partition $\mathcal{X}^{\emptyset}_{G\setminus S}$ into t sets $\{\Phi_i\}_{i=1}^t$ and rewrite Eq. (7) in the proof of Thm. 5 as:

$$\sum\nolimits_{i=1}^{t}\sum\nolimits_{X\in\Phi_i} \Pr[\widetilde{X}|G\setminus S]\cdot\left(r(a, \widetilde{X}) - r(a, X)\right) \quad (8)$$

Using similar reasoning to that in Eq. (7) in the proof of Thm. 5 for $G\setminus(S\cup\{g\})$, we have

$$\sigma(a, G\setminus(S\cup\{g\})) - \sigma(a, G\setminus(S\cup\{g, e\}) \quad (9)$$

$$= \sum\nolimits_{X\in\mathcal{X}^{\emptyset}_{G\setminus(S\cup\{g\})}} \Pr[\widetilde{X}|G\setminus(S\cup g)]\cdot\left(r(a, \widetilde{X}) - r(a, X)\right)$$

Then we need only compare Eq. (9) and (8) term by term for each $X_i \in \mathcal{X}^{\emptyset}_{G \setminus (S \cup \{g\})}, i = 1, \ldots, t$. Clearly, when $\Phi_i = \{X_i\}$, the terms from the two equations are equal. When $\Phi_i = \{X_i, X_i'\}$, we need to show

$$\Pr[\widetilde{X}_i | G \setminus S] \cdot \Big(r(a, \widetilde{X}_i) - r(a, X_i) \Big)$$
$$+ \Pr[\widetilde{X}_i' | G \setminus S] \cdot \Big(r(a, \widetilde{X}_i') - r(a, X_i') \Big)$$
$$\geqslant \Pr[\widetilde{X}_i | G \setminus (S \cup \{g\})] \cdot \Big(r(a, \widetilde{X}_i) - r(a, X_i) \Big) \quad (10)$$

Based on the probability mapping property in Prop. 4, we have $\Pr[\widetilde{X}_i | G \setminus (S \cup \{g\})] = \Pr[\widetilde{X}_i | G \setminus S] + \Pr[\widetilde{X}_i' | G \setminus S]$. Then to establish Eq. (10), it suffices to show that

$$r(a, \widetilde{X}_i') - r(a, X_i') \geqslant r(a, \widetilde{X}_i) - r(a, X_i).$$

Recall that $X_i' = (V, E_{X_i} \cup \{g\})$. Since live-edge graphs are constructed in a way that each node has at most one incoming edge, each reachable node y has a unique path from the source node a to node y. Furthermore: (1) a reachability path in $\widetilde{X}_i$ is clearly also present in $\widetilde{X}_i'$, hence if removing edge $e = (u, v)$ from $\widetilde{X}_i$ results in unreachability of some nodes in X_i then those same nodes become unreachable when removing e from $\widetilde{X}_i'$; (2) removing edge e from $\widetilde{X}_i'$ may disconnect some additional nodes whose paths from the source a include edge g. Therefore the reduction in reachable nodes when removing edge e from $\widetilde{X}_i'$ is the same or larger than the reduction when removing edge e from $\widetilde{X}_i$. This completes the proof. □

4.2 Edge Addition Problem

In this section, given a *partial* influence graph $G'(V, E', w)$ and a larger *potential* influence graph $G = (V, E, w)$ with $E' \subseteq E$, we want to add to G' a set of edges S^* of size k from $E \setminus E'$ such that the resulting susceptibility is maximized:

$$S^* := \underset{S' \subseteq E \setminus E' : |S'| = k}{\operatorname{argmax}} \sum_{a \in A} \sigma(a, G' \cup S'), \quad (11)$$

where the objective function is a set function over the edges S' to be added. We will show that each $\sigma(a, G' \cup S')$ is monotone and supermodular, and hence their positive combination, $\sigma(A, G' \cup S')$, is also monotone and supermodular.

THEOREM 7. *The function $\sigma(a, G' \cup S')$ is a monotone and supermodular function of the set of S' edges to be added.*

PROOF. We will prove the results by relating the objective function to that in the edge deletion problem and then apply the results from the edge deletion problem. More specifically, let $S' \subseteq T'$ and $e \in E \setminus T'$. If we define $S = E \setminus (S' \cup E' \cup \{e\})$, then

$$\sigma(a, G' \cup (S' \cup \{e\})) = \sigma(a, G \setminus S)$$
$$\sigma(a, G' \cup S') = \sigma(a, G \setminus (S \cup \{e\})),$$

since $G' \cup (S' \cup \{e\}) = G \setminus S$ and $G' \cup S' = G \setminus (S \cup \{e\})$. Similarly, if we define $T = E \setminus (T' \cup E' \cup \{e\})$, then

$$\sigma(a, G' \cup (T' \cup \{e\})) = \sigma(a, G \setminus T)$$
$$\sigma(a, G' \cup T') = \sigma(a, G \setminus (T \cup \{e\})).$$

Note that $S' \subseteq T'$ implies that $T \subseteq S$. Then we apply the supermodularity of $\sigma(a, G \setminus S)$ as a function of the edges S to be deleted in Thm. 6, and obtain

$$\sigma(a, G' \cup (S' \cup \{e\})) - \sigma(a, G' \cup S')$$
$$\leqslant \sigma(a, G' \cup (T' \cup \{e\})) - \sigma(a, G' \cup T'),$$

which completes the proof. □

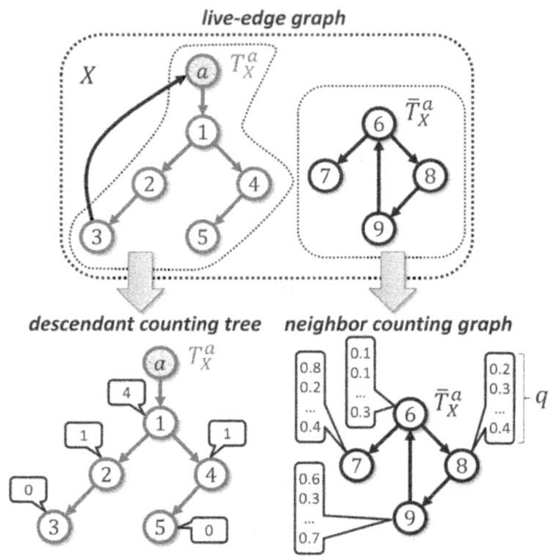

Figure 3: Illustration of a live-edge graph X, the tree T^a_X induced by BFS rooted at a, the part of the graph $\overline{T}^a_X$ which is the complement to T^a_X. For the edge deletion problem, we build a descendant counting tree data structure for each live-edge tree T^a_X where each node stores its number of descendants. For the edge addition problem, we build a neighbor-counting graph data structure for each complement $\overline{T}^a_X$, where each node stores a list of q least labels $\{l_i^*(v)\}$ obtained over q random labelings.

5. SCALABLE ALGORITHMS

Given that the edge deletion and addition problems are supermodular, we can, in principle, solve the network topology optimization problems using the state-of-the-art supermodular optimization algorithms. However, there remain great challenges in scaling these algorithms up to diffusion networks with millions of nodes. First, supermodular optimization requires evaluating the influence function many times. The problem of computing the influence function $\sigma(a, G)$ exactly has been shown to be #P-Hard [4]. Thus there is a need to design methods to approximately compute the influence function in near-linear time. To tackle this problem, we will estimate $\sigma(a, G)$ using *empirical averaging* (EA) over a *fixed* set of live-edge graphs, pre-sampled using the LT live-edge graph generation process described in section 2.2. That is

$$\sigma(a, G) \approx \widehat{\sigma}(a, G) := \frac{1}{|\mathcal{L}|} \cdot \sum_{X_i \in \mathcal{L}} r(a, T^a_{X_i}) \quad (12)$$

where $\mathcal{L} = \{X_i\}_{1 \leq i \leq l}$ is the set of sampled *live-edge graphs* from G. Recall $T^a_{X_i}$ is the tree rooted at a induced from X_i.

Second, typically, the marginal change of the influence function for each candidate edge needs to be computed. This imposes the additional requirement that each marginal change computation has to be nearly constant-time to handle the large number of candidate edges. To address these challenges, we will design an efficient descendant-counting tree data structure for the edge deletion problem, and use it as part of a greedy algorithm to minimize the supermodular objective function. For the edge addition problem, we will employ an efficient randomized neighbor-counting graph data structure, and use it inside a modular approximation algorithm to maximize the supermodular objective function. Fig. 3 illustrates the data structures. In both cases, time and space complexities are linear in the network size.

5.1 Edge Deletion

It is easy to see that the empirical average influence function $\widehat{\sigma}(a, G \setminus S)$ under edge deletion is also supermodular and monotonically decreasing. To solve the problem at hand, we adopt a simple greedy approach: at each iteration, given the current solution S_t, add to the solution the element e with the largest *marginal loss* $\Delta(e|S_t)$ defined using Eq. (12)

$$\frac{1}{\mathcal{L}}\sum_{a\in A}\sum_{X_i\in\mathcal{L}} r(a, T^a_{X_i}\setminus S_t) - r(a, T^a_{X_i}\setminus(S_t\cup\{e\})) \qquad (13)$$

where $T^a_{X_i}\setminus S_t$ means deleting edges S_t from tree $T^a_{X_i}$. Based on this expansion, we notice that the edge with largest marginal loss is the edge whose deletion results in the largest decrease in the average number of descendants over all source nodes and the set of induced live-edge trees T^a_X. Note that we use the terminology "marginal loss" rather than "marginal gain" because our objective function is monotone *decreasing*, hence $\Delta(e|S_t)$ measures the marginal loss resulting from removing e after edges S_t have been removed.

Naïvely applying the greedy algorithm is computationally intensive and will not scale to networks with millions of nodes. Basically, at iteration t, for every edge $e\in E\setminus S_t$ and every T^a_X, we need to compute $\Delta(e|S_t)$ by performing a Breadth-First-Search (BFS) traversal from the source a, and count the number of nodes reachable in $T^a_{X_i}\setminus S_t$ and $T^a_{X_i}\setminus(S_t\cup\{e\})$. It is easy to see that such an approach will lead to an $O(|V|^2+|V||E|)$ complexity algorithm: BFS is $O(|V|+|E|)$ and we need to check $O(|E|)$ edges in $E\setminus S_t$. Such quadratic dependence on the network size motivates us to design a more efficient solution.

Scaling Up. Can we avoid the many BFS traversals? To answer this question, we first make the following observation

OBSERVATION 1. *Given an edge $e=(u,v)$ to be deleted where v is reachable from the source a, the marginal loss $\Delta(e|S_t)$ can be computed as*

$$r(a,T^a_X\setminus S_t) - r(a,T^a_X\setminus(S_t\cup\{e\})) = r(v,T^a_X\setminus S_t)+1 \quad (14)$$

This observation implies that, if we can compute $r(v,T^a_X)$ for all $v\in V$ in the original live-edge tree T^a_X, we can then compute the marginal gain of each edge e efficiently.

Can we compute the number of descendant, $r(v,T^a_X)$, efficiently, for *all* $v\in V$? Fortunately, since we are dealing with trees of at most $|V|$ edges each, this can be done in time $O(|V|)$ using a single BFS traversal. More specifically, after initializing $r(v,T^a_X)=0$, $\forall v\in V$,

1. Perform a BFS starting from the source a of T^a_X, adding each traversed edge e to a stack H; at the end of the BFS, the top of the queue is the last edge traversed.
2. While stack H is not empty, pop edge $e=(u,v)$ and increment $r(u,T^a_X)$ by $r(v,T^a_X)+1$.

The correctness of the above procedure is easy to verify: the number of descendants of a node is equal to the sum of the number of descendants of its children, plus the number of children it has, which is exactly what we are computing.

Suppose we have already maintained the descendant counts $r(v,T^a_X\setminus S_t)$ for all node $v\in V$. Then after deleting edge $e=(u,v)$, there are two types of nodes for which need to update the descendant counts: the ancestors u' of node v, and the nodes that have become unreachable. For the former, we update their descendant counts by subtracting out the number of descendants of node v plus 1. Similar to Eq. (14), $r(u',T^a_X\setminus(S_t\cup\{e\})) = r(u',T^a_X\setminus S_t) - r(v,T^a_X\setminus S_t)-1$. For the latter, we simply set their descendant counts to zero, *i.e.*, $r(u',T^a_X\setminus(S_t\cup\{e\}))=0$. Last, the marginal loss of each edge can also be updated according to Eq. (14).

Overall Algorithm: GREEDYCUTTING is summarized in Algorithm 1. It first samples live-edge graphs and obtains the corresponding live-edge trees for the input sources A. Lines 4–12 compute the initial descendant counts variables $r(u,T^a_X)$ for each node u and each T^a_X, and the edge marginal loss variables $\Delta(e)$ for all edges in E. For each iteration, line 15 adds to the solution set the edge with largest marginal loss, and lines 16–27 locally update the descendant count variables for nodes, and marginal loss variables for edges. Finally, the solution set S^* is returned.

If we assume the number of source nodes to be poly-logarithmic in $|V|$, then Algorithm 1 has computational complexity $O(k|\mathcal{L}||V|)$, which is linear (up to poly-logarithmic factors) in the size of the network. As for space complexity, our main data structures store the node descendant counts for each induced live-edge tree on one hand, and the marginal losses of the edges on the other, requiring space of complexity $O(|E|+|V||\mathcal{L}|)$, linear in the network size.

LEMMA 8. *Let $S^*\in\operatorname{argmin}_{S\subseteq E:|S|=k}\sum_{a\in A}\sigma(a,G\setminus S)$, and $h(S)=\sum_{a\in A}\sigma(a,G)-\sigma(a,G\setminus S)$, the reduction in influence when S is deleted from E. Let α be the approximation factor for influence estimation by EA. The solution $\widehat{S}$ returned by* GREEDYCUTTING *satisfies*

$$h(\widehat{S})\geqslant(1-1/e-\alpha)h(S^*)$$

PROOF. Straightforward based on [18] □

Algorithm 1: GREEDYCUTTING

Input: Influence Graph $G(V,E,w)$, Sources A, k
Output: Edges S^*

1 Sample a set of live-edge graphs $\mathcal{L}=\{X\}$ from G
2 Obtain the set of induced live-edge trees $\{T^a_X\}$ from $\mathcal{L}$
3 Initialize $\Delta(e)=0$ for all $e\in E$, $r(u,T^a_X)=0$ for all $u\in V$ and T^a_X
4 **for** *each* T^a_X **do**
5   Initialize queue Q, stack H, $Q.enqueue(a)$, $visited=\{a\}$
6   **while** Q *is not empty* **do**
7     $s=Q.dequeue()$
8   **for** $u\in V$ *and* (s,u) *is an edge in* T^a_X **do**
9   **if** $u\notin visited$ **then**
10         $visited=visited\cup\{u\}$, $Q.enqueue(u)$, $H.push((s,u))$
11   **while** H *is not empty* **do**
12     $(u,v)=H.pop()$, $r(u,T^a_X)\mathrel{+}=r(v,T^a_X)-1$, $\Delta((u,v))\mathrel{+}=r(v,T^a_X)+1$
13 $S^*=\emptyset$
14 **for** t=*1 to* k **do**
15   $e_t=(u_t,v_t)=\operatorname{argmax}_{e\in E\setminus S^*}\Delta(e)$, $S^*=S^*\cup\{e_t\}$
16   **for** *each* T^a_X **do**
17   **if** e_t *is an edge in* T^a_X **then**
18       $s=u_t$
19   **while** s *is not the source* a **do**
20         $r(s,T^a_X)\mathrel{-}=r(v_t,T^a_X)+1$, $\Delta((parent(s),s))\mathrel{-}=r(v_t,T^a_X)-1$, $s=parent(s)$
21   Initialize queue Q, $Q.enqueue(u_t)$, $visited=\{u_t\}$
22   **while** Q *is not empty* **do**
23         $s=Q.dequeue()$
24   **for** $u\in V$ *and* (s,u) *is an edge in* T^a_X **do**
25   **if** $u\notin visited$ **then**
26             $visited=visited\cup\{u\}$, $Q.enqueue(u)$, $\Delta((s,u))\mathrel{-}=r(u,T^a_X)+1$, $r(s,T^a_X)=0, r(u,T^a_X)=0$
27 **return** S^*

5.2 Edge Addition

We now turn to our algorithmic framework for solving the problem of adding edges. Recently, Iyer et al. [11] proposed a simple approach for constrained submodular minimization with approximation guarantees, which we will adapt for our (analog) supermodular maximization problem. Recall that given a *partial* influence graph $G'(V, E', w)$ and a larger *potential* influence graph $G = (V, E, w)$ with $E' \subseteq E$, we want to add to G' a set of edges S^* of size k from $E \setminus E'$ such that the resulting susceptibility is maximized (Eq. (11)). The algorithm constructs a *modular lower bound* (MLB) of the objective function, and then adds edges that maximize this lower bound, instead of the original objective. That is,

$$\frac{1}{|\mathcal{L}|}\sum_{a\in A}\sum_{X_i\in\mathcal{L}} r(a, T^a_{X_i}\cup S) \geqslant \frac{1}{|\mathcal{L}|}\sum_{a\in A}\sum_{X_i\in\mathcal{L}}\sum_{e\in S} r(a, T^a_{X_i}\cup\{e\}),$$

where $\mathcal{L} = \{X_i\}_{1\leq i\leq l}$ is the set of sampled *live-edge graphs* from G', and $T^a_{X_i}$ is the tree rooted at a induced from X_i. Then, $T^a_{X_i} \cup S$ refers to the live-edge tree resulting from adding new edges S to $T^a_{X_i}$. Note that the resulting tree may allow the source a to reach some nodes originally not reachable in $T^a_{X_i}$.

The MLB approach has several nice properties. First, the modular lower bound function is simple, essentially requiring us to compute the reachability score $r(a, T^a_{X_i} \cup \{e\})$ for each candidate edge to be added. Second, maximizing the MLB for a budget k reduces to simply finding the top k edges which lead to the largest function value

$$\sum_{a\in A}\widehat{\sigma}(a, G'\cup\{e\}) = \frac{1}{|\mathcal{L}|}\sum_{a\in A}\sum_{X_i\in\mathcal{L}} r(a, T^a_{X_i}\cup\{e\}). \quad (15)$$

However, naïvely applying the MLB algorithm is computationally intensive and can not be scaled up to networks with millions of nodes. Basically, for every candidate edge e to be added and for every T^a_X, we need to compute the reachability $r(a, T^a_{X_i} \cup \{e\})$ by performing a BFS traversal from the source a, and count the number of nodes reachable in $T^a_{X_i} \cup \{e\}$. It is easy to see that such an approach will lead to an $O(|V||E|)$ complexity algorithm: BFS is $O(|V|)$ (since trees T^a_X have at most $|V|$ edges), and we need to check $O(|E|)$ edges in $E \setminus E'$. Again, we are motivated to design a more efficient solution.

Scaling Up. Can we avoid the many BFS traversals? To answer this question, we first make the following observation

OBSERVATION 2. *Given an edge $e = (u, v)$ to be added, where node v is originally not reachable from the source a, but becomes reachable with the addition of e, the reachability of a can be updated as*

$$r(a, T^a_X\cup\{e\}) = r(a, T^a_X) + w(e)\cdot(r(v, \overline{T}^a_X) + 1) \quad (16)$$

where $\overline{T}^a_X$ is the complement of T^a_X containing those nodes and edges not reachable from a.

We note that the term $r(v, \overline{T}^a_X) + 1$ is multiplied by the weight $w(e)$ of edge e to account for the *probability* of that edge being actually picked by node v in the live-edge generation process of the new influence graph $G' \cup \{e\}$. Furthermore, note that $\overline{T}^a_X$ may contain cycles.

Can we compute the number of reachable nodes, $r(v, \overline{T}^a_X)$, efficiently, for all v in $\overline{T}^a_X$? Fortunately, this problem has been extensively studied in the theoretical computer science literature as the neighborhood size-estimation problem [5], and was recently applied in the context of influence estimation for a continuous-time diffusion model [7]. We will adapt a linear-time algorithm by Cohen [5] for our problem.

We apply the algorithm to $\overline{T}^a_X$ as follows: first, we assign to each node u a label $l(u)$ drawn from the exponential distribution with parameter (mean) 1. Then, we exploit the fact that the minimum $l^*(v)$ of the set of exponential random labels $\{l(u)\}$ for nodes u reachable from v will itself be an exponential random variable, with its parameter equal to $r(v, \overline{T}^a_X)$. If we repeat the random labeling q times and obtain q such *least labels* $\{l^*_i(v)\}^q_{i=1}$, then the neighborhood size is estimated as

$$r(v, \overline{T}^a_X) \approx \frac{q-1}{\sum_{i=1}^q l^*_i(v)}. \quad (17)$$

Can we find the least labels efficiently for all nodes v given each random labeling? In fact, this can be done using a modified BFS traversal which requires time only linear in the network size. More specifically, For a given labeling, we start from the node v with the smallest label, and perform a BFS traversal in the reverse direction of the graph edges. For each node u encountered in the BFS, we set $l^*(u) = l(v)$. Once a node has been encountered in a BFS and its least label has been set, it is marked as *visited*, not only for this particular BFS, but across all subsequent BFS runs. After the BFS traversal from node v is complete, we move to the *unvisited* node with the next smallest label, and repeat the procedure iteratively until all nodes have been marked as visited. It is easy to see why this algorithm correctly assigns the appropriate least label $l^*(v)$ to each node v: since we order the BFS runs by minimum labels, and traverse the edges in reversed direction, then once a node u has been visited, we are guaranteed that the $l^*(u)$ we assign to it is the smallest, and any subsequent BFS that can reach u will have a label larger than $l^*(u)$.

Overall Algorithm: MODULARADDING is summarized in Algorithm 2: we first generate the live-edge graphs, induce the live-edge trees, and draw q labels for each node $v \in V$ from the exponential distribution with mean 1 (lines 1-5). Then, for each source node $a \in A$, we iterate over the induced live-edge trees T^a_X, collecting the estimated neighborhood size of each node v in the complement $\overline{T}^a_X$ of each such tree, by applying Cohen's algorithm (lines 7-20). After iterating over the live-edge trees, we compute the final score for each edge $e \in \mathcal{C}$ in the candidate set $\mathcal{C}$ as the sum over v's neighborhood size estimates, weighted by the edge's diffusion probability $w(e)$ (lines 21-22). Finally we sort the scores vector in descending order, and return the top k edges.

We assume the number of sources $|A|$ is poly-logarithmic in $|V|$ and hence ignored in the complexity analysis. Then Algorithm 2 has computational complexity $O(q|\mathcal{L}||V|)$ and space complexity $O(q|V|)$. This is because the Cohen's algorithm has complexity $O(q|V|)$, and is invoked $O(|\mathcal{L}|)$ times. The final sorting of the scores can be done in $O(|E \setminus E'|)$. As for space, we only require data structures of sizes linear in the number of nodes $O(q|V|)$ to hold the least labels.

LEMMA 9. *Let $S^* \in \mathrm{argmax}_{S'\subseteq E\setminus E':|S'|=k}\sum_{a\in A}\sigma(a, G'\cup S')$, and $g(S) = \sum_{a\in A}\sigma(a, G) - \sigma(a, G'\cup S')$, the difference between the influence in the potential graph G and the influence when S is added to E'. Let κ_g be the* curvature *[11] of g, and β be the approximation factor of our two estimation subroutines (1) EA and (2) Cohen's algorithm. The solution $\widehat{S}$ returned by* MODULARADDING *satisfies*

$$g(\widehat{S}) \leqslant \beta/(1-\kappa_g)\cdot g(S^*)$$

PROOF. Straightforward based on Thm. 5.4 in [11]. □

6. EXPERIMENTS AND RESULTS

We now present our experimental setting and results.

6.1 Setting

Synthetic networks. We generate three types of networks using the Kronecker graph model[2] [17], known to

[2]http://snap.stanford.edu/data/

Algorithm 2: MODULARADDING

Input: $G'(V, E', w), k$, Sources A, Candidates $\mathcal{C}$
Output: Edges S^*

```
Sample a set of live-edge graphs L = {X} from G'
Obtain the set of induced live-edge trees {T_X^a} from L
for each v ∈ V do
    for each i = 1, ..., q do
        l_i(v) ~ exp(-x)
for each a ∈ A do
    for each T̄_X^a do
        for each i = 1, ..., q do
            visited = ∅
            for nodes v in T̄_X^a ordered according to argsort({l_i(v)}) do
                if v ∉ visited then
                    visited = visited ∪ {v}
                    Initialize Q, Q.enqueue(v)
                    while Q is not empty do
                        u = Q.dequeue(), l_i^*(u) = l(v)
                        visited = visited ∪ {u}
                        for each parent s of u in T̄_X^a do
                            Q.enqueue(s)
        for each node v in T̄_X^a do
            r(v, T̄_X^a) = (q - 1) / Σ_{i=1}^{q} l_i^*(v)
    for each e = (u, v) ∈ C do
        score(e) += w(e) · Σ_{X_i ∈ L} (r(v, T̄_X^a) + 1)
S* = argsort(score, k, descending)
return S*
```

Table 1: Datasets summary. Numbers outside (inside) bracket are for edge deletion (addition) experiments. Last column is for Kronecker parameter matrices.

Dataset	#Nodes	#Edges	Kronecker
COREPERIPHERY			[.9 .5; .5 .3]
ERDOSRENYI	1M(65K)	2M (131K)	[.5 .5; .5 .5]
HIERARCHICAL			[.9 .1; .1 .9]
HEPPH	35K	420K	
EPINIONS	75K	509K	—
MEMETRACKER	1.8K	5K	

generalize a number of realistic graph models: (1) COREPERIPHERY, (2) ERDOSRENYI and (3) HIERARCHICAL. These three graph models have very different structural properties, allowing us to test for sensitivity to network structure.

Real-world networks. We choose three publicly available real-world datasets[2] that are amenable to diffusion processes and hence suitable for our problems: (1) HEPPH: a whom-cites-whom citation network based on the Arxiv *High-energy Physics* papers over the period 1993-2003; (2) EPINIONS: a who-trusts-whom online social network of the consumer review site Epinions.com; (3) MEMETRACKER: a who-copies-from-whom network of news media sites and blogs. The statistics of the datasets are summarized in Table 1.

Assigning probabilities. Given a network $G(V, E)$, we populate the weight vector representing the probabilities on the edges E according to the LT model, as follows: for a given node $v \in V$, we draw a probability value $\widetilde{w}(u, v)$ for each edge $e = (u, v) \in E$ that is incoming into v, uniformly at random from the interval $[0, 1]$. In addition, we draw from the same interval a probability value $\overline{w}_v$ representing no infection, i.e the probability that v's infected parents fail

Table 2: Parameter values used in the experiments of Fig. 4 (1st row), and Fig. 5 (2nd row): A is the set of sources, $\mathcal{L}_{\texttt{opt}}$ is the set of live-edge graphs used by our algorithm, $\mathcal{L}_{\texttt{eval}}$ is the set of live-edge graphs used for evaluation of all algorithms and heuristics, t refers to the budget of edges deleted for which diffusion stops completely, q is the number of random labelings used in Algo. 2.

	Parameters for Experiments				
Problem	$\lvert A\rvert$	$\lvert\mathcal{L}_{\texttt{opt}}\rvert$	$\lvert\mathcal{L}_{\texttt{eval}}\rvert$	k	q
Edge Deletion	100	1,000	5,000	$[0, t]$	–
Edge Addition				$[0, 2000]$	20

to activate it. Since the probabilities on the edges plus the probability of no infection must sum to 1, we then normalize each probability over the sum of all the probabilities, *i.e.*, we obtain $w(u, v) = \widetilde{w}(u, v)/(\sum_{u \in V} \widetilde{w}(u, v) + \overline{w}_v)$. We apply this method for all datasets except for MEMETRACKER.

For MEMETRACKER, we make use of the median transmission time, also provided as part of the dataset. Let $\widetilde{t}(u, v)$ be the median transmission time between two nodes u and v, then we set $w(u, v) \propto \widetilde{t}(u, v)^{-1}$, rewarding smaller transmission times with higher diffusion probabilities, and vice versa. We assign a probability of $\overline{w}_v = 0.2, \forall v \in V$, and normalize the weights for all nodes v such that $\sum_{u \in V} w(u, v) + \overline{w}_v = 1$.

Competing heuristics. To evaluate the efficacy of the solutions provided by our algorithms, we compare against other heuristic measures that are not based on the dynamics entailed by the LT diffusion model. These heuristic strategies can be described as follows: (1) `Random`: select k edges uniformly at random from the input set of edges, (2) `Weights`: select the k edges with highest diffusion probability (weight) $w(u, v)$, (3) `Betweenness`: select k edges with highest *edge betweenness centrality* [2, 20], (4) `Eigen`: select the k edges that cause the maximum decrease (increase) in the leading eigenvalue of the network when removed from it, or added to it [22], (5) `Degree`: select the k edges whose destination nodes have the highest out-degrees [8].

6.2 Deleting Edges

We carry out each experiment as follows: given an influence graph $G(V, E, w)$, a set of source nodes A chosen uniformly at random from V, and a budget k of edges to delete, we run GREEDYCUTTING and the five heuristics and obtain a set of edges from each. Then, for each algorithm or heuristic, we simulate the LT diffusion process by generating a set of live-edge graphs $\mathcal{L}_{\texttt{eval}}$ based on G, and then deleting the proposed set of edges S^* from all live-edge graphs in $\mathcal{L}_{\texttt{eval}}$. The efficacy of each proposed set of edges is measured by I_k, the average number of infected nodes over $\mathcal{L}_{\texttt{eval}}$. These parameters are summarized in Table 2. The budget k is increased until diffusion is no longer possible, *i.e.*, the source nodes are completely isolated.

Synthetic networks. The results are shown in Fig. 4 (a-c). First, we observe that our algorithm clearly outperforms *all five* other heuristics: for *any* budget k of edges to delete, our algorithm minimizes the graph susceptibility ratio (I_k/I_0) better than any of the heuristics for all three synthetic network types, implying that it produces good solutions *independently* of the structural properties of the input network. On the other hand, the considered heuristics perform arbitrarily good or bad, as we vary the type of synthetic network. At last, we observe that even for $|\mathcal{L}_{opt}| = 1,000$, a quantity much smaller than the typical 10,000 used in the literature, the green and red lines are almost indistinguishable, meaning our solution generalizes well to the larger evaluation set of 5,000 live-edge graphs.

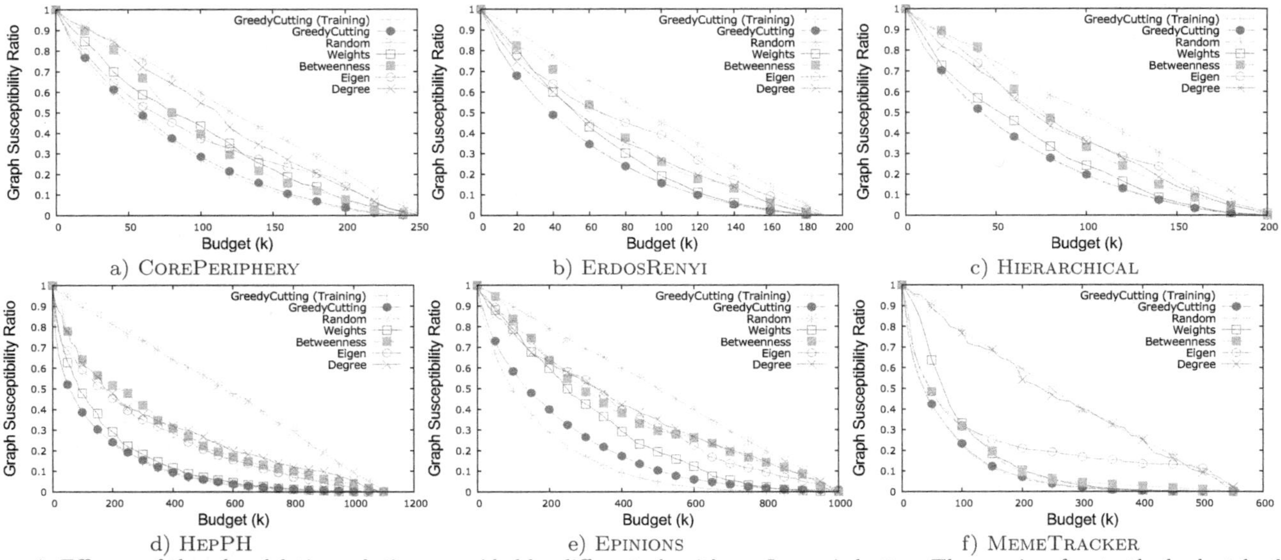

a) COREPERIPHERY b) ERDOSRENYI c) HIERARCHICAL

d) HEPPH e) EPINIONS f) MEMETRACKER

Figure 4: Efficacy of the edge deletion solutions provided by different algorithms. Lower is better. The x-axis refers to the budget k; the y-axis refers to the *graph susceptibility ratio*, defined in the range $[0, 1]$ as: I_k/I_0.

Real-world networks. We observe similar performance for real-world networks (Fig. 4 (d-f)). For instance, for the EPINIONS dataset (Fig. 4(e)), our method has decreased the graph susceptibility to 40% of its original value at $k = 200$, whereas the best performing heuristic at the same k is `Weights` with 60% (here, lower is better).

6.3 Adding Edges

The experimental procedure for evaluating our MODULARADDING algorithm and other heuristics is analogous to that described in 6.2 for edge deletion. We compare our algorithm to all previously described heuristics, for the exception of the `Betweenness` heuristic, as it is not obvious how meaningful it would be to compute this metric for edges that do not initially exist in the network. Results are in Fig. 5.

Synthetic networks. Our algorithm is almost always *twice as effective* as the next best heuristic, be it `Weights` or `Degree`. This efficacy gap is consistent across all three types of networks, confirming yet again the robustness of the solutions we find to varying structural properties of networks.

Real-world networks. Similarly to the synthetic setting, our algorithm significantly outperforms all four heuristics in the real-world setting, for all three datasets. For instance, for the HEPPH dataset in Fig. 5(d), the `Degree` heuristic requires adding 2,000 edges to the set A of 100 sources in order to increase the graph susceptibility by twice its initial value (*i.e.*, at $k = 0$), whereas our algorithm increases the graph susceptibility by the same amount for $k = 200$ edges, a small fraction of 2000. This superior performance implies that our algorithm is more amenable to real-world applications, where the budget is typically very small relative to the number of nodes, possibly representing humans in a social network, blogs on the web, etc.

6.4 Scalability

Scalability is a major concern in the industrial setting. We experimentally verify the scalability of both our edge deletion and addition algorithms. All experiments were executed on a laptop with a 2.7GHz quad-core i7 CPU and 16Gb RAM. The results presented in Fig. 6 measure the runtime of our algorithms on synthetic COREPERIPHERY networks of increasing number of nodes, and fixed average degree of 2.

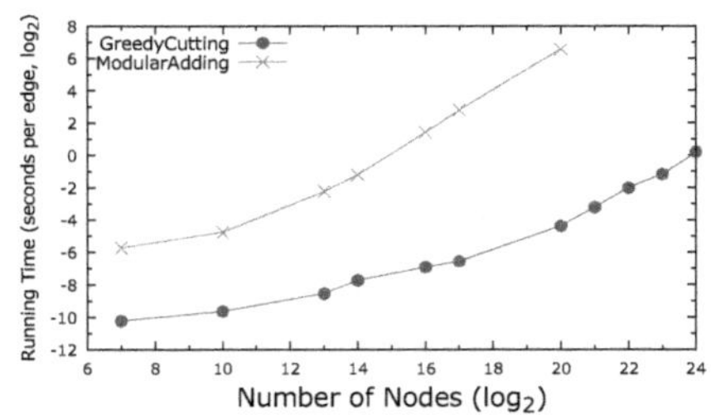

Figure 6: Runtime on synthetic core-periphery networks: for both lines, each point represents the average time in seconds per edge deleted or added. The number of sources is poly-logarithmic in the number of nodes and the number of live-edge graphs used is 100, for both problems. For MODULARADDING, $q = 5$.

We vary the number of nodes, starting at $2^7 = 128$ nodes, and up to $2^{23} = 8,388,608$ nodes (16,777,216 edges). The experimental results show that our algorithms scale linearly in the size of the network. As expected, MODULARADDING, while also having a linear scaling, is more time-consuming than GREEDYCUTTING, due to the repeated linear-time algorithm for building the neighbor-counting graph.

7. ACKNOWLEDGEMENTS

This research was supported in part by NSF/NIH BIGDATA 1R01GM108341-01, NSF IIS1116886, NSF CAREER IIS1350983 and a Raytheon faculty fellowship to L. Song.

References

[1] I. Bogunovic. Robust protection of networks against cascading phenomena. Master's thesis, ETHZ, 2012.

[2] U. Brandes. A faster algorithm for betweenness centrality. *Journal of Mathematical Sociology*, 25(2), 2001.

[3] W. Chen, L. V. Lakshmanan, and C. Castillo. Information and influence propagation in social networks. *Synthesis Lectures on Data Management*, 2013.

[4] W. Chen, Y. Yuan, and L. Zhang. Scalable influence maximization in social networks under the linear threshold model. In *IEEE ICDM*, pages 88–97, 2010.

[5] E. Cohen. Size-estimation framework with applications to transitive closure and reachability. *Journal of Computer and System Sciences*, 55(3):441–453, 1997.

[6] P. Domingos and M. Richardson. Mining the network value of customers. In *ACM KDD*, pages 57–66, 2001.

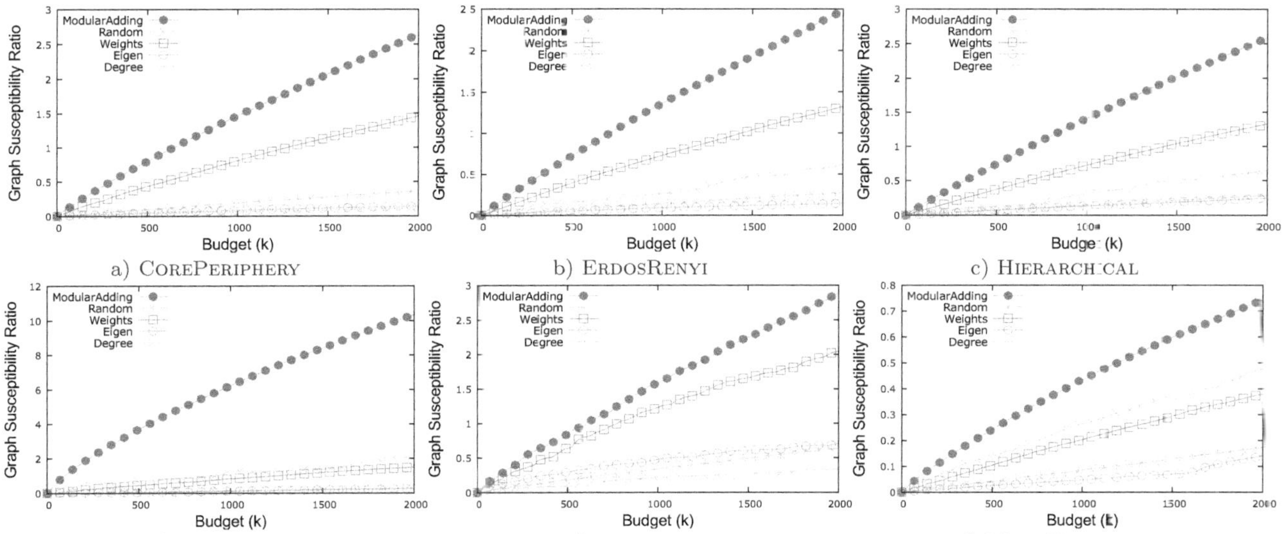

a) COREPERIPHERY b) ERDOSRENYI c) HIERARCHICAL

d) HEPPH e) EPINIONS f) MEMETRACKER

Figure 5: Efficacy of the edge addtion solutions provided by different algorithms. Higher is better. The x-axis refers to the budget of edges to add; the y-axis refers to the *graph susceptibility ratio*, defined in the range $[0, n]$ as: $(I_k - I_0)/I_0$.

[7] N. Du, L. Song, H. Zha, and M. Gomez Rodriguez. Scalable influence estimation in continuous time diffusion networks. In *NIPS*, 2013.

[8] C. Gao, J. Liu, and N. Zhong. Network immunization and virus propagation in email networks: experimental evaluation and analysis. *KAIS*, 27(2):253–279, 2011.

[9] X. He, G. Song, W. Chen, and Q. Jiang. Influence blocking maximization in social networks under the competitive linear threshold model. In *SDM*, 2012.

[10] H. W. Hethcote. The mathematics of infectious diseases. *SIAM review*, 42(4):599–653, 2000.

[11] R. Iyer, S. Jegelka, and J. Bilmes. Fast semidifferential-based submodular function optimization. In *ICML*, 2013.

[12] D. Kempe, J. Kleinberg, and É. Tardos. Maximizing the spread of influence through a social network. In *ACM KDD*, pages 137–146. ACM, 2003.

[13] M. Kimura, K. Saito, and H. Motoda. Solving the contamination minimization problem on networks for the linear threshold model. In *PRICAI*. 2008.

[14] M. Kimura, K. Saito, and H. Motoda. Blocking links to minimize contamination spread in a social network. *ACM TKDD*, 3(2):9, 2009.

[15] C. J. Kuhlman, G. Tuli, S. Swarup, M. V. Marathe, and S. Ravi. Blocking simple and complex contagion by edge removal. In *IEEE ICDM*, 2013.

[16] J. Leskovec, L. Backstrom, and J. Kleinberg. Meme-tracking and the dynamics of the news cycle. In *ACM KDD*, pages 497–506. ACM, 2009.

[17] J. Leskovec, D. Chakrabarti, J. Kleinberg, C. Faloutsos, and Z. Ghahramani. Kronecker graphs: An approach to modeling networks. 11(Feb):985–1042, 2010.

[18] G. Nemhauser, L. Wolsey, and M. Fisher. An analysis of the approximations for maximizing submodular set functions. *Mathematical Programming*, 14, 1978

[19] S. Peng, S. Yu, and A. Yang. Smartphone malware and its propagation modeling: A survey. *IEEE Communications Surveys Tutorials*, PP(99):1–17, 2013.

[20] C. M. Schneider, T. Mihaljev, S. Havlin, and H. J. Herrmann. Suppressing epidemics with a limited amount of immunization units. *Physical Review E*, 84(6), 2011.

[21] D. Sheldon, B. Dilkina, A. N. Elmachtoub, R. Finseth, et al. Maximizing the spread of cascades using network design. *UAI*, 2010.

[22] H. Tong, B. A. Prakash, T. Eliassi-Rad, M. Faloutsos, and C. Faloutsos. Gelling, and melting, large graphs by edge manipulation. In *ACM CIKM*, 2012.

APPENDIX

PROOF OF PROP. 1. Since edge $e \notin S$, we can always find two live-edge graphs within $\mathcal{X}_{G\setminus S}$ which differ by the edge e. The first live-edge graph X does not contain e, and the second live-edge graph X' contains the additional edge e. □

PROOF OF PROP. 2. Since $S \subset S \cup \{e\}$, the influence graph $G\setminus(S\cup\{e\})$ has one less edge than $G\setminus S$, while other parameters of the two graphs remain the same. This implies that any live-edge graph X generated from the former influence graph can always be generated from the latter one, which establishes the first part of the proposition. Furthermore, $\mathcal{X}_{G\setminus(S\cup\{e\})}$ contains those live-edge graphs without edge e, which is essentially the union of $\mathcal{X}^{\bar{e}}_{G\setminus S}$ and $\mathcal{X}^{\emptyset}_{G\setminus S}$ by definition. □

PROOF OF PROP. 3. We will explicitly construct a set $\Phi_i \subseteq \mathcal{X}^{\emptyset}_{G\setminus S}$ for each element $X_i \in \mathcal{X}^{\emptyset}_{G\setminus(S\cup\{g\})}$. There are two types of elements in $\mathcal{X}^{\emptyset}_{G\setminus(S\cup\{g\})}$, and we will construct Φ_i respectively as follows: (1) If node v' has an incoming edge in X_i, then $\Phi_i = \{X_i\}$. Φ_i is contained in $\mathcal{X}^{\emptyset}_{G\setminus S}$ since $\mathcal{X}^{\emptyset}_{G\setminus(S\cup\{g\})} \subseteq \mathcal{X}^{\emptyset}_{G\setminus S}$ using a similar argument as in the space inclusion property. (2) Otherwise, $\Phi_i = \{X_i, X_i'\}$, where $X_i' = (V, E_{X_i} \cup \{g\})$ is obtained by extending X_i with edge g. Φ_i is also contained in $\mathcal{X}^{\emptyset}_{G\setminus S}$ since $g \notin S$ and hence X_i' is a valid live-edge graph in $\mathcal{X}^{\emptyset}_{G\setminus S}$. It is easy to see that the Φ_is are pairwise disjoint and form a partition of the space $\mathcal{X}^{\emptyset}_{G\setminus S}$. □

PROOF OF PROP. 4. We will consider two cases. When $\Phi_i = \{X_i\}$ is a singleton, $\Pr[X_i|G\setminus(S\cup\{g\})] = \Pr[X_i|G\setminus S]$ and hence the statement holds true trivially. When $\Phi_i = \{X_i, X_i'\}$, the difference $\Pr[X_i|G\setminus(S\cup\{g\})] - \sum_{H\in\Phi_i}\Pr[H|G\setminus S]$ is proportional to $p(v', X_i, G\setminus(S\cup\{g\})) - p(v', X_i, G\setminus S) - p(v', X_i', G\setminus S)$, where we only need to consider the contribution of the terminal node v' of edge $g = (u', v')$, since all other nodes contribute the same amount to the probability of each live-edge graph involved. Based on Eq. (3), the difference between the first two terms, $w(u', v')$, cancels out with the third term, $w(u', v')$, which shows that the difference $\Pr[X_i|G\setminus(S\cup\{g\})] - \sum_{H\in\Phi_i}\Pr[H|G\setminus S]$ is zero, and completes the proof. □

Probabilistic Latent Network Visualization: Inferring and Embedding Diffusion Networks

Takeshi Kurashima*, Tomoharu Iwata+, Noriko Takaya* and Hiroshi Sawada*
*NTT Service Evolution Labs., NTT Corporation
+NTT Communication Science Labs., NTT Corporation
*1-1 Hikari-no-oka, Yokosuka-Shi, Kanagawa, 239-0847 Japan
+2-4 Hikaridai, Seika-Cho, Soraku-gun, Kyoto, 619-0237 Japan
*+{kurashima.takeshi,iwata.tomoharu,takaya.noriko,sawada.hiroshi}@lab.ntt.co.jp

ABSTRACT

The diffusion of information, rumors, and diseases are assumed to be probabilistic processes over some network structure. An event starts at one node of the network, and then spreads to the edges of the network. In most cases, the underlying network structure that generates the diffusion process is unobserved, and we only observe the times at which each node is altered/influenced by the process. This paper proposes a probabilistic model for inferring the diffusion network, which we call *Probabilistic Latent Network Visualization* (PLNV); it is based on cascade data, a record of observed times of node influence. An important characteristic of our approach is to infer the network by embedding it into a low-dimensional visualization space. We assume that each node in the network has latent coordinates in the visualization space, and diffusion is more likely to occur between nodes that are placed close together. Our model uses maximum a posteriori estimation to learn the latent coordinates of nodes that best explain the observed cascade data. The latent coordinates of nodes in the visualization space can 1) enable the system to suggest network layouts most suitable for browsing, and 2) lead to high accuracy in inferring the underlying network when analyzing the diffusion process of new or rare information, rumors, and disease.

Categories and Subject Descriptors

H.2.8 [**Database Management**]: Database Applications—*Data Mining*; I.5.1 [**Pattern Recognition**]: Models

Keywords

Diffusion network; network visualization; survival analysis

1. INTRODUCTION

In a broad range of domains such as viral marketing, information propagation in social network, and disease infection, there has been a great interest in analyzing the diffusion process with respect to the underlying network or, equivalently, a graph. Diffusion starts at one node and then spreads from node to node to the edge of the network. Understanding the mechanism that causes the diffusion process helps to optimize advertising strategies, predict meme propagation, or counter infection. Some existing methods assume that the network structure (i.e. a set of connectivities) is predefined [5, 6]. However, in most cases, the exact path of the diffusion of information, influence, and disease over networks is unknown, and we only observe when a node mentions information, makes a decision, or becomes infected. Inferring and understanding the underlying network that causes the diffusion process is quite challenging and remains an interesting subject for study [14, 16, 7, 21, 3, 4].

We propose a probabilistic model that processes observed cascade data to infer diffusion networks, which we call *Probabilistic Latent Network Visualization* (PLNV). A cascade is, for one process, a record of when nodes are altered/influenced by the process. We have two criteria for designing a method that can estimate diffusion networks. First, suggesting a network that is embedded into a low-dimensional visualization space is important. In general, visualization techniques are very useful for understanding high-dimensional and complex data such as networks since they enable us to browse intuitively through huge numbers of nodes. The desired property of the diffusion network layout in terms of the visualization space is as follows; each node attempts to place its influential nodes relatively closer than non-influential ones in the visualization space, we call this the *influence preservation principle*. For example, a marketer, who wants to trigger a chain reaction of people into ordering goods for sale, can, from the initial sight of the layout, identify communities wherein the nodes strongly influence each other. A visualization space that satisfies this principle also serves as a vehicle for suggesting the growth process of the cascade since it seems that diffusion spreads over the visualization space gradually. Second, inferring the underlying diffusion network accurately is important, particularly when many cascades remain hidden. When we analyze the diffusion process of new information, disease, and rumors, only a little amount of cascade data might be available. Understanding the underlying diffusion network soon after its occurrence leads to a quick response to a crisis such as the spread of false rumors or disease.

With these criteria in mind, we develop a method for inferring diffusion networks. An important feature of our approach is to infer the network by embedding it into a low-dimensional visualization space. We assume that each node in the network has latent coordinates in the visualization space, and diffusion is more likely to occur between nodes that are placed close together. Our model learns the latent coordinates of nodes that best explain the observed cascade data. By incorporating this assumption into the generative process of diffusion, our model can suggest the diffusion network layout in the visualization space that fulfills the influence preserva-

KDD'14, August 24–27, 2014, New York, NY, USA.
Copyright 2014 ACM 978-1-4503-2956-9/14/08 ...$15.00.
http://dx.doi.org/10.1145/2623330.2623646.

tion principle. Moreover, our proposed model can recognize latent influence relationships between nodes even if we have not observed the common events linking the nodes, since the distances between nodes in the low-dimensional visualization space implies the presence of an influence relation.

There has been great interest in processing cascade data to infer underlying networks. Some approaches infer only the network structure [15, 17], while others infer not only the network structure but also the strength of every edge in the network [13, 14, 16, 7, 21, 3, 4]. The strength of each edge, called transmission rate, represents how quickly or likely information is to spread from one node to another. The network structure estimated by existing diffusion models is complex when the network is large. Visualization methods such as Multi-Dimensional Scaling (MDS) [20], Isomap [19], and the spring method [9], can embed high-dimensional networks into low dimensional spaces, and help in the study of the inferred network. Existing visualization methods can employ a set of distances in the inferred diffusion network as input. The separation distance for each node pair is obtained from the transmission rate of the two nodes.

However, the distances between nodes in the network may not be suitable when they are embedded in the visualization space since the distances are estimated in a space different from the visualization space. Furthermore, the objective function maximized by existing visualization methods is not the likelihood of all cascades, but rather that of input distances. Thus it is impossible for existing visualization methods to determine which distance should be preferentially restored in the visualization space based on the likelihood function of all cascades. Moreover, the accumulation of errors in the network inference process cannot be corrected in the embedding process with existing visualization methods since they are modulated, which may result in poor visualization. Our proposal simultaneously infers and visualizes the diffusion network in one probabilistic framework. Therefore, latent coordinates are estimated so as to be optimal in terms of the likelihood of all cascades when nodes are embedded in the low-dimensional visualization space.

Additionally, when analyzing diffusion networks of new information, disease, and rumors, the network inference performance of existing models is likely to be poor since there are few events that can provide clues as to the influence relations. In existing network inference models, the influence relation of each pair of nodes is recognized only after observing common events that link the pair members. The number of parameters (i.e. transmission rates) to be estimated by existing models is the square of the number of nodes. Thus a lot of cascades are required to estimate all parameters. On the other hand, the proposed model has far fewer parameters. Thus it can capture the essential features of the underlying diffusion network even if the number of cascades is small.

We demonstrate the effectiveness of the proposed model on the *MemeTracker* dataset, which records information diffusion among Web sites. We conduct two quantitative experiments. The first quantitatively shows that the network layout yielded by our proposed model satisfies the influence preservation principle. The second experiment compares its network inference performance against that of the existing network inference model, and shows that ours yields better performance when the number of cascades is small. Our qualitative experiments show that the visualization space learned by our model is not only useful for browsing the underlying network layout intuitively, but also serves as a vehicle for suggesting the growth process of the observed diffusion data.

Table 1: Notation

Symbol	Description
n	node (e.g. person, news article, and blog post)
N	number of nodes
c	cascade (event)
$\boldsymbol{C}$	set of cascades
$\boldsymbol{t}^c$	observed infection times of cascade, $c \in \boldsymbol{C}$
T^c	length of the observation window of cascade c
β	scale parameter for the width of the visualization space
D	dimensionality of the visualization space

2. PROBABILISTIC LATENT NETWORK VISUALIZATION

2.1 Preliminaries

Our model is based on survival analysis [10, 11]. By utilizing time information, survival analysis provides a powerful way to model event occurrence such as infection and information diffusion. We first present the basic concept of basing diffusion models on survival analysis.

We start with a set of cascades $\boldsymbol{C} = \{\boldsymbol{t}^1, ..., \boldsymbol{t}^{|\boldsymbol{C}|}\}$. A cascade is represented by N-dimensional vector $\boldsymbol{t}^c = (t_1^c, ..., t_N^c)$, where N is the number of nodes. Cascade $\boldsymbol{t}^c$ is the history of event c within the population during time interval $[0, T^c]$. For example, when we analyze the spread of an infection, a certain infectious disease (say influenza) corresponds to an event, and people are represented by nodes. When we analyze information diffusion in Web space, a news topic of a newly-released mobile phone is an event, and a personal blog site that refers to it can be represented by a node. t_n^c of event c records the time stamp when event c occurs at or to node n, and $t_n^c \in [0, T^c] \cup \{\infty\}$. The symbol ∞ labels nodes that are not reached in a cascade within observation window $[0, T^c]$. The clock is set to 0 at the start of each cascade (i.e. the time stamp of the node where each event happens first is set to 0). The notations used are summarized in Table 1.

The transmission function $f(t_i|t_j)$ is the conditional likelihood of transmission time from node j to node i; it represents the likelihood of an event happening to node i at time t_i given that the same event has already happened to node j at time t_j. If $f(t_i|t_j)$ is the probability density function of time, $F(t_i|t_j) = \int_{t_j}^{t_i} f(t)dt$ and is thus its cumulative distribution function. Given that node j was infected at time t_j, $F(t_i|t_j)$ represents the probability that node i was infected by node j within the period of time t_j to time t_i. Only if $t_j < t_i$ can node j, which was infected at time t_j, infect node i at time t_i.

The *survival function* is defined as the probability that node i is *not* infected by node j before time t_i; it is calculated by

$$S\left(t_i|t_j\right) = 1 - F\left(t_i|t_j\right) = \int_{t_i}^{\infty} f\left(t\right) dt. \tag{1}$$

The survival function is a monotonically decreasing function with $S\left(\Delta_{ji} = 0\right) = 1$ and $S\left(\Delta_{ji} = \infty\right) = 0$, where $\Delta_{ji} = t_i - t_j$ is the time difference between node j and node i.

The *hazard function* is the instantaneous infection rate, the rate at which node i, which has not been infected yet (up to time t_i), will become infected within a small interval after time t_i. It is calculated by

$$h\left(t_i|t_j\right) = \frac{f\left(t_i|t_j\right)}{S\left(t_i|t_j\right)}. \tag{2}$$

Table 2: Model

Model	Transmission function $f(t_i \mid t_j)$	Log survival function $\log S(t_i \mid t_j)$	Hazard function $h(t_i \mid t_j)$
Weibull	$\mu\,\alpha(\boldsymbol{x}_i,\boldsymbol{x}_j)(\Delta_{ji})^{\mu-1}\exp(-\alpha(\boldsymbol{x}_i,\boldsymbol{x}_j)(\Delta_{ji})^{\mu})$	$-\alpha(\boldsymbol{x}_i,\boldsymbol{x}_j)(\Delta_{ji})^{\mu}$	$\mu\,\alpha(\boldsymbol{x}_i,\boldsymbol{x}_j)(\Delta_{ji})^{\mu-1}$
Exponential	$\alpha(\boldsymbol{x}_i,\boldsymbol{x}_j)\exp(-\alpha(\boldsymbol{x}_i,\boldsymbol{x}_j)\Delta_{ji})$	$-\alpha(\boldsymbol{x}_i,\boldsymbol{x}_j)\Delta_{ji}$	$\alpha(\boldsymbol{x}_i,\boldsymbol{x}_j)$
Rayleigh	$\alpha(\boldsymbol{x}_i,\boldsymbol{x}_j)\Delta_{ji}\exp\left(-\alpha(\boldsymbol{x}_i,\boldsymbol{x}_j)\frac{(\Delta_{ji})^2}{2}\right)$	$-\alpha(\boldsymbol{x}_i,\boldsymbol{x}_j)\frac{(\Delta_{ji})^2}{2}$	$\alpha(\boldsymbol{x}_i,\boldsymbol{x}_j)\Delta_{ji}$

Here we focus on the shift-invariant transmission function whose value only depends on the time difference Δ_{ji}. That is to say, $f(t_i|t_j) = f(\Delta_{ji})$, $F(t_i|t_j) = F(\Delta_{ji})$, $S(t_i|t_j) = S(\Delta_{ji})$, and $h(t_i|t_j) = h(\Delta_{ji})$.

The likelihood $\ell(\boldsymbol{t}^c)$ of a cascade induced by event c is the product of all individual likelihoods $\ell_n(\boldsymbol{t}^c)$ of event c occurring to each node n. If we do not observe event c happening to node n in observation window $[0, T^c]$, the individual likelihood is calculated as the product of survival functions,

$$\ell_n^{\text{survive}}(\boldsymbol{t}^c) = \prod_{\{j \mid t_j^c \le T^c\}} S(\Delta_{jn}^c), \tag{3}$$

since node n is not infected by nodes that have already been infected up to T^c. Δ_{ji}^c is the time difference between node j and node i as recorded in cascade c; it is calculated by

$$\Delta_{ji}^c = \begin{cases} T^c - t_j^c & \text{if } t_i^c > T^c \\ t_i^c - t_j^c & \text{otherwise.} \end{cases} \tag{4}$$

The observation of infection plays a much more prominent role in determining the likelihood of transmission. Let us consider that event c happens to node n at t_n^c in observation window $[0, T^c]$. In this case, we consider all possible transmission routes. One possibility is that node n was infected by already-infected node j (i.e. $t_j^c < t_n^c$), and is not infected by any other infected node. The likelihood is calculated as the sum of all possibilities:

$$\ell_n^{\text{infected}}(\boldsymbol{t}^c) = \sum_{\{j \mid t_j^c < t_n^c\}} f(\Delta_{jn}^c) \prod_{\{k \mid k \ne j, t_k^c < t_n^c\}} S(\Delta_{kn}^c). \tag{5}$$

The likelihood $\ell(\boldsymbol{t}^c)$ of a cascade induced by event c can be calculated by the product of these two scenarios:

$$\ell(\boldsymbol{t}^c) = \prod_{\{n \mid t_n^c > T^c\}} \ell_n^{\text{survive}}(\boldsymbol{t}^c) \times \prod_{\{n \mid t_n^c \le T^c\}} \ell_n^{\text{infected}}(\boldsymbol{t}^c). \tag{6}$$

Finally, the likelihood of all cascades $\boldsymbol{C}$ is the product of individual cascade likelihoods. The negative log likelihood of all cascades can be described using the hazard and the survival functions as follows:

$$L(\boldsymbol{C}) = -\sum_i \sum_j \sum_{\{c \mid t_j^c < t_i^c\}} \log S(\Delta_{ji}^c) - \sum_i \sum_{\{c \mid t_i^c \le T^c\}} \log \sum_{\{j \mid t_j^c \le t_i^c\}} h(\Delta_{ji}^c). \tag{7}$$

2.2 Proposed Model

The proposed model infers the diffusion network by embedding it into a low-dimensional visualization space. Our model estimates node coordinates $\boldsymbol{X} = \{\boldsymbol{x}_n\}_{n=1}^N$, where $\boldsymbol{x}_n = (x_{n1}, ..., x_{nD})$ are the coordinates of the nth node in the visualization space; D is its dimensionality, usually $D = 2$ or 3. We assume that information is more likely to be propagated between nodes that are located close together in the visualization space. We estimate coordinates $\boldsymbol{X}$ such that we can explain the observed cascade data. By incorporating this assumption into the generative process of diffusion, our model suggests the diffusion network layout in the visualization space that fulfills the influence preservation principle.

We assume that the transmission function $f(\Delta_{ji})$ from node j to i is determined by the Euclidean distance between them in the visualization space. Here, we use the Weibul model to define the transmission function as follows;

$$f(\Delta_{ji}|\boldsymbol{x}_i,\boldsymbol{x}_j) = \mu\alpha(\boldsymbol{x}_i,\boldsymbol{x}_j)(\Delta_{ji})^{\mu-1}\exp(-\alpha(\boldsymbol{x}_i,\boldsymbol{x}_j)(\Delta_{ji})^{\mu}), \tag{8}$$

where $\alpha(\boldsymbol{x}_i,\boldsymbol{x}_j) \ge 0$ is the transmission rate (represents how likely node j with coordinates $\boldsymbol{x}_j$ is to infect node i with $\boldsymbol{x}_i$); μ determines the shape of the probability density function. As $\alpha(\boldsymbol{x}_i,\boldsymbol{x}_j)$ approaches zero, the expected diffusion time becomes arbitrarily long (i.e. node j does not infect node i). The transmission rate $\alpha(\boldsymbol{x}_i,\boldsymbol{x}_j)$ is assumed to be determined by the Euclidean distance in the visualization space as follows:

$$\alpha(\boldsymbol{x}_i,\boldsymbol{x}_j) = \exp\left(-\frac{\beta}{2}||\boldsymbol{x}_j - \boldsymbol{x}_i||^2\right), \tag{9}$$

where β is the scale parameter of the visualization space. The assumption underlying our model appeals to our intuition. Consider an outbreak of influenza in the real world. The infection rate is high among those people in close proximity. For example, when a person has been infected, her/his family, friends, and colleagues are also likely to be infected since she/he often meets them in the real world. However, the risk of infection fades over time since the infected person recovers from her/his illness. In this example, the likelihood of infection depends on the individual's activity area like her home, school, and office. Thus the learned visualization space is expected to reflect the geographical closeness between people in the real world.

By plugging (8) and (9) into (1) and (2), the log survival and hazard functions of our model are

$$\log S(\Delta_{ji}|\boldsymbol{x}_i,\boldsymbol{x}_j) = -\exp\left(-\frac{\beta}{2}||\boldsymbol{x}_j - \boldsymbol{x}_i||^2\right)(\Delta_{ji})^{\mu}, \tag{10}$$

$$h(\Delta_{ji}|\boldsymbol{x}_i,\boldsymbol{x}_j) = \mu\exp\left(-\frac{\beta}{2}||\boldsymbol{x}_j - \boldsymbol{x}_i||^2\right)(\Delta_{ji})^{\mu-1}. \tag{11}$$

Our model has the capacity to deal with a wide variety of cascade data since its definition is based on the Weibull distribution. Some existing network inference methods use exponential or Rayleigh distributions for modeling the process of diffusion [14, 16, 21, 3]. The exponential distribution is a special case of the Weibull distribution where $\mu = 1$. Furthermore, the Weibull distribution with $\mu = 2$ is a good approximation of the Rayleigh distribution. Parameter μ is predefined by the user of our system to suit the cascade type. Table 2 summarizes the transmission, survival, and hazard functions of each distribution.

2.3 Inference

We use maximum a posteriori (MAP) estimation to determine the unknown parameters $\boldsymbol{X}$ in the proposed model that yield best fits to the observed cascade data. The number of dimensions, D, is assumed to be specified for visualization.

The negative log likelihood of parameters $\boldsymbol{X}$ for the given set of cascades, $\boldsymbol{C}$, with prior is as follows:

$$L(\boldsymbol{X}|\boldsymbol{C}) = \sum_i \sum_j \sum_{\{c|t_j^c<t_i^c\}} \exp\left(-\frac{\beta}{2}||\boldsymbol{x}_j - \boldsymbol{x}_i||^2\right) (\Delta_{ji}^c)^\mu$$
$$-\sum_i \sum_{\{c|t_i^c \le T^c\}} \log \sum_{\{j|t_j^c \le t_i^c\}} \mu \exp\left(-\frac{\beta}{2}||\boldsymbol{x}_j - \boldsymbol{x}_i||^2\right) (\Delta_{ji}^c)^{\mu-1}$$
$$-\sum_i \log\left(\left(\frac{\gamma}{2\pi}\right)^{\frac{D}{2}} \exp\left(-\frac{\gamma}{2}||\boldsymbol{x}_n||^2\right)\right), \quad (12)$$

where γ is a hyper-parameter. In order to control the size of the resultant embedding, we use a Gaussian prior with zero mean and spherical covariance for coordinates $\boldsymbol{x}_n$. We use $\gamma = 0.1$ in all experiments described in Section 4. The objective function can be minimized through the use of a gradient-based numerical optimization method such as the quasi-Newton method [12].

The gradient of $\boldsymbol{x}_n$ used in gradient-based numerical optimization can be calculated by considering two cases as follows: If $i = n$, the gradient of $\boldsymbol{x}_n$ is calculated by

$$\frac{\partial L}{\partial \boldsymbol{x}_n} = \sum_j \sum_{\{c|t_j^c<t_n^c\}} \beta(\boldsymbol{x}_j - \boldsymbol{x}_n) \exp\left(-\frac{\beta}{2}||\boldsymbol{x}_j - \boldsymbol{x}_n||^2\right) (\Delta_{jn}^c)^\mu$$
$$- \sum_{\{c|t_n^c \le T^c\}} \frac{\sum_{\{j|t_j^c<t_n^c\}} \beta(\boldsymbol{x}_j - \boldsymbol{x}_n)\exp(-\frac{\beta}{2}||\boldsymbol{x}_j - \boldsymbol{x}_n||^2)(\Delta_{jn}^c)^{\mu-1}}{\sum_{\{j|t_j^c<t_n^c\}} \exp(-\frac{\beta}{2}||\boldsymbol{x}_j - \boldsymbol{x}_n||^2)(\Delta_{jn}^c)^{\mu-1}}$$
$$+ \gamma \boldsymbol{x}_n. \quad (13)$$

If $j = n$, the gradient of $\boldsymbol{x}_n$ is calculated by

$$\frac{\partial L}{\partial \boldsymbol{x}_n} = \sum_i \sum_{\{c|t_n^c<t_i^c\}} \beta(\boldsymbol{x}_i - \boldsymbol{x}_n) \exp\left(-\frac{\beta}{2}||\boldsymbol{x}_n - \boldsymbol{x}_i||^2\right) (\Delta_{ni}^c)^\mu$$
$$-\sum_i \sum_{\{c|t_i^c \le T^c\}} \frac{\beta(\boldsymbol{x}_i - \boldsymbol{x}_n)\exp(-\frac{\beta}{2}||\boldsymbol{x}_n - \boldsymbol{x}_i||^2)(\Delta_{ni}^c)^{\mu-1}}{\sum_{\{j'|t_{j'}^c<t_i^c\}} \exp(-\frac{\beta}{2}||\boldsymbol{x}_{j'} - \boldsymbol{x}_i||^2)(\Delta_{j'i}^c)^{\mu-1}}. \quad (14)$$

Combining the two above scenarios, yields the gradient of $\boldsymbol{x}_n$ as follows:

$$\frac{\partial L}{\partial \boldsymbol{x}_n} = \sum_j \sum_{\{c|t_n^c \ne t_j^c\}} \beta(\boldsymbol{x}_j - \boldsymbol{x}_n) \exp\left(-\frac{\beta}{2}||\boldsymbol{x}_j - \boldsymbol{x}_n||^2\right) (\Delta_{jn}^c)^\mu$$
$$- \sum_{\{c|t_n^c \le T^c\}} \sum_{\{j|t_j^c<t_n^c\}} \beta(\boldsymbol{x}_j - \boldsymbol{x}_n) P(n|j)$$
$$-\sum_j \sum_{\{c|t_j^c \le T^c\}} \beta(\boldsymbol{x}_j - \boldsymbol{x}_n) P(j|n) + \gamma \boldsymbol{x}_n, \quad (15)$$

where $P(n|j)$ is the conditional probability of infection from node j to node n, and $P(j|n)$ is the conditional probability of infection from node n to node j. These values are calculated by

$$P(n|j) = \frac{\exp\left(-\frac{\beta}{2}||\boldsymbol{x}_j - \boldsymbol{x}_n||^2\right) (\Delta_{jn}^c)^{\mu-1}}{\sum_{\{i|t_i^c<t_n^c\}} \exp\left(-\frac{\beta}{2}||\boldsymbol{x}_i - \boldsymbol{x}_n||^2\right) (\Delta_{in}^c)^{\mu-1}}, \quad (16)$$

$$P(j|n) = \frac{\exp\left(-\frac{\beta}{2}||\boldsymbol{x}_n - \boldsymbol{x}_j||^2\right) (\Delta_{nj}^c)^{\mu-1}}{\sum_{\{i|t_i^c<t_j^c\}} \exp\left(-\frac{\beta}{2}||\boldsymbol{x}_i - \boldsymbol{x}_j||^2\right) (\Delta_{ij}^c)^{\mu-1}}. \quad (17)$$

Scale parameter β can be estimated by using cross validation.

Existing network inference models directly infer transmission parameter α_{ji}, which represents how likely information is to spread from node j to node i. The number of parameters to be estimated is $N \times N$, and the number of parameters increases as the square of N. Thus a lot of cascades are required to learn all parameters. On the other hand, the number of parameters to be estimated by our model is $D \times N$. In general, D, the dimensionality of the visualization space, is considerably smaller than the number of nodes N. Thus the proposed model has significantly fewer parameters than existing models. Accordingly, our model can capture the essential features of underlying diffusion networks even if the number of cascades is small.

3. RELATED WORK

A great deal of effort has been expended to model diffusion processes with respect to the underlying network structure; published techniques are used for viral marketing, information propagation in social network, and following the spread of infectious diseases. Independent cascade models [5] and linear threshold models [6], two representative diffusion models, are mainly used for analyzing activities in online social communities. These models treat time in discrete steps rather than as a continuous variable although real events happen in continuous time. Some prior work treats time as a continuous variable. NETINF uses submodular optimization to estimate network connections [15]. NETINF assumes that the transmission rates between all nodes are predefined and not inferred. On the other hand, [14] proposed a continuous model called NETRATE; it allows different transmission rates across different edges. [14] provides a basic and simple framework for solving the network inference problem, and has been extended as follows; [16] uses stochastic gradients to estimate the time-varying transmission rates of edges and thus capture the temporal dynamics of the network. TOPICCASCADE proposed by [3] estimates topic-dependent transmission rates of edges by using LDA to represent topic structure of memes. MoNET considers additional features of nodes; it uses a predefined similarity measure between meme contents [21]. [7] used shared cascade Poisson processes to model information diffusion in online social communities, and proposed a Baysian inference procedure. However, in the existing diffusion models, The influence relation of each node pair is recognized only after observing common events linking them. The performance of network inference decreases when the number of cascades is small since there are few events that can provide clues as to the influence relations. Our model infers the network embedded into a low-dimensional visualization space. Since the proposed model has significantly fewer parameters than existing models, ours accurately infers the underlying network even when there are few observed cascades. The distance in the visualization space indicates the strength of the influence relation between nodes even if we have not observed common event(s) that link them. The method proposed by [4] estimates a block matrix of transmission rates by combining ideas from stochastic block modeling and network inference models. The method by [4] is similar to ours in that it reduces the dimensionality of the diffusion network, but differs in that it can not visualize the diffusion network. Ours not only infers the low-dimensional representation of diffusion network but also visualizes it in a Euclidean space, which is a metric space that most closely corresponds to our intuitive understanding of space.

The network structure estimated by existing diffusion models is complex when the network is large. This complexity hinders the scientific discovery of knowledge or principles from the results since we can not understand the results in an intuitive way. In order to embed and visualize high-dimensional data such as diffusion networks, a number of visualization methods have been proposed [19, 20, 18, 9]. These methods attempt to embed nodes into a low-dimensional Euclidean space in order to restore predefined pairwise distances between nodes. However, the 2-step process frequently results in poor visualization for the reasons noted in Section 1. In order to best explain the observed diffusion process, our model simultaneously estimates the latent coordinates of nodes and visualizes them in the same probabilistic framework.

In the sense of utilizing latent coordinates for modeling generative probabilistic models, the proposed model is related to *Probabilistic Latent Semantic Visualization* (PLSV), which extracts topics by embedding documents in a low-dimensional space [8]. While PLSV is designed for visualizing documents, our proposal, PLNV, is designed for visualizing networks.

4. EXPERIMENTS

4.1 Data

We evaluated the proposal by analyzing the information diffusion process occurring in Web space. For this we used the MemeTracker dataset of [16]. In this dataset, a cascade is represented by a set of time-stamps. Each time-stamp represents when a news article or blog post referred to a keyword (an event), and is recorded at the time scale of seconds. Each cascade in the dataset is categorized into topics based on what type of keyword it referred to. We chose eight types of cascade data related to eight topics; "iPhone", "Jobs", "Baseball", "Basketball", "Earthquake", "Fukushima", "Sept. 11", and "Syria". Each topic-dependent-dataset consisted of the top 500 sites and contained about 1,000 cascades.

4.2 Baseline methods

We compared the proposed method against various existing network inference and visualization methods. We used NETRATE as the state-of-the-art network inference method for estimating the weight for each edge in the directed graph based on observed cascade data. NETRATE directly estimates transmission parameter α_{ji} which represents how likely information is to spread from node j to node i. For both our proposed model and NETRATE, we define the transmission function as an exponential model for simplicity. That is to say, our model was defined based on the Weibull distribution with $\mu = 1$. Based on an $N \times N$ matrix of transmission rates estimated by NETRATE, we embedded N nodes into a D-dimensional visualization space using the KK spring method [9], MDS [20], or Isomap [19] as existing visualization methods.

Although NETRATE outputs a similarity matrix where each element is the degree of similarity, the visualization method expects a distance matrix as its input. In the distance matrix, as an element approaches infinity, it is much less likely to be infected. Thus, as a pre-processing step, α_{ji} is converted into its inverse $\hat{\alpha}_{ji}$, which represents how far j is from i.

$$\hat{\alpha}_{ji} = \frac{1}{\alpha_{ji} + \epsilon}, \tag{18}$$

where ϵ is a smoothing factor (this yields a value when $\alpha_{ji} = 0$). We used $\epsilon = 10^{-3}$ in this experiment.

The KK spring method is a visualization method that uses a pairwise graph-theoretic distance matrix. We define the graph-theoretic distance from node j to node i as $\hat{\alpha}_{ji}$. The method determines the coordinates of each node in the visualization space such that the following objective function is minimized.

$$L_{KK} = \frac{1}{2}\sum_{j}\sum_{\{i|i\neq j\}} \frac{(\hat{\alpha}_{ji} - ||\boldsymbol{x}_j - \boldsymbol{x}_i||)^2}{\hat{\alpha}_{ji}^2}. \tag{19}$$

MDS is a linear dimensionality reduction method, and can embed nodes so as to minimize the discrepancy between pairwise distances in the visualization space and those in the original space. We also used Isomap as a non-linear dimensionality reduction method; it first constructs a graph connecting h-nearest neighbors, and then embeds nodes so as to preserve the shortest path distances in the graph by MDS. Note that MDS and Isomap require the input to be a symmetric matrix (i.e. $\alpha_{ji} = \alpha_{ij}$). We calculated distance $\overline{\alpha}_{ji}$ (= $\overline{\alpha}_{ij}$), used as input to MDS and Isomap, by two methods listed below.

- $\overline{\alpha}_{ji} = Minimum(\hat{\alpha}_{ji}, \hat{\alpha}_{ij})$
- $\overline{\alpha}_{ji} = Average(\hat{\alpha}_{ji}, \hat{\alpha}_{ij})$

$Minimum$ chooses and returns the minimum value from among the arguments; $Average$ calculates and returns the average score of arguments.

Finally, we compared our method with six baselines; the KK spring method, Minimum-MDS, Average-MDS, Minimum-Isomap, and Average-Isomap.

4.3 Quantitative Experiments

4.3.1 Performance of Visualization

This experiment quantitatively shows that our method can output a visualization space wherein each node is placed closer to its influential nodes than non-influential ones. We consider that j is an influential node for node i if i is likely to be infected by j. That is to say, we determine if the visualization space as estimated by our method satisfies the influence preservation principle.

We divided cascades into training and test sets, and evaluated whether or not the visualization space learned from the training data could predict the influence relations present in the test data. We considered that the influence relation between nodes is true (there exists a influence relation between nodes) if test data has an event (cascade) wherein both of them are infected.

We designed an evaluation metric to evaluate embedded diffusion network layouts in terms of how well the influence relations were preserved. We adopted the idea of the *F-measure*, which is widely used in the research field of information retrieval [1]. The method of calculating the F-measure score for the results of the visualization space is as follows: The F-measure combines *precision* and *recall*. For each node n, we consider a D-dimensional ball $B_n(r_n)$ with center $\boldsymbol{x}_n$ and radius r_n. The precision for node n is the fraction of nodes that are contained in the D-dimensional ball $B_n(r_n)$ that have influence relations to node n; it is calculated by

$$Precision_n(r_n) = \frac{\#\{k|\boldsymbol{x}_k \in B_n(r_n), I(n,k) = 1, k \neq n\}}{\#\{k|\boldsymbol{x}_k \in B_n(r_n), k \neq n\}}, \tag{20}$$

where $I(n,k) = 1$ if there is an influence relation and $I(n,k) = 0$ otherwise. The recall evaluates the sensitivity of the method. The recall for node n is the fraction of nodes that have influence relations that are successfully contained in $B_n(r_n)$; it is calculated by

$$Recall_n(r_n) = \frac{\#\{k|\boldsymbol{x}_k \in B_n(r_n), I(n,k) = 1, k \neq n\}}{\#\{k|I(n,k) = 1, k \neq n\}}. \tag{21}$$

The *F-measure* for node n is the weighted harmonic average of precision and recall as follows

$$F\text{-}measure_n(r_n) = 1/\left(\frac{1}{2} \cdot \frac{1}{Precision_n(r_n)} + (1 - \frac{1}{2}) \cdot \frac{1}{Recall_n(r_n)}\right). \tag{22}$$

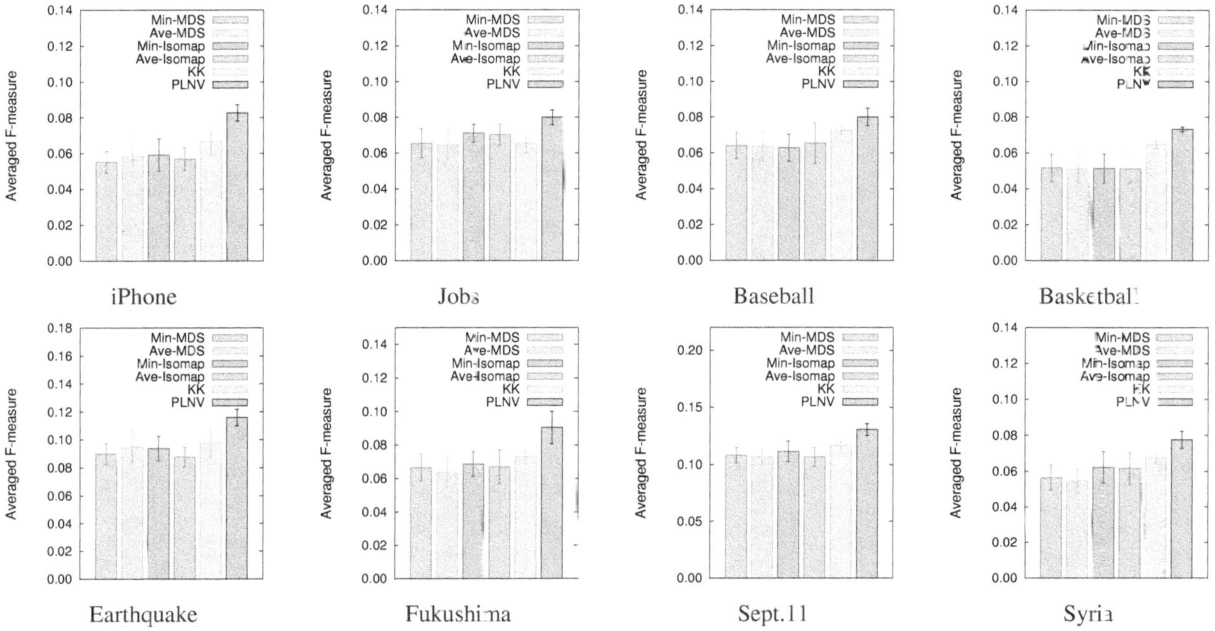

Figure 1: Comparisons of averaged F-measure in terms of the visualization task. The number of dimensions, D, is 2.

The final score for a visualization space is the averaged F-measure over all N nodes. In general, a small r_n leads to high precision and low recall, while a large one leads to low precision and high recall. For each method and node n, we chose r_n that yielded the best F-measure.

Figures 1 and 2 show the results of the F-measures so as to compare methods with different dimensions, $D = 2$ and 3. For more reliable results, 5-fold cross validation was used for testing: We divided the cascades into five subsets. One subset was used for testing, and the others were used for training. This was repeated using each of the subsets as the test set. Thus, the Y-axis in these figures shows the averaged score over all trials. We set $86,400$ seconds (a day) as T^c for our model and baseline methods. For simplicity, we assume $T^c = 86,400$ for all cascades. Parameter β of our model was set to the best parameter value based on the results of 5-fold cross validation; β was chosen from 10^1, 10^2, 10^3, 10^4, 10^5, and 10^6. As shown, for each dataset (topic), our model yielded better performance than the baseline methods. The results show that the proposed method ensured that node pairs likely to be infected in the same event were placed close to each other. The performance of each baseline method strongly depends on the topic. Based on the type of analyzed data, a user of baseline method may have to find the right combination of distance metric and visualization method which would demand a lot of effort. Our model allows the user to avoid this trial and error process since it simultaneously estimates the coordinates of nodes in one probabilistic framework.

4.3.2 *Performance of Network Inference*

This experiment evaluates our proposed model in terms of network inference performance. When only few cascades are observed, the $N \times N$ matrix output by existing network inference models is likely to be sparse since there are few events available to provide clues as to the underlying diffusion network. However, inferring underlying the network with few observations is important. As noted before, our method can infer robust models even when there are few cascades. Our model predicts an unknown element in the sparse matrix (i.e. transmission rate between nodes) based on the distance in the low-dimensional space. More intuitively, even if two nodes have not experienced infection in the same event, the proposed method can predict the existence of connectivity between them from whether the existence of their common influential nodes. This experiment shows that our proposal can accurately predict connections between users even when relatively few cascades have been observed.

We evaluated the diffusion network estimated by the network inference model from the training data in terms of how well it explains the influence relations present in the test data. As in the previous experiment, we used the F-measure as the evaluation metric. Let w_{kn} be the distance from node k to node n as estimated by each network inference method, and d_n be its threshold which determines whether node k is an influential node for node n or not. The precision for node n represents the probability that the influential node for node n is located within d_n; it is calculated by

$$Precision_n(d_n) = \frac{\#\{k|w_{kn} \leq d_n, I(n,k) = 1, n \neq k\}}{\#\{k|w_{kn} \leq d_n, n \neq k\}}. \quad (23)$$

Recall for node n is the fraction of its influential nodes that are actually located within d_n; it is calculated by

$$Recall_n(d_n) = \frac{\#\{k|w_{kn} \leq d_n, I(n,k) = 1, n \neq k\}}{\#\{k|I(n,k) = 1, n \neq k\}}. \quad (24)$$

The F-measure score is calculated by (22). We compared the averaged F-measures of our model against those of an existing network inference model, NETRATE. We used $\hat{\alpha}_{kn}$ for w_{kn} when calculating the F-measure of NETRATE, and $||\boldsymbol{x}_k - \boldsymbol{x}_n||$ for w_{kn} when calculating the F-measure of the proposed model. One parameter that also influences the performance of our method is the number of dimensions D. Although the number of dimensions D in our model is set to 2 or 3 for visualization, a larger number of dimensions can be set in our model. This experiment considered four values of D (2,3,5, and 10).

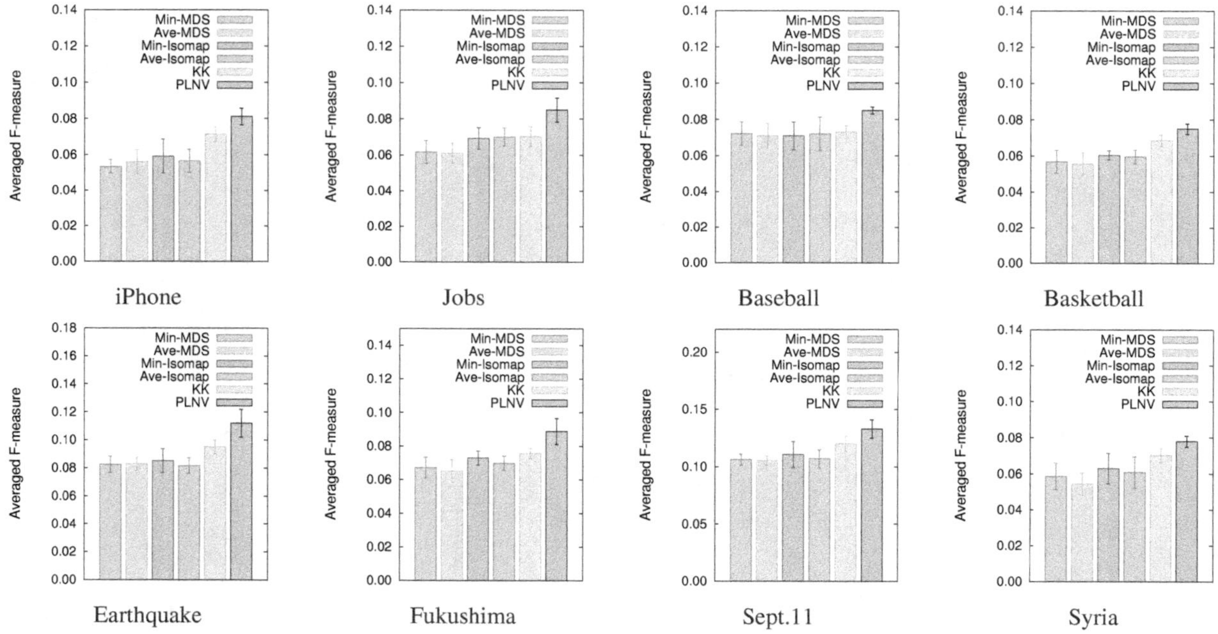

Figure 2: Comparisons of averaged F-measure in terms of the visualization task. The number of dimensions, D, is 3.

We studied the influence of the number of cascades on the performance of network inference. Figure 3 shows the performance of each model at different cascade sizes. We changed the number of cascades from 100 to 1,000 in steps of 100. For each step, we calculated the averaged F-measure. As shown, the proposed model demonstrated better network inference performance than NETRATE when the number of cascades was less than 300. The results suggest that our model is appropriate for solving network inference problems with sparse cascade data. In some datasets ("Earthquake" and "Sept.11"), even when the number of cascades is relatively large, the proposal inferred connections with the same or better accuracy than NETRATE. In the previous experiment, we tested the performance of visualization on the condition that a lot of cascades were used in training (the number of cascades was set to 1,000). The low accuracy of NETRATE in terms of network inference with the sparse training data implies low accuracy in terms of visualization, since the existing visualization method learns the visualization space by maximizing the likelihood of the given parameters (i.e. transmission rates) from NETRATE. Even if it succeeds in constructing a low-dimensional representation of NETRATE parameters, the existing visualization method yields only inferior visualization performance, particularly when few cascades are observed.

4.4 Qualitative Experiments

This experiment qualitatively discusses the value of our model for two different application scenarios.

Browsing network layout: While it remains difficult to evaluate whether a given network layout is suitable for browsing or not, we observed the characteristic features of each method. Figure 4 illustrates the 2- and 3-dimensional layout yielded by each method examined. We used the cascades related to "Baseball". Based on the results of the quantitative experiments, we adopted the minimum function as the distance measure for MDS and Isomap since it yields better performances than the average function for most datasets. In the layouts created by MDS and Isomap, many nodes are collapsed to a single point, which is not desirable for browsing. As shown, the layout created by the KK spring method avoids the node collapse problem, but many nodes tend to be placed on the circumferences of circles. This phenomenon is referred to as the *dandelion effect* [2]. Our model is superior to the KK spring method in terms of its support for community-finding. Our visualization space exhibits several densely-populated areas, which we call communities. The nodes in a community are likely to influence each another. An event experienced by a member is likely to be propagated throughput the community. When we use our method for the purpose of viral marketing, the marketer can get key information from the layouts created by the proposed method since the marketer can trigger a chain reaction of people wanting to the goods for sale. Even if the goods are new releases, for which there are few cascades, the proposed method can suggest the network layout that best explains the mechanism of the diffusion process to the marketer.

Browsing growth process of cascade: The visualization space output by our model serves as a vehicle for suggesting the growth process of a cascade since it satisfies the influence preservation principle. An event that occurs at one node in a community is expected to spread like an epidemic from node to node. Figure 5 shows examples of cascade visualizations yielded by the network layout. We used the cascade datasets related to three topics; "iPhone", "Basketball", and "Sept. 11". For each topic, we chose the most widely propagated event (cascade), and show the infected and survival nodes at four different time points. In these figures, colored and uncolored nodes indicate infected and survival nodes, respectively. For example, the node that was the first to experience an event related to iPhone is plotted on (a). The nodes which became infected within 1200, 2400, and 3600 seconds of the start of the event are marked by the colored nodes in (b), (c), and (d), respectively. We compared our proposed method against the combination of NETRATE and the KK spring model. As shown, in the layout created by the KK spring method, each event seems to prop-

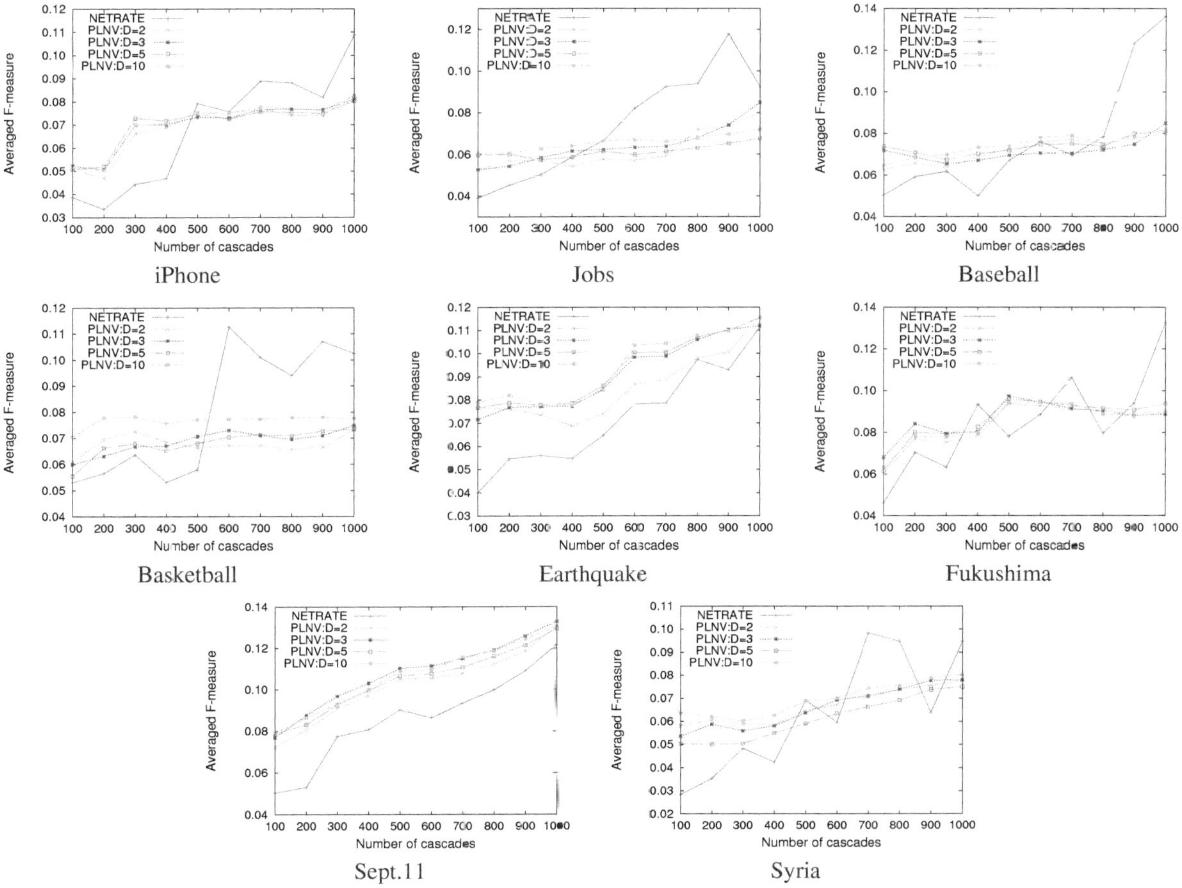

Figure 3: Comparisons of averaged F-measure in terms of the network inference task.

agate along the circumference of a circle since many nodes tend to be arranged on circles. On the other hand, in the layout created by the proposed model, each event propagates within a narrow space at an early stage, but diffusion eventually covers a much wider area. The structure enables us to grasp an appropriate understanding of the present situation since we can characterize each diffusion event by its speed, coverage, and density. Thus we can gain an understanding of the big picture through the visualization. Furthermore, an analysis of a diffusion process is expected to establish a reasonable understanding of future infection patterns since diffusion gradually spreads over the visualization space. For example, to prevent the initial carrier from spreading his infectious disease or spreading a rumor, the people in his community can be put on their guard.

5. CONCLUSION

This paper proposed a probabilistic model for estimating diffusion networks and embedding them into low-dimensional visualization spaces. We consider that the desired property of the layout of the diffusion network is that each node should be more closely co-sited with its influential nodes than with non-influential ones in the visualization space; we call this the influence preservation principle. This property is realized by the proposed model through the following assumption; each node in a network has latent coordinates in the visualization space, and propagation is more likely to occur between nodes that are placed closer together. Our model learns the latent coordinates in the visualization space that best explain the observed cascade data; our model is fitted to the given cascade data by using maximum a posteriori estimation. Different from previous works, our model simultaneously estimates the latent coordinates of nodes in the visualization space in one probabilistic framework. As a result, the coordinates of nodes are optimal in terms of the likelihood of all cascades. Another important feature of our model is its robustness. The parameters in our model can be learned accurately even when there are few cascades since the number of parameters to be estimated is significantly smaller than that in existing network inference models. Our model can accurately predict unknown influence-relations between nodes based on the distance in the learned space, even if we have not yet observed a common event which both nodes are infected.

We used the histories of information diffusion in a Web space to evaluate the performance of network visualization, and quantitatively showed that the visualization results of the proposed model satisfy the influence preserving principle, unlike the existing methodology; it combines existing network inference and visualization methods. The visualization space learned by our model is not only useful for browsing the underlying network layout intuitively, but also serves as a vehicle for suggesting the growth process of the observed cascade. The second experiment showed that our model addresses the sparsity problem better than existing network inference models. We compared its performance in the network inference task to that of an existing network inference method, and showed that ours yields better performance when there are few cascades.

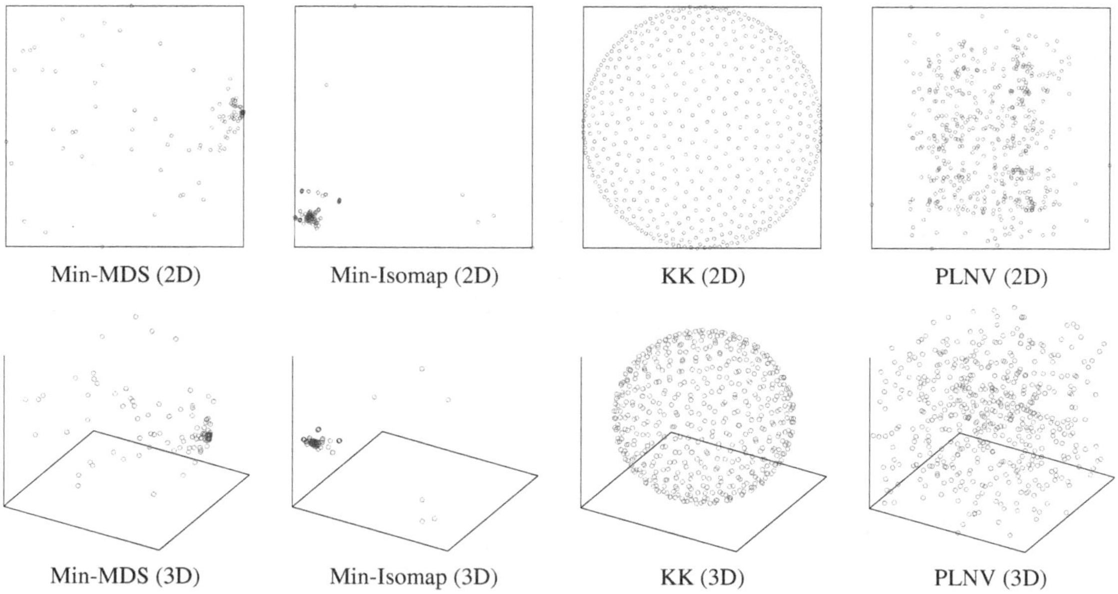

Figure 4: Comparisons of 2-, and 3- dimensional visualizations of each method. Each visualization space was learned from a set of cascades related to "Baseball".

This is because our model allows us to associate nodes based on the distance in the visualization space, even in the absence of any event that involves both nodes.

Our experiments, offline evaluations using observed cascade data, are an important starting point for exploring the validity of our model, but are only one approach to evaluating visualization methods. We will let real users in realistic settings evaluate the real strengths of our approach. Another future direction is to use other types of cascade data for evaluating the effectiveness of our model. We will analyze diffusion process with respect to information propagation in social networks, and the spread of infectious diseases.

6. REFERENCES

[1] R. Baeza-Yates, B. Ribeiro-Neto, et al. *Modern information retrieval*, volume 463. ACM press New York, 1999.

[2] A. Buja, D. F. Swayne, M. L. Littman, N. Dean, H. Hofmann, and L. Chen. Data visualization with multidimensional scaling. *Journal of computational and graphical statistics*, 17(2):444–472, 2008.

[3] N. Du, L. Song, H. Woo, and H. Zha. Uncover topic-sensitive information diffusion networks. In *AISTATS'13*, pages 229–237, 2013.

[4] C. DuBois, C. Butts, and P. Smyth. Stochastic blockmodeling of relational event dynamics. In *AISTATS'13*, pages 238–246, 2013.

[5] J. Goldenberg, B. Libai, and E. Muller. Talk of the network: A complex systems look at the underlying process of word-of-mouth. *Marketing letters*, 12(3):211–223, 2001.

[6] M. Granovetter. Threshold models of collective behavior. *American journal of sociology*, 83(6):1420, 1978.

[7] T. Iwata, A. Shah, and Z. Ghahramani. Discovering latent influence in online social activities via shared cascade poisson processes. In *KDD'13*, pages 266–274, 2013.

[8] T. Iwata, T. Yamada, and N. Ueda. Probabilistic latent semantic visualization: Topic model for visualizing documents. In *KDD'08*, pages 363–371, 2008.

[9] T. Kamada and S. Kawai. An algorithm for drawing general undirected graphs. *Information processing letters*, 31(1):7–15, 1989.

[10] J. F. Lawless. *Statistical models and methods for lifetime data*, volume 362. John Wiley & Sons, 2011.

[11] E. T. Lee and J. W. Wang. *Statistical methods for survival data analysis*. John Wiley & Sons, 2013.

[12] D. C. Liu and J. Nocedal. On the limited memory BFGS method for large scale optimization. *Mathematical programming*, 45(1-3):503–528, 1989.

[13] S. A. Myers and J. Leskovec. On the convexity of latent social network inference. In *NIPS'10*, pages 1741–1749, 2010.

[14] M. G. Rodriguez, D. Balduzzi, and B. Schölkopf. Uncovering the temporal dynamics of diffusion networks. In *ICML'11*, pages 561–568, 2011.

[15] M. G. Rodriguez, J. Leskovec, and A. Krause. Inferring networks of diffusion and influence. In *KDD'10*, pages 1019–1028, 2010.

[16] M. G. Rodriguez, J. Leskovec, and B. Schölkopf. Structure and dynamics of information pathways in online media. In *WSDM'13*, pages 23–32, 2013.

[17] M. G. Rodriguez and B. Schölkopf. Submodular inference of diffusion networks from multiple trees. In *ICML'12*, pages 1019–1028, 2012.

[18] S. T. Roweis and L. K. Saul. Nonlinear dimensionality reduction by locally linear embedding. *Science*, 290(5500):2323–2326, 2000.

[19] J. B. Tenenbaum, V. De Silva, and J. C. Langford. A global geometric framework for nonlinear dimensionality reduction. *Science*, 290(5500):2319–2323, 2000.

[20] W. S. Torgerson. Theory and methods of scaling. 1958.

[21] L. Wang, S. Ermon, and J. E. Hopcroft. Feature-enhanced probabilistic models for diffusion network inference. In *ECML/PKDD'12*, pages 499–514, 2012.

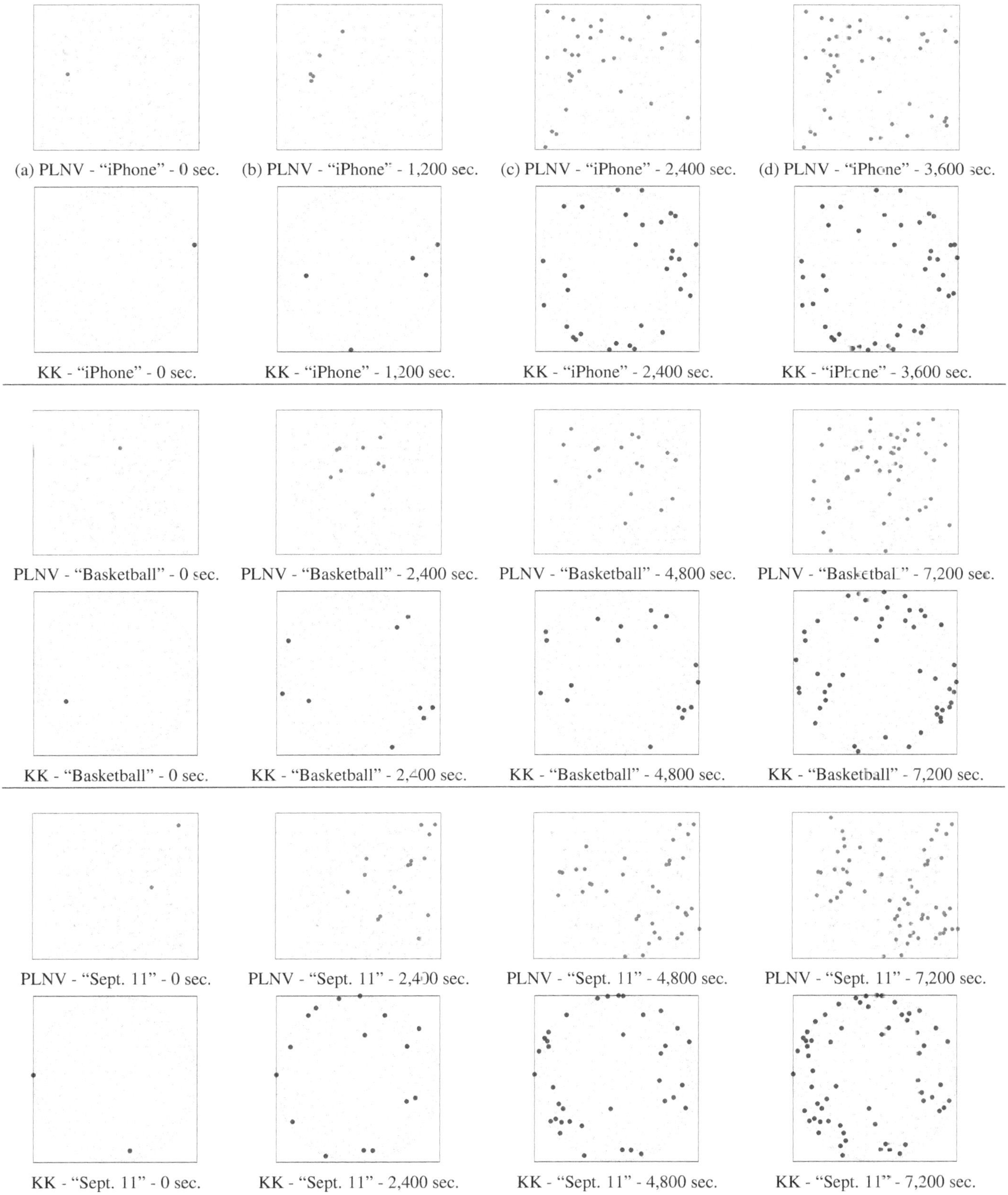

(a) PLNV - "iPhone" - 0 sec. (b) PLNV - "iPhone" - 1,200 sec. (c) PLNV - "iPhone" - 2,400 sec. (d) PLNV - "iPhone" - 3,600 sec.

KK - "iPhone" - 0 sec. KK - "iPhone" - 1,200 sec. KK - "iPhone" - 2,400 sec. KK - "iPhone" - 3,600 sec.

PLNV - "Basketball" - 0 sec. PLNV - "Basketball" - 2,400 sec. PLNV - "Basketball" - 4,800 sec. PLNV - "Basketball" - 7,200 sec.

KK - "Basketball" - 0 sec. KK - "Basketball" - 2,400 sec. KK - "Basketball" - 4,800 sec. KK - "Basketball" - 7,200 sec.

PLNV - "Sept. 11" - 0 sec. PLNV - "Sept. 11" - 2,400 sec. PLNV - "Sept. 11" - 4,800 sec. PLNV - "Sept. 11" - 7,200 sec.

KK - "Sept. 11" - 0 sec. KK - "Sept. 11" - 2,400 sec. KK - "Sept. 11" - 4,800 sec. KK - "Sept. 11" - 7,200 sec.

Figure 5: Comparisons of 2-dimensional cascade visualization. We compared the proposed method against the combination of NETRATE and the KK spring model. The infected and survival nodes at four different time points are shown.

MMRate: Inferring Multi-aspect Diffusion Networks with Multi-pattern Cascades

Senzhang Wang*, Xia Hu‡, Philip S. Yu†, Zhoujun Li*
* Beihang University, Beijing, 100191, China
‡ Arizona State University, Tempe, AZ 85287, USA
† University of Illinois at Chicago, Chicago, IL 60607, USA
{szwang@cse., lizj@}buaa.edu.cn, psyu@uic.edu, xia.hu@asu.edu

ABSTRACT

Inferring diffusion networks from traces of cascades has been extensively studied to better understand information diffusion in many domains. A widely used assumption in previous work is that the diffusion network is homogenous and diffusion processes of cascades follow the same pattern. However, in social media, users may have various interests and the connections among them are usually multi-faceted. In addition, different cascades normally diffuse at different speeds and spread to diverse scales, and hence show various diffusion patterns. It is challenging for traditional models to capture the heterogeneous user interactions and diverse patterns of cascades in social media. In this paper, we investigate a novel problem of *inferring multi-aspect diffusion networks with multi-pattern cascades*. In particular, we study the effects of various diffusion patterns on the information diffusion process by analyzing users' retweeting behavior on a microblogging dataset. By incorporating aspect-level user interactions and various diffusion patterns, a new model for inferring **M**ulti-aspect transmission **R**ates between users using **M**ulti-pattern cascades (MMRate) is proposed. We also provide an Expectation Maximization algorithm to effectively estimate the parameters. Experimental results on both synthetic and microblogging datasets demonstrate the superior performance of our approach over the state-of-the-art methods in inferring multi-aspect diffusion networks.

Categories and Subject Descriptors

H.2.8 [**Database Management**]: Database Application: *data mining*

General Terms

Algorithms; Experimentation

Keywords

Information Diffusion; Graph Mining; Social Network

KDD '14, August 24-27 2014, New York, NY, USA
Copyright 2014 ACM 978-1-4503-2956-9/14/08$15.00.
http://dx.doi.org/10.1145/2623330.2623728.

1. INTRODUCTION

The increasing popularity of social networking websites, such as Twitter and Sina Weibo, has greatly promoted the research on social network analysis due to the massive real data available. A ubiquitous problem of social network analysis is how the information, idea, and innovation diffuse in the networks. Studying the process of information dissemination, cascading behavior and influence spreading in social networks is fundamental in many applications, such as technological innovations spreading [12], word of mouse effects in viral marketing [2, 13] and personalized recommendation in E-commerce websites [17].

As a fundamental research issue in information diffusion, inferring the network structure from a collection of diffusion cascades has been studied in many domains, such as the hyperlink network of on-line news articles [6, 7, 8] and the collaboration network of scientists [18]. Existing models can be roughly divided into inferring the network connectivity, such as NetInfer [7] and MulTree [9], and inferring not only the network structure but also the transmission rates over the edges, like NETRATE [6] and InfoPath [8]. These methods normally use a continuous time distribution to model the cascade diffusion process, and try to find the optimal homogeneous network which can maximize the likelihood of all the observed cascades.

Existing studies assume the network connections are homogeneous and have only one aspect [6, 8, 18]. This assumption does not hold in social media. The interactions on social networks are usually heterogeneous and have many aspects. For example, the research on social trust showed that the trust relationship between online users has many facets [22]. One user tends to trust different users in terms of different facets. Similarly, social theories [11, 15] demonstrated that the effect of social influence from different angles such as topics may vary significantly. Users tend to interact with different friends in terms of different angles in society. People's multi-aspect interests and influence of different types suggest people may adopt different types of information from different people in social networks.

Figure 1 shows a toy example of a network with two aspects: research and sports. The entire network can be decomposed into two subgraphs. Each subgraph is associated with one aspect. The width of the edges represents the relationship strength. For different aspects, the corresponding relationship strength is different. For example, user 1 and 2 are researchers working on data mining related topics. They might interact with each other intensively on data mining related cascades, but they do not necessarily share similar

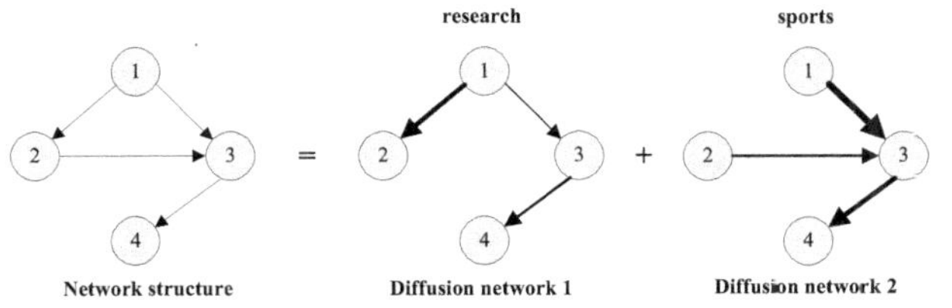

Figure 1: Example of a 2-Aspect Diffusion Network

interests on sports. It is challenging to infer the multi-aspect diffusion network due to the fact that the aspects are usually not explicitly observed. Though the toy example suggests we can consider each topic as an aspect, it is hard to verify whether different topics can be integrated as one aspect due to similar diffusion cascades. Moreover, the topics in different social network websites may differ significantly. For example, topics a user discusses on Twitter could be different from the topics he/she discusses on Epinions. To address this challenge, we need a general model to automatically distinguish the aspects of the cascades and infer the aspect-sensitive diffusion networks.

Meanwhile, the underlying reasons driving a piece of information spreading from node to node is more complex in social networks than those in traditional networks. Social theories showed that information and influence can be transmitted by various mechanisms, such as *conformity*, *social learning*, and *social contagion* [19]. In medical science, it is also well-established that more infectious disease, compared against less infectious ones, can spread to a wider scale in a short period of time [14]. In social networks, cascades usually spread at different speeds and to diverse scales, and thus present various diffusion patterns. Inspired by the sociological and epidemiologic theories, we are particularly interested in investigating the following question: *do various diffusion patterns of the cascades reflect users' retweeting behavior in social networks?* Distinguishing diverse diffusion patterns of the cascades in social networks may potentially help us better understanding information diffusion and more accurately inferring the diffusion networks.

In this paper, we propose a new model to infer the multi-aspect diffusion networks by taking advantage of both aspect-sensitive user interactions and various diffusion patterns. In particular, we investigate 1) whether different cascades present distinct diffusion patterns in social networks, and 2) how their diffusion patterns reflect users' behavior in information diffusion. Then we discuss how to incorporate the aspect-sensitive transmission rates and diffusion patterns of cascades into a new model to more effectively infer the multi-aspect diffusion networks. Finally, we conduct extensive experiments to evaluate the proposed model. The main contributions of this paper can be summarized as follows:

- We formally define the problem of inferring the multi-aspect diffusion networks to enable the utilization of multi-aspect user interactions and the various diffusion patterns of cascades in social networks;
- By analyzing 300,000 retweeting cascades in Sina Weibo, we study 1) the existence of various diffusion patterns of the microblogs; and 2) users' retweeting behaviors when encountering the cascades with remarkably different diffusion patterns;
- By incorporating the aspect-sensitive diffusion cascades and various diffusion patterns, we present a new model MMRate. Moreover, to effectively estimate the parameters, an Expectation Maximization algorithm is given;
- We empirically evaluate MMRate on both synthetic and real-world microblogging datasets and study the application of MMRate to help other data mining tasks, such as aspect-sensitive influential mining.

The remainder of the paper is organized as follows: in Section 2, we formally define the studied problem. Section 3 describes the dataset and analyzes how the diffusion patterns reflect users' retweeting behavior. Section 4 introduces the proposed model MMRate and gives an EM-algorithm to effectively infer the parameters. In Section 5, we evaluate our approach and report the results. We discuss related work in Section 6, and conclude this paper in Section 7.

2. PROBLEM FORMULATION

In this section, we will first introduce some notations, and then we will give a formal definition of the studied problem.

Cascade: A cascade $\mathbf{t}^c$ can be denoted as a N-dimensional vector $\mathbf{t}^c = (t_1^c, ..., t_N^c)^T$, where N is the number of nodes. The i_{th} dimension of $\mathbf{t}^c$ records the time stamp when information c infects node i, and $t_i^c \in [0, T^c] \cup \{\infty\}$. The symbol ∞ labels nodes that are not infected during the observation window $[0, T^c]$. The time stamp is set to 0 at the start of each cascade.

A cascades dataset $\mathbb{C}$ consists of a collection of cascades, i.e. $\mathbb{C} = \{\mathbf{t}^1, ..., \mathbf{t}^M\}$, where M is the number of cascades. To simplify the problem formulation, we make the following two assumptions. First, within a cascade $\mathbf{t}^c$, a node i with a time stamp t_i^c can only be infected by the node j with an earlier time stamp, i.e. $t_j^c < t_i^c$. In a cascade $\mathbf{t}^c$, if $t_j^c > t_i^c$, we refer node j as one of node i's child node and node i as one of node j's parent node, though there may not exist an edge between them on the true network. Second, similar to the Independent Cascade model [5], we assume the child node is infected once its first parent succeeds in infecting it, and it can not be infected again. All the parents try to infect their child nodes independently.

Aspect distribution: Assuming there are K aspects in $\mathbb{C}$, the aspect distribution of $\mathbb{C}$ can be represented as $\Pi = \{\pi_1, ..., \pi_K\}$, and $\sum_{i=1}^K \pi_i = 1$, where π_i is the probability of the k_{th} aspect. Each cascade c_i is associated with a K-dimensional vector $\mathbf{z}_i = (z_{i1}, ..., z_{iK})$ and $\sum_{k=1}^K z_{ik} = 1$, with the k_{th} element z_{ik} denoting the probability of the cascade $\mathbf{t}^{c_i}$ belonging to the k_{th} aspect.

Diffusion patterns: Each cascade $\mathbf{t}^c$ presents a unique diffusion pattern which is independent of the network structure. To model the diffusion pattern of $\mathbf{t}^c$, we use a function $g(\Delta t; \delta^c)$ to represent the probability distribution of the decaying time Δt between two successively infected node (t_i^c, t_j^c) in cascade $\mathbf{t}^c$, where δ^c is the distribution parameter. The parameter δ^c determines the spreading speed of the cascade. We will describe the function $g(\Delta t; \delta^c)$ in detail later.

Aspect-sensitive information diffusion graph: An information diffusion graph $\mathbb{G} = (\mathbb{N}, \mathbb{E})$ can be decomposed as K aspect-sensitive subgraphs $\mathbb{G} = \cup_{k=1:K} G_k$ with $G_k = (\mathbb{N}, \mathbb{E}_k)$. $\mathbb{N}$ is the node set, $\mathbb{E}$ is the edge set, and $\mathbb{E}_k$ is the edge set associated with aspect k. $\mathbb{E}_k$ can be further denoted as $\mathbb{E}_k = \cup_{i,j=1:N}\{\alpha_{ij}^k\}$, where α_{ij}^k is the k-aspect

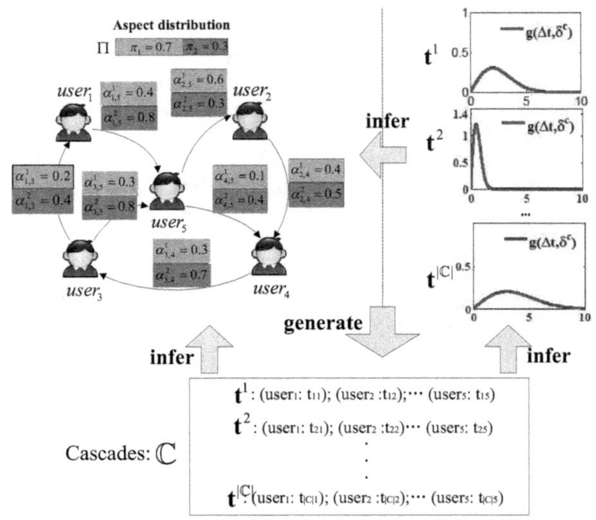

Figure 2: An Illustration of the Studied Problem

transmission rate from node i to j. In most cases, the aspect-sensitive pairwise transmission probability is asymmetric, i.e., $\alpha_{ij}^k \neq \alpha_{ji}^k$.

We provide an illustration of the studied problem in Figure 2. The upper left part of Figure 2 shows a 2-aspect network, the upper right part presents various diffusion patterns of the cascades, and the lower part is the collection of cascades $\mathbb{C}$. In the network, the green and red bars denotes the two aspects with probabilities $\pi_1 = 0.7$ and $\pi_2 = 0.3$, respectively. Each connected pair of users have two transmission rates α_{ij}^1 and α_{ij}^2 with each one associated with an aspect. The diffusion pattern of cascade $\mathbf{t}^c$ is modeled by the distribution function $g(\Delta t, \delta^c)$ shown in the upper right part. The x-axis is the decaying time of the cascades during spreading, and the y-axis is the probability. Each cascade $\mathbf{t}^c$ in $\mathbb{C}$ is composed by the tuples $(user_i : t_{ic})$, where $user_i$ is the node and t_{ic} is the time when $user_i$ is infected by the cascade $\mathbf{t}^c$. Given the multi-aspect network $\mathbb{G}$ with heterogeneous relationships between users, the aspect distribution Π and the diffusion patterns $\delta^{\mathbb{C}}$, a set of corresponding cascades $\mathbb{C}$ can be generated. Conversely, given the cascades data $\mathbb{C}$, the task here is inferring the aspects distribution Π, the diffusion patterns $\delta^{\mathbb{C}}$ and the multi-aspect diffusion network $\mathbb{G}$.

Based on the above definitions, we define the task of *inferring the multi-aspect diffusion networks with multi-pattern cascades* as follow.

PROBLEM 1. *Given 1) a network $\mathbb{G} = \{\mathbb{N}, \mathbb{E}\}$ with hidden edges, where $\mathbb{N}$ represents nodes in the graph and $\mathbb{E}$ are the edges which are unknown, and 2) a collection of observed cascades $\mathbb{C} = \{\boldsymbol{t}^1, ..., \boldsymbol{t}^M\}$ spreading with various diffusion patterns, our goal is to accurately 1) infer the edges $\mathbb{E}$ of $\mathbb{G}$, and 2) estimate the aspect-sensitive information transmission rates $(\alpha_{ij}^1, ..., \alpha_{ij}^K)^T$ over each edge $\boldsymbol{e}_{ij}$.*

3. DATASET AND DATA ANALYSIS

In this section we will first introduce the dataset studied in this paper. Then we will study the difference of the diffusion patterns and investigate the effect of different patterns on information diffusion via real data.

Table 1: Statistics of the Datasets

	DPU	*DUNF*
# of nodes	1,038	750
# of edges	11,385	2,974
#of cascades	5,124	4,206
average # of cascades per edge	1.9	6.8

3.1 Datasets

We study the large microblogging network dataset crawled from Sina Weibo[1] [25]. This dataset is crawled to study the retweeting behaviors in the microblogging network. It contains 1,776,950 users, 308,489,739 following relationships, 300,000 original microblogs, and 23,755,810 retweets. On average, each microblog has been retweeted for about 80 times in the dataset. For the purpose of this study, we build the following two datasets from the initial dataset.

The first dataset is built as follows. As more popular Sina Weibo users can transmit information to a wider scale, we first select the users with over 1,500 followers as nodes and extract corresponding relationships among them as edges. In this way, we obtain a network with 1,624 nodes and 23,097 corresponding directed connections. Then for each microblog, we extract its diffusion path in the extracted network. As a result, 5,124 microblogs are extracted as diffusion cascades. Some nodes or edges have not participated in any of the selected diffusion cascades are then eliminated. Finally, we obtain the first diffusion network with 1,038 users and 11,385 following relationships. For simplicity, we name this dataset *DPU* (Dataset of Popular Users).

For the second dataset, we select the users with a large number of friends as the nodes, because such users can usually receive more posts and hence have more chances to participate in more cascades. Similarly, we extract corresponding relationships among them and obtain a network with 1,345 nodes and 5,874 edges. In the similar way as *DPU*, we extract 4,206 cascades, After eliminating some isolate nodes and edges, we obtain the second dataset with 750 nodes and 2,974 edges. We name this dataset *DUNF* (Dataset of Users with Numerous Friends). The statistics of the two datasets are given in Table 1.

3.2 Study the Diffusion Patterns in Microblogging Network

In this subsection, we will study the diffusion patterns of the cascades and investigate how these patterns reflect users' retweeting behavior in microblogging network. More specifically, we want to answer the following two questions: *Are the diffusion patterns of some cascades significantly different from others in microblogging networks? How does the various diffusion patterns of the cascades reflect users' retweeting behavior during information diffusion?* To answer the two questions, we conduct the following two groups of t-tests.

To answer the first question, we conduct a group of two-sample t-tests to verify whether more popular posts spread faster than ordinary ones. We first rank the microblogs according to their numbers of retweets, then we select the top

[1] http://arnetminer.org/Influencelocality.

k% microblogs from the ranking results as the first group of samples. The entire dataset are considered as the second group of samples. From each group, we randomly select 1000 posts composing two test samples S_1 and S_2. Then we compute the average spreading speed sc_t, sc_r of S_1 and S_2, respectively. sc_t can be computed by $sc_t = \frac{1}{1000}\sum_{i=1}^{1000}\frac{n_i}{t_i}$, where n_i denotes the repost number of the post p_i and t_i is the time span of p_i. sc_r can be computed in the similar way. The null hypothesis is that there is no significant difference between the two spreading speeds, $H_0 : sc_t = sc_r$; while the alternative hypothesis is the average spreading speed of S_1 is faster than that of S_2, $H_1 : sc_t > sc_r$. The null hypothesis is rejected at the significant level $\alpha = 0.01$. The p-values of the t-test with various k are shown in Table 2. The star next to the p-value means that there is statistical evidence to reject the null hypothesis. One can see that the null hypothesis can be rejected when k is 5, 10 and 20. In others words, the top 5%, 10% and 20% popular posts spread significantly faster than the random selected posts.

Table 2: Hypothesis Testing Results (P-Values) to Verify More Popular Posts Spread Faster.

p (k=5)	p (k=10)	p (k=20)	p (k=40)
3.1259e-10*	1.9653e-4*	6.8347e-4*	1.39e-2

To answer the second question, we conduct the second groups of two-sample $t-$tests to investigate 1) whether the spreading of popular posts counts on the closeness of the senders and recipients, and 2) whether the user's retweeting behavior is related to the diffusion patterns of the posts. Before describing the detail of the t-test, we first give a definition as follow.

Definition 1. **Closeness**: the closeness from $user_i$ to $user_j$ is defined as $closeness_{ij} = \frac{t_j}{t_{all}}$, where t_j denotes the number of posts $user_i$ retweeting from $user_j$, and t_{all} denotes the total number of retweeted posts by $user_i$.

To obtain enough data for the t-test, we tend to choose the users with larger number of friends and posts. Hence we first randomly select 100 users who posted more than 1000 microblogs and have more than 200 friends. Then for each selected user $user_i$, we rank all his/her friends according to the closeness to them. We select top k% friends from the ranking as the first group of samples S_1, and bottom k% friends as the second group of samples S_2. Then we compute the average number of retweet sp_t, sp_l of the posts $user_i$ retweeted from the friends in S_1 and S_2, respectively. The null hypothesis is that there is no significant difference between sp_t and sp_l, $H_0 : sp_t = sp_l$; while the alternative hypothesis is sp_t is significantly smaller than sp_l, $H_1 : sp_t < sp_l$. The null hypothesis is rejected at the significant level $\alpha = 0.01$. The p-values of the t-test with various k are shown Table 3. The t-test result reveals that there is statistical evidence to reject the null hypothesis when k is 2, 5 and 8. That is, the average popularity of posts retweeted from the top 2%, 5% and 8% close friends is significantly smaller than that from those less close friends. Note that the t-test result does not mean popular tweets spread mostly through less close friends. It just means that if a user retweets a post

Table 3: Hypothesis Testing Results (P-Values) to Verify Diffusion Patterns Reflect Users Behavior

p (k=2)	p (k=5)	p (k=8)	p (k = 50)
8.2723e-8*	2.9124e-8*	7.4367e-6*	3.65e-2

from a less close friend, the retweeted post is more likely to be popular.

In summary, the evidence from the two groups of t-test results suggests the following answers to the questions: *1) The more popular microblogs are more likely to spread faster, and this infers that different cascades may present significantly different diffusion patterns. 2) Users' retweeting behavior is related to the diffusion patterns of the posts. With a higher probability, a post spreading through two users who are not closed is more popular than a post spreading through two very close users.* Based on these findings, we next will introduce how to exploit the diffusion patterns of cascades to help us better infer diffusion networks.

4. MMRATE: INFERRING MULTI-ASPECT DIFFUSION NETWORKS

In this section, we will start by briefly describing some preliminaries. Then we will give the multi-aspect information diffusion model and present how to compute the likelihood of a collection of cascades using the proposed model. To estimate the parameters, we next will give a EM-algorithm to effectively infer both the aspect-sensitive diffusion networks and the aspect of each cascade belonging to.

We first revisit some basic concepts and introduce some standard notations. We define a nonnegative random variable T to be the time when an event happens, such as $user_i$ adopting a piece of information. Let $f(t)$ be the probability density function of T, then the cumulative density function can be denoted as $F(t) = P(T \leq t) = \int_0^t f(x)dx$.

Survival function. The survival function $S(t)$ is the probability that an event does not happen to a node by time t:

$$S(t) = P(T \geq t) = 1 - F(t) = \int_t^\infty f(x)dx.$$

Hazard function. Given functions $f(t)$ and $S(t)$, we can further define the *hazard function* $H(t)$, which means the instantaneous rate that an event will happen to a particular node within a small interval just after time t if it has not happened to the node yet by time t.

$$H(t) = \lim_{\Delta t \to 0} \frac{p(t \leq T \leq t + \Delta t | T \geq t)}{\Delta t} = \frac{f(t)}{S(t)}.$$

4.1 Incorporating Patterns and Aspects

In this subsection, we will introduce the proposed model MMRate. For each cascade, we use the decaying time distribution function to model its diffusion pattern. We consider that each cascade is also associated with a hidden aspect. By a liner combination of the diffusion pattern and aspect, the MMRate is proposed.

To model information diffusion, first we need to consider how to compute the diffusion probability between two nodes in a specific cascade. In our model, the pairwise diffusion probability is aspect-sensitive and related to the diffusion

Table 4: Notations

SYMBOL	DESCRIPTION
N	the number of nodes in the network
M	the number of cascades
K	the number of aspects
$\mathbf{t}^c$	a cascade, $\mathbf{t}^c = (t_1^c, ..., t_N^c)^T$
$\mathbb{C}$	the collection of cascades, $\mathbb{C} = \{\mathbf{t}^1, ..., \mathbf{t}^M\}$
$\mathbb{G}$	the hidden multi-aspects diffusion network
Π	the aspects distribution, $\Pi = \{\pi_1, ...\pi_K\}$
$\mathbb{Z}$	the aspect matrix of the cascades, $\mathbb{Z} = (\mathbf{z}_i, ..., \mathbf{z}_M)$
Θ	the variable set, $\Theta = \{\mathbb{G}, \mathbb{Z}\}$
G^k	the diffusion network associated with aspect k
α_{ij}^k	the transmission rate from node i to j in aspect k
$\mathbf{z}_i$	the aspects distribution of cascade c_i
z_{ik}	if c_i belongs to aspect k, $z_{ik} = 1$; otherwise, $z_{ik} = 0$
π_k	the probability of the k_{th} aspect
$\delta^{\mathbb{C}}$	the diffusion pattern parameters, $\delta^{\mathbb{C}} = \{\delta^1, ...\delta^M\}$

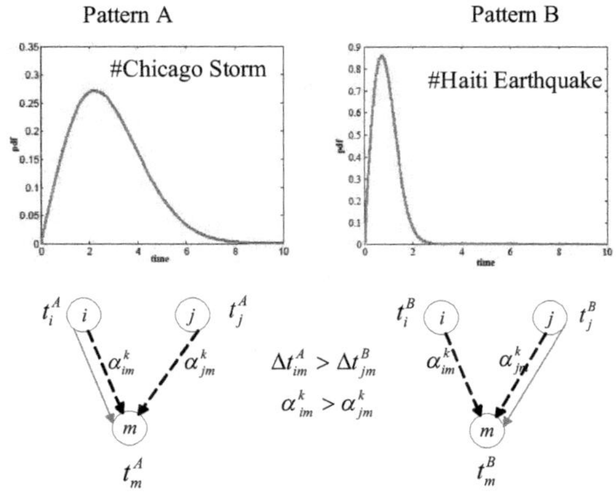

Figure 3: An Illustration to Show How the Diffusion Patterns Reflect Information Propagation

patterns. Hence we decompose the probability of one node i activating one of its neighbors j in the cascade $\mathbf{t}^c$ into two parts: the aspect-sensitive transmission rate α_{ij}^k, and the probability that cascade $\mathbf{t}^c$ with a pattern parameter δ^c takes time Δt_{ij}^c to infect a new node. Before describing MMRate in detail, we first give some notations in Table 4.

Probability of node i infecting node j. The probability of node i infecting node j in the cascade $\mathbf{t}^c$ with aspect k and pattern δ^c can be represented as :

$$f(\Delta t_{ij}^c; k, \delta^c) = g_1(\Delta t_{ij}^c; g_2(\alpha_{ij}^k, \delta^c)). \quad (1)$$

Here, $g_1(\cdot)$ is the distribution to model the conditional likelihood of node i infecting j given the aspect-sensitive transmission rate α_{ij}^k, diffusion pattern parameter δ^c and the time gap Δt_{ij}^c. $g_2(\cdot)$ is a mapping function. Given α_{ij}^k and δ^c, $g_2(\cdot)$ combines the two values. Here we simply sum the two values, i.e. $g_2(\alpha_{ij}^k, \delta^c) = \alpha_{ij}^k + \delta^c$.

In this paper, we apply the following three distributions to model the diffusion probability function $g_1(\cdot)$: exponential, power-law and Rayleigh. The exponential and power-law distributions are widely used to model information diffusion in social networks [7, 18]. Rayleigh distribution is a non-monotonic parametric model used in epidemiology [24]. Recently the Rayleigh model is also adopted to model information diffusion [6, 8]. For simplicity, we assume the diffusion pattern function $g_2(\cdot)$ of the cascade $\mathbf{t}^c$ also follows one of the three distributions with a distribution parameter δ^c, and the maximum likelihood estimation (MLE) of δ^c can be derived from the distribution function. The mathematical expressions of the three models and the corresponding MLE of δ^c are given in Table 5.

Further explanation of MMRate. Intuitively, the probability that node i transmits the information c to node j depends on both their aspect-sensitive transmission rate α_{ij}^k and the diffusion pattern with the parameter δ^c. As we studied previously, the diffusion patterns of cascades can reflect users' retweeting behavior. The propagation of microblogs are also related to their diffusion patterns, and those popular ones can spread between two users independent of their *closeness*. Figure 3 gives an example to show how different diffusion patterns reflect information propagation. The upper two figures show the diffusion patterns of the two hashtags in Twitter: "#Chicago Storm" and "#Haiti Earthquake", and the lower two figures show the corresponding diffusion paths. The dashed black lines in the lower two figures represent the underlying possible diffusion paths, and the red solid ones are the real diffusion paths. The transmission rate from i to m is larger than that from j to m ($\alpha_{im}^k > \alpha_{jm}^k$), but the time interval between j and m is smaller than that between i and m ($\Delta t_{im}^A > \Delta t_{jm}^B$). One can see that the diffusion paths of the two hashtags are different. For the hashtag "#Chicago Storm", the transmission rate contributes more to its diffusion, but for the spreading of "#Haiti Earthquake", time plays a more important role.

Likelihood of node i infecting j in cascade $\mathbf{t}^c$. In a cascade, we assume 1) one node gets infected once the first parent infects it, and 2) all the parents infect their child nodes independently. Based on the two assumptions, the likelihood of the parent node i infecting the child node j in the cascade $\mathbf{t}^c$ with aspect k and pattern δ^c can be computed by

$$f(\Delta t_{ij}^c; \alpha_{ij}^k, \delta^c, G^k) \times \prod_{i \neq u, t_u^c < t_j^c} S(\Delta t_{uj}^c; \alpha_{uj}^k, \delta^c, G^k). \quad (2)$$

In the cascade $\mathbf{t}^c$, the node j could possibly infected by any one of its parent nodes. Hence the likelihood of j getting infected in the cascade $\mathbf{t}^c$ can be calculated by summing over the likelihoods of each potential parent being the first one to infect it.

$$\Gamma_j^+(\mathbf{t}^c; k, \mathbb{G}, \delta^c) = \sum_{i: t_i^c < t_j^c} f(\Delta t_{ij}^c; \alpha_{ij}^k, \delta^c, G^k) \times \prod_{i \neq k, t_u^c < t_j^c} S(\Delta t_{uj}^c; \alpha_{uj}^k, \delta^c, G^k). \quad (3)$$

Likelihood of node survived from the cascade $\mathbf{t}^c$. If node j is survived from all the parents by the time T^c, we say the node is survived from the cascade $\mathbf{t}^c$. The likelihood that node j is survived from the cascade $\mathbf{t}^c$ can be represented by the following product of survival function

$$\Gamma_j^-(\mathbf{t}^c; k, \mathbb{G}, \delta^c) = \prod_{t_i^c < T^c} S(T^c - t_j^c; \alpha_{ij}^k, \delta^c, G^k). \quad (4)$$

Table 5: Three Distributions to Model the Edge Transmission Likelihoods

Model	Propagation likelihood $f(\Delta t^c_{ij}; k, \delta^c, \mathbb{G})$	Log survival function $\log S_{ij}(\Delta t^c_{ij}; k, \delta^c, \mathbb{G})$	Hazard function $H_{ij}(\Delta t^c_{ij}; k, \delta^c, \mathbb{G})$	MLE of δ^c $\hat{\delta}^c$
EXP	$\begin{cases}(\alpha^k_{ij}+\delta^c)\cdot e^{-(\alpha^k_{ij}+\delta^c)\Delta t^c_{ij}} \text{ if } t_i < t_j \\ 0 \text{ otherwise}\end{cases}$	$-(\alpha^k_{ij}+\delta^c)\cdot\Delta t^c_{ij}$	$\alpha^k_{ij}+\delta^c$	$\frac{1}{\overline{\Delta t}}$
POW	$\begin{cases}\frac{(\alpha^k_{ij}+\delta^c)}{\sigma}\cdot(\frac{\Delta t^c_{ij}}{\sigma})^{-1-(\alpha^k_{ij}+\delta^c)} \text{ if } t_i+\sigma < t_j \\ 0 \text{ otherwise}\end{cases}$	$-(\alpha^k_{ij}+\delta^c)\cdot\log(\frac{\Delta t^c_{ij}}{\sigma})$	$(\alpha^k_{ij}+\delta^c)\cdot\frac{1}{\Delta t^c_{ij}}$	$1+n[\sum_{i=1}^{n} ln\frac{\Delta t_i}{\sigma}]^{-1}$
RAY	$\begin{cases}(\alpha^k_{ij}+\delta^c)\cdot\Delta t^c_{ij}\cdot e^{-\frac{1}{2}(\alpha^k_{ij}+\delta^c)(\Delta t^c_{ij})^2} \text{ if } t_i < t_j \\ 0 \text{ otherwise}\end{cases}$	$-(\alpha^k_{ij}+\delta^c)\cdot\frac{\Delta t^2_{ij}}{2}$	$(\alpha^k_{ij}+\delta^c)\cdot\Delta t^c_{ij}$	$\overline{\Delta t}\sqrt{\frac{2}{\pi}}$

Likelihood of the cascade $\mathbf{t}^c$. Given a cascade $\mathbf{t}^c := (t^c_1, ..., t^c_N)$, its likelihood can be computed by multiplying the likelihoods of all the infected and survived nodes in the cascade. By Eq. (3) and Eq. (4), the likelihood can be represented as

$$f(\mathbf{t}^c; k, \mathbb{G}, \delta^c) = \prod_{t^c_j < T^c} \Gamma^+_j(\mathbf{t}^c) \times \prod_{t^c_j < T^c} \Gamma^-_j(\mathbf{t}^c)$$

$$= \prod_{t^c_j < T^c} \prod_{t^c_m > T^c} S(T^c - t^c_j; \alpha^k_{jm}, \delta^c, G^k) \times$$

$$\prod_{u: t^c_u < t^c_j} S(\Delta t^c_{uj}; \alpha^k_{uj}, \delta^c, G^k) \sum_{i: t^c_i < t^c_j} H(\Delta t^c_{ij}; \alpha^k_{ij}, \delta^c, G^k). \quad (5)$$

Assuming the cascades spread independently in the network, the likelihood of a set of cascades $\mathbb{C} = \{\mathbf{t}^1, ..., \mathbf{t}^M\}$ is the product of the likelihoods of all the individual cascades.

$$\prod_{\mathbf{t}^c \in \mathbb{C}} f(\mathbf{t}^c; \mathbb{Z}, \delta^c, \mathbb{G}). \quad (6)$$

Inferring the network. Given a set of cascades $\mathbb{C} = \{\mathbf{t}^1, ..., \mathbf{t}^M\}$ with estimated diffusion patterns $\delta^{\mathbb{C}}$, our goal here is to find the aspect matrix of the cascades $\mathbb{Z} = (\mathbf{z}^1, ..., \mathbf{z}^M)$ and the graph $\mathbb{G}$ to maximize the likelihood of generating the cascades collection $\mathbb{C}$. This problem can be reduced to solve the following convex optimization problem

$$\min\nolimits_{\mathbb{G},\mathbb{Z}} - \sum_{c \in C} \log f(\mathbf{t}^c; \mathbb{Z}, \delta^c, \mathbb{G}) \quad (7)$$

$$\text{s. t.} \quad \alpha^k_{ij} \geq 0, z_{ik} \in \{0,1\} \text{ and } \sum_{k=1:K} z_{ik} = 1$$

$$i, j = 1, ..., N, i \neq j; k = 1, ..., K$$

where α^k_{ij} is the aspect-sensitive transmission rate variable in the multi-aspect graph $\mathbb{G}$; $\mathbb{Z} = \{z_{ik} | i, k = 1, ..., N\}$ is the matrix of the aspect variables. The edges of the k-aspect network are those pairs of nodes with transmission rate $\alpha^k_{ij} > 0$.

4.2 Parameter Estimation

To solve Eq. (7), we have to infer the aspect matrix $\mathbb{Z}$ and the graph $\mathbb{G}$. In this subsection, we propose an Expectation Maximization method to infer the two groups of parameters.

Similar to the Gaussian mixture model, we first consider the aspect matrix $\mathbb{Z} = (\mathbf{z}_1, .., \mathbf{z}_M)$ as hidden variables, where $\mathbf{z}_i$ denotes the aspect vector of cascade c_i. If cascade c_i belongs to the k_{th} aspect, only the k_{th} element z_{ik} of $\mathbf{z}_i$ is 1 and all the other elements z_{im} $(m \neq k)$ are 0. In addition, we use π_k to denote the probability of the k_{th} aspect in $\mathbb{C}$.

The complete likelihood of all the cascades can be represented as

$$\begin{aligned}
&\log\mathbb{L}(\mathbb{G}, \Pi | \mathbb{C}, \mathbb{Z}, \delta^{\mathbb{C}}) \\
=&\log p(\mathbb{C}, \mathbb{Z} | \mathbb{G}, \Pi, \delta^{\mathbb{C}}) \\
=&\log \prod_{i=1}^{M} p(\mathbf{t}^{c_i}, \mathbf{z}_i | \mathbb{G}, \Pi, \delta^{c_i}) \quad (8) \\
=&\sum_{i=1}^{M} \log \sum_{k=1}^{K} p(\mathbf{t}^{c_i} | z_{ik} = 1, G^k, \delta^{c_i}) \cdot p(z_{ik} = 1 | \mathbb{G}) \\
=&\sum_{i=1}^{M} \log \sum_{k=1}^{K} p(\mathbf{t}^{c_i} | z_{ik} = 1, G^k, \delta^{c_i}) \cdot \pi_k
\end{aligned}$$

The E-Step: For simplicity, we user Θ to denote the variables $\mathbb{G}$ and $\mathbb{Z}$. That is, $\Theta = \{\mathbb{G}, \mathbb{Z}\}$. Then the E-step can be formulated as

$$\begin{aligned}
&Q(\Theta, \Theta^{(t-1)}) \\
=&Q[(\mathbb{G}; \mathbb{Z}), (\mathbb{G}; \mathbb{Z})^{(t-1)}] \\
=&E_{f(\mathbb{Z})|\mathbb{C},\Theta^{(t-1)}}[\mathbb{L}(\mathbb{G}, \Pi | \mathbb{C}, \mathbb{Z}, \delta^{\mathbb{C}}) | \mathbb{C}, \Theta^{(t-1)}] \\
=&\int_{\mathbf{z}} \log[\mathbb{L}(\mathbb{G}, \pi | \mathbb{C}, \mathbf{z})] p(\mathbf{z} | \mathbb{C}, \Theta^{(t-1)}, \delta^{\mathbb{C}}) d_{\mathbf{z}} \\
=&\int_{\mathbf{z}} \sum_{i=1}^{M} \log[p(c_i | z_{ik} = 1, \delta^{c_i}) \cdot \pi_k] \prod_{j=1}^{N} p(z_{jk} = 1 | c_i, \Theta^{(t-1)}) d_{\mathbf{z}} \\
=&\sum_{k=1}^{K} \sum_{i=1}^{M} \log[p(c_i | G_k, \delta^{c_i}) \cdot \pi_k] p(z_{ik} = 1 | c_i, \Theta^{(t-1)}) \quad (9) \\
=&\sum_{k=1}^{K} \sum_{i=1}^{M} \log(\pi_k) \cdot p(z_{ik} = 1 | c_i, \Theta^{(t-1)}) + \\
&\sum_{k=1}^{K} \sum_{i=1}^{M} \log[p(c_i | G_k, \delta^{c_i})] \cdot p(z_{ik} = 1 | c_i, \Theta^{(t-1)}).
\end{aligned}$$

Using Bayes's rule, we can compute

$$p(z_{ik} = 1 | c_i, \Theta^{(t-1)}) = \frac{\pi^{(t-1)}_k p(c_i | G^{(t-1)}_k, \delta^{c_i})}{\sum_{m=1}^{K} \pi^{(t-1)}_m p(c_i | G^{(t-1)}_m, \delta^{c_i})} \quad (10)$$

and

$$p(\mathbb{Z} | \mathbb{C}, \Theta^{(t-1)}) = \prod_{i=1}^{M} p(\mathbf{z}_i | c_i, \Theta^{(t-1)}). \quad (11)$$

In order to get the estimation for π_k, we need to maximize

$\mathbb{Q}^{(\Theta,\Theta^{(t-1)})}$. Introducing Lagrange multiplier λ, we get:

$$\frac{\partial}{\partial \pi_k}[\mathbb{Q}^{(\Theta,\Theta^{(t-1)})} + \lambda(\sum_{k=1}^{K} \pi_k - 1)] = 0. \quad (12)$$

That is

$$\sum_{i=1}^{M} \frac{1}{\pi_k} p(z_{ik} = 1 | c_i, \Theta^{(t-1)}) + \lambda = 0. \quad (13)$$

Thus, combing Equ. (10) and (13). We get the new estimation for π_k given previous $\Theta^{(t-1)}$

$$\pi_k = \frac{\sum_{i=1}^{M} \pi_k^{(t-1)} p(c_i | G_k^{(t-1)}, \delta^{c_i})}{\sum_{i=1}^{M} \sum_{m=1}^{K} \pi_k^{(t-1)} p(c_i | G_m^{(t-1)}, \delta^{c_i})}. \quad (14)$$

M-Step: In the M-Step, we maximize the expectation of the parameter Θ

$$\text{maximize } Q(\Theta, \Theta^{(t-1)}). \quad (15)$$

5. EXPERIMENTAL RESULTS

In this section, we will conduct extensive experiments to evaluate the proposed model MMRate. More specifically, we want to evaluate: 1) the effectiveness of MMRate in recovering multi-aspect network structure; 2) the effectiveness of MMRate in estimating the aspect-sensitive transmission rates between each pair of connected nodes; and 3) the application of MMRate to other data mining tasks.

We begin with introducing the experimental setup, and then compare the performance of MMRate against baselines on both synthetic and real-world datasets. Finally, we give a case study to show how MMRate can be applied to help us rank aspect-sensitive influential user in microblogging.

5.1 Experimental Setup

Dataset. Besides the real social network datasets described in Section 3, we also use various synthetic datasets to evaluate our approach. We use the popular Kronecker Graph model [16] to generate the following three types of graphs with different topological structures: random graph, hierarchical graph, and core-periphery graph. For each type of graph, we first set the aspect size K. For each aspect k, we generate an aspect-sensitive graph G_k by drawing the pairwise transmission rate α_{ij}^k for edge e_{ij} from a uniform distribution. In this way, we obtain a K-aspect graph $\mathbb{G}$. Next, over each aspect-sensitive graph G_k we generate cascades over it. We first generate the aspect distribution $\Pi = \{\pi_1, ..., \pi_K\}$. Each time we randomly draw an aspect k from the distribution, and then over the corresponding graph G_k, we generate a cascade. Root nodes of cascades are chosen uniformly at random. Once a node is infected, the propagation probabilities of outgoing edges of the node determine the infection of its neighbors. The diffusion process continues until some terminating conditions are satisfied, such as reaching the maximum time window T or no more nodes getting infected.

Baselines. As MMRate infers both the connectivity of the network and the transmission rates over each edge, we compare MMRate with the following two state-of-the-art baselines which also infer both the network structure and pairwise transmission rates between nodes.

- **NETRATE**[2] [6]. This is an effective and representative model for inferring the hidden diffusion networks.
- **InfoPath**[3] [8]. InfoPath is an approach proposed recently to infer the dynamic diffusion networks. It can also work on static networks as long as the networks at each time step are the same.
- **Multi-aspect Model** This method is included to examine whether incorporating the diffusion patterns can improve the performance. Multi-aspect model only incorporates the multi-aspects, but ignores the diffusion patterns. That is, the parameter δ^c is set to 0.

Evaluation Metrics. We evaluate the performance via the following two metrics,

- F_1-*measure*. F_1-*measure* is defined as F_1-*measure* $= \frac{2 \cdot precision \cdot recall}{precision + recall}$, where precision is the fraction of edges in the inferred network $\hat{\mathbb{G}}$ present in the true network $\mathbb{G}$, and recall is the fraction of edges of the true network $\mathbb{G}$ present in the inferred network $\hat{\mathbb{G}}$;
- *Mean Absolute Error*. To access the accuracy of the estimated transmission rates α_{ij}, we compute the mean absolute error as follows: $MAE = E(\frac{|\alpha_{ij} - \hat{\alpha}_{ij}|}{\alpha_{ij}})$, where $\alpha_{ij} = \sum_{k=1}^{K} \alpha_{ij}^k$ is the true transmission rate and $\hat{\alpha}_{ij} = \sum_{k=1}^{K} \hat{\alpha}_{ij}^k$ is the estimated transmission rate.

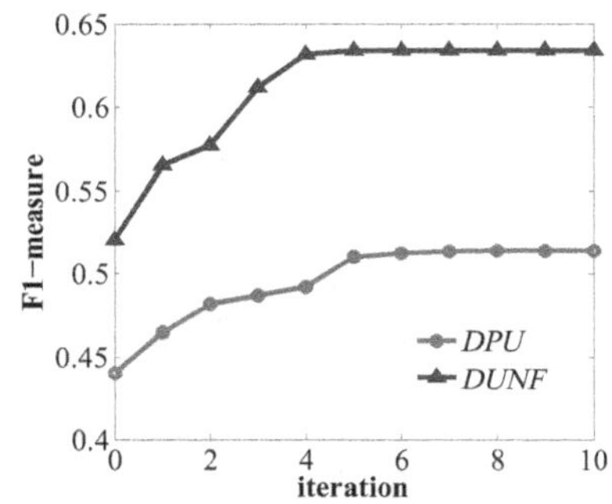

Figure 4: Convergence Curves

Convergence analysis. Before evaluation, we first examine the convergence of MMRate. Figure 4 shows the convergence curves of MMRate on the datasets *DPU* and *DUNF*. One can see that the F_1-*measure* on both datasets first keeps increasing, and then stabilizes after 5 or 6 iterations, which means MMRate can effectively converge. Through the iterations, the F_1-*measure* improvement for *DPU* is about 0.08 (from 0.44 to 0.52), and about 0.12 (from 0.52 to 0.64) for *DUNF*.

5.2 Performance Evaluation on Synthetic Data

To evaluate the effectiveness of MMRate on recovering the network structure as well as estimating the transmission rates of each aspect, we compare it with NETRATE and InfoPath on various synthetic data. Since the latent network and corresponding transmission rates for generating

[2]http://people.tuebingen.mpg.de/manuelgr/netrate/
[3]http://snap.stanford.edu/infopath/index.html

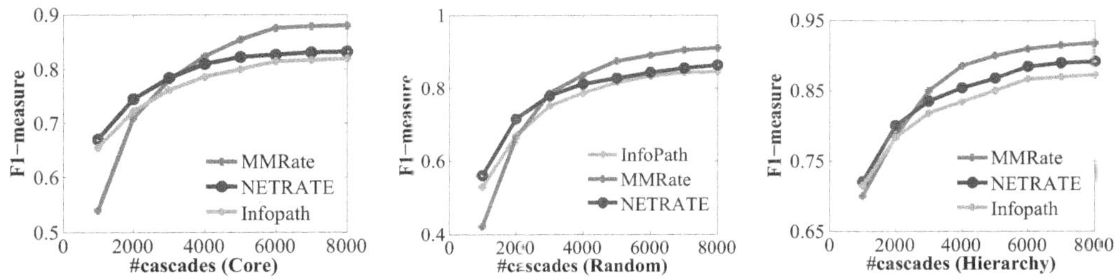

Figure 5: F_1-*measure* of the Three Methods on 3-Aspect Networks with 512 Nodes and 1024 Edges

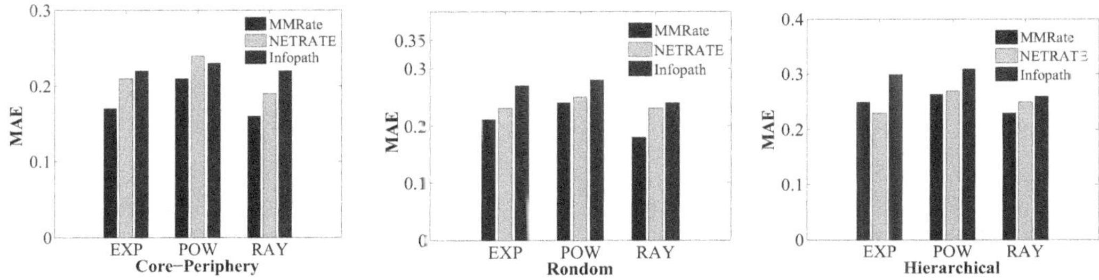

Figure 6: Mean Absolute Error of the Three Methods on 3-Aspect Networks with 512 Nodes and 1024 Edges

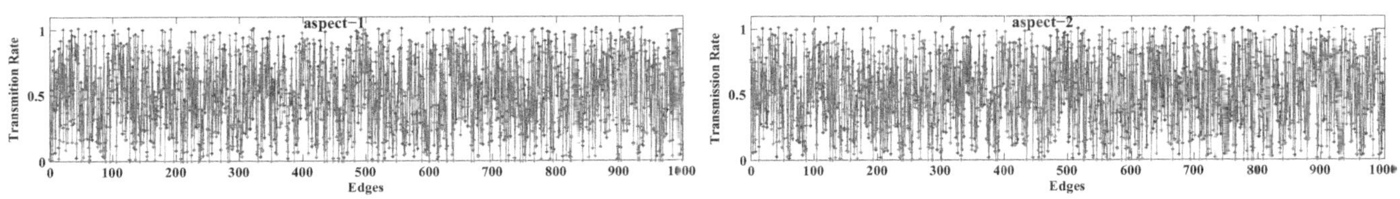

Figure 7: Visualization of the True Transmission Rates (Red Lines) *vs* the Estimated Transmission Rates (Blue Lines) Over a 2-Aspect Diffusion Network

cascades are known in advance, we can perform quantitive comparisons with the two baselines.

Figure 5 shows the F_1-*measure* of the three methods over the three types of generated networks with 512 nodes and 1024 edges. We can observe that MMRate performs inferior to the baselines when the number of cascade is less than 3,000, but with the increase of the number of cascades, MMRate outperforms NETRATE and InfoPath by up to 8%. This is because our model aims to infer the multi-aspect network, and hence each aspect of the network needs enough data to be inferred. One can also see that the F_1-*measure* steadily increases as we increase the number of cascades, and stabilizes with around 6,000 cascades.

Figure 6 shows the mean absolute error (MAE) between the estimated networks and the true networks with 5,000 cascades. One can see that in almost all the cases (with only one exception), the MAE of MMRate is smaller that the two baselines. It means that our method can not only more accurately infer the network structure, but also more precisely estimate the transmission rates over the edges.

To further test the effectiveness of MMRate on estimating the transmission rates of each aspect on the multi-aspect diffusion networks, we visualize the estimated and the true transmission rates over the edges of a 2-aspect network in Figure 7. We can observe that MMRate first recovers most edges for each aspect network. MMRate only fails to infer the edges whose estimated transmission rates are zero. Second, the transmission rates of each aspect estimated by MMRate seem good. The mean absolute error of estimated aspect-sensitive transmission rates are mostly less than 0.3. It indicates that MMRate can effectively estimate the transmission rates over the edges for each aspect network.

5.3 Performance Evaluation on Real Data

To evaluate the performance of MMRate on real data, we compare the F_1-*measure* achieved by MMRate and three baselines on *DPU* and *DUNF* datasets.

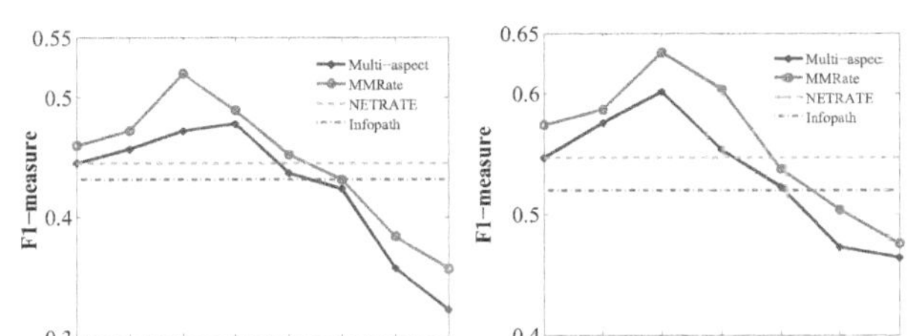

Figure 8: Comparison of F_1-*measure* on two Datasets

Figure 8 shows the best experimental results of the three diffusion models on the two datasets. For the dataset *DPU*, the exponential model achieves the best result and for the dataset *DUNF*, the best result is achieved by the Rayleigh

Table 6: Aspect-Sensitive Top-5 Users of the 3-Aspect *DPU* Dataset

aspect	User ID	# of followers	# of posts	description (occupation or tags)
k=1	1830438495	529,837	10,551	**Occupation:** a famous writer
	1496850204	3,647,584	13,307	**Occupation:** the chief editor of *New Weekly*
	1733596871	198,192	6,381	**Occupation:** a famous columnist
	1737694433	828,899	10,529	**Occupation:** a columnist of *The Wall Street Journal* (Chinese version)
	1641428154	175,533	10,698	**Occupation:** a famous columnist
k=2	1266321801	29,382,466	7,043	**Occupation:** a famous actress
	1656809190	27,000,777	2,911	**Occupation:** a famous actress
	1704116960	24,796,098	1,069	**Occupation:** a famous TV show host
	1645826702	1323179	7,985	**Occupation:** writer, screenwriter and director
	1282005885	25,020,327	1,650	**Tags:** entertainment, art, literature and media
k=3	1813080181	11,709,072	85,012	**Tags:** mobile internet, Start Your Business (SYB)
	1558226504	1,819,724	8,877	**Tags:** CEO, design, Start Your Business (SYB)
	1737694433	828,899	10,529	**Occupation:** a columnist of *The Wall Street Journal* (Chinese version)
	1653689003	8,350,338	17,520	**Occupation:** *New Weekly* (the microblog site of the *New Weekly* journal)
	1641983193	204,420	11,095	**Tags:** Internet, E-Commerce and social media

model. The first observation from Figure 8 is that with the increase of cascade number, the F_1-*measure* achieved by MMRate first increases, and then gradually decreases. The best performance is achieved with around 3 or 4 aspects. More aspects make the performance worse due to over-fitting. Second, by differentiating the cascades into a small number of aspect groups, MMRate can significantly outperform the baselines. For *DPU*, MMRate outperforms baselines by 15% with K equals to 3; for *DUNF*, the improvement can be up to 20%. Moreover, the performance of MMRate is always better than the multi-aspect model. It indicates that considering the diffusion patterns of the cascades can better capture the information diffusion process in social networks; and therefore, help us more accurately recover the diffusion networks.

5.4 Application of MMRate: A Case Study

MMRate can also be applied to help other data mining tasks, such as aspect-sensitive influential mining and aspect-level influence maximization. Here we give a case study to show how MMRate can be used to help us mining aspect-sensitive influential users in social networks.

Given a diffusion graph G^k with the aspect k, the influence of its users can be ranked by a weighted PageRank algorithm as follows

$$\mathbf{R}^k = (1-d)\cdot\frac{\mathbf{E}}{N^k} + d\cdot\mathbf{A}^k\cdot\mathbf{R}^k \qquad (16)$$

where the vector $\mathbf{R}^k$ denotes the authorities of the nodes, $\mathbf{E}$ is a column vector containing only ones, $\mathbf{A}^k$ is the weighted adjacency matrix with each entry $A^k_{ij} = \alpha^k_{ij}$, d is the damping factor, and N^k is the number of nodes.

Due to space limitation, we only report the ranking result of the dataset *DPU*. Table 6 lists the top-5 users of each aspect in the 3-aspect network of *DPU*. For each user, we show the user ID, the number of followers, the number of posts and the descriptions for this user. We use the tags or occupations of the users to describe them. As not all the users make their occupations public available, for such users we give their tags. We can see that the ranking result seems reasonable. First, most of the top ranked users have a large number of followers, which implies they are very popular. Some top uses in aspect 2 even have tens of millions followers. Second, most of these users have published more than 6,000 posts. This means these users are also very active and have more chances to interact with their friends or followers. Therefore, we can infer more connections to these users and rank them high. Moreover, top users in different aspects are mostly different. The top-5 users of aspect-1 are famous writers, columnists, or editors; the users of aspect-2 are mostly famous actors, TV show hosts, or directors; and users of aspect-3 are mostly interested in commerce, Internet, or new media. Some users are famous in multiple aspects. For example, the user with ID 1737694433 ranks in the top-5 of both aspect-1 and aspect-2. For most top ranking users, however, they are only very influential in just one aspect. It implies that MMRate can effectively categorize different types of users into different diffusion networks.

6. RELATED WORK

The problem of inferring the diffusion networks and estimating the diffusion probabilities has been intensively studied in social network analysis [6, 7, 8, 9, 10, 20, 21]. Earlier work in [10, 20, 21] considers the network structure is known and as an input to estimate the diffusion probabilities on the edges through the spreading events. Kazumi et al. proposed a likelihood maximization approach for the learning of the information diffusion probabilities for the Independent Cascade Model [21]. To estimate the diffusion probabilities for a continuous time delay independent cascade (CTIC) model, Saito el. al also proposed an approach to maximize the likelihood of the observed diffusion cascades [20].

Recently, some work has focused on inferring the diffusion networks with hidden structures from the time logs of a collection of cascades [6, 7, 8, 9, 18]. These work can be roughly divided into inferring the network connectivity [7, 9] and inferring both the network structure and the transmission rates between nodes [6, 8, 18]. The representative work on inferring the network structure is NetInfer [7], which formulates this problem as a submodular function maximization problem. A variant of NetInfer to tradeoff between accuracy and scalability is MulTree [9]. NETRATE is a representative approach to infer not only the connectivity of the network, but also to estimate the transmission rates of infections between two connected nodes [6]. This method tries to find the optimal network that maximizes the likelihood of the observed cascades by using convex optimization. A further work based on NETRATE is InfoPath [8], which aims to infer the dynamic diffusion networks.

It has long been studied both in social theories [11, 15] and computer society [1, 22, 23] that influence diffusion and information propagation are related to the types of relationships between users. Tang et al. [22] discerned multi-faceted trust on social media, and proposed a model mTrust to estimate the trust strengths of different facets. To differentiate the social influences from different topics, Tang et al [23] proposed Topic Affinity Propagation (TAP) to model the topic-level social influence on large networks. However, distinguishing different types of cascades for inferring diffusion networks with multiple aspects is less studied. An effort devoted to differentiate cascades with different topics recently is TopicCascade [3]. However, TopicCascade uses topic model to find the topics each cascade related to instead of inferring them from the diffusion data.

7. CONCLUSIONS AND FUTURE WORK

Different from tradition network data which are mostly homogeneous, the user interactions on social networks are usually multi-aspected and the cascades show various diffusion patterns, which present challenges to infer the heterogeneous diffusion networks in social media. In this paper, we proposed a novel model MMRate to handle multi-aspect and multi-pattern cascades for inferring multi-aspect diffusion networks. In particular, we studied the existence of various diffusion patterns of cascades and the effects of the different patterns on information diffusion. By incorporating the aspects and patterns of the cascades, the fine-grained model MMRate was proposed. To effectively estimate the parameters, an EM-algorithm was also provided. Experimental results on both synthetic and real social network datasets showed the effectiveness of MMRate compared against state-of-the-art approaches.

For future work it would be interesting to study whether MMRate can be applied to other domains, such as the virus propagation networks. Similar to information diffusion in social networks, the virus propagation networks are also multi-aspected due to the facts that people's immunity differs for different viruses [4]. Different viruses may tend to propagate among different groups of people. We are also interested in applying our model to help other social media applications, such as predicting trending topics with different aspects in social media. In the future, we will investigate whether the aspect-level transmission rates between users estimated by MMRate can help us more accurately predict the future popularity of the topics with different aspects.

8. ACKNOWLEDGMENTS

This work is supported by NSFC (Grand Nos. 61170189, 61370126, 61202239), the Research Fund for the Doctoral Program of Higher Education (Grand No. 20111102130003), the Innovation Foundation of BUAA for PhD Graduates (Grand No. YWF-14-YJSY-021), Microsoft Research Asia Fund (Grand No. FY14-RES-OPP-105), NSF through grants CNS-1115234, DBI-0960443, and OISE-1129076, and the Pinnacle Lab at Singapore Management University.

9. REFERENCES

[1] N. Barbieri, F. Bonchi, and G. Manco. Topic-aware social influence propagation models. *Knowledge and information systems*, 37(3):555–584, 2013.

[2] W. Chen, C. Wang, and Y. Wang. Scalable influence maximization for prevalent viral marketing in large-scale social networks. In *KDD, 2010*.

[3] N. Du, L. Song, H. Woo, and H. Zha. Uncover topic-sensitive information diffusion networks. In *AISTATS, 2013*.

[4] D. D. Erdman. Propagation and identification of viruses. *Topley and Wilson's Microblology and Microblal Infections*, 2010.

[5] J. Goldenberg, B. Libai, and E. Muller. Using complex systems analysis to advance marketing theory development: Modeling heterogeneity effects on new product growth through stochastic cellular automata. *Academy of Marketing Science Review*, 2001.

[6] M. Gomez-Rodriguez, D. Balduzzi, and B. Scholkopf. Uncovering the temporal dynamics of diffusion networks. In *ICML, 2011*.

[7] M. Gomez-Rodriguez, J. Leskovec, and A. Krause. Inferring networks of diffusion and influence. In *KDD, 2010*.

[8] M. Gomez-Rodriguez, J. Leskovec, and B. Scholkopf. Structure and dynamics of information pathways in online media. In *WSDM, 2013*.

[9] M. Gomez-Rodriguez and B. Scholkopf. Submodular inference of diffusion networks from multiple trees. In *ICML, 2012*.

[10] A. Goyal, F. Bonchi, and L. V. S. Lakshmanan. Learning influence probabilities in social networks. In *WSDM, 2010*.

[11] M. S. Granovetter. The strength of weak ties. *American Journal of Sociology*, 78(6):1360–1380, May 1973.

[12] M. Herlihy. Diffusion in organizations and social movements: From hybrid corn to poison pills. *Annual Review of Sociology*, 24:265–290, August 1998.

[13] D. Kempe, J. Kleinberg, and E. Tardos. Maximizing the spread of influence through a social network. In *KDD, 2003*.

[14] A. Klovdahl, J. J. Potterat, D. E. Woodhouse, J. B. Muth, S. Q. Muth, and W. W. Darrow. Social networks and infectious disease: The colorado springs study. *Social Science and Medicine*, 38(1):79–88, January 1993.

[15] D. Krackhardt. *The Strength of Strong ties: the Importance of Philos in Organization.* Harvard Business School Press, 1992.

[16] J. Leskovec, D. Chakrabarti, J. Kleinberg, C. Faloutsos, and Z. Ghahramani. Kronecker graphs: An approach to modeling networks. *Journals of Machine Learning Research*, 11:985–1042, 2010.

[17] J. Leskovec, A. Singh, and J. Kleinberg. Patterns of influence in a recommendation network. In *PAKDD, 2006*.

[18] S. A. Myers and J. Leskovec. On the convexity of latent social network inference. In *NIPS, 2010*.

[19] J. Oh, A. Suasarla, and Y. Tan. Examining the diffusion of user-generated content in online social networks. *Social Science Research Network*, 2008.

[20] K. Saito, M. Kimura, K. Ohara, and H. Motoda. Learning continuous-time information diffusion model for social behavioral data analysis. In *ACML, 2009*.

[21] K. Saito, R. Nakano, and M. Kimura. Prediction of information diffusion probabilities for independent cascade model. In *KES, 2008*.

[22] J. Tang, H. Gao, and H. Liu. mtrust: Discerning multi-faceted trust in a connected world. In *WSDM, 2012*.

[23] J. Tang, J. Sun, C. Wang, and Z. Yang. Social influence analysis in large-scale networks. In *KDD, 2009*.

[24] J. Wallinga and P. Teunis. Different epidemic curves for severe acute respiratory syndrome reveal similar impacts of control measures. *American Journal of Epidemiology*, 15(6):509–516, Sep 2004.

[25] J. Zhang, B. Liu, J. Tang, T. Chen, and J. Li. Social influence locality for modeling retweeting behaviors. In *IJCAI, 2013*.

Stability of Influence Maximization

Xinran He
University of Southern California
941 Bloom Walk
Los Angeles, CA, United States
xinranhe@usc.edu

David Kempe
University of Southern California
941 Bloom Walk
Los Angeles, CA, United States
dkempe@usc.edu

ABSTRACT

In the well-studied Influence Maximization problem, the goal is to identify a set of k nodes in a social network whose joint influence on the network is maximized. A large body of recent work has justified research on Influence Maximization models and algorithms with their potential to create societal or economic value. However, in order to live up to this potential, the algorithms must be robust to large amounts of noise, for they require quantitative estimates of the influence which individuals exert on each other; ground truth for such quantities is inaccessible, and even decent estimates are very difficult to obtain.

We begin to address this concern formally. First, we exhibit simple inputs on which even very small estimation errors may mislead *every* algorithm into highly suboptimal solutions, motivating a need for algorithms that can determine whether a given instance is vulnerable to noise. Analyzing the susceptibility of specific instances to estimation errors leads to a clean algorithmic question which we term the Influence Difference Maximization problem, and for which we present an approximation algorithm based on maximizing a non-monotone submodular function.

Using the proposed techniques, we investigate the susceptibility of synthetic and real-world social network data sets. Roughly, when perturbations are on the order of 10% of the observed parameter values, the objective function is fairly stable, while relative perturbations above 20% may lead to significant instability. Our results thus suggest caution in the use of algorithmic Influence Maximization results.

Categories and Subject Descriptors

[**Human-centered computing**]: Social networks

Keywords

Influence Maximization, Uncertainty, Noise, Submodular Optimization, Robust Optimization

KDD'14, August 24–27, 2014, New York, NY, USA.
Copyright 2014 ACM 978-1-4503-2956-9/14/08 ...$15.00.
http://dx.doi.org/10.1145/2623330.2623746 .

1. INTRODUCTION

The processes and dynamics by which information and behaviors spread through social networks have long interested scientists within many areas. Understanding such processes has the potential to shed light on human social structure, and to impact the strategies used to promote behaviors or products. While the interest in the subject is long-standing, recent increased availability of social network and information diffusion data (through sites such as Facebook, Twitter, and LinkedIn) has raised the prospect of applying social network analysis at a large scale to positive effect. Consequently, the resulting algorithmic questions have received widespread interest in the computer science community.

Among the broad algorithmic domains, Influence Maximization has been repeatedly held up as having the potential to be of societal and financial value. The high-level hope is that based on observed data — such as social network information and past behavior — an algorithm could infer which individuals are likely to influence which others. This information could in turn be used to effect desired behavior, such as refraining from smoking, using superior crops, or purchasing a product. In the latter case, the goal of effecting desired behavior is usually termed *viral marketing.*

Consequently, both the problem of inferring the influence between individuals [10, 11, 18] and that of maximizing the spread of a desired behavior have been studied extensively. For the Influence Maximization problem, a large number of models have been proposed, along with many heuristics with and without approximation guarantees [5, 23, 8, 13, 14, 17]. (See the monograph [7] for a recent overview of work in the area.)

However, one crucial aspect of the problem has — with very few execeptions discussed in Section 1.6 — gone largely unstudied. Contrary to many other algorithmic domains, *noise in social network data is not an exception, but the norm.* Indeed, one could argue that the very notion of a "social link" is not properly defined in the first place, so that any representation of a social network is only an approximation of reality. This issue is much more pronounced for a goal such as Influence Maximization. Here, the required data include, for every pair (u, v) of individuals, a numerical value for the strength of influence from u to v and vice versa. This influence strength will naturally depend on context (e.g., what exact product or behavior is being spread); furthermore, it cannot be observed directly, and must therefore be inferred from observed behavior or individuals' reports; all of these are inherently very noisy.

When the inferred influence strength parameters differ from the actual ground truth, even an optimal algorithm is bound to return suboptimal solutions, for it will optimize the wrong objective function: a solution that appears good with respect to the incorrect parameters may be bad with respect to the actual ones. If relatively small errors in the inferred parameters could lead to highly suboptimal solutions, this would cast serious doubts on the practical viability of algorithmic influence maximization. *Therefore, in the present paper, we begin an in-depth study of the effect of noise on the performance of Influence Maximization algorithms.*

1.1 The Independent Cascade Model

We study this question under two widely adopted models for influence diffusion [13]: the *Independent Cascade (IC) Model* and the *Linear Threshold (LT) Model*. Both of these models fit in the following framework: The algorithm selects a *seed set* A_0 of k nodes, which begin *active* (having adopted the behavior). Starting with A_0, the process proceeds in discrete time steps: in each time step, according to a probabilistic process, additional nodes may become active based on the influence from their neighbors. Active nodes never become inactive, and the process terminates when no new nodes become active in a time step. The goal is to maximize the expected number of active nodes when the process terminates; this expected number is denoted by $\sigma(A_0)$.

To illustrate the questions and approaches, we describe the IC model in this section. (A formal description of the LT model and general definitions of all concepts are given in Section 2.) Under the IC model, the probabilistic process is particularly simple and intuitive. When a node u becomes active in step t, it attempts to activate all currently inactive neighbors in step $t+1$. For each neighbor v, it succeeds with a known probability $p_{u,v}$. If it succeeds, v becomes active; otherwise, v remains inactive. Once u has made all these attempts, it does not get to make further activation attempts at later times. It was shown in [13] (see Lemma 3) that the set of nodes active at the end can be characterized alternatively as follows: for each ordered pair (u, v) independently, insert the directed edge (u, v) with probability $p_{u,v}$. Then, the active nodes are exactly the ones reachable via directed paths from A_0.

1.2 Can Instability Occur?

Suppose that we have inferred all parameters $p_{u,v}$, but are concerned that they may be slightly off: in reality, the influence probabilities are $p'_{u,v} \approx p_{u,v}$. Are there instances in which a seed set A_0 that is very influential with respect to the $p_{u,v}$ may be much less influential with respect to the $p'_{u,v}$? It is natural to suspect that this might not occur: when the objective function σ varies sufficiently smoothly with the input parameters (e.g., for linear objectives), small changes in the parameters only lead to small changes in the objective value; therefore, optimizing with respect to a perturbed input still leads to a near-optimal solution.

However, the objective σ of Influence Maximization does not depend on the parameters in a smooth way. To illustrate the issues at play, consider the following instance of the IC model. The social network consists of two disjoint bidirected cliques K_n, and $p_{u,v} = \hat{p}$ for all u, v in the same clique; in other words, for each directed edge, the same activation probability $\hat{p}$ is observed. The algorithm gets to select exactly $k = 1$ node. Notice that because all nodes look the same, any algorithm essentially chooses an arbitrary node, which may as well be from Clique 1.

Let $\hat{p} = 1/n$ be the sharp threshold for the emergence of a giant component in the Erdős-Rényi Random Graph $G(n, p)$. It is well known [4, 9] that the largest connected component of $G(n,p)$ has size $O(\log n)$ for any $p \le \hat{p} - \Omega(1/n)$, and size $\Omega(n)$ for any $p \ge \hat{p} + \Omega(1/n)$. Thus, if unbeknownst to the algorithm, all true activation probabilities in Clique 1 are $p \le \hat{p} - \Omega(1/n)$, while all true activation probabilities in Clique 2 are $p \ge \hat{p} + \Omega(1/n)$, the algorithm only activates $O(\log n)$ nodes in expectation, while it could have reached $\Omega(n)$ nodes by choosing Clique 2. Hence, small adversarial perturbations to the input parameters can lead to highly suboptimal solutions from any algorithm.[1]

1.3 Diagnosing Instability

The example of two cliques shows that there exist *unstable instances*, in which an optimal solution to the observed parameters is highly suboptimal when the observed parameters are slightly perturbed compared to the true parameters. Of course, not every instance of Influence Maximization is unstable: for instance, when the probability $\hat{p}$ in the Two-Clique instance is bounded away from the critical threshold of $G(n, p)$, the objective function varies much more smoothly with $\hat{p}$. This motivates the following algorithmic question, which is the main focus of our paper: *Given an instance of Influence Maximization, can we diagnose efficiently whether it is stable or unstable?*

To make this question precise, we formulate a model of perturbations. We assume that for each edge (u, v), in addition to the observed activation probability $p_{u,v}$, we are given an interval $I_{u,v} \ni p_{u,v}$ of values that the *actual probability* $p'_{u,v}$ could assume. The *true values* $p'_{u,v}$ are chosen from the intervals $I_{u,v}$ by an adversary; they induce an objective function σ' which the algorithm would like to maximize, while the observed values induce a different objective function σ which the algorithm actually has access to.

An instance $(p_{u,v}, I_{u,v})_{u,v}$ is *stable* if $|\sigma(S) - \sigma'(S)|$ is small for all objective functions σ' induced by legal probability settings, and for all seed sets S of size k. Here, "small" is defined relative to the objective function value $\sigma(A_0^*)$ of the optimum set.

When $|\sigma(S) - \sigma'(S)|$ is small compared to $\sigma(A_0^*)$ for all sets S, we will show in Section 3 that a user can have confidence that his optimization result will provide decent performance guarantees even if his input was perturbed. The converse is of course not necessarily true: even in unstable instances, a solution that was optimal for the observed input *may* still be very good for the true input parameters.

[1]The example reveals a close connection between the stability of an IC instance and the question whether a uniform activation probability p lies close to the edge percolation threshold of the underlying graph. Characterizing the percolation threshold of families of graphs has been a notoriously hard problem. Successful characterizations have only been obtained for very few specific classes (such as d-dimensional grids [15] and d-regular expander graphs [2]). Therefore, it is unlikely that a clean characterization of stable and unstable instances can be obtained. The connection to percolation also reveals that the instability was not an artifact of having high node degrees. By the result of Alon et al. [2], the same behavior will be obtained if both components are d-regular expander graphs, since such graphs also have a sharp percolation threshold.

1.4 Influence Difference Maximization

Trying to determine whether there is a function σ' and a set S for which $|\sigma(S) - \sigma'(S)|$ is large motivates the following optimization problem: Maximize $|\sigma(S) - \sigma'(S)|$ over all feasible functions σ' and all sets S. For any given set S, the objective is maximized either by making all probabilities (and thus $\sigma'(S)$) as small as possible, or by making all probabilities (and thus $\sigma'(S)$) as large as possible.[2] We denote the resulting two objective functions by σ^- and σ^+, respectively. The following definition then captures the optimization goal.

DEFINITION 1 (INFLUENCE DIFFERENCE MAXIMIZATION). *Given two instances with probabilities $p_{u,v} \geq p'_{u,v}$ for all u, v, let σ and σ' be their respective influence functions. Find a set S of size k maximizing $\delta(S) := \sigma(S) - \sigma'(S)$.*

The Influence Difference Maximization problem subsumes the Influence Maximization problem, by setting $p'_{u,v} \equiv 0$ (and thus also $\sigma' \equiv 0$). Notice that δ is generally not monotone, as $\delta(\emptyset) = \delta(V) = 0$, while $\delta(S) > 0$ for some sets S. Our main theoretical result is that while δ is not generally monotone, it is *submodular*.[3]

THEOREM 1. *Under the IC (and also LT) model, the influence difference objective function $\delta(S)$ is a non-negative and submodular function of the set S, whenever the functions σ, σ' satisfy the conditions of Definition 1.*

The proof of Theorem 1 is given in Section 4. It lets us leverage known efficient algorithms for non-monotone submodular function maximization subject to a cardinality constraint [6, 22]. In particular, we rely on the recent simple Random Greedy approximation algorithm of Buchbinder et al. [6], which guarantees an approximation factor of at least 0.266, but gets a guarantee close to $1/e$ when $k \ll n$.

If we use the Random Greedy algorithm and determine that the maximum influence difference is significantly smaller than the objective value of Influence Maximization, we can be confident that the solution determined by the Influence Maximization algorithm is a constant-factor approximation. Otherwise, the solution may still be good; however, the algorithm cannot provide a guarantee, as the deviation from parameter misestimates may drown out the objective value.

1.5 Experiments

Next, we investigate how pervasive instabilities are in real data. We evaluate frequently used synthetic models (2D grids, random regular graphs, small-world networks, and preferential attachment graphs) and real-world data sets (computer science theory collaborations and retweets about the Haiti earthquake). We focus on the IC model, and vary the influence strengths over a broad range of commonly studied values. We consider different relative perturbation levels Δ, ranging from 1% to 50%. The adversary can thus choose the actual activation probability to lie in the interval $[p_{u,v}(1-\Delta) \cdot p_{u,v}, p_{u,v} + \Delta \cdot p_{u,v}]$.

Our experiments suggest that perturbations can have significantly different effects depending on the network structure and observed values. As a general rule of thumb, unless the parameters are carefully chosen to lie right at the percolation threshold (in which case even tiny perturbations can have huge effects), perturbations with relative errors below 10% tend to not have huge impacts, while perturbations above 20% could significantly distort the optimum solution.

Since errors above 20% should be considered quite common for estimated social network parameters, our results suggest that practitioners exercise care in evaluating the stability of their problem instances, and treat the output of Influence Maximization algorithms with a healthy dose of skepticism.

1.6 Adversarial vs. Random Perturbations

One may question why we choose to study adversarial instead of random perturbations. This choice is for three reasons:

Theoretical: Worst-case analysis provides stronger guarantees, as it is not based on particular assumptions about the distribution of noise.

Practical: Most random noise models assume independence of noise across edges. However, we believe that in practice, both the techniques used for inferring model parameters as well as the data sources they are based on may well exhibit systematic bias, i.e., the noise will not be independent. For instance, a particular subpopulation may systematically underreport the extent to which they seek others' advice, or may have fewer visible indicators (such as posts) revealing their behavior.

Modeling Interest: Perhaps most importantly, most natural random noise models do not add anything to the IC and LT models. As an illustration, consider the random noise models studied in recent work by Goyal, Bonchi and Lakshmanan [12] and Adiga et al. [1]. Goyal et al. assume that for each edge (u, v), the value of $p_{u,v}$ is perturbed with uniformly random noise from a known interval. Adiga et al. assume that each edge (u, v) that was observed to be present is actually absent with some probability ϵ, while each edge that was not observed is actually present with probability ϵ; in other words, each edge's presence is independently flipped with probability ϵ.

The standard IC model subsumes both models straightforwardly. Suppose that a decision is to be made about whether u activates v. In the model of Goyal et al., we can first draw the actual (perturbed) value of $p'_{u,v}$ from its known distribution; subsequently, u activates v with probability $p'_{u,v}$; in total, u activates v with probability $\mathbb{E}\left[p'_{u,v}\right]$. Thus, we obtain an instance of the IC model in which all edge probabilities $p_{u,v}$ are replaced by $\mathbb{E}\left[p'_{u,v}\right]$. In the special case when the noise has mean 0, this expectation is exactly equal to $p_{u,v}$, which explains why Goyal et al. observed the noise to not affect the outcome at all.

In the model of Adiga et al., we first determine whether the edge is actually present; when it was observed present, this happens with probability $1-\epsilon$; otherwise

[2]This observation relies crucially on the fact that each $p_{u,v}$ can independently take on any value in $I_{u,v}$. If the adversary were constrained by the total absolute deviation or sum of squares of deviations of parameters, this would no longer be the case. This issue is discussed in Section 6.

[3]Recall that a function f is submodular if it has "diminishing returns:" $f(S+x) - f(S) \geq f(T+x) - f(T)$ for any element x whenever $S \subseteq T$.

with probability ϵ. Subsequently, the activation succeeds with probability p. ([1] assumed uniform probabilities). Thus, the model is an instance of the IC model in which the activation probabilities on all observed edges are $p(1-\epsilon)$, while those on unobserved edges are $p\epsilon$. This reduction explains the theoretical results obtained by Adiga et al.

More fundamentally, practically all "natural" random processes that independently affect edges of the graph can be "absorbed into" the activation probabilities themselves; as a result, random noise does not at all play the result of actual noise.

2. MODELS AND PRELIMINARIES

The social network is modeled by a directed graph $G = (V, E)$ on n nodes. All parameters for non-existing edges are assumed to be 0. We first describe models of influence diffusion, and then models of parameter perturbation.

2.1 Influence Diffusion Models

Most of the models for Influence Maximization have been based on the Independent Cascade Model (see Section 1.1) and Linear Threshold Model studied in [13] and their generalizations. Like the Independent Cascade Model, the Linear Threshold Model also proceeds in discrete rounds. Each edge (u, v) is equipped with a weight $c_{u,v} \in [0, 1]$, satisfying $\sum_{u \to v} c_{u,v} \leq 1$ for all nodes v. (By $u \to v$, we denote that there is a directed edge (u, v).) Each node v initially draws a threshold ψ_v independently and uniformly at random from $[0, 1]$. A set A_0 of nodes is activated at time 0, and we use A_t to denote the set of nodes active at time t. In each discrete round t, each node v checks if $\sum_{u \in A_{t-1}, u \to v} c_{u,v} \geq \psi_v$. If so, v becomes active at time t, and remains active subsequently.

Any instance of the Influence Maximization problem is characterized by its parameters. For the LT model, the parameters are the n^2 edge weights $c_{u,v}$ for all edges (u, v). Similarly, for the IC model, the parameters are the edge activation probabilities $p_{u,v}$ for all edges (u, v). To unify notation, we write $\boldsymbol{\theta} = (\theta_{u,v})_{(u,v) \in E}$ for the vector of all parameter values, where $\theta_{u,v}$ could be either $c_{u,v}$ or $p_{u,v}$.[4]

Both the IC and LT model define random processes that continue until the diffusion process quiesces, i.e., no new activations occur. Let $\tau \leq n$ be the (random) time at which this happens. We denote the stochastic process by $\boldsymbol{P}_{\boldsymbol{\theta}}^{\text{Mod}}(A_0) = (A_t)_{t=0}^{\tau}$, with Mod $\in$ {IC, LT} denoting the model. The final set of active nodes is A_τ. We can now formally define the Influence Maximization problem:

DEFINITION 2 (INFLUENCE MAXIMIZATION). *The Influence Maximization problem consists of maximizing the objective $\sigma(A_0) := \mathbb{E}[|A_\tau|]$ (i.e., the expected number of active nodes in the end[5]), subject to a cardinality constraint $|A_0| \leq k$.*

[4]Some models besides IC and LT have more or fewer or different parameters. We will briefly see one such example in Section 4.2, but prefer to avoid unnecessarily general notation for now.

[5]Our results carry over unchanged if we assign each node a non-negative value r_v, and the goal is to maximize $\sum_{v \in A_\tau} r_v$. We focus on the case of uniform values for notational convenience only.

The key insight behind most prior work on algorithmic Influence Maximization is that the objective function $\sigma(S)$ is a monotone and submodular function of S. This was proved for the IC and LT models in [13], and subsequently for a generalization called Generalized Threshold Model (proposed in [13]) by Mossel and Roch [17].

2.2 Models for Perturbations

To model adversarial input perturbations, we assume that for each of the edges (u, v), we are given an interval $I_{u,v} = [\ell_{u,v}, r_{u,v}] \subseteq [0, 1]$ with $\theta_{u,v} \in I_{u,v}$. For the LT model, to ensure that the resulting activations functions are always submodular, we require that $\sum_{u \to v} r_{u,v} \leq 1$ for all nodes v. We write $\boldsymbol{\Theta} = \times_{(u,v) \in E} I_{u,v}$ for the set of all allowable parameter settings. The adversary must guarantee that the ground truth parameter values satisfy $\boldsymbol{\theta}^* \in \boldsymbol{\Theta}$; subject to this requirement, the adversary can choose the actual parameter values arbitrarily.

Together, the parameter values $\boldsymbol{\theta}$ determine an instance of the Influence Maximization problem. We will usually be explicit about indicating the dependence of the objective function on the parameter setting. We write $\sigma_{\boldsymbol{\theta}}$ for the objective function obtained with parameter values $\boldsymbol{\theta}$, and only omit the parameters when they are clear from the context. For a given setting of parameters, we will denote by $A^*_{\boldsymbol{\theta}} \in \operatorname{argmax}_S \sigma_{\boldsymbol{\theta}}(S)$ a solution maximizing the expected influence under parameter values $\boldsymbol{\theta}$.

2.3 Influence Difference Maximization

In order to capture to what extent adversarial changes in the parameters can lead to misestimates of any set's influence, we are interested in the quantity

$$\max_S \max_{\boldsymbol{\theta}' \in \boldsymbol{\Theta}} |\sigma_{\boldsymbol{\theta}}(S) - \sigma_{\boldsymbol{\theta}'}(S)| , \tag{1}$$

where $\boldsymbol{\theta}$ denotes the observed parameter values. For two parameter settings $\boldsymbol{\theta}, \boldsymbol{\theta}'$ with $\boldsymbol{\theta} \geq \boldsymbol{\theta}'$ coordinate-wise, it is not difficult to show using a simple coupling argument (see Lemma 6) that $\sigma_{\boldsymbol{\theta}}(S) \geq \sigma_{\boldsymbol{\theta}'}(S)$ for all S. Therefore, for any fixed set S, the maximum is attained either by making $\boldsymbol{\theta}'$ as large as possible or as small as possible. Hence, solving the following problem is sufficient to maximize (1).

DEFINITION 3. *Given an influence model and two parameter settings $\boldsymbol{\theta}, \boldsymbol{\theta}'$ with $\boldsymbol{\theta} \geq \boldsymbol{\theta}'$ coordinate-wise, define*

$$\delta_{\boldsymbol{\theta},\boldsymbol{\theta}'}(S) = \sigma_{\boldsymbol{\theta}}(S) - \sigma_{\boldsymbol{\theta}'}(S). \tag{2}$$

Given the set size k, the Influence Difference Maximization (IDM) problem is defined as follows:

$$\begin{array}{ll} \textit{Maximize} & \delta_{\boldsymbol{\theta},\boldsymbol{\theta}'}(S) \\ \textit{subject to} & |S| = k. \end{array} \tag{3}$$

3. MAIN THEOREM AND APPLICATIONS

Maximizing $\delta_{\boldsymbol{\theta},\boldsymbol{\theta}'}(S)$ (approximately) lets us evaluate how susceptible an instance is to noise. Hence, we would like to exhibit useful properties of the function $\delta_{\boldsymbol{\theta},\boldsymbol{\theta}'}$ making it amenable to optimization. This is accomplished by Theorem 1, which we restate here using the notation from Section 2.

THEOREM 1. *Under the IC and LT models, the function $\delta_{\boldsymbol{\theta},\boldsymbol{\theta}'}(S)$ is a non-negative submodular function of S whenever $\boldsymbol{\theta} \geq \boldsymbol{\theta}'$ pointwise.*

As we show in Section 3.2, Theorem 1 implies that we can leverage known results on the maximization of submodular functions (see [6, 22] and references therein) in order to approximately maximize $\delta_{\theta,\theta'}(S)$, and thus gain an understanding of how large the changes in objective function values are. The proof of Theorem 1 is presented in Section 4.

3.1 Approximation for Perturbed Objectives

We have several times alluded to the idea that if the maximum influence difference is "small," the seed set found by an Influence Maximization algorithm for the *observed* parameters will have useful guarantees even for the *unobserved* actual parameters. We now make the notion of "small" precise and derive a guarantee on the performance vis-à-vis unobserved actual parameters. We consider four different parameter settings and their associated objective functions:

- $\boldsymbol{\theta}$ is the observed/inferred vector of parameters, and $\sigma = \sigma_{\boldsymbol{\theta}}$ is the resulting objective function. Let A^* be a seed set maximizing $\sigma(S)$ subject to $|S| = k$, and A the seed set returned by the greedy algorithm for Influence Maximization. Thus, A satisfies

$$\sigma(A) \geq (1 - 1/e) \cdot \sigma(A^*). \qquad (4)$$

- $\hat{\boldsymbol{\theta}}$ is the vector of ground truth parameters chosen by the adversary, and $\hat{\sigma} = \sigma_{\hat{\boldsymbol{\theta}}}$ the associated objective function. $\hat{A}$ denotes the seed set maximizing $\hat{\sigma}(S)$.
- $\boldsymbol{\theta}^+$ is the vector making each parameter as large as possible, and $\sigma^+ = \sigma_{\boldsymbol{\theta}+}$ the associated objective function.
- $\boldsymbol{\theta}^-$ is the vector making each parameter as small as possible, and $\sigma^- = \sigma_{\boldsymbol{\theta}-}$ the associated objective function.

Since the observed objective value $\sigma(A)$ is the only "scale" that an algorithm has available for measuring the impact of perturbations, we relate all deviations to this quantity. Specifically, assume that running the greedy Influence Difference Maximization algorithm has revealed the following[6] for all sets S with $|S| = k$:

$$\delta_{\boldsymbol{\theta}+,\boldsymbol{\theta}}(S) \leq \alpha^+ \cdot \sigma(A). \qquad (5)$$

In addition to the Influence Difference Maximization estimate, assume that explicitly evaluating the difference for the set A has revealed that

$$\delta_{\boldsymbol{\theta},\boldsymbol{\theta}-}(A) = \alpha^- \cdot \sigma(A). \qquad (6)$$

Our goal is now to lower-bound $\hat{\sigma}(A)$ in terms of $\hat{\sigma}(\hat{A})$. We begin by lower-bounding $\sigma(A^*)$:

$$\begin{aligned}\sigma(A^*) &= \Big(\sigma(A^*) - \sigma(\hat{A})\Big) + \Big(\sigma(\hat{A}) - \hat{\sigma}(\hat{A})\Big) + \hat{\sigma}(\hat{A}) \\ &\geq \Big(\sigma(\hat{A}) - \sigma^+(\hat{A})\Big) + \hat{\sigma}(\hat{A}) \\ &\overset{(5)}{\geq} -\alpha^+ \cdot \sigma(A) + \hat{\sigma}(\hat{A}).\end{aligned}$$

[6]Notice that to reveal such a bound, the algorithm's observed maximum function value $\delta_{\boldsymbol{\theta}+,\boldsymbol{\theta}}(S)$ must be smaller than $\sigma(A)$ by a constant factor (roughly e), to compensate for the approximation factor of the Influence Difference Maximization algorithm.

For the first inequality, we used that the first term is nonnegative by the optimality of A^* for σ, and that $\sigma^+(S) \geq \hat{\sigma}(S)$ for all sets S. We can now combine Inequality (4) with the previous derivation and solve for $\sigma(A)$:

$$\sigma(A) \geq \frac{1 - 1/e}{1 + \alpha^+ \cdot (1 - 1/e)} \cdot \hat{\sigma}(\hat{A}).$$

Finally, we use this inequality to bound $\hat{\sigma}(A)$ as follows:

$$\begin{aligned}\hat{\sigma}(A) &= (\hat{\sigma}(A) - \sigma(A)) + \sigma(A) \qquad (7)\\ &\geq \big(\sigma^-(A) - \sigma(A)\big) + \sigma(A) \\ &\overset{(6)}{=} (1 - \alpha^-) \cdot \sigma(A) \\ &\geq \frac{(1 - \alpha^-) \cdot (1 - 1/e)}{1 + \alpha^+ \cdot (1 - 1/e)} \cdot \hat{\sigma}(\hat{A}), \qquad (8)\end{aligned}$$

where the first inequality used that $\hat{\sigma}(S) \geq \sigma^-(S)$ for all sets S.

Thus, whenever α^-, α^+ are small enough, we can guarantee that the calculated seed set A is within a constant factor of the best seed set for the unknown ground truth influence parameters.

3.2 Maximizing Submodular Functions

While the maximization of monotone submodular functions is essentially a solved problem (the widely known and used $1 - 1/e$ approximation algorithm due to Nemhauser et al. [19] is best possible unless P=NP), approximation algorithms for the maximization of *non-monotone* submodular functions subject to a cardinality constraint have only more recently received significant attention. (See [6, 22] and references therein.)

In our work, we use the *Random Greedy* algorithm of [6], given as Algorithm 1 below. It is a natural generalization of the simple greedy algorithm widely used for maximizing monotone submodular functions.[7] Instead of picking the *best* single element to add in each iteration, it first finds the set of the k individually best single elements (i.e., the elements which when added to the current set give the largest, second-largest, third-largest, ..., k^{th}-largest gain). Then, it picks one of these k elements uniformly at random and continues.

The approximation guarantee for Random Greedy is captured by Theorem 2 below. The current best approximation guarantee — a factor 0.356 (slightly less than $1/e$) — is achieved by running Random Greedy and another algorithm called "Continuous Double Greedy" and keeping the better of the two solutions. While taking the better of the two algorithms gives a better approximation guarantee, in our experiments, we prefer to just use the Random Greedy algorithm due to its simplicity and efficiency. Notice that when $k \ll n$, the approximation guarantee of Random Greedy is very close to $1/e$; since $k \ll n$ for all of our experiments, we treat the approximation guarantee as $1/e$ in our discussion for simplicity.

THEOREM 2 (BUCHBINDER ET AL. [6]). *Let g be a nonnegative submodular (not necessarily monotone) function. Consider the problem of maximizing $g(S)$ subject to the constraint that $|S| = k$; let S_k^* be the optimum set of size k.*

[7]Buchbinder et al. [6] show that for non-monotone submodular functions, the traditional greedy algorithm can perform arbitrarily poorly.

1. *The set S_k returned by the Random Greedy Algorithm guarantees $\mathbb{E}[g(S_k)] \geq \max(0.266, \frac{1}{e} \cdot (1 - \frac{k}{en})) \cdot g(S_k^*)$, where the expectation is taken over the random choices of the algorithm.*

2. *By taking the better of the outputs of the Random Greedy Algorithm and the "Continuous Double Greedy Algorithm," the resulting set $\hat{S}$ guarantees that $\mathbb{E}\left[g(\hat{S})\right] \geq 0.356 \cdot g(S_k^*)$.*

Algorithm 1 Random Greedy Algorithm

Initialize: $S_0 \leftarrow \emptyset$
for $i = 1, \ldots, k$ **do**
  Let $M_i \subseteq V \setminus S_{i-1}$ be the subset of size k maximizing $\sum_{u \in M_i} g(S_{i-1} \cup \{u\}) - g(S_{i-1})$.
  Draw u_i uniformly at random from M_i.
  Let $S_i \leftarrow S_{i-1} \cup \{u_i\}$.
end for
Return S_k

The running time of the Random Greedy Algorithm is $O(kC|V|)$, where C is the time required to estimate $g(S \cup \{u\}) - g(S)$. In our case, the objective function is #P-hard to evaluate exactly [23, 8], but arbitrarily close approximations can be obtained by Monte Carlo simulation. Since each simulation takes time $O(|V|)$, if we run M iterations of the Monte Carlo simulation in each iteration, the overall running time of the algorithm is $O(kM|V|^2)$. In order to accelerate the algorithm in practice, we use the CELF optimization proposed by Leskovec et al. [16]. It exploits submodularity to avoid computation of $g(S_{i-1} \cup \{u\}) - g(S_{i-1})$ whenever the value of $g(S_{i-2} \cup \{u\}) - g(S_{i-2})$ is sufficiently small that u cannot be the optimal element to add in iteration i.

4. PROOF OF THEOREM 1

We exploit and extend the *Triggering Set* technique from [13]. The idea of the Triggering Set technique is to characterize the outcome A_τ of the dynamic and stochastic activation process $\boldsymbol{P}_{\boldsymbol{\theta}}^{\text{Mod}}(A_0)$ by a more static process called a Triggering Model: Generate a random graph G according to a particular distribution, and let $R_G(A_0)$ be the set of nodes reachable from A_0 in G. ([13] calls the edges in G *live* and the edges missing from G *blocked.*) The Triggering Set technique then consists in showing that for each of the models {IC, LT}, one can identify a Triggering Model (i.e., a distribution over random graphs G) such that the random set $R_G(A_0)$ has precisely the same distribution (under the random graph G) as the random set A_τ under the random process $\boldsymbol{P}_{\boldsymbol{\theta}}^{\text{Mod}}(A_0)$. More specifically, [13] proves the following two lemmas:

LEMMA 3 (CLAIM 2.3 FROM [13]). *Given an instance of the IC model with edge probabilities $\boldsymbol{\theta} = (p_{u,v})$, let $\mathcal{G}_{\boldsymbol{\theta}}^{IC}$ be the random graph model in which each directed edge (u, v) is present (or live) independently with probability $p_{u,v}$, and blocked otherwise. Then, for all sets A_0, S,*

$$\text{Prob}_{G \sim \mathcal{G}_{\boldsymbol{\theta}}^{IC}}[R_G(A_0) = S] = \text{Prob}_{\boldsymbol{P}_{\boldsymbol{\theta}}^{IC}(A_0)}[A_\tau = S].$$

LEMMA 4 (CLAIM 2.6 FROM [13]). *Given an instance of the LT model with edge weights $\boldsymbol{\theta} = (c_{u,v})$, let $\mathcal{G}_{\boldsymbol{\theta}}^{LT}$ be the random graph model in which each node v picks the incoming edge (u, v) with probability $c_{u,v}$; the presence of the edges is mutually exclusive, so that each node v has at most one incoming live edge, and with probability $1 - \sum_u c_{u,v}$ has no incoming live edge. Then, for all sets A_0, S,*

$$\text{Prob}_{G \sim \mathcal{G}_{\boldsymbol{\theta}}^{LT}}[R_G(A_0) = S] = \text{Prob}_{\boldsymbol{P}_{\boldsymbol{\theta}}^{LT}(A_0)}[A_\tau = S].$$

These lemmas imply that instead of studying a dynamic process, we can randomly generate graphs, and then study reachability on those graphs. When we consider two parameter settings $\boldsymbol{\theta} \geq \boldsymbol{\theta}'$ (pointwise), it seems intuitive that we should be able to generate two corresponding graphs G, G' (on the same vertex set V) according to the respective distributions, such that $E(G) \supseteq E(G')$ *always holds*. More formally, below, we will show the following coupling lemma:

LEMMA 5 (COUPLING OF RANDOM GRAPHS). *For any instances $\boldsymbol{\theta}, \boldsymbol{\theta}'$ of the IC Model (or LT Model) with $\boldsymbol{\theta} \geq \boldsymbol{\theta}'$, there is a distribution D over pairs (G, G') of graphs on the same vertex set V, with the following properties:*

1. *$E(G) \supseteq E(G')$ always holds.*

2. *$\sum_{G'} \text{Prob}_D[(G, G')] = \text{Prob}_{G \sim \mathcal{G}_{\boldsymbol{\theta}}^{Mod}}[G]$. That is, the first graph in isolation follows the random graph distribution $\mathcal{G}_{\boldsymbol{\theta}}^{Mod}$ (where Mod could be IC or LT).*

3. *$\sum_{G} \text{Prob}_D[(G, G')] = \text{Prob}_{G' \sim \mathcal{G}_{\boldsymbol{\theta}'}^{Mod}}[G']$. That is, the second graph in isolation follows the random graph distribution $\mathcal{G}_{\boldsymbol{\theta}'}^{Mod}$ (where again Mod could be IC or LT)*

Finally, we analyze "reachability difference" between two arbitrary graphs with $E(G) \supseteq E(G')$.

LEMMA 6 (COMPARISON OF REACHABILITY). *Let G, G' be two fixed graphs with $E(G) \supseteq E(G')$. Then, $R_G(S) \supseteq R_{G'}(S)$.*

Furthermore, let $\rho(S) := |R_G(S) \setminus R_{G'}(S)|$ be the number of nodes reachable from S in G, but not in G'. $\rho(S)$ is a submodular function of S.

To complete the proof, we can decompose the influence difference objective into a distribution over individual graphs as follows:

$$\begin{aligned}
\delta_{\boldsymbol{\theta},\boldsymbol{\theta}'}(A_0) &= \mathbb{E}_{G \sim \mathcal{G}_{\boldsymbol{\theta}}^{\text{Mod}}}[|R_G(A_0)|] - \mathbb{E}_{G' \sim \mathcal{G}_{\boldsymbol{\theta}'}^{\text{Mod}}}[|R_{G'}(A_0)|] \\
&= \mathbb{E}_{(G,G') \sim D}[|R_G(A_0)| - |R_{G'}(A_0)|] \\
&= \mathbb{E}_{(G,G') \sim D}[|R_G(A_0) \setminus R_{G'}(A_0)|] \\
&= \sum_{G,G'} \text{Prob}_{(G,G') \sim D}[(G, G')] \cdot |R_G(A_0) \setminus R_{G'}(A_0)| \\
&= \sum_{G,G'} \text{Prob}_{(G,G') \sim D}[(G, G')] \cdot \rho(A_0).
\end{aligned}$$

The second equality used that D defines a valid coupling over pairs of graphs; the third equality used that $E(G) \supseteq E(G')$, and the fourth equality used the definition of the expectation.

Notice that the final form is a non-negative linear combination of submodular and non-negative functions, which is known to be submodular. This completes the proof. ■

4.1 Proof of Lemmas

Proof of Lemma 6. Fix two graphs G, G' on the same vertex set V, with $E(G) \supseteq E(G')$. $R_G(S) \supseteq R_{G'}(S)$ is obvious, so we focus on the second part of the lemma. To show that $\rho(S)$ is submodular, we will show a slightly stronger statement. Let $\Delta R(S) := R_G(S) \setminus R_{G'}(S)$ be the actual *set* of nodes reachable from S in G, but not in G'. We will show that for all sets $S \subseteq T$ and nodes v, we have $\Delta R(T+v) \setminus \Delta R(T) \subseteq \Delta R(S+v) \setminus \Delta R(S)$. This directly implies submodularity of $\rho(S) = |\Delta R(S)|$.

By definition, a node u is in $\Delta R(S)$ if and only if there exists a path from S to u in G, but not in G'. Thus, a node u is in $\Delta R(T+v) \setminus \Delta R(T)$ if and only if there is (1) a path from $T+v$ to u in G, (2) no path from $T+v$ to u in G', and (3) no path from T to u in G.

By the first and third condition, there must be a path from v to u in G (since the addition of the source node v is the only difference between those conditions). Hence, there is a path from $S+v$ to u in G. Second, because there is no path from $T+v$ to u in G', and $S \subseteq T$, there cannot be a path from $S+v$ to u in G'. Third, because there is no path from T to u in G, and $S \subseteq T$, there cannot be a path from S to u in G. Hence, by definition, u is in $\Delta R(S+v) \setminus \Delta R(S)$. In other words, $u \in \Delta R(T+v) \setminus \Delta R(T)$ implies that $u \in \Delta R(S+v) \setminus \Delta R(S)$, completing the proof. ∎

Proof of Lemma 5. We begin by proving the lemma for the IC model, for which the coupling is simpler. We need to decide, for each edge (u, v) independently, whether to include (u, v) in G and G'. To do so, we generate, independently for each (u, v), a number $x_{u,v}$ uniformly from $[0, 1]$. The edge (u, v) is included in G iff $x_{u,v} \leq p_{u,v}$; similarly, (u, v) is included in G' iff $x_{u,v} \leq p'_{u,v}$. Thus, the inclusion probabilities are correct. Furthermore, because $p_{u,v} \geq p'_{u,v}$ by assumption, whenever (u, v) is included in G', it is also included in G. Thus, the proposed generative process is a valid coupling for the IC model.

Next, we exhibit a valid coupling for the LT model. We need to decide, for each node v independently, which single incoming edge (u, v) (if any) to include in G and G'. We use the following generative process. For each node v, we consider the interval $[0, 1]$. For every edge (u, v) into v, we place an interval J_u of length $c_{u,v}$ into the $[0, 1]$ interval, such that the intervals $J_u, J_{u'}$ for $u \neq u'$ are disjoint. This is possible because $\sum_u c_{u,v} \leq 1$. Then, for each node u, we pick a subinterval $J'_u \subseteq J_u$ of length $c'_{u,v}$.

Finally, a random number x_v is drawn uniformly at random from $[0, 1]$. If x_v lies in J_u, then (u, v) is inserted into G, and if it lies in J'_u, then (u, v) is inserted into G'. If x_v does not lie in any of the J_u, then v has no incoming edge in G; similarly for G'. Notice that the incoming edge in both graphs is chosen with the correct distribution, proving that we have a valid coupling. Furthermore, because $J'_u \subseteq J_u$, whenever the edge (u, v) is included in G', it is also included in G, so that $E(G) \supseteq E(G')$, as desired. ∎

4.2 A more general view

The Triggering Set technique we used in the proof of Theorem 1 can be applied to prove a more general version of the theorem. It shows that $\delta_{\boldsymbol{\theta},\boldsymbol{\theta}'}(A_0)$ is submodular whenever the following two hold:

1. The diffusion model is equivalent to a Triggering Model.
2. Whenever $\boldsymbol{\theta} \geq \boldsymbol{\theta}'$ holds pointwise, the random graphs (G, G') with parameters $\boldsymbol{\theta}, \boldsymbol{\theta}'$ can be coupled such that $E(G) \supseteq E(G')$ always holds.

For example, [13] defined the "Only Listen Once" model: in it, a node v is activated with some probability p_v by the first neighbor trying to convince it; if the attempt is unsuccessful, all subsequent activation attempts deterministically fail. [13] showed that this model is equivalent to a Triggering Model in which a node has live incoming edges from all of its neighbors with probability p_v, and from none of its neighbors with probability $1 - p_v$. When $p_v \geq p'_v$ for all v, these decisions can be coupled like the presence of single edges in the IC model. Thus, Influence Difference Maximization is also submodular for the "Only Listen Once" model.

More generally, the conditions under which a coupling is possible are characterized by Strassen's Monotone Coupling Theorem [21]:

THEOREM 7 (STRASSEN [21]). *Let $(\mathcal{X}, \preceq)$ be a finite partially ordered set, and let μ, ν be probability distributions on $\mathcal{X}$. If μ stochastically dominates ν[8], then there exist (coupled) random variables $M \sim \mu, N \sim \nu$ such that $M \succeq N$ always holds.*

Strassen's Theorem can be applied with $\mathcal{X}$ being the set of all subsets of edges, ordered by the $\subseteq$ order. We obtain the following corollary:

COROLLARY 8. *Consider any Influence Maximization model equivalent to a Triggering model, and instances with parameters $\boldsymbol{\theta}, \boldsymbol{\theta}'$. The Influence Difference Maximization objective function $\delta_{\boldsymbol{\theta},\boldsymbol{\theta}'}(S)$ is submodular whenever $\mathcal{G}^{Mod}_{\boldsymbol{\theta}}$ stochastically dominates $\mathcal{G}^{Mod}_{\boldsymbol{\theta}'}$.*

5. EXPERIMENTS

While we saw in Section 1.2 that examples highly susceptible (with errors of magnitude $\Omega(n)$) to small perturbations exist, the goal of this section is to evaluate experimentally how widespread this behavior is for realistic social networks.

5.1 Experimental Setting

We carry out experiments under the IC model, for six classes of graphs — four synthetic and two real-world. In each case, the model/data give us a simple graph or multigraph. Multigraphs are converted to simple graphs by collapsing parallel edges to a single edge with weight c_e equal to the number of parallel edges; for simple graphs, all weights are $c_e = 1$. The observed probabilities for edges are $p_e = c_e \cdot p$; across experiments, we vary the base probability p to take on the values $\{0.01, 0.02, 0.05, 0.1\}$. The resulting parameter vector is denoted by $\boldsymbol{\theta}$.

The uncertainty interval for e is $I_e = [(1-\Delta)p_e, (1+\Delta)p_e]$; here, Δ is an uncertainty parameter for the estimation, which takes on the values $\{1\%, 5\%, 10\%, 20\%, 50\%\}$ in our experiments. The parameter vectors $\boldsymbol{\theta}^+$ and $\boldsymbol{\theta}^-$ describe the settings in which all parameters are as large (as small, respectively) as possible.

[8] We say that μ stochastically dominates ν if for every set $A \subseteq \mathcal{X}$ which is upward-closed (i.e., $x \in A$ and $y \succeq x$ implies $y \in A$), $\mu(A) \geq \nu(A)$.

5.2 Network Data

We run experiments on four synthetic networks and two real social networks. Synthetic networks provide a controlled environment in which to compare observed behavior to expectations, while real social networks may give us indications about the prevalence of vulnerability to perturbations in real networks that have been studied in the past.

Synthetic Networks. We generate synthetic networks according to four widely used network models. In all cases, we generate undirected networks with 400 nodes. The network models are: (1) the 2-dimensional grid, (2) random regular graphs, (3) the Watts-Strogatz Small-World (SW) Model [24] on a ring with each node connecting to the 5 closest nodes on each side initially, and a rewiring probability of 0.1. (4) The Barabási-Albert Preferential Attachment (PA) Model [3] with 5 outgoing edges per node. For all synthetic networks, we select $k = 20$ seed nodes.

Real Networks. We consider two real networks to evaluate the susceptibility of practical networks: one (*STOCFOCS*) is a co-authorship network of theoretical CS papers; the other (*Haiti*) is a Retweet network.

The co-authorship network, *STOCFOCS*, is a multigraph extracted from published papers in the conferences STOC and FOCS from 1964–2001. Each node in the network is a researcher with at least one publication in one of the conferences. For each multi-author paper, we add a complete undirected graph among the authors. As mentioned above, parallel edges are then compressed into a single edge with corresponding weight. The resulting graph has 1768 nodes and 10024 edges. Due to its larger size, we select 50 seed nodes.

The *Haiti* network is extracted from tweets of 274 users on the topic *Haiti Earthquake* in Twitter. For each tweet of user u that was retweeted by v, we add a directed edge (u, v). We obtain a directed multigraph; after contracting parallel edges, the directed graph has 383 weighted edges. For this network, due to its smaller size, we select 20 seeds.

In all experiments, we work with uniform edge weights p, since — apart from edge multiplicities — we have no evidence on the strength of connections. It is a promising direction for future in-depth experiments to use influence strengths inferred from real-world cascade datasets by network inference methods such as [10, 11, 18].

5.3 Results

In all our experiments, the results for the Grid and Small-World network are sufficiently similar that we omit the results for grids here. As a first sanity check, we empirically computed $\max_{S:|S|=1} \delta_{\theta^+,\theta^-}(S)$ for the *complete graph* on 200 nodes with $I_e = [1/200 \cdot (1 - \Delta), 1/200 \cdot (1 + \Delta)]$ and $k = 1$. According to the analysis in Section 1.2, we would expect extremely high instability. The results, shown in Table 1, confirm this expectation.

Δ	σ_{θ^+}	σ_{θ^-}
50%	66.529	1.955
20%	23.961	4.253
10%	15.071	6.204

Table 1: Instability for the clique K_{200}.

Next, Figure 1 shows the (approximately) computed values $\max_{S:|S|=k} \delta_{\theta^+,\theta^-}(S)$, and — for calibration purposes — $\max_{A_0:|A_0|=k} \sigma_{\theta}(A_0)$ for all networks and parameter settings. Notice that the figure shows the *computed* values in reality, $\max_S \delta_{\theta^+,\theta^-}(S)$ could be up to about a factor e larger than the displayed values due to the loss of an approximation factor.

While individual networks vary somewhat in their susceptibility, the overall trend is that larger estimates of baseline probabilities p make the instance more susceptible to noise, as do (obviously) larger uncertainty parameters Δ. In particular, for $\Delta \geq 20\%$, the noise (after scaling) dominates the Influence Maximization objective function value, meaning that optimization results should be used with care. On the other hand, when $\Delta \leq 10\%$, even the scaled-up misestimation is noticeably less than the Influence Maximization objective, so that reasonable approximation guarantees are obtained even for perturbed data.

Next, we compute what approximation guarantees could be given for the instances using Formula (8). Specifically, using $\boldsymbol{\theta}$ as the observed edge probabilities, we run the standard greedy algorithm for Influence Maximization to determine a set A_0. Based on this set and the lower bounds $\boldsymbol{\theta}^-$, the value α^- is directly computed. To compute α^+ we run the Random Greedy Influence Difference Maximization algorithm on $\delta_{\theta^+,\theta}(S)$ and scale up the maximum value it finds by a factor e. We use the best solution of 10 independent runs of the Influence Difference Maximization algorithm. The objective function value is approximated using $M = 2000$ iterations of the Monte Carlo simulation. As discussed in Section 3.2, since $k \ll n$ in all our experiments, the approximation guarantee is very close to $1/e$, so that this scaling ensures that α^+ does not underestimate the effect of perturbations. Using all of these values, we can now estimate the approximation guarantee using Formula (8). The results are shown in Figure 2.

In interpreting Figure 2, notice that even with perfect data, one cannot exceed an approximation guarantee of $1 - 1/e \approx 0.63$. As indicated already by Figure 1 when the baseline probability is large and the error exceeds 20%, the approximation guarantee begins to deteriorate significantly. According to Formula (8), Influence Maximization can tolerate $\alpha^+ > 1$, which corresponds to significant perturbations that make parameter values *larger*. On the other hand, for deviations that make parameter values *smaller* (which would indicate that the solution A_0 may only *appear* good based on an overestimate of some parameters), a value of α^- close to 1 would have devastating effects. ($\alpha^- > 1$ is impossible by definition.) Fortunately, α^- is computed only for one specific set A_0, and thus not subject to the $1/e$ approximation factor for Influence Difference Maximization.

Next, we evaluate the dependence of the noise tolerance on the degrees of the graph, by experimenting with random d-regular graphs whose degrees vary from 5 to 25. It is known that such graphs are expanders with high probability, and hence have percolation thresholds of $1/d$ [2]. Accordingly, we set the base probability to $(1 + \alpha)/d$ with $\alpha \in \{-40\%, -20\%, 0, 20\%, 40\%\}$. We use the same setting for uncertainty intervals as in the previous experiments. Figure 3 shows the ratio between Influence Difference Maximization and Influence Maximization, i.e., $\frac{\max_S \delta_{\theta^+,\theta^-}(S)}{\max_S \sigma_{\theta}(S)}$, with $\alpha = 0$. (The results for $\alpha \neq 0$ are similar and omitted due to space constraints.) It indicates that for random regular graphs, the degree does not appear to significantly affect stability, and that again, noise around 20% begins to pose

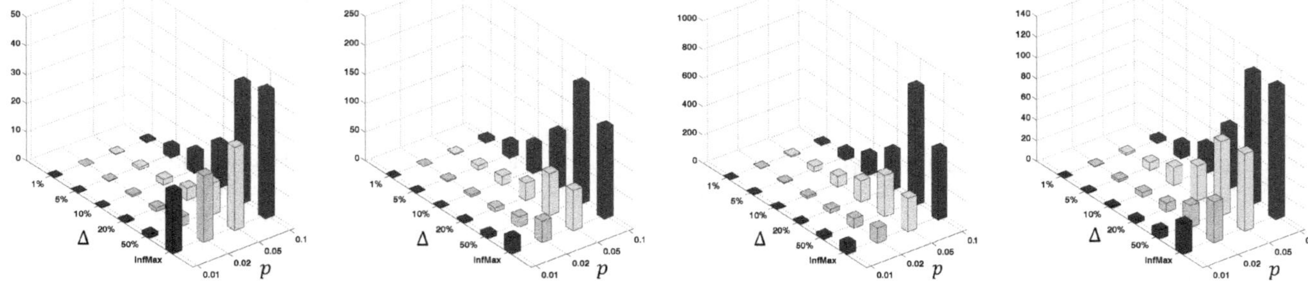

(a) Small World (b) PA (c) STOCFOCS (d) Haiti

Figure 1: Comparison between Influence Difference Maximization and Influence Maximization results for four different networks.

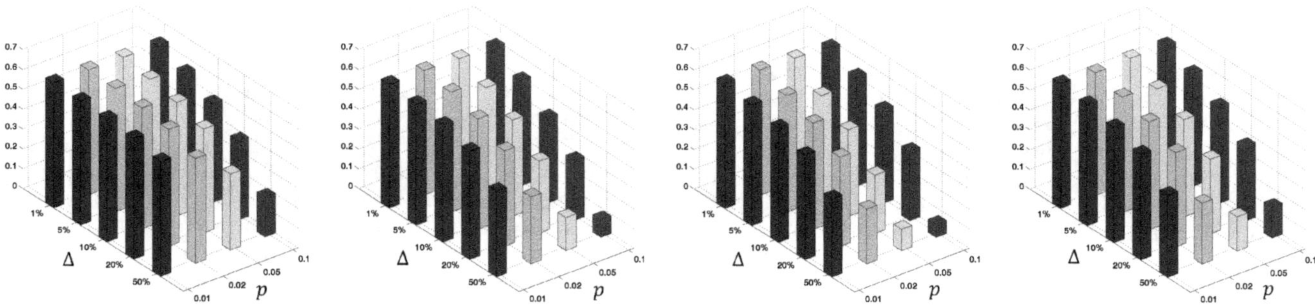

(a) Small World (b) PA (c) STOCFOCS (d) Haiti

Figure 2: Approximation Guarantees according to the bound in (8), for four different networks.

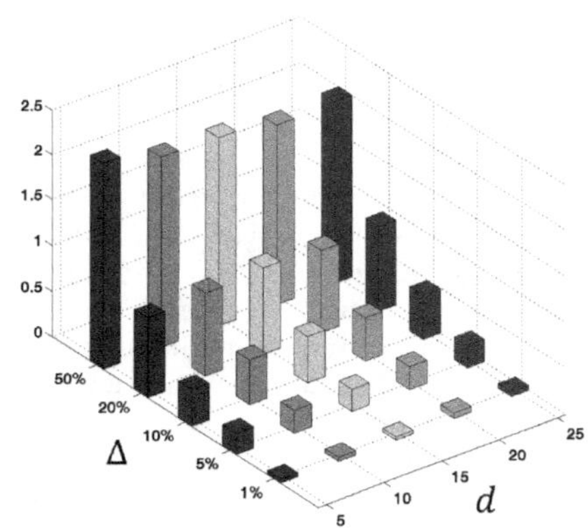

Figure 3: Ratio between Influence Difference Maximization and Influence Maximization under random regular graphs with different degree.

a significant challenge. Moreover, we observe that the approximation guarantee reaches its minimum when the edge activation probability is exactly at the percolation threshold $1/d$. This result is in line with percolation theory and also the analysis of Adiga et al. [1].

As a general takeaway message, decent approximation guarantees are obtained when the noise is below 10%, and in some cases even for noise around 20%. However, for larger amounts of noise — which may well occur in practice — a lot of caution is advised in using the results of algorithmic Influence Maximization.

6. DISCUSSION

We began a study of the stability of Influence Maximization when the input data are adversarially noisy. We showed that estimating the susceptibility of an instance to perturbations can be cast as an Influence Difference Maximization problem with a non-monotone submodular objective function. This let us leverage known algorithms for maximizing such functions to evaluate the susceptibility of real and synthetic data sets. In the examples we studied, typically, relative perturbations of less than 10% still lead to satisfactory solutions for Influence Maximization, while relative perturbations above 20% lead to significant risk of wrong outputs. Given the noise inherent in all estimates of social network data, this suggests applying extreme caution before relying heavily on results of algorithmic Influence Maximization.

Our work raises a number of interesting questions for follow-up work. First, while we prove submodularity of Influence Difference Maximization for the IC and LT models, it is an interesting question whether Influence Difference Maximization is submodular under more general models, such as the General Threshold Model [13, 17], and how general of an adversarial perturbation model can be tolerated. A path towards an extension to Triggering Models is suggested by Corollary 8. However, while a full characterization of models equivalent to Triggering Models was achieved by Salek et al. [20], it is not clear how to leverage such a characterization to determine what pairs of parameter vectors lead to stochastic domination.

Second, our adversarial model specified a valid range of parameters for each parameter of the model, and allowed the adversary to perturb the parameters arbitrarily within that range. Instead, we may posit an upper bound on the *total* (or *total squared*) perturbation the adversary can apply; such a bound creates dependencies between the perturbations at different nodes, making it much harder to even determine which legal parameter setting would maximize $|\delta_{\theta,\hat{\theta}}(S)|$ for a given set S.

While we begin an investigation of how pervasive susceptibility to perturbations is in Influence Maximization data sets, our investigation is necessarily limited. Most importantly, ground truth data are by definition impossible to obtain, and even good and reliable inferred data sets of actual influence probabilities are currently not available. The values we assigned for our experimental evaluation cover a wide range of parameter values studied in past work, but the community does not appear to have answered the question whether these ranges actually correspond to reality.

At an even more fundamental level, the *models* themselves have received surprisingly little thorough experimental validation, despite having served as models of choice for hundreds of papers over the last decade. In addition to verifying the susceptibility of models to parameter perturbations, it is thus a pressing task to verify how susceptible the optimization problems are to incorrect models. The verification or falsification of sociological models for collective behavior likely falls outside the expertise of the computer science community, but nonetheless needs to be undertaken before any significant impact of work on Influence Maximization can be truthfully claimed.

Acknowledgments

We would like to thank Shaddin Dughmi for useful pointers and feedback, Shishir Bharathi and Mahyar Salek for useful discussions, and anonymous reviewers for useful feedback. Xinran He was supported in part by the grant ONR MURI W911NF-11-1-0332 and DARPA SMISC W911NF-12-1-0034.

7. REFERENCES

[1] A. Adiga, C. J. Kuhlman, H. S. Mortveit, and A. K. S. Vullikanti. Sensitivity of diffusion dynamics to network uncertainty. In *Proc. 28th AAAI Conf. on Artificial Intelligence*, 2013.

[2] N. Alon, I. Benjamini, and A. Stacey. Percolation on finite graphs and isoperimetric inequalities. *Annals of Probability*, 32:1727–1745, 2004.

[3] A.-L. Barabási and R. Albert. Emergence of scaling in random networks. *Science*, 286:509–512, 1999.

[4] B. Bollobás. *Random Graphs*. Cambridge University Press, second edition, 2001.

[5] C. Borgs, M. Brautbar, J. T. Chayes, and B. Lucier. Maximizing social influence in nearly optimal time. In *Proc. 25th ACM-SIAM Symp. on Discrete Algorithms*, pages 946–957, 2014.

[6] N. Buchbinder, M. Feldman, J. S. Naor, and R. Schwartz. Submodular maximization with cardinality constraints. In *Proc. 25th ACM-SIAM Symp. on Discrete Algorithms*, pages 1433–1452, 2014.

[7] W. Chen, L. V. Lakshmanan, and C. Castillo. *Information and Influence Propagation in Social Networks*. Synthesis Lectures on Data Management. Morgan & Claypool, 2013.

[8] W. Chen, Y. Yuan, and L. Zhang. Scalable influence maximization in social networks under the linear threshold model. In *Proc. 10th Intl. Conf. on Data Mining*, pages 88–97, 2010.

[9] P. Erdős and A. Rényi. On the evolution of random graphs. *Publ. Math. Inst. Hung. Acad. Sci.*, 5:17–61, 1960.

[10] M. Gomez-Rodriguez, D. Balduzzi, and B. Schölkopf. Uncovering the temporal dynamics of diffusion networks. In *Proc. 28th Intl. Conf. on Machine Learning*, pages 561–568, 2011.

[11] A. Goyal, F. Bonchi, and L. V. S. Lakshmanan. Learning influence probabilities in social networks. In *Proc. 3rd ACM Intl. Conf. on Web Search and Data Mining*, pages 241–250, 2010.

[12] A. Goyal, F. Bonchi, and L. V. S. Lakshmanan. A data-based approach to social influence maximization. *Proc. VLDB Endow.*, 5(1):73–84, Sept. 2011.

[13] D. Kempe, J. Kleinberg, and E. Tardos. Maximizing the spread of influence in a social network. In *Proc. 9th Intl. Conf. on Knowledge Discovery and Data Mining*, pages 137–146, 2003.

[14] D. Kempe, J. Kleinberg, and E. Tardos. Influential nodes in a diffusion model for social networks. In *Proc. 32nd Intl. Colloq. on Automata, Languages and Programming*, pages 1127–1138, 2005.

[15] H. Kesten. Asymptotics in high dimension for percolation. In G. Grimmett and D. Welsh, editors, *Disorder in Physical System*, pages 219–240. Oxford University Press, 1990.

[16] J. Leskovec, A. Krause, C. Guestrin, C. Faloutsos, J. VanBriesen, and N. S. Glance. Cost-effective outbreak detection in networks. In *Proc. 13th Intl. Conf. on Knowledge Discovery and Data Mining*, pages 420–429, 2007.

[17] E. Mossel and S. Roch. Submodularity of influence in social networks: From local to global. *SIAM J. Comput.*, 39(6):2176–2188, 2010.

[18] S. A. Myers and J. Leskovec. On the convexity of latent social network inference. In *Proc. 22nd Advances in Neural Information Processing Systems*, pages 1741–1749, 2010.

[19] G. L. Nemhauser, L. A. Wolsey, and M. L. Fisher. An analysis of the approximations for maximizing submodular set functions. *Mathematical Programming*, 14:265–294, 1978.

[20] M. Salek, S. Shayandeh, and D. Kempe. You share, I share: Network effects and economic incentives in P2P file-sharing systems. In *Proc. 6th Workshop on Internet and Network Economics (WINE)*, 2010.

[21] V. Strassen. The existence of probability measures with given marginals. *The Annals of Mathematical Statistics*, 36(2):423–439, 1965.

[22] J. Vondrák. Symmetry and approximability of submodular maximization problems. In *Proc. 50th IEEE Symp. on Foundations of Computer Science*, pages 651–670, 2009.

[23] C. Wang, W. Chen, and Y. Wang. Scalable influence maximization for independent cascade model in large-scale social networks. *Data Mining and Knowledge Discovery Journal*, 25(3):545–576, 2012.

[24] D. J. Watts and S. Strogatz. Collective dynamics of 'small-world' networks. *Nature*, 393:440–442, 1998.

Who to Follow and Why: Link Prediction with Explanations

Nicola Barbieri
Yahoo Labs
Barcelona, Spain
barbieri@yahoo-inc.com

Francesco Bonchi
Yahoo Labs
Barcelona, Spain
bonchi@yahoo-inc.com

Giuseppe Manco
ICAR-CNR
Rende, Italy
manco@icar.cnr.it

ABSTRACT

User recommender systems are a key component in any on-line social networking platform: they help the users growing their network faster, thus driving engagement and loyalty.

In this paper we study *link prediction with explanations* for user recommendation in social networks. For this problem we propose WTFW ("Who to Follow and Why"), a stochastic topic model for link prediction over directed and nodes-attributed graphs. Our model not only predicts links, but for each predicted link it decides whether it is a "topical" or a "social" link, and depending on this decision it produces a different type of explanation.

A topical link is recommended between a user interested in a topic and a user authoritative in that topic: the explanation in this case is a set of binary features describing the topic responsible of the link creation. A social link is recommended between users which share a large social neighborhood: in this case the explanation is the set of neighbors which are more likely to be responsible for the link creation.

Our experimental assessment on real-world data confirms the accuracy of WTFW in the link prediction and the quality of the associated explanations.

Categories and Subject Descriptors: H.2.8 [Database Management]: Database Applications - *Data Mining*
Keywords: social networks; link prediction

1. INTRODUCTION

Link prediction is the task of estimating the likelihood of the existence of an unobserved link between two nodes, based on the other observable links around the two nodes and, when available, the attributes of the nodes [8]. It finds application in any context in which the network is only partially observable and we want to guess the unobserved part. A typical setting is when we consider the network evolving along time, so that the unobservable part of the network is the set of links which are not yet created: given the graph observed at time t, we want to predict the set of links which will be created in the time interval $[t, t+1]$[17].

KDD'14, August 24–27, 2014, New York, NY, USA.
Copyright 2014 ACM 978-1-4503-2956-9/14/08 ...$15.00.
http://dx.doi.org/10.1145/2623330.2623733 .

Link prediction has been applied in a variety of domains, ranging from bioinformatics to web sites management, from bibliography to e-commerce [12, 18, 5]. However, the most immediate and prominent application of link prediction is the recommendation of users to other users of a social network. This is one of the most fundamental functionalities common to all on-line social networking platforms[1]: it helps the users having a quicker start in building their network, thus driving engagement and loyalty. It is a key component for growth and sustenance of a social network: for instance, the WTF ("Who to Follow") service at Twitter is claimed to be responsible for millions of new links daily [11]. Given that growing the user base and maintaining a high level of engagement are key factors for the success (or the death) of these billion-dollar businesses, one can easily figure out the importance of user recommendation systems.

In this paper we study *link prediction with explanations for user recommendation systems* in on-line social networks. Enriching recommendations with explanations has the benefit to increase the trust of the user in the recommendation, and thus the likelihood that the recommendation is adopted. While these benefits are well understood in classic collaborative-filtering recommender systems [14, 25, 30], providing explanations in the context of user recommendation systems is still largely underdeveloped: in fact, in most of the real-world systems, the unique explanations given for user recommendations are of the type "you should follow user Z because your contacts X and Y do the same".

Our starting observation is that a link creation is usually explainable by one of two main reasons: interest identity or personal social relations. This observation is rooted in sociology, where it goes under the name *common identity and common bond theory* [24, 26]. Identity-based attachment holds when people join a community based on their interest in a well-defined common theme shared by all of the members of that community. The goal in this case is information collecting and sharing in the specific theme of interest. People joining a community through identity-based links may not even directly participate, e.g., by producing content or by engaging with other members, and instead only passively consume information.

Conversely, bond-based attachment is driven by personal social relations with other specific individuals (e.g., family, friends, colleagues), and thus it does not require a common theme of interest to be justified. Bond-based links are usu-

[1]E.g., *"People You May Know"* in Facebook and LinkedIn, *"Recommended Blogs"* in Tumblr, or *"Who to Follow"* in Twitter, just to mention a few.

ally reciprocated, while identity-based links are much more directional, where the direction is given by the level of authoritativeness of the user on the theme. The two types of links create two different types of communities, that for simplicity we name "topical" for identity-based and "social" for bond-based [10].

Based on this observation we define a stochastic model, dubbed WTFW ("Who to Follow and Why"), which not only predicts links, but *for each predicted link it decides whether it is a topical or a social link, and depending on this decision it produces a different type of explanation.*

A topical link $u \rightarrow v$ (u should follow v) is usually recommended to u when v is authoritative in a topic in which u has demonstrated interest. In this case the explanation is a set of the top-k binary features (e.g., tags in `Flickr` or hashtags in `Twitter`) describing the topic of authoritativeness of v, which makes v a potential source of interesting information for u. A social link $u \rightarrow v$ instead is recommended when u and v are already part of the same social community, i.e., they have many contacts in common. In this case the explanation is the set of the top-k common neighbors w.r.t. the likelihood of being responsible for the link creation. As an important by-product, WTFW also *implicitly detects communities and their type (social or topical).*

More in details WTFW is a bayesian topic model defined over directed and nodes-attributed graphs. In WTFW each link creation and each attribute adoption by a node are explained w.r.t. a finite number of latent factors. These latent factors can be abstractly thought as *topics* or *communities*: in the rest of the paper we will use the three terms (latent factor, topic, and community) interchangeably. Each community is characterized by a level of sociality/topicality: social communities are characterized by high density and reciprocity of links, whereas topical communities are characterized by low entropy in the features and by the presence of authoritative users on the relevant topic. Each user tend to be involved in different communities to different extent and with different roles. These components are modeled by three different multinomial distributions over the set of users, modeling their sociality, authoritativeness and interest in each topic. Finally, each topic is characterized by a multinomial distribution over the feature set, which provide a semantic interpretation of the topic.

Paper contributions. The contributions of this paper are summarized as follows:

- We study for the first time the problem of *link prediction with explanations*, which is motivated by the real-world application of user recommender systems in online social networks.
- We introduce WTFW ("Who to Follow and Why") a stochastic topic model which not only predicts links, but for each predicted link it decides whether it is a topical or a social link, and depending on this decision it produces a different type of explanation.
- As a by-product, WTFW also implicitly extract communities that can be labeled as either topical or social.
- Our experimental assessment on two real-world datasets (`Twitter` and `Flickr`) confirms that our model is very accurate in link prediction and in labeling the predicted link as social or topical. The experiments also highlight the high quality of the topics extracted and their coherence with the topical Vs. social labeling.

2. RELATED WORK

Link prediction has attracted a great deal of attention in the last decade (the interested reader may refer to [12, 18] for a comprehensive survey): however, to the best of our knowledge, no previous work has studied *link prediction with explanations for user recommendation systems.* Our proposal can also be collocated in the literature on relational learning methods that are able to leverage attribute information on nodes [29, 34, 19]. The main drawback of those approaches is scalability, which seriously prevents their application on real-world networks.

The *Supervised Random Walk* algorithm for link prediction [1], exploits edge features to learn the edge strength that is then used random walk transition probability. Alternative random-walk approaches rely on merging the social graph and node attributes in a unique graph with person-nodes and attribute-nodes linked among them [33, 9].

The joint factorization of social links and node attributes is closely related to the task of detecting communities in nodes-attributed graphs. [35] uses node attributes to augment the social graph by generating "attribute edges" between nodes that are similar on a given attribute, and then identify communities in the augmented graph. [21] introduces the problem of *finding cohesive patterns*, defined as connected subgraphs whose density exceeds a given threshold, and with homogeneous values on node-attributes. [31] proposes a co-clustering framework based on users and tags. Users are implicitly connected by their common interests, as expressed by the tags they use. [23] studies the problem of finding communities with *concise descriptions* based on the nodes attributes.

Several stochastic models for community detection in networks with node attributes have been proposed in the literature. In *Link-LDA* [6] social connections and user attributes are generated by a mixture of user-specific distributions over topics. In [22, 15, 32] the community-membership vectors are used to factorize both links and the attribute-profile of each user. [27] extends the author-topic model to communication networks in which the sender and recipient of each post are known. [2] proposes a generative stochastic model to detect communities from the social graph and a database of information propagations over the social graph.

3. WHO TO FOLLOW AND WHY

In this section we introduce the WTFW model for link prediction with explanations. Our application scenario is that of online social networking platforms, where users build and maintain social connections, share information, and follow updates from other users. We represent this as a directed graph, where each node is a user and it has associated a set of binary features, representing the interests of the user.

More formally, let $G = (V, E)$ be the social graph where V is a set of n users, $E \subseteq V \times V$ is a set of m *directed* arcs, and (u, v) indicates that u follows v and hence he is notified of v's activities. We also denote the neighborhood of a node u as $N(u) = \{v \in V : (u, v) \in E \vee (v, u) \in E\}$. Moreover let $\mathcal{F}$ denote a set of h binary features. We are given a binary $n \times h$ matrix F such that $F_{u,f} = 1$ when user u is interested in the feature f. For simplicity we denote this case also as $(u, f) \in F$. Finally, we denote all the features of the node u as $F(v) = \{f \in \mathcal{F} : (u, f) \in F\}$ and the set of all the nodes having attribute f as $V(f) = \{u \in V : (u, f) \in F\}$.

1. sample $\mathbf{\Pi} \sim Dir\left(\vec{\xi}\right)$
2. For each $k \in \{1, \ldots, K\}$ sample

$$\delta_k \sim Beta(\delta_0, \delta_1) \qquad \tau_k \sim Beta(\tau_0, \tau_1)$$
$$\mathbf{\Phi}_k \sim Dir(\vec{\gamma}) \qquad \boldsymbol{\theta}_k \sim Dir(\vec{\alpha})$$
$$\boldsymbol{A}_k \sim Dir\left(\vec{\beta}\right) \qquad \boldsymbol{S}_k \sim Dir(\vec{\eta})$$

3. For each link $l \in \{l_1, \ldots, l_m\}$ to generate:
   (a) Choose $k \sim Discrete(\mathbf{\Pi})$
   (b) Sample $x_l \sim Bernoulli(\delta_k)$
   (c) if $x_l = 1$
      - sample source $u \sim Discrete(\boldsymbol{\theta}_k)$
      - sample destination $v \sim Discrete(\boldsymbol{\theta}_k)$

   (d) else
      - sample source $u \sim Discrete(\mathbf{S}_k)$
      - sample destination $v \sim Discrete(\mathbf{A}_k)$
4. For each feature pair $a \in \{a_1, \cdots, a_t\}$ to associate
   (a) sample $k \sim Discrete(\Pi)$
   (b) Sample $y_a \sim Bernoulli(\tau_k)$:
      - if $y_a = 1$ then $u_a \sim Discrete(\boldsymbol{A}_k)$
      - otherwise $u_a \sim Discrete(\boldsymbol{S}_k)$

   (c) sample $f_a \sim Discrete(\mathbf{\Phi}_k)$

Figure 1: Generative process for the WTFW model

Following the *common identity and common bond theory* discussed in Section 1, we assume two main types of behavior in creating connections in a social network. The "topical" behavior, in which a user u decides to follow another user v because of u's interest in a topic in which v is authoritative; and the "social" behavior in which u follows v because they know each other in the real world, or they have many common contacts in the social network. In the topical behavior case we can further identify two distinct roles for a user, either as authoritative ("influential") for the topic or just interested ("susceptible") in the topic. In the social case instead there are no specific roles, but a generic tendency to connect among the users of a close-knit circle.

Following these considerations, we propose to explain the structure of the network (the links) and the features of the nodes, by introducing a set of latent factors representing users' interests, and by labeling the links as either social or topical. This is done by means of a unique stochastic topic model, which is based on the following assumptions:

- Links can be explained by different latent factors (overlapping communities);
- Social links tend to be reciprocal and communities characterized by a high level of sociality exhibit *high density*;
- Topical links tend to exhibit a clear directionality and communities that are highly topicality have *low entropy* on the set of features assigned to nodes.

More in details, the degree of involvement and role of user u in the community/topic k is governed by three parameters: (1)$A_{k,u}$ which measures the degree of the authoritativeness of u in k; (2)$S_{k,u}$ which measures the degree of interest u in the topic k, or in other terms, the likelihood of following users that are authoritative in k (susceptibility to social influence); and (3)$\theta_{k,u}$ denotes the social tendency of u, i.e., her likelihood to connect to other social peers within community k. Moreover, each latent factor k is characterized by

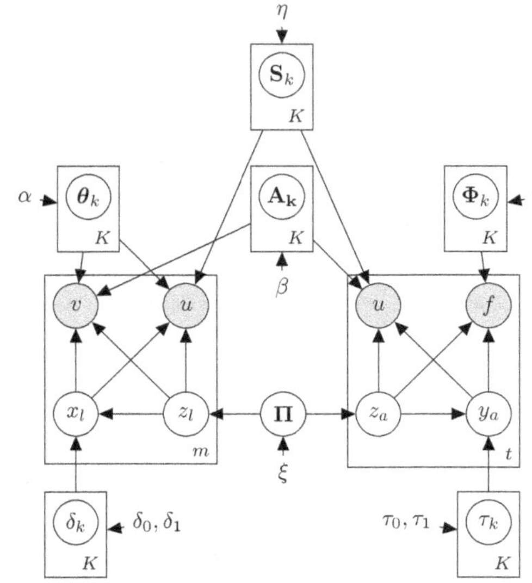

Figure 2: The WTFW model in plate notation.

a propensity to adopt certain features in $\mathcal{F}$ over others. We can formalize such a propensity by means of a weightΦ $_{k,f}$, denoting the importance of feature f within k.

All these components are accommodated in a mixture membership model expressed in a Bayesian setting [4], to define distributions governing the stochastic process, given some prior hypotheses. Bayesian modeling is better suited when the underlying data is characterized by high sparsity (like in our case), as it allows a better control of the priors which govern the model and it prevents overfitting.

In particular, we directly model each *observed* social link $(u, v) \in E$ or adoption of feature by a node $(u, f) \in F$ and introduce random variables on the source/destination of these observations. That is, for each link $(u, v) \in E$ we model the likelihood that there exists a latent factor k, such that u has high probability of being a source, while v has high probability of being a destination. We further introduce a latent variable $x_{u,v}$, which encodes the (social/topical) nature of an existing link. Analogously, the adoption of an observed feature association $(u, f) \in F$ will be explained by a latent factor k and by the status of the latent variable $y_{u,f}$ which represent the role of the user u, either as authoritative or just interested, when adopting the feature f.

The underlying generative process for social links and adoption of features depends jointly on the components $\boldsymbol{\theta}$, $\mathbf{A}$, $\mathbf{S}$ and $\mathbf{\Phi}$, as described in Figure 1 and depicted in plate notation in Figure 2. The overall generative process is governed by the following components:

- A multinomial distribution $\mathbf{\Pi}$ over a fixed number of K latent factors, which generate latent community-assignments z_l and z_a, for each link $l \in E$ and for each adoption of feature $a \in F$;
- The multinomial distributions $\boldsymbol{\theta}_k, \mathbf{A}_k$ and $\mathbf{S}_k$ over the set of user V, which specify, respectively, the degree of sociality, authority and susceptibility of each user within k;
- The multinomial probability $\mathbf{\Phi}_k$ over $\mathcal{F}$ which specify the likelihood of observing each feature within the community k.

- The degree of "sociality" δ_k (or "topicality", $1-\delta_k$) which measures the likelihood of observing social/topical connections within each community k;
- The "authoritative attitude" τ_k of observing the adoption of an attribute by authoritative subject in k (or, dually, the "susceptible attitude", $1-\tau_k$).

Since the whole model relies on multinomial and Bernoulli distributions, a full Bayesian treatment can be obtained by adopting Dirichlet and Beta conjugate priors.

Let $\Theta = \{\mathbf{\Pi}, \boldsymbol{\delta}, \boldsymbol{\tau}, \boldsymbol{\theta}, \mathbf{A}, \mathbf{S}\}$ denote the status of the distributions described above. Both the probability of observing link $l = (u, v)$ and a feature assignment $a = (u, f)$ can be expressed as mixtures over the latent community assignments z_l and z_a:

$$\Pr(l|\Theta) = \sum_{k=1}^{K} \pi_k \Pr(l|z_l = k, \Theta) \tag{1}$$

$$\Pr(a|\Theta) = \sum_{k=1}^{K} \pi_k \Pr(a|z_a = k, \Theta) \tag{2}$$

The generation of a link changes depending on the status of the latent variable x_l. A social connection $l = (u, v)$ can only be observed if, by picking a latent community k, u and v have high degrees of social attitude $\theta_{k,u}$ and $\theta_{k,v}$, that is

$$\Pr(l|z_l = k, x_l = 1, \Theta) = \theta_{k,u} \cdot \theta_{k,v}.$$

Conversely, a topical connection $l = (u, v)$ can only be observed if, by picking a latent community k, u has a high degree of activeness $A_{k,u}$ and v have a high degree of passive interest $S_{k,u}$, that is

$$\Pr(l|z_l = k, x_l = 0, \Theta) = S_{k,u} \cdot A_{k,v}.$$

Note that the likelihood of observing the reciprocal link (v, u) is equally likely in case of social connection, while it is different in a topical context, and hence reflect our design assumption on the directionality of links in social/topical communities. Each link is finally generated by taking into account the social/topical mixture of each community:

$$\begin{aligned}\Pr(l|z_l = k, \Theta) =& \delta_k \Pr(l|z_l = k, x_l = 1, \Theta) \\ &+ (1-\delta_k) \Pr(l|z_l = k, x_l = 0, \Theta) \\ =& \delta_k \cdot \theta_{k,u} \cdot \theta_{k,v} + (1-\delta_k) \cdot S_{k,u} \cdot A_{k,v}\end{aligned}$$

Similarly, the probability of observing a node-feature pair $a = (u, f) \in F$ depends on the degree of authoritativeness/susceptibility of the user and by the likelihood of observing the attribute f within each latent factor k:

$$\Pr(a|z_a = k, \Theta) = (\tau_k A_{k,u} + (1-\tau_k) \cdot S_{k,u})\, \Phi_{k,f}.$$

Here, the term $\tau_k \mathbf{A}_k + (1-\tau_k)\mathbf{S}_k$ defines a multinomial distribution over users, which encodes the joint (both susceptible and authoritative) attitude of users within that community.

3.1 Learning

We have described the intuitions behind our joint modeling of links and feature associations and now we focus on defining a procedure for inference and parameter estimation under WTFW.

Let $\Xi = \{\vec{\xi}, \vec{\alpha}, \vec{\beta}, \vec{\gamma}, \vec{\eta}, \vec{\delta} = \{\delta_0, \delta_1\}, \vec{\tau} = \{\tau_0, \tau_1\}\}$ denote the set of hyperparameters of the Dirichlet/Beta priors. Also, let $\mathbf{Z}^e$ represents a binary $m \times K$ matrix where $z_{l,k} = 1$ denotes that link l has been associated with the k-th latent factor (i.e., $z_l = k$). Analogously, $\mathbf{Z}^f$ denotes the $t \times K$ binary matrix where $z_{a,k} = 1$ denotes that feature assignment $a \in F$ is associated with the k-th latent factor ($z_a = k$). Finally, $\mathbf{X}$ and $\mathbf{Y}$ denote the vectors of assignments x_l and y_a. With an abuse of notation, we also introduce the counters described in Tab. 1, relative to these matrices.

The key problem in inference is to compute the posterior distribution of latent variables given the observed data. We start by expressing the joint likelihood as:

$$\begin{aligned}\Pr(E, F, \Theta, \mathbf{Z}^e, \mathbf{Z}^f, \mathbf{X}, \mathbf{Y}|\Xi) =& \\ &\Pr(E|\Theta, \mathbf{X}, \mathbf{Z}^e) \Pr(F|\Theta, \mathbf{Y}, \mathbf{Z}^f) \\ &\Pr(\mathbf{Z}^e|\Pi) \Pr(\mathbf{Z}^f|\Pi) \\ &\Pr(\mathbf{X}|\mathbf{Z}^e, \boldsymbol{\delta}) \Pr(\mathbf{Y}|\mathbf{Z}^f, \boldsymbol{\tau}) \Pr(\Theta|\Xi)\end{aligned} \tag{3}$$

where

$$\begin{aligned}\Pr(E|\Theta, \mathbf{X}, \mathbf{Z}^e) &= \prod_u \prod_k \theta_{k,u}^{c_{k,u}^{s,s} + c_{k,u}^{s,d}} S_{k,u}^{c_{k,u}^{t,s}} A_{k,u}^{c_{k,u}^{t,d}} \\ \Pr(F|\Theta, \mathbf{Y}, \mathbf{Z}^f) &= \prod_u \prod_k A_{k,u}^{d_{k,u}^a} S_{k,u}^{d_{k,u}^s} \prod_f \prod_k \Phi_{k,f}^{d_{k,f}} \\ \Pr(\mathbf{Z}^e|\Pi) &= \prod_k \pi_k^{c_k} \\ \Pr(\mathbf{Z}^f|\Pi) &= \prod_k \pi_k^{d_k} \\ \Pr(\mathbf{X}|\mathbf{Z}^e, \boldsymbol{\delta}) &= \prod_k \delta_k^{c_k^s} (1-\delta_k)^{c_k^t} \\ \Pr(\mathbf{Y}|\mathbf{Z}^f, \boldsymbol{\tau}) &= \prod_k \tau_k^{d_k^a} (1-\tau_k)^{d_k^s}\end{aligned}$$

and $\Pr(\Theta|\Xi)$ represents the product of all the Dirichlet and Beta priors. By marginalizing over Θ, we can obtain a closed form for the joint likelihood $\Pr(E, F, \mathbf{Z}^e, \mathbf{Z}^f, \mathbf{X}, \mathbf{Y}|\Xi)$. The latter is the basis for developing a stochastic EM strategy [3, section 11.1.6], where the E-step consists of a collapsed Gibbs sampling procedure [13, 3] for estimating the matrices $\mathbf{Z}^e, \mathbf{Z}^f, \mathbf{X}$ and $\mathbf{Y}$, and the M-step estimates both the predictive distributions in Θ and the hyperparameters of interest in Ξ. In particular, the sampling step consists of a sequential update of each arc and feature-assignment, of the status of the corresponding latent variables in $\mathbf{Z}^e, \mathbf{Z}^f, \mathbf{X}$ and $\mathbf{Y}$. A possible sampling strategy for each arc $l \in E$ and adoption $a \in F$ is based on the following chain: $\Pr(z_l = k|\mathit{Rest}), \Pr(z_a = k|\mathit{Rest}), \Pr(x_l = 1|\mathit{Rest})$ and $\Pr(y_a = 1|\mathit{Rest})$[2]. By algebraic manipulations, we can devise the sampling equations expressed in Tab. 8. The overall learning scheme is shown in Alg. 1. Lines 5-12 of the algorithm represent the Gibbs sampling steps, while line 14 represents the update of the multinomial distributions which are collapsed in the derivation of the sampling equations:

$$A_{k,u} = \frac{c_{k,u}^{t,d} + d_{k,u}^a + \eta_u}{c_k^t + d_k^a + \sum_u \eta_u} \tag{4}$$

$$\theta_{k,u} = \frac{c_{k,u}^{s,s} + c_{k,u}^{s,d} + \alpha_u}{2c_k^s + \sum_u \alpha_u} \tag{5}$$

$$S_{k,u} = \frac{c_{k,u}^{t,s} + d_{k,u}^s + \eta_u}{c_k^t + c_k^s + \sum_u \eta_u} \tag{6}$$

$$\phi_{k,f} = \frac{d_{k,f} + \gamma_f}{d_k + \sum_f \gamma_f} \tag{7}$$

$$\pi_k = \frac{c_k + d_k + \xi_k}{m + t + \sum_k \xi_k} \tag{8}$$

In line 15 we update the Beta ($\vec{\delta}$, $\vec{\tau}$) and Dirichlet $\vec{\xi}$ hyperparameters, according to the fixed point iterative procedure

[2] The term *Rest* denotes the remaining variables in the set $\{E, F, \mathbf{Z}^e, \mathbf{Z}^f, \mathbf{X}, \mathbf{Y}, \Theta, \Xi\}$ after the explicit variables in both the conditioning and conditioned part have been removed.

Symbol	Description	Expression
c_k	Number of links associated with community k	$\sum_{l\in E} z_{l,k}$
c^s	Number of social links	$\sum_{l\in E} x_l$
c^t	Number of topical links	$\sum_{l\in E}(1-x_l)$
c_k^s	Number of social links associated with community k	$\sum_{l\in E} x_l \cdot z_{l,k}$
c_k^t	Number of topical links associated with community k	$\sum_{l\in E}(1-x_l)\cdot z_{l,k}$
$c_{k,u}^{s,s}$	Number of social links associated with community k where u is the source	$\sum_{l=(u,\cdot)\in E}\{x_l \cdot z_{l,k}\}$
$c_{k,u}^{s,d}$	Number of social links associated with community k where u is the destination	$\sum_{l=(\cdot,u)\in E}\{x_l \cdot z_{l,k}\}$
$c_{k,u}^{t,s}$	Number of topical links associated with community k where u is the source	$\sum_{l=(u,\cdot)\in E}\{(1-x_l)\cdot z_{l,k}\}$
$c_{k,u}^{t,d}$	Number of topical links associated with community k where u is the destination	$\sum_{l=(\cdot,u)\in E}\{(1-x_l)\cdot z_{l,k}\}$
d_k	Number of feature-assignments associated with community k	$\sum_{a\in F} z_{a,k}$
d^a	Number of authoritative feature-assignments	$\sum_{a\in F} y_a$
d^s	Number of susceptible feature-assignments	$\sum_{a\in F}(1-y_a)$
d_k^a	Number of feature-assignments within community k on authoritative users	$\sum_{a\in F} y_a \cdot z_{a,k}$
d_k^s	Number of feature-assignments within community k on susceptible users	$\sum_{a\in F}(1-y_a)\cdot z_{a,k}$
$d_{k,f}$	Number of recipients associated with community k relative to feature f	$\sum_{a=(\cdot,f)\in F}\{(1-y_a)\cdot z_{a,k}\}$
$d_{k,u}^a$	Number of features associated with community k where u is the authoritative source	$\sum_{a=(u,\cdot)\in F}\{y_a \cdot z_{a,k}\}$
$d_{k,u}^s$	Number of features associated with community k where u is the susceptible source	$\sum_{a=(u,\cdot)\in F}\{(1-y_a)\cdot z_{a,k}\}$

Table 1: Counters adopted in the Gibbs Sampling and their meaning.

described in [20]. The final predictive distributions $\mathbf{A}$, $\mathbf{S}$, $\boldsymbol{\theta}$ and $\boldsymbol{\Pi}$, $\boldsymbol{\delta}$ and $\boldsymbol{\tau}$ are averaged along all the steps of the Gibbs sampling procedure.

A single iteration of the sampler performs $\mathcal{O}((m+t)\cdot K)$ computations and hence it is linear on the size of observed data. In Alg. 1 we assume that the number K of topics is given as input; typically this value is determined experimentally as the number of topics that maximizes the predictive performances. However, it is possible to automatically devise the number of topics by relying on Bayesian nonparametrics. In fact, as shown in [7], it is possible to adapt the sampling equations in order to make explicit the annihilation of some topics as well the generation of new ones, according to the *Chinese Restaurant Process* principle.

Algorithm 1 Gibbs-sampling with parameter estimation

```
Require: G and F,the number of latent features K,
         initial hyperparameter set Ξ.
Random initialization for the matrices Z^e, Z^f, X and Y;
it ← 0
converged ← false
while it < nMaxIt and ¬converged do
    for all observed link l do
        Sample z_l according to Eq. 13 and 14
        Sample x_l according to Eq. 15 and 16
    end for
    for all observed attribute-assignment a do
        Sample z_a according to Eq. 17 and 18
        Sample y_a according to Eq. 19 and 20
    end for
    if (it > burn-in) and (it%sampleLag = 0) then
        Sample A (Eq. 4) ,θ (Eq. 5), S (Eq. 6), Φ (Eq. 7), and Π
        (Eq. 8);
        Update hyperparameters δ̄, τ̄ and ξ̄;
    end if
    it ← it + 1
end while
```

3.2 Producing explanations

The success of a recommender system does not only depend on its accuracy in inferring and exploiting users' interests, but it also relies on how the deployed recommendations are perceived by the users. Explanations increase the transparency of the recommendation process and may positively contribute in gaining users' trust and satisfaction.

When generating explanations for social recommendations, the first step is to understand if the proposed connection $l=(u,v)$ is social (i.e., such that $x_l=1$) or topical (i.e., $x_l=0$). WTFW provides a natural way to do this:

$$\Pr(x_l=1|l,\Theta)\propto\sum_k \pi_k\delta_k\theta_{k,u}\theta_{k,v} \tag{9}$$

$$\Pr(x_l=0|l,\Theta)\propto\sum_k \pi_k(1-\delta_k)S_{k,u}A_{k,v}, \tag{10}$$

Social connections have a natural explanation in terms of close-knit circles. Thus, for a given link $l=(u,v)$ predicted as social (i.e., such that $x_l=1$), we can provide an explanation as the set of the *most prospective common neighbors*, ranked according to the following score:

$$rank(w;l)=\sum_k \pi_k\delta_k\theta_{k,u}\theta_{k,v}\theta_{k,w}. \tag{11}$$

This rank promotes common neighbors that have high degree of involvement in social communities where both u and v are involved as well. Interestingly, the score finds an explanation in terms of the probability of observing a social triangle among u, v and w. In fact, the joint probability of observing $(u,v),(u,w)$ and (v,w) within community k is proportional to $\theta_{k,u}\theta_{k,v}\theta_{k,w}$. And, since by definition both (u,w) and (v,w) hold in the data, the score explain the prospective new link (u,v) in terms of the common neighbors which are more likely to devise a triangle in the data.

Conversely, topical links can be explained through a list of attributes which are representative of the topics of interest by the current user and for which the recommended connection has high authority. For each feature common to the two nodes, we define the following score:

$$rank(f;l)=\sum_k \pi_k(1-\delta_k)\Phi_{k,f}A_{k,v}\cdot (\tau_k A_{k,u}+(1-\tau_k)S_{k,u}). \tag{12}$$

Here, the latter term represents the topical involvement of the user u within community k. Again, the score has an interpretation in terms of the prospective triangle among $(u,v),(u,f)$ and (v,f). Notice, however, that the directionality plays a role here, since we are only interested in those features for which v is authoritative.

The procedure for producing explanations for a recommended link is summarized in Alg. 2. In short, the procedure predicts the nature (either social or topical) of the prospective link, hence providing the list of most prominent neighbors/common features.

Algorithm 2 Producing explanations

Require: The social network G, the WTFW model, a recommended link $l = (u, v)$ and the number of explanations L;
Ensure: a list $\mathcal{L}$ of either social or topical explanations for the link.

$\mathcal{L} \leftarrow \emptyset$
Compute x_l according to equations 9 and 10
if $x_l = 1$ **then**
  $\mathcal{L}_N \leftarrow \emptyset$
  for all $w \in N(u) \cap N(v)$ **do**
    Compute $rank(w, l)$ according to Eq. 11
    $L_N \leftarrow L_N \cup (w, rank(w, l))$
  end for
  Sort L_N and compute $\mathcal{L} = top(L_N, L)$
else
  $L_F \leftarrow \emptyset$
  for all $f \in F(u) \cap F(v)$ **do**
    Compute $rank(f, l)$ according to Eq. 12
    $L_F \leftarrow L_F \cup (f, rank(f, l))$
  end for
  Sort L_F and compute $\mathcal{L} = top(L_F, L)$
end if

4. EXPERIMENTAL EVALUATION

In this section we report the empirical assessment of the proposed WTFW model on real networks. The experimentation is aimed at assessing the following:

- The accuracy of the model for what concerns both *link prediction* and *label prediction*, where the latter refers to the classification of a link as either social or topical.
- The scalability and stability of the learning procedure by studying learning time and performance varying the number of iterations of the Gibbs sampler.
- The quality of the associations between links and features, that we show by means of anecdotal evidence in the reconstruction of the data through the model.

Datasets. For our purposes we need datasets coming from social networking platforms in which links creation can be explained in terms of interest identity and/or personal social relations. This requirement is satisfied, among the others, by two popular social networking platforms, namely **Twitter** and **Flickr**. On both platforms, the underlying network is inherently directed to reflect interest of users towards important, and authoritative, information sources. Moreover, in these systems the role of users may naturally change with respect to different topics. The **Twitter** dataset we use is publicly available[3] and it includes information from 973 ego-networks crawled from the public API. The resulting network contains roughly 80 thousand nodes and 1.7 million directed links. Attribute information consists in all the hashtags (e.g. #sanfrancisco) and mentions (e.g. @BarackObama), used by those users.

Flickr data has been obtained by querying **Flickr** public API in the time window 2004 – 2008 and then by performing forest fire sampling [16] on the resulting network. Features are generated by crawling all the tags used by each users. **Flickr** also contains a form of ground-truth for the label prediction task. Specifically, for each link in the dataset there are two flags, namely *friend* and *family*, that a user can specify. We naturally interpret these flags as follows: a link is labeled as "social" if it is either marked as family or friend. Conversely, a link is "topical" if none of the two flags are set. It is important to stress that this ground-truth is expectedly very noisy as it is any user-declared information on the internet. As such, it is likely to produce an underestimation of the accuracy in the label prediction task.

In order to keep the experimental setting as close as possible to the original data (high dimensionality and exceptional sparsity), no further pre-processing has been performed. Basic statistics about these two datasets are given in Table 2. These datasets are characterized by different properties. The social graph in **Twitter** is much more directed and sparse than in **Flickr**, while the number of attributes per user is much higher in **Flickr**.

	Twitter	Flickr
Number of nodes	81,306	80,000
Number of links	1,768,149	14,036,407
Number of one-way links	1,342,311	9,604,945
Number of bidirectional links	425,838	4,431,462
Number of social links	-	6,747,085
Number of topical links	-	7,289,322
Avg in-degree	21	175
Avg out-degree	25	131
Number of features	211,225	819,201
Number of feature assignments	1,102,000	37,316,862
Avg. features per user	15	613
Avg. users per feature	5	45

Table 2: Datasets statistics.

Experimental setting. In all the experiments we assume a partial observation of the network and a complete set of user features.[4] The learning algorithm starts with a random assignments to latent variables, it performs a burn-in phase (burn-in=500) to stabilize the Markov chain, and the parameters of the model are updated at regular intervals (sampling lag=20) for the next 2000 iterations. We initialize hyperparameters with the following (symmetric) values: $\alpha = \beta = \eta = \frac{1}{n}$, $\gamma = \frac{1}{h}$, $\tau_0 = \tau_1 = \delta_0 = \delta_1 = \xi = 2$.

4.1 Model Assessment

Evaluation on link prediction. In a first set of experiments, we measure the accuracy of the model in predicting new links. On **Twitter**, we perform a Monte Carlo Cross-Validation in 5 folds, by randomly splitting the network into training and test data. We also measure the accuracy of the learned models for different proportions of training/test, namely 60/40, 70/30, 80/20. This allows us to stress the robustness of the link prediction task for different proportions, and to mitigate the effects of the random splits. In **Flickr** instead the dataset contains the timestamp of creation of the link, allowing us to perform a chronological split, where older links (70% of the data) are used for learning the model, while the most recent 30% are used as prediction target.

The accuracy of link prediction is measured by computing the area under the ROC curve (AUC) over a set of positive and negative examples drawn from the test set. In principle, we can consider all links in the test-set as positive examples, and all non-existing links as negative example. However, the sparsity of the networks poses two major issues: (*i*) the number of non-existing links can be enormous, thus making the computation of the AUC infeasible; (*ii*) missing links do not necessarily represent negative information, but rather unseen information [28]. Following [1], we thus limit the negative examples to all the 2-hops non-existing links.

[3] `http://snap.stanford.edu/data/egonets-Twitter.html`

[4] The task of predicting/recommending missing features is not investigated here and it is left as future work

Method	Split	8	16	32	64	128	256
		Number of latent factors					
WTFW	60/40	0.567	0.615	0.667	0.707	0.739	**0.792**
	70/30	0.565	0.631	0.680	0.713	0.749	**0.798**
	80/20	0.586	0.639	0.692	0.732	0.760	**0.812**
JSVD	60/40	0.439	0.471	0.525	0.588	0.660	0.768
	70/30	0.446	0.48	0.537	0.602	0.679	0.744
	80/20	0.454	0.495	0.545	0.617	0.693	0.763
CNF		0.7025/0.7125/0.7199					
AA-NF		0.7301/0.7397/0.7472					

Table 3: AUC on link prediction - `Twitter`

Method	8	16	32	64	128	256
	Number of latent factors					
WTFW	0.6467	0.6488	0.6534	0.6576	0.661	**0.677**
JSVD	0.598	0.596	0.597	0.609	0.619	0.624
CNF	0.53					
AA-NF	0.58					

Table 4: AUC on link prediction - `Flickr`

Method	8	16	32	64	128	256
	Number of latent factors					
WTFW	0.7393	0.7548	**0.7603**	0.6883	0.6618	0.6582
Baseline	0.6545					

Table 5: AUC on link labeling - `Flickr`.

We compare the performance of the WTFW model with some popular baseline approaches from the literature, which perform well on a range of networks [18, 9]: *Common Neighbors/Features (CNF)* and *Adamic-Adar (AA-NF)*. CNF is a local similarity index that produces a score for each link (u, v), which is given by the number of common neighbors/features:

$$score(u, v) = |N(u) \cap N(v)| + |F(u) \cap F(v)|.$$

AA-NF represents a refinement of the simple counting of common neighbors/features, which is achieved by assigning more weight to less-connected components.

$$score(u, v) = \sum_{w \in N(u) \cap N(v)} \frac{1}{|N(w)|} + \sum_{f \in F(u) \cap F(v)} \frac{1}{|V(f)|}$$

In addition, we compare WTFW with a matrix factorization approach based on SVD, dubbed *Joint SVD (JSVD)* [9]. In practice, the approach computes a low-rank factorization of the joint adjacency/feature matrix $\mathbf{X} = [E\ F]$ as $\mathbf{X} \approx \mathbf{U} \cdot diag(\sigma_1, \ldots, \sigma_K) \cdot \mathbf{V}^T$, where K is the rank of the decomposition and $\sigma_1, \ldots, \sigma_K$ are the square roots of the K greatest eigenvalues of $\mathbf{X}^T\mathbf{X}$. The matrices $\mathbf{U}$ and $\mathbf{V}$ provide substantial interpretation in terms of connectivity of both E and F. The term $U_{u,k}$ can be interpreted as the tendency of u to be either a source in E or an adopter in F, relative to factor k. Analogously, $V_{u,k}$ represents the tendency of u to appear as a destination in E, and $V_{f,k}$ represents the likelihood that item f is adopted in k. The link prediction score can hence be computed as:

$$score(u, v) = \sum_{k=1}^{K} U_{u,k} \sigma_k V_{v,k}.$$

Tables 3 and 4 summarize the results of the evaluation, for increasing values of the number of latent topics/factors. On `Twitter` data, both WTFW and JSVD underperform when the number of latent factors is limited, but exhibit a competitive advange over the baselines for higher values of K. WTFW outperforms the other considered approaches and these results are stable on different training/test set proportions. The prediction on `Flickr` is in general weaker for all

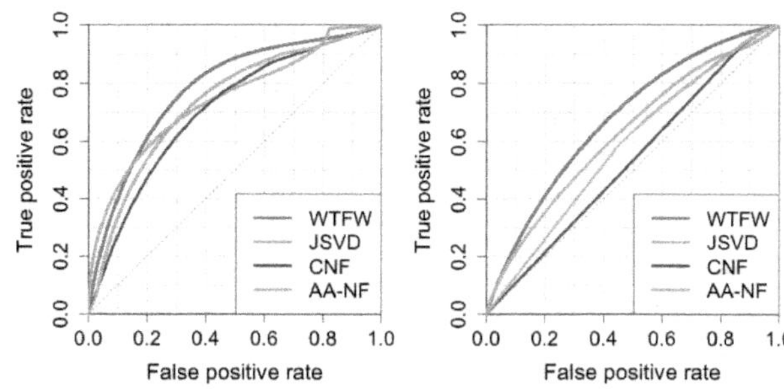

Figure 3: Link prediction: `Twitter` (left) and `Flickr` (right).

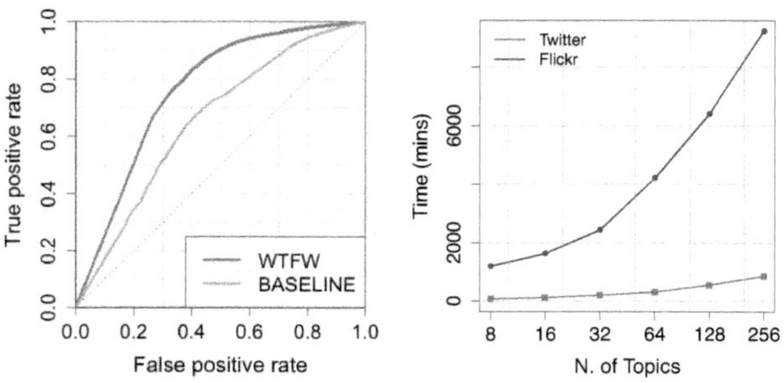

(a) (b)

Figure 4: (a) Accuracy of link labeling on `Flickr`. (b) Learning times on the 70/30 split for both `Flickr` and `Twitter`.

methods. However, the results seems stabler, since the difference with regards to JSVD remains constant for increasing values of K. The standard baselines perform poorly on this dataset. Figure 3 shows the slope of the ROC curves on both datasets for $K = 256$. On `Twitter`, there are some limited areas where the JSVD is skewed but, in general, WTFW clearly outperforms the other methods. This is even more evident on the `Flickr` dataset.

Evaluation on link labeling. We next turn our attention to the task of discriminating between social and topical links, thanks to the ground truth that we have in the `Flickr` dataset. Again, we measure the accuracy by computing the AUC on the prediction, and by comparing the result with a baseline based on common neighbors/features. That is, a link $l = (u, v)$ is deemed social if the weight of the common neighbors is higher than those of the common features, and topical otherwise. Formally:

$$\Pr(x_l = 1|l) = \frac{|N(u) \cap N(v)|}{|N(u) \cap N(v)| + |F(u) \cap F(v)|}.$$

Table 5 reports the results for increasing values of K. The best results are obtains on a lower number of topics, and in particular for $K = 32$. This is somehow surprising if we compare this results with the results on link prediction discussed above. In an attempt to explain such a behavior, we analysed the values of $\mathbf{\Pi}$ and $\boldsymbol{\delta}$ in the model, and we noticed that all models exhibit a strongly dominant latent factor. We will discuss this component also in the next subsection: it is worth mentioning, however that the associated probability δ_k leans towards 0.5 (a clear sign that the community tends to mix topical and social contributions). Clearly, the balanced value of δ_k does not affect the performance in link prediction (as it only depends on whether any of the social/topical components is strong enough to trigger

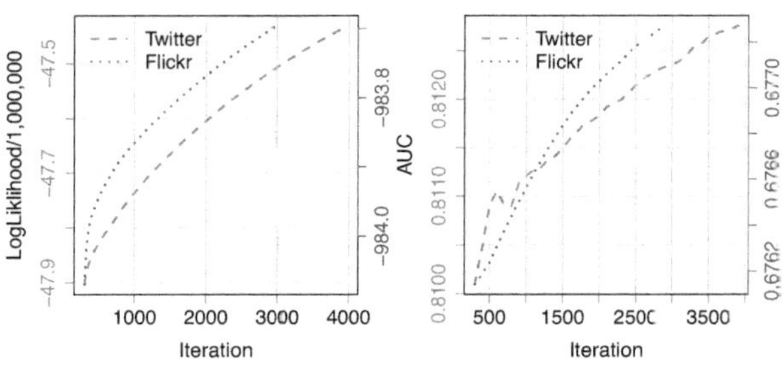

Figure 5: log likelihood and accuracy along the iterations.

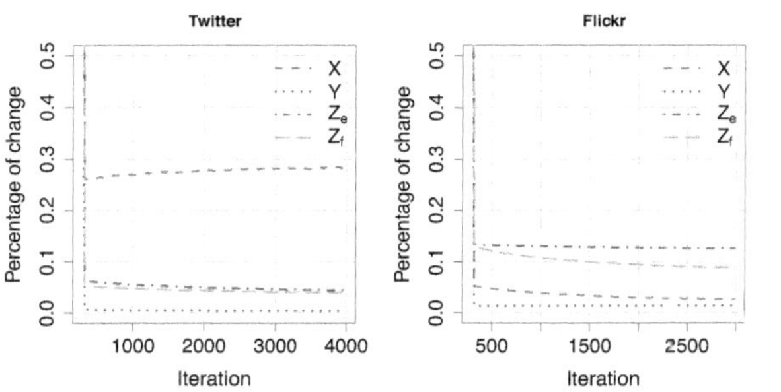

Figure 6: Changes in the matrices $\mathbf{Z}^e$, $\mathbf{Z}^f$, $\mathbf{X}$ and $\mathbf{Y}$.

the link), but it can negatively affect the label prediction. The degradation of the performance for higher values of K can find a justification in the split of this giant component: apparently, the splitting seems to produce a reallocation of the links in the other communities, thus causing the overfitting. Besides this anomalous behavior, WTFW outperforms the baseline prediction for each considered value of K, as shown in Fig. 4(a).

Scalability and sensitivity analysis. We next discuss how the model parameters affect the learning time and the quality of the results. As already mentioned, we chose to perform 2,000 Gibbs sampling iterations. Figure 4 shows that the learning is substantially linear in the number of topics. Figure 5 shows the behavior of the log-likelihood (on the left) and the AUC values on the validation data, along the iterations. We can see that, although the likelihood increases substantially, the improvements on the AUC is marginal, and the algorithm tends to converge to a stable accuracy value quite rapidly. Hence, limiting the number of iterations to 2,000 seems to be a good compromise between learning time and accuracy in prediction.

Finally, Figure 6 shows the percentage of relocations in latent factors assignments in the sampling steps of the Gibbs sampler, along iterations. After an initial phase, the latent factor matrices tend to become stable, except for the matrix $\mathbf{X}$ on `Twitter`, for which there is constant 25% change along all iterations. Also, it is interesting to notice that the changes in $\mathbf{Z}^e$ and $\mathbf{Z}^f$ tend to be higher on `Flickr`.

4.2 Qualitative analysis

We next turn to a more qualitative analysis of the models produced. Here we consider the latent structure corresponding to $K = 64$ on `Twitter` and $K = 32$ on `Flickr`. These values are chosen for presentation readability sake.

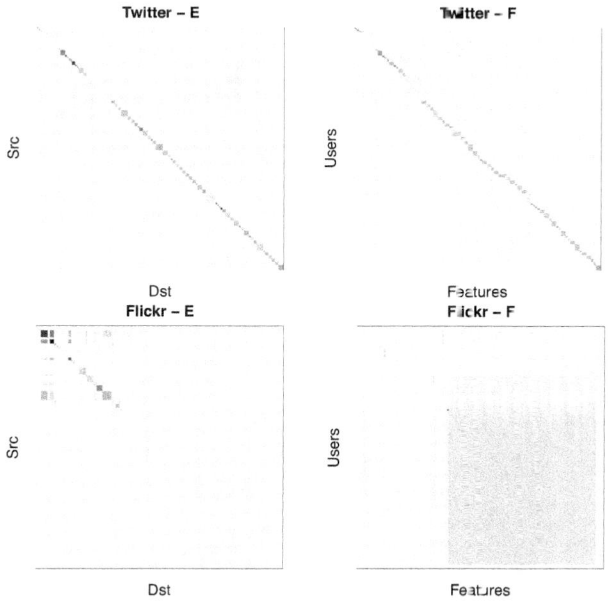

Figure 7: Density plot of the blocks within $\mathbf{E}$ and $\mathbf{F}$.

Figure 7 shows the block adjacency and feature matrices, where both users and features are grouped according to their likelihood to belong to each community. Specifically, for each user, we compute the probability $\Pr(k|u) \propto \sum_k \pi_k \Pr(u|k)$, where $\Pr(u|k)$ is the probability that a user is associated to community k as either source/destination of a connection, or as adopter of a feature. Analogously, $\Pr(k|f) \propto \sum_k \pi_k \Phi_{k,f}$ represents the likelihood that the feature f is observed in the context of the community k. Each user/feature is then associated with the community k for which the probability is higher.

Darker colors in the block matrices denote higher relative density. As witnessed by the diagonal structure on the block adjacency matrix, the discovered communities capture neat patterns of connectivity among users. The joint analysis of the two block matrices supports the following findings.

- Connections in `Twitter` tend to be strongly topical; each community is strongly characterized by a corresponding set of features. The only exception is given by two communities (4 and 15) in which associations tend to be looser (and in fact the corresponding features tend to entropically spread along all communities).
- The connectivity behavior of users on `Flickr` is more social. The block adjacency matrix exhibits high density blocks, and by contrast the feature block matrix exhibits higher entropy. Apparently, it seems that there is not a strong characterization in terms of features for the detected communities. While few communities are specialized in a very limited set of features, a larger number of tags is popular in the remaining ones. The dominant community mentioned before, where most of the features association hold is very visible.

The above hypotheses are supported by the analysis in Figure 8, where we report for each community the percentage of users who qualify as either authoritative, susceptible or social. The authoritiveness score for the user u within k

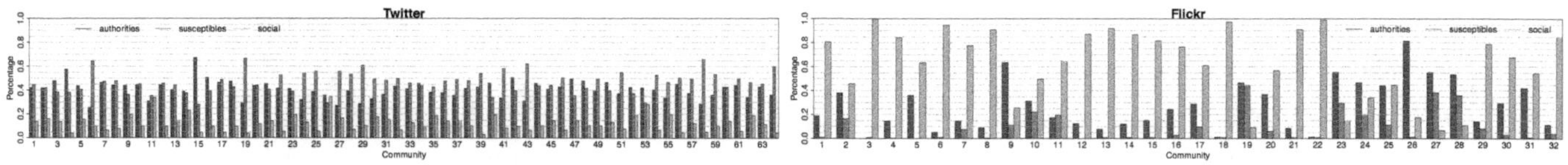

Figure 8: Proportion of authoritative, susceptible and social users in both Twitter and Flickr.

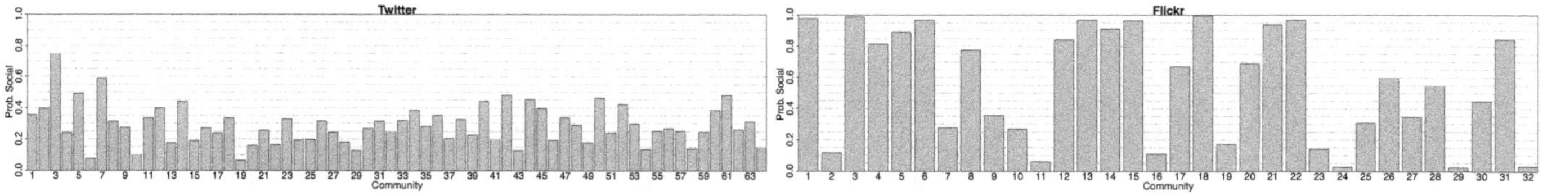

Figure 9: Distribution of δ_k for each community.

is computed as:

$$\Pr(Auth|u,k) = \frac{(1-\delta_k)A_{k,u}}{\delta_k\theta_{k,u} + (1-\delta_k)(A_{k,u}+S_{k,u})}.$$

Scores for measuring the degree of susceptibility and sociality can be computed likewise. Again, Twitter tends to exhibit a predominant amount of authorities/followers, whereas the great majority of the communities in Flickr tend to include social users. Finally, Figure 9 shows the estimated values of δ_k within the communities. As already observed before, Flickr tends to be more clearly social than Twitter. Moreover, the distinction between social and topical latent factors is very clear in Flickr with almost all communities having probability of being "social" either above 0.9, or below 0.2. This discriminating attitude is even more evident when we increase the number of latent topics.

Finally, a further assessment of the correct identification of social and topical latent factors can be performed by measuring, for a given feature f, the probability of observing it in a social/topical context, computed as follows:

$$\Pr(Social|f) \propto \sum_k \pi_k \delta_k \Phi_{k,f}$$

$$\Pr(Topical|f) \propto \sum_k \pi_k (1-\delta_k) \Phi_{k,f}.$$

In Table 6 we validate the accuracy of the feature-labeling task on two small sets of tags. The first set contains keywords notably associated with social events, such as *family*, and *wedding*. The second set contains keywords specific to photographic techniques, e.g. *hdr* and *polaroid*, which are likely to generate topical interest in the users. The results confirm the capability of the model to discriminate between social and topical features.

Finally, Table 7 summarizes the top keywords detected by our approach on both datasets in some representative communities/topics: highly social communities (large δ) have characteristic features (e.g., *family*, *christmas* on Flickr, and *followback* on Twitter) which are clearly social.

Feature	Prob. Social
birthday	0.69
family	0.67
wedding	0.69
party	0.67
puppy	0.69

Feature	Prob. Social
hdr	0.40
vintage	0.29
collage	0.24
nude	0.08
polaroid	0.28

Table 6: Social/Topical connotations of selected tags on Flickr.

Flickr			
Topic 1 $\delta = 0.98$	*Topic 5* $\delta = 0.98$	*Topic 18* $\delta = 0.17$	*Topic 22* $\delta = 0.14$
Christmas, esther, passenger, Birthday, eros, party, stories, apple, curling, homemade	family, mom, dog, driving, vitus, bakery, woods, birthday, friends, halloween, shirt, brothers, baby	handmade, warehouse, vintage, knitting, craft, green, pansies, doll, sewing	bird, art, design, illustration, drawing, fotoincatenate, sketch, street, painting, ink, graffiti
Twitter			
Topic 3 $\delta = 0.74$	*Topic 9* $\delta = 0.27$	*Topic 64* $\delta = 0.16$	*Topic 47* $\delta = 0.33$
TeamFollowBack TFB FollowNGain fb InstantFollowBack nowplaying lastfm TeamAutoFollow Follow4Follow 500aDay anime 4sqDay	Autodesk BIM AutoCAD Revit AU2012 Civil3D AEC adsk_sf2012 SWTOR revit CAD au2011 cloud 3dsMax AU2011 C3D2013	ISS space science Discovery Mars nasa spottheshuttle ESA astronomy Enterprise Soyuz	GameofThrones FakeWesteros GoT ooc SXSWesteros TheGhostofHarrenhal GardenofBones asoiaf GRRM GOT

Table 7: Most representative features of selected communities.

5. CONCLUSIONS AND FUTURE WORK

This paper introduces WTFW, a novel stochastic generative model that jointly factorizes both social connections and feature associations. The model provides accurate link prediction and contextualized socio/topical explanations to support the predictions. Our approach is based on latent factors which can be interpreted as communities of people sharing a similar behavior, and on the explicit modeling of the underlying latent nature behind each observed connection. The result is a decoupling of social and topical connections to reflect the idea that social communities should have high density and reciprocal connections, whereas topical communities should exhibit clear directionality and a low entropy over user attributes.

Our work can be extended in several directions. First, we deliberately omitted to quantify the quality of the communities that the model produces. Some initial results based on modularity look promising (we measured 0.55 and 0.37 on Twitter and Flickr, respectively). Also, the qualitative analysis in Section 4 clearly denotes the capability of the model to group users according to both connectivity and common features. However, we plan to devote to future work a more detailed treatment, as well a thorough comparison with other approaches in the literature.

Second, the approach explored in this paper is rooted on mixture membership topic modeling. However, other alternatives are possible, which can be based on probabilistic matrix factorization. We plan to explore and compare these different strategies in a future work.

Table 8: Equations for the Gibbs Sampling.

$$Pr(z_l = k|x_l = 1, Rest) \propto (c_k + d_k + \xi_k - 1) \cdot \frac{c^s_k + \delta_0 - 1}{c_k + \delta_0 + \delta_1 - 1} \cdot \frac{\left(c^{s,s}_{k,u_l} + c^{s,d}_{k,u_l} + \alpha_{u_l} - 1\right) \cdot \left(c^{s,s}_{k,v_l} + c^{s,d}_{k,v_l} + \alpha_{v_l} - 1\right)}{\left(2c^s_k + \sum_u \alpha_u - 1\right)\left(2c^s_k + \sum_u \alpha_u\right)} \tag{13}$$

$$\Pr(z_l = k|x_l = 0, Rest) \propto (c_k + d_k + \xi_k - 1) \cdot \frac{c^t_k + \delta_1 - 1}{c_k + \delta_0 + \delta_1 - 1} \cdot \frac{c^{t,s}_{k,u_l} + d^s_{k,u_l} + \eta_{u_l} - 1}{c^t_k + d^s_k + \sum_u \eta_u - 1} \cdot \frac{c^{t,d}_{k,v_l} + d^a_{k,v_l} + \beta_{v_l} - 1}{c^t_k + d^a_k + \sum_u \beta_u - 1} \tag{14}$$

$$\Pr(x_l = 1|Rest) \propto \frac{\left(c^{s,s}_{k,u_l} + c^{s,d}_{k,u_l} + \alpha_u - 1\right) \cdot \left(c^{s,s}_{k,v_l} + c^{s,d}_{k,v_l} + \alpha_v - 1\right)}{\left(2c^s_k + \sum_u \alpha_u - 1\right)\left(2c^s_k + 1 + \sum_u \alpha_u - 1\right)} \cdot \frac{c^s_k + \delta_0 - 1}{c^s_k + c^t_k + \delta_0 + \delta_1 - 1} \tag{15}$$

$$\Pr(x_l = 0|Rest) \propto \frac{c^{t,s}_{k,u_l} + d^s_{k,u_l} + \eta_{u_l} - 1}{c^t_k + d^s_k + \sum_u \eta_u - 1} \cdot \frac{c^{t,d}_{k,v_l} + d^a_{k,v_l} + \beta_{v_l} - 1}{c^t_k + d^a_k + \sum_u \beta_u - 1} \cdot \frac{c^t_k + \delta_1 - 1}{c^s_k + c^t_k + \delta_0 + \delta_1 - 1} \tag{16}$$

$$\Pr(z_a = k|y_a = 1, Rest) \propto (c_k + d_k + \xi_k - 1) \cdot \frac{d^a_k + \tau_0 - 1}{d^a_k + d^s_k + \tau_0 + \tau_1 - 1} \cdot \frac{c^{t,d}_{k,u_a} + d^a_{k,u_a} + \beta_{u_a} - 1}{c^t_k + d^a_k + \sum_u \beta_u - 1} \cdot \frac{d_{k,f_a} + \gamma_{f_a} - 1}{d_k + \sum_f \gamma_f - 1} \tag{17}$$

$$Pr(z_a = k|y_a = 0, Rest) \propto (c_k + d_k + \xi_k - 1) \cdot \frac{d^s_k + \tau_1 - 1}{d^a_k + d^s_k + \tau_0 + \tau_1 - 1} \cdot \frac{c^{t,s}_{k,u_a} + d^s_{k,u_a} + \eta_u - 1}{c^t_k + d^s_k + \sum_u \eta_u - 1} \cdot \frac{d_{k,f_a} + \gamma_{f_a} - 1}{d_k + \sum_f \gamma_f - 1} \tag{18}$$

$$\Pr(y_a = 1|Rest) \propto \frac{c^{t,d}_{k,u_a} + c^a_{k,u_a} + \beta_{u_a} - 1}{c^t_k + d^a_k + \sum_u \beta_u - 1} \cdot \frac{d^s_k + \tau_1 - 1}{d^a_k + d^s_k + \tau_0 + \tau_1 - 1} \tag{19}$$

$$\Pr(y_a = 0|Rest) \propto \frac{c^{t,s}_{k,u_a} + d^s_{k,u_a} + \eta_{u_a} - 1}{c^t_k + d^s_k + \sum_u \eta_u - 1} \cdot \frac{d^a_k + \tau_0 - 1}{d^a_k + d^s_k + \tau_0 + \tau_1 - 1} \tag{20}$$

Acknowledgments. This work was partially supported by MULTISENSOR project, funded by the European Commission, under the contract number FP7-610411.

6. REFERENCES

[1] L. Backstrom and J. Leskovec. Supervised random walks: Predicting and recommending links in social networks. In *WSDM*, 2011.

[2] N. Barbieri, F. Bonchi, and G. Manco. Cascade-based community detection. In *WSDM*, 2013.

[3] C. Bishop. *Pattern Recognition and Machine Learning*. Springer-Verlag New York, Inc., Secaucus, NJ, USA, 2006.

[4] D. Blei, A. Ng, and M. Jordan. Latent dirichlet allocation. *J. Mach. Learn. Res.*, 3:993–1022, 2003.

[5] F. Bonchi, C. Castillo, A. Gionis, and A. Jaimes. Social network analysis and mining for business applications. *ACM TIST*, 2(3):22, 2011.

[6] E. Erosheva, S. Fienberg, and J. Lafferty. Mixed-membership models of scientific publications. *PNAS*, 101:5220–5227, 2004.

[7] S. Gershman and D. Blei. A tutorial on bayesian nonparametric models. *Journal of Mathematical Psychology*, 56:1–12, 2012.

[8] L. Getoor and C. P. Diehl. Link mining: a survey. *SIGKDD Explorations*, 7(2):3–12, 2005.

[9] N. Z. Gong, A. Talwalkar, L. W. Mackey, L. Huang, E. C. R. Shin, E. Stefanov, E. Shi, and D. Song. Joint link prediction and attribute inference using a social-attribute network. *ACM TIST*, 5(2), 2014.

[10] P. A. Grabowicz, L. M. Aiello, V. M. Eguiluz, and A. Jaimes. Distinguishing topical and social groups based on common identity and bond theory. In *WSDM*, 2013.

[11] P. Gupta, A. Goel, J. Lin, A. Sharma, D. Wang, and R. Zadeh. Wtf: the who to follow service at twitter. In *WWW*, 2013.

[12] M. A. Hasan and M. J. Zaki. A survey of link prediction in social networks. In *Social Network Data Analytics*, 2011.

[13] G. Heinrich. Parameter Estimation for Text Analysis. Technical report, University of Leipzig, 2008.

[14] J. L. Herlocker, J. A. Konstan, and J. Riedl. Explaining collaborative filtering recommendations. In *CSCW*, 2000.

[15] M. Jamali, T. Huang, and M. Ester. A generalized stochastic block model for recommendation in social rating networks. In *RecSys*, 2011.

[16] J. Leskovec and C. Faloutsos. Sampling from large graphs. In *KDD*, 2006.

[17] D. Liben-Nowell and J. M. Kleinberg. The link prediction problem for social networks. In *CIKM*, 2003.

[18] L. Lü and T. Zhou. Link prediction in complex networks: A survey. *Physica A*, 390(6):1150 – 1170, 2011.

[19] K. T. Miller, T. L. Griffiths, and M. I. Jordan. Nonparametric latent feature models for link prediction. In *NIPS*, 2009.

[20] T. Minka. Estimating a Dirichlet distribution. Web, 2000.

[21] F. Moser, R. Colak, A. Rafiey, and M. Ester. Mining cohesive patterns from graphs with feature vectors. In *SDM*, 2009.

[22] R. M. Nallapati, A. Ahmed, E. P. Xing, and W. W. Cohen. Joint latent topic models for text and citations. In *KDD*, 2008.

[23] S. Pool, F. Bonchi, and M. van Leeuwen. Description-Driven Community Detection. ACM TIST 5(2): 28, 2014.

[24] D. A. Prentice, D. T. Miller, and J. R. Lightdale. Asymmetries in Attachments to Groups and to their Members: Distinguishing between Common-Identity and Common-Bond Groups. *Personality and Social Psychology Bulletin*, 20(5):484–493, 1994.

[25] P. Pu and L. Chen. Trust building with explanation interfaces. In *IUI*, 2006.

[26] Y. Ren, R. Kraut, and S. Kiesler. Applying Common Identity and Bond Theory to Design of Online Communities. *Organization Studies*, 28(3):377–408, 2007.

[27] M. Sachan, D. Contractor, T. A. Faruquie, and L. V. Subramaniam. Using content and interactions for discovering communities in social networks. In *WWW*, 2012.

[28] V. Sindhwani, S. Bucak, J. Hu, and A. Mojsilovic. One-class matrix completion with low-density factorizations. In *ICDM*, 2010.

[29] B. Taskar, M. F. Wong, P. Abbeel, and D. Koller. Link prediction in relational data. In *NIPS*, 2003.

[30] N. Tintarev and J. Masthoff. Effective explanations of recommendations: user-centered design. In *RecSys*, 2007.

[31] X. Wang, L. Tang, H. Gao, and H. Liu. Discovering overlapping groups in social media. In *ICDM*, 2010.

[32] Z. Xu, Y. Ke, Y. Wang, H. Cheng, and J. Cheng. A Model-based Approach to Attributed Graph Clustering. In *SIGMOD*, 2012.

[33] Z. Yin, M. Gupta, T. Weninger, and J. Han. Linkrec: a unified framework for link recommendation with user attributes and graph structure. In *WWW*, 2010.

[34] K. Yu, W. Chu, S. Yu, V. Tresp, and Z. Xu. Stochastic relational models for discriminative link prediction. In *NIPS*, 2006.

[35] Y. Zhou, H. Cheng, and J. X. Yu. Graph clustering based on structural/attribute similarities. *PVLDB*, 2(1):718–729, 2009.

Activity-edge Centric Multi-label Classification for Mining Heterogeneous Information Networks

Yang Zhou
College of Computing
Georgia Institute of Technology
Atlanta, GA 30332
yzhou@gatech.edu

Ling Liu
College of Computing
Georgia Institute of Technology
Atlanta, GA 30332
lingliu@cc.gatech.edu

ABSTRACT

Multi-label classification of heterogeneous information networks has received renewed attention in social network analysis. In this paper, we present an activity-edge centric multi-label classification framework for analyzing heterogeneous information networks with three unique features. First, we model a heterogeneous information network in terms of a collaboration graph and multiple associated activity graphs. We introduce a novel concept of vertex-edge homophily in terms of both vertex labels and edge labels and transform a general collaboration graph into an activity-based collaboration multigraph by augmenting its edges with class labels from each activity graph through activity-based edge classification. Second, we utilize the label vicinity to capture the pairwise vertex closeness based on the labeling on the activity-based collaboration multigraph. We incorporate both the structure affinity and the label vicinity into a unified classifier to speed up the classification convergence. Third, we design an iterative learning algorithm, AECLASS, to dynamically refine the classification result by continuously adjusting the weights on different activity-based edge classification schemes from multiple activity graphs, while constantly learning the contribution of the structure affinity and the label vicinity in the unified classifier. Extensive evaluation on real datasets demonstrates that AECLASS outperforms existing representative methods in terms of both effectiveness and efficiency.

Categories and Subject Descriptors

H.2.8 [**Database Applications**]: Data Mining

Keywords

Multi-label Classification; Heterogeneous Network; Activity-based Edge Classification; Collaboration Multigraph; Label Vicinity

1. INTRODUCTION

Multi-label classification has received increasing attention in both data mining and machine learning over the last decade [10–22]. In contrast to single-label classification, multi-label classification analysis adopts a more realistic view that entities in the real world are often associated with multiple class labels simultaneously. For example, most people in a social network belong to multiple social groups and participate in multiple types of activities with different degrees of engagement. Most of web pages in the web graph may cover multiple topics at different intensities.

Existing multi-label classification efforts for networked data focus on designing effective and yet scalable algorithms [17–22]. Although previous studies differ from one another in the concrete approaches to mining the linkage structure, to the best of our knowledge, they all suffer from two weaknesses: (1) None of previous studies separate different types of activity graphs from the heterogeneous information networks and exploit the correlations among the set of class labels within each activity graph and across multiple activity graphs; and (2) None of previous works combine both the vertex-centric multi-label classification and the edge-centric multi-label classification to boost the effectiveness and efficiency.

In this paper we show that by utilizing activity-edge centric approach, we can incorporate the two missing dimensions to improve both the accuracy and the complexity of multi-label classification analysis. First, we argue that entities in the real world may involve themselves in multiple activity networks. These activity networks may provide abundant information about heterogeneous entities and links, and how entities are linked in the context of each of activity networks. We aim to utilize these activity networks to find a natural and cheap way to identify the inter-dependencies among labels. Second, based on different activity networks, an entity can be tagged by a subset of K labels with different class-membership distributions. We model the class-membership distribution for each of activity networks as multi-labeled edges. Third, we consider not only the labels of related vertices but also the possible labels of associated edges to further enhance the accuracy of multi-label classification. We integrate the vertex-centric labeling and edge-centric labeling into a unified classifier with different weights. An iterative method is proposed to learn the weights towards the classification objective.

This paper makes the following original contributions to multi-label classification for networked data.

- We model a heterogeneous information network in terms of a collaboration graph and multiple associated activity graphs, and cluster activity vertices in each activity graph into K categories with the given K class labels. Clustering each activity graph provides a natural way to capture the dependencies among activity categories within activity graphs.
- We introduce a novel concept of vertex-edge homophily in terms of both vertex labels and edge labels, and transform a general collaboration graph into an activity-based collaboration multigraph by augmenting its edges with class labels from each activity graph through activity-based edge classification.
- We utilize the structure affinity to capture the pairwise topological similarity of vertices and the label vicinity to capture the pairwise vertex closeness based on the labeling on the activity-based collaboration multigraph. We incorporate both the struc-

KDD'14, August 24–27, 2014, New York, NY, USA.
Copyright 2014 ACM 978-1-4503-2956-9/14/08 ...$15.00.
http://dx.doi.org/10.1145/2623330.2623737.

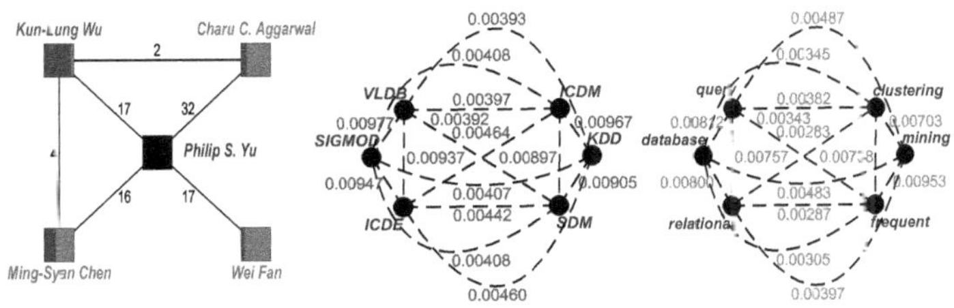

(a) Coauthor Graph (b) Conference Graph (c) Term Graph

Figure 1: An Illustrating Example from DBLP

ture affinity and the label vicinity into a unified classifier to speed up the classification convergence.

- We design an iterative learning algorithm, **AEClass**, to dynamically refine the classification result by continuously adjusting the weights on different activity-based edge classification schemes from multiple activity graphs, while constantly learning the contribution of the structure affinity and the label vicinity in the unified classifier. To make the classification process converge fast, a sophisticated nonlinear fractional programming problem with multiple weights is transformed to a straightforward parametric programming problem of a single variable.
- Empirical evaluation over real multi-label datasets demonstrates the competitiveness of AEClass against state-of-the-art methods in terms of both inference performance and time complexity.

2. PROBLEM DEFINITION

We address the problem of multi-label classification for networked data by employing our activity-edge centric multi-label classification algorithm. First, we model a heterogeneous information network in terms of two types of information networks: (1) a collaboration graph at the instance level, which is the target of multi-label classification, and (2) a collection of its associated activity graphs at the category level. For example, the DBLP bibliography dataset may consist of three types of vertices: authors, publication venues (e.g., conferences, journals), and title terms in the publications. An author can publish in multiple venues and his papers may contain multiple terms. If the target of multi-label classification is to infer author's labels, then we transform the DBLP dataset into a primary collaboration network for authors at the instance level and two associated activity networks (conference-similarity network and term-similarity network) at the category level. The collaboration network is defined based on both labeled and unlabeled instances with the given K class labels, where each vertex represents one instance and each edge reflects the collaborative relationships between pairwise instances, e.g., the number of co-authored publications. Each of associated activity networks is constructed with all the associated activities as vertices. Similar activities are linked together with each edge value indicating the similarity between pairwise activities, such as product purchasing activity network, sport activity network or conference activity network. Given that each entity in the collaboration network may participate in multiple activities in each of activity networks, we cluster all activities in each activity networks into K categories. Then we construct a collaboration multigraph by augmenting the original collaboration graph based on N activity networks as follow: For each pair of vertices with an edge in the collaboration graph, if both have participated in at least one of N activity networks, then we will add up to K edges between this pair of vertices.

Figures 1 gives an illustrative example extracted from the DBLP dataset, consisting of three graphs: a collaboration graph of authors, a conference activity graph and a term activity graph. For ease of presentation, we only choose the co-authored papers published in three top DB conferences of *SIGMOD*, *VLDB* and *ICDE*, and three top DM conferences of *KDD*, *ICDM* and *SDM*. In Figure 1 (a), ochre labels and green labels represent that authors are given predefined class labels of *DB* and *DM* respectively. In addition, ochre block or green block in each vertex rectangle represents the proportion of an author belonging to class *DB* or *DM*. We want to use the label information of four labeled authors to learn the class-membership probabilities of *Philip S. Yu* over classes *DB* and *DM*. In Figure 1 (b), blue numbers measure the similarity scores between pairwise conferences. We utilize a multi-typed soft clustering framework, NetClus [25], to cluster conferences and terms into 24 CS research areas [31] simultaneously. According to conference's clustering distribution over 24 categories and ranking score in each category, we calculate the similarities between conferences in the conference activity graph. Similarly, red numbers in Figure 1 (c) measure the similarity scores between terms. We then choose a category with the highest probability for each conference or each term as its primary category and put them into the corresponding primary categories. This operation actually produces a hard clustering result for each activity network. As shown in Figure 2, the conferences and terms in Figures 1 (b) and (c) are put into their individual primary categories respectively.

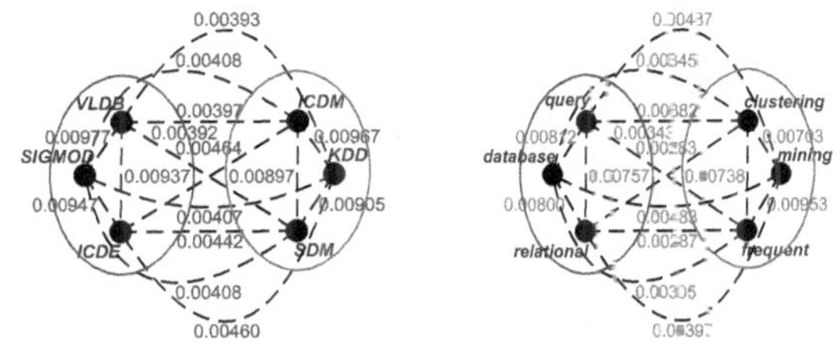

(a) Conference Clusters (b) Term Clusters

Figure 2: Activity Graph Partition

We formally define the above concepts as follows.

A *collaboration graph* is denoted as $CG = (V, F)$, where V is the set of vertices representing the entities in CG, such as customers or authors, and F is the set of edges denoting the collaborative relationships between members. We use N_{CG} to represent the size of V, i.e., $N_{CG} = |V|$.

An *activity graph* is defined by $AG_i = (U_i, F_i)$, where $u \in U_i$ denotes an activity vertex in the ith associated activity network AG_i, and $f \in F_i$ is a weighted edge representing the similarity between two activity vertices, such as functional or manufacture similarity. We denote the size of each activity vertex set as $N_{AG_i} = |U_i|$. The vertex set U_i is partitioned into K disjoint primary categories, denoted by U_{ip} ($1 \leq p \leq K$), such that $U_i = \bigcup_{p=1}^{K} U_{ip}$ and $U_{ip} \bigcap U_{iq} = \phi$ for $\forall 1 \leq p, q \leq K, p \neq q$ and each activity category U_{ip} is labeled with one of the K class labels, c_p.

Given a collaboration graph $CG = (V, F)$ and its N associated activity graphs $AG_i = (U_i, F_i)$ $(1 \leq i \leq N)$, a *collaboration multigraph* denoted as $MG = (V, E)$, is an activity-edge augmented multigraph, where V has the same definition in CG and E is the set of edges satisfying the following condition for each edge $(v_i, v_j) \in F$ in CG, we create a set of parallel edges between the pair of vertices in E. Each set of edges has up to K labeled edges and each edge corresponds to one activity category labeled by c_p $(p \in \{1, \cdots, K\})$ in each of the N activity graphs.

The problem of multi-label classification of multigraph is defined as follows: let $C = \{c_1, c_2, \cdots, c_K\}$ be a finite set of K possible class labels. Given a collaboration multigraph $MG = (V, E)$ with a set of multi-label training instances $V_l \subset V$ initially labeled using the given K class labels, and a set of multi-label testing instances $V_u = V - V_l$ unlabeled. For presentation brevity we assume that the vertices in V are ordered and the first l vertices are labeled and the remaining vertices are unlabeled. Thus we have $V = \{v_1, \cdots, v_l, v_{l+1}, \cdots, v_{N_{CG}}\}$. Let an instance $v_i \in V$ be associated with a subset of labels in C ,i.e., we use a binary vector

$y_i = (y_i^1, y_i^2, \cdots, y_i^K) \in \{0,1\}^K$, in which $y_i^j = 1$ iff the label c_j is in the label set of v_i. We use $Y = \{y_1, \cdots, y_l, y_{l+1}, \cdots, y_{N_{CG}}\}$ to denote a possible labeling for the instance set V. $Y_l = \{y_1, \cdots, y_l\}$ indicates the observed multi-label set assigned to V_l and $Y_u = Y - Y_l$ represents the multi-label set to be determined. The task of our **activity-edge centric multi-label classification of multigraph** is to use the label information of the training instances in V_l to predict the label set Y_u for the testing instances in V_u.

3. THE AEClass APPROACH

Compared to existing multi-label relational classifiers outlined in Section 1, AECLASS improves both the accuracy and the efficiency of multi-label classification by incorporating four mining strategies: (1) activity-based edge classification; (2) edge label dependency; (3) vertex label vicinity; and (4) weight learning. We first introduce the overall design of AECLASS. We then describe each part of AECLASS in detail in the next subsections.

- Activity-based edge classification, which consists of five tasks. (1) given a collaboration graph CG, choose N suitable activity graphs AG_i based on the specific context defined by the classification objective; (2) cluster all AG_is into K activity categories; (3) construct an label dependency graph based on the clustering of each AG_i to identify inter-dependencies among K class labels; (4) based on K categories of each AG_i, split and classify each unlabeled edge in CG into at most K labeled edges; and (5) transform CG and all AG_is into a unified multigraph MG by integrating N edge classification schemes of CG based on each AG_i weighted by $\omega_1^{(1)} = \cdots = \omega_N^{(1)} = \frac{1}{N}$.
- Activity-edge centric vertex classification, which includes four tasks. (1) initialize a transition probability $\mathbf{T}_j^{(1)}$ of MG; (2) initialize a classification kernel $\mathbf{K}_j^{(1)}$; (3) infer the class-membership vector $\mathbf{X}_j^{(1)}$ on each class c_j; and (4) produce the class-membership vector $\mathbf{Y}_j^{(1)}$ by refining $\mathbf{X}_j^{(1)}$ with label dependency graphs.
- Iterative learning, which has four steps. (1) solve the parametric programming problem for classification objective to update $\alpha^{(t)}, \beta^{(t)}, \omega_1^{(t)}, ..., \omega_N^{(t)}$ ($\alpha^{(t)}, \beta^{(t)}$ are updated if t>2); (2) adjust the structure affinity $\mathbf{T}_j^{(t+1)}$ of CG with $\omega_1^{(t)}, ..., \omega_N^{(t)}$; (3) update $\mathbf{K}_j^{(t+1)}$ by combining the structure affinity $\mathbf{T}_j^{(t+1)}$ and the label vicinity $(\mathbf{T}_j^{(t+1)}\mathbf{Y}^{(t)})(\mathbf{T}_j^{(t+1)}\mathbf{Y}^{(t)})^T$ weighted by $\alpha^{(t)}$ and $\beta^{(t)}$ ($\alpha^{(t)} = \beta^{(t)} = \frac{1}{2}$ if t=2); and (4) do classification $\mathbf{X}_j^{(t+1)} = \mathbf{K}_j^{(t+1)}\mathbf{X}_j^{(t)}$ and enter the next round.

3.1 Activity-based Edge Classification

Existing classification models assume the existence of vertex homophily, namely, similar vertices in nature are connected to each other with social links. For example, *Philip S. Yu* and *Wei Fan* have many co-authored works published on *DM* conferences, as shown in Figure 4 (a). However, the truth is not always like this. entities that are connected together may be similar in different ways with respect to a given set of K class labels. As is known to all, *Philip S. Yu* and *Ming-Syan Chen* are experts on data mining, i.e., they both have more research publications in the area of data mining than in any other academic area such as database. However, as seen in Figure 4 (a), they have more co-authored papers published on *DB* conferences. Thus the vertex homophily is insufficient to accurately infer the possible labels of an author. This motivates us to propose the concept of vertex-edge homophily, the principle that both links and their associated vertices should be similar and likely belong to the same classes, to further improve the accuracy of multi-label classification.

In order to capture the vertex-edge homophily in the multi-label classification, we first perform activity-based edge classification.

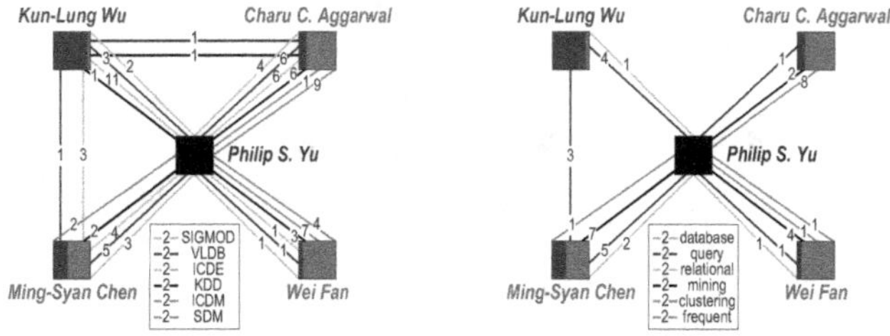

(a) Conference-based Splitting (b) Term-based Splitting

Figure 3: Edge Splitting

For each activity graph and the original collaboration graph CG, we first construct an activity-edge augmented collaboration graph CG_i by examining each edge and the pair of connected entities in CG and splitting each edge into a set of parallel edges based on each activity in AG_i that this pair of entities have in common. The size of each set of parallel edges is at most N_{AG_i}, i.e., the number of activity vertices in AG_i. Figures 3 (a) and (b) present the activity-edge augmented collaboration graphs of Figure 1 (a) based on conference activities in Figure 1 (b) and term activities in Figure (c) respectively. Each edge in Figure 1 (a) is divided into multiple edges in terms of the common conference venues or the common title terms in co-authored publications between the pair of co-authors.

However, such activity-based edge augmentation may lead to substantial increase in size of activity-edge augmented collaboration graphs. We address this issue by introducing activity-based edge augmentation with edge classification to efficiently improve the scalability of classification. Concretely, we utilize the clustering result by NetClus, i.e., the probability distribution of each activity over K categories, to infer the class labels of parallel edges in each CG_i over the K categories.

Given the probability of the mth activity in AG_i belonging to cluster (class) c_j produced by NetClus, denoted by $P(L_m = c_j|AG_i)$, we can compute the class-membership probability of edge $(v_p, v_q) \in E$ belonging to class c_j based on AG_i, denoted by $P(L_{pq} = c_j|AG_i)$.

$$P(L_{pq} = c_j|AG_i) = \frac{1}{W(p,q)} \sum_{m=1}^{N_{AG_i}} W_m^i(p,q) P(L_m = c_j|AG_i) \qquad (1)$$

where $W(p,q)$ represents the value on edge $(v_p, v_q) \in E$ in CG, and $W_m^i(p,q)$ denotes the value on the mth edge between v_p and v_q in CG_i, which is based on the mth activity in AG_i. If there does not exist such an edge between v_p and v_q, then $W_m^i(p,q)$ is equal to 0.

After generating the class-membership distribution of each edge in CG_i, we reduce CG_i to an activity-edge augmented collaboration graph $\overline{CG_i}$ with classified edges by grouping at most N_{AG_i} parallel edges between any pair of vertices in CG_i into at most K parallel edges in $\overline{CG_i}$.

$$\overline{W}_j^i(p,q) = W(p,q) P(L_{pq} = c_j|AG_i) \qquad (2)$$

where $\overline{W}_j^i(p,q)$ represents the value on the edge with label c_j between v_p and v_q in $\overline{CG_i}$. For ease of presentation, assuming that *SIGMOD*, *VLDB*, *ICDE*, *database*, *query* and *relational* only belong to class *DB* with the probability of 1, and *KDD*, *ICDM*, *SDM*, *mining*, *clustering* and *frequent* just belong to class *DM* with the probability of 1, two $\overline{CG_i}$s in Figure 4 present the edge-classification results of two CG_is in Figures 3 respectively.

3.2 Activity-edge Centric Vertex Classification

As N edge classification schemes of CG, i.e., $\overline{CG_i}$s ($1 \le i \le N$), may have different degree of contributions to vertex classification, we propose to integrate N edge classification schemes into a unified collaboration multigraph with different weighting factors $\omega_1^{(t)}, \cdots, \omega_N^{(t)}$ through dynamic weight tuning mechanism. Thus the unified weight value on the edge with label c_j between v_p and v_q in MG at the tth iteration, denoted by $\mathbf{W}_j^{(t)}(p,q)$, can be computed as follow.

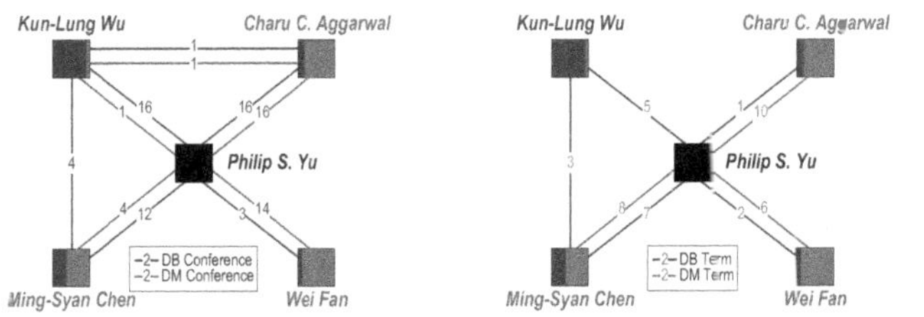

(a) Conference-based Classification (b) Term-based Classification

Figure 4: Edge Classification

$$\mathbf{W}_j^{(t)}(p,q) = \sum_{i=1}^{N} \omega_i^{(t)} \overline{W}_j^i(p,q) = \sum_{i=1}^{N} \omega_i^{(t)} \sum_{m=1}^{N_{AG_i}} W_m^i(p,q) P(L_m = c_j | AG_i),\ 1 \le j \le K \quad (3)$$

subject to $\sum_{i=1}^{N} \omega_i^{(t)} = 1, \omega_i^{(t)} \geqslant 0, i = 1, \cdots, N$.

Note that $\mathbf{W}_j^{(t)}(p,q)$ keeps changing with $\omega_1^{(t)}, \cdots, \omega_N^{(t)}$ through dynamic weight learning. We set the initial $\mathbf{W}_j^{(1)}(p,q)$ with equal weighting factors of $\omega_1^{(1)}, \cdots, \omega_N^{(1)} = \frac{1}{N}$.

Figure 5 (a) shows the unified multigraph for our running example in Figure 1 by combining the links with the same labels between the same vertex pair from two activity-based edge classification schemes in Figure 4 with equal weighting factor of 0.5.

With the unified multigraph MG, we below describe the activity-edge centric vertex classification, which integrates the activity-edge labels with the vertex labels among structurally relevant instances through transition probability on collaboration multigraph.

Definition 1. [Transition Probability on Collaboration Multigraph] Let $MG = (V, E)$ be a *collaboration multigraph* where V is the set of entity vertices and E is the set of parallel edges denoting the collaborative relationships on different classes between entities of MG. The transition probability on MG at the tth iteration can be defined by normalizing the edge values as follows.

$$\mathbf{T}_j^{(t)}(p,q) = \begin{cases} \dfrac{\mathbf{W}_j^{(t)}(p,q)}{\sum_{r=1}^{N_{CG}} \sum_{m=1}^{K} \mathbf{W}_m^{(t)}(p,r)}, & p > l, \\ 1, & p = q \le l, \\ 0, & otherwise. \end{cases} \quad (4)$$

where $\mathbf{T}_j^{(t)}(p,q)$ represents the transition probability on the edge with label c_j between v_p and v_q in MG. Here, we assume that Y_l, i.e., the labels of the vertices in V_l, are fixed during the classification process. Figure 5 (b) presents the transition probabilities of parallel edges from *Philip S. Yu* to other authors based on the collaboration multigraph in Figure 5 (a).

We express the above transition probability in a matrix form.

$$\mathbf{T}_j^{(t)} = (\mathbf{D}^{(t)})^{-1} \mathbf{W}_j^{(t)} \quad (5)$$

where $\mathbf{D}^{(t)}$ is a diagonal matrix $\mathbf{D}^{(t)} = \mathrm{diag}(1, \cdots, 1, d_{l+1}, \cdots, d_{N_{CG}})$, $1, \cdots, 1$ specifies l ones, and $d_p = \sum_{r=1}^{N_{CG}} \sum_{m=1}^{K} \mathbf{W}_m^{(t)}(p,r)$ $(l+1 \le p \le N_{CG})$. $\mathbf{T}_j^{(t)}$ determines the transition probability on those edges with the class label of c_j in MG.

Instead of decomposing the multi-label classification problem into a set of binary classification problems, we construct a unified multi-label classifier by using a single normalizing factor $\mathbf{D}^{(t)}$ to normalize parallel edges with different class labels. The original transition operation is actually divided into two steps: (1) choose those edges with the objective class label in terms of classification objective; and (2) select an edge with the largest value from the above edges to jump.

Now we define the initial unified classification kernel $\mathbf{K}_j^{(1)}$, which only utilizes the structure information of MG, i.e., those edges with label c_j, due to the lack of label vicinity at initialization.

$$\mathbf{K}_j^{(1)} = \mathbf{T}_j^{(1)} \quad (6)$$

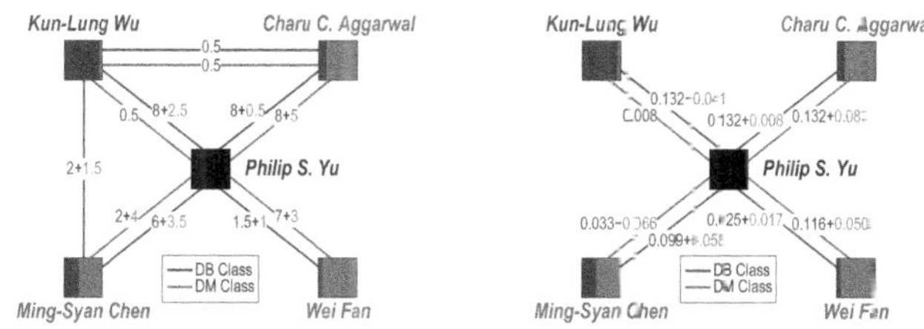

(a) Coauthor Multigraph (b) Transition Probability

Figure 5: Multigraph Representation

Since we have ordered the vertices in V such that the labeled nodes V_l are indexed before the unlabeled nodes V_u, we rewrite the unified classification kernel $\mathbf{K}_j^{(1)}$ as a block matrix.

$$\mathbf{K}_j^{(1)} = \begin{bmatrix} \mathbf{K}_{jll}^{(1)} & \mathbf{K}_{jlu}^{(1)} \\ \mathbf{K}_{jul}^{(1)} & \mathbf{K}_{juu}^{(1)} \end{bmatrix} = \begin{bmatrix} \mathbf{I} & \mathbf{O} \\ \mathbf{K}_{jul}^{(1)} & \mathbf{K}_{juu}^{(1)} \end{bmatrix} \quad (7)$$

where $\mathbf{K}_{jll}^{(1)}$ is an $l \times l$ identity matrix representing the transition probability among labeled vertices, we set the $l \times (N_{CG} - l)$ block matrix $\mathbf{K}_{jlu}^{(1)}$ to be zero matrix since the labels on the vertices in V_l are fixed, the $(N_{CG} - l) \times l$ matrix $\mathbf{K}_{jul}^{(1)}$ specifies the transition probability from unlabeled vertices to labeled vertices, and $\mathbf{K}_{juu}^{(1)}$ is an $(N_{CG} - l) \times (N_{CG} - l)$ matrix denoting the transition probability among unlabeled vertices.

Suppose that the class-membership matrix is denoted by $\mathbf{X} = [\mathbf{X}_1, \mathbf{X}_2, \cdots, \mathbf{X}_K] \in \mathbb{R}^{N_{CG} \times K}$, for each class-membership vector $\mathbf{X}_j (1 \le j \le K)$ based on class c_j, we use its individual classification kernel $\mathbf{K}_j^{(t)}$ to iteratively infer the probabilities of vertices on class c_j.

$$\mathbf{X}_j^{(t)} = \mathbf{K}_j^{(t)} \mathbf{X}_j^{(t-1)} \quad (8)$$

Let $\mathbf{X}_j = [\mathbf{X}_{jl}; \mathbf{X}_{ju}]$ be the class-membership vector, where $\mathbf{X}_{jl}$ indicates the probabilities of the labeled vertices in V_l belonging to class c_j, and $\mathbf{X}_{ju}$ represents the probabilities of the unlabeled vertices in V_u belonging to class c_j. Due to the labels on the vertices in V_l are fixed, Eq. (8) is equivalent to the following formula.

$$\mathbf{X}_{ju}^{(t)} = \mathbf{K}_{jul}^{(t)} \mathbf{X}_{jl}^{(t-1)} + \mathbf{K}_{juu}^{(t)} \mathbf{X}_{ju}^{(t-1)} \quad (9)$$

After the tth iteration, the class-membership matrix is updated as follow.

$$\mathbf{X}^{(t)} = [\mathbf{X}_1^{(t)}, \mathbf{X}_2^{(t)}, \cdots, \mathbf{X}_K^{(t)}] = \begin{bmatrix} \mathbf{X}_{1l} & \mathbf{X}_{2l} & \cdots & \mathbf{X}_{Kl} \\ \mathbf{X}_{1u}^{(t)} & \mathbf{X}_{2u}^{(t)} & \cdots & \mathbf{X}_{Ku}^{(t)} \end{bmatrix} \quad (10)$$

Compared to existing multi-label relational classifiers, we argue that AEClass based on the activity-edge augmented collaboration multigraph can significantly improve the performance of multi-label classification: (1) accuracy improvement. Based on the vertex-edge homophily, we classify each edge in CG into at most K parallel edges in MG. During the classification process, AEClass only picks up those vertices and links with the same label as the current objective class c_j, i.e., $\mathbf{K}_j^{(t)}$ and $\mathbf{X}_j^{(t-1)}$, to execute the inference. For example, given the class-membership probabilities of *Ming-Syan Chen* on classes *DB* and *DM* in Figure 5 (a), we want to infer the class-membership probabilities of *Kun-Lung Wu* on *DB* and *DM*. AEClass will produce a positive probability on *DB* and a zero probability on *DM* since there exists no edge with label *DM* between these two authors. In contrast, existing classifiers will output a higher probability on *DM* than on *DB* for any positive edge value between two authors in the original CG in Figure 1 (a). In fact, *Kun-Lung Wu* is known as a database researcher without any data mining publications. (2) efficiency improvement. Based on the vertex homophily, no matter which class the current objective is, existing classifiers need to check each neighbor of a vertex and summarize the labels of all neighbors. In comparison, AEClass performs the similar summary at lower cost. When we classify an edge in CG into m parallel edges in MG, m is often much smaller than the number of K class labels. Suppose that the current objective

(a) Conference Dependency (b) Term Dependency

Figure 6: Edge Label Dependency by Category Similarity

class is c_j, for a neighbor of a vertex, there may not exist an edge with label c_j between the vertex and this neighbor. Thus, the number of neighbors of a vertex with edge label c_j can be much smaller than the number of its neighbors, thus reducing the amount of unnecessary computations. Concretely, by utilizing the vertex-edge homophily, AEClass only needs to consider those links with label c_j and associated neighbors and further stops label propagation to the circle of those irrelevant neighbors (without link with label c_j) in the next iterations. For the above example, we can safely ignore the operation of inferring the probability of *Kun-Lung Wu* on *D-M* since there exists no edge with label *DM* between two authors. More importantly, AEClass prevents the probability of *Ming-Syan Chen* on *DM* from being diffused to both *Kun-Lung Wu* and the neighbor-based circle of *Kun-Lung Wu*.

3.3 Improvement by Edge Label Dependency

We argue that the underlying correlations among different activity categories can have significant impact on the performance of multi-label classification. Based on activity graph partition, we first define the edge label similarity to capture the inter-dependencies among K activity categories within each of N activity graphs.

Definition 2. [Edge Label Similarity] Let $AG_i = (U_i, F_i)$ be the ith activity graph ($1 \leq i \leq N$), $S_i(u_m, u_n)$ be the similarity score between two activities $u_m, u_n \in U_i$ in AG_i, and U_{ip} and U_{iq} be two categories of U_i with class labels of $c_p, c_q \in C$ respectively. The activity category similarity between c_p and c_q with respect to AG_i is also referred to as the edge label dependency between two edge labels c_p and c_q, and is defined as follow.

$$S_i(c_p, c_q) = \begin{cases} \sum_{u_m \in U_{ip}, u_n \in U_{iq}} \frac{S_i(u_m, u_n)}{|U_{ip}| \times |U_{iq}|}, & p \neq q, \\ 1, & p = q. \end{cases} \tag{11}$$

Figure 6 shows two edge label dependency graph by activity category similarity based on two class labels *DB* and *DM* with respect to the conference graph and the term graph in Figure 2 respectively.

We thus incorporate them into our AEClass framework to adjust the class-membership matrix $\mathbf{X}^{(t)}$. The adjusted class-membership vector on class c_j, denoted by $\mathbf{Y}^{(t)}_{ju}$, can be defined by integrating class-membership vectors on other classes in terms of the similarity scores between class c_j and other classes.

$$\mathbf{Y}^{(t)}_{ju} = \sum_{m=1}^{K} \sum_{i=1}^{N} \omega_i^{(t)} S_i(c_j, c_m) \mathbf{X}^{(t)}_{mu}, \ 1 \leq j \leq K \tag{12}$$

where the weight $\omega_i^{(t)}$ for AG_i is the same as in Eq. (3). The adjusted class-membership matrix is thus defined as follow.

$$\mathbf{Y}^{(t)} = [\mathbf{Y}^{(t)}_1, \mathbf{Y}^{(t)}_2, \cdots, \mathbf{Y}^{(t)}_K] = \begin{bmatrix} \mathbf{X}_{1l} & \mathbf{X}_{2l} & \cdots & \mathbf{X}_{Kl} \\ \mathbf{Y}^{(t)}_{1u} & \mathbf{Y}^{(t)}_{2u} & \cdots & \mathbf{Y}^{(t)}_{Ku} \end{bmatrix} \tag{13}$$

3.4 Refinement by Vertex Label Vicinity

One disadvantage of conventional iterative classifiers is that they often need lots of iterations to converge to a stationary distribution and the repeated label propagation causes a non-trivial computational cost. Wang et al. [22] proposed a dynamic label propagation (DLP) model by fusing both data features and data labels to improve the effectiveness on multi-class/multi-label classification. However, the DLP model failed to quantify the weighted contributions from data features and data labels such that it often can not work well on real classification tasks. We model the label vicinity to capture the pairwise vertex closeness based on the labeling on the activity-based collaboration multigraph by following the similar idea. To improve both effectiveness and efficiency of classification, we design an iterative learning method to dynamically refine the classification results by continuously quantifying and adjusting the weights on the structure affinity and on the label vicinity towards the classification objective.

Based on the transition probability $\mathbf{T}^{(t)}_j$ on CG, we define a diffusion process to map the multigraph space into an N_{CG}-dimensional space $\mathbb{R}^{N_{CG}}$, where each element $\phi^{(t)}_j(i) \in \mathbb{R}^{N_{CG}}$ represents the transition probabilities on the edges with label c_j from vertex v_i to the other vertices and $P(\phi^{(t)}_j(i)) = \mathcal{N}(\phi^{(t)}_j(i)|\mathbf{T}^{(t)}_j)$. On the other hand, based on a heuristics rule: two instance vertices with highly similar class-membership distributions are likely to be highly similar to each other in the input multigraph space, $\mathbf{Y}^{(t)}(\mathbf{Y}^{(t)})^T$ can be viewed as the similarity between vertices based on the class-membership distribution. Similarly, we map this label-based similarity space into an N_{CG}-dimensional space $\mathbb{S}^{N_{CG}}$, where each entry $\varphi^{(t)}(i) \in \mathbb{S}^{N_{CG}}$ specifies the label-based similarity between vertex v_i and the other vertices and $P(\varphi^{(t)}(i)) = \mathcal{N}(\varphi^{(t)}(i)|\mathbf{Y}^{(t)}(\mathbf{Y}^{(t)})^T)$. We then define a linear projection operation based on $\mathbf{T}^{(t+1)}_j$.

$$\phi^{(t+1)}_j = \mathbf{T}^{(t+1)}_j \varphi^{(t)} \tag{14}$$

where $\phi^{(t+1)}_j = [\phi^{(t+1)}_j(1); \phi^{(t+1)}_j(2); \cdots; \phi^{(t+1)}_j(N_{CG})]$ and $\varphi^{(t)} = [\varphi^{(t)}(1); \varphi^{(t)}(2); \cdots; \varphi^{(t)}(N_{CG})]$.

With the linear projection, we generate the following formula.

$$P(\phi^{(t+1)}_j|\varphi^{(t)}) = \mathcal{N}(\phi^{(t+1)}_j|\mathbf{T}^{(t+1)}_j \varphi^{(t)}) \tag{15}$$

The corresponding marginal distribution is given below.

$$\begin{aligned} P(\phi^{(t+1)}_j) &= \int \mathcal{N}(\varphi^{(t)}|\mathbf{Y}^{(t)}(\mathbf{Y}^{(t)})^T)\mathcal{N}(\phi^{(t+1)}_j|\mathbf{T}^{(t+1)}_j \varphi^{(t)})d\varphi^{(t)} \\ &= \mathcal{N}(\phi^{(t+1)}_j|\mathbf{T}^{(t+1)}_j \mathbf{Y}^{(t)}(\mathbf{Y}^{(t)})^T(\mathbf{T}^{(t+1)}_j)^T) \end{aligned} \tag{16}$$

Since directly combining $\varphi^{(t)}(\varphi^{(t)})^T$ into the unified classification kernel $\mathbf{K}^{(t+1)}_j$ may lead to a degeneration at the beginning of classification if the learned label information of vertices in V_u is not enough to infer the label-based similarity scores, we adjust $\mathbf{K}^{(t+1)}_j$ by integrating the label-based similarity through $\mathbf{T}^{(t)}_j$.

$$\mathbf{K}^{(t+1)}_j = \alpha^{(t+1)}\mathbf{T}^{(t+1)}_j + \beta^{(t+1)}(\mathbf{T}^{(t+1)}_j \mathbf{Y}^{(t)})(\mathbf{T}^{(t+1)}_j \mathbf{Y}^{(t)})^T \tag{17}$$

subject to $\alpha^{(t+1)} + \beta^{(t+1)} = 1, \alpha^{(t+1)}, \beta^{(t+1)} \geq 0$.

$\alpha^{(t+1)}$ and $\beta^{(t+1)}$ are weighting factors to balance two kinds of similarity scores. The label vicinity $(\mathbf{T}^{(t+1)}_j \mathbf{Y}^{(t)})(\mathbf{T}^{(t+1)}_j \mathbf{Y}^{(t)})^T$ quantitatively measures the extent of similarity between vertices and their neighbors based on the current labeling.

3.5 Weight Learning

Classification analysis often utilizes the F1 score, i.e., the harmonic mean of precision and recall, to evaluate the accuracy of testing instances. The objective of multi-label classification of multigraph is to maximize the Macro-F1 score [32], i.e., the unweighted mean of F1 score on classes. To define the Macro-F1 score, we first introduce an indicator function.

$$\mathcal{I}(\hat{y}^j_i = 1) = \begin{cases} 1, & \hat{y}^j_i = 1, \\ 0, & \hat{y}^j_i = 0. \end{cases} \tag{18}$$

where $\mathcal{I}(\hat{y}^j_i = 1)$ indicates whether the label c_j is assigned to an instance vertex v_i.

Definition 3. [Macro-F1] Let $MG = (V, E)$ be a collaboration multigraph, y_i be the true label vector of the ith instance vertices in V and $\hat{y}_i$ be the predicted label vector, and the Macro-F1 score is defined below.

$$Macro\text{-}F1 = \frac{1}{K} \sum_{j=1}^{K} \frac{2\sum_{i=l+1}^{N_{CG}} \mathcal{I}(\hat{y}^j_i = 1)y^j_i}{\sum_{i=l+1}^{N_{CG}} \mathcal{I}(\hat{y}^j_i = 1) + \sum_{i=l+1}^{N_{CG}} y^j_i} \tag{19}$$

Assuming $\theta = \max_{i,j}\{\mathbf{Y}(i, j) : l + 1 \leq i \leq N_{CG}, 1 \leq j \leq K\}$, we define an s-shape function to approximate the indicator function.

$$\mathcal{S}(\mathbf{Y}(i, j)) = \begin{cases} 1, & \mathbf{Y}(i, j) = \theta, \\ 0, & \mathbf{Y}(i, j) = 0, \\ \mathbf{Y}(i, j)/\theta, & otherwise. \end{cases} \tag{20}$$

The decision rule determining $\hat{y}_i^j = 1$ if $\mathbf{Y}(i,j) > \theta/2$, i.e., $S(\mathbf{Y}(i,j)) > 0.5$ is represented as follow.

$$I(\hat{y}_i^j = 1) = I(\mathbf{Y}(i,j) > \theta/2) = I(S(\mathbf{Y}(i,j)) > 0.5) \approx S(\mathbf{Y}(i,j)) \quad (21)$$

The Macro-F1 score is thus approximated as follow.

$$Macro\text{-}F1 \approx \frac{1}{K}\sum_{j=1}^{K} \frac{2\sum_{i=l+1}^{N_{CG}} \mathbf{Y}(i,j) y_i^j}{\sum_{i=l+1}^{N_{CG}} \mathbf{Y}(i,j) + \sum_{i=l+1}^{N_{CG}} \theta y_i^j} \quad (22)$$

According to Eqs.(3)-(17), the Macro-F1 score is a fractional function of multi variables $\alpha, \beta, \omega_1, \cdots, \omega_N$ with non-negative real coefficients. On the other hand, the numerator and the denominator of Macro-F1 are both polynomial functions of the above variables. Without loss of generality, we rewrite Eq.(22) as follow.

$$Macro\text{-}F1 \approx \frac{\sum_{i=1}^{m} a_i(\alpha)^{b_i}(\beta)^{c_i} \prod_{j=1}^{N}(\omega_j)^{d_{ij}}}{\sum_{i=1}^{n} o_i(\alpha)^{p_i}(\beta)^{q_i} \prod_{j=1}^{N}(\omega_j)^{r_{ij}}}, \quad (23)$$

$$a_i, b_i, c_i, d_{ij}, o_i, p_i, q_i, r_{ij} \geq 0, b_i, c_i, d_{ij}, p_i, q_i, r_{ij} \in \mathbb{Z}$$

where there are m polynomial terms in the numerator and n polynomial terms in the denominator, a_i and o_i are the coefficients of the ith terms respectively, and $b_i, c_i, d_{ij}, p_i, q_i, r_{ij}$ are the exponents of corresponding variables in the ith terms respectively.

Definition 4. [Multigraph Classification Objective] Let $MG = (V, E)$ be a collaboration multigraph, $\alpha, \beta, \omega_1, \cdots, \omega_N$ are the weighting factors defined in Eqs.(3) and (17), respectively. The goal of multi-label classification of multigraph is to maximize the Macro-F1 score.

$$\max_{\alpha,\beta,\omega_j} Macro\text{-}F1 \approx \max_{\alpha,\beta,\omega_j} \frac{\sum_{i=1}^{m} a_i(\alpha)^{b_i}(\beta)^{c_i} \prod_{j=1}^{N}(\omega_j)^{d_{ij}}}{\sum_{i=1}^{n} o_i(\alpha)^{p_i}(\beta)^{q_i} \prod_{j=1}^{N}(\omega_j)^{r_{ij}}} \quad (24)$$

subject to $\alpha + \beta = 1, \alpha, \beta \geqslant 0, \sum_{j=1}^{N} \omega_j = 1, \omega_j \geqslant 0, j = 1, \cdots, N$.

For ease of presentation, we revise the original objective as the following nonlinear fractional programming problem (NFPP).

Definition 5. [Nonlinear Fractional Programming Problem] Let $f(\alpha, \beta, \omega_1, \ldots, \omega_N) = \sum_{i=1}^{m} a_i(\alpha)^{b_i}(\beta)^{c_i} \prod_{j=1}^{N}(\omega_j)^{d_{ij}}$ and $g(\alpha, \beta, \omega_1, \ldots, \omega_N) = \sum_{i=1}^{n} o_i(\alpha)^{p_i}(\beta)^{q_i} \prod_{j=1}^{N}(\omega_j)^{r_{ij}}$, the classification goal is revised below.

$$\max_{\alpha,\beta,\omega_1,\ldots,\omega_N} \frac{f(\alpha, \beta, \omega_1, \ldots, \omega_N)}{g(\alpha, \beta, \omega_1, \ldots, \omega_N)} \quad (25)$$

subject to $\alpha + \beta = 1, \alpha, \beta \geqslant 0, \sum_{i=1}^{N} \omega_i = 1, \omega_i \geqslant 0, i = 1, \cdots, N$.

Our classification objective is equivalent to maximize a quotient of two polynomial functions of multiple variables. It is very hard to perform function trend identification and estimation to determine the existence and uniqueness of solutions. Therefore, we want to transform this sophisticated NFPP into a easily solvable problem.

THEOREM 1. *The NFPP in Definition 5 is equivalent to a polynomial programming problem with polynomial constraints (PPPPC).*

$$\max_{\alpha,\beta,\omega_1,\ldots,\omega_N,\pi} \pi f(\alpha, \beta, \omega_1, \ldots, \omega_N) \quad (26)$$

subject to $\alpha + \beta = 1, \alpha, \beta \geqslant 0, \sum_{i=1}^{N} \omega_i = 1, \omega_i \geqslant 0, i = 1, \cdots, N$, $0 \leqslant \pi \leqslant 1/g(\alpha, \beta, \omega_1, \ldots, \omega_N)$.

Proof. If $(\overline{\alpha}, \overline{\beta}, \overline{\omega}_1, \ldots, \overline{\omega}_N, \overline{\pi})$ *is an optimal solution of PPPPC, then* $\overline{\pi} = 1/g(\overline{\alpha}, \overline{\beta}, \overline{\omega}_1, \ldots, \overline{\omega}_N)$. *Thus* $\overline{\pi} f(\overline{\alpha}, \overline{\beta}, \overline{\omega}_1, \ldots, \overline{\omega}_N) = f(\overline{\alpha}, \overline{\beta}, \overline{\omega}_1, \ldots, \overline{\omega}_N)/g(\overline{\alpha}, \overline{\beta}, \overline{\omega}_1, \ldots, \overline{\omega}_N)$. *For any feasible solution* $(\alpha, \beta, \omega_1, \ldots, \omega_N)$ *of NFPP, the constraints of PPPPC are satisfied by setting* $\pi = 1/g(\alpha, \beta, \omega_1, \ldots, \omega_N)$, *so* $\pi f(\alpha, \beta, \omega_1, \ldots, \omega_N) \leqslant \overline{\pi} f(\overline{\alpha}, \overline{\beta}, \overline{\omega}_1, \ldots, \overline{\omega}_N)$, *i.e.* $f(\alpha, \beta, \omega_1, \ldots, \omega_N)/g(\alpha, \beta, \omega_1, \ldots, \omega_N) \leqslant f(\overline{\alpha}, \overline{\beta}, \overline{\omega}_1, \ldots, \overline{\omega}_N)/g(\overline{\alpha}, \overline{\beta}, \overline{\omega}_1, \ldots, \overline{\omega}_N)$.

Conversely, if $(\overline{\alpha}, \overline{\beta}, \overline{\omega}_1, \ldots, \overline{\omega}_N)$ *solves NFPP, then for any feasible solution* $(\alpha, \beta, \omega_1, \ldots, \omega_N, \pi)$ *of PPPPC we have* $\pi f(\alpha, \beta, \omega_1, \ldots, \omega_N) \leqslant f(\alpha, \beta, \omega_1, \ldots, \omega_N)/g(\alpha, \beta, \omega_1, \ldots, \omega_N) \leqslant f(\overline{\alpha}, \overline{\beta}, \overline{\omega}_1, \ldots, \overline{\omega}_N)/g(\overline{\alpha}, \overline{\beta}, \overline{\omega}_1, \ldots, \overline{\omega}_N) = \overline{\pi} f(\overline{\alpha}, \overline{\beta}, \overline{\omega}_1, \ldots, \overline{\omega}_N)$ *with* $\overline{\pi} = 1/g(\overline{\alpha}, \overline{\beta}, \overline{\omega}_1, \ldots, \overline{\omega}_N)$.

Although PPPPC is a polynomial programming problem, the polynomial constraints make it very hard to solve. We further simplify it as an nonlinear parametric programming problem (NPPP).

Definition 6. [Nonlinear Parametric Programming Problem] Let $f(\alpha, \beta, \omega_1, \ldots, \omega_N) = \sum_{i=1}^{m} a_i(\alpha)^{b_i}(\beta)^{c_i} \prod_{j=1}^{N}(\omega_j)^{d_{ij}}$ and $g(\alpha, \beta, \omega_1, \ldots, \omega_N) = \sum_{i=1}^{n} o_i(\alpha)^{p_i}(\beta)^{q_i} \prod_{j=1}^{N}(\omega_j)^{r_{ij}}$, the NPPP is defined below

$$F(\gamma) = \max_{\alpha,\beta,\omega_1,\ldots,\omega_N} f(\alpha, \beta, \omega_1, \ldots, \omega_N) - \gamma g(\alpha, \beta, \omega_1, \ldots, \omega_N) \quad (27)$$

subject to $\alpha + \beta = 1, \alpha, \beta \geqslant 0, \sum_{i=1}^{N} \omega_i = 1, \omega_i \geqslant 0, i = 1, \cdots, N$.

THEOREM 2. *The NFPP in Definition 5 is equivalent to the NPPP in Definition 6, i.e.,* $\gamma = \max_{\alpha,\beta,\omega_1,\ldots,\omega_N} \frac{f(\alpha,\beta,\omega_1,\ldots,\omega_N)}{g(\alpha,\beta,\omega_1,\ldots,\omega_N)}$ *iff* $F(\gamma) = \max_{\alpha,\beta,\omega_1,\ldots,\omega_N} f(\alpha, \beta, \omega_1, \ldots, \omega_N) - \gamma g(\alpha, \beta, \omega_1, \ldots, \omega_N) = 0$.

Proof. If $(\overline{\alpha}, \overline{\beta}, \overline{\omega}_1, \ldots, \overline{\omega}_N)$ *is a feasible solution of* $F(\gamma) = 0$, *then* $f(\overline{\alpha}, \overline{\beta}, \overline{\omega}_1, \ldots, \overline{\omega}_N) - \gamma g(\overline{\alpha}, \overline{\beta}, \overline{\omega}_1, \ldots, \overline{\omega}_N) = 0$. *Thus* $f(\alpha, \omega_1, \ldots, \omega_N) - \gamma g(\alpha, \omega_1, \ldots, \omega_N) \leqslant f(\overline{\alpha}, \overline{\beta}, \overline{\omega}_1, \ldots, \overline{\omega}_N) - \gamma g(\overline{\alpha}, \overline{\beta}, \overline{\omega}_1, \ldots, \overline{\omega}_N) = 0$. *We have* $\gamma = f(\overline{\alpha}, \overline{\beta}, \overline{\omega}_1, \ldots, \overline{\omega}_N)/g(\overline{\alpha}, \overline{\beta}, \overline{\omega}_1, \ldots, \overline{\omega}_N) \geqslant f(\alpha, \omega_1, \ldots, \omega_N)/g(\alpha, \omega_1, \ldots, \omega_N)$. *Therefore,* γ *is a maximum value of NFPP and* $(\overline{\alpha}, \overline{\beta}, \overline{\omega}_1, \ldots, \overline{\omega}_N)$ *is an optimal solution of NFPP.*

Conversely, if $(\overline{\alpha}, \overline{\beta}, \overline{\omega}_1, \ldots, \overline{\omega}_N)$ *solves NFPP, then we have* $\gamma = f(\overline{\alpha}, \overline{\beta}, \overline{\omega}_1, \ldots, \overline{\omega}_N)/g(\overline{\alpha}, \overline{\beta}, \overline{\omega}_1, \ldots, \overline{\omega}_N) \geqslant f(\alpha, \omega_1, \ldots, \omega_N)/g(\alpha, \omega_1, \ldots, \omega_N)$. *Thus* $f(\alpha, \omega_1, \ldots, \omega_N) - \gamma g(\alpha, \omega_1, \ldots, \omega_N) \leqslant f(\overline{\alpha}, \overline{\beta}, \overline{\omega}_1, \ldots, \overline{\omega}_N) - \gamma g(\overline{\alpha}, \overline{\beta}, \overline{\omega}_1, \ldots, \overline{\omega}_N) = 0$. *We have* $F(\gamma) = 0$ *and the maximum is taken at* $(\overline{\alpha}, \overline{\beta}, \overline{\omega}_1, \ldots, \overline{\omega}_N)$.

Now the original NFPP has been successfully transformed into the straightforward NPPP. This transformation can efficiently speed up the classification convergence due to the following properties.

THEOREM 3. $F(\gamma)$ *is convex.*

Proof: Suppose that $(\overline{\alpha}, \overline{\beta}, \overline{\omega}_1, \ldots, \overline{\omega}_N)$ *is an optimal solution of* $F((1-\lambda)\gamma_1 + \lambda\gamma_2)$ *with* $\gamma_1 \neq \gamma_2$ *and* $0 \leqslant \lambda \leqslant 1$. $F((1-\lambda)\gamma_1 + \lambda\gamma_2) = f(\overline{\alpha}, \overline{\beta}, \overline{\omega}_1, \ldots, \overline{\omega}_N) - ((1-\lambda)\gamma_1 + \lambda\gamma_2) g(\overline{\alpha}, \overline{\beta}, \overline{\omega}_1, \ldots, \overline{\omega}_N) = \lambda(f(\overline{\alpha}, \overline{\beta}, \overline{\omega}_1, \ldots, \overline{\omega}_N) - \gamma_2 g(\overline{\alpha}, \overline{\beta}, \overline{\omega}_1, \ldots, \overline{\omega}_N)) + (1-\lambda)(f(\overline{\alpha}, \overline{\beta}, \overline{\omega}_1, \ldots, \overline{\omega}_N) - \gamma_1 g(\overline{\alpha}, \overline{\beta}, \overline{\omega}_1, \ldots, \overline{\omega}_N)) \leqslant \lambda \max_{\alpha,\beta,\omega_1,\ldots,\omega_N} f(\alpha, \beta, \omega_1, \ldots, \omega_N) - \gamma_2 g(\alpha, \beta, \omega_1, \ldots, \omega_N) + (1-\lambda) \max_{\alpha,\beta,\omega_1,\ldots,\omega_N} f(\alpha, \beta, \omega_1, \ldots, \omega_N) - \gamma_1 g(\alpha, \beta, \omega_1, \ldots, \omega_N) = \lambda F(\gamma_2) + (1-\lambda) F(\gamma_1)$. *Thus,* $F(\gamma)$ *is convex.*

THEOREM 4. $F(\gamma)$ *is monotonically decreasing.*

Proof: Suppose that $\gamma_1 > \gamma_2$ *and* $(\overline{\alpha}, \overline{\beta}, \overline{\omega}_1, \ldots, \overline{\omega}_N)$ *is an optimal solution of* $F(\gamma_1)$. *Thus,* $F(\gamma_1) = f(\overline{\alpha}, \overline{\beta}, \overline{\omega}_1, \ldots, \overline{\omega}_N) - \gamma_1 g(\overline{\alpha}, \overline{\beta}, \overline{\omega}_1, \ldots, \overline{\omega}_N) < f(\overline{\alpha}, \overline{\beta}, \overline{\omega}_1, \ldots, \overline{\omega}_N) - \gamma_2 g(\overline{\alpha}, \overline{\beta}, \overline{\omega}_1, \ldots, \overline{\omega}_N) \leqslant \max_{\alpha,\beta,\omega_1,\ldots,\omega_N} f(\alpha, \beta, \omega_1, \ldots, \omega_N) - \gamma_2 g(\alpha, \beta, \omega_1, \ldots, \omega_N) = F(\gamma_2)$.

THEOREM 5. $F(\gamma) = 0$ *has a unique solution.*

Proof: Based on the above-mentioned theorems, we know $F(\gamma)$ *is continuous as well as decreasing. In addition,* $\lim_{\gamma \to +\infty} F(\gamma) = -\infty$ *and* $\lim_{\gamma \to -\infty} F(\gamma) = +\infty$.

The procedure of solving this NPPP includes two parts: (1) find such a reasonable parameter γ ($F(\gamma) = 0$), making NPPP equivalent to NFPP; (2) given the parameter γ, solve a polynomial programming problem about the original variables $\alpha, \beta, \omega_1, \ldots, \omega_N$. Our weight adjustment mechanism is an iterative procedure to find the solution of $F(\gamma) = 0$ and the corresponding weights after each iteration of the classification process. We first generate an initial unified classification kernel $\mathbf{K}_j^{(1)}$ with equal weights of $\frac{1}{N}$ to produce an initial classification result on the collaboration multigraph. According to the initial classification result, we then calculate an initial $F(\gamma)$. Since $F(\gamma)$ is a monotonic decreasing function and $F(0) = \max_{\alpha,\beta,\omega_1,\ldots,\omega_N} f(\alpha, \beta, \omega_1, \ldots, \omega_N)$ is obviously non-negative, we start with an initial $\gamma = 0$ and solve the subproblem $F(0)$ by using existing fast polynomial programming model to update the weights $\alpha, \beta, \omega_1, \ldots, \omega_N$. The parameter γ is gradually increased by $\gamma = f(\alpha, \beta, \omega_1, \ldots, \omega_N)/g(\alpha, \beta, \omega_1, \ldots, \omega_N)$ to help the algorithm enter the next round. The algorithm repeats the above-mentioned iterative procedure until $F(\gamma)$ converges to 0.

By assembling different pieces together, we provide the pseudo code of our **AEClass** classifier in Algorithm 1.

Algorithm 1 Activity-Edge Centric Multi-label Classification

Input: a collaboration graph CG, N activity graphs AG_i, a class number K, initial weights $\alpha^{(2)}=\beta^{(2)}=\frac{1}{2}$, $\omega_1^{(1)}=\cdots=\omega_N^{(1)}=\frac{1}{N}$ and a parameter $\gamma^{(1)}=0$.
Output: the predicted label Y_u for the testing instances V_l.

1: Invoke NetClus to partition each of N kinds of activities into K clusters simultaneously;
2: Calculate the category similarity on each AG_i in Eq.(11);
3: Execute the edge classification on CG based on each AG_i in Eqs.(1)-(2);
4: Construct the collaboration multigraph MG;
5: Compute the unified weight $\mathbf{W}_j^{(1)}$ of MG for each c_j in Eq.(3);
6: Calculate the transition probability $\mathbf{T}_j^{(1)}$ for each c_j in Eqs.(4)-(5);
7: Generate the classification kernel $\mathbf{K}_j^{(1)}$ for each c_j in Eq.(6);
8: **for** t=1 **to** $F(\gamma^{(t)})$ converges to 0
9: Calculate the class-membership matrices $\mathbf{X}^{(t)}$ in Eqs.(8)-(10) and $\mathbf{Y}^{(t)}$ in Eqs.(12)-(13);
10: Compute the Macro-F1 score in Eq.(22);
11: Solve $F(\gamma^{(t)})$ in Eq.(27);
12: Update $\omega_1^{(t+1)}, ..., \omega_N^{(t+1)}$ if t=1, or update $\alpha^{(t+1)}, \beta^{(t+1)}, \omega_1^{(t+1)}, ..., \omega_N^{(t+1)}$ if t>1;
13: Refine $\gamma^{(t+1)}=f(\alpha^{(t+1)},\beta^{(t+1)},\omega_1^{(t+1)},...,\omega_N^{(t+1)})/g(\alpha^{(t+1)},\beta^{(t+1)},\omega_1^{(t+1)},...,\omega_N^{(t+1)})$;
14: Update $\mathbf{W}_j^{(t+1)}$ in Eq.(3);
15: Adjust $\mathbf{T}_j^{(t+1)}$ in Eqs.(4)-(5);
16: Update $\mathbf{K}_j^{(t+1)}$ in Eq.(17);
17: Return $\mathbf{Y}^{(t)}$ and Y_u.

4. EXPERIMENTAL EVALUATION

We have performed extensive experiments to evaluate the performance of our **AEClass** classifier on real graph datasets.

4.1 Experimental Datasets

The first real-world dataset is extracted from the DBLP Bibliography data [1]. We build a coauthor graph with highly prolific 100,000 authors from all research areas and 712,834 associated links where vertices represent authors and edges represent their coauthor relationships, and two associated activity graphs: conference graph and term graph. According to [31], we categorize research areas into 24 fields: AI, AIGO, ARC, BIO, CV, DB, DIST, DM, EDU, GRP, HCI, IR, ML, MUL, NLP, NW, OS, PL, RT, SC, SE, SEC, SIM, WWW. We utilize a multi-typed soft clustering framework, NetClus [25], to cluster conferences and terms into 24 categories simultaneously. According to conference's or term's clustering distribution over 24 categories and ranking score in each category, we calculate the similarities between conferences or terms. The classification goal is infer research areas of each author.

Last.fm [2] is a music-oriented online social network. We use the API call *user.getfriends* to collect the list of friends and construct a friendship graph with 50,000 users and 496,611 associated links where vertices represent users and edges denote their friendships. The two activity networks: artist graph and track graph are generated by invoking the API calls *artist.getSimilar* and *track.getSimilar* respectively. By calling the API calls *user.getTopArtists* and *user.getTopTracks*, we classify each friendship edge in terms of the same artists or the same tracks shared by two users. The classification task is to assign each user to a subset of 21 music genres in the database: acoustic, ambient, blues, classical, country, electronic, emo, folk, hardcore, hip hop, indie, jazz, latin, metal, pop, pop punk, punk, reggae, rnb, rock, soul.

[1]http://dblp.uni-trier.de/xml/
[2]http://www.last.fm/api

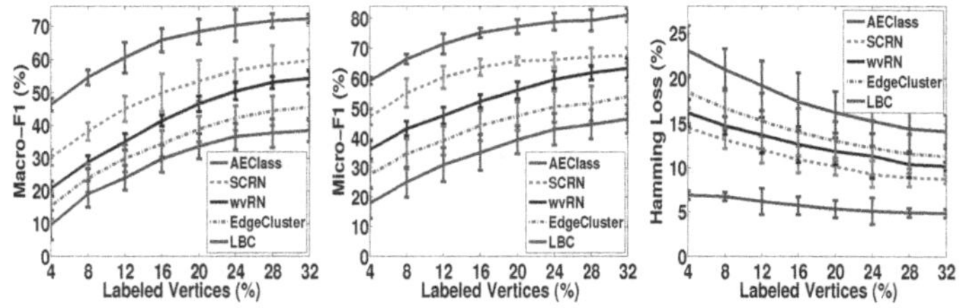

(a) Macro-F1 (b) Micro-F1 (c) Hamming Loss

Figure 7: Classification Quality on DBLP

The third real dataset is extracted from the Internet Movie Database (IMDb) [3]. We construct a collaboration graph with 10,000 highly prolific actors and 270,227 links where vertices represent actors and edges specify their costar relationships in terms of co-appearance of actors in the same movies. We build a movie activity graph where edges denote co-direct relationship between movies, i.e., movies are directed by the same directors. The objective is to associate each actor with a subset of 22 movie genres: Action, Adventure, Animation, Biography, Comedy, Crime, Documentary, Drama, Family, Fantasy, Film-Noir, History, Horror, Music, Musical, Mystery, Romance, Sci-Fi, Sport, Thriller, War, Western.

4.2 Comparison Methods and Evaluation

We compare **AEClass** with two representative link-based classification algorithms, **LBC** [1], **wvRN** [2], and two recently developed multi-label classifiers, **EdgeCluster** [18], **SCRN** [20]. All four methods perform multi-label classification on a single weighted graph based on the assumption of vertex homophily. The detailed introductions for four methods are presented in Section 5. Note that LBC is originally a multi-class classifier. In order to compare all algorithms, we modify the last step in LBC and use the posterior probability distribution over K classes as the multi-label classification result. AEClass integrates multiple information networks into a unified multigraph with combining both the vertex-centric multi-label classification and the edge-centric multi-label classification based on vertex-edge homophily. It also integrates both the structure affinity and the label vicinity into a unified classifier through dynamic weight tuning mechanism.

Evaluation Measures We use three measures to evaluate the quality of classification results generated by different methods. The first measure is Macro-F1 defined in Definition 3. Given the same definitions in Eq.(18), other two metrics are defined as follows.

$$Micro\text{-}F1 = \frac{2\sum_{j=1}^{K}\sum_{i=l+1}^{N_{CG}} \mathcal{I}(\hat{y}_i^j = 1)y_i^j}{\sum_{j=1}^{K}\sum_{i=l+1}^{N_{CG}} \mathcal{I}(\hat{y}_i^j = 1) + \sum_{j=1}^{K}\sum_{i=l+1}^{N_{CG}} y_i^j} \quad (28)$$

Micro-F1 [32] represents the harmonic mean of micro average of precision and recall. The larger the value, the better the quality.

$$HammingLoss = \frac{1}{N_{CG}-l}\sum_{i=l+1}^{N_{CG}} \frac{1}{K}\|\mathcal{I}(\hat{y}_i = 1) \oplus y_i\|_1 \quad (29)$$

where $\oplus$ represents the XOR operation, and $\|\cdot\|_1$ specifies the $l1$-norm. Hamming Loss [33] measures the loss between true labels and predicted labels. The smaller the value, the better the quality.

4.3 Classification Quality

Figures 7-9 exhibit the classification quality on DBLP, Last.fm and IMDb by varying the proportion of labeled vertices respectively. For each proportion of labeled vertices, we average the performance scores over 10 cross-validation folds. The average performance scores with standard deviations of five multi-label classification methods are reported with respect to three evaluation measures of Macro-F1, Micro-F1 and Hamming Loss. We make the following observations on the performances by different methods.

[3]http://www.imdb.com/interfaces

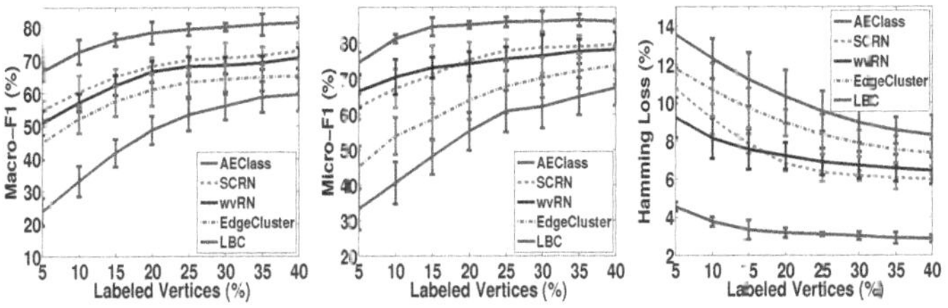

(a) Macro-F1 (b) Micro-F1 (c) Hamming Loss

Figure 8: Classification Quality on Last.fm

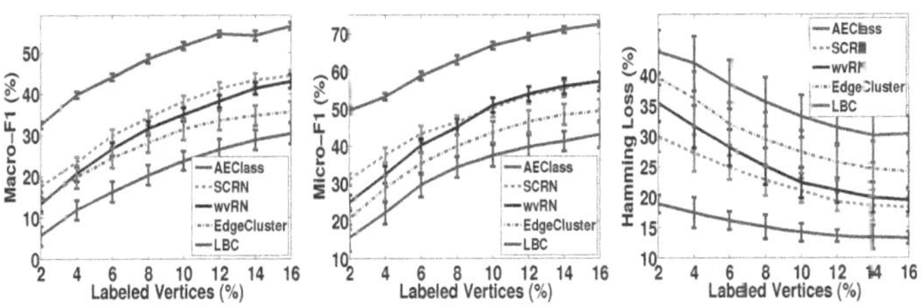

(a) Macro-F1 (b) Micro-F1 (c) Hamming Loss

Figure 9: Classification Quality on IMDb

First, AEClass, SCRN and wvRN significantly outperform LBC and EdgeCluster on all three evaluation measures. We first categorize five multi-label classification methods into non-transductive learning methods and transductive learning methods, based on how they utilize topological structure information. As non-transductive learning methods, both LBC and EdgeCluster only utilize the direct links between vertices in the graph, i.e., one-hop structure information, to produce vertex's features. As transductive learning approaches, AEClass, SCRN and wvRN make full use of both direct links and indirect edges (the circle of friends) between vertices through iterative graph propagation, i.e., multiple-hop structure information, to further improve the classification quality. These results demonstrate the importance of exploiting both direct links and indirect edges for multi-label classification in networked data.

Second, SCRN always outperforms wvRN on three graph datasets. Although SCRN and wvRN exploit the very similar relational inference framework, SCRN improves wvRN by integrating both the network topology and the social context features extracted by EdgeCluster into the classifier. A careful examination reveals that these two approaches are very close in terms of prediction performance in many situations, in spite of the optimization adopted by SCRN. A reasonable explanation is that both of them are only based on the assumption of vertex homophily, i.e., the principle that similar vertices in nature are connected to each other with social links.

Finally, among all five classification methods, AEClass achieves the best classification performance on all three real datasets for all three evaluation measures. Compared to other algorithms, AEClass averagely achieves 14.6% Macro-F1 increase, 12.1% Micro-F1 boost and 5.2% loss reduction on DBLP, 10.2% Macro-F1 growth, 9.9% Micro-F1 increase and 4.1% loss decrease on Last.fm, and 16.7% Macro-F1 increase, 16.2% Micro-F1 boost and 7.5% loss reduction on IMDb, respectively. Note that even if the proportion of labeled vertices is very small, such as 2% and 4%, AEClass still can achieve comparable accuracy on all datasets. Concretely, there are four critical reasons for high accuracy of AEClass: (1) the structure information from associated activity networks boosts the effectiveness of classification. Activity network partition provides us with additional activity labels; (2) the multigraph organization integrates both the vertex-centric multi-label classification based on vertex homophily and the edge-centric multi-label classification based on vertex-edge homophily to leverage the classification performance; (3) Activity network partition captures the inter-dependencies among multiple class labels; and (4) the iterative learning algorithm help the classifier achieve a good balance among different activity-

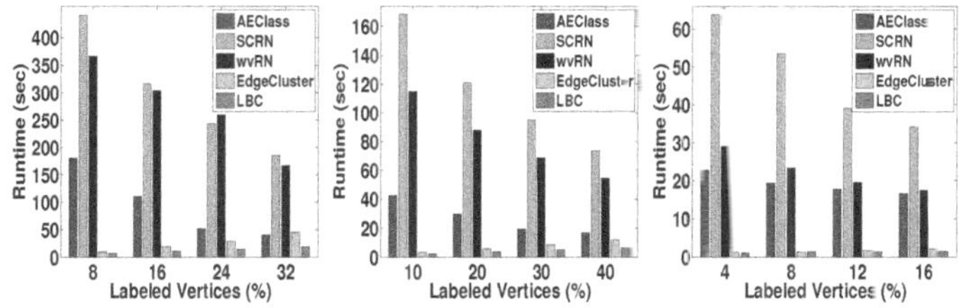

(a) DBLP (b) Last.fm (c) IMDb

Figure 10: Classification Efficiency

based edge classification schemes and an effective integration of the structure affinity and the label vicinity.

4.4 Classification Efficiency

Figures 10 (a), (b) and (c) present the classification time on DBLP, Last.fm and IMDb with different proportions of labeled vertices respectively. First, LBC has lowest runtime in seconds compared to all other algorithms in all experiments, since it is a logistic regression classifier by aggregating the labels of neighbors as vertex's feature vector. Second, EdgeCluster, a linear SVM classifier with an edge clustering scheme to extract sparse social dimensions, is slightly slower than LBC since the linear SVM approaches generally fall behind the LR methods in speed. Both LBC and EdgeCluster are faster than other three methods because both only utilize the direct links between vertices, i.e., one-hop structure information. In comparison, AEClass, SCRN and wvRN use both direct links and indirect edges (the circle of friends) between vertices, i.e., multiple-hop structure information. Thus, the last three classifiers have higher time complexity than the first two models but they achieve better classification quality. Third, wvRN is consistently faster than SCRN on all three datasets. SCRN improves wvRN by integrating the social dimensions extracted by EdgeCluster into the classifier. This improvement results in an additional computational cost for calculating the class propagation probability of each vertex on each class. Finally, AEClass significantly outperforms the other two transductive learning based multi-label classifiers: SCRN and wvRN. Although SCRN and wvRN execute the classification on a general graph, AEClass does classification on an activity-based collaboration multigraph by augmenting its edges with class labels from each activity graph. There are three main reasons for high efficiency of AEClass: (1) the multigraph organization increases the size of dataset but reduces the computational cost of classification. As we discussed in Subsection 3.2, based on the vertex homophily, no matter which class the current objective is, both SCRN and wvRN need to check each neighbor of a vertex and summarize the labels of all neighbors. In contrast, AEClass only picks up those vertices and links with the same label as the current objective class to execute the inference. Most importantly, AEClass stops the label propagation through irrelevant neighbors (without a link with the same label as the current objective class) in the future iterations; (2) the label vicinity between vertices based on the class-membership distribution over K classes is integrated into the classifier; and (3) we transform the original nonlinear fractional programming problem of multiple weights into a nonlinear parametric programming problem of single variable. According to Theorems 2-5, solving $F(\gamma)$ for a given γ is a polynomial programming problem which can be sped up by existing fast polynomial programming model.

4.5 Classification Convergence

Figure 11 (a) and (b) exhibit the trend of classification convergence in terms of Macro-F1, Micro-F1, and Hamming Loss on DBLP with 4% label nodes and Last.fm with 5% label vertices. Both the Macro-F1 values and the Micro-F1 scores in two figures keep increasing and have concave curves when we iteratively perform the tasks of vertex labeling, weight update and kernel adjustment

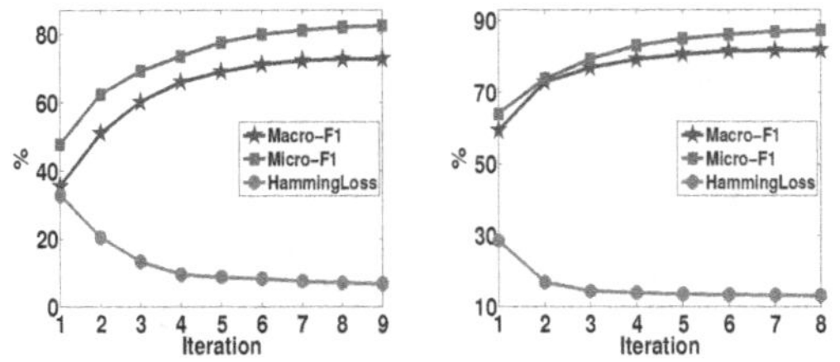

(a) DBLP (b) Last.fm

Figure 11: Classification Convergence

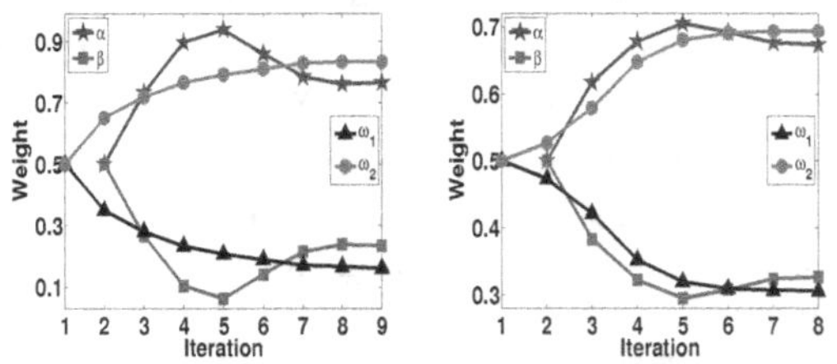

(a) DBLP (b) Last.fm

Figure 12: Weight Update

during the classification process. On the other hand, the Hamming Loss values decrease with the classification iterations and have a convex curve. The classification process converges very quickly, usually in eight iterations for Last.fm and nine iterations for DBLP.

Figure 12 (a) and (b) show the tendency of weight update on DBLP and Last.fm respectively. α and β in two figures represent the weights of structure affinity and label vicinity in the unified classifier $\mathbf{K}_j^{(t+1)}$ in Eq.(17) respectively. ω_1 and ω_2 in Figure 12 (a) denote the weights of the conference graph and the term graph respectively. ω_1 and ω_2 in Figure 12 (b) represent the weights of the artist graph and the track graph respectively. We keep the constraints $\alpha+\beta=1$ and $\omega_1+\omega_2=1$ during the classification process. We observe that all the weights converge as the clustering process converges. An interesting phenomenon is that α first increases and then decreases with the iterations and the β curve has a converse trend. A reasonable explanation is that there is lack of enough labeling information at the beginning of classification such that the unified classifier has to rely mostly on the structure affinity to achieve a good classification performance. After a few iterations, we have enough labeling information to utilize both the structure affinity and the label vicinity to classify vertices. An interesting finding is that the term weight is increasing but the conference weight is decreasing with more iterations. A reasonable explanation is that people who have many publications on the same conferences may have different research topics but people who have many papers with the same terms usually have the same research topics. For example, both database papers and data mining papers are published on *VLDB*. Similarly, the track weight increases but the artist weight decreases with more iterations. This is because users who favor the same artists may belong to different music genres since the artists are often related to multiple genres but users who like the same tracks usually belong to the same music genres.

4.6 Case Study

We examine some details of the experiment results on DBLP 100,000 Authors when the proportion of labeled vertices is equal to 32% based on the coauthor graph, the conference graph and the term graph. Table 1 shows the set of authors and their class-membership probabilities after seven iterations based on 24 conference categories and 24 term categories. We only present most prolific DBLP experts in the area of database (DB), data mining (DM), machine learning (ML) and information retrieval (IR). The class-membership scores in Table 1 are normalized by different (conference or term) categories for each author. We observe that the predicted class memberships of authors are consistent with their

Author/Class	DB	DM	ML	IR
Peter L. Bartlett	0.019	0.039	0.938	0.004
Elisa Bertino	0.738	0.054	0.028	0.180
Andrei Z. Broder	0.037	0.097	0.015	0.851
Michael J. Carey	0.965	0.029	0.006	0.023
W. Bruce Croft	0.054	0.007	0.037	0.902
David J. DeWitt	0.912	0.057	0.004	0.027
Inderjit S. Dhillon	0.030	0.409	0.457	0.104
Christos Faloutsos	0.321	0.500	0.031	0.147
Jiawei Han	0.391	0.463	0.045	0.100
H. V. Jagadish	0.850	0.056	0.009	0.048
Michael I. Jordan	0.007	0.062	0.917	0.014
Daphne Koller	0.026	0.045	0.915	0.013
Vipin Kumar	0.120	0.622	0.199	0.059
Bing Liu	0.086	0.427	0.266	0.220
Hector Garcia-Molina	0.788	0.010	0.016	0.186
C. J. van Rijsbergen	0.003	0.051	0.024	0.922
Michael Stonebraker	0.946	0.013	0.007	0.034
Jeffrey D. Ullman	0.824	0.065	0.064	0.047
Philip S. Yu	0.342	0.496	0.044	0.118
Mohammed J. Zaki	0.148	0.672	0.057	0.123

Table 1: Class-membership Probabilities of Authors Based on Conference and Keyword Partitions from DBLP

actual research areas. For those experts with unique research areas, such as *Michael J. Carey* and *Michael Stonebraker*, the primary research areas for them in the predicted result are obviously consistent with their actual research areas; For those researchers known to work in multiple research areas, the predicted class-membership distributions also correspond to their current research activities. For example, both *Jiawei Han* and *Philip S. Yu* are experts on data mining and database, though their *DM* probabilities are slightly higher since each of them and their circle of co-authors have more *DM* papers. This table also shows that each author has a class-membership score in each category. This demonstrates that our AEClass model can make each author quickly reach each class label.

5. RELATED WORK

Node classification in networked data has attracted active research in the last decade [1–9]. LBC [1] is a network-only derivative of the link-based classifier which creates a feature vector for a node by aggregating the labels of neighboring nodes, and then uses logistic regression to build a discriminative model based on these feature vectors. wvRN [2] presented a weighted-vote relational neighbor classifier to solve link-based classification problems based solely on the class labels of linked neighbors. DYCOS [6] exhibited a node classification model in dynamic information networks with both text content and links. RankClass [7] integrates classification and ranking in a mutually enhancing process to provide class summaries for heterogeneous information networks.

Multi-label classification is gaining attention in recent years [10–16]. Read et al. [12] reduces the complexity and potential for error with a pruning procedure to focus on core relationships within multi-label sets. IBLR [13] proposed a multi-label classification approach to combine model-based and similarity-based inference with the estimation of optimal regression coefficients. LEAD [15] decomposes a multi-label learning task into a set of single-label classification problems with a Bayesian network to encode the conditional dependencies of labels as well as the feature set. Guo and Gu [16] proposed a generalized conditional dependency network for model training using binary classifiers and label predictions using Gibbs sampling inference.

Multi-label classification in networked data has been extensively studied in recent years [17–22]. Sun et al. [17] presented a hypergraph spectral learning formulation for multi-label classification, where a hypergraph is constructed to exploit the correlation information among different labels. EdgeCluster [18] presented a social-dimension based approach for collective behavior prediction with an edge clustering scheme to extract sparse social dimensions and a linear SVM classifier for discriminative learning. SCRN [20] is a multi-label iterative relational neighbor classifier by considering both network topology and social context features. PIPL [21] facilitates the multi-label learning process by mining label correlations and instance correlations from the heterogeneous networks.

Recent works on heterogeneous social network analysis [7,9,23–30] combine links and content into heterogeneous information networks to improve the quality of querying, ranking and clustering. Cai et al. [23] proposed to learn an optimal linear combination of different relations on heterogeneous social networks in terms of their importance on a certain query. GenClus [28] proposed a model-based method for clustering heterogeneous networks with different link types and different attribute types. Yu et al. [29] presented a query-driven discovery system for finding semantically similar substructures in heterogeneous networks.

To our knowledge, this work is the first one to address the problem of activity-edge centric multi-label classification of heterogeneous multigraph with the prior knowledge of multiple activity graphs by dynamically adjusting their individual contributions.

6. CONCLUSIONS

We have presented an edge-centric multi-label classification approach for mining heterogeneous information networks. First, we integrate the primary social network and multiple associated activity networks into a unified multigraph with edge classification. Second, we combine both the structure affinity and the label vicinity based on multiple activity networks into a unified classifier. Third, an iterative learning algorithm is proposed dynamically refine the classification result by continuously adjusting the weights on different activity-based edge classification schemes from multiple activity graphs, while constantly learning the contributions of the structure affinity and the label vicinity in the unified classifier.

Acknowledgement. This material is based upon work partially supported by the NSF under Grants IIS-0905493, CNS-1115375, IIP-1230740, and a grant from Intel ISTC on Cloud Computing.

7. REFERENCES

[1] Q. Lu and L. Getoor. Link-based classification. In *ICML'03*.

[2] S. A. Macskassy and F. Provost. A simple relational classifier. In *MRDM*, pages 64–76, 2003.

[3] D. Zhou, O. Bousquet, T. N. Lal, J. Weston, and B. Scholkopf. Learning with local and global consistency. In *NIPS*, 2003.

[4] J. Neville and D. Jensen. Relational dependency networks. *Journal of Machine Learning Research*, 8:653–692, 2007.

[5] S. A. Macskassy and F. Provost. Classification in networked data: A toolkit and a univariate case study. *Journal of Machine Learning Research*, 8:935–983, 2007.

[6] C. C. Aggarwal and N. Li. On Node Classification in Dynamic Content-based Networks. In *SDM*, 2011.

[7] M. Ji, J. Han, and M. Danilevsky. Ranking-based classification of heterogeneous information networks. In *KDD*, pages 1298–1306, 2011.

[8] S. Bhagat, G. Cormode, and S. Muthukrishnan. Node classification in social networks. *Social Network Data Analytics*, pages 115–148, 2011.

[9] X. Kong, P. S. Yu, Y. Ding, and D. J. Wild. Meta path-based collective classification in heterogeneous information networks. In *CIKM*, pages 1567–1571, 2012.

[10] S. Godbole and S. Sarawagi. Discriminative methods for multi-labeled classification. In *PAKDD*, 2004.

[11] G. Chen, Y. Song, F. Wang, and C. Zhang. Semi-supervised multi-label learning by solving a sylvester equation. In *SDM*, Atlanta, GA, April 24-26 2008.

[12] J. Read, B. Pfahringer, and G. Holmes. Multi-label classification using ensembles of pruned sets. In *ICDM'08*.

[13] W. Cheng and E. Hullermeier. Combining instance-based learning and logistic regression for multilabel classification. *Machine Learning*, 76(2-3):211–225, 2009.

[14] K. Dembczynski, W. Cheng, and E. Hullermeier. Bayes optimal multilabel classification via probabilistic classifier chains. In *ICML*, Haifa, Israel, June 21-24 2010.

[15] M.-L. Zhang and K. Zhang. Multi-label learning by exploiting label dependency. In *KDD*, 999–1008, 2010.

[16] Y. Guo and S. Gu. Multi-label classification using conditional dependency networks. In *IJCAI*, 2011.

[17] L. Sun, S. Ji, and J. Ye. Hypergraph spectral learning for multi-label classification. In *KDD*, 668–676, 2008.

[18] L. Tang and H. Liu. Scalable learning of collective behavior based on sparse social dimensions. In *CIKM*, 2009.

[19] S. Peters, Y. Jacob, L. Denoyer, and P. Gallinari. Iterative multi-label multi-relational classification algorithm for complex social networks. *Social Network Analysis and Mining*, 2(1):17–29, 2012.

[20] X. Wang and G. Sukthankar. Multi-label relational neighbor classification using social context features. In *KDD*, 2013.

[21] X. Kong, B. Cao, and P. S. Yu. Multi-label classification by mining label and instance correlations from heterogeneous information networks. In *KDD*, pages 614–622, 2013.

[22] B. Wang, Z. Tu, and J. K. Tsotsos. Dynamic label propagation for semi-supervised multi-class multi-label classification. In *ICCV*, 2013.

[23] D. Cai, Z. Shao, X. He, X. Yan, and J. Han. Community mining from multi-relational networks. In *PKDD*, 2005.

[24] Y. Zhou, H. Cheng, and J. X. Yu. Graph clustering based on structural/attribute similarities. In *VLDB*, 718–729, 2009.

[25] Y. Sun, Y. Yu, and J. Han. Ranking-based clustering of heterogeneous information networks with star network schema. In *KDD*, pages 797–806, 2009.

[26] T. Yang, R. Jin, Y. Chi, and S. Zhu. Combining link and content for community detection: a discriminative approach. In *KDD*, pages 927–936, 2009.

[27] Y. Zhou, H. Cheng, and J. X. Yu. Clustering large attributed graphs: An efficient incremental approach. In *ICDM*, 2010.

[28] Y. Sun, C. C. Aggarwal, and J. Han. Relation strength-aware clustering of heterogeneous information networks with incomplete attributes. *PVLDB*, 5(5):394–405, 2012.

[29] X. Yu, Y. Sun, P. Zhao, and J. Han. Query-driven discovery of semantically similar substructures in heterogeneous networks. In *KDD*, 1500–1503, 2012.

[30] Y. Zhou and L. Liu. Social influence based clustering of heterogeneous information networks. In *KDD*, 2013.

[31] T. Chakraborty, S. Sikdar, V. Tammana, N. Ganguly, and A. Mukherjee. Computer science fields as ground-truth communities: Their impact, rise and fall. In *ASONAM*, 2013.

[32] R.-E. Fan and C.-J. Lin. A study on threshold selection for multi-label classification. In *Tech Report*, National Taiwan University, 2007.

[33] X. Zhang, Q. Yuan, S. Zhao, W. Fan, W. Zheng, and Z. Wang. Multi-label classification without the multi-label cost. In *SDM*, 2010.

Meta-path based Multi-Network Collective Link Prediction

Jiawei Zhang
Big Data and Social Computing (BDSC) Lab
University of Illinois at Chicago
Chicago, IL, USA
jzhan9@uic.edu

Philip S. Yu
Big Data and Social Computing (BDSC) Lab
University of Illinois at Chicago
Chicago, IL, USA
psyu@cs.uic.edu

Zhi-Hua Zhou
National Key Laboratory for Novel Software Technology,
Nanjing University
Nanjing 210023, China
zhouzh@lamda.nju.edu.cn

ABSTRACT

Online social networks offering various services have become ubiquitous in our daily life. Meanwhile, users nowadays are usually involved in multiple online social networks simultaneously to enjoy specific services provided by different networks. Formally, social networks that share some common users are named as partially aligned networks. In this paper, we want to predict the formation of social links in multiple partially aligned social networks at the same time, which is formally defined as the multi-network link (formation) prediction problem. In multiple partially aligned social networks, users can be extensively correlated with each other by various connections. To categorize these diverse connections among users, 7 "intra-network social meta paths" and 4 categories of "inter-network social meta paths" are proposed in this paper. These "social meta paths" can cover a wide variety of connection information in the network, some of which can be helpful for solving the multi-network link prediction problem but some can be not. To utilize useful connection information, a subset of the most informative "social meta paths" are picked, the process of which is formally defined as "social meta path selection" in this paper. An effective general link formation prediction framework, MLI (Multi-network Link Identifier), is proposed in this paper to solve the multi-network link (formation) prediction problem. Built with heterogenous topological features extracted based on the selected "social meta paths" in the multiple partially aligned social networks, MLI can help refine and disambiguate the prediction results reciprocally in all aligned networks. Extensive experiments conducted on real-world partially aligned heterogeneous networks, Foursquare and Twitter, demonstrate that MLI can solve the multi-network link prediction problem very well.

Categories and Subject Descriptors

H.2.8 [**Database Management**]: Database Applications-Data Mining

KDD'14, August 24–27, 2014, New York, NY, USA.

http://dx.doi.org/10.1145/2623330.2623645.

Keywords

Link Prediction; Social Networks; Classification; Transfer Learning; Data Mining

1. INTRODUCTION

Nowadays, online social networks with specific characteristics have become an essential part in our daily life. Users in online social networks can usually enjoy a wide variety of social services, e.g., establish social connections with friends, write online posts, check in at locations. Meanwhile, social networks which provide these various services can usually contain heterogeneous information, which include multiple kinds of information entities, e.g., users, posts and locations, and complex links among these entities, e.g., social links among users [25, 26] and location checkin links between users and locations [26].

Via these diverse links in online social networks, users can be connected with each other closely. Consider, for example, given two users, *Alice* and *Bob*, who both have checked in at the "*Lincoln Memorial*" in Foursquare[1], the location checkin links "*Alice– Lincoln Memorial– Bob*" can form a path from *Alice* to *Bob* in the network. Formally, the sequences of links starting and ending with users in online social networks are defined as the *social paths*. The length of social paths is defined as the number of links that constitute them. For instance, path "*Alice – Lincoln Memorial – Bob*" is a social path of length 2 connecting *Alice* and *Bob* in Foursquare.

In all possible connections among users, social links, which are one kind of social paths of length 1 as well, among users have received lots of attention in recent years [21, 22, 23]. The problem of predicting social links to be formed in the near future based on a snapshot of online social networks is formally defined as the *social link (formation) prediction* problem. Many concrete social services in social networks can be cast as *social link prediction* problems, e.g., friend recommendation. Meanwhile, as pointed out in [25], users' "loyalty" to a social network is positively correlated to the number of friends they have in the network. As a result, *social link formation prediction* problem, which can help introduce more social connections for users, can be very important for online social networks.

Traditional link prediction problems which aim at predicting one single kind of links in one network [16, 20, 24, 3] have been studied for many years. Dozens of different link prediction methods have been proposed so far [1, 14, 19, 16, 20, 24, 3]. Conventional link prediction methods usually assume

[1]https://foursquare.com

that there exists sufficient information within the network to compute features (e.g., common neighborhoods [9]) for each pair of nodes. However, as proposed in [25, 26], such assumption can be violated seriously when dealing with social networks containing little information because of the "new network" problems.

The *new network problem* can be encountered when online social networks branch into new geographic areas or social groups [26] and information within the new networks can be too sparse to build effective link prediction models. Meanwhile, Zhang et al. [10, 25, 26] notice that users nowadays can participate in multiple online social networks simultaneously. Users who are involved in a new network can have been using other well-developed networks for a long time, in which they can have plenty of heterogeneous information. To address the new network problem, Zhang et al. [25, 26] propose to transfer information from the well-developed networks to overcome the shortage of information problem in the new network. Formally, networks that share some common users are defined as the "*partially aligned networks*" and the common users shared across these "*partially aligned networks*" are named as the "*anchor users*" [10, 25, 26]. In this paper, we define the unshared users as the "*non-anchor users*" between the *aligned networks*.

Social networks aligned by the "anchor users" can share common information. Meanwhile, as proposed in [15, 23], different online social networks constructed to provide different services usually have distinct characteristics. Moreover, information in various social networks may be of different distributions [15, 23], which is named as the "*network difference problem*" in this paper. The "*network difference problem*" will be a obstacle in link prediction across *multiple partially aligned networks*, as it is likely that information transferred from other aligned networks could deteriorate the prediction performance in a given network.

In this paper, we want to predict the formation of social links in multiple *partially aligned networks* simultaneously, which is formally defined as the *multi-network link prediction* problem in this paper. As introduced at the beginning of this section, the *multi-network link prediction* problem can have very extensive applications in real-world social networks. As a result, the *multi-network link prediction* problem studied in this paper is very important for *multiple partially aligned social networks*.

The *multi-network link prediction* problem studied in this paper is a novel problem and totally different from other existing link prediction problems. Moreover, link prediction methods proposed in [25, 26] cannot be applied to solve the *multi-network link prediction* problem directly because these existing methods: (1) are proposed to transfer useful information for *anchor users* only; (2) fail to consider the *network difference problem*; (3) can only predict links in each network independently. A more detailed comparison of the *multi-network link prediction* problem with these correlated problems, e.g., social link prediction for new users [25], transfer heterogeneous links across networks [26], anchor link prediction [10] and multi-transfer with multiple views and sources [18], is available in Table 1.

Despite of its importance and novelty, the *multi-network link prediction* problem studied in this paper is also very challenging to solve due to the following reasons:

- *lack of features*: Networks studied in this paper can contain different kinds of information. Proper definition of heterogeneous features extracted for social links from the networks is a prerequisite for addressing link formation prediction tasks.
- *partial alignment*: To overcome the "new network problem", we propose to transfer information from other aligned networks. Existing information transferring methods proposed in [25, 26] can only work well for *anchor users*. Method that can transferring information for both *anchor users* and *non-anchor users* is what we desire in this paper.
- *network difference problem*: Different networks usually have different characteristics and information transferred from other *aligned networks* can be different from that of the given network, which could deteriorate the link prediction performance in the given network.
- *simultaneous link prediction in multiple networks*: The *multi-network link prediction* problem covers multiple *link prediction* tasks in multiple *partially aligned networks* simultaneously. Analysis and utilization the correlations among these tasks to enhance the prediction performance in each network mutually is very challenging.

To solve all these above challenges in the *multi-network link prediction* problem, a novel link prediction framework, MLI, is proposed in this paper. Inspired by Sun's [17] work on meta path as a means to capture similarity of nodes, which are not directly connected in heterogeneous information networks, MLI explores the meta path concept to generate useful features. MLI can generate not only intra-network features via "intra-network meta paths", but also inter-network features via "inter-network meta paths" through the *anchor links*. By judiciously selecting the "inter-network meta paths", MLI can take advantage of the commonality among the *multiple partially aligned networks*, while contain the potential negative transfers from network differences. These derived features can greatly improve the effectiveness of MLI in predicting links for each network. Furthermore, MLI is a general link formation prediction framework that solves the *multi-network link prediction* problem and the *link prediction* tasks in different networks can help each other mutually.

The rest of this paper is organized as follows. In Section 2, we formulate the problem. Detailed description of the methods is available in Section 3. We show the experiment results in Section 4. Related works are given in Section 5. Finally, we conclude the paper in Section 6.

2. PROBLEM FORMULATION

In this section, we will give the formal definitions of many important concepts used in this paper and the formulation of the *multi-network link prediction* problem.

2.1 Terminology Definition

Definition 1 (Heterogeneous Social Network): A social network is *heterogeneous* if it contains multiple kinds of nodes and links. *Heterogeneous social networks* can be represented as $G = (V, E)$, where $V = \bigcup_i V_i$ is the union of different node sets and $E = \bigcup_i E_i$ is the union of heterogeneous link sets.

Networks used in this paper are Twitter and Foursquare, which are both heterogeneous social networks. Users in

Table 1: Summary of related problems.

Property	**Mutual Social Link Prediction in Multiple Aligned Networks**	**Transfer Heterogeneous Links across Networks [26]**	**Multi-Transfer with Multi-View & Multi-Domain [18]**	**Social Link Prediction for New Users [25]**	**Inferring Anchor Links across Networks [10]**
information sources	multiple **networks**	multiple **networks**	multiple **domains**	multiple **networks**	multiple **networks**
source type	heterogeneous	heterogeneous	multi-view	heterogeneous	heterogeneous
sources aligned?	partially aligned	partially aligned	no	fully aligned	fully aligned
source differences	solved	not solved	solved	not solved	not solved
predicted links	social links in all aligned networks	heterogeneous links in the target network	n/a	social links in the target network	anchor links across networks
settings	semi-supervised learning and transfer learning	supervised learning and transfer learning	supervised learning and transfer learning	supervised learning and transfer learning	supervised learning and transfer learning
knowledge to transfer	network structure via meta paths	network structure through anchor links	domain information via common feature space	network structure through anchor links	network structure through anchor links

both Twitter and Foursquare can make friends with other users, write posts online, which can contain text content, timestamps and attach location check-ins. Both Twitter and Foursquare can be formulated as $G = (V, E)$, where $V = U \cup P \cup L \cup T \cup W$, and U, P, L, T and W are the sets of user, post, location, timestamp and word nodes in the network respectively, while $E = E_{u,u} \cup E_{u,p} \cup E_{p,l} \cup E_{p,t} \cup E_{p,w}$ are the sets of heterogeneous links in G, which include the *social links* among users, *write link* between users and posts, links between posts and locations, timestamps and words.

Definition 2 (Aligned Heterogeneous Social Networks): If two different social networks share some common users, then these two networks are called *aligned networks*. *Multiple aligned heterogeneous social networks* can be formulated as $\mathcal{G} = ((G^1, G^2, \cdots, G^n), (A^{1,2}, A^{1,3}, \cdots, A^{1,n}, A^{2,3}, \cdots, A^{(n-1),n}))$, where $G^i, i \in \{1, 2, \cdots, n\}$ is a *heterogeneous social network* and $A^{i,j} \neq \emptyset, i, j \in \{1, 2, \cdots, n\}$ is the set of undirected *anchor links* between G^i and G^j.

Definition 3 (Anchor Links): Let U^i and U^j be the user sets of G^i and G^j respectively. Link (u^i, v^j) is a undirected *anchor link* between G^i and G^j iff($u^i \in U^i) \wedge (v^j \in U^j) \wedge$ (u^i and v^j are the accounts of the same user in G^i and G^j respectively).

Definition 4 (Anchor Users): User $u^i \in U^i$ is an *anchor user* in G^i between G^i and G^j iff $\exists v^j \in U^j, (u^i, v^j) \in A^{i,j}$. The set of *anchor users* in G^i between G^i and G^j can be represented as $U^i_{A^{i,j}} = \{u^i | u^i \in U^i, \exists v^j \in U^j, (u^i, v^j) \in A^{i,j}\}$.

Definition 5 (Non-Anchor Users): User $u^i \in U^i$ is an *non-anchor user* between G^i and G^j iff $u^i \notin U^i_{A^{i,j}}$. The set of *non-anchor users* in G^i between G^i and G^j can be represented as $U^i_{-A^{i,j}} = U^i - U^i_{A^{i,j}}$.

Definition 6 (Full Alignment): Networks G^i and G^j are *fully aligned* if users in both G^i and G^j are all anchor users. In other words, G^i and G^j are *fully aligned* iff($U^i_{A^{i,j}} = U^i) \wedge (U^j_{A^{i,j}} = U^j)$.

Definition 7 (Partial Alignment): Networks G^i and G^j are *partially aligned* if there exist users in G^i or G^j who are *non-anchor users*. In other words, G^i and G^j are partially aligned iff $((U^i_{-A^{i,j}} \neq \emptyset) \vee (U^j_{-A^{i,j}} \neq \emptyset)) \wedge (A^{i,j} \neq \emptyset)$.

Considering that *fully aligned networks* can hardly exist in the real world, different from the strict full alignment assumption of networks proposed in [10, 25], networks used in this paper are *partially aligned* instead. In addition, there exists no restriction about the constraint on *anchor links*, which means that the *anchor links* can be either *one-to-one* [10] or *many-to-many*.

2.2 Multi-PU Link Prediction

Let $G^i, i \in \{1, 2, \cdots, n\}$ be a *heterogeneous online social network* in the multiple *aligned networks*. The user set and existing social link set of G^i can be represented as U^i and $E^i_{u,u}$ respectively. In network G^i, all the existing links are the formed links and, as a result, the formed links of G^i can be represented as $\mathcal{P}^i$, where $\mathcal{P}^i = E^i_{u,u}$. Furthermore, a large set of unconnected user pairs are referred to as the unconnected links, $\mathcal{U}^i$, and can be extracted from network G^i: $\mathcal{U}^i = U^i \times U^i - \mathcal{P}^i$. However, no information about links that will never be formed can be obtained from the network. In this paper, with $\mathcal{P}^i$ and $\mathcal{U}^i$, we formulate the *link formation prediction* as a *PU link prediction* problem.

Similarly, let $\{\mathcal{P}^1, \cdots, \mathcal{P}^n\}$, $\{\mathcal{U}^1, \cdots, \mathcal{U}^n\}$ and $\{\mathcal{L}^1, \cdots, \mathcal{L}^n\}$ be the sets of formed links, unconnected links, and links to be predicted of $G^1, G^2, \cdots, G^n$ respectively. With the formed and unconnected links of $G^1, G^2, \cdots, G^n$, we can solve the *multi-network link prediction* problem as a *multi-PU link prediction* problem.

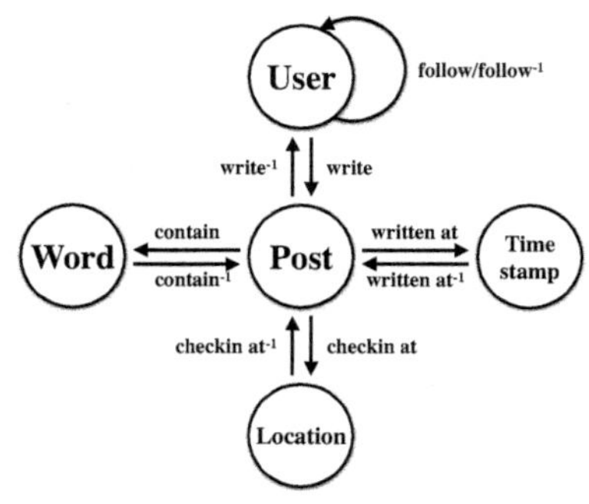

Figure 1: Schema of heterogeneous network.

3. PROPOSED METHODS

In this section, we will introduce MLI to solve the *multi-network link prediction* problem. This section includes 3 parts: (1) social meta path based feature extraction and selection; (2) PU link prediction; (3) multi-network link prediction framework.

3.1 Social Meta Path Definition and Selection

Before talking about the link prediction methods, we will introduce the features extracted from the *partially aligned networks* in this subsection at first.

3.1.1 Intra-Network Social Meta Path

Users in heterogeneous online social network can be extensively connected to each other via different paths. In this part, we will categorize the diverse paths connecting users in one single network with the *intra-network social meta paths* concept.

For a given heterogeneous online social network, e.g., G, to describe its structure more clearly, we define its *schema* to be $S_G = (T, R)$, where T, R are the sets of node types and link types in G. For example, if $G = (V, E)$, where $V = U \cup P \cup L$ contains user, post and location nodes, $E = E_{u,u} \cup E_{u,p} \cup E_{p,l}$ contains the social links, write links and location links, then $S_G = (T, R)$, T = {User, Post, Location} and R = {Social Link, Write Link, Location Link}. A complete schema of networks studied in this paper is shown in Figure 1. In network G, nodes can be connected with each other via extensive paths consisting of various links. To categorize all possible paths in heterogeneous networks G, we define the concept of *intra-network meta path* based on schema S_G as follows:

Definition 8 (Intra-Network Meta Path): Based on the given the network schema, $S_G = (T, R)$, $\Phi = T_1 \xrightarrow{R_1} T_2 \xrightarrow{R_2} \cdots \xrightarrow{R_{k-1}} T_k$ is defined to be a *meta path* in network G, where $T_i \in T, i \in \{1, 2, \cdots, k\}$ and $R_i \in R, i \in \{1, 2, \cdots, k-1\}$.

Meanwhile, depending on types of nodes and links that constitute it, Φ can be divided into two different categories.

Definition 9 (Homogeneous and Heterogeneous Intra-Network Meta Path): For a given meta path $\Phi = T_1 \xrightarrow{R_1} T_2 \xrightarrow{R_2} \cdots \xrightarrow{R_{k-1}} T_k$ defined based on S_G, if $(T_1, \cdots, T_k$ are all the same $) \wedge (R_1, \cdots, R_{k-1}$ are all the same), then Φ is a *homogeneous meta path*; otherwise P is a *heterogeneous meta path*.

In this paper, we are mainly concerned about meta paths connecting user nodes, which can be defined as the *intra-network social meta path*.

Definition 10 (Intra-Network Social Meta Path): For a given meta path $\Phi = T_1 \xrightarrow{R_1} T_2 \xrightarrow{R_2} \cdots \xrightarrow{R_{k-1}} T_k$ defined based on S_G, if T_1 and T_k are both the "User" node type, then P is defined as a *social meta path*. Depending on whether $T_1, \cdots, T_k$ and $R_1, \cdots, R_{k-1}$ are the same or not, P can be divided into two categories: *homogeneous intra-network social meta path* and *heterogeneous intra-network social meta path*.

Based on the schema of networks studied in this paper, shown in Figure 1, we can define many different kinds of *homogeneous and heterogeneous intra-network social meta paths* for network G, whose physical meanings and notations are listed as follows:

Homogeneous Intra-Network Social Meta Path

- *ID 0. Follow*: User $\xrightarrow{follow}$ User, whose notation is "$U \to U$" or $\Phi_0(U, U)$.
- *ID 1. Follower of Follower*: User $\xrightarrow{follow}$ User $\xrightarrow{follow}$ User, whose notation is "$U \to U \to U$" or $\Phi_1(U, U)$.
- *ID 2. Common Out Neighbor*: User $\xrightarrow{follow}$ User $\xrightarrow{follow^{-1}}$ User, whose notation is "$U \to U \leftarrow U$" or $\Phi_2(U, U)$.
- *ID 3. Common In Neighbor*: User $\xrightarrow{follow^{-1}}$ User $\xrightarrow{follow}$ User, whose notation is "$U \leftarrow U \to U$" or $\Phi_3(U, U)$.

Heterogeneous Intra-Network Social Meta Path

- *ID 4. Common Words*: User $\xrightarrow{write}$ Post $\xrightarrow{contain}$ Word $\xrightarrow{contain^{-1}}$ Post $\xrightarrow{write^{-1}}$ User, whose notation is "$U \to P \to W \leftarrow P \leftarrow U$" or $\Phi_4(U, U)$
- *ID 5. Common Timestamps*: User $\xrightarrow{write}$ Post $\xrightarrow{contain}$ Time $\xrightarrow{contain^{-1}}$ Post $\xrightarrow{write^{-1}}$ User, whose notation is "$U \to P \to T \leftarrow P \leftarrow U$" or $\Phi_5(U, U)$.
- *ID 6. Common Location Checkins*: User $\xrightarrow{write}$ Post $\xrightarrow{attach}$ Location $\xrightarrow{attach^{-1}}$ Post $\xrightarrow{write^{-1}}$ User, whose notation is "$U \to P \to L \leftarrow P \leftarrow U$" or $\Phi_6(U, U)$.

3.1.2 Social Meta Path based Features

Meta paths introduced in the previous part can actually cover a large number of path instances connecting users in the network. Formally, we denote that node n (or link l) is an instance of node type T (or link type R) in the network as $n \in T$ (or $l \in R$). Identity function $I(a, A) = \begin{cases} 1, & \text{if } a \in A \\ 0, & \textit{otherwise}, \end{cases}$ can check whether node/link a is an instance of node/link type A in the network. To consider the effect of the unconnected links when extracting features for social links in the network, we formally define the *Intra-Network Social Meta Path based Features* to be:

Definition 11 (Intra-Network Social Meta Path based Features): For a given link (u, v), the feature extracted for it based on meta path $\Phi = T_1 \xrightarrow{R_1} T_2 \xrightarrow{R_2} \cdots \xrightarrow{R_{k-1}} T_k$ from the network is defined to be the expected number of formed path instances between u and v in the network:

$$x(u, v) = I(u, T_1) I(v, T_k) \sum_{n_1 \in \{u\}, n_2 \in T_2, \cdots, n_k \in \{v\}} \prod_{i=1}^{k-1} p(n_i, n_{i+1}) I((n_i, n_{i+1}), R_i),$$

where $p(n_i, n_{i+1}) = 1.0$ if $(n_i, n_{i+1}) \in E_{u,u}$ and otherwise, $p(n_i, n_{i+1})$ denotes the *formation probability* of link (n_i, n_{i+1}) to be introduced in Subsection 3.2.

Features extracted based on $\Phi = \{\Phi_1, \cdots, \Phi_6\}$ are named as the *intra-network social meta path* based social features (Φ_0 will be used in Subsection 3.1.4 only.)

3.1.3 Anchor Meta Path

When a network is very new, features extracted based on *intra-network social meta paths* can be very sparse, as there exist few connections in the network. Consider, for example, in Figure 2, we want to predict whether social link (A^1, B^1) in network G^1 will be formed or not. Merely based on the *intra-network social meta paths*, the feature vector of extracted for link (A^1, B^1) will be $\mathbf{0}$. However, we find that A^1 and B^1 can be correlated actually with various inter-network paths, e.g., $B^1 \to B^2 \to A^2 \to A^1$, $B^1 \to B^2 \to F^2 \to A^2 \to A^1$ and $B^1 \to B^2 \to E^2 \to A^2 \to A^1$.

By following this idea, we propose to transfer useful information from aligned networks with the following *anchor meta path* and the *inter-network social meta paths* to be introduced in Subsection 3.1.4.

Definition 12 (Anchor Meta Path): Let U^i, U^j be the user nodes of G^i and G^j respectively and $A^{i,j}$ be the anchor links between G^i and G^j. Meta path $\Upsilon = T_1 \xleftrightarrow{R_1} T_2$ is an *anchor meta path* between network G^i and G^j iff $T_1 = U^i$ and $T_2 = U^j$ and $R_1 = A^{i,j}$. The notation of *anchor meta*

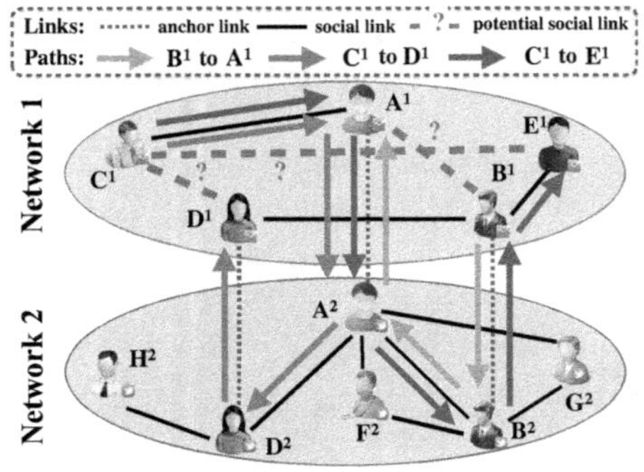

Figure 2: Meta Path across Aligned Networks.

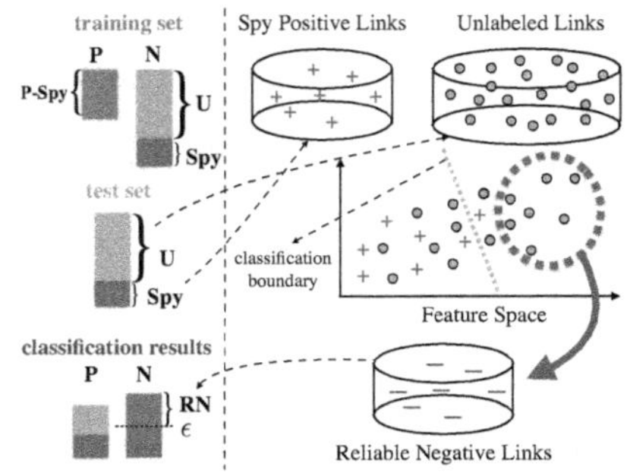

Figure 3: PU Link Prediction.

path from G^i to G^j is $\Upsilon(U^i, U^j)$ and the length of $\Upsilon(U^i, U^j)$ is 1.

3.1.4 Inter-Network Social Meta Paths

Based on the definition of *anchor meta path*, we can describe the inter-network paths from B^1 to A^1 in Figure 2 with the following *inter-network meta path*.

Definition 13 (Inter-Network Meta Path): Meta path $\Psi = T_1 \xrightarrow{R_1} T_2 \xrightarrow{R_2} \cdots \xrightarrow{R_{k-1}} T_k$ is an *inter-network meta path* across G^i and G^j iff $\exists m \in \{1, 2, \cdots, k-1\}$, $T_m \xleftrightarrow{R_m} T_{m+1} = \Upsilon(U^i, U^j)$.

In this paper, we are concerned about *inter-network meta path* starting and ending with users, which are named as the *inter-network social meta path*. The 4 specific *inter-network social meta paths* used in this paper include:

Category 1: $\Upsilon(U^i, U^j) \circ (\Phi(U^j, U^j) \cup \Phi_0(U^j, U^j)) \circ \Upsilon(U^j, U^i)$, whose notation is $\Psi_1(U^i, U^i)$;

Category 2.: $(\Phi(U^i, U^i) \cup \Phi_0(U^i, U^i)) \circ \Upsilon(U^i, U^j) \circ (\Phi(U^j, U^j) \cup \Phi_0(U^j, U^j)) \circ \Upsilon(U^j, U^i)$, whose notation is $\Psi_2(U^i, U^i)$;

Category 3.: $\Upsilon(U^i, U^j) \circ (\Phi(U^j, U^j) \cup \Phi_0(U^j, U^j)) \circ \Upsilon(U^j, U^i) \circ (\Phi(U^i, U^i) \cup \Phi_0(U^i, U^i))$, whose notation is $\Psi_3(U^i, U^i)$;

Category 4.: $(\Phi(U^i, U^i) \cup \Phi_0(U^i, U^i)) \circ \Upsilon(U^i, U^j) \circ (\Phi(U^j, U^j) \cup \Phi_0(U^j, U^j)) \circ \Upsilon(U^j, U^i) \circ (\Phi(U^i, U^i) \cup \Phi_0(U^i, U^i))$, whose notation is $\Psi_4(U^i, U^i)$;

where $\Phi(U^i, U^i) \cup \Phi_0(U^i, U^i) = \{\Phi_0(U^i, U^i), \cdots, \Phi_6(U^i, U^i)\}$ denote the 7 *intra-network social meta paths* of network G^i introduced in Subsection 3.1.1.

Let $\Psi = \{\Psi_1, \Psi_2, \Psi_3, \Psi_4\}$. Ψ is a comprehensive *inter-network social meta path* set and features extracted based on Ψ can transfer information for both anchor users and non-anchor users from other aligned networks. For example, in Figure 2, by following path "$B^1 \to B^2 \to A^2 \to A^1$", we can go from *anchor user* B^1 to *anchor user* A^1 and such path is an instance of $\Psi_1(U^1, U^1)$; by following path $C^1 \to A^1 \to A^2 \to D^2 \to D^1$, we can go from *non-anchor user* C^1 to *anchor user* D^1, which is an instance of $\Psi_2(U^1, U^1)$; in addition, by following path $C^1 \to A^1 \to A^2 \to B^2 \to B^1 \to E^1$, we can go from *non-anchor user* C^1 to *non-anchor user* E^1, which is an instance of $\Psi_4(U^1, U^1)$.

3.1.5 Social Meta Path Selection

As introduced in Section 1, information transferred from aligned networks is helpful for improving link prediction performance in a given network but can be misleading as well, which is called the *network difference problem*. To solve the *network difference problem*, we propose to rank and select top K features from the feature vector extracted based on the *intra-network* and *inter-network social meta paths*, $[\mathbf{x}_\Phi^T, \mathbf{x}_\Psi^T]^T$, from the multiple *partially aligned heterogeneous networks*.

Let variable $X_i \in [\mathbf{x}_\Phi^T, \mathbf{x}_\Psi^T]^T$ be a feature extracted based on a meta path in $\{\Phi, \Psi\}$ and variable Y be the *label*. $P(Y = y)$ denotes the *prior probability* that links in the training set having label y and $P(X_i = x)$ represents the *frequency* that feature X_i has value x. Information theory related measure *mutual information* (mi) is used as the ranking criteria:

$$mi(X_i) = \sum_x \sum_y P(X_i = x, Y = y) \log \frac{P(X_i = x, Y = y)}{P(X_i = x) P(Y = y)}$$

Let $[\bar{\mathbf{x}}_\Phi^T, \bar{\mathbf{x}}_\Psi^T]^T$ be the features of the top K *mi* score selected from $[\mathbf{x}_\Phi^T, \mathbf{x}_\Psi^T]^T$. In the next subsection, we will use the selected feature vector $[\bar{\mathbf{x}}_\Phi^T, \bar{\mathbf{x}}_\Psi^T]^T$ to build a novel PU link prediction model.

3.2 PU Link Prediction

In this subsection, we will propose a method to solve the *PU link prediction* problem in one single network.

As introduced in Section 2, from a given network, e.g., G, we can get two disjoint sets of links: connected (i.e., formed) links $\mathcal{P}$ and unconnected links $\mathcal{U}$. To differentiate these links, we define a new concept "*connection state*", z, in this paper to show whether a link is connected (i.e., formed) or unconnected in network G. For a given link l, if l is connected in the network, then $z(l) = +1$; otherwise, $z(l) = -1$. As a result, we can have the "*connection states*" of links in $\mathcal{P}$ and $\mathcal{U}$ to be: $z(\mathcal{P}) = \mathbf{+1}$ and $z(\mathcal{U}) = \mathbf{-1}$.

Besides the "*connection state*", links in the network can also have their own "*labels*", y, which can represent whether a link is to be formed or will never be formed in the network. For a given link l, if l has been formed or to be formed, then $y(l) = +1$; otherwise, $y(l) = -1$. Similarly, we can have the "*labels*" of links in $\mathcal{P}$ and $\mathcal{U}$ to be: $y(\mathcal{P}) = \mathbf{+1}$ but $y(\mathcal{U})$ can be either $+1$ or -1, as $\mathcal{U}$ can contain both links to be formed and links that will never be formed.

By using $\mathcal{P}$ and $\mathcal{U}$ as the positive and negative training sets, we can build a *link connection prediction model* $\mathcal{M}_c$, which can be applied to predict whether a link exists in the original network, i.e., the *connection state* of a link. Let l be a link to be predicted, by applying $\mathcal{M}_c$ to classify l, we can get the *connection probability* of l to be:

Definition 14: (Connection Probability): The probability that link l's *connection states* is predicted to be *connected* (i.e., $z(l) = +1$) is formally defined as the *connection probability* of link l: $p(z(l) = +1 | \mathbf{x}(l))$, where $\mathbf{x}(l) = [\bar{\mathbf{x}}_\Phi(l)^T, \bar{\mathbf{x}}_\Psi(l)^T]^T$.

Meanwhile, if we can obtain a set of links that "will never be formed", i.e., "-1" links, from the network, which together with $\mathcal{P}$ ("+1" links) can be used to build a *link formation prediction model*, $\mathcal{M}_f$, which can be used to get the *formation probability* of l to be:

Definition 15: (Formation Probability): The probability that link l's *label* is predicted to be *formed or will be formed* (i.e., $y(l) = +1$) is formally defined as the *formation probability* of link l: $p(y(l) = +1|\mathbf{x}(l))$.

However, from the network, we have no information about "links that will never be formed" (i.e., "-1" links). As a result, the *formation probabilities* of potential links that we aim to obtain as proposed in Section 2 can be very challenging to calculate. Meanwhile, the correlation between link l's *connection probability* and *formation probability* has been proved in existing works [5] to be:

$$p(y(l) = +1|\mathbf{x}(l)) \propto p(z(l) = +1|\mathbf{x}(l)).$$

In other words, for links whose *connection probabilities* are low, their *formation probabilities* will be relatively low as well. This rule can be utilized to extract links which can be more likely to be the reliable "-1" links from the network. We propose to apply the the *link connection prediction model* $\mathcal{M}_c$ built with $\mathcal{P}$ and $\mathcal{U}$ to classify links in $\mathcal{U}$ to extract the *reliable negative link set*.

Definition 16: (Reliable Negative Link Set): The *reliable negative links* in the *unconnected link* set $\mathcal{U}$ are those whose *connection probabilities* predicted by the *link connection prediction model*, $\mathcal{M}_c$, are lower than threshold $\epsilon \in [0, 1]$:

$$\mathcal{RN} = \{l | l \in \mathcal{U}, p(z(l) = +1|\mathbf{x}(l)) < \epsilon\}.$$

Some Heuristic methods have been proposed to set the optimal threshold ϵ, e.g., the *spy technique* proposed in [13]. As shown in Figure 3, we randomly selected a subset of links in $\mathcal{P}$ as the spy, $\mathcal{SP}$, whose proportion is controlled by $s\%$. $s\% = 15\%$ is used as the default sample rate in this paper. Sets $(\mathcal{P} - \mathcal{SP})$ and $(\mathcal{U} \cup \mathcal{SP})$ are used as positive and negative training sets to the *spy prediction* model, $\mathcal{M}_s$. By applying $\mathcal{M}_s$ to classify links in $(\mathcal{U} \cup \mathcal{SP})$, we can get their *connection probabilities* to be:

$$p(z(l) = +1|\mathbf{x}(l)), l \in (\mathcal{U} \cup \mathcal{SP}),$$

and parameter ϵ is set as the minimal *connection probability* of spy links in $\mathcal{SP}$:

$$\epsilon = \min_{l \in \mathcal{SP}} p(z(l) = +1|\mathbf{x}(l)).$$

With the extracted *reliable negative link set* $\mathcal{RN}$, we can solve the *PU link prediction* problem with *classification based link prediction methods*, where $\mathcal{P}$ and $\mathcal{RN}$ are used as the positive and negative training sets respectively. Meanwhile, when applying the built model to predict links in $\mathcal{L}^i$, the optimal labels, $\hat{\mathcal{Y}}^i$, of $\mathcal{L}^i$, should be those which can maximize the following *formation probabilities*:

$$\begin{aligned}\hat{\mathcal{Y}}^i &= \arg\max_{\mathcal{Y}^i} p(y(\mathcal{L}^i) = \mathcal{Y}^i|G^1, G^2, \cdots, G^k) \\ &= \arg\max_{\mathcal{Y}^i} p(y(\mathcal{L}^i) = \mathcal{Y}^i| \left[\bar{\mathbf{x}}_\Phi(\mathcal{L}^i)^T, \bar{\mathbf{x}}_\Psi(\mathcal{L}^i)^T\right]^T)\end{aligned}$$

where $y(\mathcal{L}^i) = \mathcal{Y}^i$ represents that links in $\mathcal{L}^i$ have labels $\mathcal{Y}^i$.

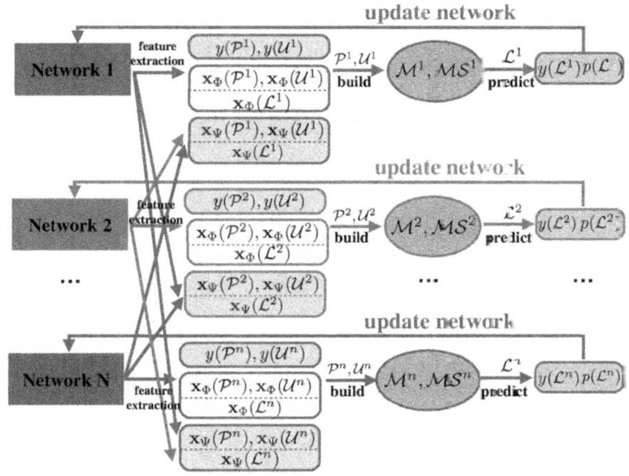

Figure 4: Multi-PU Link Prediction Framework.

3.3 Multi-Network Link Prediction Framework

Method MLI proposed in this paper is a general link prediction framework and can be applied to predict social links in n *partially aligned networks* simultaneously. When it comes to n partially aligned network formulated in Section 2, the optimal labels of potential links $\{\mathcal{L}^1, \mathcal{L}^2, \cdots, \mathcal{L}^n\}$ of networks $G^1, G^2, \cdots, G^n$ will be:

$$\begin{aligned}\hat{\mathcal{Y}}^1, \hat{\mathcal{Y}}^2, \cdots, \hat{\mathcal{Y}}^n = \arg\max_{\mathcal{Y}^1, \mathcal{Y}^2, \cdots, \mathcal{Y}^n} p(y(\mathcal{L}^1) = \mathcal{Y}^1, y(\mathcal{L}^2) = \mathcal{Y}^2, \\ \cdots, y(\mathcal{L}^n) = \mathcal{Y}^k|G^1, G^2, \cdots, G^n)\end{aligned}$$

The above target function is very complex to solve and, in this paper, we propose to obtain the solution by updating one variable, e.g., $\mathcal{Y}^1$, and fix other variables, e.g., $\mathcal{Y}^2, \cdots, \mathcal{Y}^n$, alternatively with the following equation [26]:

$$\begin{cases} (\hat{\mathcal{Y}}^1)^{(\tau)} & = \arg\max_{\mathcal{Y}^1} p(y(\mathcal{L}^1) = \mathcal{Y}^1|G^1, G^2, \cdots, G^n, \\ & \quad (\hat{\mathcal{Y}}^2)^{(\tau-1)}, (\hat{\mathcal{Y}}^3)^{(\tau-1)}, \cdots, (\hat{\mathcal{Y}}^n)^{(\tau-1)}) \\ (\hat{\mathcal{Y}}^2)^{(\tau)} & = \arg\max_{\mathcal{Y}^2} p(y(\mathcal{L}^2) = \mathcal{Y}^2|G^1, G^2, \cdots, G^n, \\ & \quad (\hat{\mathcal{Y}}^1)^{(\tau)}, (\hat{\mathcal{Y}}^3)^{(\tau-1)}, \cdots, (\hat{\mathcal{Y}}^n)^{(\tau-1)}) \\ \cdots\cdots & \\ (\hat{\mathcal{Y}}^n)^{(\tau)} & = \arg\max_{\mathcal{Y}^n} p(y(\mathcal{L}^n) = \mathcal{Y}^n|G^1, G^2, \cdots, G^n, \\ & \quad (\hat{\mathcal{Y}}^1)^{(\tau)}, (\hat{\mathcal{Y}}^2)^{(\tau)}, \cdots, (\hat{\mathcal{Y}}^{(n-1)})^{(\tau)}) \end{cases}$$

The structure of framework MLI is shown in Figure 4. When predicting social links in network G^i, we can extract features based on the *intra-network social meta path*, $\mathbf{x}_\Phi$, extracted from G^i and those extracted based on the *inter-network social meta path*, $\mathbf{x}_\Psi$, across G^1, G^2, $\cdots$, G^{i-1}, G^{i+1}, $\cdots$, G^n for links in $\mathcal{P}^i$, $\mathcal{U}^i$ and $\mathcal{L}^i$. Feature vectors $\mathbf{x}_\Phi(\mathcal{P})$, $\mathbf{x}_\Phi(\mathcal{U})$ and $\mathbf{x}_\Psi(\mathcal{P})$, $\mathbf{x}_\Psi(\mathcal{U})$ as well as the labels, $y(\mathcal{P})$, $y(\mathcal{U})$, of links in $\mathcal{P}$ and $\mathcal{U}$ are passed to the PU link prediction model $\mathcal{M}^i$ and the meta path selection model $\mathcal{MS}^i$. The formation probabilities of links in $\mathcal{L}^i$ predicted by model $\mathcal{M}^i$ will be used to update the network by replace the weights of $\mathcal{L}^i$ with the newly predicted formation probabilities. The initial weights of these potential links in $\mathcal{L}^i$ are set as 0 (i.e., the *formation probability* of links mentioned in Definition 11). After finishing these steps on G^i, we will move to conduct similar operations on G^{i+1}. We iteratively predict links in G^1 to G^n alternatively in a sequence until the results in all of these networks converge.

Table 2: **Properties of the Heterogeneous Networks**

	property	network Twitter	Foursquare
# node	user	5,223	5,392
	tweet/tip	9,490,707	48,756
	location	297,182	38,921
# link	friend/follow	164,920	76,972
	write	9,490,707	48,756
	locate	615,515	48,756

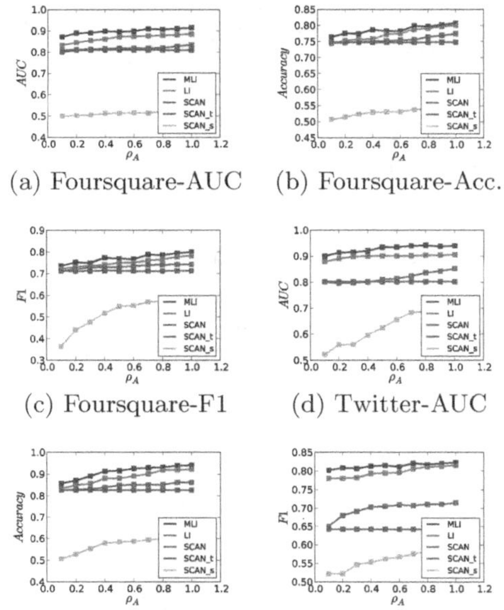

(a) Foursquare-AUC (b) Foursquare-Acc.

(c) Foursquare-F1 (d) Twitter-AUC

(e) Twitter-Acc. (f) Twitter-F1

Figure 5: Effects of anchor link ratio ρ_A on prediction results in different networks evaluated by different metrics.

4. EXPERIMENTS

To demonstrate the effectiveness of MLI in dealing with real-world multiple *partially aligned heterogeneous networks*, we will conduct extensive experiments in this section. This section includes 3 parts: (1) dataset description; (2) experiment setting; (3) experiment results.

4.1 Datasets

The datasets used in this paper are Foursquare and Twitter, both of which are famous heterogeneous online social networks. These two networks were crawled during November of 2012 [10, 25, 26]. The structures of both Foursquare and Twitter have been introduced in Section 2. Statistical information about these two datasets is available in Table 2:

- **Foursquare**: 5,392 users, 48,756 tips and 38,921 locations are crawled from Foursquare. The social links among the crawled users is 76,972 and each user has about 14 friends in Foursquare.
- **Twitter**: 5,223 users together with their tweets are crawled from Twitter, whose number is 9,490,707. Among these 5,223 users, there exist 164,920 follow links. Among all these tweets, about 615,515 have location checkins, accounting for about 6.48% of all the tweets.

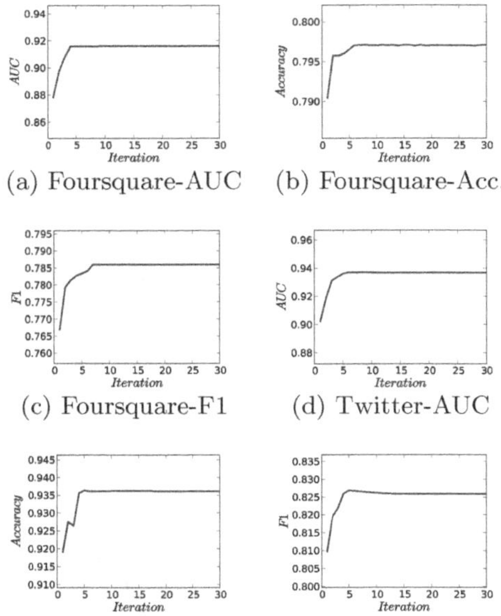

(a) Foursquare-AUC (b) Foursquare-Acc.

(c) Foursquare-F1 (d) Twitter-AUC

(e) Twitter-Acc. (f) Twitter-F1

Figure 6: Convergence analysis in different networks under the evaluation of different metrics.

4.2 Experiment Setting

4.2.1 Comparison Methods

To show the advantages of MLI, we compare MLI with many other baseline methods, which include:

- MLI: Method MLI is the multi-network link prediction framework proposed in this paper, which can predict social links in multiple online social networks simultaneously. The features used by MLI are extracted based on the meta paths selected from Φ and Ψ across aligned networks.
- LI: Method LI (Link Identifier) is identical to MLI except that LI predict the formation of social links in each network independently.
- SCAN: Method SCAN (Cross Aligned Network link prediction) proposed in [25, 26] is similar to MLI except that (1) SCAN predicts social links in each network independently; (2) features used by SCAN are those extracted based on meta paths Φ and Ψ_1 without meta path selection.
- SCAN-S: Method SCAN-S (SCAN with Source Network) proposed in [25, 26] is identical to SCAN except that the features used by SCAN-S are those extracted based on Ψ_1 without meta path selection.
- SCAN-T: Method SCAN-T (SCAN with Target Network) proposed in [25, 26]) is identical to SCAN except that the features used by SCAN-S are those extracted based on Φ without meta path selection.

4.2.2 Evaluation Metrics

The social links in both Foursquare and Twitter are used as the ground truth to evaluate the prediction results. SVM

Table 3: Performance comparison of different methods for inferring social and location links for Foursquare of different remaining information rates. The anchor link sample rate ρ_A is set as 1.0.

network	measure	methods	0.1	0.2	0.3	0.4	0.5	0.6	0.7	0.8
			Remaining information rates ρ_F of Foursquare.							
Foursquare	AUC	MLI	**0.677±0.023**	**0.776±0.011**	**0.844±0.008**	**0.887±0.005**	**0.906±0.003**	**0.912±0.005**	**0.912±0.003**	**0.916±0.004**
		LI	0.573±0.019	0.68±0.023	0.806±0.01	0.853±0.004	0.866±0.003	0.874±0.007	0.881±0.003	0.878±0.005
		SCAN	0.549±0.009	0.56±0.009	0.662±0.03	0.745±0.009	0.786±0.014	0.804±0.01	0.812±0.005	0.82±0.004
		SCANT	0.5±0.083	0.503±0.007	0.613±0.012	0.739±0.008	0.764±0.013	0.787±0.007	0.8±0.006	0.81±0.007
		SCANS	0.524±0.013	0.524±0.017	0.524±0.012	0.524±0.005	0.524±0.002	0.524±0.01	0.524±0.003	0.524±0.005
	Accuracy	MLI	**0.632±0.01**	**0.692±0.007**	**0.755±0.005**	**0.769±0.004**	**0.779±0.002**	**0.798±0.006**	**0.799±0.004**	**0.797±0.005**
		LI	0.568±0.013	0.624±0.053	0.699±0.004	0.722±0.006	0.761±0.01	0.782±0.01	0.789±0.005	0.791±0.006
		SCAN	0.558±0.007	0.6±0.006	0.683±0.071	0.714±0.009	0.721±0.007	0.736±0.007	0.75±0.008	0.765±0.009
		SCANT	0.491±0.019	0.568±0.004	0.65±0.008	0.685±0.007	0.714±0.007	0.727±0.009	0.736±0.012	0.747±0.003
		SCANS	0.548±0.011	0.548±0.055	0.548±0.007	0.548±0.008	0.548±0.007	0.548±0.01	0.548±0.003	0.548±0.006
	F1	MLI	**0.644±0.01**	**0.695±0.022**	**0.722±0.013**	**0.742±0.005**	**0.761±0.005**	**0.789±0.006**	**0.788±0.00[illegible]**	**0.786±0.006**
		LI	0.63±0.017	0.635±0.015	0.66±0.007	0.684±0.01	0.715±0.016	0.753±0.014	0.764±0.007	0.766±0.009
		SCAN	0.6±0.02	0.609±0.006	0.614±0.031	0.632±0.018	0.645±0.018	0.676±0.016	0.70[illegible]±0.01	0.726±0.013
		SCANT	0.534±0.196	0.559±0.004	0.565±0.016	0.584±0.011	0.645±0.011	0.674±0.016	0.696±0.019	0.712±0.01
		SCANS	0.56±0.016	0.56±0.041	0.56±0.015	0.56±0.015	0.56±0.013	0.56±0.013	0.56±0.005	0.56±0.01
Twitter	AUC	MLI	**0.884±0.004**	**0.891±0.003**	**0.915±0.003**	**0.917±0.003**	**0.923±0.002**	**0.929±0.003**	**0.927±0.003**	**0.937±0.003**
		LI	0.841±0.003	0.847±0.002	0.852±0.003	0.862±0.002	0.873±0.002	0.884±0.003	0.894±0.003	0.904±0.003
		SCAN	0.801±0.003	0.814±0.002	0.819±0.003	0.817±0.002	0.819±0.002	0.823±0.003	0.831±0.002	0.837±0.003
		SCANT	0.802±0.002	0.802±0.002	0.802±0.002	0.802±0.002	0.802±0.002	0.802±0.002	0.802±0.002	0.802±0.002
		SCANS	0.508±0.002	0.543±0.002	0.584±0.003	0.531±0.001	0.653±0.002	0.666±0.003	0.673±0.003	0.686±0.003
	Accuracy	MLI	**0.92±0.003**	**0.927±0.002**	**0.927±0.003**	**0.929±0.004**	**0.93±0.003**	**0.932±0.003**	**0.936±0.003**	**0.936±0.004**
		LI	0.899±0.004	0.904±0.004	0.908±0.004	0.913±0.002	0.916±0.003	0.918±0.003	0.918±0.003	0.92±0.004
		SCAN	0.831±0.005	0.835±0.003	0.837±0.006	0.842±0.001	0.844±0.002	0.848±0.004	0.848±0.002	0.849±0.004
		SCANT	0.827±0.003	0.827±0.003	0.827±0.003	0.827±0.003	0.827±0.003	0.827±0.003	0.827±0.003	0.827±0.003
		SCANS	0.568±0.004	0.577±0.003	0.585±0.002	0.587±0.002	0.591±0.003	0.594±0.003	0.596±0.003	0.598±0.004
	F1	MLI	**0.804±0.002**	**0.808±0.002**	**0.809±0.003**	**0.811±0.003**	**0.812±0.003**	**0.818±0.003**	**0.826±0.003**	**0.826±0.004**
		LI	0.776±0.005	0.785±0.005	0.792±0.005	0.8±0.003	0.804±0.003	0.808±0.003	0.809±0.003	0.811±0.004
		SCAN	0.682±0.006	0.686±0.004	0.69±0.006	0.699±0.001	0.703±0.003	0.707±0.004	0.709±0.002	0.711±0.005
		SCANT	0.683±0.003	0.683±0.003	0.683±0.003	0.683±0.003	0.683±0.003	0.683±0.003	0.683±0.003	0.683±0.003
		SCANS	0.53±0.006	0.546±0.006	0.559±0.004	0.564±0.004	0.571±0.004	0.575±0.004	0.581±0.004	0.583±0.005

[2] with linear kernel and optimal parameters is used as the base classifier of all comparison methods. *Accuracy*, *AUC* and *F1* score are used as the evaluation metrics in this paper.

4.2.3 Experiment Setups

All the existing links in Foursquare are used as the positive link set and a proportion of unconnected links among users except the positive links are sampled as the negative link set, which is of the same size as the positive link set. Both the positive and negative link sets are divided into 5 folds: 4 folds as the training set and 1 fold as the test set. To represent different degrees of newness (available information users have in the networks), a fraction of information, which include posts, location checkins, temporal records, is randomly sampled from Foursquare as the available information under the control of parameter $\rho^F \in [0, 1]$ and the remaining information are deleted. Meanwhile, ρ^F proportion of the positive links are randomly sampled as the final positive link set and the remaining $(1 - \rho^F)$ proportion of positive links are mixed with the negative links to form the final unlabeled link set: $\mathcal{U}^F$. A subset of links in $\mathcal{U}^F$ are extracted as the reliable negative link set, $\mathcal{RN}^F$, with the spy technique. In a similar way, we can obtain the positive and reliable negative links in Twitter to be $\mathcal{P}^T$ and $\mathcal{RN}^T$, controlled by the sampling parameter $\rho^T \in [0, 1]$.

Supervised models, $\mathcal{M}^F$, built with $\mathcal{P}^F$ and $\mathcal{RN}^F$, are applied to classify links in the test set, $\mathcal{L}^F$. Depending on the specific methods, features used to build the models can be different and *social meta path* selection model $\mathcal{MS}^F$ is applied to select the most useful *social meta path* based features (K is set as 7 in the experiment) to build model $\mathcal{M}^F$. The predicted formation probabilities of links in $\mathcal{L}^F$ will be used to update their link weights in Foursquare. Based on the updated aligned networks, supervised models, $\mathcal{M}^T$, built with $\mathcal{P}^T$ and $\mathcal{RN}^T$, will be applied to classify links in the test set, $\mathcal{L}^T$, in which *social meta path* selection model $\mathcal{MS}^T$ is applied as well. And the predicted formation probabilities of links in $\mathcal{L}^T$ will also used to update their weights in Twitter. Only the weights of potential social links in $\mathcal{L}^F$ and $\mathcal{L}^T$ will be updated in each iteration and this process continues until the predicted formation probabilities of links in $\mathcal{L}^T$ and $\mathcal{L}^F$ converge.

4.3 Experiment Results

To denote different degrees of network newness in Table 3, we fix ρ^T as 0.8 but changes ρ^F within $\{0.1, 0.2, \cdots, 0.8\}$. Table 3 has two parts: the upper part is the link prediction results in Foursquare and the lower part is that in Twitter, as MLI is an integrated PU link prediction framework. The link prediction results in each part are evaluated by different metrics: *AUC*, *Accuracy* and *F1*. As shown in Table 3, MLI can outperform all other comparison methods consistently for $\rho^F \in \{0.1, 0.2, \cdots, 0.8\}$ in both Foursquare network and Twitter network. For example, in Foursquare when $\rho^F = 0.5$, the *AUC* achieved by MLI is about 5% better than LI, 15% better than SCAN, 19% better than SCAN-T and 73% better than SCAN-S; the *Accuracy* achieved by MLI is about 2.3% better than LI, 8% better than SCAN, 9.1% higher than SCAN-T and over 40% higher than SCAN-S the *F1* of MLI is 6.4% higher than LI, 18% higher than SCAN and SCAN-T and 36% higher than SCAN-S. When $\rho^F = 0.5$, the link prediction results of MLI in Twitter are also much better than all other baseline methods. For instances, in Twitter the *AUC* of MLI is 0.923 ± 0.002, which is about 6% better than LI, over 13% better than SCAN, SCAN-T and over 40% better than SCAN-S. Similar results can be obtained when evaluated by *Accuracy* and *F1*.

In Table 4, we fix $\rho^F = 0.8$ but change ρ^T with values in

Table 4: **Performance comparison of different methods for inferring social and location links for Foursquare of different remaining information rates. The anchor link sample rate ρ_A is set as 1.0.**

network	measure	methods	Remaining information rates ρ_T of Twitter 0.1	0.2	0.3	0.4	0.5	0.6	0.7	0.8
Foursquare	AUC	MLI	**0.862±0.003**	**0.867±0.004**	**0.87±0.003**	**0.873±0.005**	**0.885±0.003**	**0.891±0.003**	**0.895±0.004**	**0.916±0.004**
		LI	0.831±0.005	0.834±0.004	0.846±0.004	0.853±0.005	0.855±0.005	0.867±0.004	0.868±0.005	0.87±0.005
		SCAN	0.81±0.007	0.81±0.008	0.812±0.005	0.817±0.007	0.816±0.01	0.815±0.007	0.822±0.006	0.82±0.004
		SCANT	0.81±0.007	0.81±0.007	0.81±0.007	0.81±0.007	0.809±0.007	0.809±0.007	0.81±0.007	0.81±0.007
		SCANS	0.504±0.007	0.51±0.003	0.511±0.005	0.516±0.005	0.522±0.004	0.53±0.005	0.53±0.004	0.53±0.005
	Accuracy	MLI	**0.78±0.003**	**0.786±0.005**	**0.789±0.004**	**0.794±0.005**	**0.793±0.004**	**0.789±0.004**	**0.796±0.005**	**0.797±0.005**
		LI	0.745±0.011	0.762±0.005	0.768±0.007	0.772±0.007	0.777±0.008	0.783±0.008	0.789±0.006	0.791±0.006
		SCAN	0.749±0.007	0.754±0.006	0.754±0.007	0.757±0.006	0.758±0.007	0.761±0.008	0.763±0.009	0.765±0.009
		SCANT	0.748±0.003	0.748±0.003	0.747±0.003	0.748±0.003	0.748±0.003	0.748±0.003	0.748±0.003	0.747±0.003
		SCANS	0.692±0.011	0.717±0.008	0.725±0.008	0.746±0.008	0.741±0.006	0.746±0.004	0.75±0.007	0.758±0.006
	F1	MLI	**0.768±0.004**	**0.774±0.005**	**0.778±0.006**	**0.784±0.006**	**0.785±0.005**	**0.777±0.004**	**0.785±0.006**	**0.786±0.006**
		LI	0.721±0.02	0.734±0.01	0.734±0.012	0.736±0.012	0.744±0.012	0.755±0.011	0.764±0.01	0.766±0.009
		SCAN	0.717±0.01	0.718±0.007	0.714±0.009	0.715±0.009	0.718±0.011	0.72±0.012	0.721±0.013	0.726±0.013
		SCANT	0.713±0.01	0.712±0.01	0.712±0.01	0.713±0.01	0.713±0.01	0.712±0.01	0.713±0.01	0.712±0.01
		SCANS	0.509±0.02	0.514±0.014	0.524±0.014	0.529±0.013	0.54±0.009	0.542±0.007	0.559±0.012	0.559±0.01
Twitter	AUC	MLI	**0.837±0.004**	**0.858±0.004**	**0.905±0.005**	**0.926±0.003**	**0.924±0.002**	**0.932±0.003**	**0.934±0.002**	**0.937±0.003**
		LI	0.772±0.009	0.829±0.008	0.871±0.009	0.887±0.002	0.887±0.002	0.897±0.003	0.899±0.003	0.904±0.003
		SCAN	0.706±0.008	0.771±0.012	0.799±0.009	0.817±0.002	0.819±0.002	0.829±0.003	0.83±0.003	0.834±0.003
		SCANT	0.555±0.133	0.678±0.006	0.753±0.044	0.754±0.019	0.764±0.014	0.781±0.004	0.794±0.003	0.802±0.002
		SCANS	0.687±0.008	0.687±0.002	0.687±0.005	0.687±0.002	0.687±0.002	0.687±0.004	0.687±0.003	0.687±0.003
	Accuracy	MLI	**0.821±0.005**	**0.864±0.001**	**0.892±0.008**	**0.914±0.004**	**0.925±0.002**	**0.926±0.004**	**0.936±0.002**	**0.936±0.004**
		LI	0.706±0.002	0.834±0.011	0.877±0.003	0.898±0.005	0.912±0.001	0.92±0.004	0.924±0.002	0.92±0.004
		SCAN	0.594±0.006	0.716±0.009	0.781±0.005	0.801±0.003	0.823±0.002	0.831±0.004	0.842±0.002	0.849±0.004
		SCANT	0.547±0.062	0.645±0.038	0.723±0.048	0.786±0.004	0.8±0.002	0.815±0.005	0.824±0.002	0.827±0.003
		SCANS	0.59±0.009	0.59±0.007	0.59±0.004	0.59±0.004	0.59±0.002	0.59±0.004	0.59±0.003	0.59±0.004
	F1	MLI	**0.713±0.009**	**0.762±0.005**	**0.791±0.006**	**0.81±0.004**	**0.81±0.002**	**0.819±0.004**	**0.821±0.002**	**0.826±0.004**
		LI	0.651±0.006	0.671±0.023	0.749±0.014	0.779±0.007	0.801±0.003	0.813±0.005	0.818±0.003	0.811±0.004
		SCAN	0.6±0.017	0.633±0.023	0.657±0.013	0.684±0.004	0.703±0.004	0.714±0.005	0.716±0.002	0.711±0.005
		SCANT	0.552±0.113	0.574±0.016	0.604±0.031	0.618±0.003	0.63±0.001	0.641±0.004	0.67±0.002	0.686±0.003
		SCANS	0.575±0.025	0.575±0.016	0.575±0.005	0.575±0.006	0.575±0.004	0.575±0.004	0.575±0.003	0.575±0.005

$\{0.1, 0.2, \cdots, 0.8\}$. Similar to the results obtained in Table 3 where ρ_F varies, MLI can beat all other methods in both Twitter and Foursquare when the degree of newness of the Twitter network changes.

MLI can perform better than LI in both Foursquare and Twitter, which shows that predicting social links in multiple networks simultaneously in MLI framework can do enhance the results in both networks; the fact that LI can beat SCAN shows that features extracted based on cross network meta paths can do transfer useful information for both anchor and non-anchor users; SCAN works better than both SCAN-T and SCAN-S denotes that link prediction with information in two networks simultaneously is better than that with information in one single network.

4.4 Parameter Analysis

An important parameter that can affect the performance of all these methods is the rate of anchor links existing across networks. In this part, we will analyze the effects of the anchor link rate, $\rho_A \in [0, 1.0]$. To exclude other parameters' interference, we fix ρ^F and ρ^T as 0.8 but change ρ^A with values in $\{0.1, 0.2, \cdots, 1.0\}$ and study the link prediction results in both Foursquare and Twitter under the evaluation of *AUC*, *Accuracy* and *F1*. The results are shown in Figure 5.

As shown in Figure 5, where Figures 5(a)-5(c) are the link prediction results in Foursquare and the Figures 5(d)-5(f) are those in Twitter, almost all the methods can perform better as ρ^A increases, except SCAN-T as it only utilizes information in the target network only. It shows that with more anchor links, MLI, LI, SCAN and SCAN-S can transfer much more information from other aligned source networks to the target network to enhance the results. In addition, MLI can work better than LI consistently as ρ^A varies, which can show the effectiveness of MLI in dealing with networks with different ratios of anchor links

4.5 Convergence Analysis

MLI need to predict the links in all the aligned networks alternatively and iteratively until convergence. In this part, we will analyze whether MLI can converge as this process continues. We show the link prediction results achieved by MLI in both Foursquare and Twitter under the evaluation of *AUC*, *Accuracy* and *F1* when ρ^F, ρ^T and ρ^A are all set as 0.8 in Figure 6. Figures 6(a)-6(c) are the results in Foursquare network from iteration 1 to iteration 30 and Figures 6(d)-6(f) are those in Twitter network. As shown in these figures, results achieved by MLI can converge in less than 10 iterations in both Foursquare and Twitter evaluated by all these three metrics.

5. RELATED WORK

Link prediction in online social networks first proposed by D. Liben-Nowell *et al.* [12] has been a hot research topic in recent years and many different methods have been proposed. D. Liben-Nowell *et al.* [12] propose many unsupervised link predicators to predict the social connections among users. M. Hasan *et al.* [8] propose to predict links by using supervised learning methods. An extensive survey of other link prediction methods is available in [9, 7].

Meanwhile, some works have also been done on predicting multiple kinds of links simultaneously. I. Konstas *et al.* [11] propose to recommend multiple kinds of links with collaborative filtering methods. F. Fouss *et al.* [6] propose to use a traditional model, random walk, to predict multiple kinds of links simultaneously in networks. M. Bilgic *et al.* [1] propose an approach to address two problems by interleaving object classification and link prediction in a collective algorithm. P. Domingos *et al.* [4] propose a unifying framework, Markov Logic, for collective classification problems in social networks.

PU learning techniques have been proposed for many years and have been widely used in many different areas. B. Liu *et al.* [13] propose many different settings to obtain the reliable negative instance set from unlabeled instances in text mining tasks. Y. Zhao *et al.* [28] propose to apply PU learning techniques to graph mining area.

Nowadays, the researchers' focus start shifting to study multiple aligned heterogeneous online social networks simultaneously. X. Kong *et al.* [10] are the first to propose the concept of "multiple aligned heterogeneous social networks" and "anchor links" . They propose a two-phase method to predict the anchor links across networks. J. Zhang *et al.* [25] propose to transfer useful information across aligned networks to help predict social links for new users and they are the first to study social link prediction across aligned networks. J. Zhang *et al.* [26] propose to predict multiple kinds of links for new networks with information transferred across partially aligned networks and they are the first to study collective link prediction across partially aligned networks. J. Zhang *et al.* also gives a survey about link prediction problems and methods across social networks in [27].

6. CONCLUSION

In this paper, we have studied the *multi-network link prediction* problems across partially aligned networks. An effective general link prediction framework, MLI, has been proposed to solve the problem. Heterogeneous features can be extracted from the network based on both *intra-network* and *inter-network social meta paths*. Useful features are selected and transferred to aligned networks to enhance the prediction results mutually. Extensive experiments conducted on two real-world *aligned networks* demonstrate that MLI can work very well in predicting social links in multiple *partially aligned networks* simultaneously.

7. ACKNOWLEDGEMENT

This work is supported in part by NSF through grants CNS-1115234, DBI-0960443, and OISE-1129076, US Department of Army through grant W911NF-12-1-0066, and the Pinnacle Lab at Singapore Management University, NSFC (61333014, 61321491) and 111 Program (B14020).

8. REFERENCES

[1] M. Bilgic, G. Namata, and L. Getoor. Combining collective classification and link prediction. In *ICDMW*, 2007.

[2] C.-C. Chang and C.-J. Lin. *LIBSVM: a library for support vector machines*, 2001. Software available at http://www.csie.ntu.edu.tw/~cjlin/libsvm.

[3] E. Cho, S. Myers, and J. Leskovec. Friendship and mobility: user movement in location-based social networks. In *KDD*, 2011.

[4] P. Domingos and M. Richardson. Markov logic: A unifying framework for statistical relational learning. In *ICML Workshop*, 2004.

[5] C. Elkan and K. Noto. Learning classifiers from only positive and unlabeled data. In *KDD*, 2008.

[6] F. Fouss, A. Pirotte, J. Renders, and M. Saerens. Random-walk computation of similarities between nodes of a graph with application to collaborative recommendation. *TKDE*, 2007.

[7] L. Getoor and C. P. Diehl. Link mining: A survey. *SIGKDD Explorations Newsletter*, 7(2), 2005.

[8] M. Hasan, V. Chaoji, S. Salem, and M. Zaki. Link prediction using supervised learning. In *SDM*, 2006.

[9] M. Hasan and M. J. Zaki. A survey of link prediction in social networks. In Charu C. Aggarwal, editor, *Social Network Data Analytics*. 2011.

[10] X. Kong, J. Zhang, and P. Yu. Inferring anchor links across multiple heterogeneous social networks. In *CIKM*, 2013.

[11] I. Konstas, V. Stathopoulos, and J. M. Jose. On social networks and collaborative recommendation. In *SIGIR*, 2009.

[12] D. Liben-Nowell and J. Kleinberg. The link prediction problem for social networks. In *CIKM*, 2003.

[13] B. Liu, Y. Dai, X. Li, W. Lee, and P. Yu. Building text classifiers using positive and unlabeled examples. In *ICDM*, 2003.

[14] Z. Lu, B. Savas, W. Tang, and I. Dhillon. Supervised link prediction using multiple sources. In *ICDM*, 2010.

[15] S. Pan and Q. Yang. A survey on transfer learning. *TKDE*, 2010.

[16] S. Scellato, A. Noulas, and C. Mascolo. Exploiting place features in link prediction on location-based social networks. In *KDD*, 2011.

[17] Y. Sun, J. Han, X. Yan, P. Yu, and T. Wu. Pathsim: Meta path-based top-k similarity search in heterogeneous information networks. *PVLDB*, 2011.

[18] B. Tan, E. Xiang, Q. Yang, and E. Zhong. Multi-transfer: Transfer learning with multiple views and multiple sources. In *SDM*, 2013.

[19] J. Tang, T. Lou, and J. Kleinberg. Inferring social ties across heterogenous networks. In *WSDM*, 2012.

[20] D. Wang, D. Pedreschi, C. Song, F. Giannotti, and A. Barabasi. Human mobility, social ties, and link prediction. In *KDD*, 2011.

[21] K. Wilcox and A. T. Stephen. Are close friends the enemy? online social networks, self-esteem, and self-control. Journal of Consumer Research, 2012.

[22] Y. Yao, H. Tong, X. Yan, F. Xu, and J. Lu. Matri: a multi-aspect and transitive trust inference model. In *WWW*, 2013.

[23] J. Ye, H. Cheng, Z. Zhu, and M. Chen. Predicting positive and negative links in signed social networks by transfer learning. In *WWW*, 2013.

[24] M. Ye, P. Yin, and W. Lee. Location recommendation for location-based social networks. In *GIS*, 2010.

[25] J. Zhang, X. Kong, and P. Yu. Predicting social links for new users across aligned heterogeneous social networks. In *ICDM*, 2013.

[26] J. Zhang, X. Kong, and P. Yu. Transfer heterogeneous links across location-based social networks. In *WSDM*, 2014.

[27] J. Zhang and P. Yu. Link prediction across heterogeneous social networks: A survey. 2014.

[28] Y. Zhao, X. Kong, and P. Yu. Positive and unlabeled learning for graph classification. In *ICDM*, 2011.

Fast Influence-based Coarsening for Large Networks

Manish Purohit† manishp@cs.umd.edu

B. Aditya Prakash* badityap@cs.vt.edu

Chanhyun Kang† chanhyun@cs.umd.edu

Yao Zhang* yaozhang@cs.vt.edu

V. S. Subrahmanian† vs@cs.umd.edu

*Computer Science Department, Virginia Tech., USA
†Department of Computer Science, University of Maryland - College Park, USA

ABSTRACT

Given a social network, can we quickly 'zoom-out' of the graph? Is there a smaller equivalent representation of the graph that preserves its propagation characteristics? Can we group nodes together based on their influence properties? These are important problems with applications to influence analysis, epidemiology and viral marketing applications.

In this paper, we first formulate a novel Graph Coarsening Problem to find a succinct representation of any graph while preserving key characteristics for diffusion processes on that graph. We then provide a fast and effective near-linear-time (in nodes and edges) algorithm COARSENET for the same. Using extensive experiments on multiple real datasets, we demonstrate the quality and scalability of COARSENET, enabling us to reduce the graph by 90% in some cases without much loss of information. Finally we also show how our method can help in diverse applications like influence maximization and detecting patterns of propagation at the level of automatically created groups on real cascade data.

Categories and Subject Descriptors

H.2.8 [**Database Management**]: Database Applications—*Data Mining*

Keywords

Graph Mining; Propagation; Diffusion; Coarsening

1. INTRODUCTION

The unprecedented popularity of online social networking websites, such as Facebook, Google+, Flickr, and YouTube, has made it possible to analyze real social networks. Word of mouth marketing and viral marketing strategies have evolved to take advantage of this network structure by utilizing network effects. Similarly, understanding large-scale epidemiological datasets is important for designing effective propagation models and containment policies for public health. The sheer size of today's large social networks makes it challenging to perform sophisticated network analysis.

Given a propagation graph, possibly learnt from cascade analysis, is it possible to get a smaller nearly diffusion-equivalent representation for it? Getting a smaller equivalent graph will help multiple algorithmic and data mining tasks like influence maximization, immunization, understanding cascade data and data compression. In this paper, we study a novel graph coarsening problem with the aim of approximating a large social network by a much smaller graph that approximately preserves the network structure. Our primary goal is to find a compact representation of a large graph such that diffusion and propagation processes on the large graph can be studied by analyzing the smaller representation. Intuitively, most of the edges in a real network are relatively unimportant; hence we propose characterizing and "contracting" precisely such edges in a graph to obtain a coarse representation.

The main contributions of this paper are:

(a) *Problem Formulation:* We carefully formulate a novel *Graph Coarsening Problem* (GCP) to find a succinct representation of a given social network so that the diffusion characteristics of the network are mostly preserved.
(b) *Efficient Algorithms:* We develop COARSENET, an efficient (near-linear time) and effective algorithm for GCP, using careful approximations. We show that due to our novel scoring technique, the coarsened graph retains most of the diffusive properties of the original network.
(c) *Extensive Experiments:* We show that COARSENET is able to coarsen graphs *up to* 90% without much loss of key information. We also demonstrate the usefulness of our approach via a number of interesting applications. A major application we consider in this work is that of influence maximization in the Independent Cascade model. We propose a framework CSPIN that involves coarsening the graph and then solving influence maximization on the smaller graph to obtain high quality solutions. As the coarsened graph is much smaller than the original graph, the influence maximization algorithm runs orders of magnitude faster on the coarsened graph. Further using real cascade data from Flixster, we show how GCP can potentially help in understanding propagation data and constructing non-network surrogates for finding nodes with similar influence.

KDD'14, August 24–27, 2014, New York, NY, USA.
Copyright 2014 ACM 978-1-4503-2956-9/14/08 ...$15.00.
http://dx.doi.org/10.1145/2623330.2623701.

The rest of the paper is organized as follows: Section 2 gives related work and Section 3 briefly gives the notation and explains some technical preliminaries. Section 4 provides a formal definition of the Graph Coarsening Problem that we introduce, while Section 5 presents our approach and solution. In Section 6, we show how our coarsening framework can be applied to solve influence maximization on large networks. Finally, Section 7 gives experimental results while we conclude in Section 8.

2. RELATED WORK

The idea of coarsening a network for some task is not new, and has been used extensively in the popular community detection techniques (METIS [21] and GRACLUS [9]): nevertheless, they use different metrics for coarsening like cut-based, flow-based or heavy-edge matching-based conditions. In contrast we study diffusion-based metrics, and do not aim to find communities.

The related problem of graph sparsification has also been well studied in the theory community under the notion of "spanners" [10]. A spanner is a sparse subgraph that maintains the pairwise distances between all nodes within a multiplicative or additive factor. Fung et al. [12] study the cut-sparsifier problem which asks for a sparse weighted subgraph such that the weight of all cuts is maintained within a small multiplicative factor. Graph sparsification for influence analysis has emerged as a new tool for analyzing large networks. Mathioudakis et al. [28] propose an algorithm to find the sparse backbone of an influence network. The major difference is that graph sparsification *removes* edges (so the nodes stay the same), while we *coarsen* and *contract* node-pairs to reduce the graph. Another line of very recent work [30] tries to learn influence models at community-scale, using groups supplied by graph-partitioning algorithms like METIS. Our work is related in the sense that we also aim to 'group' nodes, but not based on link-based communities, instead automatically based on nodes' diffusion characteristics. In that sense we believe our work provides a complementary viewpoint: learn models directly at the node level, and then try to group them appropriately automatically.

The rest of the related work can be categorized into Epidemic Thresholds, Influence Maximization, Other Optimization problems, and General Information Diffusion.

Epidemic Thresholds. The classical texts on epidemic models and analysis are May and Anderson [1] and Hethcote [20]. Much research in virus propagation focuses on the so-called epidemic threshold, i.e. determining the conditions under which an epidemic will not break out. Widely-studied epidemiological models include *homogeneous models* [2, 29, 1] which assume that every individual has equal contact with others in the population. While earlier works [23, 31] focus on some specific types of graph structure (e.g., random graphs, power-law graphs, etc), Chakrabarti et al. [6] and Ganesh et al. [13] found that, for the flu-like SIS model, the epidemic threshold for any arbitrary graph depends on the leading eigenvalue of the adjacency matrix of the graph. Prakash et al. [32] further extended the result to a broad class of epidemic models.

Influence Maximization: The influence maximization problem was introduced by Domingos and Richardson [34]. Kempe et al. [22] formulated it as a combinatorial optimization problem under the Independent Cascade Model, proved it is NP-Hard and gave a simple $1 - 1/e$ approximation based on the submodularity of expected spread of a set of starting seeds. Numerous follow-up papers have looked at speeding-up the algorithm (e.g., [27, 16, 8, 24, 7]).

Other Optimization Problems. Another related problem is immunization, i.e, the problem of finding the best vertices for removal to stop an epidemic, with effective immunization strategies for static and dynamic graphs [19, 38, 4]. Other such problems where we wish to select a subset of '*important*' vertices on graphs, include 'outbreak detection' [27] and finding most-likely starting points ('culprits') of epidemics [26, 33].

General Information Diffusion. There is a lot of research interest in studying dynamic processes on large graphs, (a) blogs and propagations [18, 25, 22], (b) information cascades [3, 14, 17] and (c) marketing and product penetration [35]. These dynamic processes are all closely related to virus propagation. General algorithms for information diffusion based optimization include [36].

3. PRELIMINARIES

Table 1 gives some of the notation.

Table 1: Symbols

Symbol	Definition and Description
$\mathbf{A}, \mathbf{B}, \ldots$	matrices (bold upper case)
$\vec{a}, \vec{b}, \ldots$	column vectors
a_j or $a(j)$	j^{th} element of vector a
n	number of vertices in the graphs
m	number of edges in the graphs
α	the reduction factor
$\lambda_{\mathbf{G}}$	first eigenvalue (in absolute value) of adjacency matrix of graph $\mathbf{G}$
$\vec{u}_{\mathbf{G}}, \vec{v}_{\mathbf{G}}$	Right and left first eigenvectors (for $\lambda_{\mathbf{G}}$) of adjacency matrix $\mathbf{G}$
IC Model	The Independent Cascade Model
GCP	Graph Coarsening Problem (see Definition 4.3)
COARSENET	Our algorithm for GCP

IC Model. A social network is a directed, weighted graph $G = (V, E, w)$. Usually each vertex $v \in V$ represents an individual of the network and edges represent influence relationships between these individuals. The Independent Cascade (IC) model is a popular diffusion model used to model the way influence propagates along the edges of a social network. In this setting, a vertex $v \in V$ is called *active* if it has been influenced and *inactive* otherwise. Once an inactive vertex becomes active, it always stays active, i.e. we focus only on *progressive* models. Given a seed set $S \subset V$ of initially active vertices, the Independent Cascade model proceeds in discrete time steps as follows. At time step t, let S_t denote the set of vertices activated at time t. Every vertex $u \in S_t$ is given a *single* chance to activate each currently inactive neighbor v with probability of success $w(u, v)$ independently of all other interactions. If u succeeds, then v becomes active at time $t + 1$. This diffusion process continues until no more activations are possible. The *influence spread* of seed set S, denoted by $\sigma(S)$, is the expected number of activated vertices at the end of the process.

4. PROBLEM FORMULATION

Motivated by the fact that in any real network, *most* edges and vertices are not important (due to the heavily skewed degree distributions), we propose a graph coarsening problem which involves pruning away precisely such edges (and vertices). We aim to coarsen the graph to obtain a much smaller representation which retains the diffusive properties. We *coarsen* a graph by successively merging adjacent node pairs. We attempt to quickly find "good" edges which have little effect on the network's diffusive properties. At first glance, this seems impossible as the diffusive properties of a graph are highly dependent on the connectivity of the vertices and edge weights. Further, determining which node pairs to merge and analyzing the effect of merging two nodes on diffusion are non-trivial. Informally, we study the following problem in this paper:

DEFINITION 4.1 (INFORMAL PROBLEM).
INPUT: *Weighted graph* $G = (V, E, w)$ *and a target fraction* $0 < \alpha < 1$
GOAL: *Coarsen* G *by repeatedly merging adjacent node pairs to obtain a weighted graph* $H = (V', E', w')$ *such that*

- $|V'| = (1 - \alpha)|V|$
- *Graph* H *approximates graph* G *with respect to its diffusive properties*

Role of Eigenvalues. In order to address the informal problem described above, we need a tractable way to characterize the diffusive properties of a network. Recent work [32] shows that for almost any propagation model (including the IC model), important diffusion characteristics (in particular the so-called epidemic threshold) of a graph (after removing self loops) are captured by the spectrum of the graph, specifically, by the first eigenvalue of the adjacency matrix. Thus it is natural to believe that if the first eigenvalue of the coarsened graph H (its adjacency matrix) is close to that of the original graph G, then H indeed approximates G well. Although the work of [32] deals with undirected graphs, their findings are also applicable to strongly connected directed graphs.
Merging node pairs. To explicitly formulate the problem in Definition 4.1, we also need to define what happens when a node pair is merged (i.e. an edge is contracted) in a weighted graph. More precisely, after merging neighboring vertices a and b to form a new node c, we need to determine the *new* edge weights of all incoming and outgoing edges of c. In order to maintain the diffusive properties of the network, we need to reweight the new edges appropriately.

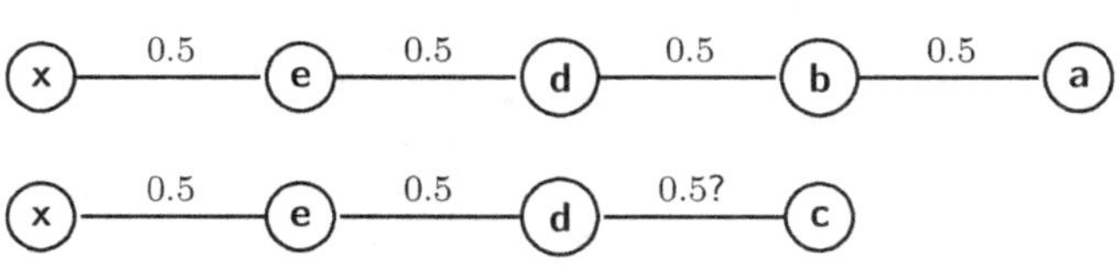

Figure 1: Why reweight?

To see why this is crucial, consider Figure 1. Assume that the IC model is being run. Suppose we need to pick the two best seeds (i.e. two nodes with the maximum influence spread as defined in the previous Section) from the top 5-vertex chain. Further assume that the graph is undirected and each edge has the same weight $\beta = 0.5$. Clearly, vertices b and e are the best. If we merge vertices $\{a, b\}$, we get the bottom 4-vertex chain. To still match the original solution, we correspondingly want $\{c, e\}$ to be the best seed-set in the new chain—but if edge $\{d, c\}$ remains the same weight, any of the pair of vertices $\{e, c\}$ or $\{x, d\}$ are the best seed sets in the 4-vertex chain. This motivates the need to reweight suitably so that new coarsened graph still retains the original characteristics.

The main insight is that if we select c as a seed, we are in-effect intending to choose only *one* of vertices a and b to be seeded (influenced); which suggests that the likelihood of d being influenced from c is *either* 0.5 or 0.25 (corresponding to when a or b is chosen respectively). Hence the weight of edge (c, d) should be modified to reflect this fact.

We propose the following solution: Suppose $e = (a, b)$ is contracted and a and b are merged together to form "supervertex" c (say). We reweight the edges adjacent to a and b while coarsening so that the edges now represent the average of the transmission probabilities via a or b. So in our example of Figure 1, edge $\{c, d\}$ would have weight 0.375 (average of 0.5 and 0.25). Further, we can verify that in this case $\{e, c\}$ will be the best seed-set, as desired.

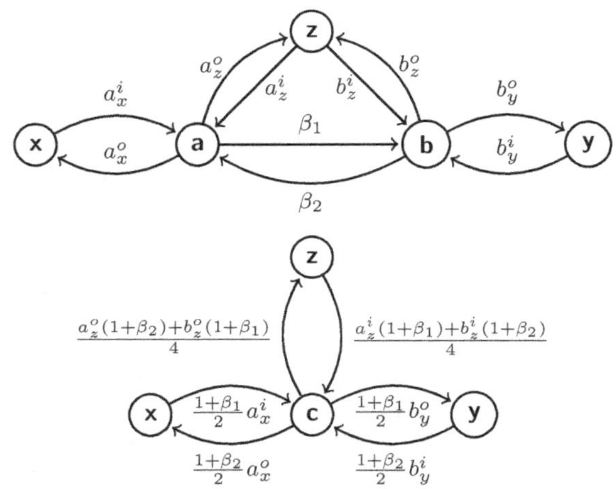

Figure 2: Reweighting of edges after merging node pairs

Extending the same principle, Figure 2 shows the general situation for any candidate node pair (a, b) and how a merge and re-weight (= contract) operation will look like. More formally, our contract operation is as follows:

DEFINITION 4.2 (MERGING NODE PAIRS). *Let* $Nb^i(v)$ *(respectively* $Nb^o(v)$*) denote the set of in-neighbors (resp. out-neighbors) of a vertex* v*. Let* $v_u^i = w(u, v)$ *and* $v_u^o = w(v, u)$ *denote the weight of the corresponding edges. If the node pair*(a, b) *is now contracted to a new vertex* c*, and* $w(a, b) = \beta_1$ *and* $w(b, a) = \beta_2$*, then the new edges are weighted as -*

$$c_t^i = \begin{cases} \dfrac{(1+\beta_1)a_t^i}{2} & \forall t \in Nb^i(a) \backslash Nb^i(b) \\ \dfrac{(1+\beta_2)b_t^i}{2} & \forall t \in Nb^i(b) \backslash Nb^i(a) \\ \dfrac{(1+\beta_1)(a_t^i)+(1+\beta_2)(b_t^i)}{4} & \forall t \in Nb^i(a) \cap Nb^i(b) \end{cases}$$

$$c_t^o = \begin{cases} \frac{(1+\beta_2)a_t^o}{2} & \forall t \in Nb^o(a)\backslash Nb^o(b) \\ \frac{(1+\beta_1)b_t^o}{2} & \forall t \in Nb^o(b)\backslash Nb^o(a) \\ \frac{(1+\beta_2)(a_t^o)+(1+\beta_1)(b_t^o)}{4} & \forall t \in Nb^o(a) \cap Nb^o(b) \end{cases}$$

Graph Coarsening Problem. We are now ready to state our problem formally. Motivated by the connections between the diffusive and spectral properties of a graph, we define the following Graph Coarsening Problem to find the set of node pairs which when merged (according to Definition 4.2) lead to the least change in the first eigenvalue. Further, since a vertex cannot influence itself, we assume without loss of generality that the graph G has no self loops.

DEFINITION 4.3 (GRAPH COARSENING PROBLEM). INPUT: *Directed, strongly connected, weighted graph $G = (V, E, w)$ without self loops and a target fraction $0 < \alpha < 1$* OUTPUT: $E^* = \arg\min_{E' \subset E, |E'|=\alpha|V|} |\lambda_G - \lambda_{G'}|$, *where G' is obtained from G by merging all node pairs in E'.*

A related problem is Edge Immunization [37] that asks for a set of edges whose *removal* leads to the *greatest drop* in the first eigenvalue. In contrast, GCP seeks to find a set of edges whose *contraction* (Definition 4.2) leads to the *least change* in the first eigenvalue. The Edge Immunization problem is known to be NP-hard [37].

5. OUR SOLUTION

As obvious algorithms to GCP are clearly exponential, we propose a greedy heuristic that repeatedly merges a node pair which minimizes the change in the first eigenvalue. Let $G_{-(a,b)}$ denote the graph G after merging nodes a and b (and incorporating the re-weighting strategy), and λ_G denote the first eigenvalue of the adjacency matrix of G. We define the score of a node pair(a, b) as follows -

DEFINITION 5.1 (SCORE). *Given a weighted graph $G = (V, E, w)$ and an adjacent node pair(a, b), score(a, b) is defined by:*

$$score(a, b) = |\lambda_{G_{-(a,b)}} - \lambda_G| = \Delta\lambda_{(a,b)}$$

Intuitively, if $score(a, b) \approx 0$, it implies that edges (a, b) and (b, a) do not play a significant role in the diffusion through the graph and can thus be contracted. Figure 3 shows an example of our approach.

Naïve Algorithm: The above intuition suggests the following naïve algorithm for selecting node pairs for merging. At each stage, calculate the change in the eigenvalue due to merging each adjacent node pair, choose the node pair leading to the least change, merge the chosen nodes, and repeat until the graph is small enough. An implementation for this, even using the Lanczos algorithm for eigenvalue computation for sparse graphs, will be too expensive, taking $O(m^2)$ time. Can we compute (maybe approximately) the scores of each node pair faster?

Main Idea: We use a matrix perturbation argument to derive an expression for the change in eigenvalue due to merging two adjacent nodes. Using further information about the specific perturbations occurring due to merging two adjacent nodes, we show that the change in the eigenvalue can be approximated well in constant time. Thus, we obtain a linear ($O(m)$) time scheme to estimate the score of every pair of adjacent nodes.

5.1 Score Estimation

Let a and b denote the two neighboring vertices that we are trying to score. We assume that the first eigenvalue of the graph λ_G and the corresponding right and left eigenvectors $\vec{u}, \vec{v}$ are precomputed. Further since the graph G is strongly connected, by the Perron-Frobenius theorem, the first eigenvalue λ_G and the eigenvectors $\vec{u}$ and $\vec{v}$ are all real and have positive components. When it is clear from the context, we drop subscripts G and (a, b). In the proofs that follow $\lambda = \lambda_G$ and $\Delta\lambda = \Delta\lambda_{(a,b)}$ as there is no ambiguity. Let $\mathbf{A}$ denote the adjacency matrix of the graph. Further as $\vec{u}$ denotes the eigenvector of $\mathbf{A}$, let $u_a = u(a)$ denote the component of $\vec{u}$ corresponding to vertex a. Merging nodes changes the dimensions of the adjacency matrix $\mathbf{A}$ which we handle by viewing merging nodes a, b as adding b's neighbors to a and isolating node b.

Approximation 5.1 provides an equation for the change in the eigenvalue by a matrix perturbation argument. Proposition 5.2 and Proposition 5.3 show how our reweighting strategy helps us to approximate the $score(a, b)$ in constant time.

APPROXIMATION 5.1. *The change in eigenvalue $\Delta\lambda$ can be approximated by $\Delta\lambda = \frac{\vec{v}^T\Delta\mathbf{A}\vec{u} + \vec{v}^T\Delta\mathbf{A}\Delta\vec{u}}{(\vec{v}^T\vec{u} + \vec{v}^T\Delta\vec{u})}$ where $\Delta\mathbf{A}$ denotes an infinitesimally small change in the adjacency matrix $\mathbf{A}$ and $\Delta\vec{u}$ denotes the corresponding change in the eigenvector $\vec{u}$.*

JUSTIFICATION. By the definition of an eigenvalue and eigenvector of a matrix, we have

$$\mathbf{A}\vec{u} = \lambda\vec{u} \quad (1)$$
$$\vec{v}^T\mathbf{A} = \vec{v}^T\lambda \quad (2)$$

Perturbing all values of (1) infinitesimally, we get

$$(\mathbf{A} + \Delta\mathbf{A})(\vec{u} + \Delta\vec{u}) \approx (\lambda + \Delta\lambda)(\vec{u} + \Delta\vec{u})$$
$$\mathbf{A}\Delta\vec{u} + \Delta\mathbf{A}\vec{u} + \Delta\mathbf{A}\Delta\vec{u} \approx \lambda\Delta\vec{u} + \Delta\lambda\vec{u} + \Delta\lambda\Delta\vec{u}$$

Premultiplying by $\vec{v}^T$ and using (1) and (2),

$$\Delta\lambda(\vec{v}^T\vec{u} + \vec{v}^T\Delta\vec{u}) \approx \vec{v}^T\Delta\mathbf{A}\vec{u} + \vec{v}^T\Delta\mathbf{A}\Delta\vec{u}$$
$$\Delta\lambda \approx \frac{\vec{v}^T\Delta\mathbf{A}\vec{u} + \vec{v}^T\Delta\mathbf{A}\Delta\vec{u}}{(\vec{v}^T\vec{u} + \vec{v}^T\Delta\vec{u})} \quad (3)$$

□

Using expression (3) along with prior knowledge about the perturbations to the adjacency matrix $\mathbf{A}$ and the eigenvector $\vec{u}$, we obtain an expression for computing the score of the node pair.

PROPOSITION 5.2 (SCORE ESTIMATE). *Under Approximation 5.1, the score of a node pair score(a, b) can be approximated as*

$$\Delta\lambda_{(a,b)} = \frac{-\lambda(u_a v_a + u_b v_b) + v_a \vec{u}^T\vec{c^o} + \beta_2 u_a v_b + \beta_1 u_b v_a}{\vec{v}^T\vec{u} - (u_a v_a + u_b v_b)}$$

(ignoring second order terms).

PROOF. Approximation 5.1 provided an expression for $\Delta\lambda$ in terms of the change in the adjacency matrix and the eigenvector. Now $\Delta\mathbf{A}$, i.e., change in the adjacency matrix

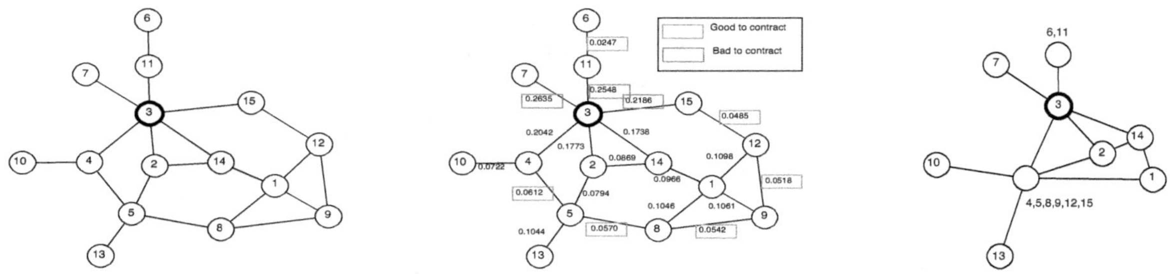

(a) Original Network (b) Assigning scores to each edge (c) Coarsened Network

Figure 3: Our approach on an example network. All edges have weight 0.5 in the original graph. We do not show the new edge weights in the coarsened graph for clarity.

can be considered as occurring in three stages namely (i) Deletion of a, (ii) Deletion of b, (iii) Insertion of c. Assume that c is inserted in place of a. Thus we obtain,

$$\begin{aligned}\Delta\mathbf{A} = &-\left(\vec{a^i}\vec{e_a}^T + \vec{e_a}\vec{a^o}^T\right) - \left(\vec{b^i}\vec{e_b}^T + \vec{e_b}\vec{b^o}^T\right) \\ &+ \left(\vec{c^i}\vec{e_a}^T + \vec{e_a}\vec{c^o}^T\right)\end{aligned} \tag{4}$$

where $\vec{e_v}$ denotes a vector with a 1 in the vth row and 0 elsewhere. Further, as we modify only two rows and columns of the matrix, this change $\Delta\mathbf{A}$ is very small.

Also, deletion of vertices a and b cause a^{th} and b^{th} components of $\vec{u}$ and $\vec{v}$ to be zero. $\Delta\vec{u}$, i.e, change in the eigenvector $\vec{u}$ can thus be considered as setting u_a and u_b to zero, followed by small changes to other components and to u_a due to addition of c. Thus we obtain,

$$\Delta\vec{u} = -u_a\vec{e_a} - u_b\vec{e_b} + \vec{\delta} \tag{5}$$

Although $\Delta\vec{u}$ cannot be considered as small, we assume that the changes $\vec{\delta}$ after setting u_a and u_b components to zero are very small.

Substituting for $\Delta\mathbf{A}$, we get

$$\begin{aligned}\vec{v}^T\Delta\mathbf{A}\vec{u} = \vec{v}^T(&-(\vec{a^i}\vec{e_a}^T + \vec{e_a}\vec{a^o}^T) - (\vec{b^i}\vec{e_b}^T + \vec{e_b}\vec{b^o}^T \\ &+ (\vec{c^i}\vec{e_a}^T + \vec{e_a}\vec{c^o}^T))\vec{u}\end{aligned}$$

Since $\vec{v}^T\vec{e_a} = v_a$ and similarly,

$$\begin{aligned}\vec{v}^T\Delta\mathbf{A}\vec{u} = &-u_a\vec{v}^T\vec{a^i} - v_a\vec{a^o}^T\vec{u} - u_b\vec{v}^T\vec{b^i} - v_b\vec{b^o}^T\vec{u} \\ &+ u_a\vec{v}^T\vec{c^i} + v_a\vec{c^o}^T\vec{u}\end{aligned}$$

But $\vec{v}^T\vec{a^i} = \lambda v_a$ and $\vec{a^o}^T\vec{u} = \lambda u_a$ and similarly,

$$\vec{v}^T\Delta\mathbf{A}\vec{u} = -2\lambda\left(u_a v_a + u_b v_b\right) + u_a\vec{v}^T\vec{c^i} + v_a\vec{c^o}^T\vec{u} \tag{6}$$

Now using (4) and (5) consider,

$$\vec{v}^T\Delta\mathbf{A}\Delta\vec{u} = \vec{v}^T\Delta\mathbf{A}(-u_a\vec{e_a} - u_b\vec{e_b} + \vec{\delta})$$

Since $\Delta\mathbf{A}$ and $\vec{\delta}$ are both very small, we ignore the second order term $\vec{v}^T\Delta\mathbf{A}\vec{\delta}$.

$$\begin{aligned}\Rightarrow \vec{v}^T\Delta\mathbf{A}\Delta\vec{u} &= \vec{v}^T\Delta\mathbf{A}(-u_a\vec{e_a} - u_b\vec{e_b}) \\ &= \vec{v}^T(-(\vec{a^i}\vec{e_a}^T + \vec{e_a}\vec{a^o}^T) - (\vec{b^i}\vec{e_b}^T + \vec{e_b}\vec{b^o}^T \\ &\quad + (\vec{c^i}\vec{e_a}^T + \vec{e_a}\vec{c^o}^T))(-u_a\vec{e_a} - u_b\vec{e_b})\end{aligned}$$

Since self loops do not affect diffusion in any way, we can assume without loss of generality that G has no self loops. Further, simplifying using definitions of eigenvalue we get,

$$\begin{aligned}\vec{v}^T\Delta\mathbf{A}\Delta\vec{u} = &\lambda(u_a v_a + u_b v_b) + \beta_2 u_a v_b \\ &+ \beta_1 u_b v_a - u_a\vec{v}^T\vec{c^i}\end{aligned} \tag{7}$$

Ignoring small terms, we also have,

$$\vec{v}^T\Delta\vec{u} = \vec{v}^T(-u_a\vec{e_a} - u_b\vec{e_b} + \vec{\delta}) = -(u_a v_a + u_b v_b) \tag{8}$$

Substituting (6),(7) and (8) in Approximation 5.1, we get

$$\Delta\lambda = \frac{-\lambda\left(u_a v_a + u_b v_b\right) + v_a\vec{u}^T\vec{c^o} + \beta_2 u_a v_b + \beta_1 u_b v_a}{\vec{v}^T\vec{u} - (u_a v_a + u_b v_b)}$$

□

Note that every term in this expression is a simple product of scalars, except for the $\vec{u}^T\vec{c^o}$ term. We now show that even $\vec{u}^T\vec{c^o}$ can in fact be expressed in terms of scalars and can thus be computed in constant time.

Proposition 5.3. *Using the re-weighting scheme as defined in Definition 4.2, if c denotes the new vertex created by merging nodes $\{a, b\}$ and $\vec{c^o}$ denotes the out-adjacency vector of c, $\vec{u}^T\vec{c^o} = \frac{(1+\beta_2)}{2}(\lambda u_a - \beta_1 u_b) + \frac{(1+\beta_1)}{2}(\lambda u_b - \beta_2 u_a)$ where β_1 is the weight of edge (a, b) and β_2 is the weight of the edge (b, a).*

Proof. Let $X = Nb^o(a) \backslash Nb^o(b), Y = Nb^o(b) \backslash Nb^o(a), Z = Nb^o(a) \cap Nb^o(b)$. Since, c is adjacent only to neighbors of a and b, we have

$$\vec{u}^T\vec{c^o} = \sum_{t\in X} u_t c_t^o + \sum_{t\in Y} u_t c_t^o + \sum_{t\in Z} u_t c_t^o + u_c W$$

where W is the weight of a self loop added at c. Note that a self loop does not affect diffusion in any way (as a node can not influence itself). We use a self loop only in the analysis so as to compute the scores efficiently.

As per our reweighting scheme (See Definition 4.2)

$$\begin{aligned}\vec{u}^T\vec{c^o} = &\sum_{t\in X}\frac{(1+\beta_2)}{2}u_t a_t^o + \sum_{t\in Y}\frac{(1+\beta_1)}{2}u_t b_t^o \\ &+ \sum_{t\in Z}\left(\frac{(1+\beta_2)}{4}a_t^o + \frac{(1+\beta_1)}{4}b_t^o\right)u_t + u_c W\end{aligned} \tag{9}$$

But, by definition of eigenvalues, we know that

$$\lambda u_a = \sum_{t \in V} u_t a_t^o = \sum_{t \in X} u_t a_t^o + \sum_{t \in Z} u_t a_t^o + u_b \beta_1$$

$$\begin{aligned}\sum_{t \in X} u_t a_t^o &= \lambda u_a - \sum_{t \in Z} u_t a_t^o - \beta_1 u_b \\ &= \lambda u_a - a^o(Z) - \beta_1 u_b \end{aligned} \quad (10)$$

where $a^o(Z) = \sum_{t \in Z} u_t a_t^o$

Similarly, we get

$$\sum_{t \in Y} u_t b_t^o = \lambda u_b - b^o(Z) - \beta_2 u_a \quad (11)$$

Substituting Equations (10), (11), in (9),

$$\begin{aligned}\vec{u}^T \vec{c^o} = &\frac{(1+\beta_2)}{2}(\lambda u_a - a^o(Z) - \beta_1 u_b) \\ &+ \frac{(1+\beta_1)}{2}(\lambda u_b - b^o(Z) - \beta_2 u_a) \\ &+ \frac{(1+\beta_2)}{4} a^o(Z) + \frac{(1+\beta_1)}{4} b^o(Z) + u_c W\end{aligned}$$

We now choose $W = (-\frac{(1+\beta_2)}{4} a^o(Z) - \frac{(1+\beta_1)}{4} b^o(Z))/u_c$, so that we get

$$\vec{u}^T \vec{c^o} = \frac{(1+\beta_2)}{2}(\lambda u_a - \beta_1 u_b) + \frac{(1+\beta_1)}{2}(\lambda u_b - \beta_2 u_a)$$

□

COROLLARY 5.1. *Given the first eigenvalue λ and corresponding eigenvectors $\vec{u}, \vec{v}$, the score of a node pair $score(a, b)$ can be approximated in constant time.*

PROOF. Substituting for $\vec{u}^t \vec{c^o}$ in Proposition 5.2 using Proposition 5.3, we obtain an expression for $score(c, b)$ that is composed entirely of scalar terms. Thus we can estimate the edge score in constant time. □

5.2 Complete Algorithm

Using the approximation described in the previous section, we assign a score to every pair of adjacent nodes of the graph. We then sort these node pairs in ascending order of the absolute value of their scores. Intuitively, we would like to merge a node pair if it has minimal score. Given an upper bound of α, the graph is then coarsened by contracting αn node pairs one by one in this order ignoring any pairs that have already been merged. We give the pseudo-code of our algorithm COARSENET in Algorithm 1.

LEMMA 5.1 (RUNNING TIME). *The worst case time complexity of our algorithm is $O(m \ln(m) + \alpha n n_\theta)$ where n_θ denotes the maximum degree of any vertex at any time in the coarsening process.*

PROOF. Computing the first eigenvalue and eigenvector of the adjacency matrix of the graph takes $O(m)$ time (for example, using Lanczos iteration assuming that the spectral gap is large). As shown in Section 5.1, each node pair can be assigned a score in constant time. In order to score all m adjacent pairs of nodes of the graph, we require linear i.e. $(O(m))$ time. The scored node pairs are sorted in $O(m \ln(m))$ time. Merging two nodes (a, b) requires $O(deg(a) + deg(b)) = O(n_\theta)$ time. Since we each

Algorithm 1 Coarsening Algorithm - COARSENET (G, α)

Input: A directed, weighted graph G=(V,E,w), a reduction factor α
Output: Coarsened graph G^α_{coarse}=(V',E',w')

$i = 0$
$n = |V|$
$G' = G$
for each adjacent pair of nodes $a, b \in V$ **do**
  Compute $score(a, b)$ using Section 5.1
$\pi \leftarrow$ ordering of node pairs in increasing order of $score$
while $i \leq \alpha n$ **do**
  $(a, b) = \pi(i)$
  $G' \leftarrow Contract_{G'}(a, b)$
  $i{+}{+}$
return $G^\alpha_{coarse} = G'$

merge at most αn pairs of nodes, the merging itself has time complexity $O(\alpha n n_\theta)$.

Therefore, our worst-case time complexity is $O(m \ln(m) + \alpha n n_\theta)$. □

6. SAMPLE APPLICATION: INFLUENCE MAXIMIZATION

The eigenvalue based coarsening method described above aims to obtain a small network that approximates the diffusive properties of the original large network. As an example application, we now show how to apply our graph coarsening framework to the well studied influence maximization problem. Recall that given a diffusion model (IC model in our case) and a social network, the influence maximization problem is to find a small seed set of k nodes such that the expected number of influenced nodes is maximized.

Since we have designed our coarsening strategy such that nodes and edges important for diffusion remain untouched, we expect that solving influence maximization on the coarsened graph is a good proxy for solving it on the much larger original network. The major challenge in this process is to determine how to map the solutions obtained from the coarsened graph back onto the vertices of the original network. But due to the carefully designed coarsening strategy which tries to keep important, candidate vertices unmerged, we observe that a simple random pull back scheme works well in practice.

More formally, we propose the following multi-stage approach to solve influence maximization:

1. **Coarsen** the social network graph G by using Algorithm 1 to obtain a much smaller graph G_{coarse}. Let $\mu : V \rightarrow V_{coarse}$ denote a mapping from vertices of the original graph to those of the coarsened graph.
2. **Solve** the influence maximization problem on G_{coarse} to get k vertices $s_1, \ldots, s_k$ in the coarsened graph that optimize the desired objective function. We can use any off-the-shelf algorithm for influence maximization in this step. Since G_{coarse} is much smaller than G, traditional algorithms for influence maximization can provide high quality solutions in little time.
3. **Pull back** the solutions on to the vertices of the original graph. Given a seed s_i in G_{coarse} we need to select a vertex $v \in \mu^{-1}(s_i)$ from G as a seed. Multiple strategies can be considered here such as $v =$

$\arg\max_{u \in \mu^{-1}(s_i)}(\sigma(u))$ where $\sigma(u)$ is the expected influence by seeding u. However, thanks to our careful coarsening framework, we show that a simple strategy of selecting a seed uniformly at random from $\mu^{-1}(s_i)$ for every seed s_i performs very well in practice.

Algorithm 2 describes our strategy to solve influence maximization problems. Note that a similar strategy can be applied to study other problems based on diffusion in networks.

Algorithm 2 CSPIN: Influence Maximization Framework

Input: A weighted graph G=(V,E,w), the number of seeds k, a reduction factor α
Output: A seed set S of k seeds
1: G^{α}_{coarse}, $\mu \leftarrow$ COARSENET (G,α) (See Algorithm 1)
2: $s'_1, s'_2, \ldots, s'_k \leftarrow$ InfluenceMaximization(G^{α}_{coarse}, k)
3: **for** $i = 1, \ldots, k$ **do**
4: $s_i \leftarrow$ random sample from $\mu^{-1}(s'_i)$
5: return $S = \{s_1, s_2, \ldots, s_k\}$

7. EXPERIMENTAL EVALUATION

We performed several experiments to show the effectiveness of COARSENET algorithm and also the GCP framework for cascade analysis.

Table 2: Datasets: Basic Statistics

Dataset	#Vertices	#Edges	Mean Degree
Flickr_small	500,038	5,002,845	20.01
Flickr_medium	1,000,001	14,506,356	29.01
Flickr_large	2,022,530	21,050,542	20.82
DBLP	511,163	1,871,070	7.32
Amazon	334,863	1,851,744	11.06
Brightkite	58,228	214,078	7.35
Portland	1,588,212	31,204,286	39.29
Flixster	55,918	559,863	20.02

Datasets. All experiments were conducted on an Intel Xeon machine (2.40 GHz) with 24GB of main memory[1]. We used a diverse selection of datasets from different domains to test our algorithm and framework (see Table 2). These datasets were chosen for their size as well as the applicability to the diffusion problem. COARSENET was tested on data from Flickr, DBLP, Amazon, Brightkite and Portland epidemiology data. In the Flickr data, vertices are users, and links represent friendships [5]. In the DBLP data, vertices represent authors and edges represent co-authorship links. Brightkite is a friendship network from a former location-based social networking service provider Brightkite. In the Amazon dataset, vertices are products and an edge represents that the two products are often purchased together. The Portland dataset is a social contact graph of vertices representing people and edges representing interactions—it represents a synthetic population of the city of Portland, Oregon, and has been used in nation-wide smallpox studies [11]. Finally, we also used a *real* cascade dataset Flixster[2], where cascades of movie ratings happen over a social network.

[1]Code at:
`http://www.cs.vt.edu/~badityap/CODE/coarsenet.tgz`
[2]`http://www.cs.ubc.ca/~jamalim/datasets/`

7.1 Performance for the GCP problem

We want to measure the performance of COARSENET algorithm on the GCP problem. In short, we can coarsen up to 70% of node-pairs using COARSENET, and still retain almost the same eigenvalue.

7.1.1 Effectiveness

As a baseline we used RANDOM, a random node-pair coarsening algorithm (randomly choose a node-pair and contract), used in some community detection techniques. Figure 4 shows the values of λ as the reduction factor α increases when we ran COARSENET and RANDOM on three datasets (we set a weight of 0.02 for this experiment). We observed that in all datasets, as the reduction factor α increases, the values of λ barely change for COARSENET, showing that the diffusive properties are maintained even with almost 70% contraction; while RANDOM destroyed the eigenvalue very quickly with increasing α. This shows that (a) large graphs *can* in fact be coarsened to large percentages while maintaining diffusion; and (b) COARSENET effectively solves the GCP problem. As we show later, we apply the GCP problem and COARSENET on a detailed sample application of influence maximization.

7.1.2 Scalability

Figure 5 shows the running times of COARSENET w.r.t. α and n. To analyze the runtime of COARSENET with respect to graph size (n), we extracted 6 connected components (with 500K to 1M vertices in steps of 100K) of the Flickr_large dataset. As expected from Lemma 5.1, we observe that in all datasets, as the reduction factor α increases, the running time increases linearly (figures also show the linear-fit, with R^2 values), and scale near-linearly as the size of the graph increases. This demonstrates that COARSENET is scalable for large datasets.

7.2 Application 1: Influence Maximization

Here we demonstrate in detail a concrete application of our GCP problem and COARSENET algorithm to diffusion-related problems. We use the well-known Influence Maximization problem. The idea as discussed before is to use the Coarsen-Solve-Project CSPIN framework (see Section 6). In short we find that we obtain 300× speed-up on large networks, while maintaining the quality of solutions.

Propagation probabilities: Since accurate propagation probabilities for these networks are not available, we generate propagation probabilities according to two models following the literature.

- **Uniform:** Each edge is assigned a low propagation probability of 0.02. In most real social networks, the propagation probabilities are known to be low. For example, [5] find that the propagation probability in the Flickr network is about 1-2%.
- **Trivalency:** We also test on the trivalency model studied in [7]. For every edge we choose a probability uniformly at random from the set $\{0.1, 0.01, 0.001\}$ which correspond to the edge having high, medium and low influence respectively.

Algorithms and setup: We can use any off-the-shelf algorithm to solve Inf. Max. problem on the smaller coarsened network. Here, we choose to use the fast and popular PMIA [7] algorithm. We then compared the influence spreads

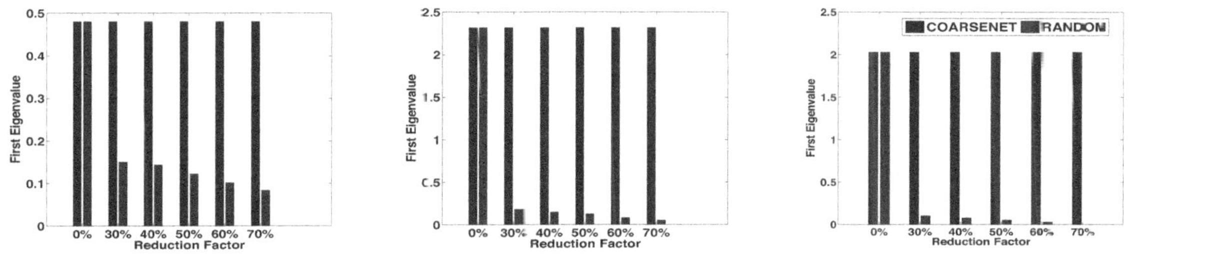

(a) Amazon (b) DBLP (c) Brightkite

Figure 4: Effectiveness of COARSENET for GCP. λ vs α for COARSENET and RANDOM. COARSENET maintains λ values.

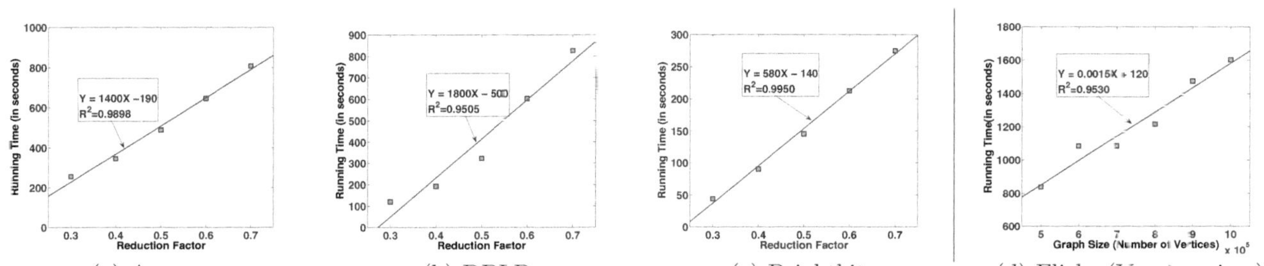

(a) Amazon (b) DBLP (c) Brightkite (d) Flickr (Varying sizes)

Figure 5: Scalability of COARSENET for GCP. (a,b,c) Linear w.r.t. α. (d) Near-linear w.r.t. size of graph.

and running-times of the CSPIN framework with the plain PMIA algorithm to demonstrate gains from using GCP.

7.2.1 Effectiveness

Quality of solution (Influence spread). In all experiments, the influence spread generated by our CSPIN approach is within 10% of the influence spread generated by PMIA. In some cases, we even perform slightly better than PMIA. Figure 6(a) shows the expected spread obtained by selecting $k = 1000$ seeds on five datasets. For these experiments, the percentage of edges to merged is set at 90% and we use the uniform propagation model.

Quality w.r.t α. We find that we can merge up to 95% of the edges while still retaining influence spread. As more edges are merged, the coarsened graph is smaller so the superseeds in G^{α}_{coarse} can be found faster and thus we expect our running time to decrease. We ran tests on the Flickr_medium dataset for 1000 seeds and varied α from 80% to 95%. Figure 6(b) shows the ratio of the expected influence spread obtained by CSPIN to that obtained by PMIA is almost 1 with varying α.

Quality of solution: Effect of unbiased random pullback. COARSENET groups nodes which have similar diffu-

Table 3: Insensitivity of CSPIN to random pullback choices : Expected influence spread does not vary much.

#Trials	Maximum Spread	Minimum Spread	Coefficient of variation ($\frac{\sigma}{\mu}$)
100	58996.6	58984.8	5.061×10^{-5}

sion effects, hence choosing *any one* of the nodes randomly inside a group will lead to similar spreads (hence we do the random pullback in CSPIN). Note we do not claim that these groups belong to link-based communities—only that their diffusive effects are similar. To demonstrate this, we performed 100 trials of the random pullback phase for the Flickr_small graph. For these trials, 1000 superseeds were found by coarsening 90% of the edges. In each trial, we use these same superseeds to find the 1000 seeds independently and uniformly at random. Table 3 shows that the coefficient of variation of the expected spread is only 5.061×10^{-5}.

7.2.2 Scalability

Scalability w.r.t number of seeds (k). As the budget k increases, we see dramatic performance benefits of CSPIN over PMIA. We run experiments on Flickr_small, and Portland by setting $\alpha = 90\%$, and k varied from 0.01% to 1% of $|V|$. Figure 7(a,b) shows the total running times (including the coarsening). Due to lack of space we show only the results for the trivalency model (the uniform case was similar). In all datasets, as k increases, the running time of CSPIN increases very slowly. Note that we get *orders of magnitude* speed-ups: e.g. on Flickr PMIA takes *more than 10 days* to find 200+ seeds, while CSPIN runs in 2 minutes.

Scalability w.r.t α. We can see that the running time also drops with increased coarsening as seen in Figure 6(c).

Scalability w.r.t n. We ran CSPIN on the components of increasing size of Flickr_large with $k = 1000$ and $\alpha = 90\%$. Figure 7(c) plots the running times: CSPIN obtains a speed up of around 250× over PMIA consistently.

7.3 Application 2: Diffusion Characterization

We now briefly describe how the GCP problem can help in understanding cascade datasets in an exploratory setting.

Methodology: We used a Flixster dataset, where users can share ratings of movies with friends. There is a log-file which stores ratings actions by each user: and a cascade is supposed to happen when a person rates the same movie soon after one of her friends. We use the methodology of [15] to learn influence probabilities of a IC-model over the edges of the friendship network from the traces. We then coarsen

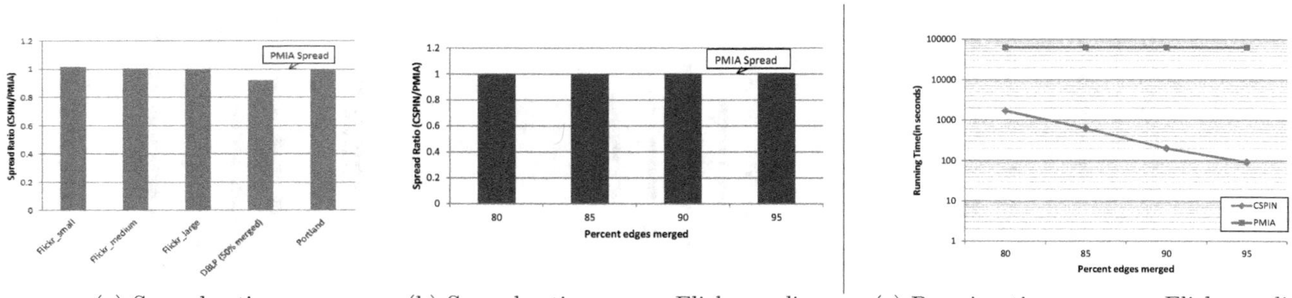

(a) Spread ratio (b) Spread ratio vs α on Flickr_medium (c) Running times vs α on Flickr_medium

Figure 6: Effectiveness of CSPIN. Ratio of influence spread between CSPIN and PMIA for (a) different datasets; (b) varying α. (c) Running time vs α.

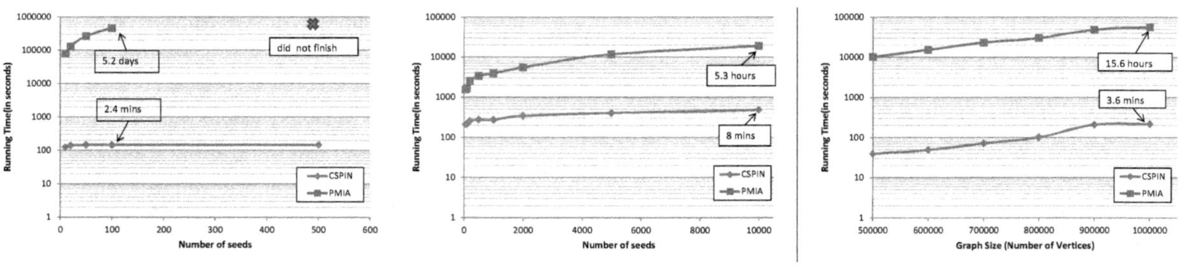

(a) Flickr_small (trivalency model) (b) Portland (trivalency model) (c) Flickr (Varying sizes)

Figure 7: Scalability of CSPIN. (a,b) vs k; (c) vs size of graph. CSPIN gets increasing orders-of-magnitude speed-up over PMIA.

the resulting directed graph using COARSENET to $\alpha = 50\%$, and study the formed groups (supernodes). Note that this is in contrast to the approaches where the group information is supplied by a graph-partitioning algorithm (like METIS), and then a group-based IC model is learnt. The base network had 55,918 nodes and 559,863 edges. The trace-log contained about 7 *million* actions over 48,000 movies. We get 1891 groups after removing groups with only one node, with mean group size 16.6 with the largest group having 22061 nodes (roughly 40% of nodes).

Distribution of movies over groups: Figure 8 shows the histogram of the # of groups reached by the movie propagations (following [30], we assume that a movie reaches a group if at least 10% of its nodes rated that movie). We show only the first 100 points of the distribution. We observe that a very large fraction of movies propagate in a small number of groups. Interestingly we observe a *multi-modal* distribution, suggesting movies have multiple scales of spread.

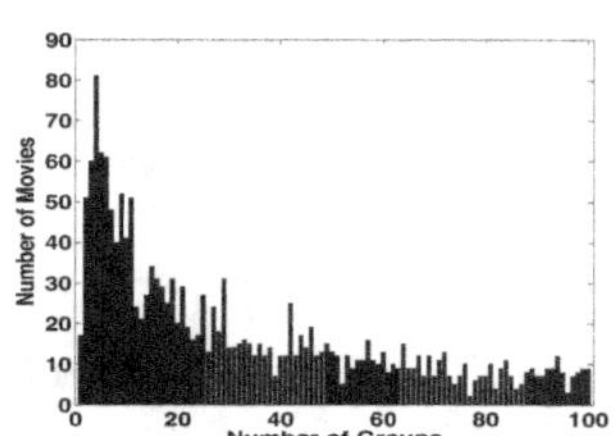

Figure 8: Distribution of # groups entered by movie traces.

Groups through the lens of surrogates: An important point to note is that our groups *may not* be link-based communities: we just ensure that nodes in a group have the same diffusive properties. We validated this observation in the previous section (Table 3). Hence a natural question is if groups found in Flixster have any other natural structure (e.g. demographics)—if they do, we can get a non-network external *surrogate* for similar diffusive characteristics. Fortunately, the Flixster does contain a couple of auxiliary features for its users (like ID, Last Login, Age). We calculated the Mean Absolute Error (MAE) for 'Age' *inside* each group, and compared it with the MAE across groups. We found that the average MAE inside the group is very small (within 2 years) compared to a MAE of almost 8 outside, which implies that ages are concentrated within groups and can act as surrogates for diffusive characteristics.

8. CONCLUSIONS

We propose influence-based coarsening as a fundamental operation in the analysis of diffusive processes in large networks. Based on the connections between influence spread and spectral properties of the graph, we propose a novel Graph Coarsening Problem and provide an effective and efficient heuristic called COARSENET. By carefully reweighting the edges after each coarsening step, COARSENET attempts to find a succinct representation of the original network which preserves important diffusive properties.

We then describe the CSPIN framework to solve influence maximization problems on large networks using our coarsening strategy. Experimental results show that CSPIN indeed outperforms traditional approaches by providing high quality solutions in a fraction of the time.

Finally we show that our COARSENET framework can also be used for examining cascade datasets in an exploratory setting. We observe that in our case study the nodes merged together form meaningful communities in the sense of having similar diffusive properties which can serve as surrogates using external demographic information.

Future work can consist of resolving the complexity of GCP and investigating more applications of our framework to tasks where spectral properties may need to be preserved.

Acknowledgements. The authors would like to thank Christos Faloutsos for discussions. This material is based upon work supported by the US Army Research Office under Grant No. W911NF0910206, by the NSF under Grant No. IIS-1353346, by the NSA (under a 'Science of Security' lablet) and by the VT College of Engineering.

9. REFERENCES

[1] R. M. Anderson and R. M. May. *Infectious Diseases of Humans*. Oxford University Press, 1991.

[2] N. Bailey. *The Mathematical Theory of Infectious Diseases and its Applications*. Griffin, London, 1975.

[3] S. Bikhchandani, D. Hirshleifer, and I. Welch. A theory of fads, fashion, custom, and cultural change in informational cascades. *Journal of Political Economy*, 100(5):992–1026, October 1992.

[4] L. Briesemeister, P. Lincoln, and P. Porras. Epidemic profiles and defense of scale-free networks. *WORM 2003*, Oct. 27 2003.

[5] M. Cha, A. Mislove, and K. P. Gummadi. A Measurement-driven Analysis of Information Propagation in the Flickr Social Network. In *In Proceedings of the 18th International World Wide Web Conference (WWW'09)*, Madrid, Spain, April 2009.

[6] D. Chakrabarti, Y. Wang, C. Wang, J. Leskovec, and C. Faloutsos. Epidemic thresholds in real networks. *ACM TISSEC*, 10(4), 2008.

[7] W. Chen, C. Wang, and Y. Wang. Scalable influence maximization for prevalent viral marketing in large-scale social networks. *KDD*, 2010.

[8] W. Chen, Y. Wang, and S. Yang. Efficient influence maximization in social networks. In *Proceedings of the 15th ACM SIGKDD international conference on Knowledge discovery and data mining*, pages 199–208. ACM, 2009.

[9] I. S. Dhillon, Y. Guan, and B. Kulis. Weighted graph cuts without eigenvectors a multilevel approach. *IEEE Trans. Pattern Anal. Mach. Intell.*, 29(11):1944–1957, 2007.

[10] M. Elkin and D. Peleg. Approximating k-spanner problems for k> 2. *Theoretical Computer Science*, 337(1):249–277, 2005.

[11] S. Eubank, H. Guclu, V. S. Anil Kumar, M. V. Marathe, A. Srinivasan, Z. Toroczkai, and N. Wang. Modelling disease outbreaks in realistic urban social networks. *Nature*, 429(6988):180–184, May 2004.

[12] W. S. Fung, R. Hariharan, N. J. Harvey, and D. Panigrahi. A general framework for graph sparsification. In *Proceedings of the 43rd annual ACM symposium on Theory of computing*, pages 71–80. ACM, 2011.

[13] A. Ganesh, L. Massoulié, and D. Towsley. The effect of network topology on the spread of epidemics. In *IEEE INFOCOM*, Los Alamitos, CA, 2005. IEEE Computer Society Press.

[14] J. Goldenberg, B. Libai, and E. Muller. Talk of the network: A complex systems look at the underlying process of word-of-mouth. *Marketing Letters*, 2001.

[15] A. Goyal, F. Bonchi, and L. V. Lakshmanan. Learning influence probabilities in social networks. WSDM '10, 2010.

[16] A. Goyal, W. Lu, and L. V. S. Lakshmanan. Simpath: An efficient algorithm for influence maximization under the linear threshold model. *ICDM*, 2011.

[17] M. Granovetter. Threshold models of collective behavior. *Am. Journal of Sociology*, 83(6):1420–1443, 1978.

[18] D. Gruhl, R. Guha, D. Liben-Nowell, and A. Tomkins. Information diffusion through blogspace. In *WWW '04*, 2004.

[19] Y. Hayashi, M. Minoura, and J. Matsukubo. Recoverable prevalence in growing scale-free networks and the effective immunization. *arXiv:cond-mat/0305549 v2*, Aug. 6 2003.

[20] H. W. Hethcote. The mathematics of infectious diseases. *SIAM Review*, 42, 2000.

[21] G. Karypis and V. Kumar. METIS: Unstructured graph partitioning and sparse matrix ordering system. *The University of Minnesota*, 2, 1995.

[22] D. Kempe, J. Kleinberg, and E. Tardos. Maximizing the spread of influence through a social network. In *KDD '03: Proceedings of the ninth ACM SIGKDD international conference on Knowledge discovery and data mining*, pages 137–146, New York, NY, USA, 2003. ACM.

[23] J. O. Kephart and S. R. White. Measuring and modeling computer virus prevalence. *IEEE Computer Society Symposium on Research in Security and Privacy*, 1993.

[24] M. Kimura and K. Saito. Tractable models for information diffusion in social networks. *Knowledge Discovery in Databases: PKDD 2006*, pages 259–271, 2006.

[25] R. Kumar, J. Novak, P. Raghavan, and A. Tomkins. On the bursty evolution of blogspace. In *WWW '03: Proceedings of the 12th international conference on World Wide Web* pages 568–576, New York, NY, USA, 2003. ACM Press.

[26] T. Lappas, E. Terzi, D. Gunopulos, and H. Mannila. Finding effectors in social networks. In *Proceedings of the 16th ACM International Conference on Knowledge Discovery and Data Mining (SIGKDD), Washington, DC*, pages 1059–1068, 2010.

[27] J. Leskovec, A. Krause, C. Guestrin, C. Faloutsos, J. VanBriesen, and N. S. Glance. Cost-effective outbreak detection in networks. In *KDD*, pages 420–429, 2007.

[28] M. Mathioudakis, F. Bonchi, C. Castillo, A. Gionis, and A. Ukkonen. Sparsification of influence networks. In *Proceedings of the 17th ACM SIGKDD international conference on Knowledge discovery and data mining*, pages 529–537. ACM, 2011.

[29] A. G. McKendrick. Applications of mathematics to medical problems. In *Proceedings of Edin. Math. Society*, volume 44, pages 98–130, 1925.

[30] Y. Mehmood, N. Barbieri, F. Bonchi, and A. Ukkonen. Csi: Community-level social influence analysis. In *Machine Learning and Knowledge Discovery in Databases*, volume 8189 of *Lecture Notes in Computer Science* 2013.

[31] R. Pastor-Santorras and A. Vespignani. Epidemic spreading in scale-free networks. *Physical Review Letters 86*, 14, 2001.

[32] B. A. Prakash, D. Chakrabarti, M. Faloutsos, N. Valler, and C. Faloutsos. Threshold conditions for arbitrary cascade models on arbitrary networks. In *ICDM*, 2011.

[33] B. A. Prakash, J. Vreeken, and C. Faloutsos Spotting culprits in epidemics: How many and which ones? In *ICDM*, 2012.

[34] M. Richardson and P. Domingos. Mining knowledge-sharing sites for viral marketing. In *Proceedings of the eighth ACM SIGKDD international conference on Knowledge discovery and data mining*, pages 61–70. ACM, 2002.

[35] E. M. Rogers. *Diffusion of Innovations, 5th Edition*. Free Press, August 2003.

[36] P. Shakarian, M. Broecheler, V. Subrahmanian, and C. Molinaro. Using generalized annotated programs to solve social network optimization problems. *ACM Transactions on Computational Logic*, 2012.

[37] H. Tong, B. A. Prakash, T. Eliassi-Rad, M. Faloutsos, and C. Faloutsos. Gelling, and melting, large graphs by edge manipulation. In *ACM CIKM*, 2012.

[38] H. Tong, B. A. Prakash, C. E. Tsourakakis, T. Eliassi-Rad, C. Faloutsos, and D. H. Chau. On the vulnerability of large graphs. In *ICDM*, 2010.

Minimizing Seed Set Selection with Probabilistic Coverage Guarantee in a Social Network

Peng Zhang
Purdue University
zhan1456@purdue.edu

Wei Chen
Microsoft
weic@microsoft.com

Xiaoming Sun*
Institute of Computing Technology, CAS
sunxiaoming@ict.ac.cn

Yajun Wang
Microsoft
yajunw@microsoft.com

Jialin Zhang
Institute of Computing Technology, CAS
zhangjl2002@gmail.com

ABSTRACT

A topic propagating in a social network reaches its tipping point if the number of users discussing it in the network exceeds a critical threshold such that a wide cascade on the topic is likely to occur. In this paper, we consider the task of selecting initial seed users of a topic with minimum size so that *with a guaranteed probability* the number of users discussing the topic would reach a given threshold. We formulate the task as an optimization problem called *seed minimization with probabilistic coverage guarantee (SM-PCG)*. This problem departs from the previous studies on social influence maximization or seed minimization because it considers influence coverage with *probabilistic* guarantees instead of guarantees on *expected* influence coverage. We show that the problem is not submodular, and thus is harder than previously studied problems based on submodular function optimization. We provide an approximation algorithm and show that it approximates the optimal solution with both a multiplicative ratio and an additive error. The multiplicative ratio is tight while the additive error would be small if influence coverage distributions of certain seed sets are well concentrated. For one-way bipartite graphs we analytically prove the concentration condition and obtain an approximation algorithm with an $O(\log n)$ multiplicative ratio and an $O(\sqrt{n})$ additive error, where n is the total number of nodes in the social graph. Moreover, we empirically verify the concentration condition in real-world networks and experimentally demonstrate the effectiveness of our proposed algorithm comparing to commonly adopted benchmark algorithms.

*This work was supported in part by the National Natural Science Foundation of China Grant 61170062, 61222202 and the National Program for support of Top-notch Young Professionals.

KDD'14, August 24–27, 2014, New York, NY, USA.

Categories and Subject Descriptors

H.4 [**Information Systems Applications**]: Miscellaneous; F.2.2 [**Analysis of Algorithms and Problem Complexity**]: Nonnumerical Algorithms and Problems

General Terms

Algorithms, Experimentation, Performance

Keywords

social networks, influence diffusion, independent cascade model, seed minimization

1. INTRODUCTION

With online social networks such as Facebook and Twitter becoming popular for people to express their thoughts and ideas, or to chat with each other, online social networks provide a platform for triggering a hot topic and then influencing a large population. Different from most traditional media (such as TV and newspapers), information spread on social networks mainly base on the trust relationship between individuals. Consider the following scenario: when someone publishes a topic on the online social network, his/her friends will see this topic on the website. If they think it is interesting or meaningful, they may write some comments to follow it or just forward it on the website as a response. Similarly, the comments or forwarding from these friends will attract their own friends, leading to more and more people on the social network paying attention to that topic. When the number of users discussing about this topic on the online social network reaches certain critical threshold, this topic becomes a *hot topic*, which is likely to be surfaced at the prominent place on the social networking site (e.g. 10 hot topics of today), and is likely to be picked up by traditional media and influential celebrities. In turn this will generate an even wider cascade causing more people to discuss about this topic.

Therefore, making a topic reach the critical threshold (also called the *tipping point* [10]) is the crucial step to generate huge influence on the topic, which is desirable by companies large and small trying to use social networks to promote their products, through the so called *viral marketing campaigns*. Besides making the content of the topic attractive and viral, another key aspect is to select seed users in the network that initiate the topic discussion effectively to trigger a large cascade on the topic. Due to the cost incurred for engaging seed users (e.g. providing free sample products), it is desirable that the size of seed users is minimized. Moreover, the marketers also need certain probabilistic guarantee on how likely the viral marketing campaign could reach the desired critical threshold in order to trigger an even larger cascade via hot topic listings, traditional media coverages, and celebrity followings. Hence, the problem at hand is how to select a seed set of users of minimum size to trigger a topic cascade such that the cascade size reaches the desired critical threshold with guaranteed probability.

In this paper, we formulate the above problem as the following optimization problem and call it *seed minimization with probabilistic coverage guarantee (SM-PCG)*. A social network is modeled as a directed graph, where nodes represent individuals and directed edges represent the relationships between pairs of individuals. Each edge is associated with an *influence probability*, which means that once a node is activated, it can activate its out-neighbors through the outgoing edges with their associated probabilities at the next step. Our analytical results work for a large class of influence diffusion models that guarantee submodularity (the diminishing marginal return property in terms of seed set size), but for illustration purpose, we adopt the classic *independent cascade (IC) model* [14] as the influence diffusion model. In the IC model, initially all seed nodes are activated while others are inactive, and at each step, nodes activated at the previous step have one chance to activate each of its inactive out-neighbors in the network. The total number of active nodes after the diffusion process ends is referred as the *influence coverage* of the initial seed set. Given such a social network with influence probabilities on edges, given a required coverage threshold η and a probability threshold P, the SM-PCG problem is to find a seed set S^* of minimum size such that the probability that the influence coverage of S^* reaches η or beyond is at least P.

The formulation of the SM-PCG problem significantly departs from previous optimization problems based on social influence diffusion (e.g. [14, 5, 4, 12]) in that it requires the selected seed set to satisfy a *probabilistic* coverage guarantee, while previous research focuses on *expected* coverage guarantee. For the application of generating a hot topic, we believe that it is reasonable to ask for a guarantee on the probability of influence coverage exceeding a given threshold, since this provides direct information on the likelihood of success of the viral marketing campaign, which is very helpful for marketers to gauge their cost and benefit trade-offs for the campaign. Merely saying that the expected influence coverage exceeds the required coverage threshold is not enough in this case. To the best of our knowledge, this is the first work that focuses on probabilistic influence coverage guarantee among existing studies on social network influence optimization problems.

In this paper, we first show that the set functions based on the SM-PCG problem are not submodular, which means that it is more difficult than most of the existing social influence optimization problems that rely on submodular set function optimizations. Next, we investigate two computation tasks related to SM-PCG problem, one is to fix a seed set S and a coverage threshold η and compute the probability of influence coverage of S exceeding η, and the other is to fix a seed set S and a probability threshold P, and compute the maximum coverage threshold η such that the probability of influence coverage of S exceeding η is at least P. We show that the first problem is #P-hard but can be accurately estimated, while the second one is #P-hard to even approximate the value within any nontrivial ratio. These results further demonstrate the hardness of the problem.

We then adapt the greedy approximation algorithm targeted for expected influence coverage problem (which is submodular) to the SM-PCG problem. Although the adapted algorithm still follows the greedy approach, our main contribution is on a detailed analysis, which proves that our algorithm approximates the optimal solution with both a multiplicative ratio and an additive error. The multiplicative ratio is due to the greedy approximation algorithm for expected influence coverage and is tight, while the additive error is determined by the concentration property (in particular the standard deviations) of influence coverage distributions of two specific seed sets. For one-way bipartite graphs where edges are directed from one side to the other side, we analytically show that the influence coverage distributions are well concentrated and we could reach an additive error of $O(\sqrt{n})$ where n is the total number of nodes in the graph.

Finally, using several real-world social networks including a network with influence probability parameters obtained from prior work, we empirically validate our approach by showing that (a) influence coverage distributions of seed sets are well concentrated, and (b) our algorithm selects seed sets with sizes much smaller than commonly adopted benchmark algorithms.

To summarize, our contributions include (a) we propose the study of seed minimization with probabilistic coverage guarantee (SM-PCG), which is more relevant to hot topic generation in online social networks and has not been studied before; (b) we show that neither of the two versions of set functions related to SM-PCG is submodular, one version is #P-hard to compute but allows accurate estimation while the other version is #P-hard to even approximate to any nontrivial ratio; (c) we adapt the greedy algorithm targeted for expected coverage guarantee to SM-PCG, and analytically show that the adapted algorithm provides an approximation guarantee with a tight multiplicative ratio and an additive error depending on the influence coverage concentrations of certain seed sets; and (d) we empirically demonstrate the effectiveness of our algorithm using real-world datasets.

1.1 Related Work

Influence maximization, as the dual problem of seed minimization, is to find a seed set of at most k nodes to maximize the expected influence coverage of the seed set. Domingos and Richardson are the first to formulate influence maximization problem from an algorithmic perspective [7, 17]. Kempe et al. first model this problem as a discrete optimization problem [14], provide the now classic independent cascade and linear threshold diffusion models, and establish the optimization framework based on submodular set function optimization. A number of studies follow this approach and provide more efficient influence maximization algorithms (e.g. [5, 4, 6, 13]). In [16], Long et al. first study independent cascade and linear threshold diffusion models from a minimization perspective. In [12], Goyal et al. provide a bicriteria approximation algorithm to minimize the size of the seed set with its expected influence coverage reaching a given threshold. Recently, a continuous time diffusion model is proposed and studied in [18] and [8]. All these existing studies focus on expected influence coverage, and rely on the submodularity of expected influence coverage function for the optimization task. In contrast, we are the first to address probabilistic coverage guarantee for the seed minimization problem, which is not submodular.

Seed minimization with non-submodular influence coverage functions under different diffusion models have been studied. Chen [3] studies the seed minimization problem under the fixed threshold model, where a node is activated when its active neighbors exceed its fixed threshold. He shows that the problem cannot be approximated within any polylogarithmic factor (under certain complexity theory assumption). Goldberg and Liu [11] study another variant of fixed threshold model and provide an approximation algorithm based on the linear programming technique. Influence coverage functions in both models are deterministic and non-submodular. However, these models are quite different from the model we study in this paper, and thus their results and techniques are not applicable to our problem.

The rest of this paper is organized as follows. We define the diffusion model and the optimization problem SM-PCG in Section 2, and provide related results and tools in Section 3, including the non-submodularity of the set functions for SM-PCG. In Section 4 we investigate the computation problems related to SM-PCG. In Section 5 we provide our algorithm for general graphs and analyze its approximation guarantee. In Section 6 we provide algorithmic and analytical results for one-way bipartite graphs. We empirically validate our concentration assumption on influence coverage distributions and the effectiveness of our algorithm in Section 7, and conclude the paper in Section 8 with a discussion on potential future directions. Due to the space constraint, some of the technical proofs and empirical results are omitted, and they are included in our full technical report [20].

2. MODEL AND PROBLEM

In our problem, a social network is modeled as a directed *social graph* $G = (V, E)$, where V is the set of n nodes representing individuals in a social network, and E is the set of directed edges representing influence relationships between pairs of individuals. Each edge $(u, v) \in E$ is associated with an *influence probability* $p_{u,v}$. Intuitively, $p_{u,v}$ is the probability that node u activates node v after u is activated. The influence diffusion process in the social graph G follows the independent cascade (IC) model, a randomized process summarized in [14]. Each node has two states, *inactive* or *active*. The influence diffusion proceeds in discrete time steps, and we say that a node u *is activated at time* t if t is the first time step at which u becomes active. At the initial time step $t = 0$, a subset of nodes $S \subseteq V$ is selected as active nodes, defined as the *seed set*, while other nodes are inactive. For any time $t \geq 1$, when a node u is activated at step $t-1$, u is given a single chance to activate each of its inactive out-neighbors v through edge (u, v) independently with probability $p_{u,v}$ at step t. Once activated, a node stays as active in the remaining time steps. The influence diffusion process stops when there is no new activation at a time step.

Given a target set $U \subseteq V$, let $Inf_U(S)$ be the random variable denoting the number of active nodes in U after the diffusion process starting from the seed set S ends. When the context is clear, we usually omit the subscript U and use $Inf(S)$ to represent this random variable, and we refer $Inf(S)$ as the *influence coverage* of seed set S (for target set U). The optimization problem we are trying to solve is to find a seed set S of minimum size such that the influence coverage of S is at least a required threshold with a required probability guarantee. The formal problem is defined below.

Definition 1 (Seed minimization with probabilistic coverage guarantee) *We define the problem of* seed minimization with probabilistic coverage guarantee (SM-PCG) *as follows. The input of the problem includes the social graph $G = (V, E)$, the influence probabilities $p_{u,v}$'s on edges, the target set U, a coverage threshold $\eta < |U|$,*[1] *a probability threshold $P \in (0, 1)$. The problem is to find the minimum size seed set S^* such that S^* can activate at least η nodes in U with probability P, that is,*

$$S^* = \operatorname*{argmin}_{S:\Pr(Inf(S)\geq\eta)\geq P} |S|.$$

The following theorem shows the hardness of the SM-PCG problem.

THEOREM 1. *The problem SM-PCG is NP-hard, and for any $\varepsilon > 0$, it cannot be approximated within a ratio of $(1-\varepsilon)\ln n$ unless NP has $n^{O(\log\log n)}$-time deterministic algorithms.*

PROOF (SKETCH). We show that the NP-complete problem Set Cover is a special case of SM-PCG, and the lower bound on approximation ratio is due to the result in [9] on the Set Cover problem. □

With the above hardness result, we set our goal as to find algorithms that solve the SM-PCG problem with approximation ratio close to $\ln n$.

3. USEFUL RESULTS AND TOOLS

In this section, we provide some useful results and tools in preparation for our algorithm design.

Almost all previous work on social influence maximization or seed minimization is based on submodular function optimization techniques. Consider a set function $f(\cdot)$ which maps subsets of a finite ground set into real number set $\mathbb{R}$. We say that $f(\cdot)$ is *submodular* if for any subsets $S \subseteq T$ and any element $u \notin T$, $f(S \cup \{u\}) - f(S) \geq f(T \cup \{u\}) - f(T)$. Moreover, we say that $f(\cdot)$ is *monotone* if for any subsets $S \subseteq T$, $f(S) \leq f(T)$.

Consider a monotone and submodular function $f(\cdot)$ on subsets of nodes in the social graph $G = (V, E)$. Suppose that each node $v \in V$ has a cost $c(v)$, given by a cost function $c : V \to \mathbb{R}^+$. The cost of a subset S is defined as $c(S) = \sum_{v\in S} c(v)$. In [12], Goyal et al. investigate the problem of finding a subset $S \subseteq V$ with minimum cost such that $f(S)$ is at least some given threshold η. As in many optimization tasks for submodular functions, the following greedy algorithm is applied to solve the problem: starting from the emptyset $S_0 = \emptyset$, in the i-th iteration with

[1]We believe that $\eta < |U|$ is reasonable for the application scenarios we described since typically it requires only a fraction of the entire target node set to make a topic hot. For the case of $\eta = |U|$, we also worked out a separate solution for one-way bipartite graphs, but due to page limit, we omit it in this paper.

$i = 1, 2, \ldots$, find a node v_i that provides the largest marginal gain on f per-unit cost, that is find

$$v_i = \underset{v \in V \setminus S_{i-1}}{\operatorname{argmax}} \frac{f(S_{i-1} \cup \{v\}) - f(S_{i-1})}{c(v)},$$

and add v_i to S_{i-1} to obtain S_i; continue this process until iteration j in which $f(S_j) \geq \theta$, where θ is a threshold that could be η or some other value chosen by the algorithm as the stopping criteria, and output S_j as the selected subset S. However, generally computing $f(\cdot)$ exactly is #P-hard, but for most influence spread models, it can be estimated by Monte Carlo simulation as accurately as possible. We say an estimation $\hat{f}(\cdot)$ is a *γ-multiplicative error estimation* of $f(\cdot)$, if for any subset S, $|\hat{f}(S) - f(S)| \leq \gamma f(S)$. Goyal et al. show a bicriteria approximation result for the above greedy algorithm when $\gamma = 0$ [12]. For the case of uniform node cost and $\eta < f(V)$, we slightly improve the above result by removing the bicriteria restriction and generalizing to the case of $\gamma \geq 0$.

THEOREM 2. *Let $G = (V, E)$ be a social graph, and let $f(\cdot)$ be a nonnegative, monotone and submodular set function on the subsets $|V|$. Given a threshold $0 < \eta < f(V)$, let $S^* \subseteq V$ be a subset of minimum size such that $f(S^*) \geq \eta$, and S be the greedy solution using a γ-multiplicative error estimation function $\hat{f}(\cdot)$ with the stopping criteria $\hat{f}(S) \geq (1+\gamma)\eta$. For any $0 \leq \varepsilon_0 \leq 1$, for any $0 \leq \gamma \leq \frac{\varepsilon_0 (f(V)-\eta)}{8|V|(f(V)+\eta|V|)}$, we have $f(S) \geq \eta$, and $|S| \leq \alpha|S^*| + 1$ where $\alpha = \max\{\left\lceil \ln \frac{(1+\varepsilon_0)\eta|V|}{f(V)-\eta} \right\rceil, 0\}$.*

Note that when $\eta = \Theta(f(V))$, we have $\gamma \leq \frac{\varepsilon_0 (f(V)-\eta)}{8|V|(f(V)+\eta|V|)} = \Theta(\frac{\varepsilon_0}{|V|^2})$.

Kempe et al. show that set function $E[Inf(S)]$ for *expected influence coverage* is monotone and submodular under the IC model [14]. Therefore, if our problem is to find a seed set of minimum size such that the expected influence coverage is at least a threshold value η, Theorem 2 already provides the approximation guarantee of the greedy algorithm. We call this problem the *seed minimization with expected coverage guarantee (SM-ECG)*, to differentiate with the problem concerned in this paper — seed minimization with *probabilistic* coverage guarantee (SM-PCG).

For the SM-PCG problem, we want the influence coverage to be at least η with a guaranteed probability P. This seemingly minor change from SM-ECG actually alters the nature of the problem. The SM-PCG corresponds to two variants of set functions, but neither of them is submodular. In the first variant, we fix influence threshold η, and define $f_\eta : 2^{|V|} \rightarrow \mathbb{R}^+$ where $f_\eta(S) = \Pr(Inf(S) \geq \eta)$. In the second variant, we fix probability P, and define $g_P : 2^{|V|} \rightarrow \mathbb{R}^+$ where $g_P(S) = \max_{\eta' : \Pr(Inf(S) \geq \eta') \geq P} \eta'$. Neither $f_\eta(\cdot)$ nor $g_P(\cdot)$ is submodular, as shown by the two examples below. For f_η, see Figure 1(a), G is a bipartite graph where all edges are associated with probability 1, and U contains all the nodes in the lower part. We fix $\eta = 5$. Let $S = \{a\}$ and $T = \{a, b\}$, then $f_\eta(S \cup \{u\}) - f_\eta(S) = 0$, since neither S nor $S \cup \{u\}$ could reach 5 nodes in U. Similarly, $f_\eta(T) = 0$. However, $f_\eta(T \cup \{u\}) = 1$, since 5 nodes are reached by $T \cup \{u\}$. Therefore, $f_\eta(T \cup \{u\}) - f_\eta(T) > f_\eta(S \cup \{u\}) - f_\eta(S)$, and thus $f_\eta(\cdot)$ is not submodular. For g_P, see Figure 1(b), G is a bipartite graph where all edges are associated with probability 0.5, and $U = \{u\}$. We set $P = 0.8$. Let $S = \{a\}$ and $T = \{a, b\}$,

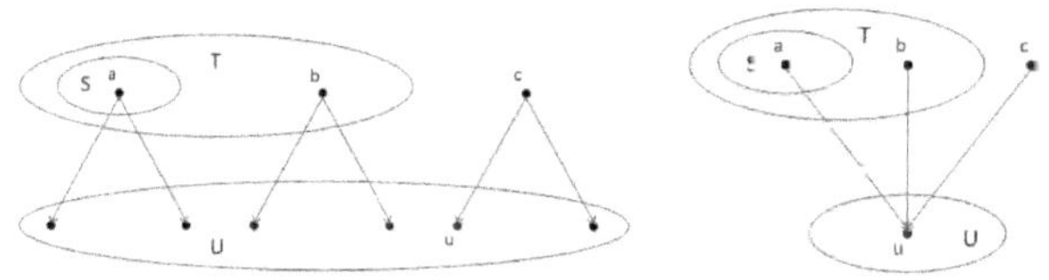

(a) f_η (b) g_P

Figure 1: Function f_η and g_P are nonsubmoduar.

Algorithm 1 Function MC-CompProb[R]: R is a tuning parameter controlling the accuracy of the estimate

Input: $G = (V, E), \{p_{u,v}\}_{(u,v) \in E}, U, S, \eta$
Output: estimate of $P = \Pr(Inf(S) \geq \eta)$

```
t = 0
for i = 1 to R do
    simulate IC diffusion with seed set S
    N_i = number of final active nodes in U
    if N_i ≥ η then
        t = t + 1
    end if
end for
return t/R
```

then $g_P(S \cup \{c\}) - g_P(S) = 0$ and $g_P(T \cup \{c\}) - g_P(T) = 1$. Since $g_P(S \cup \{c\}) - g_P(S) < g_P(T \cup \{c\}) - g_P(T)$, g_P is not submodular.

Since neither $f_\eta(\cdot)$ nor $g_P(\cdot)$ is submodular, we cannot apply Theorem 2 on $f_\eta(\cdot)$ or $g_P(\cdot)$ to solve the SM-PCG problem. In this paper, we address this non-submodular optimization problem by relating it to the SM-ECG problem through a concentration assumption on random variable $Inf(S)$ for certain seed sets S.

4. INFLUENCE COVERAGE COMPUTATION

Before working on the SM-PCG problem directly, we first address the related computation issue when a seed set S is given. As we mentioned in last section, there are two variants in influence coverage computation. The first variant is that, given a seed set S and a coverage threshold η, we need to compute the probability $f_\eta(S)$ that S can activate at least η nodes in U. Note that we have $E[Inf(S)] = \sum_{i=1}^{n-1}(f_i(S) - f_{i+1}(S)) \cdot i + f_n(S) \cdot n$. Thus the exact computation of $f_\eta(S)$ must be #P-hard in the IC model since computing expected influence coverage $E[Inf(S)]$ of seed set S has shown to be #P-hard in the IC model [4]. However, we can use Monte Carlo simulation to compute an accurate estimate of the probability. Algorithm 1 shows the procedure MC-CompProb[R] for this task, which simulate the diffusion from seed set S for R runs and use the fraction of runs in which the number of active nodes in U reaches η as the estimate of the probability.

The following lemma shows the relationship between the number of simulations R and the accuracy of the estimate.

LEMMA 1. *Let $\hat{P}$ be the estimate of true value $P = \Pr(Inf(S) \geq \eta)$ output by* MC-CompProb[R] *in Algorithm 1. To guarantee an error of at most ε, i.e. $|\hat{P} - P| \leq \varepsilon$*

[2], *with probability at least* $1 - 1/n^\delta$, *it is sufficient to set* $R \geq \ln(2n^\delta)/(2\varepsilon^2)$.

PROOF (SKETCH). This is a direct application of Hoeffding's Inequality since Monte Carlo simulation runs are mutually independent. □

The second variant is that, given a seed set S and a specified probability P, we need to compute the maximum influence coverage η of S with at least probability P, that is, $\eta = \max_{\eta':\Pr(Inf(S)\geq\eta')\geq P} \eta'$. Unlike the first variant, we show below that this problem is #P-hard to approximate to any non-trivial ratio. We say that an algorithm approximates a true value v for a computing problem with ratio $\alpha > 1$ if the output of algorithm $\hat{v}$ satisfies $v/\alpha \leq \hat{v} \leq \alpha v$. Note that if the range of value v is from 1 to n, then using $\hat{v} = n^{1/2}$ gives a trivial approximation ratio of $\alpha = n^{1/2}$.

THEOREM 3. *For any fixed probability* $P \in (0, 1)$, *the problem of computing* $\eta = \max_{\eta':\Pr(Inf(S)\geq\eta')\geq P} \eta'$ *given a directed social graph* $G = (V, E)$, *influence probabilities* $\{p_{u,v} \mid (u, v) \in E\}$, *target set* $U = V$, *and a seed set* S *is #P-hard to approximate within a ratio of* $|V|^{1/2-\varepsilon}$ *for any* $\varepsilon > 0$.

Note that we treat P as a fixed parameter of the problem rather than as part of the input to the computation problem, which makes the result stronger.

PROOF (SKETCH). We prove the theorem by first reducing the #P-complete counting problem of *s-t* connectivity in a directed graph [19] to its decision version, and then reducing the decision version to our computation problem. □

5. APPROXIMATION ALGORITHM

In this section, we overcome the nonsubmodularity nature of the SM-PCG problem discussed in Section 3 by connecting it with the submodular problem SM-ECG. We first provide the general algorithm, and then show that the algorithm returns a seed set that approximates the optimal solution with both a multiplicative ratio and an additive error. The multiplicative ratio is due to the connection with the SM-ECG problem. For the additive error term, we show that it would be nontrivial when certain concentration assumption on influence coverages holds.

Algorithm 2 illustrates algorithm MinSeed-PCG for solving the SM-PCG problem. The algorithm builds up a sequence of subsets $S_0, S_1, S_2, \ldots$, where for each $i \geq 1$, S_i contains one more element u than S_{i-1} such that u provides the largest marginal increase in *expected* influence coverage to seed set S_{i-1}. The way of constructing seed sets S_i's is in line with the greedy approach as discussed in Section 3. In our algorithm, $\hat{E}[Inf(\cdot)]$ is a γ-multiplicative error estimation of exact expected influence $E[Inf(\cdot)]$. Every time a new set S_i is constructed, we compute the probability that the influence coverage of S_i is at least η (line 5). The CompProb in line 5 is a generic function computing $\Pr(Inf(S_i) \geq \eta)$, which could be MC-CompProb[R] in Algorithm 1 for general graphs, or Bi-CompProb in Algorithm 3 for one-way bipartite graphs, or some other functions for this purpose. If the probability computed is at least $P + \varepsilon$, where $\varepsilon \in [0, (1 - P)/2)$ is a parameter of the algorithm, we stop and return S_i as the seed set found by the algorithm. Parameter ε is related to the accuracy of the function CompProb. If CompProb accurately computes $\Pr(Inf(S) \geq \eta)$ (e.g. Bi-CompProb for one-way bipartite graphs), we set ε to 0. If CompProb only provides an estimate (e.g. MC-CompProb[R] for general graphs), we set ε to be an appropriate value related to the error term of the estimate given by the function. We will discuss parameter ε with more technical details later.

[2]This lemma holds when $\varepsilon > P$. However, we usually set ε smaller than P to make the estimate more reasonable.

Algorithm 2 MinSeed-PCG[ε]: $\varepsilon \in [0, (1-P)/2)$ is a control parameter

Input: $G = (V, E), \{p_{u,v}\}_{(u,v)\in E}, U, \eta, P$
Output: seed set S, which is an approximation to $S^* = \operatorname{argmin}_{S':\Pr(Inf(S')\geq\eta)\geq P}\{|S'|\}$
1: $S_0 = \emptyset$
2: **for** $i = 1$ to n **do**
3: select $u = \operatorname{argmax}_v\{\hat{E}[Inf(S_{i-1} \cup \{v\})] - \hat{E}[Inf(S_{i-1})]\}$
4: $S_i = S_{i-1} \cup \{u\}$
5: $prob = \mathsf{CompProb}(G, \{p_{u,v}\}_{(u,v)\in E}, U, S_i, \eta)$
6: **if** $prob \geq P + \varepsilon$ **then**
7: **return** S_i
8: **end if**
9: **end for**

Let S^* be the optimal seed set for the SM-PCG problem, that is, $S^* = \operatorname{argmin}_{S:\Pr(Inf(S)\geq\eta)\geq P} |S|$. Let $n = |V|$ and $m = |U|$. Let $\mathcal{S} = \{S_1, S_2, \ldots, S_n = V\}$ be the sequence of greedy seed sets computed by algorithm MinSeed-PCG[ε] (considering the entire sequence even when MinSeed-PCG[ε] actually stops). Let S_a be the output of MinSeed-PCG[ε] and a is its index in sequence $\mathcal{S}$, and thus S_{a-1} is the set in $\mathcal{S}$ just before S_a.

We define $c = \max\{\eta - E[Inf(S^*)], 0\}$ and $c' = \max\{E[Inf(S_{a-1})] - \eta, 0\}$. Intuitively, we know that $\Pr(Inf(S^*) \geq \eta) \geq P$, and c indicates how much $E[Inf(S^*)]$ could be smaller than η. If $Inf(S^*)$ concentrates well, c should be small. Similarly, we also know that $\Pr(Inf(S_{a-1}) \geq \eta) < P + \varepsilon$, since S_a is the first set satisfying $\Pr(Inf(S_a) \geq \eta) \geq P + \varepsilon$. Thus, c' indicates how much $E[Inf(S_{a-1})]$ could be larger than η, and if $Inf(S_{a-1})$ concentrates well, c' should be small.

The following theorem shows that the output S_a of MinSeed-PCG[ε] approximates the optimal solution S^* with c and c' included in the additive error term.

THEOREM 4. *For any* $0 \leq \varepsilon_0 \leq 1$ *and any* $0 \leq \gamma \leq \frac{\varepsilon_0(m-(\eta+c'))^2}{8mn(m+\eta n)}$. *If* $\hat{E}[Inf(\cdot)]$ *is a* γ*-multiplicative error estimation of* $E[Inf(\cdot)]$ *for any subset of nodes, the size of the output by algorithm* MinSeed-PCG[ε] *approximates the size of the optimal solution in the following form:*

$$|S_a| \leq \left\lceil \ln \frac{(1+\varepsilon_0)\eta m}{m-\eta} \right\rceil \cdot |S^*| + \frac{(c+c')n}{m-(\eta+c')} + 3 + \varepsilon_0. \quad (1)$$

First, note that we assume $m > \eta$, so the multiplicative term above is well defined. Moreover, $\eta + c'$ must be less than m, because otherwise $E[Inf(S_{a-1})] = m = |U|$, which implies $\Pr(Inf(S_{a-1}) = m) = 1$, contradicting the fact that $\Pr(Inf(S_{a-1}) \geq \eta) < P + \varepsilon < 1$. Second, for the multiplicative ratio of $\lceil \ln \frac{\eta n}{m-\eta} \rceil$, when η is a constant fraction of m, i.e. $\eta = \beta m$ where β is a constant independent of m and n, it is

$\ln n + O(1)$, which is tight, since Theorem 1 already states that the ratio cannot be better than $\ln n$. The additive error term involves c and c', and we will discuss it in more detail after providing the proof to the theorem below. Third, when $\eta+c'$ is a constant fraction of m, $\gamma \leq \frac{\varepsilon_0(m-(\eta+c'))^2}{8mn(m+\eta n)} = \Theta(\frac{\varepsilon_0}{n^2})$. Fourth, by Chernoff bound, to achieve a γ-multiplicative error estimation of expected influence with probability $1-1/n$ for all subsets computed in our algorithm, it is sufficient to sample $\Theta(\gamma^{-2} n \log n)$ number of graphs for each set.

PROOF. We only prove the case of $\gamma = \varepsilon_0 = 0$ in this paper. Let i be the minimum index such that $S_i \in \mathcal{S}$ and $E[Inf(S_i)] \geq \eta - c$, and S_i^* be the minimum-sized seed set such that $E[Inf(S_i^*)] \geq \eta - c$. Since $E[Inf(S^*)] \geq \eta - c$, we know that $|S_i^*| \leq |S^*|$. By Theorem 2, since $\left\lceil \ln \frac{(\eta-c)n}{m-(\eta-c)} \right\rceil > 0$, we have that

$$|S_i| \leq \left\lceil \ln \frac{(\eta-c)n}{m-(\eta-c)} \right\rceil \cdot |S_i^*| + 1 \leq \left\lceil \ln \frac{\eta n}{m-\eta} \right\rceil \cdot |S^*| + 1.$$

Let j be the minimum index such that $S_j \in \mathcal{S}$ and $E[Inf(S_j)] \geq \eta + c'$. Since $E[Inf(S_{a-1})] \leq \eta + c'$ we know that $|S_j| \geq |S_{a-1}|$. To bound the difference between $|S_{a-1}|$ and $|S_i|$, it is sufficient to compute the difference between $|S_j|$ and $|S_i|$.

By the definition of j, we have that $E[Inf(S_{j-1})] < \eta + c'$, thus $E[Inf(S_{j-1})] - E[Inf(S_i)] < c + c'$. Moreover, by the submodularity of $E[Inf(\cdot)]$, we know that for each $i < t < j$,

$$\begin{aligned} E[Inf(S_t)] - E[Inf(S_{t-1})] &\geq \frac{m - E[Inf(S_{t-1})]}{n} \\ &> \frac{m-(\eta+c')}{n}. \end{aligned}$$

Thus, we have that

$$\begin{aligned} |S_{j-1} \setminus S_i| &\leq \frac{E[Inf(S_{j-1})] - E[Inf(S_i)]}{\min_{i<t<j}\{E[Inf(S_t)] - E[Inf(S_{t-1})]\}} \\ &< (c+c') \cdot (\frac{m-(\eta+c')}{n})^{-1} \\ &= \frac{(c+c')n}{m-(\eta+c')}. \end{aligned}$$

It means that

$$|S_j \setminus S_i| < \frac{(c+c')n}{m-(\eta+c')} + 1.$$

Since $|S_a| \leq |S_j| + 1 = |S_i| + |S_j \setminus S_i| + 1$, we have

$$|S_a| \leq \left\lceil \ln \frac{\eta n}{m-\eta} \right\rceil \cdot |S^*| + \frac{(c+c')n}{m-(\eta+c')} + 3.$$

The theorem holds. □

We now discuss the additive term in Inequality (1). To make it nontrivial, we need the additive term to be $o(n)$ as n grows. This means first that the target set size m should be increasing with n, which is reasonable. Then we should have $c + c' = o(m)$ in order to make the additive term $o(n)$. In the following theorem, we bound c and c' by the variances of the influence coverage of S^* and S_{a-1} respectively using Chebyshev's inequality, and thus linking the above requirement on c and c' to the requirement on the variances of influence coverages.

THEOREM 5. *For algorithm* MinSeed-PCG[ε] *with any parameter* ε, *we have*

$$c \leq \sqrt{\frac{Var(Inf(S^*))}{P}}. \tag{2}$$

If we use MC-CompProb[R] *for function* CompProb *and set* $R \geq \ln(2n^2)/(2\varepsilon^2)$, *then algorithm* MinSeed-PCG[ε] *finds a seed set* S_a *such that, with probability at least* $1 - 1/n$, $\Pr(Inf(S_a) \geq \eta) \geq P$ *and*

$$c' \leq \sqrt{\frac{Var(Inf(S_{a-1}))}{1-P-2\varepsilon}}. \tag{3}$$

Theorem 5 shows that the variances of influence coverages of seed sets, or more exactly the standard deviations of influence coverages, determine the scale of the additive error term of the algorithm MinSeed-PCG[ε]. If influence coverages concentrate well with small standard deviations, the algorithm would have a good additive error term. Consider the common case where target set size $m = \Theta(n)$, and η is a constant fraction of m, and P is a normal probability requirement not too close to 0 or 1 (e.g. 0.1 or 0.5), if we could have $Var(Inf(S^*)) = O(m)$ and $Var(Inf(S_{a-1})) = O(m)$, then $c + c' = O(\sqrt{m})$, and the additive error term is $O(n/\sqrt{m}) = O(\sqrt{n})$. Together with Theorem 4, we would know that

$$|S_a| \leq (\ln n + O(1))|S^*| + O(\sqrt{n}).$$

In the next section, we analytically show that for one-way bipartite graphs indeed $c+c' = O(\sqrt{m})$. We also empirically verify that in real-world graphs the standard deviations of influence coverages are indeed small, close to $\sqrt{m}$. Therefore, our algorithm are likely to perform well in practice.

We remark that our theorems in this section can be applied to a class of models with the following characteristics:

1. the influence coverage function of a seed set (i.e., $Inf(\cdot)$) is nonnegative, monotone and submodular, thus greedy algorithm gives an $O(\log n)$-approximation ratio for SM-ECG (Theorem 2) and provides a tight multiplicative ratio.
2. the influence coverage when choosing the whole set of nodes as seeds is the size of the targeted set (i.e., $Inf(V) = |U|$), which guarantees that the additive error is reasonable.

The above class includes many diffusion models, such as linear threshold model, general threshold model and continuous time diffusion model.

6. RESULTS ON BIPARTITE GRAPHS

In this section, we solve the SM-PCG problem on a one-way bipartite graph $G = (V_1, V_2, E)$, where all edges in E are from V_1 to V_2. For the sake of convenience, we just assume that $U = V_2$ in this section. It is easy to remove this assumption and make U to be any subset of $V_1 \cup V_2$.

One-way bipartite graphs provide two significant advantages over general graphs. First, it allows a dynamic programming method to compute the exact influence coverage distribution given any seed set S. Second, it allows a theoretical analysis on the concentration of influence coverages of seed sets. We illustrate both aspects below.

We first show how to implement exact computation of function CompProb. We assign indices for nodes in V_2:

$v_1, v_2, \ldots, v_m$. Let $A(S,i,j)$ denote the probability that seed set S can activate exactly j nodes in the first i nodes of V_2: $v_1, \ldots, v_i$, where $j \leq i$. Let $p(S,v)$ be the probability that v can be activated by S. When $i = 1$, it is trivial to get $A(S,1,j)$. When $i > 1$, we can use $A(S,i-1,j-1)$ and $A(S,i-1,j)$ to compute $A(S,i,j)$. If $j = 0$, it means $v_1, \ldots, v_{i-1}$ and v_i are all inactive. If $0 < j < i$, there are two cases: j nodes are activated in the first $i-1$ nodes while v_i is not activated; $j-1$ nodes are activated in the first $i-1$ nodes and v_i is activated. If $j = i$, both $v_1, \ldots, v_{i-1}$ and v_i are activated. Thus, we have the following recursion,

$$A(S,1,j) = \begin{cases} p(S,v_1), & j = 1 \\ 1 - p(S,v_1), & j = 0 \end{cases}$$

and

$$A(S,i,j) =$$

$$\begin{cases} A(S,i-1,j) \cdot (1 - p(S,v_i)), & j = 0 \\ A(S,i-1,j) \cdot (1 - p(S,v_i)) & \\ +A(S,i-1,j-1) \cdot p(S,v_i), & 0 < j < i \\ A(S,i-1,j-1) \cdot p(S,v_i), & j = i \end{cases}$$

For IC model, $p(S,v_i) = 1 - \prod_{u \in S}(1 - p_{u,v_i})$; for LT model, $p(S,v_i) = \sum_{u \in S} p_{u,v_i}$. Using the above dynamic programming formulation, we can implement function CompProb as function Bi-CompProb given in Algorithm 3.

Algorithm 3 Function Bi-CompProb for bipartite graphs

Input: $G = (V_1, V_2, E), \{p_{u,v}\}_{(u,v) \in E}, S, \eta$
Output: $P = \Pr(\mathit{Inf}(S) \geq \eta)$
1: **for** i from 1 to n, and j from 1 to i **do**
2: compute $A(S,i,j)$ via dynamic programming
3: **end for**
4: **return** $\sum_{j=\eta}^{m} A(S,m,j)$

One-way bipartite graphs have an important property that the activation events of nodes in V_2 are mutually independent. This allows us to bound c and c' defined in Section 5 using Hoeffding's Inequality, and get the following result.

THEOREM 6. *For one-way bipartite graphs, algorithm* MinSeed-PCG[0] *using function* Bi-CompProb *returns seed set S_a such that $\Pr(\mathit{Inf}(S_a) \geq \eta) \geq P$, and when we consider the probability threshold P as a constant independent of n and m, we have*

$$|S_a| \leq (\ln n + O(1)) \cdot |S^*| + O(\frac{n}{\sqrt{m}}). \tag{4}$$

We note that one-way bipartite graphs are a restricted class of graphs, where the influence cascading is a 1-hop cascading process and cannot be generated to a cascade with greater depth. However, we believe their analytical results can shed lights on more realistic networks when most of node activations in the network are independent.

7. EXPERIMENTS

We conduct experiments on real social networks for the following purposes: (1) test the concentration of influence coverage distributions of seed sets; (2) validate the performance of our algorithm against baseline algorithms.

7.1 Experiment setup

Datasets. We conduct experiments on three real social networks. The first one is wiki-Vote [15], a network relationship graph from Wikipedia community with totally 7,115 nodes and 103,689 edges. In wiki-Vote graph, each node represents a user, and an edge (u,v) represents user u votes for user v, which means that v has an influence on u. Thus, in our experiment, we reverse all edges to express the influence between pairs of nodes. We use weighted cascade (WC) model [14] to assign the influence probabilities on edges. For each edge (u,v), we assign its probability to be $1/d_{in}(v)$, where $d_{in}(v)$ is the in-degree of node v.

The second network is NetHEPT, which is a standard dataset used in [5, 4, 6, 13, 12]. NetHEPT is an academic collaboration network from arXiv (http://www.arXiv.org), with totally 15,233 nodes and 58,891 edges. In NetHEPT graph, each node represents an author, and each edge represents coauthor relationship between two authors. NetHEPT is an undirected graph, and in our experiment we add two directed edges between two nodes if there exists at least one edge between these two nodes in NetHEPT. Similar to wiki-Vote, we use WC model to assign edge influence probabilities. We assign the probability on directed edge (u,v) to be $d(u,v)/d(v)$, where $d(u,v)$ is the number of papers collaborated by u and v, and $d(v)$ is the number of papers published by v.

The last one is Flixster, an American movie rating social site. Each node is a user, and edges describe the friendship between users. In this network, we use a Topic-aware Independent Cascade Model from [1] to learn the real influence probabilities on edges for different topics. We simply use two different topics, say topic 1 and topic 2, and get the edge probabilities that one user influences his/her friend on the specific topic. In both topics, we remove edges with probability 0 and isolated nodes. For topic 1, there are 28,317 nodes and 206,012 edges. The mean of edge probabilities is 0.103, and the standard deviation is 0.160. For topic 2, there are 25,474 nodes and 135,618 edges. The mean of edge probabilities is 0.133, and the standard deviation is 0.205.

Experiment methods. In the experiment, for the sake of convenience, we set $U = V$.

Our first task is to test the concentration of influence coverage distributions of seed sets. To do so, we test the variances (or their square roots, i.e. standard deviations). According to Theorem 5, small standard deviations imply small c and c' and thus small additive errors of the MinSeed-PCG[ε] algorithm output. By Inequality (3), to verify that c' is small, we just need to test the standard deviations of all seed sets generated by the algorithm. For quantity c, we need to test the standard deviation of the influence coverage of the optimal seed set, according to Inequality (2). However, finding the optimal seed set is NP-hard, therefore we cannot fully verify the bound on c. To compensate, we test randomly selected seed sets as follows. For each fixed seed set size k, we independently select 10 seed sets of size k at random, and compute the maximum standard deviations of the influence coverage distributions of these selected seed sets. Although randomly selected seed sets may be far from the optimal seed set, what we hope is that by testing standard deviations on both randomly selected sets and greedily selected sets by algorithm MinSeed-PCG[ε], we have a general understanding of standard deviations of influence coverages of seed sets, which may provide us with hints for other seed sets, such as the optimal seed set. To estimate the standard deviations of influence coverage of a seed set S, we use 10,000 times Monte Carlo simulation and compute the standard deviation.

Our second task is to test the performance of seed selection algorithm MinSeed-PCG[ε]. We compare the performance with three baseline algorithms: (a) Random, which generates the seed set sequence in random order; (b) High-degree, which generates the seed set sequence according to the decreasing order of the out-degree of nodes; and (c) PageRank, which is a popular method for website ranking [2]. We use $p_{v,u}/\sum_{(w,u)\in E} p_{w,u}$ as the transition probability for edge (u,v). Higher $p_{v,u}$ means that v is more influential to u, indicating that u ranks v higher. We use 0.15 as the restart probability and use the power method to compute PageRank values. When two consecutive iterations are different for at most 10^{-4} in L_1 norm, we stop. As for our MinSeed-PCG[ε] algorithm, to speed up the algorithm, we use the state-of-the-art PMIA algorithm of [4] to greedily generate the seed set sequence. For all the above algorithms, we use the same MC-CompProb[R] algorithm to compare whether a seed set S in the sequence satisfies the condition $\Pr(\mathit{Inf}(S) \geq \eta) \geq P + \varepsilon$. Since the seed set sequence generations in all the above algorithms are fast comparing to the Monte Carlo simulation based MC-CompProb[R] algorithm, our implementation actually generates the sequence first and then uses binary search to find the seed set in the sequence satisfying $\Pr(\mathit{Inf}(S) \geq \eta) \geq P + \varepsilon$.

We set parameters $R = 10,000$ and $\varepsilon = 0.01$. One may see that these settings do not satisfy the condition $R \geq \ln(2n^2)/(2\varepsilon^2)$ in Theorem 5 for our datasets: in our datasets, n is around 10^4, and thus $\ln(2n^2)/(2\varepsilon^2)$ is around 9.6×10^4. However, we can justify our choice as follows. First, the condition $R \geq \ln(2n^2)/(2\varepsilon^2)$ is a conservative theoretical condition for obtaining high probability of $1 - 1/n$ for our approximation guarantee. In practice, a smaller R of 10,000 is good enough for illustrating our results. Second, all algorithms use the same MC-CompProb[R] algorithm, so the comparison is fair among them, and is focused on the difference in their generations of seed set sequences, not on the accuracy of the estimate of function CompProb. Third, the seed selections actually depends only on the combined parameter $P' = P + \varepsilon$, and not on P and ε separately. Thus setting $\varepsilon = 0.01$ is only for intuitive understanding and setting it to some other value would not change the results as long as P' remains the same.

7.2 Experiment results

Concentration of influence coverages. Figure 2 shows the standard deviations of influence coverages of randomly selected seed sets and greedily selected seed sets (by algorithm MinSeed-PCG[ε]) on wiki-Vote, NetHEPT and Flixster. We can see that in all graphs, standard deviations for greedily selected seed sets quickly drop, while for randomly selected seed sets sometimes it has a small increase when the seed set size is small, and then quickly drop too. The maximum value is about 130 for wiki-Vote ($|V| = 7,115$), 105 for NetHEPT ($|V| = 15,233$), 750 for Flixster with topic 1 ($|V| = 28,317$), and 270 for Flixster with topic 2 ($|V| = 25,474$). Thus by observation the standard deviation is at the order of $\sqrt{|V|}$. As discussed after Theorem 5, this means that the additive error of our algorithm would be $O(\sqrt{|V|})$, a small and satisfactory value.

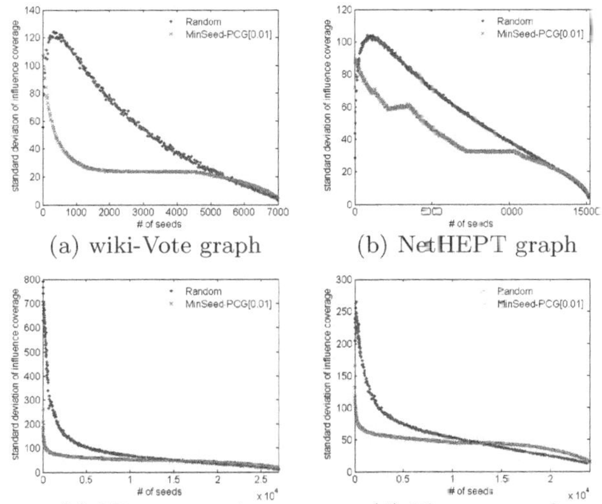

(a) wiki-Vote graph (b) NetHEPT graph (c) Flixster graph with topic 1 (d) Flixster graph with topic 2

Figure 2: Standard deviations of influence coverages of seed sets.

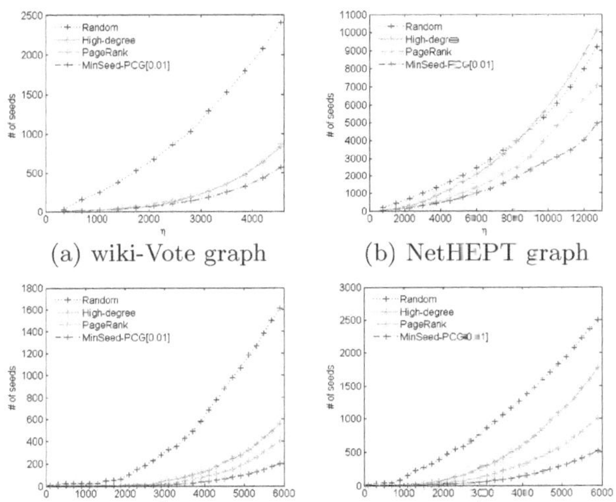

(a) wiki-Vote graph (b) NetHEPT graph (c) Flixster graph with topic 1 (d) Flixster graph with topic 2

Figure 3: Size of selected seed sets vs. coverage threshold η under a fixed probability threshold $P = 0.1$.

The standard deviations for wiki-Vote are larger than those for NetHEPT at small seed set size even though the number of nodes of wiki-Vote is smaller. We believe this is because wiki-Vote has more edges (103,689) than NetHEPT (58,891), and thus when the seed set size is small more edges could cause larger variances in influence coverage. This can also explain why in Flixster topic 1 (with 206,012 edges) has larger standard deviations than topic 2 (with 135,618 edges).

Performance of MinSeed-PCG[ε] compared with baselines. We conduct two sets of tests for this purpose. First, we fix the probability threshold P to 0.1 and 0.5, and vary the coverage threshold η to compare the size of seed sets selected by various algorithms. Figure 3 and Figure 4 show

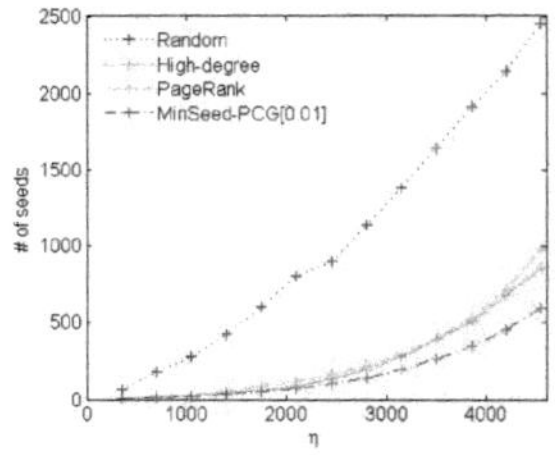

(a) wiki-Vote graph

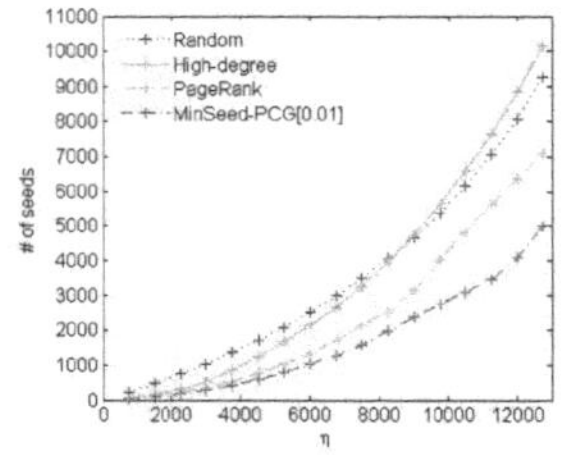

(b) NetHEPT graph

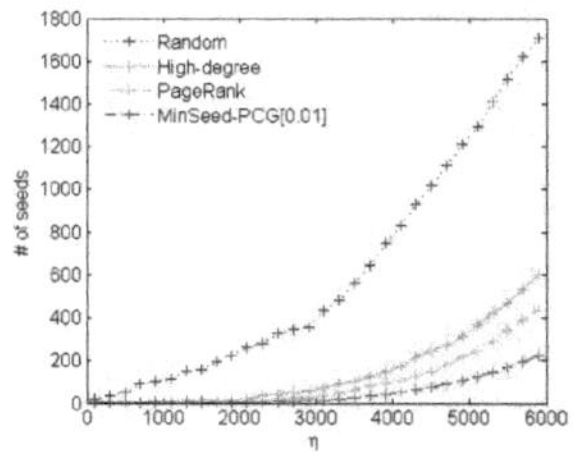

(c) Flixster graph with topic 1

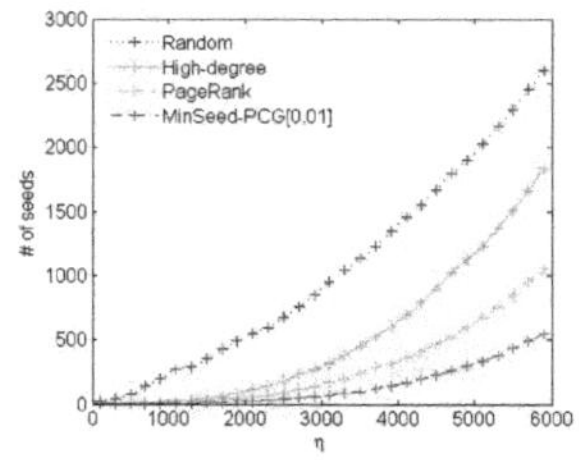

(d) Flixster graph with topic 2

Figure 4: Size of selected seed sets vs. coverage threshold η under a fixed probability threshold $P = 0.5$.

the test results on three datasets. All test results consistently show that our algorithm performances the best, and sometimes with a significant improvement over the Random, High-degree and PageRank heuristics. In particular, for wiki-Vote and $P = 0.1$ (Figure 3(a)), on average our algorithm MinSeed-PCG[ε] selects seed sets with size 88.2% less than those selected by Random, 20.2% less than High-degree, and 30.9% less than PageRank. For NetHEPT and $P = 0.1$ (Figure 3(b)), on average our algorithm selects seed sets with size 56.7% less than Random, 46.0% less than High-degree, and 24.4% less than PageRank. The High-degree heuristic performs close to MinSeed-PCG[ε] in wiki-Vote, but performs badly in NetHEPT, even worse than Random when η is large. This shows that High-degree is not a good and stable heuristic for this task. For Flixster with topic 1 and $P = 0.1$ (Figure 5(c)), on average MinSeed-PCG[ε] selects seed sets with size 94.4% less than Random, 54.0% less than High-degree, and 29.2% less than PageRank. For Fixster with topic 2 and $P = 0.1$ (Figure 5(d)), on average MinSeed-PCG[ε] selects seed sets with size 91.1% less than Random, 73.0% less than High-degree, and 24.4% less than PageRank. Figures 4 show the results for $P = 0.5$. The curves are almost the same as the corresponding ones for $P = 0.1$. This can be explained by the sharp phase transition to be observed in the next set of tests, which is due to concentration of influence coverage, such that typically only a few tens of more seeds would satisfy probability threshold P from 0.1 to 0.5.

Our second set of tests is to fix a coverage threshold η, and observe the change of coverage probability $\Pr(Inf(S) \geq \eta)$ as the seed set S grows as computed by various algorithms. Figure 5 shows the test results. Wiki-Vote, NetHEPT and Flixster with topic 2 (Figure 5(a), (b), (d)) have sharp phase transition: there is a short range of seed set size where the probability increases very fast from 0.01 to very close to 1 (only several nodes are needed to reach a 0.1 increment in probability). While Filxster with topic 1 (Figure 5(c)) has a relatively smooth phase transition. This phase transition

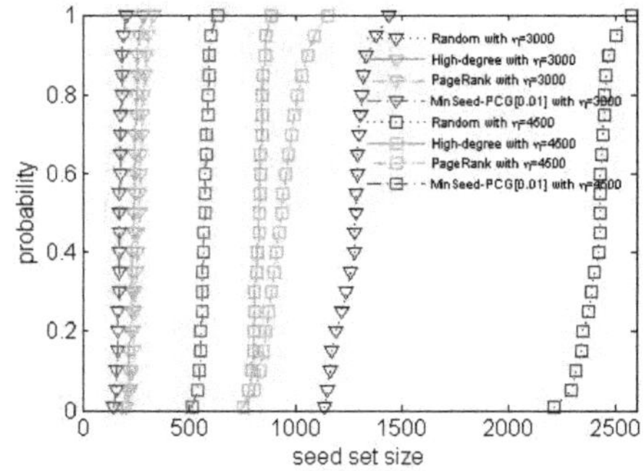

(a) wiki-Vote graph, $\eta = 3000, 4500$

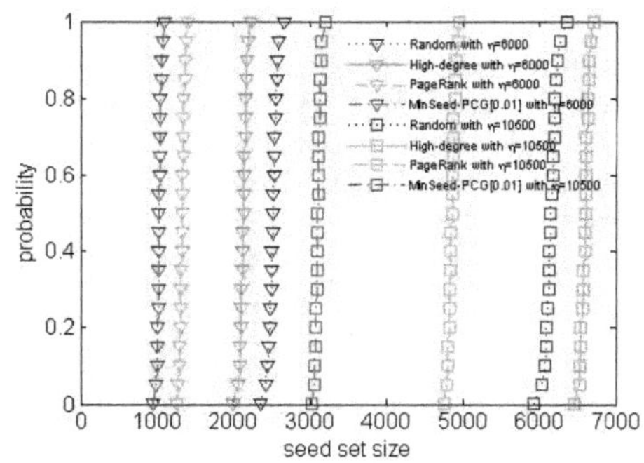

(b) NetHEPT graph, $\eta = 6000, 10500$

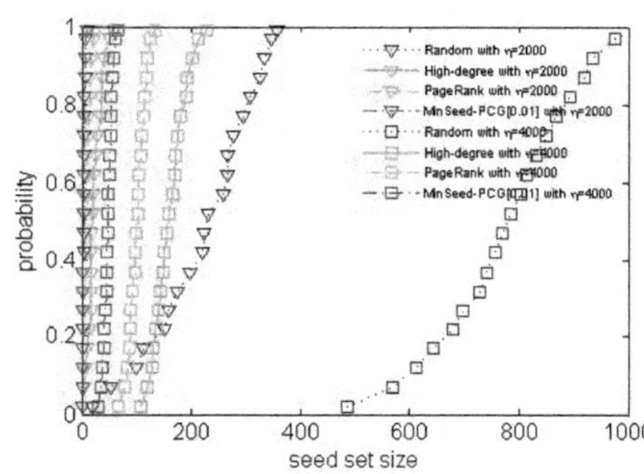

(c) Flixster graph with topic 1, $\eta = 2000, 4000$

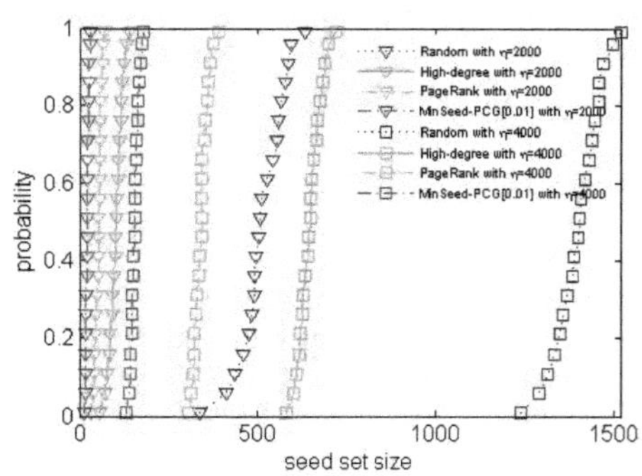

(d) Flixster graph with topic 2, $\eta = 2000, 4000$

Figure 5: Size of selected seed sets vs. probability threshold P under a fixed coverage threshold η.

phenomenon is clearly due to the concentration of influence coverages of seed sets, as already verified in Figure 2.

In all our tests, MinSeed-PCG[ε] performances the best: its phase transition comes first before the other algorithms, which means it uses less number of seeds to achieve the same probability threshold P. Random performs much worse than MinSeed-PCG[ε], while PageRank and High-degree perform close to MinSeed-PCG[ε] when η is small, but noticeably worse than MinSeed-PCG[ε] when η gets larger. For wiki-Vote, on average MinSeed-PCG[ε] selects a seed set with size 34.1% less than PageRank, 27.7% less than High-degree, and 86.4% less than Random when $\eta = 3,000$. When $\eta = 4,500$, MinSeed-PCG[ε] selects a seed set with size on average 38.8% less than PageRank, 30.8% less than High-degree, and 76.3% less than Random. For NetHEPT, when $\eta = 6,000$, on average MinSeed-PCG[ε] selects a seed set with size 22.8% less than PageRank, 51.8% less than High-degree, and 59.2% less than Random. When $\eta = 10,500$, on average MinSeed-PCG[ε] selects a seed set with size 36.1% less than PageRank, 52.9% less than High-degree, and 49.6% less than Random. For Flixster with topic 1, when $\eta = 2,000$, on average the output number of seeds by MinSeed-PCG[ε] is 44.1% less than PageRank, 78.9% less than High-degree, and 98.3% less than Random. When $\eta = 4,000$, the corresponding results are 53.2%, 70.7% and 93.9%. For topic 2, when $\eta = 2,000$, the output number of seeds by MinSeed-PCG[ε] is 59.0% less than PageRank, 78.6% less than High-degree, and 95.8% less than Random. When $\eta = 4,000$, the corresponding results are 54.9%, 76.2% and 89.0%.

For all these graphs, we do not test the case when η is very close to the number of nodes. Since in this case a large seed set close to the full node set is needed, and greedy-based seed selection loses its advantage comparing to simple random or high-degree heuristics when a large number of seeds are needed. Moreover, we believe that requiring η to be close to the full network size is not a realistic scenario in practice.

As a summary, our experimental results validate that influence coverages of seed sets are concentrated well in real-world networks, and thus support the claim that our algorithm provides good approximation guarantee. Moreover, our algorithm performs much better than simple baseline algorithms, achieving significant savings on seed set size.

8. FUTURE WORK

This study may inspire a number of future directions. One is to study the concentration property of other classes of graphs, especially graphs close to real-world networks such as power-law graphs, to see if we can analytically prove that a large class of graphs have good concentration property on influence coverage distributions. Another direction is to speed up the estimation of $\Pr(\mathit{Inf}(S) \geq \eta)$, which is done by Monte Carlo simulation in this work and is slow. One may also study influence maximization problem where reaching the tipping point is the first step, which is followed by further diffusion steps. Our algorithm and results may be an integral component of such influence maximization tasks.

9. REFERENCES

[1] N. Barbieri, F. Bonchi, and G. Manco. Topic-aware social influence propagation models. In *Data Mining (ICDM), 2012 IEEE 12th International Conference on*, pages 81–90. IEEE, 2012.

[2] S. Brin and L. Page. The anatomy of a large-scale hypertextual web search engine. *Computer networks and ISDN systems*, 30(1):107–117, 1998.

[3] N. Chen. On the approximability of influence in social networks. *SIAM Journal on Discrete Mathematics*, 23(3):1400–1415, 2009.

[4] W. Chen, C. Wang, and Y. Wang. Scalable influence maximization for prevalent viral marketing in large-scale social networks. In *KDD'10*, pages 1029–1038. ACM, 2010.

[5] W. Chen, Y. Wang, and S. Yang. Efficient influence maximization in social networks. In *KDD'09*, pages 199–208, 2009.

[6] W. Chen, Y. Yuan, and L. Zhang. Scalable Influence Maximization in Social Networks under the Linear Threshold Model. In *ICDM'10*, pages 88–97, 2010.

[7] P. Domingos and M. Richardson. Mining the network value of customers. In *KDD'01*, pages 57–66. ACM, 2001.

[8] N. Du, L. Song, M. Gomez-Rodriguez, and H. Zha. Scalable influence estimation in continuous-time diffusion networks. In *Advances in Neural Information Processing Systems*, pages 3147–3155, 2013.

[9] U. Feige. A threshold of $\ln n$ for approximating set cover. *J. ACM*, 45(4):634–652, 1998.

[10] M. Gladwell. *The Tipping Point:How Little Things Can Make a Big Difference.* Back Bay Books, 2002.

[11] S. Goldberg and Z. Liu. The Diffusion of Networking Technologies. In *SODA'13*, pages 1577–1594, 2013.

[12] A. Goyal, F. Bonchi, L. V. Lakshmanan, and S. Venkatasubramanian. On minimizing budget and time in influence propagation over social networks. *Social Network Analysis and Mining*, pages 1–14, 2012.

[13] A. Goyal, W. Lu, and L. V. S. Lakshmanan. SIMPATH: An Efficient Algorithm for Influence Maximization under the Linear Threshold Model. In *ICDM'11*, pages 211–220, 2011.

[14] D. Kempe, J. Kleinberg, and É. Tardos. Maximizing the spread of influence through a social network. In *KDD'03*, pages 137–146. ACM, 2003.

[15] J. Leskovec. Wiki-vote social network. `http://snap.stanford.edu/data/wiki-Vote.html`.

[16] C. Long and R.-W. Wong. Minimizing seed set for viral marketing. In *Data Mining (ICDM), 2011 IEEE 11th International Conference on*, pages 427–436. IEEE, 2011.

[17] M. Richardson and P. Domingos. Mining knowledge-sharing sites for viral marketing. In *KDD'02*, pages 61–70. ACM, 2002.

[18] M. G. Rodriguez and B. Schölkopf. Influence maximization in continuous time diffusion networks. In *Proceedings of the 29th International Conference on Machine Learning (ICML-12)*, pages 313–320, 2012.

[19] L. G. Valiant. The complexity of enumeration and reliability problems. *SIAM Journal on Computing*, 8(3):410–421, 1979.

[20] P. Zhang, W. Chen, X. Sun, Y. Wang, and J. Zhang. Minimizing seed set selection with probabilistic coverage guarantee in a social network. *arXiv preprint arXiv:1402.5516*, 2014.

Core Decomposition of Uncertain Graphs

Francesco Bonchi[1] Francesco Gullo[1] Andreas Kaltenbrunner[2] Yana Volkovich[2]

[1]Yahoo Labs, Spain
{bonchi,gullo}@yahoo-inc.com

[2]Barcelona Media - Innovation Centre, Spain
{andreas.kaltenbrunner,yana.volkovich}@barcelonamedia.org

ABSTRACT

Core decomposition has proven to be a useful primitive for a wide range of graph analyses. One of its most appealing features is that, unlike other notions of dense subgraphs, it can be computed linearly in the size of the input graph.

In this paper we provide an analogous tool for uncertain graphs, i.e., graphs whose edges are assigned a probability of existence. The fact that core decomposition can be computed efficiently in deterministic graphs does not guarantee efficiency in uncertain graphs, where even the simplest graph operations may become computationally intensive. Here we show that core decomposition of uncertain graphs can be carried out efficiently as well.

We extensively evaluate our definitions and methods on a number of real-world datasets and applications, such as *influence maximization* and *task-driven team formation*.

Categories and Subject Descriptors

H.2.8 [**Database Management**]: [Database Applications-Data Mining]; G.2.2 [**Discrete Mathematics**]: [Graph Theory-Graph Algorithms]

Keywords

uncertain graphs; dense subgraph; core decomposition

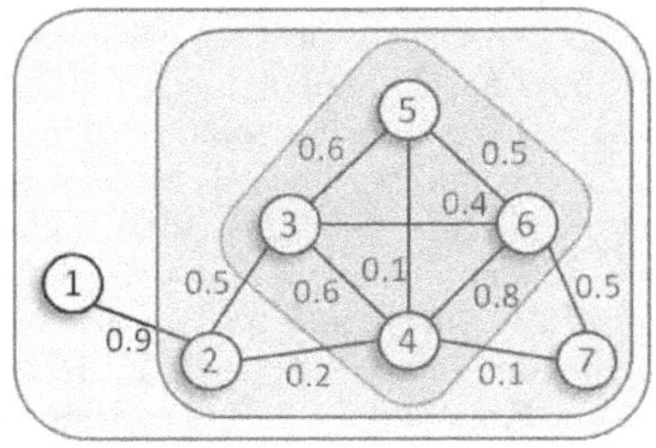

Figure 1: An uncertain graph and its (k, η)-*core decomposition* for $\eta = 0.04$. Vertex 1 has core number 1, vertices 2 and 7 have core number 2, and vertices 3, 4, 5 and 6 have core number 3.

1. INTRODUCTION

Uncertain graphs, i.e., graphs whose edges are assigned a probability of existence (see an example in Figure 1), arise in several emerging applications [24, 14, 15]. For instance, in *biological networks* and *protein-interaction networks* vertices represent genes and/or proteins, while edges represent interactions among them. Since the interactions are derived through noisy and error-prone laboratory experiments, the existence of each edge is uncertain [4, 26, 24]. In *social networks* uncertainty arises for various reasons [1]. Edge probabilities may represent the outcome of a *link-prediction* task [20] or the influence of one person on another, like in *viral marketing* [11]. Uncertainty can also be intentionally injected for privacy purposes [7].

KDD'14, August 24–27, 2014, New York, NY, USA.
Copyright 2014 ACM 978-1-4503-2956-9/14/08 ...$15.00.
http://dx.doi.org/10.1145/2623330.2623655.

Finding dense subgraphs is a fundamental primitive in many graph-analysis tasks [21]. There exist many different definitions of what a dense subgraph is, e.g., *cliques, n-cliques, n-clans, k-plexes, f-groups, n-clubs, lambda sets*, most of which are **NP**-hard to compute or at least quadratic in the size of the input graph. In this respect, the notion of *core decomposition* is particularly appealing as (*i*) it can be computed in linear time [5], and (*ii*) it is related to many other definitions of a dense subgraph (as discussed later).

The *k-core* of a graph is defined as a maximal subgraph in which every vertex is connected to at least k other vertices within that subgraph. The set of all k-cores of a graph G forms the *core decomposition* of G [25]. The fact that core decomposition can be performed in linear time in deterministic graphs does not guarantee efficiency in uncertain graphs. Indeed, in such graphs even the simplest tasks may become hard. As an example, consider the *two-terminal-reachability* problem, which asks whether two query vertices are connected. In a deterministic graph the solution to this problem requires a simple scan of the graph. Instead, in uncertain graphs, computing the probability that two vertices are connected is a #**P**-complete problem [28].

Thus, a major question we aim at answering in this paper is: *can the core decomposition of an uncertain graph be computed efficiently?*

Related work and applications. Existing research on uncertain graphs has mainly focused on querying [15, 33, 24, 31] and mining, particularly on extracting frequent subgraphs [34] or subgraphs that are connected with high probability [14], and clustering [22, 18].

Core decomposition of deterministic graphs has been exploited to analyse the nature of a network and discover dense substructures [2, 17]. It has been applied in many different domains, such as bioinformatics [30], software engineering [32], and social networks [17]. Core decomposition has been also used to speed-up the computation of more complex definitions of a dense subgraph. For instance, it serves to find maximal cliques more efficiently [10], and it is at the basis of linear-time approximation algorithms for the *densest-subgraph* problem [19] and the *densest at-least-k-subgraph* problem [3]. It is also used to approximate *betweenness centrality* [13]. A core-decomposition tool for uncertain graphs would thus provide a natural extension of all these applications to the context of uncertain graphs. Other direct applications of core decomposition of uncertain graphs include *influence maximization* and *task-driven team formation*, which we showcase in Section 6 and 7, respectively.

In *influence maximization* [16], the probability of an edge (u, v) represents the influence that u exerts on v, i.e., the likelihood that some action/information propagates from u to v. The greedy algorithm [12] traditionally used to find the users that maximize the information spread over the network requires a number of Monte Carlo simulations that largely limit its efficiency. In Section 6 we show how our probabilistic core-decomposition tool can be used to speed-up the influence-maximization process.

In *task-driven team formation*, the input is a collaboration graph $G = (V, E, \tau)$, where vertices are individuals and edges exhibit a probabilistic topic model τ representing the topic(s) of past collaborations. A query is a pair $\langle T, Q\rangle$, where T is a set of terms describing a new task, and Q is a set of vertices. The goal is to find an answer set of vertices A, such that $A \supseteq Q$ is a good team for the task described by T. The given query task T, along with the topic model τ, induces a (single) probability value p^T for each edge $(u, v) \in E$, such that $p^T(u, v)$ represents the likelihood that u and v collaborate on T. This gives rise to an uncertain graph to which one can naturally apply core decomposition in order to find the desired team (Section 7).

Challenges and contributions. In this paper we study the problem of core decomposition of uncertain graphs, which, to the best of our knowledge, has never been considered so far. We introduce (Section 2) the notion of (k, η)-*core* as a maximal subgraph whose vertices have at least k neigbours in that subgraph with probability no less than η; here $\eta \in [0, 1]$ is a threshold defining the desired level of certainty of the output cores.

Let the η-degree of a vertex v be the maximum degree such that the probability for v to have that degree is no less than η. We design an algorithm for finding a (k, η)-core decomposition that iteratively removes the vertex having the smallest η-degree and prove its correctness (Section 3). The proposed algorithm resembles the traditional algorithm for computing the core decomposition of a deterministic graph [5]; however, as usual when the attention is shifted from the deterministic context to uncertain graphs, the adaptation of that algorithm is non-trivial. A major challenge is the capability of handling large graphs.

Two main critical steps affect our algorithm: computing initial η-degrees and updating η-degrees whenever a vertex is removed from the graph. While the corresponding steps in the deterministic case (i.e., computing and updating the degree of a vertex) are straightforward, performing them efficiently in uncertain graphs needs a great deal of attention; approaching them naïvely, indeed, may even lead to intractable (exponential) time complexity. We show how to overcome the exponential-time complexity by devising a novel yet efficient dynamic-programming method to compute η-degrees from scratch. We also exploit the same intuition underlying the dynamic-programming algorithm so as to efficiently update η-degrees after a vertex removal. As a result, we show that computing a (k, η)-core decomposition takes $\mathcal{O}(m\Delta)$ time, where m is the number of edges in the input uncertain graph and Δ is the maximum η-degree.

As a further contribution, we devise a novel method to improve the efficiency of the proposed (k, η)-core-decomposition algorithm (Section 4). The idea is to exploit a fast-to-compute lower bound on the η-degree that can be used as a placeholder during the first iterations while being replaced with the actual η-degree only when the vertex at hand is selected and the graph has become smaller.

Finally, we report experiments on efficiency and numerical stability on real-world graphs (Section 5) and show our proposal at work in two real-life applications (Sections 6–7).

2. PROBLEM DEFINITION

Cores of deterministic graphs. Before focusing on uncertain graphs, we briefly recall the problem of computing cores of deterministic graphs. Let $G = (V, E)$ be an undirected graph, where V is a set of n vertices and $E \subseteq V \times V$ is a set of m edges. For every vertex $v \in V$, let $deg(v)$ and $deg_H(v)$ denote the degree of v in G and in a subgraph H of G, respectively. Also, given a set of vertices $C \subseteq V$, let $E|C$ denote the subset of edges induced by C, i.e., $E|C = \{(u, v) \in E \mid u \in C, v \in C\}$.

Definition 1 (k-core). *The* k-core *(or* core of order *k) of G is a* maximal *subgraph $H = (C, E|C)$ such that $\forall v \in C : deg_H(v) \geq k$. The* core number *(or* core index*) of a vertex v, denoted $c(v)$, is the highest order of a core that contains v. The set of all k-cores of G, for all k, is the* core decomposition *of G.* □

The notion of k-core is strictly related to the notion of k-*shell*, that is the subgraph induced by the set of all vertices having core number equal to k. Note that neither k-cores nor k-shells are necessarily connected subgraphs. Also, while these two notions usually refer to subgraphs of the input graph, in the remainder we slightly abuse of notation and denote by k-core (or k-shell) both the subgraph $H = (C, E|C)$ itself and the vertex set C that induces H.

All k-shells of a graph G form a partition of the vertex set V, while all k-cores are nested into each other: $G = C_0 \supseteq C_1 \supseteq \cdots \supseteq C_{k^*}$ ($k^* = \max_{v \in V} c(v)$). As a result, the core decomposition of G is *unique* and fully determined by the core number $c(v)$ of all vertices v in G: the k-core of G simply corresponds to (the subgraph induced by) the set of all vertices v having core number $c(v) \geq k$.

Batagelj and Zaveršnik [5] show how to compute the core decomposition of a graph G in linear time (Algorithm 1). The algorithm iteratively removes the smallest-degree vertex and sets the core number of the removed vertex accordingly. Vertices are thus required to be ordered based on their degree. Defining the initial vertex ordering and keeping vertices ordered during the execution of the algorithm take $\mathcal{O}(n)$ and $\mathcal{O}(1)$ time, respectively. The idea is to employ an n-dimensional vector $\mathbf{D}$ whose single cells $\mathbf{D}[i]$ store all vertices having degree equal to i in the current graph. The overall time complexity of the algorithm is hence $\mathcal{O}(n + m)$.

Algorithm 1 k-CORES

Input: A graph $G = (V, E)$.
Output: An n-dimensional vector $\mathbf{c}$ containing the core number of each $v \in V$.

```
c ← ∅,  d ← ∅,  D ← [∅, ..., ∅]
for all v ∈ V do
    d[v] ← deg(v)
    D[deg(v)] ← D[deg(v)] ∪ {v}
end for
for all k = 0, 1, ..., n do
    while D[k] ≠ ∅ do
        pick and remove a vertex v from D[k]
        c[v] ← k
        for all u : (u, v) ∈ E, d[u] > k do
            move u from D[d[u]] to D[d[u] − 1]
            d[u] ← d[u] − 1
        end for
        remove v from G
    end while
end for
```

Cores of uncertain graphs. Let $\mathcal{G} = (V, E, p)$ be an uncertain graph, where $p : E \rightarrow (0, 1]$ is a function that assigns a probability of existence to each edge.[1] For the sake of brevity, we hereinafter denote the probabilities $p(e)$ with p_e. For every vertex $v \in V$, let $N_v = \{(u, v) \in E\}$ denote the set of edges incident to v, and $d_v = |N_v|$ its size.

To define our notion of core decomposition of an uncertain graph, we resort to the well-known *possible-world semantics*, which has been recognized as a sound principle to define queries on probabilistic data [9]. Broadly, such a principle interprets the probabilistic data as a set of deterministic instantiations, called *possible worlds*, each of which associated with its probability of being observed. In the context of uncertain graphs, the bulk of the literature assumes the probabilities of existence of the edges independent from one another [24, 14, 15]. Under this assumption, the possible-world semantics interprets an uncertain graph $\mathcal{G}$ with m edges as a set of 2^m possible deterministic graphs (worlds), each of which containing a subset of the edges in E. More precisely, an uncertain graph $\mathcal{G} = (V, E, p)$ yields a set of possible graphs $\{G = (V, E_G)\}_{E_G \subseteq E}$, and the probability of observing a possible graph $G = (V, E_G) \sqsubseteq \mathcal{G}$ is:

$$\Pr(G) = \prod_{e \in E_G} p_e \prod_{e \in E \setminus E_G} (1 - p_e). \tag{1}$$

According to the possible-world semantics, answering a probabilistic query q means to derive a probability distribution over all possible deterministic answers a to the query q, where the probability of an answer a corresponds to the sum of the probabilities of all worlds where a is the answer to q. As this answer distribution is usually too large and sparse to be explicitly interpreted or computed/stored, the general turnaround adopted is to assign a score to each domain object based on its probability of being part of an answer to the probabilistic query q, and return the objects having highest scores as a final answer to q [9].

We cast such a general framework to our context by defining the score of each vertex v to be part of a k-core $\mathcal{H}$ as the probability that v has degree no less than k in $\mathcal{H}$, i.e., $\Pr[deg_{\mathcal{H}}(v) \geq k]$. Then, we employ a classic threshold-based approach to decide which vertices should actually form a k-core based on their scores. As a result, the notion of *probabilistic (k, η)-core* we come up with is the following:

DEFINITION 2 (PROBABILISTIC (k,η)-CORES). *Given an uncertain graph $\mathcal{G} = (V, E, p)$, and a threshold $\eta \in [0, 1]$, the* probabilistic (k, η)-core *of $\mathcal{G}$ is a maximal subgraph $\mathcal{H} = (C, E|C, p)$ such that the probability that each vertex $v \in C$ has degree no less than k in $\mathcal{H}$ is greater than or equal to η, i.e., $\forall v \in C : \Pr[deg_{\mathcal{H}}(v) \geq k] \geq \eta$.* □

The notion of *η-core number* immediately follows from the definition of (k,η)-core and is defined as the highest order k of a (k,η)-core containing v.

The problem we address in this work is the following.

PROBLEM 1 (PROBCORES). *Given an uncertain graph $\mathcal{G}$ and a probability threshold $\eta \in [0, 1]$, find the (k, η)-*core decomposition *of $\mathcal{G}$, that is the set of all (k,η)-cores of $\mathcal{G}$.* □

Our definition of core decomposition of an uncertain graph, has the desirable feature of being unique, as formally shown in the next theorem.

THEOREM 1. *Given an uncertain graph $\mathcal{G}$ and a probability threshold η, the (k, η)-core decomposition of $\mathcal{G}$ is unique.*

PROOF. We prove the theorem by showing that $\mathcal{G}$ cannot have more than one (k, η)-core, for all k. Assume that $\mathcal{G}$ has two (k, η)-cores and denote them by $\mathcal{H}_1$ and $\mathcal{H}_2$, respectively. According to Definition 2, it holds that $\mathcal{H}_1$ is a maximal subgraph of $\mathcal{G}$ such that $\forall v \in \mathcal{H}_1 : \Pr[deg_{\mathcal{H}_1}(v) \geq k] \geq \eta$, and the same happens for $\mathcal{H}_2$. Combining the (k, η)-core conditions of $\mathcal{H}_1$ and $\mathcal{H}_2$ leads to the subgraph $\mathcal{H}_1 \cup \mathcal{H}_2$ to satisfy the (k, η)-core condition too, as $\forall v \in \mathcal{H}_1 : \Pr[deg_{\mathcal{H}_1}(v) \geq k] \geq \eta \wedge \forall v \in \mathcal{H}_2 : \Pr[deg_{\mathcal{H}_2}(v) \geq k] \geq \eta$ clearly implies that $\forall v \in \mathcal{H}_1 \cup \mathcal{H}_2 : \Pr[deg_{\mathcal{H}_1 \cup \mathcal{H}_2}(v) \geq k] \geq \eta$. This means that neither $\mathcal{H}_1$ nor $\mathcal{H}_2$ are maximal, thus contradicting the hypothesis. The theorem follows. □

An example of *(k, η)-core decomposition* of an uncertain graph is provided in Figure 1.

3. COMPUTING PROBABILISTIC CORES

For a vertex v of the input uncertain graph $\mathcal{G}$, the probability $\Pr[deg(v) \geq k]$ can be expressed as:

$$\Pr[deg(v) \geq k] = \textstyle\sum_{G \sqsubseteq \mathcal{G}_v^{\geq k}} \Pr(G), \tag{2}$$

where $\mathcal{G}_v^{\geq k}$ is the set of all possible graphs drawn from $\mathcal{G}$ where v has degree $\geq k$, i.e., $\mathcal{G}_v^{\geq k} = \{G \sqsubseteq \mathcal{G} \mid deg_G(v) \geq k\}$.

It is easy to see that such a probability value is monotonically non-increasing with k, i.e., $\Pr[deg(v) \geq 0] \geq \Pr[deg(v) \geq 1] \geq \ldots \geq \Pr[deg(v) \geq d_v]$. Then, given a threshold η, for every vertex v in the graph, there exists a value $\hat{k} \in [0..d_v]$ such that $\Pr[deg(v) \geq h] \geq \eta$, for all $h \leq \hat{k}$, and $\Pr[deg(v) \geq h] < \eta$, for all $h > \hat{k}$. We call this value the *η-degree* of vertex v.

DEFINITION 3 (η-DEGREE). *Given an uncertain graph $\mathcal{G} = (V, E, p)$ and a threshold $\eta \in [0, 1]$, the* η-degree *η-$deg(v)$ of a vertex $v \in V$ is defined as*

$$\eta\text{-}deg(v) = \max\{k \in [0..d_v] \mid \Pr[deg(v) \geq k] \geq \eta\}.$$

Let also η-$deg_{\mathcal{H}}(v)$ be the η-degree of v in a subgraph $\mathcal{H}$. □

[1] We consider undirected graphs for the sake of presentation and consistency with the literature on core decomposition. However, all our definitions/methods apply to directed graphs too, by simply replacing the notion of degree with either in-degree or out-degree. Indeed, in Section 6, where we focus on *influence maximization*, the graph is directed and we define probabilistic cores based on out-degree.

Algorithm 2 (k,η)-CORES

Input: An uncertain graph $\mathcal{G} = (V, E, p)$, a threshold $\eta \in [0, 1]$.
Output: An n-dimensional vector $\mathbf{c}$ containing the η-core number of each $v \in V$.

```
1: compute η-deg(v) for all v ∈ V
2: c ← ∅,  d ← ∅,  D ← [∅, ..., ∅]
3: for all v ∈ V do
4:   d[v] ← η-deg(v)
5:   D[η-deg(v)] ← D[η-deg(v)] ∪ {v}
6: end for
7: for all k = 0, 1, ..., n do
8:   while D[k] ≠ ∅ do
9:     pick and remove a vertex v from D[k]
10:    c[v] ← k
11:    for all u : (u, v) ∈ E, d[u] > k do
12:      recompute η-deg(u)
13:      move u from D[d[u]] to D[η-deg(u)]
14:      d[u] ← η-deg(u)
15:    end for
16:    remove v from G
17:  end while
18: end for
```

Intuitively, the notion of η-degree gives an idea of the degree of a vertex given a specific threshold η. We exploit the notion η-degree to adapt the k-CORES algorithm used for deterministic graphs to the context of uncertain graphs. The proposed algorithm, called (k,η)-CORES (Algorithm 2), follows the same scheme as in the deterministic case with the main difference of the use of the η-degree. The soundness of the proposed algorithm is shown in the following theorem.

THEOREM 2. *Given an uncertain graph $\mathcal{G}$ and a threshold η, Algorithm 2 provides the (k,η)-core decomposition of $\mathcal{G}$.*

PROOF. For every $v \in V$ and every subgraph $\mathcal{H} = (C, E_C, p|C)$ of $\mathcal{G}$, it is easy to see that $\eta\text{-}deg_{\mathcal{H}}(v) \leq \eta\text{-}deg(v)$, as the η-degree computation in $\mathcal{G}$ relies on more successful events than those encountered in $\mathcal{H}$. This implies that $\eta\text{-}deg_{\mathcal{H}}(v)$ is a *monotonic vertex property function* [5], where, for every $v \in V$ and $C \subseteq V$, a vertex property function on $\mathcal{G}$ is a function $\phi(v, C) : V \times 2^V \to \mathbb{R}$, and the monotonicity property holds if $\forall\, C_1, C_2 \subseteq V : C_1 \subseteq C_2$ implies that $\forall\, v \in V : \phi(v, C_1) \leq \phi(v, C_2)$. The proof is completed by the result by Batagelj and Zaveršnik [5], who show that, for a monotonic vertex property function $\phi(v, C)$, the algorithm that repeatedly removes a vertex with the smallest ϕ value gives the desired core decomposition.[2] □

Instead of computing/updating standard degrees, in the probabilistic case one thus needs to (i) compute all η-degrees at the beginning of the algorithm (Line 1), and (ii) update the η-degree of a neighbour of the currently being processed vertex v (Line 12). While computing/updating degrees in the deterministic case is straightforward, for the η-degrees such steps are non-trivial, as shown next.

Computing initial η-degrees

To show how to derive η-degrees from scratch, we first focus on the computation of $\Pr[deg(v) \geq k]$ for a vertex v, and note that $\Pr[deg(v) \geq k]$ is equal to the sum of the probabilities $\Pr[deg(v) = i]$ either for all $i \in [k..d_v]$ or, equivalently for all $i \in [0..k-1]$:

$$\Pr[deg(v) \geq k] = \sum_{i=k}^{d_v} \Pr[deg(v) = i] = 1 - \sum_{i=0}^{k-1} \Pr[deg(v) = i]. \quad (3)$$

Furthermore, we observe that each individual $\Pr[deg(v) = i]$ can in turn be computed considering all subsets of edges $N \subseteq N_v$ of size i and summing over the probabilities that all and only the edges in these various N exist:

$$\Pr[\deg(v) = i] = \sum_{\substack{N \subseteq N_v,\\ |N| = i}} \prod_{e \in N} p_e \prod_{e \in N_v \setminus N} (1 - p_e). \quad (4)$$

The sum in the above formula is over all subsets $N \subseteq N_v$, $|N| = i$; thus, a naïve computation would lead to a time complexity exponential in the size of N_v. We can however manage this by rearranging the formula as

$$\Pr[deg(v) = i] = P_v R(i, N_v),$$

where $P_v = \prod_{e \in N_v}(1 - p_e)$, $R(i, N_v) = \sum_{N \subseteq N_v, |N|=i} \prod_{e \in N} \tilde{p}_e$, and $\tilde{p}_e = \frac{p_e}{1-p_e}$. This rearrangement allows us to exploit the next recursive formula, which has originally been introduced in [8] for sampling from a finite population with unequal probabilities and without replacement:

$$R(i, N_v) = \frac{1}{i} \sum_{j=1}^{i} (-1)^{j+1} T(j, N_v) R(i - j, N_v), \quad (5)$$

where $T(j, N_v) = \sum_{e \in N_v} (\tilde{p}_e)^j$. Now, it is easy to see that Equation (5) allows for computing all individual $\Pr[\deg(v) = i]$ values, for all $i \in [0..k-1]$ (which, according to Equation (3), are needed to derive the desired $\Pr[\deg(v) \geq k]$) in polynomial time, precisely in $\mathcal{O}(kd_v)$ time.

A dynamic-programming method. Although the above way of computing $\Pr[\deg(v) = i]$ solves a seemingly exponential-time problem, it still has weaknesses due to the recursive formula in Equation (5). Firstly, as the formula involves both products and sums of $\tilde{p}_e$ values that can be either very large (when $p_e \to 1$) or very small (when $p_e \to 0$), it may incur numerical-stability issues, which might make the computation of $\Pr[\deg(v) = i]$ problematic when executed by a computer. Secondly, using such a formula, the η-degree of a vertex v when one of its incident edges is removed cannot be recomputed faster than a from-scratch computation.

For the above reasons, we propose here an alternative way of computing $\Pr[\deg(v) = i]$. Consider a vertex v and an edge e incident to v, and let $\mathcal{G}_{\setminus\{e\}}$ denote the subgraph of $\mathcal{G}$ where e is not present. The method is based on the following key observation: the event "v has degree k in $\mathcal{G}$" implies that either "e exists *and* v has degree $k-1$ in $\mathcal{G}_{\setminus\{e\}}$" or "$e$ does not exist *and* v has degree k in $\mathcal{G}_{\setminus\{e\}}$". This way, the probability for v to have degree k in the original graph $\mathcal{G}$ can be computed as a linear combination of the probabilities that v has degree either $k-1$ or k in the subgraph $\mathcal{G}_{\setminus\{e\}}$.

The above reasoning can be generalised to every subgraph of $\mathcal{G}$ and formally expressed in the next theorem (for which we omit a formal proof due to limited space).

THEOREM 3. *Given an uncertain graph $\mathcal{G} = (V, E, p)$ and a vertex $v \in V$, let $N_v = \{e_1, \ldots, e_{d_v}\}$ be the set of all edges incident to v ordered in some way. Also, given a subset*

[2] That work states that the time complexity of such an algorithm is $\mathcal{O}(m \times \max\{D, \log n\})$, where D is the maximum degree. But this is a general result for vertex property functions that can be updated linearly in the degree of a vertex. For any specific vertex property function, such as our η-degree, the complexity can be higher or lower.

$N \subseteq N_v$, *let* $deg(v|N)$ *denote the degree of* v *in the subgraph* $\hat{\mathcal{G}} = (V, E \setminus (N_v \setminus N), p)$. *For all* $h \in [1..d_v - 1]$ *it holds that:*

$$\begin{aligned} &\Pr[deg(v|\{e_1, \ldots, e_{h+1}\}) = i] = \\ &= \ p_{e_{h+1}} \Pr[deg(v|\{e_1, \ldots, e_h\}) = i - 1] + \\ &\quad +(1 - p_{e_{h+1}}) \Pr[deg(v|\{e_1, \ldots, e_h)\} = i]. \quad \square \end{aligned} \tag{6}$$

Theorem 3 provides a principled way to efficiently compute $\Pr[deg(v) = i]$ based on the dynamic-programming paradigm. Particularly, we take an arbitrary ordering of the edges incident to the vertex v being currently under consideration and define a proper recursive formula that allows for computing partial solutions relying only on the first i edges. The ultimate score (i.e., the actual value of $\Pr[deg(v) = i]$) is available only when all the edges have been considered; this makes the overall computation independent from the specific ordering of the edges. Formally, let $X(h, j) = \Pr[deg(v|\{e_1, \ldots, e_h\}) = j]$, for all $h \in [0..d_v]$, $j \in [-1..i]$. We set the following base cases:

$$\begin{cases} X(0,0) &= 1, \\ X(h,-1) &= 0, \quad \text{for all } h \in [0..d_v], \\ X(h,j) &= 0, \quad \text{for all } h \in [0..d_v], j \in [h+1..i], \end{cases}$$

while we exploit Equation (6) to compute the generic dynamic-programming recursive step as

$$X(h,j) = p_{e_h} X(h-1, j-1) + (1 - p_{e_h}) X(h-1, j),$$

for all $h \in [1..d_v]$, $j \in [0..h]$. We need to compute all $X(\cdot,\cdot)$ values so as to get to $X(d_v, i)$, which corresponds to the desired probability $\Pr[deg(v) = i]$. This requires $\mathcal{O}(id_v)$ time.

Moreover, one can notice that the values of the *entire set* $\{X(d_v, j)\}_{j=0}^{i}$ (not just $X(d_v, i)$) correspond to the actual probability values $\{\Pr[deg(v) = j]\}_{j=0}^{i}$. Thus, employing the proposed dynamic-programming method and setting $i = k-1$, the probability values $\Pr[deg(v) = 0], \ldots, \Pr[deg(v) = k-1]$, which are required for computing $\Pr[deg(v) \geq k]$ according to Equation (3), can all be derived in $\mathcal{O}(kd_v)$ time.

Thus, the dynamic-programming method just described has the same complexity as the method based on Equation (4). But, at the same time, it (*i*) alleviates the numerical-stability shortcomings, as the numbers involved into Equation (6) are all probabilities ≤ 1 (unlike the numbers $\tilde{p}_e$ which range from $[0, \infty)$), and (*ii*) can easily be employed for efficiently updating η-degrees when an edge is removed from the graph, as described next.

Time complexity. The η-degree of a vertex v can be computed incrementally. We start with $k = 0$ and $\Pr[deg(v) \geq 0] = 1$. Then, we increase k one by one and compute $\Pr[deg(v) \geq k]$ as $\Pr[deg(v) \geq k-1] - \Pr[deg(v) = k-1]$. We stop once $\Pr[deg(v) \geq k] < \eta$, and we set $\eta\text{-}deg(v) = k - 1$. This way, we need to compute probabilities $\Pr[deg(v) = k]$ only for $k = 0, ..., \eta\text{-}deg(v) + 1$, which, according to the findings reported above, leads to a time complexity of $\mathcal{O}(\eta\text{-}deg(v) \times d_v)$. Clearly, in the worst case, such a complexity equals $\mathcal{O}(d_v^2)$, but we expect in practice $\eta\text{-}deg(v)$ reasonably lower than d_v, especially for those vertices having very large d_v and/or large enough η values.

Computing all η-degrees hence takes $\mathcal{O}(\sum_{v \in V} \eta\text{-}deg(v) \times d_v)$. Denoting by Δ the maximum η-degree over all vertices in the graph, i.e., $\Delta = \max_{v \in V} \eta\text{-}deg(v)$, the complexity can be more compactly expressed as $\mathcal{O}(\sum_{v \in V} d_v \Delta) = \mathcal{O}(m\Delta)$.

Updating η-degrees

We now consider the case where the η-degree of a vertex v needs to be updated because an edge incident to v has been removed. We recall that this is the other crucial step of our (k,η)-CORES algorithm (Algorithm 2, Line 12).

As anticipated, we can exploit Theorem 3 to avoid from-scratch recomputations. The problem can be reduced to (efficiently) updating the probabilities $\Pr[deg(v) = 0], \ldots, \Pr[deg(v) = \eta\text{-}deg(v)]$, whose earlier values are available because of the computation of the earlier η-degree. Once all these new probabilities are computed, the new η-degree can be derived by the same incremental process described in the previous paragraph "Time complexity".

Let e denote the edge to be removed and let $\Pr[deg(v|\neg e) = i]$, for all $i \in [0, \ldots, \eta\text{-}deg(v)]$, be a shorthand for the new probabilities $\Pr[deg(v|N_v \setminus \{e\}) = i]$ to be computed. Such $\Pr[deg(v|\neg e) = i]$ values can be derived by rearranging Equation (6) as follows:

$$\Pr[deg(v|\neg e) = i] = \frac{\Pr[deg(v) = i] - p_e \Pr[deg(v|\neg e) = i-1]}{1 - p_e}. \tag{7}$$

This way, one can set $\Pr[deg(v|\neg e) = 0] = \frac{1}{1-p_e} \Pr[deg(v) = 0]$, and apply Equation (7) to compute the remaining $\Pr[deg(v|\neg e) = i]$ values, for all $i \in [1..\eta\text{-}deg(v)]$. Each probability $\Pr[deg(v|\neg e) = i]$ takes constant time. Computing all the new probabilities, and, hence, updating the η-degree of v, globally takes $\mathcal{O}(\eta\text{-}deg(v))$ time, thus improving upon the $\mathcal{O}(\eta\text{-}deg(v) \times d_v)$ time of a from-scratch recomputation.

Overall running time of (k,η)-CORES

We analyse now the overall time complexity of our (k,η)-CORES algorithm. The initialisation phase (Lines 1–6) is dominated by the computation of the initial η-degree for all vertices, which takes $\mathcal{O}(m\Delta)$ time (Δ is the maximum η-degree over all vertices). In the main cycle (Lines 7–18), like the deterministic case, each vertex is visited only once and then removed from the graph. For each visited vertex v, the η-degree of all its neighbours has to be updated. As reported above, for a single neighbour u, this takes $\mathcal{O}(\eta\text{-}deg(u))$. Thus, the main cycle globally takes $\mathcal{O}(\sum_{v \in V} \sum_{u:(u,v) \in N_v} \eta\text{-}deg(u)) = \mathcal{O}(\sum_{v \in V} d_v \Delta) = \mathcal{O}(m\Delta)$. In conclusion, the running time of the (k,η)-CORES algorithm is therefore $\mathcal{O}(m\Delta)$.

4. SPEEDING-UP (k,η)-CORES

In this section we show how to further speed-up our (k,η)-CORES algorithm. Our key observation is that the main bottleneck of (k,η)-CORES is the computation of initial η-degrees (experimentally confirmed in Section 5): although this step is asymptotically as fast as updating η-degrees after a vertex removal, the latter is in practice faster as it is performed on a graph that gets progressively smaller. In this regard, we derive a fast-to-compute lower bound on the η-degree and use it as a placeholder during the first iterations, while replacing it with the actual η-degree only when the vertex at hand is going to be processed. This way, the initial η-degrees can be computed only when actually needed and on a smaller graph, thus leading to the desired speed-up.

In the following we provide the details of our lower bound on the η-degree and show how to efficiently update this bound after vertex removals. Then, we describe how to incorporate such findings into the enhanced algorithm.

Lower bound on the η-degree. We define our lower bound on the η-degree in terms of the *regularised beta function*. Given a real number $z \in [0,1]$ and two integers a and b, the regularized beta function $I_z(a,b)$ is defined as the ratio between the *incomplete beta function* $B(z;a,b)$ and the *beta function* $B(a,b)$ [29]:

$$I_z(a,b) = \frac{B(z;a,b)}{B(a,b)} = \sum_{i=a}^{a+b-1} \binom{a+b-1}{i} z^i (1-z)^{a+b-1-i}.$$

Given a vertex v in the input graph, let $p_{min}(v)$ denote the minimum probability on the edges incident to v, i.e., $p_{min}(v) = \min_{e \in N_v} p_e$. The next lemma shows how the probability for v to have degree no less than k can be lower-bounded by using the regularised beta function I.

LEMMA 1. *Given an uncertain graph $\mathcal{G} = (V,E,p)$, for every vertex $v \in V$ and for all $k \in [0..d_v]$ it holds that*

$$\Pr[deg(v) \geq k] \;\geq\; I_{p_{min}(v)}(k, d_v - k + 1).$$

PROOF. Consider a vertex v' having as many incident edges as v, and assume that each edge incident to v' has probability $p_{min}(v)$. It is easy to see that $\Pr[\deg(v) = i] \geq \Pr[\deg(v') = i]$, for all i. Exploiting Equation (4) we get:

$$\begin{aligned}\Pr[\deg(v) = i] &\geq \Pr[\deg(v') = i] = \\ &= \sum_{\substack{N \subseteq N_{v'},\\ |N|=i}} \prod_{e \in N} p_{min}(v) \prod_{e \in N_{v'} \setminus N} (1 - p_{min}(v)) = \\ &= \binom{d_v}{i} (p_{min}(v))^i (1 - p_{min}(v))^{d_v - i}.\end{aligned}$$

Combining such a result with Equation (3) we obtain:

$$\Pr[deg(v) \geq k] = \sum_{i=k}^{d_v} \Pr[deg(v) = i] \geq$$

$$\geq \sum_{i=k}^{d_v} \binom{d_v}{i} (p_{min}(v))^i (1 - p_{min}(v))^{d_v - i} = I_{p_{min}(v)}(k, d_v - k + 1).$$

The lemma follows. □

The desired lower bound on η-degree can now immediately be derived by exploiting Lemma 1. We denote such a lower bound by η-LB and formally state it in the next theorem.

THEOREM 4. *Given an uncertain graph $\mathcal{G} = (V,E,p)$, for every vertex $v \in V$ it holds that*

$$\eta\text{-}deg(v) \geq \eta\text{-LB}(v) = \max\{k \in [0..d_v] \,|\, I_{p_{min}(v)}(k, d_v - k + 1) \geq \eta\}.$$

The computation of the above lower bound is very fast. For a fixed z, the values $I_z(a,b)$ of the regularised beta function are monotonically non-increasing as a increases and/or b decreases. Therefore, the lower bounds on $\Pr[deg(v) \geq k]$ are monotonically non-increasing as k increases and one can thus perform binary search to derive the maximum k such that $I_{p_{min}}(k, d_v - k + 1) \geq \eta$, which, according to Theorem 4, corresponds to the lower bound η-LB(v). The computation of η-LB(v) requires a logarithmic (in the number of edges of v) number of evaluations of I_z. Each evaluation of I_z can be computed in constant time using tables [23]. Thus, computing η-LB(v) for a vertex v takes $\mathcal{O}(\log d_v)$ time

A major feature of the lower bound η-LB is its fast from-scratch computation. Here we show that it can also be updated very efficiently (i.e., in constant time) when an edge is removed from the graph. To this end, we first need to report a couple of results. We start by showing that the η-degree of a vertex v can decrease at most by one when an edge incident to v is removed (Lemma 2).

LEMMA 2. *Given an uncertain graph $\mathcal{G} = (V,E,p)$ and a vertex $v \in V$, let $e \in N_v$ be an edge incident to v and let $\mathcal{H} = (V, E \setminus \{e\}, p)$ be the subgraph of $\mathcal{G}$ where e is missing. Also, let η-$deg_{\mathcal{H}}(v)$ be the η-degree of v in $\mathcal{H}$. It holds that η-$deg_{\mathcal{H}}(v) > \eta$-$deg(v) - 2$.*

PROOF.

$$\Pr[deg(v) \geq k] = \sum_{i=k}^{d_v - 1} \Pr[deg_{\mathcal{H}}(v) = i] + p_e \Pr[deg_{\mathcal{H}}(v) = k-1] =$$

$$= \underbrace{\sum_{i=k-1}^{d_v - 1} \Pr[deg_{\mathcal{H}}(v) = i]}_{\Pr[deg_{\mathcal{H}}(v) \geq k-1]} - (1 - p_e)\Pr[deg_{\mathcal{H}}(v) = k-1] \leq$$

$$\leq \Pr[deg_{\mathcal{H}}(v) \geq k - 1].$$

By the definition of η-degree we know that $\Pr[deg_{\mathcal{H}}(v) \geq \eta\text{-}deg_{\mathcal{H}}(v) + 1] < \eta$; thus, setting $k = \eta\text{-}deg_{\mathcal{H}}(v) + 2$ in the above inequality, we get

$$\Pr[deg(v) \geq \eta\text{-}deg_{\mathcal{H}}(v) + 2] \leq \Pr[deg_{\mathcal{H}}(v) \geq \eta\text{-}deg_{\mathcal{H}}(v) + 1] < \eta.$$

Then, η-$deg(v) < \eta$-$deg_{\mathcal{H}}(v) + 2$, or, equivalently, η-$deg_{\mathcal{H}}(v) > \eta$-$deg(v) - 2$. The lemma follows. □

Based on the above lemma, we can also prove that the lower bound η-LB(v) of a vertex v can decrease at most by one when an edge incident to v is removed.

THEOREM 5. *Given an uncertain graph $\mathcal{G} = (V,E,p)$ and a vertex $v \in V$, let $e \in N_v$ be an edge incident to v and let $\mathcal{H} = (V, E \setminus \{e\}, p)$ be the subgraph of $\mathcal{G}$ where e is missing. Also, let η-LB$_{\mathcal{H}}(v)$ be the lower bound on the η-degree of v in $\mathcal{H}$. It holds that η-LB$_{\mathcal{H}}(v) > \eta$-LB$(v) - 2$.*

PROOF. Consider a vertex v' having as many incident edges as v, and assume that each edge incident to v' has probability $p_{min}(v)$. It is easy to see that the η-degree η-$deg(v')$ of v' equals the lower bound η-LB(v). Combining this with Lemma 1, we get η-LB$_{\mathcal{H}}(v) = \eta$-$deg_{\mathcal{H}}(v') > \eta$-$deg(v') - 2 = \eta$-LB$(v) - 2$. The theorem follows. □

Theorem 5 can be exploited for safely updating η-LB in constant time. Let e denote again the edge incident to v to be removed and let $\mathcal{H}$ be the subgraph of $\mathcal{G}$ where e is missing. Thus, η-LB(v) denotes the earlier lower bound of v, while η-LB$_{\mathcal{H}}(v)$ denotes the new lower bound to be computed after the e's removal. The idea is to compute (in constant time) just the value $I_{p_{min}(v)}(\eta\text{-LB}(v), (d_v - 1) - \eta\text{-LB}(v) + 1) = I_{p_{min}(v)}(\eta\text{-LB}(v), d_v - \eta\text{-LB}(v))$. Lemma 1 ensures that

$$\Pr[deg_{\mathcal{H}}(v) \geq \eta\text{-LB}(v)] \geq I_{p_{min}(v)}(\eta\text{-LB}(v), d_v - \eta\text{-LB}(v)).$$

Thus, if $I_{p_{min}(v)}(\eta\text{-LB}(v), d_v - \eta\text{-LB}(v))$ is still $\geq \eta$, then the lower bound has not changed, i.e., η-LB$_{\mathcal{H}}(v) = \eta$-LB(v). Otherwise, it means that the lower bound has decreased. According to Theorem 5, this decreasing can be at most by one, hence we can safely set η-LB$_{\mathcal{H}}(v) = \eta$-LB$(v) - 1$.

A major shortcoming of updating η-LB as described above is that, for each vertex v, we need to load/keep-in-memory $\mathcal{O}(d_v^2)$ values of I_z (i.e., all values within $\{I_{p_{min}(v)}(k, h-k+1) \mid h \in [0..d_v], k \in [0..h]\}$). This would penalize too much both time and space complexity of the algorithm. However, this can be overcome by still relying on Theorem 5. The idea is to simply set $\eta\text{-LB}_{\mathcal{H}}(v) = \max\{0, \eta\text{-LB}(v) - 1\}$ *every time* an edge e incident to v is removed, no matter whether $I_{p_{min}(v)}(\eta\text{-LB}(v), d_v - \eta\text{-LB}(v)) \geq \eta$ or not. Indeed, Theorem 5 guarantees that $\eta\text{-LB}(v) - 1$ is still a lower-bound for $\eta\text{-}deg(v)$, even though possibly less tight. This way our algorithm would require only $\mathcal{O}(d_v)$ values of I_z for each vertex v, i.e., just the values $\{I_{p_{min}(v)}(k, d_v - k + 1) \mid k \in [0..d_v]\}$.

The E-(k,η)-cores algorithm. We now provide the details of our ENHANCED-(k,η)-CORES (for short, E-(k,η)-CORES) algorithm (pseudocode omitted for space reasons). The algorithm follows the scheme of the basic (k,η)-CORES algorithm (Algorithm 2). The main difference is that, for each vertex v, the lower bound η-LB(v) is computed in the initialisation phase, rather than the exact η-degree. A set $\widetilde{V}$ keeps trace of the vertices for which the exact η-degree has not been computed yet. Right after initialisation, $\widetilde{V}$ corresponds to the whole vertex set V. In the main cycle, vertices are processed based on their (lower bound on) η-degree. When a vertex v is being processed, it is primarily checked whether its exact η-degree is already available. If not, the exact η-degree of v is computed and v is moved to the proper set of the vector $\mathbf{D}$, so that it can be processed in the correct (possibly later) iteration. Otherwise, if the exact η-degree of v is available, the η-core number of v is set and the η-degrees (either the exact or the lower bounds) of all v's neighbours are updated.

The worst-case time complexity of E-(k,η)-CORES is the same as the basic (k,η)-CORES algorithm, i.e., $\mathcal{O}(m\Delta)$. However, smaller running times are expected in practice due to the lazy computation/updating of η-degrees in reduced versions of the input graph.

5. EXPERIMENTS

In this section we report quantitative experiments on efficiency and numerical stability of our (k,η)-CORES and E-(k,η)-CORES algorithms (Sections 3 and 4).[3] For this task we use the following real-world uncertain graphs.

Flickr (www.flickr.com, $|V| = 24\,125$, $|E| = 300\,836$). We borrowed the dataset from [24], where the probability of an edge between two users is defined based on *homophily*, the principle that similar interests indicate social ties. Particularly, [24] uses as a measure of homophily the Jaccard coefficient of the interest groups shared by the two users.

DBLP (www.informatik.uni-trier.de/~ley/db/, $|V| = 684\,911$, $|E| = 2\,284\,991$). The dataset was borrowed from [24, 15]. Two authors are connected if they co-authored at least once, and the probability on an edge expresses the fact that the collaboration has not happened by chance: the more the collaborations, the larger the probability. Precisely, [24, 15] define the probability of each edge based on an exponential function to the number of collaborations.

BioMine (biomine.org, $|V| = 1\,008\,200$, $|E| = 6\,742\,939$). A snapshot of the database of the BioMine project [26] containing biological interactions. Edges inherently come with probabilities. The probability of any edge provides evidence that the interaction actually exists.

Table 1: Times (secs) of the proposed methods for computing (k,η)-core decomposition (precision 64 bits). The column "*gain (%)*" reports the gain of the E-(k,η)-cores algorithm over the (k,η)-cores algorithm.

η	*initial η-degrees*	*main cycle*	*total*	*initial η-degrees*	*main cycle*	*total*	*gain (%)*
	Flickr, (k,η)-CORES			Flickr, E-(k,η)-CORES			
0.1	15.45	8.88	24.33	14.41	7.98	22.39	7.99%
0.3	13.73	7.89	21.61	12.90	7.22	20.12	6.89%
0.5	12.56	7.33	19.89	11.86	6.71	18.57	6.62%
0.7	11.45	6.64	18.09	10.82	6.14	16.96	6.25%
0.9	9.86	5.72	15.58	9.34	5.32	14.66	5.87%
	DBLP, (k,η)-CORES			DBLP, E-(k,η)-CORES			
0.1	53.81	36.92	90.73	38.23	26.45	64.68	28.71%
0.3	49.08	33.16	82.24	36.28	25.21	61.48	25.24%
0.5	44.74	31.14	75.88	33.98	24.45	58.43	23.00%
0.7	40.65	28.40	69.05	31.86	23.07	54.92	20.46%
0.9	35.54	24.42	59.96	28.40	21.06	49.46	17.51%
	BioMine, (k,η)-CORES			BioMine, E-(k,η)-CORES			
0.1	4801	1549	6350	4388	1404	5792	8.78%
0.3	4704	1542	6246	4333	1447	5780	7.46%
0.5	4645	1538	6183	4281	1404	5685	8.05%
0.7	4568	1523	6091	4240	1403	5643	7.35%
0.9	4498	1478	5977	4151	1423	5575	6.72%

Efficiency. Table 1 reports on the running times exhibited by our (k,η)-CORES (left) and E-(k,η)-CORES (right) algorithms on the selected datasets. Times are split by the main phases of computing initial η-degrees and running the main cycle. Both algorithms are very fast on Flickr and DBLP. They take on average around 20 and 60 seconds, respectively. On BioMine, which is much larger and denser, clearly the time increases. However, the time required by our algorithms on the latter dataset is in the order of one hour. This is reasonable for networks of such size and testifies the applicability of our methods to very large uncertain graphs.

As expected, E-(k,η)-CORES runs faster than the basic (k,η)-CORES algorithm, allowing a reduction of the total time up to around 30% (DBLP, $\eta = 0.1$). The gain is more evident on the larger datasets (i.e., DBLP and BioMine) and is generally increasing as η decreases. The latter finding is expected because the smaller η, the larger the η-degree of a vertex, and, thus, the better the chance for the lower-bound to be tighter and lead to better pruning. Larger η-degrees for smaller η is also the reason why times (for both phases and both algorithms) are increasing with smaller η.

Numerical stability. As discussed in Section 3, probabilities may lead to numerical instability. To prevent this, one can exploit native solutions provided by modern programming languages to enlarge range and/or precision of the numerical representation. As a side effect, this would slow down the overall computation as larger precision implies slower arithmetic computations. Thus, the goal is to minimise the number of critical operations that may lead to numerical instability, to avoid using a too large precision with the aim of achieving reasonable accuracy. As reported in Section 3, a major feature of the novel dynamic-programming method we employ in our algorithms to compute/update η-degrees is to alleviate such numerical issues. We next provide experimental evidence on this.

First, we report results by varying the precision used for representing numbers (we consider 32, 64, 128, and 256 bits

[3]We implemented our code in Java and run experiments on a 2.83GHz, 32GB Intel Xeon server.

Table 2: **Accuracy of (k,η)-core index for $\eta = 0$ w.r.t. deterministic core index (ground truth) for different values of precision (bits).**

dataset	*pr=32*	*pr=64*	*pr=128*	*pr=256*
	avg absolute error			
Flickr	6.17	5.12	3.4	2.26
DBLP	0.27	0.1	0.03	0.01
BioMine	2.18	1.25	0.41	0.14
	% vertices with non-zero error			
Flickr	31.69%	18.91%	11.92%	6.00%
DBLP	17.48%	2.27%	0.51%	0.18%
BioMine	1.51%	1.11%	0.47%	0.09%

as precision levels).[4] We note that, for $\eta = 0$, the (k,η)-core decomposition of an uncertain graph $\mathcal{G}$ should ideally correspond to the core decomposition of the deterministic graph derived from $\mathcal{G}$ by ignoring probabilities. Thus, we measure accuracy by comparing, for each vertex, the 0-core number outputted by our algorithms with the core number returned by the standard k-CORE algorithm (Algorithm 1) on such a deterministic graph.

Tables 2 and 3 show accuracy results (in terms of per-vertex average absolute error and percentage of vertices with core number other than the exact one) and running times, respectively. We report times separately for (k,η)-CORES and E-(k,η)-CORES, while accuracy is the same for both. As expected, larger precision leads to better accuracy and worse efficiency. Particularly, the results show a linear trend: doubling the precision, time doubles while errors get halved.

We also compare the results of our algorithms when equipped with the proposed dynamic-programming method to the results of our algorithms equipped with the method that computes/updates η-degrees using the formula in Equation (5). We denote our proposed combination "(k,η)-CORES + dynamic-programming method" simply as (k,η)-CORES, while we refer to the "baseline" combination "(k,η)-CORES + Equation (5)-based method" as EQ5. These results are summarised in Table 4 (precision 64 bits). Our method outperforms EQ5 in terms of both average absolute error and percentage of vertices with non-zero error. Particularly, the average absolute error of the EQ5 method is reduced by 9% (Flickr), 41% (DBLP), and 40% (BioMine).

6. INFLUENCE MAXIMIZATION

The *influence-maximization* problem [16], has received a great deal of attention over the last decade. It requires to find a set of vertices S, with $|S| = s$, that maximizes the *expected spread*, i.e., the expected number of vertices that would be infected by a viral propagation started in S, under a certain probabilistic propagation model.

The *independent cascade model* [16] is a widely-used propagation model; under this model, the problem of finding a set S of s vertices that maximizes the expected spread $\sigma(S)$ is **NP**-hard. However, the submodularity of $\sigma(S)$ allows the GREEDY algorithm that iteratively adds to S the vertex bringing the largest marginal gain to the objective function to achieve a $(1 - \frac{1}{e})$ approximation guarantee. Unfortunately, finding the maximum-marginal-gain vertex requires to solve a **#P**-complete reliability problem. Hence, existing approaches usually apply sampling methods (e.g., Monte Carlo) to estimate the best seed vertex at each iteration of the algorithm. This drastically affects the efficiency of the algorithm, thus limiting its applicability only to moderately-sized networks (the time complexity of the algorithm is $\mathcal{O}(sTnm)$, where T is the number of Monte Carlo samples, with $T \in [1\,000, 10\,000]$, usually). Optimizations of the basic algorithm have been defined which exploit the submodularity of σ to avoid unneeded computations [12], but the improvement achieved is typically not enough to handle large graphs (in the experiment that we show below, on a moderately sized graph a state-of-the-art algorithm such as CELF++ [12] could not finish after several weeks).

[4]In our implementation, we use the *BigDecimal* Java API, which allows for representing numbers arbitrarily large and/or small, and with arbitrary user-defined precision (up to "unlimited" precision).

Table 3: **Times (secs) of the two proposed methods for computing (k,η)-core decomposition, for $\eta = 0.1$, for different values of precision (bits).**

prec. (bits)	*initial η-degrees*	*main cycle*	*total*	*initial η-degrees*	*main cycle*	*total*	*gain (%)*
	Flickr, (k,η)-CORES			Flickr, E-(k,η)-CORES			
32	6.96	3.83	10.79	6.63	3.73	10.36	3.94%
64	15.23	8.89	24.12	14.08	7.94	22.02	8.72%
128	25.55	14.48	40.03	23.69	12.92	36.62	8.53%
256	34.35	22.13	56.48	31.95	19.38	51.63	8.59%
	DBLP, (k,η)-CORES			DBLP, E-(k,η)-CORES			
32	26.71	20.22	46.93	19.46	15.51	34.97	25.48%
64	56.73	39.19	95.92	40.98	27.17	68.14	28.96%
128	86.65	59.81	146.5	62.84	40.40	103.2	29.51%
256	128.7	89.14	217.8	91.15	59.30	150.5	30.93%
	BioMine, (k,η)-CORES			BioMine, E-(k,η)-CORES			
32	2376	704	3080	2021	659	2681	12.97%
64	5452	1693	7145	4738	1390	6128	14.24%
128	9815	3146	12961	8153	2607	10760	16.98%
256	13296	5055	18351	11274	4515	15789	13.96%

Table 4: **Accuracy of the proposed method in terms of error w.r.t. a ground truth (precision 64 bits).**

	avg absolute error		*vertices w non-zero error*	
dataset	(k,η)-CORES	EQ5	(k,η)-CORES	EQ5
Flickr	5.12	5.62	18.91%	19.91%
DBLP	0.1	0.17	2.27%	4.42%
BioMine	1.25	2.07	1.11%	1.36%

Within this view, a useful application of our (k, η)-core decomposition is to provide a way to speed-up the execution of the GREEDY algorithm. The idea is simple: just reduce the input graph $\mathcal{G}$ by keeping only the inner-most η-shells and run the (optimized version of the) GREEDY algorithm on such a reduced graph. The rationale here is that, as experimentally observed in [17], the core decomposition of the deterministic version of $\mathcal{G}$, is a direct indicator of the expected spread of a vertex: the higher the core index is, the more likely the vertex is an influential spreader. The finding in [17] however exploits cores derived from a deterministic version of the input graph, thus completely ignoring its probabilistic nature. We conjecture that exploiting a notion of core decomposition defined ad-hoc for uncertain graphs can only positively affect the behaviour observed in [17]. We next empirically show the correctness of our conjecture.

Experiments. We use a small *directed* graph from Twitter ($|V| = 21\,882, |E| = 372\,005$), and a set of propagations of URLs in the social graph, which we use as past evidence to learn the influence probabilities (we employ the traditional method described in [11] for this). Each edge (u, v) expresses the fact that v is a follower of u and the corresponding probability provides evidence that an action performed by u will be performed by v as well.

The objective here is to show that running the standard GREEDY influence-maximization algorithm on a reduced version of the graph given by the inner-most (k, η)-shells allows to achieve high-quality results while keeping the running time small. We test our method replacing the notion of de-

Table 5: Expected spread achieved by the proposed (k,η)-cores-based method vs. some baselines with varying the output set size $|S|$.

	$\|S\| = 10$	$\|S\| = 20$	$\|S\| = 30$
(k,η)-CORES	9 570	9 606	9 610
OUT-DEGREE	9 014	9 016	9 130
η-DEGREE	9 019	9 089	9 125
EXP-DEGREE	9 012	9 093	9 123
k-CORES	9 134	9 192	9 223

gree with out-degree (given that the graph is directed) and setting $\eta = 0.5$. We obtain 8 cores and keep the three innermost (k,η)-shells. This gives a reduced graph with 2 064 vertices and 86 142 edges. We run the optimized version of the GREEDY algorithm defined in [12], i.e., the CELF++ algorithm, on such a reduced graph and take the seed vertices S outputted as our result.

For accuracy evaluation, we compute the expected spread achieved by S on *the whole graph* (using Monte Carlo sampling with 10 000 samples). As criteria for comparison, we use the top-K vertices ranked according to the following baseline ranking functions: (*i*) maximum out-degree (ignoring probabilities, as suggested in the seminal work on influence maximization [16]), (*ii*) maximum η-degree, (*iii*) maximum expected degree (computed by summing the probabilities on the edges outgoing from a vertex), and (*iv*) vertices computed by running CELF++ on the graph reduced according to *deterministic* core decomposition (ignoring probabilities). Note that we could not use the results of the direct execution of CELF++ on the whole graph due to its excessive running time (it could not finish in several weeks).

The results reported in Table 5 (we vary $|S|$ from 10 to 30) show how our (k,η)-CORES-based method evidently outperforms all the baselines, allowing to increase the spread up to 590 (OUT-DEGREE), 551 (η-DEGREE), 558 (EXP-DEGREE), and 436 (k-CORES). As far as efficiency, we report runtimes in the order of 4–5 hours (with $|S| = 30$), which are times clearly affordable—contrast to the unaffordable runtime of the direct execution of CELF++ on the whole graph.

7. TASK-DRIVEN TEAM FORMATION

In *task-driven team formation* we are given a collaboration graph $G = (V, E, \tau)$, where vertices are individuals and edges are assigned a probabilistic topic model τ, representing (a distribution on) the topics exhibited by past collaborations. The topic model can be produced by standard methods, such as the popular *Latent Dirichlet Allocation* (LDA) [6]. The input of LDA (or any other similar method) is (*i*) a number Z of topics, and (*ii*) for each edge $(u, v) \in E$, a document $d(u, v)$ representing all the past collaborations between u and v. The document $d(u, v)$ is a bag of terms coming from a finite vocabulary Σ. The output is the topic model τ, that is:

- for each edge $(u, v) \in E$ and each topic $z \in [1..Z]$, the probability $p^z_{u,v} = (z|u, v)$ that the collaborations between u and v are on the topic z, with $\sum_{z=1}^{Z} p^z_{u,v} = 1$.
- for each term $t \in \Sigma$, a distribution over topics, i.e., for each topic $z \in [1, Z]$, the probability $\gamma^z_t = P(t|z)$ that the term t has been generated by the topic z, with $\sum_{t\in\Sigma} \gamma^z_t = 1$.

A task-driven team-formation query is a pair $\langle T, Q\rangle$, where $T \subset \Sigma$ is a set of terms describing a task, and $Q \subset V$ is a set of vertices (possibly even a single vertex). The goal is to find an answer vertex set A, with $Q \subseteq A$, which is a good team to perform the task described by the terms in T. Being a good team means having a good affinity among the team members with respect to the given task. We report more formal details on this in the following.

The query task T, together with the topic model τ, induce a single probability value $p^T(u, v)$ for each edge $(u, v) \in E$, such that $p^T(u, v)$ represents the likelihood that T has been generated by a collaboration between u and v:

$$p^T(u, v) = p(u, v|T) = \prod_{t\in T} \sum_{z=1}^{Z} \gamma^z_t p^z_{u,v}. \quad (8)$$

Hence, given a task T, the input collaboration graph G yields an uncertain graph $\mathcal{G}^T = (V, E, p^T)$. This way, given $\mathcal{G}^T$ and a set of query vertices $Q \subseteq V$, the task of finding a good team for the query at hand directly translates into finding a subgraph of $\mathcal{G}^T$ that represents a good community for Q. Formally, the goal is to find a *connected* subgraph $\mathcal{H} = (V_\mathcal{H}, E_\mathcal{H})$ of $\mathcal{G}^T$ that (*i*) contains all query vertices ($Q \subseteq V_\mathcal{H}$), and (*ii*) maximizes a notion of density. Particularly, as far as the density measure, the *minimum degree* has been widely recognized as a principled choice for this kind of problem.[5] We therefore rely on this notion of density and ask for the subgraph $\mathcal{H}$ to maximize the minimum η-degree of a vertex in $\mathcal{H}$. The resulting problem statement is:

PROBLEM 2 (TASK-DRIVEN TEAM FORMATION). *Given a collaboration graph $G = (V, E, \tau)$ and a query $\langle T, Q\rangle$, let $\mathcal{G}^T$ be the uncertain graph derived from G and T as described in Equation (8). Given a threshold $\eta \in [0, 1]$, we want to find a* connected *subgraph $\mathcal{H} = (V_\mathcal{H}, E_\mathcal{H})$ of $\mathcal{G}^T$ induced by a set of vertices $V_\mathcal{H}$ such that*

$$V_\mathcal{H} = \arg\max_{Q\subseteq S\subseteq V} \min_{u\in S} \eta\text{-}deg(u). \quad \square$$

Exploiting (k,η)-cores for team formation. We now show that Problem 2 can be optimally solved by resorting to our notion of (k,η)-core decomposition. This result is stated in the next theorem (we omit the proof for space reasons).

THEOREM 6. *Given an uncertain graph $\mathcal{G}^T$ and a threshold $\eta \in [0, 1]$, let $\mathbf{C} = \{C_0, C_1, \ldots, C_{k^*}\}$ be the (k,η)-core decomposition of $\mathcal{G}^T$ (with $C_0 \supseteq C_1 \supseteq \cdots \supseteq C_{k^*}$), and, given a set of query vertices $Q \subseteq V$, let C^*_Q be the smallest-sized core in $\mathbf{C}$ such that every $q \in Q$ belongs to the same connected component of C^*_Q.*

Then, the solution to Problem 2 is given by the connected component of C^*_Q that contains Q. $\square$

Theorem 6 provides us with a principled way of solving Problem 2. The solution can be summarized as follows:

1. Given a collaboration graph $G = (V, E, \tau)$ and a task-driven team-formation query $\langle T, Q\rangle$, derive the uncertain graph $\mathcal{G}^T = (V, E, p^T)$ (Equation (8)).[6]
2. Compute the (k,η)-core decomposition $\mathbf{C}$ of $\mathcal{G}^T$;

[5] As argued in [27], maximizing the minimum degree provides a better evidence of the goodness of a community than, e.g., the maximization of the average degree, which is instead more suitable for dense-subgraph discovery.

[6] As Equation (8) can produce very small probabilities, in our implementation we prune $\mathcal{G}^T$ by removing edges with probability smaller than a threshold ϵ ($\epsilon = 10^{-16}$ in our experiments).

Table 6: Three examples of task-driven team-formation queries and corresponding results.

$T = \{gene, express\}$, $Q = \{H.V.Jagadish\}$	$T = \{xml, tree\}$, $Q = \{H.V.Jagadish, S.Muthukrishnan\}$	$T = \{auction, model\}$, $Q = \{S.Muthukrishnan\}$
Brian D. Athey, Giovanni Scardoni, Kathleen A. Stringer, Venkateshwar G. Keshamouni, Jing Gao, Terry E. Weymouth, Vasudeva Mahavisno, Charles F. Burant, Christopher W. Beecher, Maureen A. Sartor, Alla Karnovsky, Rork Kuick, Zach Wright, James D. Cavalcoli, Gilbert S. Omenn, **H. V. Jagadish**, Carlo Laudanna, Tim Hull, Barbara R. Mirel, V. Glenn Tarcea	**S. Muthukrishnan**, Panagiotis G. Ipeirotis, Lauri Pietarinen **H. V. Jagadish**, Divesh Srivastava, Nick Koudas	Uri Nadav, Noam Nisan, Jon Feldman, Vahab S. Mirrokni, Gagan Aggarwal, Tanmoy Chakraborty, Aranyak Mehta Evdokia Nikolova, **S. Muthukrishnan**, Martin Pal, Clifford Stein, Eyal Even-Dar Florin Constantin, Yishay Mansour

3. Visit the cores in **C** starting from the smallest-sized one (i.e., the inner-most core), until finding C_Q^*;
4. Return the connected component of C_Q^* containing Q as the solution to Problem 2.

Experiments. We consider task-driven team formation in the context of collaborations among computer-science researchers. We build a collaboration network from the DBLP database (`www.informatik.uni-trier.de/~ley/db/`): vertices are authors and an edge connects two authors if they co-authored at least once. The resulting graph has $|V| = 1\,089\,442$ and $|E| = 4\,144\,697$. For each edge, we take the bag of words of the titles of all papers coauthored by the two authors (words are stemmed and stop-words are removed) and apply LDA to infer the topic model τ (we set $Z = 100$).

In Table 6 we report the results of three task-driven team-formation queries. The first two queries share the query vertex `H. V. Jagadish`, but the first task is about *gene expression* while the second one is about *xml*: as expected the two proposed teams are very different. The third query shares with the second one the vertex `S. Muthukrishnan`; but, unlike the previous one that is about xml (a database topic), the third query is about *auction models* (an algorithm-theory topic): the different teams proposed correctly reflect the difference in the tasks. It is worth noticing that the extraction of these teams, following the process described above and exploiting our efficient (k,η)-core decomposition, takes approximately 2-3 seconds on a commodity laptop.

8. CONCLUSIONS

In this paper we extend the graph tool of core decomposition to the context of uncertain graphs. We define the (k,η)-core concept, and we devise efficient algorithms for computing a (k,η)-core decomposition. As a future work, we plan to investigate the relationship between (k,η)-cores and other definitions of (probabilistic) dense subgraphs, so as to exploit the former as a speeding-up preprocessing.

9. REFERENCES

[1] E. Adar and C. Re. Managing Uncertainty in Social Networks. *IEEE Data Eng. Bull.*, 30(2):15–22, 2007.

[2] J. I. Alvarez-Hamelin, L. Dall'Asta, A. Barrat, and A. Vespignani. Large scale networks fingerprinting and visualization using the k-core decomposition. In *NIPS*, 2005.

[3] R. Andersen and K. Chellapilla. Finding dense subgraphs with size bounds. In *WAW*, 2009.

[4] S. Asthana, O. D. King, F. D. Gibbons, and F. P. Roth. Predicting Protein Complex Membership using Probabilistic Network Reliability. *Genome Res.*, 14:1170–1175, 2004.

[5] V. Batagelj and M. Zaveršnik. Fast algorithms for determining (generalized) core groups in social networks. *Advances in Data Analysis and Classification*, 5(2):129–145, 2011.

[6] D. M. Blei, A. Y. Ng, and M. I. Jordan. Latent dirichlet allocation. *JMLR*, 3:993–1022, 2003.

[7] P. Boldi, F. Bonchi, A. Gionis, and T. Tassa. Injecting Uncertainty in Graphs for Identity Obfuscation. *PVLDB*, 5(11):1376–1387, 2012.

[8] X. H. Chen, A. P. Dempster, and J. S. Liu. Weighted finite population sampling to maximize entropy. *Biometrika*, 81:457–469, 1994.

[9] N. Dalvi and D. Suciu. Efficient query evaluation on probabilistic databases. In *VLDB*, pages 864–875, 2004.

[10] D. Eppstein, M. Löffler, and D. Strash. Listing all maximal cliques in sparse graphs in near-optimal time. In *ISAAC*, 2010.

[11] A. Goyal, F. Bonchi, and L. V. Lakshmanan. Learning influence probabilities in social networks. In *WSDM*, 2010.

[12] A. Goyal, W. Lu, and L. V. Lakshmanan. Celf++: optimizing the greedy algorithm for influence maximization in social networks. In *WWW*, pages 47–48, 2011.

[13] J. Healy, J. Janssen, E. E. Milios, and W. Aiello. Characterization of graphs using degree cores. In *WAW*, 2006.

[14] R. Jin, L. Liu, and C. C. Aggarwal. Discovering Highly Reliable Subgraphs in Uncertain Graphs. In *KDD*, 2011.

[15] R. Jin, L. Liu, B. Ding, and H. Wang. Distance-Constraint Reachability Computation in Uncertain Graphs. *PVLDB*, 4(9):551–562, 2011.

[16] D. Kempe, J. Kleinberg, and E. Tardos. Maximizing the spread of influence through a social network. In *KDD*, 2003.

[17] M. Kitsak, L. K. Gallos, S. Havlin, F. Liljeros, L. Muchnik, H. E. Stanley, and H. A. Makse. Identifying influential spreaders in complex networks. *Nature Physics 6*, 888, 2010.

[18] G. Kollios, M. Potamias, and E. Terzi. Clustering large probabilistic graphs. *TKDE*, 25(2):325–336, 2013

[19] G. Kortsarz and D. Peleg. Generating sparse 2-spanners. *J. Algorithms*, 17(2):222–236, 1994.

[20] D. L.-Nowell and J. Kleinberg. The Link Prediction Problem for Social Networks. In *CIKM*, 2003.

[21] V. E. Lee, N. Ruan, R. Jin, and C. C. Aggarwal. A survey of algorithms for dense subgraph discovery. In *Managing and Mining Graph Data*. 2010.

[22] L. Liu, R. Jin, C. Aggrawal, and Y. Shen. Reliable clustering on uncertain graphs. In *ICDM*, 2012.

[23] K. Pearson. *Tables of the Incomplete Beta-Function*. Cambridge University Press, 1968.

[24] M. Potamias, F. Bonchi, A. Gionis, and G. Kollios. k-Nearest Neighbors in Uncertain Graphs. *PVLDB*, 3(1):997–1008, 2010.

[25] S. B. Seidman. Network structure and minimum degree. *Social Networks*, 5(3):269–287, 1983.

[26] P. Sevon, L. Eronen, P. Hintsanen, K. Kulovesi, and H. Toivonen. Link Discovery in Graphs Derived from Biological Databases. In *DILS*, 2006.

[27] M. Sozio and A. Gionis. The community-search problem and how to plan a successful cocktail party. In *KDD*, 2010.

[28] L. G. Valiant. The Complexity of Enumeration and Reliability Problems. *SIAM J. on Computing*, 8(3):410–421, 1979.

[29] E. W. Weisstein. Binomial distribution. From MathWorld—A Wolfram Web Resource. Last visited on 16/5/2013, `http://mathworld.wolfram.com/BinomialDistribution.html`.

[30] S. Wuchty and E. Almaas. Peeling the yeast protein network. *Proteomics*, 5(2):444–449, Feb. 2005.

[31] Y. Yuan, G. Wang, L. Chen, and H. Wang. Efficient Subgraph Similarity Search on Large Probabilistic Graph Databases. *PVLDB*, 5(9):800–811, 2012.

[32] H. Zhang, H. Zhao, W. Cai, J. Liu, and W. Zhou. Using the k-core decomposition to analyze the static structure of large-scale software systems. *The Journal of Supercomputing*, 53(2):352–369, 2010.

[33] L. Zou, P. Peng, and D. Zhao. Top-K Possible Shortest Path Query over a Large Uncertain Graph. In *WISE*, 2011.

[34] Z. Zou, H. Gao, and J. Li. Discovering Frequent Subgraphs over Uncertain Graph Databases under Probabilistic Semantics. In *KDD*, 2010.

Learning Multifractal Structure in Large Networks

Austin R. Benson
Stanford University
Institute for Computational and Mathematical Engineering
arbenson@stanford.edu

Carlos Riquelme
Stanford University
Institute for Computational and Mathematical Engineering
rikel@stanford.edu

Sven Schmit
Stanford University
Institute for Computational and Mathematical Engineering
schmit@stanford.edu

ABSTRACT

Using random graphs to model networks has a rich history. In this paper, we analyze and improve the multifractal network generators (MFNG) introduced by Palla *et al.* We provide a new result on the probability of subgraphs existing in graphs generated with MFNG. This allows us to quickly compute moments of an important set of graph properties, such as the expected number of edges, stars, and cliques for graphs generated using MFNG. Specifically, we show how to compute these moments in time complexity independent of the size of the graph and the number of recursive levels in the generative model. We leverage this theory to propose a new method of moments algorithm for fitting MFNG to large networks. Empirically, this new approach effectively simulates properties of several social and information networks. In terms of matching subgraph counts, our method outperforms similar algorithms used with the Stochastic Kronecker Graph model. Furthermore, we present a fast approximation algorithm to generate graph instances following the multifractal structure. The approximation scheme is an improvement over previous methods, which ran in time complexity quadratic in the number of vertices. Combined, our method of moments and fast sampling scheme provide the first scalable framework for effectively modeling large networks with MFNG.

Categories and Subject Descriptors

H.2.8 [**Database Applications**]: Data mining

General Terms

Algorithms, Theory

Keywords

graph mining; real-world networks; multifractal; method of moments; graph sampling; stochastic kronecker graph; random graphs

KDD'14, August 24–27, 2014, New York, NY, USA.

ACM 978-1-4503-2956-9/14/08 ...$15.00.
http://dx.doi.org/10.1145/2623330.2623718.

1. RECURSIVE GRAPH STRUCTURE

Generative random graph models with recursive or hierarchical structure are successful in simulating large-scale networks [5, 15]. The recursive structure produces graphs with heavy-tailed degree distribution and high clustering coefficient. Random samples from recursive models are used to test algorithms, benchmark computer performance [13], anonymize data, and to understand the structure of networks.

A relatively new model is the multifractal network generators (MFNG, [14]). However, there are two issues that are barriers to making MFNG a practical model for large-scale networks. First, results for fitting MFNG models to graphs have been extremely limited. Current procedures can only match a single graph property, such as the number of nodes with degree d. Second, to our knowledge, all MFNG sampling techniques are $\mathcal{O}(|V|^2)$ algorithms, where V is the vertex set. This makes the generation of large graphs infeasible.

In this paper, we address both barriers and demonstrate that MFNG can be a better alternative to the more popular stochastic Kronecker graphs. In Section 3, we show how to compute several key properties of MFNG (e.g., expected number of edges, triangles, stars, etc.) with computational complexity independent of $|V|$ and the recursion depth. This result lets us develop an extremely efficient method of moments algorithm to fit networks to MFNG. We test our new method of moments algorithm on synthetic data and large social and information networks. In Section 5, we provide a heuristic fast approximate sampling scheme to randomly sample MFNG with complexity $\mathcal{O}(|E| \log |V|)$, where E is the edge set of the network. In Section 6.1, we show that our algorithm can identify model parameters in synthetic graphs sampled from MFNG, and in Section 6.2, we see that our algorithm can match the number of edges, wedges, triangles, 4-cliques, 3-stars, and 4-stars in large networks. Our contributions are summarized as follows:

- We show how to efficiently compute moments of several feature counts in random graphs generated with MFNG and use this to accelerate a method of moments algorithm for fitting large networks to MFNG.
- We provide a fast sampling algorithm for MFNG, so that large networks can be randomly generated in reasonable time.
- We empirically show that MFNG models graph feature counts better than alternatives and that global graph properties are accurately matched.

1.1 Related work

Popular recursive and hierarchical models include Stochastic Kronecker Graphs (SKG, [5]), Block Two-Level Erdős-Rényi (BTER, [15]), and Random Typing Generator (RTG, [1]). An older, popular model is the recursive matrix (R-MAT, [2]), which is a specific instance of an SKG model with a 2×2 generator matrix.

SKG is popular for several reasons including capturing degree distributions, clustering coefficients, and diameter in large networks. There are several methods for fitting SKG parameters to simulate a target network, including maximum likelihood estimation (the KronFit algorithm, [5, 6]) and the method of moments [3]. Maximum likelihood estimation is also used for the Multiplicative Attribute Graph model [4], and a simulated method of moments is used for mixed Kronecker product graph models [11, 12]. Finally, SKG produces graph samples in time complexity $\mathcal{O}(|E|\log(|V|))$ rather than $\mathcal{O}(|V|^2)$. On the other hand, SKG is constrained by a rather strong assumption on the relationship between the number of recursion levels and the number of nodes in the graph. Specifically, the number of recursive levels is $\lceil \log(|V|) \rceil$.

MFNG decouples the relationship between the recursion depth and the number of nodes and also naturally handles graphs where $|V|$ is not a power of two. While there are ad-hoc methods for SKG when $|V|$ is not a power of two, all analyses in the literature make the assumption. We do not assume that $|V|$ is a power of two in our analysis in Section 3. Furthermore, the variable interval lengths in MFNG allow for more flexibility than is offered by the SKG framework. These reasons make MFNG more flexible as a generator for graphs.

2. OVERVIEW OF MFNG

MFNG is a recursive generative model based on a generating measure, $\mathcal{W}_k$. The measure $\mathcal{W}_k$ consists of an m-vector of lengths ℓ with $\sum_{i=1}^{m} \ell_i = 1$ and a symmetric $m \times m$ probability matrix $\mathbf{P}$. The subscript k is the number of recursive levels, which we will subsequently explain. In this paper, we refer to the m indices of ℓ as *categories*. Also, since the measure is completely characterized by $\mathbf{P}$, ℓ, and k, we write $\mathcal{W}_k(\mathbf{P}, \ell)$ to explicitly describe the full measure.

An undirected graph $G = (V, E)$ is distributed according to $\mathcal{W}_k(\mathbf{P}, \ell)$ if it is generated by the following procedure:

1. Partition $[0, 1]$ into m subintervals of length ℓ_i, $i = 1, \ldots, m$. Recursively partition each subinterval k times into m pieces, using the relative lengths ℓ_i. This creates m^k intervals $\ell_{i_1,\ldots,i_k}$ of length $\prod_{r=1}^{k} \ell_{i_r}$ such that $\sum_{i_1,\ldots,i_k} \ell_{i_1,\ldots,i_k} = 1$.
2. Sample N points uniformly from $[0, 1]$ and create the nodes $V = \{x_1, \ldots, x_N\}$. Each node x_i is identified by its k-tuple of categories $c(x_i) = (i_1, \ldots, i_k)$, based on its position on $[0, 1]$ and the partitioning in Step 1.
3. For every pair of nodes x_i and x_j identified by the k-tuple of categories $c(x_i) = (i_1, \ldots, i_k)$ and $c(x_j) = (j_1, \ldots, j_k)$, add edge (x_i, x_j) to G with probability $\prod_{r=1}^{k} p_{i_r j_r}$.

While the generation is intricate, MFNG admit a geometric interpretation. Consider first the partition of the unit square into m^2 rectangles according to the lengths ℓ. The rectangle in position (q, s) has side lengths ℓ_q and ℓ_s, $1 \le q, s \le m$. The point $(x_i, x_j) \in [0, 1] \times [0, 1]$ lands in the unit square, inside some rectangle R with side lengths ℓ_{i_1} and ℓ_{j_1}. The edge 'survives' the first round with probability p_{i_1,j_1}. In the next round, we recursively partition R according to the lengths ℓ. The relative positions of x_i and x_j land the point in a new rectangle with side lengths ℓ_{i_2} and ℓ_{j_2}. The edge survives the second round with probability p_{i_2,j_2}. The process is repeated k times and is illustrated in Figure 1. If an edge survives all k levels, then it is added to the graph.

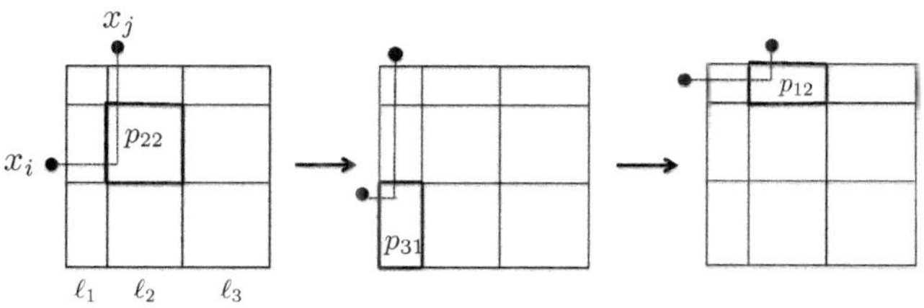

$$P((x_i, x_j) \in G) = p_{22} p_{31} p_{12}$$

Figure 1: MFNG's recursive edge generation with $m = k = 3$.

3. THEORETICAL RESULTS

The original work on MFNG [14] shows how to compute the expected feature counts for graph properties by examining the entire expanded measure $\mathcal{W}_k(\mathbf{P}, \ell)$. In other words, to count the features, the entire probability matrix of size $m^k \times m^k$ is formed. However, in some cases m^k is of the order of $\mathcal{O}(|V|)$ (see the examples in Section 6.2). Clearly, computing and storing $\mathcal{O}(|V|^2)$ probabilities is infeasible for large networks. Thus, current methods for counting and fitting features are intolerably expensive. Theorem 2 shows that we can count many of the same features by only looking at the probability matrix $\mathbf{P}$ a constant number of times (independent of $|V|$). Hence, we are able to scale these computations to graphs with a large number of nodes.

3.1 Decoupling of recursive levels

We start with a lemma that shows how to decompose a generating measure $\mathcal{W}_k$ with k recursive levels in k measures with depth one. This will make it easier to count subgraphs in Theorem 2.

LEMMA 1. *Consider generating measures $\mathcal{W}_1(\mathbf{P}, \ell)$ and $\mathcal{W}_k(\mathbf{P}, \ell)$, which are parameterized by the same probability matrix $\mathbf{P}$ and lengths ℓ but different recursion depths. Let graphs $H_1, \ldots, H_k \sim \mathcal{W}_1(\mathbf{P}, \ell)$ be independently drawn, and also denote $H_i = (V, E_i)$, with nodes labelled arbitrarily. Then the intersection graph $G = (V, \cap_{i=1}^{k} E_i) = (V, E_G) \sim \mathcal{W}_k(\mathbf{P}, \ell)$.*

PROOF. We prove the lemma by conditioning on the categories to which the nodes belong (recall that a category is the set of intervals that a node falls into at each level of the recursion). Each node $u \in V$ is identified with some real number in $[0, 1]$. The probability that the k-tuple of categories corresponding to u is $c(u) = (c_1, \ldots, c_k)$ in any graph $H \sim \mathcal{W}_k(\mathbf{P}, \ell)$ is simply $\prod_{r=1}^{k} \ell_{c_r}$. By independence of the H_i, the probability that the same node u is in the same categories $c_1, \ldots, c_k$ in the graphs $H_1, \ldots, H_k$, respectively, is also $\prod_{r=1}^{k} \ell_{c_r}$. Note that

$$\begin{aligned}
&\mathbb{P}((u, v) \in E_G | c(u) = (c_1^u, \ldots, c_k^u), c(v) = (c_1^v, \ldots, c_k^v)) \\
&= \mathbb{P}\left((u, v) \in \cap_{i=1}^{k} E_i | c(u) = (c_1^u, \ldots, c_k^u), c(v) = (c_1^v, \ldots, c_k^v)\right) \\
&= \prod_{i=1}^{k} \mathbb{P}((u, v) \in E_i | c(u) = (c_1^u, \ldots, c_k^u), c(v) = (c_1^v, \ldots, c_k^v)) \\
&= \prod_{i=1}^{k} \mathbb{P}((u, v) \in E_i | [c(u)]_i = c_i^u, [c(v)]_i = c_i^v) = \prod_{i=1}^{k} p_{c_i^u, c_i^v}.
\end{aligned}$$

In the first equality, we use the definition of E_G; in the second and third equalities, we use the independence of the H_i; and in the final equality, we use the definition of $\mathcal{W}_1$. However, for any graph

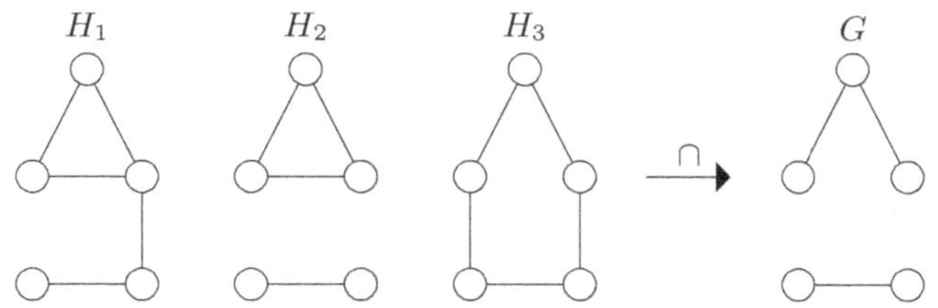

Figure 2: Illustration of Lemma 1. If three graphs H_1, H_2, and H_3 are generated from $\mathcal{W}_1(\mathbf{P}, \ell)$, then their intersection G follows the distribution of $\mathcal{W}_3(\mathbf{P}, \ell)$.

$G' \sim \mathcal{W}_k(\mathbf{P}, \ell)$, we have

$$\mathbb{P}\left((u, v) \in G' | c(u) = (c_1^u, \ldots, c_k^u), c(v) = (c_1^v, \ldots, c_k^v)\right)$$
$$= \prod_{i=1}^{k} p_{c_i^u, c_i^v}.$$

□

Figure 2 illustrates Lemma 1. Our main result is a straightforward consequence of this lemma.

THEOREM 2. *Let $\mathcal{W}_1(\mathbf{P}, \ell)$ and $\mathcal{W}_k(\mathbf{P}, \ell)$ be generating measures defined by the same probabilities $\mathbf{P}$ and lengths ℓ but with different recursion depths. Consider k multifractal graphs $H_i = (V, E_i)$ generated independently from $\mathcal{W}_1(\mathbf{P}, \ell)$ and a multifractal graph $G = (V, E_G)$ generated from $\mathcal{W}_k(\mathbf{P}, \ell)$. For any event A on G that can be written as $A = \{S \subset E_G\}$, where $S \subset \{(i, j) : i, j \in \{1, \ldots, n\}, i < j\}$,*

$$\mathbb{P}_{\mathcal{W}_k}(A) = \mathbb{P}_{\mathcal{W}_1}(A)^k.$$

PROOF.

$$\begin{aligned}
\mathbb{P}_{\mathcal{W}_k}(A) &= \mathbb{P}_{\mathcal{W}_k}(s \in E_G, \forall s \in S) \\
&= \mathbb{P}_{(\mathcal{W}_1)^k}(s \in E_i, \forall s \in S, \forall i \in \{1, \ldots, k\}) \\
&= \prod_{i=1}^{k} \mathbb{P}_{(\mathcal{W}_1)^k}(s \in E_i, \forall s \in S) \\
&= \mathbb{P}_{(\mathcal{W}_1)^k}(s \in E_1, \forall s \in S)^k \\
&= \mathbb{P}_{\mathcal{W}_1}(A)^k.
\end{aligned}$$

□

In other words, the probability that a subset of the edges exists if the graph is drawn from $\mathcal{W}_k$ is the k-th power of the probability that these edges exist if the graph is drawn from $\mathcal{W}_1$. The condition that A can be written as $A = \{S \subset E\}$ is subtle. It states that Theorem 2 holds if we can specify a subset of the edges that must be present in the graph. We can be indifferent about certain edges, but we cannot specify that an edge is *not* present in the graph.

We can now easily compute the moments of subgraph counts, such as the number of edges, triangles, and larger cliques in MFNG. The following corollary shows how to use Theorem 2 for these calculations. for graphs generated by MFNG.

COROLLARY 3. *The expected number of edges $|E|$ in a graph sampled from MFNG is*

$$\mathbb{E}[|E|] = \binom{n}{2} s^k, \tag{1}$$

where $s = \sum_{i,j \in [m]} p_{ij} \ell_i \ell_j$.

PROOF. Let u and v, $u \neq v$, be two random nodes of G. Let A denote the event $A = \{(u, v) \in E\}$, and we define A_i to denote the analogous event restricted to H_i in the multifractal generator. By Theorem 2, we have that

$$\mathbb{P}(A) = \prod_{i=1}^{k} \mathbb{P}(A_i) = \mathbb{P}(A_1)^k.$$

Now we can restrict ourselves to A_1,

$$\begin{aligned}
\mathbb{P}(A_1) &= \sum_{i,j \in [m]} \mathbb{P}(A^{(1)} | c_1^u = i, c_1^v = j)\, \mathbb{P}(c_1^u = i, c_1^v = j) && (2) \\
&= \sum_{i,j \in [m]} p_{ij}\, \mathbb{P}(c_1^u = i) \mathbb{P}(c_1^v = j) && (3) \\
&= \sum_{i,j \in [m]} p_{ij}\, \ell_i \ell_j = s. && (4)
\end{aligned}$$

We conclude that

$$\mathbb{P}(A) = \mathbb{P}((u, v) \in E) = s^k. \tag{5}$$

The expected number of edges is then given by

$$\mathbb{E}[|E|] = \binom{n}{2} s^k. \tag{6}$$

□

COROLLARY 4. *Graphs sampled from MFNG also have the following moments. The expected number of d-stars* [1] *S_d is:*

$$\mathbb{E}[S_d] = n \binom{n-1}{d} \left(\sum_{i_1, \ldots, i_{d+1} \in [m]} \prod_{j=2}^{d+1} p_{i_1 i_j} \prod_{j=1}^{d+1} \ell_{i_j} \right)^k.$$

In particular, the expected number of wedges (2-stars) is

$$\mathbb{E}[S_2] = n \binom{n-1}{2} \left(\sum_{i_1, i_2, i_3 \in [m]} p_{i_1 i_2} p_{i_1 i_3}\, \ell_{i_1} \ell_{i_2} \ell_{i_3} \right)^k.$$

The variance $\sigma_E = Var(|E|)$ of the number of edges is

$$\sigma_E = \binom{n}{2} s^k \left(1 - \binom{n}{2} s^k \right) + 2\,\mathbb{E}[S_2] + \binom{n}{2} \binom{n-2}{2} s^{2k},$$

where s is the same as in Corollary 3.

The expected number of t-cliques [2] *C_t is*

$$\mathbb{E}[C_t] = \binom{n}{t} s_t^k, \tag{7}$$

where

$$s_t := \sum_{i_1, \ldots, i_t \in [m]} \left(\prod_{\substack{j, q \in [t] \\ j < q}} p_{i_j i_q} \right) \ell_{i_1} \ell_{i_2} \cdots \ell_{i_t}. \tag{8}$$

In particular, the expected number of triangles (3-cliques) is:

$$\mathbb{E}[C_3] = \binom{n}{3} \left(\sum_{i,j,t \in [m]} p_{ij} p_{it} p_{jt}\, \ell_i \ell_j \ell_t \right)^k. \tag{9}$$

[1] A d-star is a graph with $d + 1$ vertices and d edges that connect the first node to all other vertices.

[2] A t-clique is a graph with t vertices where every possible edge between the vertices exists.

Finally, the expected number of nodes with degree d, E_d, satisfies $\mathbb{E}[E_{|V|-1}] = \mathbb{E}[S_{|V|-1}]$ *and*

$$\mathbb{E}[E_d] = \mathbb{E}[S_d] - \sum_{i=d+1}^{|V|-1} \binom{i}{d} \mathbb{E}[E_i]. \tag{10}$$

PROOF. The proofs follow the same patterns as of the proof of Corollary 3. We include the proofs in supplementary material online [3]. □

These are some examples of properties for which we can compute the *exact* expectation. However, we can also compute useful approximations. For a given measure $\mathcal{W}_k$, we could empirically compute the value of $\mathbb{E}[C_t]$ for each t until we find $\mathbb{E}[C_{t^*}] \geq 1 > \mathbb{E}[C_{t^*+1}]$, which is a good estimator of the expected maximum clique size.

Finally, we note that there are graph properties which will certainly not translate to this theoretical framework. Let $\mu(G)$ be the chromatic number of G, i.e., the smallest number of colors needed to color the vertices such that vertices connected by an edge are not the same color. Suppose we want to compute $\mathbb{P}(\mu(G) < 10)$. If the theorem is used directly, then the result is $\mathbb{P}(\mu(G) < 10) = \mathbb{P}(\mu(H_1) < 10)^k$. But $\mathbb{P}(\mu(G) < 10) \geq \mathbb{P}(\mu(H_1) < 10)$ since taking the intersection of graphs can only reduce the chromatic number. In this case, $\mathbb{P}(\mu(G) < 10)$ cannot be written as an event on the subset of the edges of the graph. Hence, the assumptions of the theorem are violated.

4. METHOD OF MOMENTS LEARNING ALGORITHM

Now we change gears and look at how we can use the theory laid out above to fit multifractal measures to real networks. Given a graph G, we are interested in finding a probability matrix $\mathbf{P}$, a set of lengths ℓ, and a recursion depth k, such that graphs generated from the measure $\mathcal{W}_k(\mathbf{P}, \ell)$ are similar to G. The theoretical results in Section 3 make it simple to compute moments for MFNG, so a method of moments is natural. In particular, given a set of desired features counts f_i (such as number of edges, 2-stars, and triangles), we seek to solve the following optimization problem:

$$\begin{aligned}
\underset{\mathbf{P},\ell,k}{\text{minimize}} \quad & \sum_i \frac{|f_i - \mathbb{E}_{\mathcal{W}_k}[F_i]|}{F_i} \\
\text{subject to} \quad & 0 \leq p_{ij} = p_{ji} \leq 1, \qquad 1 \leq i \leq j \leq m \\
& 0 \leq \ell_i \leq 1, \qquad\qquad\quad 1 \leq i \leq m \\
& \sum_{i=1}^{m} \ell_i = 1
\end{aligned} \tag{11}$$

Here, F_i denotes the actual count of feature f_i in the MFNG.

If certain features are more important to fit, then we can weight the terms in the objective function, but for simplicity of our numerical experiments, we only use an unweighted objective in this paper. Similar objective functions were proposed for SKG [3] and for mixed Kronecker product graph models [12]. In Section 6, we see that the simple objective function works well on synthetic and real data sets.

4.1 Desired features

We want to model real world networks accurately and efficiently. Theorem 2 shows that, given a generating measure $\mathcal{W}_k(\mathbf{P}, \ell)$, we can quickly compute moments of several (local) feature counts. However, (global) graph properties such as degree distribution and clustering coefficient are not covered by our theoretical results. Therefore, we use local feature counts, such as number of d-stars and t-cliques[4], as a proxy. If the number of d-stars and t-cliques are similar, then we expect the degree distribution and clustering to be similar as well. For example, the global clustering coefficient is three times the ratio of the number of triangles (3-cliques) to the number of wedges (2-stars) in the graph. In Section 6.2, we show that matching star and clique subgraph counts in social and information networks leads to a generating measure that produces graphs with a similar degree distribution.

4.2 Solving the optimization problem

Optimization problem (11) is not trivial to solve, as there are many local minima and some of them turn out to be very poor. On the other hand, if we are given the feature counts of a graph and fix k, running a standard optimization solver such as `fmincon` in Matlab, we find a critical point quickly: we only have to fit $m^2 + m + 1$ variables, where, typically, m is two or three. Thus, we solve the optimization problem with many random restarts and use the best result. For each random restart, we first choose a random k and then solve the optimization problem with k fixed. We demonstrate that this crude method works on several practical examples (see Section 6). More sophisticated methods are beyond the scope of this work. We also point out that the bottleneck of the estimation is performing the feature counts, not solving the above optimization problem (despite the many restarts).

5. FAST SAMPLING FOR SPARSE GRAPHS

In this section, we discuss a heuristic method for generating sample graphs following the multifractal measure that is effective when the graph to be generated is sparse, i.e. has relatively few edges. This is important because the naive sampling method takes $\mathcal{O}(|V|^2)$ time—it considers the edge for every pair of nodes in the graph. The fast heuristic algorithm is inspired by the "ball-dropping" scheme for SKG (see Section 3.6 of [5]). Unlike the SKG case, however, our algorithm is merely a heuristic due to the stochastic nature of the location of the nodes. The speed-up is obtained by fixing the number of edges in advance and only considering $\mathcal{O}(|E|)$ pairs of vertices. We will demonstrate that our sampling algorithm runs in time $\mathcal{O}(|E| \log(|V|))$. The pseudo-code is given in Algorithm 1. In the next sections, we give the details of the algorithm and briefly discuss the performance.

5.1 The algorithm

In order to avoid looping over all pairs of nodes, we fix the number of edges. The number of edges is sampled from a normal random variable with mean $\mathbb{E}[|E|]$ and variance σ_E, as provided by Corollaries 3 and 4. Since the number of edges is a sum of Bernoulli trials, this is well approximated using a Gaussian random variable.

Once the number of edges in the graph is fixed, we start adding edges. Because node locations are random (i.e., every node has a random category), it is nontrivial to select a candidate edge. This contrasts with SKG, where the edge probabilities for a given node is deterministic. The algorithm selects node categories level by level, for each edge. To select categories, we sample an index (c, c') of a matrix $\mathbf{Q}$:

$$\mathbf{Q}_{ij} = p_{ij}\ell_i\ell_j.$$

[3] `http://stanford.edu/~arbenson/mfng.html`

[4] From now on we implicitly mean counting subgraphs if we say counting d-stars or t-cliques.

The sampling is done proportional to the entries in $\mathbf{Q}$. The matrix $\mathbf{Q}$ reflects the relative probability mass corresponding to an edge falling into those categories. In other words, it is the probability of selecting the categories c and c' at a given level *and* the edge surviving the level. The category sampling is performed k times, one for each level of recursion. This gives two k-tuples of categories: $c = (c_1, \ldots, c_k)$ and $c' = (c'_1, \ldots, c'_k)$.

Now we want to add an edge between nodes u and u' that have the categories c and c'. However, we have to be careful about the number of nodes that have the same category. We can think of the category pair (c, c') as a box B on the generating measure. Consider two boxes B_1 and B_2 and suppose that both have the same area in the unit square, and the probability between potential boxes in B_1 and B_2 is the same.

A simple example is the following case:

- $k = m = 2$
- $p_{11} = p_{22} = p_{12} = 0.5$
- $\ell_1 = \ell_2 = 0.5$

The edge probabilities in any two boxes B_1 and B_2 in the measure are the same, and the probabilities of selecting either box (from sampling the $\mathbf{Q}$ matrix) are the same. However, because of the randomness categories for nodes, there may be 10 node pairs in B_1 and only one node pair in B_2. If we simply pick a node pair at random from a box, the probability of connecting the node pair in B_2 is much higher than in B_1.

To overcome this discrepancy, we take into account the difference between the *expected* number of nodes pairs in a box and the *actual* number of node pairs in a box. Note that the joint distribution of nodes is Multinomial$(n; l_1, l_2, \ldots, l_{m^k})$ where l_i denotes the length of interval i (after recursive expansion). Let $p_{c,c'}$ be the edge probability in the box corresponding to the category pair (c, c'). Let the box's sides have lengths l and l'. Using standard properties of the Multinomial distribution, the expected number of nodes in a box, $n_{c,c'}$, is:

$$n_{c,c'} = \begin{cases} |V|(|V|l^2 - l^2 + l) & \text{if } c = c' \\ |V|(|V| - 1)ll' & \text{if } c \neq c' \end{cases}$$

Finally, we sample

$$e_{\text{to add}} \sim \text{Poisson}\left(\frac{n_{c,c'}}{\lambda |V_c||V_{c'}|}\right),$$

where $V_c = \{v \in V | \text{category of v is } c\}$. We then add $e_{\text{to add}}$ edges to the box (c, c'). Thus, if there are more node pairs in a box than expected, we add more edges to the box.

There are a couple of details we have swept under the rug. First, we haven't discussed what to do if the box (c, c') is empty. In this case, we simply re-sample c and c'. In practice, this does not occur too frequently. Second, we have introduced some dependence between edges, and MFNG samples edges independently. For this reason, we use the accuracy factor λ. By increasing λ, the sampling takes longer, but there is less dependency between edges.

5.2 Performance

The speedup achieved by this fast approximation algorithm really depends on the type of graph. We trade an $\mathcal{O}(|V|^2)$ algorithm for an algorithm that takes $\mathcal{O}(|E| \log |V|)$ time if there are no rejected tries due to empty boxes, edges that are already present, etc. In the case that the graph is sparse and $k <\approx \log_m n$, this is fine. However, for denser graphs, this fast method will actually turn out to be slower. To arrive at a complexity of $\mathcal{O}(|E| \log |V|)$ we note that it takes $\mathcal{O}(|V| \log |V|)$ time to compute the categories for each $u \in V$. Then, assuming that the number of retries is small, the while loop of Algorithm 1 is executed $\mathcal{O}(|E|)$ times, each taking $\mathcal{O}(k) = \mathcal{O}(\log |V|)$ steps. Therefore, in total, the algorithm has complexity $\mathcal{O}(|E| \log |V|)$.

Algorithm 1 Fast approximate sampling algorithm

Input: Generating measure $\mathcal{W}_k(\mathbf{P}, \ell)$, accuracy factor λ
Output: Graph G with distribution approximately $\mathcal{W}_k(\mathbf{P}, \ell)$.
Add $|V|$ nodes by uniformly sampling on $[0, 1]$ and assigning the proper categories to each node.
Set $V_c = \{v \in V | \text{category of v is } c\}$ for each category c.
Fix number of candidate edges $|E| = \lfloor \mathcal{E} \rfloor$, where $\mathcal{E} \sim N(\mu_{|E|}, \sigma_{|E|})$.
Compute $\mathbf{Q}$, where $Q_{ij} = p_{ij}\ell_i\ell_j$ for $1 \leq i, j, \leq m$
Set $e_{\text{global}} = 0$
while $e_{\text{global}} < |E|$ **do**
  for $h = 1$ **to** k **do**
    Pick category c_h, c'_h independently and with probability proportional to $\mathbf{Q}_{c_h, c'_h}$
  end for
  $c = (c_1, \ldots, c_k), c' = (c'_1, \ldots, c'_k)$.
  Set l, l' to lengths of interval corresponding to c, c'
  if $|V_c||V_{c'}| \neq 0$ **then**
    if $c = c'$ **then**
      $n_{c,c'} = |V|(|V|l^2 - l^2 + l)$
    else
      $n_{c,c'} = |V|(|V| - 1)ll'$
    end if
    Draw $e_{\text{to add}} \sim$Poisson$(n_{c,c'}/(\lambda|V_c||V_{c'}|))$
    Set k = 0
    Set $e_{\text{local}} = 0$
    while $e_{\text{local}} < e_{\text{to add}}$ and $k < \max_k$ **do**
      Pick $u \in V_c$ and $v \in V_{c'}$ uniform at random.
      if $(u, v) \notin E$ and $u \neq v$ **then**
        Add (u, v) to E
        Set $e_{\text{local}} = e_{\text{local}} + 1$
      end if
      Set $k = k + 1$
    end while
    $e_{\text{global}} = e_{\text{global}} + e_{\text{local}}$
  end if
end while
Return $G = (V, E)$

6. EXPERIMENTAL RESULTS

In the next sections, we demonstrate the effectiveness of our approach to modeling networks. First, we show that our method is able to recover the multifractal structure if we generate synthetic graphs following the MFNG paradigm. Thereafter, we consider several real-world networks and compare the performance of our method to alternative methods that use the SKG framework.

6.1 Identifiability and learning synthetic networks

Before turning to real networks, it is important to see if our method of moments algorithm recovers the structure of graphs that are actually generated by MFNG with some measure $\mathcal{W}_k$. In other words, can our method of moments identify graphs generated from our model? There are two success metrics for recovery of the generating measure. First, we want the method of moments to recover a measure similar to $\mathcal{W}_k$. Second, even if we cannot recover the

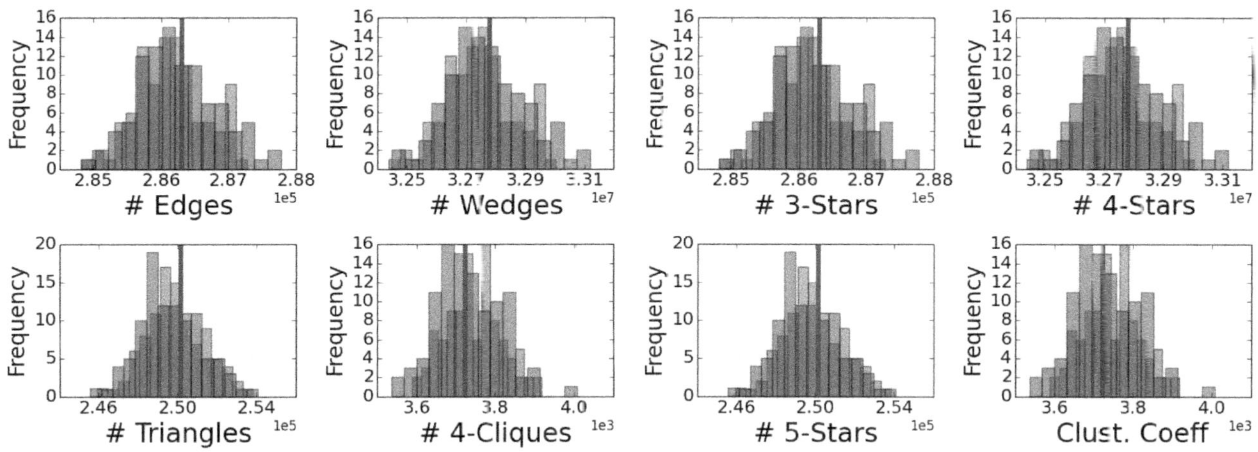

Figure 4: Empirical distributions of feature counts and clustering coefficient for the original MFNG (green) and the retrieved MFNG (red) found with the method of moments algorithm. The blue line is the feature count from the single sample of the original MFNG used in the method of moments. In this case, the original MFNG followed an Erdős-Rényi model. The original and retrieved measures produce similar distributions.

Generating Measure	$\|V\|$	m	k	ℓ_1	ℓ_2	p_{11}	p_{12}	p_{22}
Original $\mathcal{W}_k$	5,000	2	12	0.5	0.5	0.73	0.73	0.73
Retrieved $\bar{\mathcal{W}}_{\bar{k}}$	5,000	2	10	0.0574	0.9425	0.0074	0.7273	0.6829

Table 1: Comparison of original measure to the measure retrieved by using the method of moments algorithm from Section 4. The graph features used for the method of moments were: number of edges, number of d-stars for $d = 2, 3, 4, 5$, and number of t-cliques for $t = 3, 4$. The original generative measure is an Erdős-Rényi random graph model. While the recursion depth, probabilities, and lengths vector are quite different, the retrieved measure is similar to the same Erdős-Rényi model (see the discussion in Section 6.1).

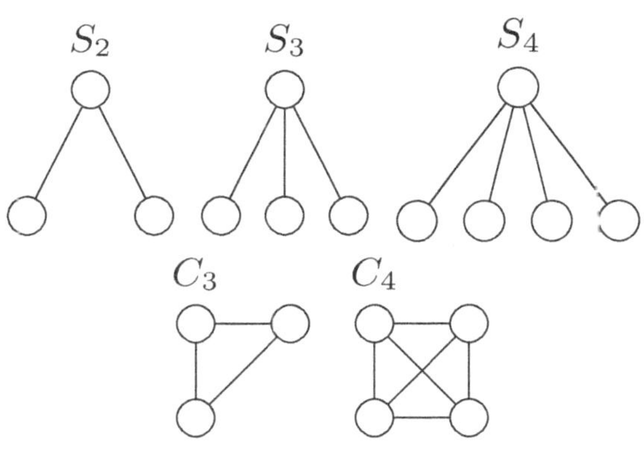

Figure 3: d-stars and t-cliques features that are counted in the experiments in Section 6.

measure, we want a measure that has similar feature counts. Our experiments in this section show that we can be successful in both metrics. If we can recover a measure with similar moments, then the new measure will be a useful model for the old one.

Our basic setup is as follows:

1. Construct a measure $\mathcal{W}_k(\mathbf{P}, \ell)$ and generate a *single* graph G from the measure.
2. Run the method of moment algorithm from Section 4 with G using 10,000 random restarts. Fit the moments for the following graph features: number of edges, number of d-stars for $d = 2, 3, 4, 5$, and number of t-cliques for $t = 3, 4$. The measure given by the method of moments is denoted $\bar{W}_k(\bar{\mathbf{P}}, \bar{\ell})$.
3. To compare $\mathcal{W}_k(\mathbf{P}, \ell)$ and $\bar{W}_k(\bar{\mathbf{P}}, \bar{\ell})$, sample 100 graphs from each measure and look at the histogram of the features that were considered by the method of moments algorithm.

We use two different measures $\mathcal{W}_k$ for testing. The first is equivalent to an Erdős-Rényi random graph. This is modeled by a generating measure $\mathcal{W}_k(\mathbf{P}, \ell)$ where every entry of $\mathbf{P}$ is identical. In this case, MFNG is an Erdős-Rényi generative model with edge probability $\mathbf{P}_{11}^k$, independent of ℓ. Table 1 shows the retrieved measure $\bar{\mathcal{W}}_{\bar{k}}(\bar{\mathbf{P}}, \bar{\ell})$ and the original Erdős-Rényi measure $\mathcal{W}_k(\mathbf{P}, \ell)$. While $\bar{\mathbf{P}}$ and $\bar{\ell}$ are quite different than $\mathbf{P}$ and ℓ, $\bar{\mathcal{W}}_{\bar{k}}(\bar{\mathbf{P}}, \bar{\ell})$ still represents a measure close to an Erdős-Rényi random graph model. The reason is that the length vector $\bar{\ell}$ is heavily skewed to the second component ($\ell_2 \approx 0.94$). In expectation, $0.94^{\bar{k}} \approx 0.53$ of the nodes correspond to the same category. These nodes are all connected with probability $0.6829^{\bar{k}} \approx 0.022$, which is nearly the same as the edge probability in the original Erdős-Rényi measure. Figure 4 shows the histograms of the features that were used in the method of moments algorithms (as well as the clustering coefficient). The green histogram is the data for graphs sampled from $\mathcal{W}_k(\mathbf{P}, \ell)$, the red histogram is the same data for graphs sampled from $\bar{\mathcal{W}}_{\bar{k}}(\bar{\mathbf{P}}, \bar{\ell})$, and the blue line is the feature count in the original graph G used as input to the method of moments. There is remarkable overlap between the empirical distribution of the features for $\bar{\mathcal{W}}_{\bar{k}}(\bar{\mathbf{P}}, \bar{\ell})$ and the distribution of the features for the original measure.

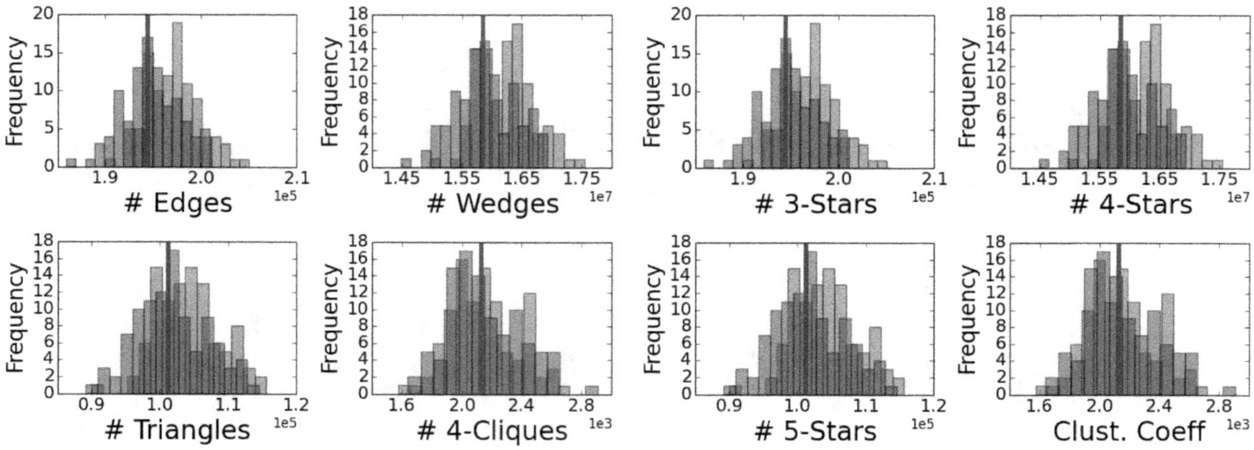

Figure 5: Empirical distributions of feature counts and clustering coefficient for the original MFNG (green) and the retrieved MFNG (red) found with the method of moments algorithm. The blue line is the feature count from the single sample of the original MFNG used in the method of moments. The original and retrieved measures produce similar distributions.

Generating Measure	$\|V\|$	m	k	ℓ_1	ℓ_2	p_{11}	p_{12}	p_{22}
Original $\mathcal{W}_k$	6,000	2	10	0.25	0.75	0.59	0.43	0.78
Retrieved $\mathcal{W}_{\bar{k}}$	6,000	2	9	0.2728	0.7272	0.5431	0.4101	0.7593

Table 2: Comparison of original measure to the measure retrieved by using the method of moments algorithm from Section 4. The graph features used for the method of moments were: number of edges, number of d-stars for $d = 2, 3, 4, 5$, and number of t-cliques for $t = 3, 4$. All parameters in the retrieved measure are remarkably similar to the parameters in the original measure.

For a second experiment, we used an original measure $\mathcal{W}_k(\mathbf{P}, \ell)$ that did not possess the uniform generative structure of Erdős-Rényi random graphs. Table 2 shows the retrieved measure and the original measure. In this case, the method of moments identified a similar generative measure. The parameters $\bar{k}$, $\bar{\mathbf{P}}$, and $\bar{\ell}$ are remarkably similar to k, $\mathbf{P}$, and ℓ. Figure 5 shows the distribution of the features in graphs sampled from the two measures. Again, there is rather significant overlap in the empirical distributions.

Finally, we compare the degree distributions of the original and retrieved measures in Figure 6. The degree distributions are nearly identical.

These results show that the method of moments algorithm described in Section 4 can successfully identify MFNG instances using a single sample.

6.2 Learning real networks

We now show how the method of moments from Section 4 performs when fitting to the following four real-world networks to MFNG:

1. The Gnutella graph is a network of host computers sharing files on August 31, 2012 [8].
2. The Citation network is from a set of high energy physics papers from arXiv [7].
3. The Twitter network is a combination of several ego networks from the Twitter follower graph [9].
4. The Facebook network is a combination of several ego networks from the Facebook friend graph [9].

All data sets are from the SNAP collection. We use the optimization procedure described in Section 4 with 2,000 random restarts. The features we use (the f_i in Section 4) are number of edges, wedges (S_2), 3-stars (S_3), 4-stars (S_4), triangles (C_3), and 4-cliques (C_4). For each network, we use $m = 2, 3$ and $k = \lceil \log_m(|V|) \rceil$. With these values of m we are able to effectively fit the networks to MFNG. We do not believe that larger values of m are useful: we would need to estimate too many parameters and we lose a lot in interpretability of results. While k can be arbitrary, a smaller value of k leads to many nodes belonging to the same categories and hence having the same statistical properties. In large graphs, this causes a "clumping" of properties such as degree distribution near a small set of discrete values. While smaller k may be satisfactory for testing algorithms, keeping k near $\log_m(|V|)$ produces more realistic graphs. In an additional set of experiments, we only fit the number of edges, wedges, and triangles. We also compare against KronFit and the SKG method of moments [3].

The results are summarized in Table 3. In addition, the online material lists all recovered parameters. Overall, for both $m = 2$ and $m = 3$, the method of moments can effectively match most feature counts. The number of 4-stars (S_4) was the most difficult parameter to fit. We see that when only fitting the number of edges, wedges, and triangles, the other feature moments can be significantly different from the original graph. In particular, the number of 4-cliques tends to be severely under- or over-estimated. Although KronFit does not explicitly try to fit moments, the results show that it severely underestimate several feature counts. The method of moments approach to SKG can fit three of the features, which is consistent with results on other networks [3].

As mentioned in Section 4.1, the clustering coefficient is three times the ratio of the number of triangles (3-cliques) to the number of wedges (2-stars) in the graph. The results of Table 3 show that

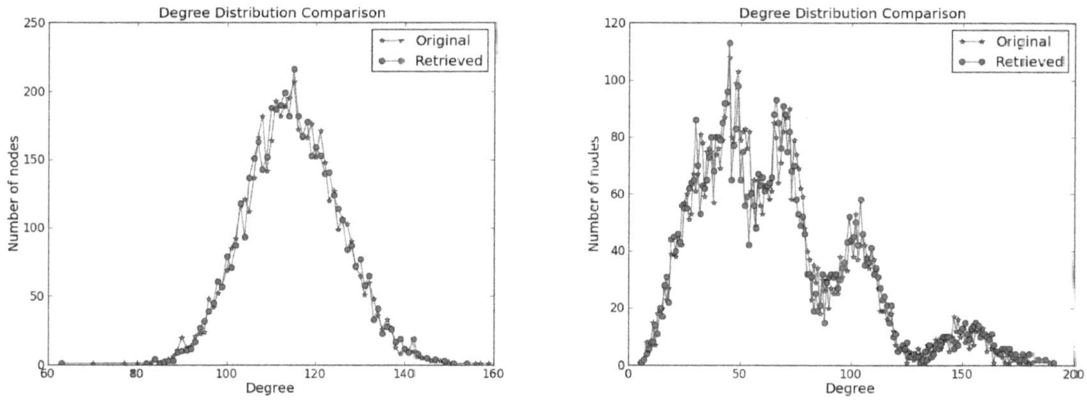

Figure 6: On the left, degree distribution of graphs generated according to the original Erdős-Rényi measure (red) given in Table 1 and the retrieved measure (green). On the right, degree distribution of graphs generated according to the original measure (red) described in Table 2 and the retrieved measure (green). The retrieved measure was found by the method of moments algorithm from Section 4. The original and retrieved measures produce almost identical distributions.

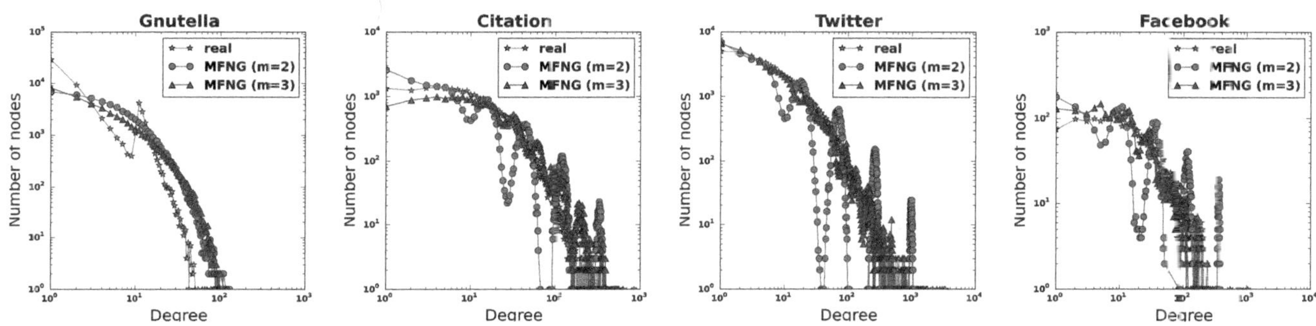

Figure 7: Degree distributions for the original graphs and MFNG graphs with $m = 2, 3$ for several networks. The degree distributions of the MFNG graphs are similar to those of the original network, even though we only fit d-star and t-clique moments. In the Twitter, Citation, and Facebook graphs, the MFNG fit with $m = 2$ results in oscillating degree distributions. In Section 6.3, we show how to add noise to dampen the oscillations. The graph samples were generated with the fast sampling algorithm in Section 5.

the method of moments can match both the number of triangles and the number of wedges in expectation. This does not make any guarantees about the *ratio* of these random variables, but the synthetic experiments (Section 6.1) demonstrated that their variances are not too large. Therefore, the expectation of the ratio is near the ratio of the expectations, and we approximately match the global clustering coefficient.

Figure 7 shows the degree distributions for the original networks and a sample from the corresponding MFNG, using the fast sampling algorithm. We see that, even though we only fit feature moments, the global degree distribution is similar to the real network. However, the MFNG degree distributions experience oscillations, especially in the case when $m = 2$. This is a well-known issue in SKG [16], and we address this issue in Section 6.3. Finally, note that we only plot the degree distribution for a single MFNG sample. The reason is that the samples tend to have quite similar degree distributions. This lack of variance has been observed for SKG [10], and addressing this issue for MFNG is an area of future work.

Table 4 shows the diameter, effective diameter, and average node eccentricity for the original networks and sampled MFNG networks. Effective diameter is the 90-th percentile of the linearly interpolated distribution of shortest path lengths [5]. The values between the original network and the MFNG samples are similar.

Network	Diameter	Eff. Diameter	Avg. Eccentricity
	original / MFNG ($m = 2$) / MFNG ($m = 3$)		
Gnutella	11 / 13 / 12	6.73 / 5.66 / 5.09	8.94 / 6.05 / 4.27
Citation	13 / 15 / 21	4.99 / 5.62 / 6.56	9.15 / 7.02 / 12.17
Twitter	7 / 11 / 21	4.52 / 4.47 / 6.47	5.92 / 5.57 / 10.94
Facebook	8 / 10 / 14	4.76 / 3.98 / 4.90	6.35 / 5.91 / 8.40

Table 4: Diameter, effective diameter and average node eccentricity for the original networks and sampled MFNG networks. For MFNG, each value is the median of five samples from the method described in Section 5. For diameter and effective diameter, 20% of the nodes were used to approximate the property.

6.3 Noisy MFNG

Figure 7 shows that the graphs generated with MFNG experience oscillations in the degree distribution. The oscillations for the degree distribution are a well-known issue in SKG [16]. Seshadhri *et*

Network method	m	features for fitting	$\|V\|$	$\|E\|$	S_2	S_3	S_4	C_3	C_4
Gnutella	–	–	62,586	147,892	1.57e+06	8.17e+06	4.38e+07	2.02e+03	1.6e+01
MFNG MoM	2	all	–	1.13	1.00	0.97	1.00	1.00	1.00
MFNG MoM	3	all	–	1.00	0.97	1.00	1.00	1.00	1.00
MFNG MoM	2	$\|E\|, S_2, C_3$	–	1.00	1.00	1.10	1.15	1.00	0.05
MFNG MoM	3	$\|E\|, S_2, C_3$	–	1.00	1.00	1.21	1.54	1.00	0.26
SKG MoM	–	$\|E\|, S_2, S_3, C_3$	–	1.14	1.00	1.00	18.34	0.30	< 0.69
KronFit	–	–	–	0.54	0.30	0.23	3.67	0.06	$<$ 0.01
Citation	–	–	34,546	420,921	2.63e+07	1.34e+09	1.04e+10	1.28e+06	2.57e+06
MFNG MoM	2	all	–	0.79	1.02	1.00	0.61	1.00	1.00
MFNG MoM	3	all	–	1.00	1.03	1.00	1.00	1.00	1.00
MFNG MoM	2	$\|E\|, S_2, C_3$	–	0.99	1.00	0.77	0.42	1.00	4.65
MFNG MoM	3	$\|E\|, S_2, C_3$	–	1.00	1.00	0.85	0.60	1.00	1.08
SKG MoM	–	$\|E\|, S_2, S_3, C_3$	–	1.00	0.89	1.00	11.60	0.02	< 0.01
KronFit	–	–	–	0.53	0.21	0.09	0.57	$<$ 0.01	$<$ 0.01
Twitter	–	–	81,306	1,342,310	2.30e+08	6.35e+10	2.99e+13	1.31e+07	1.05e+08
MFNG MoM	2	all	–	1.00	1.59	1.00	0.33	1.00	1.00
MFNG MoM	3	all	–	1.00	1.16	1.00	1.00	0.89	1.00
MFNG MoM	2	$\|E\|, S_2, C_3$	–	1.00	1.00	0.44	0.12	1.00	2.83
MFNG MoM	3	$\|E\|, S_2, C_3$	–	1.00	1.00	0.44	0.11	1.00	2.71
SKG MoM	–	$\|E\|, S_2, S_3, C_3$	–	1.00	1.05	1.00	0.01	0.03	$<$ 0.01
KronFit	–	–	–	0.69	0.30	0.10	$<$ 0.01	$<$ 0.01	$<$ 0.01
Facebook	–	–	4,039	88,234	9.31e+06	7.27e+08	9.71e+10	1.61e+06	3.00e+07
MFNG MoM	2	all	–	0.96	1.19	1.00	0.42	1.00	1.00
MFNG MoM	3	all	–	1.00	1.06	1.00	0.69	0.90	1.00
MFNG MoM	2	$\|E\|, S_2, C_3$	–	0.90	1.00	0.80	0.34	1.00	1.88
MFNG MoM	3	$\|E\|, S_2, C_3$	–	1.00	1.00	0.75	0.33	1.00	1.13
SKG MoM	–	$\|E\|, S_2, S_3, C_3$	–	1.00	1.03	1.00	0.19	0.08	0.03
KronFit	–	–	–	0.49	0.20	0.07	0.04	0.01	$<$ 0.01

Table 3: Results of method of moments (MoM) fit to MFNG for several graphs. Each column gives the ratio of the expected feature count to the true feature count. S_d is the number of d-stars in the graph, and C_t is the number of t-cliques in the graph. A value of 1.00 means that the moment is an exact fit to two decimal places. In all cases, MFNG is able to fit many of the feature counts exactly in expectation. For MFNG, we fit all feature moments listed and fitting just the number of edges, wedges, and triangles. The SKG MoM and KronFit are included for comparison. For these methods, S_4 and C_4 were estimated by taking the mean from 10 sample graphs (closed-form moment formulas are not available for these feature counts). Our MFNG MoM outperforms both KronFit and SKG MoM in fitting feature moments.

Algorithm 2 Noisy MFNG ($m = 2$)

Input: 2×2 probability matrix $\mathbf{P}$, lengths vector ℓ, number of recursive levels k, noise level b
Output: noisy MFNG matrix G
for $i = 1$ **to** k **do**
  Sample $\mu_i \sim$ Uniform$[-b, b]$.
  $\mathbf{P}^{(i)} = \begin{pmatrix} \mathbf{P}_{11} - \frac{2\mu_i \mathbf{P}_{11}}{\mathbf{P}_{11}+\mathbf{P}_{22}} & \mathbf{P}_{12} + \mu_i \\ \mathbf{P}_{21} + \mu_i & \mathbf{P}_{22} - \frac{2\mu_i \mathbf{P}_{22}}{\mathbf{P}_{11}+\mathbf{P}_{22}} \end{pmatrix}$
  $\mathbf{P}^{(i)} = \min(\max(\mathbf{P}^{(i)}, 0), 1)$ entry-wise
  Sample $H_i \sim \mathcal{W}_1(\mathbf{P}^{(i)}, \mathbf{l})$
end for
$G := \cap_{i=1}^{k} H_i$

al. present a "Noisy SKG" model that perturbs the initiator matrix at each recursive level, which dampens the oscillations. Inspired by their work, we present a similar "Noisy MFNG" in this section.

We first note that Figure 7 shows that using $m = 3$ results in less severe oscillations in the degree distribution. The intuition behind this is that more categories get mixed at each recursive level, producing a larger variety of edge probabilities. For $m = 2$, we propose a Noisy MFNG model, which is described in Algorithm 2. The idea is to perturb the probability matrix slightly at each level. In the context of Lemma 1, this means that the noisy MFNG graph is the intersection of several graphs generated from slightly different probability matrices. The fast generation method still works in this case—a different matrix at each level determines the categories instead of one single matrix. The probability perturbations are analogous to those performed by Seshadhri *et al.* We test Noisy MFNG on the citation and Twitter networks, and the results are in Figure 8. The graphs are sampled using the fast sampling algorithm. We see that increasing the noise significantly dampens the degree distribution. However, the far end of the tail still experiences some oscillations.

7. DISCUSSION

We have shown that the multifractal graph paradigm is well suited to model and capture the properties of real-world networks by building on the work of Palla *et al.* [14] and incorporating several ideas from SKG. The foundation of our theoretical work is Theorem 2, which has opened the door to quick evaluation of the expected value of a number of important counts of subgraphs, such as d-stars and t-cliques. Combined with standard optimization routines, we are

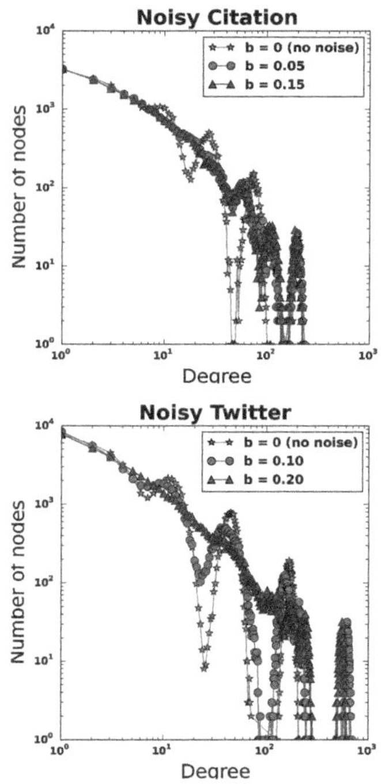

Figure 8: Degree distributions for fitting the citation and Twitter networks to Noisy MFNG with varying degrees of noise. We see that adding noise dampens the oscillations in the degree distributions. At the far end of the tail, it is still difficult to control the degree distribution. The graph samples were generated with the fast sampling algorithm in Section 5.

able to fit large graphs fast and accurately. Our method of moments algorithm identifies synthetically generated MFNG and also produces close fits for real-world networks. It is quite amazing how fitting a few 'local' properties leads to a generator that fits the overall structure of graphs well.

This would not be too useful if we were not able to also generate multifractal graphs of the same scale. For this, we presented a fast heuristic approximation algorithm that generates such graphs in $\mathcal{O}(|E| \log |V|)$ complexity, rather than the naive $\mathcal{O}(|V|^2)$ algorithm. Since many real-world networks are sparse, this is a significant improvement.

7.1 Future work

Future work includes the development of approximation formulas for the moments of global properties like graph diameter and a more tailored approach in the optimization routines for the fitting. A pressing issue is the theory behind the fast generation method. While the generation tends to produce similar graphs to the naive generation in practice, we want to prove that the approximation is good. Furthermore, it is possible to improve the generation further by considering a parallel implementation. Lastly, it would be interesting to do a theoretical analysis of the oscillatory degree distribution, similar in spirit to [16].

8. ACKNOWLEDGEMENTS

We thank David Gleich and Victor Minden for helpful discussions. Austin R. Benson is supported by an Office of Technology Licensing Stanford Graduate Fellowship. Carlos Riquelme is supported by a DARPA grant research assistantship under the supervision of Prof. Ramesh Johari. Sven Schmit is supported by a Prins Bernhard Cultuurfonds Fellowship.

9. REFERENCES

[1] L. Akoglu and C. Faloutsos. RTG: a recursive realistic graph generator using random typing. *Data Mining and Knowledge Discovery*, 19(2):194–209, 2009.

[2] D. Chakrabarti, Y. Zhan, and C. Faloutsos. R-MAT: A recursive model for graph mining. In *SDM*, volume 4, pages 442–446. SIAM, 2004.

[3] D. F. Gleich and A. B. Owen. Moment-based estimation of stochastic Kronecker graph parameters. *Internet Mathematics*, 8(3):232–256, 2012.

[4] M. Kim and J. Leskovec. Multiplicative attribute graph model of real-world networks. In *Algorithms and Models for the Web-Graph*, pages 62–73. Springer, 2010.

[5] J. Leskovec, D. Chakrabarti, J. Kleinberg, C. Faloutsos, and Z. Ghahramani. Kronecker graphs: An approach to modeling networks. *The Journal of Machine Learning Research*, 11:985–1042, 2010.

[6] J. Leskovec and C. Faloutsos. Scalable modeling of real graphs using Kronecker multiplication. In *Proceedings of the 24th international conference on Machine learning*, pages 497–504. ACM, 2007.

[7] J. Leskovec, J. Kleinberg, and C. Faloutsos. Graphs over time: densification laws, shrinking diameters and possible explanations. In *Proceedings of the eleventh ACM SIGKDD international conference on Knowledge discovery in data mining*, pages 177–187. ACM, 2005.

[8] J. Leskovec, J. Kleinberg, and C. Faloutsos. Graph evolution: Densification and shrinking diameters. *ACM Transactions on Knowledge Discovery from Data (TKDD)*, 1(1):2, 2007.

[9] J. McAuley and J. Leskovec. Learning to discover social circles in ego networks. In *Advances in Neural Information Processing Systems 25*, pages 548–556, 2012.

[10] S. Moreno, S. Kirshner, J. Neville, and S. Vishwanathan. Tied Kronecker product graph models to capture variance in network populations. In *Communication, Control, and Computing (Allerton), 2010 48th Annual Allerton Conference on*, pages 1137–1144, Sept 2010.

[11] S. Moreno and J. Neville. Network hypothesis testing using mixed Kronecker product graph models. In *ICDM*, pages 1163–1168, 2013.

[12] S. I. Moreno, J. Neville, and S. Kirshner. Learning mixed Kronecker product graph models with simulated method of moments. In *Proceedings of the 19th ACM SIGKDD international conference on Knowledge discovery and data mining*, pages 1052–1060. ACM, 2013.

[13] R. C. Murphy, K. B. Wheeler, B. W. Barrett, and J. A. Ang. Introducing the graph 500. *Cray User's Group (CUG)*, 2010.

[14] G. Palla, L. Lovász, and T. Vicsek. Multifractal network generator. *Proceedings of the National Academy of Sciences*, 107(17):7640–7645, 2010.

[15] C. Seshadhri, T. G. Kolda, and A. Pinar. Community structure and scale-free collections of Erdős-Rényi graphs. *Physical Review E*, 85(5):056109, 2012.

[16] C. Seshadhri, A. Pinar, and T. G. Kolda. An in-depth analysis of stochastic Kronecker graphs. *Journal of the ACM (JACM)*, 60(2):13, 2013.

Temporal Skeletonization on Sequential Data: Patterns, Categorization, and Visualization

Chuanren Liu
Rutgers, The State University of New Jersey
New Jersey, USA
chuanren.liu@rutgers.edu

Kai Zhang
Autonomic Management, NEC Laboratories America, Inc.
New Jersey, USA
kzhang@nec-labs.com

Hui Xiong*
Rutgers, The State University of New Jersey
New Jersey, USA
hxiong@rutgers.edu

Geoff Jiang
Autonomic Management, NEC Laboratories America, Inc.
New Jersey, USA
gfj@nec-labs.com

Qiang Yang
Hong Kong University of Science and Technology
Kowloon, Hong Kong
qyang@cse.ust.hk

ABSTRACT

Sequential pattern analysis targets on finding statistically relevant temporal structures where the values are delivered in a sequence. With the growing complexity of real-world dynamic scenarios, more and more symbols are often needed to encode a meaningful sequence. This is so-called "curse of cardinality", which can impose significant challenges to the design of sequential analysis methods in terms of computational efficiency and practical use. Indeed, given the overwhelming scale and the heterogeneous nature of the sequential data, new visions and strategies are needed to face the challenges. To this end, in this paper, we propose a "temporal skeletonization" approach to proactively reduce the representation of sequences to uncover significant, hidden temporal structures. The key idea is to summarize the temporal correlations in an undirected graph. Then, the "skeleton" of the graph serves as a higher granularity on which hidden temporal patterns are more likely to be identified. In the meantime, the embedding topology of the graph allows us to translate the rich temporal content into a metric space. This opens up new possibilities to explore, quantify, and visualize sequential data. Our approach has shown to greatly alleviate the curse of cardinality in challenging tasks of sequential pattern mining and clustering. Evaluation on a Business-to-Business (B2B) marketing application demonstrates that our approach can effectively discover critical buying paths from noisy customer event data.

Categories and Subject Descriptors

H.2.8 [**Database Management**]: Database Applications—*Data Mining*

General Terms

Algorithms, Application

Keywords

Temporal Skeletonization, Curse of Cardinality, Sequential Pattern Mining, Network Embedding

1. INTRODUCTION

Unraveling meaningful and significant temporal structures from large-scale sequential data is a fundamental problem in data mining with diversified applications, such as mining the customer purchasing sequences, motion gesture/video sequence recognition, and biological sequence analysis [11]. While there have been a large amount of research efforts devoted to this topic and its variants [1, 2, 7, 10, 25], we are still facing significant emerging challenges. Indeed, with the growing complexity of real-world dynamic scenarios, it often requires more and more symbols to encode a meaningful sequence. For example, in Business to Business (B2B) marketing analytics, we are interested in finding critical buying paths of B2B customers from historical customer event sequences. Due to the complexity of the B2B marketing processes, as well as the difficulty of manually annotating the great variety of customer activities, a large number of symbols is often needed to represent the sequential data. This is known as the "curse of cardinality", which can impose significant challenges to the design of sequential analysis methods from the following perspectives.

- **Complexity**. The computational complexity of finding frequent sequential patterns is huge for large symbol sets. Many existing algorithms have a time complexity that grows exponentially with decreasing pattern supports.
- **Rareness**. In general, the support of a specific sequential pattern decreases significantly with the growing cardinality. To see this, let us consider k symbols that appear with uniform probability in a sequence. The possibility of locating a particular pattern of length ℓ is ℓ^{-k}. In other words, the higher the cardinality, the rarer the patterns are. Since the number of unique subsequences grows with the cardinality, the number of sequences required to identify significant patterns also tends to grow drastically.

*Contact Author.

KDD'14, August 24-27 2014, New York, NY, USA
Copyright 2014 ACM 978-1-4503-2956-9/14/08$15.00.
http://dx.doi.org/10.1145/2623330.2623741

- **Granularity**. A large number of symbols in a sequence can "dilute" useful patterns which themselves exist at a different level of granularity. As we will discuss in more detail later, semantically meaningful patterns can exist at a higher granularity level, therefore pattern mining on the original, huge set of symbols may provide little clues on interesting temporal structures.
- **Noise**. Due to the stochastic nature of many practical sequential events, or the multi-modality of events, useful patterns do not always repeat exactly but instead can happen in many permutations. For example, the customers may accidentally download some trial products by mistake when they are looking for the desired information. Without dealing with such irregular perturbations, we may fail to discover some meaningful patterns.

In the literatures, there have been some related works on how to reduce the cardinality in pattern mining by performing a grouping operation on the original symbols. A commonality of these approaches is that they all exploit extra knowledge associated with the symbols as a guidance to perform clustering. For example, a taxonomy of the items may already exist in the form of domain knowledge [18] or can be derived from the structured description of the product features [9]. In Giannotti et al. [7], the 2-dimensional coordinates of spatial points are used to group them into regions to further facilitate the finding of the trajectory patterns. Generally speaking, these approaches first apply clustering on the items whose features are relatively easy to extract, and then search the patterns in different clustering levels.

While these methods have been successfully applied in some application scenarios, there are some emerging issues to be addressed when we face the overwhelming scale and the heterogeneous nature of the sequential data. First, in some applications, it might be difficult to obtain the knowledge of symbols. For example, many sequential data simply use an arbitrary coding of events either for simplicity or security reasons. Second, there are circumstances where it is difficult to define distance among symbols, and therefore clustering becomes impractical. For example, it is unclear how to define the distance between actions customers have taken in their purchasing process. Finally, the biggest concern is that the grouping in these methods is performed irrespective of the temporal content. As a result, these methods may not be able to find statistically relevant temporal structures in sequential data. Therefore, there is a need to develop a new vision and strategy for sequential pattern mining.

To this end, this paper proposes a temporal skeletonization approach to proactively reduce the representation of sequences, so as to expose their hidden temporal structures. Our goal is to make temporal structures of the sequences more concise and clarified, and thus more prone to discovery. Our basic assumption is the existence of symbolic events that tend to aggregate temporally. Then, by identifying temporal clusters and mapping each symbol to the cluster it belongs to, we can reduce not only the cardinality of sequences but also their temporal variations. This allows us to find interesting hidden temporal structures which are otherwise obscured in the original representation.

Exploring temporal clusters from a large number of sequences can be challenging. To achieve this, we have resorted to graph-based manifold learning. The basic idea is to summarize the temporal correlations in the data in an undirected graph. The "skeleton" of the graph (i.e., the temporal clusters) can then be extracted through the graph Lapacian, which serves as a higher granularity where hidden temporal patterns are more likely to be identified. A nice interpretation of such temporal grouping is that when individual symbols are replaced by their cluster labels, the averaged smoothness of all sequences is maximized. Intuitively, this can greatly improve the possibility of finding significant sequential patterns, as we shall observe empirically. In addition, the embedding topology of the graph allows us to translate the rich temporal content of symbolic sequences into a metric space for further analysis and visualization. Compared with existing methods that attempt to reduce the cardinality via clustering, our approach does not require specific knowledge about the items. Instead, it caters directly to the temporal contents of given data sequences. To the best of our knowledge, using the temporal correlations to perform clustering and reduction of representation is a novel approach in sequential pattern mining.

Temporal skeletonization can be deemed as a transformation that maps the temporal structures of sequences into the topologies of a graph. Such a dual perspective provides not only more insights on pattern mining, but also brings powerful new tools for analysis and visualization. For example, many techniques in graph theories can be used to analyze symbolic sequences, which appear as random walks on the created graph. On the other hand, due to the explicit embedding, symbolic sequences are represented as numerical sequences or point clouds in the Euclidean space for which visualization becomes much more convenient.

Experimental results on real-world data have shown that the proposed approach can greatly alleviate the problem of curse of cardinality for the challenging tasks of sequential pattern mining and clustering. Also, we show that it is convenient to visualize sequential patterns in the Euclidean space by temporal skeletonization. In addition, the case study on a Business-to-Business (B2B) marketing application demonstrates that our approach can effectively identify critical buying paths from noisy marketing data.

2. TEMPORAL SKELETONIZATION

In this section, we introduce the detail of the proposed method. The key concept is the "temporal cluster", namely group of symbols which tend to aggregate more closely together in the sequences. By transforming the sequential data into graphs, we can identify such temporal clusters to greatly simplify the representation of the sequences.

2.1 Temporal Clusters

We believe that temporal clusters often exist in practical sequence data. Otherwise, if there is no such "preferential" structures and everything becomes uniform, we may not find anything interesting. In the following, we discuss two typical scenarios. One involves stage-wise patterns where each stage can be deemed as a temporal cluster; another scenario involves frequent associative patterns.

2.1.1 Case I: Stage-Wise Patterns

First, some sequential processes exhibit stage-wise behaviors; that is, the process typically goes through a number of stages before reaching the final goal, with each stage marked by a collection of representative events. For example, in B2B markets, the business customer will go through stages such as "Investigating more product information", "Trial experience and evaluation", "Contacting customer service for specific information", and "Contacting sales to finalize the purchase". Here, each stage includes a number of events, and the global structure of the underlying process is shaped by the stages as backbones. Note that the order of stages can vary with regard to different customers. Also, events within a stage may or may not have a dominant ordering. However, collectively, we can observe that each stage forms temporally compact clusters. It will be very useful to find such clusters for understanding the global patterns of sequences.

In case of stage-like sequences, it is obviously more meaningful to detect patterns at the stage level. However, the stages are unknown and typically cannot be determined by grouping the symbols based on their features. Therefore, few existing methods could handle such situations. In the following we use one simple example to show that the large number of symbols in stage-like sequences can "dilute" useful patterns which themselves exist at a different level of granularity, posing a big challenge on existing methods.

$$\begin{aligned}1 &: \mathtt{m,h,j,f,d,a,i,k,b}\\ 2 &: \mathtt{j,l,m,a,n,f,b,o,g}\\ 3 &: \mathtt{e,h,l,c,f,n,i,b,o}\\ 4 &: \mathtt{h,l,e,c,a,f,k,o,i}\end{aligned}$$

For the four sequences above, if we apply pattern mining on the original level of symbols, we would be unable to find any frequent pattern. However, if we cleverly group the symbols in the following way

$$\begin{aligned}\mathtt{A} &= \{\mathtt{m,h,j,e,l}\}\\ \mathtt{B} &= \{\mathtt{a,f,c,d,n}\}\\ \mathtt{C} &= \{\mathtt{k,g,o,b,i}\}\end{aligned}$$

then all the four sequences read as

$$\mathtt{A,A,A,B,B,B,C,C,C}$$

It is obvious that $\mathtt{A,B,C}$ is a frequent (stage) pattern with 100% support.

2.1.2 Case II: Frequent Associative Patterns

Temporal cluster also has an interesting connection with frequent associative patterns. Since associative items tend to occur closely to each other, they are temporally more coherent and can likely form temporal clusters. In other words, there must exist temporal clusters if there are significant frequent patterns. However, temporal clusters can be more general than frequent patterns. Another challenge for finding frequent patterns is the noise in the data. If frequent sub-sequences are somewhat perturbed, special cares have to be taken in finding exact patterns. In comparison, the temporal clusters we try to discover are identified via the temporal distribution of all existing event pairs, thus our approach is inherently more resistant to noise.

2.2 Temporal Graph and Skeletonization

Since large cardinality hampers pattern mining, we propose to find meaningful temporal clusters to alleviate it. The key role of temporal clusters is that they can be used to re-encode the original sequences. Since temporal clusters are composed of symbols that are temporally more coherent, the newly encoded sequences will be temporally smoother than the original sequences. By doing this, we can greatly reduce not only the cardinality but also the temporal variations of the sequences. The latter makes it much easier to find semantically useful patterns. Specifically, we put this under the following optimization framework.

Suppose we have a set of symbols $\mathcal{S} = \{e_1, e_2, \cdots, e_{|\mathcal{S}|}\}$. The n-th sequence is denoted by $S_n = (s_1^n, s_2^n, \cdots, s_{T_n}^n)$, where $s_t^n \in \mathcal{S}$ for $t = 1, 2, \cdots, T_n$ and T_n is the length of the nth sequence.

Problem 1 (Temporal skeletonization). *Given a set of sequences $\{S_n | n = 1, 2, \cdots, N\}$, we want to find a new encoding scheme of the symbols $e \in \mathcal{S}$, denoted by the mapping $y = f(e) \in \{1, 2, \cdots, K\}$, such that when encoded with f, the temporal variation of resultant sequences is minimized*

$$\min_{y\in\{1,2,\ldots,K\}} \frac{1}{N}\sum_{n=1}^{N}\sum_{\substack{1\le p,q\le T_n\\ |p-q|\le r}} \left(f(s_p^n) - f(s_q^n)\right)^2. \quad (1)$$

Here r is a pre-defined integer that controls the range that local sequence variations are computed, and the cardinality of the encoding scheme, K, is a pre-defined integer that is much smaller than that of the original representation $|\mathcal{S}|$.

Here, in each of the N sequences, we only consider pairs of events s_p^n and s_q^n that are within r intervals to each other, such that when they are re-encoded with $f(s_p^n)$ and $f(s_q^n)$, they are similar to each other.

This is an integer programming problem which has shown to be NP-hard. Therefore, we propose to relax the integer constraint to real numbers. In addition, we will define the so-called "temporal graph" to re-phrase the problem as a graph optimization one.

Definition 1 (Temporal graph). *Let G be a weighted graph $G = \langle V, E\rangle$ with vertex set $V = \mathcal{S}$ and edges E. The i-th node of G corresponds to the i-th symbol e_i in the symbol set $\mathcal{S}$. The weight of the edge between node i and node j is defined as the ij-th entry of an $|\mathcal{S}|\times|\mathcal{S}|$ matrix W, where*

$$W_{ij} = \frac{1}{N}\sum_{\substack{1\le n\le N\\ e_i,e_j\in S_n}} \delta\left(|\ell(e_i, S_n) - \ell(e_j, S_n)| \le r\right). \quad (2)$$

Here, we say $e \in S_n$ if the symbol e can be observed in the sequence S_n and $\ell(e, S_n) \in \{1, 2, \cdots, T_n\}$ is the corresponding location of e in the sequence S_n.

We call G "temporal graph", because the edge weight of the graph captures the averaged temporal closeness between any pair of symbols/events across all the input sequences. With this definition, and let $\mathbf{y} \in \mathbb{R}^{|\mathcal{S}|}$ where $\mathbf{y}_i = f(e_i)$, Problem 1 can be written in the following compact form

$$\min_{\mathbf{y}\in\mathbb{R}^{|\mathcal{S}|}} \sum_{i,j} W_{ij}(\mathbf{y}_i - \mathbf{y}_j)^2. \quad (3)$$

Problem (3) has a standard form of graph-based optimization. Let us define the graph Laplacian of G as $L = D - W$, where D is a diagonal degree matrix with $D_{ii} = \sum_j W_{ij}$. Then, Equation 3 can be formalized as

$$\begin{aligned}\min_{\mathbf{y}\in\mathbb{R}^{|\mathcal{S}|}} \quad & \mathbf{y}'(D - W)\mathbf{y} \quad (4)\\ s.t. \quad & \mathbf{1}'D\mathbf{y} = 0\\ & \mathbf{y}'D\mathbf{y} = 1\end{aligned}$$

where $\mathbf{1}$ is a vector of all 1's. Here, the translation and scale constraints are added to avoid trivial solutions. This is also known in the literatures as Laplacian eigenmap [3], which has also been applied in spectral clustering [14]. To the best of our knowledge, it is a novel application to use graph-based algorithm to extract interesting temporal structures from multiple sequences.

Note that the more often symbol e_i and symbol e_j appear close to each other in the sequences, the higher the W_{ij} is and the larger the penalty it induces on the objective (Equation 4), and as a result, the closer $\mathbf{y}_i$ and $\mathbf{y}_j$ should be. This equivalently achieves a grouping of the symbols, which are the temporal clusters we try to extract. As can be expected, by re-encoding the sequence with the label of the temporal clusters, we can improve the temporal smoothness which is beneficial to subsequent pattern mining.

The level of smoothness can be adjusted effectively by the order parameter r. The order parameter controls the resolution on which clusters are extracted. A larger r captures the similarities among events in a longer temporal range, which potentially lead to fewer clusters, while a small r only considers directly adjacent symbols as similar, which lead to more clusters. In the extreme case when r approaches infinity, W becomes a constant matrix, and all the events will be categorized into one cluster. In practice, instead of using the delta function ($\delta\left(|\ell(e_i, S_n) - \ell(e_j, S_n)| \leq r\right)$) to measure the similarity, one can also use a smoother function such as

$$W_{ij} = \frac{1}{N} \sum_{\substack{1 \leq n \leq N \\ e_i, e_j \in S_n}} \kappa_h\left(|\ell(e_i, S_n) - \ell(e_j, S_n)|\right), \quad (5)$$

where κ_h is a non-increasing function parametrized by h. For example, we can use the exceedance of the Exponential distribution $\kappa_h(d) = \exp(-hd)$.

2.3 Embedding and Visualization

The optimal solution of Equation 4 is the eigenvector of the graph Lapacian corresponding to the second smallest eigenvalue. In practice, one usually computes several eigenvectors and applies some simple clustering algorithms such as K-means or GMM (Gaussian mixture model) in this low-dimensional space. The useful eigenvectors of the graph Lapacian not only provide a relaxed solution for finding temporal clusters, but also more interestingly, naturally connect to the manifold embedding of the graph.

Note that the eigenvectors of the graph can be deemed as a low-dimensional embedding, in which the proximity relation among objects preserves that in the original space [24]. Since the similarity measurements in W_{ij} of the graph reflect the temporal closeness of the events, the embedding eigenvectors of the graph will also inherit this configuration. Namely, if two symbols, e_i and e_j are temporally more related, their distance will also be small in the embedded space. In other words, our approach provides a direct platform for visualizing the temporal structures of sequential data. We believe that such visualization can provide interesting insights allowing domain experts to draw useful conclusions.

To provide more intuition on the temporal embedding results, in Figure 1, we give several examples. Figure 1a is the embedding of a collection of random sequences. As can be seen, the embedded symbols (each represented by one point) are distributed uniformly and there is hardly any interesting structure. Figure 1b is a simulated data containing 5 stages of events (more details in Section 4). As can be seen, there are clear clusters in the embedding, each representing exactly events belonging to one stage. In Figure 1c we used a real-world data set composed of thousands of B2B customer event sequences. As can be seen, the cluster structures are complicated: some clusters are well separated while others are diffusing. This has to do the complicated relationships between practical events in the data set. From these examples, we can see that our temporal skeletonization approach can translate the temporal structures in the sequential data into their topological counterparts. The resultant visualization can bring useful insights.

In the literatures, there are many algorithms for manifold learning. Many of these approaches rely on the eigenvalue decomposition of a similarity matrix to obtain the manifold embedding. For example, Isomap [20] is another popular method that embed a graph into an Euclidean space. In our experiments, we also use Isomap to visualize the data, and find that it can provide spatially more unfolded embedding. The details of using Isomap are provided in the Appendix.

2.4 Post-Temporal-Smoothing

By finding temporal clusters in the embedded Euclidean space, and use it to re-encode the sequence, we can obtain temporally smoother representation. For example, we can transform the original customer event sequences to sequences of stages, with each stage being defined as the groups of symbols (marketing campaigns) in the temporal clusters identified. However, although the embedded graph is estimated robustly with the integrated data from all the sequential observations, the individual sequence might still be noisy in some cases, for instance, the order parameter r is chosen too small. Thus, one might want to further smooth away the irregularities in the sequences. To this end, we propose a multi-series post-smoothing using fused lasso [21].

Specifically, we use the Gaussian mixture models to perform a soft clustering on the embedded symbols. We denote this by a partition matrix $Y \in \mathbb{R}^{|\mathcal{S}| \times K}$ where Y_{sk} is the probability that the symbol $s \in \mathcal{S}$ belongs to the k-th temporal cluster. Then we can use this partition matrix to transform each individual sequence $S_n = (s_1^n, s_2^n, \cdots, s_{T_n}^n)$ into a multiple of K sequences, denoted by $Y^n \in \mathbb{R}^{T_n \times K}$ where Y_{tk}^n is the probability that the t-th interaction s_t^n in S_n belongs to the k-th cluster. Then we try to find a smoother version of the multiple sequences Y^n, denoted by X^n. To achieve this, we encourage sparsity of the differences between the successive rows in X^n, i.e., $\sum_{t=1}^{T_n-1} \|X_t^n - X_{t+1}^n\|_1$ where $\|X_t^n - X_{t+1}^n\|_1 = \sum_{k=1}^{K} |X_{tk}^n - X_{(t-1)k}^n|$. We optimize the approximation of X^n by maximizing the alignment $\sum_{t=1}^{T_n} \sum_{k=1}^{K} X_{tk}^n Y_{tk}^n$ and with probability constraints. Thus, we would like to maximize $\sum_{t=1}^{T_n} \sum_{k=1}^{K} X_{tk}^n Y_{tk}^n$, subject to

$$\frac{1}{T_n - 1} \sum_{t=1}^{T_n - 1} \|X_t^n - X_{t+1}^n\|_1 \leq \lambda,$$

in addition to $\sum_{k=1}^{K} X_{tk}^n = 1$ and $X_{tk}^n \geq 0$. Here λ is a tuning parameter controlling smoothness of X^n.

To solve the approximation problem with the smooth constraint, we let $X_{tk}^n - X_{(t+1)k}^n = \alpha_{tk}^n - \beta_{tk}^n$ for $t = 1, \cdots, T_n - 1$ and $k = 1, \cdots, K$ where $\alpha_{tk}^n, \beta_{tk}^n \geq 0$. Let $A^n \in \mathbb{R}^{(T_n-1) \times T_n}$ with $A_{tt}^n = 1$, $A_{t(t+1)}^n = -1$ and $A_{tt'}^n = 0$ otherwise so that $A^n X^n = \alpha^n - \beta^n$. We can rewrite the smooth approxima-

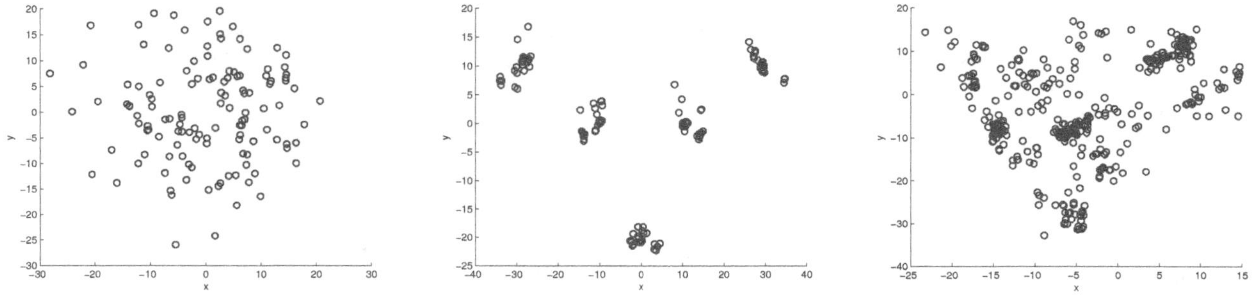

(a) Random sequences. (b) Stage-wise sequences. (c) B2B customer event sequences.

Figure 1: The embedding of symbols in different types of sequence data.

tion as a linear programming problem:

$$\begin{aligned} \max \quad & \sum_{t=1}^{T_n} \sum_{k=1}^{K} X_{tk}^n Y_{tk}^n, \\ s.t. \quad & \sum_{k=1}^{K} X_{tk}^n = 1, \forall t = 1, \cdots, T_n, \\ & A^n X^n = \alpha^n - \beta^n, \\ & \frac{1}{T_n - 1} \sum_{t=1}^{T_n - 1} \sum_{k=1}^{K} (\alpha_{tk}^n + \beta_{tk}^n) \leq \lambda, \end{aligned}$$

in addition to the non-negative constraints $X^n, \alpha^n, \beta^n \geq 0$.

3. APPLICATIONS

In this section, we discuss the applications of the proposed temporal skeletonization method in several interesting problems. The reduced representation makes it much easier to perform these tasks than on the original sequences.

3.1 Sequence Visualization

Our framework embeds symbolic events in sequence data into an Euclidean space, which allows to visualize each sequence as a trajectory. Such visualization can provide direct insights on the relationship between events, which, when subject to examination of domain expert, can greatly facilitate them making analysis and decisions. In Section 5, we will report how temporal clusters in the B2B customer event data can help to understand typical purchase patterns.

In choosing the embedding dimensions, we typically choose two or three dimensions, which correspond to the dominant components of the temporal graph. Usually, these few dimensions can encode a sufficient amount of the temporal relations. To see this, we investigate the residual variance in the Isomap with regard to the number of selected embedding dimensions. As shown in Figure 2, in both the simulation and real-world data sets, the residual variance drops most significantly with the first few dimensions.

3.2 Sequential Pattern Mining

By identifying meaningful temporal clusters, our method transforms the original sequence of events to the sequence of temporal clusters (the cluster labels are used as a new set of symbols to encode events). This helps to reduce the cardinality of the sequence representation, and the supports

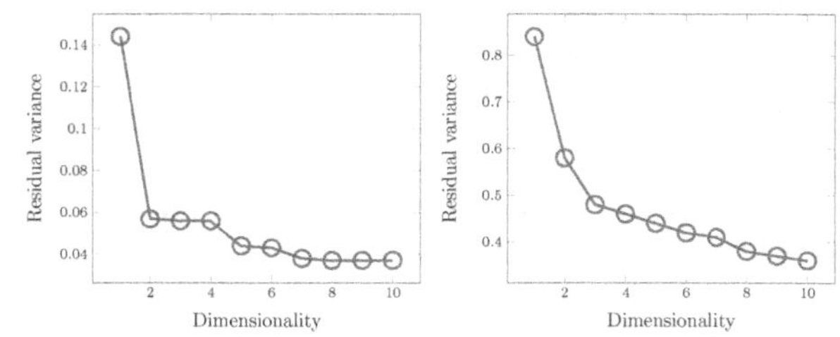

(a) Simulation data. (b) B2B customer data.

Figure 2: The residual variance vs. dimensionality.

of the sequential patterns are increased. As a result, consequent sequential pattern mining is able to discover significant knowledge which otherwise would be diluted in the raw data. Indeed, the patterns discovered in this way are defined with a higher level of granularity, i.e., the temporal clusters. Therefore, to interpret the patterns, we can first annotate the temporal clusters with domain knowledge.

For example, in the B2B customer event data, the temporal event clusters can be semantically labelled as Webinar, Tradeshow, Direct Marketing Mail, Web Marketing Ads, Trial Product Download, and Unsubscribe, etc. As we shall see, these temporal clusters correspond to stages in the purchasing route of the customers, which are much easier to understand and interpret compared with the raw sequences.

3.3 Sequence Clustering

Sequence clustering is an important task, however, it is not always easy to extract appropriate features or define distances among sequences so that clustering can be performed properly. This is particularly true when sequences are represented by a huge number of symbols. The temporal skeletonization method we have proposed can be used to tackle these difficulties. This is because the temporal skeletonization can remove noises in the sequences based on their collectively temporal behaviours. More importantly, it re-summarizes the events in the form of groups of events, therefore we will observe much more repeated subsequence on which sequential features can be more meaningful.

For example, when there is only a reasonably small number of symbols in the sequences, we can extract the following useful features, such as the counts of each temporal cluster passed by the sequence, or how many times one symbol appears in precedence of another, and so on. It turns out such a straightforward approach can effectively cluster the sequences. To incorporate more temporal information, we can also leverage the frequent sequential patterns discovered by the aforementioned sequential pattern mining, as suggested by Lee et al. [13].

4. EMPIRICAL EVALUATION

In this section, we evaluate the performances of our approach in comparison with several state-of-the-art methods. All the experiments are performed on a GNU/Linux system with 8 CPUs (Intel i7 2.93GHz) and 8G RAM.

4.1 Synthetic Data

We have simulated symbolic sequential data composed of stages of events. We define 5 stages $\{A, B, C, D, E\}$, where each contains 25 symbols. Then, we create 5000 sequences that are of two patterns. The first 2500 sequences mainly follow stage pattern $A \to B \to C \to D$; the other 2500 sequences follow $B \to E \to C$. The simulation proceeds as follows. After deciding which stage to sample from based on the two patterns, we randomly pick d symbols from that stage, where d is a random integer. Then, we inject the selected symbols into the sequence, and continue to the next stage in the pattern. Indeed, such a simulation process is equivalent to a standard Hidden Markov Model (HMM), where 5 stages correspond to 5 hidden states and symbols within each stage correspond to observations. Let the transition probability from each stage to itself be p, and that to the next stage (as specified in the two patterns) be $1-p$. Then, the stage duration d follows a geometric distribution $d \sim (1-p)p^{d-1}$, with the expected value $\mathbb{E}[d] = \frac{1}{1-p}$. To have significant stage-wise patterns in the produced sequences, we have used a large probability $p = \frac{14}{15}$, leading to $\mathbb{E}[d] = 15$. In other words, on average, we randomly pick 15 symbols for each stage in the sequences.

4.2 Baselines

First, we apply state-of-the-art Frequent Sequence Mining (FSM) algorithms, including GSP [19], SPADE [25], PrefixSpan [10], SPAM [2]. The results in Figure 3 show that, when desired pattern support drops, the time consumption of these algorithms grow super-exponentially, indicating the difficulties introduced by the large numbers of symbols. The number of detected patterns also becomes explosive, most of which are non-informative and provide no clear insight of the underlying sequence generating processes (as shown in Table 1). In comparison, using the temporal clusters identified via our approach (more details in Section 4.3), the mining process succeeds quickly in one second.

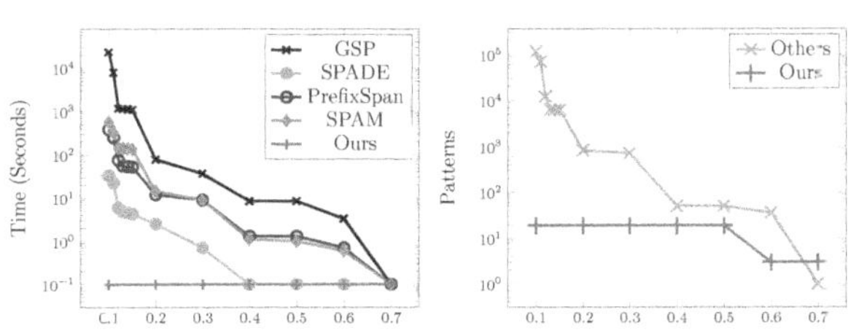

Figure 3: FSM algorithms on the simulated data.

In addition to the improvement on efficiency, we also compare the pattern mining results on the original and the re-encoded sequences via our method in Table 1. For the task of pattern mining, we compute the precision (fraction of discovered patterns that are relevant) and recall (fraction of the relevant patterns that are discovered) of the discovered patterns against the ground truth. The results show that when working on the raw data, FSM performs poorly with an F-measure around 0.281. In contrast, after re-encoding using our approach, it can lead to an 100% accuracy

Task	Pattern Mining		Sequence Clustering		Stage Recovery	
Method	FSM	Ours	HMM	Ours	HMM	Ours
Precision	0.725	**1.0**	0.997	**1.0**	0.488	**1.0**
Recall	0.174	**1.0**	0.997	**1.0**	0.448	**1.0**

Table 1: Utility comparison on the simulated data.

Since data simulation process follows the Markov property, the second baseline approach we have experimented with is the classical HMM. In our data, there are two hidden patterns, thus we adopt the HMM based clustering (HMMC) [15] to simultaneously cluster the sequences and estimate the HMM parameters for each cluster. Specifically, to group sequences into M clusters, the HMMC randomly allocates all sequences to M disjoint subsets as initial clusters, then the following two procedures are iterated until convergence. First, for all sequences in cluster C_m, we estimate a transition matrix ϕ_m and a emission matrix θ_m; Second, we reallocate each sequence S_n to the cluster C_m on whose transition and emission matrices it has the highest probability of being produced, i.e., $m = \arg\max_m \Pr(S_n|\phi_m, \theta_m)$.

We have provided the HMMC method with some ground truth parameters, i.e., the number of clusters $M = 2$, and the number of hidden states (stages) for each cluster. Table 1 shows the accuracy of the HMM based method for the task of sequence clustering and stage recovery. To be specific, for these two tasks, we first compute the so-called confusion matrix C, where C_{ij} is the number of instances in resulted group i and ground truth class j. Then, the precision is computed as $\frac{1}{N}\max_\sigma \sum_j C_{\sigma(j)j}$ where $N = \sum_{ij} C_{ij}$ and σ maps classes to different groups; the recall is computed as $\frac{1}{N}\sum_i \max_j C_{ij}$, which is also termed as clustering purity. Again, our method gives perfect results on both tasks. The HMMC only works well for sequence clustering, while its performance is almost random for the task of stage recovery.

4.3 Our Results

Here, we show that our approach can successfully recover patterns hidden in the data. In Figure 4a, we see that our approach embeds altogether 125 symbols in such a way that 5 dominant clusters emerge. This is in perfect consistency with the ground truth structure we have used in the simulation. In Figure 4b, we show that, by extracting simple features as discussed in Section 3.3, we can correctly group the 5000 sequences into two clusters (in red and green).

Our approach does not require any prior knowledge on the simulated data. We tried different ways (Equation 2 and Equation 5) to construct the temporal graph, and the results were very robust with respect to parameters (e.g., $1 \le r \le 5$ and $1 \le h \le 5$). Also, we can clearly identify the number of stages based on well clustered symbols. Finally, the post-temporal-smoothing procedure works with λ in a wide range, e.g., $1 \le \lambda \le 10$.

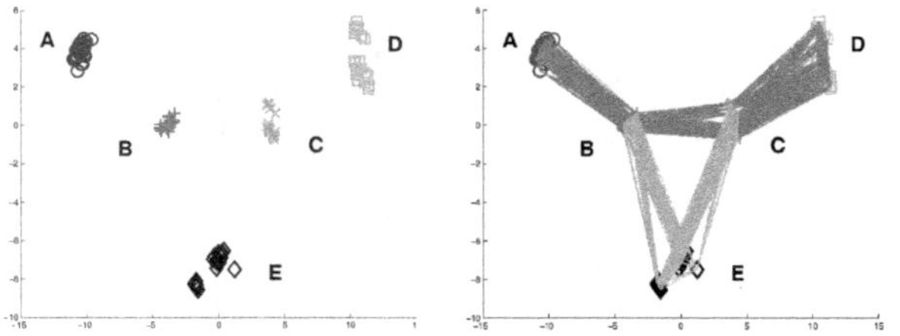

(a) The temporal clusters. (b) The sequence clusters.

Figure 4: The embedding of simulated data.

4.4 Noisy Cases

Now we examine the performances of our approach in case of noisy data. We have injected two types of noises. The first is introduced on items of each sequence, such that one stage could contain symbols that belong to other stages. Such a noisy behavior is quite natural in the buying process of customers. For example, customers might occasionally participate events not very relevant to their current buying stages. The second kind of noise is introduced as random sequences not following any certain patterns. In real world, these random sequences might correspond to event sequences of some unintended customers. We have 5% noisy observations for each type of noise. Moreover, we have added another two stage-wise patterns to make the problem more challenging.

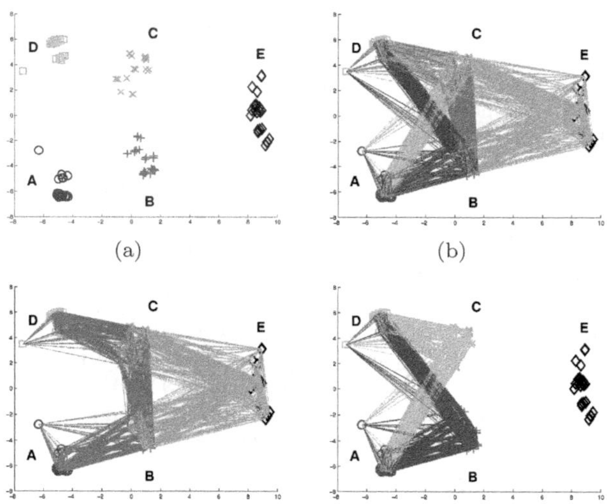

(a) (b) (c) (d)

Figure 5: The noisy simulated data. a: The temporal clusters. b: The sequences clusters. c: Pattern $A \rightarrow B \rightarrow C \rightarrow D$ and $B \rightarrow E \rightarrow C$. d: Pattern $A \rightarrow B \rightarrow D$ and $A \rightarrow C \rightarrow D$.

We can see from Figure 5a that, even in this noisy data, the temporal clusters are still identifiable, which correspond to stages of events. The reason is that, our temporal graph is estimated robustly with integrated temporal content from all the sequences, therefore a small portion of individual noisy observations cannot significantly affect the result. In particular, the post-temporal-smoothing (Section 2.4) can also be very useful in removing the random events. As shown in Figure 5b, once noisy random events are removed, we can discover important patterns (groups of sequences). Indeed, the 4 stage-wise patterns are all discovered by our approach.

We report the results of standard FSM and HMMC in Table 2. As can be seen, their performances both degrade compared with the noiseless case, while our approach still successfully returns the ground truth patterns.

Task	Pattern Mining		Sequence Clustering		Stage Recovery	
Method	FSM	Ours	HMM	Ours	HMM	Ours
Precision	0.526	**1.0**	0.688	**1.0**	0.480	**1.0**
Recall	0.134	**1.0**	0.621	**1.0**	0.416	**1.0**

Table 2: Utility comparison on the noisy cases.

5. B2B PURCHASE PATTERN ANALYSIS

In this section, we apply our method to find critical buying paths of Business-to-Business (B2B) buyers from historical customer event sequences. Since B2B purchases are often involved with strategic development of the company, and as a result, extra cautions and extensive research efforts have to be taken in making such investment, the decision process of customers in purchasing certain products or services is much more complicated than that in our daily purchasing activities. Thus, it is of significant business value if we can discover characteristic and critical buying paths from observations. These can be used to recommend directed advertising campaigns so as to increase potential profits and also reduce the marketing cost. In addition, we would also like to visually display the buying processes of the customers. By doing this, we can better understand the behavior patterns of B2B customers and accordingly develop promising marketing strategies. In the following, we show that our framework is effective for these objectives.

5.1 Data Description

We have collected huge amount of purchasing event data for the customers of a big company. In more detail, we have event sequences from $N = 88040$ customers, with the number of unique events (symbols) $|S| = 5028$, leading to altogether $T = \sum_n T_n = 248725$ event records. We construct the temporal graph using Equation 5 and $h = 5$, and then embed the graph using Isomap. In the appendix, we describe details on how to apply Isomap embedding on the temporal graph we have constructed.

5.2 Embedding Results and Buying Stages

We plot the embedding of selected 503 events (top 10% nodes with the largest degrees in the temporal graph) in Figure 6, and mark it with the clustering results. For each detected cluster, we are able to extract dominant semantic keywords for the events in that cluster, as shown in Table 3. Note that the semantic information here is only used to summarize each temporal cluster for better understanding of our results, but not for the purpose of grouping the events.

We discuss some interesting observations on the temporal clusters. First, clusters that are close to each other appear logically related, e.g., 'search engine' (C_{13}) and 'trial product download' (C_3); 'webinar' (C_{12}) and 'trade show' (C_8). Second, symbols with the same semantic meaning may not be in the same temporal cluster. For example, C_6, C_{11}, C_{12}

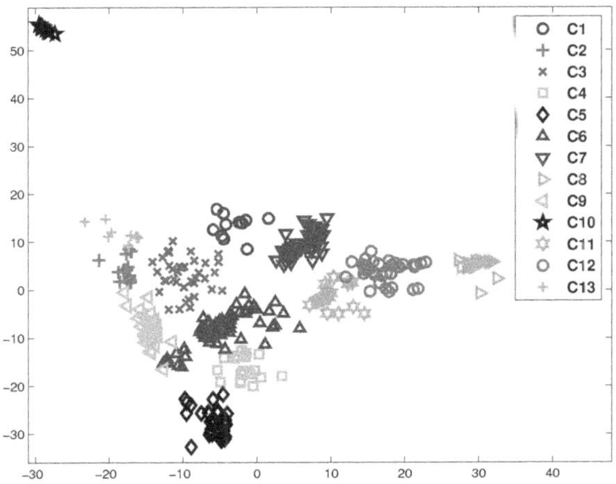

Figure 6: The customer event clusters.

Cluster	Top keywords	Size
C_1	Official Website	12
C_2	Corporate Event, Direct Marketing Mail	20
C_3	Trial Product Download	45
C_4	Conference	27
C_5	Unsubscribe	38
C_6	Webinar	101
C_7	Trial Product Download	70
C_8	Tradeshow	37
C_9	Corporate Event, Direct Marketing Mail	65
C_{10}	Web Marketing Ads	13
C_{11}	Webinar	21
C_{12}	Webinar	42
C_{13}	Search Engine	12

Table 3: The semantic annotation of event clusters.

are all marked with 'webinar' but they form 3 separate clusters. Note that these three clusters are close to 'direct marketing mail', 'trial product download', 'trade show', respectively, indicating that they have different levels of maturity towards final purchase. Thus, it is reasonable to have them separated. Nevertheless, the three clusters are still neighbors, after all, since they have the same nature ('webinar'). In other words, temporal clusters could be partially consistent with attribute-based clusters, while meanwhile revealing more fine-grained structure by exploiting the temporal correlations. This is where the extra value comes from.

5.3 Critical Buying Paths

With the detected temporal clusters, we apply the post-temporal-smoothing, since the data set we collected is very noisy and can be subject to human errors. Then, we can transform the original event sequences to sequences of temporal clusters, and apply the FSM algorithms on the re-encoded sequences. Figure 7 reports some results of pattern mining on the original and re-encoded sequences respectively. The pattern supports are generally chosen much smaller than those used in the simulation study, since we have much more symbols here and more complicated patterns. As can be observed, on the original sequences, the number of identified patterns again grows super-exponentially with decreasing support. This would indicate that it is very hard to have a conclusive and comprehensive understandings of the customers' purchasing patterns. In contrast, using the transformed sequences via temporal skeletonization, the number of detected patterns is much more reasonable.

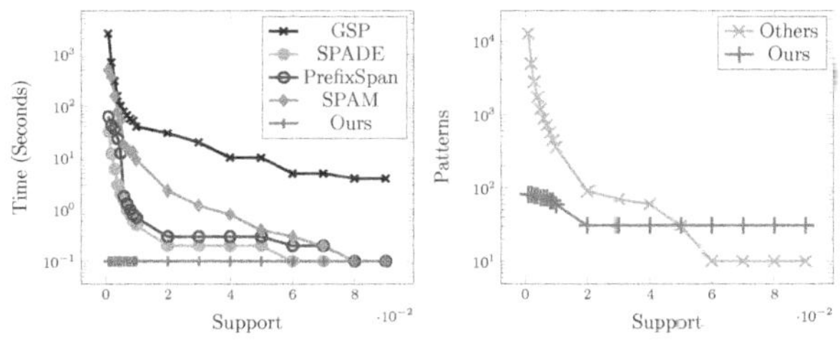

Figure 7: Sequential patterns in B2B customer event data.

We then perform clustering on the transformed sequences, using the frequent patterns detected to extract features as discussed in Section 3.3. We focus on a few dominant clusters in which the customers have relatively longer event sequences. The remaining customers only participated events in one or two buying stages and their behaviors are almost random. In Figure 8, we plot the sequences corresponding to some dominant clusters covering 3501 customers, by connecting each event of the sequence embedded in the two-dimensional plane. Here, each cluster corresponds to one type of customers with a unique buying path. We summarized these buying paths in Table 4.

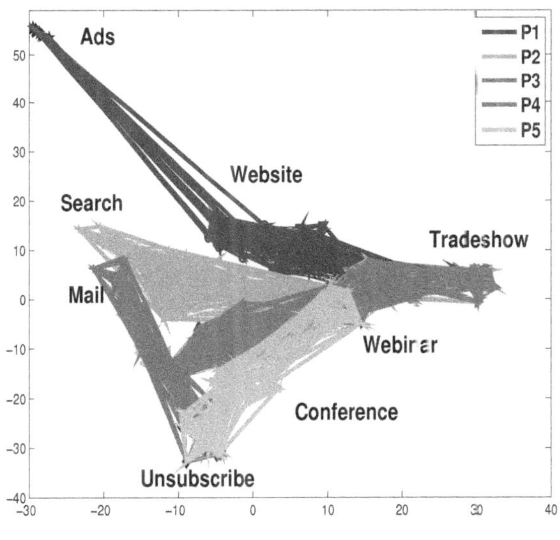

Figure 8: The customer buying paths.

With the semantic annotation in Table 3, we can see that the temporal clusters can be used to reveal several interesting buying paths. For example, the blue path P_1 passes through 5 clusters (or stages), as $C_{10} \rightarrow C_1 \rightarrow C_7 \rightarrow C_{12} \rightarrow C_8$. These customers were attracted by 'Web Marketing Ads', then they went to 'Official Website' and found the 'Trial Product Download'. When customers needed more information to make decisions, they continued to attend 'Webinar' and finally went to 'Tradeshow'. The green path P_2 also ends with 'Trade Show', but starts with 'Search Engine', indicating that these customers started from their own effort in acquiring information of the product suiting their needs. In comparison, the pattern in the red path P_3 is simpler, starting with 'Webinar' and ending with 'Tradeshow'. All these three paths can be grouped into the 'Successful' class, which leads to the higher maturity of the customers. The remaining two paths, P_4 and P_5, which end with 'Unsubscribe', indicating these customers do not want to participate further events any more.

These buying paths reveal different psychologies of B2B customers. Among the successful class, P_1 and P_2 represent customers that are comfortable with self-motivated/directed actions, e.g., searching product information themselves or browsing advertisements. In comparison, in the unsuccessful class, P_4 represents customers passively involved via 'direct marketing mail' but finally choose to give up. For paths P_3 and P_5, although they both start from webinar, they branch to opposite routes. We speculate that P_3 are easy customers; while P_5 are customers that are relatively more difficult to persuade. These uncovered patterns can be helpful in guiding the marketing campaigns, such as identifying customer groups, initiating more customer-friendly and less commercialized advertisements, and so on.

Class	Path	Path/Keyword	Size
Successful	P_1	$C_{10} \rightarrow C_1 \rightarrow C_7 \rightarrow C_{12} \rightarrow C_8$ `Ads→Website→Download→Webinar→Tradeshow`	933
	P_2	$C_{13} \rightarrow C_3 \rightarrow C_{11} \rightarrow C_{12} \rightarrow C_8$ `Search→Download→Webinar→Webinar→Tradeshow`	1110
	P_3	$C_6 \rightarrow C_{11} \rightarrow C_{12} \rightarrow C_8$ `Webinar→Webinar→Webinar→Tradeshow`	702
Unsuccessful	P_4	$C_2 \rightarrow C_9 \rightarrow C_5$ `Mail→Corporate Event→Unsubscribe`	423
	P_5	$C_{11} \rightarrow C_4 \rightarrow C_5$ `Webinar→Conference→Unsubscribe`	333

Table 4: The annotation of sequence clusters/buying paths.

From these observations, we can see that temporal clusters do represent meaningful buying stages and they greatly facilitate the description of typical buying paths. Identifying the buying paths/stages for B2B customers are critical to many marketing applications. This clearly demonstrates the advantages of our approach.

6. RELATED WORK

Sequential pattern mining [1] is an important topic in data mining. Given a database of customer transactions, where each transaction consists of customer-id, transaction time, and the items bought, sequential pattern mining finds frequent sequences of item sets. Some research efforts [25, 10, 2] focused on the computing efficiency. In addition to the customer behavior analysis, sequential data from other domains have also been exploited. For example, Giannotti et al. [7] proposed to find trajectory patterns from the location traces of moving objects to study their movement behaviors.

However, limited efforts [18, 9, 7] have been focused on the "curse of cardinality" problem. As we discussed in Section 1, these methods typically reduce the cardinality by performing a grouping of symbols, for which either a taxonomy already exists [18], or extracted from domain knowledge [9], or through clustering on the features associated with the symbols [7]. These grouping are irrespective of the temporal content in the sequences, while our approach achieves the grouping of symbols based on their temporal relations. It is worthy to note that combining the two types of clustering is a very interesting topic we shall pursue in the future.

Instead of reducing the cardinality of original symbols/items, one can also compress the discovered patterns for more concise interpretation. Pei et al. [16] computed so-called condensed frequent pattern bases to approximate the support of any frequent pattern. Xin et al. [22] proposed to compress frequent patterns with representative patterns via clustering. In these methods, an initial set of frequent patterns has to be identified first, which could suffer from the large cardinality. In comparison, our approach can be deemed as compressing the original set of symbols.

Another category of related work is rank aggregation [17], which tries to find a unified ranking of a set of elements that is "closest to" a given set of input (partial) rankings. For example, each customer event sequence can be deemed as a ranking of the participated events. Methods include position based statistics [5] and permutation optimization [6, 8], etc. However, rank aggregation is suited only when there is a dominant ordering in the data. When there are different patterns of the ordering, rank aggregation fails to give a valid result. In comparison, our approach can identify different types of orders as discussed in Section 3.3.

The HMM is another widely used method for sequence analysis. Most algorithms for HMM estimation are supervised; that is, hidden states in the training data need to be provided for model estimation. However, in the B2B customer event sequence analysis, it is very difficult to obtain labels for the buying stages corresponding to individual events. For unsupervised estimation of HMM, Expectation Maximization (EM) is often used, which could suffer from the local optimum problem. In our simulated study (Section 4), we observed that unsupervised HMM estimation often fails to recover the ground truth. In the literature, there have been convex approaches for the learning of HMM [23, 12]. However, this is achieved by avoiding explicit estimation of model parameters (transition matrix, emission matrix, etc.), hence not applicable if the model parameters are needed. Markov models were also used for clustering sequential data [4], as we also exploited in our empirical study [15]. Simultaneous clustering the sequential data and computing the temporal skeletonization shall be an interesting future work.

7. CONCLUDING REMARKS

In this paper, we proposed a novel approach of temporal skeletonization to address the problem of "curse of cardinality" in sequential data analysis. The key idea is to map the temporal structures of sequences into the topologies of a graph in a way that the temporal contents of the sequential data are preserved in the so-called temporal graph. Indeed, the embedding topology of the graph can allow to translate the rich temporal content into the metric space. Such a transformation enables not only sequential pattern mining at a more informative level of granularity, but also enables new possibilities to explore, quantify, and visualize statistically relevant temporal structures in the metric space. Finally, the experimental results showed the advantages of temporal skeletonization over existing methods. Also, the case study showed the effectiveness of the proposed method in terms of finding interesting buying paths from real-world B2B marketing data, which otherwise would be hidden.

APPENDIX

Isomap [20] is a method to embed a graph into a Euclidean space. It works on graphs weighed by a distance matrix $\mathbf{G}$, where $\mathbf{G}_{ij}$ is the distance between nodes i and j. Isomap first sparsifies the distance matrix by only preserving edges between K-nearest neighbours. Then, it computes the geodesic distance $\mathbf{D}_{ij}$'s using the Dijkstra's algorithm. The matrix $\mathbf{D}$ is (entry-wise) squared and converted to an inner product matrix via $\mathbf{K} = -\frac{1}{2}\mathbf{H}(\mathbf{D} \circ \mathbf{D})\mathbf{H}$, where $\mathbf{H}$ is the centering matrix. Finally, the eigenvectors of $\mathbf{K}$ with dominant eigenvalues are used to construct the embedding $\mathbf{X}$ that maximally preserves the manifold structure. We used the code from `http://isomap.stanford.edu`.

To apply Isomap on the temporal graph (Section 2.2), we convert temporal similarities $\mathbf{W}_{ij}$'s to distances. Since we mainly used radial basis function $\kappa_h(d) = \exp(-h \cdot d)$, which gives the relation $\mathbf{W}_{ij} = \exp(-h \cdot \mathbf{G}_{ij})$, we can transform the similarity to distance via $\mathbf{G}_{ij} = -\frac{1}{h}\log(\mathbf{W}_{ij})$.

Acknowledgements

This research was partially supported by National Science Foundation (NSF) via grant numbers CCF-1018151 and IIS-1256016.

References

[1] Rakesh Agrawal and Ramakrishnan Srikant. Mining sequential patterns. In *ICDE*, 1995.

[2] Jay Ayres, Jason Flannick, Johannes Gehrke, and Tomi Yiu. Sequential pattern mining using a bitmap representation. In *SIGKDD*, 2002.

[3] Mikhail Belkin and Partha Niyogi. Laplacian eigenmaps and spectral techniques for embedding and clustering. In *NIPS*, 2001.

[4] Igor Cadez, David Heckerman, Christopher Meek, Padhraic Smyth, and Steven White. Model-based clustering and visualization of navigation patterns on a web site. *Data Mining and Knowledge Discovery*, 7 (4):399–424, 2003.

[5] Don Coppersmith, Lisa Fleischer, and Atri Rudra. Ordering by weighted number of wins gives a good ranking for weighted tournaments. In *Symposium on Discrete algorithm*, 2006.

[6] Cynthia Dwork, Ravi Kumar, Moni Naor, and Dandapani Sivakumar. Rank aggregation methods for the web. In *WWW*, 2001.

[7] Fosca Giannotti, Mirco Nanni, Fabio Pinelli, and Dino Pedreschi. Trajectory pattern mining. In *SIGKDD*, 2007.

[8] Aristides Gionis, Heikki Mannila, Kai Puolamäki, and Antti Ukkonen. Algorithms for discovering bucket orders from data. In *SIGKDD*, 2006.

[9] Jiawei Han and Yongjian Fu. Mining multiple-level association rules in large databases. *TKDE*, 11(5): 798–805, 1999.

[10] Jiawei Han, Jian Pei, Behzad Mortazavi-Asl, Helen Pinto, Qiming Chen, Umeshwar Dayal, and MC Hsu. Prefixspan: Mining sequential patterns efficiently by prefix-projected pattern growth. In *ICDE*, 2001.

[11] Jiawei Han, Hong Cheng, Dong Xin, and Xifeng Yan. Frequent pattern mining: current status and future directions. *Data Mining and Knowledge Discovery*, 15 (1):55–86, 2007.

[12] Daniel Hsu, Sham M Kakade, and Tong Zhang. A spectral algorithm for learning hidden markov models. *Journal of Computer and System Sciences*, 78(5): 1460–1480, 2012.

[13] J-G Lee, Jiawei Han, Xiaolei Li, and Hong Cheng. Mining discriminative patterns for classifying trajectories on road networks. *TKDE*, 23(5):713–726, 2011.

[14] Andrew Y Ng, Michael I Jordan, and Yair Weiss. On spectral clustering: Analysis and an algorithm. *NIPS*, 2002.

[15] Lane MD Owsley, Les E Atlas, and Gary D Bernard. Automatic clustering of vector time-series for manufacturing machine monitoring. In *ICASSP*, 1997.

[16] Jian Pei, Guozhu Dong, Wei Zou, and Jiawei Han. On computing condensed frequent pattern bases. In *ICDM*, 2002.

[17] Frans Schalekamp and Anke van Zuylen. Rank aggregation: Together we're strong. In *ALENEX*, 2009.

[18] Ramakrishnan Srikant and Rakesh Agrawal. Mining generalized association rules. In *VLDB*, 1995.

[19] Ramakrishnan Srikant and Rakesh Agrawal. Mining sequential patterns: Generalizations and performance improvements. In *EDBT*, 1996.

[20] Joshua B Tenenbaum, Vin De Silva, and John C Langford. A global geometric framework for nonlinear dimensionality reduction. *Science*, 290(5500): 2319–2323, 2000.

[21] Tibshirani et al. Sparsity and smoothness via the fused lasso. *Journal of the Royal Statistical Society: Series B (Statistical Methodology)*, 67(1):91–108, 2005.

[22] Dong Xin, Jiawei Han, Xifeng Yan, and Hong Cheng. Mining compressed frequent-pattern sets. In *VLDB*, 2005.

[23] Linli Xu, Li Cheng, Tao Wang, and Dale Schuurmans. Convex hidden markov models. In *NIPS Workshop on Advances in Structured Learning for Text and Speech Processing*, 2005.

[24] Shuicheng Yan, Dong Xu, Benyu Zhang, Hong-Jiang Zhang, Qiang Yang, and Stephen Lin. Graph embedding and extensions: a general framework for dimensionality reduction. *TPAMI*, 29(1):40–51, 2007.

[25] Mohammed J Zaki. Spade: An efficient algorithm for mining frequent sequences. *Machine learning*, 42(1-2): 31–60, 2001.

Focused Clustering and Outlier Detection in Large Attributed Graphs

Bryan Perozzi◇, Leman Akoglu◇
◇ Stony Brook University
Department of Computer Science
{bperozzi, leman}@cs.stonybrook.edu

Patricia Iglesias Sánchez○, Emmanuel Müller○•
○ Karlsruhe Institute of Technology, • University of Antwerp
Department of Computer Science
{patricia.iglesias, emmanuel.mueller}@kit.edu

ABSTRACT

Graph clustering and graph outlier detection have been studied extensively on plain graphs, with various applications. Recently, algorithms have been extended to graphs with attributes as often observed in the real-world. However, all of these techniques fail to incorporate the user preference into graph mining, and thus, lack the ability to steer algorithms to more interesting parts of the attributed graph.

In this work, we overcome this limitation and introduce a novel user-oriented approach for mining attributed graphs. The key aspect of our approach is to infer user preference by the so-called focus attributes through a set of user-provided exemplar nodes. In this new problem setting, clusters and outliers are then simultaneously mined according to this user preference. Specifically, our FocusCO algorithm identifies the focus, extracts focused clusters and detects outliers. Moreover, FocusCO scales well with graph size, since we perform a local clustering of interest to the user rather than global partitioning of the entire graph. We show the effectiveness and scalability of our method on synthetic and real-world graphs, as compared to both existing graph clustering and outlier detection approaches.

Categories and Subject Descriptors

H.2.8 [**Database Applications**]: Data mining; I.5.3 [**Pattern Recognition**]: Clustering

Keywords

focused graph mining; infer user preference; attributed graphs; clustering; outlier mining; distance metric learning

1. INTRODUCTION

Many real-world graphs have attributes associated with the nodes, in addition to their connectivity information. For example, social networks contain both the friendship relations as well as user attributes such as interests and demographics. A protein-protein interaction network may not only have the interaction relations but the gene expressions associated with the proteins. Both types of information can be described by a graph in which nodes represent the objects, edges represent the relations between them, and feature vectors associated with the nodes represent the attributes. Such graph data is often referred to as an *attributed graph*.

KDD'14, August 24–27, 2014, New York, NY, USA.
Copyright 2014 ACM 978-1-4503-2956-9/14/08 ...$15.00.
http://dx.doi.org/10.1145/2623330.2623682

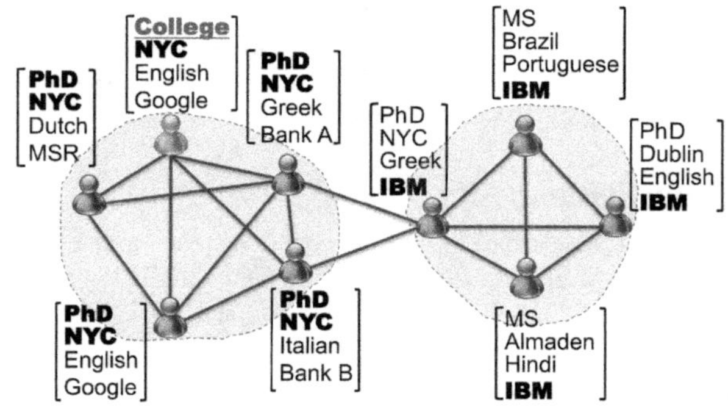

Figure 1: Example graph with two focused clusters and one focused outlier.

For attributed graphs, we see major challenges that remain unsolved by traditional graph mining techniques [4, 10, 19, 24, 31], which consider plain graphs (without attributes). Recent methods have been proposed for attributed graphs, however, they either use all the given attributes [2, 14, 20, 34] or they perform an unsupervised feature selection [16, 18, 22, 26]. In contrast to all of these graph mining paradigms (cf. Table 1), we consider a user-oriented setting where the users can control the relevance of attributes and as a consequence, the graph mining results.

In particular, we consider cluster and outlier detection based on user preference. This *focused clustering* is of particular interest in attributed graphs, where users might not be concerned with all but a few available attributes. As different attributes induce different clusterings of the graph, the user should be able to steer the clustering accordingly. As such, the user controls the clustering by providing a set of exemplar nodes (perceived similar by the user) from which we infer *attribute weights* of relevance that capture the user-perceived similarity. The essence of user preference is captured by those attributes with large weights. We call these the *focus attributes*, which form the basis of our approach for discovering focused clusters and outliers.

To elaborate on this new terminology, we give a toy example in Figure 1. The graph represents the friendship relations and the node attributes denote `degree, location, mother tongue`, and `work`. There are two focused clusters: On the

Table 1: Comparison of related work.

Property	Graph clustering	On attributed graphs	Attribute subspace	User-preferred clusters	Overlapping clusters	Outlier detection	Scalability
METIS [19], Spectral [24], Co-clustering [10]	✓						✓
Autopart, Cross-associations [7]	✓					✓	✓
PageRank-Nibble [3], [30], BigClam [33]	✓				✓		✓
Spectral Relational [20], SA-Cluster [34]	✓	✓					
CoPaM [22], Gamer [16]	✓	✓	✓				✓
PICS [2]	✓	✓					✓
CODA [14]	✓	✓				✓	
GOutRank [23], ConSub [18]		✓	✓			✓	✓
FocusCO [this paper]	✓	✓	✓	✓	✓	✓	✓

left, people know each other due to their `degrees` and `locations`. On the right, a similarity in `work` induces the second cluster. As such, different user interest in subsets of the attributes may induce different clusters. In case a user is interested in `degree` and `location`, focused clustering should only find the left cluster and not the right one. Analogously, the example outlier is deviating with a college degree among all others having PhDs, where `degree` is a focus attribute.

While our example is on a toy graph, our problem setting has several practical applications in the real-world. For instance, a marketing manager interested in selling cosmetics could aim to find communities in a large social network with its members being of a certain age, gender, and income-level. S/he could then offer deals to a few members from each community, and expect the news to propagate by the word-of-mouth. A scientist could aim to identify clusters of sky-objects that are all in close-distance to one another (assuming a graph is constructed among sky-objects by distance in space) and share certain characteristics of interest (e.g., helium level, temperature, light, etc.).

Such user-preferred clusters are likely a handful in the graph, and thus an algorithm should be able to (*i*) effectively identify user preference, (*ii*) efficiently "chop out" relevant clusters locally without necessarily partitioning the whole graph, and additionally (*iii*) spot outliers if any. In this paper, we offer the following contributions:

- **Focused Graph Mining**: We propose a new user-centric problem setting that exploits the user interest for focused mining in attributed graphs.
- **Steered Search by User Preference**: We infer user preference and steer the graph clustering and outlier detection accordingly.
- **Scaling to Large Graphs:** Our proposed method has near-linear time complexity, and with appropriate initialization can run in time sub-linear w.r.t. the size of the input graph.

In our evaluation we demonstrate the effectiveness and scalability of our method on synthetic and real-world graphs, compared to existing graph clustering and outlier detection methods. Our experiments show that existing approaches are not suitable for the new focused graph mining setting.

2. RELATED WORK

We show the highlights of related work in Table 1. The two key differences of our work are summarized as follows: (1) we introduce a new user-oriented problem setting for attributed graphs, in which we aim to find *focused* clusters and outliers based on *user preference*, and (2) we propose an algorithm that *simultaneously* extracts relevant clusters and outliers from large graphs. In the following, we discuss related work in three areas; traditional plain graph mining, attributed graph mining, and semi-supervised data mining.

Graph mining on plain graphs.

Graph partitioning has been well studied in the literature. Widely used methods include METIS [19] and spectral clustering [11, 24], which aim to find a k-way partitioning of the graph. Different from partitioning, community detection methods [12] cluster the graph into variable size communities. Autopart, cross-associations [7], and information-theoretic co-clustering [10] are parameter-free examples to graph clustering methods. Several methods [3, 30, 33] also allow clusters to overlap as observed in real-world social and communication networks. Works that aim to spot structural outliers in plain graphs include [1, 28]. However, all of these methods are limited to plain graphs (without attributes).

Graph mining on attributed graphs.

Compared to the wide range of work on plain graph mining, there has been much less work on attributed graphs. The representative methods [2, 14, 17, 20, 27, 34] aim to partition the given graph into structurally dense and attribute-wise homogeneous clusters, detect deviations from frequent subgraphs [25], or search for community outliers in attributed graphs [14]. These methods, however, enforce attribute homogeneity in all attributes. Recently some methods loosen this constraint by unsupervised feature selection [26], subspace clustering [16, 22] and subspace outlier detection [18, 23] and extract cohesive subgraphs with homogeneity in a subset of attributes. However, all of these methods either do not perform a selection of attributes or do not allow for user preference to steer the algorithm.

Semi-supervised methods.

A broad variety of methods for semi-supervised clustering consider user-given constraints like 'must-link' and 'cannot-link' referred to as constraint-based clustering [5]. There also exist methods for semi-supervised outlier mining [13]. However, these methods are based on vector data and further, not applicable to graphs with attributes.

Methods on seeded community mining [3, 8, 15, 30] find communities around (user-given) seed nodes. However, those methods find structural communities on plain graphs and neither apply to attributed graphs, nor enable user preference on attributes. Moreover, they do not provide outlier detection. In contrast, we use user-given exemplar nodes to automatically infer user preference on attributes. To the best of our knowledge this problem setting is new and we propose the first focused graph mining approach for simultaneous clustering and outlier detection in attributed graphs.

3. METHOD FocusCO

In this section we first introduce the notation and pose the focused clustering and outlier detection problem formally. Next, we discuss the main components of our approach and walk through the details of our algorithm. Lastly, we analyze the computational complexity of FocusCO.

3.1 Problem Formulation

In this paper we introduce the novel problem of *focused clustering and outlier detection* in attributed graphs, defined as follows: Given a large attributed graph $G(V, E, F)$ with $|V| = n$ nodes and $|E| = m$ edges, where each node is associated with $|F| = d$ attributes (features), extract from G only the (type of) clusters pertaining to a user u's interest (rather than partitioning the whole graph). To do so, the user provides a small set C_{ex} of exemplar nodes that s/he considers to be similar to the type of nodes the clusters of his/her interest should contain. Assuming that the nodes in a cluster "unite" or "knit up" around a few defining attributes, we then aim to infer the implicit weights $\boldsymbol{\beta_u}$ (i.e., relevance) of attributes that "define" the nodes in C_{ex}, i.e., the weights of attributes that make them as similar as possible. Thus, $\boldsymbol{\beta_u}$ is expected to be a sparse vector with large weights for only a few attributes (e.g., `degree` and `location` in Figure 1), which we call the *focus attributes.*

Having inferred the attribute weights $\boldsymbol{\beta_u}$ from user u, our first goal is to extract focused clusters $\mathcal{C}$ from G that are (1) structurally dense and well separated from the rest of the graph, as well as (2) consistent on the focus attributes with large weights. The focused clusters can be overlapping, sharing several of their nodes, as observed in real-world social and communication networks. Moreover, the set $\mathcal{C}$ is a subset of all the clusters in G since different sets of clusters are expected to unite around different attributes and we aim to extract only those that are specifically similar to the type of clusters user u is interested in. Besides focused clustering, our second goal is to also perform *outlier detection.* Outliers $\mathcal{O}$ are those nodes that structurally belong to a focused cluster (i.e., have many cluster neighbors), but deviate from its members in some focus attributes. In summary, the focused clustering and outlier detection problem in attributed graphs is given as follows:

Given a large graph $G(V, E, F)$ with node attributes, and a set of exemplar nodes C_{ex} of user u's interest;
Infer attribute *weights* $\boldsymbol{\beta_u}$ of relevance/importance,
Extract *focused* clusters $\mathcal{C}$ that are (1) dense in graph structure, and (2) coherent in heavy focus attributes,
Detect focused outliers $\mathcal{O}$, i.e. nodes that deviate from their cluster members in some focus attributes.

3.2 Approach and Algorithm Details

Next we present the details of the three main components of FocusCO: (1) inferring attribute weights, (2) extracting focused clusters, and (3) outlier detection.

3.2.1 Inferring Attribute Relevance

Our focused clustering setting is a user-oriented one, where each user is interested in extracting certain kind of clusters from a given graph. The user steers the clustering by providing a small set of exemplar nodes that are similar to one another as well as similar to the type of nodes the clusters of his/her interest should contain. Our first goal then is to identify the relevance weights of node attributes that make the exemplar nodes similar to each other. This kind of weighted similarity is often captured by the (inverse) Mahalanobis distance: the distance between two nodes with feature vectors $\boldsymbol{f_i}$ and $\boldsymbol{f_j}$ is $(\boldsymbol{f_i} - \boldsymbol{f_j})^T \boldsymbol{A}(\boldsymbol{f_i} - \boldsymbol{f_j})$. Setting $\boldsymbol{A}$ as the identity matrix yields Euclidean distance, otherwise the features/dimensions are weighted accordingly.

Given the exemplar nodes, how can we learn an $\boldsymbol{A}$ such that they end up having small distance to each other? This is known as the distance metric learning problem [29]. We adopt the optimization objective by [32]:

$$\min_{\boldsymbol{A}} \sum_{(i,j)\in P_S} (\boldsymbol{f_i} - \boldsymbol{f_j})^T \boldsymbol{A}(\boldsymbol{f_i} - \boldsymbol{f_j}) - \gamma \log \Big(\sum_{(i,j)\in P_D} \sqrt{(\boldsymbol{f_i} - \boldsymbol{f_j})^T \boldsymbol{A}(\boldsymbol{f_i} - \boldsymbol{f_j})} \Big) \quad (1)$$

which is convex and enables efficient, local-minima-free algorithms to solve it, especially for a diagonal solution.

We give the details of inferring attribute weights in Procedure P1. P_S and P_D are two sets of similar and dissimilar pairs of nodes, respectively (P1 Line 1). In our setting, all pairs of exemplar nodes constitute P_S (P1 Line 2). We create P_D by randomly drawing pairs of nodes that do not belong to the exemplar set (P1 Lines 3-7).

We remark that in creating P_D, we may also obtain samples similar to those in P_S since these draws are random. To alleviate the affect of such draws, we keep the size of P_D sufficiently large. This assumes that the number of dissimilar pairs is substantially larger than the number of similar pairs in the original distribution. This a suitable assumption, given that the number of "focused" clusters for any particular user-preference is likely small. Thus, we make the size of P_D be $|F|$ times larger than that of P_S (P1 Line 7). This also ensures that the data size exceeds dimension size, and that the learning task is feasible.

Moreover, in inferring attribute weights we learn a diagonal $\boldsymbol{A}$ matrix (P1 Line 9). The reason for this choice is twofold. First, individual weights for attributes provide ease of interpretation. Second, learning a diagonal $\boldsymbol{A}$ is computationally much more tractable (especially in high dimensions) than learning a full one, since the latter requires solving a program with a semi-definite constraint. Of course if desired, one can instead learn a full matrix (in low dimensions).

3.2.2 Focused Cluster Extraction

Having determined attribute weights $\boldsymbol{\beta}$, we extract the focused clusters of interest. The main idea in "chopping out" focused clusters from G is to first identify good candidate nodes that potentially belong to such clusters, and then to expand around those candidate nodes to find the clusters. Details are given in Algorithm A1, which we describe below.

The process of finding good candidate sets to expand is detailed in Procedure P2. Intuitively, nodes in focused clusters have high weighted similarity to their neighbors. Therefore, we first re-weigh the edges E by the weighted similarity of

Procedure P1 InferAttributeWeights

Input: exemplar set of nodes C_{ex}
Output: attribute weights vector $\boldsymbol{\beta}$
    // generate similar and dissimilar node pairs
Similar pairs $P_S = \emptyset$, Dissimilar pairs $P_D = \emptyset$
for $u \in C_{ex}, v \in C_{ex}$ **do** $P_S = P_S \cup (u, v)$ **end for**
repeat
    Random sample u from set $V \backslash C_{ex}$
    Random sample v from set $V \backslash C_{ex}$
    $P_D = P_D \cup (u, v)$
until $d|P_S|$ dissimilar pairs are generated, $d = |F|$
Oversample from P_S such that $P_S = P_D$
Solve objective function in Equ. (1) for diagonal $\boldsymbol{A}$
return $\boldsymbol{\beta} = diag(\boldsymbol{A})$

their end nodes (P2 Lines 2-4), induce G on the edges with notably large weights[1] (P2 Line 5), and consider the nodes in the resulting connected components as our candidate nodes (P2 Lines 6-7). We call each such component a *core* set.

Next, we expand around each core by carefully choosing new nodes to include in the cluster and continue expanding until there exist no more nodes that increase the quality of the cluster. There exist several measures of cluster quality including modularity and cut size [24]. In this work, we use conductance [3] as it accounts for both the cut size as well as the total volume/density retained within the cluster. The weighted conductance $\phi^{(w)}(C, G)$ of a set of nodes $C \subset V$ in graph $G(V, E, F)$ is defined as

$$\phi^{(w)}(C,G) = \frac{W_{cut}(C)}{WVol(C)} = \frac{\sum\limits_{(i,j)\in E, i\in C, j\in V\backslash C} w(i,j)}{\sum\limits_{i\in C} \sum\limits_{j,(i,j)\in E} w(i,j)}$$

where $WVol(C)$ is the total weighted degree of nodes in C. The lower the conductance of a cluster, the better its quality is with few cross-cut edges and large within-density.

The expansion operation is presented in Procedure P3. First, we enlist all their non-member neighbors as the candidate set (P3 Line 4). For each candidate node n, we compute the difference $\Delta\phi_n^{(w)}$ in cluster conductance if n was to be added to C (P3 Lines 6-16). If there exist any node with negative Δ (i.e., node improves conductance), we pick the best n with the minimum (i.e., largest absolute drop in conductance) (P3 Lines 17-23). We continue iterating until no candidate node yields negative $\Delta\phi^{(w)}$.

The node additions are based on a best-improving search strategy. While being cautious in which node to add (the best one at every step), our decisions are greedy. Thus, in the following step of our algorithm we adopt a retrospective strategy and check if there exist any nodes in C whose removal would drop conductance, presented in Procedure P4. We repeat the node addition and removal iterations until convergence, that is, when the conductance stops changing (A1 Lines 7-12).

We remark that our algorithm is guaranteed to converge; as the (weighted) conductance of a cluster is lower-bounded

[1]To identify such edges, we use hypothesis testing. We first find the top few most weighted edges, and bootstrap a Normal distribution. We then progressively subject the remaining edges to a membership-test and consider only those that pass the test. Every time an edge passes the test, model parameters are updated.

Algorithm A1 FocusCO: Focused Clusters&Outliers

Input: attributed graph $G(V, E, F)$, exemplar nodes C_{ex}
Output: focused clusters $\mathcal{C}$ and outliers $\mathcal{O}$
1: $Cores \leftarrow$ FindCoreSets($G(V, E, F), C_{ex}$)
2: $\mathcal{C} = \emptyset$, $\mathcal{O} = \emptyset$
3: **for each** core $i \in Cores$ **do**
4:     $C \leftarrow Seeds(i).getNodes()$
5:     $BSN = \emptyset$ *// holds all Best Structural Nodes to add*
6:     $\phi_{curr}^{(w)} \leftarrow \phi^{(w)}(C, G)$
7:     **repeat**
8:         $\phi_{init}^{(w)} \leftarrow \phi_{curr}^{(w)}$
9:         $(C, BSN, \phi_{curr}^{(w)}) \leftarrow$ Expand($G, C, BSN, \phi_{curr}^{(w)}$)
10:         $(C, \phi_{curr}^{(w)}) \leftarrow$ Contract($G, C, \phi_{curr}^{(w)}$)
11:         $BSN \leftarrow BSN \backslash C$
12:     **until** $\phi_{init}^{(w)} = \phi_{curr}^{(w)}$
13:     $\mathcal{C} \leftarrow \mathcal{C} \cup C$, $\mathcal{O} \leftarrow \mathcal{O} \cup BSN$
14: **end for**

Procedure P2 FindCoreSets

Input: attributed graph $G(V, E, F)$, exemplar nodes C_{ex}
Output: seed sets to expand as focused clusters
1: $\boldsymbol{\beta} \leftarrow$ InferAttributeWeights(C_{ex})
    // (re)-weigh edges by feature similarity of end-nodes
2: **for each** $(i, j) \in E$ **do**
3:     $w(i, j) = 1/(1 + \sqrt{(\boldsymbol{f}_i - \boldsymbol{f}_j)^T diag(\boldsymbol{\beta})(\boldsymbol{f}_i - \boldsymbol{f}_j)})$
4: **end for**
5: $w' \leftarrow \max_{w'} w' \notin$ distribution$f(\{w | w \geq w'\})$
6: Build induced subgraph $g(V', E', F)$ s.t.
    $\forall u, v \in V', (u, v) \in E,\ w(u, v) \geq w'$ iff $(u, v) \in E'$
7: **return** ConnectedComponents($g(V', E', F)$)

by 0 and we improve (i.e., decrease) the weighted conductance in every iteration (P3 Line 8, P4 Line 5).[2]

We omit the details of the Δ conductance computation for brevity, but remark that it is an efficient operation. Specifically, the operation of a node u to be added to or to be removed from a cluster S has complexity proportional to the degree of u, i.e. $O(d(u))$. In addition, the total volume of S is simply increased/decreased by the weighted degree $w(u)$ of u, when it is added/removed, which takes $O(1)$.

3.2.3 Focused Outlier Detection

Our algorithm also identifies outlier nodes in each focused cluster along with finding the clusters in a unified fashion. Our definition of a focused cluster outlier is quite intuitive: a node that belongs to a focused cluster structurally (having many edges to its members), but that deviates from its members in some focus attributes significantly is an outlier. To quantify this definition, the main idea is to identify the best *structural* nodes BSNs (best in terms of *unweighted* conductance) during the course of expansion (P3 Lines 3, 14, 22) and later check if there exist any BSNs which were not included in the resulting focused cluster (A1 Line 11).

In order to identify the best structural node for a cluster in each iteration, we need to also track its unweighted conductance. An advantage of our proposed approach is that the overhead of computing the unweighted $\Delta\phi$ of a node, in addition to its weighted $\Delta\phi^{(w)}$, is negligible. The reason

[2]P4 Line 5 removes a node even if conductance remains the same, however, the number of such steps is also bounded by cluster size.

Procedure P3 EXPAND

Input: attributed graph $G(V, E, F)$, focused cluster C, set BSN, current conductance $\phi_{curr}^{(w)}$

Output: a focused cluster C, its best structural nodes BSN, and its conductance $\phi_{curr}^{(w)}$

repeat
  $bestNode = NULL$,
  $bestStructureNode = NULL$
  $candidateNodes \leftarrow neighbors(C)$
  $\Delta\phi_{best}^{(w)} = 0$, $\Delta\phi_{best} = 0$
  for each node n in $candidateNodes$ **do**
    $\Delta\phi_n^{(w)}, \Delta\phi_n \leftarrow$ GETΔCONDUCTANCE(G, C, n,ADD)
    if $\Delta\phi_n^{(w)} < \Delta\phi_{best}^{(w)}$ **then**
      $\Delta\phi_{best}^{(w)} = \Delta\phi_n^{(w)}$
      $bestNode \leftarrow n$
    end if
    if $\Delta\phi_n < \Delta\phi_{best}$ **then**
      $\Delta\phi_{best} = \Delta\phi_n$
      $bestStructureNode \leftarrow n$
    end if
  end for
  if $bestNode \neq NULL$ **then**
    $C \leftarrow C \cup bestNode$
    $\phi_{curr}^{(w)} = \phi_{curr}^{(w)} + \Delta\phi_{best}^{(w)}$
  end if
  if $bestStructureNode \neq NULL$ **then**
    $BSN \leftarrow BSN \cup bestStructureNode$
  end if
until $bestNode = NULL$
return $C, BSN, \phi_{curr}^{(w)}$

is that, to compute $\Delta\phi$, we simply count the total number, instead of the total weight, of those same edges that are involved in the computation of $\Delta\phi^{(w)}$. As such, both conductances can be computed efficiently at the same time and the best structural node and the best focused cluster node can be identified simultaneously.

3.2.4 Complexity analysis

Given an attributed graph $G(V, E, F)$ and the exemplar nodes C_{ex}, we first create similar and dissimilar node pairs which we use to infer the attribute weights. As the optimization objective we adopt is convex and as we aim for a diagonal solution, local-optima-free gradient descent techniques will take $O(\frac{d}{\epsilon^2})$ for an ϵ-approximate answer [6].

To determine good core sets to expand clusters around, we re-weigh the graph edges by the weight vector $\boldsymbol{\beta}$ with complexity $O(dm)$. Assuming $\boldsymbol{\beta}$ is sparse with only a few non-zero entries for focus attributes, the multiplicative factor becomes effectively constant yielding a complexity of $O(m)$. Next, we identify the top-k edges with largest weights on which we induce G to find the core sets ($k \ll m$). To do so, we use a min-heap to maintain this top set while making a single pass over the edges. This requires $O(m \log k)$ in the worst case, assuming each edge triggers an insertion into the heap. Using these top-k edges we estimate the parameters of a Normal distribution, which takes $O(k)$. Next we make another pass over the edge set and subject each to a membership test against the Normal model in $O(m)$. We induce the graph on all the edges that pass the test, the connected components of which yield the core sets. Overall complexity for finding the core sets is thus $O(m \log k)$.

Procedure P4 CONTRACT

Input: attributed graph $G(V, E, F)$, focused cluster C, current conductance $\phi_{curr}^{(w)}$

Output: a focused cluster C and its conductance $\phi_{curr}^{(w)}$

1: **repeat**
2:   $removed \leftarrow false$
3:   **for each** node n in C **do**
4:     $\Delta\phi_n^{(w)} \leftarrow$ GETΔCONDUCTANCE(G, C, n,REMOVE)
5:     **if** $\Delta\phi_n^{(w)} \leq 0$ **then**
6:       $C \leftarrow C \backslash n$
7:       $\phi_{curr}^{(w)} = \phi_{curr}^{(w)} + \Delta\phi_n^{(w)}$
8:       $removed \leftarrow true$
9:     **end if**
10:   **end for**
11: **until** $removed = false$
12: **return** $C, \phi_{curr}^{(w)}$

For expanding a focused cluster, we enlist all the non-member neighbors as the candidate set C and evaluate their weighted Δ conductance. As discussed in §3.2.2, the complexity is $\sum_{n \in C} d(n)$. Since $C \subseteq V$, it is equivalently $O(m)$. As we add one node at each iteration, the total complexity becomes $O(|S|m)$ where $|S|$ is the size of the focused cluster, and $|S| \ll n$. Also note that focused clusters can be extracted around each core set in parallel.

We remark that scanning candidate set C for picking the best node takes $O(m)$ in the worst case. Assuming small rounded focused clusters, one can expect that not all edges of G are "touched" by C's neighbors. This implies sub-linear performance for expanding a single cluster in practice.[3]

3.2.5 Variants of FOCUSCO

We conclude this section by briefly discussing a couple of variants of our problem setting and how we can adapt our proposed algorithm to handle these variants.

In one variant of the problem, the user might explicitly ask for the exemplar nodes s/he provided to be included in the focused clusters. While it is highly likely that most of the exemplar nodes will indeed be part of the focused clusters found in Algorithm 1, inclusion of all is not guaranteed. To handle this setting, we can include the connected components induced on the exemplar nodes as additional core sets (in P2 Line 7) and later never allow the removal of any exemplar node in extracting the clusters (in P4 Lines 5-9).

Another variant involves the user asking for a sparser representation of the focus attributes. In other words, it may be practical to define the similarity among the exemplar nodes using as few attributes as possible, especially in high dimensions. In such a case, we can tune the regularization constant γ that we introduced in Equation (1) for learning the weight vector $\boldsymbol{\beta}$. Specifically, a large γ drives the second term in the objective to become large. To make the pairs in P_D as dissimilar as possible, a dense $\boldsymbol{\beta}$ is learned. The smaller the γ gets, the less the emphasis on the dissimilar pairs becomes, and a sparser weight vector is learned.[4]

In other settings, the user may choose to explicitly provide the set of dissimilar nodes or the attribute relevances (i.e., the $\boldsymbol{\beta}$ vector) directly, which can be incorporated trivially.

[3]Different ways of choosing the core sets (e.g., only using user-provided nodes) can remove the dependence on processing the entire graph, and allow FOCUSCO to run in sublinear time.

[4]For $\gamma = 0$, constraint on P_D is completely waived and $\boldsymbol{\beta}$ is zero.

4. EVALUATION

In this section we thoroughly evaluate our method[5] on clustering quality, outlier detection performance, and running time on synthetic and real-world networks. None of the existing methods address the focused clustering and outlier detection problem we pose in this paper. Nevertheless, we compare to two representative techniques, CODA [14] and METIS [19]. CODA is a graph clustering and outlier detection algorithm on attributed graphs, and treats all attributes equally. The clustering is not steered by user-preference, as such, it clusters the whole graph. METIS is a graph partitioning algorithm and does not provide outlier detection. Both methods expect the number of clusters as input.

To evaluate *focused clustering* quality, we use the Normalized Mutual Information (NMI), a widely used metric for computing clustering accuracy of a method against the desired ground truth [21]. The ground truth in our case is the true focused clusters that are relevant to a particular user's interest. The best NMI score is 1. We evaluate *outlier detection* performance by the F1-score; the harmonic mean of precision and recall for a known set of outliers.

4.1 Results on Synthetic Graphs

4.1.1 Data generation

To study the behavior of our algorithm compared to other approaches on graphs with ground truth (focused) clusters and outliers, we generated synthetic graphs with various number of clusters focusing on different subsets of the attribute space, containing various number of clusters, and with varying size ranges. Our generative algorithm is based on the planted partitions model [9].

Simply put, given the desired number of nodes in each cluster we split the adjacency matrix into blocks defined by the partitioning. For each block B_{ij}, we choose a probability p_{ij}. Using a random draw process we assign a 1, i.e. an edge, for each possible entry in the block, and 0 otherwise. In other words, p_{ij} specifies the density of each block. The diagonal blocks constitute the actual clusters and off-diagonal entries yield the cross edges. Unless otherwise noted, we set $p_{ii} = 0.35$ and $0.10 \leq p_{ij} \leq 0.25$, $i \neq j$.

We assign the graph clusters generated, either to one of two focus attribute sets (i.e. focus-1 or focus-2) or as unfocused. Please note that in real-world graphs, we expect to see more than two focuses on a variety of attribute subspaces. For each focused cluster, one of the two subsets (focus-1 or focus-2) is chosen as focus attributes. For each attribute i in this subset the attribute values are drawn from a Normal distribution $N(\mu_i, \sigma)$ with uniform random mean $\mu_i \in [0, 1]$ and a variance $\sigma = 0.001$. The variance is specifically chosen to be small such that the clustered nodes "agree" on their focus attributes. The rest of the attributes, on the other hand, are drawn from a Normal distribution with much larger variance; $N(0, 1)$. In contrast, all of the attribute values of nodes in unfocused clusters are drawn from large-variance Normals.

Focused outliers are generated by randomly choosing members from each focused cluster and "deflating" (depending on the setting) one or more of their focus attributes i; by replacing them by a value drawn from $N(\mu_i, \sigma = 1)$.

[5]A FocusCO implementation is available at `http://bit.ly/focusedclustering`

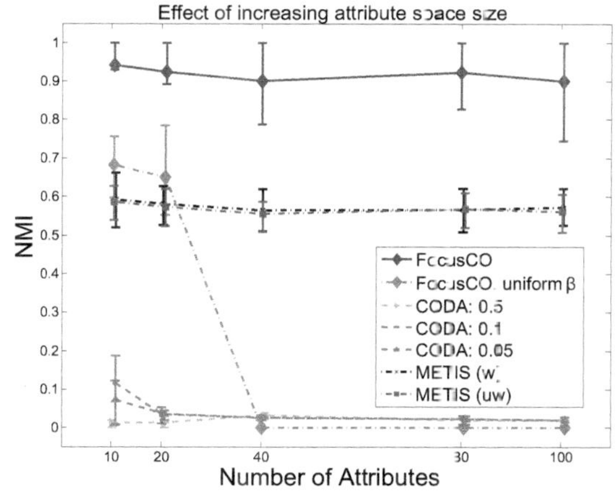

Figure 2: NMI vs. attribute size $|F|$. Results averaged over 100 runs, bars depict 25-75%.

4.1.2 Clustering quality

To study the clustering performance, we generated graphs with 3 focused clusters that are coherent in focus-1 attributes, 3 focused clusters that are coherent in focus-2 attributes, and 3 unfocused clusters, for a total of 9 clusters. The task is to extract the focus-1 clusters with the respective user preference.

For comparison we use CODA and METIS, which do not perform focused cluster extraction. They both partition the entire graph, and thus, we explicitly need to select the 3 best clusters that these methods returned, by measuring the overlap among the clusters they produced to the ground-truth clusters. Since both methods require the number of clusters to be provided as input, we asked for the correct number of (9) clusters, i.e. best performance, although in practice this number is hard to choose as the number of hidden clusters is unknown, especially for large graphs.

METIS is a graph partitioning algorithm that does not handle attributes. In one version of METIS, we ignore the attributes and use only the graph structure. In a second version, we incorporate attribute information by weighing the edges of the graph (using $\boldsymbol{\beta}$) by the attribute similarity of their end nodes. We call these two versions as weighted METIS (w) and unweighted METIS (uw). While CODA can perform clustering for attributed graphs, a main challenge with it is to carefully choose a λ parameter that controls the trade-off between structural and attribute similarity of the nodes. In our experiments we report results using 3 different λ settings, 0.05, 0.1, and 0.5, for CODA.

Figure 2 shows the clustering performance (mean NMI over 100 independent runs) of the methods when we increase the number of attributes while retaining the same number of (5) focus attributes for the focused clusters. We observe that FocusCO remains superior to all the other approaches in the face of irrelevant attributes for the clustering task.

To illustrate the importance of weight learning, we also study the performance of a variant of our FocusCO, in which we use a uniform attribute weight vector $\boldsymbol{\beta}$, i.e., we bypass weight learning and directly perform cluster extraction. We observe that the performance of this version of our algorithm drops quickly with increasing attribute size. Our analysis suggests that this occurs due to the edge weights having a more and more uniform distribution when weighted by using a uniform $\boldsymbol{\beta}$, which yields an inferior collection of

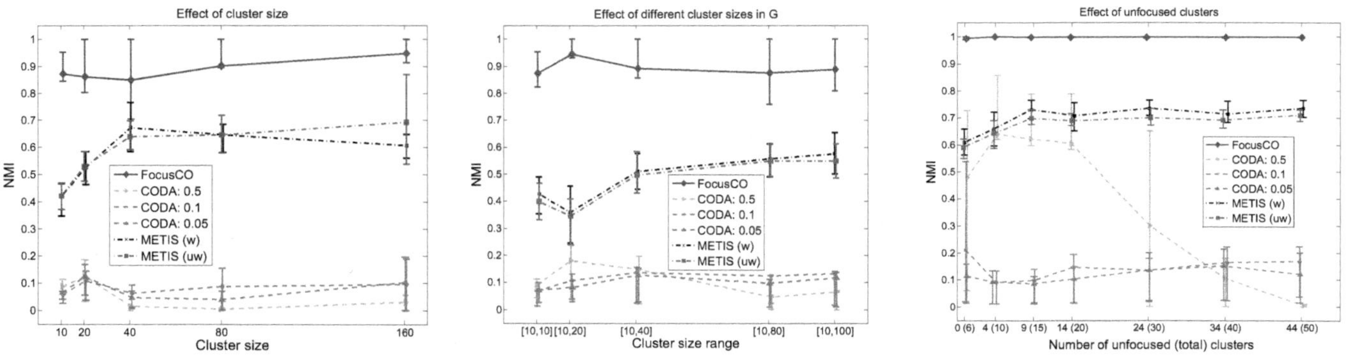

(a) NMI vs. cluster size (b) NMI vs. variable cluster size (c) NMI vs. number of unfocused clusters

Figure 3: NMI clustering quality results on synthetic graphs, for FocusCO, CODA with three different λ parameter settings, and METIS on un/weighted graphs; (a) for changing cluster sizes (all clusters have the same size), (b) for changing cluster size variance (graph has variable size clusters), and (c) for increasing number of unfocused clusters. FocusCO performs the best in all scenarios across a wide range of settings. Symbols depict the mean over 100 runs, bars depict 25-75%.

core sets around which we find clusters. Thus, we proceed with studying the performance of our original FocusCO.

Next in Figure 3 we show the clustering performance of the methods under various other settings. In (a), we increase the cluster size where we create clusters of the same size in the graph. In (b), we allow the graph to contain variable size clusters and increase the variance of the cluster sizes, by randomly drawing them from increasing ranges. Finally in (c), we increase the number of unfocused clusters in the graph, while keeping the number of focused clusters fixed.[6] Notice that recovering a few focused clusters of interest in the existence of more unfocused clusters is an increasingly challenging problem.

From all these setups, we observe that FocusCO outperforms the competing methods and their variants in all scenarios. Weighted METIS seems to achieve slightly better performance than the unweighted version, although the differences are not significant. CODA's accuracy is the lowest, as the homophily assumption it is making does not hold in the full attribute space. We note that in (c), one parameterization of CODA ($\lambda = 0.5$) achieves as high accuracy as METIS for small number of clusters. Its accuracy, however, quickly drops when many more unfocused clusters than focused ones are introduced. Other two parameterizations give low accuracy, pointing out the sensitivity of CODA to the choice of its parameter.

Finally, we study the clustering performance when focus-1 and focus-2 clusters share common focus attributes. We create 20 node attributes out of which the first 10 are assigned as focus-1 attributes and the next 10 are assigned as focus-2 attributes to the respective clusters. Then, we gradually overlap the focus attributes until they are the same set of 10 for all the focused clusters. Figure 4 shows that the performance of FocusCO remains stable and high across all overlaps. The accuracy of METIS (w) is also quite stable and stays around 0.6 (METIS (uw) is not expected to be affected in this setup). We also notice that CODA's performance starts increasing after more than 50% of the focus attributes overlap. At 100%, there is essentially only a single focus in the graph, where CODA's performance peaks. This suggests that CODA is more suitable for attributed graphs with uniform graph clusters and would suffer when the graph contains many heterogeneous focused clusters (with multiple focuses) as we would expect to see in real networks.

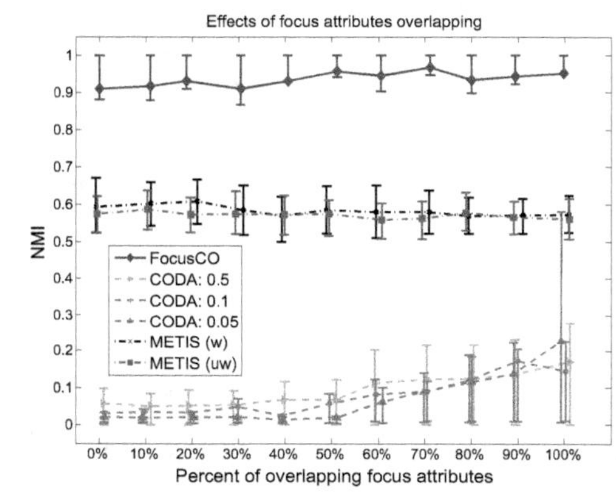

Figure 4: Clustering performance by increasing overlap on focus attributes of different focused clusters. (mean NMI over 100 runs, bars: 25-75%).

These results show the robustness of FocusCO, where its performance remains quite stable across different settings. They also illustrate that the general graph clustering methods are not suitable for our focused clustering problem, as their performance is (*i*) sensitive to the (parameter) setting, and (*ii*) lower than that of FocusCO at all settings.

4.1.3 Outlier detection

Next we evaluate outlier detection performance. Since METIS does not detect outliers, we compare to CODA. In addition to its λ parameter, CODA expects a parameter r that controls the top percentage of nodes to be returned as outliers. We report experiments for the cross-product of $\lambda = \{0.05, 0.1, 0.5\}$ and $r = \{1\%, 5\%\}$.

In the first setup, we study the performance with respect to the severity of outliers. If an outlier deviates in a larger number of focus attributes from its cluster members, it becomes more severe in outlierness, but easier to detect. To create outlier nodes with higher outlierness, we gradually in-

[6] To ensure sparsity of the growing graphs, we set $p_{ij} = 0.02$.

crease their number of focus attributes that we deflate. Figure 5 shows the F1-score and precision (averaged over 100 runs). We observe that FocusCO achieves superior performance to CODA in both metrics. We can also notice the increase in detection accuracy of FocusCO with increasing number of deflated focus attributes (i.e., increasing ease in spotting outliers), as we expected, while the same trend is not apparent for CODA potentially because it does not calibrate to attribute subspaces.

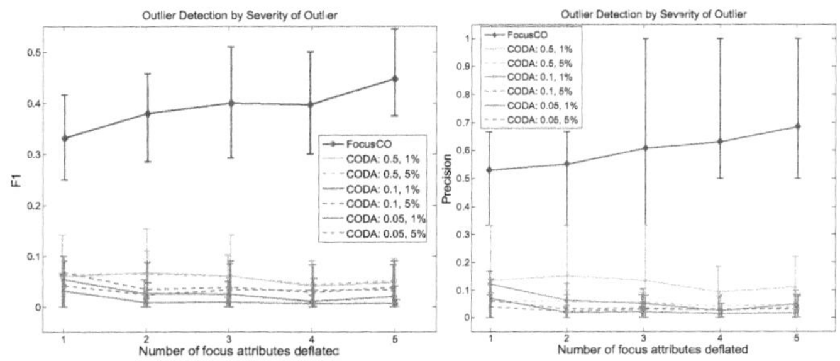

(a) F1-score (b) precision

Figure 5: Outlier detection performance by increasing number of deflated focus attributes.

We further analyze the outlier detection accuracy with respect to the attribute space size. In Figure 6 we observe that CODA's performance starts dropping after a certain number of attributes, where identifying descriptive focus attributes becomes more and more crucial to accurately spot the outliers that are hidden in different community structures. The performance of FocusCO on the other hand remains quite stable and superior to CODA.

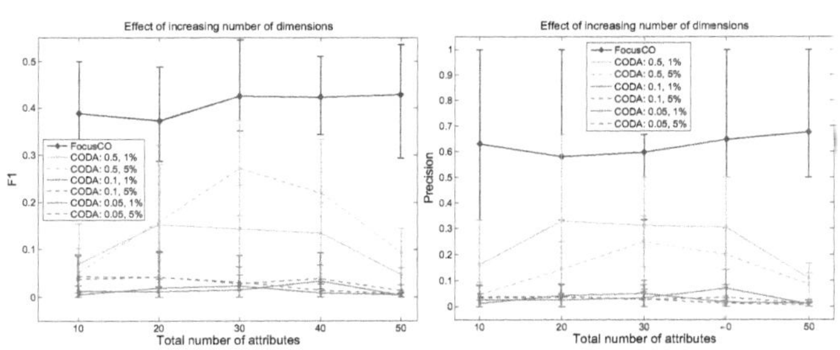

(a) F1-score (b) precision

Figure 6: Outlier detection performance by increasing number of attributes $|F|$.

Finally, we note that the precision of FocusCO is often higher than its recall, while both being superior to CODA's.

4.1.4 *Scalability*

Finally we study the scalability of the methods. Figure 7 shows the running times with increasing number of edges and attributes. CODA's inference techniques are computationally demanding, and thus, its running time is much higher than other methods. METIS on the other hand uses an extremely efficient heuristic and achieves low running times. We report the average cluster extraction time for FocusCO in addition to total running time, as each cluster extraction can be performed in parallel. In fact, we notice that while its total running time increases by graph size, average time to extract a single cluster remains stable and low. In such a case, FocusCO is also comparable to METIS.

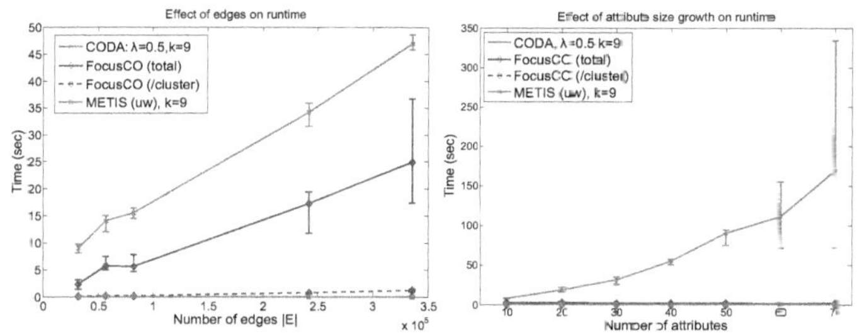

(a) time vs. #edges (b) time vs #attributes

Figure 7: Running time scalability w.r.t. (a) number of edges $|E|$ and (b) number of attributes $|F|$

4.2 Results on Real-world Graphs

4.2.1 *Dataset description*

We use several attributed networks obtained from real-world data to evaluate our approach. Disney is an *Amazon* co-purchase graph of Disney movies.[7] Each movie has 28 attributes such as price, rating, number of reviews, etc. PolBlogs is the citation network among a collection of online blogs that discuss political issues. Attributes are the keywords in their text. DBLP and 4Area are two different co-authorship networks of computer science authors. The attributes reflect the conferences which an author has published in broadly (DBLP), or just in databases, data mining, information retrieval, and machine learning (4Area). Finally, we have the friendship relations of YouTube users and the attributes depict their group memberships. Dataset statistics are given in Table 2.

Table 2: Real-world datasets used in this work. Average running time in seconds per cluster ± std (avg. number of clusters extracted).

Dataset	$\|V\|$	$\|E\|$	$\|F\|$	Running time (sec)
Disney	124	333	28	0.0017 ± 0.0022 (8.3)
PolBlogs	362	1288	44839	0.0040 ± 0.0052 (2.8)
4Area	27199	66832	4	0.0052 ± 0.0018 (3390.9)
DBLP	30599	146647	18	0.2868 ± 0.0630 (761.4)
YouTube	77381	367151	30087	2.9643 ± 0.7201 (257.4)

4.2.2 *Running time*

Our real datasets come from various domains and have different node, edge, and attribute counts. Here we report running time experiments to demonstrate the efficiency of our method on these real graphs.

We setup 10 runs of our method on each graph, each with a randomly sampled 1% of the attributes as the focus attributes. Each run returns a different number of clusters, thus we report the running time per cluster averaged over the 10 runs and their standard deviations in Table 2. Notice that similar to Figure 7, the running times are quite low. In particular, the average time to extract a cluster in our largest graph YouTube takes around 3 seconds.

4.2.3 *Case Studies*

The first case study we consider is finding two types of focused clusters in Disney. In one instance, a user wants to understand how the popularity of a movie influences its

[7]http://www.ipd.kit.edu/~muellere/consub/

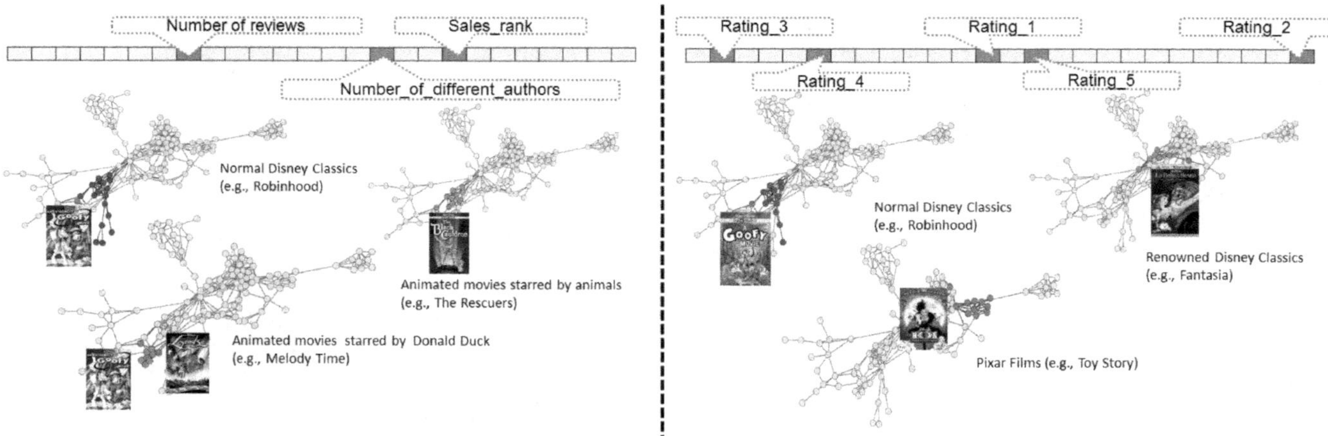

Figure 8: Two sets of focused clusters in Disney. Left clusters focus on attributes related to popularity (sales rank, number of reviews, etc.) Nodes in right clusters share similar ratings. Outliers are marked with red and illustrated. See text for discussion. (best viewed in color)

community in a co-purchase network. The user decides that the product's popularity is related to the features `Number_of_reviews` and `Sales_rank`, and so chooses a few products which have similar values in those attributes. FocusCO then uses this exemplar set C_{ex} to learn an attribute weighting $\boldsymbol{\beta_u}$. This $\boldsymbol{\beta_u}$ reflects the user's intent, and has also captured another dimension correlated with those attributes; `Number_of_different_authors`.

Several extracted focused clusters for this task are shown on the left in Figure 8. In general, the discovered clusters consist of movies of similar age and acclaim. The first focused cluster (blue) reflects traditional Disney classics such as `Robinhood`. Its outlier is a sequel (`An Extremely Goofy Movie`) that is much less popular than the other classics in the cluster. The second community (green) focuses on popular older Disney movies, and has outliers such as `American Legends` and again the Goofy sequel, that are much less popular. The third cluster (orange) *overlaps* with the first focused cluster. It is a subset of the classic Disney movies of the larger cluster that were predominantly starred by animals (e.g., `The Rescuers`). Its cluster outlier is `The Black Caldron`, which although of similar vintage, starred a human protagonist and was much less popular.

In the next instance, a user wants to examine how the differences in the distribution of consumer ratings affect the Disney clustering. In this case, the focused clusters represent collections of movies that are similarly rated (e.g., Pixar films or animated Disney classics). The outliers represent movies which are rated differently from the movies they are purchased with, and reflect consumer opinion. The results are shown in the right of Figure 8. The first focused cluster (purple) represents traditional Disney classics. Its outlier (which was included in the previous focused popularity cluster) is the movie `A Goofy Movie` which although reasonably popular, is not as high rated. The second cluster (green) is the Pixar community, featuring high-rated movies like `Toy Story`. Its focused outlier is the live action version of `101 Dalmatians`, a movie which is rated quite differently than most Pixar films. The third cluster consists of renowned Disney films such as `Fantasia`. It also contains an outlier, the Spanish version of `Beauty and the Beast`.

We consider a second case study on PolBlogs, where a user seeks to understand the difference between blog content

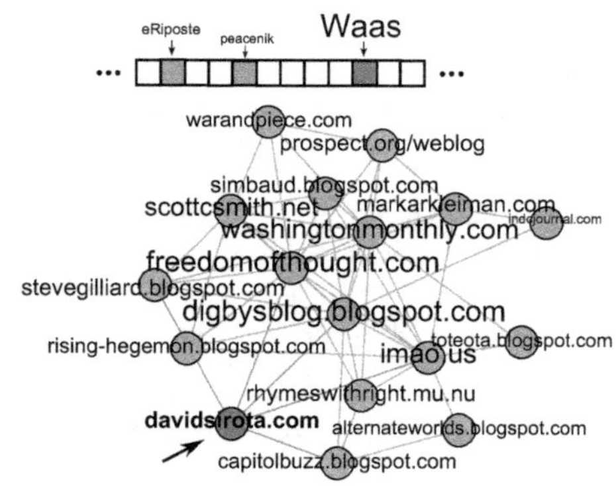

Figure 9: A focused cluster of liberal blogs in PolBlogs with a focus on Iraq war debate. Outlier `David Sirota` does not mention `Waas` in his posts.

written by different liberal bloggers during the height of the Iraq war controversy in 2005. Using several liberal blogs as an example set, the user learns a $\boldsymbol{\beta_u}$ which represents the focus of the bloggers (as shown in the top of Figure 9, text size of features proportional to weight). It contains words such as `eriposte`, an active liberal blogger, `peacenik`, a term for an anti-war activist, and most strongly `Waas`. Murray Waas was an independent journalist praised for his investigative journalism of the Bush administration.[8] The focused community outlier for this group is David Sirota, a well-connected liberal blogger who did not explicitly mention Waas in the dataset.

The third case study we consider is on the 4Area dataset. Here a user wants to understand who the outliers are in the data mining co-authorship network. S/he learns a $\boldsymbol{\beta_u}$ using `{Christos Faloutsos, Jiawei Han, Jon M. Kleinberg, Jure Leskovec, Andrew Tomkins}` as input, who focus primarily on data mining. One of the focused clusters found is around data mining researchers mostly in industry, as shown in Figure 10. The outlier is `Cameron Marlow`, the former head of Facebook's data science team, who collaborated with the researchers in the data mining community but published on information retrieval.

[8]`http://www.huffingtonpost.com/jay-rosen/murray-waas-is-the-woodwa_b_18875.html`

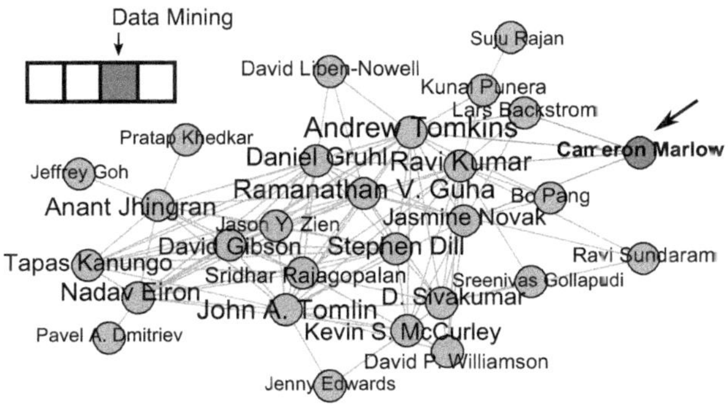

Figure 10: A focused cluster of data mining researchers in 4Area. Outlier Cameron Marlow closely publishes with them, but on information retrieval.

5. CONCLUSION

In this work we introduce a new problem of finding *focused clusters and outliers* in large attributed graphs.

Given a set of exemplar nodes that capture the user interest, our goal is two-fold: 1) "chop out" clusters of similar nodes that are densely connected and exhibit coherence in a subset of their attributes, called the focus attributes, and 2) identify focused outliers, i.e. nodes that belong to a focused cluster in network structure but show deviance in some focus attribute(s). We propose an efficient algorithm that infers the focus attributes of interest to the user, and that both extracts focused clusters and spots outliers simultaneously. Experiments on synthetic and real-world graphs show the effectiveness and scalability of our approach and that the existing graph clustering and outlier detection techniques are not suitable to handle the newly posed problem.

Acknowledgments

The authors thank the anonymous reviewers for their helpful comments. This material is based upon work supported by the ARO Young Investigator Program grant with Contract No. W911NF-14-1-0029, an ONR SBIR grant under Contract No. N00014-14-P-1155, NSF Grant IIS-1017181, the Stony Brook University Office of Vice President for Research, the Young Investigator Group program of KIT as part of the German Excellence Initiative, and by a postdoctoral fellowship by the Flanders research foundation (FWO). Any findings and conclusions expressed in this material are those of the author(s) and do not necessarily reflect the views of the funding parties.

6. REFERENCES

[1] L. Akoglu, M. McGlohon, and C. Faloutsos. OddBall: Spotting anomalies in weighted graphs. In *PAKDD*, 2010.
[2] L. Akoglu, H. Tong, B. Meeder, and C. Faloutsos. PICS: Parameter-free identification of cohesive subgroups in large attributed graphs. In *SIAM SDM*, pages 439–450, 2012.
[3] R. Andersen, F. Chung, and K. Lang. Local graph partitioning using pagerank vectors. In *FOCS*, 2006.
[4] A. Banerjee, S. Basu, and S. Merugu. Multi-way clustering on relation graphs. In *SIAM SDM*, 2007.
[5] S. Basu, I. Davidson, and K. Wagstaff. *Clustering with Constraints: Algorithms, Applications and Theory.* 2008.
[6] S. Boyd and L. Vandenberghe. *Convex Optimization.* Cambridge University Press, NY, USA, 2004.
[7] D. Chakrabarti, S. Papadimitriou, D. S. Modha, and C. Faloutsos. Fully automatic cross-associations. In *KDD*, pages 79–88, 2004.
[8] A. Clauset. Finding local community structure in networks. *Physical Review E*, 72(2):026132, 2005.
[9] A. Condon and R. M. Karp. Algorithms for graph partitioning on the planted partition model. *Random Struct. Algorithms*, 18(2):116–140, 2001.
[10] I. Dhillon, S. Mallela, and D. Modha. Information-theoretic co-clustering. In *KDD*, 2003.
[11] C. H. Q. Ding, X. He, H. Zha, M. Gu, and H. D. Simon. A min-max cut algorithm for graph partitioning and data clustering. In *ICDM*, 2001.
[12] G. W. Flake, S. Lawrence, and C. L. Giles. Efficient identification of web communities. In *KDD*. 2000.
[13] J. Gao, H. Cheng, and P.-N. Tan. Semi-supervised outlier detection. In *ACM Symp. on Appl. Comp.*, 2006.
[14] J. Gao, F. Liang, W. Fan, C. Wang, Y. Sun, and J. Han. On community outliers and their efficient detection in information networks. In *KDD*, pages 813–822, 2010.
[15] D. F. Gleich and C. Seshadhri. Vertex neighborhoods, low conductance cuts, and good seeds for local community methods. In *KDD*, pages 597–605, 2012.
[16] S. Günnemann, I. Färber, B. Boden, and T. Seidl. Subspace clustering meets dense subgraph mining: A synthesis of two paradigms. In *ICDM*, 2010.
[17] D. Hanisch, A. Zien, R. Zimmer, and T. Lengauer. Co-clustering of biological networks and gene expression data. In *ISMB*, pages 145–154, 2002.
[18] P. Iglesias, E. Müller, F. Laforet, F. Keller, and K. Böhm. Statistical selection of congruent subspaces for outlier detection on attributed graphs. In *ICDM*, 2013.
[19] G. Karypis and V. Kumar. Multilevel algorithms for multi-constraint graph partitioning. In *Proc. of Supercomputing*, pages 1–13, 1998.
[20] B. Long, Z. Zhang, X. Wu, and P. S. Yu. Spectral clustering for multi-type relational data. In *ICML*, 2006.
[21] C. D. Manning, P. Raghavan, and H. Schtze. *Intro to Information Retrieval.* Cambridge University Press, 2008.
[22] F. Moser, R. Colak, A. Rafiey, and M. Ester. Mining cohesive patterns from graphs with feature vectors. In *SDM*, 2009.
[23] E. Müller, P. I. Sanchez, Y. Mülle, and K. Böhm. Ranking outlier nodes in subspaces of attributed graphs. In *ICDE Workshops*, pages 216–222, 2013.
[24] A. Y. Ng, M. I. Jordan, and Y. Weiss. On spectral clustering: Analysis and an algorithm. In *NIPS*, 2001.
[25] C. C. Noble and D. J. Cook. Graph-based anomaly detection. In *KDD*, pages 631–636, 2003.
[26] J. Tang and H. Liu. Unsupervised feature selection for linked social media data. In *KDD*, pages 904–912, 2012.
[27] Y. Tian, R. A. Hankins, and J. M. Patel. Efficient aggregation for graph summarization. In *SIGMOD*, 2008.
[28] H. Tong and C.-Y. Lin. Non-negative residual matrix factorization with application to graph anomaly detection. In *SIAM SDM*, pages 143–153, 2011.
[29] F. Wang and J. Sun. Distance metric learning in data mining. In *SIAM SDM*. Tutorials, 2012.
[30] J. Whang, D. Gleich, and I. Dhillon. Overlapping community detection using seed set expansion. In *CIKM*, pages 2099–2108, 2013.
[31] S. White and P. Smyth. A spectral clustering approach to finding communities in graph. In *SDM*, 2005.
[32] E. P. Xing, A. Y. Ng, M. I. Jordan, and S. J. Russell. Distance metric learning with application to clustering with side-information. In *NIPS*, pages 505–512, 2002.
[33] J. Yang and J. Leskovec. Overlapping community detection at scale: a nonnegative matrix factorization approach. In *WSDM*, pages 587–596, 2013.
[34] Y. Zhou, H. Cheng, and J. X. Yu. Graph clustering based on structural/attribute similarities. *PVLDB*, 2(1):718–729, 2009.

Inside the Atoms: Ranking on a Network of Networks

Jingchao Ni [1], Hanghang Tong [2], Wei Fan [3], and Xiang Zhang [1]
[1]Department of Electrical Engineering and Computer Science, Case Western Reserve University
[2]School of Computing, Informatics, Decision Systems Engineering, Arizona State University
[3]Huawei Noahs Ark Lab
[1]{jingchao.ni, xiang.zhang}@case.edu, [2]htong6@asu.edu, [3]david.fanwei@huawei.com

ABSTRACT

Networks are prevalent and have posed many fascinating research questions. How can we spot similar users, e.g., virtual identical twins, in Cleveland for a New Yorker? Given a query disease, how can we prioritize its candidate genes by incorporating the tissue-specific protein interaction networks of those similar diseases? In most, if not all, of the existing network ranking methods, the nodes are the ranking objects with the finest granularity.

In this paper, we propose a new network data model, a Network of Networks (NoN), where each node of the main network itself can be further represented as another (domain-specific) network. This new data model enables to compare the nodes in a broader context and rank them at a finer granularity. Moreover, such an NoN model enables much more efficient search when the ranking targets reside in a certain domain-specific network. We formulate ranking on NoN as a regularized optimization problem; propose efficient algorithms and provide theoretical analysis, such as optimality, convergence, complexity and equivalence. Extensive experimental evaluations demonstrate the effectiveness and the efficiency of our methods.

Categories and Subject Descriptors

H.2.8 [**Database Management**]: Database Applications—*Data mining*

Keywords

Network of Networks; Ranking; Query

1. INTRODUCTION

How can we spot similar users, e.g., virtual identical twins, in Cleveland for a New Yorker? Given a disease, how can we prioritize its candidate genes by incorporating the tissue-specific protein interaction networks of those similar diseases? Among all the researchers in the area of bioinformatics, who is most likely to collaborate with a given data miner in the near future? In these applications, networks (or graphs[1]) provide a natural data model to capture the relationship among different objects.

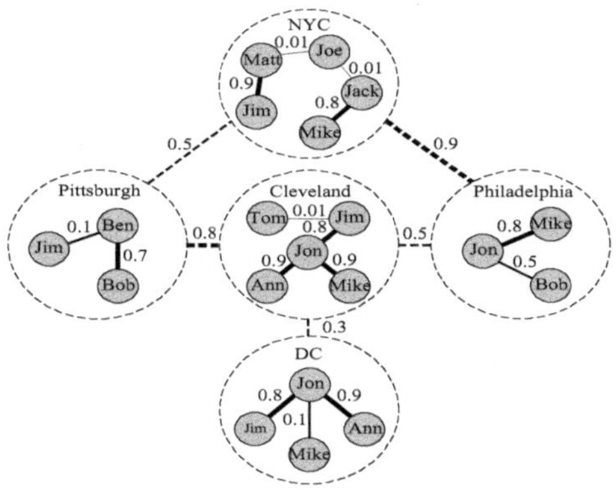

Figure 1: An example of NoN. The main network is represented by dashed nodes and edges. The domain-specific networks are represented by solid nodes and edges.

In the past decade, many graph ranking algorithms have been proposed. Please see Section 6 for a brief review. Despite their own success, a common limitation of these methods is that *ranking stops at the node (atom) level*. That is, the nodes are the ranking objects with the finest granularity in these existing ranking algorithms.

In this paper, we take one step further and propose a new data model - **a Network of Networks (NoN)**. In this NoN model, each node of the main network can be represented as another network. Let us elaborate using the example in Figure 1. Here, the dashed network represents a geo-proximity network (the main network), where the nodes are five different cities and links indicate the geo-proximity among different cities. Each node of this main network is further represented as a social network (the domain-specific network), where nodes are users and links denote their friendship. Collectively, we call this structure as a (geo-proximity) network of (social) networks.

The main advantage of this new NoN model is that it enables to compare the nodes in a broader context and rank them at a finer granularity. Take Figure 1 as the example, using the existing network models, we could either rank the geo-centrality of the cities, or the popularity of the users within each domain-specific network. On the other hand, by the NoN model, we will be able to rank all the users by considering both their popularity within each domain-specific network as well as the geo-centrality of the locations they belong to. We refer to this setting as CROSSRANK. Moreover, we

[1]In this paper, we use network and graph interchangeably.

KDD'14, August 24–27, 2014, New York, NY, USA.

http://dx.doi.org/10.1145/2623330.2623643.

Table 1: Symbols

Symbol	Definition
$\mathbf{G}$	the adjacency matrix of main network
$\mathcal{A}$	domain specific networks $\mathcal{A} = \{\mathbf{A}_1, ..., \mathbf{A}_g\}$
$\mathbf{A}_i$	the ith domain specific network
θ	the one-to-one mapping function
$\mathcal{R}$	a network of networks $\mathcal{R} =< \mathbf{G}, \mathcal{A}, \theta >$
$\mathbf{r}_i$	the ranking vector for $\mathbf{A}_i$
$\mathbf{e}_i$	the ith query vector for $\mathbf{A}_i$
$\mathbf{I}_n$	an $n \times n$ identity matrix
$\mathcal{I}_{ij}$	the set of common nodes between $\mathbf{A}_i$ and $\mathbf{A}_j$
$d_m(i)$	the degree of the ith node in $\mathbf{G}$
$\mathbf{D}_m$	the degree matrix: $\mathbf{D}_m = \text{diag}(d_m(1), ..., d_m(g))$
g	the number of nodes in the main network
n_i	the number of nodes in $\mathbf{A}_i$, $(i = 1, ..., g)$
m_i	the number of edges in $\mathbf{A}_i$, $(i = 1, ..., g)$
c, a	the parameters $0 < c < 1$, and $a > 0$

might be interested in finding who are the most similar from New York City for *Jon* from Cleveland, i.e., who are the virtual identity twins of *Jon* in New York City. In this case, the ranking targets reside in a certain domain-specific network. We refer to this setting as CROSSQUERY. The NoN model will enable much more efficient search for this problem.

The NoN model can be observed in many real-world applications. As another example, consider a NoN, where each node in the main network is a research area, and the domain-specific networks are the co-author networks in different areas. By the NoN model, we can rank authors according to their contributions to multiple areas using CROSSRANK; and find future collaborators for a researcher in a different area using CROSSQUERY.

The main contributions of this paper can be summarized as:

- **New Data Model**. We propose a novel network data model, a network of networks, which enables network ranking to go beyond the atom/node level (Section 2).
- **Algorithms and Analysis**. We propose two new ranking algorithms (CROSSRANK and CROSSQUERY) in NoN and analyze their *optimality*, *convergence*, *complexity* and *relationship* with existing ranking algorithms (Section 3 and 4).
- **Empirical Evaluations**. We perform extensive experiments on real datasets to validate the effectiveness and efficiency of the proposed algorithms (Section 5).

2. PROBLEM DEFINITIONS

Table 1 lists the main symbols used throughout this paper. We use the bold capital letters to denote matrices (e.g., $\mathbf{G}$, $\mathbf{A}$, etc.), the bold lower cases for vectors (e.g., $\mathbf{r}$) and calligraphic letters for sets (e.g., $\mathcal{A}$). In this paper, we consider weighted undirected networks. We denote the networks by their corresponding weighted adjacency matrices. For example, a network with g nodes can be denoted by a $g \times g$ adjacency matrix $\mathbf{G}$. The rows/columns of the matrix $\mathbf{G}$ represents the nodes of the network and its non-zero element $\mathbf{G}(i, j)$ measures the link strength from node i to node j. With the above notations, a network of networks (NoN) can be formally defined as follows.

Definition 1. **Network of Networks (NoN).** Given a $g \times g$ **main** network $\mathbf{G}$, a set of g **domain-specific** networks $\mathcal{A} = \{\mathbf{A}_1, ..., \mathbf{A}_g\}$ and a one-to-one mapping function θ, which maps each node in the main network $\mathbf{G}$ to a domain-specific network, a **Network of Networks (NoN)** is defined as the triplet $\mathcal{R} =< \mathbf{G}, \mathcal{A}, \theta >$. Nodes in the main network are referred to as *main nodes*, nodes in the domain-specific networks are called *domain nodes*. Each main node represents a domain-specific network through the mapping function θ. In addition, we represent the nodes in each domain-specific network as $\mathcal{V}_i (i = 1, ..., g)$. We define $\mathcal{I}_{i,j}$ as the *common nodes* between $\mathbf{A}_i$ and $\mathbf{A}_j$, i.e., $\mathcal{I}_{i,j} = \mathcal{V}_i \cap \mathcal{V}_j$.

Take Figure 1 as an example, the dashed network is the main network $\mathbf{G}$, which has five main nodes, including *NYC, Pittsburgh, Cleveland, Philadelphia, DC*. Each of these main nodes is mapped to a domain-specific network (the solid network). For example, the main node *Pittsburgh* is further represented as a domain-specific network with three nodes, including *Jim, Ben, Bob*.

Given an NoN $\mathcal{R} =< \mathbf{G}, \mathcal{A}, \theta >$, a fundamental task is to compare and rank the nodes in this network. For instance, we might be interested in ranking the importance/popularity of the individuals in each domain-specific network. Further more, given an individual, e.g., *Jim* from *Pittsburgh*, we may also want to find the similar users from *NYC* as well as other cities.

We introduce a query vector $\mathbf{e}_i$ $(i = 1, ..., g)$ for each domain-specific network, which is an $n_i \times 1$ nonnegative vector (n_i represents the number of nodes in the domain-specific network). If we are given a query node of interest from a domain-specific network (e.g., *Jim* from *Pittsburgh*), we set its corresponding entry $\mathbf{e}_i$ to 1, and all other entries to 0. Otherwise, all the entries in $\mathbf{e}_i$ are set to $\frac{1}{n_i}$. Formally, we define the CROSSRANK problem as follows.

PROBLEM 1. CROSSRANK

Given: *(1) an NoN* $\mathcal{R} =< \mathbf{G}, \mathcal{A}, \theta >$, *and (2) the query vectors* $\mathbf{e}_i$ $(i = 1, ..., g)$;

Find: *ranking vectors* $\mathbf{r}_i$ *for the nodes in the domain-specific networks* $\mathbf{A}_i$ $(i = 1, ..., g)$.

In the above definition, when all the query vectors are uniform, i.e., no query node is given, we essentially want to measure and rank the *global importance* of all the domain nodes within each domain-specific network. On the other hand, if a query node is given, we essentially want to measure the *proximity* (i.e., relevance) from the query node to all the domain nodes within each domain specific network. Note that in the latter case, sometimes, we might be interested in ranking domain nodes from a particular domain-specific network. For instance, given *Jim* from *Pittsburgh*, we might want to find out the top-3 most similar users from *NYC*. We call this special case of CROSSRANK as CROSSQUERY, which is formally defined as follows.

PROBLEM 2. CROSSQUERY

Given: *(1) an NoN* $\mathcal{R} =< \mathbf{G}, \mathcal{A}, \theta >$, *(2) a query node of interest from a* source *domain-specific network* $\mathbf{A}_s$, *(3) a* target *domain-specific network* $\mathbf{A}_d$, *and (4) an integer k,*

Find: *the top-k most relevant nodes from the* target *domain-specific network* $\mathbf{A}_d$ *w.r.t. the query node.*

In the next two sections, we give our solutions for CROSSRANK and CROSSQUERY, respectively.

3. CROSSRANK

In this section, we present our solution to CROSSRANK. We start with formulating it as a regularized optimization problem, then present an effective algorithm to solve it, followed by some theoretical analysis.

3.1 Optimization Formulation

The basic idea of our method is to formulate CROSSRANK as a regularized optimization problem by encoding the following three types of constrains. (1) *Within-network smoothness*: for a given domain-specific network $\mathbf{A}_i$, the ranking scores among the neighboring nodes should be somehow smooth. That is, for any two adjacent nodes x, y on $\mathbf{A}_i$, we want to minimize the difference of the rank scores between them, i.e., $(\mathbf{r}_i(x) - \mathbf{r}_i(y))^2$. (2) *Query preference*: the ranking vector $\mathbf{r}_i$ should also reflect the preference of the specific query node of interest from the corresponding domain-specific network. That is, we want to minimize the difference between the ranking vector $\mathbf{r}_i$ and the corresponding query vector $\mathbf{e}_i$. (3) *Cross-network consistency*: for a pair of domain-specific networks $\mathbf{A}_i$ and $\mathbf{A}_j$ that are connected with each other by the main network (i.e., $\mathbf{G}(i, j) > 0$), they may share some common nodes, i.e., $\mathcal{I}_{ij} = \mathcal{V}_i \cap \mathcal{V}_j$ is non-empty. In this case, those common nodes will receive multiple ranking scores (one from each ranking vector). Intuitively, the ranking scores for the same node should be consistent across highly similar domain-specific networks. In other words, we want to minimize the difference between $\mathbf{r}_i(\mathcal{I}_{ij})$ and $\mathbf{r}_j(\mathcal{I}_{ij})$. Here $\mathbf{r}_i(\mathcal{I}_{ij})$ can be viewed as the projection of the entire ranking vector $\mathbf{r}_i$ on the common node set $\mathcal{I}_{ij}$.

Putting everything together, we have the following regularized objective function $J(\mathbf{r}_1, ..., \mathbf{r}_g)$. The optimal ranking vectors $\mathbf{r}_i$ ($i = 1, ..., g$) are those minimize the objective function.

$$\mathrm{J}(\mathbf{r}_1, ..., \mathbf{r}_g) = c \underbrace{\sum_{i=1}^{g} \mathbf{r}_i'(\mathbf{I}_{n_i} - \tilde{\mathbf{A}}_i)\mathbf{r}_i}_{within-network\ smoothness} + (1-c) \underbrace{\sum_{i=1}^{g} \|\mathbf{r}_i - \mathbf{e}_i\|_F^2}_{query\ preference} + \underbrace{a \sum_{i=1}^{g}\sum_{j=1}^{g} \|\frac{\mathbf{r}_i(\mathcal{I}_{ij})}{\sqrt{d_m(i)}} - \frac{\mathbf{r}_j(\mathcal{I}_{ij})}{\sqrt{d_m(j)}}\|_F^2 \mathbf{G}(i, j)}_{cross-network\ consistency} \quad (1)$$

where $\|\cdot\|_F$ denotes the Frobenius norm; $\tilde{\mathbf{A}}_i$ is the symmetrically normalized adjacency matrix of $\mathbf{A}_i$; and a and c are two regularization parameters. Note that the length of different ranking vectors could be different and all entries of a given ranking vector $\mathbf{r}_i$ add up to 1. To make the ranking scores comparable with each other for the common nodes, we normalize $\mathbf{r}_i(\mathcal{I}_{ij})$ and $\mathbf{r}_j(\mathcal{I}_{ij})$ by their corresponding degrees in the main networks, respectively.

Discussions. If we ignore the third term (cross-network consistency) in Eq. (1), we can show that the objective function $J(\mathbf{r}_1, ..., \mathbf{r}_g)$ can be decoupled into g independent terms. Each of these terms becomes the same objective function of a popular ranking method on homogeneous network - random walk with restart (also called manifold ranking, the personalized pagerank, etc.) [33, 26]. From this perspective, what we essentially aim to do in Eq. (1) is to solve multiple, inter-correlated such ranking problems simultaneously.

3.2 Optimization Solutions

We first present an equivalent formulation of Eq. (1). Denote the aggregated ranking vector $\mathbf{r} = (\mathbf{r}_1', ..., \mathbf{r}_g')'$, the aggregated query vector $\mathbf{e} = (\mathbf{e}_1', ..., \mathbf{e}_g')'$. Let the aggregated adjacency matrix $\tilde{\mathbf{A}} = \mathrm{diag}(\tilde{\mathbf{A}}_1, ..., \tilde{\mathbf{A}}_g)$ be a $g \times g$ diagonal block matrix, $\mathbf{O}_{ij}$ be an $n_i \times n_j$ binary indicator matrix with $\mathbf{O}_{ij}(x, y) = 1$ if the xth node in $\mathbf{A}_i$ is the yth node in $\mathbf{A}_j$, i.e., common node. Then $\mathbf{O}$ is a block matrix whose $(i, j)^{\text{th}}$ block is $\mathbf{G}(i, j)\mathbf{O}_{ij}$.

Since $\mathbf{O}$ may be singular due to zero-rows/columns, we define $\mathbf{Y} = \mathbf{O} + \mathbf{D}_T$, where $\mathbf{D}_T = \mathrm{diag}(d_m(1)\mathbf{I}_{n_1}, ..., d_m(g)\mathbf{I}_{n_g}) - \mathbf{D}_O$ with $\mathbf{I}_{n_i} (1 \le i \le g)$ being an $n_i \times n_i$ identity matrix and $\mathbf{D}_O$ being the degree matrix of $\mathbf{O}$. $\mathbf{Y}$ is non-singular. The $(i, i)^{th}$ block of $\mathbf{D}_Y$ (i.e., $\mathbf{Y}$'s degree matrix) equals $d_m(i)\mathbf{I}_{n_i}$. Finally, we define $\mathbf{X} = \mathbf{D}_Y^{-\frac{1}{2}}(\mathbf{D}_Y - \mathbf{Y})\mathbf{D}_Y^{-\frac{1}{2}} = \mathbf{I}_n - \tilde{\mathbf{Y}}$, where $\tilde{\mathbf{Y}} = \mathbf{D}_Y^{-\frac{1}{2}}\mathbf{Y}\mathbf{D}_Y^{-\frac{1}{2}}$.

With these definitions, the objective function in Eq. (1) can be re-written as the following matrix form

$$\mathrm{J}(\mathbf{r}) = c\mathbf{r}'(\mathbf{I}_n - \tilde{\mathbf{A}})\mathbf{r} + (1-c)\|\mathbf{r} - \mathbf{e}\|_F^2 + 2a\mathbf{r}'\mathbf{X}\mathbf{r} \quad (2)$$

where $n = \sum_{i=1}^{g} n_i$ is the total number of nodes in all the domain-specific networks.

LEMMA 1. *Equation* (1) *and Equation* (2) *are equivalent.*

PROOF. We only need to prove that the third term in Eq. (1) is equal to that in Eq. (2).

By the definition of $\mathbf{X}$ and $\mathbf{r}$, we have

$$\mathbf{r}'\mathbf{X}\mathbf{r} = \mathbf{r}'\mathbf{I}_n\mathbf{r} - \mathbf{r}'\tilde{\mathbf{Y}}\mathbf{r} = \sum_{i=1}^{g} \mathbf{r}_i'\mathbf{I}_{n_i}\mathbf{r}_i - \sum_{i=1}^{g}\sum_{j=1}^{g} \mathbf{r}_i'\tilde{\mathbf{Y}}_{ij}\mathbf{r}_j$$

where $\tilde{\mathbf{Y}}_{ij}$ is the $(i, j)^{\text{th}}$ block of $\tilde{\mathbf{Y}}$ of size $n_i \times n_j$. Then

$$\mathbf{r}'\mathbf{X}\mathbf{r} = \frac{1}{2}\Big(\sum_{i=1}^{g} \frac{\mathbf{r}_i'}{\sqrt{d_m(i)}}(\mathbf{D}_Y)_{ii}\frac{\mathbf{r}_i}{\sqrt{d_m(i)}} - 2\sum_{i=1}^{g}\sum_{j=1}^{g} \frac{\mathbf{r}_i'}{\sqrt{d_m(i)}}\mathbf{Y}_{ij}\frac{\mathbf{r}_j}{\sqrt{d_m(j)}} + \sum_{j=1}^{g} \frac{\mathbf{r}_j'}{\sqrt{d_m(j)}}(\mathbf{D}_Y)_{jj}\frac{\mathbf{r}_j}{\sqrt{d_m(j)}}\Big)$$

where $(\mathbf{D}_Y)_{ii}$ is the ith diagonal block of $\mathbf{D}_Y$, and $\mathbf{Y}_{ij}$ is the $(i, j)^{th}$ block of $\mathbf{Y}$. Thus

$$\mathbf{r}'\mathbf{X}\mathbf{r} = \frac{1}{2}\Big(\sum_{i=1}^{g}(\frac{\mathbf{r}_i'}{\sqrt{d_m(i)}}(\mathbf{D}_O)_{ii}\frac{\mathbf{r}_i}{\sqrt{d_m(i)}} + \frac{\mathbf{r}_i'}{\sqrt{d_m(i)}}(\mathbf{D}_T)_{ii}\frac{\mathbf{r}_i}{\sqrt{d_m(i)}}) - 2\sum_{i=1}^{g}\sum_{j=1}^{g}(\frac{\mathbf{r}_i'}{\sqrt{d_m(i)}}\mathbf{G}(i, j)\mathbf{O}_{ij}\frac{\mathbf{r}_j}{\sqrt{d_m(j)}} + \frac{\mathbf{r}_i'}{\sqrt{d_m(i)}}(\mathbf{D}_T)_{ij}\frac{\mathbf{r}_j}{\sqrt{d_m(j)}}) + \sum_{j=1}^{g}(\frac{\mathbf{r}_j'}{\sqrt{d_m(j)}}(\mathbf{D}_O)_{jj}\frac{\mathbf{r}_j}{\sqrt{d_m(j)}} + \frac{\mathbf{r}_j'}{\sqrt{d_m(j)}}(\mathbf{D}_T)_{jj}\frac{\mathbf{r}_j}{\sqrt{d_m(j)}})\Big)$$

where $(\mathbf{D}_T)_{ij}$, $(\mathbf{D}_O)_{ij}$ and $\mathbf{O}_{ij}$ are block matrices representing $(i, j)^{th}$ block of $\mathbf{D}_T$, $\mathbf{D}_O$ and $\mathbf{O}$, respectively. Since $\mathbf{D}_T$ is a diagonal block matrix, we have

$$2\sum_{i=1}^{g}\sum_{j=1}^{g} \frac{\mathbf{r}_i'}{\sqrt{d_m(i)}}(\mathbf{D}_T)_{ij}\frac{\mathbf{r}_j}{\sqrt{d_m(j)}} = 2\sum_{i=1}^{g} \frac{\mathbf{r}_i'}{\sqrt{d_m(i)}}(\mathbf{D}_T)_{ii}\frac{\mathbf{r}_i}{\sqrt{d_m(i)}}$$

and

$$\sum_{i=1}^{g} \frac{\mathbf{r}_i'}{\sqrt{d_m(i)}}(\mathbf{D}_T)_{ii}\frac{\mathbf{r}_i}{\sqrt{d_m(i)}} - 2\sum_{i=1}^{g}\sum_{j=1}^{g} \frac{\mathbf{r}_i'}{\sqrt{d_m(i)}}(\mathbf{D}_T)_{ij}\frac{\mathbf{r}_j}{\sqrt{d_m(j)}} + \sum_{j=1}^{g} \frac{\mathbf{r}_j'}{\sqrt{d_m(j)}}(\mathbf{D}_T)_{jj}\frac{\mathbf{r}_j}{\sqrt{d_m(j)}} = 0$$

This means $\mathbf{D}_T$ does not affect the ranking results. Therefore, we have that

$$\begin{aligned}\mathbf{r}'\mathbf{X}\mathbf{r} &= \frac{1}{2}\sum_{i=1}^{g}\sum_{j=1}^{g}\mathbf{G}(i, j)\Big(\frac{\mathbf{r}_i'(\mathcal{I}_{ij})}{\sqrt{d_m(i)}}\frac{\mathbf{r}_i(\mathcal{I}_{ij})}{\sqrt{d_m(i)}} - 2\frac{\mathbf{r}_i'(\mathcal{I}_{ij})}{\sqrt{d_m(i)}}\frac{\mathbf{r}_j(\mathcal{I}_{ij})}{\sqrt{d_m(j)}} + \frac{\mathbf{r}_j'(\mathcal{I}_{ij})}{\sqrt{d_m(j)}}\frac{\mathbf{r}_j(\mathcal{I}_{ij})}{\sqrt{d_m(j)}}\Big) \\ &= \frac{1}{2}\sum_{i=1}^{g}\sum_{j=1}^{g}\mathbf{G}(i, j)\|\frac{\mathbf{r}_i(\mathcal{I}_{ij})}{\sqrt{d_m(i)}} - \frac{\mathbf{r}_j(\mathcal{I}_{ij})}{\sqrt{d_m(j)}}\|_F^2\end{aligned}$$

This completes the proof. □

Algorithm 1: CROSSRANK

Input: (1) a network of networks $\mathcal{R} =< \mathbf{G}, \mathcal{A}, \theta >$; (2) the query vectors $\mathbf{e}_i$, $(i = 1, ..., g)$; and (3) the parameters a and c

Output: the ranking vectors $\mathbf{r}_i$, $(i = 1, ..., g)$

Offline-computation: Construct $\tilde{\mathbf{A}}$ and $\tilde{\mathbf{Y}}$ from $\mathcal{R}$;
Online-ranking:
Construct the aggregated query vector $\mathbf{e} = (\mathbf{e}'_1, ..., \mathbf{e}'_g)'$;
Initialize the aggregated ranking vector $\mathbf{r} = \mathbf{e}$;
while *not convergence* **do**
  Update: $\mathbf{r} \leftarrow (\frac{c}{1+2a}\tilde{\mathbf{A}} + \frac{2a}{1+2a}\tilde{\mathbf{Y}})\mathbf{r} + \frac{1-c}{1+2a}\mathbf{e}$;
end
return the ranking vectors $\mathbf{r}_1, ..., \mathbf{r}_g$ based on $\mathbf{r}$

From Eq. (2), it can be seen that the objective function J is a quadratic function of the ranking vector $\mathbf{r}$. We have

$$\frac{\partial J}{\partial \mathbf{r}} = 2((1+2a)\mathbf{I}_n - c\tilde{\mathbf{A}} - 2a\tilde{\mathbf{Y}})\mathbf{r} - 2(1-c)\mathbf{e}$$

If we set $\mathbf{r} = \mathbf{r} - \eta\frac{\partial J}{\partial \mathbf{r}}$, where $\eta = \frac{1}{2+4a}$, we have

$$\mathbf{r} = (\frac{c}{1+2a}\tilde{\mathbf{A}} + \frac{2a}{1+2a}\tilde{\mathbf{Y}})\mathbf{r} + \frac{1-c}{1+2a}\mathbf{e} \quad (3)$$

Based on Eq. (3), we have a fixed-point approach to compute the optimal ranking vector $\mathbf{r}$ that minimizes the objective function $J(\mathbf{r})$ as illustrated in Algorithm 1.

3.3 Proofs and Analysis

In this subsection, we analyze Algorithm 1 in terms of its *convergence*, *optimality*, *complexity* and discuss its *relationship* with existing ranking algorithms.

We start with the the convergence of Algorithm 1, which is summarized in Theorem 1. It says that the proposed CROSSRANK algorithm converges to its closed-form solution.

THEOREM 1. ***Convergence of* CROSSRANK.** *Algorithm 1 converges to the closed-form solution:* $\mathbf{r} = (\mathbf{I}_n - \frac{c}{1+2a}\tilde{\mathbf{A}} - \frac{2a}{1+2a}\tilde{\mathbf{Y}})^{-1}\frac{1-c}{1+2a}\mathbf{e}$.

PROOF. First, the closed-form solution can be obtained by solving $\frac{\partial J}{\partial \mathbf{r}} = 0$. Then let $\mathbf{M} = \frac{c}{1+2a}\tilde{\mathbf{A}} + \frac{2a}{1+2a}\tilde{\mathbf{Y}}$. Eq. (3) becomes $\mathbf{r} = \mathbf{M}\mathbf{r} + \frac{1-c}{1+2a}\mathbf{e}$. Next, we show that the eigenvalues of $\mathbf{M}$ are in $(-1, 1)$.

Since $\tilde{\mathbf{A}}$ and $\tilde{\mathbf{Y}}$ are similar to the stochastic matrices $\mathbf{A}\mathbf{D}_A^{-1} = \mathbf{D}_A^{\frac{1}{2}}\tilde{\mathbf{A}}\mathbf{D}_A^{-\frac{1}{2}}$ and $\mathbf{Y}\mathbf{D}_Y^{-1} = \mathbf{D}_Y^{\frac{1}{2}}\tilde{\mathbf{Y}}\mathbf{D}_Y^{-\frac{1}{2}}$, respectively, both $\tilde{\mathbf{A}}$ and $\tilde{\mathbf{Y}}$ have eigenvalues within $[-1, 1]$.

One result of the Weyl's inequality theorem [1] states that for matrices $\hat{\mathbf{H}}, \mathbf{H}, \mathbf{P} \in \mathcal{H}_n$, where $\mathcal{H}_n$ is the set of $n \times n$ Hermitian matrices, if $\hat{\mathbf{H}} = \mathbf{H} + \mathbf{P}$ and their eigenvalues are arranged in non-increasing orders, i.e., $\lambda_1(\hat{\mathbf{H}}) \geq ... \geq \lambda_n(\hat{\mathbf{H}})$, $\lambda_1(\mathbf{H}) \geq ... \geq \lambda_n(\mathbf{H})$, $\lambda_1(\mathbf{P}) \geq ... \geq \lambda_n(\mathbf{P})$, then the following inequalities hold:

$$\lambda_n(\mathbf{P}) \leq \lambda_i(\hat{\mathbf{H}}) - \lambda_i(\mathbf{H}) \leq \lambda_1(\mathbf{P}), \forall i = 1, ..., n$$

Since $\tilde{\mathbf{A}}, \tilde{\mathbf{Y}}, \mathbf{M} \in \mathcal{H}_n$ and $\mathbf{M} = \frac{c}{1+2a}\tilde{\mathbf{A}} + \frac{2a}{1+2a}\tilde{\mathbf{Y}}$, we have

$$\lambda_1(\mathbf{M}) \leq \frac{c}{1+2a}\lambda_1(\tilde{\mathbf{A}}) + \frac{2a}{1+2a}\lambda_1(\tilde{\mathbf{Y}})$$
$$\lambda_n(\mathbf{M}) \geq \frac{c}{1+2a}\lambda_n(\tilde{\mathbf{A}}) + \frac{2a}{1+2a}\lambda_n(\tilde{\mathbf{Y}})$$

which means the eigenvalues of $\mathbf{M}$ are in the range of $[-\frac{c+2a}{1+2a}, \frac{c+2a}{1+2a}]$. Since $0 < c < 1$, the eigenvalues of $\mathbf{M}$ are in $(-1, 1)$.

Based on this property, we can show the convergence of the fixed-point approach. Without loss of generality, let $\mathbf{r}^{(0)} = \mathbf{e}$, and t be the iteration index $(t \geq 1)$. According to Eq. (3), we have

$$\mathbf{r}^{(t)} = \mathbf{M}^t\mathbf{e} + \sum_{i=0}^{t-1}\mathbf{M}^i\frac{1-c}{1+2a}\mathbf{e}$$

Since the eigenvalues of $\mathbf{M}$ are all in $(-1, 1)$, we have

$$\lim_{t\to\infty}\mathbf{M}^t = 0, \text{and} \lim_{t\to\infty}\sum_{i=0}^{t-1}\mathbf{M}^i = (\mathbf{I}_n - \mathbf{M})^{-1}$$

Therefore

$$\mathbf{r} = \lim_{t\to\infty}\mathbf{r}^{(t)} = (\mathbf{I}_n - \mathbf{M})^{-1}\frac{1-c}{1+2a}\mathbf{e}$$
$$= (\mathbf{I}_n - \frac{c}{1+2a}\tilde{\mathbf{A}} - \frac{2a}{1+2a}\tilde{\mathbf{Y}})^{-1}\frac{1-c}{1+2a}\mathbf{e}$$

which is the closed-form solution. □

Next, we show in Lemma 2 that Algorithm 1 finds the *global optimal* solution of the objective function $J(\mathbf{r})$ defined in Eq. (2).

LEMMA 2. ***Optimality of* CROSSRANK.** *At convergence, Algorithm 1 finds the global minimal solution of $J(\mathbf{r})$ defined in Eq. (2)*

PROOF. This can be proved by showing that the function in Eq. (2) is convex. The Hessian matrix of Eq. (2) is $\nabla^2 J = 2((1+2a)\mathbf{I}_n - c\tilde{\mathbf{A}} - 2a\tilde{\mathbf{Y}})$. Following the similar idea as in the proof of Theorem 1, we have that the eigenvalues of $\nabla^2 J$ are no less than $2(1-c)$. Since $0 < c < 1$, $\nabla^2 J$ is positive-definite. Therefore, Eq. (2) is convex. □

The complexity of Algorithm 1 is summarized in Lemma 3, which says that it is *linear* w.r.t. the overall number of nodes and edges in NoN in terms of both space and time cost.

LEMMA 3. ***Complexity of* CROSSRANK.** *The time complexity of Algorithm 1 is $O(T^*(m + ng))$ and its space complexity is $O(m + n)$, where $m = \sum_{i=1}^{g} m_i$, $n = \sum_{i=1}^{g} n_i$, and T^* is the total iteration number.*

PROOF. In the preprocessing stage, we need to construct $\tilde{\mathbf{A}}$ and $\tilde{\mathbf{Y}}$. The construction time of $\tilde{\mathbf{A}}$ is $O(m)$, since there are $O(m)$ nonzero entries in $\tilde{\mathbf{A}}$. The construction time of $\tilde{\mathbf{Y}}$ is $O(gn)$, since the nonzero entries of $\tilde{\mathbf{Y}}$ are pairwise intersection of node lists of all the domain-specific networks, i.e., $\sum_{i=1}^{g} gn_i = gn$. Therefore, preprocessing cost is $O(m + gn)$. The online-computation cost depends on the fix-point updating step in Eq. (3). Since there are $O(m+gn)$ nonzero entries in $\frac{c}{1+2a}\tilde{\mathbf{A}} + \frac{2a}{1+2a}\tilde{\mathbf{Y}}$, the online-computation cost is $O(T^*(m+gn))$. In Algorithm 1, we need to store $\tilde{\mathbf{A}}$ and $\tilde{\mathbf{Y}}$, with space complexity $O(m+gn)$. Usually g is much smaller than n, we can regard time and space complexities as $O(T^*(m+n))$ and $O(m+n)$ respectively. □

Finally, we show the relationship between the proposed CROSSRANK algorithm and random walk with restart (RWR).

LEMMA 4. ***Relationship between* CROSSRANK *and RWR.*** *CROSSRANK fixed-point approach is equivalent to random walk with restart with the transition matrix $\tilde{\mathbf{W}} = \frac{c}{c+2a}\tilde{\mathbf{A}} + \frac{2a}{c+2a}\mathbf{Y}\mathbf{D}_Y^{-1}$ if $\tilde{\mathbf{A}}$ is stochastic.*

PROOF. Let $\tilde{c} = \frac{c+2a}{1+2a}$ and $\mathbf{W} = \frac{c}{c+2a}\tilde{\mathbf{A}} + \frac{2a}{c+2a}\tilde{\mathbf{Y}}$, we can transform Eq. (3) to

$$\mathbf{r} = \tilde{c}\mathbf{W}\mathbf{r} + (1-\tilde{c})\mathbf{e} \quad (4)$$

and the closed-form solution of Eq. (2) to

$$\mathbf{r} = (\mathbf{I}_n - \tilde{c}\mathbf{W})^{-1}(1-\tilde{c})\mathbf{e} \quad (5)$$

These formulations have a RWR form except that $\mathbf{W}$ is not stochastic, since $\tilde{\mathbf{A}}$ and $\tilde{\mathbf{Y}}$ are symmetrically normalized. If we denote $\tilde{\mathbf{W}} = \frac{c}{c+2a}\tilde{\mathbf{A}} + \frac{2a}{c+2a}\mathbf{Y}\mathbf{D}_Y^{-1}$, we can further transform the closed-form solution to

$$\begin{aligned}
\mathbf{r} &= (\mathbf{I}_n - \frac{c}{1+2a}\tilde{\mathbf{A}} - \frac{2a}{1+2a}\tilde{\mathbf{Y}})^{-1}\frac{1-c}{1+2a}\mathbf{e} \\
&= \mathbf{D}_Y^{-\frac{1}{2}}(\mathbf{I}_n - \frac{c}{1+2a}\tilde{\mathbf{A}} - \frac{2a}{1+2a}\mathbf{Y}\mathbf{D}_Y^{-1})^{-1}\mathbf{D}_Y^{\frac{1}{2}}\frac{1-c}{1+2a}\mathbf{e} \qquad (6) \\
&= \mathbf{D}_Y^{-\frac{1}{2}}(\mathbf{I}_n - \tilde{c}\tilde{\mathbf{W}})^{-1}\mathbf{D}_Y^{\frac{1}{2}}(1-\tilde{c})\mathbf{e}
\end{aligned}$$

In the above equation, $\mathbf{D}_Y^{\frac{1}{2}}\tilde{\mathbf{A}}\mathbf{D}_Y^{-\frac{1}{2}} = \tilde{\mathbf{A}}$ since $\mathbf{D}_Y^{\frac{1}{2}}\tilde{\mathbf{A}}\mathbf{D}_Y^{-\frac{1}{2}}$ is a diagonal block matrix, of which each diagonal block can be represented as $(\mathbf{D}_Y)_{ii}^{\frac{1}{2}}(\tilde{\mathbf{A}})_{ii}(\mathbf{D}_Y)_{ii}^{-\frac{1}{2}}$ where $(\mathbf{D}_Y)_{ii}$ and $\tilde{\mathbf{A}}_{ii}$ are the ith diagonal block of $\mathbf{D}_Y$ and $\tilde{\mathbf{A}}$, respectively. Since the diagonal values of $(\mathbf{D}_Y)_{ii}$ equal to $d_m(i)$, $(\mathbf{D}_Y)_{ii}^{\frac{1}{2}}(\tilde{\mathbf{A}})_{ii}(\mathbf{D}_Y)_{ii}^{-\frac{1}{2}} = (\tilde{\mathbf{A}})_{ii}$ and $\mathbf{D}_Y^{\frac{1}{2}}\tilde{\mathbf{A}}\mathbf{D}_Y^{-\frac{1}{2}} = \tilde{\mathbf{A}}$.

Note that we can view $\tilde{\mathbf{W}}$ as the normalized matrix of a network generated by linking the common nodes between any two domain-specific networks if they are connected in the main network. Eq. (6) shows that if we normalize the initial vector $\mathbf{e}$ of CROSSRANK as $\tilde{\mathbf{e}} = \mathbf{D}_Y^{\frac{1}{2}}\mathbf{e}$, the process $\tilde{\mathbf{r}} = \tilde{c}\tilde{\mathbf{W}}\tilde{\mathbf{r}} + (1-\tilde{c})\tilde{\mathbf{e}}$ spreads information symmetrically within domain-specific networks and stochastically across domain-specific networks (note this process converges since $\tilde{\mathbf{W}}$ and $\mathbf{W}$ are similar). It gives the same ranking results as Eq. (4), since multiplying $\mathbf{D}_Y^{-\frac{1}{2}}$ on the ranking scores $\tilde{\mathbf{r}}$ does not affect the relative ranking order within the domain-specific networks. If $\tilde{\mathbf{A}}$ is stochastic, $\tilde{\mathbf{W}}$ is stochastic and $\tilde{\mathbf{r}} = \tilde{c}\tilde{\mathbf{W}}\tilde{\mathbf{r}} + (1-\tilde{c})\tilde{\mathbf{e}}$ becomes a stochastic process. This completes the proof. □

4. CROSSQUERY

In this section, we address CROSSQUERY. Note that CROSSQUERY is a special case of CROSSRANK, by (1) requiring the query node being from a source domain-specific network $\mathbf{A}_s$; (2) restricting the query results within a target domain-specific network $\mathbf{A}_d$; and (3) searching for a set of k most relevant nodes from $\mathbf{A}_d$ (as opposed to demanding the exacting ranking vectors). Thus, a default solution for CROSSQUERY is to run the CROSSRANK algorithm to get the ranking vector $\mathbf{r}_d$ for the target domain-specific network and return the top-k nodes with the highest ranking scores. In this section, we aim to further speed-up its computation.

4.1 CROSSQUERY-BASIC

According to Lemma 4, CROSSRANK has a RWR form on the integrated normalized matrix $\mathbf{W}$. This not only reveals an interesting relationship between CROSSRANK and RWR, but also opens the door to take the advantage of the vast machinery of the existing scalable algorithms for RWR [25, 5, 6]. For example, we could modify the algorithm in [6] to solve CROSSQUERY since $\lim_{t\to\infty}(\tilde{c}\mathbf{W})^t = 0$ (a prerequisite of this algorithm), which is summarized in Algorithm 2. This is an exact method that improves the basic power iteration method by estimating the node ranking scores using only a small number of iterations.

Time Complexity. Following the notations in Lemma 3, the overall time complexity of CROSSQUERY-BASIC is $O(T(bf+h) + m + gn)$, where b is the average size of the neighborhood for each node, f and h are the average size of the subtree $\mathcal{T}^{(t)}$ and the selected nodes set $\mathcal{S}^{(t)}$ over all iterations respectively, T is the total number of iterations. Compared with the CROSSRANK method, whose time complexity is $O(T^*(m+gn))$, where T^* is the total number of iterations, Algorithm 2 is more efficient since in practice $bf << m + gn$, $h << n$ and $T << T^*$.

Algorithm 2: CROSSQUERY-BASIC (adopted from [6])

Input: (1) matrices $\mathbf{W}, \mathbf{W}_{max}$ ($\mathbf{W}_{max}(u) = \max_{v\in\mathcal{N}(u)}\mathbf{W}(u,v)$ where $\mathcal{N}(u)$ is the neighbourhood of u); (2) node sets $\mathcal{V}_1, ..., \mathcal{V}_g$; (3) nodes q, s, d and (4) parameters $\tilde{c}, k$
Output: Top k relevant nodes set $\mathcal{K}$

Set $\mathbf{e}_s(q) = 1, \mathbf{e}_i = \mathbf{0}, \forall i \in (1, ..., g)\backslash s$, and the query vector $\mathbf{e} = (\mathbf{e}'_1, ..., \mathbf{e}'_g)'$;
Initialize the random walk vector $\mathbf{p} = \mathbf{e}$, the lower bound vector $\underline{\mathbf{r}}_d^{(0)} = \mathbf{0}$, and the upper bound vector $\bar{\mathbf{r}}_d^{(0)} = \mathbf{0}$;
Initialize the iteration number $t = 0$, Subtree $\mathcal{T}^{(0)} = \{q\}$, the selected nodes set $\mathcal{S}^{(0)} = \mathcal{V}_d$, the threshold $\sigma = -1$;
while $|\mathcal{S}^{(t)}| > k$ **do**
  Increase the iteration number $t = t + 1$;
  $layer^{(t)} = \{u | u.layer = t$ by BFS rooted at $q, \forall u \in \bigcup_{i=1}^{g}\mathcal{V}_i\}$;
  expand $\mathcal{T}^{(t)} = \mathcal{T}^{(t-1)} \cup layer^{(t)}$;
  update $\mathbf{p}(\mathcal{T}^{(t)}) \leftarrow \mathbf{W}\mathbf{p}(\mathcal{T}^{(t)})$;
  update lower bound: $\underline{\mathbf{r}}_d^{(t)} \leftarrow \underline{\mathbf{r}}_d^{(t-1)} + (1-\tilde{c})\tilde{c}^t\mathbf{p}(\mathcal{S}^{(t-1)})$;
  update upper bound: $\bar{\mathbf{r}}_d^{(t)} \leftarrow \underline{\mathbf{r}}_d^{(t)} + \tilde{c}^{t+1}\mathbf{W}_{max}(\mathcal{S}^{(t-1)})$;
  update threshold: $\sigma \leftarrow$ the kth largest value in $\underline{\mathbf{r}}_d^{(t)}$;
  shrink selected nodes: $\mathcal{S}^{(t)} = \{u | \bar{\mathbf{r}}_d^{(t)}(u) \geq \sigma, \forall u \in \mathcal{S}^{(t-1)}\}$;
  shrink bounds lists: $\underline{\mathbf{r}}_d^{(t)} \leftarrow \underline{\mathbf{r}}_d^{(t)}(\mathcal{S}^{(t)})$, $\bar{\mathbf{r}}_d^{(t)} \leftarrow \bar{\mathbf{r}}_d^{(t)}(\mathcal{S}^{(t)})$;
end
return $\mathcal{K} = \mathcal{S}^{(t)}$

4.2 CROSSQUERY-FAST

Next, we propose a more efficient algorithm for CROSSQUERY. The basic idea is as follows. Let the corresponding main nodes for $\mathbf{A}_s$ and $\mathbf{A}_d$ be node s and node d, respectively. Given s and d, parts of the main network $\mathbf{G}$ might have little contributions to measure the relevance for the nodes from $\mathbf{A}_d$ w.r.t. the query node, and thus can be pruned with little impact on the final query accuracy. In the context of NoN, even if we can only prune a small portion of the main network, the computational efficiency can be significantly improved since all the corresponding domain-specific networks can be filtered out during the ranking process.

Let $\mathbf{r}(v)$ be the ranking score of any node v w.r.t. a query node q by RWR. It is well known that $\mathbf{r}(v)$ can be represented by the so-called *inverse P-distance* [9].

$$\mathbf{r}(v) = \sum_{p\in\{q\rightsquigarrow v\}} Prob(p)(1-c)c^{l(p)}$$

where $p \in \{q \rightsquigarrow v\}$ is a path from q to v, and $l(p)$ is the unweighed length of p. For any path $p: v_1 \to v_2 \to ... \to v_{l(p)}$, $Prob(p) = \prod_{i=1}^{l(p)-1} Prob(v_{i+1}|v_i)$, where $Prob(v_{i+1}|v_i)$ is the transition probability from v_i to v_{i+1}. We call $Prob(p)$ the transition probability of path p.

Inspired by the relationship between CROSSRANK and RWR (as indicated by Eq. (6)), here we consider $\tilde{\mathbf{A}}$ to be stochastic (i.e., column normalized) to guide the pruning process. Then we can express the CROSSQUERY score of a node v w.r.t. the query node q as

$$\mathbf{r}(v) = \sum_{p\in\{q\rightsquigarrow v\}} \frac{\sqrt{d_m(s)}}{\sqrt{d_m(d)}} Prob(p)(1-\tilde{c})\tilde{c}^{l(p)} \qquad (7)$$

The following lemma says that $Prob(p), \forall p \in \{q \rightsquigarrow v\}$, is upper bounded by the transition probability of some path in the main network.

LEMMA 5. **Upper Bound of** *Prob(p). For any path $p \in \{q \rightsquigarrow v\}$, $\exists p' \in \{s \rightsquigarrow d\}$ s.t. $Prob(p) \leq Prob(p')$, where p' is a path con-*

necting s and d in the main network. Here $Prob(p') = \prod_{e_{ij}\in p'} \frac{\mathbf{G}(i,j)}{d_m(i)}$ *where* e_{ij} *is the edge connecting main nodes i and j in* $\mathbf{G}$.

PROOF. For any edge $e_{xy} \in p$, let i and j be the main nodes that contain domain nodes x and y respectively. We have

$$\begin{aligned} Prob(p) &= \prod_{\substack{e_{xy}\in p \\ i=j}} \frac{c}{c+2a}\tilde{\mathbf{A}}_i(y,x) \prod_{\substack{e_{xy}\in p \\ i\neq j}} \frac{2a}{c+2a}(\mathbf{YD}_Y^{-1})_{ji}(y,x) \\ &\leq \prod_{\substack{e_{xy}\in p \\ i\neq j}} (\mathbf{YD}_Y^{-1})_{ji}(y,x) \\ &= \prod_{\substack{e_{ij}\in p' \\ i\neq j}} \frac{\mathbf{G}(i,j)}{d_m(i)} = Prob(p') \end{aligned}$$

where $(\mathbf{YD}_Y^{-1})_{ji}$ is the $(j,i)^{th}$ block of $\mathbf{YD}_Y^{-1}$, which is the transition matrix from domain-specific network i to j. □

In the above lemma, p' consists of edges in p that go across domain-specific networks. Let φ be the function that maps each p to its corresponding p', i.e., $\varphi(p) = p'$, then we have the following upper bound of the ranking score $\mathbf{r}(v)$.

COROLLARY 1. **Upper Bound of $\mathbf{r}(v)$.** *The* CROSSQUERY *score of a node* $v \in \mathcal{V}_d$ *w.r.t. the query node q, i.e.,* $\mathbf{r}(v)$*, is upper bounded by*

$$\mathbf{r}(v) \leq \sum_{p\in\{q\rightsquigarrow v\}} \frac{\sqrt{d_m(s)}}{\sqrt{d_m(d)}} Prob(\varphi(p))(1-\tilde{c})\tilde{c}^{l(\varphi(p))}$$

PROOF. This can be derived directly from Eq. (7) and Lemma 5. The detailed proof is omitted. □

From Corollary 1, we have that if $Prob(\varphi(p))$ is small, the contribution from the path p to $\mathbf{r}(v)$ will be small. Based on this observation, we can extract a subnetwork of the main network consisting of paths with large $Prob(\varphi(p))$.

For any p, let $\tilde{Prob}(\varphi(p)) = \frac{\sqrt{d_m(s)}}{\sqrt{d_m(d)}} Prob(\varphi(p)) = \prod_{e_{ij}\in\varphi(p)} \frac{\mathbf{G}(i,j)}{\sqrt{d_m(i)}\sqrt{d_m(j)}}$. We define the distance between node i and node j as

$$L_{ij} = -log(\frac{\mathbf{G}(i,j)}{\sqrt{d_m(i)}\sqrt{d_m(j)}}) \quad (8)$$

Then the upper bound of the ranking score $\mathbf{r}(v)$ in Corollary 1 becomes

$$\mathbf{r}(v) \leq \sum_{p\in\{q\rightsquigarrow v\}} 10^{-\sum_{e_{ij}\in\varphi(p)} L_{ij}}(1-\tilde{c})\tilde{c}^{l(\varphi(p))} \quad (9)$$

This transformation allows us to search for short paths connecting s and d in the main network that capture high transition probabilities. We adopt a fast heuristics proposed in [12] to extract these paths. With the subgraph consisting of the extracted paths in the main network, we then apply CROSSQUERY-BASIC on the corresponding NoN to retrieve the top-k most relevant nodes from the target domain-specific network.

Algorithm 3 summarizes this approach. The algorithm starts the shortest path search rooted from s and d simultaneously in $\mathbf{G}$ (e.g., using Dijkstra's algorithm). Let $\mathcal{N}(s)$ and $\mathcal{N}(t)$ be the neighborhoods of s and d expanded by the algorithm so far. The first overlapping node in $\mathcal{N}(s)$ and $\mathcal{N}(t)$ identifies the shortest path between s and d. Denote this path as p'_{max} as it has the maximal transition probability from s to d (Steps 4 to 6). The algorithm continues expanding and adding new nodes in $\mathcal{N}(s)$ and $\mathcal{N}(t)$. The overlapping nodes in $\mathcal{N}(s)$ and $\mathcal{N}(t)$ will generate new paths. The expansion stops when the transition probability of the newly discovered path

Algorithm 3: CROSSQUERY-FAST

Input: (1) matrices $\mathbf{G}, \tilde{\mathbf{A}}, \mathbf{Y}$; (2) node sets $\mathcal{V}_1, ..., \mathcal{V}_g$; (3) nodes s, d, q and (4) parameters: ϵ, a, c, k
Output: Top k relevant nodes set $\mathcal{K}$

1 Initialize $L(p'_{max}) = \infty$, neighbourhoods $\mathcal{N}(s) = \phi, \mathcal{N}(d) = \phi$, radiuses $r_s = 0, r_d = 0$, selected nodes set $\mathcal{G} = \phi$;
2 Transform similarity in $\mathbf{G}$ into distances by Eq. (8);
3 **while** $r_s \leq \frac{L(p'_{max})-log(\epsilon)}{2} \vee r_d \leq \frac{L(p'_{max})-log(\epsilon)}{2}$ **do**
4   **if** $\mathcal{N}(s)$ *and* $\mathcal{N}(d)$ *first overlap at node u* **then**
5     $L(p'_{max}) = L(s \rightsquigarrow u \rightsquigarrow d)$;
6   **end**
7   **if** $r_s \leq \frac{L(p'_{max})-log(\epsilon)}{2}$ **then**
8   Expand $\mathcal{N}(s)$ and update r_s;
9   **end**
10   **if** $r_d \leq \frac{L(p'_{max})-log(\epsilon)}{2}$ **then**
11   Expand $\mathcal{N}(d)$ and update r_d;
12   **end**
13 **end**
14 Further prune $\mathcal{N}(s)$ and $\mathcal{N}(d)$: $\mathcal{G} = \{u|L(s,u) + L(u,d) \leq L(p'_{max}) - log(\epsilon), u \in \mathcal{N}(s) \cup \mathcal{N}(d)\}$
15 Calculate $\mathbf{W}, \mathbf{W}_{max}, \tilde{c}$ based on $\mathcal{G}, \tilde{\mathbf{A}}, \mathbf{Y}, a$ and c;
16 Apply CROSSQUERY-BASIC on the extracted NoN;
17 **return** $\mathcal{K}$

p'_{new} drops below $\epsilon \times \tilde{Prob}(p'_{max})$, where $0 < \epsilon < 1$ is an error factor. Thus we have $L(p'_{new}) > L(p'_{max}) - log(\epsilon)$, where $L(\cdot)$ is the weighed length of a path. Therefore, the neighborhoods with radius $\frac{L(p'_{max})-log(\epsilon)}{2}$ from s and d (i.e., r_s and r_d) will contain all significant paths based on ϵ (Steps 7 to 12). A node u in the neighborhoods can be pruned if $L(s,u) + L(u,d) > L(p'_{max}) - log(\epsilon)$, where $L(s,u)$ and $L(u,d)$ are the shortest distances between s and u, u and d, respectively (Step 14). Finally we apply CROSSQUERY-BASIC on the pruned NoN (Step 15 to 16).

Time Complexity. Let the number of nodes and edges in the main network be g and z respectively, and T be the number of iterations. Subgraph extraction takes $O(T(glog(g) + z))$ using Dijkstra's algorithm. The pruning step takes $O(g)$. Thus the overall complexity of subgraph extraction is $O(T(glog(g) + z))$. Note that since g and z are typically very small compared to the overall size of the domain-specific networks, this step is usually very efficient. Experimental results show that CROSSQUERY-FAST brings 4.5× to 7.5× additional speedup while preserving a high accuracy.

5. EXPERIMENTS

In this section, we perform comprehensive experiments to evaluate the performance of the proposed methods. We study NoN in two real-world applications: ranking authors in the network of co-author networks constructed from the DBLP bibliographic data, and prioritizing candidate gene in the network of tissue-specific protein interaction networks. Synthetic datasets are also generated to evaluate the efficiency of the developed optimization strategies. All experiments are performed on a 3.00 GHz desktop PC with 8G memory.

5.1 Co-Author NoN

We construct the co-author NoN from the DBLP data [24] as follows. The main network consists of 5 research areas, i.e., data mining (DM), machine learning (ML), database (DB), information retrieval (IR), and bioinformatics (BIO). Each area corresponds to a node in the main network. The conferences included in each area are summarized in Table 2. The similarity between two areas is measured by the ratio between the number of citations across these

Table 2: Areas in the main network

Area	Conference included
DM	KDD, ICDM, SDM, PKDD, PAKDD
ML	ICML, NIPS, AAAI, IJCAI, UAI, ECML
DB	VLDB, SIGMOD, ICDE, ICDT, EDBT, PODS
IR	SIGIR, WWW, ACL, ECIR, CIKM
BIO	ISMB, RECOMB, ECCB, BIBE, BIBM, WABI

two areas and the total number of cited papers in them. This is intuitive since two similar areas are more likely to cite each other's papers. The co-author network in each area is used as the domain-specific network.

5.1.1 *Effectiveness Evaluation*

To evaluate the effectiveness of the NoN model, we first apply CROSSRANK and study how the top-10 authors in DB change when varying a. Table 3 shows the ranking results for different a values. Note that when $a = 0$, the ranking result is the same as that of applying random walk with restart in each individual area independently.

From the table, we can see that the rank of three authors, Jiawei Han, Christos Faloutsos and Philip S. Yu, increases as a increases. When $a = 0$, their rank indicates their contributions to DB only. When a increases, their contributions to areas related to DB are also taken into consideration. In particular, they are the top-3 researchers in DM, which is the most similar area to DB in the main network. This indicates that CROSSRANK can effectively recognize a researcher's broader impact by incorporating his/her contribution across multiple areas.

Next, we evaluate the effectiveness of CROSSQUERY by studying an interesting cross-area link prediction task, i.e., for a given query author, we would like to identify future collaborators for this author in a relevant area. In particular, we partition the DBLP dataset into two parts, one from 2001 to 2005 (time interval T_1) and another from 2006 to 2010 (time interval T_2). We are interested in the DB researchers who have no DM publications during $T1$ but collaborate with DM researchers and publish in DM during T_2. We select such DM-DB author-pairs and use network in T_1 to predict their co-authorship in T_2.

For comparison, we select methods developed for (1) a single merged co-author network, and (2) heterogeneous information network. For a single merged network, we select the following methods. The path counting (PC) method uses the number of paths between each pair. Here we consider paths with length no longer than 5. The Katz method [11] is also a path counting method that penalizes longer paths. Personalized PageRank [9] and PropFlow [16] are random walk based methods. PathSim is designed for heterogeneous information network [22]. We use the 9 meta paths proposed in [21] for co-authorship link prediction. The parameters of the selected methods are tuned for their optimal performance.

Note that for all the selected methods, we focus on authors with at least certain number of publications, and author-pairs who are within a few hops in the merged overall co-author networks. This is reasonable since highly productive authors are more likely to cooperate with authors within a small distance [21].

We perform leave-one-out cross validation and use *accuracy* and *AUC* value as the evaluation criteria. Specifically, we test one selected DM-DB author-pair at each time. The DM researcher is used as the query node and DB is the target query area. A prediction is considered accurate if the test DB researcher is among the top-20 ranked authors in DB.

Table 4: Co-authorship prediction results

#Papers	Hops	#Pairs	Methods	AUC	Accuracy
≥ 3	$[3, 4]$	45	PC	0.7196	0.4444
			Katz	0.7439	0.5556
			PropFlow	0.7558	0.6222
			PathSim	0.5636	0.2444
			PageRank	0.7417	0.5333
			CrossQuery	**0.7685**	**0.6444**
≥ 3	$[3, 6]$	70	PC	0.6009	0.3000
			Katz	0.6243	0.3714
			PropFlow	0.6268	0.4429
			PathSim	0.5278	0.2143
			PageRank	0.6378	0.3714
			CrossQuery	**0.6632**	**0.4571**
≥ 5	$[3, 4]$	23	PC	0.6521	0.2609
			Katz	0.6717	**0.3478**
			PropFlow	0.6850	**0.3478**
			PathSim	0.4279	0.1304
			PageRank	0.6743	**0.3478**
			CrossQuery	**0.7099**	**0.3478**
≥ 5	$[3, 6]$	38	PC	0.5692	0.2105
			Katz	0.5786	0.2368
			PropFlow	0.5950	**0.2895**
			PathSim	0.4362	0.1053
			PageRank	0.5880	0.2368
			CrossQuery	**0.6308**	**0.2895**

Table 4 shows the results. From the table, we can see that CROSSQUERY outperforms all alternative methods. The performance gain becomes larger when more test author-pairs are available. The alternative methods are not suitable for this cross-area query task, since they only consider the similarity between the authors but not areas. Note that the meta paths used in PathSim do not consider the similarity between areas and conferences either.

5.1.2 *Efficiency Evaluation*

We evaluate the efficiency of the proposed methods using both the DBLP and synthetic datasets. The main network in the DBLP NoN consists of 121 conferences. The number of nodes in the conference-specific coauthor networks ranges from 88 to 14,636 depending on the size of the conferences, with a total of 259,822 nodes. The synthetic NoN are generated using the R-MAT model [2] so that the resulting networks resemble real-word networks. The main network consists of 1,023 nodes. The domain-specific networks contain 935 to 8,100 nodes with a total of 3,773,519 nodes.

Figure 2 shows the running time of CROSSQUERY-BASIC and CROSSQUERY-FAST when varying the number of returned nodes k. The running time of CROSSRANK is also reported in the figure as a reference. The running time is averaged over 10 randomly selected query nodes and target domain-specific networks. The parameters are $a = 0.2, c = 0.85$, and $\epsilon = 10^{-3}$. It can be seen that both CROSSQUERY-BASIC and CROSSQUERY-FAST are much more efficient than CROSSRANK. The running time of CROSSQUERY-BASIC and CROSSQUERY-FAST increases as k increases. The randomly selected query nodes may affect the trend, e.g., in Figure 2(b) when $k = 500$. The corresponding averaged accuracy of CROSSQUERY-FAST is shown in 2(c). From the results, we can see that CROSSQUERY-FAST achieves more than 90% accuracy for all settings and dramatically improves the efficiency.

5.2 Protein Interaction NoN

In this section, we apply the proposed NoN model to the candidate gene prioritization problem, which has recently attracted in-

Table 3: Top ranked authors in the database area when varying a

Rank	$a = 0$	$a = 0.05$	$a = 0.1$	$a = 0.3$	$a = 0.5$
1	Divesh Srivastava	**Jiawei Han**	**Jiawei Han**	**Jiawei Han**	**Jiawei Han**
2	**Jiawei Han**	Divesh Srivastava	Divesh Srivastava	**Philip S. Yu**	**Philip S. Yu**
3	**Philip S. Yu**	**Philip S. Yu**	**Philip S. Yu**	Divesh Srivastava	**Christos Faloutsos**
4	Hector Garcia-Molina	Hector Garcia-Molina	Hector Garcia-Molina	**Christos Faloutsos**	Michael Stonebraker
5	Raghu Ramakrishnan	Raghu Ramakrishnan	**Christos Faloutsos**	Michael Stonebraker	Divesh Srivastava
6	Gerhard Weikum	Gerhard Weikum	Michael Stonebraker	Hector Garcia-Molina	Hector Garcia-Molina
7	Beng Chin Ooi	**Christos Faloutsos**	Raghu Ramakrishnan	Michael J. Carey	Michael J. Carey
8	H. V. Jagadish	Michael Stonebraker	Gerhard Weikum	Raghu Ramakrishnan	Gerhard Weikum
9	Michael J. Carey	Michael J. Carey	Michael J. Carey	Gerhard Weikum	Raghu Ramakrishnan
10	Michael Stonebraker	Beng Chin Ooi	Beng Chin Ooi	Elke A. Rundensteiner	Elke A. Rundensteiner

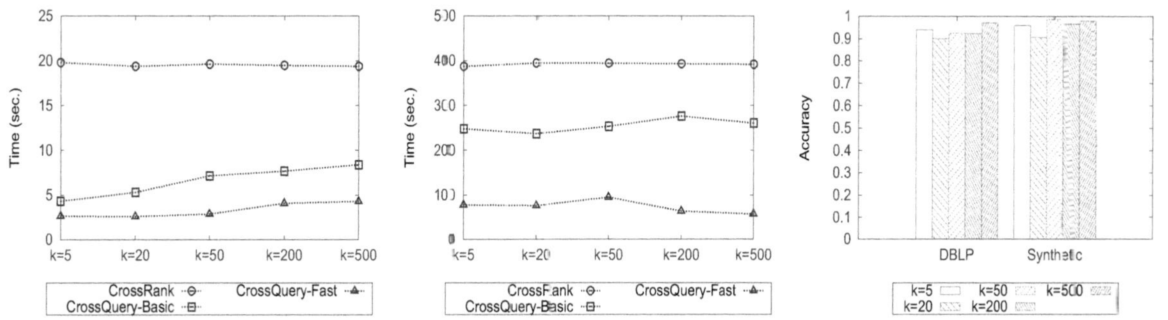

(a) Query time on DBLP NoN (b) Query time on synthetic NoN (c) Accuracy of CROSSQUERY-FAST

Figure 2: Efficiency and accuracy of the proposed techniques

tensive research interests. Various methods have been proposed including regression based methods [29], alignment based methods [30], random walk based methods [31, 14, 28], and maximum flow based methods [3].

Most of the state-of-the-art methods use a heterogeneous network as shown in Figure 3(a). The heterogeneous network consists of three components: a disease similarity network, a generic protein interaction network, and known disease-gene associations connecting the two networks. Based on the "guilt-by-association" principle, these methods utilizes similarities between diseases to infer genes that are associated with diseases [4].

Since the majority of genetic disorders tend to manifest only in a few tissues, recent studies have shown that it is more reasonable to utilize tissue-specific protein interaction networks in candidate gene prioritization [17].

We construct the tissue-specific protein interaction NoN as shown in Figure 3(b). The similarity network between 5,080 diseases is retrieved from the OMIM database [7] and used as the main network in NoN. We use the tissue-specific protein interaction network contributed in [17]. The authors generated tissue-specific protein interaction networks of 9,998 proteins for 60 human tissues using gene expression profiles in these tissues. For each disease in the main network, we use the protein interaction network in the tissue that is most relevant to the disease as its domain-specific network [13]. We collect 2,187 known associations between 1,524 diseases and 1,326 genes from the OMIM database [7] and select a subset of known disease-gene associations by filtering out diseases with the MAS (Maximum Association Score) less than 8%, which is used for selecting diseases having high associations with relevant tissues [17, 13], and diseases whose maximum similarity to all other diseases is less than 0.5 to preserve significant similarities among diseases [27]. The resulting disease-gene associations involve 147 associations between 106 diseases and 102 genes. These genes are

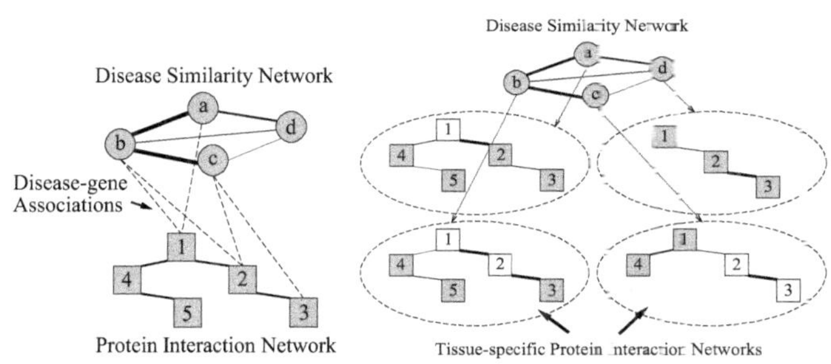

(a) Heterogeneous network structure (b) NoN structure

Figure 3: Heterogeneous network and NoN for the candidate gene prioritization problem. The protein interaction network in (a) is unweighed while those in (b) are weighed, denoting by the edge thickness

used as seed nodes in CROSSRANK which are represented by the white rectangles in Figure 3(b)

We select four state-of-the-art methods for comparison, including RWRH [14], BIRW [31], PRINCE [28] and Katz [20]. We use the standard leave-one-out cross validation to compare the prioritization accuracy of the selected methods. Specifically, at each time, we remove an association between the query disease and one causal gene, as well as all the associations involving the causal gene to avoid the trivial cases where mutations in the same gene cause two very similar diseases [28, 17]. This causal gene is used as the test gene. If the test gene is ranked within the top-k genes, where k is the total number of known genes for the query disease, this is considered as a successful prediction. This evaluation method is

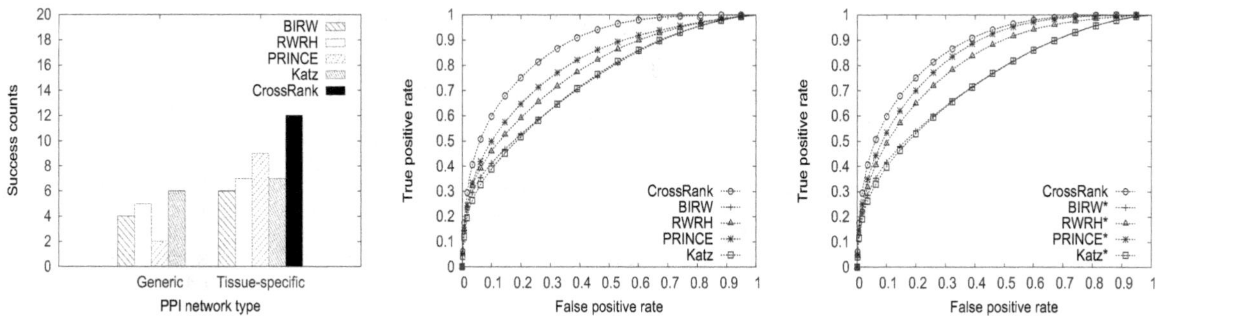

(a) # successful preditions (b) ROC using generic protein network (c) ROC using tissue-specific protein network

Figure 4: Comparison between CROSSRANK and baseline methods

Table 5: AUC value comparison

Method	AUC50	AUC100	AUC300	AUC500	AUC
RWRH	0.2222	0.2846	0.3335	0.3601	0.8049
RWRH*	0.2143	0.2616	0.3364	0.3738	0.8475
BIRW	0.2261	0.2786	0.3198	0.3381	0.7586
BIRW*	0.2233	0.2653	0.3203	0.3393	0.7672
PRINCE	0.2373	0.2799	0.3454	0.3827	0.8339
PRINCE*	0.2446	0.2899	0.3656	0.4133	0.8832
Katz	0.1869	0.2343	0.2896	0.3073	0.7594
Katz*	0.1948	0.2299	0.2804	0.3077	0.7636
CrossRank	**0.2935**	**0.3477**	**0.4280**	**0.4800**	**0.9048**

Table 6: Ranking results comparison

Method	better	tie	worse	p-value
CrossRank vs. RWRH	106	2	39	2.04×10^{-11}
CrossRank vs. RWRH*	94	6	47	2.38×10^{-6}
CrossRank vs. BIRW	106	4	37	1.82×10^{-11}
CrossRank vs. BIRW*	100	9	38	1.44×10^{-9}
CrossRank vs. PRINCE	108	4	35	1.08×10^{-10}
CrossRank vs. PRINCE*	79	6	62	1.17×10^{-2}
CrossRank vs. Katz	108	5	34	2.32×10^{-12}
CrossRank vs. Katz*	103	9	35	1.23×10^{-10}

commonly used in the candidate gene prioritization studies [28]. The parameters are tuned for their optimal performance for the selected methods.

Note that all these baseline methods use a generic (non tissue-specific) protein interaction network. For a fair comparison, we also apply these methods to tissue-specific protein interaction networks. Specifically, for each query disease, we replace the generic protein interaction network by its most relevant tissue-specific protein interaction network.

Figure 4(a) shows the number of successful predictions made by the selected methods. As we can see, using tissue-specific protein interaction networks can improve the accuracy for the baseline methods. CROSSRANK has more successful predictions than all other methods. Figures 4(b) and 4(c) show the ROC curve. The results are consistent with the previous ones. The corresponding AUC values are reported in Table 5, where AUC values are reported by considering up to 50, 100, 300, 500 and all false positives. Note that a "*" indicates the use of tissue-specific protein interaction networks.

We further study how often CROSSRANK gives higher ranks to test genes than other methods. The results are shown in Table 6. The Wilcoxon signed rank test is used to assess the statistical significance of the difference between the ranking lists given by the two compared methods. It is clear from the table that the results of CROSSRANK are significantly better than that of the alternatives.

6. RELATED WORK

Networks are ubiquitous in real-life applications. The simplest model uses a single graph to represent a network. A variety of ranking algorithms have been developed for a single network [9, 8, 19, 6, 15]. Recently, various advanced network models have been proposed, such as multi-relational network [18], heterogenous information network [23], and hypergraph [34]. The multi-relational network and heterogeneous information network can incorporate node or edge type information: in a multi-relational network, edges connecting two nodes may be of different types; while different types of objects can co-exist in a heterogenous information network. Some work uses them interchangeably [32]. A tensor based co-ranking framework is proposed in [18] for multi-relational network. In heterogeneous information network, ranking-based clustering [23] and ranking-based classification [10] frameworks are developed, where ranking and clustering/classification can be mutually enhanced. In a hypergraph, an edge can connect any subset of nodes and is similar to a main node in our NoN model. But the set of nodes connected by an edge in a hypergraph do not form any network topology. If we treat each hyperedge as a main node, hypergraph can be viewed as special case of NoN where we do not have any links among domain nodes at all.

7. CONCLUSION

Ranking is a primitive operation in network analysis. In this paper, we propose a new network data model, Network of Networks (NoN), which enables novel ranking tasks such as CROSSRANK and CROSSQUERY. We formulate ranking on NoN as a regularized optimization problem, develop efficient algorithms, and provide rigorous theoretical analysis. Experimental results on real-world datasets demonstrate the effectiveness and efficiency of the proposed methods.

8. ACKNOWLEDGEMENT

This work was partially supported by the National Science Foundation grants IIS-1162374, IIS-1218036 and IIS1017415, by the Army Research Laboratory under Cooperative Agreement Number W911NF-09-2-0053, by Defense Advanced Research Projects Agency (DARPA) under Contract Number W911NF-11-C-0200 and

W911NF-12-C-0028, by Region II University Transportation Center under the project number 49997-33 25, and by China 973 Fundamental R&D Program (No.2014CB340304).

9. REFERENCES

[1] R. Bhatia. Linear algebra to quantum cohomology: the story of alfred horn's inequalities. *American Mathematical Monthly*, pages 289–318, 2001.

[2] D. Chakrabarti, Y. Zhan, and C. Faloutsos. R-mat: A recursive model for graph mining. In *SDM*, 2004.

[3] Y. Chen, T. Jiang, and R. Jiang. Uncover disease genes by maximizing information flow in the phenome–interactome network. *Bioinformatics*, 27(13):i167–i176, 2011.

[4] Y. Chen, W. Zhang, M. Gan, and R. Jiang. Constructing human phenome-interactome networks for the prioritization of candidate genes. *STATISTICS AND ITS INTERFACE*, 5(1):137–148, 2012.

[5] Y. Fujiwara, M. Nakatsuji, M. Onizuka, and M. Kitsuregawa. Fast and exact top-k search for random walk with restart. *VLDB*, 5(5):442–453, 2012.

[6] Y. Fujiwara, M. Nakatsuji, H. Shiokawa, T. Mishima, and M. Onizuka. Efficient ad-hoc search for personalized pagerank. In *SIGMOD*, pages 445–456, 2013.

[7] A. Hamosh, A. F. Scott, J. S. Amberger, C. A. Bocchini, and V. A. McKusick. Online mendelian inheritance in man (omim), a knowledgebase of human genes and genetic disorders. *Nucleic acids research*, 33(suppl 1):D514–D517, 2005.

[8] G. Jeh and J. Widom. Simrank: a measure of structural-context similarity. In *KDD*, pages 538–543, 2002.

[9] G. Jeh and J. Widom. Scaling personalized web search. In *WWW*, pages 271–279, 2003.

[10] M. Ji, J. Han, and M. Danilevsky. Ranking-based classification of heterogeneous information networks. In *KDD*, pages 1298–1306, 2011.

[11] L. Katz. A new status index derived from sociometric analysis. *Psychometrika*, 18(1):39–43, 1953.

[12] Y. Koren, S. C. North, and C. Volinsky. Measuring and extracting proximity in networks. In *KDD*, pages 245–255, 2006.

[13] K. Lage, N. T. Hansen, E. O. Karlberg, A. C. Eklund, F. S. Roque, P. K. Donahoe, Z. Szallasi, T. S. Jensen, and S. Brunak. A large-scale analysis of tissue-specific pathology and gene expression of human disease genes and complexes. *Proceedings of the National Academy of Sciences*, 105(52):20870–20875, 2008.

[14] Y. Li and J. C. Patra. Genome-wide inferring gene–phenotype relationship by walking on the heterogeneous network. *Bioinformatics*, 26(9):1219–1224, 2010.

[15] D. Liben-Nowell and J. Kleinberg. The link-prediction problem for social networks. *Journal of the American society for information science and technology*, 58(7):1019–1031, 2007.

[16] R. N. Lichtenwalter, J. T. Lussier, and N. V. Chawla. New perspectives and methods in link prediction. In *KDD*, pages 243–252, 2010.

[17] O. Magger, Y. Y. Waldman, E. Ruppin, and R. Sharan. Enhancing the prioritization of disease-causing genes through tissue specific protein interaction networks. *PLoS Computational Biology*, 8(9):e1002690, 2012.

[18] M. K.-P. Ng, X. Li, and Y. Ye. Multirank: co-ranking for objects and relations in multi-relational data. In *KDD*, pages 1217–1225, 2011.

[19] P. Sarkar, A. W. Moore, and A. Prakash. Fast incremental proximity search in large graphs. In *ICML*, pages 896–903, 2008.

[20] U. M. Singh-Blom, N. Natarajan, A. Tewari, J. O. Woods, I. S. Dhillon, and E. M. Marcotte. Prediction and validation of gene-disease associations using methods inspired by social network analyses. *PloS one*, 8(5):e58977, 2013.

[21] Y. Sun, R. Barber, M. Gupta, C. C. Aggarwal, and J. Han. Co-author relationship prediction in heterogeneous bibliographic networks. In *ASONAM*, pages 121–128, 2011.

[22] Y. Sun, J. Han, X. Yan, P. S. Yu, and T. Wu. Pathsim: Meta path-based top-k similarity search in heterogeneous information networks. *VLDB*, 2011.

[23] Y. Sun, J. Han, P. Zhao, Z. Yin, H. Cheng and T. Wu. Rankclus: integrating clustering with ranking for heterogeneous information network analysis. In *EDBT*, pages 565–576, 2009.

[24] J. Tang, J. Zhang, L. Yao, J. Li, L. Zhang, and Z. Su. Arnetminer: extraction and mining of academic social networks. In *KDD*, pages 990–998, 2008.

[25] H. Tong, C. Faloutsos, and J.-Y. Pan. Random walk with restart: fast solutions and applications. In *ICDM*, pages 327–346, 2006.

[26] H. Tong, J. He, M. Li, W.-Y. Ma, H.-J. Zhang, and C. Zhang. Manifold-ranking-based keyword propagation for image retrieval. *EURASIP J. Adv. Sig. Proc.*, 2006.

[27] M. A. van Driel, J. Bruggeman, G. Vriend, H. G. Brunner, and J. A. Leunissen. A text-mining analysis of the human phenome. *European journal of human genetics*, 14(5):535–542, 2006.

[28] O. Vanunu, O. Magger, E. Ruppin, T. Shlomi, and R. Sharan. Associating genes and protein complexes with disease via network propagation. *PLoS computational biology*, 6(1):e1000641, 2010.

[29] X. Wu, R. Jiang, M. Q. Zhang, and S. Li. Network-based global inference of human disease genes. *Molecular Systems Biology*, 4(1), 2008.

[30] X. Wu, Q. Liu, and R. Jiang. Align human interactome with phenome to identify causative genes and networks underlying disease families. *Bioinformatics*, 25(1):98–104, 2009.

[31] M. Xie, T. Hwang, and R. Kuang. Reconstructing disease phenome-genome association by bi-random walk *Bioinformatics*, 2012.

[32] Y. Yang, N. Chawla, Y. Sun, and J. Hani. Predicting links in multi-relational and heterogeneous networks. In *ICDM*, pages 755–764, 2012.

[33] D. Zhou, O. Bousquet, T. N. Lal, J. Weston, and B. Schölkopf. Learning with local and global consistency. *Advances in neural information processing systems*, 16(16):321–328, 2004.

[34] D. Zhou, J. Huang, and B. Schölkopf. Learning with hypergraphs: Clustering, classification, and embedding. *Advances in neural information processing systems*, 19:1601, 2007.

Community Membership Identification from Small Seed Sets

Isabel M. Kloumann
Cornell University
657 Rhodes Hall
Ithaca, NY, 14853
imk36@cornell.edu

Jon M. Kleinberg
Cornell University
318 Gates Hall
Ithaca, NY, 14853
kleinber@cs.cornell.edu

ABSTRACT

In many applications we have a social network of people and would like to identify the members of an interesting but unlabeled group or community. We start with a small number of exemplar group members – they may be followers of a political ideology or fans of a music genre – and need to use those examples to discover the additional members. This problem gives rise to the seed expansion problem in community detection: given example community members, how can the social graph be used to predict the identities of remaining, hidden community members? In contrast with global community detection (graph partitioning or covering), seed expansion is best suited for identifying communities locally concentrated around nodes of interest. A growing body of work has used seed expansion as a scalable means of detecting overlapping communities. Yet despite growing interest in seed expansion, there are divergent approaches in the literature and there still isn't a systematic understanding of which approaches work best in different domains.

Here we evaluate several variants and uncover subtle trade-offs between different approaches. We explore which properties of the seed set can improve performance, focusing on heuristics that one can control in practice. As a consequence of this systematic understanding we have found several opportunities for performance gains. We also consider an adaptive version in which requests are made for additional membership labels of particular nodes, such as one finds in field studies of social communities. This leads to interesting connections and contrasts with active learning and the trade-offs of exploration and exploitation. Finally, we explore topological properties of communities and seed sets that correlate with algorithm performance, and explain these empirical observations with theoretical ones.

We evaluate our methods across multiple domains, using publicly available datasets with labeled, ground-truth communities.

Categories and Subject Descriptors: H.2.8 [**Database Management**]: Database applications—*Data mining*

Keywords: Seed set expansion; Ground-truth communities

KDD'14, August 24–27, 2014, New York, NY, USA.
Copyright 2014 ACM 978-1-4503-2956-9/14/08 ...$15.00.
http://dx.doi.org/10.1145/2623330.2623621 .

1. INTRODUCTION

There are many settings in which we are interested in accessing or studying a group of people in a social network, but instead of the full membership of the group we know only a few examples. A natural goal in this case is to expand these examples into a larger set that approximates the full extent of the group, and this goal has been the focus of recent work on *seed set expansion* in networks. Phrasing the problem slightly informally for purposes of this discussion, we are given a graph G that contains a group of nodes C whose identities we'd like to uncover, and we are told the identities of a small subset S of C. Given a budget k, can we find k additional nodes such that as many of them as possible come from C?

Examples of the seed set expansion problem are numerous. For example, recent work studying political activism has started from a small set of representatives of each competing ideology, collected through detailed field work, and then attempted to expand these representatives into the larger groups that they come from [18]. Recommendation tools for forming on-line groups have the potential to collect a few initial suggestions from a user and then produce a longer list of recommended group members. Similarly, a marketer may want to expand a set of a few interested consumers of a product into a longer list of people who might also be interested in the product. Seed set expansion has also been used to infer missing attributes in user profile data [14] and to detect e-mail addresses of spammers [20]. Nor are the applications limited to social networks; as we will see below, we could ask similar questions in which we start with a few items such as products for sale, and we then attempt to use a co-purchase network to expand these items into a product category that contains all of them.

It is useful to note a few properties of the seed set expansion problem, consistent with these sources of motivation. First, we focus on cases in which the expansion is guided by an underlying graph structure — the basic premise is that if a person or item v is "tightly linked" in the graph to many members of the group C, then this provides evidence that v may also be a member of the group. Second, the goal in the seed set expansion problem as it has been studied in prior work — and the goal we pursue here — is neither to find the full extent of the group C nor to sample uniformly from it, but instead to "collect" a fixed number of members from it with as little error as possible.

The present work: Principles for seed set expansion. The number of approaches to seed set expansion has proliferated rapidly, but there is still very little understanding of the principles through which we can reason about trade-offs between different approaches or the types of instances on which we can expect good performances. In this work we seek to begin developing some of the principles underlying the seed set expansion problem. Among the questions that guide our study, we consider the following. Do certain approaches to seed set expansion produce consistently better results than others, across a range of domains? Can characteristics of the initial seed set S help us understand when seed set expansion will be effective? And how do structural characteristics of the group C affect the quality of the solution?

We can go further in our analysis by taking into account the following issue. If we think about many of the applications that motivate the seed set expansion problem, there is a potentially rich interaction available between the expansion algorithm and the "expert" who can recognize members of the group C. Consider for example the problem of identifying members of political movements noted earlier [18]. In such a setting there is a domain expert who has provided the initial representatives of a group, and if we are trying to expand these representative members into a larger set, we may well have the ability to adaptively query the expert — a few nodes at a time — and make future choices based on the result of this feedback. There is thus an opportunity to incorporate such interaction between the algorithm and the domain expert into the formalism of seed set expansion. Such interaction clearly has a structure similar to work in active learning, although we should emphasize that unlike traditional work in that domain, we are not seeking a classification of the full underlying graph, nor do we have a subset of the data available for training; rather, we want to collect a set of nodes from C based only on the initial examples S.

The present work: Overview of results. We first consider a wide range of techniques that have been used in prior work for seed set expansion, applying them to three main datasets: two social networks (a co-authorship network among researchers and the YouTube social network among its users), and a product co-purchase network in which the groups are product categories. We find that measures based on PageRank are by far the most effective. Moreover, almost all of the performance gains from PageRank come from running just two or three iterations of the PageRank update rule — a finding that is novel to the best of our knowledge, and consistent with our analysis of where PageRank is achieving most of its relative performance gains over more local neighbor-based methods, on nodes that are outside the immediate vicinity of the seed set S.

We then consider how properties of the seed set affect performance. In thinking about trade-offs here, it is useful to consider the interaction between the expansion algorithm and the domain expert discussed above: in that context, our motivation is to identify how a domain expert should best use their knowledge to compile a seed set of members. In practice we are highly constrained by those community members about which a domain expert has knowledge. One natural question is to ask whether performance is better when S consists of the highest-degree nodes in C or a uniformly random subset of C. In choosing a large-degree seed set, we model a domain expert who returns a list of the most popular or most famous nodes in the network. In choosing a random seed set, we model a domain expert who returns a seed set that is representative of the community, to wit, one potentially consisting of high and low degree nodes. We also consider the effect of seed set size, exploring a basic trade-off: if the seed set is too large a fraction of the group, it can be hard to find the remaining members, but if it is too small, then it is not providing a sufficiently useful set of examples for the full extent of the group.

We similarly look at trade-offs in the structural properties of the group C, finding that denser groups — those with a higher ratio of edges to nodes — tend to result in better performance for seed set expansion.

Dataset	Nodes	Edges	Communities
DBLP	317080, authors	1049866, co-authorship	13477, conferences
Amazon	334863, products	925872, co-purchased	151037, product categories
YouTube	1134890, users	2987624, friendship	8385, user-defined groups

Table 1: The number and substantive interpretation of nodes, edges, and communities in each network. All sourced from [21].

Finally, we look at different ways of managing the interaction between the algorithm and the domain expert. We find contexts in which regularly interspersing expansion steps with queries to the expert can outperform approaches in which the queries are batched in larger blocks. We also find that for our objective function of collecting members of C as quickly as possible, asking the expert about nodes on the "margin" of C can be effective in finding the boundaries of the group, but this benefit is more than offset by the downside of querying the expert about a greater number of nodes that turn out not to be in C.

2. SETUP: DATA, PERFORMANCE, ALGORITHMS

Data. We use network data with ground-truth community membership from the Stanford Network Analysis Project (snap.stanford.edu). Table 1 gives a summary of the datasets used in this paper; see Yang & Leskovec [21] for additional background on these datasets.

Seed Sets and Performance. We are given a graph G that contains a collection of potentially overlapping communities $\mathcal{C}$, and we have an interest in a particular community $C \in \mathcal{C}$. We are given a set of labeled community members $S \subset C$. Thus $C - S$ consists of the unlabeled, not-yet-discovered community members We have a budget to make a prediction consisting of a set of nodes of size k, and we will call the prediction P. We wish to maximize the recall, $|P \cap C|/|C - S|$, i.e. the fraction of the unlabeled community recovered by the algorithm.

Unless otherwise specified we choose S to be a random subset of C of size $|C|/10$.

Communities. From Table 1 we see that there are roughly 10^4-10^5 labeled, ground-truth communities in each dataset. These communities vary in size from 6 to roughly 10^4. In this paper we focus on the 600 communities closest in size to $m^{3/4}$, where m is the size of the largest community; let us call this set $\mathcal{C}^{300}_{3/4}$.[1]

Stopping criteria. Here we model the scenario in which a researcher knows that there are approximately k community members, and so they select the top k results from their choice algo-

[1]Given the same number of guesses, it would be unfair to compare the recall of an algorithm on a community of size 10000 with one of size 100. We find that there are 600 communities centered about this log-space third-quartile all close enough in size that such biases do not taint our results. Rather, thanks to the large number of moderately sized communities, we are able to estimate performances with good standard error estimates. In point of fact, good statistical convergence that distinguishes the various algorithms can be achieved with only 20 communities, and so our consideration of all 600 provides a large extra margin.

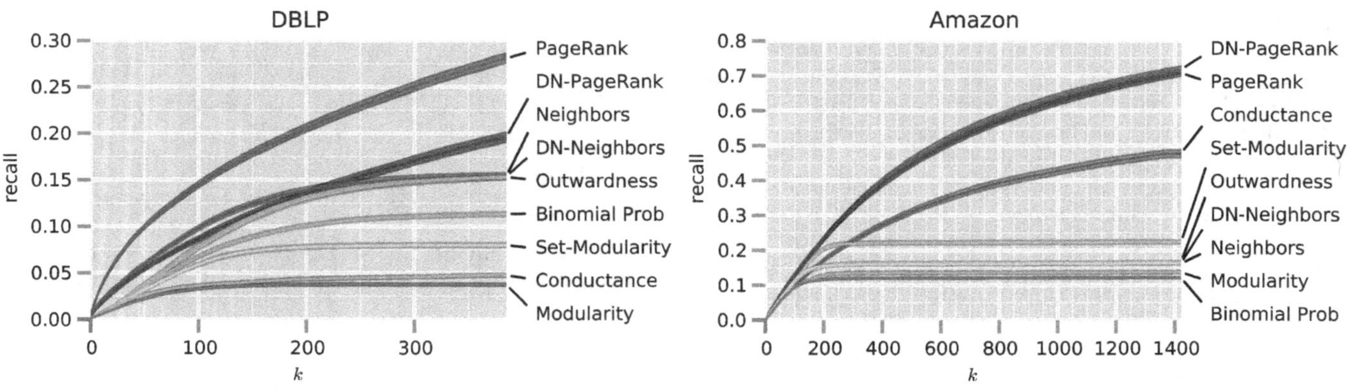

Figure 1: Recall averaged over $C^{600}_{3/4}$. Rankings for YouTube are the same as for DBLP. The envelopes represent two standard errors centered about the mean.

rithm, A, as the predicted community. That is, we choose a simple stopping criterion of a fixed number of guesses equal to the size of the central value; for example on $C^{600}_{3/4}$ we fix $k = m^{3/4}$ and set our prediction P to be the k top nodes according to A's ranking. As we will see in Figures 1, 3, and 5, the relative performance rankings are not very sensitive to the choice of k.

This stopping rule has the advantage that it is not sensitive to the topology of the prediction P, which would be undesirable given that the algorithms we compare produce communities with a variety of typical topologies (this is discussed in detail in [1]). We discuss alternate stopping criteria in §7.

3. RESULTS: PREDICTION ALGORITHMS

3.1 PageRank's success

Figure 1 shows the recall values for a wide range of algorithms detailed in §7 and the appendix. Variants of PageRank — in which we rank by the stationary probability of a random walk with restarts originating at the seed set — are the clear winners. This is consistent with PageRank's success in other applications, but it is nonetheless perhaps surprising that it is so much more powerful than other methods that have been used for this problem. We also note that in two of our three domains, pure unnormalized PageRank significantly outperforms variants such as degree-normalized PageRank (DN-PageRank); this poses an interesting contrast to the fact that DN-PageRank rather than pure PageRank has typically been the preferred method for seed set expansion.

We now consider three questions that suggest insights into the problem and how to the use these approaches in practice.

1. Why does PageRank outperform other methods such as neighbor counting?
2. In computing PageRank with the power method, how many iterations (random walk steps) does it need to take to achieve this high performance?
3. Could variations beyond DN-PageRank and PageRank achieve even better performance?

3.2 Whom does PageRank find?

In addition to the success of PageRank and its variants in Figure 1, it is also striking to see how PageRank climbs smoothly with k in contrast with neighbor-counting methods that flatten abruptly as k is increased.

Looking into this behavior helps us understand where PageRank gets some of its power. In particular, we ask which true positives

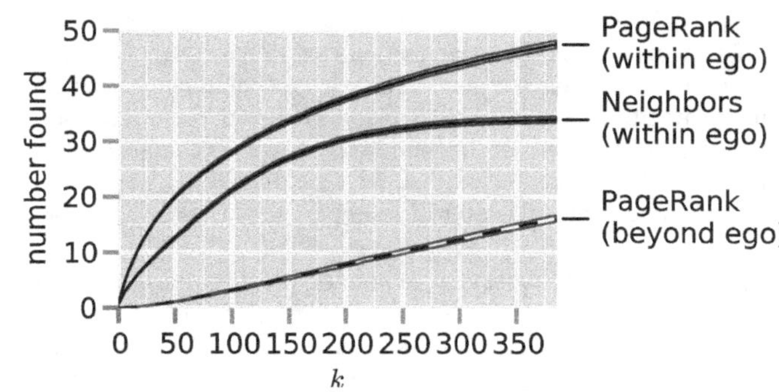

Figure 2: Number of community members found within $\text{ego}(S)$, the seed set's ego network, and outside of it for positive PageRank and positive neighbor counting. Results are averaged over $C^{600}_{3/4}$. Envelopes represent two standard errors centered about the mean.

are found by PageRank compared to Neighbors, categorizing based on whether they belong to $\text{ego}(S)$, the set of nodes directly adjacent to the seed set S. Neighbor-counting methods cannot effectively use information about nodes outside $\text{ego}(S)$. Is this hindrance the sole factor underlying PageRank's advantage over Neighbors?

Figure 2 untangles this issue: first, we see that PageRank's rate of discovery of members within $\text{ego}(S)$ is significantly higher than that of Neighbors; second, we see that it finds true positives outside the ego at a constant linear rate. So in addition to having this broad reach beyond the ego, which we expected, PageRank is even better at identifying which members of the seed set's immediate neighbors are true positives. PageRank's success over neighbor-counting is thus both inside *and* outside $\text{ego}(S)$.

3.3 How many steps does it take to get to the community?

Next we consider a question regarding PageRank itself: in computing PageRank with the power method, how many random walk steps are needed for PageRank to realize its maximum performance? This is a basic question about PageRank's iterative nature, and the concrete performance measures underlying our problem formulation make it natural to evaluate the question in this context.

The results in Figure 3 indicate that after only three random walk steps PageRank's performance has converged to its upper limit, and it is already close to this limit after two steps. It is striking that

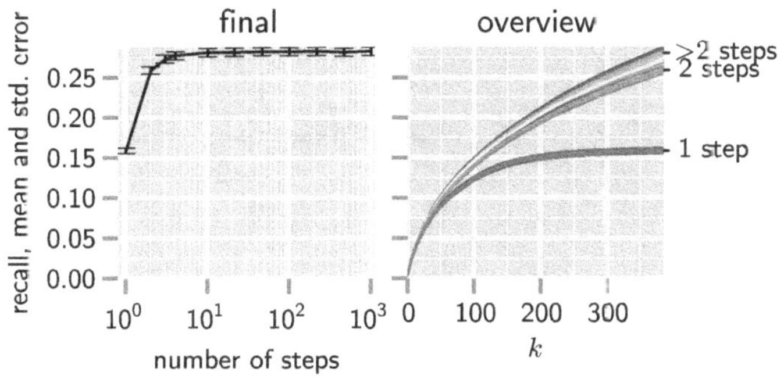

Figure 3: Comparison of PageRank performance for a variety of walk lengths. For each community the same random seed set was used as the walk length was varied. Results are averaged over $C_{3/4}^{600}$ and the envelopes represent two standard errors centered about the mean.

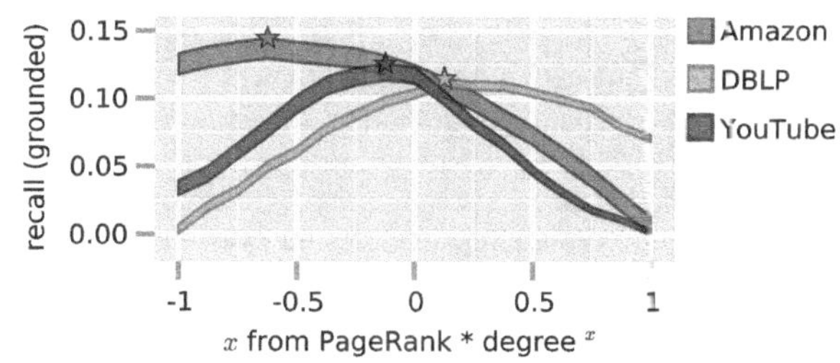

Figure 4: Mean performance as a function of x, where x is a variable exponent in the sorting heuristic PageRank*degree^x. The performances have been shifted vertically such that the lowest performance is grounded at 0, resulting in shifts for Amazon, DBLP, and YouTube of 0.52, 0.18, and 0.049, respectively. The star symbol indicates a curve's maximum. Results are averaged over $C_{3/4}^{600}$ and the envelopes represent two standard errors centered about the mean.

most of PageRank's power on these networks comes from just its first few iterations. To appreciate this we consider PageRank's interpretation at each step and the corresponding performance. 0-step PageRank represents random guessing. 1-step PageRank is closely related to DN-Neighbors[2] — and indeed the performance curve of 1-step PageRank has the same "flattening out" that stood out in the performance curve for neighbor-counting, as well as a comparable final performance value. 2-step PageRank reaches one step beyond ego(S) and in Figure 3 we see that in the transition from 1 to 2 steps PageRank's performance exhibits a dramatic increase, nearly reaching its full potential. This indicates that most of the members found by PageRank are within 2-steps of the seed set. Finally, 3-step PageRank yields PageRank's full potential, and t-step PageRank continues at this level as $t \to \infty$.

3.4 Variations on PageRank

To normalize or not to normalize. Not to normalize. As mentioned, essentially the only PageRank-derivative used in the literature for community detection by seed set expansion has been DN-PageRank [3,16,19,21]. Yet PageRank yields much higher performance than degree-normalized PageRank in DBLP and Youtube and they reach a tie on the Amazon network.

In Figure 1 we find that in DBLP and Youtube (not pictured) unnormalized PageRank, or simply PageRank, finds true community members with greater accuracy than degree-normalized PageRank does. This performance increase is robust after controlling for and considering all community sizes, and it is true in both "easy to detect" and "hard to detect" communities. Indeed, PageRank is best or tied for best on roughly 80% of the communities, on an instance-by-instance basis.

On the Amazon product network, in contrast, PageRank and DN-PageRank reach a statistical tie. It would be interesting to understand the differences in domain that lead to this, including the natural contrast that Amazon is a network on items for purchase, rather than a social network on people as in both DBLP and YouTube.

A continuum: degree-normalization to amplification. Finally we note that DN-PageRank and PageRank are two special cases of using the sorting metric $\rho \cdot d^x$ with $x = -1$ for normalization and $x = 0$ for pure PageRank. It's therefore natural to consider the performance for all values of x, and we show this for all three datasets in Figure 4.

As we see there, the optimal exponents for DBLP and YouTube are both close to 0, indicating the power of unnormalized PageRank on these two social networks, whereas in Amazon the results were statistically indistinguishable for exponents $x \in [-1, 0]$. It is interesting that the optimal exponent x in DBLP is in fact slightly positive — in other words, rather than normalizing PageRank, the optimal strategy is to inflate it slightly. This can perhaps be motivated by the fact that many of the false positives being recovered by the algorithm are low degree nodes.[3]

3.5 Combining Multiple Measures

A natural extension of the current framework is to treat each of these network measures as a feature, and to choose nodes for C by training a classifier on the labeled examples and classifying the remaining nodes each according to their corresponding feature vector. We tried this using a support vector machine (SVM) on a feature in which node v's features are the values of the network measures (PageRank, Neighbors, etc.) evaluated on v. For example, for a simple classifier that combines Neighbors and PageRank, the feature vector for a node u was $[ego(u), \rho(u)]$ and the feature matrix used to train the classifier was $(|S| + |N|) \times 2$. The result is interesting in the negative direction: we were not able to realize any performance gains by combining multiple measures. Rather, the higher-dimensional classifiers performed only as well as its best-performing single-dimensional classifier submember. For example,

[2]But instead of normalizing by the target's user degree, the normalization happens with respect to the outgoing nodes

[3]Who are the false positives?
Note that because the communities in these datasets are overlapping, the nodes recovered by the algorithm should really be classified as being one of three types: true positives, false positives, and *neutral positives*. Neutral positives are nodes that are in some community together with the seed node, simply not in the community of interest C. In that sense, when the algorithm recovers a neutral positive it is accurately discovering information about the graph's community structure. If we relabel the original group of false positives into neutral positives or false positives, we find that in DBLP the 'real' false positives have a much lower average degree and very low variance in degree compared to the neutral or true positives. This distinction is not evident if one only considers the original binary labeling of being in the target community or not. That PageRank is making most of its big mistakes on low-degree nodes motivates the slight degree-amplification that we see is optimal for DBLP in Figure 4.

the 2D SVM consisting of PageRank and Neighbors performed as well as PageRank, and the 2D SVM consisting of Neighbors and BinomProb performed as well as Neighbors.

To construct the classifier we build a feature vector for each of the PageRank-based and Neighbor-based methods, e.g. all the algorithms except Conductance and Modularity. (The latter were excluded because they do not assign attributes for every node in the graph – only for ones local to the seed set.) We build the feature vectors by seeding each of the algorithms with 25% of the input nodes; we reserve such a large fraction so as to emphasize teaching the algorithm about the attributes of 'hidden' positive members, rather than seeded ones (which will typically have much larger values of, for example, PageRank). To choose the C value for the SVM classifier we perform 3-fold cross validation with a 75/25 train/test split. We consider linear and radial basis function kernels and normalize all features to have unit $||L_2||$ norm before training.

Negative examples and information. Note that to train the SVM we require both positive and negative examples, and so for the learning framework we introduce the notion of a negative seed set, T. Much like S, the seed set of known community members, T consists of nodes that are known from the outset (e.g. thanks to a domain expert's knowledge) to be non-members. To choose the negative seed set we tested the same heuristics as we did for the positive seed set, namely random nodes as in §2 and higher degree nodes as we will see in §4.1.

The introduction of the negative examples lead us to consider the possibility that the information about their non-membership could help improve classification. For example, just as we expect nodes tightly knit with the positive seed set S to more likely be members themselves, we expect nodes tightly knit to the negative seed set T to be less likely to be members.

We used SVMs to empirically verify both of these intuitions. That is, we seed PageRank with the negative seed set T and call the resulting metric on the nodes Negative-PageRank. For the purposes of this discussion, we call the original PageRank seeded with S Positive-PageRank. We then train an SVM using these two attributes as node features, and find that the SVM's weight vector has a positive coefficient for the Positive-PageRank feature and a negative coefficient for the Negative-PageRank feature, as expected.

However, the introduction of Negative-PageRank ultimately had no significant effect, neither improving nor hurting the performance of the classifier. The same is true regarding analogous versions of Negative-Neighbors and Negative-BinomProb.

4. RESULTS: SEED SETS

Having looked at the relative performance of different algorithms for seed set expansion, we now consider the effect that different structural properties of the seed set itself can have on performance.

4.1 Heuristics for seed set selection

We begin by considering the effect of the node degrees in the seed set. In Figure 5 we see that for seeding PageRank it is highly advantageous to use a random positive seed set compared with one consisting of high-degree nodes. Though we have not pictured it here, this result holds for all domains, community sizes, and high-performing algorithms. It is true for the neighbor counting metrics as well (with the exception of binomial probability), however for the neighbor counting metrics the improvement is not as striking.

In many settings we should expect to have relatively little control over which members are in the seed set: the community is hidden to us and the seed set consists of those members for whom we happen to have labels. However, the particular contrast we analyze here,

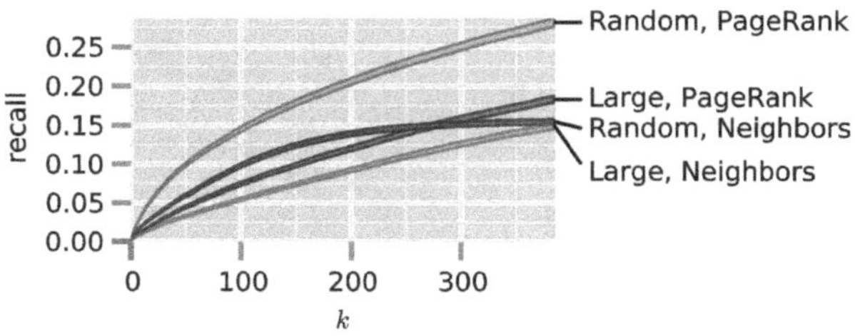

Figure 5: Comparison of algorithm performance for positive seed sets composed of random versus high-degree nodes, using PageRank and Neighbors. Results are averaged over $\mathcal{C}^{600}_{3/4}$ from DBLP and the envelopes represent two standard errors centered about the mean.

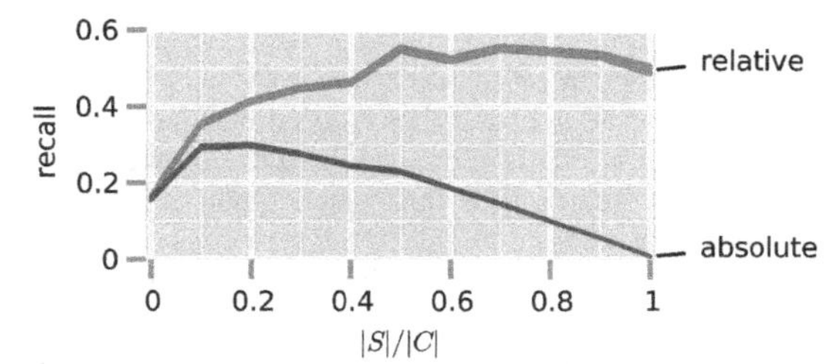

Figure 6: Performance as a function of the fraction of the community used to seed PageRank for all DBLP communities. For each community C ten seed sizes were tested, with size uniformly spaced between 1 and $\lfloor 0.99|C| \rfloor$. We distinguish between two types of recall: relative recall is $|P \cap C|/|C - S|$, i.e. the fraction of unlabeled members that were discovered; whereas absolute recall is $|P \cap C|/|C|$, the fraction of the all members recovered during the evaluation stage. Envelopes represent two standard errors centered about the mean.

between random and high-degree nodes, corresponds naturally to two distinct scenarios for interacting with a domain expert: if the expert knows the most popular or most famous nodes in the community, this would lead to a high-degree seed set, while if the expert returns a more representative seed set, this would be modeled by a set consisting of random nodes. Some experience indicates that experts will often have a tendency to identify high-degree members, which, we see here, is not in fact the most effective way to gather a seed set for further expansion.

This lesson is an important heuristic to consider. Given that our recommendation is to use PageRank over more local methods when possible, it would also be advantageous for domain experts to heuristically search for nodes with a more diverse degree distribution, rather than searching for and validating the membership of those with highest degree. Note that even when this is not possible, and PageRank is seeded with a large degree seed set, it still outperforms Neighbors as a method.

4.2 Seed set size and performance

In Figure 6 we examine the algorithm's performance as a function of the fraction of the community C used in the seed set S, $|S|/|C|$. We evaluate performance using two measures of recall: the *relative recall* $|P \cap C|/|C - S|$, and the *absolute recall* $|P \cap$

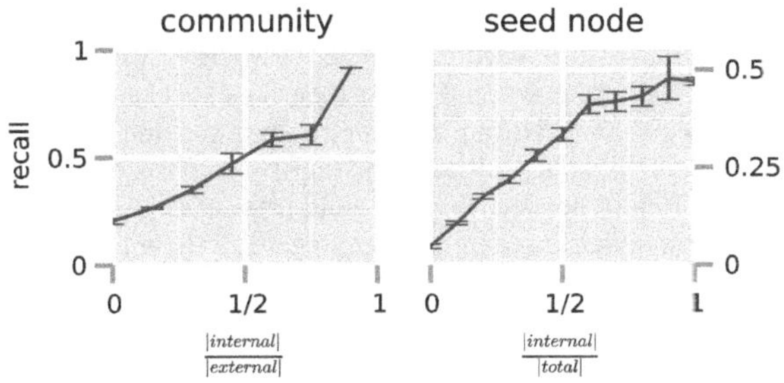

Figure 7: Left: Performance as a function of the target community's ratio of internal to external edge density. Right: Performance as a function of the fraction of edges the seed has within the community. Both plots use PageRank as the sorting metric and test on $C_{3/4}^{600}$.

$C|/|C|$. We find that the relative recall eventually plateaus as $|S|/|C|$ is increased whereas the absolute recall has an interior maximum.

Intuitively we expect this interior maximum in absolute performance: by starting off with very little of the community C we will be lacking sufficient information about C and will find it difficult to accurately characterize and identify additional members. In the other extreme, if we begin with all but a few of the members, we are inherently limited in the number of additional members we can discover. Thus we expect there to be some internal maximum in absolute performance, as we see at $|S|/|C| = 0.1$ in Figure 6.

For relative recall, in contrast, we find that performance simply plateaus after a certain point, meaning that the additional information is neither helping nor hindering our relative rate of discovery.

4.3 Internal seed set structure

Finally, we consider how well the seed set is connected both internally and to the (unobserved) remainder of the community. Although we have seen that seed nodes with overall high degree point to reduced performance, we find here that performance is significantly higher when a large fraction of the seed nodes' edges are to nodes that lie in the community. Figure 7 (right panel) shows the performance in terms of this fraction; the left panel of the figure establishes a related point, that performance is better when the community C has a high ratio of internal edge density to external edge density.

These findings highlight several points. First, it suggests that in practice one can form an *a priori* estimate of the success of seed set expansion on a per-instance basis, based on structural properties of the seed set and/or the community, if one has estimates about these edge density parameters. Second, the strong relation to performance forms an interesting connection to mathematical work on community detection. The literature has emphasized that a good mathematical definition of a community is a set of nodes whose internal edge density is higher than its external one. It is interesting then that in these communities which are defined only by a shared qualitative property of member nodes that this canonical metric emerges as being correlated with high performance.

Finally, as with some of our earlier findings about seed set structure, we cannot necessarily control the seed set properties with which we make our prediction. But it does suggest a heuristic in which one can try to elicit from the domain expert a set of seed nodes that have good internal connectivity into the rest of the community, relative to their connectivity to the rest of the graph. The community results are a reminder that when searching for nodes in a community we should only expect high prediction accuracy if we can also expect that the members for whom we are searching form a densely connected subset of the graph.

5. RICHER INTERACTIONS FOR PRODUCING LABELS

We have been thinking about seed set expansion in terms of interaction with a domain expert who is able to provide us with an initial set of examples. In this section we enrich this interaction by asking the expert to initially label some number of selected nodes beyond the seed set before we make further guesses about nodes likely to belong to the community. Thus, there are three types of nodes here, in order: (i) the initial seed set; (ii) the nodes explored in the *interactive* phase, when the expert is being actively queried; and (iii) the nodes explored in the *non-interactive* phase, when a set of nodes is guessed and only evaluated afterward for membership in C.

This second, additional round of interaction introduces several further questions. (1) How many nodes should be labeled in the interactive phase? We'll call this quantity the query budget. (2) Which nodes should be labeled in the interactive phase? We'll call this function the strategy. (3) Should the nodes in the interactive phase be labeled all at once? Or is there a performance gain to be had by introducing a feedback loop, in which at every iteration b nodes (strictly fewer than the query budget) are chosen according to the strategy, labeled, and used to refine the strategy input on the next round?

Finally, there are two ways of evaluating the algorithm, and we will consider both. One approach, in keeping with the initial motivation for seed set expansion, is to say that all nodes after the initial seed set count toward the performance of the algorithm, including those in the interactive phase. The other approach, more akin to a training/test split, is to say that the nodes in the interactive phase are purely for calibration, and the performance of the algorithm is only evaluated by its success in the non-interactive phase.

The former case is natural for settings where the goal is simply to collect members of the community — for example, in the case of a marketer who simply wants as large a set of likely purchasers as possible. In this case, there is an interesting trade-off between collecting nodes likely to belong to C in the interactive phase versus asking the expert about nodes that are less likely to belong to C, but which will help refine the boundary of C. This will be one of the main trade-offs we explore in this section.

Computational experiments. We fix the size of the query budget to be that of the size of the seed set, that is, 10% the size of the community. We now focus on questions (2) and (3) above.

We consider four heuristics for choosing which nodes to query based on the values of one of our classifiers for membership in C: (1) nodes on the boundary of the decision function; (2) nodes most likely to be positive, as predicted by the classifier; (3) nodes most likely to be negative, as predicted by the classifier; (4) random nodes. We model this selection process by viewing (1)-(4) as having the associated probabilities $(p_0, p_+, p_-, p_*) = p$, and in each step of the interactive phase selecting, for example, $b_+ = p_+b$ nodes predicted to be positive. We measure performance throughout this 3-dimensional parameter space ($p_0 + p_+ + p_- + p_* = 1$). We start with two observations that allow us to simplify our discussion and exploration of this parameter space:

1. It is never advantageous to have $p_* > 0$, that is, there is no benefit to querying random nodes instead of putting that probability mass on some other dimension. This is not sur-

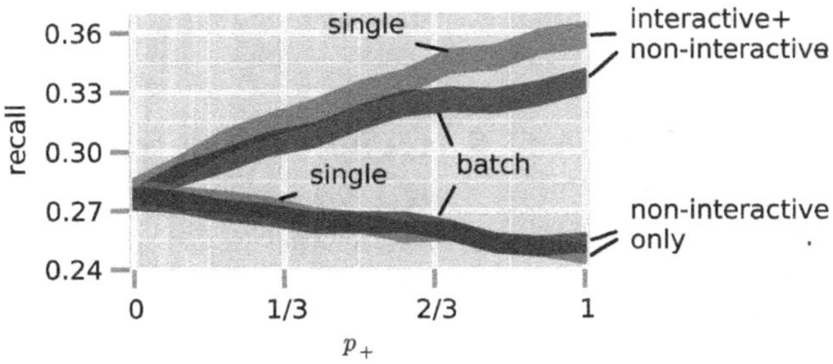

Figure 8: Performance of PageRank with two querying strategies and two evaluation metrics. In *batch* mode, we use the query budget in one sweeping request. *Single* mode is the other extreme: we query the expert for one node's label, reseed PageRank with the updated label, and repeat for as many steps as the query budget allows. Here we fix the query budget to be 10% the expected size of the community. The lower *non-interactive only* curves indicate the final performance of the classifier, not including any positive examples recovered during the interactive phase. The upper *interactive + non-interactive* curves include true positives recovered during both the interactive and non-interactive phases.

prising and in fact this parameter was introduced as a baseline.

2. It is never advantageous to have $p_- > 0$, that is, there is no benefit to querying nodes that are most certainly not in the community. While this is not very surprising we did find it worth considering the possibility that having very clear examples of what community members do not look like could improve the classifier.

These observations imply that, for the scenarios we have defined, $p_- > 0$ and $p_* > 0$ are both dominated by strategies with $p_- = p_* = 0$. Thus we are left with a one-dimensional parameter space, $1 = p_+ + p_0$. In Figure 8 we explore how the performance is affected by labeling boundary nodes (via p_0), positive nodes (via p_+), or some combination thereof. We find that the optimal strategy depends on how performance is being measured:

1. If nodes found in both the interactive and non-interactive phases are counted towards performance, then $p_+ = 1$ is optimal.

2. If only nodes from the non-interactive phase count towards performance , then querying all nodes on the classifier boundary is optimal ($p_+ = 0$).

In the next section, we will see how the trade-off between these two results is reflected in the contrast between two different ways of formulating the problem of identifying nodes in a community.

Note, however, that when the interactive phase does not count towards performance, only a small performance gain is had by $p_0 = 1$ compared to $p_0 = 0$, though the gain is statistically significant (compare the performance of the lower curve on the left and right extremes in Figure 8). In contrast, when the goal is to maximize the number of community members collected (the upper curves in Figure 8), $p_+ = 1$ is a clearly dominant strategy.

Finally we address question (3), whether there is a performance gain to be had by introducing a feedback loop in the labeling stage. We find that it is advantageous to use smaller block sizes when nodes found in the interactive phase count toward performance and the strategy $p_+ = 1$ is used (which is the optimal one for this case). In all other cases we find that the performances are statistically indistinguishable. The performance gain in the first case is all had in the interactive phase; that is, smaller block sizes do not improve the final classifier, but they do yield improved likelihood of finding positive nodes in the interactive stage. For the other scenarios there are either few positive nodes to be found by that strategy (i.e. querying on the boundary) or the nodes found in this stage do not count towards performance and so are irrelevant for evaluation purposes. This is also true in both cases that we discussed above: querying the most positive nodes ($p_+ = 1$) and querying on the boundary ($p_0 = 1$).

6. SEED SET EXPANSION: THEORETICAL RESULTS

If we abstract beyond the specific methods used for seed set expansion, our discussion thus far has highlighted a number of themes implicit purely in the formulation of the problem itself — the difference between collecting a fixed number of nodes from a group C and finding the full set C; the trade-off, as in the previous section, between exploring in the vicinity of nodes known to be in C versus exploring near the estimated boundary of C; and the role of negative information, about non-membership in C.

We now consider a theoretical framework that seeks to highlight how these trade-offs and contrasts work across the different problem formulations. At the top level, it will be based on the distinction between the following two problems: *enumeration*, in which we want to find the full set C; and *seed set expansion*, in which we want to collect "many" members of C but not the full set.

Basic Set-up. To set up these problems, let us assume we are given an undirected n-node graph $G = (V, E)$, and a subset $C \subseteq V$ is specified by a *membership oracle* that takes a node $v \in V$ and reports whether or not $v \in C$. We are also given a seed set $S \subseteq C$ of nodes that we know at the outset to belong to C. Finally, we will make the assumption that C is a connected set of nodes in G.[4]

In these terms, *enumeration* is now the problem of finding all the nodes of C using as few queries as possible to the membership oracle. *Seed set expansion*, in contrast is the problem in which, given a "budget" k, we want to find as many nodes of $C - S$ as possible using at most k queries to the membership oracle.

A Motivating Example. To get an initial picture of the contrasts between these two problem formulations, let's consider them on an extremely simple graph, the n-node cycle, which just consists of nodes $v_0, v_1, \ldots, v_{n-1}$ such that v_i is connected to v_{i-1} and v_{i+1} (addition modulo n). The group C we are trying to discover is a connected subset of the cycle (and hence a contiguous interval of nodes on it).

Suppose we are given a single seed node $v_j \in C$. Then the optimal algorithm for the seed set expansion problem it to begin querying nodes for membership in C starting at v_j and moving in a clockwise direction. The first time we come to a node $v_\ell \notin C$, we

[4] We view this as a reasonable approximation to the real problem in practice, since many of the groups C we are interested in studying will have a giant component $\tilde{C} \subseteq C$. Unless we have seed notes in the smaller components, it is not reasonable in any case to try discovering them; thus, we can view our problem as operating on this giant component. Indeed, some formulations of the seed set expansion problem have explicitly described it as searching for a specific component of the group.

know we have fallen off one end of the interval defined by C. We then go back to v_j and do the same thing in the counter-clockwise direction. In this way, either we discover all of C (if our budget k is large enough), or else we collect nodes at almost full efficiency; aside from the node v_ℓ, every node we query is in C, and so we collect at least $k-1$ nodes with our budget of k.

An efficient algorithm for the enumeration problem has a quite different structure. First, for the enumeration problem it is natural to make an extra assumption that we didn't need for the seed set expansion problem — that we also know a node $z \notin C$. (Otherwise, we would have to begin with an essentially brute-force search for a non-member of C.) Given $s \in C$ and $z \notin C$, there are two paths of C that run between them: one clockwise from s to z, and the other one counter-clockwise from s to z. We perform binary search on the first of these paths to find a pair of adjacent nodes (v, w) such that $v \in C$ and $w \notin C$. We do the same on the other path, and thus find the two endpoints of the interval defining C in $O(\log n)$ queries to the membership oracle.

Contrasting algorithms. Let us now contrast the approaches to these two problems. When $k \ll \log n$, seed set expansion collects nodes of C with almost no waste (i.e. almost no querying of non-members of C), while the efficient algorithm for enumeration could spend its first $\Omega(\log n)$ without ever identifying another member of C. On the other hand, when $k \gg \log n$, seed set expansion is collecting nodes of C one-by-one, whereas after the initial investment of $O(\log n)$ probes, the algorithm for enumeration implicitly knows all of C even though it hasn't visited all of its nodes explicitly.

These two contrasting strategies also relate to some other themes from earlier sections. As in the previous section, the seed set expansion algorithm does well by focusing attention near the nodes of C that it already knows about, whereas the enumeration algorithm focuses attention on farther-away nodes as it attempts to find the boundary of C. And negative information is not particularly relevant for the seed set expansion algorithm, whereas it is crucial for the efficiency of the enumeration algorithm — a reflection of the role that negative information played in our empirical results as well.

Thus far, however, these insights are all based on an extremely simple instance of the problem — finding a contiguous interval on the cycle. Do the same contrasts apply in other graphs? We now prove two theorems establishing that in fact they do, in a very strong sense: for *every* graph G, one can obtain contrasting and asymptotically optimal bounds for seed set expansion and enumeration that naturally extend the results we obtained for the simple case of the cycle.

We stress that in this theoretical analysis, we are focusing on comparing the consequences of the two problem formulations, seeking algorithms for each that are asymptotically optimal in the worst case, rather than trade-offs among specific heuristics for the problems.

General theorems. We continue with the set-up defined at the outset, with an arbitrary graph $G = (V, E)$, a connected set of nodes $C \subseteq V$ that we want to discover, and a given seed set $S \subseteq C$. A key structure for analyzing our algorithms will be the set of edges $\delta(C)$, consisting of all edges that have one end in C and the other end not in C; a central quantity for parametrizing the performance of the algorithms will be $c = |\delta(C)|$.

We begin with the generalization for the seed set expansion problem, essentially showing that there is an algorithm that can collect at least $k - c$ nodes of C. This is the same sense in which the algorithm on the cycle was collecting nodes a perfect efficiency except for the queries in which it fell off the end of C.

THEOREM 1. *Given a budget of k queries to the membership oracle, there is an algorithm that finds at least* $\min(k-c, |C-S|)$ *nodes in $C - S$. (In other words, it either finds at least $k - c$ nodes of $C - S$, or else it finds all of $C - S$.) This is asymptotically tight in the worst case.*

PROOF. We show that the guarantee in the statement of the theorem will be achieved by any algorithm with the following structure: for k iterations, look for a node $v \in C$ connected by an edge to a node w whose membership in C is not yet known, and query w. If at any point before the k iterations are over, there are no such pairs (v, w), then the algorithm can stop and declare that it has found all of C.

Let us first verify why the algorithm is correct when it concludes it has found all of C. Since $G[C]$ is connected, as long as some nodes of C have not yet been found, there must exist an edge (v, w) such that $v, w \in C$, with node v already known to belong to C and node w not yet known to belong to C. Hence as long as all of C has not yet been found, the algorithm can execute another iteration.

Now, in each of the k iterations for which the algorithm does not discover a new node in $C - S$, it instead finds an edge $(v, w) \in E$ for which $v \in C$ and $w \notin C$. Thus $(v, w) \in \delta(C)$. Since there are only c edges in $\delta(C)$, there can be at most c iterations in which the algorithm does not find a new node in $C - S$; in the remaining iterations, at least $k - c$ in total, it must discover a new node in $C - S$, and this establishes the performance guarantee of the algorithm.

To see why the bound of $k - c$ is tight in the worst case, consider the star graph, equal to a tree with a central node v connected to $n - 1$ other nodes $w_1, w_2, \ldots, w_{n-1}$. If $S = \{v\}$ and C consists of v plus all but c of the leaf nodes, then in the worst case the algorithm will discover all c nodes not in C before moving on to any nodes in $C - S$. $\square$

We now give the contrasting generalization for the enumeration problem — that all of C can be found with $O(c \log n)$ queries. For this algorithm, as in the case of the cycle, we need to assume the presence of negative information; in particular, we assume there is a set of nodes $Z \subseteq V - C$ that is rich enough in its coverage that Z contains at least one node from each component of $G - C$.

THEOREM 2. *Given seed set $S \subseteq V$ and negative set $Z \subseteq V$ satisfying the assumptions above, there is an algorithm to find all the nodes of C using at most $O(c \log n)$ queries to the membership oracle. This is asymptotically tight in the worst case.*

PROOF. The algorithm works as follows. Let s be any node in the given set $S \subseteq C$; we say that an *s-Z path* is any path whose first node is s and whose last node belongs to Z. Edges will get *marked* during the execution of the algorithm; initially all edges start out unmarked. While there is an s-Z path P in G consisting entirely of unmarked edges, we perform binary search over the ordered sequence of nodes on P to find an edge (v, w) on P for which $v \in C$ and $w \notin C$. We then mark this edge (v, w). This is one iteration of the algorithm, and it uses $O(\log n)$ queries to the membership oracle in order to perform the binary search.

How many iterations can there be? Each iteration marks an edge in $\delta(C)$ that was previously unmarked; since $|\delta(C)| = c$, there can be at most c iterations. It follows that in total the algorithm performs at most $O(c \log n)$ queries.

Let F be the set of marked edges when the algorithm terminates, and let $U \subseteq V$ be the connected component of $G - F$ that contains the node s. We claim that $U = C$. Indeed, suppose there were a node $u \in C$ such that $u \notin U$. Then since $G[C]$ is connected, there is an s-u path consisting entirely of nodes in C, and hence using no marked edges. This contradicts the assumption that $u \notin U$. Conversely, suppose there were a node $u \in U$ such that $u \notin C$. Let z be a node of Z that belongs to same component of $G - C$ that u does. There is a u-z path Q such that all nodes belong to $V - C$; since each marked edge contains a node of C, there are no marked edges on Q. Concatenating Q with an s-u path using no marked edges, we get an s-z path using no marked edges, contradicting the termination of the algorithm.

These arguments show that $C \subseteq U$ and $U \subseteq C$, so $U = C$ and hence the algorithm produces the correct output set C.

Finally, we argue that there exist instances with a graph $G = (V, E)$ and a set $C \subseteq V$ for which $\Omega(c \log n)$ queries are required. One such graph is a collection of c parallel paths each of length n/c, that each run from s to z, but which otherwise have no nodes or edges in common. Any set C obtained by choosing a prefix of each s-z path, and taking the union of these c prefixes, will have $s \in C$ and $z \notin C$, with $\delta(C) = c$. There are $\Omega(n^c)$ such sets C, and hence any algorithm that uniquely identifies one of them through a sequence of yes/no questions to an oracle must make at least $\Omega(\log n^c) = \Omega(c \log n)$ queries in the worst case. □

7. RELATED WORK

The seed set expansion problem has its roots in a number of overlapping areas, including the problem of identifying central nodes in social networks [6, 9] and finding related and/or important Web pages from an initial set of query results [10, 15].

In particular, the PageRank algorithm broadened from its initial focus on Web search [15] to also include methods for finding nodes "similar" to an initial root, by starting short random walks from the root and seeing which other nodes were likely to be reached [7]. Spielman & Teng developed methods that started with a seed node and sorted all other nodes by their degree-normalized PageRank with respect to this seed [17]; they also introduced ideas based on truncation of small values, leading to a method known as PageRank-Nibble. Anderson & Lang and Andersen *et al.* built on these methods to formulate an algorithm for detecting overlapping communities in networks [2, 3]; in our evaluation, their method serves as our version of DN-PageRank, short for degree-normalized, personalized PageRank. DN-PageRank was adopted by Leskovec *et al.* [11] and Yang & Leskovec for global and local community detection. In a large comparison study they established DN-PageRank as competitive with METIS [8], a sophisticated and popular graph partitioning algorithm. Finally, Abrahao *et al.* observe that from among approximately ten popular community detection algorithms, ground-truth communities are structurally most similar to the communities discovered by random walk methods [1].

In parallel with the development of PageRank-based methods, another line of work explored methods for seed set expansion by adding nodes to a growing community (or removing them) if a target measure such as conductance or modularity is improved by doing so. Clauset [5] used this idea by adding single nodes to increase modularity; Luo *et al.* [12] allowed for addition and deletion of larger sets; and Mislove *et al.* [14] used greedy node addition to reduce conductance.

Finally, a number of approaches evaluated nodes based on the number of neighbors they had in and out of the community, adding nodes to the community when they optimized a function of these two quantities. Bagrow [4] did this for a measure called *outwardness*, defined as the degree-normalized difference between neighbors inside and outside the community. Mehler & Skiena [13] used several variations of neighbor counting methods for seeded community detection, the main ones being pure neighbor count, neighbor ratio, and binomial probability of neighbor distribution. More recently in 2013 Weber *et al.* used another variation of a neighbor-counting metric to infer the political ideology of Twitter users, based on which community a user retweeted more frequently.

In an analysis of the effect of seed-set structure, Whang, Gleich, & Dillon [19] systematically compared several sophisticated approaches for choosing the seed sets with which to seed PageRank-based measures for community detection. Their methods outperform existing sophisticated methods, but do not significantly outperform the use of random nodes.

Finally, essentially all seed set expansion algorithms need to make a decision about the choice of *stopping criterion* — when does one stop expanding the set? Such a criterion can be treated relatively independently from the choice of expansion rule. Andersen & Lang [3] and Yang & Leskovec [11] choose the first nodes that represent a set with a locally minimal conductance (given that additions happen in the order induced by sorted, DN-PageRank). Mehler & Skiena continue until the mining rate of reserved labeled nodes passes below a certain threshold; Bagrow [4] looks for transitions and cusps in the modularity that one expects at a community border. Others such as Mislove *et al.* [14], Luo *et al.* [12], and Clauset [5] greedily add and subtract nodes from the predicted community until a local maximum is reached. In 2012 Yang & Leskovec used PageRank-type measures to empirically compare different topological parameters to identify community boundaries in real-world data sets. They found that the result was somewhat domain-dependent, but that either the set's conductance or its triad participation ratio were, most reliably, high accuracy stopping rules.

8. CONCLUSION

The seed set expansion problem has been gaining visibility as a general-purpose framework for identifying members of a networked community from a small set of initial examples. But subtle trade-offs in the formulation and underlying methods can have a significant impact on the way this process works, and in this paper we have identified several such principles about the relative power of different expansion heuristics, and the structural properties of the initial seed set. Our investigations have involved analyses of datasets across diverse domains as well as theoretical trade-offs between different problem formulations.

There are a number of interesting directions for further work. In particular, the power of PageRank-based methods raises the question of whether these are indeed the "right" algorithms for seed set expansion, or whether they should be viewed as proxies for a richer set of probabilistic approaches that could yield strong performance. Second, the contrast between seed sets consisting of random nodes versus those consisting of high-degree nodes suggests that deeper structural contrasts may be present as well; a richer understanding of the seed sets that lead to the most effective expansions to a larger community could provide useful insights for the application of these methods. And finally, as noted earlier in the paper, nodes in a network tend to belong to multiple communities simultaneously, and a robust way of expanding several overlapping communities together is a natural question for further study.

9. ACKNOWLEDGMENTS

We thank Michael Macy, Silvana Toska, and Shaomei Wu for useful discussions. Research supported in part by an NSF Graduate Research Fellowship, a Simons Investigator Award, a Google Research Grant, an ARO MURI grant, and NSF grant IIS-0910664.

10. REFERENCES

[1] Bruno Abrahao, Sucheta Soundarajan, John Hopcroft, and Robert Kleinberg. On the separability of structural classes of communities. In *In KDD '12*, pages 624–632. ACM, 2012.

[2] Reid Andersen, Fan Chung, and Kevin Lang. Local graph partitioning using pagerank vectors. In *Foundations of Computer Science, 2006. FOCS'06. 47th Annual IEEE Symposium on*, pages 475–486. IEEE, 2006.

[3] Reid Andersen and Kevin J Lang. Communities from seed sets. In *In WWW '06*.

[4] James P Bagrow. Evaluating local community methods in networks. *Journal of Statistical Mechanics: Theory and Experiment*, 2008(05):P05001, 2008.

[5] Aaron Clauset. Finding local community structure in networks. *Physical review E*, 72(2):026132, 2005.

[6] Charles H Hubbell. An input-output approach to clique identification. *Sociometry*, 1965.

[7] Glen Jeh and Jennifer Widom. Scaling personalized web search. In *In WWW '03*, pages 271–279. ACM, 2003.

[8] George Karypis and Vipin Kumar. Metis-unstructured graph partitioning and sparse matrix ordering system, version 2.0. 1995.

[9] Leo Katz. A new status index derived from sociometric analysis. *Psychometrika*, 18(1):39–43, 1953.

[10] Jon M Kleinberg. Authoritative sources in a hyperlink environment. In *Proc. of ACM-SIAM Symposium on Discrete Algorithms*, 1998.

[11] Jure Leskovec, Kevin J Lang, and Michael Mahoney. Empirical comparison of algorithms for network community detection. In *In WWW '10*, pages 631–640. ACM, 2010. data source.

[12] Feng Luo, James Z Wang, and Eric Promislow. Exploring local community structures in large networks. *Web Intelligence and Agent Systems*, 6(4):387–400, 2006.

[13] Andrew Mehler and Steven Skiena. Expanding network communities from representative examples. *ACM Transactions on Knowledge Discovery from Data (TKDD)*, 3(2):7, 2009.

[14] Alan Mislove, Bimal Viswanath, Krishna P Gummadi, and Peter Druschel. You are who you know: inferring user profiles in online social networks. In *In WSDM '10*, pages 251–260. ACM, 2010.

[15] Lawrence Page, Sergey Brin, Rajeev Motwani, and Terry Winograd. The pagerank citation ranking: Bringing order to the web. 1999.

[16] Jason Riedy, David A Bader, Karl Jiang, Pushkar Pande, and Richa Sharma. Detecting communities from given seeds in social networks. 2011.

[17] Daniel A Spielman and Shang-Hua Teng. Nearly-linear time algorithms for graph partitioning, graph sparsification, and solving linear systems. In *In STOC '04*, pages 81–90. ACM, 2004.

[18] Ingmar Weber, Venkata R Kiran Garimella, and Alaa Batayneh. Secular vs. islamist polarization in egypt on twitter. In *In ASONAM '13*, pages 290–297. ACM, 2013.

[19] Joyce Jiyoung Whang, David F Gleich, and Inderjit S Dhillon. Overlapping community detection using seed set expansion. In *In CIKM '13*, pages 2099–2108. ACM, 2013.

[20] Baoning Wu and Kumar Chellapilla. Extracting link spam using biased random walks from spam seed sets. In *In AIRWeb '07*, pages 37–44. ACM, 2007.

[21] Jaewon Yang and Jure Leskovec. Defining and evaluating network communities based on ground-truth. In *In MDS '12*, page 3. ACM, 2012.

APPENDIX

A. SUMMARY OF ALGORITHMS

Here we provide brief summaries of the algorithms used in the main text; for more details see citation. We distinguish between three types of algorithms:

Neighbor counting.
(a) Outwardness, the degree-normalized difference between the number of edges a node has into and out of the labeled community [4];
(b) Neighbors, the number of neighbors a node has in the labeled community [13];
(c) DN-Neighbors, the degree-normalized version of Neighbors [13];
(d) BinomProb, the binomial probability that a node is in the community, given the number of neighbors it has in the labeled community [13].

Greedy structural optimization.
(e) Modularity, greedy algorithm: in each step add the node that yields the highest increase in the set modularity of the predicted community, [5];
(f) SetModularity, greedy algorithm: in each step add the nodes that yield a positive increase in set modularity, then remove the set of all nodes whose removal precipitates an increase, [12];
(g) Conductance, greedy algorithm: in each step add the node that yields the most negative change in conductance, [14].

PageRank.
(h) PageRank, implemented here with personalization and computed using the power method and jumpback probability $\alpha = 0.10$, see [7] or footnote [5] for implementation details. For comparison with [2,21] we also implemented a version with ϵ-truncation (semi-accurate estimate of PageRank); however we found that below a $\epsilon \approx 1/|G|$) there were no significant differences in performance, and past this ϵ, the performance steeply plummets to approach that achieved by random guessing.
(i) DN-PageRank, the degree-normalized version of PageRank [17]; again, see footnote [5].

[5] Let ρ^t be the tth random walk vector given that the initialization set S is the set of known community members.
Let $\chi(S)$ be an indicator vector where $\chi_i(S) = 1$ if $i \in S$ and 0 otherwise. Let A be the adjacency matrix, where $A_{ij} = 1$ if j links to i and 0 otherwise. The degree of node j is given by $d_j = \sum_i A_{ij}$. The random walk is initialized with $\rho^0 = \chi(S)/|S|$. In step $t+1$ each node i distributes $\alpha\rho_i^t$ probability mass uniformly over the seed set S and $(1-\alpha)\rho_i^t$ probability mass over its neighbors. The corresponding probability transition matrix $M(S)$ is:

$$M_{ij}(S) = \alpha\frac{\chi_i(S)}{|S|} + (1-\alpha)\frac{A_{ij}}{d_j}.$$

Community Detection in Graphs through Correlation

Lian Duan
New Jersey Institute of Technology
Newark, NJ 07102, USA
lian.duan@njit.edu

W. Nick Street
University of Iowa
Iowa City, IA 52242, USA
nick-street@uiowa.edu

Yanchi Liu
New Jersey Institute of Technology
Newark, NJ 07102, USA
yl473@njit.edu

Haibing Lu
Santa Clara University
Santa Clara, CA 95053, USA
hlu@scu.edu

ABSTRACT

Community detection is an important task for social networks, which helps us understand the functional modules on the whole network. Among different community detection methods based on graph structures, modularity-based methods are very popular recently, but suffer a well-known resolution limit problem. This paper connects modularity-based methods with correlation analysis by subtly reformatting their math formulas and investigates how to fully make use of correlation analysis to change the objective function of modularity-based methods, which provides a more natural and effective way to solve the resolution limit problem. In addition, a novel theoretical analysis on the upper bound of different objective functions helps us understand their bias to different community sizes, and experiments are conducted on both real life and simulated data to validate our findings.

Categories and Subject Descriptors

H.2.8 [**DATABASE MANAGEMENT**]: Database Applications – Data Mining

Keywords

community detection; correlation analysis; modularity; leverage; likelihood ratio

1. INTRODUCTION

The modern science of graphs has significantly helped us understand complex systems. One important feature of graphs is community structure where nodes in the same community have a higher chance to be connected to each other than that of nodes in different communities. Such communities can be considered as relatively independent components and play a role in the system. Community detection, which attempts to identify the modules by using the graph topology, has a long history in sociology, biology, and computer science where systems are often represented as graphs. The first research on community detection was made by Weiss and Jacobson [39] to study the working relationships between members of a government agency. Nowadays, there are many different community detection methods, such as spectral-based methods [24], density-based methods [26], modularity-based methods [9, 35], divisive methods [19], statistical-inference-based methods [28], etc. Generally speaking, their progress can be categorized into the following three procedures: (1) feature selection (2) objective function (3) search procedure.

Feature selection selects relevant features, and removes irrelevant noisy information. Spectral-based methods [24] use the eigenvectors of the adjacency matrix for community detection. The Laplacian is by far the most used matrix in spectral-based methods. Though no unique matrix is exactly called the graph Laplacian [24], one commonly used Laplacian is calculated as follows. Given the adjacency matrix W of the graph G, we calculate the matrix D where the diagonal element d_{ii} is equal to $\sum_{j=1}^{n}(w_{ij})$ and non-diagonal elements are 0. The Laplacian matrix L is equal to $D-W$. We choose k eigenvectors corresponding to the k smallest eigenvalues to transform the original adjacency matrix, and then apply the traditional clustering methods like K-mean [25] on the transformed matrix. The spectral-based methods are popular because the change of representation induced by eigenvectors makes the community structure more obvious.

Objective function is the function to express our goal in mathematical terms. No matter how the community is defined, the commonly accepted goal for community detection can be boiled down to two objectives: (1) More connections are inside each community. (2) Fewer connections are across different communities. Since there are two objectives, people have proposed many different methods to strike a different balance between them. There are various kinds of objective functions for community detection [1]. For example, density-based methods [26] try to find the communities within which nodes are tightly connected with each other. We define the internal-community density $\delta_{int}(S)$ of the subgraph S as the ratio of the number of internal edges of S to the number of all possible internal edges, i.e. $\delta_{int}(S) = \frac{k_{int}(S)}{n_s*(n_s-1)/2}$ where $k_{int}(S)$ is the number of internal edges of S. Similarly, the external-community density $\delta_{ext}(S) = \frac{k_{ext}(S)}{n_s*(n-n_s)}$. For S to be a community, we expect large $\delta_{int}(S)$ and small $\delta_{ext}(S)$.

KDD'14, August 24–27, 2014, New York, NY, USA.
Copyright 2014 ACM 978-1-4503-2956-9/14/08 ...$15.00.
http://dx.doi.org/10.1145/2623330.2623629 .

Searching for the best tradeoff between $\delta_{int}(S)$ and $\delta_{ext}(S)$ is the goal of density-based methods. A simple way of doing that is to maximize the sum of the difference $\delta_{int}(S)-\delta_{ext}(S)$ [26]. Another example is modularity-based methods which search the partition that maximizes the modularity function [9]. Although the modularity function is originally introduced as a stopping criterion for hierarchical methods [19], it has rapidly become an essential element of many clustering methods by searching the partitions that maximize it

Search procedure is the way we search the optimal solution according to the objective function. However, for the most objective functions, finding the optimal value is very slow. For example, it has been proved that modularity optimization is an NP-complete problem [7]. Therefore, many different heuristic search algorithms, including greedy search [9, 38], simulated annealing [27], extremal optimization [6, 14], and genetic algorithms [31], are used.

According to different survey studies [16, 40] on community detection, modularity-based methods are considered as one classical type of methods. Despite the vast amount of expert endeavor spent on different optimization techniques to maximize the modularity function, there is little analysis on the modularity function itself, and the most analysis on the modularity function is related to the calculation of the edge probability [17] or the extension to complicated networks [3]. In addition, modularity-based methods suffer the well-known resolution limit problem [22]. This problem also cannot be solved by multi-resolution methods [33] as two concurrent biases, the tendency to merge small communities and to split large communities, are introduced.

The modularity function [9] searches for partitions that the actual number of edges is larger than the expected number of edges inside communities under the assumption of random partition, while correlation analysis on itemset mining [13, 18, 36] searches for itemsets that occur more than the expected occurrence if items are independent from each other. Since both modularity on community detection and correlation analysis on itemset mining search for patterns that actually happens more than what is expected under the assumption of independence, this paper builds the connection between the modularity function and correlation measures, and changes the modularity function from the correlation perspective, through which the resolution limit problem of the original modularity function can be solved and performance can be improved. The focus in this paper is on the improvements over the modularity function from the correlation perspective. In order to have a fair comparison within the framework of correlation, the original modularity function is treated as a baseline for the performance evaluation rather than other commonly used objective functions such as density [26] and conductance [21]. Although the modularity function can be combined with fuzzy logic for overlapping community detection [29], we limit our performance evaluation to non-overlapping community detection in this paper. The rest of the paper is organized as follows. Section 2 introduces the basic notation of correlation analysis and modularity-based community detection. We build the connection between correlation analysis and modularity-based community detection by subtly reformatting their math formulas, and introduce a novel theoretical analysis on the bias of different correlation measures by analyzing their upper bounds in Section 3. Experiments on both real life and simulated datasets are conducted to test different methods in Section 4. Finally, we draw a conclusion and point out future directions in Section 5.

2. BASIC NOTATION

Since we try to improve modularity-based methods from the correlation analysis perspective, the basic concepts of correlation and modularity-based community detection will be introduced first before connecting them.

2.1 Correlation Analysis

Most of the correlation analysis in the data mining area is conducted on the context of itemset mining. Therefore, we follow the routine to introduce the basic concept of correlation. Given an itemset $S = \{I_1, I_2, ..., I_m\}$ with m items in a dataset with sample size n, the true probability is $tp = P(S)$, the expected probability under the assumption of independence among items is $ep = \prod_{i=1}^{m} P(I_i)$. Many functions have been proposed to measure correlation [12, 13, 18, 35]. Here, we only introduce four typical correlation measures, Simplified χ^2, Probability Ratio, Leverage, and Likelihood Ratio, which are derived from the simple statistical theory and enough for generality.

2.1.1 *Simplifie* χ^2

The χ^2 test is arguably the most popular statistical check for correlation, and is specifically designed for use with categorical data. It is calculated as $\chi^2 = \sum_i \sum_j (r_{ij} - E(r_{ij}))^2/E(r_{ij})$. If an itemset contains m items, 2^m cells in the contingency table must be considered for the above χ^2 statistic. The computation of the statistic itself is intractable for high-dimensional data. However, we can still use the basic idea behind χ^2 to create Simplified χ^2 [20]: $\chi'^2 = (r-E(r))^2/E(r)$, i.e., $n \cdot (tp - ep)^2/ep$, where the cell r corresponds to the exact itemset S and n is the total number of records. Since Simplified χ^2 is more computationally desirable, we only discuss the properties and experimental results of Simplified χ^2. The value of Simplified χ^2 is always larger than 0 and cannot differentiate positive from negative correlation. Therefore, we take advantage of the comparison between tp and ep. If $tp > ep$, it is a positive correlation. Then Simplified χ^2 is equal to $n \cdot (tp-ep)^2/ep$. If $tp < ep$, it is a negative correlation. Then Simplified χ^2 is equal to $-n \cdot (tp-ep)^2/ep$. This transformed Simplified χ^2 is mathematically favorable. Larger positive numbers indicate stronger positive correlation, 0 indicates no correlation, and larger (in magnitude) negative numbers indicate stronger negative correlation.

2.1.2 *Probability Ratio/Lift/Interest Factor*

Probability Ratio (also known as Lift or Interest Factor) [8] is the ratio of an itemset's true probability to its expected probability under the assumption of independence. It is calculated as follows: $ProbabilityRatio(S) = tp/ep$. This measure is straightforward and means how many times the itemset S happens more than expected. However, this measure might not be a good correlation measure to use. The problem is that it favors the itemsets containing a large number of items rather than significant trends in the data.

2.1.3 *Leverage*

An itemset S with higher occurrence and low Probability Ratio may be more interesting than an alternative itemset S' with low occurrence and high Probability Ratio. Introduced by Piatesky-Shapiro [30], $Leverage(S) = tp - ep$. It measures the difference between the true probability of an itemset S and its expected probability if all the items in S are independent from each other. Since ep is always no less than 0, $Leverage(S)$ can never be bigger than tp. Therefore, Leverage is biased to high-occurrence itemsets.

2.1.4 Likelihood Ratio

Likelihood Ratio is similar to a statistical test based on the loglikelihood ratio described by Dunning [15]. We take the ratio of the likelihood under our hypothesis of independence to the likelihood of the best "explanation" overall. To apply the likelihood ratio test as a correlation measure, we use the binomial distribution $Pr(p, o, n) = \binom{n}{o} p^o(1-p)^{(n-o)}$, where p is the probability of a given itemset S, o is the occurrence of the itemset S, and n is the total number of transactions. Given our assumption of independence of all items, we predict that each trial has a probability of success ep. Therefore, the chance for us to observe o out n transactions contain S is $Pr(ep, o, n)$ under the assumption of independence. However, the best possible explanation for the single trial probability is tp instead of ep according to the observed data. In order to measure to what extent our assumption of item independence was violated in practice, we comparing the null hypothesis of independence with the best possible explanation. Formally, the Likelihood Ratio in this case is $LikelihoodRatio(S) = Pr(tp, o, n)/Pr(ep, o, n)$. The Likelihood Ratio strikes a balance between the Probability Ratio and the actual occurrence o. It favors itemsets with both high Probability Ratio and high occurrence. For the itemsets containing a small number of items, their occurrence tends to be high, but the Probability Ratio tends to be low, while, for the itemsets containing a large number of items, their Probability Ratio tends to be high, but the actual occurrence tends to be low. Likelihood Ratio favors middle-sized itemsets which can strike a balance between the Probability Ratio and the actual occurrence. The numerator of the Likelihood Ratio is the maximal likelihood of the real situation, so the Likelihood Ratio is always larger than 1 and cannot differentiate positive from negative correlation. Therefore, we conduct the similar transformation we do for Simplified χ^2 by comparing tp with ep.

2.2 Modularity-based Community Detection

The modularity function has several variants, but these variants share the same idea. Without the loss of generality, we introduce the original modularity-based method [9]. Given a graph with n nodes and m links represented by the adjacency matrix W, the expected number of edges falling between two nodes i and j is $k_i \cdot k_j/(2m)$ under the assumption of independence where k_i is the degree of node i. The modularity Q is calculated as $\frac{1}{2m}\sum_{ij}(w_{ij} - \frac{k_i \cdot k_j}{2m}) \cdot \delta(v_i, v_j)$. It is the sum of the difference between the actual number of edges and the expected number of edges over all the pairs of nodes in the same community. $\delta(v_i, v_j)$ is the Kronecker delta function whose value is equal to 1 if v_i and v_j are in the same community and 0 otherwise. Initially, each node is the only member of its own community. The original algorithm iteratively joins the two communities that increase the modularity most in the current round. The original algorithm will stop if the best merge cannot further increase modularity.

3. CORRELATION ANALYSIS AND MODULARITY

3.1 Connecting Modularity-based Community Detection with Correlation Analysis

In this section, we subtly transform the modularity function and connect it with correlation measures. Given a partition with l groups $\{G_1, G_2, ..., G_l\}$ for the graph G with n nodes and m links, the modularity Q is $\frac{1}{2m}\sum_{ij}(w_{ij} - \frac{k_i \cdot k_j}{2m}) \cdot \delta(v_i, v_j)$. For the node v_q in the group G_p, k_q^{int} is the number of the nodes in the group G_p that connect to v_q. The partial modularity Q_p, which all the nodes in the group G_p contribute to the overall modularity function, is $\frac{1}{2m}\sum_{i \in G_p, j \in G}(w_{ij} - \frac{k_i \cdot k_j}{2m}) \cdot \delta(v_i, v_j)$.

Therefore,

$$\begin{aligned} Q_p &= \sum_{i \in G_p, j \in G} \frac{w_{ij} \cdot \delta(v_i, v_j)}{2m} - \sum_{i \in G_p, j \in G} \frac{k_i \cdot k_j \cdot \delta(v_i, v_j)}{(2m)^2} \\ &= \sum_{i \in G_p} \frac{\sum_{j \in G} w_{ij} \cdot \delta(v_i, v_j)}{2m} - \sum_{i \in G_p} \frac{k_i \cdot \sum_{j \in G} k_j \cdot \delta(v_i, v_j)}{(2m)^2} \\ &= \sum_{i \in G_p} \frac{k_i^{int}}{2m} - \sum_{i \in G_p} \frac{k_i \cdot \sum_{j \in G_p} k_j}{(2m)^2} \\ &= \frac{\sum_{i \in G_p} k_i^{int}}{2m} - \frac{\sum_{i \in G_p} k_i}{2m} \cdot \frac{\sum_{j \in G_p} k_j}{2m}. \end{aligned}$$

It is easy to calculate that the total number of links inside G_p is $\sum_{i \in G_p} k_i^{int}/2$ and the total number of links in the graph G is m. If we randomly select a link from the graph G, the probability of the link inside G_p is $\frac{\sum_{i \in G_p} k_i^{int}/2}{m}$. Similarly, the probability of the link with at least one end inside G_p is $\frac{\sum_{i \in G_p} k_i}{2m}$ when we randomly select a link from the graph G. If the partition with l groups $\{G_1, G_2, ..., G_l\}$ for the graph G is totally random, the probability of the link with the other end inside G_p from the links with one end already inside G_p is $\frac{\sum_{i \in G_p} k_i}{2m} \cdot \frac{\sum_{j \in G_p} k_j}{2m}$. Therefore, given a partition with l groups $\{G_1, G_2, ..., G_l\}$ for the graph G, if we randomly select a link from the graph G, the true probability of the link being inside G_p, tp, is $\frac{\sum_{i \in G_p} k_i^{int}}{2m}$, and the expected probability of the link being inside G_p under the assumption of independent partition, ep, is $\frac{\sum_{i \in G_p} k_i}{2m} \cdot \frac{\sum_{j \in G_p} k_j}{2m}$. Therefore, the partial modularity function Q_p can be rewritten as: $Q_p = tp - ep$. By comparing the correlation measure $Leverage(S) = tp - ep$, we can see the modularity function shares the same idea with the correlation measure Leverage. Since the other correlation measures are also functions of tp and ep, we can change the partial modularity function Q_p by using the formula of other correlation measures. In the rest of the paper, instead of using the term modularity, we use Simplified χ^2, Probability Ratio, Leverage, and Likelihood Ratio referring to the corresponding changed partial modularity function Q_p, and Leverage is the original modularity community detection method.

3.2 Upper Bound Analysis

The performance differences among different correlation measures have been recognized since 2004 by two very influential papers [18, 36] in the data mining area. They categorized measures according to their different property satisfaction. By categorizing measures, users only need to check the performance of the typical measure in each category instead of all the possible measures. However, two measures can still generate different results even if they satisfy the same set of properties. Instead, one recent paper [37] categorized measures directly according to their final result similarity. No matter how categorizing measures, the fundamental question is still not answered. If there is a difference between results of two measures, what is the difference? In this section, we provide a novel way to understand the performance difference by analyzing the upper bound of different partial modularity functions Q_p inferred from different correlation measures. Simplified χ^2, Probability Ratio, Leverage, and Likelihood Ratio all satisfy the third correlation property proposed by Piatesky-Shapiro [30]: The correlation Measure M monotonically decreases with the increase of ep when tp remains the same. According to the above correlation property, the measures reach their upper bound when tp is fixed and ep reaches its lower bound.

THEOREM 1. *Simplified χ^2, Probability Ratio, Leverage, and Likelihood Ratio monotonically decreases with the increase of ep when tp remains the same.*

PROOF. **Simplified χ^2:** When $tp \geq ep$, $\chi^2 = n \cdot (tp - ep)^2/ep$. If we consider Simplified χ^2 as a function of ep, then $\chi^{2\prime} = n \cdot (ep^2 - tp^2)/ep^2$. Since $0 \leq ep \leq tp \leq 1$, $ep^2 \leq tp^2$. Therefore, $\chi^{2'}(S) \leq 0$. Similarly, when $tp < ep$, $\chi^2 = -n \cdot (tp - ep)^2/ep$ and $\chi^{2\prime} = -n \cdot (ep^2 - tp^2)/ep^2 < 0$ In all, Simplified χ^2 decreases with the increase of ep.

Probability Ratio: When tp is fixed, Probability Ratio, tp/ep, decreases with the increase of ep.

Leverage: When tp is fixed, Leverage, $tp - ep$, decreases with the increase of ep.

Likelihood Ratio: When $tp > ep$,

$$\begin{aligned} ln(LR(S)) &= n \cdot tp \cdot (ln(tp) - ln(ep)) \\ &\quad + n \cdot (1 - tp) \cdot (ln(1 - tp) - ln(1 - ep)) \\ &= n \cdot tp \cdot ln(tp) - n \cdot tp \cdot ln(ep) \\ &\quad + n \cdot ln(1 - tp) - n \cdot ln(1 - ep) \\ &\quad - n \cdot tp \cdot ln(1 - tp) + n \cdot tp \cdot ln(1 - ep) \\ &= n \cdot tp \cdot ln\frac{tp}{1 - tp} + n \cdot ln(1 - tp) \\ &\quad - n \cdot ln(1 - ep) + n \cdot tp \cdot ln\frac{1 - ep}{ep}. \end{aligned}$$

If we consider $ln(LR(S))$ as a function of ep, then

$$\begin{aligned} ln(LR(S))' &= \frac{n}{1 - ep} - \frac{n \cdot tp}{(1 - ep) \cdot ep} \\ &= \frac{n \cdot (ep - tp)}{(1 - ep) \cdot ep}. \end{aligned}$$

Since $tp > ep$, then $ln(LR(S))' < 0$. In other words, Likelihood Ratio decreases with the increase of ep when $tp > ep$. Similarly, when $tp < ep$, we can prove Likelihood Ratio decreases with the increase of ep. In all, Likelihood Ratio decreases with the increase of ep.

□

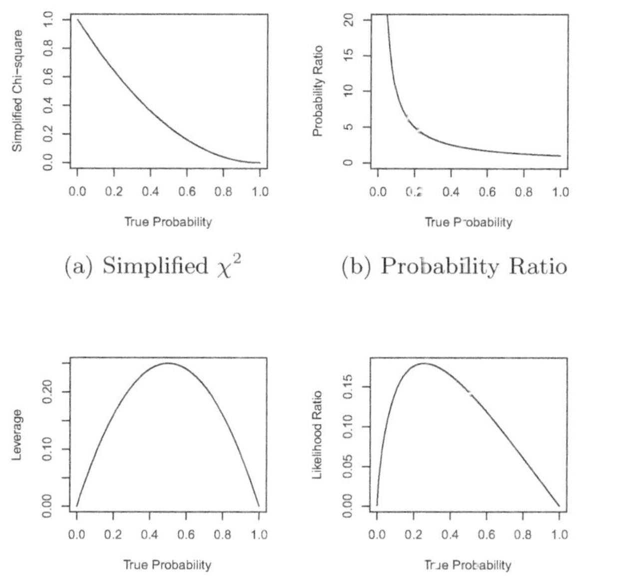

(a) Simplified χ^2 (b) Probability Ratio

(c) Leverage (d) Likelihood Ratio

Figure 1: Upper bounds of different measures for a single community

Given a partition with l groups $\{G_1, G_2, ..., G_l\}$ for the graph G, the true probability of a link being inside G_p, tp, is $\frac{\sum_{i \in G_p} k_i^{int}}{2m}$, and the expected probability, ep, is $\frac{\sum_{i \in G_p} k_i}{2m} \cdot \frac{\sum_{j \in G_p} k_j}{2m}$. If $\sum_{i \in G_p} k_i^{int}$ is fixed, the lowest possible value for $\sum_{i \in G_p} k_i$ is $\sum_{i \in G_p} k_i^{int}$ because $k_i^{int} \leq k_i$. In other words, when tp for the group G_p is fixed, the lowest possible value for ep is tp^2. When $ep = tp^2$, the measures reach their upper bound. Figure 1 shows the upper bounds of the various measures with respect to different tp for a single community. It is easy to see that different measures favor groups within different tp ranges. The upper bound of Simplified χ^2 increases to 1 and that of Probability Ratio increase to infinity when tp is close to 0, which means they favor extremely small groups rather than large groups. Leverage and Likelihood Ratio reach their highest upper bound when tp is between 0 and 1. According to the graph, Leverage does not favor the group which contains more than half of the edges in the graph since its upper bound starts to decrease even when the group size increases. Similarly, Likelihood Ratio does not favor the group which contains more than roughly one quarter of the edges in the graph. In all, Probability Ratio favors the smallest groups, followed by Simplified χ^2, Likelihood Ratio, and Leverage.

4. EXPERIMENTS

4.1 Experiment Settings

Most prior research on modularity-based methods sets modularity as their objective function and uses different optimization techniques to search for the partition that generates the highest value. In this paper, instead of exploring better optimization techniques for the same objective function, we change the objective function and study what kinds of difference the various objective functions make. In order to conduct the fair comparison for different objective functions, we choose greedy search, the simplest optimization technique, which is also used by the original modularity method and generates reasonably good results [9]. Initially, each node is the only member of its own community. The algorithm iteratively join the two communities that increase the objective function most in the current round. The algorithm will stop if the best merge cannot further increase the objective function. In this section, we conduct experiments on both real life and simulated datasets.

4.1.1 Real Life Data

The two real life datasets include Karate Club [41] and College Football [19], as shown in Figure 2 [1]. As we mentioned in Section 1, we only conduct the performance evaluation on non-overlapping community detection. The existing large datasets with ground truth that we can find are all for overlapping community detection, so we can only do the performance evaluation on large datasets of simulated data. The karate dataset contains friendships between 34 members of a karate club at a US university in the 1970s. There was a disagreement between the administrator and the instructor in the club, which resulted in two communities in this graph. The football dataset records games between Division IA colleges during regular season Fall 2000. There were 115 teams in 12 different conferences.

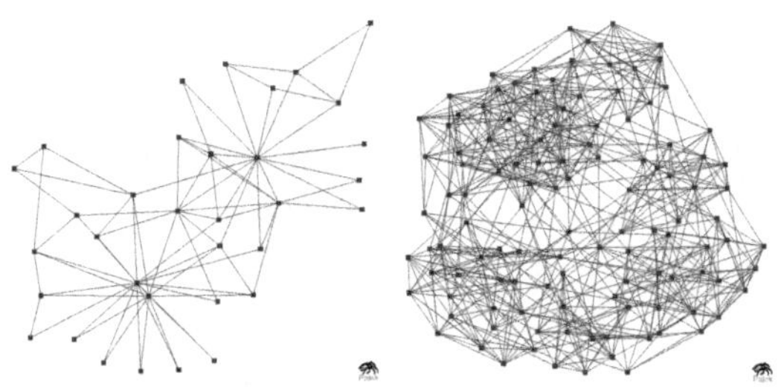

(a) Karate (b) Football

Figure 2: Real data sets

4.1.2 Simulated Data

With regard to graph simulation, the first related work is called the planted L-partition model [10]. The model simulates a graph with $n = g * l$ nodes in l groups with g nodes each. Nodes of the same group are linked with a probability $p_{internal}$, whereas nodes of different groups are linked with a probability $p_{external}$. If $p_{internal} > p_{external}$, the intra-cluster edge density exceeds the inter-cluster edge density. Then the graph has a community structure which is quite intuitive. However, by using the planted L-partition model, all nodes have approximately the same degree and all communities have exactly the same size. In the real social network data, degree distributions are usually skewed, with many nodes with low degree and a few nodes with high degree. A similar heterogeneity is also observed in the distribution of community size. Recently, Lancichinetti et al. [23] introduced a very popular LFR model. They assume that the distributions of degree and community size are power laws with τ_1 and τ_2 respectively. Each node shares a fraction of $1 - u$ of its edges with the nodes in the same community and a fraction of u with the nodes in the other communities, where u is the mixing parameter. Since the LFR model is much more realistic, we will use the graphs generated by this model to test our algorithms. The simulation procedure is as follows:

1 A set of community sizes s_j following the predefined power law parameter τ_2 is generated.

2 A set of node degrees k_i following the predefined power law parameter τ_1 is generated. The internal degree of each node is $(1-u)k_i$ where u is the mixing parameter.

3 In the beginning, nodes are not assigned to any community. Each node is assigned to a randomly-chosen community which has empty spots to accept a new node. If the community size exceeds the internal degree of the node, the node enters the community; otherwise, it enters a waiting list.

4 For each node in the waiting list, we let the node enter a random community whose size exceeds the node's internal degree and randomly kick one node in the selected community out to the waiting list. We do this step iteratively until the waiting list is empty.

5 We enforce the condition on the fraction of internal degree and external degree. The rewiring procedure in [4] is performed when needed.

However, the constraint used in the LFR model to assign the internal degree of each node in the second step is problematic because the condition imposed by a fixed u cannot guarantee $p_{internal} > p_{external}$ which must be satisfied for a community structure. For a node A in a community with n' nodes in a graph with n nodes, u must be smaller than $1 - n'/n$ to guarantee $p_{internal} > p_{external}$. Therefore, we use the following constraint to assign the internal degree of each node in the second step: $p_{internal} = \beta \cdot p_{external}$, where β is the ratio to control the community structure and must be greater than 1.

There are 8 parameters related to the LFR simulation model: the total number of nodes, the minimal node degree, the maximal node degree, the power law parameter for node degree, the minimal community size, the maximal community size, the power law parameter for community size, and the ratio β for community structure. In order to avoid bias to different objective functions, we choose greedy search, the simplest optimization technique. However, greedy search can only handle 2,000 nodes within a reasonable amount of time. Therefore, we also use a fast unfolding search technique [5] to handle the network with more than 1 million nodes, which is closer to the real world network size.

Given the number of nodes is 2,000, we conduct 9 sets of experiments and the parameter values are shown in Table 1. In order to check the performance difference on different community sizes and tightness of community structure, we only change the minimal community size and the ratio β for community structure to generate different graphs. When the minimal community size is 5, there are a lot of small communities, some mid-size communities, and a few large communities, while the graph only contains large communities

[1]All the network visualization in this paper is visualized by Pajek Software

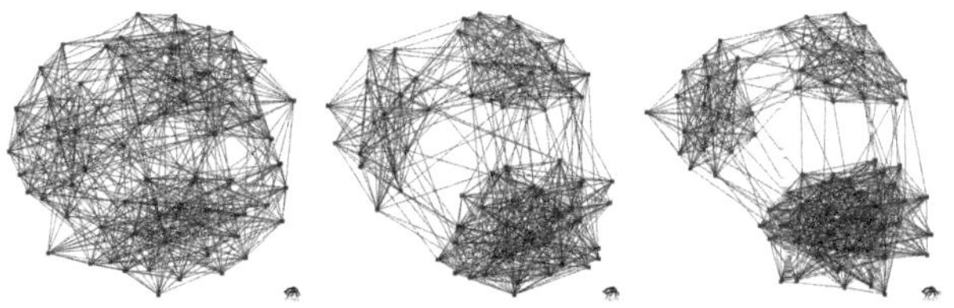

(a) β is 5 (b) β is 10 (c) β is 20

Figure 3: Simulated data sets

when the minimal community size is 100. The community structure is fuzzy when β is 5, while it is clear when β is 20. How the β affects the community structure is shown in Figure 3. Given the number of nodes is 300,000, we conduct a similar set of 9 experiments and the parameter values are also shown in Table 1.

4.1.3 Evaluation Measures

After finding communities in a given graph, we need to compare our search results with the "actual communities" (the ground truth). For two partitions $X = (X_1, X_2, ..., X_{n_x})$ and $Y = (Y_1, Y_2, ..., Y_{n_y})$ of a graph, X is determined by the algorithm with n_x communities and Y is the ground truth with n_y communities. We need a criterion to measure how similar the partition result of the algorithm is to the partition we hope to find. Many different measures, such as Normalized Mutual Information [11], Jaccard, Rand Index [32], and F-measure [34], have been proposed, and they can be divided into three categories: pair counting, community matching, and information theory [2]. Since different measures have different bias, we show the experimental results on different measures, but focus our analysis on the most widely accepted measure, Normalized Mutual Information. First, it calculates Mutual Information: $MI = \sum_i \sum_j P(X_i \cap Y_j) log \frac{P(X_i \cap Y_j)}{P(X_i)P(Y_j)}$. MI measures the amount of information by which our knowledge about the community in one partition increases when we are told what the community in the other partition is. The minimum of MI is 0 if the X partition is random with respect to the Y partition. However, given a partition Y, all partitions derived from Y by further partitioning have the same mutual information with Y, even though they are different from each other. In this case, the mutual information is equal to the entropy $H(Y) = -\sum_j P(Y_j) log(P(Y_j))$. To avoid that, Danon et al. [11] proposed the normalized mutual information: $NMI = \frac{2*MI}{H(X)+H(Y)}$. It is currently often used and reaches its maximal value 1 if X partition is identical to Y partition.

4.2 Evaluation on Real Life Datasets

The result on real life datasets is shown in Table 2 [2]. The best method for Karate dataset is Leverage. The result is consistent with our theoretical analysis. The karate dataset only contains two large communities, and Leverage is the method having the most bias to large communities. Both Simplified χ^2 and Likelihood Ratio are good for the football dataset. This dataset contains 12 almost equal size communities. According to Figure 1, Likelihood Ratio has the bias to middle-size communities, and Simplified χ^2 has the bias, but not the extreme bias, to small communities. It is why Simplified χ^2 and Likelihood Ratio work better on the football dataset.

4.3 Evaluation on Simulated Datasets

For each parameter setting, we generate the graph 10 times to test each method. We calculate the average value for each evaluation measure shown in Table 3 and 4. Since the result of 2,000 nodes is very similar to that of 300,000 nodes, we focus our analysis on the result of 2,000 nodes. In addition, different evaluation measures provide different information. Since NMI is the most widely-accepted measure, we focus our discussion on NMI in the following. The average NMI and the average number of partitioned communities generated by each method for each parameter setting are shown in Figures 4 - 7.

Figure 4 shows the NMI achieved by each method and Figure 5 shows the number of partitioned communities when fixing the minimal community size and changing the ratio β. No matter what the minimal community size and the ratio β are, the NMI and the number of partitioned communities for both Simplified χ^2 and Probability Ratio are almost the same. They always detect more than 500 communities. Since the total number of nodes is 2,000, most of the communities they detect contain 2 or 3 nodes. That supports our observation in Section 3 that Simplified χ^2 and Probability Ratio favor small size communities. No matter what the minimal community size is, both Leverage and Likelihood Ratio achieve better NMI when the community structure becomes clearer. Only when the community structure is clear and the whole graph only contains large communities, the NMI of Leverage is better than that of Likelihood Ratio. Leverage has more bias towards large communities than Likelihood Ratio according to our upper bound analysis; therefore, we are expecting Leverage is better than Likelihood Ratio when the graph only contains large communities. In practice, social networks contain a lot of small communities; therefore, Likelihood Ratio is better in the common case. The number of partitioned communities by Leverage is almost the same no matter how we change the minimal community size and the ratio β, while the number of partitioned communities by Likelihood Ratio get closer to the ground truth when the community structure becomes clearer. Another interesting observation related to Leverage is that its NMI is very low when the minimal community size is large under the fuzzy community structure. Even under the fuzzy community structure, Leverage detects the same number of large communities. Such a partition assigns many nodes in different real communities to the same partitions, which results in the low NMI. Generally speaking, the partition generated by Likelihood Ratio is better and more adaptive to the different types of graphs than that of Leverage.

Figure 6 shows the NMI achieved by each method and Figure 7 shows the number of partitioned communities when fixing the ratio β and changing the minimal community size. Since both Simplified χ^2 and Probability Ratio favor small-size communities, their NMI decreases with the increase of the minimal community size no matter the community structure is fuzzy or clear. The NMI of Likelihood Ratio decreases with the increase of the minimal community size when the

[2]RI: Rand Index; DNC: the detected number of communities; ANC: the actual number of communities; χ^2: Simplified χ^2; PR: Probability Ratio; and LR: Likelihood Ratio

Parameter	Data set A	Data set B
The total number of nodes	2000	300000
The minimal node degree	5	50
The maximal node degree	300	3000
The power law parameter for node degree	2.5	2.5
The minimal community size	5, 50, or 100	50, 500, or 5000
The maximal community size	300	10000
The power law parameter for community size	1.5	1.5
The ratio β for community structure	5, 10, or 20	5, 10, or 20

Table 1: Parameter Setting for Simulated Graphs

Data Set	Measure	NMI	Jaccard	RI	F-measure	DNC	ANC
Karate	χ^2	0.4852	0.2842	0.6453	0.4426	7	2
	PR	0.3868	0.0945	0.5561	0.1728	14	2
	Leverage	**0.6925**	**0.6833**	**0.8414**	**0.8118**	3	2
	LR	0.5385	0.3958	0.6952	0.5671	5	2
Football	χ^2	**0.9141**	0.7571	0.9793	0.8618	14	12
	PR	0.6864	0.0829	0.9240	0.1531	55	12
	Leverage	0.6977	0.3622	0.8807	0.5317	6	12
	LR	0.9086	**0.7897**	**0.9812**	**0.8825**	12	12

Table 2: Results on real life datasets

Data Set	Measure	NMI	Jaccard	RI	F-measure	DNC	ANC
MCS=5 β=5	χ^2	**0.5868**	0.0122	**0.9391**	0.0240	629.5	50.8
	PR	0.5856	0.0062	0.9390	0.0124	903.3	50.8
	Leverage	0.1222	**0.0809**	0.7749	**0.1481**	9.4	50.8
	LR	0.5515	0.0272	0.9388	0.0530	300.5	50.8
MCS=5 β=10	χ^2	**0.6023**	0.0146	0.9397	0.0289	604.8	51.2
	PR	0.5937	0.0068	0.9394	0.0136	905	51.2
	Leverage	0.2741	**0.1523**	0.7900	**0.2605**	7.5	51.2
	LR	0.5992	0.0462	**0.9406**	0.0883	263.4	51.2
MCS=5 β=20	χ^2	0.6212	0.0196	0.9436	0.0385	564.6	51.8
	PR	0.6035	0.0089	0.9432	0.0177	855.7	51.8
	Leverage	0.5349	0.2265	0.8215	0.3658	6.8	51.8
	LR	**0.7545**	**0.5136**	**0.9714**	**0.6699**	139.5	51.8
MCS=50 β=5	χ^2	**0.4775**	0.0091	**0.9177**	0.0181	586.2	16
	PR	0.4765	0.0054	0.9176	0.0107	777.6	16
	Leverage	0.1172	**0.1016**	0.7754	**0.1820**	9.2	16
	LR	0.4314	0.0194	0.9172	0.0381	283.7	16
MCS=50 β=10	χ^2	**0.5075**	0.0125	0.9240	0.0246	554.3	16.5
	PR	0.4969	0.0069	0.9237	0.0137	747.9	16.5
	Leverage	0.4318	**0.2523**	0.8302	**0.3983**	6.2	16.5
	LR	0.5040	0.0507	**0.9259**	0.0958	243.3	16.5
MCS=50 β=20	χ^2	0.5280	0.0154	0.9211	0.0303	533	15.8
	PR	0.5065	0.0076	0.9205	0.0151	758.4	15.8
	Leverage	0.7375	0.4098	0.8886	0.5773	6.5	15.8
	LR	**0.7663**	**0.6430**	**0.9703**	**0.7778**	67.9	15.8
MCS=100 β=5	χ^2	0.4210	0.0073	**0.8978**	0.0145	568.9	10.7
	PR	**0.4243**	0.0044	0.8977	0.0088	750	10.7
	Leverage	0.1471	**0.1330**	0.7710	**0.2336**	8.5	10.7
	LR	0.3727	0.0156	0.8972	0.0306	280.2	10.7
MCS=100 β=10	χ^2	0.4538	0.0092	0.9038	0.0183	571.9	11.3
	PR	0.4514	0.0053	0.9036	0.0106	774.2	11.3
	Leverage	**0.5587**	**0.3423**	0.8532	**0.5038**	6.2	11.3
	LR	0.4458	0.0287	**0.9046**	0.0558	250.8	11.3
MCS=100 β=20	χ^2	0.4844	0.0128	0.9016	0.0253	522.6	11.2
	PR	0.4657	0.0069	0.9010	0.0138	721.9	11.2
	Leverage	**0.8318**	0.5755	0.9291	0.7300	6.8	11.2
	LR	0.7614	**0.6550**	**0.9638**	**0.7851**	52.2	12

Table 3: Results on simulated datasets with 2,000 nodes

Data Set	Measure	NMI	Jaccard	RI	F-measure	DNC	ANC
	χ^2	**0.5567**	0.0007	**0.9882**	0.0057	87651.0	428.2
MCS=50	PR	0.5294	0.0002	0.9882	0.0068	117151.1	428.2
β=5	Leverage	0.0698	**0.0173**	0.6044	**0.0642**	5.6	428.2
	LR	0.5145	0.0006	0.9882	0.0088	56275.7	428.2
	χ^2	**0.5731**	0.0007	**0.9889**	0.0060	89529.1	458.4
MCS=50	PR	0.5413	0.0002	0.9889	0.0071	118370.6	458.4
β=10	Leverage	0.0941	**0.0191**	0.6488	**0.0715**	7.4	458.4
	LR	0.5349	0.0008	0.9889	0.0094	55654.8	458.4
	χ^2	0.5793	0.0007	0.9880	0.0056	91573.8	433.7
MCS=50	PR	0.5427	0.0002	0.9880	0.0067	119961.7	433.7
β=20	Leverage	0.3588	0.0486	0.7721	0.2688	11.1	433.7
	LR	**0.6270**	**0.5480**	**0.9947**	**0.2805**	38997.4	433.7
	χ^2	**0.5009**	0.0005	**0.9860**	0.0021	86258.5	135.7
MCS=500	PR	0.4730	0.0001	0.9860	0.0018	103355.6	135.7
β=5	Leverage	0.0534	**0.0182**	0.6446	**0.0661**	4.7	135.7
	LR	0.4625	0.0005	0.9860	0.0024	56536.5	135.7
	χ^2	**0.5156**	0.0005	**0.9863**	0.0022	87168.8	139.2
MCS=500	PR	0.4816	0.0002	0.9863	0.0018	104363.0	139.2
β=10	Leverage	0.2004	**0.0354**	0.7473	**0.2048**	7.3	139.2
	LR	0.4828	0.0006	0.9863	0.0026	56810.1	139.2
	χ^2	0.5234	0.0006	0.9854	0.0021	88439.6	131.2
MCS=500	PR	0.4854	0.0002	0.9854	0.0018	104308.4	131.2
β=20	Leverage	0.5731	0.0866	0.8531	0.4551	20.4	131.2
	LR	**0.7106**	**0.8050**	**0.9972**	**0.6000**	18350.4	131.2
	χ^2	**0.3747**	0.0001	**0.9751**	0.0006	81634.5	41.7
MCS=5000	PR	0.3427	0.0001	0.9751	0.0005	68326.2	41.7
β=20	Leverage	0.0099	**0.0226**	0.8037	**0.0632**	10.0	41.7
	LR	0.3456	0.0001	0.9751	0.0007	58845.6	41.7
	χ^2	0.3885	0.0002	**0.9748**	0.0007	81365.6	41.4
MCS=5000	PR	0.3521	0.0001	0.9748	0.0006	65978.2	41.4
β=20	Leverage	**0.8037**	**0.2315**	0.9099	**0.6057**	19.2	41.4
	LR	0.3726	0.0003	0.9748	0.0010	58409.5	41.4
	χ^2	0.4053	0.0002	0.9749	0.0008	80492.0	41.4
MCS=5000	PR	0.3737	0.0002	0.9749	0.0008	64004.6	41.4
β=20	Leverage	0.8964	0.4267	0.9635	0.7332	24.8	41.4
	LR	**0.9971**	**0.9962**	**0.9999**	**0.9964**	214.4	41.4

Table 4: Results on simulated datasets with 300,000 nodes

community structure is not clear. However, when the community structure is clear, Likelihood Ratio achieves almost the same performance with the increase of the minimal community size. The NMI of Leverage always increases with the increase of the minimal community size since it has the bias to large communities.

5. CONCLUSION

In this paper, we connect modularity-based methods with correlation analysis by subtly reformatting their math formulas, and make smart use of different correlation measures to change the objective function of modularity-based methods. A novel theoretical analysis on upper bounds is conducted to analyze the bias of different objective functions and the bias is validated by our experiments. Using the widely-accepted Normalized Mutual Information to compare the partitions determined by the algorithm with the ground truth, Likelihood Ratio is better and more robust. However, different measures can be used for different purposes. For example, Probability Ratio can be used if we want to fairly partition the students in the class into small groups for class projects, and we might use Leverage to find relatively large groups for marketing campaigns. As shown above, our finding provides a more natural and effective way to solve the resolution limit problem of the original modularity function by modifying it through different correlation measures. In the future, we will investigate more correlation measures, and test performance differences for detecting overlapping communities.

6. REFERENCES

[1] H. Almeida, D. O. G. Neto, W. M. Jr., and M. J. Zaki. Is there a best quality metric for graph clusters? In *15th European Conference on Principles and Practice of Knowledge Discovery in Databases*, Sep 2011.

[2] E. Amigó, J. Gonzalo, J. Artiles, and F. Verdejo. A comparison of extrinsic clustering evaluation metrics based on formal constraints. *Information Retrieval*, 12:461–486, August 2009.

[3] A. Arenas, A. FernÂÍÂćndez, and S. GÂÍÂ3mez. Analysis of the structure of complex networks at different resolution levels. *New Journal of Physics*, 10(5):053039, 2008.

[4] J. P. Bagrow. Evaluating local community methods in networks. *Journal of Statistical Mechanics: Theory and Experiment*, 2008(05):P05001+, 2008.

[5] V. D. Blondel, J.-L. Guillaume, R. Lambiotte, and E. Lefebvre. Fast unfolding of communities in large networks. *Journal of Statistical Mechanics: Theory and Experiment*, 2008(10):P10008, 2008.

[6] S. Boettcher and A. G. Percus. Extremal optimization for graph partitioning. *PHYS.REV.E*, 64:026114, 2001.

[7] U. Brandes, D. Delling, M. Gaertler, R. Gorke, M. Hoefer, Z. Nikoloski, and D. Wagner. On modularity clustering. *IEEE Trans. on Knowl. and Data Eng.*, 20:172–188, February 2008.

[8] S. Brin, R. Motwani, J. D. Ullman, and S. Tsur. Dynamic itemset counting and implication rules for market basket data. In *Proc. ACM SIGMOD Int. Conf. on Management of Data*, pages 255–264, 1997.

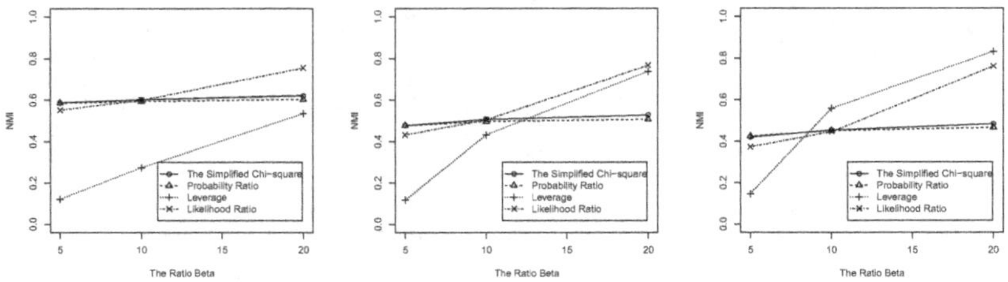

(a) The minimal community size is 5 (b) The minimal community size is 50 (c) The minimal community size is 100

Figure 4: NMI when fixing the minimal community size

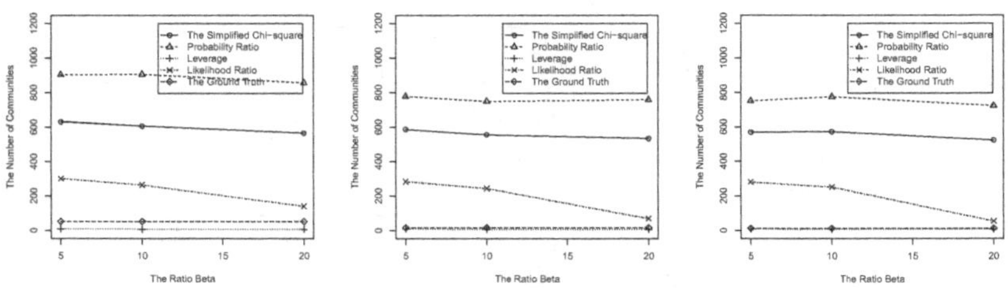

(a) The minimal community size is 5 (b) The minimal community size is 50 (c) The minimal community size is 100

Figure 5: The number of communities when fixing the minimal community size

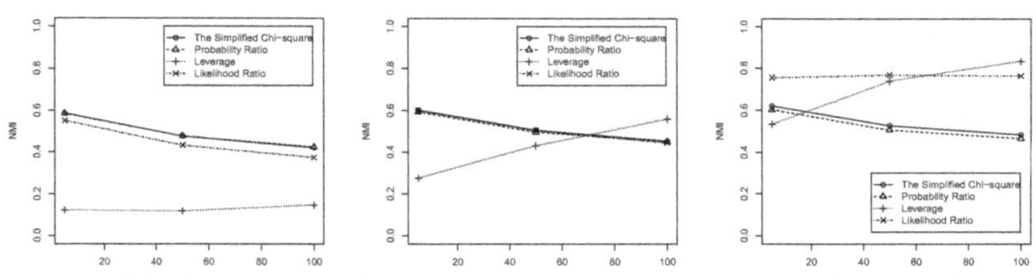

(a) The ratio β is 5 (b) The ratio β is 10 (c) The ratio β is 20

Figure 6: NMI when fixing the ratio β

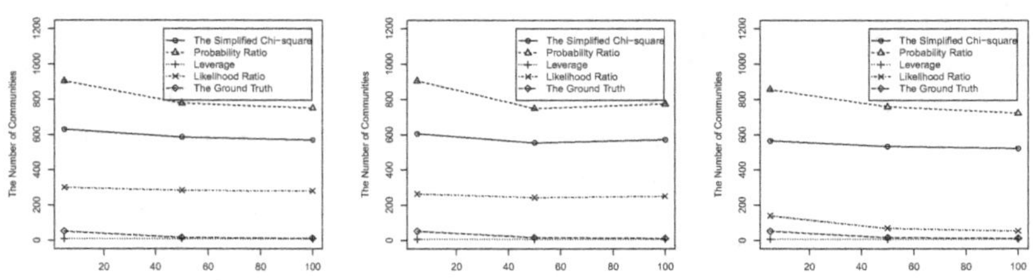

(a) The ratio β is 5 (b) The ratio β is 10 (c) The ratio β is 20

Figure 7: The number of communities when fixing the ratio β

[9] A. Clauset, M. E. J. Newman, and C. Moore. Finding community structure in very large networks. *Physical Review E*, 70(6):066111+, Dec. 2004.

[10] A. Condon and R. M. Karp. Algorithms for graph partitioning on the planted partition model. *Random Struct. Algorithms*, 18:116–140, March 2001.

[11] L. Danon, A. D. Guilera, J. Duch, and A. Arenas. Comparing community structure identification. *Journal of Statistical Mechanics: Theory and Experiment*, 2005(9):P09008–09008, Sept. 2005.

[12] L. Duan and W. N. Street. Finding maximal fully-correlated itemsets in large databases. In *ICDM '09: Proc. Int. Conf. on Data Mining*, pages 770–775, Miami, FL, USA, 2009.

[13] L. Duan and W. N. Street. Selecting the right correlation measure for binary data. *http://ssrn.com/abstract=2035491*, 2012.

[14] J. Duch and A. Arenas. Community detection in complex networks using extremal optimization. *Physical Review E*, 72(2):027104+, Aug. 2005.

[15] T. Dunning. Accurate methods for the statistics of surprise and coincidence. *Computational Linguistics*, 19(1):61–74, 1993.

[16] S. Fortunato. Community detection in graphs. *Physics Reports*, 486:75–174, 2010.

[17] M. Gaertler, R. Görke, and D. Wagner. Significance-driven graph clustering. In *Proceedings of the 3rd international conference on Algorithmic Aspects in Information and Management*, AAIM '07, pages 11–26, Berlin, Heidelberg, 2007. Springer-Verlag.

[18] L. Geng and H. J. Hamilton. Interestingness measures for data mining: A survey. *ACM Computing Surveys*, 38(3):9, 2006.

[19] M. Girvan and M. E. J. Newman. Community structure in social and biological networks. *Proceedings of the National Academy of Sciences*, 99(12):7821–7826, June 2002.

[20] C. Jermaine. Finding the most interesting correlations in a database: How hard can it be? *Information Systems*, 30(1):21–46, 2005.

[21] R. Kannan, S. Vempala, and A. Veta. On clusterings-good, bad and spectral. In *Proceedings. 41st Annual Symposium on Foundations of Computer Science*, pages 367–377, 2000.

[22] A. Lancichinetti and S. Fortunato. Limits of modularity maximization in community detection. *Phys. Rev. E*, 84:066122, Dec 2011.

[23] A. Lancichinetti, S. Fortunato, and F. Radicchi. Benchmark graphs for testing community detection algorithms. *Phys. Rev. E*, 78:046110, Oct 2008.

[24] U. Luxburg. A tutorial on spectral clustering. *Statistics and Computing*, 17:395–416, December 2007.

[25] J. B. MacQueen. Some methods for classification and analysis of multivariate observations. In L. M. L. Cam and J. Neyman, editors, *Proc. of the fifth Berkeley Symposium on Mathematical Statistics and Probability*, volume 1, pages 281–297. University of California Press, 1967.

[26] S. Mancoridis, B. S. Mitchell, and C. Rorres. Using automatic clustering to produce high-level system organizations of source code. In *Proc. 6th Intl. Workshop on Program Comprehension*, pages 45–53, 1998.

[27] C. P. Massen and J. P. K. Doye. Identifying communities within energy landscapes. 71(046101) 2005.

[28] M. E. J. Newman. Community detection and graph partitioning. *CoRR*, abs/1305.4974, 2013.

[29] V. Nicosia, G. Mangioni, V. Carchiolo, and M. Malgeri. Extending the definition of modularity to directed graphs with overlapping communities. *Journal of Statistical Mechanics: Theory and Experiment*, 2009:P03024, 2009.

[30] G. Piatetsky-Shapiro. *Discovery, Analysis, and Presentation of Strong Rules*. AAAI/MIT Press, 1991.

[31] C. Pizzuti. Community detection in social networks with genetic algorithms. In *Proceedings of the 10th annual conference on Genetic and evolutionary computation*, GECCO '08, pages 1137–1138, New York, NY, USA, 2008. ACM.

[32] W. M. Rand. Objective Criteria for the Evaluation of Clustering Methods. *Journal of the American Statistical Association*, 66(336):846–850, 1971.

[33] J. Reichardt and S. Bornholdt. Statistical mechanics of community detection. *Phys. Rev. E*, 74:016110, Jul 2006.

[34] C. V. Rijsbergen. Foundation of Evaluation. *Journal of Documentation*, 30:365–373, 1974.

[35] H. Shiokawa, Y. Fujiwara, and M. Onizuka. Fast algorithm for modularity-based graph clustering. In M. desJardins and M. L. Littman, editors, *AAAI*. AAAI Press, 2013.

[36] P.-N. Tan, V. Kumar, and J. Srivastava. Selecting the right objective measure for association analysis. *Information Systems*, 29(4):293–313, 2004.

[37] C. Tew, C. Giraud-Carrier, K. Tanner, and S. Burton. Behavior-based clustering and analysis of interestingness measures for association rule mining. *Data Mining and Knowledge Discovery*, pages 1–42, 2013.

[38] K. Wakita and T. Tsurumi. Finding community structure in mega-scale social networks. In *Proceedings of the 16th international conference on World Wide Web*, WWW '07, pages 1275–1276, New York, NY, USA, 2007. ACM.

[39] R. S. Weiss and E. Jacobson. A method for the analysis of the structure of complex organizations. *American Sociological Review*, 20(6):pp. 661–668, 1955.

[40] J. Xie, S. Kelley, and B. K. SZYMANSKI. Overlapping community detection in networks: the state of the art and comparative study. *ACM Computing Surveys*, 45, 2013.

[41] W. W. Zachary. An information flow model for conflict and fission in small groups. *Journal of Anthropological Research*, 33:452–473, 1977.

Heat Kernel Based Community Detection

Kyle Kloster
Purdue University
West Lafayette, IN
kkloste@purdue.edu

David F. Gleich
Purdue University
West Lafayette, IN
dgleich@purdue.edu

ABSTRACT

The heat kernel is a type of graph diffusion that, like the much-used personalized PageRank diffusion, is useful in identifying a community nearby a starting seed node. We present the first deterministic, local algorithm to compute this diffusion and use that algorithm to study the communities that it produces. Our algorithm is formally a relaxation method for solving a linear system to estimate the matrix exponential in a degree-weighted norm. We prove that this algorithm stays localized in a large graph and has a worst-case constant runtime that depends only on the parameters of the diffusion, not the size of the graph. On large graphs, our experiments indicate that the communities produced by this method have better conductance than those produced by PageRank, although they take slightly longer to compute. On a real-world community identification task, the heat kernel communities perform better than those from the PageRank diffusion.

Categories and Subject Descriptors

G.2.2 [**Discrete mathematics**]: Graph theory—*Graph algorithms*; I.5.3 [**Pattern recognition**]: Clustering—*Algorithms*

General Terms

Algorithms,Theory

Keywords

heat kernel; local clustering

1. INTRODUCTION

The community detection problem is to identify a set of nodes in a graph that are internally cohesive but also separated from the remainder of the network. One popular way to capture this idea is through the conductance measure of a set. We treat this idea formally in the next section, but informally, the conductance of a set is a ratio of the number of edges leaving the set to the number of edges touched by the set of vertices. If this value is small, then it indicates a set with many internal edges and few edges leaving.

In many surveys and empirical studies [47, 33, 17], the conductance measure surfaces as one of the most reliable measures of a community. Although this measure has been critized for producing *cavemen*-type communities [24], empirical properties of real-world communities correlate highly with sets produced by algorithms that optimize conductance [1]. Furthermore, state-of-the-art methods for identifying overlapping sets of communities use conductance to find real-world communities better than any alternative [52].

Virtually all of the rigorous algorithms that identify sets of small conductance are based on min-cuts [6, 46], eigenvector computations [21, 4], or local graph diffusions [5, 14]. (One notable exception is the graclus method [17] that uses a relationship between kernel k-means and a variant of conductance.) In this paper, we study a new algorithm that uses a heat kernel diffusion [14] to identify small-conductance communities in a network. (The heat kernel is discussed formally in Section 3.) Although the properties of this diffusion had been analyzed in theory in Chung's work [14], that work did not provide an efficient algorithm to compute the diffusion. Recently, Chung and Simpson stated a randomized Monte Carlo method to estimate the diffusion [16].

This paper introduces an efficient and deterministic method to estimate this diffusion. We use it to study the properties of the small conductance sets identified by the method as communities. For this use, a deterministic approach is critical as we need to differentiate between subtle properties of the diffusion. Our primary point of comparison is the well-known personalized PageRank diffusion [5], which has been used to establish new insights into the properties of communities in large scale networks [33]. Thus, we wish to understand how the communities produced by the heat kernel compare to those produced by personalized PageRank.

The basic operation of our algorithm is a coordinate relaxation step. This has been used to efficiently compute personalized PageRank [23, 36, 5] where it is known as the "push" operation on a graph; the term "coordinate relaxation" is the classical name for this operation, which dates back to the Gauss-Seidel method. What distinguishes our approach from prior work is the use of coordinate relaxation on an implicitly constructed linear system that will estimate the heat kernel diffusion, which is formally the exponential of the random walk transition matrix.

We began looking into this problem recently in a workshop paper [27], where we showed that this style of algorithm

KDD'14, August 24–27, 2014, New York, NY, USA.

ACM 978-1-4503-2956-9/14/08 ...$15.00.
http://dx.doi.org/10.1145/2623330.2623706.

successfully estimates a related quantity. This paper tackles a fundamentally new direction and, although similar in techniques, required an entirely new analysis. In particular, we are able to estimate this diffusion in constant time in a degree-weighted norm that depends only on the parameters of the diffusion, and not the size of the graph. A Python implementation of our algorithm to accomplish this task is presented in Figure 2.

In the remainder of the paper, we first review these topics formally (Sections 2 and 3); present our algorithm (Section 4) and discuss related work (Section 5). Then we show how our new approach differs from and improves upon the personalized PageRank diffusion in synthetic and real-world problems.

Summary of contributions.

- We propose the first local, deterministic method to accurately compute a heat kernel diffusion in a graph. The code is simple and scalable to any graph where out-link access is *inexpensive.*
- Our method is always localized, even in massive graphs, because it has a provably constant runtime in a degree-weighted norm.
- We compare the new heat kernel diffusion method to the venerable PageRank diffusion in synthetic, small, and large networks (up to 2 billion edges) to demonstrate the differences. On large networks such as Twitter, our method tends to produce smaller and tighter communities. It is also more accurate at detecting ground-truth communities.

We make our experimental codes available in the spirit of reproducible research:
https://www.cs.purdue.edu/homes/dgleich/codes/hkgrow

2. PRELIMINARIES

We begin by fixing our notation. Let $G = (V, E)$ be a simple, undirected graph with $n = |V|$ vertices. Fix an ordering of the vertices from 1 to n such that we can refer to a vertex by it's numeric ID. For a vertex $v \in V$, we denote by d_v the degree of node v. Let $\mathbf{A}$ be the associated adjacency matrix. Because G is undirected, $\mathbf{A}$ is symmetric. Furthermore, let $\mathbf{D}$ be the diagonal matrix of degrees ($\mathbf{D}_{ii} = d_i$) and $\mathbf{P} = (\mathbf{D}^{-1}\mathbf{A})^T = \mathbf{A}\mathbf{D}^{-1}$ be the random walk transition matrix. Finally, we denote by $\mathbf{e}_i$ the vector (of an appropriate length) of zeros having a single 1 in entry i, and by $\mathbf{e}$ the vector of all 1s.

Conductance. Given a subset $S \subseteq V$, we denote by vol(S) the sum of the degrees of all vertices in S, and by $\partial(S)$, the *boundary* of S, the number of edges with one endpoint inside of S and one endpoint outside of S. With this notation, the conductance of a set S is given by

$$\phi(S) := \frac{\partial(S)}{\min\{\text{vol}(S), \text{vol}(V - S)\}}$$

Conceptually, $\phi(S)$ is the probability that a random walk of length one will land outside of S, given that we start from a node chosen uniformly at random inside S.

Matrix exponential. The heat kernel of a graph involves the matrix exponential, and we wish to briefly mention some facts about this operation. See Higham [22] for a more in-depth treatment. Consider a general matrix $\mathbf{G}$. The exponential function of a matrix is not just the exponential applied element-wise, but rather is given by substituting the matrix into the Taylor series expansion of the exponential function:

$$\exp\{\mathbf{G}\} = \sum_{k=0}^{\infty} \frac{1}{k!}\mathbf{G}^k.$$

That said, the exponential of a diagonal matrix *is* the exponential function applied to the diagonal entries. This phenomenon occurs because powers of a diagonal matrix are simply the diagonal elements raised to the given power. For any matrix $\mathbf{G}$, if $\mathbf{G}^T\mathbf{G} = \mathbf{G}\mathbf{G}^T$ (which is a generalization of the notion of a symmetric matrix, called a *normal* matrix), then $\mathbf{G}$ has an eigenvalue decomposition $\mathbf{G} = \mathbf{X}\mathbf{\Lambda}\mathbf{X}^{-1}$ and there is a simple, albeit inefficient, means of computing the exponential: $\exp\{\mathbf{G}\} = \mathbf{X}\exp\{\mathbf{\Lambda}\}\mathbf{X}^{-1}$. Computing the matrix exponential, or even the *product* of the exponential with a vector, $\exp\{\mathbf{G}\}\mathbf{z}$, is still an active area of research [2].

3. FINDING SMALL CONDUCTANCE COMMUNITIES WITH DIFFUSIONS

A graph diffusion is any sum of the following form:

$$\mathbf{f} = \sum_{k=0}^{\infty} \alpha_k \mathbf{P}^k \mathbf{s}$$

where $\sum_k \alpha_k = 1$ and $\mathbf{s}$ is a stochastic vector (that is, it is non-negative and sums to one.) Intuitively, a diffusion captures how a quantity of s_i material on node i *flows* through the graph. The terms α_k provide a decaying weight that ensures that the diffusion eventually dissipates. In the context of this paper, we are interested in the diffusions of single nodes or neighborhood sets of a single vertex; and so in these cases $\mathbf{s} = \mathbf{e}_i$ or $\mathbf{s} = \sum_{i \in S} \mathbf{e}_i/|S|$ for a small set S. We call the origins of the diffusion the *seeds.*

Given an estimate of a diffusion $\mathbf{f}$ from a seed, we can produce a small conductance community from it using a sweep procedure. This involves computing $\mathbf{D}^{-1}\mathbf{f}$, sorting the nodes in descending order by their magnitude in this vector, and computing the conductance of each prefix of the sorted list. Due to the properties of conductance there is an efficient means of computing all of these conductances. We then return the set of smallest conductance as the community around the seeds.

The personalized PageRank diffusion. One of the most well-known instances of this framework is the personalized PageRank diffusion. Fix $\alpha \in (0, 1)$. Then $\mathbf{p}$ is defined:

$$\mathbf{p} = (1 - \alpha) \sum_{k=0}^{\infty} \alpha^k \mathbf{P}^k \mathbf{s}. \quad (1)$$

The properties of this diffusion have been studied extensively. In particular, Andersen et al. [5] establish a local Cheeger inequality using a particular algorithm called "push" that locally distributes mass. The local Cheeger inequality informally states that, *if* the seed is nearby a set with small conductance, *then* the result of the sweep procedure is a set with a related conductance. Moreover, they show that their "push" algorithm estimates $\mathbf{f}$ with an error ε in a degree-weighted norm by looking at $\frac{1}{(1-\alpha)\varepsilon}$ edges.

The heat kernel diffusion. Another instance of the same framework is the heat kernel diffusion [14, 15]. It simply replaces the weights α_k with $t^k/k!$:

$$\mathbf{h} = e^{-t}\left(\sum_{k=0}^{\infty}\frac{t^k}{k!}(\mathbf{P})^k\right)\mathbf{s} = \exp\left\{-t(\mathbf{I}-\mathbf{P}^{-1})\right\}\mathbf{s}. \qquad (2)$$

While it was known that estimating $\mathbf{h}$ gave rise to a similar type of local Cheeger inequality [15]; until Chung and Simpson's Monte Carlo approach [16], no methods were known to estimate this quantity efficiently. Our new algorithm is a deterministic approach that is more suitable for comparing the properties of the diffusions. It terminates after exploring $\frac{2Ne^t}{\varepsilon}$ edges (Theorem 1), where N is a parameter that grows slowly with ε.

Heat kernels compared to PageRank. These different sets of coefficients simply assign different levels of importance to walks of varying lengths: the heat kernel coefficients $\frac{t^k}{k!}$ decay much more quickly than α^k, and so the heat kernel more heavily weights shorter walks in the overall sum (depicted in Figure 1). This property, in turn, will have important consequences when we study these methods in large graphs in Section 6.

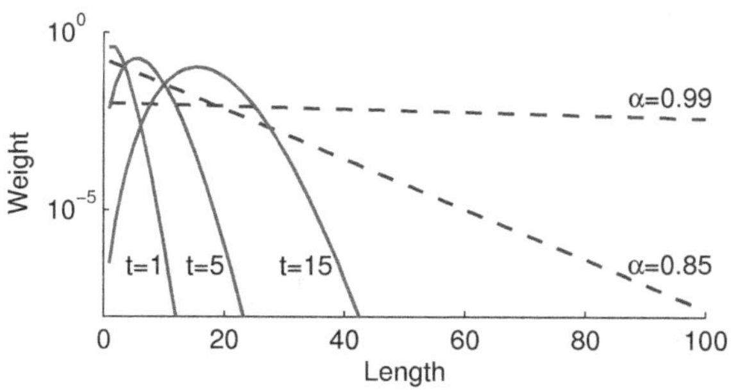

Figure 1: Each curve represents the coefficients of $(\mathbf{AD}^{-1})^k$ in a sum of walks. The dotted blue lines give α^k, and the red give $t^k/k!$, for the indicated values of α and t.

4. ALGORITHM

The overall idea of the local clustering algorithm is to approximate a heat kernel vector of the form

$$\mathbf{h} = \exp\left\{-t(\mathbf{I}-\mathbf{P})\right\}\mathbf{s}$$

so that we can perform a sweep over $\mathbf{h}$. Here we describe a coordinate-relaxation method, which we call `hk-relax`, for approximating $\mathbf{h}$. This algorithm is rooted in our recent work on computing an accurate column of $\exp\{\mathbf{P}\}$ [27]; but is heavily tuned to the objective below. Thus, while the overall strategy is classical – just as the PageRank push method is a classic relaxation method – the simplifications and efficient implementation are entirely novel. In particular, the new objective in this paper enables us to get a constant runtime bound independent of any property of the graph, which differs markedly from both of our previous methods [27, 26].

Our objective. Recall that the final step of finding a small conductance community involves dividing by the degree of each node. Thus, our goal is to compute $\mathbf{x} \approx \mathbf{h}$ satisfying the degree weighted bound:

$$\|\mathbf{D}^{-1}\exp\left\{-t(\mathbf{I}-\mathbf{P})\right\}\mathbf{s} - \mathbf{D}^{-1}\mathbf{x}\|_\infty < \varepsilon.$$

By using standard properties of the matrix exponential, we can factor $\exp\{-t(\mathbf{I}-\mathbf{P})\} = e^{-t}\exp\{t\mathbf{P}\}$ and scale by e^t so that the above problem is equivalent to computing $\mathbf{y}$ satisfying $\|\mathbf{D}^{-1}(\exp\{t\mathbf{P}\}\mathbf{s}-\mathbf{y})\|_\infty < e^t\varepsilon$. The element-wise characterization is that $\mathbf{y}$ must satisfy:

$$|e^t\mathbf{h}_i - \mathbf{y}_i| < e^t\varepsilon d_i \qquad (3)$$

for all i. A similar weighted objective was used in the push algorithm for PageRank [5].

Outline of algorithm. To accomplish this, we first approximate $\exp\{t\mathbf{P}\}$ with its degree N Taylor polynomial, $T_N(t\mathbf{P})$, and then we compute $T_N(t\mathbf{P})\mathbf{s}$. But we use a large, implicitly formed linear system to avoid explicitly evaluating the Taylor polynomial. Once we have the linear system, we state a relaxation method in the spirit of Gauss-Seidel and the PageRank push algorithm in order to compute an accurate approximation of $\mathbf{h}$.

4.1 Taylor Polynomial for exp{X}

Determining the exponential of a matrix is a sensitive computation with a rich history [39, 40]. For a general matrix $\mathbf{G}$, an approximation via the Taylor polynomial,

$$\exp\{\mathbf{G}\} = \sum_{k=0}^{\infty}\tfrac{1}{k!}\mathbf{G}^k \approx \sum_{k=0}^{N}\tfrac{1}{k!}\mathbf{G}^k,$$

can be inaccurate when $\|\mathbf{G}\|$ is large and $\mathbf{G}$ has mixed signs, as large powers $\mathbf{G}^k$ can contain large, oppositely signed numbers that cancel properly only in exact arithmetic. However, we intend to compute $\exp\{t\mathbf{P}\}\mathbf{s}$, where $\mathbf{P}$, t, and $\mathbf{s}$ are nonnegative, so the calculation does not rely on any delicate cancellations. Furthermore, our approximation need not be highly precise. We therefore use the polynomial $\exp\{t\mathbf{P}\}\mathbf{s} \approx T_N(t\mathbf{P}) = \sum_{k=0}^{N}\frac{t^k}{k!}\mathbf{P}^k$ for our approximation. For details on choosing N, see Section 4.5. For now, assume that we have chosen N such that

$$\|\mathbf{D}^{-1}\exp\{t\mathbf{P}\}\mathbf{s} - \mathbf{D}^{-1}T_N(t\mathbf{P})\mathbf{s}\|_\infty < \varepsilon/2. \qquad (4)$$

This way, if we compute $\mathbf{y} \approx T_N(t\mathbf{P})\mathbf{s}$ satisfying

$$\|\mathbf{D}^{-1}T_N(t\mathbf{P})\mathbf{s} - \mathbf{D}^{-1}\mathbf{y}\|_\infty < \varepsilon/2,$$

then by the triangle inequality we will have

$$\|\mathbf{D}^{-1}\exp\{t\mathbf{P}\}\mathbf{s} - \mathbf{D}^{-1}\mathbf{y}\|_\infty < \varepsilon, \qquad (5)$$

our objective.

4.2 Error weights

Using a degree N Taylor polynomial, `hk-relax` ultimately approximates $\mathbf{h}$ by approximating each term in the sum of the polynomial times the vector $\mathbf{s}$:

$$\mathbf{s} + \tfrac{t}{1}\mathbf{P}\mathbf{s} + \cdots + \tfrac{t^N}{N!}\mathbf{P}^N\mathbf{s}.$$

The total error of our computed solution is then a weighted sum of the errors at each individual term, $\frac{t^k}{k!}\mathbf{P}^k\mathbf{s}$. We show in Lemma 1 that these weights are given by the polynomials $\psi_k(t)$, which we define now. For a fixed degree N Taylor polynomial of the exponential, $T_N = \sum_{k=0}^{N}\frac{t^k}{k!}$, we define

$$\psi_k := \sum_{m=0}^{N-k}\tfrac{k!}{(m+k)!}t^m \text{ for } k = 0, \cdots, N. \qquad (6)$$

These polynomials $\psi_k(t)$ are closely related to the ϕ functions central to exponential integrators in ODEs [37]. Note that $\psi_0 = T_N$.

To guarantee the total error satisfies the criterion (3) then, it is enough to show that the error at each Taylor term satisfies an ∞-norm inequality analogous to (3). This is discussed in more detail in Section A.

4.3 Deriving a linear system

To define the basic step of the **hk-relax** algorithm and to show how the ψ_k influence the total error, we rearrange the Taylor polynomial computation into a linear system.

Denote by $\mathbf{v}_k$ the kth term of the vector sum $T_N(t\mathbf{P})\mathbf{s}$:

$$T_N(t\mathbf{P})\mathbf{s} = \mathbf{s} + \tfrac{t}{1}\mathbf{P}\mathbf{s} + \cdots + \tfrac{t^N}{N!}\mathbf{P}^N\mathbf{s} \tag{7}$$

$$= \mathbf{v}_0 + \mathbf{v}_1 + \cdots + \mathbf{v}_N. \tag{8}$$

Note that $\mathbf{v}_{k+1} = \frac{t^{k+1}}{(k+1)!}\mathbf{P}^{k+1} = \frac{t}{(k+1)}\mathbf{P}\mathbf{v}_k$. This identity implies that the terms $\mathbf{v}_k$ exactly satisfy the linear system

$$\begin{bmatrix} \mathbf{I} & & & & \\ \frac{-t}{1}\mathbf{P} & \mathbf{I} & & & \\ & \frac{-t}{2}\mathbf{P} & \ddots & & \\ & & \ddots & \mathbf{I} & \\ & & & \frac{-t}{N}\mathbf{P} & \mathbf{I} \end{bmatrix} \begin{bmatrix} \mathbf{v}_0 \\ \mathbf{v}_1 \\ \vdots \\ \vdots \\ \mathbf{v}_N \end{bmatrix} = \begin{bmatrix} \mathbf{s} \\ 0 \\ \vdots \\ \vdots \\ 0 \end{bmatrix}. \tag{9}$$

Let $\mathbf{v} = [\mathbf{v}_0; \mathbf{v}_1; \cdots; \mathbf{v}_N]$. An approximate solution $\hat{\mathbf{v}}$ to (9) would have block components $\hat{\mathbf{v}}_k$ such that $\sum_{k=0}^{N} \hat{\mathbf{v}}_k \approx T_N(t\mathbf{P})\mathbf{s}$, our desired approximation to $e^t\mathbf{h}$. In practice, we update only a single length n solution vector, adding all updates to that vector, instead of maintaining the $N+1$ different block vectors $\hat{\mathbf{v}}_k$ as part of $\hat{\mathbf{v}}$; furthermore, the block matrix and right-hand side are never formed explicitly.

With this block system in place, we can describe the algorithm's steps.

4.4 The hk-relax algorithm

Given a random walk transition matrix $\mathbf{P}$, scalar $t > 0$, and seed vector $\mathbf{s}$ as inputs, we solve the linear system from (9) as follows. Denote the initial solution vector by $\mathbf{y}$ and the initial $nN \times 1$ residual by $\mathbf{r}^{(0)} = \mathbf{e}_1 \otimes \mathbf{s}$. Denote by $r(i,j)$ the entry of $\mathbf{r}$ corresponding to node i in residual block j. The idea is to iteratively remove all entries from $\mathbf{r}$ that satisfy

$$r(i,j) \geq \frac{e^t \varepsilon d_i}{2N\psi_j(t)}. \tag{10}$$

To organize this process, we begin by placing the nonzero entries of $\mathbf{r}^{(0)}$ in a queue, $Q(\mathbf{r})$, and place updated entries of $\mathbf{r}$ into $Q(\mathbf{r})$ only if they satisfy (10).

Then **hk-relax** proceeds as follows.

1. At each step, pop the top entry of $Q(\mathbf{r})$, call it $r(i,j)$, and subtract that entry in $\mathbf{r}$, making $\mathbf{r}(i,j) = 0$.
2. Add $r(i,j)$ to $\mathbf{y}_i$.
3. Add $r(i,j)\frac{t}{j+1}\mathbf{P}\mathbf{e}_j$ to residual block $\mathbf{r}_{j+1}$.
4. For each entry of $\mathbf{r}_{j+1}$ that was updated, add that entry to the back of $Q(\mathbf{r})$ if it satisfies (10).

Once all entries of $\mathbf{r}$ that satisfy (10) have been removed, the resulting solution vector $\mathbf{y}$ will satisfy (3), which we prove in Section A, along with a bound on the work required to achieve this. We present working code for our method in Figure 2 that shows how to optimize this computation using sparse data structures. These make it highly efficient in practice.

```
# G is graph as dictionary-of-sets,
# seed is an array of seeds,
# t, eps, N, psis are precomputed
x = {} # Store x, r as dictionaries
r = {} # initialize residual
Q = collections.deque() # initialize queue
for s in seed:
  r[(s,0)] = 1./len(seed)
  Q.append((s,0))
while len(Q) > 0:
  (v,j) = Q.popleft() # v has r[(v,j)] ...
  rvj = r[(v,j)]
  # perform the hk-relax step
  if v not in x: x[v] = 0.
  x[v] += rvj
  r[(v,j)] = 0.
  mass = (t*rvj/(float(j)+1.))/len(G[v])
  for u in G[v]:   # for neighbors of v
    next = (u,j+1) # in the next block
    if j+1 == N: # last step, add to soln
      x[u] += rvj/len(G(v))
      continue
    if next not in r: r[next] = 0.
    thresh = math.exp(t)*eps*len(G[u])
    thresh = thresh/(N*psis[j-1])/2.
    if r[next] < thresh and \
      r[next] + mass >= thresh:
      Q.append(next) # add u to queue
    r[next] = r[next] + mass
```

Figure 2: Pseudo-code for our algorithm as working python code. The graph is stored as a dictionary of sets so that the G[v] statement returns the set of neighbors associated with vertex v. The solution is the vector x indexed by vertices and the residual vector is indexed by tuples (v,j) that are pairs of vertices and steps j. A fully working demo may be downloaded from github https://gist.github.com/dgleich/7d904a10cfd9ddfaf49a.

4.5 Choosing N

The last detail of the algorithm we need to discuss is how to pick N. In (4) we want to guarantee the accuracy of $\mathbf{D}^{-1}\exp\{t\mathbf{P}\}\mathbf{s} - \mathbf{D}^{-1}T_N(t\mathbf{P})\mathbf{s}$. By using $\mathbf{D}^{-1}\exp\{t\mathbf{P}\} = \exp\{t\mathbf{P}^T\}\mathbf{D}^{-1}$ and $\mathbf{D}^{-1}T_N(t\mathbf{P}) = T_N(t\mathbf{P}^T)\mathbf{D}^{-1}$, we can get a new upperbound on $\|\mathbf{D}^{-1}\exp\{t\mathbf{P}\}\mathbf{s} - \mathbf{D}^{-1}T_N(t\mathbf{P})\mathbf{s}\|_\infty$ by noting

$$\begin{aligned} &\|\exp\left\{t\mathbf{P}^T\right\}\mathbf{D}^{-1}\mathbf{s} - T_N(t\mathbf{P}^T)\mathbf{D}^{-1}\mathbf{s}\|_\infty \\ &\leq \|\exp\left\{t\mathbf{P}^T\right\} - T_N(t\mathbf{P}^T)\|_\infty \|\mathbf{D}^{-1}\mathbf{s}\|_\infty. \end{aligned}$$

Since $\mathbf{s}$ is stochastic, we have $\|\mathbf{D}^{-1}\mathbf{s}\|_\infty \leq \|\mathbf{D}^{-1}\mathbf{s}\|_1 \leq 1$. From [34] we know that the norm $\|\exp\left\{t\mathbf{P}^T\right\} - T_N(t\mathbf{P}^T)\|_\infty$ is bounded by

$$\frac{\|t\mathbf{P}^T\|_\infty^{N+1}}{(N+1)!}\frac{(N+2)}{(N+2-t)} \leq \frac{t^{N+1}}{(N+1)!}\frac{(N+2)}{(N+2-t)}. \tag{11}$$

So to guarantee (4), it is enough to choose N that implies $\frac{t^{N+1}}{(N+1)!}\frac{(N+2)}{(N+2-t)} < \varepsilon/2$. Such an N can be determined efficiently simply by iteratively computing terms of the Taylor polynomial for e^t until the error is less than the desired error for **hk-relax**. In practice, this required a choice of N no greater than $2t\log(\frac{1}{\varepsilon})$, which we think can be made rigorous.

4.6 Outline of convergence result

The proof proceeds as follows. First, we relate the error vector of the Taylor approximation $E_1 = T_N(t\mathbf{P})\mathbf{s}-\mathbf{x}$, to the error vector from solving the linear system described in Section 4.4, $E_2 = T_N(t\mathbf{P})\mathbf{s}-\mathbf{y}$. Second, we express the error vector E_2 in terms of the residual blocks of the linear system (9); this will involve writing E_2 as a sum of residual blocks $\mathbf{r}_k$ with weights $\psi_k(t\mathbf{P})$. Third, we use the previous results to upper-bound $\|\mathbf{D}^{-1}T_N(t\mathbf{P})\mathbf{s}-\mathbf{D}^{-1}\mathbf{x}\|_\infty$ with $\sum_{k=0}^{N}\psi_k(t)\|\mathbf{D}^{-1}\mathbf{r}_k\|_\infty$, and use this to show that $\|\mathbf{D}^{-1}T_N(t\mathbf{P})\mathbf{s} - \mathbf{D}^{-1}\mathbf{x}\|_\infty < \varepsilon/2$ is guaranteed by the stopping criterion of `hk-relax`, (3). Finally, we prove that performing steps of `hk-relax` until the stopping criterion is attained requires work bounded by $\frac{2N\psi_1(t)}{\varepsilon} \leq 2Ne^t/\varepsilon$.

5. RELATED WORK

We wish to highlight a few ideas that have recently emerged in the literature to clarify how our method differs. We discuss these in terms of community detection, the matrix exponential, fast diffusion methods, and relaxation methods.

Community detection and conductance. Conductance often appears in community detection and is known to be one of the most important measures of a community [47]. The personalized PageRank method is one of the most scalable methods to find sets of small conductance, although recent work opened up a new possibility with localized max-flow algorithms [46]. For the PageRank algorithm we use as a point of comparison, Zhu et al. [54] recently provided an improved bound on the performance of this algorithm when finding sets with high internal conductance. The internal conductance of a set is the minimum conductance of the subgraph induced by the set and we would expect that real-world communities have large internal conductance. Due to the similarity between our algorithm and the personalized PageRank diffusion, we believe that a similar result likely holds here as well.

The matrix exponential in network analysis. Recently, the matrix exponential has frequently appeared as a tool in the network analysis literature. It has been used to estimate node centrality [18, 20, 19], for link-prediction [29], in graph kernels [28], and – as already mentioned – clustering and community detection [14]. Many of these studies involve fast ways to approximate the *entire* matrix exponential, instead of a single column as we study here. For instance, Sui et al. [49] describe a low-parameter decomposition of a network that is useful both for estimating Katz scores [25] and the matrix exponential. Orecchia and Mahoney [44] show that the heat kernel diffusion implicitly approximates a diffusion operator using a particular type of generalized entropy, which provides a principled rationale for its use.

Fast methods for diffusions. Perhaps the most related work is a recent Monte Carlo algorithm by Chung and Simpson [16] to estimate the heat kernel diffusion via a random walk sampling scheme. This approach involves directly simulating a random walk with transition probabilities that mirror the Taylor series expansion of the exponential. In comparison, our approach is entirely deterministic and thus more useful to compare between diffusions, as it eliminates the algorithmic variance endemic to Monte Carlo simulations. A similar idea is used by Borgs et al. [13] to achieve a randomized sublinear time algorithm to estimate the largest PageRank entries, and in fact, Monto Carlo methods frequently feature in PageRank computations due to the relationship between the diffusion and a random walk [7, 13, 8, 9]. Most other deterministic approaches for the matrix exponential involve at least one matrix-vector product [45, 2].

Relaxation methods. The algorithm we use is a coordinate relaxation method similar to Gauss-Seidel and Gauss-Southwell. If we applied it to a symmetric positive definite matrix, then it would be a coordinate descent method [35]. It has been proposed for PageRank in a few difference cases [23, 36, 5]. The same type of relaxation method has also been used to estimate the Katz diffusion [12]. We recently used it to estimate a column of the matrix exponential $\exp\{\mathbf{P}\}\mathbf{e}_i$ in a strict, 1-norm error and were able to prove a sublinear convergence bound by assuming a very slowly growing maximum degree [27] or a power-law degree distribution [26]. This paper, in comparision, treats the scaled exponential $\exp\{-t(\mathbf{I}-\mathbf{P})\}\mathbf{e}_i$ in a degree-weighted norm; it also shows a constant runtime independent of any network property.

6. EXPERIMENTAL RESULTS

Here we compare `hk-relax` with a PageRank-based local clustering algorithm, pprpush [5]. Both algorithms accept as inputs a symmetric graph $\mathbf{A}$ and seed set $\mathbf{s}$. The parameters required are t and ε, for `hk-relax`, and α and ε for pprpush. Both algorithms compute their respective diffusion ranks starting from the seed set, then perform a sweep-cut on the resulting ranks. The difference in the algorithms lies solely in the diffusion used and the particular parameters. We conducted the timing experiments on a Dual CPU system with the Intel Xeon E5-2670 processor (2.6 GHz, 8 cores) with 16 cores total and 256 GB of RAM. None of the experiments needed anywhere near all the memory, nor any of the parallelism. Our implementation uses Matlab's sparse matrix data structure through a C++ mex interface. It uses C++ unordered maps to store sparse vectors and is equivalent to the code in Figure 2.

6.1 Synthetic results

In this section, we study the behavior of the PageRank and heat kernel diffusions on the symbolic image graph of a chaotic function f [48]. The graphs that result are loosely reminiscent of a social network because they have pockets of structure, like communities, and also chaotic behaviour that results in a small-world like property.

The symbolic image of a function f is a graph where each node represents a region of space, and edges represent the action of the function in that region of space. We consider two-dimensional functions $f(x, y)$ in the unit square $[0, 1]^2$ so that we can associate each node with a pixel of an image and illustrate the vectors as images. In Figure 3 (left), we illustrate how the graph construction works. In the remaining examples, we let f be a map that results from a chaotic, nonlinear dynamical system [48] (we use the T10 construction with $k = 0.22, \eta = 0.99$ and sample 1000 points from each region of space, then symmetrize the result and discard weights). We discretize space in a 512×512 grid, which results in a $262,144$ node graph with $2M$ edges. In Figure 3 (right), we also show the PageRank vector with uniform teleportation as an image to "illustrate the structure" in the function f.

Next, in Figure 4, we compare the vectors and sets identified by both diffusions starting from a single seed node. We chose the parameters $\alpha = 0.85$ and $t = 3$ so the two methods perform the same amount of work. These results are what would be expected from Figure 1, and what many of the remaining experiments show: PageRank diffuses to a larger region of the graph whereas the heat-kernel remains more focused in a sub-region. PageRank, then, finds a large community with about 5,000 nodes whereas the heat kernel finds a small community with around 452 nodes with slightly worse conductance. This experiment suggests that, if these results also hold in real-world networks, then because real-world communities are often small [33], the heat kernel diffusion should produce *more accurate* communities in real-world networks.

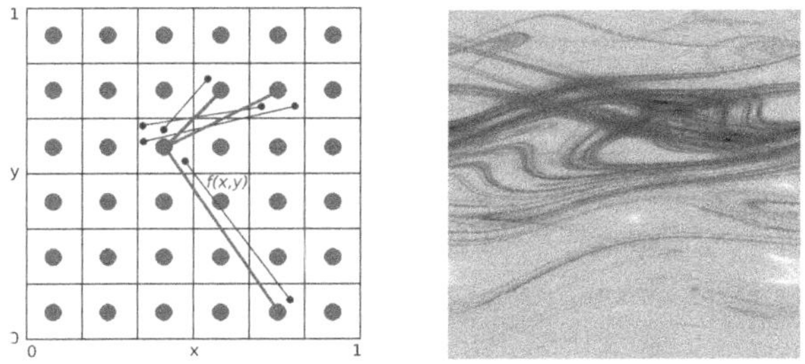

Figure 3: (Left) An illustration of the symbolic image of a function f as a graph. Each large, blue node represents a region of space. Thick, blue edges represent how the thin, red values of the function behave in that region. (Right) The global PageRank vector is then an image that illustrates features of the chaotic map f and shows that it has pockets of structure.

(a) ppr vector $\alpha = 0.85$, $\varepsilon = 10^{-5}$ (b) ppr set, $\phi = 0.31$, size $= 5510$

(c) hk vector $t = 3$, $\varepsilon = 10^{-5}$ (d) hk set, $\phi = 0.34$, size $= 455$

Figure 4: When we compare the heat-kernel and PageRank diffusions on the symbolic image of the Chirikov map (see Figure 3), pprgrow finds a larger set with slightly better conductance, whereas hk-grow finds a tighter set with about the same conductance. In real-world networks, these smaller sets are more like real-world communities.

6.2 Runtime and conductance

We next compare the runtime and conductance of the algorithms on a suite of social networks. For pprpush, we fix $\alpha = 0.99$, then compute PageRank for multiple values of $\varepsilon = 10^{-2}, 10^{-3}, 10^{-4}, 10^{-5}$, and output the set of best conductance obtained. (This matches the way this method is commonly used in past work.) For `hk-relax`, we compute the heat kernel rank for four different parameter sets, and output the set of best conductance among them: $(t, \varepsilon) = (10, 10^{-4}); (20, 10^{-3}); (40, 5 \cdot 10^{-3}); (80, 10^{-2})$. We also include in `hk-relax` an early termination criterion, in the case that the sum of the degrees of the nodes which are relaxed, $\sum d_{i_l}$, exceeds $n^{1.5}$. However, even the smaller input graphs (on which the condition is more likely to be met because of the smaller value of $n^{1.5}$) do not appear to have reached this threshold. Furthermore, the main theorem of this paper implies that the quantity $\sum d_{i_l}$ cannot exceed $\frac{2N\psi_1(t)}{\varepsilon}$. The datasets we use are summarized in Table 1; all datasets are modified to be undirected and a single connected component. These datasets were originally presented in the following papers [3, 10, 32, 41, 42, 33, 31, 50, 30, 53, 11, 38].

To compare the runtimes of the two algorithms, we display in Figure 5 for each graph the 25%, 50%, and 75% percentiles of the runtimes from 200 trials performed. For a given graph, each trial consisted of choosing a node of that graph uniformly at random to be a seed, then calling both the PageRank and the heat kernel algorithms. On the larger datasets, which have a much broader spectrum of node degrees and therefore greater variance, we instead performed 1,000 trials. Additionally, we display the 25%, 50%, and 75% percentiles of the conductances achieved during the exact same set of trials. The trendlines of these figures omit some of the trials in order to better show the trends, but all of the median results are plotted (as open circles). The figures show that in small graphs, `hk-relax` is faster than pprpush, but gets larger (worse) conductance. The picture reverses for large graphs where `hk-relax` is slower but finds smaller (better) conductance sets.

Cluster size and conductance. We highlight the individual results of the previous experiment on the symmetrized twitter network. Here, we find that `hk-relax` finds sets of better conductance than pprpush at all sizes of communities in the network. See Figure 6.

6.3 Clusters produced vs. ground-truth

We conclude with an evaluation of identifying ground-truth communities in the `com-dblp`, `com-lj`, `com-amazon`, `com-orkut`, `com-youtube`, and `com-friendster` datasets [53, 38]. In this experiment, for each dataset we first located 100 known communities in the dataset of size greater than 10. Given one such community, using every single node as an individual seed, we looked at the sets returned by `hk-relax` with $t = 5, \varepsilon = 10^{-4}$ and pprpush using the standard procedure. We picked the set from the seed that had the highest F_1 measure. (Recall that the F_1 measure is a harmonic mean of precision and recall.) We report the mean of the F_1 measure, conductance, and set size, where the average is taken over all 100 trials in Table 2. These results show that `hk-relax` produces only slightly inferior conductance

Table 1: Datasets

Graph	$\|V\|$	$\|E\|$
pgp-cc	10,680	24,316
ca-AstroPh-cc	17,903	196,972
marvel-comics-cc	19,365	96,616
as-22july06	22,963	48,436
rand-ff-25000-0.4	25,000	56,071
cond-mat-2003-cc	27,519	116,181
email-Enron-cc	33,696	180,811
cond-mat-2005-fix-cc	36,458	171,735
soc-sign-epinions-cc	119,130	704,267
itdk0304-cc	190,914	607,610
dblp-cc	226,413	716,460
flickr-bidir-cc	513,969	3,190,452
ljournal-2008	5,363,260	50,030,085
twitter-2010	41,652,230	1,202,513,046
friendster	65,608,366	1,806,067,135
com-amazon	334,863	925,872
com-dblp	317,080	1,049,866
com-youtube	1,134,890	2,987,624
com-lj	3,997,962	34,681,189
com-orkut	3,072,441	117,185,083

Table 2: The result of evaluating the heat kernel (hk) vs. PageRank (pr) on finding real-world communities. The heat kernel finds smaller, more accurate, sets with slightly worse conductance.

data	F_1-measure		conductance		set size	
	hk	pr	hk	pr	hk	pr
amazon	0.325	0.140	0.141	0.048	193	15293
dblp	0.257	0.115	0.267	0.173	44	16026
youtube	0.177	0.136	0.337	0.321	1010	6079
lj	0.131	0.107	0.474	0.459	283	738
orkut	0.055	0.044	0.714	0.687	537	1989
friendster	0.078	0.090	0.785	0.802	229	333

scores, but using much smaller sets with substantially better F_1 measures. This suggests that hk-relax better captures the properties of real-world communities than the PageRank diffusion in the sense that the tighter sets produced by the heat kernel are better focused around real-world communities than are the larger sets produced by the PageRank diffusion.

7. CONCLUSIONS

These results suggest that the hk-relax algorithm is a viable companion to the celebrated PageRank push algorithm and may even be a worthy competitor for tasks that require accurate communities of large graphs. Furthermore, we suspect that the hk-relax method will be useful for the myriad other uses of PageRank-style diffusions such as link-prediction [29] or even logic programming [51].

In the future, we plan to explore this method on directed networks as well as better methods for selecting the parameters of the diffusion. It is also possible that our new ideas may translate to faster methods for non-conservative diffusions such as the Katz [25] and modularity methods [43], and we plan to explore these diffusions as well.

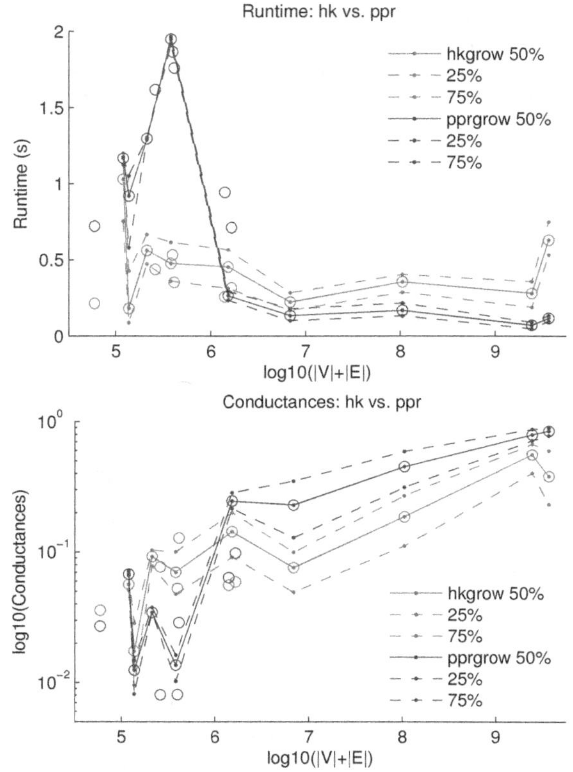

Figure 5: (Top figure) Runtimes of the hk-relax vs. ppr-push, shown with percentile trendlines from a select set of experiments. (Bottom) Conductances of hk-relax vs. ppr-push, shown in the same way.

Acknowledgements

This work was supported by NSF CAREER Award CCF-1149756.

8. REFERENCES

[1] B. Abrahao, S. Soundarajan, J. Hopcroft, and R. Kleinberg. On the separability of structural classes of communities. In *KDD*, pages 624–632, 2012.

[2] A. H. Al-Mohy and N. J. Higham. Computing the action of the matrix exponential, with an application to exponential integrators. *SIAM J. Sci. Comput.*, 33(2):488–511, March 2011.

[3] R. Alberich, J. Miro-Julia, and F. Rossello. Marvel universe looks almost like a real social network. *arXiv*, cond-mat.dis-nn:0202174, 2002.

[4] N. Alon and V. D. Milman. λ_1, isoperimetric inequalities for graphs, and superconcentrators. *J. of Comb. Theory, Series B*, 38(1):73–88, 1985.

[5] R. Andersen, F. Chung, and K. Lang. Local graph partitioning using PageRank vectors. In *FOCS*, 2006.

[6] R. Andersen and K. Lang. An algorithm for improving graph partitions. In *SODA*, pages 651–660, January 2008.

[7] K. Avrachenkov, N. Litvak, D. Nemirovsky, and N. Osipova. Monte carlo methods in pagerank computation: When one iteration is sufficient. *SIAM J. Numer. Anal.*, 45(2):890–904, February 2007.

[8] B. Bahmani, K. Chakrabarti, and D. Xin. Fast personalized pagerank on MapReduce. In *SIGMOD*, pages 973–984, New York, NY, USA, 2011. ACM.

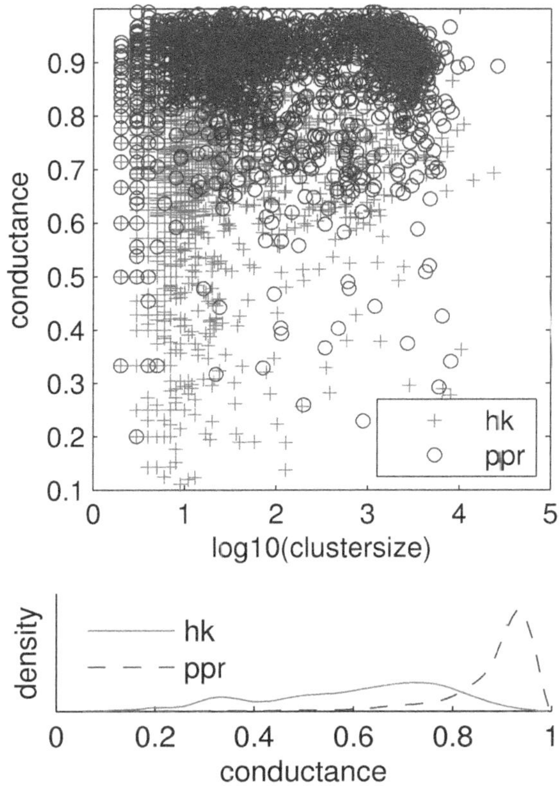

Figure 6: The top figure shows a scatter plot of conductance vs. community size in the twitter graph for the two community detection methods; the bottom figure shows a kernel density estimate of the conductances achieved by each method, which shows that hk-relax is more likely to return a set of lower conductance.

[9] B. Bahmani, A. Chowdhury, and A. Goel. Fast incremental and personalized pagerank. *Proc. VLDB Endow.*, 4(3):173–184, Dec. 2010.

[10] M. Boguñá, R. Pastor-Satorras, A. Díaz-Guilera, and A. Arenas. Models of social networks based on social distance attachment. *Phys. Rev. E*, 70(5):056122, Nov 2004.

[11] P. Boldi, M. Rosa, M. Santini, and S. Vigna. Layered label propagation: A multiresolution coordinate-free ordering for compressing social networks. In *WWW*, pages 587–596, March 2011.

[12] F. Bonchi, P. Esfandiar, D. F. Gleich, C. Greif, and L. V. Lakshmanan. Fast matrix computations for pairwise and columnwise commute times and Katz scores. *Internet Mathematics*, 8(1-2):73–112, 2012.

[13] C. Borgs, M. Brautbar, J. Chayes, and S.-H. Teng. Multi-scale matrix sampling and sublinear-time pagerank computation. *Internet Mathematics*, Online, 2013.

[14] F. Chung. The heat kernel as the PageRank of a graph. *PNAS*, 104(50):19735–19740, 2007.

[15] F. Chung. A local graph partitioning algorithm using heat kernel pagerank. *Internet Mathematics*, 6(3):315–330, 2009.

[16] F. Chung and O. Simpson. Solving linear systems with boundary conditions using heat kernel pagerank. In *Algorithms and Models for the Web Graph*, pages 203–219. Springer, 2013.

[17] I. S. Dhillon, Y. Guan, and B. Kulis. Weighted graph cuts without eigenvectors a multilevel approach. *IEEE Trans. Pattern Anal. Mach. Intell.*, 29(11):1944–1957, November 2007.

[18] E. Estrada. Characterization of 3d molecular structure. *Chemical Physics Letters*, 319(5-6):713–718, 2000.

[19] E. Estrada and D. J. Higham. Network properties revealed through matrix functions. *SIAM Review*, 52(4):696–714 2010.

[20] A. Farahat, T. LoFaro, J. C. Miller, G. Rae, and L. A. Ward. Authority rankings from HITS, PageRank, and SALSA: Existence, uniqueness, and effect of initialization. *SIAM Journal on Scientific Computing*, 27(4):1181–1201, 2006

[21] M. Fiedler. Algebraic connectivity of graphs *Czechoslovak Mathematical Journal*, 23(98):298–305, 1973

[22] N. J. Higham. *Functions of Matrices: Theory and Computation*. SIAM, 2008.

[23] G. Jeh and J. Widom. Scaling personalized web search. In *WWW*, pages 271–279. ACM, 2003.

[24] U. Kang and C. Faloutsos. Beyond 'caveman communities': Hubs and spokes for graph compression and mining. In *ICDM*, pages 300–309, Washington, DC, USA, 2011. IEEE Computer Society.

[25] L. Katz. A new status index derived from sociometric analysis. *Psychometrika*, 18(1):39–43, March 1953.

[26] K. Kloster and D. F. Gleich. A fast relaxation method for computing a column of the matrix exponential of stochastic matrices from large, sparse networks. *arXiv*, cs.SI:1310.3423, 2013.

[27] K. Kloster and D. F. Gleich. A nearly-sublinear method for approximating a column of the matrix exponential for matrices from large, sparse networks. In *Algorithms and Models for the Web Graph*, page in press, 2013.

[28] R. I. Kondor and J. D. Lafferty. Diffusion kernels on graphs and other discrete input spaces. In *ICML*, pages 315–322, San Francisco, CA, USA, 2002. Morgan Kaufmann Publishers Inc.

[29] J. Kunegis and A. Lommatzsch. Learning spectral graph transformations for link prediction. In *ICML*, pages 561–568, 2009.

[30] H. Kwak, C. Lee, H. Park, and S. Moon. What is Twitter, a social network or a news media? In *WWW*, pages 591–600, 2010.

[31] J. Leskovec, D. Huttenlocher, and J. Kleinberg. Signed networks in social media. In *CHI*, pages 1361–1370, 2010.

[32] J. Leskovec, J. Kleinberg, and C. Faloutsos. Graph evolution: Densification and shrinking diameters. *ACM Trans. Knowl. Discov. Data*, 1:1–41, March 2007.

[33] J. Leskovec, K. J. Lang, A. Dasgupta, and M. W. Mahoney. Community structure in large networks: Natural cluster sizes and the absence of large well-defined clusters. *Internet Mathematics*, 6(1):29–123, September 2009.

[34] M. Liou. A novel method of evaluating transient response. *Proceedings of the IEEE*, 54(1):20–23, 1966.

[35] Z. Q. Luo and P. Tseng. On the convergence of the coordinate descent method for convex differentiable minimization. *J. Optim. Theory App.*, 72(1) 7–35, 1992. 10.1007/BF00939948.

[36] F. McSherry. A uniform approach to accelerated PageRank computation. In *WWW*, pages 575–582, 2005.

[37] B. V. Minchev and W. M. Wright. A review of exponential integrators for first order semi-linear problems. Technical Report Numerics 2/2005, Norges Teknisk-Naturvitenskapelige Universitet, 2005.

[38] A. Mislove, M. Marcon, K. P. Gummadi, P. Druschel, and B. Bhattacharjee. Measurement and analysis of online social networks. In *SIGCOMM*, pages 29–42, 2007.

[39] C. Moler and C. Van Loan. Nineteen dubious ways to compute the exponential of a matrix. *SIAM Review*, 20(4):801–836, 1978.

[40] C. Moler and C. Van Loan. Nineteen dubious ways to compute the exponential of a matrix, twenty-five years later. *SIAM Review*, 45(1):3–49, 2003.

[41] M. Newman. Network datasets. http://www-personal.umich.edu/~mejn/netdata/, 2006.
[42] M. E. J. Newman. The structure of scientific collaboration networks. *PNAS*, 98(2):404–409, 2001.
[43] M. E. J. Newman. Modularity and community structure in networks. *PNAS*, 103(23):8577–8582, 2006.
[44] L. Orecchia and M. W. Mahoney. Implementing regularization implicitly via approximate eigenvector computation. In *ICML*, pages 121–128, 2011.
[45] L. Orecchia, S. Sachdeva, and N. K. Vishnoi. Approximating the exponential, the Lanczos method and an Otilde(m)-time spectral algorithm for balanced separator. In *STOC*, pages 1141–1160, 2012.
[46] L. Orecchia and Z. A. Zhu. Flow-based algorithms for local graph clustering. In *SODA*, pages 1267–1286, 2014.
[47] S. E. Schaeffer. Graph clustering. *Computer Science Review*, 1(1):27–64, 2007.
[48] D. L. Shepelyansky and O. V. Zhirov. Google matrix, dynamical attractors, and ulam networks. *Phys. Rev. E*, 81(3):036213, March 2010.
[49] X. Sui, T.-H. Lee, J. J. Whang, B. Savas, S. Jain, K. Pingali, and I. Dhillon. Parallel clustered low-rank approximation of graphs and its application to link prediction. In *Languages and Compilers for Parallel Computing*, volume 7760 of *Lecture Notes in Computer Science*, pages 76–95. Springer Berlin, 2013.
[50] C. (The Cooperative Association for Internet Data Analyais). Network datasets. http://www.caida.org/tools/measurement/skitter/router_topology/, 2005. Accessed in 2005.
[51] W. Y. Wang, K. Mazaitis, and W. W. Cohen. Programming with personalized pagerank: A locally groundable first-order probabilistic logic. In *CIKM*, pages 2129–2138, New York, NY, USA, 2013. ACM.
[52] J. J. Whang, D. F. Gleich, and I. S. Dhillon. Overlapping community detection using seed set expansion. In *CIKM*, pages 2099–2108, New York, NY, USA, 2013. ACM.
[53] J. Yang and J. Leskovec. Defining and evaluating network communities based on ground-truth. In *ICDM*, pages 745–754, 2012.
[54] Z. A. Zhu, S. Lattanzi, and V. Mirrokni. A local algorithm for finding well-connected clusters. In *ICML*, pages 396–404, 2013.

APPENDIX

A. CONVERGENCE THEORY

Here we state our main result bounding the work required by `hk-relax` to approximate the heat kernel with accuracy as described in (3).

THEOREM 1. *Let $\boldsymbol{P}$, t, $\psi_k(t)$, and $\boldsymbol{r}$ be as in Section 4. If steps of `hk-relax` are performed until all entries of the residual satisfy $r(i,j) < \frac{e^t \varepsilon d_i}{2N\psi_j(t)}$, then `hk-relax` produces an approximation $\boldsymbol{x}$ of $\boldsymbol{h} = \exp\{-t(\boldsymbol{I}-\boldsymbol{P})\}\,\boldsymbol{s}$ satisfying*

$$\|\boldsymbol{D}^{-1}\exp\{-t(\boldsymbol{I}-\boldsymbol{P})\}\,\boldsymbol{s} - \boldsymbol{D}^{-1}\boldsymbol{x}\|_\infty < \varepsilon,$$

and the amount of work required is bounded by

$$work(\varepsilon) \le \frac{2N\psi_1(t)}{\varepsilon} \le \frac{2N(e^t-1)}{\varepsilon t}.$$

Producing $\mathbf{x}$ satisfying

$$\|\mathbf{D}^{-1}\exp\{-t(\mathbf{I}-\mathbf{P})\}\,\mathbf{s} - \mathbf{D}^{-1}\mathbf{x}\|_\infty < \varepsilon$$

is equivalent to producing $\mathbf{y}$ satisfying

$$\|\mathbf{D}^{-1}\exp\{t\mathbf{P})\}\,\mathbf{s} - \mathbf{D}^{-1}\mathbf{y}\|_\infty < e^t\varepsilon.$$

We will show that the error vector in the `hk-relax` steps, $T_N(t\mathbf{P})\mathbf{s}-\mathbf{y}$, satisfies $\|\mathbf{D}^{-1}T_N(t\mathbf{P})\mathbf{s} - \mathbf{D}^{-1}\mathbf{y}\|_\infty < e^t\varepsilon/2$.

The following lemma expresses the error vector, $T_N(t\mathbf{P})\mathbf{s}-\mathbf{y}$, as a weighted sum of the residual blocks $\mathbf{r}_k$ in the linear system (9), and shows that the polynomials $\psi_k(t)$ are the weights.

LEMMA 1. *Let $\psi_k(t)$ be defined as in Section 4. Then in the notation of Section 4.3, we can express the error vector of `hk-relax` in terms of the residual blocks $\boldsymbol{r}_k$ as follows*

$$T_N(t\boldsymbol{P})\boldsymbol{s} - \boldsymbol{y} = \sum_{k=0}^{N} \psi_k(t\boldsymbol{P})\boldsymbol{r}_k \tag{12}$$

PROOF. Consider (9). Recall that $\mathbf{v} = [\mathbf{v}_0; \mathbf{v}_1; \cdots; \mathbf{v}_N]$ and let $\mathbf{S}$ be the $(N+1)\times(N+1)$ matrix of 0s with first subdiagonal equal to $[\frac{1}{1}, \frac{1}{2}, \cdots, \frac{1}{N}]$. Then we can rewrite this linear system more conveniently as

$$(\mathbf{I} - \mathbf{S}\otimes(t\mathbf{P}))\mathbf{v} = \mathbf{e}_1 \otimes \mathbf{s}. \tag{13}$$

Let $\mathbf{v}_k$ be the true solution vectors that the $\hat{\mathbf{v}}_k$ are approximating in (13). We showed in Section 4.3 that the error $T_N(t\mathbf{P})\mathbf{s}-\mathbf{y}$ is in fact the sum of the errors $\mathbf{v}_k - \hat{\mathbf{v}}_k$. Now we will express $T_N(t\mathbf{P})\mathbf{s}-\mathbf{y}$ in terms of the residual partitions, i.e. $\mathbf{r}_k$.

At any given step we have $\mathbf{r} = \mathbf{e}_1\otimes\mathbf{s} - (\mathbf{I}-\mathbf{S}\otimes(t\mathbf{P}))\hat{\mathbf{v}}$, so pre-multiplying by $(\mathbf{I}-\mathbf{S}\otimes(t\mathbf{P}))^{-1}$ yields $(\mathbf{I}-\mathbf{S}\otimes(t\mathbf{P}))^{-1}\mathbf{r} = \mathbf{v}-\hat{\mathbf{v}}$, because $(\mathbf{I}-\mathbf{S}\otimes(t\mathbf{P}))\mathbf{v} = \mathbf{e}_1\otimes\mathbf{s}$ exactly, by definition of $\mathbf{v}$. Note that $(\mathbf{I}-\mathbf{S}\otimes(t\mathbf{P}))^{-1}\mathbf{r} = \mathbf{v}-\hat{\mathbf{v}}$ is the error vector for the linear system (13). From this, an explicit computation of the inverse (see [27] for details) yields

$$\begin{bmatrix} \mathbf{v}_0 - \hat{\mathbf{v}}_0 \\ \vdots \\ \mathbf{v}_N - \hat{\mathbf{v}}_N \end{bmatrix} = \left(\sum_{k=0}^{N} \mathbf{S}^k \otimes (t\mathbf{P})^k\right) \begin{bmatrix} \mathbf{r}_0 \\ \vdots \\ \mathbf{r}_N \end{bmatrix}. \tag{14}$$

For our purposes, the full block vectors $\mathbf{v}, \hat{\mathbf{v}}, \mathbf{r}$ and their individual partitions are unimportant: we want only their sum, because $T_N(t\mathbf{P})\mathbf{s}-\mathbf{y} = \sum_{k=0}^{N}(\mathbf{v}_k - \hat{\mathbf{v}}_k)$, as previously discussed.

Next we use (14) to express $\sum_{k=0}^{N}(\mathbf{v}_k - \hat{\mathbf{v}}_k)$, and hence

$$T_N(t\mathbf{P})\mathbf{s}-\mathbf{y},$$

in terms of the residual blocks $\mathbf{r}_k$. We accomplish this by examining the coefficients of an arbitrary block $\mathbf{r}_k$ in (14), which in turn requires analyzing the powers of $(\mathbf{S}\otimes t\mathbf{P})$.

Fix a residual block $\mathbf{r}_{j-1}$ and consider the product with a single term $(\mathbf{S}^k\otimes(t\mathbf{P})^k)$. Since $\mathbf{r}_{j-1}$ is in block-row j of $\mathbf{r}$, it multiplies with only the block-column j of each term $(\mathbf{S}^k\otimes(t\mathbf{P})^k)$, so we want to know what the blocks in block-column j of $(\mathbf{S}^k\otimes(t\mathbf{P})^k)$ look like.

From [27] we know that

$$\mathbf{S}^m\mathbf{e}_j = \begin{cases} \frac{(j-1)!}{(j-1+m)!}\mathbf{e}_{j+m} & \text{if } 0 \le m \le N+1-j \\ 0 & \text{otherwise.} \end{cases}$$

This means that block-column j of $(\mathbf{S}^m\otimes(t\mathbf{P})^m)$ contains only a single nonzero block, $\frac{(j-1)!}{(j-1+m)!}t^m\mathbf{P}^m$, for all $0\le m\le N+1-j$. Hence, summing the $n\times n$ blocks in block-column j of each power $(\mathbf{S}^m\otimes(t\mathbf{P})^m)$ yields

$$\sum_{m=0}^{N+1-j} \frac{(j-1)!t^m}{(j-1+m)!}\mathbf{P}^m \tag{15}$$

as the matrix coefficient of $\mathbf{r}_{j-1}$ in the right-hand side expression of $\sum_{k=0}^{N}(\mathbf{v}_k-\hat{\mathbf{v}}_k) = (\mathbf{e}^T\otimes\mathbf{I})(\sum_{m=0}^{N}\mathbf{S}^m\otimes(t\mathbf{P})^m)\mathbf{r}$.

Substituting $k=j-1$ on the right-hand side of (15) yields

$$\begin{aligned}\sum_{k=0}^{N}(\mathbf{v}_k-\hat{\mathbf{v}}_k) &= (\mathbf{e}^T\otimes\mathbf{I})\left(\sum_{m=0}^{N}\mathbf{S}^m\otimes(t\mathbf{P})^m\right)\mathbf{r} \\ &= \sum_{k=0}^{N}\left(\sum_{m=0}^{N-k}\frac{k!t^m}{(k+m)!}\mathbf{P}^m\right)\mathbf{r}_k \\ &= \sum_{k=0}^{N}\psi_k(t\mathbf{P})\mathbf{r}_k,\end{aligned}$$

as desired. □

Now that we've shown $T_N(t\mathbf{P})\mathbf{s} - \mathbf{y} = \sum_{k=0}^{N} \psi_k(t\mathbf{P})\mathbf{r}_k$ we can upperbound $\|\mathbf{D}^{-1}T_N(t\mathbf{P})\mathbf{s} - \mathbf{D}^{-1}\mathbf{y}\|_\infty$. To do this, we first show that

$$\|\mathbf{D}^{-1}\psi_k(t\mathbf{P})\mathbf{r}_k\|_\infty \le \psi_k(t)\|\mathbf{D}^{-1}\mathbf{r}_k\|_\infty. \tag{16}$$

To prove this claim, recall that $\mathbf{P} = \mathbf{A}\mathbf{D}^{-1}$. Since $\psi_k(t)$ is a polynomial, we have $\mathbf{D}^{-1}\psi_k(t\mathbf{P}) = \mathbf{D}^{-1}\psi_k(t\mathbf{A}\mathbf{D}^{-1}) = \psi_k(t\mathbf{D}^{-1}\mathbf{A})\mathbf{D}^{-1}$, which equals $\psi_k(t\mathbf{P}^T)\mathbf{D}^{-1}$.

Taking the infinity norm and applying the triangle inequality to the definition of $\psi_k(t)$ gives us

$$\|\mathbf{D}^{-1}\psi_k(t\mathbf{P})\mathbf{r}_k\|_\infty \le \sum_{m=0}^{N-k} \frac{t^m k!}{(m+k)!}\|(\mathbf{P}^T)^m(\mathbf{D}^{-1}\mathbf{r}_k)\|_\infty.$$

Then we have $\|(\mathbf{P}^T)^m(\mathbf{D}^{-1}\mathbf{r}_k)\|_\infty \le \|(\mathbf{P}^T)^m\|_\infty\|(\mathbf{D}^{-1}\mathbf{r}_k)\|_\infty$ which equals $\|(\mathbf{D}^{-1}\mathbf{r}_k)\|_\infty$ because $\mathbf{P}^T$ is row-stochastic. Returning to our original objective, we then have

$$\begin{aligned}\|\mathbf{D}^{-1}\psi_k(t\mathbf{P})\mathbf{r}_k\|_\infty &\le \sum_{m=0}^{N-k} \frac{t^m k!}{(m+k)!}\|(\mathbf{D}^{-1}\mathbf{r}_k)\|_\infty \\ &= \psi_k(t)\|\mathbf{D}^{-1}\mathbf{r}_k\|_\infty,\end{aligned}$$

proving the claim in (16).

This allows us to continue:

$$\begin{aligned} T_N(t\mathbf{P})\mathbf{s} - \mathbf{y} &= \sum_{k=0}^{N} \psi_k(t\mathbf{P})\mathbf{r}_k \quad \text{so} \\ \|\mathbf{D}^{-1}T_N(t\mathbf{P})\mathbf{s} - \mathbf{D}^{-1}\mathbf{y}\|_\infty &\le \sum_{k=0}^{N} \|\mathbf{D}^{-1}\psi_k(t\mathbf{P})\mathbf{r}_k\|_\infty \\ &\le \sum_{k=0}^{N} \psi_k(t)\|\mathbf{D}^{-1}\mathbf{r}_k\|_\infty.\end{aligned}$$

The stopping criterion for `hk-relax` requires that every entry of the residual satisfies $r(i,j) < \frac{e^t\varepsilon d_i}{2N\psi_j(t)}$, which is equivalent to satisfying $\frac{r(i,j)}{d_i} < \frac{e^t\varepsilon}{2N\psi_j(t)}$. This condition guarantees that $\|\mathbf{D}^{-1}\mathbf{r}_k\|_\infty < \frac{e^t\varepsilon}{2N\psi_k(t)}$. Thus we have

$$\begin{aligned}\|\mathbf{D}^{-1}T_N(t\mathbf{P})\mathbf{s} - \mathbf{D}^{-1}\mathbf{y}\|_\infty &\le \sum_{k=0}^{N} \psi_k(t)\|\mathbf{D}^{-1}\mathbf{r}_k\|_\infty \\ &\le \sum_{k=0}^{N} \left(\psi_k(t)\frac{e^t\varepsilon}{2N\psi_k(t)}\right)\end{aligned}$$

which is bounded above by $e^t\varepsilon/2$. Finally, we have that

$$\|\mathbf{D}^{-1}T_N(t\mathbf{P})\mathbf{s} - \mathbf{D}^{-1}\mathbf{y}\|_\infty < e^t\varepsilon/2$$

implies $\|\mathbf{D}^{-1}(\exp\{-t(\mathbf{I}-\mathbf{P})\}\,\mathbf{s} - \mathbf{x})\|_\infty < \varepsilon/2$, completing our proof of the first part of Theorem 1.

Bounding work.

It remains to bound the work required to perform steps of `hk-relax` until the stopping criterion is achieved.

Because the stopping criterion requires each residual entry to satisfy

$$\frac{r(i,j)}{d_i} < \frac{e^t\varepsilon}{2N\psi_j(t)}$$

we know that each step of `hk-relax` must operate on an entry $r(i,j)$ larger than this threshold. That is, each step we relax an entry of $\mathbf{r}$ satisfying $\frac{r(i,j)}{d_i} \ge \frac{e^t\varepsilon}{2N\psi_j(t)}$.

Consider the solution vector $\mathbf{y} \approx T_N(t\mathbf{P})\mathbf{s}$ and note that each entry of $\mathbf{y}$ is really a sum of values that we have deleted from $\mathbf{r}$. But $\mathbf{r}$ always contains only nonnegative values: the seed vector $\mathbf{s}$ is nonnegative, and each step involves setting entry $r(i,j) = 0$ and adding a scaled column of $\mathbf{P}$, which is nonnegative, to $\mathbf{r}$. Hence, $\|\mathbf{y}\|_1$ equals the sum of the $r(i,j)$ added to $\mathbf{y}$, $\sum_{l=1}^{T} r(i_l, j_l) = \|\mathbf{y}\|_1$.

Finally, since the entries of $\mathbf{y}$ are nondecreasing (because they only change if we add positive values $r(i,j)$ to them), we know that $\|\mathbf{y}\|_1 \le \|T_N(t\mathbf{P})\mathbf{s}\|_1 = \psi_0(t) \le e^t$. This implies, then, that

$$\sum_{l=1}^{T} r(i_l, j_l) \le e^t.$$

Using the fact that the values of $r(i,j)$ that we relax must satisfy $\frac{r(i,j)}{d_i} \ge \frac{e^t\varepsilon}{2N\psi_j(t)}$ we have that

$$\sum_{l=1}^{T} \frac{d_{i_l}e^t\varepsilon}{2N\psi_{j_l}(t)} \le e^t.$$

Simplifying yields

$$\sum_{l=1}^{T} \frac{d_{i_l}}{\psi_{j_l}(t)} \le \frac{2N}{\varepsilon}.$$

By Lemma 1 we know $\psi_k(t) \le \psi_1(t)$ for each $k \ge 1$, so we can lowerbound $\sum_{l=1}^{T} \frac{d_{i_l}}{\psi_1(t)} \le \sum_{l=1}^{T} \frac{d_{i_l}}{\psi_{j_l}(t)} \le \frac{2N}{\varepsilon}$, giving us

$$\sum_{l=1}^{T} d_{i_l} \le \frac{2N\psi_1(t)}{\varepsilon}.$$

Finally, note that the dominating suboperation in each step of `hk-relax` consists of relaxing $r(i,j)$ and spreading this "heat kernel rank" to the neighbors of node i in block $\mathbf{r}_{j+1}$. Since node i has d_i neighbors, this step consists of d_i adds, and so the work performed by `hk-relax` is $\sum_{l=1}^{T} d_{i_l}$, which is exactly the quantity we bounded above.

On the Permanence of Vertices in Network Communities

Tanmoy Chakraborty[1,a], Sriram Srinivasan[2,b], Niloy Ganguly[3,a],
Animesh Mukherjee[4,a], Sanjukta Bhowmick[5,b]
[a]Dept. of Computer Science & Engg., Indian Institute of Technology, Kharagpur, India – 721302
[b]Dept. of Computer Science, University of Nebraska, Omaha, Nebraska 68182
{[1]its_tanmoy,[3]niloy,[4]animeshm}@cse.iitkgp.ernet.in
{[2]sriramsrinivas,[5]sbhowmick}@unomaha.edu

ABSTRACT

Despite the prevalence of community detection algorithms, relatively less work has been done on understanding whether a network is indeed modular and how resilient the community structure is under perturbations. To address this issue, we propose a new vertex-based metric called *permanence*, that can quantitatively give an estimate of the community-like structure of the network.

The central idea of permanence is based on the observation that the strength of membership of a vertex to a community depends upon the following two factors: (i) the distribution of external connectivity of the vertex to individual communities and *not* the total external connectivity, and (ii) the strength of its internal connectivity and *not* just the total internal edges.

In this paper, we demonstrate that compared to other metrics, permanence provides (i) a more accurate estimate of a derived community structure to the ground-truth community and (ii) is more sensitive to perturbations in the network. As a by-product of this study, we have also developed a community detection algorithm based on maximizing permanence. For a modular network structure, the results of our algorithm match well with ground-truth communities.

Categories and Subject Descriptors

H.2.8 [**Database Application**]: Data mining; E.1 [**Data Structure**]: Graphs and networks

Keywords

permanence; community analysis; modularity

1. INTRODUCTION

Finding accurate community structures, i.e., groups of vertices that have more connections within a group than across the groups is one of the central problems in network analysis. Several community detection algorithms have been proposed over the last decade; these algorithms are generally based on optimizing certain scoring functions (for example, modularity [21] or conductance [18]). The output of these algorithms is an assignment of the vertices to their respective communities, for which the designated parameters are optimal (or nearly-optimal)[1]. However, almost all these detection techniques will always output a set of communities, irrespective of whether the network has an inherent community structure or not. Moreover, the optimal values of the scoring functions do not provide any insight as to whether a network actually possesses community structure or not. For example, the highest modularity in the Jazz network is 0.45 [5] and that of the Western USA power grid is 0.98 [5, 13]. However, it has been observed [5, 13], that Jazz has a much stronger community structure than the power grid.

The key reason for this is that optimization metric such as modularity frequently enforces the detection algorithm to make a choice by arbitrarily breaking ties. While this indeed increases the value of the metric, each such tie-breaking obfuscates the possibility of other community assignments. In grid-like networks, where choices can occur frequently, such tie-breaking can produce inaccurate or insignificant communities, while producing a high scoring function. Although, methods for finding consensus communities [17] can indicate whether the communities are significant or not, these techniques are dependent on the number of algorithms used to find the consensus.

In this paper, we propose a novel vertex-based scoring function called *permanence* whose optimization encounters much fewer tie-breaking situations in a network. The key idea behind formulating permanence is as follows. Most optimization metrics consider either the degree of a vertex in a community or the total number of external connections of the vertex (i.e., those connections that are attached with the other neighbors of the vertex outside the community). We posit that the distribution of the external connections of a vertex is equally important. In particular, our vertex assignment decisions are based not on the total number of external connections but on the maximum number of external connections to any single neighboring community. To the best of our knowledge, we are the first to make this distinction between the total external connections and their distribution. Permanence of a vertex thus quantifies its propensity to remain in its assigned community and the extent to which it is "pulled" [5] by the neighboring communities.

The value of permanence ranges from 1 (vertex is strongly connected to its assigned community) to -1 (vertex is weakly connected to its assigned community, and possibly wrongly

KDD'14, August 24–27, 2014, New York, NY, USA.

http://dx.doi.org/10.1145/2623330.2623707.

[1]In this paper, we consider only the non-overlapping communities.

assigned). If the permanence is zero, this indicates that the vertex is pulled equally by all its neighbors, all of which are in different communities. The "pull" in the metric is modeled as the maximum number of external connections to any single neighboring community. The introduction of pull in the formulation significantly reduces the frequency of tie-breaking situations that the algorithm has to encounter. In case the "pull" from all the neighboring communities is equal for a vertex, we assign it to a *singleton* community (i.e., community containing only one vertex), rather than assigning it to one of the (larger size) neighboring communities.

The sum of the permanence of all vertices, normalized by the number of vertices, provides the permanence of the network. It indicates to what extent, on an average, the vertices of a network are bound to their communities. As with permanence, this value also ranges from 1 to (nearly) -1. Maximizing permanence can be therefore used as an alternative method for identifying communities which constitutes a by-product of the current study. This approach of combining the microscopic (vertex-level) information to obtain the mesoscopic (community-level) information provides a more fine-grained view of the modular structure of the network. As the community structure of the network degrades, so does the value of permanence of the entire network.

The principal benefits of our approach are – (i) permanence provides a quantitative estimate of the inherent community structure of the network (Section 2),**(ii)** permanence is comparable (and sometimes better) than several other popular community scoring functions in identifying good communities (Section 4), **(iii)** permanence is very sensitive to the different perturbations of the network – a desirable property for a community scoring metric (Section 5), **(iv)** for modular networks, maximizing permanence algorithm is more successful in finding ground-truth communities as compared to several other community detection algorithms (Section 6), **(v)** community detection using maximizing permanence can reduce the effect of resolution limit, degeneracy of solutions and asymptotic growth of the optimal value with network size (Section 6).

2. DEFINITION OF PERMANENCE

In this section, we explain the concepts that lead to the formulation of permanence followed by a definition of the formula.

2.1 Distribution of External Connections

In contrast to most optimization metrics that either consider the degree of the vertex in a community or the total number of external neighbors of the vertex, in permanence we consider the distribution of external connections of the vertex to its neighboring communities. A vertex that has equal number of connections to all its external communities (e.g., a vertex with total 6 external connections with 2 to each of 3 neighboring communities) has equal "pull" from each community whereas a vertex with more external connections to one particular community (e.g., a vertex with total 6 external connections with 1 connection each to two neighboring communities and 4 connections to the third neighboring community), will experience more "pull" from that community due to large number of external connections to it.

This property is demonstrated by a toy example in Figure 1(a). If the edge (a, b) is deleted and the edge (c, c) is added, then the number of external connections remains the same, and the value of modularity, conductance and cut-ratio are also the same for this change. However, in the initial graph, vertex a had more "pull" from the community of b, in fact proportional to the number of its internal connections, whereas in the modified version a has equal pull from both the communities of b and c. Our permanence formula, defined in Section 2.3, takes this distinction into account.

Figure 1(b) shows a histogram of the fraction of vertices versus the ratio between the number of total (E_{sum}) and maximum (E_{max}) external connections for two representative networks. We notice that – (i) very few vertices have (closely) similar values of E_{sum} and E_{max} (i.e., ratio=1); the majority have significantly different E_{sum} and E_{max} (ii) the ratio between these two quantities is not constant; it is spread over a wide range of values. Therefore, we cannot estimate E_{max} from the value of E_{sum}. Consequently, metrics that are based on total number of external connections lack the information as to what extent a vertex may be "pulled" by the neighboring communities which can better estimated by E_{max}. Using E_{sum} can potentially result in frequent ties that need to be arbitrarily resolved by the community detection algorithms based on such metrics.

When computing permanence, we use the maximum number of external connections, i.e., the maximum pull, to any one external community, instead of combining all the external connections.

2.2 Strength of Internal Connections

The internal connections of a community are generally considered together as a whole. However, how strongly a vertex is connected to its internal neighbors can differ. The toy example of Figure 1(c) shows two networks each having two communities. Both the networks have the same number of edges; and the modularity, conductance and cut-ratio for the two divisions are exactly the same. However, the vertices on the left-hand graph are more tightly connected to each other than the vertices on the right-hand graph. To measure this internal connectedness of a vertex, one can compute the clustering coefficient of the vertex with respect to its internal neighbors. The higher this internal clustering coefficient, the more tightly the vertex is connected to its community.

As an empirical study, we further obtain the internal clustering coefficient per vertex of the benchmark networks for their ground-truth communities. Figure 1(d) shows a histogram of the internal clustering coefficient versus the number of vertices corresponding to a specific range of internal clustering coefficient. As can be seen from the histogram, for most vertices the internal clustering coefficients are generally towards the high range. However, for LFR (μ=0.6) there is a reverse trend. In this network, there are more vertices with lower internal clustering coefficient. This network by construction has a weaker community structure than the other networks in the set, and thus quite a few of its vertices are loosely connected internally (see more in Section 6).

To represent whether vertices are tightly connected within their communities, we include the internal clustering coefficient as a factor in computing permanence.

2.3 Formulation of Permanence

Based on our observations on the distribution of external connections and the internal clustering coefficient, we for-

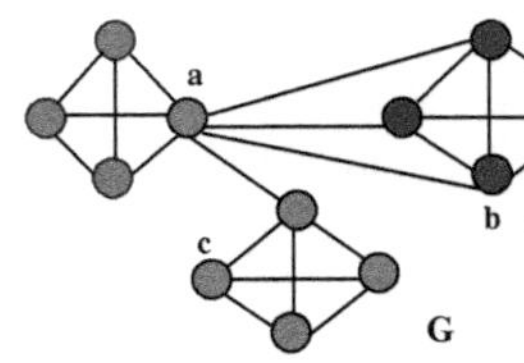

Configuration	Mod	1-Con	1-Cut	Perm
G	0.48	0.91	0.77	0.84
G - <a,b> + <a,c>	0.48	0.91	0.77	0.85

(a) Example demonstrating the importance of the distribution of external connections.

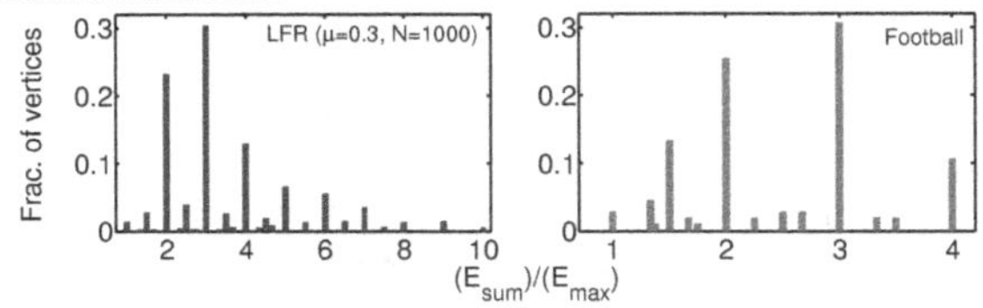

(b) Fraction of vertices versus the ratio between the number of total (E_{sum}) and maximum (E_{max}) external connections.

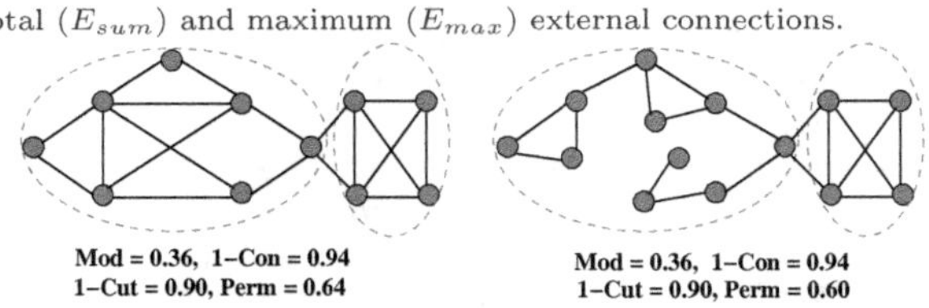

(c) Two networks with same modularity, conductance and cut-ratio, but the left one has more prominent community structure.

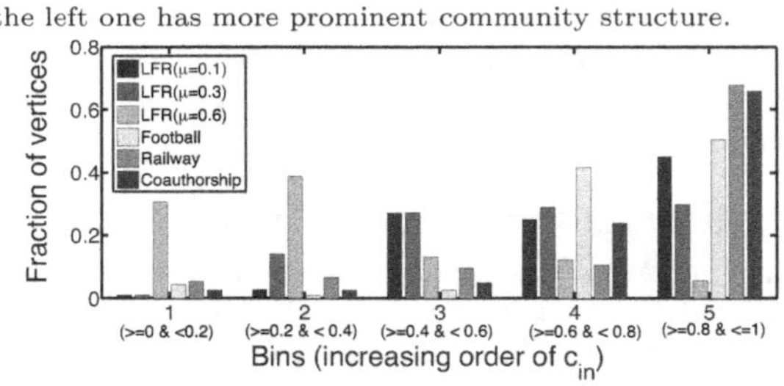

(d) Fraction of vertices with a specific range of internal clustering coefficient (c_{in}) in LFR and real-world networks.

Figure 1: (Color online) Toy examples and empirical observations demonstrating the drawbacks of existing community scoring metrics. The communities in (a) and (c) are distinguished by different colors.

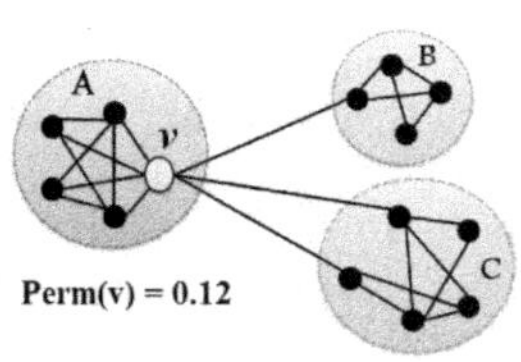

Figure 2: Toy example depicting *permanence* of a vertex v (here $I(v)$=4, $D(v)$=7, $E_{max}(v)$=2, $c_{in}(v)$=$\frac{5}{6}$).

mulate permanence of a vertex based on the following two criteria that measure the possibility of the vertex remaining in its own community:

(i) The internal connections, $I(.)$, of the vertex v should be more than the maximum connections to a single external community, $E_{max}(.)$, which results more internal pull than the maximum external pull. This criteria is represented in the permanence computation as the ratio of $I(v)$ and $E_{max}(v)$ (indicated by F1 in Equation 1). If the vertex has no external connections, F1 is just the value of the internal connections. We normalize this value by the total degree of the vertex, $D(v)$ (indicated by F2 in Equation 1), which ensures that the product of F1 and F2 will be between 0 (no internal connections) and 1 (no external connections).

(ii) Within a specific community, the internal neighbors of the vertex v should be highly connected among each other (i.e., its internal clustering coefficient[2], $c_{in}(v)$, should be high). This criteria emphasizes that a vertex is likely to be within a community if it is part of a near-clique substructure. For computing $c_{in}(v)$, we assume that each community should have at least three vertices and three internal connections; otherwise, $c_{in}(v)$ is set to 0. When computing permanence, we impose a penalty based on low internal clustering coefficient (indicated by F3 in Equation 1). The less the internal clustering coefficient, the more the penalty imposed to the final outcome of the community score. This value also ranges from 0 (no penalty) to 1 (maximum penalty).

We aggregate these two criteria to formulate permanence of a vertex v as follows:

$$Perm(v) = \Big[\underbrace{\frac{I(v)}{E_{max}(v)}}_{\text{F1}} \times \underbrace{\frac{1}{D(v)}}_{\text{F2}}\Big] - \Big[\underbrace{1 - c_{in}(v)}_{\text{F3}}\Big] \quad (1)$$

Figure 2 depicts a toy example for measuring permanence of a vertex v. Note that, this formula actually differentiates between the two cases in Figure 1(a) with higher permanence value for the case where the external pull is uniform. Similarly, the formula differentiates between the two cases in Figure 1(c) by imposing more penalty on the network that has a less tightly knit internal substructure.

2.4 Boundary Conditions of Permanence

For vertices that do not have any external connections, $Perm(v)$ is considered to be equal to the internal clustering coefficient (i.e., $Perm(v) = c_{in}(v)$). The maximum value of $Perm(v)$ is 1 and is obtained when vertex v is an internal node and part of a clique. The lower bound of $Perm(v)$ is close to -1. This is obtained when $I(v) \ll D(v)$, such that $\frac{I(v)}{D(v)E_{max}(v)} \approx 0$ and $c_{in}(v) = 0$. Therefore for every vertex v, $-1 < Perm(v) \leq 1$. The permanence of a graph $G(V, E)$, where V is the set of vertices and E is the set of edges, is given by $Perm(G) = \frac{1}{|V|}\sum_{v \in V} Perm(v)$. For a graph $G(V, E)$, the range is $-1 < Perm(G) \leq 1$.

$Perm(G)$ will be closer to 1 as more vertices have high permanence, that is more vertices are in well-defined communities. This can happen only if the network has a strong community structure. The maximum value obtained is when G consists of a series of disconnected cliques. If there is a vertex bridging between two cliques, then the highest overall permanence will be obtained if each clique acts as a separate community and bridging vertex forms a singleton community. For a grid, the best value of $Perm(G)$ will be zero, i.e., each vertex is assigned to a singleton community.

3. EXPERIMENTAL SETUP

In this section, we provide a brief overview of the datasets, metrics and comparative methods that we use for our experiments.

[2]Note that, internal clustering coefficient of v is obtained by considering the ratio of the existing connections and the total number of possible connections among the *internal neighbors* of v.

3.1 Test Suite of Networks

We use the **LFR benchmark** model [15] to generate synthetic networks along with their ground-truth communities. Users can specify the following properties: number of nodes (n), average ($< k >$) and maximum (k_{max}) degree, the degree distribution, the community size distribution, and the mixing-coefficient (μ). The mixing coefficient represents the ratio (in average) between the external connections of a node to its degree. Thus the lower the value of μ, the stronger the community in the network. For our experiments, we set the number of nodes as 1000, and μ as 0.1, 0.3 and 0.6 (unless mentioned otherwise). For the rest of the parameters, we use the default values mentioned in the authors' implementation[3] [15].

We also use three real-world networks[4] whose true community structures are known a-priori and whose properties are summarized in Table 1.

Football network was proposed by Girvan and Newman [10] which contains the network of American football games between Division IA colleges during regular season Fall of 2000. The vertices in the graph represent teams (identified by their college names), and edges represent regular-season games between the two teams they connect.

Indian Railway network proposed by Ghosh et al. [9] consists of nodes representing stations, where two stations s_i and s_j are connected by an edge if there exists at least one train-route such that both s_i and s_j are scheduled halts on that route. The weight of the edge between s_i and s_j is the number of train-routes on which both these stations are scheduled halts. We filter out the low-weight edges and then make the resultant network unweighted. We tag each station based on the state in India[5] to which that station belongs. The states act as communities since the number of trains within each state is much higher than the number of trains between two states.

Co-authorship network is derived from the citation dataset[6] developed by Chakraborty et al. [4]. This dataset contains the metadata (title, author(s), related field(s)[7] of the paper, publication venue, year of publication, references and abstract) of all the papers of computer science published between 1960 to 2009 and archived in DBLP repository. We build an aggregated undirected coauthorship network where each node represents an author, and an undirected edge between a pair of authors is drawn if they were co-authors at least once. Since each paper is marked by its related field, we assume this field as the research area of the author(s) writing that paper. Therefore, an author may possess more than one area of research interests. We resolve this by tagging each author by the major field on which she has written most of the papers. These fields act as the ground-truth communities. Besides the aggregated network, we also create some intermediate networks mentioned in Table 8 by cumulatively aggregating all the vertices and edges over each year, e.g., 1960-1971, 1960-1972, ..., 1960-1980.

Note that, the principles for constructing the Indian railway network and the co-authorship network are the same – there is an underlying bipartite structure in each case; for railway network, it is the station-train interaction network with an edge denoting if a particular train passes through a station, while for the co-authorship network it is the article-author interaction network with an edge denoting the authorship of a researcher in a scientific article. The railway network is therefore the one-mode projection of the train-station network and the co-authorship network is similarly the one-mode projection of the article-author network. Note that, although the principles of construction are same for both the networks (one clique per train/article is imposed in the one-mode projection), the results, as we shall see in Section 6 are far better for the railway network since the ground-truth here is much more fine-grained in comparison to the co-authorship network.

Table 1: Properties of real-world networks; n and e are the number of nodes and edges, c is the number of communities, $<k>$ and k_{max} its average and maximum degree, n_c^{min} and n_c^{max} the sizes of its smallest and largest communities.

Networks	n	e	$<k>$	k_{max}	c	n_c^{min}	n_c^{max}
Football	115	613	10.57	12	12	5	13
Railway	301	1224	6.36	48	21	1	46
Coauthorship	103677	352183	5.53	1230	24	34	14404

3.2 Scoring Functions for Evaluating Community Structure

The goodness of a community is often measured by how well certain scoring functions are optimized. Here we compare the optimal value of permanence for the obtained communities versus three popular scoring functions, namely modularity (Mod) [21], conductance (Con) [18] and cut-ratio (Cut) [19]. In order to make the higher the better, we measure (1-Con) and (1-Cut) for conductance and cut-ratio respectively.

3.3 Metrics to Compare with Ground-truth

A stronger test of the correctness of the community detection algorithm, however, is by comparing the obtained community with a given ground-truth structure. We use three standard validation metrics, namely Normalized Mutual Information (NMI) [7], Adjusted Rand Index (ARI) [12] and Purity (PU) [20] to measure the accuracy of the detected communities with respect to the ground-truth community structure. [14] argues that these measures have certain drawbacks in that they ignore the connectivity of the network. We therefore also use the weighted versions of these measures, namely Weighted-NMI (W-NMI), Weighted-ARI (W-ARI) and Weighted-Purity (W-PU) as proposed in [14]. Note that, all the metrics are bounded between 0 (no matching) and 1 (perfect matching).

3.4 Community Detection Algorithms

We use the following community detection algorithms for comparison with our proposed algorithm discussed in Section 6:

(i) Modularity-based: FastGreedy [22], Louvain [3] and CNM [6].

(ii) Random walk-based: WalkTrap [24].

(iii) Compression-based: InfoMod [25] and InfoMap [26].

[3] https://sites.google.com/site/santofortunato/inthepress2

[4] All the datasets are publicly available at http://cnerg.org/permanence.

[5] http://irfca.org/apps/station_codes

[6] http://cnerg.org

[7] Note that, the different sub-branches like Algorithms, AI, Operating Systems etc. constitute the different "fields" of computer science domain.

Table 2: For football network, the values of the scoring functions on the output obtained from different algorithms and the scores of the validation metrics with respect to the ground-truth communities. The ranks of the algorithms (using dense ranking) are shown within parenthesis. The average ranks of all the normal (weighted) validation measures are shown in column 9 (column 13).

Algorithms	Mod	Perm	1-Con	1-Cut	NMI	ARI	PU	Avg (N)	W-NMI	W-ARI	W-PU	Avg (W)
Louvain	0.60(1)	0.36(1)	0.77(5)	0.44(5)	0.93(1)	0.99(1)	0.89(2)	1.33	0.99(2)	0.93(2)	0.99(1)	1.67
FastGreedy	0.58(2)	0.25(3)	0.81(3)	0.59(3)	0.93(1)	0.99(1)	0.91(1)	1.00	1.00(1)	0.94(1)	0.99(1)	1.00
CNM	0.55(3)	0.20(4)	0.85(1)	0.86(1)	0.67(4)	0.75(4)	0.42(5)	4.33	0.55(5)	0.63(5)	0.71(3)	4.33
WalkTrap	0.60(1)	0.36(1)	0.82(2)	0.69(2)	0.90(2)	0.98(2)	0.84(3)	2.33	0.98(3)	0.91(3)	0.99(1)	2.33
Infomod	0.60(1)	0.35(2)	0.82(2)	0.69(2)	0.89(3)	0.97(3)	0.82(4)	3.33	0.97(4)	0.89(4)	0.98(2)	3.33
Infomap	0.60(1)	0.35(2)	0.79(4)	0.51(4)	0.89(3)	0.97(3)	0.82(4)	3.33	0.97(4)	0.89(4)	0.98(2)	3.33

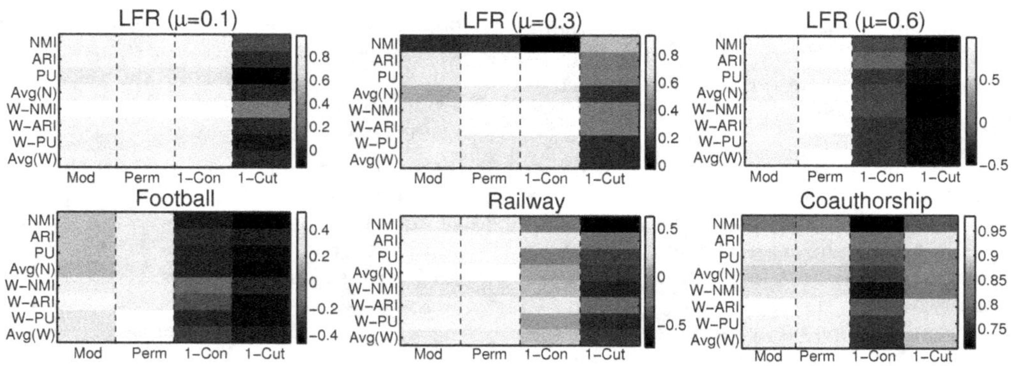

Figure 3: (Color online) Heat maps depicting the pairwise Spearman's rank correlation between four scoring functions with six validation measures for six different networks. Avg(N) and Avg(W) are the averages of the ranks of three normal and three weighted validation measures respectively as shown in Table 2.

4. PERMANENCE AS A COMMUNITY SCORING FUNCTION

In this section, we demonstrate the effectiveness of permanence as a scoring function for evaluating the goodness of detected communities, and compare it with modularity, 1-Con and 1-Cut. To do this, we perform the following experiment, on the same lines as that of [27].

These are the steps in our experiment: (i) We apply several community detection algorithms on a specified network and obtain the vertex-to-community assignment as given by each algorithm; (ii) We compute the values of all the community scoring functions for these communities; (iii) For each scoring function we rank the algorithms based on which one of these produces the most optimal (highest) value; (iv) We then compare the obtained community with the known ground-truth community and compute the respective validation measures, namely NMI, ARI, Purity and their weighted versions; (v) For each validation metric, we rank the algorithms based on the one that produces the highest value, i.e., best match with ground-truth.

Table 2 shows the results of the experiment performed on football network. Scoring functions (columns 2-5) are measures of goodness of the community set obtained. The validation metrics (columns 6-8, 10-12) measure the concurrence of the communities with the ground-truth communities. We posit that since these two types of measures are orthogonal, and because the validation metrics generally provide a stronger measure of correctness after measuring similarity with the ground-truth structure, the values of a good scoring function should "match" those of the validation metrics. That is, if a scoring function indeed identifies the correct communities, then when its value is high (low), the values of the corresponding validation metrics would also be high (low).

To compute this correlation, we compare the relative ranks, because the range of the values is not commensurate across the quantities and we are more interested in observing the "up" or "down" direction, rather than the absolute values. For each network, we measure the Spearman's rank correlation between all pairs of scoring functions and validation measures. Note that, it is not always possible to assign ranks uniquely. We used different ranking schemes to break ties. Here, we present the results using dense ranking; we have also used standard competition ranking and fractional ranking (see in [1]) and our results are consistent across all the different methods.

Results. Table 2 shows the values and ranks for the different metrics for football network. For all the networks, the rank correlations of the scoring functions and the validation metrics are shown as heat maps in Figure 3. Lighter color indicates higher correlation and hence more similarity between the scoring function and the validation metric. For the networks having distinct community structure such as LFR ($\mu = 0.1$), football and railway networks, permanence shows comparable performance as that of other scoring functions. However for LFR network, with the increase of μ, the inter-community connection density starts increasing, and it is difficult for any community detection algorithm and/or scoring function to capture the ground-truth communities. Interestingly, we observe that the rank correlation obtained through the permanence scores and those through validation metrics is exceptionally high for LFR ($\mu = 0.6$) and coauthorship networks which seem to have poor community

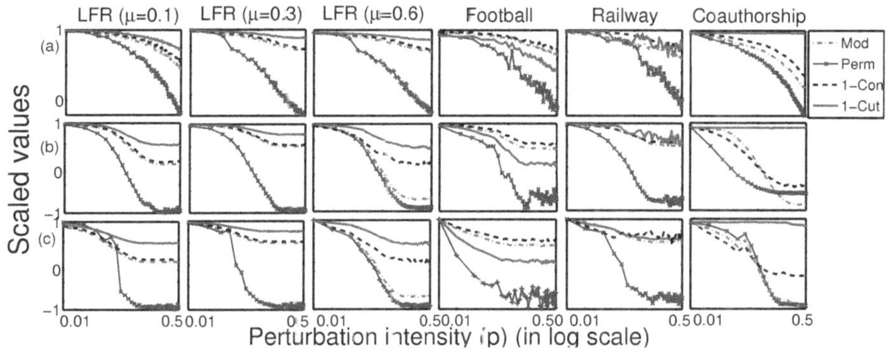

Figure 4: (Color online) Change in the value of the scoring functions with the increase of perturbation intensity (p) in (a) edge-based, (b) random and (c) community-based perturbation strategies. The values are normalized by the maximum value obtained from each function.

structure compared to the other networks (see Table 1 and Table 5). Since the ground-truth communities are not well formed, there is a wide variance in the type of community structures identified by different algorithms. Permanence score can capture this variability much better than other scoring functions. To summarize the results, in Table 3 we present the average rank correlations of these community scoring functions across all the validation metrics for each network. We observe that for all the networks, permanence on an average produces the best ranking followed by modularity, conductance and cut-ratio in order.

Table 3: Average rank correlations (over different validation metrics) of the community scoring functions for all the networks. For each network, the highest (best) correlation is in bold font.

Networks	Modularity	Permanence	Conductance	Cut
LFR(μ=0.1)	**0.88**	**0.88**	**0.88**	0.02
LFR(μ=0.3)	0.61	**0.74**	0.72	0.28
LFR(μ=0.6)	0.87	**0.96**	-0.18	-0.44
Football	0.25	**0.43**	-0.29	-0.41
Railway	0.43	**0.46**	0.08	-0.48
Coauthorship	**0.92**	**0.92**	0.76	0.86

5. SENSITIVITY OF PERMANENCE

We now evaluate the sensitivity of permanence under different perturbations of the ground-truth community structure. We posit that a good metric for evaluating communities should be stable under small perturbations of the ground-truth communities (i.e., groups of nodes that differ very slightly from the ground-truth communities). This indicates that the scoring function is robust to noise. However, if the perturbation is beyond a threshold, i.e., when the ground-truth community structure is perturbed to such an extent that it resembles a random set of nodes, then a good scoring function should assign it a low score.

Given a graph $G =< V,E >$ and *perturbation intensity* p, we start with the ground-truth community S and then modify it (i.e., change its members) by executing the perturbation strategy $p \cdot m$ times. The value of m is based on different strategies, as described below. For our experiments, we adopt three perturbation strategies motivated by the methods proposed in [28]:

(i)Edge-based perturbation picks a random inter-community edge (u,v) where $u \in S$ and $v \in S'$ (where $S \neq S'$) and then swaps the memberships (i.e., assign u to S' and v to S). It continues until $p \cdot |E|$ iterations are completed (here, $m = |E|$). This strategy preserves the size of S. However if v is not connected to any other nodes in S except u, then it makes S disconnected.

(ii) Random perturbation takes community members and replaces them with random non-members. We pick two random nodes $u \in S$ and $v \in S'$ (where $S \neq S'$) and then swap their memberships. It continues until $p \cdot |V|$ iterations are completed (here, $m = |V|$). Random perturbation maintains the size of S but may disconnect S. Generally, it degrades the quality of S faster than edge-based strategy, since edge-based strategy only affects the "fringe" of the community.

(iii) Community-based perturbation adopts a similar mechanism as in the edge-based strategy. However, it considers each community S from the ground-truth community structure one by one and continues the perturbation until $p \cdot |S|$ constituent nodes of the community are swapped with the other non-constituent nodes (here, $m = |S|$). This process is repeated for all the communities separately. This perturbation decreases the quality of the ground-truth communities the fastest among the three since the number of swaps is much higher than the others.

We perturb different networks using these three perturbation strategies for values of p ranging between 0.01 to 0.5. We compute the values of four community scoring functions, i.e., modularity, permanence, 1-Con and 1-Cut. For small values of p, small change of the original value of the scoring function is desirable since it indicates that the scoring function is robust to noise. For high perturbation intensities (i.e., for larger values of p), the value should drop significantly since the communities become more random.

Results. Figure 4 shows the results of our experiments. For a commensurate comparison, we rescale the values of each parameter by normalizing with the maximum value obtained from that function. For all three strategies, the values of the scoring functions tend to decrease with the increase of p, and the effect is most prominent in community-based strategy followed by random and edge-based strategies. For each network, once p has reached a certain threshold, the decrease is much faster in permanence. On more careful inspection, we find that this happens because the internal structure of a community completely breaks down if perturbation is taken beyond a point and thus has an avalanche effect on the value of the clustering coefficient ($c_{in}(v)$ in Equation (1)). This in turn quickly pulls the value of permanence down. Summarizing, the results indicate that permanence is a better measure for distinguishing true communities from randomized sets of nodes than the other parameters.

6. PERMANENCE MAXIMIZATION

Inspired by the effectiveness of permanence as a scoring function and its sensitivity to perturbations, we develop a community detection algorithm called **Max_Permanence**[8] (pseudocode in Algorithm 1) that identifies communities by maximizing permanence.

Our algorithm is a heuristic, that strives to obtain a high value of permanence. In this algorithm, we begin with initializing every vertex to a singleton community. A vertex is moved to a community only if this movement results in a net increase in the number of internal connections and/or a net decrease in the number of external connections to any of the neighboring communities. If such a move is not possible, then either the vertex remains as a singleton (such as in the case where moving to any one of the candidate communities will give equal permanence) or moves to the community where it is more tightly connected with its neighbors (this causes the vertex to have positive permanence). This process is repeated for each vertex and the entire relocation of all vertices is repeated over several iterations until the permanence value converges. However, convergence is not theoretically guaranteed, but we observed that the algorithm converges with high probability.

6.1 Performance Evaluation

Table 4 shows results of the improvement of our method (as differences) compared to the average and best performances of six competing algorithms (given in Section 3.4) based on six ground-truth based validation metrics.

Comparable results - in LFR ($\mu = 0.1$) and football networks, since the communities are well-separated, most algorithms efficiently capture these partitions and our method is comparable to the other algorithms as well.

Improved results - in LFR ($\mu = 0.3$) and railway networks, our method significantly outperforms other algorithms. Moreover in railway network, we observe that our algorithm detects three singleton communities (i.e., communities each containing only one vertex), one of which is also present in the ground-truth structure. None of the community detection algorithms is able to capture this singleton community.

Moderate results - our method does not work well for the LFR ($\mu = 0.6$) network. For coauthorship network, we observe that though our algorithm outperforms the average performance of the competing algorithms, it performs less well than that of the two information-theoretic approaches (Infomod and Infomap).

Reasons behind moderate performance

LFR (μ=0.6) – To understand why our algorithm is not as competitive for LFR ($\mu = 0.6$), we further observe the quality of the ground-truth communities in three LFR networks. We observe that while the average internal clustering coefficient of vertices in LFR ($\mu = 0.1$) is 0.78, it deteriorates to 0.36 for LFR ($\mu = 0.6$). Moreover, 97% of vertices in ground-truth communities of LFR (μ=0.6) have less internal connections than the external connections (while LFR (μ=0.1) and LFR (μ=0.3) hardly have any such nodes). This indicates that LFR ($\mu = 0.6$) does not have modular structure in the ground-truth communities.

[8]The code is available at `http://cnerg.org/permanence`.

Algorithm 1 Max_Permanence

Input: A graph G.
Output: Permanence of G; Detected communities

```
procedure MAX PERMANENCE(G(V, E))
    Each vertex is assigned to its seed community
    Set value of maximum iteration as maxIt
    vertices ← |V|
    Sum ← 0
    Old_Sum ← −1
    Itern ← 0
    while Sum ≠ Old_Sum and Itern < maxIt do
        Itern ← Itern + 1
        Old_Sum ← Sum
        Sum ← 0
        for all v ∈ V do
            (compute current permanence of v)
            cur_p ← Perm(v)
            if cur_p == 1 then
                Sum ← Sum + cur_p
                continue;

            cur_p_neig ← 0          ▷ Neig(v)=set of neighbors of v
            for all u ∈ Neig(v) do
                (compute current permanence of u)
                cur_p_neig ← cur_p_neig + Perm(u)

              ▷ Comm(v) is the set of neighboring communities of v
            for all C ∈ Comm(v) do
                Move v to community C
                (compute permanence of v in community C)
                n_p ← Perm(v)

                    ▷ Neighbors of v are affected for this movement
                n_p_neig ← 0
                for all u ∈ Neig(v) do
                (compute new permanence of u)
                    n_p_neig ← n_p_neig + Perm(u)
                if (cur_p < n_p) and (cur_p_neig < n_p_neig) then
                    cur_p ← n_p
                else
                    replace v to its original community
            Sum ← Sum + cur_p
    Netw_perm = Sum/vertices                  ▷ Permanence of G
    return Netw_perm
```

To further strengthen this claim, we also measure the similarity of the communities obtained by different community detection algorithms (as listed in Section 3.4) across different validation measures. The results in Table 5 clearly show the degradation of the similarity values with the increase in μ. The reason is that with the increase in μ, the communities in LFR network tend to be less well-knit, and thus the agreement of the outputs of different algorithms is also less. Therefore, the output of a good community detection algorithm should reflect such absence of modular structure in the network (hence shows poor performance).

Coauthorship network – To explain the permanence-based results obtained from coauthorship network, we further analyze the communities obtained from our algorithm. We check the title and the abstract of the papers written by the authors in each community of coauthorship network, and notice that our method splits large ground-truth communities into denser submodules. This splitting is mostly noticed in older research areas such as Algorithms and Theory, Databases etc. These submodules are actually the subfields (sub-communities) of a field (community) in computer science domain. Few examples of such sub-communities ob-

Table 4: Improvement of Max_Permanence with respect to the average (left-hand value) and the best (right-hand value) performances of the six competing algorithms (separated by semicolon). Positive (negative) values indicate that Max_Permanence outperforms (underperforms) the corresponding performances of the competing algorithms.

Validation metrics	LFR (μ=0.1)	LFR (μ=0.3)	LFR (μ=0.6)	Football	Railway	Coauthorship
NMI	0.04; 0.00	0.15; 0.05	-0.31; -0.78	0.04; 0.00	0.15; 0.11	0.04; -0.06
ARI	0.06; 0.00	0.21; 0.02	-0.39; -0.76	0.07; 0.00	0.03; 0.04	0.03; -0.08
PU	0.04; 0.00	0.17; 0.00	-0.38; -0.72	0.01; 0.00	0.13; 0.00	0.03; -0.06
W-NMI	0.02; 0.00	0.14; 0.00	-0.41; -0.78	0.09; 0.00	0.26; 0.00	0.05; -0.01
W-ARI	0.05; 0.02	0.19; 0.05	-0.35; -0.72	0.05; 0.00	0.02; -0.15	0.04; -0.06
W-PU	0.03; 0.01	0.17; 0.00	-0.45; -0.79	0.00; 0.00	0.05; -0.04	0.02; -0.15

tained from our algorithm are noted in Table 6. Thus, our algorithm, in addition to identifying well-defined communities, is also able to unfold the hierarchical organization of a network.

Table 5: Average values among pairwise similarities between outputs of the community detection algorithms on different LFR networks.

Validation measures	LFR (μ=0.1)	LFR (μ=0.3)	LFR (μ=0.6)
NMI	0.95	0.82	0.53
ARI	0.98	0.79	0.48
PU	0.99	0.85	0.56
W-NMI	0.94	0.85	0.54
W-ARI	0.97	0.78	0.50
W-PU	0.98	0.83	0.57

Table 6: Example of communities and sub-communities obtained from coauthorship network using Max_Permanence algorithm.

Communities	Sub-communities
Algorithms and Theory	Theory of computation; Formal methods; Data structure; Information & coding theory; Computational geometry
Databases	Models; Query optimization; Database languages; storage; Performance, security, and availability

Comparison of largest community size. Many optimization algorithms have the tendency to underestimate smaller size communities (known as the resolution limit problem [11]) and sometimes tend to produce very large size communities. In our test suite, we observe the similar tendency in all the competing algorithms whereas the communities obtained by permanence are smaller in size. In Table 7, we show for two representative networks that the size of the largest communities detected by the other algorithms is much larger than the size of the largest community present in the ground-truth structure. We also measure the maximum similarity (using Jaccard coefficient) between the largest-size community detected by each algorithm with the communities in ground-truth structure and notice that Max_Permanence is able to detect largest size community which is most similar to the ground-truth structure. Therefore, we hypothesize that our algorithm has the potentiality to reduce the effect of resolution limit.

6.2 Handling Modularity Maximization Issues

As discussed earlier, modularity maximization algorithms suffer from the issues including (a) resolution limit, (b) degeneracy of solution and (c) dependence on the size of the graph [11]. We now discuss how each of these problems are ameliorated by maximizing permanence.

We demonstrate that community assignments are different in a modularity-based algorithm vis-a-vis **Max_Permanence**

Table 7: Size of the largest communities obtained from different community detection algorithms and their similarities with the ground-truth structure for two networks (LFR (μ=0.3, N=1000) and football).

	Largest community size		Similarity	
	LFR ($\mu = 0.3$)	Football	LFR ($\mu = 0.3$)	Football
Ground-truth	49	12	--	--
Louvain	62	24	0.70	0.41
FastGreedy	95	18	0.32	0.65
CNM	91	32	0.52	0.31
Walktrap	83	15	0.51	0.57
Infomod	61	16	0.79	0.86
Infomap	59	16	0.74	0.86
Max_Permanence	49	13	1	0.92

algorithm using the example in Figure 5. In this figure, we assume that apart from the edges through v, there is no connection between the communities A and B.

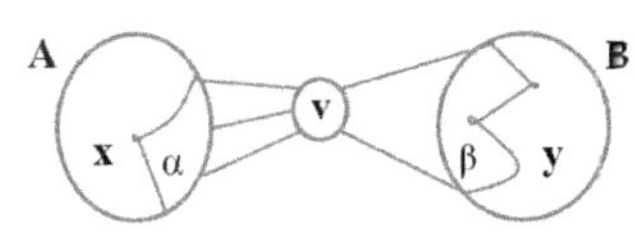

Figure 5: (Color online) An illustrative example to show the community assignment of vertex v.

Terminology. Let vertex v be connected to α (β) nodes in community A (B), and these α (β) nodes form the set N_α (N_β). The number of vertices in community A is $(x+\alpha)$, and in community B is $(y+\beta)$. Let the average internal degree of a vertex $a \in N_\alpha$ and a vertex $b \in N_\beta$, before v is assigned to any of the communities, be I_α and I_β respectively. Let the average internal clustering coefficient of the neighboring nodes in communities A and B be C_A and C_B respectively If v is added to communities A (B) then the average internal clustering coefficient of v becomes C_A^v (C_B^v), and the average internal clustering coefficient of the nodes in $N_\alpha(N_\beta)$ become C^α (C^β).

We assume that the communities A and B are tightly connected internally such that the values of C_A and C_B are very high ($>$ 0.5). To simplify the explanations, we consider the case where none of the neighbors of v are connected to each other. If v does not add any new edges to the group of neighbors, then $C^\alpha = C_A \frac{(I_\alpha - 1)}{(I_\alpha + 1)}$ (similarly, $C^\beta = C_B \frac{(I_\beta - 1)}{(I_\beta + 1)}$).

Given this scenario, we can determine the conditions (due to the lack of space detailed calculations are provided in an online appendix [1]) for which a particular assignment of v to any of the communities will give the highest permanence.

Table 8: Change in scoring functions with the (near-)symmetric growth of coauthorship network obtained in each year by adding vertices and edges till that year. N: number of nodes, c: number of communities, $< I >$: average internal degree, $< k >$: average degree, $< c_{in} >$: average internal clustering coefficient, $< E_{max} >$: average maximum external connectivity. The value of permanence is less affected by the growth.

			60-71	60-72	60-73	60-74	60-75	60-76	60-77	60-78	60-79	60-80
Coauthorship	Year		60-71	60-72	60-73	60-74	60-75	60-76	60-77	60-78	60-79	60-80
	Network properties	n	964	1515	1991	2681	3386	4836	6284	7814	9001	10386
		c	24	24	24	24	24	24	24	24	24	24
		$\frac{<I>}{<k>}$	0.082	0.095	0.093	0.091	0.089	0.104	0.111	0.112	0.115	0.113
		$\frac{1}{<E_{max}>}$ $(\times 10^{-4})$	3.8	3.2	2.9	3.9	2.8	2.11	2.39	2.92	2.69	3.22
		$< (1 - c_{in}) >$	0.239	0.248	0.246	0.251	0.251	0.260	0.265	0.269	0.270	0.274
	Modularity		0.369	0.374	0.395	0.392	0.421	0.422	0.465	0.471	0.493	0.501
	Permanence		0.094	0.092	0.092	0.096	0.095	0.095	0.097	0.097	0.097	0.098

Using these conditions, we show how permanence overcomes some of the issues related to modularity maximization.

Degeneracy of solution is a problem where a community scoring function (e.g., modularity) admits multiple distinct high-scoring solutions and typically lacks a clear global maximum, thereby, resorting to tie-breaking [11]. For our example, when $\alpha = \beta$, modularity maximization algorithm will assign v arbitrarily to A or B. However, in the case of permanence, v will remain as a separate community so long as the following condition is maintained:

Condition. If $\alpha = \beta$, $C^\beta = C_B \frac{I_\beta - 1}{I_\beta + 1}$, then communities A, B and v will remain separate rather than v joining community A, if $\alpha(\frac{2C_A - 1}{I_\alpha + 1}) + (1 - C_A^v) \geq \frac{1}{2\alpha}$.

We observe that when $\alpha = \beta = 1$, then $C_A^v = 0$ and the communities will always remain separate. Furthermore, as α increases, the left-hand side of the above condition will become larger than the right, thus increasing the chance of separate communities.

Resolution limit is a problem where communities of certain small size are merged into larger ones [11]. A classic example where modularity cannot identify communities of small size is a cycle of m cliques. Here maximum modularity is obtained if two neighboring cliques are merged.

In the case of permanence, we can determine that whether two communities A and B would merge (as in modularity) or whether v would join community A (we select A, but similar analysis can also be done for the case when v joins B), by the following condition:

Condition. Joining v to community A gives higher permanence than merging the communities A, B and v if $C^\beta = C_B$, and $(\frac{\gamma}{(\gamma+1)\beta} + \frac{C_A^v(2\gamma+1) - C_B^v}{(\gamma+1)^2} - \frac{\beta}{I_\beta+1}) > 1$; where $\gamma = \alpha/\beta$ and also if $C^\beta = C_B \frac{I_\beta - 1}{I_\beta + 1}$, and $(\frac{\gamma}{(\gamma+1)\beta} + \frac{C_A^v(2\gamma+1) - C_B^v}{(\gamma+1)^2} + \frac{\beta(2C_B - 1)}{I_\beta + 1}) > 1$.

This result is independent of the size of the communities. Moreover, so long as A and B are almost cliques (internal clustering coefficients > 0.5), C_A^v is sufficiently high and C_B^v is sufficiently small (e.g., $C_A^v > 2/3$ and $C_B^v = 0$), v will join community A rather than merging. Thus, in general, *the highest permanence is obtained if v joins the community to which it is very tightly connected rather than the one to which it is loosely connected.*

Asymptotic growth of value of a metric implies a strong dependence on the size of the network and the number of modules the network contains [11]. Rewriting Equation 1, we get the permanence of the entire network G as follows: $Perm(G) = \frac{1}{|V|} \sum_{v \in V} \left[\frac{I(v)}{D(v) E_{max}(v)}\right] - \frac{1}{|V|} \sum_{v \in V} [(1 - c_{in}(v))]$. We can notice that most of the parameters in the above formula are independent of the network size and the number of communities. Table 8 illustrates the change in modularity and permanence with the symmetric growth of the network size in coauthorship network. Note that, the intermediate networks are formed by cumulatively aggregating all the vertices and edges of coauthorship network over the years, e.g., 1960-1971, 1960-1972,..., 1960-1980. We observe that the modularity increases consistently with the symmetric growth, while the value of permanence remains almost constant.

7. RELATED WORK

A huge volume of work has been devoted to finding communities in large networks, including diverse methods such as modularity optimization [3, 6], spectral graph-partitioning [23], random-walk [24], information-theoretic [25, 26], consensus clustering [17] and many others (see [8] for the review). Recently, Chakraborty et al. [5] pointed out how vertex ordering influences the results of the community detection algorithms. They identify invariant groups of vertices (named as "constant communities") whose assignment to communities are not affected by vertex ordering.

On the other hand, several metrics for evaluating the quality of community structure have been proposed. The most popular is modularity [21]. However, community detection using modularity has certain issues including resolution limit, degeneracy of solutions and asymptotic growth [11]. To address these issues, multi-resolution versions of modularity [2] were proposed to allow researchers to specify a tunable target resolution limit parameter. Furthermore, Lancichinetti and Fortunato [16] stated that even those multi-resolution versions of modularity are not only inclined to merge the smallest well-formed communities, but also to split the largest well-formed communities.

8. DISCUSSIONS AND FUTURE WORK

In this paper, we have introduced a new vertex-based metric, permanence for evaluating the goodness of communities in networks. From our experiments we observe that the permanence score has a good correlation with the quality of the ground-truth communities (Section 4) and is sensitive to perturbations in the community structure (Section 5). In addition, permanence also provides some significant advantages compared to other popular community scoring functions.

The *value of permanence strongly correlates to the community like structure of the network.* For example, the power grid network, which is not at all modular [13], has a modularity of 0.98 and a permanence of -0.16. In contrast, community-rich networks such as a circle of 30 cliques generate permanence (modularity) of 0.92 (0.87). Therefore, permanence can also be used to identify whether the network is at all suitable for community detection.

We believe that the advantages of permanence arise because it is a local vertex-based metric as opposed to the more common global/mesoscopic metrics. At the same time, permanence also derives the benefits of a global metric to a certain extent by looking into the exact community assignments of the external neighbors of the vertex considered. Perfectly global metrics tend to aggregate the effect of the connections of all the vertices in a community. As we have seen in Section 2 we can lose information by aggregation, particularly if the distribution of the connections is skewed. A vertex-based metric is more fine-grained, and therefore allows partial estimation of communities in a network whose entire structure is not known.

In this paper we have empirically demonstrated the advantages of permanence. As an immediate future work, we plan to extend permanence metric to evaluate the quality of overlapping communities and communities in dynamic and weighted networks. We believe that this metric will help in formulating a strong theoretical foundation for identifying community structures where the ground-truth is not known. All the codes, datasets and supporting materials are publicly available at `http://cnerg.org/permanence/`.

9. ACKNOWLEDGMENTS

The first author of the paper is financially supported by Google India PhD Fellowship Grant for Social Computing. The authors from University of Nebraska are supported by College of IS&T, the Graca grant for UNO-SPR and the RISC Fellowship.

10. REFERENCES

[1] `http://cse.iitkgp.ac.in/resgrp/cnerg/Files/resources/appendix_permanence.pdf`.

[2] A. Arenas, A. Fernández, and S. Gómez. Analysis of the structure of complex networks at different resolution levels. *New Journal of Physics*, 10(5):053039, 2008.

[3] V. D. Blondel, J.-L. Guillaume, R. Lambiotte, and E. Lefebvre. Fast unfolding of communities in large networks. *J. Stat. Mech.*, 2008(10):P10008, Oct. 2008.

[4] T. Chakraborty, S. Sikdar, V. Tammana, N. Ganguly, and A. Mukherjee. Computer science fields as ground-truth communities: Their impact, rise and fall. In *ASONAM*, pages 426 – 433, 2013.

[5] T. Chakraborty, S. Srinivasan, N. Ganguly, S. Bhowmick, and A. Mukherjee. Constant Communities in Complex Networks. *Scientific Reports*, 3, May 2013.

[6] A. Clauset, M. E. J. Newman, and C. Moore. Finding community structure in very large networks. *Phys. Rev. E*, 70(6):066111, 2004.

[7] L. Danon, A. Diaz-Guilera, J. Duch, and A. Arenas. Comparing community structure identification. *J. Stat. Mech.*, 9:P09008, 2005.

[8] S. Fortunato. Community detection in graphs. *Phys. Rep.*, 486:75–174, 2010.

[9] S. Ghosh, A. Banerjee, N. Sharma, S. Agarwal, and N. Ganguly. Statistical analysis of the indian railway network: a complex network approach. *Acta Physica Polonica B Proceedings Supplement*, 4:123–137, 2011.

[10] M. Girvan and M. E. Newman. Community structure in social and biological networks. *PNAS*, 99(12):7821–7826, June 2002.

[11] B. Good, Y. D. Montjoye, and A. Clauset. Performance of modularity maximization in practical contexts. *Phys. Rev. E*, 81(4):046106, 2010.

[12] L. Hubert and P. Arabie. Comparing partitions. *Journal of classification*, 2(1):193–218, 1985.

[13] B. Karrer, E. Levina, and M. E. J. Newman. Robustness of community structure in networks. *Phys. Rev. E*, 77(4):046119, 2008.

[14] V. Labatut. Generalized measures for the evaluation of community detection methods. *CoRR*, abs/1303.5441, 2013.

[15] A. Lancichinetti and S. Fortunato. Benchmarks for testing community detection algorithms on directed and weighted graphs with overlapping communities. *Phys. Rev. E*, 80(1):016118, July 2009.

[16] A. Lancichinetti and S. Fortunato. Limits of modularity maximization in community detection. *Phys. Rev. E*, 84:066122, 2011.

[17] A. Lancichinetti and S. Fortunato. Consensus clustering in complex networks. *Scientific Reports*, 2, 2012.

[18] J. Leskovec, K. J. Lang, A. Dasgupta, and M. W. Mahoney. Community structure in large networks: Natural cluster sizes and the absence of large well-defined clusters. *Internet Mathematics*, 6(1):29–123, 2009.

[19] J. Leskovec, K. J. Lang, and M. Mahoney. Empirical comparison of algorithms for network community detection. In *WWW*, pages 631–640, New York, USA, 2010. ACM.

[20] C. D. Manning, P. Raghavan, and H. Schütze. *Introduction to Information Retrieval.* Cambridge University Press, New York, NY, USA, 2008

[21] M. E. Newman. Modularity and community structure in networks. *PNAS*, 103(23):8577–8582, June 2006.

[22] M. E. J. Newman. Fast algorithm for detecting community structure in networks. *Phys. Rev. E*, 69(6):066133, 2004.

[23] M. E. J. Newman. Spectral methods for community detection and graph partitioning. *Phys. Rev. E*, 88:042822, 2013.

[24] P. Pons and M. Latapy. Computing communities in large networks using random walks. *Journal of Graph Algortihms and Applications*, 10(2):191–218, 2006.

[25] M. Rosvall and C. Bergstrom. An information-theoretic framework for resolving community structure in complex networks. *PNAS*, 104(18):7327, 2007.

[26] M. Rosvall and C. T. Bergstrom. Maps of random walks on complex networks reveal community structure. *PNAS*, 105(4):1118–1123, 2008.

[27] K. Steinhaeuser and N. V. Chawla. Identifying and evaluating community structure in complex networks. *Pattern Recog. Lett.*, 31(5):413–421, 2010.

[28] J. Yang and J. Leskovec. Defining and evaluating network communities based on ground-truth. In *ACM SIGKDD Workshop on Mining Data Semantics*, pages 3:1–3:8, New York, USA, 2012.

The Interplay Between Dynamics and Networks: Centrality, Communities, and Cheeger Inequality

Rumi Ghosh
Robert Bosch
rumi.ghosh@gmail.com

Shang-Hua Teng
Computer Science
USC
shanghua@usc.edu

Kristina Lerman and Xiaoran Yan
Information Sciences Institute
USC
lerman/xiaoran@isi.edu

ABSTRACT

We study the interplay between a *dynamic process* and the *structure* of the network on which it is defined. Specifically, we examine the impact of this interaction on the quality-measure of network clusters and node centrality. This enables us to effectively identify network communities and important nodes participating in the dynamics. As the first step towards this objective, we introduce an umbrella framework for defining and characterizing an ensemble of dynamic processes on a network. This framework generalizes the traditional *Laplacian framework* to continuous-time biased random walks and also allows us to model some epidemic processes over a network. For each dynamic process in our framework, we can define a function that measures the quality of every subset of nodes as a potential cluster (or community) with respect to this process on a given network. This subset-quality function generalizes the traditional *conductance measure* for graph partitioning. We partially justify our choice of the quality function by showing that the classic Cheeger's inequality, which relates the conductance of the best cluster in a network with a spectral quantity of its Laplacian matrix, can be extended from the Laplacian-conductance setting to this more general setting.

1. INTRODUCTION

Two fundamental problems in network analysis involve identifying central nodes and communities in a network. The goal of centrality identification is to find central or important nodes, for example, those that control the flow of information on the network. The objective of community detection is to discover subsets of well-interacting nodes in a given network. Both of these graph mining approaches have tremendous applications in different areas, such as social network, biological network, World Wide Web analysis. For example, the centrality measure Page Rank [20] is one of the backbones of Google's search algorithm. Similarly, community detection or graph clustering is useful in potential drug-target identification [29].

KDD'14, August 24–27, 2014, New York, NY, USA.

http://dx.doi.org/10.1145/2623330.2623738 .

The first step towards finding potentially meaningful communities is to define a *quality function* that measures the degree to which a subset of network nodes tend to interact among themselves. To this end, measures such as clustering coefficients, subgraph density, and conductance, were introduced to express the quality of a subset as a good cluster. Similarly, many measures of *centrality* including Page Rank and eigenvector centrality are used to discover important nodes. However, to define a useful quality or centrality function, one needs to determine how the network structure models the interaction among nodes. Unfortunately, this can be quite challenging and is often ignored. Indeed, the aforementioned measures apply different interpretations. As a result, current network analysis methods often make implicit assumptions about the dynamic processes (and the resultant interaction) among nodes and use these assumptions to define the quality of a cluster or centrality of a node.

Explicitly taking the dynamic process into account, a node's centrality at any time describes its participation in the flow taking place on the network [5, 15]. Similarly, communities are groups of nodes that interact more frequently with each other (according to the rules of the dynamic process) than with nodes from other communities [16]. In fact, this view of modeling is not new. For instance, in choosing *conductance* as a measure of cluster quality, one may in fact implicitly assume that *unbiased random walk* is taking place on the network [12, 26, 8, 9]. Under this assumption, a measure of centrality is the *heat kernel page rank* [6].

Other dynamic processes such as the spread of information, ideas, or epidemics, induce different interactions from the unbiased random walks. An epidemic [13] is a stochastic process that, unlike a random walk, attempts to transition to (i.e., infect) every neighbor of a node. Epidemic dynamics may be specified by the *replicator* operator [16], whose stationary distribution defines *eigenvector centrality* [4, 10]. It is natural to think that the centrality of a node depends on the specifics of the dynamic process, which together with the network topology influence its activity level. For example, nodes that are visited most frequently by a random walk (specified by the heat kernel page rank) are different from nodes that are infected most often during an epidemic (specified by eigenvector centrality). Moreover, epidemics could lead to a different community formation of a network [16].

Our Contributions.

We study the interplay between a dynamic process and the underlying network on which it unfolds. We focus on the impact of this interaction on the emergence of central nodes and the formation of communities in the network, and on the design of efficient algorithms for their identification.

General framework for dynamic processes: We present an umbrella framework for describing dynamic processes on a network that generalizes the traditional Laplacian framework for diffusion and random walks. Recall that a random walk on a network is a stochastic dynamic process that transitions from a node to a random neighbor of that node. It defines a Markov chain that can be specified by the normalized Laplacian of the network. Our framework (Section 2) attempts to capture the class of dynamic processes that evolve in time according to a rule that can be defined by generalizing the normalized Laplacian.

Formal analysis of interaction dynamics: Our framework defines a class of dynamic processes with relatively simple characterization parameters, which enables rigorous analysis of the impact of these parameters on the measures of the community quality and node centrality. Its inclusion of diffusion and random walks allows us to build on the insights from previous work on mathematical analysis of random walks, conductance measures for clustering, and spectral notions for centrality, in order to derive our generalization that reflects the interaction between the dynamic process and its underlying network. We are also able to use it to define new processes whose properties may offer useful insights into community finding and graph partitioning. Although this particular framework cannot express every dynamic process of interest, the generalization allows us to model some epidemic processes over a network. Thus, we can use these well- established special cases (such as random walks and epidemics) to clarify the relationship between the parameters of the dynamic processes and their induced community qualities and centralities.

Generalized conductance: We extend conductance to a general quality-measure for clusters that reflects the dynamic process on the network. For each dynamic process, we use its characterization parameters to define this function. It measures the quality of every subset (of nodes) as a potential cluster (community) with respect to this process on the given network. This subset-quality measure generalizes traditional conductance and provides a continuous family of measures for subsets in a graph. Recall that, for each set $S \subset V$ in a weighted graph $G = (V, E)$, the *conductance* of S, $\phi_G(S)$, is equal to the ratio of the degree of the connectivities between S to $V - S$ to total degree of connectivities of S (or the total degree of connectivities of $V - S$, whichever is smaller). As each subset-quality function measures different degree to which a subset of nodes in a graph tend to cluster together and its coherence as a community, a comparative study of these subset-measures could be useful in the design and evaluation of community detection algorithms.

Generalized Cheeger's inequality: In both theory and practice, a basic problem in community detection is to justify why one quality function is better than another for modeling communities in a network. Unfortunately, this is a highly challenging problem for rigorous reasoning and justification. The interplay of dynamics and network topology further adds to its difficulty. In this paper, we will build on the wisdoms demonstrated in the past decades in spectral graph theory. To partially justify our choice of the quality function, we prove that the classical Cheeger's inequality can be extended to our generalized settings. Recall (also see Section 3) that the Cheeger's inequality relates a spectral quantity of the Laplacian matrix of the network to the conductance of the best cluster in the network. Particular it shows that if λ is the second smallest eigenvalue of the normalized Laplacian matrix of G and $S \subset V$ is a subset in G with the smallest conductance, then

$$(\phi_G(S))^2 / 2 \leq \lambda \leq 2 \cdot \phi_G(S). \tag{1}$$

Centrality, quality and community: We will show that the same relation (as in Eq. 1) holds for the generalized conductance and the extreme eigenvalue of the linear operator for each dynamic process in our framework. Each function that measures community quality can then be used to decompose the network into potential communities.

In addition, like previous work in random walks, we can also relate the convergence to stationary distribution with the quality measure in each of the dynamics in this framework. For example, the time taken by the random walk to reach its stationary distribution is bounded by conductance [11]. The Cheeger inequality provides this connection via the extreme eigenvalue of the normalized Laplacian. Similarly, using generalized Cheeger inequalities, we also show that the time it takes for each of the dynamic processes to reach its stationary is bounded by the corresponding quality function.

Efficient spectral and local partitioning algorithms: Like previous studies in Laplacian-based spectral graph theory, such as Spielman-Teng [26], Andersen-Chung-Lang [2], and Andersen-Peres [3], our analysis also leads to efficient spectral and local algorithms for identifying provably good clusters based on these new quality functions.

We hope this study will help lead to better approaches for defining and understanding the general interaction between dynamics and networks. Due to lack of space we are unable to provide the proofs of many theorems in this paper, which will be available in the extended version of this paper.

2. DYNAMIC PROCESSES ON NETWORKS

We represent a network as a weighted, undirected graph $G = (V, E, \boldsymbol{A})$, where for $i, j \in V$, $\boldsymbol{A}[i,j] = a_{i,j}$ assigns an (affinity) non-negative weight to each edge. We follow the tradition that $a_{i,j} = 0$ if and only if $(i,j) \notin E$; i.e., $\boldsymbol{A}$ is the weighted adjacency matrix. By convention we assume it is symmetric and $a_{i,i} = 0$ for all $i \in V$. In the discussion below, the *(weighted) degree* of node $i \in V$ is defined as the total weight of edges incident on it, that is, $d_i = \sum_j a_{i,j}$.

2.1 A Family of Dynamic Processes

In a dynamic process, each network node i has a dynamic variable θ_i associated with it, which can change its value based on interactions with its neighbors. The values of the variables evolve in time according to the rules of the dynamic process. We consider linear dynamic processes of the kind:

$$\frac{d\boldsymbol{\theta}}{dt} = -\boldsymbol{\mathcal{L}}\boldsymbol{\theta}, \tag{2}$$

where $\boldsymbol{\theta}$ is a column vector containing the θ entries and $\boldsymbol{\mathcal{L}}$ is a symmetric positive semi-definite matrix, the *spreading operator*, which defines the details of the dynamic process.

As discussed in the introduction, we focus on dynamic processes on a network that generalize the traditional normalized Laplacian for diffusion and random walks. Recall that the *symmetric normalized Laplacian matrix* of a weighted graph $G = (V, E, \boldsymbol{A})$ is defined as

$$\boldsymbol{D}^{-1/2}(\boldsymbol{D} - \boldsymbol{A})\boldsymbol{D}^{-1/2},$$

where $\boldsymbol{D}$ is the diagonal matrix defined by $(d_1, ..., d_n)$. We study the properties of a dynamic process whose spreading operator can be written as:

$$\boldsymbol{\mathcal{L}} = \boldsymbol{T}^{-1/2}\boldsymbol{D}_{\boldsymbol{W}}^{-1/2}(\boldsymbol{D}_{\boldsymbol{W}} - \boldsymbol{W})\boldsymbol{D}_{\boldsymbol{W}}^{-1/2}\boldsymbol{T}^{-1/2}. \tag{3}$$

Here $\boldsymbol{T}$ is the $n \times n$ diagonal matrix of *node delay factors*. Its ith diagonal element τ_i represents the average delay of node i. Another generalization from the traditional Laplacian is the use of the *interaction matrix* $\boldsymbol{W}$ instead of the adjacency matrix $\boldsymbol{A}$. In theory, $\boldsymbol{W}$ can be any $n \times n$ symmetric positive-definite matrix; however, here we restrict our attention to scaling transformations of the adjacency matrix $\boldsymbol{A}$. We also assume that the spreading operator is *properly scaled*: specifically, we assume that $\tau_i \geq 1$, for all $i \in V$. Note that the degree matrix $\boldsymbol{D}_{\boldsymbol{W}}$ is now also defined in terms of the interaction matrix, that is $d_{\boldsymbol{W}i} = \sum_j w_{i,j}$. We name this spreading operator the *generalized Laplacian*.

We study how the interplay between dynamics and topology affects clustering as $\boldsymbol{T}$ and $\boldsymbol{W}$ vary. For a better intuition, it helps to consider the random walk Laplacian matrix:

$$\boldsymbol{\mathcal{L}}^{RW} = (\boldsymbol{D}_{\boldsymbol{W}} - \boldsymbol{W})\boldsymbol{D}_{\boldsymbol{W}}^{-1}\boldsymbol{T}^{-1}.$$

This matrix is similar to our symmetric normalized Laplacian matrix, with identical spectral properties. As its name indicates, this operator defines a continuous-time unbiased random walk on the interaction graph $\boldsymbol{W}$, which according to [15] is equivalent to biased random walks on the original adjacency matrix $\boldsymbol{A}$. Under this interpretation, τ_i is the mean delay time of the random walk on node i before a transition, assuming a simple Poisson process. This intuition leads to two orthogonal parametrizations of a dynamic process: namely $\boldsymbol{W}$ controls the distribution of walk trajectories and $\boldsymbol{T}$ controls the delay time of node transitions along each trajectory. While we use symmetric operators for mathematical convenience in definitions and proofs, it is more intuitive to think from the random walk perspective.

While the generalized Laplacian does not cover all dynamic processes of interest, this family of spreading operators includes some well-known ones, such as the Laplacian or normalized Laplacian, as well as a continuous family of new operators that are not as well studied. It also contains certain operators for modeling epidemics. The consideration of this family of operators is also partially motivated by our recent experimental work in understanding network centrality [10, 16]. We conclude this subsection with some special cases that can be described in this framework.

Normalized Laplacian.

If the interaction matrix is the original adjacency matrix $\boldsymbol{W} = \boldsymbol{A}$, and node delay factor is simply the identity matrix $\boldsymbol{T} = \boldsymbol{I}$, then we recover the *normalized symmetric Laplacian*:

$$\boldsymbol{\mathcal{L}} = \boldsymbol{I} - \boldsymbol{D}^{-1/2}\boldsymbol{A}\boldsymbol{D}^{-1/2}.$$

(Scaled) Graph Laplacian.

When $\boldsymbol{W} = \boldsymbol{A}$, $\boldsymbol{T} = d_{max}\boldsymbol{D}^{-1}$, the spreading operator corresponds to the (scaled) graph *Laplacian*

$$\boldsymbol{\mathcal{L}} = \frac{1}{d_{max}}(\boldsymbol{D} - \boldsymbol{A}).$$

This operator is often used to describe *heat diffusion*-like processes.

Replicator.

Let $\boldsymbol{v}$ be the eigenvector of $\boldsymbol{A}$ associated with its largest eigenvalue λ_{max}: $\boldsymbol{A}\boldsymbol{v} = \lambda_{max}\boldsymbol{v}$. We can then construct a diagonal matrix $\boldsymbol{V}$ whose elements are the components of the eigenvector $\boldsymbol{V}$. Let us scale the adjacency matrix according to $\boldsymbol{W} = \boldsymbol{V}\boldsymbol{A}\boldsymbol{V}$ and use it as the interaction matrix. Setting the node delay factor to identity, the spreading operator is:

$$\boldsymbol{\mathcal{L}} = \boldsymbol{I} - \boldsymbol{D}_{\boldsymbol{W}}^{-1/2}\boldsymbol{W}\boldsymbol{D}_{\boldsymbol{W}}^{-1/2} = \boldsymbol{I} - \frac{1}{\lambda_{max}}\boldsymbol{A}$$

This operator is known as the replicator matrix $\boldsymbol{R}$, and it models *epidemic diffusion* on a graph [16]. It is simply the normalized Laplacian of the interaction graph $\boldsymbol{V}\boldsymbol{A}\boldsymbol{V}$ [24]. Using the random walk intuition, an unbiased random walk on this interaction graph is equivalent to a maximum entropy random walk on the original graph given by the adjacency matrix $\boldsymbol{A}$ [15].

Unbiased Adjacency Matrix.

Reweighing each edge by the inverse of square root of the degrees of the endpoints gives the unbiased adjacency matrix $\boldsymbol{W} = \boldsymbol{D}^{-1/2}\boldsymbol{A}\boldsymbol{D}^{-1/2}$. Then, the degree of node i in the scaled graph is $d_{\boldsymbol{W}i} = \sum_{j \in V} \boldsymbol{W}[i, j]$. Letting $\boldsymbol{T} = d_{\boldsymbol{W}max}\boldsymbol{D}_{\boldsymbol{W}}^{-1}$ gives a *unbiased Laplacian matrix*:

$$\boldsymbol{\mathcal{L}} = \frac{1}{d_{\boldsymbol{W}max}}(\boldsymbol{D}_{\boldsymbol{W}} - \boldsymbol{W}).$$

Similarly, many other operators can be expressed using this framework.

2.2 Network Dynamics and Centrality

Before considering the impact of spreading operators on communities, we first examine the node centralities of each operator at any time, and their stationary distribution after convergence. The community quality functions that we use are partially inspired by the stationary distribution.

Solution of Equation 2 gives the weight distribution of the dynamic process across nodes at any time based on the initial weight distribution. In the rest of the paper, for convenience we will refer to this instantaneous distribution $\boldsymbol{\theta}(t)$ as *time-dependent centrality*. Its stationary distribution is the conventional *stationary centrality*, or centrality for short.

$$\boldsymbol{\theta}(t) = e^{-\boldsymbol{\mathcal{L}}t} \cdot \boldsymbol{\theta}_0 = \sum_{k=0}^{\infty} \frac{(-t)^k}{k!}\boldsymbol{\mathcal{L}}^k\boldsymbol{\theta}_0 \tag{4}$$

If the dynamic process converges when starting from $\boldsymbol{\theta}_0$, then $\lim_{t\to\infty} \boldsymbol{\theta}(t)$ is proportional to $\boldsymbol{\pi}$:

$$\pi_i = \frac{\sqrt{d_{\boldsymbol{W}i}\tau_i}}{\sum_j \sqrt{d_{\boldsymbol{W}j}\tau_j}} \tag{5}$$

For example, the stationary distribution of $\boldsymbol{R}$ is $\boldsymbol{v}$, also known as the *eigenvector centrality*. Eigenvector centrality was introduced by Bonacich [4] to explain the importance of actors in a social network based on the importance of the actors to which they were connected, and it gives the stationary distribution of a simple epidemic at the epidemic threshold [27, 10].

2.3 Network Dynamics and Communities

In network clustering and community detection, one would like to identify subsets of nodes $S \subseteq V$ that are more similar, or behave more similarly, to each other than to nodes in other subsets. A standard approach to clustering involves defining an objective function that measures the *quality* of a cluster. For a subset $S \subseteq V$, let $\bar{S} = V \setminus S$ to denote the complement of S, which consists of nodes that are not in S. Let $\text{cut}(S, \bar{S}) = \sum_{i\in S, j\in \bar{S}} a_{i,j}$ denote the total affinity weights of all edges used by S to connect with the outside world. Let $\text{vol}(S) = \sum_{i\in} d_i = \sum_{i\in S, j\in V} a_{i,j}$ denote the volume of all affinity weights involving vertices in S.

One popular heuristic to measure the quality of a subset S as a potential good cluster (or a community) [12, 26, 8] is to use the ratio of these two quantities:

$$\phi(S) = \frac{\text{cut}(S, \bar{S})}{\min(\text{vol}(S), \text{vol}(\bar{S}))} \tag{6}$$

For example, a subset that (approximately) minimizes this quantity — the *conductance* of S — is a desirable cluster, as it maximizes the fraction of affinities within the subset. If interactions among nodes are proportional to their affinity weights, then a set with small conductance also means that its members interact significantly more with each other than with members not in the subset. Other well-known quality functions are normalized cut [23] and ratio-cut, given by

$$\frac{\text{cut}(S, \bar{S})}{\text{vol}(S)} + \frac{\text{cut}(S, \bar{S})}{\text{vol}(\bar{S})} \quad \text{and} \quad \frac{\text{cut}(S, \bar{S})}{\min(|S|, |\bar{S}|)},$$

respectively. The smallest achievable such ratio is known as the *isoperimetric number*.

Algorithmically, once a quality function is selected, one can then perform a partitioning-based algorithm or mathematical programming-based method to find a cluster or clusters that optimizes the quality function.

For the Normalized Laplacian paradigm (or when the underlying process is a random walk), there exists a relationship between clustering and dynamics: in a good (i.e., low conductance cut) cluster, a random walk starting within a cluster seldom transitions outside the cluster [17, 23, 22, 26]. Therefore, the presence of a good cluster implies that it will take a random walk a long time to reach its stationary distribution. We generalize this notion with a claim that every dynamic process has an associated function that measures the quality of the cluster with respect to that process. Optimizing the quality function leads to cohesive communities, i.e., groups of nodes that the dynamic process seldom leaves.

Generalized Conductance.

Consider a dynamic process defined by a spreading operator $\mathcal{L} = T^{-1/2} D_W^{-1/2} (D_W - W) D_W^{-1/2} T^{-1/2}$. For a set $S \subseteq V$, let $\text{vol}_{\mathcal{L}}(S) = \sum_{i\in S} d_{W\,i} \tau_i$ be the generalized volume under our framework. We define the quality of a set S with respect to $\mathcal{L}$ as:

$$h_{\mathcal{L}}(S) = \frac{\text{cut}(S, \bar{S})}{\min\left(\text{vol}_{\mathcal{L}}(S), \text{vol}_{\mathcal{L}}(\bar{S})\right)} = \frac{\sum_{i\in S, j\in \bar{S}} w_{i,j}}{\min\left(\sum_{i\in S} d_{W\,i}\tau_i, \sum_{i\in \bar{S}} d_{W\,i}\tau_i\right)} \tag{7}$$

We also define,

$$\phi_{\mathcal{L}} = \min_S h_{\mathcal{L}}(S) \tag{8}$$

Using the random walk perspective, the numerator measures the random jumps across communities, while the denominator ensures a balanced bisection. The generalized volume can be interpreted as the total time a random walk stays within a community after convergence, as it is proportional to both node degrees and node delay factors.

Below, we summarize the induced special cases discussed in the previous subsection.

Normalized Laplacian.

$W = A$ and $T = I$, and hence $h_{\mathcal{L}}(S)$ is the conductance.

(Scaled) Graph Laplacian.

$W = A$ and $T = d_{max} D^{-1}$, hence

$$h_{\mathcal{L}}(S) = \frac{\text{cut}(S, \bar{S})}{\min(d_{\max}|S|, d_{max}|\bar{S}|)} = \frac{1}{d_{\max}} \cdot \frac{\text{cut}(S, \bar{S})}{\min(|S|, |\bar{S}|)},$$

This is the ratio cut scaled by $1/d_{\max}$.

Replicator.

$W = VAV$ and $T = I$. Recall v is the eigenvector of W associated with the largest eigenvalue λ_{max}. The redefined cut size is $\sum_{i\in S, j\in \bar{S}} f_{ij} = \sum_{i\in S, j\in \bar{S}} v_i v_j$. Therefore,

$$h_{\mathcal{L}}(S) = \frac{\sum_{i\in S, j\in \bar{S}} v_i v_j}{\lambda_{\max} \min\left(\sum_{i\in S} v_i^2, \sum_{i\in \bar{S}} v_i^2\right)}$$

Since the degree of a node in an interaction graph is $d_{W\,i} = \sum_j f_{ij} = \lambda_{\max} v_i^2$, the generalized conductance of the Replicator is simply the conductance of the interaction graph [24].

Unbiased Adjacency Matrix.

$W = D^{-1/2} A D^{-1/2}$. and $T = d_{W\,max} D_W^{-1}$. The associated quality function is

$$h_{\mathcal{L}}(S) = \frac{1}{d_{W\,max}} \cdot \frac{\sum_{i\in S, j\in \bar{S}} \frac{a_{i,j}}{\sqrt{d_i d_j}}}{\min(|S|, |\bar{S}|)}.$$

We call this quality function *unbiased cohesion*.

3. GENERALIZED CHEEGER'S INEQUALITY AND SPECTRAL PARTITIONING

Cheeger inequality states that

$$\phi_G^2/2 \le \lambda_1 \le 2\phi_G$$

where λ_1 is the second largest eigenvalue of the normalized Laplacian, $\mathcal{L} = I - D^{-1/2} W D^{-1/2}$, and ϕ_G is conductance. The relationship between conductance and spectral properties of the Laplacian enables the use of its eigenvectors for partitioning graphs, particularly the nearest-neighborhood graphs and finite-element meshes [25].

In this section, we generalize Cheeger's inequality to any spreading operator under our framework and its associated generalized conductance (given by Eq. 8). Our generalization of Cheeger's inequality comes with algorithmic consequences. It leads to spectral partitioning algorithms that are efficient in finding low conductance cuts for a given operator.

3.1 Generalized Cheeger Inequality

THEOREM 1. *(Generalized Cheeger Inequality) Consider the dynamic process described by a (properly scaled) spreading operator* $\boldsymbol{\mathcal{L}} = \boldsymbol{T}^{-1/2}\boldsymbol{D}_{\boldsymbol{W}}^{-1/2}(\boldsymbol{D}_{\boldsymbol{W}}-\boldsymbol{W})\boldsymbol{D}_{\boldsymbol{W}}^{-1/2}\boldsymbol{T}^{-1/2}$. *Let* $\lambda_0 \leq \lambda_1 \leq ... \leq \lambda_{n-1}$ *be the eigenvalues of* $\boldsymbol{\mathcal{L}}$. *Then* $\lambda_0 = 0$ *and* λ_1 *satisfies the following inequalities:*

$$\phi_{\boldsymbol{\mathcal{L}}}(G)^2/2 \leq \lambda_1 \leq 2\phi_{\boldsymbol{\mathcal{L}}}(G)$$

where $\phi_{\boldsymbol{\mathcal{L}}}(G)$ *is given by Eq. 8.*

PROOF. We prove the theorem by following the approach for proving the classic Cheeger's inequality (see [8]).

Let $(\tau_1, ..., \tau_n)$ be the diagonal entries of $\boldsymbol{T}$. Note that $\boldsymbol{v}_0 = \boldsymbol{T}^{1/2}\boldsymbol{D}_{\boldsymbol{W}}^{1/2} \cdot \mathbf{1}$, where $\mathbf{1}$ denotes the vector of all 1's, is an eigenvector of $\boldsymbol{\mathcal{L}}$ associated with eigenvalue $\lambda_0 = 0$. Let $\mathrm{vol}_{\boldsymbol{\mathcal{L}}}(S) = \sum_{i\in S} d_i\tau_i$ for $S \subseteq V$, where for clarity we abuse the notation d_i and use it as $d_{\boldsymbol{W}i}$. Suppose $\boldsymbol{f}$ is the eigenvector associated with λ_1. Then, $\boldsymbol{f} \perp \boldsymbol{v}_0$. Consider vector $\boldsymbol{g}$ such that $g[u] = f[u]/\sqrt{d_u\tau_u}$. The fact that $\boldsymbol{f} \perp \boldsymbol{v}_0$ then implies $\sum_v g[v]d_v\tau_v = 0$. Then,

$$\phi_{\boldsymbol{\mathcal{L}}}(G) = \min_S \frac{\mathrm{cut}(S,\bar{S})}{\min(\mathrm{vol}_{\boldsymbol{\mathcal{L}}}(S), \mathrm{vol}_{\boldsymbol{\mathcal{L}}}(\bar{S}))}$$

$$\lambda_1 = \frac{\boldsymbol{f}^T\boldsymbol{\mathcal{L}}\boldsymbol{f}}{\boldsymbol{f}^T\boldsymbol{f}} = \frac{\sum_{u,v\in V}\left(\frac{f[u]}{\sqrt{d_u\tau_u}} - \frac{f[v]}{\sqrt{d_v\tau_v}}\right)^2 w_{u,v}}{\sum_v f[v]^2} = \frac{\sum_{u,v\in V}(g[u]-g[v])^2 w_{u,v}}{\sum_v g[v]^2 d_v\tau_v}$$

Instead of sweeping the vertices of G according to the eigenvector $\boldsymbol{f}$ itself, we sweep the vertices of the graph G according to $\boldsymbol{g}$ by ordering the vertices of G so that

$$g[v_1] \geq g[v_2] \geq \cdots \geq g[v_n]$$

and consider sets $S_i = \{v_1, \cdots, v_i\}$ for all $1 \leq i \leq n$.

Similar to [8], we will eventually only consider the first "half" of the sets S_i during the sweeping: Let r denote the largest integer such that $\mathrm{vol}_{\boldsymbol{\mathcal{L}}}(S_r) \leq \mathrm{vol}_{\boldsymbol{\mathcal{L}}}(V)/2$. Note that

$$\sum_v (g[v]-g[v_r])^2 d_v\tau_v = \sum_v g[v]^2 d_v\tau_v + g[v_r]^2 d_v\tau_v \geq \sum_v g[v]^2 d_v\tau_v.$$

where the first equation follows from $\sum_v g[v]d_v\tau_v = 0$. We denote the positive and negative part of $g - g[v_r]$ as g_+ and g_- respectively:

$$g_+[v] = \begin{cases} g[v]-g[v_r], & \text{if } g[v] \geq g[v_r]. \\ 0, & \text{otherwise.} \end{cases} \tag{9}$$

$$g_-[v] = \begin{cases} |g[v]-g[v_r]|, & \text{if } g[v] \leq g[v_r]. \\ 0, & \text{otherwise.} \end{cases} \tag{10}$$

Now

$$\lambda_1 = \frac{\sum_{u,v\in V}(g[u]-g[v])^2 w_{u,v}}{\sum_v g[v]^2 d_v\tau_v} \geq \frac{\sum_{u,v\in V}(g_+[u]-g_+[v])^2 w_{u,v} + (g_-[u]-g_-[v])^2 w_{u,v}}{\sum_v (g_+[v]^2 + g_-[v]^2) d_v\tau_v} \geq \min\left[\frac{\sum (g_+[u]-g_+[v])^2 w_{u,v}}{\sum_v g_+[v]^2 d_v\tau_v}, \frac{\sum (g_-[u]-g_-[v])^2 w_{u,v}}{\sum_v g_-[v]^2 d_v\tau_v}\right]$$

Without loss of generality, we assume the first ratio is at most the second ratio, and will mostly focus on the vertices $\{v_1, ..., v_r\}$ in the first "half" of the graph in the analysis below. Thus,

$$\lambda_1 \geq \frac{\sum_{u,v}(g_+[u]-g_+[v])^2 w_{u,v}}{\sum_v g_+[v]^2 d_v\tau_v} \geq \frac{\left(\sum_{u,v}(g_+^2[u]-g_+^2[v])w_{u,v}\right)^2}{\left(\sum_v g_+[v]^2 d_v\tau_v\right)\left(\sum_{u,v}(g_+[u]+g_+[v])^2 w_{u,v}\right)}$$

which follows from the Cauchy-Schwartz inequality.

We now separately analyze the numerator and denominator. To bound the denominator, we will use the following property of τ_i: Because $\boldsymbol{\mathcal{L}}$ is properly scaled, $\tau_i \geq 1$ for all $i \in V$. Therefore,

$$\sum_{u,v}(g_+[u]+g_+[v])^2 w_{u,v} \leq \sum_{u,v} 2(g_+^2[u]+g_+^2[v])w_{u,v} = 2\sum_{u\in V} g_+^2[u]d_u \leq 2\sum_{u\in V} g_+^2[u]d_u\tau_u.$$

Hence, the denominator is at most

$$2\left(\sum_{u\in V} g_+^2[u]d_u\tau_u\right)^2.$$

To bound the numerator, we consider subsets of nodes $S_i = \{v_1, \cdots, v_i\}$ for all $1 \leq i \leq r$ and define $S_0 = \emptyset$. First note that

$$\mathrm{vol}_{\boldsymbol{\mathcal{L}}}(S_i) - \mathrm{vol}_{\boldsymbol{\mathcal{L}}}(S_{i-1}) = d_{v_i}\tau_{v_i}. \tag{11}$$

By the definition of $\phi_{\boldsymbol{\mathcal{L}}}(G)$, we know $\phi_{\boldsymbol{\mathcal{L}}}(G) \leq \min_i h_{\boldsymbol{\mathcal{L}}}(S_i)$ for all $1 \leq i \leq r$, where recall the function $h_S(\boldsymbol{\mathcal{L}})$ is defined by Eq. 7. Since $\mathrm{vol}_{\boldsymbol{\mathcal{L}}}(S_i) \leq \mathrm{vol}_{\boldsymbol{\mathcal{L}}}(\bar{S_i})$ for all $1 \leq i \leq r$, we have

$$\mathrm{cut}(S_i, \bar{S_i}) \geq \phi_{\boldsymbol{\mathcal{L}}} \cdot \mathrm{vol}_{\boldsymbol{\mathcal{L}}}(S_i) \tag{12}$$

By orienting vertices according to $v_1, ..., v_n$, we can express the numerator

$$\begin{aligned}
\mathrm{Num} &= \left(\sum_{u,v}(g_+^2[u]-g_+^2[v])w_{u,v}\right)^2 \\
&= \left(\sum_{i<j}\sum_{k=0}^{j-i-1}\left(g_+^2[v_{i+k}]-g_+^2[v_{i+k+1}]\right)w_{v_i,v_j}\right)^2 \\
&= \left(\sum_{i=1}^{n-1}\left(g_+^2[v_i]-g_+^2[v_{i+1}]\right)\cdot \mathrm{cut}(S_i,\bar{S_i})\right)^2 \\
&\quad \text{Collecting } (v_i, v_{i+1}) \text{ terms} \\
&\geq \left(\sum_{i=1}^{n-1}\left(g_+^2[v_i]-g_+^2[v_{i+1}]\right)\cdot \phi_{\boldsymbol{\mathcal{L}}} \cdot \mathrm{vol}_{\boldsymbol{\mathcal{L}}}(S_i)\right)^2 \\
&\quad \text{By Eqn: 12} \\
&= \phi_{\boldsymbol{\mathcal{L}}}^2 \cdot \left(\sum_{i=1}^{n} g_+^2[v_i]\cdot(\mathrm{vol}_{\boldsymbol{\mathcal{L}}}(S_i)-\mathrm{vol}_{\boldsymbol{\mathcal{L}}}(S_{i+1}))\right)^2 \\
&\quad \text{By Eqn. 11 and } g_+(v_n) = 0 \\
&= \phi_{\boldsymbol{\mathcal{L}}}(G)^2 \cdot \left(\sum_{i=1}^{n} g_+^2[v_i]\cdot d_{v_i}\tau_i\right)^2.
\end{aligned}$$

Combining the bounds for the numerator and the denominator, we obtain $\lambda_1 \leq \phi_{\mathcal{L}}^2/2$ as stated in the theorem. The right hand side of the theorem follows from the same argument for the standard Cheeger Inequality. □

3.2 Spectral Partitioning for Generalized Conductance

Given a weighted graph $G = (V, E, \boldsymbol{A})$ and a operator $\mathcal{L}$, we can use the standard sweeping method in the proof of Theorem 1 to find a partition $(S, \bar{S})$. This procedure is described in Algorithm 1.

Algorithm 1 Spectral Dynamics Clustering $(G, \mathcal{L})$

Input: weighted network: $G = (V, E, \boldsymbol{A})$, and spreading operator $\mathcal{L}$ defined by the interaction matrix $\boldsymbol{W}$ and the node delay factor $\boldsymbol{T}$.
Output partition: $(S, \bar{S})$
Algorithm

- Find the eigenvector $\boldsymbol{f}$ of $\mathcal{L} = \boldsymbol{T}^{-1/2}\boldsymbol{D}_{\boldsymbol{W}}^{-1/2}(\boldsymbol{D}_{\boldsymbol{W}} - \boldsymbol{W})\boldsymbol{D}_{\boldsymbol{W}}^{-1/2}\boldsymbol{T}^{-1/2}$ associated with the second smallest eigenvalue of $\mathcal{L}$.
- Let vector $\boldsymbol{g}$ be $g[u] = f[u] \cdot \sqrt{d_{\boldsymbol{W}_u}\tau_u}$.
- Order the vertices of G into $(v_1, ..., v_n)$ such that $g[v_1] \geq g[v_2] \geq ... \geq g[v_n]$.
- Sweeping: For each $S_i = \{v_1, ..., v_i\}$, compute
$$h_{\mathcal{L}}(S_i) = \frac{\mathrm{cut}(S_i, \bar{S}_i)}{\min\left(\mathrm{vol}_{\mathcal{L}}(S_i), \mathrm{vol}_{\mathcal{L}}(\bar{S}_i)\right)}.$$
- Output the S_i with the smallest $h_{\mathcal{L}}(S_i)$.

Before stating the quality guarantee of the above algorithm, we quickly discuss its implementation and running time. The most expensive step is the computation of the eigenvalue vector f associated with the second smallest eigenvalue of $\mathcal{L}$. While one can use standard numerical methods to find an approximation of this eigenvector – the analysis would depend on the separation of the second and the third eigenvalue of $\mathcal{L}$. Since $\mathcal{L}$ is a diagonally scaled normalized Laplacian matrix, one can use the nearly-linear-time Laplacian solvers (e.g., by Spielman-Teng [26] or Koutis-Miller-Peng [14]) to solve linear systems in $\mathcal{L}$.

Following [26], let us consider the following notion of spectral approximation of $\mathcal{L}$: Suppose $\lambda_1(\mathcal{L})$ the second smallest eigenvalue of $\mathcal{L}$. For $\epsilon \geq 0$, $\bar{\boldsymbol{f}}$ is an *ϵ-approximate second eigenvector* of $\mathcal{L}$ if $\bar{\boldsymbol{f}} \perp \boldsymbol{D}^{1/2}\boldsymbol{T}^{1/2} \cdot \mathbf{1}$, and

$$\frac{\bar{\boldsymbol{f}}^T \mathcal{L} \bar{\boldsymbol{f}}}{\bar{\boldsymbol{f}}^T \bar{\boldsymbol{f}}} \leq (1+\epsilon) \cdot \lambda_1(\mathcal{L}).$$

The following proposition follows directly from the algorithm and Theorem 7.2 of [26] (using the solver from [14]).

PROPOSITION 1. *For any interaction graph $G = (V, E, \boldsymbol{W})$ and node scaling factor $\boldsymbol{T}$, and $\epsilon, p > 0$, with probability at least $1-p$, one can compute an* ϵ-approximate second eigenvector *of operator $\mathcal{L}$ in time*

$$O\left(|E| \log n \log\log n \log(1/p) \log(1/\epsilon)/\epsilon\right).$$

To use this spectral approximation algorithm (and in fact any numerical approximation to the second eigenvector of $\mathcal{L}$) in our spectral partitioning algorithm for the dynamics we will need a strengthened theorem of Theorem 1.

THEOREM 2. *(Extended Cheeger Inequality with Respect to Rayleigh Quotient)*
For any interaction graph $G = (V, E, \boldsymbol{W})$ and node scaling factor $\boldsymbol{T}$, (whose diagonals are $(\tau_1, ..., \tau_n)$), for any vector $\boldsymbol{u}$ such that $\boldsymbol{u} \perp \boldsymbol{D}^{1/2}\boldsymbol{T}^{1/2} \cdot \mathbf{1}$, if we order the vertices of G into $(v_1, ..., v_n)$ such that $g[v_1] \geq ... \geq g[v_n]$, where $\boldsymbol{g} = (\boldsymbol{DT})^{-1/2} \cdot \boldsymbol{u}$ then

$$\frac{(\min_i h_{\mathcal{L}}(S_i))^2}{2} \leq \frac{\boldsymbol{u}^T \mathcal{L} \boldsymbol{u}}{\boldsymbol{u}^T \boldsymbol{u}},$$

where $\mathcal{L} = \boldsymbol{T}^{-1/2}\boldsymbol{D}_{\boldsymbol{W}}^{-1/2}(\boldsymbol{D}_{\boldsymbol{W}} - \boldsymbol{W})\boldsymbol{D}_{\boldsymbol{W}}^{-1/2}\boldsymbol{T}^{-1/2}$ and $S_i = \{v_1, ..., v_i\}$.

The next theorem then follows directly from Proposition 1, Theorem 2 and the definition of ϵ-approximate second eigenvector of $\mathcal{L}$ that provide a guarantee of the quality of the algorithm of this subsection.

THEOREM 3. *For any interaction graph $G = (V, E, \boldsymbol{W})$ and node scaling factor $\boldsymbol{T}$, (whose diagonals are $(\tau_1, ..., \tau_n)$), one can compute in time*

$$O(|E| \log n \log\log n \log(1/\epsilon)/\epsilon)$$

a partition $(S, \bar{S})$ such that

$$\begin{aligned} h_{\mathcal{L}}(S) &= \frac{\sum_{v \in S, u \in \bar{S}} w_{u,v}}{\min\left(\sum_{v \in S} d_{\boldsymbol{W}_v}\tau_v, \sum_{v \in \bar{S}} d_{\boldsymbol{W}_v}\tau_v\right)} \\ &\leq \sqrt{2(1+\epsilon)\lambda_1(\mathcal{L})} \end{aligned}$$

where $\boldsymbol{T}^{-1/2}\boldsymbol{D}_{\boldsymbol{W}}^{-1/2}(\boldsymbol{D}_{\boldsymbol{W}} - \boldsymbol{W})\boldsymbol{D}_{\boldsymbol{W}}^{-1/2}\boldsymbol{T}^{-1/2}$, $w_{u,v}$ is the $(u,v)^{th}$ entry of the interaction matrix $\boldsymbol{W}$, and $\lambda_1(\mathcal{L})$ is the second smallest eigenvalue of $\mathcal{L}$. Consequently,

$$\begin{aligned} & h_{\mathcal{L}}(S) \leq 2\sqrt{(1+\epsilon)\phi_{\mathcal{L}}(G)} \\ = \; & 2(1+\epsilon)\sqrt{\min_{S^* \in V} \frac{\sum_{v \in S^*, u \in \bar{S^*}} w_{u,v}}{\min\left(\sum_{v \in S^*} d_{\boldsymbol{W}_v}\tau_v, \sum_{v \in \bar{S^*}} d_{\boldsymbol{W}_v}\tau_v\right)}}. \end{aligned}$$

4. LOCAL CLUSTERING ALGORITHMS

In the analysis of massive networks, it is essential to identify subsets of nodes whose induced sub-graphs have "significant" structural coherence without examining the entire network. Using clustering as an example, Spielman and Teng [26] introduced a framework of *local algorithms* for network analysis: given an input node, a local algorithm can only explore the neighbors of the nodes it has already accessed. It may occasionally access some random nodes in the network. The complexity of the local algorithm is then measured by the total number of accesses it makes, as well as the computations it performs.

In spite of lacking global access, Spielman and Teng showed that local algorithms can be effective in identifying good clusters when conductance is used as quality measure. Their work was subsequently improved by Andersen-Chung-Lang [2], Andersen-Pere [3], and Chung [6, 7]. Chung [6, 7] applied the sweeping method to the heat-kernal page rank to identify a random walk-based local cluster. Similarly, we propose a dynamic-dependent sweeping procedure to discover a local cluster of provably good generalized conductance. Due to length limit, we only state relevant theorems in this paper. For details of proofs, please refer to the full version on arXiv.

4.1 Convergence and Local $h_{\mathcal{L}}$-Clustering

For an starting vector $\boldsymbol{\mu}$, let $\theta_{t,\boldsymbol{\mu}}[i]$ denote the value of the dynamics of vertex $i \in V$ at time t when the initial vector is $\boldsymbol{\mu}$. In other words, $\boldsymbol{\theta}_{t,\boldsymbol{\mu}} = (\theta_{t,\boldsymbol{\mu}}[1], ..., \theta_{t,\boldsymbol{\mu}}[n])$ is the solution of Eq. 4 with $\boldsymbol{\theta}_0 = \boldsymbol{\mu}$.

Let $\boldsymbol{\pi} = (\pi[1], ..., \pi[n])$ denote

$$\boldsymbol{\pi} = \left(\sqrt{d_{\boldsymbol{W}1}\tau_1}, ..., \sqrt{d_{\boldsymbol{W}n}\tau_n}\right).$$

If the dynamic process converges when starting from $\boldsymbol{\mu}$, then $\lim_{t\to\infty} \boldsymbol{\theta}_{t,\boldsymbol{\mu}}$ is proportional to $\boldsymbol{\pi}$, i.e., for a constant z depending only on $\boldsymbol{\mu}$,

$$\lim_{t\to\infty} \theta_{t,\boldsymbol{\mu}}[i] = z_{\boldsymbol{\mu}} \cdot \pi[i] = z_{\boldsymbol{\mu}} \cdot \sqrt{d_{\boldsymbol{W}i}\tau_i}. \tag{13}$$

We will also use $\boldsymbol{\pi}_{\boldsymbol{\mu}}$ to denote $\lim_{t\to\infty} \boldsymbol{\theta}_{t,\boldsymbol{\mu}}$.

In this spirit, we define the *fractional volume* of a subset $S \subseteq V$ be $\text{fvol}_{\mathcal{L}}(S) = \sum_{j\in S} \sqrt{d_{\boldsymbol{W}j}\tau_j}$. Following the analysis of Theorem 1, let $\tau_{min} = \min_i \tau_i$, $\tau_{max} = \max_i \tau_i$ and $\boldsymbol{\mu}_S[i] = \frac{\sqrt{d_{\boldsymbol{W}i}\tau_i}}{\sum_j \sqrt{d_{\boldsymbol{W}j}\tau_j}}$ for $i \in S$ and is 0 otherwise. Like in the traditional Laplacian-conductance framework, we will establish that the existence of a community $S \subset V$ with small $h_{\mathcal{L}}(S)$ underscores why the dynamics may not converge rapidly from the inital distribution.

We examine the evolution of the dynamics defined by a network $G = (V, E, \boldsymbol{A})$ and a spreading operator $\mathcal{L}$. Particularly, we are interested in estimating the rate that the dynamic process converges to its stationary distribution from some initial distribution, and its relation to the generalized conductance $h_{\mathcal{L}}$ that we defined (Eqn. (7)). As each dynamic process leads to its own notion of (time-dependent) centrality, we will study and compare the corresponding community structures by its generalized conductance.

Our local clustering algorithm (Algorithm 2) explores this interplay. Here we assume the starting vector $\boldsymbol{\mu}_u$ is seeded in a single node u, i.e., it has a single one entry for node u, and other entries are all zeros. Next theorem provides a performance guarantee for the local algorithm.

THEOREM 4 (LOCAL $h_{\mathcal{L}}$-CLUSTERING). *For any $0 \le \phi \le 1$, suppose S is a subset in a interaction graph $G = (V, E, \boldsymbol{W})$ with $\text{vol}_{\mathcal{L}}(S) \le \frac{1}{12} \cdot \frac{\tau_{min}}{\tau_{max}} \cdot \text{vol}_{\mathcal{L}}(V)$ and $h_{\mathcal{L}}(S) \le \phi^2$. Then, there exists a subset $S_S \subseteq S$ with $\text{fvol}_{\mathcal{L}}(S_S) \ge \text{fvol}_{\mathcal{L}}(S)/4$ such that for any $u \in S_S$, Algorithm 2 with $s \ge 2\text{fvol}_{\mathcal{L}}(S)$ and $\epsilon = \phi^2 \cdot \frac{\tau_{min}}{\tau_{max}} \cdot \frac{1}{10\cdot s}$ will in time $O\left(s\phi^{-2} \cdot \frac{\tau_{max}}{\tau_{min}} \cdot \log n\right)$ return a set S_S with the properties that (1) the conductance of S_S is at most $O\left((1+\epsilon)\phi \cdot \sqrt{\log s + \log \frac{\tau_{max}}{\tau_{min}}}\right)$ and (2) $\text{fvol}(S_S) \le 2s$.*

Theorem 4 follows from our proofs in the following subsection 3 together with Andersen-Chung-Lang's analysis [2] of the push-based approximation scheme. Similar to its global counterpart in Theorem 3, Theorem 4 uses Theorem 2 in place of Theorem 1 to address the approximation of the dynamic process. During the approximate dynamic process with the Andersen-Chung-Lang push scheme, only $O(1/\epsilon)$ nodes have non-zero entries.

Algorithm 2 Local $h_{\mathcal{L}}$-Clustering$(G, \mathcal{L}, u, \phi, s, \epsilon)$

Input: Network: $G = (V, E, \boldsymbol{A})$, spreading operator $\mathcal{L}$ defined by the interaction matrix $\boldsymbol{W}$ and the node delay factor $\boldsymbol{T}$. The starting node: u, quality bound: ϕ, targeted fractional volume: s, and rounding approximation ϵ

Output: subset S_S

Algorithm

1. Set $t = \phi^{-2} \cdot \tau_{min} \cdot \log 2$.
2. Apply the push-based approximation scheme of Andersen-Chung-Lang [2] with rounding parameter ϵ to find an approximation $\tilde{\boldsymbol{\theta}}_{t,u,\epsilon}$ to $\boldsymbol{\theta}(t, u) = e^{-\mathcal{L}t}\boldsymbol{\mu}_u$ and adaptively maintain the set $\tilde{V}_\epsilon = \{v : \tilde{\theta}_{t,u,\epsilon}[v] > 0\}$.
3. Order the vertices of $\tilde{V}_\epsilon$ into $\{v_1, v_2, \cdots\}$ such that $\frac{\theta_{t,u}[v_1]}{\sqrt{d_{\boldsymbol{W}1}\tau_1}} \ge \frac{\theta_{t,u}[v_2]}{\sqrt{d_{\boldsymbol{W}2}\tau_2}} \ge \cdots \ge \frac{\theta_{t,u}[v_n]}{\sqrt{d_{\boldsymbol{W}n}\tau_n}}$
4. Sweeping: For each $S_i = S_{t,u}[i] = \{v_1, ..., v_i\}$ such that $\text{fvol}S_i \le 2s$, compute
$$h_{\mathcal{L}}(S_i) = \frac{\text{cut}(S_i, \bar{S}_i)}{\min\left(\text{vol}_{\mathcal{L}}(S_i), \text{vol}_{\mathcal{L}}(\bar{S}_i)\right)}.$$
5. Output the S_i with the smallest $h_{\mathcal{L}}(S_i)$.

4.2 Rate of Convergence and Local Sweeping

Define $\Theta_{t,\boldsymbol{\mu}}(S) = \sum_{i\in S} \theta_{t,\boldsymbol{\mu}}[i]\sqrt{\frac{d_{\boldsymbol{W}i}}{\tau_i}}$. We first establish a lemma showing that while the quantity $\Theta_{t,\boldsymbol{\mu}}(S)$ is reducing during every step of the dynamic process, the derivative depends on the generalized volume of S, and is bounded by a factor proportional to the generalized conductance $h_{\mathcal{L}}(S)$ of S given by Eqn. (7).

LEMMA 1. *For $S \subset V$ with $\text{fvol}_{\mathcal{L}}(S) \le \text{fvol}_{\mathcal{L}}(V)/2$ we have $\frac{d\Theta_{t,\boldsymbol{\mu}}(S)}{dt} \le 0$. Moreover, $\left|\frac{d\Theta_{t,\boldsymbol{\mu}}(S)}{dt}\right| \le \frac{h_{\mathcal{L}}(S)}{\tau_{min}}$.*

Lemma 1 then provides a lower bound on the fractional volume of a subset $S_S \subset S$ from whom the dynamic process does not converge rapidly. Let $\boldsymbol{\theta}_{t,u}$ denote $\boldsymbol{\theta}_{t,\boldsymbol{\mu}_u}$, $\boldsymbol{\pi}_u$ denote $\boldsymbol{\pi}_{\boldsymbol{\mu}_u}$, $\Theta_{t,u}(S) = \Theta_{t,\boldsymbol{\mu}_u}(S)$.

COROLLARY 1. *For any subset $S \subset V$ in a interaction graph $G = (V, E, \boldsymbol{W})$, let*

$$S_S = \left\{u \in S : \Theta_{t,u}(S) \ge \frac{1}{4} \cdot \Theta_{0,u}(S) \cdot e^{-\frac{1}{\tau_{min}} \cdot h_{\mathcal{L}}(S) t}\right\}.$$

If $t \ge \frac{\tau_{min}}{h_{\mathcal{L}}(S)}$ then $\text{fvol}_{\mathcal{L}}(S_S) \ge \text{fvol}_{\mathcal{L}}(S)/4$.

Following the intuition of the proof of the extended Cheeger inequality (Theorem 1) and the traditional Laplacian analysis [17, 26, 8, 7], we consider a sweeping process based on the time-dependent centrality with starting vertex u. At time t, the sweeping is performed according to

$$\frac{\theta_{t,u}[v_1]}{\sqrt{d_{\boldsymbol{W}1}\tau_1}} \ge \frac{\theta_{t,u}[v_2]}{\sqrt{d_{\boldsymbol{W}2}\tau_2}} \ge \cdots \ge \frac{\theta_{t,u}[v_n]}{\sqrt{d_{\boldsymbol{W}n}\tau_n}}$$

by considering $S_{t,u}[i] = \{v_1, \cdots, v_i\}$. Like in Chung [6], for a targeted size s, we define the *s-local $h_{\mathcal{L}}$-value* denoted by $\kappa_{t,u,s}$ as: $\kappa_{t,u,s} = \min_{i:\text{fvol}_{\mathcal{L}}(S_{t,u}[i])\le 2s} h_{\mathcal{L}}(S_{t,u}[i])$.

LEMMA 2. *For any subset $S \subset V$ in a interaction graph $G = (V, E, \boldsymbol{W})$ of fractional volume $s = \text{fvol}_{\mathcal{L}}(S) \leq \text{fvol}_{\mathcal{L}}(V)/4$, we have*

$$\Theta_{t,u}(S) - \Pi_u(S) \leq \frac{1}{\tau_{min}} \text{fvol}_{\mathcal{L}}(S) \cdot e^{-t\frac{\kappa_{t,u,s}^2}{4}}. \quad (14)$$

.

The following lemma is a consequence of Lemma 2 and Corollary 1, which ultimately leads to Theorem 4.

LEMMA 3 (LOCAL $h_{\mathcal{L}}$-SWEEPING). *For any $0 \leq \phi \leq 1$, suppose S is a subset in a interaction graph $G = (V, E, \boldsymbol{W})$ with $\text{vol}_{\mathcal{L}}(S) \leq \frac{1}{12} \cdot \frac{\tau_{min}}{\tau_{max}} \cdot \text{vol}_{\mathcal{L}}(V)$ and $h_{\mathcal{L}}(S) \leq \phi^2$. Then, there exists a subset $S_S \subseteq S$ with $\text{fvol}(S_S) \geq \text{fvol}(S)/4$ such that for any $u \in S_S$, the sweeping by using the vector $\boldsymbol{\theta}_{t,u}$ with $t = O(\phi^{-2} \cdot \tau_{min})$ will find a set S_S with s-local $h_{\mathcal{L}}$-value at most $O\left(\phi \cdot \sqrt{\log s + \log(\tau_{max}/\tau_{min})}\right)$.*

5. EXPERIMENTS

Through experiments we demonstrate the difference in the centralities and communities detected in a graph under different dynamic processes. Interestingly, even this simple class of processes can lead to divergent views about who the central nodes are and what are the cohesive clusters for a collection of widely studied real-world networks.

We study how the dynamic processes defined in this paper affect centrality and spectral partitioning. Our framework actually offers more freedom in designing node delay factor $\boldsymbol{T}$ and the interaction graph $\boldsymbol{W}$ and is thus a much more powerful tool. We will study these possibilities in greater detail and use the proposed local clustering algorithm for real-world applications in future work.

Table 1 lists the networks we study empirically, and their properties. We treat all networks as undirected. These networks come from different domains, and embody a variety of dynamic processes and interactions, from real world friendships (Zachary karate club [30]), to social network (Facebook [18]), to electrical power distribution (Power Grid [28]), to intra-text (Word Adjacency [19]) and inter-text (Political Blogs [1]) links.

The House of Representatives network is built from the 98th United States House of Representatives voting data [21]. Unlike the previously studied variants, here we use a special version taking account of all 908 votes. The resulting network is dense and has an unusually flat degree distribution. Originally analyzed by Smith et al. [24], this network better differentiates between the dynamics under our framework.

5.1 Centrality Profiles

We first study node (stationary) centrality rankings resulting from different dynamic processes. By construction, centrality of a node converges to Eq. 5. Given a graph, the degree sequence is fixed, and stationary centrality depends solely on the node delay factor $\boldsymbol{T}$. A centrality profile is a curve of stationary centrality values for each node given a spreading operator. Figure 1 shows the *centrality profiles* of network nodes. To improve visualization, nodes are ordered by their centrality according to the normalized Laplacian matrix, and they are rescaled to fall within the same range.

Except for "House of Representatives" and "Power Grid" networks, the centrality profiles on the other four data sets are very similar. They all have heavy-tailed degree distributions, thus their centralities under the normalized Laplacian

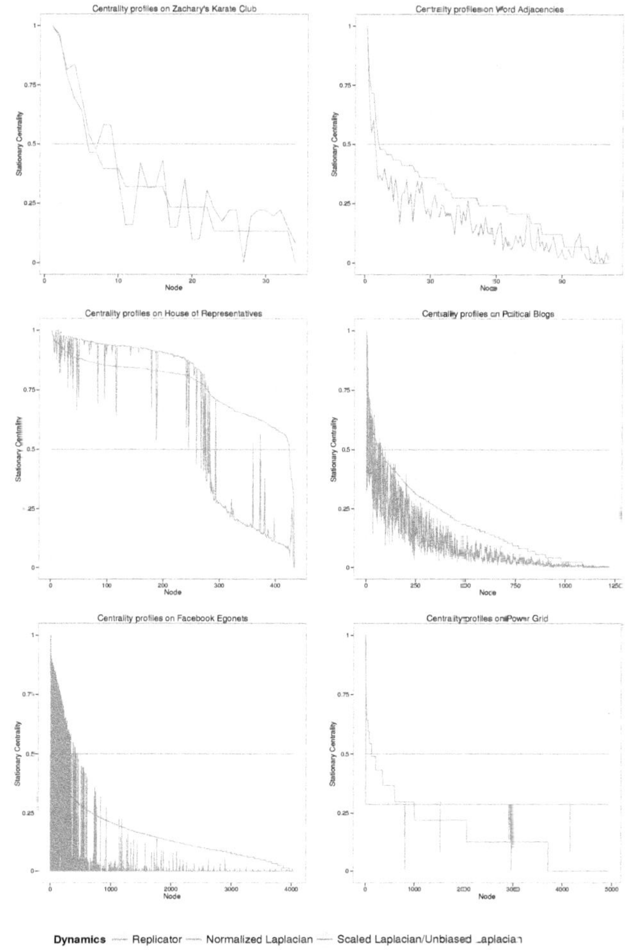

Figure 1: Centrality profiles for different networks
Comparison of stationary centrality on all six networks. The x-axes represent node indices which has been fixed for all dynamics on each network in descending order of the "Normalized Laplacian" centrality. On the y-axes, the convergent centrality has been normalized to the interval [0,1] for all dynamics on all networks.

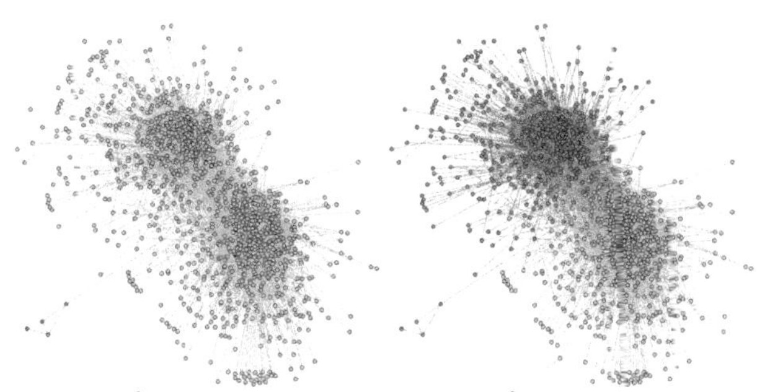

Figure 2: Optimal bisections for $\mathcal{L}$ (left) and $\boldsymbol{R}$ (right) on Political Blogs
Laplacian has the exact same bisection as Normalized Laplacian, while Unbiased Adjacency leads to similar results as Replicator. Notice the correspondence to their sweep profiles.

Table 1: Specifications of benchmark networks

Name	*#nodes*	*#edges*	*Diameter*	*Clustering*	*Properties*
Zachary's Karate Club	34	78	5	0.588	A toy social network
Word Adjacency	112	425	5	0.19	A disassortative network
House of Representatives	434	51033	4	0.882	A dense network with even degrees
Political Blogs	1490	16714	9	0.21	Has two "cores" with "whiskers"
Facebook Egonets	4039	88234	17	0.303	Combined ego networks
Power Grid	4941	6594	46	0.107	A large sparse network

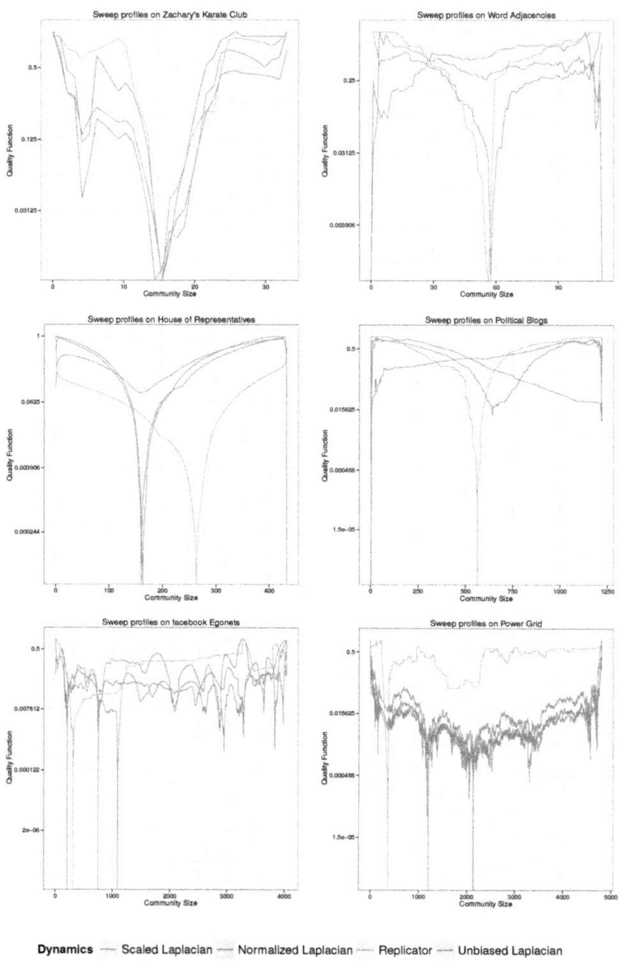

Figure 3: Sweep profiles for different networks *Sweep profiles produced according to Algorithm 1 on all six networks. The x-axes indicate the sweep point, or community size of one of the bi-sections. On the logarithmic y-axes, the quality function has been normalized to the same range for all dynamics on each network.*

behave similarly. Replicator centralities follow largely the same trend. There are important differences, however. For example, in the "House of Representatives" network, nodes in the range $[1, 50]$ considered to be highly central according to the normalized Laplacian are judged not as important by the Replicator. Since centralities and communities are closely related under our framework, this would eventually lead to the differences in community detection, as we show in the next subsection. The centrality scores of nodes in the "Power Grid" network are all the same except for a few nodes. The lack of information comes from the extreme sparsity of the network.

5.2 Communities and Sweep Profiles

We use the *sweep profile* to study differences in network partitioning using different spreading operators for the real world networks listed in Table 1. Given a spreading operator, a sweep profile is a curve of quality functions following Algorithm 1. Let $\boldsymbol{f}$ be the eigenvector associated with the second smallest eigenvalue of $\boldsymbol{\mathcal{L}}$. The vertices are ordered $(v_1, ..., v_n)$ such that $g[v_1] \geq ... \geq g[v_n]$ where $g[u] = f[u]/\sqrt{d_{\mathbf{W}_u} \tau_u}$. The x-axis plots $S_i = \{v_1, ..., v_i\}$. The y-axis plots

$$h_{\boldsymbol{\mathcal{L}}}(S_i) = \frac{\text{cut}(S_i, \bar{S}_i)}{\min\left(\text{vol}_{\boldsymbol{\mathcal{L}}}(S_i), \text{vol}_{\boldsymbol{\mathcal{L}}}(\bar{S}_i)\right)}.$$

The smallest $h_{\boldsymbol{\mathcal{L}}}(S_i)$ gives a provably good cluster S_i according to Theorem 3.

Figure 3 shows the sweep profile for each network under different dynamics. To improve visualization, we rescale community profiles to lie within the same range. Sweep profiles provide us an interesting perspective into the differences in the communities identified according to different dynamics. With the exception of Zachary's karate club, there are large differences both in the shape of the profile and, more importantly, in the location of its minimum, which corresponds to the optimal bisection of the network.

In the "Political Blogs" network, both regular and normalized versions of Laplacian split a "whisker" community from the core (Left of Figure 2). However, the Replicator identifies a community of more than 500 nodes (Right of Figure 2). While Replicator is less susceptible to "whiskers", on the "Power Grid" and "Facebook Egonets" networks, it only identifies small communities within the "core". Instead, unbiased Laplacian succeeds in finding more balanced cuts of the networks. In the "House of Representatives" network, the Replicator puts "swing nodes" into a different community from the other operators. Recall that this difference was also reflected in its centrality profiles. In future work, we plan to analyze the reasons behind these differences in more detail and in a dynamic setting.

6. CONCLUSION

The dynamics of a process occurring on a network can be succinctly described in terms of a spreading operator. The generalized Laplacian operator presented in this paper can describe the spreading operators associated with known processes, such as random walks and epidemics, but also new ones, such as the unbiased Laplacian. We generalize the relationships between the properties of random walks and normalized graph Laplacian, to other dynamic processes. Each operator leads to a distribution that gives centrality of nodes with respect to that process. In addition, we show that the generalized conductance measuring community quality with respect to the dynamic process is related to the eigenvalues of the spreading operator describing that process through a Cheeger-like inequality. These relationships can be used for spectral graph partitioning. Nodes within the same partition interact more with each other via the dynamic process than with nodes in other partitions. As in previous local clustering algorithms of Spielman-Teng, Andersen-Chung-Lang and Andersen-Peres [26, 3, 2], the mathematical structure underlying the generalized Cheeger's inequality enables efficient local clustering algorithms for the more general community qualities, whose running time is essentially linear in the size of the cluster it outputs, and does not depend on the size of the whole graph.

While our framework is flexible enough to represent several important types of dynamic processes, it does not represent all possible processes, for example, those that are locally non-conservative. In order to describe such dynamics an even more general framework is needed. We conjecture, however, that the more general spreading operators will still obey the Cheeger-like inequality, and that other theorems presented in this paper can be extended to these processes.

Acknowledgments

This work is partly supported by grants NSF CIF-1217605, AFCSR-MURI FA9550-10-1-0569, AFRL FA-8750-12-2-0186, DARPA W911NF-12-1-0034, NSF CCF-0964481, and NSF CCF-1111270.

7. REFERENCES

[1] L. A. Adamic and N. Glance. The political blogosphere and the 2004 US election: divided they blog. In *Proceedings of the 3rd international workshop on Link discovery*, pages 36–43. ACM, 2005.

[2] R. Andersen, F. Chung, and K. Lang. Using PageRank to Locally Partition a Graph. *Internet Math.*, 4(1):1–128, 2007.

[3] R. Andersen and Y. Peres. Finding Sparse Cuts Locally Using Evolving Sets. In *STOC*, pages 235–244. ACM, 2009.

[4] P. Bonacich and P. Lloyd. Eigenvector-like measures of centrality for asymmetric relations. *Social Networks*, 23(3):191–201, 2001.

[5] S. Borgatti. Centrality and network flow. *Social Networks*, 27(1):55–71, Jan. 2005.

[6] F. Chung. The heat kernel as the pagerank of a graph. *Proceedings of the National Academy of Sciences*, 104(50):19735–19740, Dec. 2007.

[7] F. Chung. A local graph partitioning algorithm using heat kernel pagerank. *Internet Mathematics*, 6(3):315–330, Jan. 2009.

[8] F. R. K. Chung. *Spectral Graph Theory (CBMS Regional Conference Series in Mathematics, No. 92)*. American Mathematical Society, Feb. 1997.

[9] J.-C. Delvenne, S. N. Yaliraki, and M. Barahona. Stability of graph communities across time scales. *ArXiv e-prints*, Dec. 2008.

[10] R. Ghosh and K. Lerman. Parameterized centrality metric for network analysis. *Physical Review E*, 83(6):066118, June 2011.

[11] M. Jerrum and A. Sinclair. Conductance and the rapid mixing property for Markov chains: the approximation of permanent resolved. In *STOC*, pages 235–244. ACM, 1988.

[12] R. Kannan, S. Vempala, and A. Vetta. On Clusterings: Good, Bad and Spectral. *J. ACM*, 51(3):497–515, May 2004.

[13] D. Kempe, J. Kleinberg, and E. Tardos. Maximizing the spread of influence through a social network. In *KDD '03*, pages 137–146. ACM, 2003.

[14] I. Koutis, G. L. Miller, and R. Peng. Approaching Optimality for Solving SDD Linear Systems. In *FOCS*, pages 235–244. IEEE, 2010.

[15] R. Lambiotte, R. Sinatra, J.-C. Delvenne, T. S. Evans, M. Barahona, and V. Latora. Flow graphs: Interweaving dynamics and structure. \pre, 84(1):017102, July 2011.

[16] K. Lerman and R. Ghosh. Network Structure, Topology and Dynamics in Generalized Models of Synchronization. *Physical Review E*, 86(026108), 2012.

[17] L. Lovász. *Random Walks on Graphs: A Survey*, pages 353–397. 1993.

[18] J. J. McAuley and J. Leskovec. Learning to Discover Social Circles in Ego Networks. In *NIPS*, volume 272, pages 548–556, 2012.

[19] M. E. J. Newman. Finding community structer in networks using the eigenvectors of matrices. *Physical Review E*, 74(3), 2006.

[20] L. Page, S. Brin, R. Motwani, and T. Winograd. The pagerank citation ranking: Bringing order to the web, 1999.

[21] K. Poole. Voteview Website. `http://voteview.com/house98.htm`.

[22] M. Rosvall and C. T. Bergstrom. Maps of random walks on complex networks reveal community structure. *Proceedings of the National Academy of Sciences*, 105(4):1118–1123, Jan. 2008.

[23] J. Shi and J. Malik. Normalized Cuts and Image Segmentation. *IEEE Transactions on Pattern Analysis and Machine Intelligence*, 22(8):888–905, 2000.

[24] L. M. Smith, K. Lerman, C. Garcia-Cardona, A. G. Percus, and R. Ghosh. Spectral Clustering with Epidemic Diffusion. *CoRR*, abs/1303.2663, 2013.

[25] D. A. Spielman and S.-H. Teng. Spectral partitioning works: Planar graphs and finite element meshes. In *IEEE FOCS*, pages 96–105, 1996.

[26] D. A. Spielman and S.-H. Teng. Nearly-linear Time Algorithms for Graph Partitioning, Graph Sparsification, and Solving Linear Systems. In *STOC*, pages 81–90. ACM, 2004.

[27] Y. Wang, D. Chakrabarti, C. Wang, and C. Faloutsos. Epidemic spreading in real networks: an eigenvalue viewpoint. In *Proceedings of the 22nd Symposium on Reliable Distributed Systems*, pages 25–34, Los Alamitos, CA, USA, Oct. 2003. IEEE.

[28] D. J. Watts and S. H. Strogatz. Collective dynamics of 'small-world'networks. *nature*, 393(6684):440–442, 1998.

[29] M. A. Yildirim, K.-I. Goh, M. E. Cusick, A.-L. Barabasi, and M. Vidal. Drug-target network. *Nat Biotech*, 25:1119–1126, Oct. 2007.

[30] W. W. Zachary. An Information Flow Model for Conflict and Fission in Small Groups. *Journal of Anthropological Research*, 33(4):452–473, 1977.

Almost Linear-Time Algorithms for Adaptive Betweenness Centrality using Hypergraph Sketches

Yuichi Yoshida
National Institute of Informatics, and
Preferred Infrastructure, Inc.
yyoshida@nii.ac.jp

ABSTRACT

Betweenness centrality measures the importance of a vertex by quantifying the number of times it acts as a midpoint of the shortest paths between other vertices. This measure is widely used in network analysis. In many applications, we wish to choose the k vertices with the maximum adaptive betweenness centrality, which is the betweenness centrality without considering the shortest paths that have been taken into account by already-chosen vertices.

All previous methods are designed to compute the betweenness centrality in a fixed graph. Thus, to solve the above task, we have to run these methods k times. In this paper, we present a method that directly solves the task, with an almost linear runtime no matter how large the value of k. Our method first constructs a hypergraph that encodes the betweenness centrality, and then computes the adaptive betweenness centrality by examining this graph. Our technique can be utilized to handle other centrality measures.

We theoretically prove that our method is very accurate, and experimentally confirm that it is three orders of magnitude faster than previous methods. Relying on the scalability of our method, we experimentally demonstrate that strategies based on adaptive betweenness centrality are effective in important applications studied in the network science and database communities.

Categories and Subject Descriptors

E.1 [**Data**]: Data Structures—*Graphs and networks*

Keywords

Adaptive betweenness centrality; Adaptive coverage centrality; Randomized algorithm

1. INTRODUCTION

The *centrality* of a vertex measures its relative importance within a graph. There is no unique way of measuring the importance of vertices. In fact, many criteria of a vertex have been used to define its centrality, such as its degree, distance to other vertices, and its eigenvalue [4].

In this paper, we consider centralities based on shortest paths. The most famous such centrality is the *(shortest-path) betweenness centrality*, which quantifies the number of times a vertex acts as a midpoint of the shortest paths between other vertices [12]. Betweenness centrality has been extensively used in network analysis, such as for measuring lethality in biological networks [17, 10], studying sexual networks and AIDS [20], and identifying key actors in terrorist networks [18, 9]. Betweenness centrality is also used as a primary routine for clustering and community identification in real-world networks [23, 15].

We also study the *(shortest-path) coverage centrality*, which measures the importance of a vertex by counting the number of pairs of vertices with a shortest path passing through it. Coverage centrality naturally arises in the study of indexing methods for determining shortest-path distances [2, 25, 1].

Although computing the betweenness centrality and coverage centrality is already quite costly, in many applications, we want to compute these centralities in an iterative way. Consider the problem of suppressing epidemics with immunization [16]. In this problem, a vertex is infected by a disease, and the disease spreads to other vertices under some stochastic process. We have a limited number k of vaccines, and the task is to find an effective strategy to vaccinate vertices to suppress the epidemic. For this task, it is known that greedily choosing k vertices with the maximum adaptive betweenness centrality often shows a good performance [16]. Here, the *adaptive betweenness centrality* denotes the betweenness centrality without considering the shortest paths that have been taken into account by already-chosen vertices.

In the indexing method for determining shortest-path distances proposed by [2], it is desirable to compute the vertex ordering obtained by greedily taking vertices with the maximum adaptive coverage centrality, where *adaptive coverage centrality* is defined analogously.

An obvious drawback of using the top-k vertices, or the vertex ordering with respect to adaptive centrality, is that obtaining these is computationally expensive. Indeed, the fastest exact methods for computing the top-k vertices with respect to adaptive betweenness and coverage centrality take $O(knm)$ time and $O(kn^2m)$ time, respectively, where n is the number of vertices and m is the number of edges. To ameliorate this issue, faster randomized approximation algorithms have been proposed for the betweenness centrality [8, 7, 14, 24]. However, because we must run the al-

KDD'14, August 24–27, 2014, New York, NY, USA.
Copyright 2014 ACM 978-1-4503-2956-9/14/08 ...$15.00.
http://dx.doi.org/10.1145/2623330.2623626.

gorithm k times to obtain the top-k vertices, we still need at least $\Omega(k(n+m))$ time. Hence, the effectiveness of the top-k vertices and the vertex ordering with respect to adaptive centrality has only been confirmed for small graphs, and dealing with larger graphs remains a challenging problem.

1.1 Our contributions

The main contribution of this paper is to present an algorithm that approximately computes the vertex ordering (and hence the top-k vertices) with respect to the adaptive betweenness and coverage centrality in almost linear time. This is remarkable, as finding the (single) vertex with the maximum centrality requires linear time.

Let us explain the idea of our algorithm using the coverage centrality. In this paper, we only consider undirected and unweighted graphs, but it is fairly straightforward to extend our result for directed and weighted graphs. For a graph $G = (V, E)$, the (shortest-path) coverage centrality of a vertex $v \in V$ is defined as

$$C(v) = \#\{(s,t) \in V \times V \mid v \in P_{st}\},$$

where P_{st} is the set of all vertices on shortest paths between s and t. In other words, $C(v)$ is the number of pairs such that some shortest path between them goes through v. For a vertex v and a vertex set $S \subseteq V$, the *adaptive coverage centrality (ACC) of v conditioned on (having chosen) S* is defined as

$$C(v \mid S) = \#\{(s,t) \in V \times V \mid v \in P_{st}, P_{st} \cap S = \emptyset\}.$$

Hence, we ignore pairs (s,t) if some shortest path between them is already covered by a vertex in S. Note that $C(v) = C(v \mid \emptyset)$ for any v. Our goal is to keep choosing vertices with the maximum ACC conditioned on the set of already-chosen vertices.

To this end, we construct a hypergraph H, which we call the *hypergraph sketch*, that encodes all information for estimating ACC as follows. First, we randomly sample $M = \Theta(\log n/\epsilon^2)$ pairs of vertices, where ϵ is an error parameter. For each sampled pair (s,t), we add to H a hyperedge with the vertex set P_{st}. Then, our algorithm for obtaining the vertex ordering is very simple: we keep choosing vertices with the maximum degree in the hypergraph after removing the hyperedges incident to already-chosen vertices. The runtime of this algorithm is almost linear, and we have a good accuracy if M is chosen to be sufficiently large.

Our idea is applicable for obtaining the vertex ordering based on the adaptive betweenness centrality. For a graph $G = (V, E)$, the (shortest-path) betweenness centrality of a vertex $v \in V$ is defined as

$$B(v) = \sum_{s,t \in V \setminus \{v\}} \frac{\sigma_{st}(v)}{\sigma_{st}},$$

where σ_{st} is the number of shortest paths between s and t, and $\sigma_{st}(v)$ is the number of shortest paths between s and t going through v. For a vertex $v \in V$ and a vertex set $S \subseteq V$, the *adaptive betweenness centrality (ABC) of v conditioned on (having chosen) S* is defined as

$$B(v \mid S) = \sum_{s,t \in V \setminus \{v\}} \frac{\sigma_{st}(v \mid S)}{\sigma_{st}},$$

where $\sigma_{st}(v \mid S)$ is the number of shortest paths between s and t passing through v, but not passing through any vertex in S. Our goal is to keep choosing vertices with the maximum ABC conditioned on the set of already-chosen vertices. Though we can use the hypergraph sketch again, the algorithm becomes more involved than the case of ACC, because we must impose weights on the vertices and update them each time we choose a vertex. However, the resulting runtime remains almost linear.

For both centralities, we prove that our method has a high probability of estimating the adaptive centrality of any vertex with additive error of ϵn^2. This additive error should not be critical in most applications, as numerous real-world graphs actually have vertices of centrality $\Theta(n^2)$, and it often suffices to obtain the correct ordering among these.

For both centralities, we can define the centrality of a vertex set, and our method can be seen as an approximation of the problem of finding a set of k vertices with the maximum centrality. We prove that our method has almost the same approximation ratio as the exact greedy method, which is known to work quite well in practice. Hence, the quality of the output of our method should be very high.

We also empirically show that our method runs two or three orders of magnitude faster than previous methods.

Now that we have a method to obtain the vertex ordering based on adaptive centrality, we investigate the two applications mentioned before: suppressing epidemics with immunizations, and constructing indices for determining shortest-path distances. Our experiments demonstrate that the strategy based on vertex ordering with respect to adaptive centrality shows a better performance than other heuristic strategies in large graphs, which we have not been able to confirm due to the prohibitively large runtime of previous methods.

1.2 Related work

As we have mentioned, there are plenty of studies on computing the betweenness centrality. Currently, the fastest known algorithm for exactly computing the betweenness centralities of all the vertices is that proposed by Brandes [6], which first solves the single-source shortest-path problem (SSSP) from every vertex. An SSSP computation from a vertex s produces a directed acyclic graph (DAG) encoding all shortest paths starting at s. By backward aggregation, the contributions of these paths to the betweenness centrality can be computed in linear time. In total, Brandes' algorithm runs in $O(nm)$ time for unweighted graphs, and $O(nm + n^2 \log m)$ time for weighted graphs.

Brandes and Pich [8] investigated how the exact algorithm can be turned into an approximation algorithm by sampling a small set of vertices, from which we solve the SSSP. A random sample of starting vertices turns out to work well. To obtain better accuracy and runtime, several sampling and aggregation methods have been studied [14, 3, 24]. However, none of these methods is sufficiently fast when we wish to obtain the vertex ordering based on the adaptive centrality.

Lee et al. [19] considered the problem of updating the betweenness centrality when the graph changes. However, their method is not sufficiently fast to handle large graphs, say, millions of vertices.

Borgs et al. [5] considered the problem of *influence maximization*. In this problem, vertices are iteratively influenced by neighbors under some stochastic process, and the objective is to find a seed set of k vertices that maximizes the expected number of influenced vertices at the end of the process. To efficiently implement a greedy algorithm, they proposed a method that constructs a hypergraph so that the degree of a vertex represents its influence. Though their method has a similar flavor to ours, we consider completely unrelated problems.

1.3 Organization

We first explain our method for ACC, and present its theoretical analysis in Section 2, because this is much simpler than for ABC. We then proceed to ABC in Section 3. In Section 4, we empirically demonstrate the accuracy and runtime of our method. Section 5 is devoted to confirming the effectiveness of the vertex ordering based on adaptive centrality using the two applications.

Notations.

For a given graph, we always use the symbols n and m to denote the number of vertices and edges, respectively.

2. ADAPTIVE COVERAGE CENTRALITY

We formalize the problem of computing the top-k vertices with respect to ACC. Let $G = (V, E)$ be a graph. For two vertices s and t, let P_{st} be the set of all vertices on any shortest path between s and t. By orienting the edges in P_{st} according to the distance from s, we can obtain a DAG rooted at s. We often identify P_{st} with this DAG. We say that a pair (s,t) is *covered* by a vertex $v \in V$ if $v \in P_{st}$. Similarly, we say that a pair (s,t) is *covered* by a vertex set $S \subseteq V$ if $S \cap P_{st} \neq \emptyset$. In other words, (s,t) is covered by v (resp., S) if some shortest path between s and t goes through v (resp., some vertex in S).

The *coverage centrality* of a vertex $v \in V$ is

$$C(v) = \#\{(s,t) \in V \times V \mid v \in P_{st}\},$$

which is the number of pairs of vertices (s,t) that is covered by v. We extend the notion to a set of vertices. For a set of vertices $S \subseteq V$, the *coverage centrality* of S is

$$C(S) = \#\{(s,t) \in V \times V \mid S \cap P_{st} \neq \emptyset\},$$

which is the number of pairs of vertices (s,t) covered by S.

Suppose that, given a parameter $k > 0$, we want to find a set of k vertices with the maximum coverage centrality. We call this problem MCC_k, which stands for the maximum coverage centrality problem with parameter k. A natural strategy for MCC_k is to keep choosing vertices that cover the maximum number of pairs that have not been covered by already-chosen vertices. This strategy motivates us to define the following notion. For a vertex v and a vertex set S, we define the *ACC of v conditioned on S* as

$$C(v \mid S) = \{(s,t) \in V \times V \mid v \in P_{st}, S \cap P_{st} = \emptyset\}.$$

Related to this definition, we say that a vertex v *covers* the pair (s,t) conditioned on S if $v \in P_{st}$ and $S \cap P_{st} = \emptyset$. The following proposition is obtained immediately from this definition.

PROPOSITION 2.1. *For any vertex v and vertex set S, we have*

$$C(S \cup \{v\}) = C(S) + C(v \mid S).$$

The greedy strategy keeps choosing vertices with the maximum ACC conditioned on the set of already-chosen vertices, or from Proposition 2.1, we can say that it keeps choosing vertices that maximize the resulting coverage centrality.

Given a set of vertices S, an obvious way to exactly compute $C(v \mid S)$ for all $v \in V$ is the following. First, for each pair (s,t), we obtain P_{st} by performing a breadth-first search (BFS). If P_{st} contains a vertex in S, then the pair is already covered. Otherwise, vertices in P_{st} cover the pair (s,t) conditioned on S. In this way, we can compute $C(v \mid S)$ for all $v \in V$ in $O(n^2 m)$ time. If we want to run the greedy algorithm to obtain a solution for MCC_k, we need $O(kn^2 m)$ time. On the other hand, our method runs in almost linear time, even when $k = n$.

2.1 Proposed method

We describe our method for computing the top-k vertices with respect to ACC. Given a graph $G = (V, E)$, we first build a hypergraph H that encodes all the information needed to compute the ACC as follows. The vertex set of H is V. Given a parameter M, we pick M pairs of vertices at random. Then, for each pair (s,t), we add P_{st} to H as a hyperedge (Algorithm 1). Let $E(H)$ denote the set of hyperedges in H, and for a hyperedge $e \in E(H)$, let $V(e)$ denote the set of vertices incident to e.

The *degree* $d_H(v)$ of a vertex $v \in V$ in H is the number of hyperedges incident to v. Similarly, we define the *degree* $d_H(S)$ of a vertex set $S \subseteq V$ in H as the number of hyperedges incident to S. That is, $d_H(S) = \#\{e \in E(H) \mid V(e) \cap S \neq \emptyset\}$. Note that $d_H(\{v\}) = d_H(v)$.

The following observation is crucial.

LEMMA 2.2. *For any vertex set $S \subseteq V$, we have*

$$\mathop{\mathbf{E}}_{H}[d_H(S)] = \frac{M}{n^2} C(S).$$

PROOF. Each time we sample a pair (s,t), the probability that P_{st} contains a vertex in S is exactly $C(S)/n^2$. Hence, the lemma holds from the additivity of expectation. □

We define $\widetilde{C}(S) = \frac{n^2}{M} d_H(S)$ for a set $S \subseteq V$. Note that $\widetilde{C}(S)$ is a random variable, and its expectation is $C(S)$. We will later show that $d_H(S)$ is highly concentrated on its expectation, and we can use $\widetilde{C}(S)$ as a good approximation to $C(S)$.

We can estimate the coverage centralities of vertices in G using the hypergraph H, and, in particular, find the vertex with the maximum coverage centrality. We now proceed to find the vertex v with the maximum $C(v \mid S)$, given a set S of already-chosen vertices. Note that $C(v \mid S) = C(S \cup \{v\}) - C(S)$ from Proposition 2.1. Hence, we can approximate $C(v \mid S)$ by

$$\begin{aligned}\widetilde{C}(v \mid S) &:= \widetilde{C}(S \cup \{v\}) - \widetilde{C}(S) \\ &= \frac{n^2}{M}(d_H(S \cup \{v\}) - d_H(S)) = \frac{n^2}{M} d_{H-S}(v),\end{aligned}$$

where $H - S$ is the hypergraph obtained from H by removing S and all hyperedges incident to S. With this observation, to estimate $C(v \mid S)$, we can simply use the degree of v in the hypergraph $H - S$. Algorithm 2 describes how to compute the top-k vertices with respect to ACC. We choose $M = O(\log n/\epsilon^2)$ to guarantee the quality of its output.

2.2 Accuracy

In this section, we first show that, for any set of vertices S, $\widetilde{C}(S)$ has a high probability of being a good approximation

Algorithm 1 Build-Coverage-Hypergraph(G, M)

Input: A graph $G = (V, E)$ and an integer $M \geq 1$.

Initialize $H = (V, \emptyset)$.
for $i = 1$ to M **do**
  Pick a pair of vertices (s, t) at random.
  Add a hyperedge with the vertex set P_{st} to H.
return H.

Algorithm 2 Top-k-ACC(G, k)

Input: A graph $G = (V, E)$ and an integer $k \geq 1$.

$M \leftarrow O(\log n/\epsilon^2)$.
$H \leftarrow$ Build-Coverage-Hypergraph(G, M).
for $i = 1$ to k **do**
  $v_i \leftarrow \arg\max_v \{d_H(v)\}$.
  Remove v_i and all hyperedges incident to v_i.
return the set $\{v_1, \ldots, v_k\}$.

to $C(S)$. Then, we examine the quality of the output of Top-k-ACC. We say that an algorithm is an (α, β)*-approximation algorithm* to a maximization problem if, for any instance of the problem, it outputs a solution whose value is at least $\alpha \cdot \mathrm{opt} - \beta$, where opt is the optimal value of the instance. When $\beta = 0$, this is simply called an α*-approximation algorithm.* We will show that Top-k-ACC is a $(1 - 1/e, \epsilon n^2)$-approximation algorithm to MCC$_k$.

To show that $\widetilde{C}(S)$ is a good approximation to $C(S)$, we recall Hoeffding's inequality:

LEMMA 2.3 (HOEFFDING'S INEQUALITY). *Let $X_1, \ldots, X_n$ be independent random variables in $[0, 1]$ and $\overline{X} = \frac{1}{n}\sum_{i=1}^{n} X_i$. Then,*

$$\Pr[|\overline{X} - \mathbf{E}[\overline{X}]| \geq t] \leq 2\exp(-2t^2 n).$$

It is not hard to show that, with high probability over the construction of H, we can estimate the coverage centrality to within a small error:

LEMMA 2.4. *For any set of vertices $S \subseteq V$, we have*

$$\Pr_H\left[|\widetilde{C}(S) - C(S)| \geq \frac{\epsilon n^2}{2}\right] < \frac{1}{n^3}$$

over the construction of the hypergraph H.

PROOF. From Lemma 2.2, we have $\mathbf{E}[\widetilde{C}(S)] = C(S)$. Because $\widetilde{C}(S)$ is the sum of M random variables whose values are in $[0, 1]$, Hoeffding's inequality implies that

$$\begin{aligned}
&\Pr\left[\left|\widetilde{C}(S) - C(S)\right| \geq \frac{\epsilon n^2}{2}\right] \\
&= \Pr\left[\left|\frac{n^2}{M}d_H(S) - \frac{n^2}{M}\mathbf{E}[d_H(S)]\right| \geq \frac{\epsilon n^2}{2}\right] \\
&= \Pr\left[\left|\frac{1}{M}d_H(S) - \mathbf{E}[\frac{1}{M}d_H(S)]\right| \geq \frac{\epsilon}{2}\right] \leq 2\exp\left(-\frac{\epsilon^2 M}{2}\right)
\end{aligned}$$

By choosing $M = 2\log(2n^3)/\epsilon^2 = O(\log n/\epsilon^2)$, we have the desired result. □

Now we show that our method is a $(1-1/e, \epsilon n^2)$-approximation algorithm to MCC$_k$. We note that the problem can be seen as a *monotone submodular function maximization problem.* A function $f : 2^V \to \mathbb{R}$ is called *monotone* if

$$f(S) \leq f(T) \text{ for any } S \subseteq T \subseteq V,$$

and is *submodular* if

$$f(S \cup \{e\}) - f(S) \geq f(T \cup \{e\}) - f(T) \quad \text{for any } S \subseteq T \subseteq V \text{ and } e \in V \setminus T.$$

In the monotone submodular function maximization problem (MSFM for short), we are given a non-negative monotone submodular function $f : 2^V \to \mathbb{R}$ and a parameter k, and the objective is to find a set $S \subseteq V$ of k elements that maximizes $f(S)$. A standard heuristic for this problem is a greedy algorithm, that is, we keep choosing elements v that produce the maximum marginal gain $f(S \cup \{v\}) - f(S)$, where S is the set of already-chosen vertices. The following fact is well known.

LEMMA 2.5 ([21, 22]). *The greedy algorithm is a $(1 - 1/e)$-approximation algorithm to MSFM, and obtaining a better approximation ratio requires an exponential number of queries in $|V|$.*

We can exploit this result to solve MCC$_k$. We need the following properties of coverage centrality

LEMMA 2.6. *The function $C : 2^V \to \mathbb{Z}$ is non-negative, monotone, and submodular.*

PROOF. As non-negativity and monotonicity are clear, we consider the submodularity. Let $S \subseteq T \subseteq V$ and $v \in V$. Then, $C(S \cup \{v\}) - C(S) = C(v \mid S)$ and $C(T \cup \{v\}) - C(T) = C(v \mid T)$. Hence, it suffices to show $C(v \mid S) \geq C(v \mid T)$, but this should be true because the number of pairs newly covered by v is larger when having chosen a smaller set of vertices. □

COROLLARY 2.7. *The greedy algorithm is a $(1 - 1/e)$-approximation algorithm to MCC$_k$.*

Of course, we do not want to run the greedy algorithm on the function C, as evaluating C would take a very long time. Instead, we show that Algorithm 2 has almost the same quality, that is, it is a $(1 - 1/e, \epsilon n^2)$-approximation algorithm. We first show the following.

LEMMA 2.8. *The function $\widetilde{C} : 2^V \to \mathbb{Z}$ is non-negative, monotone, and submodular for any realization of H.*

PROOF. As non-negativity and monotonicity are clear, we consider the submodularity. Let $S \subseteq T \subseteq V$ and $v \in V$. Then, $\widetilde{C}(S \cup \{v\}) - \widetilde{C}(S) = \widetilde{C}(v \mid S)$ and $\widetilde{C}(T \cup \{v\}) - \widetilde{C}(T) = \widetilde{C}(v \mid T)$. Hence, it suffices to show $\widetilde{C}(v \mid S) \geq \widetilde{C}(v \mid T)$, but this should be true because the number of hyperedges newly incident to v is larger when having chosen a smaller set of vertices. □

THEOREM 2.9. *Let $\widetilde{S}$ be the output of Algorithm 2, and S^* be the optimal solution to MCC$_k$. Then, with a probability of at least $1 - 1/n$,*

$$C(\widetilde{S}) \geq \left(1 - \frac{1}{e}\right) C(S^*) - \epsilon n^2.$$

PROOF. Let $\widetilde{S}^* = \arg\max_{S \subseteq V : |S| = k} \widetilde{C}(S)$. By Lemma 2.2, there is a probability of at least $1 - \frac{1}{n^3}$ that $\widetilde{C}(S^*) \geq C(S^*) - \epsilon n^2/2$. In particular, $\widetilde{C}(\widetilde{S}^*) \geq C(S^*) - \epsilon n^2/2$.

Algorithm 2 runs the greedy algorithm on the function $\widetilde{C}$, and outputs the set $\widetilde{S}$. Because $\widetilde{C}$ is a non-negative submodular function by Lemma 2.8, we have $\widetilde{C}(\widetilde{S}) \geq (1 - 1/e)\widetilde{C}(\widetilde{S}^*)$ by Lemma 2.5.

Let $\widetilde{S}_i$ be the set of vertices chosen up to and including the i-th iteration (with $\widetilde{S}_0 = \emptyset$). In particular, $\widetilde{S}_k = \widetilde{S}$. On the i-th iteration, we consider each set of the form $\widetilde{S}_{i-1} \cup \{v\}$, where v is a vertex. There are at most n of these sets, and hence the union bound implies that C and $\widetilde{C}$ differ by at most $\epsilon n^2/2$ on each of these sets, with probability at least $1 - 1/n^2$. In particular, $|\widetilde{C}(\widetilde{S}_i) - C(\widetilde{S}_i)| < \epsilon n^2/2$. Taking the union bound over all iterations, we have that $|\widetilde{C}(\widetilde{S}_k) - C(\widetilde{S}_k)| < \epsilon n^2/2$ with probability at least $1 - 1/n$. Therefore, we have

$$C(\widetilde{S}_k) \geq \widetilde{C}(\widetilde{S}_k) - \frac{\epsilon n^2}{2} \geq \left(1 - \frac{1}{e}\right)\widetilde{C}(\widetilde{S}^*) - \frac{\epsilon n^2}{2}$$
$$\geq \left(1 - \frac{1}{e}\right)C(S^*) - \epsilon n^2$$

conditioned on an event of probability $1 - 1/n$.

□

Hence, there is a high probability that Algorithm 2 outputs a $(1 - 1/e, \epsilon n^2)$-approximation. In Section 4, we will see that the output is close to that of the exact greedy algorithm.

2.3 Runtime

We finally consider the runtime of Algorithm 2.

THEOREM 2.10. *Algorithm 2 can be implemented to run in $O((n + m)\log n/\epsilon^2)$ time.*

PROOF. Build-Coverage-Hypergraph clearly runs in $O((n+m)\log n/\epsilon^2)$ time. For Top-k-ACC, we will maintain a list of vertices sorted by their degree in H; this will enable us to iteratively choose the vertex with the maximum degree in constant time. We need $O(n \log n)$ time for the initial sort. We must bound the time needed to remove an edge from H and correspondingly update the sorted list. The sorted list is implemented as a doubly linked list of groups of vertices, where each group itself is implemented as a doubly linked list containing all vertices of a given degree (with only non-empty groups present). Each edge of H will maintain a list of pointers to its vertices. When an edge is removed, the degree of each vertex in the edge decreases by 1. We modify the list by shifting any decremented vertex to the preceding group (creating new groups and removing empty groups as necessary). The time taken to remove an edge from H and update the sorted list is therefore proportional to the size of the edge. As each edge in H can be removed at most once over all iterations of Top-k-ACC, the total runtime is at most the sum of degrees in H, which is at most $O((n + m)M) = O((n + m)\log n/\epsilon^2)$. □

3. ADAPTIVE BETWEENNESS CENTRALITY

In this section, we describe our method for ABC.

We formalize the problem of computing the top-k vertices with respect to ABC. Let $G = (V, E)$ be a graph. For a vertex $v \in V$, we define the *betweenness centrality* of v as

$$B(v) = \sum_{s,t \in V \setminus \{v\}} \frac{\sigma_{st}(v)}{\sigma_{st}},$$

where σ_{st} is the number of shortest paths between s and t, and $\sigma_{st}(v)$ is the number of shortest paths between s and t passing through v. For a vertex set $S \subseteq V$, we similarly define the *betweenness centrality* of S as

$$B(S) = \sum_{s,t \in V} \frac{\sigma_{st}(S)}{\sigma_{st}},$$

where $\sigma_{st}(S)$ is the number of shortest paths between s and t passing through some vertex in $S \setminus \{s, t\}$. The betweenness centrality of a set is also called the *group betweenness centrality* in [11, 13].

Suppose that, given a parameter $k > 0$, we want to find a set of k vertices with the maximum betweenness centrality. We call this problem MBC_k, which stands for the maximum betweenness centrality problem with parameter k. Similar to the coverage centrality, a natural strategy for MBC_k is to keep choosing vertices v that maximize the resulting betweenness centrality. It is convenient to introduce some definitions. For vertices $v \in V$, $s, t \in V \setminus \{v\}$, and a vertex set $S \subseteq V$, let $\sigma_{st}(v \mid S)$ denote the number of shortest paths passing through v but avoiding all vertices in $S \setminus \{s, t\}$. In particular, $\sigma_{st}(v \mid S)$ is zero when $v \in S$. For a vertex v and a vertex set S, the *ABC of v conditioned on S* is

$$B(v \mid S) = \sum_{s,t \in V \setminus \{v\}} \frac{\sigma_{st}(v \mid S)}{\sigma_{st}}.$$

PROPOSITION 3.1. *For any vertex v and vertex set S, we have*

$$B(S \cup \{v\}) = B(S) + B(v \mid S).$$

PROOF.

$$B(S \cup \{v\}) = \sum_{s,t \in V \setminus \{v\}} \frac{\sigma_{st}(S \cup \{v\})}{\sigma_{st}}$$
$$= \sum_{s,t \in V \setminus \{v\}} \frac{\sigma_{st}(S) + \sigma_{st}(v \mid S)}{\sigma_{st}} = B(S) + B(v \cup S). \quad \square$$

By Proposition 3.1, we can say that the greedy strategy keeps choosing vertices v that maximize the ABC conditioned on the set of already-chosen vertices.

For a vertex set S, we can exactly compute $B(v \mid S)$ for all v simultaneously using the following variant of Brandes' algorithm [6]. For $s \in V \setminus \{v\}$, let $\delta_s(v \mid S) = \sum_{t \neq v} \frac{\sigma_{st}(v|S)}{\sigma_{st}}$. Because $B(v \mid S) = \sum_{s \in V \setminus \{v\}} \delta_s(v \mid S)$, it suffices to compute $\delta_s(v \mid S)$ for every $s \in V \setminus \{v\}$. Let P_s be the DAG representing the shortest paths from s, which can be constructed by performing a BFS from s. Let $\mathrm{succ}_s(v)$ be the set of successors of v in the DAG P_s. In particular, $\mathrm{dist}(s, w) = \mathrm{dist}(s, v) + 1$ for all $w \in \mathrm{succ}_s(v)$, where $\mathrm{dist}(u, v)$ is the distance between u and v. We process vertices in the DAG P_s in reverse topological order, that is, by non-increasing distance from s. We have the following recursion:

$$\delta_s(v \mid S) = \sum_{w \in \mathrm{succ}_s(v)} \left(\frac{\sigma_{sv}(v \mid S)}{\sigma_{sw}} + \frac{\sigma_{sv}(v \mid S)}{\sigma_{sw}(w \mid S)} \delta_s(w \mid S) \right).$$

The first term in the summand deals with the contribution to $\delta_s(v \mid S)$ of the pair (s, w). The second term in the summand deals with the contribution to $\delta_s(v \mid S)$ of pairs (s, t), where t ranges over all descendants of w in the DAG P_s. We need the scaling factor $\frac{\sigma_{sv}(v|S)}{\sigma_{sw}(w|S)}$, because only a

Algorithm 3 Build-Betweenness-Hypergraph(G, M)

Input: A graph $G = (V, E)$ and an integer $M \geq 1$.

```
Initialize H = (V, ∅).
for i = 1 to M do
    Pick a pair of vertices (s, t) at random.
    Make a weighted hyperedge e = {(v, σ_st(v)/σ_st) | v ∈ P_st \ {s, t}}, and add it to H.
return H.
```

Algorithm 4 Top-k-ABC(G, k)

Input: A graph $G = (V, E)$ and an integer $k \geq 1$.

```
M ← O(log n/ε²).
H ← Build-Betweenness-Hypergraph(G, M).
for i = 1 to k do
    v_i ← arg max_v {w_H(v)}.
    for Each hyperedge e incident to v_i do
        Replace it with a new weighted hyperedge
        {(v, σ_s(e)t(e)(v|v_1,...,v_i)/σ_s(e)t(e)) | v ∈ P_s(e)t(e) \ {s, t}}.
return The set {v_1, ..., v_k}.
```

$\frac{\sigma_{sv}(v|S)}{\sigma_{sw}(w|S)}$-fraction of shortest paths from s to w pass through the edge (v, w). We do not give a detailed proof of this here as the only difference from Brandes' original algorithm is that we exclude shortest paths passing through S, and the proof remains almost the same.

Let us consider the runtime of the algorithm explained above. First, we must compute P_s for every vertex s, which takes $O(nm)$ time. For each DAG P_s, we need $O(m)$ time to calculate the recursion. Hence, in total, we require $O(nm)$ time. Moreover, if we want to run the greedy algorithm to obtain a solution for MBC_k, we need $O(knm)$ time. Though this runtime is much better than the case of MCC_k, it is still quite large. On the other hand, our method runs in almost linear time, even when $k = n$.

3.1 Proposed method

In this section, we explain our method for ABC. The idea is similar to the case of ACC, but is technically more involved. Algorithm 3 describes how to construct a hypergraph sketch H for the betweenness centrality. We pick a set of M pairs of vertices (s, t), and for each pair (s, t), we add a hyperedge with a weight on each vertex. Specifically, we add to H a set of pairs $\{(v, \frac{\sigma_{st}(v)}{\sigma_{st}}) \mid v \in P_{st} \setminus \{s, t\}\}$. In what follows, we simply call the set a *hyperedge*. For a hyperedge e of H, let $V(e)$ be the set of vertices in e. For a vertex v, let $w_e(v)$ be the weight of v imposed by e. If $v \notin V(e)$, we set $w_e(v) = 0$. Let $s(e)$ and $t(e)$ denote the pair (s, t) used to make the hyperedge e.

For a vertex v, we define the *weight* of v in H as $w_H(v) = \sum_{e \in E(H)} \frac{\sigma_{s(e)t(e)}(v)}{\sigma_{s(e)t(e)}}$. Similarly, for a vertex set $S \subseteq V$, we define the *weight* of S in H as $w_H(S) = \sum_{e \in E(H)} \frac{\sigma_{s(e)t(e)}(S)}{\sigma_{s(e)t(e)}}$. Note that $w_H(\{v\}) = w_H(v)$.

We often use the following observation.

LEMMA 3.2. *For any vertex set $S \subseteq V$,*

$$\mathop{\mathbf{E}}_{H}[w_H(S)] = \frac{M}{n^2} B(S).$$

PROOF. If we have sampled a pair (s, t), then the contribution to $w_H(S)$ is $\frac{\sigma_{st}(S)}{\sigma_{st}}$. Hence, the expected contribution to $w_H(S)$ over a pair chosen at random is exactly $B(S)/n^2$. The lemma follows from the linearity of expectation. □

We define $\widetilde{B}(v) = \frac{n^2}{M} w_H(v)$ and $\widetilde{B}(S) = \frac{n^2}{M} w_H(S)$. Similar to the case of coverage centrality, we can show that $w_H(S)$ is highly concentrated on its expectation. Hence, we can use $\widetilde{B}(S)$ as a good approximation to $B(S)$.

We note that $w_H(v) = \sum_{e \in E(H)} \frac{\sigma_{s(e)t(e)}(v)}{\sigma_{s(e)t(e)}} = \sum_{e \in E(H)} w_e(v)$. Hence, we can obtain the vertex with the maximum betweenness centrality by choosing that with the maximum sum of weights imposed by hyperedges in H. We now show how to modify the hypergraph H so that we can compute ABC. Suppose that we have chosen a vertex set S. Because $B(v \mid S) = B(S \cup \{v\}) - B(S)$, we want to approximate it by

$$\begin{aligned}\widetilde{B}(v \mid S) &:= \widetilde{B}(S \cup \{v\}) - \widetilde{B}(S) \\ &= \sum_{e \in E(H)} \frac{\sigma_{s(e)t(e)}(S \cup \{v\})}{\sigma_{s(e)t(e)}} - \sum_{e \in E(H)} \frac{\sigma_{s(e)t(e)}(S)}{\sigma_{s(e)t(e)}} \\ &= \sum_{e \in E(H)} \frac{\sigma_{s(e)t(e)}(v \mid S)}{\sigma_{s(e)t(e)}}.\end{aligned}$$

The last expression suggests how we should modify the hypergraph H. That is, after choosing a vertex set S, for each hyperedge e and a vertex $v \in V(e)$, we need to change the weight $w_e(v)$ to $\frac{\sigma_{s(e)t(e)}(v|S)}{\sigma_{s(e)t(e)}}$. We can use the variant of Brandes' algorithm mentioned before to compute $\frac{\sigma_{s(e)t(e)}(v|S)}{\sigma_{st}}$. However, as we only consider shortest paths between $s(e)$ and $t(e)$, we have $\sigma_{st}(v \mid S) = \sigma_{sv}(v \mid S) \cdot \sigma_{tv}(v \mid S)$ if $v \in P_{st}$ and $v \notin S$, and we have $\sigma_{st}(v \mid S) = 0$ otherwise. Hence, we can compute $\frac{\sigma_{st}(v|S)}{\sigma_{st}}$ for all $v \in V(e)$ in linear time with respect to the number of edges in the DAG $P_{s(e)t(e)}$.

Algorithm 4 summarizes how to compute the top-k vertices with respect to ABC. We choose $M = O(\log n/\epsilon^2)$ to guarantee the quality of its output.

3.2 Accuracy

We can prove the accuracy of Algorithm 4 in a similar manner to the case of the coverage centrality:

THEOREM 3.3. *Let $\widetilde{S}$ be the output of Algorithm 4 and S^* be the optimal solution to MBC_k. Then, with a probability of at least $1 - 1/n$,*

$$B(\widetilde{S}) \geq \left(1 - \frac{1}{e}\right) B(S^*) - \epsilon n^2.$$

Hence, there is a high probability that Algorithm 4 outputs a $(1 - 1/e, \epsilon n^2)$-approximation to MBC_k.

3.3 Runtime

As opposed to the coverage centrality, we do not have a linear runtime in the worst case, because we must keep updating the vertex weights. However, we can bound the runtime with the following parameter

$$h = \mathop{\mathbf{E}}_{s,t \in V}[|P_{st}| \cdot |E(P_{st})|].$$

THEOREM 3.4. *Algorithm 4 can be implemented so that its expected runtime is $O((n + m + h \log n) \log n/\epsilon^2)$.*

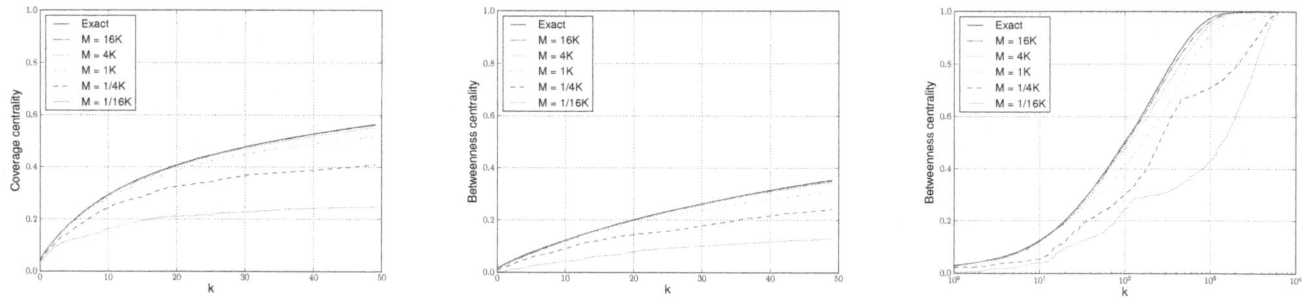

(a) Coverage centrality ($k \leq 50$) (b) Betweenness centrality ($k \leq 50$) (c) Betweenness centrality ($k \leq n$)

Figure 1: Accuracy of our method against the exact method

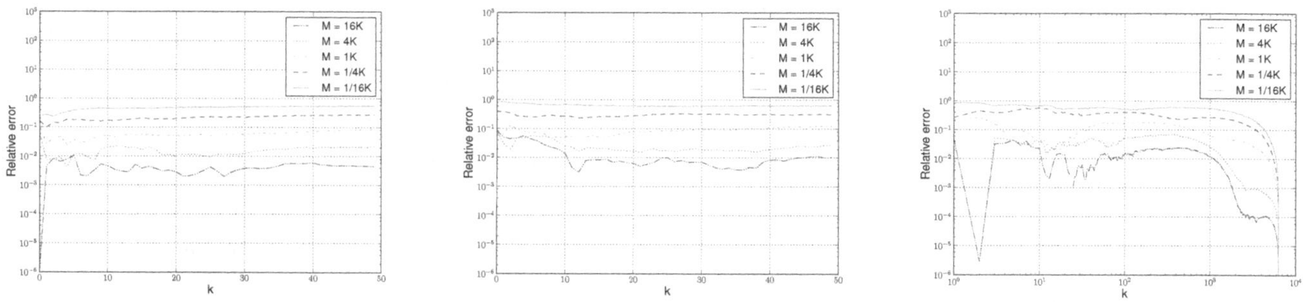

(a) Coverage centrality ($k \leq 50$) (b) Betweenness centrality ($k \leq 50$) (c) Betweenness centrality ($k \leq n$)

Figure 2: Relative error of our method against the exact method

PROOF. Build-Betweenness-Hypergraph clearly runs in $O((n+m)M)$ time.

For Top-k-ABC, we first examine the total runtime caused by updating the vertex weights. Let e be a hyperedge in H, with corresponding DAG P_{st}. When choosing a vertex $v \in V(e)$, we need $O(|E(P_{st})|)$ time to update the weights of vertices in $V(e)$. In addition, we need to update the weights of vertices in e at most $|P_{st}|$ times throughout the algorithm. As we sample M pairs of vertices at random when constructing H, the expected total runtime is $O(hM)$.

Because we must find vertices with the maximum weight at most hM times, using a standard priority queue (note that we are dealing with real values), the total time required to find vertices with the maximum weight is at most $O(hM \log n)$.

Hence, the expected total runtime is $O((n+m)M + hM + hM \log n) = O((n+m+h\log n)\log n/\epsilon^2$. □

COROLLARY 3.5. *With a probability of at least 99/100, Algorithm 4 outputs a* $(1-1/e, \epsilon n^2)$*-approximation to* MBC_k *in* $O((n+m+h\log n)\log n/\epsilon^2)$ *time.*

PROOF. By Theorem 3.5 and Markov's inequality, Algorithm 4 stops in $O((n+m+h)\log n/\epsilon^2)$ time with a probability of at least 199/200. By Theorem 3.3, we have a probability of at least 199/200 of obtaining the desired approximation. By the union bound, we have the desired result. □

In Section 4, we empirically show that h is much smaller than $n+m$ in real-world graphs, and hence our method runs in almost linear time.

Table 1: Datasets

Dataset	n	m	h
ego-Facebook	4,039	88,234	2.27×10^2
ca-GrQc	5,242	14,490	1.97×10^2
p2p-Gnutella08	6,301	20,777	5.39×10^2
email-Enron	36,692	183,831	2.63×10^3
soc-Epinions1	75,878	405,740	6.01×10^3
ego-Twitter	81,306	1,342,303	9.85×10^3
web-Google	875,713	4,322,051	3.58×10^3
roadNet-PA	1,088,092	1,541,898	2.57×10^5
roadNet-TX	1,393,383	1,921,660	4.20×10^5
as-Skitter	1,696,415	11,095,298	4.18×10^5

4. EXPERIMENTS

We conducted experiments on a Linux server with an Intel Xeon E5-2690 (2.90 GHz) processor and 256 GB of main memory. The experiments required, at most, 4 GB of memory. All algorithms were implemented in C++.

We considered various types of network, including social, computer, and road networks. All datasets utilized in this paper are available from the Stanford Network Analysis Project (`http://snap.stanford.edu/index.html`). All datasets were treated as undirected and unweighted graphs. Table 1 shows

Table 2: Runtime of algorithms for MCC_k. DNF means that the experiment did not finish in 12 h.

Dataset	$k = 50$					$k = n$				
	Exact	Sampling method		This work		Exact	Sampling method		This work	
		$M = 1$K	16K	$M = 1$K	16K		$M = 1$K	16K	$M = 1$K	16K
ego-Facebook	0.54 h	15.2 s	245 s	0.31 s	5.06 s	DNF	8.68 h	DNF	0.33 s	4.95 s
ca-GrQc	1.57 h	7.4 s	111 s	0.20 s	2.21 s	DNF	3.93 h	DNF	0.27 s	2.36 s
p2p-Gnutella08	2.91 h	14.1 s	221 s	0.30 s	4.46 s	DNF	8.17 h	DNF	0.41 s	4.69 s

Table 3: Runtime of algorithms for MBC_k. DNF means that the experiment did not finish in 12 h.

Dataset	$k = 50$					$k = n$				
	Exact	Sampling method		This work		Exact	Sampling method		This work	
		$M = 1$K	16K	$M = 1$K	16K		$M = 1$K	16K	$M = 1$K	16K
ego-Facebook	215 s	19.3 s	309 s	1.22 s	14.29 s	3.60 h	8.48 h	DNF	1.80 s	29.77 s
ca-GrQc	165 s	12.1 s	190 s	0.48 s	6.04 s	3.74 h	3.96 h	DNF	0.52 s	9.90 s
p2p-Gnutella08	392 s	28.5 s	449 s	0.70 s	11.61 s	9.58 h	7.88 h	DNF	1.33 s	22.48 s

the basic statistics of the datasets used in our experiments. To estimate the parameter $h = \mathbf{E}_{s,t \in V}[|P_{st}| \cdot |E(P_{st})|]$, we sampled 100,000 pairs of vertices (s,t) at random, and took the average of $|P_{st}| \cdot |E(P_{st})|$.

For the exact greedy algorithm for MCC_k (resp., MBC_k), we use that described in Section 2 (resp., Section 3), whose runtime is $O(kn^2m)$ (resp., $O(knm)$).

In this section, the symbol K denotes $2^{10} = 1024$.

4.1 Accuracy

To confirm the accuracy of our method, we conducted the following experiment for both MCC_k and MBC_k using the p2p-Gnutella08 dataset: For each problem, we executed the exact method to obtain the set of k vertices. We then executed our method to obtain the set of k vertices, and recomputed its exact centrality.

Figure 1 shows the accuracy of our method with various choices of k and M. For MCC_k, we could only use $k \leq 50$, as the exact method for MCC_k is very slow. Centralities are divided by n^2 so that the range becomes $[0,1]$ and we can easily see how the addtive error of ϵn^2 affects the quality. As can be observed from the figure, our method is very accurate when $M = 4$K and $M = 16$K. When $k = n$, the accuracy of our method deteriorates, as it outputs more vertices, especially when M is small. This is because our method only approximates the centrality to within ϵn^2, and the ordering among vertices with an adaptive centrality of less than ϵn^2 could be random.

Figure 2 shows the relative error of our method against the exact method using the same experimental setting as in Figure 1. As we can confirm from the figure, the relative error is less than 1% in most cases when $M = 16$K.

Note that the set (and the ordering) of vertices obtained by the exact method and our method may be very different. From these experiments, however, we can confirm that our method is accurate in the sense of solving MCC_k and MBC_k.

4.2 Runtime

Tables 2 and 3 summarize the runtime of our method and previous methods for MCC_k and MBC_k, respectively. Besides the exact greedy algorithm, we also implemented a sampling method that considers a fixed number, say M, of pairs of vertices, instead of all pairs, when computing the centrality. This can be viewed as a greedy algorithm that

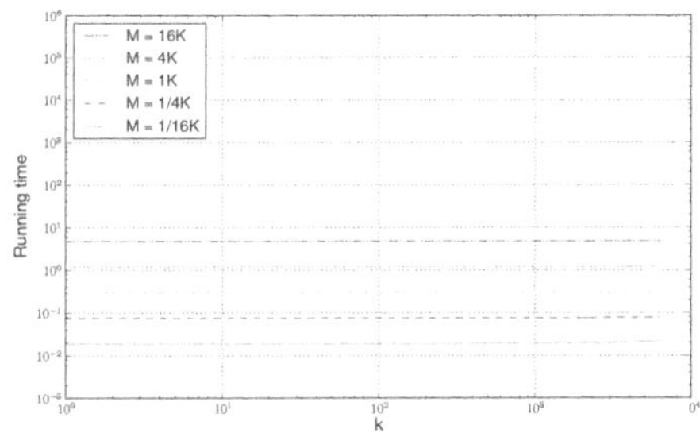

(a) Coverage centrality

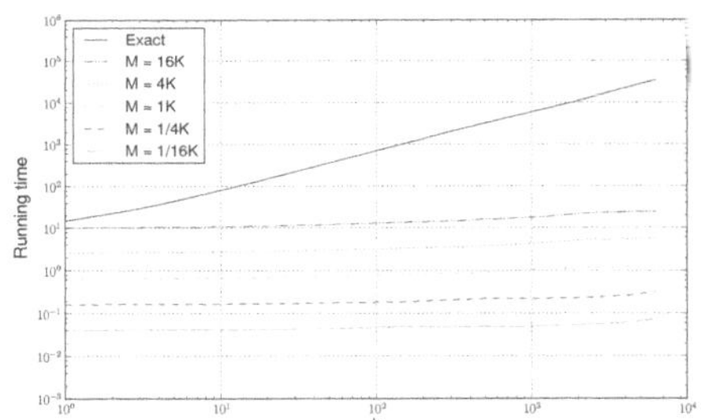

(b) Betweenness centrality

Figure 3: Runtime as a function of k

uses the method of Brandes and Pich [8] when computing the centralities.

When $k = 50$, our method runs two or three orders of magnitude faster than the exact method, and at least one order of magnitude faster than the sampling method.

The difference is even larger when $k = n$. In many cases, previous methods did not finish the computation within 12 h. As our method finishes in less than 30 s for all cases, our method runs at least three orders of magnitude faster than previous methods. The main reason for this is that the runtime of previous methods is proportional to k, whereas our method always runs in nearly linear time, no matter how large the value of k. We can confirm this observation from Figure 3, which illustrates how the runtime increases as k increases for the p2p-Gnutella08 dataset. There is no

Table 4: Runtime for large graphs

Dataset	MCC_n		MBC_n	
	$M = 1\text{K}$	16K	$M = 1\text{K}$	16K
soc-Epinions1	4.75 s	75.7 s	10.4 s	156 s
email-Enron	1.47 s	24.0 s	3.28 s	53.0 s
ego-Twitter	18.3 s	268 s	31.3 s	526 s
web-Google	148 s	2333 s	316 s	6131 s
as-Skitter	201 s	3541 s	472 s	7501 s

line corresponding to the exact method for MCC_k, as the program did not finish in 12 h.

Table 4 summarizes the runtime of our method for larger graphs, which demonstrates its scalability.

5. APPLICATIONS

In this section, we consider two applications of adaptive centralities that we have not previously been able to investigate.

5.1 Suppressing epidemics with immunization

Suppose a person is infected with a disease, and the disease spreads out through a social network. We have a limited number of k vaccines, and can immunize at most k people. The objective is to determine an effective immunization strategy that prevents an epidemic. This problem is well-studied in the network science community. It has been reported that a strategy based on ABC, that is, immunizing the top-k vertices with respect to ABC, is the most effective natural strategy [16]. However, as it is quite costly to compute ABC, its effectiveness has only been confirmed for small graphs.

We demonstrate the effectiveness of ABC for larger graphs using our method. To measure the effectiveness of immunization, we use the size of the largest connected component in the graph that results from removing vaccinated vertices, which is standard in the network science community.

Figure 4 illustrates the performance of the strategy based on ABC. We compare this with strategies based on betweenness, degree, and adaptive degree, which means the degree of the resulting graph after removing selected vertices. As we can see, the strategy based on ABC is most effective in these datasets. This improvement could have a huge impact in the context of suppressing epidemics.

5.2 Indexing methods for answering distances

Computing the distance between two vertices is a fundamental graph operation. To quickly compute the distance, it is natural to construct an index from the input graph, and use this when answering queries. Among many others, Akiba et al. [2] proposed an efficient method based on *pruned landmark labeling*. Given a vertex ordering $v_1, \ldots, v_n$, this approach performs a BFS from v_i, and records the distances from v_i for each $i = 1, \ldots, n$ in this order. A non-trivial claim of this method is that, when the BFS from v_i reaches a vertex w along the shortest path passing through some of $v_1, \ldots, v_{i-1}$, there is no need to expand vertex w in the BFS. Hence, the runtime of the i-th BFS is proportional to

$$\#\{w \mid P_{v_i w} \cap \{v_1, \ldots, v_{i-1}\} = \emptyset\}.$$

In other words, after performing (pruned) BFSs from vertices $v_1, \ldots, v_i$, we do not have to consider pairs (s, t) such

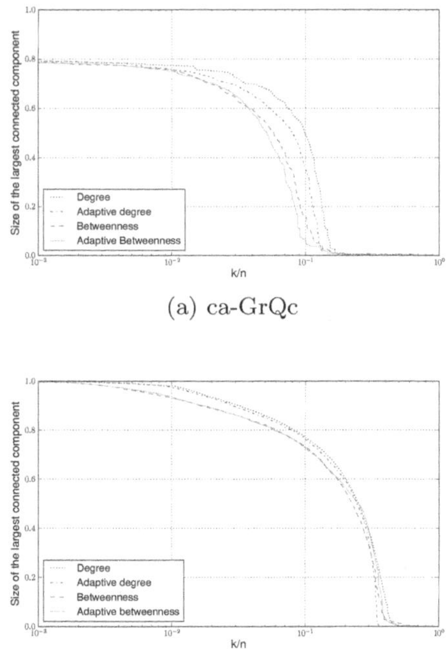

(a) ca-GrQc

(b) ego-Twitter

Figure 4: Size of the largest connected component

that $P_{st} \cap \{v_1, \ldots, v_i\} \neq \emptyset$, and s and t appear after $v_1, \ldots, v_i$ in the ordering. With this observation, it is natural to utilize the vertex ordering based on ACC.

In [2], the authors used a vertex ordering based on degree. This strategy works well when the input graph is a web graph or a social network, as the shortest paths of many pairs pass through high-degree vertices. However, the degree-based strategy does not work well for other kinds of graphs, such as road networks. For such graphs, coverage centrality might be more plausible.

Table 5 summarizes the performance of each strategy for road networks. In all datasets, we set the number of bit-parallel BFSs to be 64 (see [2] for details). The label size of a vertex means the number of distances recorded to that vertex. Note that the index size is (roughly) $(64 + \text{LN})n$, where LN is the average label size. We also chose $M = 4\text{K}$ in our method.

The best criteria with respect to the indexing time and the label size are strategies based on adaptive coverage and betweenness centrality, respectively. Adaptive centralities are better than their corresponding centralities in terms of the label size and the indexing time, and are comparable in terms of the ordering time. Thus, a strategy based on adaptive centrality may be preferable to one based on the corresponding centrality, which justifies the importance of adaptive centrality.

The label size of the degree-based strategy is larger than that of other strategies. Though its ordering time is much faster than other strategies, the combined ordering and indexing time is slightly longer than that of the ACC strategy.

To conclude, the strategy based on ACC is the best of those studied here, as it has the lowest total indexing time, and the label size is half that of the strategy developed by Akiba et al. [2].

Table 5: **Comparison of performance of the pruned landmark labeling method using various strategies. OT, IT, and LN denote the time required to obtain the vertex ordering, the indexing time excluding the vertex ordering, and the average label size of a vertex, respectively.**

Dataset	Degree			CC			ACC			BC			ABC		
	OT	IT	LN	OT	IT	LN	OT	IT	LN	OT	IT	LN	OT	IT	LN
roadNet-PA	**0.116** s	331 s	358	251 s	99.9 s	227	252 s	**71.3** s	176	578 s	316 s	411	1865 s	119 s	**166**
roadNet-TX	**0.148** s	446 s	372	303 s	180 s	256	306 s	**137 s**	208	695 s	374 s	404	2832 s	159 s	**192**

6. CONCLUSIONS

We have proposed an almost linear-time approximate method for obtaining the vertex orderings with respect to the *adaptive* coverage and betweenness centralities. Our method is remarkable, because simply obtaining the vertex with the maximum coverage or betweenness centrality requires linear time. The output quality of our method against the exact method is high in the sense of centralities, and our method is three orders of magnitude faster than previous methods.

Our method opens the door to use the vertex orderings with respect to the adaptive coverage and betweenness centralities for large graphs, say, millions of vertices. As illustrating examples, we have empirically shown the effectiveness of strategies based on these orderings in applications that arise from the network science and database communities.

Acknowledgment

The author thanks T. Akiba, C. Seshadhri, and T. Takaguchi for helpful comments.

Y. Y. is supported by JSPS Grant-in-Aid for Young Scientists (B) (No. 26730009), MEXT Grant-in-Aid for Scientific Research on Innovative Areas (No. 24106003), and JST, ERATO, Kawarabayashi Large Graph Project.

7. REFERENCES

[1] T. Akiba, Y. Iwata, K. Kawarabayashi, and Y. Kawata. Fast shortest-path distance queries on road networks by pruned highway labeling. In *ALENEX*, 2014. to appear.

[2] T. Akiba, Y. Iwata, and Y. Yoshida. Fast exact shortest-path distance queries on large networks by pruned landmark labeling. In *SIGMOD*, pages 349–360, 2013.

[3] D. A. Bader, S. Kintali, K. Madduri, and M. Mihail. Approximating betweenness centrality. In *WAW*, pages 124–137. Springer-Verlag, 2007.

[4] S. P. Borgatti and M. G. Everett. A graph-theoretic perspective on centrality. *Soc. Networks*, 28(4):466–484, 2006.

[5] C. Borgs, M. Brautbar, J. Chayes, and B. Lucier. Maximizing social influence in nearly optimal time. In *SODA*, 2014.

[6] U. Brandes. A faster algorithm for betweenness centrality. *J. Math. Sociol.*, 25(2):163–177, 2001.

[7] U. Brandes. On variants of shortest-path betweenness centrality and their generic computation. *Soc. Networks*, 30(2):136–145, 2008.

[8] U. Brandes and C. Pich. Centrality estimation in large networks. *Int. J. Bifurcat. Chaos*, 17(07):2303–2318, 2007.

[9] T. Coffman, S. Greenblatt, and S. Marcus. Graph-based technologies for intelligence analysis. *Commun. ACM*, 47(3):45–47, 2004.

[10] A. del Sol, H. Fujihashi, and P. O'Meara. Topology of small-world networks of protein-protein complex structures. *Bioinformatics*, 21(8):1311–1315, 2005.

[11] M. G. Everett and S. P. Borgatti. Extending centrality. *Models and methods in social network analysis*, 35(1):57–76, 2005.

[12] L. C. Freeman. A set of measures of centrality based on betweenness. *Sociometry*, 40(1):35–41, 1977.

[13] T. Fushimi, K. Saito, T. Ikeda, and N. Mutoh. Proposing set betweenness centrality measures focusing on nodes' collaboratative behaviors and its application. *IEICE T. Inf. Syst.*, J96-D(5):1158–1165.

[14] R. Geisberger, P. Sanders, and D. Schultes. Better approximation of betweenness centrality. In *ALENEX*, pages 90–100, 2008.

[15] M. Girvan and M. E. J. Newman. Community structure in social and biological networks. *P. Natl. Acad. Sci.*, 99(12):7821–7826, 2002.

[16] P. Holme, B. Kim, C. N. Yoon, and S. K. Han. Attack vulnerability of complex networks. *Phys. Rev. E*, 65(5):056109, 2002.

[17] H. Jeong, S. P. Mason, A. L. Barabasi, and Z. N. Oltvai. Lethality and centrality in protein networks. *Nature*, 411(6833):41–42, 2001.

[18] V. E. Krebs. Mapping networks of terrorist cells. *Connections*, pages 43–52, 2002.

[19] M.-J. Lee, J. Lee, J. Y. Park, R. H. Choi, and C.-W. Chung. Qube: a quick algorithm for updating betweenness centrality. In *WWW*, page 351, 2012.

[20] F. Liljeros, C. R. Edling, L. A. N. Amaral, H. E. Stanley, and Y. Åberg. The web of human sexual contacts. *Nature*, 411(6840):907–908, 2001.

[21] G. L. Nemhauser and L. A. Wolsey. Best algorithms for approximating the maximum of a submodular set function. *Math. Oper. Res.*, 3(3):177–188, 1978.

[22] G. L. Nemhauser, L. A. Wolsey, and M. L. Fisher. An analysis of approximations for maximizing submodular set functions—I. *Math. Program.*, 14(1):265–294, 1978.

[23] M. Newman and M. Girvan. Finding and evaluating community structure in networks. *Phys. Rev E*, 69(2):026113, 2004.

[24] M. Riondato and E. M. Kornaropoulos. Fast approximation of betweenness centrality through sampling. In *WSDM*, 2014. to appear.

[25] Y. Yano, T. Akiba, Y. Iwata, and Y. Yoshida. Fast and scalable reachability queries on graphs by pruned labeling with landmarks and paths. In *CIKM*, pages 1601–1606, 2013.

Efficient SimRank Computation via Linearization

Takanori Maehara
National Institute of Informatics
JST, ERATO, Kawarabayashi Project
maehara@nii.ac.jp

Mitsuru Kusumoto*
Preferred Infrastructure, Inc
mkusumoto@preferred.jp

Ken-ichi Kawarabayashi
National Institute of Informatics
JST, ERATO, Kawarabayashi Project
k_keniti@nii.ac.jp

ABSTRACT

SimRank, proposed by Jeh and Widom, provides a good similarity measure that has been successfully used in numerous applications. While there are many algorithms proposed for computing SimRank, their computational costs are very high.

In this paper, we propose a framework for computing SimRank accurately. Our framework is based on the novel technique, *linearized SimRank*, which provides efficient algorithms for the single-pair, single-source, and all-pairs SimRank problems, respectively. More specifically, our framework consists of two phases, a preprocessing phase and a query phase. In the preprocessing phase, we estimate a parameter for a given graph and a desired accuracy by Monte Carlo simulation, and then in the query phase, we efficiently solve SimRank problems using this preprocessed parameter. Our algorithms are efficient in both time and space. The preprocessing phase is performed in nearly linear time and the query phase requires only linear time for single-pair and single-source problems; furthermore, the space complexity is linear for both preprocessing and query phase.

We conducted experiments to evaluate our algorithms. For small networks ($n \leq 1,000,000$), our algorithm required only a few minutes for preprocessing, and then answered single-pair and single-source queries in 100 and 300 milliseconds, respectively. All-pairs computation was performed in a few days. For large networks ($n \geq 40,000,000$), our algorithm required a few hours for preprocessing, and then answered single-pair and single-source queries approximately in 10 seconds and in a half minutes, respectively.

In comparison to previous studies, for the all-pairs problem, our algorithm uses significantly less memory than any existing algorithm; thus it scales for much larger networks. For the single-pair and the single-source problems, our algorithm requires much fewer random samples than any existing Monte Carlo based algorithm for the same accuracy solution.

*supported by JST, ERATO, Kawarabayashi Project

KDD '14, August 24 - 27 2014, New York, NY, USA

http://dx.doi.org/10.1145/2623330.2623696.

Keywords

Similarity measure; SimRank; linearized SimRank

1. INTRODUCTION

1.1 SimRank

In recent years, much effort has been devoted to extracting useful information from large graphs. With the rapidly increasing amount of graph data, the *similarity search problem*, which identifies similar vertices in a graph, has become an important problem with many applications, including web analysis [16, 27], graph clustering [38, 45], spam detection [14], computational advertisement [4], recommender systems [2,39], and natural language processing [34].

Several similarity measures have been proposed [20,28,29, 30,35]. In this paper, we focus on *SimRank* [16]. SimRank is a link-based similarity measure proposed for similarity searches on the World Wide Web. The fundamental idea behind SimRank is that

> two pages are similar if they are referenced by similar pages.

This intuition is formulated as follows. Let $G = (V, E)$ be a directed graph with vertex set $V = \{1, \ldots, n\}$. *SimRank* $s(i,j)$ of vertex i and j is recursively defined by

$$s(i,j) = \begin{cases} 1, & (i = j), \\ \dfrac{c}{|\mathrm{In}(i)||\mathrm{In}(j)|} \displaystyle\sum_{i' \in \mathrm{In}(i), j' \in \mathrm{In}(j)} s(i', j'), & (i \neq j), \end{cases} \tag{1}$$

where $\mathrm{In}(i) = \{j \in V : (j, i) \in E\}$ is the set of in-neighbors of i, and $c \in (0, 1)$ is a decay factor usually set to $c = 0.8$ [16] or $c = 0.6$ [31]. SimRank and its related measures [4,9,41,43] give high-quality scores in many application areas, because it takes multi-step neighborhoods into account, whereas other similarity measures, such as the Jaccard coefficient, utilize only one-step neighborhoods.

While there are several algorithms proposed to compute SimRank scores, its computation cost is very high. More precisely, there are three fundamental SimRank problems:

Single-pair SimRank. Given two vertices $i, j \in V$, compute SimRank score $s(i, j)$.

Single-source SimRank. Given a vertex $i \in V$, compute SimRank scores $s(i, j)$ for all $j \in V$.

All-pairs SimRank. Compute SimRank scores $s(i, j)$ for all $i, j \in V$.

Table 1: Summary of SimRank algorithms on sparse graphs, where n is the number of vertices, m is the number of edges, T is the number of SimRank iterations, R and L are parameters that depend on the desired accuracy for our algorithm, and R' is the parameter for the algorithm [11].

Algorithm	Preprocessing	Query Type	Time	Memory	Technique
Proposed	$O(TRLn)$	Single-pair	$O(Tm)$	$O(m)$	Linearization
		Single-source	$O(T^2m)$		
		All-pairs	$O(T^2nm)$		
Fogaras and Rácz [11]	$O(TR'n)$	Single-pair	$O(TR')$	$O(m+nR')$	Random surfer pair (Monte Carlo)
		Single-source	$O(TR'n)$		
Li et al. [26]	—	Single-pair	$O(Tm^2)$	$O(n^2)$	Random surfer pair (Iterative)
Jeh and Widom [16]	—	All-pairs	$O(Tn^2)$	$O(n^2)$	Naive
Lizorkin et al. [31]	—	All-pairs	$O(Tnm)$	$O(n^2)$	Partial sum
Yu et al. [42]	—	All-pairs	$O(Tnm)$	$O(n^2)$	Fast matrix multiplication

Most existing algorithms solve the all-pairs SimRank problem using $O(n^2)$ space, where n is the number of vertices; thus they are impractical for large graphs. A few algorithms solve the single-pair and single-source problems, but they also have accuracy and complexity issues, which we describe in Section 5.3.

Therefore, the purpose of this paper is to propose efficient algorithms, in both time and space, for these SimRank problems.

1.2 Related work

In this subsection, we review existing algorithms for SimRank computation.

All-pairs SimRank.

In the original paper by Jeh and Widom [16], SimRank is computed by recursively evaluating equation (1) for all $i, j \in V$. This naive computation yields an $O(Tm^2)$ time algorithm, where m denotes the number of edges, and T denotes the number of iterations. Lizorkin et al. [31] proposed a *partial sum* technique to reduce the time complexity to $O(T \min\{nm, n^3/\log n\})$. Jia et al. [19] removed dangling vertices, which are vertices with no in-links, since the SimRank scores of these vertices are always zero. Yu et al. [42] introduced a matrix-based iteration approach and applied a fast matrix multiplication algorithm [36, 37] that yields an $O(T \min\{nm, n^\omega\})$ time algorithm, where $\omega < 2.373$ is the exponent of matrix multiplication. Cai et al. [8] proposed an algorithm that discards SimRank scores less than a predefined threshold, a technique already employed in previous algorithms [31, 42]. They showed that this technique works effectively on scale-free networks. Jia et al. [18] proposed an algorithm to maintain only vertex pairs of small distances and showed that this technique works effectively on small-world networks.

We emphasize that for all existing algorithms for the all-pairs problem, the space complexity of these algorithms is $O(n^2)$, since they must maintain all SimRank scores for each pair of nodes to evaluate equation (1).

Single-pair SimRank.

Jeh and Widom [16] provided a random-walk interpretation of SimRank, called a *random surfer pair model.* Consider two random walks that start from vertices i and j respectively, and follow their in-links. Let $\tau(i, j)$ be the random variable that denotes the first meeting time of i and j. Then the SimRank score is obtained by

$$s(i,j) = \mathbf{E}[c^{\tau(i,j)}], \tag{2}$$

where $\mathbf{E}$ denotes the expectation. Fogaras and Rácz [11] evaluated the right hand side via Monte Carlo simulation with a fingerprint tree data structure. This requires $O(nR')$ space to maintain R' random walks for each vertex, and computes a SimRank score $s(i, j)$ in $O(TR')$ time. Furthermore, they extended their method for single-source query that simultaneously computes single-pair queries for (possibly) similar vertices by traversing the fingerprint tree; this yields an $O(TR'n)$ time algorithm. Li et al. [26] also used the random surfer pair model, but their algorithm is deterministic; more specifically, their algorithm is an iterative algorithm for the first meeting time, and requires $O(n^2)$ space.

Note that some papers [12,25,40,41] proposed spectral decomposition (or low-rank decomposition) based algorithms; however, unfortunately, their algorithms do not actually compute SimRank, because their algorithms are based on an incorrect formula; see Remark 1 in Section 2 below.

1.3 Contribution

In this paper, we propose a framework for efficiently computing SimRank with an arbitrary accuracy ϵ (i.e., the error is less than ϵ). Our framework consists of two phases, a *preprocessing phase* and a *query phase.* In the preprocessing phase, we estimate a diagonal matrix D, which is defined in Section 2 and which plays a crucial role in our framework, for a given graph and an accuracy ϵ, and in the query phase, by using this estimated matrix D, we solve single-pair, single-source, and all-pairs SimRank problems. The obtained algorithms are efficient in both time and space, as described below.

Efficient in time. The preprocessing phase to estimate a matrix D is an iterative algorithm with Monte Carlo simulation (Subsections 4.1 and 4.2). The time complexity of this phase is $O(TLRn)$, where T is the number of iterations to compute SimRank scores, R is the number of Monte Carlo samples, and L is the number of iterations for the estimation algorithm. It can be shown that $R = O((\log n)/\epsilon^2)$ and $L = O(\log(n/\epsilon))$ (Subsection 4.3). Thus, the time complexity is expected to be nearly linear. Note that the preprocessing phase is the most computationally intensive part of our framework.

Once this matrix D is estimated, SimRank scores can be computed by deterministic algorithms (Section 3). The single-pair problem can be solved in $O(Tm)$ time, the single-source problem can be solved in $O(T^2m)$ time, and the all-pairs problem can be solved in $O(T^2nm)$ time by solving single-source problems for all vertices. Note that our all-pairs algorithm can easily be parallelized to multiple machines, i.e., if we have M machines, it can run in $O(T^2nm/M)$ time.

Efficient in space. In both the preprocessing and query phases, the algorithms only require $O(n)$ extra space to store a diagonal matrix D and vectors of length n. thus the total space complexity is $O(m)$. Note that for the all-pairs case, we do not have to *store* the similarity of all pairs of vertices. We emphasize that this is the first linear space algorithm to compute all-pairs SimRank scores.

We evaluated our algorithms using real networks in Section 5. For small networks ($n \leq 1,000,000$), our algorithm took only a few minutes for preprocessing, and then answered single-pair and single-source queries in 100 and 300 milliseconds (on average), respectively. All-pairs computation was performed in a few days. For large networks ($n \geq 40,000,000$), our algorithm required a few hours for preprocessing, and then answered single-pair and single-source queries approximately in 10 seconds and in a half minutes (on average), respectively. To the best of our knowledge, our experiment is performed on the largest datasets in the literature.

Comparison with other existing algorithms. We compare our algorithm with the existing ones in Subsection 5.3. Our algorithms have the following advantages:

1. The state-of-the-art all-pairs algorithm, proposed by Yu et al. [42], requires much more memory, and hence works only for small networks which has $n \leq$ 1,000,000 vertices. On the other hand, our algorithm requires much less memory, therefore it works for a very large networks.

2. The state-of-the-art Monte Carlo based single-pair and single-source algorithm by Fogaras and Racz [11] also requires much more space.

Our framework is based on a novel technique, named *linearized SimRank*. In Section 2, we observe that the computational difficulty of SimRank comes from its *non-linearity*. We introduced linearized SimRank to overcome this difficulty, which enabled us to compute SimRank scores via a *linear recurrence equation*.

1.4 Organization

In Section 2, we introduce the linearized SimRank, which is the main idea of our paper. In Section 3, we propose algorithms for three fundamental problems for SimRank, which are based on the linearized SimRank. In Section 4, we propose a parameter estimation algorithm, which is required for preprocessing. In Section 5, we evaluate our algorithm on several real networks in terms of accuracy and efficiency. We also give comparisons with existing algorithms. Finally in Section 6, we conclude our paper and describe future work.

2. LINEARIZED SIMRANK

Let us first observe the difficulty in computing SimRank. Let $G = (V, E)$ be a directed graph, and let $P = (P_{ij})$ be a transition matrix of transpose graph $G^\top$ defined by

$$P_{ij} := \begin{cases} 1/|\mathrm{In}(j)|, & (i,j) \in E, \\ 0, & (i,j) \notin E, \end{cases}$$

where $\mathrm{In}(i) = \{j \in V : (j,i) \in E\}$ denotes the in-neighbors of $i \in V$. Let $S = (s(i,j))$ be the *SimRank matrix*, whose (i,j) entry is the SimRank score of i and j. Then the SimRank equation (1) is represented [42] by:

$$S = (cP^\top SP) \vee I, \tag{3}$$

where I is the identity matrix, and $\vee$ denotes the element-wise maximum, i.e., (i,j) entry of the matrix $A \vee B$ is given by $\max\{A_{ij}, B_{ij}\}$.

In our view, the difficulty in computing SimRank via equation (3) comes from the element-wise maximum, which is a *non-linear* operation. To avoid the element-wise maximum, we introduce a new formulation of SimRank as follows. By observing (3), since S and $cP^\top SP$ only differ in their diagonal elements, there exists a diagonal matrix D such that

$$S = cP^\top SP + D. \tag{4}$$

We call such a matrix D the *diagonal correction matrix*. The main idea of our approach here is to split the SimRank computation problem into the following two subproblems:

1. Estimate diagonal correction matrix D, and

2. compute SimRank using D and the linear recurrence equation (4).

The second step is straightforward and can be efficiently performed (Section 3). The first step is the difficult portion of our framework. For efficient computation, we must estimate D without computing the whole part of S.

For the remainder of this paper, to simplify the discussion, we introduce the notion of *linearized SimRank*. Let Θ be an $n \times n$ matrix. A linearized SimRank $S^L(\Theta)$ is a matrix that satisfies the following *linear* recurrence equation:

$$S^L(\Theta) = cP^\top S^L(\Theta)P + \Theta. \tag{5}$$

Below, we provide an example that illustrates what linearized SimRank is.

EXAMPLE 1 (STAR GRAPH OF ORDER 4). *Let G be a star graph of order 4 (i.e., G has one vertex of degree three and three vertices of degree one). The transition matrix (of the transposed graph) is*

$$P = \begin{bmatrix} 0 & 1 & 1 & 1 \\ 1/3 & 0 & 0 & 0 \\ 1/3 & 0 & 0 & 0 \\ 1/3 & 0 & 0 & 0 \end{bmatrix},$$

and SimRank for $c = 0.8$ is

$$S = \begin{bmatrix} 1 & 0 & 0 & 0 \\ 0 & 1 & 4/5 & 4/5 \\ 0 & 4/5 & 1 & 4/5 \\ 0 & 4/5 & 4/5 & 1 \end{bmatrix}.$$

Thus, the diagonal correction matrix D is obtained by

$$D = S - cP^\top SP = \mathrm{diag}(23/75, 1/5, 1/5, 1/5),$$

Algorithm 1 Single-pair SimRank

procedure SINGLEPAIRSIMRANK(i,j)
  $\alpha \leftarrow 0$, $x \leftarrow e_i$, $y \leftarrow e_j$
  for $t = 0, 1, \dots, T-1$ **do**
    $\alpha \leftarrow \alpha + c^t x^\top D y$, $x \leftarrow Px$, $y \leftarrow Py$
  end for
  Report $S_{ij} = \alpha$
end procedure

REMARK 1. *Some papers have used the following formula for SimRank (e.g., equation (2) in [12], equation (2) in [15], equation (2) in [25], and equation (3) in [41]):*

$$S = cP^\top SP + (1-c)I. \quad (6)$$

However, this formula does not hold; (6) *requires diagonal correction matrix D to have the same diagonal entries, but Example 1 is a counterexample. In fact, matrix S defined by* (6) *is a linearized SimRank $S^L(\Theta)$ for a matrix $\Theta = (1-c)I$.*

We provide some basic properties of linearized SimRank in Appendix.

3. LINEARIZED SIMRANK COMPUTATION

In this section, we present our proposed algorithms for SimRank by assuming that the diagonal correction matrix D has already been obtained. All algorithms are based on the same fundamental idea; i.e., in (4), by recursively substituting the left hand side into the right hand side, we obtain the following series expansion:

$$S = D + cP^\top DP + c^2 P^{\top 2} DP^2 + \cdots. \quad (7)$$

Our algorithms compute SimRank by evaluating the first T terms of the above series. The time complexity of the algorithms are $O(Tm)$ for the single-pair problem, $O(T^2 m)$ for the single-source problem, and $O(T^2 nm)$ for the all-pairs problem. For all problems, the space complexity is $O(m)$.

3.1 Single-pair SimRank

Let e_i be the i-th unit vector ($i = 1, \dots, n$); then SimRank score $s(i,j)$ is obtained via the (i,j) component of SimRank matrix S, i.e., $s(i,j) = e_i^\top S e_j$. Thus, by applying $e_i^\top$ and e_j to both sides of (7), we obtain

$$e_i^\top S e_j = e_i^\top D e_j + c(Pe_i)^\top DPe_j + c^2 (P^2 e_i)^\top DP^2 e_j + \cdots. \quad (8)$$

Our single-pair algorithm (Algorithm 1) evaluates the right-hand side of (8) by maintaining $P^t e_i$ and $P^t e_j$. The time complexity is $O(Tm)$ since the algorithm performs $O(T)$ matrix vector products for $P^t e_i$ and $P^t e_j$ ($t = 1, \dots, T-1$).

3.2 Single-source SimRank

For the single-source problem, to obtain $s(i,j)$ for all $j \in V$, we need only compute vector Se_i, because its j-th component is $s(i,j)$. By applying e_i to (7), we obtain

$$Se_i = De_i + cP^\top DPe_i + c^2 P^{\top 2} DP^2 e_i + \cdots. \quad (9)$$

Our single-source algorithm (Algorithm 2) evaluates the right hand side of (9) by maintaining $P^t e_i$ and $P^t e_j$. The time complexity is $O(T^2 m)$ since it performs $O(T^2)$ matrix vector products for $P^{\top t} DP^t e_i$ ($t = 1, \dots, T-1$).

Algorithm 2 Single-source SimRank

procedure SINGLESOURCESIMRANK(i)
  $\gamma \leftarrow \vec{0}$, $x \leftarrow e_i$
  for $t = 0, 1, \dots, T-1$ **do**
    $\gamma \leftarrow \gamma + c^t P^{\top t} Dx$, $x \leftarrow Px$
  end for
  Report $S_{ij} = \gamma_j$ for $j = 1, \dots, n$
end procedure

Algorithm 3 All-pairs SimRank

procedure ALLPAIRSSIMRANK
  for $i = 1, \dots, n$ **do**
    Compute SingleSourceSimRank(i)
  end for
end procedure

3.3 All-pairs SimRank

Computing all-pairs SimRank is an expensive task for a large network, because it requires $O(n^2)$ time since the number of pairs is n^2. To compute all-pairs SimRank, it is best to avoid using $O(n^2)$ space.

Our all-pairs SimRank algorithm applies the single-source SimRank algorithm (Algorithm 2) for all initial vertices, as shown in Algorithm 3. The complexity is $O(T^2 nm)$ time and requires only $O(m)$ space. Since the best-known all-pairs SimRank algorithm [31] requires $O(Tnm)$ time and $O(n^2)$ space, our algorithm significantly improves the space complexity and has almost the same time complexity (since the cost of factor T is much smaller than n or m).

It is worth noting that this algorithm is distributed computing friendly. If we have M machines, we assign initial vertices to each machine and independently compute the single-source SimRank. Then the computational time is reduced to $O(T^2 nm/M)$. This shows the scalability of our all-pairs algorithm.

4. DIAGONAL CORRECTION MATRIX ESTIMATION

As seen in the previous section, once diagonal correction matrix D is obtained, SimRank computation is a straightforward task. In this section, we show how to estimate diagonal correction matrix D.

We first observe that the diagonal correction matrix is uniquely determined from the diagonal condition.

PROPOSITION 1. *A diagonal matrix D is the diagonal correction matrix, i.e., $S^L(D) = S$ if and only if D satisfies*

$$S^L(D)_{kk} = 1, \quad (k = 1, \dots, n), \quad (10)$$

where $S^L(D)_{kk}$ denotes (k,k) entry of the linearized SimRank matrix $S^L(D)$.

PROOF. See Appendix. □

This proposition shows that the diagonal correction matrix can be estimated by solving equation (10). Furthermore, we observe that, since S^L is a linear operator, (10) is a *linear equation* with n real variables $D_{11}, \dots, D_{nn}$ where $D = \mathrm{diag}(D_{11}, \dots, D_{nn})$. Therefore, we can apply a numerical linear algebraic method to estimate matrix D.

Algorithm 4 Diagonal estimation algorithm.

procedure DIAGONALESTIMATION
  Set initial guess of D.
  for $\ell = 1, \dots, L$ **do**
    for $k = 1, \dots, n$ **do**
      $\delta \leftarrow (1 - S^L(D)_{kk}) / S^L(E^{(k,k)})_{kk}$
      $D_{kk} \leftarrow D_{kk} + \delta$
    end for
  end for
  return D
end procedure

The problem for solving (10) lies in the complexity; a naive method (Algorithm 1) requires $O(Tm)$ time to evaluate $S^L(D)_{kk}$ for each k, but this is very expensive. To reduce the complexity, we combine an *alternating method* (a.k.a. the *Gauss-Seidel method*) with *Monte Carlo simulation*. The complexity of the obtained algorithm is $O(TLRn)$ time, where L is the number of iterations for the alternating method, and R is the number of Monte Carlo samples. We analyze the upper bound of parameters L and R for sufficient accuracy in Subsection 4.3 below.

4.1 Alternating method for diagonal estimation

Our algorithm is motivated by the following intuition:

A (k, k) diagonal entry $S^L(D)_{kk}$ is the most affected by the (k, k) diagonal entry D_{kk} of D. (11)

This intuition leads to the following iterative algorithm. Let D be an initial guess[1]; for each $k = 1, \dots, n$, the algorithm iteratively updates D_{kk} to satisfy $S^L(D)_{kk} = 1$. The update is performed as follows. Let $E^{(k,k)}$ be the matrix whose (k, k) entry is one, with the other entries being zero. To update D_{kk}, we must find $\delta \in \mathbb{R}$ such that

$$S^L(D + \delta E^{(k,k)})_{kk} = 1.$$

Since S^L is linear, the above equation is solved as follows:

$$\delta = \frac{1 - S^L(D)_{kk}}{S^L(E^{(k,k)})_{kk}}. \tag{12}$$

This algorithm is shown in Algorithm 4.

Mathematically, the intuition (11) shows the *diagonally dominant* property of operator S^L. Furthermore, the obtained algorithm (i.e., Algorithm 4) is the *Gauss-Seidel* method for a linear equation. Since the Gauss-Seidel method converges for a diagonally dominant operator [13], Algorithm 4 converges to the diagonal correction matrix[2] .

4.2 Monte Carlo based evaluation

For an efficient implementation of our diagonal estimation algorithm (Algorithm 4), we must establish an efficient method to estimate $S^L(D)_{kk}$ and $S^L(E^{(k,k)})_{kk}$.

Consider a random walk that starts at vertex k and follows its in-links. Let $k^{(t)}$ denote the location of the random walk after t steps. Then we have

$$\mathbf{E}[e_{k^{(t)}}] = P^t e_k.$$

We substitute this representation into (8) and evaluate the expectation via Monte Carlo simulation. Let $k_1^{(t)}, \dots, k_R^{(t)}$ be R independent random walks. Then for each step t, we have estimation

$$(P^t e_k)_i \approx \#\{r = 1, \dots, R : k_r^{(t)} = i\}/R =: p_{ki}^{(t)}. \tag{13}$$

Thus the t-th term of (8) for $i = j = k$ is estimated as

$$(P^t e_k)^\top D P^t e_k \approx \sum_{i=1}^{n} p_{ki}^{(t)2} D_{ii}. \tag{14}$$

We therefore obtain Algorithm 5 for estimating $S^L(D)_{kk}$ and $S^L(E^{(k,k)})_{kk}$.

Algorithm 5 Estimate $S^L(D)_{kk}$ and $S^L(E^{(k,k)})_{kk}$.

$\alpha \leftarrow 0$, $\beta \leftarrow 0$, $k_1 \leftarrow k, k_2 \leftarrow k, \dots, k_R \leftarrow k$
for $t = 0, 1, \dots, T-1$ **do**
  for $i \in \{k_1, k_2, \dots, k_R\}$ **do**
    $p_{ki}^{(t)} \leftarrow \#\{r = 1, \dots, R : k_r = i\}/R$
    if $i = k$ **then**
      $\alpha \leftarrow \alpha + c^t p_{ki}^{(t)2}$
    end if
    $\beta \leftarrow \beta + c^t p_{ki}^{(t)2} D_{ii}$
  end for
  for $r = 1, \dots, R$ **do**
    $k_r \leftarrow \delta_-(k_r)$ randomly
  end for
end for
return $S^L(D)_{kk} \approx \alpha$, $S^L(E^{(k,k)})_{kk} \approx \beta$.

Using a hash table, we can implement Algorithm 5 in $O(TR)$ time, where R denotes the number of samples and T denotes the maximum steps of random walks that are exactly the number of SimRank iterations. Therefore Algorithm 4 is performed in $O(TLRn)$ time, where L denotes the number of iterations required for Algorithm 4.

4.3 Correctness: Accuracy of the algorithm

To complete the algorithm, we provide a theoretical estimation of parameters L and R that are determined in relation to the desired accuracy. In Section 5, we experimentally evaluate the accuracy.

Estimation of the number of iterations L. The convergence rate of the Gauss-Seidel method is linear; i.e., the squared error $\sqrt{\sum_{k=1}^{n}(S^L(D)_{kk} - 1)^2}$ at l-th iteration of Algorithm 4 is estimated as $O(\rho^l)$, where $0 \le \rho < 1$ is a constant (i.e., the spectral radius of the iteration matrix). Therefore, since the error of an initial solution is $O(n)$, the number of iterations L of Algorithm 4 is estimated as $O(\log(n/\epsilon))$ for desired accuracy ϵ.

Estimation of the number of samples R. Since the algorithm is a Monte Carlo simulation, there is a trade-off between accuracy and the number of samples R. The dependency is estimated by the Hoeffding inequality, which is described below.

[1]We discuss an initial solution in Remark 2 in Appendix.

[2]Strictly speaking, we need some conditions for the diagonally dominant property of operator S^L. In practice, we can expect the estimation algorithm converges; see Lemma 1 in Appendix.

PROPOSITION 2. *Let* $p_{ki}^{(t)}$ $(i = 1, \ldots, n)$ *be defined by* (13), *and let* $p_k^{(t)} := (p_{k1}^{(t)}, \ldots, p_{kn}^{(t)})$. *Then*

$$\mathbf{P}\left\{\|P^t e_k - p_k^{(t)}\| > \epsilon\right\} \leq 2n \exp\left(-\frac{(1-c)R\epsilon^2}{2}\right).$$

where **P** *denotes the probability.*

PROOF. See Appendix. □

This shows that we need $R = O((\log n)/\epsilon^2)$ samples to accurately estimate $P^t e_k$ via Monte Carlo simulation.

By combining all estimations, we conclude that diagonal correction matrix D is estimated in $O(Tn \log(n/\epsilon)(\log n)/\epsilon^2)$ time. Since this is nearly linear time, the algorithm scales well.

Note that the accuracy of our framework only depends on the accuracy of the diagonal estimation, i.e., if D is accurately estimated, the SimRank matrix S are accurately estimated by $S^L(D)$; see Proposition 4 in Appendix. Therefore, if we want accurate SimRank scores, we only need to spend more time in the preprocessing phase and fortunately do not need to increase the time required in the query phase.

5. EXPERIMENTS

In this section, we evaluate our algorithm via experiments using real networks. The datasets we used are shown in Table 2[3]. We first evaluate the accuracy in Subsection 5.1, then evaluate the efficiency in Subsection 5.2; and finally, we compare our algorithm with some existing ones in Subsection 5.3.

For all experiments, we used decay factor $c = 0.6$, as suggested by Lizorkin et al. [31], and the number of SimRank iterations $T = 11$, which is the same as Fogaras and Rácz [11].

All experiments were conducted on an Intel Xeon E5-2690 2.90GHz CPU with 256GB memory running Ubuntu 12.04. Our algorithm was implemented in C++ and was compiled using g++v4.6 with the -O3 option.

5.1 Accuracy

The accuracy of our framework depends on the accuracy of the estimated diagonal correction matrix, computed via Algorithm 4. As discussed in Subsection 4.3, our algorithm has two parameters, L and R, the number of iterations for the Gauss-Seidel method, and the number of samples for Monte Carlo simulation, respectively. We evaluate the accuracy by changing these parameters.

To evaluate the accuracy, we first compute the *exact* SimRank matrix S by Jeh and Widom's original algorithm [16], and then compute the *mean error* [42] defined as follows:

$$\mathrm{ME} = \frac{1}{n^2}\sum_{i,j}\left|S^L(D)_{ij} - s(i,j)\right|. \quad (15)$$

[3]ca-GrQc, as20000102, Wiki-Vote, ca-HepTh, email-Enron, soc-Slashdot0811, soc-Slashdot0902, soc-Epinions1, email-EuAll, web-BerkStan web-Google, web-NotreDame, web-Stanford, and soc-LiveJournal datasets are available at `http://snap.stanford.edu/data/index.html` [3, 21, 22, 23, 24]. dblp-2011, in-2004, indochina-2004, it-2004, twitter-2010, and uk-2007-05 datasets are available at `http://law.di.unimi.it/datasets.php` [5, 6]. flickr dataset is available at `http://socialnetworks.mpi-sws.org/datasets.html` [33]. See the corresponding web pages noted above for detailed information about each of these datasets.

Table 2: Dataset information.

Dataset	n	m
ca-GrQc	5,242	14,496
as20000102	6,474	13,895
Wiki-Vote	7,155	103,689
ca-HepTh	9,877	25,998
email-Enron	36,692	183,831
soc-Epinions1	75,879	508,837
soc-Slashdot0811	77,360	905,468
soc-Slashdot0902	82,168	948,464
email-EuAll	265,214	400,045
web-Stanford	281,903	2,312,497
web-NotreDame	325,728	1,497,134
web-BerkStan	685,230	7,600,505
web-Google	875,713	5,105,049
dblp-2011	933,258	6,707,236
in-2004	1,382,908	17,917,053
flickr	1,715,255	22,613,981
soc-LiveJournal	4,847,571	68,993,773
indochina-2004	7,414,866	194,109,311
it-2004	41,291,549	1,150,725,436
twitter-2010	41,652,230	1,468,365,182
uk-2007-05	105,896,555	3,738,733,648

Since this evaluation is expensive (i.e., it requires SimRank scores for $O(n^2)$ pairs), we used the following smaller datasets: ca-GrQc, as20000102, wiki-Vote, and ca-HepTh. Results are shown in Figure 1, and we summarize our results below.

- For mean error $\mathrm{ME} \leq 10^{-5} \sim 10^{-6}$, we need only $R = 100$ samples with $L = 3$ iterations. Note that this is the same accuracy level as [42].
- If we want more accurate SimRank scores, we need much more samples R and little more iterations L. This coincides with the analysis shown in Subsection 4.3 in which we estimated that $L = O(\log(n/\epsilon))$ and $R = O((\log n)/\epsilon^2)$.

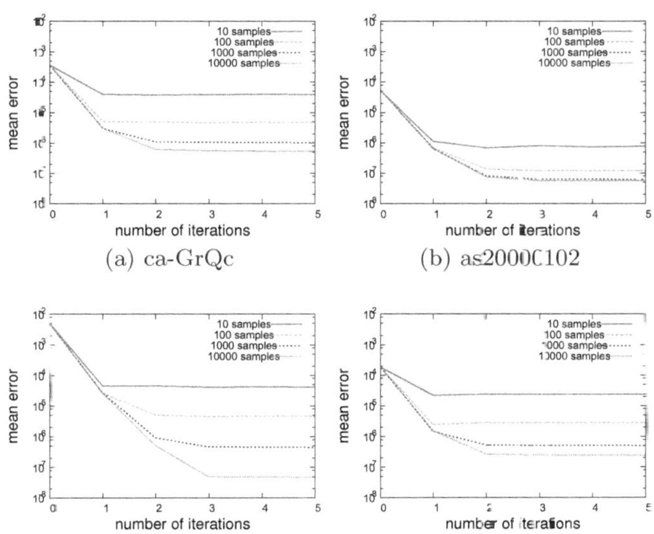

(a) ca-GrQc (b) as20000102

(c) wiki-Vote (d) ca-HepTh

Figure 1: Number of iterations L vs. mean error of computed SimRank.

5.2 Efficiency

We next evaluate the efficiency of our algorithm. We first performed preprocessing with parameters $R = 100$ and $L = 3$, respectively. We then performed single-pair, single-source and all-pairs queries for real networks. Results are shown in Table 3; we omitted results of the all-pairs computation for a network larger than in-2004 since runtimes exceeded three days. We summarize our results below.

- For small networks ($n \leq 1,000,000$), only a few minutes of preprocessing time were required; furthermore, answers to single-pair queries were obtained in 100 milliseconds, while answers to single-source queries were obtained in 300 milliseconds. This efficiency is certainly acceptable for online services. We were also able to solve all-pairs query in a few days.
- For large networks, $n \geq 40,000,000$, a few hours of preprocessing time were required; furthermore, answers to single-pair queries were obtained approximately in 10 seconds, while answers to single-source queries were obtained in a half minutes. To the best of our knowledge, this is the first time that such an algorithm is successfully scaled up to such large networks.
- The space complexity is proportional to the number of edges, which enables us to compute SimRank values for large networks.

5.3 Comparisons with existing algorithms

In this subsection, we compare our algorithm with two state-of-the-art algorithms for computing SimRank. We used the same parameters ($R = 100$, $L = 3$) as the above.

Comparison with the state-of-the-art all-pairs algorithm.

Yu et al. [42] proposed an efficient all-pairs algorithm; the time complexity of their algorithm is $O(Tnm)$, and the space complexity is $O(n^2)$. They computed SimRank via matrix-based iteration (3) and reduced the space complexity by discarding entries in SimRank matrix that are smaller than a given threshold. We implemented their algorithm and evaluated it in comparison with ours. We used the same parameters presented in [42] that attain the same accuracy level as our algorithm.

Results are shown in Table 3; the omitted results (—) mean that their algorithm failed to allocate memory. From the results, we observe that their algorithm performs a little faster than ours, because the time complexity of their algorithm is $O(Tnm)$, whereas the time complexity of our algorithm is $O(T^2nm)$; however, our algorithm uses much less space. In fact, their algorithm failed for a network with $n \geq 300{,}000$ vertices because of memory allocation. More importantly, their algorithm cannot estimate the memory usage before running the algorithm. Thus, our algorithm significantly outperforms their algorithm in terms of scalability.

Comparison with the state-of-the-art single-pair and single-source algorithm.

Fogaras and Rácz [11] proposed an efficient single-pair algorithm that estimates SimRank scores by using first meeting time formula (2) with Monte Carlo simulation. Like our approach, their algorithm also consists of two phases, a preprocessing phase and a query phase. In the preprocessing phase, their algorithm generates R' random walks and stores the walks efficiently; this phase requires $O(nR')$ time and $O(nR')$ space. In the query phase, their algorithm computes scores via formula (2); this phase requires $O(TnR')$ time. We implemented their algorithm and evaluated it in comparison with ours.

Table 4: Accuracy of the single-pair algorithm proposed by Fogaras and Rácz [11]; accuracy is shown as mean error.

Dataset	Samples	Accuracy
ca-GrQc	100	1.59×10^{-4}
	1,000	5.87×10^{-5}
	10,000	1.32×10^{-5}
	100,000	6.43×10^{-6}
	(Proposed	4.77×10^{-6})
as20000102	100	2.51×10^{-3}
	1,000	7.87×10^{-4}
	10,000	2.54×10^{-4}
	100,000	8.69×10^{-5}
	(Proposed	1.19×10^{-7})
wiki-Vote	100	1.03×10^{-3}
	1,000	3.57×10^{-4}
	10,000	1.13×10^{-4}
	100,000	3.63×10^{-5}
	(Proposed	2.81×10^{-6})
ca-HepTh	100	1.36×10^{-4}
	1,000	5.58×10^{-5}
	10,000	1.18×10^{-5}
	100,000	6.04×10^{-6}
	(Proposed	4.56×10^{-6})

We first checked the accuracy of their algorithm by computing all-pairs SimRank for the smaller datasets used in Subsection 5.1; results are shown in Table 4. From the table, we observe that in order to obtain the same accuracy as our algorithm, their algorithm requires $R' \geq 100{,}000$ samples, which are much larger than our random samples $R = 100$. This is because their algorithm estimates all $O(n^2)$ entries by Monte Carlo simulation, but our algorithm only estimates $O(n)$ diagonal entries by Monte Carlo simulation.

We then evaluated the efficiency of their algorithm with $R' = 100{,}000$ samples. These results are shown in Table 3. This shows that their algorithm needs much more memory, thus it only works for small networks. This concludes that in order to obtain accurate scores, our algorithm is much more efficient than their algorithm.

6. CONCLUSION

In this paper, we propose a framework for computing SimRank that is based on a linearized SimRank. Our framework consists of two phases, a preprocessing phase and a query phase. Once the preprocessing completes, we can efficiently solve single-pair, single-source, and all-pairs SimRank problems.

Our experiments show that our algorithm is fast and uses relatively low memory; thus it can scale up to very large networks.

For future work, it would be interesting to extend our method to dynamic networks [25]. When a network is modified by adding or removing vertices or edges, we must efficiently update matrix D. Establishing such a method will be noteworthy both in theory and practice.

Table 3: Computational results of our proposed algorithm and existing algorithms; single-pair and single-source results are the average of 10 trials; we omitted results of the all-pairs computation of our proposed algorithm for a network larger than in-2004 since runtimes exceeded three days; other omitted results (—) mean that the algorithms failed to allocate memory.

Dataset	Proposed					Yu et al. [42]		Fogaras and Rácz [11]			
	Preproc.	SinglePair	SingleSrc.	AllPairs	Memory	AllPairs	Memory	Preproc.	SinglePair	SingleSrc.	Memory
ca-GrQc	842 ms	0.236 ms	2.080 ms	10.90 s	3 MB	2.97 s	69 MB	64.7 s	87.0 ms	288 ms	23.3 GB
as20000102	96 ms	0.518 ms	0.812 ms	5.26 s	2 MB	0.13 s	8 MB	106 s	112 ms	262 ms	28.1 GB
Wiki-Vote	187 ms	0.613 ms	5.26 ms	37.4 s	6 MB	8.74 s	143 MB	43.4 s	30.4 ms	42.5 ms	24.5 GB
ca-HepTh	698 ms	0.493 ms	3.24 ms	39.0 s	4 MB	23.3 s	316 MB	205 s	61.2 ms	262 ms	44.2 GB
email-Enron	2.75 s	2.56 ms	24.13 ms	885 s	20 MB	302 s	3.47 GB	8055 s	86.9 ms	1.19 ms	162 GB
soc-Epinions1	4.12 s	5.90 ms	74.4 ms	5647 s	31 MB	777 s	6.94 GB	—	—	—	—
soc-Slashdot0811	6.14 s	4.16 ms	20.4 ms	1581 s	47 MB	747 s	7,37 GB	—	—	—	—
soc-Slashdot0902	5.87 s	4.63 ms	21.0 ms	1725 s	49 MB	694 s	7.24 GB	—	—	—	—
email-EuAll	11.3 s	14.5 ms	61.7 ms	4.54 h	57 MB	2.00 h	59.1 GB	—	—	—	—
web-Stanford	21.0 s	9.76 ms	288 ms	22.5 h	132 MB	—	—	—	—	—	—
web-NotreDame	8.07 s	14.7 ms	47.3 ms	4.28 h	107 MB	1.50 h	45.5 GB	—	—	—	—
web-BerkStan	49.6 s	35.7 ms	272 ms	51.7 h	392 MB	—	—	—	—	—	—
web-Google	52.2 s	64.2 ms	234 ms	57.0 h	325 MB	11.1 h	203 GB	—	—	—	—
dblp-2011	104 s	53.6 ms	207 ms	53.7 h	395 MB	3140 s	24.1 GB	—	—	—	—
in-2004	71.7 s	91.1 ms	335 ms	—	843 MB	—	—	—	—	—	—
flickr	160 s	137 ms	424 ms	—	1.11 GB	—	—	—	—	—	—
soc-LiveJournal	819 s	394 ms	1.19 s	—	3.74 GB	—	—	—	—	—	—
indochina-2004	391 s	487 ms	1.73 s	—	8.15 GB	—	—	—	—	—	—
it-2004	2822 s	3.51 s	12.0 s	—	49.2 GB	—	—	—	—	—	—
twitter-2010	14376 s	3.17 s	11.9 s	—	59.4 GB	—	—	—	—	—	—
uk-2007-05	8291 s	9.42 s	32.7 s	—	153 GB	—	—	—	—	—	—

In general, our linearization technique can be applied to recursively defined values with a maximum. For example, consider P-Rank [7, 43], which generalizes SimRank as follows. Let P be a transition matrix of $G^\top$ and let Q be a transition matrix of G. Then P-Rank is defined by

$$S = \Big((1-\lambda)cP^\top SP + \lambda cQ^\top SQ\Big) \vee I.$$

SimRank is the case in which $\lambda = 0$, and rvs-SimRank [43] is the case in which $\lambda = 1$; i.e., SimRank only uses the in-link information, whereas rvs-SimRank only uses out-link information, but P-Rank uses both types of links. We can establish a linear formulation of P-Rank as

$$S = \Big((1-\lambda)cP^\top SP + \lambda cQ^\top SQ\Big) + D$$

with a suitable diagonal matrix D. Therefore we can possibly extend our algorithm to P-Rank by the above formula.

References

[1] K. M. Abadir and J. R. Magnus. *Matrix Algebra*. Cambridge University Press, 2005.

[2] Z. Abbassi and V. S. Mirrokni. A recommender system based on local random walks and spectral methods. In *WebKDD/SNA-KDD*, pages 139–153. Springer, 2007.

[3] R. Albert, H. Jeong, and A.-L. Barabasi. Internet: Diameter of the World-Wide Web. *Nature*, 401(6749):130–131, 1999.

[4] I. Antonellis, H. Garcia-Molina, and C.-C. Chang. Simrank++: query rewriting through link analysis of the click graph. *PVLDB*, 1(1):408–421, 2008.

[5] P. Boldi, M. Rosa, M. Santini, and S. Vigna. Layered label propagation: a multiresolution coordinate-free ordering for compressing social networks. In *WWW*, pages 587–596, 2011.

[6] P. Boldi and S. Vigna. The webgraph framework I: compression techniques. In *WWW*, pages 595–602, 2004.

[7] Y. Cai and S. Chakravarthy. Pairwise similarity calculation of information networks. In *DaWaK*, pages 316–329, 2011.

[8] Y. Cai, G. Cong, X. Jia, H. Liu, J. He, J. Lu, and X. Du. Efficient algorithm for computing link-based similarity in real world networks. In *ICDM*, pages 734–739, 2009.

[9] Y. Cai, P. Li, H. Liu, J. He, and X. Du. S-SimRank: Combining content and link information to cluster papers effectively and efficiently. In *ADMA*, pages 317–329, 2008.

[10] L. Cao, B. Cho, H. D. Kim, Z. Li, M.-H. Tsai, and I. Gupta. Delta-SimRank computing on MapReduce. In *BigMine*, pages 28–35, 2012.

[11] D. Fogaras and B. Rácz. Scaling link-based similarity search. In *WWW*, pages 641–650, 2005.

[12] Y. Fujiwara, M. Nakatsuji, H. Shiokawa and M. Onizuka. Efficient search algorithm for SimRank. In *ICDE*, pages 589–600, 2013.

[13] G. H. Golub and C. F. Van Loan. *Matrix Computations*. 3rd eds., Johns Hopkins Studies in the Mathematical Sciences, 2012.

[14] Z. Gyöngyi, H. Garcia-Molina, and J. O. Pedersen. Combating web spam with TrustRank. In *VLDB*, pages 576–587, 2004.

[15] G. He, H. Feng, C. Li, and H. Chen. Parallel SimRank computation on large graphs with iterative aggregation. In *KDD*, pages 543–552, 2010.

[16] G. Jeh and J. Widom. SimRank: a measure of structural-context similarity. In *KDD*, pages 538–543, 2002.

[17] G. Jeh and J. Widom. Scaling personalized web search. In *WWW*, pages 271–279, 2003.

[18] X. Jia, Y. Cai, H. Liu, J. He, and X. Du. Calculating similarity efficiently in a small world. In *ADMA*, pages 175–187, 2009.

[19] X. Jia, H. Liu, L. Zou, J. He, and X. Du. A fast two-stage algorithm for computing SimRank and its extensions. In *WAIM Workshops*, pages 61–73, 2010.

[20] M. M. Kessler. Bibliographic coupling extended in time: Ten case histories. *ISR*, 1(4):169–187, 1963.

[21] J. Leskovec, D. P. Huttenlocher, and J. M. Kleinberg. Predicting positive and negative links in online social networks. In *WWW*, pages 641–650, 2010.

[22] J. Leskovec, D. P. Huttenlocher, and J. M. Kleinberg. Signed networks in social media. In *CHI*, pages 1361–1370, 2010.

[23] J. Leskovec, J. M. Kleinberg, and C. Faloutsos. Graphs over time: densification laws, shrinking diameters and possible explanations. In *KDD*, pages 177–187, 2005.

[24] J. Leskovec, K. J. Lang, A. Dasgupta, and M. W. Mahoney. Community structure in large networks: Natural cluster sizes and the absence of large well-defined clusters. *Internet Math.*, 6(1):29–123, 2009.

[25] C. Li, J. Han, G. He, X. Jin, Y. Sun, Y. Yu, and T. Wu. Fast computation of SimRank for static and dynamic information networks. In *EDBT*, pages 465–476, 2010.

[26] P. Li, H. Liu, J. X. Yu, J. He, and X. Du. Fast single-pair simrank computation. In *SDM*, pages 571–582. SIAM, 2010.

[27] D. Liben-Nowell and J. M. Kleinberg. The link-prediction problem for social networks. *JASIST*, 58(7):1019–1031, 2007.

[28] Z. Lin, I. King, and M. R. Lyu. PageSim: A novel link-based similarity measure for the World Wide Web. In *WI*, pages 687–693, 2006.

[29] Z. Lin, M. R. Lyu, and I. King. Extending link-based algorithms for similar web pages with neighborhood structure. In *WI*, pages 263–266, 2007.

[30] Z. Lin, M. R. Lyu, and I. King. MatchSim: a novel similarity measure based on maximum neighborhood matching. *KAIS*, 32(1):141–166, 2012.

[31] D. Lizorkin, P. Velikhov, M. N. Grinev, and D. Turdakov. Accuracy estimate and optimization techniques for SimRank computation. *VLDBJ*, 19(1):45–66, 2010.

[32] A. McCallum, K. Nigam, J. Rennie, and K. Seymore. Automating the construction of internet portals with machine learning. *IRJ*, 3(2):127–163, 2000.

[33] A. Mislove, M. Marcon, P. K. Gummadi, P. Druschel, and B. Bhattacharjee. Measurement and analysis of online social networks. In *IMC*, pages 29–42. 2007.

[34] C. Scheible. Sentiment translation through lexicon induction. In *ACL (Student Research Workshop)*, pages 25–30. 2010.

[35] H. Small. Co-citation in the scientific literature: A new measure of the relationship between two documents. *JASIS*, 24(4):265–269, 1973.

[36] V. Strassen. Gaussian elimination is not optimal. *Numer. Math.*, 13(4):354–356, 1969.

[37] V. V. Williams. Multiplying matrices faster than Coppersmith-Winograd. In *STOC*, pages 887–898. 2012.

[38] X. Yin, J. Han, and P. S. Yu. LinkClus: Efficient clustering via heterogeneous semantic links. In *VLDB*, pages 427–438. 2006.

[39] L. Yu, Z. Shu, and X. Yang. SimRate: Improve collaborative recommendation based on rating graph for sparsity. In *ADMA*, pages 167–174, 2010.

[40] W. Yu, X. Lin, and J. Le. Taming computational complexity: Efficient and parallel SimRank optimizations on undirected graphs. In *WAIM*, pages 280–296, 2010.

[41] W. Yu, X. Lin, W. Zhang, L. Chang, and J. Pei. More is simpler: Effectively and efficiently assessing node-pair similarities based on hyperlinks. *PVLDB*, 7(1):13–24, 2013.

[42] W. Yu, W. Zhang, X. Lin, Q. Zhang, and J. Le. A space and time efficient algorithm for SimRank computation. *WWW*, 15(3):327–353, 2012.

[43] P. Zhao, J. Han, and Y. Sun. P-Rank: a comprehensive structural similarity measure over information networks. In *CIKM*, pages 553–562. 2009.

[44] W. Zheng, L. Zou, Y. Feng, L. Chen, and D. Zhao. Efficient SimRank-based similarity join over large graphs. *PVLDB*, 6(7):493–504, 2013.

[45] Y. Zhou, H. Cheng, and J. X. Yu. Graph clustering based on structural/attribute similarities. *PVLDB*, 2(1):718–729, 2009.

APPENDIX

In this appendix, we provide details of propositions and proofs mentioned in the main body of our paper.

We first introduce a vectorized form of SimRank, which is convenient for analysis. Let $\otimes$ be the Kronecker product of matrices, i.e., for $n \times n$ matrices $A = (A_{ij})$ and B,

$$A \otimes B = \begin{bmatrix} A_{11}B & \cdots & A_{1n}B \\ \vdots & \ddots & \vdots \\ A_{n1}B & \cdots & A_{nn}B \end{bmatrix}.$$

Let "vec" be the vectorization operator, which reshapes an $n \times n$ matrix to an n^2 vector, i.e., $\mathrm{vec}(A)_{n \times i+j} = a_{ij}$. Then we have the following relation, which is well known in linear algebra [1]:

$$\mathrm{vec}(ABC) = (C^\top \otimes A)\mathrm{vec}(B). \tag{16}$$

PROPOSITION 3. *Linearized SimRank operator S^L is a non-singular linear operator.*

PROOF. A linearized SimRank $S^L(\Theta)$ for a matrix Θ is a matrix satisfies relation

$$S^L(\Theta) = cP^\top S^L(\Theta)P + \Theta.$$

By applying the vectorization operator and using (16), we obtain

$$\left(I - cP^\top \otimes P^\top\right) \mathrm{vec}(S^L(\Theta)) = \mathrm{vec}(\Theta). \tag{17}$$

Thus, to prove Proposition 3, we only have to prove that the coefficient matrix $I - cP^\top \otimes P^\top$ is non-singular.

Since $P^\top \otimes P^\top$ is a (left) stochastic matrix, its spectral radius is equal to one. Hence all eigenvalues of $I - cP^\top \otimes P^\top$

are contained in the disk with center 1 and radius c in the complex plane. Therefore $I - cP^\top \otimes P^\top$ does not have a zero eigenvalue, and hence $I - cP^\top \otimes P^\top$ is nonsingular. □

We now prove Proposition 1, which is the basis of our diagonal estimation algorithm.

PROOF OF PROPOSITION 1. Let us consider linear system (17) and let $Q := P^\top \otimes P^\top$. We partite the system (17) into 2×2 blocks that correspond to the diagonal entries and the others:

$$\begin{bmatrix} I - cQ_{DD} & -cQ_{DO} \\ -cQ_{OD} & I - cQ_{OO} \end{bmatrix} \begin{bmatrix} \vec{1} \\ X \end{bmatrix} = \begin{bmatrix} \operatorname{diag}(D) \\ 0 \end{bmatrix}, \tag{18}$$

where Q_{DD}, Q_{DO}, Q_{OD}, and Q_{OO} are submatrices of Q that denote contributions of diagonals to diagonals, diagonals to off-diagonals, off-diagonals to diagonals, and off-diagonals to off-diagonals, respectively. X is the off-diagonal entries of $S^L(D)$. To prove Proposition 1, we only have to prove that there is a unique diagonal matrix D that satisfies (18).

We observe that the block-diagonal component $I - cQ_{OO}$ of (18) is non-singular, which can be proved similarly as in Proposition 3. Thus, the equation (18) is uniquely solved as

$$(I - cQ_{DD} - c^2 Q_{DO}(I - cQ_{OO})^{-1} Q_{OD})\vec{1} = \operatorname{diag}(D), \tag{19}$$

which is a closed form solution of diagonal correction matrix D. □

REMARK 2. *It is hard to compute D via the closed form formula* (19) *because the evaluation of the third term of the left hand side of* (19) *is too expensive.*

On the other hand, we can use (19) *to obtain a reasonable initial solution for Algorithm 4. By using first two terms of* (19)*, we have*

$$\operatorname{diag}(D) \approx \vec{1} - cQ_{DD}\vec{1}, \tag{20}$$

which can be computed in $O(m)$ time.

Our additional experiment shows that the initial solution (20) *gives a slightly better (at most twice) results than the trivial guesses $D = I$ and $D = 1 - c$.*

We give a convergence proof of our diagonal estimation algorithm (Algorithm 4). As mentioned in Subsection 4.1, Algorithm 4 is the Gauss-Seidel method [13] for the linear system

$$\begin{bmatrix} S^L(E^{(1,1)})_{11} & \cdots & S^L(E^{(n,n)})_{11} \\ \vdots & \ddots & \vdots \\ S^L(E^{(1,1)})_{nn} & \cdots & S^L(E^{(n,n)})_{nn} \end{bmatrix} \begin{bmatrix} D_{11} \\ \vdots \\ D_{nn} \end{bmatrix} = \begin{bmatrix} 1 \\ \vdots \\ 1 \end{bmatrix}. \tag{21}$$

LEMMA 1. *Consider two independent random walks start from the same vertex i and follow their in-links. Let $p_i(t)$ be the probability that two random walks meet t-th step (at some vertex). Let $\Delta := \max_i \{\sum_{t=1}^{\infty} c^t p_i(t)\}$. If $\Delta < 1$ then the coefficient matrix of* (21) *is diagonally dominant*

PROOF. By definition, each diagonal entry $S^L(E^{(j,j)})_{jj}$ is greater than or equal to one. For the off diagonals, we have

$$\begin{aligned} \sum_{i:i \neq j} S^L(E^{(i,i)})_{jj} &= \sum_{i:i \neq j} \sum_{t=1}^{\infty} c^t (P^t e_j)^\top E^{(i,i)} (P^t e_j) \\ &\le \sum_{t=1}^{\infty} c^t (P^t e_j)^\top (P^t e_j) = \sum_{t=1}^{\infty} c^t p_j(t) \le \Delta. \end{aligned}$$

This shows that if $\Delta < 1$ then the matrix is diagonally dominant. □

COROLLARY 1. *If a graph G satisfies the condition of Lemma 1, Algorithm 4 converges with convergence rate $O(\Delta^l)$.*

PROOF. This follows the standard theory of the Gauss-Seidel method [13]. □

REMARK 3. *Let us observe that, in practice, the assumption $\Delta < 1$ is not an issue. For a network of average degree d, the probability $p_i(t)$ is expected to $1/d^t$. Therefore $\Delta = \sum_t c^t p_i(t) \simeq (c/d)/(1 - (c/d)) \le 1/(d-1) < 1$. This implies that Algorithm 4 converges quickly when the average degree is large.*

We now prove Proposition 2. We use the following lemma.

LEMMA 2. *Let $k_1^{(t)}, \ldots, k_R^{(t)}$ be positions of t-th step of independent random walks that start from a vertex k and follow In-links. Let $X_k^{(t)} := (1/R)\sum_{r=1}^{R} e_{k_r^{(t)}}$. Then for all $l = 1, \ldots, n$,*

$$P\left\{\left|e_l^\top \left(X_k^{(t)} - P^t e_k\right)\right| \ge \epsilon\right\} \le 2\exp\left(-2R\epsilon^2\right).$$

PROOF. Since $\mathbf{E}[e_{k_r^{(t)}}] = P^t e_k$, this is a direct application of the Hoeffding's inequality. □

PROOF OF PROPOSITION 2. Since $p_{ki}^{(t)}$ defined by (13) is represented by $p_{ki}^{(t)} = e_i^\top X_k^{(t)}$. Thus we have

$$\begin{aligned} P\left\{\|P^t e_k - p_k^{(t)}\| > \epsilon\right\} &\le nP\left\{\left|e_i^\top P^t e_k - p_{ki}^{(t)}\right| > \epsilon\right\} \\ &\le 2n\exp\left(-2R\epsilon^2\right). \end{aligned}$$

□

PROPOSITION 4. *Let $D = \operatorname{diag}(D_{11}, \ldots, D_{nn})$ and $\tilde{D} = \operatorname{diag}(\tilde{D}_{11}, \ldots, \tilde{D}_{nn})$ be diagonal matrices. If they satisfy*

$$\sup_k |D_{kk} - \tilde{D}_{kk}| \le \epsilon$$

then

$$\sup_{i,j} |S^L(D)_{ij} - S^L(\tilde{D})_{ij}| \le \frac{\epsilon}{1-c}.$$

PROOF. Let $\varDelta := D - \tilde{D}$. Since S^L is linear, we have $S^L(\varDelta) = S^L(D) - S^L(\tilde{D})$. Consider

$$S^L(\varDelta) = cP^\top S^L(\varDelta) P + \varDelta$$

By applying e_i and e_j, we have

$$\begin{aligned} S^L(\varDelta)_{ij} &= c(Pe_i)^\top S^L(\varDelta)(Pe_j) + \varDelta_{ij} \\ &\le c \sup_{i',j'} S^L(\varDelta)_{i'j'} + \epsilon. \end{aligned}$$

Here, we used $p^\top A q \le \sup_{ij} A_{ij}$ for any stochastic vectors p and q. Therefore

$$(1-c)\sup_{i,j} S^L(\varDelta)_{ij} \le \epsilon.$$

By the same argument, we have

$$(1-c)\inf_{i,j} S^L(\varDelta)_{ij} \ge -\epsilon.$$

By combining them, we obtain the proposition. □

The above proposition shows that if diagonal correction matrix D is accurately estimated, all entries of SimRank matrix S is accurately computed.

FAST-PPR: Scaling Personalized PageRank Estimation for Large Graphs

Peter Lofgren
Department of Computer Science
Stanford University
plofgren@cs.stanford.edu

Siddhartha Banerjee
Department of Management Science & Engineering
Stanford University
sidb@stanford.edu

Ashish Goel
Department of Management Science & Engineering
Stanford University
ashishg@stanford.edu

C. Seshadhri
Sandia National Labs
Livermore, CA
scomand@sandia.gov

ABSTRACT

We propose a new algorithm, FAST-PPR, for computing personalized PageRank: given start node s and target node t in a directed graph, and given a threshold δ, FAST-PPR computes the Personalized PageRank $\pi_s(t)$ from s to t, guaranteeing a small relative error as long $\pi_s(t) > \delta$. Existing algorithms for this problem have a running-time of $\Omega(1/\delta)$; in comparison, FAST-PPR has a provable average running-time guarantee of $O(\sqrt{d/\delta})$ (where d is the average in-degree of the graph). This is a significant improvement, since δ is often $O(1/n)$ (where n is the number of nodes) for applications. We also complement the algorithm with an $\Omega(1/\sqrt{\delta})$ lower bound for PageRank estimation, showing that the dependence on δ cannot be improved.

We perform a detailed empirical study on numerous massive graphs, showing that FAST-PPR dramatically outperforms existing algorithms. For example, on the 2010 Twitter graph with 1.5 billion edges, for target nodes sampled by popularity, FAST-PPR has a 20 factor speedup over the state of the art. Furthermore, an enhanced version of FAST-PPR has a 160 factor speedup on the Twitter graph, and is at least 20 times faster on all our candidate graphs.

Categories and Subject Descriptors

F.2.2 [**Nonnumerical Algorithms and Problems**]: Computations on Discrete Structures; G.2.2 [**Graph Theory**]: Graph Algorithms

General Terms

Algorithms,Theory

KDD '14, August 24 - 27 2014, New York, NY, USA.

ACM 978-1-4503-2956-9/14/08 ...$15.00.
http://dx.doi.org/10.1145/2623330.2623745.

Keywords

Personalized PageRank; Social Search

1. INTRODUCTION

The success of modern networks is largely due to the ability to search effectively on them. A key primitive is PageRank [1], which is widely used as a measure of network importance. The popularity of PageRank is in large part due to its fast computation in large networks. As modern social network applications shift towards being more customized to individuals, there is a need for similar ego-centric measures of network structure.

Personalized PageRank (PPR) [1] has long been viewed as the appropriate ego-centric equivalent of PageRank. For a node u, the personalized PageRank vector π_u measures the frequency of visiting other nodes via short random-walks from u. This makes it an ideal metric for *social search*, giving higher weight to content generated by nearby users in the social graph. Social search protocols find widespread use – from personalization of general web searches [1, 2, 3], to more specific applications like collaborative tagging networks [4], ranking name search results on social networks [5], social Q&A sites [6], etc. In a typical personalized search application, given a set of candidate results for a query, we want to estimate the Personalized PageRank to each candidate result. This motivates the following problem:

Given source node s and target node t, compute the Personalized PageRank $\pi_s(t)$ up to a small relative error.

Since smaller values of $\pi_s(t)$ are more difficult to detect, we parameterize the problem by threshold δ, requiring small relative errors only if $\pi_s(t) > \delta$. Current techniques used for PPR estimation (see Section 2.1) have $\Omega(1/\delta)$ running-time – this makes them infeasible for large networks when the desired $\delta = O(1/n)$ or $O((\log n)/n)$.

In addition to social-search, PPR is also used for a variety of other tasks across different domains: friend recommendation on Facebook [7], who to follow on Twitter [8], graph partitioning [9], community detection [10], and other applications [11]. Other measures of personalization, such as personalized SALSA and SimRank [12], can be reduced to PPR. However, in spite of a rich body of existing work [2,

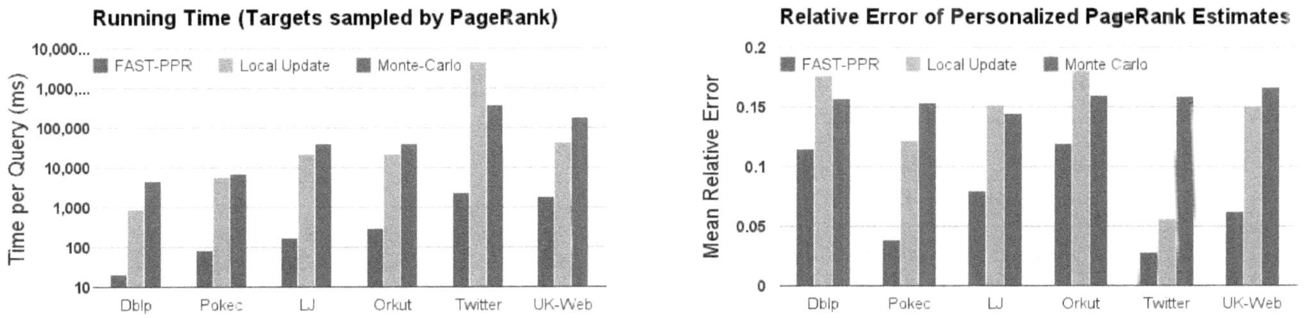

(a) Running time (in log scale) of different algorithms

(b) Relative accuracy of different algorithms

Figure 1: Comparison of Balanced FAST-PPR, Monte-Carlo and Local-Update algorithms in different networks – 1000 source-target pairs, threshold $\delta = \frac{4}{n}$, teleport probability $\alpha = 0.2$. Notice that Balanced FAST-PPR is 20 times faster in all graphs, without sacrificing accuracy. For details, see Section 6.

13, 9, 14, 15, 16, 17], estimating PPR is often a bottleneck in large networks.

1.1 Our Contributions

We develop a new algorithm, *Frontier-Aided Significance Thresholding for Personalized PageRank* (FAST-PPR), based on a new bi-directional search technique for PPR estimation:

• **Practical Contributions:** We present a simple implementation of FAST-PPR which requires no pre-processing and has an average running-time of $O(\sqrt{d/\delta})$[1]. We also propose a simple heuristic, Balanced FAST-PPR, that achieves a significant speedup in practice.

In experiments, FAST-PPR outperforms existing algorithms across a variety of real-life networks. For example, in Figure 1, we compare the running-times and accuracies of FAST-PPR with existing methods. Over a variety of data sets, FAST-PPR is significantly faster than the state of the art, with the same or better accuracy.

To give a concrete example: in experiments on the Twitter-2010 graph [19], Balanced FAST-PPR takes less than 3 seconds for random source-target pairs. In contrast, Monte Carlo takes more than 6 minutes and Local Update takes more than an hour. More generally in all graphs, FAST-PPR is at least 20 times faster than the state-of-the-art, without sacrificing accuracy.

• **Theoretical Novelty:** FAST-PPR is the first algorithm for PPR estimation with $O(\sqrt{d/\delta})$ average running-time, where $d = m/n$ is the average in-degree[2]. Further, we modify FAST-PPR to get $O(1/\sqrt{\delta})$ worst-case running-time, by pre-computing and storing some additional information, with a required storage of $O(m/\sqrt{\delta})$.

[1]We assume here that the desired relative error and teleport probability α are constants – complete scaling details are provided in our technical report [18].

[2]Formally, for (s,t) with $\pi_s(t) > \delta$, FAST-PPR returns an estimate $\widehat{\pi}_s(t)$ with relative error c, incurring $O\left(\frac{1}{c^2}\sqrt{\frac{d}{\delta}}\sqrt{\frac{\log(1/p_{fail})\log(1/\delta)}{\alpha^2\log(1/(1-\alpha))}}\right)$ average running-time; refer to our technical report [18] for complete details.

We also give a new running-time *lower bound* of $\Omega(1/\sqrt{\delta})$ for PPR estimation, which essentially shows that the dependence of FAST-PPR running-time on δ cannot be improved.

Finally, we note that FAST-PPR has the same performance gains for computing PageRank with arbitrary *preference vectors* [2], where the source is picked from a distribution over nodes. Different preference vectors are used for various applications [2, 1]. However, for simplicity of presentation, we focus on Personalized PageRank in this work.

2. PRELIMINARIES

Given $G(V,E)$, a directed graph, with $|V| = n, |E| = m$, and adjacency matrix A. For any node $u \in V$, we denote $\mathcal{N}^{out}(u), d^{out}(u)$ as the out-neighborhood and out-degree respectively; similarly $\mathcal{N}^{in}(u), d^{in}(u)$ are the in-neighborhood and in-degree. We define $d = \frac{m}{n}$ to be the average in-degree (equivalently, average out-degree).

The personalized PageRank vector π_u for a node $u \in V$ is the stationary distribution of the following random walk starting from u: at each step, return to u with probability α, and otherwise move to a random out-neighbor of the current node. Defining $D = \text{diag}(d^{out}(u))$, and $W = D^{-1}A$, the *personalized PageRank* (PPR) vector of u is given by:

$$\pi_u^T = \alpha \mathbf{e}_u^T + (1-\alpha)\pi_u^T.W, \qquad (1)$$

where $\mathbf{e}_u$ is the identity vector of u. Also, for a target node t, we define the *inverse-PPR* of a node w with respect to t as $\pi_t^{-1}(w) = \pi_w(t)$. The inverse-PPR vector $\{\pi_t^{-1}(w)\}_{w \in V}$ of t sums to $n\pi(t)$, where $\pi(t)$ is the global PageRank of t.

Note that the PPR for a uniform random pair of nodes is $1/n$ – thus for practical applications, we need to consider δ of the form $O(1/n)$ or $O(\log n/n)$. We reinforce this choice of δ using empirical PPR data from the Twitter-2010 graph in Section 6.2 – in particular, we observe that only 1% of (s,t) pairs have PPR greater than $4/n$. In order to process real-time queries, one option would be precompute all answers, and for each node u, store a list of all targets with PPR at least δ. This results in $O(1)$ running-time at query, but requires $\Omega(1/\delta)$ storage per node, which is not feasible in large networks. The other extreme is to eschew storage and compute the PPR at query time – however, as we discuss below, existing algorithms for computing PPR have a worst-case running-time of $\Omega(1/\delta)$. For the relevant values of δ, this is infeasible.

2.1 Existing Approaches for PPR Estimation

There are two main techniques used to compute PageRank/PPR vectors. One set of algorithms use the power iteration. Since performing a direct power iteration may be infeasible in large networks, a more common approach is to use *local-update* versions of the power method, similar to the Jacobi iteration. This technique was first proposed by Jeh and Widom [2], and subsequently improved by other researchers [20, 9]. The algorithms are primarily based on the following recurrence relation for π_u:

$$\pi_u^T = \alpha e_u^T + \frac{(1-\alpha)}{|\mathcal{N}^{out}(u)|} \cdot \sum_{v \in \mathcal{N}^{out}(u)} \pi_v^T \tag{2}$$

Another use of such local update algorithms is for estimating the inverse-PPR vector for a target node. Local-update algorithms for inverse-PageRank are given in [14] (where inverse-PPR is referred to as the 'contribution PageRank vector'), and [21] (where it is called 'susceptibility'). However, one can exhibit graphs where these algorithms need a running-time of $O(1/\delta)$ to get additive guarantees on the order of δ.

Eqn. 2 can be derived from the following probabilistic re-interpretations of PPR, which also lead to an alternate set of randomized or *Monte-Carlo* algorithms. Given any random variable L taking values in $\mathbb{N}_0$, let $RW(u, L) \triangleq \{u, V_1, V_2, \ldots, V_L\}$ be a random-walk of random length $L \sim Geom(\alpha)^3$, starting from u. Then we can write:

$$\pi_u(v) = \mathbb{P}[V_L = v] \tag{3}$$

In other words, $\pi_u(v)$ is the probability that v is the last node in $RW(u, L)$. Another alternative characterization is:

$$\pi_u(v) = \alpha \mathbb{E}\left[\sum_{i=0}^{L} \mathbb{1}_{\{V_i = v\}}\right],$$

i.e., $\pi_u(v)$ is proportional to the number of times $RW(u, L)$ visits node v. Both characterizations can be used to estimate $\pi_u(\cdot)$ via Monte Carlo algorithms, by generating and storing random walks at each node [13, 15, 16, 17]. Such estimates are easy to update in dynamic settings [15]. However, for estimating PPR values close to the desired threshold δ, these algorithms need $\Omega(1/\delta)$ random-walk samples.

2.2 Intuition for our approach

The problem with the basic Monte Carlo procedure – generating random walks from s and estimating the distribution of terminal nodes – is that to estimate a PPR which is $O(\delta)$, we need $\Omega(1/\delta)$ walks. To circumvent this, we introduce a new *bi-directional estimator* for PPR: given a PPR-estimation query with parameters (s, t, δ), we first work backward from t to find a suitably large set of 'targets', and then do random walks from s to test for hitting this set.

Our algorithm can be best understood through an analogy with the shortest path problem. In the bidirectional shortest path algorithm, to find a path of length l from node s to node t, we find all nodes within distance $\frac{l}{2}$ of t, find all nodes within distance $\frac{l}{2}$ of s, and check if these sets intersect. Similarly, to test if $\pi_s(t) > \delta$, we find all w with $\pi_w(t) > \sqrt{\delta}$ (we call this the *target set*), take $O(1/\sqrt{\delta})$ walks from the start node, and see if these two sets intersect. It turns out that these sets might not intersect even if $\pi_s(t) > \delta$, so we go one step further and consider the *frontier set* – nodes outside the target set which have an edge into the target set. We can prove that if $\pi_s(t) > \delta$ then random walks are likely to hit the frontier set.

Our method is most easily understood using the characterization of $\pi_s(t)$ as the probability that a single walk from s ends at t (Eqn. (3)). Consider a random walk from s to t – at some point, it must enter the frontier. We can then decompose the probability of the walk reaching t into the product of two probabilities: the probability that it reaches some node w in the frontier, and the probability that it reaches t starting from w. The two probabilities in this estimate are typically much larger than the overall probability of a random walk reaching t from s, so they can be estimated more efficiently. Figure 2 illustrates this bi-directional scheme.

2.3 Additional Definitions

To formalize our algorithm, we first need some additional definitions. We define a set B to be a blanket set for t with respect to s if all paths from s to t pass through B. Given blanket set B and a random walk $RW(s, L)$, let H_B be the first node in B hit by the walk (defining $H_B = \perp$ if the walk does not hit B before terminating). Since each walk corresponds to a unique H_B, we can write $\mathbb{P}[V_L = v]$ as a sum of contributions from each node in B. Further, from the memoryless property of the geometric random variable, the probability a walk ends at t conditioned on reaching $w \in B$ before stopping is exactly $\pi_s(t)$. Combining these, we have:

$$\pi_s(t) = \sum_{w \in B} \mathbb{P}[H_B = w] \cdot \pi_w(t). \tag{4}$$

In other words, the PPR from s to t is the sum, over all nodes w in blanket set B, of the probability of a random walk hitting B first at node w, times the PPR from w to t.

Recall we define the *inverse-PPR vector* of t as $\pi_t^{-1} = (\pi_w(t))_{w \in V}$. Now we introduce two crucial definitions:

DEFINITION 1 (TARGET SET). *The target set $T_t(\epsilon_r)$ for a target node t is given by:*

$$T_t(\epsilon_r) := \{w \in V : \pi_t^{-1}(w) > \epsilon_r\}.$$

DEFINITION 2 (FRONTIER SET). *The frontier set $F_t(\epsilon_r)$ for a target node t is defined as:*

$$F_t(\epsilon_r) := \Big(\bigcup_{v \in T_t(\epsilon_r)} \mathcal{N}_v^{in}\Big) \setminus T_t(\epsilon_r).$$

The target set $T_t(\epsilon_r)$ thus contains all nodes with inverse-PPR greater than ϵ_r, while the frontier set $F_t(\epsilon_r)$ contains all nodes which are in-neighbors of $T_t(\epsilon_r)$, but not in $T_t(\epsilon_r)$.

2.4 A Bidirectional Estimator

The next proposition illustrates the core of our approach.

PROPOSITION 1. *Set $\epsilon_r < \alpha$. Fix vertices s, t such that $s \notin T_t(\epsilon_r)$.*

1. *Frontier set $F_t(\epsilon_r)$ is a blanket set of t with respect to s.*

[3]i.e., $\mathbb{P}[L = i] = \alpha(1-\alpha)^i \, \forall i \in \mathbb{N}_0$

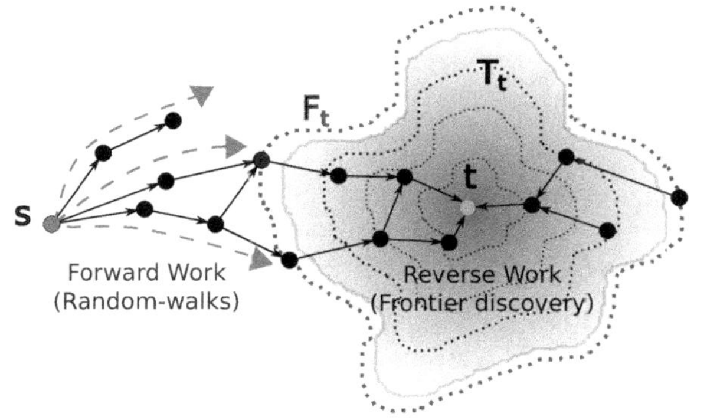

Figure 2: The FAST-PPR Algorithm: We first work backward from the target t to find the frontier F_t (with inverse-PPR estimates). Next we work forward from the source s, generating random-walks and testing for hitting the frontier.

2. *For random-walk $RW(s, L)$ with length $L \sim Geom(\alpha)$:*

$$\mathbb{P}[RW(s,L) \text{ hits } F_t(\epsilon_r)] \geq \frac{\pi_s(t)}{\epsilon_r}$$

PROOF. For brevity, let $T_t = T_t(\epsilon_r), F_t = F_t(\epsilon_r)$. By definition, we know $\pi_t(t) \geq \alpha$ – thus $t \in T_t$, since $\epsilon_r < \alpha$. The frontier set F_t contains all neighbors of nodes in T_t which are not themselves in T_t – hence, for any source node $u \notin T_t$, a path to t must first hit a node in F_t.

For the second part, since F_t is a blanket set for s with respect to t, Eqn. 4 implies $\pi_s(t) = \sum_{w \in F_t} \mathbb{P}[H_{F_t} = w] \pi_w(t)$, where H_{F_t} is the first node where the walk hits F_t. Note that by definition, $\forall w \in F_t$ we have $w \notin T_t$ – thus $\pi_w(t) \leq \epsilon_r$. Applying this bound, we get:

$$\pi_s(t) \leq \epsilon_r \sum_{w \in F_t} \mathbb{P}[H_{F_t} = w] = \epsilon_r \mathbb{P}[RW(s,L) \text{ hits } F_t(\epsilon_r)].$$

Rearranging, we get the result. □

The aim is to estimate $\pi_s(t)$ through Eqn. 4. By the previous proposition, $F_t(\epsilon_r)$ is a blanket set. We will determine the set $F_t(\epsilon_r)$ and estimate all quantities in the right side of Eqn. 4, thereby estimating $\pi_s(t)$.

We perform a simple heuristic calculation to argue that setting $\epsilon_r \approx \sqrt{\delta}$ suffices to estimate $\pi_s(t)$. Previous work shows that $T_t(\epsilon_r)$ can be found in $O(d/\epsilon_r)$ time [14, 21] – using this we can find $F_t(\epsilon_r)$. Now suppose that we know all values of $\pi_w(t)$ ($\forall w \in F_t(\epsilon_r)$). By Eqn. 4, we need to estimate the probability of random walks from s hitting vertices in $F_t(\epsilon_r)$. By the previous proposition, the probability of hitting $F_t(\epsilon_r)$ is at least δ/ϵ_r – hence, we need $O(\epsilon_r/\delta)$ walks from s to ensure we hit $F_t(\epsilon_r)$. All in all, we require $O(d/\epsilon_r + \epsilon_r/\delta)$ – setting $\epsilon_r = \sqrt{d\delta}$ we get a running-time bound of $O(\sqrt{d/\delta})$. In reality, however, we only have (coarse) PPR estimates for nodes in the frontier – we show how these estimates can be boosted to get the desired guarantees, and also empirically show that, in practice, using the frontier estimates gives good results. Finally, we show that $1/\sqrt{\delta}$ is a fundamental lower bound for this problem.

We note that bi-directional techniques have been used for estimating fixed-length random walk probabilities in *regular undirected graphs* [22, 23]. These techniques do not extend to estimating PPR – in particular, we need to consider *directed graphs, arbitrary node degrees and walks of random length.* Also, Jeh and Widom [2] proposed a scheme for PageRank estimation using intermediate estimates from a *fixed skeleton* of target nodes. However there are no running-time guarantees for such schemes; also, the target nodes and partial estimates need to be pre-computed and stored. Our algorithm is fundamentally different as it constructs *separate target sets for each target node* at query-time.

3. THE FAST-PPR ALGORITHM

We now develop the *Frontier-Aided Significance Thresholding* algorithm, or FAST-PPR, specified in Algorithm 1. The input-output behavior of FAST-PPR is as follows:

- **Inputs:** The primary inputs are graph G, teleport probability α, start node s, target node t, and threshold δ – for brevity, we suppress the dependence on G and α. We also need a *reverse threshold* ϵ_r – in subsequent sections, we discuss how this parameter is chosen.
- **Output:** An estimate $\widehat{\pi}_s(t)$ for $\pi_s(t)$.

The algorithm also requires two parameters, c and β – the former controls the number of random walks, while the latter controls the quality of our inverse-PPR estimates in the target set. In our pseudocode (Algorithms 1 and2), we specify the values we use in our experiments – the theoretical basis for these choices is provided in Section 3.2.

Algorithm 1 FAST-PPR(s, t, δ)

Inputs: graph G, teleport probability α, start node s, target node t, threshold δ

```
Set accuracy parameters c, β (in our experiments we use c = 350, β = 1/6).
Call FRONTIER(t, ε_r, β) to obtain target set T_t(ε_r), frontier set F_t(ε_r), and inverse-PPR values (π_t^{-1}(w))_{w ∈ F_t(ε_r) ∪ T_t(ε_r)}.
if s ∈ T_t(ε_r) then
    return π_t^{-1}(s)
else
    Set number of walks k = c ε_r/δ   (See Theorem 3 for details)
    for index i ∈ [k] do
        Generate L_i ~ Geom(α)
        Generate random-walk RW(s, L_i)
        Determine H_i, the first node in F_t(ε_r) hit by RW_i; if RW_i never hits F_t(ε_r), set H_i = ⊥
    end for
    return π̂_s(t) = (1/k) Σ_{i∈[k]} π_t^{-1}(H_i)
end if
```

FAST-PPR needs to know sets $T_t(\epsilon_r), F_t(\epsilon_r)$ and inverse-PPR values $(\pi_t^{-1}(w))_{w \in F_t(\epsilon_r) \cup T_t(\epsilon_r)}$. These can be obtained (approximately) from existing algorithms of [14, 21]. For the sake of completeness, we provide pseudocode for the procedure FRONTIER (Algorithm 2) that obtains this information. The following combines Theorems 1 and 2 in [21].

THEOREM 1. *FRONTIER(t, ϵ_r, β) algorithm computes estimates $\widehat{\pi}_t^{-1}(w)$ for every vertex w, with a guarantee that $\forall w$, $|\widehat{\pi}_t^{-1}(w) - \pi_t^{-1}(w)| < \beta\epsilon_r$. The average running time (over all choices of t) is $O(d/(\alpha\epsilon_r))$, where $d = m/n$ is the average degree of the graph.*

Observe that the estimates $\widehat{\pi}_t^{-1}(w)$ are used to find approximate target and frontier sets. Note that the running

Algorithm 2 FRONTIER($G, \alpha, t, \epsilon_r, \beta$) [14, 21]

```
Inputs: graph G, teleport probability α, target node t, reverse threshold ε_r, accuracy factor β
Define additive error ε_inv = βε_r
Initialize (sparse) estimate-vector π̂_t^{-1} and (sparse) residual-vector r_t as:
    π̂_t^{-1}(u) = r_t(u) = 0 if u ≠ t
    π̂_t^{-1}(t) = r_t(t) = α
Initialize target-set T̂_t = {t}, frontier-set F̂_t = {}
while ∃w ∈ V s.t. r_t(w) > αε_inv do
    for u ∈ N^in(w) do
        Δ = (1 − α) · r_t(w) / d^out(u)
        π̂_t^{-1}(u) = π̂_t^{-1}(u) + Δ, r_t(u) = r_t(u) + Δ
        if π̂_t^{-1}(u) > ε_r then
            T̂_t = T̂_t ∪ {u}, F̂_t = F̂_t ∪ N^in(u)
        end if
    end for
    r_t(w) = 0
end while
F̂_t = F̂_t \ T̂_t
return T̂_t, F̂_t, (π̂_t^{-1}(w))_{w ∈ F̂_t ∪ T̂_t}
```

time for a given t is proportional to the frontier size $|\widehat{F}_t|$. It is relatively straightforward to argue (as in [21]) that $\sum_{t \in V} |\widehat{F}_t| = \Theta(nd/(\alpha\epsilon_r))$.

In the subsequent subsections, we present theoretical analyses of the running times and correctness of FAST-PPR. The correctness proof makes an excessively strong assumption of perfect outputs for FRONTIER, which is not true. To handle this problem, we have a more complex variant of FAST-PPR that can be proven theoretically – refer to our technical report [18] for details. Nonetheless, our empirical results show that FAST-PPR does an excellent job of estimating $\pi_s(t)$.

3.1 Running-time of FAST-PPR

THEOREM 2. *Given parameters δ, ϵ_r, the running-time of the FAST-PPR algorithm, averaged over uniform-random pairs s, t, is $O(\alpha^{-1}(d/\epsilon_r + \epsilon_r/\delta))$.*

PROOF. Each random walk $RW(u, Geom(\alpha))$ takes $1/\alpha$ steps on average, and there are $O(\epsilon_r/\delta)$ such walks performed – this is the *forward time*. On the other hand, from Theorem 1, we have that for a random (s,t) pair, the average running time of FRONTIER is $O(d/(\alpha\epsilon_r))$ – this is the *reverse time*. Combining the two, we get the result. □

Note that the reverse time bound above is averaged across choice of target node; for some target nodes (those with high global PageRank) the reverse time may be much larger than average, while for others it may be smaller. However, the forward time is similar for all source nodes, and is predictable – we exploit this in Section 5.2 to design a balanced version of FAST-PPR which is much faster in practice. In terms of theoretical bounds, the above result suggests an obvious choice of ϵ_r to optimize the running time:

COROLLARY 1. *Set $\epsilon_r = \sqrt{d\delta}$. Then FAST-PPR has an average per-query running-time of $O(\alpha^{-1}\sqrt{d/\delta})$.*

3.2 FAST-PPR with Perfect FRONTIER

We now analyze FAST-PPR in an idealized setting, where we assume that FRONTIER returns *exact inverse-PPR estimates* – i.e., the sets $T_t(\epsilon_r)$, $F_t(\epsilon_r)$, and the values $\{\pi_t^{-1}(w)\}$ are known exactly. This is an unrealistic assumption, but it gives much intuition into *why* FAST-PPR works. In particular, we show that if $\pi(s,t) > \delta$, then with probability at least 99%, FAST-PPR returns an estimate with relative error at most $1/4$; furthermore, if $\pi(s,t) < \delta$, then FAST-PPR returns an estimate with additive error at most $\delta/4$. Note that the above guarantees are chosen for ease of exposition – in our main theoretical result (provided in our technical report [18]), we show that FAST-PPR can achieve any desired relative error target and success probability.

THEOREM 3. *For any s, t, δ, ϵ_r, FAST-PPR outputs an estimate $\widehat{\pi}_s(t)$ such that with probability > 0.99:*

$$|\pi_s(t) - \widehat{\pi}_s(t)| \leq \max(\delta, \pi_s(t))/4.$$

PROOF. We choose $c = \max(48 \cdot 8e\ln(100), 4\log_2(100))$; this choice of parameter c is for ease of exposition in the computations below, and has not been optimized.

To prove the result, note that FAST-PPR performs $k = c\epsilon_r/\delta$ i.i.d. random walks $RW(s, L)$. We use H_i to denote the first node in $F_t(\epsilon_r)$ hit by the ith random walk. Let $X_i = \pi_t^{-1}(H_i)$ and $X = \sum_{i=1}^{k} X_i$. By Eqn. 4, $\mathbb{E}[X_i] = \pi_s(t)$, so $\mathbb{E}[X] = k\pi_s(t)$. Note that $\widehat{\pi}_s(t) = X/k$. As result, $|\pi_s(t) - \widehat{\pi}_s(t)|$ is exactly $|X - \mathbb{E}[X]|/k$.

It is convenient to define scaled random variables $Y_i = X_i/\epsilon_r$ and $Y = X/\epsilon_r$ before we apply standard Chernoff bounds. We have $|\pi_s(t) - \widehat{\pi}_s(t)| = (\epsilon_r/k)|Y - \mathbb{E}[Y]| = (\delta/c)|Y - \mathbb{E}[Y]|$. Also, $\pi_s(t) = (\delta/c)\mathbb{E}[Y]$. Crucially, because $H_i \in F_t(\epsilon_r)$, $X_i = \pi_{H_i}(t) < \epsilon_r$, so $Y_i \leq 1$. Hence, we can apply the following two Chernoff bounds (refer to Theorem 1.1 in [24]):

1. $\mathbb{P}[|Y - \mathbb{E}[Y]| > \mathbb{E}[Y]/4] < \exp(-\mathbb{E}[Y]/48)$
2. For any $b > 2e\mathbb{E}[Y], \mathbb{P}[Y > b] \leq 2^{-b}$

Now, we perform a case analysis. Suppose $\pi_s(t) > \delta/(4e)$. Then $\mathbb{E}[Y] > c/(4e)$, and

$$\begin{aligned}\mathbb{P}[|\pi_s(t) - \widehat{\pi}_s(t)| > \pi_s(t)/4] &= \mathbb{P}[|Y - \mathbb{E}[Y]| > \mathbb{E}[Y]/4] \\ &< \exp(-c/48 \cdot 4e) < 0.01\end{aligned}$$

Suppose $\pi_s(t) \leq \delta/(4e)$. Then, $\delta/4 > 2e\pi_s(t)$ implying $c/4 > 2e\mathbb{E}[Y]$. By the upper tail:

$$\mathbb{P}[\widehat{\pi}_s(t) > \delta/4] = \mathbb{P}[Y > c/4] \leq 2^{-c/4} < 0.01$$

The proof is completed by trivially combining both cases. □

4. LOWER BOUND FOR PPR ESTIMATION

In this section, we prove that any algorithm that accurately estimates PPR queries up to a threshold δ must look at $\Omega(1/\sqrt{\delta})$ edges of the graph. Thus, our algorithms have the optimal dependence on δ. The numerical constants below are chosen for easier calculations, and are not optimized.

We assume $\alpha = 1/100\log(1/\delta)$, and consider randomized algorithms for the following variant of Significant-PPR, which we denote as *Detect-High*(δ) – for all pairs (s,t):

- If $\pi_s(t) > \delta$, output ACCEPT with probability $> 9/10$.
- If $\pi_s(t) < \frac{\delta}{2}$, output REJECT with probability $> 9/10$.

We stress that the probability is over the random choices of the algorithm, *not* over s, t. We now have the following lower bound:

THEOREM 4. *Any algorithm for* Detect-High(δ) *must access* $\Omega(1/\sqrt{\delta})$ *edges of the graph.*

PROOF OUTLINE. The proof uses a lower bound of Goldreich and Ron for *expansion testing* [25]. The technical content of this result is the following – consider two distributions $\mathcal{G}_1$ and $\mathcal{G}_2$ of undirected 3-regular graphs on N nodes. A graph in $\mathcal{G}_1$ is generated by choosing three uniform-random perfect matchings of the nodes. A graph in $\mathcal{G}_2$ is generated by randomly partitioning the nodes into 4 equally sized sets, $V_i, i \in \{1, 2, 3, 4\}$, and then, within each V_i, choosing three uniform-random matchings.

Consider the problem of distinguishing $\mathcal{G}_1$ from $\mathcal{G}_2$. An adversary arbitrarily picks one of these distributions, and generates a graph G from it. A *distinguisher* must report whether G came from $\mathcal{G}_1$ or $\mathcal{G}_2$, and it must be correct with probability $> 2/3$ regardless of the distribution chosen. Theorem 7.5 of Goldreich and Ron [25] asserts the following:

THEOREM 5 (THEOREM 7.5 OF [25]). *Any distinguisher must look at* $\sqrt{N}/5$ *edges of the graph.*

We perform a direct reduction, relating the *Detect-High*(δ) problem to the Goldreich and Ron setting – in particular, we show that an algorithm for *Detect-High*(δ) which requires less than $1/\sqrt{\delta}$ queries can be used to construct a distinguisher which violates Theorem 5. The complete proof is provided in our technical report [18]. □

5. FURTHER VARIANTS OF FAST-PPR

The previous section describes vanilla FAST-PPR, with a proof of correctness assuming a perfect FRONTIER. We now present some variants of FAST-PPR. We give a theoretical variant that is a truly provable algorithm, with no assumptions required – however, vanilla FAST-PPR is a much better practical candidate and it is what we implement. We also discuss how we can use pre-computation and storage to obtain worst-case guarantees for FAST-PPR. Finally, from the practical side, we discuss a workload-balancing heuristic that provides significant improvements in running-time by dynamically adjusting ϵ_r.

5.1 Using Approximate Frontier-Estimates

The assumption that FRONTIER returns perfect estimates is theoretically untenable – Theorem 1 only ensures that each inverse-PPR estimate is correct up to an additive factor of $\epsilon_{inv} = \beta\epsilon_r$. It is plausible that for every w in the frontier $\widehat{F}_t(\epsilon_r)$, $\pi_t^{-1}(w) < \epsilon_{inv}$, and FRONTIER may return a zero estimate for these PPR values. It is not clear how to use these noisy inverse-PPR estimates to get the desired accuracy guarantees.

To circumvent this problem, we observe that estimates $\pi_t^{-1}(w)$ for any node $w \in \widehat{T}_t(\epsilon_r)$ *are in fact accurate up to a multiplicative factor.* We design a procedure to bootstrap these 'good' estimates, by using a special 'target-avoiding' random walk – this modified algorithm gives the desired accuracy guarantee with only an additional $\log(1/\delta)$ factor in running-time. The final algorithm and proof are quite intricate – due to lack of space, the details are deferred to our technical report [18].

5.2 Balanced FAST-PPR

In FAST-PPR, the parameter ϵ_r can be chosen freely while preserving accuracy. Choosing a larger value leads to a smaller frontier and less forward work at the cost of more reverse work; a smaller value requires more reverse work and fewer random walks. To improve performance in practice, we can optimize the choice of ϵ_r based on the target t, to balance the reverse and forward time. Note that for any value of ϵ_r, the forward time is proportional to $k = c\epsilon_r/\delta$ (the number of random walks performed) – for any choice of ϵ_r, it is easy to estimate the forward time required. Thus, instead of committing to a single value of ϵ_r, we propose a heuristic wherein we *dynamically decrease* ϵ_r *until the estimated remaining forward time equals the reverse time already spent.*

We now describe this Balanced FAST-PPR algorithm in brief. Instead of pushing from any node w with residual $r_t(w)$ above a fixed threshold $\alpha\epsilon_{inv}$, we now push from the node w with the largest residual value – this follows a similar algorithm proposed in [21]. From [14, 21], we know that a current maximum residual value of r_{max} implies an additive error guarantee of $\frac{r_{max}}{\alpha}$ – this corresponds to a dynamic ϵ_r value of $\frac{r_{max}}{\alpha\beta}$. At this value of ϵ_r, the number of forward walks required is $k = c\epsilon_r/\delta$. By multiplying k by the average time needed to generate a walk, we get a good prediction the amount of forward work still needed – we can then compare it to the time spent on revere-work and adjust ϵ_r till they are equal. Thus Balanced Fast-PPR is able to dynamically choose ϵ_r to balance the forward and reverse running-time. In Section 6.5, we experimentally show how this change balances forward and reverse running-time, and significantly reduces the average running-time.

5.3 FAST-PPR using Stored Oracles

All our results for FAST-PPR have involved average-case running-time bounds. To convert these to worst-case running-time bounds, we can precompute and store the frontier for all nodes, and only perform random walks at query time. To obtain the corresponding storage requirement for these *Frontier oracles*, observe that for any node $w \in V$, it can belong to the target set of at most $\frac{1}{\epsilon_r}$ nodes, as $\sum_{t \in V} \pi_t^{-1}(w) = 1$. Summing over all nodes, we have:

$$\begin{aligned}\text{Total Storage} &\leq \sum_{t \in V} \sum_{w \in T_t} \sum_{u \in \mathcal{N}^{in}(w)} \mathbb{1}_{\{u \in F_t\}} \\ &\leq \sum_{w \in V} \sum_{t \in V : w \in T_t} d^{in}(w) \leq \frac{m}{\epsilon_r}\end{aligned}$$

To further cut down on running-time, we can also precompute and store the random-walks from all nodes, and perform appropriate joins at query time to get the FAST-PPR estimate. This allows us to implement FAST-PPR on any distributed system that can do fast intersections/joins. More generally, it demonstrates how the modularity of FAST-PPR can be used to get variants that tradeoff between different resources in practical implementations.

6. EXPERIMENTS

We conduct experiments to explore three main questions:

1. How fast is FAST-PPR relative to previous algorithms?
2. How accurate are FAST-PPR's estimates?
3. How is FAST-PPR's performance affected by our design choices: use of frontier and balancing forward/reverse running-time?

Table 1: Datasets used in experiments

Dataset	Type	# Nodes	# Edges
DBLP-2011	undirected	1.0M	6.7M
Pokec	directed	1.6M	30.6M
LiveJournal	undirected	4.8M	69M
Orkut	undirected	3.1M	117M
Twitter-2010	directed	42M	1.5B
UK-2007-05	directed	106M	3.7B

6.1 Experimental Setup

• **Data-Sets:** To measure the robustness of FAST-PPR, we run our experiments on several types and sizes of graph, as described in Table 1. Pokec and Twitter are both social networks in which edges are directed. The LiveJournal, Orkut (social networks) and DBLP (collaborations on papers) networks are all undirected – for each, we have the largest connected component of the overall graph. Finally, our largest dataset with 3.7 billion edges is from a 2007 crawl of the UK domain [26, 27]. Each vertex is a web page and each edge is a hyperlink between pages.

For detailed studies of FAST-PPR, we use the Twitter-2010 graph, with 41 million users and 1.5 billion edges. This presents a further algorithmic challenge because of the skew of its degree distribution: the average degree is 35, but one node has more than 700,000 in-neighbors.

The Pokec [28], Live Journal [29], and Orkut [29] datasets were downloaded from the Stanford SNAP project [30]. The DBLP-2011 [26], Twitter-2010 [26] and UK 2007-05 Web Graph [26, 27] were downloaded from the Laboratory for Web Algorithmics [19].

• **Implementation Details:** We ran our experiments on a machine with a 3.33 GHz 12-core Intel Xeon X5680 processor, 12MB cache, and 192 GB of 1066 MHz Registered ECC DDR3 RAM. Each experiment ran on a single core and loaded the graph used into memory before beginning any timings. The RAM used by the experiments was dominated by the RAM needed to store the largest graph using the SNAP library format [30], which was about 21GB.

For reproducibility, our C++ source code is available at: `http://cs.stanford.edu/~plofgren/fast_ppr/`

• **Benchmarks:** We compare FAST-PPR to two benchmark algorithms: Monte-Carlo and Local-Update.

Monte-Carlo refers to the standard random-walk algorithm [13, 15, 16, 17] – we perform $\frac{c_{MC}}{\delta}$ walks and estimate $\pi_u(v)$ by the fraction of walks terminating at v. For our experiments, we choose $c_{MC} = 35$, to ensure that the relative errors for Monte-Carlo are the same as the relative error bounds chosen for Local-Update and FAST-PPR (see below). However, even in experiments with $c_{MC} = 1$, we find that FAST-PPR is still 3 times faster on all graphs and 25 times faster on the largest two graphs (refer to our technical report [18] for additional plots).

Our other benchmark, Local-Update, is the state-of-the-art local power iteration algorithm [14, 21]. It follows the same procedure as the FRONTIER algorithm (Algorithm 2), but with the additive accuracy ϵ_{inv} set to $\delta/2$. Note that a backward local-update is more suited to computing PPR forward schemes [9, 2] as the latter lack natural performance guarantees on graphs with high-degree nodes.

• **Parameters:** For FAST-PPR, we set the constants $c = 350$ and $\beta = 1/6$ – these are guided by the Chernoff bounds

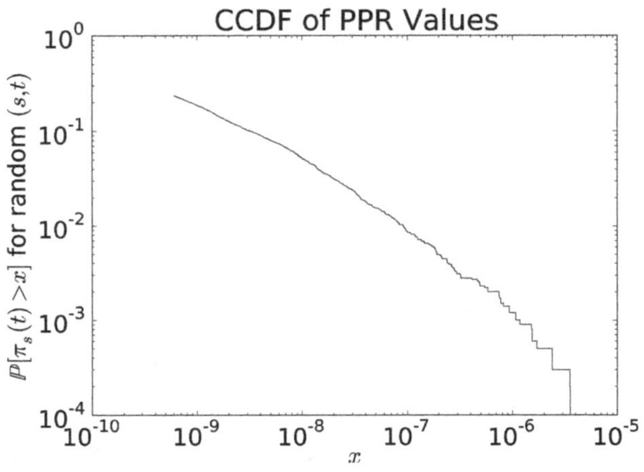

Figure 3: Complementary cumulative distribution for 10,000 (s,t) pairs sampled uniformly at random on the Twitter graph.

we use in the proof of Theorem 3. For vanilla FAST-PPR, we simply choose $\epsilon_r = \sqrt{\delta}$.

6.2 Distribution of PPR values

For all our experiments, we use $\delta = \frac{4}{n}$. To understand the importance of this threshold, we study the distribution of PPR values in real networks. Using the Twitter graph as an example, we choose 10,000 random (s, t) pairs and compute $\pi_s(t)$ using FAST-PPR to accuracy $\delta = \frac{n}{10}$. The complementary cumulative distribution function is shown on a log-log plot in Figure 3. Notice that the plot is roughly linear, suggesting a power-law. Because of this skewed distribution, only 2.8% of pairs have PPR above $\frac{1}{n}$ = 2.4e-8, and less than 1% have PPR over $\frac{4}{n}$ = 9.6e-8.

6.3 Running Time Comparisons

After loading the graph into memory, we sample 1000 source/target pairs (s, t) uniformly at random. For each, we measure the time required for answering PPR-estimation queries with threshold $\delta = 4/n$, which, as we discuss above, is fairly significant because of the skew of the PPR distribution. To keep the experiment length less than 24 hours, for the Local-Update algorithm and Monte-Carlo algorithms we only use 20 and 5 pairs respectively.

The running-time comparisons are shown in Figure 4 – we compare Monte-Carlo, Local-Update, vanilla FAST-PPR, and Balanced FAST-PPR. We perform an analogous experiment where target nodes are sampled according to their global PageRank value. This is a more realistic model for queries in personalized search applications, with searches biased towards more popular targets. The results, plotted in Figure 4(b), show even better speedups for FAST-PPR. All in all, FAST-PPR is many orders of magnitude faster than the state of the art.

The effect of target global PageRank: To quantify the speedup further, we sort the targets in the Twitter-2010 graph by their global PageRank, and choose the first target in each percentile. We measure the running-time of the four algorithms (averaging over random source nodes), as shown in Figure 5. Note that FAST-PPR is much faster than previous methods for the targets with high PageRank.

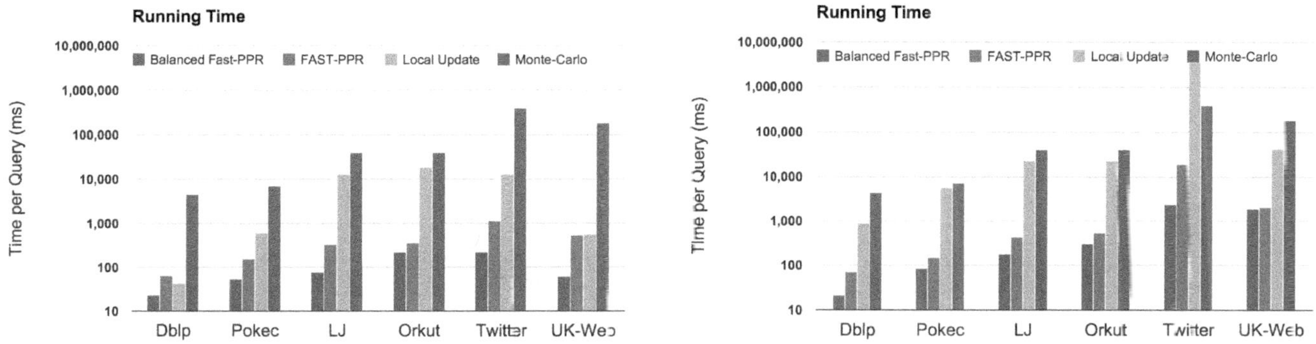

(a) Sampling targets uniformly (b) Sampling targets from PageRank distribution

Figure 4: Average running-time (on log-scale) for different networks. We measure the time required for Significant-PPR queries (s, t, δ) with threshold $\delta = \frac{4}{n}$ for 1000 (s, t) pairs. For each pair, the start node is sampled uniformly, while the target node is sampled uniformly in Figure 4(a), or from the global PageRank distribution in Figure 4(b). In this plot we use teleport probability $\alpha = 0.2$.

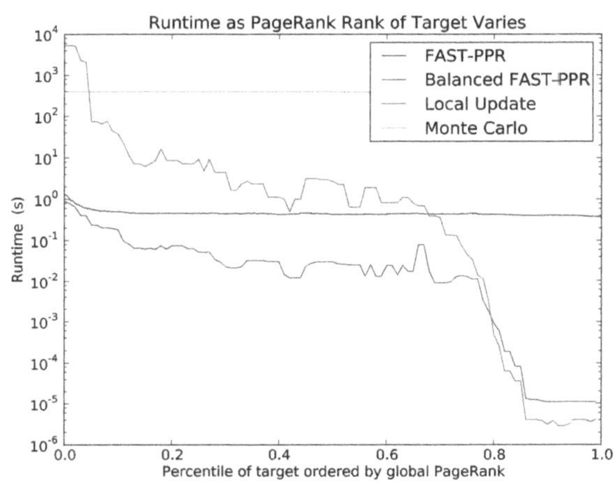

Figure 5: Execution time vs. global PageRank of the target. Target nodes were sorted by global PageRank, then one was chosen from each percentile. We use $\alpha = 0.2$, and 5-point median smoothing.

Note also that large PageRank targets account for most of the average running-time – thus improving performance in these cases causes significant speedups in the average running time. We also see that Balanced FAST-PPR has significant improvements over vanilla FAST-PPR, especially for lower PageRank targets.

To give a sense of the speedup achieved by FAST-PPR, consider the Twitter-2010 graph. Balanced FAST-PPR takes less than 3 seconds for Significant-PPR queries with targets sampled from global PageRank – in contrast, Monte Carlo takes more than 6 minutes and Local Update takes more than an hour. In the worst-case, Monte Carlo takes 3 minutes and Local Update takes 6 hours, while Balanced FAST-PPR takes 40 seconds. Finally, the estimates from FAST-PPR are twice as accurate as those from Local Update, and 6 times more accurate than those from Monte Carlo.

6.4 Measuring the Accuracy of FAST-PPR

We measure the empirical accuracy of FAST-PPR. For each graph, we sample 25 targets uniformly at random, and compute their ground truth inverse-PPR vectors by running a power iteration up to an additive error of $\delta/100$ (as before, we use $\delta = 4/n$). Since larger PPR values are easier to compute than smaller PPR values, we sample start nodes such that $\pi_s(t)$ is near the significance threshold δ. In particular, for each of the 25 targets t, we sample 50 random nodes from the set $\{s : \delta/4 \leq \pi_s(t) \leq \delta\}$ and 50 random nodes from the set $\{s : \delta \leq \pi_s(t) \leq 4\delta\}$.

We execute FAST-PPR for each of the 2500 (s, t) pairs, and measure the empirical error – the results are compiled in Table 2. Notice that FAST-PPR has mean relative error less than 15% and max relative error less than 65% on all graphs – this is sufficiently accurate to make it useful for personalized search.

To make sure that FAST-PPR is not sacrificing accuracy for improved running-time, we also compute the relative error of Local-Update and Monte-Carlo, using the same parameters as for our running-time experiments. For each of the 2500 (s, t) pairs, we run Local-Update, and measure its relative error. For testing Monte-Carlo, we use our knowledge of the ground truth PPR, and the fact that each random-walk from s terminates at t with probability $p_s = \pi_s(t)$. This allows us to simulate Monte-Carlo by directly sampling from a Bernoulli variable with mean $\pi_s(t)$ – this statistically identical to generating random-walks and testing over all pairs. Note that actually simulating the walks would take more than 50 days of computation for 2500 pairs. The relative errors are shown in Figure 1(b). Notice that FAST-PPR is more accurate than the state-of-the-art competition on all graphs. This shows that our running time comparisons are using parameters settings that are fair.

6.5 Some Other Empirical Observations

• **Necessity of the Frontier:** Another question we study experimentally is whether we can modify FAST-PPR to compute the target set $T_t(\epsilon_r)$ and then run Monte-Carlo walks until they hit the target set (rather than the frontier set $F_t(\epsilon_r)$). This may appear natural, as the target set is also a blanket set, and we have good approximations for inverse-PPR values in the target set. Further, using only the

Table 2: **Accuracy of FAST-PPR (with parameters as specified in Section 6.1)**

	Dblp	Pokec	LJ	Orkut	Twitter	UK-Web
Threshold δ	4.06e-06	2.45e-06	8.25e-07	1.30e-06	9.60e-08	3.78e-08
Average Additive Error	5.8e-07	1.1e-07	7.8e-08	1.9e-07	2.7e-09	2.2e-09
Max Additive Error	4.5e-06	1.3e-06	6.9e-07	1.9e-06	2.1e-08	1.8e-08
Average Relative Error:	0.11	0.039	0.08	0.12	0.028	0.062
Max Relative Error	0.41	0.22	0.47	0.65	0.23	0.26

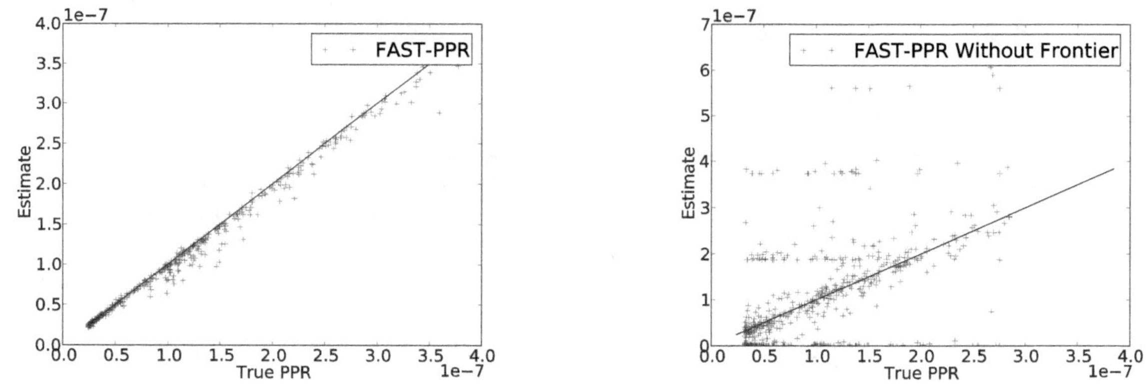

(a) FAST-PPR

(b) FAST-PPR using target set instead of frontier

Figure 6: The importance of using the frontier. In each of these plots, a perfect algorithm would place all data points on the line $y = x$. Notice how using inverse-PPR estimates from the target set rather than the frontier results in significantly worse accuracy.

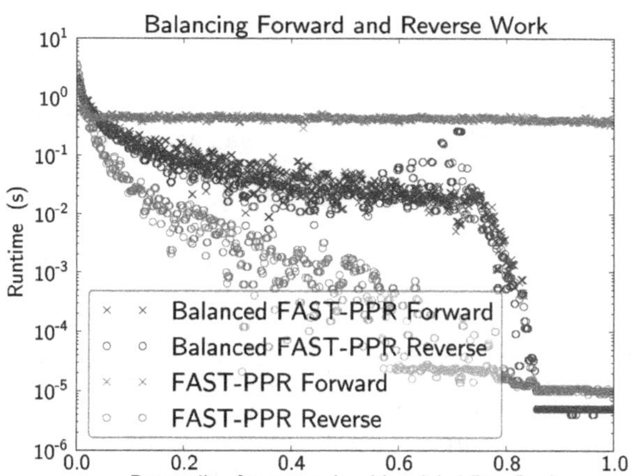

Figure 7: Forward and reverse running-times (on log-scale) for FAST-PPR (in red) and Balanced FAST-PPR (in blue) as we vary the global PageRank of the target node on the x-axis. Data is for the Twitter-2010 graph and is smoothed using median-of-five smoothing. Notice how there is a significant gap between the forward and backward work in Fast-PPR, and that this gap is corrected by Balanced Fast-PPR.

target set would reduce the dependence of the running-time on d, and also reduce storage requirements for an oracle-based implementation.

It turns out however that *using the frontier is critical* to get good accuracy. Intuitively, this is because nodes in the target set may have high inverse-PPR, which then increases the variance of our estimate. This increase in variance can be visually seen in a scatterplot of the true vs estimated value, as shown in Figure 6(b) – note that the estimates generated using the frontier set are much more tightly clustered around the true PPR values, as compared to the estimates generated using the target set.

- **Balancing Forward and Reverse Work:** Balanced FAST-PPR, as described in Section 5.2, chooses reverse threshold ϵ_r dynamically for each target node. Figure 4 shows that Balanced FAST-PPR improves the average running-time across all graphs.

In Figure 7, we plot the forward and reverse running-times for FAST-PPR and Balanced FAST-PPR as a function of the target PageRank. Note that for high global-PageRank targets, FAST-PPR does too much reverse work, while for low global-PageRank targets, FAST-PPR does too much forward work – this is corrected by Balanced FAST-PPR.

Acknowledgements

Peter Lofgren is supported by a National Defense Science and Engineering Graduate (NDSEG) Fellowship.

Ashish Goel and Siddhartha Banerjee were supported in part by the DARPA XDATA program, by the DARPA GRAPHS program via grant FA9550- 12-1-0411 from the U.S. Air Force Office of Scientific Research (AFOSR) and the Defense Advanced Research Projects Agency (DARPA), and by NSF Award 0915040.

C. Seshadhri is at Sandia National Laboratories, which is a multi-program laboratory managed and operated by Sandia Corporation, a wholly owned subsidiary of Lockheed Martin Corporation, for the U.S. Department of Energy's National Nuclear Security Administration under contract DE-AC04-94AL85000.

7. REFERENCES

[1] L. Page, S. Brin, R. Motwani, and T. Winograd, "The pagerank citation ranking: bringing order to the web.," 1999.

[2] G. Jeh and J. Widom, "Scaling personalized web search," in *Proceedings of the 12th international conference on World Wide Web*, ACM, 2003.

[3] P. Yin, W.-C. Lee, and K. C. Lee, "On top-k social web search," in *Proceedings of the 19th ACM international conference on Information and knowledge management*, ACM, 2010.

[4] S. A. Yahia, M. Benedikt, L. V. Lakshmanan, and J. Stoyanovich, "Efficient network aware search in collaborative tagging sites," *Proceedings of the VLDB Endowment*, 2008.

[5] M. V. Vieira, B. M. Fonseca, R. Damazio, P. B. Golgher, D. d. C. Reis, and B. Ribeiro-Neto, "Efficient search ranking in social networks," in *Proceedings of the sixteenth ACM conference on Conference on information and knowledge management*, ACM, 2007.

[6] D. Horowitz and S. D. Kamvar, "The anatomy of a large-scale social search engine," in *Proceedings of the 19th international conference on World wide web*, ACM, 2010.

[7] L. Backstrom and J. Leskovec, "Supervised random walks: predicting and recommending links in socialnetworks," in *Proceedings of the fourth ACM international conference on Web searchand data mining*, ACM, 2011.

[8] P. Gupta, A. Goel, J. Lin, A. Sharma, D. Wang, and R. Zadeh, "Wtf: The who to follow service at twitter," in *Proceedings of the 22nd international conference on World Wide Web*, International World Wide Web Conferences Steering Committee, 2013.

[9] R. Andersen, F. Chung, and K. Lang, "Local graph partitioning using pagerank vectors," in *Foundations of Computer Science, 2006. FOCS'06. 47th Annual IEEE Symposium on*, 2006.

[10] J. Yang and J. Leskovec, "Defining and evaluating network communities based on ground-truth," in *Proceedings of the ACM SIGKDD Workshop on Mining Data Semantics*, p. 3, ACM, 2012.

[11] H. Tong, C. Faloutsos, and J.-Y. Pan, "Fast random walk with restart and its applications," 2006.

[12] T. Sarlós, A. A. Benczúr, K. Csalogány, D. Fogaras, and B. Rácz, "To randomize or not to randomize: space optimal summaries for hyperlink analysis," in *Proceedings of the 15th international conference on World Wide Web*, ACM, 2006.

[13] K. Avrachenkov, N. Litvak, D. Nemirovsky, and N. Osipova, "Monte carlo methods in pagerank computation: When one iteration is sufficient," *SIAM Journal on Numerical Analysis*, 2007.

[14] R. Andersen, C. Borgs, J. Chayes, J. Hopcraft, V. S. Mirrokni, and S.-H. Teng, "Local computation of pagerank contributions," in *Algorithms and Models for the Web-Graph*, Springer, 2007.

[15] B. Bahmani, A. Chowdhury, and A. Goel, "Fast incremental and personalized pagerank," *Proceedings of the VLDB Endowment*, 2010.

[16] C. Borgs, M. Brautbar, J. Chayes, and S.-H. Teng, "Multi-scale matrix sampling and sublinear-time pagerank computation," *Internet Mathematics*, 2013.

[17] A. D. Sarma, A. R. Molla, G. Pandurangan, and E. Upfal, "Fast distributed pagerank computation," *Distributed Computing and Networking*, 2013.

[18] P. Lofgren, S. Banerjee, A. Goel, and C. Seshadhri, "Fast-ppr: Scaling personalized pagerank estimation for large graphs," tech. rep., Stanford University, 2014. arXiv preprint arXiv:1404.3181.

[19] "Laboratory for web algorithmics." `http://law.di.unimi.it/datasets.php`. Accessed: 2014-02-11.

[20] D. Fogaras, B. Rácz, K. Csalogány, and T. Sarlós, "Towards scaling fully personalized pagerank: Algorithms, lower bounds, and experiments," *Internet Mathematics*, 2005.

[21] P. Lofgren and A. Goel, "Personalized pagerank to a target node," *arXiv preprint arXiv:1304.4658*, 2013.

[22] O. Goldreich and D. Ron, "On testing expansion in bounded-degree graphs," in *Studies in Complexity and Cryptography. Miscellanea on the Interplay between Randomness and Computation*, Springer, 2011.

[23] S. Kale, Y. Peres, and C. Seshadhri, "Noise tolerance of expanders and sublinear expander reconstruction," in *Foundations of Computer Science, 2008 FOCS'08. IEEE 49th Annual IEEE Symposium on*, IEEE, 2008.

[24] D. Dubhashi and A. Panconesi, *Concentration of Measure for the Analysis of Randomized Algorithms*. Cambridge University Press, 2009.

[25] O. Goldreich and D. Ron, "Property testing in bounded degreegraphs," *Algorithmica*, 2002 Conference version in STOC 1997.

[26] P. Boldi, M. Rosa, M. Santini, and S. Vigna, "Layered label propagation: A multiresolution coordinate-free ordering for compressing social networks," in *Proceedings of the 20th international conference on World Wide Web*, ACM Press, 2011.

[27] P. Boldi, M. Santini, and S. Vigna, "A large time-aware graph," *SIGIR Forum*, vol. 42, no. 2, 2008.

[28] L. Takac and M. Zabovsky, "Data analysis in public social networks," in *International. Scientific Conf. & Workshop Present Day Trends of Innovations*, 2012.

[29] A. Mislove, M. Marcon, K. P. Gummadi, P. Druschel, and B. Bhattacharjee, "Measurement and Analysis of Online Social Networks," in *Proceedings of the 5th ACM/Usenix Internet Measurement Conference (IMC'07)*, (San Diego, CA), October 2007.

[30] "Stanford network analysis platform (snap)." `http://http://snap.stanford.edu/`. Accessed: 2014-02-11.

Graph Sample and Hold: A Framework for Big-Graph Analytics

Nesreen K. Ahmed[1], Nick Duffield[2*], Jennifer Neville[3], Ramana Kompella[4]
Purdue University[1,3,4], Rutgers University[2]
{nkahmed,neville,kompella}@cs.purdue.edu[1,3,4],nick.duffield@rutgers.edu[2]

ABSTRACT

Sampling is a standard approach in big-graph analytics; the goal is to efficiently estimate the graph properties by consulting a sample of the whole population. A perfect sample is assumed to mirror every property of the whole population. Unfortunately, such a perfect sample is hard to collect in complex populations such as graphs (e.g. web graphs, social networks), where an underlying network connects the units of the population. Therefore, a good sample will be representative in the sense that graph properties of interest can be estimated with a known degree of accuracy.

While previous work focused particularly on sampling schemes to estimate certain graph properties (e.g. triangle count), much less is known for the case when we need to estimate various graph properties with the same sampling scheme. In this paper, we propose a generic stream sampling framework for big-graph analytics, called Graph Sample and Hold (gSH), which samples from massive graphs sequentially in a single pass, one edge at a time, while maintaining a small state in memory. We use a Horvitz-Thompson construction in conjunction with a scheme that *samples* arriving edges *without* adjacencies to previously sampled edges with probability p and *holds* edges *with* adjacencies with probability q. Our sample and hold framework facilitates the accurate estimation of subgraph patterns by enabling the dependence of the sampling process to vary based on previous history. Within our framework, we show how to produce statistically unbiased estimators for various graph properties from the sample. Given that the graph analytics will run on a sample instead of the whole population, the runtime complexity is kept under control. Moreover, given that the estimators are unbiased, the approximation error is also kept under control. Finally, we test the performance of the proposed framework (gSH) on various types of graphs, showing that from a sample with $\leq$ 40K edges, it produces estimates with relative errors $< 1\%$.

Categories and Subject Descriptors

G.2.2 [**Graph Theory**]: Graph Algorithms; H.2.8 [**Database Applications**]: Data Mining

* Address from September 1, 2014: Department of Electrical and Computer Engineering, Texas A&M University, College Station, TX 77843-3128

KDD'14, August 24–27, 2014, New York, NY, USA.
Copyright 2014 ACM 978-1-4503-2956-9/14/08 ...$15.00.
http://dx.doi.org/10.1145/2623330.2623757.

Keywords

Network Sampling, Graph Streams, Statistical Estimation

1. INTRODUCTION

A large percentage of the world's population routinely use online applications (e.g., Facebook and instant messaging) that allow them to interact with their friends, family, colleagues and anybody else that they wish to. Analyzing the various properties of these interconnection networks is a key aspect in managing these applications; for example, uncovering interesting dynamics often prove crucial for either enabling new services or making existing ones better. Since these interconnection networks are often modeled as graphs, and these networks are huge in practice (e.g., Facebook has more than a billion nodes), efficient *big-graph analytics* has recently become extremely important.

One key stumbling block for enabling big graph analytics is the limitation in computational resources. Despite advances in distributed and parallel processing frameworks such as MapReduce for graph analytics and the appearance of infinite resources in the cloud, running brute-force graph analytics is either too costly, too slow, or too inefficient in many practical situations [33, 28]. Further, finding an 'approximate' answer is usually sufficient for many types of analyses; where the extra cost and time in finding the exact answer is often not worth the extra accuracy. *Sampling* therefore provides an attractive approach to quickly and efficiently find an approximate answer to a query, or more generally, any analysis objective [4, 3].

Many interesting graphs in the online world naturally evolve over time, as new nodes join or new edges are added to the network. A natural representation of such graphs is in the form of a stream of edges, as some prior work noted [4]. Clearly, in such a streaming graph model, sampling algorithms that process the data in one-pass are more efficient than those that process the data in an arbitrary order. Even for static graphs, the streaming model is still applicable, with a one-pass algorithm for processing arbitrary queries over this graph typically more efficient than those that involve arbitrary traversals through the graph.

1.1 Sampling, Estimation, Accuracy

In this paper, we propose a new sampling framework for big-graph analytics, called Graph Sample and Hold (gSH). gSH essentially maintains a small amount of state and passes through all edges in the graph in a streaming fashion. The sampling probability of an arriving edge can in general be a function of the stored state, such as the adjacency properties of the arriving edge with those already sampled. For example, if an arriving edge has no adjacencies to previously sampled edges we *sample* it with probability p, but if the edge has adjacencies we *hold* it with probability q. (This can be seen as an analog of the manner in which standard Sample and Hold [15] samples packets with a probability depending on whether their key matches one already sampled). Since any graph analysis algorithm involves processing only a sample of edges (and thus, nodes), gSH helps to keep runtime complexity under check.

gSH provides a generic framework for unbiased estimation of the counts of arbitrary subgraphs. By varying the dependence of sampling probabilities on previous history, one can tune the estimation of various properties of the original graph efficiently with arbitrary degrees of accuracy. For example, simple uniform sampling of edges at random may naturally lead to selecting a large number of higher-degree nodes since higher-degree nodes appear in more number of edges. For each of these sampled nodes, we can choose the holding function to simply track the size of the degree for these specific nodes, of course accounting for the loss of the count before the node has been sampled in an unbiased manner. Similarly, by carefully designing the sampling function, we can obtain a uniformly random sample of nodes (similar to the classic node sampling [4]), for whom we can choose to hold an accurate count of number of triangles each of these nodes is part of.

Our framework uses the Horvitz-Thompson construction [19] in which the count of any sampled object is weighted by dividing by its sampling probability. In gSH this is realized by maintaining along with each sampled edge, the sampling probability that was in force when it was sampled. The counts of subgraphs of sampled edges are then weighted according to the product of the selection probabilities of their constituent edges. Since the edge sampling probabilities are determined conditionally with respect to the prior sampling outcomes, this product reflects the dependence structure of edge selection. The sampling framework also provide the means to compute the accuracy of estimates, since an unbiased estimator of the variance of the count estimator can be computed from the sampling probabilities of selected edges alone. More generally, the covariance between the count estimators of any pair of subgraphs can be estimated in the same manner.

In this paper, we demonstrate applications of the gSH framework in two directions. Firstly, we formulate a parameterized family gSH(p,q) of gSH sampling schemes, in which an arriving edge with no adjacencies with previously sampled edges is selected with probability p; otherwise it is sampled with probability q. Secondly, we consider four specific quantities of interest to estimate within the framework. These are counts of links, triangles, connected paths of length two, and the derived global clustering coefficient. We also provide an unbiased estimator of node counts based on edge sampling. Note that we do not claim that these lists of examples are by any means exhaustive or that the framework can accommodate arbitrary queries efficiently.

1.2 Relation to Sample and Hold

gSH for big-graph analytics bears some resemblance to the classic Sample and Hold (SH) approach [15], versions of which also appeared as Counting Samples of Gibbons and Matias[18], and were used for attack detection by Smitha, Kim and Reddy [31]. In SH, packets carry a key that identifies the flow to which they belong. A router maintains a cache of information concerning the flows of packets that traverse it. If the key of an arriving packet matches a key on which information is currently maintained in the router, the information for that key (such as packet and byte counts and timing information) is updated accordingly. Otherwise the packet is sampled with some probability p. If selected, a new entry is instantiated in the cache for that key. SH is more likely to sample longer flows. Thus SH provides an efficient way to store information concerning the disposition of packets across the small proportion of flows that carry a large proportion of all network packets.

gSH can be viewed as an analog of SH in which the equivalence relation of packets according to their keys is replaced by adjacency relation between links. But this generalization brings many differences as well. In particular, many graph properties involve transitive properties (e.g., triangles) that are relatively uninteresting in networking measurements (and hence, under explored). For many of these properties, it is important to realize that the accuracy of the analytics depends on the ordering of edges to some extent, which was not the case for the vast majority of network measurement problems considered in the literature.

1.3 Contributions and Outline

In Section 2, we describe our general graph sampling framework and show how it can be used to provide statistically unbiased estimates of the counts of subgraph patterns. We also show how unbiased estimates of the variance of these estimators can be efficiently computed within the same framework. In Section 3, we show how counts of specific types of subgraph (links, triangles, paths of length 2) and global clustering coefficient can be estimated. In Section 4, we describe the specific gSH(p,q) graph *Sample* and *Hold* algorithms. In Section 5, we evaluate our method on a number of real world networks. We estimate the counts described in Section 3 and show that the resulting sampling distributions are centered and balanced over the actual values of interest, with low relative errors and tight error bounds as the sample size increases. We also compare with prior work and show orders of magnitude improvement in relative error with small(er) use of memory. We discuss the general relation of our work to existing literature in Section 6 and conclude in Section 7.

2. FRAMEWORK FOR GRAPH SAMPLING

2.1 Graph Stream Model

Let $G = (V, K)$ be a graph. We call two edges $k, k' \in K$ are adjacent, $k \sim k'$, if they join at some node. Specifically:

- *Directed adjacency:* $k = (k_1, k_2) \sim k' = (k'_1, k'_2)$ iff $k_2 = k'_1$ or $k_1 = k'_2$. Note that $\sim$ is not symmetric in this case.
- *Undirected adjacency:* $k = (k_1, k_2) \sim k' = (k'_1, k'_2)$ iff $k \cap k' \neq \emptyset$. Note that $\sim$ is symmetric in this case.

Without loss of generality we assume edges are unique; otherwise distinguishing labels that are ignored by $\sim$ can be appended.

The edges in K are arriving in an order $k : [|K|] \to K$. For $k, k' \in K$, we write $k \prec k'$ if k appears earlier than k' in arrival order. For $i \leq |K|$, $K_i = \{k \in K : k \preceq k_i\}$ comprises the first i arrivals.

2.2 Edge Sampling Model

We describe the sampling of edges through a random process $\{H_i\} = \{H_i : i \in [|K|]\}$ where $H_i = 1$ if k_i is selected, and $H_i = 0$ otherwise. Let $\mathcal{F}_i$ denote the set of possible outcomes $\{H_1, \ldots, H_i\}$; We assume that an edge is selected according to a probability that is a function of the sampling outcomes of previous edges. For example, the selection probability of an edge can be a function of the (random) number of previously selected edges that are adjacent to it. Thus we write

$$\mathbb{P}[k_i \text{ is selected } | \{H_1, \ldots, H_{i-1}\}] = \mathbb{E}[H_i | \mathcal{F}_{i-1}] = p_i \qquad (1)$$

where $p_i \in (0,1]$ is the *random* probability that is determined by the first $i-1$ sampling outcomes[1].

2.3 Subgraph Estimation

In this paper, we are principally concerned with estimating the frequency of occurrence of certain subsets of K within the sample. Our principal tool is the **selection estimator** $\widehat{S}_i = H_i/p_i$ of the link k_i, which indicates the presence of k_i in K. It is uniquely defined by the properties: (i) $\widehat{S}_i \geq 0$; (ii) $\widehat{S}_i > 0$ iff $H_i > 0$; and (iii) $\mathbb{E}[\widehat{S}_i|\mathcal{F}_{i-1}] = 1$, which we prove in Theorem 1 below. We recognize $\widehat{S}_i$ as a Horvitz-Thompson estimator [19] of unity.

The idea generalizes to indicators of general subsets of edges with K. We call a subset $J \subset K$ an ordered subset when written in the increasing arrival order $J = (j_{i_1}, j_{i_2}, \ldots, j_{i_m})$ with $i_1 < i_2 < \cdots < i_m$. For an ordered subset J of K we write

$$H(J) = \prod_{j_i \in J} H_i \quad \text{and} \quad P(J) = \prod_{j_i \in J} p_i \tag{2}$$

with the convention that $H(\emptyset) = P(\emptyset) = 1$. We say that J is selected if $H(J) = 1$. The selection estimator for an ordered subset J of K is

$$\widehat{S}(J) = \prod_{j_i \in J} \widehat{S}_{j_i} = H(J)/P(J) \tag{3}$$

which is our main structural result concerning the properties of $\widehat{S}(J)$.

THEOREM 1. *(i)* $\mathbb{E}[\widehat{S}_i|\mathcal{F}_{i-1}] = 1$ *and hence* $\mathbb{E}[\widehat{S}_i] = 1$.

(ii) For any ordered subset $J = (j_{i_1}, \ldots, j_{i_m})$ *of* K,

$$\mathbb{E}[\widehat{S}(j_{i_1}, \ldots, j_{i_m})|\mathcal{F}_{i_m-1}] = \widehat{S}(j_{i_1}, \ldots, j_{i_{m-1}}) \tag{4}$$

and hence

$$E[\widehat{S}(J)] = 1 \tag{5}$$

(iii) Let J, J' *be two ordered subsets of* K*. If* $J \cap J' = \emptyset$ *then*

$$\mathbb{E}[\widehat{S}(J)\widehat{S}(J')] = 1 \text{ and hence } \mathrm{Cov}(\widehat{S}(J), \widehat{S}(J')) = 0 \tag{6}$$

(iv) Let $J_1, \ldots, J_\ell$ *be disjoint ordered subsets of* K*. Let* q *be a polynomial in* ℓ *variables that is linear in each of its arguments. Then* $\mathbb{E}[q(\widehat{S}(J_1), \ldots, \widehat{S}(J_\ell))] = q(1, \ldots, 1)$.

(v) Let J, J' *be two ordered subsets of* K *with* $J\Delta J'$ *be their symmetric difference. Then* $\widehat{C}(J, J')$ *defined below is non-negative and an unbiased estimator of* $\mathrm{Cov}(\widehat{S}(J), \widehat{S}(J'))$*, which is hence non-negative.* $\widehat{C}(J, J')$ *is defined to be 0 when* $J \cap J' = \emptyset$*, and otherwise:*

$$\widehat{C}(J, J') = \widehat{S}(J \cup J')\left(\widehat{S}(J \cap J') - 1\right) \tag{7}$$

(vi) $\widehat{S}(J)\left(\widehat{S}(J) - 1\right)$ *is an unbiased estimator of* $\mathrm{Var}(\widehat{S}(J))$.

PROOF. (i) $\mathbb{E}[\widehat{S}_i|\mathcal{F}_{i-1}] = \mathbb{E}[H_i/p_i|\mathcal{F}_{i-1}] = 1$, since $p_i > 0$. (ii) is a corollary of (i) since

$$\begin{aligned} &\mathbb{E}[\widehat{S}(j_{i_1}, \ldots, j_{i_m})|\mathcal{F}_{i_m-1}] && (8)\\ &= \mathbb{E}\left[\mathbb{E}[\widehat{S}_{i_m}|\mathcal{F}_{i_m-1}]\widehat{S}(j_{i_1}, \ldots, j_{i_{m-1}})|\mathcal{F}_{i_{m-1}}\right] \\ &= \widehat{S}(j_{i_1}, \ldots, j_{i_{m-1}}) && (9)\end{aligned}$$

[1]Formally, $\{\mathcal{F}_i\}$ is the natural filtration associated with the process $\{H_i\}$, and $\{p_i\}$ is previsible w.r.t. $\{\mathcal{F}_i\}$; see [35].

(iii) When $J \cap J' = \emptyset$, then by (ii)

$$\mathbb{E}[\widehat{S}(J)\widehat{S}(J')] = \mathbb{E}[\widehat{S}(J \cap J')] = 1 \tag{10}$$

(iv) Is a direct corollary of (iii)

(v) Unbiasedness: The case $J \cap J' = \emptyset$ follows from (iii). Otherwise,

$$\begin{aligned}\mathbb{E}[\widehat{C}(J, J')] &= \mathbb{E}[\widehat{S}(J)\widehat{S}(J')] - \mathbb{E}[\widehat{S}(J \cup J')] && (11)\\ &= \mathbb{E}[\widehat{S}(J)\widehat{S}(J')] - 1 = \mathrm{Cov}(\widehat{S}(J), \widehat{S}(J'))\end{aligned}$$

since $\mathbb{E}[\widehat{S}(J)] = \mathbb{E}[\widehat{S}(J')] = 1$. Nonnegativity: $\widehat{C}(J, J') = (H(J \cup J')/P(J \cup J'))(H(J \cap J')/P(J \cap J') - 1) = (H(J \cup J')/P(J \cup J'))(1/P(J \cap J') - 1) \geq 0$, since $H(A)H(B) = H(A)$ when $B \subset A$.

(vi) is a special case of (v) with $J = J'$. ☐

3. SUBGRAPH SUM ESTIMATION

We now describe in more detail the process of estimation, and computing variance estimates. The most general quantity that we wish to estimate is a weighted sum over collections of subgraphs; for brevity, we will refer to these as **subgraph sums**. This class includes quantities such as counts of total nodes or links in G, or counts of more complex objects such as connected paths of length two, or triangles that have been a focus of study in the recent literature. However, the class of more general quantities in which a selector is applied to all subgraphs of a given type (e.g. triangles) or only subgraphs fulfilling a selection criterion (e.g. based on labels on the nodes of the triangle) are to be included in future work.

3.1 General Estimation and Variance

To allow for the greatest possible generality, we let $\mathcal{K} = 2^K$ denote the set of subsets of K, and let f be a real function on $\mathcal{K}$. For any subset $Q \subset \mathcal{K}$, the subset sum of f over Q is

$$f(Q) = \sum_{J \in Q} f(J) \tag{12}$$

Here Q represents the set of subgraphs fulfilling a selection criterion as described above. Let $\widehat{Q}$ denote the set of objects in Q that are sampled, i.e., therefore $J = (k_{i_1}, \ldots, k_{i_m}) \in Q$ for which all links are selected. The following is an obvious consequence of the linearity of expectation and Theorem 1

THEOREM 2. *(i) An unbiased estimator of* $f(Q)$ *is*

$$\widehat{f}(Q) = \sum_{J \in Q} f(J)\widehat{S}(J) = \sum_{J \in \widehat{Q}} f(J)/P(J) \tag{13}$$

(ii) An unbiased estimator of $\mathrm{Var}(\widehat{f}(Q))$ *is*

$$\sum_{J, J' \in \widehat{Q}: J \cap J' \neq \emptyset} f(J)f(J')(1/P(J \cup J'))(1/P(J \cap J') - 1) \tag{14}$$

Note that the sum in (14) can formally be left unrestricted since terms with non-intersecting J, J' are zero due to our convention that $P(\emptyset) = 1$.

3.2 Edges

As before K denotes the edges in G; let $\widehat{K}$ denote the set of sampled edges. Then

$$\widehat{N}_K = \sum_{k_i \in \widehat{K}} \frac{1}{p_i} \tag{15}$$

is an unbiased estimate of the unique edge count $N_K = |K|$. An unbiased estimate of the variance of $\widehat{N}_K$ is

$$\sum_{k_i \in \widehat{K}} \frac{1}{p_i}\left(\frac{1}{p_i} - 1\right) \tag{16}$$

3.3 Triangles

Let T denote the set of triangles $\tau = (k_1, k_2, k_3)$ in G, and $\widehat{T}$ the set of sampled triangles. Then

$$\widehat{N}_T = \sum_{\tau \in \widehat{T}} 1/P(\tau) \tag{17}$$

is an unbiased estimate of $N_T = |T|$, the number of triangles in G. Since two intersecting triangles have either one link in common or are identical, an unbiased estimate of $\mathrm{Var}(\widehat{N}_T)$ is

$$\sum_{\tau \in \widehat{T}} \frac{1}{P(\tau)}\left(\frac{1}{P(\tau)} - 1\right) + \sum_{\tau \neq \tau' \in \widehat{T}} \frac{1}{P(\tau \cup \tau')}\left(\frac{1}{P(e(\tau, \tau'))} - 1\right)$$

where $e(\tau, \tau')$ is the common edge between τ and τ'

3.4 Connected Paths of Length 2

Let Λ denote the set of connected paths of length two $L = (k_1, k_2)$ in G, and $\widehat{\Lambda}$ the subset of these that are sampled. Then

$$\widehat{N}_\Lambda = \sum_{L \in \widehat{\Lambda}} 1/P(L) \tag{18}$$

is an unbiased estimate of $N_\Lambda = |\Lambda|$, the number of such paths in G. Since two non-identical members of Λ may have one edge in common, an unbiased estimate of $\mathrm{Var}(\widehat{N}_\Lambda)$ is

$$\sum_{L \in \widehat{\Lambda}} \frac{1}{P(L)}\left(\frac{1}{P(L)} - 1\right) + \sum_{L \neq L' \in \widehat{\Lambda}} \frac{1}{P(L \cup L')}\left(\frac{1}{P(e(L, L'))} - 1\right)$$

where $e(L, L') = L \cap L'$ is the common edge between L and L'.

3.5 Clustering Coefficient

The global clustering coefficient of a graph is defined as $\alpha = 3N_T/N_\Lambda$. While we use $\widehat{\alpha} = 3\widehat{N}_T/\widehat{N}_\Lambda$ as an estimator of α, it is not unbiased. However, the well known delta-method [29] suggests using a formal Taylor expansion. But we note that a rigorous application of this method depends on establishing asymptotic properties of $\widehat{N}_T$ and $\widehat{N}_\Lambda$ for large graphs, the study of which we defer to a subsequent paper. With this caveat we proceed as follows. For a random vector $X = (X_1, \ldots, X_n)$ a second order Taylor expansion results in the approximation

$$\mathrm{Var}(f(X_1, \ldots, X_n)) \approx v \cdot Mv \tag{19}$$

where $v = (\nabla f)(\mathbb{E}[X])$ and M is the covariance matrix of the X_i. Considering $f(\widehat{N}_T, \widehat{N}_\Lambda) = \widehat{N}_T/\widehat{N}_\Lambda$ we obtain the following approximation. For computation we replace all quantities by their corresponding unbiased estimators derived previously:

$$\begin{aligned} \mathrm{Var}(\widehat{N}_T/\widehat{N}_\Lambda) \quad \approx \quad & \frac{\mathrm{Var}(\widehat{N}_T)}{\widehat{N}_\Lambda^2} + \frac{\widehat{N}_T^2\,\mathrm{Var}(\widehat{N}_\Lambda)}{\widehat{N}_\Lambda^4} \\ & -2\frac{\widehat{N}_T\,\mathrm{Cov}(\widehat{N}_T, \widehat{N}_\Lambda)}{\widehat{N}_\Lambda^3} \end{aligned} \tag{20}$$

Following Theorem 1, the covariance term is estimated as

$$\sum_{\substack{\tau \in \widehat{T}, L \in \widehat{\Lambda} \\ \tau \cap L \neq \emptyset}} \frac{1}{P(\tau \cup L)}\left(\frac{1}{P(\tau \cap L)} - 1\right) \tag{21}$$

3.6 Nodes

Node selection is not directly expressed as a subgraph sum, but rather through a polynomial of the type treated in Theorem 1(iv). Let $K(x)$ denote the edges containing the node $x \in V$. Now observe x remains unsampled if and only if no edge in $K(x)$ is sampled. This motivates the following estimator of node selection:

$$\widehat{n}_x = 1 - \prod_{k_i \in K(x)} (1 - \widehat{S}_i) \tag{22}$$

The following is a direct consequence of Theorem 1(iv)

LEMMA 1. *$\widehat{n}_x = 0$ if and only if no edge from $K(x)$ is sampled, and $\mathbb{E}[n_x] = 1$.*

4. GRAPH SAMPLE AND HOLD

4.1 Algorithms

We now turn to specific sampling algorithms that conform to the edge sampling model of Section 2.2. **Graph Sample and Hold** gSH(p, q) is a single pass algorithm over a stream of edges. The edge k is somewhat analogous to the key of (standard) sample and hold. A matching edge is sampled with probability q. If there is not a match, the edge is stored with some probability p. An edge not sampled is discarded permanently. For estimation purposes we also need to keep track of the probability with which a selected edge is sampled. We formally specify gSH(p, q) as Algorithm 1.

Algorithm 1: Graph Sample and Hold: gSH(p, q)

$\widehat{K} \leftarrow \emptyset$;
while *new edge* k **do**
  if $k \sim k'$ *for some* $(k', p') \in \widehat{K}$ **then**
    $r = q$
  else
    $r = p$
  Append (k, r) to $\widehat{K}$ with probability r

In some sense, gSH samples connected components in the same way the standard sample and hold samples flows, although there are some differences. The main difference is a single connected component in the original graph may be sampled as multiple components. This can happen, for example, if omission of an edge from the sample can disconnect a component. Clearly the order in which nodes are streamed determines whether or not such sampling disconnection can occur.

Clearly, gSH would admit generalizations that allow a more complex dependence of the sampling probability for a new edge on the current sampled edge set. This can be achieved by adapting the flexible holding function. Consequently, the details of the sampling scheme (holding function) should allow certain subgraphs to be favored for selection. In this paper, we do not delve into this matter in great detail, rather we look at a simple illustrative modification of gSH that favor the selection of triangles– called gSH$_T$. gSH$_T$ is identical to gSH except that any arriving edge that would complete a triangle is selected with probability 1; see Algorithm 2. Obviously gSH$(p, 1)$ and gSH$_T(p, 1)$ are identical

4.2 Illustration with gSH(p,1)

We use a simple example of a path of length 3 to illustrate that in Graph Sample and Hold gSH$(p, 1)$, the distribution of the random graph sample depends on the order in which the edges are presented. The graph $G = (V, K)$ comprises 4 nodes $V = a, b, c, d$

Order			Selection			Prob.	Weights			Est. Node Degree			
(a,b)	(b,c)	(c,d)	(a,b)	(b,c)	(c,d)		(a,b)	(b,c)	(c,d)	a	b	c	d
1	2	3	✓	✓	✓	p	$1/p$	1	1	$1/p$	$1/p+1$	2	1
			·	✓	✓	$(1-p)p$	0	$1/p$	1	0	$1/p$	$1/p+1$	1
			·	·	✓	$(1-p)^2p$	0	0	$1/p$	0	0	$1/p$	$1/p$
			·	·	·	$(1-p)^3$	0	0	0	0	0	0	0
2	1	3	✓	✓	✓	p	1	$1/p$	1	1	$1/p+1$	$1/p+1$	1
			✓	·	✓	$(1-p)p^2$	$1/p$	0	$1/p$	$1/p$	$1/p$	$1/p$	$1/p$
			·	·	✓	$(1-p)^2p$	0	0	$1/p$	0	0	$1/p$	$1/p$
			✓	·	·	$(1-p)^2p$	$1/p$	0	0	$1/p$	$1/p$	0	0
			·	·	·	$(1-p)^3$	0	0	0	0	0	0	0
1	3	2	✓	✓	✓	p^2	$1/p$	1	$1/p$	$1/p$	$1/p+1$	$1/p+1$	$1/p$
			✓	✓	·	$p(1-p)$	$1/p$	1	0	$1/p$	$1/p+1$	1	0
			·	✓	✓	$(1-p)p$	0	1	$1/p$	0	1	$1/p+1$	1
			·	✓	·	$(1-p)^2p$	0	$1/p$	0	0	$1/p$	$1/p$	0
			·	·	·	$(1-p)^3$	0	0	0	0	0	0	0

Table 1: Estimation on a path of length 3 using gSH$(p,1)$

Algorithm 2: Graph Sample and Hold for Triangles: gSH$_T(p,q)$

```
K̂ ← ∅;
while new edge k do
    if k would complete a triangle in K̂ then
        r = 1
    else
        if k ∼ k' for some (k', p') ∈ K̂ then
            r = q
        else
            r = p
    Append (k, r) to K̂ with probability r
```

Table 2: Statistics of datasets. n is the number of nodes, N_K is the number of edges, N_T is the number of triangles, N_Λ is the number of connected paths of length 2, α is the global clustering coefficient, and D is the density.

graph	n	N_K	N_T	N_Λ	α	D
socfb-CMU	7K	249.9K	2.3M	37.4M	0.18526	0.0114
socfb-UCLA	20K	747.6K	5.1M	107.1M	0.14314	0.0036
socfb-Wisconsin	24K	835.9K	4.8M	121.4M	0.12013	0.0029
web-Stanford	282K	1.9M	11.3M	3.9T	0.00862	5.01×10^{-5}
web-Google	876K	4.3M	13.3M	727.4M	0.05523	1.15×10^{-5}
web-BerkStan	685K	6.6M	64.6M	27.9T	0.00694	2.83×10^{-5}

connected by 3 undirected edges $K = \{(a,b),(b,c),(c,d)\}$ which are the keys for our setting. There are 6 possible arrival orders for the keys, of which we need only analyze 3, since the other orders can be obtained by time reversal. These are displayed in the "Order" columns in Table 1. For each order, the possible selection outcomes for the three edges by the check marks ✓, followed by the probability of each selection. The adjusted weights for each outcome is displayed in "Weights" followed by corresponding estimate of the node degree, i.e., the sum of weights of edges incident at each node. One can check by inspection that the probability-weighted sums of the weight estimators are 1, while the corresponding sums of the degree estimators yield the the true node degree.

5. EXPERIMENTS AND EVALUATION

We test the performance of our proposed framework (gSH$_T$) as described in Algorithm 2 (with $r = 1$ for edges that are closing triangles), on various social and information networks with 250K–7M edges. For all network datasets, we consider an undirected graph, discard edge weights, self-loops, and we generate the stream by randomly permuting the edges. Table 2 summarizes the main characteristics of these graphs, such that n is the number of nodes, N_K is the number of edges, N_T is the number of triangles, N_Λ is the number of connected paths of length two, α is the global clustering coefficient, and D is the graph density.

1. **Social Facebook Graphs**. Here, the nodes are people and edges represent friendships among Facebook users in three different US schools (CMU, UCLA, and Wisconsin, see [32] for data analysis and downloads).
2. **Web Graphs**[2]. Here, the nodes are web-pages and edges are hyperlinks among these pages in different domains.

We ran the experiments on MacPro 2.66GHZ 6-Core Intel processor, with 48GB memory. In order to test the effect of parameter settings (i.e., p and q), we perform 100 independent experiments and we consider all possible combinations of p and q in the following range,

$$p, q = \{0.005, 0.008, 0.01, 0.03, 0.05, 0.08, 0.1\}$$

Our experimental procedure is done independently for each $p = p_i, q = q_i$ as follows:

1. Given one parameter setting $p = p_i, q = q_i$, we obtain a sample of edges $\widehat{K} \subset K$ using gSH$_T(p_i,q_i)$–as described in Algorithm 2.
2. Using $\widehat{K}$, compute the unbiased estimates of the following statistics: Edge counts $\widehat{N}_K$; Triangle counts $\widehat{N}_T$; Connected paths of length two $\widehat{N}_\Lambda$; Global Clustering Coefficient $\widehat{\alpha}$.
3. Compute the unbiased estimates of the variance of the quantities mentioned above.

Note that the estimation of the count of unique edges $\widehat{N}_K$ is necessary when the graph stream is not simple (i.e., edges may occur more than once).

[2] Stanford Network Project, http://snap.stanford.edu/

Table 3: Estimates of expected value and relative error, when sample size ≤ 40K edges, with sampling probability $p, q = 0.005$ for web-BerkStan, and $p = 0.005, q = 0.008$ otherwise. First column shows the statistics of the full graph, SSize is the number of sampled edges, and LB/UB are the 95% lower and upper bounds respectively.

Edges N_K	N_K	$\widehat{N}_K$	$\frac{\lvert\widehat{N}_K - N_K\rvert}{N_K}$	SSize	LB	UB
socfb-CMU	249.9K	249.6K	0.0013	1.7K	236.8K	262.4K
socfb-UCLA	747.6K	751.3K	0.0050	5K	729.3K	773.34K
socfb-Wisconsin	835.9K	835.7K	0.0003	5.5K	812.2K	859.1K
web-Stanford	1.9M	1.9M	0.0004	14.8K	1.9M	2M
web-Google	4.3M	4.3M	0.0007	25.2K	4.2M	4.3M
web-BerkStan	6.6M	6.6M	0.0006	39.8K	6.5M	6.7M

Triangles N_T	N_T	$\widehat{N}_T$	$\frac{\lvert\widehat{N}_T - N_T\rvert}{N_T}$	SSize	LB	UB
socfb-CMU	2.3M	2.3M	0.0003	1.7K	1.6M	2.9M
socfb-UCLA	5.1M	5.1M	0.0095	5K	4.2M	6.03M
socfb-Wisconsin	4.8M	4.8M	0.0058	5.5K	4M	5.7M
web-Stanford	11.3M	11.3M	0.0023	14.8K	3.7M	18.3M
web-Google	13.3M	13.4M	0.0029	25.2K	11.7M	15M
web-BerkStan	64.6M	65M	0.0063	39.8K	45.5M	84.6M

Path. Length two N_Λ	N_Λ	$\widehat{N}_\Lambda$	$\frac{\lvert\widehat{N}_\Lambda - N_\Lambda\rvert}{N_\Lambda}$	SSize	LB	UB
socfb-CMU	37.4M	37.3M	0.0018	1.7K	32.6M	42M
socfb-UCLA	107.1M	107.8M	0.0060	5K	100.1M	115.42M
socfb-Wisconsin	121.4M	121.2M	0.0018	5.5K	108.9M	133.4M
web-Stanford	3.9T	3.9T	0.0004	14.8K	3.6T	4.2T
web-Google	727.4M	724.3M	0.0042	25.2K	677.1M	771.5M
web-BerkStan	27.9T	27.9T	0.0002	39.8K	26.5T	29.3T

Global Clustering α	α	$\widehat{\alpha}$	$\frac{\lvert\widehat{\alpha} - \alpha\rvert}{\alpha}$	SSize	LB	UB
socfb-CMU	0.18526	0.18574	0.00260	1.7K	0.14576	0.22572
socfb-UCLA	0.14314	0.14363	0.00340	5K	0.12239	0.16437
socfb-Wisconsin	0.12013	0.12101	0.00730	5.5K	0.10125	0.14077
web-Stanford	0.00862	0.00862	0.00020	14.8K	0.00257	0.01467
web-Google	0.05523	0.05565	0.00760	25.2K	0.04825	0.06305
web-BerkStan	0.00694	0.00698	0.00680	39.8K	0.00496	0.00900

5.1 Performance Analysis

We proceed by first demonstrating the accuracy of the proposed estimators for the different graph statistics we discuss in this paper across various social and web networks. Given a sample $\widehat{K} \subset K$ (collected by gSH$_T$ Algorithm 2), we consider the absolute relative error (i.e., $\frac{|\mathrm{E[est]} - \mathrm{Actual}|}{\mathrm{Actual}}$) as a measure of how far is the estimated statistic from the actual graph statistic of interest, where E[est] is the mean estimated value across 100 independent runs. Table 3 provides the estimated values in comparison to the actual statistics when the sample size is $\leq$ 40K with $p, q = 0.005$ for web-BerkStan and $p = 0.005$, $q = 0.008$ otherwise. We summarize below our main findings from Table 3:

- For edge count (N_K) estimates, we observe that the relative error is in the range of 0.03% – 0.5% across all graphs.
- For triangle count (N_T) estimates, we observe that the relative error is in the range of 0.03% – 0.95% across all graphs.
- For the number of connected paths of length two (N_Λ), we observe that the relative error of the estimates is in the range of 0.02% – 0.6% across all graphs.
- For clustering coefficient (α) estimates, we observe that the relative error is in the range of 0.02% – 0.76% across all graphs.
- Finally, we observe that the highest error is in the triangle count estimates and yet it is still $\leq 1\%$

5.2 Confidence Bounds

Having selected a sample that can be used to estimate the actual statistic, it is also desirable to construct a confidence interval within which we are *sufficiently* sure that the actual graph statistic of interest lies. We construct a 95% confidence interval for the estimates of edge (N_K), triangle (N_T), connected paths of length two (N_Λ) counts, and clustering coefficient (α) as follows,

$$\mathrm{est} \pm 1.96\sqrt{\mathrm{Var(est)}} \tag{23}$$

where the estimates 'est' and 'Var(est)' are computed using the equations of the unbiased estimators of counts and their variance as discussed in Section 3. For example, the 95% confidence interval for the edge count is,

$$\widehat{N}_K \pm 1.96\sqrt{\mathrm{Var}(\widehat{N}_K)} \tag{24}$$

where $\mathrm{UB} = \widehat{N}_K + 1.96\sqrt{\mathrm{Var}(\widehat{N}_K)}$, $\mathrm{LB} = \widehat{N}_K - 1.96\sqrt{\mathrm{Var}(\widehat{N}_K)}$ are the upper and lower bounds for the edge count respectively.

Table 3 provides the 95% upper and lower bounds (i.e., UB, LB) for the sample when the sample size is $\leq$ 40K edges. We observe that the actual statistics across all different graphs lie in between the bounds of the confidence interval (i.e., LB $\leq$ Actual $\leq$ UB). Note that the sample is collected using gSH$_T$ Algorithm 2.

Additionally, we study the properties of the sampling distribution of our proposed framework (gSH) as we change the sample size. Figure 1 shows the sampling distribution as we increase the sample size (for all possible settings of p, q in the range 0.005–0.1 as described previously). More specifically, we plot the fraction $\frac{\mathrm{E[est]}}{\mathrm{Actual}}$ (represented by blue diamond symbols in the figure), where E[est] is the mean estimated value across 100 independent runs. Further, we plot the fractions $\frac{\mathrm{UB}}{\mathrm{Actual}}$, and $\frac{\mathrm{LB}}{\mathrm{Actual}}$ (represented by green circle symbols in the figure). These plots show the sampling distribution of all statistics for socfb-UCLA, and socfb-Wisconsin graphs.

We now summarize the findings that we observe from Figure 1:

- The sampling distribution is centered and balanced over the red line ($y_{\text{axis}} = 1$) which represents the actual value of the graph statistic. This shows the unbiased properties of the estimators for the four graph quantities of interest that we discussed in Section 2.
- The upper and lower bounds contain the actual value (represented by the red line) for different combinations of p, q.
- As we increase the sample size, the bounds *converge* to be more concentrated over the actual value of the graph statistic (i.e, the estimated variance is decreasing as we increase the sample size).
- The confidence intervals for edge counts are small in the range of 0.98–1.02.
- The confidence intervals for triangle counts and clustering coefficient are larger compared to other graph statistics (in the range of 0.87–1.12).
- Samples with size = 40K edges (dashed vertical line) provide a reasonable tradeoff between sample size and unbiased estimates with low variance.

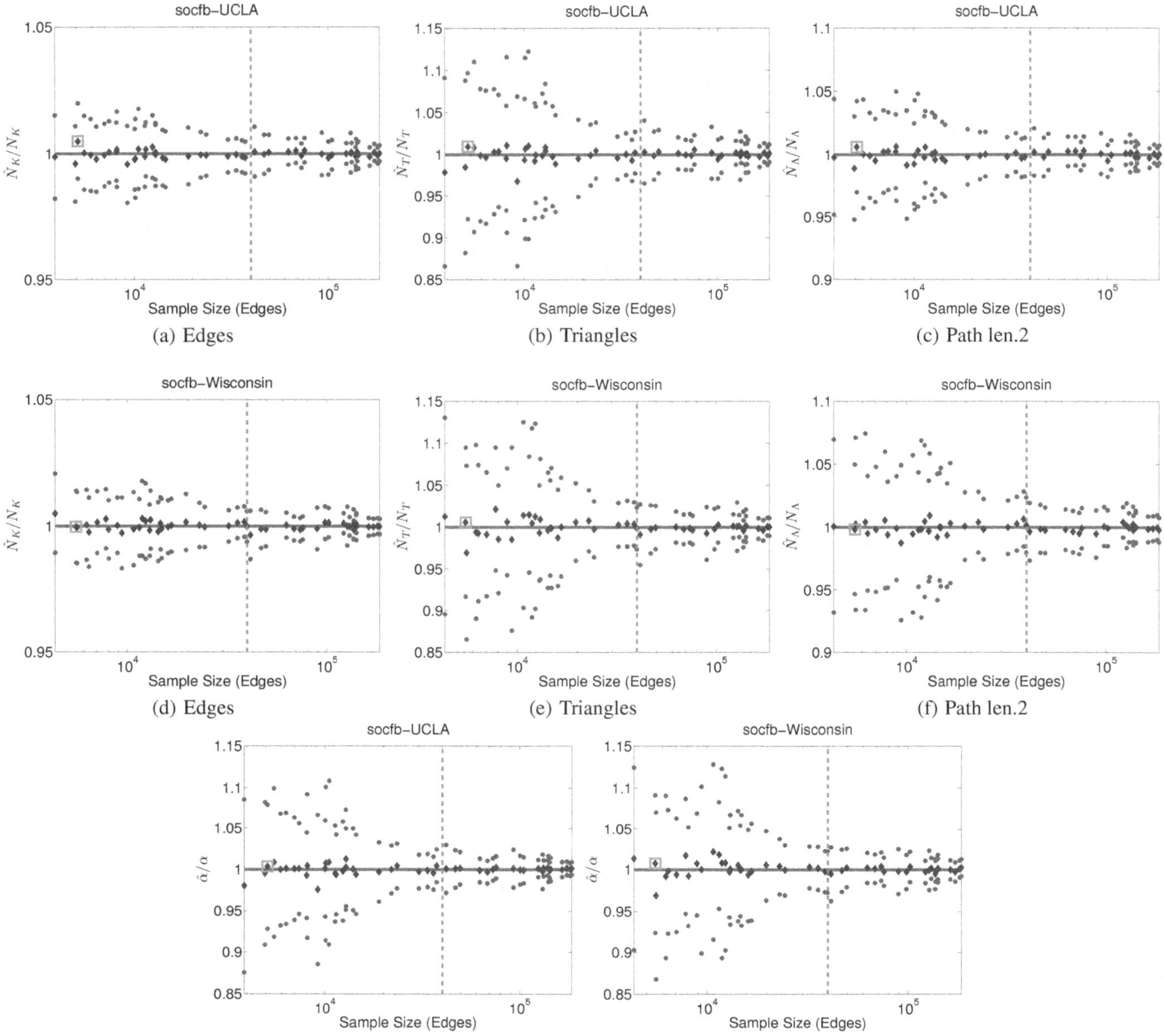

(a) Edges (b) Triangles (c) Path len.2

(d) Edges (e) Triangles (f) Path len.2

(g) Clust. (h) Clust.

Figure 1: Convergence of the estimates (N_K, N_T, N_Λ, α, upper and lower bounds) for socfb-UCLA and socfb-Wisconsin graphs, for all possible samples with p, q in the range 0.005–0.1. Diamonds (Blue): $\frac{\text{E[est]}}{\text{Actual}}$. Circles (Green): $\frac{\text{UB}}{\text{Actual}}$, $\frac{\text{LB}}{\text{Actual}}$. Square (Orange): refers to the sample in Table 3. Dashed vertical line (Grey): refers to the sample at 40K edges

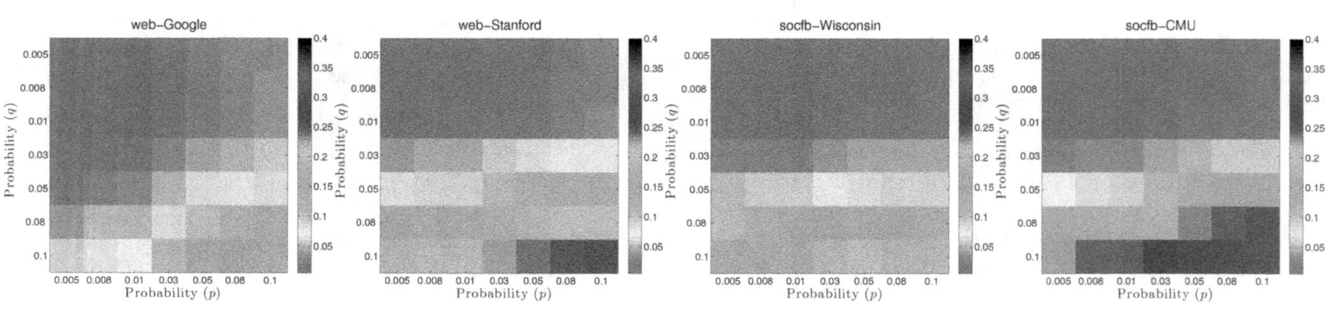

Figure 2: Sampling Fraction ($\frac{\text{SSize}}{N_K}$) as p, q changes in the range '0.005–0.1' for web and social graphs (ordered from sparse → dense).

Table 4: Coverage Probability γ for 95% conf. interval

graph	γ_{N_K}	γ_{N_T}	γ_{N_Λ}	γ_α
socfb-CMU	0.94	0.95	0.96	0.92
socfb-UCLA	0.96	0.95	0.95	0.92
socfb-Wisconsin	0.95	0.95	0.96	0.95
web-Stanford	0.97	0.92	0.95	0.92
web-Google	0.95	0.93	0.95	0.95
web-BerkStan	0.96	0.94	0.93	0.93

Table 5: The relative error and sample size of Jha *et al.* [20] in comparison to gSH$_T$ for triangle count estimation

	Jha *et al.* [20]		gSH$_T$	
graph	$\frac{\lvert\widehat{N}_T - N_T\rvert}{N_T}$	SSize	$\frac{\lvert\widehat{N}_T - N_T\rvert}{N_T}$	SSize
web-Stanford	≈ 0.07	40K	0.0023	14.8K
web-Google	≈ 0.04	40K	0.0029	25.2K
web-BerkStan	≈ 0.12	40K	0.0063	39.8K

- Thus, we conclude that the sampling distribution of the proposed framework has many desirable properties of unbiasedness and low variance as we increase the sample size.

Note that in Figure 1, we use a square (with orange color) to refer to the sample reported in Table 3. We also found similar observations for the rest of the graphs (plots are omitted due to space constraints).

In addition to the analysis above, we compute the *exact coverage* probability γ of the 95% confidence as follows,

$$\gamma = \mathbb{P}(\text{LB} \leq \text{Actual} \leq \text{UB}) \tag{25}$$

For each $p = p_i, q = q_i$, we compute the proportion of samples in which the actual statistic lies in the confidence interval across 100 independent sampling experiments gSH$_T(p_i, q_i)$. We vary p, q in the range of 0.005–0.01, and for each possible combination of p, q (e.g., $p = 0.005, q = 0.008$), we compute the exact coverage probability γ. Table 4 provides the mean coverage probability with $p, q = \{0.005, 0.008, 0.01\}$ for all different graphs. Note γ_{N_K}, γ_{N_T}, γ_{N_Λ}, and γ_α indicate the exact coverage probability of edge, triangle, paths of length two counts, and clustering coefficient respectively. We observe that the nominal 95% confidence interval holds to a good approximation, as $\gamma \approx 95\%$ across all graphs.

5.3 Comparison to Previous Work

We compare to the most recent research done on triangle counting by Jha *et al.* [20]. Jha *et al.* proposed a Streaming-Triangles algorithm to estimate the triangle counts. Their algorithm maintains two data structures. The first data structure is the edge reservoir and used to maintain a uniform random sample of edges as they streamed in. The second data structure is the wedge (path length two) reservoir and used to select a uniform sample of wedges created by the edge reservoir. The algorithm proceeds in a reservoir sampling fashion as a new edge e_t is streaming in. Then, edge e_t gets the chance to be sampled and replace a previously sampled edge with probability $1/t$. Similarly, a randomly selected new wedge (formed by e_t) replaces a previously sampled wedge from the wedge reservoir. Table 5 provides a comparison between our proposed framework (gSH) and the Streaming-Triangles algorithm proposed by Jha *et al.* [20]. Note that we compare with the results reported in their paper.

From Table 5, we observe that across the three web graphs, our proposed framework produces a relative error that is *orders of magnitude* smaller than the error produced by the Streaming-Triangles algorithm proposed in [20], and also uses a small(er) overhead storage (in most of the graphs). We note that Jha *et al.* [20] compares to other state of the art algorithms and shows that they are not practical and produce a very large error; see Section 6 for more details.

We have also compared to the work of Pavan *et al.* [25] and found their algorithm needs to store estimators, each of which stores *at least* one edge ($\approx$ 36 bytes per estimator). Their algorithm also needs at least 128 estimators to obtain good results. On the other hand, gSH$_T$ used orders of magnitude less storage to achieve even a better performance (results were omitted due to space constraints).

5.4 Effect of p, q on Sampling Rate

While Figure 1 shows that the sampling distribution of the proposed framework is unbiased regardless the choice of p, q, the question as to what effect the choice of p, q has on the sample size still needs to be explored. In this section, we study the effect of the choice of parameter settings on the fraction of edges sampled from the graph.

Figure 2 shows the fraction of sampled edges using gSH$_T$ Algorithm 2, as we vary p, q in the range of 0.005–0.1 for two web graphs and two social Facebook graphs. Note that the graphs are ordered by their density (see Table 2) going from the most sparse to the most dense graph. We observe that when $q \leq 0.01$, regardless the choice of p, the fraction of sampled edges is in the range of 0.5% – 2.5% of the total number of edges in the graph. We also observe that as q goes from 0.01 to 0.03, the fraction of sampled edges would be in the range of 2.75% – 5%. These observations hold for all the graphs we studied.

On the other hand, as q goes from 0.03 to 0.1, the fraction of sampled edges depends on whether the graph is dense or sparse. For example, for the web-Google graph, as q goes from 0.03 to 0.1, the fraction of sampled edges goes from 5% to 15%. Also, for the web-Stanford graph, as q goes from 0.03 to 0.1, the fraction of sampled edges goes from 5% to 25%. However, for the most dense graph we have in this paper (socfb-CMU), the fraction of sampled edges goes from 5% to 31%. Note that when we tried $q = 1$, regardless the choice of p, more than 80% of the edges were sampled.

Since p is the probability of sampling a fresh edge (not adjacent to a previously sampled edge), one could think of p as the probability of random jumps (similar to random walk methods) to explore unsampled regions in the graph. On the other hand, q is the probability of sampling an edge adjacent to previous edges. Therefore, one could think of q as the probability of exploring the neighborhood of previously sampled edges (similar to the forward probability in Forest Fire sampling).

From all the discussion above, we conclude that using a small p, q settings (i.e., ≤ 0.008) is better to control the fraction of sampled edges, and also recommended since the sampling distribution of the proposed framework is unbiased regardless the choice of p, q as we show in Figure 1 (also see Section 2). However, if a tight confidence interval is needed, then increasing p, q helps to reduce variance.

5.5 Implementation Issues

In practice, statistical variance estimators are costly to compute. In this paper, we provide an efficient parallel procedure to compute

Table 6: Computation time (in seconds) of graph statistics for the full graph versus the sample output of gSH$_T$

	Full Graph		Sampled Graph	
graph	Time	Graph size	Time	SSize
web-Stanford	19.68	1.9M	0.13	14.8K
web-Google	5.05	4.3M	0.55	25.2K
web-BerkStan	113.9	6.6M	1.05	39.8K

the variance estimate. As an example, we illustrate this for the task of computing the variance of the triangle estimate ($Var(\widehat{N}_T)$ from Section 3.3). Consider any pair of triangles τ and τ'. Assuming τ and τ' are not identical, the covariance of τ and τ' is greater than zero (i.e., $\text{Cov}(\tau, \tau') > 0$), if and only if the two triangles are intersecting in one edge $e(\tau, \tau')$. Since two intersecting triangles have either one edge in common or are identical, we can find intersecting triangles by finding all triangles *incident* to a particular edge e. In this case, the intersection probability of the two triangles is $P(\tau \cap \tau') = P(e(\tau, \tau'))$. Note that if τ and τ' are identical, then the computation is straightforward. The procedure is very simple as follows,

- Given a sample set of edges $\widehat{K} \subset K$, for each edge $e \in \widehat{K}$
  - find the set of all triangles 'T_e' incident to e
  - for each pair of triangles (τ, τ'), where $\tau, \tau' \in T_e$, and $\tau \neq \tau'$, compute the $Cov(\tau, \tau')$ such that $P(\tau \cap \tau') = P(e(\tau, \tau'))$

Since, the computation of each edge is independent of other edges, we parallelize the computation of the variance estimators. Moreover, since the computation of triangle counts and paths of length two can themselves be parallelized, we compare the total elapsed time in seconds used to compute these counts on both the full graph and a sampled graph of size $\leq$ 40K edges. Table 6 provide the results of this comparison for the three web graphs. Note that in the case of the sampled graph, we report the sum of the total computations of both the variance estimators and expected values of the triangle and paths of length two count statistics. Also, note that we use the sample reported in Table 3 for these computations. The results show a significant reduction in the time needed to compute triangles and paths of length two counts. For example, consider the web-BerkStan graph, where the total time is reduced from 113 seconds to 1.05 seconds. Note that all the computations of Table 6 are performed on a MacPro laptop 2.9GHZ Intel Core i7 with 8GB memory.

6. RELATED WORK

In this section, we discuss the related work on the problem of large-scale graph analytics and their applications. Generally speaking, there are two bodies of work related to this paper: (i) graph analytics in the graph stream setting, and (ii) graph analytics in the non-streaming setting (e.g. using MAPREDUCE). In this paper, we propose a generic stream sampling framework for big-graph analytics, called Graph Sample and Hold (gSH), that works in a *single pass* over the stream. Therefore, we focus on the related work for graph analytics in the graph stream setting.

Graph Analysis Using Streaming Algorithms.

Before exploring the literature of graph stream analytics, we briefly review the literature in data stream analysis and mining that may not contain graph data. For example, for sequence sampling (*e.g.*, reservoir sampling) [34, 6], for computing frequency counts [24], and for mining concept drifting data streams [16]. Additionally, the idea of *sample and hold* (SH) was introduced in [15] for unbiased sampling of network data with integral weights. Subsequently, other work explored adaptive SH, and SH with signed updates [11, 12]. Nevertheless, none of this work has considered the framework of *sample and hold* (SH) for social and information networks. In this paper, however, we propose the framework of *graph sample and hold* (gSH) for big-graph analytics.

There has been an increasing interest in mining, analysis, and querying of massive graph streams as a result of the proliferation of graph data (*e.g.*, social networks, emails, IP traffic, Twitter hashtags). For example, to count triangles [20, 25, 7, 10, 8, 21], finding common neighborhoods [9], estimating pagerank values [27], and characterizing degree sequences in multi-graph streams [13]. In the data mining field, there is the work done on clustering and outlier detection in graph streams [1, 2].

Much of this work has used various sampling schemes to sample from the stream of graph edges [4]. Surprisingly, the majority of this work has focused primarily on sampling schemes that can be used to estimate certain graph properties (e.g. triangle counts), while much less is known for the case when we need a generic approach to estimate various graph properties with the same sampling scheme with minimum assumptions.

For example, the work done in [10] proposed an algorithm with space bound guarantees for triangle counting and clustering estimation in the *incidence stream model* where all edges incident to a node are arriving in order together. However, in the incidence stream model, counting triangles is a relatively easy problem, and counting the number of paths of length two is simply straightforward. On the other hand, it has been shown that these bounds and accurate estimates will no longer hold in the case of *adjacency stream model*, where the edges arrive arbitrarily with no particular order [20, 25].

Another example, the work done Jha *et al.* in [20] proposed a practical, single pass, $O(\sqrt{n})$-space streaming algorithm specifically for triangle counting and clustering estimation with additive error guarantee (as opposed to other algorithms with relative error guarantee). Although, the algorithm is practical and approximates the triangle counts accurately at a sample size of $40K$ edges, their method is specifically designed for triangle counting. Nevertheless, we compare to the results of triangle counts reported in [20], and we show that our framework is not only generic but also produces errors with orders of magnitude less than the algorithm in [20], and with a small(er) storage overhead in many times.

More recently, Pavan *et al.* proposed a space-efficient streaming algorithm for counting and sampling triangles in [25]. This algorithm works in a single pass streaming fashion with order $O(N_K \Delta / N_T)$-space, where Δ is the maximum degree of the graph. However, this algorithm needs to store estimators (i.e., wedges that may form potential triangles), and each of these estimators stores *at least* one edge. In their paper, they show that they need at least 128 estimators (i.e., more than $128K$ edges), to obtain accurate results (i.e., large storage overhead compared to those in this paper).

Other semi-streaming algorithms were proposed for triangle counting, such as the work in [8], however, they are not practical and produce large error as discussed and analyzed by the work in [25].

Horvitz-Thompson estimation was proposed for social networks by Frank [17], including applications to subgraph sampling, but limited to a model of simple random sampling of vertices without replacement.

Graph Analysis Using Static and Parallel Algorithms.

We briefly review other research for graph analysis in non-streaming setting (i.e., static). For example, exact counting of triangles with runtime $O(N_K{}^{3/2})$ [28], or approximately by sampling edges as in [33]. Although not working in a streaming fashion, the algorithm in [33] uses unbiased estimators of triangle counts similar to our work. Moreover, other algorithms were proposed based on wedge sampling and proved to be accurate in practice, such as the work in [30]. More recently, the work done in [26] proposed a parallel framework for finding the maximum clique.

Finally, there has been an increasing interest in the general problem of network sampling. For a detailed survey and comparison, see [4]. For example, to obtain a representative subgraph [22, 4], and to preserve the community structure [23], and other sampling goals [14, 5].

7. CONCLUSION

In this paper, we presented a generic framework for big-graph analytics called graph sample and hold (gSH). The gSH framework samples from massive graphs *sequentially in a single pass*, one edge at a time, while maintaining a small state typically less than 1% of the total number of edges in the graph. Our contributions can be summarized in the following points:

- We show how to produce unbiased estimators and their variance for four specific graph quantities of interest to estimate within the framework. Further, we show how to obtain confidence bounds using the variance unbiased estimators.
- We conducted several experiments on real world graphs, such as social Facebook graphs, and web graphs. The results show that the relative error ranging from 0.02% to 0.95% for a sample with $\leq$ 40K edges. Moreover, the results show that the sampling distribution is centered and balanced over the actual values of the four graph quantities of interest, with tight error bounds as the sample size increases.
- We compare to the state of the art and our proposed framework has a relative error *orders of magnitude* less than the Streaming-Triangles algorithm proposed in [20], as well as with a small(er) overhead storage (in most of the graphs).
- We show how to parallelize and efficiently compute the unbiased variance estimators, and we discuss the significant reductions in computation time that can be achieved by gSH framework.

In future work, we aim to extend gSH to other graph properties such as cliques, communities, and others.

Acknowledgments

This research is supported by NSF under contract number(s) IIS-1017898 and IIS-1219015. The U.S. Government is authorized to reproduce and distribute reprints for governmental purposes notwithstanding any copyright notation hereon.

8. REFERENCES

[1] AGGARWAL, C., ZHAO, Y., AND YU, P. On clustering graph streams. In *SDM* (2010), pp. 478–489.

[2] AGGARWAL, C., ZHAO, Y., AND YU, P. Outlier detection in graph streams. In *ICDE* (2011), pp. 399–409.

[3] AHMED, N. K., NEVILLE, J., AND KOMPELLA, R. Network sampling designs for relational classification. In *ICWSM* (2012).

[4] AHMED, N. K., NEVILLE, J., AND KOMPELLA, R. Network sampling: from static to streaming graphs. *(to appear) TKDD* (2013).

[5] AL HASAN, M., AND ZAKI, M. Output space sampling for graph patterns. *Proceedings of the VLDB Endowment 2*, 1 (2009), 730–741.

[6] BABCOCK, B., DATAR, M., AND MOTWANI, R. Sampling from a moving window over streaming data. In *SODA* (2002), pp. 633–634.

[7] BAR-YOSSEF, Z., KUMAR, R., AND SIVAKUMAR, D. Reductions in streaming algorithms with an application to counting triangles in graphs. In *SODA* (2002), pp. 623–632.

[8] BECCHETTI, L., BOLDI, P., CASTILLO, C., AND GIONIS, A. Efficient semi-streaming algorithms for local triangle counting in massive graphs. In *KDD* (2008), pp. 16–24.

[9] BUCHSBAUM, A., GIANCARLO, R., AND WESTBROOK, J. On finding common neighborhoods in massive graphs. *Theoretical Computer Science 299*, 1 (2003), 707–718.

[10] BURIOL, L., FRAHLING, G., LEONARDI, S., MARCHETTI-SPACCAMELA, A., AND SOHLER, C. Counting triangles in data streams. In *PODS* (2006), pp. 253–262.

[11] COHEN, E., CORMODE, G., AND DUFFIELD, N. Don't let the negatives bring you down: sampling from streams of signed updates. *In SIGMETRICS 40*, 1 (2012), 343–354.

[12] COHEN, E., DUFFIELD, N., KAPLAN, H., LUND, C., AND THORUP, M. Algorithms and estimators for accurate summarization of internet traffic. In *SIGCOMM* (2007), pp. 265–278.

[13] CORMODE, G., AND MUTHUKRISHNAN, S. Space efficient mining of multigraph streams. In *PODS* (2005), pp. 271–282.

[14] DASGUPTA, A., KUMAR, R., AND SIVAKUMAR, D. Social sampling. In *KDD* (2012), pp. 235–243.

[15] ESTAN, C., AND VARGHESE, G. New directions in traffic measurement and accounting. In *SIGCOMM* (2002), pp. 323–336.

[16] FAN, W. Streamminer: a classifier ensemble-based engine to mine concept-drifting data streams. In *VLDB* (2004), pp. 1257–1260.

[17] FRANK, O. Sampling and estimation in large social networks. *Social Networks 1*, 1 (1978), 91–101.

[18] GIBBONS, P., AND MATIAS, Y. New sampling-based summary statistics for improving approximate query answers. In *SIGMOD* (1998).

[19] HORVITZ, D. G., AND THOMPSON, D. J. A generalization of sampling without replacement from a finite universe. *Journal of the American Statistical Association 47*, 260 (1952), 663–685.

[20] JHA, M., SESHADHRI, C., AND PINAR, A. A space efficient streaming algorithm for triangle counting using the birthday paradox. In *KDD* (2013), pp. 589–597.

[21] JOWHARI, H., AND GHODSI, M. New streaming algorithms for counting triangles in graphs. In *COCOON*. 2005, pp. 710–716.

[22] LESKOVEC, J., AND FALOUTSOS, C. Sampling from large graphs. In *KDD* (2006), pp. 631–636.

[23] MAIYA, A. S., AND BERGER-WOLF, T. Y. Sampling Community Structure. In *WWW* (2010), pp. 701–710.

[24] MANKU, G. S., AND MOTWANI, R. Approximate Frequency Counts over Data Streams. In *VLDB* (2002), pp. 346–357.

[25] PAVAN, A., TANGWONGSAN, K., TIRTHAPURA, S., AND WU, K.-L. Counting and sampling triangles from a graph stream. *VLDB 6*, 14 (2013), 1870–1881.

[26] ROSSI, R. A., GLEICH, D. F., GEBREMEDHIN, A. H., AND PATWARY, M. A. Fast maximum clique algorithms for large graphs. In *WWW* (2014).

[27] SARMA, A. D., GOLLAPUDI, S., AND PANIGRAHY, R. Estimating PageRank on Graph Streams. In *PODS* (2008), pp. 69–78.

[28] SCHANK, T. Algorithmic aspects of triangle-based network analysis.

[29] SCHERVISH, M. J. *Theory of Statistics*. Springer, 1995.

[30] SESHADHRI, C., PINAR, A., AND KOLDA, T. G. Triadic measures on graphs: The power of wedge sampling. In *SDM* (2013).

[31] SMITHA, KIM, I., AND REDDY, A. Identifying long term high rate flows at a router. In *High Performance Computing* (2001).

[32] TRAUD, A. L., MUCHA, P. J., AND PORTER, M. A. Social structure of facebook networks. *Physica A: Statistical Mechanics and its Applications 391*, 16 (2012), 4165–4180.

[33] TSOURAKAKIS, C. E., KANG, U., MILLER, G. L., AND FALOUTSOS, C. Doulion: counting triangles in massive graphs with a coin. In *KDD* (2009), pp. 837–846.

[34] VITTER, J. Random sampling with a reservoir. *TOMS 11* (1985).

[35] WILLIAMS, D. *Probability with Martingales*. Cambridge University Press, 1991.

Balanced Graph Edge Partition

Florian Bourse[*]
ENS
Paris, France
florian.bourse@ens.fr

Marc Lelarge
INRIA-ENS
Paris, France
marc.lelarge@ens.fr

Milan Vojnović
Microsoft Research
Cambridge, UK
milanv@microsoft.com

ABSTRACT

Balanced edge partition has emerged as a new approach to partition an input graph data for the purpose of scaling out parallel computations, which is of interest for several modern data analytics computation platforms, including platforms for iterative computations, machine learning problems, and graph databases. This new approach stands in a stark contrast to the traditional approach of balanced vertex partition, where for given number of partitions, the problem is to minimize the number of edges cut subject to balancing the vertex cardinality of partitions.

In this paper, we first characterize the expected costs of vertex and edge partitions with and without aggregation of messages, for the commonly deployed policy of placing a vertex or an edge uniformly at random to one of the partitions. We then obtain the first approximation algorithms for the balanced edge-partition problem which for the case of no aggregation matches the best known approximation ratio for the balanced vertex-partition problem, and show that this remains to hold for the case with aggregation up to factor that is equal to the maximum in-degree of a vertex. We report results of an extensive empirical evaluation on a set of real-world graphs, which quantifies the benefits of edge- vs. vertex-partition, and demonstrates efficiency of natural greedy online assignments for the balanced edge-partition problem with and with no aggregation.

Categories and Subject Descriptors

E.1 Data [**Data Structures**]: Graphs and networks; G.2.2 [**Mathematics of Computing**]: Discrete Mathematics–Graph Theory, Graph Algorithms; H.2 [**Information Systems**]: Database Management

General Terms

Algorithms, Experiments, Performance

[*]Work performed as part of a MSR-INRIA joint research centre project.

KDD'14, August 24–27, 2014, New York, NY, USA.

http://dx.doi.org/10.1145/2623330.2623660.

Keywords

Graph Edge Partition, Distributed Massive Computations, Approximation Algorithms, Streaming Heuristics

1. INTRODUCTION

A common approach to scale-out computations on large-scale input graph data is to partition the graph data and parallelize the computation on some given number of machines in a distributed cluster of machines. For example, this is of interest for iterative computations on input graph data such as computing the PageRank using the power-iteration method in systems such as Pregel [23], Giraph [8] and Spark [39], or for iterative machine learning computations such as approximate Bayesian inference in systems such as Graphlab [22, 21], or for efficiently resolving queries in large-scale databases, e.g. [3], and specifically, graph databases, e.g., Neo4j [24] and Trinity [30]. An important problem is to ensure a high-quality of a graph partition with respect to two criteria: balancing the processing load across machines and minimizing the communication cost between different machines.

A traditional approach to placing a graph on a cluster of k machines is to construct a balanced *vertex partition* that equi-partitions the set of vertices to k partitions such that the number of edges spanning the partitions is minimized. A new approach was proposed recently in [9] that advocates to perform an *edge partition* by equi-partitioning the set of edges to k partitions such that the amount of communication required to synchronize the state of vertex-copies is minimized. This new approach is motivated by the observation that standard tools, e.g., [14, 26] for constructing a balanced vertex partition perform poorly on power-law graphs [1, 19, 20]. Each cut edge contributes to storage and network overhead since both machines maintain a copy of the adjacency information, and in some cases, a ghost vertex per each cut edge is maintained [10]. Many systems resort to using hash (random) vertex placement for its simplicity of implementation. Since the graph partitioning problem is considered to be intrinsically difficult, this random partition may perform rather poorly. The design rationale of performing an edge partition is to allow for more flexibility for processing load balancing by allowing a single vertex program to span multiple machines and reduction of communication and storage overhead by evenly assigning edges to machines. Since each edge is stored exactly once, changes to edge data do not need to be communicated.

Little is known about the balanced edge-partition problem both on the grounds of theoretical computation complexity and approximation guarantees, and practical methods with good average-case performance. This is unlike to the traditional balanced vertex-partition problem which was studied rather extensively, with the best known approximation guarantee of $O(\sqrt{\log k \log n})$ for the edge-cut cost of a partition in k clusters of a size n graph [18], and with software tools being available off-the-shelf, e.g. METIS [12, 13]. An important requirement for graph partitioning at scale is to being able to produce a good-quality graph partition under restriction to make a single pass through the graph data, which is often referred to as *streaming graph partition.* Here, again, we find a number of approaches that have been studied for the vertex-partition problem, e.g. [32, 34, 25]. On the contrary, the study of streaming heuristics for the edge-partition problem is limited to the study of the PowerGraph heuristic introduced and studied in the original proposal [9] that advocates the use of edge partitions.

In this paper we study the following two fundamental questions:

Q1 *What are the quantitative performance benefits of using the edge-partition approach as opposed to using the traditional vertex-partition approach?*

and

Q2 *What are the approximation guarantees for the edge-partition problem and is it possible to achieve a good average-case performance by using some natural heuristics for the streaming version of the problem?*

The first question requires some care to ensure a fair comparison. It is important here to compare the two approaches by using a conforming definition of the cut cost, and we distinguish two different definitions of a cut cost. The first definition of a cut cost assumes no aggregation of messages. In this case for the traditional vertex partition problem, the cost of a cut corresponds to the number of edges spanning the partition boundaries, and for the edge partition problem it corresponds to the number of copies of vertices across clusters. The second definition of a cut cost assumes aggregation of messages. For the vertex-partition problem, the cost of fetching messages by a vertex from its neighbor vertices is equal to the number of distinct remote machines to which the neighbor vertices are assigned. Similarly, for the edge-partition problem, the cost of synchronizing the state of a master vertex is equal to the number of distinct remote machines that contain at least one edge with the given vertex as one of its end-points. The second question is studied by deriving theoretical approximation guaranteed and empirical evaluation of a large-set of real-world graphs.

Our main contributions can be summarized in the following points (n is the number of vertices in the graph, m the number of edges and k the number of clusters in the partition):

- We formulate the combinatorial optimization problems for the balanced vertex-partition and edge-partition problems with and without aggregation.
- We characterize the expected cost for each of these four cases under uniform random assignment policy.
- Under uniform random assignment, the expected cost of edge-partition with aggregation is always less than or equal to that of the vertex-partition with aggregation.
- For the edge-partition problem with aggregation, we show a polynomial time $O(d_{\max}\sqrt{\log k \log n})$-approximation algorithm, where $d_{\max}$ is the maximum degree of a vertex, for any graph with $m = \Omega(k^2)$ edges. From a practical point of view, we show that from any 'good' vertex partitioning algorithm, we can derive a 'good' edge partitioning algorithm for any sparse graph.
- We show that the edge-partition problem with no aggregation corresponds to a balanced vertex-partition problem with in-degree-weighted cardinality constraints. Hence, the edge-partition problem has the same approximation guarantees as that of a vertex-partition problem. Again, this implies that any algorithm for the vertex-partition can be easily turned into an edge-partition algorithm with similar performance.
- We report results of an empirical study of a large set of real-world graphs to evaluate the benefits of using the edge-partition approach vs. the vertex-partition approach, evaluate the quality of edge partitions using the approximation algorithms derived in this paper. We found that the edge partitions for the greedy assignment streaming heuristics derived from our offline problem formulations outperform previously best-known heuristics.

The paper is structured as follows. Section 2 formulates the problems of vertex- and edge-partition without and with aggregation. Section 3 provides characterizations of the expected cost for uniform random assignment of vertices of edges, and provide the comparison results. In Section 4, we provide our main results on the approximation guarantees for the edge-partition problem with and without aggregation. Streaming heuristics are discussed in Section 5. Empirical evaluation results are provided in Section 6. Related work is further discussed in Section 7. Finally, we conclude in Section 8.

2. PROBLEM FORMULATION

In this section, we describe the four different partition problems.

Given a directed graph $G = (V, E)$ with the set of vertices V and the set of directed edges $E \subset V \times V$. Let n and m denote the number of vertices and the number of directed edges, respectively. Throughout the paper, we shall use the following notation. Let $N_{\text{in}}(u) = \{v \in V, (v, u) \in E\}$ and $N_{\text{out}}(u) = \{v \in V, (u, v) \in E\}$ denote the set of vertices that have edges respectively incoming to and outgoing from $u \in V$. Let us define $d_{\text{in}}(u)$ and $d_{\text{out}}(u)$ the in-degree and out-degree of vertex $u \in V$, i.e. $d_{\text{in}}(u) = |N_{\text{in}}(u)|$. Note that $\sum_{u \in V} d_{\text{in}}(u) = \sum_{u \in V} d_{\text{out}}(u) = m$.

A partition of vertices into k clusters is defined as follows: $y_{v,i} = 1$ if vertex $v \in V$ is assigned to partition $i \in [k]$, and $y_{v,i} = 0$ otherwise. Each vertex being assigned to exactly one cluster, we have $\sum_{i=1}^{k} y_{v,i} = 1$ for all $v \in V$.

Similarly, a partition of edges into k clusters is defined as follows: $x_{e,i} = 1$ if edge $e \in E$ is assigned to cluster $i \in [k]$, and $x_{e,i} = 0$, otherwise. Each edge is assigned to exactly one cluster, thus $\sum_{i=1}^{k} x_{e,i} = 1$, for all $e \in E$.

Each partition problem is characterized by a communication cost (denoted by C) which has to be minimized under a condition of balanced loads of the clusters. If we denote by $L(i)$ the load of cluster $i \in [k]$, our partition problems can be written as:

$$\begin{array}{ll} \text{minimize} & C(x) \\ \text{subject to} & \max_{i \in [k]} L_i(x) \leq (1+\nu)\frac{\sum_{i \in [k]} L_i(x)}{k} \\ & x \text{ is a valid partition} \end{array}$$

In the sequel we call the parameter $\nu \geq 0$ the load constraint. The precise definitions of the communication cost and the load of a cluster will depend on which problem we consider: vertex or edge partition with or without aggregation. Typically, the communication cost between two clusters is assumed to be linear in the number of messages exchanged in order to synchronize the states of the replicas and the load of a cluster is assumed to be linear in the number of basic operations done by all the elements (vertices or edges) stored on a cluster. We precisely define the four different problems in the sequel.

We can also deal with undirected graphs. In this case, we create the following directed graph from the original graph: we associate to each undirected edge $\{uv\}$ two directed edges (u, v) and (v, u). The problem formulation is then the same except for the following modification: we require that for each undirected edge $\{u, v\}$, we have $x_{(u,v),i} = x_{(v,u),i}$. Note that in this case, $d_{\text{in}}(u) = d_{\text{out}}(u)$ is the degree of vertex u in the undirected graph and m is twice the number of edges in the undirected graph.

2.1 Vertex Partition with No Aggregation

In a vertex partition, the cost function to minimize is typically the number of edges with endpoints in different clusters. This case corresponds to the case with no aggregation. In the case of k clusters, the number of such edges is given by:

$$C^{\text{VP}}(y) = \sum_{i=1}^{k} \sum_{(u,v)\in E} y_{u,i}(1 - y_{v,i}). \tag{1}$$

Standard balanced graph partitioning problem asks for an optimal partitioning of vertices under a balance condition on the cardinality of clusters. Here, we consider a more general version where for some given positive weights on vertices $(a_u,\ u \in V)$, the load of a cluster is given by:

$$L_i^{\text{VP}}(y) = \sum_{u\in V} a_u y_{u,i}. \tag{2}$$

For $\nu \geq 0$, the vertex partition problem with no aggregation is formulated as the following integer programming problem denoted $(k, a) - VP$:

(k, a)-VERTEX PARTITION WITH NO AGGREGATION:

$$\begin{array}{ll} \text{minimize} & \sum_{i=1}^{k} \sum_{(u,v)\in E} y_{u,i}(1 - y_{v,i}) \\ \text{subject to} & \sum_{u\in V} a_u y_{u,i} \leq (1+\nu)\frac{\sum_{v\in V} a_v}{k},\ i \in [k] \\ & \sum_{i=1}^{k} y_{u,i} = 1,\ u \in V \\ & y \in \{0,1\}^{n\times k} \end{array}$$

The vertex cardinality constraints are accommodated as a special case with unit weights: $a_u = 1$. We shall use the notation (k, d_{in}) to refer to a balanced vertex partition with no aggregation problem where the weights correspond to in-degrees of vertices: $a_u = d_{\text{in}}(u)$, for $u \in V$.

2.2 Vertex Partition with Aggregation

When aggregation is possible, the communication cost changes as edges between two clusters can be lumped together and then incur only a cost of one. In this case, the communication cost is simply:

$$C^{\text{VPA}}(y) = \sum_{u\in V} \sum_{i=1}^{k} y_{u,i} \sum_{j\neq i} \left(1 - \prod_{v\in N_{\text{in}}(u)} (1 - y_{v,j})\right). \tag{3}$$

The balance condition remains the same as above (2) so that the vertex partition with aggregation can be formulated as the following integer programming problem denoted $(k, a) - VPA$:

(k, a)-VERTEX PARTITION WITH AGGREGATION:

$$\begin{array}{ll} \text{minimize} & \sum_{u\in V} \sum_{i=1}^{k} y_{u,i} \sum_{j\neq i} \left(1 - \prod_{v\in N_{\text{in}}(u)}(1 - y_{v,j})\right) \\ \text{subject to} & \sum_{u\in V} a_u y_{u,i} \leq (1+\nu)\frac{\sum_{v\in V} a_v}{k},\ i \in [k] \\ & \sum_{i=1}^{k} y_{u,i} = 1,\ u \in V \\ & y \in \{0,1\}^{n\times k} \end{array}$$

We shall use the notation (k, d_{out}) to refer to a balanced vertex partition with no aggregation problem where the weights correspond to in-degrees of vertices: $a_u = d_{\text{out}}(u)$, for $u \in V$.

2.3 Edge Partition with No Aggregation

We consider now a situation where each edge is assigned to exactly one cluster. As a result, a vertex might have copies in different clusters. For example in Figure 1, node u is replicated 3 times, once in each of the clusters 1, 3 and 4. For each vertex v, we assume that there is a designated *master vertex* assigned to exactly one cluster whose task is to collect messages from all neighbors vertices of v, perform a computation using the input messages, and then communicate the result to all copies of vertex v. The location of a master vertex is indicated by $z_{v,i} = 1$ if the master of vertex v is located in cluster i, and $z_{v,i} = 0$, otherwise. Note that the master of a vertex v is not necessarily located in a cluster that contains at least one copy of vertex v.

In case of no aggregation, we assume that a unit cost is incurred per each edge incident to a given vertex that resides in a cluster different from that of the master vertex of the given vertex. For example in Figure 1, suppose that the master for vertex u is located in cluster 4, then a communication cost of 4 is payed for vertex u as there are four incoming edges that reside in clusters other than 4. In a distributed iterative computation, each such copy of a vertex, will require a message to be sent to the master vertex across different partitions. More formally, the communication cost can be written as:

$$C^{\text{EP}}(x, z) = \sum_{u\in V} \left(d_{\text{in}}(u) - \sum_{i=1}^{k} z_{u,i} \left(\sum_{v\in N_{\text{in}}(u)} x_{(v,u),i}\right)\right). \tag{4}$$

Each master vertex is assumed to incur a processing cost that is equal to the number of edges incident to the corresponding vertex. In a distributed iterative computation, the processing cost of the master is assumed to be linear in the number of messages received per iteration. More formally, the load of cluster i is given by (note it is independent of x):

$$L_i^{\text{EP}}(z) = \sum_{u\in V} d_{\text{in}}(u) z_{u,i}.$$

Finally, for any $\nu \geq 0$, the edge partition problem with no aggregation denoted $k - EP$ is given by:

k-EDGE PARTITION WITH NO AGGREGATION:

$$\begin{array}{ll} \text{minimize} & \sum_{u\in V} \left(d_{\text{in}}(u) - \sum_{i=1}^{k} z_{u,i} \left(\sum_{v\in N_{\text{in}}(u)} x_{(v,u),i}\right)\right) \\ \text{subject to} & \sum_{u\in V} d_{\text{in}}(u) z_{u,i} \leq (1+\nu)\frac{m}{k},\ i \in [k] \\ & \sum_{i=1}^{k} x_{e,i} = 1,\ e \in E \\ & \sum_{i=1}^{k} z_{u,i} = 1,\ u \in V \\ & x \in \{0,1\}^{m\times k} \\ & z \in \{0,1\}^{n\times k} \end{array}$$

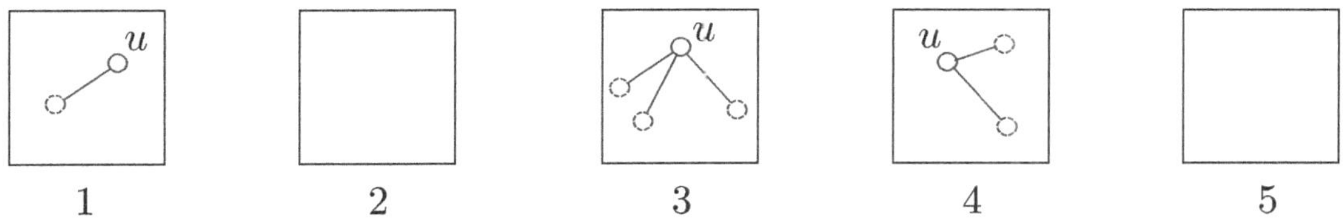

Figure 1: An edge partition (only incoming edges to u are represented).

Note that for directed graphs, the optimal communication cost is zero. Indeed for any admissible $z_{u,i}$, we can take $x_{(v,u),i} = z_{u,i}$ so that the cost becomes: $C^{\text{EP}}(x,z) = 0$. However for undirected graphs, the communication cost will generally not be zero because of the constraint $x_{(u,v),i} = x_{(v,u),i}$ for each undirected edge $\{u,v\}$.

2.4 Edge Partition with Aggregation

If aggregation is possible then both the communication cost and the load are modified as computations are done locally, the results of these computations are lumped and then sent to each master. As a result, each vertex $u \in V$ incurs a communication cost which is simply the number of clusters containing at least an edge $(v,u) \in E$ minus one (corresponding to the cluster containing the master). Summing the contribution of each vertex, we get:

$$C^{\text{EPA}}(x) = \sum_{u \in V} \sum_{i=1}^{k} (1 - \prod_{v \in N_{\text{in}}(u)} (1 - x_{(v,u),i})) - n. \quad (5)$$

Now, since computations are made locally, the load of a cluster is simply proportional to the number of edges contained in this cluster:

$$L_i^{\text{EPA}}(x) = \sum_{e \in E} x_{e,i}.$$

Finally, for any $\nu \geq 0$, the edge partition problem with no aggregation denoted $k-EPA$ is given by (note that we can remove the additive constant n in the cost function without modifying the optimal solution; we keep it to allow to make comparison with the other problems):

k-EDGE PARTITION WITH AGGREGATION:

$$\begin{array}{rl} \text{minimize} & \sum_{u \in V} \sum_{i=1}^{k} (1 - \prod_{v \in N_{\text{in}}(u)} (1 - x_{(v,u),i})) - n \\ \text{subject to} & \sum_{e \in E} x_{e,i} \leq (1+\nu)\frac{m}{k},\ i \in K \\ & \sum_{i=1}^{k} x_{e,i} = 1,\ e \in E \\ & x \in \{0,1\}^{m \times k} \end{array}$$

3. RANDOM ASSIGNMENT

In this section we consider the expected cost of random assignment policy that for the case of edge partition assigns each edge independently and uniformly at random to one of k partitions, and likewise for the case of vertex partition assigns each vertex independently and uniformly at random to one of k partitions. We shall provide exact characterizations of these expected costs for the case without and with aggregation. We then show that aggregation lowers the expected communication cost (in most cases). Moreover, also expected costs are the same for edge and vertex partition with no aggregation, we find that when aggregation is possible, edge partition has a lower expected cost than vertex partition. There are two statistics of the in-degree sequence of a given graph that play an important role here for the case without and with aggregation, respectively, the *number of (directed) edges*: $m = \sum_{v \in V} d_{\text{in}}(v)$ and

$$\psi(d_{\text{in}}, k) = \frac{1}{n} \sum_{v \in V} \left(1 - \frac{1}{k}\right)^{d_{\text{in}}(v)}.$$

The latter statistic corresponds to a *moment generating function of the degree sequence evaluated at the value* $\log(1 - 1/k)$.

3.1 Edge Partition

PROPOSITION 1. *For any given graph with sequence of in-degrees $d_{\text{in}} = (d_{\text{in}}(v))_{v \in V}$, we assign edges independently and uniformly at random across k clusters. In the case of edge partition with no aggregation, we assign the master to a random cluster. Then we have the following expected communication costs:*

$$\mathbb{E}[C^{\text{EP}}] = \left(1 - \frac{1}{k}\right) m \quad (6)$$

$$\mathbb{E}[C^{\text{EPA}}] = kn(1 - \psi(d_{\text{in}}, k)) - n. \quad (7)$$

COROLLARY 1. *As soon as $nk \geq m$, aggregation lowers the communication cost under a random edge partition, i.e. $\mathbb{E}[C^{\text{EP}}] > \mathbb{E}[C^{\text{EPA}}]$. Moreover, for any given graph, the gap between the two expected costs is at least $(n - m/k)$.*

Proofs are provided in Appendix [7].

3.2 Vertex Partition

PROPOSITION 2. *For any given graph with sequence of degrees $d_{\text{in}} = (d_{\text{in}}(v))_{v \in V}$, we assign vertices independently and uniformly at random across k clusters. Then we have the following expected communication costs:*

$$\mathbb{E}[C^{\text{VP}}] = \left(1 - \frac{1}{k}\right) m \quad (8)$$

$$\mathbb{E}[C^{\text{VPA}}] = n(k-1)(1 - \psi(d_{\text{in}}, k)). \quad (9)$$

COROLLARY 2. *Aggregation lowers the communication cost under a random vertex partition, i.e. $\mathbb{E}[C^{\text{VP}}] > \mathbb{E}[C^{\text{VPA}}]$.*

Proofs are provided in Appendix [7].

3.3 Edge vs. Vertex Partition

Note that the expected costs are the same for the edge and vertex partitions when there is no aggregation. The following easy corollary shows that the situation is different with aggregation:

COROLLARY 3. *For every given graph, the expected cost of vertex partition with aggregation is greater than the expected cost of edge partition with aggregation. Moreover, the gap between the two expected costs is at least $n\psi(d_{\text{in}}, k)$.*

PROOF. Follows directly from (7) and (9). □

4. APPROXIMATION ALGORITHMS

In this section, we restrict ourselves to the undirected case so that $N_{\text{in}}(u) = N_{\text{out}}(u) = N(u)$, $d_{\text{in}}(u) = d_{\text{out}}(u) = d(u)$ and $\sum_{u \in V} d(u) = m$ is twice the number of (undirected) edges.

4.1 Hardness Results

It is well-known that the $(2,1)$-vertex partition problem with no aggregation, i.e. the minimum bisection problem is NP-complete but efficient approximation algorithms have been obtained in [6]. The following theorem shows that it is not possible to derive a finite approximation factor for each of the four problems when k is not a constant.

THEOREM 1. *Each of the four problems with $\nu = 0$: (k,d)-vertex partition with/with no aggregation and k-edge partition with/with no aggregation, has no polynomial time approximation algorithm with finite approximation factor unless $P = NP$.*

PROOF. The case of $(k,1)$-vertex partition with no aggregation is Theorem 2.1 in [17] and the other cases follow by the same reduction from the 3-Partition problem (details omitted). □

4.2 Edge Partition with Aggregation

For edge partition with aggregation we show that there exists a polynomial-time algorithm with approximation ratio that matches that of the vertex partition problem up to a $d_{\max}$ factor, where $d_{\max}$ is the maximum degree of a vertex. Since the best known approximation ratio for the vertex partition problem is poly-logarithmic in the number of vertices of the graph, this yields a poly-logarithmic approximation algorithm for any sparse graph, i.e. such that $d_{\max} = O(\log^c n)$, for some positive constant c. The algorithm uses as a subroutine an approximation algorithm for the vertex partition problem with no aggregation and the load of a partition defined to be the sum of degree weighted vertices assigned to this partition. The algorithm can be summarized in the following two steps:

- Partition the set of vertices according to an approximation algorithm for the (k,d)-VP problem with load parameter ν, and let $S_1, S_2, \dots, S_k$ denote the output of this algorithm.
- For each pair of vertex partitions S_i and S_j, assign the set of cut edges with end-vertices in S_i and S_j to partitions i and j such that if the number of such edges is even, exactly half of edges is assigned to each partition, and otherwise, either of them gets at least half of edges (to ensure a balanced partitioning).

THEOREM 2. *There exists a polynomial-time algorithm that given a feasible solution y with load constraint ν to (k,d)-*VP *of cost $C^{\text{VP}}(y)$ outputs a feasible solution x with load constraint $\nu + \frac{k^2}{m}$ to k-*EPA *of cost $C^{\text{EPA}}(x)$ such that*

$$\frac{1}{d_{\max}} C^{\text{VP}}(y) \leq C^{\text{EPA}}(x) \leq C^{\text{VP}}(y). \tag{10}$$

PROOF. The proof consists of two steps. First, we show that given a feasible vertex partition y for the (k,d)-VP problem with the load parameter ν, the given construction of an edge partition x is a feasible solution for the k-EPA problem with the load parameter $\nu + k^2/m$. Second, we show that the objective functions $C^{\text{EPA}}(x)$ and $C^{\text{VP}}(y)$ satisfy the relations in (10).

Suppose y is a feasible solution to the (k,d)-VP problem and let $C^{\text{VP}}(y)$ denote the value of the cut. Let S_i be the set of vertices in partition i, i.e. $S_i = \{v \in V : y_{v,i} = 1\}$. The total cost of the cut can be expressed as $\frac{1}{2}\sum_{i \in [k]} |E(S_i, V \setminus S_i)|$ where for $A, B \subset V$, $E(A,B)$ denotes the set of edges with exactly one end in A and the other end in B. Now, note that

$$|E(S_i, S_i)| = \frac{1}{2}\left(\sum_{u \in V} y_{u,i} d(u) - |E(S_i, V \setminus S_i)|\right).$$

Since y is assumed to be a feasible assignment,

$$|E(S_i, S_i)| \leq (1+\nu)\frac{m}{k} - \frac{1}{2}|E(S_i, V \setminus S_i)|. \tag{11}$$

Let us define the edge-partition $P_1, P_2, \dots, P_k$ as follows: for each pair $i, j \in [k]$ such that $i \neq j$, split $E(S_i, S_j)$ into two sets $P_{i,j}$ and $P_{j,i}$ of balanced cardinalities, i.e. $P_{i,j}, P_{j,i} \subset E(S_i, S_j)$ such that $P_{i,j} \cup P_{j,i} = E(S_i, S_j)$, $P_{i,j} \cap P_{j,i} = \emptyset$, and $-1 \leq |P_{i,j}| - |P_{j,i}| \leq 1$. Define $P_i = E(S_i, S_i) \cup \cup_{j \neq i} P_{i,j}$, for $i \in [k]$.

It is easy to observe that for all $i \in [k]$,

$$-k + 1 \leq |\cup_{j \neq i} P_{i,j}| - \frac{1}{2}|E(S_i, V \setminus S_i)| \leq k - 1. \tag{12}$$

Hence

$$\begin{aligned} |P_i| &= |E(S_i, S_i) \cup (\cup_{j \neq i} P_{i,j})| \\ &= |E(S_i, S_i)| + |\cup_{j \neq i} P_{i,j}| \\ &\leq (1+\nu)\frac{m}{k} + k - 1 \\ &\leq (1 + \nu + \frac{k^2}{m})\frac{m}{k} \end{aligned}$$

where the first inequality follows by (11) and (12) and the second inequality is by the fact $k - 1 \leq (1+\nu)(k^2/m)m/k$. This implies that the given edge partitioning satisfies the constraints of the k-EPA problem.

It remains to show that the objective functions $C^{\text{EPA}}(x)$ and $C^{\text{VP}}(y)$ satisfy the relations in (10). First note that only edges cut in the vertex partition y contribute to the communication cost $C^{\text{EPA}}(x)$, indeed removing all the edges which are not cut in y will not change $C^{\text{VP}}(y)$ nor $C^{\text{EPA}}(x)$. Moreover each edge cut in y contribute to at most one in $C^{\text{EPA}}(x)$ so that $C^{\text{EPA}}(x) \leq C^{\text{VP}}(y)$.

Inversely, each vertex $u \in V$ incurs a cost of at most $d_{\max}$ in the communication cost $C^{\text{VP}}(y)$ (corresponding to the case where each incident edge to u is cut in y). A vertex $u \in V$ incurs a cost of zero in $C^{\text{VP}}(y)$ if none of the incident edge to u is cut. In this last case, the vertex will not contribute to the communication cost $C^{\text{EPA}}(x)$ by previous remark. Hence we have $C^{\text{VP}}(y) \leq d_{\max} C^{\text{EPA}}(x)$. □

COROLLARY 4. *Assume that $m = \Omega(k^2)$, then there exists a polynomial-time algorithm with approximation ratio $O(d_{\max}\sqrt{\log k \log n})$ for k-*EPA *problem with $\nu = 1$.*

PROOF. This is a corollary of Theorem 2 and an easy extension of Theorem 1.1 in [18] to the (k,d)-VP problem showing that there exists a polynomial-time approximation algorithm with the approximation ratio $O(\sqrt{\log k \log n})$. □

4.3 Edge Partition with No Aggregation

We shall show that the edge partition is in a one-to-one correspondence to a vertex partition problem. This will show that the computational complexity of the balanced edge partition with no aggregation corresponds to that of a balanced vertex partition problem (with no aggregation). This reduction will be established by the following simple two-step construction:

1. Suppose y is an optimal solution to the (k,d)-vertex partition problem.
2. Then, partition edges by assigning each edge $(u,v) \in E$ to the cluster of either of its end vertices u and v, as specified by y, arbitrarily.

THEOREM 3. *k-edge partition problem is in a one-to-one correspondence with the (k,d)-vertex partition problem.*

Proof of this theorem is provided in Appendix [7]. Again thanks to an easy extension of Theorem 1.1 in [18], we obtain the following corollary of Theorem 3:

COROLLARY 5. *There exists a polynomial-time algorithm with approximation ratio $O(\sqrt{\log k \log n})$ for the k-edge partition problem.*

5. STREAMING HEURISTICS

In this section, we discuss streaming heuristics for the balanced edge partition problem without and with aggregation. We shall first introduce a state-of-the-art heuristic for the balanced edge partition problem and point out to some of its deficiencies. We shall then move to introducing a class of novel streaming heuristics that are inspired by the analysis of the offline version of the problem in Section 4.

5.1 PowerGraph Heuristic

Suppose edges arrive in an arbitrary order. In the description of the algorithm below, $S(v)$ will be a set evolving as edges arrive and it will contain the clusters with at least one already observed edge incident to vertex v. Initially, $S(v) = \emptyset$, for all $v \in V$. The algorithm defined below requires to know for each arriving edge, the number of unassigned edges for each end-vertex of this edge. For this to be realized, it suffices to know the degree of each vertex, and then the number of the unassigned edges of a vertex can be kept as part of the algorithm state (this we omit in the description presented below).

PowerGraph heuristic Per each arrival of an edge (u,v), do the following:
1. If the intersection of $S(u)$ and $S(v)$ is non-empty, then assign edge (u,v) to a cluster I in this intersection.
2. Otherwise, assign edge (u,v) to a cluster I in $S(u) \cup S(v)$ (containing either u or v) with the most unassigned edges.
3. Otherwise, if both $S(u)$ and $S(v)$ are empty, then assign edge (u,v) to a partition I with the least number of assigned edges.
4. $S(u) \leftarrow S(u) \cup \{I\}$ and $S(v) \leftarrow S(v) \cup \{I\}$.

This heuristic can be showed to correspond to a greedy assignment that for each arriving edge minimizes the expected cut cost conditional on that all subsequent edges are assigned to partitions uniformly at random. This can be seen as a derandomization of the uniform random assignment, and is thus guaranteed to yield a cut cost that is guaranteed to be less or equal to that of the uniform random assignment.

An important observation from the definition of the Powergraph heuristic is that edges are assigned using a greedy assignment that prioritizes assignment of an edge to a partition that already contains one of the end-vertices, and the load balancing of edges is performed only if neither of the end-vertices have been already assigned. This may result in a gross imbalance of the partition sizes. For example, a worst-case is a breadth-first search traversal of a connected tree, where all edges end up being assigned to one partition, which results in an extreme imbalance.

5.2 Greedy Online Assignments

5.2.1 Edge partition

For the basic formulation, we derive a greedy online assignment for edge partition with aggregation by an irrevocable assignment of edges to clusters as they are observed in the input stream to a cluster that minimizes the marginal cost. We denote by P_i the clusters of an edge-partition. Then for any $S \subset E$, $V(S)$ is the set of vertices spanned by S, i.e. all vertices adjacent to an edge in S. Note from (5) that the marginal cost of the cut size by adding an edge (u,v) to cluster i is equal to

$$|V(P_i \cup (u,v))| - |V(P_i)| = |V(P_i \cup (u,v)) \setminus V(P_i)|.$$

It is noteworthy that in any case the marginal cost of the cut size is either 0, 1 or 2: first, it is zero if the edge is placed in a cluster in which both of its end-vertices have been already assigned, second, it is equal to 1 if exactly one of its end-vertices has been previously assigned, and third, it is equal to 2 if neither of its vertices have been previously assigned to this cluster.

Since $|V(P_i \cup (u,v)) \setminus V(P_i)| = 2 - |V(P_i) \cap \{u,v\}|$, a greedy online heuristic for minimizing the cut size is to assign each input edge (u,v) to a cluster $i \in I$ where

$$I = \text{argmax}_{j\in[k]}\{|V(P_j) \cap \{u,v\}|\} \tag{13}$$

which means that the edge is assigned to a cluster in the following priority order: (i) in a cluster that already contains both of its end-vertices, if any exists, (ii) in a cluster that already contains exactly one of its end-vertices, if any exists, and else (iii) to an arbitrary cluster. Such an assignment is greedy with respect to the cost of the cut criteria and is entirely ignorant of the load balancing criteria.

A way to define a greedy assignment that accounts for both criteria is to redefine the optimization problem as follows. Let $c: R_+ \to R_+$ be an increasing convex function such that $c(0) = 0$. Then, redefine k-EPA by moving the hard constraints into the objective function as a soft penalty function, as given in here

$$\begin{array}{ll} \text{minimize} & \sum_{i=1}^{k} |V(P_i)| + c(|P_i|) \\ & (P_1, P_2, \ldots, P_k) \in \mathcal{P}(G). \end{array}$$

The greedy online assignment with respect to this problem amounts to assigning an input edge (u,v) to a cluster $i \in I$

where

$$I = \text{argmax}_{j\in[k]}\{|V(P_j)\cap\{u,v\}| - [c(|P_j \cup (u,v)|) - c(|P_j|)]\}.$$

We refer to this class of greedy assignment policies as the least incremental cost (IC) assignment.

An alternative class of heuristics is derived by following an approach pursued for balanced vertex partitioning that amounts to discounting the marginal benefit in (13) with the cardinality of the partition. Specifically, for given decreasing function $d : R_+ \to R$, assign an input edge (u, v) to a cluster I where

$$I = \text{argmax}_{j\in[k]}\{|V(P_j)\cap\{u,v\}|d(|P_j|)\}.$$

Notice that unlike to the PowerGraph heuristic, the greedy online assignments as defined in this section do not require any extra information about the input data, such as knowing the degree of each vertex.

5.2.2 *Vertex partition*

We use as a subroutine a greedy online algorithm for approximating vertex partitioning defined in [34], which is very similar to the one described in the previous section. It supposes vertex arrival. The idea of the algorithm is to minimize the following objective function: $\sum_{i\in[k]}|E(S_i, V\backslash S_i)| + c(|S_i|)$. This can be done with this greedy online assignment: Per vertex u arrival, we assign it to a partition $i \in I$ where

$$I = \text{argmax}_{j\in[k]}\{|N_{\text{in}}(u)\cap P_j| + c(|P_j \cup u|) - c(|P_j|)\}.$$

We refer to this class of greedy vertex assignment policies as the vertex partition least incremental cost (VP-IC) assignment.

5.3 Streaming Edge Partition Based on Balanced Vertex Partition

Suppose edges arrival in an arbitrary order. Suppose we have some partitioning of the vertices S_i, for all $i \in \{1..k\}$, which are balanced with regard to degree weights. We can derive easily an edge partitioning from this vertex partitioning as follows. Per each arrival of an edge (u, v), flip a fair coin, and do either of the following: (1) assign (u, v) to partition i such that $u \in S_i$, or (2) assign (u, v) to partition i such that $v \in S_i$. This will give an edge partitioning with a communication cost lesser than the vertex partitioning's one, and should keep a maxload ratio close to the previous one thanks to random assignment.

6. EVALUATION

In this section we report results of empirical evaluation of several hypotheses on a dataset containing samples of five real-world graphs whose properties are summarized in Table 1. This dataset contains samples of real-graphs with quite some diversity along several dimensions, including the scale ranging from hundred of thousands to millions of vertices, sparsity ranging from a few to hundreds of edges per vertex, and type including social graphs, co-purchasing of products and co-authorship of scientific papers. In the first part of this section, we shall evaluate expected communication cost for edge and vertex partition problems with and without aggregation under random assignment of edges of vertices, under our benchmark random edge or vertex assignment, which is commonly deployed in practice. This part of our analysis provides empirical support to the following claims:

(H1) For balanced edge partition, aggregation of messages typically provides significant reduction of the communication cost.

(H2) Balanced edge partition with aggregation can have significantly smaller expected communication cost than balanced vertex partition with aggregation.

In the second part, we shall focus on evaluating our approximation algorithms for balanced edge partition problem, for the offline and the online version of the problem. For the online version, we shall compare with previously-proposed method for balanced edge partition problem, namely PowerGraph heuristics. Our empirical validation results provide support to the following claims:

(H3) PowerGraph heuristic provides significant reduction of the communication cost with respect to random edge partition. However, this is at the expense of a maximum load of a partition that may assume rather large values.

(H4) Least incremental cost heuristic (described in Section 5.2.1) typically has communication cost that is smaller or equal to that of PowerGraph heuristic and nearly perfectly balanced loads of partitions.

(H5) Balanced edge partition derived from a vertex partition with degree-weighted vertices using an offline solver tends to have significantly smaller communication cost than online assignment strategies.

(H6) Balanced edge partition derived from a vertex partition with degree-weighted vertices using the least marginal cost online heuristic tends to have much smaller communication cost than random edge assignment, but worse than least marginal cost strategy for balanced edge partition problem.

6.1 Communication Cost under Random Edge or Vertex Assignments

We evaluate expected communication costs under random edge or vertex assignments. In Section 3 we provided a complete characterization of the expected communication costs under random or vertex assignment, and observed that they all depend in one way or another on the degree sequence of the given input graph. The degree distributions of the graphs in our dataset are showed in Figure 2. As one would expect they all exhibit some degree of a power-law dependence. For all the examples, the 0.99-quantile of the vertex degree is in the order of 10 vertices. A notable distinction of Orkut graph data is that an approximately same portions of vertices have degrees in the range from one to order ten. In Figure 3 we show expected communication cost for edge partition with and without aggregation, and vertex partition with aggregation versus the number of partitions ranging from 2 to 32 partitions. In this figure, the circles represent empirical means computed over 10 repeated partitions. As one would expect, the empirical means are highly concentrated around the expected values computed using the degree sequence in the characterization results presented in Section 3. For all graphs in our dataset, aggregation of messages for balanced edge partition problem yields significant reduction of communication cost. For a small number of partitions, the communication cost of edge partition with aggregation can be as small as 1/10 of that with no aggregation. From Figure 3, we also observe that balanced edge partition with aggregation typically has smaller communication cost than vertex partition with aggregation, and there

	Nodes	Edges	Mean degree	Median degree	90% quantile	Max degree	Description
Amazon	334 863	925 872	5.53	3	9	549	Co-purchasing
dblp	317 080	1 049 866	6.62	3	13	343	Co-authorship
Livejournal	3 997 962	34 681 189	17.35	5	41	14 815	Social
Orkut	3 072 441	117 185 083	76.28	44	161	33 313	Social
Youtube	1 134 890	2 987 624	5.27	1	7	28 754	Social

Table 1: Datasets used in our experiments.

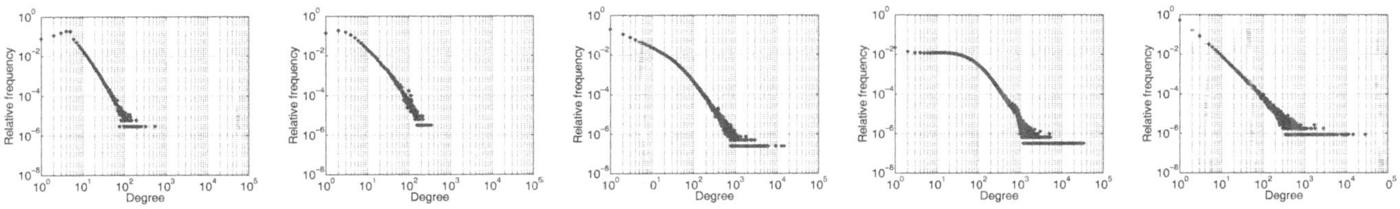

(a) Amazon (b) dblp (c) Live Journal (d) Orkut (e) Youtube

Figure 2: Degree distributions for the graphs in our dataset.

exist cases where the difference is significant. Overall, these results provide support to hypothesis (H1) and (H2) asserted at the beginning of this section.

6.2 Approximation Algorithms

We evaluated various approximation algorithms for balanced edge partition problem with respect to the two criteria of the communication cost and the maximum load of a partition. In Figure 4, we present results for different approximation algorithms for each input graph from our dataset. RND refers to random edge assignment. VP-IC refers to edge partition derived as explained in Section 5.3 from a vertex partitioning given by a greedy online assignment as defined in Section 5.2.2 with $c(x) = \alpha x^\gamma$, $\alpha = n(\frac{k}{n})^\gamma$ and $\gamma = 1.5$. PG refers to Powergraph heuristic defined in Section 5.1. IC refers to greedy online assignment as defined in Section 5.2.1 with $c(x) = \alpha(\sum_{u \in x} d_u)^\gamma$, $\alpha = m\frac{k^{\gamma-1}}{n^\gamma}$ and $\gamma = 1.5$. And, finally, VP-METIS refers to edge partitioning derived as explained in Section 5.3 from a vertex partitioning given by the offline tool METIS, which is a state-of-the-art software tool for approximating balanced vertex partition problem.

In this part of analysis we evaluate performance of three one-pass streaming algorithms for balanced edge partition, including random, least marginal cost, and PowerGraph, and the approximation algorithm for the offline version of the problem in Section 4.2. In particular, in the latter case, we use METIS solver for finding an approximate solution to the subroutine balanced vertex partition with degree-weighted vertices. For the online version of the problem, we observe that for all the graphs in our dataset, least marginal cost algorithm yields a smaller or equal communication cost than PowerGraph. We observe that PowerGraph exhibits varying quality of partition with respect to the maximum load of a partition, which in some cases attains significantly larger values than any other method. Especially, under PowerGraph assignment, the maximum load tends to increase with the number of partitions, and can achieve maximum load values of more than 10% of extra load to the mean number of edges per partition. On the other hand, the least marginal cost assignment achieves nearly perfect load balancing, and still performs better or nearly equal than PowerGraph with respect to the communication cost. Overall, these observations provide empirical support to the hypotheses (H3) and (H4). For the offline approximation algorithm described in Section 4.2, we observe that it can perform significantly superior performance with respect to the communication cost than one-pass streaming algorithms. This provides empirical support to hypothesis (H5) Finally, we also observe that using a one-pass streaming algorithm for the balanced vertex partition problem with degree-weighted vertices and then deriving an edge partition from the resulting vertex partition can provide significant reduction of the communication cost with respect to random edge assignment, but worse than the least marginal cost strategy for balanced edge partition problem. This provides empirical support to hypothesis (H6). An implication of this hypothesis is that one needs to exercise some care in designing a scalable partition strategy based on a few passes through graph data based on the approach in Section 4.2 that uses a balanced vertex partition problem as a subroutine.

7. RELATED WORK

Traditional balanced graph partitioning problem, referred to in this paper as the vertex partition problem with no aggregation, has been studied extensively by theoretical computer science and more applied communities. The best known approximation ratio for this problem is $O(\sqrt{\log k \log n})$ [17] and [18], using a semi-definite programming relaxation and a randomized rounding. The solvers used in practice rely on a combination of various heuristics, e.g. one commonly used software is METIS [12, 14, 13] that combines a number of heuristics including the well-known Kernighan and Li heuristic [15]. Graph partitioning has attracted a lot of attention recently by the systems community to scale out large-scale computations, e.g. for parallel distributed computing in distributed clusters of machines [9, 22, 21, 11, 38, 40, 16], graph databases and graph analytics platforms [30, 37, 36, 4], search and social networks [35, 5, 28], and multi-core and share memory systems [27, 2, 31, 29]. In recent

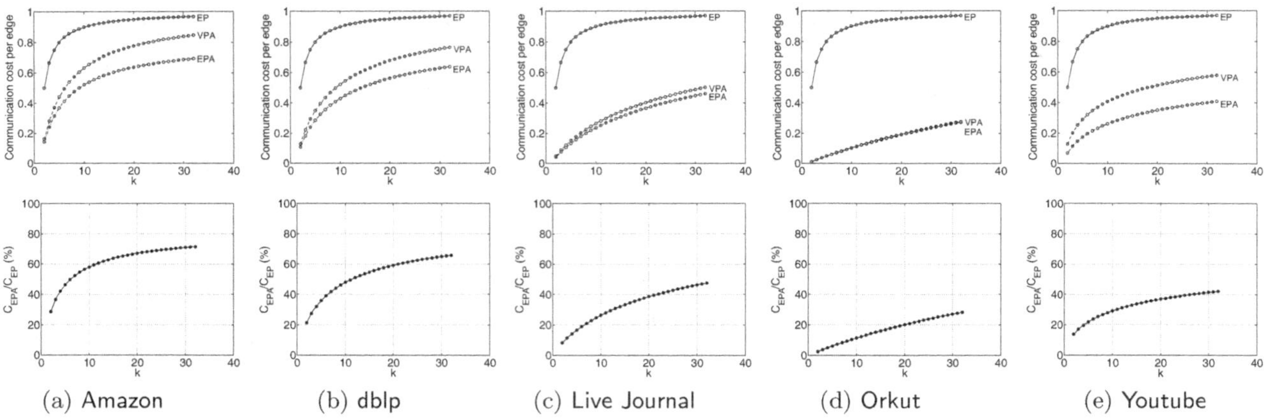

Figure 3: Expected communication costs for edge partition, edge partition with aggregation, and vertex partition with aggregation vs. the number of partitions k.

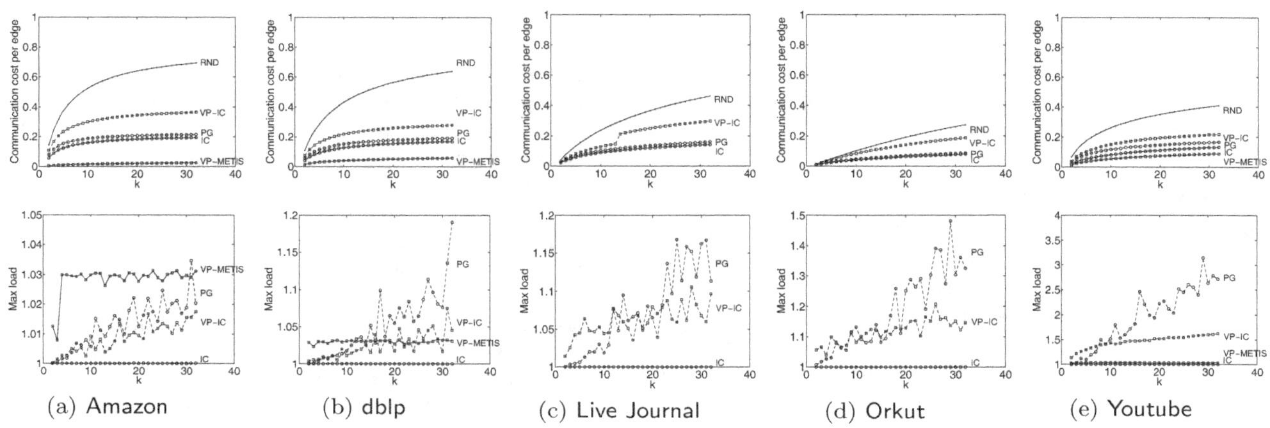

Figure 4: Approximation algorithms: (top) communication cost and (bottom) maximum load.

work, scalable strategies for graph strategies have been investigated that are based on one-pass streaming algorithms. An early work in this direction is [32] that focused on the traditional graph partitioning problem, improved strategies in [34], and a multi-pass version in [25]. [35] studied local improvements algorithms that aim at minimizing the cut subject to a budget constraint on the number of vertices to reallocate. In this recent work, novel variants of graph partitioning problems have emerged that are different from the traditional balanced graph partitioning problem with respect to the definition of the cut cost function and the load balancing constraints. One such new variant is the balanced edge partition problem, originally proposed in [9], which we have studied in this paper.

From a theoretical standpoint, the balanced edge partition problem is an instance of a submodular function minimization subject to cardinality constraints. For general class of submodular load balancing problems, the approximation guarantee of $O(\sqrt{n/\log n})$ was showed to hold in [33]. Our approximation ratio of $O(d_{\max}\sqrt{\log k \log n})$ provides a better approximation guarantee for the subclass of balanced edge partition problems for any graphs with $d_{\max} = o(\sqrt{n})$.

8. CONCLUSION

In this paper we analyzed balanced graph edge partition problem that was recently proposed as an alternative to traditional balanced graph vertex partition for scaling out distributed computations in data analytics platforms. We provided explicit characterization of the expected communication cost for different variants of the graph partition problem under commonly deployed scheme of randomly assigning edges of vertices to a given number of partitions. We provided approximation algorithms for balanced edge partition problem with and without message aggregation. Interestingly, both problems use a balanced vertex partition problem as a subroutine, thus allowing us to reutilize known techniques and off-the-shelf software for this traditional graph partition problem. For scalable partitioning based on a single pass through graph data, we showed that the least marginal cost greedy heuristic provides better performance than the best previously known heuristic with respect to both the communication cost and load balancing of partitions. The results in this paper present a first step towards a more thorough analysis of balanced edge partition problem both on the side of theoretical approximation guarantees and the design of practical algorithms with good average-case performance.

9. REFERENCES

[1] A. Abou-Rjeili and G. Karypis. Multilevel algorithms for partitioning power-law graphs. In *Proc. of the 20th Int'l Conf. on Parallel and Distributed Processing*, IEEE IPDPS'06, pages 124–124, Washington, DC, USA, 2006.

[2] V. Agarwal, F. Petrini, D. Pasetto, and D. A. Bader. Scalable graph exploration on multicore processors. In *Proc. of the 2010 ACM/IEEE Int'l Conf. for High Performance Computing, Networking, Storage and Analysis*, SC '10, pages 1–11, Washington, DC, USA, 2010.

[3] C. Curino, E. Jones, Y. Zhang, and S. Madden. Schism: a workload-driven approach to database replication and partitioning. In *VLDB '10*, 2010.

[4] M. Curtiss, I. Becker, T. Bosman, S. Doroshenko, L. Grijncu, T. Jackson, S. Kunnatur, S. Lassen, P. Pronin S. Sankar, G. Shen, G. Woss, C. Wang, and N. Zhang. Unicorn: A system for searching the social graph. In *VLDB '13*, 2013.

[5] Q. Duong, S. Goel, J. Hofman, and S. Vassilvitskii. Sharding social networks. In *ACM WSDM '13*, pages 223–232, New York, NY, USA, 2013.

[6] U. Feige and R. Krauthgamer. A polylogarithmic approximation of the minimum bisection. *SIAM J. Comput.*, 31(4):1090–1118, Apr. 2002.

[7] M. V. Florian Bourse, Marc Lelarge. Balanced edge partition. Technical Report MSR-TR-2014-20, Microsoft Research, 2014.

[8] T. A. S. F. Giraph. http://giraph.apache.org, 2014.

[9] J. E. Gonzalez, Y. Low, H. Gu, D. Bickson, and C. Guestrin. Powergraph: distributed graph-parallel computation on natural graphs. In *OSDI'12*, pages 17–30. USENIX Association, 2012.

[10] D. Gregor and A. Lumsdaine. The parallel bgl: A generic library for distributed graph computations. In *Proceedings of POOSC*, 2005.

[11] U. Kang, C. E. T., and C. Faloutsos. Pegasus: A peta-scale graph mining system. In *ICDM*, pages 229–238, 2009.

[12] G. Karypis and V. Kumar. Metis-unstructured graph partitioning and sparse matrix ordering system, version 2.0. 1995.

[13] G. Karypis and V. Kumar. Parallel multilevel graph partitioning. In *Proc. of the 10th Int'l Parallel Processing Symposium*, IEEE IPPS '96, pages 314–319, Washington, DC, USA, 1996.

[14] G. Karypis and V. Kumar. Multilevel k-way partitioning scheme for irregular graphs. *Journal of Parallel and Distributed Computing*, 48(1):96 – 129, 1998.

[15] B. W. Kernighan and S. Lin. An efficient heuristic procedure for partitioning graphs. *Bell Syst. Tech. J.*, 49(2):291–307, Feb. 1970.

[16] Z. Khayyat, K. Awara, A. Alonazi, H. Jamjoom, D. Williams, and P. Kalnis. Mizan: A system for dynamic load balancing in large-scale graph processing. In *Proc. of the 8th ACM European Conference on Computer Systems*, ACM EuroSys '13, pages 169–182, New York, NY, USA, 2013.

[17] A. Konstantin and H. Räcke. Balanced graph partitioning. In *SPAA '04*, pages 120–124, 2004.

[18] R. Krauthgamer, J. S. Naor, and R. Schwartz. Partitioning graphs into balanced components. In *SODA '09*, pages 942–949, 2009.

[19] K. Lang. Finding good nearly balanced cuts in power law graphs. Technical Report YRL-2004-036, Yahoo! Research Labs, 2004.

[20] J. Leskovec, K. J. Lang, A. Dasgupta, and M. W. Mahoney. Community structure in large networks: Natural cluster sizes and the absence of large well-defined clusters. *Internet Mathematics*, 6(1):29–123, 2008.

[21] Y. Low, D. Bickson, J. Gonzalez, C. Guestrin, A. Kyrola, and J. M. Hellerstein. Distributed graphlab: a framework for machine learning and data mining in the cloud. *Proc. VLDB Endow.*, 5(8):716–727, Apr. 2012.

[22] Y. Low, J. Gonzalez, A. Kyrola, D. Bickson, C. Guestrin, and J. M. Hellerstein. Graphlab: A new framework for parallel machine learning. In *UAI*, pages 340–349, 2010.

[23] G. Malewicz, M. H. Austern, A. Bik, J. Dehnert, I. Horn, N. Leiser, and G. Czajkowski. Pregel: a system for large-scale graph processing. In *ACM SIGMOD '10*, pages 135–146, 2010.

[24] Neo4j. http://www.neo4j.org, 2014.

[25] J. Nishimura and J. Ugander. Restreaming graph partitioning: simple versatile algorithms for advanced balancing. In *ACM KDD '13*, pages 1106–1114, 2013.

[26] F. Pellegrini and J. Roman. Scotch: A software package for static mapping by dual recursive bipartitioning of process and architecture graphs. In *High-Performance Computing and Networking*, volume 1067 of *Lecture Notes in Computer Science*, pages 493–498. Springer Berlin Heidelberg, 1996.

[27] V. Prabhakaran, M. Wu, X. Weng, F. McSherry, L. Zhou, and M. Haridasan. Managing large graphs on multi-cores with graph awareness. In *USENIX ATC'12*, pages 4–4, 2012.

[28] J. M. Pujol, V. Erramilli, G. Siganos, X. Yang, N. Laoutaris, P. Chhabra, and P. Rodriguez. The little engine(s) that could: scaling online social networks. In *ACM SIGCOMM '10*, pages 375–386, New York, NY, USA, 2010.

[29] A. Roy, I. Mihailovic, and W. Zwaenepoel. X-stream: Edge-centric graph processing using streaming partitions. In *ACM SOSP'13*, 2013.

[30] B. Shao, H. Wang, and Y. Li. Trinity: A distributed graph engine on a memory cloud. In *Proceedings of the VLDB Endowment*, VLDB '13, 2013.

[31] J. Shun and G. E. Blelloch. Ligra: a lightweight graph processing framework for shared memory. In *ACM PPoPP '13*, pages 135–146, New York, NY, USA, 2013.

[32] I. Stanton and G. Kliot. Streaming graph partitioning for large distributed graphs. In *ACM KDD '12*, pages 1222–1230, 2012.

[33] Z. Svitkina and L. Fleischer. Submodular approximation: Sampling-based algorithms and lower bounds. *SIAM J. Comput.*, 40(6):1715–1737, Dec. 2011.

[34] C. Tsourakakis, C. Gkantsidis, B. Radunovic, and M. Vojnovic. Fennel: Streaming graph partitioning for massive scale graphs. In *ACM WSDM '14* 2014.

[35] J. Ugander and L. Backstrom. Balanced label propagation for partitioning massive graphs. In *ACM WSDM '13*, pages 507–516, 2013.

[36] V. Venkataramani, Z. Amsden, N. Bronson, G. Cabrera III, P. Chakka, P. Dimov, H. Ding, J. Ferris, A. Giardullo, J. Hoon, S. Kulkarni, N. Lawrence, M. Marchukov, D. Petrov, and L. Puzar. TAO: how facebook serves the social graph. In *ACM SIGMOD '12*, pages 791–792, 2012.

[37] R. S. Xin, J. E. Gonzalez, M. J. Franklin, and I. Stoica. Graphx: a resilient distributed graph system on spark. In *First International Workshop on Graph Data Management Experiences and Systems*, ACM GRADES '13, pages 2:1–2:6, 2013.

[38] S. Yang, X. Yan, B. Zong, and A. Khan. Towards effective partition management for large graphs. In *ACM SIGMOD '12*, pages 517–528, 2012.

[39] M. Zaharia, M. Chowdhury, T. Das, A. Dave, J. Ma, M. McCauley, M. J. Franklin, S. Shenker, and I. Stoica. Resilient distributed datasets: A fault-tolerant abstraction for in-memory cluster computing. In *NSDI'12*, pages 2–2, Berkeley, CA, USA, 2012. USENIX Association.

[40] J. Zhou, N. Bruno, and W. Lin. Advanced partitioning techniques for massively distributed computation. In *ACM SIGMOD '12*, pages 13–24, 2012.

Using Strong Triadic Closure to Characterize Ties in Social Networks

Stavros Sintos
Department of Computer Science and Engineering
University of Ioannina
Ioannina, Greece
cs101919@cs.uoi.gr

Panayiotis Tsaparas
Department of Computer Science and Engineering
University of Ioannina
Ioannina, Greece
tsap@cs.uoi.gr

ABSTRACT

In the past few years there has been an explosion of social networks in the online world. Users flock these networks, creating profiles and linking themselves to other individuals. Connecting online has a small cost compared to the physical world, leading to a proliferation of connections, many of which carry little value or importance. Understanding the strength and nature of these relationships is paramount to anyone interesting in making use of the online social network data. In this paper, we use the principle of Strong Triadic Closure to characterize the strength of relationships in social networks. The Strong Triadic Closure principle stipulates that it is not possible for two individuals to have a strong relationship with a common friend and not know each other. We consider the problem of labeling the ties of a social network as strong or weak so as to enforce the Strong Triadic Closure property. We formulate the problem as a novel combinatorial optimization problem, and we study it theoretically. Although the problem is NP-hard, we are able to identify cases where there exist efficient algorithms with provable approximation guarantees. We perform experiments on real data, and we show that there is a correlation between the labeling we obtain and empirical metrics of tie strength, and that weak edges act as bridges between different communities in the network. Finally, we study extensions and variations of our problem both theoretically and experimentally.

Categories and Subject Descriptors

J.4 [**Computer Applications**]: Social and behavioral sciences; H.2.8 [**Database Applications**]: Data Mining; H.4 [**Information Systems Applications**]: Miscellaneous

Keywords

Strong Triadic Closure, Social Networks, Approximation Algorithms

KDD'14, August 24–27, 2014, New York, NY, USA.

ACM 978-1-4503-2956-9/14/08 ...$15.00.
http://dx.doi.org/10.1145/2623330.2623664.

1. INTRODUCTION

The past few years have been marked by the emergence and explosive growth of online social networks. Facebook, LinkedIn, and Twitter are three prominent examples of such online networks, which have become extremely popular, engaging hundreds of millions of users all over the world. Online social networks grow much faster than physical social networks since the "cost" of creating and maintaining connections is much lower. The average user in Facebook has a few hundreds of friends, and a sizeable fraction of the network has more than a thousands friends [20]. The social circle of the average user contains connections with true friends, but also with forgotten high-school classmates, distant relatives, and acquaintances made through brief encounters. Many of the online connections correspond to weak, or no relationships in the physical world.

Understanding the strength and nature of online relationships is paramount to anyone interested in extracting some utility out of the online social network data. For monetization purposes, knowing which relationships correspond to true friendships is of critical importance to advertisers who want to profile users based of their social circle and initiate viral marketing campaigns. For sociologists, knowing the relative importance of online relationships can have a significant effect on the way they model and interpret dynamics and norms in the social network. For friendship suggestion algorithms, knowing which friends matter more can have an important impact on the produced link recommendations.

The problem of understanding the strength and nature of social ties has been studied in the past [12, 7, 6, 22]. Previous approaches rely on user characteristics in order to estimate the true affinity between two users. In this work we use solely the graph structure in order to derive the characterization of the ties within a social network. To this end we make use of the *Strong Triadic Closure* (STC) principle [4]. The STC principle has its roots into early works in Psychology [3, 15, 8], and it has been used in the study of social networks [4, 8]. Informally, the STC principle assumes that there are two types of ties, strong and weak, and it stipulates that it is not possible for two individuals to have a strong relationship with a common friend and not know each other. That is, it is not possible to have an open triangle in the network graph where both edges of the triangle are labeled strong.

We use the STC property to characterize the ties of a social network by asking for a labeling of the edges of the social graph into strong and weak such that the STC property is satisfied. There is a trivial solution to this problem which is to label all edges weak. However, we believe that creating strong relationships is the main motivation for users to join, and actively engage with a social network, online or otherwise. Therefore, we look for a labeling that also maximizes the number of strong ties (or minimizes the number of weak ties).

We thus obtain the following two problems: the MAXSTC problem where we ask for a labeling of the graph such that the STC property holds and the number of strong edges is maximized, and the MINSTC problem where we seek to minimize the number of weak edges. These are two novel combinatorial optimization problems that are of independent theoretical interest. Both problems are NP-hard, and we thus look for efficient algorithms with approximation guarantees. We show that this is not possible for the MAXSTC problem. For the MINSTC problem, we show that it can be expressed as a graph vertex cover problem on an appropriately defined graph, a problem known to have a constant factor approximation algorithm.

We also extend our formulation to capture more complex problems where new edges may be added to the graph, or ties in the network may be of different types. Of particular interest is the MINMULTISTC problem where we seek to enforce a variant of the STC property in the presence of multiple *types* of strong edges. The problem of understanding the "type" of an edge is something that arises naturally in practice. Although there are specialized online social networks catering to different needs of the users (social, professional, informational), the boundaries between these different circles are not always clear. It is often the case that there are multiple types of relationships in a single network. Therefore, it is important to be able to not only distinguish between strong and weak ties, but also to differentiate between different types of relationships and social circles.

We test our algorithms experimentally on real datasets. Our experiments demonstrate that the labeling we obtain based on the structural graph property of Strong Triadic Closure correlates well with empirical measures of tie strength. Furthermore, our labeling agrees with the celebrated "strength of weak ties" observation [8]. The edges between different communities in the social network are usually labeled weak, while the strong edges concentrate among the nodes of the communities.

In summary, in this work we make the following contributions.

- We formulate the problem of characterizing the edges of a social network as a novel optimization problem where we seek to enforce the Strong Triadic Closure property while maximizing the number of strong edges in the graph (or minimizing the number of weak edges).

- We show that our optimization problem is NP-hard. For the minimization problem there exists an efficient approximation algorithm with constant approximation ratio, while there is no good approximation algorithm for the maximization problem.

- We propose and study two extensions to our problem. The first allows the addition of new edges in the graph in order to enforce the STC property. The second allows for multiple types of strong edges.

- We study our algorithms experimentally on real datasets. We show that there is a correlation between the label of an edge and naturally defined notions of tie strength, and that the weak edges act like bridges between different communities in the network.

The rest of the paper is structured as follows. In Section 2 we review some of the related work. In Section 3 we formally define the problems we will study. In Section 4 we study the complexity of our problem, and in Section 5 we consider approximation algorithms. Section 6 considers extensions to the basic problem. Section 7 contains the experimental evaluation, and Section 8 concludes the paper.

2. RELATED WORK

In this paper we build upon the Strong Triadic Closure principle from Psychology. Strong Triadic Closure was first defined by Granovetter [8] in his seminal paper "The Strength of Weak Ties". Previously, Davis [3] and Newcomb [15] discuss some evidence that this property exists in social networks. The Strong Triadic Closure is discussed in detail in the book of Easley and Kleinberg [4]. They discuss the effect of the property on the structure of the network, and possible relaxations, but they do not consider the problem of labeling the edges of the graph to enforce the property. In the discussion they also consider recent experiments [10, 16] which demonstrate a correlation between structural properties of an edge and a notion of strength measured in practice. We perform similar experiments in Section 7 where we study the correlation between the label of an edge and the empirical tie strength.

Recent work has considered the problem of assessing the link strength in a social network, using data from e-mails [14], phone calls [16], and social media [7]. Kahanda and Neville [12] develop a supervised learning approach to predict link strength from transactional information (communication, file transfers, etc) and differentiate between strong and weak relationships in large-scale social networks. Gilbert and Karahalios [7] develop a model for characterizing ties in a social network using features about the similarity and interaction between users. They validate their model on small-scale data collected with questionnaires. In a follow-up work, Gilbert [6] explores how well a tie-strength model developed for one social medium adapts to another in order to find relationships which transcend a particular medium. In addition, Xiang et al. [22] develop an unsupervised model to estimate relationship strength from interaction activity and user similarity. They also handle heterogeneous relationship strength (e.g. acquaintances, best friends). Their work is motivated by the theory of homophily from sociology, which postulates that people tend to form ties with other people who have similar characteristics. Jones et al. [11] found that the frequency of online interaction is a good predictor of strong ties.

Another direction of related research focuses on characterizing the type of a relationship between users. Tang, et al. [19] use user and link characteristics to build a generative model which assigns the most likely type to a specific relationship. In a follow-up work, Tang et al. [18] extend their model for classifying the type of social relationships by learning across heterogenous networks. Their model incorporates ideas from social theories such as structural balance and social status. Backstrom et al. [1] use only the structure of the Facebook graph to identify the romantic partner of a user. They propose dispersion as a new network measure for estimating tie strength.

Our work is similar to this line of research in the sense that we are also trying to characterize the strength and type of social ties. However, prior work relies heavily on user and link characteristics to derive this characterization. In our case we only make use of the graph structure. We use the Strong Triadic Closure principle to formulate our labeling problem as a discrete optimization problem.

3. PROBLEM DEFINITION

Let $G = (V, E)$ be an undirected graph that represents a social network, where the set of vertices V corresponds to individuals, and the set of edges E corresponds to the connections (ties) between these individuals. The goal is to produce a *labeling* of the ties in the social network as either *strong* or *weak*. We will denote this labeling as a function $L_G : E \rightarrow \{W, S\}$, which maps each edge $e \in E$ to a label W (Weak), or S (Strong). Abusing the notation, we will sometimes use L_E to refer to the labeling of the set of edges in E.

The goal is to find a labeling that satisfies the *Strong Triadic Closure (STC)* property, which is defined as follows.

DEFINITION 1 (STRONG TRIADIC CLOSURE). *Given a graph G, a labeling L_G of the graph satisfies the Strong Triadic Closure (STC) property, if there exists no pair of edges (u, v) and (u, w), such that $L_G(u, v) = S$ and $L(u, w) = S$, and $(v, w) \notin E$.*

Informally, the STC property requires that for every node u, it is never the case that u has strong ties with both v and w, yet there is no tie between v and w.

We want to label the edges of the graph into strong or weak, such that the labeling satisfies the STC property. It is easy to see that a trivial solution to this problem is to label all edges in the network as weak. However, we believe that people build social networks with the goal to create strong ties with other people, therefore, we ask for a labeling that satisfies the STC property while maximizing the number of strong ties. Equivalently, we can ask to minimize the number of weak ties in the network, while satisfying the STC property. Let $S(L_G)$ and $W(L_G)$ denote the number of strong and weak ties respectively produced by the labeling L_G. We are interested in the following two problems.

PROBLEM 1 (MAXIMUM STRENGTH STC (MAXSTC)). *Given a graph G, find a labeling L_G that satisfies the STC property and maximizes $S(L_G)$.*

PROBLEM 2 (MINIMUM WEAKNESS STC (MINSTC)). *Given a graph G, find a labeling L_G that satisfies the STC property and minimizes $W(L_G)$.*

In the following we show that the problems are NP-hard, and we consider approximation algorithms.

4. COMPLEXITY ANALYSIS

To establish hardness it is sufficient to consider one of the two variants. We will show that the MAXSTC problem is NP-hard, since the proof is easier.

Before going into the hardness proof, we introduce some notation and provide some intuition about the problem. Let $(u, v), (u, w) \in E$ denote pair of edges in the graph G that share a common endpoint u. We say that the edges define an *open triangle* $\langle (u, v), (u, w) \rangle$ *incident* on u, if $(v, w) \notin E$. The first observation is that, according to the definition of the STC property, a labeling L_G *violates* the STC property if and only if there exists at least one open triangle $\langle (u, v), (u, w) \rangle$ such that both (u, v) and (u, w) are labeled strong. In this case, we say that the open triangle *violates* the STC property; otherwise, we say that the open triangle *satisfies* the STC property. It is clear that a labeling L_G satisfies the STC property, if there is no open triangle that violates the STC property. Furthermore, it is also clear an edge (u, v) that does not belong to any open triangle should be labeled strong. The labeling of (u, v) does not affect the labeling of the remaining edges, since it cannot cause the STC property to be violated. Thus, when looking for the optimal solution, we only need to consider edges that participate in at least one open triangle.

For our reduction we will consider a special type of network: the *ego-network* G_u of a user u. Assuming an underlying social network G, consider a single user $u \in V$ of the network, and let N_u be the friends of u. Let E_u denote the set of edges from u to the nodes in N_u, and E_N the set of edges between the nodes in N_u. The ego-network of a user u is defined as $G_u = (\{u\} \cup N_u, E_u \cup E_N)$.

We will now define a simpler variant of the MAXSTC problem, which we will show that it is as hard as the MAXSTC problem. In our new problem, given an ego-network G_u we ask for a labeling of just the edges E_u incident on the node u such that the STC property is not violated. That is, there is no open triangle incident on u that has both edges labeled as strong.

PROBLEM 3 (MAXEGOSTC). *Given the ego-graph G_u of user u, find a labeling L_{E_u} of the edges incident on node u that satisfies the STC property and maximizes $S(L_{E_u})$.*

It is easy to show that the MAXSTC problem is at least as hard as the MAXEGOSTC problem.

LEMMA 1. *There is a polynomial-time reduction from the MAXEGOSTC problem to the MAXSTC problem.*

PROOF. Let G_u be the ego-network of node u that is given as input to the MAXEGOSTC problem. The reduction is straightforward: we create an instance of the MAXSTC problem, using the the graph G_u as input and asking for a labeling L_E that maximizes the number of strong edges. The key observation is that whether or not the labeling L_{E_u} of the edges in E_u satisfies the STC property is independent of the labeling L_{E_N} of the edges in E_N. This follows from the fact that there exists no open triangle in G_u that contains an edge from E_u and an edge from E_N. Such a triangle would have to be of the form $\langle (u, v), (v, w) \rangle$, missing the edge (u, w). However this is not possible, since by construction $(u, w) \in E_u$. Therefore, all open triangles in G_u contain either two edges from E_u, or two edges from E_N. Thus, we can label the edges E_u and E_N independently. Finding a labeling L_E that maximizes the number of strong edges in G_u while respecting the STC property requires to find labelings L_{E_u} and L_{E_N} that maximize the number of strong edges in E_u and E_N respectively. The labeling L_{E_u}

is a solution of the MAXEGOSTC problem. Note also that finding a labeling L_{E_N} that maximizes the number of strong edges in E_N is an instance of the MAXSTC problem, with the graph $G_N = (N_u, E_N)$ as input.

More formally, consider the decision problem for the MAXEGOSTC problem, where given a graph G_u, we ask if there is a labeling L_{E_u} that has $S(L_{E_u}) \geq k$. Consider also the decision version of the MAXSTC problem, where given a graph G, we ask if there is a labeling L_G that has $S(L_G) \geq \ell$. Given the graph G_u we create the graph G_N and using binary search on the value of ℓ we find the labeling $L^*_{G_N}$ that maximizes $S(L_{G_N})$. Let $S(L^*_{G_N}) = \mu$. Now we give the graph G_u as input to the MAXSTC problem and we ask if there is a labeling L_{G_u} such that $S(L_{G_u}) \geq k + \mu$. Since the labeling of E_u and E_N are independent, there is a labeling L_{E_u} with $S(L_{E_u}) \geq k$, if and only if there is a labeling L_{G_u} with $S(L_{G_u}) \geq k + \mu$. □

LEMMA 2. *The* MAXEGOSTC *problem is NP-hard.*

PROOF. We will now show that the MAXEGOSTC problem is NP-hard by reducing the MAXCLIQUE problem to it. Given an input graph $G = (V, E)$ and a value k, the decision version of the MAXCLIQUE problem asks if there exists a subset $V_c \subseteq V$ of vertices of size at least k, such that the induced subgraph $G_c = (V_c, E_c)$ forms a clique, where $E_c = \{(u, v) \in E : u \in V_c, v \in V_c\}$.

Given the input graph $G = (V, E)$ to the MAXCLIQUE problem, we create an instance of the MAXEGOSTC problem, by creating an ego-network G_u consisting of an additional node u and edges E_u that connect node u to all the nodes V of G. That is, $G_u = (\{u\} \cup V, E_u \cup E)$. We ask if there is a solution of the MAXEGOSTC problem of size at least k.

Let $S \subseteq E_u$ be the subset of edges in E_u that are labeled strong according to a labeling L_{E_u}. Each edge $(u, v) \in S$ in the ego-network defines a unique vertex $v \in V$. Let $V_S \subseteq V$ denote the set of vertices defined by the set of edges S. The labeling L_{E_u} satisfies the STC property, if and only if the set of vertices V_S defines a clique in the graph G. If the labeling of the edges in S satisfies the STC property, then no pairwise combination of edges from S can create an open triangle. Therefore, for every pair of edges $(u, v), (u, w) \in S$, we have that $(v, w) \in E$, and thus V_S defines a clique. On the other hand, if the labeling of the edges in S does not satisfy the STC property, then there must exist at least one pair of edges $(u, v), (u, w) \in S$ that define an open triangle. Therefore, the edge $(v, w) \notin E$ and hence the set V_S does not define a clique.

Therefore, there exists a labeling L_{E_u} for the MAXEGOSTC problem such that $S(L_{E_u}) \geq k$, if and only if, there exists a clique of size at least k in graph G. □

5. APPROXIMATING MIN-STC

Given that the two problems we consider are NP-hard, we look for approximation algorithms. The reduction from MAXCLIQUE to MAXEGOSTC preserves the approximation, so, following the result in [9] we cannot approximate the MAXEGOSTC solution within a factor better than $O(n^{1-\epsilon})$. Fortunately, we can do better for the case of the MINSTC problem.

THEOREM 1. *There exists a 2-approximation algorithm for the* MINSTC *problem.*

PROOF. Recall that a labeling L_G satisfies the STC property, if there exists no open triangle that violates the STC property. That is, there is no open triangle $\langle(u, v), (u, w)\rangle$ such that both (u, v) and (u, w) are labeled strong. Therefore, for every open triangle, at least one of the edges of the open triangle must be labeled weak. We say that this edge *covers* the open triangle. The goal is to find the minimum set of edges that cover all open triangles in the graph.

Using this intuition we will show how the MINSTC problem can be mapped to the *Minimum Vertex Cover* (MINVERTEXCOVER) problem. Given a graph $G = (V, E)$, a subset of vertices $C \subseteq V$ is a *vertex cover* of the graph G, if for every edge $(u, v) \in E$, $u \in C$ or $v \in C$. The MINVERTEXCOVER problem, given a graph G looks for a vertex cover of G with the smallest number of vertices.

The mapping from MINSTC to MINVERTEXCOVER proceeds as follows. Given a graph $G = (V, E)$ that is input to the MINSTC problem, let T denote the set of all open triangles in G. We create a *dual* graph $G_T = (V_E, E_T)$ that is input to MINVERTEXCOVER as follows. For every edge $e \in E$ we create a vertex $v_e \in V_E$. For every open triangle $\langle e_1, e_2\rangle \in T$, we create an edge $(v_{e_1}, v_{e_2}) \in E_T$.

Given a labeling L_G we define the set C to be the set of vertices $v_e \in V_E$ such that the corresponding edge $e \in E$ is labeled weak. If L_G satisfies the STC property, then for every triangle $\langle e_1, e_2\rangle \in T$ at least one of the edges e_1, or e_2 must be labeled weak. Therefore, for every edge $(v_{e_1}, v_{e_2}) \in E_T$ at least one of the two endpoints is included in the set C, and hence C is a vertex cover for the graph G_T.

Furthermore, given a minimum vertex cover $C \subseteq V_E$ of the graph G_T we can create a labeling L_G by labeling as weak every edge $e \in E$, such that $v_e \in C$, and the remaining edges as strong. Since C is a vertex cover for G_T, by construction of G_T it follows that every open triangle in G is covered by at least one edge labeled weak. Therefore, the labeling L_G respects the STC property. If C is the minimum vertex cover, then L_G is the labeling with the minimum number of weak edges. If C is an α-approximate solution for the minimum vertex cover, then L_G is an α-approximation of the minimum number of weak edges. It is well known that there is a 2-approximation algorithm for the MINVERTEXCOVER problem [21, 2], which implies a 2-approximation algorithm for the MINSTC problem. □

In our experiments we consider two different approximation algorithms for the MINSTC problem: A 2-approximation algorithm that relies on finding a *maximal matching* for the dual graph G_T; A greedy $O(\log n)$-approximation algorithm that constructs a vertex cover of G_T by always selecting the node that covers the most uncovered edges. We discuss the details of the algorithms in Section 7.

6. EXTENSIONS AND VARIATIONS

We will now discuss some extensions and variations to the basic MINSTC problem.

6.1 STC with edge additions

Consider the case that the graph G that we want to label consists of a full clique of n nodes, missing a single edge (u, v). Then, the best labeling we can obtain has $n-2$ weak edges (all the edges incident to either u or v). However, we could obtain a labeling with all the edges labeled strong if we simply added the missing edge (u, v). Thus, we consider a new minimization problem, where, in order to guarantee the STC property, except for labeling existing edges as weak, we can also add new edges to the graph. The goal is to minimize the number edges added to the graph, and the number of edges in the original graph that are labeled weak. We refer to this problem as MINSTC+.

PROBLEM 4 (MINSTC+). *Given a graph $G = (V, E)$, identify a set of* additional *edges $E' \subseteq V \times V \setminus E$ and a labeling $L_{G'}$ of the graph $G' = (V, E \cup E')$ that satisfies the STC property such that $W(L_E) + |E'|$ is minimized.*

The MINSTC+ problem is also NP-hard. However, we can again view it as a coverage problem, and exploit the fact that there is a known approximation algorithm.

LEMMA 3. *There is a $O(\log n)$-approximation algorithm for the* MINSTC+ *problem.*

PROOF. We will show that our problem can be modelled as an instance of the Minimum Hitting Set (MINHITSET) problem. The minimum hitting set problem is defined as follows. Given a universe of elements U and a collection of subsets of U, $\mathcal{S} = \{S_1, ..., S_n\}$, we want to find a subset $C \subseteq U$ of minimum size, such that for each $S_i \in \mathcal{S}$, $S_i \cap C \neq \emptyset$, that is, each set $S_i \in \mathcal{S}$ is *hit* by C.

We can transform an instance of the MINSTC+ problem to an instance MINHITSET problem using a construction very similar to the one we used for transforming MINSTC to the MINVERTEXCOVER problem. Given the graph $G = (V, E)$ the universe U is defined as the set of all pairs of the form (u, v) where $u, v \in V$. For every open triangle $t = \langle (u, v), (u, w) \rangle$ of the graph G, we create a set $S_t = \{(u, v), (u, w), (v, w)\}$. The goal is to find the smallest subset C of pairs in U such that we hit all the sets S_t. Given a hitting set, we define the set E' as the set of pairs $(w, u) \in C$ such that $(w, u) \notin E$. The remaining pairs in C correspond to edges in E and are labeled weak. The labeling of graph G' satisfies the STC property since every open triangle in G is either covered by a weak edge, or it is closed by an edge in E'. We can assume that the additional edges are labeled weak, therefore, they do not create any new violating open triangles.

Given a solution to the MINSTC+ problem, we can define a hitting set, by adding to the set C the pairs in E', and the edges in E that are labeled weak. Since all open triangles in G are covered, this defines a hitting set.

The MINHITSET problem is NP-hard, but the simple greedy algorithm that always selects the element that hits most sets that are not already hit is known to have a $O(\log n)$ approximation ratio. Therefore, there exists a $O(\log n)$ approximation algorithm for the MINSTC+ problem. □

6.2 STC with multiple relationship types

In the MINSTC (or MAXSTC) problem, there are only two types of edges: strong and weak. We assume that the weak edges are the "less important" ones, and we want to produce a labeling that maximizes the strong ones. We now consider the scenario where there are multiple types of strong ties. For example, when considering the social network of a specific individual it would be useful to understand which links correspond to strong family ties, strong work ties, or strong friendship ties. In this case we want to identify the strong edges of each type.

We model this problem using a natural extension of the STC property. Similar to before, the goal is to have as many strong edges as possible, such that there is no violating open triangle with both edges labeled strong. The difference is that with multiple types of strong edges, an open triangle is violating if both its edges are labeled strong *and* they are both of the same type. That is, it is ok for a user u to have strong relationships with users v, w and v, w to not be connected, as long as the type of relationship of (u, v) and (u, w) is different.

More formally, we assume a fixed number k of strong relationship types. We can view these types as k labels $\{S_1, ..., S_k\}$. We also have the additional label W for the weak edges. Given graph $G = (V, E)$, we want to produce a labeling $L_E : E \rightarrow \{W, S_1, ..., S_k\}$ of the edges of a graph G. The labeling must satisfy the *multi-Strong Triadic Closure* property (multi-STC) which is defined as follows.

DEFINITION 2 (MULTI-STRONG TRIADIC CLOSURE). *Given a graph G, a labeling $L_E : E \rightarrow \{W, S_1, ..., S_k\}$ satisfies the multi-Strong Triadic Closure (multi-STC) property, if there exists no pair of edges (u, v) and (u, w), such that $(v, w) \notin E$ and $L(u, v) = L(u, w) = S_i$, for some $i \in [1, k]$.*

Similar to the STC property, we can trivially satisfy the multi-STC property by labeling all edges as weak. Our goal is again to maximize the number of edges labeled strong (of any type), or minimize the number of edges labeled weak. The maximization problem runs again into the problem of finding the maximum clique, so we study the minimization problem.

PROBLEM 5 (MINMULTISTC). *Given a graph G, and k strong edge types, find a labeling L_E that satisfies the multi-STC property and minimizes $W(L_E)$.*

We can now prove the following theorem.

THEOREM 2. *The* MINMULTISTC *problem is NP-hard for any $k \geq 2$. There is a $O(\log n)$-approximation algorithm for $k = 2$. The problem is hard to approximate for $k \geq 3$, unless $P = NP$.*

PROOF. For the proof, we will make use of the dual graph G_T that we constructed in Section 5. We can model our problem as a coloring problem on the dual graph G_T, where we want to color the nodes of G_T with $k + 1$ colors. There are k "strong" colors $\{S_1, ..., S_k\}$, one for each strong label, plus an additional "white" color W for the weak label. We want a *legal* coloring of the nodes of the graph G_T, where no two adjacent nodes can be colored with the same strong color. It is ok if we have two adjacent nodes having a white color. We want a legal coloring that minimizes the number of white nodes.

For $k = 2$ our problem is equivalent to the odd-cycle traversal problem [17], which given a graph asks for the minimum number of vertices to be removed, so that the resulting graph becomes bipartite. This problem is also known to be NP-hard, but there is a $O(\log n)$-approximation algorithm [5].

For $k \geq 3$ we can show that the problem is not only NP-hard, but also hard to approximate unless $P = NP$. The proof follows easily by observing that for a k-colorable graph, the optimal solution to the MINMULTISTC problem has cost zero, that is, we do not need to use the white color. This implies that if there was an algorithm with bounded approximation ratio, then for an input instance for which the optimal algorithm has cost zero, the algorithm would be able to produce a solution with zero cost as well; otherwise the approximation ratio is infinite. However, for $k \geq 3$, finding a k-coloring of a k-colorable graph is NP-hard. Therefore, it is hard to decide if there is a solution to the MINMULTI-STC problem that has cost greater than zero. Therefore, the problem is hard to approximate, unless $P = NP$. □

We note that for $k = 2$, the $O(\log n)$-approximation algorithm makes use of linear programming for deriving the solution. We propose a simpler heuristic in Section 7.

7. EXPERIMENTS

The goal of the experiments is to study if the labeling we obtain by enforcing the STC property correlates with an intuitive measure of tie strength in practice. We perform a variety of experiments towards this end. Our experiments are on real data, and demonstrate the practical utility of our formulation and of the proposed algorithms.

7.1 Datasets

We use five different datsets in our experiments: *Actors*, *Authors*, *Les Miserables*, *Karate Club* and *Amazon Books*. Table 1 shows some statistics about our datasets. The column "Weights" indicates whether we can compute weights for the edges of the graph. The weight of an edge corresponds to the empirical strength of the connection The column "Community Structure" indicates whether there exists a known community structure in the graph.

Table 1: Datasets Statistics.

Dataset	Nodes	Edges	Weights	Community structure
Actors	1,986	103,121	Yes	No
Authors	3,418	9,908	Yes	No
Les Miserables	77	254	Yes	No
Karate Club	34	78	No	Yes
Amazon Books	105	441	No	Yes

We now describe the datasets in detail.

The *Actors* dataset: We create a graph from a movie dataset collected from IMDB[1], consisting of 3,125 movies made from 1945 to 2010, and 2,171 actors that participate in these movies. The actor graph contains a node for each actor in the data, and there is an edge between two actors if they have collaborated in at least one movie. For each node of the graph we also have information about the set of movies in which the actor has played. We prune actors who participated in less than 5 movies since we do not consider them to be significant members of the network.

The *Authors* dataset: This dataset was obtained from data downloaded from the DBLP site[2]. It consists of a collection of authors that have published papers in one of the major Data Mining, Databases or Theory conferences during the period between 1994 and 2013. The author graph contains a node for each author in the data, and there is an edge between two authors if they have collaborated in at least one paper. For each node in the graph we also have information about the set of papers the author has written. We prune authors who wrote less than 3 papers since we do not consider them to be significant members of the network.

The *Les Miserables* dataset: This dataset contains the network of co-appearances of characters in Victor Hugo's novel "Les Miserables" [13]. Nodes represent characters of the novel, and there is an edge between two nodes if the pair of characters appear in the same chapter of the book. For each edge we have the number of such co-appearances between the two characters.

The *Karate Club* dataset: Zachary's Karate Club dataset [23] is a social network of friendships between 34 members of a karate club at a US university in the 1970s. The information about the friendship was derived by questionnaires filled out by the members of the club.

The *Amazon Books* dataset: This dataset contains a set of books about US politics published around the time of the 2004 presidential election which are sold by the online bookseller Amazon.com[3]. Edges between books represent frequent co-purchasing of the books. In addition, each node (book) is labeled as "liberal", "neutral", or 'conservative", depending on its political viewpoint. There are 43 liberal, 13 neutral and 49 conservative books in this dataset.

7.2 Algorithms

In Section 5, we proved that MINSTC problem on the graph G can be mapped to the MINVERTEXCOVER problem on the *dual* graph G_T. Given the graph G, the dual graph G_T is constructed by creating a node for every edge of G, and connecting two nodes if the corresponding edges form an open triangle. The algorithms we consider work by constructing an approximate solution to the MINVERTEXCOVER problem. We now describe them in detail.

The Greedy Algorithm: The input to the algorithm is the graph G and its dual G_T, and the output is a labeling of the edges of the graph G as strong or weak. The algorithm works by constructing a vertex cover of graph G_T in a greedy fashion. Recall that a vertex cover of a graph is a set of vertices such that every edge of the graph has at least one endpoint in the set. Let C denotes the set of nodes which are selected by our algorithm. Initially $C = \emptyset$. At every step the algorithm selects the node v with the maximum degree in G_T, and adds it to the set C. It then deletes node v and all edges incident on v from graph G_T. The process is repeated until there are no more edges in the graph G_T. Given the set of nodes in C, we label the corresponding edges of graph G as weak. The remain edges are labeled strong. This algorithm is known to be a $O(\log n)$-approximation algorithm [21].

If at any step of the algorithm more than one nodes have the same degree, we break ties by choosing the node that corresponds to the edge in G that participates in the fewest *closed triangles* in the graph G. This way, our algorithm tends to label as weak edges that participate in many open triangles and few closed triangles, a principle that agrees with our intuition of what a weak edge should be.

The MaximalMatching Algorithm: The MaximalMatching algorithm also produces a vertex cover of the graph G_T, by constructing a maximal matching for the dual graph G_T. A matching of a graph is a collection of non-adjacent edges of the graph, while a maximal matching is one where no additional edges can be added. The algorithm constructs the matching one edge at the time. Let M denote the set

[1] http:www.imdb.com

[2] http://dblp.uni-trier.de/xml/

[3] Available by V. Krebs at http://www.orgnet.com/.

of edges selected by our algorithm. Initially $M = \emptyset$. The algorithm selects the next edge to add to the set M by first selecting the node u with the highest degree in G_T and then the neighbor v of u with the highest degree. If more than one nodes have the same degree then we break ties in the same way as in the Greedy Algorithm. We add edge (u, v) to M, and delete u, v and all edges incident on u or v from G_T. The algorithm terminates when there are no more edges in the graph G_T. Let C denote the set of vertices that are endpoints of the edges in M. Similar to before, we label as weak the corresponding edges of G, while the remaining edges are labeled as strong. This algorithm is known to be a 2-approximation algorithm [21].

Note that for both algorithms if there are vertices in the graph G_T that have no incident edges, then the corresponding edges in the graph G will be labeled strong. These correspond to edges that participate only in closed triangles, or that are isolated in the graph G.

Table 2 shows the number of edges labeled weak and strong for the two algorithms on the five datasets we consider in this paper. Despite the better approximation ratio the MaximalMatching algorithm always produces a larger number of weak edges.

Table 2: Number of strong and weak edges for Greedy and MaximalMatching algorithms.

	Greedy		MaximalMatching	
	Strong	Weak	Strong	Weak
Actors	11,184	91,937	8,581	94,540
Authors	3,608	6,300	2,676	7,232
Les Miserables	128	126	106	148
Karate Club	25	53	14	64
Amazon Books	114	327	71	370

7.3 Measuring Tie Strength

In this section we study the relationship between the assigned labels and a notion of tie strength measured in practice. Our experiments follow the line of experimentation in prior work [16, 10] where they study how structural features of an edge correlate with empirical tie strength.

For this experiment, we use the three datasets for which we can compute weights for the edges: the *Actors* dataset, the *Les Miserables* dataset and the *Authors* dataset. The weights on the edges correspond to the strength of the relationships: a strong and enduring collaboration between two nodes in the case of the *Actors* and *Authors* datasets, and high affinity in the storyline of the novel in the case of the *Les Miserables* dataset. Specifically, for the *Actors* dataset, the weight of an edge is the number of times that the two actors have collaborated; for the *Authors* dataset it represents the number of papers that they have written together; for the *Les Miserables* dataset, it is the number of co-appearances between two characters in the same chapter. The goal of this experiment is to test the validity of the edge labeling, by examining if there is a correlation between the assigned label and the weight of the edge. Mathematically, we will show that there is a statistically significant difference between the mean weight of strong and weak edges.

Table 3 shows the mean weight for the strong and weak edges for all the three datasets, using the Greedy and MaximalMatching algorithms. Clearly, for all of the datasets the strong edges have higher weight than the weak ones. The t-test reveals that the difference is statistically significant at a 5% confidence level. We can thus conclude that the labeling of our algorithm agrees with the "true" strength of the network ties.

Table 3: Mean count weight for strong and weak edges for Greedy and MaximalMatching algorithms.

	Greedy		MaximalMatching	
	S	W	S	W
Actors	1.4	1.1	1.3	1.1
Authors	1.341	1.150	1.362	1.167
Les Miserables	3.83	2.61	3.87	2.76

The frequency of common activity (e.g. collaboration) between two users is obviously a strong indicator of tie strength. However it may also be an artifact of the general frequent activity of the two users. For example, two highly prolific researchers may collaborate on higher-than-average number of papers, but this may be simply due to the fact that they produce a lot of publications in general. An alternative measure of tie strength is the fraction of the activity of the two users that is devoted to their relationship. We use Jaccard similarity to capture this idea. Recall that Jaccard similarity between two sets is defined as the ratio of their intersection over their union. In our case the sets correspond to the sets of activities in which the two users engage (e.g., movies, publications, etc), and the Jaccard similarity measures the fraction of their activities that are common.

For this experiment we use the *Actors* and the *Authors* datasets. For the *Actors* dataset the weight of an edge between two actors is the number of movies in which they have played together, over the total number of movies in which at least one of the two actors has participated. Similarly, the weight of an edge between two authors is defined as the number of papers that they have written together over the total number of their papers. We cannot compute Jaccard similarity for the *Les Miserables* dataset, since we do not have the exact chapter appearances for each character.

Table 4 shows the mean Jaccard similarity for the strong and weak edges using Greedy and MaximalMatching algorithms. Again, for all of the datasets the strong edges have higher weight than the weak ones and the t-test reveals that this difference is statistically significant at a 5% confidence level. We note that in the case of Jaccard similarity, the gap between strong and weak edges is larger than before. It seems that our labeling is more adept at capturing this focused measure of tie strength.

Table 4: Mean Jaccard similarity for strong and weak edges for Greedy and MaximalMatching algorithms.

	Greedy		MaximalMatching	
	S	W	S	W
Actors	0.06	0.04	0.06	0.04
Authors	0.145	0.084	0.155	0.088

Comparing the MaximalMatching and the Greedy algorithm we observe that they behave very similarly in terms of the mean weights of strong and weak edges. However, the Greedy algorithm produces consistently a larger number of strong edges, and it is intuitively more appealing.

7.4 Weak edges as bridges

Granovetter, in his seminal paper [8], demonstrated the importance of weak social ties in connecting individuals with information that is not readily available in their close social circle, such as new work opportunities. A possible explanation to this observation is nicely articulated in the book of David Easley and Jon Kleinberg [4], where they postulate that weak ties act as *bridges* between communities in the graph. Communities hold different types of information, and the only way for an individual to obtain access to information from a community different than her own is through weak ties.

In accordance to this interpretation, given a labeling of the edges of a graph with known community structure, we would like most of the inter-community edges to be labeled weak, while most of the strong labels to be confined to intra-community edges. That is, edges that bridge communities should be labeled weak, while strong edges should serve as a backbone of the communities.

Formally, let $G = (V, E)$ denote the input graph, and let $\mathcal{C} = \{C_1, ..., C_k\}$ denote a partition of the nodes of the graph into k communities, which is also given as part of the input. Let E_{inter} denote the set of edges (u, v) such that $u \in C_i$ and $v \in C_j$ for some $i \neq j$, and let E_{intra} denote the set of edges (u, v) such that $u, v \in C_i$ for some i. Also given the labeling L_G of the graph G let W denote the set of edges labeled weak, and let S denote the set of edges labeled strong. We define the precision P_W and recall R_W for the weak edges as follows:

$$P_W = \frac{|W \cap E_{inter}|}{|W|} \quad \text{and} \quad R_W = \frac{|W \cap E_{inter}|}{|E_{inter}|}$$

Similarly, we define precision P_S and recall R_S for strong edges as follows:

$$P_S = \frac{|S \cap E_{intra}|}{|S|} \quad \text{and} \quad R_S = \frac{|S \cap E_{intra}|}{|E_{intra}|}$$

The numbers we are mostly interested in are R_W and P_S, that is, we want the bridging edges to be labeled weak, and the strong edges to be confined within the communities.

To test our hypothesis we need graphs with known community structure. To this end, we use the *Karate Club* and *Amazon Books* datasets. For the *Karate Club* dataset it is well known [4] that there were two fractions within the members of the club, centered around the two trainers, that eventually led to the breakup of the club. For the *Amazon Books* dataset the communities are given by the political viewpoint of the books.

Table 5: Precision and Recall for strong and weak edges for Greedy and MaximalMatching algorithms.

	Greedy			
	P_S	R_S	P_W	R_W
Karate Club	1	0.37	0.19	1
Amazon Books	0.81	0.25	0.15	0.69
	MaximalMatching			
	P_S	R_S	P_W	R_W
Karate Club	1	0.2	0.16	1
Amazon Books	0.73	0.14	0.14	0.73

Table 5 shows the results for the two datasets for the Greedy and MaximalMatching algorithms. The two algorithms behave similarly, but the Greedy algorithm performs better overall in terms of both precision and recall. We now study the labeling of the Greedy algorithm in more detail.

For the *Karate Club* dataset we observe that we have perfect precision for the strong edges, and perfect recall for the weak edges. We visualize the results of the Greedy algorithm in Figure 1. The nodes are colored white and gray depending on the community to which they belong. The thick red edges correspond to the edges labeled strong, and the thin blue edges to the edges labeled weak. We can see that strong edges appear only between nodes of the same group, while all edges that cross communities are labeled weak.

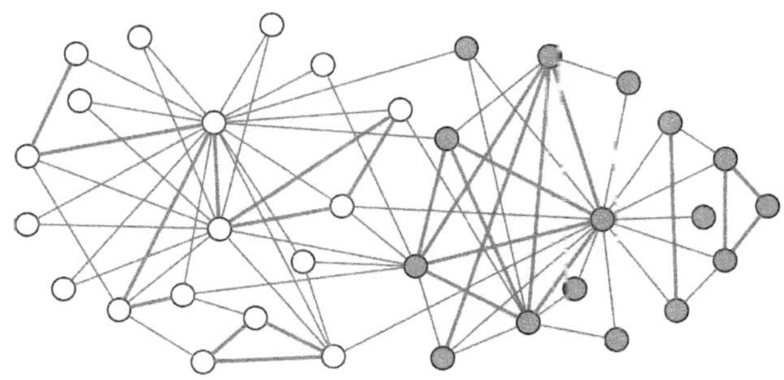

Figure 1: Karate Club graph. Blue light edges represent the weak edges, while red thick edges represent the strong edges.

For the *Amazon Books* dataset the Greedy algorithm characterizes 114 edges as strong, out of which 92 connect books of the same type, thus yielding precision $P_S = 0.81$. On the other hand, there are 70 edges that connect nodes from different groups, and 48 of those are labeled weak, yielding recall $R_W = 0.69$. Of the remaining 22 edges that cross communities and are labeled strong, 20 are edges with one of the two endpoints being a book labeled as neutral. It is intuitive that people would co-purchase books of neutral viewpoint with liberal or conservative books, thus leading to strong connections. There are only two edges that connect a liberal and a conservative pair of books, and are labeled strong by our algorithm. These pairs are: ("America Unbound", "Rise of the Vulcans"), and ("The Choice", "Rise of the Vulcans"). After some investigation, we found out that, for the first pair, although the books "America Unbound" and "Rise of the Vulcans" belong to different categories (liberal and conservative respectively), they are both about the exact same issue: George W. Bush's foreign policy. Therefore, there is a different latent dimension that groups them together, which can explain the strong relationship between them.

7.5 STC with added edges

In this section we conduct experiments for the MINSTC+ problem, where except for labeling edges as strong or weak, we can also add edges to the graph. To this end we use the greedy algorithm we described in Section 6. The algorithm works iteratively. At each step of the algorithm a pair of nodes (u, v) is selected which covers the most remaining open triangles. This pair is either an edge not currently in the graph, which, when added, closes the most remaining open triangles, or an existing edge, which, when labeled weak, covers the most remaining open triangles. We refer to this algorithm as the Greedy+ Algorithm.

Table 6 shows the number of strong, weak and added edges using the Greedy+ algorithm. We can see that, as expected, using added edges the number of strong edges increases. Table 7 shows the mean weight for the strong and weak edges for the Greedy+ algorithm. It is still the case that strong edges have higher mean weight than the weak edges, however, compared to the results in Table 3, the strong edges have lower mean weight while weak edges have higher mean weight. Therefore, although the Greedy+ algorithm labels more edges as strong, it seems that some of these edges are of low weight.

Table 6: Number of strong, weak and added edges for the Greedy+ algorithm.

	Strong	Weak	Added
Actors	12095	91026	537
Authors	4041	5867	343
Les Miserables	165	89	14
Karate Club	29	49	1
Amazon Books	158	283	29

Table 7: Mean count weight for strong and weak edges for the Greedy+ algorithm.

	S	W
Actors	1.403	1.191
Authors	1.332	1.142
Les Miserables	3.345	3.011

To obtain further insight into the effect of added edges we look at the labeling produced by the Greedy+ algorithm for networks with known community structure. Table 8 shows the results for the *Amazon Books* and *Karate Club* datasets. We observe that the recall value R_S of the Greedy+ algorithm is higher compared to that of the Greedy algorithm, while the P_S value is almost the same. This means that the algorithm is successful at introducing strong edges within the communities as it was supposed to. We also compute the precision P_A of the added edges, shown in Table 8. We define P_A as the fraction of added edges that fall within the community. Clearly, the added edges serve the purpose of "strengthening" an existing community.

Table 8: Precision and Recall for strong and weak edges for the Greedy+ algorithm

	P_S	R_S	P_W	R_W	P_A
Karate Club	1	0.43	0.2	1	1
Amazon Books	0.79	0.37	0.13	0.53	0.72

We also visualize the effect of the added edges for the case of the *Karate Club* dataset in Figure 2. For this dataset, the Greedy+ algorithm adds only one edge (the dashed black edge in the figure). Compared to Figure 1, the algorithm maintains all the inter-community weak edges, and all the intra-community strong edges produced by the Greedy algorithm, and it adds an additional four strong edges within the grey community. The added edge reveals the existence of a near-clique of seven users in the network, which can now be labeled strong.

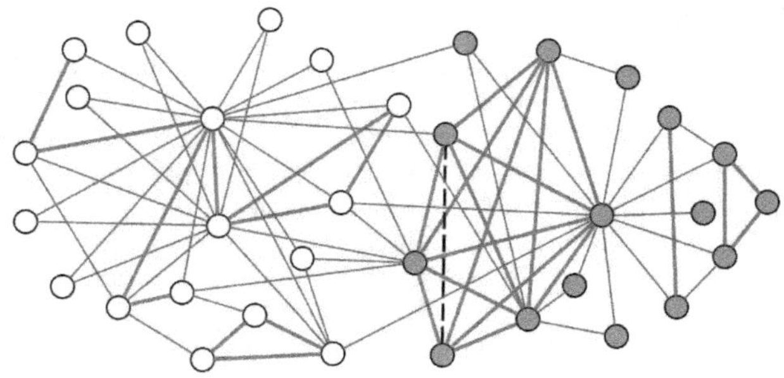

Figure 2: Karate Club graph. Blue light edges represent the weak edges, red thick edges represent the strong edges, and the black dashed edge represents the added edge

Therefore, we can conclude that the Greedy+ algorithm is better than the Greedy algorithm in revealing the backbone of an existing community in the graph. However, this comes at the price of labeling as strong more low-weight edges.

7.6 STC with multiple relationship types

We now consider the MINMULTISTC problem where we have k different types of strong ties. For this problem, there is an approximation algorithm for $k = 2$, however, it makes use of Linear Programming, making it complex to implement. There is no known algorithm for $k > 2$.

We propose a heuristic algorithm that works for any k by making iterative calls to the Greedy algorithm. The algorithm starts by running the Greedy algorithm on the graph G, producing sets S_1 and W_1 of strong and weak edges respectively. We label the edges in S_1 as "Strong 1". Given the set W_1 we compute the subgraph G_{W_1} induced by the edges in W_1. We can now repeat the same process on the graph G_{W_1} to obtain a new set of edges S_2 to label "Strong 2", and a new subgraph G_{W_2}. We continue iteratively until all k labels have been utilized.

More formally, the i-th iteration of the algorithm takes the graph $G_{W_{i-1}}$ as input (where $G_{W_0} = G$), runs the Greedy algorithm, and produces the sets of edges S_i and W_i. The set S_i is labeled as "Strong i", and the set W_i is used to produce the graph G_{W_i} for the next iteration. This process is repeated until k iterations are completed. The set W_k in the final iteration is labeled as "Weak". We refer to this algorithm as the MultiGreedy Algorithm.

We now experiment with the MultiGreedy algorithm. For simplicity we only consider the case where $k = 2$, that is, we only have two types of strong edges. For this experiment, we use as input graph an *ego-graph*, that is, the relationships of a single individual, and the edges between them. This is a common scenario in online social networks, where we want to be able to discriminate between different types of relationships of a specific individual.

Using the *Authors* dataset, we create two ego-networks centered around Jon Kleinberg, and Ravi Kumar, two researchers with diverse interests and collaborations. We prune co-authors with whom the author has less than 3 papers together, so that we focus on the more meaningful collaborations. Tables 9 and 10 show the results. For Kleinberg we observe that the "Strong 1" edges correspond to collaborations related to the early Web research, and his association with IBM Almaden, while the "Strong 2" collaborations correspond to more theoretical publications. For Ravi Kumar, the "Strong 1" ties correspond to his time at IBM Almaden, while the "Strong 2" ties to the time at Yahoo. Our algorithm is able to differentiate between these two distinct types of relationships.

Table 9: J. Kleinberg's ego-network.

Type	Names
Strong 1	R. Kumar, S. Rajagopalan, A. Tomkins, A. Sahai, P. Raghavan
Strong 2	M. Sudan, D. P. Williamson
Weak	E. Tardos, F. T. Leighton, L. Backstrom, D. P. Huttenlocher, A. Kumar, J. Leskovec, L. Lee

Table 10: R. Kumar's ego-network.

Type	Names
Strong 1	A. Tomkins, D. Sivakumar, E. Upfal, P. Raghavan, S. Rajagopalan
Strong 2	V. Josifovski, S. Vassilvitskii, A. Z. Broder
Weak	R. Rubinfeld, K. S. McCurley, M. Mitzenmacher, A. Dasgupta, A. Panconesi, K. Punera, V. Rastogi, J. Novak, J. M. Kleinberg, M. Mahdian, E. Vee, S. Lattanzi, B. Reed, A. Sahai, R. Krauthgamer, T. S. Jayram, S. Pandey, B. Pang, R. V. Guha

8. CONCLUSIONS

In this paper we addressed the problem of characterizing the connections in a social network. We made use of the Strong Triadic Closure property, and we formulated a novel optimization problem where we look for a labeling of the edges of a graph into strong or weak, such that the STC property is satisfied and the number of weak edges is minimized. We studied the complexity of the ensuing problems, and we showed that for the minimization problem we can provide a constant approximation algorithm. We also considered extensions of the basic formulation, to account for edge additions and networks where ties may have several different types. The experimental results demonstrate that the labeling we obtain makes sense in practice.

Our work leaves room for further research. More specifically, it would be interesting to consider further relaxations of the STC property. It would also be interesting to have a stochastic model where each edge has a probability of being strong or weak, rather than belonging exclusively to one class or another. These questions become more interesting when we have more than one types of strong edges.

9. ACKNOWLEDGMENTS

This work is supported by the Marie Curie Reintegration Grant project titled JMUGS which has received research funding from the European Union.

10. REFERENCES

[1] L. Backstrom and J. M. Kleinberg. Romantic partnerships and the dispersion of social ties: a network analysis of relationship status on facebook. In *CSCW*, pages 831–841, 2014.

[2] K. L. Clarkson. A modification of the greedy algorithm for vertex cover. *IPL*, 16(1):23–25, 1983.

[3] J. A. Davis. Clustering and hierarchy in interpersonal relations. *American Sociological Review*, page 845.

[4] D. Easley and J. Kleinberg. *Networks, Crowds, and Markets: Reasoning About a Highly Connected World.* Cambridge University Press, 2010.

[5] N. Garg, V. V. Vazirani, and M. Yannakakis. Multiway cuts in directed and node weighted graphs. In *ICALP*, volume 820, pages 487–498, 1994.

[6] E. Gilbert. Predicting tie strength in a new medium. In *CSCW*, pages 1047–1056, 2012.

[7] E. Gilbert and K. Karahalios. Predicting tie strength with social media. In *CHI*, pages 211–220, 2009.

[8] M. Granovetter. The strength of weak ties. *American Journal of Sociology*, 78:1360–1380, 1973.

[9] J. Hastad. Clique is hard to approximate within $n^{(1-\epsilon)}$. In *Acta Mathematica*, pages 627–636, 1996.

[10] B. A. Huberman, D. M. Romero, and F. Wu. Social networks that matter: Twitter under the microscope. *First Monday*, 14, 2009.

[11] J. J. Jones, J. E. Settle, R. M. Bond, C. J. Fariss, C. Marlow, and J. H. Fowler. Inferring tie strength from online directed behavior. *PLoS ONE 8*, 2013.

[12] I. Kahanda and J. Neville. Using transactional information to predict link strength in online social networks. In *ICWSM*, 2009.

[13] D. E. Knuth. The stanford graphbase: A platform for combinatorial computing. *Journal of Anthropological Research*, 1993.

[14] G. Kossinets and D. Watts. Empirical analysis of an evolving social network. *Science 311*, pages 88–90, 2006.

[15] T. M. Newcomb. *The Acquaintance Process.* New York: Holt, Rinehart & Winston, 1961.

[16] J.-P. Onnela, J. Saramaki, J. Hyvonen, G. Szabo, D. Lazer, K. Kaski, J. Kertesz, and A.-L. Barabasi. Structure and tie strengths in mobile communication networks. *PNAS USA*, 104:7332–7336, 2007.

[17] B. Reed, K. Smith, and A. Vetta. Finding odd cycle transversals. *Operations Research Letters*, 32(4):299 – 301, 2004.

[18] J. Tang, T. Lou, and J. Kleinberg. Inferring social ties across heterogenous networks. In *WSDM*, pages 743–752, 2012.

[19] W. Tang, H. Zhuang, and J. Tang. Learning to infer social ties in large networks. In *ECML/PKDD*, pages 381–397, 2011.

[20] J. Ugander, B. Karrer, L. Backstrom, and C. Marlow. The anatomy of the facebook social graph. *CoRR*, abs/1111.4503, 2011.

[21] V. V. Vazirani. *Approximation algorithms.* Springer, 2001.

[22] R. Xiang, J. Neville, and M. Rogati. Modeling relationship strength in online social networks. In *WWW Conference*, pages 981–990, 2010.

[23] W. W. Zachary. An information flow model for conflict and fission in small groups. *Journal of Anthropological Research*, 33:452–473, 1977.

Network Structural Analysis via Core-Tree-Decomposition

Takuya Akiba*
The University of Tokyo
JST, ERATO,
Kawarabayashi Project
t.akiba@is.s.u-tokyo.ac.jp

Takanori Maehara
National Institute of Informatics
JST, ERATO,
Kawarabayashi Project
maehara@nii.ac.jp

Ken-ichi Kawarabayashi
National Institute of Informatics
JST, ERATO,
Kawarabayashi Project
k_keniti@nii.ac.jp

ABSTRACT

The study of network analysis is still a new science; currently, the structure of real-world networks is described only in terms of the coarsest and basic details such as diameter and degree distribution. To efficiently and effectively implement network analysis techniques, a more comprehensive grasp of their finer mathematical structure is required. The seminal work by Leskovec et al. tackled this issue by decomposing networks into two parts; namely "whiskers" and "cores."

In this study, we progress toward this issue by obtaining a novel "core-tree-decomposition," which is a variant of the well-known tree-decomposition. Specifically, we perform experiments to construct core-tree-decompositions for as many as 40 publicly available datasets. Our decomposition provides more structural information than the previous method in the following ways:

1. By comparing the eigenvalue distribution of the cores obtained by our decomposition method with that of the Erdős-Rényi random graphs, we confirm that, unlike the previously defined core, our "core" behaves like a random graph, i.e., an expander graph. Thus, the intuition that the cores should be "expander-like" is confirmed by the eigenvalue distribution of our cores.

2. By deleting the core, we obtain a tree-decomposition of small width, which behaves like a tree. Therefore, we can say that whiskers are "tree-like," and can be explained in terms of "tree-width."

3. We show that the cores of real networks widely range in size, which implies that their tree-widths are also quite varied. Furthermore, we show theoretical and empirical evidence that tree-width plays a significant role in the efficiency of certain types of algorithms.

*Supported by a Grant-in-Aid for JSPS Fellows (256563).

KDD'14, August 24–27, 2014, New York, NY, USA.

ACM 978-1-4503-2956-9/14/08 ...$15.00.
http://dx.doi.org/10.1145/2623330.2623753.

Categories and Subject Descriptors

H.2.8 [**Database Management**]: Database Application—*Data Mining*

General Terms

Measurement, Theory, Algorithms

Keywords

Tree-decomposition; tree-width; core-tree-decomposition; expander; social network; web graph

1. INTRODUCTION

In recent years, considerable interest in graph structures has been arising in social and information networks, i.e., graphs in which the vertices represent underlying social entities and the edges represent interactions between pairs of vertices. However, the study of network analysis is still in its infancy; currently, the structure of real-world networks is described only in terms of the coarsest and basic details such as diameter and degree distribution. To efficiently and effectively implement network analysis techniques, a more comprehensive grasp of their finer mathematical structure is required. In fact, in most cases, we need to extract such a structural property.

The seminal work by Leskovec et al. [24] tackled this issue by decomposing web graphs and social networks into two parts; namely the "whiskers" and the "cores". We closely examine this approach first.

1.1 "Whiskers" and "Core"

In social networks and web graphs, there is a substantial fraction of vertices that are barely connected to the main part of the network, i.e., they are part of a small subgraph between 10 and 100 vertices that are attached to the remainder of the network via one or a small number of edges. In particular, a large fraction of the network comprise vertices that are not in the "core," i.e., they are in components attached to the core of the network via a single edge. In fact, according to [24], their empirical results show that a substantial fraction of vertices are connected to the main network by a single cut edge, and the largest 2-edge-connected component of this network contains only around 60% of the vertices and 80% of the edges of the original network.

This is a motivation to define a "core" and a "whisker" more precisely. The "core" of a network is the largest 2-edge-connected component. "Whiskers" are maximal subgraphs that can be detached from the rest of the network by removing a single edge. To find whiskers, we only need to detect bridges (i.e., an edge e such that $G - e$ is disconnected) and the largest 2-edge-connected component (which is the core), which can be easily achieved in linear time.

1.2 Structural Properties of Real Networks

In [24], it is stated that web graphs and social networks should have both numerous small, well-separated, whisker-like clusters and an expander-like core[1]. Specifically, the following should be considered for the structural property of web graphs and social networks.

1. They should have a relatively large number of comparatively small (except when compared with random graphs), well-connected, and distinct whisker-like communities.
2. They should have a large expander-like core graph, which may be considered as intermingled communities, possibly emerging from whisker-like communities. The boundaries of these communities become less well-defined as they grow larger, and as they gradually blend in with the rest of the network.

1.3 Our Contributions

The above two points are certainly realistic network structures; however, several important questions remain unanswered. Our main motivation is the following.

> In reality, decomposing web graphs and social networks into "whiskers" and "cores" using 2-edge-connected components does not seem to be sufficient to resolve these points.

Let us make our motivations clearer and more specific:

1. The previous "cores" of web graphs and social networks seem to have several cuts of size two. This suggests that the "core" defined by a maximal 2-edge-connected subgraph is not really an expander, because if it were, it would be globally highly connected. To construct expander-like cores, what types of operations are required for web graphs and social networks?
2. In response to the above question, whiskers do not seem to capture enough structural information. What type of structure should we define instead of the previous whiskers?

It turns out that we can answer these questions using our "core-tree-decomposition" method. This decomposition is a type of tree-decomposition, which has been extensively studied in the algorithm research community (for examples, see [3, 4, 13, 17, 18, 28, 29]). However, in this core-tree-decomposition, we shall detect a "core" of a given graph. Specifically, our method allows us to decompose any graph into two parts, "core" and "almost tree," such that

> the "almost tree" part induces a tree-decomposition of small tree-width. Specifically, it behaves like a "tree" (Subsection 2.3).

[1]For the exact definition of expander graphs, see Subsection 2.2. For the time being, we can assume that expander graphs behave like random graphs.

Moreover, such decomposition can be computed very quickly (Section 3).

We constructed core-tree-decompositions for as many as 40 publicly available datasets. Results from these experiments show that our cores provide more structural network information in the following sense:

> By comparing the eigenvalue distribution of the cores obtained by our decomposition method with that of the Erdős-Rényi random graphs, we confirm that our "core" behaves like an expander graph, whereas the "core" defined by 2-edge-connected components [24] does not. Details are given in Subsection 6.2.

The intuition behind this fact will be explained in Subsection 2.4.

In summary, our core-tree-decomposition can resolve the above two issues in such a way that whiskers are "tree-like," which can be explained in the context of tree-width, and the intuition that the cores should be "expander-like" can be explained via their eigenvalue distribution. Moreover, our core-tree-decomposition yields the following features, which are of independent interest:

1. Our analysis based on core-tree-decomposition scales to large networks with billions of edges.
2. We observe that many widely used network datasets have a small core, which implies that they are of small tree-width. For these datasets, we perform experiments to show that tree-width plays a significant role in small index space for certain types of algorithms.
3. Social networks tend to have larger cores. Indeed, for social networks, the size of cores is up to 23% of the vertices; however, for web graphs, it is at most 13% of the vertices. These facts contrast with the core defined by 2-edge-connected components [24] that contains 60% of the vertices.

This paper is organized as follows. In the next section, we introduce tree-decompositions and core-tree-decompositions that are key concepts in our study. Our decomposition algorithm is explained in Section 3, and the datasets for our experiments are explained in Section 4. We classify the networks into two classes: small and large datasets, where the former are mainly discussed in Section 5 to deal with full tree-decompositions, and the latter are only used in Section 6 to analyze the structural properties of cores. First, however, we introduce several additional related works.

Related Work on Tree-Decomposition.

A vast amount of theoretical work has been conducted using tree-decomposition and tree-width, such as [4, 13, 17, 21, 22, 28–30]. In the area of machine learning, tree decomposition is further employed to solve the probabilistic inference problem on a small tree-width graph [23, 32, 35]. Tree-width is used to characterize a polynomially solvable class of the constraint satisfaction problem (CSP); under some conditions, a CSP is solvable in polynomial time if and only if an associated graph is of small tree-width [16], and some algorithms achieve this bound [11, 19].

There are a few recent papers that propose the construction of a core-tree-decomposition in preprocessing to helping computation [25, 3, 33]. We use the algorithm presented in [25] to compute a core-tree-decomposition.

2. KEY CONCEPTS

In this section, we formally define our key concepts: core-tree-decompositions and expander graphs. Before giving their definitions, we introduce basic notations from graph theory and matrix schemes that are required in our paper.

2.1 Basic Notation

Let $G = (V, E)$ be a graph. We use symbols n and m to denote the number of vertices and edges of a chosen graph. For a vertex set $S \subseteq V$, let $e(S)$ be the set of edges between S and $V - S$. We define $d(S) := |e(S)|$. For a vertex $v \in V$, $d(\{v\})$ is simply written as $d(v)$ and is called the *degree* of v. If G is a digraph, then $d^{-}(v)$ is the number of edges whose tail is v.

In this study, we also require a matrix A that arises from a graph, because this matrix and its eigenvalues help us decide whether a given graph is close to an expander (Subsection 2.2). Formally, given a directed graph G, we are interested in the *adjacency* matrix. Set the vertex set $V(G) = \{1, \ldots, n\}$. Then $A(i,j) = 1$ if there is an edge from i to j. If G is undirected, then we assume that G is a bidirectional graph (i.e., each edge corresponds to both directions). The *transition* matrix of G is $P = AD^{-1}$, where D is a diagonal matrix and $D(i,i) = 1/d^{-}(i)$.

Let B be an $n \times n$ matrix. An eigenvalue decomposition of B is a decomposition of the form

$$B = U^{\top} \Lambda U$$

where U is an orthogonal matrix and Λ is a diagonal matrix. Each element of Λ is called *eigenvalue* and the corresponding row of U is called *eigenvector*.

2.2 Expander Graph and Tools from Spectral Graph Theory

Roughly, an *expander graph* is a sparse graph in which every subset of the vertices that is not "too large" has a "large" boundary. (i.e., "globally connected"). One of the key properties given in our paper is that our core is close to an expander graph (Subsection 6.2). In this subsection, we formally define an expander graph. Whether or not a given graph G is close to an "expander" is important in our study. We explain our method of solving this at the end of this subsection.

To formally define an expander graph, we need further definitions. For a vertex set $S \subseteq V$,

$$\mu(S) := \sum_{v \in S} d(v),$$

and the *conductance* is defined as $\phi(S) := d(S)/\mu(S)$. The *conductance* of an undirected graph G is

$$\phi(G) := \min_{S \subseteq V : \mu(S) \leq \mu(V)/2} \phi(S).$$

We say that a graph G is an η*-expander* if $\phi(G) \geq \eta$. Intuitively, if the conductance η is large, then we say that G is "globally" connected. In this case, we say that G is an *expander*. It is well-known that expander graphs behave like random graphs.

The quantity $\phi(G)$ is NP-complete to compute. However, the following result from Jerrum and Sinclair [20] says that we can approximately calculate η by considering the second eigenvalue λ_2 of the transition matrix of a graph.

$$\eta^2/16 \leq 1 - \lambda_2 \leq \eta.$$

Indeed, from spectral graph theory [10], it has been known that expander graphs and eigenvalue distribution are closely related. Therefore, to decide whether or not a given graph G is close to an expander, the easiest way seems to be the following:

> looking at the eigenvalues (and their distribution) of the transition matrix of G.

We perform this in our experiments in Section 6 (Subsections 6.1 and 6.2).

2.3 Tree-Decomposition

The main tool in this study is a core-tree-decomposition. This is based on a tree-decomposition. Let us first define tree-decomposition and tree-width. Let G be an undirected graph, T a tree and let $\mathcal{V} = \{V_t \subseteq V(G) \mid t \in V(T)\}$ be a family of vertex sets $V_t \subseteq V(G)$ indexed by the vertices t of T. Following [4,29], the pair $(T, \mathcal{V})$ (or $(V_t)_{t \in T}$) is called a *tree-decomposition* of G if it satisfies the following three conditions:

- $V(G) = \bigcup_{t \in T} V_t$,
- for every edge $e \in E(G)$ there exists a $t \in T$ such that both ends of e lie in V_t,
- if $t, t', t'' \in V(T)$ and t' lies on the path of T between t and t'', then $V_t \cap V_{t''} \subseteq V_{t'}$.

Each V_t is sometimes called a *bag*. The width of $(T, \mathcal{V})$ (or $(V_t)_{t \in T}$) is the number $\max\{|V_t| - 1 \mid t \in T\}$ and the tree-width of G is the minimum width of any tree-decomposition of G. In this way, tree-width is a measure of how close a given graph is to a tree. Specifically, if the tree-width is small, then it behaves like a tree.

Furthermore, tree-width is a measure of "global" connectivity. To support this claim, let us first observe that in the framework of tree-width, it is well-known that an expander graph cannot be of small tree-width. Therefore,

> expander graphs are a counterpart of graphs of small tree-width.

The converse is not quite true, but it is true that,

> if the tree-width of a given graph is large, it contains a "highly" connected set that behaves like an expander graph (see Section 12.4 of Diestel [12] for more details).

For more details on tree-width, we refer the reader to a survey by Reed [28]. It turns out that this intuition is very important for our core-tree-decomposition, which will be defined in the next subsection.

2.4 Core-Tree-Decomposition

We now introduce the most important concept in this paper. We say that G has a "core-tree-decomposition of width d" if a tree-decomposition $(T, \mathcal{V})$ satisfies the following:

1. r is a root of the tree T, and
2. for all $t \in T - r$, $|V_t| \leq d$.

Thus, only the bag V_r has more than d vertices, and indeed, V_r corresponds to the "core". Sometimes we call $V - V_r$ the *bounded tree-width part* or the *small tree-width part*.

The purpose of our core-tree-decomposition is the following:

Algorithm 1 Core-tree-decomposition algorithm

```
procedure DecomposeGraph(G, d)
    𝒳 ← Empty list of bags
    ▽ Reduce vertices from those with lower degree
    while G is not empty do
        v ← A vertex with minimum degree
        break if d(v) > d
        V_v ← ReduceVertex(G, v)
        Append V_v to list 𝒳
    ▽ Construct the root bag V_r
    V_r ← V(G)
    Append V_r to list 𝒳
    ▽ Compute the tree
    return ConstructTree(𝒳)
```

1. We want to extract as many vertices in the core as possible so that the extracted vertices induce a graph W of small tree-width. If the remaining core is also small (i.e., it has less than d vertices), then the tree-width is at most d.
2. Once we are left with extracting vertices from the core and the remaining core contains more than d vertices, the core no longer induces a graph of tree-width d. This suggests that it contains a highly connected subgraph that behaves like an expander graph. We want this core to be close to an expander.

Therefore, we need to choose d. In Section 3, we propose, given d, an efficient algorithm to obtain our core-tree decomposition of width d. In Subsection 6.3, we discuss how to choose d.

3. DECOMPOSITION ALGORITHM

In this section, we explain the algorithm that we use to construct a core-tree-decomposition. The algorithm is based on the *min-degree heuristic* [5, 34], which was originally designed for computing standard tree-decompositions. We use a modified version that receives a parameter d and produces a core-tree-decomposition of width d. Note that it can also compute a standard tree-decomposition by setting d as a sufficiently large value.

This algorithm is different from Bodlaender's algorithm [6] and its successor [27]. The time complexity of these algorithms is $\Omega(2^d(n+m))$ time, i.e., the exponential of tree-width. Therefore, while the algorithms run in linear time when the tree-width is very small, in practice, tree-width is not that small and thus they are impractical.

3.1 Algorithm Overview

Note that, in this section, we are only interested in undirected graphs, even if the input graphs are directed. To handle a directed graph, we apply the following algorithm to the undirected graph produced by ignoring the direction of each edge.

The total algorithm is presented as Algorithm 1. It first generates a list of bags, and then constructs a tree of these bags. To generate a list of bags, the algorithm repeatedly *reduces* a vertex with minimum degree while minimum degree is at most d.

Reducing a vertex v involves three steps, as described in Algorithm 2. First, we create a new bag V_v that includes v and all its neighbors. Then, we remove vertex v from graph G. Finally, we add edges between the neighbors to make a clique among those vertices in $V_v - v$. When no vertex with degree less than or equal to d remains, we finalize this process by creating a new bag V_r that consists of all the remaining vertices. The last bag V_r corresponds to the "core" and can be arbitrarily large.

Algorithm 2 Reduction of vertex

```
procedure ReduceVertex(G, v)
    V_v ← {v} ∪ N_G(v)
    for all x, y ∈ N_G(v) such that x ≠ y do
        ▽ Make v's neighbors a clique
        Add edge (x, y) to E(G) if it is not in E(G)
    Remove v from G
    return V_v
```

After generating the list of bags, the tree of these bags is constructed. It can be guaranteed that we obtain a valid core-tree-decomposition by setting the parent of bag V_v as bag V_p where $(V_v - v) \subseteq V_p$.

3.2 Efficient Implementation

As reducing a vertex with degree δ adds $\Theta(\delta^2)$ edges, naive implementation of the above heuristic consumes considerable space and time to compute core-tree-decompositions for today's large networks. Therefore, the following speed-up technique is employed to address this issue.

To reduce a vertex v, instead of adding a clique around v, we add a vertex with a special label, named a *hub vertex*. We add edges to make the new hub vertex incident to the neighbors of v. Note that here we add only $O(d(v))$ edges. Then, we handle the resulting graph as if there were cliques around hub vertices, i.e., we consider that there is an edge between two vertices that have a hub vertex as a common neighbor.

4. EXPERIMENTAL SETUP

All experiments are conducted on a Linux server with Intel Xeon E5-2690 2.90GHz CPU with 256GB memory. Our algorithm is implemented in C++ and compiled with g++v4.6 with -O3 option.

We conducted experiments on a number of real-world networks that are publicly available from the following sources:

- Datasets `youtube`, `flickr`, `livejournal`, and `orkut` are from the social computing group at the Max Planck Institute [26][2].
- Datasets `in-2004`, `indochina-2004`, `it-2004`, `twitter-2010`, and `uk-2007-05` are from the Laboratory for Web Algorithmics at the Università degli studi di Milano [9, 8, 7][3].
- The other datasets are from the Stanford Network Analysis Project (SNAP)[4].

We classified the networks into two classes: small and large datasets. Small datasets are mainly discussed in Section 5, and large ones are only used in Section 6.

[2] `http://socialnetworks.mpi-sws.org/datasets.html`
[3] `http://law.di.unimi.it/datasets.php`
[4] `http://snap.stanford.edu/data/`

Table 1: Information of small datasets, results of our full tree-decomposition, and sizes of 2-hop indices constructed by state-of-the-art indexing methods for shortest-path distance queries.

Dataset Information				Tree-decomposition			Distance Indices (MB)	
Name	$\lvert V\rvert$	$\lvert E\rvert$	Type	Time (s)	Width d	$d/\lvert V\rvert$	PLL [1]	ISL [14]
`ca-grqc`	5,242	28,980	social (u)	0.02	253	0.048	1.4	3.9
`ca-hepth`	9,877	51,971	social (u)	0.16	798	0.081	4.4	24.7
`wiki-vote`	7,115	103,689	social (d)	0.59	1,332	0.187	2.4	23.8
`ca-condmat`	23,133	186,936	social (u)	1.5	2,160	0.093	13.4	156.8
`ca-hepph`	12,008	237,010	social (u)	0.52	1,406	0.117	8.8	65.5
`email-enron`	36,692	367,662	social (d)	1.43	2,178	0.059	8.4	136.1
`ca-astroph`	18,772	396,160	social (u)	3.34	3,497	0.186	19.5	233.5
`email-euall`	265,214	420,045	social (d)	1.67	1,033	0.004	84.1	453.0
`soc-epinions1`	75,879	508,837	social (d)	11.43	5,504	0.073	45.5	1,033.3
`soc-slashdot0811`	77,360	905,468	social (d)	28.31	8,555	0.111	77.1	1,772.3
`soc-slashdot0902`	82,168	948,464	social (d)	29.41	9,181	0.112	85.3	2,028.5
`web-notredame`	325,729	1,497,134	web (d)	0.99	2,938	0.009	95.4	2,835.4
`web-stanford`	281,903	2,312,497	web (d)	2.82	1,611	0.006	64.3	2,086.7
`web-google`	875,713	5,105,039	web (d)	80.28	18,229	0.021	712.3	64,540.1
`web-berkstan`	685,230	7,600,595	web (d)	10.81	3,272	0.005	195.5	10,482.0
`p2p-gnutella08`	6,301	20,777	p2p (u)	0.12	1,263	0.200	5.0	26.3
`p2p-gnutella09`	8,114	26,013	p2p (u)	0.19	1,618	0.199	8.0	43.5
`p2p-gnutella06`	8,717	31,525	p2p (u)	0.66	2,199	0.252	10.2	65.2
`p2p-gnutella05`	8,846	31,839	p2p (u)	0.35	2,215	0.250	10.5	65.5
`p2p-gnutella04`	10,876	39,994	p2p (u)	0.61	2,789	0.256	15.8	102.6
`p2p-gnutella25`	22,687	54,705	p2p (u)	0.9	3,618	0.159	45.8	284.1
`p2p-gnutella24`	26,518	65,369	p2p (u)	1.59	4,320	0.163	50.0	389.6
`p2p-gnutella30`	36,682	88,328	p2p (u)	2.04	5,596	0.153	100.9	707.6
`p2p-gnutella31`	62,586	147,892	p2p (u)	5.78	9,385	0.150	233.6	2,050.2
`cit-hepth`	27,770	352,807	citation (d)	11.61	8,515	0.307	158.4	687.0
`cit-hepph`	34,546	421,578	citation (d)	10.21	10,718	0.310	178.4	1,155.1

5. TREE-DECOMPOSITIONS FOR SMALL DATASETS

First, we study tree-decompositions on smaller datasets. In this section we focus on standard tree-decompositions, and then we move to core-tree-decompositions in the next section. As computing tree-decompositions is considerably more expensive than core-tree-decompositions with moderate width parameter d, in this section, we only use small datasets with up to 7.5 million edges, for which we successfully obtained a tree-decomposition in 100 seconds. In Table 1, the information of small datasets and results of our tree-decomposition are given.

Note that our tree-decompositions are not necessarily optimal, and hence the width given in Table 1 is just an upper bound of tree-width. However, the aim of this section is to show how informative the width of a tree-decomposition obtained by our algorithm is. For this purpose, we take *shortest-path distance indexing methods* [1,14] as an example and tackle the long-standing question in this field: what is the key factor in addition to network size that has a large effect on the size of constructed shortest-path distance indices? We believe that similar results also hold for other problems where state-of-the-art methods are designed to exploit the structures of real networks.

5.1 Shortest-Path Distance Indices

There has been great interest in the database research community in indexing methods that efficiently find the distance between two arbitrary points on graphs [33,3,1,14,2]. This remains a highly challenging problem with a wide range of applications such as network-aware search and network analysis.

In the following section, we focus on two state-of-the-art indexing methods: *pruned landmark labeling* [1,2] and *IS-label* [14]. Both are based on the *2-hop cover framework*. The general framework of *2-hop cover* is as follows. For simplicity, we assume that the input graph G is undirected.

For each vertex v, we precompute a *label* denoted as $L(v)$, which is a set of pairs (u, δ_{uv}), where u is a vertex and $\delta_{uv} = d_G(u, v)$. We sometimes call the set of labels $\{L(v)\}_{v\in V}$ an *index*. To answer a distance query between vertices s and t, we compute and answer $\textsc{Query}(s, t, L)$ defined as follows,

$$\textsc{Query}(s,t,L) = \min\{\delta_{vs} + \delta_{vt} \mid (v,\delta_{vs}) \in L(s), (v,\delta_{vt}) \in L(t)\}.$$

We call L a *2-hop cover index* of G if $\textsc{Query}(s, t, L)$ is the correct distance for any pair of vertices s and t.

While both pruned landmark labeling and IS-label use further sophisticated frameworks based on 2-hop cover, they can be used to construct standard 2-hop indices. Therefore, for simplicity, in our experiments we constructed standard 2-hop indices by these methods, i.e., pruned landmark labeling was not combined with the bit-parallel labeling technique and IS-label constructed complete vertex hierarchy.

5.2 Non-Trivial Factors for Index Size

Table 1 lists the sizes of 2-hop indices constructed by the two methods, pruned landmark labeling [1] and IS-label [14] for our datasets. The results indicate that, even if two graphs are of similar size, indices constructed from these graphs by the same algorithm may be of quite different sizes.

For example, datasets **`email-enron`**, **`ca-astroph`**, **`cit-hepth`** and **`cit-hepph`** have similar sizes in terms of the number of vertices and edges. However, sizes of indices for these

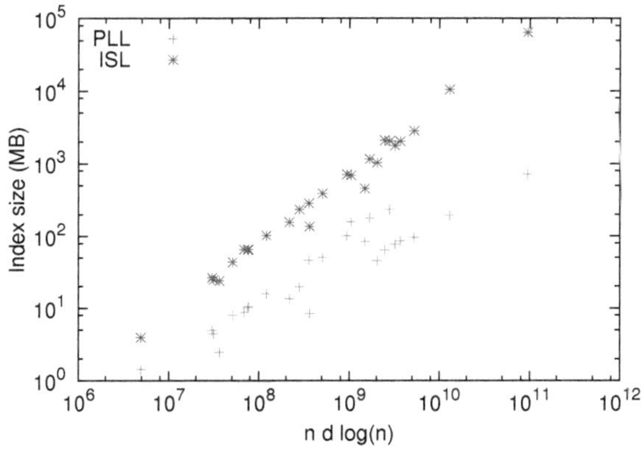

Figure 1: Actual index sizes and estimation using the widths of tree-decompositions.

datasets vary largely and, surprisingly, indices for `cit-hepph` are approximately ten times larger than those for `email-enron` for both indexing algorithms. Similar differences can be observed from datasets `ca-condmat` and `p2p-gnutella30`.

This is because these state-of-the-art indexing methods heuristically exploit the structures of real networks explicitly or implicitly, and thus they depend on the properties of each network. Indeed, it is proved that 2-hop indices may have $\Theta(n^2)$ space for general graphs [15]. Therefore, it is impossible to construct small 2-hop indices without exploiting the network structures.

However, the long-standing question among researchers in this field is that, having understood this, what is the key factor besides network size that has a large effect on the size of constructed shortest-path distance indices? In the following section, we show that obtaining the width of a tree-decomposition can take us closer to the answer.

5.3 Qualitative Empirical Analysis

Widths of tree-decompositions obtained using our algorithm are listed in Table 1. We can observe that the difference in index sizes seems to be highly related to widths. For example, widths of the tree-decompositions for datasets `email-enron` and `cit-hepph` are 10,718 and 2,178, respectively. Similarly, tree-decompositions for `ca-condmat` and `p2p-gnutella30` have widths of 1,406 and 5,596, respectively. Interestingly, from our results, index sizes for graphs with larger widths are almost always larger than those for graphs with smaller widths. Therefore, tree-width could be the key factor that has a large effect on the sizes of constructed shortest-path distance indices.

5.4 Theoretical Bound with Tree-width

To further analyze the relation between widths of tree-decompositions and sizes of distance indices, we first present theoretical analysis result. While there are no non-trivial theoretical bounds on the size of 2-hop indices that are better than $O(n^2)$ for general graphs [15], we can prove that there are small 2-hop indices for graphs of small tree-width.

In what follows, a *centroid* of a tree T denotes a node $v \in V(T)$ such that any connected component after deleting v has maximum size $V(T)/2$. It is easy to prove that any tree has at least one centroid.

Table 2: Spearman's correlation between actual index sizes and estimation with and without width d.

Methods	n	m	$n+m$	d	$nd \log n$
PLL [1,2]	0.819	0.774	0.798	0.795	**0.899**
ISL [14]	0.940	0.792	0.875	0.719	**0.983**

THEOREM 1. *Let G be a graph of tree-width d. There is a distance-aware 2-hop index for G with total size $O(nd \log n)$.*

PROOF SKETCH. We start from an empty index L. Let bag V_t be a centroid of the tree-decomposition. We add the distance $d(u, v)$ to L for all pairs (u, v) where $u \in V$ and $v \in V_t$. We then recurse to each part that can be obtained by deleting V_t. We add $O(nd)$ pairs in each depth of recursion, where the maximum depth is $O(\log n)$. □

5.5 Quantitative Empirical Analysis

Although the aforementioned methods do not necessarily yield 2-hop indices of that size (i.e., $O(nd \log n)$), we show that this theoretical bound works quite well as an estimation. Figure 1 illustrates the relation between the estimated value $nd \log n$ and actual sizes of constructed indices showing that these values correlate well.

Moreover, in Table 2, we see that Spearman's correlation coefficient between estimation $nd \log n$ and actual index sizes is significantly higher than other estimations such as n and m. This indicates that the width d of our tree-decomposition is indeed informative. Note that Spearman's correlation coefficient uses only ranks and thus, for example, the score for estimation of n^2 would be exactly the same as that of n.

6. CORE-TREE-DECOMPOSITIONS FOR LARGE DATASETS

In this section, we look at datasets of large size (between 5M and 3.6B edges). Because of the time and space constraints for our algorithm in Section 3, we cannot fully obtain a tree-decomposition for these datasets; however, we can apply our proposed algorithm to construct a core-tree-decomposition for these datasets up to $d = 1000$. The experimental results are shown in Table 3. It takes at most 45 minutes to construct a core-tree-decomposition of width

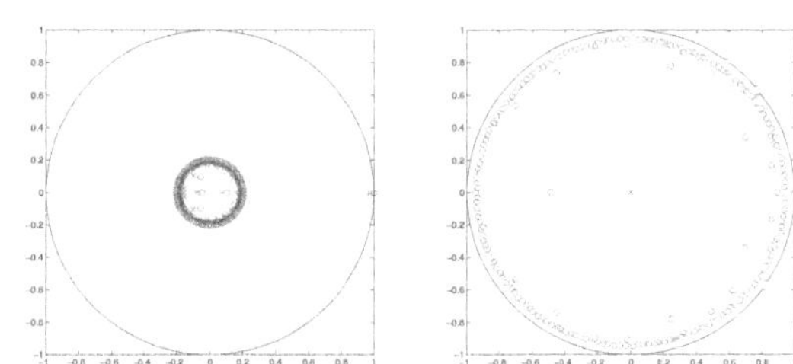

(a) Erdős-Rényi random graph ($n = 10000$, $m = 99759$)

(b) Binary tree with random edges added ($n = 100000$, $m = 115041$)

Figure 2: Extreme eigenvalues of an Erdős-Rényi random graph and a binary tree with random edges added; x axis is for the real part and y axis is for the imaginary part. Red point is for the whole network and blue point is for the core.

Table 3: **Information of large datasets, size of the largest biconnected components (BC), and results of our core-tree-decomposition.**

Dataset Information				BC Size	CT-Decomp. Time (s)			Core Size $\|V_r\|$		
Name	$\|V\|$	$\|E\|$	Type		$d = 10$	$d = 100$	$d = 1000$	$d = 10$	$d = 100$	$d = 1000$
wiki-talk	2,394,385	5,021,410	social (d)	65,778	2.21	2.75	6.45	63,366	19,047	15,966
youtube	3,238,848	18,524,095	social (u)	438,730	3.70	8.72	30.33	352,714	129,389	111,556
flickr	1,861,233	22,613,981	social (d)	504,983	2.17	5.88	27.28	318,788	156,117	131,477
soc-pokec	1,632,804	30,622,564	social (d)	1,339,202	1.10	16.17	107.42	1,023,232	648,417	574,188
livejournal	5,284,458	77,402,652	social (d)	3,046,940	6.19	46.91	220.28	2,266,055	1,221,374	1,054,805
orkut	3,072,627	223,534,301	social (u)	2,937,152	0.84	41.37	329.5	2,744,856	1,986,681	1,797,098
twitter-2010	41,652,230	1,468,365,182	social (d)	38,213,230	37.17	383.01	2514.82	24,992,877	7,767,763	5,571,211
web-notredame	325,729	1,497,134	web (d)	72,904	0.28	0.94	1.11	52,927	8,919	3,237
web-google	916,428	5,105,039	web (d)	564,705	1.27	4.81	7.75	322,633	49,645	23,450
in-2004	1,382,908	16,917,053	web (d)	670,103	0.84	3.93	5.14	547,537	47,036	5,583
indochina-2004	7,414,865	194,109,311	web (d)	4,160,949	2.97	32.45	63.02	4,109,397	470,944	53,069
it-2004	41,291,318	1,150,725,436	web (d)	30,683,202	18.00	246.96	741.07	25,771,538	4,711,353	1,366,281
uk-2007-05	105,896,435	3,738,733,648	web (d)	80,399,275	30.05	678.55	2253.75	73,394,948	13,990,744	3,995,511

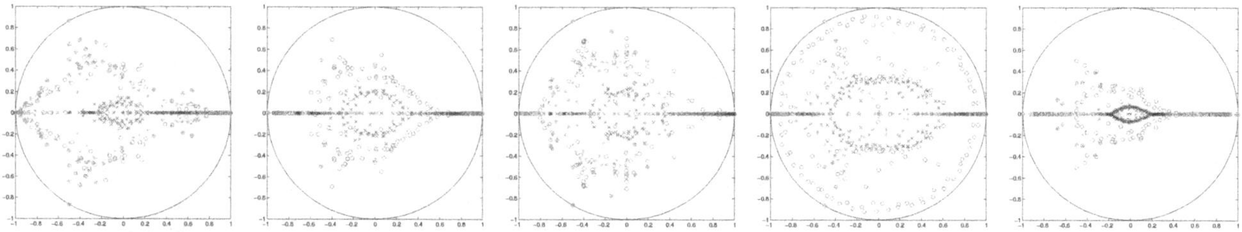

(a) flickr (b) soc-pokec (c) livejournal (d) twitter-2010 (e) wiki-talk

Figure 3: Social Networks; red points are the distribution of eigenvalues of the whole network, green points are those of the largest 2-edge-connected components, and blue points are those of our cores with $d = 100$.

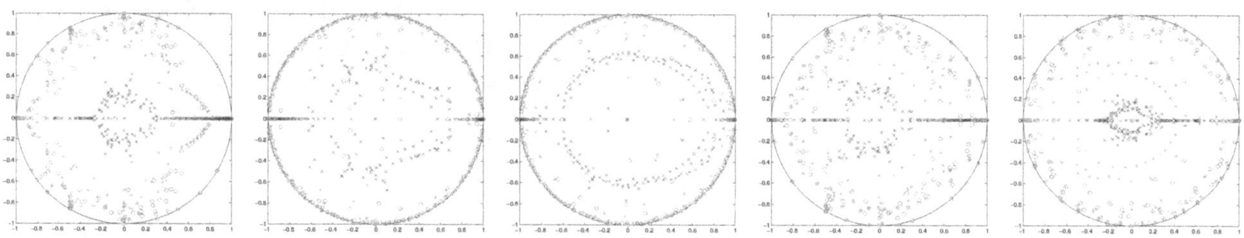

(a) in-2004 (b) it-2004 (c) uk-2007-05 (d) web-google (e) web-notredame

Figure 4: Web Graphs; red, green and blues points are the same as in Figure 3.

$d = 1000$ even for the largest dataset. Furthermore, we can confirm that there is still a large core even for the case $d = 1000$ for these datasets (Table 3). This suggests that our proposed algorithm will decompose graphs into the "core" part and the "small tree-width" part.

The main object of this section is to investigate structural properties of cores. More specifically, we look at the following points.

1. How close is the core to an expander?
2. What happens if we change d?
3. What is the density of the core?

We propose a way to answer the first question in the next subsection.

6.1 Typical Eigenvalues

In general, given a graph G, it is difficult to determine how close it is to an expander. The best way is by looking at the eigenvalues distribution, as discussed in Subsection 2.2.

For a typical expander graph (Erdős-Rényi random graph with $n = 10000$ vertices and $m = 99759$ edges) and a typical non-expander graph (binary tree with random edges added. $n = 100000$ vertices and $m = 115041$ edges), we compute 200 extreme eigenvalues of their cores and their whole networks, respectively, by the Arnoldi method [31].

We actually conduct experiments only for directed graphs because there are many more large directed graphs than large undirected graphs in the datasets, and we want to look

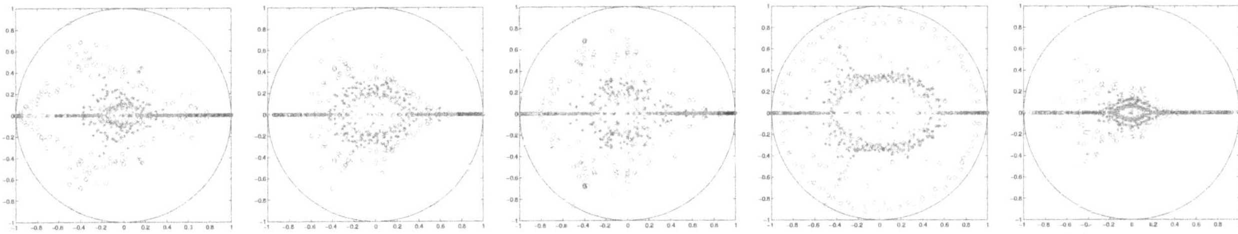

(a) flickr (b) soc-pokec (c) livejournal (d) twitter-2010 (e) wiki-talk

Figure 5: Social Networks; red points are the distribution of eigenvalues of the whole network, purple points are those of the core with $d = 10$, blue points are those of the core with $d = 100$, and green points are that of the core with $d = 1000$.

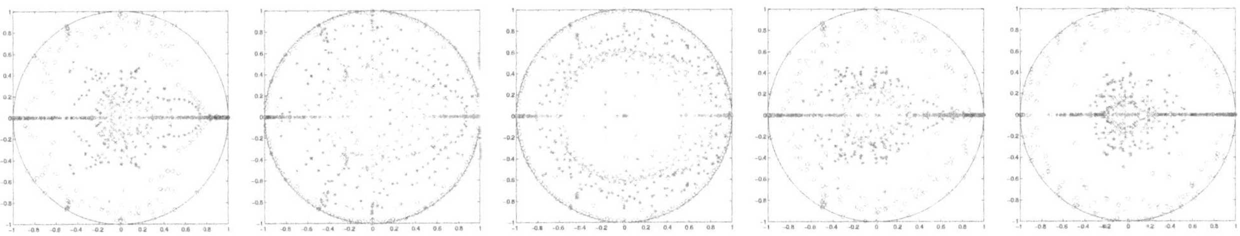

(a) in-2004 (b) it-2004 (c) uk-2007-05 (d) web-google (e) web-notredame

Figure 6: Web Graphs; red, green, purple and blue points are the same as in Figure 5.

at the eigenvalues distribution for as many "large" datasets as possible[5]; thus, it is fair to look only at digraphs.

The results are shown in Figure 2. Figure 2a is for the directed version of an Erdös-Rényi random graph, which is supposed to be a typical expander graph, and Figure 2b is for a directed complete binary tree with few random edges added, which is a typical non-expander graph (i.e., a small tree-width graph). As the transition matrices of directed graphs are not necessarily symmetric, the eigenvalues may not be real. Indeed, they contain both the real and imaginary parts, as shown in Figures 2a and 2b.

From Figures 2a and 2b, we can observe that a given network is close to an expander graph if the eigenvalues are clustered near the origin, and a given network would contain a subgraph that behaves like a tree (i.e., a small tree-width graph), if the eigenvalues were scattered. We now look at real networks.

6.2 How Close the Core is to an Expander

In this subsection, we compare our core with the core defined by Leskovec et al. [24] (i.e., the maximum 2-edge-connected component) and the original networks. More precisely, for ten real (directed) networks that contain five social networks and five web graphs, we compute 200 "extreme" eigenvalues of their cores (from our core-tree-decompositions), their maximum 2-edge-connected components, and the whole networks, by the Arnoldi method [31]. For simplicity, we fix $d = 100$, and, in the next subsection, we examine how the distribution of eigenvalues changes if we change d. The results are shown in Figure 3 for social networks and in Figure 4 for web graphs.

[5]Moreover, the eigenvalue distribution for directed graphs is considerably easier to visualize than that for undirected graphs.

We conclude that the eigenvalues of whole networks (red points) are scattered, like the distribution of a non-expander graph (Figure 2b). The eigenvalues of the maximum 2-edge-connected components (green points) are also scattered, although the green points are slightly closer to the origin than the red points. However, the eigenvalues of the cores (blue points) are clustered relatively near the origin, like the distribution of an expander graph (Figure 2a). Therefore, we can conclude that,

> neither real networks nor the maximum 2-edge-connected components are expander, but our cores of the networks are closer to expander

There is one more observation we can make from Table 3 For social networks, except for orkut and soc-pokec (which seem to have considerably bigger cores than other social networks), the size of cores is a maximum of 23% of the vertices of the original network (when $d = 100$), but for web graphs, it is at most 13% of the vertices. These facts are in contrast with the maximum 2-edge-connected component (i.e., the core defined by Leskovec et al. [24]) which contains 60% of the vertices, as previously mentioned. Therefore, we can conclude that

> social networks tend to have a larger "core" than web graphs. Moreover, our core contains a considerably smaller number of vertices than the core defined by 2-edge-connected components [24].

6.3 Changing Width Parameter d

We now look at cores with respect to the width d of our core-tree-decomposition for social networks and web graphs, respectively.

Let us first look at Figure 5 for social networks and Figure 6 for web graphs, respectively. Our process is as follows.

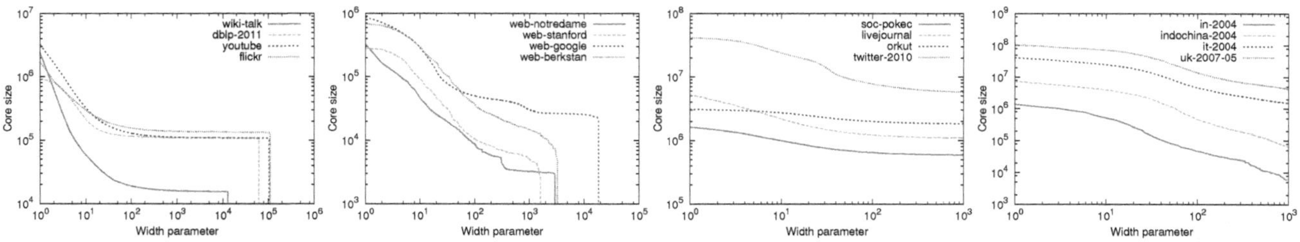

(a) Small social networks (b) Small web graphs (c) Large social networks (d) Large web graphs

Figure 7: Size of the cores of core-tree-decompositions for different width parameter d.

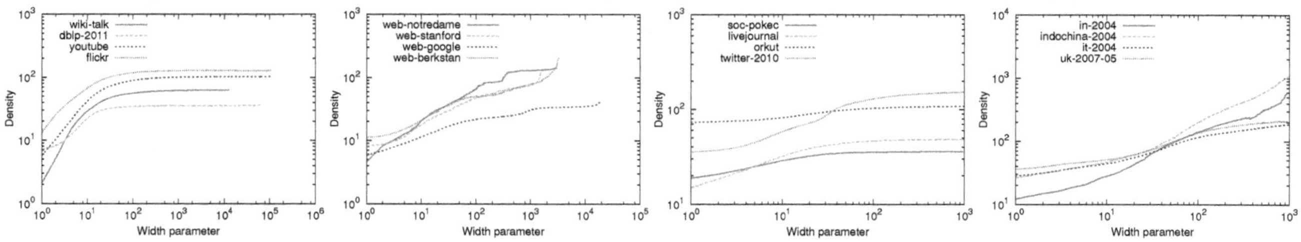

(a) Small social networks (b) Small web graphs (c) Large social networks (d) Large web graphs

Figure 8: Density of the cores of core-tree-decompositions for different width parameter d.

For ten real (directed) networks that contain five social networks and five web graphs, we compute 200 extreme eigenvalues of the whole networks and of their cores for the cases $d = 10, 100, 1000$, respectively, by the Arnoldi method [31]. The results are shown in Figure 5 for social networks and in Figure 6 for web graphs, respectively.

We can conclude that as d increases, the eigenvalues of web graph cores are clustered closer to the origin. This indicates that as d increases, the cores of web graphs gets closer to expander (like the distribution of an expander graph (Figure 2a)). On the other hand, as d increases, the eigenvalues of the social network cores are first clustered close to the origin, but then stay for a while. This indicates that for social networks, we can stop at some value of d, but for web graphs, we can increase d. Indeed, $d = 100$ seems sufficient for social networks.

This can be further explained from Figure 7 which shows the size of cores for social networks and web graphs, with respect to the width d. As the width d increases, the size of web graph cores decreases. On the other hand, the size of social network cores first decreases, but then remains constant a while until the cores of the networks form one bag of core-tree-decompositions. Indeed, for large social networks, if we consider $d \geq 100$, then the core size does not change considerably, but this is not the case for web graphs. Namely, the core size still decreases, even if d increases beyond 100. This indicates that,

> for social networks, $d = 100$ is sufficient in the sense that the core behaves like an expander, because increasing d does not affect the expander property of the core. On the other hand, for web graphs, we need to increase d (i.e., the core for the case where $d = 1000$ gets closer to an expander than that for the case where $d = 100$).

6.4 Density of Cores

Let us look at the density of a core with respect to the width d of our core-tree-decomposition for social networks and web graphs. Surprisingly, there is a large (and interesting) difference between social networks and web graphs. For web graphs, as the width d increases, the density continues to increase. On the other hand, for social networks, as the width d increases, the density first increases, but then remains constant for a while (or increase very gradually), as shown in Figure 8.

7. CONCLUSION

In this paper, using the notion of *core-tree-decomposition*, we obtained many structural properties for social networks and web graphs. Specifically, we performed experiments to construct a core-tree-decomposition for as many as 40 publicly available datasets, and we conclude that whiskers are "tree-like," which can be explained in the framework of tree-with; moreover, the intuition that the cores should be "expander-like" can be explained via their eigenvalue distribution. We have also shown that social networks tend to have larger cores. Indeed, for social networks, the size of cores is a maximum of 23% of the vertices, but for web graphs, it is at most 13% of the vertices. Additionally, we have also demonstrated the theoretical and empirical evidence that tree-width plays a significant role in the efficiency of certain types of algorithms.

8. REFERENCES

[1] T. Akiba, Y. Iwata, and Y. Yoshida. Fast exact shortest-path distance queries on large networks by pruned landmark labeling. In *SIGMOD*, pages 349–360, 2013.

[2] T. Akiba, Y. Iwata, and Y. Yoshida. Dynamic and historical shortest-path distance queries on large

evolving networks by pruned landmark labeling. In *WWW*, pages 237–248, 2014.

[3] T. Akiba, C. Sommer, and K. Kawarabayashi. Shortest-path queries for complex networks: exploiting low tree-width outside the core. In *EDBT*, pages 144–155, 2012.

[4] S. Arnborg and A. Proskurowski. Linear time algorithms for np-hard problems restricted to partial k-trees. *Discrete Appl. Math.*, 2:11–24, 1989.

[5] A. Berry, P. Heggernes, and G. Simonet. The minimum degree heuristic and the minimal triangulation process. In *WG*, volume 2880 of *LNCS*, pages 58–70. 2003.

[6] H. L. Bodlaender. A linear-time algorithm for finding tree-decompositions of small treewidth. *SIAM J. Comput.*, 25(6):1305–1317, 1996.

[7] P. Boldi, B. Codenotti, M. Santini, and S. Vigna. Ubicrawler: A scalable fully distributed web crawler. *Software Pract. Ex.*, 34(8):711–726, 2004.

[8] P. Boldi, M. Rosa, M. Santini, and S. Vigna. Layered label propagation: A multiresolution coordinate-free ordering for compressing social networks. In *WWW*, pages 587–596, 2011.

[9] P. Boldi and S. Vigna. The WebGraph framework I: Compression techniques. In *WWW*, pages 595–601, 2004.

[10] F. Chung. *Spectral Graph Theory.* Cbms Regional Conference Series in Mathematics, 1997.

[11] R. Dechter and J. Pearl. Tree clustering for constraint networks. *Artif. Intell.*, 38(3):353–366, 1989.

[12] R. Diestel. *Graph Theory, 4th Edition*, volume 173 of *Graduate texts in mathematics*. Springer, 2012.

[13] M. Frick and M. Grohe. Deciding first-order properties of locally tree-decomposable structures. *J. ACM*, 48(6):1184–1206, 2001.

[14] A. W.-C. Fu, H. Wu, J. Cheng, and R. C.-W. Wong. Is-label: an independent-set based labeling scheme for point-to-point distance querying. *PVLDB*, 6(6):457–468, 2013.

[15] C. Gavoille, D. Peleg, S. Pérennes, and R. Raz. Distance labeling in graphs. *J. Algorithms*, 53(1):85 – 112, 2004.

[16] M. Grohe. The complexity of homomorphism and constraint satisfaction problems seen from the other side. *J. ACM*, 54(1), 2007.

[17] M. Grohe, K. Kawarabayashi, and B. A. Reed. A simple algorithm for the graph minor decomposition - logic meets structural graph theory. In *SODA*, pages 414–431, 2013.

[18] R. Halin. s-function for graphs. *J. Geometry*, 8:171–186, 1976.

[19] P. Jégou and C. Terrioux. Hybrid backtracking bounded by tree-decomposition of constraint networks. *Artif. Intell.*, 146(1):43–75, 2003.

[20] M. R. Jerrum and A. Sinclair. Approximating the permanent. *SIAM J. Comput.*, 18:1149–1178, 1989.

[21] K. Kawarabayashi and P. Wollan. A shorter proof of the graph minor algorithm: the unique linkage theorem. In *STOC*, pages 687–694, 2010.

[22] K. Kawarabayashi and P. Wollan. A simpler algorithm and shorter proof for the graph minor decomposition. In *STOC*, pages 451–458, 2011.

[23] S. L. Lauritzen and D. J. Spiegelhalter. Local computations with probabilities on graphical structures and their application to expert systems. *J. R. Stat. Soc. Series B, Stat. Methodol.*, pages 157–224, 1988.

[24] J. Leskovec, K. Lang, A. Dasgupta, and M. Mahoney. Community structure in large networks: Natural cluster sizes and the absence of large well-defined clusters. *Internet Math.*, 6(1):29–123, 2009.

[25] T. Maehara, T. Akiba, Y. Iwata, and K. Kawarabayashi. Computing personalized pagerank quickly by exploiting graph structures. *PVLDB*, 7, 2014. to appear.

[26] A. Mislove, M. Marcon, K. P. Gummadi, P. Druschel, and B. Bhattacharjee. Measurement and analysis of online social networks. In *IMC*, pages 29–42, 2007.

[27] L. Perković and B. Reed. An improved algorithm for finding tree decompositions of small width. *Int. J. Found. Comput. Sci.*, 11(03):365–371, 2000.

[28] B. Reed. Tree width and tangles: a new connectivity measure and some applications. *Surveys in Combinatorics*, 241:87–162, 1997.

[29] N. Robertson and P. D. Seymour. Graph minors. iii. planar tree-width. *J. Comb. Theory, Ser. B*, 36:49–63, 1984.

[30] N. Robertson and P. D. Seymour. Graph minors .xiii. the disjoint paths problem. *J. Comb. Theory, Ser. B*, 63(1):65–110, 1995.

[31] Y. Saad. *Numerical methods for large eigenvalue problems*, volume 158. SIAM, 1992.

[32] D. Sheldon, T. Sun, A. Kumar, and T. G. Dietterich. Approximate inference in collective graphical models. In *ICML*, pages 1004–1012, 2013.

[33] F. Wei. Tedi: efficient shortest path query answering on graphs. In *SIGMOD*, pages 99–110, 2010

[34] J. Xu, F. Jiao, and B. Berger. A tree-decomposition approach to protein structure prediction. In *CSB*, pages 247–256, 2005.

[35] Y. Zheng, P. Chen, and J.-Z. Cao. Map-mrf inference based on extended junction tree representation. In *CVPR*, pages 1696–1703, 2012.

Analyzing Expert Behaviors in Collaborative Networks

Huan Sun[1] Mudhakar Srivatsa[2] Shulong Tan[1] Yang Li[1] Lance M. Kaplan[3] Shu Tao[2] Xifeng Yan[1]
{huansun, shulongtan, yangli, xyan}@cs.ucsb.edu
{msrivats, shutao}@us.ibm.com
lance.m.kaplan.civ@mail.mil
[1]University of California, Santa Barbara, [2]IBM T.J. Watson Research Center, [3]U.S. Army Research Lab

ABSTRACT

Collaborative networks are composed of experts who cooperate with each other to complete specific tasks, such as resolving problems reported by customers. A task is posted and subsequently routed in the network from an expert to another until being resolved. When an expert cannot solve a task, his routing decision (*i.e.*, where to transfer a task) is critical since it can significantly affect the completion time of a task. In this work, we attempt to deduce the cognitive process of task routing, and model the decision making of experts as a generative process where a routing decision is made based on mixed routing patterns.

In particular, we observe an interesting phenomenon that an expert tends to transfer a task to someone whose knowledge is neither too similar to nor too different from his own. Based on this observation, an *expertise difference* based routing pattern is developed. We formalize multiple routing patterns by taking into account both rational and random analysis of tasks, and present a generative model to combine them. For a held-out set of tasks, our model not only explains their real routing sequences very well, but also accurately predicts their completion time. Under three different quality measures, our method significantly outperforms all the alternatives with more than 75% accuracy gain. In practice, with the help of our model, hypotheses on how to improve a collaborative network can be tested quickly and reliably, thereby significantly easing performance improvement of collaborative networks.

Source Code
`http://www.cs.ucsb.edu/~huansun/behavemodel.htm`

Categories and Subject Descriptors

H.1.2 [**Information Systems**]: Models and Principles—*Human information processing;Human factors*

Keywords

Collaborative Network; Generative Model; Task Routing; User Modeling

KDD'14, August 24–27, 2014, New York, NY, USA.

ACM 978-1-4503-2956-9/14/08 ...$15.00.
http://dx.doi.org/10.1145/2623330.2623722.

1. INTRODUCTION

Collaborative networks are abundant in real life, where experts collaborate with each other to complete specific tasks. In service businesses, a service provider often maintains an expert network where service agents collaboratively solve problems reported by customers. Bugzilla[1] is a bug tracking system where software developers jointly fix the reported bugs in projects. In a classic collaborative network, upon receiving a task, an expert first tries to solve it; if he fails, the expert will route the task to another expert. The task is completed until it reaches an expert who can provide a solution.

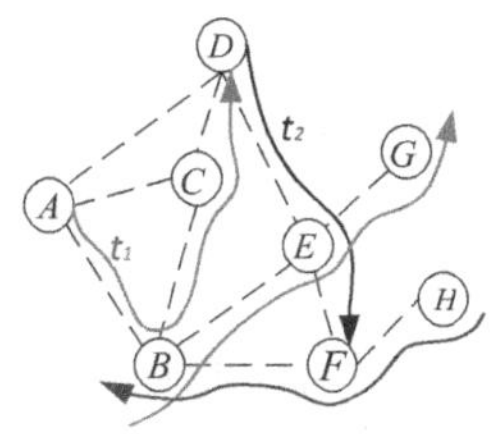

Figure 1: A Sample Collaborative Network

Figure 1 shows a sample collaborative network with task routing examples. Task t_1 starts at expert A and is resolved by expert D, and task t_2 starts at expert D and is resolved by expert F. The sequences $A \to B \to C \to D$ and $D \to E \to F$ are called *routing sequences* of task t_1 and t_2 respectively. The number of experts on a routing sequence measures the completion time of a task. The average completion time of tasks signifies the efficiency of a collaborative network in problem solving: the shorter, the more efficient.

When the number of experts in a collaborative network becomes large, to whom an expert routes a task significantly affects the completion time of the task. For example, in Figure 1, task t_1 can be directly routed to the resolver D from A. In this case the routing decision made by expert A is critical. Therefore, understanding how an expert makes a certain routing decision and detecting his routing behavioral patterns will help us identify the inefficiency of a collaborative network.

The task resolution problem in collaborative networks has been studied before. Shao *et al.*[18] propose a sequence mining algorithm to improve the efficiency of task resolution in IT service. Miao *et al.*[12] develop generative models and recommend better routing by considering both task routing sequences and task contents. In [22], Zhang *et al.* study the resolution of prediction tasks, which are to obtain probability assessments for a question of interest. All of these studies aim at developing automated algorithms that can effectively speed up a task's resolution process. However, they largely ignore human factors in real task routing. Take Figure 1 as an example. Why does expert A route task t_1 to B instead of D? Is it because he does not understand t_1 well, thus randomly distributing it to B, or he believes B has a better chance to solve it, or B has a better chance to find the right expert to solve it? Does expert A make more rational decisions than random decisions? While it is very hard to infer A's decision logic based on an individual task, it is possible to infer it by analyzing many tasks transferred and solved by A, B and D. In this work, we focus on analyzing real expert networks and try to understand experts' decision logic, *i.e.*, what kind of routing patterns an expert follows when deciding where to route a task. This understanding will help detect the inefficient spots in a collaborative network and give guidance to the management team to provide targeted expert training.

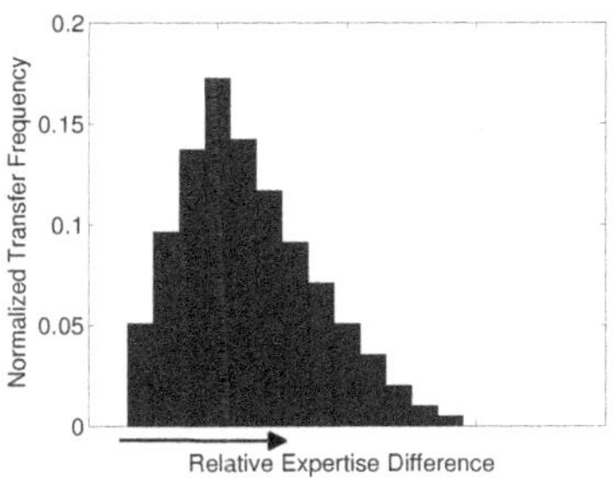

Figure 2: Task Transfer Frequency vs. Expertise Difference.

After analyzing thousands of tasks in an IBM service department, we recognize that in many cases, an expert might not route a task to the *best* candidates (in terms of the possibility to solve the task), especially when the task is far beyond his expertise. Instead, the task is transferred to an expert whose speciality is between the current expert and the best candidates. This routing pattern is clearly indicated by Figure 2. Figure 2 plots the histogram of expertise difference $\frac{\|E_A - E_B\|}{\|E_A\|}$, which is calculated when expert A transfers a task to B. E_A represents the expertise of A and is automatically learnt based on A's task resolution records. It is observed that an expert tends to transfer a task to some expert whose expertise is *neither* too similar to *nor* too different from his own. This phenomenon can be explained as follows: An expert is less likely to transfer a task to another expert whose expertise is very similar, given that the current expert already fails to resolve the task. On the other hand, if the expertise of two experts are very different, they might actually specialize in quite different domains; therefore, an expert might not be clear about the other's speciality and few tasks would be transferred between them. We conjecture that it is like the situation when a computer science professor gets a quantum physics problem, he might consult a CS professor who is working on quantum computing, rather than directly ask a physics professor who is specialized in quantum physics, though the latter might be a better candidate.

Inspired by the above observation, we introduce a routing pattern describing the general trend of expert A transferring a task to B, based on the *expertise difference* between A and B. Apart from this routing pattern, another two are also formalized. Specifically, when an expert finds there are five candidates to dispatch a task to – all of them can solve the task, who is he going to contact? A straightforward approach is to randomly pick one. An alternative is to look at the capacity of these candidates and route more tasks to an expert who can process more tasks. An expert could follow a certain pattern when deciding where to transfer a task. Different experts might adopt each routing pattern to a different degree and demonstrate different routing behavioral characteristics. This study is going to infer the routing patterns as well as experts' preferences over them, from the historical routing data, and finally give insightful analysis of experts' performance in a collaborative network.

The technical contributions of this work are three-fold: First, to the best of our knowledge, we make the first attempt to analyze the routing behaviors of experts in a collaborative network in a large-scale, quantitative manner. We present a general framework to model the decision making and cognitive process of experts, and instantiate the framework with multiple routing patterns potentially followed by an expert. A generative model is then presented to model experts' routing decisions as a result of mixed routing patterns. After trained on a historical task set, the model can uncover experts' underlying decision logic and explain real routing sequences in a held-out testing set very well.

Second, our analytical model can accurately predict the completion time of a task before actually routing it in the network. On the one hand, we verify that our analysis of experts' routing decision making reflects the real one, in the sense that a task navigated according to our model shall be completed in a similar time as in the real situation. On the other hand, estimating task completion time is important itself, because an accurate estimate of completion time can provide early signals on the "difficulty" or "abnormality" of a task, and managers can allocate more resources and take early actions to deal with such tasks and shorten customer waiting time.

Third, it is usually expensive, if not impossible, to alter real-world collaborative networks for hypothesis testing, *e.g.*, providing more training to a few critical but inefficient experts or changing network structures for better performance. Since our analytical model has shown similar characteristics to the real human routing in collaborative networks, it can be used to conduct virtual hypothesis testing. Through case studies, we discuss how to utilize our model to optimize collaborative networks.

The rest of the paper is organized as follows. In Section 2, we briefly describe our problem setting. In Section 3, we discuss multiple routing patterns potentially adopted by an expert, followed by Section 4, where a generative model combining these patterns together is presented. Section 5 details the estimation of task completion time, which serves as both an evaluation metric of our model and an important problem our model can deal with. Section 6 presents our detailed experimental results. Related work is reviewed in Section 7. We conclude this work in Section 8.

2. PRELIMINARIES

We first clarify the notations used in this work. $\mathcal{E} = \{e_1, e_2, ..., e_i, ..., e_G\}$ is a set of experts in a collaborative network. $\mathcal{N}_i$ denotes the 1-hop neighborhood of expert e_i in the network, *i.e.*, the expert set e_i has ever routed tasks to. $\mathcal{W} = \{w_1, w_2, ..., w_n, ..., w_N\}$ is a set of words used to describe the tasks. $\mathcal{T} = \{t_1, t_2, .., t_m, ..., t_M\}$ is a set of tasks resolved by the collaborative network, where each t_m is an $N \times 1$ word vector with each dimension recording the word frequency in the task description. Apart from the textual description, each task is also associated with a routing sequence starting from an initial expert to the resolver of the task.

ID	Entry	Time	Expert
599	New ticket: the available space on the /var file system is low	9/14/06 5:57:16	IN039
599	...(operations by IN039)...	...	IN039
599	Ticket 599 transferred to SAV59	...	IN039
599	...(operations by SAV59)...	...	SAV59
599	Ticket 599 transferred to SAV4F	...	SAV59
599	...(operations by SAV4F)...	...	SAV4F
599	Problem resolved: free up disk space in the file system	9/14/06 9:57:31	SAV4F

Table 1: The Lifetime of An Example Task.

Table 1 shows one example problem ticket in an IT service department. The ticket with ID 599 is a problem related to *operating system*, specifically, *the low percentage of the available file system space.* It was assigned to or initiated by expert IN039, then routed through expert SAV59, and finally resolved by expert SAV4F.

In this paper, we study the following problems: *How does an expert in a collaborative network make a routing decision? Is there any pattern an expert generally follows when routing a task?* Different from previous studies [12, 18, 22], we do not propose algorithms to perform more efficient routing. Instead, we hope to understand the routing decisions *actually* made by the experts in a collaborative network.

3. MODELING ROUTING DECISIONS

Our intuition is that an expert makes a routing decision by adopting a certain routing strategy either consciously or unconsciously. For example, an expert might decide where to route a task by evaluating the next expert's possibility to solve the task.

We advocate a general and extensible methodology to analyze the routing decision making process, which consists of two routing strategies: *Task-Neutral Routing* (TNR) and *Task-Specific Routing* (TSR). Under the Task-Neural Routing, an expert does not take into account the specificity of a task when making a routing decision, and treat different tasks equivalently. Under the Task-Specific Routing, however, an expert makes a routing decision by analyzing the specific task being transferred.

We attempt to deduce the cognitive process of an expert during task routing, and model the decision making of an expert as a generative process where a routing decision is generated based on the two routing strategies. Each routing strategy is respectively combined with three basic routing patterns, which overall produces six particular routing patterns. Our generative model, with these six routing patterns as mixture components, is then proposed to describe the process of an expert's decision making.

3.1 Routing Patterns

Given a task, we assume an expert e_i first establishes a pool of candidates, C, to dispatch the task to. The difference between the Task-Neutral Routing (TNR) and the Task-Specific Routing (TSR) lies in the composition of C. In terms of TNR, C contains all of his neighbors $\mathcal{N}_i$. In terms of TSR, C is limited to experts who are able to solve the current task in $\mathcal{N}_i$. TNR accommodates the situations when an expert does not understand a task very well, or an expert has a careless work attitude, and thereby making a routing decision irrespective of the specific task and its possible resolvers; whereas TSR mimics the situation where an expert assesses others' ability to solve a task before dispatching it.

Once C is established, e_i selects one expert from C to route the task to, based on a certain routing pattern. We identified three basic routing patterns:

Uniform Random (UR). This routing pattern implies that an expert makes a decision by randomly selecting one of the candidates in C with an equal probability.

$$P(e_i \xrightarrow{t} e_j \mid \text{UR}) = \mathbb{1}(e_j \in C)\frac{1}{|C|} \tag{1}$$

Where $e_i \xrightarrow{t} e_j$ denotes the event that expert e_i transfers task t to e_j. $\mathbb{1}$ is an indicator function: $\mathbb{1}(e_j \in C)$ picks value 1 if $e_j \in C$ holds otherwise 0.

Volume-biased (Load-based) Random (VR). Under this routing pattern, an expert also randomly dispatches tasks, but with a rate proportional to the volume of tasks previously dispatched. VR mimics the situation where the task processing capacity could vary for different experts. VR can be regarded as an expert's reaction when he finds tasks are processed slowly by some of his collaborators. Let volume v_{ij} denote the number of transferred tasks from e_i to e_j.

$$P(e_i \xrightarrow{t} e_j \mid \text{VR}) = \mathbb{1}(e_j \in C)\frac{v_{ij}}{\sum_{e_k \in C} v_{ik}} \tag{2}$$

Expertise Difference (EX). In addition to the above two routing patterns, this one is derived from the observation shown in Figure 2: An expert is more likely to send a task to another expert whose expertise is neither too close nor too far from his own. Let f_{ij} denote the general trend of expert e_i sending a task to e_j, given their expertise.

$$P(e_i \xrightarrow{t} e_j \mid \text{EX}) = \mathbb{1}(e_j \in C)\frac{f_{ij}}{\sum_{e_k \in C} f_{ik}} \tag{3}$$

To estimate f_{ij}, we build a model based on the observation in Figure 2. The relative expertise difference between expert e_i and e_j, is calculated as $\Delta(e_i, e_j) = \frac{\|e_i - e_j\|}{\|e_i\|}$, where for simplicity e_i is reused to represent the expertise vector of expert e_i. The expertise estimation problem will be discussed in Section 3.3. Based on Figure 2, we assume for those tasks transferred, the relative expertise difference between a task sender and a task receiver follows a log-normal distribution with parameters μ and σ^2. We made this assumption due to the non-negative nature of $\Delta(e_i, e_j)$ and the asymmetric shape of the distribution. However, in our experiments, we also test a model with a normal distribution to estimate f_{ij} and show that the log-normal distribution works better. Under the log-normal distribution, expert e_i is more likely to transfer tasks to e_j once $\Delta(e_i, e_j)$ obtains a higher probability density; therefore, f_{ij} is estimated by:

$$f_{ij} \propto \frac{1}{\Delta(e_i, e_j)} e^{-\frac{[\ln \Delta(e_i, e_j) - \mu]^2}{2\sigma^2}} \tag{4}$$

Note that the histogram in Figure 2 is the accumulation of all possible routing patterns, not only the *expertise difference* pattern. Later, in the experiments, we will show that the EX pattern with μ and σ^2 directly estimated from Figure 2 does not perform the best. Instead, parameters μ and σ^2 shall be estimated with more emphasis on tasks transferred following the EX pattern, which are not known a priori. We will learn them simultaneously through a mixture model with all the routing patterns considered.

To summarize, the three basic patterns {UR, VR, EX} combined with the Task-Neutral Routing and Task-Specific Routing strategy, generate six particular routing patterns: TNR^{ur}, TNR^{vr}, TNR^{ex}, TSR^{ur}, TSR^{vr}, and TSR^{ex}.

3.2 Task-Specific Routing

TNR does not take into account the distinctiveness of a specific task. In contrast, TSR means that an expert makes a routing decision based on the specific task and matches it with potential resolvers. Given expert e_i to transfer task t, his routing decision under TSR is influenced by two factors: (1) whether an expert can solve the task or not, and (2) how familiar e_i is with that expert. The first factor, only related to the task itself, can be conducted by a classification process without involving e_i. The classification identifies a subset of e_i's neighbors who can solve the task, as the candidate pool C. We build the classifier based on the task resolution records of experts in Section 3.3. The second factor is a human factor which can be modeled by the same routing patterns we previously introduced such as UR, VR, and EX. Overall, TSR will check the neighborhood of e_i, run the classifier, and establish a set of candidates C who are capable of solving t. It then selects one particular candidate from C based on one of {UR, VR, EX}. In a special case where $C = \emptyset$, TSR is reduced to TNR where we simply use the entire neighborhood $\mathcal{N}_i$ as the candidate pool.

The success of our work is related to the recognition of human factors in task routing. A straightforward routing pattern considering the specificity of a task is to transfer the task to an expert with the highest probability to solve it. Our experiments show that such a routing pattern cannot capture the real characteristics of human decision making, such as randomness, uncertainty, and sub-optimality. We observe that similar tasks are often routed to very different experts. Moreover, one usually does not search for people who are most likely to solve a problem due to, *e.g.*, unfamiliarity with those people. Instead, he might select a close collaborator who should be able to solve the problem, but not necessarily with the highest probability.

3.3 Expertise Estimation

In TSR strategy and the EX routing pattern, we need to estimate an expert's expertise and capability to solve a task. Intuitively, the capability depends on both the expert's expertise and the task description. We resort to a classic logistic regression model [6] that takes an expert's expertise vector and a task's word vector as input, and outputs the expert's capability to solve the task. In the logistic model, the probability for expert e_i to solve task t, denoted as $P(e_i, t)$, is defined as follows:

$$P(e_i, t) = \frac{1}{1 + \exp(-(W_1 t + W_2 e_i + b))} \tag{5}$$

For simplicity, the expertise vector for expert e_i is of the same length as task t, *i.e.*, an $N \times 1$ vector. W_1 and W_2 are the $1 \times N$ weights respectively associated with the word vector of a task and the expertise vector of an expert. Each component of W_1 and W_2 denotes the contribution of the corresponding dimension in t or e_i to the capability prediction. b is a bias scalar in the logistic model. The expertise vectors e_i's are not known a priori and they are to be estimated together with the model parameters $\{W_1, W_2, b\}$. We use $W = \{W_1, W_2, b, e_i's\}$ to denote all the parameters.

Given a task t and its routing sequence, *e.g.*, $e_i \rightarrow ... \rightarrow e_k$, we observe the groundtruth regarding the resolution capability: The last expert e_k solves t and any other expert on the sequence does not solve it. Therefore, we can formulate a training dataset composed of <expert, task> pairs as instances and $\{0, 1\}$ as the observed probability of an expert to solve a task, *e.g.*, 0 for $<e_i, t>$ while 1 for $<e_k, t>$.

The optimal solution of parameters in the model is obtained by minimizing the cross-entropy error function [6], based on the <expert, task> pairs in the training dataset :

$$\arg\min_{W} \sum_{<e_i,t>} [-P^*(e_i, t) \log P(e_i, t) - (1 - P^*(e_i, t)) \log(1 - P(e_i, t))] \tag{6}$$

where $P^*(e_i, t)$ is the observed probability for expert e_i to solve task t. After the parameters are learnt, given a task and an expert, one can predict the probability for the expert to solve the task using Eqn. 5. Under Task-Specific Routing, when transferring task t, expert e_i identifies a subset of his neighbors $\mathcal{N}_i$ as the candidate pool $C = \{e_j \in \mathcal{N}_i : P(e_j, t) \geq \delta\}$, where δ is set at 0.5 in our implementation. Experts in C have a probability to solve t larger than a threshold, and are estimated capable to solve the task.

Essentially, the expert capability estimation is casted as a traditional classification problem. The logistic model we employed is very similar to classification using SVM [9] with a linear kernel [6]. The difference lies in that the expertise vector of an expert is not known a priori. One might consider using the average word vector of the tasks resolved by an expert to represent the expert's knowledge. However, in practice, this method can be problematic, because we observe that there might be many experts in a network that serve as "intermediate transferrers" and did not resolve any tasks. In our case, we can also utilize those tasks unresolved by an expert to estimate his expertise in Eqn 6. Besides, by optimizing the cost function over the expertise vectors, we can give lower cost function than fixing them at somewhere non-optimal.

4. GENERATIVE MODEL

In this section, we present a generative model to put the previously discussed routing patterns together and describe an integrated decision making process.

Figure 3 shows the graphical representation of our generative model. We first clarify the notations in the figure as follows: (1) $|\mathcal{E}|$ denotes the number of experts while $|\mathcal{T}_i|$ is the number of tasks expert $e_i \in \mathcal{E}$ has ever transferred. A plate means replicating a process for multiple times. (2) θ_i is the $K \times 1$ mixture weights of different routing patterns for expert e_i, where K is the number of routing patterns. In our current setting, we have $K = 6$ routing patterns, from TNR^{ur} to TSR^{ex}. The k-th component of θ_i reveals the probability that the k-th routing pattern is adopted by e_i to transfer a task. (3) α, a $K \times 1$ vector, is parameters in a Dirichlet prior, and serves as a constraint of all the mixture

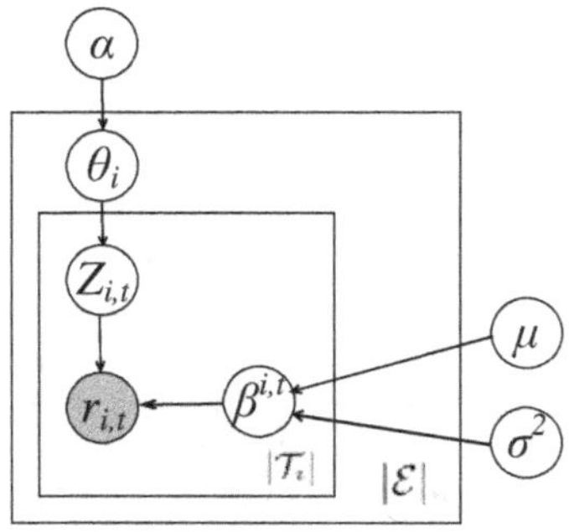

Figure 3: Graphical Representation of Our Model.

weights θ_i's. A Dirichlet prior for the mixture weights tends to alleviate over-fitting problems [7]. Besides, with the Dirichlet prior, the mixture weight θ_{new} for a new expert can be naturally assigned. (4) $Z_{i,t}$ is the label of the routing pattern employed by expert e_i when transferring task t. (5) $\beta^{i,t}$, a $K \times |\mathcal{N}_i|$ matrix, defines the probability distribution of expert e_i transferring task t to an expert in his neighborhood $\mathcal{N}_i$, under K routing patterns. Particularly, each row of $\beta^{i,t}$ is filled by a probability distribution under one of the six routing patterns, as defined in Section 3.1. For experts in $\mathcal{N}_i$ but not in the candidate pool C, the corresponding elements in $\beta^{i,t}$ are naturally filled with 0. For patterns irrelevant to EX, we pre-compute their probability distributions and fill corresponding rows of $\beta^{i,t}$, while TNR^{ex} and TSR^{ex} are parameterized with μ and σ^2. Note that $\beta^{i,t}$ is in the inner plate of the graphical model because $\beta^{i,t}$ is associated with expert e_i and task t. (6)The shaded variable $r_{i,t}$ indicates the observed receiver of task t transferred from expert e_i.

Figure 3 conveys that expert e_i decides where to route task t based on multiple routing patterns $\beta^{i,t}$ and his preference θ_i towards adopting different routing patterns. Now we formally describe the generative process as follows:

For each expert e_i to transfer tasks,

- Draw the mixture weights of K routing patterns: $\theta_i \sim \mathbf{Dir}(\alpha)$.
- For each task t to be transferred by expert e_i,
  * Draw a pattern label: $Z_{i,t} \sim \mathbf{Mult}(\theta_i)$.
  * Draw an expert from $\mathcal{N}_i$ to receive t: $r_{i,t} \sim P(e_i \xrightarrow{t} e_j | Z_{i,t}, \beta^{i,t}), \forall e_j \in \mathcal{N}_i$.

For each task $t \in \mathcal{T}_i$, the transfer relationship for t is represented by $e_i \xrightarrow{t} r_{i,t}$. We formulate the likelihood of observing all the task transfer relationships as follows:

$$\mathcal{L} = P(e_i \xrightarrow{t} r_{i,t}, \forall t \in \mathcal{T}_i, \forall e_i \in \mathcal{E} | \alpha, \mu, \sigma^2) \tag{7}$$

Since a routing decision of an expert is independent from that of another expert while the routing decisions of the same expert for different tasks are not independent from each other, we can rewrite $\mathcal{L}$ in the following way:

$$\begin{aligned} \mathcal{L} &= \prod_{e_i \in \mathcal{E}} P(e_i \xrightarrow{t} r_{i,t}, \forall t \in \mathcal{T}_i | \alpha, \mu, \sigma^2) \\ &= \prod_{e_i \in \mathcal{E}} \int_{\theta_i} P(\theta_i|\alpha) P(e_i \xrightarrow{t} r_{i,t}\ ,\ \forall t \in \mathcal{T}_i | \theta_i, \mu, \sigma^2)\, d\theta_i \end{aligned} \tag{8}$$

Here,

$$\begin{aligned} & P(e_i \xrightarrow{t} r_{i,t}\ ,\ \forall t \in \mathcal{T}_i \mid \theta_i, \mu, \sigma^2) \\ &= \prod_{t \in \mathcal{T}_i} \{ \sum_{Z_{i,t}} P(Z_{i,t}|\theta_i) P(e_i \xrightarrow{t} r_{i,t} \mid Z_{i,t}, \beta^{i,t}) \} \end{aligned} \tag{9}$$

where $P(Z_{i,t}|\theta_i) = \theta_{i,k}$ and $P(e_i \xrightarrow{t} r_{i,t} \mid Z_{i,t}, \beta^{i,t}) = \beta^{i,t}_{k,r}$, if $Z_{i,t} = k$, *i.e.*, the k-th routing pattern is adopted. $\beta^{i,t}_{k,r}$ is the probability for e_i routing task t to expert $r_{i,t}$, under the k-th pattern. $\beta^{i,t}_{k,r}$ shall contain parameters μ and σ^2 if the k-th pattern is TNR^{ex} or TSR^{ex}.

Finally, we resort to the maximum likelihood estimation approach to optimize the parameters in the model:

$$\arg \max_{\alpha, \mu, \sigma^2} \log \mathcal{L} \tag{10}$$

4.1 Inference

Now we discuss how to estimate the model parameters in detail. The latent variables $\{\theta_i$'s, $Z_{i,t}$'s$\}$ are not independent of each other, which makes their true posterior distributions computationally intractable. In this section, we employ a variational approach [6] to solve our model.

4.1.1 Variational Inference

We introduce a variational distribution Q in which the latent variables are independent of each other to approximate their true posterior distribution, *i.e.*, $Q(\theta, Z) = Q(\theta)Q(Z)$, where $\theta = \{\theta_i, \forall e_i \in \mathcal{E}\}$ and $Z = \{Z_{i,t}, \forall e_i \in \mathcal{E}, t \in \mathcal{T}_i\}$. According to the variational distribution, $Q(\theta_i) \sim \mathbf{Dir}(\gamma_i)$, $Q(Z_{i,t}) \sim \mathbf{Mult}(\phi^{i,t})$, , where γ_i and $\phi^{i,t}$ are $K \times 1$ variational parameters. γ_i and $\phi^{i,t}$ have significant meanings where γ_i represents the variational prior for θ_i and reflects which routing pattern e_i tends to adopt, while $\phi^{i,t}$ is the variational posterior mixture weights of different routing patterns adopted by e_i when transferring task t. Given the observed data, both γ_i and $\phi^{i,t}$ will be derived automatically.

Under the variational distribution and Jensen's inequality, we can maximize the lower bound of the log likelihood, instead of directly maximizing $\log \mathcal{L}$ which is intractable.

$$\log \mathcal{L} \geq E_Q \log P(\mathcal{D}, \theta, Z | \alpha, \mu, \sigma^2) + H(Q) = \lfloor \log \mathcal{L} \rfloor \tag{11}$$

where $\mathcal{D}$ denotes all the observed task transfer relationships. We expand the lower bound of the log likelihood as follows:

$$\begin{aligned} \lfloor \log \mathcal{L} \rfloor = & \sum_{e_i \in \mathcal{E}} E_Q \log P(\theta_i|\alpha) + \sum_{e_i \in \mathcal{E}} \sum_{t \in \mathcal{T}_i} E_Q \log P(Z_{i,t}|\theta_i) \\ & + \sum_{e_i \in \mathcal{E}} \sum_{t \in \mathcal{T}_i} E_Q \log P(e_i \xrightarrow{t} r_{i,t} | Z_{i,t}, \mu, \sigma^2) \\ & + H(Q(\theta, Z)) \end{aligned} \tag{12}$$

Each term on the right-hand side of the above equation, is a function over the model parameters as shown in Eqn. 13 to Eqn. 16.

$$E_Q \log P(\theta_i|\alpha) = -\log B(\alpha) + \sum_k (\alpha_k - 1)[\psi(\gamma_{i,k}) - \psi(\sum_k \gamma_{i,k})] \tag{13}$$

where $B(\alpha) = \frac{\prod_k \Gamma(\alpha_k)}{\Gamma(\sum_k \alpha_k)}$ is the normalization constant of the Dirichlet distribution $\mathbf{Dir}(\alpha)$.

$$\sum_{t \in \mathcal{T}_i} E_Q \log P(Z_{i,t}|\theta_i) = \sum_{t \in \mathcal{T}_i} \sum_k \phi^{i,t}_k [\psi(\gamma_{i,k}) - \psi(\sum_k \gamma_{i,k})] \tag{14}$$

The third term

$$\sum_{t\in\mathcal{T}_i} E_Q \log P(e_i \xrightarrow{t} r_{i,t}|Z_{i,t},\mu,\sigma^2) = \sum_{t\in\mathcal{T}_i}\sum_k \phi_k^{i,t}\log\beta_{k,r}^{i,t} \quad (15)$$

As discussed in Eqn. 9, $\beta_{k,r}^{i,t}$ contains parameters μ and σ^2 if the k-th pattern is TNR^{ex} or TSR^{ex}.
The entropy term

$$\begin{aligned} &H(Q(\theta,Z)) \\ &= -\sum_{e_i\in\mathcal{E}}[E_Q \log Q(\theta_i|\gamma_i) + \sum_{t\in\mathcal{T}_i} E_Q \log Q(Z^{i,t}|\phi^{i,t})] \\ &= \sum_{e_i\in\mathcal{E}}[\log B(\gamma_i) - \sum_k(\gamma_{i,k}-1)(\psi(\gamma_{i,k}) - \psi(\sum_k \gamma_{i,k}))] \quad (16) \\ &- \sum_{e_i\in\mathcal{E}}\sum_{t\in\mathcal{T}_i}\sum_k \phi_k^{i,t}\log\phi_k^{i,t} \end{aligned}$$

4.1.2 Parameter Estimation

The model parameters are estimated by using the variational expectation-maximization (EM) algorithm. In the E-step, we update the variational parameters $\{\gamma\text{'s}, \phi\text{'s}\}$ while in the M-step, we update the model parameters α, μ, and σ^2 so that $\lfloor \log \mathcal{L} \rfloor$ is maximized.

Specifically, the E-step updates the variational parameters according to Eqn. 17 and 18.

$$\phi_k^{i,t} \sim \beta_{k,r}^{i,t}\exp(\psi(\gamma_{i,k}) - \psi(\sum_k \gamma_{i,k}) - 1) \quad (17)$$

$$\gamma_{i,k} = \alpha_k + \sum_{t\in\mathcal{T}_i}\phi_k^{i,t} \quad (18)$$

During the M-step, we maximize the lower bound over the parameter α, μ, and σ^2, by utilizing the classic L-BFGS optimization algorithm [11]. The derivatives over the parameter α are calculated in Eqn. 19.

$$\frac{\partial\lfloor\log\mathcal{L}\rfloor}{\partial\alpha_k} = \sum_{e_i\in\mathcal{E}}[-\psi(\alpha_k) + \psi(\sum_k\alpha_k) + \psi(\gamma_{i,k}) - \psi(\sum_k\gamma_{i,k})] \quad (19)$$

Derivatives over μ and σ^2 depend on the routing pattern TNR^{ex} and TSR^{ex}, as well as the mixture weights corresponding to the two patterns.

$$\frac{\partial\lfloor\log\mathcal{L}\rfloor}{\partial\mu} = \sum_{e_i\in\mathcal{E}}\sum_{t\in\mathcal{T}_i}\sum_{k=1}^{2}(r_{i,t}\in C_k)\times\frac{\phi_k^{i,t}}{\beta_{k,r}^{i,t}}\times\frac{f_{ir}\sum_{e_j\in C_k}X_{ij}}{\sigma^2(\sum_{e_j\in C_k}f_{ij})^2} \quad (20)$$

$$\frac{\partial\lfloor\log\mathcal{L}\rfloor}{\partial\sigma^2} = \sum_{e_i\in\mathcal{E}}\sum_{t\in\mathcal{T}_i}\sum_{k=1}^{2}(r_{i,t}\in C_k)\times\frac{\phi_k^{i,t}}{\beta_{k,r}^{i,t}}\times\frac{f_{ir}\sum_{e_j\in C_k}Y_{ij}}{2(\sigma^2\sum_{e_j\in C_k}f_{ij})^2} \quad (21)$$

where we assume TNR^{ex} and TSR^{ex} are the 1st and 2nd mixture component respectively. C_k is the candidate pool established under TNR or TSR by e_i when routing task t. f_{ir} is the general trend of e_i sending a task to $r_{i,t}$, based on $\Delta(e_i, r_{i,t})$. $X_{ij} \doteq f_{ij}(\ln\Delta(e_i,r_{i,t}) - \ln\Delta(e_i,e_j))$ and $Y_{ij} \doteq f_{ij}[(\ln\Delta(e_i,r_{i,t})-\mu)^2 - (\ln\Delta(e_i,e_j)-\mu)^2]$.

The E-step and M-step are performed iteratively until the algorithm converges, which indicates that the current model parameters fit the observed training data.

5. TASK COMPLETION TIME

In a real collaborative network, a task is routed and completed as long as it reaches an expert who can solve it. The completion time (CT) of a task is defined as the number of experts in its routing sequence. Estimation of the completion time *before actually routing a task* is critically useful, as it can raise attention for those troublesome tasks and ask the network allocate more resources to handle such tasks. The estimated completion time can also be used to evaluate routing models. A good routing model shall reflect the real decision making process and give the estimation as accurate as possible.

Experts that can resolve a task are not unique and are not known before the task is actually routed. For a new task, one cannot estimate its completion time by targeting a unique "resolver". Instead, we need to consider multiple potential resolvers and multiple routing sequences.

Given a task and its initial expert, our generative model can generate a routing sequence of experts to process the task. Specifically, given a task t and its current holder, e_i, the receiver $r_{i,t}$ can be sampled according to our generative process described in Section 4. Once $r_{i,t}$ is obtained, it is treated as the current holder of t; the same procedure is repeated to produce the next receiver, until we have L experts to process t in sequence. Although the initial expert to deal with a task is important, in our work, we do not particularly deal with the assignment of an initial expert to a certain task. We assume that the initial expert to a task is given beforehand: it is either decided by the task requestor (*e.g.*, a customer) or by the system.

Task t will stop routing once an expert can solve it. Since each expert in the routing sequence has a probability to solve the task, the completion time can be estimated ($\widehat{\mathrm{CT}}_t$) as the expected number of experts having accessed the task when it is solved.

$$\widehat{\mathrm{CT}}_t = \sum_{m=1}^{L} m\prod_{n=1}^{m-1}[1-P(r_n,t)]P(r_m,t) \quad (22)$$

where r_m (r_n) is the m-th (n-th) expert in a routing sequence. $\prod_{n=1}^{m-1}[1-P(r_n,t)]P(r_m,t)$ gives the probability for the m-th expert in the sequence to solve the task while the previous $m-1$ experts fail to, where $P(r_m,t)$ s are estimated using Eqn. 5. Since the probability diminishes quite quickly, we set $L=10$ in practice. Indeed, $\widehat{\mathrm{CT}}_t$ is not going to change much when L is beyond 10. We generate multiple routing sequences for each task, estimate the completion time based on each sequence using Eqn. 22, and calculate the average as the final estimated completion time.

6. EXPERIMENTS

In this section, we validate the expertise difference routing pattern and evaluate the accuracy of our method in modeling expert behaviors on various real-life datasets. We will further demonstrate that with the help of our model, better recommendations on expert training could be automatically obtained and provided to managers for improving the performance of collaborative networks.

6.1 Datasets

We use real-world problem ticket data collected from a problem ticketing system in an IBM IT service department throughout 2006. Three datasets in different problem categories are explored: DB2, WebSphere, and AIX. DB2 contains problem tickets on database usage and management; WebSphere is a set of problem tickets on the enterprise software IBM WebSphere[2]; and AIX is the category of problem tickets on operating systems.

Datasets	# of tasks	# of experts	% of tasks with CT			
			= 2	= 3	= 4	≥ 5
DB2	26,740	55	44.2	34.3	16.5	5.0
WebSphere	65,786	234	39.0	36.2	20.0	4.8
AIX	120,780	404	40.0	39.4	14.2	6.4

Table 2: Three Datasets on Ticket Resolution.

The details of the three datasets, *i.e.*, the number of tasks, experts, and the distribution of completion time (CT), are shown in Table 2. The three datasets involve approximately 50 to 400 experts. Understanding how an expert makes a certain routing decision among many candidates is a meaningful yet potentially challenging problem. As evident in these datasets, the completion time for different tasks possesses a large diversity, which drives us to analyze expert routing behaviors that possibly lead to such diversity. For each dataset, we randomly partition it into two disjoint subsets: 75% of tasks for training, 25% for testing.

6.2 Evaluation Measures

To evaluate our generative model in capturing the real decision making process of an expert, we employ two types of measures: (1) *Routing Sequence Likelihood.* We compute the log likelihood (LL) of the routing relationships in the held-out testing dataset, according to Eqn 8. The higher the log likelihood, the better a model explains the routing decisions of experts. (2) *Predicted Completion Time.* The routing decision of an expert significantly affects the completion time of a task. Our model is considered valid if a task routed according to our generative process can achieve a similar completion time as it does in real situations. Two measures are employed to calculate the difference between the estimated, $\widehat{\mathrm{CT}}$ and the real completion time, CT.

1. Mean Absolute Error (MAE).

$$\mathrm{MAE} = \frac{1}{|\mathrm{Test\ Set}|} \sum_{t \in \mathrm{Test\ Set}} |\widehat{\mathrm{CT}}_t - \mathrm{CT}_t|$$

2. Step Loss Measure (SL). Instead of directly computing the difference between $\widehat{\mathrm{CT}}_t$ and CT_t as errors, step loss measure [15] incorporates some tolerance of the difference. If the difference is larger than the tolerance, one estimation mistake is made. We set the tolerance in our case as 1. That is, if the difference between $\widehat{\mathrm{CT}}_t$ and CT_t is within 1, the estimation is regarded as correct; otherwise, it is regarded as wrong. We calculate the percentage of the wrong estimations in the testing data set. The lower, the better.

$$\mathrm{SL} = \frac{1}{|\mathrm{Test\ Set}|} \sum_{t \in \mathrm{Test\ Set}} \mathbb{1}(|\widehat{\mathrm{CT}}_t - \mathrm{CT}_t| > 1)$$

where $\mathbb{1}$ is an indicator function: it picks value 1 if the condition $|\widehat{\mathrm{CT}}_t - \mathrm{CT}_t| > 1$ holds otherwise 0.

6.3 Evaluation Results

We compare our model with the following algorithms.
(1) Regression: For each task, to estimate its completion time, one can resort to a regression algorithm to make the prediction. We use two classic methods: Support Vector Regression (SVR) [9] and Bayesian regression method [14]. Given a task, two types of features are input to each method: (i) word frequency vector in the description of a task; (ii) the initial expert assigned to the task. 10-fold cross validation is conducted for both methods. We evaluate SVR with different kernels including a linear kernel, a polynomial kernel, an RBF kernel and a wavelet kernel. For Bayesian regression, we consider Bayesian linear regression and Bayesian logistic regression. Classification using SVM [9] or naive Bayes classifier [14] are also tested, which turns out to be worse than the regression methods. Among all the variants of SVR or Bayesian regression, we always show their best results obtained. The classification/regression approaches are employed as straightforward methods for completion time estimation. They do not attempt to understand the decision making process of experts, and their results on the sequence likelihood measure are not available.
(2) Generative models. Miao *et al.* [12] estimate the probability of an expert to solve a task and the probability of transferring a task from an expert to another. Given a task, [12] recommends a sequence of experts to route the task. Their goal is to shorten the routing as much as possible, while our goal is to characterize human routing patterns in the real network.

6.3.1 Model Accuracy

Table 3 summarizes the performance of all the methods on step loss measure, MAE, and log likelihood. From the results of SVR and Bayesian regression, we can see that the completion time of a task cannot be accurately predicted based on the straightforward regression methods. In fact, we observe that in the real datasets, similar tasks, even if assigned initially to the same expert, are often routed to different experts and resolved with a different completion time. This implies the resolution of a task is a complicated process and involves human factors. The estimated completion time in [12] is usually shorter than the real one as its goal is to shorten routing sequences. It is not surprising that it incurs a large step loss and MAE.

Now we test multiple variants of our generative model. For each variant, we select combinations of different routing patterns to train a generative model, and test the learned model under the three measures.

We first examine the performance of TNR-related and TSR-related routing patterns separately. Then they are combined together as TNR+TSR. Table 3 clearly shows both TNR and TSR play a critical role to reduce SL and MAE, indicating both types of strategies are adopted by experts in real cases. Our model does capture the decision making process of experts in a collaborative network. Our method significantly outperforms the content-focused regression methods by **75%**. Moreover, the MAE between our estimated completion time and the real one is between **0.07** and **0.15**, which shows that our method can be used to accurately predict the task completion time.

We then experiment if the expertise difference (EX) routing pattern makes sense. Specifically, we test the model that combines all the routing patterns except TNR^{ex} and TSR^{ex}, denoted as TNR+TSR-EX. The results indicates that with the EX routing pattern considered, TNR+TSR will better capture the real decision making process. This result can be attributed to our observation: an expert is more likely to transfer a task to some expert whose expertise is neither too similar nor too different.

DB2			
Models	Step Loss (%)	MAE	LL($\times 10^4$)
TNR	4.11	0.30	-0.28
TSR	4.56	0.29	-0.25
TNR+TSR	**1.77**	**0.08**	**-0.07**
TNR+TSR−EX	3.05	0.14	-0.10
Miao *et al.* [12]	9.89	0.68	-0.61
SVR	14.78	0.80	N/A
Bayesian regression	13.77	0.84	N/A
WebSphere			
Models	Step Loss (%)	MAE	LL($\times 10^4$)
TNR	4.77	0.40	-0.88
TSR	4.56	0.37	-0.80
TNR+TSR	**1.44**	**0.07**	**-0.19**
TNR+TSR−EX	2.31	0.11	-0.29
Miao *et al.* [12]	7.55	0.60	-0.81
SVR	18.20	0.71	N/A
Bayesian regression	17.02	0.80	N/A
AIX			
Models	Step Loss (%)	MAE	LL($\times 10^4$)
TNR	4.46	0.37	-0.41
TSR	4.15	0.30	-0.35
TNR+TSR	**1.99**	**0.15**	**-0.17**
TNR+TSR−EX	3.86	0.25	-0.25
Miao *et al.* [12]	11.10	0.81	-1.21
SVR	15.08	0.77	N/A
Bayesian regression	12.56	0.85	N/A

Table 3: Effectiveness of Routing Models.

6.3.2 *Resolution Efficiency*

One natural hypothesis is that under the task-specific routing, a task will be resolved quickly, since TSR directly takes into account the next expert's ability to solve the task. We now verify this hypothesis. Recall that the variational parameter $\phi^{i,t}$ in our model TNR+TSR reflects the posterior mixture weights used by expert e_i when transferring task t. If in $\phi^{i,t}$, the sum of the components corresponding to TSR-related routing patterns is larger than that corresponding to TNR-related patterns, expert e_i is regarded as using TSR to transfer task t; otherwise the expert is using TNR. Therefore, we can roughly divide experts into two groups: TNR-kind and TSR-kind. After an expert transfers a task, we count the number of remaining experts needed to resolve the task. We respectively summarize the distribution of the remaining expert number when a TSR-kind expert transfers a task, and that when a TNR-kind expert transfers a task. Figure 4 shows the results on the DB2 tickets. It clearly verifies the hypothesis. On DB2 tickets, a ticket will likely get solved with one more step when an expert favoring TSR routes it. However, if routed by a TNR-kind expert, a ticket might still need 2 or 3 more experts to get resolved. We obtain an additional implication from Table 3 and Figure 4, that is, TNR+TSR better captures the expert real routing behaviors in a collaborative network while routing based on TSR can lead to more efficient task resolution. Due to space constraints, we omit the results for AIX and WebSphere, which are very similar to that of DB2.

6.3.3 *Expertise Difference Routing Pattern*

In our EX routing pattern, given the expertise of e_i and e_j, we estimate f_{ij}, *i.e.*, the general trend of e_i sending a task to e_j, based on a log-normal distribution of $\Delta(e_i, e_j)$. The selection of log-normal is due to the non-negative nature

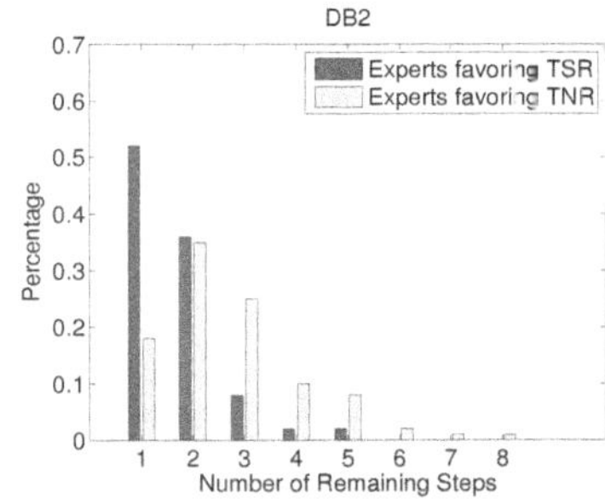

Figure 4: Efficiency of TNR vs. TSR.

of $\Delta(e_i, e_j)$ and the asymmetric shape of the distribution shown in Figure 2. However, one might consider estimating f_{ij} based on a normal distribution, since a normal distribution also seems to be quite similar to Figure 2:

$$f_{ij} \propto e^{-\frac{[\Delta(e_i, e_j) - \mu]^2}{2\sigma^2}} \tag{23}$$

Table 4 empirically justifies our selection of a log-normal distribution. (TNR+TSR)$^{\#}$ is the result corresponding to using a normal distribution to estimate f_{ij} based on Eqn. 23, which is much worse compared with TNR+TSR.

Models	Step Loss (%)	MAE	LL($\times 10^4$)
DB2			
TNR+TSR	**1.77**	**0.08**	**-0.07**
(TNR+TSR)$^{\#}$	3.54	0.22	-0.18
(TNR+TSR)*	1.90	0.10	-0.08
WebSphere			
TNR+TSR	**1.44**	**0.07**	**-0.19**
(TNR+TSR)$^{\#}$	3.67	0.24	-0.55
(TNR+TSR)*	1.59	0.08	0.20
AIX			
TNR+TSR	**1.99**	**0.15**	**-0.17**
(TNR+TSR)$^{\#}$	4.01	0.34	-0.38
(TNR+TSR)*	2.12	0.17	-0.19

Table 4: Variants of EX Routing Pattern.

Instead of optimizing μ and σ^2 during model solution, we could pre-estimate μ and σ^2 based on the distribution of the relative expertise difference in the training dataset, as shown in Figure 2, and keep them fixed during model training. We denote this setting as (TNR+TSR)*. As discussed in Section 3.1, the histogram in Figure 2 is due to the integrated effects of all the routing patterns, whereas TNR+TSR optimizes μ and σ^2 with more emphasis on tasks transferred following the EX pattern, and can further improve the accuracy. Nevertheless, given that the performance does not differ too much between TNR+TSR and (TNR+TSR)*, in practice, one might consider saving the trouble of deriving complicated derivatives over μ and σ^2 during model solution.

6.3.4 *Optimizing Collaborations*

In the management of real collaborative networks, system administrators need to optimize the current network, *e.g.*, in terms of expert training, to improve the efficiency of task execution. However, it is very expensive, if not impossible, to alter the real collaborative network just for hypothesis testing. Currently such decisions are manually made by experienced managers or consultants, without much quantitative analysis on how the resulting network will perform. Since our model accurately captures the routing behaviors of experts, it can naturally serve as a trustable simulation means for real task routing in the collaborative network. Hypotheses on whether a certain change to the network can improve the efficiency or not, can be much more easily examined with the help of our model.

Here we study optimization of the collaborative network, in terms of training experts to have more efficient routing patterns. Particularly, we examine two questions: *What kind of routing patterns might bring better resolution efficiency? Which expert(s) should be selected for more training, given a limited budget?* Section 6.3.2 implies if an expert is more likely to route a task based on TSR, the task will be resolved more quickly. We now formally verify this hypothesis. For each expert, we treat TSR and TNR as two groups of routing patterns, and set the group mixture weights respectively as $(x, 1 - x)$. When an expert transfers a task, we first randomly select TSR or TNR based on the group mixture weights, and then select a routing pattern inside the selected group according to their mixture weights previously learnt in our model TNR+TSR. Based on Section 5, we estimate the completion time of a task, and evaluate the task resolution efficiency by the average CT of all the tasks. We vary x to test the change of the task resolution efficiency. Only the results in the DB2 tickets are shown in Figure 5 since similar results on WebSphere and AIX are observed. We can see that as the mixture weight for TSR gets closer to 1, the average completion time tends to become shorter, indicating task resolution becomes more efficient. Therefore, experts in the network should be trained to route a task based on TSR.

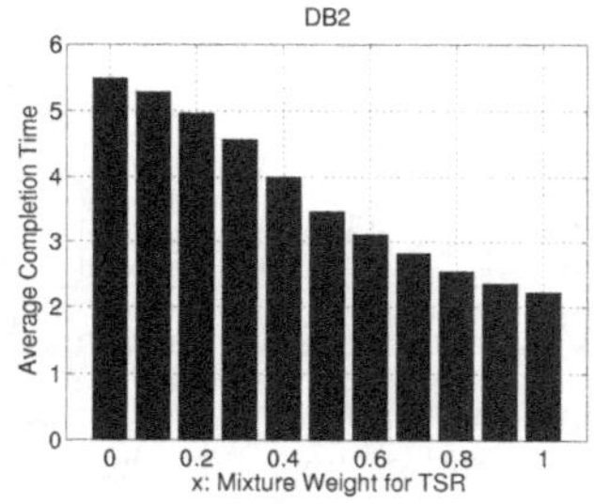

Figure 5: Effect of TSR Weights.

When the training budget is limited, which experts should be trained first to maximize the performance of the entire network, is an interesting problem. For simplicity, we consider the problem of selecting the best candidate. One can extend to top-k candidate selection by adopting a greedy method. Possible methods to recommend an expert include (1) randomly select one expert from the network, denoted as *Random*; (2) select the expert that transfers the most tasks, denoted as *Frequent Transferrer*; (3) select the expert that is the least efficient: after the expert transfers a task, the average number of remaining steps to solve a task is the highest, denoted as *Least Efficient*; (4) use our model to conduct task routing after an expert's routing pattern is changed and select the expert that can lead to the most improvement of efficiency. Efficiency improvement is evaluated by the decrease of the average CT of tasks. Methods (2)-(4) are executed on a training task set and evaluated by calculating the efficiency improvement on a testing task set. Table 5 clearly demonstrates that compared with other methods, training the expert recommended with the help of our model, can result in a much more efficiency improvement. This result is expected because through routing a training set of tasks with our model, we are able to know which expert's routing pattern plays a critical role in decreasing the average CT of tasks. This study demonstrates that our model could help conduct hypothesis testing easily and can provide valuable recommendations to decision makers during the optimization of a collaborative network.

Methods	Efficiency Improvement (%)
Random	0.27
Frequent Transferrer	0.91
Least Efficient	1.21
Recommendation with Our Model	**2.75**

Table 5: Training Recommendation

7. RELATED WORK

Our work is related to previous studies in three categories: (1)Collaborative networks; (2)User behavior modeling; (3)Multi-class classification and Markov processes.

Collaborative Networks. Camarinha-Matos *et al.*[8] propose general modeling perspectives including structural and behavioral to design and manage collaborative networks. As mentioned in Section 1, Shao *et al.*[18], Miao *et al.*[12], and Zhang *et al.*[22] propose automated routing algorithms to resolve a certain task in collaborative networks as fast as possible. The task resolution problem is also related to the expert finding problem[3, 17]: Given a keyword query, find the most knowledgeable persons regarding that query. All of them aim at proposing algorithms that can speed up the resolution of a task or a query. Our work differs from these studies: We are not aimed at building another recommendation algorithm for finding a right resolver. Instead, we try to uncover the patterns underlying human real routing decisions. Miao *et al.*[13] study a network model and a routing model to jointly simulate the structure and the task routing procedure in a collaborative network, while we directly infer the routing models in real collaborative networks. A salient feature of our model is its capability of estimating the completion time of a real task.

User Behavior Modeling. Information propagation, as one type of user behaviors, has been widely studied, such as [10] on influence maximization, [19] on propagation through e-mail forwarding, [20] on information spreading patterns in Twitter, and so on. Unlike information propagation from person to person, the purpose of task routing in a collaborative network is to find the resolver for a task instead of influencing others. Benevenuto *et al.*[5] study the clickstream data to reveal key features of user behaviors, such as how often users connect to a social network and the sequence of activities users conduct on a social network site. Retweeting behaviors of users in Twitter are investigated in [21]. Zhong *et al.*[23] leverage the knowledge of user rating behaviors in multiple social networks to enhance the predictive performance of user modeling. Different from these previous studies, in this work, we analyze experts' routing behaviors in collaborative networks: Given a task, how an expert decides where to transfer it and what kind of routing patterns an expert possesses.

Multi-class Classification and Markov Processes. In terms of methodology, our model is related to multi-class classification [16] and Markov processes [4]. When an expert considers where to route a task, the decision process can be regarded as a multi-class classification problem. One can potentially build a classifier for each expert, to decide where to route a task (*i.e.*, the label). It requires effective features and training algorithms to achieve good performance. Proposing such features for classification is not an easy problem. Actually, the routing patterns in our model can be regarded as relevant features for classification. The formalization of a mixture model gives an intuitive explanation of the decision making process of an expert. The task routing problem is also related to a Markov process, particularly, a Markov chain. States in a Markov chain correspond to experts processing a task at each step in our model. Given the current expert e_i, the next expert to access a task is independent from the experts previous to e_i, which can be regarded as the Markov property. Different from a classic Markov chain, in our case, the state (*i.e.*, expert) transition probability is with respect to a specific task and is obtained through a mixture of multiple routing patterns.

8. CONCLUSION

In this paper, we modeled the decision making and cognitive process of an expert during task routing in collaborative networks. A routing decision of an expert is formulated as a result of a generative process based on multiple routing patterns. We formalized each routing pattern in a probabilistic framework, and modeled experts' routing decision making through a generative model. Our analytical model has been verified that it not only explains the real routing sequence of a task very well, but also accurately predicts a task's completion time in the current collaborative network. In comparison with all the alternatives, our method improves the performance by more than 75% under three different quality measures. We have also demonstrated that our model can provide guidance on optimizing the performance of collaborative networks.

9. ACKNOWLEDGEMENT

This research was sponsored in part by the Army Research Laboratory under cooperative agreements W911NF-09-2-0053, NSF IIS 0917228, and 0954125. The views and conclusions contained herein are those of the authors and should not be interpreted as representing the official policies, either expressed or implied, of the Army Research Laboratory or the U.S. Government. The U.S. Government is authorized to reproduce and distribute reprints for Government purposes notwithstanding any copyright notice herein.

10. REFERENCES

[1] Bugzilla: http://www.bugzilla.org/.

[2] http://en.wikipedia.org/wiki/ibmwebsphere.

[3] K. Balog, L. Azzopardi, and M. De Rijke. Formal models for expert finding in enterprise corpora. In *SIGIR*, pages 43–50. ACM, 2006.

[4] R. Bellman. A markovian decision process. Technical report, DTIC Document, 1957.

[5] F. Benevenuto, T. Rodrigues, M. Cha, and V. Almeida. Characterizing user behavior in online social networks. In *SIGCOMM on IMC*, pages 49–62. ACM, 2009.

[6] C. M. Bishop and N. M. Nasrabadi. *PRML*, volume 1. springer New York, 2006.

[7] D. M. Blei, A. Y. Ng, and M. I. Jordan. Latent dirichlet allocation. *JMLR*, 3:993–1022, 2003.

[8] L. M. Camarinha-Matos and H. Afsarmanesh. A comprehensive modeling framework for collaborative networked organizations. *Journal of Intelligent Manufacturing*, 18(5):529–542, 2007.

[9] N. Cristianini and J. Shawe-Taylor. *An introduction to support vector machines and other kernel-based learning methods*. Cambridge university press, 2000.

[10] D. Kempe, J. Kleinberg, and É. Tardos. Maximizing the spread of influence through a social network. In *SIGKDD*, pages 137–146. ACM, 2003.

[11] D. Liu and J. Nocedal. On the limited memory bfgs method for large scale optimization. *Mathematical programming*, 45(1):503–528, 1989.

[12] G. Miao, L. E. Moser, X. Yan, S. Tao, Y. Chen, and N. Anerousis. Generative models for ticket resolution in expert networks. In *SIGKDD*, pages 733–742. ACM, 2010.

[13] G. Miao, S. Tao, W. Cheng, R. Moulic, L. E. Moser, D. Lo, and X. Yan. Understanding task-driven information flow in collaborative networks. In *WWW*, pages 849–858. ACM, 2012.

[14] T. M. Mitchell. Machine learning. 1997. *Burr Ridge, IL: McGraw Hill*, 45, 1997.

[15] H. Moskowitz and K. Tang. Bayesian variables acceptance-sampling plans: quadratic loss function and step-loss function. *Technometrics*, 34(3):340–347, 1992.

[16] J. C. Platt, N. Cristianini, and J. Shawe-taylor. Large margin dags for multiclass classification. In *NIPS*, pages 547–553, 2000.

[17] P. Serdyukov, H. Rode, and D. Hiemstra. Modeling multi-step relevance propagation for expert finding. In *CIKM*, pages 1133–1142. ACM, 2008.

[18] Q. Shao, Y. Chen, S. Tao, X. Yan, and N. Anerousis. Efficient ticket routing by resolution sequence mining. In *SIGKDD*, pages 605–613. ACM, 2008.

[19] D. Wang, Z. Wen, H. Tong, C.-Y. Lin, C. Song, and A.-L. Barabási. Information spreading in context. In *WWW*, pages 735–744. ACM, 2011.

[20] S. Wu, J. M. Hofman, W. A. Mason, and D. J. Watts. Who says what to whom on twitter. In *WWW*, pages 705–714. ACM, 2011.

[21] Z. Yang, J. Guo, K. Cai, J. Tang, J. Li, L. Zhang, and Z. Su. Understanding retweeting behaviors in social networks. In *CIKM*, pages 1633–1636. ACM, 2010.

[22] H. Zhang, E. Horvitz, Y. Chen, and D. C. Parkes. Task routing for prediction tasks. In *AAMS-Volume 2*, pages 889–896. IFAAMS, 2012.

[23] E. Zhong, W. Fan, J. Wang, L. Xiao, and Y. Li. Comsoc: adaptive transfer of user behaviors over composite social network. In *SIGKDD*, pages 696–704. ACM, 2012.

Predicting Long-Term Impact of CQA Posts: A Comprehensive Viewpoint

Yuan Yao
State Key Laboratory for Novel Software Technology, China
yyao@smail.nju.edu.cn

Hanghang Tong
Arizona State University, USA
htong6@asu.edu

Feng Xu and Jian Lu
State Key Laboratory for Novel Software Technology, China
{xf,lj}@nju.edu.cn

ABSTRACT

Community Question Answering (CQA) sites have become valuable platforms to create, share, and seek a massive volume of human knowledge. How can we spot an insightful question that would inspire massive further discussions in CQA sites? How can we detect a valuable answer that benefits many users? The long-term impact (e.g., the size of the population a post benefits) of a question/answer post is the key quantity to answer these questions. In this paper, we aim to predict the long-term impact of questions/answers shortly after they are posted in the CQA sites. In particular, we propose a family of algorithms for the prediction problem by modeling three key aspects, i.e., non-linearity, question/answer coupling, and dynamics. We analyze our algorithms in terms of optimality, correctness, and complexity. We conduct extensive experimental evaluations on two real CQA data sets to demonstrate the effectiveness and efficiency of our algorithms.

Categories and Subject Descriptors

H.2.8 [**Database Management**]: Database applications—*Data mining*

Keywords

Question answering; long-term impact; impact correlation

1. INTRODUCTION

Community Question Answering (CQA) sites, such as Stack Overflow[1], Yahoo! Answers[2], AnswerBag[3], and Ask.com[4], have become valuable platforms to create, share, and seek a massive volume of human knowledge. How can we spot an insightful question that would inspire massive further discussions in these CQA sites? How can we detect an valuable answer that benefits many users? The long-term impact of a question/answer post, which is the size of population it benefits in total, is the key quantity to answer these questions. *How can we predict the Long-term Impact of a Post (either a question or an answer) shortly after it is posted on the CQA site?* This, which we refer to as the *LIP* problem in this paper, is an essential task for the prosperity and sustainability of the CQA ecosystem that benefits all types of its users, including the information producers, spreaders, and consumers.

Despite its importance, it is not an easy task to predict the long-term impact of question/answer posts. Consequently, there are very few dedicated, existing tools for this problem (see Section 6 for a review). We summarize two major challenges below.

The first challenge lies in the *multi-aspect* of the long-term impact of question/answer posts. The user rating/voting mechanism within most of the CQA sites often provides a good measure of the long-term impact of CQA posts. For example, the voting score in Stack Overflow directly tells how many site users find the corresponding question/answer is beneficial to him/her. This naturally leads us to cast the LIP problem as a (supervised) data mining problem. Nonetheless, this problem has its own characteristics, making any off-the-shelf data mining algorithm sub-optimal for this problem. To be specific, while each of the following aspects might affect the long-term impact of question/answer posts, they require different treatments in the data mining algorithms. How can we build a comprehensive model to capture all these aspects to maximally boost the prediction accuracy?

- *A1. Non-linearity.* Both the contextual features (e.g., the reputation of the user who issues the question, etc.) and the content of the post (e.g., keywords, etc.) might affect its long-term impact; and the effect of each feature might be beyond the simple linear-relationship.

- *A2. Coupling between questions and answers.* Intuitively (which was also confirmed in our tech report [29]), the long-term impact of the questions might be correlated with that of its associated answers. Yet, the questions and answers may reside in different feature spaces.

- *A3. The dynamics (of training data sets).* While CQA sites usually offer a large size of training data set, it may arrive in a dynamic (stream-like) way for the mining algorithms.

The second challenge is the *computation*. Each of the above aspects (non-linearity, the question-answer coupling, and the dynamics) will add the extra complexity into the mining process. For example, while many machine learning algorithms (e.g., kernel regression, support vector regression, etc.) exist to capture the non-linearity between the features and outputs (long-term impact score in our case), they typically require at least $O(n^2)$ in time and space complexity, where n is the total number of the training examples.

[1]http://stackoverflow.com/
[2]http://answers.yahoo.com/
[3]http://www.answerbag.com/
[4]http://www.ask.com/

KDD'14, August 24–27, 2014, New York, NY, USA.

http://dx.doi.org/10.1145/2623330.2623649.

Moreover, when the new training examples arrive in a stream, ever-growing fashion, even an $O(n)$ algorithm might be too expensive. How can we make our prediction algorithms *scalable* to millions of CQA posts and *adaptive* to the newly arrived training examples over time?

In this paper, we aim to address both challenges by proposing a family of algorithms for predicting the long-term impact of question/answer posts. Our algorithms enjoy three key advantages. First, they are *comprehensive* in the sense that our model naturally captures all the above three key aspects (i.e., non-linearity, coupling, and dynamics) that matter with the long-term impact of a post. Second, they are *flexible* and *general*, being able to handle the special cases where only a fraction of these aspects are prominent. For example, in some CQA sites, we might be only interested in the prediction of answers posts (such as Yahoo! Answers), and/or the features may have a linear effect on the post impact, etc. Third, they are *scalable* and *adaptive* to the newly arrived examples. For example, one of our algorithms (LIP-KIMAA) has a sub-linear complexity in both time and space. On the Stack Overflow data set with more than 3 million posts, this LIP-KIMAA algorithm can build and update our model in seconds, while straightforward approaches would take hours.

The main contributions of this paper are summarized as follows:

- *A family of novel algorithms* for the prediction of the long-term impact of questions and answers in CQA sites.
- *Proofs and analysis*, showing the optimality, correctness, and computational efficiency, as well as the intrinsic relationship among different algorithms.
- *Extensive empirical evaluations*, demonstrating effectiveness and efficiency of our algorithms. For example, compared with alternative choices (e.g., KRR [25]), one of our proposed algorithm (LIP-KIMAA) (1) leads up to 35.8% improvement in prediction accuracy; (2) and is up to 390x faster while enjoying *sub-linear* scalability.

The rest of the paper is organized as follows. Section 2 describes the problem definition. Section 3 presents the proposed algorithms. Section 4 discusses some variants. Section 5 presents the experimental results. Section 6 reviews related work, and Section 7 concludes the paper.

2. PROBLEM STATEMENT

In this section, we first define the LIP problem, and then present its solution space to illustrate the relationship between our proposed algorithms and the existing work.

2.1 Problem Definitions

Table 1 lists the main symbols we use throughout the paper. For convenience, we use bold capital letters for existing matrices/vectors at time t, and bold lower case letters for newly arrived matrices/vectors at time $t+1$. We use superscript (i.e., q or a) to distinguish questions and answers, and use subscript (i.e., t, $t+1$, etc.) to indicate time. For example, we use $\mathbf{F}_t^q$ to denote the feature matrix for questions at time t, and $\mathbf{f}_{t+1}^q$ to denote the feature matrix of newly arrived questions at time $t+1$. Each row of $\mathbf{F}_t^q$ and $\mathbf{f}_{t+1}^q$ contains the feature vector for the corresponding question. Similarly, we use $\mathbf{Y}_t^q$ to denote the vector of impact scores at time t, and $\mathbf{y}_{t+1}^q$ to denote the vector of impact scores from new questions at time $t+1$. Following conventions, we use calligraphic letter $\mathcal{K}_t^q$ and $\mathcal{K}_t^a$ to denote the kernel matrix for questions and answers at time t. We will omit the subscript when the meaning of matrices/vectors is clear in the context. We use the row-normalized $n_q \times n_a$ matrix $\mathbf{M}_t$ to denote the association between questions and answers at time t, where non-zero element $\mathbf{M}_t(i,j)$ indicates that the jth answer belongs to the ith question. Thus, the matrix $\mathbf{M}_t$ is sparse since it contains only n^a non-zero elements. We also use $\mathbf{F}_t^q(i,:)$ to represent the ith row of matrix $\mathbf{F}_t^q$, $\mathbf{Y}_t^q(i)$ to represent the ith element of vector $\mathbf{Y}_t^q$, and $(\mathbf{F}_t^q)'$ to represent the transpose of $\mathbf{F}_t^q$.

Table 1: Symbols.

Symbol	Definition and Description
$\mathbf{F}_t^q, \mathbf{F}_t^a$	the features for existing questions/answers at time t
$\mathbf{f}_{t+1}^q, \mathbf{f}_{t+1}^a$	the features of new questions/answers at time $t+1$
$\mathcal{K}_t^q, \mathcal{K}_t^a$	the kernel matrix of $\mathbf{F}_t^q$ and $\mathbf{F}_t^a$
$\mathbf{k}_{t+1}^q, \mathbf{h}_{t+1}^q$	the kernel matrix of new questions at time $t+1$
$\mathbf{k}_{t+1}^a, \mathbf{h}_{t+1}^a$	the kernel matrix of new answers at time $t+1$
$\mathbf{U}_t^q, \Lambda_t^q$	the low-rank matrices to approximate $\mathcal{K}_t^q$
$\mathbf{U}_t^a, \Lambda_t^a$	the low-rank matrices to approximate $\mathcal{K}_t^a$
$\mathbf{M}_t$	the row-normalized association matrix between existing questions and answers at time t
$\mathbf{m}_{t+1}$	the row-normalized association matrix between new questions and answers at time $t+1$
$\mathbf{Y}_t^q, \mathbf{Y}_t^a$	the impact score for existing questions/answers at time t
$\mathbf{y}_{t+1}^q, \mathbf{y}_{t+1}^a$	the impact score for new questions/answers at time $t+1$
n^q, n^a	the number of existing questions/answers at time t
i^q, i^a	the number of new questions/answers at time $t+1$
d	the feature dimension
r	the rank of $\mathbf{U}_t^q$, Λ_t^q, $\mathbf{U}_t^a$, and Λ_t^a
th	the threshold for the filtering step

Based on the above notations, we define the LIP problem in its static form as:

PROBLEM 1. *Static LIP Problem*

Given: *the question/answer feature matrix* $\mathbf{F}^q/\mathbf{F}^a$, *the question/answer impact vector* $\mathbf{Y}^q/\mathbf{Y}^a$, *and the association matrix* $\mathbf{M}$;

Output: *the impact of new questions and their answers.*

In real CQA sites where questions and answers continuously arrive, we need to update the model to keep it up-to-date. To this end, we define the following dynamic form of the LIP problem:

PROBLEM 2. *Dynamic LIP Problem*

Given: *the question/answer feature matrix* $\mathbf{F}_t^q/\mathbf{F}_t^a$ *and the newly arrived question/answer feature matrix* $\mathbf{f}_{t+1}^q/\mathbf{f}_{t+1}^a$, *the question/answer impact vector* $\mathbf{Y}_t^q/\mathbf{Y}_t^a$ *and the newly arrived question/answer impact vector* $\mathbf{y}_{t+1}^q/\mathbf{y}_{t+1}^a$, *as well as the association matrix* $\mathbf{M}_t$ *and* $\mathbf{m}_{t+1}$;

Output: *the impact of new questions and their answers.*

2.2 Solution Space

Solution Space. Let us first define the solution space of the LIP problem, which is represented by a genealogy graph in Fig. 1. In this paper, we consider three key aspects that matter with the prediction performance, including (a) whether the predication models are linear or non-linear; (b) whether we treat the prediction of the questions and the answers separately (single) or jointly (coupling); and (c) whether the prediction is static or dynamic. Based on these three aspects, we could have different variants of the prediction algorithms for the LIP problem, whose intrinsic relationship is also summarized in Fig. 1. In the figure, we use the letter K, M, and I to denote non-linearity, coupling, and dynamics, respectively.

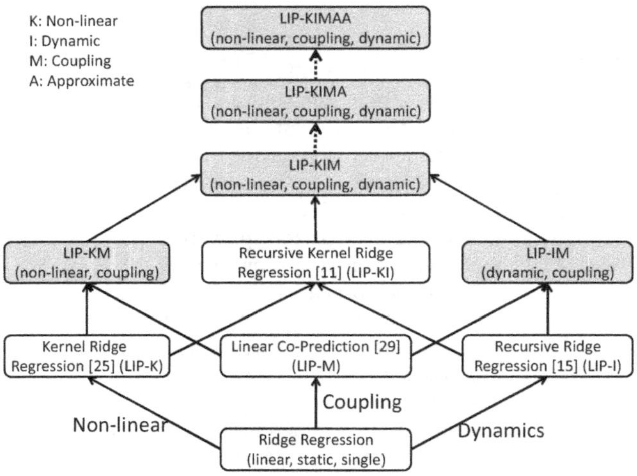

Figure 1: The solution space of LIP problem. Shaded boxes are proposed algorithms; and white boxes are existing work.

For example, LIP-KIM means that our model is non-linear and dynamic, and it jointly predict the long-term impact of questions and answers; LIP-K means that our prediction model is non-linear and static, and it treats questions and answers separately, etc.

In Fig. 1, each upward solid arrow makes the model more comprehensive by modeling more aspects in the prediction algorithms, and each dashed arrow makes the algorithms more scalable. For example, starting with the ridge regression algorithm in the bottom layer, we have the kernel ridge regression (KRR) [25] by incorporating non-linearity, and we have the recursive ridge regression [15] by incorporating dynamics. If we incorporate both non-linearity and dynamics, we have the recursive kernel ridge regression algorithm (RKRR) [11] in the third layer.

Preliminaries. In Fig. 1, we use shaded boxes to indicate the algorithms proposed in this paper, and while boxes to indicate existing work. Before presenting the proposed algorithms in the next section, we first briefly review some existing work (e.g., white boxes), which serves as the building blocks of our proposed algorithms.

(A) Linear Co-Prediction. In our tech report [29], we proposed a regularized optimization formulation to jointly predict the voting score of questions and answers

$$\begin{aligned}\min_{\alpha^q,\alpha^a} \quad & \textstyle\sum_{i=1}^{n^q}(\mathbf{F}^q(i,:)\alpha^q - \mathbf{Y}^q(i))^2 + \sum_{i=1}^{n^a}(\mathbf{F}^a(i,:)\alpha^a - \mathbf{Y}^a(i))^2 \\ & +\theta\textstyle\sum_{i=1}^{n^q}(\mathbf{F}^q(i,:)\alpha^q - \mathbf{M}(i,:)\mathbf{F}^a\alpha^a)^2 + \lambda(\|\alpha^q\|_2^2 + \|\alpha^a\|_2^2) \quad (1)\end{aligned}$$

where parameters λ and θ are used to control regularization and the importance of the coupling between questions and answers, respectively.

(B) Kernel Ridge Regression. In order to capture the non-linearity between the features and outputs, a natural choice is to user kernelized methods. Take question impact prediction as an example, the so-called kernel ridge regression [25] aims to estimate a coefficient $\boldsymbol{\beta}^q$ as follows

$$\min_{\boldsymbol{\beta}^q} \quad \textstyle\sum_{i=1}^{n^q}(\mathcal{K}^q(i,:)\boldsymbol{\beta}^q - \mathbf{Y}^q(i))^2 + \lambda(\boldsymbol{\beta}^q)'\mathcal{K}^q\boldsymbol{\beta}^q \qquad (2)$$

where $\mathcal{K}^q$ is the kernel matrix of $\mathbf{F}^q$.

3. THE PROPOSED ALGORITHMS

In this section, we propose our solutions for the LIP problem. We start with presenting two algorithms for Problem 1 (subsection 3.1) and Problem 2 (subsection 3.2), respectively; and then address the computational challenges (subsection 3.3-3.4).

3.1 LIP-KM Algorithm for Problem 1

Here, we address the static LIP problem (Problem 1). We propose an algorithm (LIP-KM) to capture both the non-linearity and the coupling aspects.

For the non-linear aspect, a natural choice is to kernelize a linear prediction model (e.g., linear ridge regression). Recall that kernel method aims to produce non-linear versions of linear learning algorithms by mapping the data points into a high-dimensional Hilbert space $\mathcal{H}$ with a non-linear function ϕ [4]. The key idea behind kernel methods is to use the kernel functions to replace the inner-product operations in the high-dimensional Hilbert space $\mathcal{H}$, and such replacement can be ensured by Mercer's Condition [6]. In other words, for two data points $\mathbf{F}(i,:)$ and $\mathbf{F}(j,:)$, the inner product of $\phi(\mathbf{F}(i,:))$ and $\phi(\mathbf{F}(j,:))$ in the Hilbert space $\mathcal{H}$ can be directly computed by a Mercer kernel $\kappa(\mathbf{F}(i,:),\mathbf{F}(j,:))$

$$\kappa(\mathbf{F}(i,:),\mathbf{F}(j,:)) =< \phi(\mathbf{F}(i,:)), \phi(\mathbf{F}(j,:)) >= \phi(\mathbf{F}(i,:))\phi(\mathbf{F}(j,:))' \quad (3)$$

where $< \cdot,\cdot >$ indicates the inner product in $\mathcal{H}$. As we can see from Eq. (3), we can derive the non-linear models without any explicit knowledge of either ϕ or $\mathcal{H}$. Common kernel functions include Gaussian kernel, polynomial kernel, cosine kernel, etc.

For the coupling aspect, LIP-KM imposes a so-called *impact consistency* on the prediction space by requiring the predicted impact of a question to be close to that of its answer (see our tech report [29] for the detailed explanations about its rationality).

Putting the non-linearity and coupling aspects together, we have the following optimization formulation for Problem 1

$$\begin{aligned}\min_{\boldsymbol{\beta}^q,\boldsymbol{\beta}^a} \quad & \textstyle\sum_{i=1}^{n^q}(\mathcal{K}^q(i,:)\boldsymbol{\beta}^q - \mathbf{Y}^q(i))^2 + \sum_{i=1}^{n^a}(\mathcal{K}^a(i,:)\boldsymbol{\beta}^a - \mathbf{Y}^a(i))^2 \\ & +\theta\textstyle\sum_{i=1}^{n^q}(\mathcal{K}^q(i,:)\boldsymbol{\beta}^q - \mathbf{M}(i,:)\mathcal{K}^a\boldsymbol{\beta}^a)^2 \\ & +\lambda((\boldsymbol{\beta}^q)'\mathcal{K}^q\boldsymbol{\beta}^q + (\boldsymbol{\beta}^a)'\mathcal{K}^a\boldsymbol{\beta}^a) \qquad (4)\end{aligned}$$

where θ is a weight parameter to control the importance of coupling, λ is a regularization parameter, and $\mathcal{K}^q$ and $\mathcal{K}^a$ are the kernel matrices of $\mathbf{F}^q$ and $\mathbf{F}^a$, respectively. $\mathcal{K}^q$ and $\mathcal{K}^a$ can computed as $\mathcal{K}^q(i,j) = \kappa(\mathbf{F}^q(i,:),\mathbf{F}^q(j,:))$, and $\mathcal{K}^a(i,j) = \kappa(\mathbf{F}^a(i,:),\mathbf{F}^a(j,:))$.

Eq. (4) can be solved by the closed-form solution

$$\begin{aligned}\boldsymbol{\beta} &= \arg\min_{\boldsymbol{\beta}^q,\boldsymbol{\beta}^a} \|\mathcal{K}^q\boldsymbol{\beta}^q - \mathbf{Y}^q\|_2^2 + \|\mathcal{K}^a\boldsymbol{\beta}^a - \mathbf{Y}^a\|_2^2 + \theta\|\mathcal{K}^q\boldsymbol{\beta}^q - \mathbf{M}\mathcal{K}^a\boldsymbol{\beta}^a\|_2^2 \\ & \quad +\lambda((\boldsymbol{\beta}^q)'\mathcal{K}^q\boldsymbol{\beta}^q + (\boldsymbol{\beta}^a)'\mathcal{K}^a\boldsymbol{\beta}^a) \\ &= \begin{bmatrix}(\theta+1)\mathcal{K}^q + \lambda\mathbf{I} & -\theta\mathbf{M}\mathcal{K}^a \\ -\theta\mathbf{M}'\mathcal{K}^q & \mathcal{K}^a + \theta\mathbf{M}'\mathbf{M}\mathcal{K}^a + \lambda\mathbf{I}\end{bmatrix}^{-1}\begin{bmatrix}\mathbf{Y}^q \\ \mathbf{Y}^a\end{bmatrix} \qquad (5)\end{aligned}$$

where $\boldsymbol{\beta} = [\boldsymbol{\beta}^q;\boldsymbol{\beta}^a]$. Once the coefficient vectors $\boldsymbol{\beta}^q$ and $\boldsymbol{\beta}^a$ are inferred from the above equation, the impact of questions/answers can then be predicted as

$$\hat{\mathbf{Y}}^q_{test} = \mathcal{K}^q_{test}\boldsymbol{\beta}^q, \quad \hat{\mathbf{Y}}^a_{test} = \mathcal{K}^a_{test}\boldsymbol{\beta}^a \qquad (6)$$

where the kernel matrices on the test set $\mathbf{F}^q_{test}$ and $\mathbf{F}^a_{test}$ can be computed as $\mathcal{K}^q_{test}(i,j) = \kappa(\mathbf{F}^q_{test}(i,:),\mathbf{F}^q(j,:))$, $\mathcal{K}^a_{test}(i,j) = \kappa(\mathbf{F}^a_{test}(i,:),\mathbf{F}^a(j,:))$.

Algorithm Analysis. Let us analyze the effectiveness and efficiency of the LIP-KM algorithm (i.e., Eq. (5)). We first summarize the optimality of LIP-KM in the following lemma, which states that LIP-KM finds (at least) a local minimum for the static LIP problem.

LEMMA 1. **Optimality of LIP-KM**. *Eq. (5) finds a local minimum for Eq. (4).*

PROOF. Omitted for brevity. □

Algorithm 1 The LIP-KIM Algorithm.

Input: $\mathbf{S}_t^{-1}, \boldsymbol{\beta}_t, \mathbf{F}_t^q, \mathbf{f}_{t+1}^q, \mathbf{F}_t^a, \mathbf{f}_{t+1}^a, \mathbf{y}_{t+1}^q, \mathbf{y}_{t+1}^a, \mathbf{M}_t$ and $\mathbf{m}_{t+1}$

Output: $\boldsymbol{\beta}_{t+1}, \mathbf{S}_{t+1}^{-1}$

1: compute the new kernels $\mathbf{k}_{t+1}^q, \mathbf{h}_{t+1}^q, \mathbf{k}_{t+1}^a$ and $\mathbf{h}_{t+1}^a$ in Eq. (7);

2: compute $\mathbf{S}_1, \mathbf{S}_2, \mathbf{S}_3, \mathbf{D}$, and $\mathbf{E}_1$ as Eq. (9) - (13);

3: update $\mathbf{S}_{t+1}^{-1}$ as $\mathbf{E}_1' \begin{bmatrix} \mathbf{S}_t^{-1} + \mathbf{S}_t^{-1}\mathbf{S}_1\mathbf{D}\mathbf{S}_2\mathbf{S}_t^{-1} & -\mathbf{S}_t^{-1}\mathbf{S}_1\mathbf{D} \\ -\mathbf{S}_3^{-1}\mathbf{S}_2\mathbf{S}_t^{-1}(\mathbf{I} + \mathbf{S}_1\mathbf{D}\mathbf{S}_2\mathbf{S}_t^{-1}) & \mathbf{D} \end{bmatrix} \mathbf{E}_1$

4: update $\boldsymbol{\beta}_{t+1}$ as $\mathbf{E}_1 \begin{bmatrix} \boldsymbol{\beta}_t + \mathbf{S}_t^{-1}\mathbf{S}_1\mathbf{D}(\mathbf{S}_2\boldsymbol{\beta}_t - [\mathbf{y}_{t+1}^q; \mathbf{y}_{t+1}^a]) \\ -\mathbf{S}_3^{-1}\mathbf{S}_2(\boldsymbol{\beta}_t + \mathbf{S}_t^{-1}\mathbf{S}_1\mathbf{D}\mathbf{S}_2\boldsymbol{\beta}_t) + \mathbf{D}[\mathbf{y}_{t+1}^q; \mathbf{y}_{t+1}^a] \end{bmatrix}$

5: **return** $\boldsymbol{\beta}_{t+1}, \mathbf{S}_{t+1}^{-1}$;

Next, we summarize the time complexity and space complexity of LIP-KM in the following lemma, which basically states that LIP-KM requires $O((n^q + n^a)^3)$ time and $O((n^q + n^a)^2)$ space.

LEMMA 2. **Complexity of LIP-KM**. *The time complexity of Eq. (5) is $O((n^q + n^a)^3 + (n^q)^2 d + (n^a)^2 d)$; the space complexity of Eq. (5) is $O((n^q + n^a)^2 + (n^q + n^a)d)$.*

PROOF. Omitted for brevity. □

3.2 LIP-KIM Algorithm for Problem 2

Here, we address the dynamic LIP problem (Problem 2). We present the LIP-KIM algorithm to incrementally update the model in Eq. (5). The basic idea of LIP-KIM is to incorporate the dynamic aspect into LIP-KM, and therefore it is adaptive to newly arrived training examples.

When new questions and answers arrive at time $t + 1$, we first need to compute the new kernel matrices $\mathcal{K}_{t+1}^q$ and $\mathcal{K}_{t+1}^a$ which are as follows

$$\mathcal{K}_{t+1}^q = \begin{bmatrix} \mathcal{K}_t^q & (\mathbf{k}_{t+1}^q)' \\ \mathbf{k}_{t+1}^q & \mathbf{h}_{t+1}^q \end{bmatrix}, \quad \mathcal{K}_{t+1}^a = \begin{bmatrix} \mathcal{K}_t^a & (\mathbf{k}_{t+1}^a)' \\ \mathbf{k}_{t+1}^a & \mathbf{h}_{t+1}^a \end{bmatrix} \tag{7}$$

where the kernel matrices involving the newly arrived examples can be computed as: $\mathbf{k}_{t+1}^q(i,j) = \kappa(\mathbf{f}_{t+1}^q(i,:), \mathbf{F}_t^q(j,:))$, $\mathbf{h}_{t+1}^q(i,j) = \kappa(\mathbf{f}_{t+1}^q(i,:), \mathbf{f}_{t+1}^q(j,:))$, $\mathbf{k}_{t+1}^a(i,j) = \kappa(\mathbf{f}_{t+1}^a(i,:), \mathbf{F}_t^a(j,:))$, and $\mathbf{h}_{t+1}^a(i,j) = \kappa(\mathbf{f}_{t+1}^a(i,:), \mathbf{f}_{t+1}^a(j,:))$.

To simplify the algorithm description, let us introduce the following matrices

$$\mathbf{S}_t = \begin{bmatrix} (\theta+1)\mathcal{K}_t^q + \lambda\mathbf{I} & -\theta\mathbf{M}_t\mathcal{K}_t^a \\ -\theta\mathbf{M}_t'\mathcal{K}_t^q & \mathcal{K}_t^a + \theta\mathbf{M}_t'\mathbf{M}_t\mathcal{K}_t^a + \lambda\mathbf{I} \end{bmatrix} \tag{8}$$

$$\mathbf{S}_1 = \begin{bmatrix} (\theta+1)(\mathbf{k}_{t+1}^q)' & -\theta\mathbf{M}_t(\mathbf{k}_{t+1}^a)' \\ -\theta\mathbf{M}_t'(\mathbf{k}_{t+1}^q)' & (\mathbf{k}_{t+1}^a)' + \theta\mathbf{M}_t'\mathbf{M}_t(\mathbf{k}_{t+1}^a)' \end{bmatrix} \tag{9}$$

$$\mathbf{S}_2 = \begin{bmatrix} (\theta+1)\mathbf{k}_{t+1}^q & -\theta\mathbf{m}_{t+1}\mathbf{k}_{t+1}^a \\ -\theta\mathbf{m}_{t+1}'\mathbf{k}_{t+1}^q & \mathbf{k}_{t+1}^a + \theta\mathbf{m}_{t+1}'\mathbf{m}_{t+1}\mathbf{k}_{t+1}^a \end{bmatrix} \tag{10}$$

$$\mathbf{S}_3 = \begin{bmatrix} (\theta+1)\mathbf{h}_{t+1}^q + \lambda\mathbf{I} & -\theta\mathbf{m}_{t+1}\mathbf{h}_{t+1}^a \\ -\theta\mathbf{m}_{t+1}'\mathbf{h}_{t+1}^q & \mathbf{h}_{t+1}^a + \theta\mathbf{m}_{t+1}'\mathbf{m}_{t+1}\mathbf{h}_{t+1}^a + \lambda\mathbf{I} \end{bmatrix} \tag{11}$$

$$\mathbf{D} = (\mathbf{S}_3 - \mathbf{S}_2\mathbf{S}_t^{-1}\mathbf{S}_1)^{-1} \tag{12}$$

With these extra notations, we present our LIP-KIM algorithm for solving Problem 2, which is summarized in Alg. 1. As we can see from the algorithm, we re-use $\mathbf{S}_t^{-1}$ and $\boldsymbol{\beta}_t$ from previous computations. Therefore, we also need to update $\mathbf{S}_{t+1}^{-1}$ and $\boldsymbol{\beta}_{t+1}$ for future iterations. After we compute the new kernels as well as the matrices (i.e., $\mathbf{S}_1$, $\mathbf{S}_2$, $\mathbf{S}_3$ and $\mathbf{D}$) that are based on the new kernels, we can update the model in Steps 3-4. In these two steps, $\mathbf{E}_1$ stands for a permutation matrix to exchange the corresponding rows/columns

$$\mathbf{E}_1 = \begin{bmatrix} \mathbf{I}_{n_q \times n_q} & \mathbf{0} & \mathbf{0} & \mathbf{0} \\ \mathbf{0} & \mathbf{0} & \mathbf{I}_{i_q \times i_q} & \mathbf{0} \\ \mathbf{0} & \mathbf{I}_{n_a \times n_a} & \mathbf{0} & \mathbf{0} \\ \mathbf{0} & \mathbf{0} & \mathbf{0} & \mathbf{I}_{i_a \times i_a} \end{bmatrix} \tag{13}$$

where i^q and i^a denote the number of questions and answers arrived at time $t + 1$, respectively.

Algorithm Analysis. The correctness of LIP-KIM is summarized in the following theorem, which states that LIP-KIM can find the same coefficients (i.e., $\boldsymbol{\beta}_{t+1}$) as if we apply the LIP-KM algorithm whenever we have new training examples.

THEOREM 1. **Correctness of LIP-KIM**. *Let $\boldsymbol{\beta}_{t+1}^*$ be the output of Eq. (5) at time $t + 1$, and $\boldsymbol{\beta}_{t+1}$ be the output of Alg. 1 updated from time t to $t + 1$, we have that $\boldsymbol{\beta}_{t+1} = \boldsymbol{\beta}_{t+1}^*$.*

PROOF. Notice that Eq. (5) can be re-written as

$$\boldsymbol{\beta}_t = \mathbf{S}_t^{-1} \begin{bmatrix} \mathbf{Y}_t^q \\ \mathbf{Y}_t^a \end{bmatrix}$$

Therefore, we need to first prove the update procedure for $\mathbf{S}_t^{-1}$ (i.e., Step 3 in Alg. 1). $\mathbf{S}_{t+1}$ can be written as

$$\mathbf{S}_{t+1} = \begin{bmatrix} (\theta+1)\mathcal{K}_{t+1}^q + \lambda\mathbf{I} & -\theta\mathbf{M}_{t+1}\mathcal{K}_{t+1}^a \\ -\theta\mathbf{M}_{t+1}'\mathcal{K}_{t+1}^q & \mathcal{K}_{t+1}^a + \theta\mathbf{M}_{t+1}'\mathbf{M}_{t+1}\mathcal{K}_{t+1}^a + \lambda\mathbf{I} \end{bmatrix}$$

where $\mathbf{M}_{t+1} = [\mathbf{M}_t, \mathbf{0}; \mathbf{0}, \mathbf{m}_{t+1}]$, and $\mathcal{K}_{t+1}^q$ and $\mathcal{K}_{t+1}^a$ are shown in Eq. (7).

By exchanging the rows and columns of $\mathbf{S}_{t+1}$ (i.e., moving all the features at time t into the upper-left corner), we have

$$\mathbf{S}_{t+1} = \mathbf{E}_1 \begin{bmatrix} \mathbf{S}_t & \mathbf{S}_1 \\ \mathbf{S}_2 & \mathbf{S}_3 \end{bmatrix} \mathbf{E}_1' \tag{14}$$

where $\mathbf{S}_1$, $\mathbf{S}_2$, $\mathbf{S}_3$ and $\mathbf{E}_1$ are specified in Eq. (9), Eq. (10), Eq. (11) and Eq. (13), respectively.

Applying Matrix Inversion Lemma [24, 14] to Eq. (14), we have that

$$\begin{aligned} \mathbf{S}_{t+1}^{-1} &= \left(\mathbf{E}_1 \begin{bmatrix} \mathbf{S}_t & \mathbf{S}_1 \\ \mathbf{S}_2 & \mathbf{S}_3 \end{bmatrix} \mathbf{E}_1'\right)^{-1} \\ &= \mathbf{E}_1 \begin{bmatrix} \mathbf{S}_t^{-1} + \mathbf{S}_t^{-1}\mathbf{S}_1\mathbf{D}\mathbf{S}_2\mathbf{S}_t^{-1} & -\mathbf{S}_t^{-1}\mathbf{S}_1\mathbf{D} \\ -\mathbf{S}_3^{-1}\mathbf{S}_2\mathbf{S}_t^{-1}(\mathbf{I} + \mathbf{S}_1\mathbf{D}\mathbf{S}_2\mathbf{S}_t^{-1}) & \mathbf{D} \end{bmatrix} \mathbf{E}_1' \end{aligned}$$

where $\mathbf{D}$ is specified in Eq. (12), and $\mathbf{E}_1^{-1} = \mathbf{E}_1'$.

Based on the updated $\mathbf{S}_{t+1}^{-1}$, we have that

$$\begin{aligned} \boldsymbol{\beta}_{t+1}^* &= \mathbf{S}_{t+1}^{-1} \begin{bmatrix} \mathbf{Y}_t^q \\ \mathbf{y}_{t+1}^q \\ \mathbf{Y}_t^a \\ \mathbf{y}_{t+1}^a \end{bmatrix} \\ &= \mathbf{E}_1 \begin{bmatrix} \mathbf{S}_t^{-1} + \mathbf{S}_t^{-1}\mathbf{S}_1\mathbf{D}\mathbf{S}_2\mathbf{S}_t^{-1} & -\mathbf{S}_t^{-1}\mathbf{S}_1\mathbf{D} \\ -\mathbf{S}_3^{-1}\mathbf{S}_2\mathbf{S}_t^{-1}(\mathbf{I} + \mathbf{S}_1\mathbf{D}\mathbf{S}_2\mathbf{S}_t^{-1}) & \mathbf{D} \end{bmatrix} \begin{bmatrix} \mathbf{Y}_t^q \\ \mathbf{Y}_t^a \\ \mathbf{y}_{t+1}^q \\ \mathbf{y}_{t+1}^a \end{bmatrix} \\ &= \mathbf{E}_1 \begin{bmatrix} \boldsymbol{\beta}_t + \mathbf{S}_t^{-1}\mathbf{S}_1\mathbf{D}(\mathbf{S}_2\boldsymbol{\beta}_t - [\mathbf{y}_{t+1}^q; \mathbf{y}_{t+1}^a]) \\ -\mathbf{S}_3^{-1}\mathbf{S}_2(\boldsymbol{\beta}_t + \mathbf{S}_t^{-1}\mathbf{S}_1\mathbf{D}\mathbf{S}_2\boldsymbol{\beta}_t) + \mathbf{D}[\mathbf{y}_{t+1}^q; \mathbf{y}_{t+1}^a] \end{bmatrix} \\ &= \boldsymbol{\beta}_{t+1} \end{aligned}$$

which completes the proof. □

The time complexity and space complexity of our LIP-KIM is summarized in the following lemma, which basically states that LIP-KIM requires $O((n^q + n^a)^2)$ time and $O((n^q + n^a)^2)$ space.

LEMMA 3. **Complexity of LIP-KIM.** *The time complexity of Alg. 1 is* $O((n^q+n^a)^2(i^q+i^a)+(n^q+n^a)(i^q+i^a)^2+(i^q+i^a)^3+(n^q i^q+n^a i^a+(i^q)^2+(i^a)^2)d)$; *the space complexity of Alg. 1 is* $O((n^q+n^a+i^q+i^a)^2+(n^q+n^a+i^q+i^a)d)$.

PROOF. Omitted for brevity. □

Since i^q and i^a are usually much smaller than n^q and n^a, and the feature dimension d is a fixed constant, the time and space complexity of LIP-KIM can be re-written as $O((n^q+n^a)^2)$. Compared with LIP-KM which is cubic in time, LIP-KIM is much more efficient. However, it is still quadratic wrt the total number of the training examples. In the next two subsections, we propose two approximate algorithms to further speed-up the computation.

3.3 LIP-KIMA Algorithm

The reason that LIP-KIM is quadratic is that we need to maintain two kernel matrices of the size $n_q \times n_q$ and $n_a \times n_a$, respectively. In order to avoid quadratic cost for both time and space, we need an efficient way to approximate/compress the full kernel matrices and update them over time.

Take the kernel matrix for questions as an example. Notice that $\mathcal{K}_t^q$ is symmetric and semi-positive definite; therefore, we can approximate it by eigen-decomposition: $\mathcal{K}_t^q \approx \mathbf{U}_t^q \Lambda_t^q (\mathbf{U}_t^q)'$, where $\mathbf{U}_t^q$ is an $n^q \times r$ orthogonal matrix, and Λ_t^q is an $r \times r$ diagonal matrix whose entries are the largest r eigenvalues of $\mathcal{K}_t^q$. By doing so, we reduce the space cost from $O(n_q^2)$ to $O(n_q r)$.

When new questions arrive at time $t+1$, we have the new kernel matrix $\mathcal{K}_{t+1}^q$ as shown in Eq. (7). We approximate $\mathcal{K}_{t+1}^q$ by Nyström method [10] as

$$
\begin{aligned}
\mathcal{K}_{t+1}^q &= \begin{bmatrix} \mathcal{K}_t^q & (\mathbf{k}_{t+1}^q)' \\ \mathbf{k}_{t+1}^q & \mathbf{h}_{t+1}^q \end{bmatrix} \\
&\approx \begin{bmatrix} \mathcal{K}_t^q \\ \mathbf{k}_{t+1}^q \end{bmatrix} (\mathcal{K}_t^q)^{-1} \begin{bmatrix} \mathcal{K}_t^q \\ \mathbf{k}_{t+1}^q \end{bmatrix}' \\
&\approx \begin{bmatrix} \mathcal{K}_t^q \\ \mathbf{k}_{t+1}^q \end{bmatrix} \mathbf{U}_t^q (\Lambda_t^q)^{-1} \Lambda_t^q (\Lambda_t^q)^{-1} (\mathbf{U}_t^q)' \begin{bmatrix} \mathcal{K}_t^q \\ \mathbf{k}_{t+1}^q \end{bmatrix}' \\
&= \begin{bmatrix} \mathbf{U}_t^q \\ \mathbf{k}_{t+1}^q \mathbf{U}_t^q (\Lambda_t^q)^{-1} \end{bmatrix} \Lambda_t^q \begin{bmatrix} \mathbf{U}_t^q \\ \mathbf{k}_{t+1}^q \mathbf{U}_t^q (\Lambda_t^q)^{-1} \end{bmatrix}' \\
&= \mathbf{X}_1 \Lambda_t^q \mathbf{X}_1'
\end{aligned}
\tag{15}
$$

where we define $\mathbf{X}_1$ as the $(n^q+i^q)\times r$ matrix $[\mathbf{U}_t^q; \mathbf{k}_{t+1}^q \mathbf{U}_t^q (\Lambda_t^q)^{-1}]$.

To make the decomposition of $\mathcal{K}_{t+1}^q$ reusable for future updates, we need to find the eigen-decomposition form of $\mathcal{K}_{t+1}^q$. To this end, we first perform the Singular Value Decomposition (SVD) on $\mathbf{X}_1$ as $\mathbf{X}_1 = \mathbf{P}\Lambda_1^q \mathbf{Q}'$, where both $\mathbf{P}$ and $\mathbf{Q}$ are orthogonal. Next, we perform eigen-decomposition on an $r\times r$ matrix $\mathbf{X}_2 = \Lambda_1^q \mathbf{Q}' \Lambda_t^q \mathbf{Q} \Lambda_1^q$, that is, $\mathbf{X}_2 = \mathbf{V}\Lambda^q \mathbf{V}'$.

Based on the above two steps, we have the approximate eigen-decomposition of the new kernel matrix $\mathcal{K}_{t+1}^q$ as follows

$$
\begin{aligned}
\mathcal{K}_{t+1}^q &\approx \mathbf{X}_1 \Lambda_t^q \mathbf{X}_1' \\
&= \mathbf{P}(\Lambda_1^q \mathbf{Q}' \Lambda_t^q \mathbf{Q} \Lambda_1^q)\mathbf{P}' \\
&= \mathbf{P}(\mathbf{V}\Lambda^q \mathbf{V}')\mathbf{P}' \\
&= \mathbf{U}_{t+1}^q \Lambda_{t+1}^q (\mathbf{U}_{t+1}^q)'
\end{aligned}
\tag{16}
$$

where we define $\mathbf{U}_{t+1}^q = \mathbf{PV}$ and $\Lambda_{t+1}^q = \Lambda^q$. Notice that $\mathbf{U}_{t+1}^q$ is orthogonal because both $\mathbf{P}$ and $\mathbf{V}$ are orthogonal.

We use the same approach to approximate and update the kernel matrix for answers: $\mathcal{K}_{t+1}^a \approx \mathbf{U}_{t+1}^a \Lambda_{t+1}^a (\mathbf{U}_{t+1}^a)'$. We further define the following notations to simplify the algorithm description

$$
\begin{aligned}
\mathbf{U} &= [\mathbf{U}_{t+1}^q, \mathbf{0}; \mathbf{0}, \mathbf{U}_{t+1}^a] \\
\Lambda &= [\Lambda_{t+1}^q, \mathbf{0}; \mathbf{0}, \Lambda_{t+1}^a] \\
\mathbf{G} &= [\mathbf{I}, -\mathbf{M}_{t+1}; -\mathbf{M}_{t+1}', \mathbf{M}_{t+1}'\mathbf{M}_{t+1}]
\end{aligned}
\tag{17}
$$

Algorithm 2 The LIP-KIMA Algorithm.

Input: $\mathbf{U}_t^q$, Λ_t^q, $\mathbf{U}_t^a$, Λ_t^a, $\mathbf{F}_t^q$, $\mathbf{f}_{t+1}^q$, $\mathbf{F}_t^a$, $\mathbf{f}_{t+1}^a$, $\mathbf{Y}_t^q$, $\mathbf{y}_{t+1}^q$, $\mathbf{Y}_t^a$, $\mathbf{y}_{t+1}^a$, $\mathbf{M}_t$ and $\mathbf{m}_{t+1}$
Output: $\boldsymbol{\beta}_{t+1}$, $\mathbf{U}_{t+1}^q$, Λ_{t+1}^q, $\mathbf{U}_{t+1}^a$ and Λ_{t+1}^a
compute the new kernels $\mathbf{k}_{t+1}^q$ and $\mathbf{k}_{t+1}^a$ in Eq. (7);
update $\mathbf{U}_{t+1}^q$, Λ_{t+1}^q, $\mathbf{U}_{t+1}^a$ and Λ_{t+1}^a as Eq. (16);
define $\mathbf{U}$, Λ and $\mathbf{G}$ as Eq. (17);
define $\mathbf{A}$ and $\mathbf{B}$ as $[\mathbf{U}, \theta\mathbf{GU}]$ and $[\Lambda\mathbf{U}'; \Lambda\mathbf{U}']$;
update $\boldsymbol{\beta}_{t+1}$ as $\frac{1}{\lambda}(\mathbf{I} - \mathbf{A}(\lambda\mathbf{I}+\mathbf{BA})^{-1}\mathbf{B})\begin{bmatrix}\mathbf{Y}_{t+1}^q \\ \mathbf{Y}_{t+1}^a\end{bmatrix}$;
return $\boldsymbol{\beta}_{t+1}$, $\mathbf{U}_{t+1}^q$, Λ_{t+1}^q, $\mathbf{U}_{t+1}^a$ and Λ_{t+1}^a;

Then, we have the following approximation for the $\mathbf{S}_{t+1}$ matrix defined in Eq. (8)

$$
\begin{aligned}
\mathbf{S}_{t+1} &= \begin{bmatrix} (\theta+1)\mathcal{K}_{t+1}^q + \lambda\mathbf{I} & -\theta\mathbf{M}_{t+1}\mathcal{K}_{t+1}^a \\ -\theta\mathbf{M}_{t+1}'\mathcal{K}_{t+1}^q & \mathcal{K}_{t+1}^a + \theta\mathbf{M}_{t+1}'\mathbf{M}_{t+1}\mathcal{K}_{t+1}^a + \lambda\mathbf{I} \end{bmatrix} \\
&= \lambda\mathbf{I} + (\mathbf{I}+\theta\mathbf{G})\begin{bmatrix} \mathcal{K}_{t+1}^q & \mathbf{0} \\ \mathbf{0} & \mathcal{K}_{t+1}^a \end{bmatrix} \\
&\approx \lambda\mathbf{I} + \mathbf{U}\Lambda\mathbf{U}' + \theta\mathbf{GU}\Lambda\mathbf{U}' \\
&= \lambda\mathbf{I} + \mathbf{AB}
\end{aligned}
\tag{18}
$$

where we define $\mathbf{A} = [\mathbf{U}, \theta\mathbf{GU}]$ and $\mathbf{B} = [\Lambda\mathbf{U}'; \Lambda\mathbf{U}']$.

Finally, applying Matrix Inversion Lemma to Eq. (18), we have the coefficients $\boldsymbol{\beta}_{t+1}$

$$
\begin{aligned}
\boldsymbol{\beta}_{t+1} &= \mathbf{S}_{t+1}^{-1}\begin{bmatrix}\mathbf{Y}_{t+1}^q \\ \mathbf{Y}_{t+1}^a\end{bmatrix} \\
&\approx (\lambda\mathbf{I}+\mathbf{AB})^{-1}\begin{bmatrix}\mathbf{Y}_{t+1}^q \\ \mathbf{Y}_{t+1}^a\end{bmatrix} \\
&= \frac{1}{\lambda}(\mathbf{I} - \mathbf{A}(\lambda\mathbf{I}+\mathbf{BA})^{-1}\mathbf{B})\begin{bmatrix}\mathbf{Y}_{t+1}^q \\ \mathbf{Y}_{t+1}^a\end{bmatrix}
\end{aligned}
\tag{19}
$$

The complete algorithm of LIP-KIMA is summarized in Alg. 2. As we can see, in addition to $\boldsymbol{\beta}_{t+1}$, the only variables we need to update are $\mathbf{U}_t^q$, Λ_t^q, $\mathbf{U}_t^a$ and Λ_t^a. Compared to Alg. 1, we do not need to store $\boldsymbol{\beta}_t$; instead we need to store $\mathbf{Y}_t^q$ and $\mathbf{Y}_t^a$. More importantly, we do not need to store $\mathbf{S}_t$; instead, we only need to store the much smaller matrices of $\mathbf{U}_t^q$, Λ_t^q, $\mathbf{U}_t^a$ and Λ_t^a.

*Algorithm Analysis.*The effectiveness of LIP-KIMA is summarized in Lemma 4. According to Lemma 4, there are two possible places where we could introduce the approximation error in the LIP-KIMA algorithm, including (a) eigen-decomposition for the $\mathcal{K}_t$ and (b) the Nyström method for $\mathcal{K}_{t+1}$. Notice that if we only do eigen-decomposition at $t=1$, such approximation error might be accumulated and amplified over time. In practice, we could 're-start' the algorithm every few time ticks, that is, to re-compute (as opposed to approximate) the eigen-decomposition for the current kernel matrix.

LEMMA 4. **Effectiveness of LIP-KIMA.** *Let* $\boldsymbol{\beta}_{t+1}^*$ *be the output of Eq. (5) at time* $t+1$, *and* $\boldsymbol{\beta}_{t+1}$ *be the output of Alg. 2 updated from time* t *to* $t+1$, *we have* $\boldsymbol{\beta}_{t+1} = \boldsymbol{\beta}_{t+1}^*$ *if* $\mathcal{K}_t = \mathbf{U}_t\Lambda_t(\mathbf{U}_t)'$ *and* $\mathbf{h}_{t+1} = \mathbf{k}_{t+1}(\mathcal{K}_t)^{-1}(\mathbf{k}_{t+1})'$ *hold for both questions and answers.*

PROOF. Omitted for brevity. □

The time complexity and space complexity of Alg. 2 is summarized in the following lemma. It basically says that the LIP-KIMA algorithm requires *linear* time and space wrt the total number of questions and answers.

LEMMA 5. **Complexity of LIP-KIMA**. *The time complexity of Alg. 2 is* $O((n^q + n^a + i^q + i^a)r^2 + r^3 + (n^q i^q + n^a i^a)d)$*; the space complexity of Alg. 2 is* $O((n^q + n^a + i^q + i^a)d + (n^q + n^a + i^q + i^a)r + r^2)$.

PROOF. Omitted for brevity. □

Since i^q and i^a are usually much smaller than n^q and n^a, and the low rank r and feature dimension d are fixed constants, the time complexity and space complexity of Alg. 2 can be re-written as $O(n^q + n^a)$ in terms of the total number of questions and answers.

3.4 LIP-KIMAA Algorithm

Compared with LIP-KIM, LIP-KIMA is much more scalable, being *linear* in terms of both time and space complexity. However, if the new training examples arrive in a stream-like, ever-growing fashion, a linear algorithm might be still too expensive. To address this issue, we further present the LIP-KIMAA algorithm to reduce the complexity to be *sub-linear*.

Our LIP-KIMAA is built upon LIP-KIMA. The main difference between LIP-KIMAA and LIP-KIMA is that we add an additional filtering step between Step 1 and Step 2 in Alg. 2. That is, when new questions and answers arrive at time $t+1$, we first treat them as test set and apply the existing model at time t on this test set. Based on the prediction results, we only add the questions and answers whose prediction error is larger than a given threshold *th*. Notice that the complexity of LIP-KIMA is linear wrt the number of questions and answers; as a result, our LIP-KIMAA scales linearly wrt the number of *remaining* questions and answers after the filtering steps. Therefore, LIP-KIMAA scales sub-linearly wrt to the total number of questions and answers in both time and space. We omit the detailed algorithm for brevity.

4. VARIANTS

The proposed LIP-KIM and its two approximate algorithms (LIP-KIMA and LIP-LIMAA) are *comprehensive*. In terms of the modeling power, they capture all the three aspects (non-linearity, coupling, and dynamics). In this section, we show that our algorithms are also *flexible*. That is, if only a subset of these three aspects matter with the prediction performance for some applications, our algorithms can be naturally adapted to these special cases. We briefly discuss some of these variants, and then summarize the algorithms in Fig. 1.

4.1 Variant 1: Linear Model LIP-IM

If we only consider the coupling and dynamic aspects (i.e., ignoring the non-linear aspect), our LIP-KIM can be simplified as the LIP-IM algorithm. Essentially, LIP-IM aims to efficiently update the solution of Eq. (1)

$$\alpha = \begin{bmatrix} (\theta+1)(\mathbf{F}^q)'\mathbf{F}^q + \lambda\mathbf{I} & -\theta(\mathbf{F}^q)'\mathbf{M}\mathbf{F}^a \\ -\theta(\mathbf{F}^a)'\mathbf{M}'\mathbf{F}^q & (\mathbf{F}^a)'\mathbf{F}^a + \theta(\mathbf{F}^a)'\mathbf{M}'\mathbf{M}\mathbf{F}^a + \lambda\mathbf{I} \end{bmatrix}^{-1} \begin{bmatrix} (\mathbf{F}^q)'\mathbf{Y}^q \\ (\mathbf{F}^a)'\mathbf{Y}^a \end{bmatrix}$$

where $\alpha = [\alpha^q; \alpha^a]$.

In this case, the $\mathbf{S}_t$ matrix becomes

$$\mathbf{S}_t = \begin{bmatrix} (\theta+1)(\mathbf{F}_t^q)'\mathbf{F}_t^q + \lambda\mathbf{I} & -\theta(\mathbf{F}_t^q)'\mathbf{M}_t\mathbf{F}_t^a \\ -\theta(\mathbf{F}_t^a)'\mathbf{M}_t'\mathbf{F}_t^q & (\mathbf{F}_t^a)'\mathbf{F}_t^a + \theta(\mathbf{F}_t^a)'\mathbf{M}_t'\mathbf{M}_t\mathbf{F}_t^a + \lambda\mathbf{I} \end{bmatrix}$$

When new questions and answers arrive at time $t+1$, we define the $\mathbf{L}$ matrix and the $\mathbf{R}$ matrix as

$$\mathbf{L} = \begin{bmatrix} (\theta+1)(\mathbf{f}_{t+1}^q)' & -\theta(\mathbf{f}_{t+1}^q)' & \mathbf{0} & \mathbf{0} \\ \mathbf{0} & \mathbf{0} & -\theta(\mathbf{f}_{t+1}^a)'\mathbf{m}_{t+1}' & \left[(\mathbf{f}_{t+1}^a)', \theta(\mathbf{f}_{t+1}^a)'\mathbf{m}_{t+1}'\right] \end{bmatrix}$$

$$\mathbf{R} = \begin{bmatrix} \mathbf{f}_{t+1}^q & \mathbf{0} \\ \mathbf{0} & \mathbf{m}_{t+1}\mathbf{f}_{t+1}^a \\ \mathbf{f}_{t+1}^q & \mathbf{0} \\ \mathbf{0} & \left[\mathbf{f}_{t+1}^a; \mathbf{m}_{t+1}\mathbf{f}_{t+1}^a\right] \end{bmatrix}$$

As we can see, both $\mathbf{L}$ and $\mathbf{R}$ are only based on new observations $\mathbf{f}_{t+1}^q$, $\mathbf{f}_{t+1}^a$ and $\mathbf{m}_{t+1}$.

Next, we further define matrix $\mathbf{C} = \mathbf{S}_t^{-1}\mathbf{L}(\mathbf{I} + \mathbf{R}\mathbf{S}_t^{-1}\mathbf{L})^{-1}\mathbf{R}$, and we can show that the model can be updated as follows

$$\begin{aligned} \mathbf{S}_{t+1}^{-1} &= (\mathbf{I} - \mathbf{C})\mathbf{S}_t^{-1} \\ \alpha_{t+1} &= (\mathbf{I} - \mathbf{C})\left(\alpha_t + \mathbf{S}_t^{-1}\begin{bmatrix} (\mathbf{f}_{t+1}^q)'\mathbf{y}_{t-1}^q \\ (\mathbf{f}_{t+1}^a)'\mathbf{y}_{t+1}^a \end{bmatrix}\right) \end{aligned}$$

Remarks. Notice that compared with LIP-KIM, LIP-IM is much more efficient since it only needs to compute the inverse of a much smaller $(3i^q + i^a) \times (3i^q + i^a)$ matrix (see the computation of matrix $\mathbf{C}$). By ignoring the smaller terms (i.e., i^q and i^a), the overall time complexity of LIP-IM is $O(d^2)$ where d indicates feature dimension; on the other hand, directly updating the model would require $O((n^q + n^a)d + d^3)$ time. In the meanwhile, by a similar procedure as the proof for Theorem 1, we can show that LIP-IM finds the *exact* solution of Eq. (1).

4.2 Variant 2: Approximate LIP-KI

If we only consider the non-linearity and dynamics aspects (i.e., ignoring the coupling aspect), our LIP-KIMA can be further simplified. Take the prediction for questions as an example. With the approximate eigen-decomposition by Eq. (16): $\mathcal{K}_{t-1}^q \approx \mathbf{U}_{t+1}^q \Lambda_{t+1}^q (\mathbf{U}_{t+1}^q)'$, we can update the coefficients β_{t+1}^q as follows

$$\begin{aligned} \beta_{t+1}^q &\approx (\mathbf{U}_{t+1}^q \Lambda_{t+1}^q (\mathbf{U}_{t+1}^q)' + \lambda\mathbf{I})^{-1}\mathbf{Y}_{t+1} \\ &= \mathbf{U}_{t+1}^q \Lambda_3^q (\mathbf{U}_{t+1}^q)'\mathbf{Y}_{t+1} \end{aligned}$$

where Λ_3^q is still a diagonal matrix with $\Lambda_3^q(i,i) = 1/(\Lambda_{t-1}^q(i,i) + \lambda)$.

Remarks. Although sharing the same linear time complexity as LIP-KIMA, this variant is even more efficient in practice since it does not need any matrix inversion at all.

4.3 Variant 3: LIP-KIM with Only Questions

Next, we discuss a special case of LIP-KIM when only new questions arrive at time $t+1$. Compared to Alg. 1, we can simplify the following notations

$$\begin{aligned} \mathbf{S}_1 &= \begin{bmatrix} (\theta+1)(\mathbf{k}_{t+1}^q)' \\ -\theta\mathbf{M}_t'(\mathbf{k}_{t+1}^q)' \end{bmatrix} \\ \mathbf{S}_2 &= \begin{bmatrix} (\theta+1)\mathbf{k}_{t+1}^q & \mathbf{0}_{i^q \times (n^q + n^a)} \end{bmatrix} \\ \mathbf{S}_3 &= (\theta+1)\mathbf{h}_{t+1}^q + \lambda\mathbf{I} \\ \mathbf{E}_1 &= \begin{bmatrix} \mathbf{I}_{n_q \times n_q} & \mathbf{0} & \mathbf{0} \\ \mathbf{0} & \mathbf{0} & \mathbf{I}_{i_q \times i_q} \\ \mathbf{0} & \mathbf{I}_{n_a \times n_a} & \mathbf{0} \end{bmatrix} \end{aligned}$$

Then the model can be updated as

$$\begin{aligned} \mathbf{S}_{t+1}^{-1} &= \mathbf{E}_1\begin{bmatrix} \mathbf{S}_t^{-1} + \mathbf{S}_t^{-1}\mathbf{S}_1\mathbf{D}\mathbf{S}_2\mathbf{S}_t^{-1} & -\mathbf{S}_t^{-1}\mathbf{S}_1\mathbf{D} \\ -\mathbf{S}_3^{-1}\mathbf{S}_2\mathbf{S}_t^{-1}(\mathbf{I} + \mathbf{S}_1\mathbf{D}\mathbf{S}_2\mathbf{S}_t^{-1}) & \mathbf{D} \end{bmatrix}\mathbf{E}_1' \\ \beta_{t+1} &= \mathbf{E}_1\begin{bmatrix} \beta_t + \mathbf{S}_t^{-1}\mathbf{S}_1\mathbf{D}(\mathbf{S}_2\beta_t - \mathbf{y}_{t+1}^q) \\ -\mathbf{S}_3^{-1}\mathbf{S}_2(\beta_t + \mathbf{S}_t^{-1}\mathbf{S}_1\mathbf{D}\mathbf{S}_2\beta_t) + \mathbf{D}\mathbf{y}_{t+1}^q \end{bmatrix} \end{aligned}$$

Remarks. The time complexity of this variant is $O((n^q + n^a)^2 i^q + (n^q + n^a)(i^q)^2 + (i^q)^3 + (n^q i^q + (i^q)^2)d)$, which can be re-written as $O((n^q + n^a)^2)$ by ignoring smaller terms of i^q and d. The correctness of this variant can also be shown by following a similar procedure as the proof for Theorem 1.

Table 2: The summarization of the algorithms from the genealogy graph in Fig. 1. The complexity is the time complexity for updating the model at each time tick, where the n is the totally number of the training examples and those smaller terms are omitted for clarity. The right five columns are the proposed algorithms in this paper.

	SVR	KRR (LIP-K)	RKRR (LIP-KI)	CoPs (LIP-M)	LIP-IM	LIP-KM	LIP-KIM	LIP-KIMA	LIP-KIMAA
Non-linearity	✓	✓	✓	x	x	✓	✓	✓	✓
Coupling	x	x	x	✓	✓	✓	✓	✓	✓
Dynamics	x	x	✓	x	✓	x	✓	✓	✓
Complexity	$\geqslant O(n^2)$	$O(n^3)$	$O(n^2)$	$O(n)$	$O(1)$	$O(n^3)$	$O(n^2)$	$O(n)$	$< O(n)$

Table 3: The statistics of SO and Math data sets.

Data	Questions	Answers	Users	Votes
SO	1,966,272	4,282,570	756,695	14,056,000
Math	16,638	32,876	12,526	202,932

4.4 Summarization

Finally, we make a comparison of different algorithms in Fig. 1 in terms of their modeling power and efficiency. The results are summarized in Table 2. In this table, we first check whether a given algorithm captures each of the three desired aspects (non-linearity, coupling, and dynamics). As we can see, only our LIP-KIM, LIP-KIMA, and LIP-KIMAA algorithms meet this requirement. We also summarize the time complexity of the algorithm for updating the model at each time tick, where the smaller terms (e.g., the feature dimensionality d, the number of new training examples i^q, i^a, etc) are omitted for clarity. For non-linear algorithms like KRR [25], support vector regression (SVR) [9, 7], RKRR [11], LIP-KM and LIP-KIM, they need at least quadratic time for the model training because they typically need to maintain the kernel matrix. Such a complexity is unaffordable in many CQA sites. On the other hand, the time complexity of the proposed LIP-KIMA and LIP-KIMAA algorithms is *linear* and *sub-linear* wrt the total number of questions and answers, respectively.

5. EXPERIMENTS

In this section, we present the experimental evaluations. The experiments are designed to answer the following questions:

- *Effectiveness*: How accurate are the proposed algorithms for predicting the long-term impact of questions/answers?
- *Efficiency*: How scalable are the proposed algorithms?

5.1 Experiment Setup

We use the data from two real CQA sites, i.e., Stack Overflow (SO) and Mathematics Stack Exchange (Math), to evaluate our algorithms. They are popular CQA sites for programming and math, respectively. The statistics of the two data sets are summarized in Table 3.

We use both content and contextual features. For content features, we adopt the "bag of words" model to extract content features after removing the infrequent words. This model is widely used in natural language processing where the frequency of each word is used as a feature for training. In addition, we adopt some commonly used contextual features in the literature, including the questioner's reputation at question creation time, the answerer's reputation at answer creation time, the length of the question/answer, the number of questioner's previous questions at question creation time, and the number of answerer's previous answers at answer creation time. For these features, we can extract them at the moment when the question/answer is posted. For other contextual features, we need to choose a short time window by the end of which the voting score is predicted. With such a fixed time window, we can include some time-related features such as the number of comments/answers received during the fixed time window. In this work, we fix this time window as 24 hours. Overall, we have 4,180 and 4,444 features for Math data and SO data, respectively (i.e., $d = 4,180$ for Math data and $d = 4,444$ for SO data). For the kernel matrix, we adopt the cosine kernel function due to the sparsity of our feature matrix.

For long-term impact, we restrict our attention to predict the impact of a question/answer after it is posted for six months. For each post in the data set, there are several choices to measure impact including the number of pageviews, the number of favorites, and the user voting score (which is the difference between the number of up-votes and the number of down-votes on the post). In this work, we choose the voting score for the following two reasons. First, we conduct a survey, asking different users about which is the best metric as the long-term impact measure of CQA posts; and most of the users (79.4%) choose the voting score. Second, to some extent, the voting score of a question/answer resembles the number of the citations that a research paper receives in the scientific publication domain. It reflects the net number of users who have a positive attitude toward it. In addition, we also measured the correlation between the three choices and found that all of them are strongly positive correlated. Thus, we expect that our algorithms could also be used to predict the other two metrics (i.e., pageviews and favorites). We normalize the voting scores into the range of $[0, 1]$.

To evaluate the dynamic aspect of our algorithms, we start with a small initial training set, and gradually add new examples into the training set in chronological order. For Math data, we start with 5% initial data, add 5% data for each update, and use the latest 10% data as the test set. For SO data whose size is much larger than the Math data, we start with 0.1% initial data, add 0.1% data for each update, and use the latest 0.1% data as the test set.

For evaluation metrics, we adopt the root mean square error (RMSE) between the real impact and the estimated impact for effectiveness, and the wall-clock time for efficiency. All the efficiency experiments were run on a machine with eight 3.4GHz Intel Cores and 24GB memory.

Repeatability of Experimental Results. Both data sets are officially published and publicly available[5]. Furthermore, we will make the code of the proposed algorithms as well as the extracted feature files publicly available. For all the results reported in this section, the specific parameter settings are as follows. We set $\lambda = \theta = 1$ for Math data and $\lambda = \theta = 0.1$ for SO data. For the low rank r in LIP-KIMA and LIP-KIMAA, we set it as 10. For LIP-KIMAA, we set $th = 0.22$ for Math data and $th = 0.18$ for SO data.

5.2 Effectiveness Results

We first compare the effectiveness of the proposed algorithms with two state-of-the-art non-linear regression methods, i.e., kernel

[5] http://blog.stackoverflow.com/category/cc-wiki-dump/

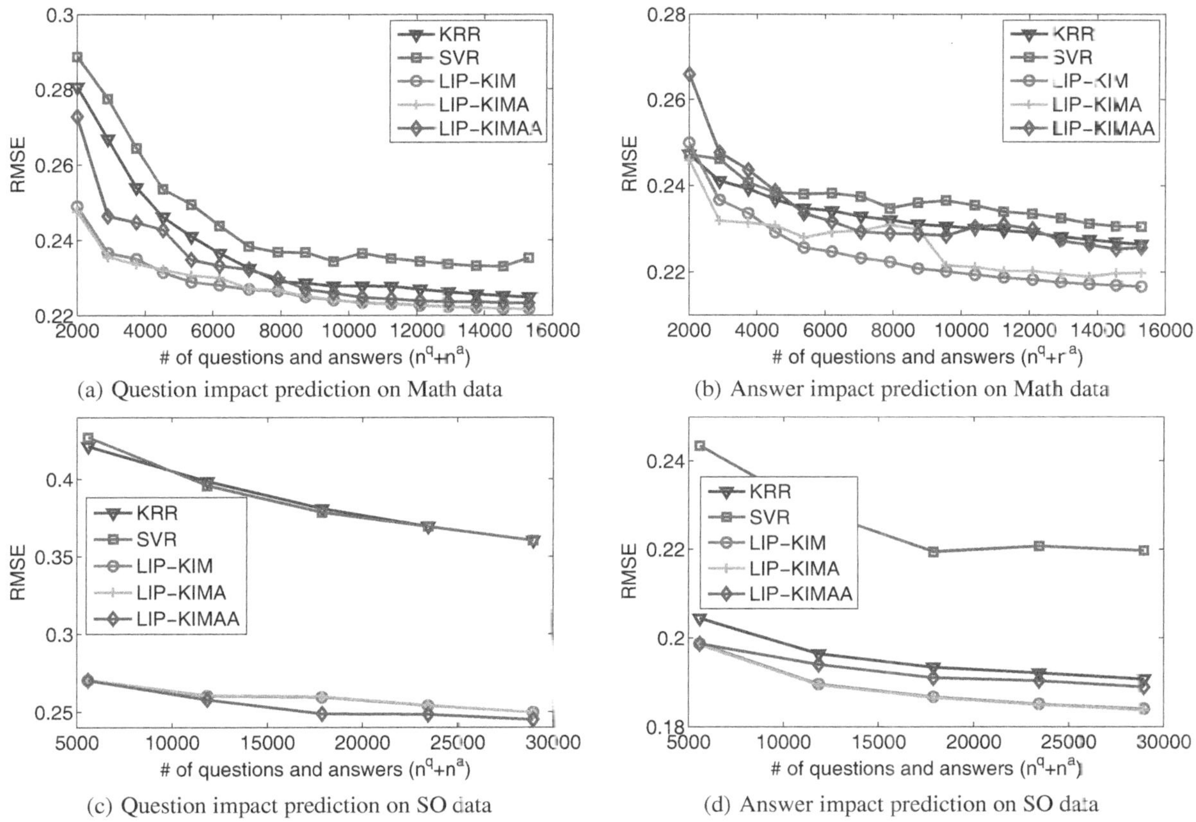

(a) Question impact prediction on Math data

(b) Answer impact prediction on Math data

(c) Question impact prediction on SO data

(d) Answer impact prediction on SO data

Figure 2: The effectiveness comparisons. Lower is better. The proposed algorithms outperform both SVR and KRR.

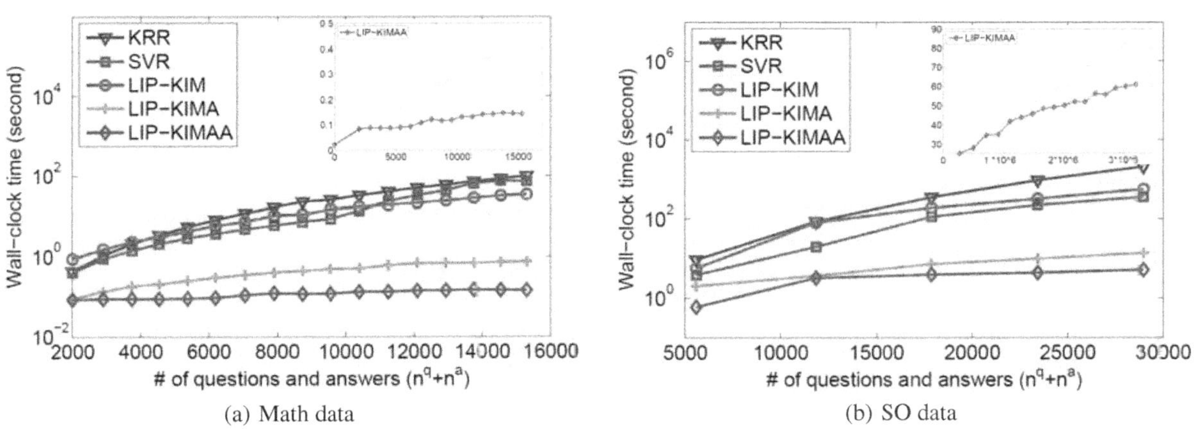

(a) Math data

(b) SO data

Figure 3: The speed comparisons. The proposed LIP-KIMA and LIP-KIMAA are much faster. Furthermore, LIP-KIMAA scales sub-linearly (in the upper-right corner).

ridge regression (KRR) [25] and support vector regression (SVR) [7]. The prediction results of questions and answers on the two data sets are shown in Fig. 2. On SO data, we only report the first few points because some of the algorithms (e.g., KRR) cannot finish training within 1 hour. We do not report the results by linear models (e.g., linear ridge regression) since their performance (RMSE) is much worse than SVR.

We make several observations from Fig. 2. First, the proposed LIP-KIM algorithm performs the best in most of the cases. For example, when the size of training set increases to 90% on the Math data, LIP-KIM improves the SVR method by 5.7% for questions and 6.0% for answers. On SO data, LIP-KIM improves the KRR method by up to 35.8% for questions and 3.6% for answers. This indicates that the coupling aspect indeed helps in impact prediction. Second, the performance of the proposed LIP-KIMA algorithm is close to LIP-KIM. This result indicates that while it reduces the time complexity from quadratic to linear, the approximation method introduces little performance loss. Finally, although not as good as LIP-KIM and LIP-KIMA, the LIP-KIMAA algo-

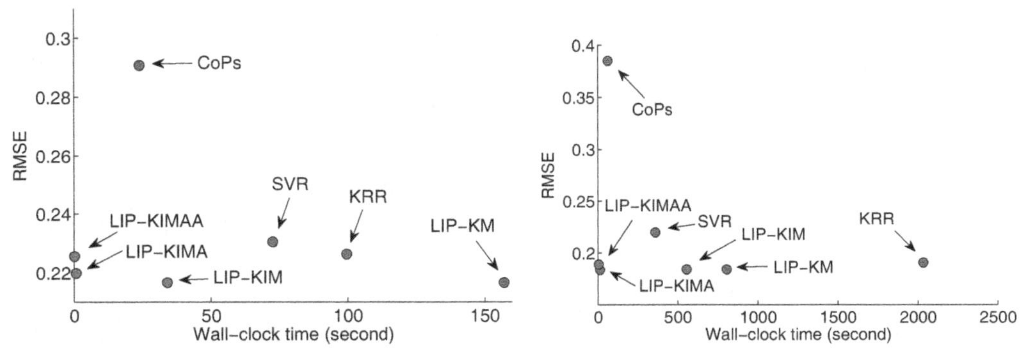

(a) Answer impact prediction on Math data (b) Answer impact prediction on SO data

Figure 4: The quality-speed balance-off. The proposed LIP-KIMA and LIP-KIMAA achieve a good balance between the prediction quality and the efficiency (in the left-bottom corner). Best viewed in color.

Table 4: Performance gain analysis. Smaller is better. All three aspects of non-linearity, coupling, and dynamics are helpful.

Questions/Answers	SO	Math
Ridge regression	0.4920/0.4409	0.2799/0.3860
LIP-K	0.4214/0.2044	0.2461/0.2368
LIP-KM	0.2704/0.1987	0.2314/0.2292
LIP-KIM	0.2595/0.1867	0.2249/0.2208

rithm is still better than the compared methods for most of the cases.

To further show the effects of all the three aspects (i.e., non-linearity, coupling, and dynamics), we analyze the performance gain in Table 4. In the table, LIP-K incorporates non-linearity into ridge regression, LIP-KM incorporates coupling into LIP-K, and LIP-KIM incorporates dynamics into LIP-KM. As we can see, all three aspects are helpful to improve the prediction performance.

5.3 Efficiency Results

Next, we compare the efficiency of the proposed algorithms with KRR and SVR in Fig. 3. Notice that the y-axis is in log scale. In Fig. 3, we also plot the results of LIP-KIMAA with y-axis in linear scale in the upper-right corner. We only report the results by LIP-KIMAA there because it is the only algorithm that can handle the entire SO data set.

As we can see from the figure, our LIP-KIMA and LIP-KIMAA are much faster than the other algorithms. In the upper-right corner, we can observe that the LIP-KIMAA scales *sub-linearly* wrt the total number of questions and answers. For instance, it only requires about 60 seconds when there are more than 3,000,000 questions and answers. In contrast, KRR requires more than 2,000 seconds when the size of the training set is about 30,000.

Finally, we study the quality-speed balance-off of different algorithms in Fig. 4. In the figure, we show the answer prediction results only. Similar results are observed in question prediction, and we omit the results for brevity. In Fig. 4, we plot the RMSE on the y-axis and the wall-clock time on the x-axis. We also plot the results of the linear co-prediction method CoPs [29] and LIP-KM. Ideally, we want an algorithm sitting in the left-bottom corner. As we can see, both our LIP-KIMA and LIP-KIMAA are in the left-bottom corner. For example, for answer impact prediction on the SO data, compared with SVR, LIP-KIMAA is 70x faster in wall-clock time and 14.0% better in RMSE. Overall, we recommend LIP-KIMAA in practice.

6. RELATED WORK

In this section, we briefly review related work including mining CQA sites and mining stream data.

Mining CQA Sites: There is a large body of existing work on mining CQA sites. For example, Li et al. [19] aim to predict question quality, which is defined as the combination of user attention, answer attempts and the arrival speed of the best answer. Jeon et al. [18] and Suryanto et al. [28] evaluate the usefulness of answer quality and incorporate it to improve retrieval performance. To predict the quality of both questions and answers, Agichtein et al. [2] develop a graph-based model to catch the relationships among users, Li et al. [20] adopt the co-training approach to employ both question features and answer features, and Bian et al. [5] propose to propagate the labels through user-question-answer graph so as to tackle the sparsity problem where only a small number of questions/answers are labeled. Recently, Anderson et al. [3] propose to predict the long-lasting value (i.e., the pageviews) of a question and its answers. How to predict the answer that the questioner will probably choose as the accepted answer is also well studied [22, 26, 1]. Overall, our work differs from these existing work at the methodology level. While most of the existing work treats the prediction problem as a single, and/or linear, and/or static problem, we view the problem from a comprehensive perspective and propose to incorporate all these important aspects into the prediction models.

Mining Stream Data: From the dynamic aspect, our LIP problem is related to stream mining [13] and time-series mining [12]. The main focus of existing stream/time-series mining work is on pattern discovery, clustering, and classification tasks. Chen et al. [8] and Ikonomovska et al. [17] study the regression problem in data streams; however, they still focus on a single and linear prediction problem. Several researchers also consider the non-linear and dynamic aspects in regression problem [11, 23]. Different from these existing work, we consider the coupling between questions and answers, and propose approximation methods to speed-up and scale-up the computation.

Other Related Work: There are several pieces of interesting work that are remotely related to our work. Liu et al. [21] propose the problem of CQA site searcher satisfaction, i.e., whether or not the answer in a CQA site satisfies the information searcher using the search engines. Shtok et al. [27] attempt to answer certain new questions by existing answers. The question routing problem (e.g., how to route the right question to the right answerer) is also an active research area [30, 16].

7. CONCLUSIONS

In this paper, we have proposed a family of algorithms to predict the long-term impact of questions/answers in CQA sites. The proposed algorithms enjoy three key advantages. First, they are *comprehensive* in the sense that our model naturally captures three key aspects (i.e., non-linearity, coupling, and dynamics) that matter with the long-term impact of a post. Second, they are *flexible* and *general*, being able to handle the special cases where only a fraction of these aspects are prominent. Third, they are *scalable* and *adaptive* to the newly arrived questions and answers. We analyze our algorithms in terms of *optimality*, *correctness*, and *complexity*, and reveal the intrinsic relationship among different algorithms. We conduct extensive experimental evaluations on two real CQA data sets to demonstrate the effectiveness and efficiency of our approaches.

8. ACKNOWLEDGMENTS

This work is supported by the National 863 Program of China (No. 2012AA011205), and the National Natural Science Foundation of China (No. 91318301, 61321491, 61100037). This material is partially supported by by the National Science Foundation under Grant No. IIS1017415, by the Army Research Laboratory under Cooperative Agreement Number W911NF-09-2-0053, by Defense Advanced Research Projects Agency (DARPA) under Contract Number W911NF-11-C-0200 and W911NF-12-C-0028, and by Region II University Transportation Center under the project number 49997-33 25.

The content of the information in this document does not necessarily reflect the position or the policy of the Government, and no official endorsement should be inferred. The U.S. Government is authorized to reproduce and distribute reprints for Government purposes notwithstanding any copyright notation here on.

9. REFERENCES

[1] L. Adamic, J. Zhang, E. Bakshy, and M. Ackerman. Knowledge sharing and yahoo answers: everyone knows something. In *WWW*, pages 665–674. ACM, 2008.

[2] E. Agichtein, C. Castillo, D. Donato, A. Gionis, and G. Mishne. Finding high-quality content in social media. In *WSDM*, pages 183–194. ACM, 2008.

[3] A. Anderson, D. Huttenlocher, J. Kleinberg, and J. Leskovec. Discovering value from community activity on focused question answering sites: a case study of stack overflow. In *KDD*, pages 850–858. ACM, 2012.

[4] N. Aronszajn. Theory of reproducing kernels. *Transactions of the American mathematical society*, 68(3):337–404, 1950.

[5] J. Bian, Y. Liu, D. Zhou, E. Agichtein, and H. Zha. Learning to recognize reliable users and content in social media with coupled mutual reinforcement. In *WWW*, pages 51–60. ACM, 2009.

[6] C. J. Burges. A tutorial on support vector machines for pattern recognition. *Data mining and knowledge discovery*, 2(2):121–167, 1998.

[7] C.-C. Chang and C.-J. Lin. Libsvm: a library for support vector machines. *ACM Transactions on Intelligent Systems and Technology*, 2(3):27, 2011.

[8] Y. Chen, G. Dong, J. Han, B. W. Wah, and J. Wang. Multi-dimensional regression analysis of time-series data streams. In *VLDB*, pages 323–334, 2002.

[9] R. Collobert and S. Bengio. Svmtorch: Support vector machines for large-scale regression problems. *The Journal of Machine Learning Research*, 1:143–160, 2001.

[10] P. Drineas and M. W. Mahoney. On the nyström method for approximating a gram matrix for improved kernel-based learning. *The Journal of Machine Learning Research*, 6:2153–2175, 2005.

[11] Y. Engel, S. Mannor, and R. Meir. The kernel recursive least-squares algorithm. *IEEE Transactions on Signal Processing*, 52(8):2275–2285, 2004.

[12] T.-c. Fu. A review on time series data mining. *Engineering Applications of Artificial Intelligence*, 24(1):164–181, 2011.

[13] M. M. Gaber, A. Zaslavsky, and S. Krishnaswamy. Mining data streams: a review. *ACM Sigmod Record*, 34(2):18–26, 2005.

[14] G. Golub and C. Van Loan. Matrix computations. 1996.

[15] S. S. Haykin. *Adaptive filter theory*. 2005

[16] D. Horowitz and S. Kamvar. The anatomy of a large-scale social search engine. In *WWW*, pages 431–440. ACM, 2010.

[17] E. Ikonomovska, J. Gama, and S. Džeroski. Learning model trees from evolving data streams. *Data mining and knowledge discovery*, 23(1):128–168, 2011.

[18] J. Jeon, W. Croft, J. Lee, and S. Park. A framework to predict the quality of answers with non-textual features. In *SIGIR*, pages 228–235. ACM, 2006.

[19] B. Li, T. Jin, M. R. Lyu, I. King, and B. Mak. Analyzing and predicting question quality in community question answering services. In *WWW*, pages 775–782. ACM, 2012.

[20] B. Li, Y. Liu, and E. Agichtein. Cocqa: co-training over questions and answers with an application to predicting question subjectivity orientation. In *EMNLP*, pages 937–946, 2008.

[21] Q. Liu, E. Agichtein, G. Dror, E. Gabrilovich, Y. Maarek, D. Pelleg, and I. Szpektor. Predicting web searcher satisfaction with existing community-based answers. In *SIGIR*, pages 415–424, 2011.

[22] Y. Liu, J. Bian, and E. Agichtein. Predicting information seeker satisfaction in community question answering. In *SIGIR*, pages 483–490. ACM, 2008.

[23] B. Pan, J. J. Xia, P. Yuan, J. Gateno, H. H. Ip, Q. He, P. K. Lee, B. Chow, and X. Zhou. Incremental kernel ridge regression for the prediction of soft tissue deformations. In *Medical Image Computing and Computer-Assisted Intervention*, pages 99–106. Springer, 2012.

[24] W. W. Piegorsch and G. Casella. Inverting a sum of matrices. *SIAM Review*, 32(3):470–470, 1990.

[25] C. Saunders, A. Gammerman, and V. Vovk. Ridge regression learning algorithm in dual variables. In *ICML*, pages 515–521, 1998.

[26] C. Shah and J. Pomerantz. Evaluating and predicting answer quality in community qa. In *SIGIR*, pages 411–418, 2010.

[27] A. Shtok, G. Dror, Y. Maarek, and I. Szpektor. Learning from the past: answering new questions with past answers. In *WWW*, pages 759–768, 2012.

[28] M. Suryanto, E. Lim, A. Sun, and R. Chiang. Quality-aware collaborative question answering: methods and evaluation. In *WSDM*, pages 142–151. ACM, 2009.

[29] Y. Yao, H. Tong, T. Xie, L. Akoglu, F. Xu, and J. Lu. Want a good answer? ask a good question first! *arXiv preprint arXiv:1311.6876*, 2013.

[30] Y. Zhou, G. Cong, B. Cui, C. Jensen, and J. Yao. Routing questions to the right users in online communities. In *ICDE*, pages 700–711. IEEE, 2009.

Who Are Experts Specializing in Landscape Photography?

Analyzing Topic-specific Authority on Content Sharing Services

Bin Bi* Ben Kao† Chang Wan† Junghoo Cho*

*University of California, Los Angeles
Los Angeles, United States
*{bbi, cho}@cs.ucla.edu

†The University of Hong Kong
Pokfulam Road, Hong Kong
†{kao, cwan}@cs.hku.hk

ABSTRACT

With the rapid growth of Web 2.0, a variety of content sharing services, such as *Flickr*, *YouTube*, *Blogger*, and *TripAdvisor* etc, have become extremely popular over the last decade. On these websites, users have created and shared with each other various kinds of resources, such as photos, video, and travel blogs. The sheer amount of user-generated content varies greatly in quality, which calls for a principled method to identify a set of authorities, who created high-quality resources, from a massive number of contributors of content. Since most previous studies only infer global authoritativeness of a user, there is no way to differentiate the authoritativeness in different aspects of life (topics).

In this paper, we propose a novel model of Topic-specific Authority Analysis (TAA), which addresses the limitations of the previous approaches, to identify authorities specific to given query topic(s) on a content sharing service. This model jointly leverages the usage data collected from the sharing log and the favorite log. The parameters in TAA are learned from a constructed training dataset, for which a novel logistic likelihood function is specifically designed. To perform Bayesian inference for TAA with the new logistic likelihood, we extend typical Gibbs sampling by introducing auxiliary variables. Thorough experiments with two real-world datasets demonstrate the effectiveness of TAA in topic-specific authority identification as well as the generalizability of the TAA generative model.

Categories and Subject Descriptors

H.4 [**Information Systems Applications**]: Miscellaneous

1. INTRODUCTION

Over the last decade, we have been witnessing the explosion of Web 2.0 applications. In the new era of Web 2.0, web users are participating not only as passive consumers of content provided by websites, but also as contributors creating content collaboratively with fellow users, commonly referred to as *user-generated content*. With the rapid growth of Web 2.0, a variety of *content sharing services*, such as *Flickr*[1], *YouTube*[2], *Blogger*[3], and *TripAdvisor*[4] etc, have become tremendously popular over the recent years. These websites enable users to create and share with each other various kinds of *resources*, such as photos, videos, and travel blogs, etc.

The sheer amount of user-generated content made available by the content sharing services can be both a blessing and a curse. From the point of user modeling, richer information content helps to build more accurate user profiles, leading to better services for consumers. On the other hand, the vast quantity of user-generated content available can often complicate the decision making process, as consumers do not have the time or ability to examine all data or compare all options [3]. On a content sharing website, the overwhelming resources vary greatly in quality, which result in confusion, sub-optimum decisions or dissatisfaction with choices made by users [27]. Therefore, it is highly significant to develop a principled method that identifies a set of authorities, who created quality-assured resources, from a massive number of contributors of content.

A lot of work has been done on authority identification in the context of social network and web structure analysis. However, most of these studies, such as typical PageRank, only infer *global* authoritativeness of each user, without assessing the authoritativeness in a particular aspect of life (topics) [24, 21, 11, 30]. It does not make sense for a user to find global authorities on a content sharing website. After all, each user has unique topical interest. For example, on Flickr, a user who is interested in photographing sunsets may look for an photographers expert in this specific topic and learn from her photos about the skill of sunset photography. On the other hand, no one is an authority on every topic. Clearly, *topic-specific* authority analysis provides a more detailed authoritativeness portfolio for a user, which is critical for authority identification on content sharing services.

A common way of distilling latent topics is to build a probabilistic topic model on the usage data collected from a *sharing log*. In a content sharing website, a *sharing log* stores users' posting and tagging history, as illustrated by Figure 1 in Section 3. However, the sharing log does not contain any information about the content quality of resources, based on which authorities are identified. It would be counterintu-

KDD'14, August 24–27, 2014, New York, NY, USA.
Copyright 2014 ACM 978-1-4503-2956-9/14/08 ...$15.00.
http://dx.doi.org/10.1145/2623330.2623752.

[1] `http://www.flickr.com`
[2] `http://www.youtube.com`
[3] `http://www.blogger.com`
[4] `http://www.tripadvisor.com`

itive to assume a high sharing frequency for every authority. Therefore, a data source in addition to the sharing log is clearly needed. Luckily, a *favorite log* made available by a content sharing website provides a valuable signal for the derivation of the content quality of resources. On current content sharing services, a resource is often presented with a *favorite* button, which a user clicks if he or she likes the resource. A *favorite click* represents an endorsement of the content quality of the resource by the user. The favorite log records the set of favorite clicks as user feedback, as illustrated by Figure 2 in Section 3.

Despite considerable research on the sharing log for various applications, little is known about the emerging favorite log. It is nontrivial to leverage a favorite log for topic-specific authority analysis in that users do not explicitly specify their topical motivates under the favorite clicks. A statistical model, built upon both the sharing log and the favorite log, is imperative to uncover each user's authoritativeness on different topics.

In this paper, we propose a novel Bayesian model to identify a list of authorities on given topic(s), which we refer to as Topic-specific Authority Analysis, abbreviated as TAA. The TAA model characterizes each user's topical authoritativeness by introducing a user-specific random vector over latent topics. To assess the topical authoritativeness, TAA exploits favorite clicks through systematically modeling the associations among users' interest and authoritativeness as well as the topics of favorited resources. We propose to learn the parameters in the TAA model from a training dataset of observations constructed from both usage logs. To this end, a novel logistic likelihood function specialized for the training set is proposed to relate the parameters to the observations. Bayesian inference for a model with a logistic likelihood has long been recognized as a hard problem. We extend typical collapsed Gibbs sampling by introducing auxiliary variables to overcome this problem. With the inferred parameters, an analysis framework is introduced to produce an ordered list of topic-specific authorities by their authoritativeness degrees that satisfy the user's query intent.

The major contributions of our work are summarized as follows:

1. We propose a novel Bayesian model, TAA, to address the new problem of topic-specific authority analysis on content sharing services by jointly leveraging the two data sources: *sharing log* and *favorite log*.

2. We propose a principled approach to training dataset construction, in which a novel logistic likelihood function is introduced.

3. We extend classic collapsed Gibbs sampling by *data augmentation* to infer the parameters in the TAA model with the new logistic likelihood.

4. We conducted thorough experiments on the datasets collected from two specific real-world content sharing websites. Experimental results confirm the effectiveness of TAA in topic-specific authority identification as well as the predictive power of the TAA generative model.

The rest of this paper is organized as follows. In Section 2, we describe the prior work related to ours. The problem statement is given in Section 3. Section 4 introduces our TAA model, for which the inference is depicted in Section 5. In Section 6, we present the experimental results. Finally we conclude the paper in Section 7.

2. RELATED WORK

Much work has been done on authority identification based on a network structure. The two most representative studies are PageRank [24] and HITS [21]. Zhang *et al.* [32] tested PageRank and HITS on a specific online community for expert identification. Jurczyk and Agichtein [19] employed the HITS algorithm to discover authorities in question answer communities. Kempe *et al.* [20] abstracted authority analysis into a influence maximization problem and pioneered the Linear Threshold (LT) Model and Independent Cascade (IC) Model to explain the spread of influence in a social network. Along with subsequent works, such as [11] and [22], all these methods are only after the identification of global authorities instead of authorities for specific topics. Although Barbieri *et al.* [2] extended the LT and IC models to be topic-aware, the topics are obtained based on the network structure, while totally neglecting valuable textual content.

A few studies have been conducted to find topic-level authorities in the context of structure analysis of the web graph and social networks. Given the popularity of PageRank, it is only natural to extend it for topical authority analysis. Topic-Sensitive PageRank (TSPR) [16] was such an extension that computes per-topic PageRank scores for webpages. TSPR biases the computation of PageRank by replacing the classic PageRank's uniform teleport vector with topic-specific ones. However, it requires an existing manually categorized topic hierarchies to derive per-topic teleport vectors. In [28], Tang *et al.* proposed a Topical Affinity Propagation (TAP) model for topic-level social influence. But, similar to TSPR, TAP requires a separate preprocess to obtain a set of topics. TwitterRank [31] extended TSPR to find topic-level influencers on Twitter. Instead of predefined topic hierarchies, a set of topics is first produced by typical LDA [8] on the tweets. Then TwitterRank applies a method similar to TSPR to compute the per-topic influence rank. Nallapati *et al.* proposed Link-PLSA-LDA [23] on a hyperlink network to estimate the influence of blogs. These studies differ from our TAA model in that they do not exploit the valuable favorite signal to model topic-specific authoritativeness. Although TwitterRank and Link-PLSA-LDA applied to the settings different from ours, we adapted them to the authority identification on content sharing services by building proper graph structures, and compared them with our TAA in empirical studies.

There also exist a few pieces of prior work on finding important users in various applications. Chen *et al.* [9] proposed a latent factor model for rating prediction, based on which reputable users are identified. Zhao *et al.* [33] found topic-level experts on community question answering services, and recommended appropriate experts to answer new questions. In [7], Followship-LDA was proposed to identify topic-specific influencers on microblogs. All these methods find important users under different contexts, with the data different from ours in nature.

In the context of recommender systems, a few topic modeling studies related to our work have been conducted. Several latent factor models were proposed for tag recommendation on social media [5, 6, 4]. Wang and Blei [29] developed the

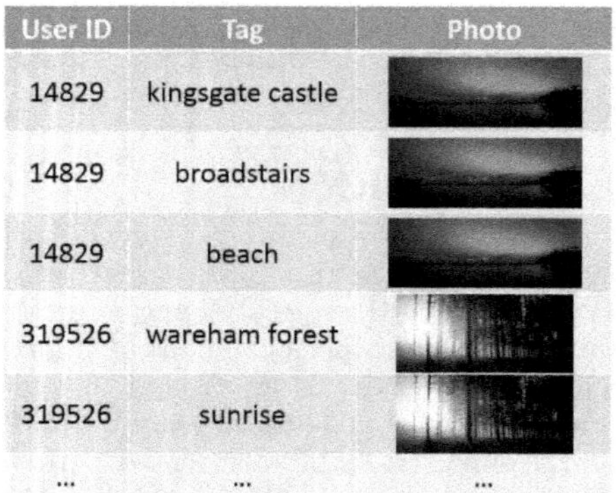

Figure 1: Sample records from the sharing log of a photo sharing website

collaborative topic regression (CTR) model to recommend scientific articles to users of an online community. Agarwal and Chen [1] proposed fLDA, which is a new matrix factorization method integrating LDA priors, to predict ratings in recommender system applications. Despite the relevance of these studies to our work, there are clear differences between them. To make recommendations, CTR utilizes scalar rating responses different from the binary favorite feedback exploited by TAA. fLDA is able to take binary responses, but it aims to predict scalar ratings of users on various items, which is different from the ultimate goal of our work.

3. PROBLEM STATEMENT

In a nutshell, the objective of this paper is developing a statistical model that identifies the authorities on a content sharing website specific to given query topic(s). A topic-specific authority is defined as a user who excels in the specified topic. For example, given *city lights* as a query topic on a photo sharing website, the topic-specific authority model is intended to retrieve a list of users who are expert in city lights shooting at night.

A content sharing website generally logs a massive number of posting and tagging records that reflect every user's unique interest and taste. These records constitute a *sharing log* that a content sharing service keeps track of. Figure 1 presents a few sample records from the sharing log of a photo sharing website. Each row in the table represents a record indicating that user u assigned tag t to resource r (i.e., a photo) which was posted by herself. For notational convenience, let L denote the total number of unique users in the log, M_u denote the number of resources posted by user u, and N_r denote the number of tags assigned to resource r. The notations used throughout this paper are given in Table 1. Some of the notations will be explained in later sections.

A feasible solution to topic-specific authority identification is adapting the classic topic model *Latent Dirichlet Allocation* (LDA) [8] to historical data in the sharing log. Specifically, we employ typical LDA on the sharing data by regarding a user as a document in a corpus, a tag as a word in a document. By fitting the topic model to observational data collected from the sharing log, we infer the optimal values of parameters θ and φ. The probabilities θ (i.e., $p(z|u)$) give the topic distribution for each user, and the probabilities φ (i.e., $p(t|z)$) give the tag distribution for each topic. As a result, topic-specific authorities can be derived from the distributions $p(z|u)$ and $p(t|z)$ by the standard *query likelihood model*, where each user is scored by the likelihood

Table 1: Notations used throughout this paper

Notation	Description
u	User identity
t	Tag identity
r	Resource identity
z	Topic assignment of a tag
f	Binary favorite feedback
L	Total number of unique users
K	Total number of unique topics
R	Total number of unique resources
V	Total number of unique tags in the vocabulary
M_u	Number of resources posted by user u
N_r	Number of tags assigned to resource r
N_u	Number of tags assigned by user u
θ	Per-user topic distribution
φ	Per-topic tag distribution
α, β	Dirichlet priors on Multinomial distributions
η	Per-user topical authoritativeness

of generating a given query. In particular, given a set of tags as a query q, we compute the likelihood $p(q|u)$ for each user u by:

$$p(q|u) = \prod_{t \in q} p(t|u) = \prod_{t \in q} \sum_{z=1}^{K} p(t|z)p(z|u). \quad (1)$$

The users with the highest likelihood $p(q|u)$ are then identified as topic-specific authorities.

The LDA-based authority analysis exploits the fact that a user is interested in a particular topic if he or she frequently labels photos with the tags specific to this topic. It further assumes that the more frequently a user uses the tags covering a specific topic, the more authoritative he or she should be on this topic . However, this is an arguable assumption which is not always valid. Tagging frequently on a particular topic does not automatically imply that the user is an authority on this topic. In fact, an authority does not have to tag more than the other users on the topic he or she excels in. For example, on a travel blogging service, a blogger who posts a number of articles tagged with *London travel* may not be an authority on blogging about traveling London, given the unknown quality of these articles. It is likely that he or she is new to blogging, in which case the articles could be at a beginner level in quality. On the other hand, an actual authority may post only a couple of blogs about London travel, but he or she can specialize in this specific topic, leading to the favorable high-quality blogs. By analyzing the usage data from a real-world sharing log, we observed that users' tag frequency is actually independent of their authoritativeness.

Since the sharing log reports posting and tagging information, but we are looking for the information about the content quality of posted resources, a supplementary data source is needed. Fortunately, a *favorite log* available in most of the content sharing services should help to infer the content quality of resources. A favorite log consists of the records of each user's favorites. Figure 2 depicts a few sample records from the favorite log of a photo sharing website. Each row in the table represents a record indicating that user u added resource r (i.e., a photo) to his or her favorites. A *favorite click* can be interpreted as the user's vote in favor of the content quality of the favorited resource. It motivates our modeling the favorite signal to infer the content quality of resources based on which topic-specific authorities are identified.

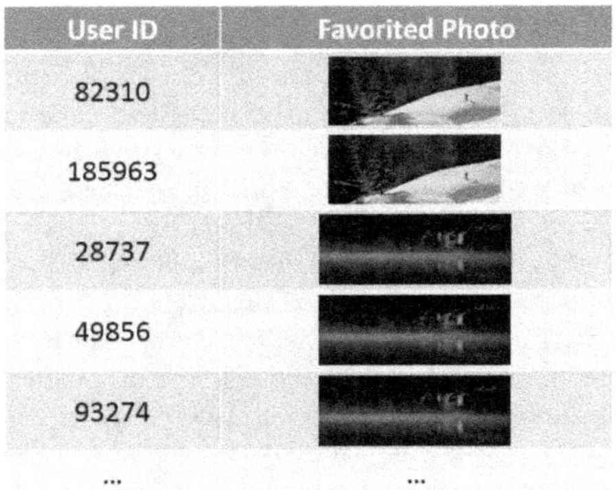

Figure 2: Sample records from the favorite log of a photo sharing website

As discussed above, users' topical interest and topical authoritativeness have different implications. A favorite log enables us to separate the analysis of users' topical authoritativeness from that of their topical interest. In order to jointly model the two factors, we need to construct a Bayesian model which specifies a generative process much more complex than that of typical LDA. The Bayesian model is intended to exploit both the sharing signal and the favorite signal by leveraging the two usage logs.

Problem Statement *Given the usage data collected from a sharing log and a favorite log, we aim to design a stochastic process that simulates how the data is generated, based on which a generative model is developed to identify authorities specific to given query topic(s) on a content sharing service.*

4. TOPIC-SPECIFIC AUTHORITY ANALYSIS

Naturally, no one is an authority on every topic, which implies that each user's authoritative degrees should be evaluated specific to individual topics. Moreover, users' topical authoritativenesses are different from each other. Therefore, in our proposed TAA model, we introduce a K-dimensional random vector over topics to characterize topical authoritativeness. The random vector is designed to be specific to individual user u, denoted by $\boldsymbol{\eta}_u$, meaning that each user has a unique topical authoritativeness. An entry of random vector $\boldsymbol{\eta}_u$ is a latent variable η_{uz} reflecting user u's authoritative degrees on topic z. We assume that $\boldsymbol{\eta}_u$ is generated from a K-dimensional Multivariate Gaussian distribution:

$$\boldsymbol{\eta}_u \sim \mathrm{MVN}(\boldsymbol{\mu}, \boldsymbol{\Sigma}), \quad (2)$$

where $\boldsymbol{\mu}$ and $\boldsymbol{\Sigma}$ are the mean vector and the covariance matrix, respectively. We choose the Multivariate Gaussian distribution due to its nice invariance property as a prior distribution. As will be discussed later, Multivariate Gaussian is a conjugate prior of our likelihood function, meaning that the posterior distribution of $\boldsymbol{\eta}_u$ will also be a Multivariate Gaussian. This trick benefits inference for our TAA model by computational convenience. The values of $\boldsymbol{\eta}_u$ for each user will be learned from the usage data collected from the sharing log as well as the favorite log.

A *favorite click* reflects a positive feedback from the user on the content quality of the specific resource. Therefore, to represent a favorite feedback, we introduce a binary random variable specific to individual user u and individual resource r, denoted by f_{ur}. The binary variable f_{ur} takes value 1 if the user u favorited the particular resource r, 0 otherwise. Introducing f_{ur} helps to relate the resource r to the user u who favorited r. More precisely, user u favorites resource r (f_{ur}=1), if the topical authoritativeness of r's owner exhibited by the resource r matches with u's topical interest. For instance, a user, who is interested in photos of Yellowstone National Park, may favorite the Yellowstone photos from a photographer who is expert in taking shots for Yellowstone National Park. On the other hand, user u does not favorite resource r (f_{ur}=0), if u's interest and the authoritativeness of r's owner exhibited by the resource r fall into different sets of topics. For example, a user, who is interested in blogs about Yellowstone travel, is unlikely to favorite the low-quality articles from a blogger who is new to this particular topic.

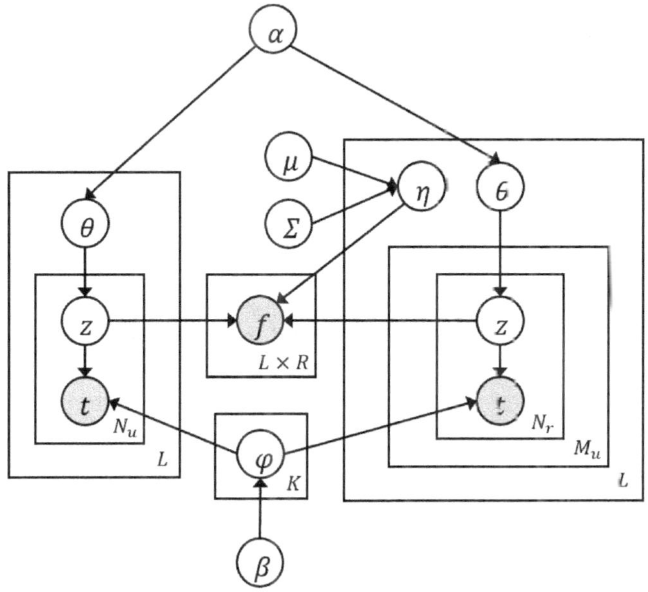

Figure 3: Graphical model for Topic-specific Authority Analysis

Since the topical motivate under each favorite click is hidden and unavailable directly, we need to identify the topics in which a user is interested as well as the topics on which a user is authoritative. To this end, we propose a novel generative model on the usage data for topic distillation. With the distilled topics, we specify the likelihood of a favorite feedback f_{ur} from user u on r with the logistic function by:

$$p(f_{ur} = 1|\boldsymbol{\eta}_{u'}, \hat{\mathbf{z}}_u, \hat{\mathbf{z}}_{u'r}) = \frac{1}{1 + e^{-\boldsymbol{\eta}_{u'}^{\mathsf{T}}(\hat{\mathbf{z}}_u \circ \hat{\mathbf{z}}_{u'r})}} \quad (3)$$

$$p(f_{ur} = 0|\boldsymbol{\eta}_{u'}, \hat{\mathbf{z}}_u, \hat{\mathbf{z}}_{u'r}) = 1 - \frac{1}{1 + e^{-\boldsymbol{\eta}_{u'}^{\mathsf{T}}(\hat{\mathbf{z}}_u \circ \hat{\mathbf{z}}_{u'r})}} \quad (4)$$

where u' denotes the user who posted resource r (i.e., r's owner); $\hat{\mathbf{z}}_u$ denotes the topic distribution for user u's interest; $\hat{\mathbf{z}}_{u'r}$ denotes the topic distribution for the resource r posted by user u', and $\circ$ denotes the Hadamard (element-wise) product. The element-wise product of $\hat{\mathbf{z}}_u$ and $\hat{\mathbf{z}}_{u'r}$ captures similarity between the topic distributions for the resource r and the interest of the user u who favorited r, which is parameterized by the owner u''s topical authoritativeness $\boldsymbol{\eta}_{u'}$. If the topic distribution for user u's interest is similar to the one for resource r, there should be the a specific set of topics prominent in both u's interest and resource r. A favorite click $f_{ur} = 1$ then indicates that this specific

For each topic $k = 1, \ldots, K$
  Sample φ_k from $Dirichlet(\beta)$
For each user $u = 1, \ldots, L$
  Sample θ_u from $Dirichlet(\alpha)$
  For the nth position of user u, where $n \in \{1, \ldots, N_u\}$
    Sample a topic z_{un} from $Multinomial(\theta_u)$, where $z_{un} \in \{1, \ldots, K\}$
    Sample a tag t_{un} from $Multinomial(\varphi_{z_{un}})$, where $t_{un} \in \{1, \ldots, V\}$
  Sample authoritativeness vector η_u from $MVN(\mu, \Sigma)$
For each tuple (u, r)
  Sample a favorite feedback f_{ur} from $Bernoulli\left(\frac{1}{1+\exp(-\eta_{u'}^{\mathsf{T}}(\hat{z}_u \circ \hat{z}_{u'r}))}\right)$,
    where $f_{ur} \in \{0,1\}$ and u' is resource r's owner

Figure 4: Generative process for Topic-specific Authority Analysis

set of topics are the ones that the resource r's owner u' is expert in, and thus should be parameterized by high authoritativeness degrees. In this way, we uncover the hidden topical motivate under each favorite click.

Figure 3 shows the graphical model for our TAA, with the notations described in Table 1. The generative process of a user's tags and favorite feedback is summarized in Figure 4. A favorite feedback is naturally associated with a tuple (u, r), where r denotes a resource, and u denotes the user who favorited r. To obtain individual user u's interest distribution over topics, each user is viewed as a mixture of topics from which tags are drawn. More specifically, for each user $u \in \{1, \ldots, L\}$, we first pick a topic distribution θ_u from a Dirichlet prior with parameter α. Then, to generate the nth tag in the resources posted by u, a topic z_{un} is sampled from θ_u, after which the tag t_{un} is drawn from the tag distribution $\varphi_{z_{un}}$ for topic z_{un}. With all the obtained topics, we compute individual user u's topical interest distribution $\hat{\mathbf{z}}_u$ by aggregating u's topic assignments. On the other hand, the topic distribution $\hat{\mathbf{z}}_{u'r}$ for individual resource r posted by user u' is obtained in a similar way, except that $\hat{\mathbf{z}}_{u'r}$ is computed by counting u''s topic assignments specific to resource r only.

The topic distributions $\hat{\mathbf{z}}_u$ and $\hat{\mathbf{z}}_{u'r}$ enable the generation of favorite feedback. In particular, for each tuple (u, r), the binary favorite feedback f_{ur} is sampled from a Bernoulli distribution with parameter $\frac{1}{1+e^{-\boldsymbol{\eta}_{u'}^{\mathsf{T}}(\hat{\mathbf{z}}_u \circ \hat{\mathbf{z}}_{u'r})}}$. More specifically, we compute the likelihoods of $f_{ur} = 1$ and $f_{ur} = 0$ using Equation (3) and Equation (4), respectively. As a result, $f_{ur} \in \{0, 1\}$ is drawn from a Bernoulli distribution of the two likelihoods.

The various parameters we can learn from TAA characterize the different factors that affect the model structure. For a user u, the K-dimensional vector $\boldsymbol{\eta}_u$ quantifies u's unique authoritativeness over topics, and the value θ_{uz} gives the probability that u is interested in topic z. For a topic z, the value φ_{zt} indicates the probability of tag t belonging to topic z. The inferred quantities serve as the inputs to our authority analysis framework, which will be described later.

5. INFERENCE FOR TAA

In this section, we present how the parameters of the TAA model are inferred from the usage data collected from the sharing log and the favorite log. More specifically, we first construct a training dataset from the usage data, with which a new Bernoulli likelihood parametrized by a logistic function is specified. Finally, an extension of traditional Gibbs sampling specialized for the logistic likelihood function is proposed to infer the optimal values of the parameters.

5.1 Preference Learning

We learn the parameters of the TAA model from a training set of observations constructed from the usage data. As mentioned above, the favorite log consists of user preferences for resources in a content sharing service. One important fact about the favorite log is that only positive observations are available – each favorite click is viewed as positive feedback for the corresponding tuple (u, r), i.e., $f_{ur} = 1$. However, there are not such clear conclusions for $f_{ur} = 0$. Considering the non-clicked tuples (u, r) (i.e., user u did not click on the *favorite* button for resource r.) as negative feedback ($f_{ur} = 0$) would misinterpret the signal of these tuples, since there are actually at least two different interpretations for any non-clicked tuple. One possibility is a negative feedback, meaning that the user did not like the resource and did not want to add it to his or her favorites. Another possibility is a missing value, indicating that the user did not even see the resource, in which case whether the user favorited the resource is unknown.

On the other hand, the non-clicked tuples should not be simply ignored, as typical machine learning models are not able to learn anything from the positive observations alone. To overcome the problem of missing negative feedback ($f_{ur} = 0$), we use tuple pairs as training data instead of individual tuples. As opposed to treating non-clicked tuples as negative observations, we assume that users prefer the resources, for which they clicked on the *favorite* buttons, over the other non-clicked resources from the same owner. More specifically, suppose that r_i and r_j represent two resources posted by a user. Given two tuples (u, r_i) and (u, r_j), user u prefers r_i over r_j if and only if r_i was favorited by u while r_j was not, which is denoted by $r_i \succ_u r_j$. Formally, we create training data $\mathcal{D}$ by including the pairwise preference relations as follows:

$$\mathcal{D} = \{(u, r_i, r_j) | r_i \succ_u r_j\}, \tag{5}$$

where each preference relation $o = (u, r_i, r_j)$ is a training sample representing the fact that user u prefers r_i over r_j. For the resources that are both favorited by a user, we cannot infer any preference. The same is true for two resources either of which a user did not favorite.

As discussed above, we construct the observational dataset $\mathcal{D}$ using the induced preference relations in place of the raw favorite feedback f_{ur}. As a result, the likelihood functions (3) and (4) need to be extended to incorporate the pairwise preference. Therefore, we reformulate the likelihood of a preference relation as:

$$p(r_i \succ_u r_j | \boldsymbol{\eta}_{u'}, \hat{\mathbf{z}}_u, \hat{\mathbf{z}}_{u'r_i}, \hat{\mathbf{z}}_{u'r_j}) = \frac{1}{1 + e^{-\boldsymbol{\eta}_{u'}^{\mathsf{T}}(\hat{\mathbf{z}}_u \circ \hat{\mathbf{z}}_{u'r_i} - \hat{\mathbf{z}}_u \circ \hat{\mathbf{z}}_{u'r_j})}}. \tag{6}$$

The probability $p(r_i \succ_u r_j | \boldsymbol{\eta}_{u'}, \hat{\mathbf{z}}_u, \hat{\mathbf{z}}_{u'r_i}, \hat{\mathbf{z}}_{u'r_j})$ gives the likelihood that user u prefers resource r_i over resource r_j, both owned by user u'. Let Θ denote the set of parameters of the TAA model. The likelihood of observing all the preference relations in training data $\mathcal{D}$ is then given by:

$$p(\mathcal{D}|\Theta) = \prod_{(u, r_i, r_j) \in \mathcal{D}} \frac{1}{1 + e^{-\boldsymbol{\eta}_{u'}^{\mathsf{T}}(\hat{\mathbf{z}}_u \circ \hat{\mathbf{z}}_{u'r_i} - \hat{\mathbf{z}}_u \circ \hat{\mathbf{z}}_{u'r_j})}}. \tag{7}$$

5.2 Bayesian Inference

Typical LDA-like generative models employ collapsed Gibbs sampling to infer their parameters [15, 17, 26]. However,

Bayesian inference for a model with the logistic likelihood function (6) has long been recognized as a hard problem, due to the analytically inconvenient form of the Gibbs sampler for a logistic likelihood [18, 12, 14]. In this section, we present an extension of traditional collapsed Gibbs sampling to infer the parameters in TAA. Our algorithm takes advantage of the *data-augmentation* idea by introducing auxiliary variables to the posterior distribution. It extends the very recent work on inference for logistic models [25, 10] to learn a Bayesian model for topic-specific authority analysis. Specifically, using the ideas of introducing Pólya-Gamma variables presented in [25, 10], we are able to derive the posterior probabilities for the Gibbs sampler analytically. Part of the derivation is provided in the appendix.

Let us first familiarize ourselves with a new family of Pólya-Gamma distributions [25].

Definition *A random variable X has a Pólya-Gamma distribution with parameters $b > 0$ and $c \in \mathcal{R}$, denoted by $X \sim PG(b, c)$, if*

$$X \stackrel{d}{=} \frac{1}{2\pi^2} \sum_{k=1}^{\infty} \frac{g_k}{(k-1/2)^2 + c^2/(4\pi^2)}, \quad (8)$$

where the $g_k \sim Gamma(b, 1)$ are independent Gamma random variables; the notation $\stackrel{d}{=}$ denotes equality in distribution.

The Pólya-Gamma family has been carefully constructed to yield a simple Gibbs sampler for the Bayesian logistic model. Let $\delta_{ur_{ij}}$ denote a Pólya-Gamma variable specific to (u, r_i, r_j). With the introduction of the auxiliary random variable $\delta_{ur_{ij}}$, the likelihood function (6) can be represented as mixtures of Gaussians with respect to a Pólya-Gamma distribution, which is rewritten as:

$$\begin{aligned} & p(r_i \succ_u r_j | \boldsymbol{\eta}_{u'}, \hat{\mathbf{z}}_u, \hat{\mathbf{z}}_{u'r_i}, \hat{\mathbf{z}}_{u'r_j}) \\ &= \frac{1}{2} e^{\frac{\boldsymbol{\eta}_{u'}^{\mathsf{T}} \hat{\mathbf{z}}_{ur_{ij}}}{2}} \int_0^{\infty} e^{-\frac{\delta_{ur_{ij}}(\boldsymbol{\eta}_{u'}^{\mathsf{T}} \hat{\mathbf{z}}_{ur_{ij}})^2}{2}} p(\delta_{ur_{ij}}|1, 0) d\delta_{ur_{ij}}, \quad (9) \end{aligned}$$

where $\hat{\mathbf{z}}_{ur_{ij}} = \hat{\mathbf{z}}_u \circ \hat{\mathbf{z}}_{u'r_i} - \hat{\mathbf{z}}_u \circ \hat{\mathbf{z}}_{u'r_j}$.

As a result, the collapsed posterior distribution of TAA augmented with the variables δ is given by:

$$\begin{aligned} & p(\mathbf{z}, \delta, \eta | \mathbf{t}, \mathbf{o}, \alpha, \beta, \mu, \Sigma) \\ & \propto \prod_{u=1}^{L} \frac{\prod_{k=1}^{K} \Gamma(c_{ku} + \alpha_k)}{\Gamma(\sum_{k=1}^{K} c_{ku} + \alpha_k)} \times \prod_{k=1}^{K} \frac{\prod_{t=1}^{V} \Gamma(g_{kt} + \beta_t)}{\Gamma(\sum_{t=1}^{V} g_{kt} + \beta_t)} \\ & \times p(\eta|\mu, \Sigma) \prod_{(u,r_i,r_j)\in\mathcal{D}} e^{\frac{\boldsymbol{\eta}_{u'}^{\mathsf{T}} \hat{\mathbf{z}}_{ur_{ij}} - \delta_{ur_{ij}}(\boldsymbol{\eta}_{u'}^{\mathsf{T}} \hat{\mathbf{z}}_{ur_{ij}})^2}{2}} p(\delta_{ur_{ij}}|1, 0) \end{aligned} \quad (10)$$

where c_{ku} is the number of user u's tags assigned to topic k, and g_{kt} is the total number of times tag t is assigned to topic k over the dataset. The detailed derivation of Equation (10) is provided in the appendix.

The univariate conditionals for a Gibbs sampler are then given as follows. The notation $\bullet$ represents all the variables other than the one to be sampled.

$[p(\boldsymbol{\eta}_x|\bullet)]$:

We impose a zero-mean isotropic Gaussian prior on the K-dimensional random vector $\boldsymbol{\eta}_x$ which characterizes user x's topical authoritativeness:

$$p(\boldsymbol{\eta}_x) = \frac{1}{\sqrt{2\pi}\sigma} e^{-\frac{\sum_k \eta_{xk}^2}{2\sigma^2}}. \quad (11)$$

Thanks to the invariance property of the conjugate prior, the posterior distribution of $\boldsymbol{\eta}_x$ is also a Multivariate Gaussian:

$$\begin{aligned} p(\boldsymbol{\eta}_x|\bullet) &\propto p(\boldsymbol{\eta}_x) \prod_{r_i\in R(x)\wedge r_j\in R(x)} e^{\frac{\boldsymbol{\eta}_x^{\mathsf{T}} \hat{\mathbf{z}}_{ur_{ij}} - \delta_{ur_{ij}}(\boldsymbol{\eta}_x^{\mathsf{T}} \hat{\mathbf{z}}_{ur_{ij}})^2}{2}} \\ &= \mathrm{MVN}(\mu_x, \Sigma_x) \end{aligned} \quad (12)$$

where $r_i \in R(x)$ represents that resource r_i is posted by user x. The posterior mean μ_x and posterior covariance Σ_x are given by:

$$\begin{aligned} \mu_x &= \Sigma_x \left(\sum_{r_i\in R(x)\wedge r_j\in R(x)} \frac{1}{2} \hat{\mathbf{z}}_{ur_{ij}} \right) \\ \Sigma_x &= \left(\frac{1}{\sigma^2} I + \sum_{r_i\in R(x)\wedge r_j\in R(x)} \delta_{ur_{ij}} \hat{\mathbf{z}}_{ur_{ij}} \hat{\mathbf{z}}_{ur_{ij}}^{\mathsf{T}} \right)^{-1} \end{aligned}$$

$[p(z_{un}|\bullet)]$:

The posterior distribution of $\mathbf{z}$ is:

$$\begin{aligned} p(\mathbf{z}|\bullet) &\propto \prod_{u=1}^{L} \frac{\prod_{k=1}^{K} \Gamma(c_{ku} + \alpha_k)}{\Gamma(\sum_{k=1}^{K} c_{ku} + \alpha_k)} \times \prod_{k=1}^{K} \frac{\prod_{t=1}^{V} \Gamma(g_{kt} + \beta_t)}{\Gamma(\sum_{t=1}^{V} g_{kt} + \beta_t)} \\ & \times \prod_{(u,r_i,r_j)\in\mathcal{D}} e^{\frac{\boldsymbol{\eta}_{u'}^{\mathsf{T}} \hat{\mathbf{z}}_{ur_{ij}} - \delta_{ur_{ij}}(\boldsymbol{\eta}_{u'}^{\mathsf{T}} \hat{\mathbf{z}}_{ur_{ij}})^2}{2}} \end{aligned} \quad (13)$$

The univariate conditional distribution of one variable z_{un} given all the other variables is then given by:

$$\begin{aligned} p(z_{un} = k|\bullet) &\propto \frac{(c_{ku}^{-(un)} + \alpha_k)(g_{kt_{un}}^{-(un)} + \beta_{t_{un}})}{\sum_{t=1}^{V} g_{kt}^{-(un)} + \sum_{t=1}^{V} \beta_t} \\ & \times \prod_{(u,r_i,r_j)\in\mathcal{D}} p(r_i \succ_u r_j | \boldsymbol{\eta}_{u'}, \mathbf{z}_{-(un)}, z_{un} = k) \end{aligned} \quad (14)$$

where $c_{ku}^{-(un)}$ bears the same meaning of c_{ku} only with the nth tag of user u excluded; similarly $g_{kt}^{-(un)}$ is defined in the same way as g_{kt} only without the count for the nth tag of user u, and $\mathbf{z}_{-(un)}$ denotes the topics for all tags except z_{un}.

$[p(\delta_{ur_{ij}}|\bullet)]$:

By definition, the posterior distribution of the auxiliary variable $\delta_{ur_{ij}}$ turns out to be a Pólya-Gamma distribution:

$$\begin{aligned} p(\delta_{ur_{ij}}|\bullet) &\propto e^{-\frac{\delta_{ur_{ij}}(\boldsymbol{\eta}_{u'}^{\mathsf{T}} \hat{\mathbf{z}}_{ur_{ij}})^2}{2}} p(\delta_{ur_{ij}}|1, 0) \\ &= \mathrm{PG}(1, \boldsymbol{\eta}_{u'}^{\mathsf{T}} \hat{\mathbf{z}}_{ur_{ij}}) \end{aligned} \quad (15)$$

The above posterior univariate distributions create a Markov chain for Gibbs sampling. It has been shown that the stationary distribution of the Markov chain is just the sought-after posterior joint distribution [13]. Specifically, the Gibbs sampler iteratively draws samples from $p(\boldsymbol{\eta}_x|\bullet)$, $p(z_{un}|\bullet)$ and $p(\delta_{ur_{ij}}|\bullet)$ using Equations (12), (14) and (15) respectively. After the Gibbs sampler has run for an appropriate number of iterations (until the chain has converged to a stationary distribution), we draw a sample $\boldsymbol{\eta}_x$ for each user x, which quantifies x's topical authoritativeness, and obtain the estimates for the distributions θ and φ via the following equations:

$$\theta_{uz} = \frac{c_{zu} + \alpha_z}{\sum_{k=1}^{K} c_{ku} + \sum_{k=1}^{K} \alpha_k} \quad (16)$$

$$\varphi_{zt} = \frac{g_{zt} + \beta_t}{\sum_{t=1}^{V} g_{zt} + \sum_{t=1}^{V} \beta_t} \quad (17)$$

5.3 Authority Analysis Framework

With the inferred parameters, we introduce an analysis framework for topic-specific authority identification. The analysis framework allows a user to issue a query q reflecting the topic(s) on which authorities are to be identified. The query q consists of a list of tags, where multi-occurrences of a tag are allowed to reflect its importance to the query topic(s). The analysis framework subsequently produces an ordered list of authorities by their authoritativeness degrees that satisfy the user's query intent.

To rank a list of authorities, the analysis framework requires **(a)** every user's topical authoritativeness: η, and **(b)** the topic(s) of query q: $\mathbf{z}_q$. When the TAA model is used as the underlying topic-specific authority analysis method, the topical authoritativeness η is produced as part of the results. To derive q's topic(s) $\mathbf{z}_q$, we use the folding-in technique on TAA by treating the query as a new user, and perform the sampling for only the tags of the pseudo user. Given the derived topical authoritativeness $\boldsymbol{\eta}_u$ and the query topic(s) $\mathbf{z}_q$, we obtain the final authoritativeness $\Psi(u, q) = \sum_{i=1}^{N_q} \eta_{u z_{qi}}$ for a user u with respect to the query q, where N_q denotes the number of tags in q. Finally, the users are returned in decreasing order of their authoritativeness $\Psi(u, q)$.

6. EMPIRICAL EVALUATION

In this section, we report the experimental results of the TAA model on real-world data collected from two specific content sharing services: *Flickr*[5] and *500px*[6]. We quantitatively compare the results of TAA with those of several competitors on both datasets. We also give real examples of Flickr authorities identified by TAA. Analysis and discussion of the experimental results are presented in this section.

6.1 Data Collections

Although TAA is a generic Bayesian model which is applicable to topic-specific authority identification on various kinds of content sharing services, we conduct experiments on the real-world datasets collected from two specific websites *Flickr* and *500px* to evaluate the quality of identified authorities. *Flickr* is one of the most popular photo sharing website, which allows users to store, share, tag and organize their photos. The huge number of Flickr users calls for an topic-specific authority model to identify the best photographers for a specified query topic. As opposed to Flickr's general user base, *500px* is a photo sharing platform catered to professional photographers. A distinct feature of 500px is the *Editors' Choice* page[7] which shows the finest photos hand-picked by the professional editors employed by 500px. These high-quality photos are used to derive the ground truth for our empirical evaluation.

[5] `http://www.flickr.com`

[6] `http://www.500px.com`

[7] `http://www.500px.com/editors`

Table 2: Statistics of Experimental Datasets

Data	#users	#photos	#tag asgmts	#fav. clicks
Flickr	21,054	204,335	3,014,813	1,562,805
500px	33,581	318,906	3,520,179	1,837,049

We collected the sharing logs and the favorite logs from both Flickr and 500px. The usage data obtained from the collected logs were processed to create training data $\mathcal{D}$, on which a TAA model was built. Extra usage information was collected to derive the ground truth for both datasets, which will be described in the next subsection. The basic statistics of the Flickr dataset and the 500px dataset are given in Table 2.

6.2 Evaluation Strategy

Quantitatively evaluating the quality of topic-specific authority analysis is a difficult task, since a content sharing service generally does not explicitly specify real authorities given a topic. Luckily, the abundant information embedded in the databases of Flickr and 500px helps to derive ground truth of topic-specific authorities.

Flickr has a large number of user-created groups that allow people who have similar interests to get together and share their photos reflecting these interests. Each of the groups is generally dedicated to a certain topic, such as food, animals, certain photo techniques, or creative commons, etc. Every group has one or more administrators which can be viewed as the real authorities specific to the group topic. On the other hand, 500px organizes photos by category, such as wedding, underwater, concert, or transportation, etc. We rank the users for each category according to their numbers of photos get selected by the editors by category. The ranked list of users for each category is instead viewed as ground truth, since unlike a Flickr group, a 500px category has no administrators specific to the category topic.

Given the different kinds of ground truth for Flickr and 500px, we used different evaluation metrics to measure the quality of the results from compared algorithms. Let Q denote a set of queries. For each query $q \in Q$, each algorithm returns an ordered list of users by their authoritativeness. For the Flickr dataset, we employed the standard Mean Reciprocal Rank (MRR). The Reciprocal Rank of a ranked list is the multiplicative inverse of the rank of the first hit in the list. The MRR score of an algorithm is the average reciprocal rank obtained by the ranked lists given by the algorithm with respect to the query set Q. Formally,

$$MRR = \frac{1}{|Q|} \sum_{q \in Q} \frac{1}{rank_q} \quad (18)$$

where $rank_q$ is the rank of the first real authority in the ranked list for query q. By definition, a higher MRR score indicates a better algorithm. For the 500px dataset, on the other hand, we employed the Spearman's rank correlation coefficient to assess the correlation between ground truth and a ranked list of users given by each algorithm. The Spearman's coefficient ρ_q for query q can take a range of values from -1 to +1 ($\rho_q < 0$ for a negative correlation, $\rho_q > 0$ for a positive correlation). The Spearman's coefficient ρ of an algorithm is the average Spearman's coefficient over the query set Q given by the algorithm. Formally,

$$\rho = \frac{1}{|Q|} \sum_{q \in Q} \rho_q \quad (19)$$

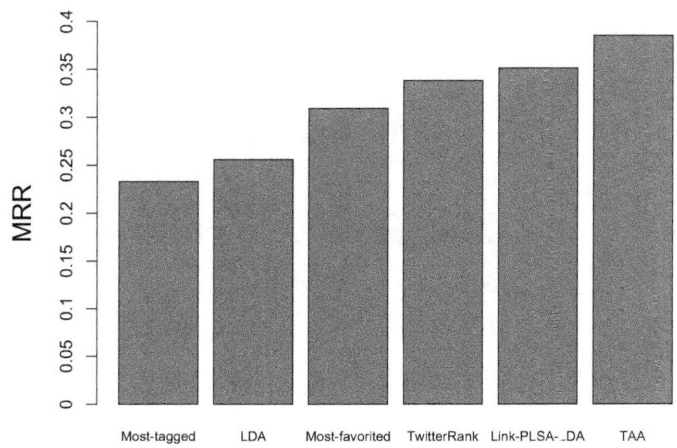

Figure 5: MRR for the Flickr dataset

6.3 Quality of Authority Analysis

In our experiments, we evaluated the quality of the authorities identified by the six algorithms, *Most-tagged*, *LDA*, *Most-favorited*, *TwitterRank*, *Link-PLSA-LDA*, and *TAA*. Given a set of tags as a query, the *Most-tagged* approach first identifies relevant photos by lexical matches against the query tags. The number of relevant photos of each user is viewed as his or her authoritativeness degree, by which *Most-tagged* produces a ranked list of users as a final result. By contrast, *LDA* identifies relevant photos using probabilistic topic modeling [8]. As a result, users are ranked in descending order of the query likelihoods given by Equation (1). Note that both *Most-tagged* and *LDA* utilize observational data from the sharing log while neglecting the valuable signal from the favorite log. On the contrary, *Most-favorited* leverages both the sharing log and the favorite log in a way that produces an ordered list of users by the numbers of times their relevant photos are favorited. As opposed to the previous three approaches, *TwitterRank* and *Link-PLSA-LDA* both build upon the graph structure constructed from the favorite log. Specifically, we construct the graph by creating a node for each user. There exists a link from node u to node v if the user corresponding to u favorited any photo of the user corresponding to v. A user's tags are associated with the corresponding node. The *TwitterRank* algorithm was originally proposed to find topic-level key influencers on Twitter [31]. It extends typical Topic-Sensitive PageRank [16] to compute per-topic influence scores. This requires a separate preprocess to create topics by running LDA on the text content associated with the nodes. The transition probability between two nodes in *TwitterRank* is defined based on the topical similarity between the corresponding users. Given the similar nature of the Twitter network and our constructed graph, we employ the *TwitterRank* algorithm to find topic-level authorities on a content sharing service. On the other hand, *Link-PLSA-LDA* is a probabilistic topic model on a hyperlink/citation network, which jointly models text and citations to estimate the influence of blogs/publications [23]. We adapt it to our constructed graph for topic-specific authority analysis. In our experiments, for every topic-sensitive algorithm, we set the number of topics to 100. We set all symmetric priors as 0.1 for every model with Dirichlet priors. For our TAA, we ran Gibbs sampling for 500 iterations. These settings are fairly typical and their tuning is beyond the scope of this paper.

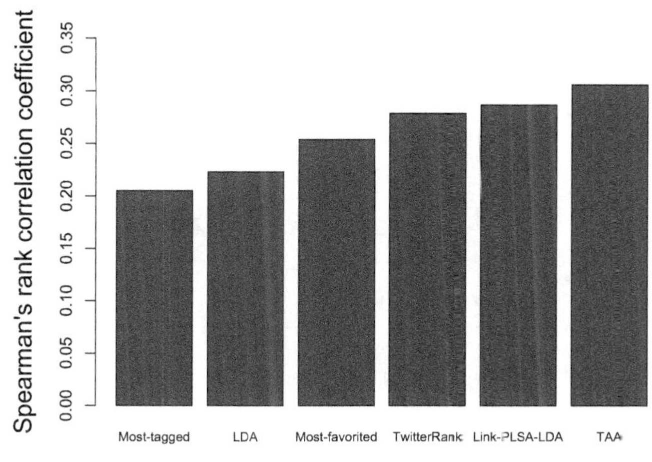

Figure 6: Spearman's rank correlation coefficient for the 500px dataset

To compute MRRs on the Flickr dataset we randomly selected 200 Flickr groups, whose administrators were treated as the real authorities on the respective group topics. The *Top Tags* generated by Flickr for each group were fed as a query to each algorithm. Figure 5 shows the MRR score of each algorithm on the Flickr dataset. It is observed that *Most-tagged* and *LDA* were inferior to the other algorithms, as neither of them models the valuable favorite signal. On the contrary, by exploiting the favorite data, the algorithms *Most-favorited*, *TwitterRank*, *Link-PLSA-LDA* and the proposed *TAA* produced higher MRR scores. In particular, *TwitterRank* underperformed *Link-PLSA-LDA* and *TAA*, due to its separation between topic modeling and authority analysis. To further measure the improvement of *TAA* over the runner-up *Link-PLSA-LDA*, we performed a paired t-test between them, which gave p-value < 0.05. It indicated that the improvement of *TAA* over *Link-PLSA-LDA* was *statistically significant*. This is not surprising because *Link-PLSA-LDA* as well as *TwitterRank* fail to uncover the latent topical motivate under each favorite click. Instead, they establish a link on the graph as long as a user favorited any photo of another, disregarding the identity of the photo as well as its underlying topics.

For 500px, we plot the Spearman's coefficient for each algorithm in Figure 6. From this figure, we observe the pattern similar to that of Figure 5. *TAA* outperformed all the other algorithms, thanks to its unified framework of topic modeling and authority analysis. In addition, *TAA* benefited from its ability to identify users' topical authoritativeness by uncovering each favorite click's underlying topical motivate and learning from pairwise resource preference.

6.4 Predictive Power Analysis

As generative models, our *TAA*, as shown in Figure 3, and the competitor *Link-PLSA-LDA* [23] are able to generate and predict unseen new data. We evaluated the predictive power and generalizability of both models using the standard *perplexity* metric [8]. The perplexity is monotonically decreasing in the likelihood of the unseen test data. Hence, a lower perplexity score indicates stronger predictive power. Formally, the perplexity is defined as:

$$perplexity(F_{\text{test}}) = \exp\left\{-\frac{\sum_{f\in F_{\text{test}}}\log p(f)}{|F_{\text{test}}|}\right\}, \qquad (20)$$

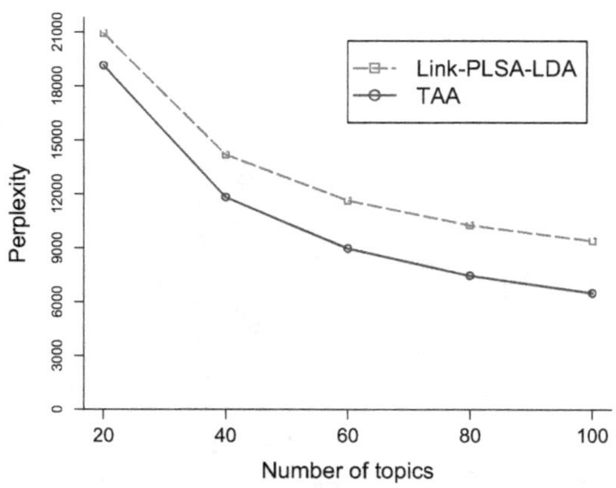

Figure 7: Perplexity for the Flickr dataset

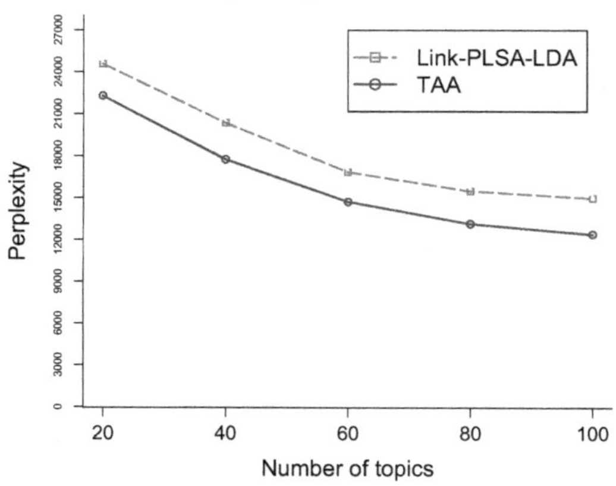

Figure 8: Perplexity for the 500px dataset

where F_{test} denotes the test set of favorites. For both Flickr and 500px, we held out 10% of the data for test purposes and trained the models on the remaining 90%.

Figure 7 and Figure 8 present the perplexity as a function of the numbers of topics for both models on Flickr data and 500px data, respectively. It is clear that the *TAA* consistently produced lower perplexity scores than *Link-PLSA-LDA* for both Flickr and 500px, indicating that our *TAA* model has stronger predictive power and better generalizability. Moreover, *TAA* predicted unseen favorites even better as the number of topics increases.

6.5 Case Visualization

For the visualization of the *TAA* model, we performed searches on Flickr data for a list of photographers who are expert in two specific topics. Figure 9 shows the examples of photographers identified by *TAA* together with their ranks in the lists. To illustrate their expertise in photography, photos on the query topics are presented as well. For the first query topic: *winter snow landscape*, we see from the photos that the first user in the ranked list demonstrated the expertise in shooting snow landscape in winter. By contrast, the user in rank 100 seemed to have broader interests, not specializing in this specific topic. The last user looked even irrelevant to the query topic. For the second query topic: *waterscape*, the user at the top was clearly superior to the others in waterscape shooting, although some photos from the last two users were somewhat related to the water topic.

7. CONCLUSION

This paper addresses the problem of authority analysis specific to given query topic(s) for users on a content shar-

Figure 9: Examples of the ranked lists of photographers identified by *TAA* on Flickr data

ing service. To model topic-specific authoritativeness, we introduce a novel method of Topic-specific Authority Analysis (TAA), which properly captures the associations among users' interest and authoritativeness as well as the topics of favorited resources to exploit the signal of favorite clicks. The parameters in the TAA model are learned from a training set of observations constructed from two data sources: *sharing log* and *favorite log*. To overcome the limitation of missing negative feedback, we propose a preference learning technique embedding a new logistic likelihood function. An extension of typical collapsed Gibbs sampling is further proposed for Bayesian inference with the logistic likelihood. With the inferred parameters, our analysis framework produces a ranked list of authorities by their authoritativeness specific to given query topic(s).

We conducted thorough experiments on the datasets collected from two specific real-world content sharing websites, Flickr and 500px. Experimental results demonstrate that the TAA model outperforms the competitors, confirming its effectiveness in topic-specific authority analysis and its generalizability to unseen data.

8. ACKNOWLEDGMENT

This research is supported by Hong Kong Research Grants Council grant HKU712712E.

9. REFERENCES

[1] D. Agarwal and B.-C. Chen. flda: Matrix factorization through latent dirichlet allocation. In *Proc. of WSDM '10*, pages 91–100, New York, NY, USA, 2010.

[2] N. Barbieri, F. Bonchi, and G. Manco. Topic-aware social influence propagation models. In *Proc. of ICDM '12*, pages 81–90, Washington, DC, USA, 2012.

[3] S. Bellman, E. J. Johnson, G. L. Lohse, and N. Mandel. Designing marketplaces of the artificial with consumers in mind: Four approaches to

understanding consumer behavior in electronic environments. *J. Interactive Marketing*, 20(1), 2006.

[4] B. Bi and J. Cho. Automatically generating descriptions for resources by tag modeling. In *Proc. of CIKM '13*, pages 2387–2392, 2013.

[5] B. Bi, S. D. Lee, B. Kao, and R. Cheng. Cubelsi: An effective and efficient method for searching resources in social tagging systems. In *ICDE*, pages 27–38, 2011.

[6] B. Bi, L. Shang, and B. Kao. Collaborative resource discovery in social tagging systems. In *Proc. of CIKM '09*, pages 1919–1922, 2009.

[7] B. Bi, Y. Tian, Y. Sismanis, A. Balmin, and J. Cho. Scalable topic-specific influence analysis on microblogs. In *Proc. of WSDM*, pages 513–522, 2014.

[8] D. M. Blei, A. Y. Ng, and M. I. Jordan. Latent dirichlet allocation. *JMLR*, 3:993–1022, Mar. 2003.

[9] B.-C. Chen, J. Guo, B. Tseng, and J. Yang. User reputation in a comment rating environment. In *Proc. of KDD '11*, pages 159–167, New York, USA, 2011.

[10] N. Chen, J. Zhu, F. Xia, and B. Zhang. Generalized relational topic models with data augmentation. In *Proc. of IJCAI '13*, pages 1273–1279, 2013.

[11] W. Chen, Y. Wang, and S. Yang. Efficient influence maximization in social networks. In *Proc. of KDD '09*, pages 199–208, New York, NY, USA, 2009.

[12] S. Fruhwirth-Schnatter and R. Fruhwirth. Data augmentation and mcmc for binary and multinomial logit models. In *Sta Mod Reg Str*, pages 111–132. 2010.

[13] A. Gelman, J. B. Carlin, H. S. Stern, and D. B. Rubin. *Bayesian Data Analysis*. November 2013.

[14] R. B. Gramacy and N. G. Polson. Simulation-based regularized logistic regression. *Bayesian Analysis*, 7(3):567–590, September 2012.

[15] T. L. Griffiths and M. Steyvers. Finding scientific topics. *PNAS*, 101(Suppl. 1):5228–5235, April 2004.

[16] T. Haveliwala. Topic-sensitive pagerank: a context-sensitive ranking algorithm for web search. *IEEE TKDE*, 15(4):784–796, July 2003.

[17] G. Heinrich. Parameter estimation for text analysis,. Technical report, University of Leipzig, 2008.

[18] C. C. Holmes and L. Held. Bayesian auxiliary variable models for binary and multinomial regression. *Bayesian Analysis*, 1(1):145–168, March 2006.

[19] P. Jurczyk and E. Agichtein. Discovering authorities in question answer communities by using link analysis. In *Proc. of CIKM '07*, pages 919–922, New York, 2007.

[20] D. Kempe, J. Kleinberg, and E. Tardos. Maximizing the spread of influence through a social network. In *Proc. of KDD '03*, pages 137–146, New York, 2003.

[21] J. M. Kleinberg. Authoritative sources in a hyperlinked environment. *JACM*, 46(5):604–632, 1999.

[22] J. Leskovec, A. Krause, C. Guestrin, C. Faloutsos, J. VanBriesen, and N. Glance. Cost-effective outbreak detection in networks. In *KDD*, pages 420–429, 2007.

[23] R. M. Nallapati, A. Ahmed, E. P. Xing, and W. W. Cohen. Joint latent topic models for text and citations. In *Proc. of KDD '08*, pages 542–550, 2008.

[24] L. Page, S. Brin, R. Motwani, and T. Winograd. The pagerank citation ranking: Bringing order to the web. In *Proc. of WWW '98*, pages 161–172, Brisbane, 1998.

[25] N. G. Polson, J. G. Scott, and J. Windle. Bayesian inference for logistic models using pólya-gamma latent variables. *JASA*, 108(504):1339–1349, 2013.

[26] I. Porteous, D. Newman, A. Ihler, A. Asuncion, P. Smyth, and M. Welling. Fast collapsed gibbs sampling for latent dirichlet allocation. In *KDD*, 2008.

[27] D. Smith, S. Menon, and K. Sivakumar. Online peer and editorial recommendations, trust, and choice in virtual markets. *J. Interactive Marketing*, 19(3), 2005.

[28] J. Tang, J. Sun, C. Wang, and Z. Yang. Social influence analysis in large-scale networks. In *Proc. of KDD '09*, pages 807–816, New York, NY, USA, 2009.

[29] C. Wang and D. M. Blei. Collaborative topic modeling for recommending scientific articles. In *KDD*, 2011.

[30] Y. Wang, G. Cong, G. Song, and K. Xie. Community-based greedy algorithm for mining top-k influential nodes in mobile social networks. In *Proc. of KDD '10*, pages 1039–1048, New York, 2010.

[31] J. Weng, E.-P. Lim, J. Jiang, and Q. He. Twitterrank: Finding topic-sensitive influential twitterers. In *Proc. of WSDM '10*, pages 261–270, 2010.

[32] J. Zhang, M. S. Ackerman, and L. Adamic. Expertise networks in online communities: Structure and algorithms. In *WWW '07*, pages 221–230, 2007.

[33] T. Zhao, N. Bian, C. Li, and M. Li. Topic-level expert modeling in community question answering. In *SDM '13*, pages 776–784. SIAM, 2013.

APPENDIX

Let us derive the collapsed posterior distribution of TAA augmented with the variables δ, as follows:

$$
\begin{aligned}
& p(\mathbf{z}, \delta, \eta | \mathbf{t}, \mathbf{o}, \alpha, \beta, \mu, \Sigma) \\
\propto\ & p(\mathbf{t}, \mathbf{z} | \alpha, \beta) p(\mathbf{o}, \delta | \mathbf{z}, \eta) p(\eta | \mu, \Sigma) \\
=\ & \int \int p(\mathbf{t}, \mathbf{z}, \theta, \varphi | \alpha, \beta) d\theta d\varphi \times p(\eta | \mu, \Sigma) p(\mathbf{o}, \delta | \mathbf{z}, \eta) \\
=\ & \int p(\mathbf{z} | \theta) p(\theta | \alpha) d\theta \times \int p(\mathbf{t} | \varphi, \mathbf{z}) p(\varphi | \beta) d\varphi \\
& \times p(\eta | \mu, \Sigma) p(\mathbf{o}, \delta | \mathbf{z}, \eta) \\
=\ & \prod_{u=1}^{L} \int \frac{\Gamma(\sum_{k=1}^{K} \alpha_k)}{\prod_{k=1}^{K} \Gamma(\alpha_k)} \prod_{k=1}^{K} \theta_{uk}^{\alpha_k - 1} \prod_{n=1}^{N_u} \theta_{u z_{un}} d\theta_u \\
& \times \prod_{k=1}^{K} \int \frac{\Gamma(\sum_{t=1}^{V} \beta_t)}{\sum_{t=1}^{V} \Gamma(\beta_t)} \prod_{t=1}^{V} \varphi_{kt}^{\beta_t - 1} \prod_{u=1}^{L} \prod_{n=1}^{N_u} \varphi_{z_{un} t_{un}} d\varphi_k \\
& \times p(\eta | \mu, \Sigma) p(\mathbf{o}, \delta | \mathbf{z}, \eta) \\
& \text{(Expand out Dirichlet and Multinomial distributions)} \\
=\ & \prod_{u=1}^{L} \int \frac{\Gamma(\sum_{k=1}^{K} \alpha_k)}{\prod_{k=1}^{K} \Gamma(\alpha_k)} \prod_{k=1}^{K} \theta_{uk}^{\alpha_k + c_{ku} - 1} d\theta_u \\
& \times \prod_{k=1}^{K} \int \frac{\Gamma(\sum_{t=1}^{V} \beta_t)}{\sum_{t=1}^{V} \Gamma(\beta_t)} \prod_{t=1}^{V} \varphi_{kt}^{\beta_t + g_{kt} - 1} d\varphi_k \\
& \times p(\eta | \mu, \Sigma) p(\mathbf{o}, \delta | \mathbf{z}, \eta) \\
\propto\ & \prod_{u=1}^{L} \frac{\prod_{k=1}^{K} \Gamma(c_{ku} + \alpha_k)}{\Gamma(\sum_{k=1}^{K} c_{ku} + \alpha_k)} \times \prod_{k=1}^{K} \frac{\prod_{t=1}^{V} \Gamma(g_{kt} + \beta_t)}{\Gamma(\sum_{t=1}^{V} g_{kt} + \beta_t)} \\
& \times p(\eta | \mu, \Sigma) \prod_{(u, r_i, r_j) \in \mathcal{D}} e^{\frac{\boldsymbol{\eta}_u^{\mathsf{T}} \hat{\mathbf{z}}_{ur_{ij}} - \delta_{ur_{ij}} (\boldsymbol{\eta}_u^{\mathsf{T}} \hat{\mathbf{z}}_{ur_{ij}})^2}{2}} p(\delta_{ur_{ij}} | 1, 0)
\end{aligned}
$$

Frontiers in E-commerce Personalization

Sri Subramaniam
Groupon
Palo Alto, CA
srisub@groupon.com

ABSTRACT

E-commerce has largely been a "Pull" model to date. Offline retailers have nailed discovery, delight, serendipity, and impulse purchases in person with greater success than online commerce sites. However, in an always-on, mobile-first world, companies like Groupon have the opportunity to push the frontier even further than offline retailers or comprehensive sites due to the fact that our smartphones are always with us. The challenge is to provide the right deals to the right user at the right time. That involves learning about the users and their locations, their personal preferences, and predicting which deals are likely to delight them, presenting diversity, discovery and engaging UX to gather user preferences and semantic graph approaches for user-deal matching. This presentation will give insight into how Groupon manages to grapple with these challenges via a data-driven system in order to delight and surprise customers.

Categories and Subject Descriptors

H.2.8 [**Database Management**]: Database Applications--*Data mining*

Keywords

E-commerce; mobile technology; geolocation data; recommender systems

Bio

Sri Subramaniam is VP of Engineering for Relevance and Search (Smart Deals) at Groupon. His responsibility is to put the right deals in front of the right consumers at the right time, for mobile, web and e-mail. Subramaniam comes to Groupon from WalmartLabs, where he was VP of Engineering, responsible for technologies such as Search, Catalog, Marketplace and Item infrastructure. WalmartLabs was created through the acquisition of Kosmix, a Semantic Tech startup, where Sri was VP, Engineering. Prior to Kosmix, Sri worked at eBay, responsible for Search and other e-commerce systems. Sri is passionate about E-commerce, Search & Personalization, and Consumer Apps. He holds a B.Tech in Electronics from the Indian Institute of Technology, Madras, and an M.S. in Computer Engineering from Rensselaer Polytechnic Institute.

KDD'14, August 24–27, 2014, New York, New York, USA.
ACM 978-1-4503-2956-9/14/08.
http://dx.doi.org/10.1145/2623330.2630820

Predictive Modeling in Practice

Tracey De Poalo
Sprint
Kansas City, MO

Jeremy Howard
Khosla Ventures
Menlo Park

ABSTRACT

It's not often we get to peer into the details of how big corporates use predictive modeling in practice. In this talk, Sprint's Head of Predictive Modeling, Tracey De Poalo, will talk about the process she developed using SAS and logistic regression to build a wide range of models. Jeremy Howard will discuss his experience as a consultant at Sprint comparing R and random forests to the existing process, and will show the pros and cons of each approach.

The talk will also cover the "real world" issues that Tracey has dealt with in creating a reusable process, including data mart development, sampling, testing, reporting, and implementation with internal customers.

Sprint's existing process is the best that Jeremy has seen in industry, and shows a lot of best practices in data structure, documentation, testing, automation, and customer interaction, and modeling.

Categories and Subject Descriptors

H.4.0 Information Systems, INFORMATION SYSTEMS APPLICATIONS: General.

Keywords

Predictive modeling; machine learning; logistic regression; random forests; real-world applications

Bio

Tracey has been managing the Predictive Analytics team at Sprint for six years. Her educational background includes a Masters in Statistics from Florida State University and a Masters in Industrial Design from Georgia Institute of Technology. A deep understanding of design methodology allows Tracey to bring creative solutions to complex analytical problems. She has introduced multiple, robust procedures that have made predictive analytics at Sprint more efficient and productive. Tracey also has extensive analytical experience in the credit industry working for Equifax and Merkle.

Jeremy Howard is an entrepreneur, business strategist, developer, and educator. He is the founder of Strategic Data Science, which aims to make machine learning accessible to non-experts, and is a Distinguished Research Scientist at the University of San Francisco. He is also a faculty member at Singularity University, and a Young Global Leader with the World Economic Forum. Previously he was the President and Chief Scientist of the data science platform Kaggle. He was the founding CEO of two successful Australian startups (FastMail, and Optimal Decisions Group). Before that, he spent 8 years in management consulting, at McKinsey & Co, and AT Kearney. Jeremy has invested in, mentored, and advised many startups, and contributed to many open source projects.

KDD'14, August 24–27, 2014, New York, New York, USA.
ACM 978-1-4503-2956-9/14/08.
http://dx.doi.org/10.1145/2623330.2630821

Medicine in the Age of Electronic Health Records

Nigam Shah
Stanford
1265 Welch Road
Stanford, CA
nigam@stanford.edu

ABSTRACT

In the era of EHRs, it is possible to examine the outcomes of decisions made by doctors during clinical practice to identify patterns of care—generating evidence based on the collective practice of experts. We will discuss methods that use unstructured patient data to monitor for adverse drug events, profile specific drugs, identify off-label drug usage, uncover 'natural experiments' and generate practice-based evidence for difficult-to-test clinical hypotheses. We will describe how to detect associations among drugs and their adverse events several years before an alert is issued as well as compute the true rate of drug-drug interactions. We will present approaches to identify novel off-label uses of drugs using the patient feature matrix along with prior knowledge about drugs, diseases, and known usage. We will review a natural experiment—where a subset of congestive heart failure patients who were prescribed Cilostazol despite its black box warning—and profile its safety. We will discuss the testing of a clinical hypothesis about an association between allergic conditions and chronic uveitis in patients with juvenile idiopathic arthritis.

KDD'14, Aug 24–27, 2014, New York, NY, USA
ACM 978-1-4503-2956-9/14/08.
http://dx.doi.org/10.1145/2623330.2630822

Categories and Subject Descriptors

J.3 [**Computer Applications**]: Life and Medical Sciences--*Health*

Keywords

Learning health system; unstructured EHR; clinical data warehouse; practice-based evidence

Bio

Dr. Nigam H. Shah is an Assistant Professor of Medicine (Biomedical Informatics) at the Stanford School of Medicine. Dr. Shah researches methods of using machine learning, text-mining, and medical ontologies to learn medical evidence from unstructured clinical data. He teaches a graduate class on data-driven medicine. Dr. Shah holds an MBBS from Baroda Medical College, India, a PhD from Penn State University, USA and completed post-doctoral training at the Stanford Medical School in 2007.

Algorithms for Interpretable Machine Learning

Cynthia Rudin
Massachusetts Institute of Technology
100 Main Street, E62, Room 576
Cambridge, MA 02142
1-617-715-4215
rudin@mit.edu

ABSTRACT

It is extremely important in many application domains to have transparency in predictive modeling. Domain experts do not tend to prefer "black box" predictive model models. They would like to understand how predictions are made, and possibly, prefer models that emulate the way a human expert might make a decision, with a few important variables, and a clear convincing reason to make a particular prediction.

I will discuss recent work on interpretable predictive modeling with decision lists and sparse integer linear models. I will describe several approaches, including an algorithm based on discrete optimization, and an algorithm based on Bayesian analysis. I will show examples of interpretable models for stroke prediction in medical patients and prediction of violent crime in young people raised in out-of-home care.

Collaborators are Ben Letham, Berk Ustun, Stefano Traca, Siong Thye Goh, Tyler McCormick, and David Madigan.

Categories and Subject Descriptors

I.2.6 [**Learning**]: *Knowledge Acquisition*

H.1.2 [**User/Machine Systems**]: *Human Factors.*

General Terms

Algorithms

Keywords

Machine Learning; Interpretability; Comprehensibility; Understandability; Sparsity, Medical Calculators

Bio

Cynthia Rudin is an associate professor of statistics at the Massachusetts Institute of Technology associated with the Computer Science and Artificial Intelligence Laboratory and the Sloan School of Management, where she directs the Prediction Analysis Laboratory. Her expertise is in machine learning and knowledge discovery, and she aims to make predictive modeling closer to decision making. Previously, Prof. Rudin was an associate research scientist at the Center for Computational Learning Systems at Columbia University, and prior to that, an NSF postdoctoral research fellow at NYU. She holds an undergraduate degree from the University at Buffalo where she received the College of Arts and Sciences Outstanding Senior Award in Sciences and Mathematics in 1999, and she received a PhD in applied and computational mathematics from Princeton University in 2004. She is the recipient of the 2013 INFORMS Innovative Applications in Analytics Award, and a 2011 NSF CAREER award. Her work has been featured in IEEE Computer, Businessweek, The Wall Street Journal, the Boston Globe, the Times of London, Fox News (Fox & Friends), the Toronto Star, WIRED Science, Yahoo! Shine, U.S. News and World Report, Slashdot, CIO magazine, and on Boston Public Radio.

KDD'14, Aug 24–27, 2014, New York, NY, USA
ACM 978-1-4503-2956-9/14/08.
http://dx.doi.org/10.1145/2623330.2630823

Data Science Through the Lens of Social Science

Drew Conway
Project Florida
New York, NY
agconway@gmail.com

ABSTRACT

In this talk, Drew will examine data science through the lens of the social scientist. He will discuss how the various skills and disciplines combine into data science. Drew will also present a motivating example directly from his work as a senior advisor to NYC's Mayor's Office of Analytics.

Categories and Subject Descriptors

H.2.8 [**Database Management**]: Database Applications--*Data mining*

Keywords

Data science; social science; local government

KDD'14, Aug 24–27, 2014, New York, NY, USA
ACM 978-1-4503-2956-9/14/08.
http://dx.doi.org/10.1145/2623330.2630824

Bio

Drew Conway is a leading expert in the application of computational methods to social and behavioral problems at large-scale. Drew is the is the Head of Data at Project Florida, and has been writing and speaking about the role of data — and the discipline of data science — in industry, government, and academia for several years.

Drew has advised and consulted companies across many industries; ranging from fledgling start-ups to Fortune 100 companies, as well as academic institutions and government agencies at all levels. Drew started his career in counter-terrorism as a computational social scientist in the U.S. intelligence community.

Information Environment Security

Rand Waltzman
DARPA
Washington, DC
Rand.Waltzman@darpa.mil

ABSTRACT

The US Department of Defense Dictionary of Military terms defines the Information Environment as "the aggregate of individuals, organizations, and systems that collect, process, disseminate, or act on information." The decisions and actions we take both as individuals and collectively simultaneously shape and are shaped by the information environment in which we live. The nature of our interaction with the information environment is rapidly evolving and old models are becoming irrelevant faster than we can develop new ones. This results in uncertainties that leave us exposed to dangerous influences without proper defenses. The purpose of this talk is to help frame a new science of Information Environment Security (IES) whose goal is to create and apply the tools needed to discover and maintain fundamental models of our ever-changing information environment and to defend us in that environment, both as individuals and collectively, against intentional as well as unintentional attempts to deceive, misinform and otherwise manipulate us. IES is an interdisciplinary science that will require bringing together experts working in areas such as cognitive science, computer science, social science, security, marketing, political campaigning, public policy, and psychology to develop a theoretical as well as an applied engineering methodology for managing the full spectrum of information environment security issues.

Categories and Subject Descriptors

K.6.5 [**Management of Computing and Information Systems**]: Security and Protection

Keywords

Information environment; security; cognitive science; computer science; social science; marketing; political campaigning; public policy; psychology

Bio

Dr. Rand Waltzman joined DARPA as a Program Manager in May 2010. His focus is on information systems security. Dr. Waltzman joined DARPA from Lockheed Martin Advanced Technology Laboratories (LM-ATL), where he served as Chief Scientist for the Applied Sciences Laboratory that specializes in advanced software techniques and the computational physics of materials. Prior to LM-ATL he was an Associate Professor in the Department of Computer Science at the Royal Institute of Technology in Stockholm, Sweden, where he taught and performed research in applications of machine intelligence technology to a variety of problem areas including digital entertainment, automated reasoning and decision support and cyber threat detection. Before his professorship he served as a DARPA Program Manager focusing on machine intelligence and image understanding. Dr. Waltzman has also held research positions at the University of Maryland, Teknowledge Corporation, and the Applied Physics Laboratory of the University of Washington.

KDD'14, Aug 24–27, 2014, New York, NY, USA
ACM 978-1-4503-2956-9/14/08.
http://dx.doi.org/10.1145/2623330.2635636

Big Data for Social Good

Nathan Eagle
Jana
Boston, MA
eagle@hsph.harvard.edu

ABSTRACT

Petabytes of data about human movements, transactions and communication patterns are being generated by everyday technologies such as mobile phones and credit cards. This unprecedented volume of information facilitates a novel set of research questions applicable to a wide range of development issues. In collaboration involving 237 mobile phone operators across 102 countries, Jana's mobile technology platform can instantly poll and compensate 3.48 billion active mobile subscriptions. This talk will discuss how insights gained from living in Kenya became the genesis of a technology company currently working with global clients in over 50 countries, including P&G, Google, Unilever, Danone, General Mills, Nestle, Johnson & Johnson, Microsoft, the World Bank, and the United Nations. After providing an overview of the mobile and social media landscapes in emerging markets, we discuss a system that implements polls and mobile subscription compensation. The presentation will conclude by emphasizing the value of consumer data in underserved and understudied regions of the world.

Categories and Subject Descriptors

H.2.8 [**Database Management**]: Database Applications--*Data mining*

KDD'14, Aug 24–27, 2014, New York, NY, USA
ACM 978-1-4503-2956-9/14/08.
http://dx.doi.org/10.1145/2623330.2630819

Keywords

Mobile technology; polling systems; social media; emerging markets

Bio

Nathan Eagle is the co-founder and CEO of Jana, a mobile technology platform that connects emerging market consumers with global brands using mobile airtime. Nathan is also an Adjunct Assistant Professor at Harvard University, where he researches how data generated by human movements, financial transactions, and communication patterns can be used for social good. He has been named to Advertising Age's 40 under 40 in 2014 and MIT's TR35, a group of the world's top innovators under 35 in 2009. Nathan current serves on the World Economic Forum as Technology Pioneer. He holds a BS and two MS degrees from Stanford's School of Engineering as well as a PhD from MIT.

Bringing Data Science to the Speakers of Every Language

Robert Munro
Idibon
San Francisco, CA
robert.munro@gmail.com

ABSTRACT

Speakers of more than 5,000 languages have access to internet and communication technologies. The majority of phones, tablets and computers now ship with language-enabled capabilities like speech-recognition and intelligent auto-correction, and people increasingly interact with data-intensive cloud-based language technologies like search-engines and spam-filters. For both personal and large-scale technologies, the service quality drops or disappears entirely outside of a handful of languages. Speakers of low-resource languages correlate with lower access to healthcare, education and higher vulnerability to disasters. Serving the broadest possible range of languages is crucial to ensuring equitable participation in the global information economy.

I will present examples of how natural language processing and distributed human computing are improving the lives of speakers of all the world's languages, in areas including education, disaster-response, health and access to employment. When applying natural language processing to the full diversity of the world's communications, we need to go beyond simple keyword analysis and implement complex technologies that require human-in-the-loop processing to ensure usable accuracy. In recent work where more than a million human judgments were collected on unstructured text and imagery data around natural disasters, I will present observations that debunk recent over-optimistic claims about the utility of social media following disasters. On the positive side, I will share results that show how for-profit technologies are improving people's lives by providing sustainable economic growth opportunities when they support more languages, aligning business objectives with global diversity.

KDD'14, Aug 24–27, 2014, New York, NY, USA
ACM 978-1-4503-2956-9/14/08.
http://dx.doi.org/10.1145/2623330.2630825

Categories and Subject Descriptors

I.2.7 [**Artificial Intelligence**]: Natural Language Processing—*Text analysis*

Keywords

Natural language processing; human-computer interaction; crowdsourcing; education; disaster-response; healthcare; employment; social development

Bio

Robert is the CEO of Idibon, a company with the objective of providing language technologies for all the world's languages. In past work he has served as Chief Information Officer for the largest solar energy company in Sierra Leone; was the Chief Technology Officer for the largest use of big data technologies to track disease outbreaks globally; worked for the UN High Commission for Refugees in Liberia; lead the crowdsourced response to the 2010 earthquake Haiti; and has helped information processing in disaster response and election monitoring in more than a dozen countries. In current work, Idibon helps everyone from Fortune 500s to disaster response organizations process language data at scale. Outside of work, he has learned about the world's diversity by cycling more than 20,000 kilometers across 20 countries. Rob has a PhD from Stanford University.

Guilt by Association: Large Scale Malware Detection by Mining File-relation Graphs

Acar Tamersoy
College of Computing
Georgia Institute of Technology
tamersoy@gatech.edu

Kevin Roundy
Symantec Research Labs
kevin_roundy@symantec.com

Duen Horng Chau
College of Computing
Georgia Institute of Technology
polo@gatech.edu

ABSTRACT

The increasing sophistication of malicious software calls for new defensive techniques that are harder to evade, and are capable of protecting users against novel threats. We present AESOP, a scalable algorithm that identifies malicious executable files by applying Aesop's moral that "a man is known by the company he keeps." We use a large dataset voluntarily contributed by the members of Norton Community Watch, consisting of partial lists of the files that exist on their machines, to identify close relationships between files that often appear together on machines. AESOP leverages locality-sensitive hashing to measure the strength of these inter-file relationships to construct a graph, on which it performs large scale inference by propagating information from the labeled files (as benign or malicious) to the preponderance of unlabeled files. AESOP attained early labeling of 99% of benign files and 79% of malicious files, over a week before they are labeled by the state-of-the-art techniques, with a 0.9961 true positive rate at flagging malware, at 0.0001 false positive rate.

Categories and Subject Descriptors

H.2.8 [**Database Applications**]: Data mining; D.4.6 [**Security and Protection**]

Keywords

Malware detection; graph mining; file graph; belief propagation; locality sensitive hashing

1. INTRODUCTION

Protection against novel malware attacks, also known as 0-day malware, is becoming increasingly important as the cost of these attacks increases. For individuals, the dollars and cents cost is rising due to the increasing prevalence of financial fraud and the increasing viciousness of malware, such as the CryptoLocker ransomware program that encrypts personal data files and holds them for a ransom of 300

KDD'14, August 24–27, 2014, New York, NY, USA.
Copyright 2014 ACM 978-1-4503-2956-9/14/08 ...$15.00.
http://dx.doi.org/10.1145/2623330.2623342.

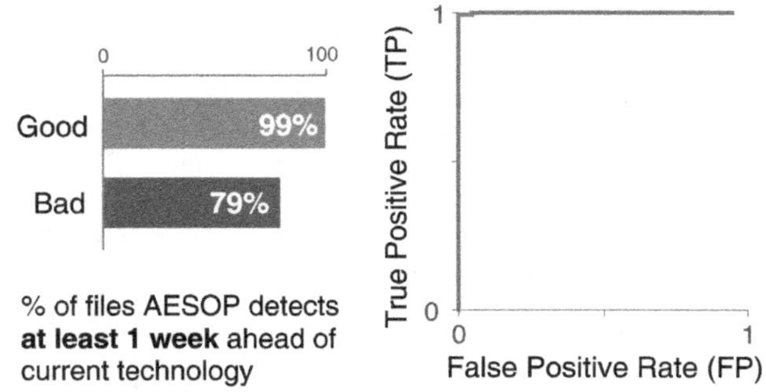

Figure 1: Left: 99% of the known good files and 79% of known bad files detected by AESOP were labeled *at least 1 week* ahead of Symantec's current technology. Right: AESOP achieves almost perfect detection for malware, with few false alarms (0.9961 TP rate at 0.0001 FP rate).

dollars [4]. Emotional and professional costs can be much higher, as when attacks result in the loss of privacy. The situation is arguably worse for governments and businesses, which find themselves under siege by well-funded attackers that routinely create devastating financial losses, and perhaps even more impactful losses of intellectual property and operational secrets [23].

Computer security providers recognize the need to respond with better protection against novel threats. The goal of these 0-day threat protections is to limit the malware's window of effectiveness, so that malicious files are detected as soon as possible after their first appearance. Another critical measure of success is a vanishingly small false positive rate, as labeling a benign file as malicious can have devastating consequences, particularly if it is a popular file or one that is essential to the stability of the system, as in the case of operating system and driver files.

We present AESOP (Figure 2), a novel approach to detecting malicious executable files by applying the well-known aphorism that "a man is known by the company he keeps," and in our case, a file's goodness may be judged by the other files that often appear with it on users' machines. More precisely, we infer unlabeled files' reputation (or goodness) by analyzing their relations with labeled peers.

AESOP is not the first attempt to detect malware by establishing file reputation scores. A representative work in this space is Polonium [7], which leverages the insight that some computer users have poor internet hygiene in that they attract many more malicious files than users that follow se-

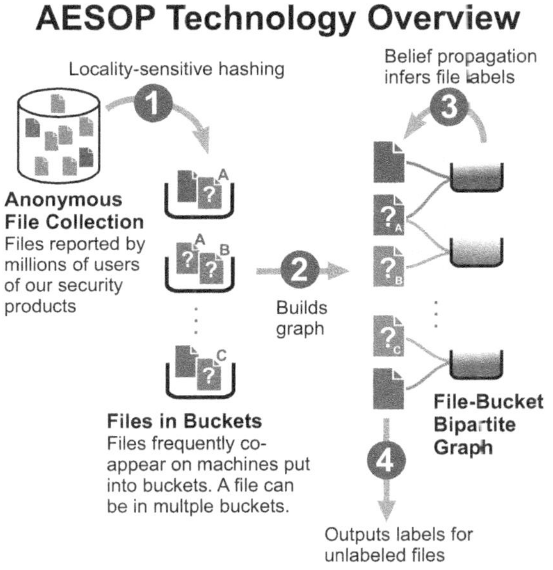

Figure 2: Overview of the AESOP technology

curity best practices. Polonium constructs a bipartite graph between files and machines, in which a file-machine edge represents the existence of a particular file on a particular machine. This approach proved to be successful Symantec has deployed Polonium; it has detected millions of malicious files. However, Polonium misses many malicious files as it can only observe malware's file-to-file relationships indirectly through the lens of low-hygiene machines. By contrast, AESOP directly captures file-to-file affinity and can therefore identify malicious files that co-occur with one another, even when they do not appear on heavily infected machines. As we shall demonstrate, AESOP is able to detect many malicious files over a week before they are labeled by Symantec's existing Polonium-based technology, with a 0.0001 false positive rate (see Figure 1).

Like Polonium, in this work we leverage Symantec's Norton Community Watch data, the most important elements of which are unique file and machine identifiers. File identifiers are SHA-256 or MD5 cryptographic hash values that are computed over the file's raw bytes. Symantec's proxy for a true machine identifier is based on the serial number of Norton security products, which is an adequate but imperfect fit because product re-installation on a single machine may result in a serial number change, and a single serial number can be carried from one machine to another. The scale of this dataset is impressive, comprising 119 million machines and 10.1 billion files.

This paper makes the following contributions:

- We formulate the malware detection problem as a large-scale graph mining and inference problem, where our goal is to identify an unknown file's relations with other files so that we can establish guilt or innocence by its association with files that are known to be benign or malicious.
- We present the AESOP algorithm that leverages locality-sensitive hashing to efficiently compute file similarity values to construct a file-relation graph for inferring file goodness based on belief propagation.
- AESOP achieved early detection of 99% of benign files and 79% of malicious files that remained unlabeled by Symantec for over a week before they were eventually labeled, with exceptionally low error rates (see Figure 1).

The remainder of this paper proceeds as follows. We begin by describing our dataset and the notation we will use throughout this paper. We then proceed to a description of AESOP and its various components, followed by the experiments we conducted to demonstrate its effectiveness. Finally, we discuss our plans to deploy AESOP in support of Symantec's malware detection capabilities, and end by presenting our conclusions.

2. NOTATION AND DATASET DESCRIPTION

In this section, we formally describe our dataset and the central notion of file co-occurrence strength.

2.1 Dataset

Our dataset D consists of records of the form $< f, M_f >$, where f is a file and M_f is the set of machines that file f appears on (i.e., M being the set of all the machines, $M_f = \{m_1, m_2, ...\}$ where $m_i \in M$). $|M_f|$ denotes the prevalence of file f, i.e., the number of machines it appears on. Each file is either *labeled* or *unlabeled*. The possible labels for a labeled file are *good* and *bad*, indicating the nature of the file, i.e., whether it is purely trusted or malicious, respectively. We refer to a labeled file with the label *good* as a *good file* and with the label *bad* as a *bad file*. The good and bad files comprise the ground-truth set. Our informal high-level problem statement can be stated as follows: *Given a dataset as defined above, assign a label (i.e. good or bad) to unlabeled files based on their co-occurrence with labeled files.*

2.2 Defining File Co-occurence Strength

We define the *strength* of co-occurrence between two files f_i and f_j based on the overlap between sets M_{f_i} and M_{f_j}, and employ the Jaccard similarity measure given by the formula $J(M_{f_i}, M_{f_j}) = \frac{|M_{f_i} \cap M_{f_j}|}{|M_{f_i} \cup M_{f_j}|}$. This measure takes values between 0 and 1 (inclusive); between files f_i and f_j, the former indicates no co-occurrence relationship and the latter indicates a perfect co-occurrence relationship.

We assume that if $J(M_{f_i}, M_{f_j}) \leq \delta_J$, this indicates a *weak* (not *strong*) co-occurrence between files f_i and f_j. Additionally, if file f has a prevalence less than or equal to δ_M, (i.e. $|M_f| \leq \delta_M$), we call file f an immature file since it did not have time to establish presence, and we deem any co-occurrence relationship it is involved in as weak. Both δ_J and δ_M must be determined based on domain knowledge— for our dataset, we set $\delta_J = 0.5$ and $\delta_M = 4$.[1]

AESOP leverages strong co-occurrence relationships between the files to label them. To achieve this, AESOP uses Jaccard similarity because it can be efficiently computed and well-approximated for our large scale dataset through locality-sensitive hashing, which we will describe in the following sections.

Table 1 lists the symbols used throughout the paper.

[1]Specifically, we set δ_M based on our experience from Polonium [7]. The study on the effects of varying δ_J is omitted due to space constraints.

Symbol	Meaning
f	File (a.k.a. executable, software, application)
m	Machine (or computer)
M_f	The set of machines that file f appears on
D	Input dataset; records consist of $< f, M_f >$
$J(M_{f_i}, M_{f_j})$	Jaccard similarity between M_{f_i} and M_{f_j}
δ_J	Jaccard similarity threshold for strong co-occurrence, set to 0.5
δ_M	Prevalence threshold, set to 4
h	Random permutation function in MinHashing
b	Number of bands in locality-sensitive hashing
r	Number of MinHash values each band contains in locality-sensitive hashing
s	Jaccard similarity between a pair of files
TP	True positive; a malware instance correctly identified as bad
FP	False positive; a good file incorrectly identified as bad

Table 1: Main symbols used throughout the paper

3. PROPOSED METHOD: THE AESOP ALGORITHM

In this section, we describe the techniques that we used in designing AESOP so that it can scale to billions of files and over a hundred million machines. Figure 2 provides an overview of the AESOP approach. We begin by describing our use of MinHashing, which allows us to approximate the Jaccard similarity between two sets efficiently. Next, we explain our application of locality-sensitive hashing to efficiently identify peer-groups of strongly co-occurring files. Finally, we describe our use of belief propagation to propagate information from labeled files to their unlabeled peers.

3.1 MinHashing for Co-occurence Strength Estimation

It is not tractable to compute the Jaccard similarity between large sets due to the expensive set intersection and union operations it involves. *MinHashing* [5], which is short for *Minwise Independent Permutation Hashing*, is a popular technique to efficiently estimate the Jaccard similarity between two sets. MinHashing has been proven to work well for large scale real-world applications, such as detecting duplicate images [8] and clustering users on Google news [10]. We will explain MinHashing using dataset D in Table 2 as a running example. MinHashing *randomly* reorders the machines in M using a bijective function h that maps the machines in M to the set $\{1, ..., |M|\}$ in a random fashion. We call function h a *random permutation function*. An example function h for $M = \{m_1, ..., m_8\}$ is given in Table 2. Notice that if we rearrange the machines in $M_f \in D$ in ascending order of the machines' values retrieved from function h, we obtain a random permutation of M_f, which we refer to as M_f^h. For instance, M_{f_2} in Table 2 is permuted as $M_{f_2}^h = \{m_7, m_3, m_5\}$ since $h(m_7) = 1 < h(m_3) = 2 < h(m_5) = 8$. The MinHash value of M_f under function h, which we refer to as $h_{min}(M_f)$, is defined as $h_{min}(M_f) = \arg\min_{m_i \in M_f} h(m_i)$. Informally, $h_{min}(M_f)$ is the first element of M_f^h. For instance, $h_{min}(M_{f_1}) = m_4$ in Table 2.

File	Set of machines containing the file
f_1	$M_{f_1} = \{m_2, m_4, m_5, m_8\}$
f_2	$M_{f_2} = \{m_3, m_5, m_7\}$
f_3	$M_{f_3} = \{m_1, m_3, m_5, m_6, m_7\}$

$$h(m_1) = 3 \quad h(m_2) = 6 \quad h(m_3) = 2 \quad h(m_4) = 4$$
$$h(m_5) = 8 \quad h(m_6) = 7 \quad h(m_7) = 1 \quad h(m_8) = 5$$

Table 2: An example dataset D and random permutation function h

The key property of MinHashing is that the probability of the MinHash values of two sets being equal is equal to the Jaccard similarity between the sets. Formally, $\Pr(h_{min}(M_{f_i}) = h_{min}(M_{f_j})) = J(M_{f_i}, M_{f_j})$ (see Cohen et al. [9] or Rajaraman and Ullman [22] for a proof). As an example, in Table 2, $h_{min}(M_{f_1}) = m_4$, $h_{min}(M_{f_2}) = m_7$, and $J(M_{f_1}, M_{f_2}) = 0.17$.

3.2 Clustering Files

Despite the use of MinHashing, the number of file pairs to be considered for strong co-occurrence still remains very large for big datasets. It is also possible that two sets may not have the same MinHash value but in fact have a high Jaccard similarity, or may receive the same MinHash value but in fact have a low Jaccard similarity. Hence, a single MinHash value is typically not sufficient to deduce whether two sets have a high Jaccard similarity or, in our case, whether two files strongly co-occur. Locality-sensitive hashing (LSH), which we describe next, addresses these points.

LSH is a technique for approximate clustering and near-neighbor search in high dimensional spaces [16, 14]. Its main idea is to use multiple hash functions to map items into buckets such that similar items are more likely to be hashed to the same bucket. LSH uses *locality-sensitive function families* to achieve this goal.[2] At a high-level, each individual function in a locality-sensitive function family should be able to provide lower and upper bounds on the probability of whether two items with a pairwise similarity (or distance) in a particular interval will receive the same hash value from the function. Therefore, locality-sensitive function families are defined for particular similarity or distance measures, such as Hamming distance [14], L_p norms [14, 11], and earth mover's distance [6]. The random permutation functions used in MinHashing (see Section 3.1) form a locality-sensitive function family for the Jaccard similarity measure [9].

A nice property of the locality-sensitive function families is that they can be amplified by combining values returned from multiple functions via logical *AND* and/or *OR* [22]. In our context, given dataset D, this means we can compute n MinHash values—using n different random permutation functions—for each $M_f \in D$. Subsequently, these n MinHash values can be combined in multiple ways. An effective and generic way is to partition n MinHash values into b bands, each consisting of r values, such that $n = b \times r$.

As an example, consider Table 3, which lists six MinHash values for M_{f_4}, M_{f_5}, and M_{f_6} obtained from six different

[2] A function family is a group of functions that share certain characteristics.

	h_{min}	M_{f_4}	M_{f_5}	M_{f_6}	Buckets
Band 1	h^1_{min}	m_1	m_1	m_1	$[f_4, f_5]$ $[f_6]$
	h^2_{min}	m_1	m_1	m_2	
Band 2	h^3_{min}	m_5	m_5	m_3	$[f_4, f_5]$ $[f_6]$
	h^4_{min}	m_8	m_8	m_4	
Band 3	h^5_{min}	m_1	m_7	m_7	$[f_4][f_5, f_6]$
	h^6_{min}	m_6	m_6	m_6	

Table 3: Hypothetical inputs and outputs for LSH. The inputs are MinHash values for each file. The outputs are buckets containing files. This LSH scheme uses three bands, each consisting of two MinHash values.

random permutation functions $h^1, ..., h^6$. These six MinHash values are partitioned into three bands, each consisting of two values. For instance, M_{f_4}'s MinHash values for Band 2 are $\{m_5, m_8\}$. If we use a cryptographic hash function, such as SHA-256, to assign files to buckets based on their MinHash values in a band, then the files will appear in the same bucket if all of their r MinHash values in that band are the same. For instance, in Band 2 of Table 3, files f_4 and f_5 appear in the same bucket because their MinHash values for Band 2, i.e., h^3_{min} and h^4_{min}, are both $\{m_5, m_8\}$, whereas file f_6 appears in a separate bucket because its MinHash values are $\{m_3, m_4\}$. In this scheme, the files have b chances of appearing in the same bucket. This type of amplification is called an *AND*-construction with r rows followed by an *OR*-construction with b bands. This is because files will hash to the same bucket at least once if *all* of their r MinHash values (*AND* operation) in *any* of the b bands are the same (*OR* operation).

Our goal with LSH is that files f_i and f_j will appear together in at least one bucket if they strongly co-occur. Based on the scheme described above, we can derive the probability that files f_i and f_j will appear in at least one bucket given their true Jaccard similarity, $J(M_{f_i}, M_{f_j}) = s$, by following the derivation steps in Rajaraman and Ullman [22]. From Section 3.1, we know that the probability that one MinHash value of M_{f_i} and M_{f_j} being equal is s. Therefore, the probability of r MinHash values of M_{f_i} and M_{f_j} being the same is s^r. Notice that s^r is the probability that files f_i and f_j will hash to the same bucket in a particular band. Therefore, the probability that files f_i and f_j will not hash to the same bucket in a particular band is $1 - s^r$. Then, the probability that files f_i and f_j will not hash to the same bucket in all of the b bands is $(1 - s^r)^b$. Finally, the probability that files f_i and f_j will hash to the same bucket in at least one of the b bands is $1 - (1 - s^r)^b$.

3.2.1 Tuning Parameters of LSH

Figure 3 illustrates the effect of b and r on $1-(1-s^r)^b$ for various values of b, r, and s. Notice that increasing r allows us to prune file pairs with low Jaccard similarity whereas increasing b allows us to retain file pairs with high Jaccard similarity. As an example, consider our Jaccard similarity threshold for strong co-occurrence, $\delta_J = 0.5$. From the figure, we see that the probability that a pair of files with $s = 0.5$ appearing in at least one bucket is 0.5 when $b = 1$ and $r = 1$. The same probability drops to almost 0 when $b = 1$ and $r = 10$. Now, consider $s = 0.9$ with which we would deem a pair of files as strongly co-occurring. With $b = 1$ and $r = 10$, we see from the figure that the probability that the files in the pair appearing in at least one bucket is less than 0.4. The same probability increases to almost 1 when $b = 10$ and $r = 10$.

Given a δ_J value, one approach to select b and r is to first determine an r value that assigns to file pairs with $s \leq \delta_J$ a very small probability of appearing in at least one bucket. Then, we can select a b value that assigns to file pairs with $s > \delta_J$ a high probability of appearing in at least one bucket. Due to the "S" shape of the function $1 - (1 - s^r)^b$ [22], it is not feasible to ensure that all the file pairs with $s > \delta_J$ have a probability close to 1 while forcing any file pair with $s \leq \delta_J$ have a probability close to 0, similar to the ideal unit step function. Another consideration is that while large b and r values are advantageous, it also means that one needs to compute a significant amount of MinHash values for LSH. Given $\delta_J = 0.5$, we set $b = 10$ and $r = 10$ since these values prune the majority of the weakly co-occurring file pairs with $s \leq 0.5$ while retaining most of the strongly co-occurring file pairs with $s > 0.5$.

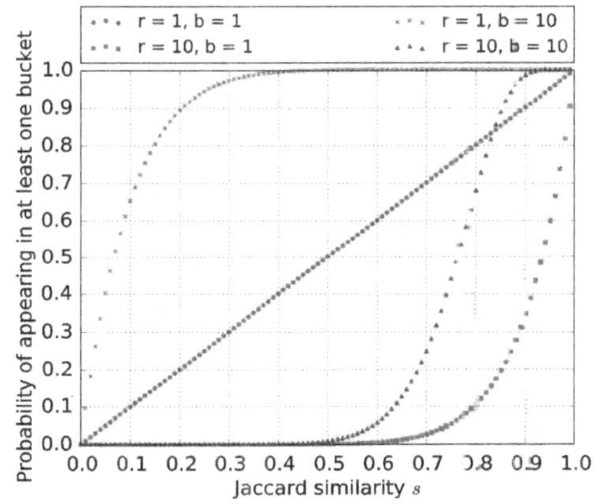

Figure 3: Effect of the number of bands, b, and MinHash values in each band, r, on the probability that two files with Jaccard similarity s will hash to the same bucket at least once in LSH. Given our Jaccard similarity threshold for strong co-occurrence $\delta_J = 0.5$, we set $b = 10$ and $r = 10$ (the blue curve with triangles) to prune the majority of the weakly co-occurring file pairs with $s \leq 0.5$ while retaining most of the strongly co-occurring file pairs with $s > 0.5$.

3.3 Labeling Files based on Co-occurrence

The outcome of LSH on dataset D is multiple bands, each consisting of a varying number of buckets that contain labeled and unlabeled files. A file appears at most once in a band, inside one of the buckets of the band. Notice that across different bands, the file might appear with a different set of files. For instance, in Table 3, file f_5 appears with file f_4 in two bands and with file f_6 in one band. In this section, we discuss how we combine the buckets from different bands into a unified "structure" and assign labels to unlabeled files using it.

Unipartite File Graph. Graphs provide a powerful representation of relationships between objects, therefore one approach to combine the buckets is to construct an undirected unipartite file graph by considering every pair of files in the buckets. In this graph, the files appear as nodes and they are connected with an edge if they *indeed* strongly co-occur. This additional check is performed to mitigate the effect of possible approximation errors incurred by LSH. The graph can then be used in a way that goodness and badness information is "sent" from the labeled files to the unlabeled files in the graph.

Our preliminary analyses showed that constructing a unipartite file graph as described above is not feasible. The reason is that a file inside a bucket typically strongly co-occurs with the majority of the other files in the bucket. This is most likely a property of the domain; there are intrinsic dependency relationships between files, e.g., the files under the "\Windows\System32" folder in the Windows operating systems. Therefore, large buckets contribute dense subgraphs to the graph during construction. In turn, the number of edges in the graph increases to billions, making it infeasible to operate on the graph.

Bipartite File-Bucket Graph. Due to this reason, AESOP instead operates on a undirected, unweighted bipartite file-bucket graph, which we also refer to as a *file-relation graph.* In this graph, there is an edge connecting a file node to a bucket node if the file appears in that bucket. Notice that the number of edges that would be included in the bipartite graph from a bucket of N strongly co-occurring files is $\mathcal{O}(N)$ in comparison to $\mathcal{O}(N^2)$ for the unipartite file graph. The bipartite graph is expected to contain more nodes than the unipartite file graph, however this is less of a concern for information propagation purposes as we will discuss. The bipartite graph is useful to assign labels to the unlabeled files; its difference with the unipartite file graph is that the files are now indirectly connected through the buckets, therefore goodness and badness information is first propagated from the labeled files to the buckets and then from the buckets to the unlabeled files.

Remarks. LSH ensures with high probability that if a file appears in a bucket consisting of more than one file, the file should strongly co-occur with at least one of the other files in the bucket. We represent this relationship by establishing an edge connecting the file to the bucket. It is, however, possible that a file does not strongly co-occur with some of the files in the bucket. In this case, the bipartite graph cannot capture the absence of strong co-occurrence between that set of files. In practice, this is a rare situation that does not pose any limitation on the effectiveness of AESOP, as we demonstrate in Section 4.

Benefits. A property of the bipartite graph is that it intrinsically captures the notion of a weight between the files. To illustrate this, consider two strongly co-occurring files f_i and f_j, and their Jaccard similarity $J(M_{f_i}, M_{f_j}) = s$. If we use a LSH scheme with b bands and r MinHash values as described in Section 3.2, the probability that files f_i and f_j appear in the same bucket in a band is s^r. Then, the number of bands files f_i and f_j appear together in a bucket is a random variable X that follows the Binomial distribution with parameters b and s^r, i.e., $X \sim B(b, s^r)$. Thus, the larger the value of s, the more bands files in which f_i and f_j will appear together inside a bucket. In the bipartite graph, this results in a larger number of paths between files f_i and f_j that go through the buckets, thereby allowing files f_i and f_j to "influence" each other more than do the other files.

Pruning. After the bipartite graph is constructed, it is possible that some of its connected components consist of one file or only unlabeled files. These components do not contribute to solving the problem of assigning labels to unlabeled files, therefore AESOP discards them from the graph to retain only the useful information in the graph.

Belief Propagation. Next, we describe our approach to assign labels to unlabeled files using the bipartite graph. Our goal is to label the nodes corresponding to unlabeled files as *good* or *bad*, along with a measure of confidence. To achieve this, we treat each file as a random variable $X \in \{x_g, x_b\}$, where x_g is the *good* label and x_b is the *bad* label. The labels are simply the possible states for the random variable X. The file's goodness and badness can then be expressed by the probabilities $\Pr(x_g)$ and $\Pr(x_b)$, respectively, such that $\Pr(x_g) + \Pr(x_b) = 1$. Based on this formulation, our goal is to determine the marginal probabilities $\Pr(X_{f_i} = x_g)$ and $\Pr(X_{f_i} = x_b)$ for unlabeled file f_i. To achieve this, there exists important background information that we can leverage. First, we know that some nodes in the graph correspond to labeled files. Second, our intuition suggests homophilic relationships between the files, i.e., good files are expected to strongly co-occur with other good files and bad files are expected to strongly co-occur with other bad files.

The above formulation converts the bipartite graph into a pairwise Markov random field (MRF). The task of inferring the marginal distribution of each node in a pairwise MRF is NP-complete [25]. The Belief Propagation algorithm (BP) is a successful approximation technique for solving this problem. BP has been adapted to various domains, such as image restoration [13] and fraud detection [20]. The algorithm is also scalable; it takes time linear in the number of edges in the graph. For this reason, AESOP adapts BP to assign labels to unlabeled files.

At a high level, BP infers the marginal distribution of a node using some prior knowledge about the node and messages arriving from the node's neighbors. The idea is to iteratively pass messages between every pair of connected nodes i and j. Typically, $m_{ij}(x_k)$ represents the message sent from node i to node j, which denotes node i's belief that node j is in state x_k. The prior knowledge, or simply the *prior*, for node i is denoted by the node potential function ϕ_i that specifies the prior probabilities of node i being in the possible states. The message passing procedure stops when the messages converge or a maximum number of iterations is reached. The final, inferred marginal probabilities are called the final beliefs. The symbol $b_i(x_j)$ denotes the final belief that node i is in state x_j.

The BP algorithm is carried out as follows in practice. An edge between nodes i and j passes a message towards each direction for each possible state. The order of the transmission can be arbitrary if all the messages are passed in every iteration. The set of beliefs that a node has for each of its neighbors is kept normalized to sum to one. This prevents any numerical underflow, i.e., a certain belief reaching 0 due to limited precision. A message from node i to its neighbor node j is generated based on node i's neighbors' messages about node i. Formally, the message update equation is:

$$m_{ij}(x_k) \leftarrow \sum_{x_\ell \in X} \phi_i(x_\ell)\, \psi_{ij}(x_\ell, x_k)\, \frac{\prod_{p \in N(i)} m_{pi}(x_\ell)}{m_{ji}(x_\ell)}$$

where $N(i)$ is the set of nodes neighboring node i, and $\psi_{ij}(x_\ell, x_k)$ is called the *edge potential*; intuitively, it is a function that transforms a node's incoming messages into the node's outgoing messages. Formally, $\psi_{ij}(x_\ell, x_k)$ specifies the probability of node i being in state x_ℓ and node j being in state x_k.

Although BP is not theoretically guaranteed to converge in general graphs, in practice the algorithm usually converges quickly. After the message passing procedure stops and the algorithm ends, the final beliefs are computed as

$$b_i(x_j) = k\ \phi_i(x_j) \prod_{p \in N(i)} m_{pi}(x_j)$$

where k is a normalizing constant.

AESOP's Adaptation of BP. Next, we describe how we map our background information into BP's context. Recall that there are two types of nodes in the bipartite graph: files and buckets. The nodes can be in either the good state or the bad state. For simplicity of exposition, we only mention the priors for the good state. For the buckets, we set their priors to 0.5. This is because we want a bucket to be initially neutral and influenced only by the files appearing in the bucket (thus connected to the bucket). For the labeled files, if the file is good we set its prior to 0.99 and if the file bad we set its prior to 0.01. For the unlabeled files, we set their priors to 0.5 so that they are initially neutral and their final beliefs are indirectly determined by the labeled files with which they strongly co-occur. We convert our intuition about homophilic file relationships into the edge potentials shown in Table 4, which indicate that a good (bad) file is more likely to be associated with a bucket consisting of other good (bad) files than a bucket consisting of bad (good) files.

$\psi_{ij}(x_\ell, x_k)$	x_ℓ = good	x_ℓ = bad
x_k = good	0.99	0.01
x_k = bad	0.01	0.99

Table 4: Edge potentials reflecting our intuition that it is more likely that good (bad) files strongly co-occur with other good (bad) files.

3.4 Time Complexity of AESOP

AESOP has two main components: LSH and BP. Given that the random permutation functions can be predetermined, LSH can be performed with a single scan of dataset D. At a high level, LSH considers each file in dataset D, maintaining a MinHash value for each permutation function while iterating over the set of machines it appears on. Assume that dataset D contains $|D|$ files. Also, recall that M denotes the set of all the machines. Then, |M| is the maximum number of machines a file can appear on. Hence, the time complexity for LSH is $\mathcal{O}(|D| \cdot |M|)$. The BP algorithm iterates over each edge in the file-relation graph a constant amount of times if the maximum number of iterations parameter is set. Assume that the graph has E edges. Then, the time complexity for BP is $\mathcal{O}(E)$. The overall time complexity for AESOP is therefore $\mathcal{O}(|D| \cdot |M| + E)$.

4. EXPERIMENTS

This section presents an experimental evaluation of AESOP. We measure its effectiveness at detecting labeled benign and malicious files as well as discovering labels for unlabeled benign and malicious files.

We conducted our experiments on a 64-bit Linux machine (RedHat Enterprise Linux Server 5.7) with 8 Opteron 2350 quad core processors running at 2.0 GHz, 64GB of RAM, and 100GB disk-quota per user.

4.1 Sampling Norton Community Watch

We leverage Symantec's Norton Community Watch data, the most important elements of which are unique file and machine identifiers. This terabyte-scale dataset contains more than 119 million machines and over 10.1 billion files. Due to the limited disk space budget, we obtained a sample of this dataset as follows.

Symantec's Worldwide Intelligence Network Environment (WINE) samples and aggregates datasets that Symantec uses in its day-to-day operations to share them with the research community [12]. The WINE sampling scheme selects machines uniformly at random and retrieves any data for the sampled machines from the production systems. Previous work showed that the uniform sampling of the machines is effective in terms of estimating or extrapolating crucial attributes of the original datasets from the samples [21].

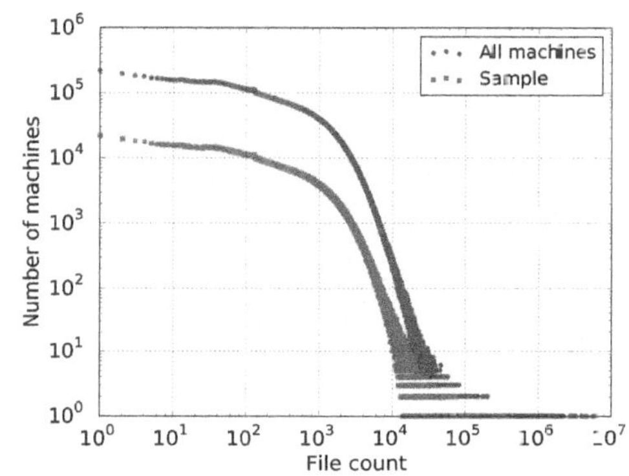

Figure 4: Distributions of the number of machines (vertical axis) with a particular file count (horizontal axis) for the full dataset (higher blue curve with circles) and the sample (lower green curve with rectangles). Our sampling strategy preserves the overall shape of the original distribution.

Motivated by this result, we employ a similar technique to sample machines from the Norton Community Watch dataset. The set of files appearing on each sampled machine is retrieved completely. Figure 4 shows the distributions of the number of machines containing a particular number of files for the original dataset and a 10% sample. More specifically, the number of machines in the sample is 10% of the total number of machines in the dataset. The uniform random sampling approach preserves the overall shape of the original distribution; both distributions are heavy-tailed with few machines containing a large number of files and a large number of machines containing few files.

We obtained the sample on November 6, 2013. After discarding the immature files with prevalence less than or equal to $\delta_M = 4$, the sample consists of 11,939,429 machines and 43,353,581 files, with labels for 7% of the files in the sample. The final sample dataset occupies 120GB space on disk.

4.2 AESOP File-relation Graph

From the sample, AESOP generates a file-relation graph of 6,056,802 nodes and 19,103,825 edges. The graph contains

1,663,506 good files, 47,956 bad files, and 1,085,937 unlabeled files, and 3,259,403 nodes that correspond to buckets. There are 40,556,182 files in the sample that do not appear in the graph because they appeared in connected components that consist of either only one file or only unlabeled files. These files are pruned from the graph for efficiency reasons as they provide no value. The number of buckets is large because AESOP uses 10 bands during LSH; each band contributes a similar set of files but a distinct set of buckets.

4.3 Sizes of Connected Components

Intuitively, AESOP's accuracy will be better if the files form small, disconnected clusters in the file-relation graph. This is because large groups of files are likely to contain a mix of good and bad files that are difficult to classify accurately. The connected components of a graph are its largest clusters, so in Figure 5 we show the graph's distribution of connected component sizes in terms of the number of files they contain. Note that the distribution is heavy tailed, indicating that most files appear in small-sized connected components. The graph's connected components that contain a very large number of files justify our selection of operating on a bipartite file-bucket graph instead of a unipartite file graph (see Section 3.3).

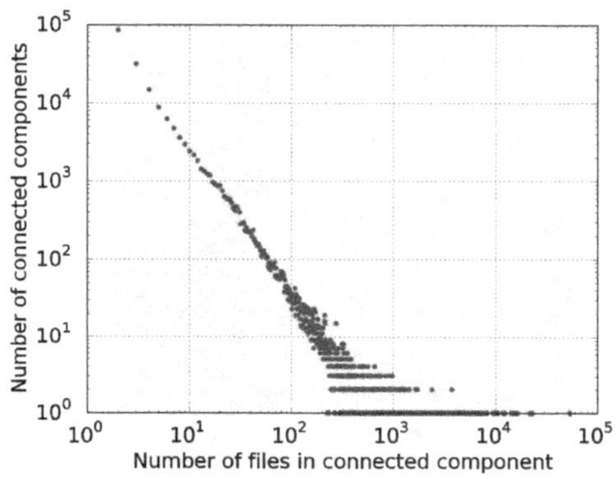

Figure 5: Distribution of the number of connected components (vertical axis) containing a particular number of files (horizontal axis) in AESOP's file-relation graph. Smaller components are less likely to contain a mix of good and bad files. The distribution is heavy tailed, indicating that most files appear in small-sized connected components.

4.4 Purity of Connected Components

It is also important that the file-relation graph's connected components are pure, i.e., they consist of files with identical labels. To test this, we turn to *entropy*, a widely used measure for determining the uncertainty or irregularity of a system [19]. We compute the entropy of a connected component as $(-\frac{e_g}{e_g+e_b}\log_2\frac{e_g}{e_g+e_b} - \frac{e_b}{e_g+e_b}\log_2\frac{e_b}{e_g+e_b})$, where e_g and e_b are the number of good and bad files in the component, respectively. Note that a smaller entropy denotes a purer connected component. Figure 6 shows the average entropy for the connected components containing a particular number of files. The error bars correspond to one standard deviation. We observe that a significant fraction of the connected components have entropies close to 0, indicating that they are pure regardless of their sizes.

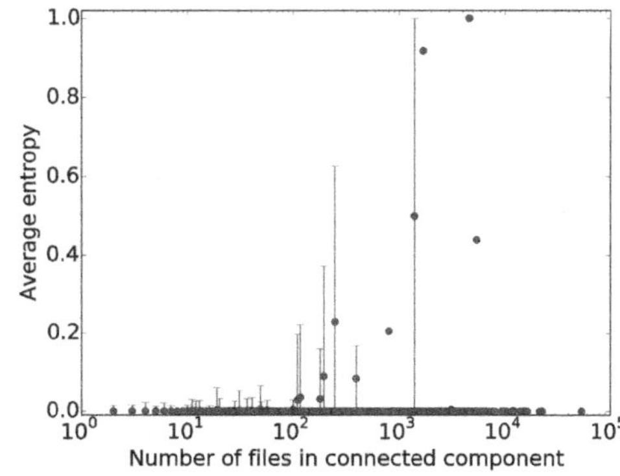

Figure 6: Average entropy for the connected components (vertical axis) containing a particular number of files (horizontal axis) in AESOP's file-relation graph. The error bars correspond to one standard deviation. A significant fraction of the connected components have 0 entropy, indicating that they consist of files with identical labels.

4.5 Performance Evaluation using Cross Validation

Next, we evaluate the effectiveness of AESOP in detecting benign and malicious files. Our evaluation scheme uses 10-fold cross validation. We treat the files in the test set as unlabeled files by setting their priors for the good state to 0.5. The files in the training set are assigned priors as described in Section 3.3. For each fold, we run the BP component of AESOP for 10 iterations and report the true positive (TP) rate at a fixed 0.0001 false positive (FP) rate. Recall that in our context a TP is a malware instance that is correctly identified as malicious and an FP is a benign file incorrectly identified as malicious.

The partitioning of the labeled files into disjoint sets may result in all of the labeled files in a connected component being assigned to the same set. When such a set is used as the test set, the corresponding connected component turns into a component consisting of only unlabeled files, which is undesirable, as it leaves behind no information to propagate in the component. For purposes of our evaluation, we prune any such connected component from the graph, as we do all the components that consist of only one file or only unlabeled files (see Section 3.3). This situation affects approximately 2% of the labeled files in the sample.

Figure 7 shows the overall and zoomed-in receiver operating characteristic (ROC) curves for this experiment. To obtain the ROC curve, we sort the final beliefs of all the files in ascending order and consider each value as a threshold; all files with final beliefs above that value are classified as good, or bad otherwise. Then, the TP rate and FP rate are computed using these classifications. We observe that AESOP achieves an impressive 0.9983 TP rate at the 0.0001 FP rate while labeling over 1.6 million files.

4.6 Early Discovery of Unlabeled Benign and Malicious Files

Next, we test the effectiveness of AESOP in assigning labels to unlabeled files. Recall that we obtained the sample on November 6, 2013. To determine to what extent AESOP labels files ahead of Symantec's current technology, which

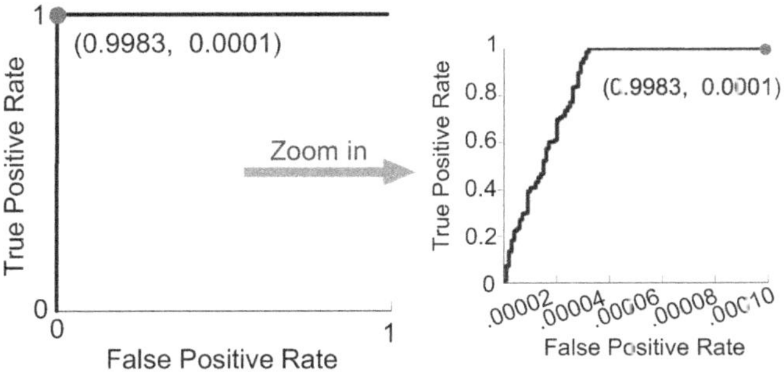

Figure 7: *Left*: ROC curve for the cross-validation experiment. AESOP achieves 0.9983 true positive rate at detecting malware, at 0.0001 false positive rate, while labeling over 1.6 million files. *Right*: Zoomed-in view.

includes the state-of-the-art Polonium approach [7], we also retrieved the file label information for November 13, 2013 and February 1, 2014. Here, we first use the labels from February 1 to obtain a list of files in AESOP'S's file-relation graph that were unlabeled by Symantec on November 6, but are labeled as of February 1. There are 774 bad and 17,997 good such eventually-labeled files. For this experiment, we run the BP component of AESOP for 10 iterations using only the file label information available on November 6 with the eventually-labeled files as the test set.

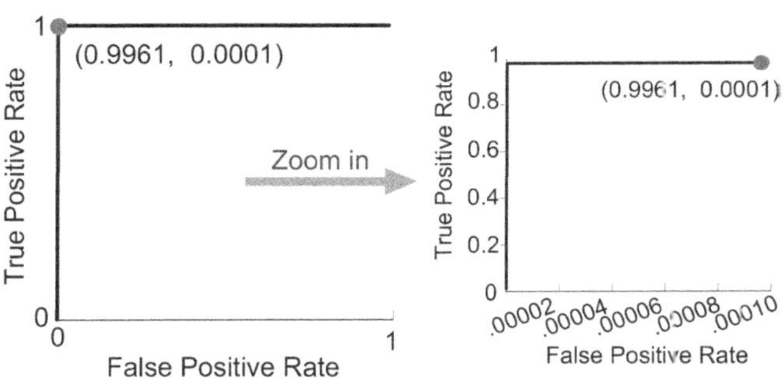

Figure 8: *Left*: ROC curve for the early discovery experiment. AESOP achieves 0.9961 true positive rate at detecting malware, at 0.0001 false positive rate, while labeling over 18 thousand originally unlabeled files. *Right*: Zoomed-in view.

Figure 8 shows the overall and zoomed-in receiver operating characteristic (ROC) curves for this experiment. We obtain the ROC curve as described in Section 4.5. We observe that AESOP achieves an impressive 0.9961 TP rate at the 0.0001 FP rate while labeling over 18 thousand originally unlabeled files.

To compare AESOP with the state-of-the-art Polonium approach [7], Figure 9 considers the file label information available on November 13 and shows the fractions of the eventually-labeled good and bad files that were still unlabeled on November 13. We observe that AESOP provides Symantec with at least a week's advantage in assigning labels to 99% and 79% of the eventually-labeled good and bad files, respectively, in comparison to Polonium.

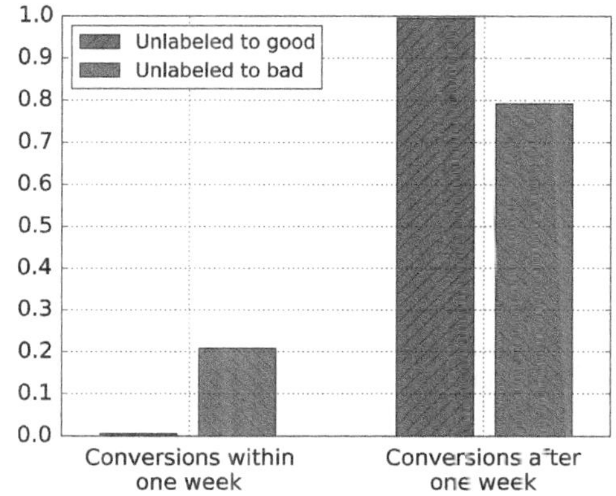

Figure 9: Fraction of unlabeled files that were and were not assigned labels within a week of the sample generation date. AESOP provides Symantec with at least a week's advantage in assigning labels to a significant amount of unlabeled files.

4.7 Running Times

Two main components of AESOP are LSH and BP. Figure 10 shows the average runtime of each component of AESOP on the sample over 3 executions, using 7 threads for LSH and a single thread for BP. The LSH step is fairly expensive, but it can be parallelized and scales linearly with the amount of input data. Also, recall that LSH processed 120GB data in this step. The BP step scales linearly with the number of edges in the file-relation graph. It can be scaled up even more through parallelization, e.g., using the MapReduce framework [17].

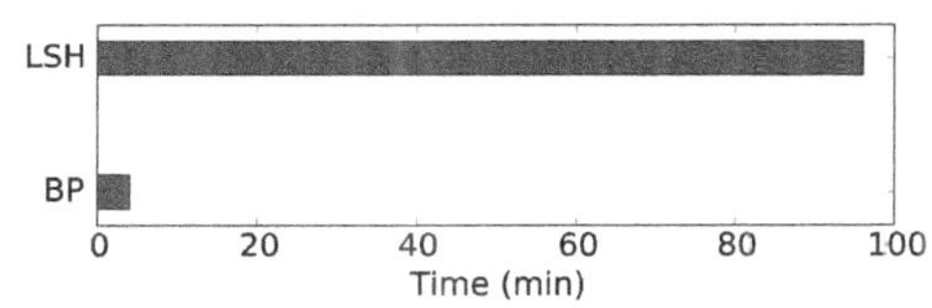

Figure 10: Average runtime for each component of AESOP on the sample occupying 120GB on disk.

5. TOWARDS DEPLOYMENT

We provide a brief discussion of the scope and limitations of our work, and then discuss our plans for integrating into Symantec's anti-malware solutions.

5.1 Scope and Limitations

It is important to describe two characteristics of this dataset that result in a significant fraction of immature files with weak co-occurrence that AESOP cannot label as benign or malicious. There are significant numbers of files that are either new or very rare, such as benign executable files created by developers that are never shared with other users, and malicious malware files that are entirely unique due to malware polymorphism. An additional limitation arises because the Norton Community Watch data provides only a partial view of the files that any given machine contains. Unfortunately, there are hundreds of thousands of machines for which our dataset only reports information about a single file (see Section 4.1). If a new or rare file only appears on a machine for which we have limited or no other information about co-occurring files, AESOP will consider it to be immature and will not be able to classify it.

Though the lack of complete machine-file data does limit AESOP's coverage, in the security space, this is a much better problem to have than that of labeling files incorrectly. In academic literature, a false positive rate of 0.1% is often considered to be good, however, this represents incorrectly labeling 1 out of a 1000 benign files as malicious. Since malicious file labels are ideally used to prevent malware infections by removing them from users' computers, this false positive rate is prohibitively high; the stability and usability of most customer machines would be impacted because of benign file removals. Ultimately, we do not expect our tool to be deployed in isolation of other techniques, but rather, that it will be an important component in Symantec's protection strategy and used to identify malicious files that cannot be identified through other techniques.

5.2 Deployment Plans

Our goal in this work was to determine how useful co-occurrence information is for malicious file detection, ultimately with an eye on integrating it into Symantec's suite of malware protection capabilities. Symantec's endpoint security products already incorporate many tiers of defence, including traditional Anti-Virus protection, Intrusion Detection, Behavioral Protection, and Insight^{TM}, of which Polonium's [7] machine-hygiene-based scores are a key component. We expect AESOP to slot easily into this existing suite of protection capabilities for the following reasons:

- Given AESOP'S exceptionally low false positive rate, its malicious vs. benign verdicts are independently useful, providing improved coverage and early detection of malware samples.
- Symantec has an infrastructure for cloud-based querying of Insight scores that we can leverage for AESOP. This infrastructure is needed because Insight scores every file that Symantec has ever seen, which represents far more information than can be replicated on individual customer devices. AESOP produces a similar amount of data, but can leverage Insight's infrastructure.
- We developed AESOP on the same database that supports Insight, so that our reputation scores can be easily incorporated into Insight's reputation scores in the same way that Polonium's [7] file-reputation scores were used. That is, AESOP scores will form a new feature used by the Insight classifier, thereby improving its coverage and creating new opportunities for early malware detection.

The next step towards the deployment of AESOP is a more detailed study of its false positives, to determine what kinds of mistakes our approach is prone to making. We are also exploring additional applications for the reputation scores obtained from AESOP, such as for false-positive mitigation of existing technologies. In parallel, we believe that the file-relation dataset that this work creates will prove to be fertile ground for additional insights. For example, we expect to see clusters of files that contain many files from a single malware family. These clusters may offer an early view of emerging malware and insights into the attackers themselves.

6. RELATED WORK

The exceptional depth and breadth of related work in the malware-detection space is a testament to the importance and difficulty of the problem. Most closely related to AESOP'S malware detection approach are reputation-based techniques and techniques that exploit similarities between files for detection.

There exist reputation systems that have been developed to address security-related problems, such as reputation scoring for IP addresses [1] and DNS entries [2, 3]. The most closely related work to ours is Polonium [7], one of Symantec's current malware detection technologies. Polonium also takes a graph-based approach to infer file reputation, however with important differences. First, AESOP infer files' goodness by directly considering file-to-file relations, which is different than Polonium's indirect approach of analyzing file-to-machine relations. Second, Polonium was not designed to pick out related files that frequently co-appear, while AESOP does; leveraging this relational information, AESOP is able to accurately label many files at least one week before the current technologies (as discussed in Section 4).

As the number of unique malware executable files has exploded due to their use of polymorphic and metamorphic techniques, security researchers are increasingly turning to techniques that identify clusters of related malware files rather than attempt to detect files individually. Symantec's MutantX-S [15] system clusters executables according to their static and dynamic properties. This approach works with low-level malware features such as sequences of machine-language opcodes, making it largely orthogonal to our approach.

Karampatziakis et al. [18] use file placement as the primary component of its malware detection technique, by leveraging unique properties of file containers that would not generalize to machines, such as the idea that the presence of any malicious file in an archive is sufficient evidence to label all files in that archive as malicious. In addition, rather than performing inference as AESOP does with belief propagation, their logistic regression classifier only looks at a file's immediate neighbors in the archives to which it belongs.

Ye et al. [24] presents a malware detection approach that combines file-to-file relationship data with features extracted at the individual file level. An important difference is the size of our dataset, which is orders of magnitude larger than their dataset of 691, 650 files. Second, due to the smaller dataset size, they do not address scalability challenges as we do. Third, while AESOP identifies malware at an extremely low false positive rate of 0.0001 by itself, their combined approach operates at a more than 0.001 false positive rate.

In summary, not only does AESOP demonstrate the independent value of calculating file-to-file similarity scores, it also provides an algorithm that addresses scalability problems while achieving impressive results compared to the state-of-the-art techniques. Furthermore, AESOP's belief propagation approach provides a reputation-based system with nuanced scores that are ideally suited for integrating and improving existing malware detection technologies.

7. CONCLUSIONS

We present AESOP, an algorithm that uses the principle of guilt by association to establish nuanced reputation scores for executable files based on the company they keep. We use a large dataset voluntarily contributed by the members of Norton Community Watch, consisting of partial lists of the files that exist on their machines. AESOP leverages locality-sensitive hashing to efficiently compute file similarity values to construct a file-relation graph for inferring file goodness based on belief propagation. Our experiments show that AESOP achieves earlier detection of unlabeled files with exceptionally low error rates in comparison to the state-of-the-art techniques.

8. REFERENCES

[1] D. S. Anderson, C. Fleizach, S. Savage, and G. M. Voelker. Spamscatter: Characterizing internet scam hosting infrastructure. In *Proceedings of the USENIX Security Symposium*, 2007.

[2] M. Antonakakis, R. Perdisci, D. Dagon, W. Lee, and N. Feamster. Building a dynamic reputation system for dns. In *Proceedings of the USENIX Security Symposium*, 2010.

[3] L. Bilge, E. Kirda, C. Kruegel, and M. Balduzzi. Exposure: Finding malicious domains using passive dns analysis. In *Proceedings of the Annual Network and Distributed System Security Symposium*, 2011.

[4] Bleeping Computer. Cryptolocker ransomware information guide and faq. October 2013. `http://www.bleepingcomputer.com/virus-removal/cryptolocker-ransomware-information`.

[5] A. Z. Broder. On the resemblance and containment of documents. In *Proceedings of the Compression and Complexity of Sequences*, 1997.

[6] M. Charikar. Similarity estimation techniques from rounding algorithms. In *Proceedings of the ACM Symposium on the Theory of Computing*, 2002.

[7] D. H. Chau, C. Nachenberg, J. Wilhelm, A. Wright, and C. Faloutsos. Polonium: Tera-scale graph mining and inference for malware detection. In *Proceedings of the SIAM International Conference on Data Mining*, 2011.

[8] O. Chum, J. Philbin, and A. Zisserman. Near duplicate image detection: min-hash and tf-idf weighting. In *British Machine Vision Conference*, 2008.

[9] E. Cohen, M. Datar, S. Fujiwara, A. Gionis, P. Indyk, R. Motwani, J. D. Ullman, and C. Yang. Finding interesting associations without support pruning. In *Proceedings of the IEEE International Conference on Data Engineering*, 2000.

[10] A. S. Das, M. Datar, A. Garg, and S. Rajaram. Google news personalization: scalable online collaborative filtering. In *Proceedings of the International conference on World Wide Web*, 2007.

[11] M. Datar, N. Immorlica, P. Indyk, and V. S. Mirrokni. Locality-sensitive hashing scheme based on p-stable distributions. In *Proceedings of the ACM Symposium on Computational Geometry*, 2004.

[12] T. Dumitras and D. Shou. Toward a standard benchmark for computer security research: The worldwide intelligence network environment (wine). In *Proceedings of the European Conference on Computer Systems BADGERS Workshop*, 2011.

[13] P. F. Felzenszwalb and D. P. Huttenlocher. Efficient belief propagation for early vision. *International Journal of Computer Vision*, 70(1):41–54, 2006.

[14] A. Gionis, P. Indyk, and R. Motwani. Similarity search in high dimensions via hashing. In *Proceedings of the International Conference on Very Large Data Bases*, 1999.

[15] X. Hu, S. Bhatkar, K. Griffin, and K. G. Shin. Mutantx-s: Scalable malware clustering based on static features. In *Proceedings of USENIX Annual Technical Conference*, 2013.

[16] P. Indyk and R. Motwani. Approximate nearest neighbors: Towards removing the curse of dimensionality. In *Proceedings of the ACM Symposium on the Theory of Computing*, 1998.

[17] U. Kang, D. H. Chau, and C. Faloutsos. Mining large graphs: Algorithms, inference, and discoveries. In *Proceedings of the IEEE International Conference on Data Engineering*, 2011.

[18] N. Karampatziakis, J. W. Stokes, A. Thomas, and M. Marinescu. Using file relationships in malware classification. In *Proceedings of the Conference on Detection of Intrusions and Malware and Vulnerability Assessment*, 2012.

[19] H. Kim and H. Park. Sparse non-negative matrix factorizations via alternating non-negativity-constrained least squares for microarray data analysis. *Bioinformatics*, 23(12):1495–1502, 2007.

[20] M. McGlohon, S. Bay, M. G. Anderle, D. M. Steier, and C. Faloutsos. Snare: A link analytic system for graph labeling and risk detection. In *Proceedings of the ACM International Conference on Knowledge Discovery and Data Mining*, 2009.

[21] E. E. Papalexakis, T. Dumitras, D. H. P. Chau, B. A. Prakash, and C. Faloutsos. Spatio-temporal mining of software adoption & penetration. In *Proceedings of the IEEE/ACM International Conference on Advances in Social Networks Analysis and Mining*, 2013.

[22] A. Rajaraman and J. D. Ullman. *Mining of Massive Datasets*. Cambridge University Press, 2012.

[23] Symantec. Internet security threat report. 18, 2013.

[24] Y. Ye, T. Li, S. Zhu, W. Zhuang, E. Tas, U. Gupta, and M. Abdulhayoglu. Combining file content and file relations for cloud based malware detection. In *Proceedings of the ACM International Conference on Knowledge Discovery and Data Mining*, 2011.

[25] J. Yedidia, W. Freeman, and Y. Weiss. *Understanding belief propagation and its generalizations*, pages 239–270. Morgan Kaufmann Publishers Inc., 2003.

Mining Text Snippets for Images on the Web

Anitha Kannan
Microsoft
ankannan@microsoft.com

Simon Baker
Microsoft
sbaker@microsoft.com

Krishnan Ramnath
Microsoft
kramnath@microsoft.com

Juliet Fiss*
University of Washington
juliet@cs.washington.edu

Dahua Lin†
TTI Chicago
dhlin@ttic.com

Lucy Vanderwende
Microsoft
lucyv@microsoft.com

ABSTRACT

Images are often used to convey many different concepts or illustrate many different stories. We propose an algorithm to mine *multiple* diverse, relevant, and interesting text snippets for images on the web. Our algorithm scales to *all* images on the web. For each image, *all* webpages that contain it are considered. The top-K text snippet selection problem is posed as combinatorial subset selection with the goal of choosing an optimal set of snippets that maximizes a combination of relevancy, interestingness, and diversity. The relevancy and interestingness are scored by machine learned models. Our algorithm is run at scale on the entire image index of a major search engine resulting in the construction of a database of images with their corresponding text snippets. We validate the quality of the database through a large-scale comparative study. We showcase the utility of the database through two web-scale applications: (a) augmentation of images on the web as webpages are browsed and (b) an image browsing experience (similar in spirit to web browsing) that is enabled by interconnecting semantically related images (which may not be visually related) through shared concepts in their corresponding text snippets.

Categories and Subject Descriptors

H.2.8g [**Information Systems**]: Database Management: Database Applications: Image Databases

General Terms

Data Mining Algorithms, Applications

Keywords

Text mining for images; Text snippets; Interestingness; Relevance; Diversity; Browsing; Semantic image browsing; Web image augmentation

*Research conducted while an intern at Microsoft.
†Research conducted while an intern at Microsoft.

KDD'14 August 24–27, 2014, New York, NY, USA

http://dx.doi.org/10.1145/2623330.2623346 .

1. INTRODUCTION

The popular adage "a picture is worth a thousand words" reflects the effectiveness of an image in conveying many different ideas or "stories." An image is typically used to illustrate one of these stories in any given webpage. However, the same image can be used in different webpages to illustrate different stories at different levels of descriptiveness and interestingness. By collecting the stories associated with an image together, we can create a host of new applications that seamlessly integrate the image and text modalities.

The focus of our paper is exactly this: We propose a mining algorithm to obtain the most relevant and interesting text snippets for images on the web. Using this database of images and their associated text snippets, we present two new applications that we have implemented at web scale. We believe, however, that these applications represent the "tip of the iceberg": many more applications are possible.

Figure 1 shows a sample of results for a few images. The images are selected to cover many of the important types of images on the web; people, travel, music, etc. For each image, we show two of the many snippets identified for it. The snippets are related to the image in the most general sense: memories or events behind the image, an analogy to establish context, or even descriptions of a historical event in the context of the image. Note, however, that the text generally goes far beyond a simple description of the visual contents of the image. For example, a visual description of Figure 1(b) might be "someone snorkeling in the Maldives." Instead, our mined snippets include interesting information about the monsoon season and the geography of the islands, information that is not apparent in the image itself.

Our first contribution is to propose a scalable solution to mine the web for multiple relevant, interesting and diverse textual snippets about the image. The scale of our solution has two dimensions: we consider *all* images on the web and for each image we consider *all* web pages that contain the corresponding image. This scale enables reliable identification of multiple high quality snippets for images that are discussed widely on the web. Note that our approach differs considerably from prior work in understanding images [7, 13, 12, 16, 20, 22, 28], where the goal is to synthesize textual descriptions of *the visual content of the image* by recognizing objects, their attributes, and possibly using similar images in image databases to borrow captions.

With the web as a repository of world knowledge, we operationalize our solution based on a key insight: if an image is interesting, multiple people will post it in webpages, including stories related to it. These stories will vary in their

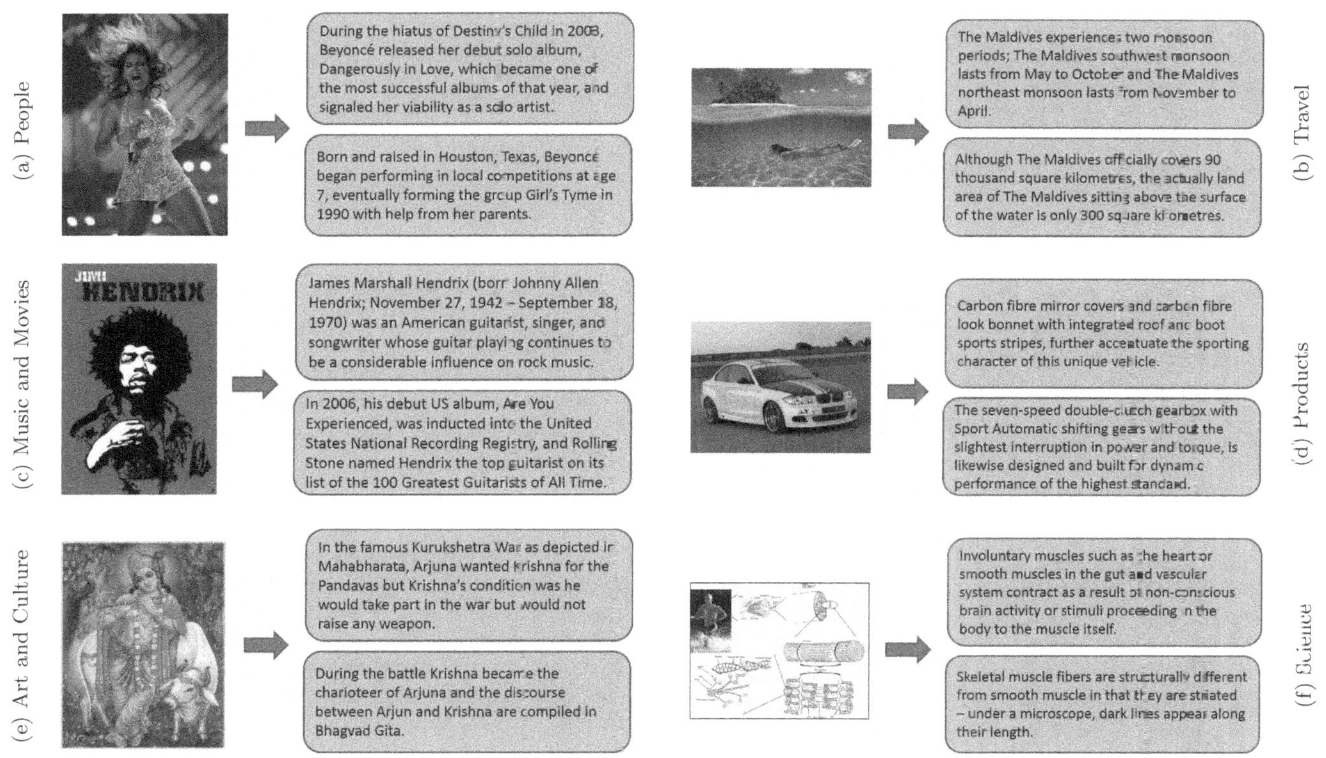

Figure 1: Examples of text snippets found by our algorithm. We just show the top two snippets, although generally many more are found. Note that the snippets are not purely descriptions of the content of the image. Instead, they contain all manner of interesting facts and stories related to the content.

content bringing about diversity. Note that these stories are generally not contained in the image captions (which are most often just descriptive), but the captions can help identify the most interesting stories. Concretely, we mine the web by first clustering all the images in the index of a Web search engine into "near duplicate" groups. For each group, we identify the top K snippets that are the most diverse, interesting and relevant, where the interestingness and relevancy are scored using learned models. The snippet selection problem is posed as the combinatorial optimization problem of subset selection. Since each image set can be processed independently, our algorithm easily parallelizes. We have run our algorithm on the entire web image index of a search engine containing billions of images.

Our second contribution is to demonstrate how the resulting database of images along with their snippets can be used to construct two new applications. Both applications are bulit at web scale(§ 5). The first application (Figure 8 and § 5.1) is a plugin to an internet browser than enables an enhanced reading experience on the web by displaying text snippets on top of images as the user passively browses the web. The second application (Figure 9 and § 5.2) is a real time web image browser that provides a seamless browsing experience through the most interesting images on the web, and their associated stories. Images are inter-connected semantically through the text snippets, unlike approaches that rely on visual similarity [10, 24].

2. RELATED WORK

There are two main bodies of related work. The first set focuses on analysing an image to generate a text description or caption. The second body of work is that of document (i.e. webpage) summarization. We discuss each in turn.

Image caption generation: Possibly the earliest work in this area is [20], which focused on associating word tags with an image by analyzing image regions at multiple granularity. Subsequently, in [12, 16, 28] the semantics of the image pixels are inferred to generate image descriptions. In particular, [12] detects objects, attributes and prepositional relationships in the image. These detections are composed to generate descriptions of the image. In [28], the image is decomposed at multiple granularity to infer the objects and attributes. The outputs of this step are then converted into a semantic ontology based representation that feeds into a text generation engine. A related line of work poses caption generation as a matching problem between the input image and a large database of images with captions [7, 13, 22]. In [7], a learned intermediate semantic space between image features and the tokens in the captions are used to generate sentences for images. In comparison, [22] constructs a data set of 1 million images spanning over 87 classes. Given an input image, this approach transfers captions from the closest matching image in the data set. In [13], phrases extracted from the caption of the matched image are used to generate a descriptive sentence. The goal of all these techniques is to describe the image content while we would like to capture the stories conveyed in the context of the image, and is not restricted by what is contained in the image.

Document Summarization: There is a large body of work in automatic text summarization. See [15, 23] for surveys. In this literature, the goal is to summarize documents, either by identifying key phrases and sentences that are reflective of the focus of the document (extractive approaches) [9, 4, 5] or by paraphrasing the content (abstractive approaches) [3]. In [9], sentences are extracted from one or more articles about the same topic. In [4] key sentences from webpages are extracted for viewing on a mobile device. In another example, [3] summarizes a webpage using a probabilistic model of the gist of the webpage. The underlying goal of all these methods is to identify the central focus of the document to be summarized. In contrast, we would like to identify content related to the image. One can think of using these techniques if we know the region of text that corresponds to image, which is a hard task by itself [2].

3. SNIPPET MINING ALGORITHM

Our algorithm is based on the insight that if an image is interesting, multiple people will embed it in a webpage and write about it. For each image (along with near-duplicates), one can mine the web for all the webpages containing it in order to identify text snippets that are relevant and interesting and also form a diverse set of text.

With this insight, we have developed a highly scalable solution to mine the web for the interesting text snippets related to an image. Figure 2 provides the overview. The web images are clustered into "near duplicate" groups (§ 3.1), referred to as "duplicate image set" or "image set," for short. While each image set corresponds to a single image, these images reside in multiple webpages, *PURL* (page URL in which the image resides) with a unique media url (*MURL*). Hence, each image set is represented by a collection of triplets {*MURL*, *PURL*, *HTML*} where *HTML* is the associated HTML source of *PURL*. Using this representation, we identify candidate snippets for each image set (§ 3.2). Then, the top K snippets that are most diverse, interesting and relevant to the image (§ 3.3) are identified by posing the problem as the combinatorial optimization problem of subset selection. We use machine-learned models of relevance and interestingness to score the snippets which are used within the optimization framework (§ 3.3.1).

3.1 Scalable Image Set Identification

We would like to cluster images such that each cluster consists of images that are near duplicate to each other. Images within a near duplicate image set can differ in their sizes, compression ratios, cropping, color transformations and other minor edits. For this purpose, we require a clustering algorithm that covers (a) large variation within a duplicate image cluster while minimizing false positives and (b) is highly scalable for clustering billions of images on the web.

To satisfy both these requirements, we use two-step clustering method [26] that is scalably implemented using hashing techniques within MapReduce framework [6]. The technique combines global and local features, with global descriptors to discover seed clusters with high precision and the local descriptors to grow the seeds to obtain good recall.

For the global descriptors, we first partition each image into 8×8 blocks and compute the mean gray value for each block. The image is then divided further into 2×2 blocks, and a histogram of edge distributions in evenly-divided 12 directions is extracted from each block, plus one dimension of non-edge pixel ratio. The histograms of mean gray values and edge distributions are cascaded into a 116-dimensional raw feature vector. A pre-learnt Principle Component Analysis (PCA) model is then applied and the first 24 dimensions of the PCA-ed vector are retained. The local descriptor of an image is a truncated set of visual words defined on a visual codebook of 1 miilion codewords. The local features proposed in [27] are first extracted and then ranked by their average Difference-of-Gaussian (DoG) responses. The top-ranked 40 features are used as the local descriptors of an image. Two images are near duplicates if they have 6 visual words in common.

Seed clusters are generated in three steps. First, each image is encoded into a 24-bit hash signature by quantizing each dimension of the global descriptor against the PCA mean. These signatures then serve as keys to divide the images in a MapReduce framework (i.e. the Map step). Second, images with identical hash signatures are assigned to the same hash buckets. Each bucket is processed within one vertex of the MapReduce machine cluster (i.e. the Reduce step). Third, pair-wise distance matching is performed within a bucket.

We grow the seed clusters by merging them using local descriptors. For computational tractability, we assume that near duplicate images reside in neighboring buckets in the global feature space, where neighboring buckets are those whose corresponding signatures are different in at most two bits. We randomly select one image from each seed cluster and add to the cluster all the images from neighboring buckets that have 6 or more visual words in common.

3.2 Forming Candidate Snippets

Each duplicate image set is represented by triplets {*MURL*, *PURL*, *HTML*} of the image url, page url and the HTML source of the page [1]. Along with this, we parse *HTML* to obtain a linear ordering of the text and image nodes and this is maintained as W^{PURL}.

Corresponding to each text node[2] in W^{PURL}, we generate a candidate snippet $< s^{n,PURL}, l^{n,PURL} >$, where $s^{n,PURL}$ is the $n, PURL^{th}$ snippet text and $l^{n,PURL}$ is its location in W^{PURL}. The set of candidate snippets generated is

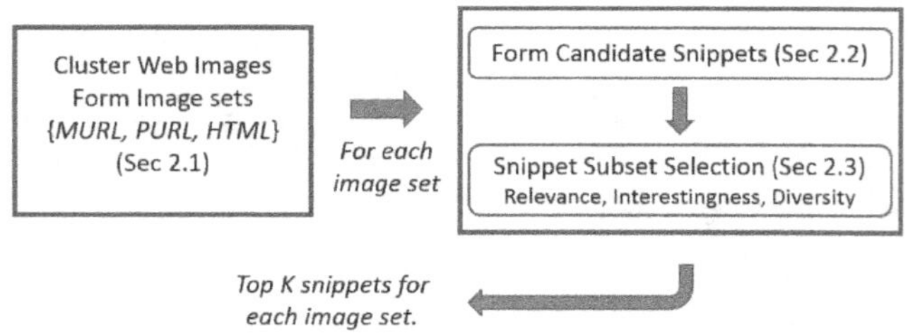

Figure 2: Overview of Snippet Mining Algorithm: We first cluster all the images on the web into "near duplicate" groups. For each set of images we extract a set of candidate snippets. We then identify the top K snippets that are relevant, interesting and diverse.

[1]We restrict triplets to be from English-language non-spam websites. We also exclude social networking and photo sharing sites that do not contain enough textual content.

[2]Non-English and/or ill-formed sentences are ignored

$\{< s^{n,PURL}, l^{n,PURL} >\}_{n=1}^{N^{PURL}}$ where N^{PURL} is the number of snippets.

Similarly, we represent an image as follows: For each image node corresponding to the $MURL$, we extract its associated "Alt" text or "Src" text. We denote this text $< m^{PURL}, L^{PURL} >$, where m^{PURL} is the text and L^{PURL} is the location of the image node in W^{PURL}.

3.3 Top K Snippet Selection

For each image, I, let $\mathcal{S}$ be the candidate set of snippets identified from the set of triples $\{MURL, PURL, HTML\}$ (§ 3.2). From this large candidate set, we would like to select K top snippets, $\mathcal{T} \subset \mathcal{S}$ which are not only *relevant* and *interesting* to I but also exhibit *diversity*. This selection can be guided by the objective function

$$\mathcal{F}(\mathcal{T}|I) = \lambda \sum_{s \in \mathcal{T}} rel(s)int(s) + (1-\lambda)H_0(\mathcal{T}), \quad (1)$$

that trades-off total gain given by the sum of the product of relevance $rel(s)$ and interestingness $int(s)$ of each snippet with their diversity as measured by the entropy of the set $H_0(\mathcal{T})$ (larger the entropy, larger the diversity).

In our objective (eq. 1), we consider the product $rel(s)int(s)$ instead of sum $rel(s)+int(s)$ because we prefer snippets that are both simultaneously relevant and interesting. We also differentiate between relevance and interestingness and not use a single term since a highly relevant snippet may not be very interesting, and vice versa (See Figure 4).

The optimal subset satisfies:

$$\mathcal{T}^* = \underset{\mathcal{T} \in 2^{|\mathcal{S}|}, |\mathcal{T}|=k}{\arg\max} \ (\mathcal{F}(\mathcal{T}|I)). \quad (2)$$

While, one can solve for the optimal subset through exhaustive search over all possible subsets of $\mathcal{S}$, this is clearly prohibitive even for a reasonable size of $\mathcal{S}$.

However, for suitable choices of $rel(s)int(s)$ and $H_0(\mathcal{T})$, Eq. 1 is submodular. That is, it exhibits the property of "diminishing returns" so that the difference in the value of the function that a single element makes when added to an input set decreases as the size of the input set increases. Mathematically, if $X \subset Y \subset \mathcal{S}$, then adding an element $z \in \mathcal{S}$ to both X and Y should satisfy:

$$\mathcal{F}(X \cup z) - \mathcal{F}(X) \geq \mathcal{F}(Y \cup z) - \mathcal{F}(Y) \quad (3)$$

As long as we choose $rel(s)int(s) \geq 0$ so that $\sum_{s \in \mathcal{T}} rel(s)int(s)$ is a monotonically increasing function, Eq. 1 will be submodular since entropy is submodular [11]. We describe one such choice for $rel(s)int(s)$ in § 3.3.1.

The advantage of submodular functions is that while being computationally difficult, we can design greedy solutions that are at most $(1 - \frac{1}{e})$ times worse than the optimal solution [21]. Using this theoretical guarantee, we design a greedy solution as follows: Initialize with a snippet that has the largest value of $rel(s)int(s)$. Then, iteratively add snippets, one at a time, such that the added snippet (along with previously chosen set of snippets) maximizes Eq. 1.

3.3.1 Relevance and Interestingness

The top-K snippet selection formulation (Eq. 1) uses separate functions to score a snippet for relevancy $rel(s)$ and interestingness $int(s)$ to the corresponding image. Here, we describe the instantiation that we use in this paper for these two components. We used separate machine learned models of regularized linear regression.

The regularized linear regressor captures the relationship between features, $\phi(\mathbf{x})$, extracted from the snippet $\mathbf{x}$ and its scores through the functional form $y = \mathbf{w}^T\phi(\mathbf{x})$. The details of the features used are provided momentarily. Given some training data $\mathbf{x}_i \in \mathcal{X}$ that has been annotated with the relevance (or interestingness) scores y_i, the corresponding parameters $\mathbf{w}$ are learned by solving the optimization function:

$$\mathbf{w}^* = \arg\min_{\mathbf{w}} \lambda||\mathbf{w}||^2 + \sum_i (\mathbf{w}^T\phi(\mathbf{x}_i) - y_i)^2 \quad (4)$$

where λ is a regularization parameter. The unique optimum of Eq. 4 can be found via gradient descent [14].

Features used:

First, we describe the vocabulary for representation:

Let $\mathcal{M} = \cup_{PURL}\left[m^{PURL} \cup \left[\cup_n s^{n,PURL}\right]\right]$ be the union of the image representation and all the candidate snippets for the image set. Let $\mathcal{V}$ be the unigrams (*sans* stop words) identified in $\mathcal{M}$.

Each snippet s is represented using a $|\mathcal{V}|$ vector, $\mathbf{s}$, such that $\mathbf{s}[k]$ is the number of times that the kth unigram in $\mathcal{V}$ occurs in s. Similarly, for image I, $\mathbf{m}$ is a $|\mathcal{V}|$ vector such that $m[k]$ is the sum of the number of times that the kth unigram in $\mathcal{V}$ occurs in the union of the representations of the images across all $PURL$, $\cup_{PURL}\left[m^{PURL}\right]$.

The feature vector, $\phi(\cdot)$, consists of nine features from the following five groups of features:

Match Score: While $\mathbf{s}$ corresponds to a single snippet, $\mathbf{m}$ is an aggregate over all image representations (captions, Alt Text) across multiple instances of the image. Therefore, we measure similarity between $\mathbf{s}$ and $\mathbf{m}$ as a dot product between $\mathbf{s}$ and normalized $\mathbf{m}$

$$\text{matchscore(s, I)} = \mathbf{s}^T \frac{\mathbf{m}}{||\mathbf{m}||} \quad (5)$$

Context Scores: When the text around a snippet is relevant, then this specific snippet is likely to be relevant too. With this intuition, we compute two features which are average of the Match Score on windows around the snippet in question. Let $\rho_{j,n,PURL} = \delta\left[l^{j,PURL} \in [l^{n,PURL} - K, l^{n,PURL} + K]\right]$ be a indicator function which evaluates to 1 if $l^{j,PURL}$ is in the range $[l^{n,PURL} - K, l^{n,PURL} + K]$. The context scores are then given by: contextScore($\mathrm{s}^{n,PURL}$, I)

$$= \frac{\sum_{j=1}^{N^{PURL}} \rho_{j,n,PURL} \text{matchscore}(\mathrm{s}^{j,PURL}, \mathrm{I})}{\sum_{j=1}^{N^{PURL}} \rho_{j,n,PURL}} \quad (6)$$

In our experiments, we used two window sizes, corresponding to $K = 5$ and $K = 30$.

HTML Parse Distance: Good snippets tend to be closer to the image location. Therefore, we also capture distance from the snippet to the image node as:

$$\text{ParseDistance}(\mathrm{s}^{n,PURL}, \mathrm{I}) = l^{n,PURL} - L^{PURL}. \quad (7)$$

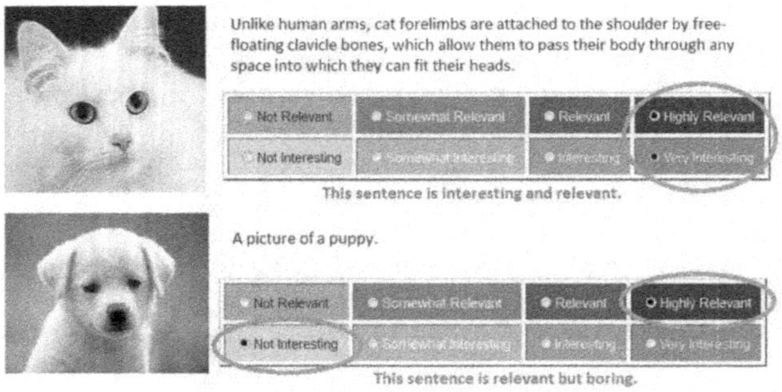

Figure 3: HIT used to collect training data to learn the snippet scoring functions. We showed image-snippet pairs to the judges and asked them to rate the snippet based on its "Relevance" to the image and on how "Interesting" it is. Some sentences are highly relevant, but not very interesting (bottom).

Measure of SPAM: When a snippet contains a lot of repeated words, it is less likely to be relevant or interesting. We use entropy of the words present to capture this idea: spamminess($s^{n,PURL}$) =

$$-\sum_{k:\mathbf{s}^{n,PURL}[k]>0} \frac{\mathbf{s}^{n,PURL}[k]}{\sum_r \mathbf{s}^{n,PURL}[r]} \log\left[\frac{\mathbf{s}^{n,PURL}[k]}{\sum_r \mathbf{s}^{n,PURL}[r]}\right]. \quad (8)$$

Linguistic Features: The interestingness of a sentence often depends on its linguistic structure. We use four linguistic features: (1) the length of the sentence with the intuition that longer sentences are more interesting (2) whether the sentence begins demonstrative (such as beginning with "this" or "these" (3) whether the sentence is first person, beginning with "I" or "we" and (4) whether the sentence is definitional, *i.e.,* begins with a pronoun and then includes the word "is" or "are" afterwards.

Data set for learning

To learn these functions, we construct a training set as follows: We randomly chose 250 images. For each image, we assembled all the snippets that are within reasonable distance to the MURL in the HTML parse tree (so that clearly irrelevant snippets are not considered). This resulted in 5443 image-snippet pairs. For each pair, we obtain human judgments independently for relevance and interestingness.

Human judgments: We designed a Human Intelligence Task (HIT) on Amazon Mechanical Turk to label each pair of image and snippet. Figure 3 shows the HIT setup for two example pairs. Given this HIT, the judges were asked to independently score the snippet for relevance and interestingness on a discrete scale between zero and three, where zero means not relevant (not interesting) and three corresponds to very relevant (very interesting). Each pair was judged by approximately 10 judges. The average relevance of the snippets is 1.57 (about half way between "Somewhat Relevant" and "Relevant"). The average interestingness score is 1.17 (a little bit higher than "Somewhat Interesting.").

(a) Somehow, between the first announcement and now The Lorax has a poster.
Relevance 2.0, Interestingness 1.0

(b) The Lorax is a children's book, written by Dr. Seuss and first published in 1971.
Relevance 2.6, Interestingness 1.7

(c) Born on March 2, 1904, Theodor Seuss Geisel, the man who would one day be published under the pen name "Dr. Seuss" began his writing career at Dartmouth College's humor paper.
Relevance 2.0, Interestingness 2.1

Numerical Scores	Not Relevant / Interesting	Somewhat Relevant / Interesting	Relevant / Interesting	Highly Relevant / Very Interesting
Relevance	0.0	1.0	2.0	3.0
Interestingness	0.0	1.0	2.0	3.0

Figure 4: An example image with three snippets and their average human labels. (a) illustrates a snippet that is relevant but not very interesting. (b) is much more interesting. (c) is more interesting than relevant; it is about the author, not his character.

In Figure 4 we include an image to illustrate the human labeling. We include three snippets together with the human scores. Snippet (a) is provided as an example of why it is important to assess the interestingness of the snippets. Snippet (a) is a fairly factual statement about the image. It is scored as relevant, but as not particularly interesting. In comparison, (b) is significantly more interesting. Snippet (c) is notable in that it has a relatively low relevance (compared to the interestingness, which is generally scored more conservatively than relevance.) The sentence is about "Dr. Seuss" whereas the image is one of his characters.

3.3.2 Entropy of Set:

The normalized entropy, $H_0(\mathcal{T})$ in Eq. 1 models the diversity of the chosen sentences. We would like to favor sentences that are diverse in two respects. First, they differ in their vocabulary usage. Second, they are derived from different webpages. Hence, the entropy $H(\mathcal{T})$ of set $\mathcal{T}$ is computed over $N+1$ binary random variables, where N of them constitute the vocabulary used in snippets in $\mathcal{T}$ and the $(N+1)^{th}$ variable models the webpage variability among $\mathcal{T}$. The probability of the nth variable to have a value of 1 is given by the fraction of times the value is observed in the set $\mathcal{T}$. The normalized entropy is given by $H_0(\mathcal{T}) = H(\mathcal{T})/log(N+1)$ which normalizes the entropy across different subsets. As we add snippets, the incremental gain in entropy will diminish due to the fact that the vocabulary is fixed.

3.4 Scaling to the Web

We have run our snippet mining algorithm on the entire web image index of a major search engine with billions of images. We provide details of scaling up the image clustering along with the details of the clustering in (§ 3.1). After the clustering step is performed, the algorithm is embarrassingly parallel and is performed independently for each image set. In fact, on a 100 core cluster, the entire processing took about 45 hours. We can also run the pipeline for delta updates to introduce clusters of new images or additional snippets for the same image set.

4. EVALUATION OF SNIPPET MINING

We now provide an experimental validation of our algorithm using a quantitative comparison with two reasonable baselines (§ 4.1) and quantitative coverage results on popular web queries for image search retrieval (§ 4.2)

4.1 Comparison with Baselines

To the best of our knowledge, there is no prior work on extracting a set of text snippets for an image on the web. There are, however, two reasonable baselines:

- **Query-by-Image and Webpage Summarization** (QbI/WS): Find all occurrences of the image on the web and then use a webpage summarization algorithm to generate a snippet for each page. We compare with a commercial system (http://images.google.com) that follows this approach for a subset of its results. In particular, we use the snippets shown for the top three results from the "Pages that include matching images."
- **Im2Text using Visual Features**: We also compare with the approach of Ordonez, Kulkarni, and Berg [22]. This algorithm matches the image to a database of 1 million Flickr images that already have captions, and transfers the captions from the best matches[3].

Data set: Web image search retrieval algorithm such as QbI/WS are most tuned for head (popular) images and their landing pages. Therefore, images that are most popular on web image search will serve as better baselines. We take the top 10,000 textual queries to a popular search engine and randomly selected 50 images that are among the top ranking results for those queries as the test set.

The results for two images are included in Figure 5. We found that the QbI/WS algorithm always found the correct image and generated plausible results. The results using purely visual features for comparison [22] are far less relevant. This algorithm never really found the correct topic of the image, due to a mismatch between their database (1 million Flickr images on narrow topics of interest) and the web (billions of images). We therefore dropped the Im2Text algorithm [22] from the subsequent quantitative comparison.

Mechanical Turk Setup: In order to perform a quantitative evaluation of our approach with QbI/WS, we conducted pairwise evaluations focused on the overall preference of one ranked list over other. We used Amazon Mechanical Turk with each Human Intelligence Test (HIT) consisting of a pair of ranked lists of snippets, corresponding to our proposed algorithm and QbI/WS. To remove the presentation bias, we considered both orderings of the lists. Each ordering is a separate HIT. We also had each HIT judged by five judges. Each judge was asked to study the two lists and specify which of the two they preferred. They also had the option of choosing "both are comparable". The judges were asked to consider multiple dimensions while making their judgements: relevancy, interestingness, diversity and repetitiveness of content. They were required to spend at least five minutes on the task (we discarded answers from judges that did not conform to this guideline).

Results: Figure 5(bottom) shows the key results. Of all the judgments, 72% exclusively preferred our approach,

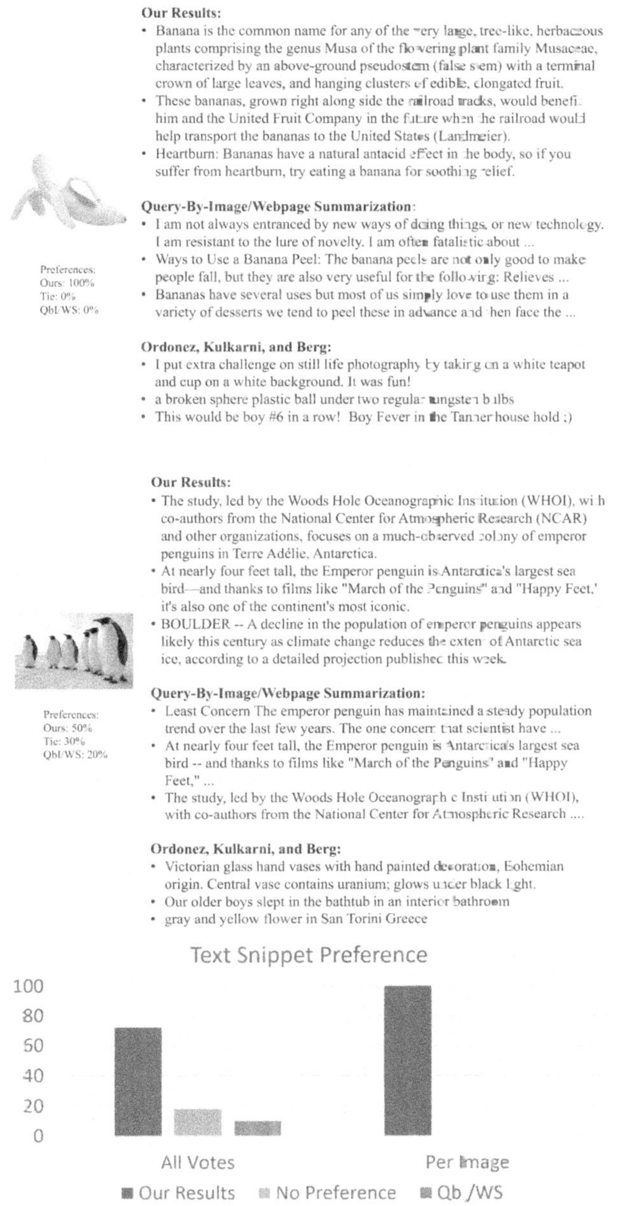

Figure 5: Top and Middle: Qualitative results from a comparison between our algorithm and two baselines. The first baseline is a Query-by-Image/Webpage Summarization algorithm that finds the image on the web and then summarizes each webpage independently. The second baseline is the algorithm of Ordonez, Kulkarni, and Berg [22]. Bottom: A quantitative comparison between our algorithm and the Query-by-Image/Webpage Summarization algorithm. We took the results for 50 images and asked judges which they preferred. No preference was also an option. Bottom Left: 72% of all votes preferred our results, compared to just 10% for the Query-by-Image/Webpage Summarization algorithm. Bottom Right: When we tally up the votes for each image, we found that the judges preferred our results for all 100 images.

[3]We used the software available at `http://vision.cs.stonybrook.edu/~vicente/sbucaptions/`

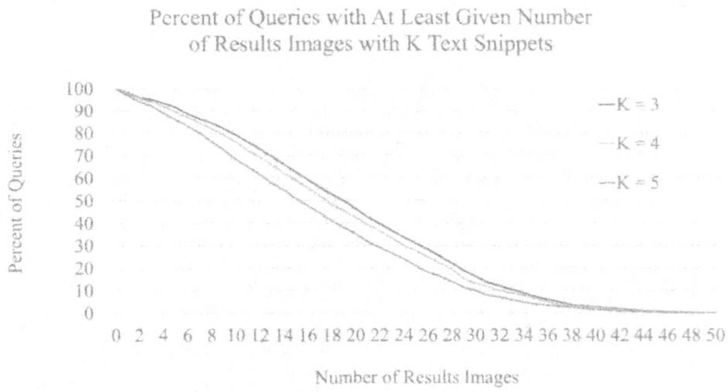

Figure 6: Results on popular queries to an image search engine. We took the top 10,000 queries and considered the top 50 result images for each query. We plot the number of result images with at least K = 3, 4, 5 text snippets (X-axis) against the page-view weighted percentage of queries (Y-axis) that have at least that number of results images with K text snippets. The results show that most queries have 10-30 results images with snippets.

Figure 7: Examples of common types of images for which our algorithm does not find enough high-quality text snippets. (a) Personal photos frequently do not have high quality text, but are often posted with a short caption. (b) We currently only process English language webpages, so foreign language images do not result in any good snippets. (c) Commercial images are often repeated across multiple webpages with very similar text and are removed as having too much text duplication. (d) Generic icons can rarely be associated with high quality text.

17.8% felt "Both are comparable," while 10.2% preferred the QbI/WS algorithm. We also looked at the individual results. For all images, a (strictly) greater number of judges preferred our approach to the QbI/WS algorithm.

The qualitative results in Figure 5 were chosen to give one example (top) where our results are unanimously preferred, and one example (middle) where a relatively high percentage of judges prefer the Query-by-Image/Webpage Summarization results (20% compared to the average of 10.2%).

4.2 Coverage for Popular Images

Although we ran our algorithm on the entire web index of a major search engine, we do not obtain results for all images. We impose a threshold on the overall score $rel(s)int(s)$ to remove poor quality results. We now present a set of experimental results to illustrate how likely a snippet will be available for the most popular images; i.e. the ones that are returned as results for the most common queries to Bing image search engine.

Experiment Setup: We consider the top 10,000 most frequent queries issued to Bing image search engine. For each query, we considered the top 50 image results, corresponding to the first page of image search results. We used our approach to identify the top K snippets. Some of these results may not have K snippets associated with them. Next, we compute a metric that captures this property.

Metric: We use the percentage of queries weighted by the frequency with which they were issued. Each query in the top 10,000 was issued by multiple users over the one month sampling interval. When computing the percentage of queries that meet a criterion, we weight by the number of times the query was issued. We refer to this metric (perhaps slightly confusingly) as "page-view weighted."

Results: The results are plot in Figure 6. On the X-axis, we plot the number of result images that have a least $K = 3, 4, 5$ text snippets. On the Y-axis we plot the page-view weighted percentage of queries that have at least that many (X-axis) results images with K text snippets. The results in Figure 6 show that for essentially all[4] queries, there are some results images with text snippets. Most queries have 10–30 results images with text snippets.

We qualitatively investigated the nature of the images for which no high quality text snippets were found. Example of the sort of images are shown in Figure 7. (a) Personal photos that are posted to blogs and photo-sharing cites rarely have high quality text associated with them, even if they are subsequently reposted multiple times. (b) As we currently only process English webpages, foreign content photos generally do not result in any snippets. (c) Photos from commercial websites often do not result in high quality snippets or are filtered out due to high repetition (often the same image is used on multiple websites with very similar text.) (d) Icons can rarely be associated with high quality text.

5. APPLICATIONS

The database of text snippets mined by our algorithm has a variety of possible applications. The snippets could be shown to users along with image search results. They can be used to improve image search relevance. It may also be possible to use the snippets to discriminate more interesting images from less interesting ones. Images for which there are a lot of interesting snippets (see Figure 1) are generally far more interesting than images for which not much text is found (see Figure 7).

We now propose two other applications. The first consists of augmenting images on the web when a user views the page (§ 5.1). The second is an image browsing application built by connecting images through their snippets (§ 5.2).

[4]We investigated the queries for which there are no results with text snippets. These were mainly cases where the top 50 results images are classified as adult content, but the query was not. We restricted our processing to non-adult images and so obtained no results in these cases.

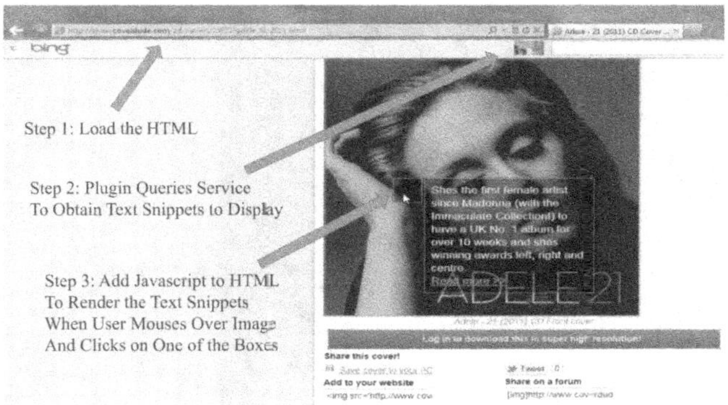

Figure 8: A screenshot of the web augmentation application (§ 5.1). The plug-in is part of the Bing Bar toolbar at the top. The text results are populated over the image as text pop-ups that show up on mouse-over. Please see http://research.microsoft.com/en-us/um/people/sbaker/i/www/augmentation.mp4 **for a video.**

These applications both follow a client-server architecture. For both application, we built a Windows Azure [19] service that hosts the database of text snippets extracted using our algorithm. This service is used by the client to query for snippets corresponding to an image and/or for images pertaining to key words that appear in a text snippet.

5.1 Web Image Augmentation

Often when an image is included in a web page, only a brief caption is provided. Enriching these images with additional interesting information can improve the web browsing experience for the user. If the information comes with associated links to its source, the user can easily choose to explore the additional information by clicking on the links. To this end, we developed a 'Bing Bar' plug-in for Internet Explorer [18] that automatically identifies all the images on the current web page, and augments them with any snippets that were found by our algorithm.

Figure 8 shows a screenshot of the application. After the webpage has been rendered, the HTML is passed to the plug-in. The plug-in parses the HTML, extracts the URLs of the images, and queries the Windows Azure service to obtain the snippets for the images. The plug-in then injects Javascript into the HTML that renders the text snippets when the user hovers over the image and then clicks on one of the boxes that are displayed. The plug-in then passes the HTML back to the browser which re-renders the page. Figure 8 shows such an example snippet for an 'Adele' image. For a detailed demo, please see the video http://research.microsoft.com/en-us/um/people/sbaker/i/www/augmentation.mp4.

There are several advantages of this system over other interfaces for viewing query-by-image results. First, the browsing experience is completely passive. The user does not need to initiate a query for every image. The query is initiated automatically, and only when there are interesting results, are they displayed in an un-obtrusive manner. Secondly, this application adds virtual hyperlink on top of the Web, from images to related content on other web pages. This can enrich the browsing experience for the user.

5.2 Semantic Image Browsing

A number of recent works have focused on building effective visualizations of a collection of images that are retrieved in response to a query of interest [10, 24]. In this section, we present a system for a *never-ending* browsing experience that revolves around images and the text snippets associated with them (found using our algorithm). The starting point for the application is either an image or a concept of interest, which can be user-provided or chosen at random. The choice of the next image is based on the text snippets, thereby allowing transitions between images that can be visually unrelated, but semantically related. In particular, we identify concepts in the snippets which are then used as the means for the user to control the choice of the next image in a semantically meaningful manner. See Figure 9.

Browse interface: The interface allows people to browse images on the web. As they browse, the system displays a set of text snippets extracted using our algorithm. These snippets provide interesting information about the current image being viewed. We also detect concepts phrases in the snippet that map to Wikipedia article titles [8, 17, 25], further refined using the techniques proposed in [illegible]. These concept phrases are used to hyperlink to other images that share the concept phrases in their snippets. Our algorithm for determining the destination of the hyperlink is randomized; if the viewer returns to the same image twice, we want them to explore a different path the second time around. Using an inverted index, we locate K=10 top images at random that have a text snippet that includes the concept being clicked on. There are typically thousands of possible destinations. We then sort these images by the frequency with which the concept appears across all the snippets associated with the image, and choose the image with the highest frequency. We found this algorithm yielded a compelling experience. More sophisticated approaches are left as future work.

Figure 9 contains an screenshot of our application. The current image is a diagram explaining how neural signals are transmitted from an axon to a dendrite in the brain. The displayed text snippet explains the process. The history of recent images is shown on the left side. We began with an image of Ernest Rutherford, then tapped on Isaac Newton, then Albert Einstein twice, once a photo of Albert and his wife, the second time just the famous physicist. We then tapped on brain and neuron before arriving at the current image. The right side of the display includes a list of all the concepts for this subset of science images. The user can tap on any concept to initiate a browsing session at a different starting point. An illustration of the browsing session in Figure 9 is contained in the web video http://research.microsoft.com/en-us/um/people/sbaker/i/www/browsing.mp4.

Evaluation using Mechanical Turk: We evaluated the effectiveness in identifying the next image to browse, based on the semantics conveyed by the snippets. In particular, are two images that are visually unrelated, indeed related through the snippets that describe them? To answer this question, we make use of an evaluation set consisting of 500 pairs, $< x_i, y_i >$, of images (along with the snippets that link x_i to y_i) constructed as follows: for each pair, we choose an image x_i at random. Then, we choose a concept associated with x_i (from the snippets of x_i) at random. We then choose the next image, y_i using the algorithm described above to compute the destination of a link within our application.

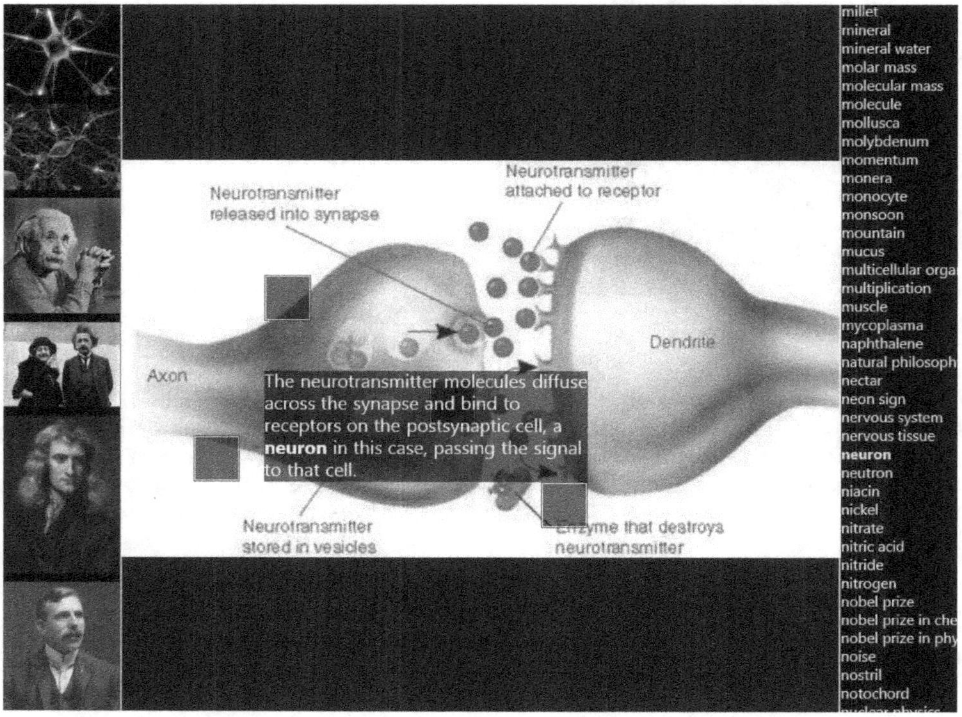

Figure 9: A screenshot of our semantic image browsing application. The current image is displayed with one of the text snippets. In the snippet, two concepts are detected, neuron and axon. Tapping on either of these concepts takes the user to a related image. The panel on the left shows the browsing history. The panel on the right contains all the concepts for this subset of images, and tapping a concept navigates to an image with that concept. See `http://research.microsoft.com/en-us/um/people/sbaker/i/www/browsing.mp4` **for a video.**

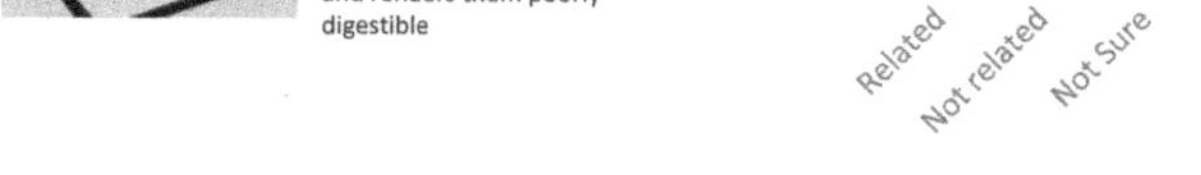

Figure 10: We validated our browsing application using Amazon Mechanical Turk. Left: We showed pairs of images that are connected with a transition in the application. The connection here is the word "calcium." Half the time we showed the corresponding text snippets. The other half we just showed the images. Right: The results show that judges are able to see connections between images more often when they are also shown the text snippets.

We conduct two sets of experiments using Amazon Mechanical Turk. In the first experiment, each Human Intelligence Task (HIT) consists of *only* the pair of images, $< x_i, y_i >$. Each judge was asked to specify if they found the pair of images to be 'related', 'not related' or 'not sure'. In the second experiment (a different HIT), the judges repeated the same experiment, but now, in addition to the pairs of images, they were also shown snippets linking the two images with the connecting concept highlighted.

Results: Figure 10 shows the average number of images that were judged in each of the categories. We can see a huge drop in fraction of 'unrelated' images from 57% to 25% showing the efficacy of our approach in linking semantically related images that are seemingly unrelated. As examples, consider the pair of images shown in Figure 10. In isolation, the connection between the two images is not obvious. With the addition of the text snippet, the viewer immediately finds both images more interesting and sees the 'semantic" relationship between them.

6. CONCLUSION

We have presented a scalable mining algorithm to obtain a set of text snippets for images on the web. The optimal set of snippets is chosen to maximize a combination of relevance, interestingness, and diversity. The relevancy and interestingness are scored using learned models.

There are a number of applications of the resulting text snippets. One possibility is to display the snippets along with image search results. In this paper we proposed two others, a plugin to an internet browser that augments webpages with snippets overlaid on images, and a tablet application that allows users to browse images on the web via hyperlinks embedded in the text snippets. The snippet data can be useful for improving image search relevance.

One suggestion for future work is to analyze the snippets in more detail, for example by clustering, to find groups of related images. The results could be used to broaden the set of snippets and concepts associated with an image, possibly leading to deeper understanding of the content of the images, and more interesting browsing experiences.

7. ADDITIONAL AUTHORS

Rizwan Ansary (Microsoft, rizwan@microsoft.com)
Ashish Kapoor (Microsoft, akapoor@microsoft.com)
Qifa Ke (Microsoft, qke@microsoft.com)
Matt Uyttendaele (Microsoft, mattu@microsoft.com)
Xin-Jing Wang (Microsoft, xywang@microsoft.com)
Lei Zhang (Microsoft, leizhang@microsoft.com)

8. REFERENCES

[1] R. Agrawal, M. Christoforaki, S. Gollapudi, A. Kannan, K. Kenthapadi, and A. Swaminathan. Mining videos from the web for electronic textbooks. *International Conference on Formal Concept Analysis*, 2014.

[2] R. Angheluta, R. De Busser, and M.-F. Moens. The use of topic segmentation for automatic summarization. In *Proceedings of the ACL-2002 Workshop on Automatic Summarization*, 2002.

[3] A. L. Berger and V. O. Mittal. Ocelot: a system for summarizing web pages. In *Proceedings of ACM SIGIR*, pages 144–151. ACM, 2000.

[4] O. Buyukkokten, H. Garcia-Molina, and A. Paepcke. Seeing the whole in parts: text summarization for web browsing on handheld devices. In *Proceedings of the 10th international conference on World Wide Web*, pages 652–662. ACM, 2001.

[5] W. T. Chuang and J. Yang. Extracting sentence segments for text summarization: a machine learning approach. In *Proceedings of ACM SIGIR*, pages 152–159. ACM, 2000.

[6] J. Dean and S. Ghemawat. Mapreduce: Simplified data processing on large clusters. In *Sixth Symposium on Operating System Design and Implementation*, pages 137–149, 2004.

[7] A. Farhadi, M. Hejrati, M. A. Sadeghi, P. Young, C. Rashtchian, J. Hockenmaier, and D. Forsyth. Every picture tells a story: Generating sentences from images. In *ECCV 2010*. Springer, 2010.

[8] E. Gabrilovich and S. Markovitch. Computing semantic relatedness using Wikipedia-based explicit semantic analysis. In *IJCAI*, 2007.

[9] J. Goldstein, V. Mittal, J. Carbonell, and M. Kantrowitz. Multi-document summarization by sentence extraction. In *Proceedings of the 2000 NAACL-ANLP Workshop on Automatic summarization*, 2000.

[10] Y. Jing, H. A. Rowley, C. Rosenberg, J. Wang, M. Zhao, and M. Covell. Google image swirl, a large-scale content-based image browsing system. In *Multimedia and Expo (ICME), IEEE International Conference on*, pages 267–267. IEEE, 2010.

[11] C.-W. Ko, J. Lee, and M. Queyranne. An exact algorithm for maximum entropy sampling. *Operations Research*, 43(4):684–691, 1995.

[12] G. Kulkarni, V. Premraj, S. Dhar, S. Li, Y. Choi, A. C. Berg, and T. L. Berg. Baby talk: Understanding and generating simple image descriptions. In *Computer Vision and Pattern Recognition (CVPR), IEEE Conference on*, pages 1601–1608. IEEE, 2011.

[13] P. Kuznetsova, V. Ordonez, A. C. Berg, T. L. Berg, and Y. Choi. Collective generation of natural image descriptions. In *Proceedings of the Association for Computational Linguistics*, pages 359–368, 2012.

[14] D. C. Liu and J. Nocedal. On the limited memory method for large scale optimization. *Mathematical Programming*, 45(3):503–528, 1989.

[15] I. Mani and M. T. Maybury. *Advances in automatic text summarization*. the MIT Press, 1999.

[16] R. Mason and E. Charniak. Annotation of online shopping images without labeled training examples. *NAACL HLT 2013*, page 1, 2013.

[17] O. Medelyan, D. Milne, C. Legg, and I. Witten. Mining meaning from Wikipedia. *International Journal of Human-Computer Studies*, 67(9), 2009.

[18] Microsoft. Internet Explorer. http://windows.microsoft.com/en-us/internet-explorer/go-explore-ie.

[19] Microsoft. Windows Azure Cloud Services. http://www.windowsazure.com.

[20] Y. Mori, H. Takahashi, and R. Oka. Image-to-word transformation based on dividing and vector quantizing images with words. In *First International Workshop on Multimedia Intelligent Storage and Retrieval Management*, 1999.

[21] G. L. Nemhauser, L. A. Wolsey, and M. L. Fisher. An analysis of approximations for maximizing submodular set functions. *Mathematical Programming*, 14(1):265–294, 1978.

[22] V. Ordonez, G. Kulkarni, and T. L. Berg. Im2text: Describing images using 1 million captioned photographs. In *Advances in Neural Information Processing Systems*, pages 1143–1151, 2011.

[23] K. Spärck Jones. Automatic summarising: The state of the art. *Information Processing & Management*, 43(6):1449–1481, 2007.

[24] G. Strong, E. Hoque, M. Gong, and O. Hoeber. Organizing and browsing image search results based on conceptual and visual similarities. In *Advances in Visual Computing*, pages 481–490. Springer, 2010.

[25] M. Strube and S. Ponzetto. WikiRelate! Computing semantic relatedness using Wikipedia. In *AAAI*, 2006.

[26] X.-J. Wang, L. Zhang, and C. Liu. Duplicate discovery on 2 billion internet images. In *Proceedings of the Big Data Workshop, IEEE CVPR*, pages 429–346. IEEE, 2013.

[27] S. Winder and M. Brown. Learning local image descriptors. In *IEEE Computer Vision and Pattern Recognition*, pages 1–8, 2007.

[28] B. Z. Yao, X. Yang, L. Lin, M. W. Lee, and S.-C. Zhu. I2t: Image parsing to text description. *Proceedings of the IEEE*, 98(8):1485–1508, 2010.

Predicting Student Risks Through Longitudinal Analysis

Ashay Tamhane
IBM Research - India
ashayuda@buffalo.edu

Shajith Ikbal
IBM Research - India
shajmoha@in.ibm.com

Bikram Sengupta
IBM Research - India
bsengupt@in.ibm.com

Mayuri Duggirala*
Tata Research Development & Design Centre, Pune, India
mayuri.duggirala@tcs.com

James Appleton
Gwinnett County Public Schools, GA, USA
jim_appleton@gwinnett.k12.ga.us

ABSTRACT

Poor academic performance in K-12 is often a precursor to unsatisfactory educational outcomes such as dropout, which are associated with significant personal and social costs. Hence, it is important to be able to predict students at risk of poor performance, so that the right personalized intervention plans can be initiated. In this paper, we report on a large-scale study to identify students at risk of not meeting acceptable levels of performance in one state-level and one national standardized assessment in Grade 8 of a major US school district. An important highlight of our study is its scale - both in terms of the number of students included, the number of years and the number of features, which provide a very solid grounding to the research. We report on our experience with handling the scale and complexity of data, and on the relative performance of various machine learning techniques we used for building predictive models. Our results demonstrate that it is possible to predict students at-risk of poor assessment performance with a high degree of accuracy, and to do so well in advance. These insights can be used to pro-actively initiate personalized intervention programs and improve the chances of student success.

Keywords

education; educational data mining; risk prediction; longitudinal data analysis

1. INTRODUCTION

One of the primary goals of any education system is to equip students with the knowledge and skills needed to transition to successful career pathways. How effectively education systems around the world are able to meet this goal acts as a major determinant of economic and social progress.

*This work was done while the author was at IBM Research-India.

KDD'14, August 24–27, 2014, New York, NY, USA.

http://dx.doi.org/10.1145/2623330.2623355.

In particular, K-12 reflects the most critical phase of an individual's lifelong learning, during which the opportunities for a successful future need to be created and nurtured. It is in recognition of this fact that increasingly, educational reforms focused around frequent and standardized testing of K-12 students are gaining acceptance as a way to monitor performance and progress at an individual and institutional level [3, 4]. For many of these assessments, a passing score is required to meet state or district standards for progression to the next grade level. Poor academic performance in such standardized assessments can thus lead to unfavorable educational outcomes such as grade retention, and when not adequately addressed, it can eventually trigger dropout or sub-optimal career pathways, which are associated with significant personal and social costs. For example, in the United States, nearly 7,000 high school students drop out of school each day; if the students who dropped out of the class of 2011 had graduated, the nation's economy would have benefited from $154 billion in additional income over the course of their lifetimes [11]. Hence, it is important to identify students at risk of poor performance in major standardized tests, and to do so well in advance, so that the right personalized intervention plans can be initiated to improve performance.

Traditionally, K-12 educators (e.g. class teachers) have relied on recent academic results of a student (e.g. in formative tests in the current grade) along with an educator's general intuition gleaned from teaching similar students in the past, to determine if the student might be at risk of poor performance in an upcoming assessment. This makes the process overly reliant on an educator's experience level, there is no objective quantification of the level of risk, and the dependence on recent data to make a prediction for the academic year may often not leave enough time to apply the right level of intervention to adequately improve performance. However, with the digitization of school records and rapid uptake of digital tools for teaching and learning, various aspects of a student's longitudinal journey through K-12 are now captured and persisted in digital form. This offers a rich repository of data that can be analyzed to detect patterns associated with unsatisfactory educational outcomes, derived from thousands of students who have progressed through the system over the years, and taking into account a holistic view of a student in terms of both academic history over a period of time, as well as other non-academic attributes (e.g. related to attendance, demographics, behavior etc.) that may influence academic performance.

The work reported in this paper has been motivated by the need to develop scientific, robust predictive models for at-risk students in a large K-12 school district in the US. An increasing number of school districts now have substantial volumes of historical data that have resulted from digitization efforts over the last decade, spurred by legislation that mandates implementation of longitudinal data systems and usage of such data to improve instruction [4]. The district in question - Gwinnett County Public Schools (also referred to as GCPS in this paper), based near Atlanta, Georgia - is the largest school system in the state of Georgia, serving more than 168,000 students across 132 schools in 2013-14 [1]. The availability of a district-wide common data system allows the progress of students to be tracked longitudinally across its 77 elementary, 26 middle and 19 high schools, besides 4 charter schools and 6 other special schools. In the course of this K-12 journey, students take a variety of standardized assessments, both state-level and national-level, and detailed performance data in these tests are persisted within the GCPS data warehouse. In addition, a variety of other data about the student such as enrollment history, various demographic indicators, discipline/behavior etc. are also stored. Over the years, such data on more than 200,000 students have been made available in the GCPS warehouse, which presents both a challenge in terms of its sheer volume, variety and complexity, and also a tremendous opportunity to develop sophisticated models of performance that can be used to improve teaching and learning programs.

Within this overall context, our specific objective was to develop predictive models to identify at-risk students in Grade 8, for two disciplines mathematics and science, in two standardized tests – a state-level assessment called Criterion Referenced Competency Test (CRCT) and a national assessment called Iowa Test of Basic Skills (ITBS). Grade 8 was specifically chosen because of its significance in the K-12 journey – as the final year in middle school, preceding the first year of high school. The specific assessments and disciplines were selected based on their importance to GCPS. The research and experimentation were driven by the following questions: (i) how accurately (and using which feature sets) can we predict students who fail Grade 8 CRCT and ITBS Mathematics and Science tests? and (ii) how early (by which grade), can we make these predictions with reasonable accuracy? The first question is important because unless at-risk students and not-at-risk students are differentiated with reasonable accuracy, significant resources may be expended on misaligned interventions for these student cohorts, without ultimately achieving the desired improvement in success rates. The importance of the second question stems from the fact that the earlier we are able to accurately identify an at-risk student, the more the time available to the school to apply interventions to reduce the risk of failure.

Our models are built based on the longitudinal data derived from the GCPS data warehouse on students who have appeared for CRCT and ITBS Grade 8 assessments in mathematics and science over the last several years, which numbered 58,361 and 43,306 students respectively for these two tests. Mean imputation was used to address missing values in the longitudinal trajectories of the students, and the models were developed employing the techniques of Logistics Regression, Naive Bayes and Decision Tree, using the IBM SPSS Modeler [2] and Weka [14]. The data attributes used for deriving the features of the predictive models relate to performance in various assessments in mathematics, science and related disciplines, several demographic indicators (e.g. gender, ethnicity, free or reduced meal eligibility, special education/gifted) and behavioral indicators (e.g. suspensions).

Our key findings may be summarized as follows:

- Our results indicate the it is possible to predict students at-risk of failing Grade 8 CRCT and ITBS assessments in Mathematics and Science with a high level of accuracy and balance between differentiating at-risk students and not-at-risk students. Of the algorithms, logistic regression gave the best results overall.
- We also observe that it is possible to predict success/failure in the Grade 8 assessments as early as Grades 4 and 5, with data from subcequent grades further improving the effectiveness of the predictions
- In terms of features, longitudinal test scores from earlier grades emerge as a strong predictor, while the set of demographic indicators taken together, are able to achieve reasonably high prediction performance as well.

The rest of the paper is structured as follows: in Section 2, we discuss related work. A detailed description of the data sets used for the analysis and its processing and feature engineering are presented in Section 3. Section 4 discusses the prediction and experimental set-up, including the data, evaluation metric and the features used. Section 5 presents the experimental results, while Section 6 has a discussion on some of the insights from the results. Finally, Section 7 outlines future work directions, and Section 8 concludes the paper.

2. RELATED WORK

There is a wealth of research available on the factors that contribute to student risk of academic performance and dropout. With the increasing availability of education related longitudinal data within K-12 and Higher Education institutions, this line of research is now becoming increasingly data-driven and evidence-based. Our study adds to this body of work, from which we review a few selected papers below to put our research in context.

Previous research has studied student risk in terms of factors such as low socioeconomic status, living in a single parent home, changing schools at non-traditional times, below average grades at specific school levels, being held back in school through grade retention, having older siblings who left high school before completion and negative peer pressure [19]. Other external factors influencing student risk, such as teacher engagement [7] and smaller class size [20] have also been studied. Several typologies have been developed for describing students at risk. Fortin et al. [12] classified at-risk students into four different subgroups: the covert behavior type, the uninterested in school type, the school and social adjustment difficulties type and the depressive type, thereby highlighting the importance of school, family and personal factors in the emergence of risk. Summarizing twenty–five years of research on influences of dropout, Rumberger and Lim [18] delineated rigorous empirical results into a typology of predictor categories. These categories included 1) individual–level factors which consisted of background, attitudes, behaviors, and performance, as well as 2) influential, but perhaps less commonly considered family–, school–

and community–level variables. At the student–level, background was focused upon demographic and health variables as well as past school experiences and performance. These influences impacted attitudes which were believed to impact behaviors and, in turn, academic performance. Such findings have influenced our selection of predictors of student performance in our study, where we have leveraged a variety of demographic and behavioral data of students, in addition to their historical academic performance record, to predict future performance.

In recent years, due to the digitization of school records and availability of instrumented digital learning environments, a wealth of student related information is now available in data warehouses, providing a fertile ground for educational data mining research. The Signals project at Purdue University [5] is a notable effort in this direction. Signals combines online academic behavior of students, such as whether they opened or completed assignments and exercises, with a student's academic performance such as standardized test scores, high school GPA and current grades, to infer the risk level of the student in the course. Other online systems make use of students' social engagement with their peers in the context of work, in addition to content-access patterns, to identify disengaged learners who can potentially be at-risk [10]. Some key variables used in predicting students at risk in online courses typically include total number of discussion messages posted, total number of mail messages sent, and total number of assessments completed. However, these models are limited in their generalizability as they focus on fully online courses alone [17]. In our current study, data from digital learning environments was not available for analysis, and we intend to extend our work with such data when available, to investigate how it influences the predictive power of our models.

In a recent study, Chen and Elliott [8] have reviewed previous research which highlights the role of early identification of students at risk. Specifically, their study found that any student who had passed the key predictor course module seemed more likely to progress to the second year successfully. Similarly, any student who failed the predictor module was more likely to repeat some of the first year modules, repeat the entire first year, or, even fail the course, i.e., drop out from a course. This pattern was valid for all of the records of the five consecutive academic years considered for the study. Our study adopts a similar approach where we attempt to examine performance (test scores) in the current grade based on test scores in previous grades, both at the micro (test strand) level and the macro (subtest) level. We also demonstrate how risks for Grade 8 standardized tests can be predicted with a reasonable degree of accuracy a few years in advance.

At the high school and undergraduate level, Hershkovitz et al [15] used a learning graph which represents the student's learning over time and was developed using a knowledge–estimation model. This model infers the degree of learning that occurs at specific moments rather than the student's knowledge at those moments. It showed substantially better student–level cross validated prediction of student's future learning than previous approaches. However, the study used a limited student sample for its research (n=181 undergraduate and high school students) thus limiting the generalizability of its conclusions. In a study on students in tertiary education by Gray, McGuinness and Owende [13], models of academic performance were found to achieve good predictive accuracy when younger students and mature students were modeled separately. Further, students with missing data were removed from analysis and the study was carried out with students having complete data. Missing data is an unavoidable characteristic of any large real-life data set, and hence we addressed the issue in our research by imputing the missing data with the mean, rather than only selecting a small number of students with complete data on a few features. Using Bayesian networks, Vihavainen et al. [21] demonstrated that students with a higher likelihood of failing their mathematics course could be detected at an early phase of their studies using data on their programming behavior. The sample comprised a large number of programming snapshots but only from 58 first year computer science students. In a recent study, Erdos et al [9] studied the extent to which first language (L1) predictors can be used to predict risk for French (L2) reading and language learning. Analyses of 86 kindergarten children revealed factors such as phonological awareness, phonological access and letter–sound knowledge in L1 were significant predictors of risk for reading difficulties in L2. Similar research has examined the relationship between oral reading fluency and success on state standardized assessments [16]. Our work builds on such examples of the use of data mining and machine learning techniques to predict academic risks, but is characterized by very large real-life data sets e.g. models built from more than 58,000 students drawn from 132 schools, and leveraging 342 features, in the case of ITBS success prediction. This gives a very broad data and evidence foundation to the study, which contributes to the robustness and generalizabilty of the results.

A review of research considered the predictive properties of 110 indicators of dropping out of high school across 36 studies and classified these on several dimensions [6]. Of these dimensions, the authors argued for sensitivity (the proportion of accurately identified future dropouts (or non–graduates) – "true positives") and specificity (the proportion of accurately identified future graduates – "true negatives") as the most important qualities of an indicator. We have adopted these metrics when evaluating the effectiveness of our predictive models.

3. DATA DESCRIPTION

Gwinnett County Public Schools (GCPS) is one of the largest school systems in the US, consisting of 132 schools and serving more than 168,000 students at present. A variety of data related to students, teachers, as well as learning and assessment activities is collected from each of the constituent schools and collated into a central data warehouse, offering a rich repository that can be mined for insights. A snapshot of this data warehouse was made available to us, which we use as the source of data for our analysis. The data snapshot consists of over a hundred tables storing various types of data including student, teacher, school, and test (assessment) data. These four broad categories are shown in Fig.1. The most important category of the available data (for the purpose of this paper) is the 'Students' category, which is a group of tables storing student data like enrollment, demography, test performance, course history and their performance in various national and state level tests they have taken so far. For the privacy of students and teachers whose data is captured, their personal information was anonymized by replacing it with hypothetical names and addresses before the data set was made available for this study.

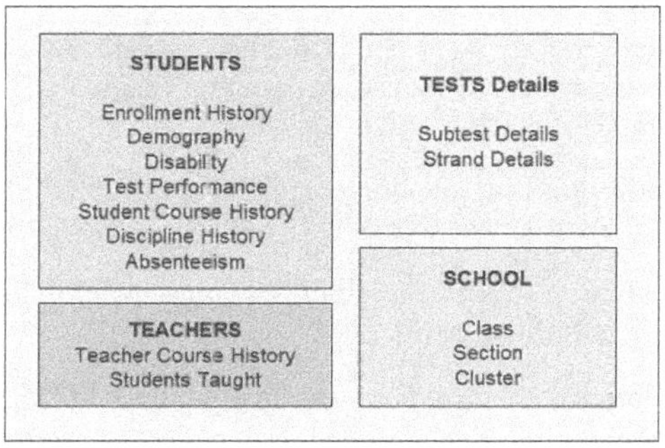

Figure 1: An Overview of the Available Data

3.1 Background On Tests and Defining Risk

It is important to understand the structure of the tests, as it will help us explain the features we use, our definition of risk, as well as understand some of the missing data challenges later in the section. Every "test" or assessment has several "sub-tests". For example, the Criterion References Competency Test (CRCT) is a test which has several sub-tests like mathematics, science and literature. Every sub-test further consists of different "strands". For example, mathematics has strands like algebra and geometry. All the test scores in the data are available both at sub-test and strand levels. Note that some tests only have sub-tests and do not have strands (for example, CogAT).

Since 2005-06, CRCT has been Georgia's annual assessment for determining how well students have acquired the skills and knowledge described in the Georgia Performance Standards (GPS). The CRCTs are currently taken across grades 3-8. In 2012-13, the CRCTs transitioned to include Common Core (CC) based items and into the (CCGPS/GPS) version. For our study, we consider the GPS version of CRCT so as to have a comparable sample of students.

Iowa Test of Basic Skills (ITBS) provides the opportunity for comparison with a nationally representative group of peers. Through ITBS, GCPS assesses students in grades 3, 5, and 8 in the areas of reading, written expression, vocabulary, conventions of writing, mathematics, science, and social studies.

The Cognitive Abilities Test (CogAT) is an assessment designed to measure acquired reasoning abilities in students, covering areas most linked to academic success in K-12 (verbal, quantitative, non-verbal). For this reason, we used CogAT results as predictors for performance in other assessments like CRCT and ITBS.

CRCTs measure performance based on predefined ranges of scores. CRCTs are structured so that the they range from 650–900s. Scores at or above 850 indicate exceeding standards, those at or above 800 indicate performance that meets test standards, where as those below 800 indicate below test standards performance. We consider a student to be at risk, if he scores below 800 in CRCT in the subtest of interest (mathematics or science). ITBS proves percentile ranks (PR) – which indicate rank within a distribution and when used with a distribution of nationally–representative peers, support inferences of relative national performance.

For our analysis, we use the national percentile ranks as an indicator of performance in the test. Being a norm-referenced test, there are no predefined performance ranges unlike CRCT. Our subject matter expert from GCPS recommended a threshold of 25 percentile to mark the risk for ITBS. We derive our target risk variables by putting corresponding thresholds on grade 8 CRCT and ITBS scores as we intend to predict risk of students performing poorly in grade 8.

3.2 Missing Data

All together, the data warehouse contains historical data of over 200,000 students. However, the data is not consistent both within and across data categories. For example, a student's performance in CRCT may be available for grades 4-8. However, ITBS scores might be available only for grades 3 and 5. There may be several reasons for such missing data. Students change counties and schools multiple times during the K–12 period. For the period when students are not part of the county, the data of their performance may not be available. A student may have not taken certain assessments. Education standards change from time to time, and so do the tests associated with them, as discussed for the case of CRCT test. Finally, data warehouse snapshot available to us may not have the complete historical data available to the school.

We now present the data processing and feature engineering pipeline which we follow to create data sets suitable for our prediction task, considering the missing data challenges.

3.3 Data Processing and Feature Engineering

We divide the task of extracting useful data from the data warehouse and converting it into usable datasets into three main phases.

3.3.1 Creation of Merged Data

As described earlier, the data warehouse contains over hundred tables. Unfortunately, the Student data which we are interested in is scattered across several tables. The first phase consists of creating a data set with features extracted and engineered from various tables and columns in the data warehouse. This phase (Fig.2) involves three main stages.

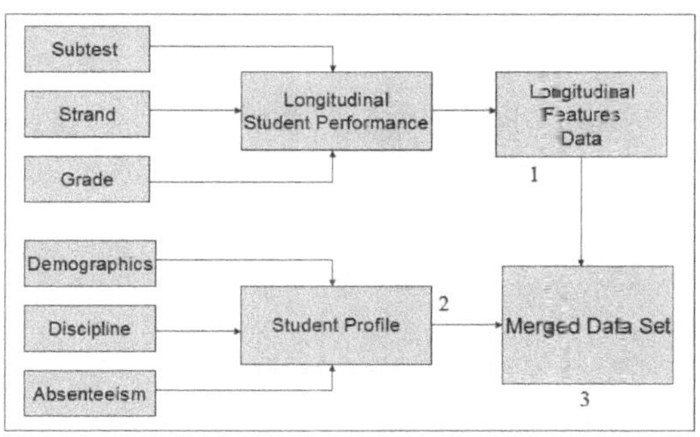

Figure 2: First Phase of Data Processing

Firstly, we create Longitudinal Features Data. This stage involves merging the different tables storing data on sub-tests and strands, as well as mapping performances to the corresponding grades in which students took the tests. This results in intermediate Longitudinal Performance Data, which contains about 19 million records as it consists of all the performances of every student. We use SPSS Modeler streams [2] to restructure the data so as to generate features for each student from the Longitudinal Performance Data. Currently, we only consider CRCT, ITBS and CogAt test features in this stage. Note that these features include both the sub-test level and the strand level scores, when applicable. The Longitudinal Features Data contains data for 158,282 students and altogether 516 different columns each containing a specific test score. However, it is important to note that large amount of entries in this data are missing and we shall discuss how we handle this in the final phase of data processing.

The second stage involves creation of the Student Profile which contain features engineered from the demographics, discipline history and absenteeism history. While the demographic features like Gender, Ethnicity, Free Meal, Gifted and Special Education Needs are available straight from the warehouse tables, features like 'Number of Discipline Incidents', 'Number of Suspensions' and 'Number of Absent Days' were created after aggregating discipline incidents and absenteeisms reported.

In the third stage, we simply merge the Longitudinal Features and the Student Profile Features, resulting in a Merged Data set which contains several missing rows and columns from the Longitudinal Features Data.

3.3.2 Creation of Target Variable Dependent Data

The second phase involves creating target variable specific data sets from the Merged Data set obtained from the first phase of data processing. Firstly, we select only those students who have no missing values for the target variable. For example, when the target variable is CRCT 8th Grade Math sub–test, we discard all those students whose data for this target variable is missing. After this step, we discard features which have more than 80% missing values. This results in 58,707 students with 342 features for ITBS test, and 43,310 students with 282 features for the CRCT test. Note that though some of the columns may contain as low as 20% values, the fact that our data covers a very large number of students ensures that at least 11,741 samples exist for each feature in the ITBS set and 8,662 samples for the CRCT set. Nonetheless, since most of the standard classifiers do not work with missing data set, we impute the missing values in the third phase.

3.3.3 Imputation of Missing Features

To make our system robust, we handle missing data which routinely exists in data warehouses of the scale similar to that of GCPS. Moreover, none of the students contain all the features in our data set. Therefore, creation of a complete data set containing features ranging over all the different grades is not possible. For the sake of simplicity in terms of method, we impute the missing values using mean value imputation. This is a common imputation technique which simply replaces each missing value with the mean of the feature. However, many advanced imputation techniques exist and exploring them for our system remains a work to be done in future.

4. RISK PREDICTION AND EXPERIMENTAL SETUP

4.1 Data

We created data sets for 3 different tasks as below to demonstrate that our approach is generalizable to various student risk prediction tasks:

1. Predicting risk of poor performance in CRCT grade 8 Mathematics subtest
2. Predicting risk of poor performance in CRCT grade 8 Science subtest, and
3. Predicting risk of poor performance in ITBS grade 8 Mathematics subtest.

During the actual experimentation, we excluded all the features related to grade 8 or above, to account for the fact that prediction will be done only using grade 7th or below features. As discussed in earlier sections, we define our risk (derive our target risk labels) using thresholds on CRCT and ITBS grade 8 Math/Science scores. Thresholds used are 800 for CRCT and the 25 percentile for ITBS. We address the problem of predicting risk by transforming this into a binary classification problem, where at-risk students are labeled as positive samples and non-risk students labeled as negative samples. As a preprocessing step, we standardized all the features to mean value of 0 and standard deviation of 1.

In our experiments, we used 5-fold cross validation settings to evaluate the accuracy of predictions made in various tasks. In this setting, the entire data set for a given task is divided into 5 equal parts. Prediction experiment is repeated 5 times, each time keeping one of the 5 parts as evaluation data and the rest as training data to build prediction model. In the end evaluation results on all 5 parts are accumulated together to compute the overall prediction accuracy.

4.2 Prediction

We used binary classifiers as risk prediction models. Specifically we used various implementations of classifiers in SPSS [2] and WEKA [14] with their default settings, such as logistic regression, naive bayes, decision tree and decision table. All the logitudinal features available per student are used as set of input features to predict a binary output namely, whether a student is at risk in various tasks listed in previous section.

4.3 Evaluation Metric

The ITBS data set contains 58,361 samples containing 15.3% positive samples and 84.7% negative samples. This shows the between-class skew that exists as students with such extreme risk are naturally rare to find. Similar is the case for the CRCT data set – which contains 43,036 students including 10.7% positive and 89.3% negative samples. This heavy skew in data has important implications on the evaluation criteria.

As described earlier, student risk prediction is effectively a binary classification task aimed at categorizing students into two groups: 1) *risk* and 2) *no-risk*, depending upon whether a student is likely to perform poorly in an important examination or not. Since the number of students falling into *risk* category is typically smaller, a simple classifier where all the students are assigned to *no-risk* class is expected to give high classification accuracy, in spite of the fact that it would result in very poor (0%) *risk* class prediction accuracy. For this reason, in this paper, we have used *receiver operating characteristic (ROC) curve* to measure the prediction performance. ROC curves show a trade-off achieved between true positive rate of the *risk* category (sensitivity) and false positive rate of the *no-risk* category (specificity) for various classification thresholds applied on classifier class probability outputs (see Figure 3 for a sample ROC curve plot). True positive (TP) rate is the percentage of actual *risk* students correctly categorized into *risk* category. False positive (FP) rate is the percentage of actual *no-risk* students wrongly categorized into *risk* category. TP rate is expected to be high for low class probability thresholds. However, this is expected to also result in high FP rate. On the other hand a high probability threshold is expected to result in lower TP and FP rates. An example ROC curve obtained for our task can be found in Figure 3.

Typically in practical systems, depending upon the task requirement, a best class probability threshold is chosen to achieve one of TP rate or FP rate requirements. However, in this paper, we use area under ROC curve (AUC-ROC) as a measure of overall prediction performance. Increase in AUC-ROC could be achieved by pushing the ROC curve shown in Figure upward left, which in turn means an improved TP and FP rates for a given class probability threshold. AUC-ROC typically varies from 0.5 to 1.0. A simple classifier choosing one of the class labels (say the majority class label) as class output would achieve an AUC-ROC value of 0.5.

4.4 Features Used

At the end of the data processing (as described in Section 3.3), total number of features available for CRCT risk prediction is 235 and for ITBS risk prediction is 280. Based on the description given in Section 3 , these features can be grouped into categories based on their type. Specifically we have grouped these features into following broad categories:

- Scores: scores obtained by students in their past grades from 1 to 7 in various tests including CRCT, ITBS and CogAt.
- Demography: student demography information such as gender, ethnicity, free meal, gifted and special education.
- Behavioral: information recorded about student behavior such as number of absent days, number of suspensions and number of discipline incidents.

We further grouped the score features into categories based on the grade at which the score is obtained (such as grade 1, grade 2, ..., grade 7) and the subject in which the score is obtained (such as maths, science, literature and others).

5. EXPERIMENTS AND RESULTS

In this section we discuss results of experiments performed to evaluate the student risk prediction system developed for GCPS. These experiments are aimed at two goals: 1) to measure risk prediction performance (described in Section 5.1), and 2) to analyze the importance of various aspects of student data and prediction in order to derive insights that would be of potential value to the educational institutions. Specifically, in such analysis we aim to explore two different aspects namely: data and prediction that might be of potential interest to educational institutions such as: 1) Feature importance (described in Section 5.2, and 2) Early prediction of the risk (described in Section 5.3).

5.1 Risk Prediction Performance

Table 2 shows a comparison of AUC-ROC values obtained using various classifiers for risk predictions in CRCT 8th grade Mathematics, CRCT 8th grade Science and ITBS 8th grade Mathematics. We used various classifier implementations in SPSS [2] and Weka [14] with their default settings. For all the tasks, a relatively simpler logistic regression model is able to consistently achieve best prediction accuracy. Hence, we have chosen to use logistic regression model in all our further experiments. As discussed in Section 4.3, ROC curve is a trade of between true positive (TP) and false positive (FP) rates. An example ROC curve obtained using logistic regression model for CRCT 8th grade Mathematics risk prediction task is shown in Figure 3. Typically, educational institutions want to keep the incorrect prediction of true risk students as low as possible. This in turn means a specification of required TP rate for the prediction task. A preferable TP rate for GCPS we are working with is 90%. Table 1 shows FP rate we could achieve using the logistic regression classifier for a minimum TP rate of 90% for various prediction tasks.

Task	Probability Threshold	True Positive TP, in %	False Positive FP, in %
CRCT 8th Mathematics	0.06	90.5	23.8
CRCT 8th Science	0.18	90.0	24.7
ITBS 8th Mathematics	0.1	90.7	28.8

Table 1: Probability threshold used to achieve minimum true positive (TP) of 90% in risk prediction. Actual values of TP and FP achieved for the thresholds used are also given.

Classifier	CRCT 8th Grade Mathematics	CRCT 8th Grade Science	ITBS 8th Grade Mathematics
Naive Bayes	0.744	0.739	0.702
Decision Tree	0.822	0.774	0.766
Decision Table	0.933	0.902	0.893
Logistic Regression	0.924	0.907	0.896

Table 2: Comparison of classifier performances for risk prediction in CRCT 8th grade Mathematics, CRCT 8th grade Science and ITBS 8th grade Mathematics.

5.2 Feature Importance

In Section 5.1 we used all available student features in order to predict risk with highest accuracy. However, educational institutions are typically interested not just in the overall prediction but also in exploring relative contribution of various features. Particularly, they are interested in finding out a subset of features that are more indicative of potential risk than others. For this purpose we have performed a feature-wise analysis of ability to predict.

Table 3 shows a performance comparison of the various feature groups described in Section 4.4. Among the broader feature groups, score features achieve the best prediction accuracy with performance almost to similar that of the entire

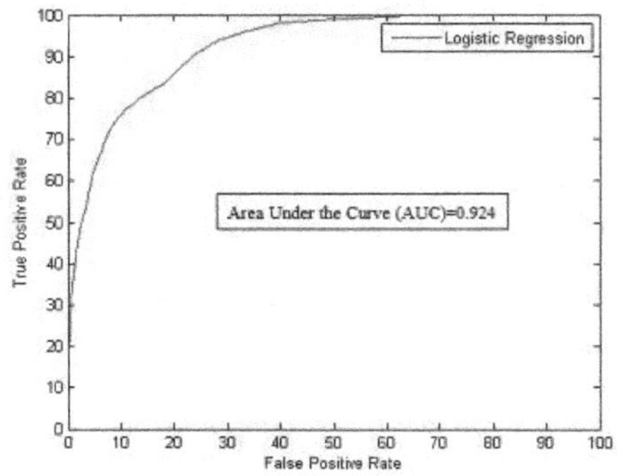

Figure 3: ROC curve for risk prediction using logistic regression for CRCT 8th grade Mathematics

feature set. This strengthens the fact that the past scores are largely indicative of the future test performance. Interestingly, the small set of demography features (5 features) are also able to achieve a reasonably good accuracy, pointing to the fact that specific patterns of demography features are typically indicative of a potential risk. However, behavioral features do not seem to correlate well with the future risk. In fact, further examination of the behavioral features show that only a few number of students are recorded for behavioral issues. Among individual demography features, ethnicity and special education needs achieve best accuracies. Table 3 also shows a comparison of importance of past subject-wise score features in predicting risk for 8th grade ITBS Mathematics. Clearly the past Mathematics scores are able to make better prediction than the other subject scores.

Feature Type	CRCT 8th Grade Mathematics	ITBS 8th Grade Mathematics
All Features	0.924	0.896
All Scores	0.902	0.882
All Demographics	0.866	0.814
All Behavioral	0.576	0.559
Scores - Maths	-	0.871
Scores - Science	-	0.828
Scores - Language	-	0.846
Scores - Others	-	0.829
Demography - Gender	0.547	0.537
Demography - Ethnicity	0.660	0.668
Demography - Gifted	0.622	0.630
Demography - Free Meal	0.646	0.640
Demography - Special Education Needs	0.721	0.637
Behavioral - Absence	0.537	0.542
Behavioral - Suspensions	0.588	0.578
Behavioral - Incidents Reported	0.583	0.569

Table 3: Comparison of feature level risk prediction performance for CRCT 8th grade Mathematics and ITBS 8th grade Mathematics.

5.3 Early Prediction of the Risk

Educational institutions are typically interested in predicting students-at-risk as early as possible so that they can pro-actively adopt early intervention plans to prevent potential failures. For this purpose, we investigated prediction of potential risk at 8th grade using only the lower grade features. Figures 4 and 5 show results of such prediction. In fact, in these figures, risk prediction performance using aggregated features as well as individual features are shown together for comparison. In case of aggregated features, all the score features from grades equal to or less than that mentioned on the x-axis are used for prediction whereas in case of individual features, scores only from grades mentioned in x-axis are used. The results show that we are able to make reasonably accurate predictions (ROC AUC of more than 0.8) as early as 4th grade for 8th grade performance. Also the prediction accuracy improves with the incremental aggregation of score features from lower grades. Individual scores from the recent past are also good predictors of the risk. However, the aggregated features are always able to predict with higher accurately than the individual features.

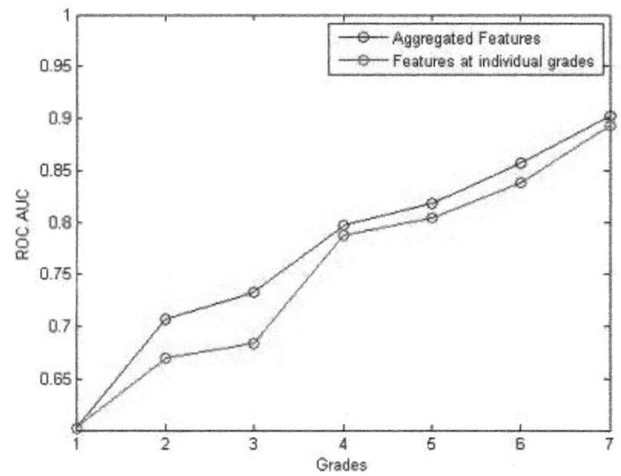

Figure 4: Early risk prediction performance for CRCT 8th grade Mathematics. In case of aggregated features all the score features equal to or less the grade mentioned in x-axis are used. For comparison, performance using individual grade scores is also given which uses just the scores from grades mentioned in the x-axis.

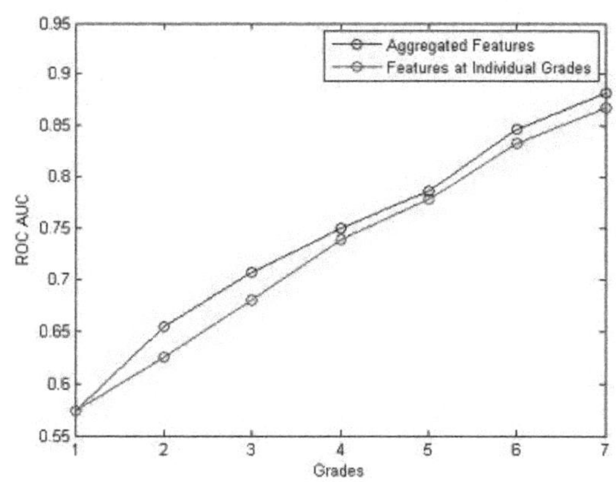

Figure 5: Early risk prediction performance for ITBS 8th grade Mathematics. In the case of aggregated features, all the score features equal to or less than the grade mentioned on the x-axis are used. For comparison, performance using individual grade scores is also given which uses just the scores from grades mentioned on the x-axis.

6. OBSERVATIONS AND INSIGHTS

In this section we discuss some of the insights derived from our experimental results that have potentially valuable implications for educators and industry practitioners.

First, our results showed that a student's risk of poor performance can be predicted with reasonable accuracy (ROC AUC of more than 0.8) in as early as grade 5. Such early prediction can allow teachers sufficient time and fewer resources to take remedial actions in a student's learning path. Additionally, we see that as the grade of prediction increases, the ROC AUC steadily increases. Apart from predicting risk with the aggregated features at a given grade (features of grades 5 and below), we also predicted the risk using individual grade features (features of grade 5). Our results showed that grade 7 features are most relevant, whereas the relevance of the earlier grades sequentially follow.

Second, we showed comparisons between several groups of features by building prediction models individually on these groups. While score features gave the best ROC AUC, demographic features were also found to be important. Yet, more in-depth examination of behavioral features could prove a useful avenue for further research. Our results also showed that while the Math features are most predictive of the risk in grade 8 Math, other subjects are also important predictors.

Third, the solid performance of the logistic regression model, when evaluated against other models, may be relevant as the model is more amenable to coefficient-by-coefficient understanding of variable influences. Additionally, the selection of classifier threshold in a realistic setting is important. Our results showed that a good balance between the true positive and false positive rates can be achieved.

In sum, the breadth of features, extent of data, and approach to modeling make this effort unique and potentially very informative for educational research and practice.

7. FUTURE WORK

We plan to continue our this work towards two fronts: 1) to improve the overall prediction accuracy, and 2) to perform more analysis aimed at deriving further valuable insights for educational institutions.

As described in earlier sections, the data used for prediction contain several missing values. Currently we use mean imputation to approximate the true values of those missing entries. This is a crude approximation and hence is likely to result in noisy predictions. More sophisticated methods to impute missing values are likely to improve the prediction accuracy further.

Currently we are building only one classifier per prediction task for the entire student data. However a divide-and-conquer approach of grouping students into clusters and building a prediction model for each cluster is likely to improve the accuracy further. An interesting aspect to explore in this direction is to group the students' data based on a subset of features that yield optimal risk prediction performance.

Apart from the feature analysis reported in the earlier section, educational institutions would be interested in an explanation of how various predictions were arrived at for each student. This requirement in our system could simply translate into an assignment of importance weights to various features in terms of their role in prediction outcome. Towards this goal, we plan to investigate a detailed feature level discriminant analysis. In addition, exploring alternate models such as hierarchical prediction models might provide an opportunity to back-trace local decisions made at various levels based on local features, thereby making it possible to derive an explanation of why a particular decision is made.

8. CONCLUSIONS

In this paper, we have reported on a large-scale study to predict students at risk of not meeting acceptable levels of performance in national and state-level Grade 8 standardized tests in Mathematics and Science. This study involved one of the largest school districts in the US (GCPS). Using a rich set of predictors related to student demographics and behavior, as well as longitudinal data on test scores through the different grades, we constructed risk prediction models that are able to identify students at risk with a high degree of accuracy. Through experimental evaluation, we also showed that the models strike a good balance between identifying and over identifying students at risk. Other key observations from our experiments include: Predictions for Grade 8 performance may be made with reasonable confidence as early as Grade 4, with data from subsequent grades further improving the accuracy. Amongst the features, longitudinal data on test scores are highly predictive of future success/failure, while a set of demographic features such as ethnicity, disability and free meal, when taken together, are able to achieve reasonably high prediction accuracies as well. Behavioral data do not come up as a strong predictor for performance in this study, and further work is needed to investigate the way behavioral data are collected and interpreted to understand if and why this is actually the case.

Overall, our study shows that longitudinal data-driven risk models for academic performance in standardized tests can lead to robust and early predictions, thereby making it possible to initiate targeted personalized intervention plans well in advance to mitigate the risks and shift a student's learning trajectory towards desired outcomes.

9. REFERENCES

[1] Gwinnet County Public Schools. http://publish.gwinnett.k12.ga.us/gcps/home/public/about.

[2] IBM SPSS Modeler. http://www-01.ibm.com/software/analytics/spss/products/modeler/.

[3] No Child Left Behind. http://www2.ed.gov/nclb/landing.jhtml.

[4] Race to the Top. http://www2.ed.gov/programs/racetothetop/index.html.

[5] Signals Project. http://www.itap.purdue.edu/studio/signals/.

[6] A. J. Bowers, R. Sprott, and S. A. Taff. Do we know who will drop out? a review of the predictors of dropping out of high school: Precision, sensitivity, and specificity. *High School Journal*, 96(2), 2012.

[7] A. B. Brewster and G. L. Bowen. Teacher support and the school engagement of latino middle and high school students at risk of school failure. *Child and Adolescent Social Work Journal*, 21(1):47–67, 2004-02-01T00:00:00.

[8] D. Chen and G. Elliott. Determining key (predictor) course modules for early identification of students at-risk. In *2013 International Conference on Advanced*

Information Engineering and Education Science (ICAIEES 2013). Atlantis Press, 2013.

[9] C. ERDOS, F. GENESEE, R. SAVAGE, and C. HAIGH. Predicting risk for oral and written language learning difficulties in students educated in a second language. *Applied Psycholinguistics*, 35:371–398, 3 2014.

[10] A. Essa and H. Ayad. Student success system: risk analytics and data visualization using ensembles of predictive models. In S. Dawson, C. Haythornthwaite, S. B. Shum, D. Gasevic, and R. Ferguson, editors, *LAK*, pages 158–161. ACM, 2012.

[11] A. for Excellent Education. The High Cost of High School Dropouts: What the Nation Pays for Inadequate High Schools. http://all4ed.org/wp-content/uploads/2013/06/HighCost.pdf, Issue Brief November 2011.

[12] L. Fortin, D. Marcotte, P. Potvin, É. Royer, and J. Joly. Typology of students at risk of dropping out of school: Description by personal, family and school factors. *European Journal of Psychology of education*, 21(4):363–383, 2006.

[13] G. Gray, C. McGuinness, and P. Owende. An investigation of psychometric measures for modelling academic performance in tertiary education.

[14] M. Hall, E. Frank, G. Holmes, B. Pfahringer, P. Reutemann, and I. H. Witten. The weka data mining software: an update. *SIGKDD Explor. Newsl.*, 11(1):10–18, 2009.

[15] A. Hershkovitz, S. M. Gowda, R. S. Baker, and A. T. Corbett. Predicting future learning better using quantitative analysis of moment-by-moment learning.

[16] J. M. Hintze and B. Silberglitt. A longitudinal examination of the diagnostic accuracy and predictive validity of r-cbm and high-stakes testing. *School Psychology Review*, 34(3), 2005.

[17] L. Macfadyen and S. Dawson. Mining lms data to develop an "early warning system" for educators: A proof of concept. *Computers & Education*, 54(2):588–599, 2010.

[18] R. Rumberger and S. A. Lim. Why students drop out of school: A review of 25 years of research, 2008.

[19] J. Spring. *American Education*. McGraw-Hill Higher Education, 2007.

[20] K. R. Stevenson. Educational trends shaping school planning and design: 2007. *National clearinghouse for educational facilities*, 2006.

[21] A. Vihavainen, M. Luukkainen, and J. Kurhila. Using students' programming behavior to predict success in an introductory mathematics course. In *Proceedings of The Fourth International Conference on Educational Data Mining 2011*, 2011.

Novel Geospatial Interpolation Analytics for General Meteorological Measurements

Bingsheng Wang
Department of Computer Science, Virginia Tech
7054 Haycock Road
Falls Church, VA 22043 USA
claren89@vt.edu

Jinjun Xiong
Smarter Energy Research Institute
IBM Thomas J. Watson Research Center
Yorktown Heights, NY 10598 USA
jinjun@us.ibm.com

ABSTRACT

This paper addresses geospatial interpolation for meteorological measurements in which we estimate the values of climatic metrics at unsampled sites with existing observations. Providing climatological and meteorological conditions covering a large region is potentially useful in many applications, such as smart grid. However, existing research works on interpolation either cause a large number of complex calculations or are lack of high accuracy. We propose a Bayesian compressed sensing based non-parametric statistical model to efficiently perform the spatial interpolation task. Student-t priors are employed to model the sparsity of unknown signals' coefficients, and the Approximated Variational Inference (AVI) method is provided for effective and fast learning. The presented model has been deployed at IBM, targeting for aiding the intelligent management of smart grid. The evaluations on two real world datasets demonstrate that our algorithm achieves state-of-the-art performance in both effectiveness and efficiency.

Categories and Subject Descriptors

H.2.8 [**Database Applications**]: Data Mining—*Machine Learning*; I.5 [**PATTERN RECOGNITION**]: I.5.4 Applications—*Miscellaneous*

Keywords

Geospatial Interpolation; Analytics; Meteorological Measurements; Bayesian Inference; Smart Grid

1. INTRODUCTION

Complete and accurate source of meteorological data are prerequisites for the efficient modelling of a wide variety of environmental processes [14]. For example, the productivity for wheat largely depends on the climate patterns, such as precipitation [24]. Crime rates are primarily driven by pleasant weather [13], while cherry blossom is mainly influenced by temperature, sunshine, etc. [20]. However, the most common source of climatic data is meteorological stations, which only supply measurements in some limited locations. Geospatial interpolation has thus attracted many researchers for the estimation of weather or climate variables at unsampled locations.

This paper looks specifically at the application of spatial interpolation to smart grid applications. Smart grid refers to a modernized utility electricity delivery systems, where the power distribution and management is enhanced by employing computer-based remote control and automation along with advanced two-way communications and pervasive computing capabilities, targeting for improved control, efficiency, reliability, safety and sustainability [5, 30]. A smart grid intelligently and bidirectionally delivers electricity between suppliers and consumers, where meteorological variables play an important role [12]. For example, temperature and precipitation are two climate measurements that have great impact on the electricity grid. From the perspective of temperature, we anticipate that when the thermometer rises in summer, so does the demand for power to achieve comfortable temperatures. The increased degree of hotness would also decrease the efficiency of power plants no matter the power is generated from stream, water, nuclear, natural resources, solar, or wind. At the same time, the increased temperatures might reduce transmission lines' efficiency and lead to line sags, which would potentially disrupt the service [8]. Considering precipitation's impacts, we expect that less precipitation might cause the drop of water level, further reducing the generation of hydro-power plants. Drought situation can pose a serious threat to the transmission lines, especially in the states where there is a fire season, such as California. Due to the lack of precipitation, fires are more like to occur and destroy the brittle infrastructure that transports power. It's of critical importance to know about the climate and weather conditions covering the power grid for intelligent peak-load management and effective measures taken to avoid lines' impairment. However, it's impossible to install weather sensors all around the transmission lines and power plants. An effective and efficient interpolation method is expected to provide maps of climatological and meteorological conditions for the whole grid.

Motivated by the needs of smart grid on weather data products, we focus on geospatial interpolation for general meteorological measurements, the procedure of estimating unsampled sites' values with a few observations. Much work has been done on estimating weather or climate variables by spatial interpolation. One branch is to apply physical-deterministic model to simulate the spatial variations in climate metrics by solving a large scale of partial differential equations. Although such models are most accurate, however, it's of high complexity and requires high performance computing, such as the national weather service [21] and the Deep Thunder system deployed by IBM [27]. To balance the efficiency and accuracy, many researchers proposed a variety of learning based interpolation techniques, ranging from inverse distance weighting, splines,

KDD '14 August 24–27 New York City USA
Copyright 2014 ACM 978-1-4503-2956-9/14/08 ...$15.00.
http://dx.doi.org/10.1145/2623330.2623367 .

regression and Kriging to neural networks and machine learning techniques [23, 17, 1]. These learning based models are easy to set up and can complete interpolation in a more efficient manner. However, they are lack of high accuracy.

The approach we present in this paper builds upon compressed sensing methods and recent work in reconstruction problems [18, 7, 31]. Specifically, the proposed model is learned with few measurements in some weather stations and then the meteorological values at all other locations are estimated and evaluated. While the interpolation procedure can be naturally formulated as such a reconstruction problem, we know of no previous application of these methods to the geospatial interpolation task. Indeed, the most common application of such algorithm is image reconstruction, which typically has small scale in spatial dimension. The large-scale geospatial interpolation task poses a new set of challenges for such methods, and existing approaches alone cannot perform well enough. Instead of applying Laplace priors to model coefficients' sparsity [26, 15, 3], we propose to use Student-t priors, and show that this improves the performance in the meteorological domain. Then, an efficient inference algorithm named Approximated Variational Inference (AVI) is developed based on Taylor series to deal with the intractability caused by the non-conjugate priors and the approximation algorithm is theoretically justified. Besides, we present a sampling based strategy as an alternative inference method to experimentally show the correctness of AVI. With respect to the task of geospatial interpolation, our model significantly outperforms the traditional methods: Thin Plate Spline (TPS) [23] and Kriging [17]. In summary, the primary contributions of this paper are as follows:

- **Provision of smarter interpolation service:** An in-depth study on the meteorological metrics is performed and our system can be potentially used to estimate the ambient weather conditions of power plants, transformers and transmission lines to support intelligent management of electrical grid.
- **Design of a novel geospatial interpolation model:** We incorporate Student-t prior into Bayesian compressed sensing to accurately model the distributions of sparse coefficients, and an efficient and effective learning algorithm is provided.
- **Comprehensive experiments to validate the effectiveness and efficiency:** We demonstrated that the proposed model outperformed the baselines, and the interpolated results are visualized to show climate patterns.

The remainder of this paper is organized as follows. In Section 2, we introduce the application deployment for the proposed approach, and the background knowledge. The Bayesian Compressed Sensing using student-T priors model (BCST) is presented in Section 3, including the introduction of the generative model and the inference algorithms. The effectiveness and efficiency of the model are illustrated with extensive experiments in Section 4. Section 5 presents our conclusions.

2. BACKGROUND & PROBLEM

2.1 Application Deployment

The intelligent management of electrical grid largely depends on the weather and climate conditions around the power plants, transformers and transmission lines. We focus on the application of smart grid asset management. For example, transformers are essential assets for utility companies, and it is impossible to construct a weather station for every transformer due to the large number of transformers. To estimate the electrical age of transformers (which

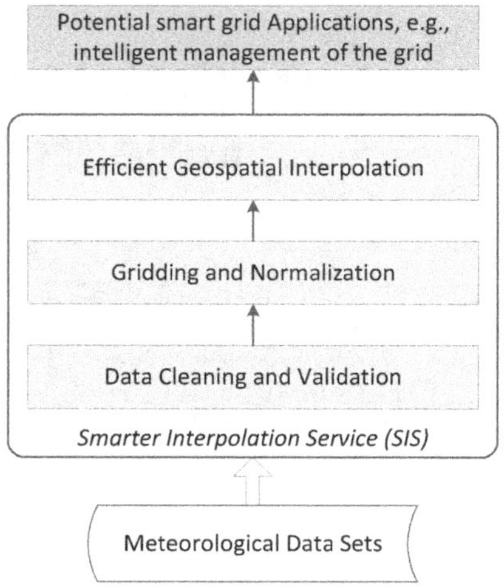

Figure 1: Overview of the deployed system: smarter interpolation service provides support for the intelligent management of power grid.

is different from calendar age) [2, 28], it is of critical importance to consider the weather conditions as input variables for modeling and computing. Acting as the smarter interpolation service, our system is capable of producing a map of meteorological measurements to potentially support the smart management of electricity grid. As shown in Figure 1, the system is consists of three key modules:

- *Data Cleaning and Validation:* This module is responsible to handle the input meteorological data. Clean the error data items, such as the data out of spatial range or containing wrong time stamp. Then we check the validity of the data, for example, the measurement of humidity (i.e., relative humidity) which is bigger than 100% or less than 0% is invalid.
- *Gridding and Normalization:* Gridding is to split the spatial region into cells, where each cell refers to the location of interest for interpolation. A large region can be divided in a recursive way and then each sub-region could be interpolated concurrently, while the edge effects caused by recursive division could be eliminated by overlapping adjacent sub-regions. Normalization is executed to provide a limited range values, which could potentially advance the process of learning spatial variations.
- *Efficient Geospatial Interpolation:* This is the core part of the system. A Bayesian compressed sensing based model is developed for fast and accurate spatial interpolation of meteorological measurements. The interpolation model is wrapped into a service provider to support smart grid. We can provide the service to detect the bottleneck of transmission lines using their ambient weather conditions. Other services can also be supplied, such as maximal workload estimation of power plants under current temperature, humidity, etc.

The preliminary evaluation results show that the deployed system can provide on-line interpolation service with very short latency. Additionally, by analysing the large amount of historical weather data, our system can discover the seasonal patterns and identify the extreme climatic conditions. An example application to smart grid is to help for wind turbine placement, since the performance and useful life of wind turbines is sensitive to wind direction/velocity, precipitation, humidity, etc. [25]. A visualization module is also developed to visualize the interpolation results. This can help to quickly recognize the places with extreme weathers, which limit the normal functionality of power grid.

2.2 Preliminaries

A spatial performance of interest, such as temperature, can be expressed as a 2-D function $g(i,j)$, where i,j denote the coordinate of a spatial location in the two-dimensional plane. We can discretize the spatial region into equal-sized grids with P rows and Q columns, and then the coordinates i and j are discrete numbers accordingly: $i \in \{1,2,\cdots,P\}, j \in \{1,2,\cdots,Q\}$.

Formally, the function $g(i,j)$ can be projected to the frequency domain by numerous 2-D transforms, such as Discrete Fourier Transform (DFT) [19], Discrete Cosine Transform (DCT) [11]. Note that DCT is used throughout the paper to illustrate the idea of our proposed model, which can be easily generalized to other transforms.

Mathematically, the DCT transform can be represented as [11],

$$G(u,v) = \sum_{i=1}^{P}\sum_{j=1}^{Q} \Gamma(u,v,i,j)g(i,j) \tag{1}$$

where $G(u,v)$ for $u = 1,2,\cdots,P$, $v = 1,2,\cdots,Q$ is the set of DCT coefficients, and

$$\begin{aligned} \Gamma(u,v,i,j) &= \alpha'_u \cdot \beta'_v \cdot \cos\frac{\pi(2i-1)(u-1)}{2P} \cdot \\ &\quad \cos\frac{\pi(2j-1)(v-1)}{2Q} \\ \alpha'_u &= \begin{cases} \sqrt{1/P} & ,u=1 \\ \sqrt{2/P} & ,1<u\le P \end{cases} \\ \beta'_v &= \begin{cases} \sqrt{1/Q} & ,v=1 \\ \sqrt{2/Q} & ,1<v\le Q \end{cases} \end{aligned} \tag{2}$$

While the Inverse Discrete Cosine Transform (IDCT) [11] can be applied to project the DCT coefficients ($G(u,v)$) to be the performance measurements in spatial domain,

$$g(i,j) = \sum_{u=1}^{P}\sum_{v=1}^{Q} \Gamma(u,v,i,j)G(u,v) \tag{3}$$

where $\Gamma(u,v,i,j)$ is defined in Eq. (2).

Compressed Sensing (CS) is an effective approach to recover original signal from few observations [6], which also has been validated to be powerful in spatial interpolation [31]:

$$\mathbf{y} = \mathbf{\Phi}\mathbf{z} + \mathbf{u} \tag{4}$$

where $\mathbf{y} \in \mathbb{R}^{M\times 1}$ denotes the few observations, $\mathbf{z} \in \mathbb{R}^{K\times 1}$ denotes the sparse coefficients, $\mathbf{\Phi} \in \mathbb{R}^{M\times K}$ is the matrix to transform from $\mathbf{z}$ to $\mathbf{y}$, and $\mathbf{u} \in \mathbb{R}^{M\times 1}$ represents the noise with zero mean and precision τ. Let $\mathbf{f} \in \mathbb{R}^{K\times 1}$ denote the unknown signal. Then we know that

$$\begin{aligned} \mathbf{f} &= [g(1,1), g(1,2), \cdots, g(P,Q)]^T \in \mathbb{R}^{K\times 1} \\ \mathbf{y} &= [g(i_1,j_1), g(i_2,j_2), \cdots, g(i_M,j_M)]^T \in \mathbb{R}^{M\times 1} \\ \mathbf{\Phi} &= \begin{bmatrix} \phi_{1,1,1} & \phi_{1,1,2} & \cdots & \phi_{1,P,Q} \\ \phi_{2,1,1} & \phi_{2,1,2} & \cdots & \phi_{2,P,Q} \\ \vdots & \vdots & \vdots & \vdots \\ \phi_{M,1,1} & \phi_{M,1,2} & \cdots & \phi_{M,P,Q} \end{bmatrix} \in \mathbb{R}^{M\times K} \\ \phi_{m,u,v} &= \Gamma(u,v,i_m,j_m) \\ \mathbf{z} &= [G(1,1), G(1,2), \cdots, G(P,Q)]^T \in \mathbb{R}^{K\times 1} \end{aligned} \tag{5}$$

Under the conditions that $\mathbf{z}$ is sparse, even when the number of measurements in $\mathbf{y}$ is far smaller than the number of coefficients in $\mathbf{z}$, i.e., $M \ll K$, the original signal $\mathbf{f}$ can be accurately reconstructed using Eq. (3), where $\mathbf{z}$ can be estimated by solving the optimization problem:

$$\mathbf{z} = \underset{\mathbf{z}}{\operatorname{argmin}} \ \{\|\mathbf{z}\|_1 + \zeta\|\mathbf{y} - \mathbf{\Phi}\mathbf{z}\|_2^2\} \tag{6}$$

The l_1-regularization formulation in Eq. (6) is equivalent to using a Laplace prior[1] on the coefficients $\mathbf{z}$ [3, 15],

$$P(\mathbf{z}) = \frac{b}{2}\exp(-\frac{b}{2}\|\mathbf{z}\|_1) \tag{7}$$

2.3 Limitations of Laplace Prior

With respect to the large-scale geospatial interpolation task, we suspect the effectiveness of Lapalce prior in Eq. (7) for modelling the distributions of the sparse coefficients. From the visualization of the coefficients' histograms in Figure 2, we observe that the Lapalce prior over-penalizes the true coefficients. Student-t is thus selected to compare with Laplace, since Student-t's heavy tail property enables it to better model large coefficients, while the peak near zero helps to keep $\mathbf{z}$ to be sparse. To explore the suitable regularizations on $\mathbf{z}$, Log-Likelihood Ratio (LLR) test is performed with two real-world meteorological datasets: KNMI dataset [16] and a dataset provided by the vendor of IBM (Vendor dataset). Let $\mathbf{z} = [z_1, z_2, \cdots, z_K]^T$, LLR is formulated as

$$LLR = \sum_{k=1}^{K} \ln\left[\frac{P(z_k \mid \mu,\sigma,\nu)}{P(z_k \mid \lambda, b)}\right] \tag{8}$$

where Student-t distribution's parameters (μ: location parameter, σ: scale parameter, ν: degree of freedoms) and Laplace distribution's parameters (λ: location parameter, b: scale parameter) are respectively estimated by maximizing corresponding likelihood functions. Table 1 shows the parameters of these two distributions and the LLR values of Student-t over Laplace. The LLR values are far greater than 0, indicating that Student-t is a better fit than Laplace. Figure 2 also illustrates similar conclusions, where we respectively use Laplace and Student-t distributions to fit the histograms of 1000 samples' Discrete Cosine Transform (DCT) coefficients. It figures out that Student-t can better fit the histograms for all of the meteorological measurements. This motivates us to extend compressed sensing by applying Student-t priors to model the sparsity of the coefficients.

[1]Using Maximum a Posterior (MAP) with Eq. (10) and (7), Eq. (6) can be achieved with $\zeta = \tau/b$.

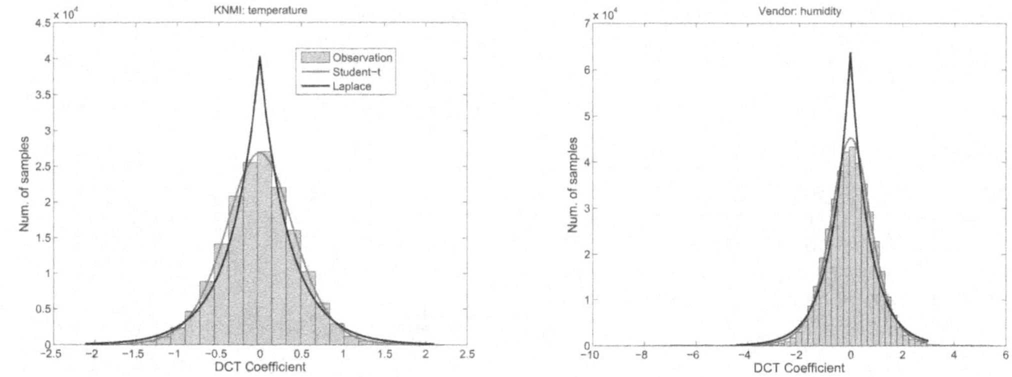

Figure 2: Histograms and distribution fitting of the normalized DCT coefficient for the two real-world meteorological datasets calculated from 100 samples for both dataset.

Table 1: Estimated parameters for Laplace distribution (λ: location parameter, b: scale parameter), and Student-t distribution (μ: location parameter, σ: scale parameter, ν: degree of freedoms) , and the log-likelihood ratio (LLR) values.

Meteorological Measurements	λ	b	μ	σ	ν	LLR
KNMI: temperature	-7.3×10^{-3}	0.3559	-8.6×10^{-3}	0.4200	11.5277	4499.0
Vendor: humidity	-5.6×10^{-3}	0.7392	-4.9×10^{-3}	0.7937	5.8467	10418

3. A NOVEL GEOSPATIAL INTERPOLATION METHOD

The geospatial interpolation of large-scale meteorological measurements has become a critical challenge since the prior of coefficients can not be captured with Laplace distribution. This section introduces a novel geospatial interpolation method by applying Student-t to model coefficient's distribution, and corresponding inference and learning algorithms are provided.

3.1 Model Definition

We begin our treatment of the generative model by expressing it as a directed graph, as illustrated in Figure 3. The measurement noise $\mathbf{u}$ is Gaussian with zero mean and unknown precision τ. With Eq. (4), we know that for each sample y_i, it depends on the latent variables $\mathbf{z}$ and τ

$$P(y_i \mid \mathbf{z}, \tau) = \mathcal{N}\left(y_i \mid \boldsymbol{\phi}_i \mathbf{z}, \tau^{-1}\right) \tag{9}$$

The M measurements are independent with each other given all the latent variables

$$P(\mathbf{y} \mid \mathbf{z}, \tau) = \prod_{i=1}^{M} \mathcal{N}\left(y_i \mid \boldsymbol{\phi}_i \mathbf{z}, \tau^{-1}\right) \tag{10}$$

The **prior on the precision** τ of noise follows a Gamma distribution governed by hyper-parameters α_0 (shape parameter) and β_0 (rate parameter)

$$\begin{aligned} P(\tau \mid \alpha_0, \beta_0) &= \text{Gamma}(\tau \mid \alpha_0, \beta_0) \\ &= \beta_0^{\alpha_0} \frac{1}{\Gamma(\alpha_0)} \tau^{\alpha_0 - 1} e^{-\beta_0 \tau} \end{aligned} \tag{11}$$

where $\Gamma(x) = \int_0^\infty t^{x-1} e^{-t} dt$.

The **prior on the coefficients** $\mathbf{z}$ is given by a Student-t distribution governed by hyper-parameters μ_0 (mean value), $\nu_0 > 0$ (degree of freedom) and $\sigma_0^2 > 0$ (scale parameter)

$$\begin{aligned} P(z_j \mid \mu_0, \nu_0, \sigma_0^2) &= t_{\nu_0}(z_j \mid \mu_0, \sigma_0^2) \\ &= c\left[1 + \frac{1}{\nu_0}\left(\frac{z_j - \mu_0}{\sigma_0}\right)^2\right]^{-\frac{\nu_0+1}{2}} \\ \text{where } c &= \frac{\Gamma(\nu_0/2 + 1/2)}{\Gamma(\nu_0/2)} \frac{1}{\sqrt{\nu_0 \pi} \sigma_0} \end{aligned} \tag{12}$$

The K sparse coefficients are independent with each other

$$P(\mathbf{z} \mid \mu_0, \nu_0, \sigma_0^2) = \prod_{j=1}^{K} P(z_j \mid \mu_0, \nu_0, \sigma_0^2) \tag{13}$$

Armed with the probabilistic formulation of BCST, the predictive density can be obtained by marginalizing over the latent variables (parameters become latent variables after applying prior dis-

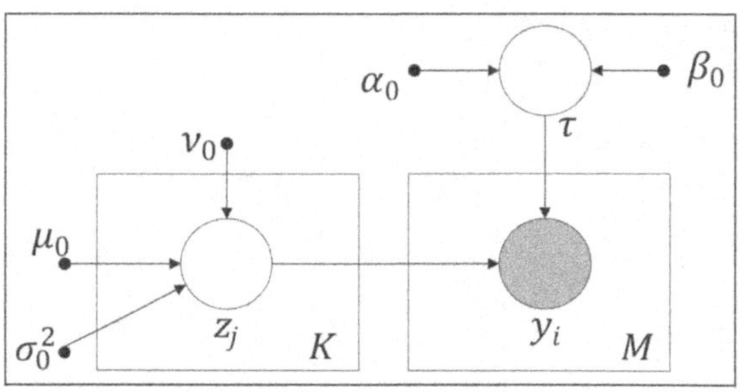

Figure 3: Representation of the generative model as a directed acyclic graph. The observed variable y_i is shown by the shaded node, while the latent variables z_j and τ are shown by circles. The right box represents the M independent measurements, while the left box represents the K independent DCT coefficients. $\alpha_0, \beta_0, \mu_0, \sigma_0$, and ν_0 are hyper-parameters.

tributions on them), so that

$$
\begin{aligned}
P(\hat{y}_i \mid \mathbf{y}) &= \int P(\hat{y}_i \mid \boldsymbol{\theta}) P(\boldsymbol{\theta} \mid \mathbf{y}) d\boldsymbol{\theta} \\
&= \int \mathcal{N}(\hat{y}_i \mid \boldsymbol{\phi}_i \mathbf{z}, \tau^{-1}) P(\boldsymbol{\theta} \mid \mathbf{y}) d\boldsymbol{\theta}
\end{aligned} \tag{14}
$$

where $\boldsymbol{\theta} = \{\mathbf{z}, \tau\}$ denotes the latent variables. To implement this framework, we must address the formulation of a tractable procedure for marginalization over the posterior distribution. Since the exact computation will inevitably cause high computational cost, approximation is required.

3.2 Approximated Variational Inference

Starting from Eq. (10), the evidence (marginal likelihood) of BCST is obtained by averaging the likelihood under priors for the latent variables (parameters which have their own hyper-parameters)

$$
P(\mathbf{y}) = \int P(\boldsymbol{\theta}) P(\mathbf{y} \mid \boldsymbol{\theta}) d\boldsymbol{\theta} \tag{15}
$$

Since the exact inference is intractable, we need to resort to some form of approximation. Let q be any functional form of $\boldsymbol{\theta}$ satisfying $\int q(\boldsymbol{\theta}) d\boldsymbol{\theta} = 1$ and $q(\boldsymbol{\theta}) > 0$. By Jensen's inequality, we have

$$
\begin{aligned}
\ln P(\mathbf{y}) &= \ln \int P(\mathbf{y}, \boldsymbol{\theta}) d\boldsymbol{\theta} \\
&\geq \int q(\boldsymbol{\theta}) \ln \frac{P(\mathbf{y}, \boldsymbol{\theta})}{q(\boldsymbol{\theta})} d\boldsymbol{\theta} \equiv \mathcal{F}(q)
\end{aligned} \tag{16}
$$

where $\mathcal{F}(q)$ forms a lower bound of $\ln P(\mathbf{y})$. The significance of this approximation is that the lower bound might be tractable by selecting suitable $q(\boldsymbol{\theta})$ although the original marginal log likelihood is not. Note that maximizing $\mathcal{F}(q)$ is equivalent to minimizing the KL-divergence between $q(\boldsymbol{\theta})$ and $P(\boldsymbol{\theta} \mid \mathbf{y})$ [4].

Without the loss of generality, let $q_j = q(z_j)$ for $j = 1, 2, \cdots, K$ and let $q_{K+1} = q(\tau)$. Similar to [4], we consider to restrict the family of distributions $q(\boldsymbol{\theta})$ by factorizing the functional form

$$
q(\boldsymbol{\theta}) = \prod_{j=1}^{K+1} q_j \tag{17}
$$

The form to maximize $\mathcal{F}(q)$ with respect to q_k is given by

$$
\begin{aligned}
\mathcal{F}(q) &= \int \prod_j q_j \{\ln P(\mathbf{y}, \boldsymbol{\theta}) - \ln q(\boldsymbol{\theta})\} d\boldsymbol{\theta} \\
&= -\mathrm{KL}\left(q_k \| \mathbb{E}_{j \neq k}[\ln P(\mathbf{y}, \boldsymbol{\theta})]\right) + \text{const}
\end{aligned} \tag{18}
$$

where $\mathbb{E}_{j \neq k}[P(\mathbf{y}, \boldsymbol{\theta})]$ is the expectation of $P(\mathbf{y}, \boldsymbol{\theta})$ with respect to the q distributions over all variables θ_j for $j \neq k$. Then the optimal q_k is

$$
q_k^\star = \frac{\exp(\mathbb{E}_{j \neq k}[\ln P(\mathbf{y}, \boldsymbol{\theta})])}{\int \exp(\mathbb{E}_{j \neq k}[\ln P(\mathbf{y}, \boldsymbol{\theta})]) d\theta_k} \tag{19}
$$

We can easily observe that $q_k^\star$ will have the same functional forms with its priors for conjugate models. However, Student-t priors are not conjugate, which leads to an analytical intractable model and infeasible for learning. Note that the Laplace priors on $\mathbf{z}$ (see Eq. (7)) are also not conjugate, two and three stage hierarchical priors are respectively considered for approximating Laplace in [15] and [3]. Instead, we consider a much faster and more effective way for the approximation of Student-t:

$$
\begin{aligned}
\ln q^\star(z_j) = &-\frac{\nu_0 + 1}{2} \ln [1 + \frac{1}{\nu_0} (\frac{z_j - \mu_0}{\sigma_0})^2] - \frac{\mathbb{E}_\tau[\tau]}{2} \times \\
&\sum_{i=1}^{M} [(\phi_{ij} z_j)^2 + 2 \sum_{k \neq j} \phi_{ik} z_k \phi_{ij} z_j - 2 y_i \phi_{ij} z_j] + \text{const}
\end{aligned} \tag{20}
$$

To deal with the intractability, under the condition that $\frac{1}{\nu_0} \left(\frac{z_j - \mu_0}{\sigma_0} \right)^2 =$

Algorithm 1 Geospatial Interpolation with BCST-AVI

Input: M geospatial locations $\{(i_1, j_1), \cdots, (i_M, j_M)\}$, and the observations $\mathbf{y} \in \mathbb{R}^{M \times 1}$ at these locations.

Output: The interpolated measurements $\mathbf{f} \in \mathbb{R}^{K \times 1}$ $(K \gg M)$.

Construct the matrix $\boldsymbol{\Phi}$ based on Eq. (5).
Randomly initialize vector $\mathbf{z} \in \mathbb{R}^{K \times 1}$
repeat
  Update μ_N, σ_N, ν_N using Eq. (22).
  Update α_N, β_N using Eq. (25).
  Evaluate the lower bound of model evidence, i.e., $\mathcal{F}(q)$, using Eq. (16).
until Convergence
Estimate the meteorological measurements at the other $(K - M)$ locations based on Eq. (27).

$\epsilon_1 \to 0$, based on Taylor series expansion, we have

$$
\ln(1 + \epsilon_1) = \frac{1}{\nu_0} (\frac{z_j - \mu_0}{\sigma_0})^2 + O(\epsilon_1^2) \approx \frac{1}{\nu_0} (\frac{z_j - \mu_0}{\sigma_0})^2
$$

Then Eq. (20) is simplified to be

$$
\ln q^\star(z_j) = -\frac{\nu_N + 1}{2} \left[\frac{1}{\nu_N} \left(\frac{z_j - \mu_N}{\sigma_N} \right)^2 \right] \tag{21}
$$

where

$$
\begin{aligned}
\mu_N &= \frac{\mu_0(\nu_0 + 1) + \varphi_2 \nu_0 \sigma_0^2}{\nu_N + 1}, \\
\sigma_N^2 &= \frac{\nu_0 \sigma_0^2}{\nu_N}, \qquad \nu_N = \varphi_1 \nu_0 \sigma_0^2 + \nu_0
\end{aligned} \tag{22}
$$

and the parameters in Eq. (22) are given:

$$
\begin{aligned}
\varphi_1 &= M \overline{\phi_{\bar{i}j}^2} \mathbb{E}_\tau[\tau], \\
\varphi_2 &= -\mathbb{E}_\tau[\tau] M \overline{(K-1) \overline{\phi_{i\bar{k}} z_{\bar{k}}} \phi_{ij}} + \mathbb{E}_\tau[\tau] M \overline{y_{\bar{i}} \phi_{\bar{i}j}}
\end{aligned}
$$

$$
\overline{\phi_{\bar{i}j}^2} = \frac{1}{M} \sum_{i=1}^{M} \phi_{ij}^2, \qquad \overline{\phi_{\bar{i}j}} = \frac{1}{M} \sum_{i=1}^{M} \phi_{ij},
$$

$$
\overline{\phi_{i\bar{k}} z_{\bar{k}}} = \frac{1}{K-1} \sum_{k \neq j} \phi_{ik} z_k = \frac{1}{K-1} (\boldsymbol{\phi}_i \mathbf{z} - \phi_{ij} z_j),
$$

$$
\overline{(K-1) \overline{\phi_{\bar{i}\bar{k}} z_{\bar{k}}} \phi_{\bar{i}j}} = \frac{1}{M} \sum_{i=1}^{M} (K-1) \overline{\phi_{i\bar{k}} z_{\bar{k}}} \phi_{ij},
$$

$$
\overline{y_{\bar{i}} \phi_{\bar{i}j}} = \frac{1}{M} \sum_{i=1}^{M} y_i \phi_{ij}
$$

Then with $\frac{1}{\nu_N} \left(\frac{z_j - \mu_N}{\sigma_N} \right)^2 = \epsilon_2 \to 0$, use Taylor series again

$$
\frac{1}{\nu_N} (\frac{z_j - \mu_N}{\sigma_N})^2 \approx \epsilon_2 + O(\epsilon_2^2) = \ln(1 + \epsilon_2)
$$

Eq. (21) thus can be converted to

$$
\begin{aligned}
&\ln q^\star(z_j) \\
&= -\frac{\nu_N + 1}{2} \ln \left[1 + \frac{1}{\nu_N} \left(\frac{z_j - \mu_N}{\sigma_N} \right)^2 \right] + \text{const}
\end{aligned} \tag{23}
$$

Following Eq. (19), the optimal $q(\tau)$ can be easily achieved since it's in conjugate form

$$
\ln q^\star(\tau) = \alpha_N \ln \tau - \beta_N \tau + \text{const} \tag{24}
$$

where

$$\alpha_N = \alpha_0 + \frac{M}{2}, \qquad \beta_N = \beta_0 + \frac{1}{2}\sum_{i=1}^{M}\mathbb{E}_{\mathbf{z}}\left[(y_i - \boldsymbol{\phi}_i\mathbf{z})^2\right] \quad (25)$$

The expected values in the above formulas are given by

$$\begin{aligned}
\mathbb{E}_\tau[\tau] &= \frac{\alpha_N}{\beta_N} \quad (\alpha_N > 0, \beta_N > 0) \\
\mathbb{E}_{z_j}[z_j] &= \mu_N \quad (\nu_N > 1) \\
\mathbb{E}_{z_j}[z_j^2] &= \frac{\nu_N \sigma_N^2}{\nu_N - 2} + \mu_N^2 \quad (\nu_N > 2)
\end{aligned} \quad (26)$$

Then the optimal $q_k^\star$ can be achieved by iteratively updating the variational parameters μ_N, σ_N, ν_N (see Eq. (22)) and α_N, β_N (see Eq. (25)) until convergence. The theoretical analysis of AVI is shown in Section A.1.

Evaluation of Predictive Density: Based on Jensen's inequality, we consider to evaluate the lower bound of the predictive density

$$\begin{aligned}
&\ln P(\hat{y}_i \mid \mathbf{y}) \approx \ln \int \mathcal{N}(\hat{y}_i \mid \boldsymbol{\phi}_i\mathbf{z}, \tau^{-1}) q(\boldsymbol{\theta}) d\boldsymbol{\theta} \\
&\geq \int q(\boldsymbol{\theta}) \ln \mathcal{N}(\hat{y}_i \mid \boldsymbol{\phi}_i\mathbf{z}, \tau^{-1}) d\boldsymbol{\theta} \\
&= \mathbb{E}_\tau[\ln \tau] - \frac{\mathbb{E}_\tau[\tau]}{2}\mathbb{E}_{\mathbf{z}}[(\hat{y}_i - \boldsymbol{\phi}_i\mathbf{z})^2] + \text{const}
\end{aligned} \quad (27)$$

where $\mathbb{E}_\tau[\ln \tau]$ is the negative entropy of $q^\star(\tau)$, and $\mathbb{E}_\tau[\tau]$ is defined in Eq. (26). The approximation in Line 1 of Eq. (27) is due to using variational distributions to replace the exact posterior distribution. The inequality in Line 2 is a simple Jensen bound.

The procedure to use BCST-AVI (Bayesian Compressed Sensing using the Approximated Variational Inference) for geospatial interpolation is summarized in Algorithm 1.

3.3 Sampling based Inference

Alternatively, we use sampling method to approximate the posterior distributions $P(\boldsymbol{\theta} \mid \mathbf{y})$ as a benchmark for testing the correctness of AVI. Gibbs sampling on $P(\boldsymbol{\theta} \mid \mathbf{y})$ can be performed by flipping the latent variables:

$$\begin{aligned}
&P(\tau \mid \mathbf{y}, \mathbf{z}) \propto \text{Gamma}(\tau \mid \alpha_s, \beta_s) \\
&P(z_j \mid \mathbf{y}, \mathbf{z} \setminus z_j, \tau) \propto \prod_{i=1}^{M} \mathcal{N}(y_i \mid \phi_i\mathbf{z}, \tau^{-1}) t_{\nu_0}(z_j \mid \mu_0, \sigma_0^2)
\end{aligned} \quad (28)$$

where $\alpha_s = \alpha_0 + \frac{M}{2}, \beta_s = \beta_0 + \frac{1}{2}\sum_{i=1}^{M}(y_i - \phi_i\mathbf{z})^2$. Since $P(z_j \mid \mathbf{y}, \mathbf{z} \setminus z_j, \tau)$ might be non log-concave, we apply Adaptive Rejection Metropolis Sampling (ARMS) for the generation of z_j [10]. Then the predictive density is evaluated by

$$P(\hat{y}_i \mid \mathbf{y}) \simeq \frac{1}{T-b}\sum_{t=s+1}^{T} \mathcal{N}(\hat{y}_i \mid \boldsymbol{\phi}_i\mathbf{z}^{(t)}, (\tau^{(t)})^{-1}) \quad (29)$$

where T is the number of total generated samples, and b is the number of abandoned starting samples, targeting for reducing the effects of unreasonable initializations.

4. EMPIRICAL EVALUATIONS

In this section, we perform the geospatial interpolation task to demonstrate the advantages of the proposed model compared to the baselines.

Table 2: Data Sets

Dataset	Metrics	Sampling Rate
KNMI	Temperature	Daily Reporting
Vendor	Temperature, Humidity, Barometric Pressure	5 Minutes

4.1 Experimental Setup

We use 2 general meteorological data sets which are summarized in Table 2. KNMI is available online [16], which contains about 12 years (2001/05 – 2013/05) climate data for 33 weather stations spreading throughout Netherlands. We use 11×17 grid to split Netherlands into equal-sized cells (edge length of one cell is about 25KM and the 33 stations can be fully separated), and consider one daily snapshot as a sample. The other dataset is provided by the vendor of IBM (Vendor dataset), reporting the climate records of 14,290 weather stations in North United States for almost 3 years (2009/04 – 2012/03). Since the entire North United States is too large for one sample, we consider a 20×20 equal-sized grid as a sample for this dataset, where edge length of each cell is about 10KM.

We compare the proposed models BCST-AVI (Bayesian Compressed Sensing using student-T priors with Approximated Variational Inference), BCST-GS (Bayesian Compressed Sensing using student-T priors with Sampling based inference) with BCSL (Bayesian Compressed Sensing using Laplace prior), CS (Compressed Sensing), TPS (Thin Plate Spline), and UK (Universal Kriging). The BCSL is implemented based on the package VB-BCS, where the Laplace prior is modelled in a hierarchical way [15]. The CS is extended to perform geospatial interpolation and implemented based on Virtual Probe (VP) solver [31]. TPS is implemented with R package "fields" [9], while UK is implemented with R package "DiceKriging" [22]. All tests run on an Intel i7-2760QM processor using up to eight cores (2.40 GHz).

Average Normalized Error (ANE) is used to measure the interpolation performance, i.e.,

$$\text{ANE} = \sqrt{\frac{\sum_i \sum_j \left[g(i,j) - \hat{g}(i,j)\right]^2}{\sum_i \sum_j g(i,j)^2}} \quad (30)$$

where $g(i,j)$ is the observed values at the evaluation weather stations, and $\hat{g}(i,j)$ is the estimated value.

4.2 Quantitative Evaluation of the Geospatial Interpolation Methods

Geospatial Interpolation Results on KNMI: With respect to KNMI, 33 weather stations almost uniformly locate in a spatial region split with a 17×11 equal-sized grid. To evaluate the performance of models with different M, we vary the number of measurements from 6 to 16 (about from 20% to 50% of 33 weather stations), and the residual sites are used for computing the ANE values. For a certain M, we repeat for 100 runs. Table 3 shows the mean±std (standard derivation) of ANE values for all models.

Geospatial Interpolation Results on Vendor Dataset: In terms of Vendor dataset, there are about 170 weather stations in a grid of size 20×20 equal-sized cells. We vary the number of measurements from 20 to 120 (about from 10% to 70% of 170 weather stations) to show how performance of models changes with M, while the remaining stations are used for evaluations. Similarly, 100 runs are repeated for any certain M. As shown in Table 4, three rows of mean±std of ANE values are reported for any M: the first row is for metric Temperature, the second is for Humidity, while the last row is for Barometric Pressure.

As shown in Tables 3 and 4, regardless of the datasets and metrics, the proposed two models (BCST-AVI and BCST-GS) significantly outperform TPS and UK, and are competitive with BCSL and CS. Specifically, under most cases, both BCST-AVI and BCST-GS perform better than BCSL and CS, indicating that the Student-t priors can more accurately model the sparsity of climate data's coefficients. We also observe that the performance of BCST-AVI, BCST-GS, BCSL and CS slightly increases with the growth of M while that of TPS and UK significantly increase, and the best performance of TPS and UK is chasing the worst of other four methods for many cases; thus conclude that the compressed sensing based methods can achieve good performance with much fewer measurements than TPS and UK. The similar performance of BCST-AVI and BCST-GS validates that the Approximated Variational Inference (AVI) can achieve as good approximation as Gibbs sampling based inference.

4.3 Efficiency Evaluation

We study the behaviour of BCST-AVI, BCST-GS, CS, TPS and UK in terms of running time. Considering the worst case for time consumption, M is set to be 16 for KNMI, and 120 for Vendor dataset. Since the varying metrics (i.e., temperature, humidity and barometric pressure) lead to very small change in the time consumption, we do not distinct them here. 10 runs are repeated to report the mean$\pm$std of the time consumption in millisecond (ms). As shown in Table 5, BCST-AVI consumes much less time than all other methods for both datasets, CS, TPS and UK can achieve acceptable performance and perform better than BCSL. As expected, BCST-GS costs quite more time than the others. Generally, increasing M (from KNMI's 16 to Vendor's 120) will inevitably cause more time consumption.

Table 5: Time consumption (mean$\pm$std, and the unit of time is ms) comparison between models: the first column is for KNMI, while the second is for Vendor dataset. The bold entries denote the best average performance.

Model \ Dataset	KNMI	Vendor
BCST-AVI	**14.162**$\pm$1.7789	**31.169**$\pm$2.0685
BCST-GS	14205$\pm$269.91	63375$\pm$1792.7
BCSL	116.20$\pm$3.1875	489.65$\pm$12.750
CS	69.073$\pm$30.499	276.31$\pm$30.312
TPS	74.000$\pm$6.6500	106.00$\pm$8.4327
UK	50.000$\pm$5.9470	160.00$\pm$10.824

4.4 Visualization of Geospatial Interpolation

Our system provides a function to visualize the geospatial interpolation results with a high resolution in a large spatial scale: using Vendor data, we are capable of estimating the meteorological measurements in a 10KM $\times$ 10KM resolution throughout USA. This allows decision makers to quickly identify the bottlenecks which limit the functionality of power grid. The detailed visualization process is implemented in a recursive way. Suppose the task is to interpolate and visualize the climate variables for USA. Since it's neither efficient nor accurate to perform interpolation with respect to the entire region, the first step we employed is to recursively grid the region until the edge-length of each cell is approximately 10KM. Then we select a size of $P \times Q$ adjacent cells as a sub-region and the size of sub-regions can vary to adapt to real scenarios. The sub-regions may also overlap with each other to reduce the edge effects. Moreover, for each sub-region, BSC-AVI is applied to perform interpolation, and this process can be concurrently executed. Finally, sub-regions' interpolation results are combined to produce the result for the whole region. Using the above stated procedure, the interpolated results would cover the sea or large water area, where the values are estimated based on the observations of sensors on land. Due to the inherent different properties of land and sea in determining climate conditions, this would inevitably lead to the inaccurate estimations for the sea area. We thus can ignore the results on the sea area in the following figures[2]. We respectively

Figure 4: Example geospatial interpolation results: temperature map in USA.

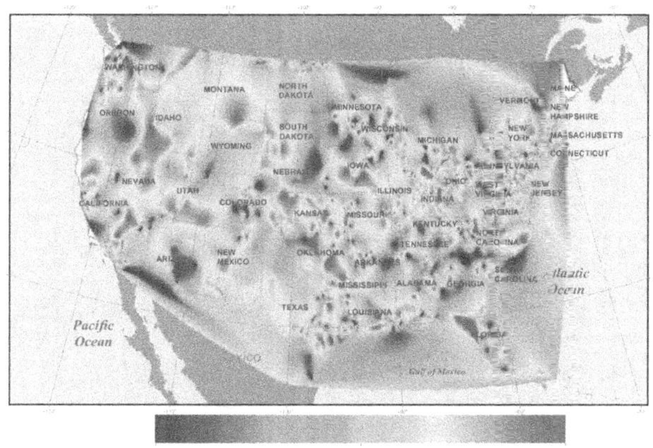

Figure 5: Example geospatial interpolation results: humidity map in USA.

show example interpolation results of temperature (in Kelvin), humidity (in %, i.e., relative humidity), barometric pressure (in 1/100 inch of mercury) in Figure 4, 5, and 6. The observations collected from nation-wide weather stations are used for interpolations. It is easy to identify the hot areas in USA (i.e., the areas with high temperature) from Figure 4. As illustrated in 5, the dry areas (i.e.,

[2] Since we don't have land boundary data, it's impossible to remove the estimations for sea area in the visualization process.

Table 3: Geospatial interpolation performance on KNMI dataset, reporting the ANE (mean±std) of Temperature (Kelvin) with varying M (the number of measurements). The bold entries denote the best average performance values.

Model / M	BCST-AVI	BCST-GS	BCSL	CS	TPS	UK
6	(**4.4655**±0.2090)%	(4.5271±0.2043)%	(6.0500±0.2360)%	(6.5341±0.2765)%	(24.075±1.0912)%	(21.531±1.2026)%
8	(4.1963±0.2071)%	(**4.0133**±0.2058)%	(5.5939±0.2126)%	(6.0756±0.2391)%	(15.071±1.1238)%	(14.295±1.2815)%
10	(3.9797±0.2077)%	(**3.9246**±0.2001)%	(5.0283±0.2247)%	(5.7360±0.2337)%	(11.676±1.0394)%	(10.578±1.2292)%
12	(**3.8415**±0.2070)%	(3.8518±0.2085)%	(4.9300±0.2586)%	(5.5593±0.2274)%	(10.209±0.9548)%	(8.0038±0.9005)%
14	(3.6969±0.2041)%	(**3.6728**±0.2097)%	(4.5629±0.2256)%	(5.3472±0.2199)%	(8.3562±0.4875)%	(6.4566±0.3853)%
16	(3.4824±0.2059)%	(**3.4815**±0.2056)%	(4.4169±0.2698)%	(5.1859±0.4248)%	(6.9671±0.4248)%	(5.2924±0.4530)%

Table 4: Geospatial interpolation performance on Vendor dataset, reporting the ANE (mean±std) of corresponding metrics with varying M (the number of measurements): the first row is for Temperature (Kelvin), the second is for Humidity (%), and the third is for Barometric Pressure (1/100 inch of mercury). The bold entries denote the best average performance values.

Model / M	BCST-AVI	BCST-GS	BCSL	CS	TPS	UK
20	(2.5943±0.2285)% (28.172±2.7023)% (**0.6073**±0.0274)%	(**2.4585**±0.2056)% (**27.414**±1.6046)% (0.6603±0.0244)%	(2.9598±0.2749)% (28.112±2.6669)% (0.7334±0.0331)%	(3.0167±0.3075)% (28.685±2.5680)% (0.7759±0.0363)%	(19.022±1.5085)% (37.721±3.2162)% (4.5072±0.2701)%	(21.263±1.9554)% (34.141±2.3860)% (5.2732±0.1194)%
40	(2.2124±0.2291)% (27.518±2.3710)% (**0.6105**±0.0282)%	(**2.1119**±0.2051)% (**26.513**±1.5725)% (0.6205±0.0201)%	(2.7849±0.3012)% (28.047±2.3536)% (0.7095±0.0318)%	(2.9782±0.2752)% (28.404±2.2523)% (0.7498±0.0326)%	(12.067±1.0984)% (32.695±2.6955)% (2.7117±0.1739)%	(13.708±1.4975)% (30.075±2.2480)% (3.4868±0.0989)%
60	(2.0481±0.2043)% (26.649±2.3825)% (0.6062±0.0199)%	(**2.0115**±0.2061)% (**26.092**±1.5882)% (**0.5866**±0.0127)%	(2.4077±0.2091)% (27.542±2.7628)% (0.6785±0.0294)%	(2.5880±0.2055)% (28.050±2.1569)% (0.7009±0.0302)%	(9.2703±1.0487)% (31.086±2.5170)% (1.9887±0.1311)%	(10.455±1.0390)% (29.257±2.2803)% (2.7652±0.0841)%
80	(**1.5401**±0.1692)% (**25.582**±1.6172)% (0.6031±0.0132)%	(1.6952±0.1347)% (25.867±1.5653)% (**0.5933**±0.0129)%	(2.1335±0.1047)% (26.796±1.7270)% (0.6284±0.0275)%	(2.2983±0.1307)% (27.068±1.9557)% (0.6729±0.0283)%	(7.5462±1.0250)% (30.229±2.4530)% (1.5779±0.1094)%	(8.3303±1.0369)% (28.942±2.2088)% (2.2954±0.0718)%
100	(1.5341±0.1056)% (25.853±1.4301)% (0.5998±0.0135)%	(**1.4843**±0.1712)% (**25.828**±1.4718)% (**0.5630**±0.0105)%	(1.8688±0.1323)% (26.541±1.3728)% (0.6199±0.0294)%	(2.0106±0.1344)% (26.891±1.9638)% (0.6706±0.0274)%	(6.4482±0.9551)% (29.776±2.4438)% (1.2842±0.0910)%	(6.6483±0.9954)% (28.800±2.2599)% (1.9843±0.0594)%
120	(1.5437±0.1257)% (**25.469**±1.7490)% (0.5944±0.0119)%	(**1.4672**±0.1041)% (25.618±1.4718)% (**0.5604**±0.0103)%	(1.7912±0.1507)% (26.339±1.8365)% (0.6132±0.0265)%	(2.0146±0.1134)% (26.933±1.9116)% (0.6573±0.0254)%	(5.4632±0.8838)% (29.534±2.4075)% (1.0383±0.0767)%	(5.4822±0.7508)% (28.661±2.1423)% (1.6784±0.0490)%

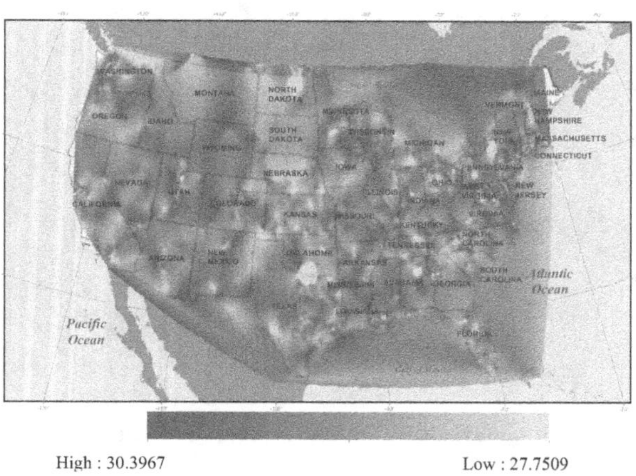

Figure 6: Example geospatial interpolation results: barometric pressure map in USA.

the areas with low humidity) have covered most of the deserts. It is expected that the barometric pressure changes very slowly with spatial locations as shown in Figure 6. The example interpolation results in New York City for temperature, humidity and barometric

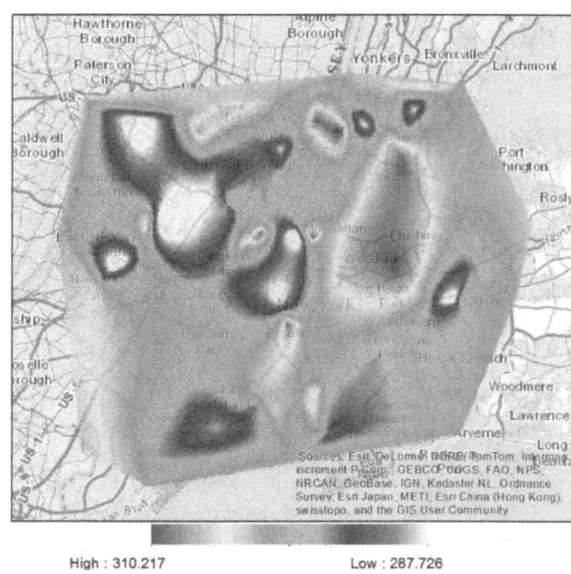

Figure 7: Example geospatial interpolation results: temperature map in New York City.

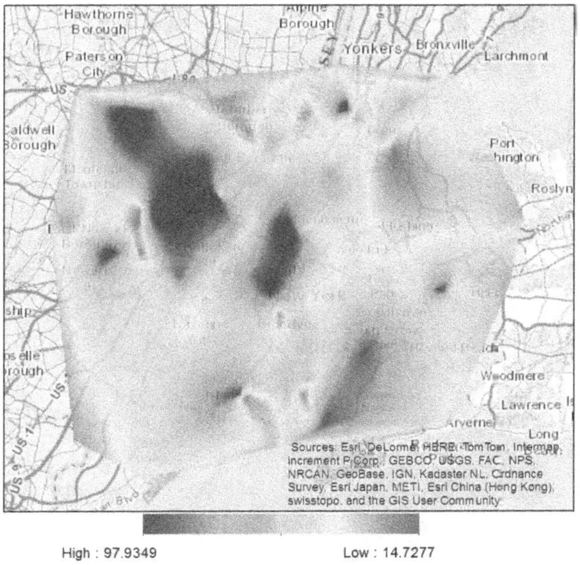

Figure 8: Example geospatial interpolation results: humidity map in New York City.

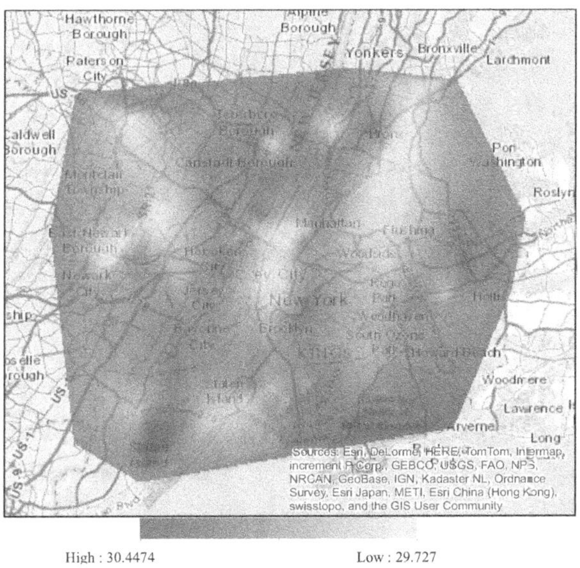

Figure 9: Example geospatial interpolation results: barometric pressure map in New York City.

pressure are respectively shown in Figure 7, 8 and 9. The city level maps of meteorological measurements convey more detailed information, which can be potentially used for city planning and guiding users to find places with pleasant weathers.

5. CONCLUSIONS

In this paper, we propose a new method to perform geospatial interpolation for large-scale meteorological measurements. Specifically, Student-t prior is incorporated into a Bayesian compressed sensing model to capture the distributions of coefficients, and the corresponding fast inference algorithm is provided. Using two real world datasets, we show that the proposed models are capable of effectively and efficiently estimating the values at unknown places with only a few measurements, while significantly outperformed the state-of-the-art methods. At the same time, our deployed system is of critical importance in supporting the intelligent management of electrical grid by providing the ambient climate conditions of power plants, transformers and transmission lines in high spatiotemporal resolutions.

References

[1] O. AntonicÂt', J. KrizËĞan, A. Marki, and D. Bukovec. Spatio-temporal interpolation of climatic variables over large region of complex terrain using neural networks. *Ecological Modelling*, 138:255 – 263, 2001.

[2] M. Arshad, S. M. Islam, and A. Khaliq. Power transformer aging and life extension. In *IEEE Conference on Probabilistic Methods Applied to Power Systems*, pages 498–501, 2004.

[3] S. Babacan, R. Molina, and A. Katsaggelos. Bayesian compressive sensing using laplace priors. *IEEE Transactions on Image Processing*, 19(1):53–63, 2010.

[4] A. Corduneanu and C. M. Bishop. Variational bayesian model selection for mixture distributions. In *Artificial Intelligence and Statistics*, pages 27–34, 2001.

[5] U. S. Department of Energy. Smart grid, 2012.

[6] D. L. Donoho. Compressed sensing. *IEEE Transactions on Information Theory*, 52(4):1289–1306, 2006.

[7] M. F. Duarte, M. A. Davenport, D. Takhar, J. N. Laska, T. Sun, K. F. Kelly, and R. G. Baraniuk. Single pixel imaging via compressive sampling. *IEEE Signal Processing Magazine*, 25:83–91, 2008.

[8] N. Farouk, L. Sheng, and Q. Hayat. Effect of ambient temperature on the performance of gas turbines power plant. *International Journal of Computer Science Issues (IJCSI)*, 10(1), 2013.

[9] R. Furrer, D. Nychka, and S. Sain. fields, 2013.

[10] W. R. Gilks, N. G. Best, and K. K. C. Tan. Adaptive rejection metropolis sampling within gibbs sampling. *Journal of the Royal Statistical Society*, 44(4):455–472, 1995.

[11] R. C. Gonzalez and R. E. Woods. *Digital Image Processing (2nd ed.)*. Prentice-Hall, Inc., Upper Saddle River, NJ, USA, 2002.

[12] L. Hernández, C. Baladrón, J. M. Aguiar, L. Calavia, B. Carro, A. Sánchez-Esguevillas, D. J. Cook, D. Chinarro, and J. Gómez. A study of the relationship between weather variables and electric power demand inside a smart grid /smart world framework. *Sensors*, 12(9):11571–11591, 2012.

[13] J. R. Hipp, D. J. Bauer, P. Curran, and K. A. Bollen. Crimes of opportunity or crimes of emotion? testing two explanations of seasonal change in crime. *Social Forces*, 82:1333–1372, 2004.

[14] S. J. Jeffrey, J. O. Carter, K. B. Moodie, and A. R. Beswick. Using spatial interpolation to construct a comprehensive archive of australian climate data. *Environmental Modelling & Software*, 16(4):309–330, 2001.

[15] S. Ji, Y. Xue, and L. Carin. Bayesian compressive sensing. *IEEE Transactions on Signal Processing*, 56(6):2346–2356, 2008.

[16] KNMI. www.knmi.nlclimatologydaily_data.

[17] M. Knotters, D. Brus, and J. O. Voshaar. A comparison of kriging, co-kriging and kriging combined with regression for spatial interpolation of horizon depth with censored observations. *Geoderma*, 67(3âĂŞ4):227–246, 1995.

[18] M. Lustig, D. Donoho, and J. Pauly. Sparse MRI: The application of compressed sensing for rapid MR imaging. *Society of Magnetic Resonance in Medicine*, 58(6):1182–1195, 2007.

[19] A. V. Oppenheim, A. S. Willsky, and S. H. Nawab. *Signals and systems (2nd ed.)*. Prentice-Hall, Inc., Upper Saddle River, NJ, USA, 1996.

[20] R. B. Primacka, H. Higuchib, and A. J. Miller-Rushing. The impact of climate change on cherry trees and other species in japan. *Biological Conservation*, 142:1943–1949, 2009.

[21] P. F. D. Roosevelt. National weather service. *Disasters, Accidents, and Crises in American History: A Reference Guide to the Nation's Most Catastrophic Events*, page 1969, 2008.

[22] O. Roustant, D. Ginsbourger, and Y. Deville. Dicekriging, 2013.

[23] A. Tait, R. Henderson, R. Turner, and X. Zheng. Thin plate smoothing spline interpolation of daily rainfall for new zealand using a climatological rainfall surface. *International Journal of Climatology*, 26(14):2097–2115, 2006.

[24] G. Tan, R. Shibasaki, and K. S. Rajan. The study of global land suitability evaluation: A case of potential productivity estimation for wheat. *International Archives of Photogrammetry and Remote Sensing*, 33:1045–1050, 2000.

[25] P. J. Tavner, D. M. Greenwood, M. W. G. Whittle, R. Gindele, S. Faulstich, and B. Hahn. Study of weather and location effects on wind turbine failure rates. *Wind Energy*, 16(2):175–187, 2013.

[26] M. E. Tipping. Sparse bayesian learning and the relevance vector machine. *Journal of Machine Learning Research*, 1:211–244, 2001.

[27] L. A. Treinish, A. P. Praino, and Z. D. Christidis. Implementation of mesoscale numerical weather prediction for weather-sensitive business operations. In *19th International Conference on IIPS*, 2003.

[28] R. Walling and G. B. Shattuck. Distribution transformer thermal behavior and aging in local-delivery distribution systems. In *Proceedings of the 19th Conference on Electricity Distribution, Vienna*, 2007.

[29] B. Wang and J. Xiong. Appendix: Novel geospatial interpolation analytics for general meteorological measurements. *http://filebox.vt.edu/users/claren89/Publications/2014/kdd2014_more.pdf*, 2014.

[30] Y. Yan, Y. Qian, H. Sharif, and D. Tipper. A survey on smart grid communication infrastructures: Motivations, requirements and challenges. *Communications Surveys & Tutorials, IEEE*, 15(1):5–20, 2013.

[31] W. Zhang, X. Li, and R. Rutenbar. Virtual probe solver, 2010.

APPENDIX

A. DERIVATIONS AND MORE RESULTS

The detailed derivations and additional experimental evaluations can be found at [29].

A.1 Proposition and Proof

PROPOSITION 1. *For any $j = 1, 2, \cdots, M$, following the schema defined in Eq.* (19), *if $\epsilon_1 \to 0$ and $\epsilon_2 \to 0$, then $q^\star(z_j)$ follows a Student-t distribution defined in Eq.* (23).

Proof: Without the loss of generality, let's take any $j = 1, 2, \cdots, M$, and we know that

$$\ln q^\star(z_j) = -\frac{\nu_0+1}{2}\ln[1+\frac{1}{\nu_0}(\frac{z_j-\mu_0}{\sigma_0})^2] - \frac{\mathbb{E}_\tau[\tau]}{2}\times \sum_{i=1}^{M}[(\phi_{ij}z_j)^2 + 2\sum_{k\neq j}\phi_{ik}z_k\phi_{ij}z_j - 2y_i\phi_{ij}z_j] + \text{const} \tag{31}$$

Note that in the following derivations, we will neglect the const factor in Eq (31) since it has nothing to do with z_j. Since $\frac{1}{\nu_0}\left(\frac{z_j-\mu_0}{\sigma_0}\right)^2 = \epsilon_1 \to 0$, applying Taylor series, we have

$$\ln(1+\epsilon_1) = \frac{1}{\nu_0}(\frac{z_j-\mu_0}{\sigma_0})^2 + O(\epsilon_1^2) \tag{32}$$

Substituting Eq. (32) into Eq. (31), we get

$$\begin{aligned}
&\ln q^\star(z_j)\\
&= -\frac{1}{2}\left(\varphi_1 + \frac{\nu_0+1}{\nu_0\sigma_0^2}\right)z_j^2\\
&\quad + \left[\frac{\mu_0(\nu_0+1)}{\nu_0\sigma_0^2} + \varphi_2\right]z_j + O(\epsilon_1^2)\\
&= -\frac{1}{2}\left(\frac{\nu_N+1}{\nu_N\sigma_N^2}\right)z_j^2 + \left[\frac{\mu_N(\nu_N+1)}{\nu_N\sigma_N^2}\right]z_j + O(\epsilon_1^2)\\
&= -\frac{\nu_N+1}{2}\left[\frac{1}{\nu_N}\left(\frac{z_j-\mu_N}{\sigma_N}\right)^2\right] + O(\epsilon_1^2)
\end{aligned} \tag{33}$$

where μ_N, σ_N, ν_N are provided in Eq. (22) in the paper. Further, with the condition that $\frac{1}{\nu_N}\left(\frac{z_j-\mu_N}{\sigma_N}\right)^2 = \epsilon_2 \to 0$, applying Taylor series again, we know

$$\frac{1}{\nu_N}(\frac{z_j-\mu_N}{\sigma_N})^2 + O(\epsilon_2^2) = \epsilon_2 + O(\epsilon_2^2) = \ln(1+\epsilon_2) \tag{34}$$

Substituting Eq. (34) into Eq. (33) we get

$$\begin{aligned}
&\ln q^\star(z_j)\\
&= -\frac{\nu_N+1}{2}\ln\left[1+\frac{1}{\nu_N}\left(\frac{z_j-\mu_N}{\sigma_N}\right)^2\right]\\
&\quad + [O(\epsilon_1^2) + O(\epsilon_2^2)]
\end{aligned} \tag{35}$$

As $\epsilon_1 \to 0$ and $\epsilon_2 \to 0$, the higher-order terms are negligible. We thus conclude

$$\begin{aligned}
&\ln q^\star(z_j)\\
&= -\frac{\nu_N+1}{2}\ln\left[1+\frac{1}{\nu_N}\left(\frac{z_j-\mu_N}{\sigma_N}\right)^2\right]\\
&= t_{\nu_N}(z_j \mid \mu_N, \sigma_N^2)
\end{aligned} \tag{36}$$

Targeting Direct Cash Transfers to the Extremely Poor

Brian Abelson
Enigma
New York, NY USA
brianabelson@gmail.com

Kush R. Varshney
IBM Research
Yorktown Heights, NY USA
krvarshn@us.ibm.com

Joy Sun*
GiveDirectly
New York, NY USA
joy@givedirectly.org

ABSTRACT

Unconditional cash transfers to the extreme poor via mobile telephony represent a radical, new approach to giving. GiveDirectly is a non-governmental organization (NGO) at the vanguard of delivering this proven and effective approach to reducing poverty. In this work, we streamline an important step in the operations of the NGO by developing and deploying a data-driven system for locating villages with extreme poverty in Kenya and Uganda. Using the type of roof of a home, thatched or metal, as a proxy for poverty, we develop a new remote sensing approach for selecting extremely poor villages to target for cash transfers. We develop an analytics algorithm that estimates housing quality and density in patches of publicly-available satellite imagery by learning a predictive model with sieves of template matching results combined with color histograms as features. We develop and deploy a crowdsourcing interface to obtain labeled training data. We deploy the predictive model to construct a fine-scale heat map of poverty and integrate this discovered knowledge into the processes of GiveDirectly's operations. Aggregating estimates at the village level, we produce a ranked list from which top villages are included in GiveDirectly's planned distribution of cash transfers. The automated approach increases village selection efficiency significantly.

Categories and Subject Descriptors

I.2.10 [**Arti cial Intelligence**]: Vision and Scene Understanding; I.5.4 [**Pattern Recognition**]: Applications; J.4 [**Social and Behavioral Sciences**]: Economics

Keywords

poverty economics; remote sensing; social good

*This project was conducted under the auspices of the DataKind DataCorps, Brooklyn, NY USA.

KDD'14, August 24–27, 2014, New York, NY, USA.

http://dx.doi.org/10.1145/2623330.2623335.

1. INTRODUCTION

GiveDirectly is a non-profit, non-governmental organization (NGO) that aims to help people living in extreme poverty by making unconditional cash transfers to them via mobile telephony. Unlike other charitable giving, unconditional cash transfers do not presuppose that food, livestock, or any other provisions are best for the recipients; recipients are free to spend the funds in any way they choose. Evidence from a randomized control trial shows that this method of charity has large positive effects on multiple measures of recipients' well-being [7]. Additionally, by forgoing large intermediary infrastructures, donations can be used extremely efficiently; to date, more than 90% of each donated dollar has reached a recipient. Currently operating in Kenya and Uganda, GiveDirectly takes an end-to-end operations model and does not outsource or subcontract work to other organizations.

Several steps comprise GiveDirectly's operations. First, funds are solicited from individual and institutional donors, and collected in GiveDirectly's bank account. Once a sufficient amount has been collected, e.g. US$ 1 million, the NGO initiates a campaign to disburse the donations to the extremely poor. The first part of a campaign is enrolling extremely poor households to be recipients; the second is transferring funds to recipients via mobile money systems such as M-Pesa [8]; and the third is conducting telephone and in-person follow-up with each recipient.

Targeting extremely poor households starts by identifying regions of the country with high poverty rates through data from the national census. Within those regions, villages and households are selected through a transparent criterion that is associated with extreme poverty. In Kenya and Uganda, where the NGO currently operates, the extremely poor tend to live in homes with thatched roofs whereas the less poor tend to live in homes with metal roofs. Villages with an abundance of low-quality housing and access to a mobile money agent are targeted.

After this selection stage, using a rigorous process of audits and security measures to prevent errors and fraud, money that has been transferred to GiveDirectly's local mobile money account is transferred directly to the recipient's account.[1] A text message is sent to the recipient who then goes to a mobile money agent — usually a shopkeeper in the village or nearby town. The recipient transfers the new funds in his or her account to the agent's account in return for cash. The

[1]SIM cards are given to those recipients that do not have mobile phones.

recipient is then free to use the cash for any purpose of his or her choosing.

In the current operations, the village selection phase involves multiple rounds of site visits with their attendant costs and logistical difficulties because governmental or other poverty data does not exist at village-level granularity. In this work, we formulate, implement, and deploy data-driven approaches to streamline this part of a campaign, thereby both increasing the efficiency of direct cash transfers and improving targeting of transfers to the extremely poor.

In particular, the main contribution of this work is a remote sensing system that estimates the quality and density of housing in large areas of central east Africa at a fine scale to facilitate village selection. Specifically, we apply a combination of image processing and machine learning methods on publicly-available electro-optical satellite imagery to construct features for a regression that estimates the number of houses of different roof types in an image patch. We use template matching to find roofs in images, and color histograms and supervised classification to differentiate roof types. We take advantage of a special characteristic of roofs in this part of the world: thresholding template matching results over a sequence of values reveals different roof types like a sieve. Therefore, all features are calculated over a sequence of thresholds.

We develop an interactive image labeling platform and deploy it to crowdsource the acquisition of training data on roof locations and types for the supervised classification and regression algorithms. We find that crowdsourcing results in rapid and high-quality completion of the labeling task, which we attribute to the intrinsic motivation of crowd members to contribute to social good. The final learned regression function allows us to construct heat maps of housing density and thatched-roof proportion from individual image patch-level estimates; areas with a preponderance of thatched-roof houses are to be targeted. From the heat maps, we aggregate village-level proportions of thatched roofs to produced a ranked list of villages to target.

Thus far, the data-driven prioritization of villages has been deployed in three districts in Kenya.[2] In total, the villages selected through the proposed approach have received or are in the process of receiving over US$ 4 million in direct cash transfers. Using the data mining approach saved approximately 100 person-hours of manual work that would have been incurred in manual ways of conducting village selection. The system offers a way to quickly scale GiveDirectly's operations and generate further cost savings in the future.

There is no specific prior work in the remote sensing literature on estimating the proportion of metal and thatched roofs in a village. However, two typical remote sensing problems are related: land use classification and building extraction. The most common feature for land use classification from single electro-optical images is color histograms as we also use [11]. Building extraction methods in the literature, including those based on the Hough transform [9], are primarily focused on urban and suburban environments having closely-spaced buildings with high variability in size and shape, and also sometimes attempt to reconstruct the three-dimensional geometry of the buildings. For our work, such approaches are excessve because we are concerned with the easier rural setting with roofs all of approximately the same size and of a similar approximately rotationally-invariant shape; therefore, we can use simpler template matching approaches with good performance.

[2]We do not report names of districts and villages in this paper to protect recipients and the process from harm.

(a) (b)

Figure 1: Homes in central east Africa with (a) metal and (b) thatched roofs.

The remainder of the paper is organized as follows. In Section 2, we further discuss the penury criterion of thatched and metal roofs. Section 3 discusses data available from satellites and previous campaigns, and the crowdsourcing we instituted to obtain further data. We present a feature construction method from satellite imagery based on template matching and use the constructed features for estimating the density of homes and the proportion that have thatched roofs in Section 4. Section 5 describes the deployment of the estimation system in GiveDirectly's campaigns for village targeting. Finally, Section 6 presents the results and impact of the deployment to GiveDirectly and Section 7 provides a summary and suggestions for future research.

2. THATCHED AND METAL ROOFS

In many villages of central east Africa, the roofs of homes are typically constructed in one of two ways: they are either made of grass, i.e., are thatched, or are made of metal like tin or iron. Photographs of the two roof types are shown in Fig. 1. Metal roofs provide many benefits over thatched roofs. For example, thatched roofs leak and collapse regularly, requiring replacement one or two times a year at a cost of US$ 100 or US$ 150 per year in materials and labor, whereas metal roofs last ten to fifteen years. Gutters to collect rain water are sometimes installed with metal roofs which lessens the incidence of waterborne diseases and reduces the labor involved with fetching water from a potentially large distance. Thatched roofs are also a comfortable habitat for mosquitoes, leading to higher incidence of mosquito-borne diseases among people living under thatched roofs [5].

Households that can afford to invest in a metal roof—which can cost as much as US$ 564 purchasing power parity in western Kenya [7]—typically do. Therefore the type of roof, thatched or metal, is a reliable proxy of the poverty level of a given area. In order to maximize operating efficiency and target the poorest, the NGO seeks to operate in administrative units with a high proportion of thatched roofs and low proportion of metal roofs.

In this work, we would like to quantify the proportion of thatched and metal roofs in administrative units as efficiently as possible. Toward this end, we turn to remote sensing because it is possible to differentiate roof type in satellite imagery. Leaving aside all other possible proxies for poverty, the remainder of the paper is concerned with estimating the

Figure 2: Example of metal roof in center of satellite image.

Figure 3: Example of thatched roof in center of satellite image.

proportion of thatched roofs in administrative units and using these estimates for village selection operations.

3. AVAILABLE DATA AND CROWDSOURCING DEPLOYMENT

In this section, we describe various data sources available to us including their limitations and also describe a crowdsourcing platform we deployed to obtain additional data.

3.1 Satellite Imagery

Various satellites take images of the earth with differing modalities (optical, hyperspectral, radar, etc.), spatial resolutions, temporal resolutions, and costs of imagery. In our application, we require the cost of obtaining imagery to be minimal, preferably zero, and the spatial resolution to be sufficient so that homes occupy more than a handful of pixels. Temporal resolution is a secondary concern for us and the electro-optical modality is sufficient. Under these desiderata, we choose to pull 400×400 pixel images at the highest zoom level available in this part of the world from the Google Maps API, which is made available for free. Metal and thatched roofs are distinguishable in these images, as seen in Fig. 2 and Fig. 3.

Satellite images from Google Maps are not without issue. In the part of Africa in which we are working, some small regions are obscured by clouds. An example is shown in Fig. 4(a). Since only one temporal snapshot is available per spatial location, we have no way of removing the clouds. Additionally, we have no indication on the provenance of the images, specifically the time stamp of acquisition. In examining the images for east central Africa, it is clear that images have been taken in different seasons, which results in different visual characteristics of roofs and the other components of the scene. As shown in Fig. 4(b)–(d), some images are from a wet season, some are from a dry season, and some are from a season in which there is an abundance of haze. These differences have a direct consequence on image processing and machine learning, as we detail in Section 4. Moreover, without a time stamp, we cannot say how out-of-date our estimates may be in various small regions.

3.2 Data from Previous Censuses and Campaigns

During the process of selecting individual households to receive cash transfers, GiveDirectly sends staff to villages to conduct censuses of the households there. Collected data includes geographic coordinates of individual homes obtained using GPS receivers and an observation on roof type. Censuses include all households in a village, irrespective of roofing material, which may have provided excellent training data for a supervised learning algorithm had it not been for the following reason. Homes are often located at close proximity to each other; the GPS coordinates did not have enough precision and accuracy to allow us to draw a correspondence between homes seen in satellite images and homes recorded in censuses. Therefore, this data was not usable as a labeled training set. This same reason prevented us from using similar data from previous campaigns along with the fact that only data on actual recipients (living under thatched roofs) was collected in campaigns. Although not amenable to supervised learning, the census coordinates proved valuable in illuminating the geographic location of typical populated villages as we discuss in Section 3.3, where we describe a crowdsourcing application we developed to obtain labeled training data.

There are several levels of administrative units in Kenya, going from coarse to fine as province, district, division, location, sublocation, and village. Prioritizing at the level of the finest administrative unit, the village level in Kenya, requires us to have the geographic coordinates of the boundaries of

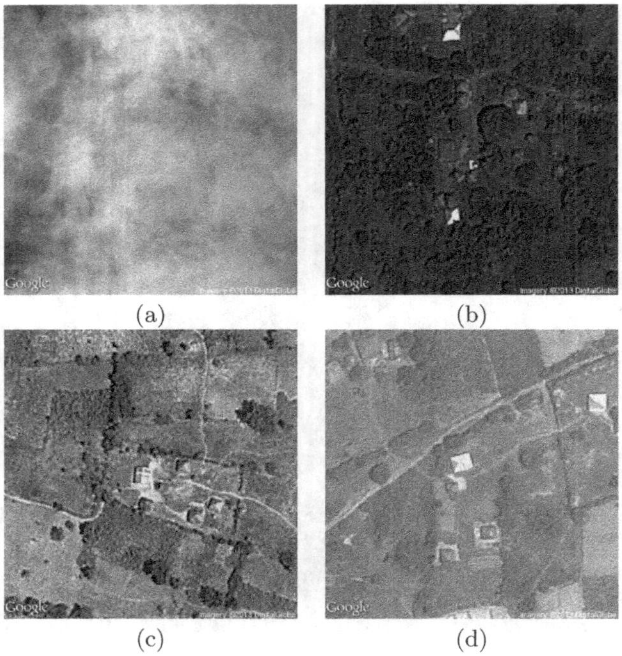

Figure 4: Satellite images taken under different conditions: (a) cloudy, (b) wet, (c), dry, and (d) hazy.

these localities. As part of previous campaigns, GiveDirectly obtained ESRI shapefiles of province, division, district, and sublocation boundaries in Kenya, but not village boundaries. The NGO also has PDF files of maps showing the village boundaries, but not in any georeferenced format, as seen in Fig. 5.

We had two options: work at the sublocation level only or try to georeference the PDF files. Since villages are the level at which the NGO desired to work, we set about converting the PDFs into shapefiles. The first step was to convert the PDF maps into a format we could open in a GIS application. Using Inkscape, an open source vector graphics editing program [1], we opened the PDF files and deleted all unnecessary features (rivers, roads, labels, etc.). We then exported the stripped-down maps as DXF files. We then opened these files in GIS—an open source mapping application—and converted the DXF files to GEOJSON. Luckily, the PDF maps had been rendered in WGS 84, a commonly-used projection system; therefore to georeference the village-level map for each division, we wrote a simple Python script that applied a linear transformation on the coordinate system of the village-level maps to fit the bounds of the division-level shapefile.

At this point, we had a fairly good geographic representation of villages. However, since villages are fairly small, any discrepancies between their actual location and their location in our shapefiles would yield innacurate results. To address this problem, we opened our transformed shapefiles in CartoDB, a web application for creating and editing maps [12], and manually aligned the shapefiles to prominent features like roads, rivers, and district boundaries. Finally, so as to ensure the interpretability of our maps, we hand-labeled each village polygon by referencing our shapefiles against the original PDF images. While this process was somewhat inexact, NGO staff members in Kenya were satisfied with the results and confident that our village polygons faithfully represented reality.

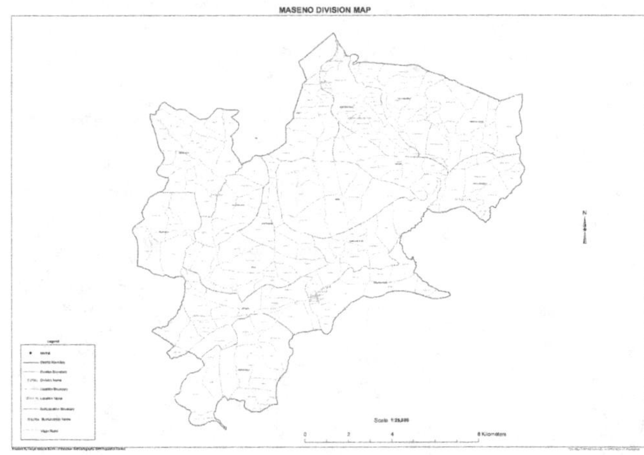

Figure 5: Example village map.

3.3 Crowdsourcing Application and Deployment

To create a collection of training data for our machine learning algorithms, we develop an interactive image labeling platform in Python using Flask—a web development framework [4]. As shown in Fig. 6, the application serves a random satellite image to a user and allows him or her to click on roofs in the image and indicate whether they are thatched or metal. When the user is done with an image, a new, unlabeled image is served and he or she replicates the process. On the backend, we record the total number of roofs of each type in each image, as well as the pixel coordinates and type of each roof in each image. The platform is deployed to the web using Heroku so that people can label images in a distributed fashion.

Working with our partners at DataKind, we recruited volunteers to help with the labeling process. DataKind initially announced the need for volunteers via meetup.com.[3] Within an hour, more than 20 people signed up. Ultimately, 10 people were selected for the crowdsourcing process. Volunteers were trained to use the platform by telephone and via a screencast we made and posted to YouTube.[4] Once volunteers were comfortable with the platform, we opened it up. Within one weekend, 10 users labeled all 1468 images in our training set.

While developing the platform, one of the authors of this paper labeled a random subset of 70 images. As a rough indication of the crowd's labeling quality, we find the correlation coefficient between the number of thatched roofs identified by the author and the crowd to be 0.783. Similarly, the correlation coefficient for iron roofs is 0.698. Both quantities are quite good; manual verification of other images also suggested that we could be highly confident in the results.

We conjecture that the excellent response time and quality are consistent with findings by Mason and Watts [10]: "When it is possible to use non-financial rewards, such as

[3]http://www.meetup.com/DataKind-NYC/events/159235222/

[4]https://www.youtube.com/watch?v=0mg-37JhAL4

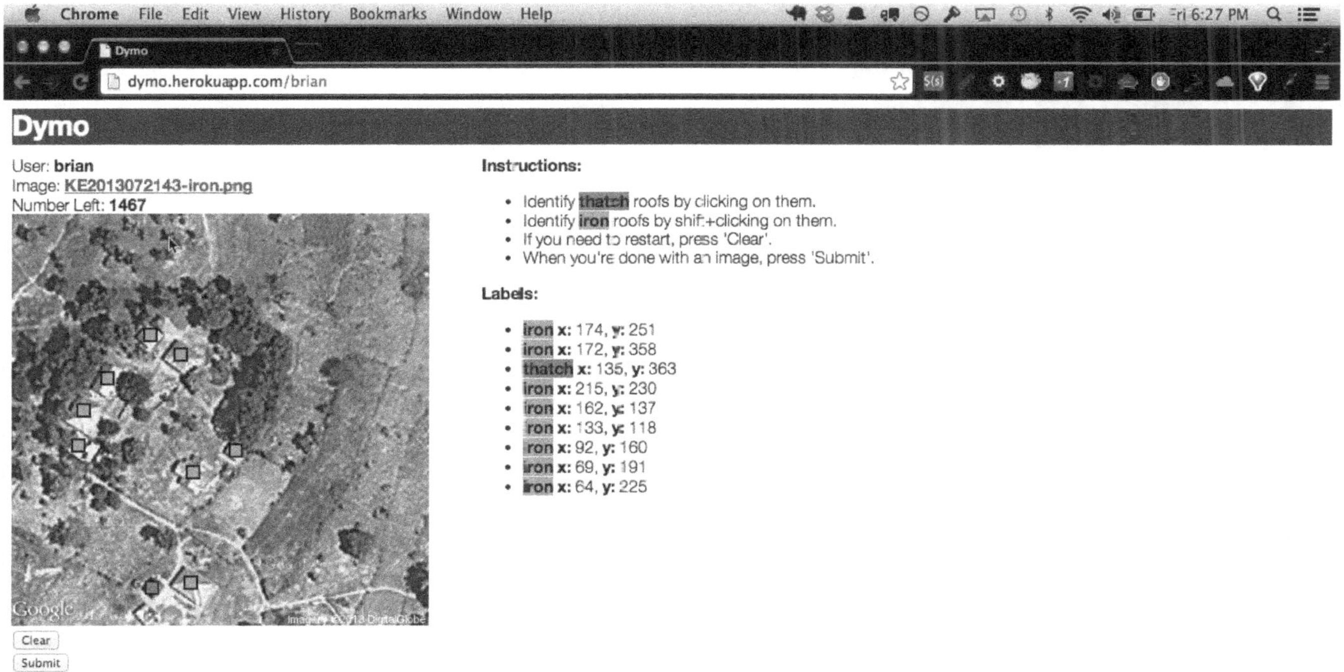

Figure 6: Screen shot of application deployed for crowdsourced labeling of roofs in satellite images.

harnessing intrinsic motivation, the quality of the work will be as good or better than using financial rewards, and therefore work can be accomplished as effectively for little to no cost." Helping to reduce poverty in the world, like other projects for social good, provides much intrinsic motivation.

4. REGRESSION OF ROOF COUNT AND ROOF TYPE PROPORTION

As we have discussed, the ultimate use of the data analytics we are performing is in selecting administrative units with the smallest proportion of metal roofs. To achieve this objective, we pose two regression problems: estimating the total number of roofs in a 400×400 pixel satellite image and estimating the proportion of metal roofs in the same image. With both estimates, we can then obtain an aggregate proportion of metal roofs for any region by taking a weighted average of estimates from a tiling of image patches from that region. Let us note that accurately classifying individual roofs is not the ultimate objective because we are tackling the village selection problem.

From the crowdsourcing, we have a training set of 1468 satellite images labeled by the number of thatched roofs and the number of metal roofs, from which we can derive the total number of roofs and the fraction that are metal. These are the response variables to predict. We use random forests with 50 trees per ensemble to perform the supervised regression because of their typical effectiveness, speed in prediction, and ease of use [2]. We note that the fraction of metal roofs response variable takes values in the range $[0, 1]$, but since all training samples fall in this range and we use random forests, the constraint does not need to be explicit in the learning. The features for the regressions are constructed from satellite image patches as we discuss next. We provide tenfold cross-validation accuracies for different feature choices at the end of the section.

4.1 Feature Construction

In constructing features that relate to the number of roofs and proportion of metal roofs in an image, we rely on two concepts: color histograms and template matching. Since metal roofs, thatched roofs, and the background all have different color distributions, we can use counts of pixels at different color values as features. In particular, we quantize each of the three color channels (red, green and blue) into eight equal-width bins to obtain twenty-four color histogram features per image patch. Color histogram features have long been used in image retrieval applications [6].

We also have a fairly good idea of the size and appearance of central east African roofs, which is fairly stationary across the region, so we can apply a basic template matching approach to find individual roofs in image patches [3]. We use the sum of absolute differences matching score on grayscale versions of image patches with two different templates: a 10×10 pixel white square and a 12×12 pixel template which is a central portion of an actual thatched roof from one of our satellite images. Specifically, denoting the image patch as I and the template as T, the matching score at pixel j of the image patch is:

$$d(I_j, T) = \sum_{i=1}^{n} |I_{i,j} - T_i|, \qquad (1)$$

where n is the total number of pixels in the template (100 for the white square template and 144 for the thatched roof template). An example of applying the white square template to a satellite image is shown in Fig. 7. The input image is shown in Fig. 7(a) and the resulting matching score is shown in Fig. 7(b).

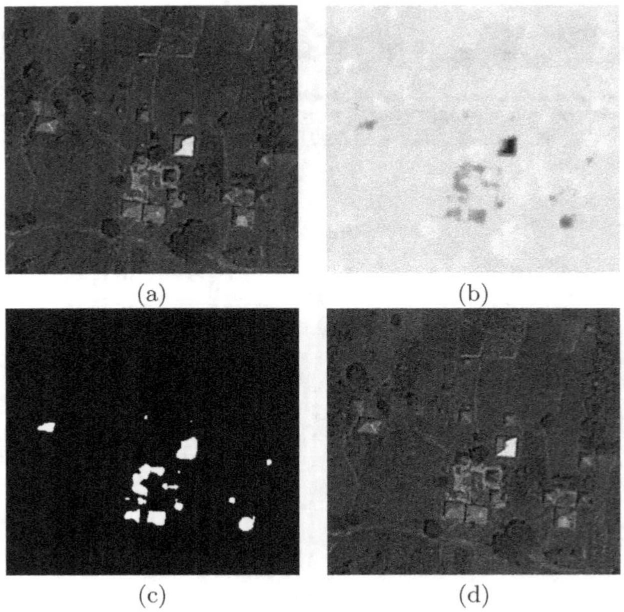

Figure 7: Template matching steps, from (a) the input image, to the (b) matching score, to the (c) thresholded matching score, to the (d) centroids of connected components in the thresholded matching score.

Once we have the template matching score for the image patch, we apply a threshold to obtain a binary image, as shown in Fig. 7(c) in which we can identify roofs. Based on morphological processing, we find all of the connected components in the binary image. The number of connected compounds is equivalent to the number of roofs identified. The centroids of the connected components that are found are superimposed on the input image in Fig. 7(d).

Of course, the number of roofs identified is a function of the threshold value applied to the template matching score, as illustrated in Fig. 8. A unique characteristic of central east African roofs that is not usually apparent in general image processing or remote sensing applications is that changing the threshold sequentially results in a sieve or filtration of roof type. When the white square template is used, as the threshold is increased, the metal roofs are revealed first and the thatched roofs are revealed later. Finally, non-roof items are revealed. The opposite is true with the thatched roof template. Therefore, the sequence of roof counts as a function of threshold is a sieve-like feature that not only provides information on the total number of roofs, but also on the proportion of metal and thatched roofs. A compound of dwellings may be identified as a single roof or as several roofs depending on the threshold, but according to our conception of the problem and our instructions to the crowd, compounds should be counted as multiple roofs.

The final set of features we construct combines template matching with color histograms within a roof classification scheme. Based on the crowdsourced labeling, we not only have the counts of thatched and metal roofs in the 1468 images, but we also have the pixel locations of all of the roofs with their labels. Among the crowdsourced image set, there are 8536 roofs: 5999 thatched and 2537 metal. Taking image patches surrounding the crowdsourced clicks, we can construct color histogram features and use those to classify the roofs. Fig. 9 shows the average color histogram by roof type in wet, dry, and hazy images. From the figure, it is apparent that on average, these color histogram features are able to distinguish thatched from metal. The baseline classification accuracy is $5999/8536 = 70.28\%$. With a random forests classifier with 50 trees (again chosen due to typical effectiveness, speed, and ease of use), we are able to achieve a tenfold cross-validation test accuracy of 89.67%.

To actually construct the final set of features, we use the output of the template matching at each threshold, take a 15×15 patch centered at each roof that is found, use the random forest classifier on color histogram features calculated on those patches, and compute the classification score output by the random forests (average vote among all constituent decision trees) [2]. The average classification score among all roofs in the image at a given template matching threshold is the feature for that image at that threshold, which is a good indicator of the proportion of metal and thatched roofs in the image.

Thus overall, we have three sets of features derived from the color pixel values in a 400×400 image patch. First is the color histogram features for the entire image patch. Second is a vector of roof counts at different template matching thresholds for two different templates. Third is the average individual roof classification score at the same thresholds for the two templates. The feature sets are summarized in Table 1.

4.2 Cross-Validation Accuracy

As mentioned at the beginning of the section, we learn regression functions for two different response variables using random forests: total roofs in an image and proportion of roofs that are metal in an image using the three sets of features described above. We examine two options for dealing with the different conditions during satellite image acquisition: learning a single estimator for all conditions, and learning separate estimators for the different conditions.

The figure of merit we use is mean absolute error (MAE) because of its easier interpretability than root mean squared error. However, we should note that MAE at the satellite image level is not the ultimate metric of interest. Since we ultimately average together estimates from all images in a village (which should reduce the error assuming that the image-level estimates are close to unbiased), and then rank the villages, the ultimate metrics of interest are MAE at the village level and especially rank correlation at the village level. However, we unfortunately have no ground truth for these quantities to report accuracy against.

Table 2 presents tenfold cross-validation testing error for different sets of features used and the two approaches for dealing with differing satellite conditions. As a point of comparison, if we use the mean value of the training response variables as the estimates for all test samples, the baseline MAEs are 2.8392 for total roofs and 0.2121 for the proportion of roofs that are metal. In examining the table, we see that separate regressions for the different conditions are better than a single regression across the board. Among the different options for feature sets, the combination of all features yields the best performance in predicting the proportion of metal roofs, with mean absolute error 0.1621. The average roof classification score feature set does not help in predicting the total number of roofs, which is expected

Figure 8: Template matching results at different thresholds.

Table 1: Summary of Feature Sets

Feature Set	Number of Features	Number of Templates	Number of Thresholds	Total
full image color histogram	24	—	—	24
template matching roof count	1	2	14	28
average classifications	1	2	14	28

because by averaging together the classification scores, we lose all information about the total number of roofs. The best performance is achieved by the combination of color histograms features and template matching roof count features with mean absolute error 1.9511. As we see in the next section, these error values are sufficiently small for our application and deployment; we use these feature sets going forward.

5. DEPLOYMENT

Having learned regression functions as described in Section 4, we now describe how we deploy the image processing and machine learning algorithm as part of the NGO's operations workflow. Based on previous experience and national-level data, GiveDirectly already identified which districts and divisions it is considering operating in. The question to answer is which villages within those divisions to target.

For any new 400×400 pixel image that was not seen by the predictive model during training, we can calculate its features and estimate the total number of roofs and the proportion metal using the learned model. The different satellite conditions in images persist over fairly large contiguous regions, so it is a quick and straightforward exercise to define bounding boxes corresponding to wet, dry, and hazy conditions, and use the appropriate regression function.

One may ask why we do not crowdsource the entire labeling effort instead of using the crowd only to provide training data for a machine learning algorithm. Our initial deployment scored approximately thirty times as many images as in the training set and future deployments may have hundreds of times as many images. Therefore relying on the crowd for the entire labeling task is not scalable, especially because we require consistency in the labels to allow comparisons between villages.

We download satellite images from the Google Maps API that tile the entire region of interest (and could do so for all of Kenya and Uganda if desired). We use equally-spaced latitudes and longitudes to do so since the API is called using latitude and longitude inputs. Since our region of interest straddles the equator, equally-spaced longitudes are an extremely close approximation to equally-spaced ground locations. We estimate the two quantities of interest for each downloaded image. We also perform a post-processing equalization step to match estimated values across satellite condition boundaries. The estimates for all image patches are visualized as heat maps, as shown in Fig. 10 and Fig. 11.

The northwest part of the region of interest contains clouds in the satellite images, which is reflected in both estimates. The estimated total number of roofs in these parts is very close to zero and the metal proportion is very high. A central large town in the middle of the region of interest shows up with a high roof count and high metal proportion. Lakes and reservoirs in the southwest appear as areas of low roof count and low metal proportion. A few thin horizontal and vertical lines in the heatmaps are artifacts of images containing a blend of satellite conditions.

The next step is to aggregate these fine-scale estimations within village boundaries. We take the average metal proportion weighted by total number of roofs of all image patches whose centers fall within the village boundary polygon. The resulting village-level metal roof proportions are mapped in Fig. 12. The cloud image patches do not contribute to the village-level metal proportion estimate because their total roof estimate is almost zero; the clouds do have the effect of occluding anything beneath them, but if the occluded portion of a village is similar to the unoccluded portion, then the effect is not too severe. The thin horizontal and vertical line artifacts have negligible effect on village-level estimates.

The village-level estimates are also presented as a ranked list, as in Table 3, which shows the top twelve (obfuscated) villages for targeting. Village C14C has the highest proportion of thatched roofs in the region of interest and is a prime village to target. Although proportion of thatched roofs is the main criterion in village targeting, there are some logistical considerations as well, such as access to M-Pesa agents and reachability from roads. We may incorporate these other criteria into an overall village score in future iterations of the algorithm for future campaigns, but in the initial campaigns for which the data-driven approach was applied, the rankings as in Table 3 were used as a priority list for manual selection that takes the other considerations into account.

In fact, many of the villages at the top of the list had already been enrolled in previous campaigns, providing a validation to the analytics. Additionally, several villages that constitute the main township area of this region were estimated to have high metal proportion, which is consistent

Table 2: Tenfold Cross-Validation Test Mean Absolute Error

Feature Set	Total Roofs (1)	Prop. Metal (1)	Total Roofs (Sep.)	Prop. Metal (Sep.)
full image color histogram (A)	2.1020	0.1755	2.0423	0.1744
template matching roof count (B)	2.0084	0.1755	1.9915	0.1755
average classifications (C)	2.4696	0.1704	2.4090	0.1670
(A) + (B)	1.9743	0.1712	1.9511	0.1720
(B) + (C)	2.0494	0.1658	2.0203	0.1630
(A) + (B) + (C)	2.0028	0.1656	1.9731	0.1621

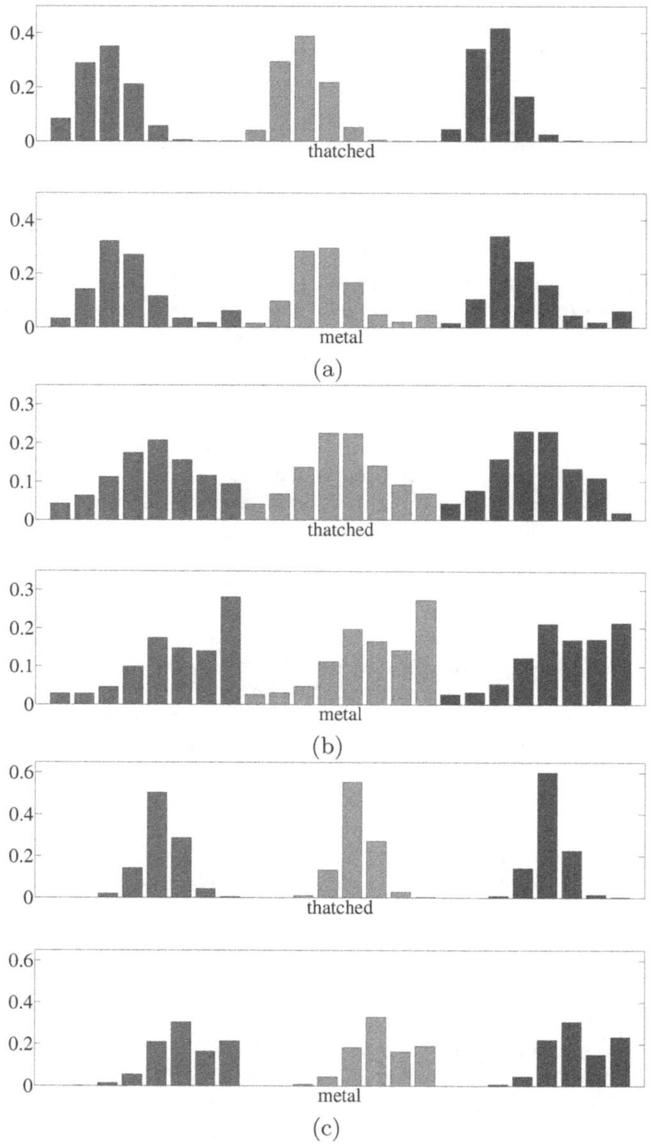

Figure 9: Average color histogram by roof type in 15×15 pixel patches of training set in (a) wet, (b) dry, and (c) hazy images.

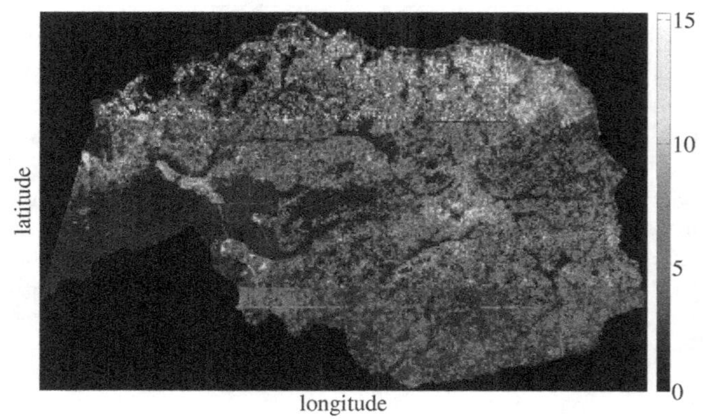

Figure 10: Heat map of number of total estimated roofs per 400×400 pixel image in the region of interest.

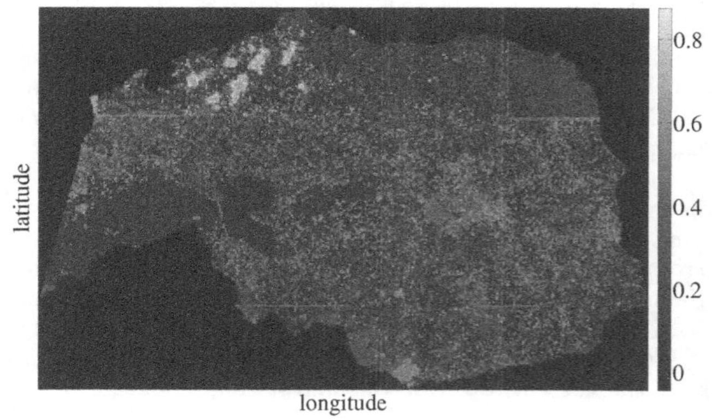

Figure 11: Heat map of proportion of roofs that are metal in the region of interest.

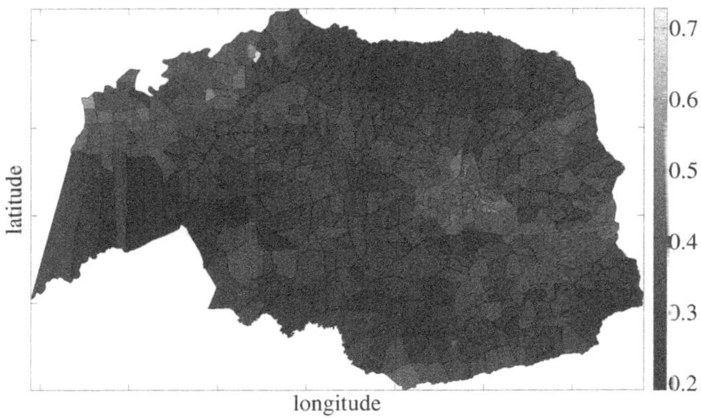

Figure 12: Estimated proportion of metal roofs in villages in the region of interest.

Table 3: Village Rankings (Names Obfuscated)

Ranking	Village Name	Proportion Metal
1	C14C	0.19039
2	C107	0.21016
3	C12E	0.21664
4	V10F	0.22197
5	V13D	0.22446
6	L180	0.22547
7	L111	0.22733
8	L106	0.22876
9	L193	0.22877
10	C14D	0.22916
11	L106	0.22934
12	C170	0.22986

with local knowledge. One small circularly-shaped village in the south central part of the region of interest is specifically delineated as a separate village by government authorities precisely bacause it is a small enclave with lower poverty; the estimation results bear this out: the predicted metal proportion is much lower than the surroundings.

6. IMPACT

In early 2014, GiveDirectly piloted the algorithm to identify approximately 50 villages in western Kenya for its largest campaign to date, which will move US$ 4 million in cash transfers. The approach immediately resulted in two major improvements: reduced staff time and reduced risk of inconsistent results.

Under the previous model, one staff member could collect requisite data on five villages per day. The 507 villages that the algorithm assessed would have required 101 person days to complete manually. This represents a cost savings of approximately US$ 4,000 in wages, which is equal to the value of cash transfers for four households (or twenty individuals) and improves overall operating efficiency by approximately ten basis points (defined as the fraction of total funds delivered directly to the poor). Reducing the person-hours required also allows implementation to move more quickly by completing the assessment in a matter of minutes rather than days, which modestly increases leverage of fixed costs like infrastructure and management time. These efficiencies will accumulate as the algorithm is applied on an ongoing basis.

The previous model also posed a risk of inconsistent results because it relied on multiple individuals, each liable to make different human errors. Although the historical error rate is unknown, it is reasonable to conclude that the algorithm improves outcomes by introducing a consistent approach to the entire task.

7. CONCLUSION

In this work, we have applied data mining for social good by developing a remote sensing approach for targeting unconditional cash transfers to the extremely poor. The algorithms and other system components we have developed have been deployed as decision support systems for planning GiveDirectly's operations. The impact of this work includes tangible benefits for the NGO including operational efficiency in cost and time, and reduction of inconsistency risk. This project also demonstrates how enthusiastic crowds can be when the goal is social good.

The machine learning and image processing components used in this work are fairly standard, but are composed in a novel way. Especially novel is the construction of sieve-like features from template matching, which was possible because of properties of thatched and metal roofs, but may find application in other settings as well. The steps taken to develop the system, its architecture, and even the results, can be applied more generally to uplift humanity beyond just targeting for unconditional cash transfers because fine-scale estimates of poverty and other social indicators in rural villages have myriad uses.

There are several avenues for future research. First, several improvements to the algorithm are possible. In this work, each image patch estimation is treated independently; Markov random field models connecting neighboring image patches, including thin-plate and thin-membrane priors often used in remote sensing, could be used to improve the estimation results [15]. Moreover, the feature engineering can be further enhanced using techniques beyond the very basic template matching and color histograms used herein. Alternative supervised learning beyond random forests could also yield improved performance.

The first deployment has been to prioritize villages in support of a human decision maker. Additional future work includes collecting data on all other considerations in village targeting and using them to fully automate the process. In this line of work, operational costs could be accounted for in the learning algorithms, cf. [14, 13], and schedules and routes for campaigns could also be constructed in a data-driven way.

One area of improvement for future campaigns relates to the fact that not all roofs seen in satellite imagery correspond to separate households. As discussed earlier, in this work, we count each structure within a compound separately. However, in the part of the world in which the NGO currently operates, it is common for kitchens to be separate structures and for there to be sleeping houses that dependent sons live in once they reach puberty, both of which should not be counted separately from the main house.

8. ACKNOWLEDGMENTS

The authors thank Jake Porway, Brian Dalessandro, Dave Goodsmith, Shubha Bala, Peter Darche, Julia Marden, Craig Barowsky, the rest of the DataKind family, Carolina Toth, Piali Mukhopadhyay, and the rest of the GiveDirectly staff for their assistance.

9. REFERENCES

[1] T. Bah. *Inkscape: Guide to a Vector Drawing Program.* Pearson, Boston, MA, 2010.

[2] L. Breiman. Random forests. *Mach. Learn.*, 45(1):5–32, Oct. 2001.

[3] R. Brunelli. *Template Matching Techniques in Computer Vision: Theory and Practice.* Wiley, Chichester, United Kingdom, 2009.

[4] R. DuPlain. *Instant Flask Web Development.* Packt Publishing, Birmingham, United Kingdom, 2013.

[5] A. C. Gamage-Mendis, R. Carter, C. Mendis, A. P. De Zoysa, P. R. Herath, and K. N. Mendis. Clustering of malaria infections within an endemic population: Risk of malaria associated with the type of housing construction. *Am. J. Trop. Med. Hyg.*, 45(1):77–85, July 1991.

[6] T. Gevers and A. W. M. Smeulders. PicToSeek: Combining color and shape invariant features for image retrieval. *IEEE Trans. Image Process.*, 9(1):102–119, Jan. 2000.

[7] J. Haushofer and J. Shapiro. Household response to income changes: Evidence from an unconditional cash transfer program in Kenya. Working paper, Abdul Latif Jameel Poverty Action Lab, Cambridge, MA, Nov. 2013.

[8] N. Hughes and S. Lonie. M-PESA: Mobile money for the "unbanked". *Innovations*, 2(1–2):63–81, Winter/Spring 2007.

[9] Z. J. Liu, J. Wang, and W. P. Liu. Building extraction from high resolution imagery based on multi-scale object oriented classification and probabilistic Hough transform. In *Proc. IEEE Geosci. Remote Sens. Symp.*, pages 2250–2253, Seoul, Korea, July 2005.

[10] W. Mason and D. J. Watts. Financial incentives and the "performance of crowds". In *Proc. ACM SIGKDD Workshop Human Comp.*, pages 77–85, Paris, France, June 2009.

[11] J. A. dos Santos, P.-H. Gosselin, S. Philipp-Foliguet, R. da S. Torres, and A. X. Falcão. Multiscale classification of remote sensing images. *IEEE Trans. Geosci. Remote Sens.*, 50(10):3764–3775, Oct. 2012.

[12] J. de la Torre. Organising geo-temporal data with CartoDB, an open source database on the cloud. In *Proc. Biodiversity Informatics Horizons*, Rome, Italy, Sept. 2013.

[13] T. Tulabandhula and C. Rudin. Machine learning with operational costs. *J. Mach. Learn. Res.*, 14:1989–2028, July 2013.

[14] T. Tulabandhula, C. Rudin, and P. Jaillet. The machine learning and traveling repairman problem. In *Proc. Int. Conf. Alg. Decision Theory*, pages 262–276, Piscataway, NJ, Oct. 2011.

[15] A. S. Willsky. Multiresolution Markov models for signal and image processing. *Proc. IEEE*, 90(8):1396–1458, Aug. 2002.

Scalable Hands-Free Transfer Learning for Online Advertising

Brian Dalessandro
Daizhuo Chen
Dstillery
470 Park Ave S
New York, NY 10016
briand,hchen@dstillery.com

Troy Raeder
Claudia Perlich
Melinda Han Williams
Dstillery
troy,claudia
melinda@dstillery.com

Foster Provost
New York University & Dstillery
44 W. 4th St
New York, NY 10012
fprovost@stern.nyu.edu

ABSTRACT

Internet display advertising is a critical revenue source for publishers and online content providers, and is supported by massive amounts of user and publisher data. Targeting display ads can be improved substantially with machine learning methods, but building many models on massive data becomes prohibitively expensive computationally. This paper presents a combination of strategies, deployed by the online advertising firm Dstillery, for learning many models from extremely high-dimensional data efficiently and without human intervention. This combination includes: (i) A method for simple-yet-effective transfer learning where a model learned from data that is relatively abundant and cheap is taken as a prior for Bayesian logistic regression trained with stochastic gradient descent (SGD) from the more expensive target data. (ii) A new update rule for automatic learning rate adaptation, to support learning from sparse, high-dimensional data, as well as the integration with adaptive regularization. We present an experimental analysis across 100 different ad campaigns, showing that the transfer learning indeed improves performance across a large number of them, especially at the start of the campaigns. The combined "hands-free" method needs no fiddling with the SGD learning rate, and we show that it is just as effective as using expensive grid search to set the regularization parameter for each campaign.

Categories and Subject Descriptors

I.5.4 [**Computing Methodologies**]: [Pattern Recognition - applications]

Keywords

Transfer Learning; Stochastic Gradient Descent; Adaptive Learning Rates; Adaptive Regularization

KDD'14, August 24–27, 2014, New York, New York, USA.
Copyright © 2014 ACM 978-1-4503-2956-9/14/08...$15.00.
http://dx.doi.org/10.1145/2623330.2623349.

1. INTRODUCTION

Online display advertising, served through real-time bidding systems, is a major source of revenue for web publishers. As media consumption continues to shift to web-hosted content, advertising dollars continue to pour into the system. Global display advertising revenues exceed 40 billion USD annually are growing at double-digit rates [7]. Real-time bidding systems are run by *ad exchanges*: auction platforms connecting sellers of ad placements (usually web publishers with ad space to monetize) and buyers (usually independent firms like Dstillery,[1] operating on behalf of consumer brands and their agencies). The goals of the buyers vary. At Dstillery, our ultimate goal is to identify the *best* possible audience for each of our individual advertising clients and advertise to this audience. What exactly "best" means depends upon the goals of the advertiser, but usually we optimize some form of *post-view conversion rate*. The definition of *conversion* is again campaign-specific, but always requires taking some action (such as visiting a site, buying a product, or signing up for a service). The *post-view* qualifier means the conversion is observed in some interval following an ad exposure but without the necessity of an ad click.

The data that we use for modeling is discussed in detail in Section 2, but the foundation of our targeting methodology is a suite of methods for high-dimensional, sparse classification (ranking) that builds multiple models for each advertising campaign individually. Training a single large-scale predictive model is no longer a rare feat. Our machine learning system trains, deploys, and continually retrains *thousands* of predictive models simultaneously. The performance requirements of display advertising customers and the need to operate many models simultaneously pose a number of technical challenges, which when combined motivate an efficient "hands-free" operation—robust performance with minimal intervention by the data science team. The specific challenges we consider are:

1. **Cold Start**: Targeting must perform well from the beginning of a campaign, even though there may be very little or even *ZERO* post-impression conversion data.
2. **Non-Stationarity**: Human browsing behavior, the basis of our models, changes over time due to natural seasonality and marketer-specific external factors.
3. **Consistency**: Since we restrict ourselves from pooling conversion data across advertisers (due to their com-

[1]Formerly Media6degrees

petitive concerns), we build separate models for each one. Each model must perform well in spite of large disparities in conversion rate and audience size.

4. **Scale and Robustness**: The system builds and maintains many different predictive models for each of hundreds of campaigns simultaneously. These models have a limited number of data scientists to monitor and validate them. Thus we need an automated and robust hands-free approach that can still learn the idiosyncrasies of individual campaigns.

Our current system addresses these issues with a number of different components, amply described in prior work (see [11] and the citations therein). The current paper explores an alternative, novel solution to the same goal by tightly integrating transfer learning [10] and scalable predictive modeling. Recent developments in adaptive learning-rate schedules [14] and adaptive regularization [13] allow for incremental training of linear models in millions of dimensions without exhaustive hyper-parameter searching. Our complications are (i) the need of transfer learning to support cold start and few available positive examples, and (ii) the application to ultra-high-dimensional modeling. This work extends the prior work first by incorporating the transfer learning steps directly into the large-scale linear models using Bayesian logistic regression (section 3) and second by combining and extending state-of-the-art methods to enable hands-free, scalable stochastic gradient descent (SGD, Section 4). The combination of these methods demonstrably improves campaign performance, especially in the early stages of the campaign, and this improvement is achievable within the throughput limitations of the system. We will discuss more specific related work in the relevant sections. We are not aware of a prior paper that describes and evaluates a production-ready combination of current state-of-the-art learning methods for efficient, hands-free transfer learning of large numbers of predictive models from extremely sparse data.

Specifically, the contributions of this paper are:

1. We develop a transfer learning system based on these methods and show that combining data from general conversions with data on post-impression conversions improves targeting performance across a large number of campaigns.
2. We derive a new update rule for the adaptive learning-rate algorithm of [14] so that it supports sparse updates and is mathematically compatible with the adaptive regularization algorithm of [13].
3. We provide an algorithm for using both adaptive learning rates and adaptive regularization simultaneously. We show that, within this framework, adaptive regularization is just as effective as an expensive grid search for the regularization parameter.
4. We use production data to show the effect of transfer learning "in vivo", specifically focusing on its ability to address the cold start problem for new campaigns. (Long-running campaigns have more natural training data and therefore derive less benefit from transferring information from other distributions.)

The remainder of the paper shows how these and other developments in linear modeling can be combined into a continuously updating, hyperparameter-agnostic ad-targeting system that transitions from learning on a proxy population (*all* conversions) to the true population (*post-impression* conversions) as more data becomes available. Our results show that this strategy is indeed effective for improving campaign performance, especially in the early stages of the campaign, and this improvement is more scalable than alternative methods.

2. DATA COLLECTION PROCESS

The data which informs our proprietary ad-targeting models comes primarily from multiple continuous data streams. One stream records general *browsing* events of users as they consume content across the web. Another similar stream records interactions between users and the brands we represent. These interactions include home page visits and conversions on their owned websites. The last data stream we consider is the actual ad serving process. We serve ads to users based on various criteria and following the ads we record whether or not these users convert. From these data streams we can construct different but related classification (ranking) tasks.

Our most obvious data asset for campaign optimization is the campaign data itself. If we want to draw training data directly from the target distribution, we can randomly target users with impressions, subsequently labeling a user as positive if she converts soon after exposure to the ad and negative otherwise. However, this poses serious challenges. Serving ads randomly at a necessary scale—to avoid the selection bias inherent in training on data resulting from targeted impressions—is something our stakeholders are often reluctant to do. Moreover, conversion rates are generally quite low (often 10^{-6} or less), which leads to the need to serve massive number of randomly targeted ads just to obtain a moderate number of conversions for training.

This paper focuses on a method to leverage other data sources for cheap and reliable "adjunct" training data. The Bayesian transfer learning approach provides a principled method for combining these data with a smaller amount of randomly sampled post-impression data.

Before a client initiates an advertising campaign, we place tracking pixels on various parts of the client's web site. Visits to these pixeled pages get logged (anonymously) for analysis and optimization. In parallel, we collect web browsing data on these same anonymous users from data partners across the web. This data is stored in our system as a set of anonymized (hashed) URL strings linked to a user's cookie. These two mechanisms, which are independent of actually serving ads, when combined give us both features and labels that we can use to build the adjunct training data. Specifically, we build training instances in a *backward looking* fashion. For a given period of time, we select all pixel events coming from the client's website and label the corresponding users as positive instances. We then select a random subset of users that were active in the same period but did not incur a pixel event and label them as negative instances. This design choice is very practical: while post-impression conversion events are typically rare, general visits or conversions on the client's website are orders of magnitude more abundant.

Thus we have two data sets for each campaign—one drawn from the target application's distribution, but which comprises relatively few positive instances, and another that is naturally more abundant and cheaper, but doesn't exactly represent the problem we are trying to solve. The challenge addressed in this paper is to use these data to build models to estimate the relative likelihood that a previously unseen user will convert after seeing an ad. The rest of the paper describes and evaluates a Bayesian transfer learning framework implemented to achieve this, as well as the modern machine learning methods we have combined and enhanced to do so at scale.

3. SCALABLE TRANSFER LEARNING

Our goal, in a nutshell, is to improve the performance of conversion-rate modeling at all points of the campaign. We do this by first initializing our model with a learned prior and then incrementally improve the prediction task by incorporating post-impression conversions as they become available. Prior work uses the term *transfer learning* [10] to refer to any situation where a model learned on one classification task (called the *source* task) is used to improve a predictive model applied to a different task, the *target* task We adopt the language and notation from [10] to present our version of transfer learning more formally.

Formally, a *classification task* $\{\chi, P(X), \gamma, P(Y|X)\}$ is composed of a feature space χ, a probability distribution $P(X)$, where $X = \{x_1, x_2, ..., x_d\} \in \chi$ is a feature vector, a label space γ, where $Y \in \gamma$ is the outcome of interest and lastly, a corresponding objective function $P(Y|X)$. In our particular situation, we refer to the campaign data as the *target* and the auxiliary data described in section 2 as the *source*. We generally assume that the source and target tasks share the same feature space χ but generally assume that $P^S(X) \neq P^T(X)$ for all X.[2] We also have different outcome spaces γ for both data sets, though they are related. In our domain γ^S represents conversion labels derived from observing general traffic on the client's website whereas γ^T is derived from post-impression conversions.

Our main estimation problem is to learn $P^T(Y^T|X)$ from the target data. We do this by first learning $P^S(Y^S|X)$ from the source data and then use that estimator as a prior on our estimator for $P^T(Y^T|X)$. We generally assume that $P^T(Y^T|X) \neq P^T(Y^S|X)$, but that the structure of the estimators (specifically the weight vectors from linear models) are similar and that is why we can use the source model as a prior on the target.

To put this more formally, consider a logistic regression model for a data set $D^S = \{(X_1, y_1^S), \dots, (X_N, y_N^S)\}$. We use the standard log-likelihood formulation and denote the sample logistic loss function as

$$\ell_t(\beta) = -y_t \log p_t(\beta) - (1 - y_t)\log(1 - p_t(\beta)), \quad (1)$$

where $p_t(\beta) = (1 + e^{-\beta X_t})^{-1}$. Again we use superscript S and T to differentiate between the source and target data. Given the source data, we define what we call the source model:

$$\hat{\mu}^S = \arg\min_{\mu} \sum_{t=1}^{N^S} [\ell_t^S(\mu) + \lambda^S r(\mu)],^3 \quad (2)$$

where $r(\mu)$ is a suitable regularization function and λ^S a regularization weight.

[2]When referring to constructs within target or source data, we use the superscripts S and T to differentiate

[3]We use μ in this equation instead of β to distinguish it as the initialization model learned on source data

We expect that the source model is relatively effective for identifying a high-performance audience even though the training data are not drawn from the "proper" (target) distribution. We want a model that will rank highly a set of users who are likely to convert following the presentation of an ad. The source model instead identifies users who are similar to a client's customer set with respect to their web browsing history, independent of the advertising process.

We can directly model the target task by first creating an appropriate dataset. Let the target data set $D^T = \{(X_1, y_1^T) \dots (X_N, y_N^T)\}$, where X_t is defined as above and y_t^T is defined as a post-impression conversion. In order to induce transfer learning from $P^S(y^S|X)$ to $P^T(y^T|X)$, we add a non-zero Gaussian or Laplace prior on the logistic regression coefficients that estimate $P^T(y^T|X)$. Our resulting optimization problem then looks like:

$$\hat{\beta}^T = \arg\min_{\beta} \sum_{t=1}^{N^T} [\ell_t^T(\beta) + \lambda^T r(\beta - \hat{\mu}^S)], \quad (3)$$

where again we are using the standard logistic loss. The differences between equations (2) and (3) are that in (3) we are training over the target data and have modified the regularization function in (3) to incorporate a non-zero informative prior. This form of knowledge transfer is highly scalable, because although we do incur the additional cost of learning μ^s, the cost of learning with equation 3 is no more than had we used a zero-mean prior. This is a major benefit in support of this method over more complicated transfer learning methods [10] and a motivating factor for putting it to use in our system.

Incorporating a source model for transfer learning as a Bayesian prior is not new. In a text-mining application, Chelba et al [5] successfully incorporate a prior model as a Bayesian prior into a maximum entropy Markov model to recover the correct capitalization of uniformly-cased text. Similarly, Arnold et al [2] use the hierarchical structure of features to learn informative priors over features to use in training conditional random fields. For transfer learning with logistic regression, Raina et al [12] perform text classification using a learned Gaussian prior. However, the formulation is quite different; we view our formulation as much more straightforward (they focus on the prior variance). In advertising applications, Chapelle et al [4] use informative priors in logistic regression models but not explicitly as a transfer learning mechanism. In their application they build models incrementally and use the previous iteration's model as the prior. We are not aware of any prior work that explicitly uses Bayesian transfer learning in a large-scale production application.

4. HYPERPARAMETER FREE LEARNING

Recall that our goal is twofold. As described above, we would like to take advantage of both the plentiful source data and the expensive-but-more-appropriate target data. We also would like to do this efficiently with minimal human curation. A popular and effective algorithm for building linear models with large-yet-sparse, data is Stochastic Gradient Descent (SGD) [4, 9, 15]. The main drawback of SGD is that it includes various hyper-parameters (learning rates, regularization parameters, etc.) that need to be carefully tuned in order to achieve good performance. Parameter tuning ultimately complicates and lengthens the model training phase. Firms that need to build hundreds or thousands of models simultaneously, in production, face a daunting task setting these hyper-parameters separately for each campaign.

To enable building many models with few data scientists, and to reduce the training load on our system, we have developed a "hands-free" approach that does not require either manual parameter setting or expensive grid-search. The methods we present here are well suited for large and sparse consumer behavior data and they integrate well with the transfer-learning described above. In particular, we present a hyper-parameter-free SGD logistic regression training algorithm based on combining and enhancing two recent developments: the adaptive learning rates [14] (which we call *NoPesky*) and adaptive regularization [13].

We made several enhancements to make NoPesky learning rates and adaptive regularization work together and efficiently in the current context. Specifically, we adapted the NoPesky learning rate method so that we can 1) take advantage of the sparse structure of the data to run efficient SGD updates, 2) explicitly integrate the regularization term in order to make NoPesky work with adaptive regularization, and 3) give the NoPesky algorithm a more robust starting point when positive samples are rare.

It is helpful to start by considering the update step of a standard SGD algorithm: at time t, we observe a new training sample with per-sample loss

$$f_t(\beta) = \ell_t(\beta) + \lambda r(\beta - \mu), \tag{4}$$

where β comprises the model coefficients; ℓ_t is the per-sample logistic loss function as defined in Section 3; λ is the regularization factor, and r is the regularization function having the form $r(\beta - \mu) = \frac{1}{2}\sum_{i=1}^{d}(\beta_i - \mu_i)^2$. We denote the average loss function by $f = \frac{1}{N}\sum_{t=1}^{N} f_t$, and the average logistic loss function by $\ell = \frac{1}{N}\sum_{t=1}^{N}\ell_t$. With each training sample, and for each dimension i of the model, we calculate the gradient $\nabla_{t,i} = \frac{\partial f_t}{\partial \beta_i}|_{\beta=\beta_t}$ and update the dimension's coefficient via

$$\beta_{t+1,i} = \beta_{t,i} - \eta_{t,i}\nabla_{t,i}, \tag{5}$$

where $\eta_{t,i}$ is the learning rate at time t for dimension i.[4] Because our algorithm works with both source and target models, we drop the superscripts S and T throughout this section.

4.1 NoPesky Learning Rates

The NoPesky learning rate method sets the SGD learning rates in a greedy manner by choosing a rate that minimizes the expected value of the average loss function f after each SGD update. It is generally impossible to solve this minimization problem exactly, but an approximate solution can be obtained and works well in practice. The method utilizes the second-order derivatives of the per-sample loss function, making it suitable for learning models with a smooth loss function, such as linear and logistic regression. Our experiments validate prior research [14], showing that SGD algorithms trained with the NoPesky learning rates perform as well as state-of-the-art adaptive learning rate schedules such as AdaGrad [6]. The difference is that NoPesky learning require no systematic parameter tuning and thus can promote faster learning.

We first sketch the core steps of the original NoPesky learning rate method that are necessary for presenting our adaptations. The method treats the stochastic gradient $\nabla_{t,i}$ as a random variable, and chooses a learning rate to minimize the expected regularized loss after one SGD update, that is:

$$\eta_{t,i} \leftarrow \arg\min_{\eta} E_{\nabla_{t,i}}[f(\beta_{t,i} - \eta\nabla_{t,i}e_i)], \tag{6}$$

where e_i is a unit vector in dimension i. In order to solve the above minimization problem, three approximations are made. First, the average loss function f is approximated by a quadratic function in the neighborhood of β_t. This is achieved by approximating its first-order derivative by $g_{t,i} \approx E[\nabla_{t,i}]$, and the second-order derivative by $h_{t,i} \approx E[\frac{\partial^2 f_t}{\partial \beta_i^2}|_{\beta=\beta_t}]$. Second, the first-order moment of $\nabla_{t,i}$ is approximated by $g_{t,i} \approx E[\nabla_{t,i}]$. And lastly, the second-order moment of $\nabla_{t,i}$ is approximated by $v_{t,i} \approx E[\nabla_{t,i}^2]$. One can then solve (6) and obtain an approximate solution, which is set as the per-sample, dimension specific learning rate.

$$\eta_{t,i} = \frac{1}{h_{t,i}}\frac{g_{t,i}^2}{v_{t,i}}. \tag{7}$$

The three approximate variables are calculated as running averages

$$\begin{aligned} g_{t,i} &= (1 - \tau_{t,i}^{-1})g_{t-1,i} + \tau_{t,i}^{-1}\nabla_{t,i}, \\ v_{t,i} &= (1 - \tau_{t,i}^{-1})v_{t-1,i} + \tau_{t,i}^{-1}\nabla_{t,i}^2, \\ h_{t,i} &= (1 - \tau_{t,i}^{-1})h_{t-1,i} + \tau_{t,i}^{-1}\left.\frac{\partial^2 f_t}{\partial \beta_i^2}\right|_{\beta=\beta_t}, \end{aligned} \tag{8}$$

where $\tau_{t,i}$ is an averaging window, that can be heuristically set by $\tau_{1,i} = 1$ and

$$\tau_{t+1,i} = (1 - \frac{g_{t,i}^2}{v_{t,i}})\tau_{t,i} + 1. \tag{9}$$

The use of a dynamic averaging window determined by equation (9) to update equation (8) enables this method to adapt to non-stationary data. When the data distributions change, τ is automatically reset to a lower number which increases the learning rate and enables more exploration.

To work within our system, we have made the following enhancements to the NoPesky method.

Sparse Updates.

As discussed above, online webpage visitation data is extremely sparse. It is desirable to take advantage of this extreme sparsity to speed up the SGD updates—specifically, we would like to enhance the NoPesky method such that at step t, we only update dimension i if $x_{t,i} \neq 0$.

In regularized logistic regression, the per-sample loss function has two components: the logistic loss function and the regularization function. The logistic loss function ℓ_t (defined in (1)) has a convenient property that its gradient in dimension i is 0 if $x_{t,i} = 0$, thus allowing for sparse updates. Unfortunately, the regularization term $\frac{\lambda}{2}\sum_i(\beta_i - \mu_i)^2$ generally does not have zero gradients. In fact, the regularization

[4]Our algorithm uses different learning rates for different dimensions, rather than a global learning rate for all dimensions. Multiple studies suggest that dimension-specific learning rates yield superior performance to global learning rates, particularly for data sets with sparse features like ours [6, 9].

term is independent of x_t and has non-zero gradient in dimension i as long as $\beta_{t,i} \neq \mu_i$. This regularization term prevents us from running efficient sparse updates.

Our solution is to rewrite the per-sample loss function as the following:

$$\tilde{f}_t(\beta) = \ell_t(\beta) + \sum_{i:x_{t,i}\neq 0} \frac{\lambda}{2}\frac{N}{N_i}(\beta_i - \mu_i)^2 \tag{10}$$

here N is the total number of training samples, and N_i is the total number of times that dimension i is present in a sample. We essentially reassigned the regularization term to the per-sample loss function. Instead of assigning equal regularization strength to every data sample, we choose to only regularize a dimension when that dimension is present, and correspondingly increase the regularization strength of that dimension in inverse proportion to the number of samples that have this dimension. In so doing, we have kept the total regularization strength unchanged, i.e., $\frac{1}{N}\sum_{t=1}^{N} f_t(\beta) = \frac{1}{N}\sum_{t=1}^{N} \tilde{f}_t(\beta) = f$.

Our learning method operates on the rewritten per-sample loss function $\tilde{f}_t$ instead of f_t. At step t, for dimension i such that $x_{t,i} = 0$, since $\nabla_{t,i} = \frac{\partial \tilde{f}_t}{\partial \beta_i}|_{\beta=\beta_t} = 0$, we can safely ignore updates on these dimensions and only run updates (7) (8) (9) on dimensions i with $x_{t,i} \neq 0$.

Explicit Handling of Regularization.

The original NoPesky method doesn't explicitly handle regularization terms, effectively putting the regularization as part of the loss function. Hence the regularization term also contributes to the running estimates $g_{t,i}$, $v_{t,i}$ and $h_{t,i}$. This inhibits the integration of NoPesky with adaptive regularization—we would like it to be capable of handling changing regularization factors.

Fortunately, since the regularization term is deterministic and can be calculated precisely, we can exclude them from the calculation of the running estimates. Thus, instead of (8), we have

$$\begin{aligned} g_{t,i} &= (1-\tau_{t,i}^{-1})g_{t-1,i} + \tau_{t,i}^{-1}\left.\frac{\partial \ell_t}{\partial \beta_i}\right|_{\beta=\beta_t}, \\ v_{t,i} &= (1-\tau_{t,i}^{-1})v_{t-1,i} + \tau_{t,i}^{-1}\left(\left.\frac{\partial \ell_t}{\partial \beta_i}\right|_{\beta=\beta_t}\right)^2, \\ h_{t,i} &= (1-\tau_{t,i}^{-1})h_{t-1,i} + \tau_{t,i}^{-1}\left.\frac{\partial^2 \ell_t}{\partial \beta_i^2}\right|_{\beta=\beta_t}, \end{aligned} \tag{11}$$

We can then modify our three approximations to

$$\begin{aligned} E[\nabla_{t,i}] &\approx g_{t,i} + \lambda_{t,i}(\beta_{t,i} - \mu_i), \\ E[\nabla_{t,i}^2] &\approx v_{t,i} + 2\lambda_{t,i}(\beta_{t,i} - \mu_i)g_{t,i} + \lambda_{t,i}^2(\beta_{t,i} - \mu_i)^2, \\ E\left[\left.\frac{\partial^2 f_t}{\partial \beta_i^2}\right|_{\beta=\beta_t}\right] &\approx h_{t,i} + \lambda_{t,i}, \end{aligned}$$

here $\lambda_{t,i} = \lambda_t \frac{N}{N_i}$ is a time-sensitive dimension-specific regularization factor (λ_t comes from adaptive regularization below). This leads us to

$$\eta_{t,i} = \frac{1}{(h_{t,i} + \lambda_{t,i})}\frac{[g_{t,i} + \lambda_{t,i}(\beta_{t,i} - \mu_i)]^2}{[v_{t,i} + 2\lambda_{t,i}(\beta_{t,i} - \mu_i)g_{t,i} + \lambda_{t,i}^2(\beta_{t,i} - \mu_i)^2]}.$$

Algorithm 1 Hyper-parameter Free Learning

Input: τ_{init}, e, α, λ_0
Data variables: $\beta_i, \bar{g}_i, \bar{v}_i, \bar{h}_i \leftarrow 0$, $\tau_i \leftarrow 1$, $\lambda \leftarrow \lambda_0$
for $t = 1$ to N **do**
  Draw a training sample
  for each dimension $i : x_{t,i} \neq 0$ **do**
    Calculate $g_i = \frac{\partial \ell_t}{\partial \beta_i}|_{\beta=\beta_t}$ and $h_i = \frac{\partial^2 \ell_t}{\partial \beta_i^2}|_{\beta=\beta_t}$
    $\bar{g}_i \leftarrow (1-\tau_i^{-1})\bar{g}_i + \tau_i^{-1} g_i$
    $\bar{v}_i \leftarrow (1-\tau_i^{-1})\bar{v}_i + \tau_i^{-1} g_i^2$
    $\bar{h}_i \leftarrow (1-\tau_i^{-1})\bar{h}_i + \tau_i^{-1} h_i$
    $\text{greg} \leftarrow \lambda_t(N/N_i)(\beta_i - \mu_i)$
    if $\tau_i < \tau_{\text{init}}$ **then**
      $\beta_i \leftarrow \beta_i - e(g_i + \text{greg})$
      $\tau_i \leftarrow \tau_i + 1$
    else
      $\text{ratio} \leftarrow (\bar{g}_i + \text{greg})^2/(\bar{v}_i + 2\bar{g}_i\text{greg} + g_{\text{reg}}^2)$
      $\eta_i \leftarrow \text{ratio}/(\bar{h}_i + \lambda_t(N/N_i))$
      $\beta_i \leftarrow \beta_i - \eta_i(g_i + \text{greg})$
      $\tau_i \leftarrow (1 - \text{ratio})\tau_i + 1$
    end if
  end for
  Draw a validation sample
  $\lambda_{t+1} = \lambda_t + \alpha\lambda_t \sum_{i=1}^{d} \frac{\partial \ell_t^{\text{val}}}{\partial \beta_i}|_{\beta=\beta_t} \beta_{t,i}$
end for

Robust Slow-Start Initialization.

Finally, we address one more limitation to the original NoPesky method, when applied to our context. The NoPesky method relies on a number of approximations that get increasingly better as it runs more updates. Unfortunately these approximations can be inaccurate in the initial stages of the training when there are few updates and the coefficients are far from the optimal solution. The original paper [14] proposed a slow-start method to process the first 0.1% of the data with a small constant learning rate in order to obtain a stable estimate of the running averages. While this method works well in their setting, where data have dense rows, it doesn't work well with data having sparse rows because many dimensions might not show up at all in the first 0.1% of the data samples!

Thus, we introduce an alternative slow-start method. We use a small learning rate (ϵ) for updates *in a particular dimension* until we have seen at least τ_{init} samples having *that dimension*. Effectively we use a fixed learning rate SGD algorithm for the first τ_{init} updates in a dimension, and only after that do we start to engage the NoPesky method. We set $\tau_{\text{init}} = 100$ and $e = 10^{-6}$ and use this for all of our experiments [5].

4.2 Adaptive Regularization

A common strategy for selecting optimal regularization weights is to perform a grid search: train multiple models using different regularization factors, and select the one that yields the best performance on the validation data. As dis-

[5]While the slow start mechanism does in fact create hyper-parameters, we found that the same settings work for a large class of similar problems (i.e., all sparse campaign data sets) and no tuning is needed once an appropriate configuration is found for that class

cussed above, this is time-consuming and prohibitive when training very large numbers of models.

Adaptive regularization [13] offers an alternative solution. It adapts the regularization factor iteratively on the validation data while learning the model on the training data. Adaptive regularization works with L^2-regularized models and can be integrated into an SGD algorithm. Instead of training multiple models with different but fixed regularization factors, with adaptive regularization we train one model with regularization factors that change over time. This is achieved by running a gradient descent algorithm on the regularization weight.

Adaptive regularization works as follows: alternatively draw one sample from the training data and one sample from the validation data then run the SGD update for the training sample. Let ℓ_t^{val} be the logistic loss function of the validation sample. Adaptive regularization then runs the following update

$$\lambda_{t+1} = \max\{\lambda_t + \alpha \sum_{i=1}^{d} \frac{\partial \ell_t^{\text{val}}}{\partial \beta_i}\bigg|_{\beta=\beta_t} \beta_{t,i}, 0\} \tag{12}$$

where α is a fixed learning rate. The max is necessary because we would like to keep the regularization factor always a non-negative quantity.

Dimension-Homogeneous Update.

There are a few undesirable features of the update in (12). First, it is difficult to choose a learning rate α that works well across multiple magnitudes of the regularization factor. Second, the need to truncate at 0 in (12) seems artificial. Finally, the dimension of the update equation doesn't match, because the dimension of $\frac{\partial \ell}{\partial \beta}\beta$ equals the dimension of ℓ, which is a logistic loss function and hence dimensionless. But λ is not dimensionless and has dimension (dimension of $\beta^2)^{-1}$ based on (4).

We fix the above issues by slightly modifying the update equation to

$$\lambda_{t+1} = \lambda_t + \alpha\lambda_t \sum_{i=1}^{d} \frac{\partial \ell_t^{\text{val}}}{\partial \beta_i}\bigg|_{\beta=\beta_t} \beta_{t,i}. \tag{13}$$

By inserting λ_t to the gradient term, we restored the dimension homogeneity of the update formula. We found this modified update formula performs more robustly in practice.

We illustrate adaptive regularization at work in Figure 1. In this example, we take a one-day sample from our training data stream (the *source* data defined in the previous section) and perform several training runs, with each one having a different initial starting point for the regularization factor. The plot shows the path that λ takes as the optimization sees more data. We see that all paths converge to the same factor, though the speed to convergence is sensitive to the initial starting point.

In practice, we set the fixed learning rate $\alpha = 0.001$. Because we will perform many updates on the regularization factor, and the model changes slowly around the optimal regularization factor, the performance of our model is not sensitive to the choice of this learning rate.

5. EMPIRICAL ANALYSIS

In this section we demonstrate empirically the improvements conferred by transfer learning, as well as the robustness of the "hands-free" design. The analysis is conducted experimentally across 100 different campaigns, across a wide variety of advertisers from different industries, with different base rates, and with different inherent predictability. A quick summary goes as follows: 1) using the transfer learning from section 3 achieves better results than not using transfer learning, and 2). doing this "hands-free" via the methods detailed in section 4 does not perform much worse than doing a full-blown grid search that is (at least) an order of magnitude less efficient. In all of these experiments, we report results on experiments conducted on data from individual campaigns, either in full detail or in aggregate. In every case, the source and target data sets used are specific to that particular campaign (as described above).

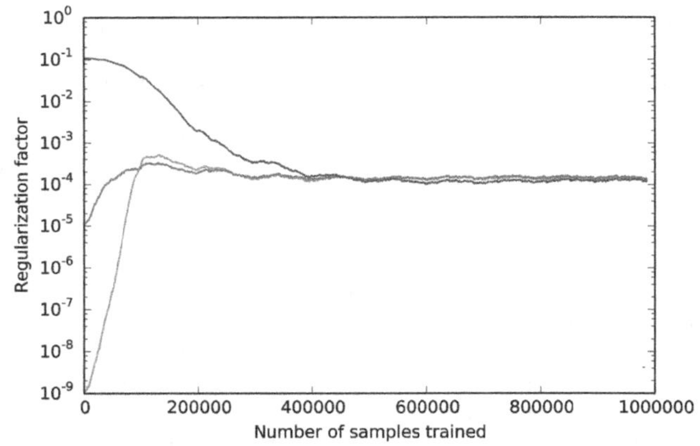

Figure 1: Adaptive regularization with dimension-homogeneous update formula (13) converges to the same regularization factor starting from a wide range of initial values.

5.1 Transfer and Hands-free Operation

Our first set of experiments was conducted on data from a single time frame spanning two time periods. We chose 100 advertisers and for each advertiser created 3 data sets: (1) a source data set D_0^S in period τ_0, (2) a target data set D_0^T in period τ_0, and (3) a target data set D_1^T in period τ_1. In this scenario periods τ_0 and τ_1 are disjoint but consecutive, and τ_0 and τ_1 span fourteen and seven days, respectively.

For this set of experiments we use a 2x2 factorial design for examining the modeling. One experimental factor is whether or not we use transfer learning. For the "Transfer Learning" variant we first learn a weight vector $\hat{\mu^s}$ using equation 2 on the source data D_0^S. We then use D_0^T, $\hat{\mu^s}$ and equation 3 to learn a source-domain-adapted model on the target data. For the "No Transfer" (control) variant, we again use D_0^T and equation 3 but without the informative prior $\hat{\mu^s}$. The second design factor represents how we tune the hyper-parameters when training the models. For the "Adaptive" variant, we use the adaptive regularization with the NoPesky learning rate schedule. For the "Grid Search" variant we use the AdaGrad learning rate formula and specifiy a fixed regularization weight. We search over a 4x9 grid of values, where we use all powers of ten between 10^0 and 10^{-3} for the initial AdaGrad learning rate and 10^2 to 10^{-6} for the regularization weight. In all training scenarios we

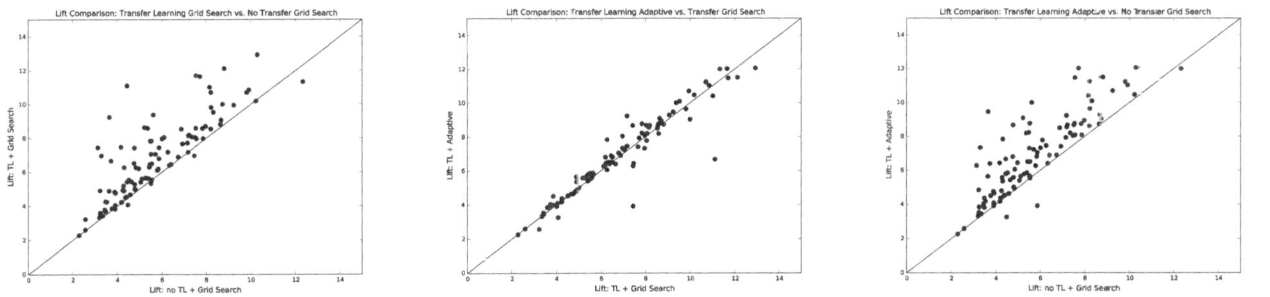

(a) (b) (c)

Figure 2: These plots show experimental results on 100 campaigns under different learning scenarios. Each point within each plot shows the lift evaluated on the same holdout set using the two methodologies listed. Plot (a) isolates the effect of using transfer learning vs. not using transfer learning using traditional grid-based hyper-parameter search for regularization and AdaGrad learning rates for both. We see that transfer learning almost always improves performance on the target data set. Plot (b) compares transfer learning using grid search vs. the hands-free methods we introduce in this paper. We see that hands-free is competitive with the more expensive approach. Plot (c) shows our main result, comparing transfer learning with adaptive learning vs. no transfer learning and traditional grid search. This combines methods from (a) and (b), and demonstrates the net performance effect from the integrated, enhanced method.

select hyper-parameters by splitting the training data into training and validation sets. We choose the hyper-parameter configuration that performs best on the validation set and then retrain on the entire training set using the selected hyper-parameters.

Figure 2 shows[6] the results of multiple tests on the different training scenarios. In figure 2 (a) we first establish that transfer learning improves performance under traditional hyper-parameter selection methods. In both axes, the models were trained using our Grid Search variant and the only difference is that transfer learning was used to produce the results in the vertical axis. Overall, we see that 91% of points fall above the identity line, meaning transfer learning improves performance for an overwhelming majority of cases.

In figure 2 (b) we hold the transfer learning variant constant and test whether our adaptive hyper-parameter selection strategies fare better or worse than traditional grid search. Overall we see a balanced and tight scatter around the identity line, with the exception of two campaigns. This suggests that in the context of our transfer learning strategy, adaptive hyper-parameter search is as effective as more traditional grid search methods. This is a powerful result, as it suggests we can indeed have a "hands-free" approach to training our models while keeping the training costs low. Our grid search optimization required 36 runs through the training data whereas the adaptive approach only takes one. In a more realistic setting, we may be able to reduce the grid space, but even then, we'd expect to still require 5-10 training runs to find an optimum. Thus, the adaptive approach significantly speeds up our ability to build transfer-enhanced models.

In figure 2 (c) we show the variants of transfer learning with adaptive hyper-parameter search against no transfer with grid search. This is our closest comparison between our proposed approach and what might be done without access to the source data. We see that 2 (a) and 2 (c) are qualitatively similar, with the difference being that (c) can be achieved up to 10 times faster because of the adaptive learning.

The results of these three comparisons are summarized in table 1. In each row we report the mean of differences when training according to the strategies specified in the first column. For AUC we measure the difference between the two strategies and for Lift we measure the ratio between the two. In our experimental design, we set our null hypothesis to be that using one variant produces no difference in performance over the other variant. We report the mean AUC difference and Lift ratio, in the 2nd and 5th columns, respectively (we take $1^{st} - 2^{nd}$ for AUC and $1^{st}/2^{nd}$ for lift). We also report the p-Values using a paired t-test on these statistics. If we think about these methods as global strategies for all campaigns, we can conclude with strong confidence that transfer learning improves campaigns on average and adaptive learning does not hurt.

5.2 Transfer and Incremental Training

In this set of experiments we explore a scenario that reflects an additional aspect of production training and model use at a firm like Dstillery. In particular, data arrives incrementally and continually from the moment a new campaign is initiated until it runs its course, and (hopefully) is replaced by a new campaign.

Since SGD trains via incremental updates, it can run naturally as an incremental learning system. For a given campaign, at any point in time we have a targeting model that has been trained using all data available up until that point; this model will then be used to target the following time period's ads. We simulate this process by creating daily samples from the advertising system for each campaign, and then incrementally updating the campaign's model using some experimental learning-algorithm variant.

[6] Note that all 3 plots in figure 2 evaluate generalization performance using lift. Using AUC instead shows the same results qualitatively. See Table 1 for summary results.

	AUC Diff. Mean	AUC Diff. % > 0	AUC Diff. p-Value	Lift Ratio Mean	Lift Ratio % >1	Lift Ratio p-Value
Transfer:Grid vs. No Transfer: Grid	2.07	86%	$< 10e^{-6}$	1.22	91%	$< 10e^{-6}$
Transfer:Adapt vs. Transfer: Grid	-0.30	50%	0.15	1.01	65%	0.09
Transfer:Adapt vs. No Transfer: Grid	1.77	80%	$< 10e^{-6}$	1.23	93%	$< 10e^{-6}$

Table 1: Each row in this table is a comparison of two methods on the 100 campaigns shown in figure 2. The table reports the mean difference of AUC (on a 100 point scale) between the first and second variants (listed in the first column) and the mean ratio of Lift for the first variant over the second variant across all the campaigns. The p-Values are a result of paired t-tests under the null hypothesis that the mean AUC difference = 0 and mean Lift ratio = 1. The columns labeled '%>k' show the number of campaigns where the metric reported was strictly greater than k. These results show that transfer learning overall improves the performance (over not using it) and that the hands-free learning does not substantially reduce predictive performance.

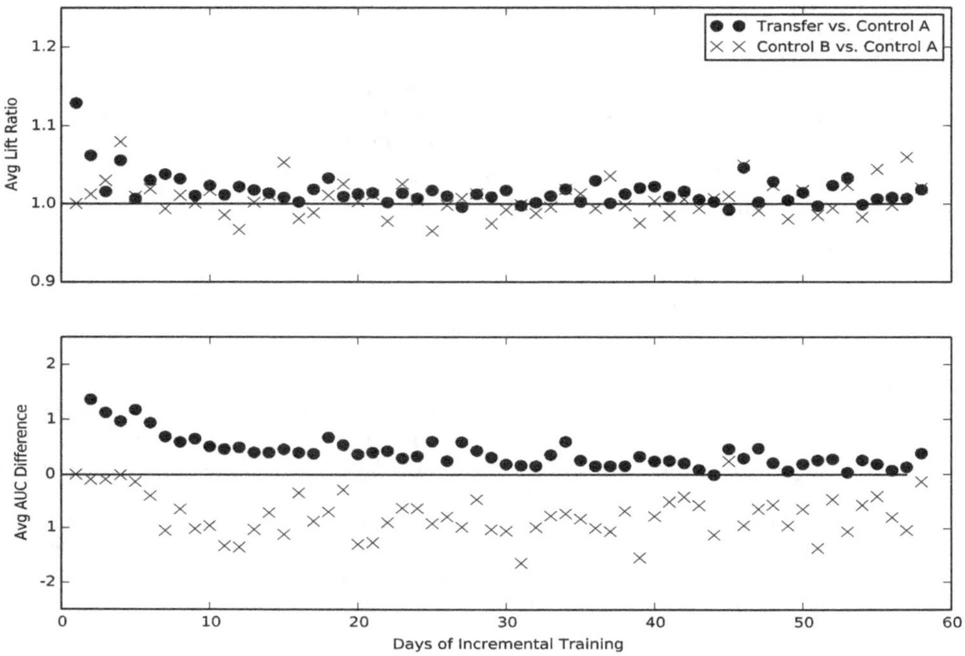

Figure 3: This figure shows the comparative results for three strategies for incremental training. For each day of analysis we initialize a model from the prior day, train on campaign data for the specified day and evaluate on campaign data for the following day. We explore 3 modeling strategies (Transfer Learning, Control A with no prior and Control B with previous day's model as a prior). Each point compares either Transfer Learning or Control B variants to the Control A variant.

We then evaluate the resultant model on the following day's sample.

We explore three variants in this set of experiments: (1) "Transfer Learning" – using equation 3 with $\hat{\mu^s}$ derived from the source data;[7] (2) "Control A" – equation 3 with $\hat{\mu^s} = 0$ (the standard regularization case), and (3) "Control B" – equation 3 with $\hat{\mu^s}$ specified as the prior day's model. This final "Control B" variant is the methodology used by [4], and is the method most similar to our work in design.[8] For each variant, on each day, we train on just the given day's data using the chosen prior with adaptive regularization and optimize using SGD with the NoPesky adaptive learning rates. When performing incremental updates using SGD, we found that performance generally improves when each day's model is initialized with the prior day's model and that the state of all parameters used to compute the learning rate are persisted and carried over to the next day (let's call this the 'warm start').

[7] In this set of experiments we learn one estimate of $\hat{\mu^s}$ for each campaign and hold that fixed throughout the 60 days of training.

[8] The work by [4] was not explicitly attempting knowledge transfer, but can be interpreted as an instance of Bayesian transfer, like ours except transferring across time periods.

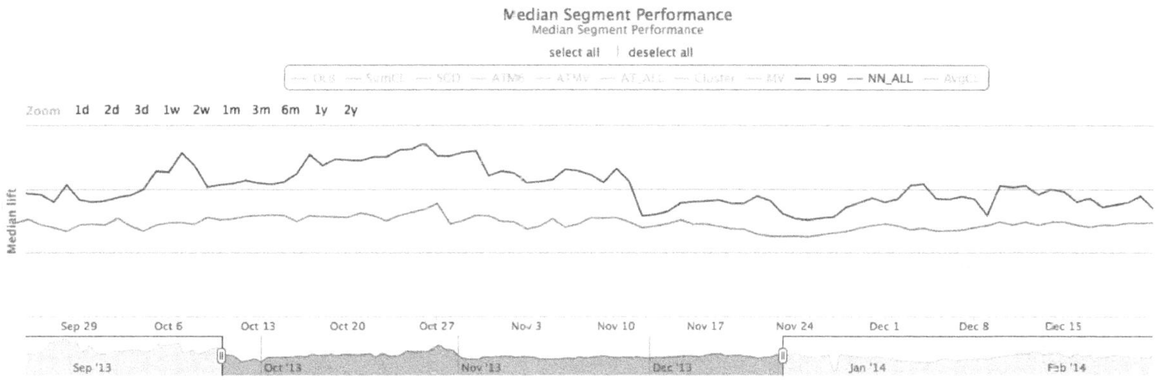

Figure 4: Snapshot of the Dstillery KPI dashboard showing median lift over an internal baseline across all active campaigns. The 'L99' line is the median Lift KPI of our transfer learning algorithm across all campaigns. The 'NN-ALL' line is the median Lift KPI across all campaigns of all of our learning algorithms combined.

Figure 3 shows aggregated results of running incremental training with daily performance evaluation across 30 randomly sampled campaigns from our production system (sampled with the one constraint that the target data had at least 5 post-impression conversions for each day of analysis). In the top chart we show the average relative Lift ratio between the variants Transfer Learning and Control B over Control A. In the bottom chart we show the average difference in AUC. Thus, in each chart a black dot above the reference line means that Transfer Learning outperformed Control A for that time period. An "X" above the line means that Control B outperformed Control A for that time period. A black dot above an "X" means that Transfer Learning outperformed Control B for that time period. And vice versa. From these results we can see multiple effects: (1) when comparing to Control A, the postive effect of transfer learning wears off over time; (2) when comparing to Control A, the transfer learning benefit is more pronounced for AUC than for Lift, although for both metrics there is a general benefit, and (3) Control B tends to underperform both variants, and this is more dramatic in AUC.

The first trend mentioned above is something we ought to expect - as more data is introduced into the system, and because the models do have some form of a memory built into them, we should expect the weights learned just with the target data will start to converge toward an optimal point. The second trend can possibly be explained by different properties of the metrics themselves. In general, Lift can be a very high variance metric in data scenarios with a low absolute number of positive outcomes. This variance comes from both (i) the model, because it is more difficult to fit the tails of the distribution, and (ii) the evaluation itself: since we are updating the models one day at a time, we have less target data per model-building and evaluation step and this increases the expected variance. As a policy, we always review both AUC and Lift, even though Lift is the more appropriate metric.

The third trend mentioned above might be the most unexpected (to us at least), and the sub-optimality of Control B warranted additional analysis. Figure 5 shows the average L2-norm of the weight vectors β learned for each variant for each day. The general trend we see is that the average

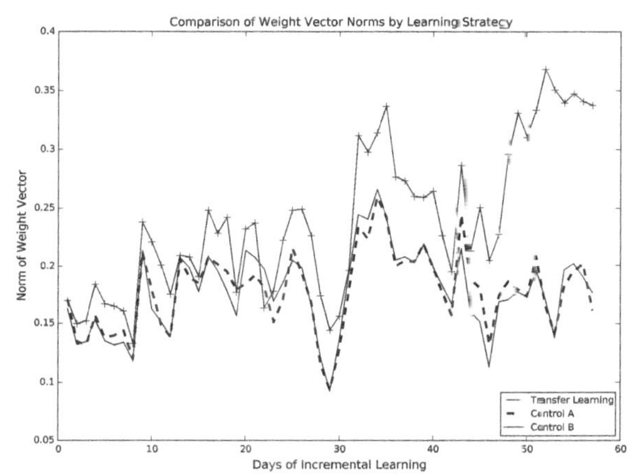

Figure 5: Average L2-norms for the models aggregated and reported in figure 3

norm of weight vectors trained using the Control B variant is bigger than that of the other two. This trend is likely an artifact of regularizing towards existing models. The issue is two-fold and manifests from the fact that the regularization prior is a moving target. Over time, the weight vector gets closer to an optimal solution and this often coincides with an increasing norm. Eventually the process begins to overfit the data and the regularization is too restrictive to let the model escape from a specific solution. Also, this regularization strategy makes it difficult to escape optimization valleys in non-stationary data. The NoPesky learning rate schedule has a built-in method for adapting to changing data distributions (i.e., by "forgetting" most of the past), but forgetting the past is difficult when the regularizer forces the model to remember it. Thus, the Transfer Learning prior might be better in our application because it doesn't increase over time and is biased enough to avoid overfitting. It is anchored close enough to a specific day's optimal solution to be useful but not too close that it over-fits in a generally noisy learning environment.

5.3 Production Performance

As additional, auxiliary support that the hands-free transfer method works well, we present its actual production performance. In the experiments above, we took care to control for the different factors that affect performance on a hold-out set so that we could isolate the different effects of our design choices. Once released 'into the wild' there are many elements that prevent a pure apples-to-apples comparison (when not doing a pure A/B test on them). Nonetheless, we find in particular that our implementation of hands-free transfer learning is in aggregate our best-performing learning method.

Figure 4 shows a screen shot taken from our internal KPI dashboard. We benchmark every targeting algorithm for every campaign against a default baseline that runs as part of the campaign. We normalize the conversion rates of each algorithm in each campaign against its respective baseline and call this our "Lift KPI." Figure 4 here shows the median Lift KPI across all campaigns for the fourth quarter of 2013. The top line (called 'L99'[9]) represents our transfer learning algorithms in action. The bottom line (called 'NN-ALL') is a blend of all our algorithms combined. While this 'L99' group might not perform best for every campaign, in general it is our best and demonstrably performs well above average across all campaigns. Many of the fluctuations in relative performance between these two lines are driven by the internal campaign allocation optimizations of the system. Each campaign starts with a set of competing algorithms. As we get live feedback we reallocate impressions to the better performing algorithms until the algorithm's performance converges to the mean of the campaign. Thus, as with production numbers generally, these should not be taken as an exact comparison between algorithms under identical conditions.

6. CONCLUSION AND DISCUSSION

We have presented a set of techniques that when applied together present a robust and scalable solution to several challenges often encountered in online display advertising. Our transfer learning approach shares intuition with prior work [1], [8], in that one can look outside of the target data set for sources of signal that can be passed to the target problem. An advantage to our formulation is that (in retrospect) it is very straightforward, which is a virtue when designing and implementing large-scale, completely automated machine learning systems. Our focus here is on producing a scalable, accurate, and robust system. We have achieved that through the combination of Bayesian transfer learning and the extension and integration of methods for adaptive, parameter-free learning. Looking forward, adaptive regularization is a recently developed strategy and more research needs to be done to understand its performance bounds and general limitations. On the transfer learning side, the effectiveness of the strategy depends on specifying an appropriate prior. This work presents a straightforward mechanism for how to transfer; more sophisticated methods could increase the advantages from inductive transfer. Additionally, within this framework, understanding *when* to transfer is necessary for developing a fully robust solution.

[9]We often use obscure terminology to refer to our internal products

7. REFERENCES

[1] D. Agarwal, R. Agrawal, R. Khanna, and N. Kota. Estimating rates of rare events with multiple hierarchies through scalable log-linear models. In *Proceedings of the 16th ACM SIGKDD international conference on Knowledge discovery and data mining*, pages 213–222. ACM, 2010.

[2] A. Arnold, R. Nallapati, and W. W. Cohen. Exploiting feature hierarchy for transfer learning in named entity recognition. In *ACL*, pages 245–253, 2008.

[3] M. Broadie, A. Zeevi, and D. Cicek. Multidimensional Stochastic Approximation: Adaptive Algorithms and Applications. 2013.

[4] O. Chapelle, E. Manavoglu, and R. Rosales. Simple and scalable response prediction for display advertising. *Transactions on Intelligent Systems and Technology*, 2013.

[5] C. Chelba and A. Acero. Adaptation of maximum entropy capitalizer: Little data can help a lot. *Computer Speech & Language*, 20(4):382–399, 2006.

[6] J. Duchi, E. Hazan, and Y. Singer. Adaptive subgradient methods for online learning and stochastic optimization. *The Journal of Machine Learning Research*, pages 2121–2159, 2011.

[7] Interactive Advertising Bureau. Q3 2013 earnings press release. `http://www.iab.net`.

[8] Y. Liu, S. Pandey, D. Agarwal, and V. Josifovski. Finding the right consumer: optimizing for conversion in display advertising campaigns. In *Proceedings of the fifth ACM international conference on Web search and data mining*, pages 473–482. ACM, 2012.

[9] H. B. McMahan, G. Holt, D. Sculley, M. Young, D. Ebner, J. Grady, L. Nie, T. Phillips, E. Davydov, D. Golovin, S. Chikkerur, D. Liu, M. Wattenberg, A. M. Hrafnkelsson, T. Boulos, and J. Kubica. Ad click prediction: a view from the trenches. In *KDD '13: Proceedings of the 19th ACM SIGKDD international conference on Knowledge discovery and data mining*, pages 1222–1230, New York, New York, USA, Aug. 2013. ACM Request Permissions.

[10] S. J. Pan and Q. Yang. A survey on transfer learning. *Knowledge and Data Engineering, IEEE Transactions on*, 22(10):1345–1359, 2010.

[11] C. Perlich, B. Dalessandro, T. Raeder, O. Stitelman, and F. Provost. Machine learning for targeted display advertising: Transfer learning in action. *Machine Learning*, pages 1–25, 2013.

[12] R. Raina, A. Y. Ng, and D. Koller. Constructing informative priors using transfer learning. In *Proceedings of the 23rd international conference on Machine learning*, pages 713–720. ACM, 2006.

[13] S. Rendle. Learning recommender systems with adaptive regularization. In *Proceedings of the fifth ACM international conference on Web search and data mining*, pages 133–142. ACM, 2012.

[14] T. Schaul, S. Zhang, and Y. LeCun. No more pesky learning rates. *arXiv preprint arXiv:1206.1106*, 2012.

[15] W. Xu. Towards optimal one pass large scale learning with averaged stochastic gradient descent. *arXiv preprint arXiv:1107.2490*, 2011.

[16] M. D. Zeiler. ADADELTA: An Adaptive Learning Rate Method. *arXiv preprint arXiv:1212.5701*, 2012.

Correlating Events with Time Series for Incident Diagnosis

Chen Luo*
Jilin University
rackingroll@163.com

Jian-Guang Lou
Microsoft Research
jlou@microsoft.com

Qingwei Lin
Microsoft Research
qlin@microsoft.com

Qiang Fu
Microsoft Research
qifu@microsoft.com

Rui Ding
Microsoft Research
juding@microsoft.com

Dongmei Zhang
Microsoft Research
dongmeiz@microsoft.com

Zhe Wang
Jilin University
wz2000@jlu.edu.cn

ABSTRACT

As online services have more and more popular, incident diagnosis has emerged as a critical task in minimizing the service downtime and ensuring high quality of the services provided. For most online services, incident diagnosis is mainly conducted by analyzing a large amount of telemetry data collected from the services at runtime. Time series data and event sequence data are two major types of telemetry data. Techniques of correlation analysis are important tools that are widely used by engineers for data-driven incident diagnosis. Despite their importance, there has been little previous work addressing the correlation between two types of heterogeneous data for incident diagnosis: continuous time series data and temporal event data. In this paper, we propose an approach to evaluate the correlation between time series data and event data. Our approach is capable of discovering three important aspects of event-timeseries correlation in the context of incident diagnosis: existence of correlation, temporal order, and monotonic effect. Our experimental results on simulation data sets and two real data sets demonstrate the effectiveness of the algorithm.

Keywords

Correlation, Incident Diagnosis, Two-sample Problem

1. INTRODUCTION

The research in this paper is motivated by a real-world application in incident investigation of online services[20]. Unlike traditional shrink-wrapped software, online service systems are designed to run continuously and be available all time(24x7). However, during the operation of an online service, live-site service incidents (unplanned interruption/outage of the service) are often unavoidable, and can lead to significant economic loss or other serious consequences. For example, many reputable online services such as those provided by Amazon, Google, and Citrix have experienced live-site incidents during the past couple of years [1, 14]. In order to minimize service downtime caused by service incidents, much effort has been invested in improving the efficiency of service-incident diagnosis.

Diagnosis of service incidents mainly depends on analyzing the telemetry data collected at the runtime of the service [20]. Unlike a desktop application, the back-end system of an online service is often a large-scale distributed system. It is usually impractical to attach a debugger to the service to investigate service incidents. In most online systems, data analysis is the only way for engineers to diagnose service incidents. Telemetry data such as service-level logs, performance counters, and machine/process/service-level events can often provide enough information for incident diagnosis. Most telemetry data can be grouped into two categories: continuous time series data and temporal event data. A time series is a sequence of real-valued data points, measured typically at successive time points equally spaced with a uniform time interval. A typical example of time series in an online service system is the performance counter of CPU usage. An event sequence in an online service is used to record the occurrences of a specific software message indicating that something has happened in the system, e.g., an event sequence of "Out of memory" contains events of "Out of memory", which occur when there is not enough memory in the system.

Among all data-driven techniques for incident diagnosis, correlation analysis between telemetry data and system states plays a very important role [7] because correlation relationships often provide hints for causality analysis. Although the correlated metrics may not exactly be the root causes of incidents, they could be intermediate useful information that pinpoints the root causes. In practice, engineers usually start their incident investigation by searching for a small set of system metrics that are correlated to the Key Performance Indicators (KPI) of the service (Here, a KPI is an indicator that can be used to manifest system's health state, e.g., service availability or request latency) [9].

---

*This work is conducted during his internship at Microsoft Research.

KDD'14, August 24–27, 2014, New York, NY, USA.

ACM 978-1-4503-2956-9/14/08 ...$15.00.
http://dx.doi.org/10.1145/2623330.2623374.

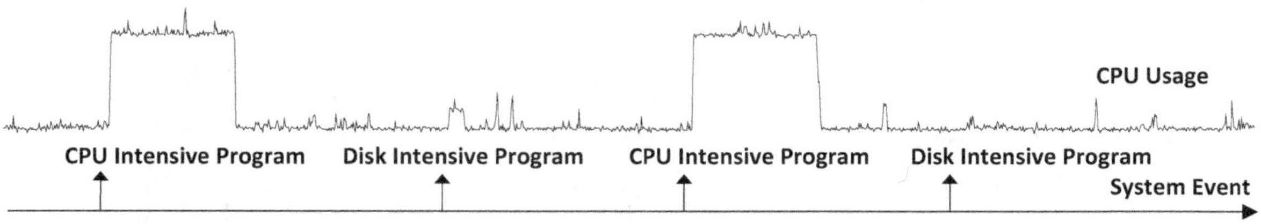

Figure 1: The relationships between CPU usage and two system tasks (*disk intensive task* and *CPU intensive task*)

Because of the importance of correlation analysis, a lot of tools have been built to analyze the correlation between time series [32] and the correlation between system events [18, 17, 2]. However, how to evaluate the correlation between a time series and an event sequence is still not well studied. Because of the heterogeneous property of these two types of data, traditional correlation analysis, such as Pearson correlation and Spearman correlation [8], often cannot provide satisfying results. Furthermore, in a large-scale system, an occurrence of an event may be related to a change of a time series during a time period rather than a point-to-point corresponding relationship in the traditional correlation analysis techniques.

In this paper, we propose an approach to evaluate the correlation between a time series and an event sequence. Motivated by the real requirement of incident management, our correlation technique tries to answer the following three questions: a. Are they correlated? b. What is the delay relationship between them? c. What is the monotonic effect between them (refer to Section 2 for the definition of monotonic effect)? In the context of service incident management, the answers to these questions can provide rich information to engineers for incident diagnosis. We formulate the correlation problem as a two-sample problem [21], and then use the nearest neighbors method to evaluate the existence of the correlation. At the same time, we identify temporal relationships and monotonic effects by analyzing the relationships between sub-series before and after the occurrence of each event(refer to Section 2).

The contributions of this paper are as follows:

1. Motivated by real applications, we articulate the correlation problem as the aforementioned three questions. To the best of our knowledge, this is the first attempt to evaluate the three aspects of correlation between a time series and an event sequence for incident diagnosis.

2. We formulate the correlation problem as a two-sample problem, and propose a novel framework to resolve the problem.

3. The experiments on simulated data and real data from Microsoft services show the effectiveness of our method.

The rest of the paper is organized as follows: The problem statement and formulation are introduced in Section 2. We propose our approach in Section 3. The Empirical evaluation is shown in Section 4. In Section 5, we introduce some related works. Finally, we conclude our work in Section 6.

2. PROBLEM STATEMENT AND FORMULATION

2.1 Problem Statement

In statistics, correlation is any statistical relationship between two random variables in which random variables do not satisfy a mathematical condition of probabilistic independence. Let us give an example first to demonstrate the correlation between event data and the time series data. Fig. 2 shows two types of events (e.g., starting a *disk intensive program and a CPU intensive program*) and a time series (e.g., *a performance counter of CPU Usage*). Every time a *CPU intensive program* starts, the performance counter of *CPU Usage* will increase significantly. On the other hand, the value of *CPU Usage* does not have any specific pattern related to the starting events of *a disk intensive program*. As a result, we can say that the starting events of *the CPU intensive program* and the performance counter of *CPU Usage* have a correlating relationship, while there is no correlation between the starting events of *a disk intensive program* and the *CPU Usage*. Such kind of correlation analysis is an important step for incident diagnosis [9, 6].

In incident diagnosis scenarios, engineers typically study the following three aspects of the correlation among telemetric data when they are investigating service incidents.

- **Existence of Dependency.** Is there a correlation between an event sequence and a time series? Although statistical correlation is not sufficient to demonstrate the presence of a causal relationship, it is still quite useful for incident diagnosis because it can often provide hints to engineers for causal analysis.

- **Temporal Order of Dependency.** Given a pair of dependent data streams, the direction of the correlation is useful information in causal analysis [23]. The temporal order of the occurrence often provides information about the cause-effect direction in the context of incident diagnosis. For example, for a given dependent pair: an event sequence E and a time series S, if events in E always occur before corresponding significant changes of S, we can often propose a hypothesis that E might be related to a cause of the changes of S, and then take actions to verify this hypothesis based on other aspects of data from the service system.

- **Monotonic Effect of Dependency.** In many cases, some event occurrence is related to a significant value-increase (or value-decrease) of a time series. Such a positive (or negative) monotonic effect between two dependent data streams is also a very important property of correlation for causal inference [30]. For example, during diagnosis, our domain knowledge tells us that significant increase of CPU usage may cause the service to violate its quality SLA (Service Level Agreement) but the decreases of CPU usage should not.

Given an event sequence (or event type) denoted as E, the timestamps of the events are denoted as $T_E = (t_1, t_2, \cdots, t_n)$, where n is the number of events that happened. A time series, denoted as $S = (s_1, s_2, \cdots, s_m)$, where m is the number of points in the time series. Unlike the timestamps of an event sequence, the timestamps of a time series, denoted as $T_S = (t(s_1), t(s_2), \cdots, t(s_n))$, have the relationship of $t(s_i) = t(s_{i-1}) + \tau$, where τ is the sampling interval.

Here, we assume that each time series has an even sampling interval, which is true in many applications. In our analysis, we also assume that the effect of an event on a time series only lasts a certain time interval that is very small compared to the total lasting time of the time series. This assumption is valid in a real-world online service system which is in a normal and healthy state most of the time. Any incident will be resolved soon after its occurrence by the system operation team.

As mentioned before, if an event type E and a time series S have a correlation relationship, every time an event E happens, there is a corresponding change of the time series S. The potential temporal relationships between an occurrence of an event $e_i \in E$ and its corresponding change of the time series are illustrated in Fig. 2. Here, each change is represented as a sub-series of S.

Supposing $\ell_k^{rear}(S, e_i)$ denotes a sub-series of S after e_i happens with length of k, and $\ell_k^{front}(S, e_i)$ denotes a sub-series of S before the e_i happens. Intuitively, if event E does not correlate to time series S, then both $\ell_k^{rear}(S, e_i)$ and $\ell_k^{front}(S, e_i)$ $(i = 1 \cdots n)$ are not related to the occurrences of e_i. In other words, the sub-series $\Gamma^{front} = \{\ell_k^{front}(S, e_i), i = 1 \cdots n\}$ (or $\Gamma^{rear} = \{\ell_k^{rear}(S, e_i), i = 1 \cdots n\}$)are not statistically different from other sub-series with length of k (denoted as Θ) that are randomly sampled from S. On the other hand, if there is a correlation relationship between E and S, the sub-series $\Gamma^{front} = \{\ell_k^{front}(S, e_i), i = 1 \cdots n\}$ (or $\Gamma^{rear} = \{\ell_k^{rear}(S, e_i), i = 1 \cdots n\}$) will be statistically different from the randomly sampled sub-series Θ.

Based on this information, we have the following definitions.

DEFINITION 1. *An event sequence E and a time series S are correlated and E often occurs after the changes of S (denoted as $S \to E$), if and only if the probabilistic distribution of $\{\ell_k^{front}(S, e_i), i = 1 \cdots n\}$ is statistically different from the randomly sampled sub-series Θ.*

DEFINITION 2. *An event sequence E and a time series S are correlated and E often occurs before the changes of S (denoted as $E \to S$), if and only if the probabilistic distribution of $\{\ell_k^{rear}(S, e_i), i = 1 \cdots n\}$ is statistically different from the randomly sampled sub-series Θ and the probabilistic distribution of $\{\ell_k^{front}(S, e_i), i = 1 \cdots n\}$ is not statistically different from Θ.*

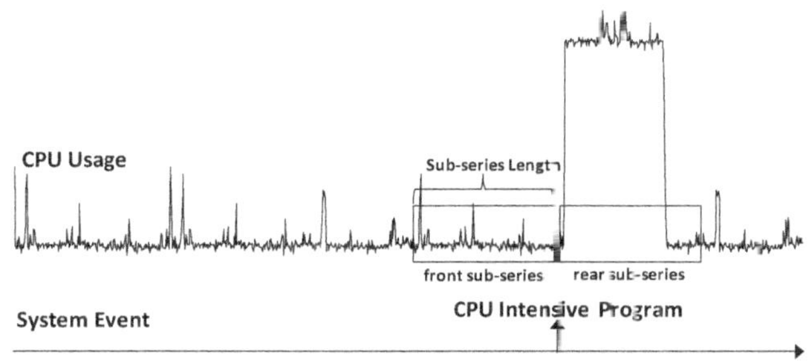

Figure 2: Example of front sub-series and rear-series

DEFINITION 3. *An event sequence E and a time series S are correlated (denoted as $E \sim S$), if there is a relationship of $E \to S$ or $S \to E$.*

DEFINITION 4. *If $E \to S$ (or $S \to E$) and the event occurrences of E are related to significant value-increases of S, we denote the correlation as $E \xrightarrow{+} S$ (or $S \xrightarrow{+} E$). If $E \to S$ (or $S \to E$) and the event occurrences of E are related to significant value-decrease of S, we denote the correlation as $E \xrightarrow{-} S$ (or $S \xrightarrow{-} E$).*

2.2 Modeling as a Two-Sample Problem

Based on the above definitions, our correlation analysis problem can be transformed to a multivariate two-sample hypothesis-testing problem. Two-sample tests are commonly used when checking whether two samples come from the same underlying distribution, which is assumed to be unknown. In our context, one sample is the set Γ^{front} or Γ^{rear}, the other sample is Θ that is the set of sub-series randomly sampled from S. Each data point is actually a sub-series, which can be represented as a vector of k dimensions. Therefore, the original problem becomes a multivariate two-sample test.

Here, we use one set Γ^{front} and Θ as our example. Let Γ^{front} and Θ be independent random samples generated from unknown distributions F and G, respectively. The distributions are assumed to be absolutely continuous with respect to Lebesgue measure. Their densities are denoted as f and g, respectively. The hypotheses of the two-sample test can be stated as follows:

$$\begin{cases} H_0 & : \quad F = G \\ H_1 & : \quad F \neq G \end{cases} \tag{1}$$

If H_1 is true, that means the probabilistic distribution of Γ^{front} is statistically different from the randomly sampled sub-series Θ. In addition, as Definition 1, time series S and event E are correlated. Otherwise, if H_0 is true, then time series S and event E may not be correlated.

3. THE APPROACH

In this section, we propose a nearest-neighbor based method algorithm to analyze the three aspects of correlation, and then analyze the complexity of the proposed approach.

3.1 Nearest Neighbor Method

Multivariate two-sample tests have been of continuous interest to the statistics community. Several different algorithms of this kind have been proposed [10, 21, 28]. To utilize some structure based distance measures such as DTW [4] or DTW-D [5], we apply the nearest neighbor statistic based method [28] in our scenario. It is worth pointing out that, other two-sample tests algorithms [10, 21] can also be used in our method.

In this subsection, we take Γ^{front} as an example. Given the two samples $\Gamma^{front} = \{\ell_k^{front}(S, e_i), i = 1 \cdots n\}$ and $\Theta = \{\theta_1, \theta_2, \cdots, \theta_{\tilde{n}}\}$, and the pooled sample by $Z = \Gamma \cup \Theta$, we label the pooled sample as $Z_1, \cdots, Z_p$ with $p = n + \tilde{n}$ where

$$Z_i = \begin{cases} \ell_k^{front}(S, e_i), & if\, i = 1, \cdots, n \\ \theta_{i-n}, & if\, i = n+1, \cdots, p. \end{cases} \tag{2}$$

For a finite set of sub-series A and a sub-series $x \in A$, let $NN_r(x, A)$ denote the r-th nearest neighbor of x within the set $\{A \backslash x\}$. For two mutually exclusive subsets A_1, A_2 and a point $x \in A$, we define an indicator function:

$$I_r(x, A_1, A_2) = \begin{cases} 1, & if\, x \in A_i \,\&\&\, NN_r(x, A) \in A_i, \\ 0, & otherwise. \end{cases} \tag{3}$$

The function $I_r(x, A_1, A_2)$ indicates whether x and its r-th nearest neighbor in $A \backslash x$ belong to the same subset.

In our problem, the nearest-neighbor based tests rely on the following quantity and its generalizations:

$$T_{r,p} = \frac{1}{pr} \sum_{i=1}^{p} \sum_{j=1}^{r} I_j(x, A_1, A_2) \tag{4}$$

Here, $p = |n + \tilde{n}|$ is the size of the sample. The test statistic $T_{r,p}$ is the proportion of pairs containing two sub-series from the same sample, among all pairs formed by a sample sub-series and one of its nearest neighbors in the pooled sample Z. Intuitively $T_{r,p}$ is small under the null hypothesis when the two samples are mixed well, while $T_{r,p}$ is large when the two underlying distributions are different.

Then, as in [28], when p is large enough, $(pr)^{1/2}(T_{r,p} - \mu_r)/\sigma_r$ obeys a standard Gaussian distribution with the following parameters:

$$\mu_r = (\lambda_1)^2 + (\lambda_2)^2 \tag{5}$$

and

$$\sigma_r^2 = \lambda_1\lambda_2 + 4\lambda_1^2\lambda_2^2 \tag{6}$$

where $\lambda_1 = n/p$ and $\lambda_2 = \tilde{n}/p$. The traditional Gaussian distribution test, Γ^{front} and Θ are significantly different when: $(pr)^{1/2}(T_{r,p} - \mu_r)/\sigma_r^2 > \alpha$, where $\alpha = 1.96$ for $P = 0.025$ (or $\alpha = 2.58$ for $P = 0.001$). For more about the hypothesis test in a Gaussian distribution, please refer to [15].

3.2 Mining Existence and Temporal Order

According to the definitions in Section 2, we can summarize that if event E and time series S are correlated, the following statement must be true: the front sub-series Γ^{front} and randomly sampled sub-series Θ are statistically different; or the rear sub-series Γ^{rear} and randomly sampled sub-series Θ is statistically different. In our approach, we use the above nearest-neighbor method to determine whether two sets of sub-series have an identical distribution.

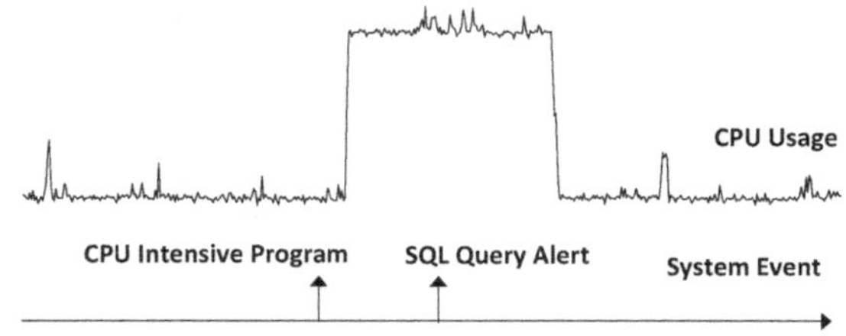

Figure 3: Example of temporal order, *CPU intensive program → CPU usage* and *CPU usage → query alert*

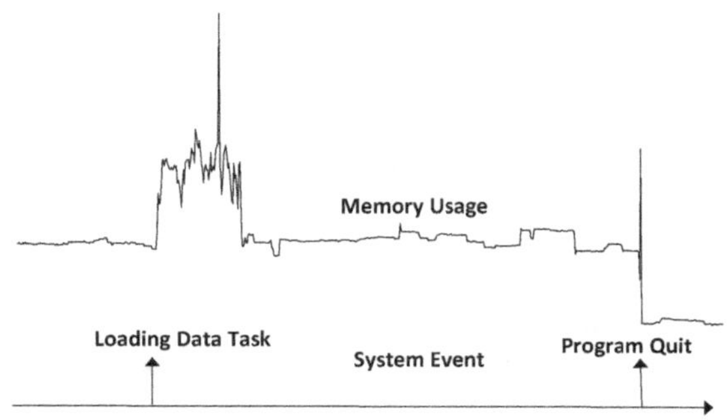

Figure 4: Effect examples: *loading data task* $\xrightarrow{+}$ *memory* and *program exiting* $\xrightarrow{-}$ *memory*

If the front sub-series Γ^{front} and randomly sampled sub-series Θ are statistically different, then $S \rightarrow E$. Otherwise, if the rear sub-series Γ^{rear} and Θ is statistically different, then $E \rightarrow S$. Fig. 3 shows an example of Correlation Temporal Order. From Fig. 3, we can see CPU Intensive Program → CPU Usage, and CPU Usage → SQL Query Alert.

3.3 Mining Effect Type

As explained in Definition 4, in order to determine the monotonic effects such as $E \xrightarrow{+} S$ (or $E \xrightarrow{-} S$) of correlation, we need to check whether there exists a significant value increase (or decrease) on the time series S after an event E happens. Similarly, it can also be formulated as a problem of statistical hypotheses testing. In this research, we use $t - test$ [15] to check whether there is a significant value increase (or decrease) from Γ^{front} to Γ^{rear}.

Here, the t_{score} between Γ^{front} and Γ^{rear} can be calculated by the following equation:

$$t_{score} = \frac{\mu_{\Gamma^{front}} - \mu_{\Gamma^{rear}}}{\sqrt{\frac{(n_1-1)\sigma^2_{\Gamma^{front}} + (n_2-1)\sigma^2_{\Gamma^{rear}}}{n_1+n_2-2}\left(\frac{1}{n_1} - \frac{1}{n_2}\right)}} \tag{7}$$

Algorithm 1: The Overall Algorithm

Input: Event $E = (e_1, e_2, ..., e_n)$, and Time Series $S = (s_1, s_2, ..., s_m)$, and the sub-series length k.
Output: The correlation flag C, the direction D, and the effect type T

Initialize Γ^{front} and Γ^{rear};
Initialize Θ;
Initialize $R = false$, $D = NULL$, $T = NULL$;
Normalize each $\ell_k^{front}(S, e_i)$ and $\ell_k^{rear}(S, e_i)$.;
Test Γ^{front} and Θ using Nearest Neighbors Method. The result is denoted as D_f.;
Test Γ^{rear} and Θ using Nearest Neighbors Method. The result is denoted as D_r.;
if $(D_r == true \&\& D_f == false)$ **then**
  $R = true$.;
  Calculate t_{score} using Equation (8).;
  if $(t_{score} > \alpha)$ **then**
    $T = E \overset{-}{\rightarrow} S$.;
  else if $(t_{score} < -\alpha)$ **then**
    $T = E \overset{+}{\rightarrow} S$.;
else if $(D_r == false \&\& D_f == true) \,||\, (D_r == true \&\& D_f == true)$ **then**
  $R = true$.;
  Calculate t_{score} using Equation (8).;
  if $(t_{score} > \alpha)$ **then**
    $T = S \overset{-}{\rightarrow} E$.;
  else if $(t_{score} < -\alpha)$ **then**
    $T = S \overset{+}{\rightarrow} E$.;
Out put R, D and T;
Algorithm End.

where $\mu_{\Gamma^{front}}$ and $\mu_{\Gamma^{rear}}$ are the mean values of Γ^{front} and Γ^{rear}. $\sigma_{\Gamma^{front}}$ and $\sigma_{\Gamma^{rear}}$ are their variance values. In our research, $n_1 = n_2 = n$, and n is the event number in E, thus Equation 7 can be reduced to:

$$t_{score} = \frac{\mu_{\Gamma^{front}} - \mu_{\Gamma^{rear}}}{\sqrt{\frac{\sigma^2_{\Gamma^{front}} + \sigma^2_{\Gamma^{rear}}}{n}}} \quad (8)$$

Then, if $t_{score} > \alpha$, we have a negative monotonic effect (e.g, $E \overset{-}{\rightarrow} S$ or $S \overset{-}{\rightarrow} E$); and if $t_{score} < -\alpha$, we have a positive monotonic effect (e.g., $E \overset{+}{\rightarrow} S$ or $S \overset{+}{\rightarrow} E$) Here, $\alpha = 1.96$ for $P = 0.025$ (or $\alpha = 2.58$ for $P = 0.001$) [15].

At the same time, for a given α,if $|t_{score}| < \alpha$, we cannot determine the effect type with a high level of confidence. However, such situations are seldom found in the real scenarios of incident diagnosis. Most services have be designed with a large certain margin to fault-tolerate. When a service incident is detected, the corresponding time-series must have a significant difference from its normal behavior (i.e., $t_{score} > \alpha$) [9].

3.4 The Overall Algorithm

The overall algorithm is then summarized as Algorithm 1. This algorithm implements the methods we have introduced in the above subsections. It performs two two-sample tests based on the sub-series Γ^{front}, Γ^{rear}, and Θ. The output of this algorithm contains all three aspects of the correlation between a time series and an event sequence. In this section, we discuss details of the algorithm implementation.

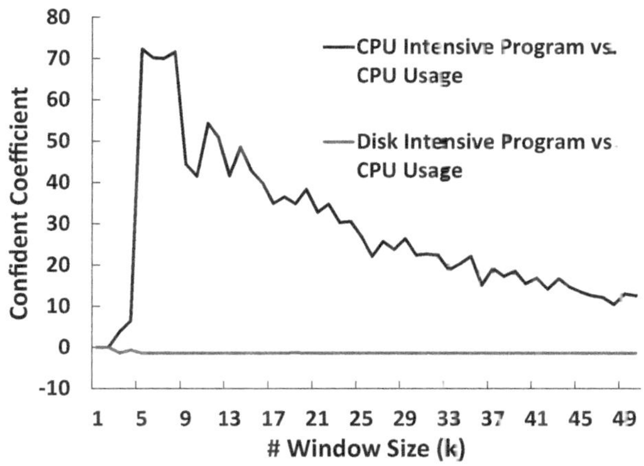

Figure 5: Confidence vs. sub-series length k.

3.4.1 Setting Parameters

The length of sub-series k is an important parameter which can directly influence the performance of our algorithm. We use one example to illustrate the influence of k. Fig. 5 shows two curves, where the vertical axis represents the value of $(Nk)^{1/2}(T_{k,N} - \mu_k)/\sigma_k^2$. For a given α, its value is directly related to the confidence of hypotheses H_1. A larger $(Nk)^{1/2}(T_{k,N} - \mu_k)/\sigma_k^2$ means a high confidence of H_1. We denote it as "Confidence Coefficient". In Fig. 5, the black curve is the confidence coefficient obtained by evaluating the correlation between a pair of "CPU Extensive Program" and "CPU Usage". We know there does exist any correlation between the pair of data. This means the higher confidence of H_1 is better. Because the front sub-series (or the rear sub-series) with a very small length (i.e., $k < 4$) only contains limited information, the confidence in testing is not high enough. As the length increases, we can see a significant increase in confidence in Fig. 5. However, when the length is larger than a certain value (e.g., 8), the confidence decreases after the maximum value. The reason is that as the sub-series length increases thereby the effect of event to time series starts to diminish which makes the subsequence closer to the population Θ. In Fig. 5, the blue curve is the confidence coefficient obtained from the pair of "Disk Transfer Extensive Program" and "CPU Usage". Domain knowledge clearly tells us this pair is not correlated. The result also confirms this fact. The curve of confidence coefficient is flat and very close to 0 for any value of k. It means the rejection of H_1 is not influenced by k if two data sets are not correlated.

In some cases, the value of k can be selected based on domain knowledge and experiments. However, in most real world situations, there are millions of time series and events, and we do not have enough domain knowledge to pre-select the values of all sub-series lengths. In this research, we design a method to auto-select the sub-series length for a time series based on the autocorrelation function [12] of the time series. Given a time series $S = (s_1, s_2, ..., s_n)$, the autocorrelation is showed as follows:

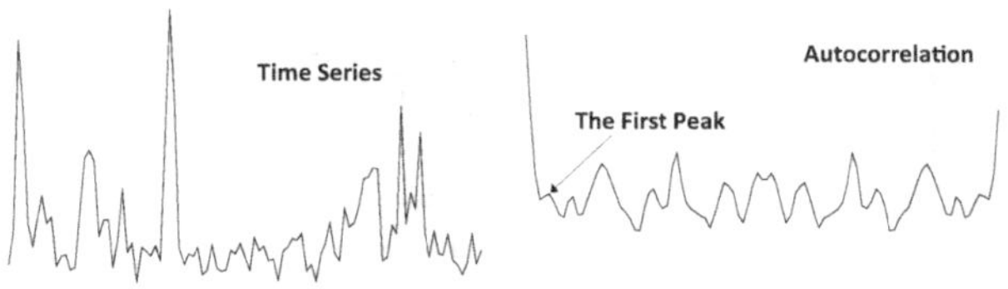

(a) Time Series (b) Autocorrelation

Figure 6: Example of a time series and the corresponding autocorrelation.

$$R(l) = E(s_i * s_{i-l}). \quad (9)$$

where l denotes the lag of the correlation. The autocorrelation function of a time series can be used to represent the energy of signals in the time series with a period of l [12]. Therefore, our length k can be assigned the value of the first peak to include the significant signal of the time series. The experiment (Section 4.5) shows the effectiveness of this method and Fig. 6 shows an example.

Besides k, the number of neighbors r is also a very important parameter. It has been demonstrated that $r = ln(p)$ is a good choice in literatures [28]. In this paper, we directly follow their suggestion.

4. EMPIRICAL EVALUATION

In this section, we make an empirical evaluation of our algorithm by performing a set of experiments on a data set from a controlled environment and two real data sets.

4.1 Baseline

In order to evaluate the effectiveness of our algorithm, we choose two baseline algorithms in our experiment. The first one is the Pearson correlation [8], which is the widely used method for correlation mining in time series. The second baseline is *J-measure* [24], which is a widely used method for correlating event data [16]. In the rest of this section, we brief introduce these two baseline algorithms.

4.1.1 Pearson Correlation

The Pearson correlation method is one of the most widely used methods for measuring the correlation between two time series. The Pearson correlation coefficient, denoted as ρ. is calculated as follows:

$$\rho_{X,Y} = \frac{cov(X,Y)}{\sigma_X \sigma_Y} = \frac{E[(X-\mu_X)(Y-\mu_Y)]}{\sigma_X \sigma_Y}$$

where cov is the covariance, σ_X is the standard deviation of X, μ_X is the mean of X and $E[*]$ denotes the expectation.

The Pearson correlation can not be directly used in the correlation evaluation between time series and event data. In order to make it comparable, we transform the event E to a time series, denoted as $S^E = (s_1^E, s_2^E, ..., s_m^E)$, where m is the size of time series S, and s_i^E is calculated as:

$$s_i^E = \begin{cases} 1, & if\, t(s_i) \in T_E \\ 0, & otherwise. \end{cases}$$

where $t(s_i)$ and T_E is the same meaning as before (see section 2.1).

After transforming the event data to the time series form, we directly calculate the Pearson correlation coefficient ρ between the S^E and S. As introduced in [8], due to our application background, we assign the threshold as 0.1 (weak correlation as in [8]). If $\rho > 0.1$, then $E \overset{+}{\sim} S$. And if $\rho < -0.1$, then $E \overset{-}{\sim} S$. Else ($|\rho| < 0.1$), E and S are not correlated.

4.1.2 J-measure Correlation

We choose the widely used event correlation method, *J-measure* [24], as the second baseline. J-measure has been used in many research efforts [16].

However, *J-measure* is proposed for the event correlation and can not be used directly. Therefore, in our experiment, we first transform each time series to an event sequence as follows: Given a time series $S = (s_1, s_2, ..., s_m)$, its corresponding event sequence is $E^S = (e_1^E, e_2^E, ..., e_n^E)$, where each e_i^E is the change point in the time series, and n is the number of changes in the time series. In this research, we use a widely used GLR algorithm [3] to detect changes in time series.

After transforming each time series to its corresponding event sequence, we can obtain a complete event sequence by combining all the event sequences from two sets: (1) event sequences transformed by time series, (2) event sequences from the original data set. Then we can directly use *J-measure* to evaluate the correlation between these complete event sequences. Similar to the first baseline (Pearson correlation), we assign a correlation threshold as 0.1 (weak correlation in [8]). If the *J-Measure* is larger than 0.1, then $E \sim S$. Otherwise, E and S are not correlated. Considering this, the Temporal Order and the Monotonic Effect Type of the correlation can not be determined using this method.

4.2 Effectiveness Study on Simulation Datasets

In this section, we introduce the experiment on the data from a controlled environment.

4.2.1 The Controlled Experiment

In this research, we setup a SQL environment for a controlled experiment to demonstrate the mutual influencing behavior in a system. For example, when a *CPU Intensive program* starts, the performance counter of *CPU usage* may increase. In a SQL server, database operations can be influenced by the increase of *CPU usage* or *memory usage*. In the experiment, three types of programs including *Disk Intensive program*, *CPU Intensive program* and *Memory Intensive program* are launched several times randomly. Each running lasts for an interval of $[5, 15]$ minutes. At the same time, we query a SQL server database every second. If the query latency exceeds the maximum latency limitation ($200ms$), the query will trigger a time-out alert.

We conduct the experiment for 6 hours. The *CPU Intensive program* run 43 times; the *Memory Intensive program* run 41 times; the *Disk Intensive program* run 38 times ; and 285 *Query Alerts* are triggered. At the same time, we collect four system events (e.g., the starting events of each program and query time-out alerts) and three system performance counters (CPU usage, memory usage, and disk I/O usage) as showed in Table 1.

Table 1: Time series and event data in the controlled experiment

Name	Type	Description
CPU Intensive program	Event	A multi-thread process, which will let the CPU Usage achieve nearly 90%
Memory Intensive program	Event	A process that will apply for a nearly 2G memory space
Disk Intensive program	Event	A copy files process which can sharply increase disk transfer rate
Query Alert	Event	When SQL query delay exceed the maximum limit, an alert occurrence.
CPU Usage	Time Series	record the CPU usage every second
Memory Usage	Time Series	record the Memory usage every second
Disk Transfer Rate	Time Series	record the Disk Transfer Rate every second

4.2.2 Result and Analysis

After obtaining the data from the controlled environment, we run the three algorithms on this data. The results produced by the proposed algorithm and two baseline algorithms are showed in Table 2.

The sub-series length k of the three time series (CPU usage, Memory Usage, Disk Transfer Rate) is assigned using the first peak of the autocorrelation (as introduced in section 3.4.1). We choose DTW distance [4] as the distance measure in Nearest neighbors method of our algorithm.

In Table 2, we see that the correlation relationship, produced using our method, can reflect real system behavior: the *CPU Intensive program* has a positive effect on the CPU usage; the *Memory Intensive program* has a positive effect on both Memory usage and CPU usage; the *Disk Intensive program* has a positive effect on the Disk Transfer rate. The *Query Alert* depends on the high usage of CPU and Memory.

On the other hand, in the results of the Pearson Correlation Algorithm, some of the correlation relations are lost (Memory Using Task $\xrightarrow{+}$ CPU usage, and Memory Usage $\xleftarrow{+}$ Query Alert). The result produced by *J-Measure* is very bad, because *J-Measure* can only encode the occurrence between event and changes. In addition, the Temporal Order and the Monotonic Effect of Dependencies can not be calculated using *J-measure*. From this view, our algorithm has great advantages compared to the baseline algorithms.

4.3 Effectiveness Study on Real Datasets

In this section, we will compare the proposed algorithm with the baseline algorithms on two real data sets.

4.3.1 Dataset

The first real world dataset is a System Monitoring Dataset. This dataset is collected from a large scale online service of Microsoft. We collect 24 different kinds of time series as our input time-series from a number of machines including performance counters of Memory usage, CPU usage, Physical Disk usage etc. The sampling interval of each time series is 5 minutes. At the same time, we also collect a set of event sequences. Each event sequence contains the starting events of a specific job that is automatically submitted by a timer in the system. There are 52 different event in this dataset. The ground truth of this data is labeled by a software engineer in the product team.

The second real world dataset is the Custom Support Dataset. In Microsoft, the customer support team is in charge of the support requests from customers about the above online service. Customers may send us support requests when they do not know how to use the service or they encounter some service quality issues. In this paper, we only collect the requests caused by service issues. The requests are grouped to different categories based on their problem phenomena and root causes (also called *support topic*) by the support team. The occurrences of requests in a single category form an event sequence in this study, because we try to understand what kind of service telemetry data is related to a specific request topic. There are 57 different events in this dataset. The time series data in this study is collected from the runtime system. The front end of our system is a Web Server. For every *HTTP* request from an end user, we have a *HTTP* status code. We group the requests from every hour based on their *HTTP* status code into 7 groups: "200 $\sim$ 300" (it means the status code is in the range from 200 to 300.), "300 $\sim$ 400", "400 $\sim$ 500", "500 $\sim$ 600", "> 600", "*Exception*" (it means no *HTTP* response, the program throws an exception.) and "*Sum*" ("*Sum*" means all the status code larger than "300"). Each group will form a time series to record the number of requests hourly.

4.3.2 Evaluation Metric

The basic model of our algorithm is a hypothesis-test model , we use the F_1 score to evaluate our method, which has been used in many research works [26] for analyzing hypothesis-test accuracy. As introduced in [26] F_1 score can be calculated as follow:

$$F_1 = \frac{2 * TruePositive}{2 * TruePositive + FalseNegative + FalsePositive}$$

In the above, $TruePositive = 1 - FalseNegative$.

Given a time series S and an event E, for the test of dependency existence, a $FalseNegative$ is a case where the algorithm result shows $S \sim E$, but actually S and E are not correlated. A $FalsePositive$ is a case where S and E are not correlated, but the result shows that $S \sim E$. For the test of temporal ordering, a $FalsePositive$ is a case where the result shows $S \rightarrow E$, while the actual temporal order is $E \rightarrow S$. A $FalseNegative$ is a case where the result does not show $S \rightarrow E$, while the actual temporal order is $S \rightarrow E$. For the Monotonic Effect Problem, a $FalsePositive$ is a case that the result shows a positive monotonic effect while the actual effect type is not positive. A $FalseNegative$ is a case that the result does not show a positive monotonic effect while the actual effect type is positive.

4.3.3 Result Analysis

We choose three distance measures for the nearest neighbor method of our algorithm, including: DTW [4] , L_1 distance and L_2 distance. The result is shown in Table 3.

For the different distance measures, we can see that there is no significant difference among them. It seems that the DTW distance has a slightly better performances than others in the experiment on Custom Support Data. When a

Table 2: Results of the data from controlled environment

Name	Proposed Method			Pearson Correlation			J-Measure		
	CPU	Memory	Disk	CPU	Memory	Disk	CPU	Memory	Disk
CPU Intensive Program	$\stackrel{+}{\rightarrow}$	NC	NC	$\stackrel{+}{\sim}$	NC [1]	NC	NC	$\sim$	$\sim$
Memory Intensive Program	$\stackrel{+}{\rightarrow}$	$\stackrel{+}{\rightarrow}$	NC	NC	$\stackrel{+}{\sim}$	NC	NC	$\sim$	$\sim$
Disk Intensive Program	NC	NC	$\stackrel{+}{\rightarrow}$	NC	NC	$\stackrel{+}{\sim}$	NC	$\sim$	$\sim$
Query Alert	$\stackrel{+}{\leftarrow}$	$\stackrel{+}{\leftarrow}$	NC	$\stackrel{+}{\sim}$	NC	NC	NC	$\sim$	$\sim$

Table 3: Result in real data set

Data Set	Methods	Existence	Temporal Order	Effect Type
		F_1 Score	F_1 Score	F_1 Score
System Monitoring Data	Correlation Mining (L1)	0.7916	0.8020	0.8016
	Correlation Mining (L2)	**0.8205**	0.7612	**0.8780**
	Correlation Mining (DTW)	0.7962	**0.8021**	0.8210
	Pearson Correlation	0.6974	N/A [2]	0.6732
	J-Measure	0.6148	N/A	N/A
Custom Support Data	Correlation Mining (L1)	0.7915	0.7659	0.7204
	Correlation Mining (L2)	0.8423	0.7870	0.8334
	Correlation Mining (DTW)	**0.8631**	**0.8205**	**0.8532**
	Pearson Correlation	0.6030	N/A	0.6501
	J-Measure	0.7398	N/A	N/A

customer encounters a problem, s/he may not call Microsoft immediately. Many of them often try several times to make sure they cannot fix by themselves before they call in. Different customers have different delay time before their calls. DTW distance can decrease the influence of latency values [5].

By comparing our algorithm with the baseline algorithms (Pearson correlation and *J-Measure*), we can see that our algorithm has significant advantages.

4.4 Efficiency Study

Now, we shall study the efficiency of our algorithm. We use synthetic datasets to evaluate the efficiency of our algorithm, because we can manipulate the size of the dataset flexibly.

In Fig. 7(a), we fix the value of sub-series length k, and vary the event data size n. We can see that the CPU execution time increased by enlarging the data size. Because we need to calculate the pair-wise distance among sub-series, the computational cost is at $O(n^2)$. In Fig. 7(b), we fix the size of event data, and vary the value of length k. Based on the results, we can see that the running time of the program is almost linear to the value of length k (note: we use L_2 as our distance measure in this experiment.).

4.5 Length of Sub-series

In this subsection, we study the influence caused by different length values of sub-series k in the algorithm. We select two event-time series pairs which are really correlated (CPU Extensive Program and CPU usage; Memory Extensive Program and Memory Usage). In this experiment, we use the confidence coefficient as an indicator to evaluate the performance of the analysis (as we have introduced in section 3.4.1). The results are shown in Fig. 8.

[1]"NC" denotes not correlated

[2]"N/A" denotes no result.

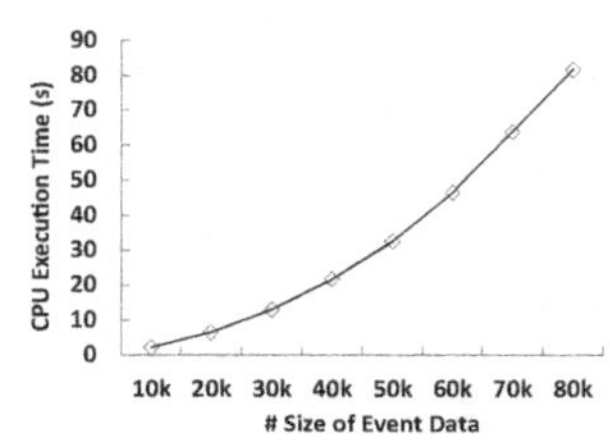

(a) Varying event data size

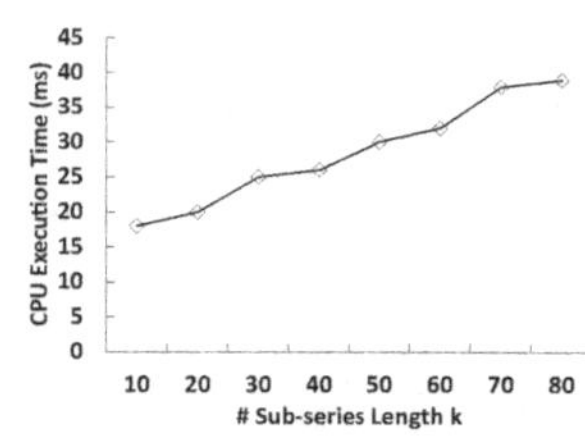

(b) Varying sub-series length

Figure 7: Efficiency by varying data size and sub-series length

The first peak of the autocorrelation of CPU usage appears at the index of 5, as shown in Fig. 8(b). In Fig. 8(a), the largest value of the Confidence coefficient appears just at the index of $k = 5$. Similarly, in Fig. 8(d), the first peak of the autocorrelation of Memory Usage appears is at the index of 11. In Fig. 8(c), the value of the Confidence Coefficient is also at a peak when $k = 11$. From these results, we can see that by using the first peak of the autocorrelation, one can obtain a good configuration of the length k.

5. RELATED WORK

In this section, we briefly introduce some related research efforts.

5.1 Correlation between Time Series Data

The correlation between two time series has been widely studied, and some of them have been included in text books [15]. The Pearson correlation [8] is a basic correlation measure

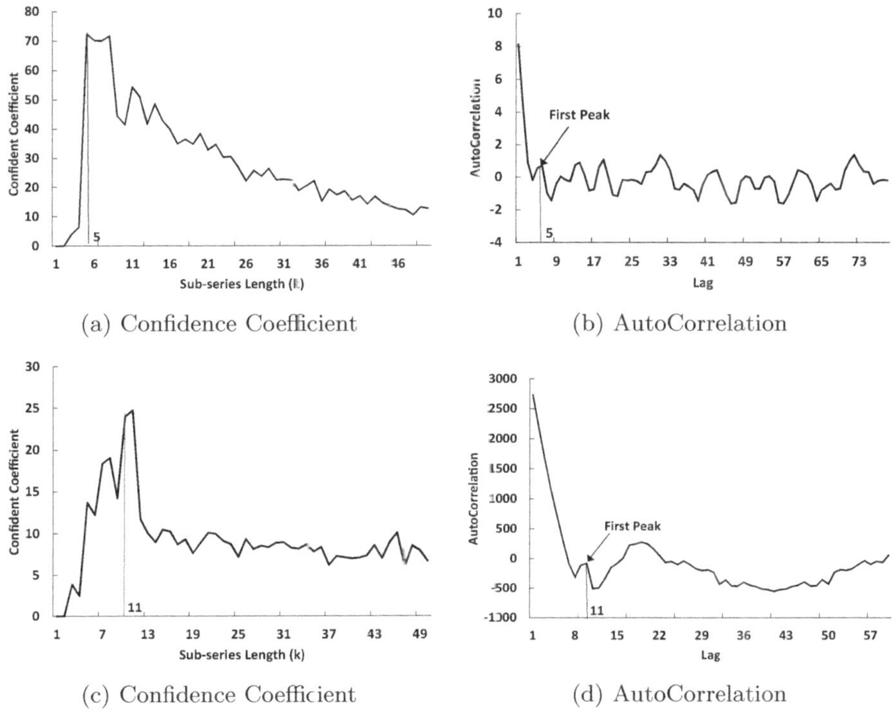

(a) Confidence Coefficient (b) AutoCorrelation

(c) Confidence Coefficient (d) AutoCorrelation

Figure 8: The confidence coefficient value vs. sub-series length k, (a) (b):*CPU intensive program* and *CPU usage*, (c) (d): *memory intensive program* and *memory usage*

between time series, which has been widely used in practice [32]. Some extensions of the Pearson correlation are also widely used. For example, lagged correlation is an extension to correlate a lagged dataset with another unlagged dataset using the Pearson product-moment method. In [31], the author uses the lagged-correlation to estimate the lead relationship between a set of time series. Because the Pearson correlation is sensitive outliers in data set, Spearman Rank correlation and Kendall Rank correlation have been used in some scenarios [27] to overcome the drawbacks of Pearson correlation. In the Spearman correlation, data is first sorted and ranked, e.g., rank 1 is assigned to the lowest value. The Spearman Rank correlation is calculated by taking the Pearson product-moment correlation of the ranks in the dataset. The Kendall correlation tries to measure the similarity of the orderings in the dataset. Because there is no ordering relationship among the different events, the above rank based algorithms cannot be directly used in our scenario.

5.2 Correlation between Event Data

Correlation between events have also been studied in many works [13, 19, 25, 22, 11]. Here, correlation mainly means the co-occurrence of different types of events. Because event data generated in online services can naturally be regarded as sequences, association rule mining algorithms [13] for sequence data can be directly used to analyze the correlation among event data. For example, [19], the authors try to construct the dependency relationships between different system components by mining the co-occurrence among the unconstructed log events generated from the system. In [22], the authors add user guided information during the event correlation mining. Therefore, this algorithm allows users to effectively navigate the result. Correlation Mining algorithms have also been used in some natural science. In [25], the authors apply a correlation mining algorithm to mine the correlation between climate events by analyzing the historical climate data of the North Atlantic and China.

5.3 Two-sample Test

Two-sample Test is an important part of our work. For univariate data, the classical two-sample test includes the nonparametric Kolmogorov-Smirnov test and Mann Whitney U test [21]. For multi-variant data, many methods have been proposed in previous works [28, 10, 29]. In [28], the author uses the proportion of all r nearest neighbors in which observations and their neighbors belong to the same sample as a statistic. The algorithm proposed in [10] is a kernel method for the two sample problem, this method maps the distance between two observations into a reproducing kernel Hilbert space (RKHS), and then uses Maximum Mean Discrepancy to solve the problem. They further propose a unifying framework by linking the two classes of statistics (i.e., energy distances in statistics and distances between distributions in RKHS) in [29]. In this paper, we use the nearest neighbor based algorithm in [28] for simplicity. In fact, the kernel based algorithms can also be applied in our scenarios.

6. CONCLUSION AND FUTURE WORKS

In this paper, we have investigated the problem of correlation mining between time series data and event data. We have defined the correlation problem and proposed a novel approach which is able to discover three important aspects of event-time-series correlation: existence of correlation, temporal ordering, and monotonic effect. In our approach, we first transform the correlation problem to a two-sample problem, use the nearest neighbors method to solve such a two-sample problem and then evaluate the correlation existence. To the best of our knowledge, this is the first work to answer the three correlation questions between event sequences and time series data for incident diagnosis. The experiments on the data from a controlled environment and two real datasets demonstrate the effectiveness and efficiency of our algorithm. The proposed method has already been implemented to an internal tool-set designed for service problem diagnosis.

Our current method does not consider the event combination problem, that only a certain combination of multiple events rather than a single type of event is correlated to a time series. This problem is much more complex, and will be a part of our future work.

7. REFERENCES

[1] Amazon's s3 cloud service turns into a puff of smoke. *Information Week*, Aug 2008.

[2] P. Bahl, R. Chandra, A. Greenberg, S. Kandula, D. A. Maltz, and M. Zhang. Towards highly reliable enter-prise network services via inference of multi-level dependencies. In *SIGCOMM*, 2007.

[3] M. Basseville, I. V. Nikiforov, et al. *Detection of abrupt changes: theory and application*, volume 104. Prentice Hall Englewood Cliffs, 1993.

[4] D. J. Berndt and J. Clifford. Using dynamic time warping to find patterns in time series. In *Knowledge Discovery and Data Mining*, pages 359–370, 1994.

[5] Y. Chen, B. Hu, E. Keogh, and G. E. Batista. Dtw-d: time series semi-supervised learning from a single example. In *KDD*, pages 383–391. ACM, 2013.

[6] I. Cohen, J. S. Chase, M. Goldszmidt, T. Kelly, and J. Symons. Correlating instrumentation data to system states: A building block for automated diagnosis and control. In *OSDI*, pages 231–244, 2004.

[7] I. Cohen, S. Zhang, M. Goldszmidt, J. Symons, T. Kelly, , and A. Fox. Capturing, indexing, clustering, and retrieving system history. In *Proc. SOSP*, pages 105–118, 2005.

[8] J. Cohen. Statistical power analysis for the behavioral sciences. 1988.

[9] Q. Fu, J.-G. Lou, Q.-W. Lin, R. Ding, Z. Ye, D. Zhang, and T. Xie. Performance issue diagnosis for online service systems. In *SRDS*, October 2012.

[10] A. Gretton, K. M. Borgwardt, M. Rasch, B. Schölkopf, and A. J. Smola. A kernel method for the two-sample-problem. volume 19, page 513. MIT; 1998, 2007.

[11] B. Gruschke et al. Integrated event management: Event correlation using dependency graphs. In *Proc. DSOM 98*, pages 130–141, 1998.

[12] J. D. Hamilton. *Time series analysis*, volume 2. Princeton university press Princeton, 1994.

[13] J. Han, M. Kamber, and J. Pei. *Data mining: concepts and techniques*. Morgan kaufmann, 2006.

[14] J. N. Hoover. Outages force cloud computing users to rethink tactics. *Information Week*, Aug 2008.

[15] R. A. Johnson and D. W. Wichern. *Applied multivariate statistical analysis*. Pearson, 2007.

[16] S. Kandula, R. Chandra, and D. Katabi. What's going on? learning communication rules in edge networks. *SIGCOMM*, 38(4):87–98, 2008.

[17] S. Kandula, R. Mahajan, P. Verkaik, S. Agarwal, J. Padhye, and P. Bahl. Detailed diagnosis in enterprise networks. In *Proc. SIGCOMM*, pages 243–254, 2009.

[18] J.-G. Lou, Q. Fu, Y. Wang, and J. Li. Mining dependency in distributed systems through unstructured logs analysis. *SIGOPS Operating Systems Review*, 41(1):91–96, 2010.

[19] J.-G. Lou, Q. Fu, S. Yang, J. Li, and B. Wu. Mining program workflow from interleaved traces. In *KDD*, pages 613–622. ACM, 2010.

[20] J.-G. Lou, Q. Lin, R. Ding, Q. Fu, D. Zhang, and T. Xie. Software analytics for incident management of online services: An experience report. In *ASE*. ACM, November 2013.

[21] H. B. Mann and D. R. Whitney. On a test of whether one of two random variables is stochastically larger than the other. *The annals of mathematical statistics*, 18(1):50–60, 1947.

[22] H. R. Motahari-Nezhad, R. Saint-Paul, F. Casati, and B. Benatallah. Event correlation for process discovery from web service interaction logs. *VLDBJ*, 20(3):417–444, 2011.

[23] J. Pearl. *Causality: Models, Reasoning, and Inference*. Cambridge University Press, 2000.

[24] G. Piateski and W. Frawley. *Knowledge discovery in databases*. MIT press, 1991.

[25] S. C. Porter and A. Zhisheng. Correlation between climate events in the north atlantic and china during the last glaciation. *Nature*, 375:305–308, 1995.

[26] D. M. Powers. Evaluation: from precision, recall and f-measure to roc, informedness, markedness & correlation. *JMLT*, 2(1):37–63, 2011.

[27] B. Rosner. *Fundamentals of biostatistics*. Cengage Learning, 2010.

[28] M. F. Schilling. Multivariate two-sample tests based on nearest neighbors. *Journal of the American Statistical Association*, 81(395):799–806, 1986.

[29] D. Sejdinovic, A. Gretton, K. Fukumizu, and B. K. Sriperumbudur. Hypothesis testing using pairwise distances and associated kernels. In *ICML-12*, pages 1111–1118, 2012.

[30] T. J. VanderWeele and J. M. Robins. Signed directed acyclic graphs for causal inference. *Journal of the Royal Statistical Society*, 72(1):111–127, 2010.

[31] D. Wu, Y. Ke, J. X. Yu, S. Y. Philip, and L. Chen. Detecting leaders from correlated time series. In *Database Systems for Advanced Applications*, pages 352–367. Springer, 2010.

[32] Y. Zhu and D. Shasha. Statstream: Statistical monitoring of thousands of data streams in real time. In *VLDB*, pages 358–369. VLDB Endowment, 2002.

Proactive Workflow Modeling by Stochastic Processes with Application to Healthcare Operation and Management

Chuanren Liu
Rutgers, The State University of New Jersey
New Jersey, USA
chuanren.liu@rutgers.edu

Yong Ge
University of North Carolina at Charlotte
North Carolina, USA
yong.ge@uncc.edu

Hui Xiong*
Rutgers, The State University of New Jersey
New Jersey, USA
hxiong@rutgers.edu

Keli Xiao
Stony Brook University
New York, USA
keli.xiao@stonybrook.edu

Wei Geng
Awarepoint Corporation
California, USA
wgeng@awarepoint.com

Matt Perkins
Awarepoint Corporation
California, USA
mperkins@awarepoint.com

ABSTRACT

Advances in real-time location system (RTLS) solutions have enabled us to collect massive amounts of fine-grained semantically rich location traces, which provide unparalleled opportunities for understanding human activities and discovering useful knowledge. This, in turn, delivers intelligence for real-time decision making in various fields, such as workflow management. Indeed, it is a new paradigm for workflow modeling by the knowledge discovery in location traces. To that end, in this paper, we provide a focused study of workflow modeling by the integrated analysis of indoor location traces in the hospital environment. In comparison with conventional workflow modeling based on passive workflow logs, one salient feature of our approach is that it can proactively unravel the workflow patterns hidden in the location traces, by automatically constructing the workflow states and estimating parameters describing the transition patterns of moving objects. Specifically, to determine a meaningful granularity for the model, the workflow states are first constructed as regions associated with specific healthcare activities. Then, we transform the original indoor location traces to the sequences of workflow states and model the workflow transition patterns by finite state machines. Furthermore, we leverage the correlations in the location traces between related types of medical devices to reinforce the modeling performance and enable more applications. The results show that the proposed framework can not only model the workflow patterns effectively, but also have managerial applications in workflow monitoring, auditing, and inspection of workflow compliance, which are critical in the healthcare industry.

*Contact Author.

KDD'14, August 24–27, 2014, New York, New York, USA.

http://dx.doi.org/10.1145/2623330.2623363

Categories and Subject Descriptors

H.4 [**Information Systems Applications**]: Miscellaneous; H.2.8 [**Database Management**]: Database Applications—*Data Mining*

General Terms

Algorithms, Application

Keywords

Indoor Location Traces, Workflow Modeling Healthcare Operation and Management

1. INTRODUCTION

Recent years have witnessed the increasing deployment of real-time location systems (RTLS) in hospitals. These RTLS solutions, as shown in Figure 1, allow people to track and monitor the movement of moving objects (e.g., medical devices, doctors and patients), and the interactions between people and medical devices. However, currently such systems are only used for basic tasks, such as simply locating a wheel chair and checking the availability of an inpatient bed. Meanwhile, hospital managers are still facing many managerial challenges. Particularly, there are three important tasks of operation and management in hospital: *workflow monitoring*, *workflow auditing*, and inspection of *workflow compliance*. For example, many healthcare providers have their own work protocols to ensure that the healthcare practices are executed in a controlled manner. Non-compliance practices may be costly and expose the healthcare providers to severe risks, such as litigation, prosecution and damage to brand reputation. However, it is not an easy task to systematically evaluate the degree to which the ongoing healthcare processes are compliant with the predefined protocols. Thus, effective inspection of workflow compliance is very needed by healthcare providers to maintain the performance and reputation of their services.

Conventionally, to accomplish these tasks, hospital managers mainly rely on inspecting detailed workflow logs, which are managerially daunting. In particular, the logs can be heterogeneous in format and stored in different media. For example, many medical records are still documented in papers, which are not easy to be systematically processed and analyzed in real time. More importantly, these workflow logs are provided passively by the personnel, which might be biased. In contrast, a proactive approach requiring minimum human intervention would be a promising complement for the workflow management tasks. Indeed, the existing RTLS and collected location traces provide unparalleled opportunities for us to develop new ways to help with the workflow management tasks. To this end, this paper provides a focused study of workflow modeling by the integrated analysis of indoor location traces in the hospital environments. One major goal is to proactively unravel the workflow patterns hidden in the location traces, by automatically constructing the workflow states and estimating parameters describing the transition patterns of medical devices. The discovered knowledge from the indoor location traces are then transformed to actionable intelligence for healthcare operation and management. Indeed, the learned workflow model is valuable in that a wide range of practical problems in hospital environments can be relieved with the modeling results.

Although modeling the workflow patterns in the hospital environments is of significant managerial value, it is a non-trivial task to systematically construct and estimate the models with the massive indoor location traces. First, there are some inherent characteristics in the indoor scenario, which pose new challenges to the workflow analysis.

- The granularity and quality of indoor location traces captured by wireless location systems might vary a lot from place to place due to several factors: the density of sensor receivers, the underlying localization techniques, and the sensor device itself (e.g., the battery power percentage).
- The topologies of indoor space are often much more complex than outdoor space. Therefore, some fundamental assumptions of outdoor scenarios may not hold for indoor scenarios. For example, the widely-used similarity measurements for outdoor trajectories based on geometry distance [4] or overlapping degree [6] are not much meaningful for indoor location traces.
- The structure of indoor space is very dynamic and the modeling framework should be automatic and adaptive accordingly. For instance, the structure and utility of many modern buildings may be frequently changed per the ongoing needs. Such dynamic changes will alter the semantic of indoor location traces.

As a result, even there are intensive works on the analysis of outdoor location traces [6, 12, 5], most of them are not suitable or practical for modeling the indoor location traces of medical devices. Moreover, the results of those methods are not very helpful towards the workflow analysis in hospital environments. For example, the method developed by Giannotti et al. [6] aims for the discovery of frequent trajectory patterns based on given thresholds, i.e., minimum support and time tolerance, from outdoor location traces. However, such frequent patterns cannot provide a parsimonious description for healthcare activities in hospitals. For example, to help with workflow compliance inspection, we need to consider all activities rather than only a subset of moving patterns, i.e., frequent patterns. Similarly, the periodic patterns mined from outdoor spatio-temporal data by Mamoulis et al. [12] are also a subset of moving activities and cannot fully meet the needs of workflow monitoring, auditing, or compliance inspection in a hospital. While Yin

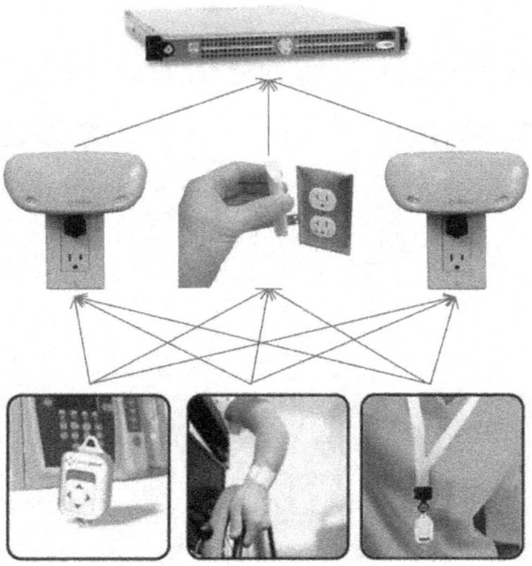

Figure 1: A demonstration of the real-time location system in hospitals. At the bottom layer, the moving objects (medical devices, patients, doctors, etc.) are attached with sensor tags, which send signals to the sensor receivers. The sensor receivers at the middle layer transmit the signal data to the network bridges. At the top layer, network bridges connected with data/application servers will collect the signal data and the data/application servers will calculate locations of the tracked objects.

et al. [17] proposed stochastic models for indoor activities, the purpose of these models is to predict the goals of activities, rather than summarize overall activity patterns in descriptive ways. Besides, their methods are mostly supervised and need sufficient training data.

To accommodate the unique characteristics of indoor location traces of medical devices in a hospital, in this paper, we propose a stochastic process-based framework to model the healthcare workflow. First, to extract each workflow state which is related to a particular type of healthcare activity, we develop a density-based clustering algorithm to partition the indoor space. Particularly, to incorporate the complex indoor topologies, we compute the neighborhood of a location record and its density in the indoor space based on the transition history rather than the geometry distance. With the clustering results, we further transform the original location traces into the sequences of workflow states. Then we analyze the workflow sequences by modeling the transitions among states with finite state machines.

Second, due to the dynamic indoor structure, we need an automatic and adaptive modeling framework to support the critical applications in real time. However, during some specific periods of observation, the estimation of parameters in the finite state machines may be unstable due to the data scarcity issue of the location traces. Meanwhile, there is some natural correlation in the location traces of a group of medical devices, which are often used together for a particular task. By leveraging such correlation, we may overcome the data scarcity issue and improve the robustness of the parameter estimation for the finite state machines. Therefore, we explore MAP (Maximum A Posteriori) estimation in the Hidden Markov Random Fields (HMRFs) to estimate the transition probabilities, which can effectively leverage the correlation in the location traces of related medical devices.

Moreover, in addition to the correlation relationship, we will be able to integrate more prior or domain information about the workflow of medical devices with the HMRFs, which will further improve the effectiveness of our workflow modeling.

Finally, we demonstrate the effectiveness of our models with the real-world data collected from multiple hospitals in US. We have also implemented and deployed a management information system, *HISflow*, based on our methods to show how the discovered knowledge can help with the three important managerial tasks in hospitals: workflow monitoring, auditing, and inspection of workflow compliance.

2. PRELIMINARIES AND PROBLEM FORMULATION

In this section, we first introduce the data format of the indoor location traces. Then, we formally formulate the problem of workflow modeling for medical devices.

2.1 Data Description and Transformation

Our location traces (trajectories) of medical devices are collected from indoor environments of several US hospitals. The location trace of an object O is represented as a sequence: $O_t = (L_1, L_2, ...)$, where L_i represents the ith record in the sequence. $L_i = (start_i, end_i; x_i, y_i, z_i)$ contains the specific coordinate and the corresponding timestamp when that record is recorded, where $start_i$ and end_i are the start time and the end time of L_i. In other words, during the time frame from $start_i$ to end_i, the object O stays at the coordinate (x_i, y_i, z_i) in a three-dimensional indoor space.

However, the indoor wireless communication may be interrupted by environmental factors and lead to some errors or noises for the localization of moving objects. Therefore, a coordinate localized by the RTLS might not indicate the exact position, but a small area surrounding the coordinate. In addition, it may not be meaningful to directly use these coordinates for workflow modeling in the indoor space. For example, for two recorded coordinates which are close to each other on the same floor, although the geometry distance of them is very small, the actual moving distance from one coordinate to another one may be very long when there is a wall between these two coordinates.

To cope with these challenges, we normalize the original location traces for workflow modeling. Specifically, we project each raw coordinate to a semantic location of the building, such as a room in the hospital, based on the floor maps of the building. For the data and maps in this study, each hallway is also treated as a room and some long hallways have been segmented into several small rooms. Then, we map $L_i = (start_i, end_i; x_i, y_i, z_i)$ to $L_i^* = (start_i, end_i, r_i)$, where r_i is the room containing the coordinate (x_i, y_i, z_i). After this projection, two neighboring coordinates of the raw location traces may be mapped into the same room. In practice, we merge these consecutive records within the same room to one union record. Specifically, if $i < j$ and $r_i = r_{i+1} = \cdots = r_j$, we replace the subsequence $(L_i, L_{i+1}, \cdots, L_j)$ with only one record $L_i^* = (start_i, end_j, r_i)$.

Now, each raw location record L_i is mapped to a symbolic room (graph node), and each location trace $Tr = (L_1^*, L_2^*, \cdots)$ is transformed to a symbolic sequence (traveling path). This data preprocessing drastically reduces the computational cost, since we significantly reduce the number of records in the data after the projection. Also, this preprocessing step greatly smooths out the noise and alleviates the impact of errors on the workflow modeling tasks.

2.2 Concepts for Workflow Modeling

The ultimate goal of our workflow pattern modeling is to automatically summarize the healthcare activities in a systematic manner. To this end, the concept of workflow patterns is actually a hierarchy with several levels. At the lowest level, the location trace itself can be seen as an instance of workflow patterns. For example, in Figure 2, we show location traces of an infusion pump with red line segments. However, it is difficult to comprehensively understand the pattern hidden in the raw location traces.

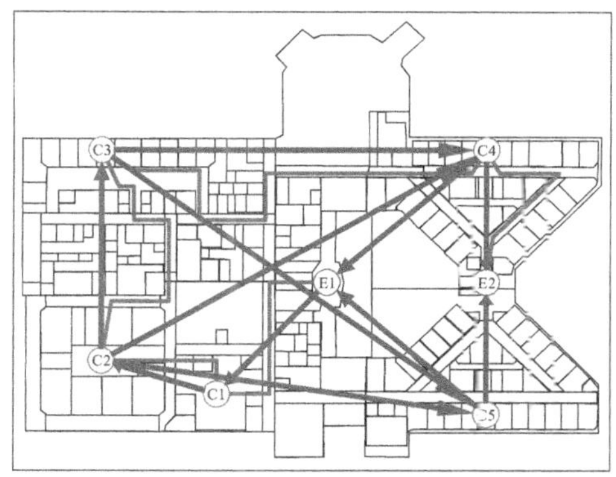

Figure 2: The workflow instances of infusion pump.

Locations	Functions
C_1	Post-anesthesia care unit (PACU)
C_2	Operating room (OR)
C_3	Intensive care unit (ICU)
C_4, C_5	Patient care unit (PCU)
E_1, E_2	Elevator

Table 1: The functions of key locations in Figure 2.

On the other hand, three workflow stages at the highest level are widely used in the healthcare industry to describe the workflow logistics: *preprocessing maintenance stage*, *in-use stage*, *postprocessing maintenance stage*. The *in-use stage* of a medical device corresponds to the period when it is used for any healthcare purpose. Before the *in-use stage*, a device is in the *preprocessing maintenance stage*, e.g., held in the storage room. After the *in-use stage*, the device must go through the *postprocessing maintenance stage* before the next circle of use. These maintenance processes include cleaning up, sterilization, disinfection, etc. However, modeling the workflow patterns based on these three stages is too coarse to get useful results to help with tasks of operation and management in a hospital. In particular, one important factor missed by the workflow stages is the spatial information, and the modeling results based on these high level stages cannot facilitate the workflow evaluation from the spatial perspectives, such as the evaluation for the utilization efficiency of the indoor space. Therefore, we need to model the workflow patterns using a middle-level representation of location traces of medical devices

2.2.1 Workflow States

To that end, we introduce an important concept, *workflow state*, which will serve as a basis for our workflow modeling at the proper level of granularity. Indeed, to better understand the location traces, we need to annotate a few key locations in these trajectories. For example, as shown in Figure 2, we annotate location traces with important location spots: C_i $(i = 1, \cdots, 5)$. The medical functions of these spots are summarized in Table 1. With these annotations, the location trace in red in Figure 2 can be represented as $C_1 \mapsto C_2 \mapsto C_3 \mapsto C_4$. Such representation with annotated spots makes it easy to understand the workflow behind the location trace.

In fact, Figure 2 is the map of the second floor of a hospital building, which is centered around E_1, the elevator connected to the basement. The red location trace of one infusion pump starts from the storage room in the basement to the elevator E_1. After E_1, the first spot C_1 is Post-Anesthesia Care Unit (PACU) where the patient is ready for medical procedures such as surgery and the medical devices are attached with the patients. Spot C_2 is the area of operating rooms (OR) where medical procedures happen. After the medical procedure, the patients and the medical devices are moved to C_3, Intensive Care Unit (ICU), based on the medical needs. When the situation of the patient becomes stable, the patient and the medical devices being used will be further moved to C_4, Patient Care Unit (PCU), before the patient is discharged. After the patient is discharged, the medical devices will be moved through elevator E_2 to the basement for cleaning up in a disinfection room and depositing into the storage rooms.

From the above example, we know that each spot with a particular healthcare purpose corresponds to a workflow state, and the location traces represented with such workflow states are very meaningful for understanding and modeling the workflow patterns. Therefore, we formally define the workflow states in the context of hospitals as follows:

DEFINITION 1 (WORKFLOW STATE). *A workflow state is a location spot in the indoor space where specific healthcare activities frequently happen.*

According to this definition, a workflow state might be a cluster of location records with specific activities. In the above example, we have workflow states C_1, C_2, C_3, C_4. By representing the location traces with workflow states, the workflow patterns are more clear to be understood and inferred than that with symbolic rooms or high level stages.

2.3 The Problem Statement of Workflow Pattern Modeling

With workflow states, a further task is to describe the transition patterns of the moving objects among the workflow states. As shown in Figure 2, the transition from one state may go to several different states. For example, when the situation of a patient is stable after the medical operation at C_2, the medical devices and the patient might be moved directly to PCU without passing through ICU (C_3). Also, there are more than one PCU spots in the hospital. For example, in addition to C_4, we have C_5 as another PCU spot in Figure 2. Note that, Figure 2 is only one floor in one building. In fact, we may have many workflow states since there might be several buildings and many floors in one hospital. Thus, the overall workflow patterns are indeed much more complex than the examples discussed above.

Furthermore, we have multiple types of medical devices moving around in the indoor space. In hospitals, many different medical devices are often used together for a particular task. Therefore, although different types of medical devices have different workflow patterns, there is some natural correlation among their location traces. Modeling such correlation not only helps reinforce the robustness of the workflow modeling, but also provides better understanding of the overall workflow patterns.

Now, we can formally state the problem of workflow pattern modeling in the indoor healthcare environments.

PROBLEM 1 (WORKFLOW PATTERN MODELING). *Given the collected location traces ($\{Tr\}$) of moving objects, such as medical devices, workflow pattern modeling is to discover the workflow knowledge including workflow states (C), and parameters (μ) describing the transition patterns of the moving objects among the workflow states. In addition, we would also like to learn the correlation measurement (s) among the transition patterns for different types of moving objects.*

To accomplish these tasks, in Section 3, we first propose a clustering algorithm to construct the workflow states. Next, in Section 4, we model the transition patterns among the workflow states with finite state machines. In Section 5, we further show how to learn the correlation measurement and build the transition models in a reinforcement way.

3. WORKFLOW STATE CONSTRUCTION

Inspired by Liu et al. [10], we develop a DBSCAN-style clustering algorithm to construct the workflow states from the location traces. This density-based method is adopted to meet the requirements for the workflow analysis. Particularly, the clustering method should be able to automatically determine the number of clusters, and detect clusters of different densities and arbitrary shapes. The detected clusters should also be spatially contiguous, since we want to identify areas of semantically meaningful locations, such as '2nd floor northeast patient rooms' and 'basement central storage rooms'. However, even if we adopt the framework in [10], we have to develop some new methods to address the challenges caused by the unique characteristics of the workflow traces. First, we need a meaningful neighborhood definition for the location records in the indoor space. Second, to cope with the definition of workflow states, we need a density definition associated with workflow activities to detect clusters of different densities.

To address these challenges, let us first introduce how to define the neighborhood of a location record by exploiting the topologies of the indoor space. Since the location traces are represented symbolically, the indoor space map can be modeled with a corresponding symbolic graph. With all the symbolic nodes V as vertices of the graph $G = (V, E)$, we can use edge E to represent neighboring relationship among the nodes. An edge is added between two vertices if a direct transition path between the corresponding pair of symbolic location nodes exists. Formally, we define the neighboring relationship based on the transition connectivity:

DEFINITION 2 (TRANSITION NEIGHBORHOOD). *For room r_0, we denote*

$$TN(r_0) = \{r \mid \exists\ Tr, (rr_0) \in Tr\}$$

as the transition neighboring rooms of r_0. One room r is said to be transition neighbor of another room r_0 if one can transit from r to r_0 without passing through other rooms.

With Definition 2, we define the neighborhood of a location record in the symbolic space:

DEFINITION 3. *The neighborhood of a location record $L_0 = (start_0, end_0, r_0)$ is a set of location records observed in the rooms that are involved in transitions to r_0, denoted by*

$$N(L_0) = \{L = (start, end, r) | r \in TN(r_0)\}.$$

Thus, instead of identifying the neighborhood of a location record based on a distance threshold as used in DBSCAN, we define the neighborhood of a location record by directly querying the transition history from the data. In this way, we avoid the use of parameters, such as the distance threshold, which DBSCAN is very sensitive to.

To detect the clusters of different densities, we propose a *weighted density* definition to measure the density of individual neighborhood and identify core location records. If we know the distribution of waiting time T in room r_0, then a natural choice to weight the location record $L = (start, end, r_0)$ is the p-value $w(L) = \Pr(T \leq d)$, where $d = end - start$ is the waiting time of L. Intuitively, a longer waiting time d will lead to a bigger weight, as it takes time to carry out medical procedures and we are identifying the spot where specific medical activities frequently happen. If we do not know the distribution of T, which often happens in reality, we propose to estimate the weight as

$$w(L) = \frac{|\{(start, end, r) | r = r_0, end - start \leq d\}|}{|\{(start, end, r | r = r_0\}|}.$$

With this formulation, we have the following definition of the weighted density for a neighborhood:

DEFINITION 4. *The weighted density of a neighborhood $N(L_0)$ is defined as:*

$$w(N(L_0)) = \frac{\sum_{L=(start,end,r)\in N(L_0)} w(L)(end - start)}{|N(L_0)|}.$$

EXAMPLE. By the definition above, suppose $N(L_0) = \{L = (start, end, r_0)\}$, let us calculate the weighted density for the following distributions of waiting times:

- $D_1 = \{1, 2, \cdots, 10\}$, 10 observations.
- $D_2 = \{5.5, 5.5, \cdots, 5.5\}$, 10 observations.
- $D_3 = \{1, 1, \cdots, 1\}$, 55 observations.

Although the total waiting time of D_1, D_2 and D_3 is the same as 55, our weighted densities are 3.85, 5.5, 1 respectively. For D_3, the neighborhood $N(L_0)$ is more likely in hallway or in front of elevator. Although the total waiting time in these places is long due to a lot of trajectories passing around, there is no long period of waiting time for carrying out medical procedures. Our weighted density definition can underrate this kind of situations. Similarly, observations with shorter waiting time in D_1 are also weighted lower. □

Finally, we compare this estimated weighted density with a user-specified threshold θ to decide if a location record is a core point or not. Although there is similar parameter in DBSCAN, i.e., minimum number of points required to form a cluster, the parameter θ is not the count of points but a weight measurement based on historical statistics. Due to the space limit, readers are referred to Liu et al. [10] for details of the algorithm, except that the neighborhood and density definitions should be replaced by Definition 3 and 4.

4. WORKFLOW TRANSITION ESTIMATION

With the constructed workflow states C, we can transform the original location trace into a workflow sequence $Tr = (s_1, s_2, \cdots, s_l)$, where $s_i = (c_i, d_i)$, $c_i \in C$ is the ith workflow state and d_i is the waiting duration in c_i. This transformation makes it feasible to model the workflow sequences of the objects moving among the indoor states with a continuous time Markov chain (CTMC). Specifically, with the constructed workflow states C as stochastic states in the workflow processes, a CTMC(μ) is defined with two sets of parameters $\mu = (P, q)$: waiting time parameters q_c for each state $c \in C$, and state transition probabilities $P_{cc'}$ from state c to c'. Let $S(t) \in C$ denote the state of the process at time $t \in [0, \infty)$. CTMC stays in $S(t) = c$ at time instant t for a random amount of duration $D_c \sim \text{Exp}(q_c)$. When CTMC finally leaves c, the next state of the system is c' with probability $P_{cc'}$ where $c' \neq c$. For $c = c'$, we let $P_{cc} = 0$. With these parameters, for the process Tr starting from s_1 and ending at time $d = \sum_{i=1}^{l} d_i$, the probability of Tr is

$$\Pr(Tr|P, q) = \exp(-q_{c_l} d_l) \prod_{i=1}^{l-1} q_{c_i} \exp(-q_{c_i} d_i) P_{c_i c_{i+1}}. \quad (1)$$

Without causing confusion, in the following, we denote states in C by integers $1, 2, \cdots, |C|$ for simplicity. For a set of processes $\{Tr\}$, the probability calculated above can also be expressed in terms of N and D, where N_{ij} is the transition count from state i to state j, and $D_i = \int [S(t) = i] dt$ is the total waiting time in state i. Specifically,

$$\prod_{Tr} \Pr(Tr|P, q) = \Pr(N, D|P, q) = \left(\prod_{ij} P_{ij}^{N_{ij}}\right) \left(\prod_i q_i^{N_i} \exp(-q_i D_i)\right),$$

Here, $N_i = \sum_j N_{ij}$ is the transition counts from state i. Note that by definition we have $N_{ii} = 0$ and we compute $P_{ii}^{N_{ii}} = 1$.

One important fact in the likelihood of parameters P, q is that, we can estimate P_{ij} and q_i separately. That is, $\Pr(N, D|P, q) = \Pr(N|P)\Pr(N, D|q)$, where:

$$\Pr(N|P) = \prod_{i,j} P_{ij}^{N_{ij}} \quad (2)$$

$$\Pr(N, D|q) = \prod_i q_i^{N_i} \exp(-q_i D_i) \quad (3)$$

The solution to maximize $\Pr(N, D|q)$ is $q_i = \frac{N_i}{D_i}$. In other words, q_i is estimated by the reciprocal of the mean waiting time at state i. In the following, we will focus on optimizing $\Pr(N|P)$ to estimate the transition probability matrix P.

Under the normalization constraints $\sum_j P_{ij} = 1$ and $P_{ij} \geq 0$, it is straightforward to estimate the parameters P using a maximum likelihood estimation approach. However, the result estimated in this way will be unstable if the training data is not sufficient (e.g., when analyzing the daily data instead of monthly or yearly data). Fortunately, the data collected from different types of moving objects may help mutually reinforce each other to estimate the moving patterns in a robust way. To leverage this potential, we introduce the Maximum A Posteriori (MAP) estimation approach which simultaneously estimates transition models for multiple types of moving objects. More importantly, with

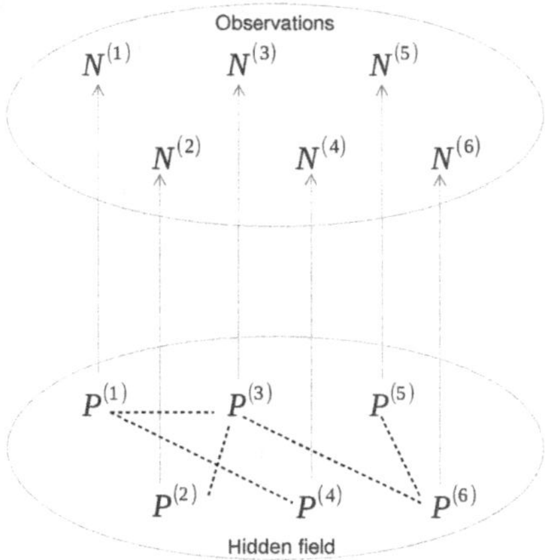

Figure 3: A Hidden Markov Random Field

this approach, we will also be able to understand the collaborating relationship among different types of medical devices.

5. MAP ESTIMATION IN HMRFS

For the healthcare procedures of one patient, multiple types of medical devices are often needed. Thus, these different types of moving objects transit together and produce the correlated location traces. Therefore, although different medical devices follow different patterns, their workflow models can be built jointly with the consideration of these correlations. To this end, we first piece together the workflow states for all the K types of moving objects:

$$C = \cup_{k=1}^{K} C^{(k)}$$

where $C^{(k)}$ is the workflow states of the kth type of moving objects. Note that, when $C_1 \in C^{(1)}$ and $C_2 \in C^{(2)}$ overlap, i.e., $C_1 \cap C_2 \neq \emptyset$, we merge them together as $C_1 \cup C_2 \in C$. Now, all the K types of transition sequences can be expressed with the common transition states C, while each type has one transition count matrix $N^{(k)}$ and one transition probability matrix $P^{(k)}$. To estimate the K transition probability matrices $\{P^{(k)}|1 \leq k \leq K\}$ together based on $\{N^{(k)}|1 \leq k \leq K\}$, we use Hidden Markov Random Fields (HMRFs) to leverage the correlation among all types of objects. Specifically, an HMRF has the following components:

Hidden field: In our model, the hidden field includes the transition matrices $P^{(k)}$ for $1 \leq k \leq K$ for all types of objects, whose values are hidden or unobservable.

Observations: The observed data includes the transition counts $N^{(k)}$ for $1 \leq k \leq K$.

As shown in Figure 3, there is also a connecting structure in the hidden field. We would like to reinforce the estimation of the connected parameters by leveraging the prior distribution of the random field. For our problem, we consider pairwise correlation among different types of objects, so the prior depends on $\sum_{k_1,k_2} V(k_1,k_2)$, where $V(k_1,k_2) \geq 0$ is the potential of the link between $P^{(k_1)}$ and $P^{(k_2)}$. Specifically, we have $\Pr(P) \propto \exp(-\sum_{k_1,k_2} V(k_1,k_2))$. By applying this prior, the objective function to be maximized is:

$$\Pr(P|N) \propto \exp(-\sum_{k_1,k_2} V(k_1,k_2)) \prod_{k,i,j} (P_{ij}^{(k)})^{N_{ij}^{(k)}}$$

or equivalently

$$\log \Pr(P|N) = -\sum_{k_1,k_2} V(k_1,k_2) + \sum_{k,i,j} N_{ij}^{(k)} \log P_{ij}^{(k)}. \quad (4)$$

Note that a normalization constant is omitted in the log-likelihood equation.

5.1 Adaptive Parameterized Correlation

HMRFs can integrate the knowledge about the neighborhood structure by formulating the potential $V(k_1,k_2)$. In the following, we demonstrate this framework by an unsupervised approach, where the neighborhood structure itself is also learned from the data. Specifically, we define the potential between them as

$$V(k_1,k_2) = w \times s(k_1,k_2) \times \mathrm{Tr}(P^{(k_1)}P^{(k_2)}), \quad (5)$$

where $w \geq 0$ is a scaling constant. Here, the correlation $s(k_1,k_2)$ measures the similarity between the transition patterns of types k_1 and k_2. The matrix trace $\mathrm{Tr}(P^{(k_1)}P^{(k_2)}) = \sum_{ij} P_{ij}^{(k_1)} P_{ji}^{(k_2)}$ is actually the probability that we can observe about the contradicting moves. For example, in the extreme case when $\mathrm{Tr}(P^{(k_1)}P^{(k_2)}) = 0$, we have $P_{ij}^{(k_1)} P_{ji}^{(k_2)} = 0$ for any given states i,j. In this case, we have $P_{ji}^{(k_2)} = 0$ only if $P_{ij}^{(k_1)} > 0$. In other words, for two types of objects that have no contradicting workflows, the probability of transition from state j to i is 0 for the second type of objects, only if we have a positive transition probability from state i to j for the first type of objects.

To measure the correlation adaptively with respect to the observed data, we propose to parameterize the Frobenius inner product using a non-negative matrix M, which leads to the following formula:

$$s(k_1,k_2) = \frac{< N^{(k_1)}, N^{(k_2)} >_M}{\|N^{(k_1)}\|_M \|N^{(k_2)}\|_M},$$

where the weighted Frobenius inner product is $< X, Y >_M = \sum_{ij} X_{ij} M_{ij} Y_{ij}$ and weighted Frobenius matrix norm is $\|X\|_M = \sqrt{< X, X >_M}$. Indeed, N is directional observation and $s(k_1,k_2)$ corresponds to a von-Mises Fisher (vMF) distribution [2] as the underlying generative model.

5.2 Iterative Optimization Algorithm

We need an iterative updating algorithm to learn the correlation from the data and optimize the objective function in Equation 4 simultaneously. Specifically, there are two sets of parameters: Frobenius weights M and transition probabilities P. To update the Frobenius weights by increasing Equation 4, a closed-form solution is unattainable. In this case, gradient ascent update can be used alternatively. Particularly, the gradients are

$$\frac{\partial \log \Pr(P|N)}{\partial M_{ij}} = -w \sum_{k_1,k_2} \frac{\partial s(k_1,k_2)}{\partial M_{ij}} \mathrm{Tr}(P^{(k_1)}P^{(k_2)}) \quad (6)$$

and

$$\frac{\partial s(k_1,k_2)}{\partial M_{ij}} = \frac{N_{ij}^{(k_1)} N_{ij}^{(k_2)}}{\|N^{(k_1)}\|_M \|N^{(k_2)}\|_M} - \frac{1}{2} \frac{< N^{(k_1)}, N^{(k_2)} >_M}{\|N^{(k_1)}\|_M \|N^{(k_2)}\|_M} \left(\left(\frac{N_{ij}^{(k_1)}}{\|N_{k_1}\|_M} \right)^2 + \left(\frac{N_{ij}^{(k_2)}}{\|N_{k_2}\|_M} \right)^2 \right).$$

With the given M, the optimal P can be obtained by solving the following KKT system:

$$-2\sum_{k'} s(k,k')P_{ji}^{(k')} + N_{ij}^{(k)}/P_{ij}^{(k)} - \lambda_{ki} = 0 \qquad (7)$$

for $1 \leq k \leq K$ and $1 \leq i,j \leq |C|$. Here λ_{ki} is a KKT multiplier. With the normalization constraints $\sum_j P_{ij}^{(k)} = 1$, this quadratic system can be numerically solved. Note that, by iteratively conducting above updates, Equation 4 will be monotonically increased and we can stop the process when a sufficiently accurate solution is reached.

6. EMPIRICAL EVALUATION

Here, we evaluate the performances of our workflow models in indoor healthcare environments. First, we show the identified workflow states and analyze the goodness-of-fit of our transition models with respect to important statistics. Then, we show that the learned correlation can reinforce the modeling performance, especially for real-time applications. The proposed models will also be compared with some baseline models. Finally, we showcase a few intelligent applications in healthcare operation and management that can benefit from the learned knowledge.

6.1 The Experimental Data

We use real-world data sets for validation. These data sets are collected from several hospitals in US. Medical devices operated in these hospitals have been attached with sensor tags and tracked by RTLS developed by Awarepoint Corporation. In Table 2, we show basic statistics of the data collected for various types of medical devices in Hospital 1. Specifically, we will build workflow models for 7 types of medical devices. The 2nd and 3rd columns show the number of medical devices of each type operated in this hospital, and the number of location records collected during the period from January 2011 to August 2011.

Type	#Objects	#Locations	#States	θ seconds
Wheelchair	121	524415	121	1200
PCA II Pump	66	4431	2	1200
Venodyne	403	1588045	74	1200
Feeding Pump	83	157370	58	3600
Heating Pad	1	211	1	1200
PCA Pump	136	231057	74	1800
ETCO2	137	220380	79	1200

Table 2: Basic data statistics in Hospital 1

6.2 The Workflow States

In Hospital 1, there are totally 123 different workflow states identified. The last two columns in Table 2 give the number of workflow states identified for each device type and the corresponding threshold for density-based clustering. We can see that different types of medical devices are used in different ranges of region. For instance, wheelchairs move among 121 workflow states, while feeding pumps transit only in 58 workflow states. We also automatically identified that PCA II Pump and Heating Pad only move in a small range, which means the workflows of these two types of devices are quite simple. Thus, in the following we focus on analyzing the remaining 5 types of devices which have more complex workflow patterns. For the threshold of clustering, we empirically specify the parameter based on the mobility of medical devices and the classical work time for treatment in order to achieve well-separated workflow states.

The identified workflow states are verified to be semantically meaningful by the domain experts. For example, in Figure 4, we show the constructed workflow states for Venodyne, which moves most frequently, on 4 building floors. A summary of these workflow states is reported in Table 3. Particularly, with the developed clustering algorithm based on the the weighted density (demonstrated as transparency), we can effectively focus on the most important location spots. For example, as shown in Figure 4a, although most of the right part on this floor is planned to be PCU (Patient Care Unit), we find that only a small subset of rooms were frequently used. This is especially surprising in the top right corner, where only one room was used efficiently. These observations lead to an important application, workflow auditing, which we will further discuss in Section 6.5.2.

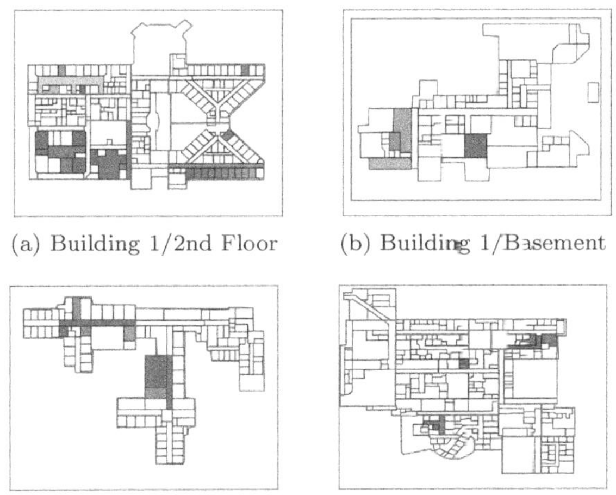

(a) Building 1/2nd Floor (b) Building 1/Basement (c) Building 2/1st Floor (d) Building 3/Basement

Figure 4: Examples of workflow states.

Building/Floor	State	Function
1/2nd	middle bottom	Post-anesthesia care unit
1/2nd	left bottom	Operating room
1/2nd	left top	Intensive care unit
1/2nd	right top	Patient care unit
1/2nd	right middle	Patient care unit
1/2nd	right bottom	Patient care unit
1/Basement	middle	Clinical Engineering
1/Basement	left middle	Storage
1/Basement	left bottom	Decontamination Service
2/1st	left top	Behavioral Health
2/1st	middle	Equipment Services
3/Basement	right top	Storage
3/Basement	middle	Nuclear Medicine
3/Basement	middle bottom	Hemodialysis

Table 3: Semantic summary of workflow states in Figure 4.

6.3 The Goodness-of-Fit

We experimented with different values of the scaling constant w in Equation 5 to build the transition models. If $w = 0$, our framework gives the maximum likelihood estimation. When $w > 0$, the scaling constant controls the tradeoff between maximizing $\Pr(N|P)$ and deconstructing the potentials in the hidden field. Users can chose a value according to the correlation degree of the workflow patterns. In this paper, we perform an exhaustive search in $[\frac{r}{2}, \frac{1+r}{2}]$

with step size 0.1 where r is the average non-weighted Frobenius inner products of the transition matrices.

To measure the goodness-of-fit of the learned transition models, we compute the *average* log-*loss* with test location traces. For a test location trace $Tr = (L_1, L_2, \cdots, L_t)$ and its corresponding workflow sequence $Tr = (s_1, s_2, \cdots, s_\ell)$ transformed with workflow states C, where $s_i = (c_i, d_i)$, the average log-loss is calculated as

$$L(Tr) = -\frac{1}{\ell} \log \Pr(Tr|P, q), \tag{8}$$

where $\Pr(Tr|P, q)$ is defined in Equation 1 and $\mu = (P, q)$ is learned from training data. According to Rissanen and Langdon [14], smaller average log-loss implies better compression of the data when using the estimated parameters.

In the following, after constructing the workflow states C, we randomly partition the data into 10 subsets and compute the average log-loss in 10 rounds. In each round, we use 9 of these subsets as training data to estimate the transition parameters $\mu = (P, q)$ and compute $L(Tr)$ for each Tr in the remaining test data. The solid green lines in Figure 5 show the average log-loss along the sequence length ℓ for different types of medical devices. We also show the performances with dashed green lines for the baseline models. The baseline model of each type straightforwardly estimates the transition parameters without considering the correlation among different types of moving objects. In the figure, we can see that our models based on HMRFs achieve lower information loss consistently for all types of moving objects.

In practice, as we will discuss in Section 6.5, sufficient observations might not be available to monitor the ongoing workflow patterns. In this case, our models can perform much better than baselines by holistic estimation. To demonstrate this, we repeat the above comparison by using only 1 subset as the training data. In Figure 5, as shown by the red lines, our models achieve much better performance. Our models not only achieve lower information losses, but also produce robust results without rigid jumps.

6.4 The Simulation Performance

In addition to the goodness-of-fit in terms of information loss, a realistic model should also be able to simulate the modeled process without breaking important characteristics. In the research of time series data, one important characteristic is the autocorrelation function, ACF, which describes the serial dependence structure in the sequence models. In our workflow models, the state space C is categorical, thus we propose to investigate the χ^2 statistic to test the homogeneity. Specifically, for a set of categorical sequences $\{Tr = (c_1, \cdots, c_l)\}$ where $c_i \in C$ and $C = \{1, 2, \cdots, |C|\}$, the *auto* χ^2 *function*, AXF, is calculated as

$$\mathrm{AXF}(h) = \sum_{i=1}^{|C|} \sum_{j=1}^{|C|} \frac{(M_{ij} - E_{ij})^2}{E_{ij}}$$

where $M_{ij} = \sum_{Tr} \sum_{k=1}^{l-h} [c_k = i, c_{k+h} = j]$, $M_{i*} = \sum_{j=1}^{|C|} M_{ij}$, $M_{*j} = \sum_{i=1}^{|C|} M_{ij}$, $M = \sum_{Tr}(l - h)$ and $E_{ij} = \frac{M_{i*} M_{*j}}{M}$. The degree of freedom of the corresponding χ^2 distribution for $\mathrm{AXF}(h)$ is $(|C| - 1)^2$. We can then calculate the p-value of the test of homogeneity with a null hypothesis that $(c_1, \cdots, c_{l-h})$ and $(c_h, \cdots, c_l)$ are independent. In Figure 6, we show the p-values of $\mathrm{AXF}(h)$ for the raw observations in solid lines. As can be seen, the serial dependence structures of the simulated processes shown in dashed lines are quite close to that of raw observations. Furthermore, we prefer the p-values that increase rapidly along h. This means the long-term dependence is little in the sequences and thus CTMC is a feasible model.

6.5 The Prototype Applications

The learned workflow model is valuable in that a range of practical problems can benefit from the results of modeling. In this paper, we have implemented a management information system, HISflow, to exploit the discovered knowledge for healthcare operation and management. In the following we elaborate on the techniques used in our implementation.

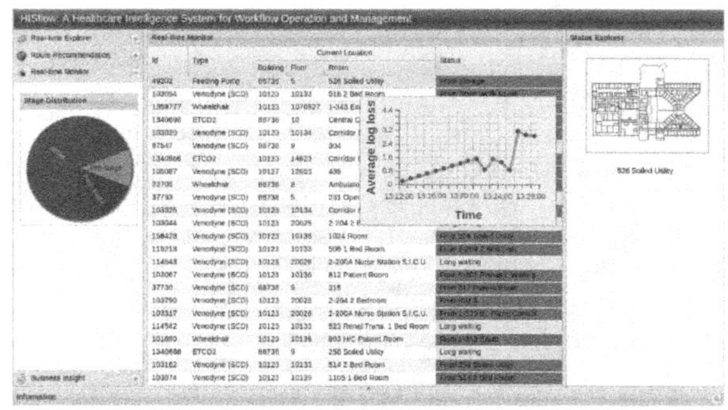

Figure 7: The screenshot of HISflow.

6.5.1 *Workflow Monitoring*

When the mined workflow patterns are legislated as procedure codes, we can identify abnormal behavior from daily healthcare activities in a real-time manner. When such anomaly occurs, warnings and alerts can be activated by the management system. Such a system helps reduce the risks of faults or accidents of healthcare services. To develop this system, a simple approach is to rank the ongoing trajectories of all monitored medical devices based on average log-loss in Equation 8. In this way, the devices ranked in the top are worth more scrutiny. However, this ranking results might not be intuitive from the management perspective. In fact, it is vital to provide more insights into the cause for the higher log-loss trajectories. To this end, we further identify the recent transition $s_i = (c_i, d_i)$ in $Tr = (s_1, s_2, \cdots, s_l)$ which causes $L(Tr)$ to increase. With the identified s_i, we can then clarify whether the increase is caused by c_i or d_i via comparing $-\log P_{c_{i-1}c_i}$ and $-\log q_{c_i} + q_{c_i} d_i$. If $-\log P_{c_{i-1}c_i}$ is larger, the increase is caused by c_i because the transition coming from c_{i-1} is unlikely to end at c_i. Otherwise, it indicates that the device stays at c_i too long.

A screenshot of the real-time monitoring is shown in Figure 7.As can be seen, the average log-loss of the selected device (Id = 49202) increases linearly at the beginning, which means the device stayed at a workflow state c and $-\log q_c + q_c d$ increases linearly with waiting time d. As shown in red, when this device is moved from Storage Room (left middle spot in Figure 4b) to 526 Soiled Utility Room (blue spot in the floor map in Figure 7), it is ranked into the top due to the unlikely transition. We also show the related information in the grid and the location status on the floor map. Such an intuitive and interpretable real-time monitor system is valuable for the hospital managers to improve the quality of healthcare services.

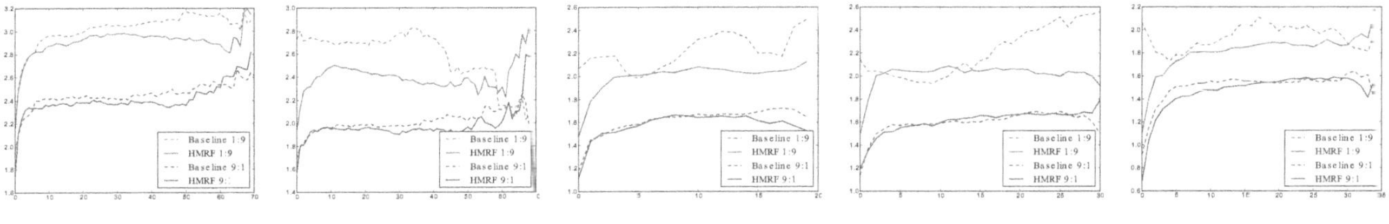

(a) Wheelchair (b) Venodyne (c) Feeding Pump (d) PCA Pump (e) ETCO2

Figure 5: A comparison of the average log-loss. X-axis: the sequence length ℓ. Y-axis: the average log-loss.

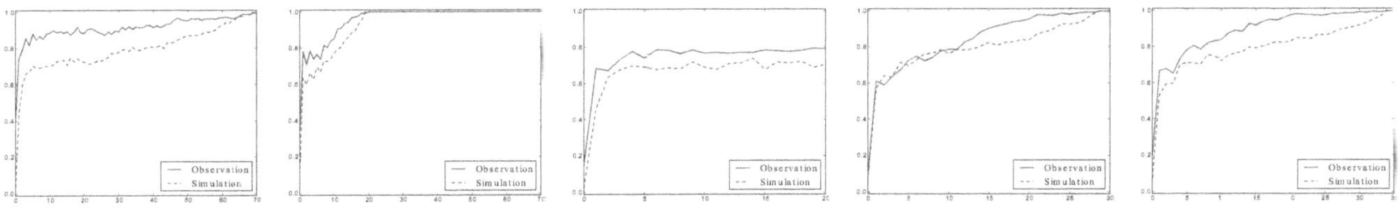

(a) Wheelchair (b) Venodyne (c) Feeding Pump (d) PCA Pump (e) ETCO2

Figure 6: A comparison of the AXF structure. X-axis: the time-lag h in AXF. Y-axis: the p-value of AXF.

6.5.2 *Workflow Auditing*

Our workflow models can also provide insights into auditing the efficiency of the healthcare services. Particularly, hospital managers would like to know how and how much the indoor spaces and the medical devices are being used. With our models, the utilization efficiency of medical devices and indoor space can be measured with sound statistics.

First, we can use waiting time parameter q in each state c to measure the utilization efficiency of the medical devices. Specifically, a small q indicates that the healthcare procedures taken in these states need a lot of time. For the workflow states corresponding to preprocessing maintenance stage (e.g., Storage rooms) and postprocessing stage (e.g., Soiled Utility Rooms, Decontamination Service Rooms), this small q means the processing procedures are not efficient. Second, to investigate the utilization efficiency of the indoor space, we would like to know the proportion of time the stochastic process spend at each state. In our CTMC model, this proportion at the ith state can be estimated by the stationary probability $r_i = \lim_{t\to\infty} Pr(S(t) = i) = \frac{\pi_i/q_i}{\sum_j \pi_j/q_j}$ where $\pi_j = \sum_i \pi_i P_{ij}$ and $\sum_j \pi_j = 1$.

Our system periodically calculates these statistics which allow hospital managers to audit the utilization efficiency of the medical devices and indoor space. By showing the trends over time and comparisons between different hospitals, one can get both intuitive understanding and quantitative measurement of the ongoing operation performance.

6.5.3 *Workflow Compliance Inspection*

The procedure of healthcare services is an operation process controlled by the science of medical treatment as well as industry legislation. Non-compliance practices lead to adverse affects such as litigation, prosecution and damage to brand reputation. To inspect the workflow compliance, we can calibrate the classical workflow sequences with respect to given workflow policies. In our stochastic model, the classical workflow sequences can be constructed by finding the most likely trajectories. Note that, in addition to providing statistic evidence on workflow compliance, the constructed classic workflow sequences are also helpful for understanding the ongoing workflow practices. Technically, given the initial state c, the final state c' and a time duration d, finding the most likely trajectory is an optimization problem to $\max_{Tr} \Pr(Tr|P, q)$, where $Tr = (s_1, \cdots, s_l)$, $s_i = (c_i, d_i)$, with constraints $c_1 = c, c_l = c'$ and $\sum_{i=1}^{l} d_i = d$. With parameters $\mu = (P, q)$ learned by our framework, this boundary value problem [13] can be solved by dynamic programming algorithms.

7. RELATED WORK

Workflow analysis conventionally relies on detailed workflow logs [1, 15, 7]. The workflow processes are typically represented by activity graphs. Given the execution logs, which are lists of activity records, the workflow mining can be formalized as a graph mining problem by deeming the execution logs as walks on the activity graphs [1]. In practice, there might be discrepancies between the actual workflow processes and the processes perceived by the management. In this case, to discover a completely specified workflow design model, Van der Aalst et al. [15] presented an algorithm to extract a process model from the workflow logs and represent it in terms of a Petri net. Instead of discovering the complete model, Greco et al. [7] later formalized the problem of discovering the most frequent patterns of executions, i.e., the workflow substructures that have been scheduled more frequently and had lead to a desired final configuration. However, these methods rely on the workflow logs which are often recorded by people in the healthcare industry. Thus, the results may be distorted due to the missed activities and bias in the logs. These distorted results can be misleading for many operation and management tasks in hospitals, such as the inspection of workflow compliance. In comparison, as we discussed in Section 1, in this paper we propose a proactive approach to workflow modeling by mining the digital location traces of moving objects automatically recorded by RTLS in the hospitals, which requires minimum amount of human intervention. The statistical modeling results provided by our approach are helpful for a range of operation and management tasks in hospital environments.

In terms of methodology, another category of related work is the modeling and prediction of human activities. For instance, Yin et al. [17] proposed stochastic process models to predict the goals of indoor human activities. Furthermore, for multiple-goal recognition, Chai and Yang [3] proposed a two-level architecture for behavior modeling and Hu and Yang [8] developed a dynamic Bayesian model where skip-chain conditional random fields were used for modeling interleaving goals. However, these approaches are supervised and require sufficient training data. Also, the activities considered in the above papers are not within the hospital environments, where specialized workflow and activities happen. In the hospital environments, the desired knowledge to be discovered is different from and more complicated than that within other environments, such as school or company.

In terms of analytics of location traces, trajectory pattern mining is also related to this work. For instance, Giannotti et al. [6] introduced trajectory patterns as frequent behaviors in terms of both time and space, where the frequent trajectory patterns are computed based on the given thresholds. In [9], methods were proposed to discover the periodic patterns from spatio-temporal data, where a periodic pattern is defined as a regular activity which periodically happens at certain locations. Also, Yang and Hu [16] proposed methods to discover sequential patterns from imprecise trajectories of moving objects. However, these methods developed for outdoor space are not designed for the purpose of workflow modeling in the indoor hospital environments, and more importantly, the mined frequent patterns cannot provide a parsimonious description of healthcare activities in hospitals and support the applications we have considered.

Finally, the last category of related work is the detection of area-of-interest with trajectory data. For instance, Liu et al. [11] proposed a non-density-based approach, called mobility-based clustering, to identify the hotspots of moving vehicles in an urban area. The key idea is that sample objects are used as "sensors" to perceive the vehicle crowdedness in nearby areas using their instant mobility, rather than the "object representatives". Moreover, Zheng et al. [18] proposed a stay point concept and identified hotspots from human moving trajectory. One location was considered as a hotspot if a lot of moving objects stay nearby over a thresholded time period. In addition, Giannotti et al. [6] used the neighborhood function to model Regions-of-Interest. Basically, they partitioned the spatial space into grids and quantified the interest of each grid with the density and the direction information of each grid. As we have discussed, even some methods mentioned above are very successful for analyzing outdoor location traces, most of them are not applicable to the proposed indoor hospital environments because of the unique characteristics of the indoor space.

8. CONCLUDING REMARKS

In this paper, we exploited the location traces of medical devices for modeling the healthcare workflow patterns in the hospital environment. Specifically, we developed a stochastic process-based framework, which provides parsimonious descriptions for long location traces. This framework provides new opportunities to understand the logistics of a large hospital in a concise manner. From the application perspective, the discovered knowledge, such as workflow states, transition patterns, and co-transiting relationships, can be integrated for use in the management information system we developed. With this system, we showed that valuable intelligent applications for healthcare operation and management can be enabled to manage, evaluate and optimize the healthcare services.

Acknowledgements

This research was partially supported by National Science Foundation (NSF) via grant numbers CCF-1018151 and IIS-1256016.

References

[1] Rakesh Agrawal, Dimitrios Gunopulos, and Frank Leymann. Mining process models from workflow logs. In *EDBT*, 1998.

[2] A. Banerjee, I. Dhillon, J. Ghosh, and S. Sra. Generative model-based clustering of directional data. In *SIGKDD*, 2003.

[3] X. Chai and Q. Yang. Multiple-goal recognition from low-level signals. In *AAAI*, 2005.

[4] Y. Ge, H. Xiong, Z.H. Zhou, H. Ozdemir, J. Yu, and K.C Lee. Top-eye: top-k evolving trajectory outlier detection. In *CIKM*, 2010.

[5] Y. Ge, H. Xiong, C. Liu, and Z.H. Zhou. A taxi driving fraud detection system. In *ICDM*, 2011.

[6] F. Giannotti, M. Nanni, D. Pedreschi, and F. Pinelli. Trajectory pattern mining. In *SIGKDD*, 2007.

[7] Gianluigi Greco, Antonella Guzzo, Giuseppe Manco, and Domenico Sacca. Mining and reasoning on workflows. *TKDE*, 17(4):519–534, 2005.

[8] D.H. Hu and Q. Yang. Cigar: concurrent and interleaving goal and activity recognition. In *AAAI*, 2008.

[9] Z.H. Li, B.L. Ding, J.W. Han, R. Kays, and P. Nye. Mining periodic behaviors for moving objects. In *SIGKDD*, 2010.

[10] C. Liu, Y. Ge, and H. Xiong. A stochastic model for context-aware anomaly detection in indoor location traces. In *ICDM*, 2012.

[11] S.Y. Liu, Y.H. Liu, L.M. Ni, J.P. Fan, and M.L. Li. Towards mobility-based clustering. In *SIGKDD*, 2010.

[13] T.J. Perkins. Maximum likelihood trajectories for continuous-time markov chains. *NIPS*, 2009.

[14] J. Rissanen and G.G. Langdon. Arithmetic coding. *IBM Journal of research and development*, 1979.

[15] Wil Van der Aalst, Ton Weijters, and Laura Maruster. Workflow mining: Discovering process models from event logs. *TKDE*, 16(9):1128–1142, 2004.

[16] J. Yang and M. Hu. Trajpattern: Mining sequential patterns from imprecise trajectories of mobile objects. In *EDBT*, 2006.

[17] J. Yin, D. Shen, Q. Yang, and Z.N. Li. Activity recognition through goal-based segmentation. In *AAAI*, 2005.

[18] Y. Zheng, L. Zhang, X. Xie, and W.Y. Ma. Mining interesting locations and travel sequences from gps trajectories. In *WWW*, 2009.

Activity Ranking in LinkedIn Feed

Deepak Agarwal, Bee-Chung Chen, Rupesh Gupta,
Joshua Hartman, Qi He, Anand Iyer, Sumanth Kolar, Yiming Ma,
Pannaga Shivaswamy, Ajit Singh and Liang Zhang
LinkedIn Corporation
Mountain View, CA, USA
{dagarwal,bchen,rugupta,jhartmain,qhe}@linkedin.com
{aiyer,skolar,yma,pshivasw,ajsingh,lizhang}@linkedin.com

ABSTRACT

Users on an online social network site generate a large number of heterogeneous activities, ranging from connecting with other users, to sharing content, to updating their profiles. The set of activities within a user's network neighborhood forms a stream of updates for the user's consumption. In this paper, we report our experience with the problem of ranking activities in the LinkedIn homepage feed. In particular, we provide a taxonomy of social network activities, describe a system architecture (with a number of key components open-sourced) that supports fast iteration in model development, demonstrate a number of key factors for effective ranking, and report experimental results from extensive online bucket tests.

Categories and Subject Descriptors

H.4 [**Information Systems Applications**]: Miscellaneous

General Terms

Design; Experimentation

Keywords

Activity Ranking; Relevance; Large Scale Learning

1. INTRODUCTION

Professional networking site LinkedIn and other social networking sites provide users an easy way to connect with other users and keep track of various updates from them. An important mechanism that helps each user keep track of such updates is through a feed of activities that is centered around her egocentric networks (her connections, people she follows, companies she follows, etc). Some examples of activities generated by a user's first degree network include job changes or profile updates, sharing of content, likes or comments on a piece of information, joining a group or connecting with another user. Since the volume of social network activities is usually large and each user has limited time to consume information in his/her feed, it is important to rank activities according their "relevance" to the user, while keeping the feed fresh and diverse.

KDD'14, August 24–27, 2014, New York, NY, USA.

ACM 978-1-4503-2956-9/14/08 ...$15.00.
http://dx.doi.org/10.1145/2623330.2623362.

The primary goal of the feed is to maximize long-term user engagement, manifested by a user visiting the site more often. However, optimizing the visit frequency of a user is difficult in practice due to long feedback loops. Proxies that are readily measurable with little feedback delay are often optimized in practice. While there are several such proxies, the most popular approach is based on the probability of a user clicking on an activity. Such a click probability is also called click-through rate (CTR).

Challenges: Ranking activities in social network feeds is challenging because of the following reasons.

- *Scalability*: The volume of activities to be ranked is high. The number of user visits is large. The data to be used for training CTR prediction models is also large. A ranking system needs to scale along all these dimensions.
- *Personalization*: There is wide variation in egocentric networks (neighborhoods) of users. Users also have different information needs and feed consumption patterns, and may prefer different types of activities. A good ranking system needs to rank activities according to each user's individual preference and provide support to test many potential signals for personalization through fast iteration of machine-learned models.

This paper describes our experience working with the production system at LinkedIn. We describe the approaches we took to address these challenges and the lessons learned. We would like to point out at the very outset that this paper is not about presentation of fundamentally new machine learning methods, but rather about practical challenges faced when deploying machine learning methods in a production environment and our attempts to address them. When studying new data mining and machine learning methods, testing out-of-sample predictive accuracy of machine-learned models on retrospective data is usually the main focus . Although useful, it does not provide the whole story of the challenges involved in deploying models in production.

Before we discuss our ranking system, we first describe a couple of potential straw man approaches that are practiced in various industrial settings when dealing with feed recommendation problems. We did not find these to be satisfactory in our problem setting.

Approach 1 – Reverse chronological ordering of feed activities: Ranking based on reverse chronological ordering (recency) of activities leads to a fresh but not necessarily a relevant feed. We conducted an online bucket test for three weeks in 2013 comparing pure recency ordering with relevance-based ranking (using our model that served the majority of users at that time), and found the CTR of relevance-based ranking to be 43% higher than that of or-

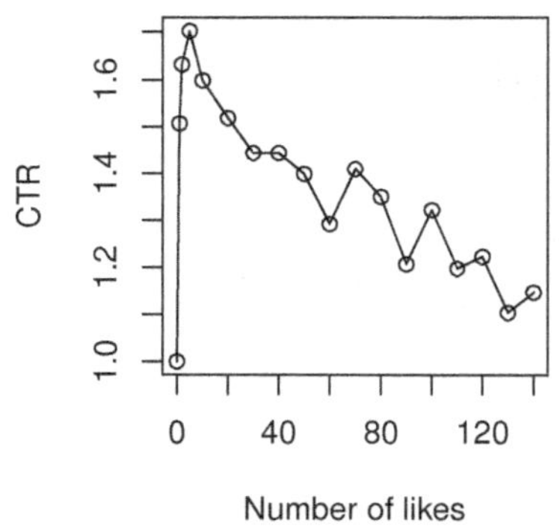

Figure 1: CTR as a function of number of likes.

dering by recency.[1] By the end of 2013, we further improved our relevance model and obtained an additional 15% gain. We believe that a well-designed relevance-based ranking system can significantly outperform recency-based ranking. In our scenario, even after achieving 60% lift (in CTR), there is still more room left for improvement.

Approach 2 – Ranking by social popularity: On LinkedIn, users can like (by clicking on the "like button") or comment on activities. Social popularity can be defined as the number of *likes* (i.e., "like button" clicks) or comments. It may seem at the first glance that ranking activities according to their social popularity is good enough. This is not true in our scenario. Firstly we note that a non-negligible fraction of activities do not receive any like or comment on LinkedIn, despite being shown to a non-negligible set of users. For those that do receive likes or comments, the CTR is not a monotonically increasing function of social popularity as shown in Figure 1. This does not imply that social popularity is not a useful signal, but that it is extremely sparse and requires systematic modeling for leverage.

Contributions: In this paper, we make the following contributions:

- We introduce a taxonomy of activities in social network feeds in Section 3.1.
- We present our system architecture and modeling process (as of 2013) that supports fast model iteration (Section 4). Our main feature storage system (Voldemort[2]) and activity indexing system (Sensei DB [3]) have already been open-sourced. We are also in the process of open-sourcing our large-scale model training library.
- We illustrate the user behavior when interacting with social network feeds based on "randomized" data in Section 3. Randomization helps reduce the bias induced by the ranking methods used during data collection.
- We report on extensive experiments based on online bucket tests (A/B experiments) in Section 5. In particular, we illustrate the effect of freshness, the benefit of impression discounting, and the gains brought in by personalization.

[1]This experiment only considers each user's first feed visit in a session. Subsequent visits in a session are served through other methods.

[2]http://www.project-voldemort.com/voldemort/

[3]http://www.senseidb.com/

Terminology: In the rest of this paper, the terms *activity* and *item* are used interchangeably both referring to a professional network activity. The term *impression* is used to refer to an item's appearance in a user's LinkedIn feed. Because users primarily respond to an activity in the feed through clicks (including clicks on links to see more information and clicks on buttons to share, like or submit a comment on the activity), we combine all these responses and denote it as the click-through rate (CTR) and use it as our primary measure to optimize in this paper.

2. RELATED WORK

Ranking activities from a user's interpersonal network has always been important in social networks. One line of work is to rank homogeneous tweet feeds in Twitter. Chen *et. al.* conducted a set of user studies for information stream recommendation on Twitter. Their purpose was to manually study how various features result in various user preferences to the Tweet feeds. They studied content sources, topic interest of users, and social voting on items in [8]; and thread length, topic relevance and tie-strength in [7], respectively. Their work paved the way for the future automated studies. For example, [1, 11] enriched user profiles with their activities on Twitter for a personalized news recommendation system; and [6] produced different rankers for different sub-communities of a user's social network, where these rankers are described as topics so that the user can rank his/her social feeds by specific topics. As this line of work mainly focused on homogeneous feeds, they are essentially close to the earlier personalized news feed recommendation work [10], except that they used additional social network features like social voting, social tie strength etc. to model the activity relevance. Furthermore, this line of work did not conduct large-scale study.

More recently, researchers started to pay attention to the heterogeneous nature of the network activity ranking problem. Starting from small-scale data, [18] identified different types of user activities from a few users' tweet feeds in Twitter; and [9] investigated the importance of diversity on the Twitter item recommendation and found that content was more relevant to users when it was highly homogeneous or highly heterogeneous. These works inferred heterogeneous activity types from Twitter's text feeds.

Subsequently, researchers started to directly study the heterogeneous data. Berkovsky *et. al.* computed the relevance of the feed items using user-user relationship strengths and user-action interest scores for the social feed personalization in the online Total Wellbeing Diet (TWD) portal [3] and an experimental eHealth portal [2] respectively. These personalized streams attracted more user attention compared to the chronologically ordered feed lists. Paek *et. al.* [19] attempted to understand how people judge the importance of their newsfeed in Facebook by asking some Facebook users to rate the importance of their newsfeed posts as well as their friends'. Classifiers were learned to identify predictive features for the newsfeed and friend relevance. Bourke *et. al.* [4] improved social stream relevance by leveraging features from messages, content source, and the users for Facebook. Soh *et. al.* [20] recommended Facebook social feeds to users by exploiting their response behavior in the past. Based on SocialBlue's news feeds, [12] computed the relevance of network activity feeds from the observed interactions of the individuals in the past. They diversified features into four types: user-user, user-action, user-object and age of activities. Some researchers also investigated the heterogeneous network activity stream personalization problem for enterprise network activity streams [13, 14]. They concluded that the activity stream based user profile is more productive than entity-based user profile for personalizing the stream. Despite the boom of this line in research, all the above work on heterogeneous activity feed ranking has not been evaluated on top of large-scale production systems.

The closest related work is [15], where various machine learning techniques including linear models on features and latent factor models (matrix factorization and tensor factorization) were applied to activity ranking in LinkedIn feed. Their focus was on offline modeling. Here, we present an overview of the end-to-end system and online bucket test results.

3. DATA ANALYSIS

In this section, we study several important aspects of activity ranking based on randomized data. In particular, we assigned a small fraction of users to the *random bucket*. For each user in the random bucket, we shuffle (uniformly at random) the top-100 activities that could appear in the user's feed and present the randomized feed to the user. For details, see Section 4.2. Such randomized data helps to reduce the *serving bias* caused by the ranking algorithm used during the data collection period and the *positional bias* caused by potential high likelihood of placing certain kinds of activities at certain positions in the feed.

We start by introducing different types of activities in the feed. We then show some interesting characteristics of our data. They motivate our relevance modeling described later.

3.1 Taxonomy of Activities

In this section, we present a taxonomy of different types of activities in a social network. In general, each activity can be represented as a triple: (actor, verb, object). For example, member A connects to member B, member A shares article C, and member A updates her profile picture D. Each user has two roles in a social network. On the one hand, a user is an *actor* who generates activities for other users to consume. On the other hand, a user is also a *viewer*, who receives a stream of activities generated by the actors in her network. The problem we study is how to rank this activity stream for each viewer. We note that, in addition to users, there may be other kinds of actors in the network. For example, in the LinkedIn network, companies, schools and content channels are actors as well, which can share different kinds of information.

The *type* of an activity, also called an *activity type*, is a triple of (actor type, verb type, object type), e.g., (member, connect, member), (member, share, article) or (member, profile-update, picture). We broadly classify activities in social networks into the following five categories and also show examples of activities on LinkedIn in Table 1.

1. Connection activities: These are the activities that add new edges in the social network. We can further classify these activities into:

- *Symmetric connection*: For example, the event of a member connecting to another member adds an undirected edge (or more precisely, a bidirectional edge) to the LinkedIn professional network.
- *Asymmetric connection*: For example, the event of a member starting to follow another member or a company (in order to receive what the followee shares) adds a directed edge to the LinkedIn network; the followee will not receive anything from the follower. Another example is the event of a member joining a group (which connects the member to the group).

2. Informational activities: These are the activities where entities in the network pass information to others. In the LinkedIn network, members and companies can share messages, articles, pictures, discussions (in groups) or jobs.

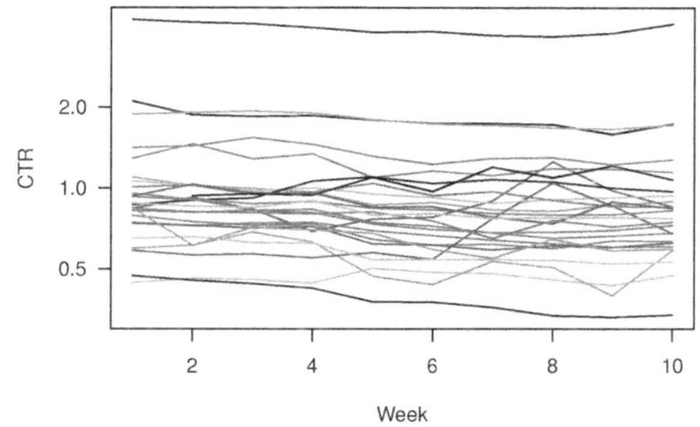

Figure 2: Relative CTRs of different activity types over a 10-week period. The y-axis is log-scaled.

3. Profile activities: These are the activities generated due to users' profile changes. Examples of such profile changes on LinkedIn include updates of profile pictures, contact information, job positions, etc.

4. Opinion activities: These are activities where users express their opinions on different kinds of objects (e.g., articles, pictures, discussions, etc.). Two kinds of opinions are common on social network sites: *like* and *comment*, where the former takes a user little effort to express his/her opinion, while the latter requires a user to put his/her opinions into words.

5. Site-specific activities: The above four categories of activities generally appear on many social network websites. However, each website may also have some activities specific to its purposes or needs. For example, LinkedIn is a professional social network and has job-related activities: job anniversaries, endorsements of users' skills and job recommendations.

Characteristics of CTR of activity types: Users' response to different activity types vary. In Figure 2, we show the CTRs of different activity types relative to the average CTR of all types for users in the random bucket. Each curve represents the CTR of an activity type over a 10-week period. Due to confidentiality reasons, we do not label the curves. However, the key message from this plot is that a few activity types have much higher CTRs than others. Also note that the CTRs of some activity types do not change much over time, while the CTRs of some other types can have large temporal variations.

3.2 Freshness

In this section, we show how freshness of activities affects click-through rate. We consider two aspects of freshness. First, the age of an activity since its creation. Second, the number of times a user has seen a particular item in the past. Note that these two notions of freshness can differ significantly for different users. For example, a heavy user might see an activity several times within the first hour of its lifetime. In contrast, a light user who did not visit the feed for a week would not have seen any activity less than 7 days old.

3.2.1 *Effect of Activity Age*

To measure the effect of age of activity on CTR, we analyzed the impression and click data collected from the random bucket (described in Section 4.2) over a period of six weeks. Even though the random shuffling mechanism used in the random bucket helps to

Table 1: Taxonomy of activities on LinkedIn

Category	Actor Type	Verb Type	Object Type
Connection	member	connect or follow	member or company
	member	join	group
Informational	member or company	share	article, picture, message, discussion, group, job
Profile	member	profile-update	picture, address, phone, snapshot, job-change
Opinion	member	like or comment	article, picture, message, discussion, group, job
Site-Specific	member	anniversary	job-anniversary
	member	endorse or endorse-by	member
	member	recommend or recommend-by	member

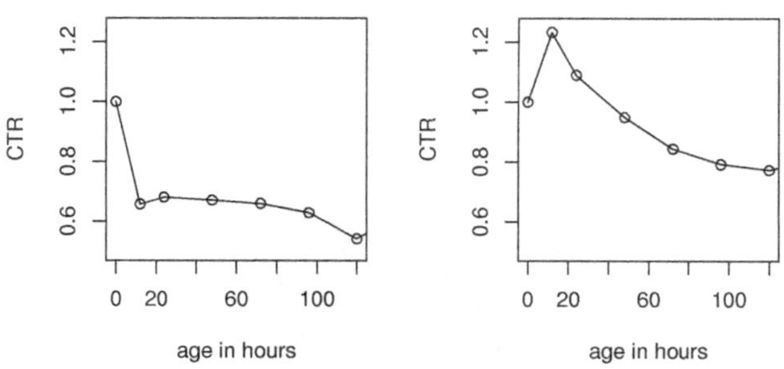

Figure 3: Effect of activity age on CTR for information sharing (left) and for profile picture updates (right). The CTRs have been normalized so that the CTR at age 0 is one.

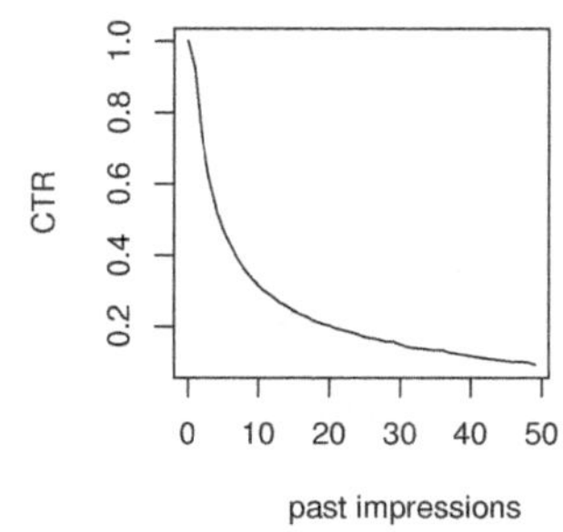

Figure 4: Effect of repeated impressions on CTR.

remove serving and positional biases, the number of times an item has been seen by a user in the past can still confound the analysis. To account for any potential bias due to user fatigue from repeated impressions, we only considered the first impression of an item for each user. The age of an item was coarsely divided into a few buckets. For example, if the age of an item was between zero and twelve hours, it was placed in the zero bucket. If the age was between 12 and 24, it was placed in the bucket corresponding to age 12 and so on. For each of these buckets, we estimated the CTR based on the items that were presented to users.

The CTR curves of two different activity types are shown in Figure 3. Due to proprietary reasons, for each activity type, the y-axis have been normalized based on the CTR of the first bucket. The plots show that the decay of CTR with age can look different for different types of activities. In the case of profile picture updates, there is a spike in CTR a few hours after the activity is created which then drops down subsequently. In contrast, in the case of information sharing there is a sharp drop in CTR initially followed by a much slower decay from there on.

3.2.2 Effect of Repeated Impressions

To determine the variation in CTR with repeated impressions, we also use the random bucket data. For each activity, we counted the number of past impressions of the activity for each user. If an item never appeared in a user's feed before, the number of past impressions for that (user, item) pair would be zero.

The behavior of CTR with the number of previous impressions of the same activity is shown in Figure 4. In this plot, the x-axis shows the number of times an activity was seen before and the y-axis shows the corresponding CTR. The plot has been normalized by the CTR of the first impression. It is obvious from the plot that the CTR of an activity decreases as it is seen multiple times. This curve suggests the need for discounting the predicted CTR based on the number of previous impressions of an activity.

3.3 Diversity of the Feed

LinkedIn feed consists of diverse types of activities as introduced in Section 3.1. In this section, we analyze how CTR changes with respect to the diversity in the feed using the random bucket data. For each feed that was presented to a user, we consider the ID of the actor of the activity at position 10 and count the number of times activities from the same actor appeared in positions 1 to 9. When this count is high, this corresponds to a scenario where most activities in the feed have the same actor. In other words, a high count reflects lack of actor diversity in the feed. Similarly, we considered the counts of the same verb type or same object type in positions 1 to 9. To avoid any bias cased by users with very few connections (thus, it is unlikely to have diverse feeds for them), we restricted this analysis to only those users who had at least 50 connections. The decay of CTR with respect to repeated actor ID, verb type and object type is shown in Figure 5. In all the plots, the y-axis have been normalized so that the CTR in the case of no repetition (i.e., #repetitions = 0) is one. It can be seen that for all the three different types of repetitions, there is a rapid initial decay in CTR.

3.4 Connection Relationship

Since members on LinkedIn are connected via a professional network, we can study how the connection relationship between a viewer and an actor affects whether the viewer would click on an activity of the actor. A few examples of connection relationship between a viewer and an actor are in the following.

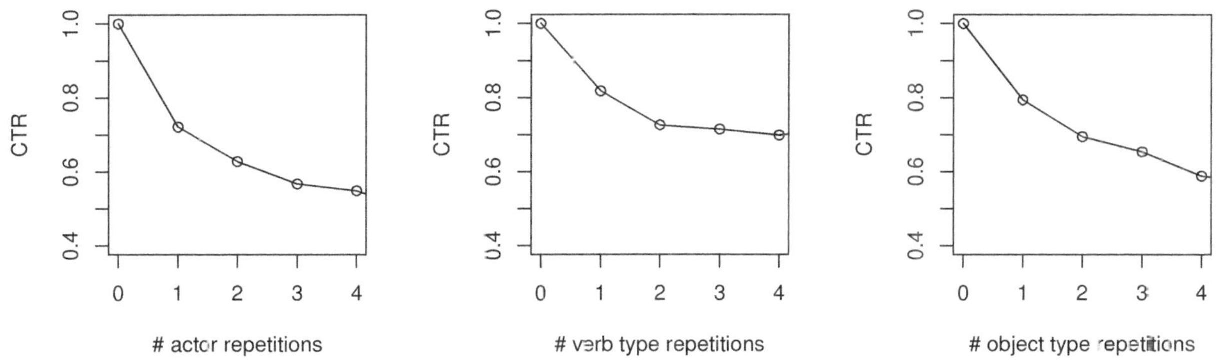

Figure 5: Effect of (lack of) diversity on CTR for actor ID, verb type and object type.

Table 2: CTR lift when the viewer and the actor have the same characteristic compared to the case where they do not.

Viewer-Actor Relationship	CTR Lift
Same Company	66%
Same Job Function	25%
Same Industry	33%
Same Geo Region	24%

Table 3: CTR lift when the viewer and the actor are in the same company for different types of activities.

Activity Type	CTR Lift
(member, post, message)	207%
(member, share, article)	111%
(member, connect, member)	72%
(member, profile-update, job-change)	-10%

- Demographic similarities based on age, gender and education, etc.
- Experience similarities based on the common companies, job positions, etc.
- Skill similarities based on the common skills and similar skills.
- Geo similarities based on the locations of the viewer and the actor at different resolutions (e.g., city, state and country).
- Social network similarities based on connections of the viewer and the actor.

Effect of connection relationship: We now present some observations from our data with respect to a couple of these similarity measures by looking at whether the viewer and the actor belong to the same company, have the same job function, are in the same industry or in the same geo-region. Table 2 shows that when the viewer and the actor have similar characteristics, there is a higher chance that the viewer would click on an activity of the actor. However, such behavior also depends on the type of activity. For example, consider whether the viewer and actor are in the same company or not. Averaged over all activity types, the CTR of "same company" is 66% higher than the CTR of "different companies". However, Table 3 shows that it is not the case for job-change type of activities. A viewer clicks more often on a job-change of an actor in a different company than a job-change of an actor in the same company, perhaps due to the high likelihood that the viewer already knew her connections in her company changed jobs.

3.5 Platform Dependence

From our analysis, we observe that users' interaction with activities differ significantly across the mobile and desktop platforms. We first looked at the impression distribution across different age

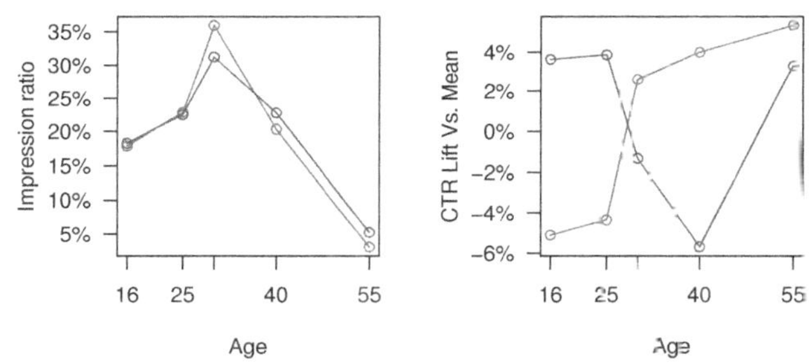

(a) Impression distributions (b) CTR lift

Figure 6: Behavior of different age groups of viewers on mobile (red) vs. desktop (blue)

groups of the viewer. It is evident from Figure 6a that the distribution of impressions is similar across age groups on the two platforms. We then looked at the CTR by age groups on these two platforms. This is shown in Figure 6b. Due to proprietary reasons, the plot only shows the deviation of CTR for an age group compared to the overall CTR on that platform. Surprisingly, although the impressions distribution is similar on the two platforms, different age groups respond differently on mobile and desktop. This example shows differences in user behavior across different age groups on different platforms. It is important to analyze users' behavioral differences on different platforms and build models that capture the behavior specific to each platform. As another example, we will show in Section 5 that a mobile specific model performs significantly better than simply using a desktop model to rank activities on our mobile feed.

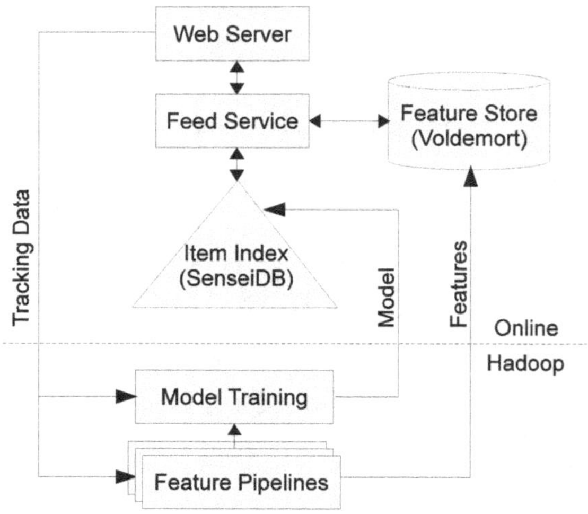

Figure 7: System architecture (simplified).

4. RELEVANCE SYSTEM

In this section, we first give an overview of our system as of 2013 and then outline our model training process which includes data collection, large-scale logistic regression and an offline replay methodology for model evaluation. The primary goal of relevance modeling is to accurately predict the CTR of a given user-item pair, i.e., the probability of the user clicking on the item. In additional to CTR prediction, it is also important to incorporate mechanisms to ensure freshness and diversity. These will be discussed in Section 4.5.

4.1 System Overview

At a high level our system consists of online components for serving users' feed requests, and also offline components for generating features and training models on Hadoop. Figure 7 shows the main components of our system and their interaction with one another. We would like to mention that two of these important components, the feature store (Voldemort) which provides large-scale feature storage and retrieval, and the item index (SenseiDB) which indexes items and ranks them according to a scoring model, have already been open-sourced and we are in the process of open-sourcing the model training component.

When a user logs in to LinkedIn, the web-server sends a request for the feed to the feed service. Activities generated on the LinkedIn professional network are stored in SenseiDB. When the feed service receives the ID of the viewer, it retrieves the appropriate model for the viewer (depending on the online bucket test running at that time) and sends the model to SenseiDB to score the candidate activities for the viewer stored in SenseiDB. The SenseiDB stores item specific features (for example: activity type, creation time etc). Some of our models incorporate additional features that are either not item specific or are derived through additional computation. For example, we use a score for the affinity of the viewer to each activity type in our models. Such features are generated by separate feature pipelines on Hadoop, and pushed to a Voldemort store which is a distributed key-value store. The feed service can then access these features efficiently from the Voldemort store. The feature pipelines generate features from the tracking data which is a log of impressions (with basic features of activities) and clicks. The features produced by the feature pipelines are also used in the training process which generates models for use in SenseiDB. More details on model training, features used and evaluation are provided next.

4.2 Training Data Collection

Collection of training data for our application can be a non-trivial exercise. In the absence of a good ranking model, a seemingly natural option is to rank activities in a reverse chronological order and present to the viewers. The response information (click/no-click) thus collected could then comprise the training dataset. However, this method of training data collection can severely suffer from serving bias in the following way. Usually viewers' attention is drawn primarily to the first few results in the feed. So if the serving scheme never serves activities of certain types to a viewer, the viewer cannot give his/her feedback on such activities. At LinkedIn, the frequencies at where different types of activities are generated are quite different. For example there are many more member connect member updates in the candidate set of activities than some other of the other types. This implies that a reverse chronologically sorted stream of a typical viewer would comprise of a large number of connection activities and other infrequent activities, like job changes, will rarely, if ever, get impressed on the viewer although they might be more relevant. This leads to data sparsity problem for a number of activity types.

The most common approach for eliminating serving bias is random serving, where activities in the candidate pool are ranked randomly. However, this scheme is likely to cause very poor user experience due to the following two reasons. First, many irrelevant and stale activities might get promoted to the top positions. Second, the set of activities presented at the first few positions would change dramatically upon each page reload. Moreover, the feed would still be dominated by a few types of activities that are more common than the others.

We overcome the aforementioned problems in the following way. We first use a ranking algorithm to rank activities. Then, the top-k results are permuted uniformly at random to prepare the final feed for the viewer. This scheme removes the serving bias from the training data to a large extent, without completely sacrificing user experience. Our training data consists of activities that were presented using this mechanism. The activities on which a viewer clicked are considered positive examples and those with which the viewer did not interact are considered negative examples. Such training data comes at the cost of reduced user experience due to randomization. Since model training/re-training is a continuous process which entails persistent availability of fresh training data, this cost must to be minimized. This is done by serving this randomized feed to only a small fraction of our viewers, and frequently changing this bucket of viewers. Also, we keep updating the underlying ranking model (which produces the top-k results for randomization) to the current best model. This ensures an improving user experience even for those viewers who happen to fall in the random serving bucket.

4.3 Model and Features

A score is required to rank the activities in the candidate pool. As discussed earlier, we use the predicted CTR as the score. To predict the CTR of each activity, we learn a logistic regression model with ℓ_2 regularization. Let y denote the click on the activity described by feature vector $\mathbf{x}$ then the corresponding Bernoulli random variable $\mathbb{Y}$ is modeled as

$$E[\mathbb{Y}] = \frac{1}{1 + \exp(-\boldsymbol{\theta}^\top \mathbf{x})} \quad (1)$$

where $\boldsymbol{\theta}$ is the parameter vector which we want to learn. Once $\boldsymbol{\theta}$ has been estimated from the training data, for any new example

$\mathbf{x}_{\text{new}}$ we simply use the mean of the Bernoulli distribution as the predicted CTR, i.e.,

$$\text{CTR}_{\text{predict}} = P(\{\mathbb{Y} = 1\}) = E[\mathbb{Y}] = \frac{1}{1 + \exp(-\boldsymbol{\theta}^\top \mathbf{x}_{\text{new}})} \quad (2)$$

We train a logistic regression model with a number of features, such as features extracted from the viewer's and actor's profile, features qualifying the connection strength and similarity between the viewer and the actor, features representing the age of an activity, features quantifying the affinity between the viewer and the type of an activity and the affinity between the viewer and the actor. Note that some of the features are generated using other models — logistic regression can be thought of as a tool to combine such base models. We also include interactions among the aforementioned features.

4.4 Model Training and Offline Evaluation

We train the logistic regression model using a Hadoop based distributed logistic regression algorithm. Our implementation of logistic regression is based on the Alternating Direction Method of Multipliers (ADMM) [5] which is a popular method for solving a convex optimization problem in a distributed fashion. We are in the process of making our implementation open source so that others facing similar challenges can benefit from it. The ADMM algorithm partitions the set of training examples into several blocks. Each block is assigned to a machine which solves (in parallel) a convex optimization problem independently on the training examples in that block. Solutions from different partitions are collected and a consensus solution is formed. The consensus solution is then sent to individual machines which update their solutions again. This process is repeated until convergence. More details can be found in [5]. This method is scalable and it allows us to train our models with a large number of training examples collected from our random bucket.

After we train a model, we need to evaluate the model before deploying it in production. For this, we use a replay methodology for unbiased offline evaluation of online serving schemes [17, 16]. We use the offline replay methodology since it is a theoretically sound way of evaluation. Typically we consider a few weeks of data from the random bucket (described in Section 4.2), starting from a point in time after the period over which the training data was collected. For replay, the activities that were presented at serve time in the random bucket are reordered using the candidate model obtained via training described above. After reordering, we only consider impressions that occur at exactly the same position as they appeared at serve time. We call these matched impressions and count the total number of clicks on such matched impressions. We call the total number of clicks on matched impressions as reward. We typically consider reward at the first feed position and the reward at the first three feed positions when comparing our models. Although the absolute value of reward may not be very meaningful, the relative rewards obtained from two different models are typically indicative of which model would perform better in production.

4.5 Reranking

Our model training described above focused only on accurately modeling the CTR of each user-activity pair. However, we pointed out in Section 3 that the click-through rate can also be influenced by aspects such as diversity and freshness.

Although relevance and diversity can be modeled jointly, such approaches typically require greedily picking the next activity based on the current set of items, which can be computationally prohibitive in a real online system serving millions of users. Hence we use a simple mechanism to enforce diversity in the feed. In this mechanism, we first score and sort all the candidate activities using the ranking model. We then go through the ranked list and count the number of times a particular actor or object appeared on the list before each item. The score of each item is discounted based on this count in a way that more prior occurrences of the same actor or object leads to a stronger discounting. In our experiments, we simply fix this reranking mechanism for all our models.

It is also important to keep the feed fresh. However, simply learning age based and impression count based coefficients from the data may not provide desired level of feed freshness. Since we also do not want to give a completely time sorted feed, we perform an additional exponential decay on the score based on the age of activities. The half lives of this decay are set in accordance with product requirements (which is influenced by user experience studies). Similarly, repeated impressions of the same activity is also discouraged by introducing an additional decay factor that takes into account past impression counts of the activity. These reranking modules allow an easy way of tuning the feed to match required characteristics.

5. EXPERIMENTS

In this section we describe several online bucket tests (A/B experiments) on the LinkedIn feed and a few offline replay experiment results. Most of our experiments are based on a large number of real users who visited LinkedIn. LinkedIn currently has more than 300 million members geographically spread across the world. A large fraction of visitors see the LinkedIn feed.

We continuously test new features and new models in our production system. We typically launch a new feature to a small fraction of users and if the feature works well compared to existing models, we slowly ramp the feature to more users. At any point in time, we are testing several models in production. It is impossible to present results from all the models that were in bucket tests. In this section, we present several interesting experiments focusing on just one aspect at a time. We also present some results where we combined a number of useful features in our production system.

5.1 Effectiveness of Replay Analysis

We described our offline replay evaluation metric in Section 4.4. In this section, we show the offline replay results and the corresponding online replay results for two models. We considered a baseline model in production that was constructed from the features mentioned in Section 4.3. We refer to this as Model A. We then added features derived from networks of viewer and actor and learned a new model using our training pipeline. We denote this model as Model B. In offline replay analysis, Model B showed a lift of 4.96% at the first feed position over Model A. When we ran these models in production for two weeks, the lifts that we observed for model B in those two weeks were 3.6% and 5.0% compared to model A. Although the absolute value of the performance improvement in the first week is slightly different from the offline lift for most of the models we tried in production, we have found that replay provides a sound way for deciding whether a model is a promising candidate for deployment. In the rest of this paper, we provide bucket test results from models deployed online rather than focusing on offline analyses.

5.2 Desktop Bucket Test Results

In this section, we show the online bucket test results using several new features that we incorporated into our modeling. First, we show the effect of adding them independently and finally we show the effect when we combined all the features.

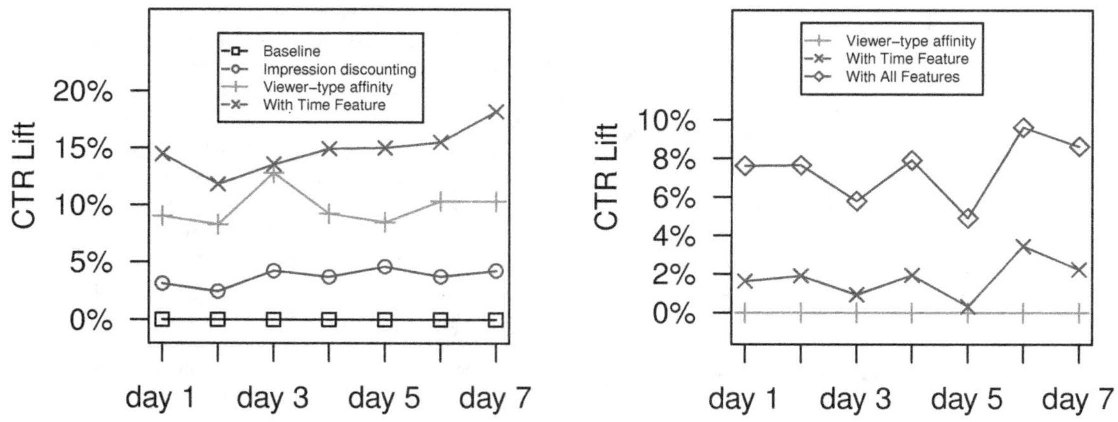

(a) Individual features

(b) All features

Figure 8: Desktop online CTR lift.

Effect of freshness.

As we discussed in Section 4.5, we control the freshness of the feed using an exponential decay on the score based on the age of the activity. To show how different segments of users behave differently to different levels of freshness, we consider two models that we had in our bucket tests. The two models were exactly the same except for the half life period on the exponential decay. Model A had an exponential decay with a half life of four days (which means the score predicted by the model halves every four days), while model B had an exponential decay with a half life of two days. Although the overall CTR for model B was slightly higher than that of model A, the results are more interesting when we segment users and look at the lifts on the individual segments. Users were divided into four segments (light, moderate, regular, heavy) based on the number of visits to LinkedIn feed. For heavy users, model B had a lift of about 25%, while for regular users model B had a smaller lift of about 7%. However, for moderate and light users, model A had a lift of 2.3 % and 6.6% respectively over model B. These results intuitively make sense. Visitors who come to LinkedIn more often expect to see fresher content, whereas visitors who visit LinkedIn less often are happy to consume older content.

Impression Discounting.

In the previous paragraph, we described bucket tests with age based freshness as the criterion. We now consider the effect based on repeated impressions of items. As we described in Section 3.2.2, we first estimated how the CTR decays with repeated impressions of activities. One challenge for impression discounting is that we have to store the number of past impressions to every activity that is served to a user. This requires a large key value store, where key is the ID of an activity and value is the number of past impressions of that activity for each viewer. We make use of a Voldemort store which was described in Section 4.1. We store the number of past impressions for several millions of activities such that these counts are available at runtime on our production systems. We then applied impression discounting to our best model at that time. By applying impression discounting, there was an improvement in CTR of about 2.2% during a period of one week. However, for our heaviest user segment (who visit our feed more than 10 times on an average per day), there was an improvement of over 5%.

Model Personalization.

In this section, we show results from couple of model improvements that we achieved through personalization. Our first approach was to develop an affinity score between viewers and activity types. As we described in Section 3.1, there are several activity types on the LinkedIn feed. Since different LinkedIn members can have different affinity towards different types of activities, we model the affinity between users and activity types. This affinity score was devised based on historic data of interaction between viewers and activity types. The basic idea of this score is to segment users based on their features (such as industry, job seniority, company size, language etc.). For each segment, we look at those user's historic data to collect how often they interacted with different activity types. From all this information, we compute an affinity score which is then used as a feature in modeling the click-through rate prediction via logistic regression. A second approach was to use a personalized age based decay for every user depending on time based features. This involved utilizing the last visit time of a user to LinkedIn. This feature effectively personalizes the feed such that heavy users tend to get fresher content. We note that the model with the time based feature also included impression discounting when we tested in production.

We trained models that consisted of each of the above feature individually combined with the features in our baseline model. The improvement from adding viewer activity type affinity features and personalized decay (with impression discounting) were 6.5% and 11.5% respectively over a period of one week. The results from our bucket tests over the days of the week are also shown in Figure 8a. While there are some variations over days, the overall trend clearly indicates performance lifts from personalization and impression discounting.

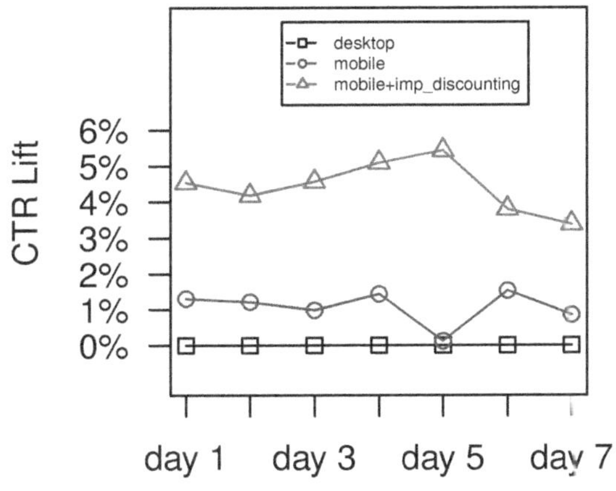

Figure 9: Mobile CTR lift over 7 days.

Combining All The Features.

Previous paragraphs showed how adding each feature individually improved user engagement. We then trained a model jointly with all the features described in the previous paragraphs (i.e., impression discounting, affinity feature and time based features) combined with the features in our baseline model. Since we usually discontinue inferior models in our production system, the result in Figure 8b only compares the all-inclusive model against the best performing models from Figure 8a which were active at the same time. As evident from Figure 8b, over a period of one week, the combined model ("With All Features" in figure) achieved a notable improvement of 7.3% over the model including only viewer activity type affinity ("Viewer-type affinity"), and 5.1% over the model including only personalized decay and impression discounting ("With Time Features").

5.3 Mobile Bucket Test Results

To understand the effectiveness of using the mobile specific models, we performed a bucket test for a period of 7 days. The results are shown in Figure 9. We first partitioned our mobile user base into 3 buckets. We then use the CTR performance of the best desktop model (trained on data from our desktop feeds) to serve traffic on mobile as the baseline (the curve labeled "desktop" in Figure 9). We also had a model which was trained using data collected from the random bucket. The mobile specific model (labeled "mobile") consistently outperformed the desktop model. A mobile model with impression discounting (labeled "mobile+imp_discount") had a significant lift over the 7 day's period.

6. CONCLUSION

We introduced the problem of ranking activities in LinkedIn feed. We showed the diverse nature of our feed through a taxonomy of activities. We analyzed various characteristics of our data and argued that a relevance system should take into account many of these characteristics to be successful in production. We then described our system architecture and showed how we collect training data, generate features, continuously train models using a distributed algorithm and evaluate those models offline before launching them in production. Finally, we showed several bucket test results which show how personalization and other modeling efforts help to improve the system.

Here are some lessons that we learned during the course of this work:

- Good ranking model are found by continuously testing of different models with different features. It is important to have a modeling framework that allows fast iteration over model training, deployment and experimentation.
- While learning from data can show impressive gains in the performance of a system, the models learned from data may not have all the characteristics we desire. For example, we learned from data that CTR decays over time. However, the learned decay factors do not always generate a fresh feed for each user visit. Other mechanisms are sometimes required to ensure certain desired user experience.
- Different platforms (such as mobile vs desktop) have different characteristics. Simply porting a desktop model to serve mobile feeds may not necessarily work well.
- Personalizing our models for user's tastes and behavior often gives large improvements in performance.

7. REFERENCES

[1] F. Abel, Q. Gao, G.-J. Houben, and K. Tao. Analyzing user modeling on twitter for personalized news recommendations. In *UMAP'11 Proceedings of the 19th international conference on User modeling, adaption, and personalization*, pages 1–12, 2011.

[2] S. Berkovsky, J. Freyne, S. Kimani, and G. Smith. Selecting items of relevance in social network feeds. In *UMAP'11 Proceedings of the 19th international conference on User modeling, adaption, and personalization*, pages 329–334, 2011.

[3] S. Berkovsky, J. Freyne, and G. Smith. Personalized network updates: Increasing social interactions and contributions in social networks. In *UMAP'12 Proceedings of the 20th international conference on User Modeling, Adaptation, and Personalization*, pages 1–13, 2012.

[4] S. Bourke, M. P. O'Mahony, R. Rafter, and B. Smyth. Ranking in information streams. In *Proceedings of the companion publication of the 2013 international conference on Intelligent user interfaces companion*, pages 99–100, 2013.

[5] S. Boyd, N. Parikh, E. Chu, B. Peleato, and J. Eckstein. Distributed optimization and statistical learning via the alternating direction method of multipliers. Technical report, Stanford University, 2010.

[6] M. Burgess, A. Mazzia, E. Adar, and M. Cafarella. Leveraging noisy lists for social feed ranking. In *AAAI*, 2013.

[7] J. Chen, R. Nairn, and E. H. Chi. Speak little and well: Recommending conversations in online social streams. In *Proceedings of the SIGCHI Conference on Human Factors in Computing Systems*, pages 217–226, 2011.

[8] J. Chen, R. Nairn, L. Nelson, M. Bernstein, and E. H. Chi. Short and tweet: Experiments on recommending content from information streams. In *Proceedings of the SIGCHI Conference on Human Factors in Computing Systems*, pages 1185–1194, 2010.

[9] M. D. Choudhury, S. Counts, and M. Czerwinski. Identifying relevant social media content: Leveraging information diversity and user cognition. In *Proceedings of the 22nd ACM conference on Hypertext and hypermedia*, pages 161–170, 2011.

[10] W. Chu and S.-T. Park. Personalized recommendation on dynamic content using predictive bilinear models. In *WWW*, 2009.

[11] G. D. Francisci, A. Gionis, and C. Lucchese. From chatter to headlines: Harnessing the real-time web for personalized news recommendation. In *Proceedings of the fifth ACM international conference on Web search and data mining*, pages 153–162, 2012.

[12] J. Freyne, S. Berkovsky, E. M. Daly, and W. Geyer. Social networking feeds: Recommending items of interest. In *RecSys*, 2010.

[13] I. Guy, I. Ronen, and A. Raviv. Personalized activity streams: Sifting through the "river of news". In *RecSys*, pages 181–188, 2011.

[14] I. Guy, T. Steier, M. Barnea, I. Ronen, and T. Daniel. Swimming against the streamz: search and analytics over the enterprise activity stream. In *Proceedings of the 21st ACM international conference on Information and knowledge management*, pages 1587–1591, 2012.

[15] L. Hong, R. Bekkerman, J. Adler, and B. D. Davison. Learning to rank social update streams. In *Proceedings of the 35th international ACM SIGIR conference on Research and development in information retrieval*, pages 651–660, 2012.

[16] J. Langford, A. Strehl, and J. Wortman. Exploration scavenging. In *Proceedings of the 25th International Conference on Machine learning*, 2008.

[17] L. Li, W. Chu, J. Langford, and X. Wang. Unbiased offline evaluation of contextual-bandit-based news article recommendation algorithms. In *Proceedings of the fourth ACM international conference on Web search and data mining*, pages 297–306. ACM, 2011.

[18] M. Naaman, J. Boase, and C.-H. Lai. Is it really about me? message content in social awareness streams. In *Proceedings of the 2010 ACM conference on Computer supported cooperative work*, pages 189–192, 2010.

[19] T. Paek, M. Gamon, S. Counts, D. M. Chickering, and A. Dhesi. Predicting the importance of newsfeed posts and social network friends. In *Proceedings of the Twenty-Fourth AAAI Conference on Artificial Intelligence (AAAI-10)*, 2010.

[20] P.-H. Soh, Y.-C. Lin, and M.-S. Chen. Recommendation for online social feeds by exploiting user response behavior. In *WWW*, 2013.

Budget Pacing for Targeted Online Advertisements at LinkedIn

Deepak Agarwal
LinkedIn
dagarwal@LinkedIn.com

Souvik Ghosh
LinkedIn
sghosh@LinkedIn.com

Kai Wei
LinkedIn
kwei@LinkedIn.com

Siyu You
LinkedIn
syou@LinkedIn.com

ABSTRACT

Targeted online advertising is a prime source of revenue for many Internet companies. It is a common industry practice to use a generalized second price auction mechanism to rank advertisements at every opportunity of an impression. This greedy algorithm is suboptimal for both advertisers and publishers when advertisers have a finite budget. In a greedy mechanism high performing advertisers tend to drop out of the auction marketplace fast and that adversely affects both the advertiser experience and the publisher revenue. We describe a method for improving such ad serving systems by including a budget pacing component that serves ads by being aware of global supply patterns. Such a system is beneficial for both advertisers and publishers. We demonstrate the benefits of this component using experiments we conducted on advertising at LinkedIn.

Categories and Subject Descriptors

H.1.0 [**Information Systems**]: Models and Principles—*General*

Keywords

budget pacing; targeted online advertising; generalized second price auction

1. INTRODUCTION

Targeted advertising is a significant source of revenue for many Internet companies. Members visiting a website are served ad impressions. Members are described by their profile which may include their demographic attributes like their geographic location, age, gender etc. Advertisers may target a segment of users specified by a combination of attributes. Advertisers are required to set up *campaigns* by specifying creatives, a target member segment, a bid value and a daily budget. As described in [7] and [18], many internet companies use a generalized second-price auction (GSP) mechanism to determine which ads to show. A GSP ad auction is one where at each opportunity of an impression, eligible campaigns are ranked based on bids and the winner pays the bid of the second highest bidder.

A second price auction mechanism used for individual auctions is a greedy algorithm. Ad campaigns participate in every eligible auction until their daily budget is used up. Here by eligible auction for a campaign, we mean an opportunity of an impression to a member who belongs to the targeted member segment of the campaign. When a campaign's budget is used up it drops out of the auction marketplace for the rest of the day. The second price auction mechanism is greedy as it tries to maximize revenue at each opportunity independent of other auctions. This greedy mechanism is not optimal and has several practical drawbacks.

- Campaigns that perform well often use up their budget fast and drop out of the marketplace early in the day.
- Advertisers often get a skewed representation from members within the audience segment they target.
- As campaigns drop out, the competition in the marketplace reduces. In a second price auction mechanism, reduced competition results in reduced revenue.
- The ad serving infrastructure may have a delay in the availability of latest spend information and campaigns spending budget fast may exceed its budget. This results in over delivery to campaigns which is essentially loss of monetizing opportunity.

In this paper we describe a *budget pacing* algorithm that improves the ad serving mechanism on each of the above mentioned issues. The budget pacing algorithm aims to spread out impressions to every campaign evenly over a budget day. The main idea is that we serve impressions to campaigns by being aware of global traffic patterns. For each campaign we obtain a forecast for the traffic pattern of eligible impressions during the day. Based on the forecasts we determine an allocation plan in which we allocate spending budget of the campaign proportional to the forecasted eligible traffic. At runtime, we monitor the spend of each ad campaign closely and for campaigns that spend faster than the allocation plan, we throttle them and do not allow them to participate in some auctions.

KDD'14, August 24–27, 2014, New York, NY, USA.

ACM 978-1-4503-2956-9/14/08 ...$15.00.
http://dx.doi.org/10.1145/2623330.2623366.

Since this algorithm slows down the spending rate of campaigns that spend faster than the plan, it increases the lifetime of campaigns and helps to mitigate the problems described above. Most importantly, this is a desired feature for many advertisers since they get a more diverse audience. This improves revenue metrics as campaigns stay alive for longer and provide higher support for other campaigns in the GSP auctions.

We describe the system we implemented and deployed at LinkedIn and the experiments we conducted that proved our claim. Targeted advertising is a significant source of revenue for LinkedIn, see [2]. Members visiting LinkedIn.com are served ad impressions and advertisers pay LinkedIn on a pay-per-view (CPM) or a pay-per-click (CPC) mode. LinkedIn has a very rich data about members and allows advertisers to target member segments by attributes like their geographic location, industry, company, education, professional skills etc., or their activity attributes on LinkedIn.com like following companies, group memberships etc. Advertisers may target a segment of users specified by any combination of such attributes. Advertisements are ranked using GSP on expected revenue from the ads where the winner pays an amount so that the expected revenue from the impression equals that of the second highest ad.

Our implementation has been deployed in two different advertising products at LinkedIn.

- *Direct Ads* is a self service advertising product where advertisers set up campaigns via a web based UI. The advertisements appear on many pages within the the LinkedIn.com domain, e.g., the top and the side panels on the home page, the profile page, the contacts page etc. Direct Ads only appears on the desktop environment.

- *Sponsored Status Update* or SSU is an advertising product that serves advertising content on the update stream of members. The update stream of a member contains content generated by the member's connections, the groups the member belongs to, the companies the member follows etc. SSUs are contents that are sponsored by companies to be promoted on the update stream of members who do not follow the company. Such content would otherwise appear naturally on the update stream of members who follow the company. Advertisers may set up campaigns via a web based UI or via interactions with sales agents. The update stream along with the SSUs appear on the desktop, mobile and the tablet environments.

In section 2 we describe the algorithm in details. In section 3 we discuss the engineering design of our implementation at LinkedIn and In section 4 we discuss the design and the results of the experiments we ran at LinkedIn. The Direct Ads and the SSU are very different in terms of their age and status. We observe beneficial but very different effects of our pacing algorithm on these two products

1.1 Literature

Targeted advertising bears a lot of similarity to the AdWords problem, also known as search advertising, where advertisers target online search keywords. There is a rich literature studying various aspects of the AdWords problem, e.g., the study of game theoretic properties of such auctions in [7], [18] and [4]; advertiser optimizations like budget optimization in [9] and selecting profitable keywords in [16]; revenue maximization for the search engine provider in [13], [10], [8] and [12].

The AdWords problem is a generalization of the online bipartite matching problem. As explained in [13], the greedy algorithm to serve ads for AdWords has a worst-case competitive ratio of 1/2. Goel and Mehta [10] though showed that the greedy algorithm has a competitive ratio of 1-1/e in the random permutation input model and in the i.i.d. input model. Mehta et.al. described a simple deterministic algorithm in [13] that achieves an optimal competitive ratio of 1-1/e. There are many other articles that study practical aspects and methods for revenue and/or relevance maximization for search ads, see e.g., [15] and [11].

Member demographics based targeted advertising is significantly different from the AdWords problem in many ways. The main difference is that advertisers in AdWords target at the very atomic target level which are search keywords-they are able to set different bids for each different keyword. In targeted advertising, such as the one in use at LinkedIn, advertisers are not able to target at the most atomic level. Advertisers set the same bid value for all members in the target audience. This adds significant complexity to the problem and makes it difficult to obtain theoretical guarantees.

Mehta et.al. [13], [6], and [1] suggest using a modified bid of campaigns in every ad auction. In an auction marketplace where the competition is low, the modified bids of campaigns exhausting their budget is likely to reduce to very low amounts. Often times though a reserve price as in [14] is used for auctions that sets a lower limit on what an advertiser can bid and pay. Having a reserve price restricts how low the bid amount can get and hence this technique might not help in increasing the life of campaigns. Instead of using a modified bid for auctions we use probabilistic throttling to filter out the high performing campaigns from some randomly chosen auctions.

Our main contribution is that we developed and deployed a simple novel algorithm that improves advertiser experience and publisher revenue for targeted advertising. We set up appropriate real-life experiments and show the benefits of our deployed algorithm.

2. THE PACING ALGORITHM

Suppose $\mathcal{S}$ is the set of all members. An ad campaign i targets a subset $\mathcal{S}_i$ of $\mathcal{S}$, has a bid b_i and a daily budget d_i. The day is discretized into T equal length time windows and $s_{i,t}$, for $0 \leq t < T$, denotes the cumulative spend of campaign i from the beginning of the day till the start of window t. We obtain a forecast for volume of eligible impressions for campaign i during each time window- $f_{i,t}$ denotes the cumulative number of eligible impressions for campaign i till the start of window t. We allocate the amount of budget we would like to spend for a campaign during each time window proportional to the forecasted volume of eligible traffic for the campaign during that window. Hence, the amount allocated to be spend from the beginning of the day till the start of window t is

$$a_{it} := \frac{f_{i,t}}{f_{i,T}} d_i, \tag{1}$$

where $f_{i,T}$ is the forecasted total volume of eligible impressions for campaign i for the entire day. We apply a filter during each ad auction. For each eligible auction a campaign is allowed to participate with probability $p_{i,t}$, the pass through rate(PTR). The value of p_{it} is updated at the start of each time window by

$$p_{i,t} = \begin{cases} p_{i,t-1} * (1 + r_t) \wedge 1 & \text{if } s_{i,t} \leq a_{i,t} \\ p_{i,t-1} * (1 - r_t) \vee 0 & \text{if } s_{i,t} > a_{i,t}. \end{cases} \quad (2)$$

Here $0 < r_t < 1$ is an adjustment rate.

For a campaign i, the allocation curve $a_{i,t}$ is fixed at the start of the day and we control the spend curve $s_{i,t}$ by modifying the PTR $p_{i,t}$. We aim to keep the spending curve $s_{i,t}$ close to the allocation curve $a_{i,t}$ for every campaign i.

Mehta et.al. [13] suggest using a modified bid of campaigns in every ad auction. They show that using b_i^*,

$$b_i^* = b_i \psi(s_{i,t}/d_i) \quad \text{where, } \psi(x) = 1 - e^{x-1}. \quad (3)$$

is an optimal choice. We have already discussed in section 1.1 why we use probabilistic throttling instead of bid modification. For probabilistic throttling, it would have been natural to use $p_{i,t}^* = \psi(s_{i,t}/d_i)$ as PTR. In a linear system this would result in same expected payoff as in [13]. The GSP auction mechanism is clearly not a linear system though. We still tried this choice of PTR. We observed an improvement in revenue but not a significant increase in campaign life. This may seem counterintuitive since $\psi(x) \to 0$ as $x \to 1$. This happens due to a combination of two reasons. Firstly, this form of PTR does not depend on the rate of budget spend and can therefore be slow to react. Secondly, system inefficiencies also reduce the effectiveness of this method. Based on this experience we developed the dynamic method of choosing PTR as described in (2) where the value at the current time window is set as a small perturbation of the value at the previous time window. We observed remarkably good results with this approach.

2.1 Implementation Details

2.1.1 Update Frequency

We update the PTR for each campaign at 1 minute intervals. This frequent updating makes the system agile and reach a steady state fast.

2.1.2 Forecasting

Forecasting the number of eligible impressions for campaigns plays an important role in our algorithm. It is used to determine the allocation curve for each campaign. Inaccurate forecasts may cause unnecessary throttling and may result in budget not being used up for some good campaigns.

We use a tool that we built at LinkedIn using the method described in [3]. Note that, in order to forecast the number of eligible impressions for campaign i, we need to forecast the number of impressions from the member segment $\mathcal{S}_i$, which is the target audience for campaign i. We maintain a large list of important member segments which we call *base profiles*. For each base profile we update the historical time series data of number of ad impression opportunities. We use an ensemble statistical time series model to fit the up-to-date time series data for each of these base profiles daily. We obtain forecasts for each targeted segment $\mathcal{S}_i$ using correlation models described in [3].

2.1.3 Adjustment Rate

We set the adjustment rate r_t at a constant 10%. This naive choice of the adjustment rate is not only the easiest to implement, but is also a very robust one. A more theoretically sound algorithm should involve the derivative $\partial s_{i,t}/\partial t$, the rate of budget spend while computing the PTR; a campaign that spends budget very fast needs to throttled more whereas a campaign spending budget just a little bit faster than the allocation curve needs to be throttled less. We chose the naive form for two main reasons. First, an estimate for $\partial s_{i,t}/\partial t$ is likely to be noisy. The budget spend curve is not smooth, especially for cost-per-click campaigns for whom it changes only when there is a click which is significantly rare compared to the impressions. Second, we adjust the PTR frequently and even if we are not at the ideal PTR at any time point we can reach there fast.

2.1.4 Slow Start

We always start with a PTR of 10% for all campaigns. We call this a *slow start*. This may be a low starting value for some campaigns and may be a high value for some other campaigns. The advantage of a low starting value is that it gives the system the time to learn about individual campaigns. On one hand, if a campaign is spending its budget too slow then it can open up fully with in 25 minutes. On the other hand if a campaign is spending too fast then having a 10% PTR to start with gives the system more time to reach the correct PTR. For such campaigns starting from a high PTR may result in using up the budget before the system learns that it needs to set a low PTR.

It is sensible to customize the starting value of the PTR for individual campaigns. We aim to do that in future developments where we plan to make the initial value of the PTR for a campaign, a function of the demand and the forecasted supply for the campaign. The demand for a campaign is the number of impressions required to spend the budget of the campaign and the supply is the total number of impressions available for the campaign. It is natural to set a low initial value of PTR for a campaign with a high demand-supply ratio.

2.1.5 Fast Finish

We use statistical models to forecast future supply of impressions for each campaign. The models typically have high accuracy but there are always statistical errors. As a result there may be situations where the algorithm continuously sets lower values of PTR for a campaign than what should have been set. We try to mitigate this issue by *fast finish*- we modify the allocation curve slightly so that the algorithm assumes there will not be any traffic during the last two hours of the day. This way the pacing algorithm attempts to exhaust budget within 22 hours. This in turn gives campaigns that have been wrongly throttled earlier in the day, more opportunities to use up their budget later.

3. ENGINEERING DESIGN

In LinkedIn's ad serving system, data on advertiser events and member events continuously flows through a tracking pipeline. Advertiser events may include creation of a new campaign or a modification to an existing one, like change in bid or daily budget etc. User events include member page views that resulted in ad request or opportunity, ad

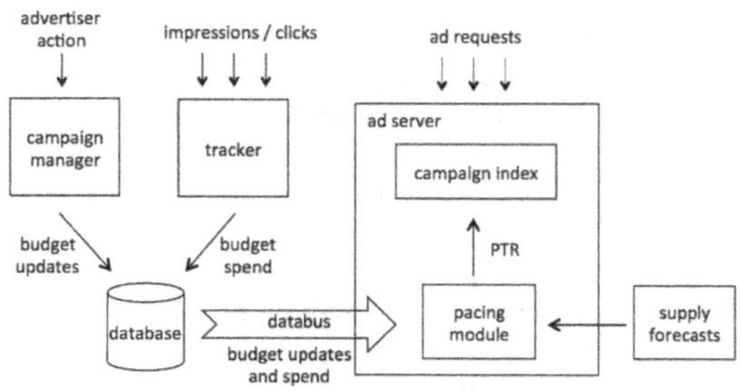

Figure 1: Engineering design

impressions served and user actions like click or share etc. This data is stored into a database.

The ad server maintains an index of all campaigns along with their current status. A pacing module that implements of our algorithm is deployed in the ad server. The pacing module receives this data from the database using a technology called databus, see [5]. Periodically the pacing module recalculates the PTR for each campaign using the latest budget/spend data and the allocation curve, and pushes it into the campaign index. The campaign index is scanned at ad matching and auction time, during which the PTR is used in a simple probability test to determine whether a given campaign should participate in the auction or not.

The forecast for eligible supply of impressions for campaigns is computed in an offline Hadoop system [17]. The forecast information is pushed to the pacing module on a daily basis.

As mentioned before, we update the PTR for each campaign at 1 minute intervals on average. The updates are randomly distributed across campaigns within each minute. That is, instead of updating all campaigns at once every minute, we update roughly 12% of all campaigns every 7 seconds. This updating frequency allows the system to reach a steady state fast and evenly spreads out the server load.

4. EXPERIMENTS

4.1 Experimental design

We designed and ran online experiments on the advertising products at LinkedIn to ascertain the benefits of deploying the budget pacing algorithm.

Experimental design, although an age-old topic of research, has been revolutionized by the Internet industry. Internet companies use experiments, often called A/B tests, to validate practically every step they take. In a typical A/B test, in order to compare control A with a treatment B, members are randomly split into two groups with one group receiving the control and the other group receiving the treatment. This approach is not directly applicable in what we wanted to test.

Randomly splitting traffic into two groups is not enough since the pacing algorithm would affect the budget spending for a campaign for an entire day and hence we would need to apply the same treatment to a campaign for the entire day. We could randomly split all campaigns into two groups and run different algorithms on two groups; this would help us determine the benefits of pacing to advertisers (like lifetime of campaigns etc.) but not the revenue benefits to the publisher since campaigns from both the groups would participate in the same auctions.

In order to observe the full benefits of the algorithm it needs to be turned on for all campaigns for an entire day. We designed the experiment to run pacing on alternate days. By running the experiment for at least 2 weeks we are able to estimate the benefits of the pacing algorithm and control for any day specific bias and weekly seasonality that may be present in the system. Table 1 describes the experimental design.

Table 1: Design of the experiment

	Sun	Mon	Tue	Wed	Thu	Fri	Sat
Week 0	Off	On	Off	On	Off	On	Off
Week 1	On	Off	On	Off	On	Off	On
Week 2	Off	On	Off	On	Off	On	Off
⋮							

In our experiments we also controlled for any bias that may result due to trend. A weekly trend is of much smaller magnitude compared to the effect of our algorithm but by controlling for it we expect to get more accurate estimates.

When running the experiment for two weeks we considered 15 days of data for computing the metrics of interest. Starting the experiment from Sunday in Week 0 we continued till Sunday in week 2. The effect of pacing is measured by averaging over the 7 days when the algorithm was turned on during this period. The metrics corresponding to the control was measured using data from 8 days where we take an average of Sunday in week 0 and Sunday in week 2 to estimate the Sunday effect. Every other day gets an equal weight of 1/7. This mechanism helps to eliminate any linear trend present in the system.

Another way to run an experiment to determine the effects of pacing would be one where we create two independent ad serving systems and put in all the ad campaigns in both the systems with half the daily budget. We can then split incoming traffic and randomly allocate to the two different systems. The advantage of this design would be that we would not have to be concerned about weekly seasonality or trend or other daily variations. We chose not to use this design for two reasons. First, It would be difficult to apply the algorithm to campaigns with small daily budget and second, it would take a lot of time and effort to implement such a two-fold ad serving system which is likely not cost effective.

4.2 Metrics of importance

The following are the main metrics we measure in our experiments. For most metrics we take the case when pacing algorithm is turned off as baseline and report the percentage change when the algorithm is turned on. The metrics are computed using all the data from LinkedIn without any sampling. LinkedIn gets tens of millions of page views regularly and has tens of thousands of advertisers advertising at LinkedIn on any day. Given the volume of the data we are confident about the statistical significance of the metrics.

- Advertiser centric metrics
  - *Campaign life time*: We use the time taken to exhaust 95% of the budget for a campaign to mea-

sure the life of the campaign in a budget day. We report the median life-time of campaigns in hours.

  - *Unique impressions per spend* is the ratio of number of unique members viewing an ad over the budget spend for the ad. An increase in this metric denotes an increase in the audience reach for advertisers with the same advertising spend.
  - *Number of campaigns served* measures the total number of ad campaigns that were served on a day.

- Publisher centric metrics
  - *Cost per request*: Ratio of total revenue with total number of requests or opportunities is measure of revenue per unit opportunity.
  - *Over delivery*: The dollar amount we delivered to a campaign beyond its daily budget as a percentage of total revenue.
- Member centric metrics
  - *Unique campaings served*: We measure the average number of unique ad campaigns viewed by members. This is a measure of diversity of advertisement content viewed by members and an increase in this metric is an improvement in member experience.

4.3 Direct Ads

Direct Ads is the advertising product that serve advertising content on various LinkedIn webpages. This product is more than 4 years old and the demand from advertisers exceed the supply. There is a high coverage in most member segments.

We ran the experiment in Direct Ads for 2 weeks during 2013 Q4. The key results are tabulated in table 2. As we mentioned before, due to privacy issues we report most metrics in relative form with the baseline being the case when the pacing algorithm in not running.

Table 2: Results for Direct Ads

Pacing	Off	On
Campaign life time (hours)	13.54	19.50
Unique impressions per spend	-	+7.74%
Number of campaigns served	-	+4.74%
Cost per request	-	+5.67%
Over delivery	3.8%	3.4%
Unique campings served	-	+0.15%

The metrics reveal that the pacing algorithm provides benefits to both advertisers and LinkedIn. The algorithm increases campaign life time by 44%. Advertisers are able to reach to a broader audience with the same budget and more advertisers are served impressions.

There is a benefit to LinkedIn as the cost per ad request increases. The pacing algorithm keeps campaigns alive for a longer time in a budget day. As discussed before, this helps increase competition later in the budget day. This is reflected in figure 2 which plots the variation in cost per click during a budget day. Cost per click (CPC) denotes what advertisers pay on average per click and in a second price auction it is a measure of support price for auctions. It is primarily used for campaigns who pay per click and they are the dominant kind in Direct Ads. In figure 2, the solid red line denotes the average CPC curve during each hour within a budget day on the days when pacing was turned on. The blue dotted line denotes the same for the days when pacing was turned off. We see that with pacing turned on, the CPC is lower during the initial part of the day but higher for a much longer period during the second half of the day. The CPC is lower at the start of the day because we throttle all the high performing campaigns during that time who otherwise all compete together and exhaust their budget fast. Again, the plot was created from all the data collected by LinkedIn during the two weeks of experimentation. Figure 3 shows the variation in cost per request during a budget day.

The loss due to over delivery of impressions to campaigns is reduced by 10%. There is a little time delay in the availability of the latest budget spent information in LinkedIn's ad serving system. In absence of pacing, the good campaigns spend at a fast rate and because of the delay in latest budget information, the system often serves impressions to such campaigns even after the budget for the day has been spent. The pacing algorithm slows down the rate of spend of such campaigns and reduces the chances of over delivery.

We do not see a statistically significant effect of pacing algorithm on the diversity of ad content seen by members. That is likely because of the long tail of the distribution of the number of unique campaigns seen by a member.

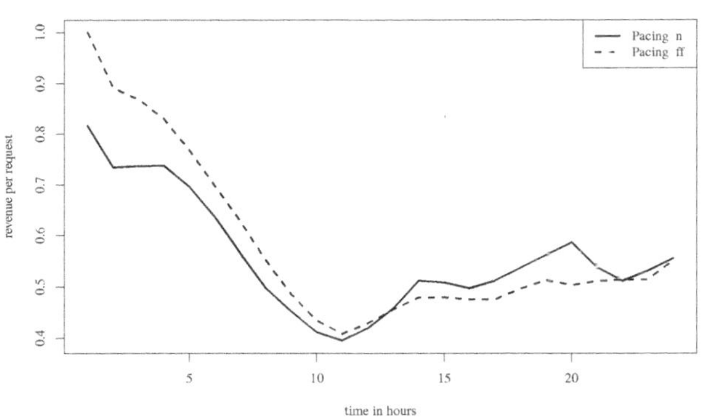

Figure 2: Variation in average cost per click during a day in Direct Ads (scaled so that the baseline at time 0 is set to 1)

4.4 Sponsored Status Updates

Sponsored Status Updates is a new advertising product from LinkedIn that was launched in mid 2013. Advertisers can sponsor a 'status update' and promote it to a specified segment of LinkedIn members. The sponsored content from an advertiser is blended with the organic content in the update stream and delivered to the members in the targeted audience.

The Sponsored Status Update marketplace was very different from Direct Ads at the time we ran the experiment. SSU is a new product, the demand to supply ratio is much lower but is growing rapidly. The SSUs appear on a prime

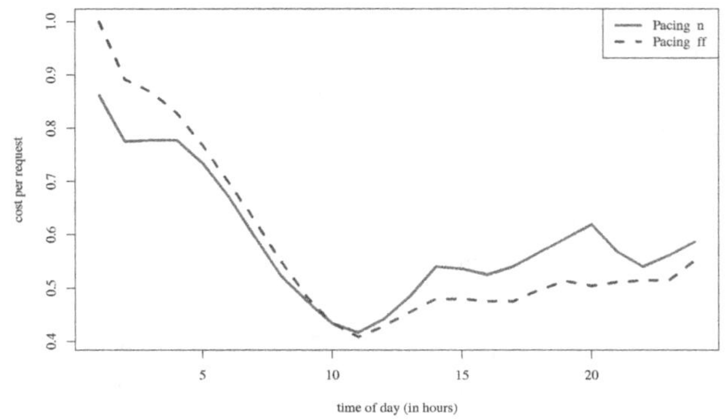

Figure 3: Variation in average revenue per request during a day in Direct Ads (scaled so that the baseline at time 0 is set to 1)

space in the LinkedIn webpage and smart phone/tablet apps. It has a higher visibility because of which campaigns can potentially exhaust the daily budget very fast. Pacing is thus very important for SSU. We ran a two week experiment on this product and the key results are tabulated in table 3.

Table 3: Results for Sponsored Status Updates

Pacing	Off	On
Campaign life time (hours)	6.92	17.25
Unique impressions per spend	-	+10.52%
Number of campaigns served	-	+0.25%
Cost per request	-	+0.96%
Over delivery	4.12%	2.39%
Unique campings served	-	-0.04%

It is expected that the pacing algorithm will have a much different effect in SSU and that is what we observe. First, we see that the increase in cost per request is of much lower magnitude compared to that in Direct Ads. The reason for that is the total revenue for SSU (at the time of the experiment) is largely determined by the advertiser demand which is lower than the supply. Second, the increase of campaign median life time is much more drastic (149%) compared to what we observed in Direct Ads.

We observe an improvement in the audience reach for advertisers as the average number of unique impressions per spend increased by 10.52%. There is a small increase in the average number of campaigns that got served per day, but this change is not statistically significant. We also observe a marked decrease in loss due to over delivery (42%). The effect on the average number of unique campaigns seen by members was slightly lower but this change is statistically insignificant.

4.5 Some Examples

Here we show the behavior of two specific campaigns during our experiments. Albeit two examples, in conjunction with the results described in sections 4.3 and 4.4, they further illustrate how well the pacing algorithm performs.

Figure 4 shows the performance of a specific campaign in SSU in two consecutive week days during the experiment. Pacing was turned off on day 1 (blue dotted line) and was running on day 2 (red solid line). On day 1 the budget was spent with in the first 30 mins of the day and there was more than 20% loss due to over delivery. On day 2, the campaign was active till the 20th hour of the day and had a significantly lower over delivery loss.

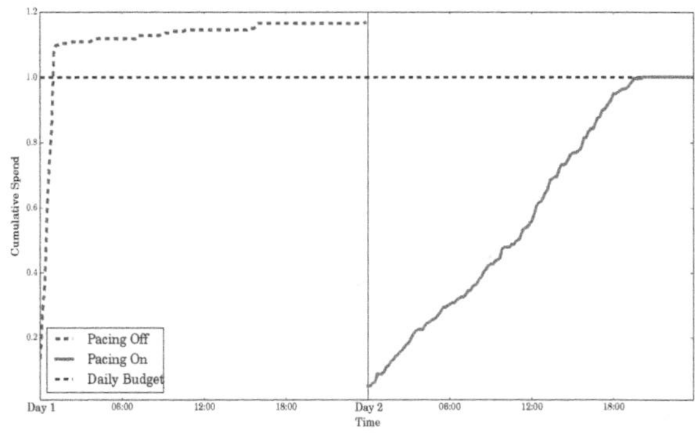

Figure 4: Cumulative budget spent for a campaign in SSU (scaled so that the total budget is 1)

Figure 5 demonstrates for a specific campaign that we are able to align the actual spending curve with the allocation curve well. The blue line is the observed spending curve and the red dotted line is the allocation curve for the campaign. This behavior is observed consistently for most campaigns with a reasonably high daily budget.

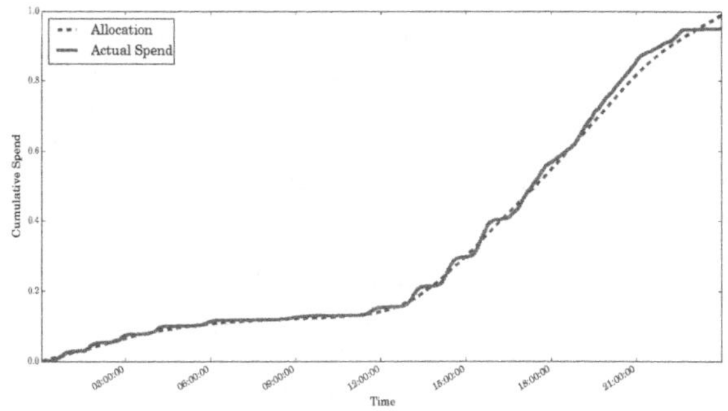

Figure 5: Actual spend curve vs. the allocation curve for a campaign in SSU(scaled so that the total budget is 1)

5. CONCLUSION

We develop a budget pacing algorithm that we use to evenly distribute the spend of advertising campaigns in a day. We implemented the algorithm and it is deployed in two advertising products at LinkedIn. The algorithm helps improve advertiser experience and provides revenue benefits to LinkedIn at the same time. We ran real life experiments at LinkedIn to demonstrate the benefit of using this algorithm. Based on the results of the experiments this algorithm was been fully deployed in both the advertising products at LinkedIn.

6. REFERENCES

[1] Z. Abrams, O. Mendelevitch, and J. Tomlin. Optimal delivery of sponsored search advertisements subject to budget constraints. In *Proceedings of the 8th ACM Conference on Electronic Commerce*, EC '07, pages 272–278, New York, NY, USA, 2007. ACM.

[2] D. Agarwal. Computational advertising: The linkedin way. In *Proceedings of the 22Nd ACM International Conference on Conference on Information & Knowledge Management*, CIKM '13, pages 1585–1586, New York, NY, USA, 2013. ACM.

[3] D. Agarwal, D. Chen, L.-j. Lin, J. Shanmugasundaram, and E. Vee. Forecasting high-dimensional data. In *Proceedings of the 2010 ACM SIGMOD International Conference on Management of Data*, SIGMOD '10, pages 1003–1012, New York, NY, USA, 2010. ACM.

[4] G. Aggarwal, A. Goel, and R. Motwani. Truthful auctions for pricing search keywords. In *7th ACM Conference on Electronic Commerce*, pages 1–7. ACM, 2006.

[5] A. Auradkar, C. Botev, S. Das, D. De Maagd, et al. Data infrastructure at LinkedIn. In *Data Engineering (ICDE), 2012 IEEE 28th International Conference on*, pages 1370–1381, April 2012.

[6] C. Borgs, J. Chayes, N. Immorlica, K. Jain, O. Etesami, and M. Mahdian. Dynamics of bid optimization in online advertisement auctions. In *Proceedings of the 16th International Conference on World Wide Web*, WWW '07, pages 531–540, New York, NY, USA, 2007. ACM.

[7] B. Edelman, M. Ostrovsky, and M. Schwarz. Internet advertising and the generalized second price auction: Selling billions of dollars worth of keywords. *American Economic Review*, 97(1):242–259, March 2007.

[8] J. Feldman, A. Mehta, V. Mirrokni, and S. Muthukrishnan. Online stochastic matching: Beating 1-1/e. In *50th Annual IEEE Symposium on Foundations of Computer Science*, pages 117–126. IEEE, 2009.

[9] J. Feldman, S. Muthukrishnan, M. Pal, and C. Stein. Budget optimization in search-based advertising auctions. In *8th ACM Conference on Electronic Commerce*, pages 40–49. ACM, 2006.

[10] G. Goel and A. Mehta. Online budgeted matching in random input models with applications to adwords. In *Proceedings of the 19th Annual ACM-SIAM Symposium on Discrete Algorithms*, pages 982–991. ACM-SIAM, 2008.

[11] S. Lahaie and D. M. Pennock. Revenue analysis of a family of ranking rules for keyword auctions. In *Proceedings of the 8th ACM Conference on Electronic Commerce*, EC '07, pages 50–56, New York, NY, USA, 2007. ACM.

[12] S. Lahaie, D. M. Pennock, A. Saberi, and R. V. Vohra. *Algorithmic Game Theory, Chapter: Sponsored Search Auctions*. Addison-Wesley Publishing Company, Reading, Massachusetts, 1986

[13] A. Mehta, A. Saberi, U. Vazirani, and V. Vazirani. Adwords and generalized on-line matching. *Journal of the ACM*, 54(5):Article no. 22, October 2007.

[14] M. Ostrovsky and M. Schwarz. Reserve prices in internet advertising auctions: A field experiment. In *Proceedings of the 12th ACM Conference on Electronic Commerce*, EC '11, pages 59–60, New York, NY, USA, 2011. ACM.

[15] F. Radlinski, A. Broder, P. Ciccolo, E. Gabrilovich, V. Josifovski, and L. Riedel. Optimizing relevance and revenue in ad search: A query substitution approach In *Proceedings of the 31st Annual International ACM SIGIR Conference on Research and Development in Information Retrieval*, SIGIR '08, pages 403–410, New York, NY, USA, 2008. ACM.

[16] P. Rusmevichientong and D. P. Williamson. An adaptive algorithm for selecting profitable keywords for search based advertising services. In *7th ACM Conference on Electronic Commerce*, pages 260–269. ACM, 2006.

[17] R. Sumbaly, J. Kreps, and S. Shah. The big data ecosystem at LinkedIn. In *Proceedings of the 2013 ACM SIGMOD International Conference on Management of Data*, SIGMOD '13, pages 1125–1134, New York, NY, USA, 2013. ACM.

[18] H. R. Varian. Position auctions. *International Journal of Industrial Organization*, 25(6):1163–1178, December 2007.

Large Scale Predictive Modeling for Micro-Simulation of 3G Air Interface Load

Dejan Radosavljevik
LIACS, Leiden University
P.O. Box 9512
2300 RA Leiden, The Netherlands
+31-71-5275778
d.radosavljevikj@liacs.leidenuniv.nl

Peter van der Putten
LIACS, Leiden University
P.O. Box 9512
2300 RA Leiden, The Netherlands
+31-71-5275778
p.w.h.van.der.putten@liacs.leidenuniv.nl

ABSTRACT

This paper outlines the approach developed together with the Radio Network Strategy & Design Department of a large European telecom operator in order to forecast the Air-Interface load in their 3G network, which is used for planning network upgrades and budgeting purposes. It is based on large scale intelligent data analysis and modeling at the level of thousands of individual radio cells resulting in 30,000 models per day. It has been embedded into a scenario simulation framework that is used by end users not experienced in data mining for studying and simulating the behavior of this complex networked system, as an example of a systematic approach to the deployment step in the KDD process. This system is already in use for two years in the country where it was developed and it is a part of a standard business process. In the last six months this national operator became a competence center for predictive modeling for micro-simulation of 3G air interface load for four other operators of the same parent company.

Categories and Subject Descriptors

H.2.8 [Database Management]: Database Applications - *Data mining*

General Terms

Algorithms, Management, Measurement, Economics, Performance, Experimentation

Keywords

Mobile Network, Air-Interface Load, Linear Regression, Simulation.

1. INTRODUCTION

This paper reports on a deployed data mining application that has been developed by one of the largest European telecom operators and has been constantly used ever since. In order to accommodate the continuing strong increase of mobile internet traffic, the operator's Radio Network Department has to persistently monitor and upgrade the 3G Radio Access Network. This requires an Air-interface Load forecast for every radio cell in the network, including indications of denial or interruption of service delivery. However, such a detailed forecast was not readily available. Furthermore, there is a need to simulate different scenarios for different parts of the network. Given the complexity of the problem, the dimension of the network and the repetitiveness of the task, a manual approach is out of the question.

In this paper we present a fully automated approach that generates multi-variate linear regression models on a grand scale, using primarily open source tools. The key business benefit of this research is that it solves a very complex and high impact business problem that cannot be approached by using general planning methods.

The traditional methods to mobile network load forecasting have a number of practical issues. They are most often analytical or Monte Carlo based approaches [1]. The load formula used is typically a general purpose analytical model, derived from physics knowledge and theory rather than from modeling on actual data, let alone being based on data from a specific operator. Furthermore, the inputs required are difficult to measure and forecast, or do not relate to changes in customer behavior such as call usage which is easier to understand and use for scenario purposes. Our approach makes it easier to translate customers and their usage into network load. To our knowledge, this is the first time a data mining approach has been used for Air Interface load prediction of a 3G mobile network.

In terms of business benefits, the exact return is confidential, but cellular network infrastructure forms a major part of an operator investment budget, and this is a key system for tactical and strategic network investment decisions. In the group where this operating company belongs, up to 50% of wireless CAPEX investments are spent on the radio access network. For reference, operators worldwide invest more than 20 billion USD into cellular network infrastructure. Our methodology is first and foremost intended to ensure that capacity is added in time and at the right place, thus avoiding inefficient investments and poor customer experience due to traffic congestion, which can ultimately lead to churn. Last but not least, Internet access is recognized as a right by law by several countries, as a part of the rights to Freedom and Expression of Opinion. By adding capacity at the right places, operators provide a valuable social service, given the growing importance of communications and social media in everyday life. This is a data mining application in telecommunications that does not raise the usual privacy concerns; on the contrary it serves a social function by mediating high quality internet access.

An early version of our approach has been published in [2]. Since then, our system has been rolled out in full use in the operator where it was developed. None of the other operator companies in this telecommunications group used a similar fine grained approach. Therefore, a more universal approach applicable to the

KDD'14, August 24–27, 2014, New York, New York, USA.

ACM 978-1-4503-2956-9/14/08…$15.00.
http://dx.doi.org/10.1145/2623330.2623339

other operators as well had to be developed.This involved dealing with complexities such as different network equipment vendors using different performance management systems and lack of certain measurements we have introduced in [2]. Nevertheless, the results of our new approach were very positive. Hence, in the past six months this operator became a competence center for Predictive Modeling of 3G Air Interface Load and it is performing this task for operators of the same telecommunications group in four countries.

Whilst the core intelligent data analysis algorithms used are not novel, we apply these on a large scale by modeling individual radio cells across a variety of dimensions (section 3 motivates why we model at cell level). This has also been embedded into a simulation framework targeted at non-data miners using tools they are familiar with, thus enabling them to run low level simulation scenarios. Hence, our goal is to provide a case example of an embedded, deployed intelligent data analysis system, dealing with real world aspects such as scale and having major business impact. Extensive simulations have been carried by the operating companies using the system, and novel use cases for scenario simulation analysis have been developed and applied.

As discussed, the technical novelty is not determined by the complexity of the base estimators used. We use simple linear regression models as data inspection has shown that the behavior to be predicted is primarily linear, and experiments confirmed that complex algorithms actually performed worse given the high variance associated with these models. This is not uncommon in real world data mining problems [3]. What makes this problem out of the ordinary is the massive number of models. For each of cell in the network we create four models to predict different kinds of outcomes, resulting in a total of 30,000-100,000 models, depending on the amounts of cells in the network. Model parameters are estimated using ten-fold cross validation, which increases the number of models estimated to over 1 million. This process is repeated on a regular basis, given that the customer base and its behavior, as well as the cellular network itself change constantly.

Finally, we do not just deploy the forecasted loads. The underlying regression formulas are provided by the data miners to the end user analysts as simple spreadsheets, which enables them to tune various simulation and forecasting scenarios without further involvement from the data miners. This turned out to be not just a practical benefit, but a major opportunity for the business as a range of simulation use cases were explored that were not envisioned by the data miners up front.

We think that this approach, including the concept of decoupling data mining from forecasting and simulation processes, can easily be replicated and applied to problems from other industries. Examples are problems that require similar predictive models and simulation of networked systems on a large scale, such as for instance sensor networks, retail outlet planning, supply chain logistics and revenue predictions for products with a complex billing process (which we have already applied).

The rest of the paper is structured as follows. Section 2 describes the load parameters. Section 3 discusses the complex nature of network load and how to approximate it, including a motivation for modeling at the granular cell level. Section 4 describes the construction of the load formulas and the forecasting of the future load of the network using simulation, as well as other simulation scenarios. Limitations and future work are discussed in section 5. Finally, we present our conclusions in section 6.

2. DEFINING THE LOAD PARAMETERS

In this section we will describe how we measure the load for a cell, plus the underlying attributes that we will use to predict future load. Both output and input parameters are measured per individual cell per hour.

2.1 Output Parameters

The communication between a network cell site (radio network element that provides access to the mobile network) and a user's mobile device is separated into downlink communication-directed from the cell to the mobile device and uplink communication- directed from the mobile device to the cell site. One cell site can serve multiple network cells.

Therefore, the Air-interface load for a cell consists of the Downlink Load (DL) and Uplink Load (UL). Multiple measures of both DL and UL can be devised. A cell is considered to be in overload if either the uplink or the downlink load is above a certain threshold. When a cell is in overload, it cannot adequately serve customers that demand its resources. Obviously, all cells in overload require an adequate upgrade.

Most of the background literature on telecom networks is related to network optimization or load control rather than load prediction [4, 5, 6, 7]. In our previous research [2] we used the following measurements of load as output parameters: *Count of RAB (Radio Access Bearer) Releases Due To Interference* [4], *Average Noise Rise (ANR)* [5] and *Average Noise Rise on Channels Dedicated to Release 99 Capable Devices* (refers to lower data transfer speed up to 384 Kbps). Two additional uplink measures were considered: *Count of RAB (Radio Access Bearer) Setup Failures* and *Count of RRC (Radio Resource Control) Setup Failures.* These measurements were discarded at later stages of the process due to the very low number of models that could be generated because of too many zero-values.

The parameters used as measures for downlink load in [2] were the following. Firstly, we used *Percentage of Consumed Downlink Power (CDP)* [6] and *Count of "No Code Available" Situations* (NCA) [7].

However, some of these measures were specific to Nokia Data Warehouse [8], a performance management tool deployed at the operator where our research originated, or were not measured by other operators that were looking to use our system. Therefore, we used universal measurements, which are applicable to performance management systems of other vendors, such as Ericsson [9], Huawei [10] or MyCom [11]. Therefore, in our new approach we picked measurements that are both compliant to the 3gpp Mobile Broadband Standard [12] and universally defined and measured across the operators which are part of this international group.

Percentage of Uplink Load, also known as UL Carrier Load Percentage [12] is the ratio between the total received power level on that carrier and the maximum acceptable level of interference.

$$\text{UL\_LOAD}=100 * \left(1 - \frac{1}{10^{\frac{\text{MeanRTWP}-\text{MinRTWP}}{10}}}\right)$$

where MeanRTWP is mean Received Total Wideband Power per cell; MinRTWP is minimum Received Total Wideband Power per cell, used as the noise floor. In other words MeanRTWP is mean of the power assigned to users, while MinRTWP is the power measured when no users are using cell resources.

Percentage of Downlink Load, also known as DL Carrier Load Percentage [12] is the ratio between the total transmitter power level on that carrier and the maximum acceptable transmitter power.

$$DL\_LOAD=100 * 10^{\frac{MeanTCP-MaxTxPower}{10}}$$

where MeanTCP is mean Total Transmitted Power per cell; MaxTxPower is maximum transmit power of the cell. In other words MeanTCP is mean of the power assigned to users, while MaxTxPower is the cell power capacity.

We used two additional measures for downlink load, based on code capacity, namely Code Utilization and Count of "No Code Available" situations. Each cell has 256 codes that can be assigned to a mobile device for a voice call or a data session. The higher the downlink bandwidth required, the higher the number of codes will be assigned. For example, voice calls require 12.2 Kbps (translates into 2 codes), while Data Sessions can require up to 14.4 Mbps (which would consume all the codes of that cell).

Code Utilization- Measures the fraction of codes used vs. codes available at the cell. It is averaged over an hour.

Count of "No Code Available" situations –After all the codes have been assigned, the next devices that requests a code from the cell, gets a "no code available" message and cannot use the cell resources. This variable measures the count of occurrences of this message per hour, and will be abbreviated as NCA.

2.2 Input Parameters

As input parameters in [2] we used different measures from the Nokia Data Warehouse [8], a tool that is used in telecom operators to monitor Radio Network Performance. Even though we included input parameters related to voice services, most of the input parameters are related to consumption of Data Services, because they require more of the cell resources. These include the following: Average Voice Call Users, Average Release 99 Uplink users, Average Release 99 Downlink users, Average High Speed Uplink Packet Access (HSUPA) users, Average High Speed Downlink Packet Access (HSDPA) users, Maximum HSUPA users, Maximum HSDPA users, Total RRC attempts, Total Active RABs, Total Voice Call RAB Attempts, Total Data Session RAB Attempts, Average Downlink Throughput, Average Uplink Throughput, Average Soft Handover Overhead Area (measures the intersection of coverage of the particular cell with other cells), Average Proportion of Voice Traffic originated in that cell (as opposed to traffic originated in other cells and handed over to that cell), Average Proportion of Data Traffic originated in that cell. Forecasts for future values of the input parameters were available at the operator.

However, due to constraints mentioned in section 2.1, namely different performance management tools from different vendors, not all these could be measured. Therefore, we reduced the input parameter set to the following:

Count of RRC attempts per hour - Radio Resource Control (RRC) attempts are related to the signaling exchange between the mobile device and the network cells. There can only be one RRC connection open per mobile device at a time.

Count of Data Session RAB Attempts per hour – Radio Access Bearer (RAB) is necessary to be assigned to a user in order to make voice call or a data session. Multiple RABs can be assigned to the same device. This variable measures the RAB **attempts** (not necessarily successful) for a data session in a cell in an hour.

Count of Voice Call RAB Attempts per hour - This variable measures the RAB **attempts** (not necessarily successful) for a voice call in a cell in an hour. It is the only variable that addresses usage of voice services exclusively.

Average Count of Release 99 Uplink users per hour- Average number of users that consumed uplink cell resources on a R99 capable device (throughput of up to 384 Kbps).

Average Count of Release 99 Downlink users per hour - Average number of users that consumed downlink cell resources on a R99 capable device (throughput of up to 384 Kbps).

Average Count of HSUPA users per hour- Average number of users that consumed uplink cell resources on a HSUPA (High Speed Uplink Packet Access) capable device (up to 5.76 Mbps).

Average Count of HSDPA users per hour - Average number of users that consumed downlink cell resources on a HSDPA (High Speed Downlink Packet Access) capable device (bandwidth up to 14.4 Kbps). Most of the current mobile devices are HSDPA[1] capable. But, an HSDPA device can also be assigned to a R99 downlink (slower) channel, if there are no HSDPA cell resources available.

Average Downlink Throughput per hour- Average per hour of the sum of downlink bandwidths consumed by all users served by the cell.

Average Uplink Throughput per hour- Average per hour of the sum of uplink bandwidths consumed by all users served by the cell.

3. APPROXIMATING THE LOAD

The traditional approaches to mobile network load forecasting are most often analytical or Monte Carlo based approaches [1]. However, the inputs required are difficult to measure and forecast, or do not relate to customer behavior such as call usage which is easier to understand and use for scenario purposes.

Most of the data mining related literature on load forecasting is related to electrical networks. A good overview is presented in [13]. Various methods have been deployed for this purpose: regression models, time series, neural networks, expert systems, fuzzy logic etc. The authors state a need for load forecasts for sub-areas (load pockets) in cases when the input parameters are substantially different from the average, which is a case similar to different cells in a mobile telecom network.

Related to mobile telecommunications, data traffic load (which is different than air interface load) focusing on a highly aggregated link has been forecasted in [14], comparing time series (moving averages and dynamic harmonic regression) with linear and exponential regression. Also, Support Vector Regression was used by [15] for link load prediction in fixed line telecommunications.

In order to forecast the future load for each cell in the network, it is necessary to understand the relationship between the input parameters (causing the load situation) and the current load. The input parameters in case of the Air Interface load are all parameters which can be made accountable for the load situation in the cell (Section 2). Therefore, the load parameter (output) can be expressed as $L=f(x_1, x_2, \dots, x_n)$. Ideally, the load of each cell x in a given time could be expressed as the sum of all users consuming

[1] Theoretically, even higher speed scan be achieved for both HSUPA and HSDPA- 21Mbps and 42Mbps, respectively

resources of that cell at the particular time multiplied by the amount of resources they use plus the interference between that cell and all the other cells in the network (in practice limited to the neighboring cells):

$$L(x) = \sum_{i=0}^{m}\sum_{j=1}^{n} \text{User}_i * \text{Resource}_j + \sum_{y=1}^{z} \text{interference}(x, y)$$

where m is the count of users that are using the resources of cell x, n is the count of resources of the cell x, z is count of all cells in the network and interference(x, y) is the interference measured between cell x and y. Unfortunately, there was no tool that would provide such a detailed overview.

In order to approximate the load function, we recorded the different load parameters (outputs) and input parameters described in section 2, on an hourly basis during 1,5-8 weeks, depending on the operator. This provided approximately between 200 and 1,000 instances per cell or 20,000,000 instances in total on a network of 20,000 cells. The operators did not store data on lower granularity than one hour. Trials on daily averages were made, but these were not successful, due to the huge the load differences between night and daytime. Also, in this case there was a trade-off between a smaller sample and a longer period of data collection, which does not yield stability given all optimization changes in the network.

One of the choices to be made was whether a distinct formula for every cell shall be built or – alternatively – a common formula valid for all cells should be used. The approach where a model is created for each cell was chosen, due to the network experts' conviction that each cell is different, and a unified approach simply would not work, because some of the parameters influencing the load of each cell were immeasurable and unpredictable.

Next, the domain experts were intrinsically interested in being able to model cells that actually do not behave like other cells, especially when these are highly loaded. Furthermore, there would be a challenge in normalizing with respect to the varying capacity of the cells, i.e. what where the cell sized to handle. Finally, we hypothesized that not just model parameters could differ by cell, but also the optimal selection of features, similar to the load pockets explained by [13].

The choice of linear regression [16] was made due to several reasons. First of all, even though the distribution of the values of each of the load measures we are trying to predict vary between close to linear and close to exponential, we are only interested in the higher values of the load curve, and this can be approximated quite well with linear regression, as shown on Figure 1. For this purpose, before constructing the regression formulas, we remove all zero instances. Furthermore, linear regression is a very fast algorithm compared to other methods, which is very useful when it is necessary to develop a large number of models in a short time. Even though it is imaginable that better results might be achieved by using non-linear regression, regression trees, or other algorithms, this might not be necessary in most cases (Figure 1).

Also, simple low variance methods such as linear regression frequently perform much better in practice than more complicated algorithms, which can very often over fit the data (e.g. high variance algorithms such as neural networks). In other words, in real world problems variance is typically a more important problem than bias when it comes to data preparation and algorithm selection [3]. Trials on a smaller sample were already made with regression trees, but apart from the visibly increased time consumption, the accuracy did not improve. On the contrary, in some instances it decreased.

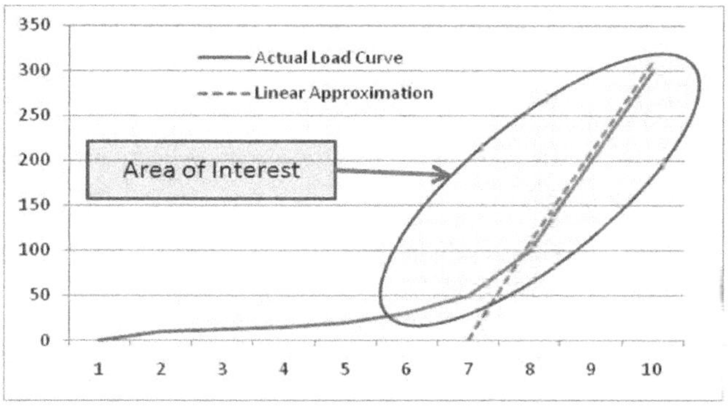

Figure 1 Actual Load vs. Linear approximation

Last but not least, linear regression is easy to implement, easy to explain and its results and models are easy to export for other use. Exporting the models to Excel was of crucial value, as analysts would use them in order to predict the future load of each cell, by scaling the input parameters, based on internal forecasting models. In other words, this allows non data miners to simulate future network load based on changes in the various type of network traffic, using simple tools they are familiar with.

4. BUILDING THE LOAD FORMULAS

In this section we will describe how the models are being generated and put to work. This includes the tools that were used, a detailed description of the approach, the results of this mass modeling process, the process of forecasting the future load and additional simulation scenarios.

4.1 Tools

The tools used in this research are either open source, or can be found in the IT portfolio of any telecom operator. These are the following:

Radio Network Performance Management System. As stated above, this research was using data from four different operators belonging to a large telecom group. Most of them have radio networks produced by different vendors, which means that also different Radio Network Performance Management Systems were used for data collection of both the input and the output parameters. In this research, we used Performance Management Systems of Nokia [8], Ericsson [9], Huawei [10] and MyCom [11], depending on the operator. These software tools were already a part of the Network/IT infrastructure of the operators. They contain technical parameters related to the mobile network performance. The most important feature of these tools for our research was that they contained hourly aggregates of all the input and output parameters we used (Section 2). These are the only domain specific tools from our process.

Load Prediction and Simulation Data Mart. This is an Oracle Database 10g- 64 bit v10.2.0.5.0 [17] used for all our task specific data preparation and manipulation.

Due to the fact that the necessary input and output parameters were stored at different tables in the respective Performance Management Systems, we needed a separate database where we could manipulate the data easier (e.g. merge tables, create indexes, and build the final flat table). In the case of Nokia Data Warehouse [8] this reduced the duration of the data collection and data preparation process from two weeks to 1 day by productizing data collection. Because we are rebuilding and rescoring models on a continuous and automated basis, this was a key improvement.

Any other database platform (commercial or open source) could have been used. We opted for Oracle based on license availability.

WEKA 3.6.4 x64, an open source data mining platform [18], was used for building the linear regression formulas and validating them. Of course, any other tool capable of deriving linear regression can also be used for this purpose. That said, this shows that even a research focused open source tool like WEKA can be used in critical commercial settings, at high complexity (e.g. 20.000 cells, 4 models each, around 1000 instances each).

Strawberry Perl for Windows v5.12.3 [19] is an open source scripting language that we used in order to create the script that is the core of this approach. Our script creates WEKA input files by querying the Oracle database, generates the regression models by executing calls to WEKA, and stores the regression formulas and the cross-validation outputs (Correlation Coefficient, Mean Absolute Error, Root Mean Squared Error, Relative Absolute Error, Root Relative Squared Error, and Total Number of Instances used to build the model) in csv files.

MS Excel 2010 [20] – part of MS Office 2010, was used to predict the future load of cells, using the regression formulas created by WEKA and extrapolations of the input values using a internet traffic model scaling factors based on handset/internet usage developments (internal to the operator).

4.2 Process Description

A graph of how our approach uses these tools to derive and store the regression models is presented on Figure 2. First, the data is extracted from the Network Performance Management Tools, e.g. Nokia Data Warehouse (NDW). The core of our approach is a Perl [21] script that automated the derivation of the regression formulas for each cell. This script executed calls to WEKA and queries the Oracle Database. It works in the following manner:

1. Get list of cells from the database
2. for each cell
   - 2.1. Run a query on the database to isolate only the data related to that cell (all the input and output parameters).
   - 2.2. Make separate files for each of the load output parameters
   - 2.3. For each of the load output parameters
     - 2.3.1. Filter out all instances where the load is 0[2].
     - 2.3.2. Select only relevant variables for the regression formula of that cell, using a wrapper approach, build the linear regression formula and store it in a separate file.
     - 2.3.3. Use 10-fold cross-validation to validate the model.
     - 2.3.4. Store the formula, the number of instances used to build the regression formula, the correlation between the predicted and actual value for load, the Mean Absolute Error (MAE) and the Root Mean Square Error (RMSE) as reported from the cross-validation.

[2] We did not want noisy data. Cells/instances with no load are of no interest.

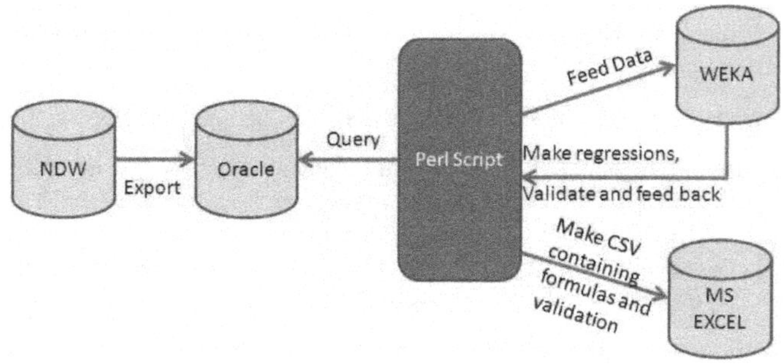

Figure 2: Communication Graph of the Tools used

While generating the models/regression formulae, we used a wrapper [22] approach. Wrapper approaches automatically select the best variables for predicting the outcome, taking into account the algorithm to be used, which in our case is linear regression. Wrapper approaches do not necessarily perform better or worse than filter approaches [23]. Our motivation to use the wrapper approach was to avoid human interaction with the model building process as much as possible, which obviously makes the process much faster.

It is worthwhile mentioning that the optimal feature and linear regression model selection were performed using 10-fold cross validation [16]. This was done in order to balance between cells with large sample of non-zero instances and cells with a smaller sample. The reported correlation coefficient, MAE and RMSE are averages from the 10 repetitions. Using 10-fold cross validation already provides a good estimate of the accuracies of these formulas. Of course, we do test them on completely new datasets, not only to confirm the accuracies achieved, but also to find out when is a good time to update the model. We expect that updates should be necessary every few months, because of the reconfiguration of the network, additions of new cells and upgrades to the existing ones.

4.3 Results and Discussion

Using this process we were able to run 30,000 regressions per day, by just one click. This does not necessarily result in 30,000 models, because in some cases it was impossible to derive a formula due to the large number of instances that were filtered out for zero load. But, in order to measure the load of a cell, it is sufficient that a model is generated for at least one output variable. Cases of cells where it was not possible to generate a model for any of the variables were rare. Furthermore, cells that do not show any load by the means of the output variables are not of interest for our problem situation. For practical purposes, we will only present the modeling results for two of the four output variables we used to describe the air interface load in section 2. We chose to present the results for the uplink and downlink load. All tables have the same structure. In the first column Bands of Averages for the respective output variables Downlink Load (DL_Load) and Uplink Load (UL_Load) are given. The second column contains the count of cells that falls into this band. The third column presents the average count of non-zero instances (NZI) in each band. In other words, it presents the number of instances used to build the regression, because we only took non-zero output values into account. The fourth column presents the average Correlation Coefficient (CC) between the predicted and actual values of the variables in the particular band. These Correlation Coefficients are the result of the 10-fold cross validation.

Table 1. Regression Modeling Results for Downlink Load (DL) for Country Operator 1

Downlink Load	Count of Cells	Avg Count of NZI	Avg Correlation Coefficient	Models Built Vs Number of Cells
DL<1	642	/	/	/
1<=DL<5	132	504.2	0.906	99%
5<=DL<10	450	528.5	0.920	100%
10<=DL<20	2995	507.7	0.914	100%
DL>=20	4120	511.1	0.955	100%

Table 2. Regression Modeling Results for Uplink Load (UL) for Country Operator 1

Uplink Load	Count of Cells	Avg Count of NZI	Avg Correlation Coefficient	Models Built Vs Number of Cells
UL<1	643	579	0.254	1%
1<=UL<5	693	513.94	0.536	96%
5<=UL<10	2880	522.06	0.676	100%
10<=UL<20	3405	516.14	0.756	100%
UL>=20	718	503.05	0.776	99%

Table 3. Regression Modeling Results for Downlink Load (DL) for Country Operator 2

Downlink Load	Count of Cells	Avg Count of NZI	Avg Correlation Coefficient	Models Built Vs Number of Cells
DL<1	683	/	/	/
1<=DL<5	2379	155.4	0.777	80%
5<=DL<10	9406	247.9	0.824	96%
10<=DL<20	4550	271.7	0.846	95%
DL>=20	1697	284.7	0.872	92%

Table 4. Regression Modeling Results for Uplink Load (UL) for Country Operator 2

Uplink Load	Count of Cells	Avg Count of NZI	Avg Correlation Coefficient	Models Built Vs Number of Cells
UL<1	431	172.8	0.554	17%
1<=UL<5	138	247.5	0.649	84%
5<=UL<10	909	273.9	0.565	87%
10<=UL<20	9649	294.7	0.617	95%
UL>=20	7816	288.8	0.801	98%

Table 5. Regression Modeling Results for Downlink Load (DL) for Country Operator 3

Downlink Load	Count of Cells	Avg Count of NZI	Avg Correlation Coefficient	Models Built Vs Number of Cells
DL<1	387	/	/	/
1<=DL<5	2447	142.5	0.854	84%
5<=DL<10	2428	155.9	0.907	95%
10<=DL<20	2114	175.5	0.935	99%
DL>=20	746	184.6	0.945	100%

Table 6. Regression Modeling Results for Uplink Load (UL) for Country Operator 3

Uplink Load	Count of Cells	Avg Count of NZI	Avg Correlation Coefficient	Models Built Vs Number of Cells
UL<1	160	56.6	0.382	11%
1<=UL<5	715	120.6	0.482	77%
5<=UL<10	1909	146.4	0.546	92%
10<=UL<20	3195	162.4	0.677	98%
UL>=20	2143	171.2	0.668	96%

Table 7. Regression Modeling Results for Downlink Load (DL) for Country Operator 4

Downlink Load	Count of Cells	Avg Count of NZI	Avg Correlation Coefficient	Models Built Vs Number of Cells
DL<1	5	952.4	0.449	100%
1<=DL<5	604	949.7	0.705	100%
5<=DL<10	3801	958.0	0.776	100%
10<=DL<20	4802	957.9	0.807	100%
DL>=20	1020	958.2	0.848	100%

Table 8. Regression Modeling Results for Uplink Load (UL) for Country Operator 4

Uplink Load	Count of Cells	Avg Count of NZI	Avg Correlation Coefficient	Models Built Vs Number of Cells
UL<1	0	/	/	/
1<=UL<5	0	/	/	/
5<=UL<10	674	948.2	0.461	98%
10<=UL<20	4187	955.5	0.598	100%
UL>=20	5371	957.2	0.669	100%

The last column presents the ratio between the number of formulas that were generated and the total count of cells in each band. Namely, for certain cells it was not possible to build the regression because of a very low number of non-zero instances.

The results of the Regression Modeling for Downlink and Uplink load for four different countries are shown in tables 1-8. In Tables 1 and 2 are the modeling results of the same operator published in [2]. However, this operator is still undergoing a full network swap, which means every cell in the network is either already replaced or will be replaced by a new one from a different network equipment vendor. At the moment, this operator is running both networks in parallel, which creates an additional level of complexity. However, the results presented in Tables 1 and 2 are referring to the modeling process on the swapped part of the network using the new vendor's equipment. Hence, the total number of cells is smaller than reported in [2]. For this reason, and the fact that we are presenting different output variables in this paper, the results of [2] and these results should not be compared.

The results can be evaluated by using two criteria: The Correlation Coefficient and The Ratio of The Models Built (the last two columns in Tables 1 to 8). Obviously, the Ratio of the Number of Formulas built for DL and UL grows alongside the number of instances for operators in all four countries, which is to be expected. We chose the correlation coefficient because it's a relative measure, and therefore more intuitive than the Mean Average Error of Root Mean Square Error. As mentioned above, we report the average correlation coefficient of each load band. The confidence intervals for the average correlation coefficient at 95% confidence level were not wider than ±0.02 in any operator in any of the Downlink or Uplink load bands, due to the relatively low standard deviations.

Furthermore, because of the choice we made at the beginning of the research, to focus on the higher levels of load and eliminate the zero values, the Average Correlation Coefficient between actual and predicted values also grows as the Load is higher, both for Downlink and Uplink. In the lowest Load bands, the performance of models is not good. However, this is of no interest, as these are not the situations that we are trying to predict. These cells are not likely to be in overload in the foreseeable future.

However, when analyzing the Average Correlation Coefficient (ACC) between the predicted and actual values there is a visible difference between Downlink and Uplink load: The ACC for Downlink Load (Tables 1, 3, 5, 7) is much higher than the ACC for Uplink Load (Tables 2, 4, 6, 8). Uplink Load seems more difficult to predict using linear regression. There are two possible reasons for this: A crucial input parameter (predictor) may be missing; or the Uplink Load has less of a linear nature.

Last but not least, model performance across operators cannot be compared due to differences in network vendors, software versions, geography, population density and smartphone penetration rates (which cause higher network load). The importance of the smartphone penetration and population density was also confirmed by the automated feature selection, where variables such as the combined throughput (uplink or downlink), which is highly influenced by smartphones and the number of HSDPA/HSUPA users per hour (which are smartphone users) were the most often selected when building the respective load formulas.

4.4 Forecasting the load

Once the load formulas have been derived it is possible to forecast the future load situation if the changes in the describing parameters are known. These changes of the input parameters are described by means of scaling factors. The scaling factors are calculated by using a traffic forecast model developed by the operator (out of scope of this paper). A cell is upgraded if any of the four output variables used as measures of Uplink or Downlink load, is above a critical value.

This is done in the following way:

```
1. for each output variable
    1.1. For each cell
        1.1.1. Select the top 100 instances of the
        output variable and its corresponding
        values for the input variable.
        1.1.2. Make averages of these input
        variables.
        1.1.3 Scale the input variables up or
        down, according to scaling factors
        developed by a traffic model.
        1.1.4. Feed the scaled values of the input
        parameters into the regression formula for
        the output variable for that cell
        1.1.5 If the resulting value is higher
        than the critical threshold for that
        output variable, the cell should be
        upgraded.
```

The forecasting model provides better and more sophisticated forecasts and as such supports better network investment decisions, which account for the major part of the entire operator CAPEX cost. In simple terms, no money is wasted by investing in unnecessary network upgrades, providing two benefits: lower cost and redirecting investments into areas that have a higher impact on a positive network experience for the customers. Also, the forecasted capacity issues are addressed and solved before they become a problem for the customers. This is a huge advantage, especially when compared to the reactive, fire-fighting like model previously deployed at the operator to address network capacity issues.

In addition, note that this part of the process is performed in a tool as simple as MS Excel. This was a key driver for the business success of the solution. In our experience the importance of the Deployment step in the data mining process is generally underestimated. By providing not just the scores but also the underlying models in a format and tool that was immediately usable and tunable to end users who are not data miners, the solution was readily accepted and also used in new ways not necessarily intended by the data miners, for instance detailed simulation scenarios. In our view, this approach may be applicable to many other domains.

4.5 Applications- Simulation scenarios

Initially, the only application of this research envisioned by the authors was the deployment scenario for forecasting future load and predicting necessary network upgrades due to "regular" traffic growth, as described in section 4.4. This has already been used in four different country operators belonging to the telecom group.

However, due to the flexibility of the approach, meaning using simple tools such as Microsoft Excel for implementation, the system developed a life of its own: the end users in the operator where this research was originally developed started creating simulation scenarios suited for different needs.

Step 1.1.3 of the algorithm described in the previous section mentions feeding scaling factors for the input parameters **based on a traffic model.** What if this traffic model is replaced by a different one? In that case, a new simulation scenario is generated. Using our approach, all it takes to generate a new scenario is to change the values of the input parameters in MS Excel. The output of the model (Downlink and Uplink Load) is automatically recalculated and the user can immediately see the effect. In the next paragraphs we will explain a few actual use case scenarios.

One of the first use cases generated was to predict future network load and evaluate network investments, based on proactive localized marketing campaigning. It was a co-operation between the Marketing and Network Technology Department. The Marketing Department provided their campaign description and expected benefits, namely new customers and increased service usage, which were trended in terms of the input parameters described in section 2. These were fed into the model as described in section 4.4, so the increased future load can be predicted and the necessary network improvements can be made, even before the marketing campaign is launched. A very similar scenario is in use for opening new stores, due to the fact that increased number of customers is expected when opening a brick-and-mortar store. This allows for the network to be prepared to accept the new customers without impacting the experience of the existing ones.

Another very powerful application of this model is evaluating a business case for adding a new wholesale client- or an MVNO (Mobile Virtual Network Operator). This is an operator that does not own a network; instead a MVNO is renting the network of a bigger telecom operator in order to provide services. In this case, the localized traffic growth for predicting the future load is based on the location (or the evaluation of) the customers of the MVNOs and their respective service usage. These are then trended and fed into our model (via MS Excel) in order to evaluate the necessary network improvements, so there is no degradation of service for the customers of the host operator. However, these upgrades come at a certain cost, which is attributed to accepting the MVNO onto the host network. If the benefit (revenues) generated by accepting the MVNO are lower than the costs incurred, the business case is negative and therefore, rejected. This approach was used in the country where the research originated to reject a business case for adding an MVNO. At the moment, a MVNO business case is being evaluated for another operator from the same telecom group.

Last but not least, this approach was used as one of the criteria to determine the strategy for the network swap and deployment of LTE (4G) network in the originating operator. As mentioned in section 4.3, this operator is undertaking a major network infrastructure investment, namely replacing the entire radio network (every cell) in order to modernize it and allow for deployment of 4G. Of course an undertaking of this size cannot be performed all at once; thus clusters of cells are being planned for replacement at a certain time. Our load prediction method was one of the criteria used for giving priority to certain clusters, thus reducing the need of unnecessary investments into the "old" network. The underlying assumption here is not only that the "new" generation radio network has more efficient resource use and therefore can handle the load better, but also that a certain amount of customers will start using 4G services, therefore offloading the 3G network.

None of the use case analyses described above were possible prior to the deployment of our method. They all require localized load predictions, which simply did not exist. The exact monetary return is once again confidential.

5. LIMITATIONS AND FUTURE WORK

The regression formulas developed by this approach can be used on a long term basis only if the mobile network stays the same (is frozen) over a longer period. But, this is not the case. The cellular network is a system of very complex dynamics. The many changes that occur, such as hardware and software updates, network reconfigurations and optimizations, as well as network upgrades and roll-out of new cell sites, which reduce the load of the existing cells, cannot be taken into account in advance. It is necessary to collect a new dataset and rebuild the regression formulas, in order to incorporate all these changes into the model. This is why the process described in this paper is scheduled for execution every 3-4 months.

Next, we intend to improve prediction for uplink load. One method would be searching for additional input parameters to improve the performance of predicting uplink load using linear regression. Alternatively, we could look for a substitute for linear regression better suited for modeling uplink load on the cells where linear regression does not deliver. However, this algorithm should not substantially slow down the whole process and must be easily transferable to MS Excel, in order to keep the flexibility and the ease of building simulation scenarios.

Further evaluation of the quality of the derived load formulas of course also involves the comparison of the predicted load with the actually measured load in the future. It should however be noted that there a lot of factors impeding a direct comparison. As noted above, all changes to the settings of a cell within the forecasting timeframe affect the load formula, which means that after such changes the derived formula is - at least to some degree - no longer correct. For this reason it will be challenging to really quantify the accuracy of the predictive model. Developing a fair method of evaluation, which would incorporate the network changes, would be beneficial. In terms of the core algorithms, we do want to keep the benefit of using a simple, fast and robust low variance approach such as linear regression.

However, we do plan to explore a methodology that would allow us to combine a global network model with local models for each cell, for instance multitask or transfer learning [24]. In principle, we have almost infinite data available for most cells, so local models cannot be improved by a global model. Nevertheless, there could be exception for a non select small number of cells. Next, a clustering approach could be devised to group cells with similar formulas or levels of load, thereby generating new knowledge for the telecom domain experts.

Furthermore, we do intend to investigate additional simulation scenarios for our approach, beyond those described in Section 4.5. Last but not least, this research has been implemented in four operators of this telecom group. Other operators from the same group are still to follow, with their use cases and applications of their own.

6. CONCLUSIONS

In this paper we presented a very simple yet effective approach of deploying data mining in commercial surroundings. Unfortunately, data mining is still seen as a black box in many industries, telecom not excluded. Even though some data mining activities are taken, typically in the Marketing/Customer

Retention field, there is a myriad of other possibilities in business where data mining can be applied. In our opinion, it is better to start with simple methods, such as regression, because it is easier to understand them. Once these simple approaches gain acceptance, and familiarize the industries with data mining, opportunities to apply more advanced techniques will arise.

In our result section we show that it is easier to accomplish a target, if one is focused on it. Namely, with our approach we wanted to target cells where some load (non-zero load) occurs, in order to predict the part that really matters more correctly: the high end part of the load curve (the cells in overload). In other words, as the network load grows, so does the quality of the model's predictions. We willingly sacrificed the models' performances within the lower loaded cells, because they are of no interest.

Next, one of the key values of the approach is that a large number of regression models (close to 30,000 per day) are developed in a very short period of time with minimum human interaction. In order to do this, we deployed a simple algorithm such as linear regression, motivated by its speed and other benefits explained earlier, a wrapper feature selection, in order to avoid human interaction, and 10-fold cross validation which makes the models statistically sound. Manually, this task would be impossible. Obviously, the possibility to generate these formulas was crucial to the operator. At the moment, the commercial tools for this purpose offer only load predictions based on single variable regressions [11], which is not as robust as our approach.

Typically, planning network upgrades is a reactive process. Our approach makes it proactive, which was acknowledged by the operator, who has fully integrated our approach into its network upgrade planning and budgeting activities. Of course, due to the fast pace network changes, the formulas need to be upgraded every 3-4 months, but this is also scheduled as a part of a standard process. Due to confidentiality, we cannot disclose the exact return of this project, but given that the network is the key resource of an operator, the investments into its upgrades are quite sizeable. To our knowledge, this is the first time a telecom operator has applied data mining in order to create a proactive network upgrade management process. This allows the operator to manage network performance better and avoid extreme congestion situations, which can result in degraded customer experience and loss of reputation for the operator. As mentioned at the beginning, the research was performed at a large telecom operator with branches in many European countries. At the moment, our research is deployed in four of the countries where this operator is present, but efforts are made to make it universal to the telecom group and replicate it in the other branches as well.

Potentially the greatest benefit of our approach is the decoupling of the data mining process from simulation scenarios. This is accomplished by exporting the models into Excel sheets after they have been have been generated by our data mining process. Then, the end users, a team of radio network analysts who are not data miners, are able to use these formulas resulting from a data mining process for forecasting the future network load. This allows them to simulate multiple traffic scenarios by scaling the current input parameters, which is as simple as changing values in their respective columns in Excel. These scenarios include "regular growth" scenarios, evaluations of network investments necessary to accommodate localized user growth due to targeted marketing campaigns, adding a new wholesale client (an MVNO- Mobile Virtual Network Operator) and prioritizing clusters for deployment of new technologies such as LTE/4G.

Next, we would like to point out the possibility of applying our research onto problems other than telecom network load. This approach would be applicable to any other industry where large scale regression models are necessary. This can be accomplished simply be replacing the data source, in this case the Radio Network Performance Management Tools, with a data source suitable for the industry that would like to apply our research. The decoupling of the data mining process from the simulation scenarios makes our approach more general to situations where detailed simulations are necessary, but the domain experts are not data miners. We already tested this approach for cluster based revenue predictions, which is a topic from the finance domain.

Last but not least, perhaps one of the most interesting aspects of our approach is the extremely low cost. Given that we used the existing IT infrastructure (Server, Radio Network Performance Management Tools, Oracle, Excel) combined with open source tools (WEKA, Perl), the only cost that incurred are the 1 week Processing Time Cost (of the Server) and the labor cost of the employees in this project. Also, the Oracle Database that we used can be replaced with a less expensive or free database alternative in order to further reduce the cost, in case the potential user of our approach does not have an Oracle License. These amounts are insignificant compared to the actual investments being made into the network.

7. REFERENCES

[1] Mäder, A., Staehle, D. 2004. Analytic modeling of the WCDMA downlink capacity in multi-service environments. In *16th ITC Specialist Seminar*. 229-238.

[2] Radosavljevik, D., van der Putten, P., Kyllesbech Larsen, K. 2012. Mass scale modeling and simulation of the air-interface load in 3G radio access networks. *Advances in Intelligent Data Analysis XI*. Springer Berlin Heidelberg. 301-312.

[3] van der Putten, P., van Someren, M. 2004. A Bias-Variance Analysis of a Real World Learning Problem: The CoIL Challenge 2000. *Machine Learning* 57(1-2), 177-195. Kluwer Academic Publishers.

[4] Yates, R. 1995. A framework for uplink power control in cellular radio systems. *IEEE JSAC* 13(7), 3141–3147

[5] Geijer Lundin, E., Gunnarsson, F., Gustafsson, F. 2003. Uplink load estimation in WCDMA. in *Proc. IEEE Wireless Communications and Networking Conference* 3, 1669-1674

[6] Muckenheim, J., Bernhard, U. 2001. A Framework for Load Control in 3rd Generation CDMA Networks. In *Proc of the IEEE Global Telecommunications Conference 6*, pp. 3738-3742

[7] Natalizio, E., Marano, S., Molinaro A. 2005. Packet scheduling algorithms for providing QoS on UMTS downlink shared channels. *IEEE VTC 4*, pp. 2597–2601

[8] Nokia Siemens Networks. 2008. Nokia Siemens Networks WCDMA RAN, Rel. RU10- System Library, v.1: RNC Counters – RNW Part. Nokia Siemens Networks. Proprietary and Confidential

[9] Ericsson. 2013. Ericsson Performance Management. DOI= http://www.ericsson.com/ourportfolio/products/performance-management

[10] Huawei.2013. iManager M2000. DOI= http://www.huawei.com/en/products/oss/mbb-om-product/imanager-m2000/

[11] MyCom. 2013. NIMS-PrOptima Service & Network Performance Management. DOI= http://www.mycom-int.com/products/nims-proptima-service-and-network-performance-solution/

[12] 3gpp.1999. RNSAP Cell Load Information procedure and message contents. DOI= http://www.3gpp.org/ftp/tsg_ran/wg3_iu/TSGR3_07/Docs/Pdfs/R3-99c57.PDF

[13] Feinberg, E.A., Genethliou, D. 2005. Load Forecasting. In: Chow, J.W., Wu, F.F., Momoh, J., (eds.) *Applied Mathematics for restructured electric power systems*, 269-285,

[14] Svoboda, P., Buerger, M., Rupp, M. 2008. Forecasting of Traffic Load in a Live 3G Packet Switched Core Network. in *Proc. of 6th International Symposium on CNSDSP*, 433 - 437

[15] Bermolen, P., Rossi, D. 2009. Support vector regression for link load prediction. *Computer Networks 53*(2), 191-201

[16] Witten, I. H., Frank, E. 2005. *Data Mining: Practical Machine Learning Tools and Technique. (2nd Ed.)*, Morgan Kaufmann, San Francisco.

[17] Oracle, 2011. Oracle Database Documentation Library. DOI= http://www.oracle.com/pls/db102/homepage

[18] Hall, M., Frank, E., Holmes, G., Pfahringer, B., Reutemann, P. Witten, I. H. 2009. The WEKA Data Mining Software: An Update; *SIGKDD Explorations* 11(1).

[19] Strawberry Perl, 2011. DOI= http://strawberryperl.com/

[20] Microsoft Corporation, 2010. Microsoft Excel. DOI= http://office.microsoft.com/en-us/excel/

[21] Christiansen, T., Torkington, N. 2003. *Perl Cookbook (2nd Ed.)*. O'Reilly, Sebastopol.

[22] Kohavi, R., John, G. 1997. Wrappers for feature subset selection. *Artificial Intelligence* 97, 273–324.

[23] Tsamardinos, I., Aliferis, C. 2003. Towards principled feature selection: Relevancy, filters and wrappers. In *Proceedings of the Ninth International Workshop on Artificial Intelligence and Statistic*

[24] Caruana, R. 1997. Multitask learning. *Machine Learning* 28, 41-75.

Unveiling Clusters of Events for Alert and Incident Management in Large-Scale Enterprise IT

Derek Lin
Pivotal Software, Inc.
3495 Deer Creek Rd
Palo Alto, CA, USA
dlin@gopivotal.com

Rashmi Raghu
Pivotal Software, Inc.
3495 Deer Creek Rd
Palo Alto, CA, USA
rraghu@gopivotal.com

Vivek Ramamurthy
Pivotal Software, Inc.
3495 Deer Creek Rd
Palo Alto, CA, USA
vramamurthy@gopivotal.com

Jin Yu
Pivotal Software, Inc.
570 Bourke street
Melbourne, VIC, Australia
jyu@gopivotal.com

Regunathan Radhakrishnan
Pivotal Software, Inc.
3495 Deer Creek Rd
Palo Alto, CA, USA
rradhakrishnan1@gopivotal.com

Joseph Fernandez
Visa Inc
900 Metro Center Blvd
Foster City, CA, USA
lazferna@visa.com

ABSTRACT

Large enterprise IT (Information Technology) infrastructure components generate large volumes of alerts and incident tickets. These are manually screened, but it is otherwise difficult to extract information automatically from them to gain insights in order to improve operational efficiency. We propose a framework to cluster alerts and incident tickets based on the text in them, using unsupervised machine learning. This would be a step towards eliminating manual classification of the alerts and incidents, which is very labor intense and costly. Our framework can handle the semi-structured text in alerts generated by IT infrastructure components such as storage devices, network devices, servers etc., as well as the unstructured text in incident tickets created manually by operations support personnel. After text pre-processing and application of appropriate distance metrics, we apply different graph-theoretic approaches to cluster the alerts and incident tickets, based on their semi-structured and unstructured text respectively. For automated interpretation and read-ability on semi-structured text clusters, we propose a method to visualize clusters that preserves the structure and human-readability of the text data as compared to traditional word clouds where the text structure is not preserved; for unstructured text clusters, we find a simple way to define prototypes of clusters for easy interpretation. This framework for clustering and visualization will enable enterprises to prioritize the issues in their IT infrastructure and improve the reliability and availability of their services.

KDD'14, August 24–27, 2014, New York, NY, USA.

http://dx.doi.org/10.1145/2623330.2623360 .

Categories and Subject Descriptors

H.2.8 [**Database Applications**]: [Data Mining]; I.5.3 [**Pattern Recognition**]: [Clustering]

Keywords

Hierarchical clustering; Connected Components; Graph cut; Complete Linkage; kd-tree; Non-Negative Matrix Factorization; Tickets Analysis; Alerts and Incidents management

1. INTRODUCTION

Organizations of all sizes struggle with a common problem in Infrastructure and Operational Management. Thousands of automated alerts with semi-structured text are generated every day from hundreds of infrastructure tools. Similarly, thousands of incident tickets (or incidents) with manually entered unstructured text are created daily by support personnel. These alerts and incidents are centrally collected (eg. IBM Netcool [5]); however, maintenance of these alerts and incidents is costly and labor intensive, and requires detailed analysis from subject matter experts. The classic problem enterprises repeatedly encounter is the identification of important alerts and incidents, on which attention can be focussed. We desire an alert and incident discovery and classification process that can be automated and is data agnostic. It benefits the downstream processing steps by helping to reduce false positive alerts [16] or improving operational efficiency to answer questions such as *What are the topics of alerts and incidents? what are the topics or clusters that generate the most volumes of alerts? What is the mean-time-to-repair for a cluster?*

Toward addressing this need, we propose two distinct frameworks: one framework to cluster alerts with semi-structured text, and another framework to cluster incidents with unstructured text. The text within alert and incident data are each preprocessed using token normalization and stop-word removal - two common approaches used in text mining. The text within each alert or incident is now represented as a bag of words.

To cluster alerts comprised of semi-structured text, we first choose a distance metric, then apply a top-down clustering approach using connected components and graph-cut. Related work in [6] used Levenshtein edit distance and DB-SCAN for text clustering; similarly [14] used Levenshtein distance for simple clustering based on dissimilarity. Resulting clusters are then visualized with a novel visualization technique for automated interpretation.

Compared to the clustering of alerts, clustering of incidents is more computationally demanding. Alerts are generated by technology components (a database, or an application) and are already broadly tagged by their component names. Alerts generated from a technology component are clustered independently from those from another technology component. Clustering of all alerts within a technology component is manageable, especially after the token normalization step which reduces the space of alerts substantially. Clustering of incidents, however, is more computationally challenging as there is no high-level grouping of incidents. To cluster incidents, we develop an approach based on matrix factorization and KD-tree to create a preliminary grouping of incidents before applying complete linkage clustering per group and later performing cluster merging in a post-processing step.

Based on the clustering output, we compute several interesting business intelligence metrics or key performance indicators per cluster and visualize them. In this paper, we also address the need for automated interpretation of alert clusters. For alert cluster interpretation, we propose a novel visualization that preserves the structure and human-readability of the text data as compared to traditional word clouds where the text structure is not preserved. For incident cluster interpretation, we simply find prototypes of clusters. KPI visualization and cluster interpretation would help enterprises prioritize the issues in their IT infrastructure and improve the reliability and availability of their services.

The rest of the paper is organized as follows. In the following two sections, we will describe the details of the framework. Then, we present the results of these clustering approaches that provide insights into the top issues in the IT infrastructure.

2. HIERARCHICAL CLUSTERING OF SEMI-STRUCTURED ALERTS TEXT BASED ON CONNECTED COMPONENTS DETECTION AND GRAPH-CUT

Figure 1 illustrates the 5 high level steps in the proposed framework to cluster semi-structured alerts text.

- Step 1: Token normalization of alert and incident summary texts.
- Step 2: Stopword removal.
- Step 3: Pairwise distance metric computation to compare any two summaries.
- Step 4: Hierarchical clustering based on computed pairwise distance matrix.
- Step 5: Post-processing and Visualization.

In the following sub-sections we will describe these steps in detail.

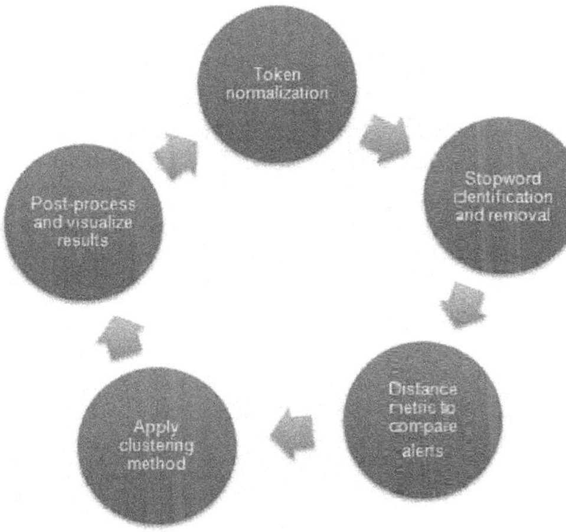

Figure 1: Steps in the clustering framework

2.1 Token Normalization of Alerts Text

Tokens are individual words within alerts. For the purpose of clustering, we are only interested in the textual structural information in alerts. Tokens exhibiting high variability such as IP address, date and time are either removed or replaced by another common string. For instance, two alerts A and B may report the same issue at specific IP address (e.g Alert A: service is not running at 10.2.34.56 and Alert B: service is not running at 10.12.2.54). For the purpose of clustering these two alerts based on the issue they refer to (a particular service not running), the specific IP address (e.g 10.12.2.54) in the alert string is not important. By replacing the IP address with a string "*ipaddr*", both of these alerts end up containing the same 'normalized' text. Which particular tokens to normalize, depends on the problem domain. In our enterprise data set, we performed the following token normalizations to bring together alerts that originally appeared to be very different.

- Replace various date formats with the text "date"
- Replace various time formats with the text "time"
- Replace various URLs with the text "url"
- Replace various file paths with the text "filepath"
- Replace various server (node) names with "nodename"
- Remove application names that provided no insight on the type of an alert
- Replace numbers with ♯, and punctuations with whitespace
- Remove trailing whitespace

Token normalization substantially reduced the alert space and eliminated a lot of noise in the data. It was now a lot easier to detect structural patterns within the normalized alerts and to apply suitable distance metrics for clustering.

2.2 Stopword Removal

Stopwords are words that commonly occur in all of the alert groups. These words do not help in clustering alerts as they are present in a large proportion of the alerts. For instance, every alert originating from a certain service component contains the word: "service". In order to cluster alerts coming out of this component based on its content, this word ("service") is not helpful and hence can be considered as a stopword and removed.

In order to identify the stopwords, we perform the following steps:

- Split the alerts text into unigrams (words or tokens)
- For each distinct unigram, compute its total count across all alerts, as well as the total number of distinct token normalized alerts that it appears in.
- Sort the unigrams in descending order of total count across all alerts, and then in descending order of total number of distinct token normalized alerts that they appear in. Choose the top "k" unigrams from this sorted list as the stopwords to be removed. "k", is chosen by visual inspection, using domain knowledge, to remove only words that are not useful for clustering.

2.3 Distance Metric to Compare Alerts

Before we can perform any clustering, we need to be able to compare any two alerts where each alert is represented as a bag of words . We propose to use Jaccard distance as a metric to compare any two alerts. In order to compute Jaccard distance, each alert is represented as a bag of words. Let us denote one such set from alert A as A and another set of words from alert B as B. Then, Jaccard distance is defined as below:

$$JaccardDistance(A, B) = 1 - (\frac{|A \cap B|}{|A \cup B|}) \quad (1)$$

Jaccard distance is a number between 0 and 1 and is not sensitive to the position of the matching word in the two alerts that are being compared.

Given N alerts that need to be clustered, we create at NxN distance matrix using the Jaccard distance metric to compare any two alerts.

It is possible to apply other distance metrics such as Rank-Biased Overlap [17], which takes into account the position of the match when comparing two alerts.

2.4 Clustering Alerts based on Distance Matrix

In the previous section, we described how we create a NxN distance matrix that summarizes how the alerts relate to each other. Given the NxN distance matrix, various clustering methods potentially apply, but each with different assumptions and advantages. For example, hierarchical clustering with minimax linkage [1] tended to produce over-fragmented clusters in our experiments by assuming that similar events within a cluster are within a certain radius distance from the centroid. Not assuming any cluster shape is a criterion in our clustering method choice. We propose using a graph-theoretic approach that uses connected component detection to generate initial clusters before applying the graph-cut algorithm to further refine the clusters.

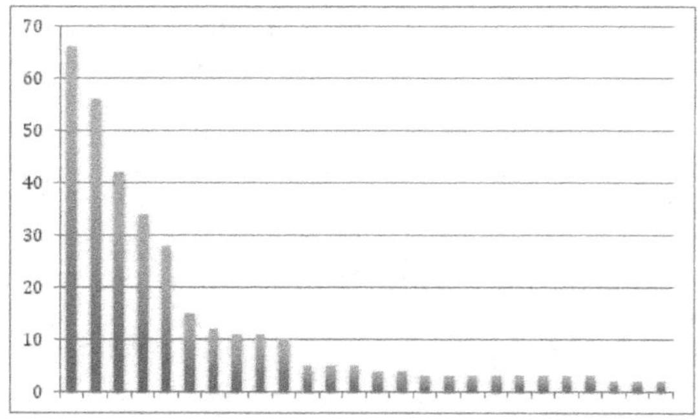

Figure 2: Size of Connected Components from a Graph (Graph A)

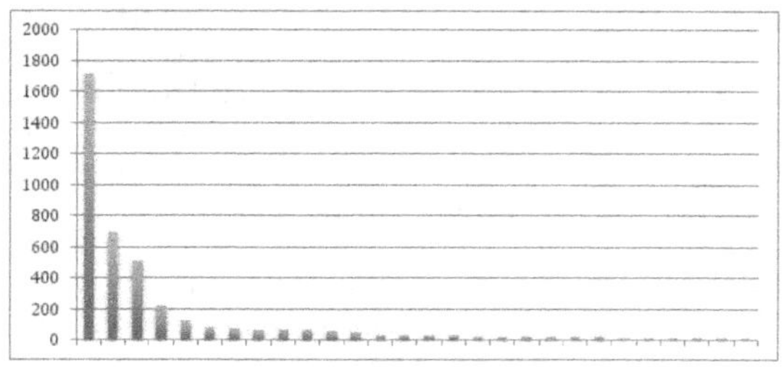

Figure 3: Size of Connected Components from a Graph (Graph B)

2.4.1 *Top-down Clustering based on Connected Components Detection*

Given the NxN distance matrix, we can create a graph where the vertices of the graph correspond to alerts. We can establish an edge between any two vertices (alerts) if the Jaccard distance between the two alerts is less than a threshold (e.g 0.5). After creating this graph, we run a connected components detection algorithm on it to identify parts of the graph that are not connected to other parts.

A connected component [4] is a sub-graph in which there exists at least one path that connects any two vertices, and which is connected to no additional vertices in the complete graph. One advantage of using connected components is that it doesn't assume any cluster shape.

Figure 2 below shows the number of connected components detected from a graph (say Graph A) representing few hundred alerts. There are 5 to 6 significant clusters or connected components detected from this group of alerts.

Similarly, we detected 196 connected components from the another graph (say Graph B) representing few thousand alerts. The size of top 3 or 4 connected components in the case of Graph B tended to be much larger than in the case of Graph A. The sizes of detected connected components from Graph B are shown below in Figure 3.

For instance, the top connected component in Graph B was of size 1717. It was desirable to break this large connected component (cluster) into smaller clusters. Toward this end, we employed normalized cut, which is a hierarchical graph partitioning algorithm. In the following subsection, we describe the details of this graph-cut algorithm.

2.4.2 *Graph Cut*

Given a NxN distance matrix (C) of a connected component, we perform the following steps to derive smaller

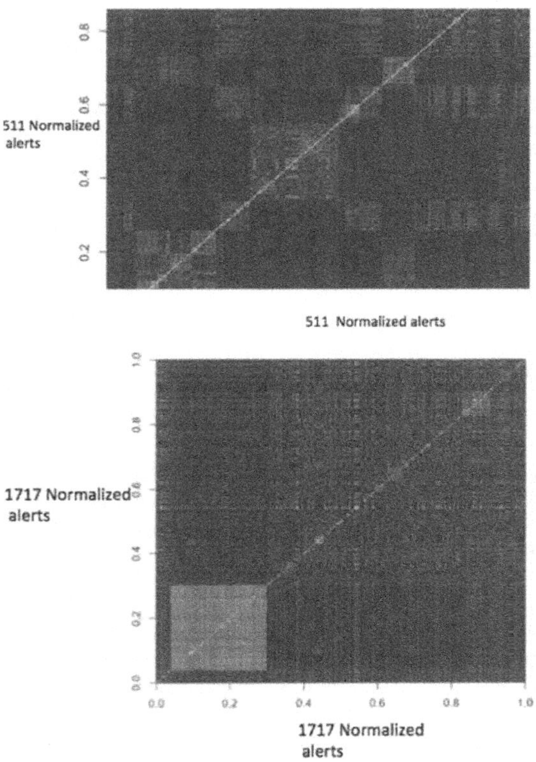

Figure 4: Affinity matrices of large connected components

clusters from this connected component:

- Compute an affinity matrix W of the same size as distance matrix where $W = exp^{(-\frac{C}{\sigma^2})}$. Here σ is a parameter that controls how quickly affinity (similarity) falls off with distance [7]. σ^2 was empirically chosen to be 0.5.

- Compute a diagonal degree matrix D whose diagonal is $d(i, i) = \sum_j W(i, j)$

- Solve the following eigen system: $D^{-1/2}(D-W)D^{-1/2}x = x$

- Here x is the cluster indicator vector that partitions the input graph into two parts A and B such that within-cluster affinity is maximized while between cluster-affinity is minimized.

- Compute cluster radii for the new partitions A and B and their sizes.

- If $clusterradius > radiusthreshold$ and $clustersize > sizethreshold$, then continue partitioning either A or B recursively.

Figure 4 below shows affinity matrices of two such large connected components (clusters). Note that the block structure along the main diagonal of the affinity matrices, indicating the presence smaller clusters within the connected component.

After recursive partitioning of Graph B, it is broken down to 4 significant smaller clusters as shown in Figure 5.The

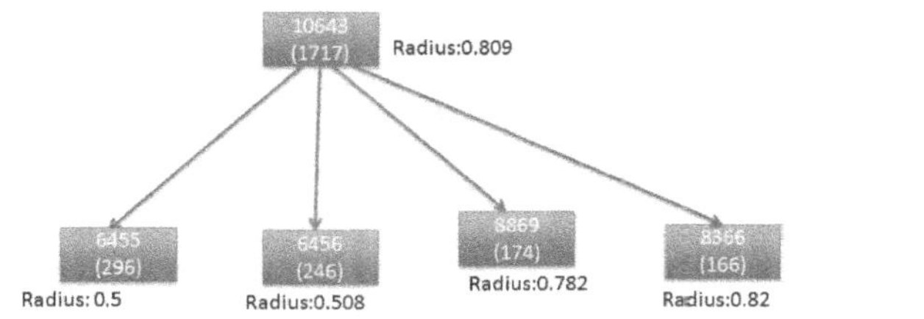

Figure 5: Graph cut based recursive partitioning of Graph B into 4 smaller clusters

connected component of size 1717 is partitioned into 4 clusters of sizes 296,246,174 and 166 respectively and other smaller clusters. Note the cluster radii for the smaller clusters from the graph-cut partitions are smaller than the radius of the large connected component.

If the largest connected component is greater than say 10000 alerts, then computing the full distance matrix and performing Graph cut may not scale. We propose to use the Nystrom method to perform graph cut, in which you randomly sample $say 5\%$ of the distance matrix and compute an approximation to the dense solution of the eigen system using the Nystrom approximation as suggested in [2]

3. HIERARCHICAL CLUSTERING OF UNSTRUCTURED INCIDENT TICKETS

To account for the complexity arising from the unstructured nature of the incident tickets, we extend the framework for clustering semi-structured Netcool alerts by incorporating two new elements: non-negative matrix factorization and KD-tree data structure. The resulting framework consists of the following high-level steps:

1. Token normalization and stopword removal.
2. High-level grouping of tickets based on non-negative matrix factorization and KD-tree.
3. Hierarchical clustering within each group of incidents.
4. A refinement step to merge similar clusters.

3.1 Token Normalization and Stopword Removal

We take the same token normalization approach as applied to Netcool alerts except that timestamps, file paths, URLs, punctuations, and digits are removed from incident summaries, instead of being replaced by common strings. This is based on the observation that unlike semi-structured alerts, ticket descriptions generally do not conform to certain formats, hence semantically non-meaningful strings like timestamps and file paths are unlikely to contribute to the formation of clusters.

In addition, we also remove common English stopwords such as "the" and "is" as well as a custom list of words such as "please" and "following" to further clean the data.

3.2 High-Level Grouping of Tickets

For Netcool data, clustering is performed within each subgroup of alerts. However, sub-group information is not available for incident tickets. This presents a potential computational challenge, due to the need to compute pairwise dis-

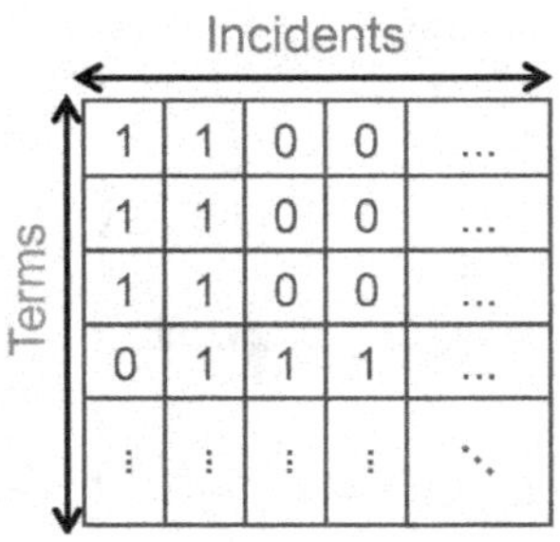

Figure 6: A binary term-incident matrix.

tances between each pair of tickets. In what follows we introduce a novel approach to the creation of high-level grouping of incident tickets. Underlying the approach are two techniques: non-negative matrix factorization and KD-tree.

3.2.1 Non-Negative Matrix Factorization

As the first step towards generating a preliminary grouping of incident tickets, we construct feature vectors to represent tickets. Using bag-of-words representation, we collect the entire set of tickets in a binary matrix. Each row represents a term (word), and each column represents an incident ticket, with the value 1 indicating the presence of a term; and 0 otherwise. As shown in Figure 6, the term-incident matrix is highly sparse. This calls for a dimensionality reduction step to obtain a more compact representation of the data. Towards this end, we factorize the term-incident matrix via non-negative matrix factorization [9, 12].

Non-negative matrix factorization (NMF) is a popular technique for dimensionality reduction and underlies a wide range of machine learning applications such as text mining [13, 15, 18], image analysis [10], recommender systems [19], etc. It refers to the factorization of a non-negative matrix $A_{m\times n}$ into the product of two low-rank matrices $W_{m\times k}$ and $H_{k\times n}$, whose elements are also non-negative. The rank parameter k is typically chosen to be much smaller than $\min(m,n)$. Given the input matrix A and the rank k, NMF can be formulated as the following constrained optimization problem:

$$\min_{W,H} \| A - WH \|_F^2, \quad \text{s.t.} \quad W, H \geq 0, \qquad (2)$$

where $\|\cdot\|_F$ denotes Frobenius norm, and the constraints: $W, H \geq 0$, enforce W and H to take only non-negative elements. This problem is non-convex in both W and H, but becomes a convex problem when either W or H is fixed.

There are many different approaches to solving (2). Alternating Least Squares (ALS) [12] is among the most popular ones, due to its simplicity and good practical performance; see Alg. 1 for an outline of the algorithm. Starting with an initial estimation of W, ALS first solves the least squares problem $\min_H \| A - WH \|_F^2$ for H, which is equivalent to solving the matrix equation at Step 5 of Alg. 1. The subsequent Step 6 is a truncation step to ensure non-negativity of the solution. It is clear that the closed-form solution to the matrix equation at Step 5 is $H = (W^\top W)^{-1} W^\top A$. Although matrix inversion is computationally expensive in general, here the size of the positive-semidefinite matrix $(W^\top W)$ is only $k \times k$. Hence, the cost of inverting this small matrix is almost negligible. The rest of the operation to obtain H involves sparse matrix multiplication, which can be

Algorithm 1 Alternating Least Squares for NMF

1: **input** a matrix $A_{m\times n} \geq 0$ and an integer $0 < k \ll \min(m,n)$.
2: **output** two low-rank factors: $W_{m\times k} \geq 0$ and $H_{k\times n} \geq 0$.
3: Initialize W, e.g. using methods introduced in [8].
4: **repeat**
5:   fix W, solve $W^\top W H = W^\top A$ for H.
6:   set all negative elements in H to 0.
7:   fix H, solve $HH^\top W^\top = HA^\top$ for W.
8:   set all negative elements in W to 0.
9: **until** a convergence criterion is met.
10: **optional** standardize the solution: normalize each column of W (resp. each row of H) to have norm 1, adjust H (resp. W) accordingly to absorb scaling coefficients.

efficiently implemented in an MPP database [3]. Similarly, given the current H, W is updated via a two-step procedure (Steps 7 and 8). The algorithm proceeds in an alternating fashion until a convergence criterion is met. In our implementation, we also standardize the solution as shown at Step 10 of Alg. 1 by normalizing H.

A known limitation of ALS is that its convergence is difficult to analyze, due to the ad-hoc enforcement of the non-negativity constraints. Nevertheless, ALS and many of its variants (see e.g. [19]) have seen great success in real-world applications. In practical implementations, it is a common strategy to monitor changes in the elements of W and H, and stop the algorithm when the changes fall below a pre-specified threshold, or the maximum number of allowed iterations is reached. Another practical aspect of ALS is initialization. Due to the non-convex nature of the NMF problem, ALS (and in fact any NMF algorithm) is bound to be sensitive to the initial estimate of W. We use an initialization strategy suggested in [8], which is to initialize each column of W by averaging a certain number of random columns in A. This simple and intuitive approach has been shown [8] to strike a good balance between performance and computational cost, and worked well in our experiments.

The resulting low-rank factors effectively encode the original matrix A (term-incident matrix) in a k-dimensional latent space. The columns of W are the basis vectors of the latent space. Let $\mathbf{a}_i$ be a column (an incident ticket) in A, and $\mathbf{h}_i$ the corresponding column in H. Then, an $\mathbf{a}_i$ can be approximated by $\mathbf{a}_i \approx W\,\mathbf{h}_i$, meaning that the approximation is an additive linear combination of the basis vectors, weighted by the entries in $\mathbf{h}_i$. Essentially, an $\mathbf{h}_i$ specifies how an incident ticket is expressed in the latent space, where tickets that share similar descriptions still remain “close”.

3.2.2 A KD-Tree of Incident Tickets

Given the low-rank factor H, we organize its columns in a KD-tree [11], a commonly used data structure for searching nearest “neighbors” in a multi-dimensional space. KD-tree partitions multi-dimensional data into non-overlapping subsets (also called subtrees) such that nearest neighbors are more likely to be within rather than outside of a subtree. A KD-tree is constructed in a recursive manner (see Fig. 7):

1. Pick a dimension.
2. Find the median along that dimension.
3. Split the data at the median.

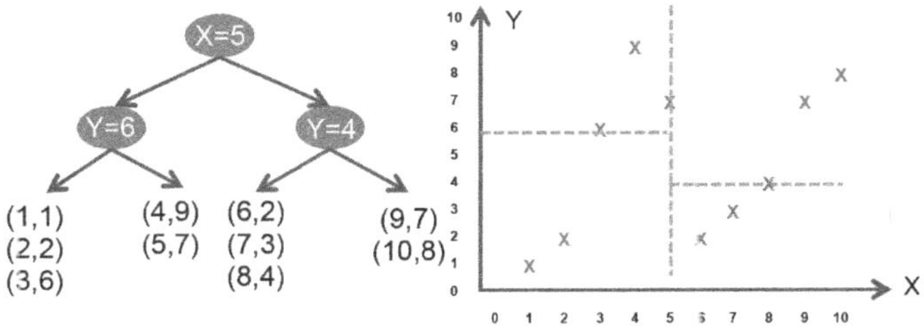

Figure 7: An example KD-tree.

4. Repeat on subtrees until they reach a desired size.

As illustrated in Fig. 7, a KD-tree creates a natural grouping of the data. This motivates our use of KD-tree to produce a high-level grouping of incident tickets

Note that at each iteration KD-tree splits the data along only one dimension. The implication is that the order of dimensions to partition the data can influence the final grouping. Our implementation gives priority to dimensions that contain more non-zero values. The assumption is that denser dimensions are more discriminative. It is also well known that "the curse of dimensionality" is a problem of KD-tree. Data points in a high-dimensional space tend to be far away from each other, hence are unlikely to form large groups. Recall that our KD-tree is constructed in the low-dimensional latent space produced by NMF. This effectively avoids the curse of dimensionality issue. Empirically, we found it sufficient to set the dimensionality (i.e., the rank parameter in NMF) to 15 to obtain a satisfactory grouping result.

3.3 Hierarchical Clustering

Having constructed a KD-tree, agglomerative hierarchical clustering is run within each subtree to obtain a refined grouping of incident tickets. Agglomerative hierarchical clustering builds a clustering tree from bottom up by merging closest clusters. In contrast to the familiar K-means clustering method, hierarchical clustering does not require the number of clusters to be specified *a priori*. Instead, a user decides at what height to cut a clustering tree, which indirectly determines the number of clusters. We find that it is often much easier to empirically find an appropriate height than the number of clusters.

Hierarchical clustering operates on pairwise distances. To measure pairwise distances between ticket descriptions, we design a distance measure as below:

$$dist(A, B) = \max_i |X_i| - |A \cap B|, \tag{3}$$

where X_i, A, and B are sets of distinct words in a ticket description, and $|\cdot|$ denotes the cardinality of a set. The first term: $\max_i |X_i|$ is a constant. It is introduced to ensure positivity of the distance measure. Note that this distance measure is based solely on the intersection of texts but not length. This is motivated by the observation that descriptions of the same issue can vary widely in length; for instance, the two examples shown in Figure 8 both describe a password related issue, but one is brief, while the other contains much more details.

For clustering, we used the complete-linkage method. It is an agglomerative hierarchical clustering method that defines the distance between two clusters by the farthest pair of data

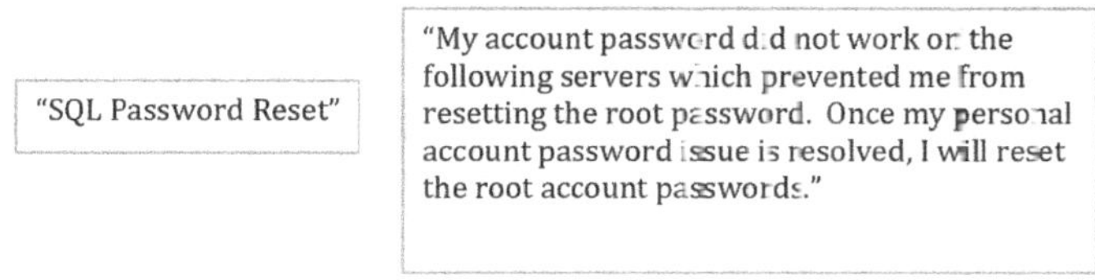

Figure 8: Tickets of the same issue can vary widely in length.

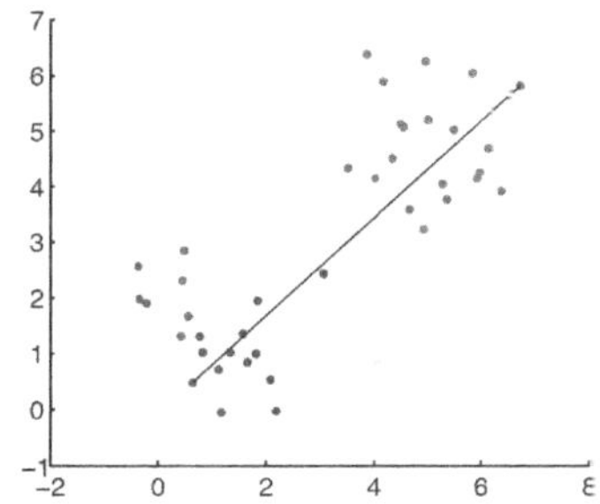

Figure 9: Complete linkage defines the distance between two clusters by the farthest pair of data points.

points (Figure 9). Combined with the intersection-based distance measure (3), complete-linkage clustering ensures that each pair of tickets in a cluster share at least some common words. The resulting clustering tree can be cut at a height to ensure a certain degree of overlap between each pair of tickets within a cluster. Suppose that the maximum length of a ticket description is 30 (i.e., $\max_i |X_i| = 30$), then setting the height to 28 guarantees an overlap of at least 2 words between any two tickets of the same cluster. Moreover, an exemplar is selected for each cluster to show the typical "look and feel" of tickets in a cluster. It is defined as the ticket that has the shortest distance to its farthest "neighbor" (Figure 10):

$$\mathbf{x}^* := \arg\min_{\mathbf{x} \in X} \max_{\mathbf{x}' \in X} d(\mathbf{x}, \mathbf{x}'). \tag{4}$$

3.4 Merging Similar Clusters

Due to the variability of ticket descriptions, the same type

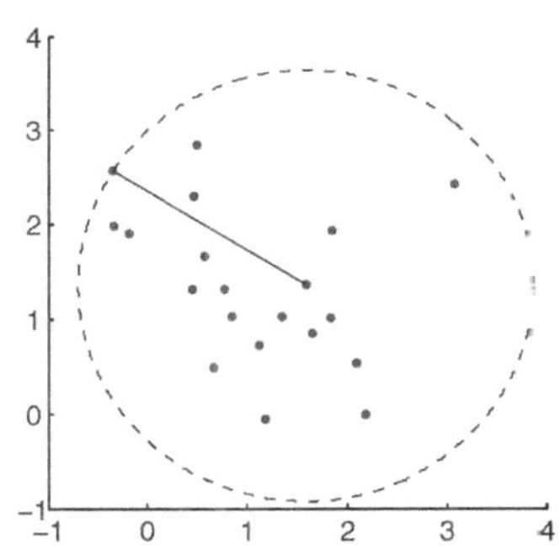

Figure 10: The exemplar (center of the encompassing circle) has the shortest distance to its farthest neighbor.

of tickets can be assigned to different subtrees, or to different clusters even within the same subtree. A refinement step was therefore developed to merge those similar clusters.

First, frequently used words (e.g. top-10 words) are extracted from each cluster to form a feature vector. The intersection-based distance measure (3) is then applied to feature vectors to quantify the dissimilarity between two clusters. Given pairwise distances of clusters, the complete-linkage clustering method is used again to create groups of clusters. For each merged cluster, a representative incident is selected as the exemplar (Figure 10). In our experiments this refinement procedure joins about 66% of clusters produced by the initial run of clustering (as described in Sec. 3.3).

4. EXPERIMENTAL RESULTS

4.1 Dataset and Compute set up

We had collected data from a large enterprise's IT infrastructure that supports several software services that are up all the time over a period of 3 months. In all, we had 5 million rows of alerts over a period of 3 months. Some of these alerts text were identical as they repeated at a certain time interval (say 1 min). Therefore, by focusing our attention only on those unique alerts we were able to reduce the 5 Million rows to about 590,000. After token normalization and stopword removal, the number of unique alerts came down to 22000 from the original count of 590000. Given these 22000 unique alerts and labels for 4 sub-groups within this set, we wanted to find clusters within 4 sub-groups. The 4 sub-groups are already known to the enterprise and hence we wanted to find clusters within each sub-group.

- Sub-Group 1 with 1408 alerts
- Sub-Group 2 with 4813 alerts
- Sub-Group 3 with 440 alerts
- Sub-Group 4 with 5388 alerts

We loaded all the data onto Pivotal's Greenplum Database (GPDB) running on a Data Computing Appliance (DCA) and implemented the clustering frameworks described above using a combination of psql scripts, MADlib (an opensource big data machine learning toolkit that runs on GPDB), PL/R code and PL/python code. GPDB has the MPP (Massively Parallel Processing) architecture with one master and several segment hosts sharing the computational load and is built for scalable big data analytics.

4.2 Clustering Results

Figure 11 presents a visualization of the clusters from each of 4 Sub-Groups of alerts. The size of the bubbles in the Figure 11 corresponds to the number of alerts belonging to a particular cluster. The intensity of the coloring of the bubbles corresponds to the number of incident tickets created from the alerts of a particular cluster. For instance, the darker the green color in the clusters corresponding to Sub-Group 4, the higher the number of incidents that got created from that cluster of alerts. Furthermore, the sizes of clusters in the 4 alert groups tend to have a long-tail distribution. That is, there are few big to medium sized clusters whereas there are a lot smaller clusters in each of the alert groups.

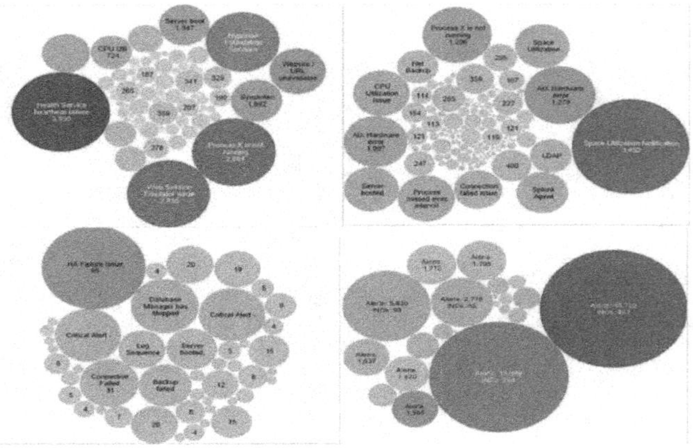

Figure 11: Visualization of clusters with the 4 Sub-Groups of Alerts

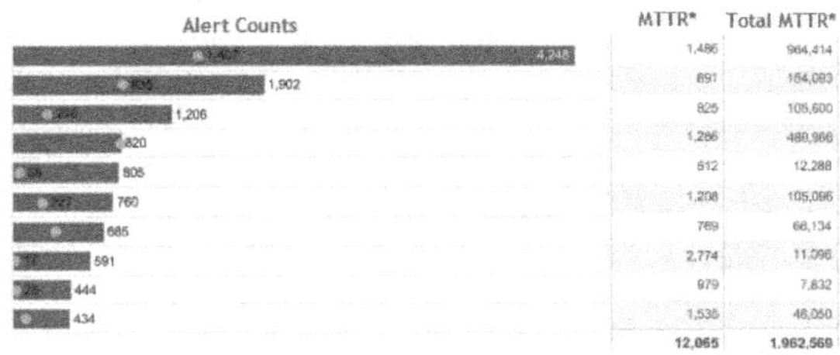

Figure 12: Key Performance Indicator (MTTR) Computed for top k clusters

In order for IT operations to focus on their top critical issues, especially events and incidents that generate major failures, it is sufficient to look at a few big-to-medium sized clusters in each of the alert groups. Furthermore, for each of incidents created we can compute a quantity called time-to-resolve which is the time taken for that particular issue to be resolved. For each of the clusters, one can then look at the mean-time-to-resolve (MTTR) from the incidents that got created from that cluster.

Figure 12 below summarizes this MTTR measure in terms of minutes for each of the top clusters across the 4 Sub-Groups. It also indicates how many of the alerts became incidents in each cluster. For instance, the first cluster has 4248 alerts of which only 1407 became incidents. This implies that there is room for improvement by paying attention to the rest of alerts before they become bigger issues.

4.3 Visualizing Clusters of Alerts

It is challenging to visualize clustered or grouped semi-structured text data such as alerts. Techniques such as word clouds are often used to visualize text data. While word clouds can show the relative frequency of different words across all alerts in a cluster they do not reveal any structure that is common across alerts.

Consider the hypothetical example of alerts shown in Table 1. Word clouds would only pick out the fact that the words 'Server', 'not'and 'responding'occur very often in the set of alerts shown but would not be able to pick out the order in which those words occur. For automated interpretation and readability of semi-structured text clusters or groups, we propose a method to visualize clusters that preserves the structure and human-readability of the text data as compared to traditional word clouds where the text structure is not preserved. This is especially necessary for large clusters and/or longer sequences of text. The proposed visualization method is also applicable to other types of semi-structured clustered/grouped text or categorical data.

Table 1: Example of semi-structured text data

Alert #	Text
1	Server A not responding
2	Server B is not responding
3	Server C not responding
4	Server D not responding

The steps in the visualization method are as follows:

1. For each alert in a given cluster generate (word, position) tuples, comprising the word and its position in the alert. Depending on whether the need is to visualize word lined up in order from left-to-right or right-to-left the text can be 'left-'or 'right-justified'prior to generating tuples.

2. For each cluster record all (word, position) tuples and the frequency with which they occur. Table 2 shows this for the example data in Table 1 with word positions in left-to-right order.

3. Visualize the frequency of (word, position) tuples from Step 2 above as shown in Figure 13. The vertical axis in the figure represents the position of the word in the alerts and the horizontal axis represents the frequency/percent occurrence of the (word, position) tuple. Each circle in the figure represents a word. Reading the words that occur most frequently in order of their positions we see the following common structure in the example: 'Server — not responding'.

Table 2: Occurrence of (word, position) tuples

Word	Position	Count	Fraction
Server	0	4	1
A	1	1	0.25
B	1	1	0.25
C	1	1	0.25
D	1	1	0.25
not	2	3	0.75
is	2	1	0.25
responding	3	2	0.75
not	3	1	0.25
responding	4	1	0.25

Figure 14 shows an example visualization of three clusters generated from real world semi-structured alerts data discussed in the previous sections. Reading the alerts with high percent occurrence off the figure we see the following elements are common within each respective cluster:

1. 'ora#: exception encountered: core dump — address not mapped to object '

2. 'time gmt positive alert harmless '

3. 'aix hardware error: '

The automatic readability of the most common theme in each cluster that this type of visualization provides is key to quick interpretation of the results.

4.4 Clustering Results of Unstructured Incident Tickets

For unstructured incident tickets, we focus on discovering the "topics" of top clusters. We find that top-25 clusters already accounts for 20% of the total tickets. (There are around 67×10^3 tickets in total.) Figure 15 provides some examples of top clusters. The keywords of each cluster are the words shared by all the ticket descriptions in a cluster, while the exemplar provides a more detailed view into what a typical ticket looks like.

5. CONCLUSIONS

This paper presents a framework to automatically cluster alerts with semi-structured text and incidents with unstructured text, generated from large enterprise IT infrastructure. Such clustering information allows IT operation staff to gain insights on issues they face everyday, based on the top clusters of alerts and incidents, allowing them to prioritize areas for problem-solving. We proposed two distinct frameworks: one framework to cluster alerts with semi-structured text, and another framework to cluster incidents with unstructured text. The text within alert and incident data are each preprocessed using token normalization and stop-word removal. The text within each alert or incident is then represented as a bag of words. To cluster alerts comprised of semi-structured text, we first choose a distance metric, then apply a top-down clustering approach using connected components and graph-cut. To cluster incidents, we proposed an approach based on matrix factorization and KD-tree to create a preliminary grouping of incidents before applying complete linkage clustering per group and later performing cluster merging in a post-processing step.

Based on the clustering output, we computed several key performance indicators per cluster such as the MTTR (Mean-Time-To-Resolve) and visualize them. For alert cluster interpretation, we propose a novel visualization that preserves the structure and human-readability of the text data as compared to traditional word clouds where the text structure is not preserved. One possible future research direction would involve incorporation of temporal information.

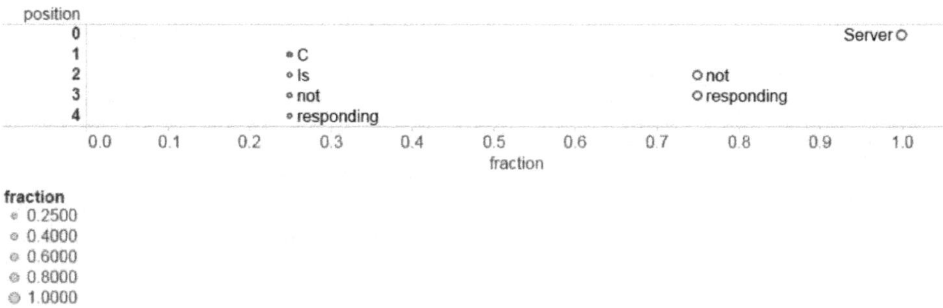

Figure 13: Visualization of the example presented in Tables 1 and 2. The 'Server __ not responding 'structure in the alerts is clearly seen

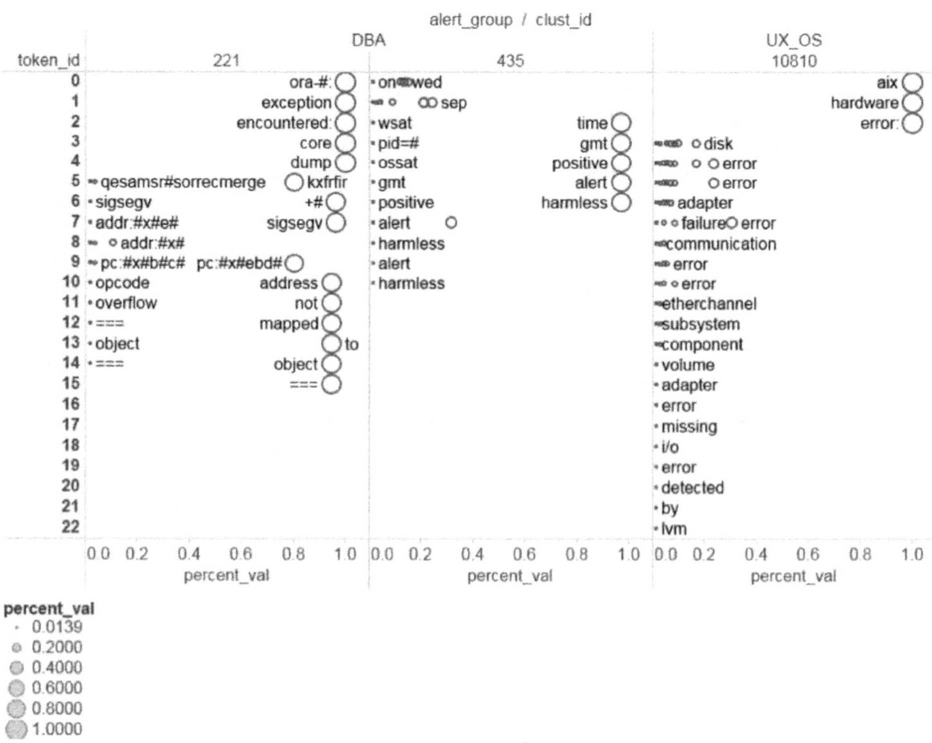

Figure 14: Visualization of clustered semi-structured alerts text

ID	Size	Cumulative Percent	keywords	Exemplar
1	2400	3.59%	ended,notok	ERR10-3E DE04 3 Q622A551 134 ENDED NOTOK 20130721 23:06:29 1064 MVS
2	1892	6.42%	alert,splunk	sdesku1-4-linux-server-splunk alert: The fileextract-primary process is not running.
3	925	7.81%	percent,utilization	sdesku1-3-aix-server-/var is at 89.93 percent utilization
4	758	8.94%	booted,ensure,running	sdesku1-4-win-server-SCOM:Server booted at 2013-09-27T21:59:41.0000000 00:00 - Please ensure critical applications are running.
5	567	9.79%	provisioning,vblock	Automated Vblock server provisioning request for linux-server [APP Files Processing System]

Figure 15: Top-5 clusters of incident tickets.

6. REFERENCES

[1] J. Bien and R. Tibshirani. Hierarchical clustering with prototypes via minimax linkage. *Journal of the American Statistical Association*, 106(495):1075–1084, 2011.

[2] S. F. C.Fowlkes and J.Malik. Spectral grouping using the nystrom method. *IEEE Trans. on Pattern Analysis and Machine Intelligence*, 26, February 2004.

[3] J. Cohen, B. Dolan, M. Dunlap, J. M. Hellerstein, and C. Welton. Mad skills: new analysis practices for big data. *Proceedings of the VLDB Endowment*, 2(2):1481–1492, 2009.

[4] P. ERDdS and A. R&WI. On random graphs i. *Publ. Math. Debrecen*, 6:290–297, 1959.

[5] IBM Netcool. http://tinyurl.com/m5v8nh2.

[6] S. Jain, I. Singh, A. Chandra, Z.-L. Zhang, and G. Bronevetsky. Extracting the textual and temporal structure of supercomputing logs. In *High Performance Computing (HiPC), 2009 International Conference on*, pages 254–263. IEEE, 2009.

[7] J.Shi and J.Malik. Normalized cuts and image segmentation. *IEEE Trans. on Pattern Analysis and Machine Intelligence*, 22, August 2000.

[8] A. N. Langville, C. D. Meyer, R. Albright, J. Cox, and D. Duling. Initializations for the nonnegative matrix factorization. In *Proceedings of ACM SIGKDD International Conference on Knowledge Discovery and Data Mining*, pages 23–26, 2006.

[9] D. D. Lee and H. S. Seung. Learning the parts of objects by non-negative matrix factorization. *Nature*, 401(6755):788–791, 1999.

[10] S. Z. Li, X. Hou, H. Zhang, and Q. Cheng. Learning spatially localized, parts-based representation. In *Proceedings of IEEE Conference on Computer Vision and Pattern Recognition*. IEEE, 2001.

[11] A. W. Moore. An introductory tutorial on KD-trees, 1991. http://tinyurl.com/cja9o9.

[12] P. Paatero and U. Tapper. Positive matrix factorization: A non-negative factor model with optimal utilization of error estimates of data values. *Environmetrics*, 5(2):111–126, 1994.

[13] V. P. Pauca, F. Shahnaz, M. W. Berry, and R. J. Plemmons. Text mining using non-negative matrix factorizations. In *Proceedings of SIAM International Conference on Data Mining*, 2004.

[14] F. Salfner and S. Tschirpke. Error log processing for accurate failure prediction. In *WASL*, 2008.

[15] F. Shahnaz, M. W. Berry, V. P. Pauca, and R. J. Plemmons. Document clustering using nonnegative matrix factorization. *Information Processing & Management*, 42(2):373–386, 2006.

[16] L. Tang, T. Li, L. Shwartz, F. Pinel, and G. Y. Grabarnik. An integrated framework for optimizing automatic monitoring systems in large it infrastructures. In *Proceedings of the 19th ACM SIGKDD international conference on Knowledge discovery and data mining*, pages 1249–1257. ACM, 2013.

[17] W. Webber, A. Moffat, and J. Zobel. A similarity measure for indefinite rankings. *ACM Transactions on Information Systems (TOIS)*, 28(4):20, 2010.

[18] W. Xu, X. Liu, and Y. Gong. Document clustering based on non-negative matrix factorization. In *Proceedings of ACM SIGIR conference on Research and Development in Information Retrieval*, pages 267–273, 2003.

[19] Y. Zhou, D. Wilkinson, R. Schreiber, and R. Pan. Large-scale parallel collaborative filtering for the Netflix prize. In *Algorithmic Aspects in Information and Management*, pages 337–348. Springer, 2008.

Style in the Long Tail: Discovering Unique Interests with Latent Variable Models in Large Scale Social E-commerce

Diane Hu
Etsy
Brooklyn, NY
dhu@etsy.com

Rob Hall
Etsy
Brooklyn, NY
rhall@etsy.com

Josh Attenberg
Etsy
Brooklyn, NY
jattenberg@etsy.com

ABSTRACT

Purchasing decisions in many product categories are heavily influenced by the shopper's aesthetic preferences. It's insufficient to simply match a shopper with popular items from the category in question; a successful shopping experience also identifies products that match those aesthetics. The challenge of capturing shoppers' styles becomes more difficult as the size and diversity of the marketplace increases. At Etsy, an online marketplace for handmade and vintage goods with over 30 million diverse listings, the problem of capturing taste is particularly important – users come to the site specifically to find items that match their eclectic styles.

In this paper, we describe our methods and experiments for deploying two new style-based recommender systems on the Etsy site. We use Latent Dirichlet Allocation (LDA) to discover trending categories and styles on Etsy, which are then used to describe a user's "interest" profile. We also explore hashing methods to perform fast nearest neighbor search on a map-reduce framework, in order to efficiently obtain recommendations. These techniques have been implemented successfully at very large scale, substantially improving many key business metrics.

Categories and Subject Descriptors

H.2.8 [**Database Applications**]: Data Mining

General Terms

Algorithms; Experimentation; Performance

Keywords

Recommender Systems; Collaborative Filtering; Topic Modeling

1. INTRODUCTION

Describing your style can be tough. There are innumerable details that constitute one's taste that elude simple description. This difficulty in describing style becomes more severe as the set of candidate content becomes larger and increasingly diverse, a "curse of dimensionality" imparted by the inability of simple words to describe what we like about all things.[1] Despite the difficulty of transcribing taste, we generally know when we like something, and often express this in our actions. These actions, if captured and measured, can be used to model taste and power new experiences.

Etsy[2] is an online marketplace for handmade and vintage items, with over 30 million active users and 30 million active listings. This is a marketplace known for its diverse and eclectic content (e.g. Figure 1); people come in order to find those unusual items that match the peculiarities of their style. Indeed, Etsy, in its entirety could be considered part of the e-commerce long tail: in addition to wide ranging functions and styles, the handmade and vintage nature of the site means that most items for sale are unique.

For any large-scale e-commerce site, helping users find relevant content can be a challenge. Sites like Ebay or Amazon surface personalized content to their users [19] by utilizing a wide range of recommendation system technologies. Etsy faces additional challenges when building such systems- the majority of users need to find items not only by category (e.g. a purse, or a desk), but also by style (e.g., modern, cottage, industrial, or geometric). Surfacing categorically relevant items for Etsy buyers is not enough: a query like "wooden desk" will match thousands of relevant listings that buyers must browse through before they find ones that match their style (industrial, rustic, mid-century modern, cottage, antique, etc.). Thus, in Etsy's setting, where there exists an extreme heterogeneity of content, and a corresponding diversity of user behaviors, capturing taste and style is particularly difficult. However, it is precisely this difficulty in describing taste and style that make accurate models for capturing this taste critical. When typical user queries or item descriptions fail to capture intent, users rely on personalization (through implicit or explicit taste modeling) to make the huge marketplace a little smaller.

While it seems that building recommender systems and personalized content at Etsy might be an almost insurmountable challenge, Etsy benefits from an extremely engaged user base, and a suite of social features that lead to the formation of a strong user community. Users connect with each other and share content – listings or shops that they like – in a way that is familiar to any user of the social web. In ad-

KDD'14, August 24–27, 2014, New York, NY, USA.

http://dx.doi.org/10.1145/2623330.2623338 .

[1]Even if you could adequately describe your taste for clothing, would that description capture your taste for furniture or home decor?

[2]`http://www.etsy.com`

dition to creating a more engaging experience, these social features have been a key data point in the development of accurate taste models for a variety of functions.

The goal of this paper is to provide a glimpse into the process of developing and operationalizing recommender systems at web scale, in the difficult setting described above. These recommender systems personalize millions of user experiences every day, and since their inception, have substantially improved some of Etsy's core business metrics.

2. RELATED WORK

Our work touches on a couple of different areas; we give background for each in turn.

2.1 Recommendation Systems

Certainly, recommender systems are nothing new, with the first papers on collaborative filtering appearing in the 1990s [18]. In the subsequent years, motivated by obvious commercial applications, developing experiences that enable shoppers to find what they're looking for more efficiently [19], recommender systems and personalization technology have advanced tremendously. In addition to commerce applications, recommender systems appear in a variety of other settings, for instance, recommending news articles to web surfers [5]. Netflix is a well-known consumer of personalization technology; the Netflix prize has led to great innovation in the recommender system community [13].

Of particular relevance to the work presented here is Gupta et al.'s description of Twitter's "Who to Follow" System [9]. Here, the authors describe the implementation details of a large-scale recommender system, focused on recommending social connections. As with our work here, the authors prescribe a single-server modeling approach in order to reduce system complexity and improve development speed.

The range of techniques available when building recommender systems is vast, too broad to cover here. For a good overview of common techniques, we urge the curious reader to read the survey of Adomavicius and Tuzhilin [1]. Also of note is the work of Koren, Volinsky and others describing the approaches that won the Netflix prize [13, 11].

2.2 Latent Dirichlet Allocation (LDA)

Latent Dirichlet Allocation (LDA) [4] is an unsupervised, probabilistic, generative model that aims to find a low dimensional description that can summarize the contents of large document collections. LDA works by positing that a summarization of a text document can be achieved by looking at the set of words used. Since words carry very strong semantic information, documents that contain similar content will most likely use a similar set of words. As such, mining an entire corpus of text documents can surface sets of words that frequently co-occur within documents, and be intuitively interpreted as topics. Each discovered topic is characterized by its own particular distribution over words, and each document is characterized as a random mixture of topics indicating the proportion of time the document spends on each topic. This random mixture of topics is essentially a summary of the document: It not only expresses the semantic content of a document in a concise manner, but also gives us a principled approach for describing documents quantitatively.

Beyond document modeling, LDA has also been adapted to numerous settings, including image segmentation [15], part-of-speech tagging [8], and automatic harmonic analysis in music [10], just to name a few. Not surprisingly, LDA has also been used in recommendation tasks, though in substantially different ways than us, to the best of our knowledge. Marlin [16] uses an LDA-like Dirichlet Multinomial model to predict user-item ratings for movie datasets. More recently, Wang et. al [21] proposes a hybrid content and collaborative-filtering based system that recommends scholarly papers and utilizes LDA for the content-based component.

2.3 Art and Style Classification

Since our work revolves around identifying aesthetic styles, we also look at literature for style-based recommendation and search tasks. We find that the majority of this kind of work relies solely on image processing features and visual cues, without any leverage from social influences or networks. Di et. al [7] seeks to match similar styles of clothing with a combination of crowd-sourced tags and bag-of-words image features. Zujovic et. al [22] uses Gabor-like image features as well as color features to try to classify digital pictures of paintings by artistic genre. Arora et. al [2] provides a survey of different methods for fine-art painting style, comparing the performance of discriminative versus generative models on various semantic-level and low-level image features. We note that our work for identifying visual style is substantially different from all of these approaches given that we use no image cues, and solely rely on observing social-network based user behavior.

3. IDENTIFYING USER INTERESTS

Etsy differs from many other e-commerce sites not only by the nature of the items which are for sale, but by the emphasis on social interaction amongst our users. Because this social component played such a pivotal role in the success of our taste models, it makes sense to start with a detailed background covering how users interact with the Etsy site, and how we gather implicit feedback from their activities.

3.1 Social E-Commerce, a Description of Etsy

On Etsy, there are three important entities:

- **User:** Anyone registered on Etsy, including sellers
- **Seller:** Etsy user who own a shop
- **Shop:** A collection of items sold by the same seller. Each shop has its own online storefront.
- **Listing:** Products/items listed in a shop, each with its unique listing id.

To give an idea of scale, we currently have approximately 1 million active sellers/shops, 30 million active listings, and 30 million active members.

Importantly, unlike many other e-commerce sites, users come to Etsy not only to purchase things – users often come to Etsy just to browse the site, with no specific intention of purchasing anything. During a recent user study, someone described browsing Etsy as "flipping through a magazine." Users will also connect with other users of similar interests, and share their discoveries though an activity feed, similar to those seen in other popular social websites. This social component is manifested in several interactions, including:

- **Favorite listing:** a way for users to bookmark listings that they like, and share their affinity with their followers. There are many possible intentions for favoriting a listing – the user may have the intention of purchasing it later, simply do it for curation purposes, or they may favorite simply to share with others.
- **Favorite shop:** a way for users to bookmark shops that they like, similar to favoriting a listing
- **Follow other user:** a way for users to keep track of what other users are favoriting (and thus being exposed to more content on the site). This will be discussed in more detail in section 4.1.

3.2 Inferring User Interests

As discussed in section 1, Etsy users not only want to find functionally/categorical relevant products – they also want to find ones that specifically match their style. The notion of a style can be very subjective, and very difficult to be describe with words. Thus, we rely on user activity patterns to define these styles for us.

While a variety of approaches were attempted, the most successful approaches for modeling user interests were based on Latent Dirichlet Allocation (LDA), an unsupervised, probabilistic, generative model for discovering latent semantic topics in large collections of text [4]. However, instead of using LDA to model listing content text (as is done traditionally), we use LDA to find patterns in user behavior and cluster them accordingly, akin to how matrix factorization is used for collaborative filtering.

Our use of LDA is based on the premise that users with similar interests will act upon similar listings. We chose to use the social action of "favoriting" listings as a a reliable signal for user style. This is done in lieu of more traditional user intent signals, for instance "purchasing" as is commonly done in collaborative filter development. The reasons for this choice are several fold: 1) user purchases only show a small subset of items that users are actually interested in, 2) user purchases are biased toward lower-priced items, and 3) the unique nature of Etsy's marketplace means that only one user has the opportunity to purchase an item. It is possible to have many users with very similar taste to have no overlap in their purchase vectors. Note that many of the techniques discussed below do not have any specific requirement that favoriting be the source of intent. Experimenting with different information sources to provide a broader picture of user intent is a subject of ongoing research.

Our treatment of LDA is as follows: Each user is represented as a "document," and each of the user's favorite listings are treated a "word". As such, each discovered topic can be interpreted as an "interest profile" – a distribution over all products, with highly weighted products belonging to a similar category or style (or sometimes both). Our model is formalized as follows: Assume there are K topics, or interests that we would like to discover, and V total listings. Then, β is a $K \times V$ matrix, where β_K is a distribution over the fixed vocabulary of listings. A user's list of favorited listings is posited to have been produced by the following generative process:

For each user u_j,

1. Draw u_j's interest profile $\theta_j \sim Dirichlet(\alpha)$.
2. For each favorited listing that u_j has,
   (a) Draw an interest group $z_{jn} \sim Multi(\theta_j)$
   (b) Draw a listing $x_{jn} \sim Mult(\beta_{z_{jn}})$

Note that the underlying model is no different from the original LDA model, making it easy to use existing libraries and implementations of LDA into our workflow. We fit the model using a multithreaded implementation of collapsed Gibbs sampling (see e.g., [17]) from Mallet[3]. Once the LDA model is fitted to our user-listings data, we obtain the topic-listing matrix β, which describes each of the K interests as a distribution over listings. Listings that have the highest weights within each topic are most indicative of the style of that group. We also obtain a K-dimensional user profile vector, θ, which indicates the proportion of time each user spends favoriting items from each interest group. This random mixture of topics gives a concise profile of each user's taste, and gives us a principled approach for describing user interests quantitatively. Section 4 describes the more practical aspects of our system and workflow in more detail.

One of the advantages of a topic-modeling approach to collaborative filtering, as we have presented here, is that the latent factors are easily visualized. In the following figures, we present some example topics in which both categories and styles are captured. For example, Figure 1 shows topics that center around a certain kind of interest, while spanning many different categories such as apparel, jewelry, home decor, etc. Here, (A) shows a fox theme, (B) shows a cephalopod theme, and (C) shows a Legend of Zelda theme. Figure 2 shows three topics that contain listings from the same furniture category, but span different styles: (A) shows a rustic, wooden style, (B) shows a french, cottage chic style, and (C) shows a mid-century modern style. Similarly, Figure 3 shows art from six very different styles: (A) botanical/hand-lettered, (B) haunting landscape photography, (C) whimsical animal illustrations, (D) abstract paintings, (E) fairytale doll prints, and (F) abstract whimsical paintings. Visualizing these topics have been imperative to understanding the different clusters of interests that users have on Etsy.

4. GENERATING RECOMMENATIONS

The interest clusters discovered in the previous section are used not only to summarize trending styles across the Etsy marketplace, but also to describe users' interests. In the LDA model, for each user u_j, we learn an interest profile vector, θ_j, that is a distribution over the discovered topics, indicating the amount of interest u_j has in each of the K groups. In the sections below, we show how the interest profiles are used in our user and shop recommendation systems.

4.1 User Recommendations

As mentioned above, Etsy combines a social experience with more traditional e-commerce. Etsy users (buyers and sellers alike) can opt to share their activity by connecting to other users, and sharing what interests them. In turn, users often discover content that is relevant to them by seeing the activities of others. To manifest this social networking behavior, Etsy has a page called the *activity feed*. The activity feed is linked from each user's signed-in homepage, and is similar to Facebook's mini-feed: a continuous stream of rectangular story cards that describe some sort of activity

[3]`http://mallet.cs.umass.edu`

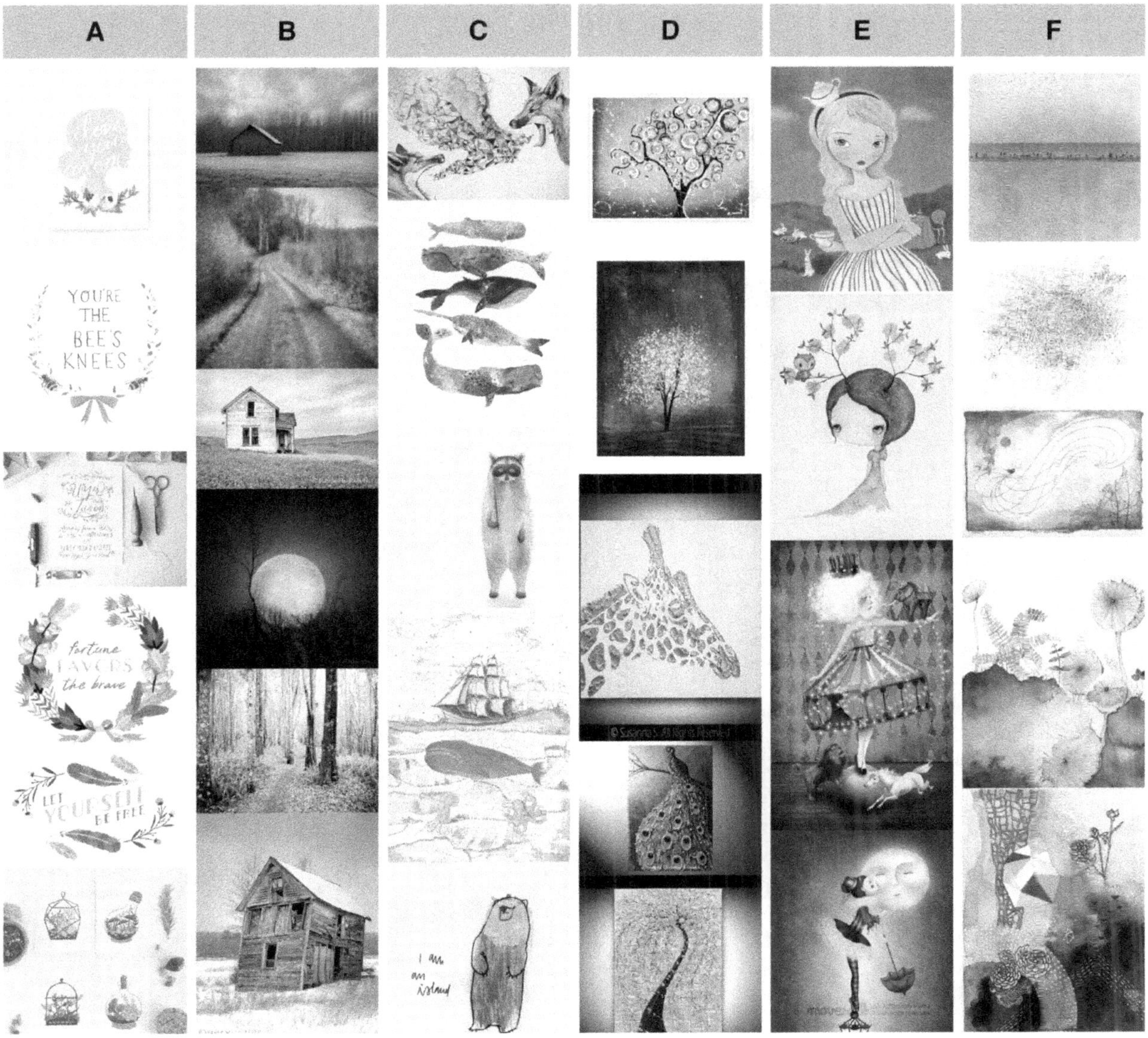

Figure 3: Six different styles of art discovered on Etsy. Each column contains high-ranking items from a topic. Note that all items come from unique sellers.

or behavior from another user that the feed owner is "following". These stories flow from the top to the bottom of the screen in the order in which the activity took place. Some examples include: "User X started following member Y" or "User X has favorited item Z", where X is a user that the feed owner follows.

More specifically, the "following" mechanism can be described as follows: Users can "follow" each other on Etsy in the same way that users can follow other users on Twitter. When user A follows user B, user B's activity (for example: products or shops that user B favorites, or even other users that user B follows) will be shown on user A's activity feed in the form of story cards (Figure 5). The idea is that a user will want to follow another user who has similar interests, so that it is more likely that user B's activity will interest user A. Before the deployment of our recommendation system, Etsy users found other users to follow by either 1) knowing the user in person, or 2) stumbling upon them while browsing the site. Thus, the purpose of the user recommendation system was to make the process of finding users with similar interests less arbitrary and more intentional.

4.1.1 *Algorithm & Implementation*

Once we obtain each user's interest profile (as described in section 3.2), we conduct a nearest neighbor search across all eligible users on Etsy (i.e. those active users who do not have private settings turned on) to find the top 100 users with the most similar θ's, which we recommend. These are users, presumably, with the most similar styles and interests.

The problem of the nearest neighbor search, of course, is that examining every pair of users to determine the distance between them (the "brute force" approach) is unfeasible due to the large number of users. Therefore, we experimented with two different hashing methods, both of which center around the idea of hashing the interest profiles θ into buckets, and then computing distances only between users that

Figure 1: Interests/styles that span different categories (clothing, stationery, jewelry, etc.).

Figure 2: Three different styles within the same furniture category.

fall into the same hash bucket. This gives an approximate nearest neighbors method where the overall time complexity is dictated by the size of the largest hash bucket, which we can manage directly. A similar nearest neighbor search on the simplex was considered in [14], but focus there was placed on the setting in which all user vectors fit into one machine in memory. In contrast, we consider using map-reduce to compute the nearest neighbors in parallel so that we may scale to millions of users and high dimensional topic models, without memory or running time becoming an issue. The two hashing methods are as follows:

Locality Sensitive Hashing. Locality Sensitive Hashing (LSH) works by splitting the input space into several cones and numbering each one (see e.g., [6]). Then the elements contained in each cone are mapped to its corresponding number. We generate m random planes which pass through the origin (in d-dimensions, the normal vector to each plane is generated from a d-dimensional isotropic Gaussian), denote these normal vectors v^i then map each point $\theta \in \mathbb{R}^d$ to

$$H_{\mathrm{LSH}}(\theta) = \sum_{i=1}^{m} 2^{i-1} \mathbf{1}\left\{\theta^T v^i \geq 0\right\}.$$

Where $\mathbf{1}\{.\}$ is a function that takes a value of 1 whenever the operand is true, and 0 otherwise. Thus each point is hashed to an m-bit integer. In our experiment we use $m = 16$. Finally, note that while this algorithm maps some nearby points to the same integer, there may be points which are close by, but separated by one of the planes. In order to mit-

Method	Number of Comparisons	20-NN Precision
Brute force	260000000	1.0
LSH-10	17711	0.37
LSH-21	38498	0.56
LSH-45	79141	0.80
TopK-5	45195	0.58
TopK-7	96630	0.68
TopK-10	197762	0.75

Table 1: Computational expense versus precision of the retrieved 20 nearest neighbors.

igate this problem, we perform the hashing multiple times, compute nearest neighbors in each hash bucket, and then combine the results of the different hashes.

"Top-K" Hashing. We propose a second hashing method which takes advantage of the sparsity that we anticipate in the topic mixture vectors from LDA. It is plausible that the nearest neighbors to a certain user will share some subset of top-k interests. Therefore, we map each topic vector to the set of all pairs of topic indices from the top-k topics. The reason for taking pairs rather than individual topic indices is to make more specific hash buckets which will have smaller capacity. Note that in this method, each vector gets mapped into several hash buckets. We compute nearest neighbors in each bucket, then combine these across buckets, and take the nearest neighbors from among those candidates.

Comparison of Hashing Methods. We compare the performance of the above nearest-neighbor search methods on the grounds of their approximation quality and computational expense. For this experiment we used a test set of approximately 800K users. Their topic vectors were inferred from a previously trained LDA model, with 1000 topics. In order to establish the performance of the above hashing methods, we compare to the exact nearest-neighbors. Since generating these for the entire set of users is computationally expensive, we restrict the experiment to a subset of 300 Etsy users.

Both hashing methods are parameterized in a way that allows control over the number of hash bins that each user is assigned to, and we test three settings for each method. For the LSH method we use 16 bit hash keys, and 10, 21, and 45 hashes per user respectively. For the top-k hashing we set k to 5, 7, and 10 and hash the vectors according to pairs of topics in the top k (leading to 10, 21 and 45 hashes per vector). We report the number of pairwise comparisons between user vectors that are computed in Table 1, and then the precision at rank n, for the 20 nearest neighbors in Figure 4. The results demonstrate that for our LDA model, both hashing methods perform adequately, although the LHS method seems to perform slightly better than the top-k hashing method, both in terms of computational cost and the quality of the approximation.

4.1.2 Extensions

In addition to the learning done in LDA, we also experimented with two extensions that modified the interest profiles, θ, slightly to better reflect or expand upon each user's interests.

Finding Correlated Interests. Many of the discovered interest groups are quite complementary; there is no doubt that users who like a certain style would be more likely to be

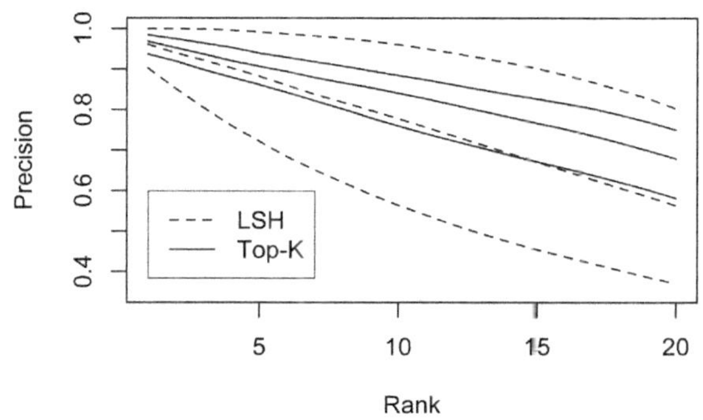

Figure 4: Precision at rank graph for experimental methods. In both cases, the higher curves correspond to higher parameter settings (i.e., the top curve is LSH-45).

interested in another, related style. In order to surface these correlations, we compute the covariance matrix, Σ, from the aggregate of the user interest profile vectors, resulting in a $K \times K$ matrix that shows which interest groups are most highly correlated. We then transform each user's θ vector by projecting it onto Σ, in order to strategically "expand" the user's interests. This can be seen as a simpler way of achieving what the Correlated Topic Model [3] does, but with an easier implementation that is trivial to do in a map-reduce framework.

Special Interest Signals. Though evaluating user recommendations can often be subjective, user feedback revealed certain recommendations that should never happen. These cases include: 1) recommending users with very feminine favorites (i.e. headbands, dresses, lingerie) to a male user, 2) recommending users with mature content to those users who have never expressed interested in mature content, and 3) recommending users with very special interests (such as wedding or baby related favorited items) to users who have no use for such item. For ease of implementation, we built several linear classifiers to predict the likelihood of each user's interest level in the above three areas, and used these as additional dimensions tacked onto the original user interest profile vector. Using the "Top-K" hashing method, these additional features were used in the hashing, as to only bucket together users with a similar level of interest in these specific areas.

4.1.3 Product Design

The final recommended users are displayed as a new story type in the activity feed, as shown in figure 5 (highlighted in orange). These user recommendation stories are inserted once every 12 hours into each user's feed, and moves down the feed over time with all of the other story cards. We chose to display the user recommendations in the activity feed specifically to encourage users who currently follow few users, in hopes that more user follows will result in more interesting feed content. Our goal here is to see an increase in the overall number of users following other users (i.e. a more connected social graph), more engagement on the Etsy site, and of course, a higher conversion rate – all of which would indicate that we are properly surfacing relevant personalized content.

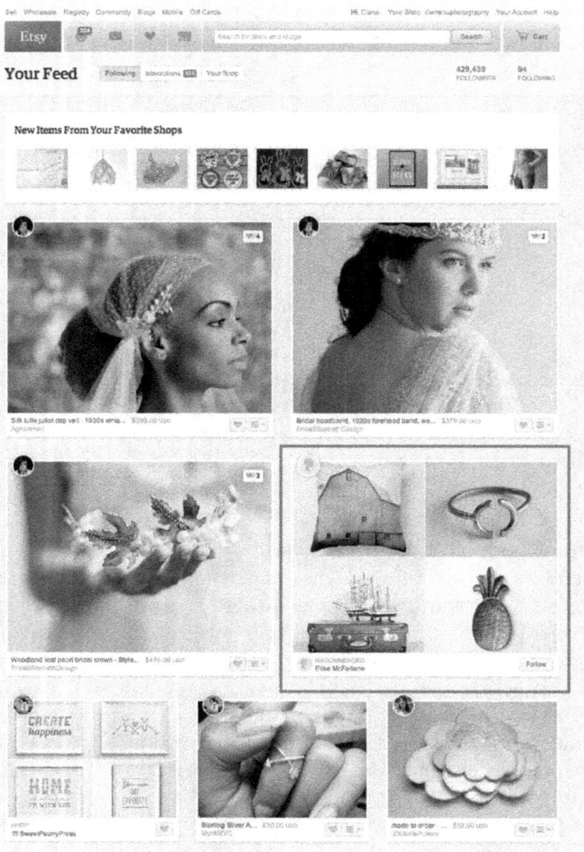

Figure 5: A section of a user's activity feed. Each story card displays an activity from a user that the feed owner is following. The story card highlighted in orange is a user recommendation story card, which highlights the recommended user's most recent favorites. A "follow" button in the bottom right-hand corner prompts the user to begin following the recommended user.

4.2 Shop Recommendations

Besides encouraging user follows, we would also like to more readily expose users to shops that are relevant to their style. Currently, users find shops by using the search engine to find specific items, through which they can find the shop that produced the item. Our goal with a shop recommendation system is to make relevant shop discovery more efficient and abundant.

4.2.1 Algorithm & Implementation

Using a very similar topic modeling approach, we developed a shop recommender system in order to encourage users to visit and favorite more shops. Here, inferring the interest profile vector, θ, is slightly different than in section 3.2. Instead of representing documents as a list of users' favorite items, we replace each favorite item with its corresponding shop id instead, and also concatenate this list with a list of shop ids of the user's favorite shops. Instead of representing listing ids as words, we use shop ids instead. The inferred topic-word matrix, β, thus becomes a distribution over shops instead items, and the resulting interest groups are described by clusters of shops instead of clusters of items.

To obtain a single shop recommendations for user u_j, we do the following:

1. Draw an interest group $z_{jn} \sim Multi(\theta_j)$
2. Recommend shop $y_{jn} \sim Mult(\beta_{z_{jn}})$

In the spirit of collaborative filtering by matrix factorization, multiplying each user's interest profile vector by the topic-shop matrix $(\theta_j \beta)$ would have been a more traditional approach. However, this matrix multiplication is quite expensive, and it is unnecessary to have a ranked list of all possible shops, as we are only concerned with highly-ranked shops for each user. Thus, we chose this sampling approach which is more efficient and theoretically, should have comparable accuracy.

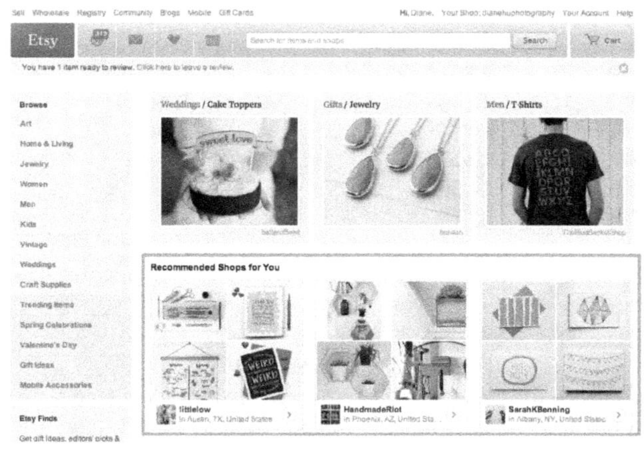

Figure 6: Shop recommendations on the homepage, highlighted in orange

4.2.2 Product Design

The shop recommendations are currently displayed as a small module on the front page of Etsy, for signed in users (Figure 6). The three shops are swapped out every two hours so that the user will always have fresh, personalized content on their homepage.

5. SYSTEM OVERVIEW

In this section, we discuss the workflow of our deployed recommender systems. Figure 7 gives an overview of the process. First, for both recommender systems, we estimate the model on all users with at least a minimum number of favorite products. After thresholding, there are approximately 4 million such users, and the resulting data is small enough that the model could be estimated on a single machine. We used a server with 100Gb of RAM and sixteen CPU cores to run the multithreaded implementation of collapsed Gibbs sampling (see e.g., [17]) from Mallet.[4]

We have experimented with topic models that consist of anywhere between 10 to 1000 topics, and found that while this number changes the content of the granularity of the interest groups greatly, it does not affect the accuracy of the

[4] `http://mallet.cs.umass.edu`

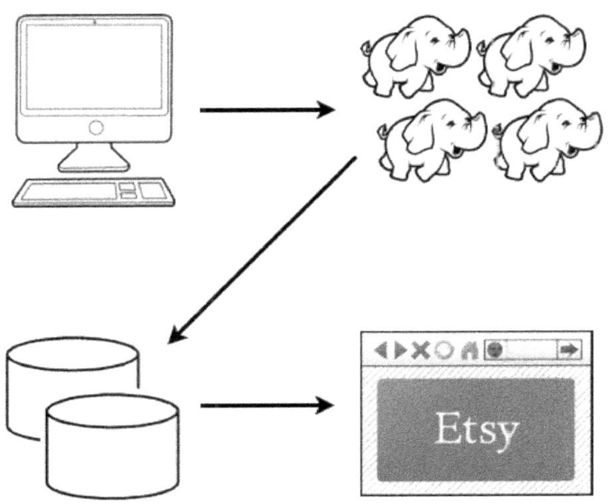

Figure 7: High-level overview of our recommendation systems: 1) Train LDA model on single machine. 2) Infer topic distributions for remaining users on Hadoop cluster; perform nearest neighbor search 3) Store recommendation datasets in Redis databases. 4) Front-end Etsy code retrieves recommendations.

user interest profiles (as evidenced from user recommendation experiments). In the end, we wound up choosing 200 and 1000 topics, depending on the specifics of the application. In both cases, the estimation of the parameters of a model takes on the order of half a day. Since the resulting model consists of a subset of all the products on Etsy, any products which are not included are treated as the nearest included product by TF-IDF distance of the text attributes of the product (the title and tags). These topic models are re-trained once a week.

Once the hyper parameters of the LDA model are learned, they are copied to our Hadoop cluster, where we infer topic distributions for the remaining users who have fewer than the necessary threshold favorite items. The inference can be done independently for each user, thus making this process completely parallelizable. For user recommendations, the top k nearest neighbors are computed on a map-reduce framework, using the techniques described in section 4.1. For shop recommendations, shops are sampled according to the algorithm in section 4.2. Both of these processes take only a couple of hours, and are computed nightly, in order to incorporate fresh user favoriting data.

The final recommendation datasets (resulting from the map-reduce jobs described above) are then stored in a shared and replicated Redis database cluster for fast retrieval by the systems used to generate Etsy's user facing web content. Earlier versions of these recommender model datasets were stored on shared mysql servers – the same servers that power crucial and complex e-commerce functionality. This proved problematic – loading the massive recommendation datasets (hundreds of millions of rows) at full speed caused a troubling performance hit for some more critical database queries. Throttling the dataset loads meant that they would take unacceptably long. Redis avoids this problem, and has the added benefit of very fast recommendation retrieval.

6. EXPERIMENTS & DISCUSSION

In the following sections, we discuss results from user studies and live experiments that were conducted for both the user and shop recommendation systems We also compare the LDA-based model to some more traditional recommender algorithms. Before we delve into the experiments though, we give an overview of the kinds of metrics we look at when evaluating a live A/B experiment like this.

6.1 Evaluation Metrics

Most of our evaluation metrics are measured per *visit*. A *visit* is defined as a consecutive sequence of page requests that are associated with a single Google cookie. The page requests must be generated by the same traffic source, and must be viewed at most 30 minutes apart. In very high-level terms, a visit is a discrete occurrence in which a user uses the Etsy site. Visit-based metrics are engrained in Etsy's experiment-driven development culture, offering increased resilience to outliers than many other numbers we could collect. The following are some relevant evaluation metrics used in our experiments:

- **Conversion Rate:** Fraction of visits that end up in at least one purchase
- **Activity Feed Visit Rate:** Fraction of visits that view the Activity Feed, the main social touchpoint on the site
- **Pages Viewed Rate:** Number of pages viewed per visit
- **User Follow Rate:** Fraction of visits in which at least one user is followed
- **Item Favorite Rate:** Fraction of visits in which at least one item is favorited
- **Shop Favorite Rate:** Fraction of visits in which at least one shop is favorited

Our user recommendation system underwent three different phases of user testing. In the first and earliest stage, we created a one-off interface (independent of the Etsy website) that would test the quality of the user recommendations. In this user study, 135 users were presented a randomly interleaved list of 30 recommended users, from 3 different models. The first model uses the topic modeling approach described in section 4.1. The other two models use common recommendation heuristics as follows: 1) *Cosine Similarity*: Represent users as a bag of favorite products, and recommend other users with high cosine similarity, and 2) *Triadic Closure*: Recommend other users who also follow the same users. Users were then asked to rate each of the 30 user recommendations, based on images of the recommended user's most recently favorited items. The possible ratings were: negative ("I would not want to follow this user's activity"), neutral ("I wouldn't mind following this user"), or positive ("I would like to follow this user"). The results shown in Table 2 show that the LDA approach was the overwhelming favorite.

Model Name	# Neg	# Neutral	# Pos	Avg
LDA	196	278	440	2.27
Cosine Similarity	361	357	315	1.96
Triadic Closure	480	248	138	1.61

Table 2: Comparison of LDA with two popular baseline methods. The weighted average attributes 1 point to negative ratings, 2 points to neutral ratings, and 3 points to positive ratings.

Metric	Control (95%)	On (Diff) (5%)
Conversion Rate	–	**+0.32%**
Pages Viewed Rate	–	**+1.18%**
Activity Feed Visit Rate	–	**+7.51%**
User Follow Rate	–	**+13.43%**
Item Favorite Rate	–	**+2.81%**
Shop Favorite Rate	–	**+2.44%**

Table 3: Stage 2 of user recommendation experiments with live A/B user testing. Bolded numbers in the *Diff* column indicate statistical significance.

In the second stage of testing, we introduced the user recommendations in the form of story cards in the activity feed (as described in section 4.1) to live traffic on the Etsy site. Users were randomly bucketed so that 95% of users would receive an unchanged experience on the activity feed (control group), and the remaining 5% would receive the new user recommendation story cards in their activity feed. The goal of this experiment was to observe the effects of this new type of story card, and how it would impact site-wide metrics such as: number of users follows, number of favorited item, overall conversion rate, etc. The experiment ran for approximately two months, and the results were overwhelmingly positive: we saw statistically significant improvements in many site-wide metrics, as shown in Table 3. After the positive results, the on group was increased to a 50% bucketing (with similar results), and later launched to 100%.

In the third and most recent stage of testing, we experimented with four different models for obtaining user recommendations. Three of these models were variations on the original LDA model, and one model implemented a traditional matrix factorization approach. We describe each of these four variants in turn:

- **LDA-1000.** This was the original LDA-based user recommendation model used in the first two experiments described above. The number of topics was set to 1000 and only users with at least 50 favorited items were used to fit the model (resulting in 700K users for model fitting). These parameter values were somewhat arbitrarily chosen based on the perceived quality of the topics shown in section 3.

- **LDA-200.** This is similar to the original LDA-based user recommendation model, but learns only 200 topics instead. Because of the smaller number of topics, we could afford to use more data when fitting the model; here, users with at least 10 favorited items were considered (resulting in a much larger dataset of 4M users).

- **LDA-INTEREST.** This is similar to LDA-200, but with the added special interest features described in section 4.1.2 .

- **SVD.** This is the only non-LDA-based user recommendation model. Here, we factorize the user-favorites matrix using the stochastic singular value decomposition (SVD) to obtain a "latent factor" vector for each user [13]. These are scaled to have unit norm, so that the direction captures the profile of their interests (as opposed to the magnitude, which is proportional to number of favorites that a user has)

For each model, we used the locality sensitive hashing (LSH) method to retrieve the nearest neighbors to each users interest profile. In order to find the optimal parameters for the hashing (both in terms of computational efficiency and the quality of the results), we tested the method with varying parameters (number of planes, number of parallel hashings) and compared the recall against the exact 100 nearest neighbors, computed via brute force, for a small subset of the users. This allowed us to arrive at a method which is tractable to compute, and yields approximately 90% precision when compared to recommendations produced by exact nearest neighbor search.

We again launched a live A/B experiment, bucketing all users into one of these four variants, where each variant is shown to 25% of all users. This experiment ran for two weeks, with Table 4 summarizing the results. We can see that the LDA-based approach (LDA_200, in particular) is almost on equal footing as the traditional matrix factorization approach; most differences are statistically insignificant. We also note that the huge improvement we see in LDA-200 over LDA-1000 tells us that more topics doesn't necessarily mean better performance for measuring user similarity, and that fitting the model on a larger dataset possibly makes a huge difference.

We note that while the A/B experiments show little difference, one advantage that the topic modeling approach has over traditional matrix factorization methods is the ability to easily visualize latent factors. We have learned from numerous studies (e.g. [20]) that users appreciate explanations of why certain content is being recommended to them. By being able to visualize each topic as a group of items (Figures 1, 2, and 3), we can show each user exactly how their interest profile were composed.

6.2 Shop Recommendations

Our shop recommendation module sits on the Etsy homepage (described in Section 4.2), and is also being A/B tested on live traffic. The most recent experiment ran for two weeks, and consisted of three variants, each shown to 33.3% of all signed-in Etsy users. The three variants are as follows: 1) No shop recommendations (control), 2) personalized shop recommendations based on LDA, and 3) generic shop recommendations (obtained by finding the most authoritative and popular shops using the well-known Hubs and Authority (HITS) algorithm [12]). Table 5 shows the impact on relevant site-wide metrics: the shop recommendations are prompting users to engage more with the site, as all desired behavior has increased by a significant amount. As predicted, personalized recommendations trump generic recommendations across all evaluation metrics.

Metric	SVD (Control) (25%)	LDA_200 (Diff) (25%)	LDA_1000 (Diff) (25%)	LDA_INTEREST (Diff) (25%)
Conversion Rate	–	-0.14%	**-2.69%**	-1.16%
Pages Viewed Rate	–	**-0.79%**	**-1.25%**	-0.08%
User Follow Rate	–	+0.10%	**-4.46%**	**-7.05%**
Item Favorite Rate	–	-0.18%	**-0.72%**	**-2.38%**
Shop Favorite Rate	–	+0.95%	**-1.13%**	-0.99%

Table 4: Stage 3 of user recommendation experiments with live A/B user testing: experimenting with multiple recommendation models. Bolded numbers in the *Diff* columns indicate statistical significance.

Metric	Control (33%)	Personalized (33%)	Generic (33%)
Conversion Rate	–	**+1.25%**	**+1.08%**
Pages Viewed Rate	–	**+3.17%**	**+2.67%**
Item Favorite Rate	–	**+7.33%**	**+6.25%**
Shop Favorite Rate	–	**+33.18%**	**+27.92%**
Shop Visit Rate	–	**+9.70%**	**+8.52%**

Table 5: Experiments from live A/B user testing of shop recommendations on the homepage. Bolded numbers in the *Diff* columns (personalized and generic) indicate statistical significance.

7. CONCLUSION AND FUTURE WORK

In this paper, we have described the challenges of building two style-based recommendation systems to a large e-commerce site. In particular, we described an untraditional usage of LDA which leverages implicit feedback of user behavior in order to accomplish collaborative filtering. As an advantage over traditional matrix factorization-based models, our LDA-based model is capable of visualizing trending interests and styles across the Etsy marketplace, and intuitively summarizing user's style preferences. We used these models to deploy a fully functional user and shop recommendation system, both of which are currently serving live traffic. We also described methods for large-scale experimentation on the Etsy site.

In the near future, we plan on several new iterations for improving the accuracy and efficiency of our recommendations systems, including: Continuing current experiments for more conclusive results of different recommendation models; incorporating user demographic, gender, and referrer urls as priors to ease the cold-start problem; incorporating text and image features for a more informed system (and also to ease the cold-start problem); and finally, figuring out more ways to utilize inferred interest groups to create a better browsing experience.

8. REFERENCES

[1] G. Adomavicius and A. Tuzhilin. Toward the next generation of recommender systems: A survey of the state-of-the-art and possible extensions. *IEEE Trans. on Knowl. and Data Eng.*, 2005.

[2] R. S. Arora and A. M. Elgammal. Towards automated classification of fine-art painting style: A comparative study. In *ICPR*, 2012.

[3] D. M. Blei and J. D. Lafferty. Correlated topic models. In *ICML*, 2006.

[4] D. M. Blei, A. Y. Ng, M. I. Jordan, and J. Lafferty. Latent dirichlet allocation. *JMLR*, 2003.

[5] A. S. Das, M. Datar, A. Garg, and S. Rajaram. Google news personalization: Scalable online collaborative filtering. In *WWW*, 2007.

[6] M. Datar, N. Immorlica, P. Indyk, and V. S. Mirrokni. Locality-sensitive hashing scheme based on p-stable distributions. In *SCG*, 2004.

[7] W. Di, C. Wah, A. Bhardwaj, R. Piramuthu, and N. Sundaresan. Style finder: Fine-grained clothing style detection and retrieval. In *CVPR Workshops*, 2013.

[8] T. Griffiths, M. Steyvers, D. Blei, and J. Tenenbaum. Integrating topics and syntax. In *NIPS*, 2005.

[9] P. Gupta, A. Goel, J. Lin, A. Sharma, D. Wang, and R. Zadeh. Wtf: The who to follow service at twitter. In *WWW*, 2013.

[10] D. J. Hu and L. K. Saul. A probabilistic topic model for unsupervised learning of musical key-profiles. In *ISMIR*, 2009.

[11] Y. Hu, Y. Koren, and C. Volinsky. Collaborative filtering for implicit feedback datasets. In *ICDM*, 2008.

[12] J. Kleinberg. Hubs, authorities, and communities. In *ACM Computer Survey*, 1999.

[13] Y. Koren, R. Bell, and C. Volinsky. Matrix factorization techniques for recommender systems. *Computer*, 2009.

[14] K. Krstovski, D. Smith, H. M. Wallach, and A. McGregor. Efficient nearest-neighbor search in the probability simplex. In *ICTIR*, 2013.

[15] F.-F. Li and P. Perona. A bayesian hierarchical model for learning natural scene categories. In *CVPR*, 2005.

[16] B. Marlin. Modeling user rating profiles for collaborative filtering. In *NIPS*, 2004.

[17] I. Porteous, A. Asuncion, D. Newman, P. Smyth, A. Ihler, and M. Welling. Fast collapsed gibbs sampling for latent dirichlet allocation. In *ACM SIGKDD*, 2008.

[18] P. Resnick, N. Iacovou, M. Suchak, P. Bergstrom, and J. Riedl. Grouplens: An open architecture for collaborative filtering of netnews. In *CSCW*, 1994.

[19] J. B. Schafer, J. Konstan, and J. Riedl Recommender systems in e-commerce. In *EC*, 1999.

[20] N. Tintarev and J. Masthoff. Evaluating the effectiveness of explanations for recommender systems. *User Modeling and User-Adapted Interaction*, 2012.

[21] C. Wang and D. M. Blei. Collaborative topic modeling for recommending scientific articles. In *ACM SIGKDD*, 2011.

[22] J. Zujovic, L. Gandy, S. Friedman, B. Pardo, and T. Pappas. Classifying paintings by artistic genre: An analysis of features & classifiers. In *MMSP*, 2009.

Corporate Residence Fraud Detection

Enric Junqué de Fortuny
University of Antwerp
Prinsstraat 13
Antwerp, Belgium
enric.junquedefortuny@uantwerp.be

Marija Stankova*
University of Antwerp
Prinsstraat 13
Antwerp, Belgium
marija.stankova@uantwerp.be

Julie Moeyersoms
University of Antwerp
Prinsstraat 13
Antwerp, Belgium
julie.moeyersoms@uantwerp.be

Bart Minnaert
Ghent University
Henleykaai 84, G-building
Ghent, Belgium
bart.minnaert@ugent.be

Foster Provost
Stern School of Business
New York University
New York, NY 10012
fprovost@stern.nyu.edu

David Martens
University of Antwerp
Prinsstraat 13
Antwerp, Belgium
david.martens@uantwerp.be

ABSTRACT

With the globalisation of the world's economies and ever-evolving financial structures, fraud has become one of the main dissipaters of government wealth and perhaps even a major contributor in the slowing down of economies in general. Although corporate residence fraud is known to be a major factor, data availability and high sensitivity have caused this domain to be largely untouched by academia. The current Belgian government has pledged to tackle this issue at large by using a variety of in-house approaches and cooperations with institutions such as academia, the ultimate goal being a fair and efficient taxation system. This is the first data mining application specifically aimed at finding corporate residence fraud, where we show the predictive value of using both structured and fine-grained invoicing data. We further describe the problems involved in building such a fraud detection system, which are mainly data-related (e.g. data asymmetry, quality, volume, variety and velocity) and deployment-related (e.g. the need for explanations of the predictions made).

Keywords

fraud detection; corporate residence fraud; transactional data; structured data

1. INTRODUCTION

The social contract [30] between governments, citizens and corporations comprises the mutual agreement between these parties on how to allocate resources for common expenses such as road construction, hospitals and the environment. Most democratic societies have implemented this social contract in the form of a taxation system in which each party agrees to contribute to the total expenditure of the country. Needless to say, the success of such a system depends on the fairness and efficiency and thus the compliance of all actors to the system in place. Falsifying or withholding information in order to limit the amount of tax liability is therefore against the law and constitutes fiscal (or tax) fraud. This is a large-scale problem that affects a multitude of entities: the public sector, the private sector and citizens [25]. Fiscal fraud exists in several forms, which can broadly be categorized as evasion of direct (income and corporate tax) and indirect (VAT) taxes. Governments are a frequent target of fraudsters, who undermine the system and abuse its benefits, grants and tax programs.

In Belgium, fiscal fraud is acknowledged as a significant problem. The State Secretary for Fraud in Belgium even stated that *"Fraud is as Belgian as beer and fries"* [9]. Estimations by the European Commission show that the Belgian government loses about €30 billion annually due to fiscal fraud, which corresponds to 6% of its GDP [9], placing Belgium's among the highest fraud rates in Western Europe. On a larger level the overall European losses due to tax evasion and avoidance are estimated to be an astonishing €1 trillion [12]. These numbers show that the fight against fraud is a crucial aspect of any fiscal system. Not only does fraud cause serious damage to society, it also has a direct financial impact on individuals. The relevance of fraud detection in the current climate of severe fiscal consolidation and social hardship is motivated in the declaration of the G20 leaders of September 2013. In this statement, they emphasize the importance of ensuring that all taxpayers pay their fair share of taxes as well as the need to tackle tax avoidance, harmful practices and aggressive tax planning [27].

Since most tax systems use audits to ensure compliance with tax laws, an accurate selection of the most likely fraudulent cases is crucial to maintain an efficient tax inspection. Given this urgent need to identify specifically the most suspicious cases, the Belgian government joined forces with academia to work on automated data mining systems that look for fraud patterns in large amounts of data to detect corporate residence fraud. This type of fraud occurs when companies deceitfully attempt to place their residency in a

*Enric and Marija contributed equally to this work.

KDD'14, August 24–27, 2014, New York, New York, USA.

http://dx.doi.org/10.1145/2623330.2623333

low-tax country in order to avoid paying the higher taxes of their real location. The data consists of two types of records: on the one hand we have structured data on the Belgian companies (sector, city, etc), on the other hand we have transactional data (invoicing logs) between Belgian and foreign companies. Although using this fine-grained transactional data can be tricky, the information that could be retrieved from it is very valuable in order to detect residence fraud. Consider the following (fictitious) example: let's say we see that a foreign company receives invoices from a golf club in Brussels. This could be an indication that the company and its owner(s) likely reside in Belgium. If this is indeed so, other foreign companies that also receive invoices from this specific golf club make for interesting suspects. Working at such a fine-grained identifier level makes available very informative data [28].

The potential of data mining techniques has also been acknowledged by governmental entities, including the Belgian government. In their action plan to strengthen the fight against tax fraud, the European Commission articulates it as follows: *"For tax administrations, the development and full use of automated tools and risk management techniques would release human and budgetary resources to concentrate on achieving targeted objectives."* [11]
The rest of the paper is structured as follows: In the next section, a literature overview is given on the importance of fraud detection, the different types of fraud, and the the main domain challenges. Section 3 looks deeper into the type and size of the data and Section 4 describes the specific methods that were used. Section 5 shows the results and the deployment, with concluding remarks in Section 6.

2. LITERATURE OVERVIEW

2.1 The Importance of Fraud Detection

As discussed above, the Belgian government is a frequent target of fraudsters. Abuse of the tax system is a very costly fraud type [25], with estimates of losses going into the billions of euros (dollars, pounds) for the EU, US and UK governments. Translating these numbers to impact on members of society is an easy exercise. For instance, Belgian estimates reveal that fraud against the public sector is estimated to be €30 billion per year and thus directly costs every adult in the country about €2,700 annually.

As mentioned before, the elementary form of damage from fraud in government-allotted resources is an immediate financial loss and thus the unfair redistribution of wealth. Note, however, that the consequences can be much broader. Fraud losses could result in cuts to thinly spread government-budgets, tax increases, less investment in the public sector (such as new roads, hospitals, schools, etc.) and eventually a slower economy altogether. Effective fraud detection, on the other hand, can lead to many benefits. Not only is there the direct impact of recovering parts of the loss of capital, increased effectiveness can also lead to enhanced deterrence [1]. That is, the increased likelihood of being captured, causes the net expected benefit from the fraudulent activities to be outweighed by their (proportionally increased) expected costs, thus decreasing the appeal of such fraud. Needless to say, governments try hard to cope with evermore creative fraud-schemes such as the ones addressed in this project.

2.2 Data Mining for Fraud Detection

In the literature, data mining has been applied to many domains for fraud detection. Some of them include the banking sector for discovering fraudulent credit card transactions or card applications [3, 6, 19, 33, 39], identifying fraudulent service subscriptions or calls in the telecommunications domain [8, 14, 15, 17], detecting false insurance claims [29], revealing websites with high level of non-intentional traffic for online advertising [35] or uncovering tax evasions in the public sector [2, 16, 41] and etc. A comprehensive overview of the complete fraud detection literature is beyond the scope of this paper (see [4, 26, 29]).

Many of the fraud detection studies need to deal, similarly to our work, with heterogeneous types of data and especially large amounts of transactional data. The applications are mainly in the banking and the telecommunications sectors, where the companies keep logs of card transactions and calls. Due to the high dimensionality of the transactional data, a very common approach in the literature is to perform some type of aggregation over the transactional data. One way to do so is to create transaction aggregates for each user account that characterize the typical legitimate behaviour of the user [5, 15]. Any new transaction that deviates from the typical behaviour of that user would be suspected as fraudulent. Other studies [3, 19, 39], take the approach of deriving RFM (Recency, Frequency, Monetary Value) attributes from the original features over a period of time. The RFM attributes are then used as inputs for a classification technique. Aggregating the transactions creates new structured data and loses the fine-grained information that is included in the transactions (cf., the golf club example from Section 1).

To our knowledge, there have been only few studies in the prior literature that take into account the information from very high-dimensional categorical attributes, especially the identifier attributes described by Perlich and Provost [28]. These attributes can represent particular identifiers as the companies accounts in our case, particular names of locations or persons and etc. The work of Fawcett and Provost [14, 15] incorporates such attributes by first searching for individual classification rules based on the transaction-level data (such as location in cell phone calls), and then building higher-level features based on these rules. The studies by Brause [6] and Sanchez [33] include these attributes by using classification based on association rules on transactional level applicable to smaller datasets Cortes et al. [8] and Stitelman et al. [35] both employ a graph representation and apply relational inference on the networks defined among persons connected if they call each other [8] and among browsers connected if they visit the same website [35]. Our study explores and combines fraud data on both levels: we apply scalable algorithms to extract fine-grained knowledge from huge amount of transactional data and also consider the structured data. By doing so, we are able to harness the predictive power of both types of data, as well as the added value of combining them.

For the purpose of tax evasion, data mining has been applied to the problem of corporate fraud [7, 20], where companies falsify their financial statements, as well as Value Added Tax (VAT) evasion [2, 16, 41], solely on structured data.

2.3 Domain Challenges

Typical challenges encountered when applying data mining techniques in the domain of corporate residence fraud detection relate to positive label scarcity and quality. Additionally, due to the way in which the data is generated nowadays, we also encounter problems related to Big Data with respect to size (volume), type (variety) and speed of data generation and stationarity-violation (velocity). Furthermore, the acceptance by stakeholders of the resulting models is highly dependent on their comprehensibility, which needs to be taken into account both during and after the modeling phase.

Data scarcity: Fraud data are usually *highly unbalanced*, as there are many more non-fraudulent instances than the number of fraudulent ones. Furthermore, limited resources and the very expensive labeling procedure (auditing) further bias the class balance. Moreover, one often encounters pollution of the data labels: data instances can have wrong labels if a fraudulent instance has not yet been discovered and therefore is marked as a legitimate one. Additionally, very little structured data is available on the foreign companies (except for the country where they are located).

Volume, variety and velocity: Every quarter, the government receives millions of tax data entries containing hundreds or even thousands of transactions as well as structured data on each of the companies involved in these entries. As such, not only do the datasets have very large *volume*, the size also continues to increase. Even so, this is not the only issue related to *velocity*. Fraudsters are known to change the way in which they commit fraud in progressively more creative and covert ways to evade the detection systems in place. This adversary effect requires continuous back-testing and updating of the models because stationarity assumptions might be violated. Needless to say, when taken as a whole, the datasets coming from our domain need fast algorithms that can cope with these challenges.

As mentioned before, the government receives both tax declarations as well as transactional data. Furthermore, the government has a database with additional information on each of these companies. Ideally, one wants to connect all these various bits of information in order to obtain the best predictions. Unfortunately, it is not trivial to do so in a sensible way. For instance, how could one combine transactional logs (e.g., foreign company FC_1 transferred money to a golf club) with a geographical location? Possible answers include hierarchical modeling, ensemble methods and stacking; clearly, this situation opens up many possible paths of model combination and design. To the best of our knowledge, we are the first to propose a solution for this corporate governance problem.

Comprehensibility: The success of a tax fraud detection system depends on more than accurately flagging suspected cases. Each suspected case is sent to an investigator who determines whether it is indeed fraudulent and collects evidence. As each investigator develops his/her own expertise on tax fraud, this expertise can conflict with the predictions. If investigators receive many cases they see as clearly non-suspect, they might reject the prediction system altogether. When the system however explains why a case is flagged as suspect, investigators can quickly determine whether this is in line with their experience or not. Further, in a confirmed match situation, the explanation provided by the system can serve as a starting point for the actual investigation. Thus a model that is comprehensible at the instance/decision level is critical both to get user acceptance and to speed up the manual investigation.

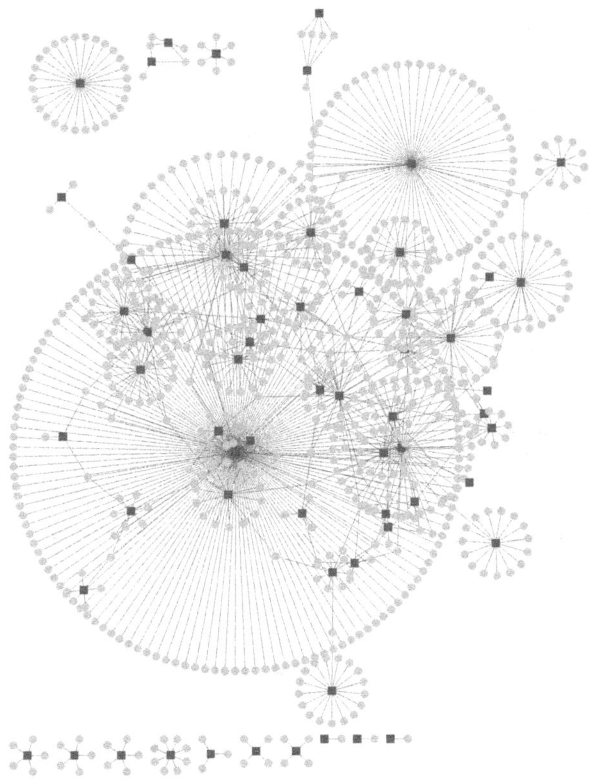

Figure 1: The structure of the invoicing network based on the incoming and outgoing transactions between the fraudulent foreign companies (red squares) and the Belgian companies they interact with (grey nodes). As can be seen from the big cluster, many of the fraudulent foreign companies are connected to the same Belgian companies.

3. DATA

Before we can dig into the modelling approaches for this domain, we must first discuss the exact data available to us. Although we received data from various sources, we can discern two main types of records. First we have invoicing records between 2,745,478 Belgian companies and 873,640 foreign companies (*transactional data, T*). Second, we also have structured information on each of the Belgian companies (*structured data, S*).

Transactional data: In terms of transactional invoicing data, we can distinguish between two types of invoices: incoming invoices from foreign companies to Belgian companies, and outgoing invoices from Belgian to foreign companies. We engineered three different datasets from these invoice logs: a dataset of incoming invoices, a dataset from outgoing invoices and a third dataset where we merged both the incoming and outgoing invoices. Additional statistics for the datasets are shown in Table 1. There can be multiple

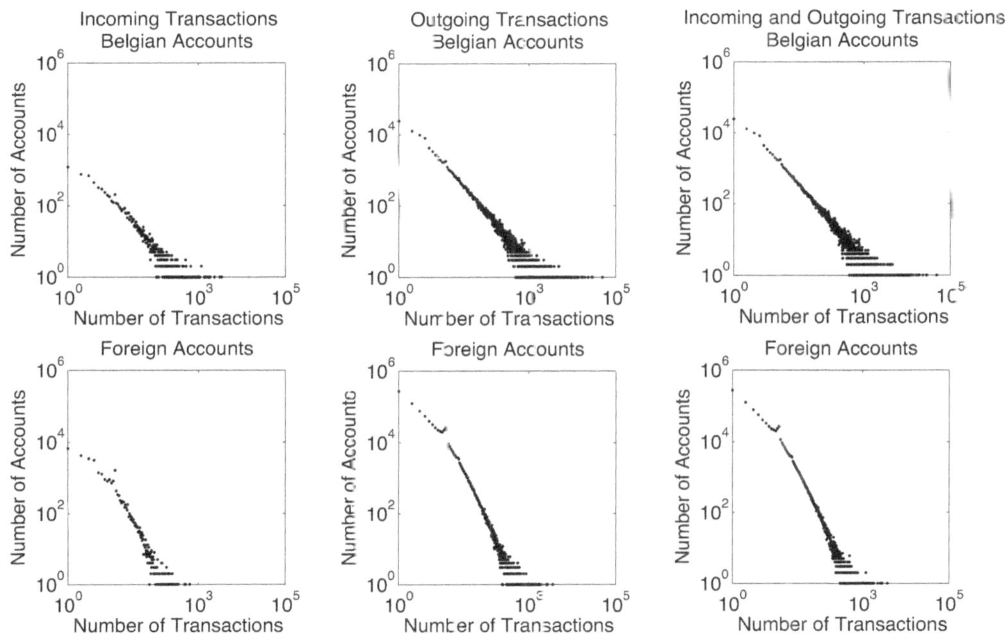

Figure 2: The number of unique transactions per account for the invoicing datasets, when considering the Belgian (top) and foreign (bottom) companies. Most of the Belgian companies typically send or receive invoices to only few foreign companies and, vice versa, most of the foreign companies interact with only few Belgian companies.

Table 1: Statistics for the three invoice datasets.

	Incoming	Outgoing	Incoming and Outgoing
Number of transactions	251,198	6,551,512	6,802,710
Number of unique transactions	73,753	1,955,912	2,029,341
Number of Belgian accounts	7,495	107,345	108,753
Number of Foreign accounts	30,541	858,131	858,703
Average number of transactions per Belgian account	9.84	18.22	18.65
Average number of transactions per foreign account	2.41	2.28	2.36

transactions between two companies, on different dates or with different amounts of money. Hence in Table 1, both the total number of transactions and the number of unique transactions between the companies are shown. The latter counts only the transactions where the sender/recipient pair is unique. Note that this transactional data can be represented both as a matrix and as a bipartite graph.

In the *matrix* representation each row i corresponds to a foreign company; column-values indicate whether the foreign company made a connection to resident company j, with entry $x_{i,j}$ equal to 1 and 0 otherwise. A *bipartite graph* (bigraph) is a graph that has two types of nodes and edges exist only between nodes of different type. A subset of the bigraph containing all of the fraudulent nodes is visualized in Figure 1 with red squares representing the fraudulent foreign nodes and the grey nodes representing Belgian companies they interact with. Figure 2 shows the degree distributions (number of transactions) of the Belgian-foreign bipartite company networks.

These graphs help us to understand the power of the fine-grained data in the modeling results presented below. Although keeping the full fine-grained data instead of aggregate values can be tricky to work with, previous studies have shown fine-grained transaction data to enhance the predictive power of models [18, 24, 28]. This is partly due to the fat tail in the degree distribution we see in Figure 2: many companies appear related to only very few other companies, but these low-connectivity companies make up the vast majority of the companies. Thus, it is relatively difficult to compress the company-related information into a small number of simple aggregate variables (that do not obscure the fine-grained connectivity information). Figure 1 in turn shows that the fraudulent foreign companies indeed do seem to interact with the same Belgian companies, as illustrated by the big cluster in which most fraudulent companies are found. Thus, it makes sense to intelligently—i.e., in a supervised fashion—examine the specific companies in the predictive modeling (note that it is informative both to be connected to one or more suspicion-inducing companies as well as to be connected to one or many suspicion-reducing companies; cf., [28]).

Structured data: Most of the available structured information is on residential companies because, to date, there is still no sharing of information between governments. This asymmetry in data is one of the challenges to overcome on the level of policy making. For each of the Belgian companies we have information on their geographical location, industry type, start-up date, etc. For foreign companies, we only know in which country they are located as well as the target label. As shown in Figure 3, we can infer certain aggregate characteristics for the foreign companies, based on what the average Belgian company that connects to it looks like.[1] For the particular foreign company shown in the figure, we can deduce that its average transaction value is a certain amount and that its usual geographical correspondence location is located in Brussels (median region in Belgium). These characteristics can be added into the input vector in order to augment the prediction information. This set-up leads to a total of 31 features per foreign company.

An important problem that arises in our scenario, due to limited resources and the very expensive labeling procedure, is skewness in the distribution of the target variable. Out of the total 873,640 available foreign companies, only 62 are marked as positive cases. Because of this skewness, we make use of AUC and lift curves and we repeat each of the experiments 10 times on different out-of-sample selections to ensure robustness and the external validity of the results.

4. METHODS

Given the variety and volume of the data, different feature engineering and modeling techniques are first applied and subsequently combined. In this section we first describe each of the different methods briefly after which we discuss their combination, displayed in Figure 4.

4.1 Structured Data

In the structured learning scenario, we are interested in predicting whether or not a foreign company is fraudulent, based on the aggregate, structured information of the associated resident companies. This turns out to be a classical predictive modeling set-up in which we predict target variable y based on vectors of structured data $\mathbf{x}$, one for each foreign company. To deal with the many-to-one variables, such as location, which appear in the transaction data, we encode them in the structured data via a "weight-of-evidence" encoding; this is a logarithmic transformation that allows one to transform a categorical variable into a variable that is monotonically related to the target variable [36, 37]. For example, if most of the Belgian companies connected to a foreign company are located in Brussels, this will be encoded as a one in the position of the dummy-encoded "Brussels" location variable. Examples of structured variables include the location of the linked company (up to town level), the main activity code of the linked company, and the legal construct type of the linked company (with a total of 31 such variables). Once the features have been engineered into a structured input vector, we train an SVM with a linear kernel. SVMs are known to work well with these kinds of data [32] and the choice of kernel is motivated by the need for comprehensibility of the model (more on this later).

[1] Due to the sensitivity of the data, all of the examples given in the figures are only illustrative; aggregate results and statistics are of course computed on the true data.

4.2 Transactional Data

The transactional data can also be represented by vectors as follows: for each of the n foreign companies we look up its previous associations with companies in Belgium. Each of the m Belgian companies is represented by a feature and the value of this feature in the foreign company's m-dimensional vector $\mathbf{x}$ will be equal to one if such a connection was made and zero otherwise. By aggregating all of these vectors we end up with a very high-dimensional, but highly sparse, matrix. There are two main approaches of handling this kind of data: (a) applying propositional learners (such as SVMs and Naive Bayes) on the huge, sparse matrix representation and (b) using relational learning/inference on the graph representation.

Propositional learners.

A first approach is to gather all of the data in a big matrix and apply *SVM* (using the LibLinear package [13]). Clearly, due to the size of the data, this will take quite a while on a standard desktop computing set-up. Further, it likely will not perform very well due to class imbalance, as explained by Wallace et al. [38]. Indeed, poor performance is revealed in the very low AUC and lift values of this approach (SVM_T, Table 1). As a first improvement, we train the SVM on a balanced subset of the data. By equally weighing the number of positive and negative examples, the SVM learns to put equal importance on each of the classes and performs much better (SVM_T(50-50)). Other improvements toward this end, could be to directly optimize for a different loss function [31]. An in-depth discussion on this matter is beyond the scope of this application-focused paper.

In a similar vein, we also apply a *binary Bernoulli Naive Bayes* (NB), specifically tailored for massive, sparse, binary data [18]; let's call that "Big Bayes." This classifier uses the same input vectors $\mathbf{x}$, but makes an estimate based on the MAP likelihood estimation of a probability parameter for each of the features. These are gathered in a vector with elements $\theta_j = P(X_j = x_{i,j}|C = c)$ and used in a 'naive' model, where all features are assumed to be conditionally independent of each other, given the class, resulting in the following probability estimate for each class (i.e., fraudulent or not):

$$P(C = c|\mathbf{x_i}) \quad \propto \quad \prod_{j=1}^{m} (\theta_j)^{x_{i,j}} (1 - \theta_j)^{(1-x_{i,j})}$$

In this formulation, fraud is encoded by class label C, and the $x_{i,j}$ indicate whether a transaction was made from foreign company j to resident company i. A decision is made by comparing the probability estimate for the fraudulence of the company ($C = 1$) and the non-fraudulence ($C = 0$). The NB modeling procedure does not suffer from the class skew problems of the SVM. The Big Bayes modifications for massive, sparse data involve only having to process the non-zero elements of the huge matrix [18]; NB does not need any further modifications to be run efficiently on the fine-grained data.

Relational learners.

Intuitively, it makes sense to apply a learner that is specifically tailored for the networks resulting from transactions like the ones described in Section 3. In order to do so, we must first realize that such transactional logs between two

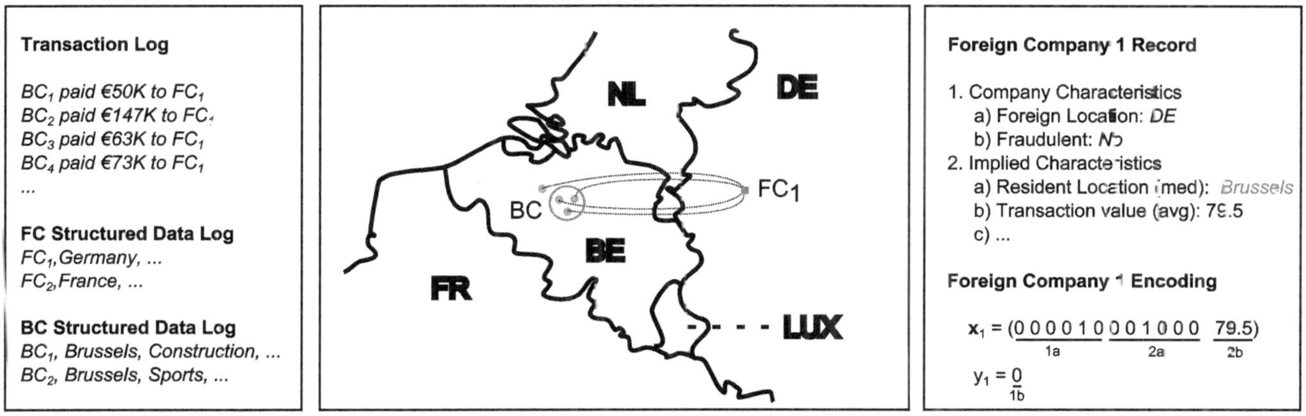

Figure 3: Example of the feature engineering for structured data. The foreign company (FC_1) has many associated Belgian companies (BC_i). Original company characteristics such as the location are combined with implied characteristics such as the average transaction values and the median resident location.

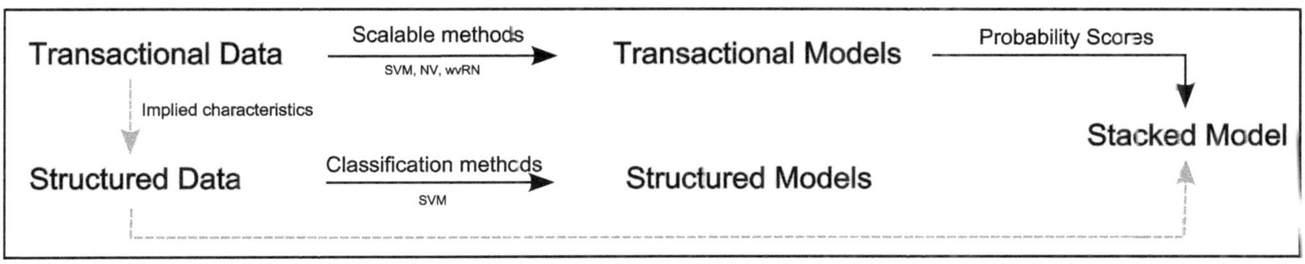

Figure 4: Overview of the system design for fraud detection. In a first step, the transactional data and structured data are engineered into features. Afterwards different modeling techniques are applied to generate both transactional and structured models. These models are evaluated separately at first, but combined in a final step as well into a stacked model.

entities (foreign and resident companies) can be represented as a bipartite graph. The visualization already suggests ("two-hop") assortativity in fraud status in the network of foreign companies.

Numerous relational learners exist for graphs with only one type of nodes. In order to make use of them, we can apply the three-step framework for classification within bigraphs proposed in [34]. The idea is to project the bigraph into a unigraph (graph with only one type of nodes) in which foreign companies are connected, based on shared Belgian company connections and then apply a relational learner. By additionally assigning weights to the edges in the projection, more information from the underlying bigraph can be preserved [34]. The resulting classification decision is then based on the posterior probability, defined as:

$$P(C = c|\mathbf{x}_i) \propto \sum_{j \in N(i)} w_{ij} \cdot P(C = c|N(\mathbf{x}_j)) \quad (1)$$

$$w_{ij} = \sum_{k \in N(\mathbf{x}_i) \cap N(\mathbf{x}_j)} \tanh\left(\frac{1}{d_k}\right) \quad (2)$$

Equation (1) presents the weighted-voted Relational Neighbor (wvRN) inference method [21]; with wvRN, the class probability of a node in the graph (a foreign company) is equal to the weighted average probabilities of all of its neighbors ($j \in N(\mathbf{x}_i)$). A neighbor is defined as a node that is linked to the node that is being investigated in the *projected graph* (in this case identified by a one in the $\mathbf{x}$ vector). As mentioned before, such a connection is made only if two foreign companies share a resident company. Equation (2) shows that the weighting (the similarity between two top-nodes) was chosen as a sum over the tanh of the inverse of the degrees of the shared nodes. That is, if say a Belgian company has connections with all of the foreign companies, this company will define a relatively low weight in the total probability calculation. If it does not, it will likely be more informative and thus should be weighted accordingly. These design choices are based on the results of the extensive experimental study on a wide variety of publicly available transactional datasets conducted by Stankova et al. [34].

4.3 Stacked model

Ideally, we want to build a model that incorporates all of the available information. As one can see from the previous sections, it is not trivial to combine these heterogeneous types of data because they require different sorts of models. One way to cope with this problem, while still preserving the variety of modeling approaches is to combine the models in a *stacked model*. The expected efficacy of such a model is explained by the fact that we are incorporating more information into one model than we did before, which should result in a lower modeling bias [40].

In our scenario, as the stacked model we use a linear SVM to produce a final model that is a linear combination of the output scores of the transactional classifiers and the structured model. An important reason for this particular design is that we do want to keep a maximum level of comprehensibility without sacrificing too much predictive performance. Specifically, the 31 variables of structured data are manageable to a human observer, but the millions of transactions clearly are not. It is much more informative to have the scores of these models encoded as variables—a human inspector can assess the contribution of the network-data component. Should this be high enough, specialized techniques can be used to inspect the underlying reasons for the predictions of the network-data component (as discussed in the next section).

Figure 4 summarizes all of the steps required to generate the complete, stacked model. First, the data is converted to (a) transactional (graph) data and (b) structured data. Next, predictive models are built on top of these data, each specifically tailored to cope with the particular aspects of the corresponding data (as explained in the previous section). Lastly, the scores of the graph models are combined with the structured data as input to the final stacked model.

5. RESULTS AND DISCUSSION

5.1 Results

The results of all of the previously explained methods in terms of predictive power (AUC) are shown in Table 2. The best performance for each dataset is denoted in boldface and underlined. Performances that are not significantly different at a 5% confidence level (according to a Wilcoxon signed rank test [10]) are tabulated in bold face. Significant differences at the 1% level are emphasized in italics, and differences at the 5% but not at the 1% level are reported in normal script. A first observation that one can make from this table is that our best models achieve very high AUC values (up to 96.22%). The somewhat high standard deviations on these percentages can be explained by the class imbalance (detecting one more or one fewer example can result in a percentage change of about 10%). Nevertheless, our results do show that our best model (the stacked combination of structured and relational models; SVM_{S+T}) performs significantly better than all of the transactional methods for the incoming and the outgoing data. Although it is still the best performing model for the combination of both data types, the variance is too large to conclude statistical significance at the 5% level using the Wilcoxon test.

Although these results are certainly interesting in terms of global predictive power and ranking ability, we should note that in the specific context of detecting fraudulent companies we are more interested in the lift (how much better than random) when targeting the highest ranking members of the dataset. This is because the fraud analysts investigate the companies deemed to be most suspicious. The lift curves (Figure 5) show the clear superiority at the highest percentiles of the models built on transactional data, where they are able to perform up to a few hundred times better as opposed to random targeting. The traditional, structured-data model and the stacked model deliver clear improvements as well, but at the highest percentiles the lifts are

Table 2: Results of different techniques in terms of AUC. Subscript S refers to models based on structured data. Subscript T refers to models based on fine-grained transaction data. Subscript $S+T$ refers to models based on both structured data and transaction data.

	Incoming data		Outgoing data		Combined data	
Technique used	AUC	std.dev.	AUC	std.dev.	AUC	std.dev.
wvRN$_T$	76.74	(±5.87)	77.32	(±6.21)	**94.55**	(±5.26)
Naive Bayes$_T$	76.64	(±5.94)	77.6	(±6.37)	**94.74**	(±5.45)
SVM$_T$	*46.88*	(±12.76)	*56*	(±9.27)	*70.26*	(±12.46)
SVM$_T$ (50-50)	*62.23*	(±21.03)	57.95	(±33.66)	74.85	(±19.97)
SVM$_S$	**82.71**	(±10.52)	**86.34**	(±7.74)	**91.77**	(±8.16)
SVM$_{S+T}$	**<u>85.92</u>**	(±7.48)	**<u>86.44</u>**	(±10.23)	**<u>96.22</u>**	(±4.8)

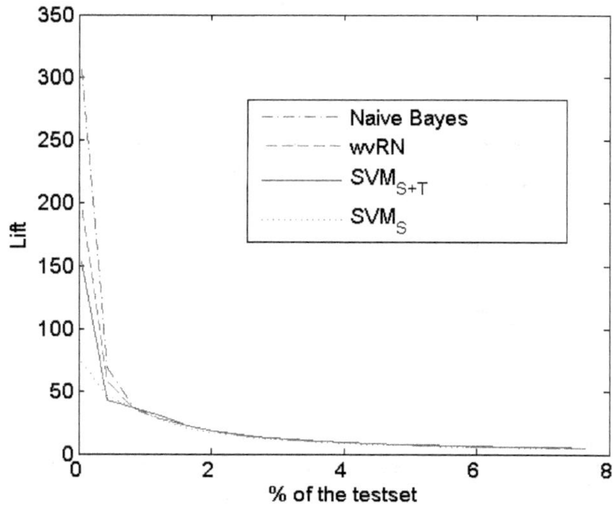

Figure 5: Lift curves of the combined dataset

not nearly as strong as those resulting from using the fine-grained transaction-based models.

As we motivated previously, we can now observe empirically that the fine-grained information included in the transactional data provides substantial gains for detecting fraudulent companies. Referring back to our example, the other fraudulent companies that transact with the Brussels golf club receive high transactional fraud scores, and rightly so apparently—as demonstrated by the very high lifts. Once these other foreign companies that transact with these suspicion-conferring Belgian companies[2] are investigated, structured data may still help to find other suspects.

In conclusion, we can say that if one is interested in a global ranking method, the stacked model would be the best design choice in our scenario, whereas the models based on transactional data are better suited for detecting the most likely frauds. The latter result highlights the importance of keeping the fine-grained information as a whole as opposed to only aggregating it into summary variables.

5.2 Comprehensibility

In the actual deployment of our model, we have been made aware of the tremendous importance of being able to explain

[2]The Belgian companies themselves are not suspicious per se, but the foreign companies that transact with them are.

the decisions made. Specifically, the auditors need to understand the exact reasons why classification models make particular decisions. Cases (even if they be few) where the model makes an obvious wrong decision can create disillusionment with the system and reluctance to use it, unless the reasons behind the decision appear to be sound. Therefore, it is essential that the decisions made by the predictive model can be explained; the auditor can decide to over-rule a specific suggestion and confidently move on to the next one. Going back to our running example of a company that has received an invoice from a golf club in Brussels: Although it might be the case that most foreign companies that receive invoices from that entity are indeed fraudsters, a foreign company such as Rolex that has sponsored a golf tournament at this specific golf club (and therefore has also received an invoice) is likely not fraudulently located abroad. So if the explanation for the classification is given (i.e., receiving an invoice from the specific golf club), an auditor can quickly see why it is or is not valid in the context of the particular focal company.

To our knowledge, the distinction between different types of comprehensibility has received relatively little attention in the data mining literature, even though it often is a crucial criterion for final acceptance and increased use of the predictive models. At least two types of explanations exist. Global explanations provide improved understanding of the complete model, and its performance over the entire space of possible instances. Instance-level explanations on the other hand provide explanations for the model's prediction regarding a particular instance. When using transactional data, the total number of variables and/or data values considered by the model (in our case, millions) is much larger than for the typical structured data. Global explanation methods, such as examining the coefficients of a linear model or using a rule-based model, are simply not applicable in such a high-dimensional context. However, an instance-level approach used for document classification [23], which faces a similar challenge with a large vocabulary, can also be used in this transactional setting: an explanation is defined as the minimal set of entities one received/sent an invoice to, such that removing all the invoices to/from this set changes the predicted class from the class of interest. For our running example, an explanation could be: *'if this company did not receive an invoice from golf club XYZ in Brussels, the predicted class would change to non-fraudulent'*. As such, instance based explanations provide an excellent tool for models that use the fine-grained invoicing data. For more on how explanations can be used both to improve acceptance and also to improve the model itself, as well as further references to related work, we refer to [23].

Global explanations do still have value, but in a different way. Decision makers need insight into the general methods used by fraudsters and their evolution. One way to do so is to list all variables of the stacked model in order, ranked according to the size of the coefficients in the linear model. Then we could see for example that the country dummies for certain countries are very high on the list, as well as the scores from the transactional models, and certain activity codes. A rule-based model could provide similar insights. These insights may then lead to different sorts of cases being discovered, which then would prime the network models to find similar instances. We are not able to show the actual global explanations, as they involve confidential information.

5.3 Deployment

In reference to this project, State Secretary for Fraud John Crombez reported: *"The interaction between the two worlds [academia and government] has proven very valuable. Other countries are now visiting Belgium to see how the Social Intelligence and Investigation Service and the Special Tax Inspection service apply this technique. That is why we need to continue to invest in this technology."* Not only is the predictive performance of our models appreciated, but also considered to be important to success is the fact that in general use this data mining technique can operate on anonymized data, whereby each company is encoded as a "random" number. A company's identity only then needs to be revealed in the context of a particular investigation of a top-suspicion instance. Further, the emphasis on the comprehensibility of the results is deemed essential.

During deployment, the system has to deal with large volumes of heterogeneous data and with new data arriving every quarter, where the underlying data generating process is non-stationary due to the problem being adversarial. The stacked model approach specifically deals with the variety of the data by combining the transactional data from invoices with structural data from tax declarations. The need to retrain the model frequently is facilitated by the scalability of the underlying (naive Bayes and wvRN) methods. They can be run (on a desktop) on the complete data and produce results in a matter of minutes.

6. CONCLUSION

In this paper we have described what to our knowledge is the first data-mining-based method for building a system for detecting corporate residence fraud. The system is based on transactional and structured data, which is gathered by the Belgian government. The success of such a detection system in practice depends on a combination of factors, including efficiency, efficacy and comprehensibility. As such, an important part of our research was to evaluate how one can cope with these conflicting requirements. When used for targeting new fraudsters, a combination of the fine-grained transactional data model and instance-based explanations results in a good trade-off between the needs of an auditor. On the other hand, combining both structured data and fine-grained data in a stacked model is more suited when the main goal is to gain macro-level insights and policy guidance.

Given the success of this pilot study, we believe further research into this application to be a logical next step. There are still many opportunities for improvement. Besides simply improving the modeling methods, one particular aspect that we did not touch upon yet is the pro-active gathering of data with active data-acquisition techniques (see e.g., [22] for a suspicion-scoring application).

It is important to continue to stress the importance of deploying counter-fraud measures for the social good of countries. Although our experiments focus on data from the Belgian government, we hope that researchers from other countries are motivated by our results to apply such methods to or to find better methods for their own countries' data, and/or to convince their governments to do so. It is important for us to understand whether and how data mining indeed can improve government fraud detection efficacy and perhaps even policy making. Once we are convinced, then we can work to remove any lingering doubt or scepticism among decision makers.

7. ACKNOWLEDGMENTS

We are very grateful to the Belgian government for allowing us to write about our work on this problem and especially for their engagement in the project and their useful feedback. David Martens also thanks the Flemish Research Council (FWO) for financial support (Grant G.0827.12N) and Foster Provost thanks NEC for a Faculty Fellowship. Note that these exact models and techniques are not necessarily those used in production.

8. REFERENCES

[1] M. H. Baer. Linkage and the Deterrence of Corporate Fraud, 2008.

[2] S. Basta, F. Fassetti, M. Guarascio, G. Manco, F. Giannotti, D. Pedreschi, L. Spinsanti, G. Papi, and S. Pisani. High quality true-positive prediction for fiscal fraud detection. In *Data Mining Workshops, 2009. ICDMW'09. IEEE International Conference on*, pages 7–12. IEEE, 2009.

[3] S. Bhattacharyya, S. Jha, K. Tharakunnel, and J. C. Westland. Data mining for credit card fraud: A comparative study. *Decision Support Systems*, 50(3):602–613, 2011.

[4] R. J. Bolton and D. J. Hand. Statistical fraud detection: A review. *Statistical Science*, pages 235–249, 2002.

[5] R. J. Bolton, D. J. Hand, et al. Unsupervised profiling methods for fraud detection. *Credit Scoring and Credit Control VII*, pages 235–255, 2001.

[6] R. Brause, T. Langsdorf, and M. Hepp. Neural data mining for credit card fraud detection. In *Tools with Artificial Intelligence, 1999. Proceedings. 11th IEEE International Conference on*, pages 103–106. IEEE, 1999.

[7] M. Cecchini, H. Aytug, G. J. Koehler, and P. Pathak. Detecting management fraud in public companies. *Management Science*, 56(7):1146–1160, 2010.

[8] C. Cortes, D. Pregibon, and C. Volinsky. *Communities of interest.* Springer, 2001.

[9] J. Crombez. *Zwart en wit.* De Bezige Bij, 2013.

[10] J. Demšar. Statistical Comparisons of Classifiers over Multiple Data Sets. *Journal of Machine Learning Research*, 7:1–30, 2006.

[11] EUR-LEX. Communication from the commission to the european parliament and the council, 2012.

[12] European Commission. Fight against tax fraud and tax evasion: A huge problem, 2013.

[13] R.-E. Fan, K.-W. Chang, C.-J. Hsieh, X.-R. Wang, and C.-J. Lin. LIBLINEAR: A library for large linear classification. *Journal of Machine Learning Research*, 9:1871–1874, 2008.

[14] T. Fawcett and F. Provost. Combining data mining and machine learning for effective user profiling. In *Proceedings of the Third KDD International Conference on Knowledge Discovery and Data Mining*, pages 8–13, 1996.

[15] T. Fawcett and F. Provost. Adaptive fraud detection. *Data Mining and Knowledge Discovery*, 1(3):291–316, 1997.

[16] P. C. González and J. D. Velásquez. Characterization and detection of taxpayers with false invoices using data mining techniques. *Expert Systems with Applications*, 40(5):1427–1436, 2013.

[17] C. S. Hilas and P. A. Mastorocostas. An application of supervised and unsupervised learning approaches to telecommunications fraud detection. *Knowledge-Based Systems*, 21(7):721–726, 2008.

[18] E. Junqué de Fortuny, D. Martens, and F. Provost. Predictive Modeling with Big Data: Is Bigger Really Better? *Big Data*, 1(4):215–226, Oct. 2013.

[19] P. Juszczak, N. M. Adams, D. J. Hand, C. Whitrow, and D. J. Weston. Off-the-peg and bespoke classifiers for fraud detection. *Computational Statistics & Data Analysis*, 52(9):4521–4532, 2008.

[20] E. Kirkos, C. Spathis, and Y. Manolopoulos. Data mining techniques for the detection of fraudulent financial statements. *Expert Systems with Applications*, 32(4):995–1003, 2007.

[21] S. A. Macskassy and F. Provost. A simple relational classifier. 2003.

[22] S. A. Macskassy and F. Provost. Suspicion scoring based on guilt-by-association, collective inference, and focused data access. In *International conference on intelligence analysis*, 2005.

[23] D. Martens and F. Provost. Explaining data-driven document classifications. *MIS Quarterly*, 38(4), 2014.

[24] D. Martens, F. Provost, J. Clark, and E. Junqué de Fortuny. Mining fine-grained consumer payment data to improve targeted marketing. Technical report, Stern School of Business, New York University, 2013.

[25] National Fraud Authority. Annual fraud indicator 2013. 2013.

[26] E. Ngai, Y. Hu, Y. Wong, Y. Chen, and X. Sun. The application of data mining techniques in financial fraud detection: A classification framework and an academic review of literature. *Decision Support Systems*, 50(3):559–569, 2011.

[27] Organisation for Economic Co-operation and Development. Tax and development themes in recent G20 discussion, 2013.

[28] C. Perlich and F. Provost. Distribution-based aggregation for relational learning with identifier attributes. *Machine Learning*, 62(1-2):65–105, 2006.

[29] C. Phua, V. Lee, K. Smith, and R. Gayler. A comprehensive survey of data mining-based fraud detection research. *arXiv preprint arXiv:1009.6119*, 2010.

[30] J.-J. Rousseau. *The Social Contract, Or Principles of Political Right (Du contrat social ou Principes du droit politique)*. 1762.

[31] C. Rudin. The p-norm push: A simple convex ranking algorithm that concentrates at the top of the list. *The Journal of Machine Learning Research*, 10:2233–2271, 2009.

[32] Y. Sahin and E. Duman. Detecting credit card fraud by decision trees and support vector machines. In *Proceedings of the International MultiConference of Engineers and Computer Scientists*, volume 1, 2011.

[33] D. Sánchez, M. Vila, L. Cerda, and J.-M. Serrano. Association rules applied to credit card fraud detection. *Expert Systems with Applications*, 36(2):3630–3640, 2009.

[34] M. Stankova, D. Martens, and F. Provost Classification over bipartite graphs through projection. *University of Antwerp, working paper*, 2013.

[35] O. Stitelman, C. Perlich, B. Dalessandro, R. Hook, T. Raeder, and F. Provost. Using co-visitation networks for classifying non-intentional traffic. 2013.

[36] L. C. Thomas. *Consumer Credit Models: Pricing, Profit and Portfolios: Pricing, Profit and Portfolios*. Oxford University Press, 2009.

[37] L. C. Thomas, D. B. Edelman, and J. N. Crook. *Credit scoring and its applications*. Siam, 2002.

[38] B. C. Wallace, K. Small, C. E. Brodley, and T. A. Trikalinos. Class imbalance, redux. In *Data Mining (ICDM), 2011 IEEE 11th International Conference on*, pages 754–763. IEEE, 2011.

[39] C. Whitrow, D. J. Hand, P. Juszczak, D. Weston, and N. M. Adams. Transaction aggregation as a strategy for credit card fraud detection. *Data Mining and Knowledge Discovery*, 18(1):30–55, 2009.

[40] D. Wolpert. Stacked generalization. *Neural networks*, 1992.

[41] R.-S. Wu, C.-S. Ou, H.-Y. Lin, S.-I. Chang, and D. C. Yen. Using data mining technique to enhance tax evasion detection performance. *Expert Systems with Applications*, 39(10):8769–8777, 2012.

Modeling Mass Protest Adoption in Social Network Communities using Geometric Brownian Motion

Fang Jin*, Rupinder Paul Khandpur*, Nathan Self*, Edward Dougherty†, Sheng Guo‡, Feng Chen§, B. Aditya Prakash*, Naren Ramakrishnan*

*Discovery Analytics Center, Department of Computer Science, Virginia Tech.
†Genetics, Bioinformatics, and Computational Biology Program, Virginia Tech.
‡LinkedIn Inc., §Department of Computer Science, University at Albany, SUNY
*{jfang8, rupen, nwself, badityap, naren}@cs.vt.edu
†edougherty@vt.edu, ‡sguo@linkedin.com, §fchen5@albany.edu

ABSTRACT

Modeling the movement of information within social media outlets, like Twitter, is key to understanding to how ideas spread but quantifying such movement runs into several difficulties. Two specific areas that elude a clear characterization are (i) the intrinsic random nature of individuals to potentially adopt and subsequently broadcast a Twitter topic, and (ii) the dissemination of information via non-Twitter sources, such as news outlets and word of mouth, and its impact on Twitter propagation. These distinct yet interconnected areas must be incorporated to generate a comprehensive model of information diffusion. We propose a bispace model to capture propagation in the union of (exclusively) Twitter and non-Twitter environments. To quantify the stochastic nature of Twitter topic propagation, we combine principles of geometric Brownian motion and traditional network graph theory. We apply Poisson process functions to model information diffusion outside of the Twitter mentions network. We discuss techniques to unify the two sub-models to accurately model information dissemination. We demonstrate the novel application of these techniques on real Twitter datasets related to mass protest adoption in social communities.

Categories and Subject Descriptors

H.2.8 [**Database Management**]: Database Applications—*Data Mining*

Keywords

Information diffusion; social networks; protests; geometric Brownian motion.

1. INTRODUCTION

In recent years social networking sites such as Twitter and Facebook have provided not just a platform for communication but also a means of mobilization and strategic interaction between key players of social movements, e.g., protests. Traditionally social movements occur within a subset of the population and have spread through on-the-ground communities and unions. With the advent of leaner communication technologies like Twitter, the way such movements form and spread through modern society has changed. With Twitter, in particular, traditional slogans have transformed into hashtags which can offer a consistent way of communicating the reason and motivation of social movements like protests and uprisings.

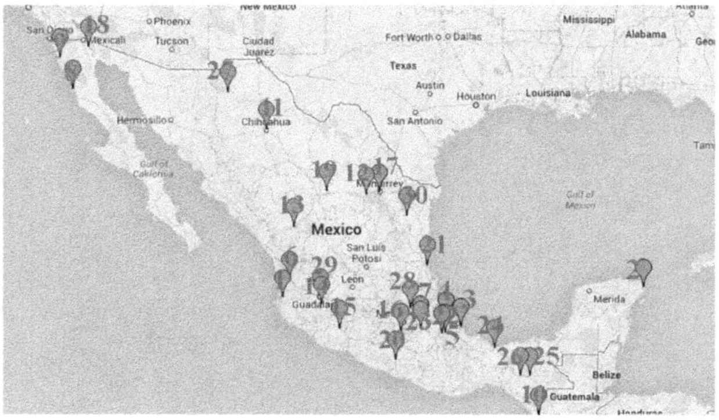

Figure 1: Mexico teacher protest events from Sep 1 to Sep 7, 2013. The blue pins denote protest cities; the numbers in red denote the sequence of protests as they spread across the country.

In this paper, we focus on Twitter's user networks during protests and similar civil unrest activities in Latin America. Our goals are to model the propagation and growth of contagion-like protest waves within a social network and to understand the social and structural dynamics underlying such phenomena. The key problem is understanding the nature of information propagation among motivated users of a social network. We have observed that such mass protests emerge very swiftly and sharply. In Twitterspeak, they would be considered trending but most such trends quickly decline on the social network even if not in the physical world. Modeling protest-related topic propagation on networks involves several challenges.

KDD'14, August 24–27, 2014, New York, NY, USA.
Copyright 2014 ACM 978-1-4503-2956-9/14/08 ...$15.00.
http://dx.doi.org/10.1145/2623330.2623376.

First, social protest propagation through online media can spread over large areas more quickly than traditional methods since users are geographically distributed. For example, on September 1, 2013, the Mexican government's education reform bill drew the wrath of teachers country-wide who opposed the reform (which required regular assessments of their performance as educators). Twitter was a virtual loudspeaker, providing a platform for organization and strategization for teachers to put forth their arguments against the bill. A series of mass teacher protests erupted and spread from city to city. As shown in Fig. 1, we see the movement spreading over time to different locations with no obvious visual mobilization pattern. The second challenge is that Twitter's user network embodies many subgraphs based on social ties which might afford different propagation rates due to subgraph-specific structures.

Thus identifying how the cause of a protest is adopted by Twitter users and how mobilization happens in the underlying network is a difficult task. To address this problem we present an integrated framework with new theoretical models as well as empirical validation on real Twitter data for actual protests witnessed in the recent past. Our key contributions are:

- We model the inherent heterogeneity in propagation using a bispace model, comprised of the Twitter mentions network (where both globally and locally influential neighbors contribute to a user's recruitment) and a latent space (where external exposure to protest-related information is captured).

- We focus on the role of community-driven information propagation over the bispace model. We use geometric Brownian motion (GBM) over the mentions network and Poisson processes over the latent space to model information propagation during mass social movements.

- We illustrate the effectiveness of our approach in modeling several key mass protest adoption scenarios in multiple countries of Latin America, viz. Argentina, Brazil, Colombia, Mexico, Uruguay, and Venezuela.

The rest of this paper is organized as follows. Section 2 covers related work in the areas of social movements, information diffusion in networks, external influences, and Brownian motion. Section 3 proposes the geometric Brownian motion propagation mechanism. Section 4 introduces the bispace propagation model, especially the model of propagation in latent space. In Section 5, we present our dataset and experimental setup, followed by initial experimental findings. Section 6 discusses the evaluation results for our approach followed by a brief discussion in Section 7.

2. RELATED WORK

We briefly review related work next, which comes from multiple areas.

Social movements: Oliver and Myers [18] develop a foundation for theoretical insights of social movements and describe the limitations of simplified models. The Arab Spring of 2010 served as a context for many researchers [6, 2, 24, 4, 20] to study the role social networking sites play in the spread and recruitment of participants in protests. A detailed anatomy of modern social protests is described by Saad-Filho [20] with the June 2013 anti-government protests in Brazil as a context. In this work, we study the processes and sociological impacts of protests in the modern era, fortified by online social networks and the communities in and around them.

Information diffusion in networks: Previous studies have approached the modeling of information propagation and diffusion in social networks through several means, e.g., contagion models (SIR [3] SISa [10]), diffusion based threshold and cascade models [12], rise-and-fall patterns [13], coverage models [22], and survival theory [19]. A good survey of different models of information diffusion is presented in [7].

External influences: We believe that the effects of influences that originate external to the observed diffusion network, such as mass media and offline spread of information, can impact the way in which information flows within the online network. Myers et al. [14] study the emergence of URLs on Twitter with a probabilistic generative process using both internal and external exposure curves in a contagion-like model. Similar attention to the role of external factors is paid by Crane and Sornette [5] for tracking the popularity of YouTube videos using a diffusion model. Iwata et al. [11] use a shared cascade Poisson process model to discover latent influences in social activities such as item adoption. Using shared parameters among multiple Poisson processes, they were able to simulate sequences of item adoption events.

Brownian motion: Zhou and colleagues (e.g., [26, 8, 27]) develop the notion of Brownian motion on networks which they use to discover communities of hierarchical structure both locally and globally. We extend this approach in this paper to formulate a propagation algorithm based on geometric Brownian motion (GBM). Borrowed from statistical physics, GBM has been used heavily in finance to model stock price movements. Scale invariance and the ability to model abrupt bumps along propagation paths are the primary motivations for using GBMs to model stochastic processes [23].

Our work builds on the concepts introduced in [8, 11, 26, 27] but differs from the other diffusion models described earlier by considering both the role of communities of users and the abrupt nature of propagation of volatile information such as mass social protests. We include the notion of bispace where both latent (attributed to external influences) and observed user network influences are considered. We infer propagation rates for communities in the observed network and allow implicit recruitment of users into protest actions through a Poisson process.

3. FORMALISMS

3.1 Basics

We model Twitter activity as a network $G(V, E)$ of mentions. Here, each vertex $v \in V$ represents a Twitter user. There is a directed edge from user v_i to user v_j if v_i mentions v_j in a tweet. We define ω_{ij} to be the number of tweets in which user v_i mentions user v_j. Note that ω_{ij} is not necessarily equal to ω_{ji}. Key players such as celebrities and politicians are more likely to be mentioned by other users, rather than the other way around. As can be seen in Fig. 2, the mentions network is a directed graph. Weight ω_{14} is the number of times Twitter user v_1 mentions user v_4, which is

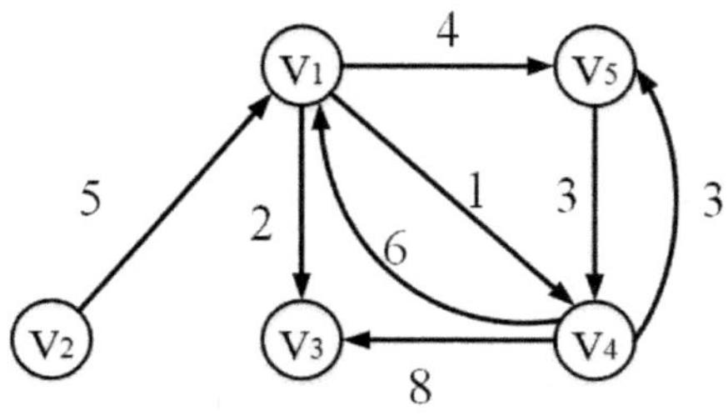

Figure 2: An example mentions network. Nodes denote Twitter users, directed edges denote direction of mentions between users, and edges are labeled with mention frequency.

1, while w_{41} is 6. Note that w_{21} is 5, while w_{12} is 0 (not shown).

We define the neighborhood $N(v_i)$ of a user v_i as the set of all users mentioned by v_i, i.e., those for whom there is a directed edge from v_i. For each user $v_j \in N(v_i)$, we define the Brownian distance from user v_i to v_j to be

$$d_{ij} = \frac{1}{(\omega_{ij}+1)(\omega_{ji}+1)^{\gamma}(\eta_{ij}+1)^{\gamma}} \tag{1}$$

Here, η_{ij} is the number of common direct neighbors shared by user v_i and user v_j [27]. In Fig. 2, node v_1 and v_4 share two common direct neighbors—v_3 and v_5—and hence η_{14} is 2.

We use the bias coefficient $\gamma \geq 1$ to heuristically weigh mentions that carry more impact. If v_i mentions v_j, meaning that $\omega_{ij} > 0$, we believe this expresses v_i's intention to propagate information to v_j. Since v_j may not know or care about v_i and consequently may seldom or never mention v_i, the return mentions, measured by ω_{ji}, are (up)weighted by γ. Furthermore, if v_i and v_j share neighbors in the mentions network, the two users may have a closer relationship than other users with no shared mentioned Twitter users, and thus this component is weighted by γ as well. A Laplacian-style (+1) correction is used when there are no counter mentions or no mutual mentions. Note that for $\gamma = 1$, d_{ij} is an unbiased Brownian distance since ω_{ij}, ω_{ji}, and η_{ij} will have the same weight.

3.2 Trust functions and GBM

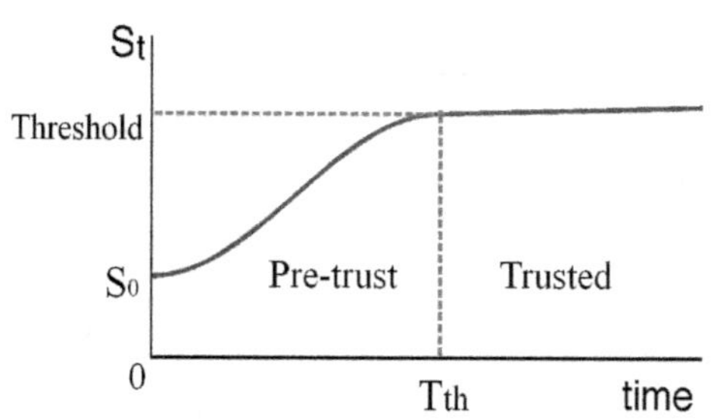

Figure 3: Trust function. A threshold defines the transition between the pre-trust and trusted period.

Next we introduce the notion of a trust function S_t which we use to model an individual user's agreement with an idea as expressed in tweets. (The trust function S_t is a function of the two entities between whom trust is modeled, but in this section we simplify the notation for ease of exposition.) We divide the trust process into a pre-trust period and a trusted period. In the pre-trust period, as a user receives new information, that user's trust, S_t, increases exponentially until S_t reaches the trust threshold at time T_{th} and enters the trusted period. In the trusted period, new information increases S_t linearly. For simplicity, an individual user cannot revoke trust once this threshold has been crossed. In our Twitter mentions network, a user's trust in a topic crosses the threshold when they have tweeted about it. During the pre-trust period, we model the trust function as follows (the coefficient μ accounts for change in the average value of this stochastic process):

$$\frac{dS_t}{S_t} = \mu dt \tag{2}$$

We then add a Wiener process W_t to account for stochasticity. According to the properties of a Wiener process [17], dW_t is essentially Gaussian white noise and contributes to our equation as:

$$\frac{dS_t}{S_t} = \mu dt + \sigma dW_t \tag{3}$$

In this way, we modeled the trust function S_t as a geometric Brownian motion (GBM) process which is a continuous-time stochastic process [17]. Per convention, we call μ the drift and σ the volatility. The drift represents deterministic trends while the volatility refers to the influence of unpredictable events in this model [25]. For simplicity, we consider μ and σ to be constant during the pre-trust period in this paper. (Our concern here primarily is with this period.)

According to Itō's theorem [17], given the initial value S_0, the above stochastic differential equation has the following analytic solution:

$$S_t = S_0 \exp\left(\left(\mu - \frac{\sigma^2}{2}\right)t + \sigma W_t\right) \tag{4}$$

The above solution for S_t is a log-normally distributed random variable with expected value and variance given as [17]:

$$E(S_t) = S_0 e^{\mu t} \tag{5}$$

$$Var(S_t) = S_0^2 e^{2\mu t}\left(e^{\sigma^2 t} - 1\right) \tag{6}$$

S_t is a geometric Brownian motion stochastic process, which is typically denoted as $\mathcal{B}(\mu, \sigma)$. In this paper we use an initial trust of $S_0 = 1$ without loss of generality.

3.3 GBM propagation

Suppose that user v_i posts a protest-related tweet at time t_0 which indicates that v_i has been recruited or infected. Whether v_i will infect its neighbor v_j depends on v_j's trust function with v_i. For instance, if v_j is a close friend of v_i, then it is more likely that v_j will be infected in a short time because of v_j's trust in v_i. But if v_j is not a very close friend of v_i, then it might take a long time to build v_j's trust with v_i and to accept v_i's status. Only after v_j's trust with v_i crosses some threshold, v_j gets infected.

For better quantitative analysis, we consider d_{ij} to be the trust threshold. After crossing this threshold, v_j will agree with v_i's opinion. According to the properties of GBMs, the trust function S_t grows continuously over time. This implies

```
input  : mentions network G(V, E), time step δt,
         propagation time T
output: infected users
for each infected user v_i ∈ V do
    for each non-infected user v_j ∈ N(v_i) do
        set t_ij = 0;
    end
    set v_i as not newly infected user
end
t = 0;
for t ≤ T do
    for each infected user v_i ∈ V do
        if v_i is a newly infected user then
            for each non-infected user v_j ∈ N(v_i) do
                set t_ij = 0;
            end
            set v_i as not newly infected user
        end
        for each non-infected user v_j ∈ N(v_i) do
            set t_ij = t_ij + δt
            ln(S_t^ij) ~ N((μ − σ²/2)t_ij, σ²t_ij)
            if ln(S_t^ij) ≥ d_ij then
                set user v_j as newly infected
            end
        end
    end
    t = t + δt;
end
```

Algorithm 1: GBM propagation algorithm

that, if some user is infected, all of that user's neighbors will eventually get infected given enough time for diffusion.

Since we assume a user cannot revoke trust, his or her status will never change once infected. Based on the above assumptions, we now detail our process for GBM propagation through the mentions network; see Algorithm 1. Since GBM is a time-continuous stochastic process, we discretize time using time steps of duration δt each. At the start of the simulation, all infected users are considered as newly infected users. Assume that the complete mass protest propagation duration is T. Once a user v_i becomes infected, the node is marked as a newly infected user, and the new status begins to affect the statuses of the neighbors, i.e., $N(v_i)$. For each user $v_j \in N(v_i)$, we use $t_{ij} = 0$ to initialize the time instant from which v_i begins to affect v_j. After all the time variables t_{ij} of $N(v_i)$ are so initialized, user v_i's status is updated to reflect that v_i is no longer a newly infected user, to avoid duplicate initializations.

Suppose that at current time t, v_j's trust with v_i is denoted as S_t^{ij}. According to the GBM properties, $ln(S_t^{ij})$ is a Gaussian variable given by:

$$ln(S_t^{ij}) \sim \mathcal{N}((\mu - \frac{\sigma^2}{2})t, \sigma^2 t) \quad (7)$$

If at time t, $ln(S_t^{ij}) \geq d_{ij}$, this means that v_j gets infected since v_j's trust with v_i is bigger than the distance d_{ij}. Now v_j begins to affect his or her own neighbors. Instead at time t, if $ln(S_t^{ij}) < d_{ij}$, then at the next time step, $t+\delta t$, the trust is still a Gaussian variable, but with higher expectation and variance:

$$ln(S_{t+\delta t}^{ij}) \sim \mathcal{N}((\mu - \frac{\sigma^2}{2})(t+\delta t), \sigma^2(t+\delta t)) \quad (8)$$

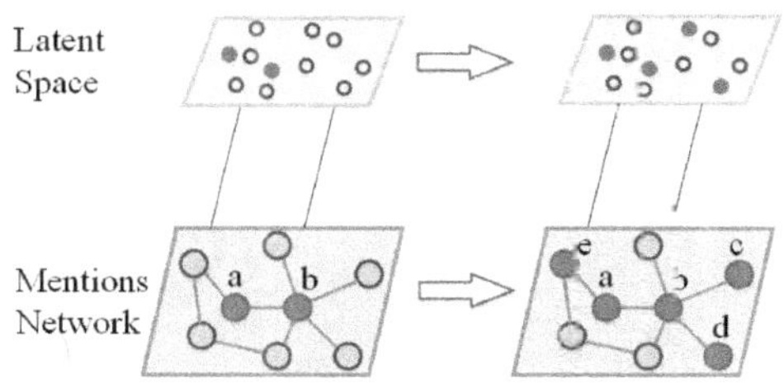

Figure 4: Bispace propagation model. In the latent space, users infections are explained by a Poisson model, and the red nodes denote the infected users from one time step to another. In the mentions network space, users are infected according to the GBM model. Here, the purple nodes (a, b, c, d, e) denote user infections explained by the GBM model.

3.4 GBM parameter estimation

We use past protest events in which Twitter played a significant role in propagation to train our GBM model parameters. For each user who gets infected we record their Brownian distance and infection time. Suppose v_j gets infected by v_i after time t_{ij}; then as per our propagation model, we claim that v_j's trust function S_t^{ij} with v_i holds:

$$ln(S_t^{ij}) \geq d_{ij} \quad (9)$$

where d_{ij} is the Brownian distance from v_i to v_j. For the convenience of parameter estimation, we can assume that $ln(S_t^{ij}) = d_{ij}$. It then follows that d_{ij} is a normally distributed random variable which can be expressed as:

$$d_{ij} \sim \mathcal{N}((\mu - \frac{\sigma^2}{2})t_{ij}, \sigma^2 t_{ij}) \quad (10)$$

Because during the parameter estimation process, for each infected user v_j, we are not interested in exactly which user gets v_j infected, we use $x_j = d_{ij}$, and $\tau_j = t_{ij}$ in the following part of this section for simplicity. The set of n users that are infected during the infection process have independent infection rates, and we get the following likelihood function:

$$\mathcal{L}(\theta, \sigma^2 \mid v_1, \ldots, v_n) = \prod_{j=1}^{n} \frac{1}{\sigma\sqrt{2\pi\tau_j}} exp(-\frac{(x_j - (\mu - \frac{\sigma^2}{2})\tau_j)^2}{2\sigma^2\tau_j})$$

The optimal estimators can be obtained by maximizing the above likelihood function. We differentiate the natural logarithm of the likelihood function above in terms of μ and σ, and set them to zeros. By solving the two equations simultaneously, we obtain the optimal estimators $\hat{\mu}$ and $\hat{\sigma^2}$.

4. BISPACE PROPAGATION MODEL

Many information diffusion models assume that propagation occurs over a single domain. However, it is hard to build a complete, exhaustive network of interactions. For instance, consider building a network based only on which Twitter users follow which other users. This network will miss interactions such as retweets and mentions and the effect of influences originating outside of Twitter. Therefore, considering only a single space will make it difficult to account for all possible factors that influence the spread of information. In this study, we propose a bispace diffusion

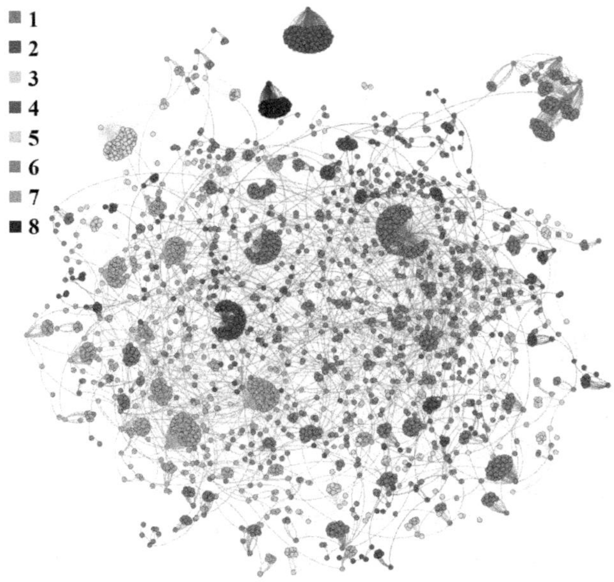

Figure 5: Major communities of teacher protest events (Sep 1 to Sep 12, 2013, Mexico).

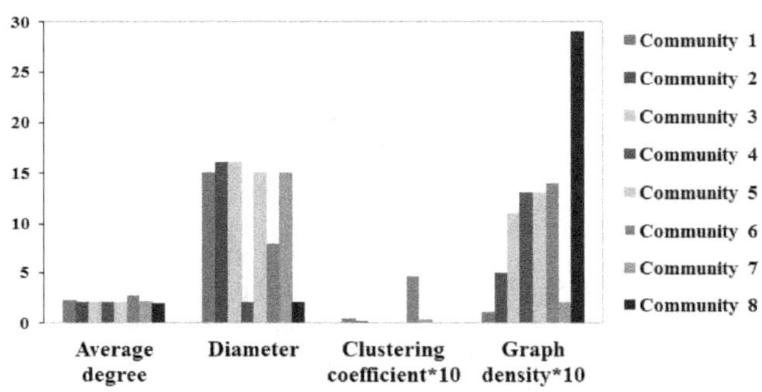

Figure 6: Key graph properties of communities underlying the Mexican teacher protest events.

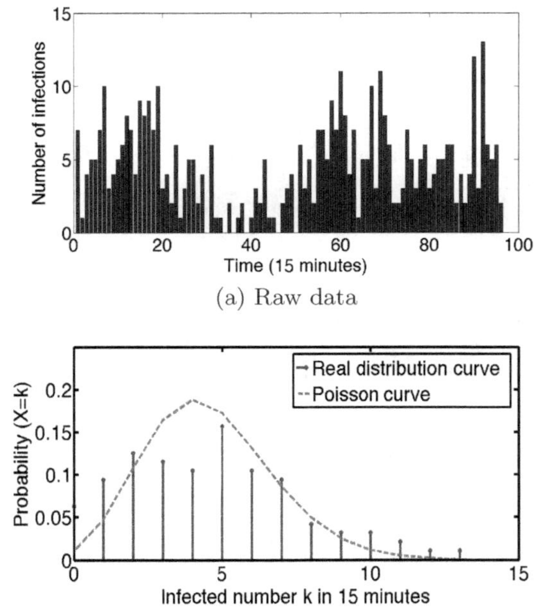

(a) Raw data

(b) Poisson distribution model

Figure 7: Poisson distribution in latent space propagation. (a) shows the raw data outside of the mentions network of teacher protest events on Sep 3, 2013. (b) shows the probability distribution of the number of infections.

model that accounts for two domains of diffusion: the observed social network and the latent space, as can be seen in Fig. 4. In our case, the observed user space is the Twitter mentions network, whereas the latent space refers to any interactions outside of this network. To account for varying diffusion dynamics, each space is intended to have its own propagation model. As described earlier, we model propagation through the Twitters mentions network as Geometric Brownian motion. We use the Poisson distribution to describe information propagation in the latent space.

4.1 GBM with Communities

Within networks, a community refers to the appearance of densely connected groups of vertices, with sparse connections between each group [16]. Instead of treating the whole network as a single propagation space, we use network structure to further split the network into communities. For our mentions network we use the Louvain method [1] for community detection to split the network into groups of users. For each community of users we can calculate classical graph features such as average degree, diameter, density, and clustering coefficient with which we can characterize them. In Fig. 6 we plot several features for each of the 8 communities found in the case study of Mexican teachers protest of 2013. Diameter $r = \max dist(v_i, v_j)$ is the length (in number of edges) of the longest geodesic path between any nodes v_i and v_j [15]. The clustering coefficient c_i is the proportion of node v_i's neighbors that are connected. Graph density is defined as $\frac{2|E|}{|V|(|V|-1)}$ where E is the number of edges and V is the number of nodes [21]. As shown in Fig. 6, diameter and graph density vary considerably.

With the observed network further split into several communities, each community is intended to have its own model parameters for GBM. In GBM, $ln(S_t^{ij})$ is a Gaussian distribution $\mathcal{N}((\mu - \frac{\sigma^2}{2})t, \sigma^2 t)$. We assume that each user within a community shares the same μ and σ so that each community has its characteristic μ and σ. As information propagates through the mentions network, it may pass through different communities. For an infected user v_i and one of the non-infected neighbors $v_j \in N(v_i)$, we assume the following propagation strategy:

- If v_i and v_j are in the same community c_i, the propagation process will follow $\mathcal{B}_{c_i}(\mu_{c_i}, \sigma_{c_i}^2)$.

- Propagation from one community to another happens as per the source community's model parameters. For instance, for propagation from community c_i to community c_j, we will use the source community c_i's GBM parameters.

- After information propagates into a different community, it will spread according to the new community's

Table 1: Mass protests studied in this paper.

No.	Event	Hashtags	Country	Affected cities	Event date(s)
1.	YoSoy132 student movement	#LaMarchaYoSoy132, #YoSoy132, #132, #soy132	Mexico	Nationwide	2012-05-17 to 2012-05-25
2.	Anti-government protests against tax reform and other policies pursued by President Juan Manuel Santos	#CacerolazoPaSantos, #5D	Colombia	Nationwide	2012-12-05
3.	Education reform protests by teachers	#ReformaEducativa	Mexico	Nationwide	2013-09-01
4.	Social protests against violence and crime	#UruguayosIndignados, #HartosDeLaViolencia	Uruguay	Montevideo	2012-05-14
5	Protests against the "media law"	#LorenzettiNoMeFalles, #MediosBuitres	Argentina	Buenos Aires	2012-11-27
6.	Protests against Senate President Renan Calheiros's election	#STFjulgueRenan, #SocorroJoaquim, #ForaRenan	Brazil	Nationwide	2013-02-22 to 2013-02-26
7.	Anti-government student protests against abuse of public media for election campaign	#ConatelCareTabla	Venezuela	Caracas	2013-03-20

parameters. Once the information has entered community c_j from community c_i, subsequent infections henceforth will use community c_j's parameters.

At each time step we use the μ and σ of any given node's current community for propagation from that node.

4.2 Propagation in Latent Space

As mentioned before, in the latent space, we are modeling unobserved interactions of users. Since there are so many factors that might affect the dissemination of information, such as news outlets, word-of-mouth, it is reasonable to assume that the probability of the number of newly infected users in a given time interval satisfies the Poisson distribution [9] in the latent space.

For each node in the mentions network, it can only be infected by the GBM process. However, for those isolated users outside the mentions network, it is only possible that they get infected via the mechanics of the Poisson process. (Recall that in the GBM process, users get infected primarily via their neighbors.) We use X to represent the number of infected users with time interval δt and so the probability of the infected users is given by:

$$\Pr(X = k) = \frac{\lambda^k e^{-\lambda}}{k!} \tag{11}$$

To obtain an estimator of λ, we can only use information about Twitter users who are outside the mentions network as our training dataset. We count the infected users outside the mentions network with time interval of 15 minutes during the Mexican teachers protest, and plot them as shown in Fig. 7(a). Adequately modelable by a Poisson distribution, we use the average value as the estimate of λ. Fig. 7(b) depicts the Poisson distribution fit with $\hat{\lambda} = 4.18$. If there are M_0 isolated users, the probability of each of these users to get infected in time interval δt is λ/M_0. To summarize, for any user not in the mentions network, infection is only possible via the Poisson process. For a user who is already in the mentions network, infection can only happen via the GBM process over the mentions network, as described earlier.

5. EXPERIMENTS

5.1 Dataset description

The study described in this paper uses two datasets: (i) a gold standard report (GSR) of social unrest events in Latin America provided by MITRE that we use to define major mass protest events, and (ii) tweets collected over 14 months from May 2012 to September 2013 from 20 Latin American countries.

The GSR documents each civil unrest event by location, date, type of protest, and specifies the national news articles that first reported the event. For protests that were prominent on Twitter, the GSR news articles often report hashtags which were used by protestors on social media. We selected only those GSR events for which we were able to find such hashtags. This process resulted in 34 unique hashtags related to 40 different protest that occurred in Latin America since May 2012. In Table 1 we list a few of these events from our study.

Our Twitter dataset was built by querying Datasift's streaming API. Each tweet payload includes crucial metadata along with the tweet's content. Though tweets from GPS-enabled devices include geographic coordinates, the percentage of such tweets in the collected sample was too low to be useful.

For this study, we further filtered tweets by removing those that do not contain hashtags relevant to a specific protest. Since most tweets do not have location data, we estimate their location by geocoding the tweet based on each tweet's content and properties of its user. We developed our own geocoding library that uses the World Gazetteer (http://archive.is/srm8P) database to lookup location names and geographic coordinates. Tweets can be geocoded to the user's location at the time of tweeting or a location of interest about which the user is tweeting. We focused on event ge-

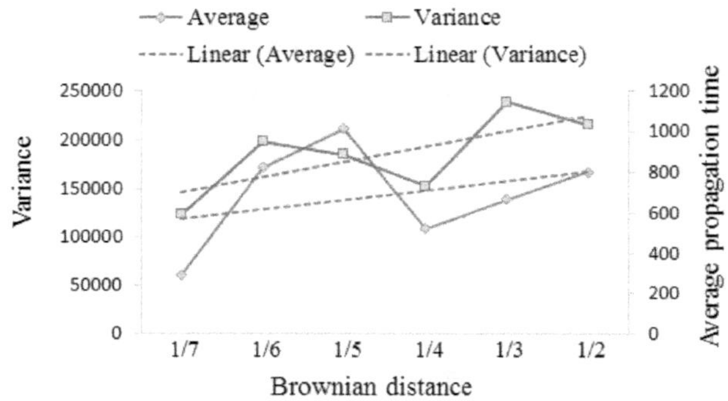

Figure 8: Brownian distance vs propagation time for teacher protest events.

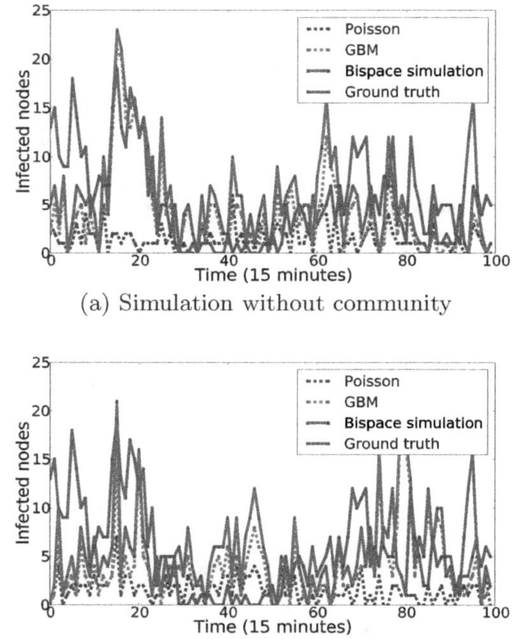

(a) Simulation without community

(b) Simulation with community

Figure 9: GBM and Poisson propagation simulation for Yosoy protests (Mexico) on May 19, 2012.

olocation, which looks for location or landmark names, such as *Plaza de la Independencia* or *Quito, Ecuador*, in a tweet's text. We generated a list of 2000 landmarks by extracting place names mentioned in GSR events which had high mutual information to civil unrest. In cases where no event location was found in a tweet's text, we use geo-coordinates or self-reported location string in the tweet's metadata.

Using the above pipeline we were able to extract and geolocate 20, 227, 830 unique users to build our mentions network from the filtered tweets that were spread over daily sub-networks.

5.2 GBM Diffusion Model

For each of our mass protest events, we filter by its specific keywords (hashtags) to obtain a set of relevant tweets and construct a mentions network from those tweets. We assume that information propagates from an initial infected user to other users through the network from one node to its neighbors. We build an adjacency matrix based on the mentions network and simulate the propagation using the GBM diffusion process as follows:

1. **Brownian distance:** The Brownian distance is intended to have an inverse relationship with mention frequency. As Fig. 8 shows, users with smaller Brownian distance have greater mention frequencies resulting in shorter mean propagation times with less variance. From Fig. 8, we can see that infection time and variance generally both increase with an increase in Brownian distance. Heuristically, more frequent mentions indicate stronger ties which leads to easier adoption of information.

2. **Propagation speed:** To evaluate our dynamic GBM infection process assumptions, we estimate the GBM parameters for different protest events and depict the GBM propagation curves in Figs. 9, 10, and 11. The blue curve depicts the Poisson propagation in latent space. The red curve depicts GBM propagation through the mentions network. The green curve is the overall simulation result while the magenta curve depicts the ground truth of the protest events process. By comparing the green and magenta curves, we can evaluate the effectiveness of our bispace model in simulating the mass protest events. As shown, we find that, given a mentions network, our bispace model can simulate the propagation speed at a reasonable scale, at the right magnitudes. As seen in Figs. 9(a), 10(a) and 11(a), we find that we can capture the burst of activity at the same time point as the ground truth during protest propagation.

5.3 GBM Diffusion with Communities

We were also able to observe the variation in μ and σ as community structure varies. In particular, community features like graph density and diameter as shown earlier in Fig. 6 may impact GBM propagation. We experimented with two modeling approaches: (i) one set of parameters for the whole network and (ii) different parameters for each community in the network. We ran simulations for both these situations, and plotted the results of the whole network vs. community-specific approach in Figs. 9, 10, and 11. Comparing these simulation results, we find the community approach performs better, especially at capturing peak values. Taking a closer look at Fig. 12, we observe that propagation time and speed of infection are different for each community and we are able to simulate local propagation more accurately, which can be seen, e.g., from Fig. 10(b), where the GBM with community method can simulate the burst propagation effectively, while the general GBM method (see Fig. 10(a)) fails to capture the exact peak time.

5.4 Latent Space Diffusion Model

We use the following steps to calculate the properties of the latent space for each event.

1. **Latent space:** The intent is to consider all possible external influences and latent interactions in this space. We split Twitter data into unique 15 minute

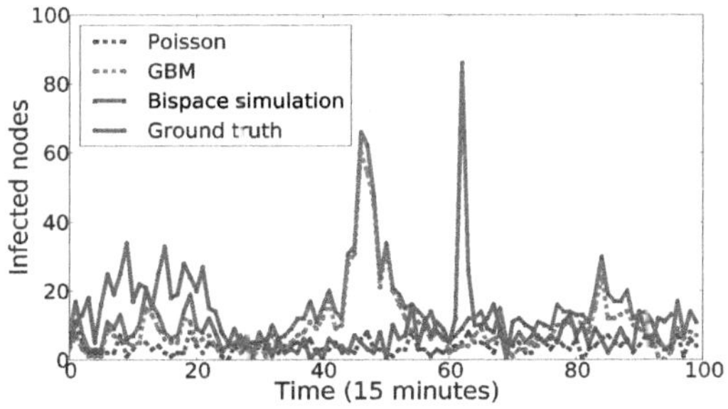

(a) Simulation without community

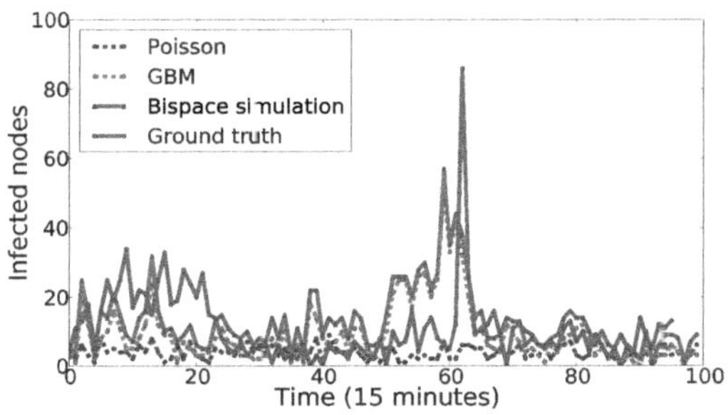

(b) Simulation with community

Figure 10: GBM and Poisson propagation simulation for teacher protests (Mexico) on Sep 1, 2013.

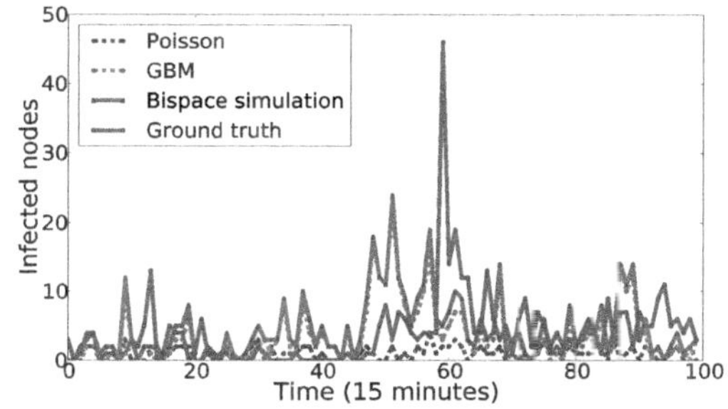

(a) Simulation without community

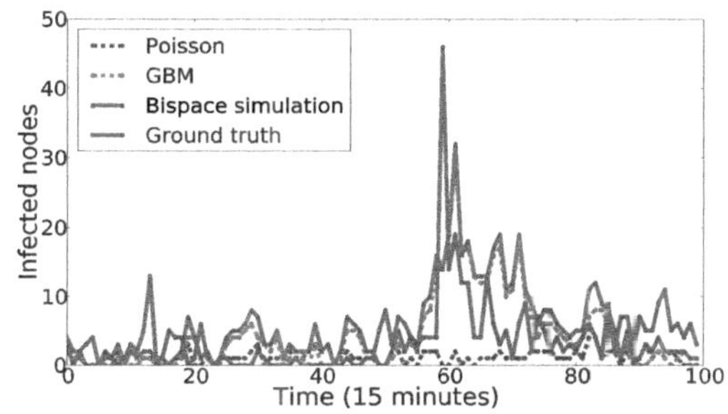

(b) Simulation with community

Figure 11: GBM and Poisson propagation simulation for Colombia protests on Dec 4, 2012.

intervals and count the total number of infected users in each interval.

2. **Normalize:** Twitter user activity varies based on time of day and day of week (see Fig. 13). For each 15 minute window from Step 1, we find the average number of tweets over a 4 week period and use this value to normalize the count. This baseline count of tweets over time in the latent space is close to the Poisson distribution. Fig. 7(a) shows an example of this baseline.

3. **Train:** Using one week's data split into 15 minute intervals, we train the Poisson distribution parameters. Fig. 7(b) shows that the training curve and ground truth curve can be matched quite well.

6. EVALUATION RESULTS

We present an exhaustive evaluation of our bispace simulation approach alongside various dimensions next

- **How effective is the performance of the bispace model?**

Recall that the bispace modeling is comprised of two independent process: the GBM simulation in the mentions network, and the Poisson process within the latent space. Given an initial mentions network, after training the GBM parameters of μ and σ, we proceed to conduct the GBM simulation. After estimating the Poisson parameter λ, we are able to do the Poisson simulation within latent space. We see that the GBM model is capable of capturing many mass protest scenarios, to the order of magnitude. Even though it cannot simulate the propagation speed accurately at every time point, the method is effective at capturing the total number of infected nodes with an accuracy of $[0.78, 0.95]$, as shown in Fig. 14.

- **How adept is the bispace model at capturing surge/burst moments? How reliable are the simulation results?**

Fig. 9 depicts the analsis of the YoSoy132 student movement, whose Twitter activity is generally tortuous, and the curve is full of surges and bursts. From Fig. 9 we see that the bispace model is capable of simulating the general surge trends. Comparing the bispace simulation results with ground truth, we can see at many time points, the bispace simulation matches the ground truth. Fig. 11 shows the second protest of people protesting against the government in Colombia; here the Twitter activity depicts a burst at a single time point which is hard to capture. We can see the bispace model did show there is a burst, but not at the precise time point, one of its current limitations.

- **Is the performance of the model better taking into account community structure?**

After numerous experiments, we plot the accuracy distribution of both approaches for all our mass protest situations in Fig. 14. Although the accuracies are sometimes interspersed, we can see that in overall the community model generally has a higher accuracy.

- **Can the bispace model simulate the propagation path?**

In addition to comparing the simulated counts of tweets over time with ground truth values, we can also compare the

Table 2: GBM simulation results for teacher protest events on Sep 2, 2013.

	Average degree	Diameter	Graph density	Connected components	Average clustering coefficient	Average path length
Simulation	1.791	11	0.002	183	0.083	4.786
Ground truth	1.726	18	0.002	204	0.008	6.261

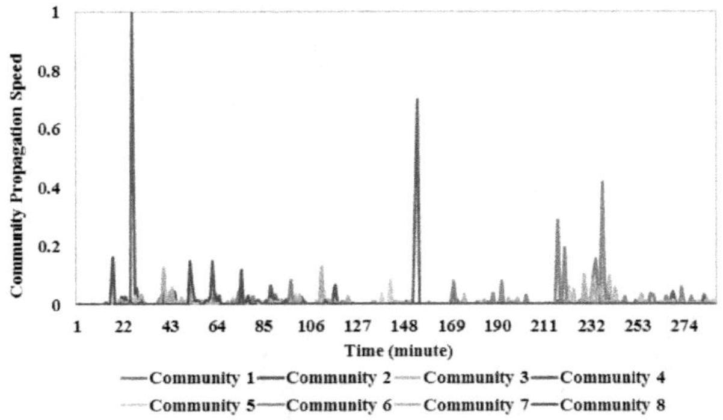

Figure 12: Normalized mass-protest propagation speed for major communities during teacher protest events.

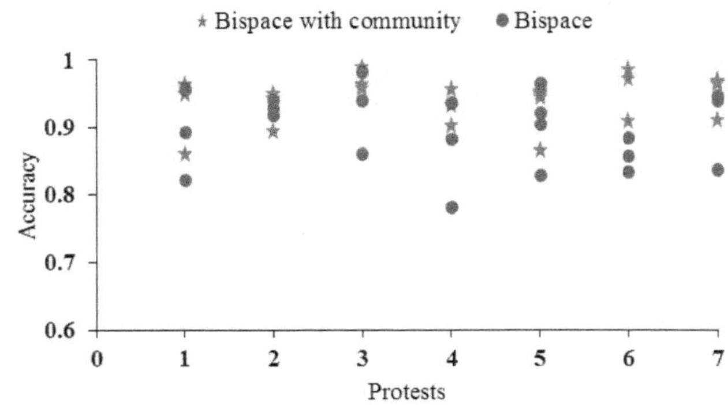

Figure 14: Performance accuracy of the bispace model for the 7 protest scenarios considered here, with and without community structure.

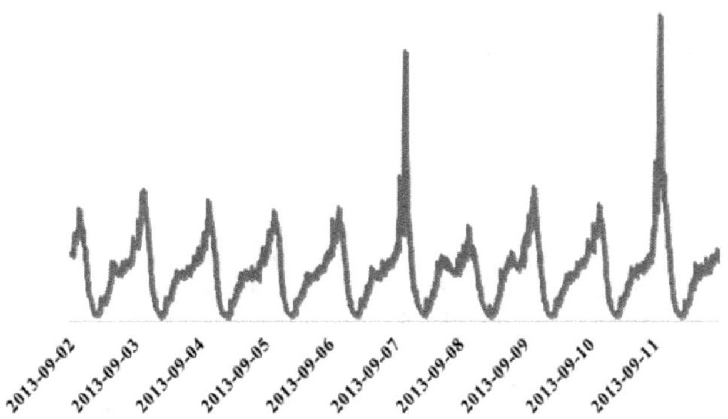

Figure 13: Total tweets over time from Sep 2 to Sep 11, 2013 (Mexico).

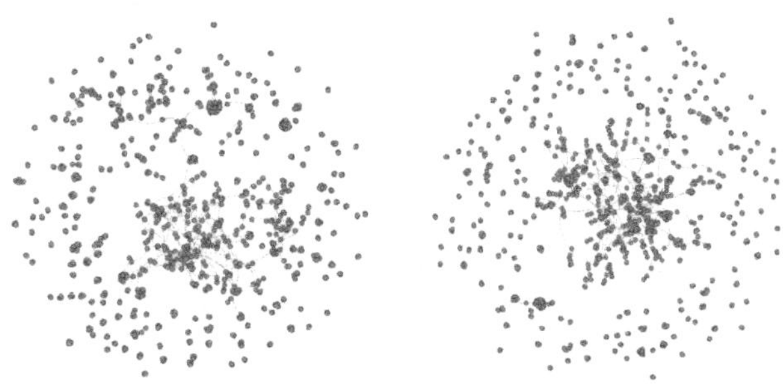

(a) Simulation results (b) Truly infected nodes

Figure 15: Bispace model simulation results compared against ground truth infected nodes for the Mexican teacher protest events.

propagation path generated by the simulation against the actual propagation path through the mentions network. In Fig. 15 we can obtain a sense of the type of infection network bispace modeling creates as compared with the actual network. The simulation produces networks with relatively accurate paths and relevant characteristics as shown in Table 2. The component to which a user belongs is that of neighbors who can be reached from connected paths running along edges of the graph [15].

- **Between the geometric Brownian model and Poisson propagation approaches, which model is more dominant during the simulation process?**

From Figs. 9, 10, 11, by observing the blue dashed line (Poisson) and red dashed line (GBM), we can see that the Poisson process shows a mild activity, while the GBM model serves as the dominant component which can capture the moments of key surges.

7. DISCUSSION

In this paper, we have characterized mass protest propagation using a bispace model comprising an observed mentions network space and a latent space. We have introduced a trust function to simulate propagation in observed space using a geometric Brownian motion diffusion process which can be further extended to support communities with different propagation parameters per community. We considered the latent space of all interactions outside the mentions network to be a Poisson distribution process. We have shown how the GBM diffusion model offers a new approach for modeling propagation through social networks like Twitter. Through our experiments, we find that the time required for spread of protest information through such networks is dependent on the network's substructures. Furthermore, we find that modeling the diffusion process on a community basis provides better results than the assumption that all nodes in the network spread information in the same way.

In future work, we hope to further characterize the hidden network with the goal of uncovering specific latent variables. Additionally, we envision applying the GBM model to other networks, such as the Twitter follower network, to identify those paths most susceptible to information dissemination. Finally, we desire to compare propagation of mass protest language against other themes, such as celebratory events, to aid in determining correlations between topic or sentiment and the resulting social media diffusion.

Acknowledgments

This work was partially supported by the NSF via grant IIS-1353346 and the Intelligence Advanced Research Projects Activity (IARPA) via Department of Interior National Business Center (DoI/NBC) contract number D12PC000337. The US Government is authorized to reproduce and distribute reprints for Governmental purposes notwithstanding any copyright annotation thereon. The views and conclusions contained herein are those of the authors and should not be interpreted as necessarily representing the official policies or endorsements, either expressed or implied, of NSF, IARPA, DoI/NBC, or the US Government.

8. REFERENCES

[1] V. D. Blondel, J.-L. Guillaume, R. Lambiotte, and E. Lefebvre. Fast unfolding of communities in large networks. *Journal of Statistical Mechanics: Theory and Experiment*, 2008(10):P10008, 2008.

[2] R. M. Bond, C. J. Fariss, J. J. Jones, A. D. Kramer, C. Marlow, J. E. Settle, and J. H. Fowler. A 61-million-person experiment in social influence and political mobilization. *Nature*, 489(7415):295–298, 2012.

[3] H. Castellini and L. Romanelli. On the propagation of social epidemics in social networks under SIR model. *eprint arXiv:nlin/0703053*, Mar. 2007.

[4] M. D. Conover, E. Ferrara, F. Menczer, and A. Flammini. The digital evolution of occupy wall street. *PloS one*, 8(5):e64679, 2013.

[5] R. Crane and D. Sornette. Robust dynamic classes revealed by measuring the response function of a social system. *PNAS*, 105(41):15649–15653, 2008.

[6] S. González-Bailón, J. Borge-Holthoefer, A. Rivero, and Y. Moreno. The dynamics of protest recruitment through an online network. *Scientific reports*, 1, 2011.

[7] A. Guille, H. Hacid, C. Favre, and D. A. Zighed. Information diffusion in online social networks: A survey. *ACM SIGMOD Record*, 42(1):17–28, 2013.

[8] H. Zhou. Network landscape from a brownian particle's perspective. *Physical Review E*, 67(4):041908, 2003.

[9] F. A. Haight and F. A. Haight. *Handbook of the Poisson distribution*. Wiley New York, 1967.

[10] A. L. Hill, D. G. Rand, M. A. Nowak, and N. A. Christakis. Emotions as infectious diseases in a large social network: the sisa model. *Proc. Royal Society B: Biological Sciences*, 277(1701):3827–3835, 2010.

[11] T. Iwata, A. Shah, and Z. Ghahramani. Discovering latent influence in online social activities via shared cascade poisson processes. In *Proc. KDD'13*, pages 266–274, 2013.

[12] D. Kempe, J. Kleinberg, and É. Tardos. Maximizing the spread of influence through a social network. In *Proc. KDD' 03*, pages 137–146. ACM, 2003.

[13] Y. Matsubara, Y. Sakurai, B. A. Prakash, L. Li, and C. Faloutsos. Rise and fall patterns of information diffusion: model and implications. In *Proc. KDD'12*, pages 6–14. ACM, 2012.

[14] S. A. Myers, C. Zhu, and J. Leskovec. Information diffusion and external influence in networks. In *Proc. KDD'12*, pages 33–41, 2012.

[15] M. E. Newman. The structure and function of complex networks. *SIAM review*, 45(2):167–256, 2003.

[16] M. E. Newman. Modularity and community structure in networks. *PNAS*, 103(23):8577–8582, 2006.

[17] B. Øksendal. *Stochastic differential equations*. Springer, 2003.

[18] P. E. Oliver and D. J. Myers. Diffusion models of cycles of protest as a theory of social movements. *Presented at the Congress of the International Sociological Association*, 1998.

[19] M. G. Rodriguez, J. Leskovec, and B. Schölkopf. Modeling information propagation with survival theory. In *Proc. ICML'13*, pages 666–674, 2013.

[20] A. Saad-Filho. Mass protests under 'left neoliberalism': Brazil, june-july 2013. *Critical Sociology*, 39(5):657–669, 2013.

[21] J. Scott and P. J. Carrington. *The SAGE handbook of social network analysis*. SAGE publications, 2011.

[22] Y. Singer. How to win friends and influence people, truthfully: influence maximization mechanisms for social networks. In *Proc. WSDM'12*, pages 733–742. ACM, 2012.

[23] P. Tankov. *Financial modelling with jump processes*. CRC Press, 2004.

[24] Z. Tufekci and C. Wilson. Social media and the decision to participate in political protest: Observations from Tahrir square. *Journal of Communication*, 62(2):363–379, 2012.

[25] U. F. Wiersema. *Brownian motion calculus*. Wiley. com, 2008.

[26] H. Zhou. Distance, dissimilarity index, and network community structure. *Physical Review E*, 67(6):061901, 2003.

[27] H. Zhou and R. Lipowsky. Network brownian motion: A new method to measure vertex-vertex proximity and to identify communities and subcommunities. In *Proc. ICCS'04*, pages 1062–1069. Springer, 2004.

Shallow Semantic Parsing of Product Offering Titles (*for better automatic hyperlink insertion*)

Gabor Melli
VigLink Inc.
539 Bryant St.
San Francisco, CA USA
gmelli@viglink.com

ABSTRACT

With billions of database-generated pages on the Web where consumers can readily add priced product offerings to their virtual shopping cart, several opportunities will become possible once we can automatically recognize what exactly is being offered for sale on each page. We present a case study of a deployed data-driven system that first chunks individual titles into semantically classified sub-segments, and then uses this information to improve a hyperlink insertion service.

To accomplish this process, we propose an annotation structure that is general enough to apply to offering titles from most e-commerce industries while also being specific enough to identify useful semantics about each offer. To automate the parsing task we apply the best-practices approach of training a supervised conditional random fields model and discover that creating separate prediction models for some of the industries along with the use of model-ensembles achieves the best performance to date.

We further report on a real-world application of the trained parser to the task of growing a lexical dictionary of product-related terms which critically provides background knowledge to an affiliate-marketing hyperlink insertion service. On a regular basis we apply the parser to offering titles to produce a large set of labeled terms. From these candidates we select the most confidently predicted novel terms for review by crowd-sourced annotators. The agreed on terms are then added into a dictionary which significantly improves the performance of the link-insertion service. Finally, to continually improve system performance, we retrain the model in an online fashion by performing additional annotations on titles with incorrect predictions on each batch.

Categories and Subject Descriptors

H.3.3 [**Information Storage and Retrieval**]: Information Search and Retrieval—*Information filtering*; I.2.7 [**Artificial Intelligence**]: Natural Language Processing—*text analysis*

KDD'14, August 24–27, 2014, New York, New York, USA
ACM 978-1-4503-2956-9/14/08.
http://dx.doi.org/10.1145/2623330.2623343.

General Terms

Algorithms, Experimentation, Case-study

Keywords

shallow semantic parsing; automated terminology extraction; composite CRF ensembles; product offer titles; hyperlink insertion

1. INTRODUCTION

With billions of database-generated pages on the Web where consumers can readily add priced product offerings to their virtual shopping cart, several opportunities will become possible once we can automatically recognize what exactly is being offered for sale on each page. While there has been a significant amount of work reported on how to extract aggregate-level information about products (and the sentiments expressed about them) from webpage content, especially for electronic products, far less work has been reported on the task of automatically reading and recognizing all of the characteristics of any individual offering. When feasible, this capability will significantly aid in such tasks as terminology extraction and cross-seller product offering searches.

A natural place to begin is to characterize the information available within product offering *titles* such as: "*The Show (Album Version)*" and "*Pro Digital Lens Hood for VIXIA HF S10, S100 Flash Camcorders (1-year wrty from e-sekuro).*" These titles, along with price, product category, and seller name, are prevalent pieces of information available on the Web [1]. While titles are a form of unstructured text, their central role in consumer decision making and search engine rank performance, sellers are motivated to ensure that its text is rich in relevant information while also being easy to read/parse. Further, we will show, these titles can be interpreted to have structure in the form of semantic terms that refer to brands, features and a few other semantic classes, along with some syntactic terms (such as "*for*"). Titles, as with full sentences, can also be understood at a higher semantic parsing structure, but simply being able to automatically identify the structure at shallow-level can be useful to real-world applications. In this paper we present a case study of a deployed data-driven system that grows a

[1]these four data items, for example, are available in a product search such as google.com/search?tbm=shop&q=Lauren+black+dress, and also in Amazon's product API service http://www.google.com/search?q=RG_Small.html

product-related terms dictionary by parsing product offering titles in order to improve an affiliate-marketing link insertion service that inserts affiliated hyperlinks to relevant offers.[2].

Although the semantic chunking of offering titles is a simpler task than the chunking of natural language sentences, even in this constrained domain there is no preexisting formal parser available to apply to the task; nor, as we will show in the experiments section, does it appear feasible to manually develop one. Given our pragmatic ambitions, we followed the best-practices approach of training a sequence BIO tagging model [19]. Further, we pursue the approach taken in natural language processing (NLP) of first chunking a text string as a preprocessing step to additional tasks [1]. As Abney writes: "*[I begin] [with an intuition]: [when I read] [a sentence], [I read it] [a chunk] [at a time]*". For us the task of shallow semantic offering title parsing appears to also be naturally commenced with a chunking step. The offering shown earlier, for example, could be semantically segmented as follows: "*[Pro Digital] [black] [Lens Hood] [for] [Canon] [VIXIA] [HF S10], [HF S100] [Flash Camcorders] ([1-year wrty.]) [from] [e-sekuro]*.". Further, just as subsequent work in NLP added the requirement to label segments with their phrase type (e.g. NP-chunk, VP-chunk, etc.) [14], the semantic segments in a title could also be mapped to semantic classes. Given a set of semantic classes such as *product category*/PC, *product feature*/PF, etc. (which we define in section 2) the sample title can now be further annotated as follows: "[*Pro Digital*]^{BN} [*black*]^{PF} [*Lens Hood*]^{PF} [*for*]^{FT} [*Canon*]^{BN} [*VIXIA*]^{PL} [*HF S10*]^{PI}, [*HF S100*]^{PI} [*Flash Camcorders*]^{PC} ([*1-year wrty.*]^{OF}) [*from*]^{FT} [*e-sekuro.com*]^{ME}".

In NLP a best-practices approach to perform chunking is to use supervised sequence tagging models, such as a linear chain conditional random fields (CRFs) [18]. Because state-of-the-art systems do not generally approximate expert-level performance, even with a significant amount of labeled and unlabeled data [8], most real-word applications need to prepare for error rates that are higher than those achieved by human annotators. One way to address this challenge is to associate a confidence score with each predicted chunk so that only high-confidence predictions are provided to consuming processes. In our case we apply a set of models (a model ensemble) to naturally produce a confidence score.

Given a system that can chunk offerings titles into rankable terms one can begin to apply it to real-world tasks, such as the growing of a domain-specific dictionary of categorized consumer product-related terms. Having such a terms database can be very useful in automation of many consumer e-commerce related tasks. Once a system knows that "*Canon*" is a brand (BN), that "*Vixia*" is a product line (PL), that "*flash camcorder*" is a product category (PC) and that "*high def*" is a product feature (PF), then a data-driven system can more easily infer the meaning of a phrase such as "*Canon Vixia high-def flash camcorder*". Unfortunately, updating and managing a terminological dictionary remains a time-consuming process [5]. With hundreds of thousands of product-related terms, it is essential to enhance the dictionary in a cost-effective manner. By parsing hundreds of thousands of titles, we believed, many high-quality candidate terms could be cheaply discovered and inserted into the dictionary.

The remainder of this paper is structured as follows: Section 2 defines the proposed annotation style in detail; Section 3 describes our algorithmic solution to the chunking task; Section 4 describes our solution to the addition of parsed terms into the dictionary, including the use of a crowdsourcing-based filter; Section 5 analyses the parser's intrinsic performance on manually annotated data; Section 6 analyses the return-on-investment from the added terms; and Section 7 concludes the paper with future possible directions.

2. ANNOTATING OFFERING TITLES

In this section we define our proposed annotation framework to the task of chunking product offering titles into their granular terms. Our main challenge is to define a term typing system that balances the requirement to handle titles from a diverse set of industries; to also identify helpful semantic characterization of the offer; and to provide intuitive guidelines to human annotators.

Based on prior work in the modeling of product databases and product data management [9] and through iterative experimentation, we propose that product offering titles can be exhaustively and beneficially decomposed into token substrings from the eight term types described below.

We observe in advance that any given title can reference zero or more of the eight term classes - no class is mandatory, though at least one must be present. Further, a given term can belong to more than one term type (famously the term "*apple*" can refer to a food category, a brand, a merchant, and even a scent-type product feature).

1. A *product identifying term* (PI) is a term that identifies any product in the offering. Electronic products, for example, are known to typically include an identifying product code, such as "*LS-606M*, "*4s*", or "*s4*" in their names. Other industries such as publishing and entertainment can use the entire title as a product identifier, such as "*Les Miserables*" (which could ambiguously refer to the book, the movie, or the recorded play by the same title). Finally, industries such as fashion typically do not include any identifying terms in their titles.

2. A *product feature term* (PF) is a term that refers to a property of any product mentioned in the offering. Typical product feature terms in offers can refer to size ("*short*","*14-42mm*"), capacity ("*50Gb*"), color ("*mustard on black*"), style ("*coupe*"), and fragrance ("*green tea*", "*apple*").

3. A *product category term* (PC) is a term that refers to a group of products with some substitutability. Examples include "*hockey helmet*", "*apple*" (the edible type). This class can require some additional level of domain-expertise to recognize, for example, that a "*hockey helmet*" is not substitutable with a "*bike helmet*" while a "*red*^{PF} *helmet*^{PC}" can be substituted for a *black*^{PF} *helmet*^{PC}" at the category-level.

4. A *product brand term* (BN) is a term that refers to a manufacturer of a product. Examples include: "*Apple*" and "*Mercedes Benz*".

[2]an affiliated hyperlink is encoded with sufficient information for a seller to reward the website publisher with some commission related to the value of "introducing" the consumer to the seller. Additional information on the service can be found here http://viglink.com/products/insert

Table 1: Examples of offering titles annotated using our framework. Square brackets indicate multi-token terms

Annotated product offering title	Industry
Tripp^{PI} *LS606M*^{PF} [*600 watt*]^{PC} [*Line Conditioner*]^{PF} [*6 Outlet*]^{PF} [*120 volt*]^{QQ}	Electronics
Samsung^{PF} *51-Inch*^{PF} *720p*^{PF} *600Hz*^{PF} *Plasma*^{PF} *HDTV*^{PC} (*Black*^{PF})	Electronics
[*Wheelskins*]^{PF} [*Genuine Deerskin*]^{PC} [*DRIVING GLOVES*]^{PC} - *Tan*^{PF} ([*Size Large*]^{PF})	Automotive
[*1990-1997*]^{PF} [*Mazda*]^{BN} [*Miata*]^{PL} *AxleBack*^{PL} [*Exhaust Bolt*]^{PC} *on*^{FT} *Muffler*^{PC}	Automotive
[*Cloudy with a Chance of Meatballs*]^{PI} (*Two-Disc*^{PF} [*Blu-ray / DVD Combo*]^{PF})	Entertainment
[*A Pius Man : A Holy Thriller*]^{PI} ([*The Pius Trilogy*]^{PL}) ([*PF*| *Volume 1*]^{PF})	Books
[*Amazing Herbs*]^{BN} [*Black Seed*]^{PF} [*Cold-Pressed Oil*]^{PC} - *32oz*^{PF}	Health & Beauty
([*180 days wrty.*]^{OF}) *ZeroLemon*^{BN} *LG*^{BN} *Nexus*^{PL} *4*^{PI} *Juicer*^{PL} [*Battery Case*]^{PC}	Mobile
[*WORLDS ONLY*]^{OF} *NEXUS*^{PL} *4*^{PI} [*BATTERY CASE*]^{PC} (*LG-N4-BattCase-black*^{PI})	Mobile
[*Kenneth Cole*]^{BN} *REACTION*^{PL} *men's*^{PF} *Cufflinks*^{PC}, *Silver*^{PF}, [*One Size*]^{PF}	Fashion

5. A *product line term* (`PL`) is a term that refers to a narrowly defined sub-brand. The term must generally be prefixable by the brand name, such as how "*Galaxy*" can be rewritten as *Samsung Galaxy*^{PL} *S4*) and "*W126*" as *1989 Mercedes Benz W126*^{PL} *v8 coupe*. The product line term type also accounts for celebrities whose name is being branded with a product, such as "*Alicia Keys*^{PL} *Rebook sneakers*". This category could be merged into the brand type, but we opted to separate it at this step.

6. A *merchant term* (`ME`) is a term that refers to a merchant/seller mentioned in the title, or the given offer of possibly of a bundled item, such as a warranty provider.

7. An *offering feature term* (`OF`) is a term added by the merchant to differentiate their offering from some other seller's offering of the same underlying product. Common terms include warranty periods, temporary discounts, and subjective attributes ("*lovely*", "*stylish*").

8. A *functional term* (`FT`) is a term that plays a syntactic role in the title. Examples include: "*of*", "*and*", "*without*", "*with*", and "*includes*".

Several examples of annotated product offering titles are presented in table 1.

3. AUTOMATICALLY CHUNKING TITLES

We opted to apply the best-practices approach of BIO tagging, in which a string is first tokenized, and then a sequential classification/tagging model is required to tag each token with either a `B`, `I`, or `O` depending on whether the given token either *begins* a chunk, is *inside* a chunk, or is *outside* of any chunk. When the task also requires that chunks be classified then the labels are updated encode the relevant term class. In our case, with eight term types, each token must be labeled with one of seventeen possible labels: {`O`, `B-PI`, `I-PI`, `B-PF`, `I-PF`, `B-PC`, ..., `I-FT`}. Specifically, we train a linear-chain conditional random field model on a manually annotated training dataset, as originally proposed in [18].

The remaining decision for applying a supervised model is to select the predictor features associated with each token and the size of the before/after token window. Here again, we leverage the best-practices of features reported to be helpful in NP-chunking [18] and named entity recognition (NER) [11, 15]. Indeed, most of features that we use are contained in the published baseline recognizer for the ICDM-2012 CPROD1 contest[3] [10].

For our task, which involves shorter text items and more varied patterns, we modified the `eosTokFeat.pl`[4] from the contest with three additional features. Two of the new features simply the offset of the token from the edge of the token string. This feature-type is used in sentence-centric chunking and was not used in the `CPROD1` contest. The other new feature is global feature based on the offerings industry (such as Electronics, Books, or Automotive). As seen in table 1, the annotation pattern for an offering's title can differ significantly based on their industry - book and movies can have long product identifiers. By introducing this feature we hope that the model can account for these patterns.

The new features are further described below:

1. *Previous Tokens* (`LEFTOFF`): The number of tokens into the title. For example, the fourth token in a title receives the label `4`.

2. *Remaining Tokens* (`RIGHTOFF`): The number of tokens remaining in the title. For example, the fourth-to-last token receives the label `4`.

3. *Industry* (`INDUSTRY`): The code of the titleś industry. For example, every token of a book title receives the code `BK`.

Clearly there are additional state-of-the-art techniques that we could apply, but we believed (given our Agile develop-

[3]the original program to generate those features `eosTokFeat.pl` can be found at http://kaggle.com/c/cprod1/forums/t/2287/crf-based-baseline2-published

[4]the updated featurization program and all code used in the experimental study is available at https://dropbox.com/sh/q8cyv0wfuyg0han/sXZ95rOUC8

ment mindset) that this best-practices approach should be good enough to prove the business value of the solution.

3.1 Sequential Tagging Model Ensembles

As presented, the trained sequence tagging model does not provide a confidence likelihood estimate with each predicted segment. Such an estimate can be helpful for many downstream tasks that may use title parser. For our dictionary population task, for example, where we require high-precision predictions, a confidence ranking score enables us to better expend our resources on predictions that will be more likely to be accepted into the dictionary. While there are methods to extract likelihood estimates from a trained CRF model, such as the Constrained Forward Backward algorithm (CFB) [3] that computes the total weight of all paths constrained by the states of our segments, these methods are not generally available in CRF software libraries and can increase the processing time.

An alternative approach that we investigate is to train an ensemble of models, and to report a confidence score based on the number of models that agree for each prediction [12]. Unfortunately, there is no agreed-on best-practice approach to combining the predictions of a set of sequence tagging models[5]. However, a simple voting approach can be naturally implemented by ranking predictions based on the proportion of models in agreement. If all models agree on a segment then associate a score of 1; if only four fifths of the models agree then associate a confidence score of 0.8. In our case, we opted to use the five models trained during a five-fold cross validation analysis which reports an in-sample F_1 (our "unit test" of each iteration is that the F_1 be higher than a threshold of 50).

4. DICTIONARY UPDATES

Now that we can parse offering titles and rank the predictions, we are ready to apply it to a real-world problem. Several business processes could benefit from this capability at our organization. The first that we explore is the addition of terms into a domain-specific dictionary that is referenced by our hyperlink-insertion service. A more complete dictionary improves the chances of recognizing mentions of product related terms in text. Managing such a large dictionary however can be a time-consuming process [16], especially if a low error-rate is required. In our case errors can result in bad user experiences to the visitors of our customer's webpages. If a term such as "*Christmas*" were accidentally inserted into our dictionary as a product category (`PC`) rather than, say, of a product feature (`PF`), then the term becomes a viable candidate for hyperlink insertion when encountered in a webpage, and then be linked to some random (if still Christmassy) product. Further, the value of adding terms diminishes over time as fewer and fewer high-value terms remain and more esoteric terms are added. Given the expectation of erroneous predictions, we opted to include a manual review step but of such high-confidence terms that the time spent per term would be very low.

We start the addition process by retrieving the titles of the most popularly clicked links to seller offerings[6] because popular destinations are more likely to contain high-value terms that are more likely to result in the insertion of additional high-value links. Each week we parse a set of approximately ten-thousand titles and retain the terms with a confidence score higher than 50% (more than half the ensemble models agree on the prediction) that are not yet present in the dictionary. This step currently produces approximately two-thousand candidate terms per week, such as: {`term=`"*table saw*", `type=PC`, `industry=HG`, `score=0.80` `quantity=72`}, ranked in descending order of their quantity (more popular terms should be entered ahead of less popular ones).

4.1 Crowd-sourced Candidate Review

Because of the requirement for low-error rate of dictionary term addition and the low marginal value per individual addition, we use a web-based crowdsourcing service to manually review each of these terms to further filter the terms that are likely to be correct[7]. These online marketplaces match *human intelligence micro-tasks* (HITs) posted by organizations with workers, and one of the areas that these services have been successfully applied to is natural language annotation [2]. A best-practice approach is to have w-workers, with typically $2 \leq w \leq 3$, perform each micro-task in order to (as with an ensemble) determine which predictions have high-confidence and to more readily identify free-riding workers. We opted for $w = 3$ workers per task.

The basic questionnaire format that we selected was for the worker to provide feedback on whether a given term was of the given offering-term type (feature, category, etc.) within a given industry (electronics, books, etc.). For example: "*Is the term <u>two-disk</u> a <u>product feature</u> in the <u>Arts & Entertainment</u> industry?*" We further experimented with whether to make it a binary-classification task (`TRUE` or `FALSE`) or to make it a multi-label classification one (`Definitely`, `Likely`, `Maybe`, `Unlikely`, and `No`). We opted for the multi-label approach because it resulted in slightly higher F_1, where agreement required two of the workers to select either `Definitely` or `Likely` for accepted predictions. Approximately six hundred terms currently survive this filtering step. The accepted terms are now manually reviewed by an internal annotator to our organization, but by now all of them are entered into the dictionary.

In terms of the fine-tuning of the crowdsourced solution, we tested three different levels of payments per micro-task: \$0.01, \$0.02 and \$0.05 and found that a payment of \$0.01 achieved the highest number of additional terms per investment. In the hope of detecting and rejecting free-riders (who sloppily speed through HITs) we identify and block any worker who replies differently than the two other annotators more than half of the time on a batch in which they attempt more than thirty HITs.

4.2 Active Iterative (Re)Training

As with many real-world predictive modeling applications, our situation benefited from continuous improvement of our models [17]. Rather than creating a single training dataset to train our model from, we iteratively updated the training set with titles in which the existing model performed poorly on. Every week we select approximately one-hundred titles that contain a term confidently predicted by the ensemble-based parser but that a majority of the crowdsourced workers agreed on as being an incorrect prediction. The dataset

[5]this topic appears to be an open research problem

[6]our click-log contains billions of seller URLs from which we can readily identify popular offerings

[7]http://mturk.amazon.com

produced by this process is further discussed in the next section on experiments.

5. INTRINSIC PERFORMANCE ANALYSIS

This section evaluates the performance of the shallow-semantic parser on a pre-annotated dataset, while the next section evaluates the impact of using the parser on a real-world application.

Our focus of the analysis is on ways to better structure the trained parser such that it produces more accurate predictions from the provided training data.[8]

5.1 Datasets

For the evaluation we used a dataset with 2,437 annotated product titles[9]. As in most real-world settings the annotated dataset evolved and grew over time, from a starting seed of records to test the feasibility of training a parser with useful accuracy. Afterwards, titles were added as described earlier in the section on iterative retraining[10]. Each record is categorized into one of nineteen typically high-level industries based on an internally managed mapping table (for example, "Computers" → "CE").

Table 2 shows the distribution of titles and of term types by the different industry labels[11]. The table shows that there is a clear skew in record distributions - with the categories of Consumer Electronics and Book accounting for more than half of the records (750+566), and product features (PF) dominating the types of terms annotated. From the product term distributions by industry we further notice a few outliers: Books and Arts & Entertainment are dominated by `PI` terms; while alternatively Fashion and Food records have relatively few `PI` terms.

5.2 Performance Measure

A standard measure of performance for systems that must segment and label text is the harmonic mean between the precision (P) and recall (R) of all predictions: $F_1 = \frac{2RP}{R+P}$. To calculate this measure we used the widely use evaluation tool from the CoNLL-2000 Shared Task [12].

5.3 Cross-validation (+ by Industry)

We performed a 5-fold cross-valuation study on the dataset. Table 3 reports the average F_1 performance of five CRF models trained and tested on different portions of the annoated data. The first row reports the F_1 performance against "*All*" test records ($F_1 = 57.7$) and against the records of the different product categories.

We had suspected that performance would vary significantly by the industry feature. This hypothesis was confirmed by the other performance results on this row. Notice how records from the books (BK) industry, , despite it having the second most number of records, performs particularly poorly ($F_1 = 41.2$). Given the relatively weak performance on some industries, we trained independent models with only records from each industry to see the effect of isolating the title data into clusters. As the table shows, two industries significantly improved F_1 performance despite the fewer available training records to the models: Books (from 41.2 to 82.0) and Arts & Entertainment (from 48.8 to 61.3).

At this point we could have decided to use three models: one for Books, on for Arts & Entertainment, and one based on *All* the training data.

Next, however we combined the `AE` and `BK` records into one training set, `BK&AE`, to determine whether these two categories could be treated as a single record cluster. Performance did improve but only for the `AE` records. This increase may be due to the relatively few `AE` records benefiting from the large number of `BK` records, while `BK` has sufficient records to diverge into its own model [13].

We tested on final permutation in this vein: Retaining the `BK` and `AE` training records to contribute to the predictions on the other industry records may be sub-optimal, so we further tested removing these records to create a `not BK|AE` model. This parsing model equaled the performance of the "All" model with lower performance on the Jewelry (`JW`) titles and higher performance on (`FS`) and (`AU`) titles.

Based on this analysis, we opted to use three models: `BK` then the title was known to be of that industry, `BK&AE` when the title was known to be from the `AE` industry, and *All* otherwise.[14].

5.4 Baseline Comparison

A natural baseline algorithm to the task is simply insert terms already found in an existing dictionary [15]. Given the overlap in terms (recall the many term types that a term such as "*apple*" can take) and the requirement that annotation occurs at a granular level (e.g. the token *2* may be from a product identifier, such as in *iPad 2* or be a product feature). After some experimentation, we opted for an iterative labeling method that proceeds from one term type, to the next. The basic pattern was to first apply brands, then product lines, then several product features, then products, black list and offer features within the record's industry [16].

The baseline algorithm describe above achieves a 30.4 F_1 overall, with high scores on FashionFS and ElectronicsCE records (40.0 and 35.7 respectively) and nearly zero on Books and Arts & Entertainment records because the dictionary only contains famous books and movies which are not found in the annotated data.

5.5 Feature Ablation Analysis

Because most of the used predictor features have been relatively well tested in other published research and none of the features are particularly time-consuming to calculate,

[8] we used MALLET as our CRF toolkit mallet.cs.umass.edu

[9] the data can be downloaded from https://dropbox.com/sh/q8cyv0wfuyg0han/sXZ95rOUC8

[10] Because of the iterative history of the datasetś development, the records are biased towards more challenging cases.

[11] The `other` label refers to titles whose merchant category did not map to one of our existing categories; the `other` label refers to titles whose merchant did not appear to provide a categorization whatsoever

[12] available and described at http://www.cnts.ua.ac.be/conll2000/chunking/output.html

[13] ideally the sequential tagging model would automatically detect and adjust for the importance of these attribute values and so avoid this time consuming and error prone creation of a composite model

[14] a demo of the service can be found at http://www.gabormelli.com/Projects/PTPv1

[15] we used an internal dictionary with nearly five-hundred thousand terms, but readers can use the term dictionary made publicly available for the CPROD1 contest

[16] the baseline program `PTPbaseline.pl` is available in the repository

Table 2: Distribution of titles in the gold dataset by industry type

	Industry	Code	Recs.	PF	PI	PC	BN	PL	BL	OF
1	Electronics	CE	760	1,618	667	596	332	283	155	3
2	Book	BK	566	103	554	7	8	68	10	0
3	Home&Garden	HG	178	502	94	231	123	28	76	2
4	Phones&Mobile	CM	127	479	151	177	80	162	121	4
5	Hobbies&Toys	HO	122	189	90	89	65	44	41	0
6	Jewelry	JW	96	253	45	50	30	22	50	2
7	Health&Beauty	HB	90	293	33	119	58	15	61	1
8	Fashion	FS	76	190	24	67	47	25	18	0
9	Automotive	AU	63	175	43	105	68	26	30	2
10	Arts&Ent.	AE	58	44	64	3	7	12	13	0
11	Gaming	GM	55	44	41	10	9	20	10	0
12	Camera&Photo.	CP	54	181	109	80	33	21	19	0
13	Sports&Fit.	SF	54	151	22	79	45	12	35	0
14	*not avail.*	na	37	77	20	33	9	8	18	5
15	Food	FD	32	87	4	41	27	1	10	0
16	Families	FB	31	82	11	41	25	14	15	0
17	Musician	MM	19	47	9	19	15	9	15	0
18	Pets	PT	12	52	6	17	11	4	10	2
19	*other*	OT	6	25	0	12	7	1	11	0

Table 3: 5-fold cross-validated F_1 performance by training and/or testing on titles from the 10 most frequent industries in the data. The statistically significant best scores are bolded.

Training Set	Test Set Category										
training set	All	CE	BK	HG	CM	HO	JW	HB	FS	AU	AE
All	**57.7**	**64.3**	41.2	**54.6**	**58.3**	48.0	**60.3**	**51.6**	55.0	46.7	48.8
CE	47.1	63.3	6.6	46.6	48.7	34.8	35.8	34.6	36.6	42.7	27.2
BK	11.1	4.0	**82.0**	2.8	4.2	2.6	2.1	3.5	3.8	2.8	37.5
HG	34.9	41.4	7.5	50.0	28.9	32.8	36.1	32.3	32.3	32.9	28.1
CM	41.2	48.9	9.1	39.7	56.5	29.8	32.5	33.1	31.0	35.7	31.5
HO	27.3	30.4	4.1	37.3	22.3	43.5	28.7	29.6	25.7	27.7	18.9
JW	27.1	30.2	7.2	31.8	19.5	23.9	56.2	29.3	31.9	26.1	15.9
HB	27.9	30.9	4.7	35.1	23.3	29.2	27.3	45.8	28.1	24.3	23.6
FS	27.0	32.0	5.8	31.7	22.1	23.1	32.1	27.6	52.3	25.0	27.8
AU	31.1	40.0	4.8	33.9	24.8	26.8	31.4	25.0	26.7	38.2	19.2
AE	13.3	9.0	59.2	6.3	7.5	7.4	4.3	9.7	11.7	4.6	61.3
BK&AE	12.9	6.2	65.2	3.6	6.0	4.0	3.0	5.2	4.9	3.3	**65.3**
not BK|AE	55.8	**64.6**	18.1	**54.3**	**59.0**	**49.3**	58.4	**52.1**	**56.3**	**49.2**	34.9

Table 4: F_1 learning curve of the *All* parser

titles	2%	5%	20%	33%	67%	80%	90%
F_1	29.1	39.8	48.2	53.1	56.9	57.7	58.2

we did not perform a thorough analysis of which features could be safely removed from the process. We did however analyze the impact of the "global" `INDUSTRY` feature that we introduced that assist the model in detecting the different patterns that apply to some of the different industries (such as long product identifier in books). What also motivated this analysis is the fact that the Books/BK and Arts&Entertainment/AE industry titles had weak performance. Table 3 suggests that the feature is not informative. This strongly suggests that the feature is not properly informing the models of the strong role that industry categories have on annotation patterns. In the future we hope to investigate the work by (Krishnan & Manning, 2006) [7] that uses two phases to introduce global features.

5.6 Learning Curve Analysis

The learning curve in table 4, in which cross-validation is used to estimate performance at different proportions of held-out data, suggests that performance has begun to plateau at the current number of training records in the annotated dataset. Given the current feature set, many more annotated titles (possibly through self-labeling approaches) would be required to noticeably impact F_1 performance. Recently, due to this analysis, we have begun to direct our annotation effort towards titles from the industries with fewer records.

6. REAL-WORLD PERFORMANCE

Given the ability to parse product titles we can now evaluate the impact on a mission-critical service. As already described in sections 3 and 4, on a weekly basis we apply the parser to a large set of product titles and filter the resulting terms with a crowdsourced service, such that approximately four-hundred terms are added weekly to the dictionary. With each batch of added terms our hyperlink insertion service has more information about the kinds of terms that relate to consumer products and may therefore be possible candidates for the insertion of a hyperlink (so long as other business rules and optimization rules are satisfied). For example, recently the process discovered that the dictionary was missing terms such as: {"table saw", "running lights", "floor mats", "suspension system", "rear derailleur"} ∈ `PC`; {"Emotiva"} ∈ `BN`; and {"Xonar", "Quadro"} ∈ `BN`. After the addition of these terms into our dictionary the linking service can be more confident that the presence of these terms in a webpage indicate a valid hyperlinkable product-related mention. For example, when the service sees a passage such as "*... the Ryobi table saw was able to ...* " in an appropriate place on a website (based on business rule restrictions) then, just like a website publisher might do manually on their own, the statistical recognizer used by the service can substitute the plain text "*Ryobi table saw*" with an affiliated hyperlink to a page that offers that type of tables saw [17] which may earn the publisher a commission each time that a visitor to their page interested in that type of product clicked on the link and soon after decided to make a purchase from the seller at the end of the link.

[17] for example to amazon.com/dp/B0050RBHQE

But, were the significant costs spent to introduce this semi-automated term-adding capability a worthwhile expense? In terms of costs and benefits, the costs to deliver the service had several dimensions, including: the time to prototype the solution, the effort to annotate the data, the effort to program a reliable weekly production system that includes crowdsourced annotating, the effort to evaluate performance, and finally the expenses of the new temporary equipment to train and evaluate models. The benefit is the increased revenue generated by the link insertion server. This can be calculated from the cumulative value each added term. Our link-insertion service has been in operation for several years so were able to retrieve significant historical evidence of past click performance for each term prior to its insertion, and from this estimate future click behavior for the term. The term "*table saw*", for example, which, being composed of a common noun "*table*" and verb "*saw*", was likely avoided by the service prior to the addition of the term, could now be more readily inserted (though still only in appropriate textual context). One unknown was whether the increase in insertions would also result in an increase in clicks - it may be that missing terms were not valuable with respect to clicks. We modeled and extrapolated the clicks for each term based on click data before and after their insertion, and from this estimated that how many weeks it would require for the incremental value (if any) would pay for the costs and from then on return a positive investment. We determined that the effort recovered its expense within the first eleven weeks of its operation, and would also continue to deliver the incremental value to our organizations and our customers who benefit from the commission associated from the previously absent links. Finally, each new batch of terms continues to identify high-value terms though, as expected, fewer with each batch. The service could also allow our organization to create one of the most comprehensive product-related dictionaries in the market quickly and cost-effectively. Finally, our organization can now apply a new capability to other mission-critical processes.

7. RELATED WORK

Given the commercial opportunity related to understanding product offerings on the Web, there has been significant published research on the automated identification of product properties from textual information. We review several publications that most closely related to our task and solution.

7.1 (Ghani & al, 2006)

One of the first published investigations in our task by Ghani & al [4] which applied a semi-supervised approach to the task of identifying attribute-value pairs in short product-related phrases.

We include three examples of the types of strings that they sought to parse:

1. "*Extended Torsion bar*"
2. "*Imported*"
3. "*Contains 2 BIOflex concentric circle magnets*"

These text items are related but differ significantly from the product offering titles listed in table 1. These short text items instead appear to be drawn from the lists of product specifications that are commonly found on the product offering description pages.

Next, they propose a general annotation structure that attempts to identify attribute-value pairs in the text. This approach is very general. It can be applied to almost all other domains, not only product offering related text. Their annotation framework involves the application of three labels to text segments: *attribute*(ATTR), *value*(VAL), and *neither*(NA), where (a TRUE value is inserted when no actual value is present in the text). As we can see in the annotated versions of the strings above, the attribute-value pairs can be readily extracted:

1. *Extended*^{NA} *Torsion*$^{VAL.}$ *bar*$^{ATTR.}$
2. *Imported*$^{ATTR.}$ TRUE$^{VAL.}$
3. *Contains*^{NA} *2*$^{VAL.}$ *BIOflex concentric circle magnet*$^{ATTR.}$

Unfortunately, their representation cannot be easily translated into our needs. As can be seen in their examples, sometimes chunks labeled as attributes and as values can both be mapped to product features. The representation, as (Ghani & al, 2006) mention, results in a significant disagreement between human annotators in the "correct" annotation structure for many cases. The example they offer is that of "*Audio/JPEG navigation menu*" which can be naturally annotated in three different ways, while for us the string naturally becomes a product feature (PF). Contrast their annotation structure to ours on their three examples:

1. *Extended*^{PF} *Torsion bar*^{PC}
2. *Imported*^{OF}
3. *Contains*^{FT} *2*^{OF} *BIOflex*^{BN} [*concentric circle*]^{PF} *magnet*^{PC}.

Aside from the annotation structure, we notice also that their input strings are already in a succinct form relative to the long descriptive product titles in our task which often contain many values with an implicit attribute. For example, when a color is mentioned in a title the color term (say *yellow*) is almost never preceded or followed by a term such as "color".

Finally, the proposed algorithm which combines semi- supervised co-training along with expectation-maximization (EM) would involve significant programming effort and has not been successfully applied in other case studies, so we did not attempt to implement it as a baseline.

7.2 (Putthividhya & Hu, 2011)

The work that most closely approximates ours, both in terms of task and approach appears to be the one by Putthividhya & Hu [13]. They propose the use of an iterative online supervised CRF approach to the task of labeling descriptive product offering titles.

Their annotation framework involves five labels: *brand* (B), *garment type* (G), *size* (S), *color* (C), and *not applicable* (NA). These labels are intentionally tailored for products from the fashion industry (from eBay's "clothing and shoes" products).

Below are two sample titles that they provide:

1. *NEXT Blue Petite Bootcut jeans size 12 BNWT*[18]
2. *Paul Smith Osmo White Plimsoll Trainers - UK 6 RRP*[19] *: £100*

Followed by their reported annotations:

1. *NEXT*^{B} *Blue*^{C} *Petite*^{NA} *Bootcut*^{NA} *jeans*^{G} [*size 12*]^{S} *BNWT*^{NA}
2. [*Paul Smith*]^{B} *Osmo*^{NA} *White*^{C} *Plimsoll*^{NA} *Trainers*^{G} -^{NA} *UK6*^{S} *RRP*^{NA} :^{NA} £^{NA} *100*^{NA}

Their labels map roughly to ours as follows: B=BN, G ∈ PC, S ∈ PF, C ∈ PF, and NA ∈ FT,PL,ME,OF.

Our annotation of their two examples is as follows:

1. *NEXT*^{BN} *Blue*^{PF} *Petite*^{PF} *Bootcut*^{PF} *jeans*^{PC} [*size 12*]^{PF} *BNWT*^{NA}
2. [*Paul Smith*]^{BN} *Osmo*^{NA} *White*^{C} *Plimsoll*^{NA} *Trainers*^{PC} - *UK6*^{PF} *RRP*^{OF} : [*£100*]^{OF}

Our proposal uses a broader term definition of product feature that encompasses their size and color labels (and is therefore applicable to other industries, but loses the granual information). We also use product line (PL) which can appear in Fashion products (such as in *Ralph Lauren* - ***Polo*** and *Tory Burch* - ***Reva***). Additionally we use the Merchant, Offering Feature, and Function Term and avoid the use of a less informative NA.

In terms of algorithm design, they also propose the use of a supervised solution and a bootstrapped solution that grows their gazetteer (seed list). Finally, they do not report on the real-world impact of their work.

7.3 (Köpcke & al, 2012)

Finally, Köpcke & al [6] address the focused task of identifying the code/identifiers in largely electronics product offering titles using information theoretic approaches. This task is too restrictive to aid in our more general needs.

8. CONCLUSION

In this paper we reviewed the design and impact of a system that can identify and label the low-level semantic structure of the billions of product offering titles that pervade consumer e-commerce websites. We leverage the current best-practices approach of supervised BIO-tagging via a trained linear CRF to train a predictive model, though we extend the approach to involve separate models based on industry information along with model ensembles that produces a voting-based ranking score. We apply the trained parser to many offering titles on a regular basis in order to grow a domain-specific dictionary of offering-related terms. To ensure a low error-rate, each candidate term is reviewed via a crowdsourcing service. Terms that pass this filter are added to the dictionary, while terms that are strongly rejected are used to select offering titles to be manually annotated and added to the training dataset for subsequent trained parsers. Finally, we assess the impact of the added terms to our affiliate hyperlink-insertion service and we find

[18] BNWT in eBay is a contraction of "*brand new with tags*"
[19] RRP in eBay is a contraction of "*recommended retail price*"

that the new capability has both paid for itself, and continues to add value to our organization, to our website-owning customers, and to their visitors.

Several enhancements to the deployed system are possible. More leading-edge mechanisms for sequential tagging and active learning should be considered such as `BILOU` (instead of `BIO`) tagging [15] as well as the two-phased approach in [7] to include global features.

Aside from enhancing the semantic parser's accuracy, there are several additional applications that we would like to deploy. These include 1) the ability to perform record linkage on product records to find substitutable products with high-accuracy and likely also data cleaning based on contradictions with what the product offerings titles suggest. Finally, these applications may also benefit from the ability to create a full parse tree from a title. For now, through this case-study, we have demonstrated the cost-effective feasibility of data-driven shallow semantic parsing of product offering titles (for better automatic hyperlink insertion).

9. ACKNOWLEDGMENTS

The author would like to thank the rest of the team at VigLink for fruitful discussions and aid with the annotation.

10. REFERENCES

[1] S. P. Abney. *Parsing by chunks.* 1989.

[2] C. Callison-Burch and M. Dredze. Creating speech and language data with amazon's mechanical turk. In *Proceedings of the NAACL HLT 2010 Workshop on Creating Speech and Language Data with Amazon's Mechanical Turk*, 2010.

[3] A. Culotta and A. McCallum. Confidence estimation for information extraction. In *Proceedings of HLT-NAACL 2004*, 2004.

[4] R. Ghani, K. Probst, Y. Liu, M. Krema, and A. Fano. Text mining for product attribute extraction. *ACM SIGKDD Explorations Newsletter*, 8(1), 2006.

[5] T. Gornostay. Terminology management in real use. In *Proceedings of the 5th International Conference Applied Linguistics in Science and Education*, 2010.

[6] H. Köpcke, A. Thor, S. Thomas, and E. Rahm. Tailoring entity resolution for matching product offers. In *Proceedings of the 15th International Conference on Extending Database Technology*, 2012.

[7] V. Krishnan and C. D. Manning. An effective two-stage model for exploiting non-local dependencies in named entity recognition. In *Proceedings of the 2006 COLING and ACL conferences*, 2006.

[8] X. Liu, S. Zhang, F. Wei, and M. Zhou. Recognizing named entities in tweets. In *Proceedings of the 2011 ACL conference*, 2011.

[9] G. Melli and J. McQuinn. Requirements specification using fact-oriented modeling: A case study and generalization. In *Object-Role Modeling Workshop at OTM 2008*, 2008.

[10] G. Melli and C. Romming. An overview of the cprod1 contest on consumer product recognition within user generated postings and normalization against a large product catalog. In *Data Mining Workshops (ICDMW), 2012 IEEE 12th International Conference on*, pages 861–864. IEEE, 2012.

[11] D. Nadeau and S. Sekine. A survey of named entity recognition and classification. *Lingvisticae Investigationes*, 30(1), 2007.

[12] R. Polikar. Ensemble based systems in decision making. *Circuits and Systems Magazine, IEEE*, 6(3), 2006.

[13] D. P. Putthividhya and J. Hu. Bootstrapped named entity recognition for product attribute extraction. In *Proceedings of the Conference on Empirical Methods in Natural Language Processing*, pages 1557–1567, 2011.

[14] L. A. Ramshaw and M. P. Marcus. Text chunking using transformation-based learning. In *Proceedings of the Third ACL Workshop on Very Large Corpora*, 1999.

[15] L. Ratinov and D. Roth. Design challenges and misconceptions in named entity recognition. In *Proceedings of the 2009 Computational Natural Language Learning conference*, 2009.

[16] F. Sclano and P. Velardi. Termextractor: a web application to learn the shared terminology of emergent web communities. In *Enterprise Interoperability II.* 2007.

[17] B. Settles and M. Craven. An analysis of active learning strategies for sequence labeling tasks. In *Proceedings of the Conference on Empirical Methods in Natural Language Processing*, 2008.

[18] F. Sha and F. Pereira. Shallow parsing with conditional random fields. In *Proceedings of the 2003 Conference of the North American Chapter of the Association for Computational Linguistics on Human Language Technology-Volume 1*, 2003.

[19] W. Wong, W. Liu, and M. Bennamoun. Ontology learning from text: A look back and into the future. *ACM Computing Surveys (CSUR)*, 44(4), 2012.

A Case Study: Privacy Preserving Release of Spatio-temporal Density in Paris

Gergely Acs
INRIA
gergely.acs@inria.fr

Claude Castelluccia
INRIA
claude.castelluccia@inria.fr

ABSTRACT

With billions of handsets in use worldwide, the quantity of mobility data is gigantic. When aggregated they can help understand complex processes, such as the spread viruses, and built better transportation systems, prevent traffic congestion. While the benefits provided by these datasets are indisputable, they unfortunately pose a considerable threat to location privacy.

In this paper, we present a new anonymization scheme to release the spatio-temporal density of Paris, in France, i.e., the number of individuals in 989 different areas of the city released every hour over a whole week. The density is computed from a call-data-record (CDR) dataset, provided by the French Telecom operator Orange, containing the CDR of roughly 2 million users over one week. Our scheme is differential private, and hence, provides provable privacy guarantee to each individual in the dataset. Our main goal with this case study is to show that, even with large dimensional sensitive data, differential privacy can provide practical utility *with* meaningful privacy guarantee, if the anonymization scheme is carefully designed. This work is part of the national project XData (`http://xdata.fr`) that aims at combining large (anonymized) datasets provided by different service providers (telecom, electricity, water management, postal service, etc.).

1. INTRODUCTION

Mobile phone datasets have become widely available in recent years and have opened the possibility to improve our understanding of large-scale social networks by investigating how people exchange information, interact, and develop social interactions. While the benefits provided by these datasets are indisputable, they unfortunately pose a considerable threat to location privacy. Not only this can impact people lives negatively, this also affects research. Because privacy is so important to people, companies and researchers are reluctant to publish mobile phone datasets by fear of being held responsible for potential privacy breaches. It is therefore urgent to develop *practical* tools for private releases and analysis of mobility datasets.

KDD'14, August 24–27, 2014, New York, NY, USA.
Copyright 2014 ACM 978-1-4503-2956-9/14/08 ...$15.00.
http://dx.doi.org/10.1145/2623330.2623361.

This paper focuses on applications that only need location counts, i.e., the repartition of visitors on a map at a given period of time. This information can typically be published by dividing a map into cells, and then releasing the count (i.e., number of users) associated to each of the cells. However, it is important to ensure that this publication does not leak any information about the mobility patterns of individual users, which might be trivial when, for example, the count values are small.

Why Differential Privacy? Privacy has different definitions and different models have been proposed. In this paper, we use *differential privacy* [10] which has emerged as a compelling privacy model. The advantage of this model, compared to the many others proposed in the literature, is two-fold. First, it provides a formal and measurable privacy guarantee regardless what other background information or sophisticated inference technique the adversary uses even in the future. Second, it is closed with respect to sequential and parallel composition, i.e., the result of the sequential or parallel combination of two differential private algorithms is also differential private.

This has particular importance in practice, since it does not only simplify the design of anonymization solutions, but also allows to measure how much privacy remains when a given dataset, or a set of correlated datasets, is anonymized (and released) several times, possibly by different entities.

Differential-private schemes often requires adding noise to the published data (e.g., to the published location counts) so that it leaks almost no information about any participating individual, but still reveals aggregated information about the population as a whole. The variance of the noise is calibrated to both the *sensitivity* of the counts (i.e., the maximal change of the counts due to the inclusion/exclusion of a single record in a dataset) and a desired privacy level ε. For large-dimensional data, such as temporal density, the sensitivity is usually so large that the added noise is much larger than the actual density count values for stringent privacy requirement (i.e. $\varepsilon < 1$). Consequently, the resultant anonymized data is often meaningless.

Contributions. In this paper, we show that, for a given privacy level (i.e., a given ε), the magnitude of noise can be substantially reduced by using several optimizations and by customizing the anonymization mechanisms to the public characteristics of datasets and applications. We observe that the temporal density, of each cell, can be characterized by a periodic time series. This is explained by the fact that aggregated mobility patterns are quite periodic. Moreover these time series follow very similar trends, as most people in nearby cells have similar calling patterns. As a consequence, time series can be compressed by sampling, clustering and low-pass filtering. Sampling and clustering reduce data sensitivity, which results in lower added noise and better performance. We further attenuate the distortion resulting from the compression and perturbation phases via novel optimization and post-processing algorithms. We show experimentally that the achieved performance is quite high and that differential privacy can be practical in real-world applications. However, we believe that there are probably no differential private anonymization techniques that fit all applications, and that anonymization algorithms have to be customized to each application and dataset.

The XData project. This work was done in the context of the French XData project. XData is a national funded project under the "Big Data program", whose goal is to study the benefit of combining and cross-processing different types of datasets provided by various service providers (such as Orange, Electricité de France, La Poste, etc.). However, according to the European Data Protection laws (Directive 95/46/EC), all datasets have to be anonymized, prior cross-processing, such that data subjects are no longer identifiable. The law does not dictate any specific privacy model, but stipulates that "*to determine whether a person is identifiable, account should be taken of all the means likely reasonably to be used either by the controller or by any other person to identify the said person*". We believe that the best existing model to achieve this goal is probably differential privacy. This paper shows how to anonymize the mobility data, provided by Orange, under the differential privacy model. In particular, we show how to release density information. Geographical density is useful in many of applications envisioned by the XData projet, such as identifying areas where to install new businesses or build new infrastructures.

2. RELATED WORK

Several recent studies have demonstrated the privacy risks of releasing location data by re-identifying individuals from geospatial data sets [8, 28, 13]. As a result, a plethora of privacy-preserving techniques have been introduced, however, most of them do not provide any formal privacy guarantee (see [6] and the references therein).

Differential privacy (DP) was first rigorously presented in [10] with the Laplace mechanism (LPA) as a first generic tool to guarantee DP. There exist two relaxations of ε-DP; (ε,δ)-probabilistic DP [20] and (ε,δ)-indistinguishability [9]. The former guarantees ε-DP with high probability ($\geq 1-\delta$), while the latter relaxes the bound of ε-DP.

Location privacy has also been addressed in the context of DP. [5] applies DP to location, and more generally, sequential data release. However, this scheme does not release time information apart from the sequentiality of locations. Another recent work [2] formalizes location privacy as protecting the users' location within a radius r with a level of privacy that depends on r. This corresponds to a generalized version of DP. They target LBS applications and add noise directly to users' GPS coordinates. Commuting patterns in U.S. were anonymized in the probabilistic DP model in [20]. This scheme has also been deployed in practice within the project called OnTheMap by the U.S. Census Bureau. Other authors [7, 19] apply different spatial decomposition techniques to partition the two dimensional domain into cells, and then obtain noisy counts for each cell. However, these techniques are not concerned with releasing multiple counts over time.

Several DP techniques have been proposed to release time series. In [12], the authors propose a framework to release real-time aggregate statistics under DP based on filtering and adaptive sampling. Some other proposals [11, 4] provide a weaker guarantee on continuous data streams; they provide event-level privacy to protect an event (i.e., one user's presence at a particular time point), rather than the presence of that user. As all these works address the *real-time* (interactive) release of aggregates, they are usually less accurate than *off-line* (non-interactive) approaches, which can access the whole time series and build more accurate models for perturbation.

The most related work to ours is [24, 17, 23]. All of them address the off-line release of time series under DP. Rastogi and Nath [24] proposed a Discrete Fourier Transform (DFT) based algorithm which guarantees DP by perturbing the discrete Fourier coefficients. This technique was further improved for DP histogram release in [1]. We reuse the improved private DFT algorithm from [1], and further improve its accuracy at the cost of some privacy. In [17], the time series are pre-processed by pre-sampling and smoothing them via averaging. These techniques diminish the global sensitivity of the data, and thereby allows to lower the injected Laplace noise. We also use a similar sampling technique to [17] in order to compress time series. However, [17] is a more general solution and targets even non-periodic time series where averaging may be a better perturbation model than DFT. As aggregated location counts are typically periodic, DFT is a more accurate perturbation model for our application. Finally, DP-WHERE [23] adds noise to the set of empirical probability distributions which is derived from the original CDR datasets, and samples from these distributions to generate synthetic CDRs. Instead of releasing the whole CDR dataset, we only aim at releasing the temporal density of IRIS cells which is a more specific problem. This mapping between CDRs and IRIS cells influences utility and is not considered in [23].

3. PRELIMINARIES

3.1 Differential Privacy

Intuitively, differential privacy [10] (DP) requires that the outcome of any computation be insensitive to the change of a single record in the dataset. Consequently, for a record owner, it means that any privacy breach will not be due to participating in the database.

Definition 1 (Differential Privacy) *A privacy mechanism $\mathcal{A}$ gives ε-differential privacy if for any database $\mathcal{D}_1$ and $\mathcal{D}_2$ differing on at most one record, and for any possible output $O \in Range(\mathcal{A})$,*

$$e^{-\varepsilon} \times Pr[\mathcal{A}(\mathcal{D}_2) = O] \leq Pr[\mathcal{A}(\mathcal{D}_1) = O] \leq e^{\varepsilon} \times Pr[\mathcal{A}(\mathcal{D}_2) = O]$$

where the probability is taken over the randomness of $\mathcal{A}$.

A relaxation of DP is probabilistic-DP [20], where privacy breaches may occur with very small probability.

Definition 2 (Probabilistic Differential Privacy [20]) *A privacy mechanism $\mathcal{A}$ gives (ε, δ)-probabilistic differential privacy if for any database $\mathcal{D}_1$ and $\mathcal{D}_2$ differing on at most one record, and for any possible output $O \in Range(\mathcal{A})$, we can partition the output space Ω into Ω_1 and Ω_2 such that (1) for all $O \in \Omega_1$,*

$$e^{-\varepsilon} \times Pr[\mathcal{A}(\mathcal{D}_2) = O] \leq Pr[\mathcal{A}(\mathcal{D}_1) = O] \leq e^{\varepsilon} \times Pr[\mathcal{A}(\mathcal{D}_2) = O]$$

and (2) for any database $\mathcal{D}$, $Pr[\mathcal{A}(\mathcal{D}) \in \Omega_2] \leq \delta$ where the probability is taken over the randomness of $\mathcal{A}$.

The latter definition guarantees that algorithm $\mathcal{A}$ achieves DP with high probability ($\geq 1-\delta$), and the set Ω_2 contains all outputs that are privacy breaches according to Definition 1. The probability of these outputs are bounded by δ. Notice that with $\delta = 0$ probabilistic DP boils down to Definition 1. Although probabilistic DP has weaker privacy guarantee than Definition 1, it provides higher utility in practice.

The definition of differential privacy enjoys the property of sequential composition, which specifies the privacy guarantee in a sequence of computation.

Theorem 1 ([21]) *Let $\mathcal{A}_i$ each provide ε_i-differential privacy. A sequence of $\mathcal{A}_i(\mathcal{D})$ over the dataset $\mathcal{D}$ provides $\sum_i \varepsilon_i$-differential privacy.*

3.2 Differential Private Mechanisms

Three principal techniques for achieving (probabilistic) DP are *Laplace mechanism* [10] (LPA), *Gaussian mechanism* [15] (GPA), and *Exponential mechanism* [22]. A fundamental concept of all these techniques is the *global sensitivity* of a function [10]:

Definition 3 (Global Sensitivity) *For any function $f : \mathcal{D} \to \mathbb{R}^d$, the sensitivity of f is $\Delta f = \max_{\mathcal{D}_1,\mathcal{D}_2} ||f(\mathcal{D}_1) - f(\mathcal{D}_2)||_1$ for all $\mathcal{D}_1, \mathcal{D}_2$ differing in at most one record.*

The global sensitivity is also called as L_1-sensitivity due to the L_1-norm used in its definition and is denoted by $\Delta_1 f$. Similarly, the L_2-sensitivity $\Delta_2 f$ of a function f, which is used later in this paper, is defined by the L_2-norm $||\cdot||_2$.

Laplace mechanism (LPA). A standard mechanism to achieve differential privacy is to add Laplace noise to the true output of a function. The noise is generated according to a Laplace distribution with the probability density function (PDF) $p(x|\lambda) = \frac{1}{2\lambda}e^{-|x|/\lambda}$, where λ is calibrated as follows.

Theorem 2 ([10]) *For any function $f : \mathcal{D} \to \mathbb{R}^d$, the mechanism $\mathcal{A}$*

$$\mathcal{A}(\mathcal{D}) = f(\mathcal{D}) + \langle \mathcal{L}_1(\lambda), \ldots, \mathcal{L}_d(\lambda)\rangle$$

gives ε-differential privacy, if $\mathcal{L}_i(\lambda)$ are i.i.d Laplace variables with scale parameter $\lambda = \Delta f/\varepsilon$.

Gaussian mechanism (GPA). An alternative technique to achieve probabilistic DP is to add Gaussian noise to the true output of a function The noise is generated according to the Gaussian distribution with the PDF $p(x|\sigma) = \frac{1}{\sqrt{2\pi}\sigma}e^{-x^2/2\sigma^2}$.

Theorem 3 ([15]) *For any function $f : \mathcal{D} \to \mathbb{R}^d$, the mechanism $\mathcal{A}$*

$$\mathcal{A}(\mathcal{D}) = f(\mathcal{D}) + \langle \mathcal{G}_1(\sigma), \ldots, \mathcal{G}_d(\sigma)\rangle$$

gives (ε, δ)-probabilistic differential privacy for any $\varepsilon \leq 1$ and $\sigma^2 \geq 2(\Delta_2 f)^2 \ln(4/\delta)/\varepsilon^2$, where $\mathcal{G}_i(\sigma)$ are i.i.d Gaussian variables with variance σ^2.

Assuming identical values of ε, a Gaussian random variable is more concentrated around 0 than a Laplace random variable thereby ensuring better utility for GPA. However, this larger accuracy also entails weaker privacy, since there is a small probability δ that ε-DP will not hold.

Exponential mechanism. The exponential mechanism [22] captures all DP mechanisms with a measurable output space. In particular, it assigns exponentially greater probabilities of being selected to outputs of higher utility so that the final output would be close to the optimum yet still differential private.

Theorem 4 ([22]) *Given a utility function $u : (\mathcal{D} \times \mathcal{R}) \to \mathbb{R}$ for a database $\mathcal{D}$, the mechanism $\mathcal{A}$,*

$$\mathcal{A}(\mathcal{D}, u) = \left\{ \text{return } r \text{ with probability} \propto \exp\left(\frac{\varepsilon u(\mathcal{D}, r)}{2\Delta u}\right)\right\}$$

gives ε-differential privacy, where $\Delta u = \max_{\forall r,\mathcal{D}_1,\mathcal{D}_2} |u(\mathcal{D}_1, r) - u(\mathcal{D}_2, r)|$.

3.3 Utility Metrics

The error between the private and original time series is measured by the following metrics. Consider counts $\mathbf{X} = \{X_0, \ldots, X_{n-1}\}$. We denote the original time series by $\mathbf{X}$, the sanitized one by $\hat{\mathbf{X}}$.

Mean Relative Error (MRE): $\text{MRE}(\mathbf{X}, \hat{\mathbf{X}}) = (1/n)\sum_{i=0}^{n-1} \frac{|\hat{X}_i - X_i|}{\max(\gamma, X_i)}$, where the sanity bound γ mitigates the effect of very small counts. Following the convention [27], we adjust γ to 0.1% of $\sum_{i=0}^{n-1} X_i$.

Pearson Correlation (PC): $\text{PC}(\mathbf{X}, \hat{\mathbf{X}}) = \frac{\sum_{i=0}^{n-1}(X_i - \sum_i X_i/n)(\hat{X}_i - \sum_i \hat{X}_i/n)}{\sqrt{\sum_{i=0}^{n-1}(X_i - \sum_i X_i/n)^2}\sqrt{\sum_{i=0}^{n-1}(\hat{X}_i - \sum_i \hat{X}_i/n)^2}}$. PC measures the linear correlation between the noisy and the original time series (i.e., whether they have similar trends), and it always falls between -1 and 1.

4. PROBLEM DEFINITION

Our goal is to release the spatio-temporal density of 989 non-overlapping areas in Paris, called IRIS cells. Each cell is defined by INSEE[1] and covers about 2000 inhabitants. The set of all IRIS cells is denoted by $\mathbb{L}$ henceforth, and are depicted in Figure 1 based on their contours[2].

We aim to release the number of all individuals who visited a specific IRIS cell in each hour over a whole week. Since human mobility trajectories exhibit a high degree of temporal and spatial regularity [14], one week long period should be sufficient for most practical applications. Therefore, we are interested in the time series $\mathbf{X}^L = \langle X_0^L, X_1^L, \ldots, X_{167}^L\rangle$ of any IRIS cell $L \in \mathbb{L}$, where X_t^L denotes the number of individuals at L in the $(t+1)$th hour of the week such that any single individual can visit a tower only once in an hour.

[1]National Institute of Statistics and Economics: http://www.insee.fr/fr/methodes/default.asp?page=zonages/iris.htm

[2]Available on IGN's website (National Geographic Institute): http://professionnels.ign.fr/contoursiris

We will omit t and L in the sequel, if they are unambiguous in the given context. $\mathbf{X}^{\mathbb{L}}$ denotes the set of time series of all IRIS cells in the sequel.

4.1 Dataset

To compute these time series, we use a CDR (Call Data Record) dataset provided by the French telecom company Orange[3], where $\mathbb{T}$ represents the set of cell towers of the operator, and a cell tower $T \in \mathbb{T}$ is visited by an individual at time t, if the operator has a recorded event at time t at tower T related to the individual. An event can be an incoming/outgoing call or message to/from the individual. This dataset contains the events of $N = 1,992,846$ users at $|\mathbb{T}| = 1303$ towers within the administrative region of Paris (i.e., the union of all IRIS cells) over a single week (10/09/2007 - 17/09/2007). Within this interval, the average number of events per user is 13.55 with a standard deviation of 18.33 (assuming that an individual can visit any tower cell only once in an hour) and with a maximum at 732. The set of all events related to an individual constitute his/her record (trajectory) in the dataset. Similarly to IRIS cells, we can create another set of time series $\mathbf{X}^{\mathbb{T}}$, where X_t^T denotes the number of visits of tower T in the $(t+1)$th hour of the week.

4.2 Computing the time series of IRIS cells

We map the counts in $\mathbf{X}^{\mathbb{T}}$ to $\mathbf{X}^{\mathbb{L}}$ as follows. First, we compute the Voronoi tesselation of the towers cells $\mathbb{T}$ which is shown in Figure 1. Then, we calculate the count of each IRIS cell in each hour from the counts of its overlapping tower cells; each tower cell contributes with a count which is proportional to the size of the overlapping area. More specifically, if an IRIS cell L overlaps with tower cells $\{T_1, T_2, \ldots, T_c\}$, then

$$X_t^L = \sum_{i=1}^{c} X_t^{T_i} \times \frac{\mathsf{size}(T_i \cap L)}{\mathsf{size}(T_i)} \tag{1}$$

at time t.

The rationale behind this mapping is that users are usually registered at the geographically closest tower at any time. We acknowledge that this mapping algorithm might sometimes be incorrect, since the real association of users and towers depends on several other factors such as signal strength or load-balancing. Nevertheless, without more details of the cellular network beyond the towers' GPS position, we are not aware of any better mapping technique.

5. PRIVACY PRESERVING RELEASE OF SPATIO-TEMPORAL DENSITY

Our aim is to transform the time series of all IRIS cells $\mathbf{X}^{\mathbb{L}}$ to a sanitized version $\hat{\mathbf{X}}^{\mathbb{L}}$ such that $\hat{\mathbf{X}}^{\mathbb{L}}$ satisfies Definition 1. That is, the distribution of $\hat{\mathbf{X}}^{\mathbb{L}}$ will be insensitive (up to ε) to all the visits of any single user during the whole week, meanwhile the error between $\hat{\mathbf{X}}^{\mathbb{L}}$ and $\mathbf{X}^{\mathbb{L}}$ is small.

Our sanitization algorithm is sketched in Algorithm 1. First, the input dataset is pre-sampled such that only ℓ visits are retained per user (Line 1). This ensures that the global sensitivity of all the time series (i.e., $\mathbf{X}^{\mathbb{L}}$) is no more than ℓ. Then, the pre-sampled time series of each IRIS cell is computed from that of the tower cells using Voronoi-tesselation

Figure 1: IRIS cells of Paris (left) and Voronoi-tesselation of tower cells (right)

Algorithm 1 Our sanitization scheme

Input: $\mathbf{X}^{\mathbb{T}}$ - input time series (from CDR), (ε, δ)-privacy parameters, $\mathbb{L}$ - IRIS cells, ℓ - maximum visits per user
Output: Noisy time series $\hat{\mathbf{X}}^{\mathbb{L}}$

1: Create $\overline{\mathbf{X}}^{\mathbb{T}}$ by sampling at most ℓ visits per user from $\mathbf{X}^{\mathbb{T}}$ (Section 5.1)
2: Compute the IRIS time series $\overline{\mathbf{X}}^{\mathbb{L}}$ from $\overline{\mathbf{X}}^{\mathbb{T}}$ (Section 4.2)
3: Compute the minimum cover $\mathbb{C} \subseteq \mathbb{T} \cup \mathbb{L}$ and the corresponding time series $\overline{\mathbf{X}}^{\mathbb{C}}$ (Section 5.2)
4: Perturb $\overline{\mathbf{X}}^{\mathbb{C}}$ into $\hat{\mathbf{X}}^{\mathbb{C}}$ (Section 5.3) `//see Algorithm 2`
5: Apply smoothing on $\hat{\mathbf{X}}^{\mathbb{C}}$ (Section 5.4)
6: Compute $\hat{\mathbf{X}}^{\mathbb{L}}$ from $\hat{\mathbf{X}}^{\mathbb{C}}$ using Formula (1)

and Formula (1) (Line 2). After the largest cells, which cover the whole city and also have large counts, from $\mathbb{T} \cup \mathbb{L}$ are identified (Line 3), their time series are perturbed to guarantee privacy (Line 4). In order to mitigate the distortion of the previous steps, we apply smoothing on the perturbed time series as a post-processing step (Line 5). Finally, the time series of all IRIS cells are computed from the post-processed time series in $\mathbb{C}$ (Line 6).

5.1 Pre-sampling

To perturb the time series of all IRIS cells, we first have to compute their sensitivity, i.e., $\Delta_1(\mathbf{X}^{\mathbb{L}})$. To this end, we first need to calculate the sensitivity of the time series of all tower cells, i.e., $\Delta_1(\mathbf{X}^{\mathbb{T}})$. Indeed, Formula (1) does not change the L_1-sensitivity of tower counts, and hence, $\Delta_1(\mathbf{X}^{\mathbb{T}}) = \Delta_1(\mathbf{X}^{\mathbb{L}})$.

$\Delta_1(\mathbf{X}^{\mathbb{T}})$ is given by the maximum *total* number of (tower) visits of a single user in *any* input dataset. This upper bound must universally hold for all possible input datasets, and is usually on the order of few hundreds; recall that the maximum number of visits per user is 732 in our dataset. This would require excessive noise to be added in the perturbation phase. We instead follow a different approach and divide the whole sanitization process into two main steps. We first perturb a pre-sample of our dataset which better withstands perturbation, and then mitigate the distortion effect of sampling in a post-processing step described later in Section 5.4.

In particular, we truncate each record of any input dataset by considering at most one visit per hour for each user, and then select at most ℓ of such visits per user uniformly at random over the whole week. This implies that a user can

[3]`http://www.orange.com`

contribute with at most ℓ to all the counts in total regardless of the input dataset, and hence, the L_1-sensitivity of the dataset always becomes ℓ. The pre-sampled dataset is denoted by $\overline{\mathbf{X}}$, and $\Delta_1(\overline{\mathbf{X}}^{\mathbb{T}}) = \Delta_1(\overline{\mathbf{X}}^{\mathbb{L}}) = \ell$.

5.2 Computing the largest covering cells

To sanitize $\overline{\mathbf{X}}^{\mathbb{L}}$, there are two basic (naive) approaches. First, we can directly perturb the IRIS counts $\overline{\mathbf{X}}^{\mathbb{L}}$ by applying the Laplace mechanism: $\hat{X}_t^L = \overline{X}_t^L + \mathcal{L}(\ell/\varepsilon)$ for all $L \in \mathbb{L}$. Alternatively, we can first perturb the tower counts $\overline{\mathbf{X}}^{\mathbb{T}}$ to obtain $\hat{\mathbf{X}}^{\mathbb{T}}$, then compute the noisy IRIS counts $\hat{\mathbf{X}}^{\mathbb{L}}$ from $\hat{\mathbf{X}}^{\mathbb{T}}$ by applying Formula (1). Although both techniques guarantee ε-DP according to Theorem 2, in terms of utility, they are suboptimal.

Cells with small counts have larger relative error, whereas larger counts better resist noise. This is due to the fact that the injected noise is independent of the magnitude of the original counts but only depends on their sensitivity. Therefore, the best approach is to first select cells having the largest counts (which can be either tower or IRIS cells) such that they cover whole Paris, perturb the counts of these cells, and then recompute the noisy counts of the smaller IRIS cells, which were not selected in the cover, from the larger (noisy) tower counts.

However, selecting the optimal cover of Paris (i.e., the set of cells having the largest counts) must also be differential private. Fortunately, a simple heuristic helps us to accurately approximate the optimal cover without using the true counts of the cells (that would require to introduce more noise): cells with large size tend to have large counts[4]. This is also confirmed by Figure 2a and 2b. Hence, we re-state the problem as follows.

How can we select the minimum cardinality subset of cells $\mathbb{C} \subseteq \mathbb{T} \cup \mathbb{L}$ such that $\mathbb{C}$ is a complete cover (i.e., covers whole Paris)?

More formally, let $G(V, E)$ denote a graph, where each vertex corresponds to a cell in $\mathbb{T} \cup \mathbb{L}$, and $(v, v') \in E$ iff cells v and v' overlap. In this setting, our problem translates to the classical minimum vertex cover problem [3]. Indeed, as $\mathbb{T}$ and $\mathbb{L}$ are also complete covers of Paris, each vertex in V has at least one edge (a tower cell is always overlapped by at least one IRIS cell, and vice-verse), and we want to compute the minimum cardinality subset of cells which cover all the overlapping areas between cells. Although the minimum vertex cover problem is NP-hard in general, our covering problem belongs to the special cases which can be efficiently solved.

Theorem 5 (Minimum cardinality cover) *Selecting the minimum cardinality subset of cells $\mathbb{C} \subseteq \mathbb{T} \cup \mathbb{L}$ such that $\mathbb{C}$ is a complete cover can be solved in $O(|\mathbb{T}||\mathbb{L}|\sqrt{|\mathbb{T}| + |\mathbb{L}|})$.*

PROOF. $G(V, E)$ is bipartite, since the IRIS cells as well as the tower cells are partitionings of Paris, i.e., there are no overlapping cells in any of the two sets. Hence, for all $(v, v') \in E$, either $v \in \mathbb{T}$ and $v' \in \mathbb{L}$, or $v' \in \mathbb{T}$ and $v \in \mathbb{L}$. For bipartite graphs, the minimum vertex cover problem is equivalent to the maximum matching problem based on König's theorem [3], which can be solved in polynomial time, e.g., with the Hopcroft-Karp algorithm [16] in $O(|E|\sqrt{|V|})$, where $|V| = |\mathbb{T}| + |\mathbb{L}|$ and $|E| \leq |\mathbb{T}||\mathbb{L}|$. □

[4]Tower cells are represented by their Voronoi polygons as it is depicted in Figure 1

Figure 2c shows the largest IRIS and tower cells covering Paris. We computed the mean count of each cell over the whole week which are illustrated by the cell colors. Apparently, the minimum cover contains cells with larger counts; the mean counts are 91 on average for the IRIS cells (Figure 2b) and 120 on average for the minimum cover (Figure 2c)

However, care must be taken before computing the cell counts in the minimum cover $\mathbb{C}$. Since $\mathbb{C}$ can contain both IRIS and tower cells which may overlap, the L_1-sensitivity of all the counts in $\mathbb{C}$ can be larger than ℓ. Indeed, if $\mathbb{C}$ contains a tower cell T and one of its overlapping IRIS cell L, then adding/removing a user who visited T at time t will change $\overline{X}_t^T$ with 1, and also $\overline{X}_t^L$ with a non-zero value. A trivial (but not optimal) solution is to modify the counts of all towers in $\mathbb{C}$ which have overlapping IRIS cells. For example, if T overlaps with IRIS cells $\{L_1, L_2, \ldots, L_c\}$, then $\overline{X}_t^T$ should be reduced by $\sum_{i=1}^{c} \overline{X}_t^{L_i} \times \frac{\text{size}(L_i \cap T)}{\text{size}(T)}$.

5.3 Perturbation

After identifying the largest covering cells, their time series (i.e., $\overline{\mathbf{X}}^{\mathbb{C}}$) can be perturbed by adding $\mathcal{L}(\ell/\varepsilon)$ to each count in all time series (see Theorem 2). Unfortunately, this naive method provides very poor results which is also illustrated in Figure 3a. Indeed, individual cells have much smaller counts than the magnitude of the injected noise; the standard deviation of the Laplacian noise is 141 with $\varepsilon = 0.3$, which is even larger than the mean count in the minimum cover.

A better approach exploits (1) the similarity of geographically close time series, as well as (2) their periodic nature. In particular, we first cluster nearby less populated cells until their aggregated counts become sufficiently large to resist noise. The key observation is that the time series of close cells follow very similar trends, but their counts usually have different magnitudes. Hence, if we simply aggregate (i.e., sum up) all time series within such a cluster, the aggregated series will have a trend close to its individual components yet large enough counts to tolerate perturbation. To this end, we first accurately approximate the time series of individual cells by normalizing their aggregated time series (i.e., divide the aggregated count of each hour with the total number of visits inside the cluster), and scale back with the (noisy) total number of visits of individual cells.

In order to guarantee DP, we also need to perturb the aggregated time series before normalization. To do so, we exploit their periodic nature and apply a Fourier-based perturbation scheme [24, 1]: we add noise to the Fourier coefficients of the aggregated time series, and remove all high-frequency components that would be suppressed by the noise. As only low-frequency components are retained and perturbed, this method preserves the trends of the original data more faithfully than LPA.

The whole perturbation process is summarized in Algorithm 2. First, the noisy total number of visits of each cell in the minimum cover $\mathbb{C}$ is computed by adding noise $\mathcal{L}(2\ell/\varepsilon)$ to $\sum_{t=0}^{167} \overline{X}_t^i$ for cell i (Line 1). These noisy total counts are used to cluster similar cells in Line 2 by invoking Algorithm 3. When the clusters are created, their aggregated time series (i.e., the sum of all cells' time series within the cluster) is perturbed with a Fourier-based perturbation scheme in Line 5 (Algorithm 4). Finally, the perturbed time series of each cell i in cover $\mathbb{C}$ is computed in Line 7 by scaling back

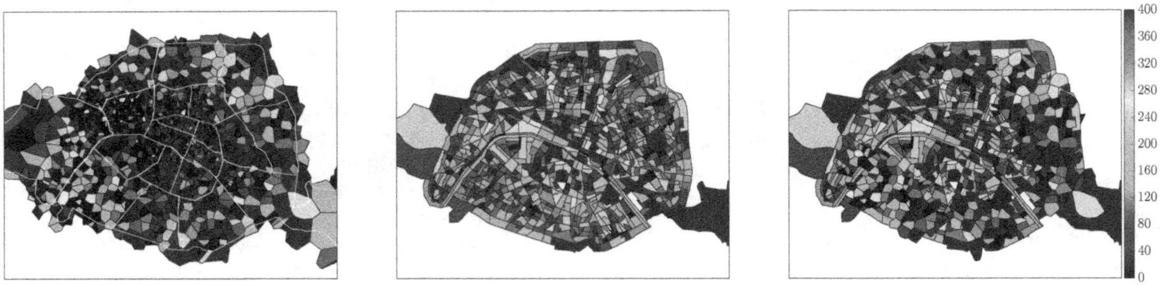

(a) Tower cells, $|\mathbb{T}| = 1303$ (b) IRIS cells, $|\mathbb{L}| = 989$ (c) Minimum cardinality cover, $|\mathbb{C}| = 826$

Figure 2: Covering Paris with the largest tower and IRIS cells. Each cell is colored based on their mean count. Large cells tend to have large counts (closer to red), while small cells are less populated (closer to blue). The minimum cover (Figure 2c) includes large, more populated cells: IRIS cells from the city center, and tower cells around the perimeter.

Algorithm 2 Perturbation

Input: Minimum cover $\mathbb{C}$, Pre-sampled time series $\overline{\mathbf{X}}^{\mathbb{C}}$, Minimum total count τ, Privacy budget ε, δ, Sensitivity $\Delta_1(\overline{\mathbf{X}}^{\mathbb{C}}) = \ell$
Output: Noisy time series $\hat{\mathbf{X}}^{\mathbb{C}}$

1: $\hat{S}_i := \sum_{t=0}^{167} \overline{X}_t^i + \mathcal{L}(2\ell/\varepsilon)$ for each $i \in \mathbb{C}$
2: $\mathbb{E} :=$ Cluster($\mathbb{C}, \tau, \hat{S}$) `//see Algorithm 3`
3: **for** each cluster $E \in \mathbb{E}$ **do**
4: $\quad \overline{\mathbf{X}}^E := \langle \sum_{i\in E} \overline{X}_0^i, \sum_{i\in E} \overline{X}_1^i, \ldots, \sum_{i\in E} \overline{X}_{167}^i \rangle$
5: $\quad \hat{\mathbf{X}}^E :=$ EFPAG($\overline{\mathbf{X}}^E, \varepsilon/2, \delta$) `//see Algorithm 4`
6: $\quad$ **for** each cell $i \in E$ **do**
7: $\quad\quad \hat{\mathbf{X}}^i := \hat{S}_i \cdot (\hat{\mathbf{X}}_t^E / ||\hat{\mathbf{X}}^E||_1)$
8: $\quad$ **end for**
9: **end for**

Algorithm 3 Cluster cells

Input: Minimum cover $\mathbb{C} = \{c_0, c_1, \ldots, c_{|\mathbb{C}|}\}$, Minimum total count τ, Noisy total counts $\hat{S}$ of cells in $\mathbb{C}$
Output: Cluster configuration $\mathbb{E} \subset 2^{|\mathbb{C}|}$

1: $\mathbb{E} := \{\{c_0\}, \{c_1\}, \{c_2\}, \ldots, \{c_{|\mathbb{C}|}\}\}$
2: $\hat{S}_E := \sum_{c_i \in E} \hat{S}_i$ for each cluster $E \in \mathbb{E}$
3: **while** $\exists E \in \mathbb{E}$ such that $\hat{S}_E < \tau$ **do**
4: $\quad E := \arg\min_{E\in\mathbb{E}} \hat{S}_E$
5: $\quad$ Let E' be the geographically closest neighbor of E
6: $\quad E := E \cup E'$
7: $\quad \hat{S}_E := \hat{S}_E + \hat{S}_{E'}$
8: $\quad$ Remove E' from $\mathbb{E}$
9: **end while**

the normalized aggregated time series with the noisy total count cell i (i.e., with $\hat{S}_i$). Since Line 1 guarantees $\varepsilon/2$-DP to the total counts ($\Delta_1(\overline{\mathbf{X}}^{\mathbb{C}}) = \ell$), it follows from Theorem 1 that Algorithm 2 is (ε, δ)-DP if EFPAG is ($\varepsilon/2, \delta$)-DP.

5.3.1 *Clustering cells*

Algorithm 3 is a simple iterative process that, in each iteration, merges the least visited cluster with its geographically closest neighboring cluster until all clusters in the resultant configuration have a total count larger than a predefined threshold τ. Initially, each cluster is a singleton composed of an individual cell in the cover. Then, in Line 4, we select the cluster which has the smallest (noisy) total count, and merge with its closest neighboring cluster in Line 5-8. The distance between two clusters are measured with the physical distance between their cluster centers[5]. In each step, the noisy total count of each cluster is computed as the sum of all (noisy) total counts of each cell within the cluster (Line 7). Since the total counts of cells are noisy, Algorithm 3 preserves DP.

5.3.2 *Perturbing aggregated time series*

To perturb aggregated time series, we build on the Fourier Perturbation Algorithm (FPA) [24]:

1. Compute the Fourier coefficients $\mathbf{F} = \langle F_0, F_1, \ldots, F_{n-1} \rangle$ of the input aggregated time series $\overline{\mathbf{X}}$ with length n by discrete Fourier transform.

2. Remove the last $n - k$ coefficients from $\mathbf{F}$, which correspond to the high-frequency components in $\overline{\mathbf{X}}$, and retain only the first k elements of $\mathbf{F}$, denoted by $\mathbf{F}^k$. Note that k is an input to the algorithm.

3. Generate the noisy version of $\mathbf{F}^k$, denoted by $\hat{\mathbf{F}}^k$, by Laplace mechanism: add i.i.d Laplace noise $\mathcal{L}(\sqrt{k}/\varepsilon)$ to each coefficient in $\mathbf{F}^k$.

4. Pad $\hat{\mathbf{F}}^k$ to be a n-dimensional vector by appending $n - k$ zeros, which is denoted by PAD$^n(\hat{\mathbf{F}}^k)$. Finally, the inverse DFT is applied to PAD$^n(\hat{\mathbf{F}}^k)$ to obtain a noisy version of $\overline{\mathbf{X}}$.

FPA provably guarantees ε-DP [24]. Enhanced FPA [1] improves basic FPA by selecting the coefficients to be removed more effectively. Specifically, in Step 2, EFPA chooses k probabilistically using the exponential mechanism such that the values of k which minimize the root-sum-squared error $\mathbb{E}||\overline{\mathbf{X}} - \hat{\mathbf{X}}||_2 \leq \sqrt{\sum_{i=k+1}^{n} |F_{i-1}|^2 + \frac{2k\Delta_2(\mathbf{X})}{\varepsilon}}$ (RSSE) have exponentially larger probability to be selected. In this paper, we improve the accuracy of EFPA in two ways. First, instead of the Discrete Fourier Transform (DFT), we

[5]The cluster center is the centroid of its consitituent cell polygons.

Algorithm 4 EFPAG

Input: Truncated time series $\overline{\mathbf{X}}$ with length n, Privacy budget ε, δ, L_2-sensitivity of $\overline{\mathbf{X}}$: $\Delta_2(\overline{\mathbf{X}})$
Output: Noisy time series $\hat{\mathbf{X}}$ with length n

1: $\mathbf{F} := \mathrm{DCT}(\overline{\mathbf{X}})$ `// Discrete Cosine Transform`
2: Compute $u_G(\overline{\mathbf{X}}, k) = \sqrt{\sum_{i=k+1}^{n} |F_{i-1}|^2} + \frac{\sqrt{2}\Delta_2(\overline{\mathbf{X}})\sqrt{k}\ln^{1/2}(4/\delta)}{\varepsilon}$ for all $1 \le k \le n$
3: Select k with probability $\propto \exp\left(-\frac{\varepsilon \cdot u_G(\overline{\mathbf{X}}, k)}{4\Delta_2(\overline{\mathbf{X}})}\right)$
4: $\hat{\mathbf{F}}^k := \mathbf{F}^k + \langle \mathcal{G}(\sqrt{2}\Delta_2(\overline{\mathbf{X}})\ln^{1/2}(4/\delta)/\varepsilon)\rangle^k$
5: **return** $\hat{\mathbf{X}} = \mathrm{IDCT}(\mathrm{PAD}^n(\hat{\mathbf{F}}^k))$ `//Inverse DCT`

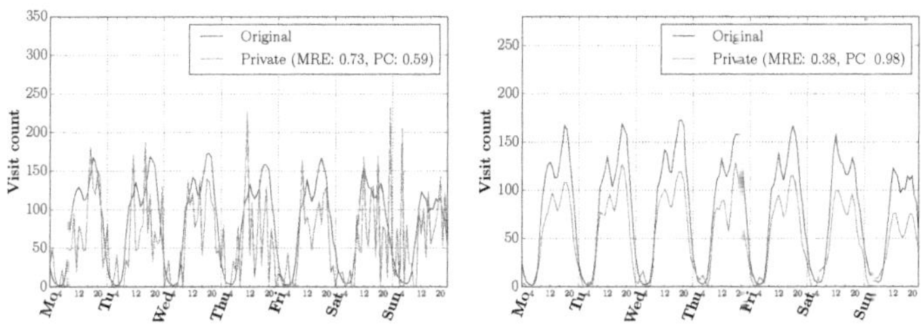

(a) LPA (b) Our approach

Figure 3: Noisy time series of an IRIS cell ($\varepsilon = 0.3$, $\ell = 30$)

apply the orthonormal version of the Discrete Cosine Transform (DCT), which tend to provide smaller high frequency components due to its different boundary conditions [26]. This can result in smaller RSSE when these components are removed in Step 2. Moreover, since we use orthonormal DCT, the resultant scheme also preserves ε-DP [1].

Second, instead of adding Laplace noise, we add properly calibrated Gaussian noise to the first k Fourier coefficients of $\overline{\mathbf{X}}$ thereby providing larger accuracy at the cost of weaker privacy. More specifically, when $\hat{\mathbf{F}}^k$ is generated in Step 3, we employ the Gaussian mechanism instead of LPA and add i.i.d Gaussian noise $\mathcal{G}(\sigma)$ to each coefficient in $\mathbf{F}^k$, where $\sigma = \sqrt{2}\Delta_2(\overline{\mathbf{X}})\ln^{1/2}(4/\delta)/\varepsilon$ to provide (ε, δ)-probabilistic DP based on Theorem 3. In addition, we select k with probability $\propto \exp\left(-\frac{\varepsilon \cdot u_G(\overline{\mathbf{X}}, k)}{4}\right)$ in Step 2, where $u_G(\overline{\mathbf{X}}, k) = \sqrt{\sum_{i=k+1}^{n} |F_{i-1}|^2} + \frac{\sqrt{2}\Delta_2(\overline{\mathbf{X}})\sqrt{k}\ln^{1/2}(4/\delta)}{\varepsilon}$ which follows from Theorem 5 in [1] and Theorem 3. When we use GPA in Step 3, the new scheme (with DCT) is denoted by EFPAG in the rest.

Since Gaussian noise has smaller variance than Laplacian, EFPAG provides better accuracy than EFPA. Specifically, the variance of the Gaussian noise added to the Fourier coefficients is $8\Delta_2(\overline{\mathbf{X}})^2\ln(4/\delta)/\varepsilon^2$, which is independent of the number of retained coefficients (i.e., k). By contrast, the variance of the Laplace noise added to the coefficients in EFPA is $8\Delta_2(\overline{\mathbf{X}})^2 k/\varepsilon^2$ which linearly increases with the number of retained coefficients. However, this improvement also leads to some privacy degradation which is measured by δ.

EFPAG is summarized in Algorithm 4, where the total budget ε is uniformly divided between GPA (Line 4) and exponential mechanism (Line 2), therefore, EFPAG is (ε, δ)-probabilistically DP due to Theorem 1.

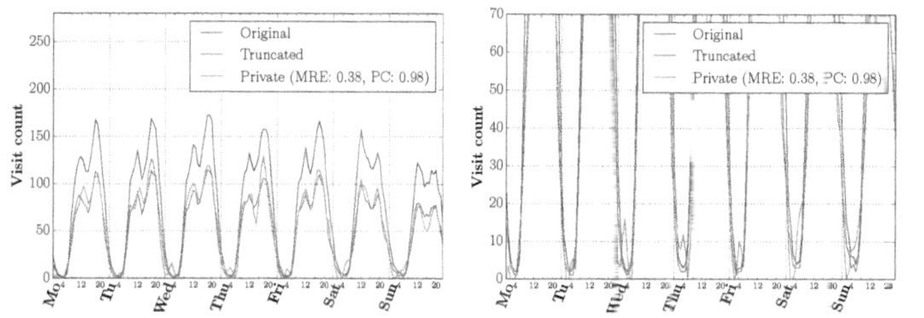

(a) Large counts (b) Small counts around local minimas

Figure 4: Our scheme before improvements ($\varepsilon = 0.3$, $\ell = 30$).

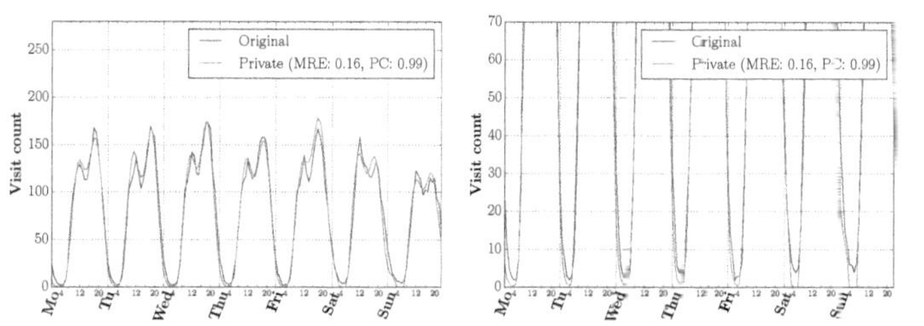

(a) Scaling (b) Smoothing

Figure 5: Our scheme after improvements ($\varepsilon = 0.3$, $\ell = 30$)

Finally, in order to employ EFPA(G), we need to compute the L_2-sensitivity of the counts in the cover $\mathbb{C}$, i.e., $\Delta_2(\overline{\mathbf{X}}^{\mathbb{C}})$. Indeed, since $\mathbb{E}$ is a partitioning of $\mathbb{C}$, $\Delta_2(\overline{\mathbf{X}}^{\mathbb{E}}) = \Delta_2(\overline{\mathbf{X}}^{\mathbb{C}})$. Recall that, as a result of pre-sampling, at most a single visit of a user is retained in any slot, and at most ℓ visits per user over the whole week. This means that, for any t, there is only a single tower whose count can change (by at most 1) by modifying a single user's data. From Formula (1), it follows that the total change of all IRIS cell counts is at most 1 at any t, and hence $\Delta_2(\overline{\mathbf{X}}^{\mathbb{L}}) \le \Delta_2(\overline{\mathbf{X}}^{\mathbb{T}}) = \sqrt{\ell}$ based on the definition of L_2-norm. Since $\mathbb{C} \subseteq \mathbb{T} \cup \mathbb{L}$, $\Delta_2(\overline{\mathbf{X}}^{\mathbb{C}}) \le \sqrt{\ell}$. Figure 3 illustrates the improvement of our approach (Clustering + EFPAG) over simple LPA.

5.4 Further improvements

Although our approach is clearly superior to LPA, Figure 4 still suggests a large error on average. This difference between $\hat{\mathbf{X}}$ and $\mathbf{X}$ is the result of two errors: the sampling error (between $\overline{\mathbf{X}}$ and $\mathbf{X}$) is attributed to pre-sampling, whereas the perturbation error (between $\hat{\mathbf{X}}$ and $\overline{\mathbf{X}}$) is due to our perturbation scheme.

As illustrated by Figure 4a, sampling error mainly distorts large counts: although the noisy counts are close to the counts of the *truncated* (pre-sampled) time series between 9:00 AM and 11:00 PM, it is still far from the original count values. This significantly increases MRE.

In addition, as Figure 4b also shows, noisy counts also deviate from pre-sampled as well as from original counts around the local minimas (close to 4:00 AM every day), which further deteriorates MRE. This perturbation error is caused by the higher frequency components that are retained and perturbed by EFPA(G).

To alleviate these errors, we propose two further improvements: first, we improve the perturbation of total cell counts (Line 1 in Algorithm 2), which is used in cell clustering (Algorithm 3) and scaling (Line 6 in Algorithm 2). Then, as a post-processing step, we smooth out small counts (i.e., between 0:00 and 6:00 AM) through non-linear least-square fitting to diminish perturbation error.

5.4.1 *Improved scaling*

Recall that we scale back the normalized aggregated time series with $\hat{S}_i$ in Line 6 (Algorithm 2), where $\hat{S}_i = \sum_{t=0}^{167} \overline{X}_t^i + \mathcal{L}(2\ell/\varepsilon)$. Since $\overline{\mathbf{X}}^i$ is the pre-sampled time series of cell i, $\hat{\mathbf{X}}^i$ (Line 6) will be a scaled down version of the original time series $\mathbf{X}^i$ due to the fact that the ℓ visits per individual are sampled *uniformly* at random. Also, as we have discussed in Section 5.1, adding Laplace noise directly to the original total count $\sum_{t=0}^{167} X_t^i$ is very inaccurate, as the sensitivity of $\sum_{t=0}^{167} X_t^i$ is $\Delta_1(\mathbf{X})$ which is too large.

We rather perturb the *original* total count $\sum_{t=0}^{167} X_t^i$ using a different approach: we first approximate the relative frequencies of each *tower* by another constraint sampling, and scale back these frequencies to count values with the (noisy) total number of visits in the dataset. The main idea is that sampling requires only a small amount of noise to guarantee privacy, while the total number of all visits is so large that it tolerates a large noise magnitude.

In particular, we estimate the histogram H where a bin H_j represents the frequency of visits at tower j, i.e., $H_j = \sum_{t=0}^{167} X_t^j / K$, where K denotes the total number of tower visits in the dataset ($K = \sum_{t=0}^{167} \sum_{T\in\mathbb{T}} X_t^T$). To do so, we sample a single visit per user uniformly at random, and create a new histogram $\tilde{H}$ from the sampled visits (with size N). Using this approximative histogram $\tilde{H}$, the total number of visits $\sum_{t=0}^{167} X_t^j$ of a tower j is computed as $(\tilde{H}_j + \mathcal{L}(2/\varepsilon')) \times \hat{K}$, where $\hat{K} = K + \mathcal{L}(2\Delta_1(\mathbf{X})/\varepsilon')$ and $\Delta_1(\mathbf{X})$ is universally fixed for all input dataset[6]. Finally, having the noisy $\sum_{t=0}^{167} X_t^j$ for each tower cell j, we can also compute the noisy $\sum_{t=0}^{167} X_t^L$ for any IRIS cell L (using Formula (1)) and calculate $\hat{S}_i$ for all cell i in $\mathbb{C}$. This technique is $2\cdot(\varepsilon'/2) = \varepsilon'$ differential private based on Theorem 1.

Figure 6a compares the accuracy of our sampling approach to perturb the relative frequencies of each tower (i.e., sampling is followed by adding $\mathcal{L}(2/\varepsilon')$ to each H_j) with the naive Laplace approach (i.e., $\mathcal{L}(2\Delta_1(\mathbf{X})/\varepsilon')$ is added to each H_j without sampling). Sampling clearly boosts the accuracy of histogram perturbation (Figure 6a) especially for smaller values of ε', and eventually yields significantly more accurate estimation of $\sum_{t=0}^{167} X_t^T$ for all towers T (Figure 6b).

The effect of scaling is illustrated in Figure 5a. Recall that the full privacy budget ε is divided equally between EFPA(G) and scaling (see Algorithm 1). Hence, our sanitization scheme is ε-DP (or (ε,δ)-prob. DP with EFPAG) based on Theorem 1.

5.4.2 *Smoothing*

In order to smooth out low (noisy) counts around the local minimas (around 4:00 AM each day), we fit an exponential curve to the noisy counts between 0:00 AM and 4:00 AM

[6] $\Delta_1(\mathbf{X})$ is fixed to 732 in this paper. Notice that although $\Delta_1(\mathbf{X})$ is large so is K: $K = 137,255,052$ in our dataset, and $|K - \hat{K}|/K$ is less than 10^{-5} on average

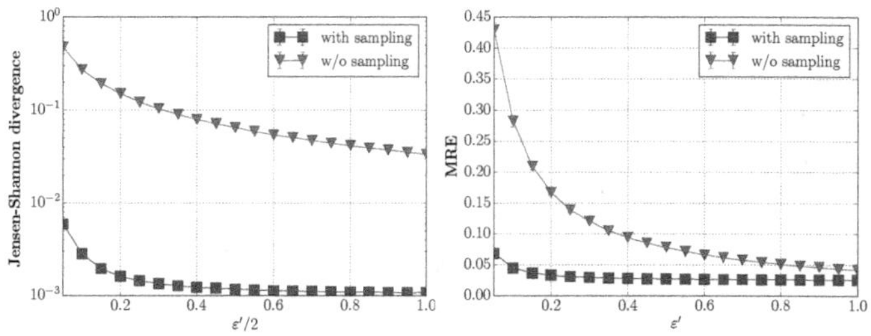

(a) Perturbing H with sampling and without sampling.

(b) MRE of the noisy $\sum_{t=0}^{167} X_t^T$ over all towers T.

Figure 6: Perturbing the total visits $\sum_{t=0}^{167} X_t^T$ of each tower cell T.

where the counts are exponentially decreasing, and another exponential curve between 4:00 AM and 6:00 AM, where the counts are exponentially increasing. In particular, we fit function $g(x,a,b) = a\cdot\exp(b\cdot x)$ to the noisy counts, i.e., compute parameters a, b such that the error $\sum_i(\hat{X}_i - g(x_i,a,b))^2$ is minimized where x_i runs over the hours of the given time intervals for each day, and then replace the noisy counts with the values of the fitted function. This is a standard non-linear least square fitting problem which can be approximated with any numerical minimization method (e.g., Levenberg-Marquardt algorithm [18]). Since this operation is performed on the noisy time series, it is already private. The effect of smoothing in illustrated in Figure 5b.

6. PERFORMANCE EVALUATION

We evaluate the utility of our scheme depending on the guaranteed privacy (i.e., ε) with EFPA and EFPAG, where $\delta = 2\cdot 10^{-6} < 1/N$. The minimum total count τ used in Algorithm 3 is adjusted such that the expected RSSE is less than 1% of the total count when all coefficients are retained in EFPA(G). That is, $\tau = \sqrt{168}\cdot\sigma/0.01$, where σ^2 is the variance of noise added to each coefficient. We compare our approaches to the naive Laplace mechanism (LPA) that adds $\mathcal{L}(\ell/\varepsilon)$ noise to each count of each time series in cover $\mathbb{C}$. We use the CDR dataset described in Section 4.

First, we analyze the utility depending on the pre-sampling size ℓ. Then, we show how pre-sampling combined with the improved scaling and smoothing boost accuracy, and also report the error distribution among individual IRIS cells. Finally, we measure the Earth Mover's Distance (EMD) which captures the error between spatial distributions in terms of geographical distances.

6.1 Utility depending on the pre-sample size

Recall that the number of visits retained per user (i.e., ℓ) determines the injected noise in the perturbation phase. In general, larger values of ℓ imply larger noise, which degrades utility. On the other hand, smaller values of ℓ preserve more information about individuals which results in a more accurate representation of the original dataset. The goal is to select a value of ℓ which yields the best trade-off. Nevertheless, we experimentally show next that our scheme exhibits stable performance with quite different values of ℓ.

In Figure 7, we report the utility of our scheme with EFPAG for three values of ℓ: 10, 30 and 168. In each case, perturbation is followed by the improvements described in

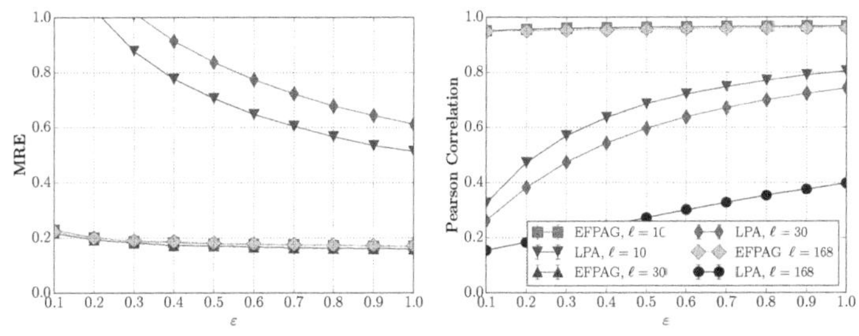

Figure 7: Utility depending on the pre-sampling size ℓ.

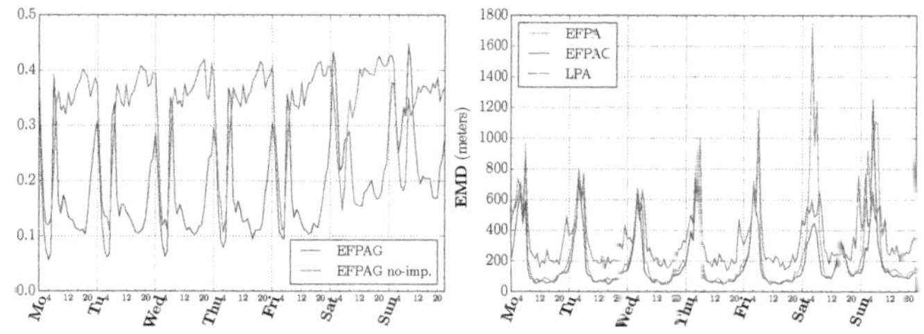

(a) Relative error

(b) EMD

Figure 9: Error depending on time with EFPAG ($\varepsilon = 0.3, \ell = 30$)

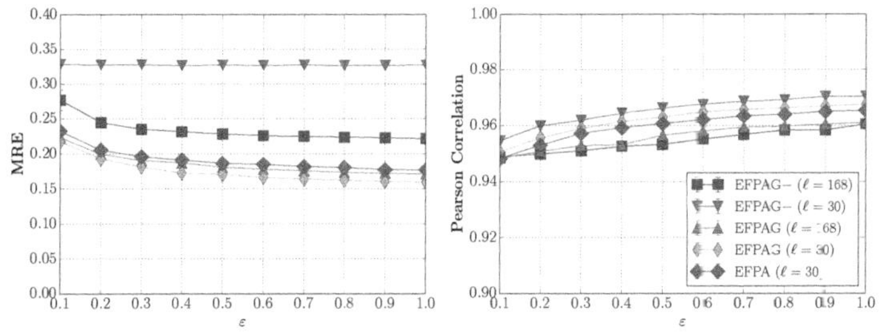

Figure 8: Utility of our scheme with different perturbation techniques.

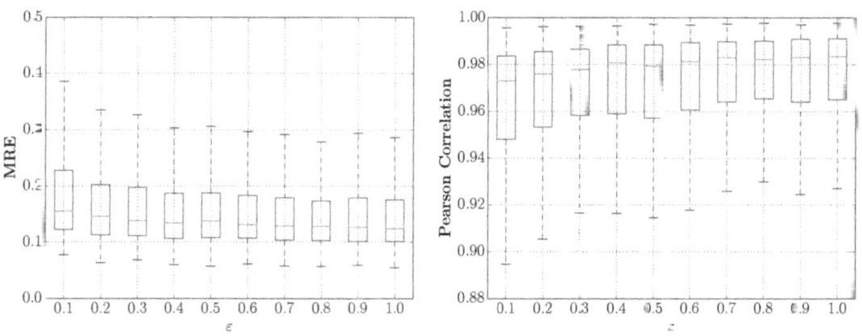

Figure 10: Error and Pearson correlation on IRIS cells with EFPAG, $\ell = 30$. The box extends from the lower to upper quartile values of the cell errors, with a red line at the median.

Section 5.4. Specifically, we computed the average of MRE and Pearson correlation over all cells. We repeated the whole process 20 times and plotted the mean and standard deviation of the average MRE and PC over all executions.

LPA has significantly larger error for all values of ℓ, and provides especially poor results for smaller values of ε. By contrast, our scheme does not only provide practical utility even for stringent privacy guarantee, but also has stable performance for different ℓ. For instance, for $\varepsilon = 0.3$, MRE is less than 20%, while PC is larger than 0.95. Therefore, the output of our scheme has almost perfect linear correlation with the original data thanks to the combination of clustering and the Fourier perturbation approach. Moreover, the variations of these values are very moderate: 0.2 ± 0.03 and 0.95 ± 0.03, respectively, for different values of ℓ. In the rest of the paper, we fix ℓ to 30.

EFPAG and EFPA[7] are compared in Figure 8. EFPAG outperforms EFPA especially for smaller ε: MRE is reduced by 0.03 and PC is increased by 0.02 on average.

6.2 Pre-sampling with scaling

The distortion effect of pre-sampling is mitigated by the improved scaling step detailed in Section 5.4.1. Our aim now is to show that scaling and smoothing indeed results in better utility. Figure 8 depicts a variation of our scheme, denoted by "EFPA−" when the improvements described in Section 5.4 are not employed after perturbation. The results show that MRE is reduced by 0.07 on average when the pre-sample size is diminished to $\ell = 30$ and improvements are employed. By contrast, PC is increased only by about 0.01 for smaller values of ε; the change is not so significant due to the fact that scaling does not influence linear correlation, and smoothing modifies relatively small number of counts in general.

In Figure 9, we also plotted the average relative error depending on the time for our scheme with and without improvements. In particular, we computed the relative error and took the average over all cells in each hour. Figure 9a confirms that scaling significantly diminishes the relative error in daylight when counts are larger. The improvement can be almost a factor of 4. This has particular importance in practice, as location counts in daylight are usually more important than at night.

6.3 Error variation among IRIS cells

Figure 10 shows through box plots how MRE and Pearson correlation change among IRIS cells; we compute these metrics for each IRIS cell, and compute the corresponding box plot over the metric values of all cells. Although medians do not change significantly for different values of ε, MRE has larger variation for smaller ε, i.e., there are more cells which have larger error.

The MRE and PC of individual IRIS cells are also illustrated by color maps in Figure 11. This figure shows that our scheme can provide practical utility for most cells with strong privacy guarantee. Specifically, the average MRE over all cells is only 0.17 with $\varepsilon = 0.3$.

6.4 Earth Mover's Distance

In order to compare the sanitized spatial probability distribution with the original one at a given time, we use Earth Mover's Distance (EMD) [25]. EMD measures the "amount of energy" (or cost) needed to transform one distribution to another, and is a metric for probability distributions (i.e., location counts have to be normalized). Formally, for any

[7]Recall that EFPAG adds Gaussian noise whereas EFPA adds Laplacian noise to the retained Fourier coefficients.

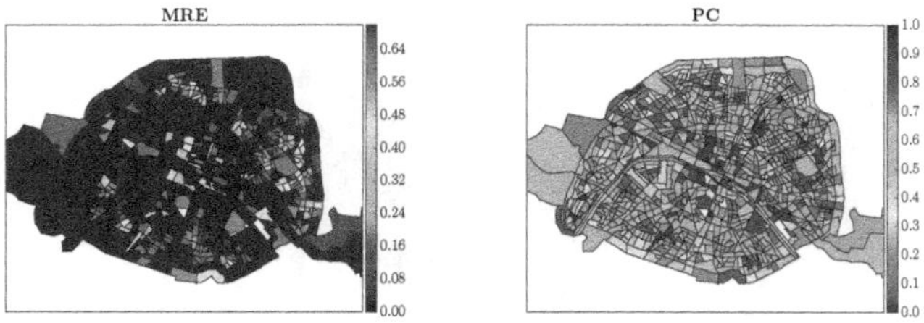

(a) LPA (Avg. MRE: 1.01, PC: 0.47)

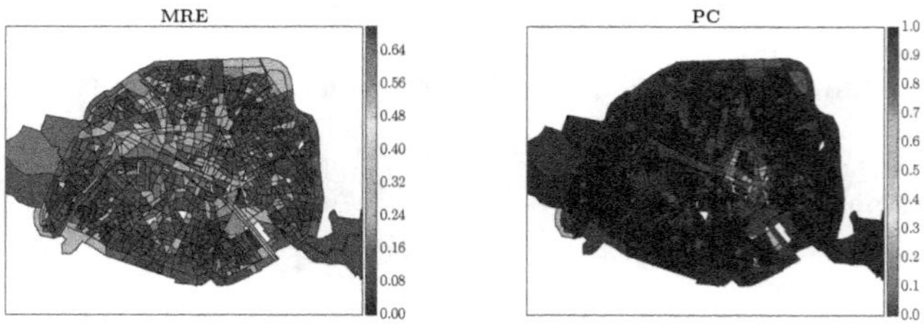

(b) Our scheme with EFPAG (Avg. MRE: 0.17, PC: 0.96)

Figure 11: MRE and PC of each IRIS cell ($\ell = 30$, $\varepsilon = 0.3$)

t, $\text{EMD}(\mathbf{X}_t^{\mathbb{L}}, \hat{\mathbf{X}}_t^{\mathbb{L}}) = \min_{\{f_{ij}\}} \sum_{i,j} f_{ij} d_{ij}$ such that $f_{ij} \geq 0$, $\sum_j f_{ij} \leq X_t^i / \sum_k X_t^k$, $\sum_i f_{ij} \leq \hat{X}_t^j / \sum_k \hat{X}_t^k$, where $\{f_{ij}\}$ denotes the set of all possible flows (each f_{ij} represents the amount of probability mass transported from IRIS cell i to j), and d_{ij} is the geographical distance between the centers of cells i and j, resp. Intuitively, EMD measures the meters of error between two spatial density maps. Figure 9b reports the EMD depending on the time. The mean EMD over the whole week is 258 meters for EFPA, 188 meters for EFPAG, and 341 meters for LPA.

7. CONCLUSIONS

The goal of this work is to demonstrate through a real-world application that differential privacy can be a practical model for data anonymization, even if the input dataset has large dimension and/or is highly sensitive. We showed that, in order to achieve meaningful accuracy, the sanitization process has to be carefully customized to the application and public characteristics of the dataset. We strongly believe that there are no "universal" sanitization solutions that fit all applications, i.e., provide good accuracy in all scenarios. In particular, achieving the best performance requires to find the most faithful and concise representation of the data, such that it withstands perturbation. In our application (i.e., spatio-temporal density), clustering and sampling with Fourier-based perturbation are seemingly the best choices due to the periodic nature and large sensitivity of location counts. We experimentally showed that our scheme can provide practical utility and strong privacy guarantee.

8. REFERENCES

[1] G. Ács, R. Chen, and C. Castelluccia. Differentially private histogram publishing through lossy compression. In *ICDM*, 2012.

[2] M. E. Andrés, N. E. Bordenabe, K. Chatzikokolakis, and C. Palamidessi. Geo-indistinguishability: Differential privacy for location-based systems. In *ACM CCS*, pages 901–914. ACM, 2013.

[3] J. A. Bondy and U. S. R. Murty. *Graph Theory with Applications*. Elsevier, New York, 1976.

[4] T.-H. H. Chan, E. Shi, and D. Song. Private and continual release of statistics. *ACM Trans. Inf. Syst. Secur.*, 14(3):26:1–26:24, Nov. 2011.

[5] R. Chen, G. Ács, and C. Castelluccia. Differentially private sequential data publication via variable-length n-grams. In *ACM CCS*, pages 638–649, 2012.

[6] C.-Y. Chow and M. F. Mokbel. Trajectory privacy in location-based services and data publication. *SIGKDD Explor. Newsletter*, 13(1):19–29, Aug. 2011.

[7] G. Cormode, C. Procopiuc, D. Srivastava, E. Shen, and T. Yu. Differentially private spatial decompositions. In *ICDE*, pages 20–31, 2012.

[8] Y.-A. de Montjoye, C. A. Hidalgo, M. Verleysen, and V. D. Blondel. Unique in the crowd: The privacy bounds of human mobility. *Scientific Reports, Nature*, March 2013.

[9] C. Dwork, K. Kenthapadi, F. McSherry, I. Mironov, and M. Naor. Our data, ourselves: privacy via distributed noise generation. In *EUROCRYPT*, pages 486–503, 2006.

[10] C. Dwork, F. McSherry, K. Nissim, and A. Smith. Calibrating noise to sensitivity in private data analysis. In *TCC*, pages 265–284, 2006.

[11] C. Dwork, M. Naor, T. Pitassi, and G. N. Rothblum. Differential privacy under continual observation. In *ACM STOC*, pages 715–724, 2010.

[12] L. Fan and L. Xiong. Real-time aggregate monitoring with differential privacy. In *ACM CIKM*, pages 2169–2173, 2012.

[13] P. Golle and K. Partridge. On the anonymity of home/work location pairs. In *Percom*, pages 390–397, 2009.

[14] M. C. Gonzalez, C. A. Hidalgo, and A.-L. Barabasi. Understanding individual human mobility patterns. *Nature*, 453, 2008.

[15] M. Götz. *On User Privacy in Personalized Mobile Services*. PhD thesis, Cornell University, May 2012.

[16] J. E. Hopcroft and R. M. Karp. An $n^{5/2}$ algorithm for maximum matchings in bipartite graphs. *SIAM Journal on Computing*, 2(4), 1973.

[17] G. Kellaris and S. Papadopoulos. Practical differential privacy via grouping and smoothing. In *VLDB*, pages 301–312, 2013.

[18] K. Levenberg. A method for the solution of certain non-linear problems in least squares. *Quarterly of Applied Mathematics*, 2:164–168, 1944.

[19] N. Li, W. Yang, and W. Qardaji. Differentially private grids for geospatial data. In *ICDE*, pages 757–768, 2013.

[20] A. Machanavajjhala, D. Kifer, J. M. Abowd, J. Gehrke, and L. Vilhuber. Privacy: Theory meets practice on the map. In *ICDE*, 2008.

[21] F. McSherry. Privacy integrated queries: an extensible platform for privacy-preserving data analysis. In *SIGMOD*, pages 19–30, 2009.

[22] F. McSherry and K. Talwar. Mechanism design via differential privacy. In *FOCS*, 2007.

[23] D. J. Mir, S. Isaacman, R. Cáceres, M. Martonosi, and R. N. Wright. Dp-where: Differentially private modeling of human mobility. In *BigData Conference*, pages 580–588, 2013.

[24] V. Rastogi and S. Nath. Differentially private aggregation of distributed time-series with transformation and encryption. In *SIGMOD*, 2010.

[25] Y. Rubner, C. Tomasi, and L. J. Guibas. The earth mover's distance as a metric for image retrieval. *Int. J. Comput. Vision*, 40(2):99–121, Nov. 2000.

[26] G. Strang. The discrete cosine transform. *SIAM Rev.*, 41(1):135–147, Mar. 1999.

[27] X. Xiao, G. Bender, M. Hay, and J. Gehrke. iReduct: Differential privacy with reduced relative errors. In *SIGMOD*, pages 229–240, 2011.

[28] H. Zang and J. Bolot. Anonymization of location data does not work: A large-scale measurement study. In *Mobicom*, pages 145–156, 2011.

Scalable Near Real-Time Failure Localization of Data Center Networks

Herodotos Herodotou
Microsoft Research
herohero@microsoft.com

Bolin Ding
Microsoft Research
bolin.ding@microsoft.com

Shobana Balakrishnan
Microsoft Research
shobanab@microsoft.com

Geoff Outhred
Microsoft
geoffo@microsoft.com

Percy Fitter
Microsoft
percyf@microsoft.com

ABSTRACT

Large-scale data center networks are complex—comprising several thousand network devices and several hundred thousand links—and form the critical infrastructure upon which all higher-level services depend on. Despite the built-in redundancy in data center networks, performance issues and device or link failures in the network can lead to user-perceived service interruptions. Therefore, determining and localizing user-impacting availability and performance issues in the network in near real time is crucial. Traditionally, both passive and active monitoring approaches have been used for failure localization. However, data from passive monitoring is often too noisy and does not effectively capture silent or gray failures, whereas active monitoring is potent in detecting faults but limited in its ability to isolate the exact fault location depending on its scale and granularity.

Our key idea is to use statistical data mining techniques on large-scale active monitoring data to determine a ranked list of suspect causes, which we refine with passive monitoring signals. In particular, we compute a failure probability for devices and links in near real time using data from active monitoring, and look for statistically significant increases in the failure probability. We also correlate the probabilistic output with other failure signals from passive monitoring to increase the confidence of the probabilistic analysis. We have implemented our approach in the Windows Azure production environment and have validated its effectiveness in terms of localization accuracy, precision, and time to localization using known network incidents over the past three months. The correlated ranked list of devices and links is surfaced as a report that is used by network operators to investigate current issues and identify probable root causes.

Categories and Subject Descriptors

C.2.3 [**Computer-Communication Networks**]: Network Operations—*Network management; Network monitoring*

KDD'14, August 24–27, 2014, New York, NY, USA.
Copyright 2014 ACM 978-1-4503-2956-9/14/08 ...$15.00.
http://dx.doi.org/10.1145/2623330.2623365.

General Terms

Algorithms; Management

Keywords

Failure localization; Data center networks

1. INTRODUCTION

Communications in data centers today are based on large-scale complex networks that concurrently support a variety of distinct services (e.g., search, email, cloud storage and compute). As an example, the Windows Azure network consists of over 7 thousand network devices (e.g., routers) and over 220 thousand links, which connect together all the servers in all Windows Azure data centers worldwide. All Windows Azure Services [14] depend on a healthy network for providing highly-available and scalable offerings. Despite the built-in redundancy in data center networks, performance issues or failures in the network can lead to *user-perceived* service interruptions. Therefore, determining and localizing user-impacting availability and performance issues in the network in near real time is crucial.

Localizing network faults is done by knowledgeable network operations teams who work with associated on-call engineers to resolve problems in real time with the help of monitoring data. Such an approach can be time consuming, tedious, and is further exacerbated by monitoring noise and the increasing size of the network. As the scale of the network grows, automated fault localization becomes increasingly important since it can reduce mean-time-to-recovery and service disruption.

Network monitoring is at the heart of failure localization and is divided into two categories: *passive* and *active* monitoring. The passive approach typically involves polling the network devices periodically to collect various telemetry data about their health and the traffic that passes by. The system will then analyze the local telemetry data and raise availability and performance alerts at the level of individual devices and links when it detects any abnormalities [4, 5, 13]. While these alerts are often useful in localizing failures, they are also noisy and not a direct signal for user-perceived failures[1], which turns troubleshooting a particular

[1]User-perceived network failures refer to network failures that have a direct effect on user traffic, where users are primarily the services running on top of the network.

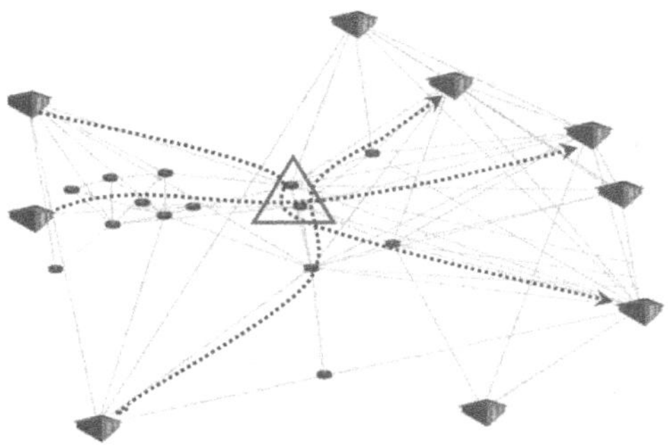

Figure 1: Failure localization approach: The successful, failed, and delayed ping data are overlaid on top of the network topology, and a statistical data mining approach is used to triangulate (i.e., localize) issues in the network.

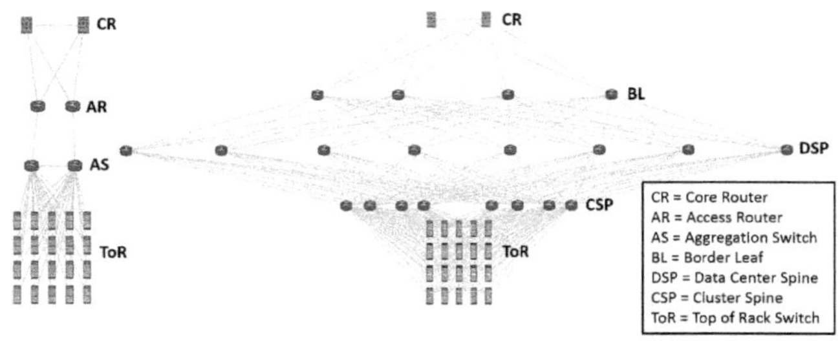

Figure 2: Common network topologies for data centers.

network issue into a time-consuming process that could take anywhere from minutes, to hours, to even days to resolve.

The active approach relies on the capability to inject test traffic into the network and to monitor the flow of that traffic. In particular, data centers typically run a *ping service* that generates large amounts of pings between pairs of end hosts in the network and acts as a proxy for user-perceived network availability and latency [15, 16]. In this setting, ping failures provide a strong signal that there is indeed an issue in the underlying network and, more specifically, that there is an issue somewhere along the path from the source to the destination of the ping. However, pings do not pinpoint the exact device or link that has caused the pings to fail since actual network routes are typically unknown.

Even though a single ping failure cannot help in identifying the culprit, the conjecture is that the combination of ping data between multiple sources and destinations will allow us to triangulate the location of an existing issue. Figure 1 provides a simple visual representation of the proposed approach, which uses statistical data mining techniques to localize user-perceived network failures based on ping data. Specifically, we (i) introduce a probabilistic model for describing the ping routes and failures, (ii) formulate the failure localization problem as a fitting problem to compute failure probabilities for devices and links in near real time, and (iii) detect statistically significant increases in the computed failure probabilities.

Our algorithm produces a short ranked list of devices and links that best explain the observed ping data. Finally, we correlate this list with passive monitoring signals, such as device and link alerts, in order to increase the confidence of the probabilistic analysis. The correlated ranked list of devices and links forms a starting point for investigating current issues in the network and can drastically reduce the time it takes for network operators to identify probable root causes and resolve network issues. Our experimental evaluation on real network incidents validates both the effectiveness and efficiency of our approach to localize network failures. In summary, our key contribution is the novel and successful application of statistical data mining techniques to localize user-impacting availability and performance issues in a worldwide data center network in near real time.

The rest of the paper is organized as follows. Section 2 presents background information for data center networks. Section 3 provides an overview of our approach, while the details are described in Section 4. The implementation and deployment details are discussed in Section 5 and the experimental evaluation is presented in Section 6. Finally, Section 7 discusses related work and Section 8 concludes the paper.

2. DATA CENTER NETWORKS BASICS

Data centers hosting Internet-scale services comprise of servers, direct attached storage, and networking infrastructure. Over the recent years, data center networks have been on the path to commoditization [1]. For example, [7] demonstrates the performance and scale that can be achieved from a network built using low-cost Ethernet switches arranged into a Clos topology that provides multiple paths between servers. The overall network consists of a densely connected mesh network within each data center as well as a core network spanning the geographies. With mega-scale data centers, the size of the network within each data center can be large connecting over 50-100 thousand servers.

Given the types of workloads that run in these data centers, the authors in [3] present the need to treat the data center as one massive warehouse-scale computer and make the appropriate design, operation, and cost tradeoffs that best support the workloads. In this paper, we have only looked at a single aspect—namely the operational aspects of the network—but from a holistic perspective of end-to-end user-perceived network performance and at the scale of these large data center networks.

2.1 Network Topology

Modern data center networks use hierarchical architectures reaching from a layer of servers in racks at the bottom to a layer of core routers at the top [1, 7]. We consider two common architectures within data centers, shown in Figure 2. In both cases, there are typically 20 to 40 servers per rack, each singly connected to a Top of Rack (ToR) switch. The data center backbone in the first topology consists of a layer of Aggregation switches (AS), whereas in the second topology it consists of two layers, namely the Cluster Spines (CSPs) and the Data Center Spines (DSPs). Here, each ToR is connected to a layer of CSPs, which in turn is connected to a layer of DSPs forming two bipartite graphs. The ASs and DSPs are then connected to the core of the network via Access Routers (ARs) and Border Leafs (BLs), respectively. Finally, ARs and BLs are connected to Core Routers (CRs).

The core network connects all data centers together forming an asymmetric wide-area network. It consists of core routers in the data centers as well as intermediate forwarding devices between the data centers. Figure 1 shows the core network between multiple data centers and forwarding stations. For this paper, we only consider the network topol-

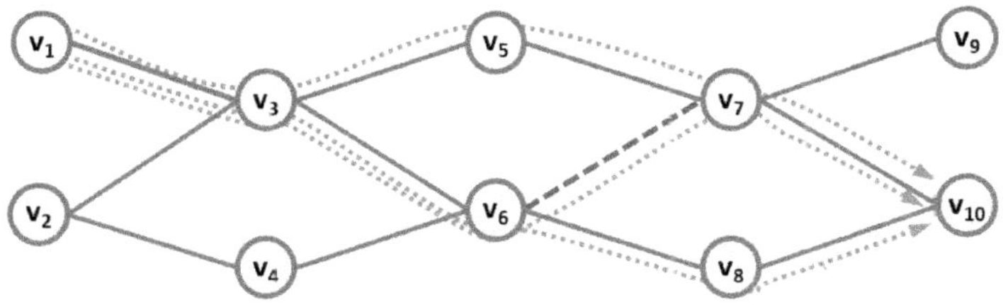

Figure 3: Example network topology. The dotted green arrows show the three possible paths between v_1 and v_{10}. The dashed red edge (v_6, v_7) represents a faulty link.

Table 1: Example ping data that lists ping successes and failures between pairs of vertices in the graph.

Source Vertex	Destination Vertex	Ping Successes	Ping Failures
v_1	v_9	45	5
v_1	v_{10}	38	2
v_2	v_8	46	0
v_2	v_9	34	6
v_2	v_{10}	37	3

ogy that is within the control of Microsoft and, therefore, do not consider peering devices or other ISP networks that connect with the core network. However, the approach can be extended beyond the Microsoft network provided we have an accurate characterization of the topology.

2.2 Routing Protocols

Large-scale data center networks typically employ *multipath routing*, which involves using multiple alternative paths through the network in order to improve fault tolerance, bandwidth, and security. In this work, we consider *Equal-Cost MultiPath (ECMP)* routing used within data centers and *Border Gateway Protocol (BGP)* used in the core network between data centers. Routers within data centers use ECMP routing to spread the traffic along multiple paths by making per-hop decisions based on routing metric calculations. For routing paths, we assume that all shortest paths are equally likely and have the same cost metric, which closely resembles the ECMP protocol.

BGP is the routing protocol that determines the routes taken in the core network. BGP is responsible for setting up Multiprotocol Label Switching (MPLS) that directs traffic from one network node to the next based on short path labels rather than long network addresses. These network paths are termed Label-Switched Paths (LSPs). For this work, we assume that all shortest paths across the core are equally likely and do not take into account the LSP information available in the core network. We plan to refine the routes in the core with this information in the future.

2.3 Network Monitoring

In passive monitoring, devices are polled periodically using various technologies (e.g., SNMP, NetFlow, RMON) and information is collected to assess network performance and status. Unfortunately, passive monitoring is known to be noisy as the generated alerts are largely threshold based and, in some cases, it suffers from a lack of signal when a device is actually faulty (*silent failures*) [6]. Hence, we leverage these signals to only increase the confidence and improve the pinpointing of the localization from our statistical analysis performed on active monitoring signals.

Our main active monitoring signal comes from the *ping service*, which runs on servers in most racks in all data centers. This service sends pings every minute to other randomly selected end hosts within the cluster, across clusters, and across data centers. Pings can fail or be delayed due to performance issues in the network or hard failures. A significant number of failed or delayed pings is an indication that there may be an issue in the physical network along the path(s) of the pings. Since the ping service runs on the same servers as the other data center services, it is a good proxy for user-perceived network availability and latency.

Another active monitoring tool is *traceroute*, which is used for displaying the path and measuring transit delays of packets across a network. A traceroute is significantly costlier than a ping since the entire history of the route is recorded. Hence, generating traceroutes to cover large-scale data center networks is prohibitively expensive and are primarily used for targeted testing [9].

3. APPROACH OVERVIEW

Our localization approach uses statistical data mining techniques on ping data to identify the links or devices that are responsible for ping failures (or significant ping delays), which typically translate into user-perceived network interruptions. This section will describe the problem formulation and provide an overview of our approach that will guide the description of our solution in Section 4.

Problem Formulation: There are two main inputs to our problem. The first input is the *network topology*, which we represent using a graph $\mathbb{G} = (\mathbb{V}, \mathbb{E})$. The vertices $\mathbb{V}$ in the graph correspond to network devices, whereas edges $\mathbb{E}$ correspond to network links. The graph contains the links and devices for all compute and storage clusters within each data center, as well as the links and devices that form the global backbone network connecting all data centers together. Figure 3 shows a simple graph with 10 vertices and 12 edges that we will use as a running example.

The second input is the *ping data*, which specifies how many pings succeeded and how many failed (or had high latency) between multiple source and destination vertices. High latency of a ping typically arises for two reasons: (a) some network device had to re-try sending the ping multiple times before succeeding or (b) the ping took a longer path than usual. In either case, significant high latency indicates an underlying issue with the network that we want to capture and localize. In our case, we consider ping latency to be significant if it belongs in the 95th percentile of the latency distribution. Table 1 shows a small example of ping data.

Our goal is to analyze the ping data overlaid on top of the topology in order to generate a short ranked list of edges and vertices associated with *failure scores*, whose potential failure would best explain the observed ping data. This list is then combined with alerts from link- and device-level telemetry data to further help network operators pinpoint a fault.

Solution Phases: The proposed failure localization approach works in 4 phases, each addressing 1 major challenge.

1. *Probabilistic Routing:* The exact ping routes through the network are unknown. Therefore, we model the underlying network protocol typically used within the data centers and then compute the most likely ping routes and their probabilities (Section 4.1).
2. *Probabilistic Failure Modeling:* Network failures are often partial. For example, a faulty link may be dropping only a small fraction of its traffic. For this reason, we model failures using a probabilistic model and formulate a corresponding data fitting problem. We solve this problem and generate a ranked list of edges and vertices associated with failure scores (Section 4.2).
3. *Deviation Detection:* There exists background noise in both the input data and the generated failure scores. To overcome this challenge, the key idea is to first look at the failure scores over time in order to establish a score baseline. We then use statistical hypothesis testing to detect significant deviations from this baseline, filtering out the noise (Section 4.3).
4. *Correlation Analysis:* In certain cases, some devices or links can be indistinguishable from each other, like in the case where multiple physical links are connecting two devices. By intersecting our probabilistic results with the current network alerts produced from passive monitoring, we can pinpoint the specific link or device causing the issue (Section 4.4)

4. FAILURE LOCALIZATION

4.1 Probabilistic Routing

Multipath routing (e.g., ECMP), which is prevalent in almost all large networks, implies that the network route of any given ping (or packet in general) is determined by the routers using local per-hop decisions and is, therefore, unknown (recall Section 2.2). Instead, only the ping source and destination devices are known.

Given a source vertex v_s and a destination vertex v_d in the network graph, the goal of probabilistic routing is to compute the most likely ping routes along with their probabilities. The computation is based on the following two principles that govern multipath routing:

- Only shortest paths (in terms of number of hops) between v_s and v_d are valid routes.
- All next hops from a single vertex are equally probable.

Consider a ping from v_1 to v_{10} in the example network graph in Figure 3. There are three possible routes indicated by the three dotted green arrows, each requiring a total of four hops. All pings from v_1 must first go through v_3. At v_3, there are two equally-likely options: v_5 and v_6. Pings that are routed to v_5 will then traverse v_7 before reaching the final destination v_{10}. On the other hand, pings that reach v_6 will be routed to either v_7 or v_8 with equal probability before reaching v_{10}. In summary, the three routes and the corresponding probabilities are:

$$Pr[v_1 \rightarrow v_3 \rightarrow v_5 \rightarrow v_7 \rightarrow v_{10}] = 0.50$$

$$Pr[v_1 \rightarrow v_3 \rightarrow v_6 \rightarrow v_7 \rightarrow v_{10}] = 0.25$$

$$Pr[v_1 \rightarrow v_3 \rightarrow v_6 \rightarrow v_8 \rightarrow v_{10}] = 0.25$$

Table 2: List of notations.

Notation	Explanation
v_i	Vertex i in the network graph
$e = (v_i, v_j)$	Edge e connecting vertices v_i and v_j
$v_i \rightarrow v_j$	Ping from vertex v_i to v_j
$P_{i,j}(e)$	The probability that a $v_i \rightarrow v_j$ ping will pass through edge e
$N_{i,j}$	The total number of pings from v_i to v_j
$F_{i,j}$	The number of failed pings from v_i to v_j
X_e	Failure score for edge e

We use the Floyd-Warshall algorithm to compute the shortest distances from all vertices to all other vertices in the graph with worse case complexity of $\mathcal{O}(|\mathbb{V}|^3)$. We then build the routes of each ping opportunistically based on the shortest distances and compute the route probabilities based on the number of forwarding edges of each vertex in each route.

We use the computed routes and probabilities to also calculate the probability $P_{s,d}(e)$ that a given $v_s \rightarrow v_d$ ping will pass through a particular edge e. Consider a $v_1 \rightarrow v_{10}$ ping and edge $e = (v_7, v_{10})$ in the example graph in Figure 3. This edge is part of two different routes, namely $v_1 \rightarrow v_3 \rightarrow v_5 \rightarrow v_7 \rightarrow v_{10}$ and $v_1 \rightarrow v_3 \rightarrow v_6 \rightarrow v_7 \rightarrow v_{10}$, with route probabilities 0.5 and 0.25, respectively. The ping will pass through edge e if it takes one of the two aforementioned routes. Therefore, the probability that the ping will pass through edge e equals the sum of the two route probabilities, i.e., $P_{1,10}(e) = 0.5 + 0.25 = 0.75$. To simplify the discussion, we present the model in terms of network edges. A similar analysis applies to vertices.

4.2 Probabilistic Failure Modeling

Network devices and links that are experiencing a failure often drop only a fraction of their overall traffic, depending on the nature of the failure. In particular, issues caused during maintenance or by device malfunctions are fairly common and typically cause small performance degradation or a small packet loss rate (less than 5%). On the other hand, catastrophic events like fiber cuts and complete hardware failures are fairly rare. We have seen only 5 such events out of the 73 real network incidents discussed in Section 6.

In order to address the challenge of partial failures, we employ a probabilistic failure model that assigns a failure probability value to each vertex and edge based on the observed ping data. We will start the discussion using a simple example before we formalize our model. Consider the network graph shown in Figure 3. Suppose edge $e = (v_6, v_7)$ is experiencing an issue and is dropping some packets. Further, suppose the total number of pings from v_1 to v_{10} is $N_{1,10} = 50$. Based on the probabilistic routing discussed in Section 4.1, we calculate the probability that any ping will go through the problematic edge e. Specifically, $P_{1,10}(e) = 0.25$. Finally, assume that this edge is dropping 20% of its traffic. In other words, the probability that any ping going through e will fail is $X_e = 0.2$. Therefore, out of the 50 pings, 25% of them will go through the problematic edge, out of which 20% will fail. Multiplying the 3 numbers together will give us the expected number of ping failures, $F_{1,10} = 5$. Table 2 summarizes the notation used in this section.

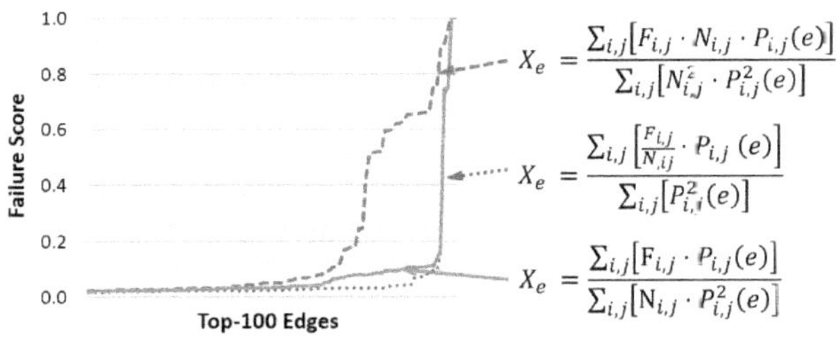

Figure 4: Distribution of failure scores for the top-100 edges for three different least squares formulations.

Equation 1 provides the basic unit of our model:

$$F_{i,j} = N_{i,j} \cdot P_{i,j}(e) \cdot X_e \quad (1)$$

The number of failed pings $F_{i,j}$ and total pings $N_{i,j}$ between vertices v_i and v_j are observed. The probability $P_{i,j}(e)$ that a $v_i \to v_j$ ping will go through a particular edge e is computed by the routing model. Finally, X_e, the failure score of edge e, is the unknown value we need to compute. This model assumes there is at most one failed edge (or vertex) on the paths from v_i to v_j, which is common in practice. However, concurrent failures on independent network paths are captured by the model. The fact that we have a long list of pings between multiple sources and destinations results in the creation of an overdetermined system of equations that can be numerically solved.

Consequently, we need to solve a data fitting problem by computing the failure score X_e for each edge e that best fits the observed data. There are several well-known techniques for solving such problems and we have chosen to use the method of *Least Squares* because it produces a linear unbiased estimator and it is computationally efficient to solve.

Least squares formulation: The best fit in the least-squares sense minimizes the sum of squared residuals; a residual being the difference between the observed value and the fitted value provided by the model. The model from Equation 1 results in the following formulation:

$$Y_e = \sum_{(\forall v_i, v_j \in V)} \Big(F_{i,j} - N_{i,j} \cdot P_{i,j}(e) \cdot X_e\Big)^2 \quad (2)$$

Solving the above least squares problem yields the equation:

$$X_e = \frac{\sum_{(\forall v_i, v_j \in V)} \Big(F_{i,j} \cdot N_{i,j} \cdot P_{i,j}(e)\Big)}{\sum_{(\forall v_i, v_j \in V)} \Big(N_{i,j}^2 \cdot P_{i,j}^2(e)\Big)} \quad (3)$$

The main drawback of this solution is that it typically assigns a wide range of failure scores to multiple edges during a network issue. In layman's terms, it is spreading the blame around, increasing the size of the output list that a network operator would have to investigate. Figure 4 shows the distribution of failure scores for the top-100 edges computed by three different least squares solutions during a real network incident. The solution from Equation 3 assigns a failure score higher than 0.5 to 25% of the edges. This behavior is partly due to the presence of the $N_{i,j}^2$ term in the denominator; the failure score is thus very sensitive to the number of total pings between each pair of vertices, which can vary between tens to hundreds of pings every 5 minutes.

Solving for $F_{i,j}/N_{i,j}$ rather than $F_{i,j}$ in the original model (Equation 1) results in a second formulation and solution:

$$Y_e = \sum_{(\forall v_i, v_j \in V)} \Big(\frac{F_{i,j}}{N_{i,j}} - P_{i,j}(e) \cdot X_e\Big)^2 \quad (4)$$

$$X_e = \frac{\sum_{(\forall v_i, v_j \in V)} \Big(\frac{F_{i,j}}{N_{i,j}} \cdot P_{i,j}(e)\Big)}{\sum_{(\forall v_i, v_j \in V)} \Big(P_{i,j}^2(e)\Big)} \quad (5)$$

The solution in Equation 5 has the desired property of high contrast in the distribution of failure scores, as can be seen in Figure 4. Only 4 edges get a failure score over 0.5. However, this solution completely ignores the presence of successful pings between two vertices when there are no failed pings, i.e., $N_{i,j}$ is ignored when $F_{i,j} = 0$.

The above observation has lead to our final formulation and solution:

$$Y_e = \sum_{(\forall v_i, v_j \in V)} \Big(\frac{F_{i,j}}{\sqrt{N_{i,j}}} - \sqrt{N_{i,j}} \cdot P_{i,j}(e) \cdot X_e\Big)^2 \quad (6)$$

$$X_e = \frac{\sum_{(\forall v_i, v_j \in V)} \Big(F_{i,j} \cdot P_{i,j}(e)\Big)}{\sum_{(\forall v_i, v_j \in V)} \Big(N_{i,j} \cdot P_{i,j}^2(e)\Big)} \quad (7)$$

Figure 4 shows that the solution from Equation 7 offers a similar contrast in failure scores as Equation 5, while the presence of $N_{i,j}$ in the denominator ensures the use of successful pings in the calculations. We use Equation 7 to compute the failure scores for all edges and vertices that are part of a possible route of any failed ping, and produce a ranked list of edges and vertices based on that score.

4.3 Deviation Detection

The presence of *background noise* in large-scale network monitoring systems is common [6]. In our case, there exists background noise in both the input ping data as well as the generated failure scores.

Noise in the ping data typically appears in the form of false ping failures or delays, even though the underlying network is not experiencing any issues. In some cases, inflated ping latency measurements are caused by increased load on the servers running the ping service. In other cases, pings might get dropped by a router—even though regular applications do not exhibit any packet loss—due to the combination of two factors: (a) traffic saturation at a link and (b) pings having the lowest priority in network traffic.

Noise in the generated failure scores is primarily attributed to the unknown nature of network routes. Since the routes for failed pings are unknown and computed using probabilities, any edge or vertex across alternative routes can potentially have a non-zero failure score.

Background noise typically manifests as low failure scores for healthy edges and vertices. A simple solution would be to introduce a threshold for filtering out the low scores. Apart from the obvious drawback of introducing an ad-hoc threshold value, we would risk filtering out low failure scores that resulted from true partial failures. By definition, partial failures cause low packet drop rates and naturally lead to low failure scores. By simply looking at the value of a failure score, we cannot distinguish these two cases

Statistical hypothesis testing: The key idea behind our solution is to look at failure scores over time in order

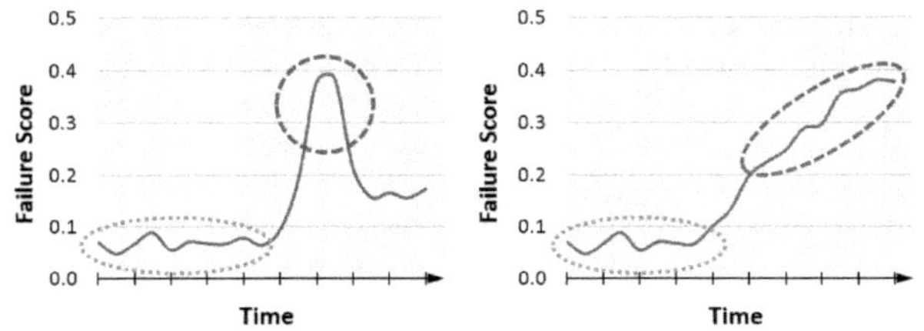

Figure 5: Detection of a spike and a gradual increase in a time sequence of failure scores.

to establish a score baseline for each edge and vertex, and then use *statistical hypothesis testing* to determine whether a current failure score is significantly different than its historical values. This approach allows us to filter out the false positives due to noise and only output edges and vertices with statistically significant failure scores.

Given a time sequence of failure scores $\mathbb{S} = \{s_0, s_1, ..., s_n\}$ for a particular edge (or vertex), we use a series of *Student's t-tests* to determine whether the addition of the latest score s_0 introduces a statistically significant change in the sequence of scores. In particular, we are interested in detecting two different score patterns over time, namely spikes and gradual increases, seen in Figure 5. Spikes are detected using *one-sample* Student's t-tests while gradual increases using *two-sample* Student's t-tests.

The one-sample Student's t-test is used to determine whether the latest score s_0 is likely to belong in the distribution of historical scores $\mathbb{S}_h = \{s_1, ..., s_n\}$, which forms the *null* hypothesis. Let n_h, μ_h, and σ_h^2 be the size, mean, and variance of $\mathbb{S}_h$, respectively. According to the t-test, the *null* hypothesis is rejected (i.e., the score is deemed significantly different) when

$$s_0 > \theta \cdot \mu_h + t_{\alpha,n_h-1} \cdot \sqrt{\frac{\sigma_h^2}{n_h}} \tag{8}$$

where θ is a scaling parameter and t_{a,n_h-1} is the t value obtained from the t-distribution table using significance level $\alpha = 99\%$ and degree of freedom equal to $(n_h - 1)$. Currently, we use a dynamic scaling parameter $\theta = 1/\sqrt{\mu_h}$, which is set based on empirical evidence.

In the two-sample Student's t-test, we divide the set of scores $\mathbb{S}$ into two independent sets, the current set $\mathbb{S}_c = \{s_0, ..., s_c\}$ and the historical set $\mathbb{S}_h = \{s_h, ..., s_n\}$. Locations c and h in the sequence are configurable and control the size and gap between the two sets.

Let n_c, μ_c, and σ_c^2 be the size, mean, and variance of $\mathbb{S}_c$, respectively. Similarly, n_h, μ_h, and σ_h^2 are the size, mean, and variance of $\mathbb{S}_h$. The *null* hypothesis is that $\mu_c \leq \theta \cdot \mu_h$, for some scaling parameter θ. We use $\theta = 1/\sqrt{\mu_h}$ as discussed above. We account for the presence of θ in the *null* hypothesis by revising $\mu_c = \mu_c/\theta$ and $\sigma_c^2 = \sigma_c^2/\theta^2$. According to the t-test, we compute the t-statistic T as:

$$T = \frac{\mu_c - \mu_h}{\sqrt{\frac{\sigma_c^2}{n_c} + \frac{\sigma_h^2}{n_h}}} \tag{9}$$

The degree of freedom *df* is computed using:

$$df = \frac{\left(\frac{\sigma_c^2}{n_c} + \frac{\sigma_h^2}{n_h}\right)^2}{\frac{\left(\frac{\sigma_c^2}{n_c}\right)^2}{n_c - 1} + \frac{\left(\frac{\sigma_h^2}{n_h}\right)^2}{n_h - 1}} \tag{10}$$

Finally, the *null* hypothesis is rejected (and the latest score is deemed significantly different) when

$$T > t_{\alpha,df} \tag{11}$$

where $t_{\alpha,df}$ is the t value obtained from the t-distribution table using significance level $\alpha = 99\%$.

Both the one-sample and two-sample Student's t-tests are invoked each time a new failure score is computed. If any of the t-tests determines the score to be significant, the corresponding edge (or vertex) is added in the final ranked list.

4.4 Correlation Analysis

The algorithms discussed so far generate a ranked list of links and devices suspected to have caused ping failures. However, it is possible for a small set of links or devices to share the same failure score due to network redundancy and multipath routing. As an example, consider the case were three physical links are connecting two network devices for redundancy purposes. Multipath routing (and our probabilistic routing) postulates that all traffic between the two devices will be equally divided among the three links. Therefore, the probability that a failed ping will go through any of the three links is the same, which in turn implies that the three links will have the same failure score.

We address this issue by taking advantage of the availability and performance alerts produced by passive monitoring (recall Section 2.3). In particular, we perform a *left outer join* between our ranked list $\mathbb{L}$ and the set of device- and link-level network alerts $\mathbb{A}$ that are triggered during the time period of the analysis. This join retains all devices and links in $\mathbb{L}$ while appending the alerting information from $\mathbb{A}$ to the matching records. We do not remove the records in $\mathbb{L}$ that do not match $\mathbb{A}$ in order to capture the cases were a device or link is dropping packets without issuing any alerts. (We discuss such cases in the experimental evaluation in Section 6.) Instead, devices and links with alerting information are pushed to the top of the list since there is more evidence that they may be responsible for the observed ping failures.

5. DEPLOYMENT

We have implemented the fault localization approach discussed in Section 4 and incorporated it into the Windows Azure network monitoring infrastructure. Figure 6 shows the relevant components of the monitoring system:

- The **Data Store** holds the network topology information, the ping data, as well as local telemetry data collected from devices and other components of the network.
- The **Ping Service** is a distributed service that runs on all compute clusters of the data centers and is responsible for collecting and sending the ping data to the Data Store.
- Multiple **Device Data Collectors** are continuously collecting, aggregating, and sending local telemetry data to the Data Store.
- The **Analysis Worker** streams the topology, ping, and telemetry data, performs the fault localization analysis, and streams the results back to the Data Store.

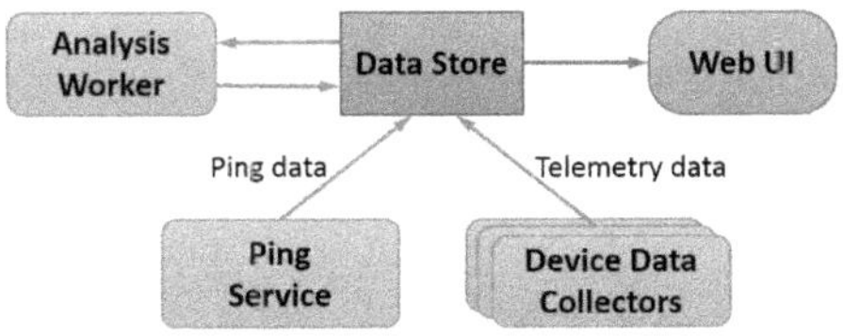

Figure 6: System architecture.

- The **Web UI** provides a web-based interface used by network operators to consume the results of the fault localization analysis in a user-friendly report.

The Ping Service and Device Data Collectors are continuously collecting large amounts of data that need to be analyzed. In particular, there are about 400 thousand pings and several hundreds to thousands of network events being generated every 15 minutes by the existing framework. In order to produce results in near real time, we process the data incrementally. Every five minutes, the Analysis Worker will (a) get the latest topology information from the Data Store and build the network graph, (b) stream in the ping and telemetry data from the last 15 minutes, (c) run the fault localization analysis presented in Section 4, and (d) stream out the ranked list of suspect links and devices, whose failures best explain the observed data.

6. EXPERIMENTAL EVALUATION

In this section, we evaluate the effectiveness and efficiency of our approach to correctly localize issues in the entire Windows Azure network. The experimental evaluation is based on 73 real network incidents that were investigated by the Windows Azure network operations team during a period of three months. After sifting through large amounts of data and reports compiled primarily by network operators, we identified the (most likely) root cause for each incident. Root causes are divided into the following 10 categories:

- **Device Issue:** A network device experienced an issue such as hardware failure or misconfiguration.
- **Fiber Cut:** The fiber cable connecting two or more devices was damaged or cut.
- **Maintenance:** Devices and links were going through planned maintenance, which may have affected their performance or availability.
- **Transient Failure:** A device or link experienced a short failure and then recovered.
- **DNS Issue:** The Domain Name System (DNS) that translates domain names to IP addresses experienced an issue like incorrect name resolution.
- **BGP Issue:** The Border Gateway Protocol (BGP) that makes routing decisions based on paths experienced an issue like BGP sessions going down.
- **Software:** A software component like a Software Load Balancer had failed or operated incorrectly.
- **False Alarm:** There was no clear evidence that a real network issue had occurred and the network appeared to be healthy during the investigation.

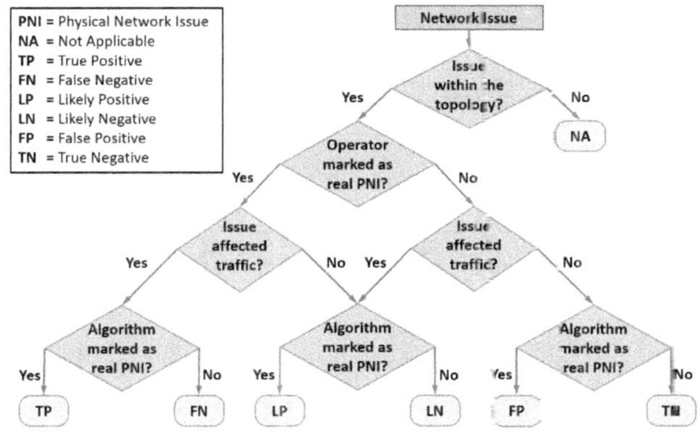

Figure 7: Derivation of localization accuracy classifications.

- **DDoS Attack:** A Distributed Denial-of-Service attack (DDoS attach) caused performance or availability issues to the network.
- **Peering Issue:** The issue was localized to outside the Windows Azure network.

Table 3 lists the total count of incidents for each root cause.

For the purpose of our evaluation, we define a real *physical network issue (PNI)* to be any issue experienced by a network device or link that resulted in dropped traffic and, therefore, has affected higher-level users. For example a fiber cut or a device failure is considered a real physical network issue; these are the type of issues our algorithm is trying to localize. On the other hand, issues with DNS or software issues are not considered physical issues, and thus our algorithm should exclude them from localization.

6.1 Localization Accuracy

In this section, we evaluate the ability of our approach to accurately localize real physical network issues (PNIs) and to correctly exclude non-physical network issues. Unfortunately, in many cases, we do not have the ground truth of whether a network incident was caused by a real PNI or not. One option would be to consider the final ruling of the network operator as the ground truth. However, issues such as transient failures can, by definition, cause loss of traffic at the time of the incident but for the network to appear healthy by the time the operator investigates the incident. Hence, to evaluate the localization accuracy of our approach, we combine two sources of truth: (a) the expertise of the network operator in marking an issue as a real PNI or not, and (b) traffic data showing whether there was a significant loss of traffic near the location and around the time of the investigated incident.

When the two sources of truth are in agreement, localization accuracy is easily established. First, suppose the operator marked the incident as a real PNI and there was significant loss of traffic at the time of the incident. Using conventional terminology from binary classification, we declare the result of our localization approach to be *true positive (TP)* when our approach correctly identifies and localizes the issue and *false negative (FN)* when it failed to identify the issue. On the other hand, suppose the operator marked the incident as not a PNI and there was no observable loss of traffic. In this case, the localization result is considered *true negative (TN)* if the algorithm did

Table 3: Localization accuracy per root cause.

Root Cause	TP	TN	FP	FN	LP	LN	NA	Total
Device Issue	4	–	–	–	–	4	1	9
Fiber Cut	3	–	–	–	–	–	1	4
Maintenance	5	5	–	–	–	–	–	10
Transient Failure	3	–	–	–	11	–	–	14
DNS Issue	–	10	–	–	–	–	–	10
BGP Issue	–	5	–	–	–	–	–	5
Software	–	7	–	–	–	–	–	7
False Alarm	–	10	–	–	–	–	–	10
DDoS Attack	–	–	2	–	–	–	–	2
Peering Issue	–	–	–	–	–	–	2	2
Total	15	37	2	0	11	4	4	73

not produce any devices or links in the topology near the investigated incident; otherwise, it is a *false positive (FP)*.

When the two sources of truth are in disagreement (i.e., the operator believes there is a real PNI but there is no significant loss of traffic, or the operator believes there is no PNI but there is loss of traffic), we define two new localization accuracy classifications. The localization result is considered a *likely positive (LP)* when the algorithm identifies an issue and either the operator has marked it as a real PNI or there was significant loss of traffic. Conversely, the result is considered a *likely negative (LN)* when the algorithm does not identify an issue and either the operator has marked it as a non-issue or there was no substantial loss of traffic. Finally, if the issue is not located within the network graph, then we classify it as *not applicable (NA)*. For example, peering links that connect Windows Azure to the outside world are not part of our topology. Figure 7 summarizes the derivation of our localization accuracy classifications.

Table 3 lists the localization accuracy of our approach for each root cause for the 73 incidents. Overall, our approach was able to correctly identify and localize 15 real physical network issues (TPs) while correctly excluding 37 non-issues (TNs). The root causes for the TPs were device issues, fiber cuts, issues during planned maintenance, and transient failures. All DNS, BGP, and software issues as well as all false alarms and some maintenance issues were correctly classified as TNs. There were only 2 cases of FPs where our algorithm incorrectly output devices and links as suspects of causing failures; both incidents were likely the result of DDoS attacks. There were no cases of FNs.

There were also 15 incidents where the network operator and the traffic data were in disagreement. In particular, there were 11 cases of transient failures where the operator did not find a physical network issue even though there was significant loss of traffic observed for a short period of time (typically 5-10 minutes). In fact, in all cases there was additional evidence in the form of device- and link-level alerts suggesting there was indeed a physical network issue. We classify these cases as likely positives (LPs) even though we believe they are probably TPs. The remaining 4 cases are classified as likely negatives (LNs) and are attributed to device misconfigurations that did not affect traffic (and by extension, did not cause any user-perceived failures). Finally, there were 4 incidents that occurred outside the Windows Azure network and are thus classified as NA.

In the absence of our algorithm, the network operators must rely on their expertise as well as device- and link-level

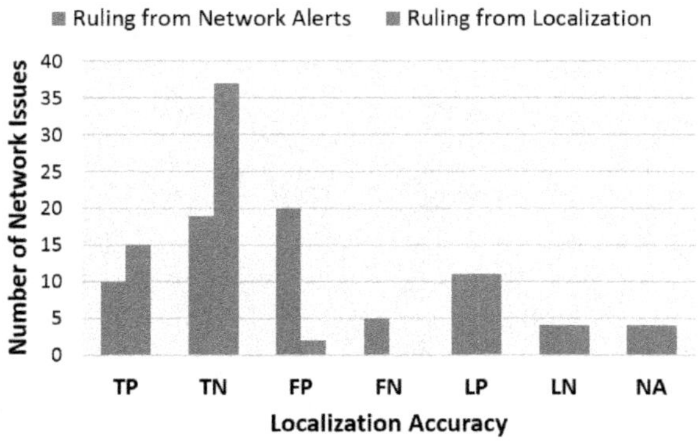

Figure 8: Localization accuracy of our approach compared to the conventional approach based on network alerts.

alerts from passive monitoring in order to localize network issues. Figure 8 compares the localization accuracy of the approach based on network alerts (we call this the *conventional* approach) and our approach. We observe that the conventional approach yields a large number of false positives; 20 compared to just 2 from our approach. It is fairly common for BGP, DNS, or software issues to cause device- and link-level alerts even though the actual devices and links are healthy and the traffic is not affected. In comparison, our approach is able to correctly determine that the issue is not related to physical devices or links.

Furthermore, the conventional approach suffered from 5 false negatives. There were 5 network incidents caused by a device (or link) malfunction but that device (or link) had no alerts associated with it (i.e., they were silent failures). We have seen this happen during device hardware failures, device misconfiguration, or planned maintenance. However, since the problematic device was causing traffic loss (and by extension ping failures or delays), our approach was able to detect and localize it correctly.

6.2 Localization Precision

While Section 6.1 demonstrated the ability of our approach to accurately localize network failures, it does not give any indication of how precise the localization is. In this section, we evaluate the precision of our approach using two metrics: one based on the size of the ranked list $\mathbb{L}$ of devices and links produced by the algorithm, and another based on the placement (i.e., rank) of the problematic device or link that caused the network issue in $\mathbb{L}$.

The first metric is termed *localization precision* and is inspired by a similar metric defined in [9]. The localization precision for a given network incident is defined as the ratio of the number of suspect devices and links after localization (i.e., the size of list $\mathbb{L}$) to that before localization. In other words, it is the fraction of devices and links that are likely to explain a particular network issue using our algorithm out of all the devices and links that can potentially cause that issue. We call the latter set the *potential set* $\mathbb{P}$.

The size of $\mathbb{P}$ depends on the scope of the investigation, which typically starts with some higher-level performance or availability alert for some part of the network. For example, suppose there is an availability alert for a particular cluster. Any ToR switch or CSP and their links could be potentially causing the issue. Table 4 lists the number of potential devices and links that might need to be checked for the 15 TP

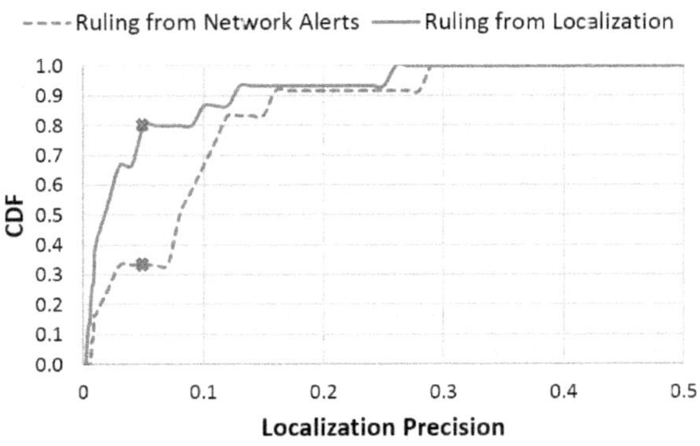

Figure 9: Localization precision of our approach compared to the conventional approach based on network alerts.

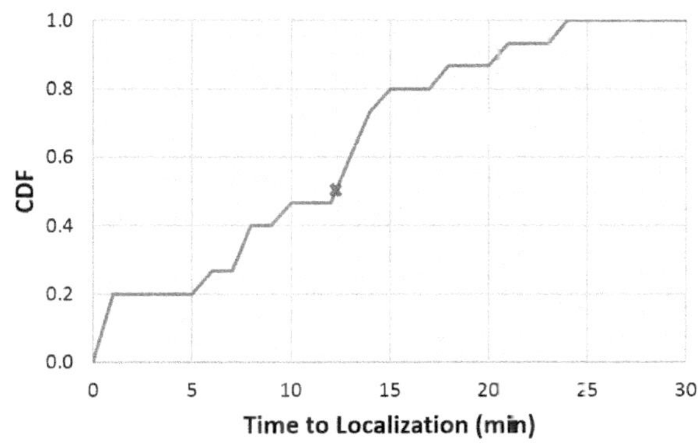

Figure 10: Time to localize real network incidents.

incidents. Of course, using domain knowledge and expertise, an operator will only check a subset of $\mathbb{P}$; but the estimate underscores the challenge faced by operators today.

Figure 9 shows the cumulative distribution functions (CDFs) of the localization precision of our approach and the conventional approach[2]. We observe that our approach localizes network issues to less than 2% for more than 50% of the failures and to less than 5% for more than 80% of the failures. On the contrary, only 33% of the failures are localized to less than 5% using the conventional approach. Table 4 further supports the poor localization precision of the conventional method as the number of distinct devices or links associated with network alerts is often much larger (up to an order of magnitude larger) than the total size of our ranked list $\mathbb{L}$. We conclude that our approach is able to localize the true issue very precisely from a large set of possible root causes for a given failure.

The second metric for evaluating the algorithm's precision is the *diagnostic rank*, which is the number of network devices or links deemed more likely culprits than the device or link that actually failed [11]. Assuming operators investigate failures in the order listed by our algorithm, the diagnostic rank reflects the overhead of identifying and resolving the issues. Table 4 lists the average diagnostic rank computed during the duration of each incident. On average, the operator will have to check less than 5 devices or links (and almost always less than 10) before identifying the real culprit, compared to 6–305 for conventional diagnosis. Hence, our approach can significantly reduce diagnosis time.

6.3 Efficiency

In this section, we evaluate the efficiency of our approach in terms of how quickly a particular network issue is localized. As discussed in Section 5, our algorithm is running continuously in real time and generates a ranked list of devices and links every 5 minutes (assuming it has identified a network issue). We compare the time the ranked list contained the problematic device or link for the first time with the starting time of the incident. Note that in most cases the exact starting time of an incident is not known, so we are using the starting time recorded in the incident report. Figure 10 shows the CDF of the time to localize real network incidents in Windows Azure. We observe that 50% of the incidents are localized within 12 minutes while the longest time to localize is 23 minutes. Typically, the time to localize depends on the severity of the incident; the higher the ping failure rate, the shorter the time to localize since the statistical hypothesis testing will quickly detect the deviation in the failure score. For example, the incident that took 23 minutes to localize had a ping failure rate between 1-2%.

It is interesting to note that in 3 incidents the device or link causing the issue was localized by our algorithm well before the starting time recorded by the operator—and presumably, before the time the operator started the investigation. Therefore, there is potential for our approach to be used in a more *proactive* way for localizing user-perceived failures. We plan to investigate this approach in the near future. Overall, our localization approach can identify and localize real physical network issues in a very short time period, significantly improving the ability of the operations team to localize and resolve network incidents.

7. RELATED WORK

In network tomography, link-level properties like link loss and packet latency are inferred using statistical approaches from end-to-end measurements [5]. In particular, BADABING [12] and Tulip [10] measure per-path characteristics to identify problems that impact network performance. These methods, along with some commercial products as well, use active testing (e.g., traceroute) to pinpoint faulty links. However, they have only been applied to smaller networks since applying an active testing technique that will sufficiently cover a worldwide network is prohibitively expensive. Our approach, on the other hand, does not require any controlled testing infrastructure and relies only on ping data, which is typically available as a connectivity signal in data center networks.

There exists a large body of work on detecting and localizing performance problems across network and services. Sherlock [2] captures the dependencies between various components of the IT infrastructure (e.g., DNS service, load balancers, network components) and tries to localize failures to a small number of components. Similarly, Shrink [8] and SCORE [9] have their own dependency model, which they use to find the most likely root causes of faults in wide-area networks. In contrast, our approach localizes failures on the underlying physical network, both within and across data centers, and as such, can complement the aforementioned tools. Furthermore, we have shown that our approach is

[2]The localization precision for the conventional approach is based on the number of distinct devices and links with network alerts within the scope of the investigation.

Table 4: Statistics for a sample of real network issues in Windows Azure. The device abbreviations are given in Figure 2.

Investigation Scope	Root Cause (Device/Link)	# Potentially Failed Devs/Links	# Devs/Links with Network Alerts	# Devs/Links in our Ranked List	Average Diagnostic Rank
Core Network	Fiber Cut (CR–CR Link)	79	6	10	9.3
Core Network	Fiber Cut (CR–CR Link)	262	–	12	10.5
Core Network	Fiber Cut (CR–CR Link)	868	85	5	1.0
Core Network	Transient (CR–CR Link)	452	72	5	3.0
Datacenter	Device Issue (DSP)	1178	132	24	3.0
Datacenter	Device Issue (CR)	951	6	9	3.0
Datacenter	Device Issue (CR)	453	–	3	2.0
Datacenter	Maintenance (CR–CR Link)	845	62	39	9.7
Datacenter	Maintenance (AR)	584	6	147	3.0
Datacenter	Maintenance (CR)	891	8	8	3.4
Datacenter	Transient (BL–DSP Link)	951	98	95	5.2
Multiple Clusters	Maintenance (CR–BL Link)	9173	228	29	3.0
Cluster	Device Issue (ToR)	1052	305	20	2.8
Cluster	Maintenance (CSP–ToR Link)	3364	287	8	6.7
Cluster	Transient (CSP)	1306	–	28	1.5

scalable, can produce results in near real time, and can handle densely connected topologies in addition to loosely connected ones such as wide-area networks.

8. CONCLUSIONS

In this paper, we described a novel and successful application of statistical data mining techniques for localizing user-impacting availability and performance issues in a worldwide data center network in near real time. A unique aspect of our work is that it is agnostic to the routing intricacies and forwarding aspects of the network and is, therefore, a scalable solution. We have deployed our solution on the Windows Azure network monitoring infrastructure with a special focus on producing a high confidence, real-time signal that can be used by operations teams to detect and localize physical network issues. Our experimental evaluation on real network incidents has validated both the efficiency and effectiveness of our approach.

9. ACKNOWLEDGMENTS

We would like to thank the Windows Azure Network teams that collaborated with us, especially Albert Greenberg for introducing us to this problem as well as Monika Machado and Tina Stewart for providing operational support.

10. REFERENCES

[1] M. Al-Fares, A. Loukissas, and A. Vahdat. A Scalable, Commodity Data Center Network Architecture. In *Proc. of the ACM SIGCOMM Conf. on Data Communication*, pages 63–74. ACM, 2008.

[2] P. Bahl, R. Chandra, A. Greenberg, S. Kandula, D. A. Maltz, and M. Zhang. Towards Highly Reliable Enterprise Network Services via Inference of Multi-level Dependencies. In *Proc. of the ACM SIGCOMM Conf. on Data Communication*, pages 13–24. ACM, 2007.

[3] L. A. Barroso and U. Hölzle. The Datacenter as a Computer: An Introduction to the Design of Warehouse-scale Machines. *Synthesis Lectures on Computer Architecture*, 4(1):1–108, 2009.

[4] Y. Bejerano and R. Rastogi. Robust Monitoring of Link Delays and Faults in IP Networks. *IEEE/ACM Transactions on Networking*, 14(5):1092–1103, 2006.

[5] N. Duffield. Network Tomography of Binary Network Performance Characteristics. *IEEE Transactions on Information Theory*, 52(12):5373–5388, 2006.

[6] P. Gill, N. Jain, and N. Nagappan. Understanding Network Failures in Data Centers: Measurement, Analysis, and Implications. In *Proc. of the ACM SIGCOMM Conf. on Data Communication*, pages 350–361. ACM, 2011.

[7] A. Greenberg, J. R. Hamilton, N. Jain, S. Kandula, C. Kim, P. Lahiri, D. A. Maltz, P. Patel, and S. Sengupta. VL2: A Scalable and Flexible Data Center Network. In *Proc. of the ACM SIGCOMM Conf. on Data Communication*, pages 51–62. ACM, 2009.

[8] S. Kandula, D. Katabi, and J.-P. Vasseur. Shrink: A Tool for Failure Diagnosis in IP Networks. In *Proc. of the ACM SIGCOMM Workshop on Mining Network Data*, pages 173–178. ACM, 2005.

[9] R. R. Kompella, J. Yates, A. Greenberg, and A. C. Snoeren. IP Fault Localization Via Risk Modeling. In *Proc. of the 2nd Symp. on Networked Systems Design & Implementation (NSDI)*, pages 57–70. USENIX, 2005.

[10] R. Mahajan, N. Spring, D. Wetherall, and T. Anderson. User-level Internet Path Diagnosis. In *Proc. of the 19th ACM Symp. on Operating Systems Principles (SOSP)*, pages 106–119. ACM, 2003.

[11] R. Niranjan Mysore. *Automated Scalable Management of Data Center Networks*. PhD thesis, University of California, San Diego, 2013. `http://escholarship.org/uc/item/7mb1w3rv`.

[12] J. Sommers, P. Barford, N. Duffield, and A. Ron. Improving Accuracy in End-to-End Packet Loss Measurement. In *Proc. of the ACM SIGCOMM Conf. on Data Communication*, pages 157–168. ACM, 2005.

[13] H. H. Song, L. Qiu, and Y. Zhang. NetQuest: A Flexible Framework for Large-scale Network Measurement. *ACM SIGMETRICS Performance Evaluation Review*, 34(1):121–132, 2006.

[14] Windows Azure Services, 2014. `http://www.windowsazure.com/en-us/services/`.

[15] H. Zeng, P. Kazemian, G. Varghese, and N. McKeown. Automatic Test Packet Generation. In *Proc. of the 8th Intl Conf. on Emerging Networking Experiments and Technologies (CoNext)*, pages 241–252. ACM, 2012.

[16] Y. Zhao, Y. Chen, and D. Bindel. Towards Unbiased End-to-end Network Diagnosis. In *Proc. of the ACM SIGCOMM Conf. on Data Communication*, pages 219–230. ACM, 2006.

Improving Management of Aquatic Invasions by Integrating Shipping Network, Ecological, and Environmental Data: Data Mining for Social Good

Jian Xu[*,1,2], Thanuka L. Wickramarathne[*,1,2,3], Nitesh V. Chawla[†,1,2,3], Erin K. Grey[3,4], Karsten Steinhaeuser[5], Reuben P. Keller[6], John M. Drake[7] and David M. Lodge[3,4]

[1]Dept. of Computer Science and Engineering, University of Notre Dame, USA
[2]Interdisciplinary Center for Network Science and Applications, University of Notre Dame, USA
[3]Environmental Change Initiative, University of Notre Dame, USA
[4]Dept. of Biological Sciences, University of Notre Dame, USA
[5]Dept. of Computer Science and Engineering, University of Minnesota, USA
[6]Institute of Environmental Sustainability, Loyola University Chicago, USA
[7]Odum School of Ecology, University of Georgia, USA

(jxu5, twickram, nchawla, egrey, dlodge)@nd.edu, ksteinha@umn.edu, rkeller1@luc.edu, jdrake@uga.edu

ABSTRACT

The unintentional transport of *invasive species* (i.e., non-native and harmful species that adversely affect habitats and native species) through the Global Shipping Network (GSN) causes substantial losses to social and economic welfare (e.g., annual losses due to ship-borne invasions in the *Laurentian Great Lakes* is estimated to be as high as USD 800 million). Despite the huge negative impacts management of such invasions remains challenging because of the complex processes that lead to species transport and establishment. Numerous difficulties associated with quantitative risk assessments (e.g., inadequate characterizations of invasion processes, lack of crucial data, large uncertainties associated with available data, etc.) have hampered the usefulness of such estimates in the task of supporting the authorities who are battling to manage invasions with limited resources. We present here an approach for addressing the problem at hand via creative use of computational techniques and multiple data sources, thus illustrating how *data mining* can be used for solving crucial, yet very complex problems towards social good. By modeling implicit species exchanges as a *network* that we refer to as the *Species Flow Network (SFN)*, large-scale species flow dynamics are studied via a *graph clustering approach* that decomposes the SFN into *clusters of ports* and *inter-cluster* connections. We then exploit this decomposition to discover crucial knowledge on how patterns in GSN affect aquatic invasions, and then illustrate how such knowledge can be used to devise effective and economical invasive species management strategies. By experimenting on actual GSN traffic data for years 1997–2006, we have discovered crucial knowledge that can significantly aid the management authorities.

*J. Xu and T.L. Wickramarathne have contributed equally.
†NV Chawla is the corresponding author.

KDD'14, August 24–27, 2014, New York, NY, USA.

http://dx.doi.org/10.1145/2623330.2623364.

Categories and Subject Descriptors

I.5 [**Pattern Recognition**]: Clustering; H.2.8 [**Database Management**]: Database Applications—*Data mining*

Keywords

Data mining, networks, clustering, risk assessment, invasive species, data mining for social good

1. INTRODUCTION

Background. Networks of human travel and trade transport different plants, animals and pathogens across the globe. Quoting from the National Invasive Species Council's 2008–2012 National Management Plan [6],

> *"Human activity such as trade, travel and tourism have all increased substantially, increasing the speed and volume of species movement to unprecedented levels. Invasive species are often unintended hitchhikers on cargo and other trade conveyances, (Page 4)." [6]*

Invasive species (i.e., non-native species that adversely affect habitats and bioregions) are among the top three drivers of global environmental change. Such invasive species include both plants and animals, and cause substantial economic and environmental harm by outcompeting or preying on native species. For instance, the impacts of *aquatic invasions* include increased diseases in humans (e.g. *cholera*) and aquaculture species (e.g., fish virus), losses of wild-caught fisheries (e.g, *comb jelly* invasion of the *Black Sea*), and losses of other ecosystem services. From an economic perspective, the estimated annual damage and control costs of invasive species in the U.S. alone amount to more than USD 120 billion [19]. These species are introduced via the networks of human trade and travel, and analyzing these networks can illuminate potential management strategies, regulatory policies, incentive structures, and risks from changing climate.

Ship-borne invasive species problem. The Global Shipping Network (GSN) is the dominant global vector for unintentional translocation of non-native aquatic species [17]: species get translocated via *ballast water* (during ballast water uptake/discharge) and *biofouling* (i.e., the accumulation of microorganisms, plants, algae, or animals) on the surfaces of ships [8]. To reduce invasion risks, authorities (e.g., International Maritime Organization (IMO)) have proposed standards for the maximum density of organisms that can be discharged in ships' ballast water. These standards are based on the premise that reducing the concentration of live organisms in ballast tanks will reduce the number of invasions, but the extent to which this approach will actually reduce the invasion risk is unknown. In addition, this approach does not address invasions via biofouling, nor does it consider many poorly known, but likely significant, biological and ecological factors that influence invasion risk. Moreover, the problem cannot be understood at a regional level, because ship-borne species can arrive from anywhere via the GSN. *With all these uncertainties in place, decisions are still needed to be made about the most efficient ways to target limited management resources.*

Significance of the problem. In the few coastal areas with good invasive species monitoring, increased shipping connecting an expanding network of global ports is correlated with an accelerating accumulation curve of established species (e.g., San Francisco Bay), and is estimated to be responsible for 69% of known aquatic invasions [17]. Although only a portion of species transported via GSN become invasive (i.e., spread, become abundant, and cause harm), environmental and economic damages from these species are often large and increase over time [13, 15]. For instance, the annual loss to the US Great Lakes regional economy due to ship-borne aquatic invasive species may be as high as USD 800 million [22]. However, GSN undoubtedly provides enormous benefits to the US economy, and is also responsible for approximately 90% of global trade. Furthermore, global trade patterns are optimized based on economic and trade considerations, but not necessarily to safeguard against aquatic invasions. Therefore, imposing expensive and cumbersome regulations on the shipping industry could cause serious adverse effects to a country's economy and trade relationships.

Motivation and Goals. It is clear that a thorough understanding of ship-borne invasion risks in terms of overall data about trade patterns, ports, vessel types, etc. is necessary to devise practices and policies that are feasible, effective and capable of bringing to bear the net long-term benefits to human welfare. With this motivation, our goal is to develop computational and data-driven frameworks that can inform invasive species management policies and practices.

1.1 Data Mining for Social Good

Ship-borne invasions are a result of a complex interplay of ship traffic, ballast uptake/discharge dynamics, species survival during transport, various environmental/biological variables, etc [28]. Incorporating these complexities into a quantitative risk assessment framework is extremely difficult, since the majority of the governing relationships are poorly quantified. The few studies that have attempted to quantify invasion risks via probabilistic approaches [14, 24] have relied on multiple simplifying assumptions. Moreover, usefulness of these approaches towards development of efficient invasion management policies is further hampered by the inability to incorporate crucial invasion mechanisms (e.g., "stepping-stone" process) into risk assessment. However, numerous streams of data that capture vessel movement patterns, ballast uptake/discharge and other environmental/biological factors (that affect species transport and establishment) are increasingly being collected by several agencies for research/commercial purposes. Therefore, one can creatively combine domain expertise and computational data analysis to understand the underlying patterns of ship-borne invasions in order to develop a sufficient understanding towards the development of effective and economical management strategies. *Our work is in fact a multi-disciplinary attempt towards utilizing this data to create insights and knowledge that can eventually lead to decision-making tools for policy makers.*

Data. We now introduce the numerous data sources utilized for the research

(i) Vessel movement data: made available by Lloyd's Maritime Intelligence Unit (LMIU) contains travel information for vessels such as `portID`, `sail_date` and `arrival_date`, along with vessel metadata, such as `vessel_type` and `DWT` (Dead Weight Tonnage), etc. This information can be readily used to build a *network* to represent species flow paths and patterns among ports. Our experiments are based on LMIU data that spans four (4) two-years-long periods starting 1st of May 1997, 1999, 2002 and 2005, totaling 6,889,748 individual voyages corresponding to a total of 50,487 vessels of various types that move among a total of 5,545 ports and regions. However, none of the existing vessel movement datasets (including LMIU) provide explicit ballast water exchange amounts (or even whether a vessel discharged ballast water).

(ii) Ballast discharge data: made available by the National Ballast Information Clearinghouse (NBIC) contains the `date` and `discharge_volume` of all ships visiting U.S. ports from Jan. 2004 to present. As suggested in [24], NBIC data can be used to estimate an average ballast discharge based on `vessel_type` and `DWT` using a linear regression model.

(iii) Ecoregion data: are available via Marine Ecoregions of the World [26] and the Freshwater Ecoregions of the World [1], where *ecoregions* are defined by species composition and shared evolutionary history [26], and are thereby capable of providing an index of native ranges. Therefore, these definitions can be used for more realistic and qualitative invasion risk analysis, in comparison to, for example, geographic distance as used in [24].

(iv) **Environmental data:** on port temperature and salinity (i.e., the two most crucial variables for identifying survivability of species in non-native coastal environments) are available via Global Ports Database (GPD) [14]. These estimates can be used for calculating species establishment risk based on environmental similarity; the missing values in GPD can also be supplemented via estimates from the World Ocean Atlas 2009 [2, 16] when necessary.

Problem Statement. Given the complexity of the problem and lack of relationships that are required for robust risk assessment, we set forth to extract knowledge on large-scale patterns of GSN in order to obtain better insight towards ship-borne invasions of non-indigenous species. Furthermore, we will illustrate how such knowledge can be used to derive efficient invasion management strategies.

Framework. Our method is devised to tackle the limitations due to lack of data and governing relationships that are required for quantitative risk assessment. Towards this, we take the following approach: **(i)** a network that represents the general species flow tendency among ports is built; then, utilizing a graph clustering method [21] that operates on the basis of flow-dynamics, **(ii)** a *map* [12, 27] of the species flow network, i.e., a cogent representation that extracts the main structure of flow while retaining information about relationships among modules (of main structure), is built; finally, using this map that summarizes the species flow dynamics in terms of *clusters* (or groups) of ports and highlights *inter-cluster* (i.e., between clusters) and *intra-cluster* (i.e., within cluster) relationships, **(iii)** the impact of GSN dynamics on aquatic invasions is studied in conjunction with ecological and environmental aspects that govern species establishment.

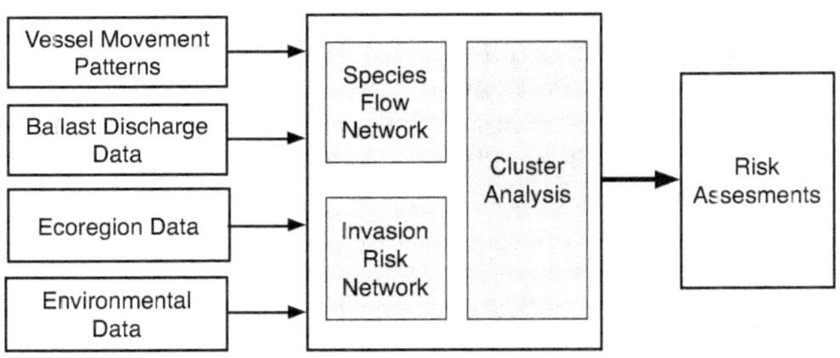

Figure 1: A **concept diagram** illustrating the integration of multiple data sources, modeling and data mining techniques for extracting useful knowledge.

1.2 Contributions and Broader Impact

We provide a data-driven foundation for more effective and efficient risk assessment and management by modeling the spread of aquatic non-indigenous species through the GSN, which is the most important vector of aquatic invasions. We have discovered vital information on patterns of GSN that can inform management strategies and regulatory policies. In a potential deployed configuration (see Fig. 2), the discovered knowledge can efficiently be used to analyze the invasion risks with respect to changing climate, policy and infrastructure. Understanding the structure of the component networks and the dynamic interactions between the different networks is crucial to the design of policies that could cost-effectively reduce invasions.

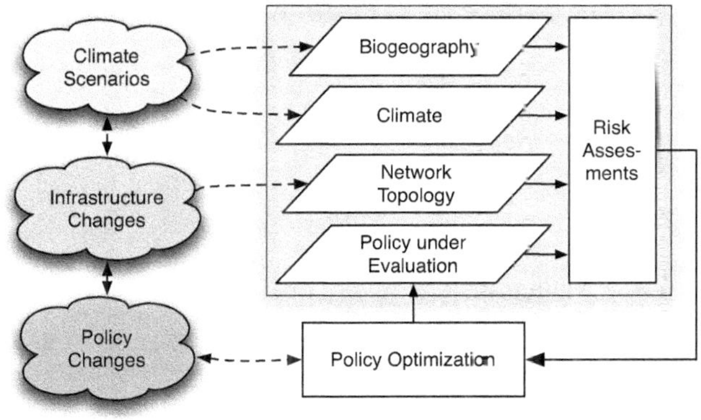

Figure 2: **Use of discovered knowledge in a potential deployed setting** for invasion risk assessment with respect to changing climate, policy and infrastructure.

This paper is organized as follows: Section 2 presents the formulation of species flow networks using LMIU and NBIC data, graph clustering approach for understanding the large-scale dynamics of GSN, and the main discoveries; Section 3 presents invasion risk assessment that incorporates ecoregion definitions and environmental conditions via a unique graphical approach; Section 4 presents how the emerging knowledge and methods can be potentially deployed towards development of species management strategies; and finally, Section 5 contains the concluding remarks

2. SPECIES FLOW ANALYSIS

The basic idea behind our work is to find patterns of species flow in order to identify ports and shipping routes for which interventions would be the most effective in stopping invasions through the entire network. Such knowledge can then be further leveraged with auxiliary information (e.g., vessel types) in order to inform management strategies in a targeted manner. Since GSN naturally forms a graph, LMIU and NBIC data can be utilized to build a network to represent species flow among ports (see Fig. 3). This network can then be analyzed via graph mining or network science techniques to extract relevant insights.

2.1 Species Flow Network (SFN)

Let $\mathcal{G} \equiv (\mathcal{N}, \mathcal{E})$ be a directed weighted graph, where $\mathcal{N} \equiv \{n_1, \ldots, n_n\}$ and $\mathcal{E} \subset \mathcal{N} \times \mathcal{N}$ denote the set of nodes and edges of $\mathcal{G}$, respectively. Let the nodes in $\mathcal{N}$ correspond to ports visited by vessels in the GSN and the *weight* of the directed edge $e_{ij} \in \mathcal{E}$ given by $w_{ij} \in (0, 1]$ represents the *total probability of species flow* corresponding to all vessels traveling from port n_i to n_j (without intermediate stopovers), for all $n_i, n_j \in \mathcal{N}$.

Species Flow Estimation. Estimation of exact amounts of species exchanged between ports is extremely difficult. However, as proposed in [24], vessel movement and ballast discharge data can be leveraged to estimate the likelihood of species exchange. We now briefly explain how LMIU and NBIC datasets are used to estimate species flow (i.e., the edge weights of $\mathcal{G}$) and refer the interested reader to [24] for a comprehensive discussion on probabilistic species flow

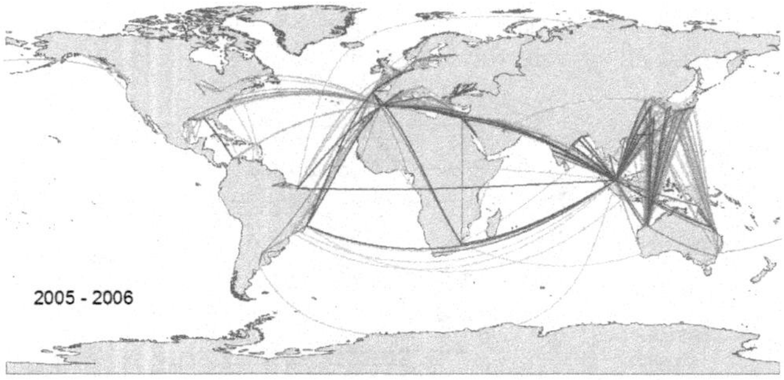

Figure 3: **Species flow between ports corresponding to vessel movements given in the LMIU 2005–2006 dataset.** The edges represent the aggregated species flow between ports, where the color intensity is proportional to the magnitude of flow. Approximately 2300 paths with the highest species flow are shown.

modeling including details on model assumptions, development and validation.

(a) Calculation of edge weights: Consider a vessel v traveling from port n_i to n_j in $\Delta t_{ij}^{(v)}$ time (without intermediate stopovers), during which the species in ballast water may die at a *mortality rate* of μ (is set to a constant average of $0.02/day$ for all routes r and vessel types). In addition, let $D_{ij}^{(v)}$, $\rho_{ij}^{(v)} \in [0,1]$ and λ denote the amount of ballast water discharged by vessel v at n_j, the efficacy of ballast water management for v for the route $n_i \to n_j$, and the characteristic constant of discharge, respectively. Then, the probability of vessel v introducing species from n_i to n_j (without intermediate stopovers) is given by:

$$p_{ij}^{(v)} = \rho_{ij}^{(v)} \, (1 - e^{-\lambda D_{ij}^{(v)}}) \, e^{-\mu \Delta t_{ij}^{(v)}}; \qquad (1)$$

the weight of the edge e_{ij} is taken to be the total probability of species introduction for all vessels traveling from n_i to n_j, and is given by:

$$w_{ij} = 1 - \prod_{\substack{r \in DB \\ r = v: n_i \to n_j}} (1 - p_{ij}^{(v)}), \qquad (2)$$

where the product is taken over all routes r in LMIU database DB s.t. a vessel v travels from port n_i to n_j.

(b) Estimation of ballast discharge: Information available on ballast discharge are incomplete, where estimation of exact quantities exchanged for each and every ship route r is impossible for most ports of the world: **(i)** ballast discharges in ports are not recorded globally, and are known to differ significantly by port and ship type; **(ii)** vessels may have intermediate stopovers, thus exchanging and mixing ballast water with existing water in ballast tanks; and **(iii)** data are largely unavailable for offshore discharges. Therefore, in order to mitigate the above difficulties, ballast discharge is estimated based on linear regression models on `DWT` per `vessel_type` as in [24]. Specifically, linear regression models on `DWT` for vessels of type `Bulk Dry`, `General Cargo`, `Ro-Ro Cargo`, `Chemical`, `Liquified Gas Tankers`, `Oil Tankers`, `Passenger Vessels`, `Refrigerated Cargo`, `Container Ships` and `Unknown/Other`). Furthermore, the relationship of ballast discharge amount to the likelihood of species introduction is not well defined. For estimation of (1), λ is chosen s.t. $p_{ij}^{(v)} = 0.80$ for a ballast discharge of $500,000\,m^3$, when $\rho_{ij}^{(v)} = 1$ and $\Delta t_{ij}^{(v)} = 0$, i.e., a discharge volume of $500,000\,m^3$ has a probability of 0.8 of introducing species if the vessel travels with zero mortalities and has no ballast management strategies in place.

Characteristics of the SFN. Summary of characteristics for SFNs generated for the four available years of data are shown in Table 1. The *path length* of a network identifies the number of stops required to reach a given port from another. An *average path length* of three (3) is observed in all four SFNs. This is perhaps mainly due to the presence of *hubs* (i.e., ports that are connected to many other ports) in GSN (e.g., Singapore). The *in-/out-degree* of a node is defined as the number of other nodes connected to/by it. Therefore, *average degree* in SFN describes the average number of direct pathways of species introduction. Furthermore, as empirical evaluations for *power law degree distribution* [5] suggest that SFNs fall under the category of *scale-free networks* [3], for degree ≥139.

Table 1: **Characteristics of Species Flow Networks**

Feature	97–98	99–00	02–03	05–06
Number of nodes	3971	4045	4264	4250
Number of edges	150479	150150	143560	145199
Average path length	2.987	2.998	3.018	3.041
Average in/out- degree	37.9	37.1	33.7	34.2
Diameter	8	7	7	9
Density	0.010	0.009	0.008	0.008

2.2 Clustering Analysis of SFN

Complex networks are efficient abstractions for highly complex systems that consist of numerous, often complex underlying patterns and relationships. However, these abstractions still remain too complex to derive useful inferences. Therefore, a decomposition that represents such complex networks via *modules* and their interactions [10, 18, 23] can be very useful in understanding the underlying patterns. We utilize a graph clustering approach in order to simplify the underlying flow dynamics of SFN. The clusters can capture the ship movement activity among ports leading to a better identification of risk corridors, which can then be used to estimate invasion risk based on ecological and environmental conditions.

Choice of Clustering Method. For the task at hand, we are interested in understanding how the structure of SFN relates to species flow across the network. Therefore, among many alternatives, *MapEquation* [21]—a graph clustering method that attempts to decompose the network with respect to *flow-dynamics* (in comparison to optimization of *modularity*)—is used. The basic principle of operation behind MapEquation-based clustering stems from the notions of information theory, which states the fact that a data stream can be compressed by a *code* that exploits regularities in the process that generates the stream [25]. Therefore, a group of nodes among which information flows quickly and easily can be aggregated and described as a single well connected module; the links between modules capture the avenues of information flow between those modules. MapE-

Table 2: **Ports that remained in the same cluster for the duration of 1997–2006**

Pacific %TP=28.33%, #P=818			Mediterranean %TP=15.61%, #P=513			W. European %TP=15.37%, #P=1117			E. North_America %TP=9.31%, #P=363			Indian_Ocean %TP=6.12%, #P=137			South_America %TP=3.41%, #P=30		
Port name	%TF	%CF	Port name	%TF	%CF	Port name	%TF	%CF	Port name	%TF	%CF	Port name	%TF	%CF	Port name	%TF	%CF
Singapore	2.82	9.96	Gibraltar	2.56	16.37	Rotterdam	0.87	5.68	Houston	0.52	5.57	Jebel Ali	0.25	4.07	Santos	0.42	12.37
Hong Kong	0.68	2.41	Tarifa	0.86	5.54	Skaw	0.60	3.93	New Orleans	0.37	3.94	Ras Tanura	0.22	3.67	Tubarao	0.33	9.70
Kaohsiung	0.58	2.05	Port Said	0.84	5.38	Antwerp	0.55	3.59	New York	0.35	3.80	Mumbai	0.20	3.29	San Lorenzo*	0.33	9.57
Port Hedland	0.52	1.83	Suez	0.48	3.09	Brunsbuttel	0.44	2.85	Baltimore	0.23	2.42	Juaymah Term.	0.19	3.12	Paranagua	0.21	6.11
Busan	0.50	1.76	Barcelona	0.29	1.83	Hamburg	0.42	2.73	Port Arthur	0.21	2.28	Kharg Is.	0.18	2.91	Rio de Janeiro	0.15	4.45
Hay point	0.49	1.72	Venice	0.24	1.52	Amsterdam	0.31	2.02	Santa Marta	0.20	2.17	Jubail	0.17	2.76	Bahia Blanca	0.15	4.31
Newcastle**	0.48	1.71	Genoa	0.23	1.47	Immingham	0.28	1.83	Tampa	0.20	2.16	New Mangalore	0.15	2.50	Rosario	0.14	4.07
Gladstone	0.47	1.67	Piraeus	0.22	1.39	St. Petersburg	0.27	1.73	Port Everglades	0.20	2.13	Mesaieed	0.13	2.08	Sepetiba	0.12	3.60
Nagoya	0.46	1.61	Leghorn	0.21	1.32	Tees	0.22	1.41	Mobile	0.19	2.04	Bandar Abbas	0.12	2.03	Rio Grande***	0.12	3.59
Incheon	0.45	1.60	Augusta	0.20	1.26	Zeebrugge	0.21	1.36	Savannah	0.18	1.95	Jebel Dhanna Term.	0.12	1.95	Praia Mole	0.12	3.50

Ports corresponding to highest %TF:=percentage flow w.r.t. total flow and %CF:=percentage flow w.r.t. flow within cluster are shown for six major clusters; for each cluster, the aggregated %TF:=percentage flow in the cluster w.r.t. total flow and number of ports in the cluster are given in the first row of table. Here, San Lorenzo*:=San Lorenzo, Argentina; Newcastle**:=Newcastle, Australia; Rio Grande***:=Rio Grande, Brazil.

quation identifies clusters by optimizing the entropy corresponding to intra- and inter-cluster in a *recursive* manner—the clusters identified cannot be further refined or partitioned.

Clusters of Ports based on Species Flow. Clustering analysis of SFN reveals several clusters of ports. These clusters represent groups of ports among which the species exchange is relatively higher; if inter-cluster pathways are controlled, species flow would be combinatorially reduced. Once such clusters are identified, species flow characteristics within clusters can be analyzed in conjunction with ecological and environmental data for invasion risk assessment. While clustering is derived based on species flow dynamics, geographical orientation of the major (in terms of aggregated flow) clusters is also intuitive (see Fig. 4). A few major clusters correspond to a significant proportion of total species flow among ports (see Table 2 for major ports that are in 6 of these major clusters). For instance, in 2005–2006, six (6) major clusters (out of 64 in total), viz., the clusters of `Pacific`, `Mediterranean`, `Western_Europe`, `Eastern_North_America`, `Indian_Ocean` and `South_America` contained 68.6% of total ports and corresponded to 76.3% of the total species flow.

Cluster Consistency. From a deployment perspective, perhaps the most crucial contribution of our analysis is that these major clusters continue to exist over the duration studied; for a given cluster, while some ports leave/join over time, the vast majority of the ports continue to remain in the same cluster (see Fig. 5). This provides a solid foundation for devising management strategies targeting clusters and inter-cluster connections to efficiently control species flow. Furthermore, evolution of clusters (or how the clustering patterns change over time) can reveal important information on how changes in vessel movement (and ballast discharge) patterns affect species flow dynamics. For instance, the exchange of the order of the two clusters `Mediterranean` and `Western_Europe` from 2002–2003 to 2005–2006 indicates a relative increase of species exchange among ports that belong to these clusters during 2005–2006, which can be attributed to the merger of a significant proportion of ports belonging to `Mediterranean` cluster with `South European Atlantic Shelf` cluster to form the `Tropical_East_Atlantic` cluster in 2005–2006. Another example is the formation of a new smaller cluster (the eighth in Fig. 5) in 1999–2000 by 21 ports in California and Hawaii, including ports such as San Francisco, Los Angeles and San Diego that previously belonged to the `Pacific` cluster in 1997–1998. Such changes can reveal large-scale trends that may be very useful in devising long term management strategies.

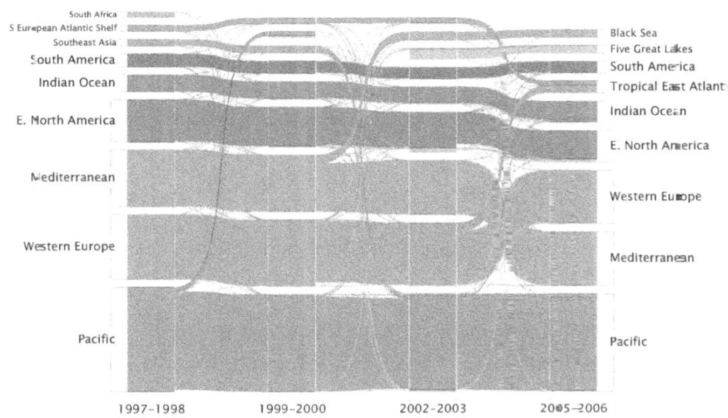

Figure 5: **Illustration of evolution of major clusters during the period of 1997–2006.** The clusters in *alluvial diagram* [21] are ranked by aggregated flow within the cluster. Here, the columns 1997, 1999, 2002 and 2005 represent the major clusters of SFN generated from LMIU datasets for 1997–1998, 1999–2000, 2002–2003 and 2005–2006, respectively.

3. INVASION RISK ANALYSIS

Quantification of invasion risk is a challenging problem because of the complex interactions between species and their abiotic and biotic environment [28]. Here, we shift our attention from inter-cluster species flow to *intra-cluster* (i.e., ports within a cluster) NIS invasion risk in order to gain insight into the plausibility of invasions in terms of environmental similarity. Previous studies have assumed that the invasion risk is proportional to *Euclidean* distance between annual averages of temperature and salinity [9,14,24]. However, this assumption may not be valid for invasive species that often exhibit broad environmental tolerances [7, 11]. We take an approach that is based on biogeographic patterns, and empirically observed temperature and salinity tolerances for ranking invasion risks.

3.1 Invasion risk modeling

For an exchange of species to become an invasion, the introduced species must be: **(i)** non-indigenous, viz., movements between non-contiguous ecoregions; and **(ii)** able to survive and establish in its new environment. Invasion risk between port environments can then be ranked by considering a species *assemblage* (or a collection) that contains "generalist" and "specialist" species. We have taken this ap-

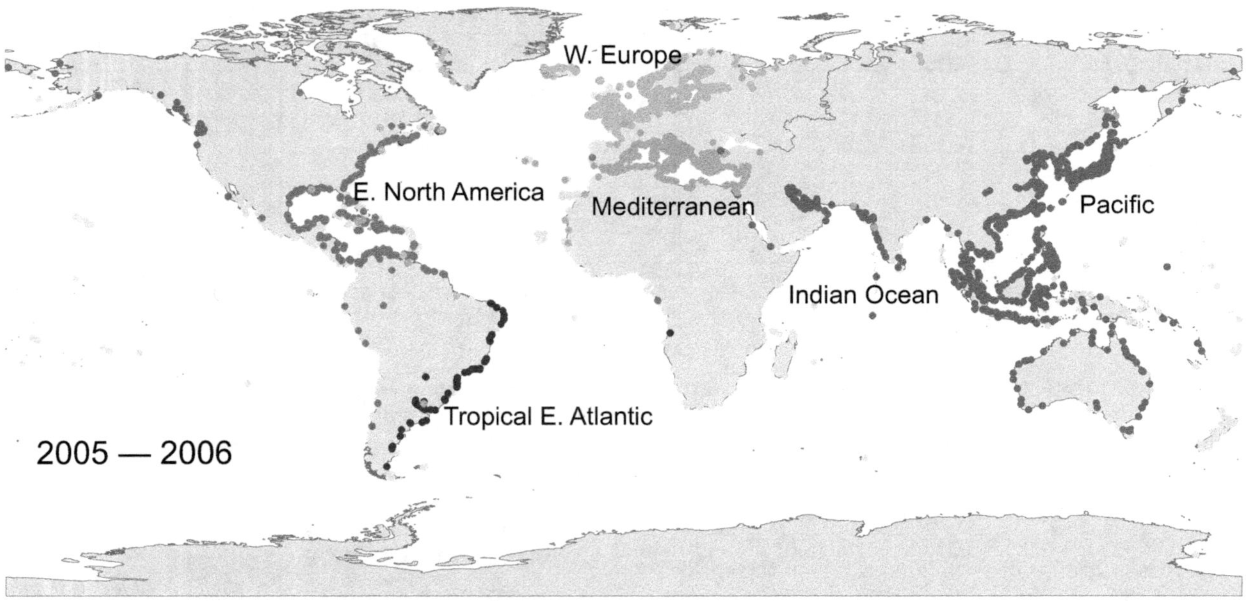

Figure 4: **The Six Major clusters of SFN during 2005–2006.** Color of dots correspond to that in Fig. 5, and white dots are not included in any of the six major clusters. Major clusters remain largely unchanged for the duration of 1997–2006, and contain a significant proportion of total species flow between ports.

proach to counteract the lack of relationships or data to calculate or estimate exact invasion risks. Based on temperature and salinity tolerance levels (empirically-estimated long term thermal tolerances of marine invertebrate taxa [20]), we define invasion risk in terms of number of species groups that can tolerate the given conditions. Specifically, six (6) different species tolerance groups based on two (2) temperature and three (3) salinity tolerance levels are considered (see Table 3). Here, salinity tolerance levels were set to capture species types that are completely intolerant to salinity (i.e., freshwater species), those that are restricted to marine waters (i.e., low tolerance), and species that can survive in a wide range of salinities (i.e., high tolerance). Risk between any two ports is then quantified as an index created by overlapping the species tolerance groups as shown in Fig. 6.

Table 3: **Grouping based on environmental tolerance**

Species Tolerance Group	Tolerance Levels	
	$\Delta T\,(°C)$	$\Delta S\,(ppt)$
Tolerance Group 1	[0, 2.9]	[0, 0.2]
Tolerance Group 2	[0, 2.9]	[0, 2.0]
Tolerance Group 3	[0, 2.9]	[0, 12]
Tolerance Group 4	[0, 9.7]	[0, 0.2]
Tolerance Group 5	[0, 9.7]	[0, 2.0]
Tolerance Group 6	[0, 9.7]	[0, 12]

3.2 Environmental Similarity Network

Quantification of port-wise invasion risk is both difficult and not very useful in terms of species control and management. In order to gain insight into what ports are at risk based on species flow and environmental similarity, we utilize a graphical representation that is referred to as the *Invasion Risk Network (IRN)*. An IRN is built for every *major* cluster in SFN to intuitively represent the invasion risk based on how easily species can establish in the new environment (based on environmental tolerance, see Table 3). Note that IRN is an undirected weighted graph, since environmental match is symmetric, and the risk level (based on number of tolerance groups at risk) can vary between port pairs, respectively.

3.3 Clustering Analysis of IRN

With the edges representing the invasion risk between ports, clustering can help detect groups of ports that have similar environmental conditions (while belonging to different ecoregions). The basic idea here is to exploit the fact that the invasion risk between groups of ports that are very dissimilar (e.g., fresh-water ports and marine ports) is lower than ports within the same group (with relatively similar conditions). Clustering analysis (Section 2.2) can therefore again be utilized on IRN to identify groups of ports that are similar in terms of invasion risk. The clusters detected here are sub-clusters of SFN clusters (that are based on species flow dynamics); therefore, if two ports are in the same cluster of IRN, then it is very likely for an invasion to occur between these two ports. Furthermore, if adequate species flow control is not in place, given the frequent species exchanges and high chances of species establishment within ports in an IRN cluster, an invasion to one single port will immediately put all the other ports in the IRN sub-cluster at risk of an invasion. Therefore, IRN clusters identify groups of ports that would most benefit from some form of species flow control to avoid invasions.

Note: Clustering based on flow-dynamics (simulating random walks) is used here for identifying ports with similar environmental conditions, since an approach only considering pair-wise distance is not capable of capturing the stepping-stone effect.

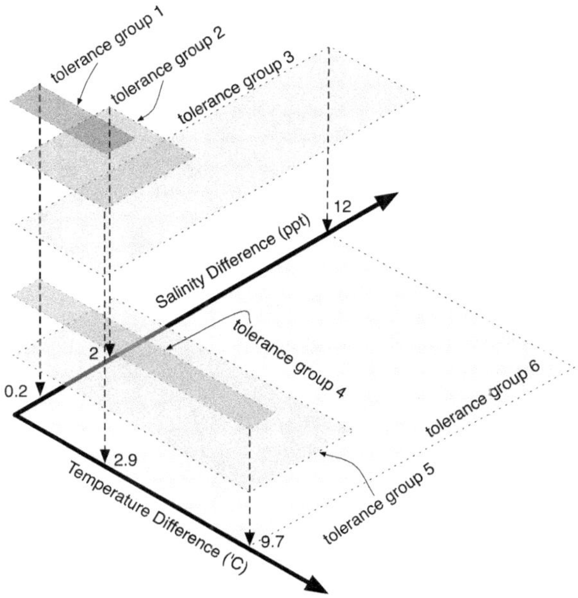

(a) Species tolerance groups

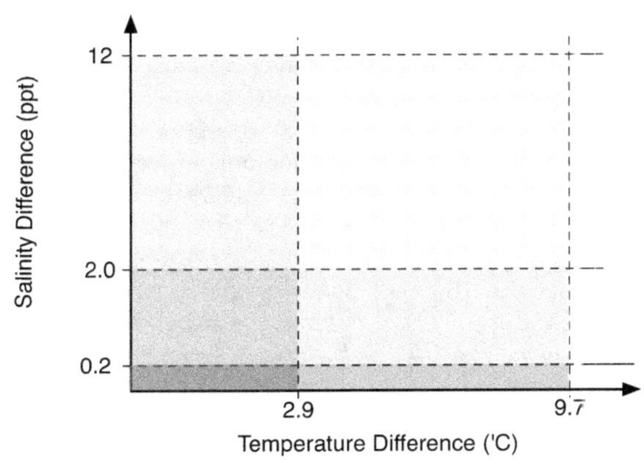

(b) Risk level definition

Figure 6: **Illustration of *risk level* definition based on species tolerance groups and between-port environmental differences.** Sub-figure (a): identifies six (6) different species groups that categorizes the risk of survival relative to given difference in temperature and salinity based on two (2) temperate tolerance levels (high = can survive up to $9.7°C$ and low = can survive up to $2.9°C$ temperature difference) and three (3) salinity tolerance levels (zero = $0.2ppt$, low = $2.0ppt$ and high = $12.0ppt$ tolerance). Sub-figure (b): definition of risk level, defined based on number of species groups as identified in (a); the colors are generated by overlapping the layers and later enhanced for clarity and ease of distinction. In this setting, risk level ranges from 0 to 6.

4. EMERGENT SPECIES FLOW CONTROL STRATEGIES

Clustering analysis on SFN has discovered a consistent pattern of port groupings in terms of potential species exchanges. One can easily identify such regions at risk, by overlaying the ecoregions to the IRN clusters above (see Fig. 9(a)). This allows one to consider the four factors of vessel movement, ballast discharge, environmental conditions, and ecoregion in a unique but an intuitive fashion. With

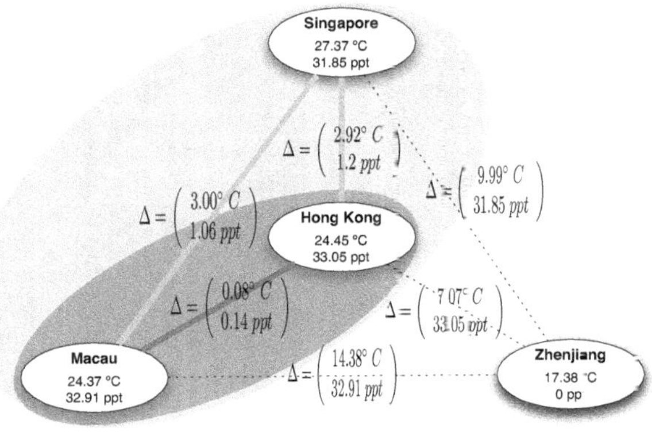

Figure 7: **Illustrating the generation of Invasion Risk Network (IRN).** The IRN is an undirected graph where nodes and edges are given by the ports visited in the GSN and invasion risk level, respectively. Shown here as examples are four ports along with annual average temperature and salinity, and pairwise salinity and temperature differences. Edges drawn in solid lines represent the risk level between ports as defined in Fig. 6; dotted-lines show zero (0) risk edges; colored-patches are used to show the overlap of species tolerance groups shared by a port-pair.

this knowledge in place, species exchange among ports can be efficiently controlled by management strategies that target high species exchange pathways in order to isolate ports and clusters of ports.

4.1 Managing inter-cluster exchanges

Consider Fig. 8 which illustrates the inter- and intra-cluster species flow among major clusters. While we observe some changes in inter-cluster connections, major clusters and species exchange pathways are virtually consistent over time. Therefore, by limiting species flow on inter-cluster connections, species exchanges among ports could be restricted to ports within clusters. This will combinatorially reduce the species introduction pathways.

For instance, consider the `Pacific` cluster in year 2005–2006. There are 37,596 inter-cluster connections, where Table 4 tabulates the strongest connections. Singapore alone

Table 4: **Highest inter-cluster flow for `Pacific` cluster in 2005–2006**

From Port	To Port
Singapore	Port Said
Singapore	Richards Bay
Mormugao	Singapore
Suez	Singapore
Paradip	Singapore
Visakhapatnam	Singapore
Tubarao	Singapore
Chennai	Singapore
Ponta da Madeira	Singapore

Table 5: **Major inter-cluster contributors in 2005–2006**

Cluster	Port
`Pacific`	Singapore
`Mediterranean`	Gibraltar
`W. Euro`	Rotterdam
`E. N. America`	New York
`Indian Ocean`	Mormugao
`S. America`	Tubarao
`Great Lakes`	Seven Islands
`Black Sea`	Istanbul
`W. N. America`	Long Beach

contributes to approximately 26% of total inter-cluster flow from/to `Pacific` cluster that contains 818 ports (see Fig. 9 for an illustration of invasion risk with respect to Singapore). Here, via targeted ballast management on inter-cluster con-

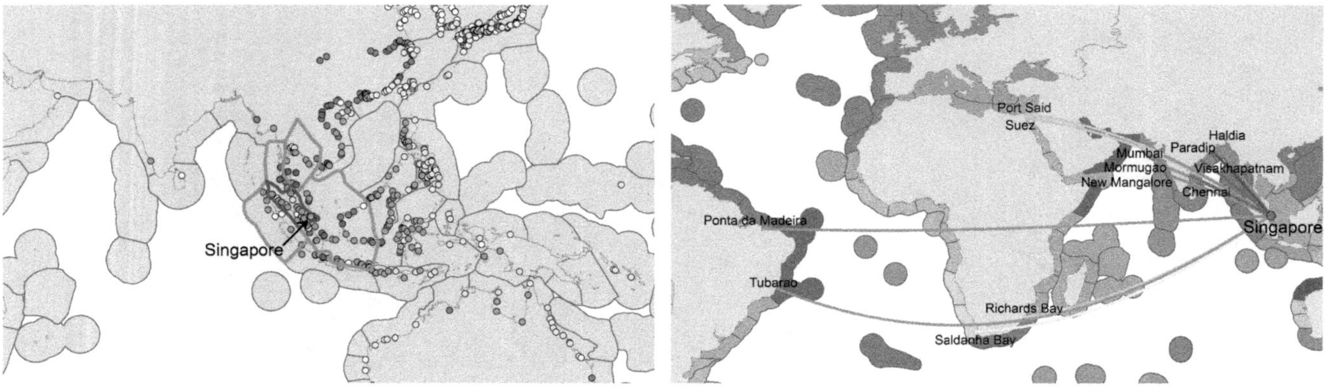

(a) Inner-Cluster Invasion Risk w.r.t. Singapore (b) Inter-Cluster Invasion Risk w.r.t. Singapore

Figure 9: **NIS invasion risk with respect to Singapore,** where the colors correspond to risk level definitions in Fig. 6.

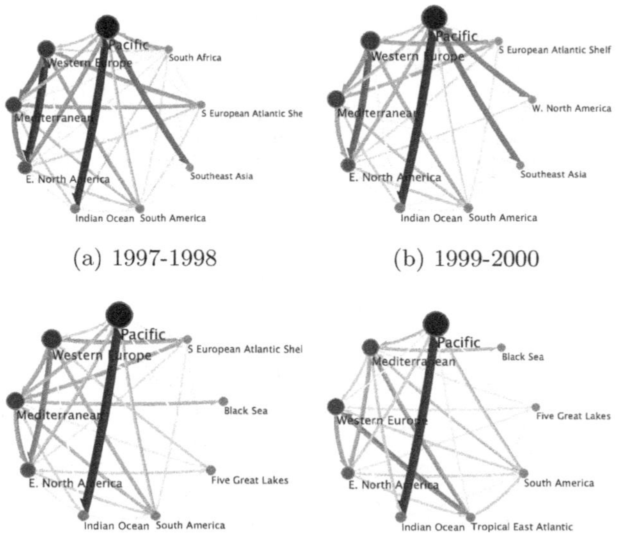

(a) 1997-1998 (b) 1999-2000

(c) 2002-2003 (d) 2005-2006

Figure 8: **Illustration of inter-cluster and intra-cluster flow.** Here, ratio of darker/lighter region explains the ratio of intra-cluster flow (i.e., flow between ports within a cluster) to inter-cluster flow (i.e., flow between ports belonging to different clusters). Therefore, in major clusters, species exchange among ports within clusters appears to be much higher compared to that of between clusters.

nections to/from Singapore and a few other "influential" ports, inter-cluster flow from/to `Pacific` cluster can be significantly reduced (see Fig. 9(b)).

Table 5 lists ports corresponding to the highest inter-cluster flow in major clusters for 2005–2006. Any practices that reduced species movements through these ports would potentially reduce a large proportion of inter-cluster species flow. Increases in species surveillance in these ports would strengthen the foundation for geographic allocation of risk management efforts. Finally, increased surveillance of ports would provide a baseline against which to measure the effectiveness of future risk reduction efforts–a baseline that is now largely absent globally (Costello et al. 2007)

4.2 Targeting hubs for species flow control

Average path length of three (3) that is observed on SFN indicates that species could be translocated between any two given ports within two (2) stopovers on average. This indicates a generally high risk of invasions in the absence of risk reduction practices. In order to understand the impact of targeted ballast management on average path length, a test scenario based on a hypothetical SFN—$\widehat{\text{SFN}}$ is derived as follows: **(i)** choose an SFN (SFN corresponding to 2005–2006 LMIU dataset was chosen for our experiment); then, **(ii)** identify 20% of all ports with the highest degree (see Table 6); and, finally **(iii)** generate $\widehat{\text{SFN}}$ by removing all edges to/from the above ports; this corresponds to ballast management with 100% efficiency, i.e., zero (0) species flow from/to these ports. *Then, the average path length increases to 6.4 indicating that it will be at least twice as difficult for species to be translocated from one port to another.* Furthermore, higher average path length also implies, **(i)** longer travel times (hence, very lower chance of survival for species during the voyage) and **(ii)** increased number of intermediate stop-overs (which is likely to dilute ballast water and expose organisms to multiple shocks).

Table 6: **Ports* with degree** > 1000 **in 2005-2006 that act as "hubs" in SFN**

Port name	Degree	Important pathways (connected ports)
Gibraltar	1882	Cape Finisterre, Tubarao
Dover Strait*	1747	Cape Finisterre, Rotterdam, Tubarao
Singapore	1569	Mormugao, Tubarao
Cape Finisterre	1387	Gibraltar, Rotterdam, Tubarao
Panama Canal*	1275	New Orleans
Tarifa	1224	Gibraltar, Cape Finisterre
Rotterdam	1126	Cape Finisterre, Dover Strait

* indicates locations in LMIU database, but do not correspond to actual ports; connected ports are listed in decreasing order of degree.

4.3 Vessel type based management strategies

The exact amount of species relocated by a vessel depends on many factors: ballast size, average duration per trip, frequently visited ports, etc. Furthermore, vessel types we observe in GSN are often chosen for specific tasks (e.g., oil transportation, vehicle transportation, etc.) and these vessels often have their respective frequent ports/routes. Therefore, we investigate the relationship of vessel types to inter- and intra-cluster species flow in order to understand existing patterns that can be helpful in devising species management strategies (based on the 2005-2006 LMIU dataset).

(i) Frequent inter-cluster travelers: While not being the most active vessel in the GSN, `container carriers` correspond to 57,909, or equivalently 24% of all inter-cluster trips in 2005-2006. Among the most frequently seen vessel types, `bulkers`, `crude oil tankers`, `refrigerated general cargo ships` and `combined bulk and oil carriers` tend to travel inter-cluster for over 25% of the time. Furthermore, among the vessel types that do not travel frequently, some vessel types tend to travel inter-cluster in a majority of their trips (e.g., `wood-chip carriers`: 40.4%, `livestock carriers`: 34.3%, `semi-sub HL vessels`: 37.4% and `barge container carriers`: 55.7%).

(ii) Frequent intra-cluster travelers: Among the most frequently travelled vessel types, `passenger carriers` tend to stay within clusters for 97.6% of their trips, thus imposing only a very minimal risk in terms of inter-cluster species translocation. Similarly, `barge ships` also stay within the cluster for 98.1% of total trips.

4.4 Impact of environmental conditions

With proper species control on inter-cluster connections, species flow can be confined to clusters. Even though ports within a cluster have higher species exchanges among them, if the environmental conditions are significantly different, invasions are less likely to occur. On the other hand, for ports in the same IRN cluster (hence, environmental conditions are very similar), if proper species flow control is not in place, invasions will be nearly unavoidable. For instance, in the `Pacific` cluster, we observe that *Hong Kong, Qingdao* and *Kaohsiung* have higher species exchanges among them; and, following clustering analysis of IRN, we also notice that Hong Kong and Kaohsiung are in the same IRN cluster. Therefore, invasions are very likely to occur in between these two ports. On the other hand, Qingdao is in a different sub-cluster to Hong Kong, indicating these two ports have significantly different environmental conditions—invasions are less likely to happen between these two ports, even with high species exchanges.

5. CONCLUDING REMARKS

Aquatic invasions via the GSN are a result of a complex interplay of ship traffic, ballast uptake/discharge dynamics, species survival during transport and numerous environmental/biological variables. The inherent complexity of the invasive species problem has made risk assessment very difficult, and thereby has severely hampered the effectiveness of species management efforts. To that end, we have developed an approach for more effective and efficient risk assessment and management by modeling the spread of aquatic non-indigenous species through the GSN, which is the most important vector of aquatic invasions. Knowledge about the patterns of GSN, within the context of species flow and invasion risk, appropriate risk assessments can be generated to help inform management strategies and regulatory policies.

In a management context, the discovered knowledge could efficiently be used to analyze the invasion risks with respect to changing climate, policy and infrastructure. Understanding the structure of the component networks and the dynamic interactions between the different networks is crucial to the design of policies that could cost-effectively reduce invasions. The analyses outlined and performed in this paper could also be used to geographically prioritize species surveillance efforts using traditional organism sampling methods (e.g., water samples, nets) and/or newer genetic approaches [4]. Furthermore, our work illustrates the value of creative use of data mining for social good via the application to a significant societal problem.

6. ACKNOWLEDGMENTS

This work is based on research supported by the Notre Dame Office of Research via the Environmental Change Initiative (ECI), the Army Research Laboratory and was accomplished under Cooperative Agreement Number W911NF-09-2-0053, the U.S. Air Force Office of Scientific Research (AFOSR) and the Defense Advanced Research Projects Agency (DARPA) grant #FA9550-12-1-0405, NOAA CSCOR and EPA GLRI grants. We are grateful to the anonymous reviewers for their constructive comments.

7. REFERENCES

[1] R. Abell, M. L. Thieme, C. Revenga, M. Bryer, M. Kottelat, N. Bogutskaya, B. Coad, N. Mandrak, S. C. Balderas, W. Bussing, M. L. J Stiassny, P. Skelton, G. R. Allen, P. Unmack, A. Naseka, R. Ng, N. Sindorf, J. Robertson, E. Armijo, J. V. Higgins, T. J. Heibel, E. Wikramanayake, D. Olson, H. L. Lopez, R. E. Reis, J. G. Lundberg, M. H. Sabaj Perez, and P. Petry. Freshwater ecoregions of the world: A new map of biogeographic units for freshwater biodiversity conservation. *BioScience*, 58(5):403–414, May 2008.

[2] J. I. Antonov, D. Seidov, T. P. Boyer, R. A. Locarnini, A. V. Mishonov, H. E. Garcia, O. K. Baranova, M. M. Zweng, and D. R. Johnson. World Ocean Atlas 2009, Volume S: Salinity. In S. Levitus, editor, *NOAA Atlas NESDIS*, volume 69, page 184. U.S. Government Printing Office, Washington, D.C., 2010.

[3] A.-L. Barabási, R. Albert, and H. Jeong. Scale-free characteristics of random networks: the topology of the world-wide web. *Physica A: Statistical Mechanics and its Applications*, 281(1-4):69–77, June 2000.

[4] K. Bohmann, A. Evans, M. T. P. Gilbert, G. R. Carvalho, S. Creer, M. Knapp, D. W. Yu, and M. de Bruyn. Environmental DNA for wildlife biology and biodiversity monitoring. *Trends in Ecology & Evolution*, 29:358–367, May 2014.

[5] A. Clauset, C. R. Shalizi, and M. E. J. Newman. Power-law distributions in empirical data. *SIAM Review*, 51:661–703, Apr 2009.

[6] N. N. I. S. Council. 2008-2012 national invasive species management plan, 2008.

[7] S. Devin and J.-N. Beisel. Biological and ecological characteristics of invasive species: a gammarid study. *Biological Invasions*, 9(1):13–24, 2007.

[8] J. M. Drake and D. M. Lodge. Global hot spots of biological invasions: Evaluating options for ballast-water management. *Proceedings: Biological Sciences*, 271(1539):575–580, Mar. 2004.

[9] O. Floerl, G. Rickard, G. Inglis, and H. Roulston. Predicted effects of climate change on potential sources of non-indigenous marine species. *Diversity and Distributions*, 19(3):257–267, 2013.

[10] M. Girvan and M. E. J. Newman. Community structure in social and biological networks. *Proceedings of the National Academy of Sciences*, 99(12):7821–7826, 2002.

[11] B. Goodwin, A. McAllister, and L. Fahrig. Predicting invasiveness of plant species based on biological information. *Conservation Biology*, 13:422–426, 1999.

[12] R. Guimera and L. A. Amaral. Functional cartography of complex metabolic networks. *Nature*, 433:895–900, Feb. 2005.

[13] B. S. Halpern, S. Walbridge, K. A. Selkoe, C. V. Kappel, F. Micheli, C. D'Agrosa, J. F. Bruno, K. S. Casey, C. Ebert, H. E. Fox, R. Fujita, D. Heinemann, H. S. Lenihan, E. M. P. Madin, M. T. Perry, E. R. Selig, M. Spalding, R. Steneck, and R. Watson. A global map of human impact on marine ecosystems. *Science*, 319(5865):948–952, Feb. 2008.

[14] R. P. Keller, J. M. Drake, M. B. Drew, and D. M. Lodge. Linking environmental conditions and ship movements to estimate invasive species transport across the global shipping network. *Diversity and Distributions*, 17(1):93–102, 2011.

[15] R. P. Keller, D. M. Lodge, M. A. Lewis, and J. F. Shogren. *Bioeconomics of Invasive Species : Integrating Ecology, Economics, Policy, and Management: Integrating Ecology, Economics, Policy, and Management*. Oxford University Press, Apr. 2009.

[16] R. A. Locarnini, A. V. Mishonov, J. I. Antonov, T. P. Boyer, H. E. Garcia, O. K. Baranova, M. M. Zweng, and D. R. Johnson. World ocean atlas 2009, volume 1: Temperature. In S. Levitus, editor, *NOAA Atlas NESDIS*, volume 68, page 184. U.S. Government Printing Office, Washington, D.C., 2010.

[17] J. L. Molnar, R. L. Gamboa, C. Revenga, and M. D. Spalding. Assessing the global threat of invasive species to marine biodiversity. *Frontiers in Ecology and the Environment*, 6(9):485–492, Feb. 2008.

[18] G. Palla, I. Derényi, I. Farkas, and T. Vicsek. Uncovering the overlapping community structure of complex networks in nature and society. *Nature*, 435(7043):814–818, June 2005.

[19] D. Pimentel, R. Zuniga, and D. Morrison. Update on the environmental and economic costs associated with alien-invasive species in the United States. *Ecological Economics*, 52(3):273–288, Feb 2005.

[20] J. Richard, S. A. Morley, M. A. S. Thorne, and L. S. Peck. Estimating long-term survival temperatures at the assemblage level in the marine environment: Towards macrophysiology. *PLoS ONE*, 7(4):e34655, Apr. 2012.

[21] M. Rosvall and C. T. Bergstrom. Maps of random walks on complex networks reveal community structure. *Proceedings of the National Academy of Sciences*, 105(4):1118–1123, 2008.

[22] J. Rothlisberger, D. Finnoff, R. Cooke, and D. Lodge. Ship-borne nonindigenous species diminish great lakes ecosystem services. *Ecosystems*, 15(3):1–15, 2012.

[23] M. Sales-Pardo, R. Guimera, A. Moreira, and L. Amaral. Extracting the hierarchical organization of complex systems. *Proc. National Academy of Sciences of the United States of America*, 104:15224–15229, Sept. 2007.

[24] H. Seebens, M. T. Gastner, and B. Blasius. The risk of marine bioinvasion caused by global shipping. *Ecology Letters*, Apr. 2013.

[25] C. E. Shannon and W. Weaver. *A Mathematical Theory of Communication*. University of Illinois Press, Champaign, IL, USA, 1963.

[26] M. D. Spalding, H. E. Fox, G. R. Allen, N. Davidson, Z. A. F. na, M. Finlayson, B. S. Halpern, K. D. Martin, E. Mcmanus, J. Molnar, C. A. Recchia, and J. Robertson. Marine ecoregions of the world: A bioregionalization of coastal and shelf areas. *BioScience*, 57(7):573–583, July 2007.

[27] E. Tufte. *Beautiful Evidence*. Graphics Press, 2006.

[28] M. Wonham, J. Byers, E. D. Grosholz, and B. Leung. Modeling the relationship between propagule pressure and invasion risk to inform policy and management. *Ecological Applications*, Mar. 2013.

FoodSIS: A Text Mining System to Improve the State of Food Safety in Singapore

Kiran Kate
IBM Research
kirankate@sg.ibm.com

Sneha Chaudhari
Language Technologies Institute,
Carnegie Mellon University, Pittsburgh, USA
sschaudh@andrew.cmu.edu

Andy Prapanca
IBM Research
andypp@sg.ibm.com

Jayant Kalagnanam
IBM Research
jayant@us.ibm.com

ABSTRACT

Food safety is an important health issue in Singapore as the number of food poisoning cases have increased significantly over the past few decades. The National Environment Agency of Singapore (NEA) is the primary government agency responsible for monitoring and mitigating the food safety risks. In an effort to pro-actively monitor emerging food safety issues and to stay abreast with developments related to food safety in the world, NEA tracks the World Wide Web as a source of news feeds to identify food safety related articles. However, such information gathering is a difficult and time consuming process due to information overload. In this paper, we present FoodSIS, a system for end-to-end web information gathering for food safety. FoodSIS improves efficiency of such focused information gathering process with the use of machine learning techniques to identify and rank relevant content. We discuss the challenges in building such a system and describe how thoughtful system design and recent advances in machine learning provide a framework that synthesizes interactive learning with classification to provide a system that is used in daily operations. We conduct experiments and demonstrate that our classification approach results in improving the efficiency by average 35% compared to a conventional approach and the ranking approach leads to average 16% improvement in elevating the ranks of relevant articles.

Categories and Subject Descriptors

H.2.8 [**Database Applications**]: Data Mining–Machine Learning; H.3.3 [**Information Search and Retrieval**]: Selection Process

Keywords

Machine Learning, Text Classification, Ranking, Semi-supervised Learning, Information Gathering

1. INTRODUCTION

The US Centers for Disease Control and Prevention (CDC) estimated that roughly 1 in 6 Americans or 48 million people fall ill, 128,000 are hospitalized and 3,000 die of food-borne diseases each year [6]. WHO estimated that the diseases caused by major food-borne pathogens alone cost up to US $35 billion annually in medical expenses and lost productivity [4]. In Singapore, the number of food poisoning cases and the number of people affected have increased significantly (by 14 and 17 times, respectively)[1] from 1965 to 2011 [14]. This increasing trend is an important public health concern as more people tend to consume meals outside of their homes. According to the Health Promotion Board (HPB), Singapore residents usually eat out at least four times a week at hawker centers, food courts and coffee shop stalls. The proportion has increased from 49% in 2004 to 60% in 2010 [5]. Food recalls also appear to be on the rise especially in the last decade [1]. Anecdotal evidence suggests similar increases food recalls in Singapore due to concerns regarding contamination in neighboring food growing and processing countries [2] or mislabeling [3]. Poor hygiene practices [14], food recalls, food contamination and mislabeling, poor food processing and related technologies are all factors that could cause food safety threats.

Government agencies such as the National Environment Agency (NEA) in Singapore are responsible for monitoring the state of food safety in the country. NEA is extremely pro-active in terms of monitoring emerging food safety issues in order to be able to take preventive actions wherever possible. One approach used by NEA to accomplish this is to constantly identify emerging food safety issues and developments by tracking the World Wide Web for articles related to food safety from a variety of local and international sources. NEA has a team to browse information including news on a daily basis from a set of identified web data sources. They sift through web articles on these sources and identify those related to food safety such that they are relevant to the function and scope of the Environmental Health Department at NEA. The identified articles are then summarized and compiled into weekly newsletters and circulated to the relevant sections in the organization. This paper describes FoodSIS, a system built for NEA to provide support for the generation of such newsletters.

The main purpose of the newsletters is to stay abreast with information such as food poisoning outbreaks happening worldwide, news about food recalls from neighboring countries, developments in food technology, and new policies/regulations about food. Each newsletter is an aggregated report of relevant information that is used by the operational teams of the agency to make tactical decisions regarding the published food safety alerts that are of rele-

KDD'14, August 24–27, 2014, New York, NY, USA.
Copyright 2014 ACM 978-1-4503-2956-9/14/08 ...$15.00.
http://dx.doi.org/10.1145/2623330.2623369.

[1]This is not a reflection of hygiene standards. Even as safety and hygiene standards go up, the sheer number of people eating out leads to higher incidents.

vance. There are two main steps in the newsletter generation process: (i) searching and identifying the content about food safety issues such that it is interesting and relevant for the agency, and (ii) summarizing the identified content and compiling it in the form of the newsletter. Due to overload of information on the web and inability of search engines to capture subtleties of an information need, the manual execution of step 1 very difficult and time consuming. After a set of relevant articles have been identified, it is then relatively straight forward to manually summarize them since they are small in number. As a result, we focus our attention to step 1 in the current system development.

As we explain in later sections, we formulate the identification of relevant content as a document classification problem and relevance ranking based on labeled data. The design of such document classification systems traditionally uses supervised learning with positive and negative labeled documents. However in real life it is rare to find sufficient number of labeled documents. As a result, the design of an operational system to classify and rank documents accurately for daily use needs to exploit two additional sources of information: (i) the sources of data and the semantic and organizational structure of these sources, and (ii) the interactive aspects of how users interact with the system to consume the results of the classification and provide feedback on the ranked list of documents classified as relevant (in order of relevance).

The news sources that need to be examined for relevant documents provide an organization by separating articles by sections (such as politics, entertainment, sports, health etc). This structure provides a way of identifying and ignoring the sections that are irrelevant (such as sports, entertainment, ...) for the topics of interest (food safety). In addition, the marginal distribution of articles from different news sources provides useful prior information for the design of an operational system.

The other important requirement is the aspect of interactive learning. FoodSIS classifies articles into *relevant* and *not relevant* and presents the *relevant* articles as a rank ordered list (in order of relevance). Based on this interface, the user provides inputs by choosing documents that are truly relevant (as per her judgment). This interaction provides information beyond the simple labeling of documents as *relevant/not relevant*. The user implicitly provides pairwise comparisons (not necessarily a total order) between documents and separation among sets of documents by his selection of relevant documents from a set of documents presented to him. This can be modeled and used to adaptively improve the ranking.

The **Food** Safety **I**nformation **S**ystem (FoodSIS) is a pilot system at NEA (National Environment Agency, Singapore) that is in operational test mode for daily operations from last 6 months. FoodSIS is based on a design of a classification and ranking engine using a variety of machine learning techniques, to account for the operational needs and the exploitation of the application specific information outlined in the paragraphs above. This system is now deployed on a pilot infrastructure and is in daily use for the past six months in an effort to evaluate its efficacy. The end users now routinely use FoodSIS as the first point of entry for navigating the web for food safety related news articles and report an increasing dependence on its availability for daily operations. FoodSIS is designed to provide a ranked list of the most relevant articles (for any food safety related search). The users routinely provide inputs both by marking the articles that are deemed as "truly relevant" and also qualitative feedback on the ease of use. This interaction provides data for continual improvement of the operational system.

The rest of the paper is organized as follows: Section 2 provides details about the data sources, data sets and the problem, and provides an analysis of the document classification problem. Section 3 describes the design and architecture of FoodSIS. Section 4 provides details regarding the technical approach for building the operationally useful classifiers using machine learning techniques. Experimental evaluation of the classifiers and results are also presented in section 4. Section 5 discusses the use of pairwise ranking inputs provided (implicitly) by the users and how this is used to improve the ranking of articles classified as *relevant*. Section 6 is a discussion of some of the challenges and lessons that were learnt from the deployment of the system. We conclude the paper with a discussion of other application areas where this approach can be used to build information gathering systems in section 7.

2. PROBLEM AND DATA DETAILS

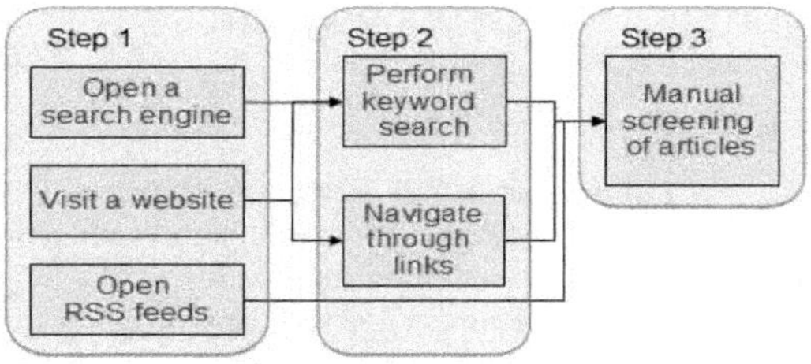

Figure 1: A manual information gathering process

Search engines are the most widely used tools for information search but there are two fundamental challenges in using them for routine, domain focused, target driven information needs: (i) Digital information overload, (ii) Inability to transform information requirements into precise keyword queries. Figure 1 captures a manual information gathering process that is commonly used today in organizations. As shown in the figure, they use three different information browsing mechanisms depending on the data sources. For example, some websites provide RSS feeds making it easier to access new content. Some websites are meant to host content on the topic of interest and users visit those directly. All other requirements are satisfied by search engines. A final step is to go through all the articles presented as search results, RSS feeds or different sections of a website and shortlist those relevant to the department.

The environmental health department of NEA also followed a similar approach to information gathering. The team identified 37 websites on which they find useful posts about food safety. These 37 data sources are categorized into 3 categories as follows:

1. **Official government websites:** Websites such as World Health Organization (WHO: http://www.who.int/en/) and websites of other government agencies.

2. **Media websites:** General global news websites.

3. **Food hygiene and safety websites:** Websites dedicated to information on food safety.

Food safety related information which is of interest to NEA can roughly be described by the following 5 categories: (i) food poisoning outbreaks/food borne diseases, (ii) developments in food technology and practices, (iii) food regulatory/policy developments, (iv) enforcement of food safety violation and recognition for food safety compliance, and (v) investigation reports on food hygiene inspections. The 5 categories only provide an idea of the kind of information that is relevant and are not used for any strict classification.

The team has a list of 19 keyword phrases they use for searching information. The keyword phrases include high level topics such as "food safety", "food hygiene", "food policy", "food poisoning". Manually crafting a detailed and complete list of keywords for a domain is a time consuming task and it is tougher for a vast domain like food safety. Also, as we try to demonstrate in the example below, the domain understanding required for correct identification of relevant articles for NEA is beyond a list of keywords.

"People have reported vomiting, diarrhoea and other symptoms of food poisoning after eating products including pizza and lasagne made by a subsidiary of Maruha Nichiro Holdings, the nation's largest seafood firm. ... Police began investigating the company last month after it revealed some of its frozen food had been tainted with malathion, an agricultural chemical often used to kill aphids in corn and rice fields."

This is a story of a major food poisoning case in Japan where over 2800 people were affected due to contamination of frozen foods with pesticide. Information about food poisoning outbreaks is one of the important categories of information relevant to NEA. However, the article with the above excerpt and all the other related articles are labeled as not relevant by the users. To understand why, one must understand the cause of contamination reported in the article as well as NEA's scope of work. The article suggests that the contamination might have happened due to pesticides during manufacturing. NEA does not oversee manufacturing stage of food products. They mainly deal with retail end of the food supply chain. So while they are interested in food poisoning outbreaks, the focus is more on food poisoning incidents which occur in food retail establishments. Extending the keyword search approach, we might need to craft complicated rules to capture these subtleties. For example, a rule such as "does not contain 'agricultur' (this word form can be obtained by stemming)" could be in the list of rules, and it should supersede the rule "contains 'food poisoning'". This needs a lot of manual effort and such an approach does not have the capability to learn over time. Machine learning techniques, in particular document classification seemed the most appropriate yet simple choice to automate the content identification step when some training data (labeled articles) is available. We also use a supervised rank learner to improve the ranked list of articles that is presented to the user as output. The next section describes the deployed system and its components.

3. SYSTEM OVERVIEW

Information gathering with FoodSIS is as simple as opening the web user interface, browsing through a ranked list of articles to identify the relevant content. The list has articles compiled from all the important data sources and ranking captures their relevance to the users. The system not only simplifies step 1 and eliminates step 2 of the manual process (figure 1), but also significantly improves the efficiency of article screening.

The overall system architecture is as shown in figure 2. The system is designed such that it is easy to use, flexible, and easily configurable. The main components of the system are: web crawler, article text extractor and indexer, document classification and ranking, and an interactive web user interface. We cover details of classification and ranking in section 4 and 5 respectively. We disuss the web interface briefly in the next paragraph. Due to space constraints, we omit the description of other components.

The web based user interface is an important component of FoodSIS which allows users to browse through the classified and ranked content. Figure 3 shows the web interface. Functionality provided by the web user interface of FoodSIS is designed with inputs from the users. Each of the features has proved very important for using FoodSIS effectively. Following are two important features available through the web interface: (i)*Ranked list of articles:* The right pane of on the web interface is a ranked list of articles. After articles are classified as *relevant*, we use a supervised ranking method to rank them in the order of relevance by making use of user feedback. Each article in the list is associated with a check box. Users can label the article as relevant or not using the check box. This feedback is saved in the system and looped back for training every week. The models are updated at the same frequency. This simple mechanism proved practically very useful, since it served as a way of obtaining more labeled data with no/little extra efforts by the domain experts, (ii) *Keyword search:* Keyword search essentially makes the system act like a custom search engine allowing users to search using keywords. For example, if they want to see all articles containing "E. coli", they can use simple keyword search. It can also be used to identify articles during bootstrapping phase of the machine learning algorithms.

FoodSIS is thus a tool for end-to-end information gathering and includes components for data collection, pre-processing, classification, ranking, and a user interface for interacting with the users effectively.

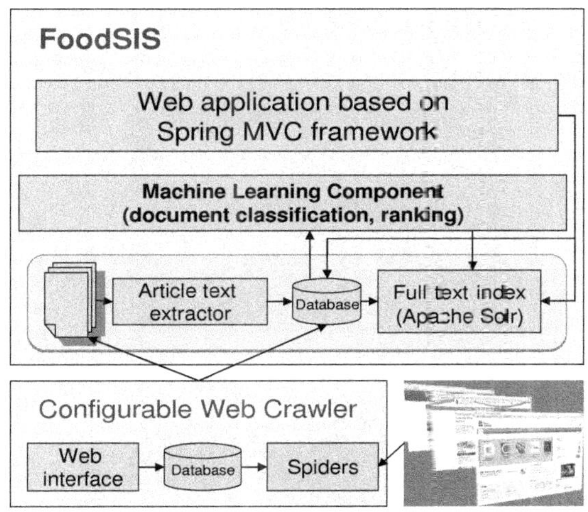

Figure 2: FoodSIS System Architecture

4. DOCUMENT CLASSIFICATION

The main challenge in making FoodSIS successful is the ability to present relevant content to the users. As illustrated in section 2, simple keyword search fails to capture the relevance effectively. Machine learning methods, in particular, document classification is well suited for such a task since the task is to separate relevant information from non-relevant. They have the ability to learn complex relationships from data and their performance improves with training. We formulate problem of identifying information relevant to food safety as a binary classification task. The class labels are *relevant* and *not relevant*. *Relevant* is a class of food safety related articles that are relevant to NEA and *not relevant* contains all the other articles that are not relevant. A quick look at the problem and the 5 types of information listed in section 2 might lead us to treating it as a multi-class classification. But we observed the domain and data carefully and noticed that the class boundaries for the 5 classes are not very clear. The 5 types are to provide guidance on the kind of information that is relevant to NEA and the information is not always strictly limited to those. Also, from system usability point of view, the agency does not necessarily need the articles to be categorized into those 5 categories.

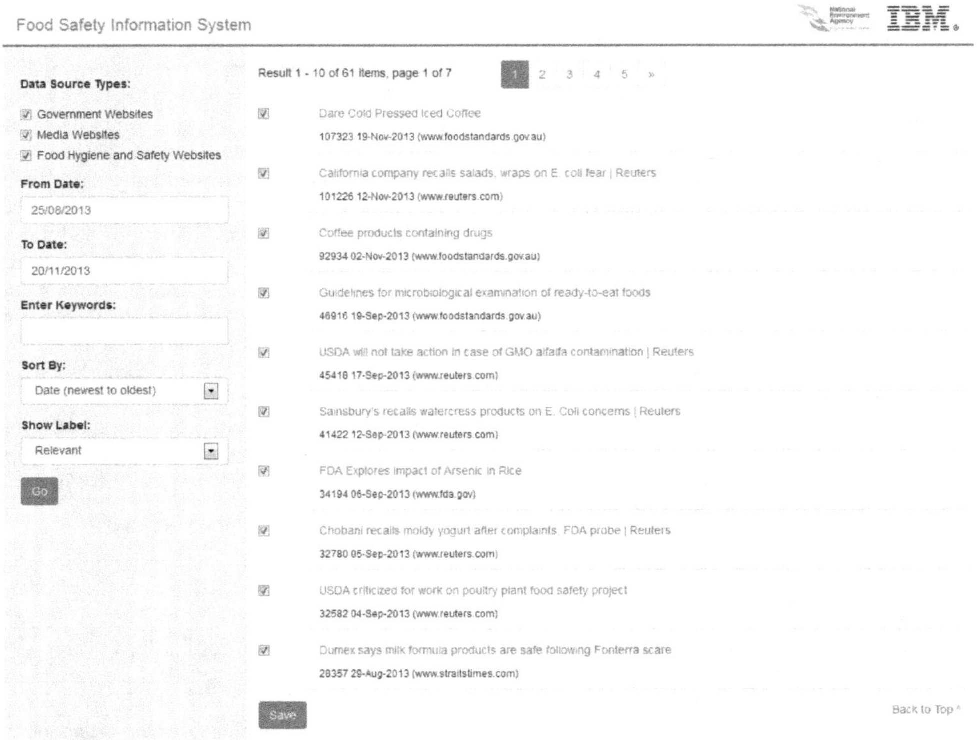

Figure 3: Screenshot of FoodSIS Web UI

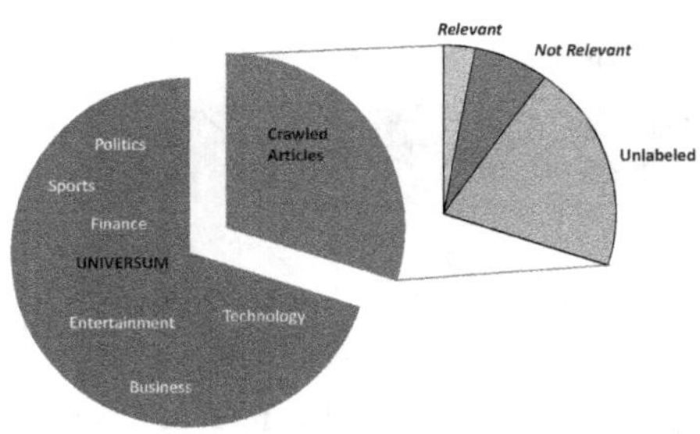

Figure 4: View of different components of the dataset

The most important consideration in a classification problem is the availability of labeled data for training. Figure 4 shows the datasets we have access to due to the nature of our problem. Each of the datasets can be interpreted and obtained as follows:

1. ***Relevant:*** We received around 6 months of food safety newsletters from NEA in e-mail format. Each newsletter has a list of *relevant* manually summarized articles. We extracted each article summary as a document of the *relevant* class. This seed data contained 53 articles of positive (i.e. *relevant*) class. We developed an initial classifier with this seed data as described in section 4.1. The users used this initial system to provide labels for more articles as discussed in 3. The labeling provided by users allows us to obtain *relevant* as well as *not relevant* articles. However, the amount of labeled data of class *relevant*, obtained after a couple of months of training is still small, specially since the real class distribution is highly skewed[2].

2. ***Not relevant:*** Our seed training data was based on the food safety newsletters and did not have samples of *not relevant* class. We obtained such samples for seed training by randomly sampling 200 articles from unlabeled articles. Though this is a standard practice, is clearly not an ideal way. Labeling by domain experts is the most ideal but expensive option. Our design of the FoodSIS web user interface allows us to obtain such labels with little extra efforts from the users. The size of our *not relevant* dataset continuously increases as users label them using the web interface.

3. **Unlabeled:** We crawl a high number of articles everyday but present only a few to the users based on their relevance. This essentially means we get user feedback only on a subset and a large portion of the crawled articles remains unlabeled. This allows us to use such unlabeled dataset for improving classification performance by employing semi-supervised techniques.

4. **UNIVERSUM:** UNIVERSUM is a set of data points that are known not to belong to any class of interest. For our setting, it is the set of articles from topics such as politics, sports, business etc. which can easily be kept out of the classification task. Websites such as news websites typically follow a categorization of news into multiple topics. This categorization is also reflected in the website structure. We can exploit

[2] just based on 4 out of 37 data sources the ratio of the number of *not relevant* articles to the number of *relevant* articles ranges from (30 to 45):1 per week

such structure and selectively choose only potential *relevant* articles for classification. For example, from news websites, data can be collected only from the "Health" sections, which then needs to be classified as *relevant* or *not relevant*. With this approach to data collection, the classifier does not have to work on articles from topics such as politics, sports, entertainment etc. and they would fall into UNIVERSUM. We followed websites' structures to collect such UNIVERSUM data set.

Following subsections explain the key settings and methods we tried, reasons behind our choices and experimental evaluation. For all the methods, we used tf-idf scores of unigrams as our features.

4.1 Supervised Learning

A simple supervised binary classification was our first attempt at solving the task. We applied a simple Naive Bayes approach to classification since it has shown to work very well for document classification and is simple to implement. The first set of training data used for building a Naive Bayes classifier contained 53 positive samples extracted from the newsletters. Negative samples were obtained by randomly sampling 200 articles from unlabeled dataset. With most of the other components of the system in place and the Naive Bayes classifier, users started to browse the articles on the web interface. The article list was ranked by the probability scores output by the classifier for membership of class *relevant* (no hard classification was performed). We had version 1 running for roughly a couple of months. This allowed us to gather training data which is used for evaluating different paradigms and methods for classification as explained below.

4.2 Semi-supervised Learning

Supervised learning works quite well assuming that there is enough training data. In real life applications, this seldom is the case. Even with our interactive setup of obtaining training data from the domain experts, the training data we collected over a couple of months is quite small to obtain good classification performance. Advances in machine learning techniques allow us to employ other learning paradigms to handle this challenge. For our setting, unlabeled articles are available in abundance. Consequently, we chose semi-supervised learning to exploit the availability of unlabeled data to improve classification performance.

Other techniques to handle scarcity of labeled training data are (i) active learning which tries to minimize the labeling effort by selecting the most informative examples for labeling [19], (ii) using domain knowledge to label features instead of examples [13], (iii) domain adaptation from a similar domain using transfer learning [7], and (iv) concept labeling which labels concepts in domain ontologies and uses concept-class associations for generating training data of reasonable quality [12]. Techniques (ii) and (iv) propose to reduce the labeling effort but require the domain experts to work on a labeling task not same as the original classification. Technique (iii) assumes the availability of training data in a similar domain. For our setting, it would be an additional task for the domain experts to understand and work on a different labeling task. The interactive learning that our system engages in with the users can be termed as a simple form of active learning.

A variety of semi-supervised techniques have been proposed and shown to work well [9], [18], [8] [20]. Transductive Support Vector Machines(TSVM)[20] is an extension of the widely used supervised Support Vector Machines (SVM). The formulation of TSVM introduces a separate term in the objective function for slack variables of unlabeled data and hence aims to find a hyperplane that separates both labeled and unlabeled data with maximum margin, maintaining the class ratio in unlabeled data. [17] discusses suitability of SVMs for information retrieval which shares many characteristics with our problem. [15] discusses the effectiveness of TSVMs for text classification where the authors mention that TSVMs are well suited for problem settings where the document vectors are sparse and input space has high dimensionality, outperforming conventional methods substantially while also being more robust. Therefore, we believe TSVMs is the best approach to apply to our case. Experimental results in section 4.5 show that TSVM performs better than SVM, specially when the amount of training data is very small.

4.3 Unlabeled Instances Selection

Incorporating unlabeled data in classification might not always be useful, as noted in [24], [10], [11]. There are many papers discussing cases where unlabeled data hurts the performance and indicating that it should be used carefully. We experimented with randomly sampling 20% to 100% of unlabeled data from the available unlabeled dataset and using it for training the TSVM. The comparison of precision, recall and F1 score for these different runs of TSVM with different amounts of randomly sampled unlabeled data did not show a clear winner. We tried a heuristic for selecting unlabeled instances based on the following property of our data sources: some data sources in our list, specially those under the category "food hygiene and safety websites" have a higher ratio of number of *relevant* articles to the number of *not relevant* articles. If we sample unlabeled data points from such sources of data, they are likely to create a dense region around *relevant* class. Following the TSVM principle, we expect such dense region to guide the separating hyperplane away from labeled data of *relevant* class, resulting in more test data points to be classified as *relevant*. Such a placement of the separating hyperplane will improve recall, reducing precision. During the first year of deployment of FoodSIS, high recall is important since it gives confidence to the users on ability of the system to provide complete results. The exact steps followed in the heuristic based selection of unlabeled data are: (i) identify a set of data source names (i.e. the hostname of the websites) corresponding to labeled examples of class *relevant*. Lets call this set W, (ii) select articles from unlabeled data based on W, i.e. select only those unlabeled instances which appear on the hosts in W. We then used this unlabeled data sample set for training a TSVM. We call this approach TSVM-Meta since it uses the meta attribute "data source name" in selecting unlabeled data. Section 4.5 compares the performance of TSVM-Meta with other methods. As demonstrated in section 4.5, though there is no formal theoretical support, TSVM-Meta performs very well empirically, due to the intuition discussed above.

4.4 Exploiting UNIVERSUM

UNIVERSUM data has been found to help improve classification performance since it encodes some useful prior knowledge and there have been many methods proposed in the recent past to exploit the availability of UNIVERSUM [22]. Yang et. al. [21] proposed a tri-class support vector machine (3C-SVM) which uses a combination of UNIVERSUM and unlabeled data together as unlabeled data for developing a maximum margin classifier, utilizing the implicit knowledge among all available data. As a by product, it also identifies the irrelevant data from the set of unlabeled examples (which, in our case is a mix of UNIVERSUM and relevant unlabeled data), which in turn helps to improve the classification performance. Further, in 3C-SVM the irrelevant data in fact plays the role of seeking a good subspace of the decision boundary based on two principles as follows: i) the confidence of prediction is related to the distance of the data point from the decision boundary i.e. if the point is farther, the data point is likely to correctly classified, however, if the data point is near the decision boundary, there is lesser probability or confidence that the data point is classified correctly. As a result, ideally, the relevant data points should lie farther from the boundary and the irrelevant class should lie near to the boundary. ii) the maximum entropy principle indicates that a classifier should rely more on the relevant data, while maximally ignore the irrelevant data. Taking these principles into consideration, 3C-SVM aims to find a maximum margin hyperplane such that irrelevant data points are closer to the hyperplane than relevant examples. As a consequence, it combines the advantages of irrelevant unlabeled data and UNIVERSUM to lead to a maximum margin hyperplane fulfilling the two assumptions.

The identification of irrelevant data points from the set of unlabeled examples is important since 3C-SVM aims to find a hyperplane in which the irrelevant data points are close to the boundary. To accomplish this, it uses two loss functions:

- Symmetric Hinge loss: $H_1(\mid u \mid) = \mid max\{0, 1-u\} \mid$, a loss function to measure risk in unlabeled data
- ϵ-sensitive loss: $I_\epsilon(u) = max\{0, \mid u \mid -\epsilon\}$, a loss function adopted to measure risk in UNIVERSUM data.

Consequently, to separate the unlabeled data into relevant and irrelevant data, 3C-SVM calculates,

$$l_{min}(x) = min\{H_1(\mid f_\theta(x_i) \mid), I_\epsilon(\mid f_\theta(x_i) \mid)\} \quad (1)$$

where, $f_\theta(x)$ is the classifier model. Hence, for an unlabeled data point, according to the value of the $l_{min}(x)$, when the error measured by the ϵ-sensitive loss is smaller than the error measured by Symmetric Hinge loss, it can be determined as irrelevant data. 3C-SVM learns a decision boundary in which irrelevant data points are closer to the boundary whereas the relevant examples are farther away from the boundary.

4.5 Experimental Evaluation

In this section, we report comparison of different classification methods on a dataset obtained by methods described earlier. The dataset we use for all the experiments has 186 *relevant*, 406 *not relevant*, 1796 unlabeled and 900 UNIVERSUM articles. Our system in its current version crawls data from a subset of the 37 different data sources. The number of articles crawled ranges from around 600 to 1300 per day. We have access to a large set of unlabeled and UNIVERSUM articles, but we intuitively feel that since labeled data is limited, using all the other available data for classification might add a lot of noise. So we randomly sampled unlabeled data to roughly 3 times the size of labeled data and UNIVERSUM data close to 1.5 times the size of labeled data. All the experiments are run 10 times with random train-test split of the labeled data and we report the average precision, recall and F1 score of the methods. Figures 5, 6 and 7 show comparison of of different classifiers based on F1 score, precision and recall respectively. The values on the x-axis are the percentages of test data in the random train-test split of labeled data. Please note that we vary test data percentage from 50% to 90% mainly because one of the objectives of comparing different methods was to find out which method performs the best with very few training examples. The motivation behind such objective is to be able to apply the system to a domain other than food safety easily. Availability of labeled data would be a major challenge to apply our methodology to a completely different domain. Hence it is important to employ a method that can work well with a small training data set. The methods we evaluate are 3C-SVM, SVM, TSVM, TSVM-Meta, and keyword search (referred to as KB in the plots). The keyword based approach uses the list of 19 keyword phrases provided by the NEA users to us and classifies an article as *relevant* if one or more of those keyword phrases occur in the article.

Figure 5 shows that 3C-SVM outperforms all other methods in F1 except the case when there are only 10% examples for training, i.e. around 18 examples of positive class and 40 examples of negative class. Improvement in F1 score due to 3C-SVM is about 10% over TSVM, in the range of 3% to 8% over TSVM-Meta, 1.5%-6% over SVM and about 27% to 39% over KB except the case with 10% labeled data for training. SVM performs as good as 3C-SVM when 50% of labeled data is used for training. But the F1 score drops drastically as the training set size becomes smaller. This is expected and is the main reason why semi-supervised learning is effective when training data is too small. Same effect can be observed in comparing SVM with TSVM and TSVM-Meta. Improvement in 3C-SVM over TSVM and TSVM-Meta can be attributed to its use of UNIVERSUM and the way it incorporates such data. An analysis of our data set using 3C-SVM provides the average distances of the 3 classes from the decision boundary (the separating hyperplane). The average absolute distance of the positive class documents from the separating hyperplane is 2.013 (σ=0.39) while the average absolute distance for the negative class is 0.65 (σ=0.23). From within the unlabeled data it is now interesting to note that the average absolute distance of the irrelevant data (UNIVERSUM) is only 0.13 (σ=0.22) while the rest of the unlabeled data has a absolute distance of about 0.72 (σ=0.31) and therefore can be considered as relevant. These numbers indicate that the underlying principle of irrelevant data being close to the decision boundary while relevant data being far from decision boundary is satisfied for our data sets and the analysis provides a good design for placing the decision boundary.

It is interesting to observe the significant lift in F1 score (4% to 20%) achieved by the unlabeled instances selection in TSVM-Meta over TSVM. As explained in section 4.3, this could be due to the proximity of the selected unlabeled instances to positive examples. It could also be due to reduction in the size of the unlabeled data resulting from the selection. To verify this, we ran experiments with random sampling of unlabeled data varying the percentage size of the sample and ran TSVM on each such dataset. We did not see any trend or conclusive effect of the size of the unlabeled dataset just based on random sampling. This leads us to believe that careful selection of unlabeled instances exploiting important properties of the dataset is effective and we are working towards formalizing such an approach. The F1 score for KB is more or less constant with different percentage of test data since there is no training phase in KB. It is important to note that the performance of most other methods matches or is lower than KB when only 10% labeled data is used for training. This case corresponds to approximately 18 *relevant* articles and 40 *not relevant* articles. It is difficult to apply machine learning techniques for such a small dataset and obtain reasonable performance.

As shown in figure 6 and 7, precision of 3C-SVM is lower than the other learning methods, but recall is very high and beats all other methods. SVM is the reverse case with highest precision and lowest recall for most data splits. TSVM and TSVM-Meta have a good balance of precision and recall compared to 3C-SVM and SVM. KB as expected has poor precision but relatively moderate recall compared to all other methods. For a system like FoodSIS, one of the challenges is to make the users comfortable with the machine learning based concepts and approach. It is difficult for domain experts to understand that it is highly unlikely for a machine learning method to be 100% accurate. The users want the system to capture all the relevant information i.e. high recall with high precision. Due to the trade-off between precision and recall, when discussed with them, they showed greater preference towards higher recall since it is important for them to see completeness in the results. 3C-SVM would still improve the precision over KB by approximately 35% in most cases. Based on high F1 scores and high recall, we chose 3C-SVM as our classifier for version 2 of FoodSIS.

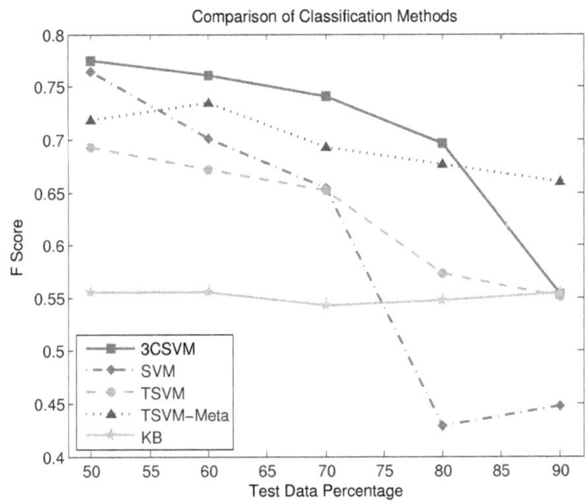

Figure 5: Comparison of different classifiers based on F1 score

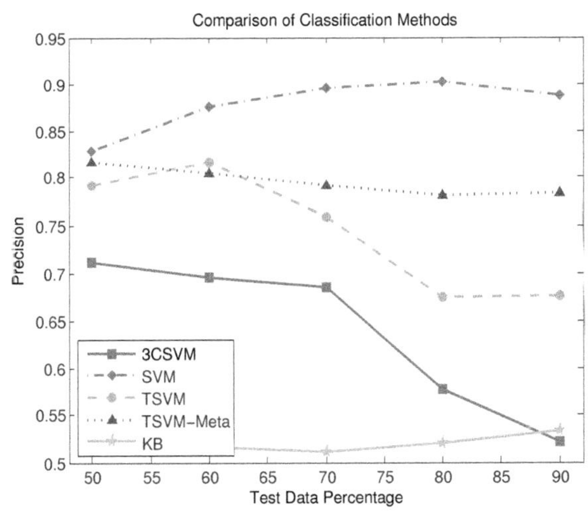

Figure 6: Comparison of different classifiers based on precision

5. LEARNING TO RANK

In this section we describe the interactive learning feature of our system. FoodSIS can actively incorporate the knowledge and preferences of users/domain experts into the system and use this feedback to improve the ranking of articles classified as *relevant* by the classifier. We saw how data for training the classifier is obtained from user feedback provided through the web interface. This feedback can also be used to infer partial pairwise comparisons between

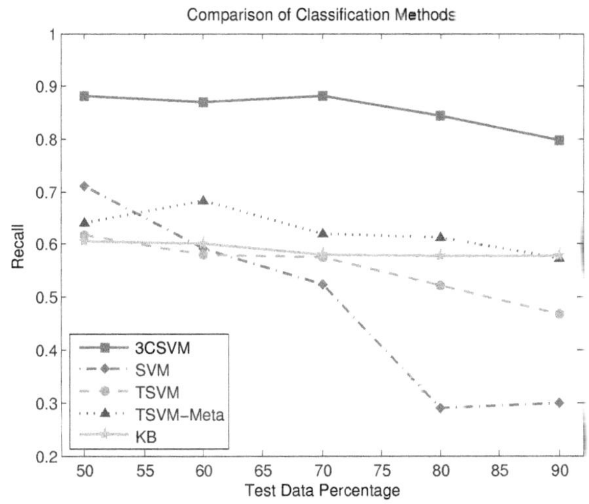

Figure 7: Comparison of different classifiers based on recall

the articles. For example, suppose a ranked list of 10 articles is presented to the user out of which, she labels the 4th and 7th article as relevant, then we can implicitly determine pairwise preferences between these articles such as :$4^{th} > 1^{st}$, $4^{th} > 2^{nd}$, $4^{th} > 3^{rd}$, $4^{th} > 5^{th}$ [3], $4^{th} > 6^{th}$, $4^{th} > 8^{th}$, $4^{th} > 9^{th}$, $4^{th} > 10^{th}$, $7^{th} > 1^{st}$, $7^{th} > 2^{nd}$, $7^{th} > 3^{rd}$, $7^{th} > 5^{th}$, $7^{th} > 6^{th}$, $7^{th} > 8^{th}$, $7^{th} > 9^{th}$ and $7^{th} > 10^{th}$. These pairwise preferences are collected and stored in the system which are then used to improve the ranked list of relevant articles in future.

This kind of feedback from domain experts has two characteristics: (i) It is in the form of pairwise preferences between articles, (ii) It is not necessarily a total order, i.e. the pairwise preferences span over a partial set of document pairs. Due to these properties, we explored ranking techniques which can learn from pairwise comparisons and a partial order over the set of articles. One of the most popular ranking techniques for this setting is the Ranking Support Vector Machine(Rank-SVM) [16][4]. Rank-SVM takes document pairs as instances for learning and transforms the problem of learning to rank into a classification problem. Moreover, it uses SVM as a classification technique to learn the model. The aim is to learn a linear ranking function $f_{\vec{w}}$ such that,

$$(d_i, d_j) \in f_{\vec{w}} \Leftrightarrow \vec{w}\phi(d_i) > \vec{w}\phi(d_j) \quad (2)$$

where, $\vec{w}$ is a weight vector of the SVM classification model and $\phi(d_i)$ is the feature vector for d_i. Specifically, for each document pair, Rank-SVM assigns a label representing the relative relevance of those documents. Then a classification model is trained using this labeled data which is equivalent to finding the weight vector so that the maximum number of pairwise preferences are fulfilled. Further, this classification model is used to obtain a ranking of the

[3]On the web interface, the user saves labels for 10 articles per page, so if on a page, 2 articles are labeled relevant, 8 others will automatically be saved as not relevant. We have an understanding with the users to label articles in batches of 10 to make this work as expected.

[4]Note that even though we can obtain a ranked list of articles using the classifiers presented in Section 4, the objective behind using Rank-SVM is to:(i) improve the ranking of articles classified as *relevant*, (ii) incorporate the active feedback/preferences give the user.

test documents. For the weight vector $\overrightarrow{w}$, the documents are ordered by their projection onto $\overrightarrow{w}$.

For FoodSIS, the *relevant* articles given by the classification model explained in Section 4 are then ordered according to the score given by the Rank-SVM model. The efficacy of this interactive learning system was evaluated with experiments that compare Average Precision(AP) [23] scores of the rankings of documents, given by the classifiers and the Rank-SVM. In particular, we compared the AP scores of ranked lists obtained by using classifiers such Naive Bayes (NB) and 3-Class SVM (3CSVM) as well as the ranked list obtained by using Rank-SVM. The ranking for NB is a descending order of probability score output for *relevant* class for the articles and 3CSVM ranking is based on descending order of the distance of the article feature vectors from the separating hyperplane.

To perform this experiment, we used the set of articles and their pairwise preferences given by the user, collected over a span of 60 days. Out of 60 days, we take out random 20 days as test set. For each day in the test set, we obtained a ranked list of articles for that day by training Rank-SVM over pairwise preferences for randomly chosen 40 days. Then, we repeated this procedure 5 times by choosing random 40 days for training Rank-SVM each time and report the average AP score for each test day corresponding to these 5 runs in Table 1. The AP scores are obtained over top 30 articles for each day in the test set. For ordering the articles in the test set using NB and 3CSVM, we sorted the documents according to the score given by the classifiers[5]. Finally, we compared the AP scores for different ranked lists given by NB, 3CSVM and Rank-SVM which were calculated as follows: For any test date,

$$AP = \frac{\sum_{k=1}^{n} P(k) \times rel(k)}{number\ of\ relevant\ documents} \quad (3)$$

where, k is the rank in the sequence of *relevant* articles, n is the number of *relevant* articles (30 for our experiments), $P(k)$ is the precision at cut-off k in the list, and $rel(k)$ is 1 if the article at rank k is a *relevant* article, zero otherwise. In Table 1 we present the corresponding results. It can be clearly seen that Rank-SVM gives significantly better AP scores for 19 days compared to NB and for 15 days compared to 3CSVM. Further, the average of AP scores over all 20 days in test set is greater for Rank-SVM and shows a 29% improvement over NB and about 16% improvement over 3CSVM. We also performed a paired t-test over these AP scores to find out if the improvement in the performance of Rank-SVM is statistically significant(overall as well as over individual days). To accomplish this, we used the AP values of 5 random runs of Rank-SVM to compute the p-value using paired t-test. We also report the p-values of *individual* days in Table 1 and highlight the values where the performance improvement was found to be statistically significant. Moreover, it was also observed that the *overall* performance improvement of Rank-SVM compared to NB and 3CSVM is statistically significant with a p-value of 1.168e-06 and 6.316e-05 respectively. Furthermore, performance improvement of 3CSVM compared to NB is statistically significant as well with a p-value of 0.0232.

	Rank-SVM	NB		3CSVM	
Day	**AP**	**AP**	**p-value**	**AP**	**p-value**
1	0.929	0.595	**8.97E-06**	0.518	**3.89E-06**
2	0.921	0.566	**6.14E-05**	0.743	**0.00089**
3	0.909	0.665	**3.49E-05**	0.647	**2.66E-05**
4	0.914	0.84	**0.00067**	0.917	0.60608
5	0.902	0.73	**4.07E-05**	0.816	**0.0006**
6	0.953	0.904	**6.23E-05**	0.901	**4.91E-05**
7	0.916	0.831	**0.0007**	0.751	**5.24E-05**
8	0.839	0.705	**0.00305**	0.642	**0.00072**
9	0.882	0.889	0.8681	0.928	0.999
10	0.901	0.817	**0.00081**	0.816	**0.00079**
11	0.903	0.842	**0.00721**	0.784	**0.00064**
12	0.947	0.632	**5.62E-07**	0.765	**5.00E-06**
13	0.832	0.68	**0.00048**	0.654	**0.00026**
14	0.577	0.452	**0.00082**	0.459	**0.00101**
15	0.846	0.721	**0.00013**	0.675	**3.90E-05**
16	0.723	0.394	**8.36E-05**	0.749	0.827
17	0.632	0.159	**0.01192**	0.583	0.3663
18	0.861	0.517	**9.24E-06**	0.725	**0.00035**
19	1.0	0.835	**1.49E-11**	0.831	**1.35E-11**
20	0.864	0.646	**0.00035**	0.934	0.981
AVG	**0.863**	0.671		0.742	

Table 1: Comparison of Average Precision(AP) scores for rankings based on different approaches

6. DEPLOYMENT

FoodSIS is developed as part of a research project between NEA and IBM. It is currently in its second version and has been deployed within NEA on a research infrastructure. NEA users are using the web interface for past 6 months and have helped us gather substantial amount of labeled data. FoodSIS is now by default the starting point for searches related to food safety within NEA. However, it is still evolving and we are adding more data sources, and more features to enhance its capability. With the current list of data sources that are crawled, we get an average of around 1000 articles a day. Note that this includes articles only from the identified websites and news from sections relevant to food safety. It is clearly impossible for the users to go through such a large number of articles per day. Employing recent advances in machine learning to classify and rank the crawled articles results in presenting a significantly smaller number of highly relevant articles to the users leading to significant improvement in the newsletter generation process efficiency. This section highlights some of the challenges of the deployment and an illustration of how the system was used to generate food safety newsletters. We also discuss the impact of the newsletters for NEA.

6.1 Challenges

Development of FoodSIS exposed us to many interesting characteristics of a real world machine learning task. The foremost being availability of labeled data. In real life, labeled data for training supervised approaches is either absent or is available but very small. We had access to very small number of articles of the positive class as seed data. Another typical situation is the lack of negatively labeled historical data. This is in large part because the users identify and store the positive examples but rarely bother to keep the negative examples especially for historically labeled data. The following 3 design choices helped us handle these challenges and provided a substantial performance lift.

1. Web application: One important decision was to build an overall architecture for FoodSIS with the web application as a key way to interact with the users. We focused on build-

[5]However, since NB and 3CSVM do not need pairwise preferences for training, the number of data points used for training of these classifiers was significantly larger than used for Rank-SVM.

	Fortnight 1	Fortnight 2	Fortnight 3	Fortnight 4
MAP	0.58	0.699	0.722	0.862

Table 2: Performance improvements with increase in labeled data

ing the web interface such that users find it useful from the beginning. In version 1, when the machine learning was not mature, users had access to all the articles (we did not filter any articles based on classification output) and they could use the keyword search feature if they wanted to query for specific terms. This allowed FoodSIS to be used as a custom search engine in absence of a high performing machine learning model. Easy use of the web interface also allowed them to provide label for each article with very little burden. It is well known that supervised approaches improve with significant increase in training data size and we observed that though such improvement was not so visible over a short time period, it can be clearly observed over longer period (in our case, training data size increases with time). Table 2 shows improvements in retrieval of top 30 relevant articles over a period of 8 weeks. It reports the MAP (MAP is Mean Average Precision i.e. AP (refer to equation 3) averaged over a time period) for top 30 ranks per day where the average is taken over 2 weeks, so we have 4 different MAP scores for the 8 week period. Observe the increasing trend in MAP scores over the 4 fortnights. Over this period, the classification method did not change and the only change was increase in the amount of training data on a weekly basis.

2. Exploiting unlabeled and UNIVERSUM datasets: The available labeled data was insignificant to get a reasonable classification performance and hence we explored several options. The first was to understand and exploit additional structural information in the data sources. The first source of structural information was semantic organization of many of the news sources which clearly organize articles under different sections (such as sports, entertainments, health etc). This provides a very clear categorization of the documents into two categories: (i) A set of documents from sections such as sports, entertainment and so forth that are clearly irrelevant for food safety related articles. This corpus of documents we can label as the UNIVERSUM. (ii) The remaining documents from the sections of the news source such as health, food, local news which might contain potential relevant documents but are unlabeled. Classification techniques which exploit the availability of unlabeled and UNIVERSUM datasets helped us achieve better classification.

3. Extracting pairwise preferences: The labeling done by users via the web interface not only provides us labels associated with individual articles, but also allows us to extract pairwise preferences as discussed in section 5. These preferences are partial since there is no extra effort involved from users in explicitly providing a correct total order of articles. As experimental evaluation demonstrates, using these preferences to learn a ranking model based on a state of the art technique results in a significant performance gain. As we reported in section 5, the use of pairwise comparisons improved the ranking engine by upto 16%.

It can be clearly seen that though we started with a very small labeled dataset, but careful design of the system and process allowed us to make the machine learning approach a viable and preferable alternative to information gathering. Another important challenge is to educate the users regarding the difference between the use of machine learning based customized search over a simple information retrieval based search. After the system was made functional, we conducted workshops to highlight this difference and the promise of continual improvement of a machine learning based technique.

6.2 Newsletter Generation

As discussed in sections 1 and 2, a team in the environmental health department of NEA generates a weekly newsletter on food safety from information posted on the web. The newsletter is circulated to the entire department. We give an example of a newsletter that was generated in the recent past and describe how FoodSIS contributed to increasing the efficiency of the process, thereby saving time and effort. This example is a real newsletter and it contains summaries of the following 3 articles on topic "mobile food vendors": (i) Food trucks cleanliness, (ii) Food trucks vs restaurants, (iii) Late night mobile food vendors.

These articles were ranked at 1, 5 and 14 on FoodSIS in that order on the day they were published. To illustrate how such a newsletter would have been generated without the use of our system, we perform search on Google under section "News" and select the exact date for each of the above 3 articles. We created 2 disjunctive queries (Google limits a search query to only 32 words) from the 19 keyword phrases provided to us by the NEA users and use those for search. Under such search setting, the first article on "food trucks cleanliness" appeared 10th in the search results and the other 2 did not even appear in the top 50. This example illustrates that FoodSIS succeeded in its objective of providing relevant information with minimum effort for the user[6].

On close observation, it can be seen that the newsletter has a central theme: "mobile food vendors" and the articles span over a period of 2.5 weeks. As part of the enhancements to the web interface, users had emphasized a need for an ability to filter articles based on whether they had been labeled as relevant, not relevant or had been left as unlabeled by the users. The drop down "Show Label" on the web interface provides such a filter. Such simple functionality provided through the web interface can facilitate browsing of articles labeled as relevant in the past and make it easier for the users to include such articles on related topics but from different time periods. As we mention in section 3, all the features of the web interface have been designed with input from the users and considering the newsletter generation process.

6.3 Impact to NEA's Operations:

The newsletters keep NEA abreast of the recent developments in topics related to food safety. They can use that information to improve their operational processes. For example, considering the newsletter on "mobile food vendors" that we discussed above, it helps NEA to understand how mobile food vendors are managed in other countries. The number of mobile food vans is on increase in Singapore and NEA wants to constantly improve its processes and regulations to handle these changes. Easy access to information about how they are handled in other countries gives them ideas that can be considered for improving NEA's processes. Newsletters about food recalls in neighboring countries act as alerts and

[6]We acknowledge that such comparison with Google search is simplistic and biased since FoodSIS might have influenced the user's choice of articles for the newsletter. But the difference in the effectiveness of the methods is significant to conclude that FoodSIS was a better tool to help with this example newsletter generation.

they can assess the impact of those recalls on Singapore. Other areas of impact of the newsletters include adopting the technology advances, policy, regulation improvements and capability development programs.

7. CONCLUSION

Many groups in an enterprise have the need for keeping up to date with news and information about their domain and they rely on the World Wide Web as a primary source of information. For example, the supply chain management organization is constantly monitoring the web for news related to various echelons of the supply network to understand potential disruptions due to weather on their logistics, impact of political, labor and natural disaster events on productivity and service levels. Similarly the marketing divisions monitor the web (and social media) for sentiment or buzz around product release or marketing campaigns. The need to build custom search engines for different enterprise functions is now a universal need.

In this paper, we have outlined our experience and a framework (leveraging machine learning) for building such systems that are tailored for a department's specific function needs. There are several operational challenges (from availability of labeled data, to leveraging interactive learning) that need to be addressed. We believe additional work and effort in streamlining the use of these techniques and the training of document classifiers would help in the adoption of these techniques broadly in daily enterprise operations.

8. ACKNOWLEDGMENTS

We would like to thank Christine Lee and Jo-Ann Lim from NEA, Singapore for labeling the articles by actively using FoodSIS. We also appreciate the valuable suggestions given by them and Christopher Goh, Atikah Rahman, Lee San Tay, Yoke Leng Toh and Kaiyun Chio from NEA, Singapore for improving the user interface. We thank Vikas Sindhwani from IBM Research for useful and insightful discussions and pointers on semi-supervised learning methods.

9. REFERENCES

[1] Last accessed on 20 Feb 2014, Available at: http://www.foodprocessing-technology.com/features/feature87576/.

[2] Last accessed on 20 Feb 2014, Available at: http://www.taipeitimes.com/News/front/archives/2013/06/02/2003563752.

[3] Last accessed on 20 Feb 2014, Available at: http://www.todayonline.com/singapore/ikea-singapore-recalls-rhubarb-crumble-pie.

[4] General information related to microbiological risks in food, world health organization. Last accessed on 20 Feb 2014, Available at: http://www.who.int/foodsafety/micro/general/en/.

[5] Health promotion board, press releases 2012. Last accessed on 20 Feb 2014, Available at: http://www.hpb.gov.sg/uploadedFiles/HPB_Online/News_and_Events/News/2012/Media%20Release%20-%20Healthier%20Coffeeshop%20Initiative%20Final.pdf.

[6] Estimates of foodborne illness in the united states, us centers for disease control and prevention. 2011. Last accessed on 20 Feb 2014, Available at: http://www.cdc.gov/foodborneburden/index.html.

[7] John Blitzer, Mark Dredze, and Fernando Pereira. Biographies, bollywood, boom-boxes and blenders: Domain adaptation for sentiment classification. In *Proceedings of the 45th Annual Meeting of the Association of Computational Linguistics*, pages 440–447, Prague, June 2007.

[8] Avrim Blum and Shuchi Chawla. Learning from labeled and unlabeled data using graph mincuts. In *Proceedings of the Eighteenth International Conference on Machine Learning*, ICML '01, pages 19–26, San Francisco, 2001.

[9] Avrim Blum and Tom Mitchell. Combining labeled and unlabeled data with co-training. In *Proceedings of the Eleventh Annual Conference on Computational Learning Theory*, COLT' 98, pages 92–100, 1998.

[10] O. Chapelle, B. Schölkopf, and A. Zien, editors. *Semi-Supervised Learning*. MIT Press, Cambridge, MA, 2006.

[11] Olivier Chapelle, Vikas Sindhwani, and Sathiya S. Keerthi. Optimization techniques for semi-supervised support vector machines. *J. Mach. Learn. Res.*, 9:203–233, June 2008.

[12] Vijil Chenthamarakshan, Prem Melville, Vikas Sindhwani, and Richard Lawrence. Concept labeling: Building text classifiers with minimal supervision. In *International Joint Conference on Artificial Intelligence*, 2011.

[13] Gregory Druck, Gideon Mann, and Andrew McCallum. Learning from labeled features using generalized expectation criteria. In *Proceedings of the 31st Annual International ACM SIGIR Conference on Research and Development in Information Retrieval*, SIGIR '08, pages 595–602, 2008.

[14] Toh HY., Hishamuddin P., and Tay J. Epidemiology and control of food poisoning outbreak in singapore, 2009-2011. 38(3):62–71.

[15] Thorsten Joachims. Transductive inference for text classification using support vector machines. In *Proceedings of the Sixteenth International Conference on Machine Learning*, ICML '99, pages 200–209, 1999.

[16] Thorsten Joachims. Optimizing search engines using clickthrough data. In *Proceedings of the Eighth ACM SIGKDD International Conference on Knowledge Discovery and Data Mining*, KDD '02, pages 133–142, 2002.

[17] Ramesh Nallapati. Discriminative models for information retrieval. In *Proceedings of the 27th Annual International ACM SIGIR Conference on Research and Development in Information Retrieval*, SIGIR '04, pages 64–71, 2004.

[18] Kamal Nigam, Andrew Kachites McCallum, Sebastian Thrun, and Tom Mitchell. Text classification from labeled and unlabeled documents using em. *Mach. Learn.*, 39(2-3):103–134, May 2000.

[19] Burr Settles. Active learning literature survey. Technical report, 2010.

[20] Vladimir Vapnik. *Statistical Learning Theory*. Wiley, 1998.

[21] Haiqin Yang, Shenghuo Zhu, Irwin King, and Michael R. Lyu. Can irrelevant data help semi-supervised learning, why and how? In *Proceedings of the 20th ACM International Conference on Information and Knowledge Management*, CIKM '11, pages 937–946, 2011.

[22] Dan Zhang, Jingdong Wang, Fei Wang, and Changshui Zhang. Semi-supervised classification with universum. In *SDM*, pages 323–333, 2008.

[23] Ethan Zhang and Yi Zhang. Average precision. In LING LIU and M.TAMER ÃŰSU, editors, *Encyclopedia of Database Systems*, pages 192–193. Springer US, 2009.

[24] Tong Zhang. The value of unlabeled data for classification problems. In *Proceedings of the Seventeenth International Conference on Machine Learning*, pages 1191–1198, 2000.

A Hazard Based Approach to User Return Time Prediction

Komal Kapoor
Department of Computer Science
University of Minnesota
Minneapolis, MN 55455
kapoo031@umn.edu

Mingxuan Sun
Pandora Media Inc.
2101 Webster Street
Oakland, CA 94612
msun@pandora.com

Jaideep Srivastava
Department of Computer Science
University of Minnesota
Minneapolis, MN 55455
srivasta@cs.umn.edu

Tao Ye
Pandora Media Inc.
2101 Webster Street
Oakland, CA 94612
tye@pandora.com

ABSTRACT

In the competitive environment of the internet, retaining and growing one's user base is of major concern to most web services. Furthermore, the economic model of many web services is allowing free access to most content, and generating revenue through advertising. This unique model requires securing user time on a site rather than the purchase of good which makes it crucially important to create new kinds of metrics and solutions for growth and retention efforts for web services. In this work, we address this problem by proposing a new retention metric for web services by concentrating on the rate of user return. We further apply predictive analysis to the proposed retention metric on a service, as a means for characterizing lost customers. Finally, we set up a simple yet effective framework to evaluate a multitude of factors that contribute to user return. Specifically, we define the problem of return time prediction for free web services. Our solution is based on the Cox's proportional hazard model from survival analysis. The hazard based approach offers several benefits including the ability to work with censored data, to model the dynamics in user return rates, and to easily incorporate different types of covariates in the model. We compare the performance of our hazard based model in predicting the user return time and in categorizing users into buckets based on their predicted return time, against several baseline regression and classification methods and find the hazard based approach to be superior.

Categories and Subject Descriptors

J.4 [**Computer Applications**]: Social and Behavioral Sciences; H.3.5 [**Online Information Services**]: Web-based services

General Terms

Human Factors, Measurement, Experimentation

KDD'14, August 24–27, 2014, New York, NY, USA.
Copyright 2014 ACM 978-1-4503-2956-9/14/08 ...$15.00.
http://dx.doi.org/10.1145/2623330.2623348 .

Keywords

online user behavior, customer relationship management, growth and retention, hazard based methods

1. INTRODUCTION

User attention is perceived as the most important resource in the internet era [12]. The web is described [23] as a *'virtual theme park where most rides are free such that revenue is generated through "selling eyeballs" to advertisers'*. The ad-supported economy of the web has the web-services vying for users' time rather than their money. Having a large loyal and dedicated user base has several indirect benefits as well. Many services grow with their users, improving themselves based on their feedback and through the power of big data analytics on their activities logs. A common example is the Google search engine, which has perfected its query auto-correct feature primarily using user click-through data, as well as improved its search performance regularly using user search histories. Furthermore, an active community can be tapped to create new content that benefits the other users of the service and the service as a whole as seen for popular social networks such as Facebook and Twitter

There is tremendous competition among the rapidly increasing number of web services for the finite and limited resource corresponding to user attention. Although, attracting new customers is crucial for any business, it is generally much easier and cheaper to retain existing customers [4, 29]. This directly results in a great deal of emphasis being placed on engaging one's current user base. Customer retention efforts have been heavily researched in sectors such as telecommunication [29], financial services [22], internet services [13] and other utilities etc. which follow the subscription based model. The methods in these domains have focused on identifying potential churners in the user population, where churners are defined as those current subscribers who are not likely to renew their subscription in the coming months. Once detected, the churner population is targeted with retention strategies like offers, customer solutions and recommendations to win them back.

However, such methods cannot be directly applied to solving the user retention problem for web services due to the following reasons:

1. **Difficult to define churn for a non-contractual setting.** A non-contractual business such as a free web service, does not receive a definitive indicator of termination from the user. To counteract this problem, some alternative definitions of churn have been proposed. Churn is defined as a significant drop in a user activity levels [16]. Another work addresses this problem by first providing a definition for a loyal user of a service and then defining churners as those users who were loyal to the service but are no longer so [21]. However, such methods remain sensitive to changes in their proposed definition of churn.

2. **Highly dynamic user visitation behavior.** Web services offer none or negligible switching costs to users. With no financial commitments towards a service, users switch quite frequently between different services. The highly dynamic nature of user visitation behavior makes it difficult to define typical activity volumes for a user and to segregate users as active and inactive with respect to the service.

To adapt to the unique incentive structures and dynamic user base, in this work we propose a novel retention metric which tracks the user return rate for addressing growth and retention in web services. The user return rate is defined as the fraction of the existing users returning to the service on a particular day. It is beneficial for a web service to improve its user return rate in order to increase its revenue. Predictive analysis of user return times can direct such improvements efforts. Return time prediction allows a service to identify indicators of earlier (longer) return times for their users. Identifying such indicators and quantifying their impact on user return times offers a service insights into its practices. It also enables a service to employ corrective measures and improve the experience to its users. Secondly, a service can identify sections of its user base that are not likely to return soon. Studies have shown that the longer the users stay away from a service, the less likely are they to return in the future [24]. Early identification of users who are not likely to return soon to the service allows the deployment of suitable marketing strategies to encourage those users to engage with the service again.

We propose a hazard model [8] from survival analysis to predict user return times. The hazard based models are preferred over the standard regression based methods for this problem due to their ability to model particular aspects of duration data such as censoring. More importantly, the Cox's proportional hazard regression model is used as it can incorporate the effects of covariates [1]. We apply the model for return time prediction on real-world datasets from two popular online music services.

We now summarize the key contributions made by us in this paper:

(a) We formally define an approach for targeting retention solutions in free web services via user return time prediction.

(b) We propose the Cox's proportional hazard to model dynamic return events and incorporate the effects of covariates for return time prediction. We develop useful return time predictors and conclude correlations between user usage patterns and their return times.

(c) The Cox's proportional hazard model outperforms state-of-the-art baselines in both return time prediction and user classification based on predicted return time.

[1]We use the term covariates to describe features or predictors in our model. The choice of terminology is based on that used in the survival analysis literature from where we adopt our model.

The rest of the paper is organized as follows. In **Section 2** we provide a brief overview of the related research in the area of churn prediction and the use of hazard based methods. We then formally define our problem and lay out our contributions in **Section 3**. In **Section 4** we describe our hazard based predictive model and provide details of the covariates used and the model estimation procedure. In **Section 5** and **Section 6** we discuss the experimentation setup and the results. We summarize the conclusions from our experimental analysis and provide future directions for our work in **Section 7**.

2. RELATED WORK

In this work, we propose a new approach for directing growth and retention solutions for web services through return time prediction. Traditionally studies have focused on the problem of churn prediction defined as a binary classification problem where users are categorized based on several behavioral and demographic features into two categories: future churners or non-churners. The popular data mining techniques used for building classifiers for churn prediction include decision trees such as CART and C4.5 etc. [29], logistic regression [4], support vector machines [7] and neural networks [28], though random forests [7, 30] are found to be better in performance. Ensemble methods have been used to combine multiple classifiers to construct powerful meta-classifiers and to handle the class imbalance problem typical to churn prediction [5]. Alternatively, approaches from survival analysis have been used to model the dynamics in the churn event rate with user tenure [14]. The churn event rate for users is found to decline with tenure such that new users are more likely to churn than tenured users.

A major hurdle to applying these methods to free-to-use services discussed in this paper is to provide an appropriate definition of churn. Studies on user lifetime modeling and retention for online environments have used different criteria for defining the loss of a customer, such as the period of inactivity [31], decrease in activity [16] or indirectly, via a definition of loyal users [21], discussed earlier. Yang et al. [31] have further studied how user participation patterns affect the length of their lifetimes on online knowledge sharing communities. However, most of these methods focus on the length of user participation rather than the volume of their activities. Instead, online businesses are increasingly paying attention to their returning users rather than the count of their registered users. Further, the research community has started concentrating on analyzing and modeling users activities on different types of websites [18, 33]. A major focus of these methods have been to understand how websites memberships, specifically measured in the number of active users, evolves with time and correlate such factors to the success or failure of the website [25]. Also, many studies on the measurement and improvement of intra-site [2, 17, 10] and inter-site engagement have emerged [32]. Many of these studies identify return time as a robust metric for user engagement. All these factors suggest that continuous tracking and improvement of user engagement, measured in terms of their return time, is crucial for the performance goals of web services. Hence, in this work we directly focus on the return time metric for organizing retention efforts for web services. We use a Cox's proportional hazard regression model [8] from survival analysis for this problem as the model can quantify the impact of covariates on the target event rate. This unique property results in the Cox's Model being a popular choice for several online user behavior studies [10, 31]. Additionally, we also define different types of return time predictors suitable for this problem.

Several types of covariates have been used for churn prediction. RFM models [11] propose the use of three variables, Recency, Frequency and Monetary value of their previous interaction for identifying potential churners. Other covariates based on demographics, contractual details, service logs, use patterns, complaints and customer service responses [3, 29] have been found useful. We use some of these covariates in our model. In addition, we also incorporate user behavior related covariates in order to understand how user interactions while engaging with the service affect the rate of their return in the future. A special feature of our model is that it can handle the recency variable implicitly by computing the expected future time of return for the users given their length of absence from the service.

3. RETURN TIME PREDICTION FOR WEB SERVICES

A user's visitation behavior on a free web service tends to be quite flexible and arbitrary post registration partially due to the lack of financial investments and constraints. Instead, the length of the tenure of users of web service displays a power law distribution with most of the users never returning back to the service [9]. In this work, we adopt a unique methodology for analyzing the dynamic user visitation data by directly modeling the user return time.

3.1 Problem Statement

We define users as belonging to either of the two activity states - the *in* and the *out* states. When users visit the service, they are said to be in the *in* state; while, when they do not visit the service, they are said to be in the *out* state.

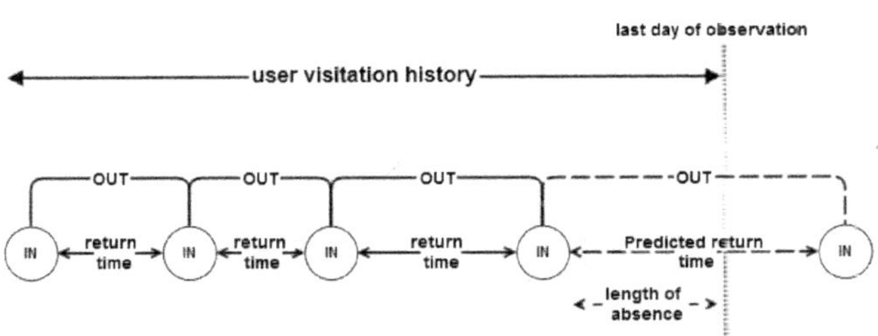

Figure 1: State Space Diagram

We focus on the problem of predicting the return time of the users which is the time the user spends in the *out* state. The return time for a user can potentially extend to infinity (for users who never return back to the service). Therefore, a threshold, t_d is defined on the return time and we predict the return time for the users up to time t_d. The return time prediction problem may be formally defined as follows:

Definition 1 Given that the last time the user was in the *in* state was at time t_0, the return time prediction problem is to predict the quantity $min(t_r, t_d)$, also called the truncated return time (T_{rd}), where t_r is the total time the user spends in the *out* state and ranges from 0 to ∞, t_d is a finite threshold on the return time and either of the following holds:

(a) the user is expected to return to the *in* state at time $t_0 + t_r$, if $T_{rd} = t_r$, or

(b) the user is expected to stay in the *out* state for at least t_d units of time, if $T_{rd} = t_d$

Figure 1 provides a diagrammatic representation of the user return time prediction problem.

3.2 Time Dependence in User Return Time

The time duration between events has been studied extensively in queuing theory, for example to study the waiting time between customer arrival and customer service events. Such events are commonly modeled to generate from a Poisson process such that the waiting times follow the exponential distribution. An attractive property of the exponential distribution is the memoryless property which entails that the future rate of occurrence of the event is independent of the elapsed time. For a random variable T denoting the time of occurrence of the event, the following equation is said to hold if the memoryless property is satisfied:

$$P(T > t + s | T > s) = P(T > t) \tag{1}$$

However, several phenomena are seen to defy the simple memoryless property in interesting ways. For example, the rate of adoption of new products is found to increase with the elapsed time [26]. Alternatively, the rate of events like responses to surveys, promotions [15] etc. is seen to decline with the elapsed time. The decline in future event rate with the elapsed time, has been referred to as '*inertia*'. We suspect similar type of inertia in user return behavior. For duration data showing time dependence, it becomes meaningful to compute the expected future time of the event given the elapsed time, $E(T|T > s)$. We, now define the problem of predicting the expected future time of return of the users given their length of absence (LOA) from the service.

Definition 2 Given that the last time the user was in the *in* state was at time t_0, and he has already been in the *out* state for time t_s, the future return time prediction problem is to predict the quantity $min(t_{fr}, (t_d - t_s))$, also called the truncated future return time T_{frd} where t_{fr} is the additional time the user spends in the *out* state and ranges from 0 to ∞, t_d is a finite threshold on the return time and either of the following holds:

(a) the user is expected to return to the *in* state at time $t_0 + t_s + t_{fr}$, if $T_{frd} = t_{fr}$, or

(b) the user is expected to stay in the *out* state for atleast $t_d - t_s$ more units of time, if $T_{frd} = t_d - t_s$

4. METHOD

We consider a time window over which user return time observations are collected. Each return time observation can be associated with a set of covariates influencing its magnitude. Hence, the data can be represented as a set of tuples

$< X, T >$ where, T is the return time observation and X is the vector of covariates associated with that observation. Since a user can return to the service multiple times during the considered time window, we can have multiple tuples corresponding to a single user.

There are two aspects of the collected data that need special attention.

1. Censoring: Duration data which is collected over a fixed time period tends to have incomplete observations corresponding to events which were yet to happen at the end of the study period. Such observations are said to be censored and this particular type of censoring is called right censoring. In order to capture censored observations as well, a special variable *status* is added to the representation of duration times. The *status* variable is set to 0 when the time variable represents the actual observation of return time whereas it is set to 1 when the time variable represents a censored observation. In the latter case the time duration represents the time gap between the user's last visit and the end of the study period. Ignoring censored observations biases one's analysis towards earlier returns. A major advantage of the hazard based methods is that they can handle censored observations quite well.

2. Recurrent observations: The collected data may contain more than one return time events, also called recurrent events, per user during the study period. The active users have many more return time observations than inactive users. Retaining these observations can bias our analysis towards the active users which is detrimental to our objective of targeting losing customers. However, we lose information if we throw away these observations. Instead, we use a simple weighting scheme for handling recurrent events. We weight each observation corresponding to a user with the inverse of the number of observations made for that user. Hence, each user has a unit weight in the data but we incorporate all observations made for him/her. Later in the paper, we discuss the sensitivity of our results to this weighting scheme. Some care needs to be taken while testing models when working with recurrent data and we discuss that in our *Experiments* section.

4.1 Hazard Based Prediction Model

Survival analysis is a branch of statistics which deals with the time of occurrence of events, also called duration modeling. It offers a rich set of methods which allow us to easily address questions like what is the probability that an event is going to happen after t units of time or what is the future rate of occurrence of the event given it has not happened in t units of time. In this work we deal with discrete measures of time. Two functions are useful for analyzing duration information:

The survival function at time t is defined as:

$$S(t) = P(T > t) \tag{2}$$

where T is a random variable denoting the time of occurrence of the event. The hazard function measures the instantaneous rate of occurrence of the event at time t, conditioned on the elapsed time t.

$$\lambda(t) = P(T = t \mid T \geq t) = -S'(t)/S(t-1) \tag{3}$$

The Cox's proportional hazard model is commonly used to incorporate the effect of covariates on the hazard rate. The model is based on the simple assumption that the covariates affect the magnitude of individual hazard rates but not the shape of the hazard function. Expressed mathematically,

$$\lambda(t) = \lambda_0(t) * \exp(\beta_1 * X_1(t) + \beta_2 * X_2(t) + ...) \tag{4}$$

where, λ_0 is the baseline hazard function, $X_1(t)$, $X_2(t)$, etc. are the covariates which may be static or may vary with time and β_1, β_2 etc. are the regression coefficients. The ability of the Cox's model to handle time-varying covariates is an important feature of the model.

One can obtain the survival function from the hazard function using the following equations:

$$\Lambda(t) = \sum_0^t \lambda(u)\, du, \tag{5}$$

$$S(t) = \exp(-\Lambda(t)), \tag{6}$$

where Λ is defined as the cumulative hazard function. The expected time of return can then be computed using the equation below:

$$E(T) = \sum_0^\infty S(t). \tag{7}$$

Furthermore, the expected future time of return given the time not returned for (t_s) can be computed as follows:

$$E(T|T > t_s) = \frac{1}{t_s} \sum_{t_s}^\infty S(t). \tag{8}$$

The survival function is truncated beyond a point of time or when the probability of survival drops below a threshold in order to prevent the return time estimate from diverging. For our prediction problem, we impose t_d as an upper bound on the return time estimate. Hence, the expected return time and the expected future return time computations can be re-defined as:

$$E(T) = \sum_0^{t_d} S(t), \tag{9}$$

$$E(T|T > t_s) = \frac{1}{t_s} \sum_{t_s}^{t_d} S(t). \tag{10}$$

4.2 Model Estimation

The Cox's proportional hazard model is a semi-parametric model as it does not assume a mathematical form for the baseline hazard function. Instead, the model can be broken down into two factors. The first factor represents the effect of the covariates on the hazard rate. The effect parameters (regression coefficients) are learnt by maximizing the partial likelihood which is independent of the baseline hazard function. Once the regression coefficients have been learnt, the non-parametric form of the baseline hazard function is estimated using the Breslow's method. Cox's seminal paper [8] is a good reference for the details of the estimation procedure.

We use the standard survival package in R for estimating the Cox's model. The survival package can handle weighted data instances. We use days as the unit of time for our analysis as most of the users in our datasets are found to return

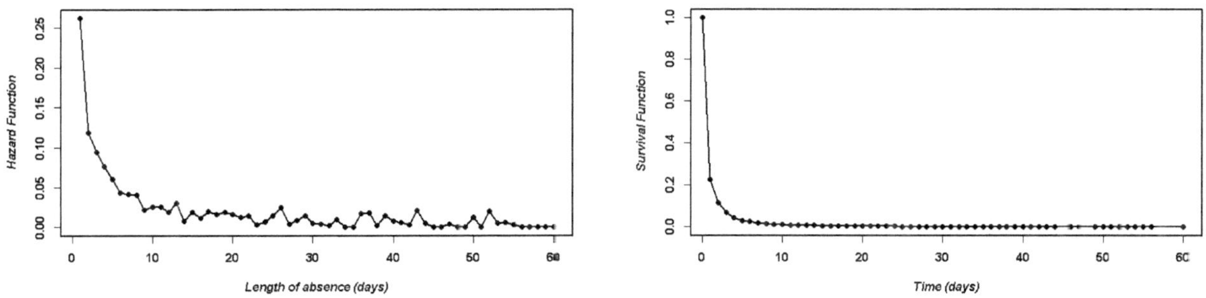

(a) Baseline Hazard Function

(b) Survival Function

Figure 2: The baseline hazard function and the survival function computed on the Last.fm training dataset.

within the first week. A user is considered to have visited the service on a day if he performed at least one activity on the service on that day. One may define more stringent criteria on user activity for this purpose, such as minimum time spent, number of interactions etc. The threshold (t_d) for the return time prediction problem is set to 60 days, which is a reasonably large value and beyond which users are already the focus of retention efforts. Return time observations larger than 60 days are hence assumed to be censored. In our experiments, we also study the performance of the model for different choices of the threshold.

5. EXPERIMENTAL SETUP

We now evaluate the performance of the Cox's proportional hazard model for solving our proposed return time prediction problem. We consider both the performance of the model at predicting the return time of the user and at classifying users based on their expected return times. Such a categorization procedure is the logical next step for a service looking to target marketing strategies to users not likely to return soon. For both the problems, we also evaluate how well the Cox's model can incorporate the LOA information by re-estimating the expected future return time given the LOA.

5.1 Data Collection

For our experiments we use a small public and a larger proprietary dataset. We briefly describe these two datasets:

- The Last.fm dataset. Last.fm, is an online music website catering to millions of active users. Recently, the service made available the complete music listening histories of around a 1000 of its users as recorded until May, 2009 [1, 6]. For every song the user listened to, the dataset includes the song title, the artist name and the timestamp at which the song was heard. We use two separate time windows for creating the training and the testing datasets. All user visits observed during Oct, 2008 - Dec, 2008 were used to test the model through cross-validation. We also tested our model on future user visits observed from Jan, 2009 - Mar, 2009.

- Large-scale dataset. Our proposed approach was applied as a part of the growth and retention efforts for a large ad-supported music service. A dataset of around 73,465 users, collected over 3 months from May, 2012 - July, 2012, was used for training and testing our model via cross-validation.

5.2 Covariates

We constructed the following covariates for the return time prediction problem.

- **Covariates related to the typical visitation patterns of a user.** Such covariates seek to predict the future return behavior of the users based on how their visitation behavior has been historically. For example, users who have been highly frequent in the past (loyal to the service) are likely to remain frequent in the future and similarly users who have been infrequent in the past (casual visitors) are likely to visit infrequently in the future.

  - Active Weeks: This covariate is defined as the ratio of the number of weeks since registration when the user visited the service at least once to the total number of weeks elapsed since registration.

  - Density of Visitation: This covariate captures the volume of user activity on the service for the weeks the user is active on the service. It is defined as the average number of days the user visited the service during the weeks the user visited the service at least once.

  - Visit Number: This covariate is used to measure how tenured the user is with the service.

  - Previous Gap: This covariate represents the most recent return time observation (which is the gap between the user's last and prior to the last visit) for the user. For first time users this covariate is set to -1.

  - Time weighted average return time (TWRT): This covariate measures the average return time for a user. The return times are further weighted by the inverse of the length of time elapsed since they were observed under the premise that the more recent return times are more informative about the user's current visitation behavior.

- **Covariates related to user satisfaction and engagement with the service.** Satisfaction and engagement related covariates are more difficult to construct as they attempt to capture latent user emotions about the service. Such can be extracted from any explicit (likes, dislikes, complaints etc.) or implicit (time spend, unique activities etc.) feedback indicators using user past interactions. In this work, we constructed these covariates based on user activities recorded on the last visit to the service (last *In* state)

- Duration: This covariate captures the time spend at the service measured by the number of songs heard by the user.
- % Distinct Songs: This covariate measures the fraction of the number of distinct songs listened by the users over the total number of songs listened by them.
- % Distinct Artists: This covariate measures the fraction of the number of distinct artists listened by the users over the total number of songs listened by them.
- % Skips: This covariate measures the fraction of the number of songs skipped by the users of the total number of songs listened by them. The skip information is not directly available for the Last.fm dataset. Instead, we indirectly identified skips by comparing the gap between two consecutive songs (s_1 and s_2) in the data with the length of the song s_1. If the time gap was found to be less than the length of song s_1 by more than 30 seconds, then song s_1 was identified to have been skipped. The API, track.getInfo made freely available by Last.fm was used to retrieve the duration for the songs in the dataset.
- Explicit feedback indicators: These covariates include information obtained directly from the users such as ratings, comments, complaints etc. Explicit feedback measures tend to be highly accurate and are an important source of information about user's satisfaction with the service. However, they are hard to acquire as providing explicit feedback requires user effort. We did not have any explicit feedback indicators for the Last.fm dataset. We had such ratings for our proprietary dataset which were included in the model.

- **Covariates used for abstracting the effects of external factors**. External factors include public holidays and weekends, marketing campaigns and promotions or personal factors which impact the rate of user return. The ability to model external factors is very useful as by modeling these covariates, we can both quantify the impact of these factors and control for these effects to improve our analysis on the other covariates. For simplicity, we have not considered any external covariates in our experiments. However, in our *Conclusion* section, we discuss how the Cox's model can be used to model the day of the month covariate which allows us to incorporate weekly effects and holiday effects in our predictions.

5.3 Evaluation Metrics and Baselines

Different baselines are used for evaluating the performance of the Cox's model at the regression and the classification tasks. All baselines are implemented using the same covariates as used in the Cox's model. For the regression problem we compared the Cox's model against simple average (trivial baseline), linear regression, decision tree regression (RepTree), Support Vector Machine (with linear kernel) and neural networks (multilayer perceptron). Support Vector Machine Regression took too long to run (more than a day) on our large scale dataset and was omitted in those results. The performance of the models were evaluated using Weighted Root Mean Square Error(WRMSE). The WRMSE is computed by weighting the error between the true return time and predicted return time with the weight of the test instance as follows:

$$WRMSE = \sqrt{\frac{\sum_{i=0}^{N} w(i) * (T^p_{rd}(i) - T_{rd}(i))^2}{\sum_{i=0}^{N} w(i)}} \tag{11}$$

where, N is the number of test instances, $T^p_{rd}(i)$ denotes the truncated return time predicted for the i-th observation and $T_{rd}(i)$ denotes the true truncated return time the i-th observation. We can replace $T^p_{rd}(i)$ with $T^p_{frd}(i)$ and $T_{rd}(i)$ with $T_{frd}(i)$ for computing the WRMSE for the expected future return time predictions.

Our classification baselines included logistic regression, random forest, support vector machine (with a linear kernel) and neural networks (multilayer perceptron). We used weighted F-measure for the minority class for measuring performance at the classification task. The weighted f-measure is defined as the harmonic mean of the weighted precision and weighted recall scores which are defined as follows. The set A denotes the instances actually belonging to the minority class and set P denotes the instances which were predicted to belong to the minority class.

$$\text{Weighted Precision} = \frac{\text{sum of weights of instances in } A \cap P}{\text{sum of weights of instances in } P} \tag{12}$$

$$\text{Weighted Recall} = \frac{\text{sum of weights of instances in } A \cap P}{\text{sum of weights of instances in } A} \tag{13}$$

The experiments for the baselines were conducted using Weka, the open source data mining software available under the GNU General Public License. The baselines were suitably tuned using a hold out set. Also, Weka provides support for handling weighted data instances allowing us to easily incorporate the weight vector while training the models. Since a direct application of cross-validation would not maintain temporal ordering between observations of the same user, for our evaluation we took special care to ensure that all recurrent data corresponding to a user belonged to the same fold. This was done by first randomly dividing users into different folds and then placing all observation associated with the user in that fold. As a result, the training and testing folds had observations from different users.

6. RESULTS

In this section we analyze the results of the experimental evaluation of the Cox's model.

6.1 Model Parameters

We only discuss the parameters of model trained on the Last.fm dataset.

The importance of the covariates for the prediction problem can be assessed using different importance indicators (Table 1). The regression coefficients and the significance score for the covariates can be obtained directly from the output of the R function for fitting the Cox's model. The regression coefficient tells us how much a unit change in the value of the covariate impacts the user's rate of return. For example, with every song the users listened during their last visit, their hazard rate was found to multiply by $\exp(1.315e-03) = 1.0013$, decreasing their return times estimates. The value of the coefficient was statistically significant at a significance level of 0.01. We found most of the covariates associated with the typical patterns of visitation (Active Weeks, Density, Previous gap) to be highly significant for predicting the return time variable. Also, some of the engagement/satisfaction related covariates, namely duration and % artists had significant effects on the hazard rate. We also computed the mean of the product of the covariate and its coefficient (MEAN($X * \beta$)) measured for all instances in the training set. This provided an average score for how much the covariate impacted the magnitude of the baseline hazard function. The density covariate impacted the rate of return the most on an average for our dataset.

Covariates	Coefficient	Significance	MEAN($X * \beta$)
Active Weeks	9.313e-02	2.140e-02*	4.370e-01
Density	2.366e-01	1.050e-13***	1.244e00
Visit Number	4.941e-05	7.318e-01	2.336e-02
Previous Gap	-5.175e-03	1.470e-03**	-1.222e-02
TWRT	-1.484e-02	2.817e-01	-2.492e-02
Duration	1.315e-03	2.538e-02 *	6.171e-02
% Distinct Songs	6.849e-02	7.653e-01	6.040e-02
% Distinct Artists	-2.251e-01	8.553e-02 .	-1.064e-01
% Skips	3.740e-01	2.322e-01	4.873e-02

Table 1: Covariate Importance Indicators for the Last.fm Dataset. Signif. codes: 0 '*' 0.001 '**' 0.01 '*' 0.05 '.'**

Figure 2 displays the baseline hazard function and the survival function computed for the training dataset from Last.fm. The baseline hazard function has a sharply declining shape typical of processes exhibiting inertia. Hence, the longer users stay away from the service the lesser likely they are of returning within sometime in the future. As a result, it is all the more important for a web service to ensure that its user are motivated to return to the service soon. The survival function has a value of 0.0009 at 60 days. This suggests that 0.09% of users for this dataset did not return within 60 days.

6.2 Return Time Prediction

Table 2 and Table 3 display the weighted root mean square error scores obtained using the hazard based approach and the standard regression based approaches for the large-scale proprietary and the Last.fm datasets, respectively. We find that the hazard based approach is superior in predictive performance than the other baselines and the improvements are highly significant (p-value$< 10^{-10}$, using two-tailed paired t-test). The hazard based approach also fares well in terms of run time. On a Intel(R) Xeon(R) CPU X5650 @ 2.67GHz 24GHz, the hazard based approach takes $\sim$ 8 minutes as compared to neural networks which take $\sim$ 16 minutes to finish one run of cross-validation. Decision tree regression ($\sim$ 4 minutes), linear regression ($\sim$ 26 seconds) and average ($\sim$ 20 seconds) are faster however, the lower run times come at the cost of performance.

As discussed earlier, the hazard based approach allows us to compute the expected future return time for a user given their length of absence (LOA) by incorporating the dynamics in the hazard function. We evaluate the performance of the hazard-based approach in updating its prediction given the LOA values. Since the standard regression approaches do not provide similar functionality, we re-learn those models by incorporating the LOA values as a separate feature. The values for this feature is generated by replicating each return time observation T, T times for all values of LOA ranging from (0) $-$ ($T-1$). The future return time is appropriately reassigned to range from (T) $-$ (1). Doing so can significantly increase the size of the dataset. The data instances are re-weighted to ensure that each user still holds a unit weight in the test and the training sets. Due to space limitations we only show the comparisons between two of our baselines: decision tree regression (best performing baseline) and linear regression (because of its ease of use), with the hazard based approach for the large-scale proprietary dataset. We find that the hazard based approach is superior than both these models in estimating the expected future return time (Fig.3).

	Training Data (10-fold Cross Validation)
Average	19.41
Linear Regression	18.54
Decision Tree Regression	18.14
Neural Networks	18.26
Hazard Based Approach	16.58

Table 2: WRMSE for User Return Time Prediction using the Proprietary Dataset.

	Training Data (10-fold Cross Validation)	Test Data
Average	10.55	10.40
Linear Regression	9.61	9.37
Decision Tree Regression	9.45	9.15
Support Vector Machine	10.76	10.33
Neural Networks	9.58	9.36
Hazard Based Approach	8.76	8.45

Table 3: WRMSE for User Return Time Prediction using the Last.fm Dataset.

6.3 Classification into User Buckets

The users are classified into different categories based on their predicted return times. For the Last.fm dataset we bucketed users based on their predicted return times being larger or within 7 days, while for the larger proprietary dataset we classified them based on their predicted return times being larger or within 30 days. The shorter time period was used for the Last.fm dataset due to scarcity of users in the test set that returned after 7 days. Table 4 and Table 5 provide the performance scores for the hazard based approach and the other baselines for classifying instances into the minority class for the proprietary and the Last.fm datasets. The proprietary dataset had 15.4% samples and the last.fm dataset had 12.2% samples belonging

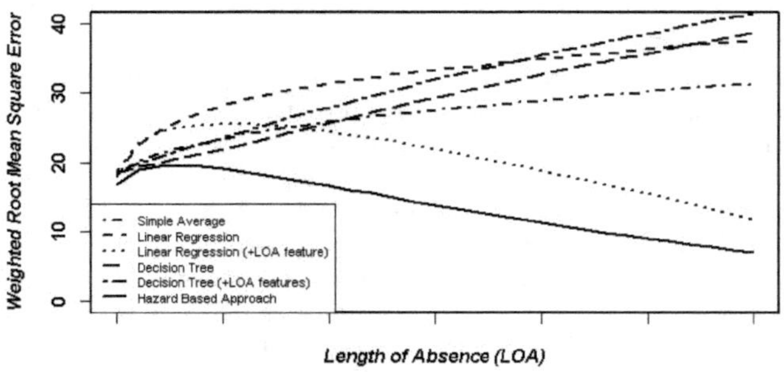

Figure 3: WRMSE for different values of LOA for the Proprietary Dataset. The units on the X-axis have been omitted.

	Training Data (10-fold Cross Validation)		
	Precision	Recall	F-Measure
Random Forest	0.47	0.10	0.18
Logistic Regression	0.52	0.08	0.15
Support Vector Machine	0	0	0
Neural Networks	0.48	0.17	0.25
Hazard Based Approach	0.41	0.23	0.29

Table 4: Weighted precision, recall and f-measure scores for the minority class (expected return time > 30) for the Large-scale Proprietary Dataset.

to the minority class. A naive classifier would have a precision of 0.154 and 0.122, respectively for these datasets. All the models perform better than a naive classifier. Although, the hazard based model is not learnt as a classification model, it still performs superior to the state-of-the-art baselines for our proprietary dataset (p-value$< 10^{-8}$, using two-tailed paired t-test) and is comparable in performance to the best performing baselines for our Last.fm dataset. The hazard based approach has the highest recall of all the models which seems to be at the cost of precision. However, for a rare class problem like ours, recall at identifying most of the at-risk users is far more important to a business and the overheads from the lower precision are low. In terms of run time, on a Intel(R) Xeon(R) CPU X5650 @ 2.67GHz 24GHz, the hazard based approach takes $\sim$ 8 minutes to finish one run of cross-validation, which is lower as compared to the other baselines: neural network classifier ($\sim$ 15 minutes), logistic regression ($\sim$ 11 minutes) and support vector machine ($\sim$ 24 minutes). Random forest has the lowest run time of all the models ($\sim$ 6 minutes).

We also evaluate the performance of the hazard based approach in classifying users into buckets given the LOA values. Again, the classification baselines do not offer similar capabilities for updating their prediction scores given LOA values. Hence, we incorporate LOA values as an additional feature for classification and replicate instances to populate the values for the feature as done for the standard regression methods earlier. We provide comparison results against the best performing baseline classification approaches - logistic regression and neural networks. We find that the hazard-based approach can incorporate the LOA information and update its prediction much effectively as compared to both logistic regression and neural networks (Fig. 4).

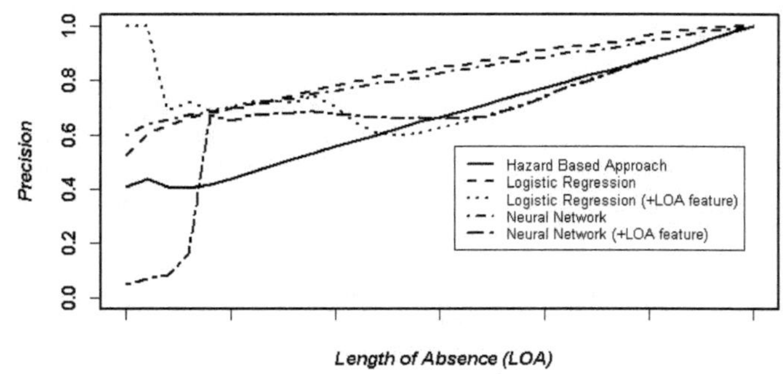

(a)

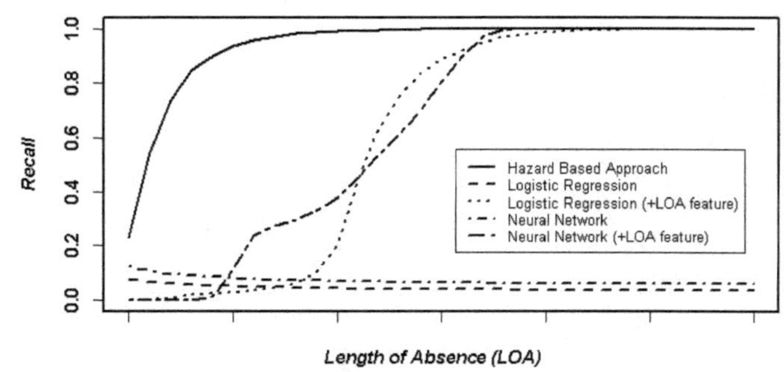

(b)

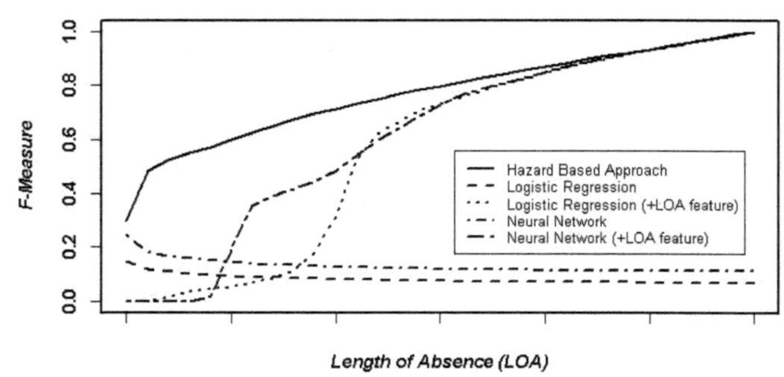

(c)

Figure 4: Figures (a), (b) and (c) are the plots of the weighted precision, recall and f-measure scores respectively, for different values of LOA for the Large-Scale Proprietary Dataset. The units on the X-axis have been omitted.

6.4 Sensitivity to the Threshold

The threshold (t_d) was set to 60 days in our experiments, which was a reasonably large value and beyond which users are already the focus of retention efforts. For completeness, we also evaluate our model for some smaller values of the threshold. Table 6 lists the performance of the models at predicting the return time for threshold values of 15, 30 and 45 days. We find that the Cox's model still performs

	Training Data (10-fold Cross Validation)			Test Data		
	Precision	Recall	F-Measure	Precision	Recall	F-Measure
Random Forest	0.64	0.24	0.35	0.72	0.29	0.41
Logistic Regression	0.68	0.44	0.53	0.66	0.40	0.50
Support Vector Machine	0.61	0.11	0.18	0.82	0.15	0.25
Neural Networks	0.77	0.39	0.52	0.71	0.36	0.48
Hazard Based Approach	0.39	0.79	0.52	0.37	0.81	0.51

Table 5: Weighted precision, recall and f-measure scores for the minority class (expected return time > 7) for the Last.fm Dataset.

better than the other baselines at the prediction task in these experiments (p-value$< 10^{-8}$, using two-tailed paired t-test).

	Training Data (10-fold Cross Validation)		
	$t_d = 15$	$t_d = 30$	$t_d = 45$
Average	6.45	11.77	16.07
Linear Regression	6.11	11.16	15.29
Decision Tree Regression	5.14	10.11	14.61
Neural Networks	5.29	10.36	15.28
Hazard Based Approach	5.04	9.54	13.41

Table 6: WRMSE for User Return Time Prediction with different values of t_d using the Proprietary Dataset.

6.5 Alternative Approaches for Handling Recurrent Observations

We use a re-weighting scheme for handling recurrent observations which allows us to retain all data instances for a user in the dataset without biasing the models towards active users. However, we now evaluate the sensitivity of our results to our weighting schemes by considering alternative approaches for handling recurrent observations. Four such approaches are defined: unweighted, using only the first observation per user, using only the last observation per user and considering only users active on a particular date chosen randomly. The last three approaches eliminate recurrent observations by data selection. We use Root Mean Square Error (RMSE) for evaluation. Due to space constraints we only report RMSE results on our proprietary dataset.

	Training Data (10-fold Cross Validation)			
	Un-weighted	First Event	Last Event	Single day
Average	7.62	17.35	26.17	7.44
Linear Regression	7.33	16.80	24.96	7.08
Decision Tree Regression	7.37	16.52	24.56	6.99
Neural Networks	7.31	17.42	24.52	7.01
Hazard Based Approach	7.31	15.955	17.76	6.87

Table 7: RMSE for User Return Time Prediction with alternative schemes for handling recurrent observations using the Proprietary Dataset.

We find that the Cox's model outperforms the other baselines when we use only the first or the last observation per user for training and testing the models (p-value$< 10^{-10}$, using two-tailed paired t-test). All the models have comparable performance when we use the un-weighted scheme or work with user observations recorded on a particular day. Both these scheme also record the lowest errors compared to the other schemes for all the models. We suspect this to happen because both these schemes are dominated by the active users and predicting the return time for such users is much easier. In order to investigate this further, we perform a pilot study in which we hold out a small sample of 1000 return time observations selectively chosen to be longer than 30 days from the proprietary dataset. The performance of different versions of the Cox model trained using the various schemes for handling recurrent observations discussed earlier is then tested at predicting these longer return time observations. The RMSE results are reported in table 8.

	Test data of long return times				
	Weighted	Un-weighted	First Event	Last Event	Single day
RMSE	32.25	40.70	32.34	32.14	41.81

Table 8: RMSE for Long Return Time Prediction for different versions of the Cox Model on the Proprietary Dataset.

These results further show that both the un-weighted scheme and choosing observations from a single day, perform poorly at predicting longer return times. Since the focus of our methods is to find users which are not likely to return soon, these approaches may not be suitable for our application. Furthermore, the weighted scheme offers a good trade-off between using just the first events or just the last events per user in our model making it more suitable for our problem.

7. CONCLUSION

In this work, we have focused on the return time performance metric for free web services. We suggest that retention solutions driven by the projected return time of users can directly address the heart of the problem for web services, which is to encourage their users to frequently engage with their service. To facilitate such efforts, we formulate the problem of user return time prediction and define several covariates relevant to the problem. The Cox's proportional hazard model is proposed as the model of choice for this prediction problem due to several reasons including the ability to handle dynamics in user return rate with time and to incorporate the LOA information. A plot of the prediction performance scores against the LOA values allows a service to identify the right amount of gap since the user's last visit needed to start retention efforts. The performance of the hazard based model is found to surpass all the state-of-the-art baselines considered by us. Finally, we find that the ability of the Cox model to quantify the impact of several important covariates, including those related to user usage patterns, on user return rates to provide important insights that can guide future decision making for the service.

The Cox's model can further accommodate several complexities of the real-world quite well. For example, our analysis till now has been limited to static covariates. However, time-varying covariates including those pertaining to external factors such as holiday and weekend effects can be important for return time prediction and can be easily incorporated in the Cox Model [27]. In our final model for the large scale music service, we incorporated the effect of the day of the month covariate (Fig. 5) on the user return rates. Another direction for future research is to account for heterogeneities among users. Several solutions exist for either controlling for such differences between users [20] or for extracting different users segments through clustering [19] can also be applied to the return time prediction problem.

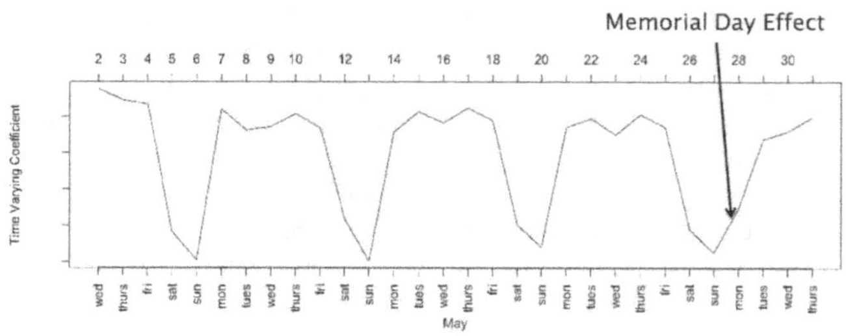

Figure 5: The regression coefficient for time-varying covariates corresponding to the different days of the month. The absolute values are omitted here.

8. REFERENCES

[1] http://www.last.fm.

[2] Simon Attfield, Gabriella Kazai, Mounia Lalmas, and Benjamin Piwowarski. Towards a science of user engagement (position paper). In *WSDM Workshop on User Modelling for Web Applications*, 2011.

[3] Alex Berson, Stephen Smith, and Kurt Thearling. *Building data mining applications for CRM*. McGraw-Hill New York, 2000.

[4] Wouter Buckinx and Dirk Van den Poel. Customer base analysis: partial defection of behaviourally loyal clients in a non-contractual fmcg retail setting. *European Journal of Operational Research*, 164(1):252–268, 2005.

[5] Jonathan Burez and Dirk Van den Poel. Handling class imbalance in customer churn prediction. *Expert Systems with Applications*, 36(3):4626–4636, 2009.

[6] O. Celma. *Music Recommendation and Discovery - The Long Tail, Long Fail, and Long Play in the Digital Music Space*. Springer, 2010.

[7] Kristof Coussement and Dirk Van den Poel. Churn prediction in subscription services: An application of support vector machines while comparing two parameter-selection techniques. *Expert systems with applications*, 34(1):313–327, 2008.

[8] David R Cox. Regression models and life-tables. *Journal of the Royal Statistical Society. Series B (Methodological)*, pages 187–220, 1972.

[9] Gideon Dror, Dan Pelleg, Oleg Rokhlenko, and Idan Szpektor. Churn prediction in new users of yahoo! answers. In *Proceedings of the 21st international conference companion on World Wide Web*, pages 829–834. ACM, 2012.

[10] Georges Dupret and Mounia Lalmas. Absence time and user engagement: evaluating ranking functions. In *Proceedings of the sixth ACM international conference on Web search and data mining*, pages 173–182. ACM, 2013.

[11] Peter S Fader, Bruce GS Hardie, and Ka Lok Lee. Rfm and clv: Using iso-value curves for customer base analysis. *Journal of Marketing Research*, pages 415–430, 2005.

[12] Rishab Aiyer Ghosh. Cooking pot markets: an economic model for the trade in free goods and services on the internet. *First Monday*, 3(2), 1998.

[13] Bing Quan Huang, M Tahar Kechadi, and Brian Buckley. Customer churn prediction for broadband internet services. In *Data Warehousing and Knowledge Discovery*, pages 229–243. Springer, 2009.

[14] Zainab Jamal and Randolph E Bucklin. Improving the diagnosis and prediction of customer churn: A heterogeneous hazard modeling approach. *Journal of Interactive Marketing*, 20(3):16–29, 2006.

[15] Michael D Kaplowitz, Timothy D Hadlock, and Ralph Levine. A comparison of web and mail survey response rates. *Public opinion quarterly*, 68(1):94–101, 2004.

[16] Marcel Karnstedt, Tara Hennessy, Jeffrey Chan, and Conor Hayes. Churn in social networks: A discussion boards case study. In *Social Computing (SocialCom), 2010 IEEE Second International Conference on*, pages 233–240. IEEE, 2010.

[17] Janette Lehmann, Mounia Lalmas, Elad Yom-Tov, and Georges Dupret. Models of user engagement. In *User Modeling, Adaptation, and Personalization*, pages 164–175. Springer, 2012.

[18] Han Liu, Atif Nazir, Jinoo Joung, and Chen-Nee Chuah. Modeling/predicting the evolution trend of osn-based applications. In *Proceedings of the 22nd international conference on World Wide Web*, pages 771–780. International World Wide Web Conferences Steering Committee, 2013.

[19] Patrick Mair and Marcus Hudec. Analysis of dwell times in web usage mining. In *Data Analysis, Machine Learning and Applications*, pages 593–600. Springer, 2008.

[20] CA McGilchrist and CW Aisbett. Regression with frailty in survival analysis. *Biometrics*, pages 461–466, 1991.

[21] Scott A Neslin, Sunil Gupta, Wagner Kamakura, Junxiang Lu, and Charlotte H Mason. Defection detection: Measuring and understanding the predictive accuracy of customer churn models. *Journal of Marketing Research*, pages 204–211, 2006.

[22] Joe Peppard. Customer relationship management (crm) in financial services. *European Management Journal*, 18(3):312–327, 2000.

[23] Jeffrey F Rayport. The truth about internet business models. *Strategy and Business*, pages 5–7, 1999.

[24] Werner J Reinartz and Vijay Kumar. On the profitability of long-life customers in a noncontractual setting: An empirical investigation and implications for marketing. *The Journal of Marketing*, pages 17–35, 2000.

[25] Bruno Ribeiro. Modeling and predicting the growth and death of membership-based websites. *Proceedings of the 23rd international conference on World Wide Web*, 2014.

[26] David C Schmittlein and Vijay Mahajan. Maximum likelihood estimation for an innovation diffusion model of new product acceptance. *Marketing science*, 1(1):57–78, 1982.

[27] Terry Therneau and Cindy Crowson. Using time dependent covariates and time dependent coefficients in the cox model. *The Survival Package (R help guide)*, 2013.

[28] Chih-Fong Tsai and Yu-Hsin Lu. Customer churn prediction by hybrid neural networks. *Expert Systems with Applications*, 36(10):12547–12553, 2009.

[29] Chih-Ping Wei, I Chiu, et al. Turning telecommunications call details to churn prediction: a data mining approach. *Expert systems with applications*, 23(2):103–112, 2002.

[30] Yaya Xie, Xiu Li, EWT Ngai, and Weiyun Ying. Customer churn prediction using improved balanced random forests. *Expert Systems with Applications*, 36(3):5445–5449, 2009.

[31] Jiang Yang, Xiao Wei, Mark S Ackerman, and Lada A Adamic. Activity lifespan: An analysis of user survival patterns in online knowledge sharing communities. In *ICWSM*, 2010.

[32] Elad Yom-Tov, Mounia Lalmas, Ricardo Baeza-Yates, Georges Dupret, Janette Lehmann, and Pinar Donmez. Measuring inter-site engagement. In *Big Data, 2013 IEEE International Conference on*, pages 228–236. IEEE, 2013.

[33] Yin Zhu, Erheng Zhong, Sinno Jialin Pan, Xiao Wang, Minzhe Zhou, and Qiang Yang. Predicting user activity level in social networks. In *Proceedings of the 22nd ACM international conference on Conference on information & knowledge management*, pages 159–168. ACM, 2013.

Predicting Employee Expertise for Talent Management in the Enterprise

Kush R. Varshney,[1] Vijil Chenthamarakshan,[1] Scott W. Fancher,[2]
Jun Wang,[1] Dongping Fang,[1] and Aleksandra Mojsilović[1]
[1]IBM Thomas J. Watson Research Center, 1101 Kitchawan Road, Yorktown Heights, New York
[2]IBM Corporate Headquarters, 1 New Orchard Road, Armonk, New York
{krvarshn,ecvijil,sfancher,wangjun,dfang,aleksand}@us.ibm.com

ABSTRACT

Strategic planning and talent management in large enterprises composed of knowledge workers requires complete, accurate, and up-to-date representation of the expertise of employees in a form that integrates with business processes. Like other similar organizations operating in dynamic environments, the IBM Corporation strives to maintain such current and correct information, specifically assessments of employees against job roles and skill sets from its expertise taxonomy. In this work, we deploy an analytics-driven solution that infers the expertise of employees through the mining of enterprise and social data that is not specifically generated and collected for expertise inference. We consider job role and specialty prediction and pose them as supervised classification problems. We evaluate a large number of feature sets, predictive models and postprocessing algorithms, and choose a combination for deployment. This expertise analytics system has been deployed for key employee population segments, yielding large reductions in manual effort and the ability to continually and consistently serve up-to-date and accurate data for several business functions. This expertise management system is in the process of being deployed throughout the corporation.

Categories and Subject Descriptors

I.2.6 [**Artificial Intelligence**]: Learning; H.2.8 [**Database Management**]: Database Applications—*Data Mining*

Keywords

expertise assessment; human resources; supervised classification; talent planning; workforce analytics

1. INTRODUCTION

The International Business Machines (IBM) Corporation is one of the largest employers of knowledge workers in the world. The global workforce is over 425,000 employees strong, with greater and greater fractions selling or delivering information technology and business consulting services every day. Two key trends in the information technology industry include a quickening pace of technological innovation and an increased customer-centrism by all employees. In the face of these trends, it is important for IBM's strategic and tactical business decision-making to be informed by complete, precise, accurate, and up-to-date information on the expertise of its employees. What team—in terms of composition of employee skills—should serve a particular client, which emerging technology areas IBM has adequate skills and experience in to support (e.g., cloud computing, cognitive computing, social business), and other similar decisions are all predicated on such information [12, 18, 1].

The human capital, or talent and expertise, of its workforce is IBM's greatest asset; only through valid and trusted data on employee expertise can this human capital be utilized to its fullest potential. Such expertise information is captured by existing expertise management systems within the IBM enterprise, but can be enhanced using digital 'breadcrumbs' and data 'exhaust' from other enterprise systems of record that have 'footprints' of employees' work activities (e.g. project claims, sales pipeline, etc.). However these pieces of data often provide only a diffuse indication of expertise. The main contribution of this work is using predictive analytics to churn such nebulous data into clear indicators of employee expertise in a way that commingles with existing IBM business processes.

Human resources (HR) departments are transforming from support functions to strategy leadership in many ways. David Bernstein, Vice President of Big Data for HR at eQuest, recently said in discussing different levels of talent analytics (operational reporting, advanced reporting, advanced analytics, and predictive analytics) that[1] "predictive analytics is where HR develops predictive models and integrates with the organization's strategic planning. The majority of organizations, however, are not doing this, yet." The fraction of organizations engaged in predictive HR analytics is reported to be as low as 4% [2]. Recent predictive modeling initiatives put IBM's HR organization into the 4% category. However like most other organizations, the newly adopted predictive HR analytics in IBM are mostly focused on recruitment and hiring, resource deployment and proactive talent retention [22, 16, 6, 21]. Predicting expertise is a much more open-ended problem than the others.

[1]`http://www.bigdatarepublic.com/author.asp?section_id=3431`

KDD'14, August 24–27, 2014, New York, NY, USA.

http://dx.doi.org/10.1145/2623330.2623337.

Extant expertise systems, such as LinkedIn's skill recommendation, are completely free-form in how skills are described. In order to operate the IBM business, however, we need a semi-structured approach which relies on IBM's existing expertise taxonomy to link to solutions and products that IBM sells and to tap into an entire ecosystem of processes and reporting tools built around the taxonomy. The existing expertise assessment system and taxonomy yield many benefits to the company, but have a few shortcomings in keeping data current and accurate as detailed in Section 2. Therefore, our goal is to start with the IBM expertise taxonomy and assessments, pull in other data sources informative of expertise, and create good predictions of employee proficiencies.

In our work, we specifically investigate the prediction of an employee's primary job role and job role specialty (which are the third and fourth levels of the five-level IBM expertise taxonomy) from enterprise systems of record and data from the internal corporate social networking site IBM Connections as features. Since employees have a single primary job role among a set of labels with not too exorbinant cardinality, we approach the predictive modeling problem as a classification problem. Since we have veracious data on a reasonable fraction of employees' job roles and job role specialties, we can further formulate the problem via supervised multi-category classification, using the veracious fraction of employees' data as a training set. We perform a comprehensive study of classification algorithms and feature sets, finding the Liblinear implementation of logistic regression using job title and HR information features to perform with best generalization accuracy [9]. Moreover, since employees tend to be grouped in the IBM organizational structure by job role and skill set, e.g. mostly strategy consultants under one manager and mostly information architects under a different manager, we attempt to improve classification accuracy taking these relationships into account, but do not find enough improvement to warrant inclusion in the deployment.

In previous work, we investigated the prediction of skills —the lowest level of the IBM expertise taxonomy—using matrix completion-based collaborative filtering with side information [24, 27], including in the cold-start regime [10]. This problem is different because unlike skills, which employees have many of, employees only have one primary job role and one primary job role specialty each. Therefore, collaborative filtering is not appropriate for job role and job role specialty prediction. Other approaches for predicting the expertise of employees within an enterprise such as IBM are focused on social media data only and importantly, are not meant to be integrated with existing business processes [13, 20, 4, 11, 5], whereas we consider other types of enterprise data as well and integrate with existing practices.

Predicting primary job roles and primary job specialties is mainly intended to improve processes related to and built upon the 'inventorying' of employees. This work represents a part of a larger effort to transform the way the IBM Corporation operates. A complimentary piece of work is enabling expertise search [23, 7, 8, 19, 14], i.e. the ability for employees to find other employees who are experts on some topic. Expertise search is driven by the need of employees to find the right person to answer a question, to bring to a client meeting, to fill out a team, and so on. Another part of the effort is the creation of enhanced profile pages known as digital business cards that better enable the collection of expertise-related information and provide enhanced user experience. These parts have been deployed within IBM through web-based and mobile-based applications.

The job role and job role specialty prediction algorithms we have developed are in various stages of deployment in IBM. Predicted job roles from our algorithm have been applied to the population of all salespeople worldwide in the company. This employee segment represents less than 10% of the employee population and is more active in maintaining accurate job roles than other employee populations. Administrators responsible for these employees used our outputs to accurately enter job role values for thousands of salespeople with either no job roles entered or an invalid or outdated job role entered. This initial single one-time deployment saved the company the equivalent of one employee's full-time effort for an entire year, not to mention all of the business benefits from current, correct data. Moreover, we are now in the process of rolling out the predictive models with a user-centered design to allow administrators in the entire company to continually maintain complete and accurate job roles and job role specialties with corresponding compounded effort savings.

The remainder of the paper is organized as follows. In Section 2, we provide a description of the expertise assessment system and processes that IBM currently uses. In Section 3, we formulate job role and job role specialty prediction as a supervised classification problem and describe the features available for making the prediction. Section 4 details our empirical study of various features and classification algorithms. We then describe the deployment of the approach within IBM in Section 5. The paper concludes in Section 6.

2. BACKGROUND AND SIGNIFICANCE

In this section, we focus on describing the problem in detail along with its significance. We first recapitulate the history of expertise assessment in IBM and show how this history motivates an evolution to predictive modeling, as developed in this work.

2.1 Expertise Taxonomy

IBM has a taxonomy of employee expertise with the following five coarse-to-fine levels: primary job category, secondary job category, job role, job role specialty, and skill. The taxonomy is a directed acyclic graph with parent-child relationships between values at different levels. We provide three examples of paths through the taxonomy with the five different levels separated by the greater than symbol: Sales > Industry Sales > Brand Client Representative > Brand Client Representative: BAO-Advanced Analytics & Optimization > Sell ILOG Optimization; Human Resources > Learning > Learning Consultant > Learning Consultant: Collaboration, Knowledge & Communities > Analyze Performance Improvement Needs; Research > Research Staff > Research Scientist > Research Scientist: Computational Biology > Develop Algorithms for Biological Data Analysis. An individual employee has a single primary job role and primary job role specialty, which are the values we predict in this work.

2.2 Existing Expertise Assessment System

IBM utilizes an internally-developed application to collect expertise assessments from employees. The system was deployed in the year 2000 and at that time, contained many leading-edge functions, numerous approaches to customize for different parts of IBM's business organizations, and a befitting user interface for employees. The basic function of the application is:

1. collecting information from the employee on what area of the business he or she works in,

2. having the employee select a primary job role and job role specialty (what he or she is assigned to do), and

3. presenting each employee with a list of expertise skills to assess on a 5 point scale.

The application interfaces directly with the IBM expertise taxonomy, which contains the relationships of expertise skills to the job role classification hierarchy. For example, each job role has a set of predefined expertise skills that are associated with it; based upon the employee-provided job role, the application asks the employee to assess the skills related to that job role.

While it is simple in concept, as IBM organizations have desired to collect finer expertise information over time, the taxonomy has grown, the number of job role specialties has grown, and the business rules that determine which employees assess which job role specialties has become quite complex. In 2000, the number of job roles was around 200 and the number of specialties 1000; today, there are around 350 job roles and 7000 specialties. The goal is to use the information collected about employees to ensure that the expertise skills which they are asked to assess directly pertain to their success in the their job: 'the right skills to the right employees.' However, the business rules sometimes deliver more than 100 skills for employees to assess, which results in a suboptimal user experience and subsequent lack of compliance.

While the current expertise assessment application has served its purpose for many years, it was designed during a time when IBM's product portfolio changed perhaps once every three or four years. Updating the taxonomy requires adding new skills to reflect new product knowledge. Updating the application's expertise delivery business rules also requires some thought to determine who should assess these new product skills. Therefore in an environment where an organization could set up the tool once every two years and have employees assess against a relatively constant set of expertise skills, the work required to set up the tool was relatively small compared to the benefit of the resulting expertise information collected.

2.3 Motivation for Predictive Modeling

Today IBM is a much more dynamically-changing company with new products, solutions, and acquisitions emerging each quarter. Thus the time and work required to set up a structured assessment begins to limit the ability to have expertise information that is responsive to the rapidly-changing needs of the business. These rapidly-changing needs of the business are actually dictating that the company evolve to a new expertise assessment approach that is much more flexible and requires much less time and effort to set up. Any information collected directly from employees requires some degree of end user design, setup, and testing. Information inferred from normal work products bypasses much of this design, setup, and testing by its very nature.

Through the proposed work, IBM is moving toward a world in which predictive analytics based upon employees' digital footprints is almost constantly updating the current inventory of expertise across the company. The eventual goal is to move from the world of counting and taking inventory once a year based upon a taxonomic system that was put in place a year earlier, to a world of instantly updated inventories: updated as soon as new terminology finds its way to the folksonomy and as soon as an employee creates digital evidence of new expertise gained. All the benefits that supply chain systems have realized over the last twenty years, with just-in-time inventories, point-of-sale inventory updates, economic order quantities, and predictive inventory demand are becoming possible for human resources and expertise management.

3. MACHINE LEARNING FORMULATION

In this section, we discuss the decisions and tradeoffs in making design choices for the data mining solution to the job role and specialty prediction problem within the IBM enterprise. In Wagstaff's three stages of a machine learning research program, this section is devoted to the necessary preparation phase: phrasing the problem as a machine learning task, collecting data, and selecting or generating features [25].

3.1 Supervised Multi-Category Classification

Several different machine learning or information retrieval formulations are possible for predicting and recommending primary job roles and job role specialties. We first lay out the desiderata of the solution and then comment on the choices made.

As mentioned earlier, an employee is supposed to have one primary job role and one primary job role specialty. Each line of business (LOB) maintains a short list, or subset, of job roles and specialties in the taxonomy that its employees may validly have. A reasonable fraction of employees throughout IBM have valid job roles and specialties, but there exists a significant fraction with values outside their LOB's short list or with no value entered at all.

The task at hand is two-fold: first, filling in the job role and specialty of any employee whose value is blank or invalid according to their LOB; and second, identifying employees whose values, although valid, are nevertheless incorrect based on their current job responsibilities and correcting them. The users of the system are not intended to be individual employees, but managers, administrators, and planners. An analytics solution is not intended to be fully automatic, but to recommend predictions and corrections that the user may or may not accept for each employee. In this mode of operation, a list of top k predicted job roles and specialties along with confidence values in the predictions may be more useful than a single prediction without an indication of confidence (wth k not more than three or four from a human factors concern).

One approach to tackle this problem is through an information retrieval formulation. We can index various data sources that provide an indication of expertise. Then, performing searches using query terms related to each job role or specialty, we can see in which search result the employee is ranked highest. However, constructing appropriate query terms that well-differentiate often-similar job roles and specialties is difficult and this approach is an indirect way of tackling the problem. The direct way of approaching the problem is via classification because the task is to label an individual from a fairly small set of labels. As discussed in Section 1, collaborative filtering (narrowly construed as predicting the preference of an individual by collecting preferences from many individuals) is not appropriate because each employee has only one primary job role and specialty.

Classification need not be based on statistical machine learning. Oftentimes, manually-specified logical classification rules developed by subject matter experts perform excellently. However, as discussed, such manual work is not sustainable in the dynamic business environment of today. For a machine learning approach, we need to have reliable training data. The reasonable fraction of employees with non-blank and valid labels is sufficient for the first task even though there is label noise (the whole reason for the second task), because this noise is not overwhelming.[2] For the second task, we can take a cross-validation approach to construct training and test sets in such a way that we can identify employees that do not fit the pattern when they are a part of the test set.

We do not consider semi-supervised learning because we want all unlabeled samples (the invalid- and blank-valued employees) to be a part of the test set in the first task. Moreover, we focus on classification rather than learning to rank because of the form of the training data and because we are typically only concerned with accurately obtaining the best one, two, three, or four labels for an employee, not the entire permutation of ranked job roles or specialties for an employee.

Thus overall for the skills analytics problem we are facing, the most direct and appropriate formulation is supervised multi-category classification. Moreover, due to the business structure, we learn separate classifiers for the different LOBs within IBM because there are different valid class labels and different feature distributions among the different LOBs. Multi-task learning could be possible in this setting to do joint training for different LOBs, but we choose not to pursue this direction because it introduces unnecessary complexity.

3.2 Data Sources

There are several potential data sources that give some indication (sometimes in a quite diffuse way) about an employee's expertise, specifically as manifested in his or her job role and job role specialty. Within the IBM context, we can divide the potential data sources into four categories. The first category is employees' descriptions of their job in their own words. For many years, one line shown underneath the employee's name in the corporate directory has been a free-text field entered and edited by the employee. This text field is known as the job title. A similar, but longer, text field on the recently deployed digital business card mentioned in Section 1 deemed 'what I'm known for' is also of this same category of data sources, but we do not use it in the work described herein because it is in its incipient stages of adoption.

The second data source category is standard HR information recorded about all employees as standard practice. Example fields include the length of service; the work location; the names of the group, department, and business unit to which the employee belongs; the job category of the employee, which is the highest level of the expertise taxonomy, but is maintained in a separate manner than job role and job role specialty; the employee's pay grade; and whether he or she is on a commission-based compensation plan.

The third category of data sources is work products, which includes artifacts produced by employees as part of their regular job responsibilities. As such, in contrast to the other data source categories, this category is job-specific. For example, researchers produce publications and patents, software developers produce documentation and code, salespeople work on and record sales opportunities, delivery personnel bill claims for their services, and so on. These days, much of this activity is captured digitally in various systems, but accessing and working with such data is often difficult. In this paper, we present empirical results on the LOB containing salespeople and show results from sales opportunity data.

Activity on the internal corporate social networking site, IBM Connections, constitutes the fourth data source category. There are several different types of social media content, including profiles, status updates, blogs, wikis, communities, forums, bookmarks, and calendars. They are also all associated with tags. Certain social media content is private whereas other content is public. For this project, we may only access public content and tags. Private material is typically confidential precisely because it relates to ongoing work activities, and thus its exclusion presents a limitation. Public content is not always work-related: there are communities for sports leagues, ethnic affinity groups, etc. too.

3.3 Feature Engineering

For each employee, we collect content from the HR information management system, business data warehouse, personal profile, and internal enterprise social network. Fig. 1 demonstrates examples of the extracted raw data, including the job title information from the HR data warehouse, sales opportunity data from the business data warehouse, and the associated tags retrieved from the social network.

The key step in processing sales data is mapping sales opportunities to employees. Several roles are associated with opportunities, including opportunity owner, supporting team, contact person, etc. In this work, we take the text descriptions of all opportunities a salesperson owns and create bag-of-words features from this text. To create a bag-of-words representation, we first convert the text into lower case and eliminate stop words. Then the text is tokenized and numerical term frequencies are computed. We compute similar bag-of-words representations for job title and social tags. Furthermore, categorical HR fields such as reporting chain and work location are processed into binary features. In summary, we have derived multiple feature representations for the employee in the feature engineering stage; the predictive power of each feature set is studied in our experiments section.

4. CLASSIFICATION ALGORITHMS

This section is devoted to the second stage of a machine learning research program, described by Wagstaff as the "machine learning contribution" [25]. We discuss the choice and development of an algorithm, discuss the choice of a

[2]We do not include any label noise correction, e.g. [17], to maintain implementational simplicity and because once the system has been deployed for some time, the label noise problem will fade away by itself.

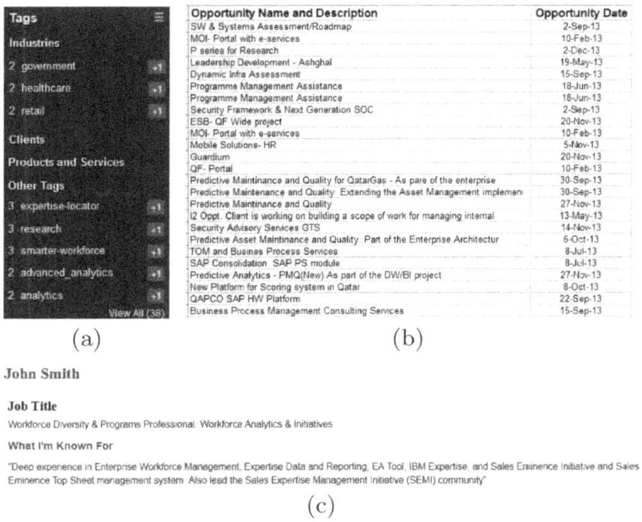

Figure 1: Examples of raw data for a single employee: (a) tags from IBM Connections, (b) sales opportunity data, and (c) job title.

metric, and conduct experiments to determine relative and absolute performance numbers.

4.1 Algorithms and Metrics

We would like to solve a multi-category classification problem with the features described in Section 3 to predict employee job role or job role specialty. Many different classification models may be applied to the problem; there is no particular a priori preference for any specific algorithm. We compare the performance of several models in the sequel. The performance metric of interest in this problem is classification accuracy. Although not the most sensible metric in many applications, it truly is the most sensible in job role prediction because the classes are not severely imbalanced and different types of misclassifications do not have different costs.

4.2 Empirical Study

In this empirical study, we focus on the job role classification problem rather than the job role specialty classification problem, but algorithmically, we treat both in the same way with the same features and evaluation criteria. The specific LOB that we focus on here is the set of all salespeople in the entire IBM Corporation worldwide. We have conducted similar empirical studies for other LOBs and populations, consistently finding similar results.

For this LOB, there are eleven valid job roles: Brand Client Representative (BCR), Client Representative (CR), Client Technical Architect (CTA), Client Technical Manager (CTM), Client Technical Specialist (CTS), Client Unit Executive (CUE), Industry Solution Representative (ISR), Mid-Market Client Representative (MCR), Solution Representative (SR), Solution Representative – Brand Specialist (SRB), and Solution Sales Manager (SSM). As may be guessed based on their names, several of these different job roles are fairly similar to each other. Due to this fact, it is not straightforward for employees to label themselves quickly and accurately, not to say anything about a machine learning algorithm.

As discussed in Section 3, we take all employees with valid labels as the training set. This amounts to 36,709 employees, which is 89% of the salesperson population. The largest class, SRB, represents 0.2633 of all sellers and thus this value is the baseline classification accuracy. We compare four one-against-the-rest multi-category classification algorithms: linear logistic regression with ℓ_2 and ℓ_1 regularization, linear support vector machine, and naïve Bayes. The regularization parameters for the first three models are found by cross-validation.

In order to estimate generalization accuracy, we calculate fivefold cross-validation test error for the different classifiers. Cross-validation provides such an estimate because there is no reason to suspect any systemic bias in employees with blank or invalid class labels. We also compare the four different feature sets individually and in combination: job title, HR information, sales opportunities, and social tags. We take the 1000 terms with the highest term frequency from the text analytics for each of the data sources except for HR information. The HR information consists of 23 categorical features converted to binary and one numeric feature. The test accuracy results are given in Table 1.

It is clear in the results table that the naïve Bayes classifier performs the worst across all feature sets and the support vector machine is consistently a little bit worse than logistic regression. The two different regularization versions of logistic regression are nearly the same across all feature sets. The most interesting thing to notice is that the classification accuracy from only social tags is actually worse than the baseline accuracy. The performance from only sales opportunities is also quite poor. This poor performance can be attributed to the words in descriptions of sales opportunities seen in Fig. 1(b) being very specific and not well matched to differentiating often-similar sales roles. More so, public social tags give a different indication of a person's activities and skills than what is required for predicting job roles.

The best performance is achieved by using the HR information and the bag-of-words features of the job title, both individually and in combination. Adding the poor-performing social tags and sales opportunity features only introduces noise and degrades accuracy. Thus we go forward with the combination of HR and job title features for the deployment. Since both logistic regressions are essentially the same and the ℓ_2-norm is easier to optimize, we choose the ℓ_2-regularized logistic regression model. The 0.8016 accuracy is quite good for this challenging eleven-class problem. The logistic regression also provides posterior probabilities or confidence scores for each of the eleven classes for each sample.

We show the confusion matrix of the cross-validation test set in Table 2. We note that most mistakes are within two clusters of very similar job roles: technical sellers {CTA, CTM, CTS}, and brand solution reps {BCR, SR, SRB, SSM}, which is to be expected due to their similarities. The classifiers evaluated here all deal with employees as statistically independent samples; subject matter expertise suggests a possible way to improve accuracy based on relationships among employees, which we explore next.

Table 1: Fivefold Cross-Validation Test Accuracy

Feature Set	ℓ_2-Reg. Logistic Regress.	ℓ_1-Reg. Logistic Regress.	Support Vec. Mach.	Naïve Bayes
Job Title (A)	0.6746	0.6749	0.6695	0.6410
HR Info (B)	0.7661	0.7641	0.7604	0.6807
Social Tags (C)	0.2320	0.2396	0.2380	0.2573
Sales Opp (D)	0.3374	0.3404	0.3473	0.2306
(A) + (B)	0.8016	0.8031	0.7899	0.7330
(A) + (B) + (C)	0.7671	0.7703	0.7504	0.6118
(A) + (B) + (C) + (D)	0.7720	0.7733	0.7655	0.3952

Table 2: Confusion Matrix (rows are actuals, columns are predictions)

	BCR	CR	CTA	CTM	CTS	CUE	ISR	MCR	SR	SRB	SSM	Total
BCR	1084	88	3	1	11	4	3	5	70	913	119	2301
CR	33	4014	7	1	4	126	8	96	72	148	50	4559
CTA	5	12	2534	40	438	4	5	0	11	9	5	3063
CTM	0	1	55	955	89	4	0	0	5	10	45	1164
CTS	0	6	286	77	7358	2	1	0	7	57	4	7798
CUE	6	247	2	0	0	600	4	18	25	11	154	1067
ISR	17	46	12	0	2	9	51	3	31	60	6	237
MCR	54	202	0	0	1	13	2	294	16	91	6	679
SR	186	164	11	4	14	19	28	20	1891	892	119	3348
SRB	310	91	11	6	70	10	5	20	247	8572	322	9664
SSM	64	76	8	16	4	115	10	9	95	358	2074	2829
Total	1759	4947	2929	1100	7991	906	117	465	2470	11121	2904	36709

4.3 Org Chart-Assisted Postprocessing

IBM, like most large corporations, is a tree-structured organization with a management chain representing the path from an employee to the Chief Executive Officer. For ease of management, employees tend to be grouped by job function within the tree. We put forth a few methods to postprocess the predicted class probabilities output by the logistic regression and examine their effects on test accuracy.

We first construct groups of employees by taking sub-trees of the organizational structure at each level except for the highest three levels because they encompass the entire salesforce. Then, in the first postprocessing method, we consider all groups having all training set employees with the same class label and change the predicted class label of all test set employees to that common class label (if they are not already). This improves the accuracy from 0.8016 to 0.8022. As a further heuristic, if we only change those predicted test set class labels with confidence score less than 0.9, then the accuracy improves to 0.8039.

Another postprocessing method is provenance-assisted classification [26]. From the same sub-tree groupings, we construct a bipartite graph with one set of nodes being the groups and the other set of nodes being the employees. Then through an iterative expectation–maximization procedure similar to that found in error-correcting codes [15], we find a maximum likelihood estimate of the class probabilities under the enforcement of consistency in groupings based on the bipartite relationships. However, such an approach with all grouping nodes decreases the accuracy significantly to 0.5982. Only including grouping nodes that have all training set samples the same, as in the previous heuristic, also decreases the accuracy to 0.7999.

Very limited improvement or even a worsening of performance occurs primarily because the HR information already includes categorical attributes indicating three levels of membership in the organizational structure and because while the grouping of employees in the tree is generally true, there are many exceptions which are identified correctly by the classifier but then smoothed out by the postprocessing.

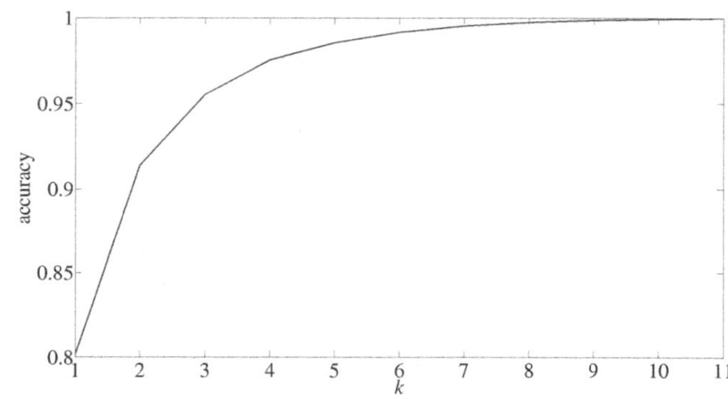

Figure 2: Fivefold cross-validation accuracy as a function of number of predictions per employee.

4.4 Discussion

As discussed earlier, one use case of the classifier outputs is showing more than one predicted job role for an employee to a system user and allowing the user to choose the correct one. In this case, we can also measure the accuracy of whether the true class label appears in the k class labels with the highest confidence scores. This accuracy value is plotted in Fig. 2, showing that with two or three predictions per employee, we can achieve very good performance: 0.9138 and 0.9553 respectively. Most of the confusion is among similar job roles, which can be alleviated by giving more than one prediction per person.

As also discussed earlier, even the labels that we use for training and cross-validation have some level of noise. We can get a rough indication of the level of noise by comparing the job role and the job role specialty values among the 36,709 salespeople in our population: if the job role specialty does not fall under the job role in the taxonomy, this mismatch indicates a possible error in the job role label. (Such a mismatch is only one possible manifestation of label noise; the job role label could be incorrect for a host of other reasons as well.) The employees with such a mismatch constitute 6.6% of the population. Among the mismatched population, the cross-validation test accuracy is 0.7207 compared to 0.8073 among the sellers with job role and job role specialty values that are in concordance. Thus in comparing 0.8073 to 0.8016, we see that label noise is not very significant, at least as manifested via job role and job role specialty discord.

Through the experimental results with different feature sets, classifiers, and predicted class probability postprocessing methods, we have seen that we can achieve approximately 80% accuracy using HR information and job title with the ℓ_2-regularized logistic regression without any postprocessing. These are the choices we go forward with in the deployment.

5. DEPLOYMENT AND IMPACT

In this section we describe the third stage of the machine learning research program: the deployment of the data mining system we have developed within the business processes of IBM. The section begins with the initial deployment among the population of all salespeople worldwide, and then discusses the deployment across the entire corporation that is currently in progress. Both of these parts discuss the business impact of the deployment. The section finishes with a discussion of lessons learned, from both the HR practioner's perspective and the data mining practitioner's perspective.

5.1 Worldwide Salespeople Deployment

We first deployed job role and speciality prediction to solve an issue with missing and incorrect job role information among IBM salespeople worldwide in the first part of 2014. The salesforce is a key segment of the IBM workforce because these employees garner the revenue for the company. Job role information is used in myriad salesforce planning and strategy functions [1].

In 2014, a new situation was encountered that required the primary job roles to be accurate and within a certain number of permitted values for 100% of the sellers. Even though sellers are asked to update job role information annually, approximately 4,000 of them fail to follow the directions or fail to provide the update. To get the employees to update this data field would have taken approximately 30 minutes per employee or manager, including contacting them, guiding them through the process, and then having them submit the update. Summed over the 4,000 employees, this is an effort of approximately 2,000 person-hours. Additional effort from corporate headquarters to create the instructions, deploy the communication, and assist with the roll out would have incurred approximately 500 person-hours.

Instead we used the result of the predictive analytics to recommend a primary job role and put that value into the primary job role field in the data. We then asked the managers to check the recommended job role and make any necessary changes. Since the predictions were accurate approximately 80% of the time, only a small number of managers had to physically make a change. Conservatively speaking, using predictive analytics saved 80% of the estimated 2,000 person-hours by employees and managers and most of the 500 person-hours by headquarters for setup and deployment, resulting in huge savings totaling approximately 2,100 person-hours, which is the equivalent of one person-year. A typical year of effort by an IBM salesperson results in revenue achievement in the range of $1 million; thus the time savings provided by the job role prediction can yield that much additional revenue for the company.

The salesforce is less than 10% of the total IBM workforce and is a population that is more compliant than many other LOBs. The less compliant an LOB is, the more time and effort savings the analytics provide. Therefore, deployment to the entire IBM workforce is expected to save more than 20 person-years of effort if used on an annual basis. However, the even greater impact is a fundamental transformation in the way the company operates Through the analytics, job role data can be refreshed at a much higher frequency than annually to support many different existing business processes and enabling new business practices with their own monetary and effort savings or revenue achievement improvements. We next discuss the deployment to the entire company that is currently in progress.

5.2 Broad Deployment

We see many other opportunities to use the job role prediction for populations besides salespeople with similar circumstances. For example, IBM has some very large populations of employees in which the primary job role field is invalid almost all of the time unlike for sellers where it is valid most of the time. For these larger employee populations with very sparse data for primary job role, the savings will be even more significant. Going forward, we are enthusiastic about the ability to predict expertise from employees' digital breadcrumbs instead of constantly asking managers or employees to fill in the data. Invariably, there are compliance challenges with an annual update; keeping job roles and specialties accurate as people transfer, change organizations, or move to new jobs is almost impossible. As discussed above, the ability to predict the primary job role and specialty and keep each continuously updated will not only save countless person-hours but will yield more up-to-date and accurate information from which to make manpower planning decisions.

The deployment to the worldwide sales organization was performed in a one-time manner without any specific thought or development given to user interface and user experience design, or to system architecture. In preparing the deployment to the entire company, we are taking a design thinking approach [3]. This process has centered around constructing user stories for the job role and specialty prediction tasks. The initial outcome has been the identification of managers and other administrators as the primary system users rather than individual employees. Also, the form of the user experience has been set forth through an expertise inventory dashboard. Two initial wireframes of the user interface are

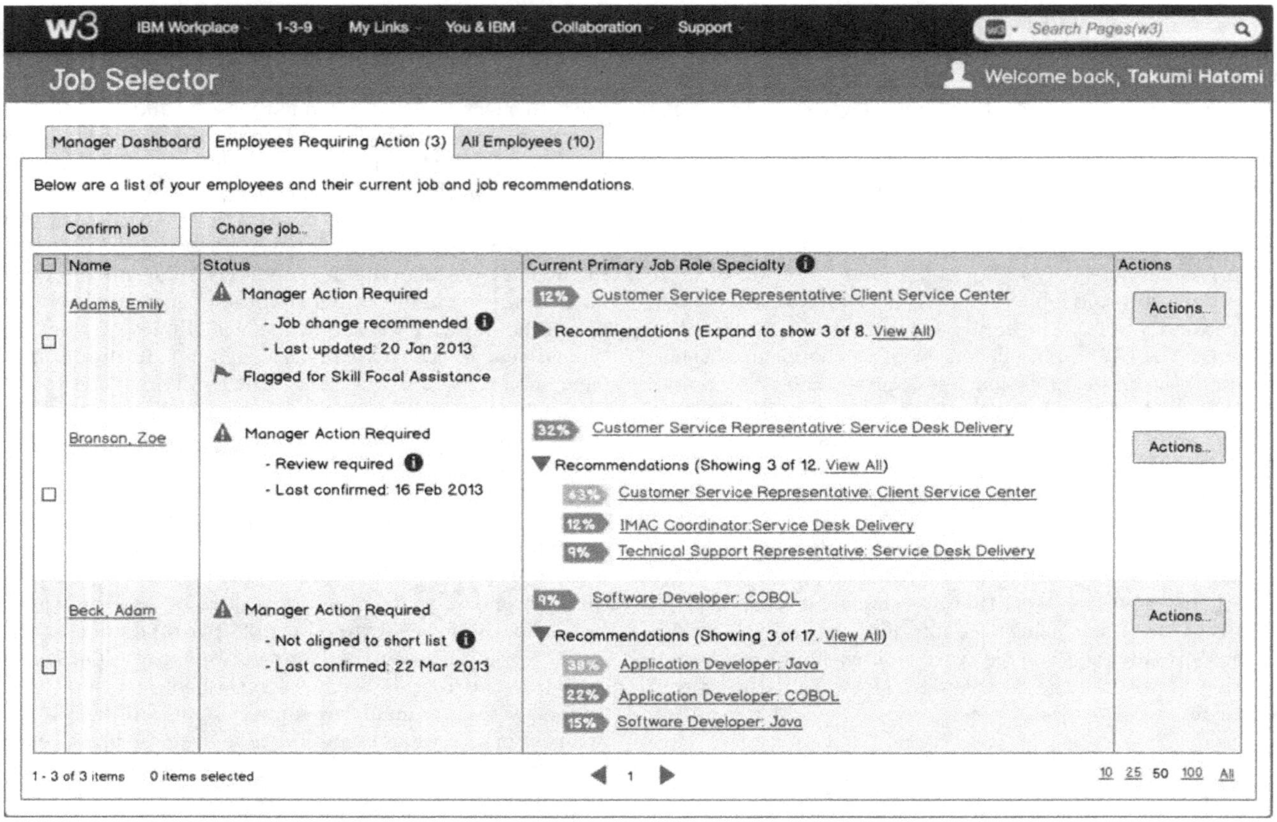

Figure 3: Wireframe of job role specialty prediction deployment.

shown in Fig. 3 and Fig. 4. The remaining work is in finalizing the user experience design and then developing the system architecture, which involves collecting and merging data from several siloed data warehouses, as well as putting together a flow of text analytics and supervised learning (through the Liblinear implementation of logistic regression) for cross-validation, training and testing. Finally, rolling out the system will require some level of education and evangelization within various business units throughout IBM.

5.3 Lessons Learned

In this section, we present lessons learned throughout the process of developing and deploying the predictive analytics from two perspectives. First, we give comments received from an HR practitioner involved in the project:

> "The prediction is only as good as the availability of data which helps the prediction. If you only have data that does not help inform the predictive analytics, you won't be able to achieve a very high accuracy level. So making data from other sources which helped us predict which specialty roles our sellers where working in was the key to success. And I think the more data that you can arm the predictive analytics with, the better the prediction will be. Determining whether different data types were useful in the prediction was a little trial and error and some sources that we thought ahead of time that would be good predictors turned out not to be. Also, adding data to the prediction algorithms which are not related to the prediction will actually make the prediction less accurate as it adds noise to the algorithm. Also, it is very important to have a pretty large control group for which you know already know the predicted value that you are trying to achieve. This is necessary to be able to validate and determine the accuracy of the predicted values."

This process also involved quite a bit of learning for the machine learning practitioners as well. One of them reports:

> "Before starting this project, I was only vaguely familiar with the expertise taxonomy. It has so many intricacies that we had to learn about just to frame the problem properly. But by doing so and by being cognizant of all of the specific business rules that are in play, we can really make an impact. In the end, we selected a fairly basic classifier, which is less exciting than something more novel would have been, but it has many desirable properties including scalability and ease of use, which will make a big difference in the final deployment. Understanding the HR folks' perspective and figuring out how we can make a transformational journey together has been enlightening and enjoyable."

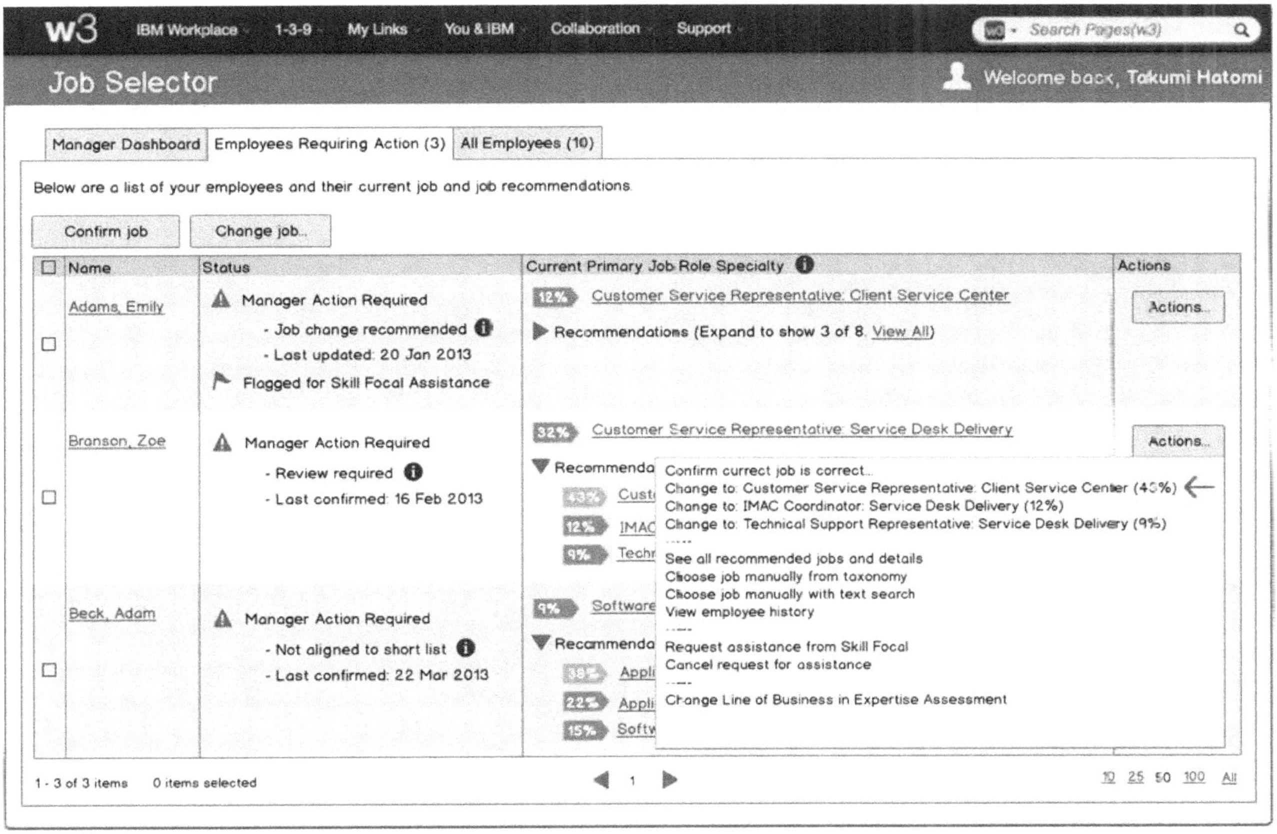

Figure 4: Wireframe of job role specialty prediction deployment with user choosing to accept the top classification.

6. CONCLUSION

The talent and human capital of IBM is its most valuable resource that must be harnessed properly using trusted expertise information. In this work, we developed a classification methodology to predict the expertise of employees based on features derived from the digital footprints of employees with the label set coming from IBM's expertise taxonomy. We deployed this system initially to fill in missing and invalid job role records and to correct erroneous records in the worldwide population of 40,000 IBM salespeople. The reduction in manual effort obtained through using predictive analytics is estimated to be one entire person-year. We are now in the process of deploying the system for use by the entire corporation, which should result in approximately twenty person-years of savings in annual updates of job roles and specialties. The impact is even greater than the savings in manual effort, because all business processes that depend on complete, accurate, and updated expertise data benefit from the predictions. Additionally, because of the steep reduction in effort, it will now be possible to update expertise assessments much more frequently than once a year, which is a transformation required to compete in today's dynamic business environment.

In developing the approach, we evaluated features from four different data sources: job title, HR information, social tags, and work products; several classification algorithms; and a few organizational chart-assisted postprocessing methods. The final choice of Liblinear ℓ_2-regularized logistic regression with bag-of-words features derived from the job title and 24 HR features yields cross-validation accuracy of 80% for a single prediction per employee and 96% accuracy if we allow three predictions per employee, which is more than enough for the application of interest. This classifier choice also allows us to present confidence values associated with predictions to the system user, which has emerged as an important feature from the user stories developed as part of the design thinking approach.

One immediate piece of future work is continued deployment and evangelization throughout the corporation. Other future work we have identified includes evaluation of additional work product data sources for different employee populations and expanding the response variable beyond job roles and job role specialties to industry specialization. Also, the simple tokenization and frequency-based word selection can be improved through advanced text analytics.

7. ACKNOWLEDGMENTS

The authors thank all of the members of the IBM Expertise team, including Karen Doherty and Anne Cunningham for support, and Derek Smith, Ed McFadden and Alison Eckholm for providing the design wireframes.

8. REFERENCES

[1] M. Baier, J. E. Carballo, A. J. Chang, Y. Lu, A. Mojsilović, M. J. Richard, M. Singh, M. S. Squillante, and K. R. Varshney. Sales-force

performance analytics and optimization. *IBM J. Res. Dev.*, 56(6):8, Nov./Dec. 2012.

[2] J. Bersin, K. O'Leonard, and W. Wang-Audia. High-impact talent analytics: Building a world-class HR measurement and analytics function, Sept. 2013.

[3] T. Brown. Design thinking. *Harvard Bus. Rev.*, 86(6):84–92, June 2008.

[4] C. Chelmis, V. Sorathia, and V. K. Prasanna. Enterprise wisdom captured socially. In *Proc. IEEE/ACM Int. Conf. Adv. Soc. Netw. Anal. Min.*, pages 1228–1235, Istanbul, Turkey, Aug. 2012.

[5] V. Chenthamarakshan, K. Dey, J. Hu, A. Mojsilovic, W. Riddle, and V. Sindhwani. Leveraging social networks for corporate staffing and expert recommendation. *IBM J. Res. Dev.*, 53(6):11, Nov. 2009.

[6] V. Chenthamarakshan, K. Dixit, M. Gattani, M. Goyal, P. Gupta, N. Kambhatla, R. Lotlikar, D. Majumdar, G. R. Parija, S. Roy, S. Soni, and K. Visweswariah. Effective decision support systems for workforce deployment. *IBM J. Res. Dev.*, 54(6):5, Nov./Dec. 2010.

[7] K. Ehrlich, C.-Y. Lin, and V. Griffiths-Fisher. Searching for experts in the enterprise: Combining text and social network analysis. In *Proc. ACM Conf. Supporting Group Work*, pages 117–126, Sanibel Island, FL, Nov. 2007.

[8] K. Ehrlich and N. S. Shami. Searching for expertise. In *Proc. SIGCHI Conf. Hum. Factors Comput. Syst.*, pages 1093–1096, Florence, Italy, Apr. 2008.

[9] R.-E. Fan, K.-W. Chang, C.-J. Hsieh, X.-R. Wang, and C.-J. Lin. LIBLINEAR: A library for large linear classification. *J. Mach. Learn. Res.*, 9:1871–1874, June 2008.

[10] D. Fang, K. R. Varshney, J. Wang, K. N. Ramamurthy, A. Mojsilović, and J. H. Bauer. uantifying and recommending expertise when new skills emerge. In *Proc. IEEE Int. Conf. Data Min. Workshops*, pages 672–679, Dallas, TX, Dec. 2013.

[11] I. Guy, U. Avraham, D. Carmel, S. Ur, M. Jacovi, and I. Ronen. Mining expertise and interests from social media. In *Proc. World Wide Web Conf.*, pages 515–525, Rio de Janiero, Brazil, May 2013.

[12] J. Hu, B. K. Ray, and M. Singh. Statistical methods for automated generation of service engagement staffing plans. *IBM J. Res. Dev.*, 51(3/4):281–293, May/Jul. 2007.

[13] A. John and D. Seligmann. Collaborative tagging and expertise in the enterprise. In *Proc. WWW Collabor. Web Tagging Workshop*, Edinburgh, UK, May 2006.

[14] C.-Y. Lin, L. Wu, Z. Wen, H. Tong, V. Griffiths-Fisher, L. Shi, and D. Lubensky. Social network analysis in enterprise. *Proc. IEEE*, 100(9):2759–2776, Sept. 2012.

[15] D. J. C. MacKay. Good error-correcting codes based on very sparse matrices. *IEEE Trans. Inf. Theory*, 45(2):399–431, Mar. 1999.

[16] S. Mehta, R. Pimplikar, A. Singh, L. R. Varshney, and K. Visweswariah. Efficient multifaceted screening of job applicants. In *Proc. Int. Conf. Extending Database Tech.*, pages 661–671, Genoa, Italy, Mar. 2013.

[17] N. Natarajan, I. S. Dhillon, P. Ravikumar, and A. Tewari. Learning with noisy labels. In *Adv. Neural Inf. Process. Syst. 26*, pages 1196–1204, Lake Tahoe, NV, Dec. 2013.

[18] Y. Naveh, Y. Richter, Y. Altshuler, D. L. Gresh, and D. P. Connors. Workforce optimization: Identification and assignment of professional workers using constraint programming. *IBM J. Res. Dev.*, 51(3/4):263–279, May/Jul. 2007.

[19] A. Perer, I. Guy, E. Uziel, I. Ronen, and M. Jacovi. Unearthing people from the SaND: Relationship discovery with social media in the enterprise. In *Proc. Int. AAAI Conf. Weblogs Soc. Med.*, pages 582–585, Barcelona, Spain, July 2011.

[20] N. S. Shami, K. Ehrlich, G. Gay, and J. T. Hancock. Making sense of strangers' expertise from signals in digital artifacts. In *Proc. SIGCHI Conf. Hum. Fact. Comput. Syst.*, pages 69–78, Boston, MA, Apr. 2009.

[21] A. Singh, R. Catherine, K. Visweswariah, V. Chenthamarakshan, and N. Kambhatla. PROSPECT: A system for screening candidates for recruitment. In *ACM Conf. Inf. Knowl. Manage.*, pages 659–668, Toronto, Canada, Oct. 2010.

[22] M. Singh, K. R. Varshney, J. Wang, A. Mojsilović, A. R. Gill, P. I. Faur, and R. Ezry. An analytics approach for proactively combating voluntary attrition of employees. In *Proc. IEEE Int. Conf. Data Min. Workshops*, pages 317–323, Brussels, Belgium, Dec. 2012.

[23] L. Terveen and D. W. McDonald. Social matching: A framework and research agenda. *ACM Trans. Comput.-Hum. Int.*, 12(3):401–434, Sept. 2005.

[24] K. R. Varshney, J. Wang, A. Mojsilović, D. Fang, and J. H. Bauer. Predicting and recommending skills in the social enterprise. In *Proc. AAAI ICWSM Workshop Social Comput. Workforce 2.0*, pages 20–23, Cambridge, MA, July 2013.

[25] K. L. Wagstaff. Machine learning that matters. In *Proc. Int. Conf. Mach. Learn.*, pages 529–536, Edinburgh, United Kingdom, Jun.–Jul. 2012.

[26] D. Wang, M. T. Al Amin, T. Abdelzaher, D. Roth, C. Voss, L. Kaplan, S. Tratz, J. Laoudi, and D. Briesch. Provenance-assisted classification in social networks. *IEEE J. Sel. Topics Signal Process.*, 8(4), Aug. 2014.

[27] J. Wang, K. R. Varshney, A. Mojsilović, D. Fang, and J. H. Bauer. Expertise assessment with multi-cue semantic information. In *Proc. IEEE Int. Conf. Serv. Oper. Logist. Informat.*, pages 534–539, Dongguan, China, July 2013.

Applying Data Mining Techniques to Address Critical Process Optimization Needs in Advanced Manufacturing

Li Zheng, Chunqiu Zeng, Lei Li,
Yexi Jiang, Wei Xue, Jingxuan Li,
Chao Shen, Wubai Zhou, Hongtai Li,
Liang Tang, Tao Li
School of Computer Science
Florida International University
{lzhen001,czeng001,taoli}@cs.fiu.edu

Bing Duan, Ming Lei,
Pengnian Wang
ChangHong COC Display Devices Co., Ltd
35 East Mianxing High-Tech Park
Mianyang, Sichuan, China 621000
{bing.duan,thunder,wpn}@changhong.com

ABSTRACT

Advanced manufacturing such as aerospace, semi-conductor, and flat display device often involves complex production processes, and generates large volume of production data. In general, the production data comes from products with different levels of quality, assembly line with complex flows and equipments, and processing craft with massive controlling parameters. The scale and complexity of data is beyond the analytic power of traditional IT infrastructures. To achieve better manufacturing performance, it is imperative to explore the underlying dependencies of the production data and exploit analytic insights to improve the production process. However, few research and industrial efforts have been reported on providing manufacturers with integrated data analytical solutions to reveal potentials and optimize the production process from data-driven perspectives.

In this paper, we design, implement and deploy an integrated solution, named `PDP-Miner`, which is a data analytics platform customized for process optimization in Plasma Display Panel (PDP) manufacturing. The system utilizes the latest advances in data mining technologies and Big Data infrastructures to create a complete analytical solution. Besides, our proposed system is capable of supporting automatically configuring and scheduling analysis tasks, and balancing heterogeneous computing resources. The system and the analytic strategies can be applied to other advanced manufacturing fields to enable complex data analysis tasks. Since 2013, `PDP-Miner` has been deployed as the data analysis platform of ChangHong COC[1]. By taking the advantages of our system, the overall PDP yield rate has increased from 91% to 94%. The monthly production is boosted by 10,000 panels, which brings more than 117 million RMB of revenue improvement per year[2].

Categories and Subject Descriptors: H.2.8[Database Applications]: Data Mining; H.4[Information Systems Applications]: Miscellaneous

Keywords: Advanced Manufacturing, Big Data, Data Mining Platform, Process Optimization

1. INTRODUCTION

The manufacturing industry involves the production of merchandise for use or sale using labor and machines, tools, chemical processing, etc. It has been the mainstay of many developed economies and remains an important driver of GDP (Gross Domestic Product). According to the Bureau of Economic Analysis data, every dollar goods in manufacturing generates $1.48 in economic activity, the highest economic multiplier among major economic sector[3]. With the advancement of new technologies, a lot of manufacturers utilize cutting-edge materials and emerging capabilities enabled by physical, biological, chemical and computer sciences. The improved manufacturing process often refers to as "advanced manufacturing" [14, 28]. For example, organizations in oil and gas industry apply new technologies to transform raw data into actionable insight to improve asset value and product yield while enhancing safety and protecting the environment.

In advanced manufacturing, a medium-sized or large manufacturing sector often arranges complex and elaborate production processes according to the product structure, and generates large volume of production data collected by sensor technologies [8], Manufacturing Execution System (MES) [13], and Enterprise Resources Planning (ERP) [22]. In practice, the production data contains intricate dependencies among a tremendous amount of controlling parameters in the production workflow. Generally, it is extremely difficult or even impossible for analysts to manually explore such dependencies, let alone proposing strategies to potentially optimize the workflow.

Fortunately, the use of data analytics offers the manufacturers great opportunities to acquire informative messages

[1]ChangHong COC Display Devices Co., Ltd is one of the world's largest display device manufacturing companies in China (http://www.cocpdp.com).

[2]http://articles.e-works.net.cn/mes/article113579.htm.

[3]JEC Democratic staff calculations based on data from the Bureau of Economic Analysis, Industry Data, Input-Output Accounts, Industry-by-Industry Total Requirements after Redefinitions (1998 to 2011).

KDD'14, August 24–27, 2014, New York, NY, USA.

http://dx.doi.org/10.1145/2623330.2623347.

Table 1: Perspective Differences Between Manufacturers and Data Analysts.

	Capacity	Capability	Knowledge
Manufacturers	• huge production output • sophisticated workflow • complex supply chain	• control yield rate • optimize production line • effective parameter setting	• private Know-How • high dependency to experts • high cost of testing
Data Analysts	• large number of samples • high-dimensional data • complex param dependencies	• process optimization • feature reduction and selection • feature association analysis	• utilize domain expertise • knowledge sharing • knowledge management
Application Gap	• utilize customized data analysis algorithms to mine the underlying knowledge; • provide configurable task platforms to allow automatic taskflow execution; • enable efficient knowledge representation and management.		

towards optimizing the production workflow. However in practice, there is a significant **application gap** between manufacturers and data analysts in observing the data and using automation tools. Table 1 highlights the perspective difference between manufacturers and analysts on three important aspects: (1) *Capacity*, i.e. what the data looks like; (2) *Capability*, i.e., how the data can be utilized; and (3) *Knowledge*, i.e., how to perform knowledge discovery and management.

To bridge the gap, it is imperative to provide automated tools to the manufacturers to enhance their capability of analyzing production data. Data analytics in advanced manufacturing, especially data mining approaches, have been targeting several important fields, such as product quality analysis [20, 26], failure analysis of production [3, 25], production planning and scheduling analysis [1, 2], analytic platform implementation [7, 8], etc. However, few research and industrial efforts have been reported on providing manufacturers with an **integrated data analytical platform**, to enable automatic analysis of the production data and efficient optimization of the production process. Our goal is to provide such a solution to practically fill the gap.

1.1 A Concrete Case: PDP Manufacturing

Plasma Display Panel (PDP) manufacturing produces over 10,000 panels for a daily throughput in ChangHong COC Display Devices Co., Ltd (COC for short). The production line is near 6,000 meters and the process contains 75 assembling routines, and 279 major production equipments with more than 10,000 parameters. The average production time throughout the manufacturing process requires 76 hours. Specifically, the workflow consists of three major procedures shown in Figure 1, i.e., *front panel*, *rear panel*, and *panel assembly*. Each procedure contains multiple sequentially executed flows, and each flow is composed of multiple key routines. The first two procedures are executed in parallel, and each pair of front and rear panels will be assembled in the assembly procedure. Figure 2 depicts the real assembly line of one routine (Tin-doped Indium Oxide, ITO) in front panel procedure, which gives us a sense of how complex the complete production process will be.

There are 83 types of equipments in the PDP manufacturing process, each of which has a different set of parameters to fulfill the corresponding processing tasks. The parameters are often preset to certain values to ensure the normal operation of each equipment. However, the observed parameter values often deviate from the preset values. Further in the production environment, external factors, e.g., temperature, humidity, and atmospheric pressure, may potentially affect

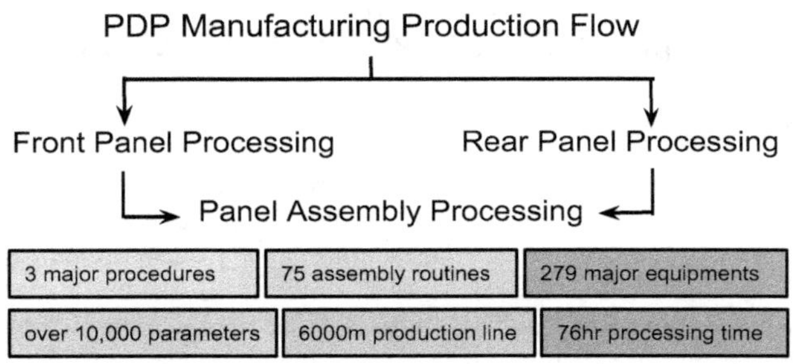

Figure 1: PDP Manufacturing Production Flow.

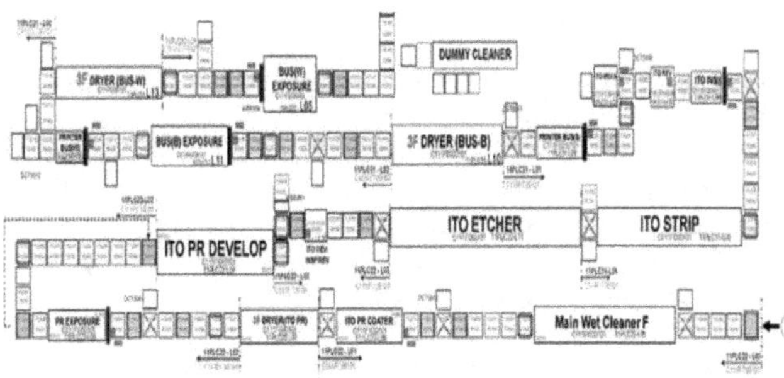

Figure 2: An Example Routine in PDP Workflow.

the product quality as the raw materials and equipments are sensitive to these factors. The observed values of external factors vary significantly in terms of sensor locations and acquisition time. The production process generates a huge amount of production data (10 Gigabytes per day with 30 Million records).

In daily operations, the manufactures are concerned with how to improve the yield rate of the production. To achieve this goal, several questions need to be carefully addressed, including

- What are the key parameters whose values can significantly differentiate qualified products from defective products?
- How the parameter value changes affect the production rate?
- What are the effective parameter recipes to ensure high yield rate?

Answering these questions, however, is a non-trivial task due to the scale and complexity of the production data, and is impossible for domain analysts to manually explore the data. Hence, it is necessary to automate the optimization process using appropriate infrastructural and algorithmic solutions.

1.2 Challenges and Proposed Solutions

The massive production data poses great challenges to manufacturers in effectively optimizing the production workflow. During the past two years, we have been working closely with the technicians and engineers from COC to investigate data-driven techniques for improving the yield rate of production. During this process, we have identified two key challenges and proposed the corresponding solutions to each challenge as follows.

In general, highly automatic production process often generates large volume of data, containing a myriad of controlling parameters with the corresponding observed values. The parameters may have malformed or missing values due to inaccurate sensing or transmission. Therefore, it is crucial to efficiently store and preprocess these data, in order to handle the increasing scale as well as the incomplete status of the data. In addition, the analytics of the production data is a cognitive activity towards the production workflow, which embodies an iterative process of exploring the data, analyzing the data, and representing the insights. A practical system should provide an integrated and high-efficiency solution to support the process.

CHALLENGE 1. *Facing the enormous data with sustained growth, how to efficiently support large-scale data analysis tasks and provide prompt guidance to different routines in the workflow?*

Existing data mining products, such as Weka [9], SPSS and SQL Sever Data Tools, provide functionalities to facilitate users to conduct the analysis. However, these products are designed for small or medium scale data analysis, and hence cannot be applied to our problem setting. To address CHALLENGE 1, we design and implement an integrated *Data Analytics Platform* based on a distributed system (*FIU-Miner*) [32] to support high-performance analysis. The platform manages all the production data in a distributed environment, which is capable of configuring and executing data preprocessing and data analysis tasks in an automatic way. The platform has the following functionalities: (1) cross-language data mining algorithms integration, (2) real-time monitoring of system resource consumption, and (3) balancing the node workload in clusters.

Besides CHALLENGE 1, in advanced manufacturing, the controlling parameters in the production workflow may correlate with each other, and potentially affect the production yield rate. Several analysis tasks identified by PDF analysts include (1) discovering the most related parameters (TASK 1); (2) quantifying the parameter correlation with the product quality (TASK 2); and (3) proposing novel parameter recipes (i.e., parameter value combinations) to improve the yield rate (TASK 3). A reasonable way to effectively fulfill these tasks is to utilize suitable data mining and machine learning techniques. However, existing algorithms cannot be directly applied to these tasks, as they may either lack the capability of handling large-scale data, or fail to consider domain-specific data characteristics.

CHALLENGE 2. *Facing various types of mining requirements, how to effectively adapt existing algorithms for customized analysis tasks that comprehensively consider the domain characteristics?*

In our proposed system, CHALLENGE 2 is effectively tackled by developing appropriate data mining algorithms and adapting them to the problem of analyzing the manufacturing data. In particular, to address TASK 1, we propose an ensemble feature selection method to generate a stable parameter set based on the results of various feature selection methods. To address TASK 2, we utilize regression models to describe the relationship between product quality and various parameters. To address TASK 3, we apply association based methods to identify possible feature combinations that can significantly improve the quality of product. To make the system an integrated solution, we also provide the functionalities of data exploration (including comparative analysis and data cube) and result management.

Our proposed solution, `PDP-Miner`, is essentially a scalable, easy-to-use and customized data analysis system for large-scale and complex mining tasks on manufacturing data. Exploitation of the latest advances in data mining and machine learning technologies unleashes the potential to achieve three critical objectives, including *enhancing exploration and production*, *improving refining and manufacturing efficiency*, and *optimizing global operations*. Since 2013, `PDP-Miner` has been deployed as the production data analysis platform of COC. By using our system, the overall yield rate has increased from 91% to 94%, which has brought more than 117 million RMB of revenue per year[4].

1.3 Roadmap

The rest of the paper is organized as follows. Section 2 presents an overview of our proposed system, starting from introducing the system architecture, followed by the details of three interleaved analysis modules, including data exploration, operational analysis and result representation. In Section 3, we explore possible feature selection strategies to identify pivotal parameters in the production process, and propose an ensemble feature selection approach to obtain robust yet predominant parameter set. In Section 4, we discuss the task of measuring the importance of parameters, and utilize regression models to examine how the parameter change will affect the yield rate. Section 5 describes our strategy of mining the knowledge of data, that is, to employ discriminative analysis (e.g., association mining) to reveal the dependencies of parameters. Section 6 represents the system deployment, in which system performance evaluation is described and some important real findings are presented. Finally, Section 7 concludes the paper.

2. SYSTEM OVERVIEW

The overall architecture of `PDP-Miner` is shown in Figure 3. The system, from bottom to top, consists of two components: *Data Analytics Platform* (including *Task Management Layer* and *Physical Resource Layer*) and *Data Analysis Modules*.

Data Analytics Platform provides a fast, integrated, and user-friendly system for data mining in distributed environment, where all the data analysis tasks accomplished by *Data Analysis Modules* are configured as workflows and also automatically scheduled. Details of this module are provided in Section 2.1.

Data Analysis Modules provide data-mining solutions and methodologies to identify important production factors, in-

[4]http://articles.e-works.net.cn/mes/article113579.htm

cluding controlling parameters and their underlying correlations, in order to optimize production process. These methods are incorporated into the platform as functions and modules towards specific analysis tasks. In PDP-Miner, there are 3 major analytic modules: *data exploration*, *data analysis*, and *result management*. In Section 2.2, more details are provided by presenting our data mining solutions customized for PDP production data. A sample system for demonstration purpose is available at http://bigdata-node01.cs.fiu.edu/PDP-Miner/demo.html.

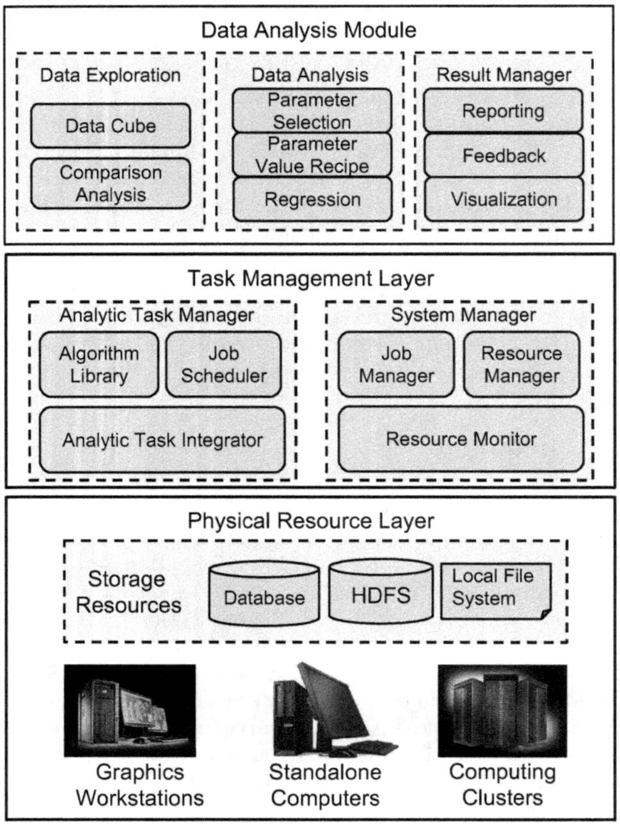

Figure 3: System Architecture.

2.1 Data Analytics Platform

Traditional data-mining tools or existing products [9, 21, 19, 18, 23, 30] have three major limitations when applied to specific industrial sectors or production process analysis: 1) They support neither large-scale data analysis nor handy algorithm plug-in; 2) They require advanced programming skills when configuring and integrating algorithms for complex data mining tasks; and 3) They do not support large scale of analysis tasks running simultaneously in heterogeneous environments.

To address the limitations of existing products, we develop the data analytic platform based on our previous large-scale data mining system, FIU-Miner [32], to facilitate the execution of data mining tasks. The data analytic platform provides a set of novel functionalities with the following significant advantages [32]:

- *Easy operation for task configuration.* Users, especially non-data-analyst, can easily configure a complex data mining task by assembling existing algorithms into a workflow. Configuration can be done through a graphic interface. Execution details including task scheduling and resource management are transparent to users.
- *Flexible supports for various programs.* The existing data mining tools, such as data preprocessing libraries, can be utilized in this platform. There is no restriction on programming languages for those programs exist or to be implemented, since our data analytic platform is capable of distributing the tasks to proper runtime environments.
- *Effective resource management.* To optimize the utilization of computing resources, tasks are executed by considering various factors such as algorithm implementation, server load balance, and the data location. Various runtime environments are supported for running data analysis tasks, including graphics workstations, stand-alone computers, and clusters.

2.2 Data Analysis Modules

2.2.1 Data Exploration

The *Comparison Analysis* and *Data Cube* are capable of assisting data analysts to explore PDP operation data efficiently and effectively.

Comparison Analysis *Comparison Analysis*, shown in Figure 6(a), provides a set of tools to help data analysts quickly identify parameters whose values are statistically different between two datasets according to several statistical indicators. *Comparison Analysis* is able to extract the top-k most significant parameters based on predefined indicators or customized ranking criteria. It also supports comparison on the same set of parameters over two different datasets to identify the top-k most representative parameters of two specified datasets.

Data Cube *Data Cube*, shown in Figure 6(b), provides a convenient approach to explore high dimensional data so that data analysts can have a glance at the characteristics of the dataset. In addition, *Data Cube* can conduct multi-level inspection of the data by applying OLAP techniques. Data analysts can customize a multi-dimensional cube over the original data. Thus, the constructed data cubes allow users to explore multiple dimensional data at different granularities and evaluate the data using pre-defined measurements.

2.2.2 Data Analysis

The data mining approaches in algorithm library can be organized as a configurable procedure in *Operation Panel*, as shown in Figure 6(c). The *Operation Panel* is a unified interface to build a workflow for executing such task automatically. The *Operation Panel* contains the following three main tasks:

Important Parameter Selection By modeling the important parameter discovery task as a feature selection problem, several feature selection algorithms are implemented adaptively based on the production data. Moreover, an advanced ensemble framework is designed to combine multiple feature selection outputs. Based on these implementations, the system is able to generate a list of important parameters, shown in Figure 6(d).

Regression Analysis The purpose of *Regression Analysis* (shown in Figure 6(f)) is to discover the correlations between the yield rate and the controlling parameters. The regression model not only indicates whether a correlation exists between a parameter and the yield rate but also quantifies the extent that the change of the parameter value will influence the yield rate.

Discriminative Analysis Discriminative analysis (See Figure 6(e)) is an alternative approach to identify the feature values that have strong indication to the target labels (panel grade). By grouping and leveraging the features of individual panels, this approach is able to find the most discriminative rules (a set of features with the values) to the target labels according to the data.

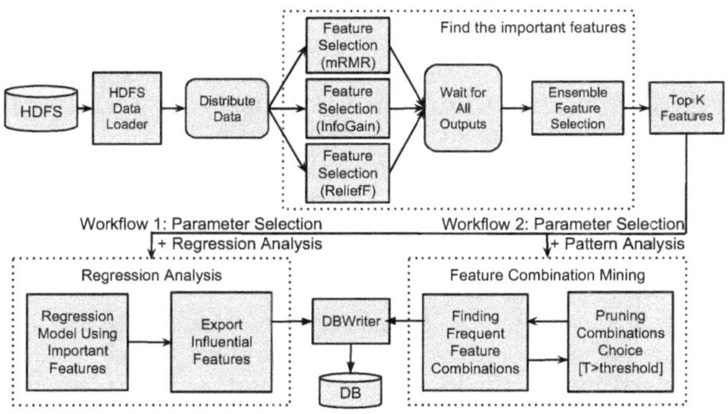

Figure 4: A Sample Workflow for PDP Manufacturing Data Analysis.

To illustrate how *Data Analysis Modules* are incorporated with the *Data Analytics Platform*, Figure 4 illustrates two example analytic tasks wrapped as two workflows. As shown, *Workflow 1* indicates an analysis procedure of building regression models with selected important parameters; *Workflow 2* indicates another procedure of identifying reasonable parameter value combinations based on previously selected parameters. The *Operation Panel* provides a user-friendly interface shown in Figure 5 to facilitate workflow assembly and configuration. Users only need to explicitly create tasks dependencies before the workflow executing automatically by our platform.

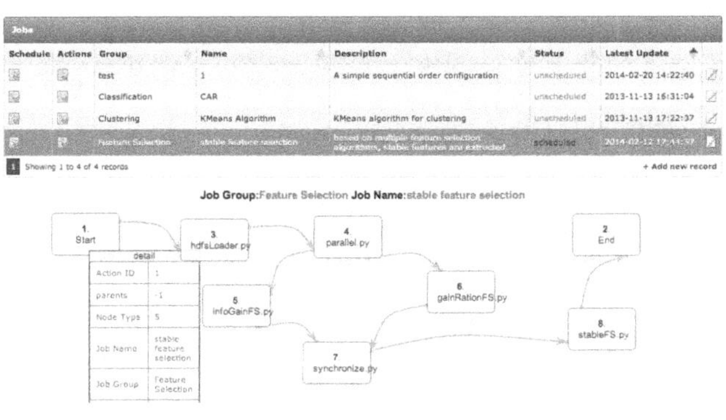

Figure 5: Data Analysis Workflow Configuration.

2.2.3 *Result Management*

The analytic results are being categorized into three types: the important parameter list, the parameter value combinations, and the regression model Templates are designed to support automatically storage, update, and retrieval of discovered patterns. Results are recorded based on analysis tasks and can be organized in terms of important equipment, top parameters, and task list. For each result, corresponding domain experts can refine and give feedback, shown in Figure 6(h). In addition, visualizations are provided to summarize the analytic results, collected feedbacks, and status of current knowledge (shown in Figure 6(g)). It provides a flexible interface for maintaining domain knowledge very efficiently.

3. ENSEMBLE FEATURE SELECTION

In manufacturing management, the primary goal is to improve the yield rate of products by optimizing the manufacturing workflow. To this end, one important question is to identify the key parameters (features) in the workflow, which can significantly differentiate qualified products from defective ones. However, it is a non-trivial task to select a subset of features from the huge feature space. To tackle this problem, we initially experimented several widely used feature selection approaches. Specifically, we use Information Gain [10], mRMR [5] and ReliefF [24] to perform parameter selection. Figure 7 shows the top 10 selected features by these three algorithms on a sampled PDP dataset.

As observed in Figure 7, the three feature subsets share only one common feature ("Char_020101-008"). Such a phenomenon indicates the instability of feature selection methods, as it is difficult to identify the importance of a feature from a mixed view of feature subsets. In general, the selected are the most relevant to the labels and less redundant to each other based on certain criteria. However, the correlated features may be ignored if we select a small subset of features. In terms of knowledge discovery, the selected feature subset is insufficient to represent important knowledge about redundant features. Further, different algorithms select features based on different criteria, which renders the feature selection result instable.

Information gain(top10)	mRMR(top10)	ReliefF(top10)
Char_110101-004	Char_020101-016	Char_110101-009
Char_110101-003	Char_020101-004	Char_110101-008
Char_110101-005	Char_020101-008	Char_100102-079
Char_110101-002	Char_020101-009	Char_100101-199
Char_110101-006	Char_020101-010	Char_100101-208
Char_110101-001	Char_020101-007	Char_100101-212
Char_020101-008	Char_020101-006	Char_100102-013
Char_020101-017	Char_020101-003	Char_100101-213
Char_100101-168	Char_020101-014	Char_100102-081
Char_020101-013	Char_020101-013	Char_020101-008

Figure 7: Selected Features by Different Algorithms.

The stability issue of feature selection has been studied recently [4, 12] under the assumption of small sample size. The results of these work indicate that different algorithms with equal classification performance may have a wide variance in terms of stability. Another direction of stable feature selection involves exploring the consensus information among different feature groups [17, 29, 31], which first identifies consensus feature groups for a given dataset, and then performs selection from the feature groups. However, these methods fail to consider the correlation between selected features and unselected ones, which might be important to guide us for feature selection.

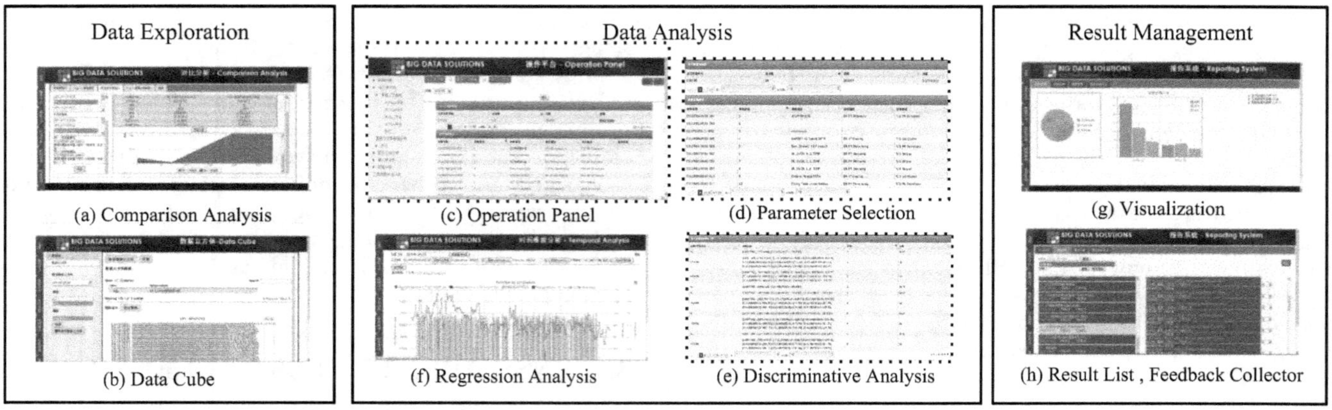

Figure 6: PDP-Miner Analysis Modules.

In our system, inspired by ensemble clustering [27, 15], we employ the ensemble strategy on the results of various feature selection methods to maintain the robustness and stability of feature selection. The problem setting of stable feature selection is defined as follows. Given a dataset with M features, we employ N feature selection methods which for an arbitrary feature i return a N-lengthed vector $\mathbf{y}_i, i = 1, 2, \ldots, M$. Each entry of $\mathbf{y}_i$ is 1 or 0 indicating whether the feature i is selected or not by the corresponding feature selection method. Since we are concerned with whether to select a feature or not, we assume a feature i, in the form of results of N feature selection methods, $\mathbf{y}_i$, is generated from a mixture of two multivariate components, indicating selected features and unselected features, i.e.,

$$p(\mathbf{y}_i) = \sum_{j=1}^{2} \pi_j p(\mathbf{y}_i|\boldsymbol{\theta}_j), \tag{1}$$

where π_j denotes the mixture probability of j-th component parameterized by $\boldsymbol{\theta}_j$, in which the n-th entry θ_{jn} means the probability of the output of n-th feature selection method equals to 1. We further assume conditional independence between feature selection methods. Therefore,

$$p(\mathbf{y}_i|\boldsymbol{\theta}_j) = \prod_{n=1}^{N} p(y_{in}|\theta_{jn}). \tag{2}$$

As the result of a feature selection method in the vector $\mathbf{y}_i$ is either selecting (1) or not selecting (0) the feature i, the probability of the feature i being selected by the n-th feature selection method, i.e., $p(y_{in}|\theta_{jn})$, could be represented by a Bernoulli distribution

$$p(y_{in}|\theta_{jn}) = \theta_{jn}^{y_{in}}(1-\theta_{jn})^{1-y_{in}}. \tag{3}$$

In addition, we assume that all the features are *i.i.d.* Then the log-likelihood of the unified probabilistic model is

$$\mathcal{L} = \sum_{i=1}^{M} \log \sum_{j=1}^{2} \pi_j p(\mathbf{y}_i|\boldsymbol{\theta}_j). \tag{4}$$

To learn the parameters π_j and $\boldsymbol{\theta}_j, j \in \{1, 2\}$, we use Expectation-Maximization (EM) algorithm. To this end, we introduce a series of hidden random variables $z_i, i = 1, 2$ to indicate $\mathbf{y}_i$ belonging to each component, i.e., the parameters of the random variable $z_{i1}, z_{z2}, z_{i1} + z_{i2} = 1$.

The iterative procedure of EM will be terminated when the likelihood of the mixture model does not change too much constrained by a predefined threshold. The hidden variable z_i indicates the probabilities of membership of feature $\mathbf{y}_i$ with respect to all mixture components. It is in some sense similar to the situation in Gaussian mixture models. The feature is assigned to the j-th component that the corresponding value z_{ij} is the largest in $z_{ij}, j \in \{1, 2\}$. As a feature selection method will eventually generate two subsets of features (selected or not), it is reasonable to make two mixture components.

After obtaining the assignments of features to components, say $\phi(z_i)$, we group features into two categories, i.e., selected/unselected. In practice, the number of selected features are significantly less than the unselected ones, and hence the features that are not selected by any feature selection method are put into a large category. The features in the other category are final feature selection results. Specifically for each component j, we pick the features that have the membership assignment, i.e., z_{ij}, greater than a predefined threshold τ, and then put these features into the selected category. In this way, we can discard features with low probabilities for selection, and hence the stability of feature selection can be achieved by assembling different feature selection results using the mixture model.

4. REGRESSION ANALYSIS

To optimize the production process, it is imperative to discover the parameters that have significant influence on the yield rate and quantify such influence. In our system, an actionable solution is to explicitly establish a relationship between controlling parameters and the yield rate, which can be achieved using regression analysis.

Formally, assume the daily observations are *i.i.d.* Then the relationship between features (parameters) and the yield rate can be modeled as a function $f(\boldsymbol{x}, \boldsymbol{w})$ with additive Gaussian noise, i.e.,

$$y = f(\boldsymbol{x}, \boldsymbol{w}) + \epsilon, \epsilon \sim \mathcal{N}(0, \beta^{-1}), \tag{5}$$

where y denotes the yield rate, $\boldsymbol{x} = (x_1, \cdots, x_d)^T$ denotes the set of features that may have impact on y, and $\boldsymbol{w}$ denotes the weight of features. The noise term is a zero mean Gaussian random variable with precision β.

In our system, we implement two linear regression based models: *ridge regression* and *lasso regression* [11]. From the perspective of maximum likelihood, the linear relationship can be expressed as

$$\ln p(y|\boldsymbol{w}, \beta) = \sum \ln \mathcal{N}(y_i|\boldsymbol{w}^T\boldsymbol{x}_i, \beta^{-1}). \quad (6)$$

For both models, we leverage least square to quantify the error, i.e.,

$$E(\boldsymbol{w}) = \begin{cases} \frac{1}{2}\sum_i(y_i - \boldsymbol{w}^T\boldsymbol{x}_i)^2 + \frac{1}{2}\lambda||\boldsymbol{w}||_2^2, \textit{ ridge regression} \\ \frac{1}{2}\sum_i(y_i - \boldsymbol{w}^T\boldsymbol{x}_i)^2 + \frac{1}{2}\lambda||\boldsymbol{w}||_1, \textit{ lasso regression} \end{cases}. \quad (7)$$

In advanced manufacturing domain, the number of features is usually large (in PDP scenario, the number of features is more than 10K), and therefore ensemble feature selection (described in Section 3) is applied before building the regression model. To conduct the regression, we incorporate three categories of features:

1. The parameters of the equipments involved in the manufacturing process. This category of features is collected from the log of the equipments.

2. The parameters of the environment, such as temperature, humidity, and pressure, etc. This category of the features is collected from the deployed sensors in each workshop.

3. The features of the materials, such as the viscosity, consistency, and concentration, etc. This category of feature is collected from material descriptions and reports.

After integrating all the features, we normalize each dimension of the features using standardization, i.e. $\frac{x-\bar{X}}{std(X)}$.

The linear regression can be solved efficiently. When the dataset is small, the closed form can be directly obtained, i.e. $\hat{\boldsymbol{w}}^{ridge} = (\lambda\boldsymbol{I} + \boldsymbol{X}^T\boldsymbol{X})^{-1}\boldsymbol{X}^T\boldsymbol{y}$ for ridge regression and $\hat{\boldsymbol{w}}^{lasso} = sgn((\boldsymbol{X}^T\boldsymbol{X})^{-1}\boldsymbol{X}^T)(|(\boldsymbol{X}^T\boldsymbol{X})^{-1}\boldsymbol{X}^T\boldsymbol{y}| - \lambda)$ for lasso regression, where $\boldsymbol{X}$ denotes the matrix of the features with ith row indicating the feature set $\boldsymbol{x}_i$. For large datasets, we train the model iteratively by using stochastic gradient descent for ridge regression and coordinate gradient for lasso regression.

The weights of the trained model can be intuitively interpreted. Firstly, the value $|\boldsymbol{w}_i|$ indicates the conditional correlation between the feature x_i and the yield rate given the other features. In general, a larger weight indicates a larger conditional correlation. Moreover, the corresponding p-value of each feature can be leveraged to measure the likelihood of the correlation. The smaller the p-value, the less likely such correlation is false.

By performing regression analysis on the PDP data, we find some interesting correlations. For example:

1. The variance of the humidity of the air has positive correlation wtih the yield rate. This provides empirical evidence to support the conjecture of PDP technicians that the variance of the humidity plays an important role in affecting the yield rate.

2. The pressure of the air has positive correlation with the yield rate, whereas its variance changes inversely. The less the pressure changes, the higher the yield rate would be.

3. The workshop temperature and its variance vary slightly within a small range, and the corresponding weight is very small. In practice, the change of the temperature may affect the usage of materials as well as the production process. Hence, it is often being carefully controlled by technicians.

5. DISCRIMINATIVE ANALYSIS

Discriminative analysis mines the feature knowledge of the PDP panel data from a different perspective. It is used as an alternative way to reveal the underlying relationship between the features and the panel grades. Specifically, it helps discover parameter recipes as well as sets of feature values which are closely related to qualified panels and defective panels. In PDP-Miner, the techniques of *association based classification* [16] and low-support discriminative pattern mining [6] are leveraged to conduct the discriminative analysis.

5.1 Association based classification

Association based classification integrates classification and association rule mining to discover a special subset of association rules called *class association rules (CARs)*. A CAR is an implication of the form $\{r : F \rightarrow y\}$, where F is a subset of the entire feature value set and y denotes the class label (the PDP panel grade in our scenario). Each CAR is associated with support s and confidence c, indicating how many records contain F and the ratio of records containing F that are labeled as y. In general, CARs contain strong discriminative information to infer the PDP panel grades. A rule-based classifier can be built by selecting a subset of the CARs that collectively cause the least error, i. e. $r_1, r_2, ..., r_n \rightarrow y$.

Compared with feature selection and regression analysis, association based classification enables the possibility of early detection due to the unique characteristics of CARs. If CARs only refer to the features in the early manufacturing process, this method can quickly identify semi-finished yet defective panels, and prevent further resource waste.

The early detection strategy is useful in the advanced manufacturing domain, as any earlier detected bad semi-finished product can directly reduce the manufacturing cost. For the production with a large number of assembling procedures, such a reduction is not trivial.

5.2 Low support discriminative pattern mining

A manufacturing process could consist of hundreds of assembling procedures with thousands of tunning parameters. When the feature dimension is high, standard association rule based methods would become time-consuming. A naïve solution for this scenario is to increase the support threshold to speed up mining. However, this strategy may miss interesting low-support patterns.

To address this problem, we adapt the idea of low support pattern mining algorithm (*SMP*) [6] and integrate the algorithm into PDP-miner. *SMP* aims at mining the discriminative patterns by leveraging a family of anti-monotonic measures called *SupMaxK*. *SupMaxK* organizes the discriminative pattern set into nested layers of subsets.

5.2.1 Discriminative Patterns Detection

Many association mining methods utilize "support" to select rules/patterns. Different from the traditional association mining, the "discriminative support" is defined to measure the quality (discriminative capability) of the rule set:

$$DisS(\alpha) = |S_{qualified}(\alpha) - S_{defective}(\alpha)|, \quad (8)$$

where α is a set of parameter values, $S_{qualified}$ and $S_{defective}$ denote the "support" of α over two classes, indicating whether the target panel is qualified or defective.

A naïve implementation using this measure suffers from low efficiency [6] when pruning frequent non-discriminative rules. To address this issue, a new measure – $SupMaxK(\alpha)$ is introduced to help prune unrelated patterns by estimating $S_{defective}(\beta)$.

$$SupMaxK(\alpha) = S_{qualified}(\alpha) - max_{\beta \in \alpha}(S_{defective}(\beta)), \quad (9)$$

where $|\beta| = K$, β is the subset of α. Three reasons make this measure useful: (1) $SupMaxK$ can help select more discriminative patterns as K increases; (2) $SupMaxK$ is a lower bound of $DisS$; (3) $SupMaxK$ is anti-monotonic.

Due to the anti-monotonic property of $SupMaxK$, SMP can naturally be utilized to mine the discriminative patterns whose support are low but have strong indication to the panel grades.

6. SYSTEM DEPLOYMENT

We evaluate our proposed system from two aspects: the system performance and the real findings. The evaluation demonstrates that our system is a practical solution for large-scale data analysis, through integrating and adapting classic data mining techniques and customizing them for specific domains, particularly, advanced manufacturing.

6.1 System performance

Our system is able to perform large-scale data analysis and can be easily scale up. To demonstrate the scalability of `PDP-Miner`, we design a series of cluster workload balance experiments in both static and dynamic computing environments. The experiments are conducted on a testbed cluster separated from the real production system. The cluster consists of 8 computing nodes with different computing performances.

In the experiments, one frequent analysis task of `PDP-Miner` is created using the job configuration interface, which consists of two sequential functions, i.e., Parameter Selection → Parameter Combination Extraction. For evaluation purpose, ten different datasets (about 30 million records) are generated by sampling from the original 1-year production datasets. The analysis task is conducted over these datasets in two types of experiments: *Exp I Workload balance in a static environment* and *Exp II Workload balance in a dynamic environment.* In the following, we describe the detailed experimental plans as well as the results.

Exp I: Each node in the cluster is deployed with one *Worker*. We configure 10 parameter selection tasks with different running times in `PDP-Miner`. Each job starts at time 0 and repeats with a random interval (< 1 minutes). Figure 8 shows how our system balances the workloads based on the underlying infrastructures. The x-axis denotes the time and the y-axis denotes the average number of completed jobs for each *Worker* at the given moment during the task execution. Clearly, the accumulated number of completed jobs (the blue solid bars) increases linearly, whereas the amortized number of completed jobs (the white empty bars) remains stable. This shows that when the cluster remains unchanged, our system achieves a good balance of the resource utilization by properly distributing jobs. The effective distribution of jobs guarantees a full use of existing resources to maximize the throughput without incurring resource bottleneck.

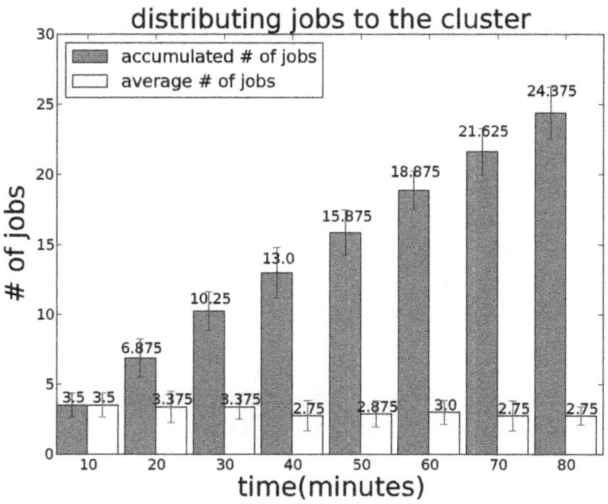

Figure 8: Load Balance in Static Environment.

Exp II: To investigate the resource utilization of `PDP-Miner` under a dynamic environment, we initially provide four nodes (node1∼4), each with 1 *Worker*, and then add the other four nodes (node5∼8) 10 minutes later. To emulate the nodes with different computing powers, the newly-added nodes are deployed with 2 to 5 *Workers*, respectively. Each *Worker* is restricted to use only 1 CPU core at a time, so the node deployed with more *Workers* can have more powerful computing resources. Figure 9 shows the number of jobs completed by each node during observing the system execution for 70 minutes. The number of jobs on each node is segmented every 10 minutes. It clearly shows that the number of completed jobs is proportional to the number of *Workers* on each node, which indicates that our system can balance the workloads in a dynamically changed cluster. It also demonstrates that the entire system can be linearly extended with resources of different computing power.

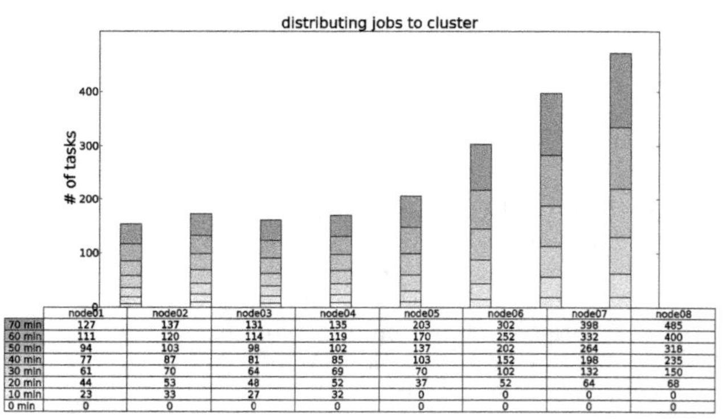

	node01	node02	node03	node04	node05	node06	node07	node08
70 min	127	137	131	135	203	302	398	485
60 min	111	120	114	119	170	252	332	400
50 min	94	103	98	102	137	202	264	318
40 min	77	87	81	85	103	152	198	235
30 min	61	70	64	69	70	102	132	150
20 min	44	53	48	52	37	52	64	68
10 min	23	33	27	32	0	0	0	0
0 min	0	0	0	0	0	0	0	0

Figure 9: Load Balance in Dynamic Environment.

6.2 Real Findings

`PDP-Miner` has been playing an important role on revealing deeper and finer relations behind big data in COC's real practice. As an example, WorkFlow1 in Figure 4 is executed to extract important parameters from a single procedure, named barrier-rib (BR). 30 selected parameters are reported

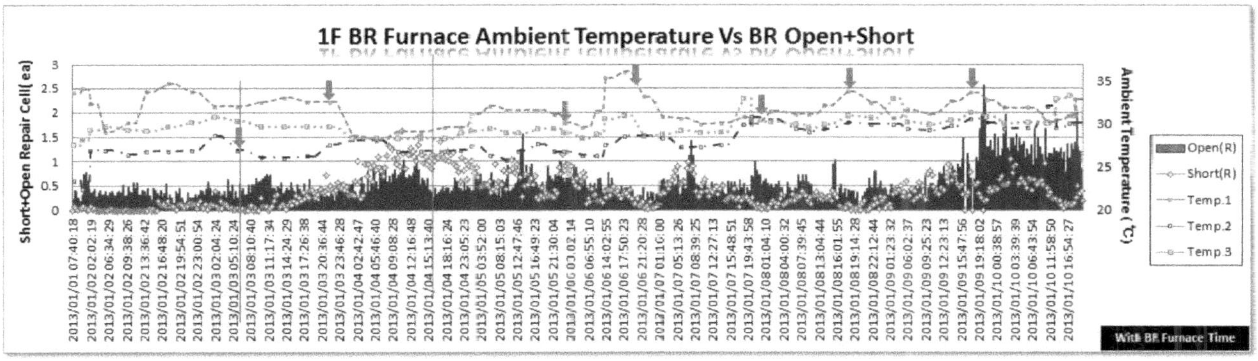

Figure 10: Real Case of Regression Analysis Results.

and verified by domain experts. Within these 30 parameters, 15 of them have already been carefully monitored by the analysts, which is consistent with domain knowledge. Another 9 parameters, which are not monitored in the previous production, are confirmed to have great impact on the product quality. After applying WorkFlow1 to the entire production data, 197 important parameters are reported by our system, among which 133 parameters are consistent with production experience, and 50 parameters are verified by domain experts to have direct impact on the product quality. The details are shown in Figure 11 (blue portion ∼ consistent with domain expertise; red portion ∼ confirmed to be important which was previously ignored; white portion ∼ excluded after verification).

To discover meaningful parameter values, WorkFlow2 in Figure 4 is used. We separate the production data to two sets by the product qualities (GOOD, i.e., qualified products, and SCRAP, i.e., defective products) and execute WorkFlow2 on these two sets, respectively. The analysis generates hundreds of frequent parameter value combinations for each given dataset (the number of outputs can be restricted by empirically setting a threshold of confidence). By extracting the frequent combinations in SCRAP that are not frequent in GOOD, we can obtain the value combinations that may result in defective products. Figure 12 shows a verification of a sample combination <para-xxxx-014=0, para-xxxx-015=0 or 24, para-xxxx-043=44 or 48> (big red crosses indicate that the values present densely on SCRAP products). Such a parameter value combination should be avoided in the production practice.

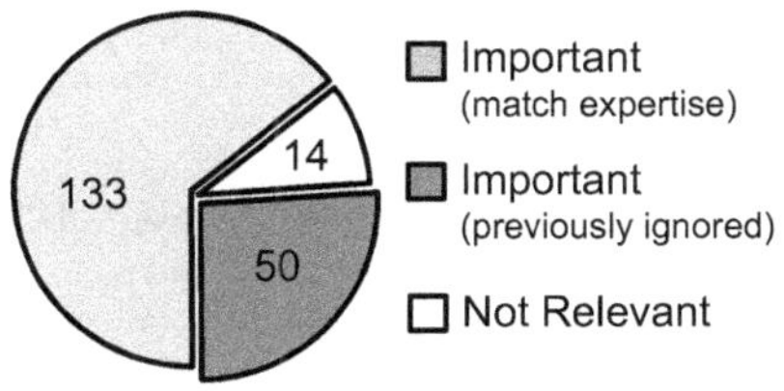

Figure 11: Important Parameters Discovered.

By applying regression analysis in WorkFlow1 of Figure 4, we discovered that environmental parameters, such as temperature and humidity, have significant correlations with the product quality. Further analysis confirmed that when the surrounding temperature of BR Furnace is under 27 °C, the

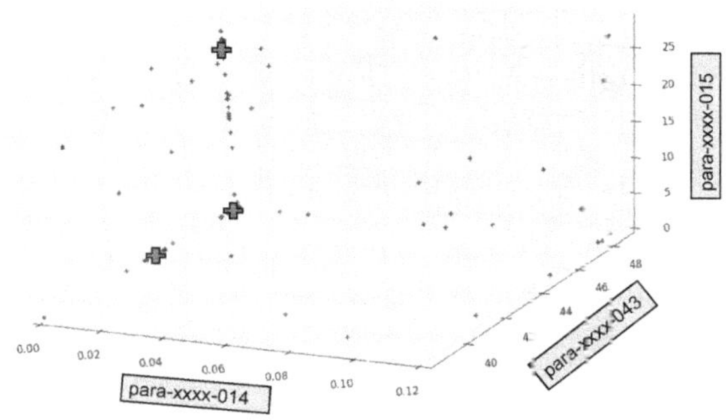

Figure 12: A Sample Parameter Combination.

number of defective products with BR Open or BR Short increases dramatically. Figure 10 depicts such findings.

The aforementioned findings are some typical examples obtained from the practical usage of our proposed system. Most of our findings have been validated by PDP technicians and are incorporated into their operational manual.

6.3 Deployment Practice

PDP-Miner has been successfully applied in ChangHong COC's PDP production line of the 3rd and 4th generations of products for manufacturing optimization. Every time the product line is upgraded, the yield rate drops significantly since previous parameter settings could not match new products requirements. The earlier parameters are tuned properly, the greater the cost will be reduced. PDP-Miner has been intensively used in such situations for problem diagnosis, including quickly identifying problematic parameter settings, detecting abnormal parameter values, and monitoring sensitive parameters.

In summary, our system brings several great benefits in optimizing the production process:

- Through establishing the relationship between parameter settings and product quality, manufacturers are more confident to properly control the production process based on analytical evidence. The cost has been greatly reduced as the number of defective products decreases.

- The prompt analysis of the production data enables the quick diagnosis on parameter values, especially when upgrading the assembly line or handling unexpected faults. As a result, the throughput increases.

- A knowledge database is constructed to manage useful analytic results that have been verified and validated by existing domain expertise. Technicians can refer to the database to look for possible solutions and control the assembly line more efficiently.

By taking advantage of our system, the overall PDP yield rate increases from 91% to 94%. Monthly production capacity is boosted by 10,000 panels, which brings more than 117 million RMB of revenue improvement per year[5]. Our system plays an revolutionary role and can be naturally transferred to other flat panel industries, such as Liquid Crystal Display (LCD) panels and Organic Light-Emitting Diode (OLED) panels, to generate great social and economic benefits.

7. CONCLUSION

`PDP-Miner` has been deployed as an important supplementary component since the year 2013. It enables prompt data analysis and efficient knowledge discovering in advanced manufacturing processes. The improved production efficacy shows that a practical data-driven solution that considers both system flexibility and algorithm customization is expected to fill the application gap between the manufacturer and data analysts. We firmly believe that, if properly being applied, the use of data analytics will become a dominating factor to underpin new waves of productivity growth and innovation, and to transform the way of manufacturings across industries in a fundamental manner.

Acknowledgement

This project is supported partially by National Science Foundation (NSF) under Grants CNS-1126619 and IIS-1213026, U.S. Department of Homeland Security under Awards 2010-ST-062-000039 and 2009-ST-061-CI0001 (VACCINE Center), Army Research Office under grants W911NF-10-1-0366 and W911NF-12-1-0431, and an FIU Dissertation Year Fellowship.

8. REFERENCES

[1] R. Belz and P. Mertens. Combining knowledge-based systems and simulation to solve rescheduling problems. *Decision Support Systems*, 17(2):141–157, 1996.

[2] I. Chen. Planning for erp systems: analysis and future trend. *Business process management journal*, 7(5):374–386, 2001.

[3] W. Chen, S. Tseng, and C. Wang. A novel manufacturing defect detection method using association rule mining techniques. *Expert systems with applications*, 29(4):807–815, 2005.

[4] C. Davis, F. Gerick, V. Hintermair, C. Friedel, K. Fundel, R. Küffner, and R. Zimmer. Reliable gene signatures for microarray classification: assessment of stability and performance. *Bioinformatics*, 22(19):2356–2363, 2006.

[5] C. Ding and H. Peng. Minimum redundancy feature selection from microarray gene expression data. *Journal of bioinformatics and computational biology*, 3(02):185–205, 2005.

[6] G. Fang, G. Pandey, W. Wang, M. Gupta, M. Steinbach, and V. Kumar. Mining low-support discriminative patterns from dense and high-dimensional data. *TKDE*, 24(2):279–294, 2012.

[7] C. Groger, F. Niedermann, H. Schwarz, and B. Mitschang. Supporting manufacturing design by analytics, continuous collaborative process improvement enabled by the advanced manufacturing analytics platform. In *CSCWD*, pages 793–799. IEEE, 2012.

[8] C. Gröger, F. Niedermann, and B. Mitschang. Data mining-driven manufacturing process optimization. In *Proceedings of the World Congress on Engineering*, volume 3, pages 4–6, 2012.

[9] M. Hall, E. Frank, G. Holmes, B. Pfahringer, P. Reutemann, and I. H. Witten. The weka data mining software: An update. *SIGKDD Explorations*, 2009.

[10] J. Han, M. Kamber, and J. Pei. *Data mining: concepts and techniques*. Morgan kaufmann, 2011.

[11] T. Hastie, R. Tibshirani, J. Friedman. *The elements of statistical learning*, volume 2. 2009.

[12] A. Kalousis, J. Prados, and M. Hilario. Stability of feature selection algorithms: a study on high-dimensional spaces. *Knowledge and information systems*, 12(1):95–116, 2007.

[13] J. Kletti. *Manufacturing Execution Systems (MES)*. Springer, 2007.

[14] D. Lei, M. A Hitt, and J. D Goldhar. Advanced manufacturing technology: organizational design and strategic flexibility. *Organization Studies*, 17(3):501–523, 1996.

[15] T. Li and C. Ding. Weighted ensemble clustering. In *SIAM Data Mining*, 2008.

[16] B. Liu, W. Hsu, and Y. Ma. Integrating classification and association rule mining. In *SIGKDD*, 1998.

[17] S. Loscalzo, L. Yu, and C. Ding. Consensus group stable feature selection. In *SIGKDD*, pages 567–576, 2009.

[18] MILK. http://pythonhosted.org/milk.

[19] MLC++. http://www.sgi.com/tech/mlc.

[20] S. Oh, J. Han, and H. Cho. Intelligent process control system for quality improvement by data mining in the process industry. In *Data mining for design and manufacturing*, pages 289–309. Springer, 2001.

[21] S. Owen, R. Anil, T. Dunning, and E. Friedman. *Mahout in Action*. Manning, 2011.

[22] R. Palaniswamy and T. Frank. Enhancing manufacturing performance with erp systems. *Information systems management*, 17(3):43–55, 2000.

[23] Z. Prekopcsak, G. Makrai, T. Henk, and C. Gaspar-Papanek. Radoop: Analyzing big data with rapidminer and hadoop. In *RCOMM*, 2011.

[24] M. Robnik-Šikonja and I. Kononenko. Theoretical and empirical analysis of relieff and rrelieff. *Machine learning*, 53(1-2):23–69, 2003.

[25] L. Shen, F. EH Tay, L. Qu, and Y. Shen. Fault diagnosis using rough sets theory. *Computers in Industry*, 43(1):61–72, 2000.

[26] V. A Skormin, V. I Gorodetski, and L. J Popyack. Data mining technology for failure prognostic of avionics. *TAES*, 38(2):388–403, 2002.

[27] A. Topchy, A. K Jain, and W. Punch. A mixture model of clustering ensembles. In *SDM*, pages 379–390, 2004.

[28] T. D Wall, J. M Corbett, R. Martin, C. W Clegg, and P. R Jackson. Advanced manufacturing technology, work design, and performance: A change study. *Journal of Applied Psychology*, 75(6):691, 1990.

[29] A. Woznica, P. Nguyen, and A. Kalousis. Model mining for robust feature selection. In *SIGKDD*, pages 913–921, 2012.

[30] L. Yu, J. Zheng, B. Wu, B. Wang, C. Shen, L. Qian, and R. Zhang. Bc-pdm: Data mining, social network analysis and text mining system based on cloud computing. In *SIGKDD*, 2012.

[31] L. Yu, C. Ding, and S. Loscalzo. Stable feature selection via dense feature groups. In *SIGKDD*, pages 803–811, 2008.

[32] C. Zeng, Y. Jiang, L. Zheng, J. Li, L. Li, H. Li, C. Shen, W. Zhou, T. Li, B. Duan, M. Lei, and P. Wang. FIU-Miner: A Fast, Integrated, and User-Friendly System for Data Mining in Distributed Environment. In *SIGKDD*, 2013.

[5]http://articles.e-works.net.cn/mes/article113579.htm.

EARS (Earthquake Alert and Report System): a Real Time Decision Support System for Earthquake Crisis Management

Marco Avvenuti
Department of Information Engineering
University of Pisa, Pisa, Italy
m.avvenuti@iet.unipi.it

Stefano Cresci
Institute for Informatics and Telematics (IIT)
National Research Council (CNR), Pisa, Italy
stefano.cresci@iit.cnr.it

Andrea Marchetti
Institute for Informatics and Telematics (IIT)
National Research Council (CNR), Pisa, Italy
andrea.marchetti@iit.cnr.it

Carlo Meletti
National Institute of Geophysics and Volcanology
Pisa, Italy
carlo.meletti@pi.ingv.it

Maurizio Tesconi
Institute for Informatics and Telematics (IIT)
National Research Council (CNR), Pisa, Italy
maurizio.tesconi@iit.cnr.it

ABSTRACT

Social sensing is based on the idea that communities or groups of people can provide a set of information similar to those obtainable from a sensor network. Emergency management is a candidate field of application for social sensing. In this work we describe the design, implementation and deployment of a decision support system for the detection and the damage assessment of earthquakes in Italy. Our system exploits the messages shared in real-time on Twitter, one of the most popular social networks in the world. Data mining and natural language processing techniques are employed to select meaningful and comprehensive sets of tweets. We then apply a burst detection algorithm in order to promptly identify outbreaking seismic events. Detected events are automatically broadcasted by our system via a dedicated Twitter account and by email notifications. In addition, we mine the content of the messages associated to an event to discover knowledge on its consequences. Finally we compare our results with official data provided by the National Institute of Geophysics and Volcanology (INGV), the authority responsible for monitoring seismic events in Italy. The INGV network detects shaking levels produced by the earthquake, but can only model the damage scenario by using empirical relationships. This scenario can be greatly improved with direct information site by site. Results show that the system has a great ability to detect events of a magnitude in the region of 3.5, with relatively low occurrences of false positives. Earthquake detection mostly occurs within seconds of the event and far earlier than the notifications shared by INGV or by other official channels. Thus, we are able to alert interested parties promptly. Information discovered by our system can be extremely useful to all the government agencies interested in mitigating the impact of earthquakes, as well as the news agencies looking for fresh information to publish.

KDD'14, August 24–27, 2014, New York, NY, USA.

http://dx.doi.org/10.1145/2623330.2623358.

Categories and Subject Descriptors

H.2.8 [**Database Management**]: Database Applications—*Data mining*; K.4.1 [**Computers and Society**]: Public Policy Issues—*Human safety*

General Terms

Design, Evaluation, Reliability

Keywords

Social sensing, social mining, decision support system, disaster management, event detection

1. INTRODUCTION

Social Media (SM) is the most effective, sophisticated and powerful way to gather preferences, tastes and activities of groups of users in the context of Web 2.0 [23]. This amount of information generates an in-depth knowledge of one or more specific issues[1]. Therefore, SM users could be regarded as social sensors, namely as a source of information about situations and facts related to the users (e.g., their preferences or experiences) and their social environment [31]. Emergency Management is a promising field of application for Social Sensing since it is possible to exploit the content shared on SM to gather up to date information on emerging situations of potential danger. These techniques allow for the acquisition of greater situational awareness which can be used to promptly alert interested parties. In the case of an emergency or a disaster, critical information needs to

[1]http://beautifuldata.net/2013/01/social-sensors/

be urgently collected so as to speed up decision making by emergency services, advising affected people, and notifying government authorities. We refer to Early Warning Systems (EWS) as those information systems able to timely detect occurring events of social concern and thus able to deliver appropriate warnings [27]. By "event" we mean a potentially dangerous situation that takes place in a finite period of time.

We aim to use spontaneous reports from users on SM as our source of information. Our focus is on reports about events causing social and safety concerns, such as natural disasters. This study is based on Social Networks (SN), a specific type of SM particularly suitable for hosting this kind of analysis. The reason for this choice is due to the large number of users involved in SN and their high level of interaction. The advantage of exploiting SN compared to traditional methods of investigation lies in the spontaneous participation of the users, in that their contribution is made without pressure or influence from others. Twitter is particularly suitable as a source of data for social sensing platforms. This is due to the fact that its users generally talk about what they are doing, and therefore what is happening around them. Analysing messages shared by Twitter users is a good way to quickly obtain details of the impact of the event.

In this paper, we will focus on reports related to earthquakes in Italy. In the Euro-Mediterranean region Italy is one of the countries with the highest seismic hazard together with Greece and Turkey. In Italy, the relationship between the damage caused by earthquakes and the energy released is much higher than in other countries with high seismicity, such as California or Japan. This is mainly due to the high population density and the considerable fragility of italian artistic and monumental heritage[2]. As suggested in [24], the highly seismic nature of Italy makes it one of the best countries where to carry out a study on the detection of earthquakes based on Twitter data. In addition, the growing use of Twitter during the last few years seems to favour a successful study (in 2013 active users increased by 40% in the world and 50% in Italy [25]).

The National Institute of Geophysics and Volcanology (INGV) is the reference scientific institution of the Italian Civil Protection for seismic and volcanic risks, as it has overall responsibility for seismic and volcanic monitoring in Italy. On the basis of specific agreements, it is in charge of detecting and communicating the occurrence of earthquakes. In addition, a protocol exists which indicates which actions must be carried out by INGV at 2, 5, 10 and 30 minute intervals after the earthquake according to the magnitude of the event. In the case of an earthquake with magnitude equal to or greater than 4, one of the products to be released is the so-called ShakeMap. A ShakeMap is an estimation of the shaking level distribution in the epicentral area in terms of peak ground-motion parameters and of instrumentally derived intensities. The application of a ShakeMap is the identification of the area where damage is probable in order to define where to concentrate the rescue teams and organize a prompt emergency response. The model is constrained with real observations coming from seismic stations connected in real-time. The limited number of stations in Italy does not allow to obtain an accurate indication of the real shaking. As a result, the opportunity to check whether damage has in fact occurred is limited. The integration of seismic station data with information discovered from social sensors will increase the number of "stations" and the reliability of a ShakeMap. This could help the Civil Protection to better evaluate the type and the degree of assistance required in the earthquake-stricken area.

The system described in this paper is aimed at providing a valuable decision support tool for INGV researchers and analysts. Our objective is to leverage experiences described in previous works in order to design and implement a system for the detection, alerting and assessment of the consequences of earthquakes. We plan to integrate the EARS (Earthquake Alert and Report System) platform with the other tools that INGV already exploits such as the ShakeMaps. Information discovered with this system can be used to acquire a greater and more fine-grained context awareness during earthquake emergencies. It can help model damage scenarios with fresh data automatically collected site by site and exploit on-the-ground community knowledge which would be otherwise inaccessible.

The remainder of this paper is organized as follows: Section 2 describes the related work. Section 3 details our design and implementation choices, Section 4 describes the frontend application. Section 5 describes the results of our study and Section 6 draws the conclusions and describes future work.

2. RELATED WORK

Several initiatives, both in scientific and in application environments, have been developed with the aim of exploiting information available on SM. Anyway despite the interest in the fields of crisis and emergency management, to date the task of the automatic assessment of the consequences of disasters has not been studied yet. To the best of our knowledge previous works have only focused on the event detection and information dissemination tasks. In literature descriptive and general approaches are opposed to practical, sector-based experiences.

2.1 Descriptive approaches

In [3] we highlighted the lack of a comprehensive approach to the problem of emergency management on SM. We described an architectural approach, we designed the components necessary for an event detection system and finally we evaluated the feasibility of the proposed solution. In [3] we did not address implementation and deployment challenges but the promising results we have achieved paved the way for the design and deployment of the EARS system which is discussed in this paper.

Researchers in [24] and [25] had the goal of creating an early warning system (EWS) for the real-time detection of earthquakes and tornadoes in Japan based on bayesian statistics. The proposed system was able to timely detect 67.9% (53 of 78) of the earthquakes with JMA (Japan Meteorological Agency) scale 2 or more which occurred in two months. In these works data acquisition is performed via the Twitter Search API[3] which accesses only a portion of all the tweets produced. This limitation can be negligible for large scale events but can impair event detection for events felt by a small number of social sensors. As described in Sec-

[2]http://www.protezionecivile.gov.it/jcms/en/homepage.wp

[3]https://dev.twitter.com/docs/api/1.1/get/search/tweets

tion 3 our approach to the data acquisition exploits the Twitter Streaming API[4] which delivers all the tweets produced worldwide that match the search criteria. Moreover the system described in [24] and [25] only focuses on the event detection task.

In [9] is described another system for the detection of earthquakes based solely on Twitter data. Again data acquisition is performed via the Twitter Search API and has the same limitations previously described. The system is evaluated with different settings according to the sensitivity of the event detection module. However, even with its best configuration the system could only detect 48 globally distributed earthquakes out of the 5,175 earthquakes reported during the same time window by the USGS.

The SMART-C project [1,2] describes a high level, multimodal framework for emergency detection and alert dissemination. The proposed solution is capable of collecting and integrating data from different sources such as SN, blogs, telephone land line communications, SMS, MMS. The project aims to improve two-way communications between the emergency response personnel and the population. Unfortunately the work presented in [1,2] mainly focuses on architectural and privacy issues without dealing with the implementation and deployment of the proposed solution.

Other works related to the emergency management have studied communication patterns and information diffusion in SN in the aftermath of disasters. The study described in [7] shows how SN can be used as a reliable source of spatio-temporal information. Researchers investigate Twitter activity during a major forest fire in the south of France in July 2009. Other similar studies have been carried out in [8,14,18] showing the importance of SN in the communications after a disaster. These studies encourage the exploitation of this information and motivate the development of systems such as the one that we are proposing.

As a generic approach, we can mention the European initiative Alert4All[5]. This project aims to create a framework to improve the effectiveness of warning messages and communications with the population in case of disasters at pan-European level. Again the focus is on the role of SM in the emergency communications [15,19].

2.2 Practical experiences

Together with the scientific studies previously described, in the last few years there has been an increasing number of applications encouraging participatory sensing in the fields of urban management and personal safety. These applications are mainly developed for mobile devices and allow users to share concise reports of civilian issues. Such tools generally perform simple tasks, lack a solid scientific background and don't employ techniques of information analysis. While a small number of these applications have become widely used in some cities or regions, the vast majority never managed to attract a significant user base. Moreover information shared on these tools is fragmented among the various applications and cannot be exploited to acquire full knowledge about the reported issues.

One of the most interesting local initiatives is represented by Emergenza24[6], the experimental version of the italian "Social Network for Emergency Management". This platform exploits a dedicated Twitter account to gather spontaneous reports of emergencies in Italy. Although reports directed to Emergenza24 are fairly common, it is clearly stated in the official website that only messages with a specific syntax are automatically captured. In Section 3 we highlight how the vast majority of emergency reports do not follow any specific format or syntax and often present grammatical mistakes or slang words. We believe that this poses a serious limitation to the effectiveness of the initiative. Similarly, the italian SMEM platform (Social Media Emergency Manager)[7] tried to promote the use of the *#smem* hashtag to report emergencies or other social issues. This initiative did not receive much interest by Twitter users and was aborted in 2012.

Authors of [5,29] describe a system to improve situational awareness during emergencies in Australia. The proposed system is interesting, but [5,29] lacks an in-depth explanation of the methodologies adopted and any kind of system evaluation. The SHIELD system [26] exploits wi-fi and bluetooth technologies to track the frequency and duration of encounters between users of the application. SHIELD exploits this information to infer the trust level between users. The system automatically selects a set of users to call with the aim of reducing the response and rescue times for victims of micro-criminality in the U.S. university campuses. Although proximity-based applications can be very effective for small scale events, this approach is hardly applicable to the field of earthquake emergency management.

3. DESIGN AND IMPLEMENTATION

In this section, we discuss the EARS system as shown in Figure 1. The system's architecture is derived from the studies we carried out in [3]. Here we turn our attention to the implementation and deployment issues and we discuss decisions and trade-offs made when making design choices for the EARS system. The main components of the EARS backend system are described in the remainder of this section. The web application frontend is discussed in Section 4.

3.1 Data Acquisition

The role of this module is very important because the system only operates on data collected in this phase. Errors at this stage, especially regarding the loss of data, have to be minimized since they will propagate throughout the system thus impairing the ability to detect events. The data acquisition module must meet both data completeness and data specificity requirements. This clearly represents a trade-off between the number of messages gathered and their relevance to the earthquake detection and damage assessment tasks. Although this module does not perform any analysis on collected data, it is possible to overcome this trade-off by fine-tuning the keywords used to collect data.

In order to select the best set of keywords we started monitoring terms reported in the literature [24], [9], [3] together with other words related to earthquakes in the italian language. We progressively restricted the initial set of 9 keywords by eliminating the ones that did not show a correlation between their frequency of usage and the seismic events reported by INGV. We discarded those keywords, such as "crollo" (wreckage) and "crepa" (crack), specifically related

[4]https://dev.twitter.com/docs/streaming-apis

[5]http://www.alert4all.eu/

[6]http://www.emergenza24.org/

[7]http://www.socialmediaemergencymanager.com

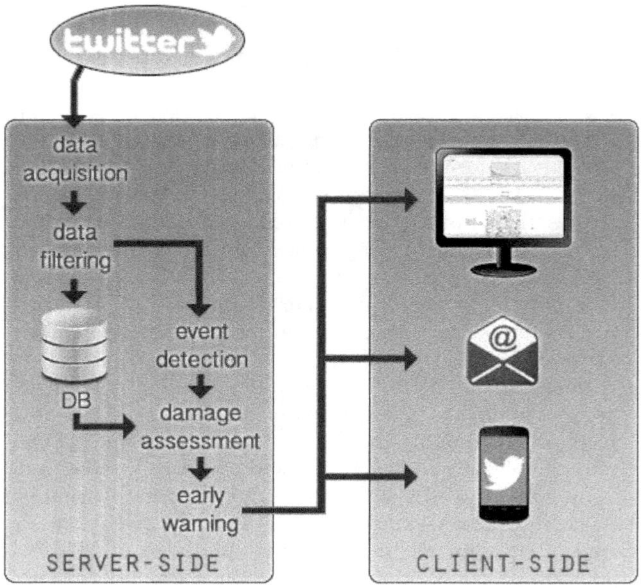

Figure 1: System architecture

to the damage assessment task; those keywords, such as "sisma" (seism) and "magnitudo" (magnitude), that are often used in official communications rather than in spontaneous user reports; and those keywords, such as "trema" (shakes) and "tremando" (shaking), that are too generic and therefore not specifically related to earthquakes. The keyword fine-tuning process lasted roughly two months. At the end of the process we concluded that the most selective italian words to collect tweets about ongoing earthquakes are "terremoto" (earthquake) and "scossa" (tremor). It is worth noticing that our set of keywords for earthquake detection differs from the sets used in [24] and [9]. Even though the keyword selection process in previous works is not thoroughly detailed, we can conclude that the best keywords for the event detection task are language specific. We believe that this poses a limitation to the possibility to easily redeploy this kind of systems to other regions of the world.

Among the methods provided by Twitter for information extraction, the EARS system exploits the Streaming API to open a persistent connection with a stream of tweets. By using this connection, new tweets containing the selected keywords can be collected. In contrast with the Search API used in the studies described in [24] and [9], which gives access only to a subset of all the tweets produced, the Streaming API potentially makes it possible to capture all the tweets matching the search criteria.

A limitation can arise considering that, as the connection can potentially access the entire flow of tweets produced in the world, Twitter delivers at most 1% of the total traffic and automatically cuts off the excess. However, our system never suffered from such a limitation over the seven month period it was used. To guarantee the robustness and the reliability of the system we also implemented additional mechanisms that manage rate-limit and generic connection problems in the use of the APIs.

3.2 Data filtering

Using keywords to query Twitter makes it possible to gather messages potentially related to an event. However, not all the messages gathered in this process relate to an ongoing earthquake. Some messages can be misleading for the event detection module and must be filtered out as noise [9]. By noise we refer to the messages containing the query keywords but which are not related to the type of event to detect. In [3] we have identified two different sources of noise: (i) messages in which the keyword is used with a different meaning from the one related to the searched event and (ii) messages in which the keyword refers to a past event. Excessive levels of noise in collected messages lead to false detections by the system. However filtering too much may result in the loss of useful messages and thus in the impossibility to detect important events. Therefore this task presents another crucial trade-off related to the accuracy of the filtering process. In EARS we overcame this trade-off by employing data mining techniques.

Our system performs data filtering by cleaning data in 2 steps. A pre-filtering phase applies raw rules to discard tweets that clearly do not refer to an ongoing seismic event. Tweets not discarded in the pre-filtering phase are then analyzed with data mining techniques to perform a more fine-grained selection. Studying the characteristics of the messages shared on Twitter in the aftermath of seismic events lead us to the observation that genuine reports of earthquakes do not follow any information diffusion model and are not influenced by other reports. This scenario rapidly evolves over time as the news of the earthquake spreads over the different medias and subsequent reports are in growing percentage influenced by other news. We concluded that the best results for the event detection task could be achieved by considering only spontaneous and independent messages. Following these guidelines we created a set of rules to apply during the pre-filtering phase. This means that EARS discards retweet messages, reply messages and messages shared by accounts belonging to a blacklist of 345 Twitter profiles that periodically publish information about past seismic events.

During the implementation and deployment of the system we also faced a challenge because the keyword "terremoto" means earthquake not only in italian but also in spanish and portuguese. Twitter natively provides a language detection mechanism that EARS exploits. Unfortunately Twitter language detection follows a best effort approach and proved to be highly inaccurate [12]. This initially lead our system to produce false detections based on messages in spanish and portuguese which contained the word "terremoto". To mitigate this issue in EARS we employ natural language processing techniques for the language detection and we discard those messages that do not appear to be in italian language.

Another possible flaw for all social mining systems lies in the vulnerability to intentional attacks performed by malicious users. Security concerns can arise if groups of people collude to generate fictitious tweets referring to an earthquake. In [3] we discussed the problem and proposed a solution based on fake account detection in order to mitigate the impact of such attacks. In the EARS system we exploit a classifier trained to distinguish between fake and real accounts [6]. The classifier has been trained on a set of 3900 equally distributed fake and real accounts and was able to correctly classify more than 95% of the accounts of the

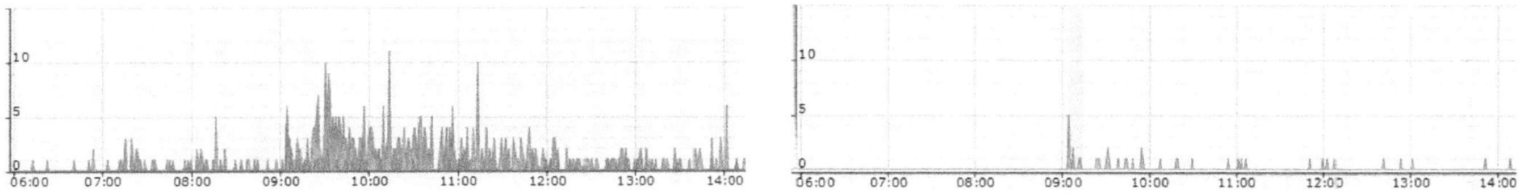

(a) *Before* filtering

(b) *After* filtering

Figure 2: Impact of the filtering phases on the number of analyzed tweets.

training set. We bought around 3000 fake accounts from 3 different sellers and randomly chose 1950 of them to be part of the training set. Similarly we created a set of 1950 verified real accounts by asking volunteers to fill a captcha or by manually checking them. The trained model is passed to the Weka tool [13] every time a new message is collected so as to infer the class (fake, real) of the user who posted it. Messages posted by fake users are automatically discarded by the system. In addition users repeatedly triggering false detections are added to the account blacklist. To further protect the system from harmful attacks we only consider for the event detection task a maximum of one message per user. In addition, messages which contain exactly the same text are only taken into consideration once. While we understand that these solutions do not fully solve the problem of malicious attacks, we are confident that our efforts represent a first response to security concerns in social mining systems. As a consequence of the adopted solutions potential attackers are required to put more effort into the creation of plausible accounts.

After the pre-filtering phase, a more sophisticated filtering process is performed by a classifier that infers the class of a tweet starting from a trained model. Again we exploited Weka to train and generate our classifier. During the offline training phase the classifier has been trained using two distinct sets of messages: tweets related and tweets not related to a seismic event in progress. Tweets of the training set were manually classified using an ad-hoc interface. Our analysis on the messages reporting earthquakes has highlighted a few interesting characteristics that help distinguish between tweets related and tweets not related to an ongoing seismic event. Tweets referring to an earthquake are generally very short, they present fewer punctuation than normal tweets and often contain slang or offensive words. This is because people reporting an earthquake are usually scared about the event and the content of the messages they write tend to represent this situation. Instead, tweets referring to official news of an earthquake or talking about a past earthquake present a longer, more structured message. Tweets not related to a recent earthquake also include a higher number of mentions and URLs than spontaneous earthquake reports. Thus we defined the following set of features that takes into account the results of the previous analysis:

- character count;
- word count;
- punctuation count;
- URL count;
- mention count;
- slang/offensive word count;

Training the classifier with this set of features produced correct classifications in more than 90% of the tweets of the training set. The classifier was obtained using the decision tree J48, corresponding to the Java implementation of the C4.5 algorithm [22] with a 10-fold cross validation [28]. The prediction is performed at run-time by invoking the classifier every time a message passes the pre-filtering phase. As Weka generally needs less than a second to predict the class of a new tweet, it is feasible to use the fine-grained classifier filter in the EARS real-time system.

Figure 2 shows the comparison between the numbers (y axis) of all collected tweets (Figure 2a) and the tweets that passed the filtering phase (Figure 2b) during a seismic event of low magnitude. The earthquake occurred in Modena, Italy, September the 4th, 2013 at 09.03 a.m. The blue plot is related to all the collected tweets. The green plot shows the tweets that passed the pre-filtering phase and, finally, the red plot represents the tweets after the filtering phase with the classifier. As shown in Figure 2 without an accurate filtering process it would have been difficult to notice the peak in the messages related to users reporting the earthquake. In fact reports for small scale events are usually overwhelmed by the number of noisy messages. In our experience the filtering process eliminated 88% of the collected messages.

3.3 Event Detection

The detection of an event is triggered by an exceptional growth in the frequency of the messages that have passed the filtering phase. The better the filtering phase the easier is the task of event detection. Event detection in social media is a topic that has been widely studied in literature. To accomplish this task researchers in [24] exploit a temporal model based on bayesian statistics, the use of peak detection algorithms is investigated in [17]. The work discussed in [21] introduces the concept of Corrected Conditional Entropy (CCE) and shows how it can be exploited to detect irregularity in time series.

In our system we adopt a novel approach based on a burst detection algorithm. A burst is defined as a large number of occurrences of a phenomenon within a short time window [30]. Burst detection techniques are commonly applied to various fields such as the detection of topics in data streams. Our system triggers the detection of a seismic event when it identifies a burst of messages referring to an earthquake. Figure 4 shows the arrival times of messages during an earthquake occurred at 00:09 a.m, August 27, 2013 in Umbria and Marche regional districts. After T1, the occurrence time of the earthquake, a big burst of tweets was recorded by our system.

Works in [10], [32] and [16] discuss various burst detection algorithms. In EARS we chose to employ a simplified version of the hierarchical algorithm proposed in [10] since it is computationally light and can adapt well to both big and small bursts. An efficient algorithm is necessary because of

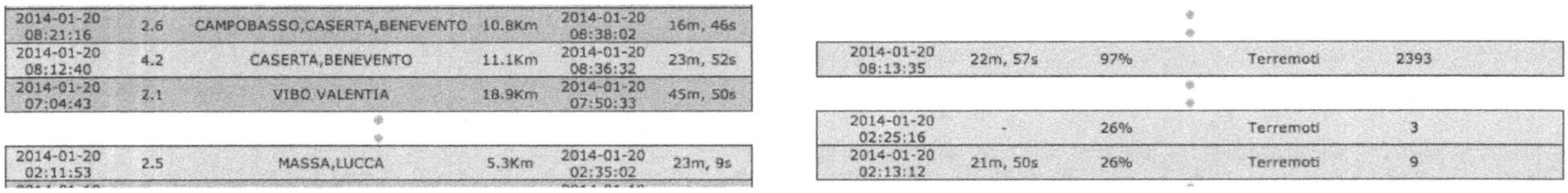

Figure 3: Chronological summary of the events

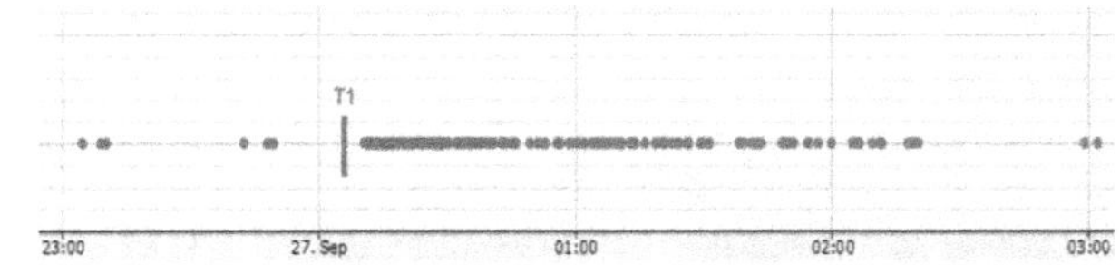

Figure 4: A burst of tweets registered after an earthquake (occurred at T1)

the real-time nature of our system and the ability to detect both big and small bursts fits well with the need to identify large scale and small scale events.

The detection of a burst is based on the calculation of the frequency (C_{freq}) of messages in a short-term time window. Assuming L_{SW} = *Length of the short-term time window* and N_{SW} = *Messages in the last short-term time window*, then:

$$C_{freq} = \frac{N_{SW}}{L_{SW}}$$

A burst is detected when such frequency exceeds a given threshold Th. The threshold to trigger a burst depends on a reference frequency (R_{freq}) calculated over a long-term time window. Assuming L_{LW} = *Length of the long-term time window* and N_{LW} = *Messages in the last long-term time window*, then:

$$R_{freq} = \frac{N_{LW}}{L_{LW}}$$

The size of both the short and long time windows along with the threshold represent implementation trade-offs and are closely linked to the characteristics of the events to detect. Shortening the short-term window makes the system respond faster since less time is required to detect a burst. However it also limits the possibility to detect events that receive a small number of reports. Widening the short-term window increases the number of events detected by the system since it is easier to reach the threshold over a longer period of time. Anyway it also exposes the system to more false detections and increases response times. Similarly, lowering the threshold allows for the detection of smaller scale events but also increases the risk of false detections.

During the fine tuning phase of the system we tried different combinations of settings. We achieved the best results with the following settings:

$$L_{SW} = \textit{1 minute}$$

$$L_{LW} = \textit{1 week}$$

$$Th = max(3, 10 * R_{freq})$$

Setting a minimum threshold of only 3 messages per minute greatly increases the sensitivity of the system. As discussed in Section 5, this setting allowed EARS to detect 100% of the earthquakes with a magnitude of 3.5 or more reported by at least one user.

3.4 Damage Assessment

Damage assessment (DA) is the process that allows emergency management personnel to determine the impact and the consequences of an emergency on communities and infrastructures. Typically, the DA process takes place in the aftermath of an emergency and involves specialized personnel who assess the consequences by visiting the location of the event. EARS exploits information shared by people directly involved in the event to automatically perform this task without the need to transport personnel over the various potentially damaged locations.

Every new message collected after the detection of an earthquake is associated to the event and contributes to the creation of a corpus of reports. As the event unfolds, the system repeatedly analyzes the growing corpus of reports to extract valuable information from it. Among the information that EARS is capable of extracting are coordinates and toponyms of locations and emerging n-grams. Locations mentioned in the reports are most likely places struck by the seismic event. To accomplish this task we make use of TagMe, a service of text annotation and disambiguation developed at the University of Pisa [11]. This tool can be specifically set to work with tweets and outputs a list of tags with the description of the terms and other related information. We then extract the coordinates associated to the toponyms disambiguated by TagMe via SPARQL [20] queries to DBpedia [4]. To further expand the set of messages associated to an earthquake the system automatically opens a new streaming connection to Twitter servers. We exploit this adaptive connection to collect messages produced in or mentioning the possible locations struck by the earthquake. This augmented message corpus is used to perform the damage assessment task by mining both the textual descriptions and the multimedial content retrieved (eg: videos, photos).

4. WEB APPLICATION

EARS is a decision support tool designed for INGV researchers and analysts. Its web frontend enables temporal, geographical and content analyses both at event and message level.

Figure 3 contains a screenshot of the web application showing a chronologically ordered summary of events of interest. Events detected by EARS are listed on the right hand side of the screen while events reported by INGV are listed on the left hand side. This screen allows for a quick evaluation of the system behavior by highlighting confirmed and unconfirmed events. Specifically, a red background is associated to events reported by INGV but not detected by EARS, an orange background is associated to events detected by our system but not yet confirmed by INGV. Finally a green background is associated to events detected by EARS and confirmed by INGV. Every listed event, both confirmed or unconfirmed, can be expanded in another window showing

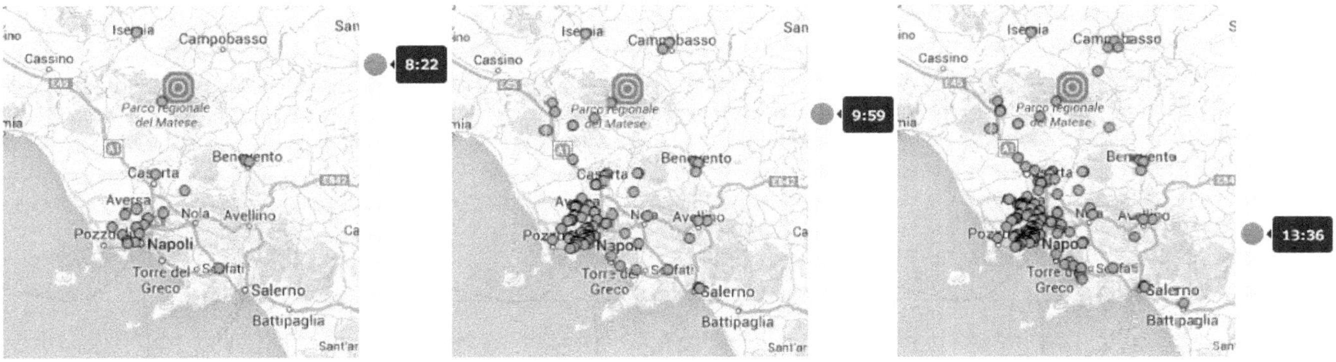

Figure 5: Geographical view: epicenter and spatial distribution of relevant messages

2014-01-20 08:30:28	**Alex__Giordanc:** Ci mancava solo il terremoto di prima mattina
2014-01-20 08:30:28	**_manuhappy:** No perché dovete sapere che io sto da giorni che tremo per il terremoto #vaffanculo
2014-01-20 08:30:31	**rinogargano:** Se c'ero dormivo. Davvero. #terremoto
2014-01-20 08:30:35	**DavideRoccio:** Di nuovo terremoto al sud. Confermate? #terremoto
2014-01-20 08:30:39	**ilfuzz:** e con questa scossa, #gennarodauria si conferma il Sommo Vegente del nostro cuore
2014-01-20 08:30:43	**asollazzo98:** PorcoDio il terremoto per la prima volta a scuola. Mi son messo paura ye
2014-01-20 08:30:49	**animaesiliata:** Come fate a dormire ancora tutti??? Non vi ha svegliati il #terremoto??
2014-01-20 08:30:53	**laccio:** mappa del #terremoto di magnitudo 4.6 http://t.co/Igw1Mo3VXS

Figure 6: Messages view: chronological list of relevant messages

all the details associated to it.

The event details window is organized in three views:

- Temporal view;
- Geographical view;
- Messages view.

The temporal view, shown in Figure 7, contains a graph of the message frequency over time. The red colored area in the graph identifies the event duration as estimated by EARS. This is not the duration of the physical event but instead the time interval in which the system collects relevant messages for the event itself. This temporal view immediately indicates the number of relevant messages and their distribution over time.

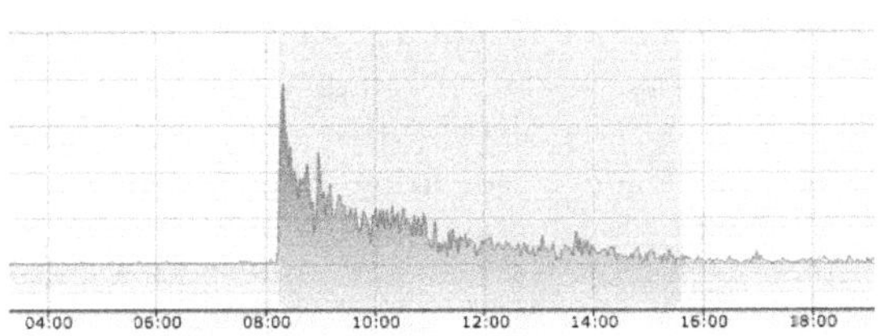

Figure 7: Temporal view: message frequency over time

The geographical view displays a map of the region affected by the event. The map contains a red marker for the epicenter of the event and a small green marker for each geocoded message. Geocoded messages include both messages carrying Twitter GPS data and messages geocoded by EARS as explained in Section 3.4. Beside the map a time slider allows to reproduce the evolution of the event from its detection time to its end. Moving the slider's handle affects information displayed in the geographical and messages views. This component shows the geographical distribution of collected messages as the event evolved in time. It also lists the the messages collected during the "lifespan" of the event. Figure 5 shows an analysis of the spatio-temporal evolution of the earthquake that struck Caserta and Benevento the 20th January 2014.

The message view provides a chronological ordered list of the relevant messages collected by EARS. Every message is described by its time of creation, the author's username and its textual content. Multimedia content is automatically displayed inside the message box. In addition an icon highlights geocoded messages. Clicking on the icon highlights the selected message in the map provided by the geographical view. Viceversa clicking on a marker in the geographical view shows the content of the related message. Figure 6 shows an excerpt of the messages view. In addition to the chronological list of messages, this view contains a list of the most used n-grams and a list of the most used annotated tags. These two lists are extracted from the whole corpus of messages associated to an event.

5. TESTING AND RESULTS

Together with the EARS system we have developed a simulator designed to read and analyze data already collected by our real-time application. The advantage of using this simulator lies in the possibility to progressively tune the system and rapidly test it against already collected data.

Magnitude	*Occurred earthquakes*	*TP*	*FP*	*FN*	*Precision*	*Recall*	*F-Measure*
> 2.0	404	17	30	387	36.17%	4.21%	7.54%
> 2.5	102	16	30	86	34.78%	15.69%	21.62%
> 3.0	26	13	17	13	43.33%	50%	46.43%
> 3.5	11	9	3	2	75%	81.82%	78.26%
> 4.0	7	5	0	2	100%	71.43%	83.33%
> 4.5	2	2	0	0	100%	100%	100%

Table 1: System evaluation against all the earthquakes registered by INGV

This approach also makes it possible to evaluate our system with stronger metrics than the ones used in other similar works [24,25], [9] and [5,29].

The evaluation dataset consists of all the messages collected by EARS over a 70 days period. By using the simulator we were able to analyze the whole evaluation dataset in less than 3 hours. The simulator performs the same analyses as the EARS system and in addition outputs a report of the performance of the system. For the system evaluation we exploited official data published by the National Institute of Geophysics and Volcanology (INGV), the authority responsible for monitoring seismic events in Italy. INGV uses different channels, including Twitter, to distribute detailed information about seismic events having magnitude 2 or more, which have been detected by their equipment. We cross-checked the events detected by the simulator against the official reports provided by INGV. We classified earthquake detection results as in the following:

- True Positives (TP), events detected by the system and confirmed by INGV;
- False Positives (FP), events detected by the system, but not confirmed by INGV;
- False Negatives (FN), events reported by INGV but not detected by the system.

True Negatives are meaningless, as it would mean counting the number of earthquakes that did not happen and that our system did not detect.

We also computed the following evaluation metrics:

- Precision, ratio of correctly detected events among the total number of detected events:

$$Precision = \frac{TP}{TP + FP}$$

- Recall, ratio of correctly detected events among the total number of occurred events:

$$Recall = \frac{TP}{TP + FN}$$

- F-Measure, harmonic mean of Precision and Recall:

$$F\text{-}Measure = 2 * \frac{Precision * Recall}{Precision + Recall}$$

Table 1 summarizes event detection evaluation against all the earthquakes registered by INGV from 2013-07-19 to 2013-09-23.

Results show that the detection of earthquakes with magnitude lower than 3 is very difficult. This is because the majority of these earthquakes are only detected by equipment and not by people. For events with a magnitude equal to or greater than 3.5, results show a good performance of the system in terms of F-Measure. This is especially significant given that seismic events of a magnitude around 3 are generally detected only by a very small number of people. In our study, for such earthquakes we always registered less than 10 tweets per event.

As the ultimate goal of the EARS system is to assess the consequences of earthquakes, light seismic events only detected by seismographs clearly do not pose any threat to communities and infrastructures. Earthquakes of interest are those actually felt by the population at large. Therefore we re-evaluated the system against those earthquakes that generated at least one report on Twitter. Results are displayed in Table 2 and show an overall improvement in the system performances. It is worth noticing that EARS achieves flawless results for earthquakes of magnitude 4.0 or more and also performs very well on earthquakes which have a magnitude in the region of 3.5.

6. CONCLUSIONS AND FUTURE WORK

EARS (Earthquake Alert and Report System) is a decision support environment for earthquake crisis management deployed for INGV researchers and analysts. The proposed system can clearly provide useful information on the consequences of seismic events. Such information is inferred from on-the-ground social sensors seconds after the detection of an earthquake. EARS can be integrated with other already established systems in order to help identify the areas where damage is probable. Information discovered by this system helps define where to concentrate the rescue teams and organize a prompt emergency response.

In Section 3 we discussed the design, implementation and deployment challenges faced during the development of EARS. These challenges are common to the majority of social mining systems even though they are not fully addressed in similar works. We proposed technical solutions for the most relevant issues which emerged from our work. Results suggest the effectiveness of such solutions although we are aware that further improvements may lead to even better performances. Among the issues we discussed is the problem of security. To the best of our knowledge EARS is the first emergency management system to employ security mechanisms in order to deter and minimize the effect of malicious attacks. Although we understand that these mechanisms are

Magnitude	*Tweeted earthquakes*	*TP*	*FP*	*FN*	*Precision*	*Recall*	*F-Measure*
> 2.0	128	17	30	111	36.17%	13.28%	19.43%
> 2.5	55	16	30	39	34.78%	29.09%	31.68%
> 3.0	21	13	17	8	43.33%	61.90%	50.98%
> 3.5	9	9	3	0	75%	100%	85.71%
> 4.0	5	5	0	0	100%	100%	100%
> 4.5	2	2	0	0	100%	100%	100%

Table 2: System evaluation against earthquakes that generated at least one report on Twitter

not sufficient on their own, we believe that they represent a good starting point towards addressing security issues of such applications. False detections are probably the most critical issue of EARS and require further investigation and effort. We manually verified that language detection problems have been the cause of several false detections by the system. These problems are primarily caused by Twitter's best effort language detection approach and by the limited length of tweets. We adopted a solution based on natural language processing but we plan to exploit user account information as well to further improve the detection. Other problems contribute to the number of false detections registered, the vast majority of which is related to mistakes in the data filtering process.

Over the past seven months we have been developing and testing the EARS system against earthquakes reported by INGV. During this period of time none of the earthquakes that struck Italy have caused serious consequences on communities or infrastructures. The highest magnitude registered since July 2013 was 4.9 degrees when two earthquakes struck Ancona and Macerata on the 21st of July 2013 and Caserta and Benevento on the 29th of December 2013. Despite the lack of significant data reporting injuries to the population or damages to the infrastructures we have developed a system capable of inferring the consequences of earthquakes. However access to historical Twitter data, especially related to the earthquakes in Emilia Romagna in 2012 and L'Aquila in 2009, could prove crucial for future improvements in the damage assessment area. For this reason we are looking forward to the upcoming Twitter Data Grants program for research[8].

In the future we will apply our system to other contexts such as wildfires, traffic jams, landslips and floods. We also plan to experiment with other sources of data like Facebook public posts and Google search activity data.

7. REFERENCES

[1] N. Adam, J. Eledath, S. Mehrotra, and N. Venkatasubramanian. Social media alert and response to threats to citizens (smart-c). In *Collaborative Computing: Networking, Applications and Worksharing (CollaborateCom), 2012 8th International Conference on*, pages 181–189. IEEE, 2012.

[2] N. R. Adam, B. Shafiq, and R. Staffin. Spatial computing and social media in the context of disaster management. *Intelligent Systems, IEEE*, 27(6):90–96, 2012.

[3] M. Avvenuti, S. Cresci, M. La Polla, A. Marchetti, and M. Tesconi. Earthquake emergency management by social sensing. In *Pervasive Computing and Communications Workshops (PERCOM Workshops), 2014 IEEE International Conference on*. IEEE, 2014.

[4] C. Bizer, J. Lehmann, G. Kobilarov, S. Auer, C. Becker, R. Cyganiak, and S. Hellmann. Dbpedia-a crystallization point for the web of data. *Web Semantics: Science, Services and Agents on the World Wide Web*, 7(3):154–165, 2009.

[5] M. A. Cameron, R. Power, B. Robinson, and J. Yin. Emergency situation awareness from twitter for crisis management. In *Proceedings of the 21st international conference companion on World Wide Web*, pages 695–698. ACM, 2012.

[6] S. Cresci, R. Di Pietro, M. Petrocchi, A. Spognardi, and M. Tesconi. A Criticism to Society (as seen by Twitter analytics). In *1st International Workshop on Big Data Analytics for Security*. IEEE, 2014.

[7] B. De Longueville, R. S. Smith, and G. Luraschi. Omg, from here, i can see the flames!: a use case of mining location based social networks to acquire spatio-temporal data on forest fires. In *Proceedings of the 2009 International Workshop on Location Based Social Networks*, pages 73–80. ACM, 2009.

[8] P. Earle, M. Guy, R. Buckmaster, C. Ostrum, S. Horvath, and A. Vaughan. Omg earthquake! can twitter improve earthquake response? *Seismological Research Letters*, 81(2):246–251, 2010.

[9] P. S. Earle, D. C. Bowden, and M. Guy. Twitter earthquake detection: earthquake monitoring in a social world. *Annals of Geophysics*, 54(6), 2012.

[10] R. Ebina, K. Nakamura, and S. Oyanagi. A real-time burst detection method. In *Tools with Artificial Intelligence (ICTAI), 2011 23rd IEEE International Conference on*, pages 1040–1046. IEEE, 2011.

[11] P. Ferragina and U. Scaiella. Fast and accurate annotation of short texts with wikipedia pages. *Software, IEEE*, 29(1):70–75, 2012.

[12] S. Hale, D. Gaffney, and M. Graham. Where in the world are you? geolocation and language identification in twitter. *Proceedings of ICWSM 2012*, pages 518–521, 2012.

[13] M. Hall, E. Frank, G. Holmes, B. Pfahringer, P. Reutemann, and I. H. Witten. The weka data

[8]https://engineering.twitter.com/research/data-grants

mining software: an update. *ACM SIGKDD Explorations Newsletter*, 11(1):10–18, 2009.

[14] A. L. Hughes and L. Palen. Twitter adoption and use in mass convergence and emergency events. *International Journal of Emergency Management*, 6(3):248–260, 2009.

[15] F. Johansson, J. Brynielsson, and M. N. Quijano. Estimating citizen alertness in crises using social media monitoring and analysis. In *Intelligence and Security Informatics Conference (EISIC), 2012 European*, pages 189–196. IEEE, 2012.

[16] J. Kleinberg. Bursty and hierarchical structure in streams. *Data Mining and Knowledge Discovery*, 7(4):373–397, 2003.

[17] A. Marcus, M. S. Bernstein, O. Badar, D. R. Karger, S. Madden, and R. C. Miller. Twitinfo: aggregating and visualizing microblogs for event exploration. In *Proceedings of the SIGCHI conference on Human factors in computing systems*, pages 227–236. ACM, 2011.

[18] A. Murakami and T. Nasukawa. Tweeting about the tsunami?: mining twitter for information on the tohoku earthquake and tsunami. In *Proceedings of the 21st international conference companion on World Wide Web*, pages 709–710. ACM, 2012.

[19] S. Nilsson, J. Brynielsson, M. Granåsen, C. Hellgren, S. Lindquist, M. Lundin, M. Narganes Quijano, and J. Trnka. Making use of new media for pan-european crisis communication. In *Proceedings of the Ninth International Conference on Information Systems for Crisis Response and Management (ISCRAM 2012)*. ISCRAM, 2012.

[20] J. Pérez, M. Arenas, and C. Gutierrez. Semantics and complexity of sparql. *ACM Transactions on Database Systems (TODS)*, 34(3):16, 2009.

[21] A. Porta, G. Baselli, D. Liberati, N. Montano, C. Cogliati, T. Gnecchi-Ruscone, A. Malliani, and S. Cerutti. Measuring regularity by means of a corrected conditional entropy in sympathetic outflow. *Biological cybernetics*, 78(1):71–78, 1998.

[22] J. R. Quinlan. *C4.5: programs for machine learning*, volume 1. Morgan kaufmann, 1993.

[23] A. Rosi, M. Mamei, F. Zambonelli, S. Dobson, G. Stevenson, and J. Ye. Social sensors and pervasive services: Approaches and perspectives. In *Pervasive Computing and Communications Workshops (PERCOM Workshops), 2011 IEEE International Conference on*, pages 525–530. IEEE, 2011.

[24] T. Sakaki, M. Okazaki, and Y. Matsuo. Earthquake shakes twitter users: real-time event detection by social sensors. In *Proceedings of the 19th international conference on World wide web*, pages 851–860. ACM, 2010.

[25] T. Sakaki, M. Okazaki, and Y. Matsuo. Tweet analysis for real-time event detection and earthquake reporting system development. *Knowledge and Data Engineering, IEEE Transactions on*, 25(4):919–931, 2013.

[26] G. S. Thakur, M. Sharma, and A. Helmy. Shield: Social sensing and help in emergency using mobile devices. In *Global Telecommunications Conference (GLOBECOM 2010), 2010 IEEE*, pages 1–5. IEEE, 2010.

[27] N. Waidyanatha. Towards a typology of integrated functional early warning systems. *International Journal of Critical Infrastructures*, 6(1):31–51, 2010.

[28] I. H. Witten and E. Frank. *Data Mining: Practical machine learning tools and techniques*. Morgan Kaufmann, 2005.

[29] J. Yin, A. Lampert, M. Cameron, B. Robinson, and R. Power. Using social media to enhance emergency situation awareness. *IEEE Intelligent Systems*, 27(6):52–59, 2012.

[30] X. Zhang and D. Shasha. Better burst detection. In *Data Engineering, 2006. ICDE'06. Proceedings of the 22nd International Conference on*, pages 146–146. IEEE, 2006.

[31] A. Zhou, W. Qian, and H. Ma. Social media data analysis for revealing collective behaviors. In *Proceedings of the 18th ACM SIGKDD International Conference on Knowledge Discovery and Data Mining*, KDD '12, pages 1402–1402, New York, NY, USA, 2012. ACM.

[32] Y. Zhu and D. Shasha. Efficient elastic burst detection in data streams. In *Proceedings of the ninth ACM SIGKDD international conference on Knowledge discovery and data mining*, pages 336–345. ACM, 2003.

Knock It Off: Profiling the Online Storefronts of Counterfeit Merchandise

Matthew F. Der, Lawrence K. Saul, Stefan Savage, Geoffrey M. Voelker
Department of Computer Science and Engineering
University of California, San Diego
{mfder, saul, savage, voelker}@cs.ucsd.edu

ABSTRACT

We describe an automated system for the large-scale monitoring of Web sites that serve as online storefronts for spam-advertised goods. Our system is developed from an extensive crawl of black-market Web sites that deal in illegal pharmaceuticals, replica luxury goods, and counterfeit software. The operational goal of the system is to identify the affiliate programs of online merchants behind these Web sites; the system itself is part of a larger effort to improve the tracking and targeting of these affiliate programs. There are two main challenges in this domain. The first is that appearances can be deceiving: Web pages that render very differently are often linked to the same affiliate program of merchants. The second is the difficulty of acquiring training data: the manual labeling of Web pages, though necessary to some degree, is a laborious and time-consuming process. Our approach in this paper is to extract features that reveal when Web pages linked to the same affiliate program share a similar underlying structure. Using these features, which are mined from a small initial seed of labeled data, we are able to profile the Web sites of forty-four distinct affiliate programs that account, collectively, for hundreds of millions of dollars in illicit e-commerce. Our work also highlights several broad challenges that arise in the large-scale, empirical study of malicious activity on the Web.

Categories and Subject Descriptors

I.5.4 [**Pattern Recognition**]: Applications—*Text processing*; K.4.4 [**Computers and Society**]: Electronic Commerce—*Security*

General Terms

Security

Keywords

Web page classification; Email spam

KDD'14, August 24–27, 2014, New York, NY, USA.

ACM 978-1-4503-2956-9/14/08 ...$15.00.
http://dx.doi.org/10.1145/2623330.2623354.

1. INTRODUCTION

The Web plays host to a broad spectrum of online fraud and abuse—everything from search poisoning [5, 20] and phishing attacks [12] to false advertising [10], DNS profiteering [4, 15], and browser compromise [17]. All of these malicious activities are mediated, in one way or another, by Web pages that lure unsuspecting victims away from their normal browsing to various undesirable ends. Thus, an important question is whether these malicious Web pages can be automatically identified by suspicious commonalities in appearance or syntax [1, 4, 8, 11, 18, 19, 21]. However, more than simply distinguishing "bad" from "good" Web sites, there is further interest in classifying criminal Web sites into groups of common origin: those pages that are likely under the control of a singular organization [3, 9, 13]. Indeed, capturing this "affiliation" property has become critical both for intelligence gathering as well as both criminal and civil interventions. In this paper, we develop an automated system for one version of this problem: the large-scale profiling of Web sites that serve as online storefronts for spam-advertised goods.

While everyone with an e-mail account is familiar with the scourge of spam-based advertising, it is only recently that researchers have come to appreciate the complex business structure behind such messages [14]. In particular, it has become standard that merchants selling illegitimate goods (e.g., such as counterfeit Viagra and Rolex watches) are organized into *affiliate programs* that in turn engage with spammers as independent contractors. Under this model, the affiliate program is responsible for providing the content for online storefronts, contracting for payment services (e.g., to accept credit cards), customer support and product fulfillment—but direct advertising is left to independent affiliates (i.e., spammers). Spammers are paid a 30–40% commission on each customer purchase acquired via their advertising efforts and may operate on behalf of multiple distinct affiliate programs over time. Such activities are big business with large affiliate programs generating millions of dollars in revenue every month [7].

Thus, while there are hundreds of thousands of spam-advertised Web sites and thousands of individual spammers, most of this activity is in service to only several dozen affiliate programs. Recent work has shown that this hierarchy can be used to identify structural bottlenecks, notably in payment processing. In particular, if an affiliate program is unable to process credit cards, then it becomes untenable to sustain their business (no matter the number of Web

GlavMed	Ultimate Rep.	SoftSales

Table 1: Screenshots of online storefronts selling counterfeit pharmaceuticals, replicas, and software.

sites they operate or spammers they contract with). Recently, a concerted effort by major brand holders and payment networks to shutdown the merchant bank accounts used by key affiliate programs demonstrated this vulnerability concretely. Over a short period of time, this effort shut down 90% of affiliate programs selling illegal software and severely disabled a range of affiliate programs selling counterfeit pharmaceuticals [13].

The success of this intervention stemmed from a critical insight—namely, that the hundreds of thousands of Web sites harvested from millions of spam emails could be mapped to a few dozen affiliate programs (each with a small number of independent merchant bank accounts). At the heart of this action was therefore a classification problem: how to identify affiliate programs from the Web pages of their online storefronts?

There are two principle challenges to classification in this domain. The first is that appearances can be deceiving: storefront pages that render very differently are often supported by the same affiliate program. The seeming diversity of these pages—a ploy to evade detection—is generated by in-house software with highly customizable templates. The second challenge is the difficulty of acquiring training data. Manually labeling storefront pages, though necessary to some degree, is a laborious and time-consuming process. The researchers in [9] spent hundreds of hours crafting regular expressions that mapped storefront pages to affiliate programs. Practitioners may endure such manual effort once, but it is too laborious to be performed repeatedly over time or to scale to even larger corpora of crawled Web pages.

Our goal is to develop a more automated approach that greatly reduces manual effort while also improving the accuracy of classification. In this paper we focus specifically on spam-advertised storefronts for three categories of products: illegal pharmaceuticals, replica luxury goods, and counterfeit software (Table 1). We use the data set from [9] consisting of 226,000 potential storefront pages winnowed from six million distinct URLs advertised in spam. From the examples in this data, we consider how to learn a classifier that maps storefront pages to the affiliate programs behind them.

We proceed with an operational perspective in mind, focusing on scenarios of real-world interest to practitioners in computer security. Our most important findings are the following. First, we show that the online storefronts of several dozen affiliate programs can be distinguished from automatically extracted features of their Web pages. In particular, we find that a simple nearest neighbor (NN) classifier on HTML and network-based features achieves a nearly perfect accuracy of 99.99%. Second, we show that practitioners need only invest a small amount of manual effort in

Figure 1: Data filtering process. Stage 1 is the entire set of crawled Web pages; stage 2, pages tagged as pharmaceutical, replica, and luxury; stage 3, storefronts of affiliate programs matched by regular expressions.

the labeling of examples: with just one labeled storefront per affiliate program, NN achieves an accuracy of 75%, and with sixteen such examples, it achieves an accuracy of 98%. Third, we show that our classifiers are able to label the affiliate programs of over 3700 additional storefront pages that were missed by the hand-crafted regular expressions of the original study. Finally, we show that even simple clustering methods may be useful in this domain—for example, to identify new affiliate programs or to reveal when known affiliate programs have adopted new software engines.

2. DATA SET

We use the data set of crawled Web pages from the measurement study of the spam ecosystem by Levchenko et al. [9]. Figure 1 depicts how they collected, filtered, and labeled the data, which we summarize in this section; we refer the reader to their paper for a more detailed explanation of their methodology.

2.1 Data Collection

Over a period of three months, Levchenko et al. [9] crawled over six million URLs from various spam feeds, including one feed from a top Web mail provider and others captured as output from live spamming bots. From the combined feeds, they obtained 1,692,129 distinct landing pages after discarding duplicate pages referenced by multiple URLs. For each landing page the crawler saved the raw HTML as well as a screenshot. In addition, a DNS crawler collected network information on the extracted domains. The first level in Figure 1 corresponds to this set of Web pages.

2.2 Data Filtering

The authors of [9] focused on three popular categories of spam-advertised goods—illegal pharmaceuticals, replica luxury goods, and counterfeit software. They used keyword matching to filter out Web pages that were unrelated to these categories of merchandise. Keywords included both brand names, such as *Viagra* and *Cialis*, in addition to more generic terms, such as *erectile dysfunction* and *drug*. This filtering removed pages whose text did not advertise for sales of pharmaceuticals, replicas, or software—an omission that runs counter to the business interest of any viable storefront. The absence of such text was found to be a reliable screen for non-storefront pages. A total of 226,439 storefront pages emerged from this filter, which were then broadly grouped into the three categories of pharmaceuticals, luxury goods, and software. These categorized pages, shown in the second level of Figure 1, comprise the universe of pages that we consider in this paper.

The filtering by domain-specific keywords may be viewed as a simple operational heuristic to narrow the massive data set of blindly crawled URLs to a subset of pages of interest. Note that the filtering in this step was purposely conservative so that legitimate storefront pages were not winnowed from the data set.

2.3 Data Labeling

Through a combination of manual inspection and heuristic pattern-matching, the authors of [9] managed to link the spam-advertised storefronts for pharmaceuticals, luxury goods, and pirated software to individual affiliate programs. An initial round of manual inspection was necessary because even the cast of affiliate programs was not known a priori. Thus the first pass over crawled Web pages focused on identifying prominent affiliate programs and collecting a moderate sample of storefront pages from each. The authors identified forty-five distinct affiliate programs in this way (although one was later discovered to be a subset of another).

The next and most time-consuming step of this process was to expand the number of storefront pages labeled for each affiliate program. The authors of [9] sought to automate this process through the use of regular expressions. Specifically, for each affiliate program, they devised a set of characteristic regular expressions that matched the HTML content of its online storefronts but not those of other programs. They also fixed an integer threshold for each affiliate program; if the Web page of an online storefront matched this number of regular expressions (or more), then it was labeled as belonging to the program. Using this approach, they were able to identify the affiliate programs of 180,690 online storefronts. The bottom level in Figure 1 represents this final set of storefront pages.

The above approach depended on the meticulous crafting of regular expressions that distinguish the storefront pages of different affiliate programs. To devise such an expression it was necessary (roughly speaking) to find a pattern that was present in all the pages of one program *and* absent in the pages of all other programs. The painstaking effort required for this approach is best illustrated by example. Here is one regular expression for storefront pages in the GlavMed affiliate program:

```
var\s+SessionType\s*=\s*"URL";\s*var\s+
SessionPrefix\s*=\s*"[0-9a-fA-F]32";\s*var\s+
SessionName\s*=\s*"USID";
```

It can take a couple hours just to hone a single regular expression such as the one above. Much more time, naturally, is required to obtain coverage of multiple affiliate programs. The full effort in [9] involved not only the careful scrutinization of HTML content, but also iterative refinement and extensive validation. In total, the authors estimated that they spent over two hundred man-hours designing and validating the regular expressions for all forty-five affiliate programs.

Examples	1st 3 months	2nd 3 months
Labeled	178,281	29,581
Unlabeled	43,442	12,756
Largest class	58,215	13,529
Smallest class	2	0

Table 2: Summary of the data from crawls of consecutive three-month periods.

In the present work, we limited our study to forty-four[1] of these affiliate programs. We also discarded pages from the above collection which lacked a screenshot (which we need for manual validation of our results). From the initial three-month Web crawl, this left us with 178,281 labeled storefronts and 43,442 unlabeled storefronts; all of these storefronts were tagged as selling pharmaceuticals, luxury goods, or software, but only the former were successfully mapped to affiliate programs by regular expressions.

We also obtained a subset of data crawled from a period of the following three months. These Web pages were collected and labeled in the same manner as before; in particular, they were labeled without updating the regular expressions from the initial crawl. It is known that storefronts evolve over time, and therefore we do not expect the labels during this time period to be as reliable as the earlier ones. Table 2 summarizes the data from each crawl. Note also the severe class imbalance: the largest affiliate program has 58,215 distinct storefronts, while the smallest has just 2. In addition, there were five affiliate programs whose regular expressions in the first period did not detect any storefront pages in the second period.

3. AN AUTOMATED APPROACH

It should be clear that the approach of Section 2.3 does not scale well with the number of storefront pages or affiliate programs. This approach is also too time-consuming to repeat on a regular basis—updating the regular expressions before they go stale—as would be necessary to maintain a working operational system. In this section we describe a faster and more highly automated approach for the classification of storefront pages by affiliate program. Our data-driven approach consists of two steps. First, we use automatic scripts to extract tens of thousands of potentially informative features from the crawl of each online storefront. Next, we represent these features in a lower-dimensional vector space and use nearest neighbor classification to identify affiliate programs from whatever labeled examples are available. Our hope with this approach is to avoid the painstaking crafting of regular expressions in favor of simple, well-tested methods in data mining and machine learning.

3.1 Feature Extraction

For each online storefront in our data set, we have both the HTML source of its Web page and the DNS record of its domain. Together these provide a wealth of information

[1]The affiliate program we exclude was later found to be a proper subset of a different program.

about the storefront that can be extracted by automatic methods. We consider each in turn.

3.1.1 HTML Features

We know from previous work [9] that the storefronts of different affiliate programs can be distinguished by properties of their raw HTML. This is likely the case because each affiliate program uses its own software engine to generate storefront templates; as a result, different storefronts within the same affiliate program often have similar DOM[2] structures. Indeed, the regular expressions of [9] only work insofar as commonalities in implementation exist among the different storefronts of individual affiliate programs.

We extract HTML features using a bag-of-words approach. This approach ignores the ordering of HTML tags and text within a Web page, but it is simple enough for the quick and automatic extraction of thousands of potentially informative features. In this respect our approach differs considerably from the manual "feature engineering" of regular expressions; we do not seek to find the most informative features ourselves, merely to extract all candidate features for a statistical model of classification.

A key consideration of our approach is how to encode HTML tags as words. Consider the following snippet of HTML code:

```
<img src="example.jpg" alt="Example pic"
  height="50" width="100">
```

The problem in encoding this snippet is how to achieve the appropriate level of granularity. It is clear that important information is carried by the context in which individual HTML tags appear. However, this information is lost if we encode the tags and tokens in this snippet as single words. On the other hand, it is clearly infeasible to encode this whole snippet, and others like it, as a single "word"; taken as a whole, the HTML element is akin to a full sentence of text. Our compromise between these two extremes is to encode each tag-attribute-value triplet as a word. We also remove whitespace. This solution, for example, parses the above HTML into the following words:

```
img:src=example.jpg
img:alt=Examplepic
img:height=50
img:width=100
```

To parse HTML element content—the text between start and end tags—we treat the text as a single string that we split on certain characters (`,;{}`) and whitespace. We then form "words" by stripping non-alphanumeric characters from the resulting substrings and converting all letters to lowercase. We parse HTML comments in the same way. Following convention, we exclude words that are either very common (e.g., stopwords) or very rare (appearing in few Web pages).

The bag-of-words approach has the potential to generate very large feature vectors: the dimensionality of the feature space is equal to the number of extracted words. We limited our vocabulary of words to the HTML of storefronts from the initial three-month crawl. From this period alone, however, we extracted over eight million unique words. Since most of these words were likely to be uninformative, we used simple heuristics to prune this space. In particular, for each of the forty-four affiliate programs, we only retained words that appeared in the HTML source of 10% (or more) of the program's online storefronts. Finally, concatenating these words we obtained a total of 34,208 HTML-based features for classification.

3.1.2 Network Features

The authors of [9] also developed a DNS crawler to enumerate all address and name server records[3] linked to the domains of spam-advertised URLs. We expect such records to help us further in identifying affiliate programs from their online storefronts. In particular, we expect different affiliate programs to use different naming and hosting infrastructures, and thus we might hope to distinguish them by the name and Web servers that support their domains. Such information may also serve to link online storefronts with different Web pages to the same affiliate program. For example, the DOM trees of two storefronts might be quite different, but if their Web pages were hosted at the same server, then we could predict with confidence that they belong to the same affiliate program.

We mined both the address and name server records of online storefronts for useful features. An address record, or A record, maps a domain name to the IP address of the machine on the Internet where the domain is hosted. For example, the A record of the domain name `ucsd.edu` maps to the IP address `132.239.180.101`. A name server record, or an NS record, identifies the name servers that provide these mappings of names to addresses. The NS record for the domain `ucsd.edu` contains the domain names of four name servers: `ns0.ucsd.edu`, `ns1.nosc.mil`, `ns1.ucsd.edu`, and `ns2.ucsd.edu`. In addition, these name servers have their own IP addresses; e.g., the A record for `ns0.ucsd.edu` maps to the IP address `132.239.1.51`. Note that a storefront's domain name may be associated with multiple A and NS records. These multiple associations are a counter-defense against security measures such as domain blacklisting.

For each storefront domain, we extracted the IP address from its A record, the IP addresses of its name servers, and the autonomous system numbers (ASNs) of both these IP addresses. (The ASN of an IP address uniquely identifies its Internet Service Provider.) All together, these IPs and ASNs yield four categorical network features for each storefront. We tallied the number of unique IPs and ASNs observed during the initial three-month crawl of storefronts: there were 17,864 unique A record IPs, 8,825 unique NS record IPs, 2,259 unique ASNs of A record IPs, and 1,853 unique ASNs of NS record IPs. We encoded each categorical feature with k uniquely occurring values as a k-dimensional binary vector (i.e., a simple unary encoding). Concatenating the elements of these vectors, we obtained a total of 30,791 binary-valued network features for each online storefront.

3.2 Dimensionality Reduction & Visualization

Table 3 shows the numbers of HTML-based and network-based features, as well as the total number of features when combined. We were interested in the different types of information contained in HTML vs. network features. To explore the value of different features, we experimented with classi-

[2]The document object model (DOM) refers to the representation of a Web page as a tree of HTML elements.

[3]Due to a technical issue, however, this information was only recorded during the first three-month crawl of online storefronts.

Features	Count	Density	PCA	Unique Exs.
Bag-of-words	34,208	2.20%	66	12.07%
Network	30,791	0.12%	665	6.09%
Both	64,999	1.21%	72	31.52%

Table 3: Feature counts, density of the data, dimensionality after principal components analysis, and percentage of unique examples.

fiers that used either one set of features or the other; this was in addition to classifiers that worked in their combined feature space.

In all of these cases, the data is very sparse and high dimensional. To reduce the dimensionality of the data we used principal component analysis (PCA) [6]: in particular, after normalizing the feature vectors to have unit length, we projected them onto enough principal components to capture over 99% of the data's variance. We did this for each of the three feature spaces. The third and fourth columns of Table 3 show, respectively, the small percentages of non-zero features before PCA and the number of principal components needed to capture 99% of the data's variance.

In the last column of Table 3 we have noted the high percentage of duplicate representations in feature space. Within a single affiliate program, it is often the case that different storefronts have identical representations as feature vectors; this is true even though every Web page in our data set has a distinct DOM tree. These duplicates arise when the extracted features do not contain the information that distinguishes actual Web pages. For example, two storefronts may have the same bag-of-words representation if their Web pages differ only slightly in their HTML (e.g., a single link, image path, or JavaScript variable name) and if, in this case, the differentiating words were too rare to be included as features. Likewise, two storefronts may have equivalent network features if they are hosted on the same server.

In Section 2 we noted that 180,690 *distinct* storefront pages were collected. The many duplicates (and many more near-duplicates) arise from the operational constraints faced by affiliate programs. To maximize their sales, affiliate programs must deploy and support many storefronts across the Internet. This process can only be streamlined by the aggressive use of template engines. Ironically, it is precisely the requirement of these programs to operate at scale that makes it possible to automate the defenses against them.

For illustration, Figure 2 plots the projections of storefront feature vectors from the largest affiliate program (EvaPharmacy) onto the data's two leading principal components. Two observations are worth noting. First, the distribution is clumpy, with some irregularly-shaped modes, evidence of the variety of storefronts in this single program. Second, some storefronts which render very differently map to nearby points. This proximity is evidence of a similar underlying structure that associates them to the same affiliate program.

3.3 Nearest Neighbor Classification

We use nearest neighbor (NN) classification [2] to identify the affiliate programs of unlabeled storefronts. In particular, we store the feature vectors of the labeled storefronts (after PCA) in memory, and for each unlabeled storefront, we compute its NN in Euclidean distance among the training examples. Finally, we identify the affiliate program from

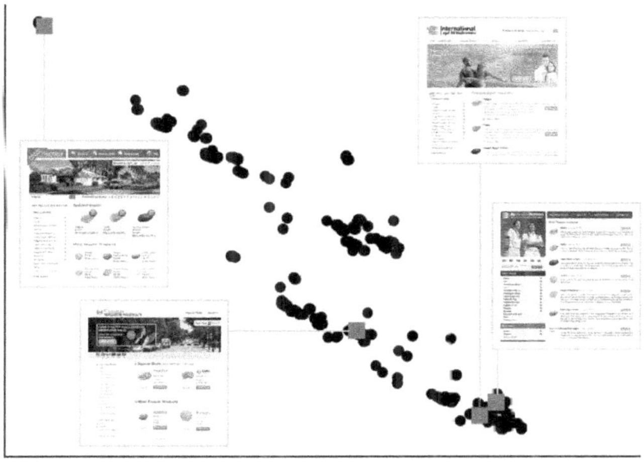

Figure 2: Projection of storefront feature vectors from the largest affiliate program (EvaPharmacy) onto the data's two leading principal components.

that of its NN. A common extension is to compute k nearest neighbors and to take the majority vote among them, but we did not find this necessary for our results in this domain.

There are many statistical models of classification—some of them quite sophisticated—but in this domain we were drawn to NN classification for reasons beyond its simplicity. A primary reason is that NN classifiers do not make any strong parametric assumptions about the data: they do not assume, for instance, that the examples in different classes are linearly separable, or that the examples in a single class are drawn from a particular distribution. The two-dimensional projection of EvaPharmacy storefronts in Figure 2 illustrates the problematic nature of such assumptions. Some affiliate programs use multiple template engines to generate a diversity of storefronts, and this in turn yields a complicated distribution in feature space. NN classification copes well with these complexities; to label examples correctly, it is only necessary to find that they are closest to others that are similarly labeled. The resulting decision boundaries can be quite nonlinear.

There are other natural advantages of NN classification for our work. It does not incur any additional complexity when there are large numbers of classes, and in our problem, there are dozens of affiliate programs. Also, NN classifiers do not need to be re-trained when new labeled data becomes available; in our problem, an operational system would need to cope with the inevitable launch of new affiliate programs. A final benefit of NN classification is that it lends itself to manual validation. For this study, we implemented a visual Web tool for validating predictions in the absence of ground truth labels. The tool displays two adjacent storefronts—one unlabeled, the other its nearest neighbor among the labeled examples—along with the distance between them and hyperlinks to their HTML source code. The tool was invaluable for ongoing validation of the classifier, a necessary part of any eventual, real-world deployment.

4. EXPERIMENTS

In this section we evaluate the potential of automated, data-driven methods for identifying the affiliate programs behind online storefronts. We take a bottom-up approach, beginning with simple diagnostics of the features in the previous section and ending with tests to measure how well a deployed NN classifier would perform in the real world. We begin with a brief overview of our experiments.

First we verify, as a proof of concept, that the online storefronts of different affiliate programs can in fact be distinguished by their HTML-based and network-based features. In these experiments, we attempt only to classify the Web pages of storefronts that belong to our previously identified set of forty-four affiliate programs. This is unrealistic as an operational setting, since in practice a working system would also need to classify Web pages that belong to other affiliate programs (or that do not even correspond to storefronts). However, as a logical first step, it is important to verify that the features we extract can—at least, in principle—separate the online storefronts of different affiliate programs.

Our next experiments remove the assumption of a "closed" universe of Web pages from previously identified affiliate programs. In these experiments we attempt to classify all Web pages that matched the category keywords of pharmaceuticals, replicas, or software (i.e., pages in the second level of Figure 1). A complication arises here in that we do not have "ground truth" labels for Web pages that were not matched and labeled by regular expressions. Many of these pages may indeed belong to other affiliate programs, but many from known programs may have simply gone undetected. (The regular expressions do not provide complete coverage; they can fail to match storefronts with slight, unforeseen variations in their HTML.) In this experiments we therefore follow NN classification with manual validation of its predictions. Here we succeed in detecting many additional storefronts from known affiliate programs that the regular expressions failed to match.

Our next experiments explore the effectiveness of NN classification at the outset of a Web crawl of spam-advertised URLs. At the outset of a crawl, practitioners must operate with very few labeled storefronts per affiliate program. While some manual labeling is unavoidable, the key question for practitioners is a simple one: how much labeling is "enough"? In particular, how many storefronts must be identified in each affiliate program before a NN classifier can take over, thereby automating the rest of the process? To answer this question we measure the accuracy of NN classification as a function of the number of labeled storefronts per affiliate program.

Our final experiments consider the most difficult scenario, one where practitioners lack the prior knowledge to label any storefronts by affiliate program. In these experiments we investigate how well (fully) unsupervised methods are able to cluster storefronts from multiple unidentified affiliate programs. We conduct two experiments to evaluate this potential. First, we cluster all the Web pages tagged as storefronts and measure how well the clusters correlate with known affiliate programs. Second, we investigate whether unsupervised methods can discover new affiliate programs among unlabeled storefronts. We also consider a closely related problem: recognizing when a known affiliate program generates storefront templates from a new software engine.

4.1 Proof of Concept

Our first experiments compare how well different features distinguish storefronts from a previously identified set of affiliate programs. In particular we experimented on the three different sets of features listed in Table 3. For each of these, we computed the accuracy of NN classification averaged over ten 70/30 training/test splits of labeled storefronts from the first three-month Web crawl. The splits were random except that we did preserve the proportion of affiliate programs across splits; this was necessary to ensure that even the smallest affiliate programs were represented in the training examples. NN classification in these experiments was extremely accurate. The classifier achieved over 99.6% (test) accuracy with just network-based features, and with HTML bag-of-word features it verged on ideal prediction: on average only 8 out of 53,484 test examples were misclassified.

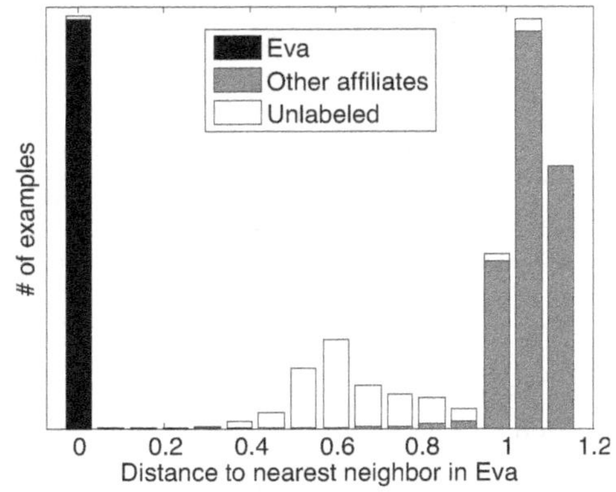

Figure 3: Histogram of three NN distances to EvaPharmacy storefronts: distances to storefronts in the same affiliate program, to those in other programs, and to unlabeled storefronts. Distances were computed using the HTML bag-of-words representation of the Web pages.

Figure 3 provides a visual explanation for the accuracy of NN classification. The distribution of NN distances illustrates how well-separated one class (EvaPharmacy) is from other classes. The shape of this distribution also reflects the large fraction of duplicates in the data set; these are different storefronts whose Web pages have the same representation in feature space.

These results demonstrate the power of very simple low-level features to distinguish the storefronts of different affiliate programs. Two points are worth emphasizing: first, that these features require no further processing for the high accuracy of NN classification, and second, that they are easy to extract automatically, requiring none of the manual effort of previous approaches.

In the experiments that follow we use only the bag-of-words features for NN classification. It is clear that these features suffice to distinguish the storefronts of different affiliate programs; they are also more readily available, as only the HTML source of a Web page is required. This consideration is important for ease-of-use as a deployed system. Also, as we have already remarked, the network-based features were not available for storefronts crawled during the second three-month period of data collection.

4.2 Labeling More Storefronts

Next we investigated whether our approach can identify the affiliate programs of storefronts whose HTML was not matched by regular expressions. One goal was to expand the

Regex matched	Not matched
 ViaGrow	 ViagPURE
 swissapotheke.net swissapotheke24.com swiss-apotheke.com	 swiss-apotheke.net

Table 4: Examples of storefronts matched by regular expressions (left column), and storefronts not matched but discovered by NN classification (right column).

number of labeled examples for subsequent evaluation of our approach. We generated bag-of-words feature vectors for the unlabeled Web pages using the vocabulary of HTML words in labeled storefronts. For each unlabeled page, we found the NN among labeled storefronts and marked it as a candidate match for that neighbor's affiliate program. Finally, for each affiliate program, we ranked the candidate pages by the proximity of their NNs and examined the rankings with the Web tool we implemented for manual validation.

In total we labeled 3,785 additional storefronts in the first three-month crawl of spam-advertised URLs; these newly labeled storefronts came from twenty-eight of the forty-four known affiliate programs. For most of these programs the new storefronts were detected as the top-ranked candidates, and a simple distance threshold separated the "hits" from the "misses." For example, Figure 3 shows that we discovered some new EvaPharmacy storefronts that were close or identical to their NN among labeled storefronts (shown by the small white segment of the first bar), but nothing beyond that. Only two affiliate programs had highly ranked candidate storefronts that belonged to a different but previously identified affiliate program.

Table 4 shows two storefronts detected by NN classification but missed by the regular expressions. In both cases, the discovered storefronts (right column) are very similar to their NN (left column) in both their HTML content and how they render in a browser. These examples expose the brittleness of the regular expressions, evading detection by a slight tweak to the domain name (`swiss-apotheke.net`) or a simple re-branding (ViaGrow → ViagPURE). Of course, a straightforward refinement of the regular expressions would rectify both these misses. However, it is precisely this need for refinement that we wish to avoid. The strength of our system is that it discovered and labeled these new storefronts automatically.

We repeated this same process to label new storefronts from the second three-month crawl of spam-advertised URLs. For this period, we found and labeled 731 new storefronts belonging to eighteen different affiliate programs. Table 5 shows how many additional storefronts we detected in all six months for certain affiliate programs. In the first time period, we detected the most new storefronts (1,467) for the RX-Promotion affiliate program, although this number only represented a 4% increase in the program's size. However, we detected an eight-fold increase in storefronts for the affiliate program Club-first.

4.3 Classification in the Wild

Our next experiments performed NN classification on all spam-advertised Web pages that were categorized as pharmaceutical, replica, or software Web sites. These are all the pages in the middle panel of Figure 1, not merely those matched by regular expressions. Most of these Web pages—the ones matched by regular expressions, and the ones detected and manually validated in the previous section—belong to the known family of forty-four affiliate programs. The others we assign to a catch-all label of "other," thereby yielding a 45-way problem in classification. With ground-truth labels for these Web pages, we can now reliably measure the performance of NN classification on this enlarged data set.

We began with experiments on the Web pages crawled during the first three-month period. As before, but now with the inclusion of an "other" label, we measured the accuracy of NN classification on ten 70/30 splits of the data. The average accuracy for 45-way classification was still remarkably high at 99.95%. These results show that NN classification can distinguish the storefronts of different affiliate programs even when many of them are collectively assigned an undifferentiated label of "other."

Next we investigated how well NN classification holds up over time. For this we performed NN classification using Web pages from the first three-month crawl as training examples and pages from the second three-month crawl as test examples. The accuracy remained high at 87.7%, a level that is still quite operationally useful for forty-five way classification of affiliate programs. But the drop of performance also indicates that a better system should adapt to affiliate programs as they evolve in time. In particular, as we detect and label new storefronts, it would behoove NN classification to augment the set of training examples and extract a larger vocabulary of HTML features.

Table 5 lists precision and recall on this task for some affiliate programs. The most startling result is the 0.25% recall for ED Express; in fact, almost 70% of the incorrect predictions involved misclassified storefronts from this affiliate program. We manually examined these storefronts and concluded that ED Express switched to a new template engine for generating storefronts. As a result the storefronts for ED Express from the second three-month crawl were rather different than those from the first. This is a valuable insight into how affiliate programs[4] operate, and we return to this case in our final set of experiments.

[4] As an aside, we learned later that these misclassified storefronts belonged to Pharmacy Express, and that Pharmacy Express and ED Express are in fact part of the same aggregate program called Mailien. Some of these errors can therefore be attributed to noisy and/or imperfect labeling of the training examples.

	1st 3 months				*2nd 3 months*			
Affiliate program	labeled	detected	precision	recall	labeled	detected	precision	recall
EvaPharmacy	58,215	434	99.98	100.00	13,529	98	99.29	99.29
Pharmacy Express	44,017	42	100.00	100.00	2,454	11	99.59	99.55
RX-Promotion	37,245	1,467	100.00	100.00	3,317	198	94.31	93.88
Online Pharmacy	16,546	758	100.00	100.00	3,457	271	92.86	92.86
GlavMed	6,616	263	99.95	100.00	176	49	77.73	76.00
EuroSoft	2,215	15	100.00	100.00	1,681	54	97.00	96.89
Ultimate Replica	79	10	100.00	100.00	121	5	96.03	96.03
ED Express	77	5	96.30	100.00	3,653	0	90.00	0.25
Club-first	14	114	100.00	100.00	6	0	100.00	100.00

Table 5: Data sizes and performance for select affiliate programs. The first five are the largest classes. EuroSoft and Ultimate Replica are representative software and replica programs. ED Express suffers drastic misprediction in the 2nd 3 months since it changed template engines. Club-first is the affiliate program whose size experiences the largest percent gain as a result of our classifier. In total, we profiled the storefronts of 29 pharmaceutical, 10 replica, and 5 software affiliate programs.

4.4 Learning with Few Labels

We next consider how many storefronts must be manually labeled before an automated system can dependably take over. In these experiments we vary the amount of labeled storefronts that are available as training examples for NN classification. In previous sections we studied the regime where there were many labeled storefronts per identified affiliate program. Here we consider the opposite regime where each affiliate program may, for instance, have no more than one labeled storefront.

We make two preliminary observations. First, in these experiments we not only have many fewer training examples; we also have many fewer features because the feature extraction is necessarily limited to counts of HTML words that appear in the training examples. Thus, to be clear, if we have just one labeled storefront per affiliate program, then we can only extract features from those forty-four labeled storefronts. In this regime we do not exclude rare words (though we still exclude stopwords).

Second, in these experiments we handle the "other" label for unidentified Web pages as a special case. At the outset of a Web crawl, we imagine that practitioners are likely to encounter numerous instances of Web pages that belong to unidentified affiliate programs or that do not represent storefronts at all. Thus in all the experiments of this section we assume that 100 Web pages are available from the undifferentiated "other" class that does not map to a previously identified affiliate program.

Figure 4 plots the balanced accuracy of NN classification per affiliate program (averaged over five random training/test splits) versus the number of labeled storefronts. Note that throughout this regime, the median accuracy holds at 100%, meaning that at least half the affiliate programs have none of their storefronts misclassified. Overall the results show that even with few labeled storefronts, NN classification is accurate enough to be operationally useful. With only one labeled storefront per affiliate program, the average 45-way classification accuracy remains nearly 75%; with two storefronts, it jumps to 85%, and with four, eight, and sixteen, it climbs respectively to 93%, 97%, and 98%.

Table 6 shows four correctly classified storefronts that render quite differently than their nearest (labeled) neighbors in this regime. Visually, it is not immediately obvious that these pairs of storefronts belong to the same affiliate program; upon inspection of their HTML source, however, it becomes apparent that their DOM trees share a similar underlying structure.

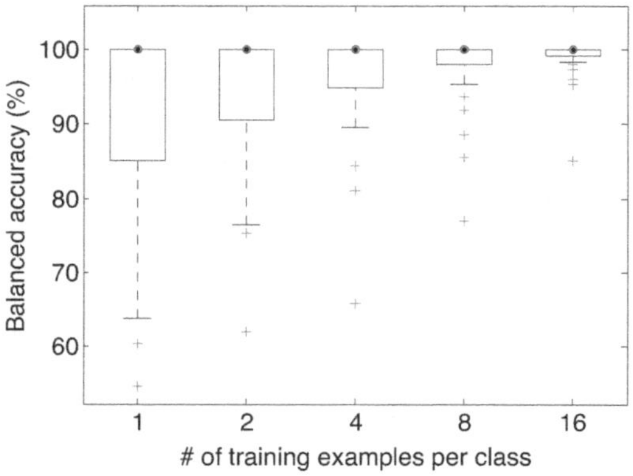

Figure 4: Boxplot showing balanced accuracy for all 45 classes as a function of training size. The top and bottom edges of the box are the 75th and 25th percentiles, respectively. The whiskers show the lowest points not considered outliers, and the outliers are individual plus marks.

We found that the affiliate program called RX-Partners suffered the worst performance throughout this regime. Upon closer examination of these errors, however, we observed that the regular expressions for RX-Partners often matched Web pages that were not storefronts at all. This mislabeling created many confusions in NN classification between RX-Partners and the undifferentiated "other" label.

These results suggest an iterative strategy for practitioners that balances the demands for high levels of both accuracy and automation. To begin, practitioners may seed NN classification with just one or two labeled storefronts per affiliate program. Then, using the preliminary predictions from NN classification in this regime, they may attempt to grow the number of labeled storefronts (and extractable features) in alternating rounds of manual validation and retraining. This "bootstrapping" strategy seems the most effective way to develop a practical, working system.

Training Example	Correct Classifications
	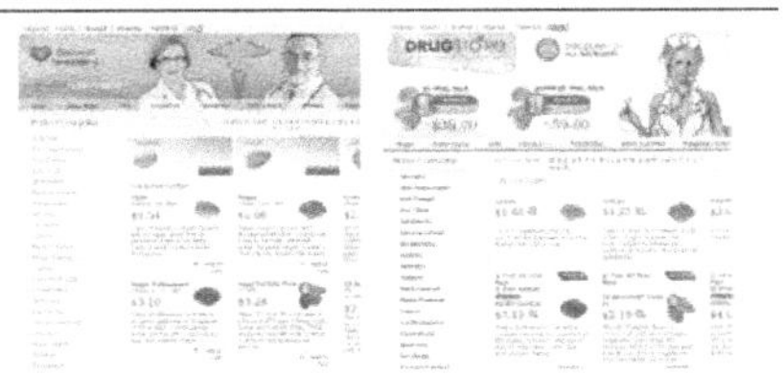
	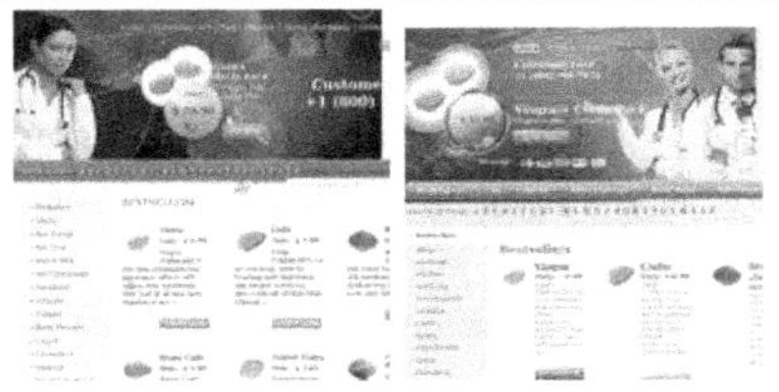

Table 6: Examples of correctly classified storefronts when there is only one training example per affiliate program. The affiliate programs shown here are 33drugs and RX-Promotion.

4.5 Clustering

Finally, we investigate the capabilities of fully *unsupervised* methods for distinguishing storefronts from different affiliate programs. We do this first for the full set of pharmaceutical, replica, and software Web pages, in the hope that these storefronts might cluster in an organic way by affiliate program. Next we do this just for the set of undifferentiated storefronts marked as "other", in the hope that we might identify new affiliate programs within this set.

4.5.1 *Clustering of Storefronts by Affiliate Program*

A preliminary clustering of online storefronts can be useful as a first step before the manual labeling of their affiliate programs. This was the approach taken in [9], and it is the operational setting that we emulate here.

We ran the k-means algorithm, one of the simplest unsupervised methods for clustering, on all the Web pages tagged as storefronts for pharmaceuticals, replica luxury goods, and software. These pages included those in the "other" class not identified with a known affiliate program. In general, the cluster labels are highly predictive of the affiliate program identities: of the 42 clusters, 22 are entirely composed of storefronts from a single affiliate program, and 32 very nearly have this property, with less than 1% of their storefronts from a competing program.

A quantitative measure of this correlation is given by the uncertainty coefficient [16], which measures the reduction of uncertainty in a Web page's class label c (e.g., affiliate program) given its cluster label d. Let C and D denote random variables for these labels. The uncertainty coefficient is computed as:

$$U(C|D) = 1 - \frac{H(C|D)}{H(C)} = 1 - \frac{\sum_{c,d} p(c,d)\,\log p(c|d)}{\sum_c p(c)\,\log p(c)},$$

where $H(C)$ is the entropy of C and $H(C|D)$ is the conditional entropy of C given D. The joint probability $p(c,d)$ is obtained by counting the number of Web pages with class label c and cluster label d, then dividing by the total number of Web pages. Note that the uncertainty coefficient is bounded between 0 and 1, where 0 indicates that the two variables are completely uncorrelated, and 1 indicates that one variable is completely determined by the other. From the results of k-means clustering we obtain an uncertainty coefficient of 0.933. This coefficient shows that very few clusters contain Web pages from more than one class.

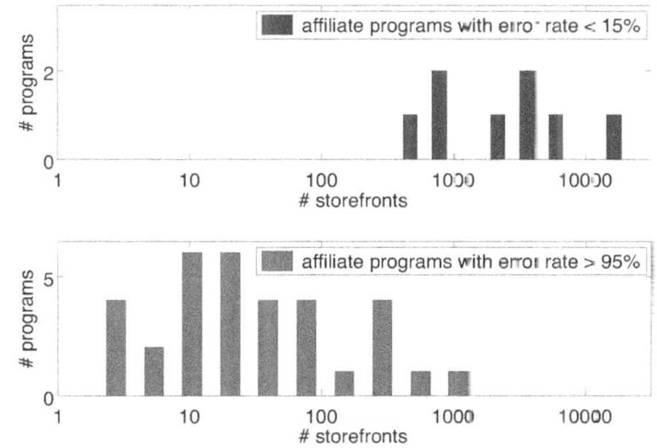

Figure 5: Number of affiliate programs of different sizes with few versus many clustering errors; see text for details. In general the larger programs have low error rates (top), while the smaller programs have very high error rates (bottom).

Another measure of cluster "purity" is obtained by computing the overall percentage of storefronts assigned to a cluster that contains more storefronts from a different affiliate program. This percentage is 3.27%, quite a low confusion rate for a problem in 45-way classification.

It must be emphasized, however, that while k-means clustering generally separates Web pages from different affiliate programs, it does so by modeling the larger affiliate programs at the expense of the smaller ones. In particular, only 11 out of 44 affiliate programs are represented as the dominant class of one or more clusters; the other 33 programs are swallowed up by the larger ones. We say a clustering "error" occurs when a storefront is mapped to a cluster that contains more storefronts from one or more different affiliate programs. The top panel of Figure 5 shows that all the largest affiliate programs (with over 2000 storefronts) have error rates less than 15%; conversely the bottom panel shows that all the smallest affiliate programs (with fewer than 100 storefronts) have error rates greater than 95%.

We conclude that unsupervised methods have high accuracy but poor coverage of affiliate programs. On one hand, by distinguishing storefronts in the largest affiliate programs (which account for over 96% of the Web pages), these methods may greatly reduce the set of pages that require manual labeling. On the other hand, for complete coverage of affiliate programs, it seems imperative to label at least one storefront per program. Once these labels are provided, moreover, we believe that the best approach will be a supervised model, such as NN classification, that exploits the information in these labels.

4.5.2 *Detecting New and Evolving Programs*

Lastly we investigate the potential of clustering methods to detect new and evolving affiliate programs. In our first experiment, we used the k-means algorithm to cluster the storefronts labeled as "other" from the first three-month crawl. We then ranked the storefronts in each cluster by their distance to the cluster centroid and manually examined the top-ranked (i.e., most "central") ones with our Web visualization tool. Using this approach, we discovered a new affiliate program called RxCashCow; the 430 top-ranked storefronts in one cluster belonged to this program, and only a small fraction of the top-ranked 1,100 did not.

Finally we revisit the interesting case of ED Express. Recall that NN classification failed to identify these storefronts during the second three-month crawl because the affiliate program switched to a new template engine. Our last experiment used the k-means algorithm to cluster all the storefronts from the second three-month crawl. Our hope was that the algorithm might separate out the evolved storefronts of ED Express, and indeed we found a cluster whose 3,580 top-ranked pages were exactly those generated by the new template engine.

5. CONCLUSION

We have described an automated approach for profiling the online storefronts of counterfeit merchandise. We evaluated our approach on hundreds of thousands of storefronts gathered from a Web crawl of spam-advertised URLs. Our methods aim to identify the affiliate programs behind these storefronts, an important first step in tracking and targeting illicit e-commerce. Our first experiments showed that these affiliate programs could be identified, with high accuracy, from simple NN classification on bag-of-words features. With an operational setting in mind, we also showed that the feature extraction and NN classification only required a small seed of labeled storefronts to be highly effective. Our final experiments investigated the potential of unsupervised methods for clustering storefronts by affiliate program. Here we found that k-means clustering could be used to discover affiliate programs with large spam footprints, but that smaller affiliate programs (i.e., those with fewer storefronts) were not cleanly identified. Overall, our work is an encouraging case study in the application of machine learning to an important class of security problems on the Web.

Acknowledgments

We thank Andreas Pitsillidis and Tristan Halvorson for making this data set accessible, as well as Cindy Moore for setting up our computing resources. This work was supported in part by National Science Foundation grant CNS-1237264, by the Office of Naval Research MURI grant N00014-09-1-1081, and by generous research, operational and/or in-kind support from Google, Microsoft, Yahoo, and the UCSD Center for Networked Systems (CNS).

6. REFERENCES

[1] S. N. Bannur, L. K. Saul, and S. Savage. Judging a site by its content: learning the textual, structural, and visual features of malicious Web Pages. In *Proc. of the 4th ACM Workshop on Security and Artificial Intelligence*, 2011.

[2] T. Cover and P. Hart. Nearest neighbor pattern classification. In *IEEE Transactions in Information Theory, IT-13*, pages 21–27, 1967.

[3] J. Drew and T. Moore. Automatic identification of replicated criminal websites using combined clustering. In *International Workshop on Cyber Crime (IWCC), IEEE Security and Privacy Workshops*. IEEE, 2014.

[4] T. Halvorson, K. Levchenko, S. Savage, and G. M. Voelker. XXXtortion? Inferring Registration Intent in the .XXX TLD. In *Proceedings of the International World Wide Web Conference (WWW)*, Apr. 2014.

[5] J. P. John, F. Yu, Y. Xie, A. K. and M. Abadi. deSEO: Combating Search-Result Poisoning. In *Proceedings of the 20th USENIX Security Symposium*, August 2011.

[6] I. T. Jolliffe. *Principal Component Analysis*. Springer-Verlag, New York, 1986.

[7] C. Kanich, N. Weaver, D. McCoy, T. Halvorson, C. Kreibich, K. Levchenko, V. Paxson, G. M. Voelker, and S. Savage. Show Me the Money: Characterizing Spam-advertised Revenue. In *Proc. of the USENIX Security Symposium*, San Francisco, CA, Aug. 2011.

[8] R. Layton, P. Watters, and R. Dazeley. Automatically determining phishing campaigns using the uscap methodology. In *eCrime Researchers Summit (eCrime), 2010*, pages 1–8, Oct 2010.

[9] K. Levchenko, A. Pitsillidis, N. Chachra, B. Enright, M. Félegyházi, C. Grier, T. Halvorson, C. Kanich, C. Kreibich, H. Liu, D. McCoy, N. Weaver, V. Paxson, G. M. Voelker, and S. Savage. Click Trajectories: End-to-End Analysis of the Spam Value Chain. In *Proceedings of the IEEE Symposium and Security and Privacy*, Oakland, CA, May 2011.

[10] Z. Li, K. Zhang, Y. Xie, F. Yu, and X. Wang. Knowing Your Enemy: Understanding and Detecting Malicious Web Advertising. In *Proc. of the ACM Conference on Computer and Communications Security (CCS)*, October 2012.

[11] J.-L. Lin. Detection of cloaked web spam by using tag-based methods. *Expert Syst. Appl.*, 36(4):7493–7499, May 2009.

[12] C. Ludl, S. McAllister, E. Kirda, and C. Kruegel. On the Effectiveness of Techniques to Detect Phishing Sites. In *Proceedings of the Conference on Detection of Intrusions and Malware & Vulnerability Assessment (DIMVA)*, 2007.

[13] D. McCoy, H. Dharmdasani, C. Kreibich, G. M. Voelker, and S. Savage. Priceless: The Role of Payments in Abuse-advertised Goods. In *Proceedings of the ACM Conference on Computer and Communications Security*, Raleigh, NC, Oct. 2012.

[14] D. McCoy, A. Pitsillidis, G. Jordan, N. Weaver, C. Kreibich, B. Krebs, G. M. Voelker, S. Savage, and K. Levchenko. PharmaLeaks: Understanding the Business of Online Pharmaceutical Affiliate Programs. In *Proceedings of the USENIX Security Symposium*, Aug. 2012.

[15] T. Moore and B. Edelman. Measuring the Perpetrators and Funders of Typosquatting. In *Proceedings of the 14th International Conference on Financial Cryptography and Data Security*, 2010.

[16] W. H. Press, S. A. Teukolsky, W. T. Vetterling, and B. P. Flannery. *Numerical Recipes 3rd Edition: The Art of Scientific Computing*. Cambridge University Press, New York, NY, USA, 2007.

[17] N. Provos, P. Mavrommatis, M. Rajab, and F. Monrose. All Your iFRAMEs Point to Us. In *Proceedings of the USENIX Security Symposium*, 2008.

[18] K. Thomas, C. Grier, J. Ma, V. Paxson, and D. Song. Design and Evaluation of a Real-Time URL Spam Filtering Service. In *Proceedings of the IEEE Symposium on Security and Privacy*, May 2011.

[19] T. Urvoy, E. Chauveau, P. Filoche, and T. Lavergne. Tracking Web Spam with HTML Style Similarities. *ACM Trans. Web*, 2(1):3:1–3:28, Mar. 2008.

[20] D. Wang, S. Savage, and G. M. Voelker. Juice: A Longitudinal Study of an SEO Campaign. In *Proc. of the Network and Distributed System Security Sympo sium (NDSS)*, San Diego, CA, Feb. 2013.

[21] Y. Zhang, J. Hong, and L. Cranor. CANTINA: A Content-Based Approach to Detecting Phising Web Sites. In *Proceedings of the International World Wide Web Conference*, pages 639–648, 2007.

Up Next: Retrieval Methods for Large Scale Related Video Suggestion

Michael Bendersky
Google, Inc.
bemike@google.com

Lluis Garcia-Pueyo
Google, Inc.
lgpueyo@google.com

Jeremiah Harmsen
Google, Inc.
jeremiah@google.com

Vanja Josifovski
Google, Inc.
vanjaj@google.com

Dima Lepikhin
Google, Inc.
lepikhin@google.com

ABSTRACT

The explosive growth in sharing and consumption of the video content on the web creates a unique opportunity for scientific advances in video retrieval, recommendation and discovery. In this paper, we focus on the task of video suggestion, commonly found in many online applications. The current state-of-the-art video suggestion techniques are based on the collaborative filtering analysis, and suggest videos that are likely to be co-viewed with the watched video. In this paper, we propose augmenting the collaborative filtering analysis with the topical representation of the video content to suggest related videos. We propose two novel methods for topical video representation. The first method uses information retrieval heuristics such as tf-idf, while the second method learns the optimal topical representations based on the implicit user feedback available in the online scenario. We conduct a large scale live experiment on YouTube traffic, and demonstrate that augmenting collaborative filtering with topical representations significantly improves the quality of the related video suggestions in a live setting, especially for categories with fresh and topically-rich video content such as news videos. In addition, we show that employing user feedback for learning the optimal topical video representations can increase the user engagement by more than 80% over the standard information retrieval representation, when compared to the collaborative filtering baseline.

Categories and Subject Descriptors

H.3.3 [**Information Storage and Retrieval**]: Information Search and Retrieval

General Terms

Algorithms, Experimentation

KDD'14, August 24–27, 2014, New York, NY, USA.

http://dx.doi.org/10.1145/2623330.2623344.

Keywords

Video retrieval, related video suggestion, video representation

1. INTRODUCTION

The World Wide Web project was originally conceived as a means to publish, share and retrieve textual information and did not aim *"to do research into fancy multimedia facilities such as sound and video"* [1]. However, with the growth of the web, video and other multimedia formats became an increasingly large and important part of it. The recent proliferation of mobile devices that enable instant video capturing, sharing and consumption, further accelerated this trend.

As an example, at the time of the writing of this paper, over 6 billion hours of video are watched monthly on YouTube, the most popular video-sharing website, an increase of 50% compared to last year. Furthermore, 100 hours of new video content are uploaded to YouTube every minute [2].

These statistics demonstrate that there is an ever-growing abundance of video content on the web. This content ranges from six-second long mobile video clips on Vine and user-uploaded footage on YouTube, to news stories on news websites and TV shows and movies on subscription-based streaming services such as Hulu and Netflix.

This abundance of content supply and demand has brought about an urgent need for increasingly sophisticated techniques for video retrieval, recommendation and discovery. In particular, in this paper, we focus on the task of *video suggestion*, which is common in many online applications.

We define *video suggestions* as a ranked list of *related videos* shown to the user in response to the video that she is currently viewing (which we refer to as the *watch video*). Video suggestions are an important part of the experience of watching video on the web today, and they are steadily becoming prevalent on more and more video websites. As an illustration, Figure 1 showcases three major use cases for video suggestions, including suggestion of (a) news stories on CNN, (b) TV show episodes on Hulu, and (c) related videos on YouTube.

As shown in previous work, successful deployment of video suggestion algorithms can result in a significant positive ef-

[1] As stated in the original HyperText proposal: `http://www.w3.org/Proposal.html`.

(a) CNN (b) Hulu (c) YouTube

Figure 1: Examples of video suggestions on the web, showcasing suggestions based on the currently watched video on CNN, Hulu and YouTube websites.

fect on user engagement and user experience [7, 13]. For instance, Davidson et al. [13] show that co-visitation based video suggestions more than double the click-through rate, compared to a baseline that does not take the watch video into account.

Video suggestions can be either based on the watch video alone [7], or can be personalized by incorporating information about the user (e.g., search history [11]). Current state-of-the-art video suggestion systems are based on the collaborative filtering analysis. Most generally, videos suggested by these systems are likely to be co-viewed with the watch video by the majority of the users [7, 11, 13].

While this approach works well for popular and often watched videos, it is less applicable to fresh videos or tail videos with few views, since they have very sparse and noisy co-view data. For these videos, collaborative filtering analysis based solely on co-views may yield either low-quality suggestions or no suggestions at all.

To address the problem of tail content in other domains such as recommendations based on textual information, researchers developed hybrid approaches [10] that combine information about the item content with the collaborative filtering information to improve recommendation. While there have been some small scale studies on hybrid recommendation systems for video suggestion [31], this paper, to the best of our knowledge, is the first published research study of a large scale deployment of such a system.

To achieve the goal of content-based video representation, we first model a video as a set of topics that are mined from a variety of sources including the video metadata, frequently used uploader keywords, common search queries, playlist names, Freebase entities and Wikipedia articles. These topics are then used to retrieve related videos for suggestion.

Thus, our approach to content-based video suggestion is akin to the standard information retrieval scenario. The topical representation of the watch video is the *query* that is issued to the inverted index that stores the topical video representations as *documents*. Since we cast the video suggestion problem as a retrieval over an inverted index, we can use query optimization algorithms [8, 14] to efficiently find the optimal video suggestions even in a very large corpus.

The highest ranked documents retrieved in response to the query are returned as content-based video suggestions. These suggestions can be either directly shown to the user, or used to augment the output of the co-view based video suggestion system.

In order to achieve an effective topical video representation, we assign weights to each topic associated with a video. We propose two techniques for topical video representation. The first technique is based on the well known information retrieval heuristics such as computing topic frequencies and topic inverse document frequencies. The second technique leverages the implicit user feedback (such as video co-watches) available in the online setting. This feedback is used for a supervised learning of the optimal topic weights.

We empirically evaluate these two topical representation methods. We find that both of these representations have a significantly positive effect on the quality of video suggestions. Furthermore, our evaluation demonstrates that learning topic weights from user feedback can increase the user engagement (compared to the collaborative filtering approach) by more than 80% over the standard information retrieval representation.

To evaluate our approaches, we conduct a large scale live experiment on millions of YouTube video. The live experiment demonstrates that a hybrid video suggestion system that incorporates topic-based retrieval significantly outperforms a purely co-view based suggestion system. These improvements are especially high for fresh videos and videos with rich topical representations.

There are several important contributions in this paper. First, we formulate the video suggestion task as an information retrieval problem and demonstrate that this formulation enables effective and efficient deployment of video suggestion on a very large scale. Previous work on video retrieval was mainly performed offline on relatively small collections such as TRECVID collections [20], or small pre-selected samples of online videos [31]. To the best of our knowledge, this is the first published study to address the challenges of real-time video retrieval using topical representation in a large scale web collection.

Second, we demonstrate that the richness of the implicit user feedback available in the online setting can be leveraged to improve the effectiveness of topical video representations. To this end we employ a novel learning technique that derives the optimal topic weights from co-view information.

Third, we describe the architecture of the hybrid video suggestion system that combines the collaborative filtering information with the topic-based video information.

Finally, we thoroughly evaluate the performance of our system using both user simulation and a large scale live experiment. This evaluation demonstrates the superiority of the proposed hybrid video suggestion system to the current state-of-the-art collaborative filtering approaches.

The rest of the paper is organized as follows. Section 2 describes video representations using topics. Section 3 describes retrieval using topics weighted by information retrieval heuristics, and Section 4 describes retrieval using topic transitions learned from user watch behavior. Section 5 provides a holistic view of the proposed video suggestion system. In Section 6 we overview the related work. Section 7 desribes the evaluation of our techniques using both user simulation and a large scale live experiment. Section 8 concludes the paper.

2. VIDEO REPRESENTATION

In this section, we discuss how a video is represented via a set of associated *topics*. These topics serve as a semantic representation of the video content, and are used by the retrieval algorithms in the next sections. The topics are derived from a variety of sources that can be associated with a video such as video metadata, uploader keywords, common search queries, playlist names, etc.

For the purpose of this paper, we use the notation V both to refer to the video itself, and the set of topics associated with it, interchangeably. Therefore, the notation $\tau \in V$ is used to state that video V is annotated with topic τ.

2.1 Topic Assignment

There is a large variety of methods described in the scientific literature (e.g., [16, 27, 28, 29, 30] among many others) on how to derive a set of annotations for images and videos. Some of these methods involve image and video analysis, while others rely on textual annotations, anchor text information and query logs.

In this paper, we follow the latter approach. This is due to the fact that there is a plethora of sources that can be utilized to annotate online videos with semantic information, including the video metadata, frequently used uploader keywords, common search queries, playlist names, and even sources from different domains such as Freebase entities and Wikipedia articles. The interested reader may refer to the YouTube official blog [1, 3] or work by Simonet [25] for more information about the YouTube video topic assignment process.

For the purpose of the retrieval algorithms discussed in the next sections, we will assume that we can reliably annotate a given video V with a set of topics using the sources described above [1, 3]. These topics represent the different semantic aspects of the video and map the video representation V into some existing concept space (e.g., Freebase concepts as shown in [3]).

As an example, Figure 2 demonstrates a movie trailer *World War Z* along with the topics associated with it and the topic weights. As can be seen in Figure 2, these topics capture several aspects of the video content including movie title, genre and leading actor, as well as information about the video itself.

In the rest of this paper, we will assume that the topical annotation can serve as a faithful representation of the video content. Therefore, we will use these annotations to retrieve videos related to the *watch video* – video that is currently being viewed by the user.

For this purpose, we will represent both the watch video and the potentially related videos as vectors of topic weights,

Figure 2: Example of topics associated with a video, and their corresponding weights.

and compute a vector dot product to determine a similarity of a <*watch video, related video*> pair. Related videos will then be ranked by their similarity score to the watch video.

2.2 Topics Versus Co-View Graph

It is important to note that the topical video representation described in the previous section has very different characteristics from the *co-view* video representation, used in previous work on related video discovery [7]. In the co-view video representation, each video is represented by a node in the co-view graph. A node is then linked to the other nodes in the graph if it is often viewed with them in the same session [7]. In this approach, related video suggestion is done based on the nodes that are in the proximity to the watch video in the co-view graph.

Therefore, in the co-view approach two videos are potentially related if and only if they have a strong connection in the co-view graph, i.e., they were often watched in the same session. This approach works well for popular videos with many views and high node connectivity. However, it is much less reliable for videos with little or no views. For these videos, using the co-view approach may lead to spurious results, or yield no candidates for suggestions.

In contrast, the topical video representation does not require an explicit co-view information to deem two video related. Instead, if two videos share (some of) the same topics they will be related, even if they were never watched in the same session before.

This semantic approach enables discovery of fresh, diverse and relevant content. It has been shown that implicit user feedback is often influenced by presentation bias [32], and click metrics do not fully correlate with relevance [21]. Topic-based video suggestion can therefore limit the *rich get richer* effect that can potentially arise when using solely the co-view information and disregarding the video content.

2.3 Topic Indexing

Video representation using topic weight vectors is akin to the *bag-of-words* document representation often used in the information retrieval applications. Therefore, we index the topic video representations in a standard inverted index structure [19] for efficient retrieval. Each video is represented using a topic weight vector, and indexed as an entry in the posting lists of its corresponding topics.

The inverted index structure enables efficient scoring of the related candidate videos in response to a watch video. Since we are only interested in a limited number of highest scoring related videos for a given watch video, we employ the WeakAnd query optimization technique first proposed by Broder et al. [8]. WeakAnd query optimization fully scores only a small fraction of the videos with score upper bound greater than a given threshold. This threshold is revised at query runtime as more videos are scored. To avoid fully scoring the document, the WeakAnd optimization maintains an upper bound of a document score, based on the maximum weight in each of the posting lists evaluated in response to the query. For more detailed description of the WeakAnd algorithm see [8, 14].

3. RETRIEVAL WITH WEIGHTED TOPICS

In Section 2.3 we described the topic indexing process. In this section, we use this topic index to develop a related video suggestion algorithm that is based on the standard information retrieval practices.

Recall that the videos in our system are represented as vectors of topic weights. Given this representation, for a watch video and related video pair $\langle V_W, V_R \rangle$ we derive the following score

$$sc(V_W, V_R) = q(V_R) \sum_{\tau \in V_W \cap V_R} \mathcal{I}_s(\tau) \frac{c(\tau, V_W)}{\log(1 + df(\tau))} c(\tau, V_R). \tag{1}$$

The score in Equation 1 has several components that are based on standard information retrieval practices.

First, the topic count function $c(\tau, V)$ returns a normalized count of videos that are annotated with the topic τ and are co-viewed with the video V. The topic count function estimates the *topicality* of video V with respect to topic τ.

Second, $\log(1 + df(\tau))$ is an inverse document frequency component that penalizes frequently occuring topics. Inverse document frequency demotes overly broad, vague and non specific topics, similarly to the *idf* term weighting in information retrieval applications.

Third, Equation 1 includes an indicator function

$$\mathcal{I}_s(\tau) = \begin{cases} 1 & df(\tau) < df_{max} \\ 0 & \text{else,} \end{cases}$$

where df_{max} is set to some large constant. The indicator function $\mathcal{I}_s(\tau)$ is inspired by the stopword removal in information retrieval applications, which removes very frequent stopwords at either indexing time or query time. We found that such stopword removal technique is useful for disregarding noisy and redundant topic matches from score computation, and improves both efficiency and effectiveness at query time.

Finally, Equation 1 takes into account the overall quality of the related video $q(V_R)$. Function $q(V_R)$ is based, among other factors on the video age, uploader, "thumbs up" and "thumbs down" counts, video popularity and freshness.

Note that since all the videos have roughly the same (small) number of topics associated with them, we do not apply any document length normalization method such as cosine similarity or pivoted length normalization [26]. Instead we simply use an unnormalized vector dot product as a scoring function in Equation 1.

4. LEARNING TOPIC TRANSITIONS

In Section 3 we described a retrieval approach that assigns topic weights based on a set of information retrieval heuristics (topic counts, inverse document frequency and stopword removal). In this section, we show that given the richness of the implicit user feedback available in the online setting, it is possible to learn the optimal transitions between the topics in the watch and the related videos. These transitions can then be directly leveraged for related video retrieval.

Consider, for instance, the example of the trailer for the *World War Z* movie shown in Figure 2. Assuming that the topic weights in Figure 2 are derived from the normalized co-occurence counts in Equation 1, the topic *Horror_Movie* is weighted lower than the topic *World_War_Z*. However, the *Horror_Movie* topic might be important for finding other related videos such as a trailer for the *Jurassic Park IV* movie. Therefore, a topic can have relatively low co-occurence counts for both the watch and the related videos, yet still be beneficial for the retrieval of relevant related videos.

Based on this intuition, we propose a novel machine learning approach that takes into account topic interactions and learns topic transition weights based on implicit user feedback. Our approach is based on pairwise classification of *<watch video, related video>* pairs.

In Sections 4.1 and 4.2 we describe how the topic transitions are represented. Then, in Section 4.3 we describe the optimization of the topic transition weights. Finally, in Section 4.4 we describe related video retrieval using topic transition weights.

4.1 Topic Transitions

Suppose that two potentially related videos are suggested to the user in response to the watch video V_W. One of the videos, $V_R^{(+)}$, was clicked and viewed by the user. The other video, $V_R^{(-)}$, was ignored by the user.

Most generally, we seek topic transition weight assignments such that the suggested related video $V_R^{(+)}$ will be preferred by the model to the suggested video $V_R^{(-)}$. This problem formulation is inspired by the pairwise classification approach which is common in learning-to-rank applications (e.g., see Burges et al. [9] or Joachims [17]).

Formally, we represent a potentially related video V_R that was suggested in response to a watch video V_W using a binary feature vector

$$\mathbf{x}_{V_R} = [\mathcal{I}_{V_R}(\tau_W, \tau_R) \colon \tau_W \in \mathbf{T}, \tau_R \in \mathbf{T}],$$

where $\mathbf{T}$ is the lexicon of all available topics, and $\mathcal{I}_{V_R}$ is a transition function from topic τ_W to τ_R such that

$$\mathcal{I}_{V_R}(\tau_W, \tau_R) = \begin{cases} 1 & \tau_W \in V_W, \tau_R \in V_R \\ 0 & \text{else} \end{cases}$$

Given a pair of related videos

$$P_R = \langle V_R^{(+)}, V_R^{(-)} \rangle,$$

we represent the pair using a ternary feature vector:

$$\mathbf{x}_{P_R} = [\mathcal{I}_{P_R}(\tau_W, \tau_R) \colon \tau_W \in \mathbf{T}, \tau_R \in \mathbf{T}],$$

where the transition function $\mathcal{I}_{P_R}(\tau_W, \tau_R)$ is defined such that

$$\mathcal{I}_{P_R}(\tau_W, \tau_R) = \mathcal{I}_{V_R^{(+)}}(\tau_W, \tau_R) - \mathcal{I}_{V_R^{(-)}}(\tau_W, \tau_R) \tag{2}$$

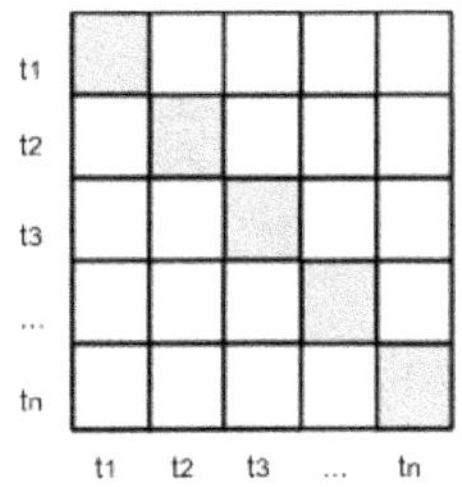

Figure 3: Topic transition matrix. Diagonal topic transitions are marked in grey.

It is easy to show that following the formulation in Equation 2, transition function $\mathcal{I}_{P_R}$ can take three values:

1. $\mathcal{I}_{P_R}(\tau_W, \tau_R) = +1$ iff τ_R is associated only with the positive example $V_R^{(+)}$.

2. $\mathcal{I}_{P_R}(\tau_W, \tau_R) = -1$ iff τ_R is associated only with the negative example $V_R^{(-)}$.

3. $\mathcal{I}_{P_R}(\tau_W, \tau_R) = 0$ in all other cases.

4.2 Diagonal Topic Transitions

Note that in the unconstrained form presented in Equation 2, we capture transitions between all pairs of topics in the lexicon $\mathbf{T}$. Therefore, given a transition matrix in Figure 3 we need to learn a transition weight for each cell in the matrix.

This approach is clearly infeasible for large open domain lexicons, which can contain millions of unique topics, since there are $\mathbf{T}^2$ possible transitions. Moreover, the transition matrix will be very sparse since there will be relatively few topic pairs with observed transitions. Even for pairs where we do observe transitions, the number of observed examples may be too small to learn a reliable model.

Therefore, we restrict ourselves to learning the transition weights only for the diagonal of the transition matrix (marked in grey in Figure 3). This makes the learning tractable, and leads to a more reliable model with less overfitting, since a diagonal transition is likely to be observed more frequently than a transition between two arbitrary topics.

Also, note that the diagonal transitions mirror the information retrieval approach described in Section 3, where only matches between topics that occur both in the watch and the related video are considered (Equation 1). This facilitates a fair comparison between the performance of these approaches, as discussed in Section 7.

4.3 Loss Miminimization

Given the diagonal topic transition representation described in Section 4.2, the train set $\mathbf{S}_P$ is defined over all the non-discordant pairs of related videos, sampled from user traffic. For the i-th pair $P_i \in \mathbf{S}_P$, a transition vector is defined as

$$\mathbf{x}_i = \{\mathcal{I}_{P_i}(\tau, \tau) : \tau \in \mathbf{T}\},$$

such that x_{ij} denotes the j-th diagonal topic transition for the i-th pair of related videos.

Then, we seek a weight vector $\mathbf{w}^*$, which minimizes the l_1- regularized logistic loss over the train set $\mathbf{S}_P$.

Algorithm 1: The *parallel-update* optimization algorithm [12] for learning topic transition weights.

```
t = 1;
repeat
    for instance i = 1, ..., |S_P| do
        q^t(i) = L(w, {x_i});
        for transition j = 1, ..., |T| do
            μ_j^+ = Σ_{i: sign(x_ij)=+1} q^t(i)|x_ij|;
            μ_j^- = Σ_{i: sign(x_ij)=-1} q^t(i)|x_ij|;
            Δ_j^t = 1/2 log (μ_j^+ / μ_j^-);
            w^{t+1} = w^t + Δ^t;
            t = t + 1;
        end
    end
until convergence or max # of iterations reached;
return w^{t+1}
```

Formally, given the loss function over an arbitrary set of examples $\mathbf{S}$, parameterized by a weight vector $\mathbf{w}$

$$\mathcal{L}(\mathbf{w}, \mathbf{S}) = \sum_{\mathbf{x} \in \mathbf{S}} \log(1 + \exp(-\mathbf{w} \cdot \mathbf{x})) + \lambda \|\mathbf{w}\|_1, \quad (3)$$

where $\lambda > 0$ is the regularization parameter, we seek an optimal vector $\mathbf{w}^*$ such that

$$\mathbf{w}^* = \arg\min_{\mathbf{w}} \mathcal{L}(\mathbf{w}, \mathbf{S}_P). \quad (4)$$

There is a wide variety of methods that could be employed to minimize the loss function in Equation 3. In this paper, we use the *parallel-update* optimization algorithm, first proposed by Collins et al. [12].

The parallel-update algorithm for finding the optimal diagonal transition weight vector $\mathbf{w}^*$ is outlined in Algorithm 1. The parallel-update algorithm iteratively updates the weight vector $\mathbf{w}^t$ at round t by vector $\mathbf{\Delta}^t$ which is computed using the loss on each individual instance $q^t(i)$.

The main advantage of the parallel-update algorithm is its scalability in the number of examples and the number of features. Note that in Algorithm 1, the $q^t(i)$ and $\mu_j^{\pm}$ parameters are computed independently for each instance i and transition j, which naturally enables parallelization of the weight updates. In addition, the parallel-update algorithm can continuously update the weight vector $\mathbf{w}^*$ as new instances are added to the train set. This property is particularly important in the online setting, where training instances are continuously added based on new user feedback.

4.4 Retrieval with Topic Transitions

Given the optimal diagonal topic transition weight vector $\mathbf{w}^*$ computed by the Algorithm 1, we use it to rank the related video suggestions in response to a watch video V_W. The scoring function is simply given by

$$sc(V_W, V_R) = \sum_{\{w_i \in \mathbf{w}^* : \tau_i \in V_W \cap V_R\}} w_i \quad (5)$$

Note that Equation 5 does not require utilizing any additional heuristics such as *idf* weighting, in addition to the transition weights. This is due to the fact the weights $\mathbf{w}^*$ are optimal for transitioning from watch video with topic τ_i to a related video with topic τ_i, according to the loss criterion defined in Equation 3.

5. SYSTEM OVERVIEW

In this section, we provide a holistic overview of the general architecture of the experimental video suggestion system, which was designed for evaluating the topic retrieval methods described in the previous sections. This system was designed specifically for the purpose of the experiments in this paper, and does not correspond to any system used in production.

We built this experimental system in order to integrate both the co-view based and the topic-based retrieval methods into a single video suggestion system, shown in Figure 4. The purpose of this integration is to demonstrate the benefits of our topic-based video suggestion approach, as compared to the standard co-view based video suggestion approaches [7, 13].

For a given watch video V_W, two retrieval processes are run in parallel. First, we retrieve a set of k related candidates based on the link structure of the co-view graph. See Baluja et al. [7] (surveyed in Section 2.2) for the detailed description of an implementation of such a process. Most generally, this process retrieves all the videos that were most oftenly co-watched with the watch video V_W, regardless of their topicality.

Second, we retrieve top-k ranking candidate videos using a topic-based retrieval process. This process is based either on the weighted topic retrieval or the diagonal topic transitions, described in Section 3 and Section 4, respectively.

This set of $k + k$ highest ranked results from both co-view and topic retrieval processes is sent to the reranking model. For fairness of our experimental setup, we ensure that the number of candidate videos from both co-view and topic retrieval processes are equal.

The final reranking model is out of the scope of this paper. However, for our purposes, it is important to make two general comments about it.

First, the reranking model takes into account a very large number of features based on the watch-related video pair. This makes the reranking model prohibitively expensive to run on the entire video corpus. Instead, the retrieval processes (based on either co-views or topics) provide a small set of tens of potentially relevant video candidates to the reranking model. By augmenting the co-view retrieval with the top results from the topic retrieval, we seek to diversify and improve this candidate set.

Second, to avoid bias in our evaluation, the reranking model excludes any topic-related features, which are used in the topic retrieval process. Therefore, we strive to ensure that the candidates from the topic retrieval process are not given an unfair advantage by the reranking model.

In the experiments in Section 7 we describe how the related video suggestion system design outlined in Figure 4 is used to evaluate the benefits of the topic-based video retrieval using both user simulation and a live traffic experiment.

6. RELATED WORK

In this paper, we propose two retrieval methods for related video suggestion. The first retrieval method, described in Section 3, is based on the standard practices in information retrieval including *idf* term weighting [23] and stopword removal [19] applied to the topical video representations.

The second retrieval method, described in Section 4, is based on learning the optimal transition weights between the watch video and the related video topics. To learn the weights, we use a pairwise classification approach, as proposed by e.g., Burges et al. [9] and Joachims [17], which is common in learning-to-rank applications [18].

The novelty of our approach is due to the fact that we are able to leverage the rich user feedback available in the online setting to learn a large scale model of topic transitions. To this end, we use a parallel-update algorithm, first proposed by Collins et al. [12], which allows continuous and scalable weight learning (see Section 4.3 for details).

Our approach to related video suggestion complements previous work by Baluja et al. [7] that uses co-view information to suggest related videos. As we show in Section 7, our approach can be used to augment the information from a co-view graph, which is especially beneficial for videos with sparse co-view data or rich topical content.

It is important to note the connection between this work and the ongoing research on hybrid recommender systems [4, 10, 15, 31]. Similar to the hybrid recommender systems, the related video suggestion system described in Section 5 combines collaborative information (retrieval from the co-view graph) with content information (topic retrieval) to improve the system performance, especially for the "cold-start" videos with sparse co-view data, or videos with rich topical representations.

Finally our work is also related to some of the current work on supervised topic weighting for video [31] and text [5] retrieval. However, this related work focuses on offline evaluation of the proposed methods. In contrast, we address the challenge of performing evaluation of our methods on live traffic, and demonstrate that our system can be successfully deployed on global scale.

7. EVALUATION

In this section, we empirically evaluate the benefits of the integration of the topic video retrieval methods into the experimental video suggestion system described in Figure 4. To this end, we first describe the methodology and the metrics used in our experiments (Section 7.1). Then, in Section 7.2 we use a simulation method to estimate the effect of the topic-based retrieval on the overall performance of our experimental video suggestion system. Finally, in Section 7.3 we describe the results of a large scale live traffic experiment.

7.1 Experimental Methods

7.1.1 Evaluation Methodology

There are several possible options for evaluating a large scale recommendation system such as the one described in this paper. These options include user simulation based on historical data, user studies and online evaluation [24]. Each of these options has its advantages and limitations, however one important consideration in the choice of the evaluation method is that the test subjects must represent as closely as possible the population of the users in the actual system [24].

This is especially true in the case of large scale web applications that are used by millions of users. In this case,

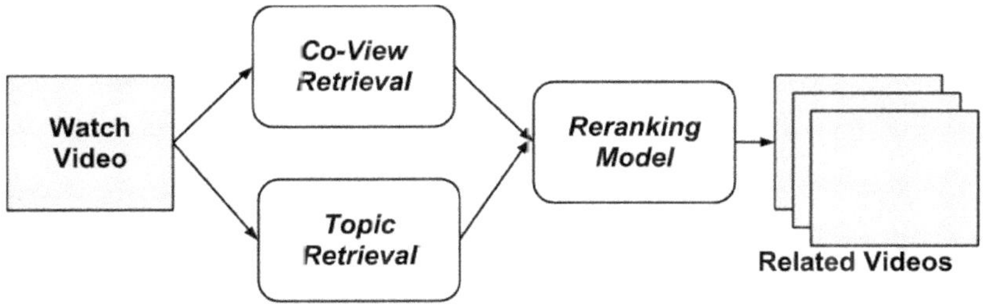

Figure 4: Overview of the related video suggestion system.

obtaining a sample of test subjects that would faithfully represent the real user population is virtually impossible. In addition to the biased sample problem, conducting a user study to evaluate a large scale video recommendation system has several other disadvantages.

First, even given a very detailed set of instructions, it would be difficult for the test subject to judge what would be the best related video to suggest, since this decision is very subjective and may be influenced by factors such as user demographics, geographic location, emotional state and cultural preferences. Even for relatively objective evaluation tasks, such as document retrieval [6] the inter-judge agreement is low. We expect the agreement rate to be even lower for rating video relatedness, which is highly subjective.

Second, as research shows [22], there is often a disconnect between what the subjects really want to watch and what they would like to *have watched.* This leads to a situation where there is little correlation between the explicitly solicited judgments and the observed user behavior in the system.

Therefore, in the next sections we evaluate the performance of the proposed methods using user simulations and a large scale online experiment, and forego evaluation of our methods on manually labeled data.

7.1.2 Metrics

Given the user-centric evaluation method of our system, in this section we address the question of what is the most suitable evaluation metric in this particular setting.

One possible choice of a metric is a click-through rate on the related video suggestions presented to the user by the system. However, research shows that the click-through rate can be highly biased by factors such as position and attractiveness of the presentation [32]. We expect this bias to be very strong in our setting, where the results are presented in ranked order, and each related result is presented as a small snapshot from the video.

Another choice of metric is based on the main functionality of the related video suggestion system, and it measures the watch times of the related videos. Intuitively, a systematic improvement in functionality will generate more relevant suggestions, which will result in a higher user engagement with the system, and lead to longer watch times of the suggested related videos.

Following this intuition, we choose a *watch time* metric, which estimates how much time the user spends watching videos during the session following a click on a related video suggestion. While the watch time metric has its limitations (e.g. it might prefer videos with longer watch times), it is a good proxy for measuring performance, since it faithfully represents the core functionality of the evaluated system.

7.1.3 Retrieval Methods

In this paper we presented two possible ways of integrating topic retrieval into the related video suggestion system. First, in Section 3 we discussed a retrieval algorithm that assigns weights to topics using co-occurence based heuristics. Second, in Section 4 we presented a novel algorithm for directly learning weights on topic transitions.

We evaluate both of these methods by integrating them into the general related video suggestion system architecture as described in Figure 4. First, the highest ranked results produced by one of the two proposed retrieval methods are introduced into the reranking model. Then we measure the changes in the overall system performance, using either a simulation experiment (Section 7.2) or an experiment using live traffic (Sectrion 7.3).

In the next sections, we refer to the retrieval algorithm presented in Section 3 as `IRTopics`, since it makes use of information retrieval heuristics. We refer to the retrieval algorithm from Section 4 as `TransTopics`, since it is based on learning transitions between the topics.

7.2 User Simulation

In this section we describe a user simulation method for estimating the performance of our retrieval methods. We exploit the reranking model described in Section 5 to simulate user interaction with the system.

Since the reranking model is trained to optimize the system performance (in terms of click-through rate and watch time) on live traffic, we use it to simulate a behavior of a typical user in the system. Then we measure how many of the results returned by the topic retrieval method will be added by the simulated user to the top related results, compared to a system that only uses co-view retrieval. By system design, if no results from the topic retrieval are selected by the simulated user, there is no benefit from performing this retrieval, since none of the results will be shown to the real users.

There are two things we are interested in measuring. First, we measure how many new results our method introduces that were not previously returned by the co-view retrieval approach. Second, and more importantly, we want to observe how many of these results are actually considered as relevant related videos by the simulated user (i.e., positioned at high ranks by the reranking model).

We run the user simulation for a large sample of videos. Figure 5(a) shows the percentage of new videos ranked among the top-K results by the simulated user that were intro-

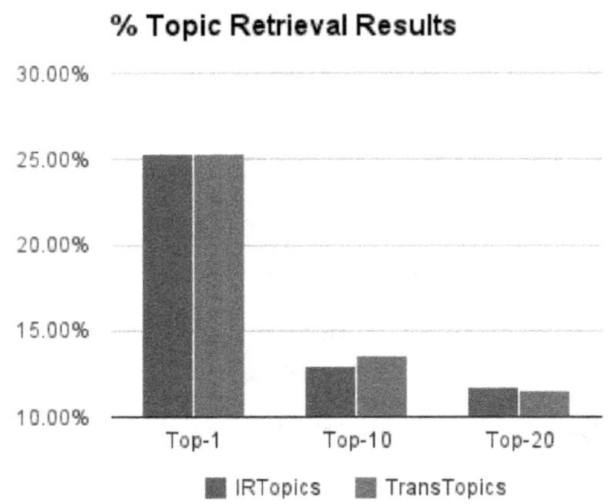

(a) Percentage of new related videos.

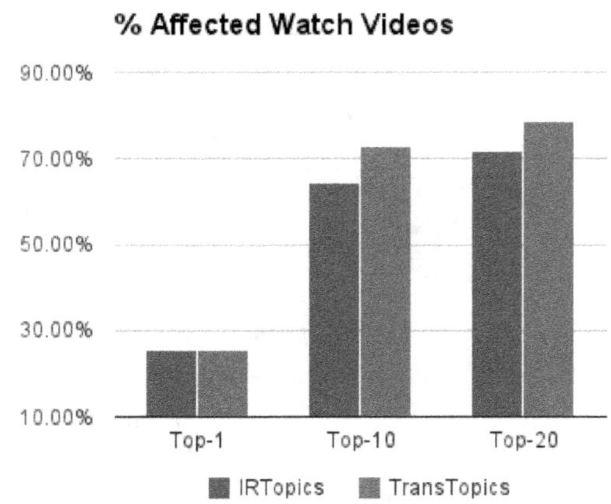

(b) Percentage of watch videos with new related videos.

Figure 5: User simulation results.

duced by the topic retrieval for either the `IRTopics` or the `TransTopics` methods. Figure 5(b) shows the percentage of watch videos that have at least one new related video among the top-K results as a result of topic retrieval.

As Figure 5(a) shows, there is a significant number of results added at the top ranks as a result of topic retrieval. Figure 5(b) demonstrates that these results are spread among watch videos. More than 70% of watch videos are affected by our retrieval, and have at least one new top-20 result coming from the topic retrieval stage.

Both of the proposed methods retrieve roughly the same number of new results, with the `TransTopics` method introducing slightly more results at the higher ranks (13.6% compared to 12.9% at the top ten results). This potentially indicates the higher relevance of the new results introduced by the `TransTopics` method.

Figure 5(b) shows a similar trend. At top ten results, the `TransTopics` method affects 73.1% of watch videos, compared to the 64.6% affected by the `IRTopics` method.

While the simulation method described in this section is suitable for the purposes of validation and testing different variants of the proposed methods, it does not provide a definitive answer whether the proposed topic-based videos will indeed have a positive effect on the actual user experience. To this end, we conduct a large scale live experiment that is described in the next section.

7.3 Live Experiment

7.3.1 Live Experiment Summary

To evaluate the performance of the `IRTopics` and the `TransTopics` methods, we conducted a large scale experiment on a random sample of live YouTube traffic. The experiment was run during a single month in 2013, and affected related video suggestions returned for millions of watch videos. The topic weights for both retrieval methods were updated on the daily basis during the experiment, according to the method descriptions in Section 3 and Section 4, respectively.

Figure 6 presents a summary of the live experiment findings. The differences in Figure 6 are reported with respect to a baseline system that does not employ a topic retrieval stage (but does employ the co-view retrieval and the reranking model, as described in Figure 4).

In Figure 6 we report the differences in three metrics related to watch time. The first metric is the *watch time* itself (as described in Section 7.1). The second metric is the *completion rate*, which measures how many of the suggested videos were fully watched from start to finish. The third metric is the *abandonment rate*, which measures the fraction of watch videos for which no related videos were watched.

As can be seen in Figure 6, the addition of the topic retrieval stage to the related video suggestion system results in improvements in all three watch metrics: watch time and completion rate increase, while the abandonment rate decreases. As the confidence intervals shown by the error bars in Figure 6 demonstrate, these improvements are statistically significant.

In absolute metrics, the `TransTopics` method achieves overall 1.3% increase in watch time over the baseline setup that does not employ topic retrieval. This is an impressive increase, given billions of hours of video watched monthly on YouTube [2].

In addition, the `TransTopics` method is significantly more effecitve compared to the `IRTopics` method. % change in the watch time is 80% higher for the `TransTopics` compared to the `IRTopics`. Similarly, % change in the completion rate is more than double, and the % change in the abandoment rate drops by more than 90% when comparing the `TransTopics` method to the `IRTopics` method.

These effectiveness improvements highlight the importance of directly learning topic transitions from user feedback. As Figure 6 clearly demonstrates, the learned weights in the `TransTopics` method can significantly improve the system performance compared to the hand-crafted heuristic weighting in the `IRTopics` method.

7.3.2 Breakdown by Video Type

In addition to the summary presented in the previous section, it is interesting to further analyze the performance of our methods by video type. In Table 1 we break down the changes in the watch time metric by *video category* (specified by the uploader of the video) and *video age*.

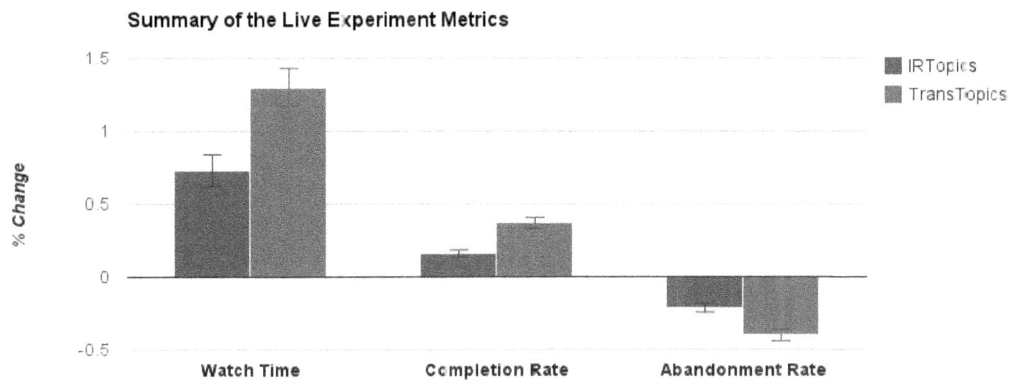

Figure 6: Summary of the live traffic experiment metrics: *watch time*, *completion ratio* and *abandonment rate*. 95% observed confidence intervals are shown by the error bars.

	IRTopics	TransTopics
Video Category		
Music	-0.64% ($\pm$0.09%)	$+0.28\%$ ($\pm$0.09%)
Gaming	$+0.86\%$ ($\pm$0.68%)	$+1.14\%$ ($\pm$0.66%)
News	$+1.61\%$ ($\pm$0.41%)	$+3.53\%$ ($\pm$0.41%)
Science and Technology	$+2.43\%$ ($\pm$0.5%)	$+3.79\%$ ($\pm$0.51%)
Pets and Animals	$+3.70\%$ ($\pm$0.68%)	$+4.16\%$ ($\pm$0.66%)
Video Age		
$<$ 1 month	$+0.99\%$ ($\pm$0.26%)	$+3.34\%$ ($\pm$0.26%)
1 month – 1 year	$+0.50\%$ ($\pm$0.11%)	$+2.24\%$ ($\pm$0.11%)
$>$ 1 year	$+0.87\%$ ($\pm$0.07%)	$+1.06\%$ ($\pm$0.08%)

Table 1: Live traffic experiment watch time metric breakdown by video category and age. 95% observed confidence intervals are shown in the parentheses.

As our retrieval methods are topic based, we expect them to be most beneficial for videos with rich topical content and videos with low co-view signal. The results in Table 1 confirm this hypothesis.

For categories with richer topical representations like *News* and *Science and Technology*, the improvements obtained by our method are approximately three times higher than the average improvement in Figure 6. The highest improvements are obtained for the *Pets and Animals* category, which has many tail videos with little co-view information. On the other hand, for *Music* and *Gaming* categories, which have more popular videos with co-view data, the topic retrieval has smaller positive benefits (or even a slight negative impact for the `IRTopics` method in the *Music* category).

Similarly, for fresh videos (e.g., less than a month old), our improvements are more significant (especially for the `TransTopics` method) than for the older videos. This is due to the fact that the fresher videos have a weaker co-view signal.

The results in Table 1 demonstrate that our topic retrieval methods improve the related video suggestions by augmenting the co-view results with fresher and more topically relevant videos. In agreement with the general results in Figure 6, the `TransTopics` method is always significantly more effective than the `IRTopics` method across different video categories and age groups.

8. CONCLUSIONS

In this paper, we focused on the task of related video suggestion, commonly found in many online applications. The majority of the current approaches to related video suggestion are based on the collaborative filtering analysis. Most generally, the collaborative filtering approaches suggest videos that are likely to be co-viewed with the currently watched video.

While such suggestions work well for popular videos with many views, it is less applicable in situations where little or no view data is available. This includes fresh videos, or tail videos with few views. To address this challenge, we propose a hybrid approach to video suggestion, which combines the video content with the co-view information to improve the related video suggestions.

To this end, we represent the video using a set of topics mined from various sources including the video metadata, frequent uploader keywords, common search queries, playlist names and Freebase entities. In order to achieve an effective topical video representation, we assign weights to each topic, and propose two approaches for topic weighting.

The first approach is based on the standard information retrieval heuristics such as topic frequency and inverse document frequency weighting and stopword removal. The downside of this approach is that it does not directly take into the account the user behavior.

Accordingly, we develop a second approach, which leverages the implicit user feedback (such as video co-watches) available in the online setting. This feedback is used for supervised learning of the optimal topic weights. Unlike the standard collaborative filtering analysis, our approach takes into account topic-to-topic rather than video-to-video co-view information. This enables suggesting a related video even if it was never explicitly viewed with the watched video.

We empirically evaluate these two topical representation methods in a large scale live experiment on YouTube traffic. We find that both of the representations have a significantly positive effect on the quality of video suggestions, compared to the standard collaborative filtering approach. This effect is especially visible for videos with rich topical representation such as videos in the *News* and *Science and Technology* categories (more than 3.5% increase in watch time), and for fresh videos with sparse co-view data (more than 3% increase in watch time).

Furthermore, our evaluation demonstrates that learning topic weights from user feedback can increase the user engagement (as compared to the collaborative filtering baseline) by more than 80% over the standard information retrieval representation. This demonstrates the importance of incorporating user feedback in content representation.

While this paper focuses on the task of related video suggestion, the findings of this work are broad, and are applicable in a variety of large scale retrieval and recommendation systems that employ topical content representations. As this work shows, learning topic weights from user feedback have the potential to significantly improve performance over the standard non-supervised weighting approaches.

9. ACKNOWLEDGMENTS

The authors would like to thank Ajith Ramanathan, Jianming He, Su-Lin Wu, Tomas Lloret Llinares and Tamas Sarlos for their advice and assistance in conducting the experiments described in this paper.

10. REFERENCES

[1] Give YouTube topics on search a whirl. `http://youtube-global.blogspot.com/2010/11/give-youtube-topics-on-search-whirl.html`.

[2] Youtube – statistics. `http://youtube.com/yt/press/statistics.html`.

[3] Youtube data API - searching with Freebase topics. `https://developers.google.com/youtube/v3/guides/searching_by_topic`.

[4] A. Ahmed, B. Kanagal, S. Pandey, V. Josifovski, L. G. Pueyo, and J. Yuan. Latent factor models with additive and hierarchically-smoothed user preferences. In *Proceedings of WSDM*, pages 385–394, 2013.

[5] B. Bai, J. Weston, D. Grangier, R. Collobert, K. Sadamasa, Y. Qi, O. Chapelle, and K. Weinberger. Supervised semantic indexing. In *Proceedings of CIKM 2009*, pages 187–196, 2009.

[6] P. Bailey, N. Craswell, I. Soboroff, P. Thomas, A. P. de Vries, and E. Yilmaz. Relevance assessment: are judges exchangeable and does it matter. In *Proceedings of SIGIR*, pages 667–674, 2008.

[7] S. Baluja, R. Seth, D. Sivakumar, Y. Jing, J. Yagnik, S. Kumar, D. Ravichandran, and M. Aly. Video suggestion and discovery for youtube: taking random walks through the view graph. In *Proceedings of WWW*, pages 895–904, 2008.

[8] A. Z. Broder, D. Carmel, M. Herscovici, A. Soffer, and J. Zien. Efficient query evaluation using a two-level retrieval process. In *Proceedings of CIKM*, pages 426–434. ACM, 2003.

[9] C. Burges, T. Shaked, E. Renshaw, A. Lazier, M. Deeds, N. Hamilton, and G. Hullender. Learning to rank using gradient descent. In *Proceedings of ICML*, pages 89–96, 2005.

[10] R. Burke. Hybrid recommender systems: Survey and experiments. *User Modeling and User-Adapted Interaction*, 12(4):331–370, Nov. 2002.

[11] B. Chen, J. Wang, Q. Huang, and T. Mei. Personalized video recommendation through tripartite graph propagation. In *Proceedings of MM*, pages 1133–1136, 2012.

[12] M. Collins, R. E. Schapire, and Y. Singer. Logistic regression, adaboost and bregman distances. *Machine Learning*, 48(1-3):253–285, Sept. 2002.

[13] J. Davidson, B. Liebald, J. Liu, P. Nandy, T. Van Vleet, U. Gargi, S. Gupta, Y. He, M. Lambert, B. Livingston, and D. Sampath. The youtube video recommendation system. In *Proceedings of RecSys*, RecSys '10, pages 293–296, New York, NY, USA, 2010. ACM.

[14] M. Fontoura, V. Josifovski, J. Liu, S. Venkatesan, X. Zhu, and J. Zien. Evaluation strategies for top-k queries over memory-resident inverted indexes. *Proceedings of the VLDB Endowment*, 4(12):1213–1224, 2011.

[15] A. Gunawardana and C. Meek. A unified approach to building hybrid recommender systems. In *Proceedings of RecSys*, pages 117–124, 2009.

[16] J. Jeon, V. Lavrenko, and R. Manmatha. Automatic image annotation and retrieval using cross-media relevance models. In *Proceedings of SIGIR*, pages 119–126, 2003.

[17] T. Joachims. Optimizing search engines using clickthrough data. In *Proceedings of KDD*, pages 133–142, 2002.

[18] H. Li. Learning to rank for information retrieval and natural language processing. *Synthesis Lectures on Human Language Technologies*, 4(1):1–113, 2011.

[19] C. D. Manning, P. Raghavan, and H. Schütze. *Introduction to Information Retrieval.* Cambridge University Press, New York, NY, USA, 2008.

[20] P. Over, G. Awad, J. Fiscus, B. Antonishek, M. Michel, A. F. Smeaton, W. Kraaij, G. Quénot, et al. TRECVID 2012 – an overview of the goals, tasks, data, evaluation mechanisms and metrics. In *TRECVID 2012-TREC Video Retrieval Evaluation Online*, 2012.

[21] F. Radlinski, M. Kurup, and T. Joachims. How does clickthrough data reflect retrieval quality? In *Proceedings of CIKM*, pages 43–52, 2008.

[22] D. Read, G. Loewenstein, and S. Kalyanaraman. Mixing virtue and vice: Combining the immediacy effect and the diversification heuristic. *Journal of Behavioral Decision Making*, 12(4):257–273, 1999.

[23] G. Salton and C. Buckley. Term-weighting approaches in automatic text retrieval. *Information processing & management*, 24(5):513–523, 1988.

[24] G. Shani and A. Gunawardana. Evaluating recommendation systems. In *Recommender systems handbook*, pages 257–297. Springer, 2011.

[25] V. Simonet. Classifying youtube channels: a practical system. In *Proceedings of WOLE 2013, in Proceedings of WWWW companion*, pages 1295–1304, 2013.

[26] A. Singhal, C. Buckley, and M. Mitra. Pivoted document length normalization. In *Proceedings of SIGIR*, pages 21–29, 1996.

[27] C. G. M. Snoek and M. Worring. Multimodal video indexing: A review of the state-of-the-art. *Multimedia Tools and Applications*, 25(1):5–35, Jan. 2005.

[28] T. Tsikrika, C. Diou, A. P. de Vries, and A. Delopoulos. Image annotation using clickthrough data. In *Proceedings of CIVR*, pages 14:1–14:8, 2009.

[29] C. Vondrick, D. Patterson, and D. Ramanan. Efficiently scaling up crowdsourced video annotation. *International Journal of Computer Vision*, pages 1–21. 10.1007/s11263-012-0564-1.

[30] J. Weston, S. Bengio, and N. Usunier. Large scale image annotation: learning to rank with joint word-image embeddings. *Machine Learning*, 81(1):21–35, Oct. 2010.

[31] B. Yang, T. Mei, X.-S. Hua, L. Yang, S.-Q. Yang, and M. Li. Online video recommendation based on multimodal fusion and relevance feedback. In *Proceedings of CIVR 2007*, CIVR '07, pages 73–80, 2007.

[32] Y. Yue, R. Patel, and H. Roehrig. Beyond position bias: examining result attractiveness as a source of presentation bias in clickthrough data. In *Proceedings of WWW*, pages 1011–1018, 2010.

Identifying Tourists from Public Transport Commuters

Mingqiang Xue #, Huayu Wu #, Wei Chen #, Wee Siong Ng #, Gin Howe Goh *
Institute for Infocomm Research, A*STAR, Singapore
{xuem, huwu, chenwei, wsng}@i2r.a-star.edu.sg
* Innovation & InfoComm Group, Land Transport Authority of Singapore
gin_howe_goh@lta.gov.sg

ABSTRACT

Tourism industry has become a key economic driver for Singapore. Understanding the behaviors of tourists is very important for the government and private sectors, e.g., restaurants, hotels and advertising companies, to improve their existing services or create new business opportunities. In this joint work with Singapore's Land Transport Authority (LTA), we innovatively apply machine learning techniques to identity the tourists among public commuters using the public transportation data provided by LTA. On successful identification, the travelling patterns of tourists are then revealed and thus allow further analyses to be carried out such as on their favorite destinations, region of stay, etc. Technically, we model the tourists identification as a classification problem, and design an iterative learning algorithm to perform inference with limited prior knowledge and labeled data. We show the superiority of our algorithm with performance evaluation and comparison with other state-of-the-art learning algorithms. Further, we build an interactive web-based system for answering queries regarding the moving patterns of the tourists, which can be used by stakeholders to gain insight into tourists' travelling behaviors in Singapore.

Categories and Subject Descriptors

I.6.4 [**Computing Methodologies**]: Simulation and Modeling; K.4 2 [**Computers and Society**]: Social Issues; H.4.0 [**Information Systems Applications**]: General

Keywords

EZ-link; tourists; data analytics; public transport

1. INTRODUCTION

1.1 Context

Using data analytics to improve the quality of various services and cares in society has attracted increasing attention from governments and private sectors in many countries. The Singapore government started promoting data analytics in different domains a few years back. Plenty of data from government agencies have been published via data.gov.sg to encourage innovative applications and R&D attempts from research institutes and private companies. On the other hand, for those data that cannot be publicly shared due to various reasons, e.g., containing sensitive information, relevant agencies often choose to work with the government-based research institutes to discover useful knowledge from the data.

Since 2013, the Land Transport Authority (LTA) of Singapore initiated a couple of projects with the Institute for Infocomm Research (I^2R) under Singapore's Agency for Science, Technology and Research, aiming to analyze public (e.g., MRT[1] and bus) and private (e.g., taxi and private car) transport data to come out with insights on areas to improve their existing services, and also to leverage on transport data analysis to get insights on social activities that would be helpful to other sectors for the benefit of Singapore's economy and development.

1.2 Motivation and Challenges

As a famous tourist city in Southeast Asia, Singapore is attracting more than 10 million foreign visitors yearly, with 23 billion Singapore dollar tourism receipts in 2012. The government is continuously making efforts to promote the tourism industry and build it into a key economic driver for Singapore.

The living places, the visited places and the travel patterns of tourists are important information for relevant public and private sectors to design and improve their services in the tourism industry. For example, souvenir store can be opened at places where tourists mostly visit, recommendations and special packages can be made if two or more places are often commonly visited, additional bus services can be introduced for popular routes seasonally, advertisement can be targeted at MRT and bus stations where tourists make transit, and etc. Such tourist information is traditionally collected by surveys and the result is reported annually by relevant agencies. The approach is not only costly, but also inflexible in two senses: first, it cannot show the tourists' dynamic behaviors timely; second, data has to be re-collected if the study plan has changed. For a concrete example, the route (by public transport) to Singapore zoo recommended on the zoo's official website was not optimal or even a bad choice for visitors staying in the west of Singapore for many years. By gathering quite a few of complaints, the website launched the interactive route recommendation module since last year. If visitor's travelling pattern could be monitored and analyzed, such services would be improved much earlier.

Despite of the existence of Hop-on Hop-off tour services, the public transport, including MRT and bus, is still the first choice by visitors to Singapore [13]. Thank to the highly efficient public

KDD'14, August 24–27, 2014, New York, NY, USA.

http://dx.doi.org/10.1145/2623330.2623352.

[1] Mass Rapid Transit (MRT) is the subway system in Singapore. The detailed description of MRT and Singapore's public transport system can be found in Section 2.

transport system, places of interest that are found widely across the Singapore island are conveniently reachable by public transport at very affordable prices. Every time when a local or a tourist rides a bus or MRT, a record that describes the time, location, fare and other information is collected in the system. Thus we see, the public transport data contain records of tourists among the records of locals. Further, if we can accurately identify these tourist records from the public transport data and analyze them, we can offer an innovative approach towards tourists' behaviors study. Compared to traditional survey-based approaches, analyzing public transport data allows complete temporal-spatial tracking of the tourists for more accurate behavior study. Furthermore, timely results can be obtained as long as the data is up-to-date.

Nevertheless, solving the tourists identification problem is non-trivial. It requires not only a comprehensive understanding about Singapore and her public transport system, but also to overcome several technical challenges: the public transport data is anonymous and the tourists records only constitute a small portion of the public transport data, yet we have to accurately differentiate them from tons of other commuter records.

1.3 Contribution and Impact

In this paper, we propose the innovative application of machine learning techniques in tourists identification from the public transport data. The public transport data that we use are provided by LTA of Singapore, and includes both MRT and bus riding records. The algorithm that we propose is based on reinforcement iterative learning: with the prior knowledge on the attractiveness of MRT stations to the tourists, which is derived from the data, and a small set of labeled data, we initiate an iterative learning process to infer potential tourists from the whole population and also update the ranking of station in each iteration. We demonstrate our model and algorithm outperforms the state-of-the-art classification methods. Furthermore, we develop an interactive web-based system that periodically discovers tourists from up-to-date public transport commuters and visualize their travel patterns to LTA and other partners from tourism industry, for better services and planning.

The research result has been recognized by LTA, and directly led the foundation of the I^{2}R-LTA Joint Laboratory, which is a long-term collaboration between I^{2}R and LTA for transport data analysis. This work also attracted interest from agencies and companies in the tourism-related industry in Singapore.

1.4 Organization

The rest of the paper is organized as follows: In Section 2, we describe the tourists identification problem that we are trying to solve. The details of our approach for the problem is presented in Section 3. We present experimental evaluation on our algorithm and other competing algorithms with real data in Section 4. Then we show a demo of the web-based system that we developed based on our learning algorithm in Section 5. We review related work in Section 6. Finally conclude this paper in Section 7.

2. PROBLEM DESCRIPTION

Before we introduce the tourist identification problem, we give an overview of Singapore's public transport system and the public transport data we own, which should be helpful for readers to understand our problem.

2.1 The Public Transport System and Dataset

In Singapore, the public transport system includes the subsystems of subway and bus. The subway system is further divided into Mass Rapid Transit (MRT) system and Light Rail Transit (LRT) system, according to the types of rails and trains. LRT uses light rails and small trains, and acts as feeder service to MRT for short-distance neighborhood railway transportation. Since the MRT and LRT share the same ticketing system, to simplify the presentation, we only use the term of MRT to represent the subway system in Singapore.

Table 1: Dataset schema

Field	Description
Card_Number_E	Card ID for this ride
Transport_Mode	BUS, LRT, or MRT
Entry_Date	Date when ride started
Entry_Time	Time when ride started
Exit_Date	Date when ride ended
Exit_Time	Time when ride ended
Payment_Mode	Method of payment
Origin_Location_ID	Starting location of the ride
Destination_Location_ID	Ending location of the ride

In Singapore, EZ-Link card is used by public transportation users to pay fare. Nearly all the residents in Singapore use EZ-Link cards tap in and tap out for bus and MRT riding. The trip fare is calculated based on the travelling distance, and deducted from a commuter's EZ-Link card when he/she tap out at a bus stop or a MRT station. For special groups of people, such as students and senior citizens, there are also concession EZ-Link cards which offers discounts. EZ-Link card is also a good choice for tourists, especially for those who stay for a few days or more and travel often, because of its convenience in use. However, buying an EZ-Link card requires a minimum payment of 12 Singapore dollars including a non-refundable 5 Singapore dollars of issuing cost. Hence, EZ-Link card might not be an economical choice for tourists who stay in Singapore for a very short period and travel with public transport in very few times. Many of such tourists may prefer using cash payment for each MRT or bus riding, as introduced later. There is also an EZ-Link day pass option for tourists, with which a tourist pays a fixed fare for unlimited rides during a whole day, and the pass turns to normal EZ-Link card after the valid period.

A commuter can also opt to use cash payment for MRT and bus riding. For MRT riding, a standard ticket need to be purchased with cash and used in a similar way as an EZ-Link card. One difference between standard ticket and EZ-Link card is that a standard ticket is disposable after one or a few times of uses. Another difference is that the per-ride price of a standard ticket is slightly higher than the EZ-Link fare for a particular trip, but the initial cost for the standard ticket is much lower compared to regular EZ-Link card as it only requires a refundable 10 cents. Therefore, the standard ticket is ideal for tourists who stay very short term or do not travel with MRT often. For bus riding, cash payment is made when a commuter boards a bus and consults the driver regarding the exact fare for his/her trip. A paper ticket will be issued to the commuter via the ticking machine after his/her payment. In Fig 2.1, we show the relationship between different payment modes and the three transport modes in Singapore's public transport system.

The public transport dataset provided by LTA consists of records generated from tap-in and tap-out activities by public transport commuters. The dataset contains records from both bus and MRT rides that are paid with regular EZ-Link card, concession EZ-Link card, standard ticket (for MRT) and paper ticket (for bus). The dataset is structured and each record follows a predefined schema. In our work, we only use a selected subset of attributes for tourists records

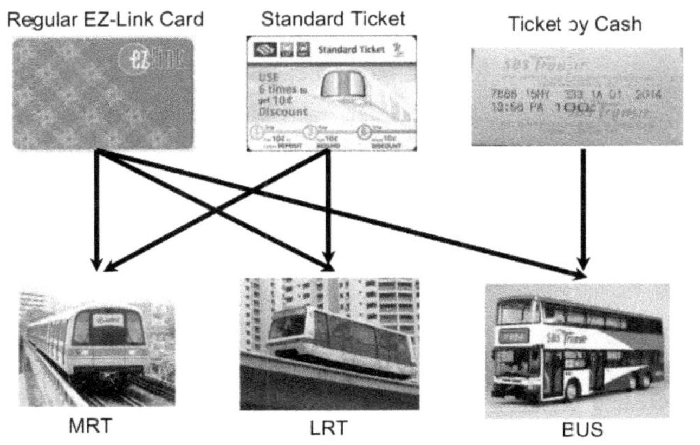

Figure 1: Singapore's public transport system

extraction, which are shown in Table 1. If the *Transport_Mode* of a record is *BUS*, the values for *Origin_Location_ID* and *Destination_Location_ID* are the corresponding IDs of bus-stops; otherwise, the values are the IDs of MRT stations. Besides of the EZ-Link records, we also have additional files for mapping a bus stop ID or MRT station ID to its names and geo-location. The *Payment_Mode* for a ride can be CSC, Pass or Standard ticket if the *Transport_Mode* is *LRT* or *MRT*. Here, *CSC* corresponds to normal adult card and the *Pass* corresponds to concession cards. As introduced above, they both belong to regular EZ-Link card. Lastly, the *Payment_Mode* for a ride can be CSC, Pass or Cash if the *Transport_Mode* is *BUS*.

2.2 Tourists Identification Problem

In this work, we target to identify records that are generated by the riding of tourists who visit Singapore from the public transport data. We assume the population can be divided into two classes, i.e., tourists and non-tourists. Sometimes, we also use locals to refer non-tourists. Tourists refer to the group of people who visit Singapore for short term, e.g., a few days, sightseeing purpose. They commonly visit places of interest of Singapore, including gardens, museums, restaurants, shopping streets, etc and stay in hotels or hostels. People who come to Singapore for other purpose such as business or medical services may also fall into the class of tourists as long as their activities satisfy our previous guideline. Non-tourists or locals are those who are not classified as tourists. Since the public transport data contains entry time, exit time, the origin and the destination, we may use these information to identify tourists from all commuters.

It might already be noticed that there are a lot of tourists records contained in the standard ticket records. This is because locals rarely use standard tickets as it is obviously not as economical, convenient and durable as EZ-Link cards. However, as a standard ticket needs to be disposed after one or a few rides, it cannot be used to reliably track the complete usages of the public transport of a tourist. On the other hand, an EZ-Link card usually stays at one's hand during one's stay in Singapore and it is good for tracking complete usages. Our focus is to identify tourist records from the entire set of EZ-Link records in the public transport data.

3. APPROACH

Our algorithm for tourist identification is a two-stages approach. In the first stage, the algorithm produces initial scores for each MRT station based on their attractiveness to the tourists. In the second stage, the scores are used to obtain initial class distributions of MRT stations. The algorithm then performs class inference for commuters, i.e., tourist or non-tourist, using an iterative process based on a graph that describes the prior class distributions of commuters and MRT stations and their interactions. There are two reasons for us to opt to use only MRT riding records rather than bus-stop ones for tourists identification. First, the standard ticket records which provide a good resource for studying tourists' travelling pattern are only available for MRT rides; Second, most places of interest in Singapore are located in walking distance. The MRT riding records should capture most of tourists' local travelling activities. Hence, it is sufficient to use them for tourist identification. Interesting, once tourists are identified, their interested places reach by bus riding can be revealed, e.g. the Singapore zoo example in Section 5.

3.1 Station Ranking

We focus on the algorithm for the initial scoring of MRT stations. The initial score s_{m_i} for the station m_i is for evaluating whether the station is more likely to be a destination for tourists or a destination for locals. Effectively, knowing someone who has visited a station with a high (or low) initial score may increase (or reduce) our belief that the person is a tourist. Thus, by considering the stations one has visited and their scores, we can differentiate tourists from locals. There are different ways to assign initial scores to stations. One ideal measurement is the probability that one is a tourist, given that he/she has visited a station. For simplicity, we denote this probability as $\Pr(t|m_i)$ in which t denotes that a commuter is a tourist and m_i denotes that the commuter has visited the station m_i. Computing the exact value of $\Pr(t|m_i)$ for each m_i is not very straightforward from the data we own. Instead, we make the transformation based on Bayes Rule:

$$\Pr(t|m_i) = \Pr(t) \cdot \frac{\Pr(m_i|t)}{\Pr(m_i)} \quad (1)$$

In the above equation, $\Pr(m_i|t)$ is the probability for one to visit m_i given that he/she is a tourist, $\Pr(m_i)$ is the prior probability for one to visit m_i and $\Pr(t)$ is the prior probability for one to be a tourist. As we see from the expression, the terms that affect the value of $\Pr(t|m_i)$ are $\Pr(m_i|t)$, $\Pr(m_i)$, and $\Pr(t)$. While $\Pr(m_i|t)$ and $\Pr(m_i)$ are dependent on the station, $\Pr(t)$ is invariant with all stations. The effect of $\Pr(t)$ can be considered as a linear scaling which does not affect the relations of the scores for different stations. In the following, we show how to estimate $\Pr(t|m_i)$ are $\Pr(m_i|t)$, $\Pr(m_i)$, and $\Pr(t)$, respectively.

The estimation for $\Pr(m_i|t)$: Ideally, to estimate $\Pr(m_i|t)$ we need to use data from tourists and summarize how often they visit each station so as to estimate the probability that they visit a particular station m_i. From prior knowledge, we already know that a lot of tourists choose to use standard tickets when taking MRT in Singapore. So it inspired us that we may obtain an estimation of $\Pr(m_i|t)$ from the standard ticket records. The main problem with using standard ticket records as tourist records is that it is incorrect to assume all standard ticket records are from tourists. Occasionally, a local may also use standard ticket in case he/she forgets to bring a regular EZ-Link card or does not have enough cash to top up the EZ-Link card that has insufficient balance. We would expect such occasions are infrequent. However, since the total rides from locals are much larger than the total rides from tourists, even if a tiny fraction of rides from locals turn to use standard tickets, they may still constitute a considerably large portion to the total standard ticket records at a station. Thus, if we need to compute $\Pr(m_i|t)$

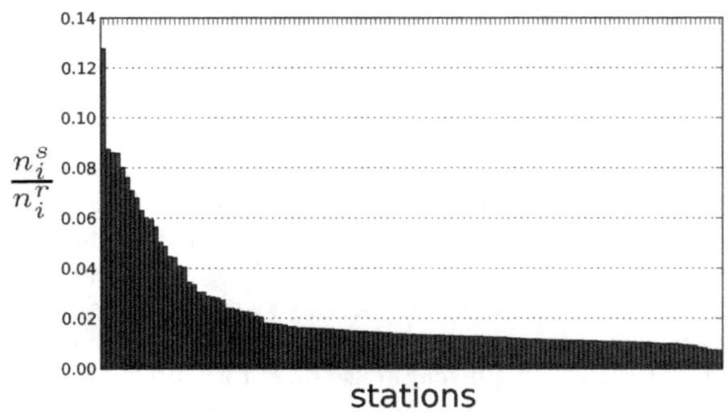

Figure 2: Stations ordered in descending c_i^s/c_i^r order

with the standard ticket records, we have to isolate the effects of locals.

To do that, we can model a parameter θ which is the expected ratio between the number of standard ticket records and the number of regular EZ-Link records from all trips made by locals. The θ is the parameter for describing how frequent a regular EZ-Link card local may turn to use standard ticket due to various reasons. For example, for a particular station m_i, we assume the total number of rides made by locals with regular EZ-Link card is 10,000. Then the number of rides from locals paid with standard tickets is estimated as $10,000 \cdot \theta$ with expected value. As we see, the θ modeling is about the behaviours of locals and is independent with stations, thus it is reasonable to assume that θ is stable for each station. Let n_i^r be the number of regular EZ-Link records and n_i^s be the number of standard ticket records at station m_i. With a fair estimation of θ, denoted as $\hat{\theta}$, we can then estimate the number of tourists who use standard tickets at m_i with its expected value $n_i^t = n_i^s - n_i^r \cdot \hat{\theta}$. In the following, we turn the attention to obtaining $\hat{\theta}$.

Table 2: Examples of non-tourist stations

Name	n_i^s	n_i^r	$\frac{n_i^s}{n_i^r}$
Marymount	6218	629435	0.009879
Yio Chu Kang	20361	2067636	0.009847
Cove	1817	189873	0.009570
Buangkok	7454	787463	0.009466
Layar	345	37211	0.00927
Oasis	489	53696	0.009107
Labrador Park	2473	292858	0.008444
Tongkang	1295	158299	0.008181
Compassvale	2705	358175	0.007552
Dover	8963	1247247	0.007186

Our idea for estimating θ is based on a key observation that tourists are very unlikely to visit stations that are located in residential areas with few shopping, hotel and restaurant facilities. Having some familiarity with the Singapore city, one can identify a few number of these stations easily. And yet, the dataset shows that there are still certain standard ticket records whose destinations are among these stations, which convinces us that these records mainly come from locals instead of tourists. Thus, by studying the ratio between the number of standard ticket records and the number of regular EZ-Link card records, we could have a fair estimation of θ. In Table 2, we show examples of these non-tourist stations with the count of standard ticket records n_i^s and the count of regular EZ-Link records n_i^r at each station and the ratio between the two. Our second observation is that, the one with the least value of $\frac{n_i^s}{n_i^r}$, which is the Dover station (the last row of the Table 2), gives the closest estimation of θ. The reason is that the smaller the $\frac{n_i^s}{n_i^r}$ value is, the less influence tourists have on the standard ticket riding records. For the information of readers who are not familiar with Singapore, Dover is a MRT station that is located next to a Polytechnic of Singapore and there is no tourist related facilities in the surrounding area. It can be imagined that most of the commuters, who exited at this station, are students or staffs from the Polytechnic. This rationale can also be explained from Figure 2, which shows the ordering of stations based on decreasing order of $\frac{n_i^s}{n_i^r}$. The values of $\frac{n_i^s}{n_i^r}$ are much higher for the stations in the first quarter than the rest stations. It indicates that the stations towards the end are non-tourist stations and their values of $\frac{n_i^s}{n_i^r}$ are getting closer the real of θ. As we see from the Table 2, the minimum value of $\frac{n_i^s}{n_i^r}$ is 0.007186. Thus, we use $\hat{\theta} = 0.007186$ as an estimation of θ, and it can be interpreted that in average 7 out of 1007 trips with MRT made by locals are payed with standard tickets. Knowing $\hat{\theta}$ allows us to estimate the number of standard tickets from tourists n_i^t at each station with the *maximum likelihood principle*, and hence estimate $\Pr(m_i|t)$ with:

$$\hat{\Pr}(m_i|t) = \frac{n_i^t}{\sum_i n_i^t} \text{ where } n_i^t = n_i^s - n_i^r \cdot \hat{\theta} \tag{2}$$

The estimation for $\Pr(m_i)$: The estimation for $\Pr(m_i)$ is much more straight-forward than $\Pr(t|m_i)$. It describes the overall probability that one may visit m_i regardless one is a local or tourist. Again the approach is based on the *maximum likelihood principle*: we count the total number of regular EZ-Link records and standard ticket records for each station m_i and divide by the total number of regular EZ-Link records and standard tickets records for all stations. Thus our estimation for $\Pr(m_i)$ is:

$$\hat{\Pr}(m_i) = \frac{n_i^s + n_i^r}{\sum_i n_i^s + n_i^r} \tag{3}$$

The estimation for $\Pr(t)$: As we have already argued, $\Pr(t)$ is a constant factor that does not affect the rankings or the relations between scores of different stations. Still, we need to estimate it for our iterative refinement algorithm to work well. Effectively, to our iterative refinement algorithm, $\Pr(t)$ acts as a tunable threshold which allows us to adjust how restrictive our algorithm is in selecting tourists records. We emphasis that a coarse estimation for $\Pr(t)$ for initial score assignment is sufficient for our algorithm to work well, as in the iterative refinement process the scores for each station will be updated to more accurate values. From our previous computation, the number of tourists arriving at an MRT station m_i using standard tickets can be estimated, i.e., n_i^t. Thus we estimate the total number of tourists arriving m_i, including both EZ-Link card users and standard ticket users, as $2n_i^t$, without any other knowledge on the percentage of the users for each type of ticket. Then our estimation for $\Pr(t)$ is:

$$\hat{\Pr}(t) = \frac{\sum_i 2n_i^t}{\sum_i n_i^s + n_i^r} \tag{4}$$

Based on the estimations of $\Pr(m_i|t)$, $\Pr(m_i)$ and $\Pr(t)$, we assign initial score for station m_i with our estimations using:

$$s_{m_i} = \hat{\Pr}(t) \cdot \frac{\hat{\Pr}(M_i|t)}{\hat{\Pr}(M_i)} \approx \Pr(t|M_i) \tag{5}$$

In Table 3 we show the top 15 stations based on the decreasing order of the initial scores. They are all famous POIs in Singapore. As we can see from the result, the top ranked station is Changi Airport which showing that visiting the airport gives the highest confidence that one is a tourist. This result perfectly matches our expectation as most tourists end their trip in the airport whereas locals do not often visit the airport. It can also be observed from the ranking that famous shopping places such as Orchard, Bugis and the CBD area City Hall are in the middle to end range of the ranking, although they are must-visit places in Singapore. Since these are also the places that are frequently visited by locals, they are not ranked so high in our scoring scheme. In other words, visiting Changi Airport gives more confidence than visiting Orchard or City Hall to infer an MRT rider as a tourist, rather than a local.

Table 3: Top ranked stations based on initial scores

Name	s_{m_i}
Changi Airport	0.213668
Marina Bay	0.145012
Clarke Quay	0.144702
Bayfront	0.128008
Little India	0.118879
Chinatown	0.113837
HarbourFront	0.106443
Bras Basah	0.104787
Esplanade	0.099637
Orchard	0.098623
Lavender	0.093104
Farrer Park	0.081844
Promenade	0.079080
Bugis	0.070973
City Hall	0.064815

3.2 Label Inference

3.2.1 *Problem Representation*

So far we have obtained the initial scores of MRT stations. In this section, we propose a graph structure, namely the Station-Commuter Relationship (SCR) graph, to encapsulate all the prior knowledge such as MRT stations and their initial scores, existing labeled and unlabeled commuters in the data, and their relationships. By representing our prior knowledge in the SCR graph, we also cast our problem into a node-labeling problem in the SCR graph. Specifically, in a SCR graph (Fig. 3), we define and distinguish two types of nodes for commuters: T are the nodes for the target users whose classes are unknown and we want to assign category class (tourist/non-tourist) and L are the nodes represent the commuters who already have high-quality classes, e.g. by human labeling. Usually, the number of labeled commuter nodes in L are much smaller than the number of unlabeled commuter nodes in T. For each $t_i \in T$, it maintains a class distribution, which is initialized to $[\hat{\Pr}(t), 1-\hat{\Pr}(t)]$ (c.f. Equation 4) at the beginning for the learning algorithm. The element of the first dimension of the distribution class for t_i describes the probability for t_i to be a tourist and the element of the second dimension is the probability for it to be a non-tourist. Similarly, each $l_i \in L$ also maintains a class distribution with the same interpretation. Differently from t_i, since the class of each s_i is already known, it is initialized to $[1,0]$ or $[0,1]$ depending whether the commuter of s_i is a tourist or a non-tourist, respectively. Besides the nodes for commuters, there are also a set of nodes M for the stations in Singapore. Similar to the nodes for commuters, each station node $m_i \in M$ also carries a class distribution which is initially set to $\phi^{0}_{m_i} = [s_{m_i}, 1-s_{m_i}]$, where the element of the first dimension represents the estimated probability for one to be a tourist if he/she visits m_i and the second is the probability for one to be a non-tourist. Let $u \in T \cup S$ be a particular commuter. The interactions between u and a station m_i, i.e. the number of times that the commuter has visited the station as a destination, represented as a weighted edge (u, m_i) where the weight w_{um_i} is the number of times that u has visited m_i.

We define and distinguish two classes. Respectively, Class 0 is the class for tourist and class 1 is the class for non-tourist. Our goal is to update the class distributions of all nodes $t_i \in T$ based on the information contained in the SCG graph, and finally assign a class label to the commuters that correspond to nodes in T.

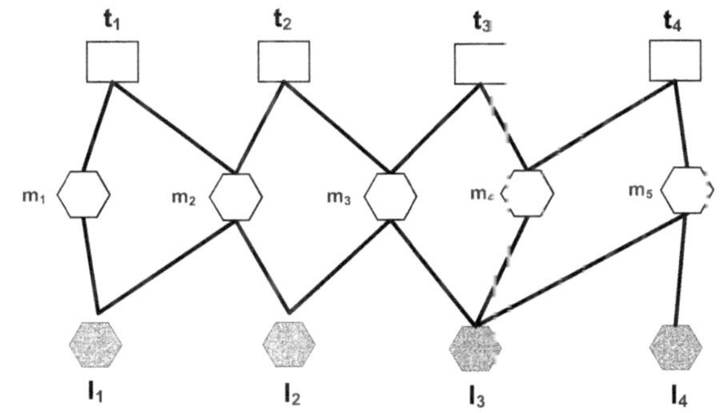

Figure 3: Example of SCR graph

3.2.2 *Algorithm*

The main resources for label inference in the SCR graph are the initial scores for stations, the limited number of labeled nodes in L and the interactions commuters and stations as denoted by the weighted edges. Considering the structure of the graph, we propose a label propagation approach to infer the classes for the nodes in T based on the nodes in L by taking the stations as bridges between T and L. The mechanisms we use for label propagation is based on the observation that commuters who have similar class (by the score) tend to travel to similar stations and vice versa. Specifically, we apply the following two mechanisms:

- *M1:* Update the class distributions of commuters based on the class distributions of the stations that they have visited. For example, in Fig. 4(a), t_1 is a node for an unlabeled tourist who visited HarbourFront and Changi Airport. As we see from Table 3, both HarbourFront and Changi Airport are very typical tourists places. Thus, in our label propagation, we may increase the confidence that t_1 is a tourist

- *M2:* Update the class distributions of stations based on the class distributions of commuters who travelled to the stations. For example, in Fig. 4(a), l_1 and l_2 are tourists, and l_3 and l_4 are non-tourists. The figure shows that the station City Hall is visited by both l_2 and l_3. Since l_2 is a tourist, it may increase the confidence that City Hall is a tourist place. On the other hand, since l_3 is a non-tourist, it may increase the confidence that City Hall is a non-tourist place. In label propagation, the class distribution for City Hall is affected by the classes of both l_2 and l_3.

With the above discussion, now we use an iterative inference algorithm to solve the classification problem. The main idea behind the algorithm is that, in each iteration, we use the class distributions of stations in M to predict the labels of commuters in T. Once the labels for the nodes in T are updated, we use the nodes in T together with the nodes in S to update the class distributions of stations in M. The process ends when the number of iterations reaches a predefined threshold (In experiments, the number of iterations we choose is 150).

Algorithm 1 Iterative Inference

Input:
Class label $C(l_i)$ for $l_i \in L$
Initial scores s_{m_i} for $m_i \in M$;
Max iteration $Maxit$;
Prior tourist probability $\hat{Pr}(t)$;
Parameter α, β, γ
Output:
Class label $C(t_i)$ where $t_i \in T$
1: // Initialization
2: **for each** $l_i \in L$ **do**
3: $\phi^0_{l_i} == [1, 0]$ if $C(l_i) == 0$ otherwise $\phi^0_{l_i} == [1, 0]$
4: **for each** $m_i \in M$ **do**
5: $\phi^0_{m_i} = [s_{m_i}, 1 - s_{m_i}]$
6: **for each** $t_i \in T$ **do**
7: $\phi^0_{t_i} = [\hat{Pr}(t), 1 - \hat{Pr}(t)]$
8: // Iterative Label Propagation
9: **for** k=1 to $Maxit$ **do**
10: // Label Propagation to L
11: **for each** $l_i \in L$ **do**
12: Update $\phi^k_{l_i}$ using equation (6)
13: // Label Propagation to T
14: **for each** $t_i \in T$ **do**
15: Update $\phi^k_{t_i}$ using equation (7)
16: // Label Propagation to M
17: **for each** $m_i \in M$ **do**
18: Update $\phi^k_{m_i}$ using equation (8)
19: // Output the Class Label
20: **for each** $t_i \in T$ **do**
21: $\hat{C}(t_i) = \underset{0 \le j \le 1}{argmax} \frac{\phi^{Maxit}_{t_i}[j]}{\sum_{t \in T} \phi^{Maxit}_{t_i}[j]}$

The complete algorithm is shown in Algorithm 1. At steps 1-7, the class distributions for nodes in L, M, and T are all initialized, based on existing-labels, initial scoring, and prior class distribution, respectively. The iterations start from step 8. In each iteration, the class distributions for each types of nodes are updated accordingly (steps 10-18). Specifically, for nodes in L (step 11 and 12), the class distribution is updated based on both the class distributions of adjacent nodes and its class distribution in the previous iteration. A configurable parameter α is used to control the rate of update. The specific updating rule is:

$$\phi^k_{l_i} \leftarrow \alpha \cdot \phi^{k-1}_{l_i} + (1 - \alpha) \cdot \frac{\sum_{m \in N(l_i)} w_{l_i m} \cdot \phi^k_m}{\sum_{m \in N(l_i)} w_{l_i m}} \tag{6}$$

In the above the edge weight $w_{l_i m}$, which is the number of times that l_i visited m, is to emphasis more important edges. $N(l_i)$ is a function for returning the neighbors of l_i in the SCR graph.

Similarity, we can define rules for updating class distributions for node $t_i \in T$, and $m_i \in M$ with different parameters β, γ for controlling the rate of update:

$$\phi^k_{t_i} \leftarrow \beta \cdot \phi^{k-1}_{t_i} + (1 - \beta) \cdot \frac{\sum_{m \in N(t_i)} w_{t_i m} \cdot \phi^k_m}{\sum_{m \in N(t_i)} w_{t_i m}} \tag{7}$$

$$\phi^k_{m_i} \leftarrow \gamma \cdot \phi^{k-1}_{m_i} + (1 - \gamma) \cdot \frac{\sum_{u \in N(m_i)} w_{u m_i} \cdot \phi^k_{m_i}}{\sum_{u \in N(m_i)} w_{u m_i}} \tag{8}$$

Note that larger values of α, β and γ imply greater trust in the original class distribution. In practice, the values for these parameters can be chosen as the ones that give best performance in cross-validation. with these updating rules, our algorithm effectively propagate the labels across the graph between nodes in L and T by taking the MRT stations as bridges.

Based on the class distribution, we can assign an node $t_i \in T$ to the class c at steps 20-21, such that:

$$\hat{C} = \underset{c}{argmax} \frac{P(t_i|c)}{P(t_i)} = \underset{c}{argmax} \frac{P(c|t_i)}{P(c)}$$

Note that the final class distribution, although has been updated for describing the probability for one to be a tourist, we cannot use it for class label assignment. The reason is that the prior distribution for tourists and non-tourist are unbalanced, if we simply choose the class that gives largest probability according to the class distribution, the best strategy for a learning algorithm is to always return non-tourist. To overcome the problem, we perform normalization with the prior distributions of each class for selecting the best class.

In summary, we can benefit from this framework for the following reasons: (1) We reduce the inference problem into a label propagation problem which be handled effectively by the iterative inference algorithm on a SCR graph. (2) The assumptions adapted behind the class distribution updating rules are very intuitive which makes the framework convincing.

Back to our running example in Figure 4(a). We initialize the class distributions based on nodes types. Particularly, Nodes in L and nodes in M are assigned class distributions according to human labels and station rankings respectively. Nodes in T are assumed to have uniform class distribution [0.5, 0.5]. The initial labels are shown in Figure 4(b). In the label propagation, the class distributions for nodes in L, T and M are updated in order. Fig. 4(c)(d)(e) show the updated result for nodes in L, M and T in the first iteration. We iterate the updates 40 times for the example. The final class distributions for nodes in T are shown in Fig. 4(f). Particularly, we can calculate the category for t_2 based on $\hat{C}(t_2)$= $argmax(0.71/(0.94 + 0.71 + 0.32 + 0.08)$,$0.29/(0.6 + 0.29 + 0.68 + 0.92))$. Hence t_2 will be classified as tourist. On the other hand, t_3 will be classified as non-tourist.

The most time consuming part of the algorithm is step 9 - step 18. In the iteration, each node is visited once and the neighbors of each node are also explored. Therefore, the time complexity of the algorithm is $\mathcal{O}(k \sum_{v \in V} degree(v))$, or $\mathcal{O}(2k|E|)$ where $|E|$ is number of edges in the graph. As such, the total time complexity of algorithm is bounded by $\mathcal{O}(|E|)$. The algorithm can be further speeded up by parallel execution of class distribution updating. For example, the updating of class distributions of each node in L and each node in T based on nodes in the M can be executed concurrently, as no two nodes in $L \cap T$ are adjacent. Further, the updating of class distributions for each m_i can also be executed in concurrently as no two station nodes are adjacent.

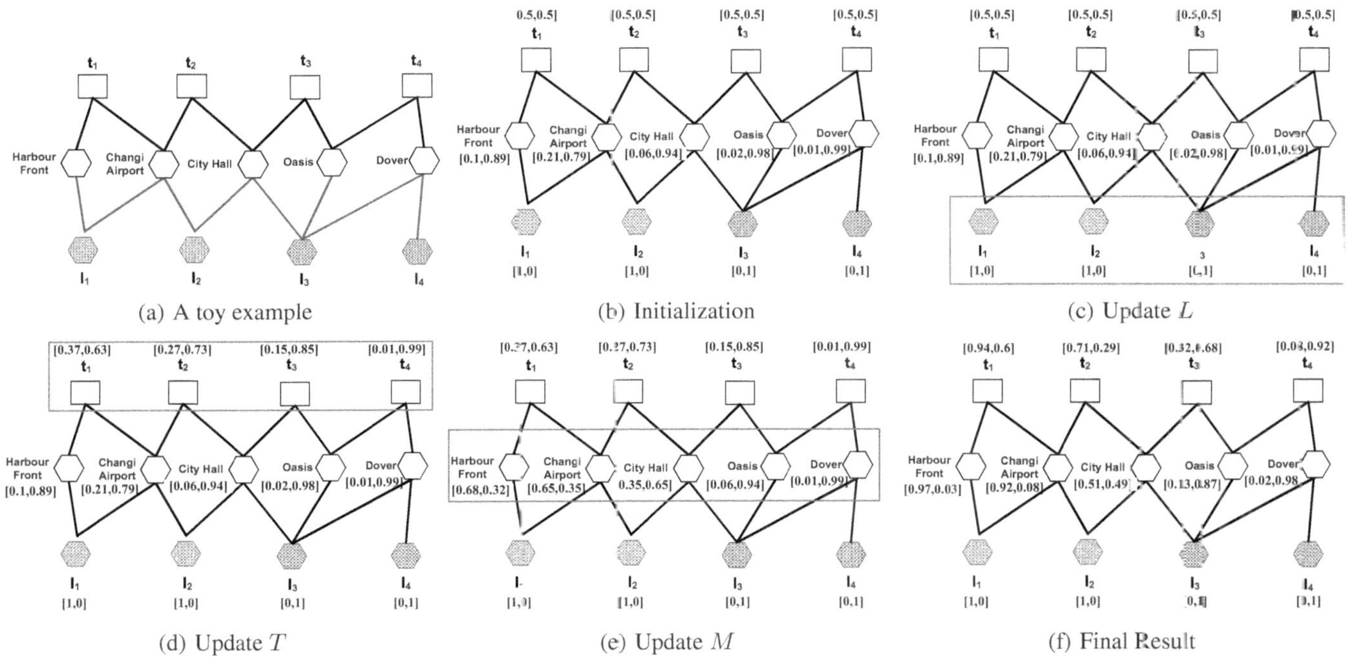

Figure 4: Example for label propagation

4. EXPERIMENTS

4.1 Data Preprocessing

The public transport data provided by LTA is securely stored in the A*DAX platform [2], and we are approved to use one-month records for January 2013 to test and report the performance of our learning algorithm publicly. We first do a preprocessing on the dataset. We exclude the commuters with less than 6 tuples of travelling records with EZ-Link card in the one month time, because these commuters do not have enough travelling information for our algorithm to learn and do the classification. Moreover, normally tourists with so few times of public transport riding would prefer using standard tickets rather than EZ-Link cards with extra issuing cost. Thus we do not consider the EZ-Link users with less than 6 records. Note that there may be tourists that use EZ-Link cards and travel less than 6 times, and our algorithm would overlook them. By assessing the trade-off between the noise brought in by the commuters with very few records and the unfound tourists with very limited travelling information, we tend to accept the latter. In fact, in tourists' travelling behavior study, the precision of identified tourists is more important than the completeness of tourist set by including those having limited travelling information.

After pre-processing, the data contains 1.7 million commuters with a total of 49.5 million transactions. We obtain a training set of 1 thousand tourists and 250 thousand locals, and their transactions. The tourists were manually labeled. We applied strict heuristics, e.g., the number of active days and spanning period to filter the EZ-Link card users and asked a group of people who know Singapore well to manually check each user's detailed origins and destinations, and finally labeled the tourists with high confidence. For validation purpose, we did not use these heuristics when training the model but in practice when building the actual model these heuristics can be applied as data preprocessing for initial prunning. The training data for locals were generated by special types of EZ-Link cards (e.g., student or senior) which require the holder to be present their local IC to purchase.

4.2 Experiment on Tourist Classification

We compare the proposed models with the following state-of-the-art classification methods for classification.

- SVM: Support Vector Machine (SVM) [5] is a well-known supervised classification algorithm, which uses a set of labeled data for learning.
- Fitting The Fits (FTF) [4] is a state-of-the-art iterative inference algorithm which uses both labeled data and unlabeled data. In specific, in each iteration the algorithm assigns predicted values to the observations whose responses are missing (unlabeled data), and then incorporates the predictions appropriately in the subsequent steps.

We will evaluate the effectiveness of our algorithm and the competing algorithms using standard F-measure, namely $F1$, whose formula is:

$$F1 = \frac{2 \times Precision \times Recall}{Recall + Precision}$$

The F measure can be interpreted as a weighted average of the precision and recall, where an F-measure reaches its best value at 1 and worst value at 0. In order to evaluate the average performance across multiple categories, the micro-averaging $F1$ and macro-averaging $F1$ are introduced. The micro-averaged scores tend to be dominated by the performance on common categories, while the macro-averaged scores are influenced by the performance in rare categories.

Table 4 shows the $F-measure$ of our proposed method against other methods by varying p, which represents the percentage of data used as training data. For example, when p equals 5%, it means 5% of labeled data is used to train the model, and 95% is used to validate the model. For all the algorithms, the more training data used, the better a model can be trained. It is clear that

Table 4: Results of F measure in the classification result

	SVM		FTF		I^2	
$p\%$	Macro F1	Micro F1	Macro F1	Micro F1	Macro F1	Micro F1
5%	0.57984	0.8415	0.6109	0.8419	**0.6267**	**0.8504**
10%	0.5917	0.8420	0.6263	0.8464	**0.6572**	**0.8538**
15%	0.6144	0.8411	0.6441	0.8433	**0.6677**	**0.8560**
20%	0.6199	0.8480	0.6758	0.8504	**0.6962**	**0.8575**
25%	0.6286	0.8402	0.6956	0.8459	**0.7154**	**0.8549**

our method is able to achieve a higher score in both Micro and Macro F1 compared to the other two methods, for all the p values we choose. With only a limited number of labeled commuters, SVM does not perform well. The reason is that the amount of labeled data is not enough to train a good model. Actually this is the problem we aim to solve in this paper. FTF is better than SVM, since it iteratively expands training set by adding predicted labels to unlabeled data and making use of these data in the next-step learning. Our algorithm is similar to FTF, but further consider the popularity of MRT stations. This information plays as a bridge to make the label propagation more accurate.

4.3 A Case Study

We apply our classification model to the entire public transport dataset, to identify tourists and analyze some patterns of tourists. In particular, we try to extract the important rules from the identified tourists and their transactions. We apply the rule-based model C5.0 decision tree [2] onto the classification result.

Due to the space limitation, we only list several rules on the top in Table 5. Take the first rule as an example. In this rule, if a commuter's visited MRT stations satisfy the seven conditions, the commuter is classified as a tourist. By examining the rule, we can see the MRT stations of Yishun, Serongoon and Sengkang are all typical residential areas in Singapore, and far away from the city center and other POIs. It can be expected that tourists rarely visit these places, as specified in the rule. On the other hand, HarbourFront and Little India are typical POIs in Singapore. Thus the rule suggests these two places as evidences to qualify a tourist. Lastly, Raffles Place is a famous place of interest for tourists, and also the CBD of Singapore. Both tourists and locals pay a lot of visit to Raffles Place. However, most locals go to Raffles Place for work. Thus the frequency a local visiting Raffles Place is expected high. Interestingly, the rule perfectly reflects this background knowledge by specifying that if a person visits Raffles Place but less than 5 times in the month, by combining with other conditions, he/she can likely be a tourist.

5. SYSTEM DEMO

To make the best use of our analytic results, we built an interactive service for users, e.g., stakeholders, to query for their interested moving patterns of tourists. In the backend, the server maintains the most up-to-date tourist records by extracting tourist data with our algorithm when there is an update to the public transport data. The public transport data is updated periodically, and the updating frequency can be configured by system users. Initially, when a user first opens the URL of the web service, a heatmap layer[3] (Fig. 5) is loaded over the Singapore's map from Google-Map to show the popular destinations by tourists. As we see from the map, the most popular destinations, i.e., the brightest spots in the map, are located in the city center of Singapore. Other POIs such as zoo, birdpark, airport, and customs are also highlighted.

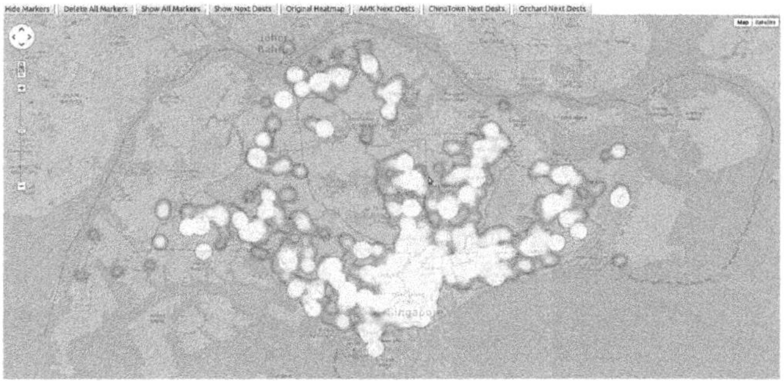

Figure 5: Heat map of tourists' favorite places in Singapore

Subsequently, a user can make queries on the next destinations of tourists by placing query landmarks with mouse clicks. The user is allowed to place multiple query landmarks at a time, and the query landmarks can be placed anywhere on the map. Once the query is issued (by clicking the "Show Next Dests" button in Fig. 5), the system automatically aligns the query landmarks to the geographically nearest bus stops or MRT stations and then return the heatmap for the next popular destinations for tourists. In addition to the heatmap, the system also returns the top 5 destination bus stops or MRT stations, by placing result landmarks, with the percentage of tourists that visit them from query landmarks. For example, in Fig. 6, we show the query results for the next destinations of tourists from the Changi airport (the red landmarks). As we see, the top destinations are all shopping, business, or leisure areas with plenty of hotels. In contrast, if we ask the same query for locals we would expect to see residential areas to come to the top. The result of this example query provide strong supports to what we find are indeed records of tourists.

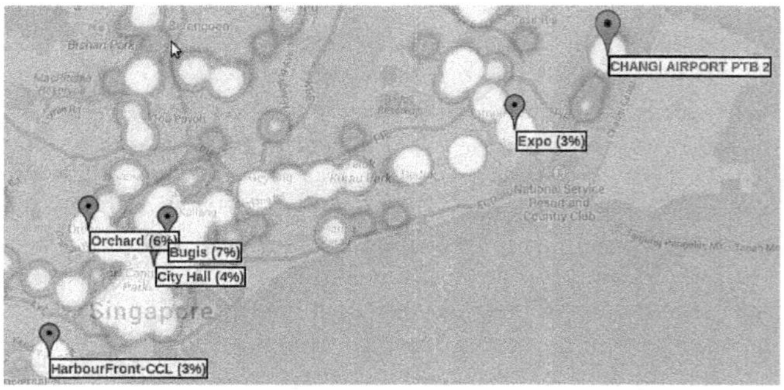

Figure 6: Destinations of tourists from the airport

[2]http://cran.r-project.org/web/packages/C50

[3]Created with gheat. url: http://code.google.com/p/gheat/

Table 5: **Results of Top 5 rules in the classification result**

Rule
Yishun <= 0, Serangoon <= 0, HarbourFront > 0,Little India > 0,Sengkang <= 0,Raffles Place > 0, Raffles Place <= 5 => Tourist
HarbourFront-CCL > 0, Lavender > 2, Changi Airport > 0 => Tourist
Hougang <= 0, Bishan <= 0, Orchard > 0, Kovan <= 0, Chinatown > 0, Serangoon <= 0, HarbourFront > 0, Clarke Quay > 0 => Tourist
HarbourFront <= 0, Clarke Quay <= 0, Marina Bay <= 0 and Changi Airport <= 0 => Non-Tourist
Orchard <= 0, Little India <= 0, Lavender <= 2, Marina Bay <= 0, Changi Airport <= 0 and Bayfront<= 0 => Non-Tourist

Continuing with the example, among the tourists favorite accommodation areas, we pick Bugis, the place on the top to issue the second query, to see what places tourists prefer going to. The result is shown in Fig. 7, from which we can see the famous POIs in Singapore, such as HarbourFront (to reach the famous Sentosa island and the Universal Studio of Singapore), Orchard, Chinatown and City Hall are among the tops. Another place, Lavender also ranks very high. The reason is that Bugis itself is also a POI in Singapore, and Lavender is near to the city and there are many cheap hotels. Many tourists staying in Lavender pay visit to Bugis and come back to hotels. Thus Lavender becomes a hot destination for tourists starting trips from Bugis.

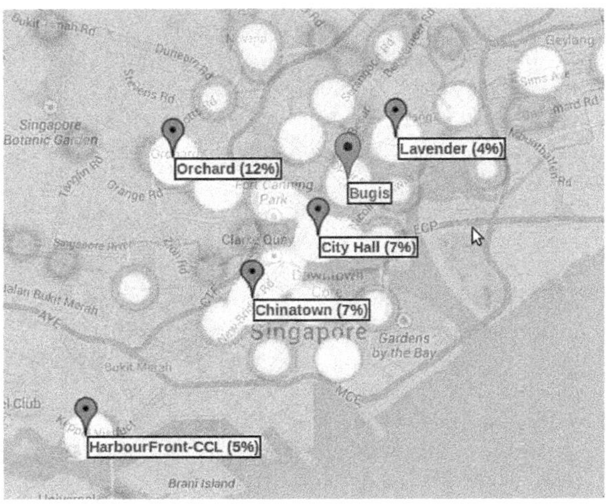

Figure 7: Destinations of tourists from Bugis

In another example, we found that the Ang Mo Kio MRT station is very frequently visited by tourists, though it is a local residential area rather than a tourism hotspot. We further investigated the reason by querying the tourist routes from Ang Mo Kio, as shown in Fig. 8. Then we found that 49% tourists went to Singapore Zoo (shown at the top left corner in Fig. 8) by bus from Ang Mo Kio. Actually, taking MRT to Ang Mo Kio and then transferring by bus was the recommended route in the Singapore Zoo's official website (this information was online for more than 10 years, and recently updated because it is not efficient for tourists staying far away from Ang Mo Kio). This explains why Ang Mo Kio became a hotspot for tourists. In fact, if this travelling pattern of tourists can be discovered earlier, the recommended routed could be revised sooner. Furthermore, if such important interchange stations as Ang Mo Kio can be discovered, services and advertisement can be set up there to target tourists.

Nevertheless, our work has opened a new door for tourists behavior analysis. There are plenty of other interesting functions one can add to the system, and the only limitation is one's imagination. In future, we would like to enhance the existing system in the following ways: 1) to support temporal constraint in the query, such

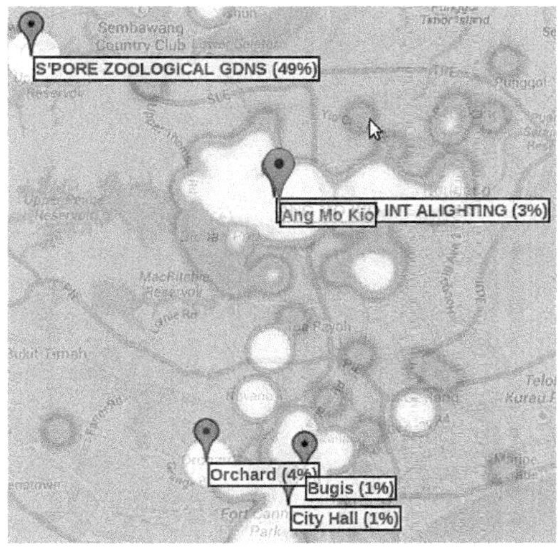

Figure 8: Destinations of tourists from Ang Mo Kio

as time of the day that tourists start their rides and time spent on trips 2) to support multi-hop queries to learn what places tourists may visited together in the same day.

6. RELATED WORK

6.1 Mining Public Transport Data

Because of the wide use of smart card for public transport fare collection in many countries, and the increasing amount of commuting data published for research, there are extensive works focusing on analyzing public transport data in recent years.

Studies have been carried out to analyze public transport data to improve public transport system in a city. [15] calculates the statistics from public transport smart card data that measure the transit supply and demand. This is a simple statistical collection. [7] proposes models to estimate the arrival time of bus runs based on the network transactions by 37 thousand commuters, which can be helpful for transit planning. [16] analyzes the riding records in Chicago during September 2004, and proposed evidence for service adjustment based on commuters' frequency and consistency. [6] introduces the OneBusAway tools to provide real-time arrival information for Seattle bus riders. [9] leverages on data mining techniques over the public transport data to promote personalized intelligent transport system. Other analysis on commuters' behaviors also have impact on the improvement of public transport services, as reviewed below.

Analyzing public transport commuters' riding behaviors is an interesting topic that attracts a lot of research attention from both transportation and data mining communities. [1] defines typical commuter types and analyze their trip habit and seasonal variability. [11] gets better knowledge of the behaviors of different groups of commuters according to the boarding patterns. [10] estimates the Origin-Destination (OD) matrix of bus routes in China, by applying trajectory search algorithms to track passengers' daily trip trajectories. [8] mines the commuting data and fare payment data in London, and address the problem and propose solutions to suggest best fare to commuters.

Some research works analyze the public transport data and find some result that are not directly related to the transportation system or commuters' travelling patterns. [3] detects the primary activities, as home and work activities and their locations based on the records of smart card fare payment. [14] investigates the encounter patterns of strangers on the same bus in Singapore. Our work falls in this category, however, we focus on finding foreign tourists, on which topic we did not find any existing work.

6.2 Mining Tourist Data

Data mining techniques have been used for extracting useful travel patterns from tourist-related data. Since the comprehensive tourist data is lowly available, most of existing works focus on exploiting tourist-related web data to discovery some patterns. From example, [12] tries to mine the information such as what places are often visited by tourists, how long they spend on these places, as well as the panoramic spots from geo-tagged images in Flickr. On the other hand, some researchers put effort in collecting such data. [17] recorded GPS tracks of 107 users for one year to identify the interestingness of tourist sites. Similar work also includes [18]. Compared to the existing attempts in tourist data analysis, our work uses more comprehensive dataset, i.e., the trips of all public transport commuters, and consequently faces more challenges, i.e., differentiate tourists from locals. Working on the public transport dataset, our work has high potential values in more accurately and timely figuring out real travel patterns of tourists.

There are also literatures published in the tourism research journals, which use simple analysis methods to report the behaviors of tourists and their impact to the tourism industry. Since the focus of this work is on mining transport data. We do not further review works on tourists' travelling pattern analysis.

7. CONCLUSION

In this paper, we propose methodologies to discover tourists from public transport commuters. Understanding tourists travelling behavior is important for both private and government stakeholders as it may help create new business opportunities or improve their existing services. In our approach, we first learn prior knowledge on tourists' favorite MRT stations based on the standard ticket users. With this knowledge and a limited set of labeled data, we design an iterative learning algorithm to infer tourists from the whole population of public transport commuters. We evaluate the performance of our algorithm in experimental test, and also validate the discovery result by perfectly matching the places visited by the discovered tourists with the real tourism POIs in Singapore. We further develop a web-based interactive system, based on our algorithm, for LTA and other partners from tourism industry in Singapore to use the discovery result to improve their services.

Our work has been recognized by LTA and other relevant agencies. It led the long-time collaboration between our research institute and LTA for transport data analytics. As future extension of this work, we will further analyze the travel patterns of the tourists discovered by the algorithm proposed in this paper, to meet the needs of government and industry partners.

Acknowledgement

This work was supported by the A*STAR Science and Engineering Research Council (SERC) Grant No. 1224200004 and 1224604057.

8. REFERENCES

[1] B. Agard, C. Morency, and M. Trl̨epanier. Mining public transport user behaviour from smart card data. In *INCOM*, pages 17–19, 2006.

[2] N. Amudha, G. G. Chua, E. S. K. Foo, S. T. Goh, S. Guo, P. M. C. Lim, M.-T. Mak, M. C. M. Munshi, S.-K. Ng, W. S. Ng, and H. Wu. A*dax: a platform for cross-domain data linking, sharing and analytics. In *DASFAA*, pages 493–502, 2014.

[3] A. Chakirov and A. Erath. Activity identification and primary location modelling based on smart card payment data for public transport. In *IATBR*, 2012.

[4] M. Culp and G. Michailidis. An iterative algorithm for extending learners to a semisupervised setting. In *The 2007 Joint Statistical Meetings (JSM*, 2007.

[5] R.-E. Fan, K.-W. Chang, C.-J. Hsieh, X.-R. Wang, and C.-J. Lin. Liblinear: A library for large linear classification. *J. Mach. Learn. Res.*, pages 1871–1874, June 2008.

[6] B. Ferris, K. Watkins, and A. Borning. Onebusaway: results from providing real-time arrival information for public transit. In *CHI*, pages 1807–1816, 2010.

[7] R. C. Ka Kee Alfred Chu. Enriching archived smart card transaction data for transit demand modeling. *Transportation Research Record: Journal of the Transportation Research Board*, (2063):63–72, 2008.

[8] N. Lathia and L. Capra. Mining mobility data to minimise travellers' spending on public transport. In *KDD*, pages 1181–1189, 2011.

[9] N. Lathia, J. Froehlich, and L. Capra. Mining public transport usage for personalised intelligent transport systems. In *ICDM*, pages 887–892, 2010.

[10] D. Li, Y. Lin, X. Zhao, H. Song, and N. Zou. Estimating a transit passenger trip origin-destination matrix using automatic fare collection system. In *DASFAA*, pages 502–513, 2011.

[11] C. Morency, M. Trepanier, and B. Agard. Analysing the variability of transit users behaviour with smart card data. In *ITSC*, pages 17–20, 2006.

[12] A. Popescu, G. Grefenstette, and P.-A. Moëllic. Mining tourist information from user-supplied collections. In *CIKM*, pages 1713–1716, 2009.

[13] Singapore Tourism Board. http://www.stb.gov.sg.

[14] L. Sun, K. W. Axhausen, D.-H. Lee, and X. Huang. Understanding metropolitan patterns of daily encounters. *PNAS*, 110, 2013.

[15] M. Trepanier, C. Morency, and B. Agard. Calculation of transit performance measures using smartcard data. *Journal of Public Transportation*, 12(1):79–96, 2009.

[16] M. Utsunomiya, J. Attanucci, and N. H. Wilson. Potential uses of transit smart card registration and transaction data to improve transit planning. *Transportation Research Record: Journal of the Transportation Research Board*, (1971):119–126, 2006.

[17] Y. Zheng, L. Zhang, X. Xie, and W.-Y. Ma. Mining interesting locations and travel sequences from gps trajectories. In *WWW*, pages 791–800, 2009.

[18] Y.-T. Zheng, Z.-J. Zha, and T.-S. Chua. Mining travel patterns from geotagged photos. *ACM Trans. Intell. Syst. Technol.*, 3(3):56:1–56:18, May 2012.

Spatially Embedded Co-offence Prediction Using Supervised Learning

Mohammad A. Tayebi
School of Computing Science
Simon Fraser University
British Columbia, Canada
tayebi@cs.sfu.ca

Martin Ester
School of Computing Science
Simon Fraser University
British Columbia, Canada
ester@cs.sfu.ca

Uwe Glässer
School of Computing Science
Simon Fraser University
British Columbia, Canada
glaesser@cs.sfu.ca

Patricia L. Brantingham
School of Criminology
Simon Fraser University
British Columbia, Canada
pbrantin@sfu.ca

ABSTRACT

Crime reduction and prevention strategies are essential to increase public safety and reduce the crime costs to society. Law enforcement agencies have long realized the importance of analyzing co-offending networks—networks of offenders who have committed crimes together—for this purpose. Although network structure can contribute significantly to co-offence prediction, research in this area is very limited. Here we address this important problem by proposing a framework for co-offence prediction using supervised learning. Considering the available information about offenders, we introduce social, geographic, geo-social and similarity feature sets which are used for classifying potential negative and positive pairs of offenders. Similar to other social networks, co-offending networks also suffer from a highly skewed distribution of positive and negative pairs. To address the class imbalance problem, we identify three types of criminal cooperation opportunities which help to reduce the class imbalance ratio significantly, while keeping half of the co-offences. The proposed framework is evaluated on a large crime dataset for the Province of British Columbia, Canada. Our experimental evaluation of four different feature sets show that the novel geo-social features are the best predictors. Overall, we experimentally show the high effectiveness of the proposed co-offence prediction framework. We believe that our framework will not only allow law enforcement agencies to improve their crime reduction and prevention strategies, but also offers new criminological insights into criminal link formation between offenders.

Categories and Subject Descriptors

H.2.8 [**Database Management**]: Database Applications—*Data Mining*

Keywords

Social Network; Link Prediction; Co-offence Prediction

KDD'14, August 24–27, 2014, New York, NY, USA.
Copyright 2014 ACM 978-1-4503-2956-9/14/08 ...$15.00
http://dx.doi.org/10.1145/2623330.2623353.

1. INTRODUCTION

Crime is a purposive deviant behavior that is an integrated result of different social, economical and environmental factors [1], and generates substantial costs to society at individual, community, and national levels. In 2007, in the United States, crimes cost $179 billion in government expenditures [2]. In 2008, the total tangible and intangible costs of crime in Canada were an estimated $100 billion [3]. Given such whopping costs, crime reduction and prevention strategies have become a priority in many countries.

Existing crime forecasting methods answer questions pertaining to spatial and temporal patterns of future crime [4, 5] These methods generally consider properties of crime incidents and behavior of single offenders to recognize criminal patterns. Over the past two decades, law enforcement and intelligence agencies have realized the importance of *co-offending network analysis* for crime investigations [6, 7]. A co-offending network links offenders who have committed crimes together [6]. Understanding co-offending is central to understanding the etiology of crime and the effects of intervention strategies [6] .

In spite of the importance of co-offending network analysis for public safety, the methodology for analyzing large-scale networks is rather premature. In this work we propose a framework for co-offence prediction using supervised learning. Even though supervised learning methods for link prediction have been studied widely [8, 9, 10, 11], to the best of our knowledge, there is no study on supervised learning for co-offence prediction. In [12], an unsupervised method for investigating top-k potential suspects is proposed.

Contrary to other social networks, concealment of activities and identity of actors is a common characteristic of co-offending networks. Still, the network topology is a primary source of information for co-offence prediction. Besides, there are two other major information sources: environmental activity and criminal activity. Offenders who are spatially close are socially close too as this increases the chance of meeting each other and forming new criminal collaborations [13]. Further, common criminal experience (with the same type of offences) also affects co-offending behavior [14].

The proposed framework builds on criminological theories [7, 15, 16, 17, 18] and, considering the available information on offenders, distinguishes three different criminal cooperation opportunities: socially-related, geographically-related and experience-related. We study the co-offence prediction problem in each of these prediction spaces separately, achieving two goals. First, the heavy class imbalance between positive (existing links) and negative samples (non-existing links) is the main challenge of the link prediction problem [10]. The restriction of the training and test data to the different prediction spaces reduces the class imbalance ratio significantly, while keeping about half of the positive samples (co-offences). Second, the prediction spaces enhance the understanding of co-offence patterns in different criminal cooperation opportunities.

We define the prediction features in four different categories, *social, geographic, geo-social* and *similarity*, and evaluate their prediction strength both individually and as a set. Social features indicate social closeness of offenders based on their position in a co-offending network. Geographic features show spatial proximity of offenders based on their residential locations and the location of offences they have committed. Geo-social features combine social and geographic characteristics of offenders. Finally, similarity features capture homophily-based characteristics of offenders. Evaluating features individually and also as a set shows that the geo-social features we define outperform other features.

Several studies show that supervised link prediction approaches outperform unsupervised methods [9, 10] that use only topological features [8]. In contrast to unsupervised methods, supervised learning methods can overcome the class imbalance problem [10]. Exploiting the geographic information provided by location-based social networks services, some recently proposed link prediction methods consider spatial characteristics of users [19, 20]. In [19], the authors use information about places visited by users, in addition to their social network features, to define prediction spaces which reduce the class imbalance ratio and improve the prediction performance.

Co-offending networks are spatially embedded similar to location-based social networks. However, the environmental effects on the formation of co-offence links and accordingly our approach in defining offenders' spatial closeness are different from those in location-based social networks [19, 20, 21, 22]. The proposed supervised learning framework aims at the public safety and security sector. Although there has been significant research on the reasons for involvement of single offenders in crime [6, 16, 18], there is no comprehensive study on the causes for offender collaboration. We argue that our study on co-offence prediction in different criminal cooperation opportunities opens up a new door to the understanding of co-offence patterns.

For the experimental evaluation, we use a large crime dataset comprising 4.4M records of police reported arrest data, made available for research purposes by the Royal Canadian Mounted Police (RCMP). The data was retrieved from the Police Information Retrieval System (PIRS), a large database keeping information for the regions of the Province of British Columbia which are policed by the RCMP. The co-offending network extracted from this dataset has more than 150k nodes. By applying different classifiers to the defined prediction spaces we can correctly predict up to 90% of all co-offences in the best case scenario.

The co-offence prediction framework proposed in this paper aims at advancing the state-of-the-art in crime data mining by making the following contributions: 1) Defining co-offence prediction spaces to reduce the class imbalance; 2) Introducing novel prediction features for co-offence prediction; and 3) Experimentally evaluating the proposed approach on large real-world crime data. Some of our main findings in this research include: a) Features evaluation have important implications. For instance, preferential attachment is a strong predictor compared to the features extracted from common friends in the network. This implies that the chance of criminal collaboration increases more with the opportunity to commit crimes than with trust or transitivity in the co-offending network. Crime locations distance is better predictor than home location distance, meaning that being criminally active in the close districts causes new criminal collaboration. b) Geo-social features are better co-offence predictors than geographic and social features. This result implies that we need to focus more on combined patterns in environmental and social features to enhance crime reduction and prevention. c) The experimental results show that the proposed supervised method outperforms the unsupervised methods. d) Although there is variability in the performance of different classifiers, the probability of predicting a co-offence for experience-related offenders is higher than for socially and geographically-related co-offenders.

Section 2 briefly introduces basic concepts and characteristics of co-offending networks as well as the crime dataset used in our work. Section 3 then explains the proposed co-offence prediction approach, and Section 4 describes the prediction feature sets. Next, Section 5 presents our experimental evaluation and results. Criminological implications and related work are discussed in Sections 6 and 7. Section 8 concludes the paper.

2. CO-OFFENDING NETWORKS

This section describes the formal co-offending network model. A crime dataset consists of a collection of crime records, each of which refers to a reported crime incident. A crime record typically identifies the date, time, location and type of a crime. To the extent known, it also identifies offenders, victims, witnesses, bystanders and their addresses, in addition to other crime specifics and circumstantial evidence. To this end, a crime dataset refers to crime incidents over some period of time.

2.1 Basic Concepts and Definitions

A *co-offending network* $G(V, E)$ is a connected graph structure. Each node represents a known offender. Offenders u and v are connected, $u, v \in V$ and $\{u, v\} \in E$, if they are known to have committed one or more offences together, and are not connected otherwise. A co-offending network is derived from a crime dataset referring to reported crime incidents over a time period.

For $G(V, E)$ and $u \in V$, let Γ_u^n be the subset of offenders in V such that their shortest path distance from u is n. $P_u = (p_u^1, p_u^2, \ldots, p_u^K)$ denotes the frequency of crimes committed by u for each of k crime types in the dataset. The subset of offenders who have committed p crime types that coincide with crime types committed by u is referred to by Θ_u^p.

For u in $G(V, E)$, let $H_u = \{h_u^1, h_u^2, \ldots, h_u^k\}$ denote the known home locations of u, and $C_u = \{c_u^1, c_u^2, \ldots, c_u^l\}$ denote the known crime locations for all offences committed by u. Finally, let $\Delta_u = \{\delta_u^1, \delta_u^2, \ldots, \delta_u^k\}$ denote the time periods (intervals) $\delta_u^i = [t_u^{i_1}, t_u^{i_2}]$ that u lived in each of the k home locations given by H_u. $D(h_u^i, h_v^j)$ is the geodesic distance between h_u^i and h_v^j.

2.2 Crime Data

Crime data mining has enormous potential as analytic tool for law enforcement agencies, criminal intelligence agencies, and beyond to facilitate crime investigations by increasing efficiency and reducing mistakes. On the other hand, access to and sharing of crime data is subject to many restrictions and can even be national security concern because of the highly sensitive nature and related personal information. Police arrest data and court-based data [23] are two important types of official crime data. Police arrest data identifies a person arrested or booked for an offense. Court-based data includes information generated by the courts. In this study we use a large real-world police arrest dataset.

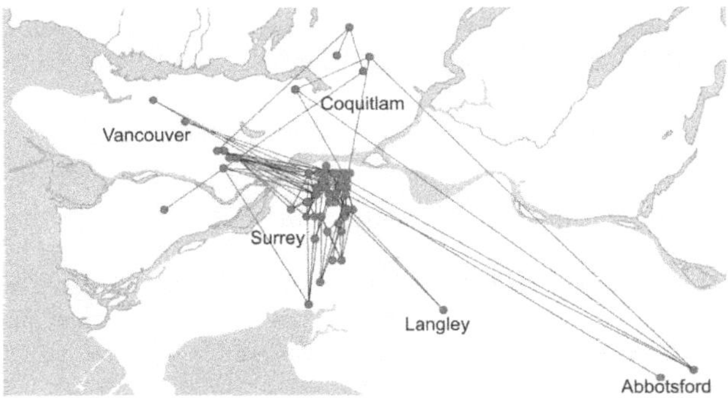

Figure 1: Spatial distance of co-offenders in the BC co-offending network.

As a result of a research memorandum of understanding between ICURS[1] and "E" Division of Royal Canadian Mounted Police (RCMP) and the Ministry of Public Safety and the Solicitor General, five years of real-world crime data was made available for research purposes. This data was retrieved from the RCMP's Police Information Retrieval System (PIRS), a large database system keeping information for the regions of the Province of British Columbia which are policed by the RCMP.

For a time period of five years (2001-2006), the BC police arrest dataset comprises $\approx$ 4.4 million crime records, one for each reported crime incident, and all persons associated with a crime, such as offenders (from complainant to charged), victims, witnesses and bystanders. In total, there are 39 different subject (person) groups. In our experiments, we consider the subjects in four main categories: *charged, chargeable, charge recommended or suspect*. Being in one of these categories means that the police were serious enough about a subjects involvement in a crime as to warrant calling them 'offenders'. From this dataset we extract , using the method described in [24], called BC co-offending network. This network comprises $\approx$ 150,000 nodes and $\approx$ 600,000 edges. The average node degree is four, and about 50% of all the nodes have degree one, meaning these offenders have committed co-offences with only one offender in their criminal life. The largest component links $\approx$ 18% of all the nodes, which is fairly big for this type of social network.

2.3 Offenders' Activity Space

The *Activity Space* of an offender has two main components: *Nodes* and *Paths*. Activity Nodes refer to locations a person frequently visits in the course of daily routine activities. Activity Path represents a common route for a routine trip to a frequently visited location. *Crime Pattern Theory* [16] contends that rather than venture into new areas to commit crimes, offenders act on criminological opportunities arising in areas they are familiar with, more specifically, areas that are part of their Activity Space.

Inverting research on crime pattern theory [16], geographic profiling [17] seeks to either estimate the location of the residence of an offender or to extrapolate locations where an offender is likely to commit future crime. Centrography is one of the most common search approaches for criminal investigation [17]. In [17], Rossmo shows that some offenders live close to the centroid of their crime locations. The "Circle Hypothesis" by Canter et. al [25] defines a circular area around the location of the first offence in a series of crimes to indicate the general area of an offender's home location.

[1]The Institute for Canadian Urban Research Studies (ICURS) is a university research centre at Simon Fraser University.

In this research our goal is consider offenders' environmental activities for co-offence prediction, while it does not fit with the bases of works in geographic profiling. Considering the definitions in the literature and the general limitations in the crime data we use a simple and safe definition in this regard. For a given offender u with home locations H_u, $A_u^R = \{a_u^1, a_u^2, \dots, a_u^k\}$ states the activity space of u, where a_u^i is defined as a circle of radius R with h_u^i at its center. We define the *common activity space* of two offenders as the area in which both are active simultaneously, if their activity spaces overlap at any time. For offenders u and v, $A_{u,v}^R = \{a_{u,v}^{1,2}, a_{u,v}^{1,3}, \dots, a_{u,v}^{p,k}\}$ is their common activity space, that is

$$A_{u,v}^R = \{a_{u,v}^{i,j} |\ a_u^i \cap a_v^j \neq \varnothing \wedge \delta_u^i \cap \delta_v^j \neq \varnothing\}.$$

Intuitively, $a_{u,v}^{i,j}$ represents the intersection of the activity space of u and v during a time they were both active at a_u^i and a_v^j. The offenders who live in $a_{u,v}^{i,j}$ and the crimes in this area are referred to by the set $\chi_{u,v}^{i,j}$ and the set $\phi_{u,v}^{i,j}$, respectively.

2.4 Geographic and Network Proximity

Neighborhood greatly influences the formation of communities and social networks. Hence, social problems are often studied in connection with neighborhoods. Many researches suggest that crime is as well strongly linked to geographical characteristics. Criminology researches use spatial analysis of crime to understand the distribution of crime incidents and why crime occurs in some places but not others [16, 17]. Figure 1 visualizes home locations of offenders for one of the connected components of the BC co-offending network. The fact that clusters can be seen in this visualization implies that many pairs of co-offenders live in the same city.

The criminology literature intensively studies modeling of offender travel to crime locations. For instance, it has been concluded that most offenders travel short distances to commit crimes [26]. But there is no definite reasoning to explain how the activity space of two offenders influences their potential collaborations. Findings in [27] suggest that co-offenders use their resources to increase the scope of their awareness space.

Generally, it is important to take into account the spatial dimension of co-offending relationships. We have studied this aspect for all observed criminal collaborations in the BC crime dataset. About 39% of the co-offenders live less than 2 km apart, and about 63% of them live less than 10 km apart. Figure 2a shows the probability distribution of home location distance for co-offenders. The probability distribution of home and crime location distance of offenders is shown in Figure 2b. 46% of the crime incidents happen in less than 2 km distance from the home location, and 70% of the crimes happen within a distance of less than 10 km. We conclude that a large percentage of the crime incidents are located close to the offenders' residence. While the maximum values for co-offenders home location distance and offenders' home and crime location distance are about 1000 km, the medians of these distances are only 5 km and 3 km, respectively. This confirms that co-offenders tend to be geographically confined.

In [13], it is concluded that socially clsoe offeners are spatially close too, meaning that offenders who are close in the co-offending network have more overlap in their activity spaces too. Criminological theories and the discussed experimental results motivated us focus more on geographic and geo-social features, besides general social features extracted from network topology for co-offence prediction.

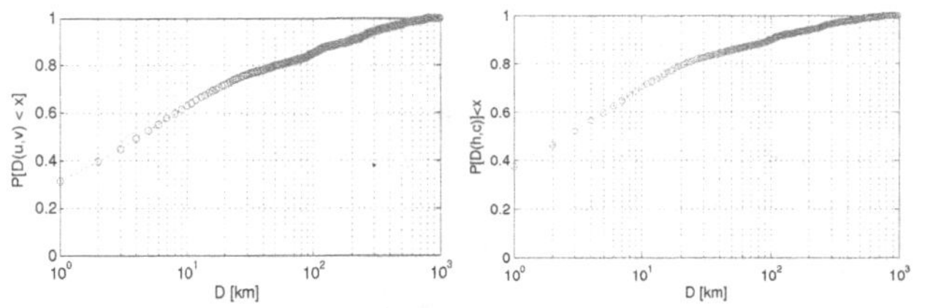

Figure 2: (a) Home location distance of co-offenders; (b) Home and crime locations distance of offenders.

3. CO-OFFENCE PREDICTION

In this section we define the *co-offence prediction problem* and propose a novel analytic framework for solving this problem.

3.1 Problem Definition

A co-offending network $G(V, E)$ refers to all co-offences within time period $[t_0, t_n]$ associated with the underlying crime dataset. For any time $t \in [t_0, t_n]$, one can derive $G_t(V_t, E_t)$ as a substructure of G, which is a co-offending network, by restricting to all crime incidents up to time t. For $G_t(V_t, E_t)$ we now define a *potential co-offence* at time $t + 1$ as any pair of offenders (u, v) such that $(u, v) \notin E_t$, meaning that offenders u and v have not committed any crime together prior to $t + 1$. A potential co-offence (u, v) is in the *positive class*, if $(u, v) \in E_{t+1}$, and it is in the *negative class*, if $(u, v) \notin E_{t+1}$. The co-offence prediction task is to predict for each potential co-offence in G_t if it belongs to the positive class or the negative class.

Co-offence prediction can be viewed as a link prediction problem for co-offending networks. This aspect is modeled using a binary classification problem that adopts a set of prediction features as described in Section 4. The major challenge in any link prediction problem is the heavily skewed distribution of negative and positive classes. Contrary to unsupervised methods, supervised methods learn class distributions to increase classification performance [10].

3.2 Criminal Cooperation Opportunities

Because of all obvious risks about committing crimes, offenders do not select their collaborators accidentally. Considering offenders' choices and selection opportunities, any co-offence can have social, environmental or experience related causes. To quantitatively model how offenders form a criminal cooperation, for each offender u, we define three opportunity spaces for criminal cooperation defined as follows:

Socially-related. Social interactions influence the behavior of individuals. This observation has been studied widely in areas such as educational choices and labor market outcomes. Arguably, this applies to criminal behavior as well, where social networks compensate for lack of formal institutions in gaining knowledge and criminal skills. Criminal behavior associated with illegal activities is influenced by informal networks and peer interactions. Sutherland, in the theory of *differential association* [18], explains individual criminality with a social-psychological process of learning crime through interaction with social groups. According to [18], criminal behavior is the result of learning an excess of definitions favorable to crime. Offenders use social interactions for sharing information, recruiting young criminals [28] and transferring criminal skills. Although co-offending networks are generally considered short-lived networks, they constitute an important source of criminal cooperation opportunities. In our definition, socially-related cooperation opportunities for an offender u, denoted by S_u, arise from offenders v such that their distance in the co-offending network is not greater than N, excluding the direct neighbors of u:

$$S_u = \{(u, v) : v \in (\bigcup_{i \leq N} \Gamma_u^i) \setminus \Gamma_u^1\}$$

Geographically-related. Activity space and social environment of offenders greatly influence their criminal decisions and are key factors in forming collaboration opportunities [29, 16]. Activity space plays a crucial role in where crimes are committed and individuals are recruited for the purpose of co-offending. Not only do offenders converge with crime victims, but they also converge with each other in order to find suitable co-offenders. Felson's "offender convergence settings" describe certain locations in which potential offenders meet each other to initiate and maintain co-offending and crime groups [29]. Based on accepted criminological theories we define geographically-related space as an important potential space for co-offending link formation.

Offender u is considered geographically related to any offender v, if they have a common (overlapping) activity space, but they are not connected to each other directly in the co-offending network.

$$G_u = \{(u, v) : v \in (\bigcup_{a_u^i \in A_u^r} \chi_u^i) \setminus \Gamma_u^1\}$$

Experience-related. Network studies on offenders have generally observed evidence of homophily like criminal experience [14]. This is so consistent that group homogeneity is considered one of the key characteristics of co-offending [14]. With similar criminal experience the chance increases that offenders forme new criminal collaborations. This can happen via implicit networks or due to demand for specific criminal expertise. All pairs of offenders who have similar criminal experience but are not directly connected to each other in the co-offending network are categorized into this class:

$$E_u = \{(u, v) : v \in (\bigcup_{i \geq P} \Theta_u^i \setminus \Gamma_u^1\}$$

We use the above criminal cooperation spaces to define the spaces which cover the prediction candidates. Prediction space division has two advantages: First, it helps to reduce the class imbalance ratio. Second, it leads to a clearer understanding of the effects of each of these categories on new co-offence formation. For $G_t(V_t, E_t)$ we generate three spaces for the co-offence prediction task:

SR: This space includes all links emerging between pairs of offenders that are socially-related: $SR^t = \{\forall u \in V_t : \bigcup_u S_u\}$. In our experiments for constructing the SR space, we consider $N = 2$. In other words, a pair of offenders who are exactly 2-hops apart are added to this space.

GR: that contains all links between pairs of offenders who are geographically-related but not socially-related: $GR^t = \{\forall u \in V_t : (\bigcup_u G_u) \setminus SR^t\}$. For constructing the activity space of offenders which defines if two offenders are geographically-related we use $R = 2km$.

ER: that includes all pair of offenders that are experience-related but not socially-related: $ER^t = \{\forall u \in V_t : \bigcup_u E_u \setminus SR^t\}$. For creating the ER space, we apply $P = 2$, meaning that (u, v) are considered experience-related offenders if both committed at least two crimes of the same type.

3.3 Reducing Class Imbalance Ratio

For a network $G(V, E)$ the number of links E is often $O(|V|)$, but the number of no-existing links is often $O(|V|^2)$. Accordingly,

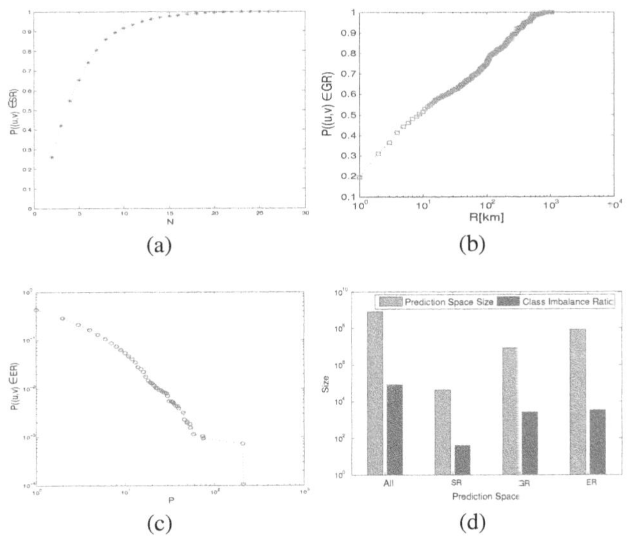

Figure 3: (a) Cumulative probability distribution of a positive sample in SR space in respect to N; (b) Cumulative probability distribution of a positive sample in GR space in respect to R; (c) Cumulative probability distribution of a positive sample in ER space in respect to P; (d) Prediction spaces size and their class imbalance ratio.

the prior probability of link formation is very small. Since the goal of supervised learning is achieving high precision, class imbalance in the training dataset leads to overfitting to negative samples which reduces the recall of positive samples. Note that in the co-offence prediction task high recall of the positive class (co-offences) is critical, so that overcoming the class imbalance is essential.

In the experimental setting defined in Section 5.1, the number of negative samples is 850M while the number of positive samples is only 11k. Therefore, the *class imbalance ratio*, the ratio of negative samples to positive samples, is about 77K. Using the prediction spaces to reduce the training and test dataset can effectively reduce the class imbalance. In [19] an efficient prediction space division schema for location-based social network is proposed, but it does not apply to co-offence prediction where environment activity of offenders are different than location-based social networks users. Furthermore we consider the homophily effects, in terms of criminal activity similarity, on forming new link which is not considered in the approach proposed in [19]. Although reducing class imbalance is an important objective, the other main concern is keeping as many positive samples as possible.

Restricting the dataset to samples with short graph distance is the most effective solution for the imbalance problem. In the SR space increasing N affects the number of negative samples set superlinearly, because we expect to see more co-offences between offenders close in the network. Figure 3a demonstrates the probability of a positive sample in the SR space for different values of N of the network distance. The probability does not grow linearly as N increases, meaning that similar to other type of social networks [10, 19] majority of positive samples are at a closer network distance. For the maximum value $N = 27$ there are 204M negative samples. But changing this to $N = 2$ decreases the number of negative samples to 47K, while keeping 25% of the positive samples.

Applying different constraints related to the other prediction spaces also helps to reduce the class imbalance ratio. Figure 3c shows the probability of a positive sample in the GR space for different values R of the radius of the activity space. With $R = 2$ km, $R = 10$ km and $R = 100$ km the GR space covers cumulative 31%, 51% and 75% of the positive samples. Figure 3b shows the probability of a positive sample in the ER space for different values of P. With $P = 2$ of the same crime type, $P = 5$ and $P = 10$ the ER space includes 29%, 13% and 5% of the positive samples. Applying $R = 2$ km and $P = 2$ reduces the $850M$ negative samples in the dataset to 8M and 82M respectively for GR and ER spaces. With these constraints we can keep 31% and 29% of the positive samples in the GR and ER spaces.

As demonstrated in Figure 3d, the original imbalance ratio of 77K for the whole prediction space reduces to 40, 2700 and 3400 respectively for SR, GR and ER spaces. While in each of three spaces roughly we can keep approximately the same percentage of positive samples (26%, 31% and 29% for the SR, GR and ER spaces), we see that the class imbalance reduction is better in the SR space. In total we are able to maintain half of positive samples for training, meaning that the likelihood of predicting a co-offence successfully increases significantly.

4. PREDICTION FEATURES

Prediction features are divided into four categories: social, geographic, geo-social and similarity features. This section describes how these features are extracted. Features are defined formally in Table 1.

4.1 Social Features

The social features set includes all features that are derived using only the topology of the co-offending network and the position of offenders in the network. Preferential is defined as the product of the node degrees of two offenders, meaning that the more connected an offender is, the more likely he forms new criminal links. Common, denotes the number of neighbors two offenders have in common. Overlap divides the number of common neighbors by the overall number of neighbors of two offenders as a normalized indication of common neighbors effect. Adamic [30] assigns higher weight to the common neighbors with smaller node degree.

4.2 Geographic Features

With increasing overlap of the activity space of offenders the chance of forming new criminal collaboration increases. Home locations distance, HDN, is the average distance between the current and past home locations of two offenders. HDT weights home location distance by the time two offenders lived in the corresponding locations. Committing crimes in the same neighborhood may cause a criminal tie between offenders. CDN is the average crime location distance of two offenders.

4.3 Geo-social Features

Geo-social features combine the social and geographical characteristics of offenders. Common activity space of offenders directly affects their behaviors. Being active in an area with many offenders living there can increase the chance that offenders meet each other directly or indirectly, and engage in co-offending. OCT denotes the number of offenders living in a common activity space of two given offenders. In the definition of common activity space time is implicitly restricted to $\delta_u^i \cap \delta_v^j$. OCTT boosts OCT if two offenders are active for a longer period of time. Without any restriction, OCN denoted the number of offenders who live in a common activity space anytime in the time interval $[t_0, t]$.

Characteristics related to the quantity of crimes in the common activity space provide another set of geo-social features. A crime hotspot located within the common activity space of offenders may increase the chance of collaboration among these offenders. CCT states the number of crimes in the common activity space of two offenders, where, similar to OCT, the time is restricted to the period over which both offenders are active simultaneously. CCTT weights the time interval of two offenders being active. And CCN refers to the total number of crime incidents in the common activity space.

4.4 Similarity Features

The homophily principle states that individuals tend to associate themselves with others in a social network who are similar [31]. This is also a very well-studied topic for co-offending [14]. Age difference, ethnic group similarity and gender similarity, represented by Age, Ethnic and Gender, are three features in this category. Finally, CrimSim also expresses similarity of criminal experience based on committed crime types.

5. EXPERIMENTS AND RESULTS

In this section we present the experimental evaluation, starting with a description of the experimental design.

5.1 Experimental Design

The spacial nature of co-offending networks makes co-offence prediction a difficult task. Offenders not only do hide their illegal activities and contacts, but their accomplice relationships are usually short-lived [6].

For our experiments, we divide the dataset into two disjoint sets of incidents, one for the first 50 months and the second one for last 10 months. Excluding noisy data, such as traffic related offenses, the number of incidents for the aforementioned time periods are 1.8M and 800K respectively. Considering only offences with more than one offender reduces these numbers to 67K and 17K. We extract the co-offending networks corresponding to each of these time periods. Next, criminal cooperation opportunities are identified and each pair of potential co-offences are assigned to one of three prediction spaces: SR, IR or ER. Eventually, the prediction features of each pairs of potential co-offenders are extracted.

We use the open-source machine-learning library Weka [32] for different classifier building. The performance of classifiers and single feature prediction are assessed based on the Receiver Operating Characteristics (ROC), which shows the trade-off between the true positive rate over the false positive rate [33]. The area under the ROC curve, called AUC, is an appropriate measure for comparing two ROC curves. AUC measures the probability that a classifier ranks a randomly chosen positive sample higher than a negative sample.

Various definitions of offender activity space are known in the literature. We use a simple definition: a circle of radius R with the home location of an offender in the center point (based on the available information on offenders in the dataset). Common activity space of two offenders is defined as the intersection of their activity space and is used for defining geo-social features. Given that there is no consensus in the criminology literature as to the appropriate value of R, we tried different values of R, ranging from 1 km to 10 km. Interestingly, for all features, a value of $R = 2$ km maximizes the prediction performance, which we therefore chose in our experiments.

5.2 Single Feature Significance

We compare the predictive power of individual features described in Section 4 in each of the prediction spaces. This is important to diagnose which features in each prediction space play a more important role in co-offence prediction. For this purpose, we compute the feature values for all negative and all positive potential co-offenders. Then, using a range of decision thresholds and computing the false/true positives ratios, we generate the ROC curves for each single feature as presented in Figure 4. Note that the social features can be extracted only for SR space.

As shown in Figure 4a, in the SR space, the Preferential feature is the best predictor with AUC value 0.82 and is superior to other social features. The performance of Adamic and Jaccard are worse than a random predictor. This shows that being a frequent offender and having broader criminal relationships, rather than common relationships, increases the chance of engaging in new criminal cooperations. Following Preferential are geo-social and geographic features CDN, OCN, CCN, and HDN, with AUC values between 0.74 and 0.79. The performance of similarity features is lower than the mentioned set.

Social Features	
Preferential	$\lvert\Gamma_u^1\rvert \times \lvert\Gamma_v^1\rvert$
Common	$\lvert\Gamma_u^1\rvert \cap \lvert\Gamma_v^1\rvert$
Overlap	$\frac{\lvert\Gamma_u^1\rvert \cap \Gamma_v^1}{\lvert\Gamma_u 1\rvert \cup \lvert\Gamma_v^1\rvert}$
Adamic	$\sum_{z \in \Gamma_u^1 \cap \Gamma_v^1} \frac{1}{log(\Gamma_z^1)}$
Geographic Features	
HDN	$\frac{\sum_{i=1}^{i=m} \sum_{j=1}^{j=n} e^{\frac{-D(h_u^i, h_v^j)}{\lambda}}}{\lvert H_u\rvert \times \lvert H_v\rvert}$
HDT	$\frac{\sum_{i=1}^{i=m} \sum_{j=1}^{j=n} e^{\frac{-D(h_u^i, h_v^j)}{\lambda}} \times \lvert(\delta_u^i \cap \delta_v^j)\rvert}{\lvert H_u\rvert \times \lvert H_v\rvert}$
CDN	$\frac{\sum_{i=1}^{i=m} \sum_{j=1}^{j=n} e^{\frac{-D(c_u^i, c_v^j)}{\lambda}}}{\lvert C(u)\rvert \times \lvert C(v)\rvert}$
Geo-social Features	
OCT	$\sum_{i=1}^{i=p} \sum_{j=1}^{i=k} \lvert\chi_{u,v}^{i,j}\rvert$
OCTT	$\sum_{i=1}^{i=p} \sum_{j=1}^{i=k} \lvert\chi_{u,v}^{i,j}\rvert \times \lvert\delta_u^i \cap \delta_v^j\rvert$
OCN	$\sum_{i=1}^{i=p} \sum_{j=1}^{i=k} \lvert\chi_{u,v}^{i,j}\rvert : [t_0, t]$
CCT	$\sum_{i=1}^{i=p} \sum_{j=1}^{i=k} \lvert\phi_{u,v}^{i,j}\rvert$
CCTT	$\sum_{i=1}^{i=p} \sum_{j=1}^{i=k} \lvert\phi_{u,v}^{i,j}\rvert \times \lvert\delta_u^i \cap \delta_v^j\rvert$
CCN	$\sum_{i=1}^{i=p} \sum_{j=1}^{i=k} \lvert\phi_{u,v}^{i,j}\rvert : [t_0, t]$
Similarity Features	
Age	$\lvert Age(u) - Age(v)\rvert$
Gender	$\begin{cases} 1, & \text{if Gender}(u) = \text{Gender}(v) \\ 0, & \text{if Gender}(u) \neq \text{Gender}(v) \end{cases}$
Ethnic	$\begin{cases} 1, & \text{if Ethnic}(u) = \text{Ethnic}(v) \\ 0, & \text{if Ethnic}(u) \neq \text{Ethnic}(v) \end{cases}$
CrimSim	$\frac{\sum_{i=1}^{K} P_u^i P_v^i}{\sqrt{\sum_i^K (P_u^i)^2} \times \sqrt{\sum_{i=1}^K (P_v^{i=1})^2}}$

Table 1: Prediction features.

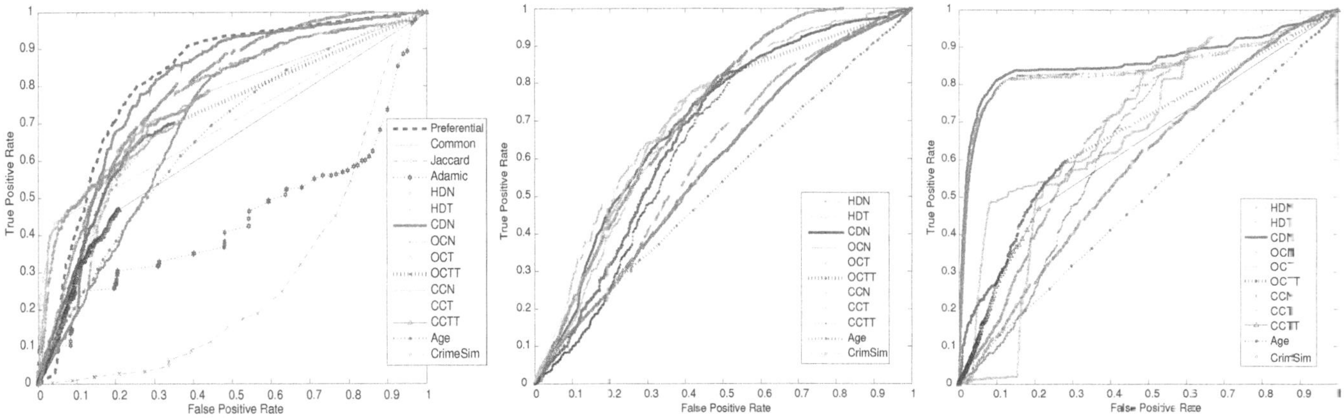

(a) SR (b) GR (c) ER

Figure 4: Single feature significance in three different predictions spaces.

In the GR space, performance of most of the features is weaker than their performance in the SR space. This is not unexpected for geographic or geo-social features, where in the negative potential class we gather all pairs that are geographically close and the predictor cannot be as successful as in the SR space. Nevertheless, the AUC values of these features fall within the range 0.60 to 0.70. Compared to the SR space, in the ER space geographic and geo-social features work better. Their AUC values are between 0.72 and 0.86.

In the similarity features generally Gender works as good as a random predictor in all three spaces. Age and Ethnic have similar performance in the ER and GR spaces. But in SR, AUC values of these two features are 0.66 and 0.60. This shows that in the SR space one can see stronger signs of the homophily principle in forming new relationships. CrimSim has the best performance in the GR space with AUC value of 0.71.

Counterintuitively, time-based features perform weaker than the original version of the corresponding feature. For instance, in the SR space, the performance of HDT compared to HDN, OCT and OCTT compared to OCN, and, finally, CCT and CCTT compared to CCN, all drop down to five percent. The same trend applies to the other prediction spaces. Parameter regularization of time-based features for promoting their prediction strength is subject to future research. An interesting pattern in all spaces is that CDN outperforms HDN, which shows that being criminally active in areas that are in close proximity is a stronger indicator for forming new criminal collaboration than living in close proximity to each other.

Each single feature can be considered an unsupervised link predictor. Unsupervised link prediction methods assign scores to potential links based on node attributes or network structural proximity measures [8]. Then, the link prediction problem is defined as a binary classification problem by choosing some probability threshold, and predicting that potential links with a probability above the threshold will be formed, whereas those below the threshold will not be formed. We use the best AUC value of the single features to compare with the supervised predictors in the next section.

As discussed in [8], the performance of unsupervised link predictors varies in different social networks, meaning that unsupervised link predictors are domain-specific. For instance, among the structural network features, preferential attachment works best for co-offending networks in our study, while this single feature predictor has the worst performance for the network of cellular phone users in[10].

5.3 Prediction Evaluation

The previous section analyzes the performance of individual features. Now, how good works a supervised method using a group of extracted features? Naturally, one would expect to see performance improvements. For this purpose, we use four different classification methods: Naïve Bayes, J48 (equivalent to C4.5), random forests (10 trees, each constructed while considering 4 random features), and bagging (10 bags).

Similar to the work in [9, 19], we run 10-fold cross validation over 10 different randomly sampled training sets for each of the three prediction spaces, SR, GR and ER. We consider the average values of AUC, and precision and recall over positive samples. The prediction results are listed in Table 2. One can see variability in the different classifier performances, and also in the results for the different prediction spaces. All classifiers for all spaces outperform single features. Generally, prediction works best in the ER space.

Two ensemble methods, bagging and random forest classifiers, work better than the other classifiers and Naïve Bayes is the weakest one in all spaces. In ensemble learning for decreasing the variance error the results of a number of classifiers are combined to make a prediction. An ensemble method improves the prediction performance if the overlap of misclassification of the single classifiers is small. On average we see 5.1% AUC improvement in random forest classifiers comparing to single decision tree classifier which shows the variance reduction influence.

Since all features are available in the SR space and the bagging classifier works better than other methods, we continue the following experiments with the SR space and bagging classifier. To study prediction strength of each of the feature sets, social, geographic, geo-social and similarity, each time we keep one of the feature sets and evaluate it using the bagging classifier with the same setting. As shown in Table 3, the geo-social features outperform the other three sets, and the geographic feature set has the worst performance. Comparing the prediction performance using all features to different subsets shows integrating all features from social, environmental and personal can contribute to co-offence prediction.

Most existing unsupervised link prediction methods assign scores to the potential links and rank them. The top-k links are categorized as new links, and the remaining as missing links. The evalua-

Algorithm	Space	Precision	Recall	AUC
J48	SR	0.888	0.807	0.907
	GR	0.869	0.834	0.901
	ER	0.935	0.81	0.898
Naïve Bayes	SR	0.836	0.514	0.825
	GR	0.825	0.441	0.817
	ER	0.945	0.706	0.895
Random Forest	SR	0.898	0.843	0.944
	GR	0.864	0.883	0.944
	ER	0.941	0.944	0.982
Bagging	SR	0.908	0.84	0.951
	GR	0.863	0.854	0.952
	ER	0.946	0.942	0.986

Table 2: Recall, precision and AUC for different classification algorithms on the three different prediction spaces, SR, GR and IR, using 10-fold cross validation over 10 different random training sets.

tion of unsupervised methods is same as single features evaluation in Section 5.2. Preferential, Jaccard and Adamic are common unsupervised link prediction methods as addressed in [8]. While Preferential has the highest the AUC value among individual features we see more then 13% improvement in the bagging classifier result, which means supervised classifiers outperform the unsupervised predictors significantly.

For a better insight into class imbalance issues, we vary the size of negative samples for the SR space using same set of positive samples, where the positive samples proportion ranges from 2% to 100%. As illustrated in Figure 5a, the AUC value is relatively stable. Unsurprisingly, with negative sample size and accordingly imbalanced ratio growth, precision increases and recall decreases. As expected, this is because of negative class overfitting, meaning that the trained classifier is more likely to predict non-existing links.

6. CRIMINOLOGICAL IMPLICATIONS

Crime forecasting models are divided into short-term and long-term categories in terms of predicted time periods. Short-term models are beneficial for tactical decision making, whereas long-term models are helpful for planning and policy development. Co-offence prediction is an important aspect for short-term models. Studying new link formation patterns can help designing effective long-term crime reduction and prevention strategies.

Based on the discussion of offenders' activity space issue in Section 2.3 for all six geo-social features we tried different values of radius R from 1 km to 10 km. As depicted in Figure 5b for all of the features and $R > 2$ km the prediction performance decreases by increasing R. This finding is consistent with a well-know criminology fact [17] which states crimes are likely to occur closer to an offender's anchor points and follow a distance-decay function.

With the settings defined in Section 5.1, $E_{t+1} \cong 120K$, while the portion of positive samples is about 9%. And in the reality the prediction is possible only in this portion where we had information about both of co-offender previously. The propose framework was able to predict 45% of all positive samples.

Figure 6a shows the cumulative degree distribution $P(k)$ in the co-offending network G_{50} for three sets of offenders: V_{50}, $\{u \mid \exists v \in V_t : (u,v) \in \text{SR} \cap E_{t+1}\}$ and $\{u \mid \exists (u,v) \in \text{SR} \wedge (u,v) \notin E_{t+1}\}$. One can see that for the same node degree k, compared to the two other sets, the set of offenders who contribute to forming co-

Features Set	Precision	Recall	AUC
Social	0.903	0.792	0.919
Geographic	0.721	0.786	0.811
Geo-social	0.863	0.853	0.942
Similarity	0.849	0.851	0.928
All Features	0.908	0.84	0.951

Table 3: Prediction strength of different feature sets for SR space using the bagging classifier with 10-fold cross validation over 10 different random training sets.

offences generally has a greater value of $P(k)$. Section 5.2 shows that Preferential for SR space is a strong predictor. This implies the relevance of co-offending networks for making new criminal cooperation.

Assume that $\tau_{u,v}$ refers to the first time that a positive co-offence (u, v) occurs in time interval $[51, 60]$, and τ is the time of the most recent offence of u or v in $[1, 50]$. Figure 6b plots the distribution of $\tau_{u,v} - \tau$ for all positive potential co-offences. We see a power law distribution, meaning that there are many offences with a small value of $\tau_{u,v} - \tau$ and few with a larger value of $\tau_{u,v} - \tau$. This results shows that offenders who were recently active have a higher potential to form new criminal cooperation.

We see some variance in the prediction strength of different prediction features, with weak and strong predictors in each of the spaces. For all spaces we see high prediction results, which shows that there are strong patterns in co-offending. This supports our idea of dividing criminal cooperation opportunities, this way, finding stronger co-offence patterns that improve predictions. However, co-offending is a product of the intricate interplay between

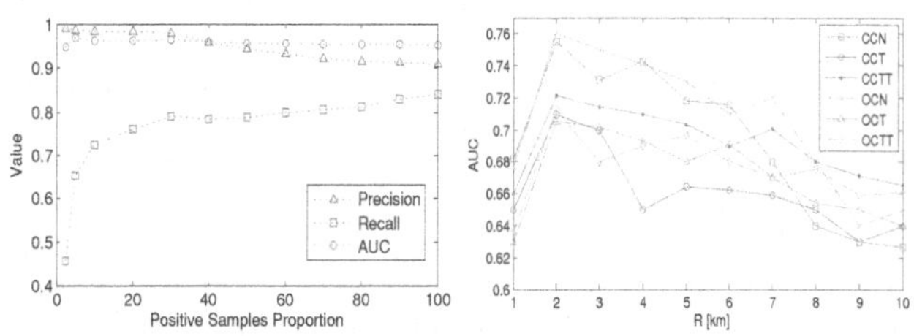

Figure 5: (a) Performance changes of the bagging classifier for different imbalance ratios. The x-axis states the ratio of the positive class size over the negative class size. (b) Single features siginicance using different activity space radius

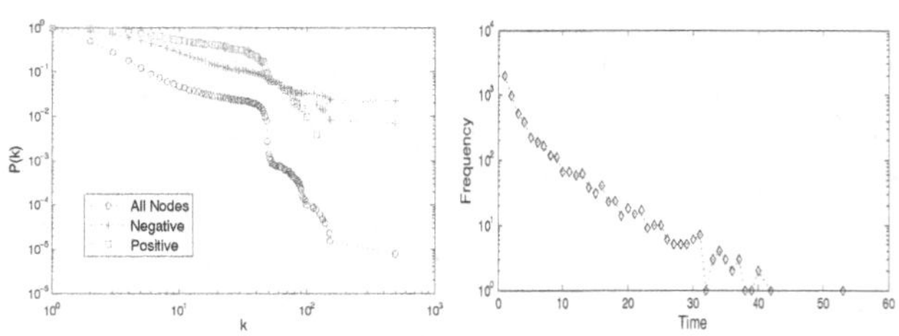

Figure 6: (a) Cumulative degree distribution of offenders (b) Frequency distribution of time difference between two offenders most recent crime and their first co-offence.

many factors, and drawing any firm conclusions requires more substantial and in-depth research beyond the scope of this paper.

Co-offending research currently is non-spatial, except in conflicting edges of gang neighborhoods [34], and usually not associated with crime signatures of crime attributes. Future research should improve the predictive power of link prediction approaches by adding more information about an individual's non-co-offending patterns and co-offending patterns with more guidance for the introduction of preventative programs to reduce gang offences. This research opens the door for advanced approaches to the co-offending networks analysis by identifying those situations where the probability of future co-offending increases. This has potential value in predictive policing by indicating the attributes of individuals who are more likely to engage in future crimes jointly.

7. RELATED WORK

This section discusses published works on co-offending network analysis, crime prediction and link prediction.

7.1 Co-offending Networks

Crime prevention and reduction is the major concern of law enforcement agencies in order to protect the lives and properties of citizens. Just like the abundance of available data on virtually all parts of society can cause an information overload for many, the rapidly growing volume of crime data makes it increasingly challenging for law enforcement and criminal intelligence agencies to analyze all of the data and extract relevant information and knowledge. Data mining constitutes the scientific foundation for managing the large volume of crime data so as to discover new insights for developing effective crime reduction and prevention strategies.

In criminology, several empirical studies that use social network analysis methods to analyze co-offending networks focus on the stability of associations in such networks. Morselli [7] offers a thoughtful insight into 'criminal organizational systems' form a criminal network perspective and applies social network analysis to a number of case studies of criminal groups and organizations. Reiss [6] concludes that the majority of co-offending groups are unstable, and their relationships are short-lived. This finding is corroborated by McGloin et al. [15], who show that there is some stability in co-offending relationships over time for frequent offenders, but delinquents do in general not tend to reuse co-offenders. However, it should be pointed out that the above findings are based on small datasets: 205 individuals in [6], and 5,600 individuals in [15], and may therefore not be representative.

Certain characteristics of co-offending networks, such as being short-lived and having hidden links, make it difficult to adopt and use social network analysis algorithms. Lack of real-world crime data for research purposes and the necessity of cross-disciplinary knowledge are further limiting factors that may explain why social network analysis studies rarely focus on criminal network analysis problems that are important for public safety, such as organized crime groups detection, criminal network destabilization and co-offence prediction.

7.2 Crime Prediction

Two main criminology theories claim that involvement in crime is the result of: 1) an individual's crime propensity, and 2) criminogenic features of the environment to which an individual is exposed. While propensity towards crime has long been studied, in the last few decades criminogenic features of the environment received specific attention. Apart from individuals, spatial aspects increasingly gain momentum, and environmental criminology [16] plays an essential role in crime reduction and prevention tactics New research areas emerge, like crime mapping [35], geographic profiling [17] and crime forecasting [4, 5], that support growing and imperative applications of this research field for law enforcement and criminal intelligence agencies.

Crime prediction methods in the literature completely ignore the role of co-offending in committing crime. Rather their goal is to spatially and temporally model observed crimes to predict the time and location of future crimes. For instance in [5], the authors use a point-pattern-based transition density model for crime space-event prediction considering criminal preferences from previous crimes. Given partial information about a crime incident, Crimewalker [12] is an unsupervised method for top-k suspect recommendation, which applies a random walk method on the co-offending network. As concluded in the link prediction literature, supervised methods always outperform the unsupervised competitors. To the best of our knowledge, the proposed approach is the first supervised learning framework for co-offence prediction.

7.3 Link Prediction

Link prediction is important aspect of social network analysis to better understand the network structure. Link prediction methods can be used to extract missing information, identify hidden interactions, evaluate network evolution mechanisms, and beyond.

Most unsupervised link prediction methods [8] rely solely on the network topology and assign scores to potential links based on structural proximity measures such as node neighborhoods or path information. On the other hand, any classification method can be used for link prediction [9, 10, 11]. In a detailed study [10], Lichtenwalter et. al. examine key factors in the link prediction problem, and propose a framework for supervised link prediction.

More recently, location-based social networking services made it possible to study and predict spatial behaviors of social network actors. Wang et. al. [20], using trajectory and communication patterns of users, concluded that combining mobility and network features enhances the link prediction results. Scellato et. al. [19], based on their study of the link prediction problem in online location-based social networks, conclude that using information about places people visited boosts the link prediction performance.

Although the challenges and concerns of our study is similar to other link prediction studies [9, 10, 19, 20], there are fundamental distinctions as well. Crime data and co-offending network characteristics are inherently different from affiliation networks, such as co-authorship networks or mobile phone networks. Although environmental activity plays an important role in creating new links, these activities are also very different from location-based social networks. Therefore the feature or prediction spaces defined based on criminological theories are different from the ones known in the literature. After all, the co-offence prediction framework proposed in this research and supported by experimental evaluation is an innovative application of social network analysis that offers a new perspective for crime reduction and prevention strategies.

8. CONCLUSIONS

This paper proposes a supervised learning framework for co-offence prediction. We define the co-offence prediction problem as a link prediction problem in co-offending networks. For our study, we use co-offending networks with more than 150K known criminal offenders. These networks were extracted from a large police-reported crime dataset containing about 4.4M offences over a period of five years in British Columbia, Canada. Considering criminological theories about social, environmental and homophily roots of offending in a comprehensive way, we assign each pair of offenders to socially-related, geographically-related or experience-related criminal cooperation opportunities. Using these sets, we create three prediction spaces. While we are able to retain half of the co-offences, the prediction space division allows us to significantly reduce class imbalance, which is a major challenge in link prediction. We do not only use homophily, social and spatial characteristics of pairs of offenders to define prediction features, but we also define novel geo-social features combining social and spatial characteristics. Evaluating single feature significance, we conclude that geo-social features generally are more effective than others, while we also observe considerable prediction strength in other features. Employing all features, our classifiers achieve a recall of 84%, 88%, and 94% respectively, for three different prediction spaces, which means that we can correctly predict roughly 90% of the co-offences. We believe that our findings provide valuable insights and novel methods for short-term and long-term crime reduction and prevention strategies.

Acknowledgements

We are thankful to RCMP "E" Division and BC Ministry for Public Safety and Solicitor General for making this research possible by providing Simon Fraser University with crime data from their Police Information Retrieval System. We further wish to thank the ICURS institute at Simon Fraser University for all their support. Finally, we also like to thank the three anonymous reviewers for their constructive criticism and helpful comments.

9. REFERENCES

[1] R. Boba. *Crime analysis and crime mapping*. SAGE Publications, 2005.

[2] U. S. Department of Justice. Crime in the United States: uniform crime reports. *Federal Bureau of Investigation; Washington, DC.*, 2008.

[3] J. Zhang. Costs of crime in canada, 2008. *Research and Statistics Division, Department of Justice Canada.*, 2011.

[4] W. Gorr and R. Harries. Introduction to crime forecasting. *International Journal of Forecasting*, 19(4):551–555, 2003.

[5] H. Liu and D. E. Brown. Criminal incident prediction using a point-pattern-based density model. *International journal of forecasting*, 19(4):603–622, 2003.

[6] A. J. Reiss Jr. Co-offending and criminal careers. *Crime and justice*, pages 117–170, 1988.

[7] C. Morselli. *Inside criminal networks*, volume 73. Springer, 2008.

[8] D. Liben-Nowell and J. Kleinberg. The link-prediction problem for social networks. *J. Am. Soc. Inf. Sci. Technol.*, 58(7):1019–1031, May 2007.

[9] M. A. Hasan, V. Chaoji, S. Salem, and M. Zaki. Link prediction using supervised learning. In *Proc. SDM'06*, 2006.

[10] R. N. Lichtenwalter, J. T. Lussier, and N. V. Chawla. New perspectives and methods in link prediction. In *Proc. KDD '10*, 2010.

[11] C. Wang, V. Satuluri, and S. Parthasarathy. Local probabilistic models for link prediction. In *Proc. ICDM '07*, 2007.

[12] M. A. Tayebi, M. Jamali, M. Ester, U. Glässer, and R. Frank. Crimewalker: a recommendation model for suspect investigation. In *Proc. RecSys'11*, 2011.

[13] M. A. Tayebi, R. Frank, and U. Glässer. Understanding the link between social and spatial distance in the crime world. In *Proc. SIGSPATIAL GIS'12*, 2012.

[14] F. M. Weerman. Co-offending as social exchange: Explaining characteristics of co-offending. *British Journal of Criminology*, 43(2):398–416, 2003.

[15] J. McGloin, C. J. Sullivan, A. R. Piquero, and S. Bacon. Investigating the stability of co-offending and co-offenders among a sample of youthful offenders. *Criminology*, 46(1):155–188, 2008.

[16] P. J. Brantingham and P. L. Brantingham. *Environmental criminology*. Sage Publications, 1981.

[17] D.K. Rossmo. *Geographic Profiling*. CRC Press, 2000.

[18] E.H. Sutherland. *Principles of criminology*. Philadelphia: Lippincott, 1947.

[19] S. Scellato, A. Noulas, and C. Mascolo. Exploiting place features in link prediction on location-based social networks. In *Proc. KDD'11*, 2011.

[20] D. Wang, D. Pedreschi, C. Song, F. Giannotti, and A. Barabasi. Human mobility, social ties, and link prediction. In *Proc. KDD'11*, 2011.

[21] C. Zhang, L. Shou, K. Chen, G. Chen, and Y. Bei. Evaluating geo-social influence in location-based social networks. In *Proc. CIKM'12*, 2012.

[22] E. Cho, S. A. Myers, and J. Leskovec. Friendship and mobility: user movement in location-based social networks. In *Proc. KDD '11*, 2011.

[23] A. Reid, M. A. Tayebi, and R. Frank. Exploring the structural characteristics of social networks in a large criminal court database. In *Proc. ISI'13*, 2013.

[24] P. L. Brantingham, M. Ester, R. Frank, U. Glässer, and M. A. Tayebi. Co-offending network mining. *Counterterrorism and Open Source Intelligence*, pages 73–102, 2011.

[25] D. V. Canter and A. Gregory. Identifying the residential location of rapists. *Journal of the Forensic Science Society*, 34(3):169–175, 1994.

[26] M. Felson. *Crime and Nature*. SAGE Publications, 2006.

[27] B. Snook. Individual differences in distance travelled by serial burglars. *Journal of Investigative Psychology and Offender Profiling*, 1(1):53–66, 2004.

[28] A. Calvó-Armengol and Y. Zenou. Social networks and crime decisions: The role of social structure in facilitating delinquent behavior. *International Economic Review*, 45(3):939–958, 2004.

[29] M. Felson. The process of co-offending. In *M. Smith and D. Cornish, eds, Theory and Practice in Situational Crime Prevention*. Monsey, NJ: Criminal Justice Press, 2003.

[30] L. A. Adamic and E. Adar. Friends and neighbors on the web. *Social networks*, 25(3):211–230, 2003.

[31] M. McPherson, L. Smith-Lovin, and J. M. Cook. Birds of a feather: Homophily in social networks. *Annual review of sociology*, pages 415–444, 2001.

[32] M. Hall, E. Frank, G. Holmes, B. Pfahringer, P. Reutemann, and I. H. Witten. The weka data mining software: an update. *SIGKDD Explor. Newsl.*, pages 10–18, 2009.

[33] F. J. Provost, T. Fawcett, and R. Kohavi. The case against accuracy estimation for comparing induction algorithms. In *Proc. ICML'98*, 1998.

[34] P. J. Brantingham, G. Tita, M. B. Short, and S. Reid. The ecology of gang territorial boundaries. *Criminology,*, 50, 2012.

[35] K. Harries. Mapping crime principle and practice. *Washington D.C, U.S. Department of Justice Office of Justice Programs*, 1999.

‘Beating the News’ with EMBERS: Forecasting Civil Unrest using Open Source Indicators

Naren Ramakrishnan*, Patrick Butler*, Sathappan Muthiah*, Nathan Self*, Rupinder Khandpur*, Parang Saraf*, Wei Wang*, Jose Cadena*, Anil Vullikanti*, Gizem Korkmaz*, Chris Kuhlman*, Achla Marathe*, Liang Zhao*, Ting Hua*, Feng Chen*††, Chang-Tien Lu*, Bert Huang†, Aravind Srinivasan†, Khoa Trinh†, Lise Getoor‡, Graham Katz§, Andy Doyle§, Chris Ackermann§, Ilya Zavorin§, Jim Ford§, Kristen Summers§, Youssef Fayed¶, Jaime Arredondo‖, Dipak Gupta**, David Mares‖

* Virginia Tech, Blacksburg, VA 24061
† University of Maryland, College Park, MD 20742
‡ University of California at Santa Cruz, Santa Cruz, CA 95064
†† University at Albany - State University of New York, Albany, NY 12222
‖ University of California at San Diego, San Diego, CA 92093
** San Diego State University, San Diego, CA 92182
¶ BASIS Technology, Herndon, VA 20171
§ CACI Inc., Lanham, MD 20706

ABSTRACT

We describe the design, implementation, and evaluation of EMBERS, an automated, 24x7 continuous system for forecasting civil unrest across 10 countries of Latin America using open source indicators such as tweets, news sources, blogs, economic indicators, and other data sources. Unlike retrospective studies, EMBERS has been making forecasts into the future since Nov 2012 which have been (and continue to be) evaluated by an independent T&E team (MITRE). Of note, EMBERS has successfully forecast the June 2013 protests in Brazil and Feb 2014 violent protests in Venezuela. We outline the system architecture of EMBERS, individual models that leverage specific data sources, and a fusion and suppression engine that supports trading off specific evaluation criteria. EMBERS also provides an audit trail interface that enables the investigation of why specific predictions were made along with the data utilized for forecasting. Through numerous evaluations, we demonstrate the superiority of EMBERS over baserate methods and its capability to forecast significant societal happenings.

Categories and Subject Descriptors

H.2.8 [**Database Management**]: Database Applications—*data mining*

Keywords

civil unrest, event forecasting, open source indicators

http://dx.doi.org/10.1145/2623330.2623373.

1. INTRODUCTION

We are constantly reminded of instabilities across the world, e.g., in regions such as Middle East and Latin America. Some of these instabilities arise from extremism or terrorism while others are the result of civil unrest, involving population-level uprisings by disenchanted citizens. Since the Arab Spring revolution began, and especially after Egypt's upheaval, many analysts (e.g., [12]) have pondered: Could we have anticipated these events? Were there precursors and signals that could have alerted us to them? Why did this happen in one country but not another?

Our team is an industry-university partnership charged with developing a system to continually monitor data sources 24x7, mine them to yield emerging trends and process these trends into forecasts of significant societal events such as protests. We refer to our system as EMBERS for Early Model Based Event Recognition using Surrogates. Although the scope of EMBERS spans a broad class of events (e.g., protests, disease outbreaks, elections), we focus our attention in this paper on only civil unrest events. Civil unrest is defined as a population-level event wherein people protest against the government or other larger organizations about specific policies, issues, or situations.

The EMBERS project is supported by the IARPA (Intelligence Advanced Research Projects Activity) OSI (Open Source Indicators) program whose objective is to forecast population-level changes using open source data feeds, such as tweets, web searches, news/blogs, economic indicators, Wikipedia, Internet traffic, and other sources. (The term ‘open source’ here refers to data sources that are openly available without requiring privileged access.) As a performer in the OSI program, EMBERS is a deployed system that has been generating forecasts since Nov 2012 and automatically emailing them in real-time to IARPA upon generation, which have been evaluated by an independent evaluation team (MITRE). Using human analysts, MITRE organizes a gold standard report (GSR) of protests by surveying newspapers for reportings of civil unrest. Our forecasts have been evaluated against this GSR every month

Warning ID: W1793
When: 01/04/2014 **Where:** Ecuador, Pinchincha, Quito **Who:** Ethnic **Why:** Energy and Resources
Probability: 0.87
Forecast Date: 12/27/13

GSR Event ID: E1859
When: 01/02/14 **Where:** Ecuador, Pinchincha, Quito **Who:** Ethnic **Why:** Energy and Resources
Reported Date: 01/05/14

Figure 1: Alerts (example, left) and events (example, right) are structured records describing protests.

since Nov 2012. Thus, unlike studies of retrospective predictability, EMBERS has been generating (and continues to generate) forecasts into the future.

Our goal in this paper is to present the design, implementation, and evaluation of EMBERS over an extended period of time. Our key contributions are:

1. We outline the system architecture and design of EMBERS, a modular 'big data' processing environment with levels of data transduction from raw feeds to warnings. EMBERS's alerts are meant for analyst consumption, but the system runs continuously 24x7 *without* a human-in-the-loop.

2. Unlike other forecasting/warning generation systems with similar motivations (e.g., [15]), EMBERS warnings are highly structured, capturing (i) when the protest is forecast to happen, (ii) where, with a city-level granularity, (iii) which subgroup of the population will protest, (iv) why will they be protesting, and (v) a probability associated with the forecast. See Fig. 1 (left) for an example of what an alert looks like.

3. EMBERS adopts a multi-model approach wherein each model harnesses different data sources to independently generate predictions and such predictions are then fused to yield final warnings. Using formalisms such as probabilistic soft logic (PSL [6]), we demonstrate how we can leverage the selective superiorities of different models and how we can employ collective reasoning to help shape predictions into a final set of warnings.

4. We illustrate the application of EMBERS to 10 countries in Latin America, viz. Argentina, Brazil, Chile, Colombia, Ecuador, El Salvador, Mexico, Paraguay, Uruguay, and Venezuela. We present an exhaustive suite of experiments evaluating EMBERS w.r.t. multiple forecasting criteria and for its capability to forecast significant societal events such as the June 2013 protests in Brazil, also known as the 'Brazilian Spring.'

2. WHAT IS CIVIL UNREST?

Event analysis of the form considered here is an established concept in social science research [3]. Civil unrest is a large concept intended to capture the myriad ways in which people express their protest against things that affect their lives and for which they assume that the government (local, regional or national) has a responsibility (e.g., cost of urban transportation, poor infrastructure, etc.). If the action is directed against private actors, there is normally a connection to government policy or behavior, e.g., a labor strike against a private company can disrupt the rhythm of everyday life for the rest of society, turn violent or lead to a series of disruptive strikes which require government involvement, and thus responsibility in the eyes of citizens. Civil unrest does not include acts by criminals for purely private gain. While authoritarian governments may outlaw civil protest and thus criminalize the participants, social scientists would distinguish illegal political protests from illegal criminal activities. Gang members stopping public buses to extort payoffs from bus owners would not be a civil unrest event, though people protesting afterward against the government's inability to control such gangs would be considered civil unrest. Regardless of a country's level of openness to citizens' expression, civil unrest may occur in carefully planned and orchestrated forms or as spontaneous responses to external events.

This expansive definition of civil unrest means that one can find it everywhere, including European protests against austerity or marches against an oil pipeline from Canada across the US to the Gulf of Mexico. Latin America, nevertheless, offers some special characteristics that make it an excellent region for study in our project. The region experiences a plethora of civil unrest events every day (providing a sufficient number of GSR events to train machine learning models), is well covered by international and national news media (facilitating the task of generating ground truth), is the object of detailed empirical research and polling (permitting the description of the social, political and economic context within which civil unrest occurs) and has a significant and growing number of social network users (thus supporting the use of modern data mining algorithms).

The forecasting problem studied here using open source indicators is a potentially powerful tool for understanding the social construction of meaning and its translation into behavior. The occurrence of an event can enhance the ability of citizens to communicate not only their views but also their priorities to those who govern them. An effective protest forecasting system can contribute to making the transmission of citizen preferences to government less costly to the economy and society, by enabling governments to respond to high priority grievances in advance of anticipated protests. If the response by the government causes a cancellation or lower turnout for the event, this decreases the costs incurred by even peaceful disruptions, such as lost work hours and the deployment of police to manage traffic and the interactions between protestors and bystanders. Given the vulnerability of large gatherings to provocation by handfuls of violence-oriented protestors (e.g., Black Box anarchists in Brazil), indications of coming protests can also enable plans to mitigate these effects.

3. RELATED WORK

Two broad classes of related work pertinent to EMBERS, are briefly surveyed here. First, there is a rich body of literature in **event extraction** [5, 17] wherein structured descriptions of events are codified from text (e.g., news reports). ICEWS [15] and GDELT [11] are two prominent systems that use the CAMEO coding taxonomy. Companies like RecordedFuture and works like [16] aim to recognize event mentions from text and Twitter. A key thread of research that has emerged is to distinguish between future and past time references in event extraction. Becker et al. [2] aim to extract details about known planned events like musical concerts from social media. Baeza-Yates [1] provides a ranking

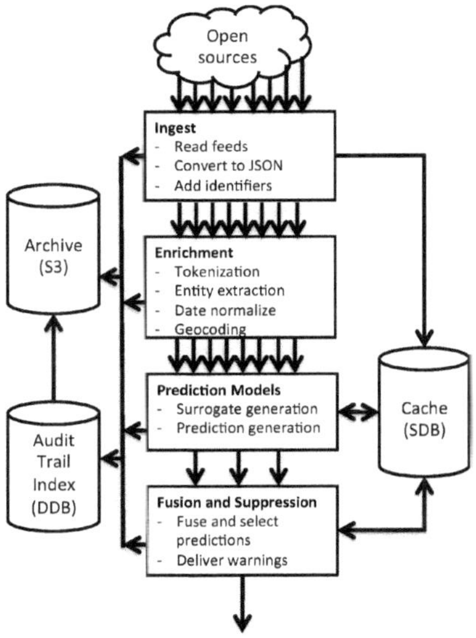

Figure 2: EMBERS system architecture

of future events retrieved from news. Dias et al. [7] extract future temporal references from text, while also distinguishing rumor from planned events using a classifier. Tops et al. [19] aim to classify a tweet talking about an event into discrete time segments and thus predict the 'time-to-event.' Kallus [10] makes use of data from RecordedFuture about planned protest events to determine if a significant protest will occur in the next three days using a random forest classifier. Other than Kallus [10], all the above cited works are primarily focused on detection (in contrast to forecasting). The second broad of thread of related research is on **civil unrest modeling** although much of this work focuses on characterization rather than forecasting. The dynamics by which volunteers are recruited via social networks to the May 2011 Spain protests was studied in [8]. Spatial and temporal distributions of civil unrest over 170 countries were studied in [4]. Our group has analyzed protests in Latin America paying specific attention to signals that manifest in social media [9]. There are many papers that aim to retrospectively analyze the breadcrumbs of information preceding significant events such as the Arab Spring [12, 10]. EMBERS distinguishes from all of the above by supporting highly structured descriptions of protests, emphasizing forecasting rather than characterization or mere detection, and utilizing a broader range of data sources than prior work. Finally, we reiterate that EMBERS is a deployed system that has been successfully issuing alerts since Nov 2012.

4. SYSTEM ARCHITECTURE

The EMBERS system is a modular, data-analytics platform for generating warnings of the form described in Fig. 1 (left). It continuously monitors streams of open source data and generates structured alerts in real time, delivered by email to IARPA/MITRE for scoring, with the date of email delivery being the *forecast date*.

The EMBERS architecture, illustrated in Fig. 2, provides a platform for the ingest and warehousing of a variety of raw data sources, and a flexible mechanism for data transfer among ingest, analytics and prediction modules. The four stages—ingest, enrichment, prediction, delivery—are described in detail, respectively, in Sections 4.1, 4.2, 5, and 6

Table 1: EMBERS system statistics

Archived data	12.4 TB
Archive size	ca. 3 billion messages
Data throughput	200-2000 messages/sec
Daily ingest	15 GB
System memory	50 GB
System core	16 vCPUs
System output	ca. 40 warnings/day

EMBERS runs in the commercial AWS cloud. It implements a share-nothing, message-based, streaming architecture using 0MQ as the underlying method of data transport. Processing components are distributed among virtual machines in a configurable, network-secure, auto-deployable, cluster of EC2 instances. With loosely coupled processes and configuration driven communication, EMBERS is able to deliver warnings reliably while facilitating rapid integration and deployment of new components and data sources. The current production cluster consists of 12 EC2 instances with two dedicated to ingest processing, three dedicated to message enrichment, four dedicated to predictive modeling and warnings selection, one each dedicated to archiving and system monitoring. EMBERS became operational in November 2012. It has ingested nearly 13TB of raw data and generated over 12,000 warnings as of this paper writing. Other notable statistics are listed in Table 1.

4.1 Ingest Processing

The EMBERS ingest module processes data from a variety of different sources: Twitter's public API, Datasift's processed Twitter feed, Healthmap's alerts and reports, RSS news and blog feeds, Talkwalker alerts, NASA satellite meteorological data, Google Flu Trends, Bloomberg financial news, TOR usage data, OpenTable's restaurant cancellation data, the PAHO health survey, and web-pages referenced Tweets. (Some of these, e.g., NASA satellite data and Google Flu Trends are used for other event classes, like disease outbreaks, as described in the introduction.) Each of these has a dedicated configurable ingest processor. Ingested data is packaged into UTF8-encoded JSON messages, assigned unique identifiers and published to a source-specific queue, allowing for simple archiving and subscription. Simple time-series and systems data, such as the store of warnings sent, are stored in a database cache.

One of our central ingest processes makes use of Datasift's Twitter collection engine. Datasift provides the ability to query and stream tweets in real time. These tweets are augmented with various types of metadata including the user profile of the tweeting user or geotagged attributes and the query can target any of these. Targeting tweets that come from a particular geographic area, e.g. Latin America, can be tricky. While some tweets use geotags to specify the location of the tweet, these tweets only comprise about 5% of the total number of tweets and may not be representative of the population overall (i.e. geotagged tweets come from people who have smart phones who also tend to be more affluent). Therefore, it is important to use other information to build a query that targets relevant tweets. In building our query we consider geotag bounding boxes (structured geographical coordinates), Twitter Places (structured data), user profile location (unstructured, unverified strings), and finally mentions of a location contained in the body of the tweet.

4.2 Message Enrichment

Messages with textual content (tweets, newsfeeds, blog postings, etc.) are subjected to shallow linguistic processing prior to analysis. Note that most of our content involves languages from the Latin American region, esp. Spanish, Portuguese, but also French (and of course, English). Applying BASIS technologies' Rosette Language Processing (RLP) tools, the language of the text is identified, the natural language content is tokenized and lemmatized and the named entities identified and classified. Date expressions are normalized and deindexed (using the TIMEN [13] package). Finally, messages are geocoded with a specification of the location (city, state, country), being talked about in the message. An example of this enrichment processing can be seen in Fig. 3.

The EMBERS system makes use of two geocoding systems, one for Tweets and one for news and blog articles. The Twitter geolocater determines not only the city, country and state, but also the approximate latitude and longitude coordinates that a tweet is referring to, or coming from. Geocoding is achieved by first considering the most reliable but least available source, viz. geotags, which give us exact geographic locations that can be reverse geocoded into place names. Second, we consider Twitter places and use place names present in these fields to geocode the place names into geographical coordinates. Finally, we consider the text fields contained in the user profile (location, description) as well as the tweet text itself to find mentions of relevant locations which can then be geocoded into geographical coordinates.

Most news articles and blog posts mention multiple locations, e.g., the location of reporting, the location of the incident, and locations corresponding to the hometown of the newspaper. We developed a probabilistic reasoning engine using probabilistic soft logic (PSL [6]) to infer the most likely city, state, and country which is the main geographic focus the article. The PSL geocoder combines various types of evidence, such as named entities such as locations, persons, and organizations identified by RLP, as well as common names and aliases and populations of known locations. These diverse types of evidence are used in weighted rules that prioritize their influence on the PSL model's location prediction. For example, extracted location tokens are strong indicators of the content location of an article, while organization and person names containing location names are weaker but still informative signals; the rules corresponding to these evidence types are weighted accordingly.

5. PREDICTION MODELS

We now outline the five different models considered in our study (see Table 2), paying specific attention to their underlying assumptions, data sources, and scenarios of applicability.

5.1 Planned Protest

Many civil unrest events are planned and organized through calls-for-action by opinion and community leaders who galvanize support for their case. The planned protest model aims at detecting such civil unrest events from traditional media (e.g., news pages, mailing lists, blogs) and from social media (e.g., Twitter, Facebook). The model filters the input streams by matching to a custom multi-lingual lexicon of expressions such as *preparación huelga*, *llamó a acudir a dicha movilización* or *plan to strike* which are likely to indicate a planned unrest event. The phrase matching is done in flexible manner making use of the lemmatized, tokenized output

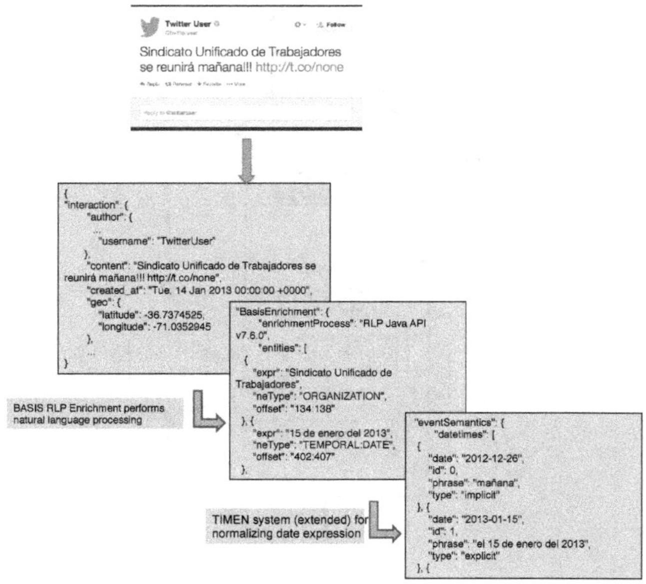

Figure 3: The process of enriching a tweet using Basis RLP enrichment and TIMEN enrichment to generate exact dates. The phrase "Sindicato Unificado de Trabajadores se reunirà manaña" gets enriched to "Sindicato Unificado de Trabajadores se reunirà January 15, 2013."

Table 2: The five different prediction models in EMBERS.

Model	Data sources
Planned protest	RSS (news, blogs), Tweets, Facebook
Volume-based	RSS (news, blogs), Tweets, Exchange rates, TOR, ICEWS, GDELT
DQE	Tweets
Cascades	Tweets
Baseline	GSR

of the BASIS enrichment module, to allow for variation and approximations in the matching. Messages that match are then screened for the mention of a future time/date occurring in the same sentence as the phrase. The event type and population are forecast using a multinomial naive Bayes classifier. Location information is determined using the enrichment geocoders. The phrase dictionary is thus a crucial aspect of the planned protest model and was populated in a semi-automatic manner using both expert knowledge and a simple bootstrapping methodology.

The planned protest model reads three kinds of input messages: standard natural language text (RSS news and blog feeds, as well as the content of web pages mentioned in tweets), microblogging text (Twitter), and Facebook Events pages. The RSS feeds and web pages are processed as discussed above. For tweets, in addition to the above processing, we require that the tweet under consideration be retweeted a minimum number of times, to avoid erroneous alerts. (This value is set to 20 in our system.) For Facebook, we use their public API to search for event pages containing the word protest or its synonyms. Most such Facebook event pages already provide significant information such as the planned date of protest, location (sometimes with resolution up to street level), and population/category of people involved.

5.2 Volume-based Model

Next, we developed a traditional machine learning model to map from a large set of volume-based features to protest characteristics. We use a logistic regression model with LASSO (Least Absolute Shrinkage and Selection Operator [18]) to select a sparse feature set, and to predict the probability of occurrence of civil unrest events in different countries. Tweets are one of the primary inputs to this model. Country-level tweets are first filtered using a keyword dictionary which includes 614 civil unrest related words (such as protest, riot), 192 phrases (e.g., right to work), and country-specific actors (public figures, political parties, etc.). For each keyword, its translations in Spanish, Portuguese and English are also used for filtering. In order to reduce the noise in the data, only tweets containing at least 3 keywords are considered. The covariates in the LASSO regression include (i) daily counts of these protest related keywords in filtered tweets, (ii) daily counts of the same keywords in news and blogs, (iii) the exchange rate (country specific currency against dollar), (iv) count of requests to TOR, i.e., the number of online users who have chosen to conceal their location and identity from the online community, (v) count of ICEWS events i.e. events identified by the "Integrated Conflict Early Warning System" [15], (vi) average intensity of the ICEWS events, (vii) the counts of events in publicly available GDELT (Global Data on Events, Location and Tone) dataset [11], which is a record of events in the international system over multiple decades, and (viii) the average tone and the Goldstein scale of these events. A threshold for the probability is determined by maximizing the area under the ROC. This methodology allows for detection as well as prediction of country-specific civil unrest events.

5.3 Dynamic query expansion (DQE)

The dynamic query expansion (DQE) model is based on the idea that the causes for protests can be quite varied and, unlike the Volume model (which uses a fixed set of keywords), we must seek emerging conditions for protests by dynamically growing our vocabularies of interest. This model relies exclusively on tweets. Given a short seed query, DQE first adopts an iterative keyword expansion strategy to dynamically generate a set of extended keywords and tweets pertinent to such keywords. In particular, the seed query consists of a small set of civil unrest related keywords like "protest" and "march.' In the initial iteration, we extract the tweets matching the seed query, and rank the terms in them by their DFIDF weights. Higher ranked terms are used to trigger the second iteration, continuing the process. The iterations are terminated once the set of keywords and their weights become stable (we have observed that DQE converges in approximately 3–5 iterations). See Fig. 4. The resulting tweets are clustered using local modularity and spatial scan statistics, and tweets in the discovered clusters are used by a classification engine to trigger an alert and to determine the event type and population.

5.4 Cascades Model

The cascades model is specifically designed to track activity on social media, especially recruitment of individuals to causes through the use of targeted campaigns, or the popularization of causes through adoption of hashtags. We characterize information diffusion on a (directed) Twitter network using activity cascades. An activity cascade is defined in the following manner: a user posts a tweet; if one of the followers of this user also posts a tweet on the same general topic within a short interval of time after the original poster, we say that the second user was influenced by the first one, and we add this second tweet to the cascade. Then, we consider the followers of the second user, and add them to the cascade if they post a tweet within a short interval of time from then, and so on. The cascade stops growing when none of the followers of the users in the cascade tweet in the general topic soon enough. In our model, we compute cascades over two different networks: the follower graph, which indicates who follows whom in Twitter, and the mention-retweet graph, where the out-neighbors of a user are those who mention or retweet that user. Activity cascades are computed for each day (which potentially could have originated from earlier days and continued growing) and their structural properties (e.g., size, number of participants, duration) are used as input to a machine learning model (generalized linear model; GLM) to forecast the probability of occurrence of a GSR event in the same topic on the following day.

5.5 Baseline model

We also developed a maximum likelihood estimate (MLE) baseline model, making heavy use of the GSR. The idea behind this model is that, even in absence of any explicit signal, the distribution of events that have appeared in the recent past is a good guide to those civil unrest events that will take place in the future. The baseline model makes predictions on the basis of the distribution of "event schema"-frequency in the most recent part of the GSR. An event schema is a combination of a location, an event type, a population and a day of the week. Some high-frequency schemas can appear as many as 10 times in a three-month window, but the vast majority of event schemas appear only once. In a typical three month interval two thirds appear once with the remaining third split evenly between those that appear twice, and those that appear three or more times. Warnings are generated with a minimum threshold of 2 and a three-month training interval, and issued with a lead time of two weeks.

6. FUSION AND SUPPRESSION

The fusion and suppression engine is responsible for the generation of the final set of warnings to be delivered. It performs several key operations:

- **Duplicate detection and warning updating:** Because our prediction models share data sources and the hypothesis space, duplicate detection is compulsory. An alert is declared as a duplicate (and discarded) if it shares the same ⟨ location, event type, population, eventDate ⟩ tuple as a previously issued alert. If two alerts differ in only the predicted event dates and those dates are at most 2 days apart, then the alerts are considered to be the same event and an update is issued to the already issued alert.
- **Filling missing values:** Certain models are incapable of predicting all details of an alert such as event type, population, or location up to the city level. In such cases, the missing information is filled in based on the likelihood of their appearance in the GSR.
- **Warning rewriting:** At times, a model produces a warning with an improbable ⟨ location, event type, population ⟩ combination. Such a prediction, could either be (1) true, (2) a result of noisy data, or (3) some inherent model error. If the last possibility, one can assume that the model would have identified the broader region correctly. Under such conditions, the fusion model aims to re-write the predicted city to a

Figure 4: Steps to building a vocabulary using the DQE model. Beginning from a few general phrases about protests, DQE hones in on keywords relevant to the particular situation being analyzed. As shown, the expanded keywords are pertinent matches to a specific GSR event.

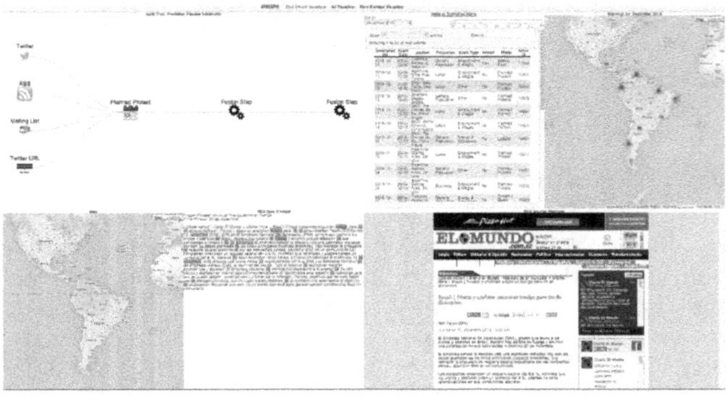

Figure 5: The audit trail visualization interface, displaying the audit trail for an alert from the planned protest model. (top left) Schema of the planned protest model. (top right) Alert chooser. (bottom panels) Data sources used in this alert, including highlighted sections.

city that is historically most probable within a given radius, and fills in other aspects accordingly.

- **Balancing the recall-quality tradeoff:** It is desirable to sacrifice some amount of recall if our overall objective is to achieve higher quality of warnings (defined in detail in the next section). We developed two classes of models to explore this tradeoff. First, we developed a random forest regression model to predict likely quality of an alert and alerts that do not pass a desired threshold are suppressed. Second, we trained a PSL engine on matched alerts and events, to learn probabilities of suppressing warnings based on characteristics of the event predicted. We explore the performance of both mechanisms in our results.

7. AUDIT TRAIL INTERFACE

In order to facilitate auditing of the warnings and further training of the models, all data that flows through the system is archived to the Amazon S3 cloud and the processing chain recorded in a NoSQL database. Using this infrastructure, the EMBERS system can produce an audit trail for any warning generated, which specifies completely which messages and analytic processes led to the warning. This audit trail can be visualized using the EMBERS web-based dashboard, shown in Fig. 5. The interface enables an analyst to rapidly search through warnings, identify the models (and post-processing) that gave rise to an alert, and the individual data sources that contributed to the alert.

8. EVALUATION METHODOLOGY

Before we describe our evaluation metrics, it is helpful to review the composition of alerts and GSR events. As introduced in Fig. 1 (left), an alert is a structured record containing four aspects: (i) the where/why/when/who of the protest, (ii) confidence associated with the forecast, and (iii) (implicitly) the date the forecast is being made (*forecast date*). The 'when' is specified in granularities of days. The **where** provides a tiered description specifying the (country, state, city), e.g., (Honduras, Francisco Morazan, Tegucigalpa). The **why** (or event type) captures the main objective or reason for a civil unrest event, and is meant to come from 7 broad classes (e.g., 'Employment & Wages', 'Housing', 'Energy & Resources' etc.) each of which is further categorized into whether the event is forecast to be violent or not. Finally, the **who** (or population) denotes common categories of human populations used in event coding [17] such as Business, Ethnic, Legal (e.g. judges or lawyers), Education (e.g. teachers or students or parents of students), Religious (e.g. clergy), Medical (e.g., doctors or nurses), Media, Labor, Refugees/Displaced, Agricultural (e.g. farmers, or just General Population.

Concomitant with the definitions in the above section, a GSR event contains again the where/why/when/who of a protest that has actually occurred and a *reported date* (the date a newspaper reports the protest as having happened). See Fig. 1 (right). As described earlier, the GSR is organized by an independent third party (MITRE) and the authors of this study do not have any participation in this activity.

8.1 Lead Time vs Accuracy of Forecast Date

Before we explain how alerts are matched to events, it is important to first understand which alerts *can* be matched to specific events. Note that there are four dates in an (alert,event) combination (see Fig. 6):

1. The date the forecast is made (*forecast date*)
2. The date the event is predicted to happen (*predicted event date*)
3. The date the event actually happens (*event date*)
4. The date the event is reported in a GSR source (*reported date*)

For an event to be qualified as having been predicted by a warning, *forecast date* < *reported date* (recall that time is measured in granularities of days). The *lead time* is given as (*reported date* − *forecast date*), i.e., the number of days by which we 'beat the news.' In contrast, the difference between *predicted event date* and *event date*, i.e., |*event date* − *predicted event date*|. is one of *quality* or accuracy. Ideally we require *lead time* to be as high as possible and |*event date* − *predicted event date*| to be as low as possible.

8.2 Other Quality Aspects

Forecasting the event date accurately is only one aspect of quality. Recall that alerts also forecast the location, event

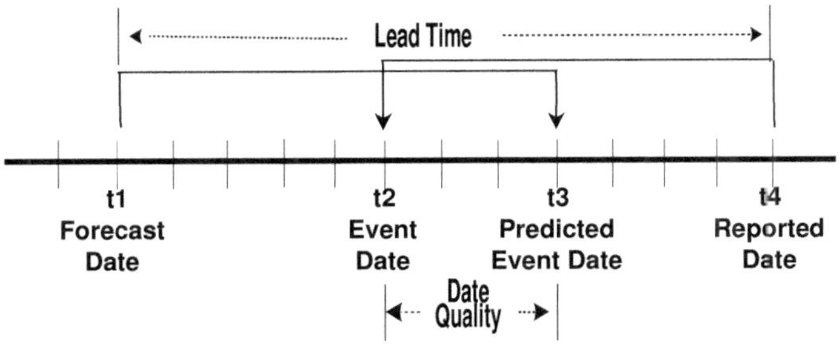

Figure 6: Alert sent at time $t1$ predicting an event at time $t3$ can be matched to a GSR event that happened at time $t2$ and reported at time $t4$ if $t1 < t4$.

type, and population. We define scores for each of these aspects and quality is defined as a sum over all these scores.

$$\text{Quality score } (QS) = DS + LS + ES + PS$$

where DS, LS, ES, and PS denote the date score, location score, event type score, and population score, respectively. Each of these scores is in turn defined next:

$$DS = 1 - \min(|\textit{event date} - \textit{predicted event date}|, 7)/7$$

If the date of the event listed in the warning is the same as the actual date of the event, then DS is 1. On the other hand, if these dates are farther than 7 days apart, then DS is 0.

Location score (LS) can be defined in many ways. Because location is defined in terms of triples of (country, state, city), one approach is to use a tiered formula. Comparing a GSR event with a warning, we can obtain a score triple of (l_1, l_2, l_3) where l_1 is the country-level score, l_2 is the state-level score, and l_3 is the city-level score. Each of these scores have a value of 0 if they do not match and 1 is they match. Then the match between submitted warning location and the GSR location is given by:

$$LS = \frac{1}{3}l_1 + \frac{1}{3}l_1 l_2 + \frac{1}{3}l_1 l_2 l_3$$

An alternative way to define location score is as:

$$LS = 0.33 + 0.66(1 - \min(\text{dist}, 300)/300)$$

where dist denotes the distance (in km) between the city predicted and the GSR city. All city location names are standardized to the World Gazetteer which provides latitude and longitude values, thus facilitating the computation of distance. The scaling and shifting values of 0.33 and 0.66 ensure that this definition of LS is compatible with the earlier definition. Cities outside a 300km radius from a GSR location will thus be scored 0.33; exact predictions will be scored 1; and cities within a 300km radius will get scores in the range [0.33,1]. We distinguish between these two criteria as the categorical LS versus physical distance-based LS.

Event type score (ES) is scored similar to categorical LS since it naturally maps to a three-level taxonomy: whether a civil unrest is forecast to happen, what objective/reason is behind the unrest, and whether it is violent. Again partial credit applies depending on the level of specification. Population score (PS) is simply a binary (0/1) score denoting whether we forecast the correct population or not. Finally, note that $QS = DS + LS + ES + PS$ is designed to take values in the range $[0, 4]$.

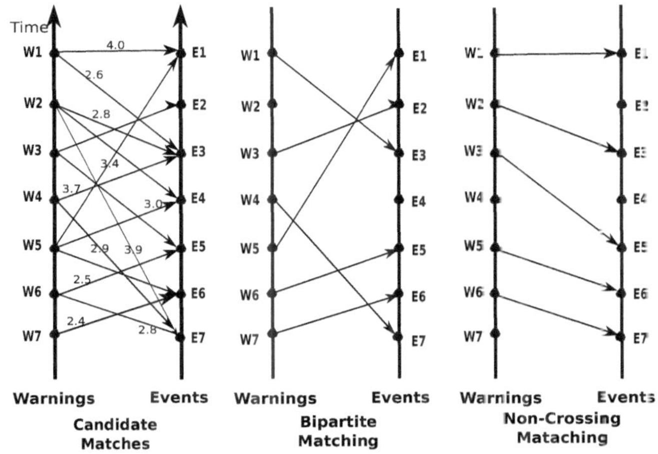

Figure 7: Given a set of candidate warning-event matches (left), we evaluate the performance of EMBERS using either a regular bipartite matching (middle) or by constructing a non-crossing matching (right).

8.3 Inclusion Criteria

Thus far we have demonstrated, given a warning-event pair, how we can score their fitness. Inclusion criteria define which W-E pairs *can* even be considered for scoring. We have already mentioned one inclusion criterion, viz. that lead time must be > 0. The full list of inclusion criteria we will consider are:

1. Lead time > 0
2. Both warning and event are for the same country.
3. The *predicted event date* and *event date* must be within 7 days of each other.

A fourth, optional (and stringent), criterion we will use is:

4. Both predicted location and event location must be within 300km of each other.

It is important to distinguish the inclusion criteria from the scoring criteria. Inclusion criteria define which W-E pairs are allowable. Scoring criteria determine, for each allowable W-E pair, what its score will be.

8.4 Matching Alerts to Events

Thus far we have assumed that we are matching an alert to a GSR event. In practice, the problem is we are given a set of issued alerts and a set of GSR events and we must determine the quality of the match: which alert would correspond to which event? One strategy is to construct a bipartite graph between the set of alerts and the set of events, where allowable edges are those that satisfy the inclusion criteria, and where weights on these allowable edges denote their quality scores. We then construct a maximum weighted bipartite matching, e.g., see Fig. 7 (middle). Such matchings are conducted on a monthly basis with a lookback period to bring in unmatched warnings from the previous month.

8.5 Non Crossing Matching

A criticism of the matching approach above is that it can lead to criss-cross matches, i.e., the matching process may not respect the temporal order in which warnings were issued or in which events unfold. A non-crossing matching is a more restrictive version of a bipartite matching. Consider two warnings w_1 and w_2 and two events e_1 and e_2. Representing them by their predicted event dates and event dates, and assuming $w_1 < w_2$ and $e_1 < e_2$, then $\{(w_1, e_2), (w_2, e_1)\}$

is a *crossing matching* since the earlier warning is paired to a later event (and vice versa). To respect the temporal order, we also investigate the computation of a maximum non-crossing matching [14] and use it as an additional evaluation criterion (see Fig. 7 (right)).

8.6 Putting it all together: Five criteria

We are now ready to identify all the evaluation criteria used in EMBERS. The overall **quality** is defined as a weighted average across all matched warning-event pairs. Similarly, **lead time** is averaged across all matched warning-event pairs. In addition, we can define **precision** in terms of the number of unmatched warnings as a fraction of the total number of sent warnings. Similarly, **recall** can be defined in terms of the number of unmatched events as a fraction of the total number of events. Finally, a **probability score** is calculated over all warnings, mapped or unmapped. For each warning, it is defined in terms of the Brier score, i.e., $1-(o-p)^2$ where p is the probability assigned to the warning, and o is 1 if the warning is mapped to some event in the GSR, and 0 is the warning is not mapped to an event in the GSR. This score is then averaged over all warnings.

9. EVALUATION RESULTS

We present an exhaustive evaluation of EMBERS against multiple aspects as follows:

How do each of our models fare for the 10 countries of interest and how well does their integration achieve the five overall metrics? Table 3 presents the performance of EMBERS models for a recent month across all the 10 countries of interest here. As is clear here, the models have selective superiorities across the countries studied. While the baseline model captures significant regularities and achieves high quality scores, models like DQE perform better for countries like Brazil, Mexico, and Venezuela, all of which have significant chatter on Twitter. Even when models have comparable performances, their integration is useful because each model will produce only a limited set of warnings and their fusion is necessary to achieve high recall. This is evident in Table 4 that demonstrates that we achieve a quality score of 3.11 with an average lead time of 8.8 days and respectable precision and recall (0.69 and 0.82, respectively). Taking a birds eye view, Fig. 8a and Fig. 8b summarize the distribution of events in the GSR and alerts sent by EMBERS over the past 15 months.

How does EMBERS's fusion and suppression engine help shape our quality distribution? Fig. 8c describes how our suppression engine can be tuned to steer the quality distribution from a mode around 2.25 to one around 3.2 by learning which warnings to suppress and which ones to issue. This capability directly helps balance the recall-quality tradeoff, as shown in Fig. 8d.

How does EMBERS fare against a baserate model with lenient versus stringent inclusion criteria for matching? To rigorously evaluate the capabilities of EMBERS, we implemented a baserate model as a yardstick for comparison. The baserate model is similar in spirit to the baseline model described earlier but functions differently. Rather than filtering for frequent combinations of event properties, it generates alerts using the rate of occurrence of events in the past three months. Table 5 compares EMBERS warnings against the baserate model. We evaluate the date and location aspects with categorical and distance-based scoring to gain further insight. Under a lenient evaluation using categorical inclusion criteria, EMBERS exhibits a quality score improvement of approximately +0.7 over baserate methods. Under a strict evaluation using distance-based inclusion criteria, this improvement is around +0.5 over baserate methods.

Table 5: Performance of EMBERS vs a baserate model.

Evaluation Type	Sep'13	Oct'13	Nov'13	Dec'13
EMBERS Categorical	3.16	3.12	3.26	3.2
Baserate Categorical	2.5	2.5	2.52	2.44
EMBERS Distance Based	3.36	3.3	3.44	3.44
Baserate Distance Based	2.9	2.84	3	2.92

How adept is EMBERS at forecasting 'surprising' events? Did EMBERS forecast significant uprisings such as the June 2013 protests in Brazil? Fig. 8e describe the performance of our system in Brazil during the summer of 2013 when Brazil witnessed significant protests that were originally triggered by bus fare increases. As can be seen, EMBERS is able to track the rise in number of protests quite accurately. More recently, Fig. 8f and Fig. 8g describe the performance of EMBERS in Brazil and Venezuela for the Jan-Feb 2014 season. Significant violent protests were witnessed in both countries, due to bus fare increases and student-led demonstrations, respectively. Finally, we also conducted a formal maximum entropy evaluation of protest counts, to determine how EMBERS fares on only those protests that are deemed to significantly higher in number relative to the past three months. As Fig. 8h shows, EMBERS demonstrates an improvement of nearly 0.5 over baserate models during months of significant uprisings (e.g., June 2013). During other months (e.g., Nov 2013) there is relatively normal activity and baserate methods perform comparably.

How reliable are EMBERS's probability scores? Fig. 8i shows that the probability scores emitted by warnings have a monotonic relationship to the likelihood of matches, indicating that EMBERS's use of confidence captures the mapping from model and warning attributes to the possibility of event matches.

How does EMBERS's lead time vary with quality scores? Fig. 8j illustrates an interesting relationship. As lead time increases from low values, as expected, quality scores decrease. But as lead time crosses a threshold, quality scores actually improve again! This is because data sources like Facebook event pages and other feeds contribute high quality planned protest warnings with high lead time.

What is the effect of adopting regular versus non-crossing matching constraints? Fig. 8k reveals that, as expected, when adopting non-crossing matching constraints, the number of matches decreases bringing down the overall quality. Nevertheless, a consistent level of improvement over baserate methods is witnessed.

How has the performance of EMBERS improved over time? Finally, Fig. 8l demonstrates the performance of our deployed EMBERS system over time. From quality scores of just over 2 in the past year, EMBERS has breached the 3.0 barrier in recent months.

10. DISCUSSION

We have presented the architecture of EMBERS, an automated system for generating forecasts about civil unrest from massive, multiple, data sources. Our evaluations over 10 countries illustrate the capabilities of EMBERS 'in the small' (matching specific events to particular warnings) as

Table 3: Comparing the forecasting accuracy of different models in EMBERS. Quality scores in this and other tables are in the range [0,4] where 4 is the most accurate. AR=Argentina; BR=Brazil; CL=Chile; CO=Colombia; EC=Ecuador; SV=El Salvador; MX=Mexico; PY=Paraguay; UY=Uruguay; VE=Venezuela. A – indicates that the model did not produce any warnings for that country in the studied period.

Model	AR	BR	CL	CO	EC	SV	MX	PY	UY	VE	All
Dynamic Query Expansion	3.1	3.31	1.88	3.1	2.43	2.94	3.26	2.88	2.72	2.9	2.97
Volume-based Model	3.0	3.11	-	2.9	-	-	3.15	-	1.72	2.9	2.88
MLE	3.33	3.0	2.37	3.15	2.29	3.11	3.11	3.1	2.57	2.77	3.0
Planned Protest	2.59	2.64	2.4	2.85	1.92	-	3.0	2.89	2.85	2.66	2.76
Cascades Model	3.13	-	-	-	-	-	-	-	-	2.93	3.0

Table 4: EMBERS metrics across multiple countries.

Metric	AR	BR	CL	CO	EC	MX	PY	SV	UY	VE	All
Quality score	3.2	3.39	2.85	2.86	2.59	3.0	3.27	2.85	3.05	3.01	3.11
Recall	1.0	1.0	0.82	0.59	1.0	1.0	0.65	1.0	1.0	0.84	0.82
Precision	0.55	0.45	0.89	0.94	0.77	0.71	1.0	0.69	0.46	0.73	0.69
Lead time (days)	10.44	11.82	6.25	7.85	8.44	8.32	8.61	10.57	8.8	6.03	8.88
Probability measure	0.71	0.66	0.87	0.87	0.75	0.74	0.94	0.74	0.72	0.72	0.76

well as 'in the large' (capturing significant upticks across countries).

Future work is targeted at three aspects. First, we are interested in social science theory-based approaches to forecasting, e.g., modeling the rise of grievances into trigger events, capturing the role of opinion leaders, and identifying whether there are both necessary and sufficient conditions for a festering sentiment to transform into a protest. Second, we plan to develop a statistical theory of tradeoffs revolving around the boundaries of precision-recall and quality-lead time. Different analysts are likely to prefer different sweet spots along these boundaries and we seek to situate EMBERS as a tunable forecasting system. Finally, for analyst consumption, we are interested in automated narrative generation, i.e., an English description of an alert providing a contextual summary of the alert (similar to automated weather report generation).

Acknowledgments

Supported by the Intelligence Advanced Research Projects Activity (IARPA) via DoI/NBC contract number D12PC000337, the US Government is authorized to reproduce and distribute reprints of this work for Governmental purposes notwithstanding any copyright annotation thereon. Aravind Srinivasan and Khoa Trinh were also supported in part by NSF Award CNS 1010789. Disclaimer: The views and conclusions contained herein are those of the authors and should not be interpreted as necessarily representing the official policies or endorsements, either expressed or implied, of IARPA, DoI/NBC, or the US Government.

11. REFERENCES

[1] R. Baeza-Yates. Searching the future. In *SIGIR Workshop on Mathematical/Formal Methods in Information Retrieval*, 2005.

[2] H. Becker, D. Iter, M. Naaman, and L. Gravano. Identifying content for planned events across social media sites. In *WSDM*, 2012.

[3] J. M. Box-Steffensmeier and B. S. Jones. *Event History Modeling: A Guide for Social Scientists*. Cambridge University press, 2004.

[4] D. Braha. Global civil unrest: contagion, self-organization, and prediction. *PLoS One*, 7(10), Jan. 2012.

[5] P. T. Brandt, J. R. Freeman, and P. A. Schrodt. Real time, time series forecasting of inter-and intra-state political conflict. *Conflict Management and Peace Science*, 28(1), 2011.

[6] M. Broecheler, L. Mihalkova, and L. Getoor. Probabilistic similarity logic. In *UAI*, 2010.

[7] G. Dias, R. Campos, and A. Jorge. Future retrieval: What does the future talk about. In *SIGIR Workshop on Enriching Information Retrieval*, 2011.

[8] S. González-Bailón, J. Borge-Holthoefer, A. Rivero, and Y. Moreno. The dynamics of protest recruitment through an online network. *Sci. Rep*, 1, 2011.

[9] T. Hua, C.-T. Lu, N. Ramakrishnan, F. Chen, J. Arredondo, D. Mares, and K. Summers. Analyzing Civil Unrest through Social Media. *Computer*, 2013.

[10] N. Kallus. Predicting crowd behavior with big public data. In *WWW*, 2014.

[11] K. Leetaru and P. Schrodt. GDELT: Global data on events, location, and tone. *ISA Annual Convention*, 2013.

[12] K. H. Leetaru. Culturomics 2.0: Forecasting large-scale human behavior using global news media tone in time and space. *First Monday*, 16, 2011.

[13] H. Llorens, L. Derczynski, R. J. Gaizauskas, and E. Saquete. TIMEN: An open temporal expression normalisation resource. In *LREC*, 2012.

[14] F. Malucelli, T. Ottmann, and D. Pretolani. Efficient labelling algorithms for the maximum noncrossing matching problem. *Discrete Applied Mathematics*, 47(2), 1993.

[15] S. P. O'Brien. Crisis Early Warning and Decision Support: Contemporary Approaches and Thoughts on Future Research. *Int. Stud. Rev.*, 12(1), Mar. 2010.

[16] A. Ritter, O. Etzioni, and S. Clark. Open domain event extraction from twitter. In *SIGKDD*, 2012.

[17] P. A. Schrodt. Automated production of high-volume, near-real-time political event data. In *American Political Science Association meetings*, 2010.

[18] R. Tibshirani. Regression shrinkage and selection via the lasso. *J. R. Stat. Soc. Ser. B*, 58, 1996.

[19] H. Tops, A. van den Bosch, and F. Kunneman. Predicting time-to-event from twitter messages. In *BNAIC*, 2013.

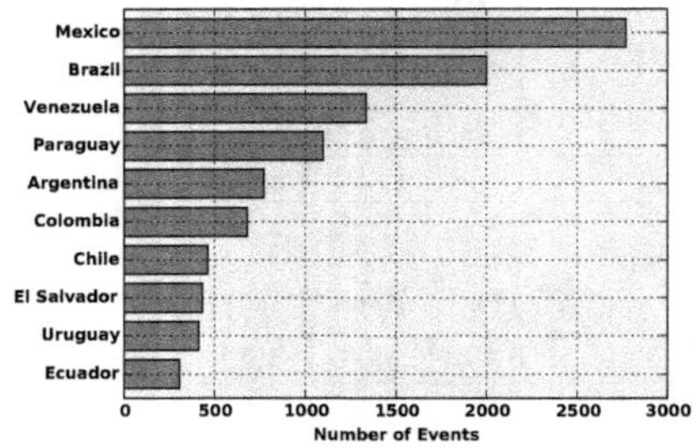

(a) GSR Distribution

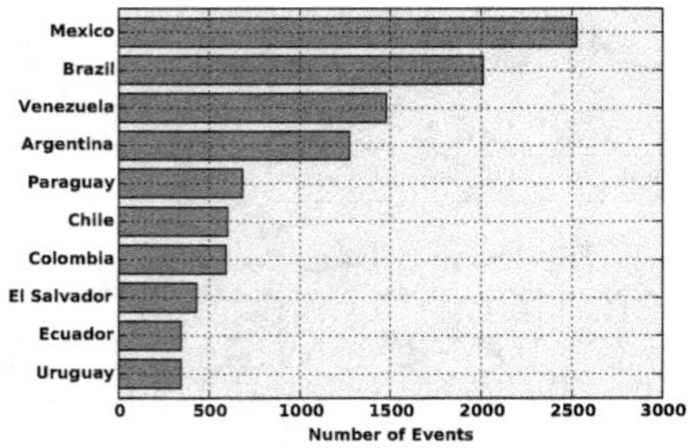

(b) EMBERS Alerts Distribution

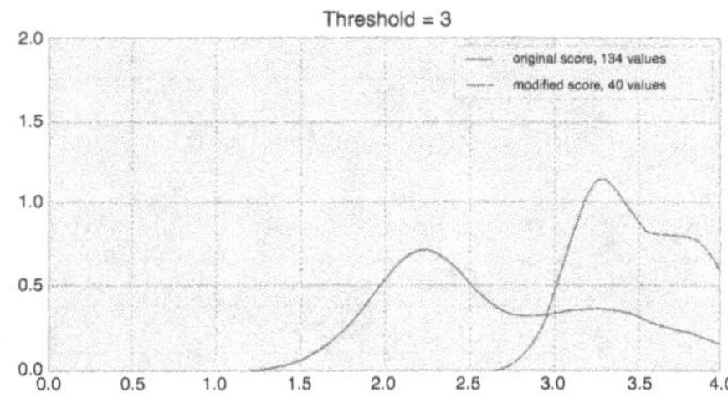

(c) Quality distributions before and after suppression

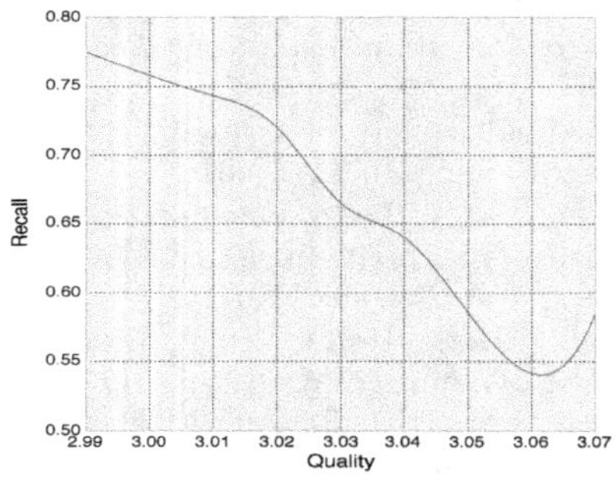

(d) Recall vs Quality Tradeoff

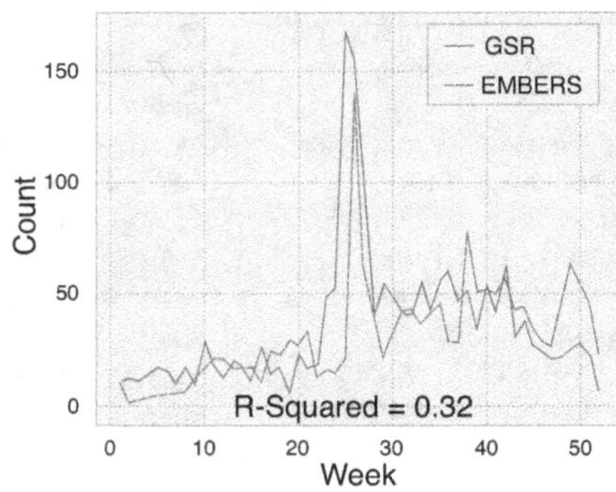

(e) The Brazilian Spring

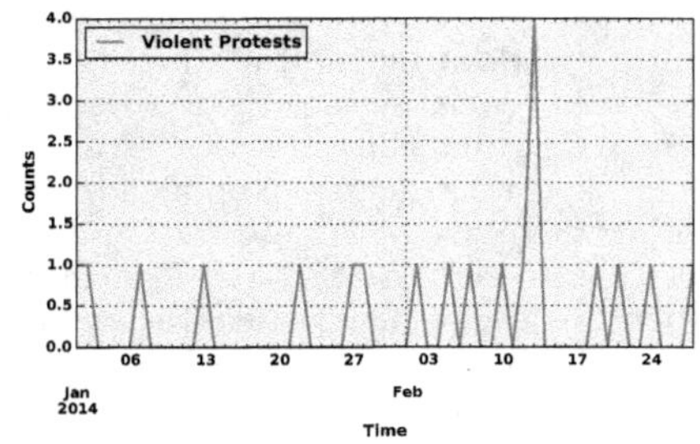

(f) Violent Protests in Brazil

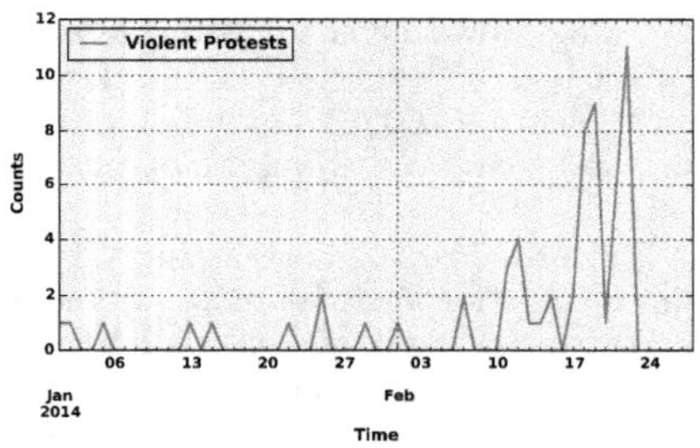

(g) Violent Protests in Venezuela

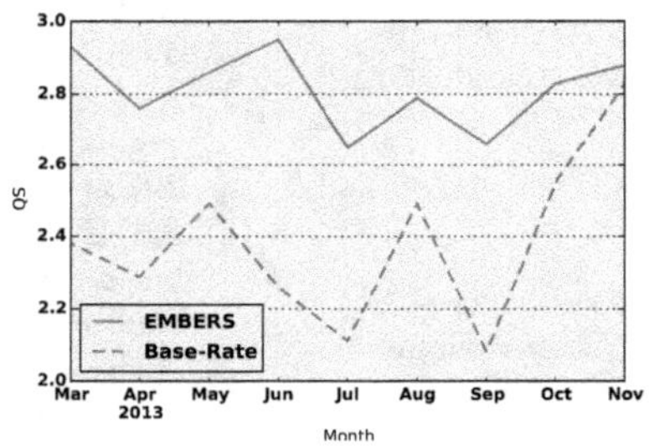

(h) MaxEnt Evaluation

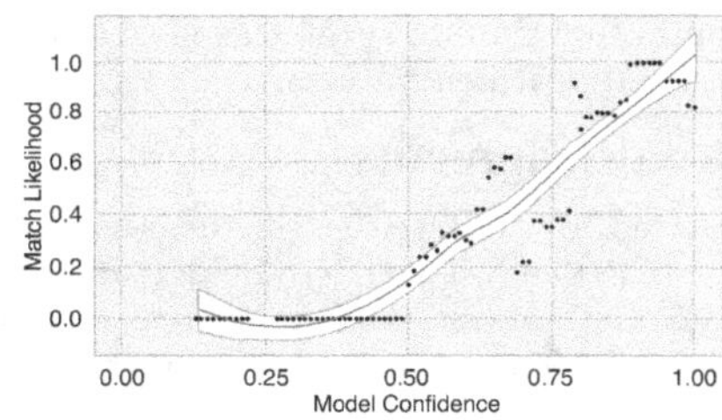

(i) EMBERS Probability Score

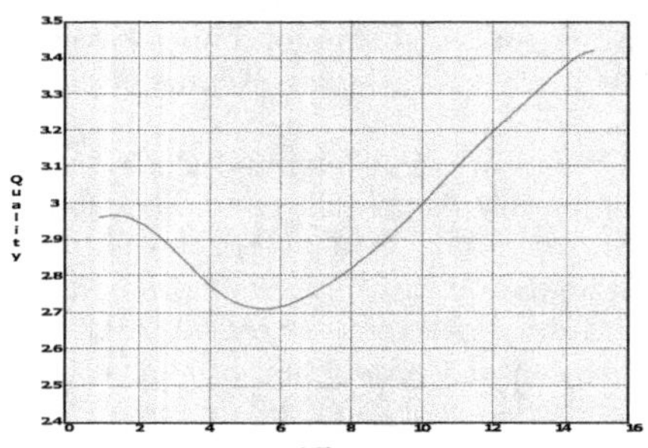

(j) Lead time vs Quality Tradeoff

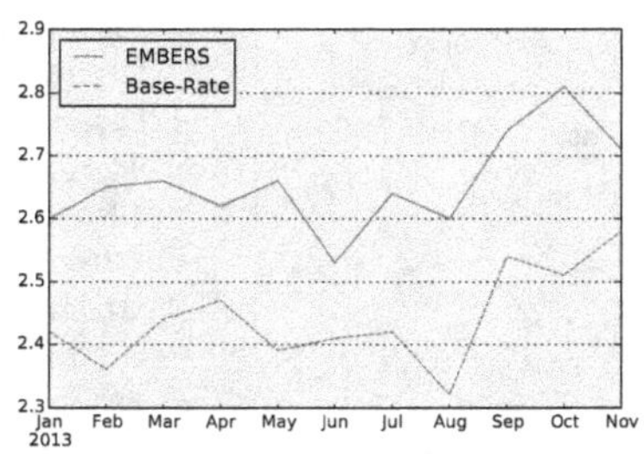

(k) Quality score with non-crossing matches (1 day interval).

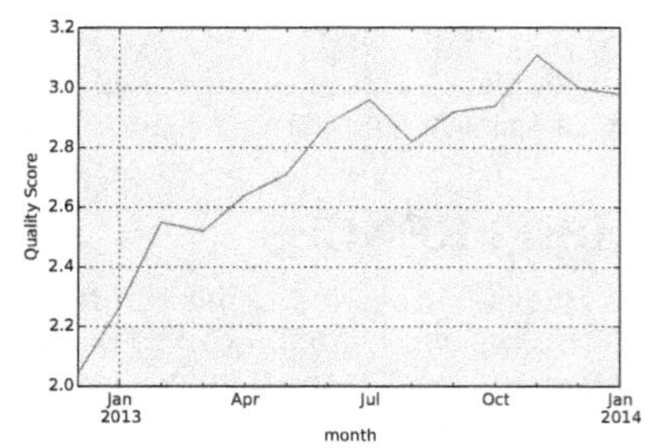

(l) Evolution of EMBERS's quality scores over time.

Figure 8: Evaluation of EMBERS

LASTA: Large Scale Topic Assignment on Multiple Social Networks

Nemanja Spasojevic, Jinyun Yan, Adithya Rao, Prantik Bhattacharyya
Klout Inc.
77 Stillman Street
San Francisco, CA 94107
{nemanja, jinyun, adithya, prantik}@klout.com

ABSTRACT

Millions of people use social networks everyday to talk about a variety of subjects, publish opinions and share information. Understanding this data to infer user's topical interests is a challenging problem with applications in various data-powered products. In this paper, we present 'LASTA' (Large Scale Topic Assignment), a full production system used at Klout, Inc., which mines topical interests from five social networks and assigns over 10,000 topics to hundreds of millions of users on a daily basis. The system continuously collects streams of user data and is reactive to fresh information, updating topics for users as interests shift. LASTA generates over 50 distinct features derived from signals such as user generated posts and profiles, user reactions such as comments and retweets, user attributions such as lists, tags and endorsements, as well as signals based on social graph connections. We show that using this diverse set of features leads to a better representation of a user's topical interests as compared to using only generated text or only graph based features. We also show that using cross-network information for a user leads to a more complete and accurate understanding of the user's topics, as compared to using any single network. We evaluate LASTA's topic assignment system on an internal labeled corpus of 32,264 user-topic labels generated from real users.

Categories and Subject Descriptors

H.3.3 [**Information Search and Retrieval**]: Information filtering; Retrieval models

Keywords

Online Social Networks; Interest Mining; Topic Assignment; Large Scale; User Modeling; Distributed Systems

1. INTRODUCTION

Mining topical interests for users from social media is an interesting and important problem to solve, because the insights gained can be applied to many applications such as recommendation and targeting systems. Such systems can deliver accurate results tailored to each individual user, only if the user's interests are well understood. The task of interest mining from social media has many challenges that mainly lie in the characteristics of the data, *viz. size, noise* and *sparsity*. While the total volume of text generated on social media is huge, the size of each individual document tends to be very short. For example, posts on Twitter (tweets) are limited to 140 characters. Often the posts are also noisy due to abbreviations, grammatically inaccurate sentences, symbols such as emoticons and misspelled words [1]. Finally, because many users on social media are inactive, sporadically active or only tend to be passive consumers of content, the textual content available for topical inference is sparse for such users.

In this study, our contributions are as follows: We describe a scalable engineering system deployed in production that mines topical interests from five social networks and assigns over 10,000 topics to hundreds of millions of users on a daily basis. dWe extract and analyze features for topic inference that extend beyond authored text. We show that using a diverse set of features and cross-network information can lead to a better understanding of a user's interests. Compared to previous studies [2, 3, 4, 5] that attempt to mine all topics for a user, we focus primarily on assigning topics for a user that other users can socially recognize and acknowledge. For example, Warren Buffett is recognized for topics like 'Business', 'Finance' and 'Money', while his personal interests may include 'Cars' and 'Airplanes'. This approach helps in building applications that are meaningful in the context of the social identity of a user.

Klout, Inc. is a social media platform that aggregates and analyzes data from social networks like Twitter, Facebook, LinkedIn, Google Plus and Instagram, and other sources like Bing Search Engine and Wikipedia. A user on Klout can connect one or more of the above social profiles to form one unique profile. We present Klout's topic system called 'LASTA', (Large Scale Topic Assignment), that focuses on inputs from four major social networking sites: Facebook (FB), Twitter (TW), GooglePlus (GP) and LinkedIn (LI).

To address the data challenges mentioned above, we consider the following approaches: We process information shared by users to get more context around individual user documents. To address data noise problems, we explode text into n-grams and map against an internal dictionary of approximately 2 million phrases to generate bags-of-phrases. We address data sparsity problems by extracting signals from

KDD'14, August 24–27, 2014, New York, NY, USA.
Copyright 2014 ACM 978-1-4503-2956-9/14/08 ...$15.00.
http://dx.doi.org/10.1145/2623330.2623350

a user's reactions, such as comments or retweets on other user's posts. We also extract signals from posts in which a user is tagged or mentioned as well as from social graph connections, to increase data coverage for a given user.

We combine the signals mentioned above to generate over 50 distinct features. The set of features are categorized as following: *Generated, Reacted, Credited* and *Graph*. Features derived from user authored posts and profile information are categorized as *Generated*. *Reacted* features come from user reactions such as comments and retweets. *Credited* features are built from signals such as lists, tags and endorsements, while *Graph* features are based on social graph connections. We evaluate LASTA's topic assignment system on an internal labeled corpus of 32,264 user-topic labels generated from real users.

The underlying infrastructure is built on the Hadoop platform[1], an open-source implementation of MapReduce. The system uses HDFS as the file system and Hive[2] as the querying infrastructure. Each day, nearly a terabyte of raw data is ingested into our data warehouse. We hope that insights gained from our experience in building LASTA will prove valuable for the community to build future topic systems.

The rest of the paper is structured as follows. Section 2 discuses related work and formally introduces the problem statement. Section 3 describes system level details and data generation steps. Section 4 presents evaluation results and some interesting and useful findings. Section 5 discusses some of the application of LASTA implemented at Klout and conclude in section 6.

2. RELATED WORK & BACKGROUND

There are a variety of topic detection systems that have been proposed, and topic inference is a well studied area. However, the effectiveness of any given system is typically dependent on the specific domain or application under consideration. For example, modeling user interests is common practice for recommendation engines such as Amazon and Netflix, where the objective is to understand user interests in a particular domain such as products or movies. The user interests are often represented as latent vectors in recommender systems [6], and are derived from either explicit feedback, such as ratings, or implicit feedback such as clicks on products. Search engines also use topic inference to personalize results [7, 8], where user interests are learnt from click-history and browsing behaviors from search logs. Similarly, clicks on ads are used to model user interests in the domain of online display advertising [9].

In many topic inference settings, the individual documents have clean data and rich context. This may include text from scientific publications [10], or text derived from a large corpus of natural language. In such scenarios, modeling user interests as unseen latent vectors, such as Latent Semantic Analysis (LSA) [11] and Latent Dirichlet Allocation (LDA) [12] have been shown to provide good results.

Recent research have focussed on topic modeling for users in social networks. User generated tags have been used to model user interests [13]. In [14], a topic of interest is described by a cluster of frequently co-occurred tags. Zheng et. al. [15] present a model to infer user topics from Weibo. Guy et. al. [16] study interests and expertise in the context of enterprise social media users. Twitter, in particular, has been the focus of many studies that aim to characterize topical interests for users. In [2], the author-topic model is proposed, and [3] describes an empirical study of the problem. [4] leverages a knowledge base to find entities in tweets, and a labeled LDA approach is presented in [5]. Twitter has also been studied as a platform for conversation between users [17, 18].

The problem we tackle here differs from the above work in three major aspects. First, in the context of short form social media messages, latent variable techniques such as LDA and LSA have a poorer performance as compared to using scientific publications or long-form text as the source. In some cases these techniques may identify topics for some users who have enough aggregated text, but they fail to do so for passive users who may not generate a lot of text themselves. Thus they cannot provide a scalable solution when identifying topics for millions of users. Second, while previous work has focused on single social networks for topic inference, as far as we are aware, this is the first attempt to incorporate multiple social profiles to form a single unique topic profile for a user. The context under which a single user creates or reacts to different messages in any given network is significantly different compared to the context in other networks. Finally, we specifically tackle the issue of identifying socially recognizable topics for a user, since this can have unique and interesting applications.

2.1 Problem Statement

At Klout, topics are represented as entries in an ontology tree, $\mathcal{T}$. The in-house ontology is manually curated and is bootstrapped using Freebase [19] and Wikipedia Concepts [20]. The ontology provides an explicit specification of topics and relationships among them and has a hierarchical tree structure as shown in Figure 1. It has three levels: super, sub and entity. The lowest level contains specific entities, including people, things and places and are regularly updated. We currently have close to 9,000 entities and includes proper nouns, popular terms in social media, and specific concepts. The sub level contains 700 sub-topics that are abstracted concepts and each corresponds to a cluster of entities. The super level is the top level abstraction and contains 15 super topics.

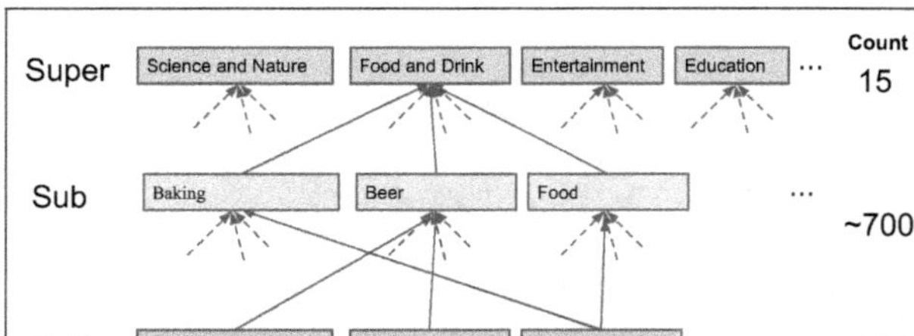

Figure 1: Hierarchical Ontology Overview

LASTA tokenizes text to generate n-grams and maps these against an internal dictionary to generate bags of phrases, $BP_u = \{BP_u^1, BP_u^2, ..., BP_u^s\}$. A user is associated with multiple bags-of-phrases where each bag-of-phrases is derived from a specific collected data source. Each of these bags-of-phrases is then mapped to a bag-of-topics, $BT_u = \{BT_u^1, BT_u^2, ..., BT_u^s\}$, from the above ontology. The mapping from a phrase to a topic ($p_j \rightarrow t_i$) is based on exact

[1]http://wiki.apache.org/hadoop/

[2]http://hive.apache.org/

match and rule-based synonym checks. Section 3.2.1 provides more details on how topics are extracted. For each user, we now obtain bags-of-topics where the kth bag-of-topics is represented as follows.

$$BT_u^k = \{t_i : (p_j \rightarrow t_i),\ \forall\ p_j \in BP_u^k\}$$

Since multiple phrases may map to a topic, the strength of each topic in BT_u^k is the sum of the occurrences of corresponding phrases.

$$count(t_i|BT_u^k) = \sum_{p_j \rightarrow t_i} count(p_j|BP_u^k)$$

The strength for each topic in BT_u^k is normalized using min-max normalization.

$$s(t_i|BT_u^k) = \frac{count(t_i|BT_u^k)}{\max_{t_j \in BT_u^k} count(t_j|BT_u^k)}$$

The problem for LASTA can be stated formally as follows: Given a set of N users, $U = \{u_1, u_2, ..., u_N\}$ and a specific user u, we wish to generate a final bag-of-topics, $T_u = \{t_1, t_2, ..., t_m\}$ where $t_i \in \mathcal{T}$, and the strength of each topic represents the user's interest towards that topic. We discuss details on how we aggregate from BT_u to the final bag-of-topics, T_u in Section 4.

2.2 Data Landscape

Klout has millions of registered users. A registered user has to connect either their Facebook or Twitter account to create an account on Klout. After that, the user may connect other social network profiles, e. g. LinkedIn, Google Plus, Instagram, etc.

One of the primary challenges faced by LASTA is the size of text created by each user to infer correctly the topical interests. We present data in Table 1 on message character counts to illustrate the challenge.

Table 1: Message sizes across networks

Percentile	FB	TW	GP	LI
0.99	564.48	140.00	1578.62	577.00
0.95	200.60	134.00	521.95	277.20
0.90	128.20	118.22	323.16	175.00
0.80	77.56	89.00	204.00	132.00
0.70	59.72	68.88	133.00	112.00
0.60	50.53	54.18	92.00	93.00
0.50	43.95	43.62	61.00	75.35

Table 2: Percentage distribution of languages across networks

FB		TW		GP		LI	
en	**67.22**	en	**34.88**	en	**74.18**	en	**80.52**
pt	6.05	ja	12.33	es	5.61	es	6.40
it	5.78	id	11.52	it	3.00	fr	2.74
es	5.39	es	8.92	de	2.55	nl	2.23
id	2.00	ar	4.44	pt	2.41	it	1.97
rest	13.54	rest	27.88	rest	12.24	rest	6.12

LASTA focuses on topic detection in the English language, and we use off-the-shelf language detectors[3] and phrase parsers to detect English text. Because English is used only by a limited number of users on social networks, this creates another sparsity problem for non-English speaking users. In Table 2, we present details on language distribution as observed by LASTA.

Figure 2 shows the distribution of phrases used by users on each social network, on log-log scale, with base 10. The x axis is the number of distinct phrases, which corresponds to the vocabulary size by users. The y axis shows the number of users as a function of their vocabulary size in past 90 days. The distribution approximately obeys the inverse power law, particularly on GooglePlus.

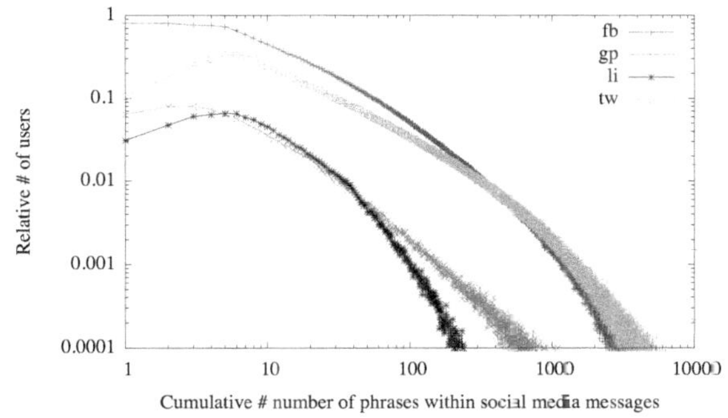

Figure 2: Registered user verbosity distribution across 90-day window

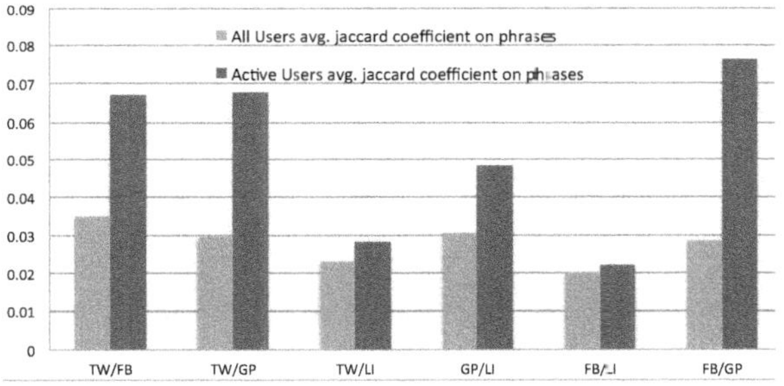

Figure 3: Phrase overlap across networks

One of LASTA's goals is to understand different behaviors presented by users in different networks. In order to illustrate different user behavior and varied vocabulary choice across social networks, we examine the phrase overlap in messages created by a user who has connected multiple social networks to their Klout profile. We use jaccard coefficient to measure phrase overlap, $PO(u, (N_i, N_j))$ as follows.

$$PO(u, (N_i, N_j)) = \frac{|\{\text{phrase in } N_i\} \cap \{\text{phrase in } N_j\}|}{|\{\text{phrase in } N_i\} \cup \{\text{phrase in } N_j\}|}$$

where N_i, N_j are i-th and j-th social network, respectively. We then average over all users for each pair of social networks. Figure 3 shows the results. The phrase overlap value is very small on each pair; the highest overlap occurs between postings across Facebook and Google Plus and is approximately 0.075. To gain deeper insights into the overlap, we narrow down to active users only. A user is considered as active in a pair of social networks if he has generated at least 100 distinct phrases in each network in last 90 days. The overlap extent increases; however it is still small and

[3]`https://code.google.com/p/language-detection/`

less than 0.1. The highest overlap occurs between postings across TW and FB and is approximately 0.035. The low phrase overlap for a single user helps LASTA aggregate topical interests from multiple social media and produce a more complete set of user interests.

3. PIPELINE OVERVIEW

Our backend system can be broken into two main components: data collection, and data processing. When a user registers at Klout, he connects one or more social networks with his 'token', and grants permission to Klout to collect and analyze his data through the network APIs. At the data collection stage Klout fetches the user's profile, activities and connection graphs from various social networks. This data is parsed and stored in normalized form. The data processing pipeline expresses topical interests for each user as a ranked list of topics. The inferred topic list is used for multiple applications including generating a unified user profile, content recommendation, targeting and question answering. Figure 4 shows an overview of collection/processing pipeline.

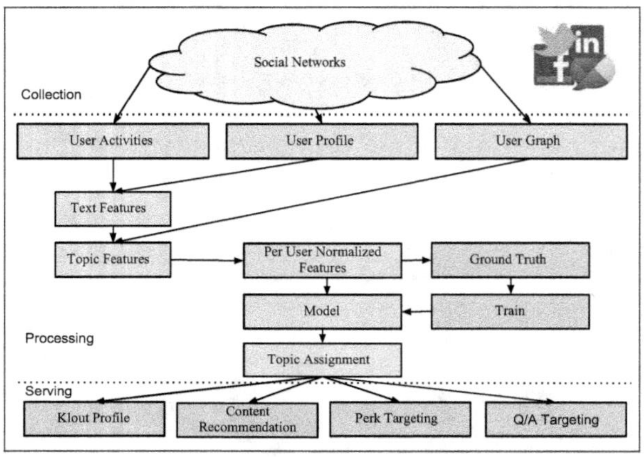

Figure 4: Data Collection and Processing Pipeline

3.1 Data Collection

LASTA focuses on collecting the following data types:

User Profile. A user may explicitly state some of his interests in his profile description on a social network. For example, the 160-character limited bio in a TW profile often contains information indicating the user's interests. On FB, users can edit their profiles to declare their interests in music, books, sports and other topics.

User Activities. Various activities on social networks provide valuable signals for topic assignment. On FB, we collect authored status updates, shared URL pages, commented and liked posts, text and tags associated with videos and pictures. On TW, we collect authored tweets, re-tweets and replies on other tweets, shared URL pages, subscribed, created and joined lists. On LI, we collect comments on posts, skills stated by the user and endorsed by connections. On GP, we collect authored messages, re-shares, comments, shared URL pages and plus-ones.

User Graph. We also collect the connection graph of a user within social networks. Such a connection graph has users as nodes and directed edges between pairs of users. This includes follower and following edges on TW, which are unidirectional relationships, and friend edges on FB, which are bidirectional relationships. The social graph also contains a hidden interest graph. For instance, if a user follows "@NBA" then it is likely that he is interested in basketball. We leverage the user graph to discover the individual's interests.

For TW in particular, Klout also partners with Gnip to collect the the public data generated in the TW Mention Stream. This includes all tweets that include re-tweets, replies or a message that contains a "mention", where a user is referenced with '@' prefixed to his username. Finally, for well-known personalities we associate their Klout profile with their Wikipedia page.

3.2 Data Processing

To reiterate, the primary goal of our system is to build a comprehensive list of user interest topics at scale. The users under consideration include registered users who connect networks on Klout, and unregistered users whose public data is available via the TW stream. Overall we assign topics to hundreds of millions of unregistered users, and the number of registered users is in the order of millions.

We use the Hadoop MapReduce infrastructure to frequently bulk process the large amount of data collected. Topic assignment is run daily as a bulk job, while machine learned models are built and improved in an offline manner regularly. The daily resource usage footprint of 'LASTA' for feature generation is: 55.42 CPU days, 6.66 PB reads, 2.33 PB writes, and for score generation is: 11.33 CPU days, 3.78 PB reads, 1.09 PB writes. These numbers refers to uncompressed HDFS data reads/writes.

In particular we use Hive which is a warehousing solution used for querying and managing large datasets residing in distributed storage. Two of the main features of Hive are – a built-in data catalog, and SQL like syntax that gets translated to a series of MapReduce jobs at runtime. Having a data catalog makes problems tractable as the number of distinct feature types in the system grows. Performing complicated data transformations with multiple joins and secondary sorts in Hive is trivial and can be expressed as a single query, saving development time and effort which would otherwise be spent on writing multiple Map-Reduce steps. The Hive Query Language abstraction allows developers to mainly focus on data transformations, leading to quick prototyping and experimentation.

We also implemented independent Java utilities for entity extraction, text to bag-of-topics mapping and language detection with Hive UDF (User Defined Function) wrappers. We have open-sourced Brickhouse [4], a collection of these utility UDFs used for data aggregation and transformation.

One of the main advantages of our data processing pipeline is that new features can be easily added and removed. Having this flexibility allows us to support large number of features, some of which are network agnostic like those derived from message reactions or connection graphs, while others are more network specific like those derived from FB likes, TW lists, LI skills and so on. Overall in our production system we generate around 50 distinct types of features. We experimented with more than 100 features over the course of the project before settling on the 50 features with the most

[4]`https://github.com/klout/brickhouse`

impact. In following section we will go in more detail about bag-of-topics generation.

3.2.1 Bag of Topics Generation

Bags-of-phrases are first extracted from textual inputs, by matching against a dictionary of approximately 2 million phrases. Phrases are extracted as n-grams where n may vary from 1 to 10. The dictionary is updated daily using Freebase [19], Wikipedia Concepts [20], manual curation and top influential users' display names on Klout. As some of these sources change daily, the dictionary dynamically updates itself to include the latest phrases in social media. Bags-of-phrases are then mapped to the topic ontology and are transformed into bags-of-topics, effectively reducing the dimensionality of the text from 2 million phrases to around 10,000 topics. A larger discussion of the ontology is beyond the scope of this paper, but we note that the system is agnostic to the ontology used, and any other ontology can also be applied in this framework. We opt for exact match and rule based synonym mapping approaches here, to avoid incorrect phrase-topic associations and to minimize false positives at this step. Alternate approaches that cluster phrases to topics, or use latent variables to perform such mappings, can be addressed in future work.

The bags-of-topics thus generated have associated strengths for each topic in the bag. For most of the text based bags-of-topics we use the cumulative phrase frequency as the topic strength. For graph based bags-of-topics we use a slightly different approach, aggregating topic strengths from the user's first degree connections. Each bag-of-topics is associated with the corresponding user id, and is identified by a name representing the data from which the bag was derived. A feature vector is generated for each user-topic pair by exploding the bags-of-topics for a user, in order to formulate the problem as a binary classification problem for matching users to topics. We describe this procedure more formally in Section 4.1. The features are identified by the same name as the bag from which the topic under consideration originated. In the remainder of the paper, we will use feature names interchangeably to represent both the individual entry in a feature vector for a topic-user pair, as well as the corresponding bag-of-topics for a user.

3.2.2 Feature Generation

We use the following naming convention for feature names: <network>_<source>_<attribution>. Each feature is represented as a combination of three characteristics that annotate – (a) the social network in which feature originated, (b) the source data type, and (c) the attribution relation of a given feature to the user. We next provide a detailed description of these feature characteristics.

Network: The social network from which the data originated, which are abbreviated as TW, FB, GP, LI, WIKI.

Source: The feature source captures the input data source, and optionally the derivation method when the same source may be interpreted in different ways. Text and social graph based sources are the two major inputs from which features are generated.

Text based sources originate from text associated with messages, posts, profiles, lists, videos, photos, or URLs shared. In addition we also fetch shared URLs and extract text from the HTML, as well as the text from meta tags annotating the title, description and keywords of a URL. This enables LASTA to gain additional context about content with respect to a user.

User graph derived features are calculated by aggregating topical interest of a user's first degree social graph. The first degree user graph topics are bootstrapped using some individual features which have high coverage and precision, for example TW Lists. Since topics are assigned daily, subsequent graph features are generated using topic assignments from the previous day. For the graph based bags-of-topics, we associate raw strengths as:

$$s(t_i|BT_u^k) = \sum_{v \in G_u} s(t_i|BT_v^k)$$

where G_u is the social graph of the user u, and v is a first-order neighbor of u. These strengths are also normalized using min-max normalization as described previously. Examples of such graph sources include FRIENDS on FB, and FOLLOWING and FOLLOWERS on TW.

The Source may optionally also include the time window considered for generating the feature. Since users' interests on social media may vary over time, some inputs may be indicators of topical interests only temporarily, while others such as country of birth, or professional interests, may indeed be long term indicators of topics associated with a user. We therefore consider inputs in a 90 day window to capture the temporal nature of changing topical interests, and an all-time window for the more permanent inputs.

Attribution: Attribution denotes the relation of the input source to the user. It may be one of the following:

1. *Generated:* Originally generated or authored content by the user, including posts, tweets and profiles. This also includes comments which are attributed as generated, to the person who authored the comment.
2. *Reacted:* Content generated by another user (actor), but as a reaction to content originally authored by the user under consideration. This includes comments, retweets, and replies.
3. *Credited:* In this case the user has no direct association with the content from which the feature was derived. Examples include text that is associated with the user because he was mentioned with tags, or added to lists and groups by other users.

The most obvious attribution is *Generated*, which is based on text that the user has authored himself. Traditionally, this has been the primary input used to infer topics, but in the context of social media, this may often be insufficient or inaccurate. Users typically talk about a variety of subjects casually, such as "I had a late lunch today", which does not necessarily indicate the user's interest in lunch or food. In addition, self-authored posts may cover only temporary or partial interests. For example, Bill Gates uses his Twitter account to primarily talk about topics like 'Philanthropy', 'Books', 'Malaria' and 'HIV infection'. While his work as a philanthropist is captured by textual input from tweets, it's essential that the system also assigns topics like 'Software industry' and 'Microsoft'. Thus generated inputs by users themselves may be inaccurate or insufficient to derive topical interests for users. To address these issues, we consider two other categories of text to derive topical signals

The first is *Reacted* text, which considers messages included in comments or replies that were created by other 'actors', in reaction to an original message created by user. In this case we attribute the text of the comment or reply to the original message author and label it with the *Reacted* attribution. For some users the amount of text generated through reactions greatly exceeds the amount of original text, thus providing a lot more context and a much better signal for topic inference.

The second attribution that we consider is *Credited.* In this case the user is only indirectly involved with the signal under consideration, and neither generates, nor directly provokes the creation of the input with which he is associated. Instead, other users in the social network associate certain messages or content to the original user. Examples of such inputs are tweets in which a user is mentioned, or posts on FB where a user is tagged, or recommendations written by colleagues on LI, or a user being listed as a member of a TW list. These messages provide strong signals for topics associated with a user, because they indicate how other members of the social network perceive the user's topical interests. This attribution is important especially in the case of celebrities who may not be regular content creators themselves, but indirectly generate text via users who talk about and mention them.

The alert reader may have also noticed that the *Generated, Reacted* and *Credited* categories are analogous to the first person, second person and third person views used in language and grammar.

3.3 Ground Truth

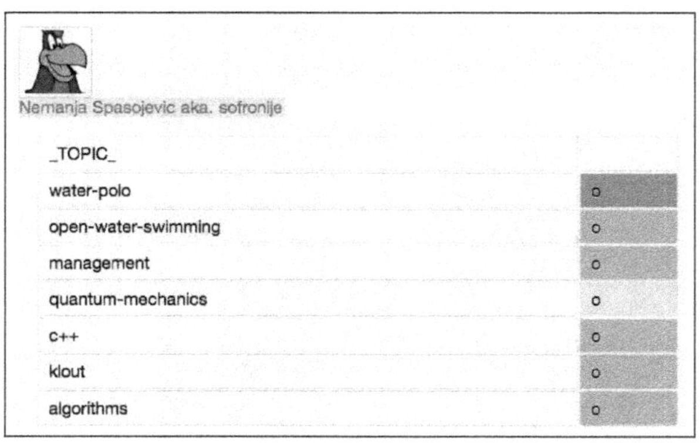

Figure 5: Ground Truth Collection Tool

In order to build models based on the features described above, we designed a simple web app to collect ground truth data with labels for user-topic interests.

Table 3: Statistics on ground truth dataset

Statistics	Value
# of participants	43
# of evaluated users	766
# of (user, topic) labels	32,264
# of positive (user, topic) labels	17,208
# of negative (user, topic) labels	15,056

We conducted controlled user studies where the evaluators in the experiment were registered Klout users. In this experimental setup, the system pulls up a set of the participant's user graph first degree connections who are also Klout users, or Twitter users whose data is available via Gnip stream. System randomly assigns topics to the users' first degree connections. The evaluator then gives positive or negative feedback, depending if the topic is good or bad match for his connection. If participants are uncertain about the relevance of the topic-user pair, they skip the evaluation for that pair. Table 3 shows the statistics of the dataset we collected through the user study. The screenshot of the tool is shown on Figure 5.

Our ground truth data is aimed at generating labels for socially recognizable user topics. A participant does not evaluate himself to ensure that personal biases are separated from the feedback. In our dataset, we found that out of all pairs of user-topic pairs that received more than one vote, only 27% have conflicting feedback. The conflicting votes contribute to only 2.2% of all the votes that were collected, suggesting that in most cases the association is clear.

4. ANALYSIS AND EVALUATION

In this section we describe our approach to solve the problem of predicting topics for a user, using supervised learning. We designed experiments and collected ground truth from real users, to acquire labeled data for matching users to topic. This labeled data is then used for training and evaluation, and the results are presented below.

4.1 Feature Analysis

As explained previously, multiple bags-of-topics are derived from different sources for each user. We explode these bags-of-topics, and for each topic-user pair (t_i, u), we build a feature vector $x_{i,u}$. The value of each feature in the vector is the topic strength of t_i given the bag-of-topics, BT_u^k:

$$x_{ik} = s(t_i | BT_u^k),$$

where BT_u^k is the kth bag-of-topics for the user. We name the kth feature with the same name as the bag BT_u^k. One of the primary contributions of this study is to analyze which features are indicative of a user's topical interests on social networks.

We find that textual input authored by users themselves accounts for at least one topic for only 58% of users on the labeled set. The remaining users either do not create enough text, or generate text that is not necessarily indicative of their topical interests. For such users we include reacted and credited signals in order to predict their topics, as described in the previous section.

We evaluate the performance of the topic prediction through traditional IR metrics:

Precision(P) measures the fraction of retrieved topics that are relevant to the user.

$$P = \frac{|\{\text{relevant topics}\} \cap \{\text{retrieved topics}\}|}{|\{\text{retrieved topics}\}|}$$

Recall(R) measures the fraction of relevant topics that are retrieved.

$$R = \frac{|\{\text{relevant topics}\} \cap \{\text{retrieved topics}\}|}{|\{\text{relevant topics}\}|}$$

Table 4 shows a selected list of important features along with their Precision (**P**) and Recall (**R**) values as evaluated on the labeled set. In this case, the predicted topics for a user are the bag-of-topics associated with the feature. We also present the coverage (**C**) in terms of percentage of registered users who have the feature.

We notice that credited List based features on Twitter and generated LinkedIn features have the highest individual predictive quality in terms of precision. Generated URL features typically have higher recall than other features, suggesting that shared URLs are a strong signal of a users topical interests. We also find that the graph based features have the highest coverage and recall values, which highlights why these features can predict topics for users who are not very active themselves.

Table 4: Feature performance and coverage

Feature Source		P	R	C
Twitter				
GEN.	MSG TEXT 90 DAY	0.22	0.15	27.37
	URL 90 DAY	0.09	0.19	14.67
	URL META 90 DAY	0.33	0.14	11.63
REAC.	MSG TEXT 90 DAY	0.26	0.12	20.81
	URL META 90 DAY	0.36	0.11	10.66
CRED.	LIST	0.68	0.21	21.19
	URL META 90 DAY	0.37	0.10	4.81
	MSG TEXT 90 DAY	0.20	0.13	21.91
	MSG #TAG 90 DAY	0.43	0.11	13.70
GRAPH	FOLLOWERS	0.08	0.26	52.41
	FOLLOWING	0.10	0.31	52.77
Facebook				
GEN.	MSG TEXT 90 DAY	0.17	0.07	29.20
	URL 90 DAY	0.08	0.12	9.52
	URL META 90 DAY	0.21	0.06	7.08
REAC.	MSG TEXT 90 DAY	0.12	0.08	45.58
	URL 90 DAY	0.05	0.12	19.82
	URL META 90 DAY	0.14	0.06	14.81
CRED.	MSG TEXT 90 DAY	0.15	0.06	13.46
GRAPH.	FRIENDS	0.08	0.25	63.66
Google Plus				
GEN.	MSG TEXT 90 DAY	0.23	0.04	1.61
	URL 90 DAY	0.09	0.15	0.34
	URL META 90 DAY	0.25	0.07	0.23
REAC.	MSG TEXT 90 DAY	0.11	0.05	1.68
	URL 90 DAY	0.05	0.08	0.46
	URL META 90 DAY	0.02	0.03	0.34
CRED.	MSG TEXT 90 DAY	0.16	0.05	0.69
LinkedIn				
GEN.	SKILLS	0.53	0.20	19.17
	INDUSTRY	0.56	0.10	16.63
Wikipedia				
CRED.	WIKI PAGE	0.18	0.28	0.11

4.2 Training and Evaluation

Given the bags-of-topics generated for users, our objective is to accurately predict the topic preference for each user. Feature vectors are generated from exploded bags-of-topics for user-topic pairs as described above. When a certain topic occurs in multiple bags for a user, then the feature vector for that pair will include all these values x_j, and 0.0 values for features where it does not occur.

We now cast the problem as a binary classification problem, in which the system must learn automatically to separate topics of interest from those that are not relevant to the user. We experimented with several classification algorithms, including those reported to achieve good performance with text classification tasks, such as support vector machines, logistic classifiers, and stochastic gradient boosted trees. We found that the best and most stable performance among the techniques we tested was obtained with the logistic classifier. We predict the label by $\hat{y} = P(y|t_i, u) = \sigma(x_{i,u} \cdot \theta)$, where $\sigma(a) = \frac{1}{1+e^{-a}}$ is the sigmoid function. The label $y \in \{0, 1\}$ assigns 1 if the topic t_i is of interest to the user u, 0 otherwise.

We train our models using the feature vectors generated for the pairs against the labels from the labeled data. The final model applies weights w_k to get the final bag-of-topics, T_u. The topic strength for a specific topic $t_i \in T_u$ is:

$$s(t_i|u) = \sum_{BT_u^k \in BT_u} w_k s(t_i|BT_u^k)$$

4.3 Results

4.3.1 *Classification Prediction Results*

In addition to precision and recall, we also use the F1 Score, $F1 = \frac{2PR}{P+R}$ to measure performance as a tradeoff between precision and recall.

Table 5 presents the performance of topic prediction using k-fold cross validation on the labeled set, where $k = 10$ and the held out set is 20% of the data. Class 1 represents positive instances where the topic was correctly predicted, and class 0 represents negative ones, where the topic was correctly discarded. We consider the predictive power of different feature sets, and how they compare to the case when the full feature set is used. The "Feature Set" column indicates the feature subset used for the prediction.

We discuss insights gained by comparing the performance of using all features versus using only subsets of features:

Single Network Comparison: The precision when all features are used is higher than when we use only features from a single network like Twitter. This shows that increasing the information available for a user by using the user's presence on other networks improves the correctness of the predicted topics in both classes. While using features from only Facebook may yield a higher precision, the recall in this case is very low, and we are able to predict fewer topics for each user. These observations together imply that because of the nature of any given social network, a user may not reveal all his interests on any single network alone, making it necessary to use features from multiple networks.

Attribution Comparison: We also compare the performance when we use only features derived from user generated input, which includes text as well as shared URLs (GEN.), or use only features from the user's reacted and credited inputs (REAC. + CRED.). The generated set of features yield a high precision, but a low recall value. The reacted and credited features give a slightly lower precision, but slightly higher recall compared to the generated input. But using all inputs together yields a much higher recall value than using them separately. This shows that using only user generated text can predict much fewer topics for the user, as compared to using the generated, reacted and credited inputs together.

Graph Comparison: Finally we also compare how the graph based features (GRAPH) play a role in topic prediction. Excluding graph based features gives a higher precision but a low recall value, and using only graph features provides a much higher recall value, with a slightly lower precision. This highlights the value of using graph features, because by the nature of the social networks, it is possible to predict topics for a user by considering the topics of the other users that he is connected to. But relying solely on graph based features gives some incorrect predictions, because of the possible noise introduced.

Thus we observe that using the complete set of features maintains a relatively high precision, while greatly improving the recall. The results show that including multiple networks, generated text input, reacted and credited signals, and graph based features together gives the best performance overall, as indicated by the F1-score in Table 5. LASTA also achieves a 92% precision k, where $k = 10$, on the full training set.

Table 5: Binary classification prediction for different feature sets

Feature Set	Class	P	R	F1	F1 Avg.
TW	1	0.703	0.484	0.573	0.613
	0	0.572	0.771	0.657	
FB	1	0.792	0.298	0.433	0.548
	0	0.538	0.912	0.677	
GEN.	1	0.799	0.335	0.472	0.568
	0	0.543	0.904	0.678	
REAC. + CRED.	1	0.733	0.373	0.495	0.572
	0	0.541	0.845	0.660	
ALL – GRAPH	1	0.792	0.411	0.541	0.610
	0	0.599	0.809	0.688	
GRAPH	1	0.739	0.501	0.597	0.633
	0	0.599	0.809	0.688	
LASTA	1	0.758	0.526	0.621	0.652
	0	0.599	0.809	0.688	

4.3.2 *Curation Evaluation*

We deployed LASTA in production at Klout, and displayed the top 10 predicted topics in ranked order on each user's profile. Users could then add, delete, or reorder the list, indicating agreement or disagreement with the predicted list. We also evaluate our system against this self-curated user data. We select the set of users who have made changes on their topic profiles, and evaluate the initially predicted list of topics against the final curated list for each user. Table 6 has the statistics of this dataset.

Table 6: Statistics of the curated dataset

Statistics	Value
# of users	19,505
# of (user, topic) pairs	196,481
Avg # of positive topics per user	7.37

We evaluate LASTA using the following metrics on the curated data:

Mean Average Precision (MAP) For a single user, average precision calculates the average of the precision of the top K topics. $AP@K = \frac{\sum_{i=1}^{K} P@i}{K^+}$, where K^+ is the number of positive samples. Here $P@i$ is the precision at cut-off i in the retrieved list. The mean average precision for N users at position K is the mean of the average precision for each user, i.e., $MAP@K = \frac{1}{N}\sum_{i=1}^{N} AP@K(i)$.

Normalized discounted cumulative gain (nDCG) Measures graded relevance of the list of topics, i.e., $DCG = \sum_i^k \frac{2^{r_i}-1}{\log_2(p_i+1)}$ where $r_i = 1$ if the topic has a positive label in the curated list, and p_i is the position of topic in the ranked list. Normalized DCG is the ratio of DCG by the model's ranking to the DCG by the ideal ranking: $nDCG = \frac{DCG}{IDCG}$.

We use these metrics to compare the output of LASTA against other approaches. In particular, we compare LASTA to approaches where the topics for a user are predicted using aggregated topic frequency (TF) from subsets of features. These subsets are those derived from generated textual input only; all generated inputs including URLs shared, LinkedIn Skills etc.; and all inputs that were generated, reacted and credited. Table 7 shows the results for ranking the top K topics of interest for each user, where $K = 10$.

Table 7: Ranking performance comparison on user curated data

Model with Features used	MAP@K	nDCG
TF - Message Text Generated	0.150	0.140
TF - All Generated	0.155	0.139
TF - All	0.160	0.141
LASTA - All	0.314	0.269

Note that the users who curate their own data are only a small fraction of users on Klout, who are self motivated to edit their topic list. Since most users do not edit their list, either because they are satisfied with it, or because they are not motivated enough to change it, we exclude such users from the dataset. On this dataset, LASTA significantly outperforms the other approaches in terms of both the MAP and nDCG metrics, showing that it does indeed produce a better set of ranked topics for a given user.

Table 8 shows some examples of topics assigned to some well known personalities according to LASTA.

Table 8: LASTA topic assignment examples

User	Top 10 Topics
Marissa Mayer	yahoo, google, technology, business, twitter, social-media, flickr, design, marketing, seo, gmail
Lady Gaga	music, lady-gaga, celebrities, art, fashion, born-this-way, venus, entertainment, radio
Barack Obama	politics, affordable-care-act, health-care, new-york-times, congress, chicago, twitter, washington, illinois

4.4 Cross Network Analysis

In our dataset, around 13% users connect to a single social networks, 40% of users to two social networks, and less than 10% users connect all four social networks. Typically it is expected that a user does not connect all four networks, since most users are only active in one or two networks. But the advantage of using four networks is that the fraction of users using at least two out of the four is higher, leading to more information about the user. The details of user behavior patterns in a cross-network setting is beyond the scope of the paper, but here we present some interesting topical insights across networks.

4.4.1 Super-topics comparison

As discussed previously in Section 2.2, we observe that phrases used by a user have low overlap across social networks. Here we examine similarities and differences between topical interests aggregated across users on different networks. To aid visualization, we roll up entities and subtopics to super-topics, reducing the topic dimension space from 10,000 to 15. We sum up the presence of user interests rolled up to super-topics in each individual social network, and plot this distribution. Table 9 shows the percentage breakdown of super-topics on each social network for the users on that network, and also the breakdown across all users according to LASTA.

We observe from the figure that users in each network have distinct topical interests. On FB and TW the super-topic "entertainment" is the most represented one, whereas "business" is the most represented super-topic on LI, and "technology" on GP. FB users are also more interested in topics related to "lifestyle" and "food-and-drink" compared to users on other networks, while a significant number of GP users show interest in "arts-and-humanities". For LI, apart from "technology" and "business", other topics are not highly represented, which is expected since it is a professional networking platform. The left-most column shows the distribution of topics as assigned by LASTA. The "business" row is an interesting one to observe. While this topic is not highly represented on TW, FB and GP, LASTA is able to assign "business" related topics to users, because it also takes into account signals from LI. This shows that using multiple networks can lead to not only a deeper understanding for each user, but also a better understanding across topics.

4.4.2 Topics distribution

While the previous section analyzes cross-network topic distributions qualitatively in terms of super-topics, here we examine the distribution quantitatively in terms of number of topics assigned to users. While assigning a very large number of topics is not necessarily the goal of the system, we analyze these distributions in order to perform cross-network comparison. In Figure 6, each plotted point represents the fraction of users who have at least x number of topics assigned to them.

We find that the number of topics assigned to users with TW and FB is much larger than that assigned using GP or LI. This is because GP and LI do not provide API access to graph data, and also have a smaller volume of textual input compared to TW and FB. We conclude from the graph that for the same number of topics, LASTA always assigns topics to more users. Also, LASTA assigns more topics to each user compared to individual networks.

5. APPLICATIONS

LASTA is serving multiple personalized services in Klout. We briefly describe some applications next.

Targeting: Given that social media is a modern means of spreading awareness among people, many brands desire to target promotional messages and campaigns to social net-

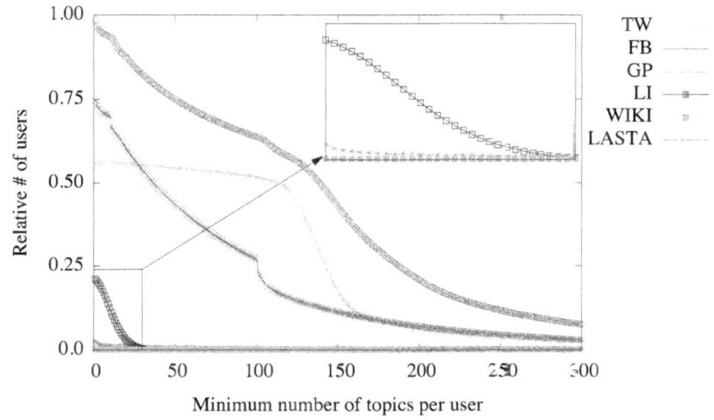

Figure 6: Distribution of registered users for minimum number of topics assigned across different networks.

work users. As an example, a car company that wants to spread awareness about a new car model, may want to target certain incentives or "perks" related to the car to some users on social media. When users interested in cars are targeted with the perk, they may be motivated to talk about the car on their respective social networks, effectively generating word-of-mouth awareness about the new model. This approach of targeting users based on topics, that can provide value to companies and brands, has been successfully implemented at Klout with LASTA.

Content Discovery: The topics deduced by LASTA provide utility to users in terms of serendipitous content discovery at Klout. This system aggregates online articles, categorized by topic, and ranks them based on relevancy to a user. The system can also identify topics that some members from the user's social graph may be interested in. A user can then be shown a customized feed of articles that he may either want to discover and read about himself, or may want to share with a wider audience on his social networks.

Question Answering: In a question answering scenario, a user in the system can ask a question pertaining to a certain topic, which can then be routed to specific users who may be able to answer the question. For example, a question such as "What is the best place to go fishing near San Francisco?", may be routed to users interested in fishing who live in San Francisco. Users to whom questions are routed are able to give credible answers to such questions, and the original asker may get multiple good answers. This system was implemented and used by users on Klout, and was again enabled by LASTA.

6. CONCLUSION AND FUTURE WORK

In this paper, we presented Klout's topic assignment system, LASTA. The system assigns overs 10,000 topics to hundreds of millions of users spread across multiple social networks on a daily basis with a high accuracy. We hope the engineering architecture and technology choice provides insights to build scalable and extendable topic mining systems.

LASTA provides the foundation to build other data-driven products that utilizes the user-topic relationships. In the future, we want to build systems that will understand topical expertise among the millions of users.

Table 9: Super-topic percentage distribution across different networks

Super-topic	LASTA	TW	FB	LI	GP	WIKI
technology	23.972	19.706	11.559	33.420	22.822	8.247
entertainment	23.987	20.049	20.866	3.406	14.377	30.669
business	15.893	10.628	7.567	41.053	12.857	10.937
lifestyle	7.910	7.403	11.409	2.328	7.969	4.810
science-and-nature	4.431	3.705	3.604	1.266	4.682	3.208
arts-and-humanities	6.605	7.056	6.836	5.765	9.392	13.373
government-and-politics	3.547	4.763	4.388	2.182	3.534	5.261
sports-and-recreation	4.379	7.503	7.591	0.659	4.913	7.921
food-and-drink	2.671	7.228	11.863	0.819	7.255	2.142
health-and-wellness	1.976	3.894	5.150	1.691	4.083	1.867
fashion	1.439	2.645	2.945	0.732	2.776	2.203
education	1.443	2.375	3.485	3.369	2.170	4.058
news-and-media	0.966	1.722	0.899	2.597	1.060	4.366
travel-and-tourism	0.535	0.779	1.155	0.614	1.041	0.654
hobbies	0.246	0.543	0.683	0.100	1.070	0.285

7. ACKNOWLEDGMENTS

We thank Sarah Ellinger for her continuous work on curating the topic ontology. We are extremely grateful to our former colleagues Yize Li, Jerome Banks, Guangle Fan and Ding Zhou who contributed towards building LASTA. We thank Joe Fernandez for his valuable feedback throughout the project and also thank Prof. S. Muthu Muthukrishnan of Rutgers University for his inputs.

8. REFERENCES

[1] Alan Ritter, Mausam Clark, Sam, and Oren Etzioni. Named entity recognition in tweets: an experimental study. In *Empirical Methods in Natural Language Processing*. Association for Computational Linguistics, 2011.

[2] Zhiheng Xu, Rong Lu, Liang Xiang, and Qing Yang. Discovering user interest on twitter with a modified author-topic model. In *Web Intelligence and Intelligent Agent Technology*, 2011.

[3] Liangjie Hong and Brian D Davison. Empirical study of topic modeling in twitter. In *Workshop on Social Media Analytics*, 2010.

[4] Matthew Michelson and Sofus A Macskassy. Discovering users' topics of interest on twitter: a first look. In *Workshop on Analytics for noisy unstructured text data*, 2010.

[5] Daniel Ramage, Susan T Dumais, and Daniel J Liebling. Characterizing microblogs with topic models. In *Weblogs and Social Media*, 2010.

[6] Yehuda Koren, Robert Bell, and Chris Volinsky. Matrix factorization techniques for recommender systems. In *Computer*. IEEE, 2009.

[7] Susan Gauch, Jason Chaffee, and Alexander Pretschner. Ontology-based personalized search and browsing. In *Web Intelligence and Agent Systems*, 2003.

[8] Feng Qiu and Junghoo Cho. Automatic identification of user interest for personalized search. In *World Wide Web*, 2006.

[9] Amr Ahmed, Yucheng Low, Mohamed Aly, Vanja Josifovski, and Alexander J Smola. Scalable distributed inference of dynamic user interests for behavioral targeting. In *Knowledge discovery and data mining*, 2011.

[10] David M Blei and John D Lafferty. A correlated topic model of science. *Annals of Applied Statistics*, 2007.

[11] Thomas K Landauer and Susan T Dumais. A solution to plato's problem: The latent semantic analysis theory of acquisition, induction, and representation of knowledge. *Psychological review*, 1997.

[12] David M Blei, Andrew Y Ng, and Michael I Jordan. Latent dirichlet allocation. *Journal of machine Learning research*, 2003.

[13] Julia Stoyanovich, Sihem Amer-Yahia, Cameron Marlow, and Cong Yu. Leveraging tagging to model user interests in del. icio. us. In *AAAI Spring Symposium: Social Information Processing*, 2008.

[14] Xin Li, Lei Guo, and Yihong Eric Zhao. Tag-based social interest discovery. In *World Wide Web*, 2008.

[15] Zheng Yang, Jingfang Xu, and Xing Li. Data selection for user topic model in twitter-like service. In *Parallel and Distributed Systems*, 2011.

[16] Ido Guy, Uri Avraham, David Carmel, Sigalit Ur, Michal Jacovi, and Inbal Ronen. Mining expertise and interests from social media. In *World Wide Web*, 2013.

[17] C Honey and Susan C Herring. Beyond microblogging: Conversation and collaboration via twitter. In *System Sciences*, 2009.

[18] Danah Boyd, Scott Golder, and Gilad Lotan. Tweet, tweet, retweet: Conversational aspects of retweeting on twitter. In *System Sciences*, 2010.

[19] Google. Freebase data dumps. `https://developers.google.com/freebase/data`, 2012.

[20] Valentin I. Spitkovsky and Angel X. Chang. A cross-lingual dictionary for english wikipedia concepts. In *Language Resources and Evaluation*, 2012.

New Algorithms for Parking Demand Management and a City Scale Deployment

Onno Zoeter Christopher Dance Stéphane Clinchant Jean-Marc Andreoli
Xerox Research Centre Europe
6 Chemin de Maupertuis
38240 Meylan
France

ABSTRACT

On-street parking, just as any publicly owned utility, is used inefficiently if access is free or priced very far from market rates. This paper introduces a novel demand management solution: using data from dedicated occupancy sensors an iteration scheme updates parking rates to better match demand. The new rates encourage parkers to avoid peak hours and peak locations and reduce congestion and underuse. The solution is deliberately simple so that it is easy to understand, easily seen to be fair and leads to parking policies that are easy to remember and act upon. We study the convergence properties of the iteration scheme and prove that it converges to a reasonable distribution for a very large class of models. The algorithm is in use to change parking rates in over 6000 spaces in downtown Los Angeles since June 2012 as part of the LA Express Park project. Initial results are encouraging with a reduction of congestion and underuse, while in more locations rates were decreased than increased.

Categories and Subject Descriptors

H.2.8 [**Database Management**]: Database Applications—*Data Mining*

General Terms

Algorithms

1. INTRODUCTION

Advances in sensor technologies and advances in information dissemination technologies, most notably the widespread use of smartphones, allow for a radical change in the way governments manage public infrastructure. The deployment of sensors allows this to be data driven, and the information channels allow this to be adaptive. It forms an interesting application domain for data mining, machine learning, and optimization techniques. And in line with this year's KDD special theme it is a good opportunity for data mining for social good since it allows scarce public utilities to be used more efficiently and helps to reduce unwanted externalities such as congestion and pollution. This paper introduces new algorithms that leverage these new sensor and dissemination opportunities to improve the way on-street parking is used.

KDD'14, August 24–27, 2014, New York, NY, USA.

ACM ACM 978-1-4503-2956-9/14/08 ...$15.00.
http://dx.doi.org/10.1145/2623330.2623359 .

On-street parking is in many city centers a scarce resource. If on-street parking is free, or priced significantly below market rates, it will be used inefficiently, because drivers are not properly incentivized to avoid peak hours and peak locations. William Vickrey [9] argued that users of on-street parking, and in fact users of any publicly owned utility, should be charged as close as possible to the externality they impose (i.e. the inconvenience they cause others).

Imagining a solution using 1950s technology, Vickrey proposed to connect 20 meters and to make them turn faster as the 20 spaces filled up. The meter could turn slowly if there were less than 17 cars parked (anybody that would want to park in the block could easily do so), would turn faster if the block filled up from there, and would turn fastest if all 20 spaces were full.

There are several problems with these ex-post (pay at the end) meters. The current infrastructure is not ready for it and the upfront uncertainty about what parking costs might not be acceptable to users. But perhaps more importantly, the ex-post meters put the burden of predicting demand for parking on the shoulders of every driver, while the overall parking system has all the data to do this best!

Several parking specialists (e.g. [8]) have suggested a more cautious approach: revise parking rates at regular intervals, say every month, based on data obtained from parking sensors. That way drivers can memorize the rates around their office, favorite restaurant, etc. and adjust their behavior accordingly.

1.1 Contributions

This paper studies the problem of iteratively improving on-street parking rates based on observed parking demand data to increase the efficiency with which these scarce resources are used and to reduce congestion and pollution It makes several contributions.

- It describes why the often proposed straightforward method of basing rate updates on average occupancy data does not correspond to a reasonable utility model and can lead to incorrect rate changes (Sec 3.1).
- It introduces an iteration scheme that is based on a trade-off between congestion and underuse. This iteration scheme is simple to communicate, fair, not based

on any model assumptions, and solves the problems with the naive scheme (Sec 3.2).

- The limiting behaviour of this iteration scheme is analyzed and proven to converge to a reasonable distribution under a very large class of models. This is particularly useful since there was no data available to build and select models before the first deployment of our methods (Sec 3.3).
- An extension of the algorithm automatically determines time-of-day windows for rates trading-off the closeness to the parking patterns and ease of communication (Sec 4).
- The paper describes the real-world deployment of these ideas. The developed methods have been used to adjust parking rates for 6300 on-street parking spaces since June 2012 in Los Angeles (Sec 5).

2. VCG PAYMENTS, POSTED PRICES AND FREE PARKING

Before we discuss iteration schemes in the next section, it is interesting to study the motivations for demand management in more detail. A simple stylized example to demonstrate the impact of parking rates on efficiency is presented in Figure 1.
This considers a single block with:

- capacity $C = 10$, a single time step
- $n \sim \text{Poiss}(\lambda = 15)$ parkers
- values for parking $v_i \overset{\text{iid}}{\sim} P(v) = \text{Gam}(\alpha = 5, \beta = 2)$ for $i = 1, \ldots, n$.

Free parking implies a first-come-first-served mechanism. A posted price mechanism will filter parkers with a very low value for parking such that spaces are kept for parkers with a high valuation. The figure shows the sum of values of parked cars (social welfare) as a function of parking rate (blue, solid line shows mean, dashed 25% and 75% quantiles). Whereas we see that a non-zero posted price can indeed improve social welfare, a too high price risks leaving spaces empty. The horizontal line shows the expected social welfare under an optimal allocation, e.g. if parking allocation could be done using a Vickrey-Clarke-Groves mechanism [10]. The green lines indicate revenue. As expected the revenue maximizing rate is higher than the welfare maximizing rate [6]. The second set of lines is added to emphasize the difference in objectives: demand management aims to increase efficiency, yield management to increase revenue.

A properly chosen take-it-or-leave-it price can provide a constant factor approximation to the optimal revenue ([1], where the same result is also claimed for social welfare). The result depends on the assumption that valuations are drawn independently. For parking several factors could break this assumption. For instance in front of a stadium all parkers will have a low-ish valuation if there is no match on, but all will have a high-ish one if there is. So if we can only set a single rate, parkers' valuations are dependent. However if we have a match-time rate and a non-match rate, for each of the two cases independence is a reasonable assumption. So for demand based pricing it is important to condition rates on important factors that significantly influences valuations.

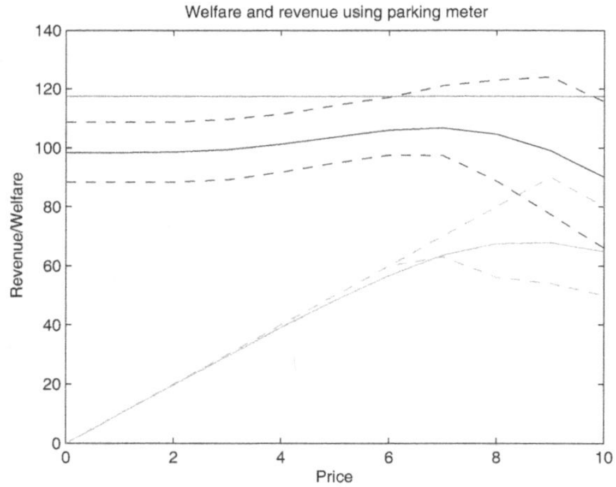

Figure 1: Welfare (dark, blue) and revenue (light, green) as function of price in a simple parking model. Solid lines represent means, dashed lines 25% and 75% quantiles. The horizontal line is the expected welfare under optimal assignment.

The work from [1] is studied in an on-line bipartite matching problem inspired by the parking problem in [5].

The stylized example of this section also makes clear that defining a utility model for a realistic parking scenario is not straightforward. In the example only the interests of the parkers have been taken into account. It could be argued that the congestion caused by drivers circling for a space should also be taken into account, or the interests of residents, shopkeepers, or others. Similarly any parking demand model will be non-trivial in a realistic setting and cannot be learned before several rate changes have been made. Even if many years worth of data is available before the first rate change, it will not distinguish between models that aim to predict how demand changes after a rate change.

3. DEMAND BASED PRICING

To get robust improvements that do not rely on a particular parking model, we use a simple iteration scheme that is inspired by stochastic approximation. Rates are on a discrete pricing ladder (in LA rates are in {\$0.5, \$1, \$1.5, \$2, \$3, ..., \$6}). At the end of every review period (say every quarter, or every month) parking data is studied and for every block-face (one side of a street in between two side streets) it is determined if the rate should go up one step, down one step, or should stay the same. The review period cannot be too short, because drivers need to learn about the new rates and change their habits, before data about the new equilibrium becomes available. Intuitively if we have observed that demand has been too high, rates should go up, if demand has been too low, rates should go down. But as we will see in the next section, care has to be taken to implement that intuition.

3.1 The problem with updates based on average occupancy

It is interesting to observe that the simplest possible approach, used e.g. in a project running in parallel in San Francisco (`sfpark.org`), basing rate changes on the average occupancy in a review period, is not true to most reasonable utility models. Most utility models would say that underuse is bad (possible shoppers or other users have been discouraged and spaces remain unused that would be used at a lower rate) and congestion is bad (parkers with a high valuation are blocked, drivers circling for a space congest and pollute). If rates are changed based on average occupancy, a period of underuse followed by congestion can lead to a perfect "neither too empty, nor too full" (Goldilocks) situation — on average, and hence mask the problems that have actually occurred. This is of particular importance if time windows are determined algorithmically based on data: a quiet morning followed by a congested afternoon risk to be grouped together, since jointly they will have a perfect average occupancy. The data from the LA deployment indicates that this is a common case in practice (See Figures 4 and 9)

3.2 Rate change rules based on congestion and underuse patterns

A simple but effective alternative is to study the number of minutes each block-face was congested and how many minutes the block-face was underused. Several practitioners (e.g. [8]) have considered 85% occupancy per block-face as an ideal occupancy target. The city of LA has decided to treat occupancies below 70% as underused, and above 90% as congested. Such a discrete classification is a simplification, but forms a reasonable and easy to communicate basis for policy change.

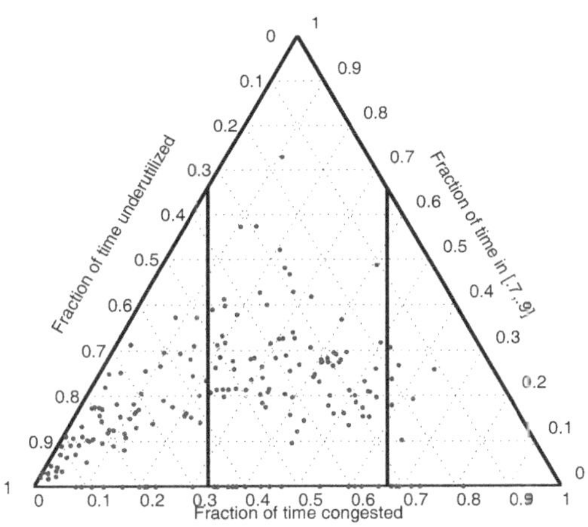

Figure 2: A ternary plot demonstrating the rate change rules. At the end of a review period each block is represented by three numbers: the fraction of time underused, the fraction of time congested, and the fraction of time just right. Since these numbers add to one, a block can be represented in a ternary plot. Blocks (dots) in the right region have a fraction of time congested minus fraction of time underused greater than 1/3 and see a rate increase. Blocks in the left region see a rate decrease. Data from April-May 2012.

At the end of every month, per block, the fractions of time spent in each of the three categories (underused, just right, congested) adds to one, and can be represented in a ternary plot. Figure 2 shows the 817 blocks in the LA project area based on data from April and May 2012 before the first rate change.

The blocks that fall close to the bottom right corner are predominantly in congested state, and a rate increase would be in order. Blocks close to the bottom left corner are predominantly underused, and rates should be reduced. Points at the top are predominantly just-right and could keep the same rate. Points in the middle close to the bottom demonstrate both non-negligible problems of congestion and of underuse. A change to a single rate can only try to improve one of the two problems at the risk of worsening the other. Studying the patterns of demand might reveal that the underuse and congestion patterns consistently appear at different parts of the day. In such cases charging different rates at different parts of the day can target the two problems appropriately. We will introduce algorithms to optimally determine such windows based on data in Section 4.

A rate change rule based on the difference between the fraction of time congested and the fraction of time underused, is a simple rule that agrees with the above sketched ideas. Rates are increased only if congestion is the predominant problem, reduced only if underuse is the predominant problem, and conservatively kept the same if both congestion and underuse form a problem. The rate changes in LA are based on thresholds 1/3 and −1/3: the regions demarked by the vertical lines in Figure 2. Algorithm 1 summarizes the method and introduces notation.

Algorithm 1 The default rate change iteration

For all blocks b

- Compute the *congestion index* $I_c^{(b)}$ as the fraction of operating hours in the review period that b is congested (occupancy > %90).
- Similarly compute the *underuse index* $I_u^{(b)}$ (underuse defined as occupancy < %70).
- Define the *congestion-underuse balance* as

$$B_{cu}^{(b)} = I_c^{(b)} - I_u^{(b)} .$$

For all b with $I_{cu}^{(b)} > 1/3$ (congestion dominant problem)

Increase the rate by one step in the ladder.

For all b with $I_{cu}^{(b)} < -1/3$ (underuse dominant problem)

Decrease the rate by one step in the ladder.

3.3 Studying the limiting distribution

The iteration scheme has a resemblance to stochastic approximation [7]. A big difference is that the updates here are restricted to a discrete set of easy-to-remember rates. Whereas stochastic approximation relies on a specific cooling schedule for the step sizes to guarantee convergence, the discrete nature of the rates prevents such convergence to a point.

In practice we observe significant mid- and long-term fluctuations in demand. In LA we see seasonal effects, changes apparently coming from the opening of new restaurants, shops, etc., and from trends that could come form general macroeconomic shifts. So one could argue that convergence to a single "perfect" rate is not desired. However it is interesting to understand the iteration scheme. To do so we study it in the context of stationary demand.

Let us denote the demand distribution $P(z|r)$, with z the sequence of observed occupancies during a review period for a particular block and $r \in \{r_1 \leq r_2 \leq \ldots \leq r_L\}$ its hourly rate. Together with the rate change rules represented in Figure 2 this defines $P_{i,i+1}$, the probability of a rate increase from i to $i+1$, and $P_{i,i-1}$, the probability of a decrease. If the demand is stationary the iteration defines a stationary Markov chain on the rates.

To be able to motivate rate changes to the general public it is very reasonable, if not required, to consider only one step up or down in the ladder. That is, the transition matrix is tri-diagonal. Any non-pathological demand distribution will have a non-zero (but possibly very small) probability of increasing or decreasing any rate and will define an aperiodic Markov chain. Hence the Markov chain will be ergodic and will have a unique stationary distribution.

This stationary distribution can be characterized under very general conditions. The only mild assumption we will make is that the combination of demand distribution and rate change rules are such that a suggestion to increase rates becomes more likely as rates go down, i.e. $P_{i+1,i+2} \leq P_{i,i+1}$. For instance for the same location we expect to see a rate increase sooner if parking costs 50 cents per hour than if it is \$1 per hour. Similarly we assume that rates are more likely to go down if the current rate is higher: $P_{i+1,i} \leq P_{i+2,i+1}$. These monotonicities are desired for any rate change rule, and will for our choice hold under many models, but cannot be formally guaranteed without specific knowledge of the underlying demand distribution.

Under these assumptions the stationary distribution is uni-modal. To show this we first observe that the stationary distribution for tri-diagonal Markov chains can be easily characterized using the transition probabilities.

LEMMA 1. *For every tri-diagonal transition matrix P there exists a vector s such that $s_i P_{i,j} = s_j P_{j,i}$ for all i and j.*

PROOF. For all diagonal and for all off-tridiagonal elements the equality holds trivially. So the only non-trivial equations that need to hold are $s_i P_{i,i+1} = s_{i+1} P_{i+1,i}$ for $i = 1, \ldots, L-1$. These can be made to hold, and we can get the stationary distribution (up to a normalizing constant) by setting $s_1 = 1$ and $s_{i+1} = s_i P_{i,i+1}/P_{i+1,i}$ for $i = 1, \ldots, L-1$. □

This allows us to demonstrate uni-modality of the stationary distribution and characterize its mode.

THEOREM 1. *If the demand distribution is stationary and the rate change rules are such that $P_{i+1,i+2} \leq P_{i,i+1}$ and $P_{i+1,i} \leq P_{i+2,i+1}$ for all i, the stationary distribution s_i over rates is uni-modal with a mode at the smallest i with $\frac{s_{i+1}}{s_i} = \frac{P_{i,i+1}}{P_{i+1,i}} < 1$, or L if there is no such i.*

PROOF. To show unimodality of the stationary distribution we look at the likelihood ratio of subsequent states. Since $s_i P_{i,i+1} = s_{i+1} P_{i+1,i}$ we have $\frac{s_{i+1}}{s_i} = \frac{P_{i,i+1}}{P_{i+1,i}}$. To check monotonicity we would like to have that as soon as this ratio becomes smaller than 1, the ratio stays below 1. So $P_{i,i+1} < P_{i+1,i} \rightarrow P_{i+1,i+2} < P_{i+2,i+1}$. This holds since $P_{i+1,i+2} \leq P_{i,i+1}$ and $P_{i+1,i} \leq P_{i+2,i+1}$ from the monotonicity of our pricing engine rules.

The ratio of the subsequent states and the unimodality leads directly to the characterization of the (not necessarily unique) mode which is given by the smallest i with $\frac{s_{i+1}}{s_i} = \frac{P_{i,i+1}}{P_{i+1,i}} < 1$, or L if there is no such i. □

With one year of data and only one or two changes up or down allowed by city ordinance limits, we have not enough data to study these properties in practice. Studies using artificially generated data demonstrate what we would expect: the stationary distribution is sharply peaked around a value that avoids both congestion and underuse (See Figure 3). A longer period between rate changes (more observations) leads, in a stationary model, to less variances in the parking patterns observed, and therefore to a more peaked stationary distribution.

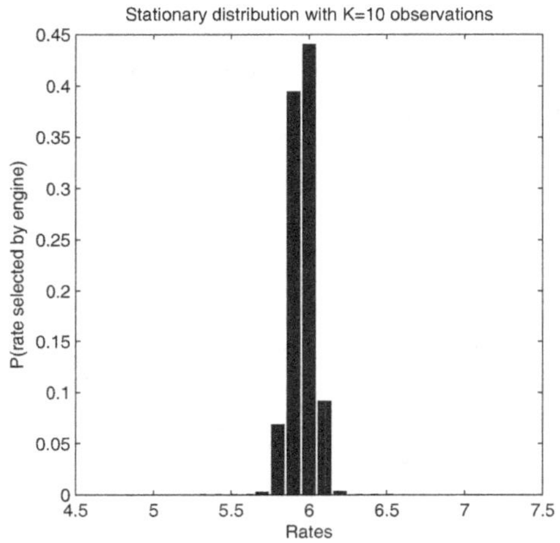

Figure 3: An empirical study of the convergence of the iteration. The plot shows the stationary distribution. The analysis is based on a truncated Poisson demand model with arrival rate function $\lambda(p) = 3(1 - 1./(1 + \exp(-(p-5)))) + 0.05$, parking price per-hour $p \in \{5, 5.1, \ldots 7\}$ and a block-face capacity of 20.

4. DEMAND DRIVEN TIME-OF-DAY WINDOWS

Parking demand clearly varies over different times of day and between weekdays and weekends. If the differences are significant, a single rate cannot be appropriate for all times. In Figure 4, the evolution of I_c (an aggregate over blocks) is shown over the week. Midday on a weekday is on average the most congested whereas parking is overall underused during nights.

If a block-face could have different rates at different times, it could potentially lead to increased effectiveness of the parking system. Following the externality based pricing principles outlined in Section 2 we would require parkers to pay a "blended rate", i.e. the integral under the rate function and not the rate at arrival time for the entire duration. In this section we introduce a suitable logic to choose nearly optimal, yet simple time-of-day windows.

Suppose we would ignore the fact that rates need to be memorized by drivers and therefore ignore the need for the

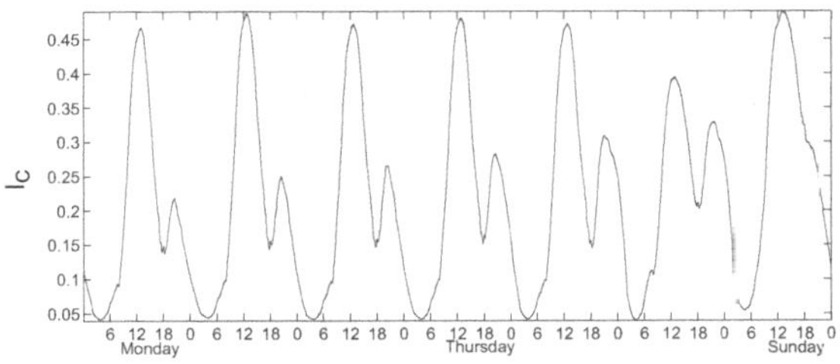

Figure 4: I_c aggregate over the blocks

rate structures to be simple. In particular suppose we could price each half-hour period differently. This is illustrated in Figure 5 on a deployment in over 800 blocks (See next section). The figure represents block-faces as rows. Every pixel represents a vote for a half hour in the week, starting with the first half hour of Monday on the left. The vote is color coded: black means a rate reduction, grey an unchanged rate or unpriced and white a rate increase. The blocks are sorted by the number of half hours that vote for an increase. An important comment is that even if B_{cu} can be low, some faces reached \$0.5 (the lowest rate allowed) so they do not get a price decrease. Secondly, one can observe that a period of low occupancy before 10 AM is common throughout the week. Finally, it is interesting to see that weekdays are rather similar, even if Mondays are slightly less busy than Fridays.

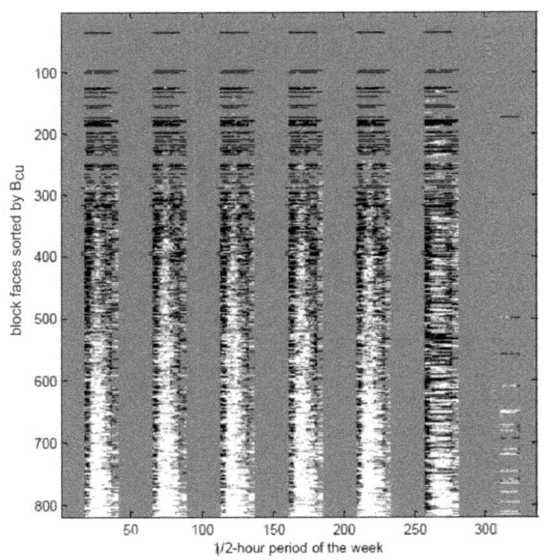

Figure 5: A matrix representing a block-faces (rows) and their vote for a rate change every half hour period in a week. Black means a suggested reduction, grey staying the same or being unpriced, white a rate increase.

Since the information about rates needs to be memorized by drivers before they can act on them, using the suggestions from Figure 5 directly is not acceptable. Encouraged by the similarity among blocks it is interesting to explore a segmentation in time-of-day windows that are *identical all over the city* while minimizing the number of half-hour periods that get the wrong price change. The fact that the windows are the same all over the city makes for a huge simplification and makes the system a natural extension of the often observed practice to have different rates for weekdays and weekends.

The optimal number of windows found is 5 and is illustrated in Figure 6 where it is compared to half-hour votes of 100 E 14th Street. For increased simplicity we add the constraint that we do not want too short segments (< two hours). The optimal partition has 5 segments, but that with the no-short-segments constraint has only 3 segments.

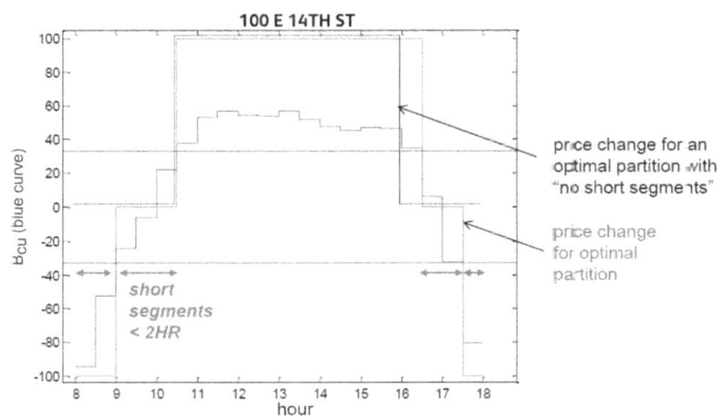

Figure 6: An example of suggested rate changes if they would be done on each half hour of the day independently (blue), and the optimal over the pilot area (red), and with an additional constraint that they cannot contain short (<2 hrs) sections.

Our full analysis on the Los Angeles pilot area, revealed that a simple partition into 3 parts for weekdays is optimal for over 90% of all stalls: (open-11:00,11:00-16:00,16:00-close) We also compared a solution with the 2 best partitions over the pilot areas but found little benefit to it. Furthermore, a single partition is much easier to communicate and to remember. We also analyzed the sensitivity of this partition to this B_{cu} threshold defined by the city of Los Angeles. If B_{cu} were concentrated near the threshold (e.g. 33%), then we would expect that the choice of partition might be rather sensitive to the choice of threshold. However, data shows the contrary. This is a pleasant property because it allows for adjustments to the thresholds on when rates increase or decrease without the data driven time-of-day windows becoming inappropriate.

In Figure 7, we show a map of block-faces where the fraction of mispriced hours with flat pricing and Time-of-Day Pricing is color-coded. Flat pricing averages the B_{cu} criterion over a large period of time and can select rates that are inappropriate to deal with congestion and underutilization (see for example blocks colored in yellow on the map). This is often the case when operating hours are not well adjusted to the typical usage of a block-face. Time-of-Day pricing greatly reduces this phenomenon as shown on the map.

So, to our surprise, we found that over 800 block-faces could be priced using only 3 time-of-day segments for weekdays and a single one for weekends while being close to what data would suggest on individual half-hours. This simplification makes it easier for drivers to remember rates, and to pre-plan parking destinations accordingly. The early morning rates (open-11am) typically can be interpreted as a "smoothed-start" to paid hours, e.g. before shops open. As a

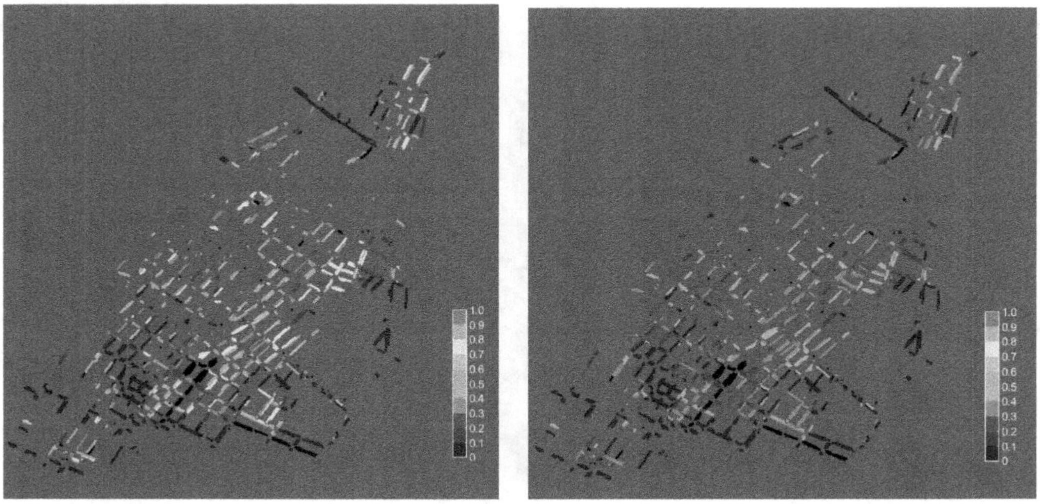

Figure 7: A map of the fraction of mispriced hours over 6 weeks of data with flat pricing (left plot) and time-of-day pricing (right plot) with 3 rates for weekdays and 1 flat rate for Saturdays. The map represents the project area as presented in Figure 8, for clarity no cartography data is shown.

last remark it is interesting to compare to a non data-driven choice of 9am-noon, noon-3pm, and 3pm-6pm as is done in e.g. San Francisco. Judging Figure 4 such a choice would lead to windows that have both underused and congestion in the same window, something that the introduction of time windows exactly tries to reduce!

5. A LARGE SCALE DEPLOYMENT: THE LA EXPRESS PARK PROJECT

The methods described in this paper are used in a large scale deployment in downtown Los Angeles in the LA Express Park project [2]. The goals of this $18.5 million federally funded project are: 1) to increase the availability of on-street parking; 2) to reduce traffic congestion and pollution and 3) to encourage a shift in travel choices. By applying the principles of demand-based parking pricing, the Los Angeles Department of Transportation (LADOT) sought to improve the distribution of parking so that ten to thirty percent of the on-street spaces on each block would be available most of the time.

Prior to LA Express Park, many block clusters had no available on-street parking spaces while others remained practically empty. Increasing the parking prices in high demand areas and lowering the prices in low demand areas shifted demand to yield a better distribution of parking within small geographic areas.

5.1 A Dedicated Sensor Infrastructure

The project depends upon the integration of new wirelessly communicating parking meters, real-time parking guidance systems (in the form of smartphone apps) and in particular upon on-street vehicle sensors that have been installed specifically for the project.

Vehicle sensors were installed in the paving for each of the 6,300 on-street parking spaces in the project area. The spaces are represented as dots in Figure 8. Measurements are based on a magnetometer. The sensors are battery operated and communicate through a wireless mesh network. A sensor provides the occupancy status of a space in real time. The real time data stream provides entries of the form ⟨Space ID, Timestamp, [Arrival, Departure, Unknown]⟩. The "Unknown" label is emitted if the sensor auto-detects that it cannot reliably determine the occupancy status. This can be due to several causes, among them interference and communication problems. It is particularly important to correct for these sensor inaccuracies, since ignoring data, or simply treating gaps to be missing at random might lead to biased estimates [11].

The sensors in the current generation have a lifetime of around three years. The sensor technology is progressing very rapidly with many manufactures supplying systems. To benefit from these rapid improvements it is important for a demand management system that it can work with any underlying sensor methodology and can automatically learn its specific failure characteristics from data. By learning the demand and noise model jointly this can be done with reasonable accuracy without detailed knowledge of the local interference sources, or the physics of the sensor [11].

The parking meters operate wirelessly as well and provide payment data. There is not a one-to-one mapping between parking and payment events due to multiple payments in one parking session ("topping up the meter"), and motorists that make use of money that is left in the meter when they arrive, and parkers that do not pay. We define *non-paying customers* to be those motorists that do not make a single payment during their stay. This concept is important because in California motorists with a reduced mobility that have a special permit can park at any space for free for an unlimited duration. In practice we see that in the very busy parts of downtown LA it is common to see over 90% of the spaces to be taken by non-paying customers. See also Section 6.2.

After correcting for sensor failures and combining with the payment data, the datasets can be processed off-line to yield entries of the form ⟨Space ID, Arrival Time, Duration, [Paying, Non-Paying]⟩.

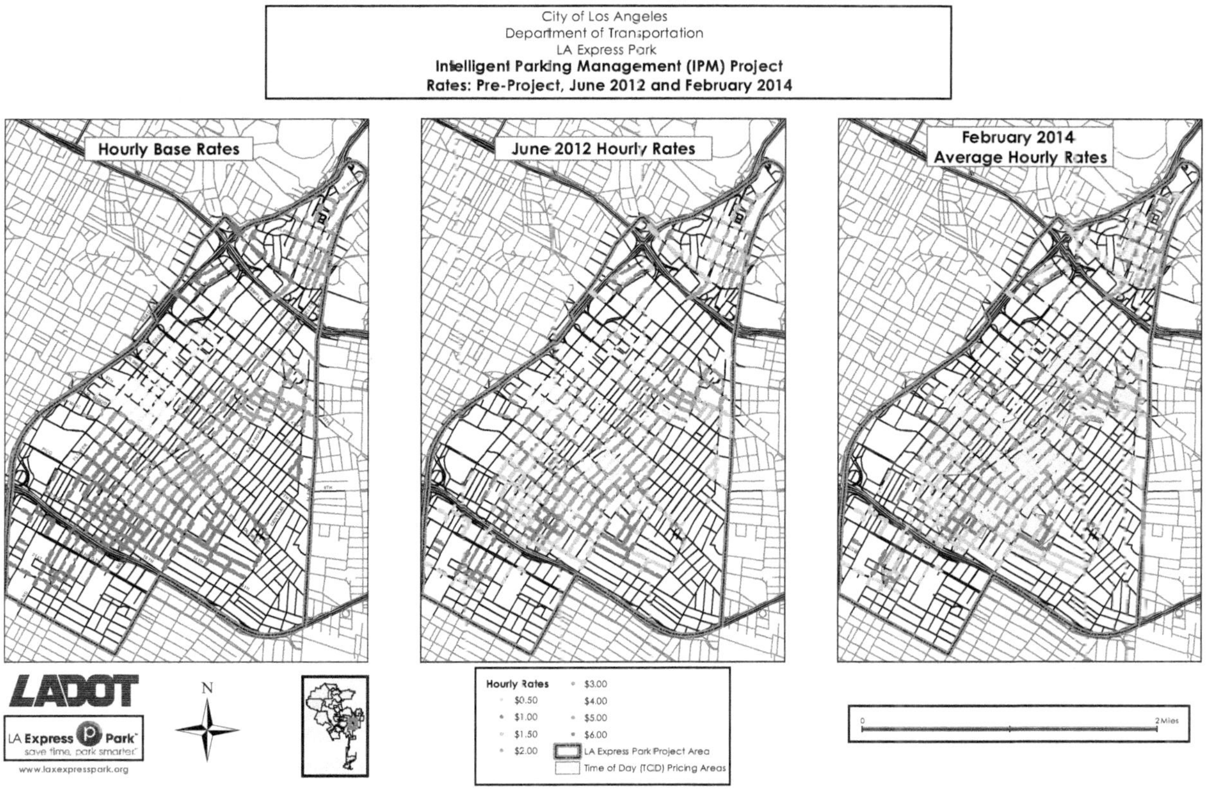

Figure 8: LA Express Park project area with pre-project rates (left) rates after the first change (middle), and rates at time of writing.

There is a large variability both in space and time, but on average a space sees close to 24 parking events per day. So with 6300 sensors and over 600 days of data our dataset consists of nearly 100 million parking events.

6. A CLOSER LOOK AT PARKING DATA

In the previous sections, we have discussed the foundations of the pricing engine: the congestion-underuse balance and its extension to time of day pricing. Parking data can be examined with different approaches:

- with simplistic raw occupancy fraction statistics;
- using arrival duration patterns for a given block-face;
- with temporal methods, assessing effects from the time of day, season, and (regular) events.

In the following sections, patterns of occupancy and arrival durations will be illustrated with block-faces from the pilot area. We then will discuss a first analysis of rate changes as reported by LADOT in [2]. We refer the interested reader to the forthcoming second report by LADOT [3] for a further analysis.

6.1 Occupancy

Figure 9 shows a year's worth of occupancy data for the 12 spaces at 701 South Olive Street in a colormap, sometimes also referred to as a "Jerry Garcia plot". Each row represents a weekday, so that from top to bottom Monday follows Tuesday and so on, with Saturday and Sunday omitted to ensure that the often different demand in the weekend does not hinder the study of the regular weekday patterns. The x-axis represents the minute of the day starting from midnight on the left, to midday in the middle, to midnight at the right. Every pixel color codes the fraction of spaces that are occupied. Blue tones represent occupancies less than 70%, green tones 70%- 90%, and red tones more than 90%. The horizontal gray lines represent policy changes. Plots like these provide a wealth of insight, we focus here on the impact of rate changes. If the change in rate is sufficiently high the change in behavior can be drastic. After the extension of operating hours from 6 p.m. to 8 p.m. in June 2012, we see a drastic change in occupancy patterns from red (congested) to blue and green (low and perfect utilization). This is a clear example that confirms the hypothesis that behavior can be changed by adjusting parking rates. We see the biggest changes in examples like these, where flat rates are maintained and operating hours are extended. The majority of rate changes are $1 up or down which leads to more subtle changes as presented in Section 6.3.

6.2 Arrival-Duration Patterns

The occupancy plots are interesting to study because they demonstrate when and where there is parking congestion

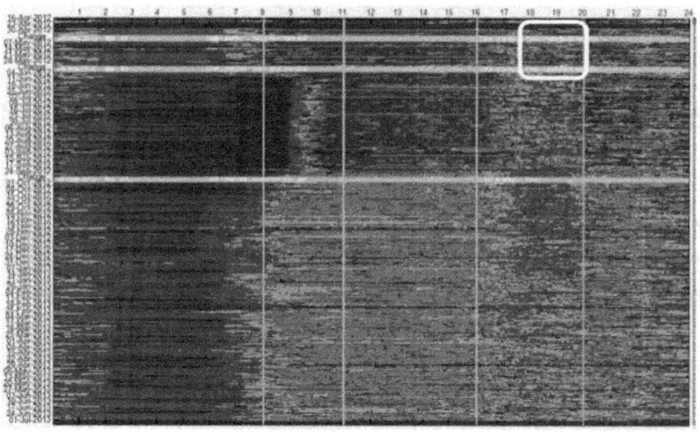

Figure 9: Occupancy data for the 12 spaces at 701 South Olive Street over a year. See text for details.

and motorists are potentially forced to circle to look for parking.

An important complementary view is one that studies arrival and duration patterns. This gives insight in how a block is used and how that use changes after a rate change. Even if occupancy stays the same, the use of the scarce resources can be improved. If for instance in front of a shop long-staying office worker is replaced by short-staying shoppers this increases the efficiency of use: one long stayer walks more, while many short stayers walk less and provide extra custom for local shops. Such a change is not directly observable in occupancy statistics.

Figure 10 shows a 2D histogram of arrival duration data for weekdays during the first year of the project on 201 North Freemont Avenue. Counts are shown in log-space (with a small offset to avoid zeros) for ease of interpretation. This example shows the significant group that arrives around 7 a.m. and parks for around 9 hours. This is longer than the 2 hour time-limit for this block. A study of the payment data confirms that this is a group of non-paying customers as defined in Section 5.1. This is a group that will not change behaviour after a change in rates.

Figure 11 shows for the same block-face and data the average occupancy, and what fractions are contributed by people that park less than 15 minutes, between 15-30 minutes, and so on. This plot shows that the long staying parkers form a significant contribution of the occupancy all throughout the day.

6.3 Analyzing Rate Changes

At the start of the project, enforcement hours (the hours during which parking needs to be paid for) were extended from 6 p.m. to 8 p.m. where there was sufficient demand. Time limits were extended from one hour to two or four hours based on the predominant use of the block.

Based on the algorithm described in Section 3.2 a major rate change was implemented on the first Monday in June 2012 impacting all blocks in the pilot area for which the sensors were successfully installed. Subsequently, rates were updated on every first Monday of the month. City officers used data of special permit use and detailed understanding of the local areas to phase the updates. For every iteration the city officials determined for which areas the recommen-

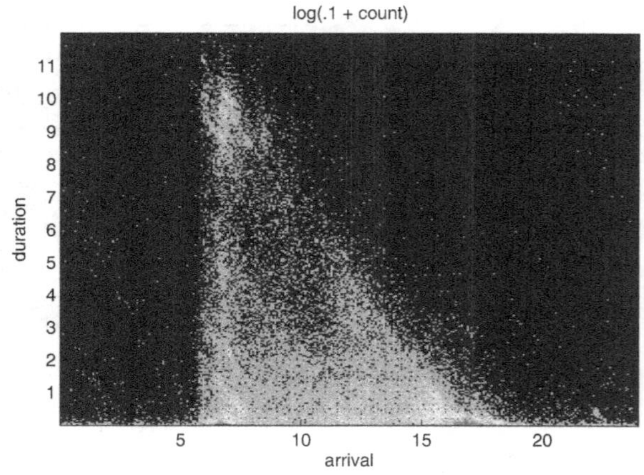

Figure 10: A 2D histogram for arrival duration patterns for 201 North Freemont Avenue. Counts are shown in logs for ease of interpretation. Note the cluster of parkers that arrive around 7 a.m. and stay for around 9 hours.

dations of the pricing engine were put into effect, and which areas "skipped a beat" to wait for more data.

For instance, Time-of-Day (ToD) pricing was introduced in the beginning of August 2012 in two areas of pilot zones (Chinatown, and Fashion District). Then, ToD was progressively applied to other parts of the project area. As of January 2014, there have been a total of nine changes.

Initial results of the first rate change have been reported in [2]. In more cases did demand patterns suggest the rates to go down than to go up (39% of blocks saw a rate decrease, 14% a rate increase), the biggest effect of rate increases in congested areas was around 7pm with a reduction in occupancy of 15%, and the biggest effect of a decrease in rate at 1pm with an average increase of occupancy of 10%.

The absolute numbers are shown for all times of day in Figure 12. We see that a rate reduction seems to effectively draw back parkers in underused areas throughout the day (8am-6pm). Increasing rates leads to a reduction in demand throughout the period 8am-6pm, but the change is subtle. The big effects are in the period from 6pm-8pm. This can be explained from the fact that in several blocks the operating hours were extended from 6pm to 8pm. The two additional hours followed the rate already in use during the day. In many places this meant an increase from 0 to 3 sometimes 4$/hr. This is a strong positive answer to the question "Can rates influence behavior?". An example of this effect was presented in Section 6.1.

6.4 Further Analysis

In the previous sections we have shown examples of the data visualization tools that can be used, and highlighted some of the insights they can give. The first analysis of the impact towards the project goals have been reported by LADOT in [2]. We refer the interested reader to the second report in [3].

In this section we would like to highlight some aspects of this forthcoming work and discuss some of the challenges and lessons learned in the analysis.

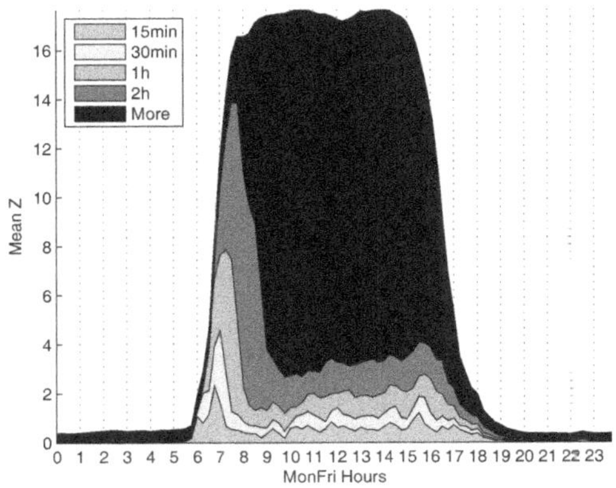

Figure 11: Average occupancy (Z) and contributions of different length parking events as a function of the time of the day. This plot shows 201 North Freemont Avenue and shows that the early arriving and long staying non-paying parkers seen in Figure 10 block a significant portion of the available spaces.

Figure 13 shows the weekly average of B_{cu} for all blocks of the project area and weeks. This is shown as a matrix where rows are block index and columns weeks. The weekly average of B_{cu} is then color coded. The bottom plot of Figure 13 displays a discretized view of the same data, where blue indicates underused (B_{cu} < -1/3), green means "just-right" or as much congested as underused ($-1/3 \leq B_{cu} < 1/3$), red means congested most of the times ($B_{cu} > 1/3$).

Overall, these plots suggests a decrease in underutilization (blue is less frequent on the right part of the matrix) with a relatively less marked increase in congestion. In addition, it is interesting to mention the seasonality effects. Near weeks 30 and 80, there are visible decrease due to Christmas. Similarly, just before these Christmas events, a less marked effect correspond to Thanksgiving.

There are several lessons we have learned while doing the analysis:

- It is important to report on weekdays and weekends independently. Parkers inherently change their behavior during the week.

- Sensors are susceptible to noise. Both in known and unknown ways. It is important that this is carefully treated to avoid biases.

- Special permit use makes that demand based pricing can only have little impact in significant parts of the project, because the main source of congestion comes from parkers that do not need to pay.

- Events such as the opening or closing of schools, seasonal effects from holidays and overall macro-economic shifts have big impacts. Empirically of at least the same order of a 1$/hr rate change. This means that when a before/after change is observed a further analysis needs to ensure that this is not due to an exogenous effect.

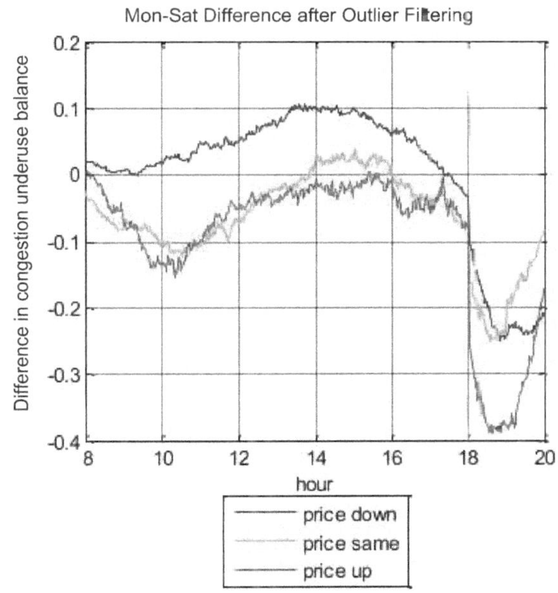

Figure 12: Difference of average B_{cu} before the first rate change (April 1 – June 4, 2012) minus average B_{cu} after rate change (June 4 – Aug 1, 2014).

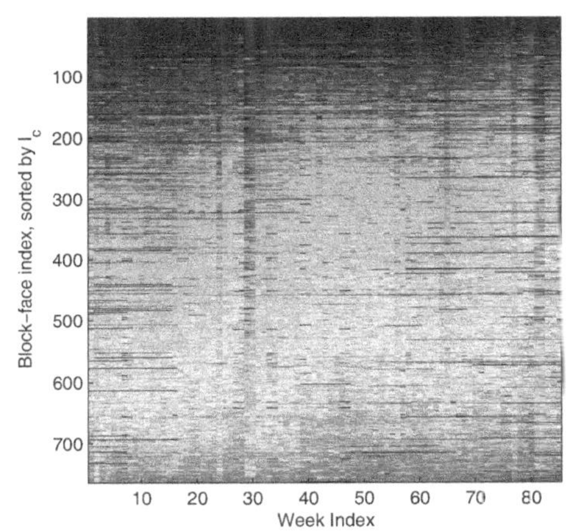

Figure 13: Weekly average of B_{cu} normalized by capacity. Week 1 starts June 4th, 2014.

- Not only the change in occupancy is of importance, but also the change in arrival duration patterns and the fraction of paying customers.

- It is important to understand overflow patterns to off-street and cheaper neighbouring alternatives.

7. DISCUSSION

New sensor technologies and learning algorithms make many new systems possible that can improve city mobility and reduce pollution. The LA Express Park project is a large scale (over 6000 spaces in over 800 blocks), multi-year project that provides a large scale implementation that tests the demand management principles set forth by Vickrey [9] and uses the iteration scheme presented in this paper.

Projects such as these do not only face technological challenges. In fact the political, and organizational challenges are at least as big, and pose important constraints on the type of methods that can be deployed. For instance the methods need to be simple to understand, easily seen to be fair, and lead to pricing policies that are easy for drivers to remember and to act upon. We have experienced that it is hard to elicit these constraints explicitly and any method needs to stand up to many different reasonable definitions of these constraints.

The demand based pricing solution deployed in LA keeps rates at simple to understand discrete values: ($0.5, $1, $1.5, $2, $3, ..., $6). Where demand patterns suggest it is best to charge different rates at different parts of the day, these periods are the same throughout downtown LA. Rates are increased only if congestion is a serious problem, and underuse is not.

Our iteration scheme is based on the fraction of time a block was congested and the fraction of the time it was underused. This "average utility" approach overcomes the basic problem of the "utility of the average" approach proposed earlier. In this method changes are based on average occupancies and can lead to obvious problems: an underused morning and a congested afternoon can lead to an average that is "just-right" even though at no point in the day the parking situation was considered to be so. We see in particular a difference between the two techniques when they are used to select time-of-day windows in a data-driven way. The average occupancy method leads to periods in the day that often exhibit both underuse *and* congestion, something that the idea of charging different rates for different times of the day expressly tries to avoid.

We have not yet seen a reason to change the simple pricing iteration. However, it can be argued that the iteration has not been tested to the fullest due to limits on the rates set by the city council. For the initial year the rates were allowed to increase or decrease by 50% from their starting values. With the pricing ladder used that meant one or at most two opportunities to inrease or decrease rates. When a larger ordinance allows more steps it might be necessary to extend the method to explicitly avoid oscillations between two rates that are nearly equally good. An obvious fix could be to keep longer periods between rate changes if such problems are detected.

Several worthwhile refinements to the basic iteration exist. An important one is to weight the occupancy status by traffic density when computing the congestion and underuse indexes. This requires accurate traffic measurements.

There are ample directions for future work. From a practical point of view, information provision can be improved. Surveys and field studies confirm our hypothesis that an understanding of drivers is a bottleneck [4]. For people to change their behavior they need to care and *know* about discounts. The aim of the techniques presented here is to be in the near future fully integrated with turn-by-turn navigation and reservation systems. Once the construction of a shortlist of options (e.g. closest, cheapest, best matched to preferences) is done by a device, the pricing systems will be more effective, and can also use more complicated rules.

To increase the impact it will also be beneficial to change the way special parking permits work. Currently motorists with a reduced mobility are allowed unlimited free parking in all on-street parking spaces. Empirically this leads to all-day use by a single car for a very high fraction of congested downtown areas. Hence for an important part of the project area smart pricing has a significantly reduced effect.

A careful and complete analysis of parking changes is a complex and challenging task as outlined in Section 6.4. The LA Department of Transportation has reported on the initial impact of the project in [2] and will report on the latest outcomes in [3].

Constructing models that describe parking behavior is an interesting challenge. In contrast to traffic flows on highways, the modeling of parking has received little attention. This is partly because data has never been available, but also because many more environment variables need to be understood and measured. Examples of such variables include the availability and price of off-street alternatives, the number of office spaces and shops in the neighborhood, and the presence of special events. A full understanding of parking behavior is useful in many applications. In the pricing problem studied here it can for instance help to anticipate the effect of changing the rates in neighboring blocks.

8. REFERENCES

[1] S. Chawla, J. D. Hartline, D. L. Malec, and B. Sivan. Multi-parameter mechanism design and sequential posted pricing. In *STOC '10*, pages 311–320, 2010.

[2] P. Ghent, D. Mitchell, and A. Sedadi. LA Express Park - curbing downtown congestion through intelligent parking management. In *Proceedings of ITS World Congress*, 2012.

[3] P. Ghent, A. Pudlin, E. Cardenas, S. Clinchant, C. Dance, and O. Zoeter. LA Express Park - Curbing downtown congestion through intelligent parking management. In *Proceedings of ITS World Congress*, 2014.

[4] J. Glasnapp, H. Du, C. Dance, S. Clinchant, A. Pudlin, D. Mitchell, and O. Zoeter. Understanding dynamic pricing for parking in Los Angeles: Survey and ethnographic results. In *HCI International*, 2014.

[5] R. Meir, Y. Chen, and M. Feldman. Efficient parking allocation as online bipartite matching with posted prices. In *Proceedings of AAMAS*, 2013.

[6] R. Myerson. Optimal auction design. *Mathematics of Operations Research*, pages 58–73, 1981.

[7] H. Robbins and S. Monro. A stochastic approximation method. *The Annals of Mathematical Statistics*, 22(3):400–407, 1951.

[8] D. Shoup. *The High Cost of Free Parking*. APA Planners Press, 2005.

[9] W. Vickrey. The economizing of curb parking space. In *Traffic Engineering Magazine*, 1954. Reprinted in Journal of Urban Economics 36, (1994), 56–65.

[10] W. Vickrey. Counterspeculation, auctions, and competitive sealed tenders. *The Journal of Finance*, 16(1):8–37, 1961.

[11] O. Zoeter, C. Dance, M. Grbovic, S. Guo, and G. Bouchard. A general noise resolution model for parking occupancy sensors. In *Proceedings of ITS World Congress*, 2012.

Reducing Gang Violence Through Network Influence Based Targeting of Social Programs

Paulo Shakarian
Arizona State University
Tempe, AZ 85281
pshakari@asu.edu

Joseph Salmento and William Pulleyblank
Network Science Center
U.S. Military Academy
West Point, NY 10996
joseph.salmento@usma.edu
william.pulleyblank@usma.edu

John Bertetto
Chicago Police Dept.
Chicago, IL 60653
john.bertetto@chicagopolice.org

ABSTRACT

In this paper, we study a variant of the social network maximum influence problem and its application to intelligently approaching individual gang members with incentives to leave a gang. The goal is to identify individuals who when influenced to leave gangs will propagate this action. We study this emerging application by exploring specific facets of the problem that must be addressed when modeling this particular situation. We formulate a new influence maximization variant - the "social incentive influence" (SII) problem and study it both formally and in the context of the law-enforcement domain. Using new techniques from unconstrained submodular maximization, we develop an approximation algorithm for SII and present a suite of experimental results - including tests on real-world police data from Chicago.

Categories and Subject Descriptors

Applied Computing [**Law, social and behavioral sciences**]: Sociology

General Terms

Algorithms, Experimentation

Keywords

complex networks, network diffusion, propagation in networks

1. INTRODUCTION

Violent street gangs are a major cause of criminal activity in the United States [2, 5]. A recent trend has been toward development of "smart policing" tactics to reduce the effectiveness of these gangs. Typically, these strategies have focused on the allocation of law enforcement resources to increase arrests and deter criminal behavior. In this paper we focus on a use of "smart policing" in a different manner: we wish to intelligently target individual gang members with incentives to leave a gang. While "pulling levers" or encouraging dis-enrollment from a gang, is already a tactic employed in cities such as Boston and Chicago, the selection of which specific gang members to focus on is still largely unanswered - and hence currently based on ad-hoc methods. In this paper, we study this emerging application as a variant of a social network influence maximization problem [14] that we refer to as the "social incentive influence" (SII) problem. We study this problem both formally and in the context of law enforcement. Then, using new techniques from unconstrained submodular maximization [7], we develop an approximation algorithm for SII and present a suite of experimental results - including tests on real-world police data.

The paper is organized as follows. In Section 2 we discuss some current methods in law-enforcement used for social program targeting. In Section 3 we introduce the SII problem an associated technical preliminaries. This is followed by a discussion of our algorithmic approach in Section 4 and associated experimental results in Section 5. Finally, we discuss related work in the literature in Section 6.

KDD'14, August 24–27, 2014, New York, NY, USA.

http //dx.doi.org/10.1145/2623330.2623331.

2. BACKGROUND

Recent successes with so called "pulling levers" (gang membership dis-enrollment) approaches to deterring violence include the Boston Gun Project and Operation CeaseFire as well as Project Safe Neighborhoods in Chicago, and continue with the on-going Group Violence Reduction Strategy in Chicago. Using this approach, law enforcement partners work with social service providers and victims advocacy groups to attempt to abate gang violence by 'pulling' whatever 'levers' need to be applied to street gangs. The types of levers applied, and the degree to which they are employed, depend upon the particular gang. Adjustments are made so that the application is both customized to the specific situation and, hopefully, more successful.

To facilitate these interactions between law enforcement, social service providers, victim's advocacy groups, and street gang members, two approaches are commonly employed. In the case of the first, law enforcement engages known street gang members on the street as part of regular patrol activities. While performed under the auspices of focused deterrence, this type of interaction is likely to have the least impact. Time spent with the gang member may be limited, the remaining levers (social service providers, victims groups, etc.) are absent so that the message conveyed to the street gang member is incomplete or biased toward criminal enforcement aspect. Moreover, the selection of target gang members is often random – the result of opportunity as the gang member is seen on the street.

In the second approach, gang members are subjected to a "call-in." The call-in sessions are prearranged meetings organized by law enforcement, social service providers, and victims groups during which messages of non-violence are conveyed. The call-in is a full-spectrum effort: law enforcement makes clear to attendees that further violence will be met with relentless police operations and enforcement efforts, social service providers offer information on how members can exit the street gang and obtain educational and vocational training, and victims groups tell stories of loss in an effort to make an emotional plea for violence cessation.

Attendees for call-in sessions are typically chosen in two ways: compulsory attendance and invitation. Gang members currently on probation or parole are compelled to attend. The remaining attendees are invitees, and it is here where the selection criteria may become a bit vague. Invitees may be selected via some form of social network analysis (as in [5]) however such concerted efforts are not entirely relied upon. Often, a large amount of discretion is afforded local law enforcement in selecting invitees. This allows for local gang experts and command staff members to identify those gang members whom they know or suspect to be influential or key members of the gang and invite them to the call-in. This can be a very successful process if the agency has access to these experts or knowledge of the gang's organizational structure. However, there is no guarantee that those persons invited are, in fact, genuinely influential in the gang or are just the "most well known to law enforcement" members of the gang. In law enforcement, where financial, personnel, and time resources are increasingly constrained, turning a more objective and analytical eye toward invitee selection grows more important.

A key aim of gang dis-enrollment programs is to enable law enforcement to invite to call-ins those gang members who, should the efforts to dis-enroll them be successful, are most likely to pull additional gang members out with them. However, there is a key challenge: are influential members also easy to encourage to leave the gang? A recent empirical study exploring non-criminal online social networks suggests that highly influential individuals are typically not susceptible [1]. However, we argue that taking both influence and susceptibility into account are necessary; identifying individuals (or groups of individuals) that possess both qualities is needed for the behavior to spread.

Though, to the best of our knowledge, influence maximization techniques have not been applied to law enforcement before, there is some anecdotal evidence that such approaches could bear fruit. For instance, there have been cases where gang members thought to be "influential" successfully convinced others to dis-enroll from the gang. In one case, in Chicago (in the summer of 20130, the district personnel (local plainclothes gang officers) knew this person to be an influential and as such targeted him for intervention. When he was contacted he indicated that he had already gotten a job, but knew several fellow gang members who could use the offered social services and dis-enrollment opportunities. He personally contacted 20 fellow gang members, of which 7 walked into the local social services facility.

In this paper we frame the problem of "pulling levers" formally as a variant of the social network maximum influence problem [14] in what we call the "social incentive influence" (SII) problem. However, there are some key nuances of the "pulling levers" strategy that we integrated into our framework that are not inherently considered in the maximum influence problem. We list these items here and address our technical approach to each in the next section.

1. **Duration of the diffusion process.** One key difference SII has from other maximum influence formulations is the length of time it takes for the diffusion process to occur. The reason for this is that gang dis-enrollment is a major life decision for an individual, hence the spread of this idea will likely take time. Further complicating the matter is that there may be changes to social network structure while the diffusion process occurs - based on events such as arrests, homicides, gang conflict and cooperation, etc.

2. **Interaction with the population during the diffusion process.** Not only does the diffusion process take time to occur in this domain, but also the law enforcement personnel will often make multiple attempts to "pull levers" as the diffusion occurs.

3. **Geographic locations and strength of connections.** Often, law enforcement data has an inherent geospatial component. In this work, we leverage this information to inform the strength of connections in the social network - as the street gangs are also inherently territorial.

4. **Notion of cost.** Cost also becomes an important factor in SII as the law enforcement personnel are attempting to encourage a major change in the life of the gang members. Conducting a call-in session with certain members costs time, money, and other resources. We also note that not all gang members will be equally susceptible to this type of intervention - some may require more or less effort to dis-enroll. Further, there are real costs associated with encouraging dis-enrollment. For example, in North Carolina personalized letters are created for the gang members that show the individual how his association with others involved in violence puts him or her at risk. A similar tactic is used in Chicago, where the letters are often delivered to the homes of the gang members. This utilizes police manpower and resources hence further increasing the cost.

5. **Pro t maximization.** As we consider cost, we also model "benefit" in SII - which is the value of each expected infectee to the diffusion process. This allows us to adopt a profit-maximizing model (similar to the ProMax problem of [15]) where we look to maximize the expected benefit minus the cost.

3. TECHNICAL PRELIMINARIES AND ANALYSIS

Throughout this paper we assume the existence of a *social network* $G = (V, E)$ where V is a set of vertices and E is a set of directed edges. We let n and m denote the cardinality of V and E respectively. For any node $v \in V$, the set of incoming neighbors is η_v^{in}, and the set of outgoing neighbors is η_v^{out}. The cardinalities of these sets (and hence the in- and out-degrees of node v) are denoted by k_v^{in}, k_v^{out} respectively. For each node v, we assume a cost of marketing to that node denoted by $c_v \in \Re^+$. We let C denote the vector of costs indexed by V. We let $\langle c \rangle$ denote the average cost $\sum_v c_v/n$. We also assume a benefit value, $b \in \Re^+$, which is the associated benefit for having marketed to a given node.

We assume that each node in G has an associated geolocation and there exists a distance function $d : V \times V \to \Re^+$ that meets the normal axioms: $d(u, u) = 0$, $d(u, v) = d(v, u)$, and $d(u, w) \leq d(u, v) + d(v, w)$.

Using this distance function, we shall assume a level of influence p_{uv} for each edge $(u, v) \in E$ that we define using an exponential distance-decay model [23, 16, 22] as follows:

$$p_{uv} = e^{-(d(u,v)/\gamma)^r}$$

where γ, r are parameters in the interval $(0, \infty)$ and e is the base of the natural logarithm. The parameter γ is used as a scaling parameter - and we shall set it to be the average distance between two nodes connected with an edge. The parameter r controls the shape of the distance decay curve, and we shall typically use $r = 2$. The use of the distance decay function as a proxy for influence is the primary way we address the geographic nature of the law-enforcement data in this application.

Diffusion Process. A key property that we utilize in our study is submodularity, which we review below:

DEFINITION 3.1 (SUBMODULARITY). *Function $f : 2^U \to \Re^+$ is* ***submodular*** *if for every $A \subseteq B \subseteq U$ and $u \in U$: $f(A \cup \{u\}) - f(A) \geq f(B \cup \{u\}) - f(B)$.*

Intuitively, the idea of submodularity represents a notion of diminishing returns: adding an element u to a set B can provide no greater benefit than that gained by adding it to any proper subset of B.

Equivalently, function $f : 2^U \to \Re^+$ is submodular if for every $A, B \subseteq U$, $f(A) - f(B) \geq f(A \cup B) + f(A \cap B)$.

A set function is *supermodular* if its negation is submodular.

Next, we define a diffusion process function (*dpf*) which accepts an initial set of vertices (called the "seed set") and returns the expected number of infectees once the diffusion process completes. In this paper, we shall require this function to be sub-modular and normalized. We provide a formal definition below.

DEFINITION 3.2 (DIFFUSION PROCESS FUNCTION). *A diffusion process function, dpf : $2^V \to [0, n]$, is any function such that: (1.) $dpf(\emptyset) = 0$ and (2.) $\forall V_1, V_2 \subseteq V$: $dpf(V_1) + dpf(V_2) \geq dpf(V_1 \cup V_2) + dpf(V_1 \cap V_2)$.*

We argue that, in general, these are reasonable restrictions. For instance, the σ function of the independent cascade and linear threshold models [14], the oracle of the MIA model [11], and the value function of the logic-programming framework of [20] are all valid diffusion process functions. We also note that these previous studies focused only on maximizing the number of expected infectees (subject to a cardinality constraint). In this work, we disregard the cardinality constraint and instead seek to maximize profit, which we formally define below.

DEFINITION 3.3 (PROFIT). *Profit, pft : $2^V \to \Re$ is defined by $pft(X) = b \times dpf(X) - \sum_{v \in X} c_v$*

The SII Problem. We now have all components necessary to formally define the social incentive influence (SII) problem:

DEFINITION 3.4 (SII PROBLEM). *We are given diffusion process function dpf, social network $G = (V, E)$, cost vector C and benefit value b. Find $SII(dpf, G, C, b) = V^* \subseteq V$ such that $pft(V^*) \geq pft(V')$ for all $V' \subseteq V$.*

Not surprisingly, the social incentive influence problem is NP-hard.

THEOREM 3.1. *SII is NP-hard.*

PROOF. We show NP-hardness by reducing SIMPLE MAX CUT [13] to SII. The SIMPLE MAX CUT problem takes as input a graph $G = (V, E)$ and returns sets $V_1, V_2 \subseteq V$ such that $|\{(u, v) \in E : u \in V_1, v \in V_2\}|$ is maximized. The following construction can be performed in polynomial time. Let $dpf(X) = \sum_{v \in X} f_v(X)$ where $f_v(X) = 1$ if $v \in X$ and $|\eta_v^{in} \cap X|$ otherwise. Note that $dpf(\emptyset) = 0$ and, because each f_v is submodular, dpf is submodular. For each v set $c_v = 1$ and set $b = 1$. Then $pft(X) = \sum_{v \in V \setminus X} : \eta_v^{in} \cap X| = |\{(u, v) \in E | u \in X, v \in V \setminus X\}|$. Hence pft becomes equivalent to the objective function for SIMPLE MAX CUT. □

However, note that our profit function pft is submodular.

PROPOSITION 3.1. *pft is submodular.*

PROOF. It is well known that subtracting a supermodular function from a submodular function yields a submodular function. Since dpf is submodular (and b is positive) and the sum of costs is supermodular, the proposition follows. □

One-Step Diffusion. As stated earlier, two key challenges in this domain are the duration of the diffusion process and the effect of the law-enforcement personnel interacting during the diffusion process. This has led us to model the diffusion process as a "one-step" influence model where we only consider the immediate effect of the diffusion process one time step in the future. Our envisioned use case is that the law-enforcement analysts will use the most current data available to make a decision as to which gang members to reach-out to based on this model. Attempts will be made to influence those individuals, after which changes to the social network (both resulting the outreach and other external factors) will be incorporated before repeating the cycle. Because we expect the time for diffusion to generally take longer, the repetition of the cycle will generally occur after about one time period. We formally define the following"one-step" influence model.

DEFINITION 3.5. *The* ***one-step diffusion model***, *$\sigma_1 : 2^V \to \Re^+$ is defined as follows:*

$$\sigma_1(V') = \sum_{u \in V} \Big(1 - \prod_{u \in \eta_v^{in} \cap V'} (1 - p_{uv})\Big)$$

Note that we also assume that a node v is infected by a node u independently of which others of its incoming neighbors were previously infected. An easy proof shows that σ_1 is a valid diffusion process function.

PROPOSITION 3.2. *σ_1 is a valid diffusion process.*

PROOF. Clearly, $\sigma_1(\emptyset) = 0$ by inspection. Next, we show that the quantity $\prod_{u\in\eta_v^{in}\cap V'}(1-p_{uv})$ is supermodular. Suppose, by way of contradiction, that it is not, then we have for V' and nodes $q, r \notin V'$ the following for each $v \in V$:

$$\prod_{u\in\eta_v^{in}\cap(V'\cup\{q,r\})}(1-p_{uv}) - \prod_{u\in\eta_v^{in}\cap(V'\cup\{r\})}(1-p_{uv}) < \prod_{u\in\eta_v^{in}\cap(V'\cup\{q\})}(1-p_{uv}) - \prod_{u\in\eta_v^{in}\cap V'}(1-p_{uv})$$

Let us assume that q, r are both neighbors of v (the other cases cause both sides to be equal). This gives us the following:

$$(1-p_{rv})\Big(\prod_{u\in\eta_v^{in}\cap(V'\cup\{q\})}(1-p_{uv}) - \prod_{u\in\eta_v^{in}\cap V'}(1-p_{uv})\Big) < \prod_{u\in\eta_v^{in}\cap(V'\cup\{q\})}(1-p_{uv}) - \prod_{u\in\eta_v^{in}\cap V'}(1-p_{uv})$$

As $\prod_{u\in\eta_v^{in}\cap(V'\cup\{q\})}(1-p_{uv}) \leq \prod_{u\in\eta_v^{in}\cap V'}(1-p_{uv})$, we have $1 < 1 - p_{rv}$ which is clearly a contradiction. Note that the supermodularity of this quantity implies the submodularity of $1-\prod_{u\in\eta_v^{in}\cap V'}(1-p_{uv})$. The rest of the statement follows from the fact that σ_1 is a positive linear combination of submodular functions. □

We note that we can cause nodes in the argument of this function to be assigned a probability of 1.0 by simply adding self-directed edges to each node in the network. We also note, that with many diffusion processes functions, the calculation of their outcome may yield an individual probability of activation for each node. Further, the one-step model also allows for the consideration of benefit as a vector - the probability for each node can obtained by inspecting the inner summation - this allows for a more customized setting of benefit on basis of each node (we are currently discussing this as a possibility with our law enforcement partners). In this case, we can identify a specific benefit for each node. The framework can be easily adapted for such a case.

4. APPROACH

While the submodularity of the *pft* function is encouraging, we note that because marketing to each node incurs an associated cost, it is possible to experience a loss by marketing to additional nodes. For instance, if we market to an additional individual who provides us no increase in the diffusion process, this reduces our profit and could lead to a loss. This is not considered in previous diffusion models designed to maximize the expected number of infectees. Hence, the greedy approximation of [17] no longer provides us an approximation guarantee. Our case can instead be viewed as an "unconstrained" submodualr function. Recently, a deterministic approximation algorithm was introduced in [7] that requires only a linear number of evaluations of the function. We recall their algorithm here (adapted for SII).

For positive, unconstrained submodular maximization, [7] proves that SII-Approx provides a result that is at least 1/3

Algorithm 1 SII-Approx[7]

INPUT: Social network $G = (V, E)$, cost vector C, benefit b, distance function d.
OUTPUT: Approximation V' to SII.

```
V' = ∅, V'' = V
for v ∈ V do
    a = pft(V' ∪ {v}) − pft(V')
    b = pft(V'' \ {v}) − pft(V'')
    if a ≥ b then
        V' = V' ∪ {v}
    else
        V'' = V'' \ {v}
    end if
end for
return V'.
```

of optimal. Note that *pft* can potentially provide a solution with negative value. However, we can leverage their results to provide the following approximation guarantee:

COROLLARY 4.1. *Given V_{ALG} as returned by SII-Approx for an instance of SII and optimal soluition V_{OPT} we have the following relationship:*

$$\frac{pft(V_{OPT})}{3} - \frac{n}{3}(\langle c\rangle - b) \leq pft(V_{ALG})$$

PROOF. In the proof of Theorem I.1 of [7], the authors show that $pft(V_{OPT}) \leq 3pft(V_{ALG}) - pft(\emptyset) - pft(V)$. We note that, by definition, $pft(\emptyset) = 0$ and $pft(V) = bn - \langle c\rangle n = -n(c-b)$, which gives the result. □

Note that if $\langle c\rangle \leq b$ then we recover the 1/3 approximation of [7].

5. EXPERIMENTAL RESULTS

All experiments were run on a computer equipped with an Intel X5677 Xeon Processor operating at 3.46 GHz with a 12 MB Cache and 288 GB of physical memory under the Red Hat Enterprise Linux version 6.1 operating system. Only one core was used for experiments. Our implementation of SII-Approx was written in Python 2.7 using the NetworkX library[1].

Police Dataset. We used a dataset consisting of arrest records of individuals from March 2010 - March 2013 in a single police district in Chicago. This data set included arrest location and relationships among the individuals. From this data, we were able to construct a social network ("arrest network") consisting of 1836 nodes and 2531 edges. Two individuals in the arrest network are connected if they were arrested together. We note that this is likely an incomplete picture of the full network, but as we move to deployment of this approach by integrating it with our GANG/ORCA analysis software [18], law enforcement personnel can easily supplement or replace an arrest network with information from additional intelligence sources, obersvations by police patrolmen, and data from correctional facilities.

Additionally, for some experiments we also generated simulated networks to supplement our analysis.

[1] http://networkx.github.io/

Dataset	Num. Sams.	Avg. Size	Min. Appx.	Max. Appx.	Avg. Appx.	Std. Dev.
Police	20	13.55	0.70	1.00	0.92	0.09
Compl.	2	22.5	1.00	1.00	1.00	0.00
E-R	9	20	0.84	1.00	0.93	0.05
SF	27	20	0.80	1.00	0.98	0.06
FF	1	15	1.00	1.00	1.00	0.00

Table 1: Empirically Determined Approximation Ratios for SII-Approx (when compared to the optimal solution)

Comparison with Optimal Solution. Our first test was to evaluate SII-Approx compared to an optimal solution found by enumeration. We did this by sampling the police dataset and by generating simulated networks. We generated 20 connected samples from the overall police network ranging in size from 11 to 20 nodes. We defined cost $c_v = 1$ for all $v \in V$ and we set benefit $b = 1$. The worst approximation ratio obtained in these tests was 0.70 - more than double the theoretical bound of 1/3 in this case. The average-case bound was better still at 0.92. Additionally, we also studied the behavior of SII-Approx on several standard generated graph types including complete graphs of size 20 and 25, Erdos-Reyni (E-R) random graphs, preferential-attachment generated scale-free graphs (SF), and the "Florentine Families" (FF) network [6]. In all of these tests, we never achieved an approximation ratio lower than 0.80. The results are shown in Table 1.

Runtime Evaluation. We evaluated runtime in two ways: (1) we compared the runtime of SII-Approx with an exact enumeration based computation and (2) we studied how SII-Approx scaled with network size. Both results are depicted in Figures 1 and 2. For the comparison with the exact computation, we studied the effect of runtime on our 20 samples from the police dataset. We studied at the speedup provided by SII-Approx (defined as the runtime for the exact approach divided by the runtime for SII-Approx on the same input) as a function of network size. We found a significant speedup in all cases and that the speedup increased exponentially with network size ($R^2 = 0.96$) - which is clearly due to the exponential runtime of the enumeration approach.

Runtime also scaled monotonically with the size of the network (quadratic fit, $R^2 = 0.97$). Hence, for the size of the datasets used by the Chicago police department (order 10^3 nodes), this is a viable approach with the current implementation. However, we think further improvement in runtime for the heuristic is possible with further practical modifications.

Cost Model Evaluation. One of the more useful characteristics of our framework is the ability to consider node costs. We studied two variants. First, we studied the case in which all nodes have the same cost, considering several different values. Second, we set the cost to be proportional to a network centrality measure. In both cases, we also varied the value of the benefit. We used the entire police dataset in these trials. The results for both sets of trials are shown in Figures 3 and 4.

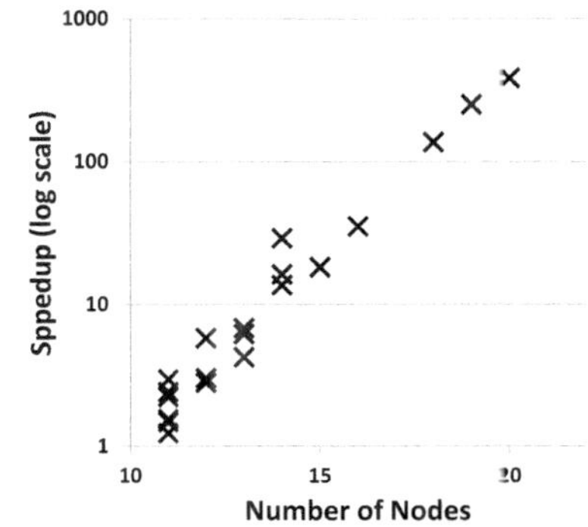

Figure 1: Network size vs. speedup obtained by SII-Approx over exact approach.

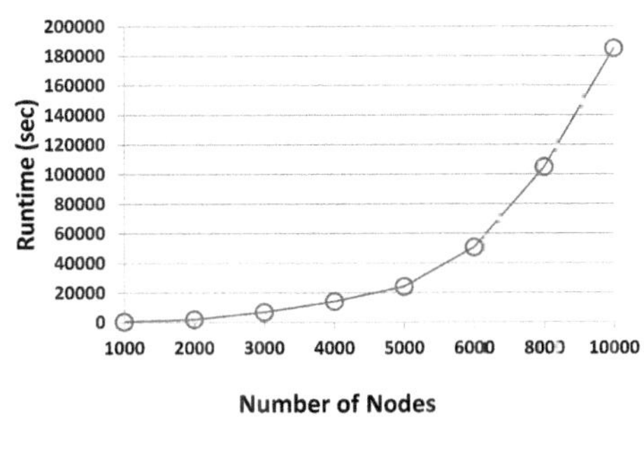

Figure 2: Network size vs. runtime for the heuristic algorithm.

We examined a fixed/uniform cost model where all nodes we assigned the same value. We examined cost values from 0.25 to 2.0 in intervals of 0.25 and compared them to uniform benefit values in the same range. In general, there was a linear relationship between the benefit and profit for all fixed cost models examined (R^2 values ranged from 0.97 to 0.99). Further, as expected, decreased cost led to increased profit.

For our centrality-based cost trials, we studied degree centrality (number of adjacent edges), closeness centrality (see [24]), eigenvector centrality (see [4]), shell number (based on shell-decomposition, see [19]), and clustering coefficient (see [24]). Cost was set to be proportional to these values for each node. We also normalized the cost so that the average would be 1.0 in each case. Just as with the fixed-cost trials, we compared the profit for various benefit values in the range $[0.25, 2.0]$ in intervals of 0.25.

For centrality-based cost models, we also observed a linear relationship between benefit and profit (R^2 values approaching 1.0). In examining the difference among centrality measures, we found the most expensive centralities were degree and shell-number followed by closeness. As these can be considered radial measures of centrality, meaning they measure centrality in terms of the number of paths that originate from a given node, then this result should be expected. Clustering coefficient was less expensive than these measures, which again was as expected as this measure is less dependent upon the number of adjacent nodes and more dependent upon the neighborhood. Perhaps most interesting was that eigenvector centrality was the "least expensive" cost model. We believe that this is due to the wide distribution of values assigned by this measure which ranged from 1.66×10^{-43} to 166.45 (compared to degree, which ranged from 0.36 to 6.17).

We note that the idea of a cost model is an important feature in our model as it has previously been shown that influential nodes are often not those who most susceptible [1]. This may imply that an individuals who may be influential in the network from a topological perspective may also be of high cost. This is why we considered cost models in our experiment where more central nodes were given a higher cost.

Heuristic for Improved Solution Quality. SII-Approx, as presented in this paper, does not take into account the order in which the vertices are selected. We found that if vertices are examined in descending order by their ClusterRank [8] then the algorithm provided a higher-profit solution when compared to our random baseline (average over 10 runs) for the case of uniform cost ($\forall v \in V, c_v = 1$) and various settings for benefit. The results are depicted in Figure 5. In [8] nodes of high ClusterRank were shown to encourage diffusion under the SIR model - which is related to the one-step process of this paper. The ClusterRank of node v is defined as follows:

$$\mathsf{cr}_v = 10^{-\mathcal{C}_v} \sum_{u \in \eta_v^{out}} (1 + k_u^{out})$$

Where $\mathcal{C}_v$ is the clustering coefficient for node v. This is particularly helpful as the computation of these measures relies only on local information and can be calculated quickly. Additionally, we examined ordering by degree, clustering coefficient, closeness centrality, shell number, and weighted degree centrality (for each $v \in V$ the quantity $\sum_{u \in V} p_{vu}$). While

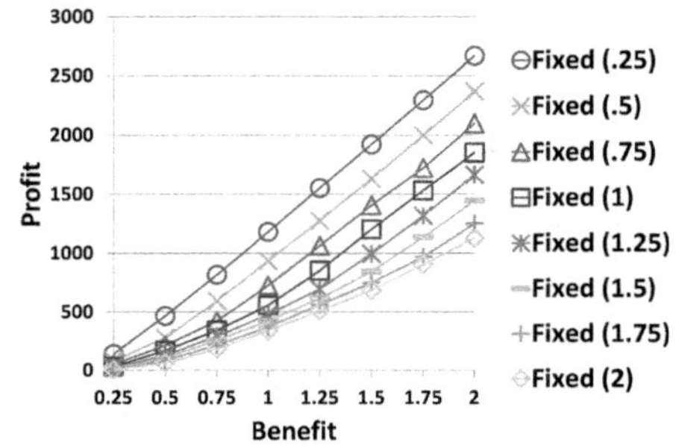

Figure 3: Pro t obtained from SII-Approx for the police dataset for xed/uniform cost models with various bene t settings.

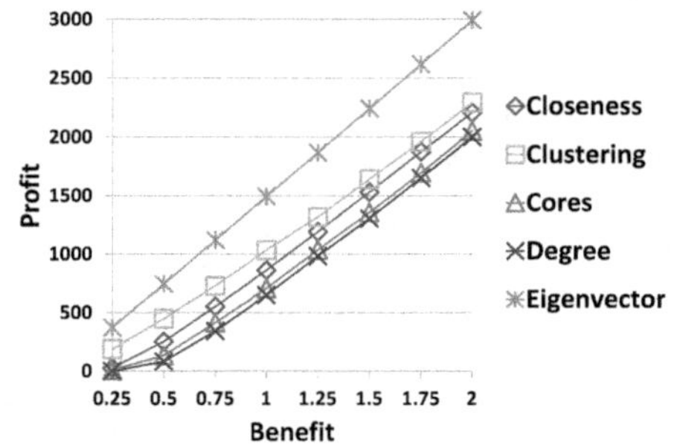

Figure 4: Pro t obtained from SII-Approx for the police dataset for centrality-based cost models with various bene t settings.

all of these measures showed some improvement over the random baseline, they were out performed by ClusterRank for all benefit values above 0.5. We are currently examining the performance of centrality-based ordering heuristics on a variety of inputs for the algorithm.

Iterative Application. We envision real-world police use of SII-Approx to occur in an iterative manner. One way this could be done is as follows: we initially consider a uniform cost model and identify initial nodes to seed. Then, we calculate the diffusion process function based on that seed set in a manner that yields the probability p_v of each node v being activated. Then, for the next iteration, we remove from the network all previously seeded nodes (or whichever subset dis-enrolled from the gang) and set the cost for each node v to be $1 - p_v$. The intuition is that it will be less expensive to seed nodes that already obtained influence from other members departing the gang. The process of re-setting the cost function and social network prior to re-running SII-Approx is then performed continually.

We applied SII-Approx iteratively five times to the police dataset in the manner described above and studied the size of the set targeted as well as the resulting profit (see Figures 6-7). We observed, under the assumption that all previously seeded members left the gang, that the profit gained decreased monotonically with the number of iterations while the number of targeted vertices increased slightly in the second iteration, followed by a steep decrease and then converged to zero. The success of the second iteration indi-

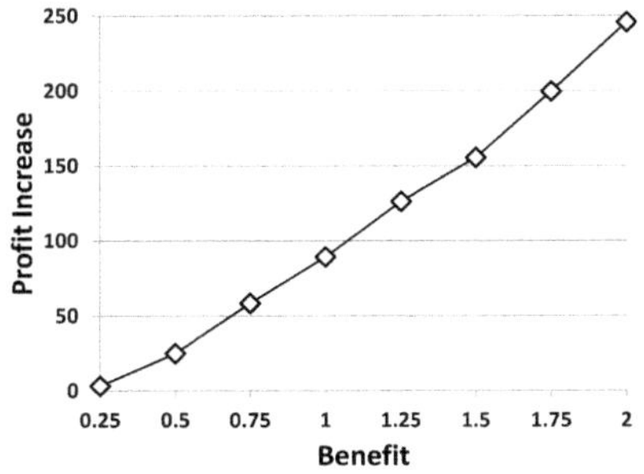

Figure 5: Improvement to pro t as returned by SII-Approx when the vertices are ordered by ClusterRank.

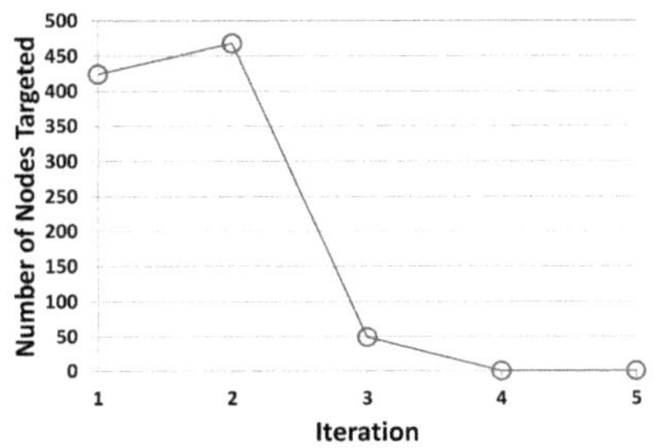

Figure 6: Iterative applications of SII-Approx – Number of nodes targetted at each iteration.

cated that viral marketing may be successful in encouraging neighboring individuals to dis-enroll. However, beyond the second step, there is limited profit to further marketing for dis-enrollment. We note that at this point, if successful, approximately half of the gang members are dis-enrolled, which would be a significant reduction. Further, we also note that topological changes to the network may become more significant after the second (and possibly even after the first) round of dis-enrollment.

Iterative application of the algorithm also opens up some new possibilities for future work. For instance, we can view our problem as a sequential decision making problem. The intuition in such an approach would be to not only to maximize the expected number of dis-enrolled gang members but also to position the law enforcement personnel to more easily influence the network in later iterations. Such an approach may also allow us to consider how the topology of the network will change over time.

6. RELATED WORK

The maximum influence problem was introduced in [14] and later studied in work such as [9, 11, 15, 21]. We refer the reader to the book [10] for a summary of recent work in this area. However, to our knowledge, no other work addresses all the challenges presented here for the SII problem simultaneously. For instance, [11] presents a model where the diffusion is restricted to shortest paths - which is a similar restriction to our one-step model, but does not consider the idea of profit. Likewise, [15] considers the idea of profit, but only applies it to the linear threshold model - which

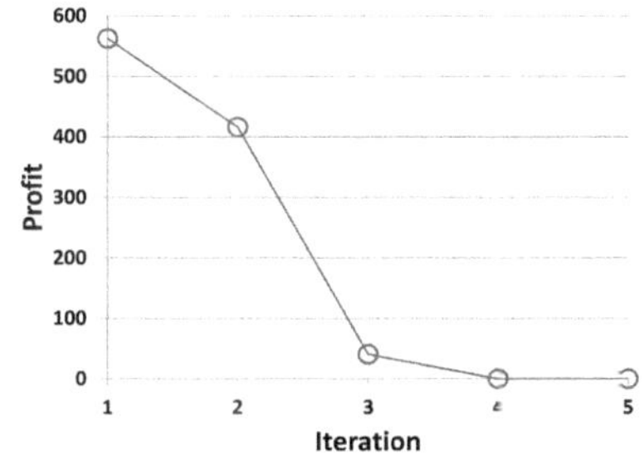

Figure 7: Iterative applications of SII-Approx – Pro t obtained at each iteration.

relies on the number of an individuals neighbors reaching a certain threshold. Another issue is that in most of these models, the diffusion process function is difficult to compute - for instance the *dpf* for the independent cascade model is shown to be P-hard in [11]. As a result, in most other pieces of work the diffusion process is approximated using simulation, which is as expensive operation. (Most law enforcement agencies we work with have limited computational power). One notable exception regarding this issue are deterministic models such as that described in [12, 21]. We note that in our previous work we have looked at utilizing this model in a law-enforcement setting [18, 3]. However the results of that work were primarily used to describe characteristics of the gangs and not to make operational decisions. This work did not study the operational issues associated with encouraging gang dis-enrollment as considered in this paper.

7. CONCLUSION

In this paper we introduced the "social incentive influence" (SII) problem, a variant of the maximum influence problem, designed to help law-enforcement personnel identify members of street gangs that they can encourage to dis-enroll. We studied this problem both formally and experimentally in the context of the law-enforcement domain. Utilizing techniques from unconstrained submodular maximization, we developed a heuristic technique to help police better identify sets of influential individuals to target with dis-enrollment incentives. We implemented our approach and performed an experimental evaluation. We currently have our approach to the SII problem integrated into our GANG/ORCA analysis software [18] that is currently in use by the Chicago Police. Our next goal is to work with law enforcement personnel to better understand how SII is employed in practice - allowing us to identify components of this framework that can be adjusted for improved results in a real-world setting.

8. ACKNOWLEDGMENTS

The authors are supported by the Army Research Office (project 2GDATXR042) and the U.S. Air Force. The opinions in this paper are those of the authors and do not necessarily reflect the opinions of the funders, the U.S. Military Academy, the U.S. Army, the U.S. Air Force, or the U.S. Department of Defense.

9. REFERENCES

[1] S. Aral and D. Walker. Identifying influential and susceptible members of social networks. *Science*, 337(6092):337–341, 2012.

[2] J. Bertetto. Countering criminal street gangs: Lessons from the counterinsurgent battlespace. *Law Enforcement Executive Forum*, 12(3):43, 2012.

[3] J. Bertetto. Counter-gang strategy: Adapted coin in policing criminal street gangs. *Law Enforcement Executive Forum*, 13(3), 2013.

[4] P. Bonacich. Factoring and weighting approaches to status scores and clique identification. *The Journal of Mathematical Sociology*, 2(1):113–120, 1972.

[5] A. Braga, D. Hureau, and A. Papachristos. Deterring gang-involved gun violence: Measuring the impact of bostonâĂŹs operation ceasefire on street gang behavior. *Journal of Quantitative Criminology*, pages 1–27, 2013.

[6] R. L. Breiger and P. E. Pattison. Cumulated social roles: The duality of persons and their algebras. *Social Networks*, 8(3):215–256, Sept. 1986.

[7] N. Buchbinder, M. Feldman, J. S. Naor, and R. Schwartz. A tight linear time (1/2)-approximation for unconstrained submodular maximization. In *Proceedings of the 2012 IEEE 53rd Annual Symposium on Foundations of Computer Science*, FOCS '12, pages 649–658, Washington, DC, USA, 2012. IEEE Computer Society.

[8] D.-B. Chen, H. Gao, L. LÃij, and T. Zhou. Identifying influential nodes in large-scale directed networks: The role of clustering. *PLoS ONE*, 8(10):e77455, 10 2013.

[9] N. Chen. On the approximability of influence in social networks. *SIAM J. Discret. Math.*, 23:1400–1415, September 2009.

[10] W. Chen, L. V. Lakshmanan, and C. Castillo. *Information and Influence Propagation in Social Networks*. Morgan and Claypool Publishers, 2013.

[11] W. Chen, C. Wang, and Y. Wang. Scalable influence maximization for prevalent viral marketing in large-scale social networks. In *Proceedings of the 16th ACM SIGKDD international conference on Knowledge discovery and data mining*, KDD '10, pages 1029–1038, New York, NY, USA, 2010. ACM.

[12] P. Dreyer and F. Roberts. Irreversible -threshold processes: Graph-theoretical threshold models of the spread of disease and of opinion. *Discrete Applied Mathematics*, 157(7):1615 – 1627, 2009.

[13] M. R. Garey and D. S. Johnson. *Computers and Intractability; A Guide to the Theory of NP-Completeness*. W. H. Freeman & Co., New York, NY, USA, 1979.

[14] D. Kempe, J. Kleinberg, and E. Tardos. Maximizing the spread of influence through a social network. In *KDD '03: Proceedings of the ninth ACM SIGKDD international conference on Knowledge discovery and data mining*, pages 137–146, New York, NY, USA, 2003. ACM.

[15] W. Lu and L. Lakshmanan. Profit maximization over social networks. In *Data Mining (ICDM), 2012 IEEE 12th International Conference on*, pages 479–488, Dec 2012.

[16] J. C. Nekola and P. S. White. Special Paper: The Distance Decay of Similarity in Biogeography and Ecology. *Journal of Biogeography*, 26(4):867–878, 1999.

[17] G. L. Nemhauser, L. A. Wolsey, and M. Fisher. An analysis of approximations for maximizing submodular set functionsï£¡i. *Mathematical Programming*, 14(1):265–294, 1978.

[18] D. Paulo, B. Fischl, T. Markow, M. Martin, and P. Shakarian. Social network intelligence analysis to combat street gang violence. In *Proceedings of the 2013 IEEE/ACM International Conference on Advances in Social Networks Analysis and Mining*, ASONAM '13, pages 1042–1049, New York, NY, USA, 2013. ACM.

[19] S. B. Seidman. Network structure and minimum degree. *Social Networks*, 5(3):269 – 287, 1983.

[20] P. Shakarian, M. Broecheler, V. S. Subrahmanian, and C. Molinaro. Using generalized annotated programs to solve social network diffusion optimization problems. *ACM Trans. Comput. Logic*, 14(2):10:1–10:40, June 2013.

[21] P. Shakarian and D. Paulo. Large social networks can be targeted for viral marketing with small seed sets. *2012 IEEE/ACM International Conference on Advances in Social Networks Analysis and Mining*, pages 1–8, 2012.

[22] H. Skov-Petersen. Estimation of distance-decay parameters: GIS-based indicators of recreational accessibility. In *ScanGIS*, pages 237–258, 2001.

[23] P. J. Taylor. Distance transformation and distance decay functions. *Geographical Analysis*, 3(3):221–238, 1971.

[24] S. Wasserman and K. Faust. *Social Network Analysis: Methods and Applications*. Number 8 in Structural analysis in the social sciences. Cambridge University Press, 1 edition, 1994.

Modeling Impression Discounting in Large-scale Recommender Systems

Pei Lee, Laks V.S. Lakshmanan
University of British Columbia
{peil, laks}@cs.ubc.ca

Mitul Tiwari, Sam Shah
LinkedIn Corporation
{mtiwari, samshah}@linkedin.com

ABSTRACT

Recommender systems have become very important for many online activities, such as watching movies, shopping for products, and connecting with friends on social networks. User behavioral analysis and user feedback (both explicit and implicit) modeling are crucial for the improvement of any online recommender system. Widely adopted recommender systems at LinkedIn such as "People You May Know" and "Endorsements" are evolving by analyzing user behaviors on impressed recommendation items.

In this paper, we address modeling impression discounting of recommended items, that is, how to model user's no-action feedback on impressed recommended items. The main contributions of this paper include (1) large-scale analysis of impression data from LinkedIn and KDD Cup; (2) novel anti-noise regression techniques, and its application to learn four different impression discounting functions including linear decay, inverse decay, exponential decay, and quadratic decay; (3) applying these impression discounting functions to LinkedIn's "People You May Know" and "Endorsements" recommender systems.

Categories and Subject Descriptors

H.3.3 [**Information Storage and Retrieval**]: Information Filtering; J.4 [**Computer Applications**]: Social and Behavior Sciences

Keywords

Impression discounting; Recommender system

1. INTRODUCTION

Analyzing and incorporating user feedback on recommended items is crucial for evolving any recommender systems, which have become important for many online activities and especially for social networks. At LinkedIn, the largest professional network with more than 300 million members, recommender systems play significant role in engaging users, discovering new content, connections, opportunities, and satisfying users needs. LinkedIn exposes connection or link recommender systems through features such as "People You May Know" (PYMK) (Figure 1(a)), which recommends other members to connect with, and skills endorsements, which recommends to endorse connections with their skills & expertise to add to their profiles (Figure 1(b)).

Modeling user behavior and incorporating feedback on live recommender systems such as PYMK and Endorsements, which are exposed to millions of users every day, are critical for enhancing these recommender systems. User feedback on recommended items viewed by users or impressions, can be explicit or implicit. User action such as inviting or dismissing a recommended member to connect with is explicit feedback in PYMK. On the other hand, viewing a recommended member or clicking to view the profile of a recommended member, but not inviting to connect, are examples of implicit feedback in PYMK. There has been extensive research on modeling explicit feedback in terms of ratings and acceptance of recommended items [9, 21, 26]. However, modeling certain implicit feedback such as no action on impressed recommended items for conversion, has been under explored. There has been some work on estimating Click-through rate (CTR) using past impressions [1], but CTR estimation is different from conversion prediction as also argued recently in [5, 17].

Usually a recommender system generates a list of items, ordered by a score, to show to users. We say a recommended item is impressed when a user views the item. Acceptance of an impressed recommended item results in conversion. No action from users on impressed recommended items can be because of multitude of reasons, for example, a user might be busy with other things, or the recommended item is not relevant or the purpose of the site visit is very different. In the impression discounting problem we aim to maximize conversion of recommended items generated by a recommender system by applying a discounting factor, derived from past impressions, on top of scores generated by the recommender system. There are two basic challenges in the impression discounting problem: (1) how can we build an effective model between conversion and various user behaviors from the large amount of past impression data? (2) how can the model be applied to improve the performance of existing recommender systems? There are various factors that can be used in modeling the impact of impressions, such as, (1) the number of times an item is impressed or recommended to a user, (2) when the item was impressed, and (3) frequency of user visits on the site or user seeing any of the recommended items.

In this work, we present models for discounting impressions of recommended items based on various factors such as the number of impressions and the last time the item was seen. The intuition behind these models is simple; for example, in the case of PYMK, a recommended member that results in a number of impressions, but does not lead to an invitation, should be removed or lowered in the recommended list of members. We performed detailed analy-

KDD '14, August 24 - 27 2014, New York, NY, USA
Copyright 2014 ACM 978-1-4503-2956-9/14/08$15.00.
http://dx.doi.org/10.1145/2623330.2623356

(a)

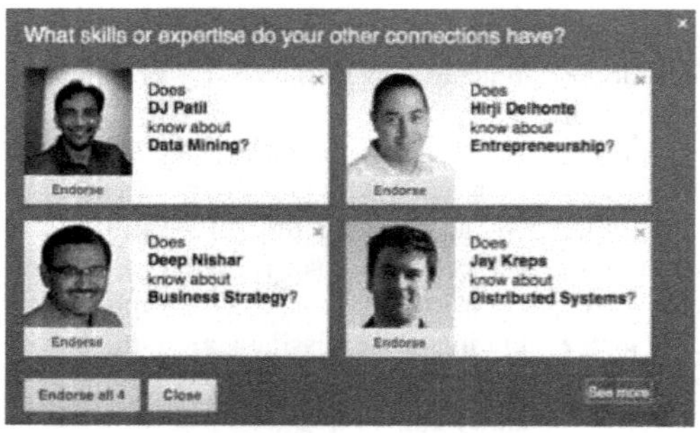

(b)

Figure 1: (a) People You May Know at LinkedIn recommends other members to connect with. (b) Suggestions for skills endorsements, a recommender system at LinkedIn to endorse connections for their skills and expertise, which can be added to their profile.

sis of past impressions over large amount of tracking data to find correlation between various factors and conversion rate, for example, invitation rate for PYMK. We learned four different regression models that represent linear decay, inverse decay, exponential decay, and quadratic decay. We developed novel anti-noise regression techniques to detect outliers and lower the effect of outliers in learning regression functions. We show empirically that our impression discounting models perform significantly better both in offline analysis using past data as well as in online A/B testing. In offline analysis for PYMK, these impression discounting models show up to 31% improvement in invitation rate, and in online A/B test experiments, the model improves invitation rate by up to 13%.

The main contributions of this paper are as follows:

- Perform large scale correlation studies between impression signals and conversion rate of impressed items;
- Design effective impression discounting models based on linear/multiplicative aggregation, and propose novel anti-noise regression model to deal with the data sparsity problem;
- Evaluate these regression models on real-world recommendation systems such as "People You May Know" and "Endorsements" to demonstrate their effectiveness both in offline analysis and in online systems by A/B testing.

The rest of the paper is organized as follows. Section 2 discusses related work. Section 3 formalizes concept of impressions in the context of recommender systems and details data sets used in this work. Section 4 presents exploratory data analysis to figure out correlations between various user behavior and conversion rate. This section also describes our impression discounting framework, and various discounting functions learned through regression. Section 4.5.3 describes our anti-noise regression techniques. Section 5 presents experimental results including offline analysis and online A/B testing results. Finally we conclude in Section 6.

2. RELATED WORK

The related work of this paper falls mainly under one of the following categories.

Implicit Feedback in CF. User implicit feedback plays an essential role in the recommendation models [2]. Collaborative filtering (CF) is a typical recommendation model, with the advantage of not needing the user/item profiles [9, 10, 21, 26]. Hu et al. [8] studied implicit feedback on CF and proposed a factor model by treating implicit feedback as the indication of positive and negative preference associated with varying confidence levels. Koren [9] discovered that incorporating implicit feedback into a neighborhood latent factor model (SVD++) could offer significant improvement. On the application side, a local implicit feedback model mining users' preferences from the music listening history is proposed in [24]. Moling et al. [15] exploited implicit feedback derived from a user's listening behavior, and modeled radio channel recommendation as a sequential decision making problem. Yang et al. [25] proposed Collaborative Competitive Filtering (CCF) to learn user preferences by modeling the choice process with a local competition effect. Gupta et al. [7] modeled user response to an ad campaign as a function of both interest match and past exposure, where the interest match is estimated using historical search/browse activities of the user. All these methods [8, 9, 25, 7] exploit implicit feedback by integrating historical signals with existing recommendation models. In contrast, our impression discounting model serves as an external plugin of the existing recommendation model, which has advantages in modularization.

CTR Estimation. The estimate of click-through rate (CTR) for online resources such as news articles, Ads or search results is a hot topic, and we categorize the related work into two types: classification-based estimate and regression-based estimate. For the first type, Agichtein et al. [2] showed that incorporating user behavior data can significantly improve the ordering of top results in real web search engines, by treating user behaviors as features and using classification to re-rank. Richardson et al. [18] employed logistic regression to predict the CTR for newly created Ads, using features of ads, terms, and advertisers. For the second type, Agarwal et al. [1] proposed a spatio-temporal model to estimate the first impression CTR of Yahoo! Front Page news articles.

Impression discounting shares some commonalities with the estimate of CTR: they both try to predict a user's future action. However, they differ in many aspects. First, impression discounting aims to improve the conversion rate of recommendations, which is a different goal from CTR estimate, as a click can happen multiple times and may not result in a conversion action. Second, the existing work on CTR estimation is mainly focused on new items; for example, the first exposure of news articles [1] or Ads [18]. The link between impression history and conversion rate is not covered in existing studies.

Density-based Approach. Density concepts, first introduced by density-based clustering [6] and recently adapted to social network and media analysis [13, 12], is a traditional way to detect noises. In the context of linear regression, Ristanoski et al. [19] proposed segmenting the input time series into groups and simultaneously optimizing both the average loss of each group and the variance of the loss between groups, to produce a linear model that has low overall error. Chen et al. [4] introduced a nonlinear logistic regression model for classification, and the main idea is to map the data to a feature space based on kernel density estimation. Kernel regression is another relevant approach, which estimates the conditional expectation of a random variable by non-parametric techniques [11]. However, all these approaches [19, 4, 11] cannot combat the noise in linear regression.

3. IMPRESSION DATA IN LARGE-SCALE RECOMMENDER SYSTEMS

In large-scale recommender systems, user actions such as impressions, are readily captured [23]. Before jumping to the modeling of impression discounting, we start to extract and formalize the impression data sets in a uniform format, crossing various application scenarios, including PYMK, Skill Endorsements, and Keyword Search Ads. These impression data sets are typically reflecting the interaction between users and popular online recommender systems.

3.1 Formalizing Impressions

Our study on the daily interaction logs of different recommender systems reveals that there is a common structure behind impression records from different sources. Without the loss of generality, we formalize each impression record as a tuple $\mathcal{T}$ with six attributes, as explained below.

Definition 1. (Impression) An impression in the recommender system is modeled as a tuple $\mathcal{T}$ with six attributes:

$$\mathcal{T} = (user, item, conversion, [behavior1, behavior2, \cdots], t, R)$$

where:

- $user$ is a user ID;
- $item$ is a recommendation item ID;
- $conversion$ is a boolean type to describe whether or not $user$ takes an action on $item$ in this impression;
- $behavior$ is an observed feature of interaction;
- t is the time stamp of impression;
- R is the recommendation score of $item$ to $user$, which is provided by the recommendation engine.

As a convention, we use $\mathcal{T}.x$ to refer to attribute x in $\mathcal{T}$.

Conversion. We use the term $conversion$ to indicate that $user$ explicitly accepts the recommendation. A $conversion$ action may differ from a user click. For example, a conversion action in PYMK means that a user does not simply click on the profile page of another user, but instead takes action to invite that user. In job recommendations, $conversion$ means that a $user$ actually applies for the job $item$.

Behaviors. User interactions with the recommender system typically follow a "see-think-do" procedure. The interaction between users and recommender systems has many facets. We aggregate the following user behaviors:

- *LastSeen*: the day difference between the last impression and the current impression, associated with the same $(user, item)$;
- *ImpCount*: the number of historical impressions before the current impression, associated with the same $(user, item)$;
- *Position*: the offset of $item$ in the recommendation list of $user$;
- *UserFreq*: the interaction frequency of $user$ in a specific recommender system.

We use X to represent the set of behaviors and use m to describe the set size, i.e., $m = |X|$.

Impression Sequence. Given a large impression data set with each record formatted as tuple $\mathcal{T}$, we can perform a "group-by" operation on $(user,\ item)$ to obtain a sequence with the same $(user,\ item)$. This sequence can be ordered by time and denoted as $seq(user, item) = (\mathcal{T}_1, \cdots, \mathcal{T}_n)$. In a given observation time window, the sequence length is indicated by *ImpCount*. Especially, if $seq(\mathcal{T}.user, \mathcal{T}.item)$ has the property $ImpCount = 1$, we call it $\mathcal{T}$ the first impression.

Conversion Rate. In most recommender systems, once the conversion is true, $item$ will not be recommended to $user$ again. So $conversion = True$ only possibly occurs once on the tail of a sequence. Thus, the overall conversion rate can be defined as the ratio between the number of impressions with $conversion = true$ and the number of all impression sequences. Let $\mathcal{S}$ denote the set of impressions. The global conversion rate is computed by

$$ConveRate = \frac{|\{\mathcal{T} \in \mathcal{S}|conversion = true)\}|}{|\mathcal{S}|} \tag{1}$$

Conversion rate can also be measured on the basis of each behavior set X. We can "group-by" all impression sequences on X, and then define the local conversion rate by the formula

$$ConveRate(X) = \frac{|\{\mathcal{T} \in \mathcal{S}|conversion = true \;\&\; behavior = X)\}|}{|\{\mathcal{T} \in \mathcal{S}|behavior = X)\}|} \tag{2}$$

We normalize conversion rates in this work as only relative changes are important.

3.2 Data Set Descriptions

To deploy the impression discounting model, we collect two real-world data sets from online recommender systems in LinkedIn and one external public data set from Tencent. In the following section, we describe the salient characteristics of these data sets.

LinkedIn PYMK Impressions. PYMK is one of the most popular recommender systems in LinkedIn. The PYMK $item$ is actually another 2nd or higher degree LinkedIn user. We select an observation time with a total of 1.08 billion impressions in tracking data. Out of them, a significant portion of impressions are multiple, which means at least half the impressions were previously presented to the users, but get no invitation action. The relatively long impression sequences in PYMK make it an ideal data set for modeling impression discounting.

LinkedIn Skill Endorsement Impressions. Skill Endorsement is another popular recommender system to recognize the skills and expertise of 1st-degree connections. We collect impressions tracking data with 0.19 billion impression tuples, and a small portion of them are multiple. The $item$ in a tuple is the combination of a user and his skill. Because endorsements are only allowed for 1st-degree connections, impression sequences are usually very short and the conversion rate is relatively high, which implies that the skill recommendations are more likely endorsed by connections in the first impression.

Tencent SearchAds Impressions[1]**.** SearchAds is a data set made publicly available for KDD Cup 2012 by the Tencent search engine. It contains various ingredients of the interaction between a user and the search engine; for example, user, query, Ad ID, depth, position, etc. In total, this data set has 0.15 billion impression sequences, and the CTR of the Ad at the 1st, 2nd and 3rd position of the search session is 4.8%, 2.7%, and 1.4% respectively.

[1] http://www.kddcup2012.org/c/kddcup2012-track2

4. IMPRESSION DISCOUNTING MODEL

There are two basic challenges in the impression discounting problem: (1) how can we learn an effective model between the *conversion* and various user behaviors from the big data? (2) how is the model applied to new impressions and improving the performance of existing recommender systems? In this section, we introduce the impression discounting model, which is learned from the actual impression data sets and integrated as a plugin in the existing large-scale recommender systems.

4.1 Conventions

For convenience of presentation, we introduce the following concepts and notations:

- **Behavior List**: a list of behaviors that describe the user's interaction with the recommender system, denoted as X. The list size is denoted by m and each element X_i can be observed from the impression records of recommender systems, e.g., X=(*LastSeen*, *ImpCount*).
- **Conversion Rate**: the actual conversion rate in data sets is defined by Eq. (2) and denoted by $y = ConveRate(X)$ for the ease of discussion. The predicted conversion rate by the model is denoted by $\hat{y}$.
- **Observation**: an observation (X, y) is composed by a behavior set X and its conversion rate y.
- **Support of Observation**: the support of an observation (X, y) is the number of impression sequences with the same X that produces the same y in Eq. (2), denoted by $support(X, y)$.
- **Observation Space**: the set of all possible observations (X, y) in the data set, denoted by D.

4.2 Impression Discounting Framework

As an example in LinkedIn PYMK, assume a common scenario that a user called Alice gets the recommendation for a connection called Bob in September 20 but takes no invitation action. This assumption has two folds of meaning: (1) the recommendation engine thinks that Bob has a relatively high recommendation score R to Alice; (2) it is very likely that Alice is not satisfied with the recommendation item Bob. If the recommender system ignores this implicit negative feedback from Alice, most likely Bob will be recommended to Alice again in another day, which only reduces the overall satisfaction of Alice. We believe that this kind of scenarios can be easily found in nearly every recommender system, e.g., Ad recommendation, job recommendation and even web search engines. Motivated by this example, we design the impression discounting framework, which serves as a module in the existing ecosystem of recommender systems, by taking full consideration of the implicit negative feedback from users. We formalize the impression discounting problem as follows.

Problem 1. (**Impression Discounting**). Given a large-scale impression data set with each record defined by Definition 1, for each unique $(user, item)$, supposing the historical impression sequence is $seq(user, item) = (\mathcal{T}_1, \cdots, \mathcal{T}_n)$ $(n \geq 1)$ and $\mathcal{T}$ is the current impression (i.e., $\mathcal{T}.t > \mathcal{T}_n.t$), the problem of impression discounting on $\mathcal{T}$ is to determine a discounting factor d $(0 < d \leq 1)$, which updates

- $\mathcal{T}^*.R = \mathcal{T}.R \cdot d$;
- $seq(user, item) = (\mathcal{T}_1, \cdots, \mathcal{T}_n, \mathcal{T})$;
- $seq^*(user, item) = (\mathcal{T}_1, \cdots, \mathcal{T}_n, \mathcal{T}^*)$;

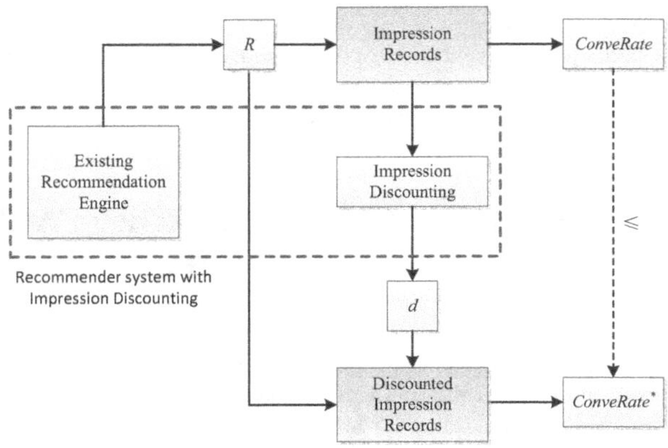

Figure 2: The impression discounting framework. Our proposed impression discounting model only relies on the historical impression records, and can be treated as a plugin for existing recommendation engines. We use the dotted rectangle to circle the newly built recommender system with impression discounting, which produces discounted impressions with a higher overall conversion rate.

and maximizes

$$Improvement = \frac{ConveRate^* - ConveRate}{ConveRate} \quad (3)$$

where $ConveRate^*$ and $ConveRate$ are computed by Eq. (1) based on $seq^*(user, item)$ and $seq(user, item)$ respectively.

To explain why impression discounting helps improve the overall conversion rate, we use the following example. Suppose that in a user interaction session, the recommendation engine fetches top 100 recommendation items ranked by $\mathcal{T}.R$ and 50 of them will be observed by the user. If without impression discounting, existing recommendation engine will present the top 50 items ranked by $\mathcal{T}.R$ to the user. However, since a large portion of item impressions are multiple, their historical negative feedback indicates that their conversion rate will be low. Now we consider a newly built recommender system with impression discounting. Since impressions are discounted properly by d where $d \leq 1$, all 100 items will be re-ranked. Ideally, items with less negative feedback will bubble up into top 50 list and be exposed to user's observation, which results in a higher overall conversion rate.

We show the impression discounting framework in Figure 2. Basically, we assume that R is already produced by the best-known recommendation method, and the computation of R is not the focus of this paper. Our proposed impression discounting model only relies on the historical impression records in the past observation time window. In other words, impression discounting can work independently with the recommendation engine. Once added as a plugin into the recommender system, impression discounting model will produce a discounting factor d, which penalizes items that not likely gain a conversion action and makes the recommendation list re-ranked. A properly designed impression discounting model will make the overall conversion rate increasing and improve user's satisfaction. The challenge of the impression discounting problem is how to design an effective model that determines the optimal d to re-rank the recommendation list with intuitive explanation.

Impression Discounting: Plugin vs. In-Model. There are typically two ways to incorporate impression discounting into an existing recommendation system: serve as an independent plugin or push in the recommendation model. The plugin approach does not change

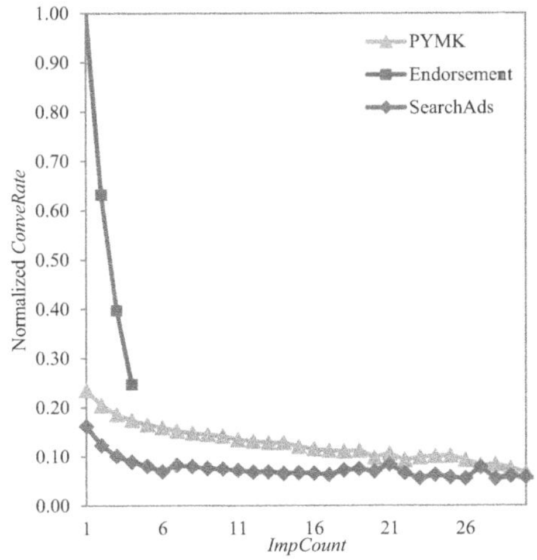

Figure 3: The change of Normalized $ConveRate$ with increasing *ImpCount* on three real-world impression data sets.

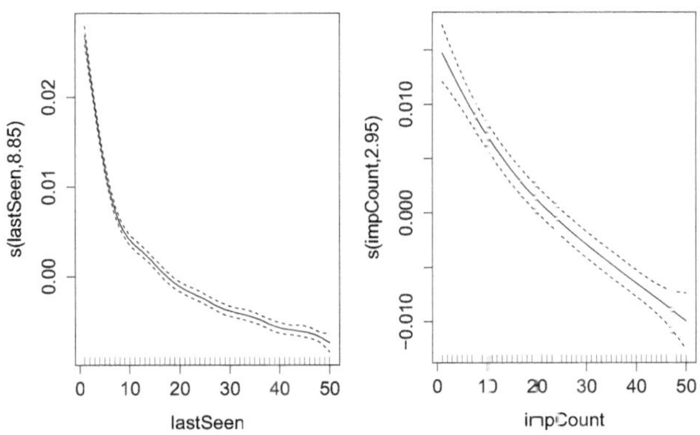

(a) *LastSeen* Correlation (b) *ImpCount* Correlation

Figure 4: Correlation confidence analysis between *ConveRate* and two behaviors on PYMK data.

the existing recommendation model, and the impression discounting is performed by multiplying a discounting coefficient d with the recommendation score. In contrast, the in-model approach modifies the existing recommendation model by adding more signals. For example, supposing the recommendation model is based on classification, the in-model approach will add signals like *impCount*, *lastSeen* as additional features. The plugin-based approach provides model independence: we can be agnostic as to the underlying recommendation model, whether it is a sophtiscated similarity ranker or simple cooccurance-based collaborative filtering, it is treated as a black box. Thus, impression discounting can be provided "as a service" for any client application. In this paper, we focus on the plugin-based approach, though these techniques can be adapted to the in-model approach without loss of generality.

4.3 Hypothesis Testing

We have a basic hypothesis for the impression discounting:

***Hypothesis** 1.* Impression $\mathcal{T}$ with $conversion = false$ is a negative feedback to the recommendation of $item$ to $user$.

If this hypothesis is false, the recommender system will always try to recommend items with a longer impression history to gain a higher conversion rate, and these long impression sequence will dominate the recommendation list, preventing new items being displayed. If this is the case, the discounting factor $d \leq 1$ in the problem definition will become invalid, as the conversion rate may increase if the impression sequence becomes longer. Thus, if this hypothesis is false, the impression discounting framework will be problematic. To verify this hypothesis on real-world impression data sets, we measure the change of $ConveRate$ with increasing impression sequence length, as shown in Figure 3. As we can see, on all three data sets, $ConveRate$ decreases very fast as increasing *ImpCount* in the beginning. Later, the decreasing trend becomes steady, and when *ImpCount* is high (which is rare in observation), there are some turbulences on the tail of the curves due to the data sparsity problem. The impression sequences of the Endorsement data set are very short in length and $ConveRate$ decreases even faster than the other two data sets. In a nutshell, Figure 3 verifies that Hypothesis 1 is true, and also reveals that the discounting factor in the Endorsement data set should be more severe and smaller than the other two data sets.

4.4 Exploratory Analysis

Correlation Analysis. It is essential to explore the correlation confidence between conversion rate and user behaviors. An effective way to tackle the correlation analysis is using non-parametric smoothers in a generalized additive model (GAM) [14] to fit the conversion rate. We perform GAM fitting on the PYMK data set and show the correlation analysis between conversion rate and *ImpCount*, *LastSeen* in Figure 4. The narrow intervals in Figure 4(a) and (b) suggest that the curvatures of the correlation are both strong. Moreover, as the interval in Figure 4(a) is even narrower than the interval in Figure 4(b), we conclude that $ConveRate$ has a stronger correlation with *LastSeen* than the correlation with *ImpCount*. In other words, *LastSeen* plays a more important role than *ImpCount* in determining conversion rate. The monotone decreasing trends suggest that the correlations are both negative. The correlation analysis for other user behaviors and in Endorsement and SearchAds data sets delivers similar messages. We omit the details due to space constraints.

Discounting Functions. Based on the correlation analysis, we define discounting functions to model the negative relationship between the conversion rate and a specific user behavior. In particular, we introduce the following four kinds of discounting functions:

- Linear Discounting: $f_L(x) = \alpha_1 \cdot x + \alpha_2$;
- Inverse Discounting: $f_I(x) = \frac{\alpha_1}{x} + \alpha_2$;
- Exponential Discounting: $f_E(x) = e^{\alpha_1 \cdot x + \alpha_2}$;
- Quadratic Discounting: $f_Q(x) = \alpha_1(x - \alpha_2)^2 + \alpha_3$.

We use PYMK as the default data set, and show the conversion rate vs. *LastSeen* and *ImpCount* in Figure 5. Since the supports of observations for a high *LastSeen* or *ImpCount* is really low, the curve tails in Figure 5(a) and (b) become fluctuant, which brings new challenges for curve-fitting, a problem we will study in Section 4.6. So far, we perform regression and show the root mean square error (RMSE) of different discounting functions to the actual observations in Table 1. As we can see, exponential discounting achieves the overall minimal RMSE with the best fitting quality. More evaluation of discounting functions can be found in Section 5. In our impression discounting model, these discounting functions will serve as the atoms in the multiple variable regression process.

4.5 Aggregated Discounting Model

Conversion rate is determined by multiple facets of user behaviors. For example, it is confirmed that *ImpCount* and *LastSeen* will

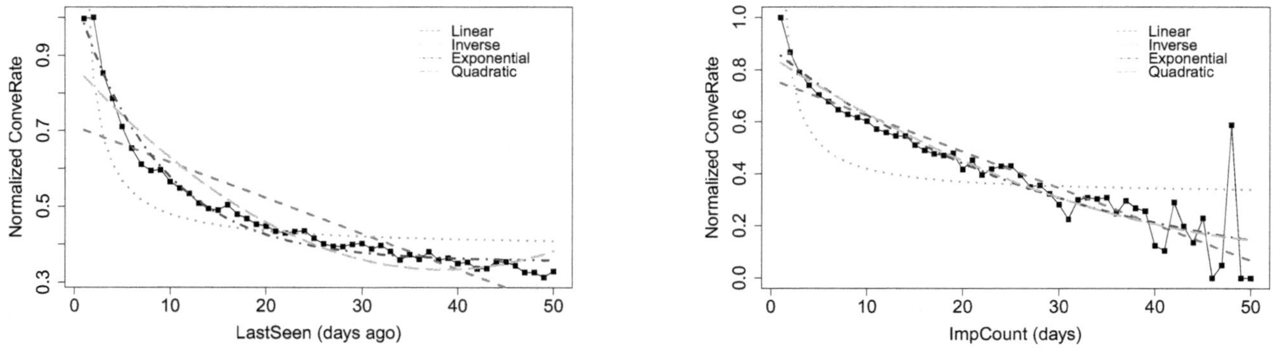

(a) Conversion rate vs. *LastSeen*

(b) Conversion rate vs. *ImpCount*

Figure 5: The change of normalized conversion rate with increasing *LastSeen* and *ImpCount*. We simulate all observations by four discounting functions, and exponential discounting achieves the minimal RMSE.

RMSE	*ConveRate∼LastSeen*	*ConveRate∼ImpCount*
Linear	0.0041	0.0032
Inverse	0.0039	0.0053
Exponential	**0.0012**	**0.0028**
Quadratic	0.0024	0.0029

Table 1: RMSEs of various discounting functions.

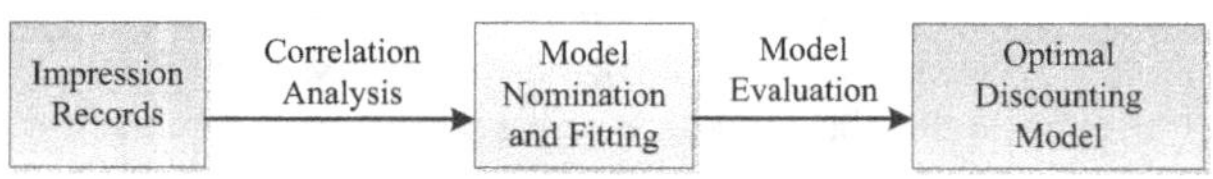

Figure 6: Impression discounting model workflow.

influence the invitation rate in PYMK. To model conversion rate accurately, we propose an aggregated discounting model in this paper, which integrates multiple discounting functions into a hybrid model. There are typically two ways to incorporate multiple variables into a model: linear or multiplicative combinations. We explore both of them in this section.

Workflow. The major workflow of the impression discounting model is presented in Figure 6. Without any prior knowledge, the correlation analysis is a great way to discover the correlation strength and polarity between the conversion rate and a specific user behavior. Correlation analysis also helps determine which discounting function fits the observations best by comparing RMSE, and narrows down the search space for the model candidates. Each candidate model will be learned by the regression from the training data set. Finally, we perform a model evaluation for each candidate on the testing data set, and the model with the best performance will be selected as the optimal discounting model for the corresponding recommender system.

Regression vs. Classification. Classification is a typical machine learning technique for decision making. Since our impression discounting framework follows the plugin approach, given that the recommendation score R is obtained from the best-available classification model, it will bring severe redundancy problem if we apply the classification model again on features in impression discounting. Besides, compared with the classification, regression can provide a better and more intuitive explanation of impression discounting by discounting functions.

4.5.1 Linear Aggregation Model

The first aggregated discounting model we explore is the linear model. Linear aggregation model combines discounting functions of different user behaviors by a linear function, in the form:

$$\hat{y} = \sum_{i=1}^{m} w_i f(X_i) \tag{4}$$

where $m = |X|$ and $f(X_i)$ is any one of discounting functions. Given a specific behavior X_i, the correlation analysis will help decide which discounting function is the best choice for $f(X_i)$. w_i is the weight for the discounting function and will be learned. It is well known that too many parameters in the linear model will result in over-fitting. Actually, once we select the specific discounting functions, the parameters in Eq. (9) can be reduced greatly. Here is an example with three different behaviors:

$$\begin{aligned} \hat{y} &= w_1 \cdot f_L(X_1) + w_2 \cdot f_I(X_2) + w_3 \cdot f_E(X_3) \\ &= w_1 \cdot (\alpha_1 X_1 + \alpha_2) + w_2 \cdot (\frac{\alpha_3}{X_2} + \alpha_4) + w_3 \cdot e^{\alpha_5 X_3 + \alpha_6} \\ &= w_1\alpha_1 \cdot X_1 + w_2\alpha_3 \cdot \frac{1}{X_2} + w_3 e^{\alpha_6} \cdot (e^{\alpha_5})^{X_3} + w_1\alpha_2 + w_2\alpha_4 \\ &= u_1 \cdot X_1 + u_2 \cdot \frac{1}{X_2} + u_3 \cdot \alpha^{X_3} + u_4 \end{aligned} \tag{5}$$

where $\alpha = e^{\alpha_5}$. In general, combing like terms in Eq. (9) can reduce the parameters from the order of $3m$ to $(m+1)$. These parameters can be learned by standard linear regression packages.

4.5.2 Multiplicative Aggregation Model

Multiplicative aggregation is another way to combine discounting functions, in the form:

$$\hat{y} = w \prod_{i=1}^{m} f(X_i) \tag{6}$$

Supposing each discounting function has two parameters on average, Eq. (6) has $(2m+1)$ parameters to learn. We try to reduce the number of parameters, by performing a linearization, in the following way:

$$\ln \hat{y} = \ln w + \sum_{i=1}^{m} \ln f(X_i) \tag{7}$$

If $f(X_i)$ is the exponential discounting, Eq. (7) degrades to a simple linear regression with $(m+1)$ parameters without accuracy loss. Otherwise, we can discard the constants or lower order terms in discounting functions and obtain an approximated version of Eq. (7) with $(m+1)$ parameters.

4.5.3 *Impression Discounting Factor*

Both linear aggregation and multiplicative aggregation can be linearized as a uniform form shown below

$$\tilde{y} = \sum_{i=0}^{m} u_i \tilde{X}_i \tag{8}$$

where $\tilde{y} = \hat{y}$ in linear aggregation and $\tilde{y} = \ln \hat{y}$ in multiplicative aggregation. We set $\tilde{X}_0 = 1$ and when $i \geq 1$, we have $\tilde{X}_i \in \{X_i, \frac{1}{X_i}, \alpha^{X_i}, X_i^2\}$ for linear aggregation and $\tilde{X}_i \in \{\ln X_i, X_i\}$ for multiplicative aggregation. It is trivial to show $support(\tilde{X}_i) = support(X_i)$. The selection of $\tilde{X}_i$ depends on the kind of discounting functions for each behavior in the model. For example, in multiplicative aggregation, if $f(X_i)$ is the inverse discounting, we have $\tilde{X}_i = \ln X_i$. Eq. (8) can be written in matrix notation as

$$\tilde{y} = \tilde{X}^T u \tag{9}$$

Once we obtain the aggregated discounting model, the impression discounting factor d for a impression tuple $\mathcal{T}$ can be computed by the normalized value of $\tilde{y}$, which falls in $(0, 1]$. That is,

$$d = \frac{\tilde{y}}{\max \tilde{y}} \tag{10}$$

4.6 Anti-Noise Regression Model

Eq. (9) transforms the aggregated discounting model as a linear regression problem, whose objective function is to minimize the mean squared error, with a form

$$RMSE^2 = \frac{1}{n}\sum_{i=1}^{n}(y_i - \tilde{y})^2 = \frac{1}{n}\sum_{i=1}^{n}(y_i - \tilde{X}_i^T u)^2 \tag{11}$$

In the practice of model-fitting, we observed a number of cases that the sparsity of observation supports may make the conversion rate go too high or too low. Examples are found on the curve tails in Figure 5(a) and 5(b). If y_i deviates from the overall trend of its neighboring observations because of sparsity, the objective function Eq. (11) will suffer a lot because it tries to minimize the difference between the local overall trend and sparse observations. Ideally, it would be perfect if outliers of observations can be removed by a well-designed mechanism and the observations with less supports can be penalized in the objective function.

Notice that the naive approach that truncates the curve tail by a threshold on the minimal support of an observation is problematic, because: (1) this will also remove the observations that don't deviate a lot from their local overall trends; (2) the threshold is difficult to decide, because on the scale of billions of records, the "sparsity" is a relative concept, where a "sparse" observation may still have millions of supports.

4.6.1 *Outlier Observation Detection*

In related work, density-based clustering [6] defines clusters as areas of higher density than the remainder of the data set, and the key idea is that for each node in the cluster, the number of neighbors within a radius ε should exceed a threshold δ. Density-based clustering has the benefit of distinguishing clusters and outliers in a data space efficiently. Recently, density-based clustering emerged into the social network and media analysis [13, 12] and demonstrated its effectiveness. In impression discounting, we model the density of an observation as the support sum in a small neighborhood of this observation. The migration of density concepts to the linear regression is a contribution of this paper. To start, we define ε-neighborhood of a behavior list X in multiple-variable linear regression as follows.

***Definition** 2.* (ε-neighborhood of a behavior). The ε-neighborhood of a behavior set X, denoted by $N_\varepsilon(X)$, is defined by $N_\varepsilon(X) = \{X' \in D | dist(X, X') \leq \varepsilon\}$.

The shape of ε-neighborhood is determined by the choice of the distance function $dist(X, X')$. Without the loss of generality, we consider the Euclidean distance is the choice for multi-dimensional feature space, that is

$$dist(X, X') = dist(X', X) = \left(\sum_{i=1}^{n}(X_i - X_i')^2\right)^{\frac{1}{2}} \tag{12}$$

Density-based clustering does not define the concept of "connection" between points. In our anti-noise regression model, as each behavior list X is associated with a response value y, we use connection to describe the relationship between two pairs of observations, as defined below.

***Definition** 3.* (Connection in ε-neighborhood). Given two different observations (X, y) and (X', y'), they are connected if $dist(X, X') \leq \varepsilon$ and $|y - y'| \leq \gamma$, where γ is the maximal tolerance for local deviation.

We compute the density of an observation (X, y) as the sum of supports connected with (X, y) in the ε-neighborhood:

$$density(X, y) = \sum_{X' \in N_\varepsilon(X), |y - y'| \leq \gamma} support(X', y') \tag{13}$$

Density score will categorize observations into three types:

- **Core Observations**: (X, y) is a core observation, if the support of connected observations within the ε-neighborhood exceeds the threshold δ. That is, $density(X, y) \geq \delta$.
- **Border Observations**: (X, y) is a border observation, if (X, y) is not a core observation but connects to at least one core observation.
- **Outlier Observations**: (X, y) is an outlier observation, if (X, y) is neither a core nor a border observation.

Intuitively, outlier observations capture those observations that are unreliable by deviating from the local trends of nearby observations. Basically, all the outlier observations can be discarded before the linear regression. We can tune density parameters $\{\varepsilon, \delta, \gamma\}$ to control the percentage of outlier observations in the observation space. As a general guideline, $\{\varepsilon, \gamma\}$ is usually fixed for a specific impression data set, and we set 5% as the percentage of outlier observations out of all observations, which can be tuned by δ.

We explain the intuition of noise detection from the graph perspective. If we view each observation as a node and a connection between observations as an edge, an observation network will be built. Core observations will be those nodes with a high connectivity to other nodes. Those nodes represent high authority ranking in the network analysis such as PageRank [16]. Outlier observations are those nodes with low degrees and no edges to any high authority nodes, and they usually represent the marginal, isolated or noisy part of the network. Removing these outlier nodes will make the whole network structure more cohesive and accurate to model.

4.6.2 *Density Weighted Regression*

In RMSE shown in Eq. (11), the error between the actual conversion rate y and predicted conversion rate $\tilde{y}$ are weighted equally. However, we argue that for observations with high supports, their errors should be emphasized in the objective function, compared with the observations with a relatively low supports. To achieve the goal, we propose the *density weighted regression*, which adds a weight v_i for each error $(y_i - \tilde{X_i}^T u)$, with a modified objective function given below

$$RMSE_v^2 = \frac{1}{n}\sum_{i=1}^{n}(v_i(y_i - \tilde{X_i}^T u))^2 \quad (14)$$

The problem is how to decide v_i. One naive solution is using the ratio between the support of an observation and the total supports to weight the corresponding error, that is $v_i^* = \frac{support(X_i)}{\sum_{X \in D} support(X)}$. The assumption of this solution is that the distribution of $support(X_i)$ is "smooth" in X_i's local neighborhood. That is to say, compared with the support of X_i's neighbors, $support(X_i)$ should not be remarkably too high or too low. However, in real-world data sets, $support(X_i)$ is likely not smooth due to the sparsity problem. Instead, we propose an advanced solution, by adopting the density parameter ε:

$$v_i = \frac{Average(\sum_{X_j \in N_\varepsilon(X_i), |y_i - y_j| \le \gamma} support(X_j))}{\sum_{X \in D} support(X)} \quad (15)$$

Notice that $X_i \in N_\varepsilon(X_i)$. The rationale behind Eq. (15) is that, the supports of all similar observations in the neighborhood of X_i contributes to the weight of (X_i, y_i). In the extreme case, if $\varepsilon = 0$, we have $N_\varepsilon(X_i) = \{X_i\}$ and v_i degrades to the naive solution. If $\varepsilon = \infty$ and $\gamma = 1$, $N_\varepsilon(X_i) = D$ and $v_i = 1$, making Eq. (14) degrades to the unweighted version (Eq. (11)). Typically, we set ε smaller than 5, making v_i as the ratio between the supports of ε-neighborhood and the total supports. v_i is smoother than v_i^* and highlights the observations with high supports effectively.

Next, we can write Eq. (14) in matrix notation as $n \cdot RMSE_v^2 = (Vy - VXu)^T(Vy - VXu)$, where $V = diag(v)$. If we take the derivative of $n \cdot RMSE_v^2$ with respect to u, we get $(VX)^T(Vy - VXu)$. By setting the derivative to zero, we solve u by the following reasoning:

$$\begin{aligned} \hat{u} &= ((VX)^T(VX))^{-1}(VX)^T(Vy) && (16)\\ &= (X^T(V^TV)X)^{-1}X^T(V^TV)y && (17)\\ &= (X^TV^2X)^{-1}X^TV^2y && (18)\end{aligned}$$

where $V^2 = diag(v \circ v)$ and $\circ$ is the Hadamard product [22] (a.k.a. entrywise product) for vectors. Eq. (18) can be actually viewed as a kind of locally weighted linear regression problem [20], where V^2 is the weighting matrix.

In the case that the matrix X^TV^2X is singular, we cannot solve $\hat{u}$ by Eq. (18) by the inverse operation. It is well known that Ridge regression [3] adds an additional matrix λI to the matrix X^TX in linear regression to make it non-singular. In our anti-noise regression model, we can apply a similar technique and estimate $\hat{u}$ by

$$\hat{u}_{ridge} = (X^TV^2X + \lambda I)^{-1}X^TV^2y \quad (19)$$

where λ is determined by minimizing RMSE.

4.7 Model Evaluation

Imagining that we have n choices for discounting functions, the number of different aggregation models can be as high as n^m for both linear aggregation and multiplicative aggregation. Although correlation analysis can rule out a large portion of aggregation models by selecting discounting functions with low RMSE, we still need standard evaluation metrics to compare different aggregation models and find the optimal discounting model for the recommender system. In this paper, we use the following evaluation metric to assess the performance of an aggregated discounting model:

- **Precision at Top** k. In the testing data set, given a $user$, we return the top k $item$ set L_k ranked by $\mathcal{T}.R \cdot d$ without looking at the $conversion$ attribute, where d is computed by the aggregated discounting model. Precision at Top k will be measured as the conversion rate of L_k, which is

$$P@k = \frac{seqSize(conversion = true)}{k} \quad (20)$$

5. EXPERIMENTAL EVALUATION

In this section, we test the proposed impression discounting model on three real online impression data sets: LinkedIn PYMK, LinkedIn Endorsement and Tencent SearchAds. The data set details are described in Section 3.2.

5.1 Correlation Analysis

Correlation analysis helps determine which discounting function fits the relationship between the conversion rate and a user behavior the best. We perform correlation visualization in both 2-D and 3-D.

5.1.1 2-D Correlation Analysis

The 2-D correlation analysis between the conversion rate and a specific behavior is an effective way to discover the strength and type of relationships between them. Figure 7 shows the conversion rate vs. *LastSeen*, *Position* and *UserFreq* on three real data sets. The conversion rate vs. *ImpCount* has already been shown in Figure 3. In Figure 7(a), we can see conversion rate in PYMK decreases faster with *LastSeen* than the conversion rate in the Endorsement data set, which reveals that *LastSeen* for Endorsement is less important than it for PYMK. *LastSeen* is not available in SearchAds data set. Figure 7(b) shows the relationships between the conversion rate and offset positions in the recommendation list. Clearly, if an $item$ is ranked lower in the recommendation list, its conversion rate will be lower. Endorsement data set has the steepest decreasing trend, compared with the other two data sets. In Figure 7(c), we show the conversion rate as the increasing of *UserFreq*. Surprisingly, we find that the conversion rate increases in both PYMK and Endorsement. The explanation may be that, a higher *UserFreq* indicates that $user$ is more active in the recommender system, and also more likely to take conversion actions. *UserFreq* does not play an important role in SearchAds, most likely because users do not have enough stickiness to a general web search engine.

5.1.2 3-D Correlation Analysis

In Figure 8, we perform the 3-D visualization between conversion rate and two user behaviors on three data sets respectively. Each ball represents an observation, which is the conversion rate with respect to a specific value of user behaviors. As we can see, on the PYMK data set (Figure 8(a)), *ConveRate* decreases with both *ImpCount* and *LastSeen*. However, on the Endorsement data set (Figure 8(b)), *ConveRate* is not very sensitive with *LastSeen*, as supported by Figure 7(a). Figure 8(b) also shows there are many outlier observations even when $ImpCount < 10$, mainly because most impression sequences in Endorsement data set are very short and the sparsity problem becomes very critical. On the SearchAds data set (Figure 8(c)), because *LastSeen* is not available, we show $ConveRate$ vs. *ImpCount* and *Position*, which clearly decreases along both dimensions.

5.2 Model Evaluation

5.2.1 Precision at Top k

We split each impression data set into training and testing sets, and the impression discounting model is learned from the training

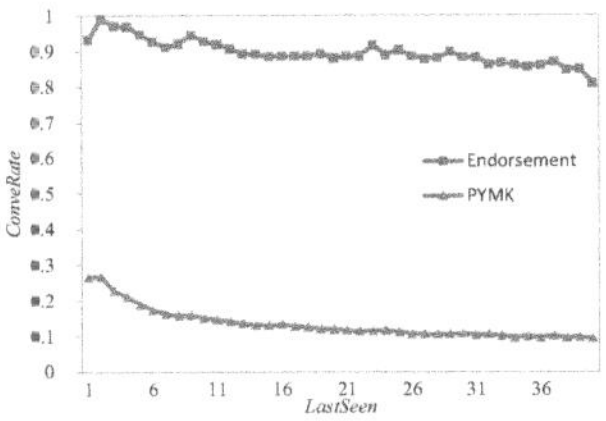

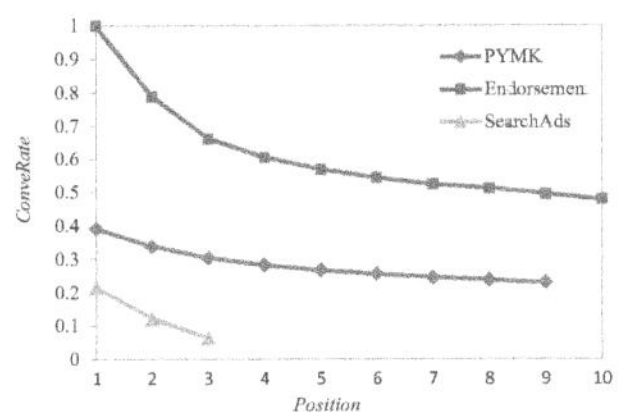

(a) Conversion rate vs. *LastSeen* (b) Conversion rate vs. *Position*

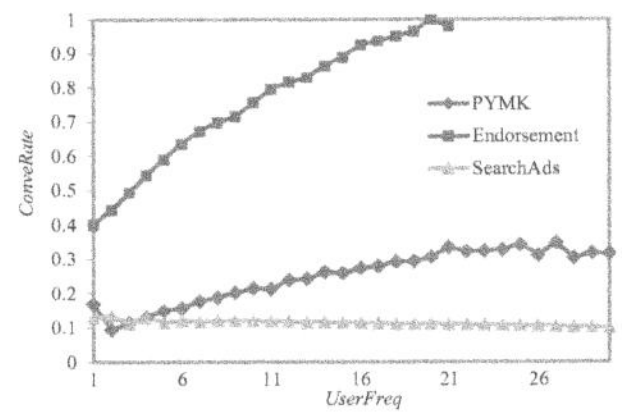

(c) Conversion rate vs. *UserFreq*

Figure 7: Conversion rate vs. *LastSeen*, *Position* and *UserFreq* on three real data sets.

Behavior Set	Precision Improvement
PYMK ($P@10$)	
LastSeen, ImpCount	13.7%
LastSeen, ImpCount Position, UserFreq	31.3%
Endorsement ($P@10$)	
LastSeen, ImpCount	1.3%
LastSeen, ImpCount Position, UserFreq	3.4%
SearchAds ($P@5$, 10)	
ImpCount	0.53%($P@10$)
ImpCount, Position	3.2%($P@10$)
ImpCount, Position	6.87%($P@5$)

Table 2: The improvement of precision at top k of the impression discounting model on different real-world data sets. The improvement rate is computed based on the precisions at top k without discounting.

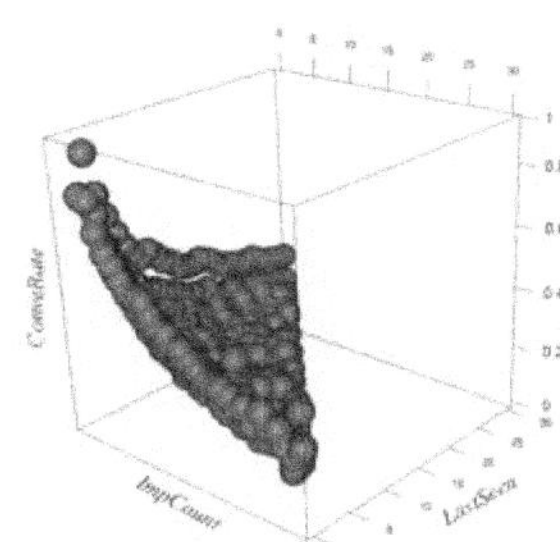

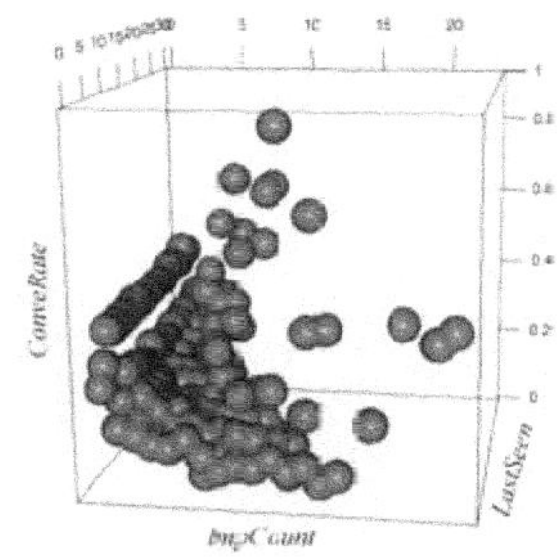

(a) PYMK 3-D (b) Endorsement 3-D

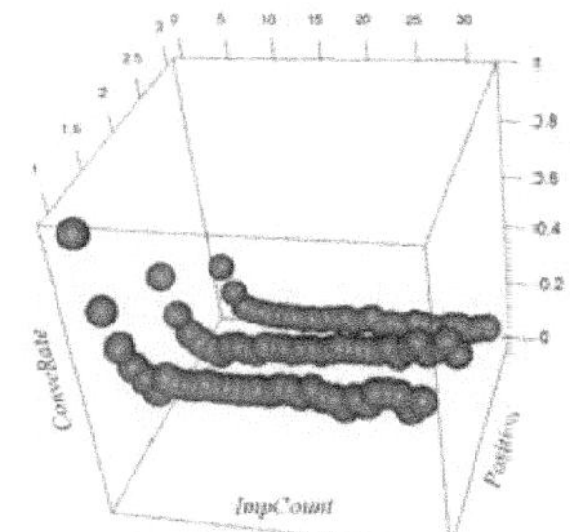

(c) SearchAds 3-D

Figure 8: The 3-D visualization between conversion rate and user behaviors on three real data sets.

X_1: *LastSeen*; X_2: *ImpCount*	
Group A: Without Impression Discounting	
Group B:	Improvement
$\alpha_1 \cdot \alpha_2^{X_1} \cdot \alpha_3^{X_2}$	$11.97\% \pm 0.2\%$
$(\frac{\alpha_1}{X_1} + \alpha_2) \cdot \alpha_3^{X_2}$	$13.26\% \pm 0.2\%$
$(\alpha_1 \cdot X_1 + \alpha_2) \cdot \alpha_3^{X_2}$	$12.18\% \pm 0.2\%$

Table 3: The A/B test results of precision at top 10 of different impression discounting models on PYMK data set, with X =(*LastSeen*, *ImpCount*).

set. We use precision at top k defined by Eq. (20) on the testing set to evaluate the performance of different aggregated discounting models. The precision improvement of the impression discounting model, compared with the baseline without a discounting model, is shown in Table 2. As we can see, if we integrate more user behaviors into the impression discounting model, the precision will be improved: the 4-behavior model on both PYMK and Endorsement gains at least two times higher precision growth compared with the 2-behavior model. Also, the precision growth on PYMK is obviously higher than the precision growth on Endorsement and SearchAds, because impression sequences in PYMK is distinctly longer than the impression sequences in the other two data sets. As proof, $P@5$ is obviously higher than $P@10$ on SearchAds, because a user has 5.8 items on average, and the precision on top 10 items of each user is not an effective evaluation metric.

5.2.2 A/B Testing

We implemented the impression discounting model in the LinkedIn PYMK recommender system, and the online A/B test results is shown in Table 3. This impression discounting model uses two behaviors, *LastSeen* and *ImpCount*. We fix the *ImpCount* dimension as the exponential discounting (as it has the minimal RMSE), and try the *LastSeen* by exponential discounting, inverse discounting, and linear discounting respectively. The results show that exponential discounting achieves a slightly better precision improvement, and all the Group B models gain significant improvements by incorporating impression discounting in recommendations.

5.2.3 Enhancing Linear Regression

In this section, we evaluate the density weighted regression proposed in Section 4.5.3. Compared with traditional linear regression, density weighted regression removes the outlier observations and assigns weights to observations based on their supports. Figure 9(a) shows the distribution of observation supports is very skewed and follows power-low distribution. If we treat these observations as unweighted, the squared error of each observation using traditional linear regression is shown in the lower line in Figure 9(b). As we can see, although linear regression minimizes the sum of squared errors by reducing the area under the curve (AUC), squared errors are high when *ImpCount* is small. Since Figure 9(a) reveals that most observations have small *ImpCount*, traditional linear regression suffers from the problem that the majority of impression sequences have high prediction error.

In contrast, density weighted regression tries to minimize the prediction error of impression sequences. In this experiment, we set $\varepsilon = 2$, $\gamma = 0.01$ and $\delta = 2$. In the preprocessing, we detect

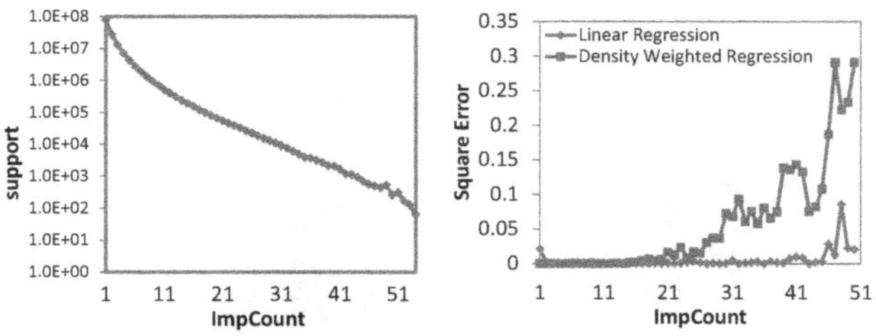

(a) (b)

Figure 9: (a) The support of observations with specific *ImpCount* in logarithmic scale. (b) The squared error of each observation by traditional linear regression and our anti-noise linear regression. Experiments are performed on PYMK data.

and remove 5 observations on the tail. We set the weights by Eq. (15), and the squared errors are shown by the upper line in Figure 9(b). Although the AUC of density weighted regression is larger than the traditional linear regression, the squared errors are minimized when *ImpCount* is small. To evaluate their performance in model-fitting, we instantiate the RMSE in Eq. (14) by

$$RMSE^2 = \frac{1}{\sum_{X \in D} support(X)} \sum_{i=1}^{n} (support(X_i, y_i)(y_i - \tilde{X_i}^T u))^2 \quad (21)$$

On PYMK data set, we compute the RMSE for traditional linear regression and density weighted regression as 0.1121 and 0.0188 respectively, which indicates density weighted regression performs much better than linear regression when the distribution of observation supports is skewed.

6. CONCLUSION

In this paper, we focuse on the impression discounting problem in large-scale recommender systems, in which a user's impressions on historical recommended items are discounted to re-rank the recommendation list. User satisfaction quantified by the conversion rate is expected to be improved due to the re-ranking. To precisely capture each facet of user interaction, we build impression discounting models by integrating discounting functions of user behaviors into a linear or multiplicative aggregation model. Moreover, to resolve the sparsity problem on observation supports, we propose anti-noise regression model to remove the outlier observations and perform a density weighted regression, which achieves a better prediction quality than the traditional linear regression. The proposed impression discounting framework is evaluated on three real-world data sets from LinkedIn and Tencent. The precision improvement on these impression data sets supports the effectiveness of our impression discounting model.

7. REFERENCES

[1] D. Agarwal, B.-C. Chen, and P. Elango. Spatio-temporal models for estimating click-through rate. In *WWW*, 2009.

[2] E. Agichtein, E. Brill, and S. T. Dumais. Improving web search ranking by incorporating user behavior information. In *SIGIR*, pages 19–26, 2006.

[3] C. Bishop. *Pattern Recognition and Machine Learning*. Information Science and Statistics. Springer, 2006.

[4] W. Chen, Y. Chen, Y. Mao, and B. Guo. Density-based logistic regression. In *KDD*, pages 140–148, 2013.

[5] B. Dalessandro, R. Hook, and C. Perlich. Evaluating and optimizing online advertising: Forget the click, but there are good proxies. In *Proceedings of Empirical Generalizations in Advertising Conference*, 2012.

[6] M. Ester, H.-P. Kriegel, J. Sander, and X. Xu. A density-based algorithm for discovering clusters in large spatial databases with noise. In *KDD*, pages 226–231, 1996.

[7] N. Gupta, A. Das, S. Pandey, and V. K. Narayanan. Factoring past exposure in display advertising targeting. In *KDD*, pages 1204–1212, 2012.

[8] Y. Hu, Y. Koren, and C. Volinsky. Collaborative filtering for implicit feedback datasets. In *ICDM*, pages 263–272, 2008.

[9] Y. Koren. Factorization meets the neighborhood: a multifaceted collaborative filtering model. In *KDD*, 2008.

[10] Y. Koren. Factor in the neighbors: Scalable and accurate collaborative filtering. *TKDD*, 4(1), 2010.

[11] S. Kpotufe and V. K. Garg. Adaptivity to local smoothness and dimension in kernel regression. In *NIPS*, pages 3075–3083, 2013.

[12] P. Lee, L. V. S. Lakshmanan, and E. E. Milios. Keysee: supporting keyword search on evolving events in social streams. In *KDD*, pages 1478–1481, 2013.

[13] P. Lee, L. V. S. Lakshmanan, and E. E. Milios. Incremental cluster evolution tracking from highly dynamic network data. In *ICDE*, pages 3–14, 2014.

[14] X. Lin and D. Zhang. Inference in generalized additive mixed models by using smoothing splines. *Journal of the Royal Statistical Society, Series B*, 61(2):381–400, 1999.

[15] O. Moling, L. Baltrunas, and F. Ricci. Optimal radio channel recommendations with explicit and implicit feedback. In *RecSys*, pages 75–82, 2012.

[16] L. Page, S. Brin, R. Motwani, and T. Winograd. The pagerank citation ranking: Bringing order to the web. Technical Report 1999-66, Stanford InfoLab, 1999.

[17] C. Perlich. Machine learning challenges in targeted advertising: Transfer learning in action. 2013.

[18] M. Richardson, E. Dominowska, and R. Ragno. Predicting clicks: estimating the click-through rate for new ads. In *WWW*, pages 521–530, 2007.

[19] G. Ristanoski, W. Liu, and J. Bailey. Time series forecasting using distribution enhanced linear regression. In *PAKDD (1)*, pages 484–495, 2013.

[20] D. Ruppert and M. P. Wand. Multivariate locally weighted least squares regression. *Annals of Statistics*, 22:1347–1370, 1994.

[21] B. M. Sarwar, G. Karypis, J. A. Konstan, and J. Riedl. Item-based collaborative filtering recommendation algorithms. In *WWW*, pages 285–295, 2001.

[22] G. P. Styan. Hadamard products and multivariate statistical analysis. *Linear Algebra and its Applications*, 6:217–240, 1973.

[23] R. Sumbaly, J. Kreps, and S. Shah. The big data ecosystem at linkedin. In *SIGMOD*, pages 1125–1134, 2013.

[24] D. Yang, T. Chen, W. Zhang, Q. Lu, and Y. Yu. Local implicit feedback mining for music recommendation. In *RecSys*, pages 91–98, 2012.

[25] S.-H. Yang, B. Long, A. J. Smola, H. Zha, and Z. Zheng. Collaborative competitive filtering: learning recommender using context of user choice. In *SIGIR*, pages 295–304, 2011.

[26] J. Zhang and P. Pu. A recursive prediction algorithm for collaborative filtering recommender systems. In *RecSys*, pages 57–64, 2007.

ISIS: A Networked-Epidemiology Based Pervasive Web App for Infectious Disease Pandemic Planning and Response

Richard Beckman*
rbeckman@vbi.vt.edu

Keith R. Bisset*
kbisset@vbi.vt.edu

Jiangzhuo Chen*
chenj@vbi.vt.edu

Bryan Lewis*
blewis@vbi.vt.edu

Madhav Marathe*†
mmarathe@vbi.vt.edu

Paula Stretz*
pstretz@vbi.vt.edu

ABSTRACT

We describe ISIS, a high-performance-computing-based application to support computational epidemiology of infectious diseases. ISIS has been developed over the last seven years in close coordination with public health and policy experts. It has been used in a number of important federal planning and response exercises. ISIS grew out of years of experience in developing and using HPC-oriented models of complex socially coupled systems. This identified the guiding principle that *complex models will be used by domain experts only if they can do realistic analysis without becoming computing experts.*

Using ISIS, one can carry out detailed computational experiments as they pertain to planning and response in the event of a pandemic. ISIS is designed to support networked epidemiology – study of epidemic processes over social contact networks. The current system can handle airborne infectious diseases such as influenza, pertussis, and smallpox. ISIS is comprised of the following basic components: (*i*) a web app that serves as the user-interface, (*ii*) a middleware that coordinates user interaction via the web app with backend models and databases, (*iii*) a backend computational modeling framework that is comprised of highly resolved epidemic simulations combined with highly realistic control strategies that include pharmaceutical as well as non-pharmaceutical interventions and (*iv*) a backend data management framework that manages complex unstructured and semi-structured data.

ISIS has been used in over a dozen case studies defined by the DoD, DHHS, NIH, BARDA and NSC. We describe three recent studies illustrating the use of ISIS in real-world settings: (*i*) uses of ISIS during the H1N1 pandemic, (*ii*) supporting a US military planning exercise, and (*iii*) distribution of limited stockpile of pharmaceuticals using public and private outlets.

Categories and Subject Descriptors

H.3.5 [**Information Storage and Retrieval**]: Online Information Services — *Web-based services*; I.6.3 [**Simulation and Modeling**]: Applications; I.6.7 [**Simulation and Modeling**]: Simulation Support Systems

Keywords

web app; computational epidemiology; simulation; HPC; public health

1. INTRODUCTION

A pandemic is an infectious disease outbreak affecting a large population across the entire globe, for example, the re-emergence of H1N1 influenza in 2009. Certain modern trends exacerbate the speed and severity of pandemics. This includes: (*i*) increased global population, (*ii*) increased mobility, both on locally and internationally, and (*iii*) increased populations of older and immunocompromised individuals. In spite of these factors, over the last 50 years, public health agencies across the world have made remarkable strides in reducing the social, economic and health impacts of such pandemics. Computational epidemiology is the development and use of computer models for understanding the spatio-temporal diffusion of disease through populations. Controlled experiments used to understand scientific phenomenon are much harder and often impossible to do when studying epidemiology, due to ethical, and often practical reasons. As a result, computational models play an important role in elucidating the space-time dynamics of epidemics. They also serve an important role in evaluating various intervention strategies, including pharmaceutical and non-pharmaceutical interventions [20, 14, 19, 18]. The role of individual behavior and public policies is critical in understanding and controlling epidemics.

Traditional mathematical models for studying epidemics focused on rate-based differential equation models [15]. In this approach, one partitions the population into subgroups based on various criteria (e.g., demographic characteristics and disease states), and use differential equation models to describe the disease dynamics across these groups. Although

*Network Dynamics and Simulation Science Laboratory, Virginia Bioinformatics Institute, Virginia Tech. Blacksburg, VA 24061, USA.

†Department of Computer Science, Virginia Tech. Blacksburg, VA 24061, USA

KDD'14, August 24–27, 2014, New York, NY, USA.

ACM 978-1-4503-2956-9/14/08 ...$15.00.
http://dx.doi.org/10.1145/2623330.2623375.

useful, the approach fails to capture the complexity of human interactions and behaviors. The diversity of human behavior makes planning and response complicated and motivates a measure-project-intervene modeling cycle. This naturally motivates an *interaction based approach*. It involves accurate modeling of the social interaction network and the disease dynamics. It uses an endogenous representations of individuals together with explicit interactions between these agents to generate and capture the disease spread across the social interaction network; see [23, 24]. In this sense, the approach goes beyond the mathematical modeling techniques discussed earlier, which assume homogeneous interactions within each segment of the population. It raises new technical difficulties though, including (*i*) synthesis of city and national scale social contact networks, (*ii*) high performance computing models to study disease spread and interventions over these networks and (*iii*) bigdata challenges spanning the ability to carry out complex computational experiments, data management and analytics. Nevertheless, recent advances in computing technology, machine learning, data mining and network science have made this approach a reality [10, 12, 22, 21, 11].

Public health epidemiology provides an important societal application to apply computational thinking and exploit big data. The big data challenges come in numerous forms: (*i*) a large number of diverse data streams pertaining to social, health, economic, policy and infrastructure realms that need to be synthesized to develop realistic social contact networks; (*ii*) the size of data sets; (*iii*) modeling the epidemics spread, and the impact of interventions, requires substantial computing resources; furthermore this produces data that is several orders of magnitude larger than the input data; (*iv*) the measure-model-analyze-act-measure loop implies that the input data and data generated by models has to be analyzed in near-real time.

2. OUR CONTRIBUTIONS

Here we describe ISIS (*Interface to Synthetic Information Systems*): a web-browser based modeling and decision support environment for public health epidemiologists. ISIS can be used for planning, situation assessment, counter-factual analysis and response as it pertains to infectious disease epidemiology. The current system can handle airborne infectious diseases such as influenza, pertussis, smallpox, etc. ISIS is a part of a larger integrated cyber-environment and is comprised of the following basic components: (*i*) a web-browser based user-interface (i.e., a web app), (*ii*) a middleware that coordinates user interaction with the UI and with the backend models and databases, (*iii*) a backend computational modeling framework that is comprised of highly resolved epidemic simulations combined with highly realistic control strategies that include both pharmaceutical as well as non-pharmaceutical interventions and (*iv*) a backend data management framework that manages complex unstructured as and semi-structured data. ISIS can support interaction based computational epidemiology discussed earlier.

ISIS is designed specifically so that public health analysts can focus on design and analysis of complex computer experiments to support planning and control of epidemics rather than becoming computer scientists. Nevertheless, the backend is comprised of powerful high performance computing based modeling and data management methods. The group has been developing models for large complex social systems for over a decade. The motivation to develop such pervasive computing web apps providing seamless access was derived from our earlier experience, wherein we realized that complex models although scientifically interesting are of little use if they cannot be made accessible to a domain expert who is usually not a computer scientist.

The supporting underlying mathematical models have been reported in our earlier work – our focus here is on computational and data infrastructure that enables the development and deployment of the pervasive and scalable web app so that it can be used by public health analysts. The focus of this paper is on problem description, design decisions, and deployment challenges.

ISIS has been used to support a number of federal planning and decision support exercises. We describe three such studies: (*i*) use of the tool during the H1N1 pandemic outbreak, (*ii*) supporting a DOD planning exercise for military preparedness, and (*iii*) socio-economic analysis of anti-viral distribution. We have chosen these examples for three reasons. First, they demonstrate the range of computational experiments that can be carried out using the tool. Second, they demonstrate the use of ISIS in important real-world settings as opposed to an academic exercise. Finally, each of the studies identified new challenges that served as requirements for further development of the tool.

3. THE WEB APP

The web app is an interactive, easy to use, graphical user interface and is designed to support the running of experiments consisting of numerous simulations that generate distributions of outcomes to gain an appreciation of the time-varying state (the dynamics) of an epidemiological event. The tool specifically supports exploration of the variability of outcomes in this highly stochastic process. Experimental outcomes are used in analysis reports, which are a kind of distribution of numerous replicates of an experiment and are generally viewable as plotted graphs. The ISIS tool is intended primarily to facilitate both the planning and course of action of analysis activities for analysts.

The ISIS web app allows a user to set up detailed factorial experiments. Using a simple interface to an underlying digital library, a user can specify the following for their experiment: (*i*) a social contact network; (*ii*) a within-host disease progression model; and (*iii*) a set of interventions. Each intervention requires additional details such as compliance level, sub-populations to which the interventions are applied and intervention triggers. An experiment consists of sweeping one or more parameters across a user-specified range of values. See Figure 1 for an illustration of ISIS experiments. After setting up the experiment, the user is provided access to the results of the simulations. A set of basic analyses are performed automatically and the results are displayed. See Figure 2 for an illustration of ISIS analyses. The standard plots and epidemic curves provide very detailed information about the epidemic. Additional information such as the spatio-temporal dynamics and disease dendrogram (how the disease moved over the social network) is also available. A key aspect of ISIS is its simplicity – we can train public health analysts to make effective use of the system in about three hours. Somewhat counter-intuitively, by hiding the computational models from the end user, ISIS makes them much more accessible. See `http://ndssl.vbi.vt.edu/apps/isis/` for further details.

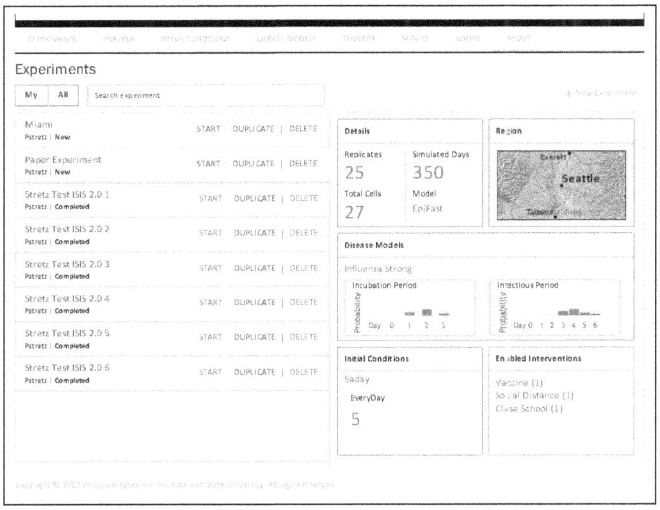

Figure 1: Experiment page of ISIS.

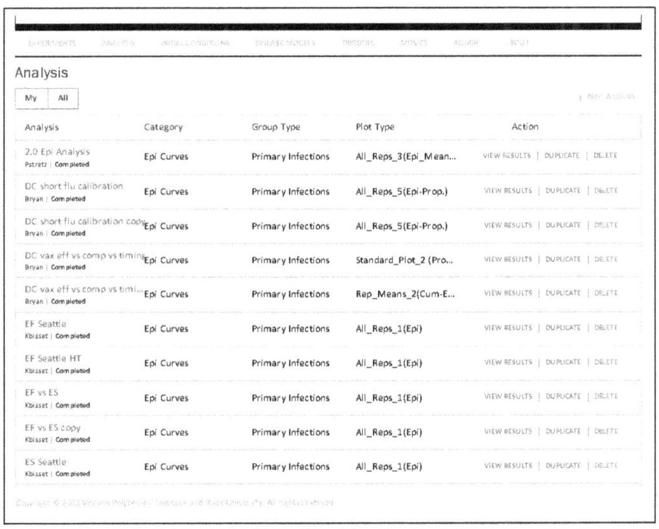

Figure 2: Analysis page of ISIS.

3.1 Designed Experiments in ISIS

ISIS is structured to easily make comparative studies of possible interventions using factorial or fractional factorial statistical designs. Rather than running and analyzing one simulation at a time, multiple simulations with differing combinations of interventions are simulated and analyzed as a way to compare the relative effectiveness of the interventions and to assess any non-linearity in these effects. The possible interventions in ISIS are: vaccinate a portion of the population, institute social distancing, close the work places or the schools, and use antivirals as a treatment or as a prophylaxis.

Figure 5 shows one screen of an experimental setup where interventions involving vaccination, social distancing, and closing schools are to be simulated and compared. The levels of vaccination required in the simulation experiment are shown in the figure: 0%, 10% or 20% of the population is vaccinated. In the experiment each of the other two interventions also has three different compliance levels. After 1% of the entire population is infected, 0%, 25% or 50% of

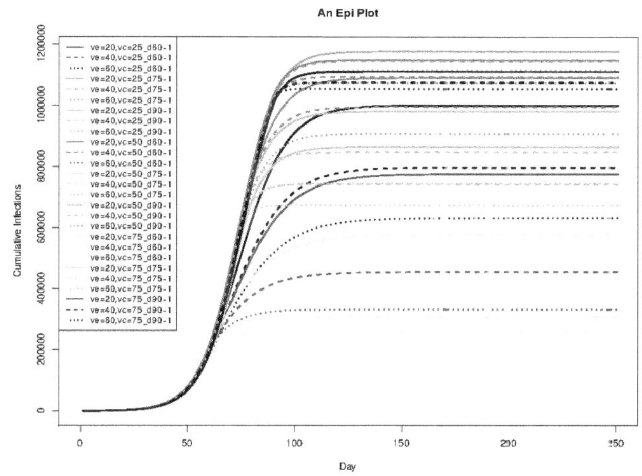

Figure 3: Analysis plots of a vaccination strategy experiment in the Washington, DC region comparing efficacy, compliance and timing of the vaccine.

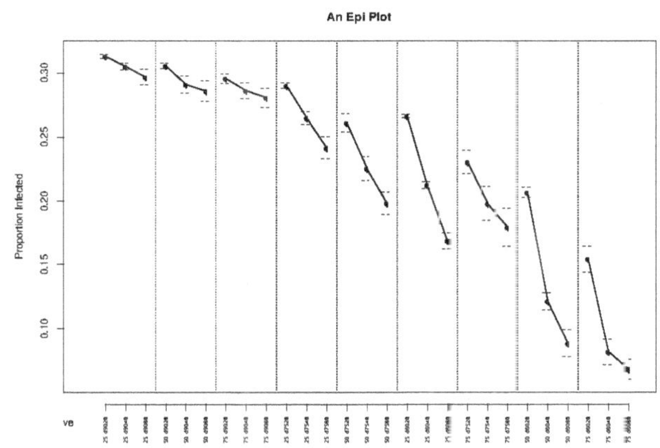

Figure 4: Analysis plots of a vaccination strategy experiment in the Washington, DC region comparing efficacy, compliance and timing of the vaccine.

the school children no longer attend school. Additionally, the entire population excludes 0%, 10% or 20% of nonessential activities. The experiment consists of simulations for all combinations of the levels of the interventions each replicated 25 times. Hence, the entire ISIS experiment is the factorial aggregate of $3 \times 3 \times 3 \times 25 = 675$ simulations.

The circles in Figure 6 are the mean number of persons infected (y-axis) for each of the treatment combinations on the x-axis. The x-axis has three rows one corresponding to each of the three interventions – vaccination (vc), close schools (sds) and general social distancing (sdg). The lines in the plot have no meaning and only serve to guide the eye. The x-axis is arranged so that the most important intervention is along the bottom row, the next most important in the next to last row, and so on. In this experiment, vaccination effects the number of infected persons the most as the infection or attack rate decreases most the as the vaccination rate

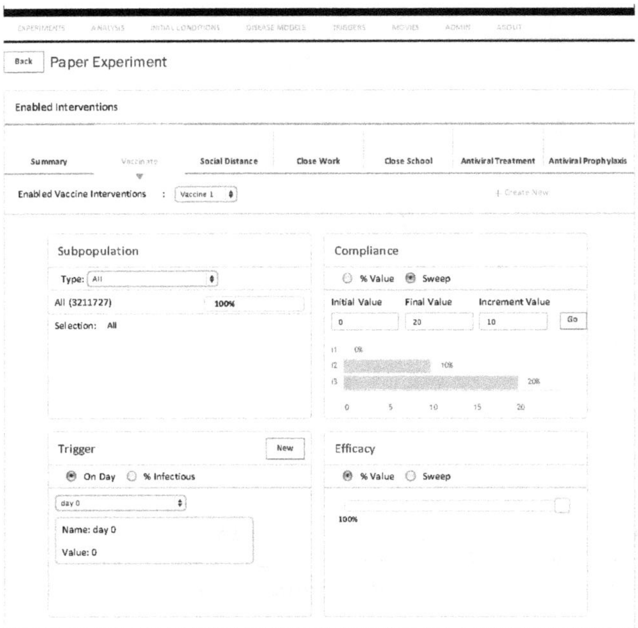

Figure 5: One of the three Isis screens for setting up a 3x3x3 experiment to assess the relative importance of vaccination, school closures, and social distancing. This figure shows that simulations are requested where 0%, 10% and 20% of the population is vaccinated. Similar screens exist for the other two interventions: social distancing and closing schools. In total 25 replicates of each of the 3x3x3=27 experimental combinations are simulated.

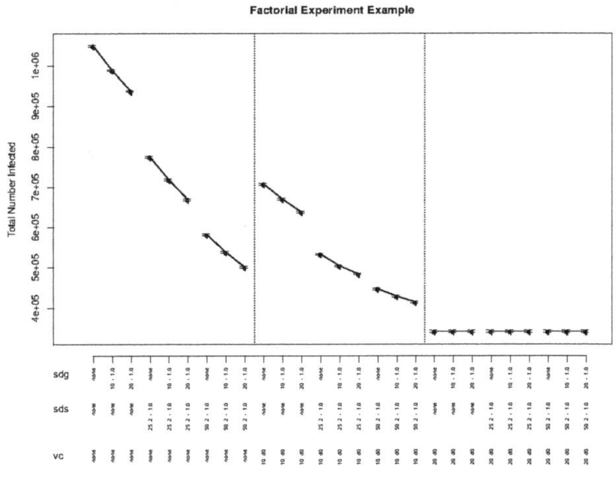

Figure 6: The attack rates (number of infected individuals) for each of the 27 intervention combinations are shown as the circles in the plot. The lines in the plot have no meaning other than to place the circles in logical groups. The x-axis has one row for each of the interventions with the most important intervention along the last row.

changes from 0% to 20%. Within each of the vaccination rates, closing schools has the largest effect at reducing the attack rate. It is interesting to note that the combination of the three interventions reveals a non-linear response in attack rates. That is, closing schools has a much larger effect on the attack rates if there is no vaccination than it does if 20% of the population is vaccinated.

3.2 Related work

Recently, there has been a flurry of activity aimed at developing easy to use interfaces to support computational infectious diseases epidemiology. Here we briefly discuss some of the prominent efforts.

1. Alex Vespignani and his colleagues at Northeastern University have developed EpiC and Gleamviz tools for global mobility and epidemic simulations. They developed a hybrid approach comprising of aggregate models for each county of interest and detailed networked connections between these counties capturing the flows of travelers based on daily airline passenger data.

2. Lauren Meyers and her group at the University of Texas at Austin have developed a set of tools DiCon for optimization and control problems related to epidemic dynamics, focusing on the logistics and supply chain [25].

3. The University of Pittsburgh group, a part of the NIH Modeling of Infectious Disease Agent Study (MIDAS) program, has developed a suite of tools for computational modeling, analysis and visualization of epidemiological processes. The tools use synthetic populations produced by RTI International [29] that are in turn based on an extension of the methodology developed by our laboratory. FRED [27] and GAIA [28] are the most related to our systems. FRED and GAIA are open sources systems and also support research in networked epidemiology.

4. The group at the University of Notre Dame is developing a cyber infrastructure for vector-borne diseases as a part of the Vector-Borne Disease Network consortium (VecNet); see [30]. VecNet is a part of the Malaria Education Research Agenda (MalERA) program established with the goal of reducing and hopefully eliminating malaria and funded by the Bill & Melinda Gates foundation.

4. HPC MODELS FOR DISEASE DIFFUSION AND BEHAVIORAL ADAPTATION

The overall approach consists of four distinct models: (*i*) a model for creating a set of synthetic individuals, (*ii*) a model for generating (time varying) interaction networks, (*iii*) a model for simulating the epidemic process, and (*iv*) a model for representing and evaluating interventions and public policies [1, 13, 2]. Mathematically, these steps can be represented by a combination of: a co-evolving graphical discrete dynamical system (CGDDS) that captures the co-evolution of disease dynamics, social network and individual behavior (first three models) and a partially observable Markov decision process (POMDP) that captures various control and optimization problems formulated on the phase space of this dynamical system. Formal descriptions on CGDDS and POMDP can be found in [6, 5, 9].

Interventions implemented in our HPC simulations can be described with the combination of a set of trigger conditions, a set of subpopulations, and a set of actions. They are usually in the form of: "when *trigger conditions* are satisfied, apply *actions* to *subpopulations*". Table 1 describes how an intervention can be represented. There may be multiple trigger conditions, subpopulations, and actions in an intervention. There may be multiple different interventions in a simulation.

Representing and analyzing disease dynamics over large unstructured and time-varying social contact networks requires new work in high performance computing as well. Table 2 shows the data sizes of a few examples of synthetic populations and networks and simulation results supported by Isis. In an effort to address the scaling problem typical in algorithms implemented for high performance computing, our group has developed three different parallel algorithms and their implementations over the last ten years: EpiSimdemics, EpiFast, and Indemics [3, 31, 7]. These differ in the traceoff they provide between computation speed, model realism and sophistication, and ease of introducing new behavior and interventions. A comparison between the simulations can be found in [5]. We briefly describe them below.

4.1 EpiSimdemics

EpiSimdemics [3], and its predecessor EpiSims [13], is an interaction-based, highly resolved modeling and simulation system for representing and reasoning about contagion diffusion across large networks. The EpiSimdemics algorithm is based on contagion diffusion across a social network. The network is represented as a bipartite graph, with people and locations as the nodes, and edges between them representing a person's presence at a location. We refer to this as a person-location graph. This representation allows location based interventions such as school closure to remove some contacts (e.g., contacts at a specific school) and replace them with contacts at a replacement location (e.g., home). EpiSimdemics can represent virtually all the existing models of between-host disease propagation. It supports fully dynamic social networks (nodes and edges can be added and removed in response to disease propagation). Through the use of its scenario scripting language [9], it also has the ability to represent a large collection of behavioral and public policy specifications, including the use of pharmaceuticals (e.g., vaccines or antivirals) and change of planned activities (e.g., school closure, quarantine). Contagion and behavior are modeled as coupled Probabilistic Timed Transition Systems (PTTS). Written in C++, EpiSimdemics initially used MPI but has recently been modified to use the Charm++ parallel framework [17, 4], which has led to improved scaling and execution time [31]. It can simulate the entire population of the United States, a person-location network with 300 million people and 1.5 billion edges. On the 352,000 core NCSA BlueWaters system, 120 days of an epidemic on this scale can be simulated in 12 seconds, as shown in Figure 7. To the best our of knowledge, this is the largest agent-based epidemic simulation, in terms of scaling.

4.2 EpiFast

EpiFast [7] differs from EpiSimdemics in the following ways: (*i*) The underlying person-person social network is explicitly given, whereas EpiSimdemics builds it implicitly using the people-location network [13]; (*ii*) EpiFast implements a simple linear multi-stage within host disease progression model, e.g., Susceptible Exposed Infectious Recovered (SEIR) disease model for epidemic simulations; (*iii*) EpiFast runs in bulk-synchronous mode; (*iv*) Interventions in EpiFast are coded as structural changes in the network (e.g., non-pharmaceutical interventions) or nodes' properties (e.g., infectivities and vulnerabilities). EpiFast is implemented in C++, using MPI for communication. It is similar to EpiSimdemics in that it can run on any distributed memory system, so long as the total of all available memory can hold the whole network and modeling parameters. The computing architecture is comprised of one master process and multiple worker processes. The system runs in a bulk synchronous parallel mode.

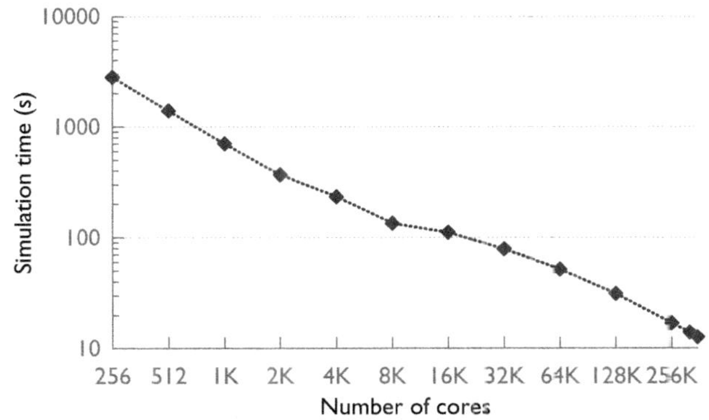

Figure 7: Execution time of EpiSimdemics on Bluewaters for United States population (300 million people) for 120 simulated days.

4.3 Indemics

Indemics [6] is an interactive, database driven HPC framework for epidemic simulations. It consists of (*i*) a simulation engine for computing epidemic dynamics, (*ii*) a situation assessment and intervention simulation engine supported by a relational database, (*iii*) a client (Indemics client) for user interactions, and (*iv*) a middleware platform (Indemics server) that connects the above components to provide online epidemic dynamics to the user for making decisions on interventions and to provide adaptive interventions to the simulation engine. Indemics uses EpiFast or EpiSimdemics as its underlying diffusion engine but is specifically designed to be interactive: a user can stop the simulation at any point, measure system state, and then proceed based on this information. The simulation is also allowed to roll-back to a previous time point if needed. Another notable feature of Indemics is its rich intervention set. In addition to a number of pre-defined interventions, a user can use SQL-based scripting language to define complex interventions [6]. The interventions can be based on the state of the disease and the dynamic, labeled people-location network (including individual attributes). Designing Isis to expose this rich set of interventions is a part of ongoing research.

5. ARCHITECTURE

Isis is hosted on the Simfrastructure service oriented middleware system [8], as shown in Figure 8. Simfrastructure serves as a multiplexer for four types of components that make up the integrated pandemic preparedness platform:

Table 1: The class of interventions provided through Isis.

component	specification	example
trigger	scheduled	winter break Dec. 21–Jan. 3
	threshold	prevalence > 0.05
subpopulation	demographic	seniors
	geographic	people in Fairfax county, Virginia
	social	critical workers
	health	diagnosed (flu) people
	combination of above	diagnosed seniors in Fairfax county
action		effects:
	vaccination	enhance immunity
	antiviral	reduce symptoms or infection probability
	school closure	remove school activities and in-school contacts
	work closure	remove work activities and at-work contacts
	isolation	remove all contacts
	combination of above	combined effects

Table 2: Examples of big data in Isis.

region	population size (million)	contacts (million)	simulation output size (per replicate)
Miami	2.2	55	15MB
Chicago	9.0	267	50MB
Delhi	13.8	210	180MB
California	33.6	962	190MB

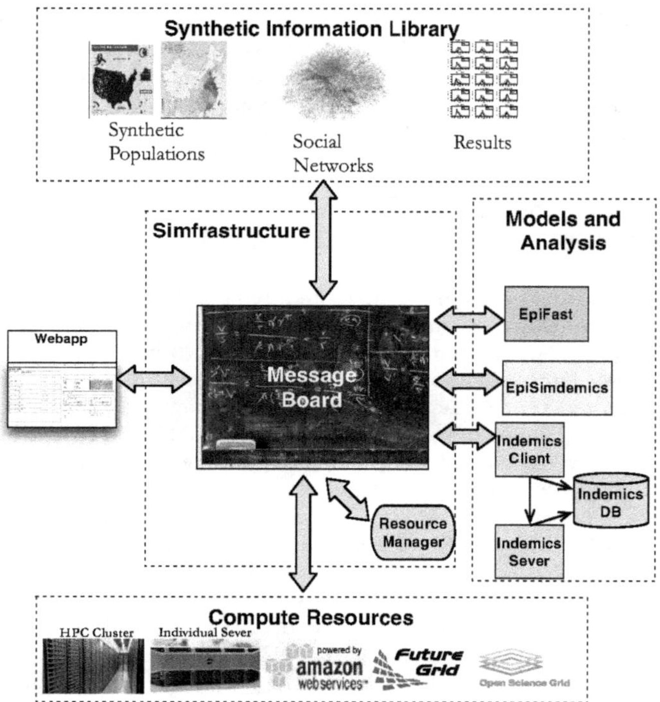

Figure 8: Architecture of Isis.

the web app, the synthetic information library, HPC models, and HPC resources, It is designed to allow any component to easily access the services provided by any other component without needing to know about the existence of any particular service provider, through the use of an asynchronous *Message Board*. The SIMFRASTRUCTURE *Resource Broker* matches service requests to appropriate service providers and computing resources, taking into account required timeliness and accuracy, as well as security, cost and other factors.

SIMDEMICS is comprised of: (*i*) high-resolution scalable models of disease transmission and behavioral adaptation; (*ii*) a service-oriented architecture and delivery mechanism for facilitating the use of these models by domain experts; (*iii*) a distributed coordinating architecture for information fusion, model execution and data processing; (*iv*) a scalable data management architecture to support model execution and analytics; and (*v*) scalable methods for visual and data analytics to support analysts [1, 2].

The challenges faced when designing and developing SIMFRASTRUCTURE include:

Scalability The cyber infrastructure must be globally scalable. The scalability comes in three forms: (*i*) allowing multiple concurrent users; (*ii*) processing huge quantities of distributed data; and (*iii*) executing large, national-scale models.

Coordination The cyber infrastructure should allow computational steering of experiments. The systems needed by stake holders are geographically distributed, controlled by multiple independent, sometimes competing, organizations and are occasionally dynamically assembled for a short period of time.

Data and Information Processing The cyber infrastructure should facilitate efficient data and information fusion and analysis. The Internet has enabled data sharing in a simple and cost effective way, from the producers' side. Consumers of the data must still locate the appropriate data and deal with multiple incompatible data formats.

User Support The cyber infrastructure should provide an appropriate analysis framework for users, including user interfaces, high level formalisms to set up experiments, and visual and data analytics that include methods for integrating heterogeneous databases to support multi-view visualization (e.g., disease spread in a geographic region and epidemic curves).

SIMFRASTRUCTURE is designed to address many of these challenges. For example, disease diffusion models have been optimized so that they can be used to undertake studies over large urban regions. Multiple concurrent users are also currently supported but further scaling is required.

5.1 Synthetic Information Library

The Synthetic Information Library (SIL) contains all of the information needed to create, run, and analyze experiments in ISIS, and well as the results of past experiments. SIL enables structured and efficient management of data sources which may be located on a collection of hardware and stored in multiple formats. A registry maintains an index of all the data sources as well as the specifications of the data. Computational methods can map existing data sets to new data sets, and the registry records these processes to track data dependencies and also to support reproducible science. The registry may be compared to a library index providing central access all methods, data sets and their full specifications along with metadata.

SIL also provides services, from very generic to application specific, that allows high level operations on the data. Some examples of these services include provenance tracking, data curation, browsing and searching. One particularly interesting service is called *memoization*. When a request for computation arrives, it is looked up to see if that computation has already been performed. If so, the stored result is returned immediately. If the request has not previously been seen, it is run and the results stored for further use.

6. CASE STUDIES

ISIS has been deployed and used in dozens of user defined studies, all mainly focused on specific pandemic planning studies and exercises. Specifically users from DHS, DoD and DHHS have used ISIS to study the impacts of a variety of interventions in response to outbreaks of influenza or other respiratory diseases, assess the characteristics of emerging epidemics, and to optimize the allocation of existing medical resources. The studies have guided the continued evolution of ISIS both in terms of its usability for the design and execution of simulations as well the delivery and consumption of the simulation results themselves. The studies also helped us identify new research questions at the interface of multi-agent modeling, data mining, network science, and high performance computing. Notable studies include:

1. **Emergence of H1N1 Influenza**. Supported modeling efforts during H1N1 pandemic. One of the only three groups nationwide that was able to provide near real time support (2009 DHHS and DTRA).
2. **Unified Combatant Command Pandemic Study**. Combined national spread of influenza with high resolution local spread for several military installations to support decision making and planning (2010 Department of Defense).
3. **Socio-Economic Impact of Pharmaceutical and Non-Pharmaceutical Interventions**. Studied impact of economic and social influence on public health mitigation strategies during epidemics (2009 NIH Modeling of Infectious Disease Agent Study).
4. **Pandemic Tabletop Exercise Support**. Modeling support for Asst. Cabinet Secretary level exercise for response to emerging pandemic (2013 National Security Council).
5. **National Planning Scenario 1**. The role of individual behavior and communications in response and recovery in the aftermath of an improvised nuclear device explosion: health effect were studied using ISIS technology (2012 Department of Defense, DTRA).
6. **Military Response to Novel Virus**. Modeling support for fervent virus two day command tabletop exercise (2011 US NORTHCOM & DTRA).
7. **Military Pandemic Preparedness**. Modeling support for military and guard preparedness in the event of an epidemic outbreak (2007, 2008 Alabama National Guard, US MEDCOM and DTRA).
8. **Non-Pharmaceutical Targeted Layered Containment Strategy**. Evaluating sensitivity to timing and compliance level of non-pharmaceutical mitigation strategies (2005, 2006 National Security Council).

See `http://ndssl.vbi.vt.edu/apps/` and `http://ndssl.vbi.vt.edu/supplementary-info/vskumar/cacm2012/` for additional examples. In the subsections below we elaborate on three of the studies.

6.1 Emergence of H1N1 Influenza

This effort was in direct response to the initial reports of the emergence of the H1N1 influenza virus in April 2009, which eventually caused a global pandemic. In the early days of the outbreak, infections were confined to Mexico, California, and Texas and then spread to New York. The rapid spread combined with initial overestimates of its mortality rate raised serious concerns of a repeat of the 1918 influenza pandemic.

Initial reports about the disease characteristics were unreliable, with wide variations placed on important disease parameters like the proportion of symptomatic individuals and the duration of infectious periods. Having developed the ISIS tool for just this purpose, we were able to quickly run a series of studies exploring the impact of the variation in these parameters in a large US population. A quick report was drafted about the impact of disease characteristics on the size and shape of the expected epidemic curve. Several variants of disease models were added to the ISIS tool.

As H1N1 influenza continued to spread in the US, the Department of Health and Human Services teamed up with the Defense Threat Reduction Agency to place the ISIS tool in the hands of US government analysts to provide day to day modeling results. This integration inside the 24-hour decision cycle running the federal government's response to this emerging crisis would not have been possible without the development of highly optimized modeling software as well as the web-enabled interface [16]. The analysts were able to perform course-of-action analyses to estimate the impact of closing schools and shutting down workplaces. Better situational awareness was also enabled by calibrating the model to newly available data from the real world about the disease's characteristics, giving a clearer picture of how many infections were likely being missed by the existing surveillance systems.

This experience demonstrates the importance and feasibility of placing sophisticated modeling tools in the hands of public health decision makers and highlights the role that highly detailed modeling can play during a response to an emerging crisis.

6.2 Unified Combatant Command Pandemic Study

This work was conducted as part of an exercise hosted by a Unified Combatant Command to prepare defense decision makers for the information and response environment likely to be encountered in future influenza pandemics. This table-top exercise sought to provide the participants with a realistic course of events, information flows and stakeholder interests that will be involved during nationwide spread of influenza. Specifically we constructed and ran a multi-scale simulation of the nation-wide spread of influenza which served as the "ground truth" of the event, guided the exercise scenario and informed the exercise white team. The results of the spread based on a national model are shown in Figures 9 and 10. The simulation was run for a total of 300 days. The figures show how influenza spreads from the west coast to the eastern parts of the United States. Figure 9 shows the state of cumulative spread three months after the initial introduction of the disease and Figure 10 shows the state of cumulative spread after it has reached all major metropolitan areas. Our high resolution models enabled enhanced situational assessment, and leveraged surveillance information available to local public health authorities.

Figure 9: This is a snapshot of cumulative infections on day 91 of the influenza epidemic. The color scale shows the number of people infected at each location.

Figure 10: This figure shows cumulative infections on day 193 of the epidemic. The color scale shows the number of people infected at each location.

For realism, since no surveillance system can capture all possible infections, we used synthetic surveillance system techniques to estimate a realistic surveillance system signal for the epidemic, thus providing a realistic "partial" set of information to the different stakeholders participating in the exercise. Additionally the nation-wide simulation was used to run simulations on a more localized (and at a highly-detailed) scale enabling more realistic estimations of the epidemic's impacts on areas of particular interest (Ft. Lewis area, Ft. Sam Houston area, and Ft. Carson / Peterson AFB / USAF Academy area). Figure 11 shows attack rate with and without interventions for the cities of San Antonio, Texas and Seattle, Washington where Fort Sam Houston and Fort Lewis are located respectively.

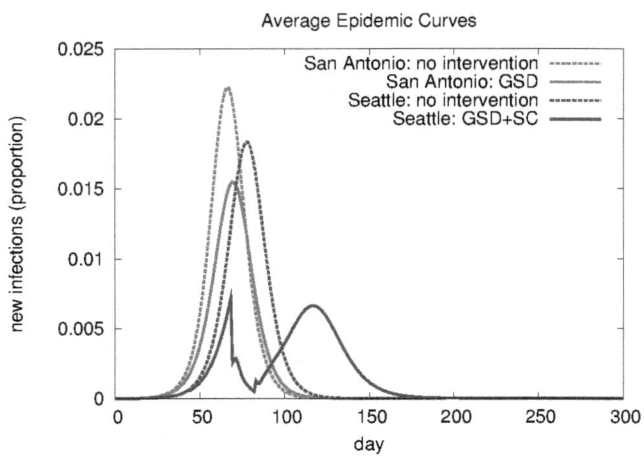

Figure 11: Mean epidemic curves for the city of San Antonio, TX and Seattle, WA. These cities were chosen because of the presence of military bases there. The "no intervention" case refers to the base case, GSD implies generic social distancing, and SC refers to school closure. The figure shows the effect of generic social distancing on the attack rate in San Antonio compared to the base case. In Seattle, generic social distancing is combined with school closure; their joint effect in controlling the attack rate is much larger.

The actual state of the epidemic, surveillance reports, detailed assessment of the impacts on the areas of interest, the interpreted actions of both public health and DoD officials, and simulation support events were all organized on a single timeline. This timeline was used to drive the table-top exercise. The timeline's interactive display concisely conveys multiple levels of information tailored to the particular interests and influence of different stakeholder communities while still enabling a vision of the overall progress of the exercise.

Requirements defined during support of this exercise led to several novel uses of existing analytical tools and techniques and to significant advances in very large scale, highly detailed social epidemiological simulation technology. This marks the first time that knowledge of existing surveillance systems was applied to simulation results to provide a realistically obscured situational awareness. This enhanced the realism for the table-top exercise for the participants. The exercise required that we integrate simulations occurring at different scales (nation-wide and regional). Technologically, this had not been done before and led to the development of a framework to enable this linkage. The use of the timeline to organize data from different sources and actions of different stakeholders while presenting a unified view of the events was important for the success of the exercise.

6.3 Socio-Economic Impact of Pharmaceutical and Non-Pharmaceutical Interventions

The goal of the project was to determine the economic and social impact of typical interventions proposed by public health officials and preventive behavioral changes adopted by private citizens in the event of an acute respiratory virus epidemic. We applied an individual-based simulation model to the New River Valley area of Virginia to address this critical problem. The economic costs included not only the loss in productivity due to sickness but also the indirect cost incurred through disease avoidance and caring for dependents.

People with different socio-economic constraints follow different behavioral strategies to avoid getting infected. These strategies are based on how individuals perceive both the state of the larger society around them and the partially observable actions taken by their immediate peer group or demographic class. The general principle being that high income individuals, young children and seniors have a lower tolerance of risk as compared to the rest of the population. Once the number of infected people in the population or in a person's class reaches the personal threshold value, the individual is triggered to modify his behavior. For members of affluent households, the modified behavior is reflected through the purchase of antivirals. The members of the middle income class eliminate non-essential activities such as shopping trips and recreational activities. Those in the poorest income class people find it too expensive to purchase antivirals, or reduce contacts and hence take no direct actions.

Public strategies include the distribution of antiviral kits and school closures. The trigger threshold for the public intervention is set at 1% of the total population becoming infected. The public stockpile of the antiviral kits is limited to 10,000. These kits are distributed to the individuals based on one of four selection criteria: randomly selected individuals, poorest individuals, first sick individuals, and the most vulnerable individuals. Each time the "close school" strategy is used, the schools are closed for a period of two weeks.

In order to assess the social and economic impact of the intervention strategies, we developed eleven distinctive scenarios based on individual and governmental actions. A base case was included to determine the size of the epidemic in the absence of interventions. The results show that the most important factor responsible for preventing income loss is the modification of individual behavior; it drops the total income loss by 62% compared to the base case. The next most important factor is the closure of schools, which reduces the total income loss by another 40%. Studies showed that the preventive behavior of private citizens is the most important factor in controlling the epidemic. The most effective interventions require school closures, public distribution of antivirals to the most vulnerable, and behavior modification by private citizens. The work appeared in [1] and was also mentioned as a part of the CDC report on school closures.

The requirements to complete a study of this nature required the extension of one of the core simulation engines used by ISIS. Specifically the need to efficiently assess the state of disease and actions across several scales, as well as delivering fine control of thresholds for different classes of individuals. This extension brings the expressive power of SQL queries to the specification of both triggering conditions and targeted populations of interventions, greatly enhancing the realism of the interventions ISIS can represent.

7. DISCUSSIONS

Data challenges. The data involved in ISIS and the backend simulations are of very large scale, and dynamic, ambiguous, and heterogeneous in nature. The experiments on ISIS usually consist of dozens of simulations, each of which simulates dynamics in synthetic contact networks of millions of nodes and billions of edges, and produces dynamics of each of the nodes during each of hundreds of simulations days. The size of the input and output data files of each simulation are in gigabytes. The output data is increasing as more experiments are run; the input data also keeps increasing because users are often interested in calibrating synthetic population, disease model, initial conditions, and interventions to do sensitivity analyses. It is impossible to consider all possible configurations users could come up with and pre-load them in ISIS.

We addressed these challenges related to data volume, velocity, variety, and veracity with the Synthetic Information Library in ISIS. This is different than the other systems, e.g., VecNet, EpiC and Gleamviz do not model person level details; DiCon does not have a GUI; FRED navigator allows one to access a database of previously computed scenarios. FRED Mobile App is the most similar to ISIS but works only at a county level. Furthermore the current version of FRED allows limited number of interventions [27].

Lessons learned. The use of ISIS in real world studies yielded important lessons and helped improve the system. First, early versions of ISIS (including the dynamical models) were slow and somewhat cumbersome to use – the current version is significantly faster and easy to use improving the overall time it takes to design and analyze a case study.

Second, what we learned in designing and using ISIS is the tradeoff between functionality and usability. While the backend HPC simulation tools (EpiSimdemics, EpiFast, and Indemics) can handle very complicated scenarios, defined by their scenario description languages, only limited features can be accommodated in a web application. We have worked with ISIS users to include only the most useful features, while allowing expert users to access a few more complex functions.

Third, we learned to distribute the computation on multiple clusters. The use of cloud computing paradigm is quite appropriate for this purpose. the SIMFRASTRUCTURE middleware achieves this goal by seamlessly mapping jobs on various clusters available for the study.

Finally, as ISIS becomes available to the broader community, there is a need to develop a scalable data management system including a digital library to support collaborative decision making. While the current system has a basic data management system, future versions will need to provide a rich set of services to achieve this goal.

Future work. Currently in ISIS, experimental data is managed by an Oracle database server and output data is written in disk files. We are exploring using parallel databases to manage the simulation output data. We are also working on integrating ISIS with FluCaster, a web app we developed for epidemic forecasting [26]. Finally, we are working on integrating optimal intervention strategies that would allow users to evaluate the efficacy of strategies that are currently implemented.

8. ACKNOWLEDGMENTS

We thank our external collaborators and members of the Network Dynamics and Simulation Science Laboratory (NDSSL) for their suggestions and comments. This work has been partially supported by DTRA Grant HDTRA1-11-1-0016, DTRA CNIMS Contract HDTRA1-11-D-0016-0001,

NIH MIDAS Grant 2U01GM070694-09, NSF NetSE Grant CNS-1011769 and NSF SDCI Grant OCI-1032677.

9. REFERENCES

[1] C. Barrett, K. Bisset, J. Leidig, A. Marathe, and M. V. Marathe. An integrated modeling environment to study the coevolution of networks, individual behavior and epidemics. *AI Magazine*, 31(1):75–87, 2010.

[2] C. Barrett, S. Eubank, and M. Marathe. Modeling and simulation of large biological, information and socio-technical systems: An interaction based approach. In *Interactive Computation*, pages 353–392. 2006.

[3] C. L. Barrett, K. R. Bisset, S. G. Eubank, X. Feng, and M. V. Marathe. EpiSimdemics: an efficient algorithm for simulating the spread of infectious disease over large realistic social networks. In *Proceedings of the ACM/IEEE conference on Supercomputing*, pages 290–294, 2008.

[4] K. Bisset, A. Aji, T. Kamal, J.-S. Yeom, M. Marathe, E. Bohm, and A. Gupta. Contagion diffusion with EpiSimdemics. In *Parallel Science and Engineering Applications: The Charm++ Approach*. 2013.

[5] K. Bisset, J. Chen, C. J. Kuhlman, V. S. A. Kumar, and M. V. Marathe. Interaction-based HPC modeling of social, biological, and economic contagions over large networks. In *Proceedings of the Winter Simulation Conference*, 2011.

[6] K. R. Bisset, J. Chen, S. Deodhar, X. Feng, Y. Ma, and M. V. Marathe. Indemics: An interactive high-performance computing framework for data intensive epidemic modeling. *ACM Transactions on Modeling and Computer Simulation*, 24(1), 2014.

[7] K. R. Bisset, J. Chen, X. Feng, V. Kumar, and M. V. Marathe. EpiFast: A fast algorithm for large scale realistic epidemic simulations on distributed memory systems. In *Proceedings of 23rd ACM International Conference on Supercomputing*, pages 430–439, 2009.

[8] K. R. Bisset, S. Deodhar, H. Makkapati, M. V. Marathe, P. E. Stretz, and C. L. Barrett. Simfrastructure: A flexible and adaptable middleware platform for modeling and analysis of socially coupled systems. In *Proc. IEEE CCGRID*, pages 506–513, 2013.

[9] K. R. Bisset, X. Feng, M. V. Marathe, and S. M. Yardi. Modeling interaction between individuals, social networks and public policy to support public health epidemiology. In *Proceedings of the Winter Simulation Conference*, pages 2020–2031, 2009.

[10] J. Brownstein, C. Freifeld, and L. Madoff. Digital disease detection – harnessing the web for public health surveillance. *N. England J. Med.*, pages 2153–2157, 2009.

[11] P. Chakraborty, P. Khadivi, B. Lewis, A. Mahendiran, J. Chen, P. Butler, E. O. Nsoesie, S. R. Mekaru, J. S. Brownstein, M. Marathe, , and N. Ramakrishnan. Forecasting a moving target: Ensemble models for ILI case count predictions. In *Proceedings of the 14th SIAM International Conference on Data Mining*, 2014.

[12] M. Dredze. How social media will change public health. *IEEE Intelligent Systems*, Vol. 27(4):81–84, July–Aug 2012.

[13] S. Eubank, H. Guclu, V. S. A. Kumar, M. Marathe, A. Srinivasan, Z. Toroczkai, and N. Wang. Modeling disease outbreaks in realistic urban social networks. *Nature*, 429:180–184, 2004.

[14] N. M. Ferguson, D. A. T. Cummings, C. Fraser, J. C. Cajka, P. C. Cooley, and D. S. Burke. Strategies for mitigating an influenza pandemic. *Nature*, 442:448–452, 2006.

[15] H. W. Hethcote. The mathematics of infectious diseases. *SIAM Review*, 42(4):599–653, 2000.

[16] N. Hupert, J. Olsen, and A. Kircher. Personal communication, 2010.

[17] L. Kalé and S. Krishnan. CHARM++: A portable concurrent object oriented system based on C++. In *Proceedings of OOPSLA'93*, pages 91–108, 1993.

[18] M. V. Kerkhove and N. Ferguson. Epidemic and intervention modelling — a scientific rationale for policy decisions? Lessons from the 2009 influenza pandemic. *Bull World Health Organ.*, pages 306–10, 2012.

[19] M. Lipsitch, L. Finelli, R. T. Heffernan, G. M. Leung, and S. C. Redd. Improving the evidence base for decision making during a pandemic: The example of 2009 influenza A H1N1. *Biosecur Bioterror.*, 9(2):89–115, 2011.

[20] I. M. Longini, A. Nizam, S. Xu, K. Ungchusak, W. Hanshaoworakul, D. A. T. Cummings, and M. E. Halloran. Containing pandemic influenza at the source. *Science*, 309(5737):1083–1087, 2005.

[21] M. Marathe and N. Ramakrishnan. Recent advances in computational epidemiology. *IEEE Intelligent Systems*, 28(4):96–101, 2013.

[22] M. Marathe and A. Vullikanti. Computational epidemiology. *Commun. ACM*, 56(7):88–96, July 2013.

[23] L. A. Meyers. Contact network epidemiology: Bond percolation applied to infectious disease prediction and control. *Bulletin of The American Mathematical Society*, 44:63–86, 2007.

[24] L. A. Meyers and N. Dimitrov. Mathematical approaches to infectious disease prediction and control. In *INFORMS, Tutorials in OPerations Research*, 2010.

[25] L. A. Meyers, N. Dimitrov, and S. Goll. DiCon: Disease control system. http://www.bio.utexas.edu/research/meyers/dicon/.

[26] Network Dynamics and Simulation Science Laboratory. FluCaster. http://ndssl.vbi.vt.edu/apps/flucaster.

[27] U. of Pittsburgh. FRED – framework for reconstructing epidemiological dynamics. http://fred.publichealth.pitt.edu/tutorials.

[28] U. of Pittsburgh. The geospatial area and information analyzer (GAIA). http://midas.pitt.edu/gaia.

[29] RTI International. Synthetic population viewer. https://www.epimodels.org/midas/synthpopviewer_index.do.

[30] VecNet. Vector-borne disease network. https://www.vecnet.org.

[31] J.-S. Yeom, A. Bhatele, K. R. Bisset, E. Bohm, A. Gupta, L. V. Kale, M. Marathe, D. S. Nikolopoulos, M. Schulz, and L. Wesolowski. Overcoming the scalability challenges of epidemic simulations on Blue Waters. In *Proc. IEEE International Parallel & Distributed Processing Symposium (IPDPS)*, 2014.

Seven Rules of Thumb for Web Site Experimenters

Ron Kohavi
Microsoft
One Microsoft Way
Redmond, WA 98052
ronnyk@live.com

Alex Deng
Microsoft
One Microsoft Way
Redmond, WA 98052
alexdeng@microsoft.com

Roger Longbotham
SW Jiaotong University
No. 111, Sec.1, N. Erhuan
Rd. Chengdu, China 610031
rogerppm@hotmail.com

Ya Xu
LinkedIn
2029 Stierlin Court
Mountain View, CA 94043
xulongya@gmail.com

ABSTRACT

Web site owners, from small web sites to the largest properties that include Amazon, Facebook, Google, LinkedIn, Microsoft, and Yahoo, attempt to improve their web sites, optimizing for criteria ranging from repeat usage, time on site, to revenue. Having been involved in running thousands of controlled experiments at Amazon, Booking.com, LinkedIn, and multiple Microsoft properties, we share seven rules of thumb for experimenters, which we have generalized from these experiments and their results. These are principles that we believe have broad applicability in web optimization and analytics outside of controlled experiments, yet they are not provably correct, and in some cases exceptions are known.

To support these rules of thumb, we share multiple real examples, most being shared in a public paper for the first time. Some rules of thumb have previously been stated, such as "speed matters," but we describe the assumptions in the experimental design and share additional experiments that improved our understanding of where speed matters more: certain areas of the web page are more critical.

This paper serves two goals. First, it can guide experimenters with rules of thumb that can help them optimize their sites. Second, it provides the KDD community with new research challenges on the applicability, exceptions, and extensions to these, one of the goals for KDD's industrial track.

Categories and Subject Descriptors
G.3 Probability and Statistics/Experimental Design: controlled experiments; randomized experiments; A/B testing.

General Terms
Measurement; Design, Experimentation

Keywords
Controlled experiments; A/B testing; Online experiments

1. INTRODUCATION

Web site owners, from small web sites to the largest properties, attempt to improve their sites. Sophisticated sites use controlled experiments (e.g. A/B tests) to evaluate their changes, including Amazon [1], eBay, Etsy [2], Facebook [3], Google [4], Groupon, Intuit [5], LinkedIn [6], Microsoft [7], Netflix [8], Shop Direct [9], Yahoo, and Zynga [10].

KDD '14, August 24–27, 2014, New York, New York, USA.

http://dx.doi.org/10.1145/2623330.2623341

Our experience in optimizing web sites comes from having worked on optimizing different sites, including Amazon, Booking.com, LinkedIn, and multiple Microsoft properties. Bing and LinkedIn, in particular, run hundreds of concurrent experiments at any point in time [6; 11]. Given the wide range and thousands of experiments, we have been involved in, we share useful "rules of thumb." These rules of thumb are supported by experiments, but they are sometimes known to have exceptions (we note known ones ourselves). The rule of 72 is a good example of a useful rule of thumb in the financial world. It states that you can divide 72 by the percent interest rate to determine the approximate amount of number of years it would take to double one's money in an investment. While it is very useful for the common interest range of 4% to 12%, it is known to be less accurate outside that range.

While these rules of thumb were generalized from controlled experiments, they are likely applicable in web optimization and analytics, including sites that do not run controlled experiments. However, sites that make changes without controlled evaluations will not be able to accurately assess the impact of the change.

Our contributions in this paper include:

1. Useful Rules of Thumb for web-site experimenters. We note that these are **emerging**, in the sense that we expect new research to refine their applicability and find exceptions. The value/payoff from utilizing controlled experiments is highly significant and was previously discussed in *Online Controlled Experiments at Large Scale* [11].
2. Refinement of prior rules of thumb. Observations like "speed matters" were previously stated by others [12; 13] and by us [14], but we describe the assumptions in the experimental design and share additional experiments that improved our understanding of where speed matters more: certain areas of the web page are more critical. Likewise, a perennial question is how many users are needed to run controlled experiments; we refine prior guidance of "thousands of users" [11].
3. Real examples of controlled experiments, most of which are being shared in a public paper for the first time. At Amazon, Bing, and LinkedIn, controlled experiments are used as part of the product development process [7; 11]. Many companies who are not yet using controlled experiments, can benefit from additional examples to handle the cultural challenges associated with a new product development paradigm [7; 15]. Companies already using controlled experiments can benefit from the insights shared.

The paper is organized as follows. Section 2 provides a brief introduction to controlled experiments and explains the data sources and the KDD process used in the examples. Section 3 is the heart of the paper with the rules of thumb, followed by conclusions in Section 4.

2. Controlled Experiments, the Data, and KDD Process

In the online controlled experiment we discuss here, users are randomly split between the variants (e.g., two different versions of the site) in a persistent manner (a user receives the same experience in multiple visits). Their interactions with the site are instrumented (e.g., page views, clicks) and key metrics computed (e.g., clickthrough-rates, sessions/user, revenue/user). Statistical tests are used to analyze the resulting metrics. If the delta between the metric values for Treatment and Control is statistically significant, we conclude with high probability that the change we introduced caused the observed effect on the metric. See *Controlled experiments on the web: survey and practical guide* [16] for details.

We have been involved in a lot of controlled experiments whose results were initially incorrect, and it took significant effort to understand why and correct them. Many pitfalls were documented [17; 18]. Given our emphasis on trust, we want to highlight a few things about the data and KDD process used in the online examples we present:

1. The **data sources** for the examples are the actual web sites discussed. There was no artificially generated data or data generated from a model; the examples are based on actual real user interactions after bot removal [16].
2. The **user samples** used in the examples were all uniformly randomly selected from the triggered population (e.g., an experiment that requires users to click a link to observe a difference limits to that population) [16]. User identification depends on the web site, and is cookie-based or login-based.
3. **Sample sizes** for the experiments are at least in the hundreds of thousands of users, with most experiments involving millions of users (numbers are shared in the specific examples) after bot removal, providing statistical power to detect small differences with high statistical significance.
4. Results noted were **statistically significant** with p-value< 0.05, and usually much lower. Surprising results (in Rule #1) were replicated at least once more, so the combined p-value, based on Fisher's Combined Probability Test (or meta-level analysis) [19] has a much lower p-value.
5. We have personal experience with each example, which was vetted by at least one of the authors and checked against common pitfalls. Each experiment ran for at least a week, the proportions assigned to the variants were stable over the experimentation period (to avoid Simpson's paradox), and the sample ratios matched the expected ratios [17].

3. RULES of THUMB

We now state the seven rules of thumb. The first three are related to impact of changes on key metrics: small changes *can* have a big impact; changes rarely have a big positive impact; and your attempts to replicate stellar results reported by others will likely not be as successful (your mileage will vary). The latter four rules of thumb are independent with no specific order; each is a very useful generalization based on multiple experiments.

Rule #1: Small Changes can have a Big Impact to Key Metrics

Anyone who has been involved in a live site knows that small changes can have a big *negative* impact on key metrics. A small JavaScript error can render checkout impossible and small bugs corrupting memory in unmanaged code can cause servers to crash. Our focus here is therefore on *positive* differences to key metrics, and the good news is that there are many such examples. Bryan Eisenberg wrote that removing the coupon code at checkout increased conversion rate by 1,000 percent at Doctor Footcare [20]. Jared Spool wrote that removing the registration requirement at checkout was worth $300 million a year to a large retailer [21].

While we have not seen such dramatic relative differences in experiments we have been involved in personally, we have seen dramatic improvements from small changes with surprisingly high Return-On-Investment (ROI).

We also want to highlight that we are discussing *sustained* impact, not a flash in the pan, or features exhibiting strong novelty/newness effects [16]. An example of something that we are *not* looking for is one told in *Yes!: 50 Scientifically proven ways to be Persuasive* [22]. In that book, the authors discuss how Colleen Szot authored a television program that shattered a nearly twenty-year sales record for a home-shopping channel. Szot changed three words to a standard infomercial line that caused a huge increase in the number of people who purchased her product: instead of the all-too-familiar "Operators are waiting, please call now," it was "If operators are busy, please call again." The authors explain that this is social proof: viewers think "If the phone lines are busy, then other people like me who are also watching this infomercial are calling, too."

Ploys, such as the above, will have a short shelf life if users recognize that it is used regularly. In a controlled experiment, the analysis will show an effect that quickly diminishes, which is why we recommend running experiments for two weeks and looking for such effects. In practice, novelty and primacy effects are uncommon [11; 18]. The situations where we observe them are in recommendation systems, where either the diversity itself causes a short-term effect, or when the Treatment utilizes a finite resource. For instance, when the algorithm for the People You May Know is changed at LinkedIn, it introduces a one-time diversity, which causes the new algorithm to evaluate better at the beginning (more clicks). Moreover, even if the algorithm is recommending better results, there is only a finite pool of people that one knows. After one connects to the top recommendations, the effect of the new algorithm dies down.

Example: Opening Links in new Tabs. A series of three experiments ran over time.

In Aug 2008, MSN UK ran an experiment with over 900,000 users, whereby the link to Hotmail opened in a new Tab (or new window for older browsers). We previously reported [7] that this trivial change (a single line of code) increased MSN users' engagement, as measured by clicks/user on the home page, by 8.9% for the triggered users (those who clicked on the Hotmail link).

In June 2010, we replicated the experiment on a larger population of 2.7M users on MSN in the US, and results were similar. This is also an example of an experiment that had novelty effects: on the first day the change deployed to all users, 20% of feedback messages were about this feature, most negative. In week two, the percentage went down to 4%, then 2% during the third and fourth week. The improvements to key metrics were sustained over time.

In April 2011, MSN in the US ran a very large experiment, with over 12M users, which opened the search results in a new tab/window, and engagement as measured by clicks per user increased by a whopping 5%. This was one of the best features that MSN has ever implemented in terms of increasing user engagement, and it was a trivial coding change.

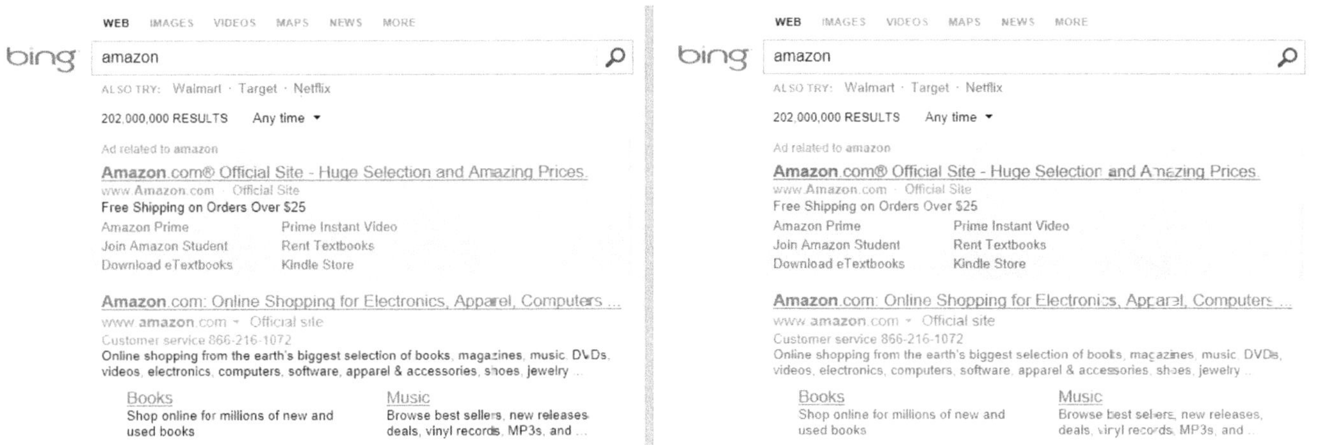

Figure 1: Font color experiment. Can you tell the difference?

All the major search engines are experimenting with opening links in new tabs/windows, but the results appear less beneficial for search engine result pages (SERPs).

Example: Font Colors. In 2013, Bing ran a set of experiments on font colors. The winning variant is shown on the right in Figure 1. To highlight the differences, the three color changes that were made are shown in this paragraph.

The cost of making such a change? Trivial: all it takes is changing several colors in the Cascading Style Sheet file (CSS). The results showed that users were more successful at completing tasks (the exact definition of success is proprietary), their time-to-success improved, and monetization improved to the tune of over $10M annually. Because such surprising results are usually viewed (rightly-so) with skepticism, this initial experiment was replicated with a much larger sample of 32 million users, and the results held.

Example: Right Offer at the Right Time. At Amazon back in 2004, the home page was split into slots, and content for the slots was tested automatically so that better content improving key metrics would be displayed more [1]. Amazon's credit-card offer was winning the top slot, which was surprising because it had very low clickthrough-rate. The reason it won was that the offer was very profitable, so despite low clickthrough-rate, the expected value was very high. But is this really the right place to offer it? No! The offer was moved to the shopping cart one sees after adding an item with some simple math shown below, highlighting the savings relative to the items in the shopping cart. Since users adding an item to the shopping cart have clear purchase intent, this offer comes at the right time.

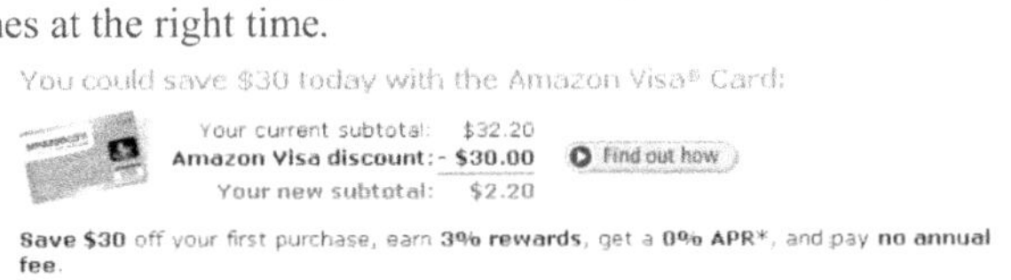

The controlled experiment showed that this simple change was worth tens of millions of dollars in profit annually.

Example: Anti-malware. Ads are a lucrative business, and "freeware" installed by users often contains malware that pollutes pages with ads. For example, Figure 2 shows what a resulting page from Bing looked like to a user with malware, where multiple ads (highlighted in red) were added to the page. Users often do not even realize that it is not the site they are on that is showing so many ads, but rather malware they inadvertently installed. This experiment was not trivial to code, but it was relatively simple: overriding the basic routines that modify the DOM (Document Object Model) and limiting who could modify the page. The experiment ran for 3.8 million triggered users, who had 3rd party code modifying the DOM, and the changes were blocked for users in the Treatment. The results showed improvements to all of Bing's key metrics, including the North-star metric Sessions/user, i.e., users came more often. In addition, users were more successful at reaching results, were quicker to succeed, and annual revenue improved by several million dollars. Page load time, a key metric discussed later in Rule #4 on speed, improved by hundreds of milliseconds for the triggered pages.

At Bing, two other small changes, which are confidential, took days to develop, and each increased ad revenues by about $100 million annually. Microsoft's Oct 2013 quarterly announcement noted that "Search advertising revenue grew 47% driven by an increase in revenue per search and volume." These two changes are responsible for a significant portion of that growth.

Given the above examples, one might think that the organization should focus on many small changes, but as the next rule shows, this is not the case. While breakthroughs due to small changes happen, they are very rare and surprising: at Bing, perhaps one in 500 experiments meets the bar of such high ROI and replicable positive impact. We also do not claim that these results will replicate to other domains, a point we make below, but rather that these and other easy-to-run experiments may be worth trying, in case they lead to a breakthrough.

The risk of focusing on small changes is Incrementalism: an organization should have a portfolio of small changes that potentially have high ROI, but also some big bets for the Big Hairy Audacious Goals [23].

Rule #2: Changes Rarely have a Big Positive Impact to Key Metrics

As Al Pacino says in the movie Any Given Sunday, winning is done inch by inch. For web sites like Bing, where thousands of experiments are being run annually, most fail, and those that succeed improve key metrics by 0.1% to 1.0%, once diluted to overall impact. While small changes with big positive impact discussed in Rule #1 do happen, they are the exception.

Two key points are important to highlight:

Figure 2: SERP with malware ads highlighted in red

1. Key metrics are not some specific feature metric, as those are easy to improve, but an all-up organizational metric, such as Sessions/user [18] and Time-to-success [24].
   For example, when building a feature, it is easy to significantly increase clicks to that feature (a feature metric) by highlighting it, or making it larger, but improving the overall page clickthrough-rate, or the overall experience is what really matters. Many times all the feature is doing is shifting clicks around and cannibalizing other areas of the page.
2. Metrics should be diluted by their segment size. It is much easier to improve metrics for a small segment. For example, a team can improve key metrics for weather-related queries on Bing, or purchases of TVs on Amazon by introducing a good comparison tool. However, a 10% improvement to key metrics must then be diluted to the overall impact, which takes into account the segment size. That 10% improvement to a 1% segment has an overall impact of approximately 0.1% (approximate because if the segment metrics are different than the average, the impact will be different).

The implication of this rule of thumb is significant because of occurrences of false positives. It is important to distinguish between two types of false positives:

1. Those that are expected from the Statistics. Because we run thousands of experiments a year, a false positive rate of 0.05 implies hundreds of false positive results for a given metric, and this is exacerbated if multiple uncorrelated metrics are used. For metrics like Sessions/user, even large sites like Bing do not have sufficient traffic to improve the sensitivity and result in very low p-values [18].
2. Those that are due to a bad design, data anomalies, or bugs, such as instrumentation errors.

Results with borderline statistically significant results should be viewed as tentative and rerun to replicate the results [11]. This can be formalized using Bayes Rule [25; 26][1]. If the probability of a true positive effect is low, i.e., most ideas fail to move key metrics in a positive direction, then the probability of a true effect when the p-value is close to 0.05 is still low. Formally, if α is the statistical significance level (usually 0.05) and β is the type-II error level (normally 0.2 for 80% power), π is the prior probability that the alternative hypothesis is true, and we denote by TP a True Positive and by SS a Statistically Significant result, then we have

$$P(TP|SS) = P(SS|TP) * \frac{P(TP)}{P(SS)} = \frac{(1-\beta)\pi}{(1-\beta)\pi + \alpha(1-\pi)}$$

Using $\alpha = 0.05, \beta = 0.20$, if we have a prior probability of success of 1/3, which is what we reported is the average across multiple experiments at Microsoft [7], then the posterior probability for a true positive result given a statistically significant experiment is 89%. However, if breakthrough results noted in Rule #1 are one in 500, then the posterior probability drops to 3.1%.

One interesting corollary to this rule of thumb is that following taillights is easier than innovating in isolation. Features that we have seen introduced by statistically-savvy companies have a higher chance of having positive impact for us. If our success rate on ideas at Bing is about 10-20%, in line with other search engines, the success rate of experiments from the set of features that the competition has tested and deployed to all users is higher. This observation is symmetric: other search engines tend to test and deploy positive changes that Bing introduces too.

One of the more interesting generalizations we have made over time is not to trust results that are too good to be true. Human reaction is naturally different to results in different directions. We are inclined to resist and question negative results to our great new feature that is being tried, so we drill deeper to find the cause. However, when the effect is positive, the inclination is to celebrate rather than drill deeper and look for anomalies. When results are exceptionally strong, we learned to call out Twyman's law [27]:

Any figure that looks interesting or different is usually wrong!

Twyman's law can be explained using Bayes Rule. We have been running thousands of experiments and know that breakthrough results are rare. For example, few experiments improve our North-star metric Sessions/user significantly. Let's assume that the distribution we see in experiments is Normal, centered on 0, with a standard-deviation of 0.25%. If an experiment shows +2.0% improvement to Sessions/user, we will call out Twyman, pointing out that 2.0% is "extremely interesting" but also eight standard-deviations from the mean, and thus has a probability of 1e-15 excluding other factors. Even with a statistically significant result, the prior is so strong against this result, that we avoid any celebration and start working on finding the bug, which is usually of the second false positive type described above (e.g., an instrumentation error). Twyman's law is regularly applied to proofs that $P = NP$. No modern editor will celebrate such a submission; instead, they will send it to a reviewer to find the bug, attaching a template that says "with regards to your proof that $P = NP$, the first major error is on page x."

[1] Ioannidis uses R as the ratio of true relationships to no relationships, so $\pi = R/(R+1)$ and our formula is equivalent to his PPV, or Positive Predictive Value.

Example: Office Online Surrogate Metric. Cook et al. [17] reported an interesting experiment ran by Microsoft Office Online. The team tested a redesign of a page with a strong call-to-action button. The key metric the team wanted to test is the actual purchases, or purchases-per-user. However, tracking the actual purchases required hooking to the billing system, which was hard at the time. So the team decided to use "clicks on revenue generating links" assuming clicks * conversion-rate = revenue, where the conversion-rate is from click to purchase.

To their surprise, there was a 64% reduction in clicks per user. This shocking result made people look deeper into the data. It turns out that the assumption of a stable conversion rate from click to purchase was flawed. The Treatment page, which showed the price of the product, attracted fewer clicks, but those users were better qualified and had a much higher conversion-rate.

Example: More Clicks from a Slower Page. JavaScript code was added to Bing's search result page. This additional script normally slows things, so one expected to see a small negative impact on key metrics measuring user engagement such as clicks-per-user. However, the results showed the opposite: users clicked more [18]! In spite of the positive movement, we followed Twyman's law and solved the puzzle. Click tracking is based on web beacons and some browsers eliminate the call when the user is navigating away from the page [28]. The additional JavaScript had a side effect of improving click tracking fidelity, not actual user clicks.

Example: Bing Edge. Over a period of several months in 2013, Bing switched its Content Delivery Network (CDN) from Akamai to its own Bing Edge. The Traffic ramp-up to Bing's Edge occurred together with many other improvements Bing deployed during this period. Several teams reported that key metrics improved over time: the Bing Home page clickthrough-rate was improving, features were used more, and our abandonment rates were coming down. It turns out that these improvements were related to click tracking fidelity: Bing's Edge improved not just page performance, but also click tracking fidelity. To quantify the impact, we ran an experiment where we replaced the beacon-based click tracking with redirects, a technique used in tracking ad clicks that has negligible click loss, but introduces a slowdown per click. The results showed that the click loss rate for some browsers dropped by more than 60%! A large portion of the gains over time were actually an artifact of improved click tracking.

Example: MSN Searches to Bing. The auto-suggest feature shows a drop-down box with possible completions and variants below a search box, as the user is typing. An experiment at MSN attempted to improve this feature with a new and better algorithm (feature teams are always able to explain a-priori why the new feature is going to be better before the experiment, but are often disappointed by the results). The experiment was a huge success with the number of searches on Bing referred from MSN dramatically improving. Given this rule of thumb, we investigated more deeply and it turns out the new code was effectively issuing two searches when users selected one of the auto-suggested options (one was always disconnected by the browser as only one SERP was displayed)

Although the explanations of many positive results may not be as exciting as if the improvements were real, our goal is to find true user impact, and Twyman's law has improved our fundamental understanding in multiple cases.

Rule #3: Your Mileage WILL Vary

There are many documented examples of successes using controlled experiments. For example, Anne Holland's "Which Test Won?" site (http://whichtestwon.com) has hundreds of case studies of A/B tests, and a new case is added about every week.

While these are great idea generators, there are several problems with such case studies

1. The quality varies. In these studies, someone at some company reported the result of an A/B experiment. Was it peer reviewed? Was it properly run? Were there outliers? Was the p-value low (we've seen tests published where the p-value was > 0.05, which is normally considered not statistically significant). There are pitfalls we have warned about [17] and many experiments do not properly check for issues.
2. What works in one domain may not work in another. For example, Neil Patel [29] recommends using the word "free" in ads and offering "30-day free trial" instead of "30-day money back guarantee." These may work for certain products and audience, but we suspect that results will vary by domain. Joshua Porter [30] reported that "Red Beats Green" for the call-to-action button "Get Started Now" on a web site. Since we do not see a lot of sites with red call-to-action buttons, we believe this is not a general result that replicates well.
3. Novelty and Primacy effects. As discussed previously, we are looking for sustained improvements, and many experiments were not run long enough to check for such effects.
4. Misinterpretation of result. Effects are often attributed to a specific factor, or the underlying reason is not understood. Below are two examples; the first is one of the earliest documented controlled experiments.

Historical Example: Lack of medical knowledge about Vitamin C. Scurvy is a disease that results from vitamin C deficiency. It killed over 100,000 people in the 16th-18th centuries, mostly sailors who went out for long-distance voyages and stayed at sea longer than perishable fruits could be stored. In 1747, Dr. James Lind noticed lack of scurvy in Mediterranean ships and gave some sailors oranges and lemons (Treatment), and others ate regular diet (Control). The experiment was very successful, but Dr. Lind did not understand the reason. At the Royal Naval Hospital in England, he treated scurvy patients with concentrated lemon juice called "rob." He concentrated the lemon juice by heating it, thus destroying the vitamin C. He lost faith in the remedy and became increasingly reliant on bloodletting. In 1793, a formal trial was done and lemon juice became part of the daily rations throughout the navy; Scurvy was quickly eliminated and British sailors are called Limeys to this day.

Example: Speed vs. more results. In a Web 2.0 talk by Marissa Mayer, then at Google, she described an experiment where Google increased the number of search results on the SERP from ten to thirty [31]. Traffic and revenue from Google searchers in the experimental group dropped by 20%. Her explanation? The page took half a second more to generate. Performance is a critical factor, but we suspect it only accounts for a small percentage of the loss. Here are three reasons:

a. Slowdown experiments that ran at Bing [11] isolated just the performance factor. Numbers showed that a 250msec delay at the server impacts revenue at about 1.5% and clickthrough-rate by 0.25%. While this is a massive impact, 500msec would impact revenue about 3% not 20%, and clickthrough-rate would drop by 0.50%, not 20% (assuming a linear approximation is reasonable). Earlier tests at Bing

[32] had similar click impact and smaller revenue impact with delays of up to two seconds.

b. Jake Brutlag from Google blogged about an experiment [12] showing that slowing down the search results page by 100 to 400 milliseconds has a measurable impact on the number of searches per user, which declined 0.2% to 0.6%, very much in line with our experiment, but far from the results reported in Marissa Mayer's talk.

c. An experiment ran at Bing, where 20 results were shown instead of 10. The revenue loss was nullified by adding another mainline ad (which slowed the page a bit more). We believe the ratio of ads to algorithmic results plays a more important role than performance.

We are skeptical of many amazing results of A/B tests reported in the literature. When reviewing results of experiments, ask yourself what trust level to apply, and remember that even if the idea worked for the specific site, it may not work as well for another. One of the best things we can do is to report replications of prior experiments (successful or not). This is how science works best.

Rule #4: Speed Matters a LOT

Web site developers that evaluate features using controlled experiments quickly realize web site performance, or speed, is critical **[13; 14; 33]**. Even a slight delay to the page performance may impact key metrics in the Treatment.

The best way to quantify the impact of performance is to isolate just that factor using a slowdown experiment, i.e., add a delay. Figure 3 shows a graph of depicting a common relationship between time (performance) and a metric of interest (e.g., clickthrough-rate per page, success rate per session, or revenue per user). Typically, the faster the site, the better (higher in this example) the metric value. By slowing the Treatment relative to Control, you can measure the impact on the metric of interest. There are a few key points about such an experiment

1. The slowdown quantifies the impact on the metric of interest at the point today, shown by the dotted vertical line in Figure 3. If the site performance changes (e.g., site is faster), or the audience changes (e.g., more international users) the impact may be different.

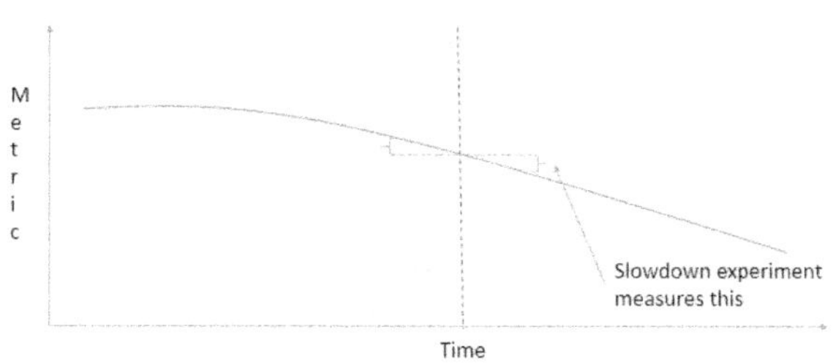

Figure 3: Typical relationship between performance (time) and a metric of interest

2. The experiment measures the impact of a slowdown. This is very useful when trying to assess the value of a feature whose first implementation is inefficient: say it moves metric M by X% and also slows the site by T%. Using the slowdown experiment, we can estimate the impact of the slowdown on metric M, and thus adjust the impact of the feature to X'% (assuming additivity), thus answering the question of its impact *if* it were implemented efficiently.
3. We can assess the impact to key metrics if the site were faster, helping us evaluate ROI (Return-On-Investment) of such efforts. Using a linear approximation (1st-order Taylor expansion), we can assume that the impact of the metric is similar in both directions (slowdown and speedup). As shown in Figure 3, we assume that the vertical delta on the right is similar to that on the left. By running slowdown experiments with different slowdown amounts, we have confirmed that a linear approximation is very reasonable for Bing.

How important is performance? Critical. At Amazon, 100msec slowdown decreased sales by 1% as shared by Greg Linden [34 p. 10]. A talk by speakers from Bing and Google [32] showed the significant impact of performance on key metrics.

Example: Server slowdown experiment. A slowdown experiment at Bing [11] slowed 10% of users by 100msec (milliseconds) and another 10% by 250msec for two weeks. The results of this controlled experiment showed that every 100msec speedup improves revenue by 0.6%. The following phrasing resonated extremely well in our organization (based on translating the above to profit): *an engineer that improves server performance by 10msec (that's 1/30 of the speed that our eyes blink) more than pays for his fully-loaded annual costs*. Every millisecond counts.

The above experiments slowed down the server's response, thus slowing down all elements of the page. It is natural to assume that some areas of the page are more important. For example, users cannot tell that elements "below the fold" (i.e., below what's visible in the current window) [35] have not been loaded yet without scrolling. Are there some elements can could be shown late, with little user impact? The following controlled experiment shows that this is indeed the case.

Example: Performance of the right pane is less critical. At Bing, some elements on the right pane (called the snapshot) are loaded late (technically, after the `window.onload` event). A recent slowdown controlled experiment was run, similar to the one described above, delaying when the right pane elements were shown by 250 milliseconds. If there was an impact on key metrics, it was not detectible, despite the experiment size of almost 20 million users.

Page Load Time (PLT) is often used to measure performance using the `window.onload` to mark the end of the useful browser activity. However, this metric has severe deficiencies with modern web pages. As Steve Souders showed [36], an Amazon page can render in 2.0 seconds above the fold, but the `window.onload` event fires at 5.2 seconds. Schurman [32] reported that being able to progressively render a page, so the header shows up early, helps. The opposite is also true with Gmail as a good example: the `window.onload` fires at 3.3 seconds, at which point only the progress bar is visible, and the above-the-fold content shows at 4.8 seconds.

There are other metrics commonly measured, such as time to first result (e.g. time to first tweet on Twitter, first algorithmic result on a SERP), but the term "Perceived performance" is often used to denote the intuitive idea that users start to interpret the page once enough of it is showing. The concept of perceived performance is easier to state abstractly than measure in practice, and `perception.ready()` isn't on any browser's roadmap [36]. Multiple proposals have been developed to estimate perceived performance, including

1. Above the Fold Time (AFT) [37], which measure the time until pixels above the fold have been painted. Implementations need to use heuristics to handle videos, animated GIFs, rotating galleries, and other dynamic content that changes the

page above the fold. Thresholds may be set for "percent of pixels painted" to avoid trivial elements of little consequence from prolonging the measured time.

2. Speed Index [38] is a generalization of AFT, which averages the time at which visible elements on the page are displayed. This does not suffer from trivial elements showing late, but still suffers from dynamic content changing above-the-fold.
3. Page Phase Time and User-Ready Time [39]. Page Phase Page Time requires identifying which rendering phase satisfies perceived performance, and phases are determined by pixel changing velocity. User-Ready time measures the time until essential elements of the page (defined for each context) are ready to use.

New W3C timing interfaces are being made available in newer HTML standards, which provide access to finer-grained events and may help understand performance issues better. The above experiments are all on desktop, and there is a lot to learn for mobile.

At Bing, we use multiple performance metrics for diagnostics, but our key time-related metric is Time-To-Success (TTS) [24], which side-steps the measurement issues. For a search engine, our goal is to allow users to complete a task faster. For clickable elements, a user clicking faster on a result from which they do not come back for at least 30 seconds is considered a successful click. TTS as a metric captures perceived performance well: if it improves, then important areas of the pages are rendering faster so that users can interpret the page and click faster. This relatively simple metric does not suffer from heuristics needed for many performance metrics. It is highly robust to changes, and very sensitive. Its main deficiency is that it only works for clickable elements. For queries where the SERP has the answer (e.g., for "time" query), users can be satisfied and abandon the page without clicking.

Rule #5: Reducing Abandonment is Hard, Shifting Clicks is Easy

A key metric that Bing measures in controlled experiment is abandonment rate on the SERP (Search Engine Results Page): the percentage of users who never click on any link. Increasing user engagement, or reducing abandonment, is considered positive, but it is a difficult metric to move. Most experiments show that there can be significant shifts in clicks from one area of the page to another, but abandonment rate rarely moves or moves very little. Below we share several examples of experiments where significant changes were made, yet abandonment rate did not change statistically significantly.

Example: **Related Searches in right column.** Some related searches were removed from the right column on Bing's SERP for an experiment with over 10 million users. If a user searches for "data mining" Bing will normally show related searches, such as "Examples of Data Mining," "Advantages of Data Mining," "Definition of Data Mining," "Data Mining Companies," "Data Mining Software," etc. These can help users modify their query (e.g., refine it) and help them be more successful. In the experiment, clicks shifted to other areas of the page, but abandonment rate did not change statistically significantly (p-value 0.64).

Example: **Related Searches below bottom ads.** Bing shows related searches inline, and these are allowed to float higher if their clickthrough-rate is better than the algorithmic results below them. In an experiment, with over 5 million users, these were pinned to the bottom of the page, below the bottom ads. The clickthrough-rate on these related searches declined 17%, but the abandonment rate did not change statistically significantly (p-value 0.71)

Example: **Truncating the SERP.** Bing dynamically sizes the SERP, not always showing the classical ten blue links. This change was motivated by the stability of the abandonment rate. For example, here are two experiments.

1. When there is a deep-link block for queries like "ebay," the click-through rate on the top block is over 75%. Showing 10 results for such queries is of little value, and the SERPs for these was truncated to show four algorithmic results in an experiment with over 8 million triggered users (triggered means at least one of their queries showed a page with a deep-links block), the abandonment rate did not change statistically significantly for these pages (p-value 0.92). These pages were therefore faster, and this feature was released
2. When users navigate from the SERP, but come back either using the browser's back button or by reissuing the query, Bing extends the page and shows more results (14 results). In an experiment with over 3 million triggered users, the page was extended to 20 results and removed related searches. There were significant changes to metrics, including: 1.8% reduction in revenue, 30msec slowdown for page load time, 18% reduction in pagination, but abandonment rate did not change statistically significantly (p-value 0.93). This change was not released.

Example: Ad background color. All major search engines have been experimenting with changing the background color for ads. In a recent experiment with over 10M users, the Treatment color caused a 12% decline in revenue (an annual loss of over $150M if this change were made). Users shifted their clicks from ads to other areas of the page, but abandonment rate did not change statistically significantly (p-value 0.83).

We have observed cases where abandonment improves, such as when we made significant improvements to relevance, and in the Anti-malware flight discussed in Rule #1, but these are uncommon and the movements are smaller than one might expect.

This rule of thumb is extremely important because we have seen many experiments (at Microsoft, Amazon, and reported by others) where a module or widget was added to the page with relatively good click-through rates. The claim is made that new module is clearly good for users because users are clicking. But if the module simply cannibalized other areas of the page, as shown in the examples above, it is only useful if those clicks are better, however "better" is defined for the site (e.g., they lead to higher success or purchases, etc.). Phrased differently: local improvements are easy; global improvements are much harder.

Rule #6: Avoid Complex Designs: Iterate

Good experimental design is vital to getting the best results from experiments. Sir R. A. Fisher once said **[40]** 'To consult the statistician after an experiment is finished is often merely to ask him to conduct a post mortem examination. He can perhaps say what the experiment died of." Our experience is that simple designs are best in the online world and given the many pitfalls **[17; 41]**, they are easier to understand, run sanity checks, and thus more trustworthy. A complex design is usually not only unnecessary, but can hide bugs. We share a couple of examples from LinkedIn.

Example: LinkedIn Unified Search. At LinkedIn, a product launch usually involves multiple features/components. One big upgrade to LinkedIn Search launched in 2013 involved improved autocomplete and suggested phrasing, and most importantly, it introduced unified search across different product categories. In the past, search had to take in a facet, whether it is "People", or "Jobs", or "Companies". With unified search, the search box is smart enough to figure out your query intent and find the relevant results. However, that was not all. Almost every single component on the search landing-page was touched, from the left rail navigation to snippets to the action buttons. The first experiment was run with all changes lumped together and many key metrics tanked. It was a lengthy process to bring back one feature at a time to realize that certain features (removed from final launch), not the unified search, were responsible for bringing down clicks and revenue. After restoring these features, unified search was shown to be positive to the user experience and deployed to everyone.

Example: **LinkedIn Contacts.** LinkedIn recently introduced the new contacts page that helps people to stay in touch better with their relationships. It was believed to be a great feature for users. However, when the results came back from the experiment, they looked horrifying. The experiment had a very complex design that made it hard to investigate what went wrong. First of all, the experiment was designed to only impact users who were not in a whitelist. To achieve that there was an eligibility check before the experiment was even triggered. Second, depending on whether a user fell into the Treatment or Control, two other experiments would be triggered that may show the new contacts page to that user. The complex design left many possibilities for error and it took days to figure out that the eligibility check was implemented with the following bug: if a user has seen the new feature once, he/she is put on the whitelist that is removed entirely from the experiment! No wonder we saw engagement dropping, as treatment users appeared to churn after one visit!

With offline experiments, where experiments are expensive relative to the design and analysis, it makes sense to make maximum use of the users (experimental units). However, online we have a continuous stream of users and we can use concurrent designs [4; 11] to run hundreds of concurrent experiments, testing one or two variables at a time. While the literature on Multi-Variable Testing (MVT) is rich, and commercial products tout their MVT capabilities, we usually find it more beneficial to run simple uni-variable (e.g., A/B/C/D variant of a feature) or bi-variable designs.

Another important reason for running simple univariable designs is to align with agile software methodologies and building minimum viable products (MVPs) [15]. Instead of building code for a complex MVTs, run an experiment as soon as a key feature is ready. There is always significant learning from exposing new features to users, such as seeing unexpected metrics move, getting verbatim feedback, finding bugs, etc. Complicated MVTs that rely on a lot of new code tend to be invalid because bugs are found in the code for at least one of the variables.

We encourage our engineering teams to deploy new code quickly and use experiments to provide a form of exposure control: start with small 1% treatments, then ramp up if there are no egregious declines in key metrics. With agile methodologies now common, without exposure control provided through controlled experiments, you run the risk of repeating a deployment like the one Knight Capital did, which in Aug 2012 caused a $440 million loss and erased 75% of Knight's equity value.

Rule #7: Have Enough Users

Experimentation methodologies typically rely on the means, which are assumed to be normally distributed. The well-known Central Limit Theorem shows that the mean of a variable has an approximately normal distribution if the sample size is large enough. Applied statistics books will suggest that small numbers usually suffice. For example, one [42] states "In many cases of practical interest, if $n \geq 30$, the normal approximation will be satisfactory regardless of the shape of the distribution." Because we are looking at statistical significance using the tails of distributions, larger sample sizes are required. Our advice in previous articles [11] is that you need "thousands" of users in an experiment; Neil Patel [29] suggests 10,000 monthly visitors, but the guidance should be refined to the metrics of interest.

Formulas for minimum sample size given the metric's variance and sensitivity (the amount of change one wants to detect) provide one lower bound [16], but these assume that the distribution of the mean is normal. Our experience is that many metrics of interest in online experiments are skewed which may require a higher lower bound before you can assume normality.

Our rule of thumb for the minimum number of independent and identically distributed observations needed for the mean to have a normal distribution is $355 \times s^2$ for each variant, where s is the skewness coefficient of the distribution of the variable X defined as

$$s = \frac{E[X-E(X)]^3}{[Var(X)]^{3/2}}.$$

We recommend the use of this rule when the |skewness| > 1. The following table shows the minimum sample size required under this rule of thumb for a few select metrics from Bing, and the sensitivity (% change detectible at 80% power) such a sample size provides.

Metric	|Skewness|	Sample Size	Sensitivity
Revenue/User	18.2	114k	4.4%
Revenue/User (Capped)	5.3	9.7k	10.5%
Sessions/User	3.6	4.70k	5.4%
Time To Success	2.1	1.55k	12.3%

At a commerce site, the skewness for purchases/customer was >10 and for revenue/customer >30. This rule of thumb gives a 95% confidence interval for the mean such that both two tail probabilities (nominally 0.025) are no greater than 0.03 and no less than 0.02. This rule was derived from the work of Boos and Hughes-Oliver [43]. Long tailed distributions are common with web data and can be quite skewed. In the table above, we found Revenue/User had a skewness of 18.2 and therefore 114k users were needed. Figure 4 shows when we only sample 100 and 1,000 users, the distribution of the sample mean is quite skewed and the 95% two-side confidence interval assuming normality would miss the true mean more than 5%. When we increase sample size to 100k, the distribution of sample mean is very close to normal for the range of -2 to 2.

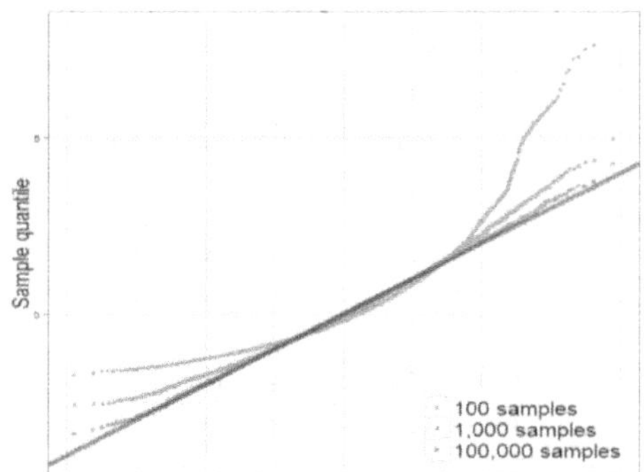

Figure 4: QQ-norm plot for averages of different sample sizes showing convergence to Normal when skewness is 18.2 for Revenue/user. Actual data used

When a metric has a large skewness, it is sometimes possible to transform the metric or cap the values to reduce the skewness so that the average converges to normality faster. After we capped Revenue/User to $10 per user per week, we saw skewness drop from 18 to 5.3 and sensitivity (i.e. power) increased. For the same sample size, Capped Revenue per user can detect a change 30% smaller than Revenue per user.

Our rule of thumb assesses the number of users needed to make the distribution of the mean be well approximated by a normal distribution. If the control and treatment are expected to have the same distribution, there is an important recommendation we can make: ensure that the control and treatment are equally sized. If the split is equally sized (e.g., 50%/50%), then the distribution of the delta will be approximately symmetric (it will be perfectly symmetric with zero skewness under the Null hypothesis) and our rule of thumb does not provide a useful lower bound (we recommended the rule be used when |skewness| > 1). Power calculations will typically provide the lower bound for sample size [16]. For skewed distributions with small samples, one can use bootstrapping techniques [44].

4. Summary

We presented seven rules of thumb for web site experiments, which we have developed based on thousands of online controlled experiments, and supported by examples. The first two show that small changes can have a big positive impact, but that they are rare and most progress is made through many small improvements over time. When results seem too good to be true, apply Twyman's law and investigate deeply before declaring an experiment as a breakthrough; most of the time, you'll find a bug. The third rule warns about claimed results "in the wild," which we learned to be cautious about. Make sure to replicate ideas, as they may not have the same effect (or even a positive effect). The fourth rule is an area we are passionate about: speed. We ran multiple experiments and better understand the relationship between performance and key metrics, showing that server speed is critical; in addition, displaying the key parts of the page faster is more important than others, such as sidebars. Despite our passion, we doubt some extreme results about performance, which we reviewed with the third rule. The fifth rule is an empirical observation that we suspect will be refined over time, but it is surprising how widely it holds: changing abandonment rate is really hard, and most experiments just shift clicks around, so one has to be careful about local optimizations. The sixth rule recommends simpler designs and quicker iterations, which aligns with modern agile software development methodologies. The seventh rule provides a lower bound for the number of users for skewed metrics, which are common in online experiments. Most examples shared here are being shared in a public paper for the first time. They support the rules of thumb, and also strengthen our conviction in the value of experimentation to help guide product development. We hope these rules of thumb will serve the community and will lead to follow-on research that will refine them and provide additional rules of thumb.

ACKNOWLEDGMENTS

We wish to thank our colleagues who have run many experiments that helped us in forming these generalized rules of thumb. Mujtaba Khambatti, John Psaroudakis, and Sreenivas Addagatla, were involved in the performance experiments and analysis. We wish to thank feedback on initial drafts from Juan Lavista Ferres, Urszula Chajewska, Gerben Langendijk, Lukas Vermeer, and Jonas Alves. Feedback on later drafts was provided by Eytan Bakshy, Brooks Bell, and Colin McFarland.

References

1. **Kohavi, Ron and Round, Matt.** *Front Line Internet Analytics at Amazon.com.* [ed.] Jim Sterne. Santa Barbara, CA : s.n., 2004. http://ai.stanford.edu/~ronnyk/emetricsAmazon.pdf.

2. **McKinley, Dan.** Design for Continuous Experimentation: Talk and Slides. [Online] Dec 22, 2012. http://mcfunley.com/design-for-continuous-experimentation.

3. **Bakshy, Eytan and Eckles, Dean.** Uncertainty in Online Experiments with Dependent Data: An Evaluation of Bootstrap Methods. *KDD 2013: Proceedings of the 19th ACM SIGKDD Conference on Knowledge Discovery and Data Mining.* 2013

4. **Tang, Diane, et al.** Overlapping Experiment Infrastructure: More, Better, Faster Experimentation. *Proceedings 16th Conference on Knowledge Discovery and Data Mining.* 2010

5. **Moran, Mike.** Multivariate Testing in Action: Quicken Loan's Regis Hadiaris on multivariate testing. *Biznology Blog by Mike Moran.* [Online] December 2008. www.biznology.com/2008/12/multivariate_testing_in_action/.

6. **Posse, Christian.** Key Lessons Learned Building LinkedIn Online Experimentation Platform. *Slideshare.* [Online] March 20, 2013. http://www.slideshare.net/HiveData/googlecontrolled-experimentationpanelthe-hive.

7. **Kohavi, Ron, Crook, Thomas and Longbotham, Roger.** Online Experimentation at Microsoft. *Third Workshop on Data Mining Case Studies and Practice Prize.* 2009. http://exp-platform.com/expMicrosoft.aspx.

8. **Amatriain, Xavier and Basilico , Justin.** Netflix Recommendations: Beyond the 5 stars. [Online] April 2012. http://techblog.netflix.com/2012/04/netflix-recommendations-beyond-5-stars.html.

9. **McFarland, Colin.** *Experiment!: Website conversion rate optimization with A/B and multivariate testing.* s.l. : New Riders, 2012. 978-0321834607.

10. **Smietana, Brandon.** Zynga: What is Zynga's core competency? *Quora.* [Online] Sept 2010. http://www.quora.com/Zynga/What-is-Zyngas-core-competency/answer/Brandon-Smietana.

11. **Kohavi, Ron, et al.** Online Controlled Experiments at Large Scale. *KDD 2013: Proceedings of the 19th ACM SIGKDD international conference on Knowledge discovery and data mining.* 2013. http://bit.ly/ExPScale.

12. **Brutlag, Jake .** Speed Matters . *Google Research blog.* [Online] June 23, 2009. http://googleresearch.blogspot.com/2009/06/speed-matters.html.

13. **Sullivan, Nicole .** Design Fast Websites. *Slideshare.* [Online] Oct 14, 2008. http://www.slideshare.net/stubbornella/designing-fast-websites-presentation.

14. **Kohavi, Ron, Henne, Randal M and Sommerfield, Dan.** Practical Guide to Controlled Experiments on the Web: Listen to Your Customers not to the HiPPO. *The Thirteenth ACM SIGKDD International Conference on Knowledge Discovery and Data Mining (KDD 2007).* August 2007, pp. 959-967. http://www.exp-platform.com/Documents/GuideControlledExperiments.pdf.

15. **Ries, Eric.** *The Lean Startup: How Today's Entrepreneurs Use Continuous Innovation to Create Radically Successful Businesses* . s.l. : Crown Business, 2011. 978-0307887894.

16. **Kohavi, Ron, et al.** Controlled experiments on the web: survey and practical guide. *Data Mining and Knowledge Discovery.* February 2009, Vol. 18, 1, pp. 140-181. http://www.exp-platform.com/Pages/hippo_long.aspx.

17. **Crook, Thomas, et al.** Seven Pitfalls to Avoid when Running Controlled Experiments on the Web. [ed.] Peter Flach and Mohammed Zaki. *KDD '09: Proceedings of the 15th ACM SIGKDD international conference on Knowledge discovery and data mining.* 2009, pp. 1105-1114. http://www.exp-platform.com/Pages/ExPpitfalls.aspx.

18. **Kohavi, Ron, et al.** Trustworthy online controlled experiments: Five puzzling outcomes explained. *Proceedings of the 18th Conference on Knowledge Discovery and Data Mining.* 2012, www.exp-platform.com/Pages/PuzzingOutcomesExplained.aspx.

19. **Wikipedia contributors.** Fisher's method. *Wikipedia.* [Online] Jan 2014. http://en.wikipedia.org/wiki/Fisher%27s_method.

20. **Eisenberg, Bryan.** How to Increase Conversion Rate 1,000 Percent. *ClickZ.* [Online] Feb 28, 2003. http://www.clickz.com/showPage.html?page=1756031.

21. **Spool, Jared.** The $300 Million Button. *USer Interface Engineering.* [Online] 2009. http://www.uie.com/articles/three_hund_million_button/.

22. **Goldstein, Noah J, Martin, Steve J and Cialdini, Robert B.** *Yes!: 50 Scientifically Proven Ways to Be Persuasive.* s.l. : Free Press, 2008. 1416570969.

23. **Collins , Jim and Porras , Jerry I.** *Built to Last: Successful Habits of Visionary Companies.* s.l. : HarperBusiness, 2004. 978-0060566104.

24. **Badam, Kiran.** Looking Beyond Page Load Times – How a relentless focus on Task Completion Times can benefit your users. *Velocity: Web Performance and Operations.* 2013. http://velocityconf.com/velocityny2013/public/schedule/detail/32820.

25. *Why Most Published Research Findings Are False.* **Ioannidis, John P.** 8, 2005, PLoS Medicine, Vol. 2, p. e124. http://www.plosmedicine.org/article/info:doi/10.1371/journal.pmed.0020124.

26. **Wacholder, Sholom, et al.** Assessing the Probability That a Positive Report is False: An Approach for Molecular Epidemiology Studies. *Journal of the National Cancer Institute.* 2004, Vol. 96, 6. http://jnci.oxfordjournals.org/content/96/6/434.long.

27. **Ehrenberg, A. S. C.** The Teaching of Statistics: Corrections and Comments. *Journal of the Royal Statistical Society.* Series A, 1974, Vol. 138, 4.

28. **Ron Kohavi, David Messner,Seth Eliot, Juan Lavista Ferres, Randy Henne, Vignesh Kannappan,Justin Wang.** *Tracking Users' Clicks and Submits: Tradeoffs between User Experience and Data Loss.* Redmond : s.n., 2010.

29. **Patel , Neil .** 11 Obvious A/B Tests You Should Try. *QuickSprout.* [Online] Jan 14, 2013. http://www.quicksprout.com/2013/01/14/11-obvious-ab-tests-you-should-try/.

30. **Porter, Joshua.** The Button Color A/B Test: Red Beats Green. *Hutspot.* [Online] Aug 2, 2011. http://blog.hubspot.com/blog/tabid/6307/bid/20566/The-Button-Color-A-B-Test-Red-Beats-Green.aspx.

31. **Linden, Greg.** Marissa Mayer at Web 2.0 . *Geeking with Greg* . [Online] Nov 9, 2006. http://glinden.blogspot.com/2006/11/marissa-mayer-at-web-20.html.

32. *Performance Related Changes and their User Impact.* **Schurman, Eric and Brutlag, Jake.** s.l. : Velocity 09: Velocity Web Performance and Operations Conference, 2009.

33. **Souders, Steve.** *High Performance Web Sites: Essential Knowledge for Front-End Engineers.* s.l. : O'Reilly Media, 2007. 978-0596529307.

34. **Linden, Greg.** Make Data Useful. [Online] Dec 2006. http://sites.google.com/site/glinden/Home/StanfordDataMining.2006-11-28.ppt.

35. **Wikipedia contributors.** Above the fold. *Wikipedia, The Free Encyclopedia.* [Online] Jan 2014. http://en.wikipedia.org/wiki/Above_the_fold.

36. **Souders, Steve.** Moving beyond window.onload(). *High Performance Web Sites Blog.* [Online] May 13, 2013. http://www.stevesouders.com/blog/2013/05/13/moving-beyond-window-onload/.

37. **Brutlag, Jake, Abrams, Zoe and Meenan, Pat .** Above the Fold Time: Measuring Web Page Performance Visually. *Velocity: Web Performance and Operations Conference.* 2011. http://en.oreilly.com/velocity-mar2011/public/schedule/detail/18692.

38. **Meenan, Patrick.** Speed Index. *WebPagetest.* [Online] April 2012. https://sites.google.com/a/webpagetest.org/docs/using-webpagetest/metrics/speed-index.

39. **Meenan, Patrick, Feng, Chao (Ray) and Petrovich, Mike .** Going Beyond onload - How Fast Does It Feel? *Velocity: Web Performance and Operations.* 2013. http://velocityconf.com/velocityny2013/public/schedule/detail/31344.

40. **Fisher, Ronald A.** Presidential Address. *Sankhyā: The Indian Journal of Statistics.* 1938, Vol. 4, 1. http://www.jstor.org/stable/40383882.

41. **Kohavi, Ron and Longbotham, Roger.** Unexpected Results in Online Controlled Experiments. *SIGKDD Explorations.* 2010, Vol. 12, 2. http://www.exp-platform.com/Documents/2010-12%20ExPUnexpectedSIGKDD.pdf.

42. **Montgomery, Douglas C.** *Applied Statistics and Probability for Engineers.* 5th. s.l. : John Wiley & Sons, Inc, 2010. 978-0470053041.

43. **Boos, Dennis D and Hughes-Oliver, Jacqueline M.** How Large Does n Have to be for Z and t Intervals? *The American Statistician.* 2000, Vol. 54, 2, pp. 121-128.

44. **Efron, Bradley and Robert J. Tibshirani.** *An Introduction to the Bootstrap.* New York : Chapman & Hall, 1993. 0-412-04231-2.

Log-based Predictive Maintenance

Ruben Sipos*
Dept. of Computer Science
Cornell University
Ithaca, NY
rs@cs.cornell.edu

Dmitriy Fradkin
Corporate Technology
Siemens Corporation
Princeton, NJ
dmitriy.fradkin@siemens.com

Fabian Moerchen*
Amazon
Seattle, WA
fabian@mybytes.de

Zhuang Wang*
Skytree
San Jose, CA
john.wang@skytree.net

ABSTRACT

Predictive maintenance strives to anticipate equipment failures to allow for advance scheduling of corrective maintenance, thereby preventing unexpected equipment downtime and improving service quality for the customers. We present a data-driven approach based on multiple-instance learning for predicting equipment failures by mining equipment event logs which, while usually not designed for predicting failures, contain rich operational information. We discuss problem domain and formulation, evaluation metrics and predictive maintenance work flow. We experimentally compare our approach to competing methods. For evaluation, we use real life datasets with billions of log messages from two large fleets of medical equipment. We share insights gained from mining such data. Our predictive maintenance approach, deployed by a major medical device provider over the past several months, learns and evaluates predictive models from terabytes of log data, and actively monitors thousands of medical scanners.

1. INTRODUCTION

Success of manufacturing companies largely depends on reliability of their products. Scheduled maintenance is widely used to ensure that equipment is operating correctly so as to avoid unexpected breakdowns. Such maintenance is often carried out separately for every component, based on its usage or simply on some fixed schedule. However, scheduled maintenance is labor-intensive and ineffective in identifying problems that develop between technician's visits. Unforeseen failures still frequently occur. In contrast, *predictive maintenance* techniques help determine the condition of in-service equipment in order to predict when and what repairs should be performed. The main goal of predictive maintenance is to enable pro-active scheduling of corrective work, and thus prevent unexpected equipment failures.

Predictive maintenance requires insight into the running condition of equipment. This can be gained by adding sensors to the equipment for recording and monitoring of signals of interest (such as temperature and voltage). The predictive maintenance module can then send alerts when sensor values deviate from normal ranges. Though sometimes an effective solution, it is impractical for in-service equipment, since major hardware upgrades, such as adding sensors, are often infeasible, especially on large fleets, due to cost, effort and potential regulatory hurdles. Alternatively, one can gain insight into the workings of a piece of equipment by studying its logs. Modern equipment is usually operated via software applications. For example, in case of medical scanners, all device operations, from warming up to scanning a patient and from generating a medical report to calibration, are controlled by various applications. These applications produce logs of their operation. These logs reflect the developers' original ideas about what are the valuable events to report, and contain informational or error messages, internal states, or exceptions. Theoretically, one can trace back how a piece of equipment was used by analyzing its logs. Mining such rich information can help in detecting potential issues in advance.

The use of equipment logs to predict failures poses many challenges and has not yet been fully explored. Since logs are mainly used for debugging purposes they (i) rarely contain explicit information for failure prediction; (ii) contain heterogeneous data including symbolic sequence, numeric time series, categorical variables and unstructured text; and (iii) contain massive amounts of data, posing computational challenges. To make use of log data, we first have to interpret the logs, filter out a large amount of noise (i.e. data irrelevant to our goal) and extract predictive features. Next, we have to collect known failure cases for learning/evaluating models, transform the problem into an appropriate learning scenario and determine a performance measure that reflects real-world needs. Then, we have to apply machine learning techniques to effectively and efficiently solve the learning problem. Moreover, we have to take into account specifics of the domain. In the following sections we discuss these points in more detail with the focus on the data and do-

*This work was done while at Siemens Corporation.

KDD'14, August 24–27, 2014, New York, NY, USA.
Copyright 2014 ACM 978-1-4503-2956-9/14/08 ...$15.00.
http://dx.doi.org/10.1145/2623330.2623340.

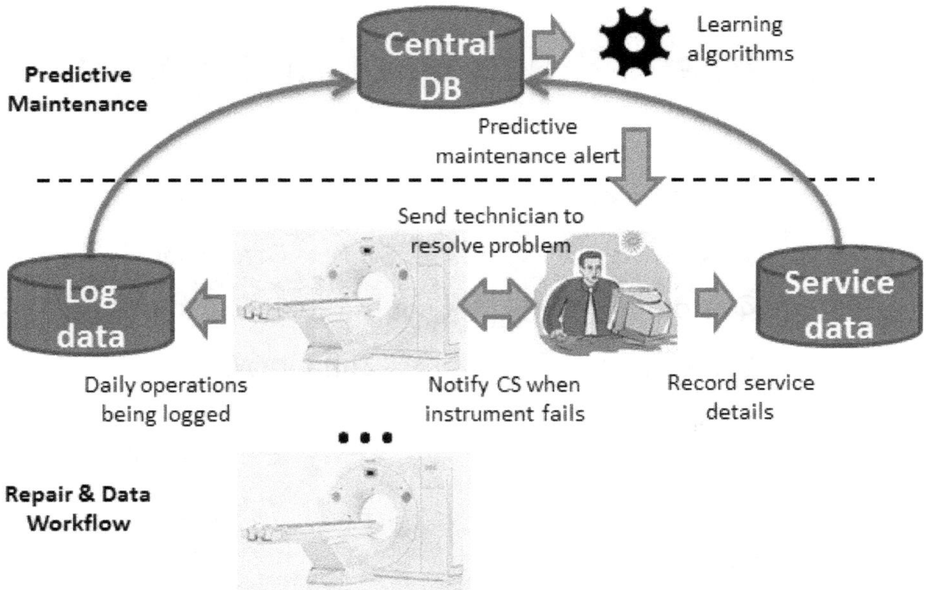

Figure 1: Predictive maintenance workflow.

main description, the problem formulation and a case study, which serve as our main contributions.

2. PROBLEM DESCRIPTION

In this section, we describe our data and application.

2.1 Data Description

A typical service life cycle looks as follows: equipment operates normally at first. When a problem occurs, the customer calls the service center for support, a "notification" is opened and repair service is scheduled. Then a technician comes on-site to resolve the problem. After resolution, the technician updates the notification with repair details such as component consumption information, hours spent, trouble-shooting or repair description, and closes the notification. Throughout the whole process, during both normal and abnormal operation, the equipment automatically records all events into log files. This cycle (illustrated in the bottom part of Figure 1) gets repeated over and over in a fleet of thousands of equipment units. The log files from such a fleet collected over the past several years form our data in this study. [1]

Log data is a collection of **events** recorded by various applications running on the equipment (see Figure 2). An event consists of a timestamp (indicating when the event occurred), a message text (either fully unstructured or generated from a template) describing the event, an event code (representing the category of a group of similar message text) and event severity. Events reflect the developers' original idea about what are the valuable states to report. In our application, we have thousands of unique event codes and a theoretically unlimited number of distinct messages texts.

[1]Although we use the data from medical devices to demonstrate our approach, our approach is also applicable to other domains, such as IT infrastructure or industrial equipment in which equipment logs are recorded.

Time Stamp	EventCode	Message
2010-09-08 20:10:51	ABC 59	ReconDone(IsvStatusSuccess) after 0 received images for ...
2010-09-08 20:10:51	ABC 49	Timer was started waiting for ...
2010-09-08 20:10:52	ABD 46	Receiving IsvMsgReconRequestDone message of size 80 Bytes from IRS.
2010-09-08 20:10:52	CDE 46	Control info CDE (E c0 03 25 20 a2 00 00)
2010-09-08 20:10:52	XYZ 10	SsqCtrl: Mode loading initiated: @PatientID@= ...
2010-09-08 20:10:52	FGH 17	SKIP button is hidden
2010-09-08 20:10:53	CDE 45	IS ImagingSystemFinished received.

Figure 2: A piece of a real log file (with renamed event codes and messages) from a medical scanner.

An equipment log is usually broken into day-long pieces. A daily log can contain tens of thousands of events since their time resolution can be as small as a few seconds.

Log data is unique in several aspects. It is temporal, and can be viewed both as symbolic sequences (over event codes) and as numeric time series, with variables extracted from messages or with event frequencies over some window, e.g. days. It can additionally include categorical features (event codes, and categorical variables in text) and fully unstructured data such as message text (some text similarity between message text may make sense, in particular in the absence of event code categories).

An experienced domain expert can scan equipment logs to identify abnormal conditions. The old-fashioned predictive maintenance approach in this domain is to manually create predictive patterns for a particular component based on the boolean combination of a few relevant event codes. Such an approach is heavily experience-based and very time consuming, but it illustrates an important concept - that component failure can be predicted by checking daily logs for patterns consisting of multiple event codes. This concept motivates us and serves as the basis for our problem formulation.

Service data is another crucial data type in predictive maintenance applications. Service notifications (or tickets) are used by the service center to record details of performed services such as the notification open date (i.e. the date customer reports a problem), the equipment involved, the component consumption and so on. Under a reasonable, though not always correct, assumption that component replacement is the consequence of a failure of that particular component, we can use this information to correlate a known component failure with its corresponding equipment, time and relevant logs.

However, service data is noisy and often includes incorrect information. A replacement of a component might be ordered but not used and later sent back to the factory; or a component may be exchanged but the repair may not have been appropriate for the problem at hand. Also, some failure modes do not involve component exchanges and need to be identified by matching certain keywords in the notification text such as "greasing" or "recalibrating". We formulate the problem using a robust learning approach (described in Section 3), which also serves to reduce the impact of low-quality data.

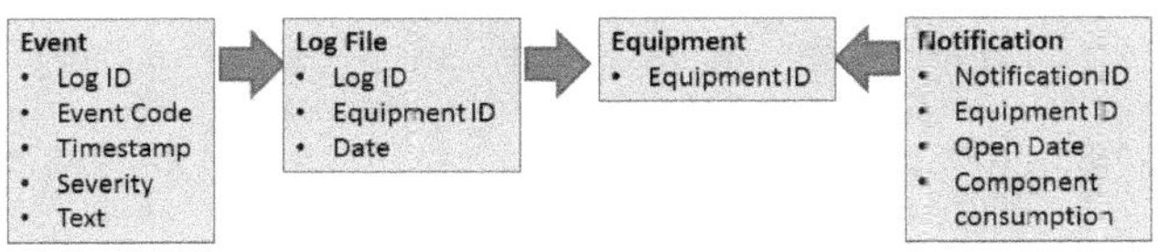

Figure 3: An ER diagram for predictive maintenance.

Figure 3 shows logical relationships between entities in predictive maintenance domains.

Given a target component and a collection of historical equipment log and service data, we can formulate a predictive maintenance problem for the target component. It consists of constructing a binary classifier for predicting failures, where training examples contain predictive features extracted from an interval of equipment's log, and the label is determined by the occurrence of the component replacement in the service data after that interval. Note that our approach is not specific to certain failure types, but targets all hardware failures (within business needs) that can be rectified by replacing or repairing the failing component and can be detected via logged data caused by aberrant or inoperable behavior. We give a more formal problem formulation in Section 3.

2.2 Predictive Maintenance Workflow

The predictive maintenance workflow is illustrated in the top part of Figure 1. A central database is at the core of a predictive maintenance platform. Data from in-service equipment and the Support Centers is collected and integrated there. The analytic module processes data from the central database. Analysis consists of the following stages: data preparation, model building, model evaluation, and monitoring. To build a model for a target component, the analytic module first pulls the relevant data from the central database, extracts predictive features (see Section 3), transforms and represents the data in a matrix format for learning algorithms. Learning algorithms build models and then pass them on for evaluation. A model is evaluated against historical data and scored by several key performance indicators. After evaluation, domain experts review the model's performance and decide whether to deploy the model into the system. In the monitoring module, the system pulls the new daily log data from monitored equipments and predict a component failure using a model. If predicted score exceeds a predefined threshold, an alert will be sent to the service center for further review.

2.3 Requirements

We worked closely with domain experts to come up with requirements that would make a log-based predictive maintenance solution practical and useful. These requirements, summarized below, served as a guideline for our design.

The timing of an alert is important for the evaluation of the quality of a model in predictive maintenance:

- **Predictive Interval**: a pre-defined time interval right before a failure. An alert occurring in this interval gives enough time for the support center to act and is considered successful.
- **Infected Interval**: a pre-defined time interval right after a failure. The equipment is breaking down or under repair. Data from this interval should not be used for modeling/evaluation.
- **Responsive Duration**: a pre-defined time length reflecting real-life action time for an alert.

True and false positives are then defined as:

- **True Positive**: an alert that occurs in the predictive interval. Note that multiple alerts in the same predictive interval only count as one true positive.
- **False Positive**: an alert that occurs outside the predictive/infected interval. Note that multiple such alerts within a responsive duration only count as one false positive.

Finally, using the definitions above, we can evaluate the performance of a model using precision and recall:

- **Precision**: True Positive / (True Positive + False Positive).
- **Recall**: True Positive / All failures.

The maintenance strategy is determined separately for different components and is influenced by many factors such as the repair cost, failure severity and the business model. Learning algorithms should balance Precision and Recall and provide user flexibility in trading these off. Without knowledge of the specific maintenance strategy, we can evaluate a model with Predictive-Maintenance-based Area Under precision-recall Curve (**PM-AUC**) score as a simple measurement. PM-AUC is computed like regular AUC but using the above definitions of Recall and Precision.

Other requirements are not defined as formally, but are present nonetheless, so we discuss them briefly.

Interpretability: It is preferable to have an interpretable model so that experts are able to review it. This allows for incorporation of expert feedback into the modeling process. We use methods with L1 regularization to build sparse linear model which the domain experts can easily review. Such a model consists of a weighted sum of a relatively small numbers of predictive features, with the weights specifying their precise contributions to the decision. Furthermore, known noisy or irrelevant features specified by experts can be easily excluded from the new modeling process. In some cases just knowing that the model is "interpretable" and understanding which features affect model performance makes experts more comfortable in adopting it.

Efficiency: The learning algorithm should be fast and capable of handling hundreds of thousands of training examples in a space of tens of thousands features. We use the state-of-the-art sparse linear classifier package Liblinear [9] to achieve this.

Handling Class Imbalance: The number of known failures is usually small. We have to be able to learn models with only tens of known failure cases. To deal with such extremely imbalanced labeled data, we apply a combination of stratified sampling, stable feature selection and large margin techniques to prevent over-fitting and learn a robust model.

3. METHODOLOGY

We view our problem as an example of Multi-Instance Learning (MIL) [8] because it is a good fit for our setting. In MIL, instead of receiving a set of independent labeled instances as in standard classification, the learner receives a set of bags which are labeled positive or negative. Each bag may contain multiple instances (equipment daily logs). A bag (all the logs from an interval, e.g. one week) is labeled negative if all the instances in it are negative (no failures according to the service notifications), and positive if it contains at least one positive. Given bags obtained from different equipment and at different dates, the goal is to build a classifier that will label either unseen bags or unseen instances correctly. The accuracy of models is here measured at the bag level.

MIL formulation captures several important aspects of our problem:

- It is more realistic to assume that at least one daily log within a short interval before a failure carries a failure signature than to assume that all the daily logs within a short interval before a failure carry a failure signature. More likely, equipment continues working irregularly, switching between normal and abnormal conditions, before a final breakdown. Therefore we should not label all instances in a pre-failure interval as positive (as we would in a non-MIL setting).
- All the daily logs are normal within a non-failure interval
- The goal is to correctly label a bag rather than every instance. This is strictly consistent with the domain-based evaluation metric.

We formally define the learning task as follows. Let D be a set of B labeled bags, $D = \{bag_j, j = 1, ..., B\}$, where $bag_j = (\{x_{ij}, i = 1, ..., b_j\}, y_j)$, $x_{ij} \in R^d$ is a feature vector of the i-th instance from the j-th bag, $y_j \in \{+1, -1\}$ is the binary label of the j-th bag and b_j is the number of instances in the j-th bag. The objective[2] is to learn a model f whose decision function $sgn(f(bag))$ accurately predicts the label of a bag.

One of the major challenges in our problem domain comes from the label imbalance and the low quality of positive labels. Since labeling is based on service notifications which are not entirely reliable, even slightly inaccurate notification dates would significantly change the identification of positive bags, if we did not take this into account. Moreover, as the known failure cases are very rare, any noisy positive bags would significantly downgrade the model quality. Recent advances in MIL resulted in many successful algorithms for learning f, but most of them are not robust to label noise in the situations with imbalanced data. Below we describe a simple algorithm which is robust to label noise for the rare class and is a more effective solution than alternatives, as evidenced by our experimental evaluation described in Section 4.

Training. Many different ways of solving MIL exist[10]; our approach combines instance-to-example, meta-examples and instance-based supervised learning.

We first transform the MIL dataset as follows: if the j-th bag is negative, we create multiple negative examples $(x_{ij}, -1)$ by an instance-to-example approach (i.e. each instance in a negative bag becomes one negative example), because all instances in negative bags are part of normal operation and not indicative of failure. If the j-th bag is positive, we create s positive example by averaging all its instances into a single positive meta example $(x_j, +1)$, where $x_j = mean(\{x_{ij}\}, i = 1, ..., b_j)$ (i.e. each positive bag becomes one positive example). One rationale for this is that the new positive meta-example (i.e. average over all instances in a positive bag) is guaranteed to be positive since we know there is at least one positive instance in the bag. Although it compromises some level of the discriminative power of positive examples due to inclusion of features from negative instances, the averaging strategy improves the label quality of positive examples which is more critical for imbalanced data.

Joining all the newly created examples from all the bags into a single training dataset $D' = \{(x_j, y_j), j = 1, ..., M\}$, we formulate the learning problem as a L1-regularized SVM optimization, $\min_w \frac{\lambda}{2}||w||_1^2 + \sum_j \max\{1 - y_j w^T x_j, 0\}$, where $\lambda > 0$ is a user-specified regularization parameter. The optimization can be efficiently solved by Liblinear [9].

Prediction. In MIL, how to apply the learned model on new instances / bags depends on the application requirement. It is not uncommon to apply different prediction strategy in training/testing phase. In our real-life deployment phase, new log data (i.e. instance) arrives on a daily base. We apply the learned model to individual instances as they arrive and trigger an alert if the prediction is beyond a pre-defined threshold (which is selected during the testing phase based on a desired precision/recall point on the PM-AUC curve). To be aligned with this setup, in the testing phase, we do not transform bags. Instead, we predict every instance of a bag and predict the bag as positive if the prediction score of a bag instance hits a given threshold[3], otherwise as negative. In the case of true pos-

[2]Actually, this 0-1-error-based objective is a surrogate as directly maximizing PM-AUC is difficult.

[3]We increment the threshold and repeat the process to calculate PM-AUC.

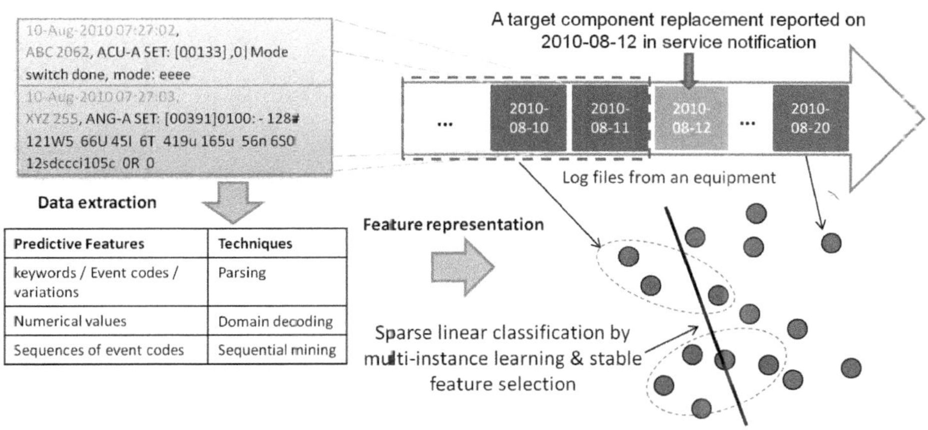

Figure 4: Our methodology.

itive prediction, our model gives an alert between one[4] to length-of-predictive-interval days in advance.

Feature Representation We use a bag-of-features approach to create feature vectors. The features that can be extracted from logs include:

- Keywords: bag-of-keyword is a fine-grained feature representation which can easily blow up the feature space to millions of dimensions. Since it poses computational challenges and is usually difficult to interpret in the final model, we do not use keywords in this paper.
- Numerical values: Numerical values are often used to record important physical or mechanical conditions. Extracting such values from text is a highly domain-dependent task because the values are often encoded to hide sensitive information. Given the high cost of domain effort for decoding, we only extract a limited number of numerical values and represent each with several statistic-based features.
- Event codes: an event code is the developer-specified category of a group of similar message texts. It is a high-level summary of the event content. Since event codes are domain-friendly (as they are widely used in traditional pattern creation process) and the extraction is fully domain-independent, we use them as basic features.
- Event code variations: textually similar messages from the same event code might be logically different. For example, "the scanning button is on" and "the scanning button is off" come from the same event code but record two opposite operations. To distinguish semantically different messages from the same event code, we decompose event codes into event code variations. For all the message text from the same event code, we first filter out embedded numerical values and then identify each distinct message template as a new event code variation. This type of feature is highly desirable by domain experts.
- Sequences: sequential features capture the logical order of events and enhance the interpretability of the final model. We have also conducted initial experiments with event-code-based sequence features generated by a novel sequential pattern-mining algorithm designed for MIL. We do not discuss details here due to space constraints and leave it for future work.

Feature Selection We use a bootstrapped feature selection algorithm to select a subset of relevant features for building robust learning models with imbalanced labels. In the spirit of [4], we perform stable feature selection by training multiple sparse linear classifiers under stratified subsampling. We create each sample of data by including all the positive bags and a set of randomly picked negative bags. We train a sparse linear classifier on the sample and learn the model weights w_i, where i is the index of a sample of data. After repeating this process multiple times, we calculate $|\sum_i w_i|$, rank features by these values and then select the features by retaining only those with the highest rankings. Afterwards, the selected features are used for another sparse linear classification on all the training data to learn the final model.

Our methodology is summarized on Figure 4. Creating the dataset, training of the model and how we test the model are described in Algorithm 1.

4. EXPERIMENTS

Our data has been collected over the several years from two large fleets of medical equipments from a major medical device provider. For each type of equipment we choose a target component of high practical interest and with a sufficient number of known failure cases. We use 7 days for the Predictive Interval, 20 days for the Infected Internal and 7 days for the Responsive Duration for both predictive maintenance tasks. All these values were agreed upon with domain experts (and we did not find significant differences in performance by slightly changing bag sizes). For each data set we create positive bags from the the daily logs of [-7 day, -1 day] interval before each failure, where day 0 is the notification open date (i.e. the noted day of the failure), and negative bags by randomly selecting about 20% of all the

[4]In the worst case the alert would be raised based on the last daily log before the failure.

C	A	description
16389	75552	#instances
3073	11238	#features
88	108	#known failures
6664	14367	#bags

Figure 5: Dataset summary.

	C	A
random	0.037 (0.004)	0.017 (0.003)
AllInst.	0.293 (0.014)	0.620 (0.013)
Agg.	0.174 (0.013)	0.498 (0.016)
MILES	0.170 (0.011)	0.427 (0.117)
MI-SVM	0.216 (0.038)	0.700 (0.014)
Ours	**0.319 (0.015)**	**0.730 (0.011)**

Figure 6: PM-AUC comparison.

Algorithm 1

Build the MIL dataset:

1. Parse daily event logs to extract features.
2. Parse service notifications to extract known failure information.
3. Create bags for MIL learning.
   (a) Group daily instances into bags using desired interval lengths.
   (b) Label bags with known failures as positive and the rest as negative.

Train the model:

1. In the training phase, transform the MIL dataset.
   (a) Each instance in a negative bag is transformed into a negative example.
   (b) For each positive bag we create a positive meta example using the average of all bag's instances.
2. Feature selection.
   (a) Create multiple subsets by randomly subsampling transformed negative bags and including all positive meta examples.
   (b) Learn a sparse linear classifier on each subset.
   (c) Average weights from all runs and select features with the highest absolute weights.
3. Train the final model.
   (a) Use the subset of features obtained in the previous step.
   (b) Learn the final model by using all the data.

Test/Apply the model:

1. In evaluation, predict a bag as positive if the prediction score of a bag instance hits a given threshold.
2. In deployment, trigger an alert if the prediction score of a new daily log hits the pre-defined threshold.

---

remaining weekly intervals. The resulting datasets A and C are summarized in Figure 5.

Domain-based Evaluation We compare our algorithm against the following methods:

- **AllInstances:** A baseline wrapper algorithm that transforms MIL into standard supervised learning by assigning the bag label to its instances (i.e. a pure *instance-to-example* way of solving MIL). It was reported to work well in some cases [18].
- **Aggregated**[23]: Another baseline wrapper algorithm that aggregates each bag into a meta-example by averaging (i.e. a pure *meta-example* way of solving MIL).
- **MILES**[6]: A popular MIL wrapper algorithm that embeds each bag into a new feature space defined by distances to training instances.
- **MI-SVM**[2]: An iterative algorithm that solves the optimization formulation of MIL as a maximum margin problem.

The PM-AUC scores of these methods are shown in Table 6. For the wrapper algorithms, L1-regularized Linear SVM with the bootstrapped feature selection is used for supervised learning[5]. Experimental results (mean and standard deviation) are reported based on bag-level 5-fold cross validation with stratified sampling for imbalanced positive labels. All hyper-parameters were selected using cross validation. These results show that our approach significantly outperforms other methods in terms of PM-AUC.

The maintenance strategy is determined by business units separately for different equipment or component, which is why predictive models have to allow trading-off between precision and recall according to the specific strategy. Figure 7 contains the PM-ROC curves (showing the mean and 90% confidence interval from 5-fold cross validation) of the models with different complexity (controlled by adjusting the L-1 regularization parameter) learned by our algorithm. In both figures, we can observe that the pink curves, representing models composed of 300 to 400 predictive features, achieve the best performance. If the business requirements are for 70% precision then our best models can cover 25% and 80%

[5]We also explored kernel SVM but did not observe significant performance improvement.

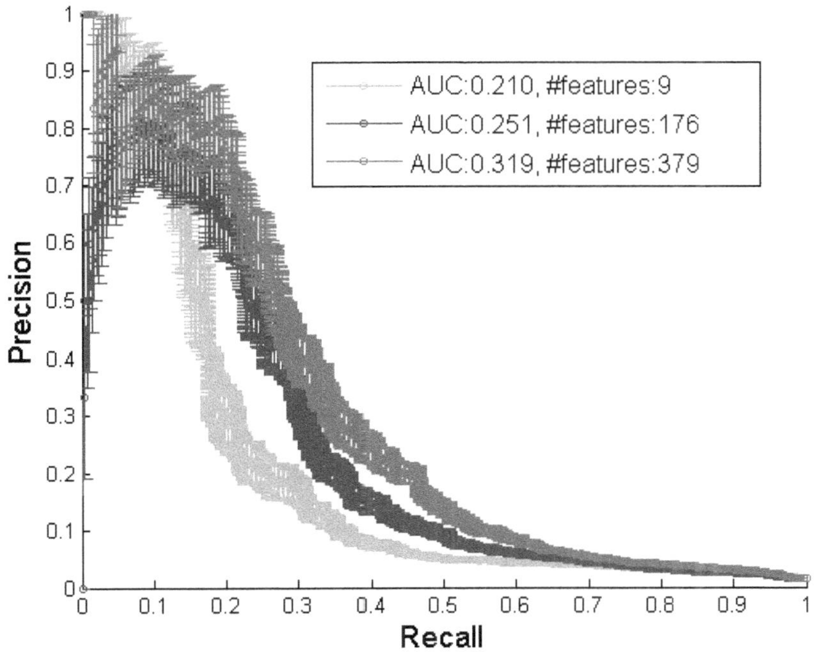

(a) Dataset C

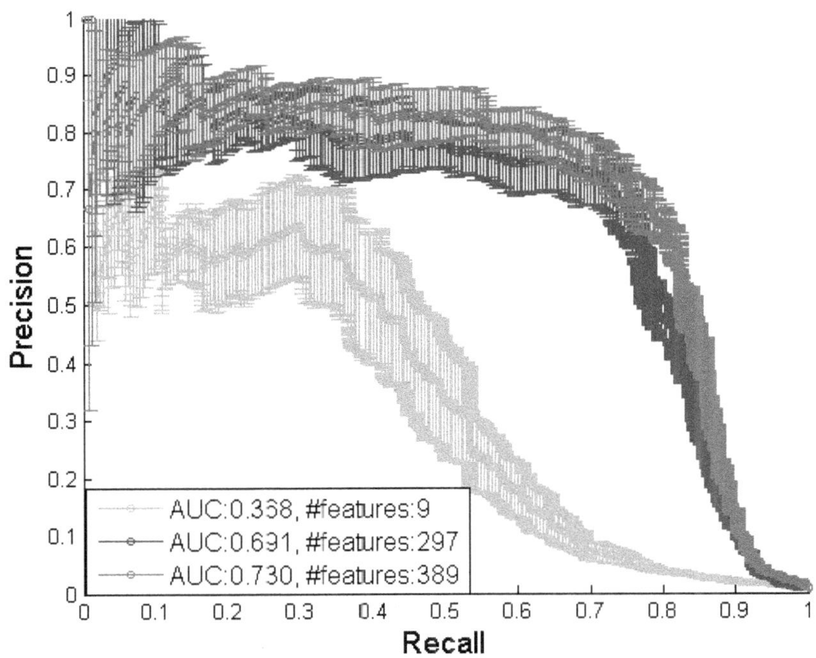

(b) Dataset A

Figure 7: PM-ROC plots with different model complexity learned by our algorithm.

of failures (i.e. recall at that precision point) within the 7-day Predictive Interval for each dataset, respectively. Considering that no existing predictive rules/models are available for these two components, our method is highly successful. Simpler models, with fewer features, are also desirable from both the machine learning and the domain points of view. Though the most complicated models (with 300 to 400 features) achieve the best PM-AUC scores on both datasets, the simpler models with less than ten features and suboptimal scores are still useful. Their simplicity, together with relatively high performance (high precision and reasonable recall), enable domain experts to understand them and thus help detect root causes of failures or identify specific failure modes.

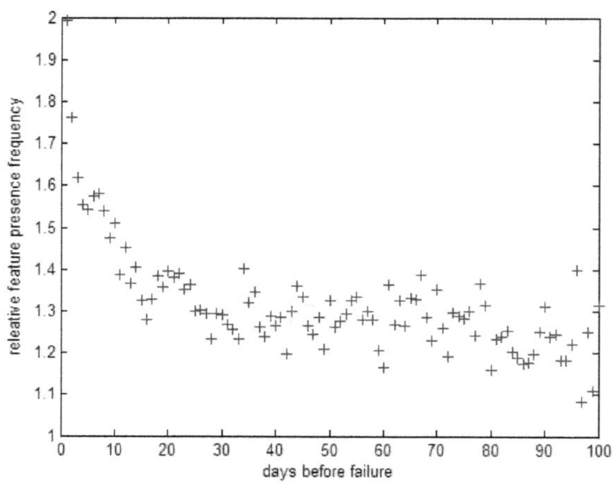

Figure 8: A plot of average (over the fleet) relative frequency of a positive feature vs. time to failure.

On Utility of Single Features An interesting question is whether the effects of an impending failure can be observed over time by looking at only a few features. Our experiments suggest that while the frequencies of some features are in aggregate correlated with approaching failures, they are not strong predictors of failures in individual instances. A plot of the relation between the (relative) frequency of one highly positive feature and the time to a failure is shown in Figure 8. There is a clear upward trend close to the failure date. However, this plot is an aggregate over multiple machines. It turns out that many positive instances do not contain this feature, and the value usually does not change smoothly or in the same direction between consequent days on the same machine. This could be an artifact of how events are logged or it could be related to utilization, which varies from day to day. In either case, we lack additional knowledge to correct for these factors. Thus this feature alone is inadequate for failure prediction. This example illustrated why simple handcrafted rules utilizing only a handful of features do not work well, while machine learning approaches that can use combined even weak signals result in decent performance.

Global vs Local Models Some types of equipment may be configured differently due to specific customer needs. The equipment with the same setup belongs to the same family. Do the equipment logs from different families behave differently? Is the model learned from one family valid for the other ones?

	I	II	III
I	0.43	0.70	0.59
II	0.45	0.87	0.70
III	0.32	0.77	0.71

Figure 9: PM-AUC of cross-testing of family-specific models. E.g. the score on the coordinate (I,II) corresponds to the model that is trained on the data from family I and tested on the data from family II.

To explore similarities between families, we performed hierarchical clustering on the equipment daily bag-of-events features and found that some families behave more similarly to each other than the others. By labeling the same features with their family types and feeding them into a multi-class classifier, we can correctly predict the family of a daily log with more than 80% accuracy on dataset A, which has 28 families. This indicates that there are noticeable differences between families. To explore the predictability of family-specific models on other families, we train a "local" classifier on each family and test on the others. The results (in terms of PM-AUCs) of this experiment on the three largest families in dataset A are summarized in Figure 9. Most of the family-specific models achieve comparable scores in the cross-testing. The fact that the family-specific predictive power is transferable and that known failure cases are very rare suggests that training a global predictive model on data from all the families make sense in our problem domain.

5. INFUSION AND IMPACT

Our approach is currently used to monitor several worldwide fleets of medical equipment. It was implemented and deployed on a SAS platform of a major medical equipment provider. The workflows were built with SAS Enterprise Miner to automate the process of model building and evaluation. Since SAS Enterprise Miner does not include L1-regularized classifiers for feature selection, we ran the proposed algorithm in our development environment to preselect the features which provide the highest PM-AUC score. Only the selected features (usually a few hundred) are used in the SAS Enterprise Miner workflows. Based on the model performance on the held-out historical data, an alert threshold is selected to balance Precision and Recall according to business requirement for a target component. When a problem is identified, an alert is sent to the user. Alerts are reviewed by domain experts to determine the next steps. The system has been deployed in early 2012 and has not been retrained in order to allow a long term real-life performance evaluation. However, it makes sense to retrain the models periodically with the new data, e.g. on a time interval basis or after a number of new failure cases are accumulated.

A real-world evaluation proceeds as follows: no corrective action is taken after receiving an alert during the evaluation period. After that, true positives, false positives and total failures are determined by the component replacement information from the Service Center. Our workflow for predicting a key medical scanner component failure was evaluated over several months on a subset of one fleet (several hundred scanners). The performance was similar to that on the experimental data (Dataset C): it successfully predicted 12 out of 31 failures within 1 week predictive interval and only generated a few (between 0 and 5) false alarms[6]

The business success cannot be measured as easily as the technical one. Evaluation would have to take into account multiple factors, such as cost saving in both spare parts and labor, improved customer satisfaction (e.g. customer return rate) and new business opportunities (e.g. the profit by selling such a service). Evaluating these factors would require intensive involvement of project stakeholders and additional time and resources which is beyond the scope of this data mining project.

6. RELATED WORK

Some recently published research focuses on using log data for anomaly detection. The main advantage is using already existing functionality to improve and better understand systems. Because many systems already include logging functionality exploiting this source of data presents a low cost alternative to augmentation with additional sensors.

Logs can be used to further the understanding of how the system behaves and what are the common patterns. The approach of [15] is aimed at discovering and understanding what the common patterns are, but does not touch upon proactive prevention of errors. In addition to understanding the normal behavior we can also try and detect anomalies. The authors of [26, 25, 24, 27] parse textual log messages and then use PCA to detect anomalies. In our data, however, the changes signaling approaching failure are weaker and noisier (we tried using PCA but did not obtain useful results). Creating event descriptions based on text messages in our logs could be done by clustering [1, 21, 22, 16, 20] but interpreting them requires unavailable domain knowledge. Another option is to use NLP and semantic web techniques to analyze text-based maintenance logs and/or problem ticket data [7, 19] to understand future events or rank events to prioritize repair. Predicting failures on a data stream processing system [13] can be done by observing system's status. This approach uses an ensemble of decision tree classifiers and is applicable in an online setting (i.e. triggering proactive actions when necessary). Taking into account the sequence of logged messages is also possible (we have explored sequence mining, but do not focus on it in this paper). For example, one can use time series of hard drive status messages in Multiple Instance Learning (MIL) setting [17] to predict failures. Finite state automata can be used to model sequential dependencies between messages and detect anomalies [11]. Moreover, temporal information can be incorporated to further improve the detection ability: for example, one could include information about bursts of events [14]. We, on the other hand, use daily aggregates and discard the possibility of fine temporal patterns to simplify the model and reduce the amount of data.

Our data bears some similarities with text represented in bag-of-words format. Machine days can be viewed as documents and events as words describing that day (with their own occurrence frequencies). We can therefore consider some research from the text mining fields as potentially relevant. In many cases, SVMs work well with text derived data which is usually high dimensional and very sparse. Special care has to be taken when dealing with highly imbalanced datasets [5].

Because we can not assign positive label to a specific day before the failure we use multi-instance learning [28, 3 10] setting to deal with this problem. Training on all individual instances using bag labels works well in many cases [18] but not on our data. Another simple approach is using distance based approaches such as k nearest neighbors (kNN). A more sophisticated approach built on top of kNN is MILES [6] which obtains state-of-the-art performance on many MIL problems by transforming the feature space using distances and then learning a supervised classifier on top of it. Performance of kNN is very poor on our data and MILES suffers from computational complexity while still achieving only mediocre performance. A very successful approach is building ensembles of classifiers [29] which can in many cases improve the results of the base classifier. This idea is partially reflected in our way of doing feature selection, but does not noticeably improve the the performance of the final classifier. MILIS [12] is an approach to MIL that similarly to our non-convex formulation formulation of selecting positive representatives selects prototype instances for positive bags and solves the optimization problem by iterating between instance selection and classifier learning.

7. CONCLUSION AND LESSONS LEARNED

We presented an approach for log-based predictive maintenance. It utilizes state-of-the-art machine learning techniques to build predictive models from log data. Our approach was developed with active involvement from domain experts and was evaluated and shown to be effective by both machine learning and domain standards. It has been deployed by a major medical equipment provider, learning and evaluating predictive models from terabytes of log data, and actively monitoring thousands of medical scanners around the world.

Appropriately formulating the problem by considering the nature of the data and incorporating the domain-based evaluation metrics are the key lessons we learned. Using MIL setting allows us to obtain a good match between data modeling and practical constraints. Data availability and quality determine the quality of the learning process and analytical results. When improving data quality is infeasible, robustness of learning algorithms becomes critical. Additionally, for the domain experts to understand and trust the machine learning algorithms and results, the learned models must be interpretable. We achieve this by building a sparse linear model with L1 regularization. We also notice that using a very small number of features is not sufficient to achieve high performance due to noise and sparsity in data. Thus hand-constructed models do not achieve our level of performance.

Acknowledgments

We thank Patrick Pyka (Siemens AG Healthcare) and Nambi Sridharan (Siemens Medical Solutions USA, Inc.) for insightful domain discussion.

8. REFERENCES

[1] Aharon, M., Barash, G., Cohen, I., Mordechai, E.: One graph is worth a thousand logs: Uncovering hidden structures in massive system event logs. In: ECML PKDD (2009)

[6]The precise number was not recorded by the customer.

[2] Andrews, S., Tsochantaridis, I., Hofmann, T.: Support vector machines for multiple-instance learning. In: NIPS (2003)

[3] Babenko, B.: Multiple instance learning: Algorithms and applications.

[4] Bach, F.R.: Bolasso: model consistent lasso estimation through the bootstrap. In: ICML (2008)

[5] Brank, J., Grobelnik, M., Milic-Frayling, N., Mladenic, D.: Training text classifiers with svm on very few positive examples. MSR-TR-2003-34 (2003)

[6] Chen, Y., Bi, J., Wang, J.Z.: Miles: Multiple-instance learning via embedded instance selection. IEEE Transactions on Pattern Analysis and Machine Intelligence **28**(12), 1931–1947 (2006)

[7] Devaney, M., Ram, A.: Preventing failures by mining maintenance logs with case-based reasoning. In: Proceedings of the 59th meeting of the society for machinery failure prevention technology (2005)

[8] Dietterich, T.G., Lathrop, R.H., Lozano-Perez, T.: Solving the multiple instance problem with axis-parallel rectangles. Artificial Intelligence **89**(3) (1997)

[9] Fan, R.E., Chang, K.W., Hsieh, C.J., Wang, X.R., Lin, C.J.: Liblinear: A library for large linear classification. Journal of Machine Learning Research **9**, 1871–1874 (2008)

[10] Foulds, J., Frank, E.: A review of multi-instance learning assumptions. The Knowledge Engineering Review **25**(1), 1–25 (2010)

[11] Fu, Q., Lou, J.G., Wang, Y., Li, J.: Execution anomaly detection in distributed systems through unstructured log analysis. In: ICDM (2009)

[12] Fu, Z., Robles-Kelly, A., Zhou, J.: Milis: Multiple instance learning with instance selection. IEEE Transactions on Pattern Analysis and Machine Intelligence **33**(5) (2011)

[13] Gu, X., Papadimitriou, S., Yu, P.S., Chang, S.P.: Online failure forecast for fault-tolerant data stream processing. In: ICDE (2008)

[14] Lahiri, B., Akrotirianakis, I., Moerchen, F.: Finding critical thresholds for defining bursts. In: DaWaK (2011)

[15] Li, T., Liang, F., Ma, S., Peng, W.: An integrated framework on mining logs files for computing system management. In: KDD (2005)

[16] Makanju, A., Zincir-heywood, A.N., Milios, E.E.: Clustering event logs using iterative partitioning. In: KDD (2009)

[17] Murray, J. F., Hughes, G. F., Kreutz-Delgado, K.: Machine learning methods for predicting failures in hard drives: a multiple-instance application. Journal of Machine Learning Research **6**, 783–816 (2005)

[18] Ray, S., Craven, M.: Supervised versus multiple instance learning: an empirical comparison. In: ICML (2005)

[19] Rudin, C., Passonneau, R.J., Radeva, A., Dutta, H., Ierome, S., Isaac, D.: A process for predicting manhole events in Manhattan. Machine Learning 80, 1–31 (2010)

[20] Taerat, N., Brandt, J., Gentile, A., Wong, M., Leangsuksun, C.: Baler: Deterministic, lossless log message clustering tool. Computer Science - Research and Development **26**, 285–295 (2011)

[21] Vaarandi, R.: A data clustering algorithm for mining patterns from event logs. In: IEEE Workshop on IP Operations and Management (2003)

[22] Vaarandi, R.: Tools and algorithms for mining patterns from event logs. In: NATO ASI Workshop on Mining Massive Data Sets for Security (2007)

[23] Wang, Z., Lan, L., Vucetic, S.: Mixture model for multiple instance regression and applications in remote sensing. IEEE Transactions on Geoscience and Remote Sensing **50**(6) (2012)

[24] Xu, W.: Detecting large scale system problems by mining console logs. Ph.D. thesis, UC Berkeley (2010)

[25] Xu, W., Huang, L., Fox, A., Patterson, D., Jordan, M.: Mining console logs for large-scale system problem detection. In: 3rd workshop on Tackling Computer Systems Problems with Machine Learning Techniques, SysML (2008)

[26] Xu, W., Huang, L., Fox, A., Patterson, D., Jordan, M.: Online system problem detection by mining patterns of console logs. In: ICDM (2009)

[27] Xu, W., Huang, L., Fox, A., Patterson, D., Jordan, M.: Using machine learning techniques in console log analysis. In: ICML (2010)

[28] Zhou, Z.H.: Multi-instance learning: A survey. Technical Report (2004)

[29] Zhou, Z.H., Zhang, M.L.: Ensembles of multi-instance learners. In: ECML (2003)

Automated Hypothesis Generation Based on Mining Scientific Literature

Scott Spangler[*,1], Angela D. Wilkins[*,3], Benjamin J. Bachman[3], Meena Nagarajan[1], Tajhal Dayaram[3], Peter Haas[1], Sam Regenbogen[3], Curtis R. Pickering[2], Austin Comer[2], Jeffrey N. Myers[2], Ioana Stanoi[1], Linda Kato[1], Ana Lelescu[1], Jacques J. Labrie[1], Neha Parikh[3], Andreas Martin Lisewski[3], Lawrence Donehower[3], Ying Chen[1], Olivier Lichtarge[3]

[1]IBM Research
San Jose, California

[2]The University of Texas MD Anderson Cancer Center
Houston, Texas

[3]Baylor College of Medicine
Houston, Texas

ABSTRACT

Keeping up with the ever-expanding flow of data and publications is untenable and poses a fundamental bottleneck to scientific progress. Current search technologies typically find many relevant documents, but they do not extract and organize the information content of these documents or suggest new scientific hypotheses based on this organized content. We present an initial case study on KnIT, a prototype system that mines the information contained in the scientific literature, represents it explicitly in a queriable network, and then further reasons upon these data to generate novel and experimentally testable hypotheses. KnIT combines entity detection with neighbor-text feature analysis and with graph-based diffusion of information to identify potential new properties of entities that are strongly implied by existing relationships. We discuss a successful application of our approach that mines the published literature to identify new protein kinases that phosphorylate the protein tumor suppressor p53. Retrospective analysis demonstrates the accuracy of this approach and ongoing laboratory experiments suggest that kinases identified by our system may indeed phosphorylate p53. These results establish proof of principle for automated hypothesis generation and discovery based on text mining of the scientific literature.

*These authors contributed equally

KDD '14, August 24 - 27 2014, New York, NY, USA

http://dx.doi.org/10.1145/2623330.2623667

Categories and Subject Descriptors

I.2.6 [**Learning**]: Concept Learning and Knowledge Acquisition

General Terms

Algorithms, Experimentation.

Keywords

Text Mining; Scientific Discovery; Hypothesis Generation.

1. INTRODUCTION

The pace of scientific publications is growing at an exponential rate [18] with over 50 million papers published so far [16], and over a million additional articles published annually [4]. This means on average a new article being published every 30 seconds. Within specific fields there may be tens of thousands of papers published every year—far more than any individual scientist can keep up with. In biomedical research, papers on specialized topics often run in the tens of thousands and topic areas contain orders of magnitude more. For example, over 70,000 papers have been published on a single protein, the tumor suppressor p53 [13]. Proteins are the fundamental machinery of the cell; understanding them is critical to advances in biology and medicine, and yet no scientist can possibly assimilate, recall and accurately process all of the known facts and relationships that could be relevant to discovering unknown protein functions, identifying relationships between proteins, or elucidating the role a particular protein may play in disease. Even recognizing new questions that should be asked can be a challenge. Instead, only a sliver of the relevant knowledge guides hypotheses: an approach that is deeply wasteful. This fundamental bottleneck is pervasive in biology and representative of every area of human endeavor in which there is a mushrooming mismatch between raw information and our analytic abilities.

Our goal is to accelerate scientific progress by combining mining, visualization, and analytics, with the hope to integrate all available content, identify the facts that are relevant to a given query, and from these facts suggest hypotheses that are new, interesting, testable and likely to be true.

Baylor College of Medicine and IBM Research have engaged in a long-term partnership to define scientific goals, build the necessary infrastructure, software, and algorithms and test the strengths and limitations of our discovery capabilities through direct experiments. We see this as a multi-year effort, but in the process of designing our approach and applying some very basic algorithms to the data, we made some early and surprising discoveries: even relatively simple approaches, when applied across enough data and with the benefit of expert domain knowledge, may quickly lead to significant discoveries in a complex domain. This paper describes our initial approach for this Knowledge Integration Toolkit (**KnIT**) for discovery and the early findings it has already led to so far.

KnIT embodies a three-phase process of Exploration, Interpretation, and Analysis. The Exploration phase surveys the relevant unstructured information, designs text queries, and extracts relevant documents for entities of interest. The entities of interest in this paper are a particular set of human proteins called kinases, detailed in Section 3. In general, each entity is modeled as a point in an abstract feature space, where the features of an entity correspond to its aggregate "text signature" in a corpus.

Next, the Interpretation phase builds a connected graph that represents the similarity relationship among entities. This helps domain experts visualize hidden connections between entities based on most of the known features and properties discussed in the literature. Coloring overlaid on top of this graph may reveal sub-graphs that correspond to clusters, typically with respect to some important property of interest. Critically, a sub-graph may contain a few "deviant" entities not known to possess the property of interest; because these entities are surrounded by others with a specific property, it is plausible to hypothesize that the deviant entities share it as well.

Finally, the Analysis phase globally diffuses annotation information among entities to rank order the best entity candidates for further experimentation of novel annotation predictions. In doing this we may compare the candidates derived analytically and rank-order the best candidates for further experimentation. The graph from the Interpretation phase can be used as a sanity check to ensure that the results correspond to common sense. Ultimately the domain expert can choose to verify only those annotation candidates that are the most analytically probable, experimentally testable, and of direct interest to the problem at hand, such as those suggesting a novel component of a disease's mechanism or a potential drug target.

Some past approaches have inferred formulas from experimental data [17]. Others have deduced direct connections based on a set of indirect associations that are obtained from highly structured, manual annotations of a corpus, such as MeSH annotations of MEDLINE data [30], hypothesis generation from unstructured text has been a hit-or-miss manual process [31] that is heavily dependent upon serendipity. Our approach leverages mining techniques for unstructured text to automatically discover hidden similarities between entities based on a corpus of scientific articles. The hope is that this approach will be robust and scalable even as entities and their multi-dimensional features create complex network relationships far beyond what human scientists can reason over, generating hypotheses that would otherwise elude domain experts.

In the rest of the paper we describe our proof of concept case study: a particular application of this methodology to a protein of singular importance across biology, the tumor suppressor p53. After discussing its role in cancer research, we describe our representation of the p53 literature and related proteins of interest. Next, we explain our knowledge visualization strategy for these proteins using a similarity graph, followed by a presentation of the analytical reasoning approach based on information diffusion. We then show in a series of retrospective validation studies that we are indeed able to create meaningful and accurate predictions. Finally, in a bona fide example of discovery, we present describe laboratory experiments that confirm several new p53 interactions predicted by KnIT, providing a proof of concept that will help direct future biological research.

2. IMPACT ON SOCIETY

In the spirit of this year's KDD emphasis on Social Good, we briefly place our work in a broader societal context. Humanity is facing a fundamental information bottleneck that overwhelms cognitive capabilities inherited from 160 million years of mammalian evolution. For most of this time, brains only had to cope with the perils posed by the physical world and by social competition. But as human language emerged, and with it the ability to pass complex abstract information across generations, a new evolutionary demand took form that was different from past constraints: now the recording, teaching and learning of facts and knowledge yielded advantages. Even so, as long as education remained oral, the body of knowledge was bounded by and matched to the cognitive abilities of each generation. Once written language emerged, however, a mere 4000 years ago, this constraint broke. Now facts and knowledge could accumulate *ex vivo* regardless of whether we could absorb them intellectually: by antiquity the library of Alexandria may have held as many as 100,000 scrolls, and by 2010 Google estimated that 130 million books were in existence. With the automated large-scale production of industrial, social, and scientific data upon us, the exponential divergence between information collections and human understanding is now as brutally vexing to all as it doubtless already was to the Alexandrian scholars.

Of course, humans overcome biological shortcomings by inventing tools, and already, many such computational aids exist. However, as empowering as they are compared to just a decade ago, their first-generation limitations are also inescapable. How often do we examine the fourth Google page, or even the third one for that matter? How deep into the literature do we read when a Medline search returns 200 papers, from the last 18 months? How much network traffic must we track to detect a lethal cancer cell, nascent electrical grid instability, or a terror target amidst anarchist chatter?

In this study, we tackle these questions. Starting from an immense corpus of knowledge, some in text and some in Big Data, we aim to extract relevant facts, represent them, and reason over them in order to generate new hypotheses that we can then test experimentally to arrive at a validated discovery. The tools and the computational framework that we develop for this purpose are entirely general, but in order to demonstrate that it may lead to immediate practical discoveries, we are focusing here on biology.

3. THE PROBLEM OF P53 KINASES

All human cells throughout an individual's body contain roughly the same genome, that is, the DNA molecules which represent the blueprints of biology inherited from one's parents. These blueprints contain the information necessary to create tens of thousands of different proteins, which are the molecular machines that are fundamental to all of cellular biology, performing a wide range actions such as metabolizing nutrients, allowing a cell to respond to its environment, and even controlling the quantities, or "expression levels", of other proteins. In this paper we investigate a particularly important protein, p53, which is often referred to as "the guardian of the genome" and is implicated in many biological processes and diseases including cancer [7; 9; 19; 22; 24; 25; 29]. As an individual grows and ages, cells must repeatedly make copies of their own genomes, which eventually results in degradation of the information contained therein. When enough errors accumulate, it is possible for a cell to enter a broken, cancerous state in which it grows continuously, damaging nearby tissue and causing harm to the organism. The p53 protein is a major player in the cell's natural defense against entering such a state: p53 responds to the detection of genomic problems by increasing the expression of hundreds of other proteins to try to fix the errors, or, if that isn't possible, it can even cause a cell to destroy itself, saving the neighboring cells and the life of the individual. One way that p53 is able to react to such problems is due to signals from a set of proteins that chemically modify p53 in response to different conditions. Each p53 modification, of which there are over 50, acts as an on/off switch, causing p53 to have one response or another [12]. The most common type of modification among all proteins, including p53 in particular, is phosphorylation, in which a phosphate molecule (PO_4^{3-}) is bonded to a specific atom in a protein molecule. The class of proteins that carries out the addition of phosphate molecules are known as kinases, which are increasingly the target of promising cancer treatments for use in these signaling mechanisms [27]. Drugs can affect the behavior of specific kinases, which can produce specific reactions in the proteins they phosphorylate, with the goal being to activate the cell's innate cancer-fighting abilities. Knowing which proteins are kinases is a well-solved problem [21]; however, knowing which proteins are modified by each kinase, and therefore which kinases would make good drug targets, is a difficult and unsolved problem. There are over 500 known human kinases and tens of thousands of possible proteins they can target. Biochemical experiments require months to establish a single novel kinase-protein relationship, and then years to fully elucidate the relationship's biological impact. Only 33 of the 500+ kinases are currently known to modify p53 [8; 12; 15; 23], but it is likely that there are many such relationships that remain unknown. In this paper, we asked as a proof of principle whether KnIT can discover novel p53 kinases.

4. REPRESENTING KINASES

To approach this problem, we first note that there are over 240,000 papers that mention one or more of 500+ known human kinases in their Medline abstract. An avid reader capable of absorbing 10 papers per day would need 70 years to go through this relevant literature—a completely unrealistic feat. Instead, however, we mine text so as to create a model for each kinase that represents all the terms present in the abstracts of the papers that specifically mention that kinase. In aggregate, and ignoring issues of errors and uncertainty, the words in these abstracts are assumed to be a useful signature of kinase features, such as details about biological process, molecular function, cellular component and specific interactions.

KnIT collects and labels the abstracts to be mined using queries against a text index of all Medline abstracts. There is one OR query for each kinase that includes the kinases canonical name along with its synonyms taken from [6; 11; 32]. KnIT submits the queries and downloads all abstracts that match each kinase up to query size. (A few kinases have well over 10,000 abstracts, which is far more than is needed to develop an accurate model.) In order to explore KnIT's predictive properties, we used several different Medline searches. In our initial exploration, we searched all kinases but removed abstracts that make any reference either to p53 or to a second kinase. We thus excluded data that would trivialize the predictions. This left us with 259 kinases in all. Of these, 23 were known to be p53 kinases.

Next we create a numeric representation that encapsulates all we know about each kinase relative to every other kinase. To facilitate this process we represent the documents in a vector space model. That is, each document is a vector of weighted frequencies of its features (words and phrases) [26]. We emphasize words with high frequency in a document, and normalize each document vector to have unit Euclidean norm.

The words and phrases that make up the document feature space are determined by counting the number of documents in which each word appears and identifying the words with the highest counts. A standard "stop word" list is used to eliminate words such as "and", "but", and "the". The top N words are retained in the first pass, where the value of N may vary depending on the length of the documents, the number of documents and the number of categories to be created. In our experiments we found that N=20000 is sufficient for the categories and documents used in this domain. After selecting the words in the first pass, we make a second pass to count the frequency of the phrases that occur using these words. A phrase is considered to be a sequence of two words occurring in order without intervening non-stop words. We again prune to keep only the N most frequent words and phrases. This becomes the feature space. A third pass through the data indexes the documents by their feature occurrences. We experimented with various methods of weighting term occurrences in this matrix and eventually determined that a Term Frequency–Inverse Document Frequency weighting (TF-IDF) [26] yielded the best overall prediction accuracy.

4.1 Kinase Space Visualization through Relative Neighborhood Graphs

Once we have a feature space we create a representation of each kinase by averaging the feature vectors of all documents that contain the kinase. This is the kinase centroid. Next we calculate a distance matrix that measures the distance between each kinase and every other kinase in the space. Such matrices are fine for computers to read and calculate properties over, but notoriously difficult for a domain expert to interpret in order to get a sense of the data's underlying validity and meaning. Interpretability is important, because an expert must be confident and insightful when proposing new hypotheses. Thus some way must be found to convert the numbers into a meaningful picture of kinase-kinase relationships.

A network graph is one approach that is often tried [10] but this requires determining when two nodes should be considered connected, when in fact all nodes are connected at some level of similarity threshold. We could pick an arbitrary similarity cutoff and draw lines whenever similarity was greater than the specified limit, but that assigns more meaning to the absolute value of the distance metric employed here than is strictly warranted. Relative distance is the more important concept to convey here.

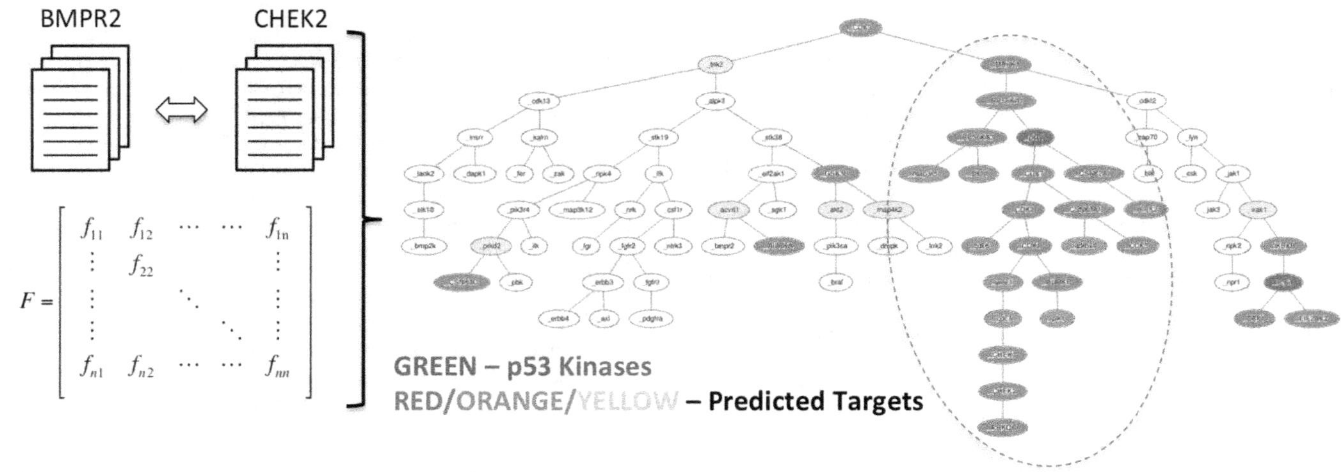

Figure 1 Kinases are clustered based on their literature distance. The clustered p53 kinases (green) suggest new kinases that may also phosphorylate p53.

To design the graph used in KnIT, we switch the goal around. What does a maximally communicative graph look like? First of all it should be minimally connected, in other words containing one less arc than the number of nodes. Secondly it should be a tree because trees are easy to navigate and communicate information based on distance from the root, which is often helpful. Third, the tree should spread connections out fairly evenly among the nodes to avoid extreme situations where one node is connected to all the others, a very uninteresting graph. This leads us to the conclusion that a binary tree (or at least low n-ary) would be highly advantageous if it can be drawn so as to accurately represent the distance matrix. To create a binary tree we must choose a meaningful root node. Does any particular entity stand out for this honor? In fact, there is one property unique and important in the text vector space—namely typicality. There is one entity whose vector is closest to the average of all the vectors. This will be the root. Now as we move down the tree we will naturally go towards less typical (more unusual nodes). This turns out to be a very intuitive concept to grasp, visually.

Algorithm 1 is used to create an n-ary similarity tree from the set of entities, where each entity is represented as a feature vector. The root of the tree is the "most typical" entity, and typicality decreases with increasing distance from the root, so that the leaves of the tree are the "least typical", i.e., unique outliers. The algorithm first computes the "most typical" feature vector as the average of the entities, and then calls the closestToFV function to select the entity closest to this typical feature vector as the root of the similarity tree. The algorithm also initializes *candidates* as a singleton set comprising the root node; here *candidates* are the set of nodes currently in the tree at which to potentially attach new child nodes. The algorithm next uses the closestPair function to find the pair (e,c) such that e belongs to *entities*, c belongs to *candidates*, and distance(e,c) is minimized over all such pairs. (Thus e is the closest entity to the current set of *candidates* and c is the candidate closest to e.) Then e is added to the tree as a child of c. Moreover, e is removed from *entities*, the set of entities that have not yet been added to the tree, and added to *candidates*. If adding e as a child to c increases the number of c's children to the limit n, then c is removed from *candidates* to ensure that its n-ary property will not be violated in the future. The algorithm continues to add elements of entities to the tree in a similar manner, until there are no more entities to add. The functions closestToFV and closestPair use Euclidean distance and break ties randomly.

In Figure 1, we show an example of this kinase network diagram with n=2. Green nodes are p53 kinases, red/orange/yellow nodes are hypothesized new p53 kinases based on their similarity to known p53 kinases. What is remarkable about this visual representation is that the green "kinase" nodes tend to be clumped together, even though the algorithm knows nothing about p53 kinases. This tends to lend credence to the supposition that those nodes in the midst of the green clumps are also likely to be p53 kinases.

Algorithm 1 *Create an n-ary similarity tree from a set of entities*

```
Input: entities, n
Output: n-ary similarity tree
mostTypicalFV = average(entities)
root = closestTo FV(entities, mostTypical FV)
entities.remove(root)
candidates = {root}
while not entities.isEmpty()
    (e, c) = closestPair(entities, candidates)
    c.addChild(e)
    if c.numChildren() == n then
        candidates.remove(c)
    end if
    candidates.add(e)
    entities.remove(e)
end while
Return: root
```

5. SELECTING CANDIDATE P53 KINASES

The visualization tool provides a set of kinases that may phosphorylate p53. However, some sort of principled ranking

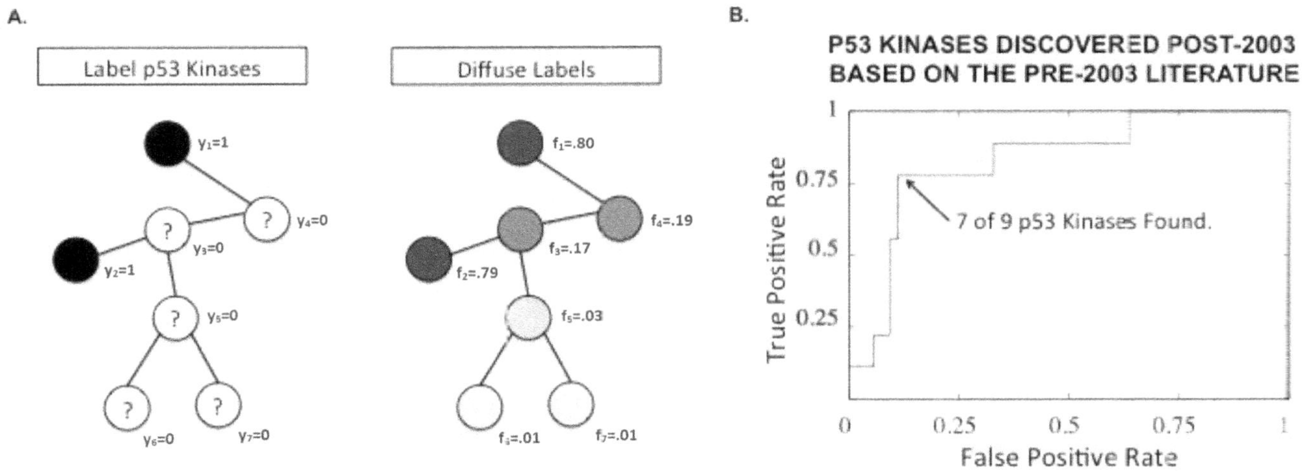

Figure 2 A) Example of graph diffusion on a network. Given a set of edges and labeled nodes, information is diffused to find additional candidate nodes for the annotation in question. B) Retrospective validation of literature vector models with graph diffusion to predict p53 kinases. Using only papers from before 2003, predictions were made for 64 other kinases, 9 of which are now known to be true positives but were not known in 2003.

scheme is needed in order to prioritize the kinases for further experimentation. To provide such a scheme, our initial prototype uses graph diffusion [34]. Graph diffusion is a semi-supervised learning approach for classification based on labeled and unlabeled data. It takes known information (initial labels) and then constrains the new labels to be smooth in respect to a defined structure (e.g. a network). In our case, we know which kinases phosphorylate p53 (initial labels); we would like to know which other proteins phosphorylate p53 (final labels). The distance matrix based on the literature gives us the structure of our kinase network. The initial labels are extracted from current knowledge found in review articles [8; 12; 15; 23].

5.1 Graph Construction and Diffusion

Graph diffusion propagates information among network nodes following the edges between them (Figure 2A). Here, human kinases are the nodes and the distance matrix of literature similarity between each kinase provides the edges. To formulate the kinase network, we defined edges between each kinase and the top ten most closely related kinases. This cutoff was determined empirically by cross-validation performance.

We can represent our knowledge of protein function as y, a fixed binary vector of labels with y_i representing whether protein i phosphorylates p53. We seek to identify a new set of continuous labels, f (*i.e.* how likely a kinase is to phosphorylate p53) by diffusing the known information in a network. We can solve for f by minimizing the sum of the loss and smoothing functions [3]:

$$(f-y)^T(f-y)+\mu f^T Lf$$

The first term, the loss function, represents the difference between initial y and final labels f. During diffusion, this function regulates and prevents the loss of the initial labels. The second term, the smoothing function, represents the smoothness of the new labels f in the context of the Laplacian matrix L. The Laplacian matrix [5] is the matrix representation of the kinase network and defined $L = D - A$. The adjacency matrix, denoted A, specifies if kinase i is connected to kinase j where $A(i,j)=1$ if the entities are connected and $A(i,j)=0$ otherwise. The degree matrix, D, is a diagonal matrix given by

$$D_{ii} = \sum_j A(i,j)$$

The diffusion coefficient μ balances the loss of the initial labels against the smoothness. The previous equation has a closed form solution [3]:

$$f = (I+\mu L)^{-1} y$$

where I is the Identity matrix. We set the diffusion coefficient μ to the inverse of the Laplacian's norm

$$\mu = \frac{1}{\max_i(\sum_{k=1}^{n} |L_{ik}|)}$$

This value insures that the Hessian is positive definite and the above function is convex [20]. In order to identify new kinases, we then look at the new labels f where the labels with the largest increase will be our targets.

5.2 Computational Validation of Performance

Leave-one-out cross-validation eliminates an observation from the original data set, and then tests whether predictions based on the remaining information can recover the observation that was removed. Each one of the known p53 kinases was relabeled as an unknown and the performance of the prediction method was evaluated by whether it could recover the information. Due to the limited availability of negative information in biology, those with no known p53 activity were treated as negatives for the purposes of computational validation.

We often used Receiver Operating Characteristic (ROC) curves to measure performance. In more detail, the diffusion scores in f, together with a threshold t, can be used to classify each protein as a "positive" (i.e., it phosphorylates p53) or a "negative" (no phosphorylation). Protein i is predicted to be positive if $f_i > t$ and a negative otherwise. Recall that the True Positive Rate (TPR) is the fraction of the True Positives found over the total possible Positives. Similarly, the False Positive Rate (FPR) is a fraction of the False Positives found over the total possible Negatives. Thus in our setting the ROC is the cumulative plot constructed by calculating TPR and FPR at all possible binary classification thresholds t. The area under this curve (AUC) summarizes prediction performance: an AUC of 1.0 represents a perfect predictor while a random prediction would lead a diagonal line and an AUC of 0.5.

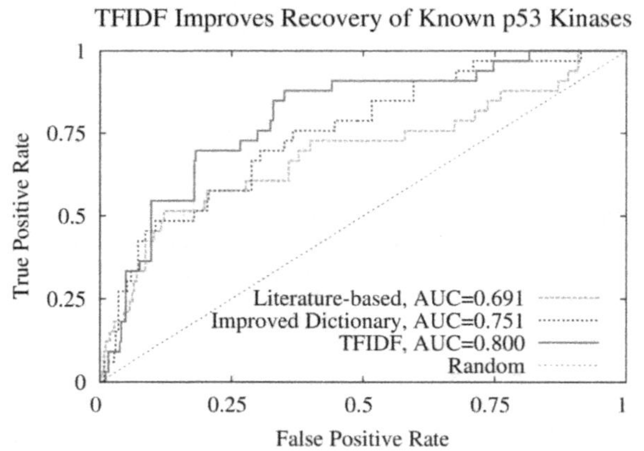

Figure 3 Graph diffusion was performed with leave-one-out-cross validation to assign scores to 33 kinases known to target p53 as well as 368 kinases not known to target p53. Of the 509 kinases included in analysis, we only included the 401 kinases reaching a minimum document count threshold. (Black) represents the average performance of a random algorithm with no predictive value. (Green) is the original algorithm's performance. (Blue) shows the improvement due to dictionary synonym refinement. (Red) is with the inclusion of the TFIDF weighting scheme.

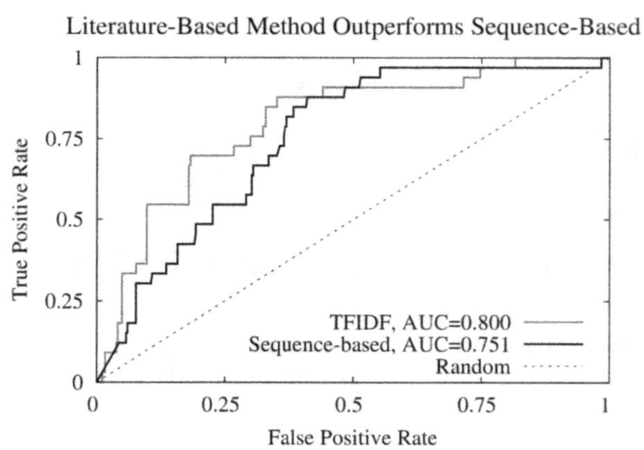

Figure 4 Comparison to sequence-based method. (Red) is predictive power of the literature vector model in a leave-one-out cross-validation analysis of known p53 kinases. (Black) is the performance of a method that uses biological sequence information to do the same task. (Black-dotted) represents the performance of a random model.

6. RESULTS

In order to test the algorithm, we first applied it in a retrospective analysis to show whether recent annotations of new p53 kinases occurring *after* a certain date could be predicted from a model that only took into account papers written *before* that date, at a time when these discoveries of p53 kinases were still unknown. Next we asked whether some variations in the algorithm could improve p53 kinase prediction as we compared its performance to the common approach used most typically to identify functionally similar proteins in biology. Finally, we expanded our analysis to a larger set of proteins to test scalability. The positive results in these retrospective controls led to a prospective study of *bona fide* predictions, discussed in section 6.

6.1 Retrospective study

If KnIT is effective, it should predict from papers published prior to a given date events that were only discovered after that date. To test this hypothesis, we mined the literature up to 2003, when only half of the 33 currently known p53 kinases had been discovered. Because we filtered out confusing abstracts that mentioned multiple different kinases and p53, the kinase search space became small: only 74 kinases. But among these 74, ten were known to phosphorylate p53 in 2003, nine were found at a later date, and the remaining 55 are for simplicity assumed to not phosphorylate p53. A kinase distance matrix and a literature vector model was developed for these 74 kinases, the ten p53 kinases that were known prior to 2003 were labeled as such, and these labels were propagated to the other 64 kinases by global graph diffusion from which we could now rank the 64 kinases by the likelihood they targeted p53. Strikingly, an ROC curve shows that seven of the nine true positives are readily predicted with this algorithm (Precision= 0.54 at Recall=0.77, with an AUC of 0.840); see Figure 2B. This time-stamped study shows that back in 2003, we could have automatically predicted many of the p53 kinases that were discovered in the subsequent decade by combining text mining with feature analysis and graph-based diffusion as KnIT does. This result is remarkable considering that for simplicity we only used a limited subset of the least ambiguous abstracts, which restricted us to studying only 74 rather than about 500 kinases.

6.2 Further Analyses of Algorithm

In order to test KnIT on a larger scale, we next sought to include more abstracts, regardless of their date or mention of multiple kinases and p53 information. This time to mitigate the most obvious problems related to incomplete or noisy information, we only filtered out those kinases having fewer than 20 abstracts. This allowed us to model 401 kinases, rather than the previous 74 kinases. Instead of a time-stamped retrospective analysis, we performed leave-one-out cross-validation of all 33 currently known p53 kinases. Specifically, a literature vector model and then a kinase distance matrix were built and we then performed 33 separate experiments. In each, one of the 33 p53 kinases was relabeled "unknown" rather than "p53 kinase," then the remaining 32 p53 kinases were diffused globally to yield a ranking for the "unknown" p53 kinase. We then diffused the label information of all 33 kinases to obtain scores for all non-p53 kinase (401-33=368). Once each kinase has a label score, we can then calculate the ROC curve treating the known p53 kinases as positives. The area under ROC curve was shown to be significant at 0.691 (Figure 3, green curve).

We first constructed a list of gene synonyms extracted form from NCBI[2; 33], UniProt KnowledgeBase[32], and Hugo Gene Nomenclature Committee [11]. We noted that some kinases have ambiguous synonyms that are likely to return more incorrect abstracts than correct ones when querying Medline:

BTK has "AT" as a synonym

TYRO3 has "TIF" as a synonym

ARUKA has "AURA" as a synonym

RIPK1 has "RIP" as a synonym (confused with "repeat induced point mutation")

ITK has "EMT" as a synonym (confused with "epithelial-mesenchymal transition")

MOK has "RAGE" as a synonym

BMP2K has "BIKE" as a synonym

KIT has a problematic main gene name

FYN has "SYN" as a synonym (common acronym for synthetic)

To improve on results, we removed these vague terms. A second issue we considered was that many of the kinases shared synonyms names (i.e. PAK1 is a synonym for PKN1, but PAK1 is a distinctly different kinase). We removed redundant gene names within the protein kinase, unless the gene name was the Hugo Approved Gene Name (As is the case of PAK1). Removing these ambiguous synonyms yields a more accurate representation of each kinase's content. After removing problematic synonyms, we resubmitted our queries and performed the analysis again with the new set of abstracts for each kinase. This improved kinase dictionary now increased the AU(ROC) from 0.591 to 0.751 (Figure 3, blue curve).

Next, we experimented with different weighting schemes for term frequencies when creating the distance matrix. We determined that a TFIDF [26] weighting, which gives a stronger weight to shared words that occur less, dramatically improves the AUC=0.800 (Figure 3, red curve). In contrast, increasing the max query size from 1600 to 3200 abstracts had virtually no impact on performance (data not shown). We also compared KnIT to a common approach for predicting biological function: protein sequence alignment. Every protein exists as a sequence of amino acid molecules, which can be represented by a series of letters using a 20-character alphabet, one letter for each type of building block in the sequence. It is well known that similar sequence often, though not always, suggests similar function of two proteins. The amino acid sequence of each kinase was aligned with the set of positives, and those with low e-value as reported by BLAST [1] were predicted to be more likely to target p53. (Roughly speaking, the BLAST e-value indicates the probability that sequences align purely by chance.) A comparison of the leave-one-out performance of these methods is shown in Figure 4. These leave-one-out control studies show over a nearly fully representative set of kinases that that KnIT is superior to a sequence-based approach with respect recovering knowledge of a true p53 kinase when this knowledge is erased. Although leave-one-out studies should not be over-interpreted, this positive result is consistent with the possibility that KnIT is predictive.

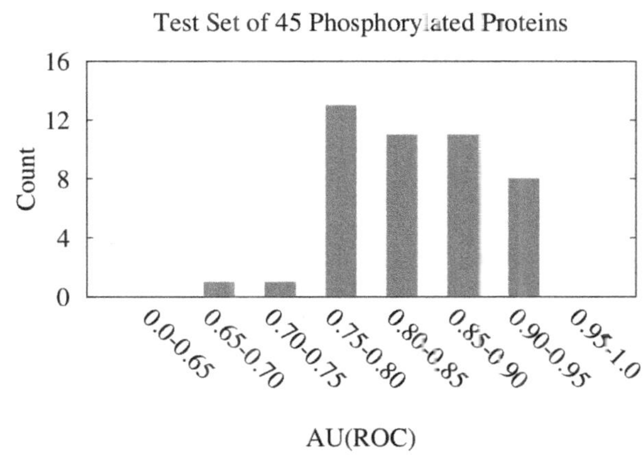

Figure 5 Summary of 45 different AU(ROC) performance measures for predictions on each of 45 different kinase targets, each with a unique set of labels for the search space of 500+ known kinases.

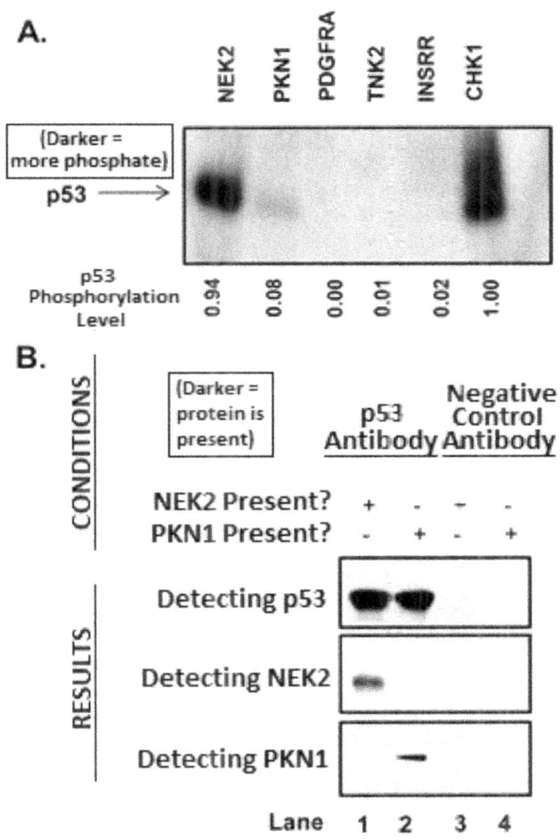

Figure 6 Experimental validation of candidate p53 kinases as *bona fide* p53 kinases. (A) *In vitro* kinase assay demonstrates phosphorylation of p53 by top ranked candidate kinases PKN1 and NEK2. Relative levels of p53 phosphorylation are indicated for each kinase normalized to positive control CHK1. Though the signal is weak for PNK1, subsequent experiments lend further support. (B) PKN1 and NEK2 shown to interact with p53 *in vivo*. A p53 antibody isolates p53 and any proteins bound to it. Antibodies detect the presence of candidate kinases in this isolate.

6.3 Large-scale Study

As a further test of scalability we next asked if KnIT could also predict kinase activity for targeted proteins other than p53. In previous experiment we exploited review articles from p53 experts. In order to extend to the larger scale analysis, we exploited the kinase-to-target knowledge base built for human kinases by PhosphoSitePlus [14]. These data are manually curated for the modifying protein, the type of modification, and the subject of the modification. So far, the curators of PhosphoSitePlus have reliably identified over 14,000 relationships between kinases and target proteins by reading the available literature. Among these, we narrowed this study to 45 unique human proteins, each modified by at least eight unique kinases belonging to our kinase network. It is likely that some sets of kinases may be easier to predict than others, for example if some have simpler biological mechanisms, therefore rather than normalizing and plotting all predictions onto a single ROC curve, each protein was evaluated independently, and the AUC was calculated for each one separately. Figure 5 shows a histogram summarizing the performance of these 45 ROC curves. We found that in all cases that the predictions were significant (AU(ROC)>0.65) and the average AUC was 0.835. These data show that KnIT does not uniquely apply to p53, but that it can extend to make predictions in many other human proteins.

6.4 Experimental Validation

Retrospective analyses are suggestive but never proof of discovery. For the latter it is critical to predict an observation that has never been made and then assess its truth in the laboratory. The algorithms described above were used to rank 252 kinases (those with at least 20 publications) by likelihood of being p53 kinases. As expected, most kinases known to phosphorylate p53 were near the top of the rankings list. Five kinases on the list not known to phosphorylate p53 were then tested by biochemical and molecular biology experiments for their ability to interact with and phosphorylate p53. Two kinases (PKN1 and NEK2) were chosen from near the top of the list and three kinases were chosen from the bottom half of the list (TNK2, INSRR, and PDGFRA). Two validation assays are shown here: an *in vitro* kinase assay and a cellular co-immunoprecipitation (IP) assay.

In Figure 6A, the *in vitro* kinase assay, p53 is combined with a kinase and a radioactive source of phosphate, gamma-^{32}P-ATP. Then a technique known as electrophoresis is used to separate the components of the mixture by weight to different positions in a gel. Because the weight of p53 is known (53 kilodaltons), we can check for radioactivity of anything that weights exactly that amount. If the predicted relationship is real, the kinase will add the radioactive phosphate to p53, and electrophoresis will move that radioactivity to a specific position in the gel, which is detectable by standard instruments. Note that in Figure 6A top ranked kinase candidates NEK2 and PKN1 exhibit a labeled p53 band, as does a known p53 kinase CHK1 [28] (used here as a positive control). The PKN1 band is faint relative to the others, but in subsequent experiments, the interaction was found to be robust. In contrast, low ranked p53 kinase candidates PDGFRA, TNK2, and INSRR exhibit no 53 kilodalton band, indicating they are unlikely to be p53 kinases.

Figure 6B shows a different approach for validating the predictions. The goal of this assay is to show that there is a physical protein-protein interaction between p53 and the predicted kinases. This is considered a strong indication that the kinase is likely to target p53. Human cells containing p53 and a candidate kinase are generated and analyzed. Proteins from the cell are isolated and a p53-specific antibody is then added; an antibody is a substance that will bind to and isolate a specific protein, in this case p53, along with any protein that is bound to it, in this case - if the prediction is correct - the kinase being tested. This isolate is then separated by size, and an additional antibody is used to test for the presence of each candidate kinase. In Figure 6B, each column, or "lane", represents a different set of experimental conditions. Lane 1 shows that p53 was indeed bound to NEK2, with lanes 2 and 3 as controls that show both NEK2 and the p53 antibody must be present to achieve this result. Lane 2 shows that p53 was bound to PKN1.

These two sets of experiments argue strongly that computationally predicted top p53 kinase candidates PKN1 and NEK1 are indeed true p53 kinases.

7. CONCLUSION AND FUTURE WORK

This early study tackles a basic problem that is challenging progress in every field of human intellectual activity: we have become much better at generation of information than at its integrative analysis. This leads to deep inefficiencies in translating research into progress for humanity. No scientist can keep up with the unrelenting flow of new studies and results, even within specialized fields. While intuition and selective reading in a highly narrowed field of work are essential and can certainly lead to breakthroughs, they are also likely to lead most scientists at one time or another towards deeply unproductive hypotheses that might have benefitted from more comprehensive insights into the data that was available but which we could not find an opportunity to learn about. Specialization also inherently limits the opportunities to find common grounds at the interface between fields, even though these interfaces are often are among the deepest areas of scientific synthesis.

Baylor College of Medicine and IBM Research have joined forces for the purpose of combining talents and technologies in many diverse fields to accelerate scientific discoveries that lead to improved patient outcomes. This research represents the first stage in this collaborative effort and as such it proves the principle that mining past literature is a viable strategy for predicting previously unknown biological events. We have shown that p53 kinases predicted with our text mining methods are supported by laboratory findings. In the future, it should be possible to make many other kinds of predictions on a much larger scale as our infrastructure and capabilities ramp up.

In the future our team will focus on a wider area of proteins and functions, building up comprehensive networks of interactions and predicting where new connections ought to exist based on everything else that is known. We believe this will ultimately accelerate the pace of cancer discoveries by an order of magnitude and allow scientists to come to a much more complete understanding of the mechanisms behind this disease. We also feel that the general approach of mining literature to identify hidden relationships between entities is not confined to cancer or even to biology, but is a general tool that can be applied in almost any science. The potential for dramatic acceleration of discovery in all sciences holds out the possibility of tremendous benefits for human health and for societal progress in the coming years. Given the enormous challenges facing science today on a global scale, with ever more complex systems of entities and networks of relationships, the acceleration of discovery is not only desirable, but also indispensable for human flourishing.

8. ACKNOWLEDGMENTS

This work was supported by the Robert and Janice McNair Foundation, DARPA (N66001-14-1-4027), National Science Foundation (NSF CCF-0905536, NSF DBI-1062455), National Institutes of Health (NIH-GM079656), and was supported in part by the IBM Accelerated Discovery Lab.

9. REFERENCES

[1] ALTSCHUL, S.F., GISH, W., MILLER, W., MYERS, E.W., and LIPMAN, D.J., 1990. Basic local alignment search tool. *J Mol Biol 215*, 3 (Oct 5), 403-410. DOI= http://dx.doi.org/10.1016/S0022-2836(05)80360-2.

[2] ASHBURNER, M., BALL, C.A., BLAKE, J.A., BOTSTEIN, D., BUTLER, H., CHERRY, J.M., DAVIS, A.P., DOLINSKI, K., DWIGHT, S.S., EPPIG, J.T., HARRIS, M.A., HILL, D.P., ISSEL-TARVER, L., KASARSKIS, A., LEWIS, S., MATESE, J.C., RICHARDSON, J.E., RINGWALD, M., RUBIN, G.M., and SHERLOCK, G., 2000. Gene ontology: tool for the unification of biology. The Gene Ontology Consortium. *Nat Genet 25*, 1 (May), 25-29. DOI= http://dx.doi.org/10.1038/75556.

[3] BELKIN, M., MATVEEVA, I., and NIYOGI, P., 2004. Regularization and Semi-supervised Learning on Large Graphs. In *Learning Theory*, J. SHAWE-TAYLOR and Y. SINGER Eds. Springer Berlin Heidelberg, 624-638. DOI= http://dx.doi.org/10.1007/978-3-540-27819-1_43.

[4] BJÖRK, B.-C., ROOSR, A., and LAURI, M., Global annual volume of peer reviewed scholarly articles and the share available via different open access options. In *Sustainability in the Age of Web 2.0 - Proceedings of the 12th International Conference on Electronic Publishing*, Toronto, Canada.

[5] CHUNG, F.R.K., 1997. Spectral Graph Theory American Mathematical Society.

[6] COORDINATORS, N.R., 2014. Database resources of the National Center for Biotechnology Information. *Nucleic Acids Res 42*, 1 (Jan 1), D7-D17. DOI= http://dx.doi.org/10.1093/nar/gkt1146.

[7] DA COSTA, C.A., SUNYACH, C., GIAIME, E., WEST, A., CORTI, O., BRICE, A., SAFE, S., ABOU-SLEIMAN, P.M., WOOD, N.W., TAKAHASHI, H., GOLDBERG, M.S., SHEN, J., and CHECLER, F., 2009. Transcriptional repression of p53 by parkin and impairment by mutations associated with autosomal recessive juvenile Parkinson's disease. *Nat Cell Biol 11*, 11 (Nov), 1370-1375. DOI= http://dx.doi.org/10.1038/ncb1981.

[8] DAI, C. and GU, W., 2010. p53 post-translational modification: deregulated in tumorigenesis. *Trends Mol Med 16*, 11 (Nov), 528-536. DOI= http://dx.doi.org/10.1016/j.molmed.2010.09.002.

[9] DERDAK, Z., VILLEGAS, K.A., HARB, R., WU, A.M., SOUSA, A., and WANDS, J.R., 2013. Inhibition of p53 attenuates steatosis and liver injury in a mouse model of non-alcoholic fatty liver disease. *J Hepatol 58*, 4 (Apr), 785-791. DOI= http://dx.doi.org/10.1016/j.jhep.2012.11.042.

[10] GOH, K.I., CUSICK, M.E., VALLE, D., CHILDS, B., VIDAL, M., and BARABASI, A.L., 2007. The human disease network. *Proc Natl Acad Sci U S A 104*, 21 (May 22), 8685-8690. DOI= http://dx.doi.org/10.1073/pnas.0701361104.

[11] GRAY, K.A., DAUGHERTY, L.C., GORDON, S.M., SEAL, R.L., WRIGHT, M.W., and BRUFORD, E.A., 2013. Genenames.org: the HGNC resources in 2013. *Nucleic Acids Res 41*, Database issue (Jan), D545-552. DOI= http://dx.doi.org/10.1093/nar/gks1066.

[12] GU, B. and ZHU, W.G., 2012. Surf the post-translational modification network of p53 regulation. *Int J Biol Sci 8*, 5, 672-684. DOI= http://dx.doi.org/10.7150/ijbs.4283.

[13] HAGER, K.M. and GU, W., 2014. Understanding the non-canonical pathways involved in p53-mediated tumor suppression. *Carcinogenesis* (Feb 3). DOI= http://dx.doi.org/10.1093/carcin/bgt487.

[14] HORNBECK, P.V., KORNHAUSER, J.M., TKACHEV, S., ZHANG, B., SKRZYPEK, E., MURRAY, B., LATHAM, V., and SULLIVAN, M., 2012. PhosphoSitePlus: a comprehensive resource for investigating the structure and function of experimentally determined post-translational modifications in man and mouse. *Nucleic Acids Res 40*, Database issue (Jan), D261-270. DOI= http://dx.doi.org/10.1093/nar/gkr1122.

[15] JENKINS, L.M., DURELL, S.R., MAZUR, S.J., and APPELLA, E., 2012. p53 N-terminal phosphorylation: a defining layer of complex regulation. *Carcinogenesis 33*, 8 (Aug), 1441-1449. DOI= http://dx.doi.org/10.1093/carcin/bgs145.

[16] JINHA, A.E., 2010. Article 50 million: an estimate of the number of scholarly articles in existence. *Learned Publishing 23*, 3 (//), 258-263. DOI= http://dx.doi.org/10.1087/20100308.

[17] LANGLEY, P., BRADSHAW, G., and SIMON, H., 1983. Rediscovering Chemistry with the Bacon System. In *Machine Learning*, R. MICHALSKI, J. CARBONELL and T. MITCHELL Eds. Springer Berlin Heidelberg, 307-329. DOI= http://dx.doi.org/10.1007/978-3-662-12405-5_10.

[18] LARSEN, P.O. and VON INS, M., 2010. The rate of growth in scientific publication and the decline in coverage provided by Science Citation Index. *Scientometrics 84*, 3 (Sep), 575-603. DOI= http://dx.doi.org/10.1007/s11192-010-0202-z.

[19] LI, M., HE, Y., DUBOIS, W., WU, X., SHI, J., and HUANG, J., 2012. Distinct regulatory mechanisms and functions for p53-activated and p53-repressed DNA damage response genes in embryonic stem cells. *Mol Cell 46*, 1 (Apr 13), 30-42. DOI= http://dx.doi.org/10.1016/j.molcel.2012.01.020.

[20] LISEWSKI, A.M. and LICHTARGE, O., 2010. Untangling complex networks: risk minimization in financial markets through accessible spin glass ground states. *Physica A 389*, 16 (Aug 15), 3250-3253. DOI= http://dx.doi.org/10.1016/j.physa.2010.04.005.

[21] MANNING, G., WHYTE, D.B., MARTINEZ, R., HUNTER, T., and SUDARSANAM, S., 2002. The protein kinase complement of the human genome. *Science 298*, 5600 (Dec 6), 1912-1934. DOI= http://dx.doi.org/10.1126/science.1075762.

[22] MAY, P. and MAY, E., 1999. Twenty years of p53 research: structural and functional aspects of the p53 protein. *Oncogene 18*, 53 (Dec 13), 7621-7636. DOI= http://dx.doi.org/10.1038/sj.onc.1203285.

[23] MEEK, D.W. and ANDERSON, C.W., 2009. Posttranslational modification of p53: cooperative integrators of function. *Cold Spring Harb Perspect Biol 1*, 6 (Dec), a000950. DOI= http://dx.doi.org/10.1101/cshperspect.a000950.

[24] MULLER, P.A. and VOUSDEN, K.H., 2013. p53 mutations in cancer. *Nat Cell Biol 15*, 1 (Jan), 2-8. DOI= http://dx.doi.org/10.1038/ncb2641.

[25] NATHANSON, J.W., YADRON, N.E., FARNAN, J., KINNEAR, S., HART, J., and RUBIN, D.T., 2008. p53 mutations are associated with dysplasia and progression of dysplasia in patients with Crohn's disease. *Dig Dis Sci 53*, 2 (Feb), 474-480. DOI= http://dx.doi.org/10.1007/s10620-007-9886-1.

[26] SALTON, G. and MCGILL, M.J., 1986. *Introduction to Modern Information Retrieval*. McGraw-Hill, Inc.

[27] SHAWVER, L.K., SLAMON, D., and ULLRICH, A., 2002. Smart drugs: tyrosine kinase inhibitors in cancer therapy. *Cancer Cell 1*, 2 (Mar), 117-123.

[28] SHIEH, S.Y., AHN, J., TAMAI, K., TAYA, Y., and PRIVES, C., 2000. The human homologs of checkpoint kinases Chk1 and Cds1 (Chk2) phosphorylate p53 at multiple DNA damage-inducible sites. *Genes Dev 14*, 3 (Feb 1), 289-300.

[29] SIGANAKI, M., KOUTSOPOULOS, A.V., NEOFYTOU, E., VLACHAKI, E., PSARROU, M., SOULITZIS, N., PENTILAS, N., SCHIZA, S., SIAFAKAS, N.M., and TZORTZAKI, E.G., 2010. Deregulation of apoptosis mediators' p53 and bcl2 in lung tissue of COPD patients. *Respir Res 11*, 46. DOI= http://dx.doi.org/10.1186/1465-9921-11-46.

[30] SRINIVASAN, P., 2004. Text mining: generating hypotheses from MEDLINE. *J. Am. Soc. Inf. Sci. Technol. 55*, 5, 396-413. DOI= http://dx.doi.org/10.1002/asi.10389.

[31] SWANSON, D.R., 1986. Fish oil, Raynaud's syndrome, and undiscovered public knowledge. *Perspect Biol Med 30*, 1 (Autumn), 7-18.

[32] UNIPROT, C., 2013. Update on activities at the Universal Protein Resource (UniProt) in 2013. *Nucleic Acids Res 41*, Database issue (Jan), D43-47. DOI= http://dx.doi.org/10.1093/nar/gks1068.

[33] WHEELER, D.L., CHURCH, D.M., FEDERHEN, S., LASH, A.E., MADDEN, T.L., PONTIUS, J.U., SCHULER, G.D., SCHRIML, L.M., SEQUEIRA, E., TATUSOVA, T.A., and WAGNER, L., 2003. Database resources of the National Center for Biotechnology. *Nucleic Acids Res 31*, 1 (Jan 1), 28-33.

[34] ZHOU, D., BOUSQUET, O., WESTON, J., and SCHOLKOPF, B., 2004. Learning with local and global consistency. In *Adnvaces in Neural Information Processing Systems (NIPS) 16* MIT, 321-328.

A System to Grade Computer Programming Skills using Machine Learning

Shashank Srikant
Aspiring Minds
shashank.srikant@aspiringminds.in

Varun Aggarwal
Aspiring Minds
varun@aspiringminds.in

ABSTRACT

The automatic evaluation of computer programs is a nascent area of research with a potential for large-scale impact. Extant program assessment systems score mostly based on the number of test-cases passed, providing no insight into the competency of the programmer. In this paper, we present a system to grade computer programs automatically. In addition to grading a program on its programming practices and complexity, the key kernel of the system is a machine-learning based algorithm which determines closeness of the logic of the given program to a correct program. This algorithm uses a set of highly-informative features, derived from the abstract representations of a given program, that capture the program's functionality. These features are then used to learn a model to grade the programs, which are built against evaluations done by experts. We show that the regression models provide much better grading than the ubiquitous test-case-pass based grading and rivals the grading accuracy of other open-response problems such as essay grading . We also show that our novel features add significant value over and above basic keyword/expression count features. In addition to this, we propose a novel way of posing computer-program grading as a one-class modeling problem and report encouraging preliminary results. We show the value of the system through a case study in a real-world industrial deployment. To the best of the authors' knowledge, this is the first time a system using machine learning has been developed and used for grading programs. The work is timely with regard to the recent boom in Massively Online Open Courseware (MOOCs), which promises to produce a significant amount of hand-graded digitized data.

Categories and Subject Descriptors: H.4 [**Information Systems Applications**]: Miscellaneous; I.2.6 [**Learning**]: General; K.3.0 [**Computers and Education**]: General

General Terms: Machine Learning; Program Analysis; Auomated Assessment

Keywords: Recruitment; Automatic grading; MOOC; Feature engineering; Supervised learning; One-class learning

KDD'14, August 24–27, 2014, New York, NY, USA.

ACM 978-1-4503-2956-9/14/08 ...$15.00.
http://dx.doi.org/10.1145/2623330.2623377 .

1. INTRODUCTION

Automatic evaluation of computer programming skills is a topic of keen interest today. It adds immense value to the recruitment processes of software development companies and also to teaching programming in training institutes, universities and Massively Open Online Courses (MOOCs) In the recruitment of software engineers, companies generally ask an applicant to solve a couple of programming problems which are subsequently discussed in an interview. The interviewer ascertains the 'closeness' of the candidate's algorithm to the correct solution and considers parameters such as programming practices used (e.g., dead-code, unused variables, etc.) and the time/space efficiency of the code to make a decision on the programming ability and algorithm design capability of the applicant. This is a non-standardized, time-consuming process and the interviewers are high-cost resources. The automatic assessment of codes can not only reduce the interview load, but also provide a report to the interviewer to assist him/her during the interview in highlighting important aspects of the candidate's performance. This would not only save time and money, but would also potentially open job opportunities to a larger set of applicants, who are missed out currently due to a lack of automated means.

In an education scenario, the benefits of such an automatic system are aplenty - first, it reduces the time and effort of graders - the number of problems given out to a candidate and the number of candidates being assessed need not be limited by the availability of graders. Second, it can provide real-time feedback. Candidates would not have to wait for the availability of teaching assistants or a faculty member to learn about the quality of their programs in order to improve themselves. Currently, the scalability of MOOCs teaching programming and algorithms is impeded by this constraint, which such an automatic system would help resolve. Third, it has the potential to lead to some standardization in the assessment of computer programs. Assessments today vary from grader to grader, with no underlying framework of reference.

A primary aspect of such an automated grading system is the ability to grade a computer program on the basis of a rubric.[1][2] Such a rubric typically maps a score (quantitative measure) to the ability of the programmer to solve a problem. For instance, a high-ranging score could mean that the candidate's program is a "correct and efficient implementation of the problem", whereas a lower grade could mean that the candidate's program "shows emergence of some of the needed control structures and data operations, but requires improvement". Such a mapping to a rubric is essential in order to provide an objective feedback, thereby helping corporations and academia in making a sound judgment of a candidate's ability and helping him/her to write better programs. For instance, an applicant at the highest level of the rubric may be hired directly for the job of a software engineer, whereas someone at an intermediate level can be hired as a trainee and be deployed on projects after a stipulated training period in or outside the corporation.[1]

The most widespread approach currently used for automatic assessment of programs is the evaluation of the number of test-cases they passed[3][4][5][6]. Unfortunately, this approach is wrought with problems. Programs which pass a high number of test-cases may not be efficient and may have been written with bad programming practices. On the other hand, programs that pass a low number of test-cases are many-a-times quite close to the correct solution; some unforced or inadvertent errors making them eventually fail the suite of test-cases designed for the problem[2]. Lastly, a score which is quantitatively defined as the number of test-cases-passed completely disregards the requirement of the score to map to a human-intuitive rubric of program quality.

Another popular approach to the automated grading of programs makes use of measuring the similarity between abstract representations (such as Control Flow Graphs and Program Dependence Graphs) of a candidate's program and representations of correct implementations for the problem[7] [8] [9]. Although promising, the theoretical elegance is damaged by the existence of multiple abstract representations for a correct solution to a given problem. Secondly, there is no underlying rubric that guides the similarity metric and neither are approaches to map the metric to a rubric discussed.[3] Apart from this, there have been publications on automatic correction of small programs [10] and peer-based assessments of programs [11], neither of which directly addresses the problem of automatic grading of programs.

We have designed an automated system to grade computer programs and produce a detailed feedback report for the student/interviewer. Firstly, the system grades how close the program's logic is to the correct solution, based on a rubric, using a novel machine learning approach. This machine learning approach, based on highly-informative features derived from abstract representations of a given program, is the subject of the present paper. Secondly, the system provides a score on the programming practices used in the program based on a rule-based system (rules as in [12]). Thirdly, it automatically detects the complexity of the program empirically by running the program for inputs of different sizes, recording the time to run and fitting a model to it. Based on these measurements, a comprehensive report is generated for each submitted program[13].

Specifically, the paper makes the following contributions:

- We demonstrate the first machine learning approach to automatically grade programs based on a rich set of features.
- We introduce a novel grammar of features which captures signature elements in a program that human experts recognize when assigning a grade. In essence, these features capture the functionality of the program. We show these features to correlate well with a proposed problem-independent rubric.
- We show empirically that the novel features add value by better modeling human-grading than an elementary keyword-counts model. (see Section 2 for details.)
- We introduce a framework with a preliminary demonstration of how learning can be used to solve the problem when one is constrained by having available an unbalanced or a small number of graded programs.
- We demonstrate, by running the algorithm on a sample of responses for programming problems and a case study, the practical usefulness of the proposed technique and program evaluation system.

The paper is organized as follows: Section 2 introduces a rubric to grade programs and proposes a grammar to generate informative features from a program. In Section 3, we discuss a machine learning framework to solve the problem. In Sections 4, 5, we present the experiment details, case study of a real-world implementation and results. Finally, Section 6 discusses the results and future work.

2. FEATURES FOR PROGRAM GRADING

2.1 Decoding the human evaluation process

Our primary motivation to address the problem of automatic evaluation was to try and understand the aspects which a manual evaluator, say an interviewer, would consider when grading a program. We understand that for a given problem, there are certain signature features which the evaluator looks for. These features are in terms of specific control structures, keywords or data dependencies being present in the program. As an illustration, we analyze a program written for a problem requiring to print a pattern (see Table 1 for problem statement and the corresponding program). The sample program is a pseudo-code in which the declaration statements of variables have been omitted and a generic syntax to print a variable has been used. This program is not fully correct as it misses out on printing a newline character at the beginning of every iteration of the outer-loop.

Given an integer ***N***, write a program to print ***N*** lines of the following pattern
 	
1
2 3
3 4 5
4 5 6 7
...
	<pre>void print_lines(int N){
	  for(i = 1; i <=N; i++){
	    count = i;
	    for(j = 0; j < i; j++){
	      print(count);
	      count++;
	    }
	  }
	}</pre>

Table 1: Pattern-printing problem with a sample program

[1]In India, large IT services companies hire 5000 to 10,000 software trainees every year, who undergo a three month training before deployment.

[2]In our own work, we see 40-50% programs falling in this category. Refer to Section 5 for details.

[3]*Janicic et al.* [8] use regression to do so, but on a very coarse set of features without much room to match the evaluation.

A human evaluator going through the sample program mentioned in Table 1 would consider the following signature features -

– Looks for basic keywords - Is a variable's value being printed? Are there loops? Are variables being incremented? If they exist, it demonstrates that the candidate has at least some basic idea of the constructs needed for the problem at hand.
– Is there a nested loop? Is a print statement included in the nested loop? If they exist, it can be inferred that the candidate has realized that a 2-dimensional printing operation primarily requires a nested loop to access each unit along the two axes.
– Is the terminating condition of the outer loop based on the input to the function? Is the terminating condition of the inner loop dependent on a variable defined in the outer loop? If yes, the candidate understands that the specific pattern in the problem demands some relationship between the two axes to exist, translating to data-dependencies between the two loops.
– Is the argument to the print function in the inner loop dependent on a variable which changes its values in each iteration? Specifically, does it increment by one and get updated to a value which is incremented by one in each outer loop? Is there a print statement in the outer loop to control the newline characters in the pattern? If yes, the candidate has a very clear understanding of the nuances demanded by the problem.

Table 2: Rubric to grade computer programs

SCORE	INTERPRETATION
5	**Completely correct and efficient:** An efficient implementation of the problem using the right control structures, data-dependencies and consideration of nuances/-corner conditions of the logic.
4	**Correct with silly errors:** Correct control structures and critical data-dependencies incorporated. Some silly mistakes fail the code to pass test-cases.
3	**Inconsistent logical structures:** Right control structures exist with few/partially correct data dependencies.
2	**Emerging basic structures:** Appropriate keywords and tokens present, showing some understanding of a part of the problem.
1	**Gibberish Code** Seemingly unrelated to the problem at hand.

It is evident that with the appearance of each set of signature features, in the order described above, a human evaluator would provide a higher score - the absence of the right keywords would receive the lowest score; the presence of the right keywords would be awarded some points; the presence of a nested loop structure would be awarded some more; the presence of data-dependencies between the loops would be awarded a relatively high score, with the best score being awarded to those programs which have all the problem-specific nuances such as the right re-initialization in the outer loops and a newline character being printed in the right loop, in addition to having all other features mentioned thus far.

This simple approach helps motivate both - the design of a grading rubric and the identification of the right features in a program which would predict it's correctness.

At this point, we urge the reader to exercise caution and not be misled by the apparent simplicity of the illustration described above. The implementation discussed above may be written with numerous variations - *while* loops replacing the *for* loops, varying number of variables and expressions, varying data-structures (use of 2-D arrays) and even varying algorithms (recursion to iterate). The question of grading the program remains hard and such a simplified illustration acts as a primer to understand the nuances involved in the process.

2.2 Evaluation Rubric

Guided by the observations mentioned in the previous Section, we present in this Section a problem-independent rubric to grade a program solving a programming problem. For any program, we define the state it is in by considering how much it has advanced in solving the given problem. The semantics used in the program i.e. the kind of keywords expressions, control structures and data-dependencies specific to the problem at hand help decide how well developed a solution it is.

The rubric is presented in Table 2. It objectively captures the program's state which, we hypothesize, links to the candidate's ability to develop an *algorithm* for a given problem. It can be used across problems and leaves scope to be more detailed and fine-grained.

2.3 Grammar of Features

In this Section, we describe a grammar of features which helps in establishing a congruence between a program and the functionality it performs. Motivated by the rubric's design, the features capture various states of expressions, control structures, data-dependencies and other properties that exist in a program. We present the features as belonging to broad classes, where each class categorises them by the underlying property they capture. Since the states mentioned in the rubric attempt to capture how well developed an *algorithm* is, these features are applicable to a program written in any programming language. Moreover, being generic, they are invariant of the underlying problem and to any particular implementation of a given problem. The details of these classes are as follows -

a. Basic Features: This class includes features obtained by counting the occurrences of various keywords and tokens appearing in the source code. These include keywords related to control structures such as *for*, *while*, *break*, etc. operators defined by a language like '+','-','*', '%', etc., character constants used in the program like '0', '1', '2', '100' etc., external function calls made like *print*() *count*(), etc.

These counts are useful to see whether the right constructs even appear in a program (characteristics of Score 2, Table 2) irrespective of whether the control-flow and data-dependencies are right.

b. Expression Features: This class includes features obtained by counting the occurrences of expressions appearing in a program. An expression in a programming language is

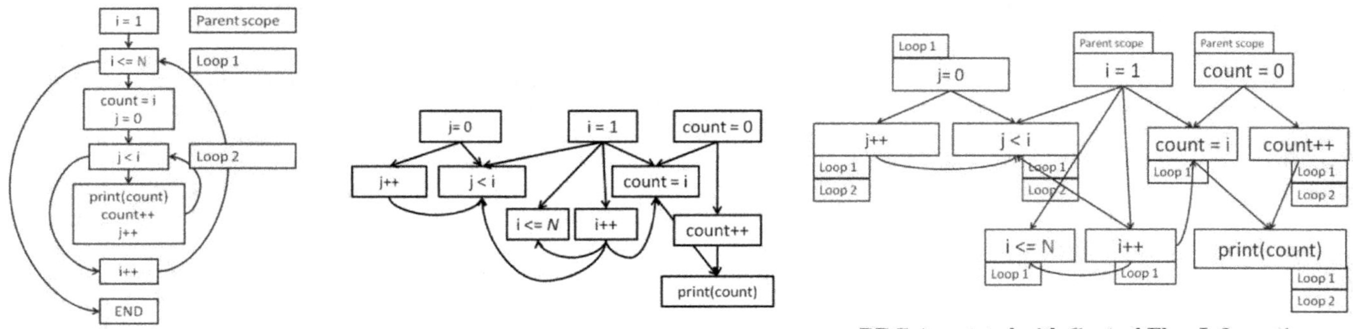

Control Flow Graph (CFG) Data Dependency Graph (DDG) DDG Annotated with Control Flow Information

Figure 1: Control & Data Information of Sample Program

a combination of explicit values, constants, variables, operators and functions. The expressions used in a program help identify arithmetic and relational operations typical of the underlying algorithm.

These expressions can be described with a varying degree of detail. For instance, the counts can either be characterized by the operators used, or by the external functions called, or by the constants used (such as '+', '-', '*print*', '100' etc.). These could further be classified by counting specific instances of each such operator, function-call etc. or by counting the total operators, function-calls etc. that appear in an expression. In our work, we capture operator-specific and data-type-specific information to count the different *types* of expressions used in a program. Table 3 illustrates a few examples of expression-features and provides their significance.

c. Basic & Expression Features in Control Context: This class includes features obtained by counting the occurrences of various expressions, keywords, tokens etc. (described in (a) and (b) above) in *context* of the control-flow structures they appear within. A *context* here signifies a block-scope extended by a control-structure to which a section of the program belongs to. A control-flow structure could include loop-statements (*for*, *while*, *do-while*, etc.) or conditional-statements (*if*, *if-else*, *switch*, etc.). In essence, these features give us the control structures the features described in (a) and (b) belong to. As in the earlier class of features, the control context too can be characterized by varying levels of details - counts could be specific to instances of loops and conditionals like *for*, *if* or could be generic to the occurrence of loops irrespective of whether it is a *for* or a *while*. Counts could also vary by the depth of the nested structures, where only the most recent context could be counted as against counting the exact context the expressions/keywords appear in. In our work, we do not differentiate between different instances of loops and conditionals and work with exact depths of contexts.

For the sample problem on printing a pattern, the CFG (see Fig. 1) reveals the presence of two occurrences of the post-increment operator (in *count++* and *j++*) appearing in a nested-loop and one occurrence (in *i++*) within a single-loop. This class of features would correlate to Score 3 in the rubric (Table 2)

d. Data-Dependency Features: This class includes features obtained by counting the occurrence of particular kinds of expressions which are dependent on other particular kinds of expression. Here, an expression refers to the features mentioned in (b). A data dependency is defined as any hierarchical ordering observed in the Data Dependency Graph (DDG) of the program. Such an ordering between two expressions generally signifies that the value of a variable(s) in one expression influences the evaluation of the other expression.

As an example illustrating this feature in the sample program, the occurrence of an edge from the node $i{+}{+}$ to $count = i$ in the DDG of the sample program (see Fig. 1) suggests that the increment on i would affect the value of the variable *count* in the expression $count = i$. Similarly, the edge from $i{+}{+}$ to $j < i$ suggests that the evaluation of the expression $j < i$ is dependent on the increment on j happening in the expression $j{+}{+}$. It is to be noted that these counts are generic and are not tagged to any particular variable in the program.

As in the previous classes of features, this class of features too can be characterized by varying levels of details - the dependencies could be listed out for an expression as a whole or could be specifically listed out for each variable appearing in an expression. The depth of the dependency captured could also vary - the dependencies could be restrained to the most recent expression which affects the current expression or could be traced back to n dependent expressions. Additionally, the various details of what constitutes an expression, as discussed in (b), can be incorporated here. In our work, we count the most recent dependency between each variable appearing in an expression separately.

e. Data-Dependency in Control Context: This class includes features obtained by counting the data-dependency features mentioned in *d.* in the context of the control structures they appear in. These features capture the specific functionality of a given program and are derived through a control-context tagged data-dependency graph of the program (see Fig. 1).
For e.g. in the illustration that has been provided in *d.*, the expressions pertaining to the edge $i{+}{+}$ to $count = i$ would additionally be annotated with a *loop* for the $count = i$ expression as it appears within a *for* loop and the expression

Table 3: Sample features and their interpretation

Feature	Interpretation
LP_LP {*Basic*}	The number of times a nested loop (a *for*-in-a-*for* or a *while*-in-a-*for* etc.) appears in the program
%::*LP_IF* {*Basic c.c** }	The number of times a modulus operator (%) appears in a nested conditional-in-a-loop. The operator appearing in a statement like *for*{.. *if*(*x*%2==0)..} would be captured by this feature
v:1::*op*:%::*c*:'2' {*Expression*}	The number of times an expression containing a modulus operator (%), one variable and the constant 2 appears in the program. An expression like *x*%2==0 would be captured by this feature
v:2::*op*:!= ::*IF* {*Expression c.c**}	The number of times an expression containing a not-equal-to operator (!=), two variables and no constants appears in an *if* block in the program. An expression like ..*if*(*x*!=*y*).. would be captured by this feature
v:2::*op*:< ↑ *v*:1::*op*:++ {*Data-dep*}	The number of times an expression containing a relational operator (<) and two variables is dependent on an expression containing a post-increment operator and one variable
v:2::*op*:<::*LP_LP* ↑ *v*:1::*op*:++::*LP* {*Data-dep c.c**}	The number of times an expression containing a relational operator (<) and two variables, which appear in a nested loop, is dependent on an expression containing a post-increment operator and one variable appearing in a loop

* c.c : in control-context

feature pertaining to *i*++ too would be annotated with a *loop* as it appears within a *for* loop.

It must be noted that the features described in (*d*) and (*e*) are of critical importance as they help identify a program belonging to a crucial level of the rubric (Score 4 and Score 5, Table 2). They identify whether a candidate has understood an algorithm and has made use of key data and control dependencies in implementing his/her understanding.

f. Other Features: In addition to the features extracted from the control and data information of a program, other metrics may be used to predict how good a given program is. Such metrics can include - the number of lines in the source code, metrics in graph theory pertaining to the generated Abstract Syntax Trees (AST), Control Flow Graphs (CFG) and/or Data Dependency Graphs (DDG) such as the number of vertices, the number of edges, the height of the tree, the number of in-edges and out-edges etc. Additionally, the number of test cases a source code passes could also be used as a feature.

All the features mentioned above can be extracted from a combination of either the AST of a program, its CFG, its DDG and its Program Dependence Graph. An implicit advantage which these structures provide is the independence of the feature extraction process with the compilability of the code. As long as the source code follows the grammar of the program strictly, these features are easily extractable. This generally is of great utility when a candidate is unable to complete his/her program in the specified time and submits a partial solution to the problem.

3. MACHINE LEARNING APPROACH

We cast the problem of automatic grading in the standard machine learning framework - where programs attempted for a given problem are rated by experts, following which a regression model is developed based on the proposed features. Given that a large number of features are generated, which include sparse features, a feature selection (or feature clustering) step may provide better modeling generalization. Clustering features in the given problem domain is intuitive, since more than one feature or feature-combinations may represent the same functionality. This can be done using techniques such as Principle Component Analysis, Factor Analysis, k-Means or by Latent Semantic Analysis (LSA)-a popular technique in the essay-grading literature.[4]

One advantage of using unsupervised methods is being able to use and extract information from ungraded samples as well. On the other hand, techniques such as forward selection, best subset selection, ridge regression, ensemble modeling can be used for supervised feature selection. In the experiments which follow, we use some simple feature selection techniques followed by the regression techniques of linear ridge regression, random forests and kernel-based SVMs. Ridge regression shrinks the feature weights leading to implicit feature selection.

One-Class Modeling: The approach of using regression to build a model entails the requirement of a domain expert to be involved to rate the programs for each problem manually. In an attempt to do away or reduce this requirement, we also explore a novel way of posing this as a problem in one-class modeling. We do so by identifying high quality codes amongst the candidate submissions using an automatic technique which looks at the number of test cases passed, programming practices used and the complexity of the code (discussed in Section 5). If the feature set indeed captures the functionality of the code and mimics the rubric, then a simple distance from these identified high-quality solutions in the feature space could provide the right grade (after some scaling). Whereas this distance approach mimics the neighborhood approaches prevalent in one-class classification (even though it is not classification), other approaches such as one-class SVMs, density estimation methods, etc. may also be used [17]. Moreover, the unsupervised clustering approaches mentioned previously may also be used to cluster these programs. In this work, we show a preliminary demonstration of using a simple one-sided, absolute distance measure to predict grades and judge the efficacy of using one-class modeling for the problem at hand.

4. SYSTEM DESIGN

We designed *Automata*, a delivery and evaluation system for testing computer programming skills. It provides an or-

[4]Such clustering may also be done using expert-knowledge as done through Wordnets etc. in Natural Language Processing [16].

line compiler-based simulated environment for applicants to code. Generally, a test contains two programming problems. Each problem has a suite of test cases which checks basic and advanced conditions of the logic of the problems. The candidates have the option to edit, compile and check the correctness of their code on these suites as many times as they chose to before submitting final solutions. Based on the programs of the candidate, a detailed report is generated[13]. The report provides a total score and one score each on *Programming Ability* and *Programming Practices*. The first score is based on the grade of the program on the rubric (based on machine learning) and also on its empirically detected time complexity. The second score is based on a rule-based system (rules similar to [12]) that identifies bad programming practices. A final total score is provided, which is an average of these scores. *Automata* has been taken by more than 200,000 students and currently used by 20+ companies for recruitment purposes.[5]

5. EXPERIMENTS

We wanted to investigate the following questions with our experiments:

- How accurately can a machine learning approach based on our novel feature set predict grades as compared to grades given by human assessors?
- Do features derived from keywords, control-structures and data-dependencies (see Section 2) add additional value in grade prediction over and above test-case based prediction?
- Do data-dependency and control-flow features add value over basic counts in the prediction and if so, by how much?
- What is the potential of one-class classification techniques in predicting accurate grades for programs, if only a set of high quality programs are available?
- What is the practical advantage of such a system in a real-world recruitment scenario?

To answer these questions, we conducted experiments on five programming problems which were graded by domain experts. The problems were chosen such that the algorithms to solve them required different control-flow structures and data-dependencies to exist in implementations. We experimented with three machine learning techniques- Ridge Regression, SVMs and Random Forest, combined with different feature selection techniques. To test the efficacy of different feature sets, we built models by various combinations of features. We also did preliminary investigations with one-class modeling techniques. We now discuss the details of the data sets used in the experiments.

5.1 Data Sets

We considered five programming problems, named in the first column of Table 4. Broadly, in *Encrypt*, one has to add numbers to each character based on its position in a string; in *Alt Sort*, one has to sort a given list of numbers and return the alternating elements, in *Find Digit*, one is given a multi-digit number and a digit and s/he has to find the number of times the digit appears in the number; in *List Primes*, one has to list out all the prime numbers less than a given number and in *Print Spiral*, one has to print N lines of a spiralling pattern of digits. The problems are above the beginners' level in programming and requires a fair amount of competence in algorithms.

We used a sample set of programs written in C solved by senior-year undergraduate engineering students majoring in Computer Science in India. Each program was rated on a scale of 1-5 following the rubric defined in Section 2. Any program with no code or less than 5-6 lines of uncorrelated code was removed from the data set. The ratings were done by two experts who had more than three years of experience in professional software development and were active participants in algorithmic programming contests. A consensus of the ratings of the two experts was taken. For programs where their grades did not match, they discussed the codes and reached a consensus. The number of graded samples for different problems varied from 84 to 294 (mentioned in first column of Table 4)[6].

The data-sets for each problem was split into two sets - training and validation. The train-set had 66% of the sample points whereas the validation-set had 33%. The split was done randomly taking care that the grade distribution in both the sets remained proportional. The total number of features generated for each problem are provided in Table 6.

Table 4: Performance across models - All features

Problem	Model	# feat	CV Correl	Val r
Encrypt (N = 106)	Ridge	80	0.85	0.79
	SVM - RBF	440	0.70	0.10
	Random Forest	87	0.96	0.29
Alt Sort (N = 84)	Ridge	68	0.93	0.91
	SVM - Linear	138	0.94	0.45
	Random Forest	56	0.98	0.68
Find Digit (N = 235)	Ridge	193	0.91	0.90
	SVM - Linear	164	0.96	0.76
	Random Forest	56	0.99	0.86
List Primes (N = 280)	Ridge	66	0.90	0.90
	SVM - RBF	85	0.90	0.60
	Random Forest	172	0.99	0.82
Print Spiral (N = 294)	Ridge	87	0.81	0.82
	SVM - RBF	123	0.90	0.60
	Random Forest	129	0.98	0.81

*N : Sample size for the problem

5.2 Regression Modeling

We used feature selection followed by a regression with 3-fold cross-validation to model the grades. We used linear ridge-regression, SVM-regression (with different kernels) and Random Forests to build the models. The best cross-validation correlation was used for selecting the model. We used some simple techniques for feature selection, which

[5]While all these candidates were tested on our delivery platform, they weren't necessarily graded by our machine learning approach. The deployment of machine learning was recent, happening at the time of writing this paper.

[6]Sample sizes are lower for the first two problems owing to their greater difficulty and removal of short/unrelated code samples

Table 5: Ridge Regression Results

Problem	Feature Type	Model Code	# Features	Cross-Val Correl	Train r	Validation r
Encrypt	Test Cases	Enc-RR-TC	3	0.39	0.39	0.54
	Basic	Enc-RR-B	60	0.62	0.87	0.41
	All, w/o Test Cases	Enc-RR-AwTC	35	0.57	0.72	0.56
	All	Enc-RR-A	80	0.61	0.85	0.79
Alt Sort	Test Cases	Sort-RR-TC	3	0.76	0.77	0.80
	Basic	Sort-RR-B	26	0.59	0.72	0.67
	All, w/o Test Cases	Sort-RR-AwTC	80	0.81	0.99	0.80
	All	Sort-RR-A	68	0.77	0.93	0.91
Find Digit	Test Cases	Digi-RR-TC	3	0.66	0.70	0.64
	Basic	Digi-RR-B	26	0.74	0.89	0.74
	All, w/o Test Cases	Digi-RR-AwTC	190	0.87	0.97	0.90
	All	Digi-RR-A	193	0.91	0.98	0.90
List Primes	Test Cases	Prime-RR-TC	3	0.74	0.75	0.80
	Basic	Prime-RR-B	35	0.83	0.88	0.69
	All, w/o Test Cases	Prime-RR-AwTC	134	0.85	0.91	0.82
	All	Prime-RR-A	66	0.90	0.94	0.90
Print Spiral	Test Cases	Spiral-RR-TC	3	0.83	0.83	0.84
	Basic	Spiral-RR-B	40	0.61	0.78	0.61
	All, w/o Test Cases	Spiral-RR-AwTC	166	0.66	0.81	0.64
	All	Spiral-RR-A	87	0.81	0.92	0.84

included choosing the most correlating features, features which were most represented in the sample programs and the most correlating/represented features in each class of features. We swept over a threshold to vary the number of features used in building a model. We also experimented with randomized sparse models (using LASSO)[18] which is supposed to work well in cases with large number of highly correlated features. Its results consistently underperformed those of our simple techniques and are hence not reported for paucity of space. Our preliminary hypothesis for its underperformance is the high sparsity of our features.[7] The method of selecting the most represented features gave best results (cross-validation correlation of final model).

Experiment parameters: For linear regression with ridge regularization, we selected the optimal ridge coefficient λ by varying it between 1 to 1000 and selecting the parameter which gave us the best cross-validation correlation. For Support Vector Machines [14][15], we tested three kernels: linear, polynomial (3rd degree) and radial basis function. In order to select the optimal SVM, we varied the penalty factor C, parameters γ and ε, the SVM kernel and selected the set of values that gave us the best correlation in cross-validation. For Random Forests [14], we varied the number of estimators from 20 to 100 and allowed for bootstrapping. MSE was used a criterion to select between models. In the feature selection step, the number of features selected was varied from selecting those which appeared at least in 5% of the data-set to at least 50% of the data-set.

The experiments were done on four sets of features: first, a set of three test case features which captured the percent of basic, advanced[8] and edge cases the program passed; second, features pertaining to counts of keywords, tokens, expressions (without control context) and other metric-based features (see Section 2); third, all features introduced in Section 2 and fourth, all features together with the test case features.

In the following subsections, the features pertaining to keyword and expression counts without control context are referred to as *basic* features while those pertaining to data-dependencies (including control context) are referred to as *advanced* features. These features collectively are referred to as *semantic* features.

5.3 Observations

The results of the experiment with different machine learning techniques are tabulated in Table 5. These are results for the models selected according to best cross-validation correlations. We report the Pearson Correlation Coefficient (r) for the different models. The number of features used in these models is mentioned in Column 3. The best cross-validation correlation in case of SVM was produced by the linear kernel for problems 2 and 3 and RBF kernels for problems 1,2 and 5.

[7]We tried PCA to cluster features which did not yield good results. We did not attempt other sophisticated clustering of features due to very small number of samples as compared to the feature set size, which we plan to do in future.

[8]Advanced Cases contain pathological input conditions which attempt to break codes implementing partially correct formulations of an algorithm.

Ridge regression consistently shows the best validation results and we consider its results (tabulated in detail in Table 5) for further analysis. We hypothesize that ridge regression's inductive bias rightly captures the problem space. For all the problems, we see that the set of semantic features (models with postfix -*AwTC*, Table 5, Column 3) does better than the set of basic features (models with postfix -*B*). The difference in performance varies from 0.13-0.16 correlation points (validation) for the problems, whereas it is 0.03 in case of *Print Spiral*. This clearly shows the utility of the advanced features in explaining the variance in human graders. To study this further, we analyze the type of features selected in the models with postfix *AwTC* (all features, without test-cases) (see Table 6). In all cases but one, the number of *advanced* features selected are more than the number of *basic* features selected, indicating their importance. The significant improvement in correlation values and considerable use of advanced features in the models demonstrate the utility of the innovative features developed.

Table 6: Class-wise selected features

Model Code	# Test-Case	# Basic	# Adv	Total
Enc-RR-A	1	39	40	80
Enc-RR-AwTC	0	24	11	35
Sort-RR-A	2	26	51	79
Sort-RR-AwTC	0	28	52	80
Digi-RR-A	3	44	146	193
Digi-RR-AwTC	0	44	146	190
Prime-RR-A	1	30	35	66
Prime-RR-AwTC	0	40	94	134
Spiral-RR-A	1	31	55	87
Spiral-RR-AwTC	0	43	123	166
Total Features				
Encrypt	3	164	4017	4184
Alt Sort	3	82	1586	1671
Find Digit	3	161	1269	1433
List Primes	3	266	1818	2087
Print Spiral	3	198	2117	2318

Additionally, we see competitive performance between test-case models (models with postfix -*TC*) and models using semantic features (models with postfix -*AwTC*). The models built using both, semantic features and test-cases (models with postfix -*A*) show better or equivalent r than test-cases-only and semantic-features-only models. The validation correlation for the models with all features range from 0.79-0.9 across the five problems and from 0.54 to 0.84 for test-cases. It may thus be concluded that the use of our new feature set considerably improves the accuracy for the problem of grading computer programs.

We now analyze how well our best models (models with suffix -*A*) do in case they were used in a real-world scenario. We find the deviation of predicted scores from their corresponding expert-assigned scores, in the validation set. As seen in Table 7, we find that more than 80% of the predicted grades are within a 1-grade shift from it's corresponding expert-rated grades. Only a maximum of three codes in every problem are predicted grades which are greater than 2-grade shifts away. We also discretized the scores to map them to a level of the rubric. The discretization was done by learning thresholds on the training-set for each score level such that the distribution of the predicted-scores vs. actual scores was the same. As an illustration, the confusion matrix of the expert-assigned scores versus the discretized predicted scores are provided for two of the five problems in Table 8 for the programs in their validation-set

Table 7: Deviation of Predicted Score : Regression

Problem	**Score Shifts vs. # of Codes**					
	#Val	0-1	1-2	2-3	3-4	>4
Encrypt	34	28	5	1	0	0
Alt Sort	27	23	4	0	0	0
Find Digit	77	72	4	1	0	0
List Primes	92	78	11	2	1	0
Print Spiral	97	79	15	2	1	0

Table 8: True vs. Discretized Predicted Scores

Encrypt	**Predicted Scores**				
	1	**2**	**3**	**4**	**5**
1	3	1	0	0	0
2	1	3	1	1	0
3	0	2	3	2	0
4	0	1	4	9	1
5	0	0	0	0	1

List Primes	**Predicted Scores**				
	1	**2**	**3**	**4**	**5**
1	20	3	2	0	1
2	2	5	1	1	0
3	0	1	8	1	1
4	0	0	2	5	4
5	0	0	0	2	33

We find that only two codes (5.8%) have more than 1 level shift for the *Encrypt* problem, whereas there are 4 (4.3%) for the *List Primes* problem. In *Encrypt*, 55.5% codes have the correct grades (owing to its lower validation correlation), whereas *List Primes* has 77.2% correct grades.

These results indicate that our approach is robust enough to be used in applications where a one-level shift is acceptable for a limited number of cases. One finds similar correlation values and confusion matrices in automatic scoring of essays wherein such methods have found their way into high-stake assessments[19]. Likewise, such confusion between adjacent levels may also be observed between two expert raters. To study this further, we would have to find correlation and confusion between multiple expert raters and also see if the automatic score has better correlation with their consensus.

5.4 Feature Insight

We wished to see what insight could be derived by looking at the features picked up by machine learning for a problem. This could not only help automatically discover important logic elements needed in a correct solution of a problem, thereby enabling us to give feedback/hints to students on what constructs to use while solving a problem, but also help design better features. As a preliminary step towards this goal, we show the most contributing feature for *Find Digit* from the high performing ridge-regression model.

Dep@Var:1,Op:!=,Const:1#input:m_LOOPc

↑

Var:1,Op:/,Const:1#input:m_LOOPb

The pseudo-code equivalent of the above described feature is shown in Table 10, left column. The algorithm to

Table 9: Correlation - Distance metric

Problem	All Features						Only Basic					
	With training			Without training			With training			Without training		
	Mean	***Min25***	*Min*	*Mean*	***Min25***	*Min*	*Mean*	***Min25***	*Min*	*Mean*	***Min25***	*Min*
Encrypt	0.57	**0.61**	0.55	0.65	**0.65**	0.51	0.52	**0.56**	0.57	0.59	**0.63**	0.54
Alt Sort	0.80	**0.83**	0.83	0.80	**0.83**	0.83	0.72	**0.75**	0.73	0.68	**0.69**	0.70
Find Digit	0.75	**0.81**	0.84	0.72	**0.80**	0.77	0.59	**0.73**	0.75	0.56	**0.67**	0.67
List Primes	0.81	**0.81**	0.66	0.76	**0.78**	0.54	0.75	**0.75**	0.63	0.65	**0.66**	0.48
Print Spiral	0.68	**0.69**	0.72	0.58	**0.58**	0.52	0.55	**0.61**	0.62	0.49	**0.51**	0.48

solve *Find Digit* (see Section 5.1 for problem details) requires each digit of the multi-digit number to be extracted and checked for equality against the input digit. The feature describes a dependency condition in control context: the input (N) is used in the condition of a loop with a $!=$ operator and a constant, which depends on an assignment made to it within the body of the same loop (dependence becomes clear if one unrolls the loop), where it is assigned an expression using a / operator and a constant. Clearly, this is a general logical structure which occurs in one of the basic implementations for the problem as illustrated in the right column of Table 10. The automatic discovery of this structure, which humans will look for in a correct implementation, illustrates the power of the technique and also a first step towards getting qualitative insight into problem solutions through machine learning.

```
...
LOOP(N! = const ){
  ...
  N = N/const
  ...
}
...
```

```
int find_digit(int N, int digit){
  while(N != 0){
    d = N %10;
    if(d == digit)
    ...
    N = N/10;
  }
}
```

Table 10: Most contributing feature - Pseudo code

5.5 One-Class Modeling

We do a preliminary investigation of using only a set of high-quality codes for the purpose of prediction. The idea is to automatically find high-scoring codes to build a predictive model thereby reducing the effort invested in hand-grading programs. We identified a set of high scoring codes for the problems in the following way- we took a subset of codes (referred to as *good set*) which passed more than 80% of the test-cases, solved the problem in the right time complexity and followed programming best practices. The number of codes this conservative filtering yielded is recorded in Table 11. Their overlap with their expert-assigned scores is also shown.

Given a small number of programs in the *good set* for some problems, the use of machine learning techniques was impeded. Thus, to predict scores, we decided to define the distance of a given code from the *good set* in the feature space. We used a simple one-sided distance metric, in which having less of a feature was penalized whereas having more was not. This was done with the intuition that having more of a particular feature was generally not indicative of an incorrect code. We kept the same weight for all features, which could have potentially been learnt had there been enough data. Our method is akin to neighbourhood approaches in one class classification.

Table 11: True Scores of Filtered Programs : One-Class Approach

Problem	True Scores					
	1	2	3	4	5	**Total**
Encrypt	0	0	0	22	5	27
Alt Sort	0	0	0	2	10	12
Find Digit	0	0	3	15	130	148
List Primes	3	0	0	9	93	102
Print Spiral	0	1	0	1	149	150

We provided scores to the programs based on the distances calculated using just the *basic* features and all the semantic features (including the test-case features). In order to calculate a score for a given program, we first sum the distance of the program from the good set. This provides a distance of the given program from each of the programs in the *good set*.We then employ three methods - a. consider the mean of these distances b. consider the minimum of these distances and c. consider the mean of the least 25% of the distances. We hypothesized that the mean metric shall be noisy given that the *good set* would have codes implementing different algorithm strategies. On the other hand, the minimum of the distances would be noisy given the presence of outlier codes (columns 1,2 and 3 of Table 11). The mean of the least distances is a good trade-off. Interpreting it differently, it attempts to identify the cluster (algorithm strategy) the current program belongs to and finds the distance from it.[9]

The correlations between the calculated distance and the expert-assigned scores are tabulated in Table 9. We provide correlations with and without including the train-set from which the distance is measured. Using the train-set is not entirely incorrect in this context since it is automatically determined (as opposed to usual machine learning applications) and has been graded automatically, mimicking a real-world scenario which the system shall encounter. Akin to our observations in the supervised learning setting, we find that scores from distances across all features outperform those only from *basic* features. Secondly, we find $Min25$ to provide the most consistently high performing results. This indicates a validation of our hypothesis regarding the existence of clusters and outliers codes in the *good set*.

[9]In future, for problems with larger sample sizes, we intend to cluster codes in the *good set* using unsupervised clustering algorithms and find distances from the clusters.

5.6 Case Study

We studied the deployment of *Automata* at a hiring event of one of Aspiring Minds' large IT-product customers. The event had a turn-up of 1050 applicants for a software engineering job. They were tested on two programming problems (*List Primes* and *Encrypt* from above set) in a 75 minutes test. The customer's default shortlisting criterion was to consider candidates who cleared at least 80% of the test-cases.

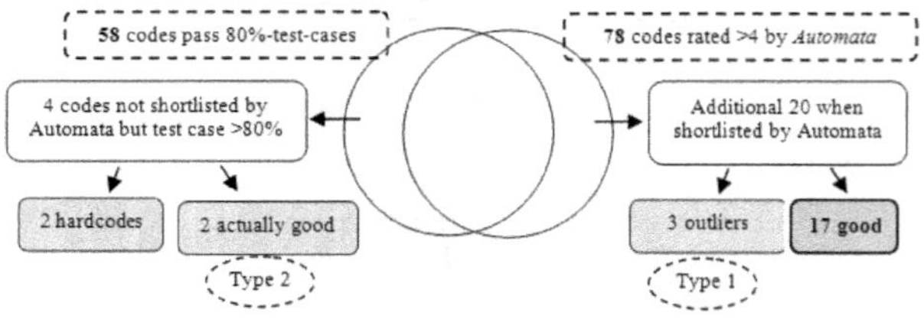

Figure 2: Case study - Extant approach vs. *Automata*

Based on the test, candidates above a programming ability score of 78 were shortlisted, which maps to score 4 on the rubric. We studied how these results would have been affected had we used the test-case pass criteria (Fig. 2). For a test-case pass rate of 80%, 58 candidates would have been shortlisted. Among the 20 extra candidates, only 3 were outliers as inspected by the interviewers. This implies that the test-case criteria would have missed 22.6% ($\frac{17}{58+17}$) of the good candidates as compared to our approach.[10] On the other hand, there were 4 candidates who were accepted by test-case, but rejected by our scoring: two of these had hard-coded the logic in their implementations(thus rightly rejected), whereas, 2 of them were outliers. Of the final offers made, 45% more selections were made from the top 50% scoring students. This preliminary case-study demonstrates how our approach gives immediate benefit and provides guidance to interviewers by reducing type-2 errors.

6. CONCLUSION

The present work proposes a system to automatically grade computer programs using machine learning. To facilitate the same, we design an objective rubric and a novel set of features that capture the program's functionality. We show that regression against expert-grades can provide much better grading than the ubiquitous test-case-pass based grading and rivals the grading accuracy of other open-response problems such as essay grading. We also show that our novel features add significant value over basic keyword/expression counts. Our preliminary investigations in one-class modeling show great promise and also indicate implicit correlation between the proposed novel features and the rubric. Finally, through a case study, we show the practical efficiency provided by a deployment of the system in the recruitment process of an IT-product company.

In future, as our data sets grow in size, we want to use more sophisticated unsupervised and supervised machine learning techniques. Given that supervised learning is hungry for graded data, we see programming classes in universities and MOOCs as an avenue to get teaching-assistants' grades effortlessly. Integration of this system into classrooms can facilitate a seamless continuous collection of data to build a powerful automated grading system. The holy grail shall remain to build problem independent grading techniques or those that reduce the need of graded data, which may be facilitated by efficient one-class modeling techniques. An interesting area to explore, preliminarily investigated in this paper, is the qualitative feedback from our techniques through feature analysis. Finally, we look forward to the large scale deployment of our system in the industry and academia to facilitate further learnings and improvements.

[10]In this case, we compare the performance of our results against the performance of test-cases and not the gold standard of expert-grades.

Acknowledgment

The authors would like to thank Vinay Shashidhar for his help in this work and for his invaluable suggestions.

7. REFERENCES

[1] V. Aggarwal, S. Srikant, V. Shashidhar. Principles for using Machine Learning in the Assessment of Open Response Items : Programming Assessment as a Case Study. 2013, NIPS Workshop on Data Driven Education

[2] S. Srikant, V. Aggarwal. Automatic Grading of Computer Programs: A Machine Learning Approach. 12th International Conference on Machine Learning Applications (ICMLA), 2013.

[3] C. Douce, D. Livingstone, and J. Orwell. Automatic test-based assessment of programming: A review. J. Educ. Resour. Comput., 5(3), Sept. 2005.

[4] M. Wick, D. Stevenson, P. Wagner. Using testing and JUnit across the curriculum. ACM SIDCSE Bulletin 37(1) (2005) 236-240

[5] Urs. Von Matt. Kassandra: the automatic grading system. SIGGUE 22(1994) 26-40

[6] M.Joy, N. Griffiths, R. Boyatt. The BOSS online submission and assessment system. Journal on Educational Resources in Computing 5(3) (2005)

[7] K. Ala-Mukta, T. Uimonen, H.M. Jarvinen. Supporting students in C++ programming courses with automatic program style assessment. Journal of Information Technology Education 3 (2004) 245-262

[8] M. Vujosevic-Janicic, M. Nikolic, Dusan Tosic, and V. Kuncak. Software verification and graph similarity for automated evaluation of students assignments. Information and Software Technology, 2012

[9] T. Wang, X. Su, Y. Wang et al. Semantic similarity-based grading of student programs. Information and Software Technology, 49(2), 99-107

[10] R. Singh, S. Gulwani, and A. Solar-Lezama. Automated feedback generation for introductory programming assignments. Programming Language Design and Implementation (PLDI) 2013.

[11] J. Sitthiworachart, and M. Joy. Web-based Peer Assessment in Learning Computer Programming. The 3rd IEEE International Conference on Advanced Learning Technologies: ICALT03, Athens, Greece, 9-11 July 2003

[12] PC-Lint Software, Gimpel Software, www.gimpel.com

[13] *Automata* sample report, `http://www.aspiringminds.in/docs/sample_report.pdf`

[14] Pedregosa et al. Scikit-learn: Machine Learning in Python. JMLR '12, pp. 2825-2830, 2011.

[15] C.C. Chang and C.J. Lin. LIBSVM: A Library for Support Vector Machines. 2001, Available: `http://www.csie.ntu.edu.tw/~cjlin/libsvm`

[16] A. Hotho, S. Staab and G. Stumme. Ontologies improve text document clustering. In Data Mining, 2003. Third IEEE International Conference on, ICDM 2003.

[17] M. Breunig, H. Kriegel, R. Ng, and J. Sander. LOF: Identifying density-based local outliers. ACM SIGMOD Record, vol. 29, no. 2, pp. 93-104, 2000

[18] N. Meinshausen, P. Buhlmann. Stability selection. Journal of the Royal Statistical Society, 72(2010)

[19] C. Leacock and M. Chodorow. C-rater: Automated Scoring of Short-Answer Questions. Computers and the Humanities, 37(4):389-405, 2003.

An Empirical Study of Reserve Price Optimisation in Real-Time Bidding

Shuai Yuan, Jun Wang, Bowei Chen
Department of Computer Science, University College London
{s.yuan, j.wang, bowei.chen}@cs.ucl.ac.uk

Peter Mason
Advance International Media
peter@advance.uk.com

Sam Seljan
AppNexus
sseljan@appnexus.com

ABSTRACT

In this paper, we report the first empirical study and live test of the reserve price optimisation problem in the context of Real-Time Bidding (RTB) display advertising from an operational environment. A reserve price is the minimum that the auctioneer would accept from bidders in auctions, and in a second price auction it could potentially uplift the auctioneer's revenue by charging winners the reserve price instead of the second highest bids. As such it has been used for sponsored search and been well studied in that context. However, comparing with sponsored search and contextual advertising, this problem in the RTB context is less understood yet more critical for publishers because 1) bidders have to submit a bid for each individual impression, which mostly is associated with user data that is subject to change over time. This, coupled with practical constraints such as the budget, campaigns' life time, etc. makes the theoretical result from optimal auction theory not necessarily applicable and a further empirical study is required to confirm its optimality from the real-world system; 2) in RTB an advertiser is facing nearly unlimited supply and the auction is almost done in "last second", which encourages spending less on the high cost ad placements. This could imply the loss of bid volume over time if a correct reserve price is not in place. In this paper we empirically examine several commonly adopted algorithms for setting up a reserve price. We report our results of a large scale online experiment in a production platform. The results suggest the our proposed game theory based OneShot algorithm performed the best and the superiority is significant in most cases.

Categories and Subject Descriptors

H.3.5 [**Information Systems**]: Information Storage and Retrieval - Online Information Services

Keywords

Display Advertising; Reserve Price; Revenue Optimisation; Online Advertising; Real-Time Bidding

KDD'14, August 24–27, 2014, New York, NY, USA.

http://dx.doi.org/10.1145/2623330.2623357.

1. INTRODUCTION

In display and mobile advertising, the most significant development in recent years is the growth of Real-Time Bidding (RTB) [34], which allows selling and buying online display advertising in real-time one ad impression at a time. It is projected to reach $8.49 billion in US alone in 2017, accounting for 29% of all digital display advertising [12].

In RTB, a publisher generates a bid request for each individual impression in real time and then sends a request to advertisers via ad exchanges [23]. In practice, the reserve price may be disclosed or not. Advertisers would submit bids for this impression based on their bidding algorithms. Usually they do so even when the bids are lower than the disclosed reserve to avoid the *time-out penalty* which reduces the bid request volume over time. Those bidding algorithms usually enquire third-party data providers to obtain the user's interest segments to assist in computing bids. When the time limit expires (usually 100ms) the exchange holds a second price auction [2], and the publisher gets the winner, saves the final price, and displays the ad from the winning advertiser to the user. The whole process is represented in Figure 1.

Along with other fixed-price advertising channels [29, 4], revenue from RTB makes an important source to support various (online) publishers, including but not limited to content providers, social networks, and personal blogs. They provide free services or content and subsidise the maintaining cost by ad revenue. Therefore, uplifting revenue by employing various yield management tools makes one of the key topics on the publisher side. An important tool among them is the *reserve price* optimisation. A reserve price defines the minimum that a publisher would accept from bidders. It reflects the publisher's private valuation of the inventory: bids will be discarded if they are below the reserve price. In the second price auction, which is commonly used in RTB, the reserve price could potentially uplift the revenue. Figure 2 illustrates how the final price is calculated from bids with a reserve price. Let $b_1, \ldots, b_K$ denote the descending bids and α the reserve price. Then, the desirable case is $b_1 \geq \alpha > b_2$ where the publisher gains extra payoff of $\alpha - b_2$; the neutral case is $b_1 > b_2 \geq \alpha$ where the publisher has no extra gain; and the undesirable case is $\alpha > b_1$ where the publisher suffers from a loss of b_2. These cases directly motivate our work.

The optimisation problem has been previously studied in the context of sponsored search [11, 13, 26, 31]. However, the

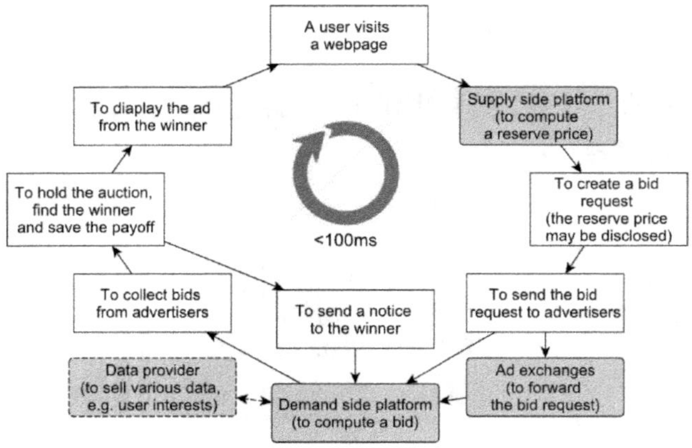

Figure 1: The simplified process of Real-Time Bidding advertising. Major entities are coloured in blue where processes are transparent. One iteration usually finishes in less than 100ms to achieve users' satisfactory.

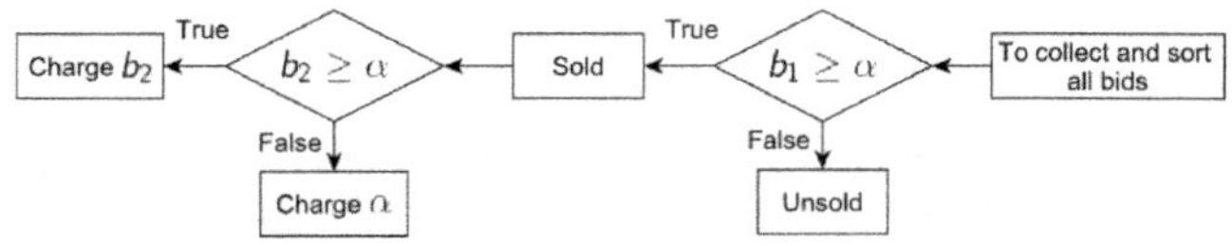

Figure 2: The decision process of second price auctions on the publisher side. The desirable case is $b_1 \geq \alpha > b_2$ where the publisher gains extra payoff of $\alpha - b_2$. We ignored *soft floor prices* which make the process a lot more complicated. Interested readers may refer to [34] for further discussion.

problem in the RTB context is different and unique. Firstly, the optimal auction theory requires to know the distribution of the advertisers' private yet true assessments of the impression before calculating the optimal reserve price [11]. In RTB, it becomes a lot harder to learn the distribution. In RTB an advertiser is required to submit a bid for each individual impression using his own algorithm, which is never disclosed to publishers and could rely heavily on privately-owned user interest segments. Besides, various practical constraints such as the budget, campaign life time, irrationality, divert advertisers from bidding at private values. This difference makes the private value based algorithm inefficient in practice. Thus, it is of great interest to empirically study the subject and examine several commonly adopted algorithms in the real-world as we report in the paper. Secondly, unlike sponsored search, an advertiser does not have the keyword constraint and faces almost unlimited supply of impressions in RTB. Setting up an aggressive reserve price would easily move the advertisers away from those placements and force them to look for something cheaper.

We analyse this possible consequence in the online experiment and reject the significant attrition hypothesis in today's RTB marketplace, which could be due to the complexity of our scheduling or less sensitivity of common bidding algorithms. The little attrition fact implies good chance of implementing the optimisation in the current eco-system.

In this paper, we represent the first field study of reserve price optimisation in the RTB context. It is based on the analysis of real-world data and online experiments on a production platform. We provide thorough discussions about the commonly adopted algorithms for reserve price optimisation including both the private-value-free and the private-value-based ones [24, 11, 26], and their variations.

2. RELATED WORK

Up to now the reserve price problem is mainly studied for sponsored search (SS). For instance, in [26], the authors first studied the reserve price problem in a real-world online advertising system (Yahoo! sponsored search). The authors test optimal auction theory on 450k keywords and the results diverge by number of impressions: for keywords with high search volume the uplift on revenue is good and statistically significant. However, for other keywords the total revenue declines by 2.2% on average. We find this result consistent with our work, although the optimisation is not helpful when there are few bidders. Additionally, we also perform the bidders' attrition analysis which is a more significant problem in RTB.

In [11] the optimal auction problem is characterised for sponsored search. The authors demonstrate the calculation of optimal reserve price for multi-item auctions and conclude that it is independent of the number of bidders. However, in [31] the authors conclude that both the number of bidders and the number of ad links affect the optimal reserve price. Some assumptions are made in the first pape: advertisers know their value per click; they have the same Click-Through Rate (CTR) at a given position; they share the common knowledge of position CTRs; they all maximise the expected profit. These assumptions might be realistic when search engines bids for advertisers, but however are far from achievable in RTB. Also in the SS context, in [13] the advertiser specific reserve prices are discussed within the generalised second-price auction (GSP) and the Vickrey-Clarke-Groves (VCG) auction [10] settings. As proved in the paper the bidder specific reserve prices could result in losing truthfulness in the VCG pricing; but could lead to envy-free equilibrium in the GSP pricing.

We plan our work in a RTB environment. In [23] the abstract model of the ad exchange is proposed and several problems are discussed, including auction mechanism, call out optimisation [8], publisher revenue optimisation [15], arbitrage bidding and risk analysis [7] etc. As mentioned by the authors, the reserve price problem taking an essential role in yield optimisation yet remains unsolved. In this paper, we study the problem at placement-level (a group of impressions) and leave the impression-level dynamic reserve prices to future work.

There is also rich literature from bidders' perspective on how to bid when a randomised reserve price in ad network is present [16, 14]. The optimal auction design is studied in [14] with two layers: central seller to intermediaries and intermediaries to bidders. The authors conclude that revenue-maximizing intermediaries will use an auction with a randomized reserve price chosen from an interval in equilibrium, and the optimal reserve price decreases with the number of buyers. In our paper, although no intermediary is employed, we also observe and discuss the relationship of the optimal reserve price and number of bidders.

Due to the similarity in mechanisms, RTB also can borrow a lot from established research on auction theories [19, 28, 22], esp. electronic commerce [3, 32]. In [18] the detection and reaction towards reserve prices cheating are first discussed for online auctions. The authors of [22] discuss the situation that an item could be resold if previous auctions fail due to high reserve price. An equilibrium reserve price was proven to approach the one in an optimal static auction. Meanwhile, there are papers on scoring inventories [27] considering unique characteristics of RTB auctions (e.g., number of bidders, bid time, bidders' identity). However, few of them take the reserve price into account.

3. THE RESERVE PRICE PROBLEM AND ALGORITHMS

Suppose a publisher tries to maximise the ad revenue for a single placement (i.e., single-item). Impressions from this placement are sold using the second price auction in RTB. The publisher could set a reserve price (also known as the hard floor price) α before an auction is conducted.

To simplify the discussion, we assume there is only one impression at each step t and the publisher is optimising the revenue over horizon T. We also assume that at each step t there are $K \geq 2$ bidders participating in the auction. If there is only one bidder it is equivalent to having the second highest bid equals to the minimal bid (usually \$0.01). Note bidders could be different each time and could change quite a lot—this introduces great noise into the system and challenges the estimation of the distribution of the private evaluation values from the advertisers, where most auction theories assume there is a fix distribution of bids.

For each auction, we denote the final bids of the placement as $b_1(t), b_2(t), \cdots, b_K(t)$. Without loss of generality we assume $b_1(t) \geq b_2(t) \geq \cdots \geq b_K(t)$. Therefore, without a reserve price ($\alpha = 0$) the payoff could be denoted as $r(t) = b_2(t)$. Now suppose the publisher sets a non-zero reserve price at each step, denoted by $\alpha(t)$. The payoff function becomes:

$$r'(t) = \begin{cases} \alpha(t), & b_1(t) \geq \alpha(t) > b_2(t) \\ b_2(t), & b_2(t) \geq \alpha(t) \\ 0, & \alpha(t) > b_1(t) \end{cases} \quad (1)$$

The overall income is $R(T) = \sum_t^T r'(t)$. We assume it is zero payoff when the reserve price is too high. In practice, publishers usually redirect these impressions to managed campaigns or other ad marketplaces for re-selling. This reduces the risk of over-optimisation.

Comparing with the original payoff function, the case $r'(t) = \alpha(t)$ provides an extra gain, whereas the case $r'(t) = 0$ incurs a loss. We plan our work at the placement level; in other words, we set up the reserve price periodically. From a control theory's point of view, throughout the planning horizon the publisher wants to explore (learn) the optimal α of the placement; the same time the publisher also exploits (predict) the known best α to get as much payoff as possible and to compensate the loss.

3.1 Optimal Auction Theory

Regardless of the existence of reserve price, bidders are encouraged to bid their private values in the second price auctions [24, 21]. Note that this dominant strategy does not hold in modern sponsored search where quality scores are generally used [10] in ad ranking. Without quality scores, the strategy of bidding at the private value forms part of the Nash equilibrium of the system, meaning as time elapses advertisers have no incentive to change their bids, given that all other factors remain the same. In this non-cooperative game [25], the winner could, but would not, lower his bid to let other competitors win because losing the auction is not beneficial in either short-term or long-term (lowering the bid while still winning has no effect since the winner always pays the second highest bid).

Suppose the publisher knows the bidders' private value distribution. The optimal auction theory mathematically defines the optimal reserve price [19, 20, 31, 24]. There is also a large scale experiment in sponsored search to test this theory [26]. We briefly introduce the theory to make the paper self-contained. Again suppose there are K bidders and they are risk-neutral and symmetric, i.e. having identical value distributions. Each bidder $k \in K$ has private information on the value of an impression, drawn from distribution $F_k(x)$, where $F_k(x)$ denotes the probability that the advertiser's private evaluation value is less than or equal to a certain number x. Usually it is assumed Log-normal [26] or Uniform distribution [24]. Assuming private values are independently distributed, the distribution over value vector is

$$F(\cdot) = F_1(\cdot) \times \cdots F_K(\cdot),$$

and then the optimal reserve price is given as (see [25] for details):

$$\alpha = \frac{1 - F(\alpha)}{F'(\alpha)} + v_P, \quad (2)$$

where $F'(\alpha)$ is the density function, the first order derivative of $F(\alpha)$ and v_P is the publisher's private value. In practice, v_P could be obtained from a guaranteed contract with a flat CPM, or from another ad network where the average revenue is known.

In the experiment we implement this theory as OPTAUC and follow the Log-normal distribution assumption of bidders' private values. We also adopt the symmetric assumption, i.e., there is only one distribution for all bidders. Under these assumptions the optimality of the auction under GSP is proved in [11]. The estimation of Log-normal's mean and standard deviation was obtained using the training dataset (impression-level logs from 14 Dec 2012 to 18 Jan 2013).

3.1.1 *Drawbacks in RTB Practice*

In practice, there are drawbacks of the optimal auction theory mostly due to the difficulty of learning bidders' private values, e.g., $F(x)$. Firstly, a bidder could have a complex private value distribution for impressions. In RTB an advertiser computes a bid for each individual impression based on the contextual [6] and behavioural [33] data. The data is fed into their private valuation models which are never disclosed to publishers or other advertisers. This is especially true in RTB comparing with SS where search engines run bidding algorithms for advertisers and host auctions as a publisher at the same time. Also, in SS the auctions are based on keywords, so the population of the bidders are relatively more stable, whereas in RTB, the auctions are in the impression level and the advertisers are more flexible in terms of choosing the impressions to bid.

We tested the Uniform distribution at placement level and Log-normal distribution at both placement and impression level. Although these distributions are widely adopted in research literature [24, 26], only a small portion of tests returned positive results as shown in Figures 7 and 8.

Secondly, it is *assumed* that advertisers bid at their private values in the second price auction [19, 26]. However, in practice, an advertiser may not know clearly his private valuation of an impression. Instead, he wants to achieve the best possible performance. Also in different stages (learning, prospecting, retargeting, etc.) of an advertising campaign, the bidding strategy could change. This makes the bidding activity vary greatly across the limited flight time of a campaign. See a plot from our experiment in Figure 5.

Thirdly, there are other practical constraints including accessibility of auction details, noise introduced by the frequent change of auction winners, c.f. Figure 6. We believe these drawbacks lead to undesirable performance of an optimal auction theory based algorithm in our real-world experiment.

3.2 A Simplified Dynamic Game

To address the above-mentioned issue, in this paper, we take an alternative view and propose a simple auction game between the publisher and auction winners and identify the dominant strategies. We simplify the game by dropping the *repeated* nature of auctions. Thus the publisher only considers the current auction and do not learn the private values from historical knowledge. In fact, the result of this simplification follows the instinct and is easy to implement; it also performs the best in most of cases in our online large scale real-world experiment.

First we give the extensive form representation of this dynamic game:

- Player: the winner of auctions (advertisers) w and the publisher p.
- The information set $\mathbb{I}$ before acting is the same for the winner and the publisher. It has two decision nodes: I_1, the winning bid b is equal to or higher than the current reserve price α; I_2, the winning bid is lower than the reserve price.
- The action set of the winner A_w: a_{w1}, to increase b to higher than α; a_{w2}, to increase b to lower than α; a_{w3}, to decrease or hold b to higher than α; a_{w4}, to decrease or hold b to lower than α.
- The action set of the publisher A_p: a_{p1}, to increase or hold α to higher than b; a_{p2}, to increase or hold α to lower than b; a_{p3}, to decrease α to higher than b; a_{p4}, to decrease α to lower than b.
- The sequence of move: first the publisher, then the winner.

The game tree representation, as well as the payoff function, is given in Figure 3. Note for some nodes the payoff of the winner consists two numbers, e.g. $30/-10$, when the winner choose to increase the bid, i.e., the action a_{w1}. The positive value stands for the case where it is still profitable to increase the bid, while the negative value stands for the possible loss if increasing the bid, since the advertiser has reached the maximum affordable price. In the latter case, an advertiser would choose other actions like a_{w2} or a_{w4}. These values have been carefully selected to reflect the positions of bidder. For example, $I_1 \to I_1|a_{p2} \to I_1|a_{w1}$ would give less payoff to the advertiser than $I_1 \to I_2|a_{p1} \to I_1|a_{w1}$ because he has been increasing bids to win auctions.

When deducing dominant strategies we assume both cases happen with an equal chance since both publishers and advertisers do not use historical knowledge but only the last state. Therefore, payoff of the publisher in these cases is discounted by 0.5 since a rational advertiser would not choose a negative payoff.

3.2.1 The Publisher's Dominant Strategy

Based on the formulation above we analyse the case where the publisher and the winner play the game for only one round. We claim the dominant strategy for the publisher is:

$$s_p^*(I) = \begin{cases} a_{p2}, & \text{if } I = I_1 \\ a_{p4}, & \text{if } I = I_2 \end{cases} \quad (3)$$

which gives the expected payoff:

$$R(s_p^*|I) = \begin{cases} 60 & \text{if } I = I_1 \\ 40 & \text{if } I = I_2 \end{cases} \quad (4)$$

We eliminate the proof here since it could be easily acquired by following nodes iteratively in the game tree, c.f. Figure 3. This strategy will serve as the foundation of the OneShot algorithm we propose in the following section. On the other hand, the dominant strategy for the winner is

$$s_w^*(I) = \begin{cases} a_{w3}, & \text{if } I = I_1 \\ a_{w1}, & \text{if } I = I_2 \end{cases} \quad (5)$$

which indicates that the bid price should be gradually reduced but increased again when lost the auction.

Based on these analysis we have the Nash equilibrium of the game: $s^* = (s_p^*, s_w^*)$. This indicates the publisher should keep the reserve price below the winning bid, while trying to approach the winning bid gradually. If the reserve price is too high, it should be reduced drastically to make sure it will be below the winning bid. Following these actions, the final state of the system comes to the second price auction without a reserve price, i.e., the reserve price is always equal to the second highest bid. In this state, the publisher does not need to lower α any more. The winner will not lower the bid otherwise he would lose the auction which gives a zero payoff. However, this state has never been observed in our experiment due to the frequent change of bidders, variation of bids, possibly different strategies adopted by advertisers (e.g. always bid at the private value).

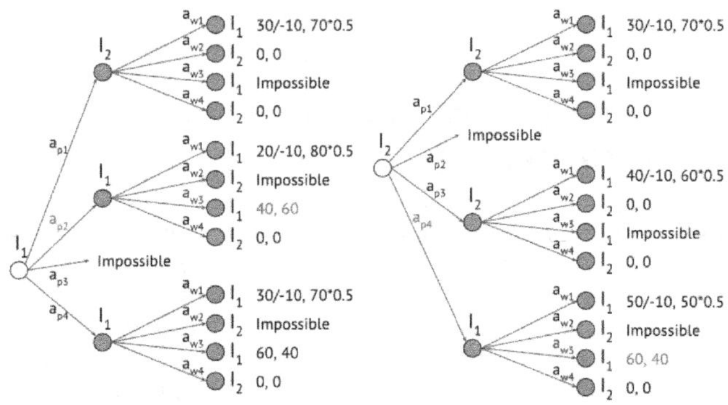

Figure 3: The game between the winner and the publisher in the reserve price problem. At the leaf nodes we give the result information set as well as the payoffs of (winner, publisher). Note for the action a_{w1} the payoff of the winner could be negative if he has already been bidding the maximal affordable price. We assume these cases happen at a chance of 50% due to no utilisation of historical data. Thus, the payoff of the publisher is discounted by 0.5 in these cases.

3.2.2 Introducing the Randomness

One may argue that since the winner of auction is constantly changing this is no longer a game between two players, but between a player and a group. The frequency of changing is indeed high. See Figure 6 from the experiment

Table 1: The payoff matrix of the publisher if the new winner bid randomly. I_1 and I_2 denote the starting information set. a_{p*} stands for publishers' actions. The publisher's dominant strategy remains the same and is illustrated in bold font.

	I_1	I_2
a_{p1}	1/3 * 70	1/3 * 70
a_{p2}	**1/3 * 80 + 1/3 * 60**	-
a_{p3}	-	1/3 * 60
a_{p4}	1/3 * 70 + 1/3 * 40	**1/3 * 50 + 1/3 * 40**

section. But, since the knowledge of auctions is not shared among the bidder group, each player of this group only possesses an imperfect information set. This could result in the randomness of winner's actions: the new winner does not have the outcome of the last auction, so has to bid randomly, which is usually based on private valuation of the impression or simply instinct.

In this case we claim that the dominant strategy of the publisher is still the one defined in Equation 3. We remove the negative payoffs of the winner from the game tree in Figure 3 and allow him to bid randomly regardless of what action has been chosen by the publisher. We remove the negative payoffs because the new winner should not bid above his private valuation of the impression in the first time step. The single-step payoff matrix of the publisher is shown in Table 1.

By playing this auction game with advertisers' random actions the publisher has the payoff:

$$R'(s_p^*|I) = \begin{cases} \frac{1}{3} * 80 + \frac{1}{3} * 60, & \text{if } I = I_1 \\ \frac{1}{3} * 50 + \frac{1}{3} * 40, & \text{if } I = I_2 \end{cases} \tag{6}$$

We consider this case describes the real-world marketplace more closely. In fact, the convergence to the second price auction state hardly happens due to two reasons. Firstly, the winner of auctions keeps changing constantly as illustrated in Figure 6, especially when there are many bidders in auctions. Secondly, the detection of the reserve price could be difficult (when it is not disclosed) and costly. It becomes even harder if certain randomisation is introduced to the final reserve price setting as we did in the experiment. The winner could suffer from distinguishing a reserve price from his competitors' bids. From the bidder's perspective, the dominant strategy of competing with other bidders (bidding the private value) and with the publisher (keep lowering the bid before losing) is clearly different.

3.2.3 *The OneShot Algorithm*

We design an algorithm based on the dominant strategy analysis above. For the publisher, if the winning bid is higher than the reserve price, slowly increase the reserve price; otherwise, decrease drastically. We make the actual implementation slightly different by introducing parameters to control the magnitude of the change under different situations. We describe the algorithm as follows.

$$\begin{cases} \alpha(t+1) = (1 - \epsilon^t \lambda_h)a(t) & \text{if } \alpha(t) > b_1(t) \\ \alpha(t+1) = (1 + \epsilon^t \lambda_e)a(t) & \text{if } b_1(t) \geq \alpha(t) \geq b_2(t) \\ \alpha(t+1) = (1 + \epsilon^t \lambda_l)\alpha(t) & \text{if } b_2(t) > \alpha(t) \end{cases}$$

where $\epsilon \in (0, 1]$ and $\lambda_h, \lambda_e, \lambda_l \in [0, 1]$. ϵ is a decay factor w.r.t. time, allowing the reserve price to converge if needed. λ_h controls the cooling speed when the reserve price is too high; λ_e controls the continued exploration when the reserve price is successfully; λ_l controls the heating up speed when the reserve price is too low.

Note the values of these parameters depend on targeting combinations (placements, date and time, geography, etc.). They need to be tuned to achieve the best result. For example, in experiments we found an effective setting of these parameters as $\epsilon = 1.0$, $\lambda_h = 0.3$, $\lambda_e = 0.01$, and $\lambda_l = 0.02$ for placement 834119 and hour-of-day=8. We obtain these parameters using the training dataset (impression-level logs from 14 Dec 2012 to 18 Jan 2013). This algorithm is denoted as ONESHOT in the experiments.

3.3 Other Private Value Based Algorithms

Although not optimal in theory, there are other algorithms which make use of private value distributions in practice. Here we propose two simple methods, which are based on Bayes' rules. An advantage of such algorithms is they could be easily tuned to be more aggressive or less according to the greediness (or risk preference) of the publisher. A disadvantage is that it does not take the future into account, so only the current payoff is maximized.

3.3.1 *Bivariate Log-normal Distribution*

To make the algorithm easier to understand we keep the Log-normal distribution assumption of private values. First we capture the first and second highest bids using a bivariate Log-normal distribution:

$$\begin{bmatrix} B_1 \\ B_2 \end{bmatrix} \sim \text{lognorm}(\boldsymbol{\mu}, \boldsymbol{\Sigma}) \tag{7}$$

where $\boldsymbol{\mu}$ and $\boldsymbol{\Sigma}$ stand for mean and variance respectively. For simplicity we consider $\boldsymbol{\Sigma}$ known and use a bivariate Gaussian distribution as the conjugate prior for $\boldsymbol{\mu}$:

$$\boldsymbol{\mu}(t) \sim \mathcal{N}(\boldsymbol{\theta}(t), \boldsymbol{\Delta}(t))$$

The priori could be learned using historical data. In our experiment, impression-level logs from 14 Dec 2012 to 18 Jan 2013 were used. During evaluation, each time the publisher observes the highest and 2nd highest bids in an auction, then updates the belief using Bayesian inference [30]:

$$\begin{bmatrix} B_1 \\ B_2 \end{bmatrix} |\boldsymbol{b}(t) \sim \text{lognorm}(\boldsymbol{\theta}(t+1), \boldsymbol{\Delta}(t+1) + \boldsymbol{\Sigma})$$

where

$$\boldsymbol{\theta}(t+1) = (\boldsymbol{\Delta}^{-1}(t) + \boldsymbol{\Sigma}^{-1})^{-1}(\boldsymbol{\Delta}^{-1}(t)\boldsymbol{\theta}(t) + \boldsymbol{\Sigma}\boldsymbol{b}(t))$$
$$\boldsymbol{\Delta}(t+1) = (\boldsymbol{\Delta}^{-1}(t) + \boldsymbol{\Sigma}^{-1})^{-1}$$

Then with $p(B_1, B_2)$ estimated at current time t, we can solve for a reserve price which has the maximum probability of sitting between the two bids:

$$\alpha(t)^* = \arg\max_{\alpha(t)} P(B_1 \geq \alpha(t) \geq \lambda B_2) \tag{8}$$

where $\alpha(t)^*$ is the current reserve price and $\frac{B_1}{B_2} \geq \lambda \geq 1$ is the risk preference parameter. It pushes the result closer to the winning bids. In experiments we set $\lambda = 1$ to mimic a risk-averse choice. The maximum could be achieved by letting the first derivative equal zero. We use a numerical solution and approximate the result in algorithm's implementation using the Broyden-Fletcher-Goldfarb-Shanno (BFGS) method, the most popular one in Quasi-Newton methods class. The BFGS method uses the first derivative and has proven good performance for smooth optimizations [5] and. We refer to this algorithm as BAYESIANB in experiments.

3.3.2 Univariate Log-normal Distribution

The most greedy choice from Equation 8 is to let $\lambda = \frac{B_1}{B_2}$: regardless of the second highest bidder, the publisher could always learn and approach the highest bid directly. It is equivalent to modelling the winning bids using a univariate Log-normal distribution, which has a simpler solution

$$B_1 \sim \text{lognorm}(\mu, \sigma^2)$$
$$\mu(t) \sim \mathcal{N}(\theta(t), \delta^2(t))$$

and still we assume that σ^2 is known. Every time we observe the highest bid b_1 we obtain

$$\theta(t+1) = \frac{\theta(t)\delta^2(t) + \sigma^2 b_1}{\sigma^2 + \delta^2(t)}$$
$$\delta^2(t+1) = \frac{\delta^2(t)\sigma^2}{\sigma^2 + \delta^2(t)}$$

where the priori was obtained using the training dataset.

Then the publisher simply chooses

$$a(t+1) = \log(\theta(t+1)) + \beta(\sigma^2 + \delta^2(t+1)) \quad (9)$$

as the new reserve price where β is the risk preference for this model which could be either positive or negative. In experiment we set $\beta = 0$ for simplicity.

We refer to this algorithm as BAYESIANU. Again, the fitting of private value distribution is beyond the scope of this paper but the ideas and algorithms always hold, allowing different models being implemented easily (it is highly likely that different models would be used for different placements, hour-of-day, and etc.).

3.4 Private Value Free Algorithms

There are algorithms based on common knowledge or intuition and do not require the assumption that each advertiser has their own private fixed valuation about the impression at hand. In fact, they play a major role in reserve price set up in real-world. Among those choices, we present two simple methods as our baselines.

The most basic one is the FIXED algorithm which sets a static reserve price for all time steps, regardless of outcome of auctions. Formally it is $\alpha(t) \equiv a$ where a denotes the pre-chosen fixed reserve price.

When $\alpha = 0$ it becomes ZERO which totally relies on the auction mechanism, in our case the second price auction, assuming that quality score (or similar factors like bid bias) is absent. It is apparently the most altruistic one in our strategy space which does not try to gain any extra benefit and could be used as a baseline to measure bidders' attrition.

The FIXED (including ZERO) is the most straightforward and easy to implement. Besides, it directly reflects the publisher's private valuation of the inventory. Before adopting the automated selling, publishers are used to negotiating contracts with advertisers or their representatives. The contract price could be easily converted to a reserve price. Also, due to simplicity this is probably the most widely adopted algorithm in today's ad marketplaces. In experiments, we consider FIXED and ZERO the most naive baselines. We show that, under certain circumstances, although simple, they performed surprisingly well.

Another family of private-value-free algorithms is based on historical payoff of auctions. For example, the AVERAGE sets the reserve price to the average of past payoff. Formally it is

$$\alpha(t) = \frac{1}{M} \sum_{i=t-M}^{t-1} r(i) \quad (10)$$

where $r(t)$ is the payoff at time step t and M is the averaging window.

A natural extension is the weighted average variation, which values more of recent payoff. Formally it is

$$\alpha(t) = \frac{1}{M} \sum_{i=t-M}^{t-1} w(i,t) r(i) \quad (11)$$

where $w(\cdot)$ is the weighting function, which could take various forms. In our experiments we used linear weights and denoted it as WEIGHTEDL.

AVERAGE and WEIGHTEDL share the similar insights with FIXED, except recognizing the fluctuation of demand and supply in the market. This fluctuation could greatly affect the reserve price setting especially at hour-of-day level. It is discussed in details in Section 4.1.

4. AN EMPIRICAL STUDY

Understanding the bidder behaviour in RTB auctions is crucial to the reserve price problem. In this section we first report our findings from an empirical study of bidders' behaviours in RTB auctions, focusing on the daily bidding pattern, the bidders' lifetime, the change of bidders and winners, and bids' distribution. Based on real-world statistics, we discuss their impact on setting reserve prices. Then we report a large scale online experiment in the same production platform to test various algorithms proposed before.

4.1 Live Experiment Setups and Dataset

First we highlight the dataset used for this empirical study:

- The dataset is obtained from a production platform in UK;
- The dataset contains 13,478,591 impressions from Dec 2012 to Feb 2013;
- These impressions are sampled from 39 placements belonging to 16 websites of different categories (e.g., finance, sports, pc & console games, news, technology & gadgets).

On average, these websites receive 1.8m impressions daily. We roughly sampled one impression every 10 seconds to construct the dataset due to the limit of computing power and storage. For each auction we have logged the following information: the venue (URL, position and size of the placement, above or below fold), date and time, demographics of visitor (geographical location, IP, browser agent, language, and segments if available), bidding activities, and current reserve price.

Parameters of tested algorithms were obtained during the training stage (14 Dec 2012 to 18 Jan 2013) then they were evaluated during the testing stage (19 Jan to 21 Feb 2013) in the live system. There were 6 placements having few bidders (less than 5) or small traffic (less than 10k impressions per day). They were dropped from the online experiment but were compared with in bidders' attrition analysis.

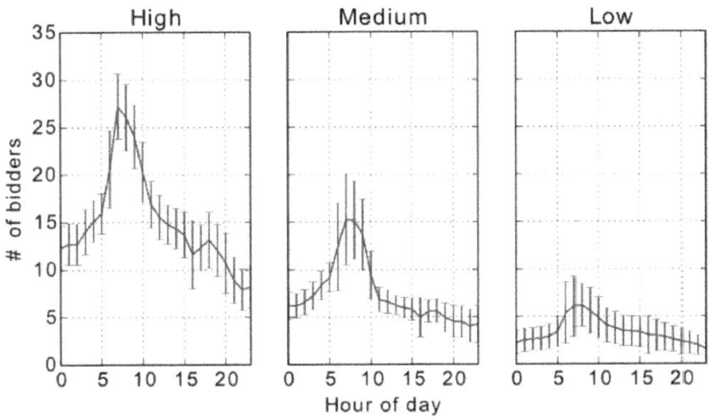

Figure 4: The average number of bidders varies across hour-of-day and placements. The error bars show standard deviation. A clear pattern emerges that for all placements the number of bidders peaks at 8-10am.

Besides, we selected 8 placements as the control group to which the optimisation had never been applied. Although we evaluated the ZERO in the experiment, having a zero reserve price at some hours is not equivalent to no optimisation at all. Having the control group makes it easier and more accurate to understand the buyers' reaction or attrition. Offline evaluation had been performed on these placements too (not reported here due to space limit).

4.2 Bidders' Behaviours

Statistically speaking, the more bidders, the higher winning bids would be. Thus, the competition level (the demand) is the first important factor we use to group the placements. In Figure 4 we illustrated the number of bidders varies across a day on different placements. By using the basic mean, std, max, and min statistics we divided placements into groups:

- Group High, 10 to 30 bidders, 6 placements;
- Group Medium, 5 to 20 bidders, 16 placements;
- Group Low, 2 to 10 bidders, 11 placements;
- Dropped, 1 to 5 bidders, 6 placements.

The experiment results confirm that for different competition levels the same policy would perform differently. Another finding is that almost on all placements the number of bidders peaks at 8-10am. With low level of competition it is still noticeable (c.f Figure 4, right). This is hard to justify from the publishers' perspective; however, we assume this is due to daily budget settings of campaigns and hour-of-day targeting.

Note that the number of bidders does not always align with the number of impressions across hour of day. It is commonly known that the number of impressions peaks at evening hours (6-11pm) as reported in [34]. Having more bidders at the morning hours (8-10am) when there are less impressions results in even higher winning bids. It implies the possibility of optimisation from both demand and supply side. In this paper, we argue it is necessary to perform at least hourly optimisation and report the results later.

Another observation is on the lifetime of bidders, sometimes referred to as the *flight time* of campaigns. There are 755 bidders (Note again that we consider each campaign a bidder) in total in the dataset. As illustrated in Figure 5 we can see two clear patterns: "learners" and "4-week campaigns", as well as a less clear pattern "6-week campaigns". This plot of lifetime is a reflection of how online advertising work: most of the campaigns are relative short, limited to

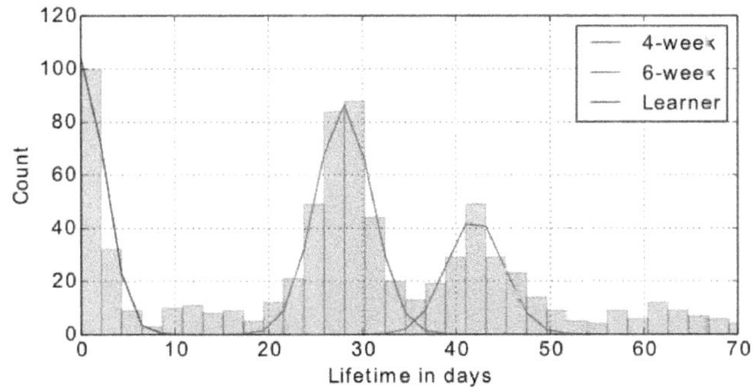

Figure 5: The histogram of 755 bidders' lifetime across all placements. *We consider each campaign a bidder.* From the figure we observe three patterns: two created by common flight-time of campaigns (4 weeks and 6 weeks) and one created by exploration of learning algorithms (0-2 days). Due to limited time of data collection there are some instances lying between 0-25 days because these bidders started their activities before the start date of our experiments.

4 weeks or 6 weeks by advertisers. Meanwhile, we observed spikes around days 0-3 that indicates the activities of *learners*: advertisers spend budget on a placement to learn its performance against a specific campaign, which is essential in demand-side optimisation.

The pattern between days 6-20 is less clear due to the limited time span of data collection. There were good quantity of campaigns already running at the beginning of the collection, and they ended randomly several days later. This could be due to the *holiday effect*, too (the data collection started on 14 Dec 2012). It is hard to identify and remove these campaigns from the dataset; however, they do not affect the result of auctions with reserve prices, and would become less significant when more data is available. The figure was created by aggregating logs across all placements. Although not reported, placements with different levels of competition showed the similar pattern; when aggregated they become easier to identify.

The impact of bidders' lifetime on reserve price algorithms is mostly indirect. However, since the optimal auction theory models auctions as iterated and dynamic games, it is preferable that bidders keep bidding for a while so that both players could learn and act properly. On the other hand, the publisher might want to set different reserve prices with respect to ages of bidders (or at least winners), esp. when lots of learners are present. We leave this discussion to the future work.

Another factor that would affect reserve prices is the change of winners of auctions, as illustrated in Figure 6. The instances of such change are in fact not negligible. Combining with the bidders' lifetime plot, a significant impact emerges. Since the winner of auctions on the same placement is constantly changing, it is difficult for buyers to detect if a reserve price is place, esp. when the reserve price is changing, too. This in turn favours publishers in the repeated and dynamic game setting, since advertisers may have only incomplete information set.

4.3 Bids' Distribution Test

An important assumption made by optimal auction theory is that bidders draw their private values from a monotonically increasing distribution. In second price auction they bid on their private values; thus the distribution of bids

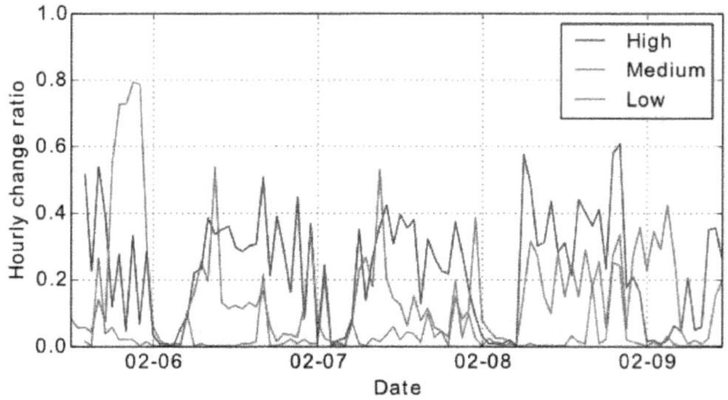

Figure 6: The change of winners for placements with different levels of competition in 4 days. The fact that a bidder does not always win could add difficulty to reserve price detection if undisclosed. The result also implies the change rate does not necessary relate to the competition level.

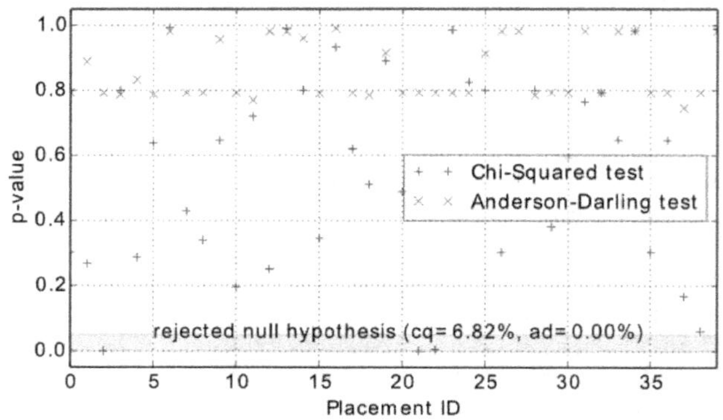

Figure 7: Only bids from 3 out of 44 placements (6.82%) accept the Uniform distribution hypothesis. The Uniform distribution is tested by Chi-Squared test and the Log-normal distribution is tested by Anderson-Darling test.

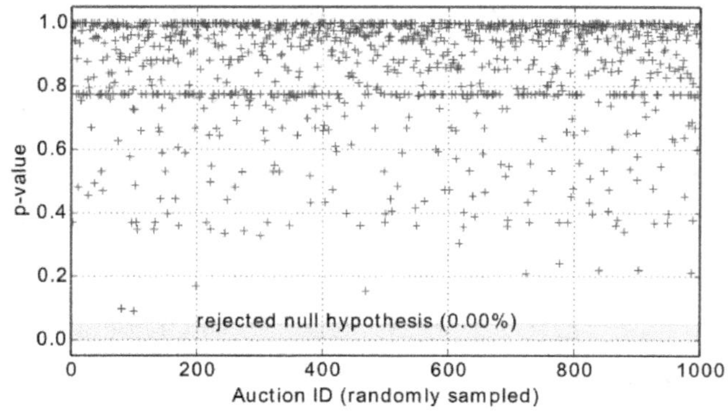

Figure 8: Only bids from less than 0.1% of all auctions accept the Log-normal distribution hypothesis. The plot shows a randomly sampled of 1000 auctions. Only the Log-normal distribution is tested by Anderson-Darling test.

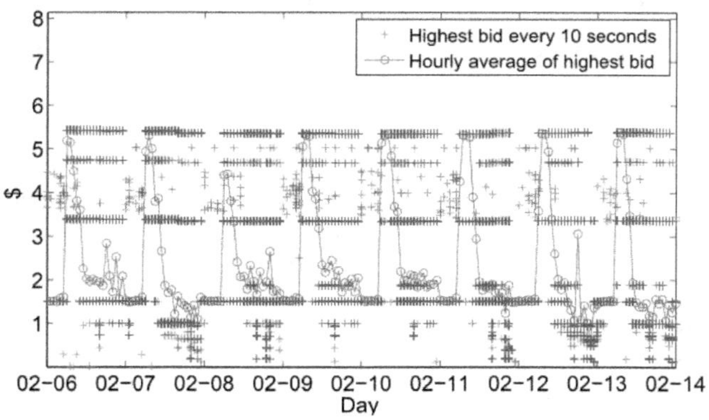

Figure 9: The plot of hourly average winning bids and bursting instances on a placement of high level of competition. Due to these bursts the model-based algorithms fitted poorly and did not perform well.

reflects their individual valuations of an impression. As introduced in Section 2 researchers often assume bidders are symmetric, and bids follow Log-normal distribution or Uniform distribution. This assumption then becomes the core of optimal auction theory based algorithms of computing reserve prices [24, 26, 31].

In our empirical study, bids are fitted to these two distributions. For the Log-normal distribution we check their normality using Anderson-Darling test [1] after taking the logarithm. We do this test at both auction level and placement level. For the Uniform distribution we use the Chi-squared test [17] only at the placement level. We use p-value< 0.05 to reject the null hypothesis.

The results are reported in Figure 8 and 7. Clearly only the acceptance of Uniform distribution assumption at placement level is noticeable yet still at a low ratio of 6.82%. The poor results are probably due to the bursts and randomness of bids as illustrated in Figure 9. However, to be consistent with the research literature, we still adopt the Log-normal assumption when implementing the optimal auction theory based algorithm in the experiment. The undesirable fitting could be the main reason that the OptAuc does not perform the best.

4.4 Live Test Results and Discussions

We carried out the online experiment in the same production platform. The experiment includes 25 placements as the treatment group and additional 8 as the control group. For each placement we have collected RTB auction logs which record bidders and their bids in every auction. The live experiments lasted from 19 Jan to 21 Feb 2013. The parameters of algorithms were trained using logs from 14 Dec 2012 to 18 Jan 2013.

4.4.1 Algorithms and Scheduling

The following algorithms and configurations were evaluated.

- Game, with publisher value set to \$1.0;
- Zero, with a fixed reserve price set to \$0.0;
- Average;
- WeightedL, with a looking back window size of 5;
- OneShot, with $\epsilon = 1$ and λ_h, λ_m, and λ_l learned individually for each placement;
- BayesianB, with $\boldsymbol{\theta}$, $\boldsymbol{\Sigma}$, and $\boldsymbol{\Delta}$ learned individually for each placement;
- BayesianU, with θ, σ, and δ learned individually for each placement.

Note that the private value of \$1.0 of the publisher was chosen based on the publisher's suggestion.

We evaluated algorithms as the following: impression-level logs were constantly sampled then fed to algorithms. We ran the experiment for 30 days. The experiment used a Round Robin scheduler at the hour level. For example, at Hour=1 and Day=1 we used Algorithm=OptAuc on Placement=1, Algorithm=Zero on Placement=2, etc.; on Hour=2 and Day=1 we used Algorithm=BayesianU on

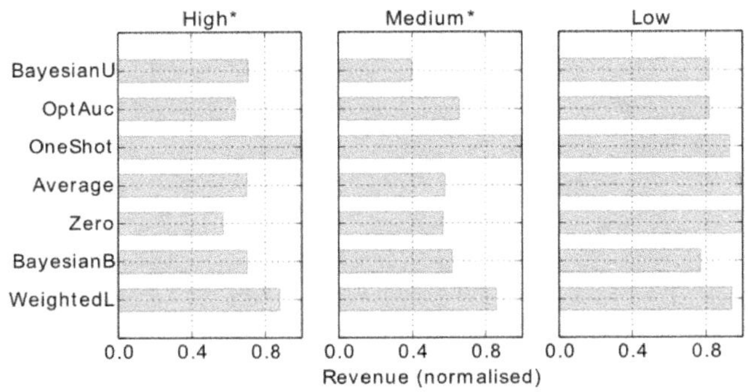

Figure 10: A snapshot of main results of the online experiment, on all placements, from 6am to 10am across all days. The * indicates the OneShot performed significantly better than others (except the WeightedL) using Wilcoxon signed-rank test. Considering the percentage of placements of high, medium, low level of competition, the OneShot performed significantly better in about 70% cases. On placements having fewer bidders it is hard to distinguish the results. Although not reported, at other hours the results are similar.

Placement=1, Algorithm=OPTAUC on Placement=2, etc. With this scheduling method the day-of-week factor does not influence the evaluation of performance of algorithms. In this way for every (hour-of-day, algorithm, level of competition) tuple we obtained 10 sets of observations. We split the results into 6 non-overlapping chunks and performed Wilcoxon signed-rank test [9] to check significance.

4.4.2 *Results*

We report the performance of algorithms with respect to levels of competition in Figure 10, where we find the private-value-free algorithms performed better than private-value-based ones. Note that the figure only includes data from 6-10am across all days but for other hours the results are similar. Considering the percentage of placements of high, medium, low level of competition, the ONESHOT performed significantly better in about 70% cases. This is very consistent with the findings made in [26].

Looking at the results and various analysis made before, we believe the undesirable fitting of Log-normal distribution led to the poor performance of private-value-based algorithms on placements with many bidders. Although there is a steady hourly average winning bids pattern on these placements, there are also lots of short periods of burst (both upward and downward) around the curve as shown in Figure 9, which could have dragged the models away from the curve easily. On the contrary the private-value-free algorithms had better chance of capturing these bursts.

The ONESHOT shares the same intuition as the WEIGHTEDL: using the observations of recent future to infer the reserve price. More specifically, we replayed the auction logs in training dataset against various parameter sets and adopted the best performing one.

4.5 Bidders' Attrition

As we argued before, a key difference of reserve price optimisation in RTB is that the inventory is not as limited as ordinary auctions or sponsored search. Thus, it is also interesting to study whether the reserve price optimisation could result in bidders' attrition [25] in long term (e.g., reduce their bid values or volume). Figure 11 compares winning bids and number of bidders before and after the reserve price optimisation experiment. It suggests that it may not

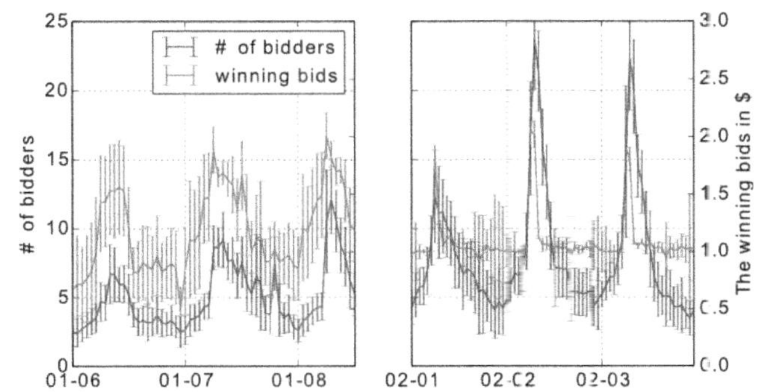

Figure 11: The comparison of winning bids and number of bidders before and after the experiment. Both factors increased after the experiment, which contradicts the attrition hypothesis that bidders would reduce their bid or volume after reserve price optimisation.

Table 2: The change of number of bidders after the experiment. On most of placements, especially ones with high level of competition, the increment is observed.

	$\leq$ -10%	-5% $\sim$ -10%	5% $\sim$ 10%	$\geq$ 10%
High	3	0	0	3
Medium	4	2	4	6
Low	3	0	0	8
Control	1	0	0	5

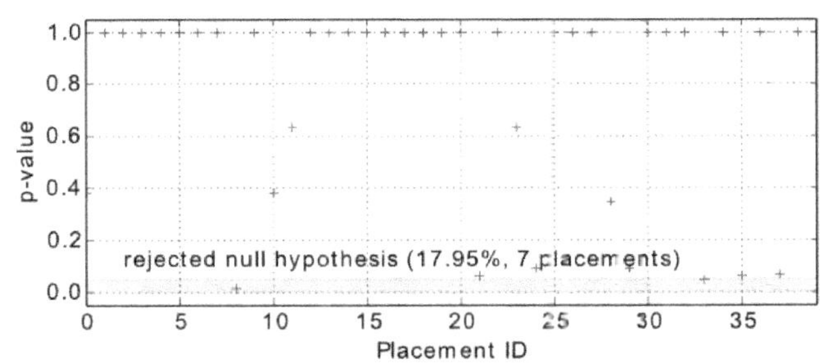

Figure 12: Bidders' attrition test after the optimisation, comparing with the number of bidders before the experiment. The t-test suggests the attrition is significant on 7 placements. 3 are placement of low level of competition and 4 of medium level. However, it is also worth noting that many more placements see an increment of number of buyers after the experiment, c.f. Table 2.

be the case in RTB. To test the statistical significance of the change, we take the mean and standard deviation of number of bidders for each placement before (12-18 Jan 2013) and after (15-21 Feb 2013) the optimisation experiment. The null hypothesis of the buyers' attrition could be denoted as H_0: $\mu_1 - \mu_2 > 0$ where $N_1(\mu_1, \sigma_1)$ and $N_2(\mu_2, \sigma_2)$ are the Normal distribution fitted from number of bidders before and after the experiment respectively. The rejection of this null hypothesis implies no significance of bidders' attrition.

The result of t-test with p-value 0.05 is summarised in Figure 12. There are only 7 placements out of 39 showed significant drop of number of bidders after the experiment. 3 of them are placements of low level of competition and 4 of medium level, where a slight change of would be significant. Interestingly, from Table 2 we see an opposite pattern emerges: the publisher was actually seeing more bidders on most of placements. This could be due to three reasons: 1) during holidays (the beginning of the experiment) there are generally less bidders because of reduced amount of Internet traffic; 2) bidders are not aware of the reserve price optimisation so no reaction is taken; 3) the campaigns' lifetime introduces fluctuation.

5. CONCLUSIONS

In this paper, we discussed a specific problem for publisher revenue optimisation in Real-Time Bidding: to find the optimal placement level reserve price for single-item display ad auctions. It is a problem of significant importance, which has been studied extensively in the game theory, but is relatively new in online advertising research literature, especially in RTB which has many unique features. In the paper we analysed drawbacks of the optimal auction theory in the RTB practice, derived dominant strategies from simplified version of the auction game, and compared it with other commonly adopted algorithms in a production platform. We also discussed the challenges of optimising reserve prices in RTB and analysed bidders' attrition in the experiment. Due to the complexity of the problem and practical constraints there are unsolved issues in this paper, including the fitting of bids, parameters tuning, and more comprehensive attrition analysis. We would like to address these in the future work.

6. REFERENCES

[1] Anderson, T. W., and Darling, D. A. A Test of Goodness of Fit. *Journal of the American Statistical Association 49* (1954), 765–769.

[2] Ausubel, L. M., and Cramton, P. Vickrey auctions with reserve pricing, 2004.

[3] Bapna, R., Goes, P., Gupta, A., and Others. Insights and analyses of online auctions. *Communications of the ACM 44*, 11 (2001), 42–50.

[4] Bharadwaj, V., Ma, W., Schwarz, M., Shanmugasundaram, J., Vee, E., Xie, J., and Yang, J. Pricing guaranteed contracts in online display advertising. In *Proceedings of the ACM CIKM* (2010).

[5] Bonnans, J. F., Gilbert, J. C., Lemaréchal, C., and Sagastizábal, C. A. *Numerical optimization: theoretical and practical aspects*. Springer, 2006.

[6] Broder, A., Fontoura, M., Josifovski, V., and Riedel, L. A semantic approach to contextual advertising. In *Proceedings of the ACM SIGIR* (2007).

[7] Cavallo, R., McAfee, R. P., and Vassilvitskii, S. Display Advertising Auctions with Arbitrage. 1–21.

[8] Chakraborty, T., Even-Dar, E., Guha, S., Mansour, Y., and Muthukrishnan, S. Selective call out and real time bidding. *Internet and Network Economics* (2010), 145–157.

[9] Crichton, N. Wilcoxon signed rank test. *Journal of Clinical Nursing, Blackwell Science Ltd* (2000).

[10] Edelman, B., Ostrovsky, M., and Schwarz, M. Internet advertising and the generalized second price auction: Selling billions of dollars worth of keywords. Tech. rep., National Bureau of Economic Research, 2005.

[11] Edelman, B., and Schwarz, M. Optimal auction design in a multi-unit environment: The case of sponsored search auctions. *Unpublished manuscript, Harvard Business School* (2006).

[12] eMarketer. RTB Ad Spend Continues Robust Growth - eMarketer.

[13] Even-Dar, E., Feldman, J., Mansour, Y., and Muthukrishnan, S. Position auctions with bidder-specific minimum prices. *Internet and Network Economics* (2008), 577–584.

[14] Feldman, J., Mirrokni, V., Muthukrishnan, S., and Pai, M. M. Auctions with intermediaries: extended abstract. In *Proceedings of the ACM EC 2010* (2010).

[15] Ghosh, A., McAfee, P., Papineni, K., and Vassilvitskii, S. Bidding for representative allocations for display advertising. *Internet and Network Economics* (2009), 208–219.

[16] Ghosh, A., Rubinstein, B. I. P., Vassilvitskii, S., and Zinkevich, M. Adaptive bidding for display advertising. In *Proceedings of the WWW 2009* (2009).

[17] Greenwood, P. E., and Nikulin, M. S. *A guide to chi-squared testing*, vol. 280. Wiley-Interscience, 1996.

[18] Kauffman, R. J., and Wood, C. A. Running up the bid: detecting, predicting, and preventing reserve price shilling in online auctions. In *Proceedings of the ACM EC 2003* (2003).

[19] Krishna, V. *Auction theory*. Academic press, 2009.

[20] Levin, D., and Smith, J. L. Optimal reservation prices in auctions. *The Economic Journal 106*, 438 (1996), 1271–1283.

[21] Matthews, S. *A technical primer on auction theory I: Independent private values*. No. 1096. 1995.

[22] McAfee, R. P., and Vincent, D. Sequentially optimal auctions. *Games and Economic Behavior 18*, 2 (1997), 246–276.

[23] Muthukrishnan, S. Ad exchanges: Research issues. *Internet and network economics 8*, 2 (2009), 1–12.

[24] Myerson, R. B. Optimal auction design. *Mathematics of operations research 6*, 1 (1981), 58–73.

[25] Osborne, M. *A Course in Game Theory*. 2011.

[26] Ostrovsky, M., and Schwarz, M. Reserve prices in internet advertising auctions: A field experiment. *Search* (2009), 1–18.

[27] Perlich, C., Dalessandro, B., Hook, R., Stitelman, O., Raeder, T., and Provost, F. Bid optimizing and inventory scoring in targeted online advertising. In *Proceedings of the ACM SIGKDD 2012* (2012), p. 804.

[28] Riley, J. G., and Samuelson, W. F. Optimal auctions. *The American Economic Review* (1981), 381–392.

[29] Roels, G., and Fridgeirsdottir, K. Dynamic revenue management for online display advertising. *Journal of Revenue & Pricing Management 8*, 5 (May 2009), 452–466.

[30] Stein, C. M. Estimation of the mean of a multivariate normal distribution. *The annals of Statistics* (1981), 1135–1151.

[31] Xiao, B., Yang, W., and Li, J. Optimal Reserve Price for the Generalized Second-Price Auction in Sponsored Search Advertising. *Journal of Electronic Commerce Research 10*, 3 (2009), 114.

[32] Xu, H., Bates, C. K., and Shatz, S. M. Real-time model checking for shill detection in live online auctions. In *Proc. Int. Conf. Software Engineering Research and Practice (SERP'09)* (2009), pp. 134–140.

[33] Yan, J., Liu, N., Wang, G., and Zhang, W. How much can behavioral targeting help online advertising? *Proceeding WWW '09 Proceedings of the 18th international conference on World wide web* (2009), 261–270.

[34] Yuan, S., Wang, J., and Zhao, X. Real-time Bidding for Online Advertising: Measurement and Analysis. In *Proceedings of the ADKDD workshop 2013* (2013).

Large-Scale High-Precision Topic Modeling on Twitter

Shuang Yang
Twitter, Inc.
syang@twitter.com

Alek Kolcz
Twitter, Inc.
ark@twitter.com

Andy Schlaikjer
Twitter, Inc.
hazen@twitter.com

Pankaj Gupta
Twitter, Inc.
pankaj@twitter.com

ABSTRACT

We are interested in organizing a continuous stream of sparse and noisy texts, known as "tweets", in real time into an ontology of hundreds of topics with *measurable* and *stringently high* precision. This inference is performed over a full-scale stream of Twitter data, whose statistical distribution evolves rapidly over time. The implementation in an industrial setting with the potential of affecting and being visible to real users made it necessary to overcome a host of practical challenges. We present a spectrum of topic modeling techniques that contribute to a deployed system. These include non-topical tweet detection, automatic labeled data acquisition, evaluation with human computation, diagnostic and corrective learning and, most importantly, high-precision topic inference. The latter represents a novel two-stage training algorithm for tweet text classification and a close-loop inference mechanism for combining texts with additional sources of information. The resulting system achieves 93% precision at substantial overall coverage.

Categories and Subject Descriptors
I.2.6 [Artificial Intelligence]: *Learning*

1. INTRODUCTION

Twitter [1] is a global, public, distributed and real-time social and information network in which users post short messages called "*tweets*". Users on Twitter *follow* other users to form a network such that a user receives all the tweets posted by the users he follows. Tweets are restricted to contain no more than 140 characters of text, including any links. This constraint fosters immense creativity leading to many diverse types of styles and information carried in the tweets. As of early 2014, Twitter has more than 240 million monthly active users all over the world. These users send more than 500 million tweets every day, which corresponds to an average of 5700 tweets per second, with spikes at up to 25 times of that velocity during special events [2].

KDD'14, August 24–27, 2014, New York, NY, USA.
Copyright 2014 ACM 978-1-4503-2956-9/14/08 ...$15.00.
http://dx.doi.org/10.1145/2623330.2623336 .

Tweets generated from all over the world are expected to be about a variety of topics. Figuring out exactly which tweet is about which topic(s) is interesting to us at Twitter in our goal to serve our users better as it enables personalization, discovery, targeted recommendations, organization of content, as well as aiding in studies and analyses to gain better insights into our platform as a whole. Such broad usefulness, and the potential of affecting and being visible to real users, however, propose demanding precision requirement. In this paper, we consider the problem of high-precision topic modeling of tweets in real-time as they are flowing through the network. This task raises a set of unique challenges given Twitter's scale and the short, noisy and ambiguous nature of tweets. We present how we address these challenges via a unique collection of techniques that we have employed in order to build a real-time high-precision tweet topic modeling system that is currently deployed in production inside Twitter. Our system achieves 93% precision on ~300 topics and 37% overall coverage on English tweets.

2. OVERVIEW & RELATED WORK

Given a tweet, and all the information associated with it (e.g., author, entities, URLs, engagements, context), we are interested in figuring out what topic(s) this tweet is about.

Topic modeling tasks have been commonly approached with unsupervised clustering algorithms (e.g., k-means, pLSI and LDA [5]), information filtering approaches (e.g., language models [19]), or weakly supervised models (e.g., supervised LDA [5], labeled LDA [22]). These approaches are effective in grouping documents into a predefined number of *coarse clusters* based on inter-document similarity or the co-occurrence patterns of terms (with help from very mild supervision). They are also cheap to train as no or very few labeled data is required. Nevertheless, they are not suitable for our use because it is very difficult to align the topic clusters produced by these approaches to a predefined ontology and perform low-latency topic inference with measurable and decent precision. In fact, *none* of these approaches could attain the precision close to what we demand.

Instead, we primarily consider supervised approaches that classifying tweets into our taxonomy with controllable high-precision. Figure 1 illustrates the overview of our system. On the training path, our "training data collector" constantly listens to the tweet stream to automatically acquire labeled training data, which, once accumulated to a certain amount, are fed into the "trainer" module to produce classification models; These models are then validated and calibrated to be used in our service. On the operation path, the classifier

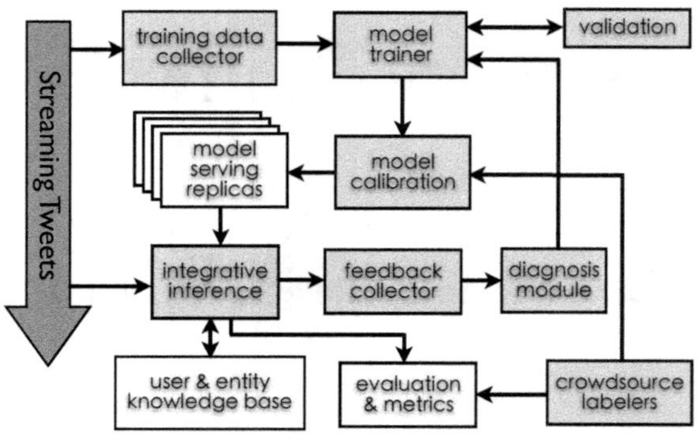

Figure 1: Overview of tweet topic inference system.

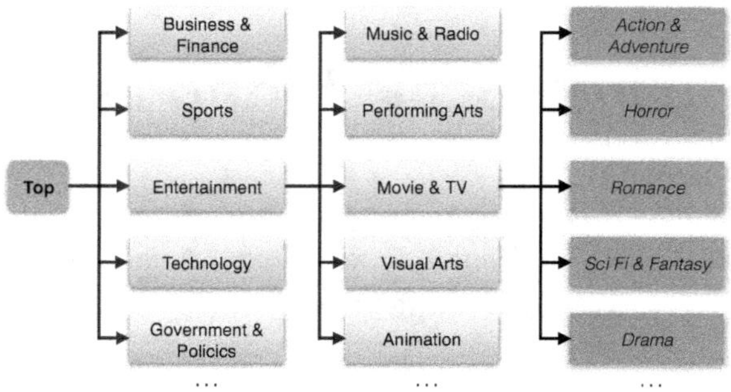

Figure 2: A subtree of our taxonomy. The deepest node is 6 hops way from the root node "Top".

models are replicated and served in parallel, together with knowledge about users and entities, in a "integrative inference" module to provide high-precision topic annotation of tweets in real time. The inference results are used to generate and refine the user-and-entity knowledge, making this a close-loop inference. The results are also scribed and used to evaluate and monitor the quality performance with help from crowd-sourced human annotation. Once the service is exposed to the user, we also employ a "feedback collector" and a "diagnosis module" to gather high-precision user curated data, which are fed back into the trainer module to fine-tune the trained models.

Related Works & Contributions. Topic modeling of tweets has been examined extensively in the literature. Most existing research has been based on un- or weekly supervised techniques such as variations of LDA [17, 27]. The inference in these approaches usually takes considerable latency, and the results are not directly controllable when precision is concerned. Recent studies employ information filtering approaches to detect tweets on specific topics of interests[19, 9]. These approaches usually have low latency and can perform inference in real-time; and when configured properly, the top-ranked results obtained by them can usually achieve a reasonable precision target. Nonetheless, because they identify only a small fraction of tweets that are *apparently relevant* to a given topic while disregarding the majority rest, the recall and coverage of these approaches are very poor, yielding heavily biased inference results that are less useful in many of our use cases. Information filtering approaches are also *only* good at specific topics, usually topics of relatively focused meanings (e.g., "San Francisco" and "NBA"), and *not* directly applicable to a broad spectrum of topics such as an ontology, as what we study here. To the best of our knowledge, this is the first published documentation of a deployed topic modeling system that infers topics of short noisy texts at high precision in real-time.

3. TAXONOMY CONSTRUCTION

We create a taxonomy represented as a fixed (and potentially deep) ontology to encode the structure and knowledge about the topics of our interest. The goal is to find a topic structure that is as complete as possible to cover as many semantic concepts (and their relationships) as we can, while focusing on topics that are frequently discussed on Twitter and are less likely to be transient. Starting from existing taxonomies such as ODP and Freebase, we undertook a number of exploratory approaches and manual curations. For example, by building topic filters based on ontology corpora (e.g., ODP, Wikipedia), we can estimate coverage of topics on Twitter and trim or merge topics that are too niche; unsupervised models such as LDA were also used to map clusters to well defined ontology (e.g., ODP, Freebase) in order to estimate coverage. This process has been iterated through multiple refinements and over different time periods to avoid bias. The current taxonomy consists of ~300 topics with a maximum of 6 levels, a fragment of which is shown in Figure 2.

4. TWEET TOPIC MODELING: TEXT CLASSIFICATION

A tweet can be associated with multiple modalities of information such as text, named entities, users (the author and people who engaged with the tweet), etc. In this section, we consider topic classification of tweets based solely on its textual features, which will be combined with other sources of information for integrative topic inference in Section 5.

High-precision tweet classification faces unique challenges because unlike ordinary documents, tweets are much sparser and noisier and the scale is daunting. The demanding precision criteria make this even more challenging. A tweet may belong to multiple topical categories at the same time, or be non-topical, which makes this a multi-label classification problem. To meet quality criteria, the participating classifier needs to be abstaining, i.e., providing topic labels only if the expected precision or confidence is sufficiently high.

4.1 Chatter detection

One key challenge for high-precision tweet classification is that a substantial proportion of tweets are non-topical [3], or at least their topics are not clear in the context of a single tweet. We use the term *chatter* to denote tweets that often primarily carry emotions, feelings or are otherwise related to personal status updates. While they are clearly an important part of user expression on Twitter, it is necessary to reject classifying these tweets (e.g., to save system latency and to control quality) and restrict the domain of interest to tweets that are *not* chatter. To that end, we build content filters to eliminate chatter tweets, as described in previous work [3].

4.2 Training data acquisition

Training high-quality tweet classification requires high-quality labeled data. Use of human annotation is prohibitive for a number of reasons. First, it is too expensive: for the scale we consider (i.e., 300 topics, millions of features) and the sparseness (i.e., only ~10s feature presence per tweet), any reliable estimation would require hundreds of millions of labeled tweets and cost millions of dollars even with the cheapest crowd-sourced service in the market. Moreover, even human-assigned labels could be too noisy. A big taxonomy like ours presents considerable *cognitive overload* to human annotators, for example, when asked to assign relevant topic labels (out of the 300 candidates) to each tweet, human raters turn to identify only a fraction of the true positive labels. While it is possible to obtain samples of data within each category, such samples are likely to be biased and to the extent that some of these instances also belong to other categories, most of these memberships will remain unknown. Human labeled data are also subject to expertise bias because a lot of niche topics (e.g., "data mining") exceed the literacy of crowd-source workers, forcing them to respond with random-guess annotations. Because of these concerns, in our system, human labeled data (with enhanced quality assurance) are only used in quality evaluation (Section 4.7). For model training, we devise scalable algorithms to collect labeled data automatically from unlabeled tweets.

The labeled data acquisition pipeline is illustrated as Figure 3. First, tweets are streamed through a set of *topic priors* to prefilter tweets that are weakly relevant to each topic. These topic priors are white-list rules that include:

User-level priors: users who tweet predominantly about a single topic (e.g., @ESPN about "Sports").

Entity-level priors: unambiguous named entities and hashtags that are highly concentrated to one or a few topics (e.g., #NBA about "Basketball"), see Section 5.2.

URL-level priors: for tweets containing URLs, the URL string usually contains topic information about the webpage it links to (e.g., `sports.yahoo.com/nba/*.html`).

We also leverage the **social annotation** functionality to extract topic priors. Many Twitter users represent authorities on a small set of topics by virtue of their profession, experience, and the fact that they tend to publish on those topics on/off Twittter. This is recognized by other Twitter users who sometimes group users "known for" a particular topic using Twitter's List feature.

The data coming through the topic prior filters are only weakly relevant to each topic and thus very noisy. To obtain high-quality positive data for each topic, we employ a *co-training* [6] based data cleaning algorithm. In particular, we consider only these tweets containing URLs, and iteratively apply the following for each topic c:

1. train a webpage classifier to remove tweets whose associated URLs satisfy: $p(c|\text{URL})$ is below ϵ_1-percentile.
2. train a tweet classifier to remove URLs whose associated tweets satisfy: with $p(c|\text{tweet})$ is below ϵ_2-percentile.

The key assumption here is that when a URL is embedded in a tweet, the webpage that the URL links to is highly likely to be on the same topics as the tweet. To make this procedure more scalable and less coupled with the final classifier models, we use Naive Bayes classifiers in this step.

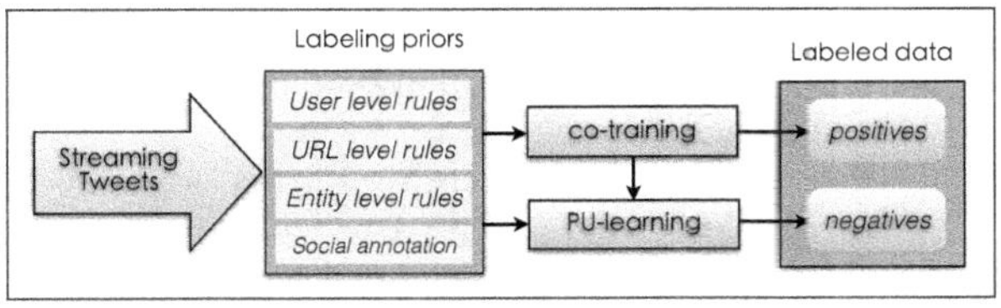

Figure 3: Training data acquisition pipeline.

Once we have positive data, for most topics, negative examples are very easy to collect, e.g., by using large-amount of randomly sampled tweets or using "*one-vs-all*" splitting of the positive data. However, for a considerable number of relatively broad topics that receive high velocity of coverage on Twitter (e.g.,"Sports", "Technology" and "News"), randomly sampled negatives are very noisy. One-vs-all doesn't work well for topics that are intercorrelated (e.g., "Sports" and "Basketball"), because semantically equivalent documents can be presented to a learner as both positive and negative examples. To this end, we employ algorithms developed for *learning from positive and unlabeled data* (or PU-learning [12]) to acquire high-precision negative examples for each topic. In particular, we select tweets / webpages as negative instances for a particular topic only when the similarity scores with the centroid of that class are below (1-ϵ_3)-percentile, i.e., via a *Rocchio* classifier [20].

4.3 Feature extraction

The effectiveness and efficiency in feature extraction are vitally important to the success of our system given our scale and quality requirement. Conventional unigram text features cannot meet our needs in both regards. First, tweets are short (bounded with 140 characters), and amount to merely ~7 unigram terms (including common stop-words) on average – very difficult for any machine learning model to infer topics with high confidence. Second, traditional implementation of unigram extraction can take considerable computational resources and dominate our system latency especially for webpages which could exceed 10K terms, which is problematic as we require real-time scoring. The latter factor is actually more critical and essentially prohibits us from using potentially more effective features such as n-grams, *word2vec* [21], or other time-consuming feature processing such as *term pre-selection* and *stemming*. Instead, in our system, we use the following two types of feature extractions for tweets and webpages respectively:

Binary hashed byte 4gram We use a circular extractor that scans through the tweet text string[1] with a sliding window of size four: every four consecutive bytes (i.e., UTF8 chars) are extracted and the binary value (4-byte integer) is hashed into the range of 0 to $d-1$, where d is chosen to be a prime number to minimize collision (e.g., $d = 1,000,081$ in our experiment). The occurrence of these hashed indices are used as binary features in tweet classifiers. This extractor (`Byte4Gram`) yields significantly denser feature vectors than unigram, e.g., for a tweet of length l, it produces exactly l feature occurrence.

[1]Tweet texts are preprocessed at the time of scoring such that less meaningful strings such as URLs and @mentions are stripped off and all strings are converted to lower case.

Hashed unigram frequency Term unigrams are extracted and hashed to integers at an extremely fast speed [13], with also a feature size d of $\sim$1 million. The term frequencies of the indices are then transformed to log-scale, i.e., $\log(1 + \text{tf}_w)$ and the feature vectors are normalized so that each webpage has the same ℓ_1-norm. This extractor (`Unigram-logTF-norm`) is extremely fast and it doesn't require any string preprocessing as Unicode conversion, lowercasing and word boundary detection are automatically taken care of.

We found that these feature extractors achieve the best balance of effectiveness and efficiency in our system.

4.4 Model pretraining

Both tweet and webpage topic inference can be casted naturally as multi-class multi-label classification problems, making *regularized logistic regression* a perfect fit. Given a set of n training instances $x_i \in \mathbb{R}^d$ together with their corresponding labels $y_i \subset \{1, 2, ..., C\}$, where C is the total number of topics, we consider two types of LR models:

Multinomial logistic regression (MLR) also known as *Multinomial logit* or *Softmax Regression* model, which models the conditional topic distribution given an instance x as the following multinomial distribution:

$$p(c \in y|x) = \frac{\exp(w_c^\top x + b_c)}{\sum_{c'=1}^{C} \exp(w_{c'}^\top x + b_{c'})}, \forall c = 1, \ldots, C.$$

One-vs-all logistic regression (LR) models "whether x belongs to a topic class c" as a Bernoulli variable:

$$p(c \in y|x) = \frac{1}{1 + \exp(-w_c^\top x - b_c)}, \forall c = 1, \ldots, C.$$

Let $l(w, b|x, y)$ be the log-likelihood of parameter (w, b) given example (x, y). To estimate the parameters (w, b), we minimize the negative log likelihood plus a penalty term:

$$\min_{w,b} \lambda(\alpha||w||_1 + \frac{1-\alpha}{2}||w||_2^2) - \frac{1}{n}\sum_{i=1}^{n} l(w, b|x_i, y_i), \quad (1)$$

where the parameter λ controls the strength of regularization. Here we consider the ElasticNet regularization which is a hybrid of ℓ_1 and ℓ_2 regularization types and includes both as special cases (when α takes 1 or 0). The non-differentiable nature of this regularization, when $\alpha > 0$, enforces sparsity of the model w, which is valuable to us because (1) a compacter model consumes less memory, loads faster and has better latency in real-time scoring; and (2) less useful (e.g., redundant or noisy) features will be automatically ruled out in training, which is important to us as we do *not* do attribute prepruning or stemming.

In our machine learning library, we provide a number of versatile model trainers on Hadoop, including distributed streaming training via SGD [18], and batch-mode training based on *L-BFGS*, *conjugate gradient* (CG) or *coordinate descent* (CD) algorithms. We also provide full regularization path sweeping for ℓ_1 and ElasticNet regularization.

The major difference between the two LR models lies in the Softmax function MLR employs to normalize the posterior scores $p(y|x)$. There are both pros and cons for doing so. On the one hand, MLR provides comparable topic scores which enables us to apply *max-a-posterior* inference to increase topic coverage. As topics are competing against one another, the inference results of MLR are less ambiguous (e.g., if topic c fires for a tweet x, topic $c' \neq c$ is less likely to fire for x due to the "*explaining-away*" effect). On the other hand, however, MLR requires the label space to be exhaustive (i.e., a tweet must belong to at least one of the topics), and it discourages usage of examples with missing label, which is not perfectly compatible to our setting. Also, because topics are coupled with one another in MLR, it is hard to train models for multiple topics in parallel, or retrain model for a subset of topics without affecting others.

Table 1: Streaming training (e.g., Pegasos) generates models with lower AUCs than batch-mode training. Increasing the number of iterations (i.e., number of scans over the data) slowly improves the AUCs but makes the training time much longer.

	#iteration	Avg AUC	Training time
Batch	NA	baseline	baseline
Streaming	1	-1.9%	-62%
Streaming	3	-1.2%	+57%
Streaming	10	-1.0%	+663%

Table 2: Comparison of MLR and LR 1-vs-all classifiers, in terms of average AUC across topics and the % of topics with improved AUCs (%topic win).

	Model	Avg AUC	%topic win
Tweet	MLR	baseline	baseline
Tweet	LR	+3.9%	86%
Webpage	MLR	baseline%	baseline
Webpage	LR	+1.7%	77%

Experiment Results. We use AUC (i.e., *area under the ROC curve*) for model validation for its independence of the choice of decision threshold – evaluation of calibrated models at their desired thresholds are reported in Section 4.9. We test models on a held-out subset of the "training data acquisition" output data, and estimate AUC with confidence intervals using standard *Bootstrap*. Because the standard errors are very small, we report here only the AUC scores.

Historically, our classifiers are trained in streaming-mode on Hadoop [18] via stochastic optimization, such as Pegasos [26]. Streaming training consumes a constant amount of memory regardless of the scale of the training data, and it is very fast when the data is scanned through only once. However, we noticed that the model generated by streaming training are significantly worse than batch-mode trained ones (e.g., via L-BFGS, CD or CG). For example, on tweet classification (with `Byte4Gram` feature), Pegasos-trained models, with 1 scan over the data, are 1.9% worse on average than batch-mode trained model, as seen in Table 1. Increasing the number of iterations helps to make the gap smaller, but at the same time, also makes the training time much longer (e.g., overhead in data I/O and communication). As we note in Section 4.10, we were able to scale up batch-mode training on massive data with distributed optimization. Hence, in the following experiments, the models are all trained in batch-mode unless noted explicitly.

Besides the advantages we mentioned previously, we found that 1-vs-all LR also performs better than MLR on both tweet and webpage classification. The results are summa-

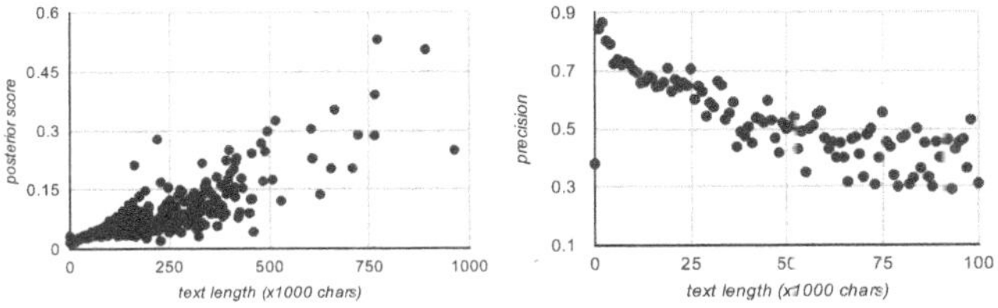

Figure 4: Effect of text length on LR classifier posterior score and precision of webpage classification. Left: longer texts receive higher posterior scores regardless of relevance; Right: precision drops as texts get longer when no feature normalization is used.

rized in Table 2, where all the models use `Byte4Gram` features. On tweets, using LR improves the AUC on 86% of the topics and by 3.9% on average across all topics. Interestingly, the improvements on webpage is relatively small, i.e., only 1.7%. This is due to LR's sensitivity to the variations in document lengths. Recall that here we use `Byte4Gram` features without normalization. When this is used in MLR, the softmax function automatically normalizes the posterior scores. However, in LR, if a text is getting longer, it gets more feature occurrences and in turn receives higher posterior scores regardless of the relevance of the documents. This effect is negligible on tweets as the lengths are bounded, but it is very dramatic on webpage and significantly deteriorates the prediction quality (e.g., precision) on lengthier webpages, as shown in Figure 4. Indeed, when we added feature normalization to webpage classifier, we observed up to 1.5% more improvement on AUC, bringing the overall improvement to 3.2%. The comparative results on feature extractors[2] are summarized in Table 3. Because of their superior performance, we use `HashedByte4Gram` for tweets and `Unigram-logTF-norm` for webpages as default features.

Finally, using ElasticNet with regularization path sweeping (i.e., optimized λ), further improves average AUC by 0.75–0.98%, as shown in Table 4. Due to the sparse nature of tweets, we found that relatively dense models have slightly better AUCs – models that are too sparse tend to generalize poorly on `Byte4Grams` that are not seen in training data. In our experiments, we found $\alpha \approx 0.05$ provides the best trade-off between test set AUC and training speed (smaller α turns to slow down the regularization sweeping).

4.5 Relational regularization

The ontological relations among topics, as defined by the hierarchical tree structure of our taxonomy, can be used to make our models smarter in learning classifiers for conceptually related topics. We consider three approaches here:

Label expansion This approach regularizes the learner by applying ontology-based label propagation to the training data, i.e., via: (1) *ancestor inclusion*: if x belongs to topic c, then it should also belong to topic c' if c' is an ancestor of c; and (2) *offspring exclusion*: if x belongs to c, then it should *not* be used as an negative example of c' in 1-vs-all splitting unless labeled so explicitly, where c' is an offspring of c. This method enables relational shrinkage via data sharing.

Cost-sensitive learning The structure of the taxonomy indicates that we should penalize mistakes involving different topic pairs differently, e.g., misclassifying a "movie" tweet as "entertainment" should receive less cost than misclassifying it as "sports". This can be done by encoding the ontological relations into a cost matrix E, where the (c, c')-th element, $e_{cc'}$, represents the cost of misclassifying an instance of topic c into topic c' and optimizing the regularized expected cost $\mathbb{E}[e(y, \hat{y})|x)] = \sum_{c=1}^{k} e_{yc} p(\hat{y} = c|x)$, where we use as $e_{cc'}$ the tree-distance between c and c' in the taxonomy.

Hierarchical regularization [28, 15] We can encode the hierarchical dependency among topics into the regularization so that the model of a topic c is shrunk towards that of its parent node parent(c), e.g. by adding a penalty term, $\frac{1}{2}\eta \sum_{c=1}^{k} ||w_c - w_{\text{parent}(c)}||_2^2$, to Eq(1).

These approaches, while tackling relational regularization in three different aspects (i.e., data sharing, relational objective, parameter sharing), usually achieve equivalent effects. Note that "cost-sensitive optimization" is more versatile as it can also handle label dependencies that are discovered from data (e.g., topic correlations) rather than prior knowledge

[2]For webpages, `Byte4Gram` consumes far more extraction time than `Unigram` and could slow down our system in real-time classification especially for very long documents.

Table 3: Comparison of feature extractors, where *-norm denotes instance-level ℓ_1-normalization.

	Feature	Avg AUC
Tweet	`Byte4Gram`	baseline
Tweet	`Unigram`	-5.7%
Tweet	`Byte4Gram-norm`	+0.0%
Webpage	`Byte4Gram`	baseline
Webpage	`Unigram`	-0.1%
Webpage	`Unigram-norm`	+1.2%
Webpage	`Unigram-logTF-norm`	+1.5%

Table 4: Comparison of regularization type. ElasticNet, with automatic regularization strength tuning, improves overall model AUC.

	Regularization	Avg AUC	%topic win	Sparsity
Tweet	ℓ_2	baseline	baseline	baseline
Tweet	ℓ_1	-0.33%	36%	1.7%
Tweet	EN, λ^*	+0.98%	100%	5.1%
Webpage	ℓ_2	baseline	baseline	baseline
Webpage	ℓ_1	-0.23%	29%	1.4%
Webpage	EN, λ^*	+0.75%	100%	4.6%

Table 5: Using relational regularization significantly improve model quality.

	Method	Avg AUC	%topic win
Tweet	Flat	baseline	baseline
Tweet	Label Exp.	+3.6%	70%
Tweet	Cost Sens.	+3.3%	66%
Tweet	Hie. Reg.	+3.6%	69%
Webpage	Flat	baseline	baseline
Webpage	Label Exp.	+2.3%	79%
Webpage	Cost Sens.	+2.2%	73%
Webpage	Hie. Reg.	+2.2%	81%

Experiment Results. In Table 5, we compared LR without relational regularization (denoted "Flat") vs the three approaches we described above. Relational regularization significantly improve model quality, e.g., over 2% boosts of average AUC. The differences among these three methods are nevertheless very small. For simplicity of implementation, hereafter, we primarily use label expansion.

4.6 Model calibration

LR models return *soft* probabilistic scores $p(y|x)$ in the range of $[0, 1]$. In order to apply them to label the topics of tweets/webpages, we need to calibrate the models towards specific quality criteria in need, i.e., a precision target in our case. There are two key questions here: (1) "over what distribution should precision be measured?" and (2) "how to find the optimal decision threshold?". For precision measurement, stratified sampling in the range of posterior scores produced by a classifier has been advocated as a way to reduce the variance of precision estimates [4]. While this method is very effective once the decision threshold are set, it is not straightforward to use when one seeks to determine the optimum thresholds.

Given a topic c, a small seed set of positive examples $\mathcal{P}_c$, an unlimited stream of unlabeled data $\mathcal{U}_c$ and a labeling oracle O, we use the following method to tune threshold θ_c:

Initial threshold Use $\mathcal{P}_c$ to estimate a rough lower bound θ_c^l for θ_c by using a much lower precision target.

Stratified sampling Apply the model to the output distribution and divide the interval $[\theta_c^l, 1]$ to equal-percentile bins[3]. Apply stratified sampling to $\mathcal{U}_c$ according to these bins and send the samples to O for confirmation labeling (Section 4.7), with results denoted $\mathcal{L}_c$.

Threshold estimation Let θ_j represent the posterior score of bin j, estimate the precision π_j for each bin j based on $\mathcal{L}_c$. The optimal threshold is the minimum breakpoint at which calibrated precision exceeds the precision target $\tilde{\pi}$, i.e.,

$$\theta_c = \arg\min \theta, \quad \text{s.t.: } \frac{\sum_{\theta_j \geqslant \theta} s_j \pi_j}{\sum_{\theta_j \geqslant \theta} s_j} \geqslant \tilde{\pi}$$

where s_j represents the size or prevalence of examples in bin j, which can be estimated using $\mathcal{U}_c$.

Note that, other than the above one-side calibration approach, a two-side approach is also possible, i.e., by initially narrowing down the range with both upper and lower bounds and applying golden section search to find optimal θ_c by progressively dividing bins (rather than fixed-size bins) and sub-stratified sampling. Although this two-side method can produce threshold estimations with arbitrary resolutions, we found in our experiments that one-side approach performs well enough and is much simpler to implement.

4.7 Quality evaluation

As we strive to achieve 90% or higher precision, high-quality gold standard data and accurate evaluation is critical to assess whether we achieve that goal. We use crowdsource human labeled data for quality evaluation. As we previously discussed in Section 4.2, human annotation is less accurate in a multi-label setting due to the *cognitive overload* caused by any nontrivial taxonomy. We instead ask for *confirmation labeling*. That is, rather than presenting the whole taxonomy to crowdsource workers and asking them to select whatever labels are relevant to a given tweet, we present a (tweet, topic) pair and ask them to provide binary answers to "whether or not the supplied topic is correct for the given tweet". As our primary goal is to estimate precision, binary judges on a sample output of our system are sufficient for our purposes. In principle, this protocol would require a lot more questions (i.e., labeling tasks) and in turn incur more costs if we were to estimate recall, e.g., for a given tweet and a 300-topic taxonomy, we need 300 labeling tasks in order to know the ground-truth topic of the tweet, compared to one task in the multi-label setting. Nevertheless, for precision assessment, this protocol has better quality assurance and it is more economical – because binary tasks are much easier, we found crowdsource workers are more willing to take the tasks at a much lower price, and more importantly, they are less likely to provide mistaking judgments.

To effectively control cost, we assign each (tweet, topic)-pair sequentially to multiple workers; once the standard error of the responses is below a certain threshold, the label is considered final and the task will be frozen without being assigned further. The quality of the response varies worker by worker. To ensure quality, when assigning tasks, we also incorporate a small set of randomly-sampled probe tasks for which we already know the true answers with high confidence. Those workers whose response accuracy consistently falls below our requirement will not be admitted for future tasks, and their response in the current batch are ignored.

Recall estimation faces challenges due to the nature of our labeling protocol, the needs for unbiased corpus and the fact that the distribution of our data evolves over time, which is the subject of another paper [7]. Instead, we use primarily precision and coverage for quality evaluation.

4.8 Diagnosis and corrective learning

Once the system is deployed in production to label the topics of tweets, it is important to be able to identify cases where the model fails, and provide diagnostic insights as well as corrective actions to fix it on the flight. To this end, we instrumented a mechanism that associate topic labels as tags to tweets and expose them to the users. When users scroll on a topic tag, two buttons will show up to allow users to provide "right or wrong" feedback about the topic tag. Clicking on a topic tag will also take you to a channel consisting of tweets all about that topic, which is useful for diagnosis of a topic model as tweets are flowing through. The UI of this feature is shown by the top chart of Figure 5. This feedback collection module makes it easy to exploit the *wisdom of crowd* in an ad hoc way to receive instantaneous feedback on the performance of our topic models and provide opportunities to identify patterns for correction. Once failing cases or trouble areas are identified, another tool is used to visualize which parts of the tweet contributed to the offending decision the strongest, as shown in the bottom charts in Figure 5. This is useful to allow the modeler to manually zoom into the model and identify potential ovefitting patterns. With all the diagnostic patterns, we then employ *corrective learning* [25, 23] to correct the mistakes of an existing topic classifier either manually or automatically on the flight. Corrective learning is used because it is desirable to adjust models *gradually* using a relatively small

[3]The boundaries of the bins can be defined based on the percentiles of the posterior scores of $\mathcal{P}_c$ or $\mathcal{U}_c$.

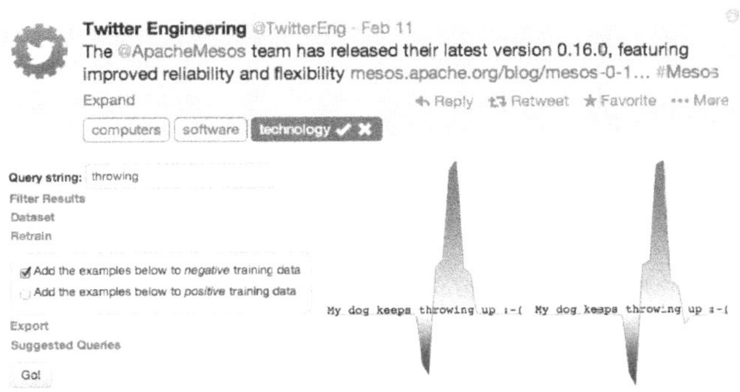

Figure 5: The diagnosis, corrective learning and feedback collection modules.Top: the feedback collection UI; Bottom: the corrective learning UI (Left), and visualization of an example tweet, which was misclassified as "rowing" before (Mid) but corrected after (Right) corrective learning.

number of new examples, and in such a way that the corrective action is limited to the area of the input space where the current models are actually misbehaving, while leaving the remainder unaffected. In Figure 5 (bottom), we show the UI for manual corrective learning, and one particular examples. The tweet was misclassified into the topic "Rowing" because of overfitting to the `Byte4Grams` extracted from the substring "-rowing", as shown in the bottom left chart (posterior score $p(c|x) = 0.97$). Fortunately, once we identify this pattern and adjust the model with corrective learning, this mistake can be corrected, as shown in the bottom right chart ($p(c|x) = 0.41$).

4.9 Model fine-tuning

Although we strive to turn down the noise in our labeled data by employing various techniques such as topic prior based pre-filtering, co-training and PU-learning, the data coming out of our training data acquisition pipeline still contains substantial noises. As a result, very few of our topic classifiers, if trained on these data, can achieve 90% precision. On the other hand, the labeled data collected from "feedback collection" and "quality evaluation" processes, albeit expensive and in relatively small amount, has very high precision as it is produced by human with controllable quality assurance. Can we use this small set of high-precision data together with the the large set of relatively noisy data to train better models? Naively training models on the combined data set is ineffective as only negligible AUC improvements were observed in our experiments (i.e., high-precision data is diluted/polluted by noisy data which is dominant in amount). We propose here a two stage training process:

Pretraining Train LR model on the larger set of noisy data as described in Section 4.4.

Fine tuning Tune the model on the small high-quality data set *in the neighborhood of* the pretrained model.

To fine tune the model, we use the pretrained model, denoted w^0, as prior and shrink w towards w^0 while minimizing the regularized loss on the high precision data:

$$\min_{w,b} \frac{\delta}{2}||w - w^0||_2^2 - \frac{1-\delta}{n}\sum_{i=1}^{n} l(w, b|x_i, y_i) + \lambda(\alpha||w||_1 + \frac{1-\alpha}{2}||w||_2^2), \quad (2)$$

where $\delta \in [0, 1]$ controls how much the model w is shrunk towards its prior w^0 *vs* w^* (i.e., the maxima of the regularized likelihood on high-precision data), we sample δ from Beta($\delta|n_0, n$), where n is the number of examples seen in the training set and n_0 is a positive number quantifying how strong we trust the prior[4]. This way, the shrinkage adaptively finds a balance between the prior and the likelihood such that the more high-precision data we supply, the less the model will be shrunk towards the prior and vice versa.

Table 6: Comparative evaluation of models on crowdsource confirmation-labeled data.

	Model	Avg AUC	%topic win
Tweet	baseline	0.7292	–
Tweet	stage-1	0.8004	89%
Tweet	stage-2	0.8415	97%
Webpage	baseline	0.7496	–
Webpage	stage-1	0.7845	85%
Webpage	stage-2	0.8051	99%

Table 7: Quality metrics of the calibrated classifiers.

	precision	coverage	topic coverage
Tweet	89.7%	33%	81%
Webpage	91.2%	53%	73%

Experimental Results. In Table 6, we report the quality of the models produced by the two-stage training process. As a reference, the very first *baseline*(i.e., the third row of Table 1) and the *stage-1* model (i.e., the third row of Table 5) are used for comparison. For more accurate assessment, we use crowdsource confirmation-labeled data (Section 4.7) in this evaluation and report the exact AUC scores. The fine-tuning (*stage-2*) consistently and significantly improves the quality of the model on both tweet and webpage, e.g., average AUC is improved by over 5% on tweets.

In Table 7, we also report the quality metrics of the calibrated models as seen in our service. The fine-tuned tweet model achieves ~90% precision with 33% tweet converge and over 80% topic coverage, a huge improvement from our first baseline, which, for example, with ~70% precision only achieves 8% tweet coverage and 21% topic coverage.

4.10 Discussions

Large-scale data. We discuss here two approaches, enabled by the prior shrinkage framework[5], which scale up our learning capability to massive data set in terabytes:

- **Sequential mini-batch learning.** With this approach, we partition the data set into multiple small segments $\{\mathcal{D}_1, \ldots, \mathcal{D}_m\}$ and train the model on each

[4]The best choices of n_0 and n can be decided by applying Laplacian approximation to the likelihood. We use cross-validation in our experiments for simplicity

[5]Note that hierarchical regularization is also enabled by prior shrinkage.

partition sequentially with prior shrinkage, i.e., suppose w^k is the model trained on $\mathcal{D}_k$, w^{k+1} will be trained on $\mathcal{D}_{k+1}$ with w^k as prior. Compared to the two extremes, i.e., pure streaming learning and single-thread batch-mode learning, this approach provide a good trade-off between computational and statistical efficiency (i.e., it takes less time than batch-mode and requires few examples to converge than streaming)[10]. Moreover, when the quality of the data is progressively improved in the partitions (e.g., sampled and labeled via active learning), we found this approach can progressively improve the quality of the model.
- **Distributed batch-mode learning** This approach is populated with the recent advances in operational research on *alternating direction method of multipliers* (ADMM) [8]. The basic idea is to maintain a global consensus $\bar{w}$ and iterate between (1) maximizing the (unregularized) log likelihood on each partition $\mathcal{D}_k$ with shrinkage towards $\bar{w}$, to obtain a local solution w_k, usually done in a distributed manner or in parallel, and (2) updating the consensus $\bar{w}$ to minimize the regularization penalty and the deviations from the local solutions $\{w_k\}$, which is usually very cheap to obtain (e.g., close-form solution in our case).

Active learning. One question one may ask is: since high-precision human labeled data is so effective in improving the model quality yet it is so expensive to acquire, would it be more efficient to apply active learning, *i.e.*, to train the model from scratch with a minimum amount of iteratively acquired training data? Unfortunately, the answer is "no". First, active learning requires integration of our machine learning capability into the API of the crowdsource agent, which is not supported by any crowdsouring services on the market. More importantly, the feature vector for each tweet is extremely sparse (e.g., only ~70 binary occurrence in a 1M space). At such sparsity, even if we were to see each feature to occur once (for each of the 300 topics), it would require millions of tweets for querying and incur a cost that easily exceeds our budget. In contrast, we find corrective learning (Section 4.8) is more suitable to our case – it provides useful diagnosis and corrective feedback to an (underperforming) existing model, and allows us to quickly fix it on the flight; moreover, it also takes advantages of the large user base of Twitter to acquire high-quality labeled data at virtually no cost by using the wisdom of the crowd.

5. BEYOND TEXT CLASSIFICATION: INTEGRATIVE TOPIC MODEL

Up to now, the topic models we present infer topics solely based on the text of tweets. However, a tweet is an envelope of different things, for example, besides (1) the text, a tweet can also contain (2) author, (3) embedded URL, (4) entities (e.g., `#hashtag`, `@mention` and named entities), (5) engagers who have interacted with the tweet (e.g., favorite, retweet, reply), (6) multi-media (e.g., image, video) and (7) other context information such as geographic, temporal and social contexts. The question is, how to harness all these sources of signals to achieve highly accurate topic inference when each single signal might fall short?

One approach is to extract feature from each source of signals and train LR models in the augmented feature space. There are some drawbacks with this approach. First, not all the features are available for every tweet (they may available at different stages or not available at all, e.g., engagements), leaving a lot of missing values. Second, the significant increase in feature dimensionality raises a lot of complications, e.g., it requires more labeled data for training and incurs significant overhead in memory consumption and runtime latency. Experiments also suggest that this approach is less effective in our system. An alternative approach is to use a hierarchical model similar to a *feed-forward neural network*, e.g., train a set of LR models on each input signal alone, and another layer of LR model on top of the output of these models. The structure doesn't have to be three layers. If needed, more hidden layers can be used to capture higher-order correlations among different features to further improve generalization performance as suggested by recent advances in neural network research [16]. Unfortunately, this model requires more complicated machine learning capabilities which are not currently supported by our infrastructure.

Instead, we present here an integrative inference approach based on *decision aggregation* (DA), where each of the signals is used as a weak decision maker to provide noisy topic labels for tweets, and the final topic labels are decided by aggregating these noisy predictions, e.g., via weighted majority voting. There is no restriction on what types of predictors to be used by each weak predictor as long as they all produce predicted labels for a given tweet. Similar methodologies have been applied successfully in the literature to handle tasks that involve multiple noisy experts or highly heterogeneous data [11, 24]. In this section, we first describe how we derive topic decisions from users and entities, we then present the integrative inference algorithm in details.

5.1 User topic model

A user is usually interested in only a few topics out of the 300+ topic space. When associated with a tweet via authorship or engagement, the user's interest topics provide a valuable signal for inferring the topic of the tweet. User interest modeling is itself an important topic. In fact, one primary use case of tweet topic modeling is to understand the interest intent of Twitter users so as to enable topic-based personalization.

Based on what a user has *produced* and *consumed* on Twitter, we derive two types of interest topics. Particularly, if a user u prominently tweets about a topic c, we call u is "*Known-for*" (KF) c. Likewise, if a user u consistently shows interest to tweets about topic c as indicated by his engagements (e.g. retweet, favorite, reply, clicks), we say u is "Interested-in" (II) c. Note that KF of u is a subset of u's II. In our system, the distribution of interest topics for each user (i.e., KF and II) are derived in real-time by running a *tfidf*-style topic-ranking algorithm on a sliding widow. The *foreground* model is a smoothed likelihood of user u producing / consuming tweets about topic c, whereas the *background* model is a population-level mean of the former. Let $r_t(c|u)$ denote the *tfidf* score of topic c to user u at time t, the topic distributions are rolled-over with a time-decay weight via $p_t(c|u) \propto \frac{1}{K(t)} \int_0^t k(t-s)\phi(r_s(c|u))ds = (k(1)p_{t-1}(c|u) + k^2(0)\phi(r_t(c|u)))/(k(1)+k^2(0))$, which is then normalized (over all the topics) and memcached for real-time access. Here $k(\cdot)$ is a time-decay kernel (e.g., the Exponential PDF $k(t) = \beta e^{-\beta t}$), $K(t) = \int_0^t k(s)ds$ is the CDF of $k(t)$, ϕ is a feature transformation function (e.g.,

Table 8: User interest models are evaluated in terms of precision at n (P@n) on user survey data.

Definition of positive interest	P@1	P@2	P@3	P@5
somewhat interested & above	0.81	0.85	0.85	0.85
interested & above	0.69	0.71	0.73	0.73

when $\phi(x) = \exp(x)$ is used, the distribution $p(c|u)$ will be a weighted softmax transformation of $r_t(c|u)$).

Another source of information for deriving user interest topics is to leverage the *social annotation* mechanism enabled by Twitter List. In particular, if a user u is *consistently* labeled by other users with lists that can be mapped to topic c, we call u is known-for c. II topics are derived from KF by using the follow graph, i.e., if a user u directly follows a user v who is unambiguously known-for topic c, we say u is interested-in c.

Interest topics derived from authorship and engagements are dynamic, and can adapt over time as users' interests evolve. In contrast, interests derived from social annotation are static. Nevertheless, we found that, especially for celebrities who don't tweet proactively, social annotation is more accurate. In our system, these two approaches are combined linearly with weight tuned on validation data.

Experimental Results. To evaluate the derived user interest topics, we conducted an online survey to collect explicit feedback from users. For each participating user, we select a set of ~ 10 topics, consisting of a subset of topics predicted by our model and a few randomly-sampled probe topics. We present these topics to users in a random order and ask them to rate how much they are interested in tweets on each topic. Users are allowed to provide their answers on 7 scale from "strongly interested (7)" to "strongly uninterested (1)", and one additional option of "not sure". Irresponsible or noisy answers which apparently conflict with what users explicitly stated in their profiles or other strong behavioral signals were filtered to reduce the noise. Based on ~ 5000 survey responses, we assess our model in terms of *precision at the top-n* topics (or P@n). The results are reported in Table 8. The average score of the top-5 predicted interest topics is around 6 (i.e., interested), significantly higher than the average score of the probe topics, which is around 3 (i.e., somewhat uninterested), indicating that the predictions by our model are consistent with what users perceive about their true interests. Overall, our model achieve up to 80% precision, and on 34% tweets, the top-5 predicted interest topics overlap with the ground-truth interests of a user.

5.2 Hashtag topic model

We present here an algorithm to infer topics from `#hashtags`, although the algorithm is applicable to other types of entities (e.g., named entities, `@mentions`) as well. Hashtag is one of the key features that define Twitter. In its essence, "*hashtag = topic*", i.e., hashtags are user-defined topics to better organize conversations. Hashtags are also way more predictive than ordinary text strings. Most hashtags span a rather narrow bandwidth out of a large spectrum of topics, e.g., `#ObamaCare`, `#TheVoice` and `#NBA`.

A straightforward approach is to use hashtag as features and train a LR model to classify tweet solely based on hashtags. This approach is, however, inherently flawed due to the huge volume (e.g., the number of hashtags are in $O(100Ms)$), the transient nature (i.e., hashtags are continuously evolving over time with new hashtags emerging every second) and the extreme sparseness (i.e., the majority of tweets usually contain no more than one hashtag). Indeed, our experiments indicate that, when hashtags are used as special unigram features together with regular text strings, only a very marginal (on some topics even negative) improvements were observed.

Instead, we infers hashtag topics via a retrieval algorithm, i.e., take a hashtag as a query, we aim to find the most representative topics for it. Unfortunately, because the hashtag-to-topic retrieval task is very different from conventional query-to-document retrieval, standard retrieval models such as pointwise mutual information (PMI), *tfidf*, BM25 and χ^2-test did not perform well in our experiments. To this end, we present a *learnable* retrieval model supervised by the output of our high-precision tweet text classifiers.

Table 9: Performance of hashtag topic model: precision at n (P@n), tweet coverage, and the ratio of output overlap with tweet classifier.

P@1	P@2	P@3	P@5	coverage	overlap ratio
32%	49%	57%	64%	6.6%	53%

Feature For hashtag h and topic c we use the following

$$p(h|c), p(h|\neg c), p(c|h), p(c|\neg h)$$

and their corresponding complement probabilities, together with the occurrences $p(h)$ and $p(c)$ as features, where $\neg a$ means the absence of a. Standard retrieval models such as PMI, *tfidf*, BM25 and χ^2 are all prescribed functions of some subsets of these 10 features.

Model We train a linear model using the logarithms of the aforementioned features: $r(c|h) = \langle\theta, \log(f)\rangle$. The parameter θ is tuned such than a retrieval metric (e.g. nDCG) is maximized on the training subset of high-precision tweet classifcation results.

Note that we can turn the direction of the retrieval model around, i.e., to find the most predictive hashtags for each topic, which is useful for a number of features such as hashtag-based topic summarization, topic-aware trends, as well as topic priors for training data acquisition (Section 4.2).

Experimental Results. In evaluation, we randomly sampled ~ 500 hashtags with 10 example tweets for each hashtag, and asked crowdsource workers whether the ground-truth topic is within the top-n topics retrieved from hashtag. The results are reported in Table 9. Overall, the model achieves 64% precision at position 5 (compared to 34% of user II topics). Moreover, hashtag topics overlap with tweet classification results on only 53% of the tweets, suggesing that they are also potentially useful for improving recall.

5.3 Integrative inference

We now have five topic predictors for a tweet, i.e,

- **Tweet text**: classification based on tweet content
- **Webpage**: classification of webpage (embedded URL)
- **Author KF**: known-for topics of the author,
- **Hashtag**: topics from the embedded `#hashtags`,
- **Engager II**: aggregated interested-in topics of the users who engaged with the tweet.

Table 10: Quality metrics of integrative inference.

Precision	Tweet Coverage	Topic Coverage
93%	37%	81%

Table 11: Importance ranks and scores of the 5 ingredient predictors in integrative inference.

1	2	3	4	5
Tweet text	Webpage	Hashtag	Author KF	Engager II
1.0	0.92	0.68	0.55	0.47

We derive the final topics for each tweet by aggregating topic labels provided by each of these predictors via *decision aggregation*. In settings where there are multiple experts providing noisy (possibly conflicting) decisions yet none of them is good enough alone, decision aggregation has been shown to beat or perform comparably to the best expert in hindsight [11, 24]. As we are primarily concerned with precision, we aggregate the noisy topic labels providing by each predictor using *weighted majority voting*: we assign a weight for each predictor and take all the topic labels to form a committee to vote, where each topic takes the sum of weights from the predictors who activate it. These topics together with their weights are then propagated according to the taxonomy tree to arrive at the final topic predictions. In our experiments, the weights are trained using the *AdaBoost* algorithm [14] on human confirmation-labeled data.

The integrative algorithm brings a close-loop inference mechanism and enables our system to dynamically adapt itself to cope with data drift, an importantly ability that a static LR classifier lacks. This is due to the fact that, by doing integrative inference, our system is running in real-time a close-loop iteration between (1) inferring topics about entities and users from tweet topics and (2) refining tweet topics using entitiy and user topics based on emerging signals.

Experimental Results While we can configure the integrative inference algorithm to improve precision and coverage (or recall) at the same time, here we exemplify with a rather conservative configuration to optimize precision (i.e., eliminate maximum false positives). The results are depicted in Table 10. At 12% higher coverage (compared to the tweet classifiers), the integrative model achieves 93% precision. Table 11 also shows the rank and importance score (normalized against the maximum score) of the 5 ingredient signals, as learned by the AdaBoost algorithm.

6. SUMMARY

We have presented a deployed large-scale topic modeling system that infers topics of tweets over an ontology of hundreds of topics in real-time and at stringently high precision. We have proposed a unique collection of topic modeling techniques that effectively helped us to address the challenges in implementing the system and satisfying the quality requirement.

Acknowledgements. We would like to thank our interns Ramnath Balasubramanyan, Mitja Trampus, Naftali Harris and Will Landecker, and the other members on the user modeling team especially Matthew Bilotti, Jake Manix, Praveen Bommannavar, Dimitar Simeonov, Dong Wang and David Burkett for their contributions to the system.

7. REFERENCES

[1] http://about.twitter.com.

[2] https://blog.twitter.com/2013/new-tweets-per-second-record-and-how.

[3] R. Balasubramanyan and A. Kolcz. Chatter in twitter: Identification and prevalence. In *ASONAM*, 2013.

[4] P. N. Bennett. Using asymmetric distributions to improve text classifier probability estimates. In *SIGIR*, 2003.

[5] D. M. Blei. Probabilistic topic models. *Commun. ACM*, 55(4):77–84, Apr. 2012.

[6] A. Blum and T. Mitchell. Combining labeled and unlabeled data with co-training. In *COLT*, 1998.

[7] P. Bommannavar, A. Kolcz and A. Rajaraman. Estimating recall for rare topic retrieval via conditionally independent classifiers. paper pending review, 2014.

[8] S. Boyd, N. Parikh, E. Chu, B. Peleato, and J. Eckstein. Distributed optimization and statistical learning via the alternating direction method of multipliers. *Found. Trends Mach. Learn.*, 3(1):1–122, Jan. 2011.

[9] M. Burgess, A. Mazzia, E. Adar, and M. Cafarella. Leveraging noisy lists for social feed ranking. *ICWSM*'13.

[10] V. Chandrasekaran and M. I. Jordan. Computational and statistical tradeoffs via convex relaxation. *PNAS*, 2013.

[11] D. Easley and J. Kleinberg. *Networks, Crowds, and Markets: Reasoning About a Highly Connected World*. Cambridge University Press, 2010.

[12] C. Elkan and K. Noto. Learning classifiers from only positive and unlabeled data. In *KDD*, 2008.

[13] G. Forman and E. Kirshenbaum. Extremely fast text feature extraction for classification and indexing. *CIKM*' 08.

[14] Y. Freund and R. E. Schapire. A decision-theoretic generalization of on-line learning and an application to boosting. In *EuroCOLT*, 1995.

[15] S. Gopal and Y. Yang. Recursive regularization for large-scale classification with hierarchical and graphical dependencies. In *KDD*, 2013.

[16] G. E. Hinton, S. Osindero, and Y.-W. Teh. A fast learning algorithm for deep belief nets. *Neural Comput.*, 2006.

[17] L. Hong and B. D. Davison. Empirical study of topic modeling in twitter. In *SOMA*, 2010.

[18] J. Lin and A. Kolcz. Large-scale machine learning at twitter. In *SIGMOD*, 2012.

[19] J. Lin, R. Snow, and W. Morgan. Smoothing techniques for adaptive online language models: Topic tracking in tweet streams. In *KDD*, 2011.

[20] C. D. Manning, P. Raghavan, and H. Schütze. *Introduction to Information Retrieval*. 2008.

[21] T. Mikolov, I. Sutskever, K. Chen, G. Corrado, and J. Dean. Distributed representations of words and phrases and their compositionality. In *NIPS*, 2013

[22] D. Ramage, D. Hall, R. Nallapati, and C. D. Manning. Labeled lda: A supervised topic model for credit attribution in multi-labeled corpora. In *EMNLP*, 2009.

[23] K. Raman, K. M. Svore, R. Gilad-Bachrach, and C. Burges. Learning from our mistakes: Towards a correctable learning algorithm. In *CIKM*, 2012.

[24] V. C. Raykar, S. Yu, L. H. Zhao, A. Jerebko, C. Florin, G. H. Valadez, L. Bogoni, and L. Moy. Supervised learning from multiple experts: Whom to trust when everyone lies a bit. In *ICML*, 2009.

[25] B. Settles. Closing the loop: Fast, interactive semi-supervised annotation with queries on features and instances. In *EMNLP*, 2011.

[26] S. Shalev-Shwartz, Y. Singer, and N. Srebro. Pegasos: Primal estimated sub-gradient solver for svm. *ICML*' 07.

[27] W. X. Zhao, J. Jiang, J. Weng, J. He, E.-P. Lim, H. Yan, and X. Li. Comparing twitter and traditional media using topic models. In *ECIR*, 2011.

[28] K. Zhou, S.-H. Yang, and H. Zha. Functional matrix factorizations for cold-start recommendation. *SIGIR*' 11.

Early Prediction of Code Blue using Electronic Medical Records

Sriram Somanchi
Carnegie Mellon University
Pittsburgh, USA
somanchi@cmu.edu

Samrachana Adhikari
Carnegie Mellon University
Pittsburgh, USA
asamrach@andrew.cmu.edu

Allen Lin
Harvard University
Cambridge, MA
allenlin@g.harvard.edu

Elena Eneva
Accenture
San Franscisco, USA
elena@elenaeneva.com

Rayid Ghani
University of Chicago
Chicago, USA
rayid@uchicago.edu

ABSTRACT

Code Blue is an emergency code in a hospital that is used to indicate when a patient goes into cardiac arrest and needs resuscitation. When Code Blue is called, an on-call medical team staffed by physicians and nurses is paged and rushes in to try to save the patient's life. It is an intense, chaotic, and resource-intensive process, and despite the considerable effort, survival rates are still less than 20% [4]. Research indicates that patients actually start showing clinical signs of deterioration some time before going into cardiac arrest[1][2][3], making early prediction, and possibly intervention, feasible. In this paper, we describe our work in partnership with NorthShore University HealthSystem that preemptively flags patients who are likely to go into cardiac arrest, using signals extracted from demographic information, hospitalization history, vitals and laboratory measurements in patient-level electronic medical records. We find that early prediction of Code Blue is possible and when compared with state of the art existing method used by hospitals (MEWS - Modified Early Warning Score) [4], our methods perform significantly better. Based on these results, this system is now being considered for deployment in NorthShore Health Systems and University of Chicago Hospital.

Categories and Subject Descriptors

I.2.1 [**Artificial Intelligence**]: Applications and Expert Systems—*Medicine and science*

Keywords

Machine Learning; Data Mining; SVM; Code Blue; Cardiac Arrest; Electronic Medical Records; Early Prediction

KDD'14, August 24–27, 2014, New York, NY, USA.
Copyright 2014 ACM 978-1-4503-2956-9/14/08 ...$15.00
http://dx.doi.org/10.1145/2623330.2623370.

1. INTRODUCTION

Code Blue is used to alert a rapid response team (RRT) in a hospital when a patient goes into cardiac arrest and needs resuscitation. The rapid response team intervenes, dropping other patients they are attending to at the time, and rushes to the Code Blue patient to possibly improve his or her deteriorating condition. More than 200,000 adult in-hospital cardiac arrests occur in the United States each year, and as many as 80% of these incidents result in death of the patient [4]. Medical professionals believe that if Code Blues can be predicted in advance, applying medical interventions can prevent some of these deaths. In addition to saving lives, early Code Blue prediction can also provide time for a hospital to plan for interventions and allocate resources accordingly, such that other patients do not suffer because of sudden shifts of resources during Code Blues.

There are some existing early warning systems [4] being used to predict which patients are at risk of entering Code Blue. However, these systems have few shortcomings: i) They require continuous monitoring of patients by clinical staff. This might be possible for patients in ICU, but around 50% of Code Blues take place in wards outside the ICU, where monitoring is only intermittent, and the interval between visits could very well be as high as 8 hours [5] ii) They use only a few characteristics of patients. With increased use of electronic medical records (EMR), we believe that using all the existing characteristics of patients can result in a more effective early warning system.

The goal of this work is to flag patients who are at risk of cardiac arrest, so that doctors can intervene early and avoid calling a Code Blue alert. The questions we consider are: i) how early can we make a prediction? ii) how precise are our predictions? and iii) how many Code Blues do we catch before they happen?

The earlier we can make a prediction, the more time a hospital has to plan interventions and adjust schedules of response teams. At the same time, our predictions need to balance the false positive rate to avoid unnecessary interventions (and associated opportunity costs) with making sure that we catch and prevent as many future cardiac arrests as possible. These factors can be considered as tradeoffs in our system since we could possibly increase the precision by waiting until a few seconds before a cardiac arrest to predict such events very accurately, but doing so makes the alert mostly useless since it may be unpreventable with just a few seconds of lead time. We model this problem as a prediction problem and use data collected by monitoring different vitals and lab results of patients leading up to the current time to flag patients who are at risk of entering Code Blue in the next several hours. We treat this as a classification problems and use support vector machines and logistic regression. We compare their performance to the early warning method currently used by hospitals (MEWS) and find that our methods significantly outperform the MEWS method and result in earlier, more precise Code Blue predictions.

The rest of the paper is organized as follows. We begin by introducing our project partner and data in section 2. We then explain the model setup and classification methods used in section 3. In section 4 we explain, in detail, our method for feature extraction. We also briefly mention other methods that could potentially improve our method, and are part of future work. In the next two sections (5 and 6), we explain construction of training and evaluation sets, along with a method for assessing the performance of different models, and for estimating variability in prediction. Finally, we end with our findings in section 7, and a short discussion about the results and deployment plans in section 8.

2. DATA AND PROJECT PARTNER

The work described in this paper was done in partnership with NorthShore University HealthSystem. This hospital system contains four individual facilities in the Chicago area. We used patient-level information for about 133,000 in-hospital patients extracted from electrical medical records (EMR) from 2006 to 2011. Code Blue was called for only 0.05% of the 133,000 patients in the hospital. These patients had multiple encounters in the hospital. The data consists of around $232K$ encounters and of these encounters Code Blue was called on only 815 encounters. This extremely skewed class distribution makes the prediction task very difficult.

The data extracted from the EMR system includes information on demographics, past hospitalization history and real-time vitals and laboratory tests for these patients. Demographic features include patient's age, gender, race and ethnicity. We have information on twenty-nine different vitals and lab tests measured at different times since the patient was admitted in the hospital. Some examples of vitals are respiratory rate, systolic and diastolic blood pressures, pulse oximetry and temperature. Lab tests include hemoglobin, platelet count, hematocrit, creatinine and sodium levels. Figure 1 is a summary plot of different vitals and labs in the data.

These measurements are neither taken at equally spaced time points nor at the same frequency for different vitals and lab tests, as demonstrated in Figure 2. We did not perform any sampling and obtained the data exactly as it was recorded in the EMR system. Figure 2, displays the readings of 5 different vitals of a patient who went into Code Blue (at the time indicated by vertical red line). As we can see in the plot, vitals like heart rate and blood pressure is recorded frequently and periodically. However, vitals like carbon dioxide level are recorded less frequently. Moreover, different patients were admitted in hospital for different lengths of time. This nature of the data makes the application of typical time series algorithms difficult. We need a good and valid procedure to incorporate temporal property of the data along with information embedded in inconsistencies in data collection. Our method for feature extraction is discussed in section 4.

We approach this problem as a two stage estimation problem. First stage is to estimate trend and temporal properties of the variables that were recorded at irregular time points in the last 24 hours. Because the length of stay is different for different patients, we use vitals information in the last 24 hours for estimating trends, and use length of stay as a feature. This truncation was necessary to have a uniform comparison across patients. Next, using the estimated trend and temporal properties along with other time constant features, we use standard classification methods like support vector machine and logistic regression, to classify patients who went into code-blue in their hospital stay. We briefly discuss the classification model in the next section.

3. CLASSIFICATION METHODOLOGY

We use classification methods to predict whether Code Blue will occur for a patient in the next h hours, from a given time point using information leading up to that time. The time point at which prediction is made is denoted as T^P. Time when the event occurs, i.e. h hours after T^P, is called event time and is denoted as T^E. We are interested in predicting the outcome (Y_i) at T^E where:

$$Y_i = \begin{cases} 1 \text{ if patient i goes into Code Blue by } T^E \\ 0 \text{ if patient i does not go into Code Blue by } T^E \end{cases}$$

We create features with medical information up to T^P for both patients who went into Code Blue at T^E (case patients) and those who did not (control patients). Next, given the features at T^P and before, we want to predict how likely a patient is going to go into Code Blue h hours after T^P, such that $T^E - T^P = h$. In our analysis, $h \in \{1, 2, 3, 4\}$, implying that we have four different classification problems. Also note that there is not a well-defined T^E for patients who never go into code-blue. It ranges from the time when a patient was admitted to when they were discharged. As this patient never went into Code Blue, they can be a negative example in the entire period. We provide an argument on why choice of T^E for control patient matters, and give some intuition on how we went about choosing it for training in the Section 5. Figure 3 is a pictorial representation of the problem setup.

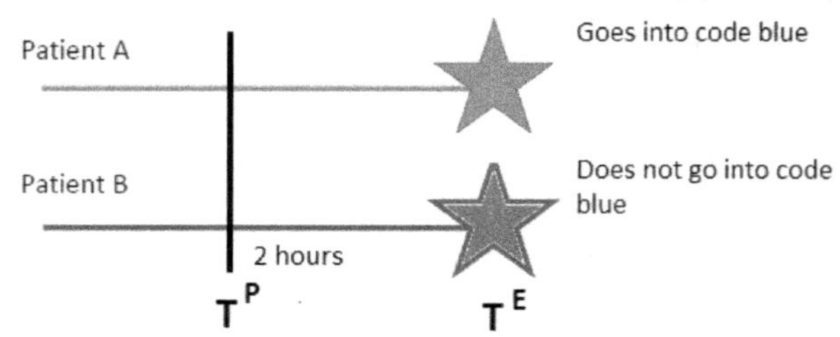

Figure 3: Pictorial representation of problem setup. We want to classify the events labeled by blue star (=1) and red star (=0), using information before T^P. Time interval between T^P and T^E in this example is 2 hours. We vary prediction time from 1 to 4 hours to see how early we can predict Code Blue.

Support vector machine (SVM) with radial kernel and logistic regression with lasso penalty are used for classification.

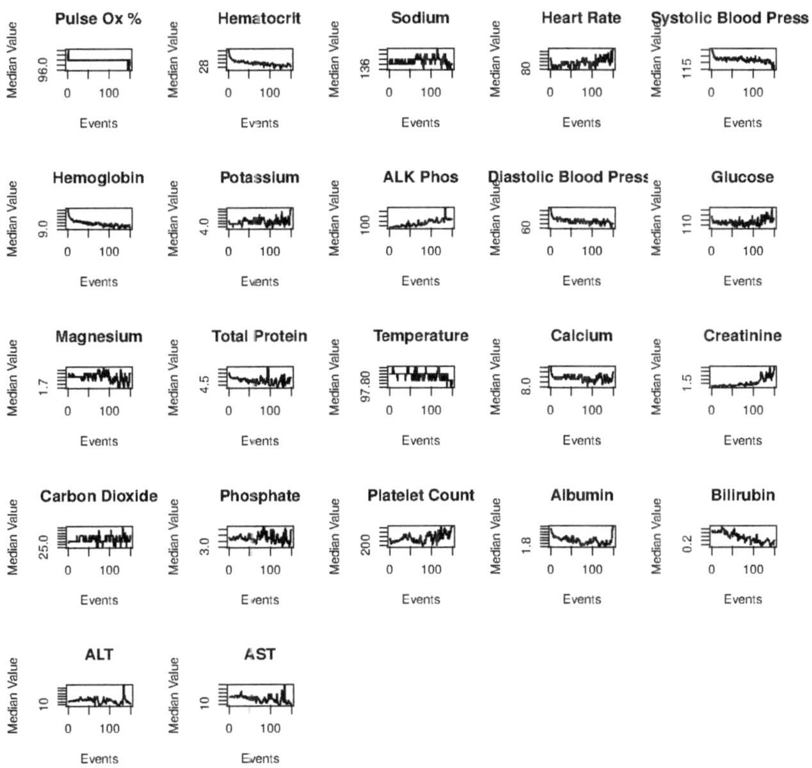

Figure 1: Summary plot of different vitals and labs for patients who go into Code Blue: Along the x-axis are different time points for which data was collected for at least one patient in the last 150 time points. Note that the event times are not regular. Along the y-axis are the median measurements for patients at that time point. This plot shows variation in population median of different vitals and lab measurements available for patients right before Code Blue.

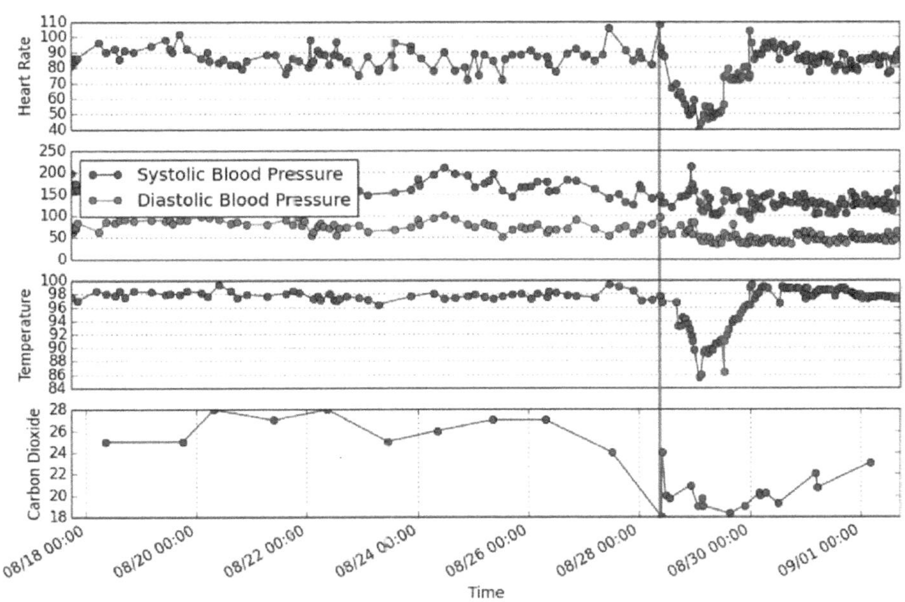

Figure 2: Example of patient-level data for five different vitals. The vertical red line represents the time of Code Blue.

We train these classifiers on training data, and evaluate their performance by making predictions on held-out test data. SVM with radial basis kernel results in better classification performance but we find that the logistic regression models are more interpretable. While the main goal of this paper is building a good predictive model, it is also of interest to explore how logistic regression perform compared to SVM and what are the important features selected by logistic regression.

Define Y^n as a vector of n outcomes and $X^{(n \times p)}$ as a matrix of p features, for each classification problem. Recall that SVM is formulated as a following optimization problem [11]:

$$\min_{\beta,\beta_0} \frac{1}{2}||\beta||^2 + C\sum_{i=1}^{N}\psi_i \quad \text{subject to } \psi_i \geq 0, y_i(x_i^T\beta + \beta_0) \geq 1 - \psi_i \forall i.$$

Here C is the cost parameter that regulates the number of overlaps in training points, ψ is the proportion by which the prediction is on the wrong side of the margin, also called slack variables. We want to maximize the separation while minimizing the overlap. For non-linear boundary in original space kernelized SVM is used. Radial basis kernel is given by $K(x, x^{'}) = exp(-\gamma||x - x^{'}||^2)$, where γ is a scale parameter. C and γ are tuning parameters chosen by 5-fold cross-validation in training data to find the best model that fits the selection criteria defined below.

Similarly, in logistic regression classification is done by estimating probability of $(Y_i = 1|X_i)$ using the model, $\text{logit}(P(Y_i = 1|X_i)) = X_i^T\beta$. When the dimension of X is large relative to the number of observation, logistic regression with lasso penalty helps to select sparse predictive model [10]. In this framework the coefficients, $\hat{\beta}$s, are estimated by solving following problem:

$$\min_{\beta} -\text{log likelihood }(\beta) + \lambda|\beta|.$$

λ is a tuning parameter of the model which controls the amount of regularization, and hence the sparsity in the estimated coefficients [11]. λ is selected by 5-fold cross-validation on training data to find the best model that fits the selection criteria.

We use F_1 score as a selection criteria. It is a measure of a test's accuracy. F_1 score can be interpreted as a weighted average of the precision and recall, where an F_1 score reaches its best value at 1 and worst score at 0. F_1 score is given by:

$$F_1 = 2\frac{\text{precision} \times \text{recall}}{\text{precision} + \text{recall}}$$

Recall (true positive rate) is computed as the proportion of true predicted Code Blue events over all the observed Code Blue, whereas FPR (false positive rate) is the ratio of false predicted Code Blue over total number of events that were observed as non-Code Blue. Since we are interested in predicting code-blue with high recall and precision, we use this criteria for model selection in cross-validation.

Finally, note that the columns of the features are centered and scaled for these methods.

3.1 Comparison with existing methods used in hospitals

Modified Early Warning Score(MEWS), is a composite index commonly used by hospital staff to determine the severity of a patient's illness. We calculate MEWS by individually scoring the aberration of five vital signs (systolic blood pressure, heart rate, respiratory rate, temperature, and level of consciousness) on a scale of 0 to 3 and summing the resulting scores [4] at the time of prediction. A score of five or more is linked to increased likelihood of Code Blue [9]. We will use 5 as a threshold for predicting whether a patient will go into Code Blue. Because MEWS is frequently used in hospitals as a criteria in activating rapid response teams, it serves as an appropriate basis to compare our results to.

4. FEATURE EXTRACTION

A key aspect in the medical domain (and in any application of data mining) is building effective features for classification. We worked with physicians from the NorthShore University HealthSystem as well as researched prior work to determine good features. For Code Blue prediction, it was important to incorporate using irregularly spaced and sparsely collected temporal data. As mentioned earlier, vitals and lab information have atypical properties that hinder in applying regular time series methods for classification. i) They are not recorded in regular time interval; ii) some vitals are recorded more regularly than others; iii) for a given vital there is more data at some time interval compared to others, and iv) since different patients stay in hospital for different period of time, length of available data is not uniform across patients. We want to incorporate these properties of the data in our feature set. Along with information like trend and range of the variables at different time intervals, we also want to use information on how often the vital was recorded and when it was missing as features. We believe that they are important to identify the features of the data and data collection process that lead to the event.

For this analysis we start with a simple approach to build features. We divide the time line of patient's stay in hospital into different windows to estimate temporal features and trends from the vitals and lab tests that change over time in an encounter [8] [6]. The time line for temporal variables before prediction time, T^P, was divided into three windows. The first window contains information up to 3 hours before T^P, the second window contains information between 3 to 9 hours before T^P, and the third one contains information between 9 to 18 hours before T^P. We truncated the data at 18 hours for uniformity across patients, since we did not have information beyond 18 hours for some of the patients. Instead, we use total length of stay of a patient as a feature. For each window and every patient, we compute first and second moment of the empirical distribution of a variable in that window, along with minimum and maximum value, and the frequency of data collection. We estimate the trend in each window by segmented regression [6]. We fit a regression line in each window and record the slope of the line to include increasing or decreasing trend information in feature set.

Using this technique dimension of our feature set is 381 variables. These include both time constant features and the features we built for time varying variables. Missing values are replaced by the feature's mean for that time window.

We realize that this is still a rather naive approach to estimate trends, but is better than taking the average over all the periods, or considering each measurement of a vital for a patient at different time points as independent (i.i.d) (which they certainly are not). Currently we are fitting separate (discontinuous) least squares in each window that is of uniform size across patients. Ideally, we would like to use all available measurements of a vital for a patient to fit a piecewise linear function that estimates underlying linear trend and use its summary as features for classification [7].

There are more sophisticated methods in the literature (mostly in economics) related to trend filtering in time series or temporal data analysis, that will be a good guidance to further advance this work. We are especially interested in implementing l_1 trend filtering approach proposed by Kim et. al [7] for continuous temporal data. We are currently exploring ways to incorporate this method in our framework.

5. TRAINING

Since our goal is to build a system that will be deployed in the hospital response system, it is critical that the classifier works in a real-time hospital setting. We train our model on historical data, and use it to predict Code Blue on future holdout data. Our goal is to classify patients who will go into Code Blue as early as possible. We train different models for each early warning time threshold: one model that predicts if a patient goes into Code Blue in the next one hour, other in the next two hours, and so on. We choose the best parameters through 5-fold cross-validation of each model on training data.

One of the important considerations in our classifier is to choose the number of negative examples that should be considered to learn the differences in two classes (Code Blue and non-Code Blue). Note that this is a highly unbalanced classification problem, where Code Blue is a rare event. We use a nested case-control approach to match control patients to every case patient, so that a classifier can learn the differences in training data easily. We match Code Blue patients to non-Code Blue patients with similar demographic features only, such that there remain differences in their physiological and hospitalization histories. We create a training set that is less skewed by sampling the data, to account for the unbalance of the two class labels. We vary the ratio of cases to controls in our training set as 1:1, 1:4 and 1:10, and we decide on the appropriate ratio based on the prediction results from the training data. It is important to note that we do not change the distribution of the test set. We only vary the number of controls samped to construct the training set for our classifiers, but we use the natural distribution of the data for the test set. This is done to make sure the models we build are applicable when put in production and the results are still consistent with the initial experiments.

Further, we need to select time of comparable event (T^E) for control patients, so that we can build up the negative examples. For patients who go into Code Blue, time when they go into Code Blue defines the positive event. However, for patients who never go into Code Blue, we have the time from when they were admitted to the time when they were discharged as a choice for the negative event. Most of the patients who get discharged are healthier at the time of discharge than they were during (or at the beginning of) their stay. This makes using time of discharge as a comparable event a bad choice, as the classification problem will become artificially easy. Using time close to admission will not give us enough information to build an accurate model. In this analysis, we vary the time of event for control patients, as the 25th, 50th and 75th percentile of their stay time in the hospital, and select the value that performs best in the training data.

We experiment with using support vector machine (SVM) with radial kernel and sparse logistic regression with lasso penalty as classifiers [11]. γ and C for SVM and λ for logistic regression are selected by cross-validation with maximizing F_1-score as a criteria. Once we select optimal parameters, we refit on the entire training set using these tuning parameters for each method, and use the estimates for prediction on test data.

6. EVALUATION AND ESTIMATION OF STANDARD ERRORS

For every hour in the evaluation set, we take the features of all the patients in the hospital present at that hour. Using these features, we predict which patients would go into Code Blue 1, 2, 3 and 4 hours from that time point. This evaluation is used to compare classifiers and compute the best parameters for those classifiers, using recall and false positive rate (FPR) as metrics. Recall is computed as the proportion of true predicted Code Blue events over all the observed Code Blue, whereas FPR is the ratio of false predicted Code Blue over total number of non-Code Blue events. Also, receiver operation characteristics (ROC) curve for aggregate monthly predictions along with area under the curve (AUC) are compared among classifiers to evaluate their performance.

Our first training set consists of data before January 1, 2011. We use events in the month following the training period as test data. We then sequentially add additional months to the existing training data, and hence create 7 new training data. Estimates from each training set is evaluated on the test data in the following month. Following this procedure we have 8 training and test data. We compute mean recall and FPR, along with the standard error of the mean, over the 8 test data. We also compute MEWS scores for patients in the test data. Patients with MEWS scores greater than or equal to 5 are predicted to go into Code Blue in the next 4 hours. Note that, the first training data is contained in the next training set and so on. This is a time dependent data, where the Code Blues in the past might affect how hospital deals with Code Blues in the future. Hence, we believe that the hospital system learns from the past, so we use the past data to predict the future events. At the same time, multiple training and testing datasets give us a valid way to estimate standard errors of the mean recall and false positive rates for different models. Also receiver operation characteristics (ROC) curve for aggregate monthly predictions along with area under the curve (AUC) are compared among classifiers to evaluate their performance.

7. RESULTS

Based on mean recall and false positive rate from predictions on multiple test data, we find that using 1:4 case to control (positive to negative class) ratio and 75% percentile time point as a comparative event for the control group in training gives the best results in terms of AUC. The rest of the results presented in this section are based on using these parameters.

We were able to predict Code Blue with around 80% recall and 20% false positive rate at 4 hours ahead of the event. We find that the SVM performs better than the current method used by medical practitioners (MEWS) in terms of mean recall and FPR, as shown in Figure 4, and in terms of ROC and AUC, as shown in Figure 5. We also ran sparse logistic

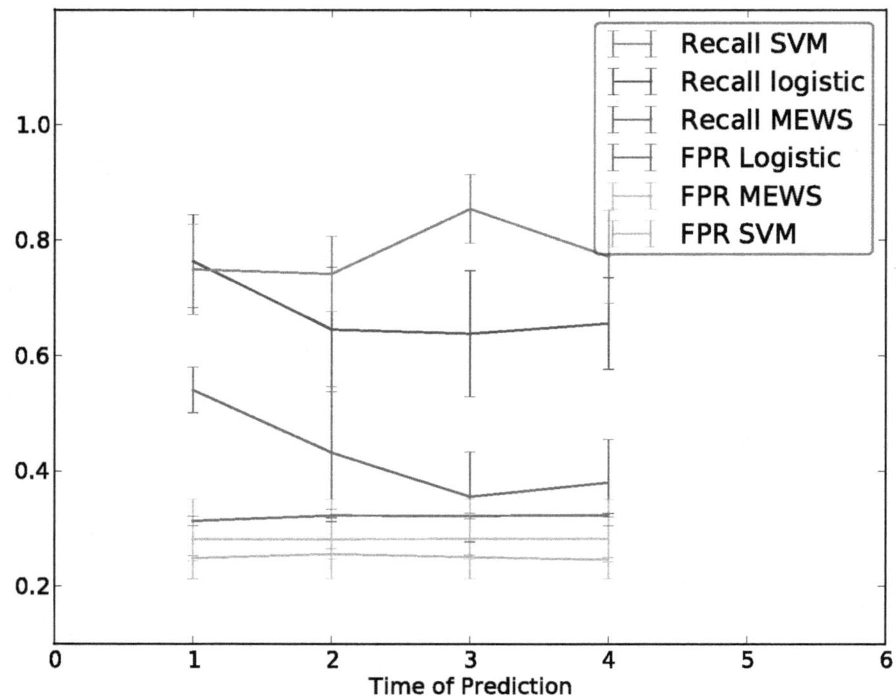

Figure 4: Comparison of the performance of SVM, Logistic Regression and MEWS. Along the x-axis is time of prediction before Code Blue. For example, 4 on the x-axis means the prediction is made 4 hours before the event. Along the y-axis is recall or false positive rate. Different colors are for different classification methods.

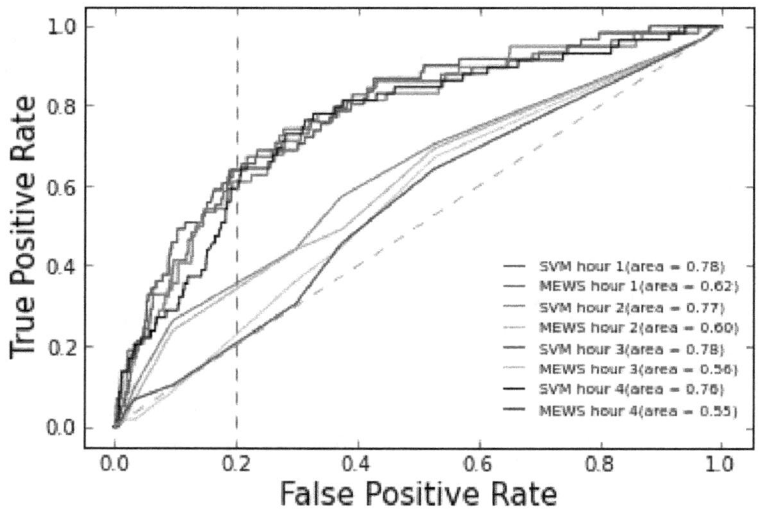

Figure 5: ROC curves for comparing the performance of SVM and MEWS. Area under the curve for each method, along with the number of hours ahead when making the prediction, is mentioned in the legend.

Feature	Coefficient
Number of Previous Code Blues	0.23
Number of Previous Discharges to Home	0.16
Emergency Admission	0.15
Number of Previous Encounters	0.13
Minimum Potassium	0.24
Platelet Count Window 0	0.22
GFR Count	0.12
Glucose Count	0.19
Glucose Count Window 2	0.11
Hematocrit Count Window 1	0.16

Feature	Coefficient
Average Respiratory Rate	0.20
Average Heart Rate Window 1	0.11
Minimum Heart Rate	0.14
SD Respiratory Rate Window 1	0.29
SD Heart Rate Window 0	0.13
SD Heart Rate Window 2	0.21
SD Diastolic Blood Pressure Window 2	0.16

Figure 6: The top features selected by our sparse logistic regression for the 1 hour ahead prediction.

regression on the similar framework. Prediction from SVM has significantly lower false positive rate compared to logistic regression. Even though predictions from SVM have higher mean recall, they are not significantly higher for all time points. Both, SVM and logistic regression performed better than MEWS in terms of recall. False positive rate estimated from MEWS has bigger standard errors, and thus we could not be certain about the performance of our method compared to MEWS. As we can observe from the results, that the benefit of using our machine learning methods increases as we make our predictions earlier. The MEWS score gets much worse (especially in terms of recall) compared to the SVM as we make our predictions earlier in time. This is critical since our goal is to make these predictions as early as possible to enable the hospital to intervene early, as well as modify the schedules for physicians and nurses to optimize overall quality of care for all patients.

One of the advantages of logistic regression is its popularity among medical practitioners because of its interpretability in terms of understanding important features. From our analysis, we see that the mean, the variability, and the trend (rate of acceleration/deceleration) of features like heart rate, respiratory rate, diastolic blood pressure, and pulse oxygen levels are important features for predictions at all hours. Moreover, the frequency at which lab measurements are taken is also a good predictive feature, and its importance increases as we make earlier predictions. Figure 6 shows the top features selected in the 1 hour ahead prediction. One interesting finding is that as we try to predict further out into the future, more features become relevant. For example, 72 features were selected as important features in the 1 hour ahead as compared to 100 features for the 2 hours ahead prediction. We think that this is because prediction gets more difficult as we try to predict Code Blue earlier, and the model needs (and uses) more features to perform effectively. However, we do not have any measure of uncertainty of these estimates, and while these features are helpful to understand their effect on Code Blue, it is difficult to make any inferences. The important features selected by our model are shown in Figure 6, where we also provide the coefficients of features in the sparse logistic regression. The coefficients represent the log odds ratio of the feature in predicting Code Blues.

8. CONCLUSIONS AND FUTURE WORK

In this paper, we described a system we are building to create an early warning prediction system for in-hospital cardiac arrests that surpasses the existing method used by medical practitioners. This gives hospital staff the ability to intervene before the patient becomes critical, thus averting some potential Code Blue occurrences (ultimately saving more lives). This also reduces the opportunity cost of dropping their current hospital activities to rush to attend to Code Blue patients and facilitates planning and scheduling. We found that this prediction can be made as early as 4 hours before the Code Blue event with high recall and relatively low false positive rate. Most importantly, we verified the hypothesis that patients show clinical signs of deterioration before going into cardiac arrest, and vital signs and lab measurements can be used to determine these signals.

We believe that there is a potential to improve the performance of these models by adding additional features that we did not have access to, like diagnosis from patient records. Also, the extreme imbalance in class labels in the data had caused some difficulties in creating test and training sets. A good future direction would be to combine data from different hospital systems, so the system can be trained on more positive examples, which should improve predictions further.

The other important future step is to assess the medical significance of this work and the implications in the medical field. While we have significantly higher recall compared to MEWS, we are only slightly better than MEWS in mean FPR. Without further consultation with medical practitioners and tests of the system in real life-like settings, it is hard to know how crucial this trade-off is in practice.

Lastly, as mentioned in feature extraction (4), there is potential for improving estimation with trends in time-varying features. Exploring more sophisticated and statistically sound time series methods is a priority for future work.

9. DEPLOYMENT PLANS

The work described here was done in partnership with NorthShore University HealthSystem. We collaborated with the team in the hospital and presented these methods and results to a set of doctors and researchers. Based on our results that outperform the currently used MEWS score, we are now in discussions with NorthShore Hospital as well as the University of Chicago hospital to determine the best way to deploy such a system. One approach we are considering is converting the classifier into a set of database queries that runs on top of the EMR system and feeds into an alerting system. This alerting system would raise an alert when a potential Code Blue is about to happen in the next n hours. In addition, the classifier would also provide input to the hospital scheduling system that will allow administrators to optimize the overall quality of care they provide to patients.

10. ACKNOWLEDGEMENTS

This work was supported by the 'Eric and Wendy Schmidt Data Science for Social Good' Summer Fellowship at the University of Chicago in 2013. We also thank Dr. Jonathan Silverstein, Vice President and Head of the Center for Clinical and Research Informatics at NorthShore University Health Systems, for his valuable inputs, access to data and supporting our efforts to deploy the methods into their hospitals.

References

[1] C. A. Alvarez, C. A. Clark, S. Zhang, E. A. Halm, J. J. Shannon, C. E. Girod, L. Cooper, and R. Amarasingham. Predicting out of intensive care unit cardiopulmonary arrest or death using electronic medical record data. *BMC Medical Informatics and Decision Making*, 13:28, 2013.

[2] M. Buist, E. Jarmolowski, P. Burton, S. Bernard, B. Waxman, and J. Anderson. Recognising clinical instability in hospital patients before cardiac arrest or unplanned admission to intensive care. a pilot study in a tertiary-care hospital. *Med Journal*, 171, 1999.

[3] P. Chan, A. Kalid, L. Longmore, R. Berg, M. Kosiborod, and J. Spertus. Hospital-wide code rates and mortality before and after implementation of a rapid response team. *JAMA*, 300, 2008.

[4] M. M. Churpek, T. C. Yuen, M. T. Huber, S. Y. Park, J. B. Hall, and D. P. Edelson. Predicting cardiac arrest on the wards, a nested case-control study. *American College of Chest Physicians*, 11-1301, 2012.

[5] D. A. Jones, M. A. DeVita, and R. Bellomo. Rapid-response teams. *New England Journal of Medicine*, 365(2), 2011.

[6] E. Keogh, S. Chu, D. Hart, and M. Pazzani. Segmenting time series: A survey and novel approach. *Data Mining in Time Series Databases*, 2004.

[7] S.-J. Kim, K. Koh, S. Boyd, and D. Gorinevsky. l1 trend filtering, 2009.

[8] C. Sian and L. David. Effective probability forecasting for time series data using standard machine learning techniques. *Proceeding of the third international conference on advances in pattern recognition*, August 2005.

[9] C. Subbe, M. Kruger, P. Rutherford, and L. Gemmel. Validation of a modified early warning score in medical admissions. *QJM*, 94(10):521–526, 2001.

[10] R. Tibshirani. Regression shrinkage and selection via the lasso. *Journal of the Royal Statistical Society, Series B*, 58:267–288, 1994.

[11] H. Trevor, T. Robert, and F. Jerome. *The Elements of Statistical Learning.* Springer Series in Statistics. Springer New York Inc., New York, NY, USA, 2001.

Large Scale Visual Recommendations From Street Fashion Images

Vignesh Jagadeesh
eBay Research Labs
2065 East Hamilton Avenue
San Jose, California, USA
vjagadeesh@ebay.com

Robinson Piramuthu
eBay Research Labs
2065 East Hamilton Avenue
San Jose, California, USA
rpiramuthu@ebay.com

Anurag Bhardwaj
eBay Research Labs
2065 East Hamilton Avenue
San Jose, California, USA
anbhardwaj@ebay.com

Wei Di
eBay Research Labs
2065 East Hamilton Avenue
San Jose, California, USA
wedi@ebay.com

Neel Sundaresan
eBay Research
2065 East Hamilton Avenue
San Jose, California, USA
nsundaresan@ebay.com

ABSTRACT

We describe a completely automated large scale visual recommendation system for fashion. Our focus is to efficiently harness the availability of large quantities of online fashion images and their rich meta-data. Specifically, we propose two classes of data driven models in the Deterministic Fashion Recommenders (DFR) and Stochastic Fashion Recommenders (SFR) for solving this problem. We analyze relative merits and pitfalls of these algorithms through extensive experimentation on a large-scale data set and baseline them against existing ideas from color science. We also illustrate key fashion insights learned through these experiments and show how they can be employed to design better recommendation systems. The industrial applicability of proposed models is in the context of mobile fashion shopping. Finally, we also outline a large-scale annotated data set of fashion images (**Fashion-136K**) that can be exploited for future research in data driven visual fashion.

Categories and Subject Descriptors

H.3.3 [**Information Storage and Retrieval**]: Information Search and Retrieval

General Terms

Data Driven Models; Fashion, Retrieval; Crowdsourcing

Keywords

visual recommenders; fashion; e-commerce; color modeling; user behavior

1. INTRODUCTION

Everybody Loves Fashion: Fashion has been and continues to be an active area of research in a variety of disciplines. Artists and designers strive to create fashionable apparel that please end users and in turn enjoy wide adoption. Economists and Statisticians have long studied the spending patterns of shoppers to understand and design market structures for fashion. Psychologists have been looking into reasoning about abstract fashion notions on what it means to be visually/aesthetically pleasing, why certain fashion trends become instantly popular while others do not. More recently data scientists have been investing considerable effort into building systems are capable of organizing and making sense of the tremendous amount of fashion data flooding the web. While the different problems appear diverse at the surface, it is fairly evident that the driving force behind each problem is in understanding fashion DNA of the target audience. The target audience could be variable: people of certain age group, people from a certain geographic location, people visiting a website at a given time of year, or at the extreme case a single user. On the other hand, the key difference between bleeding edge research into data driven fashion analytics and more traditional approaches of studying fashion is in leveraging the scale of data. For instance, perceptually motivated color science rules are a result of many small scale psychological experiments, results of which psychologists agree upon. These research studies do not leverage the scale of data which has become increasingly available over the past few years. As will become evident in later sections, purely data driven approaches proposed in this work comprehensively outperform classical rules of color science. This

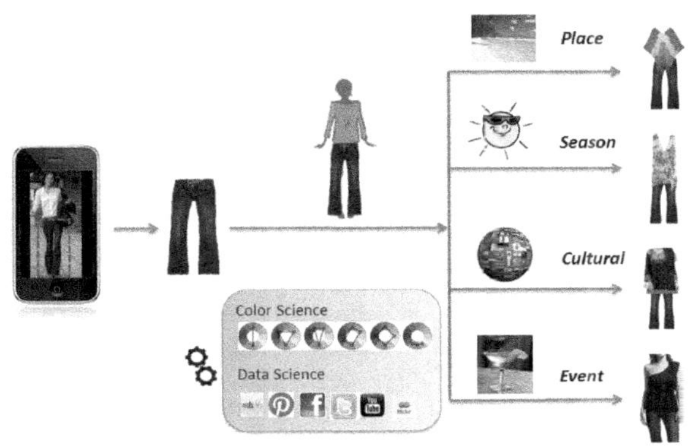

Figure 1: Illustration of context based recommendation. Different tops are recommended for the same pair of blue jeans.

KDD'14, August 24–27, 2014, New York, New York, USA.

http://dx.doi.org/10.1145/2623330.2623332

makes a strong case for re-thinking fashion rules from a bottom up data-driven perspective, from single users to groups of users to modeling fashion tastes of entire populations. **Why Large Scale Fashion Analytics → Fashion DNA ?**

- Large scale datasets increasingly available due to fashion sources from web, mobile and social networks
- Fashion choices are influenced by variety of factors eg: visual, textual, branding, seasonal, demographic, occasional
- Leveraging large scale datasets is the most promising strategy to capture these variable influencers and their correlations
- Thorough understanding of these influencers results in better personalization of fashion choices
- Fashion analytics could shed light on novel interaction mechanisms of the future

We believe there is ample scope to adopt several existing problems in the fashion domain and demonstrate the utility/gains demonstrated by a data driven thinking. We adopt the problem of "up-selling in e-commerce" where an online shopper with an item in her shopping cart is recommended other items that complement the cart. This paper proposes a similar application for fashion, where given an image of a fashion item (say "jeans"), the goal is to recommend matching fashion items (say "tops") that complement the given item (Figure 1). In order to learn the recommender we leverage large scale street fashion data, where visual experiences have strong social, cultural and commercial importance. Street fashion images typically contain full view of a street fashion model striking a pose with several fashionable accessories, see Figure 2(c) for an example. During the training phase, each image has a fashion model wearing multiple apparel (street fashion data), while the images used in test phase comprise a single apparel (e-Commerce data). Throughout this work, we stick to image data alone while noting that fusing modalities such as text, video and brands would lead to more comprehensive models.

Complementary Recommenders for e-Commerce: The computational challenges involved in complementary recommenders are two fold. Firstly, the representation of fashion item into visual features is an open problem. This problem is compounded by the task of learning inter-dependencies between such features from different items (i.e. "tops" and "jeans"). Further, a number of practical challenges that need to be addressed include obtaining high quality image data with clean background, scalability issues in terms of memory and speed requirements that can handle large image databases as well as generate real-time predictions. Such constraints are even more crucial in the context of mobile shopping which is limited by the compute, memory and network capacities. We formulate the recommendation problem as follows: Given an image i containing a set of fashion items, also referred to as "parts" (i.e. sunglasses, tops, skirts, shoes, handbags), the holistic description H_i of an image i is given by $\underline{H}_i^T := [\underline{h}_{i1}^T, \underline{h}_{i1}^T, \dots, \underline{h}_{iP}^T] \in \Re^{PK}, \underline{h}_{ij}^T \mathbf{1}_K = 1, \forall j \in [1, 2, ..P]$, where P is the number of parts, K is the size of code book to represent a part and $\underline{h}_{ij} \in \Re^K$ denotes the representation of part j for image i. Our task is to learn a predictive model $M(\mathbf{H}, \mathbf{q})$ where $\mathbf{H} = [\underline{H}_1, \underline{H}_2, \dots, \underline{H}_N]^T$ for N number of images in the data set and $\mathbf{q} = [\underline{h}_{q1}^T, \underline{h}_{q2}^T ... \underline{h}_{qm}^T, \dots, \underline{h}_{qP}^T] \in \Re^{PK}$ represents an input query description with a missing part m. Given an input query vector with a missing column entry, the problem of model learning reduces to predicting the value of empty column in the vector using Model M. Once the model is learned, it can be used to transform the input query which can then be used in applications such as recommendation systems, retrieval and personalization.

Table 1: Summary of fashion data sets in our study.

Data set	Comments
Fashion-136K	135893 street fashion images with annotations by fashionistas, brand, demographics.
Fashion-Toy	Subset of Fashion-136K. $n = 600$, $n_{train} = 500, n_{test} = 100$.
Fashion-63K	Subset of Fashion-136K. $n = 63K$, $n_{train} = 53K, n_{test} = 10K$
Fashion-350K	350K images of just tops & blouses to test retrieval performance using fashionistas.
Fashion-Q1K	1K images of skirts used to retrieve images from Fashion-350K. Skirts have one of the following different patterns: animal-print (100), floral (200), geometric (100), plaids & checks (150), paisley (50), polka dots (100), solid (200), stripes (100).

Product Deployment: The techniques described in this work are currently being deployed for internal testing through the eBay Mobile Fashion App, building on the eBay Image Swatch [1], see (https://itunes.apple.com/in/app/ebay-fashion/id378358380?mt=8). We estimate that the next version of the Fashion App with visual recommendation technology will be available for download later this year through the App Store for users in the United States. The system is implemented in such a way that the user first takes a picture of either top/bottom clothing using a mobile phone, and the algorithms described in this work respond with real time recommendations of complementary bottom/top clothing after searching through millions of images indexed by our system.

2. DATA DRIVEN VISUAL RECOMMENDERS

In order to place our ideas in context, we have divided the scope of data driven fashion analytics into four main stages where one stage naturally leads to another.

1. The Datasets: We use 3 datasets in our experiments, namely: *Fashion-136K*, *Fashion-350K* and *Fashion-Q1K*. *Fashion-136K* is a data set created by crawling the web for photographs of fashion models. It consists of 135893 street fashion images with annotations by fashionistas, brand, demographics. Hence, all images comprise top and bottom clothing co-occurring in the same image. This dataset is used for the training phase. See Table 2 for the list of tags present in *Fashion-136K*, and their mapping to corresponding human body parts. *Fashion-Q1K* dataset consists of 1000 skirt images which are used as input queries to recommender. Given these queries, the recommender searches and returns matches from *Fashion-350K*. The result of retrieval is a ranked list of the Fashion-350K images sorted by relevance to a query from Fashion-Q1K. *Fashion-350K* images are from a clothing inventory containing only top clothing (without model or mannequin). In a mobile setting, it is assumed that the user takes a photograph of a single apparel of interest (or guides the recommender by drawing a bounding box around the apparel), say bottom clothing image patches used as queries for top clothing. With advancements in computer vision, it might be possible in the near future to automatically detect query apparel patches from images of people wearing fashion accessories.

Low-Level Representation: We utilize two low-level representations of image, namely (i) HSV Histograms: Given P parts of interest characterized by P distinct bounding boxes, a normalized 40

Item	Quantity
Initial size of corpus	196974
Final size after cleanup ($H \geq 400, H/W > 1$)	135893
Number of unique tags	71
Number of unique users	8357
Number of unique brands	20110
Number of known cities	115
Number of known regions	136

(a) Images, tags, geo-location.

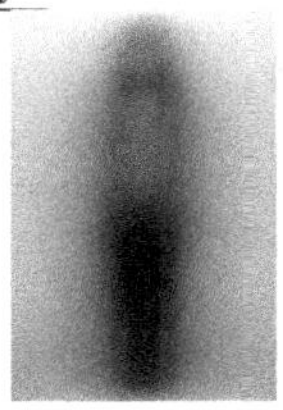

(b) Average image.

(c) Exemplars showing various pose and complex background.

Figure 2: Basic summary of street fashion corpus Fashion-136K. Images were posted and tagged by fashion designers and fashionistas. There are about 3-4 annotations per image, with each user posting anywhere from 8 to 524 images. Most contain full view of model.

Table 2: From accessory tags to semantic attributes of human body. The tags highlighted in bold are those which are most popular, and are listed with the number of occurrences in the dataset.

Semantic Group	Tags in Corpus
1 - Head (7069)	beanies / berets, hats, headbands, headdress
2 - Face (13738)	earrings, glasses / sunglasses
3 - Neck (32278)	**jewelry-25255**, necklaces, scarves / echarpes
4 - Chest (1514)	bodysuits, bustiers / bras, corsets, swimwears
5 - Hand (60584)	**bags-43864**, bracelets, clutches, gloves, rings, watches
6 - MidTorso (113506)	**dresses-33253**, jumpsuits, little black dresses, little white dresses, long dresses, minidresses, **shirt / blouses - 33923**, sweaters, **t-shirts-24907**, tanks, tartan, tunics, turtlenecks
7 - SideTorso (49961)	blazers, brooches, capes, cardigans, coats, hoodies sweatshirts, **jackets-18016**, trenches, vests
8 - Waist (11669)	belts
9 - UpperThigh (34906)	miniskirts, **skirts-20732**, tutus, shorts
10 - LowerThigh (48028)	boyfriend pants, harem / baggy pants, **jeans-21663**, jeggings, leggings, over the knee, **pants-17928**, rolled-up, skinny pants
11 - Knee (5881)	color tights, socks / tights
12 - Foot (84745)	ankle boots / booties, ballerinas, biker boots, boots, cowboy boots, flats, gladiators, **heels / wedges-38447**, lace ups, mary janes, oxfords / derbies, peep toes, sandals, sneakers

dimensional color histogram is computed by quantizing Hue Saturation and Value into 24, 8, 8 uniformly spaced bins respectively, (ii) Color BoW: A K-dimensional feature vector is obtained by randomly sampling fixed size (15×15) patches from the bounding box and quantizing them to a learned code book of K code book entries. We performed extensive experiments with texture features such Gabor Wavelets [10], Textons [12], Dense-SIFT[3] and found them to be unstable for texture classification in clothing. A preliminary analysis suggests that deformable nature of clothing often leads to unreliable texture estimation where even wrinkles and folds on solid clothes can be misinterpreted as texture. Further, we also looked at style based features based on attributes of clothing like cuts, sleeve etc., but were unable find a robust style descriptor in the vision literature. Hence, in this paper we focus our attention to using only color based image representations.

Parsing Fashion Accessories using Computer Vision: Given a database of images of fashion models (see Figure 2(c)), we are required to parse the image of the fashion model into constituent apparel being worn. In other words, the aim is to identify or localize every apparel from a label set purse, sunglass, shirt, pant etc ... Attempting to get these labels through a crowdsourcing would quickly turn out to be infeasible since the number of images are fairly large along with large label sets. Automating this by computer vision is the only feasible method to leverage the utility of this large scale data. Over the past two years there have been a couple of efforts to approach this very problem of automating image parsing. While the progress shown by these successive papers are indeed very impressive they are still not scalable to very large datasets. In this work, we utilize the x,y coordinates of top and bottom clothing tagged by fashionistas as a *weak label* to extract swatches from the image. Ensuing discussions will focus on modeling pairwise relationships between top and bottom clothing using color descriptors.

2. Preliminary Data Analysis: Once the data has been acquired, figuring out the right questions to ask from the data would lead to mechanisms for understanding the data well. For instance, how many red shirts occur with blue pants in street fashion images? These questions can be trivially answered by database queries on the collected datasets. Since we predominantly focus on color modeling, the question we ask is "Is there signal in the empirical co-occurrence of color patterns between top and bottom clothing of fashion models in images we collect?" The empirical co-occurence of color patterns street fashion dataset (*Fashion-136K*) in Figure 3. The result is intuitively satisfying since there is a clear signal of some co-occurrence of color patterns being preferred a lot more than others. Estimating these patterns would help one understand fashion tastes better, and sits at the foundation of discussions to follow.

3. Predictive Modeling: The goal of predictive modeling would be to forecast, or predict what might be interesting to the user based on past history. Our assumption in this paper is that street fashion images contain co-occurrence patterns which reflect the current fashion tastes of shoppers. This constitutes historical (training) data from which a visual recommender is to be learnt for predicting co-occurring patterns that are potentially interesting to shoppers. Further, we design two classes of models DFR (Deterministic Fashion

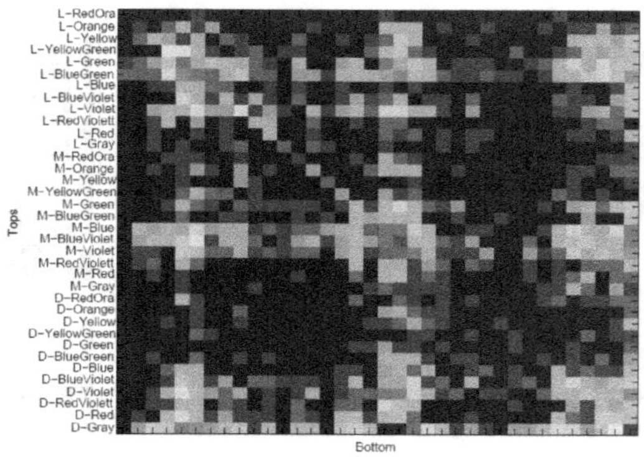

Figure 3: Empirical co-occurrence matrix of tops along rows, and bottom clothing along columns. Some intuitive patterns that can be read off the above matrix are green and blue tops go well with green and blue bottoms respectively. Further, the last column indicates that dark gray (black) bottoms go well with any colored top.

Recommender) and SFR (Stochastic Fashion Recommender). As the names suggest, results from DFR are reproducible, while those from SFR are not. Our intuition behind designing SFR was that fashion is inherently exploratory, and injecting randomness into recommenders would serve to capture this exploratory nature. We propose a suite of algorithms under each category, and comprehensively benchmark their relative pros and cons. Section 4 discusses these issues in detail.

4. User Interaction with Predictive Models: Finally, it is of considerable interest to understand how the predictive models interact with users. In other words, the aim is to perform extensive validation of these predictive models through end user studies. More on this in Section 5.

3. BACKGROUND AND RELATED WORKS

There have been only handful attempts to solve the problem of visual fashion recommendation. We are aware of only two existing works in this area. Iwata et al. [6] study this problem in isolation where they propose a topic model based approach to solve this problem. However, given the small dataset size of their experimentation it is difficult to ascertain the relative merits of their system. Liu et al. [8] propose a latent SVM based formulation to handle both "wear properly" and "wear aesthetically" criteria in their model. However most of their experimentation is tailored towards solid colored clothing and their qualitative analysis fails to demonstrate the efficacy of system performance on a variety of clothing patterns. Other related papers on fashion domain [4, 9, 13, 14, 15] work on the problem of fashion parsing and similarity retrieval where the goal is to retrieve similar fashion image for a given query. These methods either employ the mixture of parts based pose estimator or use the poselets based part detectors after applying the deformable parts based detector for person detection. Yamaguchi et al.[14] utilize a superpixel labeling approach on a CRF for inferring part labels from a labeled dataset of fashion apparel. The Street to Shop system [9] attempts to solve the cross domain discrepancy between catalogue images and images captured in the wild sent in as a query. Gallagher et al. [4] utilize attribute based classifiers regularized by a CRF that models interactions between attributes. We believe such methods are limited by their ability to accurately parse humans from real-world images since the problem of person detection and subsequent pose estimation is still largely unsolved [16].

There exists a vast amount of literature on learning aesthetically pleasing color contexts which can provide a great insight for a deeper understanding of this problem. In these papers [5, 7] the goal is to present the user with matches that are perceptually pleasing along with the query item. As a result of this research, the Matsuda templates have emerged as a popular choice for representing color basis functions. This allows for a straightforward retrieval mechanism by rotating the color wheel according to some preconceived rule. For instance, complementary color retrieval simply shifts the hue wheel by 180 degrees and subsequently retrieves nearest neighbors. In this paper, we propose to use these techniques as baselines and compare their performance against multiple data driven approaches.

4. PREDICTIVE MODELS FOR FASHION RECOMMENDATION

In order to set the context, imagine a shopper who has bought an apparel (say pants) and is not sure about what shirt would go well with the pant they have bought. It would be very useful is a trained model could leverage the scale of data and recommend relevant items from the online inventory.

We think about recommenders in two main ways: 1. Determinisitic Fashion Recommenders 2. Stochastic Fashion Recommenders

Since very limited research exists for investigating the full spectrum for solving the problem of visual recommendation, we propose the following set of algorithms to address this issue. This also allows to exploit the relative merits of each algorithm for designing a better solution. We split a data set of n images into n_{train} training and n_{test} testing images where each image has a set of parts, such as head, foot, torso, etc. Let us assume part indices to be represented by $p = \{1, 2, 3, \ldots, P\}$. For example, $p = 1, 2, P$ could correspond to head, torso and foot, respectively. Some of these parts are observable to the algorithm, while the rest are hidden. The aim of the algorithm is to infer features related to the hidden parts. On a similar note, let us assume visible part indices to be $p_v = \{1, 2, ..., |p_v|\}$ and hidden part indices to be $p_h = \{1, 2, ...|p_h|\}$. Note that $|p_v| + |p_h| = P$.

We assume each part j of image i to have an associated part descriptor $\underline{h}_{ij} \in \Re^K$. The feature $\underline{h}_{ij}$ can be color, texture, or any other visual descriptor such as bag of words (BoW). An ith image can now be described by the concatenation of all part descriptors:

$$\underline{H}_i^T := [\underline{h}_{i1}^T, \underline{h}_{i2}^T, \ldots, \underline{h}_{iP}^T] \quad (1)$$

In case of a K-dimensional HSV histogram, K is the number of bins, while in case of bag of words, K is the size of code book.

4.1 Deterministic Fashion Recommenders (DFR)

Deterministic Fashion Recommender (DFR) aims to harness the power of data in recommending co-ordinating fashion items. For each co-ordinating clothing piece in our training data (e.g. *skirts,tops*), we extract color features in form of a K-dimensional HSV histogram [1]. This generates 40-dimensional feature vector for each clothing piece. Features from <*skirt,top*> tuple are then indexed in a database. During testing time, when a query *skirt* image is presented, a 40-dimensional query feature vector is computed and searched across the *skirt* portion of all indexed tuples. Finally, *top* portions of all nearest tuples are returned as the recommended *tops*. Since, the proposed model is based on a nearest-neighbor principle, the quality of recommendation depends on the size and quality of the data. With large and diverse data, DFR can provide better recommendations and can also be interpreted as being more objective with its fashion choices.

4.1.1 Tuned Perceptual Retrieval (PR)

This baseline uses the popular perceptually motivated Matsuda templates [5] and the transformation is either a complementary or triad pattern for the hue histogram. The saturation and value channels are simply reflected on the intuition that people prefer wearing contrasting styles.

4.1.2 Complementary Nearest Neighbor Consensus (CNNC)

Let us define a fixed metric on the space, say $dist$. The metric could be $||.||_1$, $||.||_2$, KL-divergence, or Earth Mover's distance. We stick to $||.||_1$ for simplicity. The problem we are faced with is predicting the hidden P^{th} part. Denoting a single test query sample as q,

$$N_q = \underset{i:1 \leq i \leq n_{train}}{\text{argmin}_{\mathcal{K}}} \sum_{j \in p_v} dist(\underline{h}_{qj}, \underline{h}_{ij}) \tag{2}$$

The above equation simply picks those images that are similar to the input query image q in the visible parts. If a simple $argmin$ was defined, it would return the closest neighbor. However, we want the $\mathcal{K}$ closest neighbors and hence the notation $argmin_{\mathcal{K}}$.

Once nearest neighbors are picked, the goal is to infer the hidden parts. For this purpose, we accumulate representations for hidden part as $\{\underline{h}_{ij} | i \in N_q, j \in p_h\}$.

We infer the missing part as, $\underline{h}_{qj} = C_j(\underline{h}_{ij}); i \in N_q, j \in p_H$. Here $C_j : \Re^{|N_q \times K|} \rightarrow \Re^K$ is the consensus function for part j. We use the simplest average consensus function:

$$\{\underline{h}_{ij} | i \in N_q, j \in p_h\} \xmapsto{C_j(\underline{h}_{ij})} \underline{h}_{qj} = \frac{1}{N_q} \sum_{i \in N_q} \underline{h}_{ij} \tag{3}$$

Corollary: *KNN Consensus-Diversity* - In a generic shopping experience, a shopper would not like to be presented with the same type of clothing multiple times. As a result, a "diverse" retrieval is required. We propose the following generic optimization for generating diverse transformed queries, each of which can be used to query the inventory for similar images. The following optimization is proposed for the purpose:

$$\mathbf{I}_q^{diverse} = Div(\{\underline{h}_{ij} | i \in N_q, j \in p_H\}) \tag{4}$$

Div is an operator that returns a subset $\mathbf{I}_q^{diverse}$ of images from the set N_q that are as different as possible from one another on the hidden part features. In our case Div is a non-linear operator that clusters the data points and samples points, one from each cluster.

4.2 Stochastic Fashion Recommender (SFR)

Fashion choices can sometimes be highly subjective. For instance, a typical user may like polka dots so he or she may always prefer a match with polka dots over other matches. Such behavior cannot be modeled with DFR-like approaches. To address this issue, we propose Stochastic Fashion Recommender (SFR) that aims to explore the space of user biases in recommending matches. Computationally, the space of all such possible biases is huge and impractical to model. Hence, we constrain these biases to a smaller set of fashion choices. In our study, this constraint is achieved by the common notion that *solid* and *patterned* clothing co-ordinate well together. In other words, having busy patterns in both top and bottom clothing is less popular. To model this, we parameterize our desired output space (e.g. *solids*) with a probability distribution. This ensures that given a *patterned* query, all output choices from the model will be *solids*. Given this particular output space, user biases can be modeled by a distribution sampling process. In our case, we perform a uniform sampling of the distribution (i.e. randomly pick a solid color). Hence, not only does this model ensure "stochasticity" for the same input, it also relaxes computational complexity and allows us to closely mimic the human subjectivity in fashion.

4.2.1 Texture Agnostic Retrieval (TAR)

We propose the Texture Agnostic Retrieval technique, based on the notion of consumers preferring *solid* colors to go well with *patterned* clothing. In other words, having busy patterns in the top and bottom clothing seems counter-intuitive. The recommender can be stated as follows: $\underline{h}_{ij} \sim P(\underline{h}, \alpha)$ where α parameterizes the distribution which can be sampled efficiently. Since the bias has to be towards solid colors, we sample with a constraint that

$$\underline{h}_{ij} \sim P(\underline{h}, \alpha), \text{ s.t. } \underline{h}_{ij}^T \mathbf{1}_K = 1 \tag{5}$$

For our application of interest, we select $P(\underline{h}, \alpha) = U([0, 1])$, while we note any other distribution that can be efficiently sampled can be employed.

4.2.2 Mixture Models

Gaussian Mixture Models (GMM): An alternative way of viewing the above problem is using mixture models. Assuming each dimension of the space in which the Gaussian mixture model (GMM) is defined to correspond to part features, the GMM intuitively captures the part features that co-occur most frequently. At test time, the goal is to efficiently sample these high density regions using features from visible parts to recommend clothing on the hidden parts.

The learning module aims to learn the parameters of a mixture of multivariate Gaussian distribution parameterized by a random variable $\underline{H}$, and denoted by:

$$p(\underline{H}|\lambda) = \sum_{i=1}^{M} w_i g(\underline{H}\mu_i, \mathbf{\Sigma}_i) \tag{6}$$

In the above equation, $g(\underline{H}|\mu_i, \Sigma_i) = \mathcal{N}(\mu_i, \mathbf{\Sigma}_i), \lambda = (\underline{\mu}, \mathbf{\Sigma}, \underline{w})$ denotes the parameters of the Gaussian mixture distribution having M mixture components, $\underline{\mu} = [\underline{\mu}_1 ... \underline{\mu}_M], \mathbf{\Sigma} = [\mathbf{\Sigma}_1 ... \mathbf{\Sigma}_M]$ and $\underline{w} = [w_1 ... w_M]$ respectively denote the means, co-variance matrices and mixture weights of the M Gaussian mixture components.

Assume query vector $\underline{H}_q^T = [\underline{h}_{q1}^T, ..., \underline{h}_{qj}^T, ..., \underline{h}_{qP}^T]$, with a missing part m, the goal is to infer the most probable value $\underline{h}_{qm}$ of missing part m.

We cast it as the following problem:

$$\hat{\underline{h}}_{qm} = \underset{\underline{h}_{qm} : \underline{H}_q^T = [\underline{h}_{q1}^T, ..., \underline{h}_{qm}^T, ..., \underline{h}_{qP}]^T}{\text{argmax}} p(\underline{H}|\lambda) \tag{7}$$

This is a constrained conditional maximization and will fix values of parts that have already been observed and will only search over unknown variables for a maximum likelihood assignment score. Since the mixture model defined above requires high dimensional density estimation, we first vector quantize the part feature space Assuming that P parts share a common code book of size, a mixture model in P dimensions results. In other words, we utilize the code word to which a part feature is most closely associated with as an input to learn the mixture model.

Markov Chain - LDA (MCL): An approach for retrieval using inherent cluster structure of the data is to utilize topic models. In essence, what we require is a topic model where words have a specific structure. In other words, even though words are drawn

Table 3: **Comparison of different models: + (Easy), o (Medium), x (Hard)**

Model:	CNNC	GMM	TAR	MCL	PR
Learn Ease	+	+	+	x	+
Test Ease	x	x	+	+	+
Scalability	o	+	+	o	+
Generalization	+	o	o	+	x

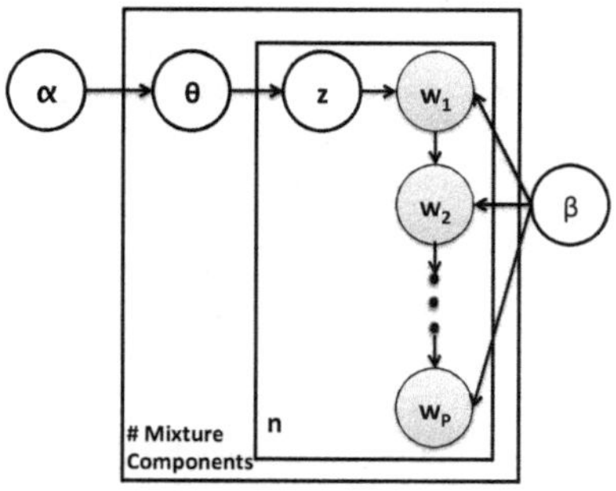

Figure 4: Markov Chain LDA model for learning fashion co-occurrences, with w_i as the word for part i.

from a code book, certain word combinations (say, color combinations) have a much higher probability of occurrence than others. We propose to model the structure in word combinations by a Markov Chain (Figure 4). It is useful to observe that a Markovian assumption may not reflect the true dependencies in fashion co-occurrence. However, the conditional independence properties yielded by a Markov Chain significantly reduces the computational needs for structured word generation.

The generative model for the original LDA model [2] for words w, topics θ and hyper parameters α and β is given by:

$$p(w|\alpha,\beta) = \int p(\theta|\alpha) \prod_{i=1}^{n} \sum_{z_i} p(z_i|\theta) p(w|z_i,\beta) d\theta \tag{8}$$

We propose the following generalization of basic LDA to Markov chains on words, thus modifying the model to:

$$p(\underline{w}|\alpha,\beta) = \int p(\theta|\alpha) \prod_{i=1}^{n} \sum_{z_i} p(z_i|\theta) p(\underline{w}|z_i,\beta) d\theta \tag{9}$$

where $\underline{w} = [w_1, w_2, \ldots, w_P]$. Inference over the joint distribution is computationally expensive. Hence we make the following simplifying assumption:

$$p(\underline{w}|\alpha,\beta) = \int p(\theta|\alpha) \prod_{i=1}^{n} \sum_{z_i} p(z_i|\theta) \cdot \underbrace{p(w_1) \prod_{j=2}^{P} p(w_j|w_{j-1},\beta,z_i)}_{p(\underline{w}|z_i,\beta)} \, d\theta \tag{10}$$

This modified model is now learned offline using training data. When a new query comes in, say a shirt, the topic most likely to have this word is now picked and the Markov chain is sampled to generate a new transformed sample that can be utilized for retrieving complementary nearest neighbors.

The methods described till now are summarized based on ease of training, ease of testing, scalability, and generalization in Table 3. The requirements for a specific application would dictate the method of choice for recommendation. We also attempted adopting

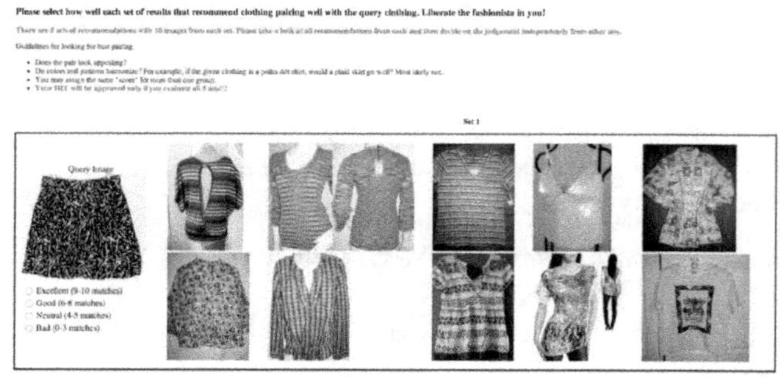

Figure 5: Illustration of crowdsourcing evaluation interface

the collaborative filtering formulation of [11], but do not describe it in detail due to practical difficulties we encountered in scaling the algorithm to large data sets. We note that there is rich literature on scaling collaborative filtering approaches to large scale datasets, which we do not investigate in this work.

5. USER BEHAVIOR/INTERACTION WITH PREDICTIVE MODELS

Crowd-sourcing Fashion: Since the primary objective is to understand user preferences in fashion, we require user ratings on recommendations provided by DFR and SFR. We propose to use crowd-sourcing to obtain these ratings. This scheme also aligns well with our goal of understanding "Street Fashion", where a layman user's (i.e. fashionista on crowd sourcing platform) rating can be used as a ground-truth dataset. This validation procedure is in line with the established validation protocols for image retrieval [17]. Figure 5 outlines the proposed crowd-sourcing experiment. A user is presented with an input query image on left side (polka skirt) and the top-10 recommended matches (tops) on the right side. User rates these matches as one of -1 (bad match), 0 (neutral match), 1 (good match), 2 (excellent match). To ensure consistency in ratings, each query was evaluated by 5 different users leading to a total of 5000 users ratings. A total of 140 unique users participated in the experiment of which majority of users had a 100% approval ratings from their previous experiments. However, since fashion tastes vary greatly across people, it is usually hard to get a consensus on which algorithm performs the best from all 5 fashionistas. As a result, we only retain ratings from fashionistas who *agree* on algorithm performance. Since there are inadvertent errors by fashionistas, the total number of ratings that result after a preliminary filtering of ratings was 937, split across 187 solid queries and 750 patterned queries. We note here that since fashion is very subjective, a rigorous evaluation using principles from psychology is a very interesting line of future work.

Agreement Among Users: Understanding users is a logical first step in designing a user-driven fashion recommendation system. This can be done by gathering useful and interesting signals from user preferences that can be captured to replicate user choices in fashion. We study this effect by introducing the notion of disagreement between user preferences over visual recommendations. Our hypothesis is that presence of strong signals in user preferences will lead to lower disagreement among their preferences. Denoting each rating of 2 algorithms (DFR, SFR) for a query q using a 2-dimensional vector $\underline{\zeta}_{qi} \in \{-1, 0, 1, 2\}^2$, where each entry is a rating from -1 to +2, the score for disagreement across users is defined as, $\gamma_{qi} = \sum_{j=1}^{2} ||\underline{\zeta}_{qi} - \underline{\zeta}_{qj}||_1$. Further, an agreement threshold is defined to be the median of disagreement scores across all

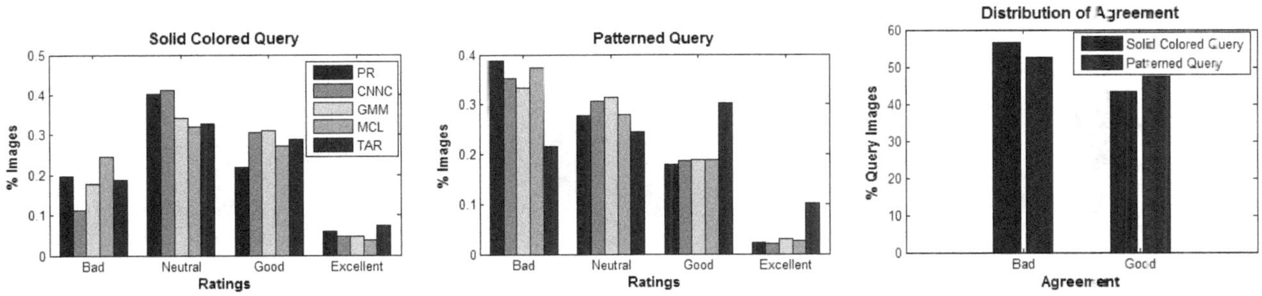

(a) (b) (c)

Figure 6: Performance comparison of algorithms. CNNC performs the best for solid colored queries (20% of query set Fashion-Q1K) and TAR for patterned queries. (a) Ratings by fashionistas for solid colored queries. (b) Ratings for patterned queries. (c) Overall performance for the complete query set (includes both solid colors and patterns). The hybrid approach uses CNNC for solids and TAR for patterned queries, based on the decision of a solid vs pattern classifier.

queries, $A_T = median(\gamma_{qi}); q \in [1, 1000], i \in [1, 2]$. User ratings are retained only if $\gamma_{qi} < A_T$. This is done to filter outlier ratings from observations to account for spam in crowd-sourcing experiments. Finally, a query rating confidence is computed as $C_q = \frac{\text{Number of Users Retained for a Query}}{\text{Total Number of Users for a Query}}$. The final rating R_m for a model m is computed as:

$$R_m = \sum_{q=1}^{1000} C_q \frac{\sum_{i=1}^{5} \zeta_{qi}(m)\delta(\gamma_{qi} < A_T)}{\sum_{i=1}^{5} \delta(\gamma_{qi} < A_T)} \quad (11)$$

where $\delta(x)$ is the Dirac-delta function, $\zeta_{qi}(m)$ refers to the rating provided by fashionista i on query q for model m. As shown in Figure 7(a), majority of the users have lower disagreement score (below 0.5) suggesting that there is enough consensus among their fashion choices that can be investigated in more detail. We now take a closer look at all these ratings where users have sufficient agreement as determined empirically through a threshold over disagreement score. These ratings are further split across solid and patterned queries to further isolate the particular section of queries which have greater rating agreements. Results shown in figure 7(b) suggest that users agree more on patterned queries, evidenced by the higher magnitude of red bars on the good agreement bin. In the case of solids, the users agreed that the retrieval was either *Neutral* or *Good* (evidenced by the higher weights to the yellow and blue bars). However, on patterned queries, users overwhelmingly agreed that the retrievals were not favorable (evidenced by the higher weights on the red bar). This result has two major conclusions: (i) *There is a strong consensus among seemingly arbitrary fashion choices made by users* (ii) *It is possible to identify a specific category of visual recommendations (i.e. solid colored bottom and patterned top combination) where such consensus is stronger.*

5.1 Retrieval Experimentation

In the past sections, we presented methods to learn the missing part of a query image. For instance, given a descriptor for skirt, what is the recommended descriptor for blouse? Thus the query descriptor is essentially mapped to a new space (say, from skirt to blouse). This mapped query now serves as an input query to a content based image retrieval (CBIR) system, for retrieving images similar to the mapped query.

Training: The Fashion-136K is a data set created by crawling the web for photographs of fashion models. Hence, all images comprise top and bottom clothing co-occurring in the same image. Further, their spatial location (x, y) coordinates are also manually annotated by fashionistas. We use this data set for training all data-driven models described previously. While studying the data, we observed interesting co-occurrence relationships between top and bottom clothing such as dark gray/black bottoms going well with any colored top. It is such interesting patterns that the data driven models attempt to learn. In scenarios that require recommendations to be driven by context (Figure 1), it is possible to learn a separate co-occurrence matrix for every context.

Retrieval: Images of skirts (bottom clothing) from the Fashion-Q1K dataset are utilized as queries to retrieve top clothing from the Fashion-350K data set. Fashion-350K images are from a clothing inventory containing only top clothing (without model or mannequin). As a result, we utilize Fashion-136K where top and bottom clothing *co-occur* to learn models that are used while querying Fashion-350K. It is useful to note that this procedure trains the retrieval system on images on a data set (Fashion-136K) that is completely different from the test data (Fashion-350K). The result of retrieval is a ranked list of the Fashion-350K images sorted by relevance to a query from Fashion-Q1K. Since there are multiple SFR/DFR algorithms proposed in this work, the results of retrieval are multiple ranked lists where each list corresponds to a different algorithm's output. The running time and scalability of the system is dominated by the time taken for retrieval [1]. Efficient schemes for indexing and retrieving image features enable real time responses in a mobile setting.

As shown in results from Figure 6(a-c), data driven models outperform perceptual retrieval. We study the performance of algorithms on solid colored and patterned clothing separately to gain better insight into the workings of each algorithm. Further, it is useful to note that we had initially given the fashionistas an option to rate on a scale from Bad-Excellent (-1 to +2). Visual results of the various retrieval algorithms are presented in Figure 9.

Retrieval for Solid Colored Query: On solid clothing queries, it was observed that CNNC had the best normalized score of 0.418 on a scale from 0 to 1, followed by TAR 0.402, GMM 0.393, PR 0.383 and MCL 0.370. As seen in Figure 9, CNNC tends to retrieve patterned clothing. This is in fact favored by fashionistas in our study, for solid colored queries. The strength of adding diversity to a method like CNNC, as in Equation 4, is also shown qualitatively in Figure 8.

Retrieval for Patterned Query: On pattern clothing queries, TAR performed the best with a normalized score of 0.40 on a scale from 0 to 1, followed by GMM 0.31, CNNC 0.30, MCL 0.30 and PR 0.29. The impressive performance of TAR can be attributed to the general preference for solid colored clothing to go with another patterned clothing. Recall that by construction TAR is agnostic to texture and recommends only solid colors. Further, the simplicity

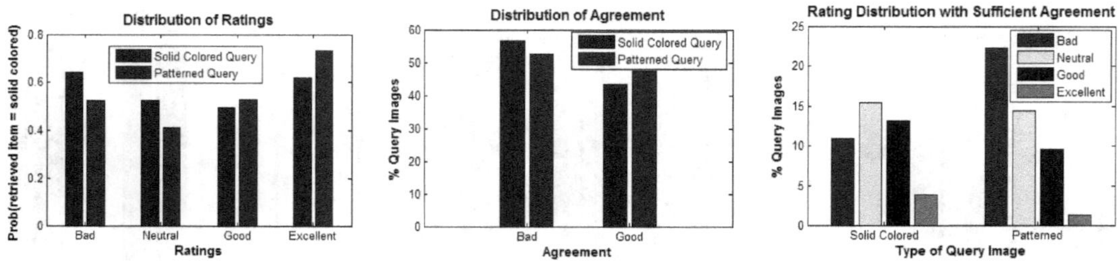

(a) (b) (c)

Figure 7: (a) A solid vs pattern classifier was used to estimate probability of solid colored clothing in the top retrievals. Fashionistas prefer patterned recommendations for solid colored queries and vice versa. (b) Illustration of rating agreement on solid colored and patterned queries. Fashionistas tend to agree more on retrievals of patterned queries, than they agree on solid queries. (c) This expands the second half of (b). Depicts common agreement amongst fashionstas based on retrieved results. Results for solid colored queries are generally more favorable than for patterned queries.

of TAR leads to a fairly robust query transformation. Finally, the query for solid colors by TAR leads to a lot more relevant retrievals from Fashion-350K, since it is much easier to match and retrieve solid clothing from an inventory in comparison to patterned clothing. See Figure 10 for examples of multiple query-retrieval pairs.

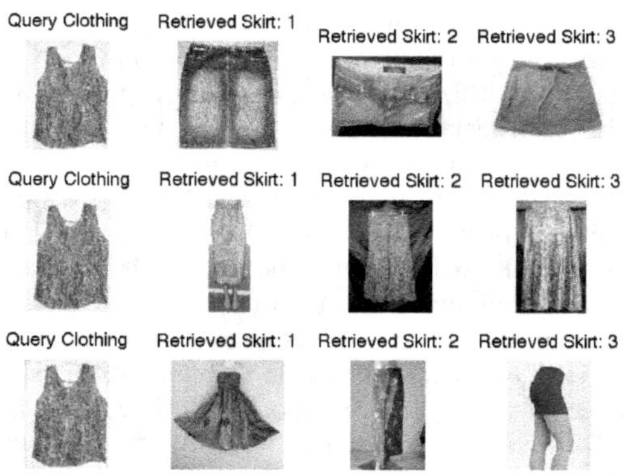

Figure 8: Illustration of diverse retrievals using CNNC, corresponding to a sample query. Each row corresponds to different set of results, while being relevant to the query.

The Hybrid Classifier: Based on our findings, we observe that CNNC performs the best for solid queries, while TAR performs best on pattern queries. Since a query could either be a solid or patterned, we propose using a single hybrid recommender that resorts to using CNNC for solid queries and TAR for patterned queries. The switching can be determined at the beginning of the retrieval procedure using a simple pattern classifier that labels a query as either solid or patterned. Experimental results on the overall query set (solid+patterns) indicate that the hybrid classifier which switches between CNNC and TAR yields the highest overall performance of 0.403, see Figure 6(c).

Ratings for Solid Colored Retrievals: The previous quantitative experiments seem to offer an insight that fashionistas prefer solid retrievals for patterned queries (evidenced by the impressive performance of TAR), which we validate in this experiment by exploring how fashionistas respond to solid colored retrievals. In other words, we run a binary classifier on the retrieval set to obtain the average probability of the retrieval set to be solid. When considering solid queries in Figure 7(a), we infer that fashionistas do not favor solid colored retrievals. This is evidenced by the higher magnitude of the blue bars on *Bad* and *Neutral* ratings. On the other hand, when considering patterned queries in Figure 7(a), we infer that fashionistas tend to favor solid colored retrievals. Observe the higher magnitude of the red bars on *Good* and *Excellent* ratings. This provides an intuitive justification behind the impressive performance of TAR on the pattern queries, since solids are retrieved by construction.

Distribution of Rating Agreement: Next, we study the rating agreement on solid and patterned queries. In other words, we measure how *agreeable* the recommendation algorithm's results are across solid and patterned queries, see Figure 7(b). It can be readily observed that fashionistas tend to agree more on patterned queries, evidenced by the higher magnitude of red bars on the good agreement bin. On the other hand, fashionistas tend to disagree more on the solid queries in comparison to patterns. It would be interesting to study whether rating agreement was on retrievals that were rated as *Good*, or on retrievals they thought were *Bad*. Figure 7(c) shows the split of among the ratings that fashionistas agreed on. In the case of solids, the fashionistas agreed that the retrieval was either *Neutral* or *Good* (evidenced by the higher weights to the yellow and blue bars). However, on patterned queries, the fashionistas overwhelmingly agreed that the retrievals were not favorable (evidenced by the higher weights on the red bar). This finding indicates that the performance of the algorithms on pattern queries can be further enhanced. A major reason for this result is the fact that the proposed system is purely color based, and integration of novel texture features devoid of drawbacks mentioned in previous sections could possibly yield a significant performance boost. This is a promising avenue for future research.

Insights into Street Fashion: Our experimental analysis leads to the following insights on street fashion, (i) Fashion Cues: Analyzing fashionista ratings for different algorithms suggest an intuitive fashion cue that a pair of patterned and solid colored clothing is more perceptually pleasing than other combinations. It also suggests that even among matches for patterned clothing, color is more important than the type of texture (i.e. plaids, polka dots), which also underscores the importance of simple yet visually strong descriptors such as color, (ii) Among all the patterns, we observed that fashionistas agree the most on recommending matches for paisley and stripes. However, fashionistas have more well-defined preferences for stripes as compared to paisley. Our initial analysis suggests this behavior can be attributed to the structure of pattern: stripes have strong structural information as compared to paisley. Hence, it is easier to recommend matches for stripes than paisley.

5.2 Understanding Users

Insights From Visual Recommendations: We observe from the previous section that CNNC gives superior performance among the DFR class of methods, and TAR performs best among the SFR

Figure 9: Top 3 retrieved items from "tops", recommended by each algorithm for query "skirts". Rows correspond to a query from a given pattern. Recommendations by TAR are more preferred than those by PR and MCL. Recommendations by CNNC and GMM have more patterns, even for patterned queries. Note that code words and modes in GMM yield identical retrievals for multiple queries.

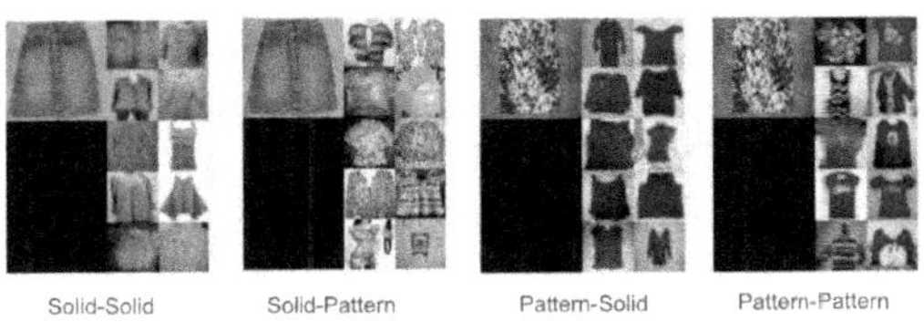

Figure 10: Illustration of the different combinations of retreivals, namely Solid-Solid, Solid-Pattern, Pattern-Solid and Pattern-Pattern

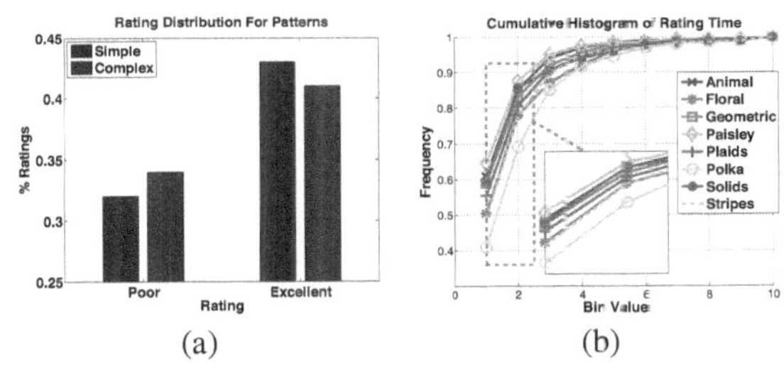

Figure 11: (a) Rating Distribution. Simple patterns are rated higher than complex patterns. (b) Cumulative Histogram of Rating Time for Each Pattern. Simple Patterns take more time due to more relevant matches as compared to complex patterns.

class of methods. Henceforth, comparisons of DFR/SFR methods utilize CNNC/TAR as exemplar techniques. The previous results provide an interesting cue that deeper insights can be revealed by segmenting fashion choices into classes such as solids or patterned queries. Our goal is to further analyze this behavior to ascertain its possible causes. One possible explanation can be found in similar results studied in computational neuroscience and vision science. These results directly correlate the complexity of an image to the visual processing time as well as image aesthetics. Motivated by this intuition, we look at the amount of time it takes to rate queries corresponding to different pattern. We hypothesize that since each pattern has a varying level of visual complexity, it should also reflect in the fashion preferences of the users. Figure 11(b) illustrates the cumulative histogram of time taken to annotate queries from each pattern class. As shown, two patterns - Polka and Paisley occupy the ends of the spectrum. Annotations from Polka take more time, whereas it's relatively faster to annotate Paisley queries. This behavior can also be understood in terms of quality of matches for each pattern. Our qualitative results suggest that in general Polka queries tend to return more relevant matches as compared to Paisley which has mostly obvious incorrect matches. A typical user takes more time to carefully rate higher number of relevant matches in Polka and hence higher annotation time as compared to Paisley. Further, it can also be concluded that quality of matches are a func-

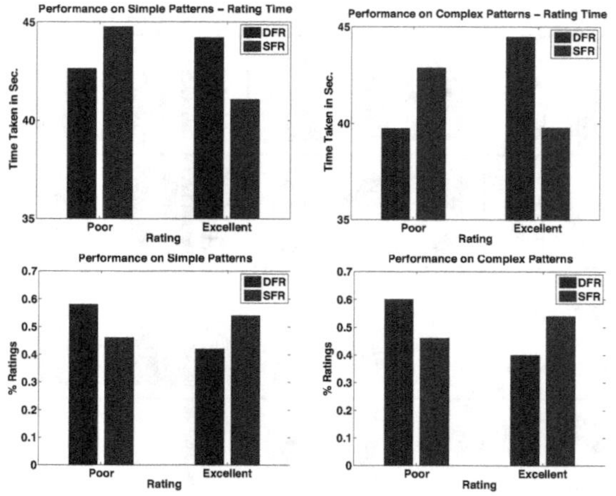

(a) (b)

Figure 12: (a) Rating Time and Model Performance on Simple Patterns. Matches from SFR are visually more appealing and hence take much less time for rating as compared to DFR. (b) Rating Time and Model Performance on Complex Patterns. SFR matches for complex patterns are more appealing as compared to simple patterns.

tion of pattern complexity - Polka is a simple pattern that Paisley, hence it returns better matches. This leads us to generate a weak categorization of all 8 patterns into 2 categories - Simple Patterns (Polka, Solids, Stripes, Plaids) and Complex Patterns (Animal, Floral, Geometric, Paisley) inspired by simple and complex cells in visual cortex. Using this scheme, we further analyze user ratings on these two categories. Figure 12(a) demonstrates that a larger proportion of users provide excellent ratings for matches corresponding to simple patterns. This result has the following conclusion: (i) *Fashion preferences tend have a strong correlation to associated complexities in visual perception.*

Enhancing Recommendations With User Understanding: All the above results provide a great insight into the role of users in fashion recommendation. However, they still do not answer if computer models can be built to replicate this understanding. To demonstrate this aspect, we evaluate two proposed models, DFR and SFR over the simple and complex pattern classes. Specifically, we look at two primary aspects, *time to rate recommendations* and *rating of recommendation* to illustrate this result. As shown in the top row of Figure 12(a&b), for all excellent ratings, users take much less time to rate recommendations from SFR as opposed to DFR. This is a strong indicator of the fact that visual recommendations from SFR have lower visual complexity and hence faster processing time for users. Moreover, the gain in time between SFR and DFR is even more pronounced for complex pattern classes. This again strengthens the argument that in the case of complex classes (when the visual complexity of the images are higher), more elastic modeling techniques such as SFR provide better aesthetically pleasing visual recommendations as opposed to pure data-driven techniques like DFR. Hence, this result illustrates that users prefer visual recommendations from SFR over DFR models. Next, we look at the distribution of user ratings for both these models over different fashion classes. The bottom row in Figure 12(a),(b) illustrates the performance of both the models. As shown, SFR outperforms DFR as it gets a much higher ratio of excellent user ratings and lower ratio of poor ratings for all the pattern classes. This result has following conclusions: (i)*Incorporating user preference by incorporating stochasticity in recommendation model makes the results visually more pleasing and relevant.*(ii) *Stochastic models are able to generalize well to different fashion segments as recommendations from both simple and complex patterns improve from it.*

6. CONCLUSION

In summary, this work approached the problem of visual recommendation by learning from street fashion data and transferring learnt knowledge to e-Commerce data. Two classes of recommenders, namely Deterministic (DFR) and Stochastic (SFR) recommenders were proposed. Initially, a thorough benchmarking of retrieval performance was presented. The results observed motivated the creation of a hybrid classifier which combines the best of SFR and DFR. Finally, the interaction of users with the recommender in terms of rating scores, user agreement, and query complexity were presented. Future work includes utilization of style based visual descriptors to enhance the existing color based descriptors. On the data curation side, an interesting line of investigation would be in collecting images at different times of the year to capture seasonal trends. Further, extension of recommendations from top-bottom clothing to multiple fashion apparel is an interesting avenue for future investigation.

7. REFERENCES

[1] A. Bhardwaj, A. Das Sarma, W. Di, R. Hamid, R. Piramuthu, and N. Sundaresan. Palette power: Enabling visual search through colors. In *KDD*, 2013.

[2] D. M. Blei, A. Y. Ng, and M. I. Jordan. Latent dirichlet allocation. *JMLR*, 3:993–1022, 2003.

[3] A. Bosch, A. Zisserman, and X. Muñoz. Scene classification via plsa. In *ECCV*, pages 517–530, 2006.

[4] H. Chen, A. Gallagher, and B. Girod. Describing clothing by semantic attributes. In *ECCV*, pages 609–623, 2012.

[5] D. Cohen-Or, O. Sorkine, R. Gal, T. Leyvand, and Y. Xu. Color harmonization. In *SIGGRAPH*, 2006.

[6] T. Iwata, S. Wanatabe, and H. Sawada. Fashion coordinates recommender system using photographs from fashion magazines. In *IJCAI*, pages 2262–2267, 2011.

[7] C. Li and T. Chen. Aesthetic visual quality assessment of paintings. *Selected Topics in Signal Processing, IEEE Journal of*, 3(2):236–252, 2009.

[8] S. Liu, J. Fen, Z. Song, T. Zhang, H. Lu, C. Xu, and S. Yan. Hi, magic closet, tell me what to wear! In *ACMMM*, 2012.

[9] S. Liu, Z. Song, G. Liu, C. Xu, H. Lu, and S. Yan. Street-to-shop: Cross-scenario clothing retrieval via parts alignment and auxiliary set. In *CVPR*, 2012.

[10] W.-Y. Ma and B. S. Manjunath. Texture features and learning similarity. In *CVPR*, pages 425–430, 1996.

[11] R. Salakhutdinov and A. Mnih. Probabilistic matrix factorization. In *NIPS*, 2008.

[12] M. Varma and A. Zisserman. A statistical approach to texture classification from single images. *IJCV*, 62(1), 2005.

[13] M. Weber and M. Bauml. Part-based clothing segmentation for person retrieval. In *AVSS*, pages 361–366. IEEE, 2011.

[14] K. Yamaguchi, M. H. Kiapour, L. E. Ortiz, and T. L. Berg. Parsing clothing in fashion photographs. In *CVPR*, 2012.

[15] M. Yang and K. Yu. Real-time clothing recognition in surveillance videos. In *ICIP*. IEEE, 2011.

[16] Y. Yang and D. Ramanan. Articulated pose estimation with flexible mixtures-of-parts. In *CVPR*, pages 1385–1392, 2011.

[17] B. Yao, A. Khosla, and L. Fei-Fei. Classifying actions and measuring action similarity. *ICML*, 2011.

We Know What You Want to Buy: A Demographic-based System for Product Recommendation On Microblogs

Wayne Xin Zhao[1], Yanwei Guo[2], Yulan He[3], Han Jiang[2], Yuexin Wu[2] and Xiaoming Li[2]
[1]School of Information,Renmin University of China, China
[2]School of Electronic Engineering and Computer Science,Peking University, China
[3]School of Engineering & Applied Science, Aston University, UK
batmanfly@gmail.com, pkuguoyw@gmail.com, y.he@cantab.net,
jianghan08@gmail.com, wuyuexin@gmail.com, lxm@pku.edu.cn

ABSTRACT

Product recommender systems are often deployed by e-commerce websites to improve user experience and increase sales. However, recommendation is limited by the product information hosted in those e-commerce sites and is only triggered when users are performing e-commerce activities. In this paper, we develop a novel product recommender system called METIS, a MErchanT Intelligence recommender System, which detects users' purchase intents from their microblogs in near real-time and makes product recommendation based on matching the users' demographic information extracted from their public profiles with product demographics learned from microblogs and online reviews. METIS distinguishes itself from traditional product recommender systems in the following aspects: 1) METIS was developed based on a microblogging service platform. As such, it is not limited by the information available in any specific e-commerce website. In addition, METIS is able to track users' purchase intents in near real-time and make recommendations accordingly. 2) In METIS, product recommendation is framed as a learning to rank problem. Users' characteristics extracted from their public profiles in microblogs and products' demographics learned from both online product reviews and microblogs are fed into learning to rank algorithms for product recommendation. We have evaluated our system in a large dataset crawled from Sina Weibo. The experimental results have verified the feasibility and effectiveness of our system. We have also made a demo version of our system publicly available and have implemented a live system which allows registered users to receive recommendations in real time.

Categories and Subject Descriptors

I.2.7 [**Arti cial Intelligence**]: Natural Language Processing—*Text analysis*; H.3.1 [**Information Storage and Retrieval**]: text mining

KDD'14, August 24–27, 2014, New York, NY, USA.

http://dx.doi.org/10.1145/2623330.2623351.

Keywords

E-commerce; product recommender; product demographic; microblog

1. INTRODUCTION

Recent years have witnessed a great success of e-commerce websites such as Amazon and eBay as they transcend geophysical barriers and allow individuals or business to form transactions anywhere and anytime. A technique widely adopted by e-commerce companies is to exploit *product recommender systems* to improve user experience and increase sales. Research has found that product recommendation largely influences consumers' purchase decisions and is likely to boost sales [23, 26, 14].

Generally speaking, there are two major challenges in the design of product recommender systems. Firstly, it is difficult to find out users' demographic information, which is essential for making right recommendations to right persons. Existing recommender systems relying on collaborative filtering explore techniques for matching users with similar interests and make recommendations on this basis. Nevertheless, it is well-known that collaborative filtering suffers from the "cold-start" problem when a recommender system knows little about a new user. Secondly, existing recommender systems embedded in e-commerce websites can only make recommendations when users are performing e-commerce activities in those websites, which cannot capture users' instantaneous purchase intents outside those websites.

Although there has been much research work on online product recommendation [24, 10, 14], most studies only focus on constructing solutions for certain e-commerce websites and are thus constrained by the information available there. In our work here, rather than relying on limited information available in any specific e-commerce website, we aim to develop a generic online product recommender system by exploring vast amount of information available externally such as that on social media platforms.

Online social media has already become the new arena of our lives and involved different aspects of our social presence from day to day. Through online activities such as chatting with friends and posting short status updates, online social networks (OSNs) have become important platforms where users discuss their needs and desires [11], and even disclose their personal information [3]. Thus, in this paper, we propose to capture users' purchase intents from OSNs and develop a generic product recommender system not limited to any specific e-commerce website. In particular, we develop our recommender system based on a microblogging service platform due to the following reasons: 1) Microblogs contain abundant data from which users' purchase intents can be easily discovered; 2) Microblogs are continuously updated which implies that users' purchase intents are also updated in real time. This is especially attractive for developing an effective product recommender system; 3) Microblogs contain public profiles of users, including age, sex and/or professions, from which we can extract users' demographic characteristics.

In this paper, we present the development of a novel product recommender system called *METIS*, a MErchanT Intelligence recommender System. The main characteristics of METIS that distinguishes itself from traditional product recommender systems are as follows: 1) METIS was developed based on a microblogging service platform which naturally addresses the aforementioned two challenges. First, users' public profiles on microblogs can be used to extract their demographic characteristics. Second, users' purchase intents can be instantaneously discovered from their tweets and the constantly updated purchase intents allow the development of a more effective recommender system not constrained by the limited information available in any specific e-commerce website. 2) The core to the METIS system is a novel demographic based recommendation algorithm which learns product demographics by leveraging knowledge from online social media. Product demographic, sometimes called the target audience, of a product or service is a collection of the characteristics of the people who buy that product. The features derived from both product demographics and the extracted users' characteristics can be fed into any learning to rank algorithm for real-time product recommendation. 3) We also propose an effective method for semi-automatic acquisition of training data for the learning to rank algorithms. This makes our system more practical since it does not rely on actual transaction records from any e-commerce website.

2. OVERVIEW OF THE SYSTEM

Our system, METIS, aims to link users' purchase intents with the real-world products in an online fashion. In specific, when a user published a tweet describing her purchase intent, METIS will first identify her purchase intent, then extract her demographic characteristics, and finally return a list of recommended products based on some similarity measurement between user's demographic and products' demographic information. The architecture of METIS is shown in Figure 1 which consists of three major components:

- *Purchase intent detection.* This component aims to detect users' purchase intents in near real-time. In order to reduce noise, irrelevant tweets are first filtered using a manually constructed keyword list. Then a classification-based method [11] is employed to identify tweets containing purchase intents. While only textual features were used to learn classifiers in [11], we propose to consider users' demographic information in addition to the lexical and syntactic information derived from tweets.
- *Demographic information extraction.* This component is divided into two parts: user demographics extraction and product demographics extraction. In the user side, we extract users' demographic information from their public profiles in a microblogging site; while in the product side, we propose two ways to leverage information from social media by extracting online product reviews on e-commerce websites and the followings/mentions information on microblogs. For both users and products, we map their demographic information into the same demographic attribute feature space.
- *Product recommendation.* This is the core component of the system which returns a list of recommended products to a user. We propose a novel demographic-based recommendation algorithm where similarity measurement is performed between a user and products based on features derived from their demographic information which are subsequently combined in a learning to rank framework for making product recommendation with high accuracy.

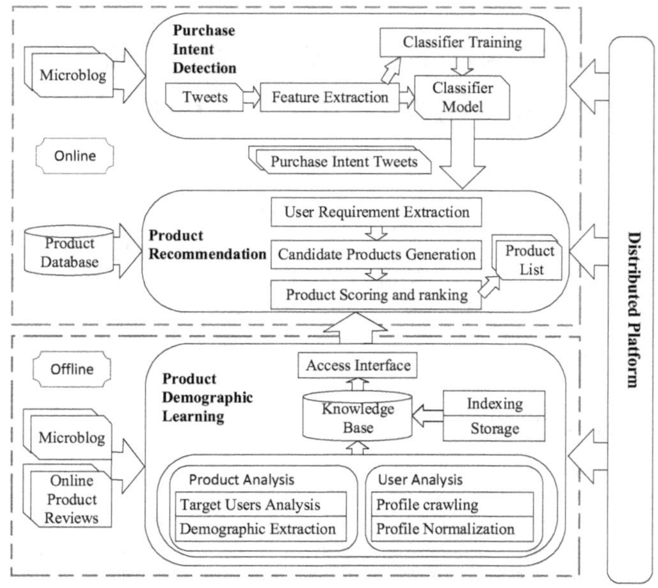

Figure 1: Architecture of METIS.

For the development of our system, we choose a microblogging platform, Sina Weibo[1], which is the largest Chinese microblogging site. We have crawled all the information for a set of 5 million active users on Weibo via an authenticated API, including their tweets, following relationships and public profiles. We have retrieved a total of 1.7 billion tweets from these 5 million active users within a half-year time span from January 2013 to June 2013. We also choose a e-commerce website, Jingdong[2], the largest B2C e-commerce website, for the selection of products for making recommendations. It is worth mentioning that our system can be easily extended to cover multiple e-commerce websites. For our experiments, we choose three popular product types in Jingdong: laptop, camera and phone. In total, these three product categories contain 3,155 products and 1.13 million user reviews. To deal with such big data, we build our backend system based on distributed indexing which allows the retrieval of information of users or products in a quick way.

Preliminary concepts

We present some preliminary concepts before delving into the details of our system.

[1] `http://weibo.com`

[2] `http://jd.com`

Purchase-intent tweet. By following the definition in [11], a tweet is defined as a *purchase-intent tweet* if it explicitly expresses a desire or interest of buying some product. Here we only consider explicit expressions of buying desires and ignore implicit purchase intents since the latter is more difficult to detect. Note that we do not assume that the author of a tweet is the one who wants to buy a potential product. In an example tweet below:

> Please recommend! *My son* wants to buy a *Samsung phone* less than $200.

The potential customer of *Samsung phone* is *My son*, not the author of the tweet.

Product demographics. The product demographics [3], sometimes called the target audience, of a product or service is a collection of the characteristics of the people who buy that product or service. A demographic profile (often shortened as "a demographic") provides enough information about the typical member of this product to create a mental picture of this hypothetical aggregate. For example, a product demographic might refer to the single, female, middle-class, age 18 to 24, college educated.

Knowing information such as the income status, age and tastes of users can help companies sell more, branch out to other groups and create more products that appeal to target buyers. Instead of identifying these useful demographic attributes manually, we start with the attributes in users' public profile on Weibo. With reference to the marketing studies [20, 28], we have identified six major demographic attributes: gender, age, marital status, education, career and interests. To quantitatively measure these attributes, we have further discretized them into different bins. We summarize the details of the demographic attributes in Table 1.

We use probabilities to characterize the demographics of a product. Formally, let $\mathcal{A}$ denote the set of attributes and $\mathcal{V}_a$ denote the set of values for an attribute a. For a product e, its demographic distribution of an attribute a is $\theta^{(e,a)} = \{\theta_v^{(e,a)}\}_{v \in \mathcal{V}_a}$, where $\theta_v^{(e,a)}$ is the proportion of the target consumers with the value v for attribute a. Since $\theta^{(e,a)}$ is a distribution, we have $\sum_{v \in \mathcal{V}_a} \theta_v^{(e,a)} = 1$. Furthermore, we use the set of attribute distributions to represent the product demographics, i.e. $\{\theta^{(e,a)}\}_{a \in \mathcal{A}}$.

Table 1: List of demographic attributes.

Attribute	Values
Gender	male, female
Age	1-11, 12-17, 18-30, 31-45, 46-59, 60+
Marital Status	single, engaged, loving secretly, married, relationship seeking, bereft of one's spouse, separated, divorced, ambiguous, loving
Education	literature, natural science, engineering, social sciences, medical science, art, others
Career	internet technology, designing, media, service industry, manufacturing, medicine, scientific research, management, others
Interests (Weibo tags)	travel, photographing, music and movie, computer games, Internet surfing, other

User pro le. *User profile*, which is also called *user demographics*, is similar to *product demographics*. Formally, given a user u and the considered attribute set $\mathcal{A}$, we use $\mathcal{D}_u = \{v_a^{(u)}\}_{a \in \mathcal{A}}$ to denote the user's profile, where $v_a^{(u)}$ is the value of attribute a. On Sina Weibo, a user is required to fill in some attributes in her public profile during registration, which can be modified later.

[3]http://www.ehow.com/info_10015346_product-demographic.html

3. PURCHASE INTENT DETECTION

The task of purchase intent detection on microblogs was first studied in [11] where a classification model is learned to classify a tweet automatically into one of the two categories (containing or not containing purchase intents). While only textual features were used in [11] for classifier training, we additionally explore users' demographic information in learning classifiers for purchase intent detection. Furthermore, only a small set of 1,335 tweets were tested in [11]. Instead, we have explored several ways to improve the efficiency of purchase intent detection in order to achieve the near real-time performance when dealing with large amount of social stream data.

3.1 Fast Generation of Candidate Purchase-Intent Tweets

Tweets are produced at a dramatic rate. There are on average 100 million tweets generated within a day on Sina Weibo. It is not feasible to directly apply purchase intent classification on such a huge amount of data. Thus, a keyword filtering method is first used to only keep tweets that are likely to contain purchase intents. An annotator major in commerce service is invited to compile a list of *purchase indicator keywords* which is shown in Table 2. We process the data stream in an online mode by distributing the data into multiple servers. We use a fast string search algorithm to keep tweets that contain at least one purchase indicator keyword in our list for subsequent processing.

Table 2: List of purchase indicator keywords and their English translations.

buy (买), recommend (推荐), change (换), which is better (哪个更好), cheap (便宜), cost (价值), auction (拍), on sale (降价), price (价格), need (需要), shopping (购物)

3.2 Intent Classification

We train an intent classifier based on the following features:

Textual features. Hollerit et al. [11] used highly discriminative n-gram features which consist of consecutive words (e.g. "buy cheap") or Part-of-Speech (POS) tags (e.g. "VB JJ") ranked by the chi-squared statistic for training intent classifiers. Intuitively, a word together with its POS tag in a tweet can represent more complete semantics than a single word or POS tag. Thus, we consider a word together with its POS tag as a feature unit. For example, for a phrase "buy VB cheap JJ", instead of generating two separate features "buy cheap" and "VB JJ", we only generate a single feature "buy-VB cheap-JJ" and call it *lexical-POS* feature.

Demographic features. The second type of features we consider is users' demographic information which is incorporated as additional context to supplement the textual evidence. For example, given two tweets respectively from a female and a boy, both tweets have mentioned "transformer model". Intuitively, the boy's tweet is more likely to contain a purchase intent. As such, we also extract users' demographic features containing the six attributes presented in Table 1 for intent classifier training.

4. PRODUCT DEMOGRAPHICS LEARNING

It is relatively easy to obtain users' demographic information from their public profiles in Sina Weibo. In this section, we focus on extracting product demographic information, also called *target audience* or *target consumer*, from social media. Previously, product demographics are derived from either user surveys [1] or commercial purchase records [10]. As have been discussed earlier, we focused on the six demographic attributes shown in Table 1. We propose to leverage demographic related knowledge from online product reviews and the followings/mentions information on microblogs.

4.1 Demographics Extraction from Online Product Reviews

The first resource we consider is *online product reviews*. We have found that users might explicitly mention demographic related information in their reviews in addition to their opinions. For example, in a sentence "I *bought my son* this phone" from a product review, the phrase "buy my son" indicates that the current product is suitable for the author's son, who is a potential target consumer. In this example, we can see that "*buy somebody something*" is an important pattern for deriving the demographic knowledge which is embedded in a phrase *my son* which we call a *demographic phrase*. We want to collect statistics of such demographic related phrases in order to reliably derive patterns expressing demographic information.

We first propose to use a bootstrap algorithm to iteratively extract frequent patterns and demographic phrases. Then we further study how to convert these patterns into demographic statistics. The bootstrapping algorithm for the extraction of demographic phrases is presented in Algorithm 1, in which we iteratively extract new patterns and identify demographic phrases with the extracted patterns. The function ExtractDemographicPhrase (p,s) aims to identify the demographic phases in a review sentence s by using the pattern p. Here we only consider extracting nouns, noun phrases, adjectives, and numbers. Note that this algorithm is very flexible to deal with data in an online mode by setting the set of identified patterns $\mathcal{P}$ as the seed set for new data.

Given a product e, we obtain a set of its related demographic phrases $\mathcal{R}_e$ which have at least 10 occurrences in our data. We then map these phrases into six demographic dimensions as has been previously described in Table 1 using a list of pre-defined rules. For example, given a phrase "my little son", we can map it into two dimensions "male"(sex) and "12∼17"(age)". We maintain a counter (a, v) which counts the number of times phrases being mapped to value v of the attribute a. Finally, we use Laplace smoothing (a.k.a add-one smoothing) to estimate the demographic distribution of a product e for an attribute a as follows

$$\theta_{a,v}^{(e)} = \frac{\#(a,v)+1}{\sum_{v' \in \mathcal{V}_a} \#(a,v') + |\mathcal{V}_a|}, \tag{1}$$

where $\mathcal{V}_a$ is the set of all possible values of attribute a. $\theta_{a,v}^{(e)}$ is a valid probability since $\sum_{v \in \mathcal{V}_a} \theta_{a,v}^{(e)} = 1$. Thus, for each attribute of a product, we can model the aggregated statistics as a distribution over a set of all possible attribute values, and a higher probability value indicates a more prominent characteristic of the product for that attribute.

4.2 Demographics Extraction from Microblogs

The second type of resources we consider is the information collected from *microblogs*. The rationale behind is that given a product, we could capture the "like" evidence, i.e. positive opinions, of users on the product. Such users can be treated as potential target audience for that particular product. As a result, the profiles of these users can be aggregated as the product demographics. We detect users' endorsements on a certain product in microblogs by considering the following two most common user behaviors:

- *following*: a brand or a product usually has its official account on microblogs. We take the followers of these official accounts as the potential target audience.
- *mentioning*: if a user is interested in a product, she may publish tweets to explicitly express her positive opinions on the product. Given a product, we retrieve the tweets containing the product name through simple keyword matching. We then use the machine learning based approach proposed in [17] for the detection of polarity $\{positive, negative\}$ of the tweet. We used review sentences with users' five-star ratings as training data: positive (>3 stars) and negative (<3 stars). Only tweets with *positive* polarity are treated as the supporting evidence, and their authors are considered as the product's target audience.

Given a product e, let $\mathcal{U}_e$ denote the set of its target users who are selected from either the *following* or the *mentioning* categories mentioned above. It is worth noting that in both *following* and *mentioning* categories, users may not be directly related to a specific product (e.g., "iPhone 5S"), instead they may be related to a brand (e.g., "iPhone") or a company (e.g., "Apple"). We introduce b_e to denote the brand or company of a product e. We then aggregate the target audience of b_e by following the similar approach, and denote it as $\mathcal{U}_{b_e}$. Also, for users in $\mathcal{U}_e$ and $\mathcal{U}_{b_e}$, we further perform spam user filtering by considering their followings/followers, tweet contents and interactions with other users.

The demographic distribution of a product e for attribute a taking the value v is calculated by combing the estimation

Algorithm 1: Bootstrapping algorithm for extracting demographic phrases from online reviews.

Input: review sentence corpus $\mathcal{C}$, seed purchase-intent patterns
Output: an set of identified demographic patterns $\mathcal{P}$ and a set of identified demographic phrases $\mathcal{R}$;
$\mathcal{P}' \leftarrow$ seed demographic patterns;
$\mathcal{P} \leftarrow$ seed demographic patterns;
$\mathcal{R}' \leftarrow \emptyset$;
$\mathcal{R} \leftarrow \emptyset$;
repeat
    $\mathcal{R}' \leftarrow \emptyset$;
    for *each pattern* $p \in \mathcal{P}'$ **do**
        for *each sentence* $s \in \mathcal{C}$ **do**
            if *p exists in s* **then**
                $\mathcal{R}' \leftarrow \mathcal{R}' \cup$ ExtractDemographicPhrase (p,s);
            end
        end
    end
    $\mathcal{P}' \leftarrow \emptyset$;
    for *each sentence* $s \in \mathcal{C}$ **do**
        for *each demographic phrase* $i \in \mathcal{R}'$ **do**
            $\mathcal{P}' \leftarrow \mathcal{P}' \cup$ GeneratePatterns(s, i);
        end
    end
    $\mathcal{P}' \leftarrow$ ExtractTopFrequentPatterns$(\mathcal{P}')$;
    $\mathcal{P} \leftarrow \mathcal{P} \cup \mathcal{P}'$;
    $\mathcal{R} \leftarrow \mathcal{R} \cup \mathcal{R}'$;
until *No new pattern is identified*;
return *An set of identified demographic patterns $\mathcal{P}$ and a set of identified demographic phrases $\mathcal{R}$;*

computed from $\mathcal{U}_e$ and $\mathcal{U}_{b_e}$ through the Jelinek-Mercer (JM) smoothing method:

$$\theta^{e}_{a,v} = (1-\lambda)\times\frac{\sum_{u\in\mathcal{U}_e}\mathbf{1}[u.a=v]}{\sum_{v'}\sum_{u\in\mathcal{U}_e}\mathbf{1}[u.a=v']}+\lambda\times\frac{\sum_{u\in\mathcal{U}_{b_e}}\mathbf{1}[u.a=v]}{\sum_{v'}\sum_{u\in\mathcal{U}_{b_e}}\mathbf{1}[u.a=v']}, \quad (2)$$

where $\mathbf{1}[\cdot]$ is the indicator function which returns 1 only when the condition is true and λ is the interpolation coefficient, which is empirically set to be 0.3 in our experiments. The target audience of a product is constructed based on both the information related to itself and that related to its corresponding brand or company.

Summary

In this section, we have presented two methods to leverage information from social media for product demographics learning. As such, we have two types of feature representations for product demographics. We do not attempt to combine them into a unified representation, instead, we keep them separate. As will be discussed later, the learning to rank algorithms can automatically assign optimal weights to these two feature types.

5. LEARN TO RANK FOR PRODUCT RECOMMENDATION

Now we discuss how to devise the product recommendation algorithm. A good recommendation algorithm should satisfy two main criteria [2]: 1) it is flexible to incorporate various types of useful information. 2) the algorithm is easy to understand for future extension and the ranking results are intuitive to explain. For the first criterion, we develop a learning to rank framework for product recommendation, which can be used on any types of features. For the second criteria, we represent products and users in the same demographic feature space, which makes our results easy to explain. Our proposed framework is generic and can be deployed with any ranking algorithms.

Our algorithm consists of two main steps: 1) candidate product generation; 2) learning to rank.

5.1 Candidate product generation

Recall that we have identified the purchase-intent tweets in *Purchase Intent Detection*. The authors of these tweets are treated as potential consumers, and the tweets reveal purchasing needs from users. In this section, we study how to generate candidate products based on users' profiles and their purchase-intent tweets.

Requirement identification. A user's requirement of a certain product can be derived from the identified purchase-intent tweets. We consider an example here:

> Please recommend! I want to buy a *Samsung phone* less than $200.

In this example, we need to detect the user's requirement of *price* < $200 for a brand, *Samsung phone*. To build a product knowledge base for products, we have indexed all the product related information such as brand, price, and screen size. Regular expressions have been compiled for each information field and users' requirements are identified by using the regular expression patterns. We generate a list of candidate products which fulfil the identified requirements.

Complicated query analysis. By default, the author of a purchase-intent tweet will be the potential customer of its related product. However, we have noticed that there are a considerable number of purchase-intent tweets, in which the potential consumer is not the author of the tweets. See the following example:

> Please recommend! I want to buy my son a *Samsung phone*.

The author of this tweet is a female, and if simply taking her as the potential customer of the phone, the recommender system would generate inappropriate recommendations. Although it is very challenging to solve this problem, our current approach naturally address this issue. Recall that we have extracted a set of demographic phrases such as "my son". We can create a set of virtual users with the profiles of this specific identity ("my son"). Once we have found that a tweet contains such an identify indicator, we will take its corresponding profile for product recommendation.

Candidate product list pruning. Although we only select the products which fulfil the identified requirements, the number of candidate products is still large which is not suitable for the learning to rank algorithms. For this reason, we select at most 30 best-sale products among the candidate products as the input to the learning to rank algorithms in the next step.

5.2 Learning to Rank

Having identified the purchase requirements of a potential consumer, we now discuss how to recommend products with the demographic information of both users and products. We formulate the task as a ranking problem and adopt the learning-to-rank algorithm as our solution. We first introduce the learning to rank framework briefly

A brief introduction to learning to rank. In learning (training), a number of queries and their corresponding retrieved documents are given. Furthermore, the relevance levels of the documents with respect to the queries are also provided. The relevance levels are represented as ranks. The objective of learning is to construct a ranking function (model) which achieves the best results in ranking of the training data by minimizing a loss function. Ideally the loss function is defined on the basis of the performance measure used in testing. In retrieval (testing), given a query, the system returns a ranked list of documents in a descending order of the relevance scores which are calculated using the ranking function.

Ranking for product recommendation. Learning to rank was originally proposed for information retrieval. We first make a connection between product recommendation and information retrieval. In our task, a purchase-intent tweet can be understood as a query and an adopted product can be understood as a relevant document. For convenience, we use the term "*query*" to denote a purchase-intent tweet.

To formulate our product recommendation problem as a ranking task, we assume that there are a set of purchase-intent tweets (i.e. queries) $\mathcal{Q} = \{q^{(1)}, q^{(2)}, ..., q^{(m)}\}$ during training. A purchase-intent tweet (query) $q^{(i)}$ is associated with a set of $n^{(i)}$ candidate products $\{p_1^{(i)}, ..., p_{n^{(i)}}^{(i)}\}$ For each candidate product, let $y_j^{(i)}$ denote the judgment on product $p_j^{(i)}$ with respect to query $q^{(i)}$. The value of $y_j^{(i)}$

can be either discrete or continuous, and a higher value indicates a better recommendation for the query $q^{(i)}$. A feature vector $\boldsymbol{x}_j^{(i)}$ can be constructed for each query-product pair $(q^{(i)}, p_j^{(i)})$. The aim of the learning task is to derive a ranking function f such that, for each feature vector $\boldsymbol{x}_j^{(i)}$ (corresponding to $q^{(i)}$ and $p_j^{(i)}$), it outputs a recommendation score $f(\boldsymbol{x}_j^{(i)})$ for product ranking.

To learn the ranking function f, there are three general approaches [15]:

- Pointwise approach. It reduces ranking to regression or classification on single documents. That is, we build the ranking function f by approximating $f(\boldsymbol{x}_j^{(i)})$ to the corresponding relevance score $y_j^{(i)}$.
- Pairwise approach. It no longer assumes absolute relevance, which reduces ranking to classification on product pairs w.r.t. the same query. That is, given a query $q^{(i)}$, we only focus on the relative preference order between a pair of candidate products $p_j^{(i)}$ and $p_k^{(i)}$.
- Listwise approach. Instead of reducing ranking to regression or classification, it performs learning directly on product lists, and an entire ranked list is treated as a learning instance. That is, for query $q^{(i)}$, the ranking function focuses on learning a list of relevance scores $(y_1^{(i)}, ..., y_{n^i}^{(i)})$ given the list of feature vectors $(\boldsymbol{x}_1^{(i)}, ..., \boldsymbol{x}_{n^i}^{(i)})$.

We define our task in a generic way such that all the above approaches can be used. Another important problem is how to construct the feature vector for each instance, which is usually the basis of good performance for learning to rank algorithms. We mainly consider two types of features:

Query-independent product features. This type of features are independent of the specific query. Intuitively, the product sale follows "rich-gets-richer", i.e. a user is more likely to buy a product with more successful sales history and more positive comments. Based on this intuition, we use the following features: the sales history of a product (*sale*) and the overall rating score of a product (*rating*). We also incorporate the overall polarity score of a product (*polarity*) as the third feature. In our dataset, we have found that popular products usually have similar high rating scores. Thus, we consider looking into the reviews and derive the polarity scores based on the opinionated user reviews. Here we follow the unsupervised method in [22] with an open Chinese opinion lexicon to transform review content into polarity scores within the interval of $[-1, 1]$. For new products, we can smooth these features with the generalized information at the brand level.

Query-dependent product features. uery-dependent product features are extracted based on a potential user and a candidate product. We quantify the match degree between a user and a product based on their six-dimensional demographic attribute values (see Table 1). Formally, given a user u and a candidate product e, we set the feature value of attribute a as the probability in the demographic distribution of e:

$$x_a^{u,e} = \theta^{(e)}_{a, v_a^u}, \tag{3}$$

where $v_a^{(u)}$ denotes the value of attribute a for user u and $\theta_{a,\cdot}^{(e)}$ is the demographic distribution defined in Equation 1 and 2. Intuitively, if a user closely matches a product, the user will be a representative of the target consumers of the product. Note that we have learnt the demographic distributions from both online reviews and microblogs, and for each attribute, we can obtain two different feature values. Instead of simply combining both values, we keep them separate and let the ranking function learn the weights automatically. The weights of the demographic features learned by a ranking function provide an intuitive way to explain the results. Although we have only evaluated our proposed recommender algorithm on the aforementioned features, the algorithm can be easily extended to incorporate other types of features.

Semi-automatic acquisition of training data. The performance of learning to rank algorithms highly relies on the amount of training data. Previous studies tend to use transaction records (users' actual purchase decisions) from online e-commerce websites as supervised information [24]. However, such data are not always available as e-commerce companies could choose not to reveal their transaction data. Even with the availability of transaction data, it is still difficult to link users across microblogs and e-commerce websites, which makes it infeasible for the evaluation of our current task. Here, we propose a novel approach to acquire training data semi-automatically which is motivated by the following two example tweets from the same user:

> *Oct 1, 2012* Please recommend! I want to buy my son a Samsung phone.
> *Oct 4, 2012* Done! I *have bought* Galaxy II for my lovely son!

In the first tweet, a user expressed her desire to buy a Samsung phone for her son. The user subsequently reported that she has purchased a product. The above example forms a query-decision pair, which can be naturally converted into a training instance.

To extract such query-decision pairs, we first identify purchase-intent tweets. Then for each tweet, a set of tweets from the same author which were subsequently published in a week time have also been retrieved. We compile some cue phrases which are indicative of reporting purchase decisions, e.g., "*have bought* something". With such cue phrases, we can then identify those tweets potentially reporting purchasing decisions. We subsequently invite a human judge to manually examine whether these tweets actually report buying decisions. The query-decision pairs can then be used as training instances for the learning to rank algorithms.

6. EXPERIMENTS

In our work here, we chose Sina Weibo, the largest Chinese microblogging service, as the microblogging platform, and Jingdong, the largest Chinese B2C e-commerce company, as the e-commerce product database. Our recommender system aims to recommend products on Jingdong to users who have expressed explicit purchase intents on microblogs. We evaluate our recommender system in two aspects: purchase intent detection and product recommendation. **All the data used in our experiments will be made available.**

6.1 Evaluation on Purchase Intent Detection

Construction of the dataset. To construct the dataset for the evaluation of purchase intent detection, we first randomly select 10,000 tweets which contain at least one keyword expressing purchase intent as listed in Table 2. Then two annotators are asked to label the tweets as containing purchase intents or not by following the guidelines introduced in [11]. The Cohen's Kappa agreement coefficient between annotators is 0.85, which indicates a high-level agreement. By only keeping the tweets which receive the same labels from both annotators, we end up with 4,434 purchase intent tweets and 5,352 non-purchase intent tweets.

Methods to compare. We evaluate the following methods for purchase intent detection:

- $Baseline_T$. Use textual features as proposed in [11].
- $Baseline_{T+D}$. Textual features + demographic features.
- $Ours_T$. Lexical-POS features.
- $Ours_{T+D}$. Lexical-POS features + demographic features.

We train the Support Vector Machines (SVMs) with two different kernels, linear and RBF, on the feature sets mentioned above.

Results and analysis. It can be observed from the results presented in Table 3 that using our proposed lexical-POS features ($Ours_T$) outperforms the baseline model using textual features only ($Baseline_T$). In particular, the improvement is more significant with the RBF kernel where over 13% improvement is observed. Adding demographic features to textual features ($Baseline_{T+D}$) improves upon $Baseline_T$ by 1% with the linear kernel and 4.7% with the RBF kernel. However, additionally incorporating demographic features into our proposed lexical-POS features ($Ours_{T+D}$) only gives marginal improvements compared to $Ours_T$. Overall, the best performance of 81.8% in F-measure is achieved using a combination of lexical-POS and demographic features trained on SVMs with the RBF kernel.

Table 3: Performance comparison for purchase intent detection with SVM.

Kernel	Methods	Precision	Recall	F-value
Linear	$Baseline_T$	0.738	0.771	0.754
	$Baseline_{T+D}$	0.743	0.788	0.765
	$Ours_T$	0.762	0.802	0.782
	$Ours_{T+D}$	0.77	0.806	0.788
RBF	$Baseline_T$	0.81	0.582	0.678
	$Baseline_{T+D}$	0.725	0.726	0.725
	$Ours_T$	0.796	0.829	0.812
	$Ours_{T+D}$	0.805	0.832	0.818

6.2 Evaluation on Product Recommendation

Construction of the dataset. We choose three popular product types, phone, camera and laptop, for the construction of our dataset for the evaluation of product recommendation. We follow the method of semi-automatic acquisition of query-decision pairs described in Section 5.2 to build our dataset. The statistics of these three product types is summarized in Table 4.

Table 4: Statistics of the dataset for product recommendation.

Types	#brands	#models	#query-decision pairs
phone	57	1,584	170
camera	25	724	496
laptop	25	829	437

Methods to compare. We evaluate our proposed recommender system using two representative learning to rank algorithms from each of the categories, pointwise, pairwise and listwise:

- *Pointwise*: MART [9], RandomForest (RF) [5];
- *Pairwise*: Ranksvm [12], RankBoost [8];
- *Listwise*: Listnet [6], AdaRank [27].

These learning to rank algorithms are trained on two types of features, query-independent features and query-dependent features. We use product sales (*sale*), product polarity scores (*polarity*), and product rating scores (*rating*) as query-independent features. The query-dependent features, or demographic based features, are derived from online reviews in the Jingdong website and microblogs from Sina Weibo, which are denoted as *JD* and *Weibo* respectively.

The open source toolkit, RankLib[4] is used for the implementation of these learning to rank algorithms. For each algorithm, five-fold cross-validation is performed and the results are averaged over five such runs.

In our task, the purchase history on e-commerce websites is not available. Thus, existing approaches relying on purchase history [24, 14] are not suitable to be used as baselines. For comparison, we built three baselines with each of them using one of the three query-independent features to rank products from our generated candidate product list.

Evaluation metrics. The evaluation metrics adopted here are precision at k ($p@k$) and Normalized Discounted Cumulative Gain (NDCG), which are commonly used in information retrieval. For $p@k$, we consider the relevance at the product model level, i.e. the specific product actually purchased as described in a tweet is treated as the only relevant product. To compute $p@k$, we calcuate the proportion of queries for which we have made the correct recommendations in the top k positions. NDCG takes into account both the ranking positions and the quality grade of products, and is defined as follows:

$$NDCG(\mathcal{Q}, k) = \frac{1}{|\mathcal{Q}|} \sum_{j=1}^{|\mathcal{Q}|} Z_{k,j} \sum_{m=1}^{k} \frac{2^{R(j,m)} - 1}{\log_2(1+m)}, \quad (4)$$

where $\mathcal{Q}$ is the set of queries, $Z_{k,j}$ is the normalizer for the jth query which denotes the ideal ranking score for the top k positions, and $R(j,m)$ is the relevance level of the mth product for the jth query. For $R(j,m)$, we mainly consider three relevance levels: relevant (2), partially-relevant (1) and non-relevant (0). For each query, there is only one relevant product which matches a user's final purchase decision. If a product model does not match the final product purchased but has the same brand, it is treated as partially-relevant. For all the other cases, products are treated as non-relevant

Overall performance comparison. It can be observed from Table 5 that the learning to rank methods are much more effective than the three simple baselines. Furthermore, the performance of the pointwise approach is much better than that of pairwise and listwise approaches. The listwise approaches perform the worst due to the difficulty in obtaining the full product ordered list for training since there is usually only one correct product decision and the ordering of irrelevant products is not available. In the pointwise category, *MART* works very well and nearly achieves the best performance for both $p@k$ and $NDCG@k$ in all the three categories, except that it is slightly worse than *RandomForest* for $p@5$ in the "Laptop" category. Overall, for all methods, the performance in the "Phone" category is much

[4]https://sourceforge.net/p/lemur/wiki/RankLib/
RankLib might assign an equal score to some items in the returned ranked list. In such cases, we order items with an equal score by their sales performance.

Table 5: Performance comparison of product recommendation on three datasets for $p@k$ and $NDCG@k$.

Types	Metrics	Baselines			Pointwise		Pairwise		Listwise	
		sale	polarity	rating	MART	RF	RankSVM	RankBoost	Listnet	AdaRank
PHONE	p@1	0.006	0.006	0.006	**0.106**	0.041	0.018	0.012	0.006	0.006
	p@5	0.041	0.018	0.029	**0.282**	0.253	0.141	0.112	0.124	0.047
	NDCG@1	0.094	0.094	0.015	**0.226**	0.126	0.085	0.097	0.129	0.165
	NDCG@5	0.170	0.093	0.099	**0.256**	0.239	0.168	0.165	0.176	0.176
CAMERA	p@1	0.000	0.000	0.004	**0.606**	0.466	0.041	0.062	0.033	0.004
	p@5	0.238	0.004	0.018	**0.688**	**0.688**	0.183	0.310	0.152	0.244
	NDCG@1	0.128	0.128	0.008	**0.641**	0.515	0.092	0.140	0.073	0.127
	NDCG@5	0.254	0.094	0.061	**0.495**	0.466	0.146	0.232	0.115	0.253
LAPTOP	p@1	0.019	0.000	0.000	**0.608**	0.599	0.140	0.055	0.133	0.017
	p@5	0.026	0.014	0.012	0.653	**0.665**	0.439	0.102	0.302	0.026
	NDCG@1	0.239	0.002	0.002	**0.695**	0.686	0.145	0.228	0.138	0.220
	NDCG@5	0.212	0.073	0.059	**0.573**	0.559	0.223	0.219	0.172	0.202

worse than that of "Camera" and "Laptop". This is because there are more brands and models but much fewer training instances in the "Phone" category compared to the other two categories as shown in Table 4.

Feature selection and analysis. As have been previously mentioned, we have a set of three query-independent features, sale, polarity and rating, denoted as *spr*. We also have two types of query-dependent features *Weibo* generated from microblogs in Sina Weibo, and *JD* derived from online reviews in Jingdong. We build our recommender systems using the best learning to rank algorithm, *MART*, trained from different types of the features. The results are presented in Table 6. We can see that 1) the combination of all the features achieves the best performance; and 2) demographic features derived from online reviews in Jingdong and those extracted from microblogs are effective to improve the recommendation performance. Combining these two types of demographic features (Weibo + JD) yields a competitive performance compared to that of using all the features.

Table 6: Performance comparison with different type of features for *MART*. *Both* denotes *Weibo* + *JD*.

Types	Metrics	spr	Weibo	JD	Both	all
p@5	PHONE	0.194	**0.282**	0.224	0.259	**0.282**
	CAMERA	0.680	0.485	0.476	0.676	**0.688**
	LAPTOP	0.606	0.245	0.520	0.537	**0.653**
NDCG@5	PHONE	0.157	0.247	0.199	0.228	**0.256**
	CAMERA	0.471	0.346	0.331	**0.495**	**0.495**
	LAPTOP	0.525	0.258	0.343	0.452	**0.573**

Table 7: Samples of the learnt product demographics based on online reviews. Real numbers denote the learned weights for the corresponding attribute values.

Galaxy S4 (White)	$(SEX, [\text{"}male\text{"}, 0.271], [\text{"}female\text{"}, 0.729])$
Galaxy S4 (Blue)	$(SEX, [\text{"}male\text{"}, 0.688], [\text{"}female\text{"}, 0.312])$
Galaxy S4 (Black)	$(SEX, [\text{"}male\text{"}, 0.852], [\text{"}female\text{"}, 0.148])$
Galaxy S4 (White)	$(Age, [\text{"} < 45\text{"}, 0.931], [\text{"} \geq 45\text{"}, 0.069])$
Galaxy S4 (Blue)	$(Age, [\text{"} < 45\text{"}, 0.755], [\text{"} \geq 45\text{"}, 0.245])$
Galaxy S4 (Black)	$(Age, [\text{"} < 45\text{"}, 0.650], [\text{"} \geq 45\text{"}, 0.350])$

Qualitative analysis of demographic features. Table 6 shows that demographic features are very effective in product recommendation. Here we present in Table 7 some learned demographic features for a phone product, Samsung Galaxy S4. In specific we only show the associated demographic features for "color". It can be observed that the demographic distributions indeed varies with different colors. Young females prefer *white* phones while young males like *black* phones more.

Table 7 shows some learned product demographic features of two different phone brands, Apple and Samsung. We have a couple of interesting observations, 1) Samsung has a more balanced sex distribution; 2) Apple products are more preferred by the consumers in the IT field.

Table 8: Samples of the learnt product demographic based on microblogs.

Apple	$(SEX, [\text{"}male\text{"}, 0.593], [\text{"}female\text{"}, 0.407])$
	(CAREER, ["IT", 0.28], ["management", 0.219] , ["media", 0.172], ["industry", 0.139])
	(TAG, ["music&movie", 0.316], ["travel", 0.249] , ["Internet surfing", 0.163], ["computer games", 0.161])
Samsung	$(SEX, [\text{"}male\text{"}, 0.503], [\text{"}female\text{"}, 0.497])$
	(CAREER, ["management", 0.252], ["IT", 0.223] , ["industry", 0.252], ["media", 0.223])
	(TAG, ["computer games", 0.281], ["travel", 0.27] , ["music&movie", 0.209], ["Internet surfing", 0.188])

Impact of the completeness of user pro les. In Table 1, we have presented the six demographic attributes. It is worth noting that not all users will fill in all the attributes in their public profiles. We want to check how the system performance is affected by the completeness of user profiles. We first analyze the dataset of three product categories in Table 4, where a query-decision pair corresponds to a unique Weibo user. The average number of attributes a user has filled in for each product category is as follows: 2.73 ± 1.10 (laptop), 2.66 ± 1.12 (camera) and 2.81 ± 1.07 (phone). Our evaluation results show that our system generally works well when a user has filled in three or more attributes, and *age*, *sex* and *interest tags* have been identified as the top three most important attributes by using the leave-one-out evaluation test. To examine the applicability of our system on a large Weibo user population, we compute the proportions of the user demographic attributes that can be found in the public profiles of the 5 million Weibo users: sex (100%), age (36.7%), marital status (4.6%), education (26.3%), career (12.9%) and tags (65.7%). It can be seen that apart from marital status, all the other attributes have considerable filled-in values, especially the identified top three most important attributes. Among the 5 million Weibo users, 44.1% of them have filled in at least three attributes and 26.5% of them have filled in all the identified top three most important attributes. These statistics provide a support evidence to our demographic based approach.

6.3 Efficiency analysis

Our dataset consists of 5 million users and 1.7 billion tweets, and about 113 tweets are published every second. As mentioned in Section 3, we use keyword filtering to reduce the number of tweets for subsequent processing. That is, tweets that do not contain any of the keywords expressing purchase intents are filtered. After keyword filtering, 3,380,894 tweets have been retained. By averaging this statistics into seconds, there would be 0.216 tweet generated per second. Our dataset covers roughly 10% of the entire Weibo data stream from active users. In this case, our purchase intent detection module will need to deal with about $0.216 \times 10 = 2.16$ tweets per second. We conduct the experiments on servers equipped with an uad-core AMT opteron(tm) processor 8380 operating at 2.5 GHz running Red Hat Linux version 9.1 and equipped with 70 GB of physical memory. Table 9 shows the running time performance of various steps in our recommender system by running on a single server with a single thread. Here, we chose linear kernel for SVM for the trade-off between accuracy and speed for purchase intent detection. It can be observed from Table 9 that our approach has a very competitive throughout of tweets per second, which is much larger than 2.16.

Table 9: Running time performance of each step in our recommender system. "t/s" denotes "tweets per second".

Step	Throughput
Purchase intent keyword filtering	751,880 t/s
Feature extraction for intent detection	301.16 t/s
Purchase intent classification (SVM linear)	217.10 t/s
Requirement identification & Feature extraction for recommendation	233.48 t/s
Ranking with MART	204.29 t/s

7. DEPLOYMENT OF THE REAL SYSTEM

We have implemented two versions of the aforementioned product recommender system (in Chinese).

Demo system. We have implemented a demo system which simulates the Weibo stream by processing our canned data collected between January and June of 2013. The system processes each tweet in turn and when it identifies a purchase-intent tweet, it will make an alert in the user interface. If we put the mouse over the tweet, the system will display the product recommendation results. The demo system is available at `http://sewm.pku.edu.cn/metis`.

Weibo service. To allow our recommender system deal with live tweets, we have set up *an official account* of our system (`http://weibo.com/u/3926085440`) and *a system response* account (`http://weibo.com/u/3802166078`). If a user wants to receive the recommendation service from our system, she can follow our official Weibo account. Our system maintains a pool of followers, and constantly monitors their tweets. Once we have detected a purchase-intent tweet, our system will generate a tweet which contains the recommendation results and a short URL link pointing to the detailed product information via the response account. The tweet contains a mention to the author of the original purchase-intent tweet. Note that the our Weibo service is limited by Sina Weibo API, and it can only deal with a small amount of requests per day.

Architecture description. A distributed platform is constructed for parallel processing, which consists of a master server and five child servers with the same configuration described in Section 6.3. Each child server keeps a local copy of all the product information. The master node coordinates the activities of the child nodes for load balancing. On each child server, an incrementally distributed index system has been implemented for storing and retrieving tweets, users profiles and product information. Each child server runs a *purchase intent detection* module and a *product recommendation* module in a pipeline mode, i.e. the identified purchase intent tweets are directly forwarded into the *product recommendation* module on the same server as shown in Figure 1. Finally, the master server collects and returns the results. User privacy has also been considered in the system design: all the user profiles are encrypted in our system and are transparent to the developers.

8. RELATED WORK

Our work is mainly related to three lines of research:

Product recommendation. Early work on product recommendation mainly relies on collaborative filtering which makes recommendations based on matching users with similar interests [19, 2, 14]. Collaborative filtering suffers from the "cold start" problem. Recently, there have been some attempts to incorporate information from online social networks into recommendation [21]. In particular, demographic information has been shown to be useful to improve the recommendation performance [13, 18, 10]. Our work is related to the aforementioned research. Nevertheless, we presented the first study which identifies users with purchase needs on social networks and make product recommendations by jointly considering both users' and products' demographic information. Some design issues and suggested guidelines for the development of product recommender systems have been previously discussed in [23, 26]. We have followed the suggested guidelines but proposed different methodologies for the implementation of our system.

Learning to rank. Learning to rank was originally proposed in information retrieval, where it aims to incorporate various features in a formal way to improve the ranking performance of the retrieved results [15]. In this paper, we formulate the product recommendation task as a learning to rank problem and evaluate various learning to rank algorithms on both the query-dependent and query-independent features derived from social media data. The learning to rank algorithms we tested include pointwise approaches, MART [9] and RandomForest [5], pairwise approaches, RankSVM [12] and RankBoost [8], and listwise approaches, ListNet [6] and AdaRank [27].

Social networking mining. Commercial intent detection and analysis has been performed on the Web data [7 and social media data such as Twitter [11]. The correlation between external events and commercial intents on microblogs have been studied in [25]. We also consider automatically detecting purchase intents from microblogs but with different feature representation and with an additional incorporation of users' demographic features. Furthermore, we have explored efficient implementation of purchase intent detection in order to achieve the near real-time performance when dealing with large amount of social stream data.

In recent years, there has also been some work on identifying individual's demographic characteristics such as age, gender and interests from social media data [16, 4]. In this paper, we directly extract users' demographic information from their public profiles in Sina Weibo. We will explore automatic methods in inferring users' demographic attributes as future work.

9. CONCLUSIONS

In this paper we have presented a novel demographic based product recommender system which detects users' purchase intents from their microblogs in near real-time and makes product recommendations based on matching the users' demographic information extracted from their public profiles with product demographics learned from microblogs and online reviews. Unlike traditional product recommender systems which are often designed for some specific e-commerce websites and can only make recommendations when users are performing e-commerce activities in those websites, our system is not constrained by any particular e-commerce website and can make instantaneous product recommendations to users who have expressed their purchase intents in micoblogs.

We have conducted extensive experiments on large-scale microblog data crawled from Sina Weibo. The experimental results have verified the feasibility and effectiveness of our proposed recommender system. We have also made a demo version of our system publicly available and have implemented a live system which allows registered users to get recommendations whenever they need. We believe our study will have profound influence on both research and industrial communities. In future work, apart from exploring methods to automatically infer users' demographic information from social media data, we will also investigate other potentially useful features to be incorporated into our recommender system.

ACKNOWLEDGEMENTS We thank the anoymous reviewers for his/her thorough review and highly appreciate the comments. We thank Prof. Ming Zhang for the help with the data collection. This work was partially supported by the National Key Basic Research Program (973 Program) of China under grant No. 2014CB340403, 2014CB340405, NSFC Grant 61272340. Yulan He was supported by the UK' s EPSRC grant EP/L010690/1. Xin Zhao was supported by MSRA PhD fellowship. Xin Zhao and Yanwei Guo contributed equally to this work and should be considered as joint first authors. Xin Zhao is the corresponding author.

10. REFERENCES

[1] Us demographic and business summary data. *Product guide*, 2012.

[2] Gediminas Adomavicius and Alexander Tuzhilin. Toward the next generation of recommender systems: A survey of the state-of-the-art and possible extensions. *IEEE TKDE*, 17(6), June 2005.

[3] Jin Yeong Bak, Suin Kim, and Alice Oh. Self-disclosure and relationship strength in twitter conversations. ACL '12, 2012.

[4] Bin Bi, Milad Shokouhi, Michal Kosinski, and Thore Graepel. Inferring the demographics of search users: Social data meets search queries. WWW '13, 2013.

[5] Leo Breiman. Random forests. *Mach. Learn.*, 45(1), October 2001.

[6] Zhe Cao, Tao in, Tie-Yan Liu, Ming-Feng Tsai, and Hang Li. Learning to rank: From pairwise approach to listwise approach. ICML '07, 2007.

[7] Honghua (Kathy) Dai, Lingzhi Zhao, Zaiqing Nie, Ji-Rong Wen, Lee Wang, and Ying Li. Detecting online commercial intention (oci). In *WWW '06*, 2006.

[8] Yoav Freund, Raj Iyer, Robert E. Schapire, and Yoram Singer. An efficient boosting algorithm for combining preferences. *J. Mach. Learn. Res.*, pages 933–969, 2003.

[9] Jerome H. Friedman. Greedy function approximation: A gradient boosting machine. *Annals of Statistics*, 29:1189–1232, 2000.

[10] Michael Giering. Retail sales prediction and item recommendations using customer demographics at store level. *SIGKDD Explor. Newsl.*, 10(2), December 2008.

[11] Bernd Hollerit, Mark Kröll, and Markus Strohmaier. Towards linking buyers and sellers: Detecting commercial intent on twitter. WWW '13 Companion, 2013.

[12] Thorsten Joachims. Training linear svms in linear time. KDD '06, 2006.

[13] Nikolaos Korfiatis and Marios Poulos. Using online consumer reviews as a source for demographic recommendations: A case study using online travel reviews. *Expert Syst. Appl.*, 40(14), 2013.

[14] Greg Linden, Brent Smith, and Jeremy York. Amazon.com recommendations: Item-to-item collaborative filtering. *IEEE Internet Computing*, 7(1), January 2003.

[15] Tie-Yan Liu. Learning to rank for information retrieval. *Found. Trends Inf. Retr.*, 3(3), March 2009.

[16] Alan Mislove, Bimal Viswanath, Krishna P. Gummadi, and Peter Druschel. You are who you know: Inferring user profiles in online social networks. WSDM '10, 2010.

[17] Bo Pang and Lillian Lee. A sentimental education: Sentiment analysis using subjectivity summarization based on minimum cuts. ACL '04, 2004.

[18] Lingyun iu and Izak Benbasat. A study of demographic embodiments of product recommendation agents in electronic commerce. *Int. J. Hum.-Comput. Stud.*, 68(10):669–688, October 2010.

[19] Badrul Sarwar, George Karypis, Joseph Konstan, and John Riedl. Item-based collaborative filtering recommendation algorithms. WWW '01, 2001.

[20] G. Sridhar. Consumer involvement in product choice - a demographic analysis. *XIMB Journal of Management*, 2007.

[21] Panagiotis Symeonidis, Eleftherios Tiakas, and Yannis Manolopoulos. Product recommendation and rating prediction based on multi-modal social networks. RecSys '11, 2011.

[22] Peter D. Turney. Thumbs up or thumbs down?: Semantic orientation applied to unsupervised classification of reviews. ACL '02, 2002.

[23] Felix von Reischach, Florian Michahelles, and Albrecht Schmidt. The design space of ubiquitous product recommendation systems. MUM '09, 2009.

[24] Jian Wang and Yi Zhang. Opportunity model for e-commerce recommendation: Right product; right time. SIGIR '13, 2013.

[25] Jinpeng Wang, Wayne Xin Zhao, Haitian Wei, Hongfei Yan, and Xiaoming Li. Mining new business opportunities: Identifying trend related products by leveraging commercial intents from microblogs. In *EMNLP*, 2013.

[26] Bo Xiao and Izak Benbasat. E-commerce product recommendation agents: Use, characteristics, and impact. *MIS Quarterly*, 31:137–209, 2007.

[27] Jun Xu and Hang Li. Adarank: A boosting algorithm for information retrieval. SIGIR '07, 2007.

[28] Valarie A Zeithaml. The new demographics and market fragmentation. *Journal of Marketing*, 49:64–75, 1985.

Modeling Professional Similarity by mining Professional Career Trajectories*

Ye Xu[1], Zang Li[2], Abhishek Gupta[2], Ahmet Bugdayci[2], Anmol Bhasin[2]
[1]Dartmouth College, ye@cs.dartmouth.edu
[2]LinkedIn Corporation, {znli, agupta, abugdayci,abhasin}@linkedin.com

ABSTRACT

For decades large corporations as well as labor placement services have maintained extensive yet static resume databanks. Online professional networks like LinkedIn have taken these resume databanks to a dynamic, constantly updated and massive scale professional profile dataset spanning career records from hundreds of industries, millions of companies and hundreds of millions of people worldwide. Using this professional profile dataset, this paper attempts to model profiles of individuals as a sequence of positions held by them as a time-series of nodes, each of which represents one particular position or job experience in the individual's career trajectory. These career trajectory models can be employed in various utility applications including career trajectory planning for students in schools & universities using knowledge inferred from real world career outcomes. They can also be employed for decoding sequences to uncover paths leading to certain professional milestones from a user's current professional status.

We deploy the proposed technique to ascertain *professional similarity* between two individuals by developing a similarity measure *SimCareers* (Similar Career Paths). The measure employs sequence alignment between two career trajectories to quantify professional similarity between career paths. To the best of our knowledge, *SimCareers* is the first framework to model professional similarity between two people taking account their career trajectory information. We posit, that using the temporal and structural features of a career trajectory for modeling profile similarity is a far more superior approach than using similarity measures on semi-structured attribute representation of a profile for this application. We validate our hypothesis by extensive quantitative evaluations on a gold dataset of similar profiles generated from recruiting activity logs from actual recruiters using LinkedIn. In addition, we show significant improvements in engagement by running an A/B test on a real-world application called *Similar Profiles* on LinkedIn, world's largest online professional network.

*This work was done when Ye Xu interned in LinkedIn.

KDD'14, August 24–27, 2014, New York, NY, USA.
Copyright 2014 ACM 978-1-4503-2956-9/14/08 ...$15.00..

Categories and Subject Descriptors

H.2.8 [**Database Applications**]: Data Mining

Keywords

Social Networks, Similarity, User Profiles, Career Paths

1. INTRODUCTION

Online professional networks are coming of age and are becoming an important tool for maintaining one's professional profile of record and discovering new career opportunities. LinkedIn maintains the professional profile for over 238 million members. With such a large number of profiles, quality profile discovery at scale becomes a challenging problem.

Recruiting is a massive use case exercised by premium users of LinkedIn. *Similar Profiles Recommender System* helps recruiters and hiring managers discover other similar quality talent by pivoting of a model user profile. It models each member profile, as illustrated in Fig.2, by extracting a labeled bags of canonicalized keywords from profile fields such as summary, skills, companies worked at, schools attended, job titles etc. Given the bags of keywords representation for user profiles, *Similar Profiles* measures the similarity between pairs of LinkedIn members by matching keywords across field pairings, and then comes up with a normalized similarity score. While relatively powerful, this approach does not leverage a critical aspect, which is fundamental to assessing professional similarity - the temporal information encoded in series of positions held by the individuals through their careers.

Let us take Fig.1 as a motivating example[1] to highlight the importance of using Career Trajectory information for finding similar people. Here, we present the top several members who are most similar to a particular user as returned by *Similar Profiles*. When we peruse through the returned list, we find that both Member 1 (ranked 1st) and Member 7 (ranked 7th) are similar to the model profile in terms of overall semantic keyword similarity. However, if we examine the appeared time of matched keywords in both profiles, we observe that the matched keywords (e.g., "Data analysis") between model profile and Member 7 (ranked 7th) both appear in their most recent position, while the matched keywords (e.g., "Data Mining") between model profile and Member 1 (ranked 1st) appear in past positions. From a recruiting standpoint, it is opined that recent experience is more applicable to profile similarity in addition to length of the experience with particular skillsets. Hence, it is intuitive to seek that the model profile is more similar to Member 7 (ranked 7th) than Member 1 (ranked 1st) in terms of career trajectory. Since the current *Similar Profiles Recommender System*

[1]For the purpose of privacy protection, we anonymize the name and profile pictures of returned results.

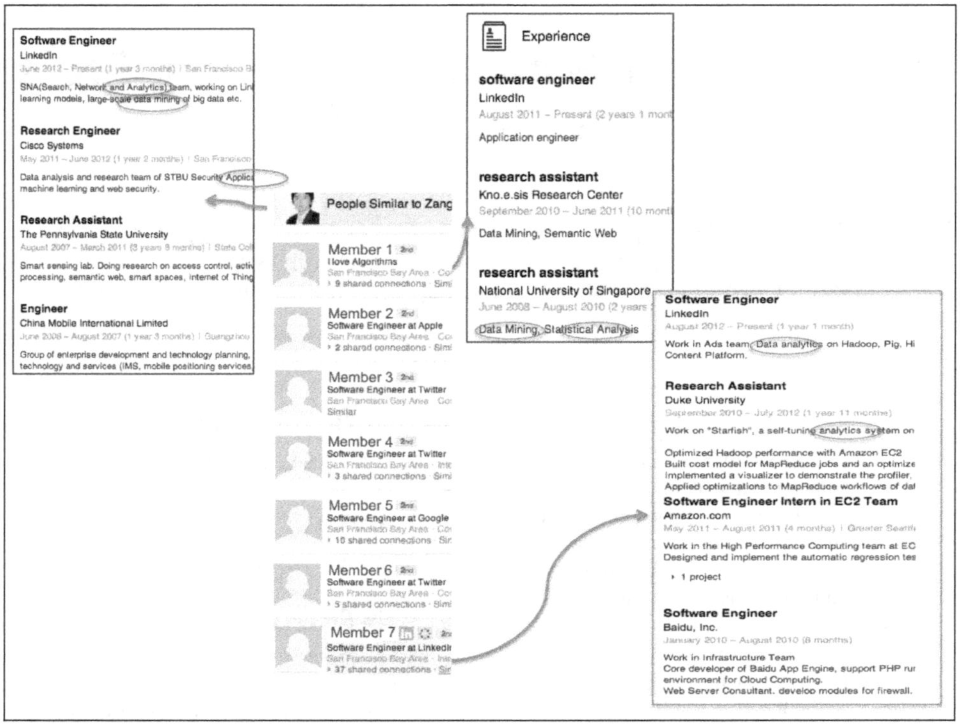

Figure 1: An example of *Similar Profiles*. All the returned results are similar in terms of keyword matching. However, because *Similar Profiles* fails to consider career trajectory information when calculating the profile similarity, a portion of returned results are not similar in terms of career trajectory.

ignores temporal information, we miss this subtle yet important signal.

To address this problem, we propose the *SimCareers* (Similar Career Paths) framework, a new approach to modeling LinkedIn member profiles by leveraging the concept of career trajectory. The *SimCareers* treats every individual member profile as a sequence of nodes, each of which records all information of the position, such as company, title, industry, time duration, and keyword summary. Then, based on the profile modeling method, the similarity between two member profiles is calculated by aligning the two sequences of nodes. At the node level, similarity is ascertained by using a generalized linear model but other approaches could be easily substituted.

The aforementioned approach is an effective way to model professional profiles, under which a comprehensive view of member's professional information is exhibited in a time-series manner. Its most immediate application is to help improve *Similar Profiles Recommender System*. This framework can be extended to help professionals do career planning. For example, by comparing career paths between young professionals and the early stage profiles from those of more successful senior individuals, we can give people a look-ahead of possible future career trajectories based on where they currently are. This can help them decide which school to choose, area of specialization to pursue and skills to acquire in order to achieve the desired outcome.

In summary, the key contributions of this paper are as follow: (1) To the best of our knowledge, *SimCareers* is the first framework that models professional profiles as time-series of career positions for any online professional network or resume databank. (2) We propose a similarity measure as a sequence alignment exercised over professional user profiles to ascertain professional similarity between two professionals from a recruiting standpoint. (3) We reveal and validate the important insight that career trajectory information is of paramount importance in modeling similarity over professional profiles. The validation is facilitated by running real-world *Similar Profiles* application experiments on the world's largest professional network - LinkedIn.

2. BACKGROUND

Similar Profiles Recommender System is used in LinkedIn for profile modeling and quality candidate discovery. In addition to serving as an independent product, it also powers *People You May Want to Hire* which is a personalized candidate discovery engine for recruiters that takes into account all of the context with regards to recruiting activity [21].

Formally speaking, the *Similar Profiles Recommender Problem* can be defined as follows:

PROBLEM 1 (SIMILAR PROFILES RECOMMENDER PROBLEM). *Given all LinkedIn members $u \in \mathcal{U}$, where each member u is associated with a member profile f^u, and a source member s, the Similar Profiles Recommender System outputs a list of k target members $t_1, t_2, ..., t_k$ who have top-k highest similarity scores to the source member, and the list of members is ranked by the similarity value in a descending order.*

Similar Profiles algorithm works as follows: (An illustration is given in Fig. 2.) It models member profiles by extracting keywords from each field in member's LinkedIn profile. A few example fields are summary, skills, current position summary, past position summary, companies worked at, schools attended, etc. These fields are placed on the member's profile on LinkedIn where members have manually entered free form text. The extracted keywords form lists of bags of keywords. We use cosine-similarity to find similarity scores for field-pairs corresponding to the two member profiles in consideration. An overall similarity score is calculated using a weighted linear combination of these scores to get the final *Similar Profiles* similarity measure between the two members. This measure is symmetric and is normalized using a logit function, so that it can be interpreted as a probability of being similar. Here, weights reflect the relative importance of field pairs that are matched. These weights are learned by fitting a logistic regression model on training data obtained from active recruiter usage of *Similar Profiles* product.

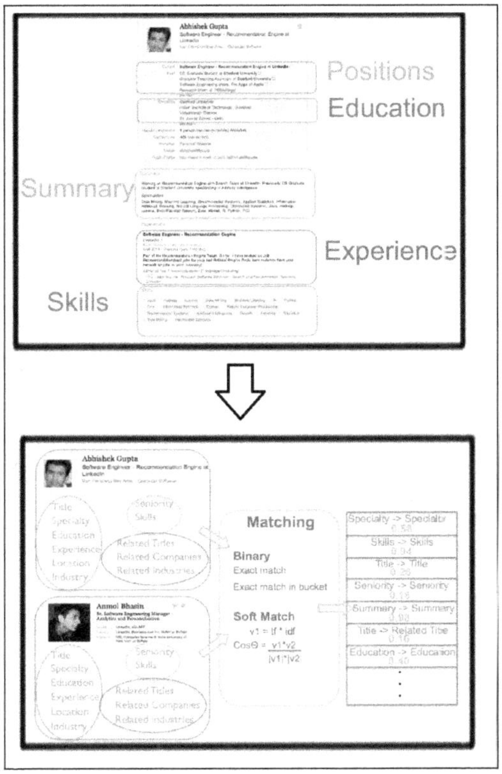

Figure 2: The procedure of *Similar Profiles*. First, keywords are extracted for every field from LinkedIn profile page for each member. Then, given two bags of keywords, we match keywords at the field level. Finally, we come up with a similarity score.

3. SIMILAR CAREER PATHS

In what follows, we give the description of Similar Career Paths framework, which models LinkedIn member profiles as career sequences. We use sequence alignment to measure overall profile similarity. For every node in the sequence, we use keyword based matching to evaluate node-level similarity.

3.1 Problem Description

For each LinkedIn member, we maintain a profile webpage[2] that records his/her professional information, e.g., title, company, seniority, overall summary, experience, skills and expertise, education, courses, languages, additional personal information, connections, groups etc. An example is shown in Fig.3. Given the profile

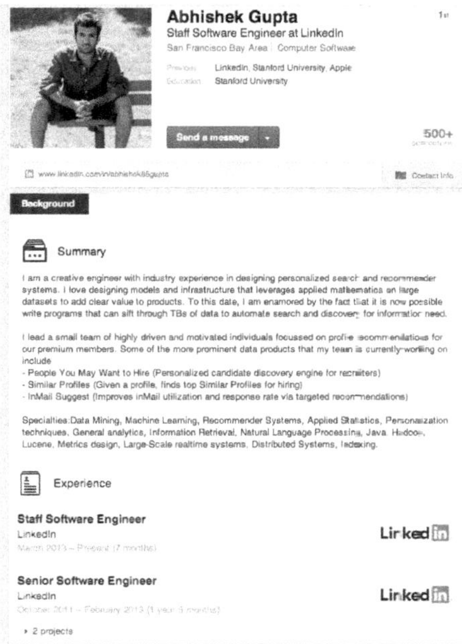

Figure 3: An example of LinkedIn member profile page: it contains professional information of the member such as job tittle, seniority, company, location, education, summary, experience etc. All these information will be extracted to learn the similarity metric between two members.

pages from two LinkedIn members, we aim to measure the similarity between them. In other words, all the information with regards to member profile can be used to calculate the similarity score between them.

3.2 Model Member Profiles

In what follows, we describe how we model LinkedIn member profiles. Like many other online social networks [7, 11, 4], *Similar Profiles*, models member profiles purely by keywords matching. It ignores the temporal order of keywords and thus fails to capture the career trajectory information, which is extremely important in a professional network.

To solve this problem, we introduce the concept of timeline. In *SimCareers*, each member profile is treated as a time sequence of nodes. In this modeling scheme, firstly, we provide a clear view for each member's career trajectory. Secondly, we explain how we divide the whole bag of keywords in the original *Similar Profiles* into finer granularity. Finally, we also describe how the temporal factor is taken into account in the similarity computation. Intuitively, the matched keywords at the closest timestamp implies that the profiles are more similar with respect to more recent work experience. Hence, it should lead to higher overall similarity. More concretely, we employ the following schemes to model the node corresponding to a job position.

Sequence of Positions: In this scheme, each node represents one particular position of the member's professional experience, e.g., position summary, company, title, seniority, industry, job function, and time durations of the position. An example is given in Fig.4.

Sequence of Compositions: In this scheme, we still model each LinkedIn member's profile using a sequence of node. For each node, in addition to using position information mentioned before, we also incorporate transition information associated with the given

[2]http://www.linkedin.com/profile/

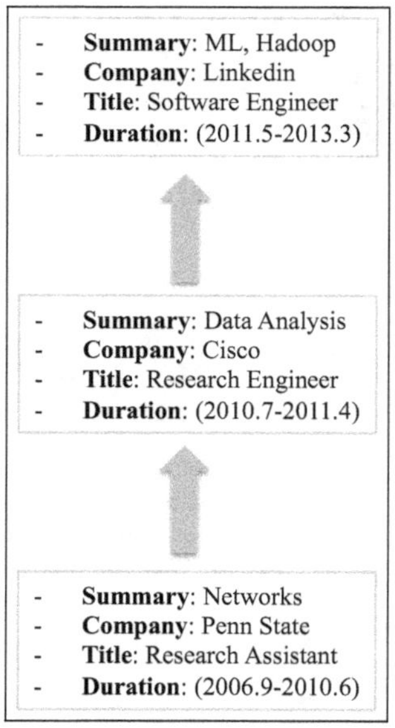

Figure 4: Sequence of positions modeling method: each node in the sequence contains information about the position, such as position summary, company, title, seniority, and time durations.

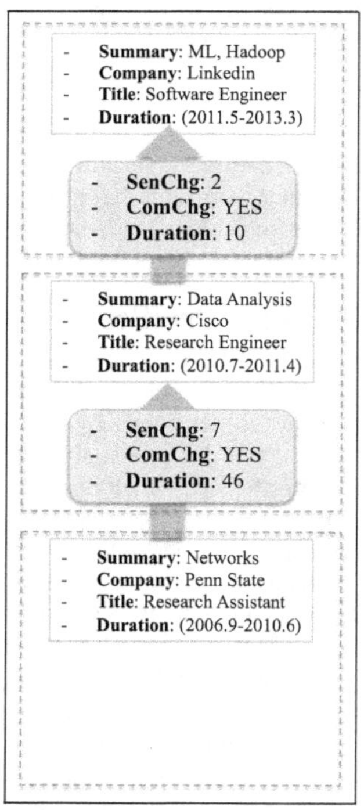

Figure 5: Sequence of compositions modeling method: each node in the sequence is the composition of position information and transition related information. Incorporating transition information enhances the representation of each node. Note that the first composition node is associated with the earliest position. It has no previous positions, thus this node does not have any transition related features.

position and the previous one. In other words, the position information, along with transition related information, together composes a node. Transition information, (i.e., whether title changes in this transition, whether company changes, how the seniority changes, and the time of years used in this transition) enhances the representation of the *Sequence of Compositions* modeling scheme by further disclosing information of the changing trend between previous and the given position. An example is given in Fig. 5.

3.3 Model Career Path Similarity

In this work, we design a similarity metric based on the sequence of nodes modeling scheme. Generally speaking, given two sequences of nodes (profiles), we conduct sequence alignment to calculate the similarity between them. Sequence alignment [22] originated in bioinformatics domain. It can identify the similarity between two sequences of DNA, RNA or protein by finding an optimal way to arrange the node-level alignment from two sequences respectively. In our profile similarity learning scenario, we need to match and align career nodes from two career sequences (i.e., member profiles) according to the similarity between them. Thus, this is naturally associated with the classic sequence alignment problem. When it comes to the specific alignment between each pair of node, we propose a node-level similarity metric. We discuss the node-level Similarity metric in more detail in Section 3.3.2.

3.3.1 Profile-Level Similarity by Sequence Alignment

We aim to evaluate the similarity between two career paths – two sequences of nodes. Each node here is a representation of one particular work experience. For overall similarity score, we want all the work experience in the career sequence to contribute. In order to compute overall similarity between two career sequences, we decompose the score into the sum of the similarity between several pairs of aligned nodes from each of the two sequences respectively [8]. We now need a scheme to find an optimal alignment between pairs of nodes from the two career paths. This naturally relates to the classic sequence alignment problem.

In sequence alignment algorithm [16], the sequence level similarity is measured by calculating the sum of the optimal alignment of node pairs. We conduct the sequence alignment in a local manner [8]. The two sequences are aligned incrementally. The sequence alignment scheme can be formulated as a dynamic programming procedure. Suppose, we have two career sequences $\mathbf{P_1} = [\mathbf{X_1}, \mathbf{X_2}, , \mathbf{X_m}]$ and $\mathbf{P_2} = [\mathbf{Y_1}, \mathbf{Y_2}, , \mathbf{Y_n}]$. ($\mathbf{X_i}$ and $\mathbf{Y_j}$ are position/composition nodes from two career sequences respectively.) Let us further imagine that we have come to the step of aligning subsequences $P_1[1 : i-1]$ and subsequence $P_2[1 : j-1]$. (In other words, shorter subsequences have been aligned previously.) The subsequences $P_1[1 : i]$ and $P_2[1 : j]$ can be aligned in three ways according to the following cases:

- The node $\mathbf{X_i}$ is similar to node $\mathbf{Y_j}$. This leads to this pair of positions being aligned and results in an overall increase in sequence similarity score as contributed by this node similarity value. Here, $\mathbf{P_1}[1 : i]$ represents the subsequence $\mathbf{X_1}$, $\mathbf{X_2}$, .., $\mathbf{X_i}$ from career sequence $\mathbf{P_1}$.

- The node $\mathbf{X_i}$ is not much similar to node $\mathbf{Y_j}$. Thus, $\mathbf{X_i}$ will be skipped. Note that although a node is allowed to be skipped during sequence alignment, we encourage contiguous alignment for the purpose of career path completeness. Therefore, we impose a gap penalty on sequence level similarity score when skipping a node. (We will further discuss this point in later section)

- And vice versa, if the node $\mathbf{X_i}$ is not much similar to node $\mathbf{Y_j}$, we impose the same gap penalty.

It is worth noting that the position-level similarity function that we employ is symmetric. Hence, $S^{node}(X_i, Y_j)$ is the same as $S^{node}(Y_j, X_i)$. More formally, given the above two career sequences $\mathbf{P_1}$ and $\mathbf{P_2}$, the similarity between two career sequences can be solved using the following scheme:

$$S^{seq}(\mathbf{P_1}[1:i], \mathbf{P_2}[1:j]) = \max \begin{cases} S^{seq}(\mathbf{P_1}[1:i-1], \mathbf{P_2}[1:j-1]) + S^{node}(\mathbf{X_i}, \mathbf{Y_j}) \\ S^{seq}(\mathbf{P_1}[1:i-1], \mathbf{P_2}[1:j]) - \lambda \\ S^{seq}(\mathbf{P_1}[1:i], \mathbf{P_2}[1:j-1]) - \lambda \end{cases} \quad (1)$$

Therein, S^{seq} is the similarity function at the career sequence level, S^{node} is the similarity function at the position/composition node level, and λ is the gap penalty parameter. We will discuss S^{node} and λ in later sections.

3.3.2 Node-Level Similarity Model

The *SimCareers* framework aligns two career sequences by incrementally aligning two position/composition nodes or skipping the node in either of the two sequences. In order to compute S^{seq}, we need to first define S^{node}. We propose to learn a similarity model at the node level by using Logistic Regression model [3]. In what follows, we will discuss the node-level similarity model in detail.

Data and Labels. We first extract position/composition node data features from LinkedIn member profile. We gather training data from active recruiter usage of the *Similar Profiles Recommender System*. Recruiters use this recommender system to discover more profiles similar to the query[3]. *Similar Profiles Recommender System* that is powered by *SimProfiles* algorithm, as discussed in Section 2, can guarantee the returned candidate profiles are similar to the query profile. Once recruiters find desired candidates, the most common way for them to reach out to candidates is via *InMail*. InMail is a paid product provided by LinkedIn that allows recruiters to reach out to members outside their existing network. In the absence of ground truth data for position similarity, we employ the following heuristic to gather quality training data for position similarity model.

We only consider profile-pairs that were discovered via *Similar Profiles Recommender System* and then contacted by recruiters. In other words, we only look at *inMails* sent as a result of *Similar Profiles Recommender* search. We regard the current position of such profile pairs, the original profile looked at and the subsequent one contacted, as similar. The assumption used here in collecting data is that if a recruiter contacts this newly discovered profile immediately after discovering the original one then presumably at-least the current position of these profiles is similar. Empirically speaking, most recruiters in LinkedIn behaves in this manner. With this scheme, we sample about 300,000 candidate profile pairs with a non-empty current position from data collected over all LinkedIn Recruiter accounts within 3 months (from March 2013 to May 2013). Note that the intuition of introducing recruiter contact here is that current Similar Profiles Recommender System is not perfectly accurate and could return some dissimilar pairs. Thus by examining recruiter contact, we can refine the quality and purity of data.Such scheme, along with the amount of data processed, can guarantee the quality of the collected data.

As a further refinement for model training, we only consider those profile-pairs as positives where more than 3 recruiters contact the profiles discovered via *Similar Profiles Recommender System*. The intuition is that if enough recruiters contact the newly discovered profile then this profile pair is more likely to be similar. Amongst the rest of the recommended profiles, all the ones that were ranked higher but were not reached out to be any recruiter are regarded as negative profile-pairs for the purpose of model training for node-level similarity. After employing this additional constraint, we get about 80,000 profile-pairs as positive labels for position similarity model training and 220,000 negative labels. During the model training, we use all 80,000 positive position pairs and randomly sample 80,000 negative position pairs from the 220,000 candidate negative labels.

[3]Here, the query member profile is often the ideal candidate they have found or already hired.

Features. Based on the discussion in Section 3.2, we have two schemes to model member profiles in *Similar Career*: (1) sequence of positions; and (2) sequence of compositions. For each of the two methods, we consider different feature sets to train the corresponding node level similarity model.

For the sequence of positions modeling scheme, we extract the following features from each pair of positions

- *CurrentTitle:* The feature indicates whether the two positions share the same title name.
- *CurrentCompany:* The feature indicates whether the two positions are from the same company.
- *CurrentCompanySize:* At LinkedIn, each company is categorized into a bucket based its employee size (e.g., less than 100 employees, 100 to 1000 employees, 1000 to 10000 employees, and more than 10000 employees.) This feature measures the difference between two positions in the aspect of company size.
- *CurrentIndustry:* This feature indicates whether the two positions are from the same industry. E.g., of some industries are Internet, Venture Capital, Hardware.
- *CurrentFunctions:* This feature indicates whether the two positions have the same job function. E.g., of some job functions are Engineering, HR.
- *JobSeniority:* This is a derived feature that takes into account overall work experience in terms of titles held in the past, companies worked at and number of years of work experience. E.g., Director of Engineer at LinkedIn would have a higher seniority than Engineering Manager at LinkedIn.
- *CurrentPositionSummary:* This feature extracts key words from the position summary field.
- *TittleSim:* This feature indicates whether the titles of the two positions are similar or not. E.g., Applied Research Engineer and Data Scientist are similar titles.
- *CompanySim:* This feature indicates whether the companies of the two positions are similar or not. E.g., from an employability standpoint, LinkedIn, Facebook and Google are considered similar.
- *IndustrySim:* This feature indicates whether the industries of the two positions are similar or not. E.g., Computer Software and Internet are more similar to each other than Internet and Civil Engineering.
- *Duration:* This feature describes the difference of time durations between the two positions.

It deserves mentioning that we normalize each feature value and make them between 0 and 1.

For the sequence of composition nodes modeling scheme, we treat the node as a composition of position and its associated transition. Therefore, in addition to the above mentioned position related features, we also consider a few transition related features, namely, features from the transition associated with the position and its immediately previous position. The following additional features are extracted for each pair of composition nodes:

- *IsSameCompany:* This feature indicates whether both of the two transitions happen within the same company or not.
- *IsSameIndustry:* This feature indicates whether both of the two transitions happen within the same industry or not.
- *SeniorityChange:* This feature indicates whether the seniorities changed for both of the two transitions.
- *TitleChange:* This feature indicates whether the titles change for both of the two transitions.
- *TimeGap:* This feature indicates the difference of how many year durations pass during the two transitions.

Similar to position node features, we also normalize the feature values.

Model: A variety of classification methods can be used to train the similarity model given the data and labels. Note that, we aim to propose a general framework to train the node level similarity model, and our setup is not limited in any way to any particular training algorithm. Without loss of generality, in this work, we employ Logistic Regression (LR) algorithm [3] for model training. In logistic regression model, the logit of the probability of relevance of the outcome is modeled as a linear function of feature values. The model is trained via maximum likelihood estimation. Due to its effectiveness, logistic regression is widely used in many application domains such as recommender systems [2, 15] and advertisement prediction [19, 5]. Logistic regression predicts the outcome of a value between 0 and 1 according to the feature values. In our scenario, the similarity value is bounded between 0 and 1. Therefore, logistic regression is ideally suitable to train the node level similarity model. Furthermore, since existing keyword based *Similar Profiles* also employs logistic regression so this mechanism provides an easy way to combine these 2 scores. We discuss a need to do so in section 3.5.

3.4 Other Factors in the Framework

In this section, we discuss the parameters used in the *SimCareer* framework.

3.4.1 Gap Penalty

In the process of aligning career sequences, the dissimilar position/composition nodes are allowed to be skipped. However, for the purpose of career path completeness, contiguous alignments are more desirable. Therefore, to encourage contiguity in career sequence alignment, we introduce the idea of gap penalty, as shown in Eq.1. The sequence alignment is computed in an incremental manner. As we encounter node pair $\mathbf{X_i}$ and $\mathbf{Y_j}$, if the node level similarity between $\mathbf{X_i}$ and $\mathbf{Y_j}$ is high enough as determined by the *Dynamic Programming* algorithm shown in Eq.1, we continue to align them. However, if $\mathbf{X_i}$ is dissimilar to node $\mathbf{Y_j}$ in sequence $\mathbf{P_2}$, we allow the possibility of skipping the alignment of the node with a penalty called *Gap Penalty* because it impairs the contiguity in sequence alignment.

In this setting, value of the gap penalty parameter λ needs to be determined. If the value of λ is too small, many nodes can be skipped during alignment and the contiguity will be impaired. On the other hand, if it is too large, no skip could happen during alignment. As disclosed in [22], in absence of any prior knowledge, grid search is a reasonable way to determine the *Gap Penalty* parameter λ. We apply 10−fold cross validation to determine the optimal gap penalty value. It deserves mentioning that the node level similarity score in our framework is bounded between 0 and 1. Therefore, it is relatively convenient to guess candidate values for λ since it should have the same order of magnitude. In section 4.1.3, we will show that the performance of the proposed *SimCareers* is not sensitive to the λ value.

3.4.2 Position Recency and Duration

SimCareers aims to detect the similarity between two career paths under the scenario of professional social networks. In discovering professional candidates, more recent experiences are more highly valued than old experiences. Furthermore, longer period of job experiences are more convincing than shorter ones. Therefore, the duration and the recency of positions are worth considering when we calculate the similarity between career sequences.

As discussed in section 3.3.2, we try to incorporate duration information as a feature when training the node level similarity model. However, note that the training data used to calculate position similarity is for latest positions only. This implies that all these job experiences are ongoing, and we cannot reliably predict when these current job positions will terminate for each member. Therefore, with our scheme of gathering training data it is inaccurate to apply the duration of current positions as a feature to train the node level similarity model. By the same argument, the recency for current positions are always 0 (i.e., 0 years from today) in our training data. Due to lack of an automated way to generate large amounts of training data, we propose to incorporate these signals as boosts to the node-level similarity for both sequence of positions and sequence of compositions method.

As mentioned above, we incentivize alignment on more recent positions and longer duration nodes. More specifically, while computing similarity between two career sequences, we impose different weights on aligned position/composition nodes according to the recency and duration of the aligned node pair. Thus, the modified sequence alignment can be formulated as follows:

$$S^{seq}(\mathbf{P_1}[1:i], \mathbf{P_2}[1:j]) =$$
$$\max \begin{cases} S^{seq}(\mathbf{P_1}[1:i-1], \mathbf{P_2}[1:j-1]) + w(i,j)S^{node}(\mathbf{X_i}, \mathbf{Y_j}) \\ S^{seq}(\mathbf{P_1}[1:i-1], \mathbf{P_2}[1:j]) - \lambda \\ S^{seq}(\mathbf{P_1}[1:i], \mathbf{P_2}[1:j-1]) - \lambda \end{cases}$$

Therein, $w(i,j)$ is the weight for aligned node pair $\mathbf{X_i}$ and $\mathbf{Y_j}$. Intuitively, longer duration and more recent nodes should have larger weight so that they can impose stronger influence on the final sequence level similarity score. Additionally, if the difference between two nodes in terms of recency and duration is smaller, we assume that the two nodes are more similar. Thus, in our scheme this weight incorporates four terms: (i) The duration difference between two nodes; (ii)The recency difference between two nodes; (iii) The duration sum of two nodes; (iv) The recency sum of two nodes.

In this work, we apply the Half-life in exponential decay [13] as the weight. Half-life exponential decay is widely used to describe a quantity undergoing exponential decay with the following formulation:

$$N(t) = e^{-\tau \cdot t} \tag{2}$$

Therein, τ is the mean lifetime parameter. Using Eq.2, the weight $w(i,j)$ in sequence alignment formulation can be written as follow:

$$w(i,j) = e^{-\tau_1|r_i-r_j|}e^{-\tau_2|d_i-d_j|}e^{-\tau_3(r_i+r_j)}(1-e^{-\tau_4(d_i+d_j)}) \quad (3)$$

Therein, d_i is the duration of node $\mathbf{X}_i$ and r_i is the recency of node $\mathbf{X}_i$. Note that we encourage small difference of duration and recency, small value of recency but large value of duration. The mean lifetime parameters τ_1, τ_2, τ_3 and τ_4 are determined by using 10−fold cross validation.

By assigning higher weights to recent or longer duration positions, their importance in discovering the similarity between professional sequences are highlighted.

3.4.3 Career Sequence Length Bias

Various LinkedIn members have different lengths for their career sequences. A very small fraction of LinkedIn members have a large sequence length due to their long career. Note that when recruiters are discovering profiles for hiring, member's more recent positions are given more importance. With this in mind, we limit the number of past positions that we consider for overall profile similarity in the *SimCareers* framework. In other words, if a member has more than L position/composition nodes in his/her career sequence, we only consider the latest L nodes for analysis.

Choosing a proper L value is important. If it is too small, important position nodes are missed. On the other hand, a large L value makes *SimCareers* consider unimportant position nodes, and also may lead to inaccurate results. Instead of using cross validation, we analyze the sequence length distribution over all LinkedIn members and pick the value for L. A significant proportion of our members have at-most 9 positions, so we choose $L = 9$.

3.5 Incorporate Similar Profiles

In our final scoring, we incorporate the existing *Similar Profiles* score into the proposed *SimCareers* framework. In what follows, we explain the motivation of considering this keyword based score.

3.5.1 Sparse Position Problem

On our member's LinkedIn profiles, it is common for members to have comprehensive and detailed descriptions in their overall summary field. However, when it comes to the position-level summary section there is huge variability in the amount of content our members provide, from hundreds of keywords to nothing at all. Furthermore, overall summary provides important information about member's skills and speciality as it stands today. In *Similar Profiles Recommender System*, this is one of the most important features. Hence, incorporating keyword based similarity score is desirable.

3.5.2 Ensemble Approach

After generating member similarity score using two separate signals, i.e., the approach discussed above and the *Similar Profiles* score, the next step is to create a unified scheme that incorporates the two signals.

Ensemble learning [25] that uses multiple models to obtain better predictive performance naturally fits our scenario. Because of its powerful generalization ability, ensemble learning has been used in many applications [17]. Based on how to combine the results from each weak classifier, ensemble methods can be divided into a few categories: bagging, boosting, stacking, and cascading [25]. In this paper, we apply Bagging scheme to incorporate *Similar Profiles* score into the proposed *SimCareers* due to its simplity and efficiency. Specifically speaking, we apply the weighted combination of *SimilarProfiles* score and sequence alignment score using the method discussed in section 3.3. Note that *Similar Profiles* score is normalized between 0 and 1. However, the sequence alignment score is not because most people have career sequences of with more than 1 position. Thus, we normalize the sequence alignment score by dividing by the total number of sequence length of source person. Fig.6 shows the probability density function (PDF) of normalized sequence alignment score and *Similar Profiles* score over *LinkedIn member dataset* from March 2013 to May 2013 (i.e., the current position data we use for training node level similarity model). It implies that after normalization sequence alignment score have similar distribution to *Similar Profiles* score, and thus validates that applying this ensemble approach in *SimCareers* is reasonable.

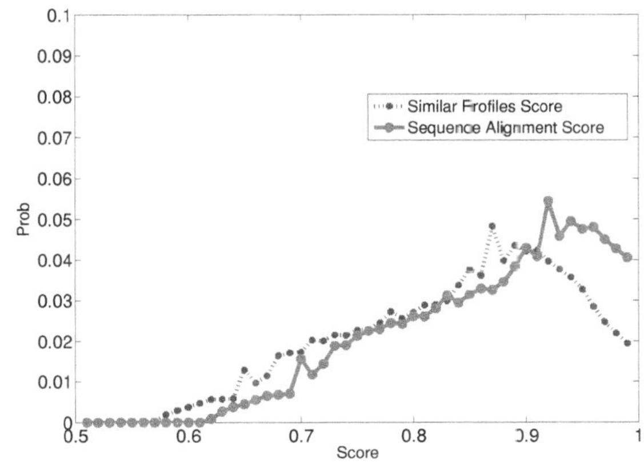

Figure 6: The Probability Density Function (PDF) of sequence alignment score and *Similar Profiles* score over *LinkedIn member dataset* within three months. Note that LinkedIn Member data is from *Similar Profiles Recommender System*.

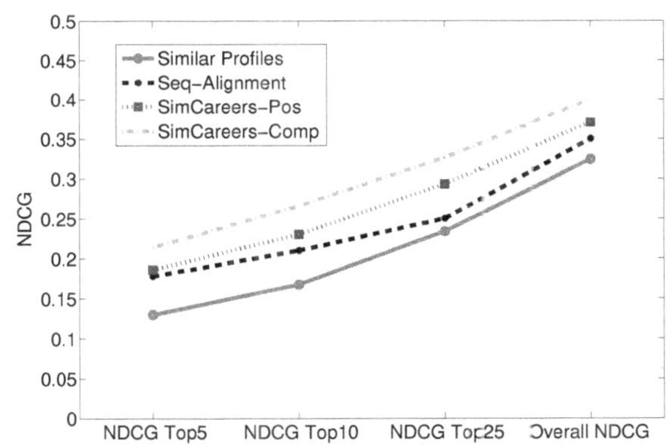

Figure 7: The NDCG scores of each method: the two *SimCareers* framework achieves much better NDCG scores than *Similar Profiles*.

4. EVALUATION

In what follows, we discuss the evaluations for the proposed *SimCareers* framework. In the first evaluation approach, we apply an offline measure of Normalized Discounted Cumulative Gain (NDCG) [10]. This measure is widely used to gauge the effectiveness of web search engines or recommender systems. Then, we also test the effectiveness of *SimCareers* by performing online AB tests and measuring the impact on our business metrics.

4.1 Offline Evaluation

The offline evaluation scheme offers a reasonable and easily repeatable mechanism for verifying performance and tuning model parameters. As a classic metric for search engine and recommender system, NDCG is used to measure the accuracy of the proposed *SimCareer* framework.

4.1.1 Experimental Setup

Dataset: We get the testing data from *Similar Profiles Recommender System* on LinkedIn. As discussed in section 3, once a recruiter account uses this recommender system to discover candidates based on a source profile, the source profile and the returned 100 recommended candidates are recorded. Note that here we only look at the candidates returned from *Similar Profiles Recommender System*. The results are shown to recruiters in descending order of *Similar Profiles* score. To demonstrate the effectiveness of our proposed framework, we use *SimCareers* to evaluate the similarity between each of the 100 pairs (i.e., source profile and each of the 100 returned results) and obtain a reranked list. Note that when calculating NDCG metric, the ground truth order of the 100 profiles is needed. Here, we employ *InMail* sending and receiving to infer this ground truth.

Similar to the scheme discussed in section 3, if after seeing Similar Profiles results for a source profile the recruiter contacts one or more of these recommended results, then we regard the source profile and the profiles that were contacted as *Similar*. As a further refinement, we only consider those cases as positives where at least 3 recruiters contacted the recommended profile. Meanwhile, within the top 100 results, the recommended profiles which were ranked higher, were seen by the recruiter and were not contacted are regarded as *Not Similar* for the purpose of collecting labeled dataset. All other recommended profiles are ignored from the labeled dataset.

In this experiment, we use data collected over all LinkedIn Recruiter accounts within one month (June 2013) for testing. We denote the base *Similar Profiles* score by *sp* and sequence alignment scores derived by *SimCareers* by *sc*. As discussed in section 3.5.2, we do a linear combination of *sp* and *sc* score via parameter δ i.e. unified relevance score = *sp* + δ * *sc*. We report offline numbers for $\delta = 1.0$.

Metric: We use Normalized Discounted Cumulative Gain (NDCG) [10], a classic metric used for evaluating search and recommender systems. The NDCG score is calculated using the following formulation:

$$nDCG = \frac{DCG}{IDCG} \tag{4}$$

Here, Discounted Cumulative Gain (DCG) is defined as follows,

$$DCG = rel(1) + \sum_{i=2}^{N} \frac{rel(i)}{log_2 i} \tag{5}$$

Therein, $rel(i)$ is the relevance score of position i. In our scenario, if the ith returned profile is similar in terms of inMail validation, $rel(i) = 1$. Otherwise, $rel(i) = 0$. $IDCG$ in Eq.4 is calculated using the same equation as DCG based on the ground truth ranking list.

Similar Profiles Recommender System is used by recruiters for discovering quality candidates given a source profile. Intuitively, doing well on the top results is better than doing well on the bottom results. Thus, the quality of top returned results is more important. To demonstrate the effectiveness of *SimCareers* we compute

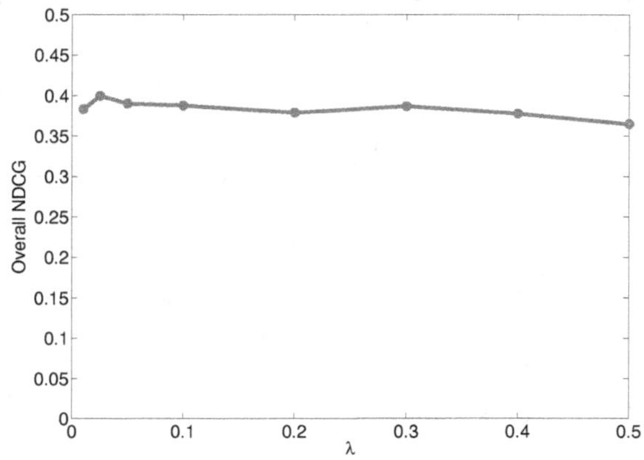

Figure 8: The NDCG scores of *SimCareers-Comp* under different λ values: (Other parameters are fixed here.) The results demonstrate that the proposed *SimCareers* framework is not sensitive to gap penalty parameter λ.

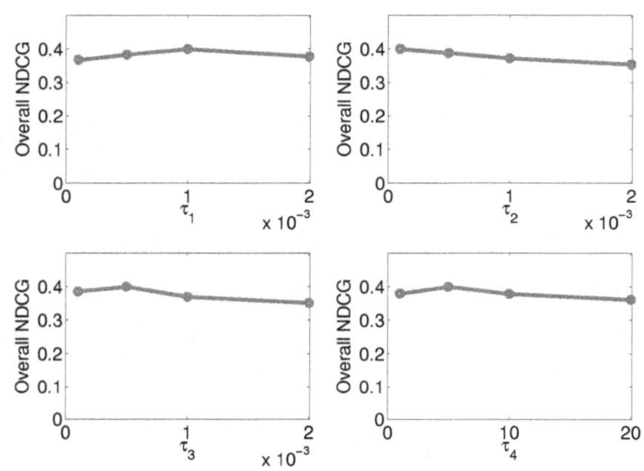

Figure 9: The NDCG scores of *SimCareers-Comp* under different τ values: each time we vary one parameter while fixing the rest.

NDCG top5, NDCG top10, and NDCG top25. (i.e., let $N = 5$, 10, and 25 respectively in Eq.5.) in addition to overall NDCG (i.e., let $N = 100$ in Eq.5).

Baseline: We use the ranking results from *Similar Profiles* as the baseline to evaluate *SimCareers*. Moreover, we compute the NDCG score using purely the sequence alignment method (*Seq-Alignment*), i.e., without resorting to the ensemble approach mentioned in Section 3.5.2. To validate the importance of using transition related information when modeling career sequence similarity, we calculate the NDCG score for sequence of positions modeling method (*SimCareers-Pos*) and sequence of compositions modeling method (*SimCareers-Comp*) respectively.

4.1.2 Experimental Results

Fig.7 shows the results of NDCG top5, NDCG top10, NDCG top25, and overall NDCG score for *SimCareers-Pos*, *SimCareers-Comp*, *Seq-Alignment* and *Similar Profiles*. These numbers validate our intuition that capturing temporal information of career trajectory is crucial in computing profile similarity for hiring. More specifically, pairwise t-tests at 95% significance level indicate that the *SimCareers* framework is significantly better than *Similar Profiles* under all the four NDCG scores. Meanwhile, the two *SimCareers* framework achieves high NDCG scores than *Seq-Alignment*, demonstrating the effectiveness of the ensemble approach. By comparing the curves of *Seq-Alignment* and two *SimCareers* methods, we can reach the conclusion that incorporating keyword based similarity score is effective and desirable. It deserves mentioning that compared with overall NDCG, the difference between *SimCareers* and *Similar Profiles* under NDCG top5 and NDCG top10 is larger. It means in the more realistic setting where top recommended profiles will end up getting contacted more often, the proposed *SimCareers* will perform even better. Note that under all the four metrics, *SimCareers-Comp* obtains higher NDCG scores than *SimCareers-Pos*. Incorporating transition related information into the position node provides a more comprehensive description and captures the dynamic changes of the work experience nodes, thus leading to higher quality *Similar Profiles*.

4.1.3 Parameter Insensitivity

To further demonstrate that *SimCareers* is not sensitive to the parameters we define in the model, i.e., the gap penalty λ and mean lifetime parameter τ_1, τ_2, τ_3, and τ_4, we report the overall NDCG score of *SimCareers-Comp* under different parameter settings. Each time we vary one parameter, and fix the rest. The NDCG scores under different λ values are shown in Fig.8, and the results under different mean lifetime parameter values are shown in Fig.9. The two figures indicate that the *SimCareers* framework is not sensitive to these parameters. It is worth noting that the dataset used for parameter estimation is a mutually disjoint dataset from the training dataset. This dataset spans March 2013 to May 2013 and serves as a validation dataset to tune these additional parameters. The difference in dataset accounts for the difference in absolute value of overall NDCG in Fig. 7.

4.2 A/B Test

We performed online AB tests[12] for a few variants of *SimCareers* model on independent segments of LinkedIn member populations. When combined with offline NDCG score for the similarity model, A/B Test provides for a deeper understanding of user behavior. We focus on the following metric for the online evaluation:

- Profile Views: This describes the profile views generated via *Similar Profiles Recommender System* from recruiters looking to hire talent. For every candidate that a recruiter discovers, we allow him to discover more profiles via *Similar Profiles* recommendations. Viewing one or more of these recommended results indicates that the recommendations are relevant.

- InMails : This describes contact between recruiters and the candidate discovered via *Similar Profiles Recommender System*. The assumption is that the more candidates recruiters reach out to via recommendations the more similar the recommendations are to the source profile that lead them to discover newer profiles.

Since combining *Similar Profiles* score and sequence alignment score significantly increases the performance for NDCG metric, we perform four A/B Tests using different parameter configurations when combining the two scores (i.e., the parameter deciding the proportion between *Similar Profiles* score and sequence alignment score used in the bagging scheme). We ran the AB test for one month. Results of *Profile Views* and *InMails* are summarized in Table 1. We denote the base *Similar Profiles* score by *sp* and sequence alignment scores derived by *SimCareers* by *sc*. As discussed in section 3.5.2, we do a linear combination of *sp* and *sc* score via parameter δ i.e. unified relevance score = $sp + \delta * sc$.

Table 1: The results of A/B Tests under different parameter configurations: the number in the table indicates the percentage increase (+) or decrease (-) in metrics using *SimCareers* compared with the baseline – *Similar Profiles*.

δ	Profile Views	InMails
0.01	−1.52%	+0.83%
0.10	−10.33%	−7.51%
1.00	**+21.14%**	+8.77%
10.0	**+20.12%**	**+12.11%**

Table.1 demonstrates the impact of A/B test results on our business metrics namely, *Profile Views* and *InMails*. These results further validate our hypothesis that capturing temporal information of career trajectory is crucial in computing profile similarity for hiring. More specifically, the δ value indicates the weight of the *SimCareers* score in the final unified relevance score. The results indicate that when the δ value is small, the difference between *SimCareers* score and *SimProfiles* score is negligible. It is because *sp* score dominates the *SimCareers* results with a small δ value. However, as we give more weight to the *SimCareers* score, we get a larger increase in both *Profile Views* and *InMails* sent. It is because that sequence alignment methodology captures the career trajectory information and thus can better measure the similarity between two profiles.

5. RELATED WORK

In this paper, we design a framework to model the similarity over a professional network. Although there are many studies on modeling similarity on social networks, none of them have taken temporal information into account in their models.

Similarity modeling over social networks is a hot topic, especially for online social networks such as Facebook, LinkedIn and Twitter. A few traditional metric can be used to model similarity based on the network structure information, such as common neighbor (CN) [14] and Adamic-Adar (AA) [1]. Note that these methods are only based on network structure. Recently, a few algorithms have been proposed to model similarity using user profile information on social networks. The most relevant one along this line was done by Centinatas et al. [4]. This work aimed to model similarity for professional networks by extracting keywords from member profiles, and then treating keywords as features to train a discriminative model. This work, as well, only considers keyword based similarity. There are also a few similarity modeling methods [7, 11] that are proposed for other online social networks. All these profile based algorithms only use keywords extracted from user profiles and fail to consider temporal information of keywords

Our paper also relates to sequence and time series data similarity [16, 6]. During past few years, due to its effectiveness, time series data similarity modeling have been widely applied in a many application domains. For instance, sequence alignment is used for detecting similarity between DNA, RNA or protein sequences [16]. In speech recognition, a few algorithms such as Dynamic Time Warping [20], have been proposed to measure similarity between audio sequences. Reyes et al. [18] applied time series data similarity in gesture recognition and achieved nice accuracy. He [9] used sequence alignment to learn features for natural language processing. Yamano et al. [24] employed sequence alignment algorithm to analyze financial data. Although time series similarity is well-established problem in various fields, in this paper it is the first trial to apply sequence alignment to a field where each sequence is used to model the professional career in professional social networks. Moreover, different from many state-of-the-art methods, not only first-order features (i.e., position features) but also second-order features (i.e., transition features) are extracted from nodes of each sequence when training the node level similarity.

6. CONCLUSION AND FUTURE WORK

In this paper, we propose an approach *SimCareers*, to model member similarity over professional networks. In *SimCareers*, the member profile is modeled as a sequence of work experiences, while the career sequence similarity is evaluated using sequence alignment. To the best of our knowledge, *SimCareers* is the first similarity learning framework over online social networks that considers the career trajectory information. We use both offline and online experiments to demonstrate the effectiveness of *SimCareers*.

We believe *SimCareers* can be further refined in a variety of ways. Firstly, we intend to strengthen node-level similarity measure by incorporating per position geo information. In our existing profile dataset, we only have geo information with regards to member's current position. In the baseline keyword-based *Similar Profiles* system, geo is one of the important signals so we believe having per-position geo information would greatly improve *SimCareers*. Secondly, while aligning sequences in addition to skipping and matching the nodes we intend to allow the possibility of merging two similar nodes into one. A large number of career transitions are either lateral moves where the member changes company but does similar work at the same/similar role. Or they are promotions where the broad responsibility remains the same with a minor change in title. In both the scenarios, the core role & responsibility of the individual remains roughly the same. The hypothesis is that such a merge will help make the similarity measure more robust w.r.t. differences in how people fill their LinkedIn profile. Last but not least, while we are using the features listed in Section 3.3.2 to model the career positions, techniques such as feature selection [23] or feature interaction could be employed to explore better solutions at the feature level.

Furthermore, we wish to leverage *SimCareers* to help professionals do career planning. More concretely, by comparing career paths between young professionals and the early stage profiles from those of more successful senior individuals, we can give people a preview of possible career trajectories based on where they are currently. Furthermore, we can help young professionals decide which schools to choose, area of specialization to pursue and skills to acquire based on their desired success criterion as reified by an existing LinkedIn profile that these professionals wish to have as a role model.

7. REFERENCES

[1] L. A. Adamic and E. Adar. Friends and neighbors on the web. *Social Networks*, 25(3):211–230, 2003.

[2] K. Bartz, V. Murthi, and S. Sebastian. Logistic regression and collaborative filtering for sponsored search term recommendation. In *EC*, 2006.

[3] C. Bishop. *Pattern Recognition and Machine Learning*. Springer, NY, 2006.

[4] S. Cetintas, M. Rogati, L. Si, and Y. Fang. Identifying similar people in professional social networks with discriminative probabilistic models. In *SIGIR*, 2011.

[5] D. Chakrabarti, D. Agarwal, and V. Josifovski. Contextual advertising by combining relevance with click feedback. In *WWW*, pages 417–426, 2008.

[6] Z. Chen. Mining individual behavior pattern based on significant locations and spatial trajectories. In *PerCom*, 2012.

[7] J. Golbeck. Trust and nuanced profile similarity in online social networks. *ACM Trans. Web*, 3(4):1–33, 2009.

[8] A. K. Hartmann. Sampling rare events: Statistics of local sequence alignments. *Physical Review E*, 65(5), 2002.

[9] J. He. Improving sequence alignment based gene functional annotation with natural language processing and associative clustering. In *ISNN*, 2010.

[10] K. Jarvelin and J. Kekalainen. Cumulated gain-based evaluation of ir techniques. *TIST*, 20(4):422–446, 2002.

[11] A. Jeckmans, Q. Tang, and P. Hartel. Privacy-preserving profile similarity computation in online social networks. In *ACM conference on Computer and communications security*, pages 793–796, 2011.

[12] R. Kohavi, R. Longbotham, D. Sommerfield, and R. M. Henne. Controlled experiments on the web: survey and practical guide. *Data Mining and Knowledge Discovery*, 18(1):140–181, 2009.

[13] D. Kreider, D. Lahr, and S. Diesel. *Principles of Calculus Modeling: An Interactive Approach*. Springer, NY, 2005.

[14] D. Liben-Nowell and J. Kleinberg. The link prediction problem for social networks. In *CIKM*, 2003.

[15] E. Montanes, J. R. Quevedo, I. Diaz, and J. Ranilla. Collaborative tag recommendation system based on logistic regression. In *ECML*, 2009.

[16] D. Mount. *Bioinformatics: Sequence and Genome Analysis*. Cold Spring Harbor, NY, 2004.

[17] A. Reda, Y. Park, M. Tiwari, C. Posse, and S. Shah. Metaphor: a system for related search recommendations. In *CIKM*, pages 664–673, 2012.

[18] M. Reyes, G. Dominguez, and S. Escalera. Featureweighting in dynamic timewarping for gesture recognition in depth data. In *ICCV*, 2011.

[19] M. Richardson, E. Dominowska, and R. Ragno. Predicting clicks: Estimating the click-through rate for new ads. In *WWW*, pages 521–529, 2007.

[20] S. Salvador and P. Chan. Toward accurate dynamic time warping in linear time and space. In *KDD Workshop*, 2004.

[21] `http://www.forbes.com/sites/georgeanders/2013/04/10/whoshould-you-hire-linkedin/-says-try-our-algorithm/`.

[22] M. Vingron and M. S. Waterman. Sequence alignment and penalty choice: Review of concepts, case studies and implications. *J. Molecular Biology*, 235(1):1–12, 1994.

[23] Y. Xu and D. Rockmore. Feature selection for link prediction. In *PIKM*, 2012.

[24] T. Yamano, K. Sato, T. Kaizoji, J.-M. Rost, and L. Pichi. Symbolic analysis of indicator time series by quantitative sequence alignment. *Journal of Computational Statistics and Data Analysis*, 53(2):486–495, 2008.

[25] Z.-H. Zhou. *Ensemble Methods: Foundations and Algorithms*. Chapman and Hall, 2012.

Filling Context-Ad Vocabulary Gaps with Click Logs

Yukihiro Tagami
Yahoo Japan Corporation
Tokyo, Japan
yutagami@yahoo-corp.jp

Toru Hotta
Yahoo Japan Corporation
Tokyo, Japan
thotta@yahoo-corp.jp

Yusuke Tanaka
Yahoo Japan Corporation
Tokyo, Japan
yuustana@yahoo-corp.jp

Shingo Ono
Yahoo Japan Corporation
Tokyo, Japan
shiono@yahoo-corp.jp

Koji Tsukamoto
Yahoo Japan Corporation
Tokyo, Japan
kotsukam@yahoo-corp.jp

Akira Tajima
Yahoo Japan Corporation
Tokyo, Japan
atajima@yahoo-corp.jp

ABSTRACT

Contextual advertising is a form of textual advertising usually displayed on third party Web pages. One of the main problems with contextual advertising is determining how to select ads that are relevant to the page content and/or the user information in order to achieve both effective advertising and a positive user experience. Typically, the relevance of an ad to page content is indicated by a tf-idf score that measures the word overlap between the page and the ad content, so this problem is transformed into a similarity search in a vector space. However, such an approach is not useful if the vocabulary used on the page is expected to be different from that in the ad. There have been studies proposing the use of semantic categories or hidden classes to overcome this problem. With these approaches it is necessary to expand the ad retrieval system or build new index to handle the categories or classes, and it is not always easy to maintain the number of categories and classes required for business needs. In this work, we propose a translation method that learns the mapping of the contextual information to the textual features of ads by using past click data. The contextual information includes the user's demographic information and behavioral information as well as page content information. The proposed method is able to retrieve more preferable ads while maintaining the sparsity of the inverted index and the performance of the ad retrieval system. In addition, it is easy to implement and there is no need to modify an existing ad retrieval system. We evaluated this approach offline on a data set based on logs from an ad network. Our method achieved better results than existing methods. We also applied our approach with a real ad serving system and compared the online performance using A/B testing. Our approach achieved an improvement over the existing production system.

KDD'14, August 24–27, 2014, New York, NY, USA.

ACM 978-1-4503-2956-9/14/08 ...$15.00.
http://dx.doi.org/10.1145/2623330.2623334.

Categories and Subject Descriptors

H.3.5 [**Information Storage and Retrieval**]: Online Information Services—*Commercial services*; I.2.6 [**Artificial Intelligence**]: Learning

Keywords

Contextual advertising, Learning-to-rank, Click feedback, Modeling.

1. INTRODUCTION

Online advertising is a key component supporting today's Internet ecosystem and is growing into a multi-billion dollar industry. Many different types of advertising are used: sponsored search advertising, contextual advertising, display advertising, real-time bidding auctions, and more [28]. In this paper, we focus on contextual advertising, which consists of short text messages that are usually displayed on third party Web pages such as news sites or blogs. The advertiser is primarily interested in targeting relevant users and the publisher is concerned with keeping the user experience pleasant. To satisfy these two objectives, an ad-networking service selects ads that are relevant to the page content and/or the user information. In this paper, we focus on increasing the click-through rate (CTR), as this metric directly relates to the user experience, publisher revenue, and advertising effectiveness objectives.

The relevance of an ad to page content is typically determined using a tf-idf score that measures the word overlap between the page content and the ad content. This task is therefore regarded as a similarity search using an inverted index. This is an effective technique when the expected word overlap rate is high, but it falters if the vocabulary used on the page is different from the vocabulary used in the ad. For example, an ad for "SIM-free smartphones" would be related to a Web page comparing of Mobile Virtual Network Operator (MVNO) services, but the word overlap might not be very high. Another example could be an ad for "HTC One" and a page about "New Nexus 7."

Some previous studies have used a semantic taxonomy in the matching function [4] or introduced a page-ad probability model with hidden classes [21]. However, in these approaches, it is necessary to expand the ad retrieval system or build new index to handle the categories or classes. In addition, a review of the number and hierarchical structure of categories or a re-creation of clusters is periodically required in the operation of the ad serving system, and these tasks are not always easy to perform.

To overcome the above problems, we have developed an approach that calculates a matching score between two term vectors using an inverted index and does not require modification of an ordinary ad retrieval system. In other words, this approach translates ad request information into the textual space of ads. With this translation table, the feature vector of ad requests is transformed into the input term vector of the ad retrieval system. The process is illustrated in Fig. 1.

This translation table will become very large because the two spaces are typically quite large. We can efficiently learn the translation table from past click data with low-rank approximation of the matrix. However, even if the learning can be done efficiently, it is necessary to make the transformed term vector sparse because the performance of the ad retrieval system gets progressively worse in accordance with the number of nonzero values in the input vector. Therefore, we first select ad features related to each query feature according to our metric based on the past CTR, and then we learn the translation matrix. In other words, we choose a subset of the matrix elements and learn only the weights with past click logs.

We reported an overview of this method and preliminary experimental results in our work-in-progress paper [23]. In the current paper, we describe the details of the improved method and report the extensive evaluations. Our main contributions are as follows.

- We propose a method of translating contextual information into the textual features of ads by using past click data.
- Our approach is easy to implement and maintain because there is no need to modify the existing ad retrieval system.
- We evaluated our approach using a real-world data set from an ad network and obtained better results than existing methods.
- We applied our approach to a real ad serving system and achieved an improvement over the existing production system.

The rest of this paper is organized as follows. Section 2 provides a general overview of the contextual advertising system. Section 3 presents our method of translating query information into ad term vector space. Section 4 details the experimental setup and results. We conclude our paper in Section 5 by summarizing our findings and making a brief mention of future work.

2. OVERVIEW AND RELATED WORKS

This section provides a general overview of contextual advertising and related studies.

2.1 Overview of Contextual Advertising

There are four players in contextual advertising: the publisher, the advertiser, the ad network, and the user. The publisher owns Web pages and reserves some space on these pages for ads. An ad network supplies the ads that an advertiser provides. In the common pay-per-click model, which is

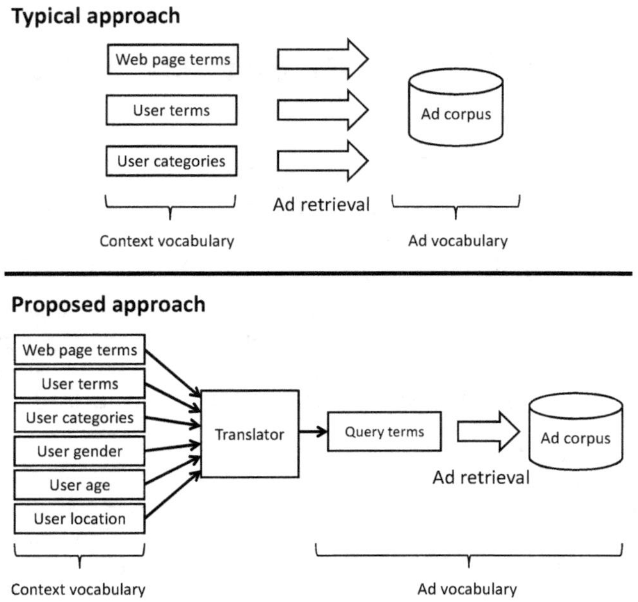

Figure 1: Typical approach (top) vs. our proposed approach (bottom). Proposed method is a translation of request features into the input term vector of an ad retrieval system.

the prevalent pricing model for contextual advertising, the advertiser pays the Web publisher and the ad network a fee only if a user clicks on their advertisement and visits their website. Thus, the expected revenue from displaying each ad is a function of both the bid price and the CTR. The bid price is the cost that the advertiser agrees to pay per click, so the advertising system already knows this. In contrast, the CTR for each ad can vary significantly depending on a variety of factors ranging from the Web page to the user. Consequently, one of the main problems in contextual advertising is determining how to accurately predict CTR and efficiently retrieve ads with a high CTR from an ad corpus.

2.2 Related Works

Some previous works have focused on developing methods to match ads to pages, since ads that are related to the page content are more likely than generic ads to provide a better user experience. That in turn increases the probability of users clicking on the ads. In these studies, the problem of matching ads with pages is transformed into a similarity search in a vector space. The relevance of an ad to page content is indicated by a tf-idf score that measures the word overlap between the page content and the ad content. Chakrabarti et al. [6] and Karimzadehgan et al. [16] introduced methods to learn the weights of each word in a page and an ad using HTML tags and ad sections. They use an inverted index to efficiently retrieve top-K items from ad corpora.

While both pages and ads are mapped to the same space, there is a discrepancy (impedance mismatch) between the vocabulary used in the ads and on the pages. Various approaches have been proposed to overcome this problem. Broder et al. [4] used a 6000-node semantic taxonomy in the matching function between pages and ads. In addition, Ratna-

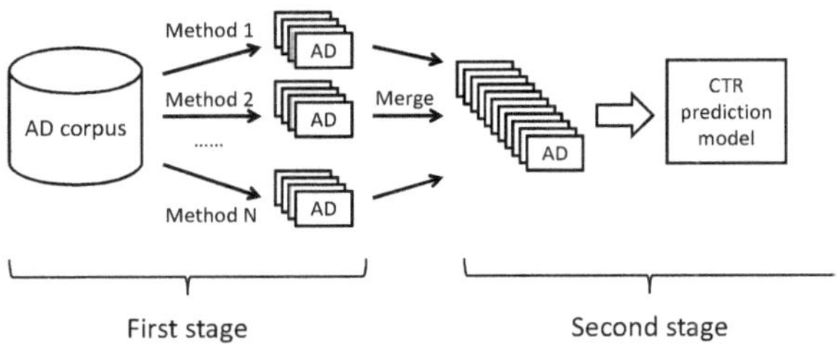

Figure 2: Two-stage approach in the ad serving system. Ads are retrieved by multiple methods in the first stage. The ads are merged and passed on to the second stage for CTR prediction.

parkhi [21] introduced a page-ad probability model in which semantic relationships between page terms and ad terms are modeled with hidden classes. Yih and Jiang [27] proposed an approach to map the original term vectors to a "concept space" so that semantically close words would be captured by the same concept. Wang et al. [26] formulated and tackled the problem of relevance learning for online targeting in heterogeneous social networks. They inferred user interests and ad concepts from heterogeneous sources and links, and developed a user-ad relevance feature based on weighted matching between any pair of concept classes. Murdock et al. [20] applied machine translation techniques to improve the matching between pages and ads.

Joshi et al. [15] presented a method to leverage user information including a user's demographic information (e.g., age, gender, and location) and behavioral information (e.g., the user's recent search history, page visits, and ad clicks) in a content match advertising setting. They mapped the non-textual user features to the textual space of ads.

In the cases where ad relevance cannot easily be gleaned from the page text alone, the "clickable terms" approach has been proposed [13]. This approach involves matching a Web site directly with a set of ad side terms, independent of the page content.

Another line of research attempts to predict the CTR of ads. These studies are not only related to contextual advertising but also to sponsored search advertising because both typically employ the pay-per-click model. Predictions of CTR for ads are generally based on a statistical model trained by using past click data. Examples of such models include logistic regression [7, 8, 19], probit regression [12], and boosted trees [9, 25]. The accuracy of the model depends greatly on the design of the features. Cheng and Cantú-Paz [7] presented a framework for the personalization of click models. These authors developed user-specific and demographic-based features that reflect the click behavior of individuals and groups. These features are based on observations of the search and click behaviors of a large number of users of a commercial search engine. Other recent works [1, 17, 22] have proposed models to estimate conversion rates (CVR).

2.3 Our Ad Serving System

Although machine-learned CTR prediction models are more accurate, as described in Section 2.2, evaluating all the items in an ad corpus is too time-consuming if we want to ensure that Web page loads quickly [2]. Our ad serving system therefore adopts a two-stage approach similar to some other studies [2, 6]. The first stage retrieves top-K items from an ad corpus using an inverted index. The second stage selects the desired top-k using brute force CTR prediction on the K retrieved ads ($k \ll K$). In the first stage, ads are independently retrieved by multiple methods in parallel. The retrieved ads in the first stage are merged and passed on to the second stage for CTR prediction. Ads are ranked and displayed on the basis of the predicted CTR and the bid price. This process is illustrated in Fig. 2. We refer to the "ad retrieval system" as a part of the first stage and focus on the part. We have used a heavily tuned search engine that employs the WAND algorithm [5, 11, 10].

In this paper, we propose a method to efficiently retrieve ads with high CTR using the search engine without any changes, even building new index. Unlike the method proposed by Agarwal and Gurevich [2] or approaches with semantic categories [4] or hidden classes [21], our method simply utilize the existing index used by typical similarity search in a vector space.

3. METHODS

In this section, we first define the matching function between a query and an ad and then describe our approach to mapping the query information to the textual space of ads.

3.1 Matching Function

We define a query feature vector as $\boldsymbol{q} = (q_1, \ldots, q_{D_q})^{\mathrm{T}}$ and an ad feature vector as $\boldsymbol{a} = (a_1, \ldots, a_{D_a})^{\mathrm{T}}$. $\boldsymbol{q}$ is a query feature vector of an ad request, which includes Web page and user information. We also define a general form of the matching function for $\boldsymbol{q}$ and $\boldsymbol{a}$ using translation matrix $\boldsymbol{W} = [w_{ij}]_{D_q \times D_a}$, as:

$$mscore(\boldsymbol{q}, \boldsymbol{a}) = \boldsymbol{q}^{\mathrm{T}} \boldsymbol{W} \boldsymbol{a} = \sum_{i=1}^{D_q} \sum_{j=1}^{D_a} w_{ij} q_i a_j, \qquad (1)$$

where D_q is a dimension of query feature space and D_a is a dimension of ad feature space.

Equation (1) is a general form of the matching function. If D_a is the same as D_q and $\boldsymbol{W}$ is the identity matrix $\boldsymbol{I}$, score$(\boldsymbol{q}, \boldsymbol{a})$ turns out to be a simple dot product:

$$mscore(\boldsymbol{q}, \boldsymbol{a}) = \boldsymbol{q}^{\mathrm{T}} \boldsymbol{I} \boldsymbol{a} = \sum_{i=1}^{D_q} q_i a_i$$

Of course, the cosine similarity can be calculated if $\boldsymbol{q}$ and $\boldsymbol{a}$ are normalized. Also, in general cases, by multiplying the query feature vector $\boldsymbol{q}$ by the translation matrix $\boldsymbol{W}$ and using $\boldsymbol{q}' = \boldsymbol{W}^{\mathrm{T}} \boldsymbol{q}$ as an input vector, we calculate the score $mscore(\boldsymbol{q}, \boldsymbol{a}) = \boldsymbol{q}^{\mathrm{T}} \boldsymbol{W} \boldsymbol{a} = \boldsymbol{q}'^{\mathrm{T}} \boldsymbol{a}$ with an ordinary inverted index based ad retrieval system.

When categories or classes are used, translation matrix $\boldsymbol{W}$ is decomposed as:

$$\boldsymbol{W} = \boldsymbol{\Gamma}_q^{\mathrm{T}} \boldsymbol{W}_c \boldsymbol{\Gamma}_a,$$

where $\boldsymbol{\Gamma}_q \in \mathbb{R}^K \times \mathbb{R}^{D_q}$, $\boldsymbol{\Gamma}_a \in \mathbb{R}^K \times \mathbb{R}^{D_a}$, $\boldsymbol{W}_c \in \mathbb{R}^K \times \mathbb{R}^K$, and K is the number of categories or classes. Here, $\boldsymbol{\Gamma}_q$ and $\boldsymbol{\Gamma}_a$ are the respective matrices that convert query feature vector $\boldsymbol{q}$ and ad feature vector $\boldsymbol{a}$ into categories or classes vector $\boldsymbol{q}_c$ and $\boldsymbol{a}_c$. Thus, the matching function in this case is expressed as:

$$\begin{aligned} mscore(\boldsymbol{q}, \boldsymbol{a}) &= (\boldsymbol{\Gamma}_q \boldsymbol{q})^{\mathrm{T}} \boldsymbol{W}_c (\boldsymbol{\Gamma}_a \boldsymbol{a}) \\ &= \boldsymbol{q}_c^{\mathrm{T}} \boldsymbol{W}_c \boldsymbol{a}_c, \end{aligned}$$

where $\boldsymbol{q}_c = \boldsymbol{\Gamma}_q \boldsymbol{q}$ and $\boldsymbol{a}_c = \boldsymbol{\Gamma}_a \boldsymbol{a}$. This decomposition can also be viewed as a matrix factorization or low-rank approximation.

3.2 Learning a Translation Matrix

As described in Section 1, we need to learn the translation matrix $\boldsymbol{W}$ efficiently and make the transformed term vector sparse for efficient ad retrieval. The translation matrix $\boldsymbol{W}$ can be learned directly with a large hash table and L1 regularization, as Wang et al. did [26]. In this paper, we propose another approach, in which we can directly control the sparseness of the matrix by considering the performance of the ad retrieval system. We first select a subset of the matrix elements and then learn the corresponding w_{ij}.

We calculate the following score m_{ij} for each pair of q_i and a_j presented in the training data:

$$m_{ij} = \frac{ctr(q_i, a_j)}{\max(ctr(q_i), ctr(a_j))},$$

where $ctr(q_i)$ denotes the CTR when the query feature vector includes q_i and $ctr(a_j)$ denotes the CTR of ads that include feature a_j. Similarly, $ctr(q_i, a_j)$ represents the CTR of ads that include feature a_j when the query feature vector includes q_i. A large m_{ij} value means that ads that include feature a_j are more likely to be clicked when the query feature vector includes q_i. A set of the pairs that has a larger m_{ij} is selected:

$$P = \{(i, j) \mid m_{ij} > T\},$$

where T is a thresholding hyper-parameter. The number of non-zero elements in $\boldsymbol{W}$ decreases as a function of T. We use P and replace the matching function (1) as follows.

$$mscore(\boldsymbol{q}, \boldsymbol{a}) = \sum_{(i,j) \in P} w_{ij} q_i a_j$$

If we perform an ordinary feature selection using mutual information or L1 regularization, we obtain features that lead negative w_{ij}'s as well as positive w_{ij}'s. However, we retrieve top-K ads which have larger $mscore(\boldsymbol{q}, \boldsymbol{a})$ from an ad corpus as described in Section 2.3. We cannot retrieve ads that have higher $mscore(\boldsymbol{q}, \boldsymbol{a})$ even if we use the negative w_{ij}'s. Thus, we employ the above approach in the hope of selecting the features to lead the positive w_{ij}'s.

We learn the above w_{ij} by using past click data. A score proportional to the click-through rate (CTR) for $\boldsymbol{q}$ and $\boldsymbol{a}$ is therefore defined as having the following linear form:

$$\begin{aligned} score(\boldsymbol{q}, \boldsymbol{a}) &= mscore(\boldsymbol{q}, \boldsymbol{a}) + bscore(\boldsymbol{q}, \boldsymbol{a}) \\ &= \sum_{(i,j) \in P} w_{ij} q_i a_j + \boldsymbol{w}_{basic}^{\mathrm{T}} \boldsymbol{x}_{basic} \\ &= \boldsymbol{w}_{match}^{\mathrm{T}} \boldsymbol{x}_{match} + \boldsymbol{w}_{basic}^{\mathrm{T}} \boldsymbol{x}_{basic} \\ &= \boldsymbol{w}^{\mathrm{T}} \boldsymbol{x}, \end{aligned} \quad (2)$$

where $bscore(\boldsymbol{q}, \boldsymbol{a})$ is a basic score as $bscore(\boldsymbol{q}, \boldsymbol{a}) = \boldsymbol{w}_{basic}^{\mathrm{T}} \boldsymbol{x}_{basic}$. $\boldsymbol{x}_{basic}$ is a feature vector that includes features such as the ad's own clickability. $\boldsymbol{w}_{basic}$ is a weight vector corresponding to $\boldsymbol{x}_{basic}$. For $(i, j) \in P$, $\boldsymbol{w}_{match}$ and $\boldsymbol{x}_{match}$ are defined as $\boldsymbol{w}_{match} = [\cdots, w_{ij}, \cdots]^{\mathrm{T}}$ and $\boldsymbol{x}_{match} = [\cdots, q_i a_j, \cdots]^{\mathrm{T}}$. $\boldsymbol{w} = \left[\boldsymbol{w}_{match}^{\mathrm{T}}, \boldsymbol{w}_{basic}^{\mathrm{T}}\right]^{\mathrm{T}}$ and $\boldsymbol{x} = \left[\boldsymbol{x}_{match}^{\mathrm{T}}, \boldsymbol{x}_{basic}^{\mathrm{T}}\right]^{\mathrm{T}}$ are concatenated vectors. The reason for adding $bscore(\boldsymbol{q}, \boldsymbol{a})$ to $mscore(\boldsymbol{q}, \boldsymbol{a})$ is that the score proportional to CTR consists of not only a matching score between query and ad but also other factors such as the ad's own clickability and display position on the Web page.

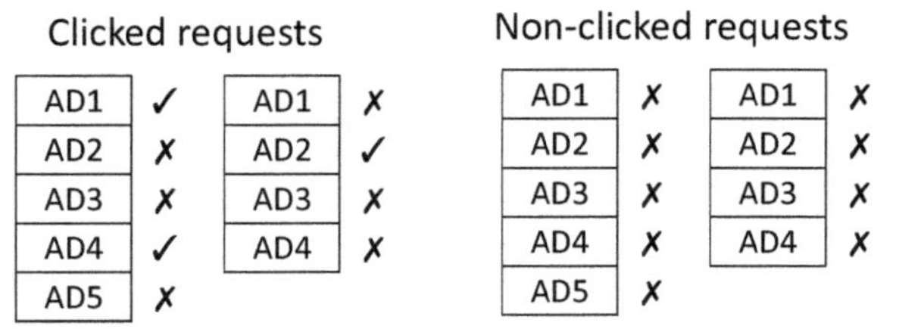

Figure 3: Examples of clicked requests and non-clicked requests. Ticks denote clicked impressions and x's represent non-clicked impressions.

As described in Section 2.3, our focus is improving the first stage of the two-staged ad serving system. We learn w_{ij} with click logs instead of simply using m_{ij}, as we expect that first retrieving top-K ads based on a score approximating the second stage score leads to better top-k results at the second stage.

We then describe how to utilize click logs to learn weights. In the contextual advertising setting, a Web publisher typically requests some ads simultaneously because more than one ad is displayed on a page at the same time. In other words, one ad request r in the logs includes $N^{(r)}$ impressions of ads:

$$(\boldsymbol{q}^{(r)}, \boldsymbol{a}_1^{(r)}, y_1^{(r)}), (\boldsymbol{q}^{(r)}, \boldsymbol{a}_2^{(r)}, y_2^{(r)}), \ldots, (\boldsymbol{q}^{(r)}, \boldsymbol{a}_{N^{(r)}}^{(r)}, y_{N^{(r)}}^{(r)})$$

Each impression of an ad consists of a tuple $(\boldsymbol{q}^{(r)}, \boldsymbol{a}_i^{(r)}, y_i^{(r)})$. Here, $\boldsymbol{q}^{(r)}$ represents the query feature vector of the request r and $\boldsymbol{a}_i^{(r)}$ represents the ad feature vector of the ith impression in request r. The output variable $y_i^{(r)} = 1$ if a user clicked the ad and $y_i^{(r)} = 0$ if not.

As described in our previous work [24], we focus on a kind of ad request and apply the learning-to-rank approach to learn the weights.

There are two kinds of ad requests in data R:

$$\begin{aligned} R^+ &= \{r \mid \exists i (y_i^{(r)} = 1)\} \\ R^- &= \{r \mid \forall i (y_i^{(r)} = 0)\} \end{aligned}$$

R^+ denotes a set of ad requests that includes at least one clicked impression; hence we refer to R^+ as **clicked requests**. R^- is called **non-clicked requests** since no ad requests in R^- include clicked impressions. Of course, $R = R^+ \cup R^-$ and $R^+ \cap R^- = \emptyset$. Examples of these two kinds of ad request are shown in Fig. 3.

We regard ad impressions in an ad request as documents related to a query in an information retrieval context and apply the learning-to-rank approach to learn the weights. We make pairwise preferences from each clicked request $r \in R^+$.

$$\{(\boldsymbol{a}_i^{(r)}, \boldsymbol{a}_j^{(r)}) \mid \forall i, j (y_i^{(r)} = 1 \wedge y_j^{(r)} = 0)\}$$

This process is illustrated in Fig. 4.

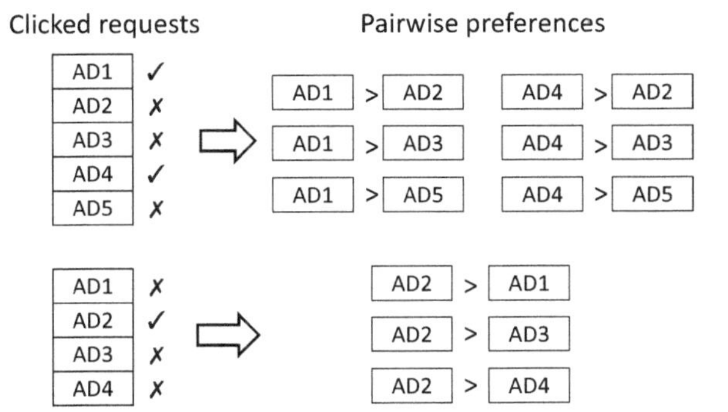

Figure 4: Making pairwise preferences from clicked requests.

The preference $(\boldsymbol{a}_i^{(r)}, \boldsymbol{a}_j^{(r)})$ indicates that a score proportional to the CTR of $\boldsymbol{a}_i^{(r)}$ for $\boldsymbol{q}^{(r)}$ is expected to be higher than that of $\boldsymbol{a}_j^{(r)}$. We represent the above preference using $score(\boldsymbol{q}, \boldsymbol{a})$ and transform using (2) as follows:

$$\begin{aligned} & score(\boldsymbol{q}^{(r)}, \boldsymbol{a}_i^{(r)}) > score(\boldsymbol{q}^{(r)}, \boldsymbol{a}_j^{(r)}) \\ \Leftrightarrow\ & score(\boldsymbol{q}^{(r)}, \boldsymbol{a}_i^{(r)}) - score(\boldsymbol{q}^{(r)}, \boldsymbol{a}_j^{(r)}) > 0 \\ \Leftrightarrow\ & \boldsymbol{w}^{\mathrm{T}}\boldsymbol{x}_i^{(r)} - \boldsymbol{w}^{\mathrm{T}}\boldsymbol{x}_j^{(r)} > 0 \\ \Leftrightarrow\ & \boldsymbol{w}^{\mathrm{T}}(\boldsymbol{x}_i^{(r)} - \boldsymbol{x}_j^{(r)}) > 0 \end{aligned}$$

Using the squared hinge loss, we define a pairwise loss function $L(\boldsymbol{w})$ like RankSVM [14], as follows:

$$L(\boldsymbol{w}) = \sum_{r \in R^+} \sum_{i: y_i^{(r)}=1} \sum_{j: y_j^{(r)}=0} \max(0, 1 - \boldsymbol{w}^{\mathrm{T}}(\boldsymbol{x}_i^{(r)} - \boldsymbol{x}_j^{(r)}))^2$$

We add a regularization term and seek the weight vector $\hat{\boldsymbol{w}}$ that minimizes the following optimization problem:

$$\hat{\boldsymbol{w}} = \arg\min_{\boldsymbol{w}} \frac{1}{2}\|\boldsymbol{w}\|_2^2 + C \cdot L(\boldsymbol{w}),$$

where $C \geq 0$ is a penalty parameter. The translation matrix $\boldsymbol{W}$ is restored from the weight vector $\hat{\boldsymbol{w}}_{match}$, where $\hat{\boldsymbol{w}} = \left[\hat{\boldsymbol{w}}_{match}^{\mathrm{T}}, \hat{\boldsymbol{w}}_{basic}^{\mathrm{T}}\right]^{\mathrm{T}}$. Note that we set $w_{ij} = 0$ for $(i, j) \notin P$.

We conducted preliminary experiments using hinge loss and logistic loss in addition to the above squared hinge loss. We decided to use the squared hinge loss as it was found to have a favorable balance between accuracy and training time.

3.3 Retrieval from AD Corpus and Implementation

With the learned matrix $\mathbf{W}$, the query feature vector $\boldsymbol{q}$ is transformed into the input term vector of the ad retrieval system for each ad request.

$$\boldsymbol{q}_{input} = \boldsymbol{W}^{\mathrm{T}}\boldsymbol{q}$$

Our proposed method only require this transformation. Thus it is easy to implement and maintain because there is no need to modify the existing inverted index or add new index

This input term vector includes some non-zero values, which are proportional to the number of non-zero values in the query feature vector. However, the performance of the ad retrieval system declines in accordance with the number of non-zero values in the input vector. Therefore, we need to limit the number of these values with hyper-parameter M:

$$\|\boldsymbol{q}_{input}\|_0 \leq M$$

$\|\boldsymbol{q}_{input}\|_0$ is the L_0-norm of $\boldsymbol{q}_{input}$, which is the number of its non-zero elements. We simply choose top-M elements, which have larger values.

4. EXPERIMENT

This section describes offline and online evaluations. Due to business confidentiality, we report only relative performance when showing experimental results.

4.1 Offline Evaluation

In this section, we first describe experimental settings such as data sets, features, models, and evaluation metric. Next, we compare our approach with existing methods and present model performances when changing the hyper-parameters T and M.

4.1.1 Data Sets and Features

We compare the models using data sampled from an ad network for a period of eight weeks. Data from the first six weeks are used as a training set, data from the fifth week are used as a validation set, and data from the last week are treated as a testing set. This ad network is for the Japanese market[1], so all ads and pages are written in Japanese, with a few exceptions.

As described in Section 3.2, each sample of the data sets is an impression of an ad and consists of a tuple $(\boldsymbol{q}^{(r)}, \boldsymbol{a}_i^{(r)}, y_i^{(r)})$. The output variable $y_i^{(r)} = 1$ if a user clicks the ad and 0 if not. The query features $\boldsymbol{q}^{(r)}$ include Web page and user information. The Web page features are extracted terms. These terms are scored on the basis of their position on the page and HTML tags. Some terms are chosen by the score. The user features are terms and categories in which the user is interested, as well as gender, age, and location. The user's gender falls into three classes: male, female, and unknown. Similarly, the user's age is categorized into thirteen groups. As in the study by Aly et al. [3], these terms and categories are extracted from user behavior events such as page visits, search queries, and ad clicks. These categories are similar to the hierarchical taxonomy in the work of Broder et al. [4]. Number of the categories is about 900. We simply use textual features as the ad features $\boldsymbol{a}_i^{(r)}$, which are tf-idf weighted terms based on the title and description in this paper. These features are summarized in Table 1.

The basic features $\boldsymbol{x}_{basic}$ described in Section 3.2 include the display position on the Web page and the historical CTR of the ad and advertiser. These features are also summarized in Table 1.

We chose eight diverse Web sites, including news, blogs, question-and-answer, finance, sports, weather, and travel sites. The models we evaluate are constructed with respect to each Web site, since the Web pages and the users that visit them are different. The data statistics for each Web site are summarized in Table 2. The number of clicked requests $|R^+|$ and the average number of impressions per

[1]`http://promotionalads.yahoo.co.jp/service/ydn/index.html`

Table 1: Summary of features

Feature type	Source	Details
Query features $\boldsymbol{q}$	Web page	Terms extracted from Web page
	User	Terms extracted from behavioral events, categories based on behavioral events, gender, age, location
Ad features $\boldsymbol{a}$	Ad	Tf-idf weighted terms
Basic features $\boldsymbol{x}_{basic}$	Past click log	Historical CTR of ad and advertiser, display position on the Web page

Table 2: Data statistics for Web sites used in evaluation.

Web site	Type	$\lvert R^{+}\rvert$	$\overline{N^{(r)}}$	$\overline{\#clicks}$
A	training	711,539	6.97	1.03
	validation	142,649	7.03	1.03
	testing	119,464	7.11	1.02
B	training	2,676,577	4.99	1.03
	validation	429,760	4.99	1.03
	testing	356,578	4.99	1.01
C	training	1,648,118	4.64	1.02
	validation	137,646	3.09	1.02
	testing	134,168	3.15	1.01
D	training	919,870	4.11	1.01
	validation	92,547	4.05	1.01
	testing	81,077	4.07	1.00
E	training	905,842	4.07	1.01
	validation	217,165	4.94	1.01
	testing	169,627	4.94	1.01
F	training	153,849	5.00	1.04
	validation	23,836	5.00	1.04
	testing	17,879	5.00	1.02
G	training	297,814	8.13	1.03
	validation	53,306	8.10	1.02
	testing	42,098	8.05	1.02
H	training	4,644,350	4.48	1.02
	validation	780,037	4.54	1.02
	testing	498,407	4.15	1.01

clicked request $\overline{N^{(r)}}$ changed over the six weeks, due to seasonal trends, changes in the budget of the advertisers, and actions carried out by publishers to achieve sales targets. $\overline{\#clicks}$, which is the average number of clicked impressions per clicked request, is approximately 1.

4.1.2 Existing Methods and Evaluation Metric

We compared the proposed method with three existing in production methods: *existing 1*, *2*, and *3*. *Existing 1* utilizes only terms extracted from Web page for ad retrieval and *existing 2* and *3* use terms and categories based on user's behavioral events respectively. Please also refer Section 4.1.1 and Table 1.

In the comparison, we use the following $score_{existing}(\boldsymbol{q}, \boldsymbol{a})$ instead of $score(\boldsymbol{q}, \boldsymbol{a})$ in Equation (2):

$$score_{existing}(\boldsymbol{q}, \boldsymbol{a}) = w \cdot escore(\boldsymbol{q}, \boldsymbol{a}) + bscore(\boldsymbol{q}, \boldsymbol{a}),$$

where $escore(\boldsymbol{q}, \boldsymbol{a})$ is a matching score calculated by an existing method. Each existing method has a different $escore(\boldsymbol{q}, \boldsymbol{a})$.

As described in Section 3.3, we need to limit the number of query terms because of the performance of the ad retrieval system. In the experiment, we carried out our evaluation by changing the value of M. Thus, we rewrite the scoring function for the prediction as:

$$t\text{-}score(\boldsymbol{q}, \boldsymbol{a}) = t\text{-}mscore(\boldsymbol{q}, \boldsymbol{a}) + bscore(\boldsymbol{q}, \boldsymbol{a}), \tag{3}$$

where $t\text{-}mscore(\boldsymbol{q}, \boldsymbol{a})$ is a matching function using truncated $\boldsymbol{q}_{input} = \boldsymbol{W}^{\mathrm{T}}\boldsymbol{q}$. We change M and truncate the query term vector $\boldsymbol{q}_{input}$ during the evaluation, not during training. This means the same translation matrix $\boldsymbol{W}$ is used. Note that this evaluation does not reflect the actual online setting very well when the value of M is limited. We use $t\text{-}score(\boldsymbol{q}, \boldsymbol{a})$ in the offline evaluation, although ads are retrieved by $t\text{-}mscore(\boldsymbol{q}, \boldsymbol{a})$ from an ad corpus in the actual online setting. Because of $bscore(\boldsymbol{q}, \boldsymbol{a})$, the order by $t\text{-}mscore(\boldsymbol{q}, \boldsymbol{a})$ and $t\text{-}score(\boldsymbol{q}, \boldsymbol{a})$ is not the same for some ad requests in the testing set.

We evaluated the performance of the model by using mean average precision (MAP) [18]:

$$\begin{aligned} MAP &= \frac{1}{|R^{+}|}\sum_{r \in R^{+}} AP^{(r)} \\ AP^{(r)} &= \frac{\sum_{k=1}^{N^{(r)}} P_k^{(r)} y_{\pi^{(r)}(k)}^{(r)}}{\sum_{k=1}^{N^{(r)}} y_{\pi^{(r)}(k)}^{(r)}} \\ P_k^{(r)} &= \frac{\sum_{l=1}^{k} y_{\pi^{(r)}(l)}^{(r)}}{k}, \end{aligned}$$

where $AP^{(r)}$ is the averaged precision over all relevant documents for request r, and $P_k^{(r)}$ is the precision up to rank position k. Here, $\pi^{(r)}(k) = i$ means that the ith impression ranks in the kth position by the predicted score $score(\boldsymbol{q}^{(r)}, \boldsymbol{a}_j^{(r)})$.

We normalize the scores of the method by a basic model that uses only $bscore(\boldsymbol{q}, \boldsymbol{a})$ during both the training and evaluation. All values of metrics in this paper are transformed by

$$\Delta MAP = \left(\frac{MAP}{MAP_{basic}} - 1\right) \times 100.$$

Note that this MAP_{basic} is reasonably high because the display position included in $\boldsymbol{x}_{basic}$ is a very beneficial feature.

4.1.3 Results

We first evaluated our approach when changing the thresholding hyper-parameter T. As described in Section 3.2, the number of non-zero elements in $\boldsymbol{W}$ decreases as a function of T. This means that model performance is expected to improve with decreasing T. In this setting, M is not limited during the evaluation. The experimental results are summarized in Table 3. The **bold** elements indicate the best performance of the methods. Our proposed method achieved an improvement over the existing methods. As expected, MAPs are improved with decreasing T. For Web sites B and H, which has a lot of training data, ΔMAP is larger than other Web sites and the impact of changes in T is relatively small. For Web site A, the MAPs of *existing 1* are higher than the scores when $T = 0.20$ and 0.15. The impact of changes in T is large. This result indicates that the model trained with more data achieves larger and robust improvement. In comparing the existing methods, there are strong and weak points for each Web site. *Existing 1* was superior to the other two methods for Web sites A, E, and F. Conversely, *existing 2* achieved better results for Web sites B, C, D, G, and H. What this means is that the importance of the features used to retrieve ads is significantly different depending on the Web site. In contrast with these existing methods, our proposed method uses both Web page and user information for ad retrieval, which is why it had the better results.

Next, we investigated the model performance of each T when changing M. As described in Section 4.1.2, we change M and truncate the query term vector $\boldsymbol{q}_{input}$ during the evaluation, not during the training. The experimental results are shown in Fig. 5. As expected, the MAPs decay in response to a decrease of M. One might think that our proposed method is quite a bit worse than the basic model in situations where the ΔMAP is a negative value, such as $T = 0.05$ and $M = 50$ on Web site H. However, such offline evaluation results do not reflect the actual online performance very well because of the difference between $t\text{-}score(\boldsymbol{q}, \boldsymbol{a})$ and $t\text{-}mscore(\boldsymbol{q}, \boldsymbol{a})$, as described in Section 4.1.2. In the next section, the comparison of the existing methods and our proposed method when M is limited is carried over to the online evaluation. Here, we claim that M is first determined by the performance of the ad retrieval system and that T then needs to be tuned for each Web site in a real ad serving setting.

Tables 4 and 5 are examples of the mapping tables used on Web site B for user terms and categories, respectively. As expected, user terms are translated into the same term and related terms. In addition, the weight of the same term is larger than that of related terms in almost all cases. Similarly, user categories are translated into related terms.

4.2 Online Evaluation

The data sets used in the offline evaluation are based on past click data, which are results of ad serving by an existing system. Therefore, the results of offline evaluation might not reflect actual online performance because ads retrieved by our approach in the online setting are possibly different from those in the logs.

To measure the online performance, we applied our approach to a real ad serving system. This ad serving system adopts a two-stage approach, as described in Section 2.3 and shown in Fig. 2. We added the proposed method to the first stage and compared the online performance by conducting A/B testing. Hyper-parameters are set as ($T = 0.20, M = 20$). For a fair comparison, the total number of ads retrieved in the first stage is set to be the same because CTR can be higher even if the number of ads just increases. The CTR prediction model used for each version in the second stage was also the same. This prediction model was a statistical model trained by using the past click data [24]. We ran the online test over 1-week period in November 2013 for each Web site.

We use three metrics for the online test: CTR, cost per click (CPC), and revenue per request (RPR). These metrics are defined as follows:

$$
\begin{aligned}
CTR &= \frac{\#clicks}{|R|} \\
CPC &= \frac{revenue}{\#clicks} \\
RPR &= \frac{revenue}{|R|},
\end{aligned}
$$

where $|R|$ denotes the number of ad requests. Revenue is the total amount of the fee that advertisers paid.

The experimental results are summarized in Table 6. These percentages also represent the relative gain. The CTR was improved for all Web sites expect site A. We simply set hyper-parameter as ($T = 0.20, M = 20$) for all Web sites although the result of $T = 0.20$ is worse than the result of *existing 1* and *2* on Web site A in Table 3. Thus, this result is reasonable and indicates that hyper-parameters need to be tuned for each Web site. For Web sites B and H, which has a lot of training data, the improvement of CTR is larger than other Web sites as well as offline test. We performed chi-squared test on the CTR results. The results of the Web sites A, B, D, E, and H are statistically significant at the 5% level (p-value < 0.05). The RPR was also improved for all Web sites expect A, whereas the CPC was decreased for Web sites B, E, G, and H. This drop in CPC is usually favored by the advertisers. In this online testing, ads were ranked and displayed by considering revenues. Ads retrieved by our proposed method had a high CTR and relatively low bid price, which is why the Web sites had the result. As described in Section 1, we focus on increasing CTR in this paper. Consequently, our proposed method improve revenue. This result indicates that our proposed method achieved an improvement in the online setting as well as the offline setting.

5. CONCLUSION AND FUTURE WORK

Contextual advertising is a form of textual advertising usually displayed on third party Web pages. Because of the need to achieve both effective advertising and a positive user experience, one of the main problems with contextual advertising is determining how to select ads that are relevant to the page content and/or the user information. In this paper, we introduced a translation method that learns a mapping of contextual information to the textual features of ads. The contextual information includes the user's demographic and behavioral information as well as Web page content information. Our proposed method only require the transformation of the context feature vector with a learned matrix into the input vector of the ad retrieval system. So it is easy to implement and there is no need to modify the existing inverted index or add new index. We evaluated this approach offline on a real-world data set from an ad network and obtained better results compared to existing methods. We also applied our approach with a real ad serving system and achieved improvement over the existing production system.

Table 3: Experimental results. Values are ΔMAP. The bold elements indicate the best performance of the methods.

Method	Web site							
	A	B	C	D	E	F	G	H
Existing 1	+1.90%	+0.01%–	0.04%	+0.01%	+0.87%	+1.22%	+0.31%	+0.00%
Existing 2	+0.85%	+2.71%	+0.53%	+0.24%	+0.85%	+0.59%	+0.98%	+1.00%
Existing 3	+0.04%	+0.37%	+0.04%	+0.03%	+0.02%	+0.38%	+0.01%	+0.11%
$T = 0.20$	+0.60%	+6.18%	+1.42%	+0.50%	+1.70%	+1.66%	+1.73%	+2.60%
$T = 0.15$	+1.16%	+6.60%	+1.50%	+0.60%	+1.79%	+2.14%	+1.86%	+2.90%
$T = 0.10$	+2.97%	+6.83%	**+1.55%**	+0.64%	**+1.84%**	+2.32%	+2.00%	+3.13%
$T = 0.05$	**+3.56%**	**+6.93%**	+1.54%	**+0.68%**	+1.81%	**+2.56%**	**+2.12%**	**+3.24%**

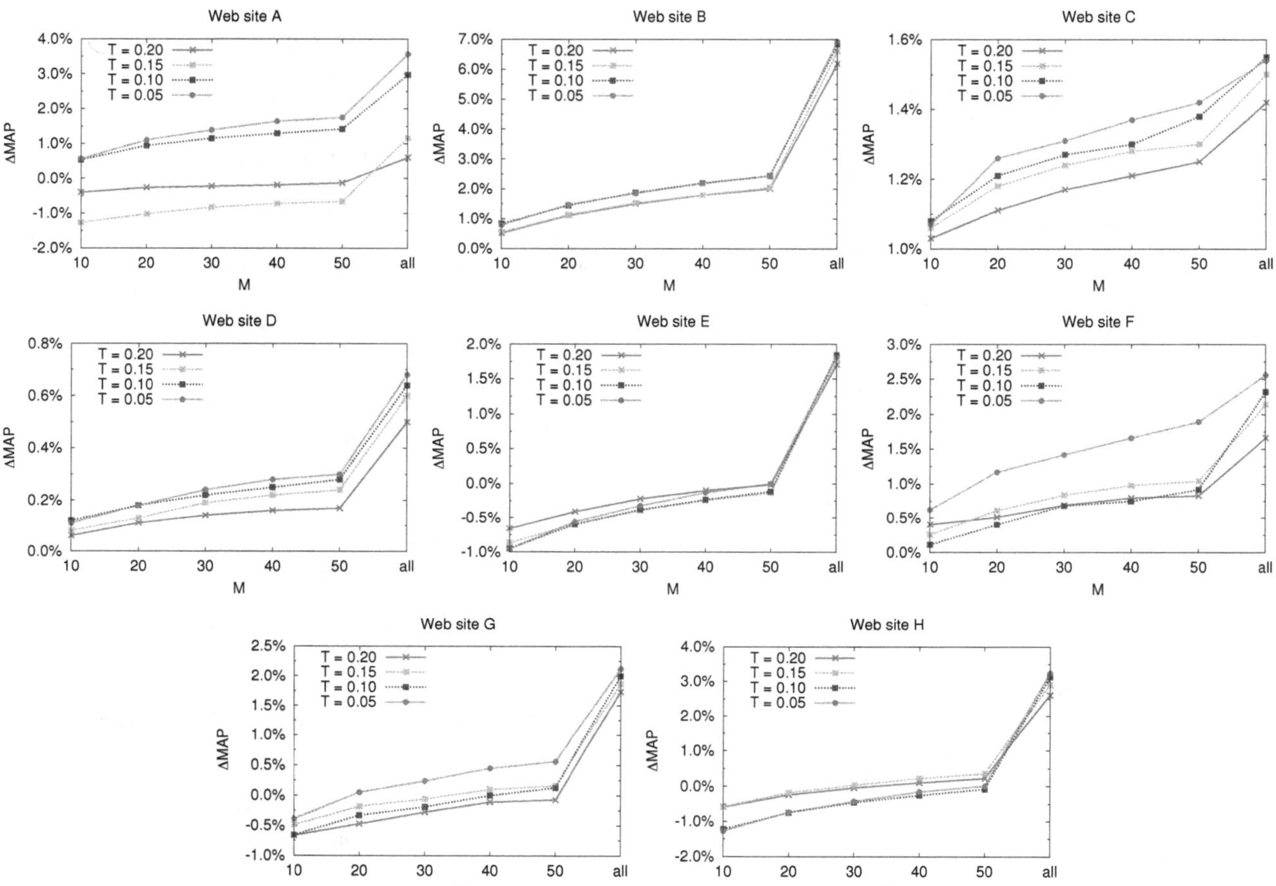

Figure 5: Experimental results when changing M.

Our future work will take three directions. First, we want to study the use of various types of context features such as ad request time and weather. Second, we plan to investigate sophisticated regularization term in objective function for making the weight matrix sparse. Finally, distributed online learning of the translation matrix is an interesting challenge that we wish to explore.

6. ACKNOWLEDGMENTS

We would like to thank our colleagues for their assistance with data collection, model evaluation, and many insightful discussions.

7. REFERENCES

[1] D. Agarwal, R. Agrawal, R. Khanna, and N. Kota. Estimating rates of rare events with multiple hierarchies through scalable log-linear models. In *Proceedings of the 16th ACM SIGKDD international*

Table 4: Example of Web site B's mapping table for user terms.

User term	Translated term	Weight
iPhone	iPhone	0.2114
	ケース (case)	0.1534
	iPad	0.0868
プリウス (Toyota Prius)	プリウス (Toyota Purius)	0.2600
	燃費 (mileage)	0.0732
	HV (Hybrid Vehicle)	0.0607
歯科 (dentistry)	歯科 (dentistry)	0.3297
	歯科医師 (dentist)	0.1892
	インプラント (implant)	0.1035
毛穴 (pores)	毛穴 (pores)	0.2319
	洗顔 (face washing)	0.1001
	化粧品 (cosmetics)	0.0663
温泉 (hot spring)	温泉 (hot spring)	0.1730
	旅館 (Japanese inn)	0.1272
	露天風呂 (outdoor hot spring)	0.0809
カーナビ (car navigation system)	カーナビ (car navigation system)	0.1229
	トヨタ (Toyota)	0.0906
	ホンダ (Honda)	0.0720

Table 5: Example of Web site B's mapping table user interest category.

User category	Translated term	Weight
Automotive/Domestic/Toyota	クラウン (Toyota Crown)	0.2605
	トヨタプリウス (Toyota Prius)	0.2171
	ランクル (Toyota Land Cruiser)	0.2053
Health Pharma/Adult Disease/Hypertensive Disease	血圧 (blood pressure)	0.1784
	高血圧 (high blood pressure)	0.1196
	食事法 (diet)	0.0531
Travel and Transportation/Overseas/Europe	海外 (overseas)	0.1181
	ヨーロッパ (Europe)	0.1168
	海外旅行 (foreign travel)	0.0868
Miscellaneous/Sex and Romance/Personals	婚活 (marriage hunting)	0.1100
	出会い (matchmaking)	0.0742
	カップル (couple)	0.0546
Life Stage/Wedding	ウェディング (wedding)	0.1398
	婚約 (engagement)	0.1391
	ドレス (dress)	0.1024

conference on Knowledge discovery and data mining, KDD '10, 2010.

[2] D. Agarwal and M. Gurevich. Fast top-k retrieval for model based recommendation. In *Proceedings of the fifth ACM international conference on Web search and data mining*, WSDM '12, 2012.

[3] M. Aly, A. Hatch, V. Josifovski, and V. K. Narayanan. Web-scale user modeling for targeting. In *Proceedings of the 21st international conference companion on World Wide Web*, WWW '12 Companion, 2012.

[4] A. Broder, M. Fontoura, V. Josifovski, and L. Riedel. A semantic approach to contextual advertising. In *Proceedings of the 30th annual international ACM SIGIR conference on Research and development in information retrieval*, SIGIR '07, 2007.

[5] A. Z. Broder, D. Carmel, M. Herscovici, A. Soffer, and J. Zien. Efficient query evaluation using a two-level retrieval process. In *Proceedings of the twelfth international conference on Information and knowledge management*, CIKM '03, 2003.

[6] D. Chakrabarti, D. Agarwal, and V. Josifovski. Contextual advertising by combining relevance with click feedback. In *Proceedings of the 17th international conference on World Wide Web*, WWW '08, 2008.

[7] H. Cheng and E. Cantú-Paz. Personalized click prediction in sponsored search. In *Proceedings of the third ACM international conference on Web search and data mining*, WSDM '10, 2010.

[8] H. Cheng, R. van Zwol, J. Azimi, E. Manavoglu, R. Zhang, Y. Zhou, and V. Navalpakkam. Multimedia features for click prediction of new ads in display advertising. In *Proceedings of the 18th ACM SIGKDD international conference on Knowledge discovery and data mining*, KDD '12, 2012.

[9] K. S. Dave and V. Varma. Learning the click-through rate for rare/new ads from similar ads. In *Proceedings*

Table 6: **Online A/B testing results. Metrics are click-through rate (CTR), cost per click (CPC), and revenue per request (RPR). Values represent the relative gains. We performed chi-squared test on the CTR results. * : p-value < 0.05, ** : p-value < 0.01, *** : p-value < 0.001**

Metric	Website							
	A	B	C	D	E	F	G	H
CTR	−3.67% **	+4.60% ***	+0.48%	+2.82% *	+2.47% **	+1.42%	+3.27%	+4.02% ***
CPC	+3.63%−	2.00%	+1.62%	+1.31%−	1.01%	+7.51%−	2.42%−	2.94%
RPR	−0.18%	+2.51%	+2.10%	+4.17%	+1.44%	+9.04%	+0.77%	+0.97%

of the 33rd international ACM SIGIR conference on Research and development in information retrieval, SIGIR '10, 2010.

[10] S. Ding and T. Suel. Faster top-k document retrieval using block-max indexes. In *Proceedings of the 34th International ACM SIGIR Conference on Research and Development in Information Retrieval*, SIGIR '11, 2011.

[11] M. Fontoura, V. Josifovski, J. Liu, S. Venkatesan, X. Zhu, and J. Zien. Evaluation strategies for top-k queries over memory-resident inverted indexes. In *Proceedings of the 37th International Conference on Very Large Data Bases*, volume 4, 2011.

[12] T. Graepel, J. Q. Candela, T. Borchert, and R. Herbrich. Web-scale bayesian click-through rate prediction for sponsored search advertising in microsoft's bing search engine. In *Proceedings of the 27th International Conference on Machine Learning*, 2010.

[13] A. Hatch, A. Bagherjeiran, and A. Ratnaparkhi. Clickable terms for contextual advertising. In *ADKDD*, 2010.

[14] T. Joachims. Optimizing search engines using clickthrough data. In *Proceedings of the eighth ACM SIGKDD international conference on Knowledge discovery and data mining*, KDD '02, 2002.

[15] A. Joshi, A. Bagherjeiran, and A. Ratnaparkhi. User demographic and behavioral targeting for content match advertising. In *Proceedings of the fifth international workshop on Data mining and audience intelligence for advertising*, ADKDD '11, 2011.

[16] M. Karimzadehgan, W. Li, R. Zhang, and J. Mao. A stochastic learning-to-rank algorithm and its application to contextual advertising. In *Proceedings of the 20th international conference on World wide web*, WWW '11, 2011.

[17] K.-C. Lee, B. Orten, A. Dasdan, and W. Li. Estimating conversion rate in display advertising from past performance data. In *Proceedings of the 18th ACM SIGKDD international conference on Knowledge discovery and data mining*, KDD '12, 2012.

[18] C. D. Manning, P. Raghavan, and H. Schtze. *Introduction to Information Retrieval*. Cambridge University Press, 2008.

[19] H. B. McMahan, G. Holt, D. Sculley, M. Young, D. Ebner, J. Grady, L. Nie, T. Phillips, E. Davydov, D. Golovin, S. Chikkerur, D. Liu, M. Wattenberg, A. M. Hrafnkelsson, T. Boulos, and J. Kubica. Ad click prediction: A view from the trenches. In *Proceedings of the 19th ACM SIGKDD International Conference on Knowledge Discovery and Data Mining*, KDD '13, 2013.

[20] V. Murdock, M. Ciaramita, and V. Plachouras. A noisy-channel approach to contextual advertising. In *Proceedings of the 1st international workshop on Data mining and audience intelligence for advertising*, ADKDD '07, 2007.

[21] A. Ratnaparkhi. A hidden class page-ad probability model for contextual advertising. In *Workshop on Targeting and Ranking for Online Advertising at the 17th International World Wide Web Conference*, 2008.

[22] R. Rosales, H. Cheng, and E. Manavoglu. Post-click conversion modeling and analysis for non-guaranteed delivery display advertising. In *Proceedings of the fifth ACM international conference on Web search and data mining*, WSDM '12, 2012.

[23] Y. Tagami, T. Hotta, Y. Tanaka, S. Ono, K. Tsukamoto, and A. Tajima. Translation method of contextual information into textual space of advertisements. In *Proceedings of the Companion Publication of the 23rd International Conference on World Wide Web Companion*, WWW Companion '14, 2014.

[24] Y. Tagami, S. Ono, K. Yamamoto, K. Tsukamoto, and A. Tajima. Ctr prediction for contextual advertising: learning-to-rank approach. In *Proceedings of the Seventh International Workshop on Data Mining for Online Advertising*, ADKDD '13, 2013.

[25] I. Trofimov, A. Kornetova, and V. Topinskiy. Using boosted trees for click-through rate prediction for sponsored search. In *Proceedings of the Sixth International Workshop on Data Mining for Online Advertising and Internet Economy*, ADKDD '12, 2012.

[26] C. Wang, R. Raina, D. Fong, D. Zhou, J. Han, and G. Badros. Learning relevance from heterogeneous social network and its application in online targeting. In *Proceedings of the 34th international ACM SIGIR conference on Research and development in Information Retrieval*, SIGIR '11, 2011.

[27] W.-t. Yih and N. Jiang. Similarity models for ad relevance measures. In *MLOAD - NIPS 2010 Workshop on online advertising*, 2010.

[28] S. Yuan, A. Z. Abidin, M. Sloan, and J. Wang. Internet advertising: An interplay among advertisers, online publishers, ad exchanges and web users. *CoRR*, 2012.

Does Social Good Justify Risking Personal Privacy?

Raghu Ramakrishnan
Microsoft
raghu@microsoft.com

Geoffrey I. Webb
Monash University, Australia
geoff.webb@monash.edu

Categories and Subject Descriptors

H.2.8 [**Database Applications**]: Data mining

Keywords

Privacy; Social Good

Panel Overview

When data-driven improvements involve personally identifiable data, or even data that can be used to infer sensitive information about individuals, we face the dilemma that we potentially risk compromising privacy. As we see increased emphasis on using data mining to effect improvements in a range of socially beneficial activities, from improving matching of talented students to opportunities for higher education, or improving allocation of funds across competing school programs, or reducing hospitalization time following surgery, the dilemma can often be especially acute.

The data involved often is personally identifiable or revealing and sensitive, and many of the institutions that must be involved in gathering and maintaining custody of the data are not equipped to adequately secure the data, raising the risk of privacy breaches. How should we approach this tradeoff? Can we assess the risks? Can we control or mitigate them? Can we develop guidelines for when the risk is or is not worthwhile, and for how best to handle data in different common scenarios?

Chairs Raghu Ramakrishnan and Geoffrey I. Webb bring this panel of leading data miners and privacy experts together to address these critical issues.

KDD'14, August 24–27, 2014, New York, NY, USA.
ACM 978-1-4503-2956-9/14/08.
http://dx.doi.org/10.1145/2623330.2630814.

Scaling Up Deep Learning

Yoshua Bengio
University of Montreal
Montreal, Canada
yoshua.bengio@umontreal.ca

ABSTRACT

Deep learning has rapidly moved from a marginal approach in the machine learning community less than ten years ago to one that has strong industrial impact, in particular for high-dimensional perceptual data such as speech and images, but also natural language. The demand for experts in deep learning is growing very fast (faster than we can graduate PhDs), thereby considerably increasing their market value. Deep learning is based on the idea of learning multiple levels of representation, with higher levels computed as a function of lower levels, and corresponding to more abstract concepts automatically discovered by the learner. Deep learning arose out of research on artificial neural networks and graphical models and the literature on that subject has considerably grown in recent years, culminating in the creation of a dedicated conference (ICLR). The tutorial will introduce some of the basic algorithms, both on the supervised and unsupervised sides, as well as discuss some of the guidelines for successfully using them in practice. Finally, it will introduce current research questions regarding the challenge of scaling up deep learning to much larger models that can successfully extract information from huge datasets.

Categories and Subject Descriptors

I.2.6 [**Artificial Intelligence**]: Learning—*Connectionism and neural nets*

Keywords

deep learning; neural networks; conditional computing; big data

KDD'14, August 24–27, 2014, New York, NY, USA.
ACM 978-1-4503-2956-9/14/08.
http://dx.doi.org/10.1145/2623330.2630802

Bio

Yoshua Bengio is Full Professor of the Department of Computer Science and Operations Research,head of the Machine Learning Laboratory (LISA), CIFAR Fellow in the Neural Computation and Adaptive Perception program, Canada Research Chair in Statistical Learning Algorithms, and he also holds the NSERC-Ubisoft industrial chair. His main research ambition is to understand principles of learning that yield intelligence. He teaches a graduate course in Machine Learning (IFT6266) and supervises a large group of graduate students and post-docs. His research is widely cited (over 16000 citations found by Google Scholar in early 2014, with an H-index of 55).

Yoshua Bengio is currently action editor for the Journal of Machine Learning Research, editor for Foundations and Trends in Machine Learning, and has been associate editor for the Machine Learning Journal and the IEEE Transactions on Neural Networks.

Yoshua Bengio was Program Chair for NIPS'2008 and General Chair for NIPS'2009 (NIPS is the flagship conference in the areas of learning algorithms and neural computation). Since 1999, he has been co-organizing the Learning Workshop with Yann Le Cun, with whom he has also created the International Conference on Representation Learning (ICLR). He has also organized or co-organized numerous other events, such as the ICML'2012 Representation Learning Workshop, the NIPS'2011 Deep Learning and Unsupervised Feature Learning Workshop, the NIPS'2010 Deep Learning and Unsupervised Feature Learning Workshop, the ICML'2009 Workshop on Learning Feature Hierarchies and the NIPS'2007 Deep Learning Workshop.

Constructing and Mining Web-Scale Knowledge Graphs

KDD 2014 Tutorial

Antoine Bordes
Facebook
770 Broadway
New York, NY 10003
abordes@fb.com

Evgeniy Gabrilovich
Google
1600 Amphitheatre Parkway
Mountain View, CA 94043
gabr@google.com

ABSTRACT

Recent years have witnessed a proliferation of large-scale knowledge graphs, such as Freebase, YAGO, Google's Knowledge Graph, and Microsoft's Satori. Whereas there is a large body of research on mining homogeneous graphs, this new generation of information networks are highly heterogeneous, with thousands of entity and relation types and billions of instances of vertices and edges. In this tutorial, we will present the state of the art in constructing, mining, and growing knowledge graphs. The purpose of the tutorial is to equip newcomers to this exciting field with an understanding of the basic concepts, tools and methodologies, available datasets, and open research challenges. A publicly available knowledge base (Freebase) will be used throughout the tutorial to exemplify the different techniques.

Who should attend

Over the recent years, multiple large-scale knowledge bases have come to existence, from purely academic projects such as YAGO to major commercial projects such as Facebook's Open Graph, Google's Knowledge Graph, and Microsoft's Satori. These knowledge bases are an enabling resource for a plethora of new knowledge-rich applications. The tutorial is designed to provide an overview of such applications and use-cases, as well as equip newcomers to this area with solid understanding of the basic techniques, research challenges, and pointers to relevant literature. This tutorial will bridge together three top-level areas of the KDD 2014 Call for Papers, namely, algorithms, applications, and big data.

Prerequisites

The tutorial will be self-contained, and is designed to be accessible to researchers and practitioners in related disciplines who want to learn more about mining large-scale knowledge graphs. An undergraduate degree in CS or statistics should be sufficient to understand most of the content in the tutorial.

KDD'14, August 24–27, 2014, New York, NY, USA.
ACM 978-1-4503-2956-9/14/08.
http://dx.doi.org/10.1145/2623330.2630803.

Instructors

Antoine Bordes is a staff research scientist at Facebook Artificial Intelligence Research. Prior to joining Facebook in 2014, he was a CNRS research staff in the Heudiasyc laboratory of the University of Technology of Compiègne in France. In 2010, he was a postdoctoral fellow in Yoshua Bengio's lab at Universite de Montreal. He received his PhD in machine learning from Pierre & Marie Curie University in Paris in early 2010. From 2004 to 2009, he collaborated regularly with the Machine Learning department of NEC Labs of America in Princeton. He received two awards for best PhD from the French Association for Artificial Intelligence and from the French Armament Agency as well as a Scientific Excellence Scholarship by CNRS in 2013. Antoine is a pioneer in the use of embedding models for modeling knowledge bases and co-authored many papers on the topic in recent years. He is also a specialist of natural language processing, deep learning and large-scale learning.

Evgeniy Gabrilovich is a senior staff research scientist at Google, where he works on knowledge discovery from the web. Prior to joining Google in 2012, he was a director of research and head of the natural language processing and information retrieval group at Yahoo! Research. Evgeniy is an ACM Distinguished Scientist (2012), and is a recipient of the 2010 Karen Sparck Jones Award for his contributions to natural language processing and information retrieval. He is also a recipient of the 2014 IJCAI-JAIR Best Paper Prize. Evgeniy serves as a PC chair for WSDM 2015, and has served as an area chair or senior program committee member at numerous major conferences, including SIGIR, KDD, WWW, WSDM, AAAI, IJCAI, ACL, EMNLP, CIKM, ICDM and ICWSM. He has organized a number of workshops and taught multiple tutorials at SIGIR, ACL, WWW, WSDM, ICML, IJCAI, AAAI, CIKM, and EC. Evgeniy earned his PhD in computer science from the Technion - Israel Institute of Technology.

Bringing Structure to Text: Mining Phrases, Entities, Topics, and Hierarchies

Jiawei Han, Chi Wang, Ahmed El-Kishky
Department of Computer Science
University of Illinois at Urbana-Champaign
Urbana, IL, USA
hanj@illinois.edu, chiwang1@illinois.edu, elkishk2@illinois.edu

ABSTRACT

Mining phrases, entity concepts, topics, and hierarchies from massive text corpus is an essential problem in the age of big data. Text data in electronic forms are ubiquitous, ranging from scientific articles to social networks, enterprise logs, news articles, social media and general web pages. It is highly desirable but challenging to bring structure to unstructured text data, uncover underlying hierarchies, relationships, patterns and trends, and gain knowledge from such data.

In this tutorial, we provide a comprehensive survey on the state-of-the art of data-driven methods that automatically mine phrases, extract and infer latent structures from text corpus, and construct multi-granularity topical groupings and hierarchies of the underlying themes. We study their principles, methodologies, algorithms and applications using several real datasets including research papers and news articles and demonstrate how these methods work and how the uncovered latent entity structures may help text understanding, knowledge discovery and management.

Why Bring Structure to Text?

In the big data age, vast amount of data generated in the world is unstructured or loosely structured, in the form of text, ranging from news to social media, business, government, and scientific documents, web pages, social networks, and enterprise logs. It is highly desirable to mine such huge amount of text data to discover its underlying thematic structures, hierarchies, and relationships.

Transforming vanilla unigrams into a richer information-rich phrases, uncovering real-world entities such as people, locations, and organizations, creation of heterogenous information networks, and constructing semantically rich conceptual and topical groupings of data can take intractable quantities of unstructured data and provide a rigid organization that can facilitate human exploration and understanding. This induced order provides application to information retrieval, information summarization, knowledge-base construction, and a wide-spectrum of new applications.

KDD'14, August 24–27, 2014, New York, NY, USA.
ACM 978-1-4503-2956-9/14/08.
http://dx.doi.org/10.1145/2623330.2630804.

Tutorial Outline

Phrase Mining and Phrase Topical Modeling
We discuss the limitations of unigrams and the 'bag-of-words' assumption to effective big-data analysis of text. We will provide examples from within the community to move forward from unigrams to multi-grams and demonstrate the value added from n-gram and 'bag-of-phrases' formulation of text data. We focus specifically on the problem of topic modeling and demonstrate the benefits of various phrase, n-gram, and bi-gram statistical topic models over unigram varieties.

Mining Topical Hierarchies: Topics at Multiple Granularities
Often times, flat topical structures fail to capture the subtleties in topics. We demonstrates efforts to more naturally model text corpora as topical hierarchies with a topic/subtopics schema. We argue that such a natural structure can allow for a more systematic drill-down approach to exploring corpora based on topical criterion.

Mining Latent Structures for Heterogenous Information Network Construction
We outline the benefits creating heterogenous information networks that embody the interrelation between the multi-typed entities found in text. We outline how mining latent structures from text can assist in constructing quality heterogenous information networks (HIN) and how these HIN allow for a principled and user-guided organization, exploration, and understanding large quantities of text.

Acknowledgments

The work was supported in part by the U.S. Army Research Laboratory under Cooperative Agreement No. W911NF-09-2-0053 (NS-CTA), the U.S. Army Research Office under Cooperative Agreement No. W911NF-13-1-0193, U.S. National Science Foundation grants IIS-1017362, IIS-1320617, IIS-1354329, DTRA, MIAS, a DHS-IDS Center for Multimodal Information Access and Synthesis at UIUC. Ahmed El-Kishky is supported by a National Science Foundation Graduate Research Fellowship grant number DGE-1144245.

Computational Epidemiology

Madhav Marathe, Anil Kumar S. Vullikanti
Virginia Bioinformatics Institute and
Department of Computer Science
Virginia Tech, Blacksburg, VA 24060
{mmarathe,akumar}@vbi.vt.edu

ABSTRACT

As recent pandemics such as SARS and the Swine Flu outbreak have shown, diseases spread very fast in today's interconnected world, making public health an important research area. Some of the basic questions are: How can an outbreak be contained before it becomes an epidemic, and what disease surveillance strategies should be implemented? These problems have been studied traditionally using differential equation methods, which are amenable to analysis and closed form solutions. However, these models are based on complete mixing assumptions, which do not hold for realistic populations, thereby limiting their utility.

In this tutorial, we focus on an approach based on diffusion processes on complex networks. This captures more realistic populations, but leads to novel mathematical and computational challenges. The structure of the underlying networks has a significant impact on the dynamical properties, motivating the need for improved network models, and efficient algorithms for computing network and dynamical properties that scale to large networks. We provide an overview of the state of the art in computational epidemiology, which is a multi-disciplinary research area, that overlaps different areas in computer science, including data mining, machine learning, high performance computing and theoretical computer science, as well as mathematics, economics and statistics. Specifically, we will discuss mathematical and computational models, problems of inference, forecasting and state assessment, and epidemic containment.

Target audience and prerequisites

The tutorial is suitable for both novice and expert researchers working in the areas of social and information networks, link prediction and public health. Problems of big data, including large scale optimization and novel statistical techniques are inherent aspects of this area. Public health is an area of great societal importance, with novel problems arising out of the use of network models. Recent advances in network modeling and agent based simulation tools, combined with the use of new datasets, such as social media data, have led to new challenges and opportunities. The tutorial will introduce this emerging area, and will identify some of the key research topics. It will be at a level that is accessible to most KDD attendees who work in these areas.

KDD'14, August 24–27, 2014, New York, NY, USA.
ACM 978-1-4503-2956-9/14/08.
http://dx.doi.org/10.1145/2623330.2630805.

Instructors

Madhav V. Marathe is a Professor of Computer Science and Director, Network Dynamics and Simulation Science Laboratory, Virginia Bioinformatics Institute, Virginia Tech. He obtained his Bachelor of Technology in 1989 in Computer Science and Engineering from the Indian Institute of Technology, Madras, and his PhD in 1994 in Computer Science from the University at Albany. He is the recipient of the Distinguished Copyright award for TRANSIMS software, LANL's achievement award, and a recipient of the University at Albany's Distinguished Alumni Award. His research interests are in high-performance computing, modeling & simulation of socio-technical systems, service oriented architectures, computer and communication networks, theoretical computer science, social networks and graph theory, computational epidemiology and computational economics. He is a fellow of the IEEE and ACM.

Anil Kumar S. Vullikanti is an Associate Professor in the Dept. of Computer Science and the Virginia Bioinformatics Institute at Virginia Tech. He received his undergraduate degree from the Indian Institute of Technology, Kanpur, and his Ph.D. from the Indian Institute of Science, Bangalore. He was a post-doctoral researcher at the Max-Planck Institute for Informatics, and a Technical Staff Member at the Los Alamos National Laboratory. His research interests are in the broad areas of approximation and randomized algorithms, dynamical systems, computation epidemiology, wireless networks, social networks, data mining and the modeling, simulation and analysis of socio-technical systems.

Acknowledgments

The authors have been partially supported by the following grants: DTRA Grant HDTRA1-11-1-0016, DTRA CNIMS Contract HDTRA1-11-D-0016-0010, NSF Career CNS 0845700, NSF ICES CCF-1216000, NSF NETSE Grant CNS-1011769 and DOE DE-SC0003957.

Management and Analytic of Biomedical Big Data with Cloud-based In-Memory Database and Dynamic Querying

A Hands-on Experience with Real-world Data

Mengling Feng
Massachusetts Institute of Technology
mfeng@mit.edu

Mohammad Ghassemi
Massachusetts Institute of Technology
ghassemi@mit.edu

Thomas Brennan
Massachusetts Institute of Technology
tpb@mit.edu

John Ellenberger
SAP Research
john.ellenberger@sap.com

Ishrar Hussain
SAP Research
ishrar.hussain@sap.com

Roger Mark
Massachusetts Institute of Technology
rgmark@mit.edu

ABSTRACT

Analyzing Biomedical Big Data (BBD) is computationally expensive due to high dimensionality and large data volume. Performance and scalability issues of traditional database management systems (DBMS) often limit the usage of more sophisticated and complex data queries and analytic models. Moreover, in the conventional setting, data management and analysis use separate software platforms. Exporting and importing large amounts of data across platforms require a significant amount of computational and I/O resources, as well as potentially putting sensitive data at a security risk. In this tutorial, the participants will learn the difference between in-memory DBMS and traditional DBMS through hands-on exercises using SAP's cloud-based HANA in-memory DBMS in conjunction with the Multi-parameter Intelligent Monitoring in Intensive Care (MIMIC) dataset. MIMIC is an open-access critical care EHR archive (over 4TB in size) and consists of structured, unstructured and waveform data. Furthermore, this tutorial will seek to educate the participants on how a combination of dynamic querying, and in-memory DBMS may enhance the management and analysis of complex clinical data.

Instructors

Mengling Feng is currently a visiting scholar at MIT in Harvard-MIT Health Sciences and Technology Division. Dr. Feng was awarded the Ministry of Education Scholarship for his undergraduate studies and the A*STAR Graduate Scholarship for his PhD study. His research was recognized with the *Bi-annual Best Paper Award* from the Institute for Infocomm Research. Dr. Feng's research focus is to develop data mining and machine learning methods to discover or infer casual phenomenon among real-life practices.

Mohammad Ghassemi is a PhD student in Electrical and Computer Engineering at the Massachusetts Institute of Technology with a research interest in statistical signal processing and medical informatics. In 2010, Mohammad received the Gates-Cambridge Scholarship to fund his MPhil at the University of Cambridge in Information Engineering. He was also awarded the Goldwater scholarship while pursuing two undergraduate degrees in Electrical Engineering and Applied Mathematics.

Thomas Brennan is currently a post-doctoral Research Engineer in the Laboratory of Computation Physiology, MIT. With a background in electrical and computer engineering, Thomas Brennan was awarded the Rhodes Scholarship from South Africa in 2004. In 2009 he completed his D.Phil. in Biomedical Engineering from the University of Oxford. In 2010, he accepted a Wellcome Trust post-doctoral research fellowship at Oxford.

John Ellenberger currently works in the "Chairman's Special Projects" group at SAP Labs where he serves as the liaison to MIT where he focuses on Big Data Topic including medical analytics, machine learning and data privacy and architecture. John has worked in SAP's research function for 10 years in both strategic and technical research roles.

Ishrar Hussain is working as a Machine Learning Researcher at SAP Research Labs, Montreal, and developing state-of-the-art machine learning solutions for Big Data applications using the SAP HANA's in-memory DBMS. He received his Master' degree in Computer Science in 2007 from Concordia University in Montreal, Canada. He is now also a Ph.D. Candidate at the same university and is expecting to graduate in 2014.

Roger G. Mark earned the SB and PhD degrees in electrical engineering from Massachusetts Institute of Technology and the MD degree from Harvard Medical School. At present Dr. Mark is Distinguished Professor of Health Sciences and Technology, and Professor of Electrical Engineering at MIT. His current research activities include *Integrating Data, Models, and Reasoning in Critical Care* and *PhysioNet* (http://www.physionet.org), both of which involve the development, use and open distribution of large physiological and clinical databases.

KDD'14, August 24–27, 2014, New York, NY, USA.
ACM 978-1-4503-2956-9/14/08.
http://dx.doi.org/10.1145/2623330.2630806.

The Recommender Problem Revisited

[Morning Tutorial]

Xavier Amatriain
Netflix
100 Winchester Cr.
Los Gatos, CA, USA
xavier@netflix.com

Bamshad Mobasher
De Paul University
243 South Wabash Avenue
Chicago, IL, USA
mobasher@cs.depaul.edu

ABSTRACT

In 2006, Netflix announced a $1M prize competition to advance recommendation algorithms. The recommendation problem was simplified as the accuracy in predicting a user rating measured by the Root Mean Squared Error. While that formulation helped get the attention of the research community in the area, it may have put an excessive focus on what is simply one of possible approaches to recommendations. In this tutorial we will describe different components of modern recommender systems such as: personalized ranking, similarity, explanations, context-awareness, or search as recommendation. In the first part, we will use the Netflix use case as a driving example of a prototypical industrial-scale recommender system. We will also review the usage of modern algorithmic approaches that include algorithms such as Factorization Machines, Restricted Boltzmann Machines, SimRank, Deep Neural Networks, or Listwise Learning-to-rank. In the second part, we will focus on the area of context-aware recommendations where the two dimensional user-item recommender problem is turned into an n-dimensional space.

1. WHO WHOULD ATTEND

This tutorial targets two different kinds of audience. On the one hand, the tutorial content should appeal to academic researchers who are interested in understanding the practical applications of some of the latest machine learning and data mining approaches for building recommender systems. On the other hand, it will appeal to industry practitioners who want to understand how latest algorithmic approaches can be applied.

The tutorial assumes basic understanding of supervised and non-supervised machine learning approaches. Some prior knowledge of traditional recommendation techniques such as collaborative filtering is not required but is encouraged in order to obtain the most out of the tutorial.

Just as the Netflix Prize helped bring the Recommender Problem into the spotlight of the KDD research community, we think this tutorial will help expanding the somewhat shallow view the researchers now have of recommender systems. We therefore anticipate a big interest and impact in the KDD community.

2. INSTRUCTORS

Xavier Amatriain (PhD) is Director of Algorithms Engineering at Netflix. He leads a team of researchers and engineers designing and implementing the next wave of machine learning approaches to power the Netflix product. Previous to this, he was a Researcher in Recommender Systems and neighboring areas such as Data Mining, Machine Learning, Information Retrieval, and Multimedia. He has authored more than 50 papers including book chapters, journals and articles in international conferences. He was General Chair for the 2010 ACM Recommender Systems Conference. He is often invited speaker at conferences, universities, and companies. He has also lectured in different universities including the University of California Santa Barbara and UPF in Barcelona, Spain, where he is originally from.

Bamshad Mobasher is a Professor of Computer Science and the director of the Center for Web Intelligence at the School of Computing of DePaul University in Chicago. His research areas include Web mining, Web personalization, recommender systems, predictive user modeling, and information retrieval. He has published five edited books as well as more than 170 scientific articles, including several seminal papers in Web mining and Web personalization that are among the most cited in these areas. Most recently, has served as the program chair and steering committee member of the ACM International Conference on Recommender Systems, as a program chair for the International Conference on User Modeling, Adaptation and Personalization, and as local organizing chair for the ACM Conference on Knowledge Discovery and Data Mining. As the director of the Center for Web Intelligence, Dr. Mobasher is directing research in Web mining, predictive analytics, and recommender systems, as well as overseeing several related joint projects with the industry. Dr. Mobasher serves as an associate editor for the ACM Transactions on the Web, ACM Transactions on Intelligent Interactive Systems and the ACM Transactions on Internet Technology. He also serves on the editorial board of User Modeling and User-Adapted Interaction, The Journal of Personalization Research.

KDD'14, August 24–27, 2014, New York, NY, USA.
ACM 978-1-4503-2956-9/14/08.
http://dx.doi.org/10.1145/2623330.2630807.

Correlation Clustering: from Theory to Practice

Francesco Bonchi
Yahoo Labs
Barcelona, Spain
bonchi@yahoo-inc.com

David García-Soriano
Yahoo Labs
Barcelona, Spain
davidgs@yahoo-inc.com

Edo Liberty
Yahoo Labs
New York City, USA
edo@yahoo-inc.com

ABSTRACT

Correlation clustering is arguably the most natural formulation of clustering. Given a set of objects and a pairwise similarity measure between them, the goal is to cluster the objects so that, to the best possible extent, similar objects are put in the same cluster and dissimilar objects are put in different clusters. As it just needs a definition of similarity, its broad generality makes it applicable to a wide range of problems in different contexts, and in particular makes it naturally suitable to clustering structured objects for which feature vectors can be difficult to obtain.

Despite its simplicity, generality and wide applicability, correlation clustering has so far received much more attention from the algorithmic theory community than from the data mining community. The goal of this tutorial is to show how correlation clustering can be a powerful addition to the toolkit of the data mining researcher and practitioner, and to encourage discussions and further research in the area.

In the tutorial we will survey the problem and its most common variants, with an emphasis on the algorithmic techniques and key ideas developed to derive efficient solutions. We will motivate the problems and discuss real-world applications, the scalability issues that may arise, and the existing approaches to handle them.

Target audience and prerequisites

The tutorial is aimed at researchers interested in the theory and applications of clustering. No special knowledge will be assumed other than familiarity with algorithmic techniques from a standard computer science background.

Outline

The tutorial is structured in three main technical parts, plus a concluding part where we will discuss future research agenda. All three technical parts will contain both theory and real-world applications.

KDD'14, August 24–27, 2014, New York, NY, USA.
ACM 978-1-4503-2956-9/14/08.
http://dx.doi.org/10.1145/2623330.2630808.

1. **Introduction and fundamental results:** Motivating examples; problem formulation; hardness; maximization and minimization versions; relationship with agnostic learning; approximation algorithms; applications.
2. **Correlation clustering variants:** Clustering aggregation/consensus clustering; bipartite correlation clustering; overlapping correlation clustering; chromatic correlation clustering; online correlation clustering; existence of a ground truth clustering; planted partition models; random noise; connections to other problems.
3. **Scalability for real-world instances:** Empirical approaches to overcome the all-pairs barrier; sublinear query complexity via relative regret approximations; neighborhood oracles; local correlation clustering; examples of real-world applications on Big Data.
4. **Challenges and directions for future research**

Instructors

Francesco Bonchi is leading the "Web Mining" research group at Yahoo Labs in Barcelona, Spain. He is member of the ECML PKDD Steering Committee, member of the Editorial Board of ACM Transactions on Intelligent Systems and Technology (TIST), and Associate Editor of IEEE Transactions on Knowledge and Data Engineering (TKDE). He has been program co-chair of ECML PKDD 2010, PinKDD 2007 and 2008, PADM 2006, and KDID 2005. More information can be found at
`http://www.francescobonchi.com/`

David García-Soriano is a postdoctoral researcher at Yahoo Labs in Barcelona. He received his PhD from the University of Amsterdam under the supervision of Harry Buhrman. His research interests include sublinear-time algorithms, learning, approximation algorithms, and large-scale problems in data mining and machine learning. More information can be found at
`https://sites.google.com/site/elhipercubo/`

Edo Liberty is leading the "Scalable Machine Learning" research group at Yahoo Labs in New York. He received his PhD in Computer Science from Yale University, under the supervision of Steven Zucker. After that, he joined the Program in Applied Mathematics at Yale as a Post-Doctoral fellow. In 2009 he joined Yahoo Labs. He received the best paper award at SODA 2011 and KDD 2013. More information can be found at `http://www.cs.yale.edu/homes/el327/`

Deep Learning

Ruslan Salakhutdinov
University of Toronto
Toronto, Canada
rsalakhu@cs.toronto.edu

ABSTRACT

Building intelligent systems that are capable of extracting high-level representations from high-dimensional data lies at the core of solving many AI related tasks, including visual object or pattern recognition, speech perception, and language understanding. Theoretical and biological arguments strongly suggest that building such systems requires deep architectures that involve many layers of nonlinear processing. Many existing learning algorithms use shallow architectures, including neural networks with only one hidden layer, support vector machines, kernel logistic regression, and many others. The internal representations learned by such systems are necessarily simple and are incapable of extracting some types of complex structure from high-dimensional input. In the past few years, researchers across many different communities, from applied statistics to engineering, computer science, and neuroscience, have proposed several deep (hierarchical) models that are capable of extracting meaningful, high-level representations. An important property of these models is that they can extract complex statistical dependencies from data and efficiently learn high-level representations by re-using and combining intermediate concepts, allowing these models to generalize well across a wide variety of tasks. The learned high-level representations have been shown to give state-of-the-art results in many challenging learning problems and have been successfully applied in a wide variety of application domains, including visual object recognition, information retrieval, natural language processing, and speech perception. A few notable examples of such models include Deep Belief Networks, Deep Boltzmann Machines, Deep Autoencoders, and sparse coding-based methods. The goal of the tutorial is to introduce the recent developments of various deep learning methods to the KDD community. The core focus will be placed on algorithms that can learn multi-layer hierarchies of representations, emphasizing their applications in information retrieval, object recognition, and speech perception.

KDD'14, August 24–27, 2014, New York, NY, USA.
ACM 978-1-4503-2956-9/14/08.
http://dx.doi.org/10.1145/2623330.2630809

Categories and Subject Descriptors

I.2.6 [**Artificial Intelligence**]: Learning—*Connectionism and neural nets*

Keywords

Deep Learning; Graphical Models; Boltzmann Machines; Autoencoders; Sparse Coding

Bio

Ruslan Salakhutdinov received his PhD in computer science from the University of Toronto in 2009. After spending two post-doctoral years at the Massachusetts Institute of Technology Artificial Intelligence Lab, he joined the University of Toronto as an Assistant Professor in the Department of Computer Science and Department of Statistics. Dr. Salakhutdinov's primary interests lie in statistical machine learning, Deep Learning, probabilistic graphical models, and large-scale optimization. He is an action editor of the Journal of Machine Learning Research and served on the senior programme committee of several learning conferences including NIPS and ICML. He is the recipient of the Early Researcher Award, Connaught New Researcher Award, Alfred P. Sloan Research Fellowship, Microsoft Research Faculty Fellowship, Google Faculty Research Award, and a is Fellow of the Canadian Institute for Advanced Research. A major focus on Dr. Salakhutdinov's work is Deep Learning, an active research area that stems, in large part, from his 2006 Science article co-authored with Geoffrey Hinton. This work developed a formulation for stacked Restricted Boltzmann Machines (RBMs), showing an algorithm capable of learning large-scale multi-layer networks. Dr. Salakhutdinov subsequently pioneered a new class of deep generative models, called Deep Boltzmann Machines (DBMs). These are probabilistic graphical models that contain multiple layers of latent variables. Each nonlinear layer captures progressively more complex patterns of data, which is a promising way of solving visual object recognition, language understanding, and speech perception problems. Dr. Salakhutdinov's contributions to Deep Learning have already received over 5000 citations according to Google Scholar, and have been applied broadly in speech, language, and image analysis.

Afternoon Tutorial
Network Mining and Analysis for Social Applications

Feida Zhu[1] Huan Sun[2] Xifeng Yan[2]
fdzhu@smu.edu.sg
{huansun, xyan}@cs.ucsb.edu
[1]Singapore Management University, [2]University of California, Santa Barbara

Abstract

The recent blossom of social network and communication services in both public and corporate settings have generated a staggering amount of network data of all kinds. Unlike the bio-networks and the chemical compound graph data often used in traditional network mining and analysis, the new network data grown out of the social applications are characterized by their rich attributes, high heterogeneity, enormous sizes and complex patterns of various semantic meanings, all of which have posed significant research challenges to the graph/network mining community. In this tutorial, we aim to examine some recent advances in network mining and analysis for social applications, covering a diverse collection of methodologies and applications from the perspectives of *event, relationship, collaboration, and network pattern.* We would present the problem settings, the challenges, the recent research advances and some future directions for each perspective. Topics include but are not limited to correlation mining, iceberg finding, anomaly detection, relationship discovery, information flow, task routing, and pattern mining.

Who Should Attend

This tutorial will be self-contained and is accessible to all data mining researchers, students and practitioners who are interested in network mining and analysis.

Prerequisites

No special prerequisite knowledge is needed to attend this tutorial.

Categories and Subject Descriptors

H.3.4 [**Information Systems**]: Systems and Software—*Information networks*

Keywords

Network Mining; Network Analysis; Social Applications

KDD'14, August 24–27, 2014, New York, NY, USA.
ACM 978-1-4503-2956-9/14/08.
http://dx.doi.org/10.1145/2623330.2630810 .

Instructors

Feida Zhu is an assistant professor at the School of Information Systems of Singapore Management University (SMU). He obtained his Ph.D. in Computer Science from the University of Illinois at Urbana-Champaign (UIUC) in 2009 and his B.Sc. in Computer Science from Fudan University, China, in 2001. His current research interests include large-scale data mining, graph/network mining and social network analysis. His research on large-scale frequent pattern mining has won the Best Student Paper Awards at 2007 IEEE International Conference on Data Engineering (ICDE) and 2007 Pacific- Asia Conference on Knowledge Discovery and Data Mining (PAKDD). He has founded the Pinnacle Lab, a joint lab with China Ping An Insurance Group to focus on social media mining and analysis for finance industry.

Huan Sun is currently a fourth-year Ph.D. student working with Prof. Xifeng Yan in the Department of Computer Science at the University of California, Santa Barbara. Her research works focus on statistical machine learning and data mining with emphasis on network analysis, text mining, and user modeling. She received the Regents' Special Fellowship in 2010 and the Ph.D. Progress Award in the Computer Science Dept. in 2014. She obtained her B.S. degree in Electronic Engineering and Information Science from the University of Science and Technology of China in 2010, and received Excellent Undergraduate Thesis Award.

Xifeng Yan is an associate professor at the University of California at Santa Barbara. He holds the Venkatesh Narayanamurti Chair of Computer Science. He received his Ph.D. degree in Computer Science from the University of Illinois at Urbana-Champaign in 2006. He was a research staff member at the IBM T. J. Watson Research Center between 2006 and 2008. He has been working on modeling, managing, and mining graphs in information networks, computer systems, social media and bioinformatics. His works were extensively referenced, with over 9,000 citations per Google Scholar and thousands of software downloads. He received NSF CAREER Award, IBM Invention Achievement Award, ACM-SIGMOD Dissertation Runner-Up Award, and IEEE ICDM 10-year Highest Impact Paper Award.

Sampling for Big Data: A Tutorial

Graham Cormode
University of Warwick*
g.cormode@warwick.ac.uk

Nick Duffield
Rutgers University / DIMACS†
nick.duffield@rutgers.edu

ABSTRACT

One response to the proliferation of large datasets has been to develop ingenious ways to throw resources at the problem, using massive fault tolerant storage architectures, parallel and graphical computation models such as MapReduce, Pregel and Giraph. However, not all environments can support this scale of resources, and not all queries need an exact response. This motivates the use of sampling to generate summary datasets that support rapid queries, and prolong the useful life of the data in storage. To be effective, sampling must mediate the tensions between resource constraints, data characteristics, and the required query accuracy. The state-of-the-art in sampling goes far beyond simple uniform selection of elements, to maximize the usefulness of the resulting sample. This tutorial reviews progress in sample design for large datasets, including streaming and graph-structured data. Applications are discussed to sampling network traffic and social networks.

1. INTRODUCTION

Research in big data draws from many disciplines, both from areas of analysis (including probability, data analysis, machine learning and algorithms) and also systems (including distributed systems, database architectures, and programming models). This tutorial addresses several target audiences, all of whom may want to benefit from a greater understanding of the use of probabilistic methods for sampling and estimation in big data:

Researchers in big data who background is not primarily concerned with probabilistic methods, but wish to learn about these as a complement to their current expertise.

Researchers with a more classical background in statistics who wish to refocus to apply their expertise to problems in big data.

Researchers in big data methodologies who wish to learn more about current applications of sampling in big data in the field.

*Supported in part by a Yahoo! Research FREP award.

†Address from September 2014: Department of Electrical and Computer Engineering, Texas A&M University, College Station, TX 77843-3128

KDD'14, August 24–27, 2014, New York, NY, USA.
ACM 978-1-4503-2956-9/14/08.
http://dx.doi.org/10.1145/2623330.2630811.

2. OUTLINE

Fundamentals of Sampling. Summarization as a means to control resource usage, sampling as special case of summarization. General comparison of sampling with other summarization techniques, including aggregation and sketching: different tradeoffs between scalability, flexibility, and ability for post-hoc exploration. Sampling as a mediator between data characteristics. Unbiased estimation and the Horvitz-Thompson approach. Variance and Covariance Estimators. General purpose samples vs. targeted estimators.

Sampling from Streams of Data. Uniform Stream Sampling, and generalizations to weighted streams, via Reservoir Sampling, Sample and Hold and Counting Samples. Inclusion Probability Proportional to Size Sampling, including Threshold Sampling, Priority Sampling, Variance Optimal Sampling, and Bottom-k Sampling Sketch guided sampling, Structure Aware Sampling, Sampling from the distinct objects via ℓ_0 sampling, and ℓ_p sampling.

Hashing and Coordinated Sampling. Hash functions as a source of Permanent Random Numbers (PRN). Hashing algorithms, including Universal Hashing and implementations. Advanced topics may include Minwise hashing, Consistent Weighted Hashing, Hashing with Timeouts, Coordinated Sampling, or Trajectory Sampling

Graph Sampling. Network sampling, ego-net sampling, and why simple edge or node centric sampling fails for more complex properties. Topics may include Biased sampling methods, Random walks, Snowball and respondent driven sampling, forest fire sampling, Graph stream sampling, Horwitz-Thompson estimation in graphs, or Triangle counting.

Sampling Applications. Network Traffic Measurement (Netflow, IPFIX, PSAMP); Sampling and Approximate Database Queries (Priority Sampling in Databases, BlinkDB) Social Networks (Social activity streams, Sampling and information diffusion).

3. TUTORS

Graham Cormode is a Professor in Computer Science at the University of Warwick in the UK.
Nick Duffield is a Research Professor at Rutgers University/DIMACS, New Jersey, USA.

Statistically Sound Pattern Discovery

Wilhelmiina Hämäläinen
University of Eastern Finland
whamalai@cs.uef.fi

Geoffrey I. Webb
Monash University, Australia
geoff.webb@monash.edu

ABSTRACT

Pattern discovery is a core data mining activity. Initial approaches were dominated by the frequent pattern discovery paradigm – only patterns that occur frequently in the data were explored. Having been thoroughly researched and its limitations now well understood, this paradigm is giving way to a new one, which can be called *statistically sound pattern discovery*. In this paradigm, the main impetus is to discover statistically significant patterns, which are unlikely to have occurred by chance and are likely to hold in future data. Thus, the new paradigm provides a strict control over false discoveries and overfitting.

This tutorial covers both classic and cutting-edge research topics on pattern discovery combined to statistical significance testing. We start with an advanced introduction to the relevant forms of statistical significance testing, including different schools and alternative models, their underlying assumptions, practical issues, and limitations. We then discuss their application to data mining specific problems, including evaluation of nested patterns, the multiple testing problem, algorithmic strategies and real-world considerations. We present the current state-of-the art solutions and explore in detail how this approach to pattern discovery can deliver efficient and effective discovery of small sets of interesting patterns.

Categories and Subject Descriptors

H.2.8 [**Database Applications**]: Data mining

Keywords

Pattern Discovery, Association Mining, Statistics

Who Should Attend

The tutorial is aimed at anyone interested in finding useful and reliable patterns in data. It is likely to inspire both practical data miners (how to test and improve the quality of discovered patterns) and algorithm designers (how to target the search into the most reliable patterns). The main contents are easy-to-understand to anyone who wants to get an overview of this new paradigm, but there is also deeper analysis, open problems and controversial questions which should interest experienced researchers, as well.

Prerequisites

General data mining/pattern discovery background, familiarity with basic mathematical concepts, including probability theory and statistics (undergraduate level mathematics).

Instructors

Dr. Wilhelmiina Hämäläinen is a postdoctoral researcher by the Academy of Finland, currently working in the School of Computing, University of Eastern Finland. She received a Ph.D. degree 2010 (Computer Science) from the University of Helsinki. She has worked as a teacher, lecturer, and researcher in the university since 1996, including 2 years as a university researcher of biology (applied data mining). She has often worked with interdisciplinary problems, involving computer science, statistics, and mathematics. Her main achievements in data mining are efficient algorithms for finding reliable statistical dependency patterns (a related award from The Finnish Society for Computer Science and Research Foundation of the Finnish Information Processing Association). Her research interests include statistical dependency analysis and significance testing, optimization algorithms, applied knowledge discovery (biology, educational technology) and general number crunching.

Dr. Geoff Webb is a Professor of Information Technology Research at Monash University. He has developed numerous algorithms and techniques for machine learning, data mining and computational structural biology. His commercial data mining software, Magnum Opus, incorporates many techniques from his association discovery research. Many of his learning algorithms are included in the widely-used Weka machine learning workbench. He is editor-in-chief of *Data Mining and Knowledge Discovery*, co-editor of the *Springer Encyclopedia of Machine Learning*, on the *Statistical Analysis and Data Mining* advisory board, and has served on numerous editorial boards including *Machine Learning* and *ACM Transactions on Knowledge Discovery from Data*. He is PC Co-Chair of SIGKDD 2105, was PC Co-Chair of ICDM 2010 and co-General Chair of ICDM 2012. He has received the 2013 *IEEE ICDM Service Award* and a 2014 *Australian Research Council Discovery Outstanding Researcher Award*.

KDD'14, August 24–27, 2014, New York, NY, USA.
ACM 978-1-4503-2956-9/14/08.
http://dx.doi.org/10.1145/2623330.2630812.

Recommendation in Social Media: Recent Advances and New Frontiers

Jiliang Tang
Computer Science & Eng
Arizona State University
Jiliang.Tang@asu.edu

Jie Tang
Computer Science & Tech
Tsinghua University
jietang@tsinghua.edu.cn

Huan Liu
Computer Science & Eng
Arizona State University
Huan.Liu@asu.edu

ABSTRACT

The pervasive use of social media generates massive data in an unprecedented rate and the information overload problem becomes increasingly severe for social media users. Recommendation has been proven to be effective in mitigating the information overload problem, demonstrated its strength in improving the quality of user experience, and positively impacted the success of social media. New types of data introduced by social media not only provide more information to advance traditional recommender systems but also manifest new research possibilities for recommendation. In this tutorial, we aim to provide a comprehensive overview of various recommendation tasks in social media, especially their recent advances and new frontiers. We introduce basic concepts, review state-of-the-art algorithms, and deliberate the emerging challenges and opportunities. Finally we summarize the tutorial with discussions on open issues and challenges about recommendation in social media. Updated information about the tutorial can be found at `http://www.public.asu.edu/~jtang20/Recommendation.htm`.

Who Should Attend

The intended audience for this tutorial mainly includes researchers, graduate students, and professionals who are new to this area or who already have some experience with data mining. The audience is expected to have some basic understanding of social network analysis, data mining, and machine learning. However, the tutorial will be presented at college junior/senior level and should be comfortably followed by academic researchers and practitioners from the industry.

Instructors

Jiliang Tang is a senior PhD student of Computer Science and Engineering at Arizona State University. He was awarded the 2014 ASU President's Award for Innovation, Best Paper Shortlist in WSDM13, the 3rd Place Dedicated Task 2 Next Location Prediction of Nokia Mobile Data Challenge 2012, University Graduate Fellowship, and various Student Travel Awards and Scholarships. His research interests are in computing with online trust and distrust, recommendation, mining social media data, data mining and feature selection. He co-presents tutorials in KDD14, WWW14 and Recsys14, and has published innovative works in highly ranked journals and top conference proceedings. He worked as a research intern in Yahoo!Labs and IBM Research.

Jie Tang is an associate professor at the Department of Computer Science and Technology, Tsinghua University. He serves as the director of Scientific Office of the Department of Computer Science. His main research interests include social network analysis and data mining. He has been a visiting scholar at Cornell University, Chinese University of Hong Kong, Hong Kong University of Science and Technology, and Leuven University. He has published over 100 research papers in major international journals and conferences. He serves as PC Co-Chair of WSDM'15, ADMA'11, SocInfo'12, Poster Co-Chair of KDD'14, Workshop Co-Chair of KDD'13, Local Chair of KDD'12, Publications Co-Chairs of KDD'11, and also serves as the PC member of more than 50 international conferences. He is now leading the project Arnetminer.org for academic social network analysis and mining, which has attracted millions of independent IP accesses from 220 countries/regions in the world. He was honored with the CCF Young Scientist Award, NSFC Excellent Young Scholar, and IBM Innovation Faculty Award.

Huan Liu is a professor of Computer Science and Engineering at Arizona State University. He obtained his Ph.D in Computer Science at University of Southern California and B.Eng. in Computer Science and Electrical Engineering at Shanghai JiaoTong University. Before he joined ASU, he worked at Telecom Australia Research Labs and was on the faculty at National University of Singapore. He was recognized for excellence in teaching and research in Computer Science and Engineering at Arizona State University. His research interests are in data mining, machine learning, social computing, and artificial intelligence, investigating problems that arise in many real-world, data-intensive applications with high-dimensional data of disparate forms such as social media. His well-cited publications include books, book chapters, encyclopedia entries as well as conference and journal papers. He serves on journal editorial boards and numerous conference program committees, and is a founding organizer of the International Conference Series on Social Computing, Behavioral-Cultural Modeling, and Prediction. He is an IEEE Fellow and an ACM Distinguished Scientist.

Acknowledgments

Jiliang Tang and Huan Liu are supported by NSF (#IIS-1217466), ARO (#025071), and ONR(N000141410095). Jie Tang is supported by the National High-tech R&D Program of China (#2014AA015103), Natural Science Foundation of China (#61222212, 61073073), and National Basic Research Program of China (2013CB329603) and a research fund supported by Huawei Inc.

KDD'14, August 24–27, 2014, New York, NY, USA.
ACM 978-1-4503-2956-9/14/08.
http://dx.doi.org/10.1145/2623330.2630813 .

Author Index

www.ingramcontent.com/pod-product-compliance
Lightning Source LLC
LaVergne TN
LVHW080100011026
849160LV00013B/1003

* 9 7 8 1 4 5 0 3 3 2 7 1 2 *